Greens Annotated Rules of the Court of Session 2024/2025

REPRINTED FROM DIVISION C (COURT OF SESSION PRACTICE) OF THE PARLIAMENT HOUSE BOOK

GREENS ANNOTATED RULES OF THE COURT OF SESSION

by

NIGEL MORRISON, KC
formerly Sheriff of Lothian and Borders at Edinburgh formerly First Counsel to the Lord President of the Court of Session

DAVID BARTOS, LLB
Advocate
formerly Legal Assistant to the Lord President of the Court of Session

NEIL CRICHTON, WS
formerly Auditor of the Court of Session

THE LATE THOMAS HIGGINS
Depute Clerk of Session and Justiciary and formerly Clerk to the First Division of the Court of Session

IAIN MACLEAN, LLB, LLM, MSc
Advocate
formerly Legal Assistant to the Lord President of the Court of Session

THE LATE J. HALDANE TAIT, SSC
formerly Auditor of the Court of Session

MATTHEW WEIR
formerly Depute Clerk of Session and Justiciary and Clerk to the First Division of the Court of Session

THE HON. LADY WOLFFE
formerly a Senator of the College of Justice

W. Green

Published in 2024 by Thomson Reuters, trading as W. Green.
Thomson Reuters is registered in England & Wales, Company No.1679046
Registered Office and address for service:
5 Canada Square, Canary Wharf, London, E14 5AQ
For further information on our products and services, visit *http://
www.sweetandmaxwell.co.uk/wgreen*

ISBN (print) 9780414122772

ISBN (e-book) 9780414122802

ISBN (print and e-book) 9780414122789

Printed and bound by CPI Group (UK) Ltd, Croydon, CR0 4YY
A CIP catalogue record for this book is available from the British Library.
For orders, go to: *http://www.tr.com/uki-legal-contact*; Tel: 0345 600 9355.

FSC
www.fsc.org
MIX
Paper | Supporting
responsible forestry
FSC® C013604

Greens Annotated Rules of the Court of Session 2024/2025

Reprinted from the *Parliament House Book*, published in looseleaf form and updated five times a year by W. Green, the Scottish Law Publisher

The following paperback titles are also available in the series:

Sheriff Court and Sheriff Appeal Court Rules 2024/2025

Solicitors Professional Handbook 2024/2025

Parliament House Book consists of the following Divisions:

A Fees and Stamps

B Courts, Upper

C Court of Session Practice

D Courts, Lower

E Licensing

F Solicitors

G Legal Aid

H Bankruptcy and other Mercantile

I Companies

J Conveyancing, Land Tenure and Registration

K Family Law

L Landlord and Tenant

M Succession, Trusts, Liferents and Judicial Factors

S Sheriff Appeal Court Practice

MAIN TABLE OF CONTENTS

Volume 1

Volume 2

TABLES

OTHER ACTS OF SEDERUNT

COURT FEES

DIRECTIONS

PRACTICE NOTES

INDEX

Index

ACT OF SEDERUNT (RULES OF THE COURT OF SESSION 1994) 1994

(SI 1994/1443)

31 May 1994.

The Lords of Council and Session, under and by virtue of the powers conferred on them by section 5 of the Court of Session Act 1988, the provisions specified in Schedule 1 to this Act of Sederunt and of all other powers enabling them in that behalf, do hereby enact and declare:

Citation and commencement

1.—(1)   This Act of Sederunt may be cited as the Act of Sederunt (Rules of the Court of Session 1994) 1994 and shall come into force on 5th September 1994.

(2)   This Act of Sederunt shall be inserted in the Books of Sederunt.

Rules of the Court of Session

2.   The provisions of Schedule 2 to this Act of Sederunt shall have effect for the purpose of providing new rules for the Court of Session.

Amendments, repeals, revocations and savings

3.—(1)   The enactments mentioned in Schedule 3 to this Act of Sederunt shall have effect subject to the amendments there specified.

(2)   The enactments mentioned in Schedule 4 to this Act of Sederunt, being enactments relating to matters in respect of which the rules specified in the fourth column of that Schedule are made, are repealed to the extent specified in the third column of that Schedule.

(3)   Subject to paragraphs (5) and (6) below, the Acts of Sederunt mentioned in Schedule 5 to this Act of Sederunt are revoked to the extent specified in the third column of that Schedule.

(4)   All Acts of Sederunt to the extent that they relate to practice or procedure in the Court of Session made before 10th November 1964 (being the date on which the Act of Sederunt (Rules of Court, consolidation and amendment) 1965 was made) are, in so far as still in force, revoked.

(5)   No revocation, by virtue of sub-paragraph (3) above, of an Act of Sederunt relating to fees and outlays of solicitors, witnesses' fees and allowances or shorthand writers' fees shall affect fees or allowances in respect of anything done, or outlays incurred, before the date on which this Act of Sederunt comes into force.

(6)   No revocation, by virtue of sub-paragraph (3) above, of an Act of Sederunt relating to interest on decrees or extracts shall affect interest included in or exigible under a decree pronounced or an extract extracted before the coming into force of this Act of Sederunt.

(SI 1994/1443)

21 March

The Lords of Council and Session, under and by virtue of the powers conferred on them by section 5 of the Court of Session Act 1988, the provisions specified in Schedule 1 to this Act of Sederunt and of all other powers enabling them in that behalf, do hereby enact and declare:

Citation and commencement

1.—(1) This Act of Sederunt may be cited as the Act of Sederunt (Rules of the Court of Session 1994) 1994 and shall come into force on 5th September 1994.

(2) This Act of Sederunt shall be inserted in the Books of Sederunt.

Rules of the Court of Session

2. The provisions of Schedule 2 to this Act of Sederunt shall have effect for the purpose of providing new rules for the Court of Session.

Amendments, repeals, revocations and savings

3.—(1) The enactments mentioned in Schedule 3 to this Act of Sederunt shall have effect subject to the amendments there specified.

(2) The enactments mentioned in Schedule 4 to this Act of Sederunt, being enactments relating to matters in respect of which the rules specified in the fourth column of that Schedule are made, are repealed to the extent specified in the third column of that Schedule.

(3) Subject to paragraphs (5) and (6) below, the Acts of Sederunt mentioned in Schedule 5 to this Act of Sederunt are revoked to the extent specified in the third column of that Schedule.

(4) All Acts of Sederunt, to the extent that they relate to practice or procedure in the Court of Session made before 16th November 1934 (being the date on which the Act of Sederunt (Rules of Court, consolidation and amendment) 1965 was made) are, in so far as still in force, revoked.

(5) The revocation by virtue of sub-paragraph (3) above of an Act of Sederunt relating to fees and liability of solicitors, witnesses, fees, and allowances of shorthand writers' fees shall not affect fees or allowances in respect of anything done or outlays incurred before the date on which this Act of Sederunt comes into force.

(6) No revocation by virtue of sub-paragraph (3) above of an Act of Sederunt relating to interest on decrees or extracts shall have effect in regard to interest payable under a decree pronounced or an extract extracted before the coming into force of this Act of Sederunt.

2

SCHEDULE 1: PREAMBLE

POWERS UNDER AND BY VIRTUE OF WHICH THIS ACT OF SEDERUNT IS MADE

C1.1

Preamble

Column 1 Relevant enactment conferring power	Column 2 Relevant amending enactment	Column 3 Relevant provision in Schedule 2
Section 34A of the Judicial Factors Act 1849 (c.51)	Inserted by section 67 of the Law Reform (Miscellaneous Provisions) (Scotland) Act 1990 (c.40)	Rules 61.31 and 61.32
Section 40 of the Judicial Factors Act 1849	Amended by paragraph 15 of Schedule 1 to the Age of Legal Capacity (Scotland) Act 1991 (c.50)	Chapter 61
Section 11B of the Judicial Factors Act 1889 (c.39)	Inserted by paragraph 4 of Schedule 7 to the Bankruptcy (Scotland) Act 1985 (c.66)	Rules 61.9 and Part II of Chapter 61
Section 21 of the Judicial Factors Act 1889		Chapter 61
Section 4 of the Court of Session Consignations (Scotland) Act 1895 (c.19)		Rule 33.12(4)
Section 11 of the Administration of Justice Act 1920 (c.81)		Part II of Chapter 62
Section 12(b) of the Foreign Judgments (Reciprocal Enforcement) Act 1933 (c.13)		Part II of Chapter 62
Section 1(1) of the Public Records (Scotland) Act 1937 (c.43)	Amended by section 1(3) and (7) of the Public Registers and Records (Scotland) Act 1948 (c.57)	Rule 9.1
Section 1(2) of the Public Records (Scotland) Act 1937		Rule 9.2
Section 58C of the Trade Marks Act 1938 (c.22)	Inserted by section 300 of the Copyright, Designs and Patents Act 1988 (c.48)	Rules 55.17
Section 8(4) of the Law Reform (Miscellaneous Provisions) (Scotland) Act 1966 (c.19)	Amended by section 52(5) of the Court of Session Act (c.36)	Rules 32.3 and 32.7

Column 1 Relevant enactment conferring power	Column 2 Relevant amending enactment	Column 3 Relevant provision in Schedule 2
Section 7(b) of the Arbitration (International Investment Disputes) Act 1966 (c.41)		Part III of Chapter 62
Section 1(3) of the Administration of Justice (Scotland) Act 1972 (c.59)		Chapter 64
Paragraph 5 of Schedule 3 to the Domicile and Matrimonial Proceedings Act 1973 (c.45)		Rule 49.1(3)
Sections 47(6) and 102(1) and (3) of the Children Act 1975 (c.72)	Section 102 was amended by Schedule 4 to the Adoption Act 1976 (c.36)	Rule 49.20
Section 48(1) of the Children Act 1975	Amended by Schedule 2 to the Law Reform (Parent and Child) (Scotland) Act 1986 (c.9)	Rules 49.8(3)(g) and 49.20
Section 11 of the Divorce (Scotland) Act 1976 (c.39)		Rule 49.17
Section 15 of the Presumption of Death (Scotland) Act 1977 (c.27)		Chapter 50
Section 92(4) of the Patents Act 1977 (c.37)		Rule 66.7
Section 59(1) of the Adoption Act 1978 (c.28)		Chapter 67
Section 57(4) of the Solicitors (Scotland) Act 1980 (c.46)	Amended by Schedule 2 to the Solicitors (Scotland) Act 1988 (c.42) and section 37(2) of the Law Reform (Miscellaneous Provisions) (Scotland) Act 1990	Rules 68.2(1) and 68.3
Section 4 of the Civil Jurisdiction and Judgments Act 1982 (c.27)	Extended by the Civil Jurisdiction and Judgments (Authentic Instruments and Court Settlements) Order 1993 [S.I. 1993/604]	Rule 62.28
Section 12 of the Civil Jurisdiction and Judgments Act 1982	Extended by the Civil Jurisdiction and Judgments (Authentic Instru-	Rule 62.40

4

Column 1 **Relevant enactment conferring power**	Column 2 **Relevant amending enactment**	Column 3 **Relevant provision in Schedule 2**
	ments and Court Settle- ments) Order 1993	
Section 48 of the Civil Jurisdiction and Judg- ments Act 1982		Part V of Chapter 62
Section 9(5) of the Merchant Shipping (Liner Conferences) Act 1982 (c.37)		Part VI of Chapter 62
Sections 121(3) and (4) and 185 of the Representation of the People Act 1983 (c.2)		Rules 69.2 and 69.3
Sections 136(2)–(4) and (7) and 185 of the Representation of the People Act 1983	Amended by paragraph 48 of Schedule 4 of the Representation of the People Act 1985 (c.50)	Rule 69.4
Sections 138(1) and 185 of the Representation of the People Act 1983		Rule 69.8
Sections 139(1) and 185 of the Representation of the People Act 1983		Rule 69.9
Sections 146(1) and 185 of the Representation of the People Act 1983		Rule 69.18
Sections 147(1) and (2) and 185 of the Representation of the People Act 1983		Rule 69.19
Sections 152(3) and 185 of the Representation of the People Act 1983		Rule 69.20
Sections 153(1) and 185 of the Representation of the People Act 1983		Rule 69.25
Section 10 of the Child Abduction and Custody Act 1985 (c.60)		Parts I and II of Chapter 70
Section 24 of the Child Abduction and Custody Act 1985		Parts I and III of Chapter 70
Section 1A(1)(b) of the Bankruptcy (Scotland) Act 1985 (c.66)	Inserted by section 1(1) of the Bankruptcy (Scotland) Act 1993 (c.6)	Rule 72.6(1)

Column 1 Relevant enactment conferring power	Column 2 Relevant amending enactment	Column 3 Relevant provision in Schedule 2
Section 14(4) of the Bankruptcy (Scotland) Act 1985	Amended by paragraph 3 of Schedule 1 to the Bankruptcy (Scotland) Act 1993	Rule 72.6(3)
Section 62(2) of the Bankruptcy (Scotland) Act 1985		Rule 72.5
Paragraph 2 of Schedule 5 to the Bankruptcy (Scotland) Act 1985		Rule 72.6(3) and (4)
Section 27 of the Family Law Act 1986 (c.55)		Rule 71.3
Section 28 of the Family Law Act 1986		Rule 71.6
Section 90(4) of the Debtors (Scotland) Act 1987 (c.18)		Rule 16.15(1)(i)
Section 102 of the Debtors (Scotland) Act 1987		Part II of Chapter 16
Section 8(4) of the Criminal Justice (Scotland) Act 1987 (c.41)		Rule 76.4(2)
Section 22 of the Criminal Justice (Scotland) Act 1987		Rules 76.10 to 76.14
Section 28(1) of the Criminal Justice (Scotland) Act 1987		Part VII of Chapter 62
Section 46 of the Criminal Justice (Scotland) Act 1987		Rules 76.3(2) and 76.7(2)
Section 7(e) of the Multilateral Investment Guarantee Agency Act 1988 (c.8)		Part VIII of Chapter 62
Section 91(1) and (2) of the Criminal Justice Act 1988 (c.33)		Part VII of Chapter 62
Section 6(i) of the Court of Session Act 1988		Chapter 3
Section 6(ii) of the Court of Session Act 1988		Rules 14.2 and 14.3

Column 1 Relevant enactment conferring power	Column 2 Relevant amending enactment	Column 3 Relevant provision in Schedule 2
Section 6(iii) of the Court of Session Act 1988		Rules 46.2, 46.3 and 46.5
Section 6(iv) of the Court of Session Act 1988		Rules 46.2 and 46.4
Section 6(v) of the Court of Session Act 1988		Chapter 25
Section 6(vi) of the Court of Session Act 1988		Part II of Chapter 63
Section 6(vii) of the Court of Session Act 1988		Rule 13.6(b)
Section 26(2) of the Court of Session Act 1988		Rule 77.10
Section 26(3) of the Court of Session Act 1988		Rule 77.3
Sections 28 and 51 of the Court of Session Act 1988		Chapter 38
Sections 29(1) and 51 of the Court of Session Act 1988		Rules 39.1 to 39.5
Sections 34 and 51 of the Court of Session Act 1988		Rule 53.1 and Chapter 60
Sections 48(2)(b) and 51 of the Court of Session Act 1988	Section 48(2)(b) was substituted by paragraph 38 of Schedule 8 to the Law Reform (Miscellaneous Provisions) (Scotland) Act 1990	Rule 23.14
Sections 49(1) and 51 of the Court of Session Act 1988		Rule 58.1(3)
Section 114(3) of the Copyright, Designs and Patents Act 1988 (c.48)		Rule 55.17(2)
Section 204(3) of the Copyright, Designs and Patents Act 1988		Rule 55.17(2)
Section 231(3) of the Copyright, Designs and Patents Act 1988		Rule 55.17(2)
Paragraph 11(2) of Schedule 4 to the Preven-		Rule 76.24

Column 1 Relevant enactment conferring power	Column 2 Relevant amending enactment	Column 3 Relevant provision in Schedule 2
tion of Terrorism (Temporary Provisions) Act 1989 (c.4)		
Paragraph 19(1)–(3) of Schedule 4 to the Prevention of Terrorism (Temporary Provisions) Act 1989		Part VII of Chapter 62
Section 8(1) to the Access to Health Records Act 1990 (c.23)		Rule 79.3

SCHEDULE 2: TABLE OF ARRANGEMENT

SCHEDULE 2

THE RULES OF THE COURT OF SESSION 1994

Paragraph 2

Arrangement of Rules

Preliminary
Chapter 1
Citation, Application, Etc.

Chapter 2
Relief from Compliance with Rules

General and Administration
Chapter 3
Offices of the Court

Chapter 4
The Process

Chapter 14
Petitions

Chapter 14A
Interim Diligence

Chapter 14B
Determination of the Value of an Order

13

15

Part II
Undefended Family Actions

Part III
Defended Family Actions

Other Proceedings in Relation to Statutory Applications
Chapter 62
Recognition, Registration and Enforcement of Foreign Judgments, etc.
Part I
General Provisions

Part II
Registration and Enforcement under the Administration of Justice Act 1920 and the Foreign Judgments (Reciprocal Enforcement) Act 1933

Part III
Registration of Awards under the Arbitration (International Investments Disputes) Act 1966

Chapter 68
Applications under the Solicitors (Scotland) Act 1980

Chapter 69
Election Petitions

Chapter 95
Scottish Commission for Human Rights

Chapter 96
Counter-terrorism Act 2008 Financial Restrictions Proceedings

Chapter 97
Applications for Parental Orders under the Human Fertilisation and Embryology Act 2008

Part I

Preliminary

Chapter 1

Citation, Application, Etc.[1]

Citation

1.1. These Rules may be cited as the Rules of the Court of Session 1994.

1.1

General note.

The current rules of the Court of Session are to be found in Sched. 2 to the A.S. (R.C.S. 1994) 1994 [S.I. 1994 No. 1443]. They are a consequence of the reports of the Rules Review Group set up by the Lord President of the Court of Session in 1984 to examine the rules, Acts of Sederunt, statutes and practice notes, and, in light of, inter alia, experience of their use, (i) to recommend what changes in the layout of the rules were necessary and what changes in the rules were desirable, with a view to the simplification of procedure and to the promotion of the speedier and more economical despatch of court business; and (ii) to make proposals for an appropriate A.S. for consideration by the Rules Council and the court. The layout, order and numbering of the R.C.S. 1994 do not follow recommendations of the Rules Review Group but more the idea of the draftsman (NMP Morrison QC). Not all the new provisions are recommendations of the Group. The Rules were made on 31st May, and came into force on 5th September 1994.

1.1.1

The general statutory power of the Court of Session to make rules regulating its procedure is to be found in ss.5 and 6 of the C.S.A. 1988 (formerly ss.16 and 17 of the Administration of Justice (Scotland) Act 1933). It includes a power to make rules to carry out the provisions of any other Act conferring powers or imposing duties on the court or relating to proceedings in the court. An Act may include specific rule-making powers for the purposes of that Act in addition to this general power. The original statutory power was in the College of Justice Act 1540.

Apart from its statutory powers, the court has an inherent right to regulate its business and procedure. This was confirmed in *Tonner v. Reiach and Hall* , 2008 S.C. 1 (Extra Div.), 31, para. [99] (though this passage was overlooked) where the court held that the Rules are not coextensive with the practice of the court; and the fact that a particular power is not mentioned in the Rules does not necessarily mean that the power is not available to be used in appropriate cases.

The court has power, under s.5 (m) of the C.S.A. 1988, to modify, amend or repeal the provisions in any enactment relating to its procedure. There is often a power in particular statutes to make rules in respect of provisions contained in them.

Acts of Sederunt and practice notes.

The court regulates its procedure by Acts of Sederunt. By s.10 of the Law Reform (Miscellaneous Provisions) (Scotland) Act 1966, an A.S. made under a statute passed after the commencement of the Statutory Instruments Act 1946 is to be by statutory instrument; and the provisions of the 1946 Act apply to such Acts of Sederunt. In practice, all Acts of Sederunt are made by statutory instrument. Practice notes are administrative directions indicating, where necessary, the way in which, for administrative purposes only, a particular rule in the R.C.S. or an administrative requirement may be complied with. They should not be used for any other purpose, such as to amend or suspend a rule of the R.C.S.

1.1.2

Rules Council.

The Rules Council, set up under s.18 of the A.J.A. 1933 (now s.8 of the C.S.A. 1988), meets from time to time to consider draft rules (formerly prepared by the Counsel to the Lord President (who are also the clerks to the Rules Council)) or to frame them. Acts of Sederunt in the form of statutory instruments are signed by the Lord President (or, in his absence, the Lord Justice-Clerk) in the presence of a quorum of the judges. The procedure for statutory instruments is followed for bringing the Acts of Sederunt into force. Interested persons may submit suggestions for reform of the R.C.S. to the Lord President's Private Office to be considered. The Lord President's Court of Session Procedure Committee occasionally suggested reforms but fell into abeyance when the Rules Review Group was set up: see note 1.1.1. The Group was disbanded after it completed its review of the rules in 1992.

1.1.3

Application

1.2. These Rules apply to any cause whether initiated before or after the coming into force of these Rules.

1.2

---

[1] Chapter heading amended by S.I. 1999 No. 1386 (effective 19th May 1999).

1.2.1

There are no transitional or savings provisions in the rules. In relation to savings, note the effect of ss.16 and 17, by virtue of s.23, of the Interpretation Act 1978 with regard to the revocation of the R.C.S. 1965. There are savings in relation to fees of solicitors, witnesses' fees and shorthand writers' fees in para. 3(5) of the A.S. (R.C.S. 1994) 1994, above, for work done before that A.S. came into force.

Interpretation etc.

1.3

1.3.—(1)[1] In these Rules, unless the context otherwise requires—

"the Act of 1988" means the Court of Session Act 1988;

[2]"the Act of 2014" means the Courts Reform (Scotland) Act 2014;

"act" means an order of the court which is extractable, other than a decree;

"agent", except in rule 16.2(2)(e)(service furth of United Kingdom by party's authorised agent) and rule 16.14(1) (arrestment of cargo), means a solicitor or person having a right to conduct the litigation;

"attend" and "attendance" are construed in accordance with Chapter 12C (mode of attendance at hearings);

"the Auditor" means the Auditor of the Court of Session;

"cause" means any proceedings;

"clerk of court" means the clerk of session acting as such;

"clerk of session" means a depute clerk of session or an assistant clerk of session, as the case may be;

"counsel" means a practising member of the Faculty of Advocates;

"depute clerk of session" means a depute clerk of session and justiciary;

"Deputy Principal Clerk" means the Deputy Principal Clerk of Session;

"document" has the meaning assigned to it in section 9 of the Civil Evidence (Scotland) Act 1988;

"the Extractor" means the Extractor of the Court of Session or the Extractor of the acts and decrees of the Teind Court, as the case may be;

"Keeper of the Records" means the Keeper of the Records of Scotland;

"Keeper of the Registers" means the Keeper of the Registers of Scotland;

"other person having a right of audience" means a person having a right of audience before the court by virtue of Part II of the Law Reform (Miscellaneous Provisions) (Scotland) Act 1990 (legal services) in respect of the category and nature of the cause in question;

"party" means a person who has entered appearance in an action or lodged a writ in the process of a cause (other than a minuter seeking leave to be sisted to a cause); and "parties" shall be construed accordingly;

"period of notice" means—

    (a) in relation to service, or intimation on a warrant for intimation before calling, of a summons, the period determined in accordance with rule 13.4 (period of notice in summonses); and

    (b) in relation to service of any other writ, intimation of a writ other than intimation referred to in sub-paragraph (a), or the period for lodging answers to a writ, the period determined in accordance with rule 14.6 (period of notice for lodging answers);

"person having a right to conduct the litigation" means a person having a right to conduct litigation by virtue of Part II of the Law Reform (Miscellaneous Provisions) (Scotland) Act 1990 in respect of the category and nature of the cause in question;

---

[1] As amended by S.S.I. 2023 No. 168 para. 2 (effective 3rd July 2023).
[2] Definition inserted by S.S.I. 2015 No. 227 para. 2(2) (effective 22nd September 2015).

"Principal Clerk" means the Principal Clerk of Session and Justiciary;

"principal writ" means the writ by which a cause is initiated before the court;

"proof" includes a proof before answer;

"rolls" means the lists of the business of the court issued from time to time by the Keeper of the Rolls;

"send" includes deliver; and "sent" shall be construed accordingly;

"simple procedure case" has the meaning given by section 72(9) of the Courts Reform (Scotland) Act 2014;[1]

"step of process" means a document lodged in process other than a production;

"summons" includes the condescendence and pleas-in-law annexed to it;

"vacation judge" means a judge of the court sitting as such in vacation;

"writ" means summons, petition, note, application, appeal, minute, defences, answers, counterclaim, issue or counter-issue, as the case may be.

(2) For the purposes of these Rules—

(a) "affidavit" includes an affirmation and a statutory or other declaration; and

(b) an affidavit shall be sworn or affirmed before a notary public or any other competent authority.

(3) Where a power is conferred in these Rules on the Lord President to make directions, the power may be exercised in his absence by the Lord Justice-Clerk.

(4) Where a provision in these Rules imposes an obligation on a principal officer, the obligation may be performed in his absence by a clerk of session authorised by him or by another principal officer; and in this paragraph "principal officer" means the Principal Clerk, Deputy Principal Clerk, Deputy Principal Clerk (Administration), Keeper of the Rolls or Principal Extractor.

(5) Unless the context otherwise requires, where a provision in these Rules requires a party to intimate, give written intimation or send a document, to another party, it shall be sufficient compliance with that provision if intimation is given or the document is sent, as the case may be, to the agent acting in the cause for that party.

(6) Unless the context otherwise requires, anything done or required to be done by a party under a provision in these Rules may be done by the agent for that party acting on his behalf.

(7)[2] Where a provision in these Rules requires a document to be lodged in an office or department of the Office of Court within or not later than a specified period and the last day of that period is a day on which that office or department is closed, the period shall be extended to include the next day on which that office or department, as the case may be, is open or on such other day as may be specified in a notice published in the rolls.

(8) Unless the context otherwise requires, a reference to a specified Chapter, Part, rule or form is a reference to the Chapter, Part, rule, or the form in the appendix, so specified in these Rules; and a reference to a specified paragraph, sub-paragraph or head is a reference to that paragraph of the rule or form, that sub-paragraph of the paragraph or that head of the sub-paragraph, in which the reference occurs.

Deriv. R.C.S. 1965, r. 68G (r. 1.3(3)) and r. 168(3) (r. 1.3(2))

---

[1] As inserted by S.S.I. 2016 No. 315 para.2 (effective 28th November 2016).

[2] R. 1.3(7) amended by S.I. 1996 No. 2587 (effective 1st November 1996)

GENERAL NOTE.

1.3.1   Under s.11 of the Interpretation Act 1978, where a statute confers power to make subordinate legisla-tion, expressions used in that legislation have the same meaning as they bear in the Act. Hence, words and expressions in the C.S.A. 1988 (under which Act the R.C.S. 1994 are made) have the same meaning in the R.C.S. 1994 unless a contrary intention appears. Further, in the R.C.S. 1994, words and expres-sions listed in Sched. 1 to the 1978 Act are, unless the contrary intention appears, to be construed accord-ing to that Schedule: Interpretation Act 1978, s.5. Not all words and expressions having special meaning in the R.C.S. 1994, however, are defined in the 1978 Act or the C.S.A. 1988; accordingly, unless the contrary intention appears, those of common application in the R.C.S. 1994 are defined here. Rules may specifically import the meaning of words used in a particular enactment, although not made under that enactment. Particular rules may be made under particular statutes (apart from under the general power in the C.S.A. 1988); and where this is the case, it is not necessary to import the meaning of a word used in that statute. It will not be always readily apparent, however, that a rule has been made under reference to a statute other than the C.S.A. 1988; therefore, the meaning of a word is specifically defined in such a rule by a further interpretation rule where appropriate. Rules made under powers in enactments other than the C.S.A. 1988 can be ascertained from Sched. 1 to the A.S. (R.C.S. 1994) 1994, above.

The words defined by s.51 of the C.S.A. 1988 for the purposes of that Act and the R.C.S. 1994 (unless the context otherwise requires or the R.C.S. 1994 provide otherwise) are as follows: "action", "the court", "enactment", "the Inner House", "the Lord President", "prescribed" and "solicitor". Although "action" is defined as a cause initiated by summons, under the R.C.S. 1994 (a) a cause transmitted or remitted from the sheriff court proceeds as if it had been initiated by summons (r. 32.4(2)) and (b) a peti-tion for suspension, suspension and interdict or suspension and liberation also proceeds as an action (r. 60.5(2)).

"ACT".

1.3.2   An act is an interlocutor that does not contain a decerniture (i.e. the word "decern(s)", which is inserted only where the interlocutor finally determines a part, or the whole, of a cause); and, therefore, is an interlocutory or procedural order.

"DOCUMENT".

1.3.2A   A document is defined by reference to the inclusive definition in s.9 of the Civil Evidence (Scotland) Act 1988.

"PERIOD OF NOTICE".

1.3.3   The period of notice in a summons is the period *before* the last day of which the summons may not be lodged for calling (see r. 13.13(1)), whereas the period of notice in a petition or other writ (for the defini-tion of which (see r. 1.3(1)) is the period *within* which any answers must be lodged.

"OTHER PERSON HAVING A RIGHT OF AUDIENCE" AND "PERSON HAVING A RIGHT TO CONDUCT THE LITIGATION".

1.3.4   A solicitor, under and by virtue of s.25A of the Solicitors (Scotland) Act 1980 (inserted by the Law Reform (Miscellaneous Provisions) (Scotland) Act 1990, s.24), may obtain an extended right of audience to appear (as an advocate) before the court. He also has the right to conduct litigation and instruct counsel: see s.25 of the 1980 Act. The rights of other persons, other than an advocate, to have a right of audience or to conduct litigation (i.e. act as a solicitor) depend on any scheme made in respect of them under s.25 of the 1990 Act: none has been made. "Solicitor" is defined in s.51 of the C.S.A. 1988.

The rule that non-natural or artificial persons, such as companies, firms, etc, must be represented by a practising member of the Faculty of Advocates or a person having a right of audience before the court (i.e. a solicitor advocate) was re-affirmed in *Secretary of State for Business, Enterprise and Regulatory Reform v. UK Bankruptcy Ltd* , 2011 S.C. 115 (Second Div.). The question of what the position would be if a non-natural person could not afford representation was left open. In *Apollo Engineering Ltd (In Liquidation) v. James Scott Ltd* 2012 S.C. 282 (Extra Div), Lady Paton considered that the court had a discretionary power in certain circumstances, provided certain conditions were met (the minimum being those specified in the UK Bankruptcy case, above, paras. [45] and [46]). The majority held that it was compatible with art. 6 of ECHR that a legal person should be legally represented, particularly in an appeal. Section 97 of the Courts Reform (Scotland) Act 2014, however, introduced lay representation of a non-natural person. The rules governing an application to the court for representation by a lay person under s. 97 of the 2014 Act, and for representative's functions, conditions and duties, are in a free-standing A.S., A.S. (Lay Representation for Non-Natural Persons) 2016 [S.S.I. 2016 No. 243]. See Chap. 12B and note 12B.1.1. Presumably, a lay representative of a non-natural person may be given permission to sign a writ on behalf of the non-natural person.

"ROLLS".

1.3.5   The rolls for the court are: (1) The General Roll, consisting of the registers of causes of the (a) General Department (the Ordinary, Admiralty and Commercial, and Family (including Consistorial) Rolls) and (b) the Petition Department. (2) The Daily Rolls—the printed rolls issued each weekday during term showing the causes in the General Roll appearing for business on a particular day, consisting of (a) in the Inner House (i) Single Bills, (ii) By Order Roll, (iii) Summar Roll and (iv) Advisings; and (b) in the Outer House (i) Calling List, (ii) Motion Roll, (iii) Diet Roll, (iv) Commercial Roll, (v) Adjustment Roll (and Continued Adjustment Roll), (vi) By Order (Adjustment) Roll, (vii) By Order Roll, (viii) Procedure

Roll, (ix) Jury Trials, Proofs, Proofs before Answer and Hearings, (x) For Judgment and (xi) Undefended Consistorial Causes (in fact undefended divorce actions). In the Daily Rolls there are also printed notices of Acts of Sederunt, practice notes and other matters of administration. Rolls issued in vacation contain details of (2)(a)(i) and (iv) and (b)(i), (iii)–(xi).

LODGING DOCUMENTS IN A DEPARTMENT OF THE OFFICE OF COURT.

For office hours of the Office of Court and holidays, see note 3.1.2.

1.3.6

"AFFIDAVIT".

An affidavit required by a rule of court or by order of the court is lodged as a step of process. An affidavit not so required is lodged as a production.

1.3.7

On lodging an affidavit as a step of process, see r. 4.4. It may be lodged by post: P.N. No. 4 of 1994, paras. 1 and 8; and see note 4.4.10. On lodging an affidavit as a production, see r. 4.5. A production may be lodged by post: P.N. No. 4 of 1994, para. 1, and see note 4.5.5.

An affidavit should be in the form of a statement of evidence written in the first person. The affidavit should contain evidence in support of, and expanding on, the averments in the pleadings. It should be sworn or affirmed and signed by the deponent before any person who may competently take an oath. Such a person includes a notary, a justice of the peace, a sheriff or any judge (or in England a commissioner for oaths (includes any barrister or solicitor)). The person taking the oath or affirmation should also sign the affidavit. Witnesses are unnecessary. A child under the age of 14 should not swear an affidavit.

Where there are contradictions between affidavits, and no other evidence to support a conclusion one way or another, no conclusion can be drawn by the court: *D v. D* , 2002 S.C. 33, 37D (Extra Div.).

Forms

1.4. Where there is a reference to the use of a form in these Rules, that form in the appendix to these Rules, or a form substantially to the same effect, shall be used with such variation as circumstances may require.

1.4

GENERAL NOTE.

A form should normally be followed, but, as each form does not cover every eventuality, changes may have to be made or more than one version of a form produced: each form is a style.

1.4.1

A form has the same number as the rule to which it relates. Where there is more than one form referred to in a rule the forms are also marked sequentially by letters of the alphabet: e.g. "13.2-A" and so on.

Direction relating to Advocate General

1.5.[1] The Lord President may, by direction, specify such arrangements as he considers necessary for, or in connection with, the appearance in court of the Advocate General for Scotland.

1.5

GENERAL NOTE.

This rule was inserted by A.S. (R.C.S.A. No. 5) (Miscellaneous) 1999 [S.I. 1999 No. 1386] to enable the Lord President to make a direction (if indeed a direction were necessary) providing for where the Advocate General may sit in court. By Direction No. 4 of 1999 the Advocate General shall be entitled, in court, to sit at the table within the Bar immediately below the Bench at the left hand side of the Chair (where the presiding judge sits), i.e. on the right hand side if facing the bench.

1.5.1

By convention the Lord Advocate is entitled to sit on the right hand side of the Chair at the table (i.e. on left if facing the bench). The Solicitor General is entitled to sit on the left hand side of the Chair at the table (i.e. on the right if facing the bench).

---

[1] R.1.5 inserted by S.I. 1999 No. 1386 (effective 19th May 1999) and correctly numbered by S.S.I. 2000 No. 66 (effective 7th April 2000).

CHAPTER 2 RELIEF FROM COMPLIANCE WITH RULES

Relief for failure to comply with rules

2.1.—(1) The court may relieve a party from the consequences of a failure to comply with a provision in these Rules shown to be due to mistake, oversight or other excusable cause on such conditions, if any, as the court thinks fit.

(2) Where the court relieves a party from the consequences of a failure to comply with a provision in these Rules under paragraph (1), the court may pronounce such interlocutor as it thinks fit to enable the cause to proceed as if the failure to comply with the provision had not occurred.

Deriv. A.S. (Rules of Court, consolidation and amendment) 1965, para. (4) [S.I. 1965 No. 321]

GENERAL NOTE.

This rule provides the court with an overriding discretion to excuse a failure to comply with a rule where justice demands in the circumstances. The provision is substantially the same as the words used in para. (4) in the R.C.S. 1948 (in A.S. (Rules of Court, consolidation and amendment) 1948 [S.I. 1948 No. 1691]) and R.C.S. 1965, para. (4) and similar to that in the proviso to R.C.S. 1934 (in A.S. approving and embodying the Rules of Court [S.R. & O. 1934 No. 772]), in which it was first introduced, with this important difference: the phrase "mistake, oversight or other cause, not being wilful non-observance of the same" is replaced by the phrase "mistake, oversight or other excusable cause" (on which see note 2.1.2).

The power has been narrowly construed: "That dispensing power has been scantily applied, and generally where it is thought the novelty of the new procedure, or legitimate doubts as to the changes introduced, partly justified an oversight. Generally it requires for application some overlook or reasonable mistake" (*Richardson v. Ministry of Pensions* 1945 S.C. 363, 370 per Lord Mackay (motion for new trial not enrolled timeously)—R.C.S. 1934). "That discretion is conferred upon the Court not with a view to enabling the Court, wherever it thinks fit, to disregard the express provisions of the Rules. That provision is inserted to deal with some highly special circumstances, which may arise in some unusual case, and this discretion should only very rarely be employed" (*Grieve v. Batchelor and Buckling* 1961 S.C. 12, 16 per L. P. Clyde (late lodging of appeal after expiry of reponing days)—R.C.S. 1948, disapproved in *Grier v. Wimpey Plant & Transport Ltd* 1994 S.C. 385 and not followed in *X v. Galloway R.C.* 1994 S.C. 498). The dispensing power may be less likely to be exercised where there is a peremptory rule or a rule containing its own provision for relief (cf. *Flynn v. Morris Young (Perth) Ltd* 1996 S.C. 255 (relief from r. 37.1(6))). It has been suggested, obiter, in *Robertson v. Robertson's Trs* 1991 S.L.T. 875 that the dispensing power does not apply to R.C.S. 1965, r. 89(f) (now R.C.S. 1994, r. 19.2(2)–(4)), but it is not clear why; and the decision may be doubted: cf. *Thomson v. Omal Ltd* 1994 S.L.T. 705, per Lord MacLean and note 19.2.2. Because r. 37.1(2) (late lodging of proposed issue on cause shown) contains its own provision for granting relief, the court will not exercise the dispensing power in r. 2.1 unless in extraordinary circumstances: *McGee v. Matthew Hall Ltd* 1996 S.L.T. 399.

But it has been more widely construed: "... one finds the meaning of the proviso by paying attention to the words 'not being wilful non-observance of' the Rules. I think that the dispensing power was meant to enable the Court to do justice" (*Dalgety's Trs v. Drummond* 1938 S.C. 709, 715 per L. P. Normand (late lodging of appeal)—R.C.S. 1934); see also *Carroll v. Glasgow Corporation* 1965 S.L.T. 95 (failure to lodge closed record timeously). In *Graham v. John Tullis & Son (Plastics) Ltd (No. 1)* 1992 S.L.T. 507, 509, L.P. Hope said that the power extends to the time within which anything required or authorised to be done shall or may be made or done: in other words it applies not only to obligations imposed by the rules but to permissive powers. In *McDonald v. Kwok* 1999 S.L.T. 593, 595J and 596C, Lord Macfadyen said that the recent trend of authorities has been towards the view that it is always competent to invoke the dispensing power and that the terms of r. 2.1 were wholly unqualified as to the nature of the failure to comply. *McDonald* was overruled in *Brogan v. O'Rourke Ltd* , 2005 S.L.T. 29 (Extra Div.) where it was held that rr. 13.13(6) and 43.3(2) were plain and the meaning of "the instance shall fall" was perfectly understood: where the summons has not called within the specified period the instance falls and it is incompetent to apply to the court under r. 2.1.

There was always an inherent power of the court (superseded by the rule) to depart from the rules where justice demanded: "I doubt greatly whether the Court ... is precluded by any Act of Sederunt from doing what it thinks according to justice and equity in any individual case before it" (*Boyd, Gilmour & Co. v. Glasgow & South Western Railway Co.* (1888) 16 R. 104, 109 per Lord Young (failure to lodge and box prints timeously); see also *Hutcheson v. Galloway Engineering Co.* 1922 S.C. 497 (note of objections to Auditor's report not timeously lodged)). In light of the (earlier) inherent power, the power in this rule should not receive, perhaps, too strict or rigid a construction. The new phrase "mistake, oversight or other excusable cause" may have resolved most of the former difficulties of interpretation and application of the provision: see further, note 2.1.2.

Non-compliance with the Rules is not necessarily to be excused simply because no particular prejudice can be identified. The rules are designed to regulate the general conduct of business, not just to suit the convenience of the parties: *Smith v. Smith* (I.H.), 23rd June 1995, unreported.

It is not usually justifiable to apply a lower standard of compliance with the rules to party litigants than is applied to represented litigants. See *AW, Applicant* [2018] CSIH 25, para. 13 referring to *Barton v.*

Wright Hassall LLP [2018] 1 W.L.R. 1119 (UKSC), paras 18 and 42. In *AW* the question was whether the party litigant's failures to comply with the rules in the court below (the SAC) raised a compelling reason for an appeal under s. 113(2)(b) of the Courts Reform (Scotland) Act 2014; it did not.

The power applies only in relation to the Court of Session rules: *G.A.S. Construction Co. Ltd v. Schrader* 1992 S.L.T. 505; *Graham*, above. It cannot, for example, be used to excuse the failure to comply with a statutory time-limit in other legislation. It has been used where the form of citation in r. 13.7 had not been signed by the process server in England, that rule repeating the requirement of the Citation Acts of 1592 and 1686 (see note 13.7.1).

Where a rule provides a specific relief from its requirements, the court should hesitate to apply the wider power of relief in r. 2.1: *McGee v. Matthew Hall Ltd* 1996 S.L.T. 399 per Lord Caplan. In *Robertson v. Robertson's Trs* , 1991 S.L.T. 875 (OH), Lord Weir held that the dispensing power (now r. 2.1) could not apply where there was a provision containing its own dispensing power (in that case what is now r. 19.2(2)). In *Thomson v. Omal Ltd* , 1994 S.L.T. 705 (OH) Lord MacLean did not agree that exercise of the general dispensing power in r. 2.1 was incompetent in relation to r. 19.2(2) but, since that latter provision contained its own dispensing power the general dispensing power, the general dispensing power could be exercise only in exceptional circumstances. In *Semple Cochrane plc v. Hughes* , 2001 S.L.T. 1121 (OH) Lord Carloway was reluctant to qualify r. 2.1 by reading into it words such as "exceptional or extraordinary circumstances". It was applied in *Little Cumbrae Estate Ltd v. Rolyat1 Ltd,* 2014 S.L.T. 1118 (OH) without there being exceptional circumstances.

The dispensing power in r. 2.1 will not be exercised to allow, without leave, a reclaiming motion which required leave to proceed as that would frustrate the object of the rule requiring leave: *Robertson v. Robertson's Exr* 1991 S.C. 21.

Occasionally an A.S. is passed giving the court a discretion to relieve a party from the consequences of a failure to comply with the provisions of a rule or other enactment as a result of some particular emergency: see, for example, A.S. (Extension of Prescribed Time) 1971 [S.I. 1971 No. 356] (postal strike); A.S. (Emergency Powers) 1972 [S.I. 1972 No. 221] (coalminers' strike; see also A.S. (Suspension of Business) 1979 [S.I. 1979 No. 226] (civil service strike).

"MISTAKE, OVERSIGHT OR OTHER EXCUSABLE CAUSE".

2.1.2 The replacement by this phrase of the phrase "mistake, oversight or other cause, not being wilful non-observance of the same" is intended to deal with the not uncommon situation, not explicitly authorised by the previous rules, of the court granting authority, often in advance, for the deliberate non-observance of a rule because the rule cannot be complied with. The amendment has wider implications than to legitimise such a necessary practice.

In relation to the previous rule, it was held in *Anderson v. British Coal Corporation* 1992 S.L.T. 398 that the dispensing power was normally exercised where there had been an excusable mistake and not where a deliberate decision had been taken.

Ignorance of a rule may be an excusable cause: *Sutherland v. Duncan* 1996 S.L.T. 428 (case concerned the equivalent O.C.R 1993, r. 2.1).

Circumstance where aspect of procedure unsuitable

2.2 **2.2.**—[1](1) Subparagraph (2) applies where, for any reason, the Lord President is of the opinion that an aspect of the procedure which would otherwise apply to particular proceedings, or proceedings of a particular description, is unsuitable for the efficient disposal of those proceedings.

(2)   The Lord President may direct that that aspect of the procedure is not to apply in respect of those proceedings and that such other procedure as he directs is to apply instead.

(3)   Before making such a direction the Lord President must consult—

(a)   in the case of particular proceedings, the parties;

(b)   in the case of proceedings of a particular description, the parties of any proceedings falling within the description which have already been raised.

GENERAL NOTE.

2.2.1 A direction has been made under this rule in relation to actions of damages for and arising from personal injuries or death through taking the drug Vioxx or Celebrex (see Direction No. 2 of 2010); in relation to pleural plaques cases (Direction No. 2 of 2012); in relation to personal injury actions re Watling Street Development (Direction No. 1 of 2013); and in relation to personal injury actions or product liability relating to vaginal tape and mesh (Direction No. 2 of 2015 and No. 2 of 2016).

The vires of this rule is questionable.

---

[1] R. 2.2 inserted by S.S.I. 2010 No. 205 (effective 15th June 2010).

Office of Court

3.1.—(1) The Office of Court shall comprise—

    (a) the General Department,

    (b) the Petition Department,

    (c) the Rolls Department,

    (d) the Extracts Department, and

    (e) the Teind Office;

but shall not include the office of the Accountant of Court or the Auditor.

(2) Each department of the Office of Court shall be under the charge of an officer who shall act under the direction of the Principal Clerk in consultation with the Lord President.

Deriv. A.J.A. 1933, s.24(2); R.C.S. 1965, r. 12(a) (part) and (b) (part)

GENERAL NOTE.

There is provision in s.24 of the Administration of Justice (Scotland) Act 1933 (as originally enacted) for the offices of the court and the business of the departments. This was repeated and extended (the Rolls Department) in the R.C.S. 1965, r.12.

OFFICE HOURS AND HOLIDAYS.

The offices of the court are open during the following hours:

Monday .... 10.30 a.m. to 1 p.m. and 2 p.m. to 4 p.m.
Tuesday to Friday 10 a.m. to 1 p.m. and 2 p.m. to 4 p.m.

The offices are not open on Saturdays, Sundays or on public or local holidays. The public and local holidays during the calendar year are as follows:

New Year's Day (1st January), or the following Monday if on a Saturday or Sunday (bank holiday),
2nd January, or the following Monday (or Tuesday) if on a Saturday (or Sunday) (bank holiday),
Spring Weekend (third Monday in April) (local holiday).
Good Friday (bank holiday),
Easter Monday,
May Day Holiday (first Monday in May) (bank holiday),
Victoria Day (local holiday),
September Weekend (third Monday in September),
Christmas Eve (24th December)—half day,
Christmas Day (25th December), or the following Monday if on a Saturday or Sunday (bank holiday),
Boxing Day (26th December), or the following Monday (or Tuesday) if on a Saturday (or Sunday).

The arrangements for urgent business when the offices are closed are as follows. Telephone the Court of Session (0131-225 2595). The telephone is manned at all times. On telephoning, leave a contact number. The security staff will contact a clerk who will contact you and make the necessary arrangements. At weekends in session there is a rota for stand-by judges. In vacation the vacation judge is the stand-by judge.

ACCOUNTANT OF COURT.

First appointed by s.9 of the Judicial Factors Act 1849 to superintend the conduct of judicial factors, tutors and curators, the office was re-appointed, and the office of Accountant in Bankruptcy was subsumed under it, by ss.1 and 5 of the Judicial Factors (Scotland) Act 1889; but, by s.1 of the Bankruptcy (Scotland) Act 1985, the Accountant of Court is the Accountant in Bankruptcy created under that Act. The Accountant of Court is not, however, an officer of the court.

The duties of the Accountant of Court are:

1.   Injudicial factories—(a) to superintend the conduct of all judicial factors, curators, tutors, guardians and others appointed by the court or the sheriff court to hold, administer and protect property belonging to persons or estates in Scotland and to audit their accounts: Judicial Factors Acts 1849, 1880 and 1889; (b) to superintend factors appointed to administer damages awarded to a child under 16 under r.43.16(a); (c) to prepare an annual report on all judicial factories: 1849 Act, above, s.18.

2.   Formerly in sequestrations as Accountant in Bankruptcy—(a) to supervise interim and permanent trustees and commissioners in their functions, to maintain the register of insolvencies and to prepare an annual report of sequestrations, etc: Bankruptcy (Scotland) Act 1985, s.1(1); (b) to audit accounts of trustees under voluntary trust deeds for creditors where sought:

1985 Act, Sch.5, para. 1; and (c) to receive deposit receipts in respect of unclaimed dividends and unapplied balances: 1985 Act, s.57(1). These functions have been transferred to the Accountant in Bankruptcy: 1985 Act, ss.1, 1A and 1C inserted by the Bankruptcy (Scotland) Act 1993, s.1.

3. In liquidations—to determine the time of the release of liquidators: Insolvency Act 1986, ss.173 and 174 and Insolvency (Scotland) Rules 1986, r.4.25 [SI 1986/1915].

4. In relation to caution—(a) to fix the caution to be found by judicial factors, curators and guardians: r.61.9(3); (b) to receive all bonds of caution lodged in any process: r.33.12(1).

5. In relation to consignation—(a) to receive all monies consigned under order of the court or otherwise: Court of Session Consignations (Scotland) Act 1895, s.3; (b) to receive consignation receipts or other deposits in respect of (i) unclaimed dividends and unapplied balances in judicial factories under his own supervision (Judicial Factors (Scotland) Act 1849, s.35) and in liquidations (Insolvency Act 1986, s.193), and (ii) sums representing consideration for shares acquired under s.430 of the Companies Act 1985 (as substituted by the Financial Services Act 1986, Sch.12) in respect of person who cannot be found after 12 years (s.430(13)); (c) miscellaneous sums held at his discretion; (d) to maintain in the Consignation Book a record of consignations: 1895 Act, above, s.4; and (e) to lodge detailed annual returns with the Lord President: 1895 Act, above, s.9.

6. To make reports on remits from the court.

7. To superintend trusts in relation to arrestment and distribution of trust funds on the order of the court on the application of a trustee: Trusts (Scotland) Act 1921, s.17.

8. To supervise administrators appointed under the Prevention of Terrorism (Temporary Provisions) Act 1989 or the Proceeds of Crime (Scotland) Act 1995.

9. To perform any other special duties imposed by statute: e.g. War Loan (Supplemental Provisions) Act 1915, s.9 (investment of funds under any trade union rules).

THE AUDITOR.

3.1.4   This is the Auditor of the Court of Session: r.1.3(1) (definition of "the Auditor"). See further, r.3.7 and note 3.7.1.

General Department

3.2   **3.2.**—(1) The General Department shall be under the charge of the Deputy Principal Clerk.

(2) There shall be lodged in the General Department all processes in—

(a)   causes originating in the court and initiated by summons or simplified divorce application;

(b)[1]   appeals from inferior courts, remits from the sheriff court and the Sheriff Appeal Court, appeals, including references, submissions and applications of the nature of appeals under statute, stated cases and special cases;

(c)   causes transmitted from the sheriff court on contingency; and

(d)   appeals to the Lands Valuation Appeal Court.

(3) All processes lodged in the General Department shall be classified as—

(a)   ordinary actions;

(b)   Admiralty and commercial actions;

(c)   family (including consistorial) actions; or

(d)   lands valuation causes.

Deriv. A.J.A. 1933, s.24(2) and (3) and C.S.A. 1988, s.6(i) (r.3.2(3)); R.C.S. 1965, rr.12(b) (part) (r.3.2(1)), 13(a) amended by SI 1982/1679 (r.3.2(2)) and 15 (r.3.2(3))

GENERAL NOTE.

3.2.1   The General Department is divided into three sections. The sections are:

A-F

G-Mac

Mad-Z.

A cause is assigned to a particular section according to (a) in the case of an individual, the initial letter of the surname of the pursuer, and (b) in the case of a firm or company, usually the initial letter of the first word where a descriptive name is used or the initial letter of the surname where a proper name is used, of the pursuer.

---

[1] Rule 3.2(2)(b) as amended by S.S.I. 2015 No. 419 para.7(2) (effective 1 January 2016).

Causes originating in the court are commenced by summons except (a) those commenced by petition (see rr.14.2 and 14.3), (b) special cases (see Chap. 77), (c) certain applications and references treated as appeals under various statutes (see note 3.2.3(d)(iii) and (iv)), (d) applications for divorce under the simplified divorce procedure (see r.49.73), and (f) applications (by minute, note or motion) treated as part of the original process.

R. 3.2(2)(H).

3.2.2

(A) Appeals from inferior courts.

(1) The sheriff court:Sheriff Courts (Scotland) Act 1907, s.28 as substituted by the Sheriff Courts (Scotland) Act 1913, s.2 and as amended by the Sheriff Courts (Scotland) Act 1971, Sch.2; 1971 Act, s.38(b) as amended by the Law Reform (Miscellaneous Provisions) (Scotland) Act 1985, s.18(4) (summary causes other than small claims) and s.37(3) as amended by the Law Reform (Miscellaneous Provisions) (Scotland) Act 1980, s.16(c) (appeals *re* remits of ordinary cause to summary cause and vice versa). (2) *The Lyon Court: Cunninghame v. Cunyngham* (1849) 11 D. 1139; Erskine, I.iv.32.

3.2.3

(B) Remits from sheriff court:

1971 Act, above, s.37(b) as amended by the 1980 Act, above, s.16 (ordinary cause), s.37(2A) as amended by the 1980 Act, above, s.16(b) and the Divorce Jurisdiction, Court Fees and Legal Aid (Scotland) Act 1983, Sch.1, para. 12 (actions for divorce or relating to custody or adoption); Presumption of Death (Scotland) Act 1977, s.1(6) (action of declarator), s.4 (variation of declarator).

(C) Appeals, etc., under particular statutes.

1.   *Appeals.* These include—Taxes Management Act 1970, ss.53, 100B(3) and 100C(4) (appeals *re* penalties from General or Special Commissioners); Inheritance Tax Act 1984, s.222 (against determination of Commissioners of Inland Revenue), and ss.249(3) and 251(2) (appeals *re* penalties from Special Commissioners); Oil Taxation Act 1975, s.1 and Sched.2, para. 1 (from Commissioners *re* penalties); Stamp Duty Reserve Tax Regulations 1986 [S.I. 1986 No. 1711], reg.8 (against determination of Commissioners of Inland Revenue); Tribunal and Inquiries Act 1992, s.11 (from VAT Tribunals); Burial Grounds (Scotland) Act 1855, s.10; Sheep Stocks Valuation (Scotland) Act 1937, s.2(2) (from sheriff from arbiter); Pharmacy Act 1954, ss.10 and 24(2) (against directions); Therapeutic Substances Act 1956, ss.2(4) and 6 (from suspension of licence); Teaching Council (Scotland) Act 1965, s.12 as substituted by Standards in Scotland's Schools etc. Act 2000 (appeal against direction *re* registration); Fair Trading Act 1973, s.42 (*re* protection of consumers from Restrictive Practices Court); Consumer Credit Act 1974, s. 41A inserted by Consumer Credit Act 2006, s. 57 (on point of law from Consumer Credit Appeals Tribunal); Control of Pollution Act 1974, s.85 (from sheriff); Restrictive Practices Court Act 1976, s.10(2) (from RPC in proceedings under Pt III of the Fair Trading Act 1973 (*re* protection of consumer)); Licensing (Scotland) Act 1976, s.39(8) (from sheriff from licensing board); Patents Acts: 1949 Act, s.87(3) and 1977 Act, Sched.4 (*re* decision of comptroller under 1949 Act, s.55), 1977 Act, s.97 (from comptroller); Estate Agents Act 1979, s.7(4) (from Secretary of State from Director General of Fair Trading *re* estate agency work); Education (Scotland) Act 1980, s.112(8) as amended by the Education (Scotland) Act 1981, s.1 and Sched.2, para. 3 (from Council *re* issue of practising certificate), ss.16 (from Council *re* restoration to roll) and 54 (from discipline tribunal); Public Passenger Vehicles Act 1981, s.51 (from Secretary of State from Traffic Commissioners); Civic Government (Scotland) Act 1982, s.4 and Sched.1, para. 12 (from sheriff from licensing authority), s.54 and Sched.2, para. 24(12) (from sheriff *re* licence of sex shop), s.64(9) (from sheriff *re* holding of procession), s.88(4) (from sheriff *re* installation of pipes through neighbouring property), s.106(5) (from sheriff *re* notices and expenses under Pt VIII); Representation of the People Act 1983, ss.56 and 57 (from sheriff from registration officer *re* registration to three judges of the court); Medical Act 1983, s.40 as amended by the NHS Reform and Health Care Professionals Act 2002, s.30 (from General Council); Dentists Act 1984, s.29 as amended by the NHS Reform and Health Care Professionals Act 2002, s.31 (appeal from Professional Conduct and Health Committees); Mental Health (Scotland) Act 1984, s.66A (appeal from sheriff); Transport Act 1985, s.117(2) and Sched.4, para. 14(1) (from Transport Tribunal); Legal Aid (Scotland) Act 1986, s.31(4) (*re* exclusion of lawyer from selection in legal aid cases); Building Societies Act 1986, s.49(1) and (2) (from tribunal from B.S. Commission); Banking Act 1987, s.31 (from Banking Appeal Tribunal); Copyright, Designs and Patents Act 1988, s.152(1) (from Copyright Tribunal) and s.251(2) (from Comptroller General *re* design rights); Opticians Act 1989, s.23 as amended by the NHS Reform and Health Care Professionals Act 2002, s.32 (from Disciplinary Committee); Human Fertilisation and Embryology Act 1990, s.21 (*re* determination of licence by HFEA); Environmental Protection Act 1990, s.73 (from sheriff *re* waste on land); Child Support Act 1991, s.25 (from the Child Support Commissioner); Agricultural Holdings (Scotland) Act 1991, s.61 and Sched.7 (from sheriff from arbiter); Social Security Administration Act 1992, ss.18(3) and 58 (from decisions or determinations by the Secretary of State) and 24 (from the SS Commissioner); Local Government Finance Act 1992, s.82(4) (from valuation appeal committee *re* council tax); Friendly Societies Act 1992, s.61 (from tribunal *re* decision of Commission); Tribunal and Inquiries Act 1992, s.11 and Sched.1 (from vari-

ous tribunals); Pension Schemes Act 1993, s.151(4) (from Pensions Ombudsman) and s.173(3) (from Occupational Pensions Board); Osteopaths Act 1993, ss.24 and 25 (against interim suspension order), s.29 (from Registrar); and s.31 as amended by the NHS Reform and Health Care Professionals Act 2002, s.33 (from Professional Conduct Committee); Chiropractors Act 1994, s.31 as amended by the NHS Reform and Health Care Professionals Act 2002, s.34 (from Professional Conduct Committee or appeal tribunal); Trade Marks Act 1994, s.76(2) (from registrar); Drug Trafficking Act 1994, s.45 (from forfeiture order by sheriff); Pensions Act 1995, s.97(3) (from Occupational Pensions Regulatory Authority); Industrial Tribunals Act 1996, s.37(1) (from Employment Appeal Tribunal); Architects Act 1997, s.22 (appeals *re* registration); Nurses, Midwives and Health Visitors Act 1997, s.12 (*re* removal from register); Special Immigration Appeals Commission Act 1997, s.7 (from Special Immigration Appeals Commission); Social Security Act 1998, s.15 (appeal from Social Security Commissioner with leave); Data Protection Act 1998, s.49(6) (on point of law from Data Protection Tribunal); Competition Act 1998, s.49 (on point of law from appeal tribunal); Social Security Act 1998, s.15 (from Social Security Commissioner); Road Traffic (NHS Charges) Act 1999, s.9(2) (on point of law from appeal tribunal); Immigration and Financial Services and Markets Act 2000, s.137(1) (from Financial Services and Markets Tribunal); Terrorism Act 2000, s.6(1) (from Proscribed Organisations Commission); Postal Services Act 2000, s.36(2) (by person aggrieved); Freedom of Information (Scotland) Act 2002, s.56 (from Scottish Information Commissioner on point of law); Proceeds of Crime Act 2002, s.299 (from sheriff); Enterprise Act 2002, s.114 (from Competition Appeal Tribunal); Nationality, Immigration and Asylum Act 2002, s.103 (from Immigration Appeal Tribunal).

2. *References.* These include—Defamation Act 1952, s.4(4) (*re* steps in fulfilment of offer of amends): see r. 54.1; Copyright, Designs and Patents Act 1988, s.251(1) (from Comptroller General) and s.252 (disputes *re* Crown use of designs): see r. 55.14; Social Security Administration Act 1992, ss.18(1) and 58 (from Secretary of State: by stated case by virtue of r. 41.34); Pension Schemes Act 1993, ss.150(7) (from Pensions Ombudsman: by stated case by virtue of r. 41.34) and 173(1) (from Occupational Pensions Board: by stated case by virtue of r. 41.34); Trade Marks Act 1994, s.76(3) (from appointed person); Pensions Act 1995, s.97(1) (from Occupational Pensions Regulatory Authority by stated case by virtue of r. 41.34). Certain references are by petition and are therefore assigned to the Petition Department: see note 3.3.1.

3. *Applications (of the nature of appeals).* These include—Public Order Act 1936, ss.2(3) and 8(2) (*re* property of an association); Acquisition of Land (Authorisation Procedure) (Scotland) Act 1947, s.1 and Sched. 1, para. 15 (*re* validity of compulsory purchase order); Housing (Scotland) Act 1966, ss.36, 38, 43 and Sched. 2, para. 2 (*re* clearance orders); Fair Trading Act 1973, s.85 (*re* default of requirement to give evidence or produce documents to Monopolies and Mergers Commission); Ancient Monuments and Archaeological Areas Act 1979, s.55(1) (*re* validity of designation orders); Wildlife and Countryside Act 1981, ss.29, 34 and Sched. 11, para. 7 (*re* validity of order *re* areas of scientific interest), s.36 and Sched. 12, para. 8 (*re* validity of order *re* marine nature reserves); Civil Aviation Act 1982, Sched. 7, para. 7 (*re* validity of orders); Telecommunications Act 1984, s.18 (*re* orders of Secretary of State); Roads (Scotland) Act 1984, Sched. 2, para. 2 (*re* validity of orders and schemes); Films Act 1985, Sched. 2, para. 9 (from decision of Secretary of State to refuse to certify or to revoke certification for purposes of s.72 of the Finance Act 1982); Gas Act 1986, s.30 (*re* orders of Secretary of State); Petroleum Act 1998, s.42 (from decisions of the Secretary of State); National Heritage (Scotland) Act 1991, Sched. 5, para. 10 (*re* validity of irrigation control order); Railways Act 1993, s.57 (*re* validity of order); Coal Industry Act 1994, s.33 (*re* validity of enforcement order); Town and Country Planning (Scotland) Act 1997, s.238 (*re* validity of structure or local plan), s.239 (*re* validity of other orders, etc.); Planning (Listed Buildings and Conservation Areas) (Scotland) Act 1997, s.58 (*re* validity of orders etc.); Planning (Hazardous Substances) (Scotland) Act 1997, s.20 (*re* validity of decisions) Petroleum Act 1998, s.42 (from decisions of the Secretary of State).

(D) Stated cases.

These include—Stamp Act 1891, s.13 (from Commissioners of Inland Revenue *re* assessment of duty); Taxes Management Act 1970, s.56 (from General or Special Commissioners); Inheritance Tax Act 1984, s.225 (from Special Commissioners); Stamp Duty Reserve Tax Regulations 1986 [S.I. 1986 No. 1711], reg. 10 (from Special Commissioners); Tribunals and Inquiries Act 1992, s.11 and Sched. 1 and Tribunals and Inquiries (Value Added Tax Tribunals) Order 1972 [S.I. 1972 No. 1210] (from VAT Tribunals); Pensions Appeal Tribunal Act 1943, ss.6 and 13 (from PAT); Lands Tribunal Act 1949, s.3(3) (from LT); Agricultural Marketing Act 1958, s.12(2) (from disciplinary committee); Building (Scotland) Act 1959, s. 16(3) (from sheriff); Industrial and Provident Societies Act 1965, s.60(9) (*re* disputes involving registered society); Social Work (Scotland) Act 1968, s.50 (from sheriff from children's hearing); Administration of Justice (Scotland) Act 1972, s.3 (from arbiter); Town and Country Planning (Scotland) Act 1972, s.234 (from Secretary of State in determining planning permission under s.51); Social Security Act 1973, s.86 (from Occupational Pensions Board: by stated case by virtue of r. 41.34); Local Government (Scotland) Act 1973, s.103(2) (on special report to Commission by Controller of Audit); Friendly Societies Act 1974, s.78 (*re* certain disputes); Restrictive Practices Court Act 1976, s.10 (from RPC); Iron and Steel Act 1982, s.26(5)(a) (from Iron and Steel Arbitration Tribunal); Representation of the People Act 1983, s.134(1) (from sheriffs principal who cannot agree *re* election of councillors) and s.146(4) (from election court on admissibility of evidence, etc.); New Roads and Street Works Act 1991, s.158(2) (from arbiter); Social Security Administration Act 1992, ss.18(1) and 58 (from Secretary of

State: by stated case by virtue of r. 41.34); Friendly Societies Act 1992, s.80(4) (from arbiter); Tribunal and Inquiries Act 1992, s.11 and Sched. 1 (from various tribunals).

(E) Special cases.

These include—Compensation (Defence) Act 1939, ss.7 and 18(2) (from Shipping Tribunal or General Tribunal); Crofters (Scotland) Act 1961, s.4(3) (from Land Court); Control of Pollution Act 1974, s.39(8); Representation of the People Act 1983, s.146(1) (from election court); C.S.A. 1988, s.27: see Chap. 77; Scottish Land Court Rules 1992, r. 88 [S.I. 1992 No. 2656].

TRANSMISSION FROM SHERIFF COURT ON CONTINGENCY.

For the meaning of contingency, see note 32.2.3. **3.2.4**

LANDS VALUATION APPEAL COURT.

The appeals to the Lands Valuation Appeal Court are under the following statutory provisions: Lands **3.2.5** Valuation (Scotland) Act 1854, s.24 (as amended by the Railways (Valuation for Rating) Act 1930, s.22(4)) (against valuations of assessors of public undertakings); Lands Valuation (Scotland) Act 1857, as amended by the Valuation of Lands (Scotland) Amendment Act 1867, s.8 and the Valuation of Lands (Scotland) Amendment Act 1879, s.7 (both as amended by the Rating and Valuation (Amendment) (Scotland) Act 1984, s.13) (appeals against entries in valuation roll) (applied to the Rating (Scotland) Act 1926, s.14); Rating and Valuation (Apportionment) Act 1928, s.9(9); Local Government (Scotland) Act 1966, s.22(3); Rating (Disabled Persons) Act 1978, s.4(8); Water (Scotland) Act 1980, s.45(2).

The judges of the Lands Valuation Appeal Court are Lords Gill, Lady Dorrian, Lords Malcolm, Woolman, Tyre and Docherty: A.S. (Lands Valuation Appeal Court) 2013 [S.S.I. 2013 No. 161].

CLASSIFICATION OF GENERAL DEPARTMENT PROCESSES.

Causes initiated by summons are so classified by virtue of the C.S.A. 1988, s.6(i), which provides for **3.2.6** (a) an Ordinary Roll, (b) an Admiralty and Commercial Roll and (c) a Family (including Consistorial) Roll. The classification is determined as follows: (i) an Admiralty cause is one defined by r. 46.1; (ii) a commercial action is one defined by r. 47.1(2); (iii) a family action is one defined by r. 49.1(1) (a consistorial cause is an action between husband and wife involving status); (iv) an ordinary action is any other cause initiated by summons; and (v) a lands valuation cause is an appeal to the Lands Valuation Court: see note 3.2.5.

Petition Department

3.3.—(1) The Petition Department shall be under the charge of the Deputy **3.3** Principal Clerk.

(2) There shall be lodged in the Petition Department all processes in causes which are initiated by petition.

Deriv. A.J.A. 1933, s.24(2); R.C.S. 1965, r. 12(b) (part) (r. 3.3(1)) and r. 13(b) (r. 3.3(2))

PETITION DEPARTMENT PROCESSES.

The processes belonging to the Petition Department are: **3.3.1**

1. Those listed in rr. 14.2 and 14.3.
2. Certain references under particular statutes. These are— Railway and Canal Commission (Abolition) Act 1949, s.1(1): by petition by virtue of r. 14.2(h); Mines (Working Facilities and Support) Act 1966, s.4(3) (grant of right *re* minerals and compensation): by petition by virtue of r. 14.2(h); Defamation Act 1952, s.4(4) (*re* steps in fulfilment of offer of amends where no action for defamation taken): r. 54.2.

PETITION REGISTER.

For the 17 categories of petitions, see note 4.1.5. Petitions are kept and recorded alphabetically ac- **3.3.2** cording to subject-matter but recorded in the Petition register chronologically. To trace a process when the subject-matter under which the process has been recorded is not known the chronological register will have to be searched if the year is known. Alternatively, if there has been a final interlocutor or a year and a day has passed with no interlocutor, a search may be made in the index of processes in the process records department but only where the record number is known and the process is not a judicial factory or liquidation in which there has been no final discharge (r. 9.1(3)). See also note 7.1.5.

Rolls Department

3.4.—(1) The Rolls Department shall be under the charge of the Keeper of the **3.4** Rolls, who shall be assisted by a clerk of session known as the Assistant Keeper of the Rolls.

(2) The Keeper of the Rolls shall be responsible for keeping the rolls of the court in consultation with the Lord President, the Lord Justice-Clerk and the Principal Clerk.

Deriv. R.C.S. 1965, r. 14 (r. 3.4(2))

GENERAL NOTE.

3.4.1   The Rolls Department did not previously exist in name, though the Keeper, and the Assistant Keeper, of the Rolls and the work of the department did.

"ROLLS".

3.4.2   These are the lists of business of the court: r. 1.3(1) (definition of "rolls"). The rolls are: (1) The General Roll, consisting of the registers of causes of the (*a*) General Department (the Ordinary, Admiralty and Commercial, and Family (including Consistorial) Rolls) and (*b*) the Petition Department. (2) The Daily Rolls—the printed rolls issued each weekday during term showing the causes in the General Roll appearing for business on a particular day, consisting of (*a*) in the Inner House (i) Single Bills, (ii) By Order Roll, (iii) Summar Roll and (iv) Advisings; and (*b*) in the Outer House (i) Calling List, (ii) Motion Roll, (iii) Diet Roll, (iv) Commercial Roll, (v) Adjustment Roll and Continued Adjustment Roll, (vi) By Order (Adjustment) Roll, (vii) By Order Roll, (viii) Procedure Roll, (ix) Jury Trials, Proofs. Proofs before Answer and Hearings, (x) For Judgment and (xi) Undefended Consistorial Causes (in fact undefended divorce actions). In the Daily Rolls there are also printed notices of Acts of Sederunt, practice notes and other acts of administration. Rolls issued in vacation contain details of (2)(*a*)(i) and (iv) and (*b*)(i), (iii)–(xi).

Extracts Department

3.5   **3.5.—**(1)   The Extracts Department shall be under the charge of the Principal Extractor who shall be assisted by a clerk of session known as the Extractor.

(2)   The Principal Extractor shall be responsible for extracting the acts and decrees of the court except those in teind causes.

(3)   Subject to rule 3.6(3) (duties of clerk of teinds), the Extractor shall be the Keeper of—

    (a)   the Register of Acts and Decrees;

    (b)   the Register of Edictal Citations and Executions of Diligence; and

    (c)   the Register of Decrees in Consistorial Causes.

(4)   As Keeper of the Register of Edictal Citations and Executions of Diligence, the Extractor shall—

    (a)   record on the copy of the schedule of diligence received by him the date of its receipt at his office;

    (b)   record the details of that schedule and its receipt in the register;

    (c)   preserve that schedule and any citation for a period of three years from the date of receipt of the schedule or citation, as the case may be;and

    (d)   make the register and schedules of diligence and citations executed on him available for inspection at his office during its normal business hours.

Deriv. R.C.S. 1965, r. 12(b) (part) (r. 3.5(1)); Debtors (Scotland) Act 1838, s. 18 and A.S. (Edictal Citations, Commissary Petitions and Petitions of Service) 1971 [S.I. 1971 No. 1165], para. 1(2) and (3) (r. 3.5(4))

GENERAL NOTE.

3.5.1   The business of the extractors was given to one Principal Extractor by the Court of Session (No. 2) Act 1838, s. 18. These officials are now appointed under the Public Records (Scotland) Act 1937, s. 31(1). The duty of the Principal Extractor, with the assistance of the Extractor, is to prepare and issue extracts of the acts and decrees of the court as required. The Extractor of acts and decrees in teind causes is the clerk of teinds: see note 3.6.4(*d*).

DUTIES OF EXTRACTOR.

3.5.2   These are:

    1.   To assist the Principal Extractor in extracting the acts and decrees of the court including decrees of the inferior courts (the sheriff court, Lyon Court and Employment Appeal Tribunal) appealed to the Court of Session and not transmitted back after disposal of the appeal (because no further procedure is necessary in the lower court). In fact, all applications for extracts are made to the Extractor: see r. 7.1(3).

2. To keep the Register of Acts and Decrees of the court: see Public Records (Scotland) Act 1937, s. 31(1). This is transmitted annually to the Keeper of the Records: r. 9.1(1).
3. To receive executions of diligence on persons resident furth of Scotland, whose residence is not known and cannot reasonably be ascertained or on whom diligence cannot otherwise be executed: see r. 16.12(4).
4. To edit and keep the Register of Edictal Citations and Executions of Diligence: r. 3.5(4); and see (A) below and note 3.5.3.
5. To edit and keep the register of decrees of divorce, nullity and dissolution of marriage as Keeper of the Register of Decrees of Consistorial Causes. This register contains decrees dissolving marriage and all other decrees in consistorial causes which used to be recorded in the Minute Book (now no longer kept, having been discontinued in January 1993). The register may be inspected at the Extracts Department.
6. To receive offers in relation to rights of pre-emption of superiors: Conveyancing Amendment (Scotland) Act 1938, s. 9(2).
7. To receive any notices of a requirement to grant a feu right under the Long Leases (Scotland) Act 1954, s. 23(1)(c).
8. To receive notices of calling up or default in relation to standard securities: Conveyancing and Feudal Reform (Scotland) Act 1970, ss. 19(6) and 21(2).

The Extractors are not responsible for the Teind Court Minute Book or for teind extracts, the clerk of teinds being so responsible: see rr. 3.5(2) and 3.6(3).
The Extractor used to have the following duties:

(A) To receive all edictal citations, services and intimations as Keeper of the Register of Edictal Citations: Reorganisation of Offices (Scotland) Act 1928, s. 8. As Keeper, the Extractor (*a*) received citations and orders for service against persons whose whereabouts were unknown under R.C.S. 1965. r. 75A (a procedure discontinued under R.C.S. 1994: see r. 16.5 (service by advertisement)); and (b) received citations, charges, publications and orders for service under para. 1 of the A.S. (Edictal Citations, Commissary Petitions and Petitions of Service) 1971 [S.I. 1971 No. 1165] (revoked by A.S. (R.C.S. 1994) 1994 [S.I. 1994 No. 1443], Sched. 5).
(B) To edit and keep the Minute Book as Keeper of the Minute Book: Reorganisation of Offices (Scotland) Act 1928, s. 8 and the Order as to Transfer of Powers and Duties of the Office of Keeper of Minute Book and Record of Edictal Citations [S.R. & O. 1929 No. 588]. The Minute Book contained the minutes of the judicial business of the court—Acts of Sederunt. Practice Notes, minutes of General, and Petition, Department business including entries of intimations, decrees, acts admitting solicitors and notaries. The Minute Book was compiled weekly and published for subscribers and transmitted annually to the Scottish Record Office. It was discontinued in January 1993 because it was not cost effective and little used.

REGISTER OF EDICTAL CITATIONS AND EXECUTIONS OF DILIGENCE.

Although edictal citation has been abolished for citation of persons furth of Scotland or whose address is not known (see r. 16.5), the register of edictal citations has to be maintained for three years: r. 3.5(4)(c) and (d). Furthermore, although edictal citation has been abolished, a means had to continue to be provided for execution of diligence on such persons. Edictal execution of diligence was retained being the simplest, practical and inexpensive means rather than resort to advertisement. For this purpose edictal execution by executing a document of diligence on the Extractor of the Court of Session is used and for which purpose the Extractor must keep a Register of Edictal Executions of Diligence; after three years from the coming into force of the R.C.S. 1994 there will be no need for a register of edictal citations. The otiose provisions of s. 18 of the Debtors (Scotland) Act 1838 (edictal execution of arrestment) and para. 1(2) and (3) of the A.S. (Edictal Citations, Commissary Petitions and Petitions of Service) 1971 [S.I. 1971 No. 1165], are replaced by r. 3.5(4) and new rules for execution of diligence in r. 16.12.

3.5.3

Teind Office

3.6.—(1) The Teind Office shall be under the charge of a clerk of session known as the clerk of teinds.

3.6

(2) There shall be lodged in the Teind Office all processes which are dealt with by the Teind Court or the Lord Ordinary in teind causes.

(3) The clerk of teinds shall—

(a) keep and index the records and processes in the Teind Office; and

(b) be the Keeper of the Teind Rolls and the Keeper of the Minute Book of the Teind Court.

Deriv. R.C.S. 1965, rr. 12(b) (part) and 13(c) (r. 3.6(2))

TEIND COURT.

The Kirk and Teinds Act 1706 transferred the powers of various commissions appointed to deal with teinds to the Court of Session. The judges of the Inner House and a Lord Ordinary as Lord Ordinary in teind causes, acting in their capacity as Lords Commissioners for teinds, are the judges of the Teind

3.6.1

Court. Any five are a quorum of the Court of Commissioners for Teinds: C.S.A. 1839, s. 8 as amended by C.S.A. 1868, s. 9. Though known as the Teind Court, the court is not a separate court from the Court of Session; and the jurisdiction of the Court of Session sitting as the Teind Court includes the original jurisdiction of the Court of Session: *Presbytery of Stirling v. Heritors of Larbert & Dunpace* (1900) 2 F. 562.

The court meets once a fortnight on a Friday during session (when there is business) at such time as is convenient; the Lord Ordinary in teind causes sits every Friday at 10.00 am (when there is business), the roll of business is made up the preceding Tuesday: Church of Scotland (Property and Endowments) Act 1925, s.41; A.S. Procedure under Church of Scotland (Property and Endowments) Act 1925, s.10, etc. [S.R. & O. 1925 No. 1062], and C.A.S. 1913, H,I,7 [S.R. & O. 1913 No. 638]. The Lord Ordinary in teind causes is currently Lord Bonomy.

JURISDICTION.

3.6.2   The Teind Court has jurisdiction—(a) to modify, settle and appoint teinds and determine all points concerning teinds: Teinds Act 1690; (b) in respect of the teind rolls: Church of Scotland (Property and Endowments) Act 1925, s.11 and Sched. 5, and A.S. Procedure relating to Preparation of Teind Rolls etc., [S.R. & O. 1925 No. 1063]; over valuation and surrender of teinds under the 1925 Act, above, s.16 and Sched. 6; (c) in relation to disjunction and erection of parishes: New Parishes (Scotland) Act 1844, ss. 1–6 and 8–11 and United Parishes (Scotland) Act 1868, ss.2 and 3; (d) in appeals in relation to (i) churches, manses and glebes: Ecclesiastical Buildings and Glebes (Scotland) Act 1868, s.14 and (ii) value of victual stipends: 1925 Act, above, s.2; (e) over the feuing of glebes: Glebe Lands (Scotland) Act 1866; and (f) over the transfer of a glebe to a new parish: United Parishes (Scotland) Act 1876.

PROCEDURE.

3.6.3   (1) In relation to teind rolls, see Church of Scotland (Property and Endowments) Act 1925, s.11 and Sched. 5, and A.S. Procedure relating to Preparation of Teind Rolls, etc. [S.R. & O. 1925 No. 1063]. (2) In relation to other teind causes, see C.A.S. 1913, H, I,III–VII [S.R. & O. 1913 No. 638].

CLERK OF TEINDS.

3.6.4   Originally appointed under the C.S.A. 1821, the clerk is now appointed under the Administration of Justice (Scotland) Act 1933, s.24 and this rule. The duties of the clerk are—(a) to prepare the teind rolls: Church of Scotland (Property and Endowments) Act 1925, s.11 and Sched. 5; (b) to officiate as clerk to the Teind Court: r. 3.6(3); (c) to keep and index the records and processes in the Teind Office: r. 3.6(3); (d) to act as extractor of acts and decrees of the Teind Court: Court of Session (No. 2) Act 1838, s.27. He is Keeper of the Teind Rolls and Keeper of the Minute Book of the Teind Court: r. 3.6(3).

Registers kept by the court[1]

3.6A   **3.6A.** Any register kept by the court, whether or not under or by virtue of these Rules, may be kept either—

3.6A.1   (a)   in documentary form; or

(b)   in electronic form (that is to say in a form accessible only be electronic means).

GENERAL NOTE.

3.6A.2   This new rule, inserted by A.S. (R.C.S.A. No. 2) (Miscellaneous) 1998 [S.I. 1998 No. 2637], will enable the court to put its registers on computer in due course.

The Auditor

3.7   **3.7.** The Auditor shall be responsible for the taxation of accounts of expenses in any cause.

THE AUDITOR.

3.7.1   This is the Auditor of the Court of Session: r. 1.3(1) (definition of "the Auditor"). First appointed by A.S. 6th February 1806, the Auditor was made a permanent official and member of the College of Justice, formerly holding his appointment *ad vitam aut culpam* by s.32 of the C.S.A. 1821. He is now appointed under s.25 of the Administration of Justice (Scotland) Act 1933 until the age of 65 unless extended (1933 Act, s.26).

The duties of the Auditor are:

1.   To tax accounts of expenses in civil causes remitted by the court: rr. 3.7 and 42.1(b)(ii).

2.   To tax accounts incurred to solicitors under (a) the Legal Aid (Scotland) (Fees in Civil Proceedings) Regulations 1989, reg. 9 [S.I. 1989 No. 1490], (b) Criminal Legal Aid (Scotland) (Fees) Regulations 1989, reg. 11 [S.I. 1989 No. 1491] and (c) Legal Aid in Contempt of Court Proceed-

---

[1] R.3.6A inserted by S.I. 1998 No. 2637 (effective 1st December 1998) and numbered correctly by S.I. 1999 No. 1386 (effective 19th May 1999).

ings (Scotland) (Fees) Regulations 1992, reg. 9 [S.I. 1992 No. 1228], if required.

3. To tax accounts incurred to solicitors by (a) judicial factors (see Notes for Guidance of J.F.s by Accountant of Court, n. 14(a)); (b) permanent trustees on sequestrated estates of debtors (see Bankruptcy (Scotland) Act 1985, s.53(2)); and (c) by administrators and liquidators of companies (under the Insolvency (Scotland) Rules 1986, rr. 2.16(3) and 4.32 [S.I. 1986 No. 1915] and applying s.53(2) of the 1985 Act, above; on the interpretation of s.53(2A) of the 1985 Act, see *Rankin, Noter* , 2003 S.L.T. 107 (OH)).

4. To tax accounts incurred in private legislation procedure: Private Legislation Procedure (Scotland) Act 1936, s.6(6).

5. To tax the accounts of returning officers in Parliamentary elections, if required: Representation of the People Act 1949, s.20(7).

6. To fix the remuneration of a receiver where remuneration has not been agreed or is disputed: Insolvency Act 1986, s.58(2).

7. To tax non-legal aid fees of counsel where not agreed under the Scheme for Accounting for and Recovery of Counsel's Fees between the Faculty of Advocates and the Law Society 1987, para. 5(4).

8. To adjudicate on a reasonable fee where counsel's fee is challenged under the Standard Terms for Direct Professional Access to Counsel, para. 3.7.

The Auditor may also tax:

1. Extra-judicial accounts remitted to him with consent of the parties.
2. Accounts incurred to solicitors where client requires.

CHAPTER 4 THE PROCESS

Form, size, etc., of documents forming the process

4.1.—(1) In an action or petition, the principal summons or petition, as the case may be, shall be on a printed form approved by the court, completed in writing, typescript or print and backed with a printed backing approved by the court.

(2) A writ, other than a principal summons or petition, bringing a cause before the court shall be in writing, typescript or print, on paper of a texture and size approved by the court and backed with cartridge paper or paper of similar durability.

(3) A step of process lodged in a cause shall be in writing, typescript or print, on paper of a texture and size approved by the court and, except in the case of a motion, backed with cartridge paper or paper of similar durability.

(4) A step of process other than a motion shall be securely fastened, folded and backed lengthwise and shall bear, on the first page and on the backing, a delimited square for the cause reference number assigned to the principal writ on being lodged.

Deriv. R.C.S. 1965, r. 19

"PRINTED FORM APPROVED BY THE COURT".

The printed forms of summons, petition and respective backings approved by the court are those in the form supplied by HMSO, Oyez Scotland, Clydebank and other stationers in accordance with Forms 13.2-A and 14.4 respectively. Only the first page and the backing are printed; additional pages must be inserted of such paper as is approved by the court—i.e. A4 paper (see note 4.1.3).

Any firm of solicitors wishing to produce forms on a word processor should contact the Deputy Principal Clerk of Session. Agents may now reproduce a facsimile of the Royal Arms in Scotland in order to produce a principal summons or petition.

For an experimental period from 23rd September, 1997, the following provision will apply instead of r. 4.1 (See P.N. No. 2 of 1997):—

(a)   In an action or petition the principal writ or other writ bringing a cause before the court shall be in the appropriate or prescribed form; it and all steps of process, except motion sheets, shall be completed in writing, transcript or print on durable quality paper of A4 size and shall be backed and securely fastened with a two-piece filing clip.

(b)   Motion sheets shall be in A4 size and consist of a backing sheet and two-piece filing clip.

"WRIT".

This means summons (including a condescendence and pleas-in-law annexed to it), petition, note, application, appeal, minute, defences, answers, counterclaim or issue: r. 1.3(1).

"PAPER ... APPROVED BY THE COURT".

A4 paper is now the approved paper and not foolscap. A process will not be accepted except in A4 size paper. There is no specified quality.

"STEP OF PROCESS".

This is any document lodged in process, other than a production (r.1.3(1)), including those listed in r.4.4(1) and any inventory of productions.

"CAUSE REFERENCE NUMBER".

The first part of the reference is a letter determined by the nature of the cause: i.e.:

O = Ordinary;
C = Family, including Consistorial;
A = Admiralty and Commercial; and
P = Petitions.

(The letter "C" has been retained for family actions whether consistorial or not.) Next is a number determined by the chronological order in which a cause is lodged and the year in which it is lodged. In the case of actions there follows the year in which the cause is lodged.

In the case of petitions, before the year is the number of the category of the petition in the petition register. The categories are:

1 — Inner House *nobile officium*;	8 — Entails;
	9 — Outer House company petitions;
2 — Curatories and Factories;	10 — Inner House company petitions;

4.1

4.1.1

4.1.2

4.1.3

4.1.4

4.1.5

3 — Adoptions;

4 — Custody of children;

5 — Sequestrations;

6 — Outer House trust petitions;

7 — Suspensions, and Interdict;

15 — Admission of solicitors;

16 — Admission of notaries;

17 — Admission of Advocates.

11 — Petitions by trustees for directions and variation of trusts;

12 — Other Outer House petitions (e.g. judicial review);

13 — Other Inner House petitions;

14 — Dissolution of marriage (now obsolete as such causes are by action);

Petitions are filed alphabetically, however, in one of the following categories according to subject-matter:

(a) Curatories and Factories;
(b) Inner House;
(c) Company;
(d) Outer House.

Signature of documents

4.2   **4.2.**—(1) Subject to paragraph (5), each page of a summons and the condescendence and pleas-in-law annexed to it shall be signed by an agent.

(2) Subject to paragraph (5), a letter passing the signet shall be signed by an agent.

(3) Subject to paragraphs (5) and (9), a petition, note, application or minute shall be signed by counsel or other person having a right of audience, except that—

    (a) a petition for the sequestration of the estates of the petitioner, or for recall of his sequestration, may be signed by the petitioner or an agent;

    (b) a petition for suspension, suspension and interdict or suspension and liberation may be signed by an agent;

  (bza)[1] an application in Form 26A.5 or Form 26A.8 may be signed by the applicant or an agent;

  (ba)[2] an application in Form 40.2 or Form 41A.2 may be signed by the applicant or an agent;

    (c) a simplified divorce application under rule 49.73 shall be signed by the applicant;

  (ca)[3] a petition in Form 58.3 which requires to be lodged urgently and where counsel or other person having a right of audience, as the case may be, is unavailable to sign, may be signed by an agent if—

    (i) the agent adds a docquet to the petition providing the name of the agent and confirming that the agent signed the petition on behalf of and with the authority of that counsel, or other person having a right of audience; and

    (ii) there is lodged with the petition a declaration by counsel or other person having a right of audience that he or she authorised the agent named to sign the petition as it required to be lodged urgently and that counsel or other person having a right of audience was unavailable to sign;

---

[1] Rule 4.2(3)(bza) as inserted by S.S.I. 2020 No. 208 para.2(2) (effective 31 July 2020).
[2] Rule 4.2(3)(ba) as inserted by S.S.I. 2016 No. 102 para.2(2) (effective 21 March 2016).
[3] Rule 4.2(3)(ba) as inserted by S.S.I. 2019 No. 293 (effective 16th October 2019).

(cc)[1]   a petition in Form 61.2 shall be signed only by the Accountant of Court;

(d)   an application for registration under Chapter 62 (recognition, registration and enforcement of foreign judgments, etc.) may be signed by the petitioner or an agent;

(dd)[2]   a petition by the Council of the Law Society of Scotland for a person's admission as (either or both)—

    (i)   a solicitor;

    (ii)   a notary public,

    may be signed by any officer of the Society who is authorised by the Council to do so; and

(e)   a minute for variation of custody may be signed by a party litigant.

(f)[34]   [...]

(4)[5] Subject to paragraphs (9) and (10), defences, answers and other writs (other than appeals) not referred to in paragraphs (1), (2) and (3), shall be signed by counsel or other person having a right of audience, or, in the case of a party litigant, the party litigant.

(5) Where a party litigant is unable to obtain the signature of counsel or other person having a right of audience or an agent on a document as required by paragraph (1), (2) or (3), he may request the Deputy Principal Clerk to place the document before the Lord Ordinary for leave to proceed without such signature; and the decision of the Lord Ordinary shall be final and not subject to review.

(6) Where the Lord Ordinary grants leave to proceed under paragraph (5), the interlocutor granting leave shall be written and signed on the face of the document and the party litigant shall sign the document.

(7) Where an agent signs a document under this rule, he shall append to his signature his business address—

(a)   in the case of a summons, at the end of the first page and on the last page after the pleas-in-law; and

(b)   in the case of any other document, at the end of the last page.

(8)[6] Where a writ has been signed—

(a)   by counsel;

(b)   by a person having a right of audience; or

(c)   on behalf of and with the authority of counsel or other person having a right of audience in accordance with paragraph (3)(ca),

he or she is to be regarded as the drawer of it and answerable for what it contains.

(9) The following documents shall not require any signature—

(a)   a minute of amendment;

(b)   answers to a minute of amendment;

(c)   a minute of sist;

(d)   a minute of transference;

(e)   a minute of objection to a minute of transference;

(f)   a note of objection.

(10)[7] Paragraph (3)(ca) applies in respect of answers requiring to be lodged under rule 58.6(1), subject to the following modifications—

---

[1] Rule 4.2(3)(cc) inserted by S.I. 1997 No. 1720 (effective 1st August 1997).

[2] Rule 4.2(3)(dd) inserted by S.I. 1997 No. 3059 (effective 23rd December 1997).

[3] Rule 4.2(3)(f) inserted by S.I. 2014 No. 371 (effective 11th January 2015).

[4] Rule 4.2(3)(f) revoked by S.S.I. 2022 No. 329 para. 2 (effective 1st December 2022).

[5] Rule 4.2(4) as amended by S.S.I. 2019 No. 293 (effective 16th October 2019).

[6] Rule 4.2(8) as substituted by S.S.I. 2019 No. 293 (effective 16th October 2019).

[7] Rule 4.2(8) as substituted by S.S.I. 2019 No. 293 (effective 16th October 2019).

(a)   the reference to "petition in Form 58.3"; and

(b)   the references to "petitions",

are to be read as references to "answers requiring to be lodged under rule 58.6(1)".

Deriv. R.C.S. 1965, r. 28(1) amended by S.I. 1991 No. 2483 (r. 4.2(3), (4) and (8)), r. 28(2) inserted by S.I. 1991 No. 2483 (r. 4.2(9)), r. 73(a) amended by S.I. 1991 No. 2483 (r. 4.2(1) and (7)),r. 73(b) (r. 4.2(2)), r. 193 amended by S.I. 1986 No. 514 and 1991 No. 2483 (r. 4.2(3) and (4).

SIGNATURE.

4.2.1

(1) A party litigant may *not* normally sign (a) a summons, (b) a letter passing the signet, or (c) a petition for suspension, suspension and interdict, suspension and liberation, or a petition under the Bankruptcy (Scotland) Act 1985 other than one for his own sequestration or recall of that sequestration: but see r. 4.2(5) for exception and note 4.2.8. He may sign any other writs. (2) An agent (i.e. a solicitor or a person having a right to conduct litigation: see r. 1.3(1)) may *not* sign (a) a simplified divorce application for the applicant or (b) a writ required to be signed by counsel under r. 4.2(3) and (4). (3) Counsel may not sign (a) a summons, (b) a letter passing the signet or (c) a simplified divorce application for the applicant. (4) Special kinds of petitions may be signed only by a particular officer: see r. 4.2(3)(ce) and (dd).

Rule 4.2(3)(ca) allows an agent to sign a petition for judicial review where counsel or other person having a right of audience is unavailable to sign it.

A minute which concludes part or the whole of a cause may only be signed by counsel or other person having a right of audience (for the meaning of which see r. 1.3(1)); it cannot be signed on his behalf. Such a minute is a minute of abandonment, tender, acceptance or joint minute.

"AGENT".

4.2.2

This means a solicitor or a person having a right to conduct the litigation: see r. 1.3(1) (definition of "agent") and note 1.3.3. "Solicitor" is defined in s. 51 of the C.S.A. 1988.

"LETTER PASSING THE SIGNET".

4.2.3

There were latterly two kinds of letters passing the signet to note (letters of loosing of arrestments were rare as recall or restriction is usually sufficient and in any event are now abolished by s. 171 of the Bankruptcy and Diligence etc. (Scotland) Act 2007). These were:

1.   Letters of inhibition. Letters were required for (a) inhibition in security for a future or contingent debt (unless sought in a depending family action: for which, see now s.19 of the Family Law (Scotland) Act 1985 and r. 49.7) where there are special circumstances, e.g., the debtor is *vergens ad inopiam or in meditatione fugae* or putting away his funds to avoid fulfilling his obligations (*Symington v. Symington* (1875) 3 R. 205); (b) on a document of debt except possibly where the document is registered for execution; (c) inhibition on the dependence of an action in the sheriff court; and (d) inhibition in execution of a decree of the sheriff court or a decree of the Court of Session where inhibition was not sought on the dependence. Letter of inhibition will soon be no longer competent in the Court of Session; decrees and extracts of documents registered in the Books of Council and Session or in sheriff court books will authorise inhibition; and inhibition on the dependence in an action in the sheriff court may now be obtained in that court: 2007 Act, s. 146 and Debtors (Scotland) Act 1987, s. 15A. Inhibition on the dependence of an action in the Court of Session is now obtained by motion: See Chap. 14A.

2.   Letters of arrestment. Letters are required (for arrestment in security) for a future or contingent debt (unless sought in a depending family action: for which, see now s.19 of the Family Law (Scotland) Act 1985 and r. 49.7) where there are special circumstances (see (1) above). Letters will be required on a document of debt not registered for execution. Letters of arrestment on the dependence of an action (in security) are rare because an arrestment may be applied for by motion (Chap.14A) or on a counterclaim (r. 25.2(1)) or third party notice (r. 26.3(1)). Letters in execution are rare as the warrant in the extract decree can be relied on: r. 7.10 and note 7.10.2.

Letters of inhibition or arrestment with warrant are obtained by application under r. 59.1. There may then be execution of the letters under r. 16.12. Letters of inhibition with warrant, once obtained, may be registered in the Register of Inhibitions and Adjudications under ss. 155 and 156 of the Titles to Land Consolidation (Scotland) Act 1868.

"COUNSEL".

4.2.4

This means a practising member of the Faculty of Advocates: r. 1.3(1) (definition of "counsel").

"OTHER PERSON HAVING A RIGHT OF AUDIENCE".

4.2.5

See r. 1.3(1) (definition) and note 1.3.4.

"PARTY LITIGANT".

4.2.6

In the Court of Session only a natural person in his own cause may be a party litigant. A company, firm, other artificial entity or non-natural person may not be a party litigant: see *Gordon v. Nakeski-Gumming* 1924 S.C. 939, 941–942 per L.P. Clyde; *Equity and Law Life Assurance Society v. Tritonia Ltd*

1943 S.C.(H.L.) 88; such artificial persons must be represented by a practising member of the Faculty of Advocates or other person having a right of audience (i.e. a solicitor advocate with a right of audience before the Court of Session).

The rule that non-natural or artificial persons, such as companies, firms, etc, must be represented by a practising member of the Faculty of Advocates or a solicitor advocate was reaffirmed in *Secretary of State for Business, Enterprise and regulatory reform v. UK Bankruptcy Ltd* , 2011 S.C. 115 (Second Div.). The question of what the position would be if a non-natural person could not afford representation was left open. In *Apollo Engineering Ltd (In Liquidation) v. James Scott Ltd*, 2012 S.C. 282 (Extra Div), Lady Paton considered that the court had a discretionary power in certain circumstances, provided certain conditions were met (the minimum being those specified in the UK Bankruptcy case, above, paras. [45] and [46]). The majority held that it was compatible with art. 6 of ECHR that a legal person should be legally represented, particularly in an appeal. Section 97 of the Courts Reform (Scotland) Act 2014, however, introduced lay representation of a non-natural person. The rules governing an application to the court for representation by a lay person under s. 97 of the 2014 Act, and for representative's functions, conditions and duties, are in a free-standing A.S., A.S. (Lay Representation for Non-Natural Persons) 2016 [S.S.I. 2016 No. 243]. See further note 12B.1.1.

For rules for law support for party litigants, see Chap. 12A; for lay representation of party litigants, see Chap. 12B.

"WRIT".

This means summons (including a condescendence and pleas-in-law annexed to it), 4 petition, note, application, appeal, minute, defences, answers, counterclaim or issue: r. 1.3(1) (definition of "writ").   **4.2.7**

LEAVE FOR PARTY LITIGANT TO PROCEED WITHOUT SIGNATURE.

A party litigant may normally not sign for certain documents such as a summons, letter passing the   **4.2.8**
signet and other writs: see r. 4.2(1), (2) and (3) and note 4.2.1. It was acknowledged in *Rennie v. Murray* (1850) 13 D. 36 that if counsel would not sign a petition the petitioner might apply to the court; but no procedure was mentioned or ever laid down. R. 4.2(5) introduces a procedure allowing a party litigant to seek leave of the court to proceed although he has not been able to obtain the necessary signature. A process is not required at this stage: see r. 4.3. Once leave has been obtained the interlocutor will be written on the face of the document and the party litigant must then sign it and, if he wishes to proceed, present the document in the appropriate department for registration and, where appropriate, signeting together with any necessary process. The document will be checked, against a copy of the original placed before the Lord Ordinary for leave to proceed, before it is registered.

The rule does not indicate what test the court would apply in considering whether to grant leave. The court may well wish to be satisfied that (a) there is a prima facie case, (b) the signature of counsel or agent has been unsuccessfully sought (for which the court may require documentary evidence) and (c) the litigant has not been declared a vexatious litigant under the Vexatious Actions (Scotland) Act 1898. Para. (b) was confirmed in *G, Ptnr.*, 2015 S.L.T. 461 (Extra Div.).

Where the party litigant is a vexatious litigant he must also seek leave to proceed with the proceedings by virtue of s.1 of the 1898 Act. An application for such leave is made by presenting the proposed writ to the Deputy Principal Clerk who puts it before the Lord Ordinary in chambers. A process is not required at this stage: see r. 4.3. A decision by the Lord Ordinary to refuse leave is final: 1898 Act, above, s.1A (inserted by the Law Reform (Miscellaneous Provisions) (Scotland) Act 1980, s.19). This application for leave may be dealt with at the same time as an application for leave to proceed without a signature of counsel or agent. On vexatious litigants, see further note 14.3.12.

"FINAL AND NOT SUBJECT TO REVIEW".

The decision of the Lord Ordinary may not be reclaimed against.   **4.2.9**

DOCUMENTS NOT REQUIRING SIGNATURE.

The documents listed in r. 4.2(9) which formerly required to be signed are accompanied by a motion.   **4.2.10**
As certain motions and any document accompanying it may be faxed (see r. 23.2), the original document will not be lodged where the motion is faxed; and for this reason these documents need not be signed.

For minutes of amendment and answers to a minute of amendment, see r. 24.2. For minutes of sist, see r. 31.1. For minutes of transference, see r. 31.2. For minutes of objection to minutes of transference, see r. 31.2(2)(b). A note of objection may be lodged in relation to a report of the Auditor (r. 42.4) or to a state of funds or scheme of division prepared by a judicial factor in a factory on the estate of a deceased person (r. 61.26(1)).

Applications for leave under section 1 of the Vexatious Actions (Scotland) Act 1898

4.2ZA.[1](1)   This rule applies where a person ("the applicant") who is the subject   **4.2ZA**
of an order under section 1 (power of Court of Session to prohibit institution of ac-

---

[1] Rule 4.2ZA as inserted by S.S.I. 2017 No. 131 (effective 1st June 2017).

tion without leave) of the Vexatious Actions (Scotland) Act 1898(a) seeks leave under that section to institute legal proceedings.

(2) The applicant must apply for leave by letter addressed to the Deputy Principal Clerk.

(3) The letter must—

  (a) state the full name and address of the applicant;

  (b) be accompanied by a copy of the document by which it is proposed to institute legal proceedings;

  (c) set out briefly why the applicant considers that leave should be granted;

  (d) set out details of any previous application for leave which relates to any extent to the same matter (including, in particular, the outcome of such applications).

(4) The Deputy Principal Clerk must—

  (a) in a case where the applicant has previously submitted an application for leave in relation to the same matter and that application has been refused, reject the application and notify the applicant accordingly;

  (b) otherwise, place the application before a Lord Ordinary.

(5) The Lord Ordinary may, without a hearing, make an order granting or refusing the leave sought.

(6) The interlocutor of the Lord Ordinary is to be sent to the applicant by letter at the address given in the application.

(7) An interlocutor of a Lord Ordinary granting leave to institute legal proceedings constitutes permission to proceed without a signature under rule 4.2(5) (signature of documents).

GENERAL NOTE.

4.2ZA.1 Section 1 of the Vexations Actions (Scotland) Act 1898 provided that the Lord Advocate could apply to either Division of the Inner House for an order, if he satisfies the court that any person has habitually and persistently instituted vexatious legal proceedings without any reasonable ground for instituting such proceedings, whether in the Court of Session or in any inferior court, and whether against the same person or against different persons, that no legal proceedings shall be instituted by that person in the Court of Session or any other court unless he obtains the leave of a judge sitting in the Outer House that such legal proceeding is not vexatious, and that there is prima facie ground for such proceeding.

The 1898 Act was repealed by the Courts Reform (Scotland) Act 2014 but orders made under the 1898 Act continue to have effect: Courts Reform (Scotland) Act 2014 (Commencement No. 7, Transitional and Savings Provisions) Order 2016 [S.S.I. 2016 No. 291].

Applications under section 100 (vexatious litigation orders) of the Courts Reform (Scotland) Act 2014

4.2A **4.2A.**[1](1) This rule applies where a person ("the applicant") who is the subject of an order under section 100 (vexatious litigation orders) of the 2014 Act seeks permission under section 101(4) of the 2014 Act to—

  (a) institute civil proceedings; or

  (b) take a specified step in specified ongoing civil proceedings (within the meaning of section 100 of the 2014 Act).

(2) The applicant may apply for permission only by letter addressed to the Deputy Principal Clerk.

(3) The application must—

  (a) state the full name and address of the applicant;

  (b) where permission is sought to institute civil proceedings, be accompanied by a copy of the document by which it is proposed to institute proceedings;

---

[1] Rule 4.2A inserted by S.S.I. 2016 No. 229 (effective 28th November 2016).

    (c)   an where permission is sought to take a step in ongoing proceedings—
          (i)   state the step the applicant wishes to take;
         (ii)   be accompanied by copies of any documents in the process of those proceedings which the applicant considers relevant to the permission sought;
    (d)   state briefly why the applicant considers that permission should be given;
    (e)   include details of any previous application under section 101 of the 2014 Act which relates to any extent to the same matter (including, in particular, the outcome of such applications).

   (4)   The Deputy Principal Clerk must—
    (a)   in a case where the applicant has previously submitted an application under section 101 of the 2014 Act in relation to the same matter and that application has been refused, reject the application and notify the applicant accordingly;
    (b)   otherwise, place the application before a Lord Ordinary.

   (5)   The Lord Ordinary may, without a hearing, make an order granting or refusing the permission sought.

   (6)   The interlocutor of the Lord Ordinary is to be sent to the applicant by letter at the address given in the application.

   (7)   An interlocutor of a Lord Ordinary granting permission to initiate proceedings constitutes permission to proceed without a signature under rule 4.2(5) (signature of documents).

GENERAL NOTE.

   Under s. 100 of the Courts Reform (Scotland) Act 2014, the Inner House may, on the application of the Lord Advocate, make a vexatious litigation order in relation to a person which may provide that the vexatious litigant may institute civil proceedings only with the permission of a judge of the Outer House and, or, take a specified step in specified ongoing civil proceedings (which must be specified in the order) only with such permission. The order may be for a fixed period or indefinitely.   **4.2A.1**
   Under s. 101(1) of the 2014 Act, the Inner House may make a vexatious litigant order if satisfied that a person "has habitually and persistently, without any reasonable ground for doing so (a) instituted vexatious civil proceedings, or (b) made vexatious applications to the court in the course of civil proceedings (whether or not instituted by the person)." In *Lord Advocate v. Aslam*, [2019] CSIH 17 (Second Div.), para. [10] Lady Dorrian, LJ-C, stated "it is not enough for an individual to be classed as a vexatious litigant that actions which he has instituted, or applications made, have not succeeded or been abandoned: it is not persistent failure which is the key, rather that the failure in question has been based on there being no merit even to commence the litigation or make the application. The critical finding will be that repeated litigation sand applications have failed for reasons of competence, irrelevance and the like. It is the fact that repeated actions were commenced with there being no reasonable grounds for doing so which can render them vexatious". In *Lord Advocate v. Politakis*, 2021 S.L.T. 1321 (Extra Div.), it was held that there were two questions to be asked: (1) has the s. 100 test been met and (2) is it in the interests of justice to exercise the court's discretion?

Lodging of processes

   4.3.   A process shall be lodged in every cause commenced by summons or petition when—   **4.3**
    (a)   in the case of a summons, the summons is presented for signeting; and
    (b)   in the case of a petition, the petition is presented to the Petition Department;
except that the foregoing provisions of this rule shall not apply where the petition is in Form 61.2.[1]

   Deriv. P.N. No. 3 of 1976, para. 3(i).

---

[1] Rule 4.3 amended by S.I. 1997 No. 1720 (effective 1st August 1997).

4.3.1   A process is required for causes commenced by summons or petition. A summons is presented when lodged for signeting and registration (r. 13.5(3)); a petition, when presented for lodging in the Petition Department. A process is also required in other causes such as appeals.

The agent for the pursuer or petitioner should write his reference on the backing of the principal writ in order to improve communications between him and court staff: see Notice, 11th December 1987 (pp. 2001 et seq.).

A process or step of process may be lodged by post: P.N. No. 4 of 1994, paras 1 and 8.

For an experimental period from 23rd September, 1997, the following provision will apply instead of r. 4.3 (see P.N. No. 2 of 1997):—

(a)   A process shall be lodged in every cause commenced by summons or petition when—
    (i)   in the case of a summons, the summons is presented for signeting; and
    (ii)   in the case of a petition, the petition is presented to the Petition Department.

(b)
    (i)   Subject to (b)(ii) below, a black process box shall be lodged by the agent for the pursuer or petitioner
        •   along with the Open Record prescribed by rule of court 22.1 in a cause commenced by summons or
        •   within 3 days of answers having been intimated in a cause commenced by petition.

    (ii)   A red process box shall be lodged by the agent for the pursuer
        •   within 3 days of defences having been intimated in a Commercial Action or
        •   along with the Open Record prescribed by rule of court 22.1 in any cause relating to Intellectual Property.

(c)   A process box shall conform to the following specification:
    (i)   of durable plastic with secure fastener;
    (ii)   depth 245 mm x width 60 mm x height 330 mm;
    (iii)   with space for names of parties and a finger hole on its spine.

Steps of process

4.4   **4.4.**—(1) A process shall include the following steps of process—
    (a)   an inventory of process;
    (b)   the principal writ;
    (c)   an interlocutor sheet;
    (d)   a motion sheet; and
    (e)   a minute of proceedings.

(2) A step of process referred to in paragraph (1), other than the principal writ, shall contain at least two pages.

(3) A step of process shall be assigned a number of process which shall be marked on the backing with the cause reference number of the principal writ and recorded in the inventory of process.

Deriv. R.C.S. 1965, r. 20 (r. 4.4(1) and (2)); r. 78(d) amended by S.I. 1990 No. 705, and r. 194 (r. 4.4(3))

4.4.1   When a process is lodged (that is, when a summons is presented for signeting or a petition is presented) it must include the steps specified in this rule. A duplicate inventory of process and a certified copy summons are no longer required: it was rarely completed and the latter is no longer acceptable as a substitute for a principal writ which has been lost; although it was relied on by the clerks of court if the principal had been borrowed. Additional pages may be added to the steps mentioned in r. 4.4(1) as required.

A step of process may be lodged by post: P.N. No. 4 of 1994, paras 1 and 8; and see note 4.4.10.

For an experimental period from 23rd September 1997, the following provision will apply instead of r.4.4 (see P.N. No. 2 of 1997):—

(a)   The process shall include the following steps enumerated thus:
    (1)   the principal writ;
    (2)   certified copy principal writ;
    (3)   the interlocutor sheets;
    (4)   a motion sheet;
    (5)   a minute of proceedings;
    (6)   *(number reserved for pursuer's productions)*
    (7)   *(number reserved for defender's productions)* an inventory of process.

(b)   A step of process referred to in paragraph 2(a) above other than the principal writ, certified copy writ and motion sheet shall contain at least 2 pages.

(c)   A step of process shall be assigned a number corresponding to (a) above where appropriate or another number consecutive thereto and said number shall be marked on the backing along with the cause reference number and recorded in the inventory of process.

"STEP OF PROCESS".

This is any document lodged in process, other than a production (r. 1.3(1)), including those listed in r. 4.4(1) and any inventory of productions.   **4.4.2**

"INVENTORY OF PROCESS".

In this inventory there is listed every step of process lodged (together with its number of process in the margin). Details of productions lodged with an inventory of productions are not given, merely their number (e.g. "9 Inventory of productions and 6 writs"). The first five entries in the inventory of process (Nos 1–5 of Process), and any other step in the process when it is first lodged, are entered by the pursuer (the first four in a petition by the petitioner); thereafter all entries are made by the clerks of session. In this inventory there are written the receipts for any paper borrowed and the marking of any paper returned: r. 4.12.   **4.4.3**

"PRINCIPAL WRIT".

This means the writ by which a cause is initiated before the court: r. 1.3(1) (definition of "principal writ").   **4.4.4**

"INTERLOCUTOR SHEET".

In the interlocutor sheet the clerk of court writes the orders of the court, and each of these is then signed: see rr. 4.15 and 4.16 on interlocutors.   **4.4.5**

"MOTION SHEET".

To the motion sheet there is appended any application to the court for any order not made at the Bar: see r. 23.2.   **4.4.6**

"MINUTE OF PROCEEDINGS".

In the minute of proceedings the clerk of court keeps a record of hearings, proofs, etc., in the cause, including the time taken, the counsel who addressed the court, the witnesses led and whether the judge made avizandum. Other information may be inserted at the request of the court or parties, e.g. the terms of an undertaking given.   **4.4.7**

"NUMBER OF PROCESS".

The inventory of process has no number. The principal writ is number 1 of process and (during the experimental period mentioned in note 4.4.1) the certified copy principal writ is number 2, the interlocutor sheet is number 3, the motion sheet is number 4 and the minute of proceedings is number 5. Subsequent steps of process lodged are numbered consecutively.   **4.4.8**

While an inventory of productions is numbered consecutively with other steps of process, the productions in it are numbered from "1" prefixed by the number of the inventory (e.g. 5/1): P.N. No. 4 of 1994, para. 8(1).

"CAUSE REFERENCE NUMBER".

See r. 4.1(4) and note 4.1.5.   **4.4.9**

STEPS OF PROCESS LODGED BY POST.

A step of process may be lodged by post: P.N. No. 4 of 1994, para. 1. Where a step of process is lodged by post the party lodging it must contact the appropriate section of the General Department or the Petition Department to ascertain the correct number of process and mark the step of process accordingly before posting it: P.N. No. 4 of 1994, para. 8(3).   **4.4.10**

FEES.

A court fee for lodging a step of process may be payable. For fee, see Court of Session etc. Fees Order 1997 [S.I. 1997 No. 688, as amended, pp.C1201 et seq.]. Certain persons are now exempt from fees: see the 1997 Fees Order, art.5 substituted by S.S.I. 2002 No. 270. A fee exemption certificate must be in existence in process: see P.N. No.1 of 2002.   **4.4.11**

Where the party enrolling a motion is represented, the fee may be debited under the credit scheme introduced on 1st April by P.N. No.4 of 1976 to the account (if one is kept or permitted) of the party's agent by the court cashier, and an account will be rendered weekly by the court cashier's office to the agent for all court fees due that week for immediate settlement. Party litigants, and agents not operating the scheme, must pay (by cash, cheque or postal order) at the time of lodging at the counter of the appropriate department.

Productions

4.5

4.5.—(1) On each occasion a production is lodged in process—

    (a) an inventory of productions shall be lodged in process; and

    (b) a copy of the inventory of productions shall be sent to every other party.

(2) A production shall be—

    (a) marked with a number of process with the cause reference number assigned to the principal writ; and

    (b) if consisting of more than one sheet, securely fastened together.

Deriv. R.C.S. 1965, r. 25

"LODGED IN PROCESS".

4.5.1

A production may be lodged by hand, or by post (P.N. No. 4 of 1994, paras. 1 and 8). For lodging a production by post, see note 4.5.5. For faxing productions in support of motions, see r. 23.2 and note 23.2.9.

"INVENTORY OF PRODUCTIONS".

4.5.2

The inventory has its own number of process and productions lodged with it are numbered within it from "1" prefixed by the number of the inventory (e.g. 9/1): P.N. No. 4 of 1994, para. 8. The numbers of the productions must also be marked in the inventory in the margin beside the description of the production. Only a copy of the inventory is required to be delivered to any other party (who may borrow up the productions to peruse or copy: see r. 4.12).

For an experimental period from 23rd September, 1997, the following provision will apply instead of r. 4.5 (See P.N. No 2 of 1997):—

    (a)   On each occasion a production is lodged in process:

        (i)   an inventory of productions shall be lodged in process; and

        (ii)   a copy of the inventory of productions shall be sent to every other party.

    (b)   A production shall be:

        (i)   marked with a number of process with the cause reference number assigned to the principal writ; and

        (ii)   if consisting of more than one sheet, securely fastened together.

    (c)   Productions should be numbered as follows:

        (i)   where there is only one pursuer, all pursuer's productions will be assigned number 6 of process and will be numbered consecutively thereafter e.g. 6/1-6/x;

        (ii)   where there is only one defender, all defender's productions will be assigned number 7 and will be numbered consecutively thereafter e.g. 7/1-7/x;

        (iii)   where there are further pursuers/defenders another number of process will be assigned to each and productions should be enumerated as at (i) and (ii) above.

In a defended action the back of the backing of the inventory must be docquetted with the word "Intimated" as evidence of intimation to the other parties required under r. 4.6.

"SENT".

4.5.3

This includes delivered: see r. 1.3(1) (definition of "send").

"CAUSE REFERENCE NUMBER".

4.5.4

See r. 4.1(4) and note 4.1.5.

PRODUCTIONS LODGED BY POST.

4.5.5

A production may be lodged by post: P.N. No. 4 of 1994, para. 1. Where a production is lodged by post the party lodging it must contact the appropriate section of the General Department or the Petition Department to ascertain the correct number of process and mark the inventory of productions and the productions accordingly before posting them: P.N. No. 4 of 1994, para. 8(3).

REDACTION OF PRODUCTIONS.

4.5.6

There is no privilege attaching to "sensitive commercial information". While there is no objection to redacting that kind of information, care must be taken against unnecessary redaction which, if it caused delay to the proceedings, could result in expenses against the redacting party: *Alliance Trust Savings Ltd v. Currie* [2016] CSOH 154, 2017 S.C.L.R. 685.

Intimation of steps of process

4.6

4.6.—(1) A party lodging a step of process shall—

    (a) give written intimation of the lodgment of it to every other party; and

    (b) subject to any other provision in these Rules, send a copy of the step of process lodged to every such party.

(2) A clerk of session shall not mark a step of process as received until a certificate of intimation has been endorsed on it.

Deriv. R.C.S. 1965, r. 21 (r. 4.6), r. 83(d) (r. 4.6(1)(b))

General note.

Formerly it was not necessary to deliver a copy of the step of process to every other party as well as intimating the lodgment, though it has been the practice to do so. The practice is now the rule.   **4.6.1**

"step of process".

This is any document lodged in process, other than a production (r. 1.3(1)), including those listed in r.   **4.6.2**
4.4(1) and any inventory of productions.

"written intimation".

For method see r. 16.9.   **4.6.3**

"subject to any other provision".

Not less than four copies of an open record (r. 22.1(a)) and six copies of a closed record (r. 22.3(2)(a))   **4.6.4**
must be delivered to each other party; and four copies of an open record after a third party notice (r.
26.7(1)(b)).

"send".

This includes deliver: r. 1.3(1) (definition of "send").   **4.6.5**

"certificate of intimation".

The back of the step of process is marked (docquetted) "Intimated" followed by the date of intimation.   **4.6.6**

Lodging of documents in Inner House causes

4.7.[1](1)   A party, on lodging in a cause in the Inner House—   **4.7**

   (a)   a petition or note,
   (b)   an appeal, stated case, special case, case, reference or submission,
   (c)   answers,
   (d)[2, 3]   a reclaiming print required under rule 38.5(2) (reclaiming prints for reclaiming motions),
   (e)   a print of the whole pleadings and other documents required under r. 39.1(4) (print of pleadings, etc., for motion for new jury trial),
   (f)[4]   an appeal print required under rule 40.7(2)(b) (appeal print in appeal from inferior court), or
   (g)[5]   an appendix required under rule 38.19 (lodging of appendices in reclaiming motions), 39.8 (lodging of appendix) or 40.19 (lodging of appendices in appeals),

shall lodge in process three copies of the document.

(1A)   A party, on lodging an application for leave to appeal in the Inner House, must—

   (a)   lodge in process a copy of the application; and
   (b)   unless otherwise agreed, send a copy to every other party.

(1B)   A party who has lodged an application for leave to appeal in the Inner House must, if notified by a clerk of session that the application will be dealt with by a Division of the Inner House under rule 37A.2(3), lodge in process two additional copies of the application within the period of 7 days beginning with the date of notification.

---

[1] Rule 4.7 amended by S.S.I. 2016 No. 102 para. 2(3) (effective 21 March 2016).
[2] Rule 4.7(d) amended by S.I 1996 No. 1756 (minor correction).
[3] Rule 4.7(1)(d), (f), and (g) amended by S.S.I. 2010 No. 30 (effective 5th April 2010).
[4] Rule 4.7(1)(d), (f), and (g) amended by S.S.I. 2010 No. 30 (effective 5th April 2010).
[5] Rule 4.7(1)(d), (f), and (g) amended by S.S.I. 2010 No. 30 (effective 5th April 2010).

(2)[1] Where a party intends to refer to a document, other than one mentioned in paragraph (1), at a hearing before a Division of the Inner House, he shall lodge three copies of it in process by 12 noon on the second sitting day before the hearing.

(3)[2] Unless rule 37A.2(3) applies, where a party intends to refer to a document (other than the application itself) at a hearing on an application for leave to appeal, the party shall lodge a copy of it in process by 12 noon on the second sitting day before the hearing.

Deriv. R.C.S. 1965, r. 26(b)

COPIES OF DOCUMENTS FOR INNER HOUSE.

4.7.1   As well as the principal, six copies of a document listed in this rule must be lodged. One copy is for the Scottish Council of Law Reporting (*Session Cases*), one for W. Green & Son Ltd (*Scots Law Times*), three are for the court (it is rare now for four judges to sit in a Division) and one is the process copy.

"REFER TO A DOCUMENT".

4.7.2   Only four copies of documents to be referred to other than those mentioned in rule 4.7(1) must be lodged: but note the terms of rule 4.8 on documents which do not conform to a standard.

Copies of documents for use of court

4.8   **4.8.**—(1) A clerk of session shall refuse to accept a copy of a document for the use of the court which does not conform to a standard approved by the court in size, spacing, lettering, legibility, quality of paper or otherwise.

(2) A party tendering a document which is refused by a clerk of session shall have the right to appeal in writing to the Deputy Principal Clerk.

(3) Where the Deputy Principal Clerk refuses an appeal under paragraph (2), he may extend the time for lodging the document.

(4) A decision of the Deputy Principal Clerk under this rule shall be final and not subject to review.

Deriv. R.C.S. 1965, r. 26(a)

GENERAL NOTE.

4.8.1   The right of appeal against the refusal of a copy has rarely been exercised. This may be because the clerks have not been rigorous in refusing illegible copies rather than because copies have been perfect.

"FINAL AND NOT SUBJECT TO REVIEW".

4.8.2   The decision cannot be appealed, reduced or otherwise reviewed by the court.

Documents ordered or allowed to be lodged

4.9   **4.9.**—(1) Where the court pronounces an interlocutor ordering or allowing a document to be lodged in process, it shall specify a time within which the document shall be lodged.

(2) The time for lodging a document referred to in paragraph (1) may be prorogated by the court on an application by motion enrolled before the time for lodging has expired.

(3) A document lodged in process, in terms of an interlocutor ordering or allowing it to be lodged, shall have marked on it—

(a)   the date of the interlocutor ordering or allowing it to be lodged;

(b)   the date of any interlocutor prorogating the time originally allowed; and

(c)   the time allowed for lodging it.

Deriv. R.C.S. 1965, r. 27

---

[1] R. 4.7(2) amended by S.S.I. 2017 No. 414 r. 3(2) (effective 1st January 2018).
[2] R. 4.7(3) amended by S.S.I. 2017 No. 414 r. 3(2) (effective 1st January 2018).

The opportunity for prorogating the time to lodge a document only arises where an interlocutor has been pronounced specifying a time within which that document must be lodged. It does not normally apply, therefore, to the lodging of defences, where the time for the lodging of which depends on r. 18.1(2) and not on an interlocutor. **4.9.1**

The former rule stated that cause must be shown for an extension of time. The requirement to show cause has been omitted from the rule as it did not accord with current practice. It does not follow, however, that the court may not require cause to be shown in a particular case, as prorogation is in the discretion of the court.

Application to lodge a document late must be made by motion to the court under r. 2.1(1) (relief for failure to comply with rules).

"MOTION".

For motions, see Chap. 23. **4.9.2**

DATE OF INTERLOCUTOR.

It is no longer necessary to set out the interlocutor prescribing the time for lodging the document: only the date of the interlocutor(s) and the time for lodging are required. **4.9.3**

Receipt of documents

4.10.—(1)   Subject to paragraph (2), a clerk of session shall mark the date of receipt on every document lodged in process other than a production. **4.10**

(2)   A clerk of session shall not accept, or mark as received, a document after the day on which it is due to be lodged.

Deriv. R.C.S. 1965, r. 29

GENERAL NOTE.

The time for lodging a document may be prorogated: see r. 4.9(2). Application to lodge a document late must be made by motion to the court under r. 2.1(1) (relief for failure to comply with rules). **4.10.1**

Documents not to be borrowed

4.11.—(1)   Subject to paragraph (2), a writ shall remain in the Office of Court and shall not be borrowed from process, but may be inspected by any person having an interest. **4.11**

(2)   Paragraph (1) shall not apply to—

    (a)   *[Revoked by S.S.I. 2008 No. 122 (effective 1st April 2008).]*

    (b)   a party borrowing his principal writ for the purpose of service or intimation; or

    (c)   a party borrowing his writ for the purpose of writing on it and authenticating an amendment which has been made.

(3)   The following steps of process shall not be borrowed from process—

    (a)   the inventory of process;

    (b)   the interlocutor sheet;

    (c)   the motion sheet;

    (d)   the minute of proceedings;

    (e)   any inventory of productions;

    (f)   the principal copy of a report ordered by the court and lodged in process;

    (g)   the principal or any copy of a bond of caution or a consignation receipt lodged in process; and

    (h)   the principal copy of any other document by which an order of the court to find caution or give security is satisfied and lodged in process until the order is recalled.

Deriv. R.C.S. 1965, r. 31(a) (r. 4.11(1) and (2))

GENERAL NOTE.

While all writs lodged may be inspected, r. 4.11(2) provides for only two situations in which they may be borrowed: (*a*) to have a principal writ served or intimated by a messenger-at-arms (r. 16.3); and (*b*) to write on the writ, e.g. a restriction of a conclusion (r. 7.3), a minute of election of expenses (r. 42.16, Table of Fees, Chap. III, Pt. I, para. 1) or an amendment (r. 7.3) before extract; and to authenticate any **4.11.1** amendment (e.g. initialling by counsel). A certified copy interlocutor, for arrestment to found jurisdiction, in rem or to dismantle a ship (r. 13.8A), on the dependence (r. 14A.2), is required where diligence is to be done after allowance of a counterclaim on that counterclaim (r. 25.2(1) and (5)), or on a third party notice (r. 26.3(1) and (3)). A defender or respondent may not (now) borrow the principal writ on entering the process; there was never any need to do so: borrowing the summons prevented the pursuer from obtaining a decree in absence when defences were not lodged timeously.

Documents other than writs may be borrowed except the steps of process in r. 4.11(3). Documents no longer require to be borrowed for transmission to the Auditor for taxation as the process is transmitted by the clerks of session.

No document or step of process may be borrowed after final extract: r. 4.13.

"WRIT".

4.11.2   This means summons (including a condescendence and pleas-in-law annexed to it), petition, note, application, appeal, minute, defences, answers, counterclaim or issue: r. 1.3(1) (definition of "writ").

"ANY PERSON HAVING AN INTEREST".

4.11.3   A party to the cause has an interest. Whether other persons have a sufficient interest is in the discretion of the Principal Clerk. The phrase might include a person who could be called in the cause. It is unlikely it would include a person, merely seeking information for the purposes of another cause, for whom there are procedures for recovery of documents in Chap. 35.

"PRINCIPAL WRIT".

4.11.4   This means the writ by which a cause is initiated before the court: r. 1.3(1) (definition of "principal writ").

DOCUMENTS NOT TO BE BORROWED.

4.11.5   The principal copy of a report ordered by the court must remain in process; copies may be borrowed or made available. Bonds of caution and consignation receipts may not be borrowed but the principal of each is transmitted to the Accountant of Court and may be uplifted on discharge: see r. 33.12.

"STEP OF PROCESS".

4.11.6   This is any document lodged in process, other than a production (r. 1.3(1)), including those listed in r. 4.4(1) and any inventory of productions.

Borrowing and returning documents

4.12   **4.12.**—(1)   A party borrowing a document which may be borrowed shall give a receipt for it, dated and signed, on the inventory of process.

(2)   Subject to paragraph (3), before a clerk of session accepts a document for return to process, he shall—

   (a)   compare it with the inventory of process and receipt in the presence of the person returning it, delete the receipt and initial and date the deletion; or

   (b)   in the case of a partial return, mark on the inventory of process the document so returned and initial and date the entry.

(3)   Where the document being returned is bulky so that it cannot be examined conveniently at the time—

   (a)   a clerk of session shall not accept the document without a separate slip accompanying it, dated and signed by the party returning it, specifying the number of process so returned; and

   (b)   the clerk of session receiving it shall examine it before the close of the following business day and give written intimation to the party returning it of any inaccuracy in the slip accompanying it.

(4)   Where written intimation is not given under paragraph (3)(b), the accuracy of the slip shall be presumed and the party returning the document shall be exonered as if the receipt had been deleted under paragraph (2)(a) or marked under paragraph (2)(b), as the case may be.

(5)   A party returning more than one document shall ensure that the documents returned are arranged in consecutive order according to the inventory of process; and a clerk of session may refuse to accept documents which are not so arranged.

(6)   The court may, on the motion of a party, ordain any other party who has borrowed a document to return that document within such period as the court thinks fit.

Deriv. R.C.S. 1965, r. 32(a) (r. 4.12(1) to (4)) and 32(6) (r. 4.12(5))

"WRITTEN INTIMATION".

For methods, see r. 16.9.   **4.12.1**

Finally extracted processes not to be borrowed

4.13. No step of process may be borrowed after a final extract has been issued.   **4.13**

GENERAL NOTE.

The reason for this rule is that the court is functus after final extract and the process must remain with   **4.13.1**
the Extractor for subsequent transmission to the Keeper of the Records under r. 9.1. It may be retransmitted to the Office of Court from the Keeper: r. 9.2(1).

"STEP OF PROCESS".

This is any document lodged in process, other than a production (r. 1.3(1)), including those listed in r.   **4.13.2**
4.4(1) and any inventory of productions.

FINAL EXTRACT.

This is a final extract of an interlocutor which concludes the cause, leaving nothing to be done, and   **4.13.3**
after which the court is functus (*Taylor v. Jarvis* (1860) 22 D. 1031, 1034 per L.J.-C. Inglis) except for
the possible rectification of errors (see note 7.9.2). See also notes 4.15.2(2) and 7.1.2(2).

Lost documents

4.14.—(1) Where—   **4.14**

    (a)   a principal writ,

    (b)   other pleadings, or

    (c)   an interlocutor sheet,

is lost or destroyed, a copy of it may be substituted which is proved in the cause to
the satisfaction of the court and authenticated in such manner as the court thinks fit.

(2) A copy of a document substituted under paragraph (1) shall be equivalent to
the original for the purposes of the cause and the process of which it forms a part,
including the use of diligence.

Deriv. R.C.S. 1965, r. 23

GENERAL NOTE.

Application to substitute a copy for a lost document is made to the court by motion. The court is usu-   **4.14.1**
ally satisfied on the explanation made at the Bar. Authentication is normally a signed certification on each
page that the substituted document is a true copy. A copy of any citation, notice or intimation sent with
any writ lost and which was served or intimated should also be produced.

This rule and R.C.S. 1965, r. 23 are derived from s.15 of the C.S.A. 1868 which was repealed by the
C.S.A. 1988 as superseded by the rule.

Outer House interlocutors

4.15—[1](1) This rule applies to interlocutors pronounced in the Outer House.   **4.15**

(2) Subject to paragraphs (3) and (3A), an interlocutor pronounced by the Lord
Ordinary may be written by the clerk of court and shall be signed by the Lord
Ordinary.

(3) Subject to any direction he may be given by the Lord Ordinary, a depute
clerk of session may sign an interlocutor, other than a final interlocutor, in respect of
a motion which is not starred; and that interlocutor shall be treated for all purposes
as if it had been signed by the Lord Ordinary.

(3A) Subject to any direction he may be given by the Lord Ordinary, an assistant
clerk of session may sign an interlocutor, other than a final interlocutor, in respect of
a motion which is intimated and enrolled in accordance with Part 2 of Chapter 23
and which is not starred; and that interlocutor shall be treated for all purposes as if it
had been signed by the Lord Ordinary.

(4) An interlocutor may be signed during session or in vacation.

---

[1] R. 4.15 amended by S.S.I. 2009 No. 387 (effective 1st February 2010 otherwise).

(5)   An extract of an interlocutor which is not signed in accordance with the provisions of this rule shall be void and of no effect.

(6)   An interlocutor may, on cause shown, be corrected or altered at any time before extract by—

(a)   the Lord Ordinary who signed it or on whose behalf it was signed; or

(b)   in the event of the death, disability or absence of the Lord Ordinary, any other judge of the court.

Deriv. R.C.S. 1965, r. 30(1) substituted by SI 1984/472 (r. 4.15(2) and (5)), r. 30(2) substituted by SI 1984/472 and amended by SI 1986/1937 (r. 4.15(6)), r. 30(3) substituted by SI 1984/472 (r. 4.15(4)), and r. 93A inserted by SI 1978/799 and amended by SI 1984/472 (r. 4.15(3))

GENERAL NOTE.

4.15.1   Interlocutors are minutes (see *Clark & Macdonald v. Bain* (1895) 23 R. 102, 104) of the official expressions of all orders of the court; where an extract is issued, the extract becomes the official expression. Originally, "interlocutor" meant an incidental order; the interlocutor determining a cause being called a decree: Stair, IV.46.2. Nowadays, and in the R.C.S. 1994, "interlocutor" is used for all orders of the court. A finding of the court not made in the form of an order is not an interlocutor: *Ranken v. Ranken* 1971 S.L.T. (Notes) 55 (entry in interlocutor sheet of findings sought on construction of an agreement not an interlocutor).

CLASSIFICATION OF INTERLOCUTORS.

4.15.2   A distinction has to be made between interlocutory orders (interlocutory decrees or incidental orders), interim decrees and final decrees. The distinction between interlocutory orders and final decrees is of importance (*a*) because, as a general rule, no motion can be made to the court after final decree (the principal exceptions being (i) to correct an error and (ii) to refer the cause to an opponent's oath) and (*b*) to ascertain whether leave is required to reclaim or to appeal to the House of Lords. It should be noted that all interlocutors are "final" in the Outer House: C.S.A. 1988, s.18.

1.   An interlocutory order (interlocutory decree or incidental order) is one pronounced before the final decision disposing of the merits and expenses of the cause and is usually procedural. Many of these may be reclaimed against only with leave of the court: see r. 38.3(5); but there are a number of exceptions: see r. 38.3(4). In relation to appeal against interlocutory judgments to the House of Lords, see s.40 of the C.S.A. 1988.

2.   A final decree or interlocutor is one, taken by itself or along with previous interlocutors, by which the whole subject-matter of the cause is disposed of: formerly C.S.A. 1868, s.53. It has been authoritatively decided that the whole subject-matter of the cause is disposed of when both the merits and the question of expenses have been determined, though expenses may not have been taxed or decerned for: *Baird v. Barton* (1882) 9 R. 970 (subject-matter of cause includes expenses); *Burns v. Waddell & Co.* (1897) 24 R. 325 (interlocutor which did not deal with expenses not an interlocutor disposing of whole subject-matter of the cause and could not be reclaimed against without leave); *Caledonian Railway Co. v. Corporation of Glasgow* (1900) 2 F. 871 (as also reserved expenses). Subject to the correction of errors (see note 4.15.5) the decree is not capable of alteration (*U.C.B. Bank plc v. Dundas & Wilson, C.S.* 1990 S.L.T. 90) and further motions in relation to expenses cannot be entertained (*Henderson v. Peeblesshire C.C.* 1972 S.L.T. (Notes) 35; *Wilson v. Pilgrim Systems plc* 1993 S.L.T. 1252). Since 1983, in a cause in which the person liable for the expenses is not legally aided there are usually two interlocutors at the conclusion of a cause (or wherever expenses are dealt with): one disposing of the merits and the other decerning for expenses as taxed, the latter being strictly the last or final decree. An interlocutor awarding expenses against a non-legally aided party has a decerniture pronounced at the time the finding of expenses is made. Where a party liable in expenses is legally aided there is no decerniture when the finding is made: a finding of liability in expenses is made with a remit to the Auditor to tax and report. A decerniture is only made thereafter, after consideration of any objections or applications for modification. The reason for the difference in the case of a legally aided party is that it is not competent to modify expenses after decerniture: *Gilbert's Tr. v. Gilbert* 1988 S.L.T. 680 (modification incompetent after decerniture for expenses). The court is, as a general rule, bound to determine expenses when giving judgment on the merits; though it may do so later if, for instance, expenses are reserved (in which case the interlocutor is not final). An interlocutor, or the rules, may reserve to the parties the right to make further applications to the court (e.g. in cases of custody or aliment of children), in which case such an interlocutor cannot be a final decree and any extract is only an interim extract: *Sanderson v. Sanderson* 1921 S.C. 686, 692 per L.P. Clyde.

Final decrees are classified as follows: (*a*) decrees in absence: i.e. those pronounced against a defender who has not entered appearance or lodged defences (see r. 19.1); and (*b*) decrees *in foro contentioso* ("in a defended action"), i.e. decrees pronounced after defences have been lodged, including a decree by default (Court Act 1672, art. 19; and see further r. 20.1). Decrees in absence are not, and decrees *in foro* (except a decree of dismissal) are, res judicata. Note that a decree in absence may become a decree *in foro*: r. 19.1(7)). Final decrees may also be classified as (i) of dismissal (where the cause as laid is put out of court but is not res judicata), (ii) of absolvitor (a decree *in foro* in favour of the defender on the merits which is res judicata), (iii) of condemnator (a decree *in foro* against a defender which is res judicata) and (iv) a mixed decree of more than one of (i)-(iii) and a decree of refusal of a petition (for interdict): *Luxmoore v. The Red Deer Commission* 1979 S.L.T. (Notes) 53 (equivalent to decree of absolvitor). On res judicata, see note 18.1.4(B)(5).

3. An interim decree is one which (*a*) makes some interim provision until the merits of the cause are determined (e.g. interim aliment or interim interdict) or (*b*) decides part of the merits (e.g. for payment of an admitted part of a debt): *Crawfurd v. Ballantine's Trs.* (1833) 12 S. 113.

SIGNATURE.

An interlocutor is merely a minute of the judgment pronounced intended for use in preparing an extract. No authentication is necessary other than the judge's signature (or that of the clerk, where permitted): *Clark & Macdonald v. Bain* (1895) 23 R. 102, 104; though a correction ought to be initialled. Where an essential interlocutor is not signed, any extract is void: *Smith v. McAuley & Co.* (1846) 9 D. 190. The date of a decree is the date when it was signed: *Cruickshank v. Williams* (1848) 11 D. 601, 614 (date of signature different from date of interlocutor).

Whenever an interlocutor is pronounced it may be signed during session, or in vacation: r. 4.15(4).

4.15.3

SIGNING OF UNSTARRED MOTIONS.

The signing of interlocutors in unstarred motions by depute clerks of session was introduced by A.S. (R.C.A. No.5) (Depute Clerks of Session) 1978 [SI 1978/799] (as amended by A.S. (R.C.A. No.2) (Miscellaneous) 1984 [SI 1984/472]) to facilitate the expedition of business. Signature by assistant clerks of session was introduced by A.S. (R.C.S.A. No. 8) (Motions Procedure) 2009 [S.S.I. 2009/387].

In fact interlocutors on unstarred motions granting interim aliment or the approval (and authentication) of issues and counter-issues are signed by the Lord Ordinary. In practice any interlocutor seen by the Lord Ordinary before signing will be signed by him.

For motions which are unstarred, see notes 23.2.15 and 23.2.17.

4.15.4

CORRECTION OF INTERLOCUTORS BEFORE EXTRACT.

This does not include clarifying an ambiguity in a previous interlocutor: *Davidson & Syme W.S. v. Booth* 1971 S.L.T.(Notes) 11. It has been observed by Lord Penrose in *Laing v. Scottish Arts Council* 2000 S.L.T. 338, 341F (OH) that the former statement here, citing *Campbell v. Campbell* 1934 S.L.T. 45 as authority for the proposition that the power to correct did not apply to a motion for expenses not timeously made, is wrong and that *Campbell* is not authority for that proposition. Formerly at common law an interlocutor could be modified only if application was made *de recenti*: *Kennedy v. Clyde Shipping Co. Ltd* 1908 S.C. 895 (motion made some six weeks after interlocutor refused), *Bruce v. Bruce* 1945 S.C. 353; and not even then when the interlocutor has been acted upon if there would be prejudice. It would appear that now delay is just one of the factors to be taken into account, along with prejudice, in determining whether to allow correction: *Martinez v. Grampian Health Board* , 1995 S.C. 428; though the new rule merely repeats the old and the court appears to have overlooked the rule that a re-enactment does not change the law. In *Laing*, above, Lord Penrose distinguished between the word "corrected" in r.4.15(6), which implied that the interlocutor contained or reflected an error, and the word "altered" in r.4.15(6) which carries no such implication and that an interlocutor could be "altered" at least *de recenti* where there was a mistake. In that case the mistake was that the defender9s counsel forgot to move for expenses from the date of the tender when the pursuer unexpectedly accepted the tender during a proof and moved for expenses to the date of the tender. It is not clear that "altered" is intended to be so different from "corrected". The latter clearly deals with a clerical error; but "altered" is intended to deal with an error of expression that would require more than correcting a word. Lord Penrose appeared to open up again the argument whether the rule replaces the common law or whether the rule and the common law exist side by side. But Lord Penrose was overruled by an Extra Division: *Laing v. Scottish Arts Council* , 2001S.C. 493.

The general rule is that a Lord Ordinary cannot alter the substance of a prior interlocutor. Clerical errors may be corrected: *Hope v. Hamilton* (1851) 13 D. 1268 (wrong date of trust disposition). The rule is not limited to clerical errors (see dicta of L.P. Dunedin in *Kennedy*, above) and applies to errors of expression; however, although errors or mistakes in figures or expression may be corrected, a judgment cannot be altered in substance after it has been pronounced: *Cuthill v. Burns* (1862) 24 D. 849, 859 per L.J.-C. Inglis; *Campbell v. James Walker Insulation Ltd* 1988 S.L.T. 263; *Walker v. Walker (No. 2)* 1990 S.L.T. 248 *Laing v. Scottish Arts Council* , 2001 S.C. 493 (Extra Div.). In *Laing*, at p.498H para. 14, the Inner House confirmed that the intention of the rules is to give power to bring an interlocutor into line with the court's original intention: "[T]he limited changes which are envisaged in this context are changes which, like correction, will not involve any departures from what the court was trying to do when it issued the interlocutor." In *Burke v. Harvey* 1916 2 S.L.T. 315 a correction was made where there had been an oversight in seeking expenses for the pursuer's agent as agent disburser (to which he would have been entitled); but in *Bailey, Petrs* 1969 S.L.T.(Notes) 70, a motion to recall an interlocutor pronounced in ignorance of the existence of an interested party was refused as not being a mere mistake of fact (cf. *Rottenburgh v. Duncan* (1896) 24 R. 35 (interlocutor pronounced on undertaking in ignorance of circumstances making its fulfilment impossible)). In *Finlayson v. Turnbull, (No. 2)* 1997 S.L.T. 619 Lord Milligan altered an interlocutor on the ground of procedural error to delete an award of interest made in the mistaken belief that there had been no challenge to it. In *Carnegie v. Lord Advocate (No. 2)* 1999

4.15.5

S.L.T. 521 it was held that an interlocutor could be altered which failed to repel a plea on a point expressly dealt with in the judgment. In *Ewos Ltd v. Mainland* , 2005 S.L.T. 1227 (OH) two interlocutors were altered to reflect the intention that expenses were to be taxed on an agent and client basis and two were not.

A joint application or motion of consent is not enough, if not relating to a correction of a mistake, clerical error or omission which was not in any event put forward *de recenti*: see *Hutchison* 1965 S.C. 240.

The decision in *McIlwham v. Secretary of State for Scotland* 1989 S.L.T. 167 that apart from this rule the court has power at common law to review its own interlocutor de recenti must be wrongly decided: the common law is replaced by the rule. In *Hamilton Academical Football Club Ltd v. Flayest Ltd* , 29th November 1996, unreported (1997 G.W.D. 2-45), the defender had wished to go to procedure roll but the interlocutor (which stated that it was represented when it was not) allowed a proof which the pursuer said could not now be varied, altered or revoked by the Lord Ordinary. The Lord Ordinary, while accepting that no rule in the R.C.S. 1994 allowed him to revoke the interlocutor, was concerned that the court's general power to do justice between the parties did not enable him to rectify a genuine mistake, and appears to have exercised such a power to appoint the case to procedure roll. The Lord Ordinary's decision is clearly wrong in principle because he has no power either to alter the substance of his own interlocutor or to recall or revoke it except where the rules permit. The view expressed here, that the cases of *McIlwham* and *Hamilton Academical* have been wrongly decided, has been endorsed by Lord Eassie in *Black v. Somerfield Stores Ltd* , 1998 S.L.T. 1315.

Exceptionally a Lord Ordinary may (in effect) recall his own interlocutor, although an interlocutor of the Lord Ordinary is final in the Outer House (C.S.A. 1988, s.18): (1) Where a particular mode of inquiry has been allowed, the court is not precluded from reconsidering and altering the mode of inquiry following a minute of amendment (and answers) by which the pleadings are altered (this is not a true recall): *Bendex v. James Donaldson & Sons Ltd* 1990 S.C. 259. (2) Where the R.C.S. 1994 or other enactment permits: e.g. recall of a decree in absence (r. 19.2).

The rule states that a correction may be made *before* extract. It does not necessarily follow, however, that a correction may *not* be made *after* extract: see note 7.9.2.

UNITS OF MEASUREMENT.

4.15.6   The Units of Measurement Directive (Council Directive 80/181 of 20th December 1979) was adopted by the E.C. in 1989 [Official Journal, 7th December 1989, L357/28]. From 1st January 1995 member states must use the metric system of measurement and, subject to certain transitional arrangements and exceptions, must cease to use imperial measurements for economic, public health, public safety and administrative purposes. Where a unit of measurement is used in pleadings it should be expressed as a metric unit, and court orders must be so expressed.

Exceptions are as follows: The nautical mile and knot are to be used for sea and air traffic and the foot is to be used for aircraft heights. Until 31st December 1999, fathom may be used for marine navigation; therm for gas supply; pint and fluid ounce for beer, cider, waters, lemonade and fruit juices on returnable containers; and ounce and pound for goods sold loose from bulk. In perpetuity, acre may be used for land registration; troy ounce for transactions in precious metals; mile, yard, foot and inch for road traffic signs, distances and speed measurements; pint for draught beer, cider and milk in returnable containers.

ISSUING OF JUDGMENTS.

4.15.7   Unless otherwise ordered, judgments are issued without the necessity of the attendance of counsel or solicitor. A clerk of session will give agents notice of the date an opinion is to be issued (usually two days in advance). A copy of the opinion may be collected on or after the date of issue from the Opinions desk during office hours on payment of the prescribed fee. See Notice (*sic*) 4th September 1997.

Agents may obtain a copy in advance of the date of issue. Neither the opinion nor any of its contents may be revealed by agents or examined by any other person including a party in advance of the date of issue. See P.N. No. 4 of 1991.

Where the opinion does not deal with expenses, a party seeking expenses will have to enrol a motion. Unless opposed, or starred by the court, a motion for expenses will be dealt with in chambers: See Notice (*sic*) 4th September 1997.

Opinions or judgments of the court, from September 1998, are available on the Internet at The Scottish Courts Web Site at *www.scotcourts.gov.uk*. The site is updated at 2 p.m. every day on which opinions are issued.

There is a growing trend to anonymise published judgments. In *MH v. Mental Health Tribunal for Scotland* 2019 S.C. 432 (First Div.), 438, para. [16] *et seq.* considered the principles to be applied under the Court of Session Act 1693 and at common law (as distinct from the powers under s. 11 of the Contempt of Court Act 1981 about reporting restrictions). The starting point is open justice, that proceedings are heard and determined in public and that the public has access to judicial determinations including reasons and the identity of parties. There are exceptions from the general principle of open justice, some statutory. Per Lord President (Carloway) "[24] ... There are situations in which the court can, and sometimes must, withhold information, and in addition make a reporting restriction, but these must be set against the background of the general principle. They should be rare events and depend not upon categories of case but individual circumstances." For a recent example of consideration and argument about whether a judgment should be anonymised (and published) as distinct from an anonymity order, see *Oil States Industries (UK) Ltd v. "S" Ltd* 2022 S.L.T. 919 (OH), 937–938, paras. [96] to [103].

SCHEDULE OF DAMAGES.

Under P.N. No. 3 of 1997 parties seeking decree in an action of reparation for personal injuries (except where that decree is sought of consent, e.g. because of a joint minute) must lodge in process a schedule of damages for the purposes of s.15(2) of the Social Security (Recovery of Benefits) Acts 1997 stating the amount of any compensation in respect of the relevant period under the heads of compensation in column 1 of Sched. 2 to the 1997 Act. It is apparent that the interlocutor subsequently pronounced will not itself specify the amounts under each head but will refer to a (or the) appended schedule which does. Clerks of Session have been issuing blank schedules in the following form:—

4.15.8

Schedule to interlocutor of even date (*amend as necessary*)

1. Solatium—

        To date:

        Future:

2. Loss of Earn-ings—

        To end of relevant period (date):

        Subsequent to end of relevant period:

3. Compensation for

        (1) cost of care

            to end of relevant period (date):

            subsequent to end of relevant period (date):

        (2) loss of mobility

            to end of relevant period (date):

            subsequent to end of relevant

                period (date):

4. Section 8 services:

5. Section 9 services:

6. Medical expenses:

7. Loss of pension rights, etc.:

                        TOTAL:

Less (number)% due to contributory negligence:

Sum decerned for:

Inner House interlocutors

4.16—(1)[1] This rule applies to interlocutors pronounced in the Inner House, except interlocutors mentioned in rule 4.16A (Inner House interlocutors relating to procedural business).

4.16

(2) Subject to paragraph (3), an interlocutor of the Inner House may be written by the clerk of court and shall be adjusted and signed by—

    (a) the judge who presided in the Division of the Inner House when the matter to be dealt with in the interlocutor was determined, or

    (b) in the event of the death, disability or absence of that judge, the next senior judge who sat in that Division when the matter to be dealt with in the interlocutor was determined, as soon as reasonably practicable and after such consultation as may be necessary with the other members of the Division who sat.

(3) An interlocutor of the Inner House in respect of a motion which is not starred shall be adjusted and signed by the judge presiding at the time when the motion was brought before the Division of the Inner House.

(4) An interlocutor may be signed during session or in vacation.

---

[1] Rule 4.16(1) amended by S.S.I. 2010 No. 30 (effective 5th April 2010).

(5)   The judge signing an interlocutor of the Inner House shall append the letters "I.P.D." to his signature as conclusive evidence that the requirements of the preceding paragraphs of this rule have been complied with.

(6)   An extract of an interlocutor which is not signed in accordance with the provisions of this rule shall be void and of no effect.

(7)   An interlocutor may, on cause shown, be corrected or altered at any time before extract by—

    (a)   the judge who signed it; or

    (b)   in the event of the death, disability or absence of that judge, the next senior judge of the same Division of the Inner House.

Deriv. R.C.S. 1965, r. 30(1) substituted by S.I. 1984 No. 472 (r. 4.16(6)), r. 30(2) substituted by S.I. 1984 No. 472 (r. 4.16(7)), r. 30(3) inserted by S.I. 1986 No. 1937 (r. 4.16(4)), and r. 295 (r. 4.16(2), (3) and (5))

GENERAL NOTE.

4.16.1   See notes to r. 4.15.

"I.P.D.".

4.16.2   These initials mean *in praesentia dominorum*, and originally meant that the interlocutor had been read and signed before a quorum of the judges as once required by the Interlocutors Act 1693.

CORRECTION OR ALTERATION ON CAUSE SHOWN.

4.16.3   In assessing whether a party has shown cause the court will take into account any undue delay in seeking the alteration and any prejudice which the alteration may cause to the other party: *Martinez v. Grampian Health Board* 1995 S.C. 428. Prejudice to the other party includes prejudice in presenting an appeal against the interlocutor in question: *Martinez*, above.

ISSUING OF JUDGMENTS.

4.16.4   Unless otherwise ordered, judgments are issued without the necessity of the attendance of counsel or solicitor. A clerk of session will give agents notice of the date an opinion is to be issued (usually two days in advance). A copy of the opinion may be collected on or after the date of issue from the Opinions desk during office hours on payment of the prescribed fee. See Notice (*sic*) 4th September 1997.

Agents may obtain a copy in advance of the date of issue. Neither the opinion nor any of its contents may be revealed by agents or examined by any other person including a party in advance of the date of issue. See P.N. No. 4 of 1991.

Where the Opinion does not deal with expenses, a party seeking expenses will have to enrol a motion. Unless opposed, or starred by the court, a motion for expenses will be dealt with in chambers: See Notice (*sic*) 4th September 1997.

Opinions or judgments of the court, from September 1998, are available on the Internet at The Scottish Courts Web Site at *www.scotcourts.gov.uk*. The site is updated at 2 p.m. every day on which opinions are issued.

Inner House interlocutors relating to procedural business

4.16A   **4.16A.**—[1](1)   This rule applies to interlocutors pronounced in the Inner House in relation to procedural business dealt with by a procedural judge within the meaning of rule 37A.1 (quorum of Inner House for certain business) and rule 37A.2 (procedural judges in the Inner House).

(2)   An interlocutor may be written by the clerk of court and shall be adjusted and signed by the procedural judge who determined the matter dealt with in the interlocutor.

(3)   An interlocutor may be signed during session or in vacation.

(4)   An extract of an interlocutor which is not signed in accordance with the provisions of this rule shall be void and of no effect.

(5)   An interlocutor may, on cause shown, be corrected or altered at any time before extract by—

    (a)   the judge who signed it; or

---

[1] R. 4.16A inserted by S.S.I. 2010 No. 30 (effective 5th April 2010).

(b) in the event of the death, disability or absence of that judge, any other procedural judge.

GENERAL NOTE.

Under new rules for Inner House business, certain procedural business (defined in r. 37A.1(2)) may be dealt with by one judge (the procedural judge). Rule 4.16A provides for interlocutors signed by that judge. **4.16A.1**

CORRECTION OR ALTERATION OF EXTRACT.

See note, 4.16.3. **4.16A.2**

CHAPTER 5 CAVEATS

Orders against which caveats may be lodged

5.1.[1] Without prejudice to rule 5.1A, a person may only lodge a caveat against—

   (a)   an interim interdict sought in an action before he has lodged defences;

   (b)   an interim order sought in an action before the expiry of the period within which he could enter appearance;

   (c)   an interim order (other than an order under section 1 of the Administration of Justice (Scotland) Act 1972 (orders for inspection of documents and other property, etc.)) sought in a petition before he has lodged answers;

   (d)   an order for intimation, service and advertisement of a petition to wind up, or to appoint an administrator to, a company in which he has an interest;

   (e)   an order for intimation, service and advertisement of a petition for his sequestration; and

   (f)[2]   an order permitting the bringing of group proceedings (within the meaning given in Chapter 26A).

Deriv. R.C.S. 1965, r. 68H inserted by S.I. 1990 No. 2118 and r. 218A(1) inserted by S.I. 1986 No. 2298 (r. 5.1(d))

GENERAL NOTE.

A caveat is a document lodged in the Petition Department (r. 5.2(1)) by a person to ensure that certain orders may not be made against him without his receiving intimation of the application for the order and having an opportunity to be heard before the order may be made (r. 23.9 (motions where caveat lodged)).

A caveat may be general (affecting any order in r. 5.1) or particular (i.e. certain specified orders in r. 5.1).

The orders against which caveats could be lodged were never clear before A.S. (R.C.S. No. 5) (Miscellaneous) 1990 [S.I. 1990 No. 2118] (inserting R.C.S. 1965, r. 68H). This rule sets out the orders against which caveats may be lodged, and no caveat may be lodged against any other order.

MULTIPLE CAVEATS.

These are single caveats lodged on behalf of a multiplicity of parties. The onus is on the caveator to justify such a caveat, for, as a general rule, such a caveat is not readily acceptable. It is justification that the parties named are liable to be sued together or in the alternative in the same cause: e.g. a company in receivership and its receiver; a partnership and the partners; the common owners of the same property. The Secretary of State for Scotland may lodge a caveat in his own behalf in respect of the departments he represents in the Scottish Office. It will not be permitted for a caveator to lodge a caveat in respect of all his clients.

"INTERIM ORDER".

This would include interim interdict, custody or aliment, an interim judicial factor, an interim administrator or liquidator of a company, or interim suspension, interim liberation, or interim possession under s.47(2) of the C.S.A. 1988.

It is not permissible to lodge a caveat against an arrestment or inhibition on the dependence as they are not truly interim orders although granted "on the dependence" and because the pursuer is entitled, in general, as of right to preserve assets of the defender to satisfy any decree. It would defeat the purpose of not giving the defender prior warning so that he cannot dispose of his assets (see s.17 of the Debtors (Scotland) Act 1838 and s.18 of the C.S.A. 1868 which introduced execution of these diligences before service of the summons): see *Mackinlay* , 20th December 1988, unreported, per Lord Cullen (inhibition). It is possible to obtain interim interdict against the use of diligence on the dependence where it would be instantly verifiable as wrongful—i.e. without warrant, irregularly or with malice and want of probable cause (*Beattie & Son v. Pratt* (1880) 7 R. 1171) or the defender has consigned the principal sum (*Duff v. Wood* (1858) 20 D. 1231). An application for letters of arrestment or inhibition is not included in r. 5.1 as something against which a caveat may be lodged. A caveat may not be lodged against an application for arrestment or inhibition under s.27 of the C.J.J.A. 1982 (on which, see, e.g. *Stancroft Securities Ltd v. McDowall* 1990 S.C. 274).

A caveat may not be lodged against an order in an application for judicial review (as formerly under authority of *Kelly v. Monklands District Council* 1986 S.L.T. 165, 166F-G per Lord Ross (obiter)) except one which is truly interim: an order for production of documents in a first order is not an interim order.

---

[1] Rule 5.1 amended by S.S.I. 2001 No. 92, r.3 (effective 1st April 2001).
[2] Rule 5.1(f) inserted by S.S.I. 2020 No. 208 r.2(3) (effective 31 July 2020).

A caveat against an order under s.1 of the Administration of Justice (Scotland) Act 1972 is also not competent under r. 5.1(c); but if another interim order under r. 5.1 is sought as well, a caveat will give notice of the 1972 Act application. On applications under s.1 of the 1972 Act, see r. 35.2 and note 35.2.6 and Chap. 64.

Interim orders relate mostly to the merits of the cause in which they are sought: *Kelly*, above, per Lord Ross at p. 167. An order is interim because of its character not merely because it is expressly granted "ad interim". "Interim" means for the time being or in the meantime.

Further restriction as to caveats

5.1A   **5.1A.**—[1](1)   *[Omitted by S.S.I. 2011 No. 288 (effective 21st July 2011).]*

(2)[2,3]   A caveat shall not be lodged against an order for intimation, service and advertisement of a petition for—

   (a)   a bank insolvency order under rule 74.35;
   (b)   a bank administration order under rule 74.45;
   (c)   a building society special administration order under rule 74.51;
   (d)   a building society insolvency order under rule 74.52; or
   (e)   a payment or electronic money institution special administration order under rule 74.64.

GENERAL NOTE.

5.1A.1   Rule 5.1A(1) prohibited a caveat against a petition under r. 83.2 by authorised officials of the E.U. seeking assistance in an investigation by them into a breach of Art. 81(1) or 82 of the EC Treaty (bringing to light an agreement, decision or concerted practice prohibited by those articles). Chapter 83 was erroneously numbered Chap. 82 in the first S.S.I; hence the subsequent amendment. Chapter 83 has since been revoked.

Rule 5.1A(2) applies to the legislation following the banking crisis and the Banking Act 2009.

Form, lodging and renewal of caveats

5.2   **5.2.**—(1)   A caveat shall be in Form 5.2 and shall be lodged in the Petition Department.

(2)   A caveat shall remain in force for a period of one year from the date on which it was lodged and may be renewed on its expiry for a further period of a year and yearly thereafter.

Deriv. R.C.S. 1965, r. 681 inserted by S.I. 1990 No. 2118

GENERAL NOTE.

5.2.1   A caveat is not a step of process in a process. It is given an index number and year number, placed in a folder and entered in an alphabetical card index register in the Petition Department. A copy of the caveat is transmitted to the Signet Officer who retains a similar index register for use in the General Department. The register is consulted by the clerks before any order under r. 5.1 is applied for ex parte.

"ONE YEAR AFTER".

5.2.2   The date of lodging is not counted in calculating the period.

MOTIONS WHERE CAVEAT LODGED.

5.2.3   When a motion is enrolled in a cause ex parte for an order against which a caveat may be lodged the clerk of session in the General or Petition Department, as the case may be, checks the register of caveats to see if a caveat has been lodged. If a caveat has been lodged he informs the Keeper of the Rolls who arranges a hearing of the motion (day or night) at a time when both parties can attend: see r. 23.9. Where the motion is enrolled by a pursuer before the calling of the summons or by a petitioner before the granting of the first order, r. 23.8 will apply.

If the duty clerk of session has to be contacted after 5pm, ring the Court of Session (0131-225 2595), leave your name and telephone number, and the duty security guard will contact the duty clerk who will contact you.

---

[1] Rule 5.1A inserted by S.S.I. 2001 No. 92 r. 3 (effective 1st April 2001) and amended by S.S.I. 2001 No. 305 para. 16 (effective 18th September 2001) and S.S.I. 2009 No. 63 para. 3 (effective 25th February 2009).
[2] Rule 5.1A substituted by S.S.I. 2010 No. 417 (effective 1st January 2011).
[3] As amended by the Act of Sederunt (Rules of the Court of Session 1994 Amendment) (Payment and Electronic Money Institution Special Administration) 2024 S.S.I. 2024 No. 75 r. 2(2) (effective 12th April 2024).

FEE.

There is a fee for lodging a caveat: see Court of Session etc. Fees Order 1997, Table of Fees, Pt I, C, item 5 [S.I. 1997 No. 688, as amended, pp. C1201 et seq.].

Where the party enrolling a motion is represented, the fee may be debited under the credit scheme introduced on 1st April by P.N. No.4 of 1976 to the account (if one is kept or permitted) of the party's agent by the court cashier, and an account will be rendered weekly by the court cashier's office to the agents for all court fees due that week for immediate settlement. Party litigants, and agents not operating the scheme, must pay (by cash, cheque or postal order) at the time of lodging at the counter of the appropriate department.

5.2.4

CHAPTER 6 THE ROLLS

Printing and publishing of rolls

6.1. The rolls shall be printed and published, and delivered to subscribers, under directions made from time to time by the Lord President.

Deriv. R.C.S. 1965, r. 18

"ROLLS".

These are the lists of business of the court: r. 1.3(1) (definition of "rolls"). The rolls are: (1) The General Roll, consisting of the registers of causes of the (*a*) General Department (the Ordinary, Admiralty and Commercial, and Family (including Consistorial) Rolls) and (*b*) the Petition Department; (2) The Daily Rolls—the printed rolls issued each weekday during term showing the causes in the General Roll appearing for business on a particular day, consisting of (*a*) in the Inner House (i) Single Bills, (ii) By Order Roll, (iii) Summar Roll and (iv) Advisings; and (*b*) in the Outer House (i) Calling List, (ii) Motion Roll, (iii) Diet Roll, (iv) Commercial Roll, (v) Adjustment Roll and Continued Adjustment Roll, (vi) By Order (Adjustment) Roll, (vii) By Order Roll, (viii) Procedure Roll, (ix) Jury Trials, Proofs, Proofs before Answer and Hearings, (x) For Judgment and (xi) Undefended Consistorial Causes (in fact undefended divorce actions). In the Daily Rolls there are also printed notices of Acts of Sederunt, practice notes and other acts of administration. Rolls issued in vacation contain details of (2)(a)(i) and (iv) and (b)(i), (iii)–(xi).

The importance of the By Order Roll in the Inner and Outer Houses is that the court itself may order a cause put out on that Roll and require parties to appear before it. A court fee is now payable for a By Order Roll hearing under the Court of Session etc. Fees Order 1997, Table of Fees, Pt I, B, item 19 or 20, or C, item 18 or 19 for every 30 minutes [S.I. 1997 No. 688 as amended, pp. C1201 et seq.]. Certain persons are exempt from payment of fees: see 1997 Fees Order, art.5; substituted by S.S.I. 2002 No. 270. A fee exemption certificate must be lodged in process: see P.N. No. 1 of 2002.

Fixing and allocation of diets in Outer House

6.2.—(1) This rule applies to the fixing and allocation of diets in the Outer House.

(2) The court shall not proceed to fix a diet where—

  (a) a proof is allowed;

  (b) issues are approved; or

  (c) a cause is appointed to the Procedure Roll.

(2A)[1] Where a party enrols a motion for a cause to be appointed to the Procedure Roll he shall include in the enrolled motion his estimate of the likely duration of the Procedure Roll hearing.

(2B)[2] If any other party considers that the estimate included under paragraph (2A) is too low, he shall record upon the enrolled motion his own estimate.

(2C)[3] On such papers (whether or not the closed record) as are transmitted to the Keeper of the Rolls for the purposes of his carrying out the functions conferred on him by paragraphs (3) and (4), the clerk of court shall note the estimate provided in pursuance of paragraph (2A) unless a higher estimate is recorded under paragraph (2B), in which case the note shall only be of the higher (or as the case may be the highest) estimate so recorded.

(3) Subject to paragraph (4), a cause appointed to the Procedure Roll may be put out for hearing by the Keeper of the Rolls in the course of any week where, unless the parties otherwise agree, the diet has been published in the rolls on Thursday of the preceding week.

(4) Where a hearing on the Procedure Roll is anticipated to be of some length or complexity, the parties may arrange a fixed diet with the Keeper of the Rolls.

---

[1] Paragraphs (2A) to (2C) and (7A) to (7C) of r. 6.2 inserted by S.S.I. 2007 No. 548 (effective 7th January 2008).

[2] Paragraphs (2A) to (2C) and (7A) to (7C) of r. 6.2 inserted by S.S.I. 2007 No. 548 (effective 7th January 2008).

[3] Paragraphs (2A) to (2C) and (7A) to (7C) of r. 6.2 inserted by S.S.I. 2007 No. 548 (effective 7th January 2008).

(5)[1]   When a party enrols for a proof to be allowed or issues to be approved in a cause depending before the Outer House he shall include in the enrolled motion his estimate of the likely duration of the proof or jury trial and request that the diet be allocated accordingly.

(6)[2]   If any other party considers that the estimate so included is too low, he shall record upon the enrolled motion his own estimate.

(7)[3]   On such papers (whether or not the closed record) as are transmitted to the Keeper of the Rolls for the purpose of his allocating the diet, the clerk of court shall note the estimate provided in pursuance of paragraph (5) unless a higher estimate is recorded under paragraph (6), in which case the note shall only be of the higher (or as the case may be the highest) estimate so recorded; and the Keeper of the Rolls shall allocate the diet of proof or jury trial accordingly and give written intimation of it to each party.

(7A)[4]   Any estimate included or recorded by a party under paragraph (2A), (2B), (5) or (6) shall be certified in Form 6.2 by any counsel or other person having a right of audience instructed by that party to represent him at the Procedure Roll hearing, proof, or jury trial, as the case may be.

(7B)[5]   A certificate under paragraph (7A) shall be lodged—

   (a)   where it relates to an estimate included under paragraph (2A) or (5), at the time of enrolling the motion mentioned in that paragraph;

   (b)   where it relates to an estimate recorded under paragraph (2B) or (6), at the time of recording that estimate.

(7C)[6]   Where a party's original estimate of the duration of any diet changes, that party shall lodge a further Form 6.2 no later than 14 days before the date of any Procedure Roll hearing, proof or jury trial.

(8)   *[Revoked by S.I. 1998 No. 890]*

(9)   *[Revoked by S.I. 1998 No. 890]*

(10)   *[Revoked by S.I. 1998 No. 870]*

(11)   *[Revoked by S.I. 1998 No. 870]*

(12)   *[Revoked by S.I. 1998 No. 870]*

(13)   An application for the allocation of a special diet may be made to the Keeper of the Rolls—

   (a)   on cause shown;

   (b)   of consent of all parties; and

   (c)   before a diet has been allocated under a preceding paragraph of this rule.

(14)   Where an application under paragraph (13) is refused, the parties may bring the application before the Lord President; and the Lord President, or a judge nominated by him, shall determine the application in chambers.

(15)   Parties shall attend on the Keeper of the Rolls for the purpose of fixing a diet for—

---

[1] Paras (5) to (7) of r. 6.2 substituted, and paras (8) to (12) revoked, by S.I. 1998 No. 890 (effective 21st April 1998).

[2] Paras (5) to (7) of r. 6.2 substituted, and paras (8) to (12) revoked, by S.I. 1998 No. 890 (effective 21st April 1998).

[3] Paras (5) to (7) of r. 6.2 substituted, and paras (8) to (12) revoked, by S.I. 1998 No. 890 (effective 21st April 1998).

[4] Paragraphs (2A) to (2C) and (7A) to (7C) of r. 6.2 inserted by S.S.I. 2007 No. 548 (effective 7th January 2008).

[5] Paragraphs (2A) to (2C) and (7A) to (7C) of r. 6.2 inserted by S.S.I. 2007 No. 548 (effective 7th January 2008).

[6] Paragraphs (2A) to (2C) and (7A) to (7C) of r. 6.2 inserted by S.S.I. 2007 No. 548 (effective 7th January 2008).

(a) a proof or jury trial in a cause of exceptional length or complexity;
(b) an undefended proof;
(c) a continued proof;
(d) a continued hearing; or
(e) a hearing on evidence.

Deriv. R.C.S. 1965, r. 17 (r. 6.2(2)), r. 94(a) (r. 6.2(3)); P.N. 5th May 1972 (r. 6.2(4)), P.N. 29th May 1975 (r. 6.2(13) and (14)), P.N. No. 2 of 1987, para. 5 (r. 6.27 (part))

GENERAL NOTE.

The former Form 6.2 procedure, introduced in 1987 by S.I. 1987 No. 1206 and amended by S.I. 1990 No. 2118, has been abolished and a new procedure provided for by A.S. (R.C.S.A.) (Miscellaneous) 1998 [S.I. 1998 No. 890]. Further amendments were made in A.S. (R.C.S.A. No. 10) (Miscellaneous) 2007 [S.S.I. 2007 No. 548]. The procedure is for a party seeking a debate on the Procedure Roll, a proof or jury trial to specify in the motion for proof or issues his estimate of the likely duration of the proof or jury trial: r. 6.2(2A) and (5). Any other party who considers that that estimate is too low must mark *on the motion* his estimate (r. 6.2(2B) and (6)) and the Keeper of the Rolls will allocate a diet in relation to a Procedure Roll hearing on the highest estimate (r. 6.2(7)). In theory the new procedure dispenses with the need for a form because the information will be in the motion. Estimates now have to be certified by counsel or person having a right of audience: r. 6.2(7A)–(7C).

In practice the procedure may be thought to have a number of drawbacks. (1) There is no sanction for failing to comply: one assumes that a motion without an estimate will be refused (to be accepted by the clerk of session) as incompetent. (2) Any higher estimate must be marked on the motion, not a notice of opposition, and accordingly cannot be done by fax but requires attendance at the General or Petition Department (as the case may be). (3) There is no provision for supplementary information of use to the Keeper, as in Form 6.2, such as the total number of witnesses, expert witnesses or witnesses from abroad (such information was, apparently, rarely given or used) or that a witness was disabled or that video equipment was to be used (regarded as necessary information). (4) The provisions omit the former reference to the "fixing" of diets; accordingly, on a strict application of the canons of statutory interpretation, the fixing of diets has been abolished. Apparently, however, the Keeper of the Rolls will take note of revised estimates he receives; information about witnesses, etc., may be intimated by letter or telephone; and the fixing of diets continues. It is unfortunate that the provisions do not even reflect the practice which they are intended to authorise and provide for, a situation which the R.C.S. 1994 had been intended by the Rules Review Group to overcome and avoid.

The purpose of the rule remains the same as before, namely, to ensure that, under our system of fixing or allocating diets, court time is not wasted by hearings going off for one reason or another or a hearing is adjourned to another date because it has taken longer than the time allocated.

Before making the weekly allocation of cases to the judges sitting in the Outer House for that week, the Keeper of the Rolls consults the senior Outer House judge. No later than 12 noon on the Friday of the week preceding the diet of their case, parties may inform the Keeper of any factors they consider may have a bearing on setting the priorities of their case: P.N. No.1 of 2001. The reason for this is that few cases are allocated to a particular judge and there are insufficient judges to hear the cases set down for hearing.

FIXING AND ALLOCATION OF DIETS.

The former provision in r. 6.2(5) referred to diets being "fixed or allocated". The amendments and new provisions inserted by A.S. (R.C.S.A.) (Miscellaneous) 1998 [S.I. 1998 No. 890] omit the reference to the fixing of diets. Accordingly, applying strictly the canons of statutory interpretation, the fixing of diets has been abolished. Apparently, however, this is not so in practice and was not intended: the practice of fixing continues. It would be better if the rule reflected the practice.

A diet is "allocated" where the Keeper of the Rolls arranges a diet without consultation with parties: he normally does so in the case of (a) causes appointed to the Procedure Roll and (b) causes in which proof has, or issues have, been allowed. A diet is "fixed" where (a) the allocated diet is inconvenient and application is made to the Keeper to arrange an alternative diet (which will be done only on cause shown) or (b) the diet is arranged before or instead of allocation because (i) parties' estimated length varies substantially, (ii) the parties apply to the Keeper under r. 6.2(4) because a procedure roll hearing is anticipated to be of some length or complexity, (iii) the parties apply under r. 6.2(13) for a special diet, or (iv) the parties are required to attend the Keeper of the Rolls to fix diets in those causes to which r. 6.2(15) applies.

In relation to causes appointed to the Procedure Roll, the Keeper will publish in the rolls a Procedure Roll warning list two weeks before the Thursday's roll on which diets are allocated for hearing the following week. Such hearings will be put out for one day unless, in response to the warning list, the Keeper is requested to fix more than one day under r. 6.2(4) ("some length" in r. 6.2(4) means, in practice, more than one day). Where a party seeks to discharge a diet fixed by the Keeper under r. 6.2(4), a motion for discharge must now be enrolled: P.N. No. 7 of 2004.

In actions of damages for personal injuries or death of a person from personal injuries, proof diets are fixed by the Keeper on the lodging of defences: r. 43.6(1)(a). In existing actions the Keeper is reviewing diets for after 31st October 2003 and parties may apply for early or accelerated diets: P.N. No.3 of 2003.

6.2.1

6.2.2

"THE COURT SHALL NOT PROCEED TO FIX A DIET".

6.2.3   The interlocutor allowing a proof or issues for jury trial or appointing a cause to the Procedure Roll will provide for such a hearing "on the…day of…", but the Keeper of the Rolls will be responsible for fixing and inserting the actual date of the hearing: see note 6.2.2.

"ESTIMATE OF THE LIKELY DURATION".

6.2.4   The party seeking a debate, proof or jury trial must specify in his motion for proof or issues his estimate of the likely duration of the debate, proof or jury trial and request allocation of a diet: r. 6.2(2A) or (5). One assumes that if he fails to comply, the motion will not be accepted by the clerk of session in the General or Petition Department (as the case may be) because it is incompetent.

Any other party who considers that that estimate is too low must mark *on the motion* his estimate: r. 6.2(2B) or (6). He does not do so by or on a notice of opposition in Form 23.4. Accordingly this cannot be done by fax and attendance at the General or Petition Department will be required. It is understood, however, that, contrary to the *express* terms of the provision, account will be taken of a fax indicating a higher estimate from another party.

Parties are expected to have discussed the duration of the proceedings before enrolling a motion (and to keep it under review) and, if necessary, lodge a further Form 6.2 at least 14 days before the diet: P.N. No. 3 of 2007.

The Keeper of the Rolls allocates a diet (see note 6.2.2) on the basis of the highest estimate: r. 6.2(7). The Keeper will take account of a revised estimate intimated to him. Also, contrary to the apparently express terms of r. 6.2(7) the Keeper may still fix a diet in consultation with the parties instead of allocating it in accordance with the highest estimate: see note 6.2.2.

ARRANGING DIETS.

6.2.5   The Keeper relies primarily on the information provided in the motion as required by r. 6.2(2A), (2B), (5) and (6). He compares the information provided by each party. Where there is an estimate that the length of a proof or jury trial will not be more than four days, the Keeper will normally allocate a diet of the length sought. Where there is an estimate of more than four days or there is a substantial variation in the estimates given by each party, the Keeper will communicate with parties with a view to ascertaining a better estimate and fixing a diet. R.6.2(15) lists those hearings or proofs for which parties must attend on the Keeper to fix diets on the list printed on a Thursday for allocation of diets.

"ENROLS".

6.2.6   This means enrols a motion. This style is not used elsewhere in the R.C.S. 1994 (except in Chap. 23), and to be consistent with the other rules the phrase "applies by motion" should have been used.

On motions, see Chap. 23.

"WRITTEN INTIMATION".

6.2.7   For methods, see r. 16.9.

SPECIAL DIETS.

6.2.8   Parties may apply to the Keeper of the Rolls for a special diet under r. 6.2(13) for a procedure roll hearing, proof, jury trial or other hearing; this will only be done (a) on cause shown, (b) with consent of parties and (c) before allocation of a diet by the Keeper (in the case of proofs or jury trials): r. 6.2(1). "Cause shown" should include complexity of the case, urgency or importance.

A decision on an application for a special diet which has been referred by the Keeper to the Lord President under r. 6.2(14) may not be reclaimed against: C.S.A. 1988, s.28.

"EXCEPTIONAL LENGTH".

6.2.9   This means, in practice, a cause requiring over eight court days.

FEE.

6.2.10   The court fee for fixing a proof or jury trial in an action is payable on the diet being fixed. For fee, see Court of Session etc. Fees Order 1997, Table of Fees, Pt I, B, item 15 [S.I. 1997 No. 688, as amended, pp. C1201 et seq.]. Certain persons are exempt from payment of fees: see 1997 Fees Order, art.5 substituted by S.S.I. 2002/270. A fee exemption certificate must be lodged in process: see P.N. No.1 of 2002.

Where a party is legally represented, the fee may be debited under a credit scheme introduced on 1st April 1976 by P.N. No. 4 of 1976 to the account (if one is kept or permitted) of the agent by the court cashier, and an account will be rendered weekly by the court cashier's office to the agent for all court fees due that week for immediate settlement. Party litigants, and agents not operating the scheme, must pay (by cash, cheque or postal order) on each occasion a fee is due at the time of lodging at the counter at the appropriate department.

Allocation of diets in Inner House

6.3   **6.3.** *[Revoked by S.S.I. 2010 No. 30 (effective 5th April 2010; subject to transitional and savings provisions).]*

GENERAL NOTE.

The former Form 6.3 procedure, introduced in 1987 by S.I. 1987 No. 1206 and amended by S.I 1990/ 2118, has been abolished and a new procedure provided for by A.S. (R.C.S.A.) (Miscellaneous) 1998 [S.I. 1998 No. 890]. Further amendments were made by A.S. (R.C.S.A. No. 10) (Miscellaneous) 2007 [S.S.I. 2007 No. 548]. The procedure is for a party seeking a hearing on the Summar Roll to specify in the motion for the hearing his estimate of the likely duration of the hearing: r. 6.3(2). Any other party who considers that that estimate is too low must mark on the motion his estimate (r. 6.3(3)) and the Keeper of the Rolls will allocate a diet on the highest estimate (r. 6.3(4)). In theory the procedure dispenses with the need for a form because the information will be in the motion. Estimates now have to be certified by counsel or person having a right of audience: r. 6.3(7) and (8).

In practice the procedure may be thought to have a number of drawbacks. (1) There is no sanction for failing to comply: one assumes that a motion without an estimate will be refused (to be accepted by the clerk of session) as incompetent. (2) Any higher estimate must be marked on the motion, not a notice of opposition, and accordingly cannot be done by fax but requires attendance at the General or Petition Department (as the case may be). (3) There is no provision for supplementary information of use to the Keeper, as in Form 6.3. (4) The new provisions omit the former reference to the "fixing" of diets; accordingly, on a strict application of the canons of statutory interpretation, the fixing of diets has been abolished. Apparently, however, the Keeper of the Rolls will take note of revised estimates he receives; supplementary information may be intimated by letter or telephone; and the fixing of diets continues. It is unfortunate that the new provisions do not even reflect the practice which they are intended to authorise and provide for, a situation which the R.C.S. 1994 had been intended by the Rules Review Group to overcome and avoid.

The purpose of the rule remains the same as before, namely, to ensure that, under our system of fixing or allocating diets, court time is not wasted by hearings going off for one reason or another or a hearing is adjourned to another date because it has taken longer than the time allocated.

The procedure applies only where a hearing is sought on the Summar Roll. It does not apply if the reclaimer or appellant seeks early disposal on the Single Bills under r. 38.13 (for reclaiming motions) or 40.11 (for appeals from inferior courts).

The stage at which consideration should be given to the grounds on which the reclaiming motion or appeal is to be argued, so that the court can be told whether the hearing is to proceed and the dates set down registered, is at the time of the By Order hearing under r. 6.3(5): *Noble Organisation Ltd v. Kilmarnock and Loudoun District Council* 1993 S.L.T. 759, 761I. A sufficient opportunity must be given for the case to be reviewed before the By Order roll hearing for counsel to confirm that the grounds of appeal are adequate: *Eurocopy Rentals Ltd v. Tayside Health Board* 1996 S.L.T. 1322, 1324J.

6.3.1

"ENROLS".

This means enrols a motion. This style is not used elsewhere in the R.C.S. 1994 (except in Chap. 23), and to be consistent with the other rules the phrase "applies by motion" should have been used.

On motions, see Chap. 23.

6.3.2

"DEPENDING".

A cause is depending from the time it is commenced (i.e. from the time an action is served or a first order in a petition is made) until final decree, whereas a cause is in dependence until final extract. For the meaning of commenced, see note 13.4.4 (action) or 14.6.1 (petition). For the meaning of final decree, see note 4.15.2(2). For the meaning of final extract, see note 7.1.2(2).

6.3.3

"SUMMAR ROLL".

There was formerly a Summar Roll and a Short Roll in the Inner House. The former was for causes dealt with summarily (speedily) and the latter was for causes heard in ordinary course. The latter roll no longer exists and all causes for hearing are appointed to the Summar Roll if not dealt with in the Single Bills or on the By Order Roll.

6.3.4

FIXING AND ALLOCATION OF DIETS.

The former provision in r. 6.3(1) referred to the "fixing and allocation" of diets. The amendments and new provisions inserted by A.S. (R.C.S.A.) (Miscellaneous) 1998 [S.I. 1998 No. 890] omit the reference to the fixing of diets. Accordingly, applying strictly the canons of statutory interpretation, the fixing of diets has been abolished. Apparently, however, this is not so in practice and was not intended: the practice of fixing continues. It would be better if the rule reflected the practice.

A diet is allocated where the Keeper of the Rolls arranges a diet without consultation with parties. A diet is fixed where (a) the allocated diet is inconvenient and application is made to the Keeper to arrange an alternative diet (which will be done only on cause shown) or (b) the diet is arranged before or instead of allocation because the parties' estimated length varies substantially.

6.3.5

"ESTIMATE OF THE LIKELY DURATION".

The party seeking a hearing on the Summar Roll specifies in his motion for the hearing his estimate of the likely duration of the hearing: r. 6.3(2). One assumes that if he fails to comply the motion will not be accepted by the clerk of session in the General or Petition Department (as the case may be) because it is incompetent.

6.3.6

Any other party who considers that that estimate is too low must mark *on the motion* his estimate: r. 6.3(3). He does not do so by or on a notice of opposition in Form 23.4. Accordingly this cannot be done by fax and attendance at the General or Petition Department will be required. It is understood, however, that, contrary to the express terms of the provision, account will be taken of a fax indicating a higher estimate from another party.

Parties are expected to have discussed the duration of the proceedings before enrolling a motion (and to keep it under review) and, if necessary, lodge a further Form 6.2 at least 14 days before the diet: P.N. No. 3 of 2007.

The Keeper of the Rolls allocates a diet (see n. 6.3.5) on the basis of the highest estimate: r. 6.3(5). The Keeper will take account of a revised estimate intimated to him. Also, contrary to the apparently express terms of r. 6.3(5) the Keeper may still fix a diet in consultation with the parties instead of allocating it in accordance with the highest estimate: see note 6.3.5.

ARRANGING DIETS.

6.3.7   The Keeper relies primarily on the information provided in the motion as required by r.6.3(2). He compares the information provided by each party. Where there is an estimate that the length of a hearing will not be more than four days, the Keeper will normally allocate a diet of the length sought. Where there is an estimate of more than four days or there is a substantial variation in the estimates given by each party, the Keeper will communicate with parties with a view to ascertaining a better estimate and fixing a diet. In certain cases, even though a diet may have been allocated, a cause may be the subject of a short notice diet or peremptory short notice diet: see notes 6.3.8 and 6.3.9.

SHORT NOTICE DIETS.

6.3.8   Parties may agree with the Keeper that, notwithstanding the allocation of a diet, notice may be given of an early diet. Intimation is by letter what notice they would require for an early diet. When a diet is cancelled agents are either contacted about the possibility of an early diet according to the notice required or a notice appears periodically in the rolls of the short notice diets available. An offer of a short notice diet by the Keeper is not to be treated as a fixed diet until written intimation has been made by the Keeper: P.N. No. 2 of 1992. Certain sheriff court and statutory appeals may be subject to peremptory short notice diets: see note 6.3.9.

PEREMPTORY SHORT NOTICE DIETS.

6.3.9   In relation to certain sheriff court and statutory appeals the Keeper may issue peremptory diets where the estimated length of the hearing is not more than two days. This provision applies generally to cases requiring some urgency. A minimum of two days notice of a diet will be given. A notice of causes to which this provision applies will be published periodically in the rolls. The fact that a later diet has been allocated does not preclude the issue of a short notice diet. See P.N. No. 6 of 1992.

"WRITTEN INTIMATION".

6.3.10   For methods, see r.16.9.

R.6.3(5).

6.3.11   The cause is put out by order not less than five weeks before the date arranged for the hearing so that the court can discover (a) whether the hearing is to proceed and (b) the current estimated length of the hearing. On the basis of this information the court may be able to rearrange other business. There is little prospect of other business being arranged where a hearing goes off within two weeks of the diet.

It is at the stage of the by order hearing that consideration should be given to the grounds on which an appeal or reclaiming motion is to be argued. A sufficient opportunity must be given for the case to be reviewed prior to its appearance on the by order roll to enable counsel to confirm that the grounds of appeal are adequate and to provide a reasonably accurate forecast of the time which will be required: *Eurocopy Rentals Ltd v. Tayside Health Board* 1996 S.C. 410, 413-414 per L. P. Hope.

No court fee will be payable for this hearing on the By Order Roll.

Putting out causes for proof, jury trial or hearing

6.4   **6.4**—(1)   The Keeper of the Rolls shall prepare and publish in the rolls from time to time lists of all causes in which diets have been fixed or allocated—

    (a)   in the Summar Roll, or

    (b)   for proof, jury trial or other hearing,

and put out such causes before such Division of the Inner House or Lord Ordinary, as the case may be, as may be convenient.

(2)   Without prejudice to rule 6.2(3) (causes appointed to procedure roll put out for hearings), a cause published in the rolls for hearing on any roll or at any diet shall be published not later than the second day before the day on which the cause is to be heard.

Deriv. R.C.S. 1965, r.16

General note.

Shortly after a proof, jury trial or other hearing has been allowed the Keeper puts out a list in the daily rolls on a Thursday of the cases in which diets are to be fixed or allocated. The lists of fixed or allocated diets appear on a Thursday in the daily rolls within a few weeks thereafter.

6.4.1

CHAPTER 7 EXTRACTS AND OFFICIAL CERTIFIED COPY INTERLOCUTORS

Applications for extracts

7.1.—(1) Subject to the provisions of this Chapter mentioned in paragraph (2), an application may be made for an extract of an act or a decree after the expiry of seven days after the date of the act or decree, as the case may be.

(2) The provisions referred to in paragraph (1) are—

paragraph (4) of this rule,

rule 7.2 (extracts of decrees in certain family actions),

rule 7.3 (amendments to principal writ),

rule 7.4 (return of steps of process and borrowing productions).

(3) An application under paragraph (1) shall be made by note to the Extractor in Form 7.1 lodged in the appropriate department of the Office of Court.

(4) The court may authorise immediate extract or supersede extract for such period as it thinks fit.

Deriv. P.N. 9th July 1980, reg.1 (r.7.1(2) and (3)) and reg.3 (r.7.1(2))

General note.

An extract is a written instrument proceedings in the name of the Lords of Council and Session, signed by the Principal Extractor or the Extractor of the Court of Session in the case of Court of Session decrees or the Extractor of the acts and decrees of the Teind Court in the case of teind causes, containing a brief narrative of the cause and the procedure in it ending with the decision of the court (the interlocutor of which extract is sought) and, where appropriate, a warrant for execution. It is not a document of debt, but a certificate of the Extractor that such a decree exists in the records of the court: *Inglis v. McIntyre* (1862) 24 D. 541. It is the authority for doing diligence on a decree.

An extract is the proper evidence of the decree of the court and, if ex facie valid, proves itself: Stair, IV.xlii.10. It may be challenged, for example, on the ground that it does not conform to the decree or that it has been issued before time: *McKellar v. Dallas's Ltd*, 1928 S.C. 503.

This rule does not apply to extracts of decrees of divorce or declarator of nullity of marriage: r.7.1(2); for these, see r.7.2.

Classification of extracts.

Extracts may be classified as (1) interim extracts or (2) final extracts.

(1) An interim extract is of an act or decree during the dependence of a cause which does not dispose of the whole of the cause: *Crawfurd v. Ballantyne's Trs.* (1833) 12 S. 113. Such an act or decree is extractable ad interim unless the court otherwise directs: C.S.A. 1988, s.47(3) (formerly C.S.A. 1850, s.28). In general, if something remains to be done in the cause after extract, the extract is an interim extract: *Smith v. Smith* 1927 S.L.T. 462, 463 per Lord Moncreiff; *Brunt v. Brunt* 1958 S.L.T. (Notes) 41. An extract of a decree disposing only of the merits is an interim extract and does not preclude a subsequent decree and extract for expenses: *Crichton Brothers v. Crichton* (1901) 4 F. 271. Nowadays the decrees on the merits and for expenses are invariably in separate interlocutors: in this way extract of the former is not held up pending taxation and, if necessary, a decree for a principal sum can be enforced before waiting for taxation of expenses.

(2) A final extract is an extract of an interlocutor which concludes the cause, leaving nothing to be done and there being no other extractable interlocutor still outstanding. Since 1983, in a cause in which the person liable for the expenses is not legally aided there are usually two interlocutors at the conclusion of a cause (or wherever expenses are dealt with); one disposing of the merits and the other decerning for expenses as taxed (and when taxed, the amount of expenses authorised by the Auditor is inserted by the Extractor in the extract), the latter being the last or final interlocutor. An interlocutor awarding expenses against a non-legally aided party has a decerniture pronounced at the time the finding of expenses is made. Where a party liable in expenses is legally aided there is no decerniture when the finding is made: a finding of liability in expenses is made with a remit to the Auditor to tax and report. A decerniture is only made thereafter, after consideration of any objections or application for modification. The reason for the difference in the case of a legally aided party is that it is not competent to modify expenses after decerniture: *Gilbert's Tr. v. Gilbert* 1988 S.L.T. 680. The interlocutor awarding expenses as taxed (or as varied) is extractable. A final extract is not necessarily, but usually will be, an extract of a final decree; a final decree is one, taken by itself or along with previous interlocutors, by which the whole subject-matter of the cause is disposed of (including expenses: *Baird v. Barton* (1882) 9 R. 970): see note 4.15.2(2) ("taking it out of Court"). The court is functus after a final extract (see *Taylor v. Jarvis* (1860) 22 D. 1031, 1034 per L.J.-C. Inglis) except for the possible rectification of errors (see note 7.9.2). In *Carr v RH Independent Healthcare Ltd* 2018 S.L.T. 1050 (OH), Lord Brailsford held that this rule that the court was functus was merely a practice, had no basis in principle, was no more than a

7.1

7.1.1

7.1.2

document evidencing what the court had done, did not bring a process to an end and the action remained extant (thus avoiding a fresh action being time-barred). Parties cannot be deprived of their rights by the erroneous issue of a final, instead of an interim, extract: *Brunt*, above. If an interlocutor, or the rules, reserves to the parties the right to make a further application to the court (e.g. in cases of custody or aliment of children), it cannot be a final decree and the extract is only an interim extract: *Sanderson v. Sanderson* 1921 S.C. 686, 692 per L.P. Clyde.

ACT OR DECREE.

7.1.3   An act is an interlocutor which does not contain a decerniture (i.e. the inclusion of the word "decern(s)" which is inserted only where the interlocutor finally determines a part or the whole of a cause) and, therefore, is an interlocutory or procedural, and not a determinative, order. A decree is a determinative order, an interlocutor which disposes of a part or the whole of the cause and, therefore, includes the word "decern(s)". The word "decern(s)" does not just give authority for extract; it gives effect to all that has gone before it: *Greig v. Lamb's Trs.* (1830) 8 S. 908.

"EXPIRY OF SEVEN DAYS".

7.1.4   Under s. 23 of the C.S.A. 1868 and then R.C.S. 1965, r. 89(aa) (inserted by A.S. (R.C.A. No. 2) (Miscellaneous) 1984 (S.I. 1984 No. 472)), a decree in absence could be extracted only after 10 days whereas other interlocutors (other than divorce and nullity decrees—which are not treated as decrees in absence) were extractable after seven days. Now that a defender or respondent has at least 21 days notice of the calling of a summons (r. 13.4(1)) or of a petition (r. 14.6(1)), seven days before extract is thought to be sufficient in all cases except divorce and nullity decrees. The date of the act or decree is not counted in calculating the period.

As an act or decree may be extracted before the expiry of the reclaiming days where leave is not required (21 or 14 days: see r. 38.3(2)-(4)), a party seeking to reclaim should notify his opponent of his intention as soon as possible: for, while the successful party cannot be prevented from obtaining an extract, execution and enforcement cannot be pursued without leave of the court except in the case of orders for custody, access or aliment (r. 38.8(5)).

APPLICATION FOR EXTRACT.

7.1.5   The persons entitled to apply for an extract are: (a) the party in whose favour the act or decree is made; (b) his solicitor holding a decree for expenses (to obtain payment of his account and outlays); (c) his assignee, on production of the assignation and evidence of intimation; and (d) his executor, on production of the confirmation.

The following paragraphs apply to applications for extracts of Court of Session decrees: for extracts of decrees in teind causes, application at any time is made to the Extractor of the acts and decrees of the Teind Court.

1.   Application for extract within five years of last interlocutor or, if none, date of calling of summons or presentation of petition (because after that a process is transmitted to the Keeper of the Records: see r. 9.1(2)). Where the process has gone to the process records department, it must first be ordered up to the General or Petition Department, as the case may be, on a transmission slip (which must show (i) year of last interlocutor, (ii) full names of parties, (iii) name of person making application and (iv) date of application). The clerks of session are responsible for the transmission of the process. A process goes to the process records department after the final interlocutor or after a year and a day in which no interlocutor has been pronounced (except injudicial factories and liquidations: r. 9.1(3)): an index is maintained of processes alphabetically, each process having a record number. In fact, the first year of all processes in the process records department are kept in the General or Petition Department, as the case may be, and not in the process record department itself.

(a)   Application is made by note in Form 7.1 (see note 7.1.5A) to the Extractor: r. 7.1(3). Rule 15.2 (applications by note) does not apply: r. 15.2(4). A note may contain more than one interlocutor sought to be extracted. Only one principal extract will be issued. Where more than one extract is required, the additional extracts will be extracts from the Register of Acts and Decrees.

The process, together with the note to the Extractor, has to be transmitted by the party applying for the extract from the General or Petition Department by way of the transmission book to the Extracts Department. The book is receipted by the Extractor's staff and returned by the party to the appropriate department.

When an extract is ready for issue, written intimation is sent to the party who applied together with a note of the fee payable in cash: for fees, see Court of Session etc. Fees Order 1997, Table of Fees, Pt. I, G, item 1 [S.I. 1997 No. 688 as amended, pp. C1201 et seq.].

Where the extract is a final extract, the process is retained in the Extracts Department; otherwise, the process is returned to the appropriate department by the Extracts Department by way of the decreets (now decree) book kept by the Extractor. The book is receipted and returned.

(b)   If the interlocutor sought to be extracted has been extracted previously and the record copy has not yet been transmitted to the Keeper of the Records (which is done within six months after the end of the calendar year (see r. 9.1(1)), application for an extract is made to the Extractor for an extract from the Register of Acts and Decrees on payment of the appropriate fee (see Table of Fees, above, Pt. I, G, item 6). It is helpful to quote the extract number on the principal extract or from the decreets (decree) book or the Register of Extracted Processes kept by the Extractor.

(c)   If the interlocutor sought to be extracted has been extracted previously and the record copy has been transmitted to the Keeper of the Records, application for an extract is made by letter or in person to the Keeper of the Records, Scottish Record Office, General Register House: see Public Records (Scotland) Act 1937, s. 9. The Register of Acts and Decrees containing the record copies of extracts (except extracts in cases of divorce, nullity or dissolution of marriage unless a full extract has been ordered under r. 7.1) for each calendar year is sent to the Keeper within six months of the end of each year: r. 9.1(1). It is helpful to quote the reference number in the Extract Book (which is the number allocated to it in the decreets book). This number and a process can also be traced through the Register of Extracted Processes kept by the Keeper of the Records (alphabetically by year and giving the extract number), a copy of which is also kept by the Extractor for the years up to 1982 (the Extractor keeps his own register from 1985 through which finally extracted processes may be traced). The Keeper will issue an extract prepared from the record copy in the Register on payment of the appropriate fee: for fees, see A.S. (Fees in the Scottish Record Office) 1990, Sched., Pt. III [S.I. 1990 No. 44].

2.   Application for extract after five years from last interlocutor or, if none, date of calling of summons or presentation of petition (because after that a process is transmitted to the Keeper of the Records: see r. 9.1(2)).

(a)   Where extract is sought of an interlocutor not previously extracted in a process not finally extracted (i.e. for a first or principal extract), application must be made by the party seeking extract either in the General or Petition Department on a slip provided for that purpose or to the Keeper of the Records for the retransmission of the process to that department from the Keeper of the Records (see r. 9.2(1) and notes); there is a fee for transmission from the Keeper: see A.S. (Fees in the Scottish Record Office) 1990, above, Sched., Pt. IV, para. 1. Note that petitions for the appointment of judicial factors and winding up of companies are not transmitted to the Keeper until final discharge: r. 9.1(3). It is helpful to quote the reference number in the Register of Unextracted Processes kept by the Keeper when seeking retransmission (the Extractor has a copy of this register back to 1959 available for tracing processes). The process together with a note to the Extractor in Form 7.1 is then transmitted from the General or Petition Department to the Extracts Department by way of the transmission book by the party seeking extract and the book is receipted by the Extractor's staff and returned by the party to the appropriate department. When the extract is ready for issue, written intimation is sent to the party who applied together with a note of the fee payable in cash; for fees, see Court of Session etc. Fees Order 1997, Table of Fees, Pt. I, G, item 1 [S.I. 1997 No. 688, as amended, pp. CI201 et seq.]. The process is then returned to the Keeper of the Records by the Extractor.

(b)   Where there has been a previous extract, application is made to the Keeper of the Records as in (c) above.

FORM 7.1.

A new Form 7.1 was provided for by A.S. (R.C.S.A. No. 3) (Miscellaneous) 1996 [S.I. 1996 No. 1756]. It is no longer necessary to set out the interlocutor(s) to be extracted. Part A is completed by the applicant; Part B by the Extracts Department.

Copies of the form are available from the Extracts Department.

"IMMEDIATE...OR SUPERSEDE EXTRACT".

7.1.5A

The court may order that any interim or final extract (see note 7.1.2) is extractable immediately, notwithstanding r. 7.1(1) which provides that seven days must elapse after decree before extract. Immediate extract will be granted only on cause shown where the justice of the case requires: see, e.g. *Gavin v. P. Henderson & Co.* 1910 S.C. 357. The provision under s. 28 of the Exchequer Court (Scotland) Act 1856 for the immediate extract of decrees in exchequer causes was repealed by the C.S.A. 1988 for lack of use.

7.1.6

Extract may be superseded until a certain event or for a specified period of time: see, e.g. *Fry v. North Eastern Railway Co.* (1882) 10 R. 290; this is often done in divorce cases in relation to the payment of a capital sum. The issue of an extract does not of itself preclude review by the Inner House: r. 38.9. Accordingly there is no need to supersede extract where, e.g. the court grants decree by default under r. 20.1: but see *Munro & Miller (Pakistan) Ltd v. Wyvern Structures Ltd* 1996 S.L.T. 135 where it was thought superseding extract might have some value; though this was commented on adversely by the First Division at 1997 S.C.1, 3C.

Extracts of decrees in certain family actions

7.2.—(1) Subject to paragraph (2), a decree—

    (a)   of divorce,

    (b)   of declarator of nullity of marriage, or

7.2

113

    (c)   in an action to which rule 49.28 (evidence in certain undefended family actions) applies,

shall be extracted automatically after the expiry of 21 days after the date of the decree unless a reclaiming motion has been enrolled.

(2)   A decree of divorce in a simplified divorce application shall be extracted immediately.

(3)   An extract under paragraph (1) or (2) shall be issued by the Extractor to the pursuer and a copy of it sent by the Extractor by first class post to the defender where his address is known.

(4)   Additional extracts under this rule may be obtained from the Extracts Department.

Deriv. R.C.S. 1965, r. 168(11) substituted by S.I. 1978 No. 106 (r. 7.2(1)), r. 170K inserted by S.I. 1982 No. 1679 (r. 7.2(2)); P.N. 9th July 1980, regs. 6 to 8 (r. 7.2(3) and (4))

GENERAL NOTE.

7.2.1   An extract under this rule shows the ground of decree, findings as to custody, access, reservation date, interdict, orders under the Matrimonial Homes (Family Protection) (Scotland) Act 1981, any order for financial provision under s. 8 of the Family Law (Scotland) Act 1985 (but not findings for capital sums unless also decerned for in the divorce interlocutor—this is to avoid the possibility of wrongful diligence should the decerniture be superseded but the extract contain warrant for diligence in respect of some other order) and any order for expenses. Extracts since 21st March 1985 should include all the necessary information of the decree and findings (and are to that extent full or complete) but are not "full" extracts as they are not obtained under rule 7.1 Between 23rd September 1975 and 21st March 1985 an extract showed only the divorce or nullity decree and findings as to custody, access, aliment and periodical allowance. Prior to 23rd September 1975 only a certificate of divorce was issued automatically.

1.   Accordingly, if a full extract is sought of a decree not previously extracted (prior to 23rd September 1975) or not fully extracted (between 23rd September 1975 and 21st March 1985, or possibly after 21st March 1985), application for a full extract may be made by the party seeking extract either to the appropriate section of the General Department or to the Keeper of the Records for retransmission of the process to that section from the Keeper of the Records (see r. 9.2(1) and note 9.2.1); there is a fee for retransmission from the Keeper: see A.S. (Fees in the Scottish Record Office) 1990, Sched., Pt. IV, para. 1 [[S.I. 1990 No. 44]. It is helpful to quote the reference number in the Register of Unextracted Processes kept by the Keeper when seeking retransmission (the Extractor has a copy of this register back to 1959). The process together with a note to the Extractor in Form 7.1 where a full extract is required is then transmitted from the General Department by the party seeking extract to the Extracts Department by way of the transmission book (which is receipted by the Extractor's staff and returned to the General Department). When the extract is ready for issue, written intimation is sent to the party who applied together with a note of the fee payable in cash: for fees, see Court of Session etc. Fees Order 1984, Table of Fees, Pt. I, G, item 1 [S.I. 1984 No. 256, Table as amended, pp. 1153 et seq.]. The process is then returned to the Keeper of the Records by the Extractor.

        Alternatively, in a decree prior to 23rd September 1975, application can be made for an extract from the Register of Decrees in Consistorial Causes kept by the Extractor; but it will not be a full extract. A note to the Extractor is not required, but the process must be obtained and transmitted direct to the Extractor as above. For fees, see Court of Session etc. Fees Order 1984, Table of Fees, Pt. I, G.

2.   If an extract is sought of such a decree which has been fully extracted, application is made to the Keeper of the Records in writing or in person to the Keeper of the Records, General Register House: see Public Records (Scotland) Act 1937, s. 9. The Register of Acts and Decrees containing the record copies of extracts for each calendar year is sent to the Keeper within six months of the end of each year: r. 9.1(1). It is helpful to quote the reference number in the extract (which is the number allocated in the Decreets Book). This number and the process can also be traced through the Register of Extracted Processes kept by the Keeper of the Records (alphabetically by year, giving the extract number) a copy of which is kept by the Extractor for the years up to 1982. The Keeper will issue an extract prepared from the record copy in the Register on payment of the appropriate fee: for fees, see A.S. (Fees in the Scottish Record Office) 1990, Sched., Pt. III [S.I. 1990 No. 44].

        The clerks of court are responsible for the transmission of the process to the Extracts Department after decree for automatic and immediate extracts under this rule.

        The pursuer has paid for an extract from the Register of Decrees in Consistorial Causes with the signeting dues: see Court of Session etc. Fees Order 1997, Table of Fees, Pt. I, B, items 3 and 4 [S.I. 1997 No. 688, as amended, pp. C1201 et seq]. The defender is issued a copy free of charge.

"EXPIRY OF 21 DAYS".

21 days must elapse after decree of divorce or declarator of nullity of marriage because, as extract is automatic, the period of the reclaiming days must expire (21 days): see r. 38.3(2). The date of the decree is not counted in calculating the period.

7.2.2

EXTRACT OF DIVORCE IN SIMPLIFIED DIVORCE APPLICATION.

Simplified divorce applications are undefended actions on the ground of two years separation with consent, or five years separation, where there are no children and no financial provision sought: see r. 49.72. An extract is issued immediately (i.e. after 4 p.m. on the date of decree).

7.2.3

"ADDITIONAL EXTRACTS".

1. Decrees prior to 23rd September 1975. (a) Where a full extract has been obtained previously and is sought, proceed as in note 7.1.5(c). (b) Otherwise, application is made by letter to the Extractor for an extract from the Register of Decrees in Consistorial Causes.
2. Decrees after 23rd September 1975. (a) Where a full extract has been obtained previously and is sought, proceed as in note 7.1.5(1)(c) (in fact all extracts after 21st March 1985 should be "full" or complete extracts), (b) Otherwise, application is made by letter to the Extractor for an extract from the Register of Decrees in Consistorial Causes.
3. Decrees after 1st May 1984. (a) Where a full extract has been obtained previously and is sought, proceed as in note 7.1.5(c) (in fact all extracts after 21st March 1985 should be "full" or complete extracts), (b) Otherwise, application is made (i) by letter to the Extractor for an extract from the Register of Decrees in Consistorial Causes or (ii) in divorce cases to the Keeper of the Records for an extract from the Central Divorce Registry kept by him of all decrees of divorce granted in Scotland (which is a copy of the extract decree issued under r. 7.2).
    For fees, see Court of Session etc. Fees Order 1984, Table of Fees, Pt. I, G, item 5(a) [S.I. 1984 No. 256, Table as amended, pp. C1202 et seq.].

7.2.4

Amendments to principal writ

7.3. An amendment which has been allowed to the instance or a conclusion of a summons, or to a petition, shall be written on the principal writ before the process is transmitted to the Extracts Department for an extract.

7.3

Deriv. P.N. 9th July 1980, reg. 1

GENERAL NOTE.

This rule is required because (a) an error in an extract cannot be altered (see r. 4.15(6) and note 4.15.5) and (b) the Extractor proceeds primarily on the basis of the information in the principal writ and interlocutor to be extracted. Although the Extractor checks all the interlocutors and pleadings for amendments, he may overlook an amendment not actually made on the principal writ, and would be reluctant to proceed without the amendment having been made because the extract cannot be altered: the responsibility must be that of the party.

In relation to a petition, it is any amendment which must be written on the principal writ before transmission to the Extracts Department.

Amendment may be allowed at any time up to final judgment: r. 24.1(1). "Final judgment" is not the same as final decree (see note 4.15.2(2)) and must mean the last or final decree or judgment after any appeal to the House of Lords or expiry of the days of appeal without an appeal: see note 24.1.3(7). Appeal to the House of Lords must be made within three months of the interlocutor appealed against: House of Lords Directions, Direction 8.1.

7.3.1

Return of steps of process and borrowing productions

7.4. Before an application is made under rule 7.1 for a final extract—

(a) any step of process which has been borrowed shall be returned; and

(b) each party shall borrow the productions lodged by him.

7.4

Deriv. P.N. 9th July 1980, reg.2

GENERAL NOTE.

A process sent for final extract is not returned to the General or Petition Department, but is kept by the Extractor for five years and then transmitted to the Keeper of the Records under r. 9.1(2) and cannot be retransmitted. Accordingly, all steps of process must be returned to process and all productions borrowed from process. Where productions are not borrowed in an action of divorce or declarator of nullity of marriage (where extract is automatic or immediate: see r. 7.2), they are returned by post by the Office of Court to the party who lodged them.

7.4.1

"FINAL EXTRACT".

See note 7.1.2(2).

7.4.2

Decrees for payment in foreign currency

7.5   **7.5.**—(1)   Where an application is made under rule 7.1 for an extract of a decree for payment in a foreign currency, the applicant shall lodge with the note to the Extractor a certified statement of the rate of exchange prevailing at—

(a)   the date of the decree sought to be extracted,

(b)   the date on which the note to the Extractor is lodged, or

(c)   a date within three days before the date on which the note to the Extractor is lodged,

and the sterling equivalent of the principal sum, interest and expenses decerned for.

(2)   The certified statement required under paragraph (1) shall be by an official in the Bank of England or an institution authorised under the Banking Act 1987.

Deriv. P.N. 9th July 1980, reg.5A

GENERAL NOTE.

7.5.1   In *Commerzbank AS v. Large* 1977 S.C. 375, it was decided that a creditor entitled to payment of a debt due in a foreign currency could conclude for and obtain decree in a foreign currency. The form of conclusion is usually "for payment of (*state sum in foreign currency*) with interest at the rate of…per cent a year or the sterling equivalent thereof at the date of payment or the date of extract whichever is the earlier". For the purposes of enforcement in Scotland it is necessary to provide for conversion into sterling at a particular date. For practical purposes the latest date is the date on which a note to the Extractor is lodged. The applicant must choose either the date of decree, the date the extract is applied for or (in the case of difficulty at a weekend) a date within three days before extract is applied for. This rule achieves fairness to both parties while giving the applicant some flexibility in converting at a favourable or not disadvantageous rate. As Lord President Emslie observed in *Commerzbank*, above at p. 383 "the search must be for the latest practical date for conversion in order to reduce to a minimum the risk that the foreign creditor who has to enforce his decree will suffer by reason of an adverse fluctuation of the value of sterling as against the currency of account."

A foreign pursuer in an action of delict may obtain decree in a foreign currency if that was the one in which he suffered his loss: *Fullemann v. Mdnnes's Exrs.* 1993 S.L.T. 259.

"CERTIFIED STATEMENT".

7.5.2   This must be a certificate signed by a bank official (of a bank which is an institution authorised under the Banking Act 1987 or the Bank of England) stating the exchange rate and the sterling equivalent of the principal and of the interest and any expenses on a stated day. The certificate should be in the following form:

"I, (*state name and position of certifier*), hereby certify that the rate current in London for the purchase of (*state foreign currency*) at the close of business on the (*state date in prose*) was (*state rate*) to the Pound Sterling. At this rate, the principal sum of (*state sum*) amounts to (*state sterling equivalent*), interest of (*state sum*) amounts to (*state sterling equivalent*) and expenses of (*state sum*) amounts to (*state sterling equivalent*).

Signed for and on behalf of

(*name of bank*)

(Signature)

Dated this day of.".

The bank does not have to be an Edinburgh, or a Scottish, bank; but it may be more convenient if it is an Edinburgh bank. The Scottish banks are authorised institutions under the Banking Act 1987.

The certificate should accompany the note to the Extractor.

The Extractor will insert a docquet at the end of the extract as follows: "In terms of a certificate dated at [Edinburgh] the (*date*), the Sterling equivalent of the principal sum is £......, the interest on that sum is £......, and the expenses is £......, at the rate of exchange prevailing at that date.".

Decrees of adjudication

7.6   **7.6.**   Where an application is made under rule 7.1 for an extract of a decree of adjudication for debt, the applicant shall lodge with the note to the Extractor a statement of the accumulated sum in Form 7.6.

Deriv. P.N. 9th July 1980, reg.5

GENERAL NOTE.

7.6.1   There are two forms of adjudication in execution to be noted here: (a) adjudication on a *debitum fundi* against heritable property for a debt is available to a creditor of a heritable security, feuduty or ground annual in order to accumulate the debt with its interest into capital bearing interest: *Bell's Comm.*, i.753, and see further Graham Stewart on *Diligence*, pp. 592 et seq.; and (b) adjudication against heritable, or moveable (where other diligence not competent), property in satisfaction of a debt constituted by decree (or a document of debt).

Where it has been necessary first to take a decree of constitution of the debt, the expenses of that action may be added to the claim in the action of adjudication. As adjudication is a diligence, the action of adjudication should not include a claim for expenses of process; and such expenses do not form part of the accumulated sum in the action and are not adjudged for. The court may award expenses where the debtor opposes the action unnecessarily; but these expenses are taken and extracted in a separate decree: see Graham Stewart, p. 589.

Adjudication for debt will be abolished by s. 79 of the Bankruptcy and Diligence etc. (Scotland) Act 2007. There will be a new form of diligence called "land attachment" introduced in Pt IV of the 2007 Act to enforce payment of a debt constituted by decree or document of debt which enables a creditor to register the land attachment in the register of Sasines or Land Register and Register of Inhibitions. It enables the creditor to apply to the sheriff to sell all or part of the land attached to pay the debt. This is more powerful than inhibition (whereby the creditor cannot force a sale) and less draconian than sequestration or liquidation (which affects the debtor's whole estate).

"STATEMENT OF THE ACCUMULATED SUM".

This brings into one (total) amount the various items of debt—i.e. principal, interest to the date of decree, any liquid penalty (the purpose of which is to cover expenses) or expenses in the action of constitution (including dues of extract). Payments to account must be deducted. Different debts should be accumulated separately; there should be separate conclusions in the action and separate statements of accumulated sum. The accumulated sum bears interest from the date of decree at the rate concluded for.

7.6.2

Interest

7.7. Where interest is included in, or payable under, a decree, it shall be at the rate of 8 per cent a year unless otherwise stated.

7.7

Deriv. R.C.S. 1965, r. 66

GENERAL NOTE.

Until 1970 the rate of interest on any decree or extract was 5 per cent. Since then the rate has changed as follows:

7.7.1

In an action commenced on or after 6th January 1970:	7%
A.S. (R.C.A. No.5) 1969 [SI 1969/1819]	
In an action commenced on or after 7th January 1975:	11%
A.S. (R.C.A. No.7) 1974 [SI 1974/2090]	
On a decree or extract on or after 6th April 1983:	12%
A.S. (R.C.A. No.2) 1983 [SI 1983/398]	
On a decree or extract on or after 16th August 1985:	15%
A.S. (R.C.A. No.5) 1985 [SI 1985/1178]	
On a decree on or after 1st April 1993:	8%
A.S. (R.C.S.A.) 1993 [SI 1993/770]	

Until 5th April 1983 any increase in the rate of interest applied only in an action *commenced* on or after the date of the increase. From 6th April 1983 any increase in the rate of interest applies to any decree pronounced, or in any extract issued, on or after the date of the increase, whenever the cause was commenced; there was no satisfactory reason for linking an alteration in the rate to the date that caused commenced rather than the date of the decree. From 1st April 1993, with interest rates coming down and to avoid any confusion arising where the interest rate changes between decree and extract, it is stated that the only relevant date is the date of decree: the parties should be in no better or worse position than that at the date of decree caused by the date on which extract was obtained; and the Extractor, in a case where the decree specified the rate, would not change the rate in the extract even though the rate had changed since the decree.

It is now sought to maintain a rate of interest, as the "judicial rate" under this rule, which is about 1 per cent above the minimum lending rate of the clearing banks. This is the principle applied by the Lord Chancellor, with the concurrence of the Treasury, for interest on judgment debts (in England and Wales) under the Judgments Act 1838, s.17. The same rate as is applied to judgment debts is fixed for awards by certain tribunals in the U.K. sitting in Scotland: e.g. Employment Appeal Tribunal and industrial tribunals, fixed by the Secretary of State for Employment with approval of the Treasury (Industrial Tribunals Act 1996, ss.14 and 36(3)).

The phrase "per cent a year" is now more appropriate than "per centum per annum".

"UNLESS OTHERWISE STATED".

7.7.2   The interlocutor allowing decree will usually state the rate of interest. It will not always be the case that the rate current in the rule and concluded for when the summons was signeted is the rate of the rule at the date of decree. A summons may be amended at any time before final judgment to conclude for the current rate (sometimes referred to (erroneously) as the legal rate). But, particularly when interest rates are or may be increasing, to avoid frequent amendment or amendment in an undefended cause (which would have to be re-served if a higher rate is sought than that originally claimed), it would seem appropriate to frame a conclusion for interest in the following or similar terms where the current rate is sought: "For interest from (*state date from which interest sought*) until payment" or "For interest at the rate in rule 7.7 of the Rules of Court of Session 1994 applicable at the date of decree from (*state date from which interest sought*) until payment". Strictly, it is not necessary to mention, or refer to, the rate in the conclusion because the rule applies the current rate where interest is included or payable; and it is not necessary to conclude for interest at all from the date of decree, for interest is due *ex lege* on the principal sum and expenses from the date of decree: *Dalmahoy and Wood v. Magistrates of Brechin* (1859) 21 D. 210. But it is the practice to have a conclusion for interest, and good practice to refer to the rate or the rule, as it is then clear to a defender what has full liability is alleged to be.

Where interest is concluded for from the date of decree, or where the conclusion is silent, and the cause has been reclaimed, the date of decree means the date of the interlocutor of the appellant court and not the date of the original degree. Interest from the date of the original decree will be considered only where there has been unjustifiable delay by the party liable: *McCormack v. National Coal Board* 1957 S.C. 277; cf. Maclaren on *Court of Session Practice*, p. 298. The House of Lords has a discretion whether to award interest on appeal to it, and if it does not award interest the Court of Session cannot do so in applying the judgment: *Roger v. J. P. Cochrane & Co.* 1910 S.C. 1.

The effect of s.1(1A) of the Interest of Damages (Scotland) Act 1958 (inserted by the Interest of Damages (Scotland) Act 1971, s.1) is mandatory, so that interest on damages for personal injuries must be included in a decree unless there are special reasons for not doing so. Therefore, the sum sued for must be deemed to cover all heads of damage and interest under that section. Accordingly, it is unnecessary to conclude for this element of interest specifically; a conclusion for £X (sufficient to cover this element of interest as well as damages) "with interest at Y per cent a year [or the rate in rule 7.7 of the Rules of the Court of Session 1994 applicable at the date of decree] from the date of decree until payment" is adequate and proper: *Orr v. Metcalfe* 1973 S.C. 57.

It is permissible to conclude for interest at a variable rate where this has been contracted for—e.g. "at X per cent a year above bank rate": *Bank of Scotland v. Forsyth* 1969 S.L.T.(Sh.Ct) 15; cf. *Royal Bank of Scotland plc v. Geddes* 1983 S.L.T.(Sh.Ct) 32.

THE FULL RATE OR LESS OR MORE.

7.7.3   Where interest is sought from the date of decree, normally the rate allowed will be the rate sought in the summons or the rate current in the rule ("the judicial rate"). Where the rate in the rule is sought from a date earlier than the date of decree, interest will not necessarily be allowed at that rate because there may be fluctuations over the period for which interest is sought (in which case an average rate may be applied) or the sum awarded is for a cumulative loss (in which case half the rate applicable to that period may be applied). The judicial rate in r.7.7 has been unaltered since April 1, 1993, although, for example, the market rate plummeted in the late 2008 and early 2009 from 5 per cent to 0.5 per cent. In *Farstad Supply AS,*, it was confirmed that, in exercise of the discretion under s.1 of the Interest on Damages (Scotland) Act 1958, the court could take into account the mismatch between the judicial rate and the market rate over recent years, and, adopting a broad brush approach, awarded 2 per cent from December 31, 2002 and December 4, 2008 when the official bank rate fell to 2 per cent, then 4 per cent to the date of decree and 8 per cent from the date of decree. Interest is compensatory and the judicial rate is an approximation of compensation for loss of income that the expended funds could have generated. The decision in *Farstad Supply AS*, above, was upheld by an Extra Division at 2013 S.C. 302. In the Division it was confirmed that the judicial rate was the guiding rate for both pre- and post- decree interest. The Division rejected adopting the approach of the Commercial Court and the Admiralty Court of England and Wales of awarding interest at 1 per cent above base rate as more reflective of the view that account should be taken of the cost of borrowing rather than the loss of a return on funds invested.

In actions of reparation for personal injuries or death, the position appears to be as follows: (1) *Pre-decree loss of earnings and loss of support.* Since the Interest on Damages (Scotland) Act 1958, s.1 (as amended by the Interest on Damages (Scotland) Act 1971, s.1), the practice has been to award interest at half the judicial rate (or half the average rate where the rate has changed over the period in question) from the date the loss began (date of accident) to the date the loss ceased or, if it did not, to the date of decree: see, e.g. *Smith v. Middleton*, 1972 SC 30; *McCuaig v. Redpath Dorman Long Ltd*, 1972 S.L.T.(Notes) 42; *Ward v. Tarmac Civil Engineering Ltd*, 1972 S.L.T.(Notes) 52; *Wilson v. Chief Constable, Lothian and Borders Police*, 1989 S.L.T. 97 (an adjusted average of two rates). (2) *Pre-decree solatium or loss of society*. In the early years of the 1971 Act amendment to the 1958 Act, interest on past solatium was (because of the change in rates between the dates of accident and degree) an average rate: see *Smith*; *McCuaig*; *Ward*, above. Since then, though the rate remained at 11 per cent for eight years, the practice has been—(a) normally to adopt a similar rule to (1) above and award half the judicial rate; (b) where most solatium was before the proof, to award a higher rate than half; and (c) where all solatium was post solatium, to award the full rate. In considering what is fair, *J.M. v. Fife Council*, 2009 S.C. 163 (First Div.) sets out factors to be considered. In *Starkey v. National Coal Board*, 1987 S.L.T. 103, Lord Morison held that there was no logical justification for the practice of calculating interest without regard to changes in the rate during the relevant period; instead of awarding half the judicial rate he adjusted the rate to take account of an increase in the rate during the latter part of the relevant period: see also *Wilson*, above. The award and payment of interim damages may affect the award of interest: see *Redman v. McRae*, 1991 S.L.T. 785; *Jarvie v. Sharp*, 1992 S.L.T. 350. (3) *Future loss*. No pre-decree interest can be awarded: *Macrae v. Reed & Mallik Ltd*, 1961 S.C. 68; *McCuaig*, above. Section 1(1) and (2) of the Damages Act 1996 provide that, in determining the rate of return to be expected from investment of a sum awarded as damages for future pecuniary loss, the court shall take into account such rate of return as may be prescribed by Scottish Ministers; but that shall not prevent the court taking a different rate of return into account if any party shows that it is more appropriate in the case in question. The current rate is 2.5 per cent (discerned from an assumed net return on ILGSs): Damages (Personal Injury) (Scotland) Order 2002 (S.S.I. 2002/46). This rate is the discount (reflecting the opportunity to invest and obtain an annual return) applied in reaching the multiplier (the number of years during which the loss is likely to subsist) by which the multiplicand (annual rate of future loss) is multiplied. There must be something special or exceptional to justify a different rate; general changes to the economic climate are not special features of a particular case and involve an attack on the prescribed rate itself: *Tortolano v. Ogilvie Construction Ltd*, 2013 S.C. 313 (Second Div). (4) Interest on the total award (including pre-decree interest) is at the judicial rate in the rule. (5) *A selective and discriminating approach must be made* in relation to interest claimed under the 1958 Act: *Macrae*; *Smith*, above. The court may refuse to award interest if there are special reasons: 1958 Act, s.1(1A). The reasons must be special to the case—e.g. undue delay or abuse of process; and see further, note 7.7.8.

The Social Security (Recovery of Benefits) Act 1997 repeals s.103 of the Social Security (Administration) Act 1992 which provided that in assessing interest the award of damages is reduced by a sum equal to the amount of relevant benefits received. Section 81(5) of the 1992 Act has been re-enacted in s.17 of the 1997 Act which provides that in assessing damages the amount of any listed benefits paid is to be disregarded. The question arises whether, now, in assessing interest the whole of the listed benefits received should be deducted and interest applied only to the balance or that no deduction should be made and interest applied to the gross award. There is a divergence of judicial opinion. In *George v. George C. Peebles & Son*, 1998 S.L.T. 685, Lord Nimmo Smith held that, since the primary purpose of an award of interest is to compensate a pursuer for being deprived of the use of money which he would have received but for the accident, it was inappropriate to leave out of account the fact that he had received benefits in place of earnings he would have received. The inference was that Parliament intended that the discretion conferred by s.1(A) of the Interest on Damages (Scotland) Act 1958 should continue to be exercised; and interest was awarded in that case on the difference between the loss of earnings and income support received. In *Spence v. Wilson*, 1998 S.C. 433, Lord Eassie came to the opposite opinion. He held that s.103 and its statutory predecessor innovated on the preceding common law and that the repeal of s.103 and omission of a re-enactment implied a legislative intention that the receipt of benefits was to be disregarded in the assessment of interest just as in the assessment of damages (notwithstanding, it must be supposed, that there is an express provision for the latter). The issue has now been determined by the Inner House in a report from the Lord Ordinary in *Wisely v. John Fulton (Plumbers) Ltd*, 1998 S.C. 910 and confirmed by the House of Lords (2000 S.C.(H.L.) 95). It was held that, by virtue of s.17 of the 1997 Act, the court disregards any benefits received by the pursuer when working out interest and, therefore, calculates interest on the whole amount of the damages for past loss of earnings. The case of *George*, above, was wrongly decided because it is inconsistent with the scheme of the 1997 Act.

Interest may be sought at a rate which is more or less than that current in the rule. Little difficulty will be encountered in seeking a lower rate. Allowance of a rate which is higher will depend on the circumstances. A rate contracted for will be allowed (see, e.g. *Bank of Scotland v. Davies*, 1982 S.L.T. 20) subject to the application of the Consumer Credit Act 1974, ss.134-140 to credit bargains, as to which, see *A. Ketley v. Scott* [1981] I.C.R. 241; otherwise, the court always has a discretion and will have regard to the circumstances of the case (*Ross v. Ross* (1896) 23 R. 802 (legitim)) and the court may refuse interest where it would normally be payable (*Waddell's Trs v. Crawford*, 1926 S.C. 654 (legacy)). Interest on a foreign debt may be allowed at the rate of the *lex loci contractus*. In *Presslie v. Cochrane McGregor Ltd (No.2)*, 1999 S.L.T. 1242, the question was left open whether the pursuer could charge interest on outlays at the bank rate on the overdraft he had to take out to fund them.

The Late Payment of Commercial Debts (Interest) Act 1998 (Commencement No. 1) Order 1998 [S.I. 1998 No. 2479], which came into force on 1st November 1998, brought into force the Late Payment of Commercial Debts (Interest) Act 1998 in relation to commercial contracts for the supply of goods or services where the supplier is a small business and the purchaser is a large business or a U.K. public authority. The Late Payment of Commercial Debts Act 1998 (Transitional Provisions) Regulations 1998 [S.I. 1998 No. 2481] provide that in any proceedings it shall be presumed, unless the contrary is proved, that the business of the purchaser is a large business. The Late Payment of Commercial Debts (Interest) Act 1998 (Commencement No. 2) Order 1999 [S.I. 1999 No. 1816] applies the Act to contracts between a small business supplier (as defined in art. 2(2) of the Order and not as in the first commencement order (S.I. 1998 No. 2479)) and a United Kingdom public authority (defined as the Scottish Parliamentary Corporate Body, the Scottish Administration, the Auditor General for Scotland, the National Assembly, and the Auditor General, for Wales). The Late Payments of Commercial Debts (Interest) Act 1998 (Commencement No. 4) Order 2001 (S.I. 2000 No. 2740) applies the 1998 Act to commercial contracts for the supply of goods or services where the supplier and the purchaser are both small businesses. The Late Payment of Commercial Debts (Rate of Interest) Order 1998 [S.I. 1998 No. 2480] sets the statutory interest which may be claimed at 8 per cent above the official dealing rate of the Bank of England. The official dealing rate, also called the U.K. clearing banks base lending rate, is announced from time to time by the Bank's Monetary Policy Committee and is published daily in the *Financial Times* (under London Money

Rates), *The Scotsman* and elsewhere. The Late Payment of Commercial Debts (Interest) Act 1998 (Commencement No.6) (Scotland) Order 2002 [S.S.I. 2002 No.337] brought the remainder of the 1998 Act into force from 7th August 2002 for all remaining commercial contracts for the supply of goods and services.

DATE FROM WHICH INTEREST MAY BE SOUGHT.

7.7.4   Interest may be sought as follows: (1) From the date of decree, as money wrongfully withheld: *Dalmahoy and Wood v. Magistrates of Brechin* (1859) 21 D. 210; *Macrae v. Reed & Mallik Ltd* , 1961 S.C. 68. (2) From the date of citation. This is where—(a) the debt is not liquid; (b) interest was not stipulated for; or (c) the principal sum was not due to be paid by agreement or custom of trade at a particular time: *Blair's Trs v. Payne* (1884) 12 R. 104. It is a rule of law that interest from the date of citation runs on claims for debt in these circumstances and cannot be modified by the exercise of any judicial discretion: *Dean Warrick Ltd v. Borthwick* , 1983 S.L.T. 533. The general rule that interest runs on contractual debts from judicial demand (i.e. citation) was confirmed in *Elliott v. Combustion Engineering Ltd* , 1997 S.C. 127, 131F (Extra Div.). In *Gaelic Assignments Ltd v. Sharp* , 2001 S.L.T. 914 (OH) the question arose as to whether a judicial demand had to be made by bringing a petitory action (or at least not earlier that the introduction of a petitory conclusion into an action). Lord Hamilton held that petitory form was not a prerequisite to a judicial demand and that bringing an action for declarator that a debt was due constituted a judicial demand. (3) From a date earlier than citation. For example, (a) where interest runs *ex lege* by statute—e.g. on bills of exchange and promissory notes from the date of presentation or maturity. Bills of Exchange Act 1882, s.57 or under the Late Payment Commercial Debts (Interest) Act 1998 (see further at the end of this note); (b) where interest is due by contract from a stipulated date; (c) where damages are claimed, interest is awarded from a date on or after the date when the right of action arose: Interest on Damages (Scotland) Act 1958, s.1 (substituted by the Interest on Damages (Scotland) Act 1971, s.1) (whereas at common law, it was only from the date damages were quantified and decree pronounced). And see "interest on interest" in note 7.7.6. For a recent exposition of the law on interest, see *Wilson v. Dunbar Bank plc* , 2008 S.C. 457 (Extra Div.).

Interest may be restricted to a period shorter than that for which it might otherwise have been due because of unreasonable delay in proceeding with the action: *Nacap Ltd v. Moffat Plant Ltd*, 1986 S.L.T. 326 (limited to five years); *M. & I. Instrument Engineers Ltd v. Varsada*, 1991 S.L.T. 106 (from date of citation only).

Interest cannot be sought after final decree either at common law or under the 1958 Act: *Handren v. Scottish Construction Co. Ltd*, 1967 S.L.T.(Notes) 21.

The general rule is that interest is due by virtue of a contract express or implied or by virtue of the principal sum of money having been wrongfully withheld and not paid when it ought to have been paid *Carmichael v. Caledonian Railway Co.* (1870) 8 M.(H.L.) 119, 131 per Lord Westbury. Where, as in an arbitration, the Interest on Damages (Scotland) Act 1958 does not apply, a sum of damages is wrongfully withheld and unpaid only once it is liquidated to a specific figure: *Farrans (Construction) Ltd v. Dunfermline D.C.*, 1988 S.L.T. 466. Where a pursuer raises an action in England for payment of a liquid debt which he abandons and reraises an action for the same debt in Scotland, the debt may be deemed to have been wrongfully withheld from the date of the raising of the English action: *Trans Barwil Agencies (U.K.) Ltd v. John S. Braid & Co. Ltd (No. 2)*, 1990 S.L.T. 182. For a peculiar case where interest was awarded on a liquid debt in a building contract from before the date of citation, see *Robertson Construction Co. (Denny) Ltd v. Taylor*, 1990 S.L.T. 698. The general rule still applies following the 1958 Act; and, in relation to damages, interest may reasonably be held to run from the date when damages may reasonably be regarded as quantifiable or capable of ascertainment: *Boots the Chemist Ltd v. G.A. Estates Ltd*, 1992 S.C. 485. That will usually be the point at which the judge quantifies it (the interlocutor awarding it) or the jury determines it (application of the verdict). In *Sheridan v News Group Newspapers Ltd*, 2019 S.C. 203 (First Div.), it was held that the interpolation of an unsuccessful reclaiming motion or motion for a new trial by a defender did not affect this principle. It was also held in that case, at para. [46], that there is little room for exercise of the discretion in s.1(1) or 1(1A) of the 1958 Act to fix a later date where there has been intercession of appellate proceedings. For a discussion of the circumstances and occasions where interest is due, see Erskine, III.iii.76 et seq.; Bell, *Comm.*, i,691 et seq. For interest on salvage awards, see *The "Ben Gairn"* 1979 S.C. 98; cf. *The "Rilland"* [1979] 1 Lloyd's Rep. 455; *Fairbairn v. Vennootschap G. Ver Vreis Zn* , 1987 S.L.T. 498.

It is an implied term, in a contract for the supply of goods or services (defined in s.2(2)) where the purchaser and supplier are each acting in the course of a business other than an excepted contract (see s.2(5)), that any qualifying debt carries simple statutory interest: Late Payment of Commercial Debts (Interest) Act 1998, s.1(1) A "qualifying debt" is one created by virtue of an obligation under a contract to pay the whole or part of the contract price unless (when created) the whole debt is prevented by s.3 from carrying statutory interest: 1998 Act, s.3. In certain circumstances contract terms to oust or vary the right to statutory interest are permitted by Pt II of the Act. Interest runs from the last day of 30 days beginning with the day of performance or the day on which the purchaser has notice of the amount of the debt (the relevant day), whichever is the later, unless another date has been agreed or the debt relates to an obligation to make an advance payment: 1998 Act, s.4. Statutory interest starts to run on the day after the relevant day at the rate prevailing in s.6 at the end of the relevant day: 1998 Act, s.4(2). The rate of statutory interest is fixed by the Secretary of State by statutory instrument: 1998 Act, s.6 (see end note 7.7.3). There may be remission of interest in the interests of justice: 1998 Act, s.5 (a provision providing a rich soil for litigation).

INTEREST ON JUDICIAL EXPENSES.

As a general rule an award of expenses bears interest from the date of the interlocutor decerning for the taxed expenses (*Dalmahoy and Wood v. Magistrates of Brechin* (1859) 21 D. 210; *McCormack v. N.C.B.*, 1957 S.C. 277) or on an interim decree when extracted and charged upon (*Wallace v. Henderson* (1876) 4 R. 264). Interest is not allowed on an award of expenses prior to decerniture for their payment: *Phee v. Gordon,* [2014] CSIH 50 (Extra Div), the principle being established in *Carmichael v. Caledonian Railway Co.,* (1870) 8 M (H.L.) 119, 131. Once expenses have been taxed the Extractor would issue extract decree for the taxed amount with interest from the date of the Auditor's report (the court already having decerned for the expenses as taxed). Now, consistent with the principle, interest on expenses will be postponed until the final interlocutor, because, e.g., the right of appeal removes the concept of withholding of the expenses being wrongful (see *Roger v. J & P Cochrane & Co.,* 1910 S.C. 1 aff'd in *McGovern v James Nimmo & Co. Ltd,* 1938 S.C. (H.L.) 18. In Maclaren on Expenses in the Supreme and Sheriff Court (1912), p.505, it is stated that in exceptional circumstances interest may be awarded prior to decree in relation to outlays but not professional work: see e.g. *McDowall v. McDowall* (1821) 1 S. 200; *Whitehead & Morton v. Cullen* (1861) 24 D. 86; *Phillips v. Upper Clyde Shipbuilders*, 1990 S.L.T. 887 (interest on outlays refused); and see *Presslie v. Cochrane McGregor Group Ltd (No. 3)*, 15th October 1998, unreported (1998 G.W.D. 35-1810).

That decerniture is usually in the final decree or interlocutor. A "final decree" is one, taken by itself or along with previous interlocutors, by which the whole subject-matter of the cause is disposed of including expenses (see note 4.15.2(2)). Where the person liable in expenses is not legally aided there is (since 1983) a decerniture for expenses in an interlocutor separate from that dealing with the merits decerning for expenses as taxed (the sum to be determined by the Auditor); whereas if the person liable is an assisted person there is no decerniture at that stage (merely a finding of expenses). The fact that the amount of expenses has not been determined should make no difference, and interest on expenses should be payable from a date no later than the date of the interlocutor finding a party liable in expenses (whether or not decerned for or the amount determined). Where the interlocutor is reclaimed, the relevant date is the date of the interlocutor affirming the original decree: *Roger v. J. & P. Cochrane & Co.*, 1910 S.C. 1.

Interim execution of expenses pending appeal to the House of Lords has not been allowed to include interest: *Dunlop v. Spier* (1825) 4 S. 179, though this may now be doubted. The House of Lords may award interest (simple or compound) in its discretion, but the expenses do not carry interest unless it has so ordered: C.S.A. 1988, s.42.

INTEREST ON INTEREST AND COMPOUND INTEREST.

It is competent to sue for a principal sum and for a fixed sum of interest due on it with interest on both from the date of citation where both the principal and the interest are the subject-matter of the action because interest was due prior to citation, usually by contract (the interest also being money wrongly withheld): *Napier v. Gordon* (1831) 5 W. & S. 745. This is often done. In *Jolly v. McNeill* (1829) 7 S. 666 it was stated that such accumulation of interest on interest was not to be allowed in ordinary contract debts where interest was not due but might be allowed in certain cases. Such accumulation has been allowed: *Napier,* above (defender in mora for refusing to pay arrears of interest); *Maclean v. Campbell* (1856) 18 D. 609; cf. *Clyde Navigation Trs v. Kelvin Shipping Co.*, 1927 S.C. 622 (thought to be compound interest being claimed); and for a recent discussion where interest on interest allowed, see *Nash Dredging (U.K.) Ltd v. Kestrel Marine Ltd*, 1986 S.L.T. 67; and see Bell's *Comm.,* i,695. *Wilson v. Dunbar Bank plc*, 2008 S.C. 457 (Extra Div.), which contains an exposition on the law relating to interest, explains the basis for interest on interest as being where interest is due on a debt before citation, usually because of a contractual provision. It is permissible to sue for the principal sum and the accrued interest in separate conclusions with interest on both, or to sue for the principal sum with interest at the (agreed) rate from the date interest became due until payment.

But compound interest proper, as a general rule, is not allowed: *Maclean v. Campbell* (1856) 18 D. 609 (interest from citation on principal and interest calculated to date of citation allowed but no compound interest after that date); and in *Douglas v. Douglas's Trs* (1867) 5 M. 827, 836, L.J.-C. Patton said: "A claim for compound interest, with annual rests, is a demand which can only be maintained, either in the case of a fixed usage in commercial dealings, or where there has been an abuse in a party trusted with funds and violating his trust". Exceptions to the general rule are—(a) express agreement; (b) as a penalty for breach of trust or where a person fails in an obligation to invest and accumulate: *Cranston & Hay v. Scott* (1826) 5 S. 62 (judicial factor *loco tutoris*); (c) where there is a fixed commercial usage (e.g. bank loans: *Reddie v. Williamson* (1863) 1 M. 229, 237) but not on interest not yet applied (*Bank of Scotland v. Davies*, 1982 S.L.T. 20); (d) where advances are made by a factor on a trust estate, but not on solicitor's cash advances unless agreed or where as usually made: *Graham's Exrs v. Fletcher's Exrs* (1870) 9 M. 298.

INTEREST IN TENDERS.

Where a tender is lodged in an action for damages the tender is deemed to to be in full satisfaction of any claim to interest unless otherwise stated: Interest on Damages (Scotland) Act 1958, s.1(1B) (inserted by the Interest on Damages (Scotland) Act 1971, s.1). Thus, if the total of principal and interest awarded exceeds the tender, the pursuer has beaten the tender: *The "Devotion 11"* 1979 S.C. 80. In considering whether the tender is beaten the court may take into account such part of the interest it awarded as it thinks appropriate: 1958 Act, s.1(1B). Hence, if the tender were lodged some time before the proof so that the interest which accrued between the date of tender and the date of the award took the award over the tender, the pursuer might not be held to have beaten the tender: cf. *Quinn v. Bowie (No. 2)*, 1987

7.7.5

7.7.6

7.7.7

S.L.T. 576. A defender may expressly exclude interest from a tender—e.g. where he intends to argue that there are special reasons for refusing interest under s.1(1A) of the 1958 Act.

Where the 1958 Act does not apply, the rule is that interest must be expressly referred to in the tender if it is to be a tender including interest: *Riddell v. Lanarkshire & Ayrshire Railway Co.* (1904) 6 F. 432; *The "Devotion II"*, above.

See further, note 36.11.8.

RESTRICTION OF INTEREST.

7.7.8   As interest is in the discretion of the court, it may be restricted or modified. This may be done, for example, where there has been unreasonable delay in pursuing a claim: *Nacap Ltd v. Moffat Plant Ltd* , 1986 S.L.T. 326 (limited to five years); *M. & I. Instrument Engineers Ltd v. Varsada* , 1991 S.L.T. 106 (from date of citation only).

Even inordinate delay in prosecuting an action should not result, however, in a pursuer being deprived of interest on items of property damage which were capable of being ascertained in respect of which expenditure had been incurred (*Boots the Chemist Ltd v. G.A. Estates Ltd* , 1992 S.C. 485—because the defenders have had use of money for a longer period than they should have had—per L.J.-C. Ross at p. 497) or on past loss of support and services (*Bhatia v. Tribax Ltd* , 1994 S.L.T. 1201).

Fees for extracts to be included in extracts

7.8   **7.8.**—(1) Where the court pronounces an interlocutor awarding a sum of expenses, the interlocutor shall be deemed to include, in addition to such sum, the fees for any extract required to enforce the award.

(2) In an extract of an interlocutor containing an award of expenses, the Extractor shall include the amount of the fee for the extract.

Deriv. R.C.S. 1965, r. 63A inserted by S.I. 1986 No. 1937

GENERAL NOTE.

7.8.1   The source of this rule in so far as it relates to modified expenses is s.33 of the C.S.A. 1821 (repealed by A.S. (R.C.A. No. 8) (Miscellaneous) 1986 [S.I. 1986 No. 1937]).

Since 1983, when the court grants decree for expenses against a non-legally aided party, it pronounces one interlocutor finding a party entitled to expenses and another decerning against the party liable in expenses as taxed by the Auditor, although the amount has not then been determined (and when taxed, the amount of expenses authorised is inserted by the Extractor in the extract). In the case of a legally aided party being found liable in expenses the first interlocutor remits to the Auditor for taxation and there is no decerniture at that stage. The interlocutor decerning for expenses is only pronounced after the Auditor's report and after consideration of any objections or application for modification. The reason for the difference in the case of a legally aided party is that it is not competent to modify expenses after decerniture: *Gilbert's Tr. v. Gilbert* , 1988 S.L.T. 680. The fees for an extract of a decree for expenses are included automatically by the Extractor when preparing the extract.

For fees for extracts, see Court of Session etc. Fees Order 1984, Table of Fees, Pt I, G [S.I. 1984 No. 256, Table as amended, pp. C 1202 et seq]. The credit scheme introduced by P.N. No. 4 of 1976 for debiting accounts of agents does not apply to extracts and the Extracts Department.

Form of extracts

7.9   **7.9.**—(1) Subject to paragraphs (2) and (3), the extract of an act or a decree shall be in such form as the Extractor thinks fit.

(2) An extract shall be—

(a) partly or wholly written,

(b) typewritten,

(c) printed,

(d) lithographed, or

(e) photographed,

and subscribed on the last page by the Extractor and have each page impressed with the stamp of the Extractor.

(3) An alteration in an extract shall be authenticated by the initials of the Extractor.

(4) In this rule, a reference to the Extractor includes the Principal Extractor.

Deriv. R.C.S. 1965, r. 63(2) and (3) substituted by S.I. 1986 No. 1937

GENERAL NOTE.

7.9.1   Until A.S. (R.C.A. No. 8) (Miscellaneous) 1986 [S.I. 1986 No. 1937], the form of an extract was governed by the Court of Session (Extracts) Act 1916 (repealed by that A.S.). R. 7.9 is substantially the same.

Extracts are usually typewritten. Where there is more than one page, the pages are numbered and the total is stated in the extract. The place and date of the extract are stated at the end. The date of the act or decree extracted is stated at the beginning of the extract; where there are two decrees extracted together as one (e.g. a decree for a principal sum and another for the expenses as taxed or a decree and an interlocutor of the Inner House adhering to the interlocutor of the court below), the dates of both are stated. There will no longer be a recital of the claim and procedure in the cause. The extract will be in such form as will reflect the decree of the court and enable its execution.

Extracts are issued in the name of the Lords of Council and Session as a judgment of the whole court, even where the interlocutor is that of a Lord Ordinary.

In preparing an extract, the Extractor may refer to the opinion(s) of the court in construing the interlocutor to be extracted: *McKellar v. Dallas's Ltd* , 1928 S.C. 503.

Extracts are backed, but an extract will no longer be stitched unless specifically requested.

RECTIFICATION OF ERRORS.

Rules 4.15(6) and 4.16(7) apply to the correction of errors before extract: and see note 4.15.5 on correction before extract. It does not necessarily follow that an interlocutor may not be corrected or altered after extract. An action of reduction may have to be brought. It may be possible to obtain an order by petition to rectify an error in an extract (though not where the error originates from the interlocutor): see, e.g. *Brown, Petr* (1840) 2 D. 1467; *Mitchell's Trs, Petrs* , 1930 S.C. 180. But corrections have been made after extract. The grounds for doing so must be no better than for correction before extract: see note 4.15.5. Where there is an error in the summons which is repeated in the extract, an order may be obtained by (petition) or motion to rectify the error: *Miller v. Lindsay* (1850) 12 D. 964; *Small's Trs, Petrs* (1856) 18 D. 1210; *Provan's Trs v. Provan* , 1987 S.L.T. 405. The application should be by petition where the record copy of the extract has reached the Keeper of the Records or the extract has been otherwise registered or recorded; otherwise it may be by motion.

An extract ex facie regular is a probative writ. It may be reduced (with difficulty), and any charge suspended, on the ground, for example, of not being in conformity with the decree: *McKellar v. Dallas's Ltd* , 1928 S.C. 503.

7.9.2

UNITS OF MEASUREMENT.

The Units of Measurement Directive (Council Directive 80/181 of 20th December 1979) was adopted by the E.C. in 1989 [Official Journal, 7th December 1989. L357/28]. From 1st January 1995 member states must use the metric system of measurement and, subject to certain transitional arrangements and exceptions, must cease to use imperial measurements for economic, public health, public safety and administrative purposes. Where a unit of measurement is used in pleadings it should be expressed as a metric unit, and court orders must be so expressed.

7.9.3

Exceptions are as follows: The nautical mile and knot are to be used for sea and air traffic and the foot is to be used for aircraft heights. Until 31st December 1999, fathom may be used for marine navigation; therm for gas supply; pint and fluid ounce for beer, cider, waters, lemonade and fruit juices on returnable containers; and ounce and pound for goods sold loose from bulk. In perpetuity, acre may be used for land registration; troy ounce for transactions in precious metals; mile, yard, foot and inch for road traffic signs, distances and speed measurements; pint for draught beer, cider and milk in returnable containers.

Warrants for execution

7.10. An extract of a decree on which execution may proceed shall include a warrant for all lawful execution in the following terms: "and the Lords grant warrant for all lawful execution on this decree".

7.10

Deriv. R.C.S. 1965, r. 64

GENERAL NOTE.

By virtue of the warrant under this rule, an extract is its own warrant for all lawful execution (for which see note 7.10.2).

7.10.1

Decrees for the payment of money may be enforced by a charge and diligence following on this warrant. Exchequer decrees are enforced in the same manner, the forms of exchequer diligence under the Exchequer Court (Scotland) Act 1856 having been abolished by the Debtors (Scotland) Act 1987.

A charge for enforcing a decree *ad factum praestandam* (to perform a specific act) is no longer competent: 1987 Act, s. 100(2). If it is sought to enforce such a decree by imprisonment, application must be made to the court by minute for a warrant of imprisonment under s. 1(2) of the Law Reform (Miscellaneous Provisions) (Scotland) Act 1940. The court has power to substitute payment of damages in lieu of imprisonment or to make such other order as appears to be just and equitable.

"ALL LAWFUL EXECUTION".

1. In the case of a decree for payment of money, the extract is warrant for charging the debtor to pay, within 14 days if the debtor is in the UK (28 days if he is not or his whereabouts are unknown: Debtors (Scotland) Act 1987, s. 90(3)), the sums mentioned in the extract and any interest accrued; and, in the event of failure to pay, the execution of an earnings arrestment, the attachment of articles belonging to the debtor (including opening lockfast places in order to execute poinding), inhibition, a land attachment, a residual attachment, a money attachment, arrestment other

7.10.2

than an earnings arrestment and, in the case of a maintenance order, a current maintenance arrestment: 1987 Act, s. 87(2). An "earnings arrestment" means a diligence under Part III of the 1987 Act (to enforce payment of a debt including maintenance) against the earnings of the debtor in the hands of his employer. A "current maintenance arrestment" means a diligence to enforce payment of maintenance as it falls due under Part III of the 1987 Act. The rules for attachment and auction sales are laid down in Parts 2 and 3 of the Debt Arrangement and Attachment (Scotland) Act 2002, and for arrestments in Part III of the 1987 Act.

Inhibition in execution is authorised on an extract decree, or document of debt registered in the Books of Council and Session or sheriff court books: Bankruptcy and Diligence etc. (Scotland) Act 2007, s. 146 and s. 87(2) of the 1987 Act (amended by s. 146 of the 2007 Act). Arrestment or furthcoming is authorised on a decree authorising it: Debtors (Scotland) Act 1987, s. 73A inserted by s. 206 of the 2007 Act.

2.   An extract of a decree in an action of poinding of the ground is warrant for a poinding of the ground: 1987 Act, s. 87(5).

With two exceptions, an extract is necessary to do diligence. The exceptions are (a) an official certified copy interlocutor for interim aliment (s. 7.11(2)) and (b) an interlocutor granting warrant for recovery of expenses in a matter before the Solicitors Disciplinary Tribunal (see note 68.2.1A).

There is no civil imprisonment for debt (Debtors (Scotland) Act 1880), even for Crown taxes (1987 Act, s. 74(2)), except on application by minute to the sheriff in the case of alimentary debts (Civil Imprisonment (Scotland) Act 1882, s. 4—which does not include failure to pay periodical allowance: *White v. White* , 1984 S.L.T. (Sh.Ct.) 30), or for rates (Local Government (Scotland) Act 1947, s. 247(5)), the community charge (Abolition of Domestic Rates Etc. (Scotland) Act 1987, Sched. 2, para. 7) or the council tax (Local Government Finance Act 1992, Sched. 8, para. 2): see *Hardie v. Hardie* , 1984 S.L.T. (Sh.Ct.) 49. There must be wilful refusal to pay (which is presumed until the contrary is proved by the debtor); mere want of means is not enough (unless the debtor can prove he has not been able to earn the means of paying the debt since the decree): 1882 Act, s. 4.

Adjudication to attach heritable property, though a diligence, required the raising of an action of adjudication to obtain a decree for it. Inhibition in execution, though so called, is still a preventive diligence. There will be a new diligence of land attachment to enforce payment of a debt constituted by decree or document of debt. Application to sell land attached will be made to the sheriff: see note 7.6.1.

Official certified copy interlocutors

7.11

7.11.—(1) An application may be made to the appropriate department of the Office of Court for an official certified copy of an interlocutor in respect of—

(a)   the appointment of a judicial factor;

(b)   the approval of a scheme of arrangement in a petition for variation of a trust under section 1(1) of the Trusts (Scotland) Act 1961;

(c)   the approval of a cy près scheme or a scheme for the variation or reorganisation of a public trust; or

(d)   a decree for interim aliment.

(2)   The Principal Clerk, the Deputy Principal Clerk, or a clerk of session authorised by either of them, may append to an official certified copy of an interlocutor granting decree for interim aliment a warrant for all lawful execution in the following terms: "and the Lords grant warrant for all lawful execution on this decree for interim aliment".

Deriv. R.C.S. 1965, r. 170D(6) inserted by S.I. 1976 No. 1994 (r. 7.11(2))

GENERAL NOTE.

7.11.1

A certified copy interlocutor (a "CCI") may be obtained for any interlocutor (the certification being applied by the clerk of session to the copy prepared by the party), but in four instances an official copy may be obtained from the court—(a) the appointment of a judicial factor, (b) approval of a trust variation scheme, (c) a cy près scheme or a scheme of variation or reorganisation of a public trust under s.9 of the Law Reform (Miscellaneous Provisions) (Scotland) Act 1990 and (d) a decree for interim aliment (pending determination of the cause). These are permitted because it is quicker than an extract. An official CCI is required to enable the judicial factor to intromit with the estate of his ward; and to enforce a decree for interim aliment on a warrant for execution. The official CCI is on headed paper and backed. To the CCI of the appointment of a judicial factor there is a sheet containing the schedule of the estate of the ward; and more than one CCI may be obtained.

On judicial factors, see Chap. 61. On variation of trusts, see Chap. 63, Pt. I. On cy près schemes and variation and reorganisation of public trusts, see Chap. 63, Pt. III. On interim aliment, see Chap. 49.

"ALL LAWFUL EXECUTION".

7.11.2

The warrant in a decree for interim aliment enables the creditor to charge the debtor to pay, within 14 days if the debtor is in the UK (28 days if he is not or his whereabouts are unknown: Debtors (Scotland) Act 1987, s. 90(3)), the sums mentioned in the extract and any interest accrued; and, in the event of failure to pay, to execute an earnings arrestment, to attach articles belonging to the debtor (including opening lockfast places in order to execute poinding), arrestment other than an earnings arrestment and, as a maintenance order, a current maintenance arrestment: 1987 Act, s. 87(2). An "earnings arrestment" means a diligence under Part III of the 1987 Act (to enforce payment of a debt including maintenance) against the earnings of the debtor in the hands of his employer. A "current maintenance arrestment" means a diligence to enforce payment of maintenance as it falls due under Part III of the 1987 Act. The rules for attachment and auction are laid down in Parts 2 and 3 of the Debt Arrangement and Attachment (Scotland) Act 2002, and for arrestments in Part III of the 1987 Act.

Because the official CCI contains the words "all lawful execution", an extract is not necessary in order to do diligence.

Civil imprisonment for failure to pay may be sought on application by minute to the sheriff: Civil Imprisonment (Scotland) Act 1882, s. 4. There must be wilful refusal to pay (which is presumed until the contrary is proved by the debtor); mere want of means is not enough (unless the debtor can prove he has not been able to earn the means of paying the debt since the decree); 1882 Act, s.4.

FEES.

7.11.3

See Court of Session etc. Fees Order 1997, Table of Fees, Pt IV, J, items 2 and 3 [S.I. 1997 No. 688, as amended, pp.C1201 et seq.]. Certain persons are exempt from payment of fees: see 1997 Fees Order, art.5 substituted by S.S.I. 2002 No. 270. A fee exemption certificate must be lodged in process: see P.N. No.1 of 2002.

Where a party is legally represented, the fee may be debited under a credit scheme introduced on 1st April 1976 by P.N. No. 4 of 1976 to the account (if one is kept or permitted) of the agent by the court cashier, and an account will be rendered weekly by the court cashier's office to the agent for all court fees due that week for immediate settlement. Party litigants, and agents not operating the scheme, must pay (by cash, cheque or postal order) on each occasion a fee is due at the time of lodging at the counter at the appropriate department.

CHAPTER 8 TAXES ON FUND UNDER CONTROL OF COURT

Certificates by officer of Revenue and Customs[1]

8.1.—[2](1) Subject to paragraph (2), no—

(a) decree or other interlocutor for payment to a person of any money consigned in the name of the Accountant of Court under the Court of Session Consignations (Scotland) Act 1895,

(b) decree or other interlocutor for payment of consigned money, or for transfer or conveyance to a person of any heritable or moveable property, in a cause which seeks the distribution of the estate of a deceased person, or

(c) decree of exoneration and discharge of a judicial factor appointed by the court to administer and distribute an estate, unless appropriate steps have been taken for the continued administration of a lapsed trust, intestate estate, partnership estate or other estate, heritable or moveable,

shall be pronounced until there has been lodged with the clerk of court a certificate by an authorised officer of the Revenue and Customs stating that all taxes or duties payable to the Commissioners for Her Majesty's Revenue and Customs have been paid or satisfied.

(2) In relation to paragraph (1)(*b*), in an action of multiplepoinding it shall not be necessary for the issue of such a certificate that all of the taxes or duties payable on the estate of a deceased claimant have been paid or satisfied.

Deriv. R.C.S. 1965, r. 36

MONEY CONSIGNED WITH ACCOUNTANT OF COURT.

Under the Court of Session Consignations (Scotland) Act 1895, s. 3, the Accountant of Court is custodian of all sums lodged by order of the court. Consignation may be ordered—(*a*) in lieu of caution for expenses: *Morrison v. Morrison's Exrx.* 1912 S.C. 892; (*b*) in lieu of sisting a mandatory: *Bell v. Strathearn & Blair* 1953 S.L.T. (Notes) 23; (*c*) in lieu of caution in suspensions, suspension and interdict, and suspension and liberation: r. 60.3. For consignation, see note 33.4.3.

CERTIFICATE OF REVENUE AND CUSTOMS.

A certificate is required notwithstanding, in the case of consignation, that income tax on interest in the hands of a deposit-taker (including an institution authorised under the Banking Act 1987) is deducted at source before payment: Income and Corporation Taxes Act 1988, s. 479. This deduction at source provision does not apply, however, where the beneficial owner of the deposit is not ordinarily resident in the UK.

---

[1] Heading and r. 8.1 amended by S.S.I. 2005 No. 268 (effective 7th June 2005).
[2] Heading and r. 8.1 amended by S.S.I. 2005 No. 268 (effective 7th June 2005).

Certificates by officer of Revenue and Customs

8.1.—(1) Subject to paragraph (2), no—

(a) decree or other interlocutor for payment to a person of any money consigned in the name of the Accountant of Court under the Court of Session (Consignations) (Scotland) Act 1895;

(b) decree of other interlocutor for the payment of consigned money, or for transfer or conveyance to a person of any heritable or movable property in a cause which seeks the distribution of the estate of a deceased person; or

(c) decree of exoneration and discharge of a judicial factor appointed by the court to administer and distribute an estate, unless appropriate steps have been taken for the continued administration of a lapsed trust, intestate estate, partnership estate or other estate heritable or movable,

shall be pronounced until there has been lodged with the clerk of court a certificate by an authorised officer of the Revenue and Customs stating that all taxes or duties payable to the Commissioners for Her Majesty's Revenue and Customs have been paid or satisfied.

(2) In relation to paragraph (1)(c), in an action of multiplepoinding it shall not be necessary for the issue of such a certificate that all of the taxes or duties payable on the estate of a deceased claimant have been paid or satisfied.

Rule: RCS 1965, r.86.

Note: consignation in Account of the Court

8.1.1 Under the Court of Session (Consignations) (Scotland) Act 1895, s.3, the Accountant of Court is custodian of all sums lodged by order of the court. Consignation may be ordered—(a) in lieu of caution for expenses: *Maxwell v Controller of Motor Cars* 1912 S.C. 467; (b) in lieu of finding a mandatory: *De Mulder v Steele* 1936 S.L.T. ... (loss of ...); ... in lieu of caution in sequestration, suspension and interdict, and suspension: see rule 33.4.3.

Cautioners or Revenue and Customs

8.1.2 A certificate required with the drawing up, in the case of consignation, that income tax or interest in the hands of a depositary, including on transaction authorised under the Finance Act 1981 is deducted at source before payment (Income and Corporation Taxes Act 1988, s.470), his deduction at source provision does not apply, however, where the beneficial owner of the deposit is not ordinarily resident in the UK.

Heading and r.8.1 amended by S.S.I. 2005 No... (effective 1st June 2005).
Heading and r.8.1 amended by S.S.I. 2005 No.268 (effective 7th July 2005).

CHAPTER 10 COURT SITTINGS

Session of the court[1]

10.1.—(1) Except in vacation, the court shall be in session throughout the year and, subject to paragraph (2), shall—

    (a) normally sit on Tuesday, Wednesday, Thursday and Friday of each week;

    (b) normally sit between 1000 hours and 1600 hours, with an appropriate adjournment for lunch;

    (c) not sit—

        (i) on a public holiday;

        (ii) on such other days as the Lord President may, in exceptional circumstances, direct.

  (2) The court may sit—

    (a) on a Monday where it is considered desirable to do so;

    (b) on a Saturday, Sunday or public holiday where it is desirable to do so to determine a matter of urgency.

  (3) For the purposes of these Rules, a "sitting day" is a day on which the court sits under paragraph (1)(a) or a vacation sitting day.

GENERAL NOTE.

The forerunner of this Chapter was introduced by A.S. (R.C.A. No. 5) (Miscellaneous) 1987 [S.I. 1987 No. 2160] replacing and repealing ss. 6, 7, 8 and 11 of the C.S.A. 1868, s.4(2), (3) (part) and (5) of the Administration of Justice (Scotland) Act 1933, s.2 of the Administration of Justice (Scotland) Act 1948, and s.3 (part) of the Exchequer Court (Scotland) Act 1856 (see r. 10.6).

R.C.S. 1994 when introduced by A.S. (R..C.S. 1994) [S.I. 1994 No. 1443] in recognition of the fact that the business of the court continued in vacation (except the hearing of proofs, jury trials and procedure roll hearings) and to avoid public misconception of the meaning of vacation, this rule provided for the court to be in session for most of the year (except in practice for one vacation at Christmas and New Year).

In A.S. (R.C.S.A) (Court Sittings) 2017 [S.S.I. 2017 No. 414], Chap. 10 was replaced and now provides for the court to sit all year round (but not normally Mondays, Saturdays and Sundays) except on public holidays and such other days as the Lord President may direct. The vacation sitting days and public holidays are now set out in tables to r. 10.3 and no longer in Directions. The current Direction No. 1 of 2016 is therefore otiose.

The legal year begins in September.

"SITTING DAY".

Previously there were terms of the court which were formerly called the sessions of the court. Now we have the more mundane "sitting days". These are defined in r. 10.1.3.The legal year begins in September: see Direction No. 1 of 2016 pp. C1501 et seq.

"VACATION SITTING DAYS".

Vacation sitting days are now defined in r.10.2 and specified in a table in r. 10.3. As the court now sits throughout the year, vacations (set out in a table in r. 10.3) are short and vacation sitting days few.

Vacation

10.2.—[2](1) During vacation, the court—

    (a) shall normally sit on a vacation sitting day;

    (b) may sit, on days other than vacation sitting days, where it is desirable to do so.

  (2) The court shall not sit on—

    (a) a public holiday;

    (b) such other days as the Lord President may, in exceptional circumstances, direct.

10.1

10.1.1

10.1.2

10.1.3

10.2

---

[1] Heading and r. 10.1 substituted by S.S.I. 2017 No. 414 r. 2(2) (effective 1st January 2018).
[2] Heading and r. 10.2 substituted by S.S.I. 2017 No. 414 r. 2(2) (effective 1st January 2018).

(3)   During vacation, one or more of the judges of the court shall act from time to time as a vacation judge sitting in court or in chambers.

(4)   The vacation judge shall deal with the business of the vacation judge under rule 11.1(1) on such days and at such times as it is desirable to do so.

(5)   A Division of the Inner House may sit during vacation, whether or not on a vacation sitting day, to determine urgent business which cannot competently be determined by the vacation judge.

GENERAL NOTE.

10.2.1   See note 10.1.1 for statutory history. For the first time, under R.C.S. 1965, r. 68C, a sederunt day was defined. The sederunt days during session were Tuesdays, Wednesdays, Thursdays and Fridays (see r. 10.3(1)). The directions which provided for the annual session and terms of the court (r. 10.1) also provided for the sederunt days in vacation under r. 10.2(2): these were invariably every Wednesday and Thursday. Historically, the business of the court could only be conducted on sederunt days.

On vacations, see note 11.1.2.

[THE NEXT PARAGRAPH IS 10.3]

Holiday dates, periods and vacation sitting days

10.3   **10.3.**[1, 2, 3, 4]   In these Rules—

"public holiday" means any of the dates or parts of days in the following table—

Table

2024	2025	2026
Monday 1st January 2024	Wednesday 1st January 2025	Thursday 1st January 2026
Tuesday 2nd January 2024	Thursday 2nd January 2025	Friday 2nd January 2026
Friday 29th March 2024	Monday 14th April 2025	Friday 3rd April 2026
Monday 1st April 2024	Friday 18th April 2025	Monday 6th April 2026
Monday 15th April 2024	Monday 21st April 2025	Monday 20th April 2026
Monday 6th May 2024	Monday 5th May 2025	Monday 4th May 2026
Monday 20th May 2024	Monday 19th May 2025	Monday 18th May 2026
Monday 16th September 2024	Monday 15th September 2025	Monday 21st September 2026
Monday 2nd December 2024	Monday 1st December 2025	Monday 30th November 2026
The afternoon of Tuesday 24th December 2024	The afternoon of Wednesday 24th December 2025	The afternoon of Thursday 24th December 2026

---

[1] Heading and r. 10.3 substituted by S.S.I. 2017 No. 414 r. 2(2) (effective 1st January 2018).

[2] As amended by S.S.I. 2019 No. 227 Sched. 1 para. 1 (effective 1st January 2021), Sched. 2 para. 1 (effective 6th January 2021) and Sched. 3 para. 1 (effective 1st January 2021) and also by S.S.I. 2021 No. 153 r. 2(2) (effective 20th April 2021).

[3] As amended by the Act of Sederunt (Rules of the Court of Session 1994 Amendment) (Court Sittings) 2023 (S.S.I. 2023 No. 57) r. 2(2) (effective 31st March 2023).

[4] As amended by Act of Sederunt (Rules of the Court of Session 1994 Amendment) (Court Sittings) 2022 (S.S.I. 2022 No. 250) r. 2 (effective 1st and 6th January 2024, per r. 1(2) and (3)).

2024	2025	2026
Wednesday 25th December 2024	Thursday 25th December 2025	Friday 25th December 2026
Thursday 26th December 2024	Friday 26th December 2025	Monday 28th December 2026;

"vacation" is any of the periods in the following table beginning with the date in the first column and ending with the date in the corresponding second column—

Table

First column	Second column
Saturday 23rd March 2024	Friday 5th April 2024
Saturday 21st December 2024	Friday 3rd January 2025
Saturday 12th April 2025	Friday 25th April 2025
Saturday 20th December 2025	Monday 5th January 2026
Saturday 28th March 2026	Friday 10th April 2026
Saturday 19th December 2026	Tuesday 5th January 2027;

"vacation sitting day" means any of the dates in the following table—

Table

2024	2025	2026
Wednesday 3rd January 2024	Wednesday 16th April 2025	Wednesday 1st April 2026
Wednesday 27th March 2024	Wednesday 23rd April 2025	Wednesday 8th April 2026
Wednesday 3rd April 2024	Tuesday 23rd December 2025	Wednesday 23rd December 2026
Wednesday 23rd December 2024	Tuesday 30th December 2025	Wednesday 30th December 2026
Wednesday 30th December 2024.		

GENERAL NOTE.

See note 10.1.1 for statutory history. The court does not normally sit on the following public holidays: **10.3.1**

New Years Day (1st January), or the following Monday if on a Saturday or Sunday (bank holiday)
2nd January, or the following Monday (or Tuesday) if on a Saturday (or Sunday) (bank holiday)
Spring Weekend (third Monday in April) (local holiday)
Good Friday (bank holiday)
Easter Monday
May Day Holiday (first Monday in May) (bank holiday)
Victoria Day (local holiday)
September Weekend (third Monday in September)
Christmas Eve (24th December)—half day
Christmas Day (25th December), or the following Monday if on a Saturday or Sunday (bank holiday)
Boxing Day (26th December), or the following Monday (or Tuesday) if on a Saturday (or Sunday).

CHAPTER 11 VACATION JUDGE

Powers of vacation judge

11.1.—(1) Subject to any other provision in these Rules and paragraph (2) of this rule, the vacation judge may, during vacation, hear and determine—

(a) a motion which might be determined during session by the Lord Ordinary;

(b) an application which might be determined during session by the Lord Ordinary in chambers; and

(c) a motion which does not affect the merits, in a cause in dependence in the Inner House.

(1A)[1] Subject to paragraph (2) of this rule, the vacation judge may, during vacation, in a case where early disposal of a reclaiming motion or appeal is sought by virtue of rule 38.7A or 40.7A make any order or refusal, or give any direction, under rule 38/14(6) or 40.12(6) which might be made or given during session by the nominated judge.

(2) The vacation judge shall not be bound to hear or determine any matter if, in his opinion, it would be more appropriate for the matter to be dealt with in the session of the court after the vacation.

Deriv. R.C.S. 1965, r. 1 amended by S.I. 1987 No. 1206

11.1

GENERAL NOTE.

The foundation of R.C.S. 1965, r. 1 was s.4(3) of the Administration of Justice (Scotland) Act 1933, the relevant part of which was repealed by A.S. (R.C.A. No.5) (Miscellaneous) 1987 [SI 1987/2160].

Any solicitor has a right of audience before the vacation judge: see C.S.A. 1988, s.48 (substituted by the Law Reform (Miscellaneous Provisions) (Scotland) Act 1990, Sch.8, para.38) and s.51.

11.1.1

"VACATION".

See r. 10.2; or, for vacation sitting days, r. 10.3.

11.1.2

"APPLICATION".

This includes a motion or other application, such as an application for letters of arrestment or inhibition under r. 59.1, for a simplified divorce under r. 49.73 or an application by petition.

11.1.3

"IN DEPENDENCE".

A cause is depending from the time it is commenced (i.e. from the time an action is served or a first order in a petition is made) until final decree, whereas a cause is in dependence until final extract. For the meaning of commenced, see note 13.4.4 (action) or 14.6.1 (petition). For the meaning of final decree, see note 4.15.2(2). For the meaning of final extract, see note 7.1.2(2).

11.1.4

"DOES NOT AFFECT THE MERITS".

Interlocutory business of the Inner House may be dealt with in vacation, but not anything which will affect the merits of the cause.

In *Shell U.K. Exploration and Production Ltd v. Innes* , 1995 S.L.T. 807, it was held that the question whether the respondents were in breach of interdict (on a minute and answers) was a question which arose in the same cause as that in which the interim interdicts were pronounced and it was not possible to regard the breach of interdict as a matter which did not affect the merits of the cause, and the vacation judge or Lord Ordinary outwith a term could not deal with the breach of interdict.

The vacation judge cannot deal, e.g., with breach of interim interdict where a decision not to recall the interim interdict has been reclaimed, because the minute and answers about breach of interdict are part of the same process as that in which the interdict was pronounced, and it is not possible to regard the breach of interdict as an interlocutory matter not affecting the merits: *Shell U.K. Exploration and Production Ltd v. Innes* , 1995 S.L.T. 807.

The question of expenses not dealt with by the Inner House following a claiming motion is a substantial issue outwith the powers that a vacation judge has in relation to interlocutory business of the Inner House: *Alliance & Leicester Building Society v. Lindsays W.S.* , 25th July 1997 (1997 G.W.D. 36-1862).

11.1.5

"IN A CASE WHERE EARLY DISPOSE ... IS SOUGHT".

Early disposal of a reclaiming motion may be sought under r. 38.13 or 40.11 respectively. Rules 38.7A and 40.7A state that in certain cases the reclaimer or appellant must enrol for early disposal.

11.1.5A

---

[1] R. 11.1(1A) inserted by S.I. 1997 No. 2692 (effective 1st December 1997).

Rule 11.1(1A) empowers the vacation judge (and a Lord Ordinary sitting in session outwith a term by virtue of r. 10.4(3)(a), to deal with questions of competency under r. 38.14(6) or 40.12(6).

"MORE APPROPRIATE".

11.1.6   A vacation judge is not bound to deal with every matter brought before him; but vacation business is not limited to urgent matters as is sometimes thought: there is a discretion where it would be more appropriate for the matter to be dealt with in the next term. The vagueness of the rule is unfortunate as it cannot be certain that any particular motion will necessarily be heard. The word "appropriate" may be less equivocal than the former word "conveniently"; it carries no sense of personal convenience.

VACATION BUSINESS UNDER STATUTE.

11.1.7   Certain statutes make express reference to matters being dealt with by a vacation judge:

(a)   Companies Clauses Consolidation (Scotland) Act 1845, ss.3 and 134 (application for appointment of an umpire in an arbitration), incorporated in the Insolvency Act 1986, s.111(4);

(b)   Land Clauses Consolidation (Scotland) Act 1845, ss.3 and 27 (application for appointment of an oversman in an arbitration), incorporated in, e.g. Acquisition of Land (Authorisation Procedure) (Scotland) Act 1947, Sched. 2, Town and Country Planning (Scotland) Act 1997, s. 188(2), Land Compensation (Scotland) Act 1973, s.63, Roads (Scotland) Act 1984, s.110(5);

(c)   Judicial Factors Act 1849, ss.1, 7 and 34 (application by judicial factor for special powers or petition for discharge of judicial factor, tutor or curator);

(d)   Titles to Land Consolidation (Scotland) Act 1868, s. 158 (application for recall or restriction of inhibition on the dependence);

(e)   Representation of the People Act 1983, s. 134(2) (discharge or variation of penalty by election court for local election);

(f)   Companies Act 1985, s. 425(5) (order on summary application for compromise or arrangement);

(g)   Insolvency Act 1986, ss. 111(4) (see (a) above) and 120(2) (jurisdiction to wind up companies).

VACATION BUSINESS UNDER THE RULES.

11.1.8   Certain rules (other than r. 11.1(1)) make express reference to matters being dealt with in vacation:

(a)   r. 10.5(3) and (4) (sittings of Inner House or Lord Ordinary to conclude a hearing commenced in term, or of Inner House to hear urgent business);

(b)   r. 10.6 (Exchequer causes);

(c)   r. 14.5(1)(b) (first order in petitions);

(d)   r. 38.5(2) (leave to reclaim against certain interlocutors);

(e)   r. 41.21(1) (orders for service and answers in statutory appeals);

(f)   r. 43.20 (Optional Procedure in certain actions of damages heard by vacation judge (subject to r. 11.1));

(g)   r. 47.2 (commercial actions heard by vacation judge (subject to r. 11.1));

(h)   r. 55.2 (causes relating to intellectual property heard by vacation judge (subject to r. 11.1));

(i)   r. 58.5 (applications for judicial review heard in vacation (subject to r. 11.1));

(j)   r. 77.3(4) (summary trial).

ORDERS OF VACATION JUDGE WHICH ARE FINAL.

11.1.9   Certain orders of a vacation judge are by statute expressly final and not subject to review:

(a)   an order giving a judicial factor special powers or discharging or removing a judicial factor: Judicial Factors Act 1849, ss. 1, 7 (final and not subject to appeal) and 34 (final and conclusive);

(b)   an order in relation to a sanction of compromise or scheme of arrangement: Companies Act 1985, s. 425(5) (not subject to review, reduction, suspension or stay of execution);

(c)   orders under the following sections of the Insolvency Act 1986 (by virtue of s. 162(2) of that Act—(not subject to review, reduction, suspension or stay of execution)):
    (i)   s. 153 (as to time for proving debts and claims);
    (ii)   s. 195 (as to meetings for ascertaining wishes of creditors and contributories);
    (iii)   s. 198 (as to examination of witnesses in regard to property or affairs of company).

ARRANGEMENT OF BUSINESS.

11.1.10   All motions requiring appearance in session will require appearance in vacation—i.e. starred motions; for such motions, see notes 23.2.14, 23.2.16 and 23.2.17(2). Unopposed motions are dealt with first, then opposed motions, all in alphabetical order. Motions of length or complexity (e.g. an application for judicial review) will usually be heard separately by another vacation judge if pressure of business requires it.

SITTINGS OF THE VACATION COURT.

11.1.11   For the power, see rr. 10.2 and 10.3. A vacation court sits at 10.30am, or as soon as possible thereafter. More than one judge may sit as a vacation judge if pressure of business requires it.

EXCHEQUER CAUSES.

An Exchequer cause may be dealt with in vacation by the Lord Ordinary in Exchequer Causes: r. 10.6. In his absence or inability an Exchequer cause may be dealt with by the vacation judge: C.S.A. 1988, s. 3 and r. 11.1(1)(a). Where this occurs any interlocutor begins with the words "The Vacation Judge in room and stead of the Lord Ordinary in Exchequer Causes".

11.1.12

RIGHTS OF AUDIENCE.

Counsel or other person having a right of audience before the Court of Session may appear before the vacation judge. On the meaning of "counsel" and "other person having a right of audience", see definitions in r. 1.3(1). A solicitor also has a right of audience before the vacation judge: C.S.A, 1988, s. 48(2)(a) substituted by the Law Reform (Miscellaneous Provisions) (Scotland) Act 1990, Sched. 8, para. 38.

11.1.13

CHAPTER 12 ASSESSORS

Summoning of assessors

12.1.—(1) Subject to the following provisions of this Chapter, the court may, at its own instance or on the motion of a party, summon to its assistance a qualified person to sit with the court to act as an assessor at a proof or hearing in any cause.

(2) Where the court considers summoning an assessor at its own instance, it shall hear the parties on the matter before making a decision.

(3) Where an interlocutor is pronounced summoning an assessor, the court shall remit to the Deputy Principal Clerk to arrange for the attendance of the assessor selected.

Deriv. Nautical Assessors (Scotland) Act 1894, s. 2; R.C.S. 1965, r. 37 amended by S.I. 1978 No. 955, r. 38 (r. 12.1(1)), r. 40 (r. 12.1(2)) and r. 41 (r. 12.1(3))

GENERAL NOTE.

Under R.C.S. 1965, rr. 37 and 38, the court (*a*) could summon an assessor in any maritime or patent cause at its own instance, (*b*) had to summon an assessor in any maritime or patent cause on the application of any party and (*c*) could summon an assessor on the joint motion of parties in any other cause. The rule has been simplified and now is that the court may summon an assessor in any cause at its own instance or on the motion of a party. The Nautical Assessors (Scotland) Act 1894 is repealed in its application to the Court of Session.

The summoning of an assessor is appropriate where there are technical matters to be decided requiring special knowledge. In maritime matters, the functions of an assessor include advising on seamanship, the interpretation and application of the Regulations for Preventing Collisions at Sea, and whether the course of action taken was one which would have been taken by a skilful seaman: *McLean v. Johnstone* (1906) 8 F. 836, 838. The trustworthiness of the evidence is a matter for the judge: *Cambo Shipping Co. Ltd v. Dampskibssellskadet Carl* 1920 S.C. 26. See also generally *Owners of SS Australia v. Owners of Cargo of SS Nautilus* [1927] A.C. 145. The assessor does not determine the issues of fact: he provides expert advice on which the court may rely in determining the issues. The court is not bound to follow the advice; but it cannot follow the advice of the assessor on which there was no evidence: *Cambo Shipping Co. Ltd*, above.

"MOTION OF A PARTY".

For motions, see Chap. 23.

"PROOF OR HEARING".

"Hearing" includes a reclaiming motion or appeal in the Inner House or a hearing on evidence. Jury trial is excluded as it is not an appropriate mode of inquiry where an assessor is appointed, because questions appropriate for the assessor are unsuitable for a jury: *McLean v. Johnstone* (1906) 8 F. 836; *Leadbetter v. Dublin & Glasgow Steam Packet Co.* 1907 S.C. 538; *Kerr v. The Screw Collier Co. Ltd* (1907) 15 S.L.T. 444; *Rodger v. Glen-Coats* 1913 1 S.L.T. 434; *Williamson v. Richard Irvin & Sons Ltd* 1960 S.L.T. (Notes) 34.

ARRANGEMENTS FOR ATTENDANCE OF ASSESSOR.

The remit to the Deputy Principal Clerk to make the necessary arrangements is contained in the interlocutor. Where the parties select an assessor under r. 12.5(1), the pursuer should inform the Deputy Principal Clerk by letter of his name and address. Where the court selects an assessor (failing agreement by the parties) under r. 12.5(1), the clerk of court will inform the Deputy Principal Clerk.

Consignation of money for fees of assessors

12.2. An interlocutor summoning an assessor in a cause other than a cause under the Patents Act 1977 shall only be pronounced subject to the condition that there shall be consigned into court such sum as the court thinks fit to meet the fees and expenses of the assessor by—

(a) the party enrolling the motion; or

(b) where an assessor is summoned by the court at its own instance, the pursuer or petitioner, as the case may be, unless the court otherwise directs.

Deriv. R.C.S. 1965, r. 44(c)

12.1

12.1.1

12.1.2

12.1.3

12.1.4

12.2

PATENTS ACT 1977.

12.2.1   The remuneration of an assessor in a cause under the Patents Act 1977 is governed by s. 98(2) of that Act which provides that the remuneration is to be determined by the Lord President with the consent of the Minister of the Civil Service to be defrayed out of monies provided by Parliament (and not by a party).

CONSIGNATION.

12.2.2   The purpose of consignation is to ensure that the assessor is paid. It is not clear, however, how the court can assess with accuracy what the sum to be consigned should be as the total fees and expenses will not be known in advance. A better provision might have been to make the agent for a party liable in the first instance to the assessor for his fees. The remuneration of an assessor (except in a patent action) is treated as expenses in the cause unless the court otherwise directs: r. 12.9. Once the remuneration and expenses of the assessor have been paid, the consigned money may be recovered.

For procedure for consignation, see r. 33.4 and note 33.4.3 and r. 33.12.

Motions to summon assessors

12.3   **12.3.** A party seeking to summon an assessor shall—

(a) enrol a motion for that purpose not less than 28 days before the diet of the proof or hearing at which the presence of an assessor is sought; and

(b) give written intimation of the motion to every other party not less than seven days before it is enrolled.

Deriv. R.C.S. 1965, r. 39(a)

GENERAL NOTE.

12.3.1   The purpose of this rule is to ensure that applications do not come so late as to make arrangements for summoning the assessor difficult.

"MOTION".

12.3.2   For motions, see Chap. 23.

"NOT LESS THAN 28 DAYS BEFORE" AND "NOT LESS THAN SEVEN DAYS BEFORE".

12.3.3   The date from which the period is calculated is not counted.

"PROOF OR HEARING".

12.3.4   See note 12.1.3.

Copies of pleadings for use of assessors

12.4   **12.4.**—(1) Where an assessor is summoned by the court at its own instance, the pursuer or petitioner, as the case may be, shall lodge in process such copy of the closed record or other pleadings in the cause as the court directs for the use of the assessor.

(2) Where a motion under rule 12.3 (motions to summon assessors) has been granted, the party who enrolled the motion shall lodge in process a copy of the closed record or other pleadings in the cause for the use of the assessor.

Deriv. R.C.S. 1965, r. 39(c)

Selection of assessors

12.5   **12.5.**—(1) Subject to paragraph (2), an assessor shall be selected by agreement between the parties, failing which, by the court on the motion of a party.

(2) A nautical assessor shall be selected from the list of persons—

(a) approved by the Lord President;

(b) kept by the Principal Clerk; and

(c) published as the Lord President shall direct.

(3) *[Revoked by S.S.I. 2007 No. 7 (effective 29th January 2007).]*

Deriv. Nautical Assessors (Scotland) Act 1894, s. 4; R.C.S. 1965, r. 38 (r. 12.5(1)) and r. 46(a) (r. 12.5(2))

GENERAL NOTE.

12.5.1   Where the parties cannot agree on the person to be appointed, one party will have to enrol a motion to have the court appoint an assessor. The motion should include the names of one or more persons from whom the appointment may be made.

For motions, see Chap. 23.

12.5.2

"LIST OF NAUTICAL ASSESSORS".

[*Omitted by the* Act of Sederunt (Rules of the Court of Session Amendment) (Miscellaneous) 2007 (S.S.I. 2007 No. 7), para. 2(2) *(effective 26th February 2007).*]

12.5.3

Number of assessors

12.6.—(1) For a proof or hearing in the Outer House, only one assessor shall be summoned.

12.6

(2) In the case of—

(a) a proof or hearing ordered by a Division of the Inner House to be taken by one of the judges of the Inner House, or

(b) a hearing in the Inner House,

the number of assessors to be summoned shall be such number as the court thinks fit.

Deriv. R.C.S. 1965, r. 43

GENERAL NOTE.

Application of paragraph (2) of this rule is even more rare than the appointment of an assessor in the Outer House. A proof or hearing in the Inner House is also rare.

12.6.1

Skilled witnesses where assessors summoned

12.7.—(1) In a cause arising out of a collision at sea where the court is assisted by a nautical assessor at a proof, no party may lead a skilled witness on nautical matters.

12.7

(2) In a cause other than one to which paragraph (1) applies, where the court is assisted by an assessor at a proof, a party may not lead evidence from more than one skilled witness on any matter within the special qualifications of the assessor.

(3) Where a question arises at a proof in relation to the application of paragraph (2), the decision of the Lord Ordinary shall be final and not subject to review.

(4) In a cause to which paragraph (2) applies, the court may, on the motion of a party—

(a) enrolled not less than 14 days before the diet of proof, and

(b) of which written intimation has been given to every other party not less than seven days before the motion is enrolled,

on cause shown, allow evidence to be led from a greater number of skilled witnesses.

Deriv. R.C.S. 1965, r. 146 (r. 12.7(1)) and r. 42 (r. 12.7(2) to (4))

GENERAL NOTE.

The limitation on the number of skilled witnesses, other than one arising out of a collision at sea, is subject to the right to seek leave to allow additional skilled witnesses (r. 12.7(4)).

12.7.1

"NAUTICAL MATTERS".

In a cause arising out of a collision at sea where a nautical assessor is appointed, there can be no skilled witness on nautical matters: r. 12.7(1). "Nautical matters" must mean the matters on which a nautical assessor may advise: see *McLean v. Johnstone* (1906) 8 F. 836, 838; and see notes 12.1.1 and 12.7.3.

12.7.2

"ANY MATTER WITHIN THE ... QUALIFICATIONS OF THE ASSESSOR".

A nautical assessor's special qualifications are as a seaman. In *The Nerano v. The Dromedary* (1895) 22 R. 237, it was held that deductions about the speed of a vessel were a matter of engineering and not of nautical skill and experience.

12.7.3

"FINAL AND NOT SUBJECT TO REVIEW".

The decision of the Lord Ordinary cannot be reclaimed against.

12.7.4

"NOT LESS THAN 14 DAYS BEFORE" AND "NOT LESS THAN 7 DAYS BEFORE".

The date from which the period is calculated is not counted.

12.7.5

"WRITTEN INTIMATION".

12.7.6   For methods, see r. 16.9.

"MOTION".

12.7.7   For motions, see Chap. 23.

Note of questions submitted to assessors

12.8   **12.8.** The judge who presides at a proof or hearing to which an assessor is summoned shall make a note of each question submitted to the assessor and of the answer; and the note shall be lodged in process.

Deriv. Nautical Assessors (Scotland) Act 1894, s.3; R.C.S. 1965, r. 45

GENERAL NOTE.

12.8.1   The importance of compliance with this rule was stressed by L.P. Clyde in *SS "Rowan" v. "West Camak"* 1923 S.C. 316, 342, because it is necessary for the appeal court (and parties considering reclaiming) to know precisely what advice was given. An example of questions put to an assessor can be found in *Hoek van Holland Maatschappij v. Clyde Shipping Co. Ltd* (1902) 5 F. 227, 231.

Remuneration of assessors

12.9   **12.9.** The remuneration to be paid to an assessor, other than in a cause under the Patents Act 1977, shall, unless the court otherwise directs, be treated as expenses in the cause.

Deriv. Nautical Assessors (Scotland) Act 1894, s.5; R.C.S. 1965, r. 44(b)

GENERAL NOTE.

12.9.1   The remuneration of an assessor in a cause under the Patents Act 1977 is governed by s.98(2) of that Act which provides that the remuneration is to be determined by the Lord President with the consent of the Minister of the Civil Service to be defrayed out of monies provided by Parliament (and not by a party). The remuneration of any other assessor will have to be agreed between the assessor and the party (or parties) seeking to appoint him. A sum which the court thinks fit to meet the fees and expenses of the assessor has to be consigned into court: r. 12.2. R.C.S. 1965, r. 46(b) which provided for an assessor to be paid £6.30 per day has not been re-enacted.

Lay Support for Party Litigants

Lay support

12A.1.—[1](1) At any time during proceedings a party litigant may apply to the court for permission to have a named individual assist the litigant in the conduct of the proceedings by sitting beside or behind (as the litigant chooses) the litigant at hearings in court or in chambers and doing such of the following for the litigant as he or she requires—

12A.1

(a) providing moral support;

(b) helping to manage the court documents and other papers;

(c) taking notes of the proceedings;

(d) quietly advising on—

(i)   points of law and procedure;

(ii) issues which the litigant might wish to raise with the court;

(iii) questions which the litigant might wish to ask witnesses.

(2) It is a condition of such permission that the named individual does not receive from the litigant, whether directly or indirectly, any remuneration for his or her assistance.

(3) The court may refuse an application under paragraph (1) only if—

(a) it is of the opinion that the named individual is an unsuitable person to act in that capacity (whether generally or in the proceedings concerned); or

(b) it is of the opinion that it would be contrary to the efficient administration of justice to grant it.

(4) An application under paragraph (1) is to be made by motion and accompanied by a document, signed by the litigant and the named individual, in Form 12.A-A.

(5) Permission granted under paragraph (1) endures until the proceedings finish or it is withdrawn under paragraph (6); but it is not effective during any period when the litigant is represented.

(6) The court may, of its own accord or on the motion of a party to the proceedings, withdraw permission granted under paragraph (1); but it must first be of the opinion that it would be contrary to the efficient administration of justice for the permission to continue.

(7) Where permission has been granted under paragraph (1), the litigant may—

(a) show the named individual any document (including a court document); or

(b) impart to the named individual any information,

which is in his or her possession in connection with the proceedings without being taken to contravene any prohibition or restriction on the disclosure of the document or the information; but the named individual is then to be taken to be subject to any such prohibition or restriction as if he or she were the litigant.

(8) Any expenses incurred by the litigant as a result of the support of an individual under paragraph (1) are not recoverable expenses in the proceedings.

GENERAL NOTE.

A supporter to help a party litigant present his or her case is not new, though heretofore more common in the sheriff court where there are already rules (Summary Cause Rules 2002 and Small Claims Rules 2002) that allow party litigants even to be represented by an unpaid lay representative. Recent political enthusiasm for lay support stems from the report of the Civil Courts Review in September 2009 which

12A.1.1

---

[1] Chapter 12A and r. 12A.1 inserted by S.S.I. 2010 No. 205 (effective 15th June 2010).

encourages its use and has led to the formal rules in Chap. 12A. Rule 12A.1 fortunately does not use the term "McKenzie friend", which is the term used in England following the case of *McKenzie v. McKenzie* [1971] 33 from which it derives its name.

Under r. 12A.1 the party litigant must apply by motion for permission to have a particular person as a lay supporter. The lay supporter assists the litigant but does not speak for the litigant and must not be remunerated. The permission may be withdrawn if it is contrary to the efficient administration of justice for the particular supporter to continue to assist.

In *Khaliq v. Gutowski* [2018] CSIH 66; 2019 S.C. 136,147 at [41], it was pointed out that the court is not to act as an adviser to a party litigant: in that case, this was said in relation to what grounds of appeal should be advanced.

"MOTION".

12A.1.2   For motions, see Chap. 23.

CHAPTER 12B LAY REPRESENTATION

Lay Representation

Application and interpretation

12B.1.—[1](1) This Chapter is without prejudice to any enactment (including any other provision in these Rules) under which provision is, or may be, made for a party to a particular type of case before the court to be represented by a lay representative.

(2) In this Chapter, a "lay representative" means a person who is not—

    (a) a solicitor;

    (b) an advocate; or

    (c) someone having a right to conduct litigation, or a right of audience, by virtue of section 27 of the Law Reform (Miscellaneous Provisions) (Scotland) Act 1990.

GENERAL NOTE.

This chapter has been inserted following the creation of the rule-making power in s. 5A of the Act of 1988 for lay representation inserted by s. 126(b) of the Legal Services (Scotland) Act 2010. As noted in note 12A.1.1, political enthusiasm for lay assistance following the report of the Civil Court review in September 2009 was met first by rules for lay support in Chap. 12A (which recognised an existing informal practice) and now by this Chap. 12B for lay representation following the statutory power in the 2010 Act. The difference is that the lay representative may speak for the party litigant. Lay representation may increase as the availability of legal aid decreases.

It is the rule at common law that a non-natural person, such as a company, must be represented by a lawyer: see note 4.2.6. Section 97 of the Courts Reform (Scotland) Act 2014 introduced lay representation of a non-natural person. The rules governing an application to the court for representation by a lay person under s. 97 of the 2014 Act, and for representative's functions, conditions and duties, are in a free-standing A.S., A.S. (Lay Representation for Non-Natural Persons) 2016 [S.S.I. 2016 No. 243]. Paragraph 2 of the A.S. limits the category of person who may act for a non-natural person, and there are restrictions in s. 97 as to suitability. The court has a discretion whether to grant permission and may impose conditions. The application is made in the form in the Schedule to the A.S.

"WITHOUT PREJUDICE TO ANY ENACTMENT"

For example, s. 95 of the Courts Reform (Scotland) Act 2014 (see note 12B.1.1 above) provides for lay representation of non-natural persons.

Lay representation for party litigants

12B.2.—[2, 3](1) In any cause depending before the court in respect of which no provision as mentioned in rule 12B.1(1) is in force, a party litigant may apply to the court for permission for a named individual (a lay representative) to appear, along with the litigant, at a specified hearing for the purpose of representing the litigant at that hearing.

(2) An application under paragraph (1) is to be made—

    (a) by motion and accompanied by a document, signed by the litigant and the named individual, in Form 12B.2; and

    (b) subject to paragraph (3), prior to the date of the hearing at which the litigant wishes the lay representative to represent the litigant.

(3) The court may grant an application made on the day of the hearing at which the litigant wishes the lay representative to represent the litigant if it is satisfied that there are exceptional reasons why the application could not have been made prior to that day.

(4) The court may grant an application under paragraph (1) only if it is of the opinion that it would be in the interests of justice to grant it.

---

[1] Chapter 12B and r. 12B.1 inserted by S.S.I. 2012 No. 189 (effective 9th July 2012).

[2] Rule 12B.2 inserted by S.S.I. 2012 No. 189 (effective 9th July 2012).

[3] As amended by S.S.I. 2017 No. 186 (effective 3rd July 2017).

(5)   It is a condition of permission granted by the court that the lay representative does not receive directly or indirectly from the litigant any remuneration or other reward for his or her assistance.

(6)   The court may grant permission under paragraph (1) in respect of one or more specified hearings in the cause; but such permission is not effective during any period when the litigant is legally represented.

(7)   The court may, of its own accord or on the motion of a party to the proceedings, withdraw permission granted under paragraph (1).

(7A)   Where permission is granted under paragraph (1), the lay representative may do anything in the preparation or conduct of the hearing that the litigant may do.

(8)   Where permission has been granted under paragraph (1), the litigant may—

(a)   show the lay representative any document (including a court document); or

(b)   impart to the lay representative any information,

which is in his or her possession in connection with the proceedings without being taken to contravene any prohibition or restriction on the disclosure of the document or the information; but the lay representative is then to be taken to be subject to any such prohibition or restriction as if he or she were the litigant.

(9)   Any expenses incurred by the litigant in connection with lay representation under this rule are not recoverable expenses in the proceedings.

GENERAL NOTE.

12B.2.1   Under Ch.12A a party litigant may have the support of someone who assists the litigant but may not speak for the party litigant. Ch.12B permits a lay representative to speak for the party litigant, by making oral submissions, in certain circumstances. These circumstances are: (1) it is only if the court is of the opinion that it would assist the court; (2) it is for one or more specified hearings; (3) application is made before the hearing or, if made at the hearing, there are exceptional reasons for not having applied before the hearing; (4) the application is made by motion; (5) the motion is accompanied by a document signed by the party litigant and the lay representative in Form 12B.2 which requires certain information and declarations; and (6) the lay representative does not receive directly or indirectly from the litigant any remuneration or other reward.

The background to Chap 12B is dealt with in note 12B.1.1.

"MOTION".

12B.2.2   For motions, see Ch.23.

Confidentiality of documents in process

12B.3   **12B.3.**[1]   Rules 67.3 and 97.4 (confidentiality of documents in process) apply to an individual permitted to act as lay representative under this Chapter as they apply to a curator ad litem and reporting officer.

---

[1] Rule 12B.3 inserted by S.S.I. 2012 No. 189 (effective 9th July 2012).

CHAPTER 12C MODE OF ATTENDANCE AT HEARINGS

Chapter 12C[1]

Mode of Attendance at Hearings

Application

12C.1. This Chapter is without prejudice to any enactment under which provision has been made regarding the mode of attendance of persons at hearings.

GENERAL NOTE

During the Covid 19 pandemic since the lockdown in March 2020, most hearings took place by electronic means. Paragraphs 6 and 8 to the Schedule to the Coronavirus (Recovery and Reform) (Scotland) Act 2022, introduced by s. 50 of the Act, contain temporary provisions to allow for non-attendance at court for hearings (other than for giving evidence) and attendance by electronic means. By s. 52 of the Act, the temporary measures expire on 30th November 2024; however, Chap. 12C was inserted in R.C.S. 1994 by A.S. (R.C.S. 1994 and O.C.R. 1993 Amendment) (Attendance at Hearings) 2023 [S.S.I 2023/168] to make permanent provision for hearings to be conducted by electronic means or by physical presence.

Mode of attendance at hearings – procedural business

12C.2.—(1) Hearings at which only procedural business is to be considered are to be attended by electronic means.

(2) Paragraph (1) does not apply to hearings at which a party is unrepresented or utilising an interpreter.

GENERAL NOTE

The facility for business to be conducted by electronic means, as a general rule, applies only to "procedural" business (see note 12C.2.2). Such business may not, however, by so conducted (a) at which a party is unrepresented or utilises an interpreter or (b) the court on its own motion or the motion of a party orders physical attendance at a hearing for procedural business (r. 12C.3(1)(a)).

As a general rule (by inference), at any hearing other than for procedural business, physical presence will be required. However, on the motion of a party or by the court at its own instance, a hearing for any other kind of business may be ordered to be by electronic means.

But note r. 12C4, under which any hearing may be partly by electronic means and partly by physical presence.

"PROCEDURAL."

The term "procedural" is not defined. Proofs, debates, and "substantive" hearings (at which decisions may be made on part or all of the substance of a cause) are clearly excluded from business that may be conducted by electronic means.

Alternative mode of attendance at hearings

12C.3.—(1) The court may, at its own instance or on the motion of a party on cause shown—

    (a)   in relation to hearings to which rule 12C.2(1) applies, order physical attendance at a hearing;

    (b)   in relation to any other hearings, order attendance at a hearing by electronic means.

(2) The court may revoke an order granted under paragraph (1) or this paragraph and, where it does so, it may make such further order as it thinks fit.

(3) Before the court makes an order under paragraph (1) or (2), it is to give parties the opportunity to make representations about the mode of attendance.

GENERAL NOTE

Under r. 12C.3, on the motion of a party or at the court's own instance, physical presence may be ordered at a hearing for procedural business and electronic means may be ordered for any other kind of hearing (at which physical presence is normally required). And see note 12C.4.1.

---

[1] Inserted by S.S.I. 2023 No. 168 para. 2 (effective 3rd July 2023).

Hybrid hearings

12C.4. An order under rule 12C.3(1) or (2) may include provision for a person to attend a hearing—

(a) both physically and by electronic means;

(b) by one mode and another person to attend by the other mode,

and at different times or dates.

GENERAL NOTE

To add to the confusion that procedural hearings are by electronic means but may not be, and that at other hearings physical presence is required but may not be, at any hearing both methods may be used by virtue of r. 12C.4.

PART III INITIATION AND PROGRESS OF PROCEEDINGS: CHAPTER 13 SUMMONSES, NOTICE, WARRANTS AND CALLING

Initiation of causes by summons

13.1.   Subject to any other provision in these Rules, all causes originating in the court shall be commenced in the Outer House by summons.

Deriv. R.C.S. 1965, r. 69 (part)

"SUBJECT TO ANY OTHER PROVISION".

The other provisions are: (a) petitions (rr. 14.2 and 14.3); (b) a counterclaim (r. 25.1); (c) a third party notice (r. 26.1); (d) special cases under s.27 of the C.S.A. 1988 (r. 77.2); (e) applications and references treated as appeals or stated cases—see note 3.2.3; (f) applications made as part of an existing process—i.e. by minute, note or motion; (g) applications for letters of inhibition or arrestment: r. 59.1.

"SUMMONS".

A summons is a writ running in the name of the Sovereign whereas a petition, minute, note or other application is simply addressed to the court. A summons is the appropriate form for seeking to establish a right or remedy against a person; a petition is an ex parte application seeking the authority of the court for something to be done which otherwise the petitioner would not be able to do or cause to be done: see Maclaren on *Court of Session Practice*, p. 825. "The object of the summons is to enforce a pursuer's legal right against a defender who resists it, or to protect a legal right which the defender is infringing; the object of a petition, on the other hand, is to obtain from the administrative jurisdiction of the court power to do something or to require something to be done, which it is just and proper should be done, but which the petitioner has no legal right to do or to require, apart from judicial authority": *Report of the Royal Commission on the Court of Session* 1927 (Cmd. 2801), pp. 49–50. A summons involves a more formal procedure than a petition.

The signeting of a summons confers authority, without more, to execute forms of diligence on the dependence and intimations stated in the warrant (see r. 13.6); in any other case the authority has to be applied for (see r. 13.8).

Form of summonses

13.2.—(1)   Subject to any other provision in these Rules, a summons shall be in Form 13.2-A.

(1A)[1]   A summons in an action to which Chapter 26A (group procedure) applies is to be in Form 13.2-AA.

(2)   A conclusion in a summons shall be stated in accordance with the appropriate style, if any, in Form 13.2-B.

(3)   Subject to rule 46.6(3) (no condescendence or pleas-in-law in ship collision actions), there shall be annexed to a summons—

<ul style="list-style:none">
<li>(a)   a statement, in the form of numbered articles of the condescendence, of the averments of fact which form the grounds of the claim; and</li>
<li>(b)   appropriate pleas-in-law.</li>
</ul>

(4)   A condescendence shall include averments stating—

<ul style="list-style:none">
<li>(a)   in an action to which the Civil Jurisdiction and Judgments Act 1982 applies, the domicile of the defender (to be determined in accordance with the provisions of that Act) so far as known to the pursuer;</li>
<li>(b)   the ground of jurisdiction of the court, unless jurisdiction would arise only if the defender prorogated the jurisdiction of the court without contesting jurisdiction;</li>
<li>(c)   unless the court has exclusive jurisdiction, whether or not there is an agreement prorogating the jurisdiction of a court in another country;</li>
<li>(d)   whether or not there are proceedings involving the same cause of action in subsistence between the parties in a country to which the convention in Schedule 1 or 3C to the Civil Jurisdiction and Judgments Act 1982 applies and the date any such proceedings commenced; and</li>
</ul>

13.1

13.1.1

13.1.2

13.2

---

[1] Rule 13.2(1A) inserted by S.S.I. 2020 No. 208 r. 2(4) (effective 31st July 2020).

(e)[1] if applicable, any special capacity in which the pursuer is suing or any special capacity in which the defender is being sued.

(5)[2] A summons may include warrants and intimation in so far as permitted under these Rules.

(6)[3] A summons may include a draft interlocutor in Form 43.1A (actions based on clinical negligence: authority to raise as ordinary action).

Deriv. R.C.S. 1965, r. 70(1)(a), (b) and (2) amended by S.I. 1984 No. 472 (r. 13.2(1) to (3) and (5)) and r. 70(1)(c) inserted by S.I. 1986 No. 1941 and amended by S.I. 1987 No. 1206 (r. 13.2(4))

General note.

13.2.1

Before 1850 a summons was in four parts—the Address, Instance, Conclusions and the Will. S. 1 of the C.S.A. 1850 introduced the addition of a condescendence and pleas-in-law annexed to the summons. A summons is now commonly referred to as including these additional parts, as also in these Rules: see r. 1.3(1) (interpretation of "summons"). The form of a summons now is (1) Instance, (2) Address and Charge, (3) Warrants, (4) Conclusions, (5) Condescendence and (6) Pleas-in-law. The official heading before the instance since at least 1934 as set out in Form 13.2-A, is "In the Court of Session"; but this form has, unfortunately been ignored, and for some reason the subject heading for the Court of Session in the Statutory Instruments Index has been inappropriately used.

Form 13.2-A (in the form approved by the court: r. 4.1(1)) is to be used for every action commenced by summons except where otherwise provided. Variants are provided for in r. 43.19 (optional procedure in certain actions of damages), r. 46.2(2) (Admiralty actions) and r. 47.3 (election of procedure in commercial actions).

The form approved by the court is an official printed form of the first page and backing: see note 4.1.1.

For the use of Form 43.1A to transfer a personal injury action involving clinical negligence actions from the Chap. 43 procedure to ordinary procedure, see r.43.1A.

Instance.

13.2.2

The instance is dealt with in this note under four headings.

(A)   Names, designation and addresses of parties.

The better practice is to state full names, but this is not essential. The test is that there must be such specification as identifies the parties intended: *Joel v. Gill* (1859) 22 D. 6, 12 per L.J.-C. Inglis; *Anderson v. Stoddart* 1923 S.C. 755; *Kay v. Morrison's Reps.* 1984 S.L.T. 175 ("the representatives of John Morrison" not sufficient). The defender should be a named individual or legal persona: *McLaren v. Procurator Fiscal for the Lothian and Borders* 1992 S.L.T. 844; cf. (D)(15) below. A person suing or being sued in a special character, such as a trustee, must have that character set forth: *Bell v. Trotter's Trs.* (1841) 3 D. 380; *Hunter v. L.M.S. Railway Co.* 1938 S.L.T. 598, 599 per Lord Jamieson. The requirement for proper disclosure in the instance of any special capacity in which a party sues or is sued was re-affirmed in *Royal Insurance (UK) Ltd v. AMEC Construction Scotland Ltd* , 2008 S.C. 201 (O.H.), 216, para. [21] per Lord Emslie. There is now a rule to that effect: see r. 13.2(4)(e). The practice of stating the occupation (other than a professional one) of parties has generally died out and is not essential.

The current address must be given. Where there has been a recent change of address there is a convenient practice to state the former address also; but a last known address alone where the current address is not known will not be sufficient for service (note repeal of s.3 of the Citation Amendment (Scotland) Act 1882 by the A.S. (R.C.S. 1994) 1994, Sched. 4) and the rules for service where the address is not known must be followed (see r. 16.5). An accommodation address is generally not sufficient, but disclosure of the actual address may be dispensed with by the court in certain circumstances (e.g. persistent harassment), the reason for non-disclosure being set out in the condescendence: *Doughton v. Doughton* 1958 S.L.T. (Notes) 34. In a family action, a party may be ordered to disclose an address where it has been withheld to enable access arrangements to work or to disclose a telephone number where the court cannot judge whether the fear of harassment was well-founded; *McLean v. McDonald* , 20th June, 1997, unreported (1997 G.W.D. 25-1236) (order on party's agent to disclose number overturned). Where a party is in prison it is desirable that he should not be designed "at present a prisoner in": P.N. 23rd July 1952; the home address should be stated.

Where a summons is posted to a person in HM Forces Northern Ireland to his private billet the envelope should be addressed as if he were a private citizen and should not disclose his rank and number; where the address of the barracks is known the summons should be sent there: P.N. 17th December 1974. Where the address of the defender is unknown this must be stated: r. 13.3(b); and see note 13.3.2.

---

[1] Rule 13.2(4)(e) inserted by S.S.I. 2008 No. 349 (effective 1st December 2008).
[2] Rule 13.2(5) amended by S.S.I. 2008 No. 122 (effective 1st April 2008).
[3] Rule 13.2(6) inserted by S.S.I. 2007 No. 282 (effective 2nd May 2007).

A substantial error in the instance will invalidate the cause: *Brown v. Rodger* (1884) 12 R. 340; *Overseas League v. Taylor* 1951 S.C. 105, 107 per L.J.-C. Thomson; but not if not material (*Anderson v. Stoddart*, above) or if permitted by amendment under r. 24.1(2)(b)(i) (to correct or supplement designation of party).

(B) Capacity.

As a general rule any adult person, sovereign power, corporate body, partnership, trade union or friendly society may, as such, invoke the jurisdiction of the court.

(B)(1)   Aliens.

(a) An alien outside British territory cannot sue the state for a wrong in the national interest (act of state). (b) A friendly alien may not sue the state in respect of wrongs in the national interest: *Poll v. Lord Advocate* (1897) 1 F. 823, 827 per Lord Kyllachy. But this dictum is of doubtful authority. The exception here is probably limited to (a) above: *Johnstone v. Pedler* [1921] 2 A.C. 262. (c) An enemy alien—i.e. a person of whatever nationality whose residence or place of business is in a foreign country with which the UK is at war (from the date of declaration) or occupied by such country—cannot sue: *Arnauld v. Boick* (1704) Mor. 10159; *Blomert v. Earl of Roxburgh* (1664) Mor. 16091; *Van Uden v. Burrell* 1916 S.C. 391; *Schulze* 1917 S.C. 113. An assignee is in no better position than the enemy alien: *Arnauld*, above; *Johnston Wright v. Goldsmid* 15 Feb. 1809 F.C. Where the pursuer is an enemy alien, the action is sisted until the end of the war: *Craig Line Steamship Co. Ltd v. North British Storage & Transit Co.* 1915 S.C. 113. An enemy alien may defend an action, including bringing a counterclaim arising out of the same cause: *Burgess v. Guild* 12 Jan. 1813 F.C.; but he cannot defend where his real character is that of pursuer: *Weber's Trs. v. Reimer* 1947 S.L.T. 295. A national of an enemy country resident or having a place of business here and complying with residence requirements may sue: *Schulze, Gow & Co. v. Bank of Scotland* 1914 2 S.L.T. 455; *Weiss v. Weiss* 1940 S.L.T. 447.

(B)(2)   Foreign states, diplomats, etc.

Jurisdiction over states is governed by the State Immunity Act 1978 which enabled the UK to ratify the *Brussels Convention on Immunity of State-owned Vessels 1926 and Protocol (Cmnd. 7800 (1980))* and the *European Convention on State Immunity 1972 (Cmnd. 7742 (1979))*. A state (see s.14) is generally immune from the jurisdiction of the court: 1978 Act, s.1, but there are exceptions relating to submission (s.2), commercial transactions (s.3), contracts of employment (s.4), reparation for death, personal injury or damage to property (s.5), immoveable property in the UK (s.6), patents, trade marks, designs or plant breeder's rights (s.7), membership of corporate or unincorporated bodies or partnerships (s.8), disputes which the state has agreed to submit to arbitration (s.9), actions in rem or in personam against a ship of the state or against a cargo of that state in admiralty causes (s.10) and liability for VAT, customs and excise duty, agricultural levies or rates of commercial premises (s.11). There are exceptions to the exceptions: see ss.3, 4, 8, 9 and 10(6).

Heads of state, their families and servants are assimilated (s.20) to that of diplomatic missions under the Diplomatic Privileges Act 1964 which divides diplomats into three categories (agents with immunity except for actions relating to immoveables, succession and activities outside their official functions; administration and technical staff with the same immunity but which does not extend to acts outside their duties; service staff with immunity for acts in the course of their duties). Consular staff of foreign and Commonwealth states and the Republic of Ireland are governed by the Consular Relations Act 1968. International organisations may be granted similar immunities under the International Organisations Act 1968 and 1981 by Order in Council under s.1 or 4 of the 1968 Act.

Section 14(2) states "A separate entity is immune from the jurisdiction of the courts of the United Kingdom if, and only if—(a) the proceedings relate to anything done by it in the exercise of sovereign authority; and (b) the circumstances are such that a State ... would have been so immune." This was recently considered in *Morrison v. Mapfre Middlesea Insurance plc* 2022 S.L.T. 1131 (First Div.), 1136, para. [22] "The manner in which section 14(2) is to be interpreted was set out in [*Kuwait Airways Corporation v Iraqi Airways Co* [1995] 1 W.L.R. 1147 (H.L.)]. The reference to 'a separate entity' is not to some body which is independent of the state, but one which remains 'an entity or separate entity of a state' (ibid Lord Goff at 1158). That would include a statutory corporation which is under the control of the state, including the third parties. Although the statutory provision refers to acts 'done ... in the exercise of sovereign authority', this is simply a reference to what were previously regarded as *acta jure imperii* as distinct from *acta jure gestionis* (ibid at 1159–1160). Thus, the ultimate test is 'whether the act in question is of its own character a governmental act, as opposed to an act which any private citizen can perform ... where an act done by a separate entity of the state on the directions of the state does not possess the character of a governmental act, the entity will not be entitled to state immunity ...' (ibid at 1160, following [*I Congreso* [1983] 1 A.C. 244, per Lord Wilberforce at p. 267])".

In *Forth Tugs Ltd v. Wilmington Trust Co.* 1987 S.L.T. 153 the court held that the adjudicative jurisdiction of the court which arose in a petitory action by reason of the possession in Scotland of heritable property was not ousted by s.13(2)(b) (as applied by s.13(6)(b)) of the 1978 Act which applied only to enforcement jurisdiction. On enforcement, under s.13(2) of the 1978 Act the property of a State is not subject to diligence for enforcing a judgment unless the property is in use for commercial purposes: 1978

Act, s.13(4). A joint stock company in which a State has a contributing interest does not make the company or the property the property of the State: *Coreck Maritime GmbH v. Sevrybokholodflot* 1994 S.L.T. 893.

(B)(3) Adults.

A person of 18 years or more (Age of Majority (Scotland) Act 1969, s.1) with ability to manage his own affairs has capacity to sue or be sued.

(B)(4) Children.

The general rule is that a child (i.e. a person under the age of 16 years) has no legal capacity to bring or defend civil proceedings on or after 25th September 1991; the former law will apply to transactions entered into before that date: Age of Legal Capacity (Scotland) Act 1991, ss.1 and 9(e); "transaction" is defined in s.9. The right of a person under the age of 21 years to apply to the court to set aside a transaction entered into while he was over 16 but under 18 and which is a prejudicial transaction does not apply to the bringing or defending of legal proceedings: 1991 Act, s.3(3). A child under 16 does have legal capacity to enter into transactions commonly entered into by persons of his age and circumstances on terms which are reasonable or to consent to medical treatment; a person under 16 has legal capacity to instruct a solicitor in connection with a civil matter and to sue, or defend, if he has a general understanding of what it means to do so, and a child of 12, or over, is presumed to have that understanding; a child of 12 or over has testamentary capacity or capacity to consent to adoption: 1991 Act, s.2. Where a child has a guardian, proceedings may be taken in his or her name. A mother is guardian of her child (as is the father if married to the mother at the time of conception or subsequently), or a person appointed by the court or a person appointed by a parent to be guardian after his death: Law Reform (Parent and Child) (Scotland) Act 1986, ss. 1, 3, 4, and 8 (definition of "parental rights"). The existing law in relation to a child who has no guardian, or whose guardian is unable because of a conflict of interest or otherwise or refuses to bring or defend civil proceedings, is retained: 1991 Act, s.1(3)(f). (a) Where a child has no guardian he may sue alone: *Hill v. City of Glasgow Bank* (1879) 7 R. 68, 74–75 per L.P. Inglis (a minor); *Ward v. Walker* 1920 S.C. 80. Once the action is in court he may seek appointment of a curator ad litem: *Young* (1828) 7 S.220. A defender is entitled to object to the action proceeding until the guardian is added or until the appointment of a curator ad litem: *Sinclair v. Stark* (1828) 6 S.336, 338. If the guardian refuses to act (*McConochie v. Binnie* (1847) 9 D. 791; *Kirk v. Scottish Gas Board* 1968 S.C. 328), has an adverse interest (*Bogie v. Bogie* (1840) 3 D. 309) or is incapacitated (*Rankine* (1821) 1 S.118), the action may be brought in the name of the child and the court may appoint a curator ad litem. Appointment of a curator ad litem is discretionary: *Kirk*, above; and may be made by the court at its own instance: *Drummond's Trs. v. Peel's Trs.* 1929 S.C. 481, 518 per Lord Murray. If there is no concurrence and no curator ad litem and the defender makes no objection, the defender is barred from contending that a decree against him is void: *Sinclair*, above. (b) Where a child defender has a guardian, the guardian (if known) should be called as defender as well as the child (*King's Trs. v. McLay* (1901) 8 S.L.T. 413) and the conclusions be against both: Stair, I.6.20. If the identity of the guardian is not known, or it is known the child has no guardian or it is not known whether he has a guardian, the action must be brought against the child and "his guardians if he any has"; if not, and it was known that the child had a guardian though his identity was not known, any decree will be null: *Earl of Craven v. Lord Elibank's Trs.* (1854) 16 D. 811. If the guardian cannot or should not act or does not appear, or the child has no guardian, the court will appoint a curator ad litem. If the guardian appears, the child is bound by any decree: *Earl of Craven*, above. If the guardian is called but does not appear and a curator ad litem was appointed, a decree will be valid (*Agnew v. Earl of Stair* (1822) 1 Shaw's App. 333); if no curator ad litem was appointed, the decree will be a valid decree in absence: *Sinclair*, above; *Drummond's Trs.*, above, per Lord Hunter at p. 505.

(B)(5) Incapaces.

A person of unsound mind and incapable of managing his own affairs or of giving instructions for their management has no *persona standi in judicio*: *Reid v. Reid* (1839) 1 D. 400; *Moodie v. Dempster* , 1931 S.C. 553. In family actions special rules apply: see r. 49.17. *I.* The new law:—From 1st April 2002 it is not competent to appoint a curator bonis, tutor-dative or tutor-at-law to a person who is aged 16 or over: Adults with Incapacity (Scotland) Act 2000. Existing curators, tutor-dative or tutor-at-law become guardians under the 2000 Act: 2000 Act, Sched.4, para. 1. Under Pt 2 (continuing attorneys and welfare powers of attorney) and Pt 6 (intervention and guardianship orders), there are already in force, there are continuing attorneys, welfare attorneys, withdrawers, holders of intervention orders and guardians. The scheme of the Act is that incapable adults need measures only to the extent of their incapacity. So, e.g. if they can manage their own affairs but need support in their personal welfare they may require one of these persons with powers only in respect of personal welfare either short term or long term. Unlike curators, a guardian may be appointed over property, financial affairs or personal welfare or all such matters. A guardian has power to act as the legal representative in relation to any matters within the scope of the guardianship: 2000 Act, s.64(3). A guardianship order lasts for such period, including an infinitive period, as the sheriff determines unless renewed. Intervention and guardianship orders are made on application to a sheriff. Accordingly, if an incapable adult is incapable of initiating or defending a particular cause, a guardian (or interventioner) may be appointed for that purpose. "Incapable" under the 2000 Act means incapable of acting, making discussions, communicating decisions or retaining the memory of decisions by reason of mental disorder or inability to communicate because of physical disability: 2000 Act, s.1(6). *II.* The old law:—(a) Where an incapax has a guardian the action should be brought in the name of the guardian, i.e. a tutor-at-law (under the Curators Act 1585), a tutor-dative (under the common law; Stair

1.6.25), or a curator bonis (see note 61.1.2); the action should be brought in the name of the tutor, failing whom the curator bonis: *Young v. Rose* (1839) 1 D.1242. If the tutor is unwilling to raise the action, a curator bonis may be appointed to do so (see note 61.1.2). Where an incapax has neither a tutor nor a curator bonis, the proper course is to petition for the appointment of a tutor-at-law, failing whom a tutor-dative, failing whom a curator bonis who may bring the action. It remains competent to petition for the appointment of the nearest male agnate as tutor-at-law under the Curators Act 1585: *Britton v. Britton's Curator Bonis* 1996 S.C. 178; and see note 14.2.11. A petition for the appointment of a curator bonis is made under Chap. 61. It is not competent to bring the action in the name of the incapax and thereafter seek appointment of a curator ad litem: *Moodie*, above. (b) Where an incapax defender has a tutor (at law or dative) or a curator bonis, the action is brought against both the incapax and his tutor, failing whom his curator bonis. Where, despite the appointment of a tutor (at law or dative) a curator bonis continues to have authority to manage the estate of the incapax (as in *Dick v. Douglas* 1924 S.C. 787), the action should be raised against both tutor and curator bonis. If an incapax defender has neither tutor (at law or dative) nor curator bonis, a curator bonis (and perhaps a curator ad litem) should be appointed before the action comes into court. If neither the incapax nor a relative is willing to petition for the appointment, the pursuer, having an interest in the estate of the incapax may do so: see note 61.1.2(1). (c) Where a person becomes incapax during the dependence of an action a curator bonis should be appointed by petition: *Anderson's Trs v. Skinner* (1871) 8 S.L.R. 325; or possibly a curator ad litem: *Moodie*, above.

(C) Title and interest.

A pursuer must have title and interest to sue. The pursuer must have title at the date of bringing the action; if not, the lack of it cannot subsequently be made good by assignation (*Symington v. Campbell* (1894) 21 R. 434) or by retrocession (*Bentley v. Macfarlane* 1964 S.C. 76), though a qualified title may be cleared or a title completed (*Bentley*, above). Title may be contingent: *Roe v. Meek* (1888) 15 R. 1033; affd (1889) 16 R.(H.L.) 31, 33. Title must be pled: *Bentley*, above; *Microwave Systems (Scotland) Ltd v. Electro-Physiological Instruments Ltd* 1971 S.C. 140; and must continue until judgment: *Donaghy v. Rollo* 1964 S.C. 278.

There must be interest as well as title, though to some extent they run into each other: *Summerlee Iron Co. Ltd v. Lindsay* 1907 S.C. 1161, 1165 per L.P. Dunedin. Provided there is title the interest need not be large or pecuniary: *Strang v. Steuart* (1864) 2 M. 1015, 1029 per L.J.-C. Inglis, obiter, but see *Smith v. Shields* (1830) 8 S. 553 (pursuer could recover nothing); *School Boards of Dunlop & Stewarton v. Patrons of Cunninghame Graham Endowment Fund* 1910 S.C. 945 (interest too remote). A person may have an interest but no title to enforce it: *Adams v. Johnson* 1920 2 S.L.T. 328.

Title to sue involves some legal relation which gives the pursuer some right which the defender either infringes or denies: *D. & J. Nicol v. Dundee Harbour Trs* 1915 S.C.(H.L.) 7, 12 per Lord Dunedin; *Simpson v. Edinburgh Corporation* 1960 S.C. 313. Interest means some benefit from asserting the right. In establishing interest, it is no longer necessary to show that the question at issue involves pecuniary rights or status as was stated by Lord Ardwell in *Swanson v. Manson* 1907 S.C. 426, at p. 429. There must be a real issue, the existence of a sufficient interest being essentially a matter depending on the circumstances of the case: *Lennox v. Scottish Branch of the British Show Jumping Association* 1996 S.L.T. 353 applying *Scottish Old People's Welfare Council, Ptrs* 1987 S.L.T. 179 (see also *Watson v. Independent Broadcasting Authority* 1979 S.C. 351; *Gunstone v. Scottish Women's Amateur Athletic Association* 1987 S.L.T. 611). In *Shariff v. Hamid* 2000 S.L.T. 294 (OH), Lord Nimmo Smith held that a person who regularly worshipped at and contributed financially to an Islamic Studies Centre had title and interest to sue in a petition for removal of trustees of the centre which was in public trust.

Every person called as a defender has title to defend, though the defence may not prevail as being irrelevant or because the defender has no interest. A person who has title and interest may be sisted as a defender. All interested persons should be called as defenders and a defender may plead that all parties have not been called (see note 18.1.4(A)(1)); but there is an equitable discretion in the court not to enforce this where it would defeat the action: *Gibson v. Smith* (1849) 11 D. 1024.

A defender objecting to the title or interest of the pursuer (see note 18.1.4(A)(7)) or to the fact that all parties are not called (see note 18.1.4(A)(1)) must state a preliminary plea to that effect: *Lade v. Largs Baking Co.* (1863) 2 M. 17.

(D) Title of particular persons.

(D)(1)   Administrator of company.

See corporate bodies, (D)(6) below.

(D)(1A)   Advocate General.

See Lord Advocate, (D)(12) below.

(D)(2)   Agent and principal.

An agent acting ostensibly as principal may sue or be sued in his own name; the principal may disclose himself and sue, or be sued if discovered, in which case the pursuer must elect which to sue as liability is alternative and not joint and several: Bell's *Comm.*, i,540; *Bennett v. Inveresk Paper Co.* (1891) 18 R. 975. It is suggested by Gloag that an undisclosed principal can sue only if the contract is assignable: *Gloag on Contract*, pp. 128–129; and see *Salton v. Clydesdale Bank* (1898) 1 F. 110. In the case of an agent acting as agent for an undisclosed principal there is little authority (Gloag, p. 138); but see *Ferrier v. Dods* (1865) 3 M. 561. A disclosed principal and not his agent, as a general rule, must sue or be sued in his own name: Bell's *Comm.*, i,540; *McIvor v. Roy* 1970 S.L.T.(Sh.Ct) 58; but the general rule does not apply if the agent has an interest in the transaction (*MacKenzie v. Cormack* 1950 S.C. 183), where obligations are undertaken by the agent (*Johnston v. Little* 1960 S.L.T. 129), where the principal is an unincorporated body which cannot be sued as a club (*Thomson v. Victoria Eighty Club* (1905) 43 S.L.R. 628) or where the agent acts for a company not yet formed (*Tinnevelly Sugar Refining Co. Ltd v. Mirrlees, Watson & Yaryan Co. Ltd* (1894) 21 R. 1009). There is a presumption of fact that an agent acting for a disclosed foreign principal intends to be bound and may sue and be sued in his own name: *Millar v. Mitchell* (1860) 22 D. 833.

(D)(3)   Assignee.

An assignee may sue in his own name or that of his cedent or sist himself as pursuer in his cedent's action: *Fraser v. Duguid* (1838) 16 S. 1130. It is permissible for persons to assign their right to sue to a person who sues as their assignee. He should sue as "assignee of (*name of cedent*)".

(D)(4)   Bankrupt.

The permanent trustee may sue or be sued or sist himself to a current action in relation to the debtor's estate vested in him (with consent of commissioners, creditors or the court where there are commissioners): Bankruptcy Act 1985, s.39(2)(b); but not in actions in respect of the debtor's status or personal affairs unless his estate is affected: *Corbidge v. Somerville* 1913 S.C. 858. He cannot initiate a claim for solatium, which is personal to the debtor (*Muir's Tr. v. Braidwood* 1958 S.C. 169); but once litiscontestation has taken place, the personal quality of the claim is shed so that it is capable of being acquired by the trustee (*Watson v. Thompson* 1991 S.C. 447). The bankrupt until discharged and reinvested with his estate (*Flett v. Mustard* 1936 S.C. 269) has no title to pursue actions which his trustee may and does pursue (*Dickson v. United Dominion Trusts Ltd* 1988 S.L.T. 19). The bankrupt may sue or be sued in respect of certain dealings with his sequestrated estate, e.g. where his trustee has abandoned to the bankrupt the property to which the dealing relates or he has authorised the dealing or is personally barred and the third party was unaware of the sequestration (1985 Act, s.32(9)); or he has abandoned the right to pursue the claim (*Dickson*, above); the right must be averred: *Grindall v. John Mitchell (Grangemouth) Ltd* 1984 S.L.T. 335. The trustee may sue or be sued in his own name as "trustee in sequestration of (*name of bankrupt*)".

(D)(5)   Beneficiary.

Where there is a trustee, or an executor, a beneficiary cannot sue the estate's debtor: *Hinton & Co. v. Connell's Trs* (1883) 10 R. 1110; *Morrison v. Morrison's Exrx* 1912 S.C. 892; though a special legatee may sue if he makes the executor a defender: *Young v. Ramage* (1838) 16 S. 572, 578 per Lord Corehouse. The beneficiary may compel the trustee to give the use of his name on security for expenses or to grant an assignation of his claim: *Morrison*, above. He has title to sue one or more of his trustees for breach of trust; if there are other beneficiaries, intimation should be made to the others as a decision might be res judicata against them: *Allen v. McCombie's Trs* 1909 S.C. 710.

(D)(6)   Corporate bodies.

(a) Corporations are constituted by Royal Charter, letters patent or by or under Act of Parliament (e.g. the Companies Acts). As a general rule an incorporated body alone and not its members has title to sue or be sued in respect of matters affecting them as a body. The majority of members has title to sue in respect of an act done irregularly without their approval (and not illegally or ultra vires) and the action is brought in the name of one against the corporation; if the act is ultra vires, illegal or a fraud on the minority, a member of the minority may sue: *North West Transportation Co. v. Beatty* (1887) 12 App.Cas. 589; and where a member complains that the affairs of a company are being conducted in a manner unfairly prejudicial to the interests of some of its members, he may apply to the court for certain orders including an order to authorise civil proceedings: Companies Act 1985, s.461. A company cannot sue for damages on a contract entered into on its behalf before it came into existence: *Tinnevelly Sugar Refining Co. Ltd v. Mirrlees, Watson & Yaryan Co. Ltd* (1894) 21 R. 1009. The means of incorporation should be stated in the instance. A registered company is a body corporate: 1985 Act, s. 13(3). Industrial and provident societies are bodies corporate: Industrial and Provident Societies Act 1965, s.3. Building societies are incorporated under the Building Societies Act 1986. The Universities of St Andrews, Glasgow, Aberdeen and Edinburgh may sue and be sued as such: Universities (Scotland) Act 1858, s.25. The University courts of each university are corporate bodies: Universities (Scotland) Act 1889, s.5(3). The Scottish Parliament is a corporate body, Scotland Act 1998, s.21, the Scottish Parliamentary Corporate Body. A company in receivership which sues may be required to find caution for expenses as the receiver is not personally liable: Companies Act 1985, s.726(2). (b) Administrators and receivers. An administrator of a company appointed under s.8 or 13 of the Insolvency Act 1986 acts as agent of the company (s.14(5)) and may sue or be sued in the name of the company (Sched. 1, para. 5). Proceedings cannot be commenced or continued against a company without the consent of the administrator or the court: 1986 Act, s.11(3)(d); and on the meaning of "proceedings", note *Air Ecosse Ltd v. Civil Aviation Authority* 1987 S.L.T. 751, *Re Barrow Borough Transport Ltd* [1990] Ch. 227 and *Carr v. British International Helicopters Ltd* [1993] B.C.C. 855, and see further note 74.10.1. A receiver appointed under s.51 or s.54 of the 1986 Act para. 5). Proceedings cannot be commenced or continued against a company without the consent of the administrator or the court: 1986 Act, s.11(3)(d); and on the meaning of "proceedings", note *Air Ecosse Ltd v. Civil Aviation Authority* 1987 S.L.T. 751, *Re Barrow Borough Transport Ltd* [1990] Ch. 227 and *Carr v. British International Helicopters Ltd* [1993] B.C.C. 855, and see further note 74.10.1. A receiver appointed under s.51 or s.54 of the 1986 Act acts as agent of the company (s.57(1)) and may sue or be sued in the name of the company (Sched. 2, para. 5). An administrator or receiver has the right to take proceedings to take possession of and get in the property of the company (Scheds 1 and 2, para. 1) and this has been interpreted as giving either officer title to sue in his own name for possessory purposes; but where he seeks recovery of a debt due to the company in respect of a contract entered into before the receivership he must sue in the company's name: *Taylor v. Scottish and Universal Newspapers Ltd* 1981 S.C. 408; *Myles J. Callaghan Ltd v. City of Glasgow D.C.* 1988 S.L.T. 227. (c) Liquidators. The liquidator of a company sues or is sued in the name of the company: 1986 Act, s.165(3) and Sched. 4, Pt II. Proceedings against a company in liquidation may not be proceeded with or commenced without leave of the court (1986 Act, s.130(2)) but leave is not required for a counterclaim for set off against the sum due (*G. & A. (Hotels) Ltd v. T.H.B. Marketing Services Ltd* 1983 S.L.T. 497).

(D)(7) Crown.

See Lord Advocate and Advocate General for Scotland, and Secretary of State for Scotland, (D)(12) and (15) below.

(D)(8) Executors.

Executors hold the estate of the deceased *pro indiviso* and must concur in suing together in an action relating to the estate, though if any refuse or are called as defenders their consent is dispensed with: Stair, III.viii.59. The powers of an executor, nominate or dative, are the same as those of a trustee: Trusts (Scotland) Act 1921, s.2; Succession (Scotland) Act 1964, s.20. Where executors refuse to sue, beneficiaries may sue in name of the executors, giving indemnity for expenses: *Morrison v. Morrison's Exrx* 1912 S.C. 892. An executor has title before confirmation so long as he confirms before extract: *Eyffe v. Fergusson* (1842) 4 D. 1482; *Mackay v. Mackay* 1914 S.C. 200. As a general rule a cause of action which A has against B is not extinguished by the death of either A or B and the right survives in the executors; but there are exceptions: (a) In uncompleted contracts involving delectus personae: *Hoey v. McEwan & Auld* (1867) 5 M. 814. (b) A right to damages under s.1 of the Damages (Scotland) Act 1976 (as amended by s.1 of the Damages (Scotland) Act 1993) which is vested in a relative of the deceased transmits to the executor of the relative in respect of the period to the relative's death: 1976 Act, s.1A as amended by the 1993 Act, s.2. (c) A right to damages in respect of personal injuries including solatium sustained by the deceased and vested in him before his death transmits to his executor, other than patrimonial loss or solatium after the date of death: 1976 Act, s.2(1)–(3) as amended by the 1993 Act, s.3. (d) A right to sue in respect of defamation or other verbal injury or other injury to reputation if the action to enforce that right had been brought by the deceased and concluded before his death: 1976 Act, ss.2(4) and 2A(2) as amended by the 1993 Act, ss.3 and 4. Executors sue or are sued as "(name and address) the executor(s) [—nominate *or as the case may he*] of (*name of deceased*)".

(D)(9) Insured person.

A person indemnified under an insurance policy against damage may sue or be sued. On the principle of subrogation, on payment under the policy to the insured, the insurer may sue in the name of the insured; if the insured, after payment, recovers from the third party he must account to the insurer: *Castellain v. Preston* (1883) 11 Q.B.D. 380; see also *Napier v. Hunter* [1993] 2 W.L.R. 42.

(D)(9A) Guardian.

A guardian appointed to a person aged 16 or over under the Adults with Incapacity (Scotland) Act 2000 normally has the power to act as the legal representative in relation to any matter within the scope of the power conferred by the guardianship order: 2000 Act, s.64(3). A guardian appointed under the 2000 Act may have conferred on him the power to pursue or defend an action of declarator of nullity of marriage or divorce or separation: 2000 Act, s.64(c). A guardian to a child under 16 may be appointed to be the legal representative of the child: Children (Scotland) Act 1995, s.11(2)(b). A person given power under an intervention order under s. 53(1) of the 2000 Act, to make decisions and give instructions in respect of an action, does not require to be sisted as a party to the action, the order being sufficient authority: *Riley v. James Beaton & Co (Plumbers) Ltd* 2004 S.L.T. 1083 (OH).

(D)(10) Landlord and tenant.

Each has title to sue in respect of a nuisance by a third party and may sue in the same action if both are affected: *Jolly v. Brown* (1828) 6 S. 872.

(D)(11) Liquidator.

See corporate bodies, (D)(6) above.

(D)(12) Lord Advocate and Advocate General for Scotland.

Civil proceedings brought by or against any part of the Scottish Administration on or after 1st July 1999 are brought by or against the Lord Advocate; in any other case (including any U.K. Government department), the proceedings are brought by or against the Advocate General: Crown Suits (Scotland)

Act 1857, ss.1–4A as amended by Sched. 8, para. 2 of the Scotland Act 1998. The "Scottish Administration" is defined by s. 126(6)–(8) of the Scotland Act 1998 as meaning the officeholders (Scottish Executive, junior ministers and non-ministerial offices (e.g. Registrar General of Births, Deaths and Marriages for Scotland, Keeper of the Registers of Scotland, Keeper of the Records for Scotland) and staff). The Lord Advocate will retain most of his statutory and other functions he currently has of representing the public interest in litigation (because they are not reserved matters for the U.K. Government). But some functions are transferred to the Advocate General: see Transfer of Functions (Lord Advocate and Advocate General for Scotland) Order 1999 (S.I 1999/679). During the transitional period of 20th May (the date on which the Scottish Law Officers cease to be members of the U.K. Government: Scotland Act 1998 (Commencement) Order 1998, Art. 2(2) and Sched. 4 (S.I 1998/3216)) to 1st July 1999, unnecessarily complicated provisions apply. Devolved matters remain the responsibility of the U.K. Government; however, *new* civil proceedings brought by or against the U.K. Government during this period should be brought by or against the Advocate General and not the Lord Advocate. During this transitional period any interest of the Lord Advocate in pending civil proceedings by or against the Lord Advocate will (unless it relates to crime or deaths) transfer to the Advocate General: Scotland Act 1998 (General Transfer, Transitional and Savings Provisions) Order 1999, Art. 6 (S.I. 1999 No. 901); but, by virtue of Art. 8 of that Order it may not be necessary to amend the pleadings. From 1st July 1999 any interest of the Advocate General in civil proceedings will transfer to the Lord Advocate if they would have been taken by or against the Scottish Administration if they had been commenced on that date: S.I. 1999 No. 901, Art. 7. The Advocate General is, therefore, after 1st July 1999 the person to sue and be sued on behalf of the Crown and government departments in relation to matters for which he has authority to act: (a) Exchequer causes—i.e. all revenues and duties of customs and excise and all other revenues, duties, debts and profits of the Crown and fines, forfeitures and penalties arising to the Crown, except where otherwise provided in an enactment (e.g. the Inland Revenue Commissioners who sue and are sued as such in relation to matters under s.13 of the Stamp Act 1891 or s.56 of the Taxes Management Act 1970): C.S.A. 1988, s.22; (b) causes by or against the Crown or a public department other than the Scottish Administration (generally the U.K. or English departments including the Treasury and the Admiralty (*Lord Advocate v. Argyllshire C.C.* 1950 S.C. 304)): Crown Suits (Scotland) Act 1857, ss.1–4A (the sections are permissive and not exclusive; see also (D)(15) below and *Cameron v. Lord Advocate* 1952 S.C. 165, 169 per Lord Mackay. S.17 of the Crown Proceedings Act 1947 (which provides for government departments in England to sue and be sued in their own names) does not apply to Scotland: 1947 Act, s.42. It is not competent to challenge the title of the Lord Advocate or the Advocate General on the ground that he has produced no authority: 1857 Act, s.3. The Lord Advocate is styled "[The Rt Hon.] (*name*), The Lord Advocate, [as representing (*name of government department*)], Lord Advocate's Chambers, Crown Office, 25 Chambers Street, Edinburgh EH1 1LA". (The Lord Advocate is no longer styled "Her Majesty's Advocate" in the Crown Suits Act 1857, no doubt because a distinction has to be made between him and the Advocate General.) The Advocate General is styled "[The Rt Hon. (*if that is the case*)] (*name*), The Advocate General for Scotland [as representing (*name of Government department*)], Office of the Solicitor to the Advocate General for Scotland, Victoria Quay, Edinburgh, EH6 6QQ". It would appear that, in Exchequer causes (unless otherwise provided) by virtue of s.22 of the C.S.A. 1988 and in causes in relation to the interest of the Crown or a public department by virtue of s.1 of the 1857 Act (see *Lord Advocate v. Black* 1995 S.L.T. 540), the Law Officers may in fact sue or be sued as "The Lord Advocate" or "The Advocate General for Scotland", as the case may be, and need not be named.

Formerly, the Lord Advocate was immune from suit in connection with proceedings on indictment: *Hester v. Macdonald* 1961 S.C. 370 (First Div.). In *Whitehouse v. Lord Advocate* 2020 S.C. 133, a Court of Five Judges decided that *Hester* was wrongly decided and that the Lord Advocate was not immune from suit for malicious prosecution.

(D)(13)   Partnership.

A firm (an association of persons carrying on business in common with a view to profit: Partnership Act 1890, ss.1, 4 and 45) has a legal persona distinct from its partners. A firm with a social name (the names of its partners past or present) may sue or be sued in the firm name alone: *Forsyth v. John Hare & Co.* (1834) 13 S. 42; cf. *Brims & Mackay v. Pattullo* 1907 S.C. 1106 (new firm cannot sue for debts of old firm unless suing under arrangement for debts of old firm when that capacity must be set forth in the instance). An individual partner may sue in the firm name for firm debts: *Kinnes v. Adam & Sons* (1882) 9 R. 698, 699 per Lord McLaren. A firm with a descriptive name may sue or be sued in the firm name together with three of its partners (or all if less than three): *Antermony Coal Co. v. Walter Wingate & Co.* (1866) 4 M. 1017. There is now no Business Names Register, but a duty to disclose the names of persons using business names was introduced by the Companies Act 1981, s.29 (now the Business Names Act 1985, s.4). A person in breach of these provisions may have a claim of his dismissed if a defender was unable to pursue his claim against that person: 1985 Act, s.5. Where surviving partners sue for a debt due to the firm it is good practice to name the dissolved firm in the instance. A limited liability partnership (LLP or llp) is a body corporate (see (D)(6), above), a legal personality separate from its members: Limited Liability Partnership Act 2000.

(D)(14)   Receiver.

See corporate bodies, (D)(6) above.

(D)(14A) Scottish Administration.

Proceedings by or against the Scottish Administration are brought by or against the Lord Advocate (subject to transitional provisions): see (D)(12) above.

(D)(14B) Scottish Parliament.

Proceedings by or against the Parliament are instituted by or against the Scottish Parliamentary Corporate Body: Scotland Act 1998, s.40. Proceedings by or against the Presiding Officer or a member of the staff of the Parliament are instituted by or against the corporate body on his behalf: 1998 Act, s.40(2). A member of the public does not have title to interdict a member of the Parliament to secure that the member complies with the rule about members' interests. In art.6 of the Scotland Act 1998 (transitory and Transitional Provisions) (Members' Interests) Order 1999 [S.I. 1999 No.1350]: *Whaley v. Lord Watson of Invergowrie* 2000 S.C. 340.

(D)(15) Secretary of State for Scotland.

It is customary for him to sue and be sued (as an officer of state) for the Scottish Office and the departments for which he is responsible. The departments within the Scottish Office, which are not separate legal entities (Reorganisation of Offices (Scotland) Act 1939) are the Scottish Office Agriculture and Fisheries Department, the Scottish Office Education Department, the Scottish Office Environment Department, the Scottish Office Home and Health Department and the Scottish Office Industry Department. He sues or is sued as "The Secretary of State for Scotland"; it is not necessary to name him: 1939 Act, s.1(8).

(D)(16) Several defenders.

A pursuer may not, as a general rule, sue more than one defender in one action with separate conclusions based on separate and independent debts: Maclaren on *Court of Session Practice*, p. 388; *Liquidators of the Western Bank of Scotland v. Douglas* (1860) 22 D. 447; *Treadwell's Drifters Inc. v. RCL Ltd*, 1996 S.L.T. 1048. An exception arises where there is sufficient connection between individual defenders having regard to the subject-matter of the case and the circumstances before the court: *Yoker Housing Association Ltd v. McGurn Logan Duncan & Opfer*, 1998 S.L.T. 1334. Joint or conjunct obligants must be called together and each is liable pro rata for his share ("A and B jointly"): *Coats v. Union Bank* 1929 S.C. (H.L.) 114. One pursuer cannot sue two or three defenders for separate causes of action and put in his summons a conclusion for a lump sum: *Ellerman Lines Ltd v. Clyde Navigation Trustees*, 1909 S.C. 690, 691 per Dunedin, LP; where there is a single wrong it is competent for a pursuer to ask for a decree for a lump sum against joint delinquents jointly and severally, but not where there are separate wrongs: Maclaren, *Court of Session Practice*, p. 266. On the other hand, distinct claims founded on different grounds may not be incompetent where considerations of convenience favour allowing it to proceed, as in Yoker, above; see *Toner v. Kean Construction (Scotland) Ltd*, 2009 S.L.T. 1038 (OH); cf *Treadwell's Drifters Inc v. RCL Ltd*, 1996 S.L.T. 1048 (OH). The guiding principle, where an objection to competency is taken (so long as the rule that it is incompetent for a pursuer to seek decree in a lump sum for separate wrongs is not broken) is whether the action is likely to lead to manifest inconvenience and injustice: *Ruddy v. Chief Constable, Strathclyde Police*, 2013 S.C. (UKSC) 126, 136, para. [32]. The general rule is that joint (or conjunct) and several obligants must be sued together if the debt has not been constituted in a decree or is not in a liquid document of debt (*Neilson v. Wilson* (1890) 17 R 608, 614) and each is liable for the whole debt ("A and B jointly and severally"), with a right of relief for payment of others' shares of the debt. The general rule is enforced by a defence of "all parties not called" but if it is open for the defender to serve a third party notice on the omitted co-obligant and there is no prejudice to the defender in an omitted joint and several obligant not being sued, the general rule may not apply (*Lang v. Ure*, 1994 S.L.T. 1235). Given that third party procedure involves the defender incurring expense against the third party which would otherwise be incurred by the pursuer under the general rule, there must presumably be a point at which non-compliance with the general rule causes prejudice to the defender which cannot be cured by third party procedure. Where the obligation is in writing or a decree, one may be sued as each is liable in solidum. There is a general presumption in favour of liability pro rata: Stair, I.xvii.20; but there are many exceptions: parties to a bill or promissory note, partners (Partnership Act 1890, s.9), parties to an obligation *ad factum praestandum*: *Rankine v. Logic Den Land Co.* (1902) 4 F. 1074. Joint proprietors must all be called together. Proprietors in common should be called together. Joint delinquents may be sued together jointly and severally or severally, or any one of them may be sued as each is liable for the whole damage arising from the combined wrong; and where they are both liable the pursuer gets a joint and several decree he can enforce against any, or if one only is held liable, a decree against that one: *Ellerman Lines Ltd v. Clyde Navigation Trs*, 1909 S.C. 690. If defenders are responsible for different acts for which they may be sued in one action, they may not be sued jointly and severally but separately for the wrong by each: *Barr v. Neilsons* (1868) 6 M. 651.

Where two or more defenders are sued "jointly" each is sought to be made liable for his share; "severally" means each is liable for the whole; "jointly and severally" means each is sought to be made liable for the whole debt (in solidum), but between each other the defenders are each liable for his share (pro rata). A decree against defenders jointly and severally means that the pursuer can seek the whole debt or part of it against one defender and "jointly" means that that defender has a right of relief against those defenders who have not paid where he has paid more than his share: *Fleming v. Gemmill*, 1908 S.C. 340, 345 per Lord McLaren. It is possible to sue against defenders "jointly and severally or severally", but, according to Lord McLaren, adding the words "or severally" adds nothing. Where, in an action competently raised against several defenders jointly and severally and decree is obtained against one defender but not satisfied (*Arrow Chemicals Ltd v. Guild,* 1978 S.L.T. 206) or a defender is assoilzied (*Gavin v. Henderson & Co,* 1910 S.C. 357) or the case against a defender is irrelevant (*Robinson v. Reid's Trustees,*(1900) 2 F. 928, 931 per Lord Moncreiff) and the case against the other is relevant (Mackersy v. Davis & Sons, (1895) 22 R. 368) or a defender settles with the pursuer (*Arrow Chemicals Ltd v. Guild,* 1978 S.L.T. 206), the pursuer may proceed with the action against the other defenders.

(D)(17) Several pursuers.

The rule is that parties cannot conjoin in the same action unless there is some connection between the parties in the matters pursued for or they have been aggrieved by the same act: *H.M. Feuers of Orkney v. Steuart,* (1741) Mor. 11986; *Paxton v. Brown,* 1908 S.C. 406, 412-413 (1907) 15 S.L.T. 662, 666 per Dunedin, L.P; *Boulting v. Elias ,* 1990 S.C. 135, 1990 S.L.T. 597 (First Div.). Although in Paxton, the L.P. said that the connection did not mean the same thing as joint interest in its legal sense, in *Boulting* the court held that the connection must be one in respect of the legal basis on which the claims in the action are made. Joint proprietors (one estate vested in them *pro indiviso*), proprietors of common property or parties having a joint title to enforce a debt or other obligation, as a general rule, must join in one action: *Lawson v. Leith & Newcastle Steam Packet Co.* (1850) 13 D. 175; *Johnston v. Crauford* (1855) 17 D. 1023; *Lade v. Largs Baking Co. Ltd* (1863) 2 M. 17, 21 per Lord Deas. But one of them may sue to protect the property from trespass or encroachment (*Warrand v. Watson* (1905) 8 F. 253) or where it would cause injustice not to allow him to do so (Lawson, above at 178 per L.J.-C. Hope (part-owner of ship entitled to sue for his share of damage)). Unconnected pursuers may sue together for protection of a common right or interest against different defenders (*Cowan & Sons v. Duke of Buccleuch* (1874) 4 R.(HL) 14); but not for the same wrong to different parties in respect of different interests (*Arthur v. Aird* 1907 S.C. 1170; *Smith-Shand's Trs v. Forbes* 1921 S.C. 820; *Concrete Products (Kirkcaldy) Ltd v. Anderson and Menzies* 1996 S.L.T. 587. Where several pursuers sue together the ground of action must be identical and there must be no material prejudice to the defender: *Buchan v. Thomson* 1976 S.L.T. 42, 44 per Lord Fraser. Several pursuers having a claim arising out of one injury and the same wrong may sue together; and for claims arising out of the death of a relative, must do so: *Darling v. Gray* (1892) 19 R.(HL) 31, 32 per Lord Watson; and see also rules for intimation to connected persons in actions of damages in respect of the death of a relative in Chap. 43, Pt I.

(D)(18) Trustees.

A majority (other than those having an adverse interest) or all trustees, unless the truster specified a quorum, may sue: *Blisset's Trs v. Hope's Trs* (1854) 16 D. 482. Normally one trustee has no title to sue: *Neilson v. Mossend Iron Co.* (1884) 12 R. 499, 525; *Neilson v. Neilson's Trs* (1885) 12 R. 670, 673; unless to challenge the other trustees or to protect the estate. When suing trustees, all should be called as defenders; though it is competent to sue one trustee for breach of trust of all of them: *Allen v. Mc-Combie's Trs* 1909 S.C. 710. Trustees must sue or be sued as "(*names and addresses*), the trustees of (*name of truster*)": *Bell v. Trotter's Trs* (1841) 3 D. 380.

(D)(19) Unincorporated bodies.

A trade union or an unincorporated employers' association may sue or be sued in its own name: Trade Union and Labour Relations (Consolidation) Act 1992, ss.10(b) and 127(2)(b). Other unincorporated bodies (but see next para.) must sue in their own name with the addition of the names of members authorised to sue, the test being that they should be persons "responsible for the proper prosecution of the action and for giving obedience to the decrees that may be given under it": *Rent on Football Club v. McDowall* (1891) 18 R. 670, 674 per Lord McLaren; it is sufficient when suing such a body to call the body with its office-bearers or a sufficient number of members to defend its interests: *Somerville v. Rowbotham* (1862) 24 D. 1187, 1189 per Lord Neaves. In relation to churches the position is somewhat complicated: on non-established churches, see Lyall, *Of Presbyters and Kings: Church and State in the Law of Scotland* (1980), Chap. 6.

A community council is a hybrid body that may sue or be sued in its own name: *Kershaw v. Connel Community Council* 2019 S.L.T. 121 (OH).

"CONCLUSIONS".

13.2.3 Styles are to be found in Form 13.2-B. A summons may contain any number of different conclusions. Decree for more than has been concluded for cannot be granted without amendment except in optional procedure reparation cases (see Form 43.18) or in actions of count, reckoning and payment where the words "or such other sum as may be found due" have been added (*Spottiswoode v. Hopkirk* (1853) 16 D. 59).

A single conclusion for payment of a lump sum may include within it a number of heads of specific non-random amounts arising from different events and on different grounds, provided that these are detailed in the condescendence and supported by adequate pleas in law: *Lord Advocate v. Duncan Logan (Construction) Ltd.,* 1964 S.L.T. 64; *Western SMT Co. Ltd. v. Magistrates of Greenock,* 1957 S.L.T. (Notes) 22. It is competent to have alternative conclusions: e.g. for implement with damages in the alternative, or for payment failing which declarator of breach of contract and damages; where one conclusion is not satisfied declarator may be sought for the alternative conclusion and the first cannot be enforced further: *Bosco Design Services Ltd v. Plastic Sealant Services Ltd,* 1979 S.L.T. (Notes) 33. Alternative conclusions may be mutually incompatible: see *Norwich Union Life Insurance Society v. Tanap Invest-*

ments V.K. Ltd (in liquidation) (No. 1), 1998 S.L.T. 623, 628C per Lord Penrose (conclusions for declarator that sums were due under a minute of agreement and also for rectification of the agreement to reflect that this was the contractual intention). An ancillary conclusion (which fails if the main conclusion fails) is also competent: *Harvey v. Smith* (1904) 6 F. 511, 523.

Expenses as an incident of process may be awarded without being concluded for: *J. Heggie & Co. v. Stark & Selkrig* (1826) 4 S. 510; but it is usual to conclude for expenses, and wise to do so to give notice and if the case is undefended. Interest runs *ex lege* from the date of decree, but it is advisable to conclude for it and this must be done if claimed from a date earlier than decree or for a rate other than that in r. 7.7 (rate of interest on decrees): on interest, see notes 7.7.1-7.7.8. A conclusion for expenses only in the event of appearing and opposing or appearing and occasioning expense is competent, but mere appearance in such a case does not infer liability for expenses: *Henderson v. Innes*, 1922 S.L.T. 550.

It is not competent for a defender to enrol a motion for decree in favour of the pursuer in terms of the conclusions of the summons: *Auld & Macdonald v. George Wimpey & Co.*, 1977 S.L.T.(Notes) 23.

The absence of any conclusions in a summons is not a fundamental nullity where it is plain to the defender from the pleadings what the nature of the claim against him is, and amendment to add conclusions has been allowed under rr. 2.1 and 24.1.2(a): *Wilson v. Lothian R.C.*, 1995 S.L.T. 991.

"CONDESCENDENCE".

Formerly each article of condescendence was very short. An unfortunate modern practice has developed of making articles long and cumbersome. Articles should be as short and concise as possible: different facts or events should be stated in separate articles, and a matter known or likely to be disputed should be in a separate article rather than amongst uncontroversial material; this forces a defender clearly to admit or deny and explain facts without hiding behind a general denial. Our whole system of pleading and disposal of cases upon preliminary pleas must depend upon each party stating with candour what are the material facts upon which he relies and admitting the facts stated by his opponent which he knows to be true: *Ellon Castle Estates Co. Ltd v. Macdonald* 1975 S.L.T.(Notes) 66 per Lord Stewart.

"It is not the function of pleadings to justify an inquiry which may result in evidence being led which might establish the pleader's case: on the contrary the pleadings must set forth clearly and specifically the facts upon which the pleader aims to succeed in his pleas, so that the other party may have notice of the case against him and the facts upon which it is founded: *Morrison v. Rendall* 1986 S.C. 69, 78 per Lord Robertson.

The condescendence must state the facts which, if true, entitle the pursuer to the decree concluded for. Averments are sufficient for relevancy if according to their primary meaning they are sufficient to support the conclusions: *Hope v. Hope's Trs* (1898) 1 F.(H.L.) 1, 3 per Lord Watson. The parties and their capacities must be identified. Any special capacity must be stated: r. 13.2(4)(e); the express provision in the Rules was probably inspired by *Royal Insurance (UK) Ltd v. AMEC Construction Scotland Ltd* , 2008 S.C. 201 (O.H.), in which Lord Emslie at p. 216, para. [21] re-affirmed the requirement for proper disclosure in the instance of any special capacity in which a party sues or is sued. Title to sue must be set forth: *Bentley v. Macfarlane* 1964 S.C. 76, 83 per Lord Guthrie; *Microwave Systems (Scotland) Ltd v. Electro-Physiological Instruments Ltd* 1971 S.C. 140, 143 per Lord Thomson. The domicile of the defender, the ground of jurisdiction, whether there is an agreement prorogating another jurisdiction and whether there are proceedings elsewhere must be stated: r. 13.2(4). An account of the circumstances must be given. The legal grounds of the action must be set forth, each in separate articles (*Keenan v. Glasgow Corporation* 1923 S.C. 611, 621 per Lord Ormidale) and any statutory provision founded on specified (although this is not always essential: *NV Devos Gehroeder v. Sunderland Sportswear Ltd* 1987 S.L.T. 331). An averment which is essential must be stated: *Brown v. Redpath & Co. Ltd* 1963 S.L.T. 219, 222 per L.J.-C. Thomson and 224 per Lord Mackay (essential to prove reasonable practice). As evidence is relevant if logically connected with the matters in dispute (*Inland Revenue Commissioners v. Stenhouse's Trs* 1993 S.L.T. 248, 251E-F per Lord Coulsfield), "collateral" issues may to that extent be averred: *Strathmore Group Ltd v. Credit Lyonnais* 1994 S.L.T. 1023.

"Believed and averred" is not sufficient except in relation to inferences drawn from facts already stated, or non-essential facts, within the defender's knowledge but not the pursuer's: *McCrone v. Macbeth, Currie & Co.* 1968 S.L.T.(Notes) 24 (facts within pursuer's knowledge); *McCrindle v. Sandelands* 1980 S.L.T.(Notes) 12 (non-essential averment); and see *Brown*, above, at 222 per L.J.-C. Thomson, *Strathmore Group Ltd*, above, at 1032K per Lord Osborne, *Littlejohn v. Wood & Davidson Ltd* , 1996 G.W.D. 3-168, unreported. Lord Osborne in Strathmore, described it as a formula which ought to be used where the pleader is averring, as a matter of inference, a fact which was sought to be inferred from other averments of primary fact: see also *Burnett v. Menzies Dougal WS* , 2006 S.C. 93 (Extra Div).

Alternative and even inconsistent averments of fact may be made: e.g. they may be alternative where the precise way in which an accident occurred is not known: *Finnie v. Logie* (1859) 21 D. 825, 829 per L. P. McNeill; *Clarke v. Edinburgh & District Tramways Co. Ltd* 1914 S.C. 775, 781 per L. P. Strathclyde; see also *M v. M* 1967 S.L.T. 157 (nullity on ground of impotence of pursuer or defender); *Safdar v. Devlin* 1995 S.L.T. 530. The relevancy of alternative averments is tested by reference to the weakest alternative, and if the weakest is irrelevant in law the whole action is irrelevant because the weakest alternative is the only one which the pursuer absolutely offers to prove: *Hope*, above. In *Haig & Ringrose Ltd v. Barrhead Buildings Ltd* 1981 S.L.T. 157, Lord Stott explained the "weakest alternative" test as meaning that if liability arises only on proof of A and the pursuer avers that the fact is A or B, the pleadings are irrelevant; but if both are relevant though one is irrelevant because of lack of specification the court is entitled to sever the irrelevant alternative. The rule that a party perils his case on the weaker alternative applies only where the alternative is weaker in law: *Stewart's Exrs v. Stewart* 1993 S.C. 427, 457A per L.P. Hope. If

13.2.4

not alternative, averments must not be self-contradictory: Maclaren on *Court of Session Practice*, p. 31. Facts should not be averred for which there is no evidence: *Boasted v. Gardner* (1879) 7 R. 139, 145 per L.J.-C. Moncreiff.

In a case of fault, there must be specific averments of fault: *Thomson & Co. v. Pattison, Elder & Co.* (1895) 22 R. 432.

Where fraud is alleged, averments of fraud must be specific: *Shedden v. Patrick* (1852) 14 D. 721, 727 per Lord Fullerton. Averments of fraud in a commercial action must meet the same standard: *Kaur v. Singh* , 1998 S.C. 233. For what must be averred in a case of fraud, see *Royal Bank of Scotland plc v. Holmes* 1999 S.L.T. 563, 569K-L, per Lord Macfadyen.

The special mention of one thing may operate to exclude things differing from it (*expressio unius est exclusio alterius*): *Buglass v. British Railways Board* , 18th June 1997 (1997 G.W.D. 26-1303) (reference to working at a particular place would exclude evidence about any other place).

Evidence should not be pled (i.e. the manner in which the facts averred will be proved): *Tulloch v. Davidson* (1858) 20 D. 1045, 1056 per Lord Cowan. So, e.g. the contents of an affidavit should not be incorporated into the pleadings, the proper course being to plead the facts on which proof would be led: *Tough v. SPS (Holdings) Ltd* , 8th December 1998 (O.H.), unreported. An expert's opinion or report should not be pled. Similarly, law should not be pled except (a) as a matter of practice, the duties owed in a reparation action; (b) a private Act of Parliament before 1850 (Interpretation Act 1978, s.3); and (c) foreign law if different from Scots law, otherwise it will be presumed to be the same as Scots law (*Emerald Stainless Steel Ltd v. South Side Distribution Ltd* 1982 S.C. 61) unless judicial knowledge must be taken of it (Macphail on *Evidence*, paras 2-04 to 2-07).

The presumption that foreign law complies with Scots law is not displaced by a European Community (or Union) regulation which has no effect on the procedural rules applicable to the ascertainment of the proper law: *Kraus v. Sullivan* , 1998 S.L.T. 963 (averments of German law required). But foreign law does not have to be pled and proved where the purpose is not to determine an issue according to the foreign law but to assist in construing a remedy derived from that foreign law: *Roy v. MR Pearlman Ltd* 1999 S.C. 459, 469 per Lord Hamilton. In that case it was held proper to look at French law without averment or proof because, in the context of an E.U. directive which provided a remedy drawn from French law, assistance towards a harmonised approach might be obtained by having regard to the experience of the French courts in applying the remedy. Two recent cases on proof of foreign law are *DNO Oman Ltd v Clouston* 2019 S.L.T. 395 and *Ted Jacob Engineering Group Inc v Morrison* 2019 S.C. 487 (First Div).

The condescendence must give fair notice of the pursuer's case: *Hope*, above; *Eadie Cairns v. Programmed Maintenance Painting Ltd* 1987 S.L.T. 777. Thus, e.g. an averment, that certain matters were stated to "several friends" who were not named, did not give adequate notice and was not admitted to probation: *Boulting v. Elias* 1990 S.C. 135. Also, in pleading vicarious liability, the person who is said to have been negligent should be named or identified; or, if not known, that fact and other circumstances from which the defender would be able to establish by inference that the negligent act had been committed by an employee of the defender should be averred: *Davaney v. Yarrow Shipbuilders Ltd*, 4th December 1998 (O.H.), unreported.

One cannot make a new case at proof for which there is no record: *Morrison's Associated Companies Ltd v. James Rome & Sons Ltd* 1964 S.C. 160, 182 per L.P. Clyde (when a duty in general terms is averred followed by a particularisation of the way in which it is alleged that the duty was breached, proof is restricted to the breach of which notice has been given and evidence directed to some other way is excluded); *Carroll v. Scott's Shipbuilding and Engineering Co. Ltd* 1969 S.L.T.(Notes) 46. In *Gibson v. British Rail Maintenance Ltd* 1995 S.L.T. 953 it was held that the breach of duty proved, although taking a different form from that which appeared in the averments, was within the case pled on record. A pursuer is entitled to rely, however, on the defender's averments of fact even if he does not succeed on his own facts so long as it does not involve more than a variation or modification of his own case on the ground pled by him: *O'Hanlon v. John G. Stein & Co.* 1965 S.C.(H.L.) 23. A variation, modification or development of what is averred in one's pleadings is permissible, but not something which is new, separate and distinct: *Burns v. Dixon's Iron Works Ltd* 1961 S.C. 102, 107 per L.J.-C. Thomson. The ultimate test is one of fairness: *Maclean v. Forestry Commission* 1970 S.L.T. 265, 272 per Lord Wheatley.

As no reference can be made to productions on procedure roll without agreement of parties, if reliance is to be placed for relevancy or specification on documents they must be "adopted and held as repeated herein *brevitatis causa*": see *Gordon v. Davidson* (1864) 2 M. 758, 769 per L.J.-C. Inglis; *Eadie Cairns*, above per Lord Avonside at p. 780E and Lord Jauncey at p. 2783F. The wholesale incorporation of lengthy documents, only parts of which are relevant, is generally unsatisfactory, however, and may well be held not to give the specification required: *Royal Bank of Scotland plc v. Holmes* 1999 S.L.T. 563. In *Prophit v. BBC* 1997 S.L.T. 745, Temporary Judge T. G. Coutts refused to listen to a tape recording of a programme because the issues at procedure roll had to be tested solely on the averments and the tape had not been incorporated into the pleadings. The implication is that if it had been so incorporated, the court would have listened to it. Bearing in mind the rule that evidence should not be pled, there should not be wholesale adoption of documents, such as expert reports. There should only be adoption of material that is required to make the case relevant.

In general, what a party avers he undertakes the evidential burden of proving. In a reparation case founding on the statutory duty of an employer to provide a safe place of work so far as reasonably practicable, it is for the employer to aver and prove non-practicability: *Nimmo v. Alexander Cowan & Sons* 1967 S.C.(H.L.) 79. A pursuer may plead a particular method of reasonable practicability or no particular method; in the former case this does not discharge the onus on the defender and still entitles the pursuer to cross-examine on other methods: *Gibson v. B.C.C. Co. Ltd* 1963 S.C.(H.L.) 15. So also when the onus of showing that due diligence was exercised transfers to the defender on a case of fault against him: *Gunn v. John McAdam & Son Ltd* 1949 S.C. 31, 40 per L.P. Cooper.

In relation to damages, consideration should be given, in a complex case, to whether details of the heads of claim could be set out in a schedule attached to the summons: see, e.g., Scott schedules in building contract cases in England.

A pursuer or a defender, in the pleadings, may "call" on the other to be specific or more specific about an averment or lack of one. Guidance was given by the LJ-C Inglis in *Gordon*, above, at p. 768 about the circumstances in which a call may properly be made and requires to be answered: "When a pursuer's statement is irrelevant or verging on irrelevancy, I could understand a call of this kind as a warning to call the pursuer's attention to the state of his averments, that he might have no reason afterwards to complain that he was taken by surprise, or that he understood that no greater specification was wanted." A failure to answer a call could, in certain circumstances, result in an implied admission that the other party's position is correct: see, e.g., *Marine & Offshore (Scotland) Ltd v Robert Jack* [2017] CSOH 89, para. [56].

"PLEAS-IN-LAW".

These were first required by ss. 9 and 11 of the C.S.A. 1825. A plea-in-law ought to be a distinct legal proposition, applicable to the facts of the case: *J. & R. Young & Co. v. Graham* (1860) 23 D. 36 per L.J.-C. Inglis. "In the circumstances condescended upon, the pursuer is entitled to decree in terms of the conclusions with expenses" and "The defender being due and resting owing to the pursuer in the sum sued for, decree therefor should be pronounced as concluded for" are not legal propositions. **13.2.5**

"DOMICILE OF THE DEFENDER".

This is required to be stated in actions to which the C.J.J.A. 1982 applies; it does not apply to causes excluded by Sched. 1, Art. 1 (substituted by the Civil Jurisdiction and Judgments Act 1982 (Amendment) Orders 1990 [S.I. 1990 No. 2591] and 2000 [S.I. 2000 No. 1824]) (the 1968 (or Brussels) Convention which applies between Denmark and the Member States of the European Community), Art.1 of the "Brussels I" Regulation in E.C. Council Regulation No.44/2001 or Regulation (EU) No. 1215/2012 in civil and commercial matters (Brussels I bis) which replaces the Brussels I Council Regulation which applies between the Member States of the E.U. except Denmark, Sched. 3C, Art. 1 (the Lugano (or "Parallel") Convention, inserted by s. 1(3) of the C.J.J.A. 1991, which applies between the E.C. countries and the Member States of the European Free Trade Association which have ratified it and any other State which accedes to it, and very closely modelled on the 1968 Convention), Sched.4, substituted by the Civil Jurisdiction and Judgments Order 2001 [S.I 2001 No.3929] based on the Brussels I Regulation (inter-U.K. jurisdiction) or Sched. 9 (proceedings excluded from Sched. 8 (jurisdiction of Scottish courts)). The importance of this provision is that the court must know in such actions which Schedule to apply; e.g. if the defender is domiciled in a country outside the U.K. to which Sched. 1 or 3C applies or in another part of the U.K., the court must sist the cause if it is not shown that the defender has been able to receive the summons (or that all steps have not been taken to this end) in sufficient time to arrange his defence: C.J.J.A. 1982, Scheds 1, 3C, Art. 20(2), and Sched. 4, r. 15(2); and Brussels I Regulation, Art.26(2), Brussels I bis, art. 28(2). Furthermore the defender is made aware of what the court is being told about the jurisdiction alleged. **13.2.6**

1.   Under the 1968 Convention and the Lugano Convention, whether a person is domiciled in the Contracting State whose courts are seized of a matter is determined in the case of individuals (natural persons) by applying its internal law (1982 Act, Scheds 1 and 3C, Art. 52(1)) and of other persons by applying its rules of private international law (1982 Act, Scheds 1 and 3C, Art. 53). Under the Brussels I Regulation the domicile of individuals (natural persons) is determined by the internal law, in order to determine whether a party is domiciled in a Member State whose courts are seized of a matter (Art. 59) similarly, Brussels I bis, art. 62; and in the case of other persons, the domicile is the place where it has its statutory seat, central administration or principal place of business (Art. 60(1); Brussels I bis, Art. 63(1), Brussels I bis, Art. 63(3)), but in the case of a trust domicile is determined by the court applying its private international law (Art. 60(3)).

2.   If a party who is a natural person is not domiciled in a contracting state to which the 1968 Convention or the Lugano Convention applies or a Member State to which the Brussels I Regulation or Brussels I bis applies whose courts are not seized of the matter, then, in order to determine whether that person is domiciled in another contracting or Member State, the court applies the law of that state: C.J.J.A. 1982, Scheds 1 and 3C, Art. 52(2); Brussels I Regulation, Art. 59(2); Brussels I bis, Art. 62(2). A person cannot be sued in Scotland under either convention or the Brussels I Regulation by virtue of rules which confer jurisdiction on the basis of the presence of property or arrestment of moveables in Scotland (C.J.J.A. 1982, Scheds 1 and 3C, Art. 3; Brussels I Regulation, Art. 3(2)).

3.   Subject to (1) and (2) above, the domicile of an individual (natural person) for the purposes of the 1968 Convention, the Lugano Convention or under U.K. jurisdiction or the general jurisdiction of the Scottish courts (C.J.J.A. 1982, Scheds 1, 3C, 4 and 8) or, for the purposes of the Brussels I Regulation or Brussels I bis, is determined by para. 9 of Sched. 1 to the Civil Jurisdiction and Judgments Order 2001 [S.I 2001 No.3929], is determined by s. 41 of the C.J.J.A. 1982 according to where he resides: i.e. (a) he is resident there and (b) the nature and circumstances of his residence indicate that he has a substantial connection with that place ((b) is presumed if he has been resident there for the last three months).

4.   The domicile of a company or other legal person is, in general, its seat. Under the C.J.J.A. 1982, a corporation or association has its seat (in the U.K. or elsewhere) in the place where it was

incorporated or formed and has its registered office or other official address, or where its central management and control is exercised: C.J.J.A. 1982, s. 42 (in the case of a trust in the U.K., domicile is determined by s. 45). For the purposes of the Brussels I Regulation, a company or other legal person or association is domiciled at the place where it has its statutory seat, central administration or principal place of business: Brussels I Regulation, Art. 60, similarly, Brussels I bis, art. 63 (in the U.K. and Ireland, "statutory seat" is the registered office or, if none, the place of incorporation or, if none, the place under the law of which formation took place). Under the C.J.J.A. 1982, in relation to proceedings concerning the validity of the constitution, nullity or dissolution of companies, other legal persons or associations or their decisions (C.J.J.A. 1982, Scheds 1 and 3C, Art. 16(2), Sched. 4, rr. 4 and 11(b) and Sched. 8, rr. 2(16) and 5(1)(b); Brussels I Regulation, Art. 22(2); Brussels I bis, Art. 24(2)), a corporation or association has its seat in a country to which the 1968 or Lugano Convention applies, or in the U.K., under whose laws it was incorporated or formed or where its central management and control is exercised, and has its seat in Scotland if it has its registered office or other official address there or where its central management and control is exercised: C.J.J.A. 1982, s. 43; Civil Jurisdiction and Judgments Order 2001 [S.I 2001 No. 3929], Sched. 1, para. 10.

5.   The domicile of the Crown is dealt with in s. 46 of the C.J.J.A. 1982. Note that, whatever the domicile of the defender, there may be exclusive jurisdiction of a court under the 1968 or Lugano Convention (Scheds 1 and 3C, Art. 16), under Sched. 4, r. 11 (inter-U.K. jurisdiction), Sched. 8, r. 5 (Scottish jurisdictional rules) or the Brussels I Regulation, Art. 22 or Brussels I bis, Art. 24).

"GROUND OF JURISDICTION".

13.2.7   The general jurisdiction of the court over persons who may be sued there is contained in Sched. 8 to the C.J.J.A 1982: C.J.J.A. 1982, s.20 (Sched.8 was substituted by the Civil Jurisdiction and Judgments Order 2001 [S.I. 2001 No. 3929]). Sched. 8 does not apply to (a) proceedings subject to the jurisdictional rules in the 1968 (or Brussels) Convention on jurisdiction and enforcement in civil and commercial matters between Denmark and the Member States of the European Community, or the similar 2007 Lugano Convention between the E.C. Member States and Member States of the European Free Trade Association which ratify it (and any other State which accedes to it; currently Denmark, Iceland, Norway and Switzerland), in Sched. 1 to the 1982 Act (C.J.J.A. 1982, s. 20); (b) proceedings subject to the jurisdictional rules in the EC Council Regulation No.44/2001 on jurisdiction and enforcement of judgments in civil and commercial matters (known as the "Brussels I Regulation") or Regulation (EU) No. 1215/2012 ("Brussels I bis" or "Brussels I Regulation (Recast)") which replaces the Brussels I Regulation between Member States of the EU; (c) proceedings subject to the jurisdictional rules in Sched. 4 to the C.J.J.A. 1982 which determines the allocation of jurisdiction between the different courts of the U.K. (C.J.J.A. 1982, s. 20); (d) proceedings in respect of which any other enactment confers jurisdiction (C.J.J.A. 1982, s. 21(a)) and (e) proceedings listed in Sched. 9 as proceedings excluded from Sched. 8 (C.J.J.A. 1982, s. 21(b)). See notes 13.2.8 to 13.2.14 on the various grounds of jurisdiction.

Denmark signed up to the Brussels I Regulation on 1st July 2007 and to the Brussels I Regulation (Recast) on 1st June 2013.

Rule 13.2(4)(a) assumes the defender will only prorogate jurisdiction when he lodges answers and does not contest jurisdiction. But he might have prorogated jurisdiction in advance in which case the ground of jurisdiction can (and must) be averred.

The position before Brexit (31st December 2020) was that (1) in relation to jurisdiction in an EU country (including Denmark which implemented it on 1st June 2013), one looked to the Brussels 1 Regulation (Recast); (2) in relation to Iceland, Norway and Switzerland, one looked to the 2007 Lugano Convention; (3) in relation other countries one looked to Sched. 8 to the C.J.J.A. 1982. The Regulation and the Convention were revoked by the Civil Jurisdiction and Judgments (Amendment) (EU Exit) Regulations 2019 [S.I. 2019 No. 479] at 11pm on 31st December 2020.

The current position is as follows:

(1)   The starting point for jurisdiction is Sched. 8 to the C.J.J.A. 1982.

(2)   In relation to jurisdiction in proceedings not concluded before 11pm on 31st December 2020, Council Regulation EC No. 1215/2012 (Brussels I Regulation (Recast)) and other specified regulations and the 2007 Lugano Convention apply: Civil Jurisdiction and Judgments (Amendment) (EU Exit) Regulations 2019 [SI 2019/479].

(3)   As the U.K. has left the EU, in relation to jurisdiction in relation to EU, and Lugano Convention, countries, after 11pm on 31st December 2020 one will fall back on other law.

(4)   Where there is a contract between a party in the U.K. and a party in another contracting state, there may be a choice of law agreement to which the 2005 Hague Convention on Choice of Court Agreements applies: see C.J.J.A. 1982, Sched. 3F inserted by the Private International Law (Implementation of Agreements) Act 2020. There is a disagreement between the EU and the U.K. as to whether the 2005 Hague Convention applies to agreements on or after 1st January 2021 (EU position) or on or after 1st October 2015 when the UK acceded to the Convention as an EU state (U.K. position).

(5)   There may be another bilateral convention with another country that may apply: see e.g., those listed in note 13.2.12.

(6)   The U.K. has applied to join the 2007 Lugano Convention. That applies between the EU Member States and Iceland, Norway and Switzerland. Denmark joined separately on 24th September 2009 (it had not signed up to the Brussels I Regulation (Recast) at that time).

(7)   In relation to children under 18, jurisdiction for parental responsibilities, custody, residence etc and protection (but not e.g. maintenance) is governed by Sched. 3D of the C.J.J.A. 1982 inserted by the Private International Law (Implementation of Agreements) Act 2020, in force from 31st December 2020.

(8)   There may be special statutory rules about jurisdiction, such as in the Domicile and Matrimonial Proceedings Act 1973.

JURISDICTION UNDER THE C.J.J.A. 1982, SCHED. 8.

Before 1st March 2002, Sched. 8 was based on the 1968 European (or Brussels) Convention. From that date, Sched. 8, substituted by the Civil Jurisdiction and Judgments Order 2001 [S.I 2001 No. 3929], was based on the EC Council Regulation No.44/2001 (known as the "Brussels I Regulation"). Sched. 4 to the C.J.J.A. 1982 is also substituted by the same S.I and is now based on the Brussels I Regulation. Sched. 8 has been further amended by the Civil Jurisdiction and Judgments (Amendment) (EU Exit) Regulations 2019 [2019/479]. In determining the meaning and extent of Sched.8 derived to any extent from Title II (Jurisdiction) of the 1968 Convention, (a) regard must be had to the relevant principles laid down by the European Court in connection with the jurisdictional rules in the 1968 Convention (though not necessarily followed as in a case under the 1968 Convention) and (b) the Jenard and Schlosser reports on that convention must be given such weight as is appropriate: C.J.J.A. 1982, s. 20(5).

The following paragraphs deal with the rules of jurisdiction under Sched. 8 to the C.J.J.A. 1982 as amended by S.I 2001 No.3929 with references to Scheds 1 (the 1968 Convention) and 4 (inter-U.K.), to the Brussels I Regulation on which Scheds 4 and 8 were based, Brussels I Regulation (Recast) and the 2007 Lugano Convention. Discussion of jurisdiction under the Brussels I Regulation (Recast) can be found in note 13.2.12A.

It should be noted that Sched. 1 to the C.J.J.A. 1982 (1968 Brussels Convention) was repealed by the Civil Jurisdiction and Judgments (Amendment) (EU Exit) Regulations 2019 [S.I. 2019/479], but had in any event been replaced successively by the freestanding Brussels I Regulation and the Brussels I Regulation (Recast). Sched. 3C to that Act (the 1988 Lugano Convention) was repealed by the Civil Jurisdiction and Judgments Regulations 2009 [S.I. 2009/3131], but had in any event been replaced by the freestanding 2007 Lugano Convention. The Brussels I Regulation (Recast) ceased to have effect after 31st December 2020, as did the 2007 Lugano Convention, by virtue of the Civil Jurisdiction and Judgments (Amendment) (EU Exit) Regulations 2019 [SI 2019/479] except in relation to proceedings not concluded before 11pm on 31st December 2020. The U.K. has applied to join the 2007 Lugano Convention.

(A)   Domicile.

The general and principal ground of jurisdiction is that a person shall be sued in the place of his domicile (C.J.J.A. 1982 (amended by S.I. 2001 No. 3929) Sched. 8, r. 1; see also Sched. 1, Art. 2, Brussels I Regulation, Art. 2 Brussels I Regulation (Recast), Art. 4, 2007 Lugano Convention, Art. 2), that is a defender must be domiciled in Scotland. This rule is subject to the rules of special jurisdiction, jurisdiction over consumer contracts, exclusive jurisdiction, prorogation of jurisdiction, submission to jurisdiction and the proceedings excluded under Sched. 9. Domicile is defined in ss. 41, 42, 43, 45 and 46 of the C.J.J.A. 1982 and is to be ascertained at the time when the cause is commenced, that is the time of citation: Erskine, III.iv.3; *Alston v. Macdougall* (1887) 15 R. 78; *Smith v. Stewart & Co.* 1960 S.C. 329, 334 per L.P. Clyde. (But this statement may have to be reconsidered: see *Canada Trust Co v. Stolzenberg (No.2)* 2000 All E.R. 481, 502C per Lord Hope of Craighead.)

(B)   Rule 2 (special jurisdiction)

provides that a person may also be sued in the Court of Session on 17 different grounds subject to rules concerning consumer contracts, exclusive jurisdiction, prorogation of jurisdiction, submission to jurisdiction and the proceedings excluded by Sched. 9. On the meaning of "special", see *Bank of Scotland v. Seitz* 1990 S.L.T. 584, 587H per L.P. Hope. A clear prima facie relevant case for the jurisdiction of the court must be averred: *Eddie v. ALPA slv*, 2000 S.L.T. 1062.

Rule 2(a)

(no fixed residence: where personally cited). This was a common law jurisdiction and earlier case law will be relevant; it was available in respect of itinerant defenders who had no fixed place of residence anywhere: Erskine, I.ii.16.

Rule 2(b)

(contract: place of performance of the obligation; see also C.J.J.A. 1982, Scheds 1, Art. 5(1), Sched.4, r. 3(a), Brussels I Regulation, Art. 5(a), Brussels I Regulation (Recast), Art. 7(1), 2007 Lugano Convention, Art. 5(1)). This rule is concerned with contractual obligations for which a particular place of performance is provided expressly or by implication: *Bank of Scotland v. I.M.R.O. Ltd* 1989 S.L.T. 432. Where not express the implication is that debts must be paid at the creditor's residence: *Bank of Scotland v. Seitz* 1990 S.L.T. 584. The court decides the place of performance in accordance with its own conflict of law rules: *Tessili v. Dunlop* [1976] E.C.R. 1473; *Custom Made Commercial v. Stawa Metallbau GmbH* [1994] E.C.R. 1-2913. The assumption in Art. 5 of the 1968 Convention is that the obligation has to be performed in one place: *Bank of Scotland v. Seitz*, above. The sole place of performance has to arise as a

13.2.8

matter of obligation and of choice by the debtor as to where he would pay: *Montague Evans v. Young* , 2000 S.L.T. 1083 (OH). In Sched. 1 whether an obligation is contractual under the 1968 Convention is a matter of community law: *Peters v. Zuid Nederlandse Aannemers Vereniging* [1983] E.C.R. 987; *Arcado v. Haviland* [1988] E.C.R. 1539. The existence of the contract is a matter relating to a contract: *Effer v. Kantner* [1982] E.C.R. 825. The words "relating to contract" do not apply to a non-contractual claim such as the condictio indebiti: *Strathaird Farmers Ltd v. Chat away & Co.* 1993 S.L.T. (Sh.Ct.) 36. In employment contracts, the obligation is the obligation which characterises the contract: *Ivenel v. Schwab* [1982] E.C.R. 1891. In other contracts, the obligation is that forming the basis of the proceedings: *De Bloos v. Bouyer* [1976] E.C.R. 1497 followed in *Shenavai v. Kreischer* [1987] 3 C.M.L.R. 782 and supported by Lord Maxwell in *Bank of Scotland v. I.M.R.O. Ltd* 1989 S.L.T. 432, 446; see also *Engdiv Ltd v. G. Percy Trentham Ltd* 1990 S.C. 53. In *Kleinwort Benson Ltd v. Glasgow City Council (sic)* [1999] 1 A.C. 153, [1997] 4 All E.R. 641 (HL) it was held that a claim fell within Art. 5(1) of Sched.4 (now r. 3(a)) if it was based on a particular contractual obligation, the place of performance of which was within the jurisdiction of the court; it did not under a supposed contract whereby the claim was for restitution based on unjust enrichment and not contract. The fact that the place at which a bill of lading fell to be delivered was within the jurisdiction did not mean that the location of the place of delivery was also within the jurisdiction: *Eddie v. Alpa srl*, 2000 S.L.T. 1062 (OH). Where there is a choice between the laws of different countries in a contractual obligation, the parties may choose the law by which the contract is to be governed failing which the law will be that of the country with which the contract has the closest connection (assumed to be that of the habitual residence of the person to effect performance): see the Contracts (Applicable Law) Act 1990, Sched. 1, Art. 4 (this presumption in Art. 4(2) has material weight: *Caledonia Subsea Ltd v. Microperi Srl.* , 2001 S.C. 716, aff'd. 2003 S.C. 71 (First Div.)). It has been held in England, by a majority of the House of Lords in *Agnew v. Lansförsäkringsbølagens AB* [2000] All ER. 737, that an obligation to disclose in pre-contract negotiations can constitute "the obligation in question" for the purposes of Art. 5(1) of the Lugano Convention. The approach to a jurisdiction issue involving Art. 4 of the Rome Convention in Sched. 1 to the 1990 Act and art. 5(1) of the 1968 Brussels Convention in the C.J.J.A. 1982 was dealt with by Lord Hamilton in *William Grant & Sons International Ltd v. Marie Brizard Espana SA* 1998 S.C. 536. First, determine by Scottish choice of law rules what system of law is applicable to the legal relation in question (i.e. which system under art. 4(3) of the Rome Convention); and secondly, apply the substantive rules of the legal system so ascertained to determine the place of performance of the contractual obligation under art. 5(1) of the 1968 Convention: see, e.g. *Ferguson Shipbuilders Ltd v. Voith Hydro GmbH & Co. KG* 2000 S.L.T. 229. Where a party relies on the special and derogative provisions of art. 5(1) of Sched. 1, he has to set out a sufficient exposition of the contractual terms to show that there is a stateable basis for maintaining that the place of performance is within the jurisdiction of the court: *Eddie v. Alpa srl* , 2000 S.L.T. 1062 (OH); see also *Montague Evans v. Young* , 2000 S.L.T. 1083 (OH); and *Atlantic Telecom Gmbh, Noter* , 2004 S.L.T. 1031 (OH).

Rule 2(c)

(delict and quasi-delict: place where harmful event occurred or may occur; see also C.J.J.A. 1982, Sched. 1, Art. 5(3) and Sched.4, r. 3(c), Brussels I Regulation, Art. 5(3), Brussels I, Art. 7(2)). The words "or may occur" do not appear in Sched. 1 of the C.J.J.A. 1982 but are derived from Art. 5(3) of the Brussels I Regulation, Art. 5(3), Brussels I Regulation (Recast), Art. 7(2) and the 2007 Lugano Convention Art. 5(3) in which they do appear. Matters relating to "delict and quasi-delict" in Art. 5(3) of the 1968 Convention in Sched. 1 mean all actions which seek to establish the liability of the defender which are not related to contract: *Kalfelis v. Schroder, Miinchmeyer, Hengst & Co.* [1988] E.C.R. 5565. An action based on a statutory right of recovery following an unsatisfied judgment in a delictual action is not a matter relating to delict or quasi-delict: *Davenport v. Corinthian Motor Policies at Lloyds* 1991 S.C. 372. Article 5(3) does not apply to a claim based on unjust enrichment, since such a claim does not generally presuppose either a harmful event or a threatened wrong: *Kleinwort Benson Ltd v. Glasgow City Council (sic)* [1997] 4 All E.R. 641; and *Compagnie Commercial Andre SA v. Artibell Shipping Co Ltd* 1999 S.L.T. 1051. Under the former Law Reform (Jurisdiction in Delict) Act 1971 it was held that the court had jurisdiction if there were a material element of delict in Scotland: *Russell v. F.W. Woolworth & Co. Ltd* 1982 S.L.T. 428. Under this ground the defender may be sued where the damage occurred or where the harmful event occurred which gave rise to the damage: *Beir v. Mines de Potasse d'Alsace* [1976] E.C.R. 1735. The place "where the harmful event occurred" means the place where the event giving rise to the damage directly produced its harmful effects on the person who is the immediate victim of the event: *Dumez France and Tracoha v. Hessiche Landesbank (Helaba)* [1990] E.C.R. 1-49. In *Docherty's Exrs v Secretary of State for Business, Innovation and Skills* 2019 S.C. 50 (First Div), it was held that the lex loci delicti was the place of the act of the defender which constituted the wrong, and not the place where any resultant harm happened to emerge. The Conventions and the Brussels I Regulation (Recast) do not specify what constitutes a "harmful event" and, accordingly, that is a matter to be determined by the national court applying the substantive law: *Shevill v. Presse Alliance SA* [1996] A.C. 959. The extension of jurisdiction to include harmful events that "may occur" is intended to cover interim remedies for threatened wrongs. In relation to delicts on the internet, a person setting up a website potentially commits a delict in any country where it can be seen; but whether he does so in any particular country depends on the de minimis principle, so that if the impact in a given country is insignificant, no delict is committed there: *Bonnier Media Ltd v Smith* 2003 S.C. 36. Note that, under EU law in relation to delict, the law applicable to an event giving rise to damage occurring after 11th January 2009 is, as a general rule, the law of the country in which the damage occurs irrespective of the country in which the event giving rise to the damage occurred and irrespective of the country in which indirect consequences occurred: Regulation (EC) No. 864/2007 on the law applicable to non-contractual obligations (Rome II), arts. 4 and 31.

Rule 2(d)

(damages or restitution based on criminal act: court seized of criminal proceedings to extent it can entertain civil proceedings); see also C.J.J.A. 1982, Sched. 1, Art. 5(4) and Sched. 4, r. 3(d), Brussels I Regulation, Art. 5(4), Brussels I Regulation (Recast), Art. 7(3) and the 2007 Lugano Convention, Art. 5(4)). A Scottish criminal court does not deal with civil proceedings.

Rule 2(e)

(maintenance: where creditor domiciled or habitually resident or if ancillary to proceedings concerning status; see also C.J.J.A. 1982, Sched. 1, Art. 5(2) and Sched. 4, r. 3(b), Brussels I Regulation, Art.5(2) 2007 Lugano Convention, Art. 5(2)). Rule 2(e) of Sched.8 does not include the provision in the other conventions or Regulation that jurisdiction over maintenance, if ancillary to an action about status, is excluded if based on the nationality of one of the parties.). An action of affiliation and aliment is not ancillary to proceedings concerning status (Sched. 8, r. 2(d) and Sched. 9, r. 1). Proceedings concerning status include divorce, separation, declarator of marriage, nullity and custody. Maintenance includes aliment, periodical allowance and lump sum payments: see *De Cavel v. De Cavel (No. 2)* [1980] E.C.R. 731. Jurisdiction in relation to maintenance was governed by the Civil Jurisdiction and Judgments (Maintenance) Regulations 2011 [S.I. 2011/1484] and rule 2(e) was deleted from Sched. 4 by those Regulations. The equivalent no longer appears in Brussels 1 Regulation (Recast). These Regulations were repeated by S.I. 2019 No. 519 for proceedings after 31st December 2020.

Rule 2(f)

(disputes from operations of a branch, agency or other establishment: where branch, agency or establishment is situated; see also C.J.J.A. 1982, Scheds. 1 and 3C, Art. 5(5) and Sched. 4, r. 3(e), Brussels I Regulation, Art. 5(5), Brussels I Regulation (Recast), art. 7(5) 2007 Lugano Convention, Art. 5(5). "Operations" means actions relating to rights and contractual or non-contractual obligations concerning the management of the establishment, actions relating to undertakings which have been entered into there and actions concerning non-contractual obligations arising from activities in which the establishment has engaged at the place in which it is established: *Somafer v. Saar-Ferngas* [1978] E.C.R. 2183. A parent company may be acting as a branch etc. of one of the subsidiaries: *SHR Schotte GmbH v. Parfums Rothschild SARL* [1987] E.C.R. 4905. "Situated" is not the same as domicile. "Establishment" implies a place of business which has the appearance of permanence. The expression "dispute arising out of operations of a branch" in Art. 5(5) of Sched. 1 does not mean that undertakings giving rise to a dispute entered into by a branch in the name of a parent body have to be performed in the contracting state in which the branch is established: *Lloyd's Register of Shipping v. Societe Compenon Bernard* [1995] E.C.R. 1-961.

Rule 2(g)

(in capacity as settler, trustee or beneficiary of an (express) trust domiciled in Scotland; see also C.J.J.A. 1982, Sched. 1, Art. 5(6) and Sched. 4, r. 3(f), Brussels I Regulation, Art. 5(6), Brussels I Regulation (Recast), Art. 7(5), 2007 Lugano Convention, Art. 5(6)). A trust is domiciled in a part of the U.K. only if the system of law of that part is the system with which the trust has the most real connection: C.J.J.A. 1982, s. 45 (for the purposes of Scheds 1, 3C, 4 and 8); and Civil Jurisdiction and Judgments Order 2001, Sched. 1, para. 12(3) [S.I. 2001 No. 3929] (for the purposes of the Brussels I Regulation).

Rule 2(h)

(where defender not domiciled in the U.K. and moveable property is arrested, or immoveable property is situated, in Scotland: cf. C.J.J.A. 1982, Sched. 1, Art. 3(2); Brussels I Regulation, Art. 2(2) Brussels I Regulation, Art. 5(2) 2007 Lugano Convention, Art. 3(2) and Annex I). These were common law grounds of jurisdiction. At common law arrestment to found jurisdiction was available only in an action with conclusions to enforce pecuniary claims (*Union Electric Co. v. Holman & Co.* 1913 S.C. 954) and not to actions affecting status (*Morley v. Jackson* (1888) 16 R. 78), a bare declarator (*Williams v. Royal College of Veterinary Surgeons* (1897) 5 S.L.T. 208) or sequestration (*Crail, Petrs* (1863) 1 M. 509) and probably not in actions for a decree ad factum praestandum alone (cf. *Powell v. Mackenzie & Co.* (1900) 8 S.L.T. 182 and *Union Electric Co.*, above, per L.P. Dunedin at p. 958). The property arrested must be in the hands of a third party, be arrestable in execution (*Leggat Bros v. Gray* 1908 S.C. 67; *Stenhouse London Ltd v. Allright* 1972 S.C. 209) and have some commercial value (*Shaw v. Dow and Dobie* (1867) 7 M. 449, 455 per L.P. Inglis; *Trowsdale's Tr. v. Forcett Railway Co.* (1870) 9 M. 88). The subjects arrested must belong to the common debtor in the capacity in which he is being sued. Arrestment originally unauthorised may be ratified (*Alexander Ward & Co. Ltd v. Samyang Navigation Co. Ltd* 1975 S.C.(H.L.) 26. It is available to the pursuer's representatives but not against the defender's representatives as it is personal to the defender and does not transfer against his successor: *Cameron v. Chapman* (1838) 16 S. 907. It establishes jurisdiction only in the action in which it is used: *Cameron*, above. The pursuer must arrest on the dependence also if he wishes to secure the subjects arrested, as the effect of the arrestment is complete once the summons is served and creates no nexus over the subjects arrested: *Leggat Bros.*, above; *Fraser-Johnston Engineering Co. v. Jeffs* 1920 S.C. 222. At common law the ownership or tenancy of heritable property in Scotland founded jurisdiction in causes relating to that heritage (proprietary or possessory claims) or in petitory actions (personal claims). The basis of jurisdiction was effectiveness, though the value was immaterial: *McArthur v. McArthur* (1842) 4 D. 354, 362 per Lord Fullerton. The defender must have a beneficial interest (*Caledonian Fish-Selling and Marine Stores Co. Ltd v. Allard Hewson & Co.* 1970 S.C. 168; cf. *Embassy Picture House (Troon) Ltd v. Cammo Developments Ltd* 1971 S.C. 25; *Llewellyn v. Hebbert* 1983 S.C. 112 (existence of missives established only a personal right but no beneficial interest)), though he need not be infeft (*Fraser v. Fraser & Hibbert* (1870) 8 M. 400); a personal right under an unrecorded disposition is sufficient (*Embassy Picture House (Troon) Ltd*, above), as is a right under a lease (*Weinschel* 1916 2 S.L.T. 91, 205), a contingent right of reversion (*Smith v. Stuart* (1894) 22 R. 130) or a right of a trust beneficiary to a conveyance (*Caledonian Fish-Selling and Marine Stores Co. Ltd*, above). The heritage must be held by the defender in the same capacity in which he is sued: *Mackenzie v. Drummond's Exrs.* (1868) 6 M. 932.

Rule 2(i)

(proprietary and possessory causes relating to moveables in Scotland: in the place where the property is situated; see also Sched. 4, r. 3(h)(ii)). These are causes in respect of the property itself. At common law jurisdiction applies not to moveables merely found in Scotland but to moveables fixed in a legal or practical sense within Scotland: e.g. moveables of a foreigner held in virtue of a landlord's hypothec in sequestration for rent (*Duncan v. Lodijensky* (1904) 6 F. 408); and also enforcement of rights in rem against ships and multiplepoindings (*Bell v. Stewart* (1852) 14 D. 837).

Rule 2(j)

(interdict: in the place where wrong likely to be committed). This was a common law jurisdiction: *Toni Tyres Ltd v. Palmer Tyre Co.* (1905) 7 F. 477. The Maxwell Committee (*Report on Jurisdiction and Enforcement* 1980, pp.246-247) recommended this rule because it was not clear that Art. 5(3) of Sched. 1 (the 1968 Convention) (and r. 2(3) of Sched. 8 in its original form) to the C.J.J.A. 1982, which deals with jurisdiction for delicts, included prospective wrongs. New Art.5(3) of the Brussels I Regulation, Art 7(2) of Brussels I bis and new r. 2(c) of Sched. 8 of the C.J.J.A. 1982, refer expressly to delicts that "may occur".

Rule 2(k)

(debts over immoveable property in Scotland: in the place where the property is situated; see also Sched. 4, r. 3(h)(i)). This was thought to be a useful jurisdiction by the Maxwell Committee (*Report on Jurisdiction and Enforcement* 1980, pp. 248-249). This ground is not fully covered by Sched. 8, r. 2(h)(ii) or r. 5(1)(a).

Rule 2(l)

(decision of an organ of a company, other legal person or association in the place where it has its seat in Scotland; see also C.J.J.A. 1982, Sched. 4, r. 4). Rule 2(l) (formerly r. 2(12)) was modelled on Art. 16(2) of the 1968 Convention which is an exclusive jurisdiction concerning constitution, whereas r. 2 is a special but non-exclusive jurisdiction relating to decisions. In constitutional matters there is an exclusive jurisdiction in Sched. 8, r. 4(b); winding up is excluded by Sched. 9, para. 5.

Rule 2(m)

(arbitration in Scotland or where procedure governed by Scots law: in the Court of Session). The 1968 and Lugano Conventions, the Brussels I Regulation and the Brussels I Regulation (Recast) do not apply to arbitration. The rule enables the court to appoint an arbiter or deal with a stated case.

Rule 2(n)

(registration or validity of patents, trade marks, designs: in the Court of Session). Art. 16(4) of the 1968 Convention and Art. 22(4) of the Brussels I Regulation and Art. 24(4) of Brussels I Regulation (Recast) and Art. 22(4) of The 2007 Lugano Convention give an exclusive jurisdiction to the State of application or registration. There is no exclusive jurisdiction in Scotland in r. 5 of Sched. 8 because the registers are in London, but r. 2(n) gives a special non-exclusive jurisdiction.

Rule 2(o)

(several defenders, third parties and counterclaims; see also C.J.J.A. 1982 Sched. 1, Art. 6 and Sched. 4, r. 5, Brussels I Regulation, Art.6, and Brussels I Regulation (Recast), Art. 8, 2007 Lugano Convention, Art. 6(3)). In relation to several defenders, there must be, when the proceedings are instituted, a connection between the claims by the pursuer against the several defenders of such a kind that it is expedient to determine the claims together in order to avoid the risk of irreconcilable judgments resulting from separate actions: r. 2(o)(i) which is derived from *Kalfelis v. Schroder, Münchmeyer, Hengst & Co.* [1988] E.C.R. 5565. In *Compagnie Commercial Andre SA v. Artihell Shipping Co. Ltd* 1999 S.L.T. 1051 (OH). Lord Macfadyen held that in most cases the presence or absence of the risk of irreconcilable judgments will be obvious from the nature of the claims against the domiciled and non-domiciled defenders; but if not, a pursuer may have to make averments to demonstrate the risk.

In *Stewart v. Trafalgar House Steamship Co Ltd,* 2013 S.L.T. 834 (OH), the pursuer raised an action against three companies of which one was domiciled in Scotland and the other two in England; the action was later abandoned against the Scottish company. It was held that jurisdiction against the English companies was not thereby lost.

The rule in relation to counterclaims is narrower than reconvention at common law (which applied not only to claims arising out of the same transaction but also where the claims arose ex diversis causis provided they were claims which could fairly be set against one another: *Thompson v. Whitehead* (1862) 24 D. 331; *Clydedock Engineering Ltd v. Cliveden Campania Naviera SA* 1987 S.L.T. 762). On counterclaims, see note 25.1.6.

On third parties, see note 26.1.2.

(C) Jurisdiction in consumer contracts

(C.J.J.A. 1982, Sched. 8, r. 3; see also C.J.J.A. 1982, Sched. 1, Arts 13, 14 and 15, and Sched. 4, r. 7, Brussels I Regulation, Art. 15, Brussels I Regulation (Recast), Art. 17 and The 2007 Lugano Convention, Art. 15, 16 and 17). This rule is subject to the rules of exclusive jurisdiction, prorogation of jurisdiction, submission to jurisdiction and the proceedings excluded by Sched. 9. A consumer may sue (a) in the place where the other party is domiciled, (b) where he himself is domiciled or (c) in the courts having jurisdiction under r. 2(f) or (i) of Sched. 8. The reference to instalment credit in Sched. 8, r. 3(1) means a transaction in which the price is paid by a series of payments or which is limited to a financing contract in Sched. 1, Art. 13 (Brussels I Regulation, Art. 15(a) and presumably Brussels I Regulation (Recast) and The 2007 Lugano Convention, Art. 15(i), Art. 17): *Bertrand v. Ott* [1978] E.C.R. 1431.

Sched. 8, r. 3 (and Sched. 4, r. 7) follows Art. 15(c) of the Brussels I Regulation, and the court has jurisdiction in relation to contracts concluded by a consumer with a person pursuing commercial activities in Scotland or, by any means, "directs such activities" to Scotland. This phrase is intended to cover contracts concluded through a website accessible in the consumer's domicile. The exclusion of transport contracts does not apply to such contracts which for an inclusive price provide for travel and accommodation (they are now treated as consumer contracts).

The jurisdiction of courts in a cause where the defender is not domiciled in a contracting state is governed not by the Brussels I Regulations or Lugano Convention but by the law of the contracting state of the court in which the cause is brought. The only exception in consumer contracts is in (Brussels I Regulation, Art. 15(2); Brussels I Regulation (Recast), Art. 17(2), or The 2007 Lugano Convention, Art. 15(2), Art. 11(2)) which applies where a consumer enters into a contract with a party not domiciled in a contracting state but which has a branch, agency or other establishment there and the dispute arises out of its operations: *Brenner and Noller v. Dean Witter Reynolds Inc.* [1994] E.C.R. I-4275.

(CA) Jurisdiction in contracts of employment

(C.J.J.A. 1982, Sched. 8, r. 4; see also Sched. 4, r. 10, Brussels I Regulation, Arts 18–21 and Brussels I Regulation (Recast), Arts 20–23 and The 2007 Lugano Convention, Arts 18–21). This rule is subject to r. 2(f) in Sched. 8 (operations of a branch etc). These rules replace those in former r. 5(1). They may be departed from by agreement entered into after the dispute has arisen or which allows the employee to sue in another court. An employer may be sued (a) where he is domiciled, (b) where the employee habitually carries or carried out his work or (c) if the employee did not do so in one place, where the business employing him is situated. An employer may sue only in the courts where the employee is domiciled.

(D) Exclusive jurisdiction of courts of country in which property is situated

(C.J.J.A. 1982, Sched. 8, r. 5; see also C.J.J.A. 1982, Scheds 1, Art. 16 and Sched. 4, r. 11, Brussels I Regulation, Art. 22 and Brussels I Regulation (Recast), Art. 24 with 2007 Lugano Convention, Art. 22). Rule 5(1) of Sched. 8 does not include reference to jurisdiction over six-month tenancies found in the other documents. In *Sanders v. Van der Putte* [1977] E.C.R. 2383, the European Court opined that the exclusive jurisdiction of Art. 16 of the 1968 Convention related to disputes as to the existence, interpretation, the giving up of, or of compensation for damage under, a lease but held that it did not cover a dispute arising out of an agreement to take over the running of a florist's shop as the principal aim of the agreement was of a different nature, namely, the operation of a business; it also determined that the denial by the defender of the existence of the agreement was immaterial to the issue; see also *Barratt International Resorts Ltd v. Martin* 1994 S.L.T. 434. Art. 16(1) applies to actions which seek to determine the extent, content, ownership or possession of immoveable property or the existence of other rights in rem in it and does not cover a personal claim by a creditor seeking to have a donation of immoveable property rendered ineffective: *Reichert & Others v. Dresdner Bank* [1990] E.C.R. I-27.

The exclusive jurisdiction in Art. 16(1) of the 1968 Convention includes lettings (between two natural persons one of whom owns the property): *Rosier v. Rottwinkel* [1985] E.C.R. 99. It does not include a holiday let arranged between a natural person and a travel agent in a country other than where the property is situated: *Hacker v. Euro-Relais GmbH* [1992] E.C.R. I-1111 where the European Court held that Art. 16(1) did not apply to a contract concluded in a Contracting State whereby a travel business with its seat in that State undertakes to procure for a client domiciled in the same State the use for several weeks of holiday accommodation not owned by it in another Contracting State and to book the travel arrangements.

It is not sufficient that a right in rem in immoveable property is involved or that the action has a link with immoveable property; the action must be founded on a right in rem and not on a right in personam (except in relation to tenancies): *Webb v. Webb* [1994] E.C.R. 1-1717 (proceedings for declaration that French property held as trustee for plaintiff and to execute documents to vest the property not an action in respect of such a right); *Lieber v. Göbel* [1994] E.C.R. 1-2535 (claim for compensation for use of a flat after a settlement of an action transferring ownership was declared void was not a right in rem).

Art. 16(1) of Sched. 1 (the 1968 Convention) was amended by the 1989 Accession Convention (Spain and Portugal) by providing that, in the case of proceedings which have as their object tenancies of immoveable property for temporary private use for a maximum of six months, the courts of the Contracting State in which the defender is domiciled also have jurisdiction if the landlord and tenant are natural persons domiciled in the same Contracting State. (In the Lugano Convention in Sched. 3C only the tenant has to be a natural person and neither party must be domiciled in the Contracting State in which the property is situated. In the Brussels I Regulation, Art. 22 proviso Brussels I Regulation (Recast) Art. 24(1) proviso, 2007 Lugano Convention, Art. 22(1) proviso, and the C.J.J.A. 1982, Sched. 4, r. 1(a)(ii) and Sched. 8, r. 5(3), only the tenant need be a natural person but both landlord and tenant must be domiciled in the same Member State/Lugano Convention country/part of the U.K./Scotland.)

(E) Prorogation of jurisdiction

(C.J.J.A. 1982, Sched. 8, r. 6; see also C.J.J.A. 1982, Sched. 1, Art. 17, Sched. 4, r. 12, Brussels I Regulation, Art. 23 and Brussels I Regulation (Recast), Art. 25 and The 2007 Lugano Convention, Art. 23). Such an agreement must be evidenced in writing or in a form which accords with a practice. A communication by electronic means which provides a durable record is now a "writing". The court had previously adopted a restrictive approach to prorogation agreements in that they must be clear and express (*Scotmotors (Plant Hire) Ltd v. Dundee Petrosea Ltd* 1980 S.C. 351; *Morrison v. Panic Link Ltd* 1993 S.C. 631) as has the European Court (*Estasis Salotti v. RüWA* [1976] E.C.R. 1831; cf. England where inference is sufficient in matters relating to contract: RSC 1965, Ord. 11, r. 1(d)(iii)). But in *McGowan v. Summit at Lloyds* , 2002 S.L.T. 1259 (Ex Div), a case under old Sched.4, it was held that *Scotmotors*, even if still authoritative, did not lay down any general rule of law that a contractual clause will only be construed as conferring exclusive jurisdiction on a foreign court if it does so expressly. The only general principal is that the same canons of construction are to be applied to jurisdiction clauses as any other material contractual provision: it is a matter of construing the words used in accordance with their natural meaning and in the light of the surrounding circumstances in which the contract was made. A choice of law does not imply a choice of court: *Blasquez v. Levy & Sons* (1893) 1 S.L.T. 14. A prorogated jurisdiction under r. 12(1) of Sched. 4 and r. 6(1) of Sched. 8 (which omit the word "exclusive") of the C.J.J.A. 1982 is not an exclusive jurisdiction. A clause that "all disputes ... shall be governed in London" does not prorogate the jurisdiction of the English courts: *Compagnie Commercial Andre SA v. Artibell Shipping Co. Ltd* 1999 S.L.T. 1051. In *McGowan*, above, it was held that the English courts did not have exclusive jurisdiction under a contractual clause that provided that "This Document shall be governed by the laws of England whose courts shall have jurisdiction ..." The European Court has held that where an insurance contract between an insurer and a policy-holder for the benefit of a third party contains a prorogation clause, the third party can rely on it even though he has not signed it: *Gerling v. Amministrazione del Tesoro dello Stato* [1983] E.C.R. 2503; as can a third party acquiring a bill of lading issued by a carrier to a shipper containing such a clause: *Partenreederei ms Tilly Russ and Ernest Russ v. NV Haven & Vervoerbedrijf Nova* [1984] E.C.R. 2417. Art. 17 of the 1968 Convention applies to an oral agreement confirmed in writing: *Berghoefer v. ASA* [1985] E.C.R. 2699. A clause in the statutes or articles of a company limited by shares conferring jurisdiction on a court to settle disputes between the company and its shareholders is an agreement prorogating jurisdiction (binding any shareholder): *Powell Duffryn plc v. Petereit* [1991] E.C.R. 1-1745. See also note 13.2.14.

Art. 17 of the 1968 Convention prevails over Art. 21 (*lis pendens*: see note 13.2.11): *Bank of Scotland v. S.A. Banque Nationale de Paris* , 1996 S.L.T. 103.

It is not clear whether the prorogated jurisdiction of another or foreign court means that the proceedings before this court should be dismissed or sisted. For a discussion, see *Compagnie Commercial Andre SA*, above. It should depend on the circumstances. In *Belgian International Insurance Group SA v. McNicoll* , 4th June 1999 (OH), unreported, it was indicated, obiter, that in that case, if, as a result of the prorogation clause, some questions had to be decided in the first instance by a Belgian court, that would not warrant dismissal, but a sist.

(F) Submission to jurisdiction

(C.J.J.A. 1982, Sched. 8, r. 7; see also C.J.J.A. 1982, Sched. 1, Art. 18, Sched. 4, r. 13, Brussels I Regulation, Art. 24 and Brussels I Regulation (Recast), Art. 26 and The 2007 Lugano Convention, Art. 24). A defender who enters appearance and lodges defences contesting jurisdiction and the merits is not taken to have submitted to jurisdiction on the merits: R.C.S. 1994, r. 18.2(a) following *Elefanten Schuh v. Jacqmain* [1981] E.C.R. 1671 and *Rohr v. Ossberger* [1981] E.C.R. 2431. The English text of Art. 24(1) of the Brussels I Regulation accords with this interpretation of Art. 18 of the 1968 Convention (by omitting the word "solely" from the phrase "solely to contest jurisdiction" which appears in the English but not the French text of the latter convention).

Article 26(2) of Brussels I Regulation (Recast), for jurisdiction in insurance, consumer contracts and employment, provides in relation to the policyholder, insured, beneficiary of insurance, injured party, consumer or employee who is a defender, the court must ensure that he has been informed of his right to contest jurisdiction and the consequences of entering or not entering appearance.

(G) Verification of jurisdiction and admissibility

(C.J.J.A. 1982, Sched. 8, rr. 8 and 9; see also C.J.J.A. 1982, Sched. 1, Arts 19 and 20, Sched. 4, rr. 14 and 15, Brussels I Regulation, Arts 25 and 26, Brussels I Regulation (Recast), Arts 27 and 28 and The 2007 Lugano Convention, Arts 25 and 26. The court must itself examine the question of jurisdiction for, (a) if another court has exclusive jurisdiction or (b) where the defender has not entered appearance, is not domiciled in Scotland and there is no ground of jurisdiction compatible with the C.J.J.A. 1982, the court must declare at its own instance that it has no jurisdiction. The reason for this is that in relation to the 1968 Convention in proceedings for recognition and enforcement of judgments there shall be no examination of the jurisdiction of the original court, and this principle is extended under Scheds 4 and 8.

PROCEEDINGS EXCLUDED FROM SCHED.8.

(A)   Where jurisdiction is conferred by any other enactment: C.J.J.A. 1982, s. 21 (1)(a); e.g. **13.2.9** Continental Shelf Act 1964, s. 3 superseded by the Oil and Gas (Enterprise) Act 1982, ss. 22 and 23 and consolidated in ss. 10 and 11 of the Petroleum Act 1998 (see *Johnston v. Heerema Offshore Contractors Ltd* 1987 S.L.T. 407); Domicile and Matrimonial Proceedings Act 1973; Council Regulation (EC) No. 2201/2003 of 27th November 2003 (new Brussels II, replacing No. 1347/2000 of 29th May 2000 (Brussels II); Council Regulation (EC) No. 4/2009 (maintenance obligations)); Debtors (Scotland) Act 1987; and see statutes bringing the conventions into effect listed in note 13.2.12.

(B)   Proceedings listed in Sched. 9: C.J.J.A. 1982, s. 21(b).

FORUM NON CONVENIENS.

This is a basis for excluding jurisdiction. Sections 22 and 49 of the C.J.J.A. 1982 save the application **13.2.10** of this doctrine in relation to the jurisdiction of the court under Sched. 8, but it has no application to causes to which the 1968 Convention, The 2007 Lugano Convention, Brussels I Regulation, or Brussels I Regulation (Recast) applies where the defender is domiciled in another Convention country (or Member State in the case of Brussels I, or art. 24 of Brussels I Regulation (Recast)) or where Art. 16 of Sched. 1, or Sched. 4, r. 11 to the C.J.J.A. 1982, Art. 22 of the Brussels I Regulation Art. 24 of the Brussels I Regulation (Recast) or Art. 22 of the 2007 Lugano Convention, applies (exclusive jurisdiction). Under these provisions the doctrine of *lis pendens* applies. The doctrine of forum non conveniens applies "whenever it can be shown that the case cannot, consistently with fairness and justice, be tried in this country" (per Lord Low) and the court must be satisfied "that there is some other tribunal, having competent jurisdiction, in which the case may be tried more suitably for the interests of all the parties and for the ends of justice" (per Lord Kinnear): *Sim v. Robinow* (1892) 19 R. 665; see also *Clements v. Macauley* (1866) 4 M. 583, 592 per L.J.-C. Inglis. Where the jurisdiction of the court is competently founded, the court has no discretion whether to exercise it or not: *Clements*, above; *Sim*, above, per Lord Kinnear at p. 668. Something more than mere practical inconvenience is required to sustain a plea of forum non conveniens. The proper translation of "conveniens" is "appropriate"; the actual convenience of the parties is not to be considered but that which is the appropriate forum for securing the ends of justice, and the decision must be taken in the light of the whole surrounding circumstances: *Société du Gaz de Paris v. Société Anonyme de Navigation "Les Armateurs Francois"* 1926 S.C.(HL) 13, 18 per Lord Dunedin. The general principles were set out by Lord Jauncey in *Credit Chimique v. James Scott Engineering Group Ltd* 1979 S.C. 406 and more recently in *R.A.B. v. M.I.B.*, 2009 S.C. 58 (Extra Div.) applying *Spiliada Maritime Corp. v. Cansulex Ltd* [1987] 1 A.C. 460 (which drew on the Scottish authorities for settling the law in England). The initial onus is on the defender to raise and justify the plea: *De Mulder v. Jadranska Linijska (Jadrolinija)* 1989 S.L.T. 269. The mere fact that evidence of foreign law is required is not enough. It is not enough to show that the defence will have a better chance of succeeding elsewhere, as one must look to the interests of the pursuer as well as those of the defender "and the thing to be shown is not that there will be a disadvantage in that sense, but that there will be unfair disadvantage, so that justice is unlikely to be done": *Longworth v. Hope* (1865) 3 M. 1049, 1057 per Lord Deas. Once the defender has satisfied the initial onus it is for the pursuer to establish that to litigate abroad would deprive him of an advantage of such importance that it would cause injustice to deprive him of it: *De Mulder*, above. The plea will usually be inappropriate in causes relating to immoveables as the court of the *lex situs* will be the only court competent to grant decree in rem: *Foster v. Foster's Trs* 1923 S.C. 212.

LIS ALIBI PENDENS.

This is a basis for excluding jurisdiction. The common law plea of *lis alibi pendens* does not apply **13.2.11** where the prior action is in a foreign court: *Martin v. Stopford-Blair's Exrs* (1879) 7 R. 329, 331 per L.P. Inglis. Where the 1968 (Brussels) or The 2007 Lugano Convention, Brussels I Regulation, or the Brussels I Regulation (Recast) applies, the provisions of those conventions for *lis pendens* and related actions apply: C.J.J.A. 1982, Sched. 1, Arts 21, 22 and 23, Brussels I Regulation, Arts 27–30, Brussels I Regulation (Recast), Arts 29–34 or The 2007 Lugano Convention Arts 27–30; and see notes 13.2.12 and 13.2.15. Where the prior action is in a foreign country to which those conventions do not apply or another part of the U.K., the plea of forum non conveniens must be relied on to exclude jurisdiction: see note 13.2.10. The plea is available unless jurisdiction is prorogated by the defender: *Longmuir v. Longmuir* (1850) 12 D. 926. If the plea is upheld the court dismisses the second action. When the plea is considered, which must be supported by relevant averments (*Flannigan v. British Dyewood Co.* 1971 S.C. 110, 111 and 114 per Lord Fraser), there must be (a) a prior action in dependence—after service of the summons and before the action is finally disposed of (including expenses) (*Aitken v. Dick* (1863) 1 M. 1038), and even if the action is asleep (*Denovan v. Cairns* (1845) 7 D. 378)—(b) in another or the same court in Scotland (*Martin*, above) of competent jurisdiction, (c) between the same parties in the same legal capacities or interest (*Longmuir*, above; *Alston v. Alston's Trs* 1912 2 S.L.T. 22), (d) in which the same question is raised (*Wilson v. Dimlop, Bremner & Co. Ltd* 1921 1 S.L.T. 35). Where the prior action is in the same court the plea is *lis pendens*. See also notes 13.2.15 and 18.1.4(A)(5).

JURISDICTION UNDER THE 1968 AND LUGANO CONVENTIONS (C.J.J.A. 1982, SCHEDS 1 AND 3C).

13.2.12   The 1968 Brussels (or European) Convention in Sched. 1 to the C.J.J.A. 1982 was substituted by the Civil Jurisdiction and Judgments Act 1982 (Amendment) Order 1990 [S.I. 1990 No. 2591]. It was replaced by EU Council Regulations. See note 13.2.12A. The Lugano (or Parallel) Convention in Sched. 3C to the C.J.J.A. 1982 was inserted by s. 1(3) of the C.J.J.A. 1991. Sched. 3C was replaced by S.I. 2009 No. 3131. It was replaced by The 2007 Lugano Convention. The conventions apply to "civil and commercial matters", a phrase which appears to limit jurisdiction to matters of private as opposed to public law. They supersede the conventions listed in Art. 55. They do not cover a public authority acting in the exercise of its statutory powers as distinct from it acting in the exercise of private law obligations: *LTU v. Eurocontrol* [1976] E.C.R. 154; *Netherlands State v. Rüffer* [1980] E.C.R. 3807. They do not extend to revenue, customs or administrative matters, the status or legal capacity of natural persons, rights in property arising out of a matrimonial relationship, wills, succession, bankruptcy, winding up, judicial arrangements, compositions and analogous proceedings, social security or arbitration (including proceedings concerning the appointment of an arbiter or the existence or validity of an arbitration agreement: *Marc Rich and Co. v. Societá Italiana Impianti* [1991] E.C.R. 1-3855): Scheds 1 and 3C, Art. 1. They do not apply to prevent a court assuming jurisdiction under the provisions of another convention even where the defender is domiciled in another Contracting State which is not a party to the other convention: Scheds 1 and 3C, Art. 57. Such other conventions will be those implemented by the U.K. under any statutory provision or rules of law: C.J.J.A. 1982, s. 9(1). These include:

the Warsaw Convention on international carriage by air, 1929, Protocol (1975): see Carriage by Air Act 1961, Sched. 1, Art. 28(1),

the Guadalajara Convention on international carriage by air by a person other than a contracting carrier, 1961: see Carriage by Air (Supplementary Provisions) Act 1962, Sched., Art. VIII.

the Brussels Convention on matters of collision, 1952, arts 1, 2 and 3: see Administration of Justice Act 1956, Pts I and V, s. 45,

the Brussels Convention relating to arrest of sea-going ships, 1952; see Administration of Justice Act 1956, Pts I and V,

the Vienna Convention on Civil Liability for Nuclear Damage, 1963, Art. 11

the Geneva Convention on carriage of goods by road, 1956: see Carriage of Goods by Road Act 1965, Sched., Art. 31(1),

the Paris Convention on third party liability in the field of nuclear energy, 1960 (with Protocol (1964), Supplement (1960), Annex (1963), Protocol to Supplement (1964)), s. 13 and Art. 14: see Nuclear Installations Acts 1965 and 1969,

the Brussels Conventions on liability for oil pollution damage, 1969 and 1984 (now 1992): see Merchant Shipping Act 1995, s.166,

the Geneva Convention on international carriage of passengers and luggage by road, 1973: see Carriage of Passengers by Road Act 1974, Sched., Art. 21(1),

the Athens Convention on carriage of passengers and luggage by sea, 1974: see Merchant Shipping Act 1995, Sched. 6, Art. 17,

the Berne Convention on international carriage by rail, 1980, App. A, Arts 52 and 60, App. B, Arts 56 and 63: see International Transport Conventions Act 1983,

the UN Convention on the Law of the Sea 1982, Art. 28 (Cmnd 8941): see Merchant Shipping Act 1995, s. 129,

the Brussels Conventions for international oil pollution damage fund, 1971 and 1984 (now 1992): see Merchant Shipping Act 1995, s. 177,

the Seoul Convention establishing the multilateral investment guarantee agency, 1985: see Multilateral Investment Guarantee Agency Act 1988, Sched., Art. 44.

the International Convention on Liability and Compensation for Damage in Connection with the Carriage of Hazardous and Noxious Substances by Sea 1996: see Merchant Shipping and Maritime Security Act 1997, Sched. 3, Arts 38 and 39 inserted in the Merchant Shipping Act 1995 as Sched. 5A.

Art. 57 precludes the application of the Brussels or Lugano Convention only in relation to questions governed by the specialised convention. Thus, if the specialised convention has rules for jurisdiction but no provision as to *lis pendens* or related actions, Arts 21 and 22 of the Brussels or Lugano Convention (as the case may be) will apply: *Owners of Cargo lately laden on Board Tatry v. Owners of Maceij Rataj* [1994] E.C.R. 5439.

The pre-eminent rule of jurisdiction is that a person shall be sued in the courts of the Contracting State in which he is domiciled (as defined by ss. 41–46 of, and Sched. 1, Arts 52 and 53 to, the C.J.J.A. 1982: see note 13.2.6 above). A person domiciled in one Contracting State may be sued in another Contracting State only by virtue of the rules set out in ss.2 (special jurisdiction: Arts 5, 6 and 6A), 3 (insurance: Arts 7–12A), 4 (consumer contracts: Arts 13–15), 5 (exclusive jurisdiction: Art. 16) and 6 (prorogation of, and submission to, jurisdiction: Arts 17 and 18) of the conventions: C.J.J.A. 1982, Sched. 1, Art. 3. Where a defender is not domiciled in a Contracting State jurisdiction shall, subject to Sched. 1, Art. 16

(exclusive jurisdiction), be determined by the laws of the country in which he is sued (in Scotland this is determined by Sched. 8 to the 1982 Act). The court may decline jurisdiction under Arts 21–23 (*lis pendens* and related actions). In relation to *lis pendens*, where proceedings involving the same cause of action and the same parties are brought, any court other than the court first seized shall sist its proceedings until jurisdiction of the court first seized is established. The court first seized is the one before which the requirements for proceedings to become definitely pending are first fulfilled: *Zelger v. Salinitri (No. 2)* [1984] E.C.R. 2397; in Scotland this is once service had been executed and the action was therefore commenced: Erskine, III.iv.3; *Alston v. Macdougall* (1887) 15 R. 78; *Smith v. Stewart & Co.* 1960 S.C. 329, 334 per L.P. Clyde. As well as the same cause of action and same parties, there must also be the same subject-matter: *Gubisch Maschinenfabrik v. Palumbo* [1987] E.C.R. 4861; *Bank of Scotland v. S.A. Banque Nationale de Paris* , 1996 S.L.T. 103.

See also discussion in note 13.2.8 of various grounds of jurisdiction in Sched. 8 to the C.J.J.A. 1982.

The Lugano Convention did not prejudice the application by the E.C. Member States of the 1968 Convention; however, the Lugano Convention applied (a) in matters of jurisdiction where the defender is domiciled in a Contracting State which is not a member of the E.C. or where Art. 16 (exclusive jurisdiction) or 17 (prorogation of jurisdiction) of the Lugano Convention confers jurisdiction on the courts of such a State, or (b) in relation to *lis pendens* or related actions as provided for in Arts 21 and 22 of the Lugano Convention, when proceedings were instituted in a Lugano Contracting State which was not a member of the E.C. and in a Lugano Contracting State which was.

The 1968 Brussels Convention was superseded by the Council Regulation (EC) No. 44/2001 (Brussels I Regulation), and then by Council Regulation (EC) No. 1215/2112 (Brussels I Regulation (Recast)). for participating Member States to the Regulation: i.e. all the Member States of the E.U. Denmark subsequently signed up to the Council Regulations on 1st July 2007 and 1st June 2013 respectively. Accordingly the 1968 Convention applies only to *Denmark*, and has to be used in relation to that country. For the Council Regulation, and participating Member States of the E.U., see note 13.2.12A.

The Lugano Convention was superseded by the Brussels I Regulation and then the Brussels I Regulation (Recast) for EU States. The 2007 Lugano Convention applies between the EU and the following countries:

Denmark
Iceland
Norway
Switzerland.

The Council Regulation will apply to the Member States of the E.U.

JURISDICTION UNDER THE BRUSSELS I REGULATION (COUNCIL REGULATION (EC) No.44/2001) OR BRUSSELS I RECAST (EU) No. 1215/2012.

Jurisdiction in civil and commercial matters between the Member States of the EU, are governed by these Regulations. They are substantially similar to the 1968 Convention, but there are significant differences (some based on 1968 Convention case law), some of which have been noted in note 13.2.8 above. These differences are— **13.2.12A**

1. In Art. 5(1) of Brussels I Regulation or Art. 7(1) of Brussels I Regulation (Recast), the place of performance of a contract is now defined, unless otherwise agreed, as (i) where under the contract the goods were or should have been delivered and (ii) in the case of services, where under the contract the services were or should have been provided.

2. In Art. 5(3) of Brussels I Regulation or Art. 7(2) of Brussels I Regulation (Recast), in delict, a defender may now also be sued in the courts for the place where the harmful event occured or may occur.

3. In Art. 6(1) of Brussels I Regulation or Art. 8(1) of Brussels I Regulation (Recast), where there is more than one defender, jurisdiction where any of them is domiciled applies only where the claims are so closely connected that it is expedient to hear and determine them together to avoid risk of irreconcilable judgments. This follows the decision in *Kalfelis v. Schröder, Münchmeyer, Hengst & Co.* , [1988] E.C.R. 5565.

4. In Arts 8–14 of Brussels I Regulation or Arts 10–16 of Brussels I Regulation (Recast), there are modifications to jurisdiction in insurance contracts.

5. In Art. 15(c), in consumer contracts, there is provision for jurisdiction where a person who pursues commercial or professional activities in a Member State or, by any means, directs such activities to that Member State. This is to cover e-commerce.

6. Transport contracts providing for travel and accommodation are not now excluded from being consumer contracts (Art. 15(1) of Brussels I Regulation or art. 17(1) of Brussels I Regulation (Recast)).

7. In Arts 18–21 of Brussels I Regulation or Arts 20–23 of Brussels I Regulation (Recast) there are now rules for individual contracts of employment.

8. In Art. 22(2) of Brussels I Regulation or Art. 24(2) of Brussels I Regulation (Recast), exclusive jurisdiction in relation to decisions of organs of companies, other legal persons or associations of persons is now limited to the validity of those decisions.

9. In relation to exclusive jurisdiction over six-month tenancies, only the tenant need be a natural person although both landlord and tenant must still be domiciled in the same Member State.

10. In Art. 23(1) of Brussels I Regulation or Art. 25(1) of Brussels I Regulation (Recast) (prorogation), there is an express statement that parties are allowed to give non-exclusive jurisdiction to the courts of a particular Member State.

11. In relation to related actions (*lis pendens*), Art. 30 of Brussels I Regulation or art. 32(1) of Brussels I Regulation (Recast) provides an autonomous rule that the court is seized of proceedings (a) at the time the document instituting the proceedings is lodged with the court (i.e. in Scotland, when the summons is presented for signeting (R.C.S. 1994, rr. 4.3, 4.4 and 13.5) or the petition is presented for a first order (R.C.S. 1994, rr. 4.3, 4.4 and 14.5) provided that the pursuer has not subsequently failed to take the steps he was required to take to effect service; or (b) if it has to be served before being lodged in court, when it is received by the authority responsible for service provided that the pursuer has not subsequently failed to take the steps required to have the document lodged in court. (In *Zelger v. Salinitri (No.2)* [1984] E.C.R. 2397 it had been held under the 1968 Convention that it was for the courts of each State to determine when a court was seized of an action.) In Scotland, the common law rule is that an action commences when it is served: see notes 13.2.5, 13.2.8(A) and 13.4.4.

The Member States of the EU to which the Brussels I Regulation (Recast) applies are—

Austria	Latvia
Belgium	Lithuania
Bulgaria	Luxembourg
Croatia	Malta
Cyprus	Netherlands
Czech Republic	Poland
Denmark	
Estonia	Portugal
Finland	Romania
France	Slovakia
Germany	Slovenia
Greece	Spain
Hungary	Sweden
Ireland	
Italy	

ALLOCATION OF JURISDICTION BETWEEN U.K. COURTS (C.J.J.A. 1982, ss.16 AND 17 AND SCHED. 4).

13.2.13 These provisions determine which U.K. court has jurisdiction where the subject-matter is within the scope of the Brussels I Regulations and the defender is domiciled in the U.K. or the proceedings are of a kind mentioned in the Brussels I Regulation, Art. 22 or Brussels I and the Brussels I Regulation (Recast), art. 24 (exclusive jurisdiction). Sched. 4 is subject to the 1968 Convention, Lugano Convention and the Brussels I Regulation. In interpreting Sched. 4, (a) regard must be had to relevant principles laid down by the European Court in connection with the jurisdictional rules in the 1968 Convention or Chap. II of the Brussels I Regulation and (b) the Jenard and Schlosser reports on the 1968 convention may be considered and, of relevant, must be given such weight as is appropriate in the circumstances: C.J.J.A. 1982, s.16(3). Sched. 4 does not apply (a) to proceedings listed in Sched. 5 or (b) to proceedings in Scotland under any enactment which confers jurisdiction on a Scottish court in respect of a specific subject-matter on specific grounds: C.J.J.A. 1982, s.17(1). Sched. 4 to the C.J.J.A. 1982 has been substituted by the Civil Jurisdiction and Judgments Order 2001 [S.I. 2001 No.3929]. Sched. 4 is a modified version of Chap. II of the Brussels I Regulation. There are the following differences—

1. Only Art. 5(1)(a) of the Regulation appears in para. 3(a) of Sched.4 (place of performance of contract and not also place of obligation). The reason for this, apparently, is that it was thought that the additional ground would cause uncertainty initially. Certainty was considered to be more important within the U.K.

2. The special rules for insurance contracts in Arts 8–15 of the Regulation are not included.

3. Paragraph 4 of Sched.4 deals with proceedings which have as their object a decision of an organ or a company, etc., and not merely the validity of such decisions as in Art. 22(4) of the Regulation.

4. As before, the exception of contracts of transport from the rules for consumer contracts extends to insurance contracts in para. 7(2) of Sched.4. The application of the rules for consumer contracts to contracts for an exclusive price which provide for a combination of travel and accommodation, which appear in Art.15(3) of the Regulation, appear in para. 7(2) of Sched.4.

5. As before, the detailed provisions for the form that an agreement to prorogate jurisdiction, which appear in Art.23(1) of the Regulation, do not appear in para. 12(1) of Sched.4. The law of the courts, the jurisdiction of which is prorogued, applies. In Scotland, that law is in para. 6(2) of new Sched. 8: that provision repeats the text of Art. 23(1) of the regulation. The express

statement in Art. 23(1) of the Regulation about agreeing non-exclusive jurisdiction does not appear in para. 12(1) of Sched.4. The absence of this statement would not seem to preclude agreeing a non-exclusive jurisdiction.

6. The provisions of Arts 27–30 of the Regulation (Arts 21–23 of the 1968 Convention) relating to *lis pendens* and related actions are omitted; the principles of forum non conveniens must be applied (see note 13.2.10).

In relation to Sched. 4, Art. 6 (5(a) of the Brussels I Regulation) (where the defender is one of a number of defenders) it has been held in England (following the test in *Kalfelis v. Schröder, Münchmeyer, Hengst & Co.* [1988] E.C.R. 5565) that a number of separate unconsolidated actions (one of which involved a Scottish local authority) not heard together would not lead to irreconcilable decisions because the final arbiters would be the House of Lords whose decision would be binding in England and Scotland: *Barclays Bank Plc v. Glasgow City Council* [1994] Q.B. 404.

"AGREEMENT PROROGATING THE JURISDICTION OF A COURT" (R. 13.2(4) (c)).

Under the 1968 or 2007 Lugano Convention, the Brussels I Regulation, Brussels I Regulation (Recast) **13.2.14** or Scottish rules of jurisdiction (Sched.8), an agreement must be evidenced in writing or in a form which accords with a practice and gives the court exclusive jurisdiction unless it purports to exclude an exclusive jurisdiction or it does not satisfy the requirements of departure by agreement from the jurisdictional rules in consumer contracts (in which case it is invalid): C.J.J.A. 1982, Sched. 1, Art. 17 and Sched. 8, r. 6, Brussels I Regulation, Art. 23, Art. 23(2) of the Regulation adds "writing" by electronic means, Brussels I Regulation (Recast), Art. 25. Under Sched. 1, Art.17, if the agreement was concluded for the benefit of one party, that party may, notwithstanding, bring proceedings in another court having jurisdiction under the 1968 Convention. That provision is not repeated in Art. 23 of the Brussels I Regulation, Art. 25 of Brussels I Regulation (Recast) or Art. 23 of the 2007 Lugano Convention. In relation to trust instruments, agreements or provisions conferring jurisdiction have no legal force if contrary to the provisions on agreements in insurance contracts, consumer contracts, contracts of employment or which purport to exclude exclusive jurisdiction: Brussels I Regulation, Art. 23(5), Brussels I Regulation (Recast), art. 25(4) and the 2007 Lugano Convention, Art. 23(5). See also note 13.2.8(E).

In connection with the allocation of jurisdiction within the U.K., parties may agree to prorogate the jurisdiction of a court. There is no rule that the agreement must be in writing, the only requirement being that the agreement would be treated as effective under the law of the court whose jurisdiction is prorogated (Sched. 8 does not apply where Sched. 4 applies); there are no rules of formal validity of such an agreement in Scots law. The court had previously adopted a restrictive approach to prorogation agreements in that they must be clear and express (*Scotmotors (Plant Hire) Ltd v. Dundee Petrosea Ltd* 1980 S.C. 351 *Morrison v. Panic Link Ltd* 1993 S.C. 631) as has the European Court (*Estasis Salotti v. RüWA* [1976] E.C.R. 1831; cf. England where inference is sufficient in matters relating to contract: RSC 1965, Ord. 11, r.1(1)(d)(iii)). But in *McGowan v. Summit at Lloyds*, 2002 S.L.T. 1259 (Extra Div), a case under Sched. 4, it was held that *Scotmotors*, even if still authoritative, did not lay down any general rule of law that a contractual clause will only be construed as conferring exclusive jurisdiction on a foreign courts if it does so expressly. The only general principal is that the same canons of construction are to be applied to jurisdiction clauses as any other material contractual provision: it is a matter of construing the words used in accordance with their natural meaning and in the light of the surrounding circumstances in which the contract was made. A choice of law does not imply a choice of court: *Blasquez v. Levy & Sons* (1893) 1 S.L.T. 14. A prorogated jurisdiction under Art. 17 of Sched. 4 (which omits the word "exclusive") is not an exclusive jurisdiction. A clause in the statutes or articles of a company limited by shares conferring jurisdiction on a court of a Contracting State to settle disputes between the company and its shareholders is an agreement prorogating jurisdiction (binding any shareholder): *Powell Duffryn plc v. Petereit* [1991] E.C.R. 1-1745. A clause that "all disputes ... shall be governed in London" does not prorogate the jurisdiction of the English courts: *Compagnie Commercial Andre SA v. Artibell Shipping Co. Ltd* 1999 S.L.T. 1051. In *McGowan*, above, it was held that the English courts did not have exclusive jurisdiction under a contractual clause that provided that "This Document shall be governed by the laws of England whose courts shall have jurisdiction ..."

It is not clear whether the prorogated jurisdiction of another or foreign court means that the proceedings before this court should be dismissed or sisted. For a discussion, see *Compagnie Commercial Andre SA*, above.

Article 17 of the 1968 or Lugano Convention prevails over Art. 21 of those conventions (*lis pendens*: see note 13.2.11): *Bank of Scotland v. S.A. Banque Nationale de Paris* 1996 S.L.T. 103.

Rule 13.2(4)(b) assumes the defender will only prorogate jurisdiction when he lodges answers and does not contest jurisdiction. But he might have prorogated jurisdiction in advance in which case the ground of jurisdiction can (and must) be averred.

"PROCEEDINGS INVOLVING THE SAME CAUSE OF ACTION".

Where proceedings involving the same cause of action between the same parties are brought in the **13.2.15** courts of different Contracting States to the 1968 Convention in Sched. 1, to the C.J.J.A. 1982, the Brussels I Regulation or Brussels I Regulation (Recast) or the 2007 Lugano Convention any court other than the court first seized of the proceedings shall at its own instance sist the proceedings until the jurisdiction of the court first seized is established: C.J.J.A. 1982, Sched. 1, Art. 21(1); Brussels I Regulation, Art. 27; Brussels I Regulation (Recast) or the 2007 Lugano Convention, Art. 29; 2007 Lugano Convention, Art. 27(1).

This provision applies irrespective of the domicile of the parties, and the court other than the court first seized cannot examine the jurisdiction of the court first seized: *Overseas Union Insurance Ltd v. New Hampshire Insurance Co.* [1991] E.C.R. 1-3317. As the court has to consider jurisdiction (and particularly if decree in absence is sought), the court must know (ex facie of the summons) whether it has jurisdiction.

Proceedings will have been brought in a court if the proceedings have commenced according to the procedural rules of that court: *Zelger v. Salinitri (No. 2)* [1984] E.C.R. 2397. In Scotland this is the date of execution of citation of the defender (Erskine, III.iv.3; *Alston v. Macdougall* (1887) 15 R. 78; *Smith v. Stewart & Co.* 1960 S.C. 329, 334 per L.P. Clyde; though in relation to the plea of forum non conveniens it has been affirmed that priority of process in terms of litiscontestation (when defences are lodged) is the normal test (*Argyllshire Weavers Ltd v. A. Macauley (Tweeds) Ltd* 1962 S.C. 388, 400 per L.P. Clyde). Under the Brussels I Regulation, Art. 30 provides an autonomous rule for when a court is seized of proceedings, see also Brussels I Regulation (Recast), art. 32 (see note 13.2.12A(11) above); and The 2007 Lugano Convention, Art. 30.

The nature and factual basis of the claim must be the same. As well as the same cause of action and same parties, there must also be the same subject-matter: *Gubisch Maschinenfabrik v. Palumbo* [1987] E.C.R. 4861; *Bank of Scotland v. S.A. Banque Nationale de Paris* 1996 S.L.T. 103. Actions do not cease to have the same cause of action and same object just because one was brought in personam and the other in rem: *Owners of Cargo lately laden on board Tatry v. Owners of Maceij Rataj* , E.C.J., 6th December, 1994. Article 21 applies even where there is a partial overlap in the bases of the actions in order to avoid irreconcilable judgments on similar facts in two contracting states: *William Grant & Sons Ltd v. Marie-Brizard & Roger International SA* , 16th May 1996, unreported (1996 G.W.D. 23-1347).

When jurisdiction of the first court is established the second court must decline jurisdiction (to the extent to which the parties to the action before it are also parties to the first action: *Owners of Cargo lately laden on Board Tatry*, above): C.J.J.A. 1982, Sched. 1 (1968 Convention), Art. 21(2); Brussels I Regulation, Art. 27(2). Where the concurrent proceedings do not involve the same parties or cause of action they may yet be related actions: in the case of related actions the second court may sist the action before it (Sched. 1, Art. 22(1); Brussels I Regulation, Art. 28(1); Brussels I Regulation (Recast), Art. 30(1); 2007 Lugano Convention, Art. 28(1)) or, on the application of a party, decline jurisdiction if the actions can be consolidated and there is jurisdiction over both actions in the first court (Art. 22(2); Brussels I Regulation, Art.28(2); Brussels I Regulation (Recast), Art. 30(2); 2007 Lugano Convention, Art. 28(2)). "Related actions" means actions so closely connected that it is expedient to hear and determine them together to avoid the risk of irreconcilable judgments (Art. 22(3); Brussels I Regulation, Art.28(3); Brussels I Regulation (Recast), Art. 30(3); 2007 Lugano Convention, Art. 28(3)). Where more than one court has exclusive jurisdiction any court other than the court first seized shall decline jurisdiction: Sched. 1 , Art. 23; Brussels I Regulation, Art. 29; Brussels I Regulation (Recast), art. 31(1). In *Sarrio SA v. Kuwait Investment Authority* [1997] 4 All E.R. 929, the House of Lords held in an English appeal that the application of art. 22 was not limited to the primary issues necessary to establish a cause of action, but that the court should apply the simple wide test in art. 22 which was designed to cover a range of circumstances from cases where matters before the courts were virtually identical to those where the connection was close enough to make it expedient for them to be heard together to avoid the risk in question. For the application of the 1968 Convention in Sched. 1 to the C.J.J.A. 1982, see note 13.2.12; and for the application of the Brussels I Regulation and Brussels I Regulation (Recast), see note 13.2.12A.

Arts 21–23 of Sched. 1 are not repeated in Scheds 4 and 8. The principles of forum non conveniens will apply: see note 13.2.10.

"WARRANTS FOR DILIGENCE AND INTIMATION".

13.2.16   See r. 13.6A and notes, and Chap. 14A.

SIGNING OF SUMMONS.

13.2.17   A summons must be signed on every page by an agent (for definition of whom, see r. 1.3(1)): r. 4.2(1). There is a special procedure for a party litigant who cannot obtain the signature of an agent: see r. 4.2(5) and (6) and note 4.2.8.

UNITS OF MEASUREMENT.

13.2.18   The Units of Measurement Directive (Council Directive 80/181 of 20th December 1979) was adopted by the E.C. in 1989 [Official Journal, 7th December 1989, L357/28]. From 1st January 1995 member states must use the metric system of measurement and, subject to certain transitional arrangements and exceptions, must cease to use imperial measurements for economic, public health, public safety and administrative purposes. Where a unit of measurement is used in pleadings it should be expressed as a metric unit, and court orders must be so expressed.

Exceptions are as follows: The nautical mile and knot are to be used for sea and air traffic and the foot is to be used for aircraft heights. Until 31st December 1999, fathom may be used for marine navigation; therm for gas supply; pint and fluid ounce for beer, cider, waters, lemonade and fruit juices on returnable containers; and ounce and pound for goods sold loose from bulk. In perpetuity, acre may be used for land registration; troy ounce for transactions in precious metals; mile, yard, foot and inch for road traffic signs, distances and speed measurements; pint for draught beer, cider and milk in returnable containers.

DECLINATURE OF JURISDICTION.

13.2.19   A judge may have to decline to hear a case. The grounds of objection are (1) pecuniary interest of the judge in the cause; and (2) personal interest including enmity, partiality, bribery or corruption. The objection may be taken by the judge or a party. Parties may agree to waive a declinature. It is not essential that the waiver be recorded in a joint minute or other document.

1. *Pecuniary Interest.* No man may be a judge in his own cause: *Wildridge v. Anderson* (1892) 2 Adam 399, 410–411 per Lord Moncrieff. In general, a pecuniary interest, however small, will disqualify. The rule does not apply where the judge is a partner in a life or fire insurance company, or the holder as trustee of shares in an incorporated company, which is a party to the litigation: Court of Session Act 1868, s.103.

2. *Personal Interest.* Where the interest is personal and not pecuniary, the interest must be substantial or calculated to cause bias in the mind of the judge: *Wildridge,* above; *Gorman v. Wright* , 1916 S.C. (J.) 44, 47 per L.J.-C. Scott Dickson. The test for declinature of jurisdiction by a judge on the ground of partiality is whether the fair-minded and informed observer, having considered the facts, would conclude that the tribunal was biased: *Gillies v. Secretary of State for Work and Pensions* , 2006 S.C. (H.L.) 71, 73, para. [3]. In that case Lord Hope of Craighead adopted the test he had formulated in the English case of *Porter v. Magill* , [2002] 2 A.C. 357, 494, para. 103 resolving a problem in England where the test was "real danger" (rather than "real likelihood" involving the objective test of the reasonable person) which placed England out of step with ECtHR, the rest of the Commonwealth and Scotland (where the test was whether there is a legitimate apprehension of a lack of impartiality, judged objectively: *Unity Trust Bank Plc v. Frost (No. 2)* , 2001 S.C.L.R. 350 (Extra Div.)).

Address of defender

13.3. In a summons, the pursuer shall—   **13.3**

   (a) set out in the instance the known residence, registered office, other official address or place of business of the defender where he is to be served; or

   (b) where that residence, office, address or place, as the case may be, is not known and cannot reasonably be ascertained, set out in the instance that the whereabouts of the defender are not known and aver in the condescendence what steps have been taken to ascertain his present whereabouts.

Deriv. R.C.S. 1965, r. 71

GENERAL NOTE.

R.C.S. 1965, r. 71 applied only where the defender was not designed as having an address in Scotland   **13.3.1**
although in practice the substance of the rule applied in any case. The address can be amended: see r. 24.1(2)(b)(i). For the domicile of defenders, see note 13.2.6; and for jurisdiction, see notes 13.2.7 to 13.2.15.

"NOT KNOWN".

The word "known" refers not to the pursuer's knowledge but to that of persons generally who had   **13.3.2**
business or social dealings with the defender (*Young v. Harper* 1970 S.C. 174, 177 per Lord Fraser); accordingly the pursuer must take some steps to ascertain an address, and this is required for a motion in respect of service where the address of the defender is not known: r. 16.5(1)(c). Where the address is not known service by advertisement will be required unless dispensed with: r. 16.5.

Period of notice in summonses

13.4.—(1) Subject to any other provision in these Rules, the period of notice in   **13.4**
a summons shall be—

   (a) in the case of service within Europe, 21 days from whichever is the later of the date of execution of service or the giving of intimation before calling on a warrant for intimation;

   (b) in the case of service furth of Europe under rule 16.2(2)(d) or (e) (service by an *huissier,* etc., or personally), 21 days from whichever is the later of the date of execution of service or the giving of intimation before calling on a warrant for intimation;

   (c) in the case of service furth of Europe other than under sub-paragraph (b), 42 days from whichever is the later of the date of execution of service or the giving of intimation before calling on a warrant for intimation; and

   (d) in the case of service by advertisement under rule 16.5 (service where address of person not known), other than in an action to which rule 49.12 (notice of family actions by advertisement) applies, six months from the date of publication of the advertisement.

(2)   An application may be made by motion to shorten or extend the period of notice in a summons.

(3)   Where a motion under paragraph (2) is made after signeting of the summons but before service—

    (a)   the summons shall be produced to the court; and

    (b)   the decision of the Lord Ordinary on the motion shall be final and not subject to review.

Deriv. R.C.S. 1965, r. 72(1) (r. 13.4(1)(a)–(c)), r. 72(3) (r. 13.4(3)) and r. 75(7) (r. 13.4(1)(d)), all substituted by S.I. 1986 No. 1941

GENERAL NOTE.

13.4.1   The phrase "period of notice" has replaced the word "*induciae*", but its effect is the same: the summons may not be called until after expiry of the period. The period of 21 days was introduced by A.S. (R.C.A. No. 9) (Jurisdiction and Enforcement) 1986 [S.I. 1986 No. 1941]. The former period of 14 days was the shortest in Europe; it was increased to 21 days following Art. 20 of the 1968 Convention in Sched. 1 (and of the Lugano Convention in Sched. 3C) to the C.J.J.A. 1982 and Art. 15 of the Hague Convention of 15th November 1965 on the Service Abroad of Judicial and Extrajudicial Documents in Civil or Commercial Matters (Cmnd. 3986 (1969)) which deal with the sisting of proceedings where it is not shown that the defender has been able to receive the document in sufficient time to arrange for his defence, and Art. 27(2) of the 1968 or Lugano Convention which entitles a court of a Contracting State to refuse to recognise a judgment in default of appearance for enforcement if the defender was not served with the summons in sufficient time to enable him to arrange for his defence: C.J.J.A. 1982, Scheds 1 and 3C, Art. 27(2). See also the Brussels I Regulation (Recast), Art. 28 and the 2007 Lugano Convention, Art. 26.

The relevant period of notice is specified in the summons. Where there is more than one defender and for one of whom the period of notice is longer than 21 days, the period of notice will be the longer period. In *Hoe International Ltd v Anderson*, 2015 S.C. 507 (Extra Div.), the period of notice was 42 days because one of the defenders resided in the USA; but solicitors in Scotland accepted service within the 21 days applicable to the other defender. The period of notice was not dispensed with. A question arose whether the summons had not called within a year and a day of the expiry of the period of notice (it would not have if the period were 42 days but would have if it were 21 days). The Lord Ordinary held that, since service was effected in Europe, the period of notice was 21 days. The Extra Division corrected this erroneous conclusion and held that the period of notice in the summons (42 days) bound the pursuer that the summons would not call before the expiry of 42 days, no dispensation of the period or application to shorten the period having been made. The instance had not therefore fallen.

"SUBJECT TO ANY OTHER PROVISION IN THESE RULES".

13.4.2   The period of notice where (a) notice is by advertisement in a family action, is 21 days and not six months (r. 49.12) and (b) service is by advertisement in an action of declarator of death, is 21 days unless the court otherwise orders (r. 50.2(2)).

"WHICHEVER IS THE LATER".

13.4.3   The period of notice expires on the last day of the period of notice, which is calculated from (but excluding) the date on which the last execution of service or giving of intimation was made; the summons may be called on that last day (r. 13.13(1)). Usually service and intimation on a warrant for intimation are made at the same time; but they may not be, or service or intimation may have to be attempted again if at first unsuccessful.

See also, *Hoe International Ltd v Anderson*, 2015 S.C. 507 (Extra Div.).

"EXECUTION OF SERVICE".

13.4.4   The date of execution of service (citation) marks the commencement of the action: Erskine, III.iv.3; *Alston v. Macdougall* (1887) 15 R. 78; *Smith v. Stewart & Co.* 1960 S.C. 329, 334 per L.P. Clyde. The period of notice will begin to run from midnight of that day; except where service is by post when time begins to run from midnight of the day after the date of posting (r. 16.4(6)). All days of the week are included in the period of notice, including Sundays and other public holidays.

For methods of service, see Chap. 16, Pt I.

"INTIMATION BEFORE CALLING".

13.4.5   A summons may not be called until the last day of the period of notice: r. 13.13(1). A summons is called by appearing in the rolls in the calling list of causes called, i.e. brought into court.

Intimation on a warrant in a summons is provided for in r. 13.6(d): and see also note 13.6.6.

Intimation on a warrant for intimation is given in the same manner as service: see r. 16.8.

"EUROPE".

13.4.6   This word has not been defined; but probably means as far east as (the Ural mountains in Russia and) the Black Sea but not Asian Russia or the Asian Republics of the former U.S.S.R., south to the Mediterranean islands but not Africa, and north to Norway, Iceland and Finland. It includes the whole of the British Isles. The word obviously includes all Member States of the European Union (though not their dependencies). Note also "Europe" for the purposes of the Royal Mail: leaflets, available in Post Offices, on mailing abroad, list the countries treated as in Europe by the Royal Mail.

APPLICATION TO SHORTEN OR EXTEND THE PERIOD OF NOTICE.

Such an application after signeting and before service will be made before calling and the procedure for such is in r. 23.8. A motion which is made (i.e. heard) before service will have been enrolled before service.

13.4.7

DISPENSING WITH PERIOD OF NOTICE.

Where the defender's agent accepts service he may dispense with the period of notice: see r. 16.10.

13.4.8

"FINAL AND NOT SUBJECT TO REVIEW".

The decision of the Lord Ordinary may not be reclaimed against.

13.4.9

Signeting

13.5.—(1)   A summons shall pass the signet.

13.5

(2)   No summons shall bear any date but the date of signeting, which date shall be treated as the date of the summons.

(3)   A summons shall be signeted and registered by a clerk of session acting under authority from the Principal Clerk (by virtue of a commission granted to him by the Keeper of the Signet).

(4)   Subject to paragraph (5), a summons shall be presented to the General Department during its normal office hours for signeting and registration.

(5)   In an emergency, a summons may be signeted and registered out with the normal office hours.

Deriv. R.C.S. 1965, r. 74 (preamble (part)) (r. 13.5(1) and (2)); P.N. No. 3 of 1976 (r. 13.5(2) to (5))

GENERAL NOTE.

A summons must have the signet or seal of the sovereign bearing the Royal Coat of Arms embossed upon it to authorise execution (service of the summons). The Keeper of the Signet, the Lord Clerk Register, granted a commission on 3rd May 1976 to the Principal Clerk of Session to signet summonses and diligence letters which was formerly done by members of the Society of Writers to the Signet. Summonses are signeted by an assistant clerk of session acting with authority from the Principal Clerk as provided in the commission. Although signeting is carried out by clerks of session, it is not a function of the court and remains a function of the Keeper of the Signet; it is not therefore a judicial act: see *Wall's Trs v. Drynan* (1888) 15 R. 359, 362 per L.P. Inglis.

13.5.1

"SIGNETING AND REGISTRATION".

A summons may be lodged in person for signeting (r. 4.3) in the appropriate section in the General Department (see note 3.2.1) where the process is registered in the appropriate roll (see r. 3.2(3)), given a cause reference number (see r. 4.1(4) and note 4.1.5), signeted (if in order) and the principal summons will be available for collection the following day (by 10.30am if lodged before 4pm the preceding day). A summons may be lodged by post by a Court of Session account holder or if accompanied by a cheque for the fee (see note 13.5.5: P.N. No. 4 of 1994, paras 2 and 4) and if there are any defects which cannot be dealt with by telephone the summons will be returned by post by the Signeting Officer.

13.5.2

A summons must be executed (served) within a year and a day after being signeted or the instance will fall and a fresh action would have to be brought: r. 13.7(2).

On signeting, the summons will be returned to the pursuer for the purpose of service and diligence.

"NORMAL OFFICE HOURS".

For office hours and holidays, see note 3.1.2.

13.5.3

"EMERGENCY".

An emergency would be the need for an interim interdict, suspension or imminent expiry of prescription or limitation period. To contact one of the clerks to obtain a signet and, if necessary, a judge after 5pm, ring the Court of Session (0131-225 2595), leave your name and telephone number and the duty security guard will contact a clerk who will contact you.

13.5.4

FEE.

The court fee for signeting and all work up to the closed record (or determination of mode of inquiry) is payable at this stage. If signeting is out with normal hours there is an extra fee. For fee, see Court of Session etc. Fees Order 1997, Table of Fees, Pt I, A, and B, item 1, [SI 1997/688, as amended, pp. C1201

13.5.5

et seq.]. Certain persons are exempt from payment of fees: see 1997 Fees Order, art.5 substituted by S.S.I. 2002 No.270. A fee exemption certificate must be lodged in process: see P.N. No.1 of 2002.

Where the pursuer is legally represented, the fee may be debited under a credit scheme introduced on 1st April 1976 by P.N. No. 4 of 1976 to the account (if one is kept or permitted) of the pursuer's agent by the court cashier, and an account will be rendered weekly by the court cashier's office to the agent for all court fees due that week for immediate settlement. Party litigants, and agents not operating the scheme, must pay (by cash, cheque or postal order) on each occasion a fee is due at the time of lodging at the counter at the General Department.

Authority for service and intimation on signeting

13.6   **13.6.**[1]   When signeted, a summons shall be authority for—

(a)   service on the defender designed in the instance; and

(b)   intimation of the summons on any person on whom intimation is required in these Rules where a warrant for that purpose has been inserted in the summons.

Deriv. R.C.S. 1965, r. 74 (preamble (part))

GENERAL NOTE.

13.6.1   Rule 13.6 as originally in R.C.S. 1994, has been divided into two by A.S. (R.C.S. A. No.6) (Diligence on the Dependence) 2003 [S.S.I. 2003 No. 537] and the automatic right to diligence on the dependence, or to found jurisdiction, has been abolished. The reason is that, following *Karl Construction Ltd v. Palisade Properties plc* , 2002 S.C. 270 (OH) and *Advocate General v. Taylor* , 2003 S.L.T. 1340 (Extra Div), concerning inhibition on the dependence, such diligence must now be applied for and considered by the court. Rule 13.6A provides the new procedure for application for such diligence. See note 13.6A.1A for a discussion of these cases.

"SIGNETED".

13.6.2   For signeting, see r. 13.5.

"SERVICE".

13.6.3   For service, see Chap. 16.

"INTIMATION".

13.6.4   For procedure for intimation see r. 16.8. For forms, see the particular rules. Intimation of a summons is required for example:

(a)   in actions relating to heritable property on persons having an interest as holders of heritable securities over it: r. 13.12;

(b)   in actions for damages for death of a relative, on connected persons: r. 43.3;

(c)   in an action under s.1 of the Merchant Shipping (Oil Pollution) Act 1971 (now s.153 of the Merchant Shipping Act 1995), to the International Oil Pollution Compensation Fund: r. 46.9;

(d)   in family actions:

(i)   where defender's address is unknown, on children and next of kin: see r. 49.8(1)(a);

(ii)   on person with whom defender is alleged to have committed adultery: r. 49.8(1)(b);

(iii) where defender is suffering from a mental disorder, on children and next of kin and Mental Welfare Commission: r. 49.8(1)(c);

(iv)   where a party has more than one spouse, on any additional spouse: r. 49.8(1)(d);

(v)   where court may make an order about parental rights, on third parties concerned: r. 49.8(1)(e), (f) and (g);

(vi)   where court may make an order which affects a child, to that child, if not a party to the action: r. 49.8(1)(h);

(vii) where order sought for transfer of property under s.8(1)(aa) of the Family Law (Scotland) Act 1985, on consenters and creditors in respect of a security over the property: r. 49.8(1)(i);

(viii) where order sought under s.18 the Family Law (Scotland) Act 1985 relating to avoidance transactions, on third parties in whose favour a transaction is made: r. 49.8(1)(j);

(ix)   where order sought under the Matrimonial Homes (Family Protection) (Scotland) Act 1981, on interested persons: r. 49.8(1)(k);

(x)   where pursuer alleges a relevant (improper) association between defender and another, on that other person: r. 49.9;

(e)   in an action of declarator of death, to the missing person's spouse and children, any other person having an interest and the Lord Advocate: r. 50.2(4).

---

[1] R. 13.6 substituted by S.S.I. 2003 No. 537 (effective 10th November 2003).

Authority for diligence etc. before calling

13.6A.—[1](1)   Before the calling of a summons, the pursuer may apply by motion for authority for—

(a)   arrestment to found jurisdiction; or

(b)   diligence by—

    (i)   *[Revoked by S.S.I. 2008 No. 122 (effective 1st April 2008).]*

    (ii)   *[Revoked by S.S.I. 2008 No. 122 (effective 1st April 2008).]*

    (iii)   arrestment in rem; or

    (iv)   dismantling a ship,

where a warrant in the appropriate form in Form 13.2-A has been inserted in the summons.

(2)   Where a Lord Ordinary pronounces an interlocutor granting a motion under paragraph (1)—

(a)   he shall record his interlocutor by signing the warrant in the summons; and

(b)   the signed warrant shall be sufficient authority for execution of the arrestment to found jurisdiction or, as the case may be, the diligence.

13.6A

GENERAL NOTE.

Rule 13.6 as originally in R.C.S. 1994, has been divided into two by A.S. (R.C.S. A. No.6) (Diligence on the Dependence) 2003 [S.S.I. 2003 No. 537] and the automatic right to diligence on the dependence, or to found jurisdiction, has been abolished. The reason is that, following *Karl Construction Ltd v. Palisade Properties plc* , 2002 S.C. 270 (OH) and *Advocate General for Scotland v. Taylor* , 2003 S.L.T. 1340 (Extra Div), concerning inhibition on the dependence, such diligence must now be applied for and considered by the court. Rule 13.6A provided a procedure for application for such diligence. Following a somewhat unnecessary statutory statement of diligence on the dependence in the Bankruptcy and Diligence (Scotland) Act 2007, diligence by arrestment or inhibition on the dependence is now dealt with in Chap. 14A.

The previous rule dealt with warrants for diligence before signeting. Rule 13.6A deals with authority for certain diligence before calling, which is by an unintimated motion. After calling (see r. 13.8A), authority will be sought, as before, by motion.

The appropriate warrant must be inserted in the summons. In *Anglo-Dutch Petroleum International Inc. v. Ramco Energy Plc* , 2006 S.L.T. 334 (OH), the warrant was for "warrant for inhibition and warrant on the dependence" on the basis of which arrestments were made. The defender obtained recall of the arrestments as the omission of the word "arrestment" was held to be critical.

13.6A.1

"ARRESTMENT TO FOUND JURISDICTION".

Subject to exceptions in Admiralty causes, arrestment to found jurisdiction is available where the defender is not domiciled in the UK or a country to which the 1968 or Lugano Convention in Sched. 1 or 3C to the C.J.J.A. 1982 applies: C.J.J.A. 1982, Scheds 1 and 3C, Art. 3(2), Sched.4, Art.3 and Sched.8, r. 2(8). In relation to Admiralty actions (defined in r. 46.1), however, see notes 16.13.1, 16.13.3 and 16.14.1 to 16.14.4. There must be a pecuniary claim: *Leggat Bros v. Gray* 1908 S.C. 67; *Union Electric Co. v. Holman & Co.* 1913 S.C. 954. The schedule of arrestment executed must state that it is to found jurisdiction: *Sutherlands of Peterhead (Road Hauliers) Ltd v. Allard Hewson & Co.* 1972 S.L.T. (Notes) 83. The arrestment is personal to the defender, does not transfer against his successors and establishes jurisdiction only for the action in which it is used: *Cameron v. Chapman* (1838) 16 S. 907. The arrestment must be executed before service of the summons: *Wall's Trs v. Dryman* (1988) 15 R. 359; cf. arrestment or inhibition on the dependence. It creates no nexus over the property arrested: *Craig v. Burnsgaard Kjosternd & Co.* (1896) 23 R. 500, 503 per Lord McLaren. If the pursuer wishes to secure the subjects arrested for enforcement of any decree he must also arrest on the dependence: *Leggat Bros.*, above; *Fraser-Johnston Engineering Co. v. Jeffs* 1920 S.C. 222. See further note 13.2.8(B), Ground (8) on jurisdiction. See also Graham Stewart on *Diligence*, pp. 246 et seq. For subjects arrestable, see notes 13.6.3(5), and 13.6.4 (arrestment of ships).

A schedule of arrestment must be served on the arrestee in Form 16.15—A (for ships, it is Form 16.15—AA). For methods of execution of the schedule of arrestment, see r. 16.12.

13.6A.2

ARRESTMENT OF SHIPS, CARGO AND ARRESTMENT IN REM.

Arrestment of a ship or vessel is a real diligence: the ship is arrested and is fixed in the place in which it is arrested (*Carlberg v. Borjesson* (1877) 5 R. 188, 195 per Lord Shand), there is not an arrestment in the hands of an arrestee (*Barclay Curle & Co. Ltd v. Sir James Laing & Sons Ltd* 1908 S.C. 82, 89 per

13.6A.3

---

[1] R.13.6A added by S.S.I. 2003 No. 537 (effective 10th November, 2003).

Lord McLaren). The exception in relation to ships does not extend to aircraft: *Emerald Airways Ltd v. Nordic Oil Services Ltd* 1996 S.L.T. 403. The diligence is completed not by an action of furthcoming but by an action of sale.

1. There may be arrestment of a ship (a) on a warrant to found jurisdiction (see notes 13.6.1 and 16.13.1(1)) or (b) on the dependence of an Admiralty action in personam where the ship is the ship with which the action is concerned (and is partly owned by the defender: see, e.g., *William Batey & Co (Exports) Ltd v. Kent* , 1985 S.L.T. 490 affd. 1987 S.L.T. 557), or all the shares are owned by the defender, to enforce or secure a claim in s.47(1) of the Administration of Justice Act 1956, or to enforce a claim in s. 47(2)(p)–(s) by virtue of s. 47(3)(a) of the 1956 Act if the conclusion is a pecuniary conclusion and the ship is a ship to which the conclusion relates. In *Oceaneering International AG, Ptnrs.* , 2011 S.L.T. 667 (OH), it was held that the supply of remotely operated vehicles, systems, services and personnel for an offshore intervention vessel was the supply of marine equipment and services to a ship for the operational benefit of it and fell within s.47(2)(k) and (l) of the 1956 Act. An admiralty action is defined in r. 46.1. It used not to be clear whether s. 47(1) limits the common law right to arrest a sister ship: see e.g. *Sheaf Steamship Co. Ltd v. Compania Transmeditteranea* , 1930 S.C. 660; cf. Brussels Convention relating to the Arrest of Seagoing Ships, May 10, 1952, art. 3(3), *The "Banco"* [1971] P. 137 (English law) and comments in *Gatoil International Inc. v. Arkwright-Boston Manufacturers Mutual Insurance Co.* 1985 S.C.(H.L.) 1, 15 per Lord Keith of Kinkel. It has now been held in the Outer House that only one ship (the ship concerned or a sister ship) per action may be arrested on the dependence under s.47(1) of the 1956 Act: *Interatlantic (Namibia) (Pty) Ltd v. Okeasnki Ribolov Ltd* 1996 S.L.T. 819; reported as *The "Afala"* in [1995] 2 Lloyd's Rep. 286.

   There may also be an arrestment of a ship on the dependence of a foreign action on a petition to the Court of Session for such a warrant: see C.J.J.A. 1982, s.27. The petitioner is not, however, entitled to the warrant to arrest as of right: *Stancroft Securities Ltd v. McDowall* , 1990 S.C. pp. 274, 277 per L.J.-C. Ross. The pursuer in the foreign action must comply with s.27 and demonstrate a colourable care in the foreign action: *Clipper Shipping Co. Ltd v. San Vincente Partners* 1989 S.L.T. 204, 207D per Lord Coulsfield and *Stancroft Securities Ltd*, above. An affidavit of the foreign lawyer conducting the action may be sufficient: see e.g. *Clipper Shipping Co. Ltd*, above.

   It is good practice to mention the name of the ship in the warrant though not essential. A schedule of arrestment on the dependence in Form 16.15—B is attached to the mainmast (or if none, another prominent part) and the Royal initials chalked above it: see r. 16.13(1) and (2). A schedule of arrestment to found jurisdiction is in Form 16.15—AA.

2. There may be an arrestment in rem (a) of a ship or cargo in an Admiralty action in rem (an action to enforce a maritime lien over a ship, cargo or freight for money due, but in respect of the ship, only where the claim is one in s.47(2) of the 1956 Act); or (b) of a ship in an Admiralty action in personam involving a claim in s.47(2)(p) to (s) of the 1956 Act in respect of a non-pecuniary claim (whether or not there is a lien) by virtue of s.47(3)(b) of that Act. In an Admiralty action in rem to arrest the res (ship or cargo) there must be an arrestment in rem, arrestment on the dependence is not sufficient: r. 46.2(1)(a); and see *Clan Line Steamers Ltd v. Earl of Douglas Steamship Co. Ltd* 1913 S.C. 967, 973 per L.P. Dunedin, *Mill v. Fildes* 1982 S.L.T. 147. In an action in rem an arrestment in rem founds jurisdiction. An arrestment in rem must be executed before service: *Mill*, above, at p. 150. The expenses of an arrestment in rem are recoverable as part of the expenses of the action: *Hatton v. A/S Durban Hansen* 1919 S.C. 154. A warrant for arrestment in rem must specify the particular res. A schedule of arrestment in Form 16.15-C (to enforce lien) or Form 16.15-D (to enforce non-pecuniary claim) is attached to the mainmast (or if none, a prominent part): rr. 16.13(1) and 16.15((1)(c) and (d). An arrestment in rem of cargo is competent on board ship or anywhere on dry land: r. 16.13(1) or 16.14. Arrestment in Form 16.15-C where the cargo is on board is made by fixing to the mainmast, etc., or, where the cargo is landed, is made in the hands of the custodian (or harbour master where in the harbour): rr. 16.13(1), 16.14 and 16.15(1)(c). There is some doubt whether cargo may be arrested at sea: cf. *Carron Co. v. Currie & Co.* (1896) 33 S.L.R. 578 and Graham Stewart on *Diligence*, p. 108.

3. There may be arrestment of a cargo on board ship (a) on a warrant to found jurisdiction or (b) on the dependence of an Admiralty action in personam or an ordinary action. There is some doubt whether cargo may be arrested at sea: cf. *Carron Co. v. Currie & Co.* (1896) 33 S.L.R. 578 and Graham Stewart on *Diligence*, p. 108.

4. A ship may be arrested in the harbour or at anchor in the roadstead, but not when she is on passage (set sail): *Carlberg v. Borjesson* (1877) 5 R. 188 and (H.L.) 215. Where the vessel has set sail and is in territorial waters it may be possible to seek a warrant (by motion) to take possession: Graham Stewart, p. 42; but this has been doubted: *The "Grey Dolphin"* 1982 S.C. 5, 7 per Lord Wylie. Alternatively caution or consignation may be sought: *Meron v. Umland* (1896) 3 S.L.T. 286. Once arrested the ship must remain where it is: *Carlberg* above, at p. 195 per Lord Shand. If any interested person seeks to remove the vessel to a safer place or for any other reason a special warrant must be obtained by motion under r. 13.11: see *Turner v. Galway* (1882) 19 S.L.R. 892.

See further, arrestment of ships and cargo in rr. 16.13 and 16.14, and Admiralty actions in Chap. 46.

"DISMANTLING A SHIP".

Where an arrestment of a ship might be disregarded an additional warrant to dismantle may be inserted. The warrant authorises the taking of the sails, rudders, anchors or a necessary part of the machinery. Dismantling is usually effected by a marine engineer under the superintendence of the messenger-at-arms executing the warrant.

13.6A.4

"CALLING".

For calling, see r. 13.13. Calling may not occur earlier than the day on which the period of notice of the summons expires: r. 13.13(1).

13.6A.5

"MOTION".

For motions, see Chap. 23.

The motion need not be intimated to any prospective defender: see r. 23.3(1).

Rule 23.8 (motions by pursuer before calling or petitioner before first order) will apply. Rule 13.6A(1) is silent as to whether a hearing before the Lord Ordinary is required. Following the dicta in *Advocate General v. Taylor* , 2003 S.L.T. 1340 (Extra Div) at para. [33], a hearing will not normally be required unless the Lord Ordinary requires it. A hearing will not be required if the summons or the motion or other information before the Lord Ordinary contains averments which prima facie justify the diligence sought and are proportionate to the claim (see *Advocate General v. Taylor* at para. [34]).

13.6A.6

"WARRANT".

If the Lord Ordinary grants warrant for diligence, the blank warrant on the summons (see Form 13.2-A as amended) is completed and signed by the Lord Ordinary.

13.6A.7

Service and intimation of summonses

13.7.—(1)   Where a summons is to be executed, a copy of the summons which has passed the signet shall be—

(a)   served on the defender with a citation in Form 13.7 attached to it; and

(b)   intimated to any person named in a warrant for intimation.

(2)   Where service of a summons is not executed within a year and a day after the date of signeting, the instance shall fall.

13.7

Deriv. A.S. 8th July 1831, para.III (r. 13.7(2))

GENERAL NOTE.

Citation is the proper term for the step which brings an action into existence by giving the defender notice of it—i.e. by service of a copy of the summons on him. The word "service" has replaced "citation" in common usage and is used in these Rules.

13.7.1

The date of execution of service (citation) marks the commencement of the action: Erskine, III.iv.3; *Alston v. Macdougall* (1887) 15 R. 78; *Smith v. Stewart & Co.* 1960 S.C. 329, 334 per L.P. Clyde. The period of notice before which the summons may not be lodged for calling will begin to run from midnight of that day; except where service is by post when time begins to run from midnight of the day after the date of posting (r. 16.4(6)). For service and intimation, see Chap. 16, Pt. I. Service may be by advertisement: r. 16.5.

It may be necessary to serve other notices with the summons and citation on the defender, e.g., the notice and form in relation to time to pay directions where there is a conclusion for a sum of money less than £10,000: see r. 44.2 and note 44.1.1.

The form of citation served must be signed by the person executing it: Citation Act 1592. It is also a requirement of Form 13.7 provided for in r. 13.7(1). It had been held that the dispensing power in r. 2.1 was not available where a citation had been signed to cure a failure to comply with the 1592 Act: *Blackfriars (Scotland) Ltd v. Shetland Salmon Co's Trustees*, 2001 S.L.T. 315 (OH) (citation not signed; decree *de plano* granted). In *Colley v. Celtic Pacific Ship Management (Overseas) Ltd*, 6th October 2000, unreported (2000 G.W.D. 331260) the summons was served without any citation. Lord Macfadyen distinguished *Blackfriars*, above, holding that, while anomalously, service of an unsigned citation remained dependent on the 1592 Act, service of a summons was made under r. 13.7 and failure to serve a citation could be cured under r. 2.1 (in that case relief was granted as the failure was due to a genuine oversight). Relief was granted under r. 2.1 in *Greenwoods Ltd v. Ans Homes Ltd*, 2007 S.L.T. 149 (OH) where service by a process server in England was not witnessed. In *Tarmac Trading Ltd v Hamilton's Executrx*, 2018 S.C. 599 (First Div.), an English process server failed to sign the Form 13.7 citation. The pursuer raised an action of declarator, reduction and interdict Blackfriars, above, was disapproved. It was held that, although the 1592 Act had not been repealed, it did no violence to those statutory provisions (which were incorporated into RCS 1994, r. 13.7) if the dispensing power under r. 2.1 were applied to the failure to comply with r. 13.7 in an appropriate case (such as this); it would be bizarre if the dispensing power were available where there was no form (*Colley*, above) but not available where there was an unsigned one). It was observed at para. [9] that allowing a party to advance objections to the defender's action for damages was inconsistent with r. 16.11. The observation, however, overlooks the fact that the pursuer did not raise the issue in the defender's action for damages to which r. 16.11 would have applied to prevent an objection, by a party who has entered the process, to an irregularity in the execution of service. It does not apply to the objection being raised in a separate action, which the pursuer had adopted and was the only way in which the objection could be and was raised by the pursuer.

"SERVED".

13.7.2 For methods of service, see Chap. 16, Pt. I.

"INTIMATED".

13.7.3 For methods, see r. 16.8.

"EXECUTED WITHIN A YEAR AND A DAY".

13.7.4 The summons must be served by the end of the last day a year and one day later. The reason for the additional day is historical, to ensure that a whole year has elapsed. Thereafter, a fresh action must be brought.

The laws of prescription and limitation may, however, have the effect of restricting the period for execution (service). Not only must a summons be executed within a year and a day, it must also be served within a year and a day, of the date of signeting: r. 13.13(6). See the discussion on the meaning of the instance falling in note 13.13.9.

Authority for intimation after signeting

13.8 **13.8.**[1] Where a warrant for intimation referred to in rule 13.6(b) is not obtained when the summons is signeted, the pursuer may apply by motion for authority for intimation of the summons on any person on whom intimation is required in these Rules.

GENERAL NOTE.

13.8.1 The previous r. 13.8 dealt with warrants for diligence after signeting. New r. 13.8 deals with intimation after signeting, a subject not previously tackled in the Rules. The R.C.S. 1994 and R.C.S. 1965 were silent about the subject. The rule conforms to the practice that intimation to persons not mentioned in the warrant for intimation at the time of signeting is applied for by motion.

Authority for diligence after calling is now dealt with in r. 13.8A.

"INTIMATION ".

13.8.2 For procedure for intimation, see r. 16.8. For forms, see the particular rules. See also note 13.6.4 for the rules in which intimation of a summons is required.

"MOTION".

13.8.3 For motions, see Chap. 23.

Authority for diligence etc. after calling

13.8A **13.8A.**—[2](1) After the calling of a summons, a pursuer may apply by motion for authority for—

    (a)   arrestment to found jurisdiction; or

    (b)   diligence by—

        (i)   *[Revoked by S.S.I. 2008 No. 122 (effective 1st April 2008).]*

        (ii) *[Revoked by S.S.I. 2008 No. 122 (effective 1st April 2008).]*

        (iii) arrestment in rem; or

        (iv) dismantling a ship.

    (2) A certified copy of an interlocutor granting a motion under paragraph (1) shall be sufficient authority for execution of the arrestment to found jurisdiction or, as the case may be, the diligence.

Deriv. R.C.S. 1965, r. 74(d) (r. 13.8A(1))

GENERAL NOTE.

13.8A.1 New r. 13.8A deals with authority for diligence sought by a pursuer after calling. As before, authority is sought by motion.

Diligence by arrestment or inhibition on the dependence is now dealt with in Chap. 14A.

On intimation of motions, see note 13.8A.3 below.

---

[1] R.13.8 substituted by S.S.I. 2003 No. 537 (effective 10th November 2003).
[2] R.13.8A inserted by S.S.I. 2003 No. 537 (effective 10th November 2003).

For calling, see r. 13.13. Calling may not occur earlier than the day on which the period of notice of the summons expires: r. 13.13(1).   **13.8A.2**

"MOTION".

For motions, see Chap. 23. Where the defender has not entered appearance, intimation is not required: r. 23.3(1). Following the dicta in *Advocate General v. Taylor*, 2003 S.L.T. 1340 (Extra Div) at para. [33], it is likely that a hearing will not normally be required unless the Lord Ordinary requires it. A hearing will not, presumably, be required if the summons or the motion contains averments which prima facie justify the diligence sought and are proportionate to the claim (see *Advocate General v. Taylor* at para. [34]).   **13.8A.3**

"ARRESTMENT TO FOUND JURISDICTION".

See note 13.6A.1.   **13.8A.4**

"INHIBITION".

See note 14A.2.8.   **13.8A.5**

"ARRESTMENT ON THE DEPENDENCE".

See note 14A.2.7.   **13.8A.6**

"ARRESTMENT IN REM".

See note 13.6A.4.   **13.8A.7**

"DISMANTLING A SHIP".

See note 13.6A.5.   **13.8A.8**

"CERTIFIED COPY INTERLOCUTOR".

A CCI is a copy of the interlocutor prepared by the party seeking the CCI, stamped and signed by a clerk of session in the General Department.   **13.8A.9**

Effect of authority for inhibition on the dependence

13.9.   [Revoked by S.S.I. 2008 No. 122 (effective 1st April 2008).]   **13.9**

GENERAL NOTE.

See new r. 14A.3 and notes to that rule.   **13.9.1**

Recall etc. of arrestment or inhibition

13.10.   *[Revoked by S.S.I. 2008 No. 122 (effective 1st April 2008).]*   **13.10**

GENERAL NOTE.

New r. 13.10(1) was substituted by A.S. (R.C.S.A. No.5) (Diligence on the Dependence) 2003 [S.S.I. 2003 No. 537]. The substance of r. 13.10(1) was the same, namely, that loosing, restricting or recalling was by motion. Recall, etc., of arrestment or inhibition on the dependence is now dealt with in r. 14A.4.   **13.10.1**

Movement of arrested property

13.11.—(1)[1]   Any person having an interest may apply by motion for a warrant authorising the movement of a vessel or cargo which is the subject of an arrestment mentioned in rule 13.6A.   **13.11**

(2)   Where the court grants a warrant sought under paragraph (1), it may make such further order as it thinks fit to give effect to that warrant.

(3)   A warrant granted on a motion under paragraph (1) shall be without prejudice to the validity and subsistence of the arrestment.

Deriv. R.C.S. 1965, r. 74(g) and (h), and r. 140(d) and (dd), amended by S.I. 1990 No. 705

GENERAL NOTE.

Rule 13.11(1) was amended by A.S. (R.C.S.A.No.5) (Diligence on the Dependence) 2003 [S.S.I. 2003 No. 537] to include a reference to new r. 13.6A.   **13.11.1**

This rule was introduced to overcome difficulties associated with someone having an interest in a ship or cargo seeking to move a ship or cargo. A vessel might be obstructing or causing loss to an innocent third party.

This is really a species of loosing of an arrestment, but is dealt with separately for the reasons above

---

[1] R.13.11(1) amended by S.S.I. 2004 No. 537 (effective 10th November, 2003).

and because in the case of arrestment of a ship there is no arrestee. If a cargo is arrested but cannot be unloaded the ship is effectively immobilised. See *Svenska Petroleum A.B. v. H.O.R. Ltd* 1982 S.L.T. 343; *West Cumberland Farmers Ltd v. Director of Agriculture of Sri Lanka* 1988 S.L.T. 296. Authority may be obtained to bring an arrested vessel into a safe harbour: *Turner v. Galway* (1882) 19 S.L.R. 892; *The "Grey Dolphin"* 1982 S.C. 5.

Where the motion is made by an interested person before the defender has entered appearance, the motion does not have to be intimated to the defender: see r. 23.3. There is no provision for intimation to the pursuer, but the Deputy Principal Clerk will inform the pursuer of the motion (whether made by the defender or an interested person) and the Keeper of the Rolls will arrange a hearing at short notice for both parties to attend, usually the next day; but it could be the same day or night: see r. 23.10. To obtain a judge after 5pm, ring the Court of Session (0131-225 2595), leave your name and telephone number and the duty security guard will contact a clerk who will contact you.

"MOTION".

13.11.2   For motions, see Chap. 23.

RECLAIMING.

13.11.3   An interlocutor granting authority to move an arrested vessel or cargo may be reclaimed against without leave within 14 days: r. 38.3(4)(i).

Intimation of actions relating to heritable property

13.12   **13.12.**—(1)   In an action relating to heritable property, it shall not be necessary to call a person as a defender by reason only of any interest he may have as the holder of a heritable security over the heritable property; but intimation of the summons shall be given to that person by a notice of intimation in Form 13.12 attached to a copy of the summons.

(2)   A warrant for intimation under paragraph (1) shall be inserted in the summons by the pursuer in the following terms: "Warrant to intimate to (*name and address*) as a person who is believed to be a heritable creditor of the defender.".

(3)   A person on whom intimation has been made under this rule may apply by motion for leave to be sisted as a party and to lodge defences.

Deriv. R.C.S. 1965, r. 76 amended by S.I. 1991 No. 2483

GENERAL NOTE.

13.12.1   The proper defender in an action is the person who has the real title and interest to prevent the pursuer from obtaining decree. A person having a security over heritable property may have an interest in the action, but he is not the real owner of the property, hence the rule for intimation only.

The rule applies even in a family action where an order is sought in respect of heritable property.

A heritable creditor to whom intimation has been made under this rule may seek by motion to enter the process: r. 13.12(3). Defences (not a minute) should be lodged when the motion is enrolled. On defences, see Chap. 18.

"INTIMATION".

13.12.2   For procedure, see r. 16.8. Where the warrant is not inserted in the summons before signeting it may be applied for by motion: r. 13.8.

Calling

13.13   **13.13.**—(1)   A summons shall not be called earlier than the day on which the period of notice expires.

(2)   A summons shall be lodged for calling not later than 12.30 p.m. on the second day before that on which it is to be called.

(3)   A summons may be called—

(a)[1]   during session, on a sitting day; or

(b)   in vacation, on a calling day of which notice has been given in the rolls.

(4)   A summons lodged for calling shall be accompanied by a typewritten slip containing the instance, subject to the following provisions—

(a)   where there is more than one pursuer or defender, the slip shall contain

---

[1] R. 13.13(3)(a) amended by S.S.I. 2017 No. 414 r. 3(2) (effective 1st January 2018).

only the name and designation of the first pursuer or defender, as the case may be, followed by the words "and Another [or Others, *as the case may be]*"; and

(b) in naming and designing a pursuer or defender which is a body of persons (such as a trust or partnership), whether individual members are also parties or not, it shall be sufficient to use the collective name of that body.

(5) The calling of a summons shall be published in the rolls on the date on which the summons calls.

(6) Where a summons has not called within a year and a day after the expiry of the period of notice, the instance shall fall.

Deriv. A.S. 8th July 1831, para. III, (r. 13.13(6)); R.C.S. 1965, r. 78(a) to (c) and (e) (r. 13.13(1) to (5)); P.N. No. 3 of 1976, para. 3(vi) (r. 13.13(1) and (2))

GENERAL NOTE.

The calling of a summons brings the action into court. This must be done within a year and a day of the expiry of the period of notice (r. 13.13(1) and (6)) by publication in the calling list in the rolls (r. 13.13(5)).

For the summons to call the pursuer must return the summons to the process (which was lodged for signeting and registration (see rr. 4.3 and 13.5(3)) in the appropriate section of the General Department (see note 3.2.1) either in person or by post (P.N. No.4 of 1994, paras 1 and 4). Where the summons is lodged for calling by post the pursuer will be informed by letter if it is accepted for calling; where there are any defects which cannot be dealt with by telephone, the summons will be returned by post: P.N. No. 4 of 1994, para. 4(3).

"NOT EARLIER THAN THE DAY ON WHICH THE PERIOD OF NOTICE EXPIRES".

The summons may call on the last day of the period of notice. The period of notice runs (a) where service is by post, from midnight of the day after the day of posting: r. 16.3(6); and (b) in any other case, from midnight of the day on which service is executed.

"PERIOD OF NOTICE".

See r. 13.4.

SESSION AND VACATION.

On sessions of the court, see rr. 10.1, 10.3 and 10.4. On vacations, see rr. 10.1 and 10.5.

"SEDERUNT DAY".

This is a day on which the court sits: see r. 10.2.

CALLING DAYS.

A summons may be called on a sederunt day: in session, Tuesday to Friday (see rr. 10.2(1) and 10.3(1)); or, in vacation, a day of which notice is given in the rolls about four weeks before the end of the preceding term, being a sederunt day specified by direction by the Lord President under r. 10.2(2) (usually every Thursday). For the office hours of the General Department and holidays, see note 3.1.2.

CALLING SLIP.

The typewritten slip referred to in r. 13.13(4) is a calling slip. It provides the information required for publication in the calling list (on the noticeboard at the top of the main corridor of Parliament House after the reception area at door 11). The list is published every sederunt day and contains the names and addresses of the parties in the summons including any capacity in which they sue or are sued (it is usually a repetition of the instance).

"CALLED WITHIN A YEAR AND A DAY".

The period of notice expires at midnight on the last day of that period and time runs from then. The summons must call at the latest by the end of the last day a year and a day later. The reason for the additional day is historical, to ensure that a whole year elapsed. Thereafter a fresh action must be brought. Where the last day falls on a Saturday, Sunday or a public holiday on which the Office of Court is closed, the next available day is allowed: r. 1.3(7). For office hours and holidays, see note 3.1.2.

"THE INSTANCE SHALL FALL".

This rule repeats the rule in para.III of the A.S. of 8th July 1831 that if a summons is not called within a year and a day of the expiry of the period of notice the instance falls. The instance falling means, or meant, that the summons thereafter is at an end and has no existence: *Cumming v. Munro* (1833) 12 S. 61, 63 per Lord Cringletie; *McKidd v. Manson* (1882) 9 R. 790, 791 per L.P. Inglis. The consequence of the decision of Lord Macfadyen in *McDonald v. Kwok* 1999 S.L.T. 593 was that it could no longer be said or relied upon that an action has ceased to exist in that situation. In that case it was held that r. 2.1 (relief for

13.13.1

13.13.2

13.13.3

13.13.4

13.13.5

13.13.6

13.13.7

13.13.8

13.13.9

failure to comply with rules) was a power that it was always competent to invoke and the terms of which were wholly unqualified. A motion, therefore, to invoke the power in r. 2.1 to enable a summons to call was, despite the terms of r. 13.13(6) according to Lord Macfadyen, competent. This decision was, to say the least, unfortunate as it negated the spirit and intention of r. 13.13(6); a defender would have hanging over him indefinitely (subject to prescription) an action which is capable of resuscitation. The remedy which Lord Macfadyen says the defender has, namely, protestation under r. 13.14, is not so much a remedy for the defender as a reminder to the pursuer. *McDonald*, above, was followed in *Kilna v. De La Salle* , 2005 S.C.L.R. 154 but fortunately overruled in *Brogan v. O'Rourke Ltd* , 2005 S.L.T. 29 (Extra Div.) where it was held that rr. 13.13(6) and 43.3(2) were plain and the meaning of "the instance shall fall" was perfectly understood: where the summons has not called within the specified period the instance falls and it is incompetent to apply to the court under r. 2.1.

DOCUMENTS FOUNDED ON OR ADOPTED.

13.13.10   Any document founded on or adopted as incorporated in the summons must be lodged as a production when the summons is lodged for calling: see r. 27.1(1)(a). For lodging of productions, see r. 4.5. For the meaning of documents founded on or adopted, see note 27.1.2.

Protestation for not calling summons

13.14   **13.14.**—(1)   Where the pursuer does not lodge the summons for calling within seven days after the date on which the period of notice expires, the defender, on production of the service copy summons, may apply by motion for an order ordaining the pursuer to lodge the summons for calling within seven days, or such other period as the court thinks fit, after the date of the order.

(2)   Where the court pronounces an interlocutor under paragraph (1), the defender shall serve a certified copy of that interlocutor on the pursuer.

(3)   Where the pursuer fails to lodge the summons within the period ordered by the court under paragraph (1), the defender may apply by motion—

(a)   for declarator that the instance has fallen;

(b)   for recall of any diligence mentioned in rule 13.6(c) which has been executed; and

(c)   for payment to the defender of his expenses of process under this rule.

(4)   An interlocutor granting a motion under paragraph (3) shall be final and not subject to review.

Deriv. R.C.S. 1965, r. 80(a)

GENERAL NOTE.

13.14.1   Protestation is the means by which a defender compels the pursuer who has not lodged the summons for calling to proceed with his action or have the court bring the process to an end. The principle of protestation in R.C.S. 1965, r. 80 is retained, but the procedure is new.

"MOTION".

13.14.2   For motions, see Chap. 23.

"WITHIN SEVEN DAYS".

13.14.3   The date of expiry of the period of notice or of the order is not counted in calculating the period; and the seventh day is included in the period. When the last day falls on a public holiday, Saturday or Sunday or on which the Office of Court is closed, the next available day is allowed: r. 1.3(7). For office hours and holidays, see note 3.1.2.

"DILIGENCE MENTIONED IN RULE 13.6(c)".

13.14.4   The diligences are arrestment and inhibition on the dependence, arrestment in rem and dismantling of a ship. Recall is not restricted to diligence executed on a warrant inserted in a summons under r. 13.6.

CERTIFIED COPY INTERLOCUTOR.

13.14.5   For fee, see Court of Session etc. Fees Order 1984, Table of Fees, Pt. IV, J, item 2 [SI 1984/256, Table as amended, pp. C 1202 et seq.].

"SERVED".

13.14.6   For service, see Chap. 16, Pt. I. A certificate of service must be lodged: r. 16.1(3).

EXPENSES.

13.14.7   The expenses will usually be the judicial expenses of process. Expenses are in the discretion of the court and, where awarded, are on a party and party basis unless otherwise ordered: *Fletcher's Trs. v.*

Fletcher (1888) 15 R. 862. Expenses may be modified (r. 42.5); modification being the exact ascertainment of the precise sum that is to be paid: *Kintore v. Pirie* (1904) 12 S.L.T. 385, 386 per Lord Kinnear.

FINALITY OF PROTESTATION.

A pursuer cannot now be reponed against a protestation. He receives intimation of the order of the court (r. 13.14(2)) and can oppose the subsequent motion under r. 13.14(3) (the decision on which is final (r. 13.14(4)). Protestation does not prevent the pursuer raising the action again because the plea of res judicata does not arise. **13.14.8**

CHAPTER 14 PETITIONS

Application of this Chapter

14.1. Subject to any other provision in these Rules, this Chapter applies to a petition presented to the court.

GENERAL NOTE.

This Chapter provides the general rules for applications by petition. But there are a number of Chapters in the Rules providing special provisions for particular applications by petition. The rules in this Chapter do not apply where they are excluded expressly or by implication in a Chapter providing particular rules.

DISTINCTION BETWEEN PETITION AND SUMMONS.

A petition is an ex parte application addressed to the Lords of Council and Session and seeks their aid for some purpose or other, by exercising some statutory jurisdiction or the *nobile officium* in a variety of matters: *Tomkins v. Cohen* 1951 S.C. 22, 23 per Lord Keith. A petition involves a less formal procedure than a summons. "The object of the summons is to enforce a pursuer's legal right against a defender who resists it, or to protect a legal right which the defender is infringing; the object of a petition, on the other hand, is to obtain from the administrative jurisdiction of the court power to do something or to require something to be done, which it is just and proper should be done, but which the petitioner has no legal right to do or to require, apart from judicial authority": Report of the Royal Commission on the Court of Session 1927 (Cmd. 2801), pp. 49–50. See also Encyclopaedia of the Laws of Scotland (Dunedin edition), Vol.11, sv. "Petition", para. 696.

A recent analysis of the difference between actions and petitions, and where petition procedure is appropriate, is to be found in *Hooley Ltd v. Ganges Jute Private Ltd* 2019 S.C. 632 (Second Div.):

> "[15] The essential feature of the ordinary action is therefore that it involves adjudication on the existing rights and obligations of the parties. What the court does is to decide what those rights and obligations (or powers and liabilities) are and to provide mechanisms for their enforcement. Petition procedure, by contrast, involves intervention by the court that goes beyond the determination of existing rights and obligations. The need for intervention by the court is in our opinion the critical feature that determines whether or not petition procedure is required. If petition procedure is required, it must obviously be competent. The court's intervention will normally involve an important element of judgment, in some cases going as far as a discretion. While in ordinary procedure, especially in granting equitable remedies, the court may have a discretion as to whether to grant the remedy sought, that is exceptional. In petition procedure, on the other hand, the element of judgment or discretion will usually be central.
>
> [16] The reason for the court's intervention will typically take one of two forms. First, in some cases the intervention is required because the court is asked to innovate on the parties' existing rights and obligations. This is the basis for the use of petition procedure for applications to the nobile officium .... Secondly, the court's intervention may be required because the order sought has what may be described as 'real' effects, in the sense that the consequences of the court's decision go beyond the rights and obligations of the parties who are represented and affect third parties who are not represented. In such a case, if the effect on third parties is direct and reasonably significant, it is clearly desirable that the court should give independent consideration to the potential consequences of its order to ensure that such third parties are not unfairly affected by it.
>
> [17] The majority of the cases where petition procedure is used in preference to an ordinary action probably fall into this second category ...
>
> [21] Accordingly, in our opinion petition procedure will be competent in any case where either it is necessary to innovate on existing legal norms or the court's order is likely to have an effect on parties who are not represented in the proceedings (or in some cases, as in company petitions relating to schemes of arrangement, who dissent from the proposals made). We do not suggest that these are the sole criteria that may justify the use of petition procedure, but those two categories perhaps cover the great majority of such cases. The critical feature is that in such cases the court is obliged to exercise an independent element of judgment, or discretion, that goes beyond the interests of the parties and the submissions that they may make in the litigation. Furthermore, as Lord Keith indicates in Tomkins v Cohen , a petition is an application addressed to the court and seeking the aid of the court. The grant of such aid is justified primarily in the foregoing two categories of application, where the court is asked for good reason to go beyond the existing law or where it is asked to pronounce an order that may have an effect on third parties."

Applications by petition in the Outer House

14.2   **14.2.** Subject to any other provision in these Rules, the following applications to the court shall be made by petition presented in the Outer House:—

    (a)   an application for the appointment of a judicial factor, a factor *loco absentis*, a factor pending litigation or a curator *bonis*;

    (b)   an application for the appointment of a judicial factor on the estate of a partnership or joint adventure;

    (c)   an application to the *nobile officium* of the court which relates to—

        (i)   the administration of a trust;

        (ii)   the office of trustee; or

        (iii)   a public trust;

    (d)   a petition and complaint for breach of interdict;

    (e)   an application to the supervisory jurisdiction of the court;

    (f)   an application for suspension, suspension and interdict, and suspension and liberation;

    (g)   an application to recall an arrestment or inhibition other than in a cause depending before the court;

    (ga)[1]   an application made under an enactment to report a matter to the court due to obstruction or for enforcement;

    (h)   a petition or other application under these Rules or any other enactment or rule of law; and

    (i)[2]   an application to the court in exercise of its *parens patriae* jurisdiction.

Deriv. R.C.S. 1965, r. 69, and r. 189(a) (preamble) (amended by SI 1970/134), (i), (ii), (iii) (substituted by SI 1987/1206), (iv) (amended by SI 1987/1206) and (xxxvii) (inserted by SI 1990/705), (r. 14.2(a)–(h))

GENERAL NOTE.

14.2.1   Most petitions are dealt with at first instance in the Outer House. Rule 14.2(h) is intended to catch applications to the court under primary or subordinate legislation, or the common law, whether or not specified to be by petition under the particular enactment or these Rules, except where specified to be an action or an application by minute (see, e.g. certain applications in family actions in Chap. 49), note (see, e.g. certain applications relating to companies in Chap. 74) or motion (see r. 23.11 (statutory applications by motion in causes depending before the court unless otherwise provided)). This rule is subject, therefore, to other provisions in the Rules and in particular to r. 14.3 which provides for Inner House petitions.

The list in r. 14.2(a)–(g) consists mostly of the common law petitions. All statutory applications by petition are Outer House petitions unless listed in r. 14.3 as Inner House petitions: r. 14.2(h). Rule 14.2(ga) was inserted by A.S. (Rules of the Court of Session 1994 Amendment) (Miscellaneous) (No.2) 2021 [S.S.I. 2021 No. 434] to cover the increasing number of odd matters that have to be brought to the court's attention for action but are not referred to in legislation as an "application" which might be covered by r. 14.2(h). See for example, a report for possible enforcement action for obstruction or contempt under para. 4(3) of Sched. 2 to the Scottish Commission for Human Rights Act 2006 or s. 17 or 27 of the Scottish Biometrics Commissioner Act 2020.

"PRESENTED IN THE OUTER HOUSE".

14.2.2   A petition is presented by being lodged for the first order (granting warrant for all or any of service, intimation and advertisement): see r. 14.5. All petitions when presented to the court are lodged in the Petition Department: r. 3.3. The petition is given a cause reference number when presented: r. 4.1(4) and note 4.1.5.

A petition is presented when it is tendered at the Petition Dept. and lodged when it is accepted. In *Tor Corporate AS v. Simopec Group Star Petroleum Corporation Ltd* , 2008 S.C. 303 (Extra Div.) it was held that a petition is presented or lodged on the date it is accepted in the Petition Dept. (with the necessary process and fee (unless there is an account arrangement)) and not handed back or stated as not being accepted as being lodged, and not when it is later date-stamped and registered. It is important, therefore, for evidential purposes that the clerk of session at least date-stamps if not registers a petition when presented.

---

[1] As inserted by the Act of Sederunt (Rules of the Court of Session 1994 Amendment) (Miscellaneous) (No.2) 2021 (S.S.I. 2021 No. 434) art.2(2) (effective 1st January 2022).

[2] Rule 14.2(i) inserted by S.I. 1996 No. 1756 (effective 5th August 1996).

JUDICIAL FACTORS.

See Chap. 61.

14.2.3

FACTOR ON ESTATE OF PARTNERSHIP OR JOINT ADVENTURE.

As the court has a common law power to sequestrate the estate of a partnership, a judicial factor may be appointed to protect the firm's assets until the firm is dissolved (*McCulloch v. McCulloch* 1953 S.C. 189) or where there is a dispute between the partners which may materially prejudice the affairs of the partnership (*Carabine v. Carabine* 1949 S.C. 521). (Sequestration is a judicial order divesting the person sequestrated of his estate by a judicial conveyance in favour of the trustee in the sequestration.) Where such an appointment is sought a crave for sequestration should be included: *Booth v. Mackinnon* (1908) 15 S.L.T. 848. When all the partners are dead the court will appoint a factor: *Dickie v. Mitchell* (1874) 1 R. 1030, 1033 per L.P. Inglis. Where there are surviving partners but they are by fault or incapacity unfitted to carry on the partnership or to wind it up, the court will appoint a judicial factor: *Dickie*, above. There must be some compelling cause to wind up a partnership or joint adventure such as fraud, abuse of power or unreasonable delay: Bell's *Comm.*, ii,527 (McLaren's note 3); *Collins v. Young* (1853) 1 Macq. 385. A petition to dissolve a partnership under s.35 of the Partnership Act 1890 is an Outer House petition: r. 14.2(h).

Jurisdiction. The court may have jurisdiction under Sched.8 to the C.J.J.A. 1982 (jurisdiction of Scottish courts), r. 1 (domicile), r. 2(9) (moveable property) or r. 4(1) (exclusive jurisdiction); see also the 1968 and Lugano Conventions, Scheds. 1 and 3C, Arts. 2 and 16, and Sched.4 (inter-UK jurisdiction), Arts. 1, 5A and 16, in the C.J.J.A. 1982.

14.2.4

ADMINISTRATION OF TRUST OR OFFICE OF TRUSTEE.

(1) Jurisdiction.

The court has jurisdiction over Scottish trusts. For what constitutes a Scottish trust, see *Clarke's Trs., Petrs.* 1966 S.L.T. 249, 251 per L.P. Clyde. A trust may also be a trust of another legal system. Jurisdiction over a trust for certain proceedings is determined by the C.J.J.A. 1982. Under Sched.8 (jurisdiction of Scottish courts) jurisdiction depends on where the trust is domiciled, but whether another court has exclusive jurisdiction in relation to particular proceedings has to be considered: see C.J.J.A. 1982, Sched.8, r. 4; see also jurisdiction under the 1968 and Lugano Conventions in C.J.J.A. 1982, Scheds. 1 and 3C. For the purposes of Scheds. 1, 3C and 8 to the C.J.J.A. 1982 a trust is domiciled in Scotland if it has its closest and most real connection there: C.J.J.A. 1982, s.45 (as amended by the C.J.J.A. 1991, Sched.2, para. 20). Not every aspect of a trust will be determined by the domicile of the trust, but the appointment and removal of a trustee will be where the C.J.J.A. 1982 applies. Sched.8 to that Act does not determine jurisdiction where no decree is sought against a person: Sched.9, para. 13. Accordingly, where the C.J.J.A. 1982 does not apply the common law is still relevant. At common law jurisdiction is determined by the principle that every person beneficially interested ought to seek his remedy in that court in which it is most for the benefit of the trust and all concerned that the litigation should be carried on: *Orr Ewing's Trs v. Orr Ewing* (1885) 13 R.(H.L.) 1, 31 per Lord Watson. Arts 6 and 7 of the Sched. to the Recognition of Trusts Act 1987 determines the choice of law governing a trust.

The court will assist the administration of an English trust in an ancillary role: *Evans-Freke's Trs, Petrs* 1945 S.C. 382.

14.2.5

(2) Administration of trust.

See Wilson & Duncan on *Trusts, Trustees and Executors*, pp. 298–317. This does not include a petition for directions under Chap. 63, Part II, which is an Inner House petition (see r. 14.3(e)).

(3) Office of trustee.

This relates to the appointment and removal of trustees. The court has a common law power and a statutory power (ss.22 and 23 of the Trusts (Scotland) Act 1921). A person interested in the trust estate may petition. Where the ground is mental incapacity, two medical certificates (one from each of two medical practitioners following examination of the incapax dated within 30 days of the examination and one month of the presentation of the petition; the certificates do not have to be on soul and conscience: P.N. of 6th June 1968) are required as in the case of appointment of a curator bonis in similar circumstances: *Lees, Petr* (1893) 1 S.L.T. 42. If an appointment of a new trustee is of a person not resident in Scotland (see Wilson & Duncan on *Trusts, Trustees and Executors*, pp. 277–278) a bond of prorogation should be lodged: for a style, see McBryde & Dowie on *Petition Procedure*, 2nd ed., p. 164. Applications to the court under the 1921 Act are to the Lord Ordinary in the Outer House: 1921 Act, s.26. See Wilson & Duncan, pp. 270–280 and 293–297.

BREACH OF INTERDICT.

Breach of interim interdict in a depending cause is dealt with by minute in that process: C.S.A. 1988, s.47(1). In any other case it is by petition and complaint. A cause is depending until final decree, whereas a cause is in dependence until final extract. For the meaning of final decree, see note 4.15.2(2). For the meaning of final extract, see note 7.1.2(2).

14.2.6

The petition (or minute) must have the concurrence of the Lord Advocate as public prosecutor because of its quasi-criminal character: *Gribben v. Gribben* 1976 S.L.T. 266. His concurrence is written on the principal petition (or minute). It is not necessary to intimate to the Lord Advocate all adjustment or amendments to the pleadings if these are averments which are part of the same course of conduct averred: *Byrne v. Ross* 1992 S.C. 498. Proceedings for breach of interdict are civil proceedings to which s.1(1) of the Civil Evidence (Scotland) Act 1988 (rule requiring corroboration abolished) applies: *Byrne*, above.

Care must be taken to name and design the respondent correctly as a material error will invalidate the petition: *Overseas League v. Taylor* 1951 S.C. 105; cf. *Anderson v. Stoddart* 1923 S.C. 755 (immaterial error). As breach of interdict constitutes a contempt of court which might lead to punishment, it is necessary in the interests of fairness that the alleged contempt is clearly and distinctly averred, and the proceedings for contempt should be confined to the averments: *Byrne*, above.

Jurisdiction. If the court has jurisdiction to grant the interdict it will have jurisdiction to deal with a breach unless jurisdiction has been lost. The court has jurisdiction under Sched.8 of the C.J.J.A. 1982 (jurisdiction of Scottish courts), r. 1 (domicile) and r. 2(j) (interdict where wrong to be committed). See also jurisdiction under Sched. 1 (1968 Convention), Sched.3C (Lugano Convention) and Sched.4 (inter-U.K. jurisdiction), Art. 5(3) (jurisdiction in delict) and Art. 24 (protective measures), and s.24(2) (protective measures where jurisdiction doubtful) and s.27 (protective measures), and under the Brussels I Regulation, Arts.5(3) and 31.

SUPERVISORY JURISDICTION OF THE COURT.

14.2.7   This phrase is nowhere defined but describes a superintending authority over inferior jurisdictions to keep inferior jurisdictions and administrative bodies right: see *McCreadie v. Thomson* 1907 S.C. 1176, 1183 per L.J.-C. Macdonald; *Moss's Empires v. Assessor for Glasgow* 1917 S.C.(H.L.) 1, 11 per Lord Shaw of Dunfermline. This jurisdiction is now exercised on an application for judicial review by petition: see Chap. 58. It includes an application for an order for specific performance of a statutory duty under s.45(b) of the C.S.A. 1988.

SUSPENSION, SUSPENSION AND INTERDICT, SUSPENSION AND LIBERATION.

14.2.8   See Chap. 60.

RECALL OF ARRESTMENT OR INHIBITION.

14.2.9   Where the arrestment or inhibition has been executed in a depending action an application for recall may be made by motion: r. 13.10. Recall of arrestment or inhibition obtained by petition under s.28 of the Proceeds of Crime (Scotland) Act 1995 or para. 13 of Sched.4 to the Prevention of Terrorism (Temporary Provisions) Act 1989, must be made by note: rr. 76.4(1)(c) (1987 Act) and 76.22(4)(c) (1989 Act). A cause is depending until final decree, whereas a cause is in dependence until final extract. For the meaning of final decree, see note 4.15.2(2). For the meaning of final extract, see note 7.1.2(2).

On recall of arrestment and inhibition, see note 13.10.4.

PETITIONS OR APPLICATIONS UNDER THESE RULES OR ANY OTHER ENACTMENT.

14.2.10   Rule 14.2(h) is intended to catch applications to the court under primary or subordinate legislation, or the common law, whether or not specified to be by petition under the particular enactment or these Rules, except where (specified to be) an action or an application by minute (see, e.g. certain applications in family actions in Chap. 49), note (see, e.g. certain applications relating to companies in Chap. 74) or motion (see r. 23.11 (statutory applications by motion in causes depending before the court unless otherwise provided)).

It is not always clear whether a statutory application should be by petition or summons, even from the apparent distinction between a petition and a summons mentioned in note 4.1.1.

Statutory applications include: Public Order Act 1936, ss.2(3) and 8(2) (re property of an association); Fair Trading Act 1973, s.85 (re default of requirement to give evidence or produce documents to Monopolies and Mergers Commission); Building Society Act 1986, s.36A* inserted by the Building Societies Act 1997 (prohibition orders); Access to Health Records Act 1990 (re failure to comply with requirements of the Act—see r. 79.2); Law Reform (Miscellaneous Provisions) (Scotland) Act 1990, ss.17(6), 18(7) and 20(11) (re review of decisions of Conveyancing and Executry Services Board—see r. 80.2) and s.21 (in relation to Board's intervention powers—see r. 80.2); Proceeds of Crime (Scotland) Act 1995, s. 17(1) compensation to person who held realisable property); Olympics Association Right (Infringement Proceedings) Regulations 1995, reg.3 (order for delivery up of infringing goods, materials or articles) and reg.5 (order as to disposal—see r. 55.17); United Nations (International Tribunal) (Former Yugoslavia) Order 1995, reg.20 (enforcement of orders for preservation or restoration of property) and reg.21 (decision as to the ownership of property); Adults with Incapacity (Scotland) Act 2000, s.50(6) (application to determine whether treatment should be given).

Section 36A of the Building Societies Act 1986 provides for the Building Societies Commission to "certify" a contravention of a prohibition order (prohibiting an activity) to the Court of Session which the court may inquire into and deal with as if it were contempt of court. Parliament has made no attempt to explain how certification is done in the context of this court's civil procedure. It is submitted that the Commission would have to present a petition under Chap. 14 by virtue of r. 14.2(h).

Applications under s.49 of the Insurance Companies Act 1982 and ss.136 and 425 of the Companies Act 1985 were Inner House petitions. By A.S. (R.C.S.A.) (Miscellaneous) 1998 [SI 1998/890] they are Outer House petitions if presented on or after 21st April 1998. On applications under the 1982 Act, see further note 14.2.12; and on the applications under the 1985 Act, see note 14.2.13. Although there is no provision for nominating a judge to deal with such petitions, Lord Eassie has been nominated to deal with them.

Previously it was thought that declarator was not available in ordinary petition procedure, but only where expressly provided for by statute or rules, e.g. judicial review: see r. 58.13(3). In *Hooley Ltd v. Ganges Jute Private Ltd* 2019 S.C. 632 (Second Div.), where an analysis of the difference between petitions and actions, and a "definition" of what petitions are for, was made, held that a declarator could be sought in an ordinary petition where what was sought went beyond a declaration of parties' existing rights and obligations which may affect third parties not represented.

"APPLICATION TO THE COURT IN EXERCISE OF ITS PARENS PATRIAE JURISDICTION".

Such applications in the Outer House were provided for by A.S. (R.C.S.A. No. 3) (Miscellaneous) 1996 [SI 1996/1756].

14.2.11

The continuing existence of the *parens patriae* jurisdiction of the court, to grant authority for taking steps in the best interests of those incapable of giving their authority or consent for that purpose, was confirmed in *Law Hospital N.H.S. Trust v. Lord Advocate* , 1996 S.C. 301; for a review of the history of this jurisdiction, see the opinion of Lord Cullen. In exercise of this jurisdiction the court has appointed tutors-dative and recently has given them particular powers to consent to medical treatment. It is now confirmed that the jurisdiction extends to the court to authorise the discontinuation of medical treatment, at least in relation to a person in a persistent vegetative state.

(1) Tutors-dative and guardians.

In 1856, the duties previously performed by or incumbent upon the Court of Exchequer with regard to the nomination, appointment and control of tutors-dative were transferred to the Court of Session (as successor to the Court of Exchequer in exercise of the right of the Crown as *pater patriae*, Erskine, I.vii.8), involving a special procedure of summary petition to the Inner House: Exchequer Court (Scotland) Act 1856, s.19. That provision was repealed by the C.S.A. 1988, Sched.2 because it was thought the procedure was not used in practice and was superseded by the power of the court to appoint a factor *loco tutoris* by petition to the Outer House (see r. 14.2(a)). Such a factor, however, has no authority over the person of his ward (unlike a tutor-dative). The appointment of tutors-dative to pupil children was effectively rendered obsolete by the Age of Legal Capacity (Scotland) Act 1991: see note 61.1.2(4). The appointment of tutors-dative to adults who are mentally *incapax* is noted in two articles in the *Scots Law Times* (referring to a number of recent unreported cases): see *"Revival of Tutors-Dative"* 1987 S.L.T.(News) 69, and *"Tutors to Adults Development"* 1992 S.L.T.(News) 325. With the repeal of s.19 of the 1856 Act, such an appointment was thought to be incompetent because Parliament repealed that section in the belief that it was a substantive provision which had fallen into desuetude. Ironically, by the time the recommendation of the Scottish Law Commission had been enacted (indeed before its report) the appointment of tutors-dative to mentally incapacitated adults had, as disclosed by the above articles, revived. Fortunately in *Law Hospital N.H.S. Trust*, above, it was authoritatively expressed that s.19 of the 1856 Act was only a procedural provision and the power of the Court of Exchequer to make such appointments in exercise of its parens patriae jurisdiction remains and was transferred to the Court of Session by the unrepealed s.1 of that Act.

On such appointments, see the cases cited in the articles in the *Scots Law Times* mentioned above. For a recent example of a tutor-dative appointed with power to consent to medical treatment on his ward's behalf, see *L v. L's curator ad litem* , 1997 S.L.T. 167 and *Britton v. Britton's Curator Bonis* 1996 S.C. 178. For the distinction between a tutor-at-law and a tutor-dative, see Stair I.vi.25.

The position of a tutor dative is gratuitous: *AB v. CD* (1890) 18 R. 90, 97. A tutor dative will be appointed only where it is necessary for decisions to be taken about a person's personal welfare: *Chapman, Petrs* 1993 S.L.T. 955. A tutor dative may be appointed in respect of the ward's person and a curator *bonis* appointed in respect of the ward's estate: *Dickie v. Douglas* 1924 S.L.T. 578. Although in the majority of cases in which the appointment of a tutor dative is sought the only powers applied for will be concerned with the personal welfare of the ward, a tutor dative may be given powers with respect to the ward's estate such as power to make certain decisions or claims which may affect the amount of the ward's estate or the way in which it is administered. Where powers are sought only in relation to the ward's welfare, and not in relation to or such as to affect the administration of the ward's estate, there is no need for the petition to be intimated to the Accountant of Court. Where powers are sought which relate to any part of the ward's estate or to the making of any claim or the taking of any decision which will or may affect the amount of the ward's estate or the manner in which or purposes for which any part of it is administered or expended, intimation to the Accountant of Court will be required. In such a case the court will have to consider whether the tutor dative should be required to find caution. All petitions for the appointment of a tutor dative require to be served on the Mental Welfare Commission: P.N. No. 11 of 1994.

As from 1st April 2002 it is not competent to appoint a tutor-dative to a person aged 16 or over: Adults with Incapacity (Scotland) Act 2000, s.80. A guardian will have to be appointed under s.57 of the 2000 Act. A person who has been appointed a tutor-dative to an adult becomes a guardian under the 2000 Act with the powers he had as a tutor-dative: 2000 Act, Sched.4, para. 1(4). The guardian would have the power to apply to the court to withdraw medical treatment as his legal representative.

(2) Petitions to withdraw medical treatment.

In *Law Hospital N.H.S. Trust*, above, it was held that the court would authorise the withdrawal of treatment where a person is in a persistent vegetative state. The procedure to be followed in such an application was set out in the opinion of L.P. Hope and is as follows:

(a) All such application should be made by petition presented to the Outer House in the same way as if they were applications to which rule 14.2 apply: see now r. 14.2(i).

(b) The application may be presented by the area health authority or N.H.S. trust in whose care the patient is for the time being, or by any relative of the patient within the meaning of Sched. 1 of the Damages (Scotland) Act 1976.

(c) The application should be for the court to authorise the treatment or the withdrawal of treatment from the patient as the case may be.

(d) The proposed treatment or withdrawal of treatment should be specified in a statement of facts and in the prayer setting out the order which is being sought.

(e) The petition should be served on the Lord Advocate for the public interest, and it should also be served on the relevant area health authority or N.H.S. trust and on the relatives of the patient unless these parties are already petitioners.

(f) There should be lodged with the petition as productions at least two medical reports on the patient's condition, describing the treatment which it is proposed to carry out or to discontinue and, if treatment is to be discontinued, the steps which will be taken to allow the patient to die peacefully and with dignity.

(g) In view of the advice given in the B.M.A. Guidelines on Treatment Decisions for Patients in Persistent Vegetative State (July 1993) that life-prolonging treatment should continue until the patient has been insentient for at least twelve months, the statement of facts should include a narrative as to when the persistent vegetative state was first diagnosed and for how long life-prolonging treatment has been continued since that date.

(h) If the view of the patient about the giving of treatment or the discontinuing of treatment have previously been expressed in writing or otherwise, the statement of facts should include averments about the views which the patient has expressed.

(i) The court should be asked, in the prayer of the petition, to appoint a curator *ad litem* to the patient so that the application may be considered separately on behalf of the patient and the curator's views made known to the court after such inquiry as the curator may consider appropriate in the circumstances.

(j) Intimation on the walls of the court will be dispensed with and any proof or other hearing will be conducted in chambers, unless the public interest otherwise requires: see now . 14.7(3).

APPLICATIONS UNDER S.49 OF THE INSURANCE COMPANIES ACT 1982.

14.2.12

Formerly there had been doubt whether a petition under this provision was appropriately an Inner or Outer House petition. That doubt was settled in the R.C.S. 1994 as originally enacted which made it an Inner House petition. By A.S. (R.C.S.A.) (Miscellaneous) 1998 [S.I. 1998 No. 890] such a petition is now presented to the Outer House.

Section 49 of the 1982 Act provides for the court sanctioning a scheme transferring long term business from one insurance company to another and is useful where the transferor is in difficulty (thus avoiding liquidation).

The petition must be (i) accompanied by a report by an actuary (s.49(2)), (ii) served on the Secretary of State (Trade and Industry) (s.49(3)(c)) and (iii) open for inspection at the company's offices (s.49(3)(d)). A notice must be inserted in the London, Edinburgh and Belfast Gazettes and two national newspapers: s.49(3)(a). A statement will have to be sent to every policyholder unless the court otherwise directs (s.49(3)(b)); and the court may so direct if there has already been a statement or something similar or a meeting to consider the proposal. The minimum period of notice of the petition is 21 days: effect of s.49(3)(c) and (d).

Jurisdiction. The court has jurisdiction if either the transferor or transferee company has its registered office in Scotland or if both have: s.49(8). This is consistent with the C.J.J.A. 1982.

APPLICATIONS UNDER SS.136 AND 425 OF THE COMPANIES ACT 1985, NOW SS.645 AND 899 OF THE COMPANIES ACT 2006.

14.2.13

Jurisdiction. The court of the country which has jurisdiction to wind up the company—i.e. the court of the country in which the company is registered—has jurisdiction: Companies Act 1985, s.744 and Insolvency Act 1986, s.120. Jurisdiction under the C.J.J.A. 1982 is excluded: C.J.J.A. 1982, Scheds 1 and 3C, Art.1, Sched. 5, para. 1 and Sched. 9, para. 4.

(1) Reduction of capital:

Companies Act 2006, s.645, formerly Companies Act 1985, s.136. Whether a company can apply for confirmation of a special resolution to reduce capital is determined by s.135(1) of the 1985 Act; there must be a power in the Articles. A special resolution requires not less than 21 days' notice, which does not mean, unless the Articles say so (see Companies (Tables A to F) Regulations 1985 [S.I. 1985 No. 805], Table A, reg. 38), 21 clear days: *Neil McLeod & Sons Ltd, Petrs* 1967 S.C. 16 (i.e. the day the notice is served is not, but the last day is, included in the calculation). Any provisions for a quorum at a meeting must be complied with (*Neil McLeod & Sons Ltd*, above) and the procedure laid down for it followed and minuted: *Citizens Theatre Ltd, Petrs* 1946 S.C. 14; *Fraserburgh Commercial Co. Ltd, Petrs* 1946 S.C. 444. The special resolution must be registered with the Registrar of Companies within 15 days: 1985 Act, s.380(1).

There should be produced with the petition (a) a draft minute of reduction for approval by the court (1985 Act, s.138(1)) which, with the order of the court, is registered (s.138(4)); (b) a copy of the Memorandum and Articles; (c) a certified copy of the notice calling the meeting to consider the special resolution; (d) a certified copy of the minute of that meeting; (e) the receipt of the Registrar of Companies of the registering of the resolution; and (f) a certified copy of the latest annual report and accounts.

The first order under r. 14.5 will include a requirement to advertise in the *Edinburgh Gazette* and appropriate newspapers (for which there should be craves in the prayer). Normally there will be no one on whom to serve the petition. After expiry of the period of notice a motion should be enrolled to remit to a reporter and if necessary to dispense *in hoc statu* with the requirements of s.136(3)–(5) of the 1985 Act (objections by and lists of creditors, etc.). Any objections will be postponed until after the report of the reporter. It is the invariable practice to remit to a reporter (usually one of two solicitors nominated by the Lord President): *Scottish Stamping and Engineering Co. Ltd, Petrs* 1928 S.C. 484; *J. Hay & Sons Ltd, Petrs* 1928 S.C. 622. The petitioner is responsible for lodging four copies of the report in process for the hearing to approve the report: r. 4.7(2) (lodging of documents in Inner House). If there are no objections by creditors the petitioner may enrol for approval of the report and if necessary for a direction that s.136(3)–(5) of the 1985 Act does not apply and to grant the prayer of the petition. It there are objections a hearing will be required on the Summary Roll. The court can dispense with a list of creditors entitled to object in certain circumstances: 1985 Act, s.136(6). In considering whether to dispense with the list the question is whether the interests of creditors are prejudiced: *Anderson, Brown & Co. Ltd, Petrs,* 1965 S.C. 81; *Martin Currie Ltd, Ptnrs,* 2008 S.L.T. 57, 59 para.[10] (whether there is a significant risk of prejudice in that debts may not be paid in ordinary course). It has been the practice of the court to disapply the requirement for a list of creditors on obtaining satisfactory assurances that their interests have been protected: *Royal Scottish Assurance Plc, Ptnr,* 2011 S.L.T. 264, 267 para.[8]. On the forms of assurance, see *uayle Munro Ltd, Ptnr,* 1992 S.C. 24 (undertaking); *Martin Currie Ltd, Ptnr,* above (book value of subsidiaries). If a list is required, motions are required to fix a date for the list to be made up and lodged and for the list to be advertised in the Gazette and appropriate newspapers with a date by which creditors not listed can claim to be put on the list or be excluded.

In confirming the reduction the court has to consider the interests of creditors, shareholders and the public: (1985 Act, s.137(1); *Westburn Sugar Refineries Ltd, Petrs,* 1951 S.C.(H.L.) 57) and whether the reduction is fair and equitable between different classes of shareholders (*Wilsons and Clyde Coal Co Ltd v Scottish Insurance Corporation Ltd,* 1949 S.C.(H.L.) 90).

Before a creditor can object to a reduction of capital, he must show that "there is a real likelihood that the reduction would result in the company being unable to discharge his debt or claim when it fell due": 2006 Act s.646(1)(b). On "real likelihood", see *Sportech Plc, Ptnr,* 2012 S.L.T. 895 (OH) adopting the approach of Norris, J., in *Re Liberty International Plc* [2010] 2 B.C.L.C. 665.

Where the petition is combined with a scheme of arrangement the procedure is modified: *Wilson Brothers and D.G. Howat & Co. Ltd, Petrs,* 1939 S.L.T. 68.

(2) Compromise or scheme of arrangement:

Companies Act 2006, s.899, formerly Companies Act 1985, s.425. This provision provides for a compromise or arrangement between a company and its creditors or members. "Compromise" means settlement of a claim where there is a dispute: Stair, I.xvii.2: but it may be more broadly interpreted: see *City of Glasgow Bank v. Geddes' Trs* (1880) 7 R. 731. In England there must be some dispute about rights: *Sneath v. Valley Gold Ltd* [1893] 1 Ch. 477. In relation to arrangement, there must be an element of give and take: *Re N.F.U. Development Trust Ltd* [1972] 1 W.L.R. 1548; *Re Savoy Hotel Ltd* [1981] Ch. 351. The section is interpreted broadly: *Singer Manufacturing Co v Robinow,* 1971 S.C. 11, 13–14 per L.P. Clyde.

The petition should include a crave for class meetings of classes of shareholders whose interests are affected by the scheme but not a general meeting of all members of the company as the company has power to do that: *Cayzer Irvine & Co. Ltd, Petrs,* 1963 S.L.T. 94. Notice of the scheme is given by advertisements in newspapers. After the meetings, a motion may be enrolled for sanction of the scheme. Before doing so the court will have to be satisfied that (a) the statutory provisions have been complied with, (b) those who attended the class meetings were fairly representative of the class, (c) the arrangement is such that a man of business would reasonably approve, (d) the majority has been acting bona fide and (e) the minority has not been overridden by the majority: *Edinburgh American Land Mortgage Co. Ltd v. Lang's Trs* (1909) S.C. 488; *Shandon Hydropathic Co Ltd, Petrs,* 1911 S.C. 1153, 1155 per L.P. Dunedin; *Re Anglo-Continental Supply Co Ltd* [1922] 2 Ch. 723, 736 per Astbury J.

Applications for the sanction of a solvent scheme are in principle to be dealt with in the same way as those where the company is insolvent or on the verge of insolvency: *Scottish Lion Insurance Co Ltd v Goodrich Corporation,* 2010 S.C. 349 (First Div.).

APPLICATIONS UNDER S.266 TO RAISE DERIVATIVE PROCEEDINGS UNDER S.265 OF THE COMPANIES ACT 2006.

This replaces and replicates the common law right of a member of a company to recover a loss suffered by the company (see *Anderson v. Hogg* , 2000 S.L.T. 634 (OH) and 2002 S.L.T. 354 (Extra Div.); *Wilson v. Inverness Retail and Business Park Ltd* , 2003 S.L.T. 301 (OH)) but now requires leave to be

14.2.14

sought from the court to do so. Circumstances for the refusing or granting of leave are set out in s.268. These provisions were considered in *Wishart v. Castlecroft Securities Ltd* , 2010 S.C. 16 (Extra Div.). The purpose of ss. 265 and 266 of the Companies Act 2006 was to sweep away uncertainties surrounding the circumstances in which derivative actions could be brought including those arising from the rule in *Foss v. Harbottle* and there was no basis for applying a test of exceptionality: *ICU (Europe) Ltd v. Ibrahim*, 2016 S.L.T. 1182 (Second Div.).

Applications by petition in the Inner House

14.3

14.3. Any of the following applications shall be made by petition presented in the Inner House:—

(a) a petition and complaint other than for breach of interdict;

(b) an application under any enactment relating to solicitors or notaries public;

(c) an application which is, by virtue of these Rules or any other enactment, to be by petition and is incidental to a cause depending before the Inner House;

(d) an application to the *nobile officium* of the court other than an application mentioned in rule 14.2(c) (applications relating to the administration of a trust, the office of trustee or a public trust);

(e) a petition by trustees for directions under Part II of Chapter 63;

(f) an application under section 1 of the Evidence (Proceedings in Other Jurisdictions) Act 1975 (assistance in obtaining evidence for civil proceedings in another jurisdiction);

(g) an application under section 1 of the Trusts (Scotland) Act 1961 (variation or revocation of trusts);

(h) *[Revoked by S.I. 1998 No. 890 (effective 21st April 1998).]*

(i) *[Revoked by S.I. 1998 No. 890 (effective 21st April 1998).]*

(j) an application under section 17(6), 18(7), 20(7), 20(11)(b), 21(5), 21(7) or 21(10) of, or under paragraph 20 of Schedule 1 to, the Law Reform (Miscellaneous Provisions) (Scotland) Act 1990 (orders in relation to conveyancing or executory practitioners); and

(k) an application required to be made to the Inner House under any enactment.

Deriv. RCS 1965, r. 190 (preamble) (amended by S.I. 1970 No. 134), (i) (amended by S.I. 1980 No. 1144), (iv) (amended by S.I. 1992 No. 1422), (vi) (amended by S.I. 1976 No. 283 and 1987 No. 1206), (vii) (amended by S.I. 1976 No. 283 and 1977 No. 1621), (viii)–(x) substituted by S.I. 1987 No. 1206, and (xi) (inserted by S.I. 1992 No. 1422), (r. 14.3(a) to (j))

GENERAL NOTE.

14.3.1

The number of petitions reserved to the Inner House has in recent years been reduced.

"PRESENTED IN THE INNER HOUSE".

14.3.2

A petition is presented by being lodged for the first order (granting warrant for all or any of service, intimation and advertisement): see r. 14.5. All petitions when presented to the court are lodged in the Petition Department: r. 3.3. The petition is given a cause reference number when presented: r. 4.1(4) and note 4.1.5.

A petition is presented when it is tendered at the Petition Dept and lodged when it is accepted. In *Tor Corporate AS v. Simopec Group Star Petroleum Corporation Ltd* , 2008 S.C. 303 (Extra Div.) it was held that a petition is presented or lodged on the date it is accepted in the Petition Dept. (with the necessary process and fee (unless there is an account arrangement)) and not handed back or stated as not being accepted as being lodged, and not when it is later date-stamped and registered. It is important, therefore, for evidential purposes that the clerk of session at least date-stamps if not registers a petition when presented.

PETITION AND COMPLAINT OTHER THAN FOR BREACH OF INTERDICT.

14.3.3

Such a petition is rare. The jurisdiction covers malversation, misconduct and gross neglect of inferior judges (other than sheriffs) and officers of court, the purpose of the petition being removal from office or the imposition of a penalty. Much may now be done by judicial review of the decision made by the inferior judge or officer of court. Otherwise these cases may be covered by statutory employment law rules.

The procedure is similar to a petition and complaint for breach of interdict: see note 14.2.6. Being of a quasi-criminal character, the petition requires the concurrence of the Lord Advocate.

SOLICITORS AND NOTARIES.

See Chap. 68.   **14.3.4**

NOBILE OFFICIUM OTHER THAN ADMINISTRATION OF TRUSTS AND TRUSTEES.

The *nobile officium* is an extraordinary equitable jurisdiction of the court to exercise jurisdiction in   **14.3.5**
circumstances which would not be justified except by the necessity of intervening in the interests of
justice; and although the court tends to limit the exercise of its jurisdiction to cases in which the power
has already been exercised, it is neither possible nor desirable to define all the circumstances in which
resort may be had to it: *Royal Bank of Scotland plc v. Gillies* 1987 S.L.T. 54, 551 per L.J.-C. Ross. It does
not exist to deal with matters of disputed right; its chief object is to provide a means of rectifying obvious
errors or omissions, principally of an administrative character, which cannot be dealt with in any other
way: *London and Clydeside Estates Ltd v. Aberdeen D. C.* 1980 S.C.(H.L.) 1, 45 per Lord Keith of
Kinkel. "The jurisdiction associated with the *nobile officium* in this court gives us a right to come to the
assistance of the petitioners where no other remedy is available": *Glasgow Magdalene Institution, Petrs*
1964 S.C. 227, 229 per L.P. Clyde. It is reserved for cases of necessity or very strong expediency where
the ordinary procedure would provide no remedy: *Gibson's Trs* 1933 S.C. 190, 205 per L.J.-C. Alness. It
may be used to meet a casus improvisus in a statute: *Skinner, Petr* 1976 S.L.T. 60; *Sloan, Petr* 1991 S.C.
281. It cannot be used to extend or derogate from the scope of a statute (*Smart v. Registrar General for
Scotland* 1951 S.C. 81, 85 per L.J.-C. Thomson); to supplement a statutory procedure which would in effect be an amendment of the statute (*Maitland, Petr* 1961 S.C. 291, 293 per L.P. Clyde); or to conflict
with or defeat a statutory intention express or implied (*R., Petr* 1993 S.L.T. 910, 912 per L.P. Hope; a rehearing of a referral under s.42 of the Social Work (Scotland) Act 1968 where the circumstances were
unforeseen was not expressly or impliedly excluded by statute (*L., Petr (No. 1)* 1993 S.L.T. 1310 and *L.,
Petr (No. 2)* 1993 S.L.T. 1342). It cannot be invoked where the law already provides a remedy: *Central
Motor Engineering Co. v. Gibbs* 1917 S.C. 490, 493 per Lord Skerrington. See also Stair, IV.iii.1 and
Erskine, I.iii.22.

Jurisdiction. Nothing in Sched. 8 to the C.J.J.A. 1982 affects the jurisdiction of the court in exercise of
its nobile officium: C.J.J.A. 1982, s.22(3).

PETITIONS BY TRUSTEES FOR DIRECTIONS.

See Chap. 63, Pt II.   **14.3.6**

APPLICATIONS UNDER S.L OF THE EVIDENCE (PROCEEDINGS IN OTHER JURISDICTIONS) ACT 1975.

See Chap. 66.   **14.3.7**

APPLICATIONS UNDER S.L OF THE TRUSTS (SCOTLAND) ACT 1961.

See Chap. 63, Pt I.   **14.3.8**

APPLICATIONS UNDER S.49 OF THE INSURANCE COMPANIES ACT 1982.

Formerly there had been doubt whether a petition under this provision was appropriately an Inner or   **14.3.9**
Outer House petition. That doubt was settled by this rule, by which paragraph (h) made it an Inner House
petition. But A.S. (R.C.S.A.) (Miscellaneous) 1998 [S.I. 1998 No. 890] transferred such applications to
the Outer House. This does not apply to a petition presented before 21st April 1998. See further, note
14.2.12.

APPLICATIONS UNDER SS.136 AND 425 OF THE COMPANIES ACT 1985.

By A.S. (R.C.S.A.) (Miscellaneous) 1998 [S.I. 1998 No. 890] these applications have been transferred   **14.3.10**
to the Outer House. This does not apply to a petition presented before 21st April 1998. See further, note
14.2.13.

CONVEYANCING AND EXECUTRY PRACTITIONERS.

For applications in relation to conveyancing and executry practitioners under the Law Reform (Miscel-   **14.3.11**
laneous Provisions) (Scotland) Act 1990, see Chap. 81.

APPLICATIONS TO INNER HOUSE UNDER ANY OTHER ENACTMENT.

R. 14.3(k) is a new provision and refers to any statute or statutory instrument. Another enactment may   **14.3.12**
provide expressly for a petition to be presented to the Inner House.

For example, an application to prevent vexatious legal proceedings must be made to the Inner House:
Vexatious Actions (Scotland) Act 1898. The application is made by the Lord Advocate who has to satisfy
the court that the respondent has habitually and persistently instituted vexatious legal proceedings without
any reasonable ground for instituting them whether in the Court of Session or any inferior court. The Act
was introduced to deal with such vexatious litigations which can obviously be oppressive and unfair to
defenders: *Lord Advocate v. Rizza* 1962 S.L.T.(Notes) 8. An order under the Act is not compatible with
Art. 6 of the ECHR: *Lord Advocate v. Bell* , 23rd March 2001 (IH), unreported. Whether a person is vexatious does not depend simply on the number of actions he has raised, it includes the manner in which he
has conducted himself in the legal process, the taking of a succession of hopeless appeals and abuse of
process: *Lord Advocate v. Cooney* 1984 S.L.T. 434; see also *Lord Advocate v B,* 2012 S.L.T. 121 (OH).
Where an order has been granted, leave must be obtained from the Lord Ordinary to pursue any cause in

the Court of Session or an inferior court. The application is made by presenting the proposed writ to the Deputy Principal Clerk who puts it before the Lord Ordinary in chambers. The decision of the Lord Ordinary is sent by letter to the applicant. A decision of the Lord Ordinary to refuse leave is final: Vexatious Actions (Scotland) Act 1898, s.1A (inserted by the Law Reform (Miscellaneous Provisions) (Scotland) Act 1980, s.19). A process is not required: see r. 4.3 (lodging of processes). It may be necessary to combine such an application with an application for leave to proceed in a petition without counsel or other person having a right of audience, or an agent, having signed the petition: see note 4.2.8.

Form of petitions

14.4

14.4.—(1) A petition shall be in Form 14.4.

(2) A petition shall include—

  (a) a statement of facts in numbered paragraphs setting out the facts and circumstances on which the petition is founded;

  (b) a prayer setting out the orders sought; and

  (c)[1] the name, designation and address of the petitioner and a statement of any special capacity in which the petitioner is presenting the petition.

(3) In a petition presented under an enactment, the statement of facts shall expressly refer to the relevant provision under the authority of which the petition is presented.

(4) Where a petition is one to which the Civil Jurisdiction and Judgments Act 1982 applies, the statement of facts shall include averments stating—

  (a) the ground of jurisdiction of the court, unless jurisdiction would arise only if the respondent prorogated the jurisdiction of the court without contesting jurisdiction;

  (b) unless the court has exclusive jurisdiction, whether or not there is an agreement prorogating the jurisdiction of a court in another country; and

  (c) whether or not there are proceedings involving the same cause of action in subsistence between the parties in a country to which the convention in Schedule 1 or 3C to that Act applies and the date any such proceedings commenced.

(5) The prayer of a petition shall crave warrant for such intimation, service and advertisement as may be necessary having regard to the nature of the petition, or as the petitioner may seek; and the name, address and capacity of each person on whom service of the petition is sought shall be set out in a schedule annexed to, and referred to in, the prayer of the petition.

(6) Where it is sought in a petition—

  (a) to dispense with intimation, service or advertisement, or

  (b) to shorten or extend the period of notice,

the appropriate order shall be craved in the prayer, and the grounds on which the order is sought shall be set out in the statement of facts.

Deriv. R.C.S. 1965, r. 191 amended by SI 1987/1206

GENERAL NOTE.

14.4.1

A petition consists of (1) the Address, (2) a statement of facts, (3) the prayer, (4) a schedule for service and, where necessary, (5) an appendix containing any scheme or document requiring approval by the court. An Inner House petition should be marked "Inner House" on the backing.

A petition must, unless otherwise provided, be on the official printed form in Form 14.4 approved by the court: r. 4.1(1); and see notes 4.1.1 and 4.1.3.

THE ADDRESS.

14.4.2

Petitions are addressed "Unto the Right Honourable the Lords of Council and Session". The name, designation and address of the petitioner must be correctly stated: *Maccallum, Petrs.* (1883) 11 R. 60. The better practice is to state full names, but this is not essential. The capacity in which the petitioner presents the petition must be stated: this often identifies the subject-matter of the petition, e.g. as where the petitioner is a trustee; this is particularly important because petitions are kept in the Petition Depart-

---

[1] R. 14.4(2)(c) inserted by S.S.I. 2008 No. 349 (effective 1st December 2008).

ment alphabetically within the categories under which petitions are filed (see note 4.1.5) according to the subject-matter (though recorded chronologically in the Petition Register)—e.g. the name of the trust, truster, incapax or company. Any special capacity must be stated: r. 13.2(4)(e); the express provision in the Rules was probably inspired by *Royal Insurance (UK) Ltd v. AMEC Construction Scotland Ltd* , 2008 S.C. 201 (O.H.), in which Lord Emslie at p. 216, para. [21] reaffirmed the requirement for proper disclosure in the instance of any special capacity in which a party sues or is sued. The practice of stating the occupation of the petitioner (other than a professional one) has generally died out and is not essential. The current address must be given. Where there has been a recent change of address there is a convenient practice to state the former address also; but a last known address alone where the current address is not known will not be sufficient for service (note repeal of s.3 of the Citation Amendment (Scotland) Act 1882 by the A.S. (R.C.S. 1994) 1994, Sched.4) and the rules for service where the address is not known must be followed (see r. 16.5).

It is not usual to name a respondent in the Address, as he is specified in the schedule for service, except (but it is not essential) in petitions where an order is sought against or in relation to a particular person, e.g. suspension and interdict and breach of interdict.

There should then follow a brief description of the general nature of the petition, e.g. "for appointment of a judicial factor".

STATEMENT OF FACTS.

This is the narrative, preceded by the words "Humbly sheweth", in numbered paragraphs (each **14.4.3** properly beginning with "That") setting out the facts, circumstances and grounds on which the petition is based. The first paragraph usually should identify the petitioner and the capacity in which he petitions. Where there has been a previous petition in relation to the same subject-matter reference should be made to it. One paragraph should refer to the persons to be served with the petition and the schedule for service. A paragraph should state the ground of jurisdiction where the C.J.J.A. 1982 applies: r. 14.4(4); and see further note 14.4.4. A paragraph (usually the last) specifies whether the petition is presented at common law or under statute (in which case the statutory provision must be stated: r. 14.4(3)). Paragraphs should be as short and concise as possible: different facts or events should be stated in separate paragraphs.

JURISDICTION.

Formerly the ground of jurisdiction always had to be specified; now it is only required where the **14.4.4** C.J.J.A. 1982 applies. Sched.8 to the C.J.J.A. 1982 contains the general grounds of jurisdiction of the court: C.J.J.A. 1982, s.20. Sched.8 does not apply to (a) proceedings subject to the jurisdictional rules in the 1968 (or Brussels) Convention on jurisdiction and enforcement in civil and commercial matters between the Member States of the European Community, or the similar Lugano (or "Parallel") Convention between the EC Member States and Member States of the European Free Trade Association which ratify it (and any other State which accedes to it), in Scheds. 1 and 3C respectively to the 1982 Act (C.J.J.A. 1982, s.20(1)), (b) proceedings subject to the jurisdictional rules in Sched.4 to the C.J.J.A. 1982 which determines the allocation of jurisdiction between the different courts of the UK (C.J.J.A. 1982 s.20(1)), (c) proceedings in respect of which any other enactment confers jurisdiction (C.J.J.A. s.21(1)(a)) and (d) proceedings listed in Sched.9 as proceedings excluded from Sched.8 (C.J.J.A. 1982, s.21(1)(b)). Sched.9 excludes, e.g. proceedings regulating the custody of children, in respect of sequestration in bankruptcy, the winding up of a company, judicial arrangements or compositions with creditors, proceedings not in substance proceedings in which a decree against any person is sought, and proceedings in pursuance of a convention which in relation to particular matters govern jurisdiction other than the 1968 Convention. The C.J.J.A. 1982 will apply, therefore, where jurisdiction depends on Scheds. 1, 3C, 4 or 8. On jurisdiction, see further notes 13.2.6 (domicile) and 13.2.7 to 13.2.12 (grounds of jurisdiction).

R. 14.4(4)(a) assumes the respondent will only prorogate jurisdiction when he lodges answers and does not contest jurisdiction. But he might prorogate jurisdiction in advance, in which case the ground of jurisdiction can (and must) be averred.

"AGREEMENT PROROGATING JURISDICTION OF A COURT".

See note 13.2.14 on this subject in relation to actions. **14.4.5**

"PROCEEDINGS INVOLVING THE SAME CAUSE OF ACTION".

See note 13.2.15 on this subject in relation to actions. The word "action" is not a term of art in the **14.4.6** Conventions and will apply also to proceedings by petition. As the court has to examine jurisdiction itself (and particularly if it is sought to have the prayer granted without any respondent lodging answers), the court must know (*ex facie* of the petition) whether it has jurisdiction.

PLEAS-IN-LAW.

It is not necessary to insert pleas-in-law in a petition unless answers are lodged by a respondent op- **14.4.7** posing the grant of the prayer. A practice has grown up of including pleas-in-law in a petition, when it is drawn, in petitions for suspension and interdict and the like, no doubt because it is expected that the respondent will appear to oppose the petition.

THE PRAYER.

The prayer of the petition consists of a series of craves setting out all the orders to be sought in the **14.4.8** order in which they are sought.

The first order is for intimation, service and advertisement: see r. 14.4(5). (1) Intimation. In a petition this usually means intimation on the walls of the court: see r. 14.7(1) and note 14.7.1. (2) Service on all persons having an interest (and specified in the schedule for service: r. 14.4(5)) has to be made and may include service by advertisement where a person's address is not known (see r. 14.7(2)). On service, see Chap. 16, Pt. I. (3) Advertisement. Certain petitions require public notice in one or more of the London, Edinburgh and Belfast Gazettes and national or local newspapers. Where it is sought to dispense with intimation, service or advertisement or to shorten or extend the period of notice this must be craved and the grounds stated in the statement of facts: r. 14.4(5). The prayer craves interested persons (whether the petition was served on them or not) to lodge answers, if so advised, within the period of notice: r. 14.6(1).

There will be a crave for the orders sought whether the petition has been presented whether or not answers have been lodged and after any inquiry or remit to a reporter the court may order. The prayer concludes with a crave "to do further or otherwise in the premises as to your Lordships shall seem proper" which permits the court to make orders not sought in the prayer: see, e.g. *Davidson v. Bogle & Co.* (1837) 15 S. 421. There are limits as to what the court can do where notice of such an order has not been given. There then follow before the signature of the person signing the petition the words "According to justice, etc." which is a short form of a longer historical text.

THE SCHEDULE.

14.4.9   The schedule specifies the persons to be served with the petition. It should also include anyone to whom the petition is to be intimated. The names and addresses must be accurate as a substantial error will invalidate the cause: *Overseas League v. Taylor* 1951 S.C. 105, 107 per L.J.-C. Thomson.

SIGNING OF PETITION.

14.4.10   The petition must be signed. On who should sign, see r. 4.2 and notes. It was stated in *Marshall & Others, Petrs.* 1938 S.N. 18 that an appendix containing any facts which would normally form part of the petition and any scheme should also be signed; but this rule has not been followed for many years.

"INTIMATION".

14.4.11   See note 14.7.1(1).

"SERVICE".

14.4.12   For methods, see Chap. 16, Pt I.

"ADVERTISEMENT".

14.4.13   See note 14.7.1(2).

UNITS OF MEASUREMENT.

14.4.14   The Units of Measurement Directive (Council Directive 80/181 of 20th 14. December 1979) was adopted by the E.C. in 1989 [Official Journal, 7th December 1989, L357/28]. From 1st January 1995 member states must use the metric system of measurement and, subject to certain transitional arrangements and exceptions, must cease to use imperial measurements for economic, public health, public safety and administrative purposes. Where a unit of measurement is used in pleadings it should be expressed as a metric unit, and court orders must be so expressed.

Exceptions are as follows: The nautical mile and knot are to be used for sea and air traffic and the foot is to be used for aircraft heights. Until 31st December 1999, fathom may be used for marine navigation; therm for gas supply; pint and fluid ounce for beer, cider, waters, lemonade and fruit juices on returnable containers; and ounce and pound for goods sold loose from bulk. In perpetuity, acre may be used for land registration; troy ounce for transactions in precious metals; mile, yard, foot and inch for road traffic signs, distances and speed measurements; pint for draught beer, cider and milk in returnable containers.

First order in petitions

14.5   **14.5.—(1)[1]** Subject to paragraph (2), on a petition being lodged, the court shall, without a motion being enrolled for that purpose, pronounce an interlocutor for such intimation, service and advertisement as may be necessary.

(2) Where a petitioner seeks—

(a)   to dispense with intimation, service or advertisement on any person, or

(b)   any interim order,

he shall apply by motion for such order as appears appropriate.

(3) On disposing of a motion under paragraph (2), the court shall make such order as it thinks fit.

Deriv. R.C.S. 1965, r. 195(a) (part)

---

[1] R. 14.5(1) substituted by S.I. 1996 No. 2168 (effective 23rd September 1996).

GENERAL NOTE.

The first order (often called the first deliverance) is for intimation, service and any advertisement or interim order.

14.5.1

Formerly, during term a petition appeared in the rolls (motion roll or single bills) for a first order. The A.S. (R.C.S.A. No. 4) (Miscellaneous) 1996 [SI 1996/2168] abolished this requirement following a recommendation of the Cullen *Review of Outer House Business* in December 1995. Now, whether a petition is lodged in or out of a term, it will not appear in the rolls for a first order.

In certain petitions there is no first order, other provisions apply and this rule is disapplied. These are: petitions for judicial review (r. 58.2), applications for recognition and enforcement of foreign judgments (r. 62.2), applications under the Evidence (Proceedings in Other Jurisdictions) Act 1975 (r. 66.2), adoption petitions (r. 67.2), causes under the Proceeds of Crime (Scotland) Act 1995 (r. 76.2), causes under the Prevention of Terrorism (Temporary Provisions) Act 1989 and the Enforcement of External Orders Order of 1995 under the Act (r. 76.20), summary trials (r. 77.2) and applications for parental orders under the Human Fertilisation and Embryology Act 1990 (r. 81.2).

"ON A PETITION BEING LODGED".

A petition is lodged in the Petition Department: r. 3.3(2). A process must be lodged with it: rr. 4.3 and 4.4. In Inner House petitions six copies of the petition must be lodged in addition to the principal: r. 4.7(1) and note 14.7.1. In Outer House petitions, although there is no rule to this effect, one copy of the petition must be handed to the clerk of session at the department's public counter for the Advocates' Library (see P.N. No. 2 of 1988).

14.5.2

On being lodged the petition is assigned a cause reference number: see r. 4.1 (4) and note 4.1.5.

A petition may be lodged in person in the Petition Department, or by post by a Court of Session account holder (see note 14.5.11) or if accompanied by a cheque (P.N. No. 4 of 1994, paras 1 and 2). Where lodged by post it should be accompanied by the motion in Form 23.2 for the first order: P.N. No. 4 of 1994, para. 6(1). Where an interlocutor for intimation and service is pronounced, a copy of it will be sent by post to the petitioner: P.N. No. 4 of 1994, para. 6(2).

A fee is payable on lodging a petition: see note 14.5.11.

DOCUMENTS FOUNDED ON OR ADOPTED.

Any document founded on or adopted as incorporated in the petition must be lodged as a production when the petition is lodged: see r. 27.1(1)(a). For lodging of productions, see r. 4.5. For the meaning of documents founded on or adopted, see note 27.1.2.

14.5.3

"WITHOUT A MOTION BEING ENROLLED".

The first order is automatic and no motion or appearance is required unless an application under r. 14.5(2) (to dispense with service, etc., or for an interim order) or 14.6(2) (to shorten or extend the period of notice) is made.

14.5.4

"DISPENSE WITH INTIMATION, SERVICE OR ADVERTISEMENT".

Where dispensation is sought a motion must be enrolled, and if sought at the time of the first order that order will not be granted without enrolment under r. 14.5(1). On intimation, see note 14.7.1.

14.5.5

"INTERIM ORDER".

Interim orders relate mostly to the merits of the cause in which they are sought: *Kelly v. Monklands D.C.* 1986 S.L.T. 165, 167 per Lord Ross. An order is interim because of its character not merely because it is expressly granted *"ad interim"*. "Interim" means for the time being or in the meantime. Interim orders would include interim interdict, an interim judicial factor, an interim administrator or liquidator of a company, interim suspension, interim liberation, or interim possession under s.47(2) of the C.S.A. 1988. For urgent applications for interim orders when the petition is lodged, see r. 23.8.

14.5.6

"MOTION".

For motions, see Chap. 23. The procedure for urgent motions before the first order under r. 14.5 is in r. 23.8.

14.5.7

FEE.

The court fee for lodging a petition is payable on lodging. An additional fee is payable when the petition is presented out with normal hours. For fee, see Court of Session etc. Fees Order 1997, Table of Fees, Pt I, C, item 1 and 2 [SI 1997/688, as amended, pp. C 1201 et seq.]. Certain persons are exempt from payment of fees: see 1997 Fees Order, art.5, substituted by SSI 2002/270. A fee exemption certificate must be lodged in process: see P.N. No.1 of 2002.

14.5.8

Where the petitioner is legally represented, the fee may be debited under a credit scheme introduced on 1st April 1976 by P.N. No. 4 of 1976 to the account (if one is kept or permitted) of the agent by the court cashier, and an account will be rendered weekly by the court cashier's office to the agent for all court fees due that week for immediate settlement. Party litigants, and agents not operating the scheme, must pay (by cash, cheque or postal order) on each occasion a fee is due at the time of lodging at the counter at the Petition Department.

Period of notice for lodging answers

14.6   **14.6.**—(1) Subject to any other provision in these Rules, the period of notice for lodging answers to a petition shall be—

   (a)   in the case of service, intimation or advertisement within Europe, 21 days from whichever is the later of the date of execution of service, the giving of intimation or the publication of the advertisement;

   (b)   in the case of service or intimation furth of Europe under rule 16.2(2)(d) or (e) (service by an *huissier* etc. or personally), 21 days from whichever is the later of the date of execution of service or the giving of intimation;

   (c)   in the case of service or intimation furth of Europe other than under sub-paragraph (b), or advertisement furth of Europe, 42 days from whichever is the later of the date of execution of service, the giving of intimation or the publication of the advertisement;

   (d)   in the case of service by advertisement under rule 16.5 (service where address of person is not known), six months from the date of publication of the advertisement.

(2) An application may be made by motion to shorten or extend the period of notice.

(3) Where a motion under paragraph (2) is made in a petition at the time that an order for intimation, service or advertisement is made under rule 14.5 (first order in petitions), the decision of the court on the motion shall be final and not subject to review.

Deriv. R.C.S. 1965, r. 75(7) (r. 14.4(1)(d)), r. 192(1) (r. 14.6(1)(a) to (c)), and r. 192(3) (r. 14.6(2)), all substituted by SI 1986/1941.

GENERAL NOTE.

14.6.1   The phrase "period of notice" has replaced the word "*induciae*", but its effect is the same: the prayer of the petition may not be granted until after expiry of the period. The period of 21 days was introduced by A.S. (R.C.A. No.9) (Jurisdiction and Enforcement) 1986 [SI 1986/1941]. The former period of 14 days was the shortest in Europe; it was increased to 21 days following the application of Art. 20 of the 1968 Convention in Sch.1 (and of the Lugano Convention in Sch.3C) to the C.J.J.A. 1982 and Art. 15 of the Hague Convention of 15th November 1965 on the *Service Abroad of Judicial and Extrajudicial Documents in Civil or Commercial Matters (Cmnd. 3986 (1969))* which deal with the sisting of proceedings where it is not shown that the respondent has been able to receive the document in sufficient time to arrange for his defence (oppose the petition), and Art. 27(2) of the 1968 or Lugano Convention which entitles a court of a Contracting State to refuse to recognise a judgment in default of appearance for enforcement if the respondent was not served with the petition in sufficient time to enable him to arrange for his defence (oppose the petition): C.J.J.A. 1982, Scheds.1 and 3C, Art. 27(2).

This rule applies generally to all periods of notice other than the period of notice in a summons (before the expiry of which the summons cannot be called) by virtue of r. 1.3(1) (definition of "period of notice").

A petition is commenced when the first order is made under r. 14.5. Cf. the date on which an application is made to the court, for the purpose of determining whether it falls within the two year period under s.7 of the Company Directors Disqualification Act 1986, which is the date on which the petition is lodged: *Secretary of State for Trade and Industry v. Normand* 1994 S.L.T. 1249.

"SUBJECT TO ANY OTHER PROVISION IN THESE RULES".

14.6.2   Other provision is expressly made for the following petitions:—

r. 57.2 (disapplication of petition rules in petitions for admission of Advocates);

r. 62.2 (disapplication of r. 14.6 in petitions to register foreign judgments, etc.);

r. 66.2 (disapplication of r. 14.6 in applications under the Evidence (Proceedings in Other Jurisdictions) Act 1975);

r. 67.2 (disapplication of r. 14.6(1)(d) in adoption petitions);

r. 69.4(1)(a) (period of notice in election petitions);

rr. 70.4(1) and 70.8(1) (period of notice of four days to lodge answers to petition under the Child Abduction and Custody Act 1985);

rr. 76.2 and 76.20 (disapplication of r. 14.6(1) to petitions relating to confiscation of proceeds of crime).

rr. 74.55(2) (building society insolvency petitions).

The period of notice where notice is given by advertisement in an action (other than in the summons: see definition of "period of notice" in r. 1.3(1)) is not six months (*a*) in a family action (r. 49.12) or (*b*) in an action of declarator of death (r. 50.2(2)).

"WHICHEVER IS THE LATER".

The period of notice expires on the last day of the period of notice which is calculated from (but excluding) the date on which the last execution of service, giving of intimation or advertisement was made. Usually service and intimation are made at the same time; but they may not be, or service or intimation may have to be attempted again if at first unsuccessful. Intimation to named persons is rare in petitions, service being the general rule.

14.6.3

"EXECUTION OF SERVICE".

The period of notice will begin to run from midnight of the day on which service is executed; except where service is by post when time begins to run from midnight of the day after the date of posting (r. 16.4(6)). All days of the week are included in the period of notice, including Sundays and other public holidays.For methods of service, see Chap. 16, Pt. I.

14.6.4

A petition is commenced when the first order is made under r. 14.5 and not later when service is executed.

"INTIMATION".

Intimation to named persons is rare in a petition, service being the general rule. A petition in a judicial factory has to be intimated to the Accountant of Court: r. 61.5(1). Intimation on the walls of the court has to be made: r. 14.7; and see note 14.7.1. On intimation by advertisement, see note 14.6.6.

14.6.5

"ADVERTISEMENT".

Certain petitions require public notice in one or more national or local newspapers either as a matter of practice or by the statute under which the petition is presented.

14.6.6

"EUROPE".

This word has not been defined; but probably means as far east as (the Ural mountains in Russia and?) the Black Sea but not Asian Russia or the Asian Republics of the former U.S.S.R., south to the Mediterranean islands but not Africa, and north to Norway, Iceland and Finland. It includes the whole of the British Isles.Note also "Europe" for the purposes of the Royal Mail.

14.6.7

APPLICATION TO SHORTEN OR EXTEND THE PERIOD OF NOTICE.

Such an application is made by motion and accordingly the first order will not be granted automatically without enrolment: for motions, see Chap. 23. The decision of the court on such an application is final (r. 14.6(3)) as is an application before service in an action (r. 13.4(3)).

14.6.8

DISPENSING WITH PERIOD OF NOTICE.

Where the respondent's agent accepts service he may dispense with the period of notice: see r. 16.10 and note 16.10.1.

14.6.9

PROROGATION OF TIME FOR LODGING ANSWERS.

Ths period within which answers have to be lodged may be prorogated: r. 4.9(2). The former rule (R.C.S. 1965, r. 21(a)) stated that cause must be shown for an extension of time. The requirement to show cause has been omitted from the rule as it did not accord with current practice. It does not follow, however, that the court may not require cause to be shown in a particular case, as prorogation is in the discretion of the court.

14.6.10

Application to lodge a document late must be made by motion to the court under r. 2.1(1) (relief for failure to comply with rules).

Intimation and service of petitions

14.7.—(1)   A petition shall be intimated—

    (a)   on the walls of the court; and

    (b)   in such other manner as the court thinks fit.

(2)   A copy of the petition shall be served on every person, specified in the petition or by the court as a person on whom the petition is to be served, with a citation in Form 14.7 attached to it.

(3)[1]   A petition to the court in exercise of its *parens patriae* jurisdiction shall not be intimated on the walls of the court.

14.7

Deriv. R.C.S. 1965, r. 195(a) (past) (r. 14.7(1)), and r. 195(c) amended by SI 1986/1941 (r. 14.7(2))

---

[1] R. 14.7(3) inserted by SI 1996/1756 (effective 5th August 1996)

14.7.1   In a petition intimation usually refers only to intimation on the walls of the court as intimation to named persons is rare (service on named persons being the general rule). Intimation in the Minute Book was discontinued in January 1993 when the Minute Book was discontinued: on the Minute Book, see note 9.1.1. A petition in a judicial factory has to be intimated to the Accountant of Court: r. 61.5(1).

1.   Intimation on the walls of the court. A typed slip containing the details of the petition or a copy of the first page is handed to the clerk of session in the Petition Department or sent by post or fax: P.N. No.7 of 1994. The details required are (a) the nature of the application (i.e. "petition" or "note"), (b) the name and address of the petitioner, (c) the general purposes of the petition and (d) the name of the petitioner's solicitor. The Petition Department is responsible for placing the slip, on the day the first order under r. 14.5 is pronounced, on a hook at the top of the main corridor of Parliament House nearest the reception area at door 11.

This form of intimation may be dispensed with by order of the court: *Low, Petr.* 1920 S.C. 351 (fear of mother disappearing with child). In certain petitions, intimation is expressly excluded or dispensed with: see—
r. 57.2 (disapplication of petition rules in petitions for admission of Advocates);
r. 62.2 (disapplication of r. 14.7 in petitions to register foreign judgments etc.);
r. 66.2 (disapplication of r. 14.7 in applications under the Evidence (Proceedings in Other Jurisdictions) Act 1975; r. 67.2 (disapplication of r. 14.7 in adoption petitions);
rr. 76.2 and 76.20 (disapplication of r. 14.7 to petitions relating to confiscation of proceeds of crime).

2.   Intimation in such other manner as the court thinks fit (r. 14.7(1)(i)). This includes advertisement and notices in the Gazettes. Certain petitions require advertisement in one or more of the London, Edinburgh and Belfast Gazettes and national or local newspapers either as a matter of practice or by the statute under which the petition is presented.

14.7.2   A petition is normally brought to the attention of all interested persons by service: for methods of service, see Chap. 16, Pt. I. Intimation in the sense in which it is used in actions is uncommon. Intimation of a petition (or note) relating to a judicial factory has to be made, however, to the Accountant of Court: r. 61.5(1).

14.7.3   On expiry of the period of notice the petitioner must lodge in process an execution copy of the petition (r. 16.1(4)) with a copy of the first order attached to it and the certificate of service attached to that: r. 16.1(3). A copy of any notice or advertisement ordered to be made must be lodged as a production and referred to in the certificate of service. A walling certificate is no longer required: P.N. No.7 of 1994, para.4.

14.7.4   See note 14.2.11.

Procedure where answers lodged

14.8   **14.8.**   Where answers to a petition have been lodged, the petitioner shall, within 28 days after the expiry of the period of notice, apply by motion for such further procedure as he seeks, and the court shall make such order for further procedure as it thinks fit.

14.8.1   Where a petition is opposed it may proceed in the same way as an action, being 1 appointed to the Adjustment Roll, the subsequent closing of the record and appointment to the Procedure Roll or to proof. In the case of suspensions this is expressly provided: r. 60.5.

The Lord Ordinary has statutory powers under s.25 of the C.S.A. 1988 (1) to determine a petition himself, (2) to make such investigation and require such assistance from professional person or persons of science or of skill as he thinks fit or (3) to grant commission to take the deposition of havers and the evidence of witnesses as provided by s.10 of the 1988 Act (evidence on commission in actions). Evidence on commission in an Inner House petition may similarly be taken: C.S.A. 1988, s.38. Under the R.C.S. 1994 all of Chap. 35 (recovery of evidence) is available. Particular rules or practice may provide for a particular form of inquiry such as by remit to a reporter.

Strictly, a person becomes a respondent only by lodging answers.

14.8.2   For the form and lodging of answers, see r. 18.3 and notes.

"WITHIN 28 DAYS".

The date from which the period is calculated is not counted. Where the last day falls on a Saturday or Sunday, or a public holiday on which the Office of Court is closed, the next available day is allowed: r. 1.3(7). For office hours and public holidays, see note 3.1.2.

14.8.3

LODGING OF EXECUTION COPY OF PETITION.

Before proceeding with a motion under this rule the execution copy of the petition certified as a true copy must be lodged with the certificates of service and any Post Office receipts for, or certificates of, posting attached, and a copy of the interlocutor ordering service, and there should be lodged as productions copies of the *Gazettes* and newspapers containing any advertisement ordered to be published: r. 16.1(3) and (4). A walling certificate is not required: P.N. No.7 of 1994, para.4. The position of the advertisement should be clearly marked on the front of the document lodged and at the place of the advertisement; alternatively, on analogy with r. 16.5(6)(b), a certificate of publication by the publisher stating the date of publication and the text of the advertisement may be accepted.

14.8.4

"MOTION".

For motions, see Chap. 23.

14.8.5

HEARINGS AND PROOFS.

A hearing in a petition may be a proof (or proof before answer) or simply a hearing.

14.8.6

At a hearing the court may consider reports, affidavits and other documentary evidence and be addressed by the parties, but parole evidence is not led. A hearing is not a proof. The interlocutor appointing a petition to a hearing will not grant authority to cite witnesses; whereas an interlocutor appointing the cause to a proof would do so. It is, therefore, important to be clear whether a hearing or a proof is sought; and the depute clerk of session should inquire if this information is not volunteered so that any necessary warrant to cite may be included (where proof is sought).

In the Inner House where a proof is ordered the proof is taken by a judge of the Inner House and any ruling by him on the admissibility of evidence may be reviewed by the Inner House in the discussion of his report on the evidence: C.S.A. 1988, s.37.

Unopposed petitions

14.9.—(1) Subject to paragraph (2), where the period of notice has expired without answers being lodged, the court shall, on the motion of the petitioner, after such further procedure and inquiry into the grounds of the petition, if any, as it thinks fit, dispose of the petition.

14.9

(2) Where—

(a) the prayer of the petition seeks an order directed against a person,

(b) service of the petition has been made on that person furth of the United Kingdom under rule 16.2, and

(c) such order has been granted without that person having lodged answers,

a certified copy of the interlocutor granting the order shall be served forthwith by the petitioner on that person.

(3) The court may, on the motion of a person to whom paragraph (2) applies, recall the interlocutor and allow answers to be lodged if—

(a) that person—

(i) without any fault on his part, did not have knowledge of the petition in sufficient time to lodge answers;

(ii) has disclosed a prima facie answer to the petition on the merits; and

(iii) has enrolled the motion for recall within a reasonable time after he had knowledge of the petition; and

(b) a certified copy of thethe motion is enrolled before the expiry of one year from the date of the interlocutor sought to be recalled.

(4) The recall of an interlocutor under paragraph (3) shall be without prejudice to the validity of anything already done or transacted, of any contract made or obligation incurred, or of any appointment made or power granted, in or by virtue of that interlocutor.

(5) The provisions of this rule are without prejudice to the power of the court to make any interim appointment or order at any stage of the cause.

Deriv. R.C.S. 1965, r. 197 (preamble) (r. 14.9(1)), r. 197(a) (r. 14.9(2)), r. 197(6) (r. 14.9(3)), r. 197(c) (r. 14.9(4)), all substituted by SI 1986/1941, and r. 191(d) (r. 14.9(5))

LODGING OF EXECUTION COPY OF PETITION.

14.9.1 Before proceeding with a motion under this rule the execution copy of the petition certified as a true copy must be lodged with the certificates of service and any Post Office receipts for, or certificates of, posting attached, and a copy of the interlocutor ordering service, and there should be lodged as productions copies of the *Gazettes* and newspapers containing any advertisement ordered to be published: r. 16.1(3) and (4). The position of the advertisement should be clearly marked on the front of the document lodged and at the place of the advertisement; alternatively, on analogy with r. 16.5(6)(b), a certificate of publication by the publisher stating the date of publication and the text of the advertisement may be accepted.

"MOTION".

14.9.2 For motions, see Chap. 23.

COURT MUST BE SATISFIED ABOUT SERVICE.

14.9.3 This is established by the appropriate certificates of service and copies of any notices or advertisements: see note 14.9.1.

In relation to an unopposed petition in which an order is sought against a person there is this significance to this requirement. Under Art. 20(2) of Scheds. 1, 3C and 4, to the C.J.J.A. 1982 the court must sist the cause so long as it has not been shown that that person has been able to receive the petition in sufficient time to enable him to defend or that all necessary steps have been taken to effect service: "all necessary steps" means that all necessary approaches have been made to the competent authorities of the country in which that person is domiciled to reach him in sufficient time (Jenard report on 1968 Convention, p. 40). Art. 20 does not apply where his whereabouts are unknown.

Under Art.15 of the Hague Convention on *Service Abroad of Judicial and Extrajudicial Documents in Civil or Commercial Matters*, 1965 (Cmnd. 3986 (1969)), which may be used in a country to which the 1968 Convention applies (Art. 20(3) of Scheds. 1 and 3C to the C.J.J.A. 1982), the court must be satisfied that service was executed by a method prescribed by the internal law of the country concerned or delivered by a method provided for under the convention in sufficient time to enable the respondent to defend. Decree may be granted, however, even if no certificate of service or delivery has been received where the petition was transmitted by a method under the convention, six months have elapsed since the date of transmission and no certificate has been received even though every reasonable effort has been made to obtain it: the UK has made the necessary declaration to bring this provision into effect. Art.15 does not apply where the whereabouts of the respondent are unknown: Art.1(2). For the countries to which the Hague Convention applies, see note 16.2.3.

In relation to any other civil procedure convention with a foreign country, regard will require to be had to its terms, if any, about the court's satisfaction about service. Where there is no convention, the court will be satisfied by any form of service under r. 16.2; it may not enquire whether, or require a certificate that, the form of service used is permitted by the laws of the country concerned, leaving it to the petitioner to take care to use a method which will enable him to enforce the decree there.

COURT MUST BE SATISFIED IT HAS JURISDICTION.

14.9.4 Averments about jurisdiction are required in a petition to which the C.J.J.A. 1982 applies: r. 14.4(4)(a); the requirement is limited to such petitions because not many petitions will be subject to that Act. Under Art. 20(1) of Scheds.1, 3C and 4, and r. 8 of Sch.8, to the C.J.J.A. 1982 the court must be satisfied that it has jurisdiction in causes to which that Act applies where the defender has not entered appearance (the respondent does not lodge answers) or it must declare at its own instance that it has no jurisdiction. Notice also that under the C.J.J.A. 1982 where it appears to the court that a court in another country has exclusive jurisdiction it must at its own instance decline jurisdiction: Art. 19 of Scheds. 1, 3C and 4, and r. 7 of Sched.8, to the C.J.J.A. 1982. The former requirement (R.C.S. 1965, r. 197(e)), to state the ground of jurisdiction in the motion for the prayer of the petition to be granted, is no longer required as it is considered unnecessary because the ground (except prorogation unless agreed in advance) is stated in the petition in those petitions to which the C.J.J.A. 1982 applies (see r. 14.4(4)).

INQUIRY IN UNOPPOSED PETITIONS.

14.9.5 Some unopposed petitions may require a hearing (e.g. adoption petitions (Chap. 67)) or some other form of inquiry such as a remit to a reporter (e.g. in applications for schemes in relation to public trusts (Chap. 63, Pt. III) or confirmation of reduction of capital of a company (see note 14.3.10)) or a proof.

SERVICE OF INTERLOCUTOR GRANTING ORDER.

14.9.6 R. 14.9(2) requires service of an order directed against a person furth of the UK and is equivalent to the rule for decrees in absence in r. 19.1(6). The purpose of this rule stems from Art. 47(1) of Sched. 1 to the C.J.J.A. 1982 which requires a judgment to have been served on the defender before an order for enforcement can be obtained in cases to which that Schedule applies. The provision is extended in this rule to all orders against persons furth of the UK.

"ANSWERS".

For form and lodging of answers, see r. 18.3 and notes. **14.9.7**

RECALL OF INTERLOCUTOR GRANTING ORDER.

R. 14.9(3) enables a person furth of the UK, served with an order required by r. 14.9(2), to seek to **14.9.8**
recall it and is equivalent to the rule for recall of decrees in absence in r. 19.2. The basis for the procedure
for recall under r. 14.9(3) is Art. 16 of the *Hague Convention on Service Abroad of Judicial and
Extrajudicial Documents in Civil or Commercial Matters*, 1965 (Cmnd. 3986 (1969)) which is applied in
this rule to any country furth of the UK whether or not one to which the convention applies. The UK
made a declaration in relation to Scotland under Art.16 limiting the period within which application may
be made for recall to one year and this is enshrined in r. 14.9(3)(b). Although such a person has a year
within which to seek recall, the decree may be extracted by the petitioner under r. 7.1.

Recall does not affect the validity of things done or transacted, or appointments made, in or by virtue
of the decree: r. 14.9(4) and (5).

Disposals in petitions

14.10.—[1](1) The court may make such order to dispose of a petition as it thinks **14.10**
fit, whether or not such order was sought in the petition.

(2) An order referred to in paragraph (1) is any order that could be made if
sought in any action or petition.

---

[1] Rule 14.10 inserted by S.S.I. 2012 No. 126 para. 2 (effective 28th May 2012).

CHAPTER 14A INTERIM DILIGENCE

Interim Diligence

14A.1.[1] In this Chapter—   **14A.1**

"the 1987 Act" means the Debtors (Scotland) Act 1987; and

"the 2002 Act" means the Debt Arrangement and Attachment (Scotland) Act 2002.

Application for interim diligence

14A.2.—[2](1) The following shall be made by motion—   **14A.2**

   (a) an application under section 15D(1) of the 1987 Act for warrant for diligence by arrestment or inhibition on dependence of an action or petition or warrant for arrestment on the dependence of an admiralty action;

   (b) an application under section 9C of the 2002 Act for interim attachment.

(2) Such an application must be accompanied by a statement in Form 14A.2.

(3) A certified copy of an interlocutor granting a motion under paragraph (1) shall be sufficient authority for execution of the diligence concerned.

GENERAL NOTE.

The Bankruptcy and Diligence etc. (Scotland) Act 2007 unnecessarily, and following the modern   **14A.2.1**
trend of governments to micro-manage, sets out rules of procedure for diligence on the dependence. A perfect example of the error of such interference in rule making is the requirement (and unnecessary expense to parties and the time of the court) that, where the court grants diligence before a hearing (i.e. ex parte), there must be a hearing thereafter even if the party against whom the order is made or a person having an interest does not seek to recall or restrict the diligence.

The Act inserts ss. 15A–15N to the Debtors (Scotland) Act 1987. The statutory procedure in these sections supersedes much that was said and done by *Karl Construction Ltd v. Palisade Properties plc* , 2002 S.C. 270 (O.H.) and *Advocate General for Scotland v. Taylor* , 2003 S.L.T. 1340 (Extra Div.).

In *Karl Construction Ltd*, above, on a motion for recall of an inhibition, Lord Drummond Young held that four requirements must be satisfied if a right of protective attachment of immoveable property during litigation is to conform to Art. 1 of the First Protocol to the ECHR. These are: (1) The pursuer must establish a prima facie case on the merits of the action. (2) The pursuer must establish that there is a specific need for an interim remedy; this will generally involve demonstrating either that there is a significant risk of the defender's insolvency or that the defender is taking steps to conceal or dissipate his assets or that there is a significant risk that the defender will remove his assets from the jurisdiction. (3) A hearing must take place before a judge at which the previous two matters are discussed. (4) If protective attachment is used without an objective justification, and in particular if the pursuer is unsuccessful in the action, the defender should be entitled to damages for any loss that he has suffered in consequence of the attachment. He held that the present law on inhibition on the dependence failed to meet these requirements and that the automatic right to inhibition conferred by Scots law (with very limited right to compensation) did not strike a fair balance between the interests of the pursuer in having assets available to satisfy his claim and the right of the defender recognised by Art.1 of the 1st Protocol to dispose of his property as he wants; the requirement of proportionality was not satisfied. In *Amalgamated Roofing and Building Co v. Wilkie* , 2004 S.L.T. 509 (OH), it was held that *Karl Construction*, above, applied prospectively and did not make invalid diligence obtained before that case.

In *Advocate General v. Taylor*, above, the Extra Division on a report to the Inner House on a motion for a warrant for inhibition following *Karl Construction*, held at para. [34] that for a warrant for inhibition (and it would also apply to arrestment) the applicant need only establish a prima facie case on the merits of the action; the necessity for diligence need not be demonstrated, although it may no doubt assist. The court also held that r. 13.6 was not compatible with ECHR. To bring the rule within art. 1 of the First Protocol, the grant of a warrant for any diligence on the dependence required a judicial act, and that it had to be judicially considered before being granted. The court did not consider that a hearing was required in every case as suggested in *Karl Construction*, above. The court recommended that the rules be changed.

The authority for the court to grant warrant for arrestment or inhibition on the dependence is now s. 15A of the 1987 Act in relation to an action and s. 15B in relation to a petition.

"MOTION".

For motions, see Chap. 23.   **14A.2.2**

---

[1] Chap. 14A and r.14A.1 inserted by S.S.I. 2008 No. 122 (effective 1st April 2008).
[2] R. 14A.2 inserted by S.S.I. 2008 No. 122 (effective 1st April 2008).

"APPLICATION UNDER SECTION 15D(1)".

14A.2.3   Under s. 15D(1) of the 1987 Act a creditor (not only the pursuer?) may at any time during the dependence of an action or petition (i.e. from the time it is commenced—that is, served or, in a petition, a first order is made—until final extract) apply for arrest or inhibition on the dependence, or interim attachment under s.9C of the Debt Arrangement and Attachment (Scotland) Act 2002. The motion must be accompanied by a statement in Form 14A.2. The application must include—and this is done in the statement—details of the debtor and any other person having an interest, whether the creditor seeks the warrant before intimation and before a hearing under s. 15F which has been intimated to interested persons.

Neither the statutory provisions nor Chap. 14A makes provision for how the application is dealt with before a hearing under s. 15F. Presumably *Advocate General for Scotland v. Taylor* , 2003 S.L.T. 1340 (Extra Div.) will apply and the application will be considered by a Lord Ordinary who may require to be addressed on the application.

The order, if granted, will last only until the hearing under s. 15K. Where diligence is refused and the creditor insists on his application, there will be a hearing under s. 15F. Whether diligence is granted or refused, the hearing under s. 15F or 15K must be intimated to the debtor and any person having an interest: 1987 Act, s. 15E(4). Neither the statutory provisions nor Chap. 14A provide for any period within which the hearing under s.15F must take place. It should not be more than 7 days.

GROUNDS FOR DILIGENCE ON THE DEPENDENCE.

14A.2.4   The court must be satisfied that (a) the creditor has a prima facie case on the merits; (b) there is a real and substantial risk that enforcement of any decree in favour of the creditor would be defeated or prejudiced by reason of (i) the debtor being insolvent or verging on insolvency or (ii) the likelihood of the debtor removing, disposing of, burdening, concealing or otherwise dealing with all or some of his assets; and (c) it is reasonable in all the circumstances, including the effect granting warrant may have on any person having an interest. The onus is on the creditor to satisfy the court that the warrant should be granted at any application without a hearing and again at any hearing under s.15F or 15K. See 1987 Act, ss.15E(2) (warrant without a hearing), 15F(3) (warrant at a hearing) and 15K(9) (recall or restriction).

The terms "insolvent" and "insolvency" are not defined in the 1987 Act. In *McCormack v. Hamilton Academical Football Club Ltd* , 2009 S.C. 313 (Extra Div.), it was held that the terms included absolute insolvency (excess of liabilities over assets) as well as practical insolvency (inability to pay debts as they fall due).

SECTION 15K HEARING.

14A.2.5   Where the application is granted before a s.15F hearing (ie ex parte) a hearing under s.15K *must* be fixed (and intimated to the debtor and any other person having an interest: 1987 Act, s.15E(4). Neither the statutory provisions nor Chap. 14A provide for any period within which the hearing under s.15K must take place. There will thus be a hearing even if no one seeks to have the diligence recalled or restricted. Any person on whom intimation has been made, and any other person the court is satisfied has an interest, must be heard.

At the hearing, even if no one seeks to have the diligence recalled or restricted, the creditor must satisfy the court all over again that the order should be granted, the grounds being the same as where it is dealt with before the s.15F hearing (se note 14A.2.4). Where the court refuses diligence it may do so on conditions including requiring the debtor to consign money, find caution or give any other security: 1987 Act, s.15F(7).

Where the court refuses diligence before intimation of a hearing under s.15F, and the creditor insists on his application, the court must fix a hearing under s.15F: 1987 Act, s.15E(6) which must be intimated to the debtor and any other person having an interest. Again, neither the statutory provisions nor Chap. 14A provides for a period within which the hearing must take place. It ought not to be more than 7 days.

TIME-LIMIT FOR EXECUTING WARRANTS.

14A.2.6   If the summons is not served on the defender before the end of 21 days beginning with the day on which the diligence is executed, the diligence ceases to have effect: 1987 Act, s.15G(2), Debt Arrangement and Attachment (Scotland) Act 2002, s.9G. The court may extend the period, having regard to the efforts to serve the summons and any special circumstances preventing or obstructing service: 1987 Act, s.15G(3) and (4), and 2002 Act, s.9G(3) and (4). This provision will also apply in petitions: 1987 Act, s.15B(3).

ARRESTMENT ON THE DEPENDENCE.

14A.2.7   This is a preventive diligence restraining a debtor (arrestee) from making payment of a debt or satisfying an obligation to the defender (common debtor). As a general rule, prior to the incorporation of the ECHR into Scots law a pursuer was entitled to insert a warrant for arrestment as a right in respect of a debt due. An arrestment on the dependence could be recalled or restricted with or without conditions; and the pursuer would be liable in damages only for its wrongful use where executed on a defective warrant, in an irregular manner, or with malice or without probable cause: see *Wolthekker v. Northern Agricultural Co.* (1862) 1 M. 211, 212 per L.J.-C. Inglis; *Grant v. Magistrates of Airdrie* 1939 S.C. 738, 758-759 per L.P. Normand. The granting, recall and restriction of arrestment on the dependence is now governed by ss.15A–15N of the Debtors (Scotland) Act 1987 inserted by the Bankruptcy and Diligence etc. (Scotland) Act 2007. The grounds on which arrestment on the dependence can be granted are set out in note 14A.2.4.

Pursuers in certain foreign actions which have been commenced, but not concluded, may present a petition to the Court of Session for a warrant to arrest on the dependence of the foreign action: see C.J.J.A. 1982, s.27. They are not, however, entitled to the warrant to arrest as of right: *Stancroft Securities Ltd v. McDowall* 1990 S.C. 274, 277 per L.J.-C. Ross. The pursuer in the foreign action must comply with s.27 and demonstrate a colourable care in the foreign action: *Clipper Shipping Co. Ltd v. San Vincente Partner* , 1989 S.L.T. 204, 207D per Lord Coulsfield and *Stancroft Securities Ltd*, above. An affidavit of the foreign lawyer conducting the action may be sufficient: see e.g. *Clipper Shipping Co. Ltd*, above.

Use of diligence on the dependence against foreign state agencies is uncommon as they could normally be expected to meet any decree, and the use of such diligence in those circumstances would be oppressive. But a distinction is to be drawn in the case of bodies merely controlled or supported by foreign governments such as state-owned companies: *Tor Corporate AS v. China National Star Petroleum Corporation* , 27th July 2000 (OH), unreported.

1. Warrant for arrestment on the dependence is competent only where an action contains a conclusion, or a petition contains a prayer, for a sum other than expenses: 1987 Act, ss.15A(2) and 15B(2)
The position at common law was as follows. The summons must contain pecuniary conclusions, even if alternative or subsidiary: *Burns v. Burns* (1879) 7 R. 355, 356 per L.P. Inglis. Arrestment cannot be used in an action only for divorce (*Burns*, above), declarator or reduction (*Stafford v. McLaurin* (1875) 3 R. 148) or where the only conclusion which can be secured is one for expenses (*Weir v. Otto* (1870) 8 M. 1070). In an action involving commercial activities the pursuer had to provide at least basic specification of factual grounds and, where that was the case, it was proper to proceed on the basis that responsible counsel had evidence which warranted the basic averments: *Interconnection Systems Ltd v. Holland* 1994 S.L.T. 777, 781A-C per Lord Penrose; cf. *Beton v. Beton* 1961 S.L.T.(Notes) 19, and see comments of Lord Cameron in a different context in *Moore v. Greater Glasgow Health Board* 1978 S.C. 123, 130.

2. A schedule of arrestment must be served on the arrestee in Form 16.15-B (or 16.15-BB in the case of a ship). For methods of execution, see r. 16.12. It may be executed at any time after it is granted, before, at the same time or after service of the summons or petition. If the summons or petition is not served before 21 days beginning with the day on which the arrestment is executed the arrestment ceases to have effect: 1987 Act, s.15G(2); and see note 14A.2.6. The 21 days may be extended. Arrestment may be executed after calling at any time until the action is disposed of by a final decree. It may not be used if the action has fallen asleep (i.e. where the action has been in court for a year and a day with no interlocutor having been pronounced). An arrestment will fall if the summons is not called within a year and a day of the expiry of the period of notice: *Thorburn v. Cox* (1830) 8 S. 945. It must not be executed before an arrestment to found jurisdiction, because the defender will not be subject to the jurisdiction until the latter has been effected: *Dramgate Ltd v. Tyne Dock Engineering Ltd* , 2000 S.C. 43 (Ex Div).

3. Arrestment is competent on the dependence where the sum concluded for is a future or contingent debt: 1987 Act, s.15C(1). The grounds will be set those set out in ss.15E and 15F of the 1987 Act: see note 14A.2.4.
The position at common law was as follows. Payment of future or contingent debt (i.e. liquid debt payable at a certain future date or on the occurrence of an uncertain future event: *Mitchell v. Scott* (1881) 8 R. 875, 879 per L.P. Inglis). Arrestment is competent in respect of a debt due (i.e. due for payment immediately *ex hypothesi* of the pursuer's case). If the debt is a future debt, although arrestable by a creditor of the common debtor, arrestment is not competent in security of another debt in an action to enforce the claim: *Costain Building & Civil Engineering Ltd v. Scottish Rugby Union plc* 1993 S.C. 650, overruling, on this point *Taylor Woodrow Construction (Scotland) Ltd v. Sears Investment Trust Ltd* 1991 S.C. 140; cf. *Rippin Group Ltd v. ITP Interpipe SA* 1995 S.C. 302. Arrestment will only be granted at common law on a claim for a future debt where there are special circumstances averred, e.g. that the defender is *vergens ad inopiam or in meditatione fugae* or considering putting away his funds with the intention of not implementing any decree or not fulfilling his obligations: *Symington v. Symington* (1875) 3 R. 205; *Gillanders v. Gillanders* 1966 S.C. 54; *Wilson v. Wilson* 1981 S.L.T. 101.

4. Arrestment must be made in the hands of a person other than the pursuer or defender who is indebted, holds goods belonging, or is liable to account, directly not indirectly, to the defender: Graham Stewart on *Diligence*, pp. 105 et seq.; *McDonald v. Mize* 1989 S.L.T. 482. Exceptions to the rule that the arrestment must be in another's hands are (a) arrestment of ships or cargo (see note 13.6.4; but not aircraft: *Emerald Airways Ltd v. Nordic Oil Services Ltd* , 1996 S.L.T. 403, (b) arrestment by a pursuer in his own hands where he holds in a different character to that in which he is pursuer: *Landcatch Ltd v. Sea Catch plc* 1993 S.L.T. 451. The arrestee must be subject to the jurisdiction of the court: *Brash v. Brash* 1966 S.C. 56. The statement in Graham Stewart on *Diligence*, p. 37, that, where arrestment is directed against an arrestee in a fiduciary capacity, this must be stated in the schedule (*Graham v. Macfarlane & Co.* (1869) 7 M. 640) was disapproved in *Huber v. Banks* 1986 S.L.T. 58. The arrestment is valid if there is, at the time it is laid, a present obligation on the arrestee to account to the defender: *Commercial Bank of Scotland Ltd v. Eagle Star Insurance Co. Ltd* 1950 S.L.T. (Notes) 30. Where the arrestee is an agent, such as a solicitor, and not a trustee he is under no obligation to account until he has received the funds; no debt exists, therefore, until then and any arrestment in his hands before then is ineffective: *Royal Bank of Scotland plc v. Law* 1996 S.L.T. 83. Where the cheque is lodged with a

bank, no obligation to account arises until the bank (the collecting bank) has presented the cheque for payment to the paying bank and the cheque is honoured, and there is no arrestable obligation until then: *McLaughlin v. Allied Irish Bank* , 2001 S.C. 485.

5.   Subjects arrestable, as a general rule, are all personal debts due to the defender or his moveable property: Stair, III.i.25; Erskine, III.vi.4; Graham Stewart on *Diligence*, pp. 44 et seq. Cargo on board ship may be arrested: see *Svenska Petroleum A.B. v. H.O.R. Ltd* 1982 S.L.T. 343; *West Cumberland Farmers Ltd v. Director of Agriculture of Sri Lanka* 1988 S.L.T. 296; and if the cargo cannot be discharged, the ship cannot be moved. Certain property is not arrestable: (a) wages or salary (including fees, bonuses and commissions) and pensions (including annuities for past services, any periodical payments in compensation for loss of employment and any disability pension): Law Reform (Miscellaneous Provisions) (Scotland) Act 1966, s.1; (b) property specially appropriated; (c) alimentary provision; (d) bills and negotiable instruments (though the debt may be); (e) joint property for debt of one of the joint owners; (f) in relation to a personal bank account, the minimum balance specified in Sch. 2 to the 1987 Act. See generally, Graham Stewart on *Diligence*, pp. 78 et seq.; Wilson on the *Scottish Law of Debt*, 2nd ed., pp. 192–195. A book debt ceases to be arrestable where a receiver is appointed over the common debtor before the arrestment because the floating charge has effect as an assignation in security of the right to receive the debt in favour of the holder of the floating charge: *Forth & Clyde Construction Co. Ltd v. Trinity Timber & Plywood Co. Ltd* 1984 S.L.T. 94.

6.   Effect of arrestment. When executed it arrests all the readiest moveable goods and gear, debts, sums of money and other moveable effects belonging or due to the defender wherever and in whosoever's hands to remain under arrestment until sufficient caution be found that the same may be forthcoming to the pursuer: see Debtors (Scotland) Act 1838, s.16. It prohibits the arrestee from parting with the subjects to the prejudice of the pursuer: see Graham Stewart on *Diligence*, pp. 125 et seq. The arrestment covers the principal debt, interest on it, the expenses of the action but at common law not expenses of the arrestment as they are not an expense of process (which had to be sought in the action of furthcoming): *Symington v. Symington* (1874) 1 R. 1006. Expenses of obtaining and executing arrestment are now expenses of process and are such as may be awarded by the court: 1987 Act, s.15M; and see note 14A.2.10. The court may limit the sum to be arrested to funds not exceeding such amount as it may specify, and the maximum it may specify when limiting the amount is the aggregate of (a) the principal sum, (b) a sum equal to 20% of that sum or such other percentage as Scottish Ministers may specify by regulations, (c) a sum equal to one year's interest on the principal sum at the judicial rate, and (d) any sum prescribed by Scottish Ministers in relation to the expenses of executing the arrestment: 1987 Act, s.15H. Arrestments are preferred according to their date of service, those on the same day rank pari passu. Arrestments within 60 days before or four months after apparent insolvency rank pari passu with the insolvency as if all used on the same day: Bankruptcy (Scotland) Act 1985, Sched. 7, para. 24. Arrestments within 60 days of sequestration or winding up are ineffectual to secure a preference in competition with other creditors: 1985 Act, s.37(4); Insolvency Act 1986, s.185 (companies). The effect of arrestment continues after final decree (even after decree of absolvitor if pursuer reclaims: *Countess of Haddington v. Richardson* (1822) 1 S.362) during the three-year prescriptive period (Debtors (Scotland) Act 1987, s.95A; and the arrestment remains in effect while a time to pay direction is in force: Debtors (Scotland) Act 1987, s.2(2). The pursuer does not have a complete right unless it is followed by decree in an action of furthcoming: *Lucas's Trs. v. Campbell* (1894) 21 R. 1096, 1103 per Lord Kinnear; but in relation to an earnings arrestment, a current maintenance arrestment or a conjoined arrestment order within the meaning of Part III of the 1987 Act an action of furthcoming is not competent and such a diligence is subject to the provisions of that Part.

7.   An arrestment will fall if the summons is not called within a year and a day of the expiry of the period of notice: *Thorburn v. Cox* (1830) 8 S.945. An arrestment not insisted in prescribes at the end of three years beginning with the day on which a final interlocutor is obtained by the creditor for payment of all or part of the principal sum concluded for or, in the case of a future or contingent debt, at the end of three years beginning with the day on which the debt becomes due: 1987 Act, s.95A.

Inhibition on the dependence.

14A.2.8   This is a preventive diligence in security restraining a debtor from burdening, alienating or otherwise affecting his heritable property to the prejudice of the inhibitor: Erskine, II.xi.2. See generally, Graham Stewart on *Diligence*, pp. 530 et seq. As a general rule prior to the incorporation of the ECHR into Scots law, a pursuer was entitled to insert a warrant for inhibition as of right in respect of a debt due. An inhibition on the dependence could be recalled in whole or in part with or without conditions; and the pursuer would be liable in damages only for its wrongful use where executed on a defective warrant, in an irregular manner or its use was unjustifiable, or with malice and without probable cause: see *Wolthekker v. Northern Agricultural Co.* (1862) 1 M. 211, 212 per L.J.-C. Inglis: *Grant v. Magistrates of Airdrie* 1939 S.C. 738, 758–759 per L.P. Normand. The granting, recall and restriction of inhibition on the dependence is now governed by ss.15A–15N of the Debtors (Scotland) Act 1987 inserted by the Bankruptcy and Diligence etc. (Scotland) Act 2007.

The grounds on which inhibition on the dependence can be granted are set out in note 14A.2.4.

Pursuers in certain foreign actions which have been commenced, but not concluded may present a petition to the Court of Session for a warrant to inhibit on the dependence of the foreign action: see

C.J.J.A. 1982, s.27. They are not, however, entitled to the warrant to inhibit as of right: *Stancroft Securities v. McDowell* 1990 S.C. 274, 277 per L.J.-C. Ross. The pursuer in the foreign action must comply with s.27 and demonstrate a colourable case in the foreign actions: *Clipper Shipping Co. Ltd v. San Vincente Partners* 1989 S.L.T. 204, 207D, per Lord Coulsfield and *Stancroft Securities Ltd*, above. An affidavit of the foreign lawyer conducting the action may be sufficient: see e.g. *Clipper Shipping Co. Ltd*, above.

1. Warrant for inhibition on the dependence of an action s competent only where it contains a conclusion for a sum other than expenses: 1987 Act, s.15A(2). Warrant for inhibition on the dependence is competent in a petition which contains a prayer for a sum other than expenses or for specific implement of an obligation to convey heritable property to the creditor or grant him a real right on security or some other right over such property: 1987 Act, s.15B(2).

    The position at common law was as follows. The summons need not contain pecuniary conclusions: it is necessary only that there is a conclusion which can be secured by inhibition, e.g. implement of an obligation in respect of heritage: *Barstow v. Menzies* (1840) 2 D. 611; *Seaforth's Trs v. Macauley* (1844) 7 D. 180. It cannot be used in an action only for divorce (*Burns v. Barns* (1879) 7 R. 355), declarator or reduction (*Stafford v. McLaurin* (1875) 3 R. 148) or where the only conclusion which can be secured is one for expenses (*Weir v. Otto* (1870) 8 m. 1070). The preventive diligence in security in an action of reduction or adjudication is the registration of a notice of litigiosity in the Register of Inhibitions and Adjudications: Titles to Land Consolidated (Scotland) Act 1868, s.159.

2. A schedule of inhibition must be served on the defender in Form 16.15—F. It may be executed after it was granted, before, at the same time as service of the summons or at any time thereafter until the action is disposed of by a final decree. If the summons or petition is not served before 21 days beginning with the day on which the inhibition is executed, the inhibition ceases to have effect: 1987 Act, s.15G; and see note 14A.2.6. The 21 days may be extended by the court. For methods of execution, see r. 16.12. It may not be used if the action has fallen asleep (i.e. where the action has been in court with no interlocutor having been pronounced for a year and a day: r. 13.7(2)). The inhibition must be registered in the Register of Inhibitions and takes effect from the beginning of the day of such registration; except that, where a notice of issued inhibition is registered before the schedule of inhibition is served on the debtor and the inhibition is registered before the expiry of 21 days after the notice, the inhibition takes effect from the beginning of the day on which the schedule of inhibition is served: Titles to Land Consolidation (Scotland) Act 1868, s.155. The time when registration was deemed to have taken place under s.155 of the 1868 Act was unclear, but in *Park, Ptnrs* 2008 S.L.T. 1026 (O.H.) it was held to be the conclusion of the day on which the inhibition or notice was registered. The register is in Meadowbank House (open 10am to 4pm Monday to Friday).

3. Payment of future or contingent debt. Inhibition is competent on the dependence where the sum prayed for is a future or contingent debt: 1987 Act, s.15C(1). As in arrestment; see note 14A.2.7.

4. Property which can be inhibited is heritable property (corporeal or incorporeal) which may be affected by adjudication (Bell's *Comm.*, ii, 135) but not heritable bonds where there has been no infeftment (Graham Stewart on *Diligence*, pp. 548–549).

5. Effect of inhibition. When executed and registered it prevents the debtor voluntarily alienating or affecting his heritable property (whether he is infeft or not) to the prejudice of the inhibiter and renders any such deed voidable. It effectively prevents any sale or creation of a heritable security. It secures a ranking in preference to that of ordinary creditors who have taken no steps to secure their debts and to that of creditors who have post-dated preferences: *Bank of Scotland v. Lord Advocate* 1977 S.L.T. 24. If decree in the action is not subsequently obtained by the pursuer the inhibition is of no effect: *Gordon v. Duncan* (1827) 5 S. 602. It has no effect on prior debts. It affects property belonging to the defender at the time of registration except property acquired after registration of the inhibition destined to him under an indefeasible title, which is then inhibited, but otherwise does not affect property acquired after registration: 1868 Act, s.157; cf. *Leeds Permanent Building Society v. Aitken Malone & Mackay* 1968 S.L.T. 338. It secures principal and interest and any expenses decerned for (*Weir v. Otto* (1870) 8 m. 1070) but at common law not the expenses of the inhibition. Expenses of obtaining and executing the inhibition are now expenses of process and are such as may be awarded by the court: 1987 Act, s.15M; and see note 14A.2.10. At present, an inhibition within 60 days before sequestration or winding up of the defender does not create a preference: Bankruptcy (Scotland) Act 1985, s.37(2), Insolvency Act 1986, s.185 (companies); otherwise the inhibiter has a preference over debts contracted subsequently: *Baird & Brown v. Stirrat's Tr.* (1872) 10 M. 414. Inhibition is personal to the inhibiter and unless followed by a separate action of adjudication gives no real right or title. Under s.154 of the Bankruptcy and Diligence etc. (Scotland) Act 2007, inhibition does not confer any preference in any sequestration, insolvency proceeding or other process in which there is a ranking. When the provisions of the 2007 Act creating land attachment following a decree or document of debt are brought into force, this will replace adjudication which will be abolished. In an action for specific implement of an obligation to convey heritable property or to grant a real right over such property in favour of the creditor, the court *must* limit the property inhibited to that property; in any other case the court *may* limit the property inhibited: 1987 Act, s.155. Once decree has been obtained, any inhibition in execution of the decree is not limited to that property: 1987 Act, s.152.

6.　An inhibition will fall if the summons is not called within a year and a day of the expiry of the period of notice: *Thorburn v. Cox* (1830) 8 S. 945; r. 13.7(2). An inhibition relating to land, a lease or a heritable security prescribes within five years from the date of registration: Conveyancing (Scotland) Act 1924, s.44(3)(a).

7.　An inhibition will be invalid if there is not strict accuracy (e.g. an error or misdescription in relation to the inhibiter or the person inhibited): *Walker v. Hunter* (1853) 16 D. 226; and see, e.g. *Allied Irish Bank plc v. G.P.T. Sales and Services Ltd* 1995 S.L.T. 163; *Modern Housing Ltd v. Love* 1998 S.L.T. 1188 (misdescription of registered office address as that of a place of business, held trivial). Where there is a disparity between the name used in the Register of Inhibitions and the Register of Sasines the test is whether the disparity is capable of misleading a third party inspecting or instructing a search: *Atlas Appointments Ltd v. Tinsley* 1994 S.C. 582; for the sequel after proof, see *Atlas Appointments Ltd v. Tinsley* 1997 S.C. 200.

"INTERIM ATTACHMENT".

14A.2.9　Sections 9A–9S of the Debt Arrangement and Attachment (Scotland) Act 2002 (inserted by s.173 of the Bankruptcy and Diligence etc. (Scotland) Act 2007) when brought into force will introduce and provide for a new concept of interim attachment similar to that of arrestment and inhibition on the dependence. The court may grant warrant for diligence by interim attachment of corporeal moveable property on the dependence of an action where the action contains a conclusion, or a petition which contains a prayer, for payment of money other than expenses. Interim attachment may be granted before a hearing or, if refused and insisted in by the creditor, at a hearing intimated to the debtor and interested persons. The grounds for granting or recall are the same as for arrestment or inhibition: see notes 14A.2.4 and 14A.4.3.

1.　A warrant for interim attachment is competent over corporeal moveable property owned alone or in common by the debtor on the dependence of an action or petition (i.e. from the time it is commenced—that is, served or, in a petition, a first order is made—until final extract) where there is conclusion, or prayer in a petition, for payment of a sum of money other than expenses: 2002 Act, s.9A.

2.　Sections 12, 13 and 15 of the Debtors (Scotland) Act 1987 apply to the execution of an interim attachment: 2002 Act, s.9F. The schedule will be in Form 2a in Appendix 1 of Sch.1 to the Act of Sederunt (Debt Arrangement and Attachment (Scotland) Act 2002) 2002 [SSI 2002/560]. It may be executed at any time after it is granted, before, at the same time as or after service of the summons or petition; but if executed before service it ceases to have effect if the summons is not served on the debtor before the end of 21 days beginning with the day on which the interim attachment is executed: 2002 Act, s.9G. The period may be extended by the court.

3.　Subjects attached. The property that may be attached is any corporeal moveable property owned alone or in common by the debtor: 2002 Act, s.9A(1). Certain property is exempt, including any article within a dwelling (!), any perishable item or article to be sold in the course of the debtor's trade: 2002 Act, s.9B.

4.　Effect of attachment. Section 21 (except subsections (3) and (15)) applies so that the debtor or person in possession of an attached article may not move it from the place it is attached, sell it, make a gift of it or otherwise relinquish ownership.

5.　Duration. Interim attachment, unless recalled, has effect, where the creditor obtains a relevant decree, until the expiry of six months after the action or petition is disposed of (but only if the article is attached in execution within that period) or, where the decree is absolvitor or dismissal and no expenses are recoverable by attachment, the date of the decree: 2002 Act, s.9L.

EXPENSES OF DILIGENCE.

14A.2.10　The creditor is entitled to expenses in obtaining warrant for arrestment, inhibition or interim attachment on the dependence and, where executed, the expenses of executing it: 1987 Act, s.15M(1); 2002 Act, s.9P(1). A debtor is entitled to expenses in opposing the warrant where the creditor acted unreasonably in applying for it: 1987 Act, s.15M(2); 2002 Act, s.9P(2). The court has power to modify the expenses. Expenses incurred in obtaining or opposing a warrant are expenses of process.

ARRESTMENT OF SHIPS ETC. ON THE DEPENDENCE; AND ARRESTMENT TO FOUND JURISDICTION.

14A.2.11　For arrestment of a ship or cargo on the dependence of an Admiralty action, see note 13.6A.4. For arrestment in rem of a ship or cargo, see note 13.6A.4(2); and for dismantling a ship, see 13.6A.5.

The provisions of the 1987 Act relating to arrestment on the dependence (apart from ss.15H (the sum attached), 15J (property affected) and 15M(expenses)) apply to arrestment on the dependence of an Admiralty action in so far as not inconsistent with Pt. V of the Administration of Justice Act 1956.

For arrestment to found jurisdiction, see note 13.6A.1.

Effect of authority for inhibition on the dependence

14A.3.—[1](1)   Where a person has been granted authority for inhibition on the dependence of an action or petition, a certified copy of the interlocutor granting the motion may be registered with a certificate of execution in the Register of Inhibitions and Adjudications.

(2)[2]   A notice of a certified copy of an interlocutor granting authority for inhibition under rule 14A.2 may be registered in the Register of Inhibitions and Adjudications; and such registration is to have the same effect as registration of a notice of inhibition under section 155(2) of the Titles to Land Consolidation (Scotland) Act 1868.

14A.3

REGISTRATION IN REGISTER OF INHIBITIONS.

To be effectual the inhibition and execution of service of it on the defender must be registered in the Register of Inhibitions and Adjudications (sometimes known as the "personal" or "diligence" register). The certified copy interlocutor granting the inhibition must be taken to the office of the register in Meadowbank House (open 10am to 4pm Monday to Friday) to be recorded.

An inhibition takes effect from the beginning of the day of registration: Titles to Land Consolidation (Scotland) Act 1868, s. 155. Where a notice of inhibition is registered before the schedule of arrestment is served on the debtor and the inhibition is registered before the expiry of 21 days after the date of the recording of the notice, the inhibition takes effect from the date on which the schedule of inhibition is served: 1868 Act, s.155. By virtue of r. 14A.3(2) the same applies to notice of the certified copy of the interlocutor granting warrant for inhibition. The Keeper of the Records must enter on each title in the Land Register any subsisting entry in the Register of Inhibitions and Adjudications adverse to the interest: Land Registration (Scotland) Act 1979, s.6(1). A title registered under this Act is subject, generally, only to such rights as are entered in the title sheet (s.3) and an inhibition will not take effect until it is so entered. Practical difficulties arising out of these provisions are discussed in Halliday on *Conveyancing Law and Practice*, Vol. II, (2nd ed.), para. 38–35 and Gretton on Law of Inhibition and Adjudication (2nd ed.), pp.39–43.

14A.3.1

Recall etc of arrestment or inhibition

14A.4.—[3](1)   An application by any person having an interest—

(a)   to loose, restrict, vary or recall an arrestment or an interim attachment; or

(b)   to recall, in whole or in part, or vary, an inhibition,

shall be made by motion.

(1A)[4]   A motion under paragraph (1) shall—

(a)   specify the name and address of each of the parties;

(b)   where it relates to an inhibition, contain a description of the inhibition including the date of registration in the Register of Inhibitions and Adjudications.

(2)   Any person having an interest may apply by motion for a warrant authorising the movement of a vessel or cargo which is the subject of arrestment on the dependence, and paragraphs (2) and (3) of rule 13.11 (movement of arrested property) shall apply in such a case as they apply to the case of that rule.

14A.4

GENERAL NOTE.

Recall or restriction or any determination of a question relating to the validity, effect or operation of a warrant for arrestment or inhibition on the dependence of an action or petition is now governed by s. 15K of the Debtors (Scotland) Act 1987. Identical provisions are made for recall, restriction, etc., of an interim attachment of land in s. 9M of the Debt Arrangement and Attachment (Scotland) Act 2002.

The debtor has to intimate any order made by the court to the creditor and any other person appearing to the court to have an interest.

14A.4.1

LOOSING OF ARRESTMENT.

This means a permission to the defender (or other person) to obtain, or for the release of, the arrested property but which does not extinguish the arrestment of the legal nexus created until the property is

14A.4.2

---

[1] R. 14A.3 inserted by S.S.I. 2008 No. 122 (effective 1st April 2008).
[2] R. 14A.3(2) substituted by S.S.I. 2009 No. 104 (effective 22nd April 2009).
[3] Rule 14A.4 inserted by S.S.I. 2008 No. 122 (effective 1st April 2008).
[4] Rule 14A.4(1A) inserted by S.S.I. 2014 No. 291 (effective 8th December 2014).

uplifted by the defender. If a later arrestment is laid by another creditor before the property is uplifted, the loosing is ineffectual when the pursuer is notified of the later arrestment. In relation to ships, loosing means a permission to move the ship and does not recall the arrestment but postpones the arrestment until after the move: *Svenska Petroleum A.B. v. H.O.R. Ltd* 1982 S.L.T. 343; and see r. 13.11. Loosing is distinguished from restriction, and from recall which extinguishes the arrestment.

RESTRICTION OR RECALL.

14A.4.3   Section 15K of the Debtors (Scotland) Act 1987 in relation to arrestment or inhibition on the dependence, and s. 9M of the Debt Arrangement and Attachment (Scotland) Act 2002 in relation to interim attachment, provide for the recall, restriction, or for the determining of any question about the validity, effect or operation of the warrant for or the diligence on the dependence in an action or petition. A motion for recall etc. must be intimated to the creditor and any other person having an interest, and at the hearing the court must give any such person to whom intimation was given, and any other person the court is satisfied has an interest, an opportunity to be heard.

There is now no onus on the debtor or any other person having an interest to establish that the warrant or diligence should be recalled or restricted. The onus is on the creditor to satisfy the court, as the case may be, that the warrant is not invalid, is not incompetent, is not irregular or ineffective, or should not be recalled or restricted: 1987 Act, s. 15K(10) and 2002 Act, s. 9M(10). As with the granting of the warrant before a hearing, or at a hearing whether opposed or not, the creditor must satisfy the court that (a) he has a prima facie case on the merits; (b) there is a real and substantial risk that enforcement of any decree in favour of the creditor would be defeated or prejudiced by reason of (i) the debtor being insolvent or verging on insolvency or (ii) the likelihood of the debtor removing, disposing of, burdening, concealing or otherwise dealing with all or some of his assets; and (c) it is reasonable in all the circumstances, including the effect granting warrant may have had on any person having an interest, for the warrant or any diligence executed in pursuance of the warrant to continue to have effect.

The position at common law in relation to restriction or recall of arrestment or inhibition on the dependence was as follows.

1.   *Where the arrestment or inhibition is nimious or oppressive*: Examples are: (a) Where the conclusions are extravagant or the sum arrested far exceeds the claim: *Shanks v. Thomson* (1838) 16 S. 1353 (arrestment); *Mylne v. Blackwood* (1832) 10 S. 430 (inhibition); *McInally v. Kildonal Homes Ltd* 1979 S.L.T. (Notes) 89. (b) Where the pursuer already has sufficient security: *Magistrates of Dundee v. Taylor and Grant* (1863) 1 M. 701 (arrestment); *Cullen v. Buchanan* (1862) 24 D. 1280 (inhibition). (c) Where there are more than sufficient funds to meet the claim and there are no prospects of it being defeated by other creditors: *Magistrates of Dundee*, above; *West Cumberland Farmers Ltd v. Director of Agriculture of Sri Lanka* 1988 S.L.T. 296 (arrestment); although this may be a ground for rejecting a plea of nimiety or oppression: *Mendok BV v. Cumberland Maritime Corporation* 1989 S.L.T. 192, 193 per Lord McDonald. The critical question to consider when determining the issue of insolvency in the context of recall of inhibition is whether a significant risk of insolvency exists at the time when the claim, if sustained by the court, falls to be paid; accordingly the future has to be considered and a balance sheet is not conclusive: *Barry D Trentham Ltd v. Lawfield Investments Ltd* , 2002 S.C. 401, 406, para.[13] (OH), (d) Where there is excessive delay in pursuing the action, where the defender has consigned the sum, where the purpose is not to protect legitimate interests but to embarrass the defender: *Levy v. Gardiner* 1964 S.L.T. (Notes) 68; *Conoco Speciality Products (Inc.) v. Merpro Montassa Ltd (No. 2)* 1991 S.L.T. 513; *Hydraload Research Ltd v. Bone Council & Baxters Ltd* 1996 S.L.T. 219. (e) Where there is no colourable case or no intelligible and discernible cause of action, though the averments are not examined with the scrutiny of a procedure roll debate: *West Cumberland Farmers Ltd v. Ellon Hinengo Ltd* 1988 S.L.T. 294 per Lord Weir; *Clipper Shipping Co. Ltd v. San Vincente Partners* 1989 S.L.T. 204 (affidavit of foreign lawyer accepted); *Stratmail Ltd v. D. & A. Todd (Building Contractors) Ltd* 1990 S.L.T. 493 (unanswerable plea of lis alibi pendens); *Hydraload*, above. Indeed, the court is not confined to the pursuer's averments but may look at the material but may look at the material before it: *Stiell Facilities Ltd v. Sir Robert McAlpine Ltd* , 2001 S.L.T. 1229 (OH), (f) Where the diligence had only a nuisance value: *Taymech Ltd v. Rush & Tompkins Ltd* 1990 S.L.T. 681. (g) Where arrestment unduly interferes with ordinary trading activities without legitimate advantage: *Matheson v. Matheson* 1995 S.L.T. 765. (h) Use of diligence on the dependence against foreign state agencies is uncommon as they could normally be expected to meet any decree, and the use of such diligence in those circumstances would be oppressive. But a distinction is to be drawn in the case of bodies merely or supported by foreign governments such as state-owned companies: *Tor Corporate AS v. China National Star Petroleum Corporation* , 27th July 2000 (OH), unreported.

2.   *Where the debt is future or contingent and there are no averments of special circumstances—e.g. that the debtor is vergens ad inopiam or in meditatione fugae*—the diligence is in fact incompetent: see note 13.6.3(3).

3.   *Where there is a defect or irregularity in execution: e.g. Richards & Wallington (Earthmoving) Ltd v. Whatlings Ltd* 1982 S.L.T. 66 (action and arrestment in wrong name, the company having changed its name before the action; arrestment recalled). In *Dramgate Ltd v. Tyne Dock Engineering Ltd* , 2000 S.C. 43 (Ex Div.), an arrestment on the dependence was held wrongful because it had been executed before the arrestment to found jurisdiction (before which there was no jurisdiction). The arrestment on the dependence in that case being defective, it was not necessary to aver malice and want of probable cause.

4. *Where the property arrested is not arrestable: Forth & Clyde Construction Co. Ltd v. Trinity Timber & Plywood Co. Ltd* 1984 S.L.T. 94; though this is usually determined in the action of furthcoming.

5. *Where the property arrested is not that of the defender. Barclay Curie & Co. Ltd v. Sir James Laing & Sons Ltd* 1908 S.C. 82; *Blade Securities Ltd, Petrs.* 1989 S.L.T. 246; *Sunrise Trading Co. Ltd v. Mobil Sales and Supply Corporation* , 27th October 1995, unreported, 1996 G.W.D. 2-111 (separate companies allegedly a single economic unit).

6. *Where caution or consignation is offered in lieu,* as diligence is simply to provide a security: see note 13.10.5.

7. *Where the pursuer has not made out a prima facie case on the merits of the action.* In *Advocate General v. Taylor* , 2004 S.C. 339, 2003 S.L.T. 1340, para. [34], it was held by an Extra Division that for a warrant for inhibition (and it would also apply to arrestment) the applicant need only establish a prima facie case on the merits of the action; the necessity for diligence need not be demonstrated, although it may no doubt assist. In that event, a ground for recall must now be that the pursuer has not made out a prima facie case on the merits. The prima facie test is a substantial hurdle for the pursuer to surmount: *Gillespie v. Toondale Ltd* , 2006 S.C. 304, 308, para. [13] (Extra Div. approving Lord Drummond Young in *Barry D Trent ham Ltd v. Lawfield Investments Ltd* , 2002 S.C. 401, 2002 S.L.T. 1094, at para. [6] on the meaning of "prima facie", i.e. a good arguable case).

If there is a disputed question of right to the subjects arrested it will not be decided in the application for recall unless instantly verifiable without a proof, or caution is offered for the recall: *Vincent v. Chalmers & Co.'s Tr.* (1877) 5 R. 43; *William Batey (Exports) Ltd v. Kent* 1987 S.L.T. 557.

Recall of arrestments could be of all arrestments used and to be used (general recall), or specified arrestments or those used (special recall); the warrant for arrestment being rarely recalled. In the recall of inhibitions, the warrant itself is recalled because the warrant authorises one diligence. Interim recall of diligence is not competent. When an inhibition has been recalled a certified copy interlocutor should be obtained (prepared by the applicant for certification by a clerk of session in the appropriate section of the General Department) and recorded in the Register of Inhibitions and Adjudications. If there is a partial recall, the interlocutor should contain an adequate description of the subjects excluded. This is to enable the Keeper of the Registers to make the appropriate entry in the Register of Inhibitions and Adjudications and, if appropriate, the Land Register. It is preferable for the interlocutor to specify the subjects excluded rather than those included for it is only in respect of the former that the defender has satisfied the court that the inhibition should be recalled. The recall ought not to be recorded until after the reclaiming days have expired (14 days: see r. 38.3(4)(h)).

Certain statutes confer particular powers for recall, loosing or restriction of arrestments and inhibitions. These include: Administration of Justice Act 1956, s. 47(5), proviso (arrestment of ship in rem for non-pecuniary claim); Merchant Shipping (Liability of Shipowners and Others) Act 1958, s.6 (arrestment for claim for which limit is set by the Merchant Shipping Act 1894, s.503); Merchant Shipping Act 1995, s.159 (arrestment on dependence or in rem where defender can limit his liability); Debtors (Scotland) Act 1987, ss.2(3) and 3(1) (arrestments in relation to time to pay directions); Criminal Justice Act 1988, s.92(4) (arrestment or inhibition of property affected by restraint orders relating to the proceeds of crime); Prevention of Terrorism (Temporary Provisions) Act 1989, Sched.4, paras. 16 and 16A (inhibition or arrestment of property affected by restraint orders relating to property liable to forfeiture); Proceeds of Crime (Scotland) Act 1995, ss.32(1) and 33(1) (inhibition or arrestment of property affected by restraint orders or interdict relating to the proceeds of crime).

Caution, other security or consignation.

Under s. 15K(11) and (12) of the Debtors (Scotland) Act 1987 in relation to arrestment or inhibition on the dependence, and s. 9M(120 and (13) of the Debt Arrangement and Attachment (Scotland) Act 2002 in relation to interim attachment, the court may in granting recall, restriction, etc., impose conditions. Those conditions may include consignation, caution or other security.

14A.4.4

The position at common law was as follows. This may not be required where the diligence was nimious or oppressive: e.g. where there is no colourable case; where its use is merely to embarrass the defender (*Levy v. Gardiner* 1964 S.L.T. (Notes) 68); where the debt is future or contingent and there are no special circumstances averred; where there was irregularity in execution; where the property arrested was not arrestable or was not the property of the defender (and this is instantly verifiable). Where the conclusions are extravagant or the sum arrested is excessive or the claim is for a random sum, caution will be fixed having regard to the nature of the action, the extent of the subjects affected by the diligence and the circumstances of the defender. Where the defender has ample funds he may be required to find caution or consignation as a condition of recall (cf. *West Cumberland Farmers Ltd v. Director of Agriculture of Sri Lanka* 1988 S.L.T. 296). Failure to offer caution may be regarded as grounds for doubting an ability to meet the claim.

Caution in lieu of arrestment may be for the arrested property or its value, but usually for the whole debt including expenses; where caution is for the whole debt a general recall should be obtained, and where a general recall is sought caution must be for the whole debt including expenses. Where recall is made on caution for the whole debt the interlocutor recalls only the arrestments used and not future arrestments (special recall), future arrestments are not ineffectual or incompetent. Caution in lieu of inhibition is usually for the whole debt including expenses.

In deciding whether a guarantee offered is an adequate alternative security to replace that held by an arrestment, the relevant comparison is between the security afforded by the proposed guarantee on the one hand and that afforded by the arrestment (and not a guarantee by an independent financial institution) on the other: *Global Marine Drilling Co. v. Triton Holdings Ltd (No.2)* , 26th January 2000, (2000 G.W.D. 5-210) (OH). There is no rule that recall should normally be on the provision of a guarantee by such an institution: *Global Marine Drilling Co*, above. Another form of security other than caution may be allowed: r. 33.4(2). Consignation may be ordered in lieu of caution: see *Fisher v. Weir* 1964 S.L.T. (Notes) 99.

EXPENSES.

14A.4.5   Under s. 15K of the Debtors (Scotland) Act 1987 in relation to arrestment or inhibition on the dependence, and s. 9M of the Debt Arrangement and Attachment (Scotland) Act 2002 in relation to interim attachment, the debtor is entitled to such expenses as the court thinks fit in opposing a warrant for diligence on the dependence where it has been granted and the creditor was acting unreasonably in applying for it. The expenses are expenses of process. The Acts are silent in relation to recall or restriction on a ground other than unreasonableness.

The position at common law was as follows. This depends on the circumstances of the arrestment or inhibition not the merits of the action: *Clark v. Loos* (1855) 17 D. 306. Where arrestment or inhibition was improperly used (nimiously, oppressively, incompetently or irregularly), the pursuer pays the judicial expenses incurred in the recall. Where properly used but loosed, restricted or recalled on caution, the defender may be required to pay the expenses. Expenses may be reserved where diligence is properly used and recalled on caution or consignation (*Dobbie v. Duncanson* (1872) 10 M. 810, 816 per L.P. Inglis). The expenses of an unsuccessful application for recall are borne by the applicant. See also Graham Stewart on *Diligence*, pp. 212 and 573; Gretton on the *Law of Inhibition and Adjudication*, pp. 39–41.

"MOTION".

14A.4.6   For motions, see Chap. 23.

RECLAIMING.

14A.4.7   An interlocutor loosing, recalling or restricting an arrestment or recalling, in whole or in part, an inhibition or refusing such, may be reclaimed without leave within 14 days: r. 38.3(4)(h).

Incidental applications in relation to interim diligence, etc

14A.5   **14A.5.**[1]   An application to the Court under Part 1A of the 1987 Act or Part 1A of the 2002 Act not otherwise provided for shall be made by motion.

"MOTION".

14A.5.1   For motions, see Chap. 23.

---

[1] R. 14A.5 inserted by S.S.I. 2008 No. 122 (effective 1st April 2008).

CHAPTER 14B DETERMINATION OF THE VALUE OF AN ORDER

Chapter 14B[1]

Determination of the Value of an Order

Application and interpretation

14B.1.—[2](1) This Chapter makes provision about determining, for the purposes of section 39 of the Act of 2014—

(a) the value of an order sought in a cause; and

(b) the aggregate total value of all the orders sought in a cause.

(2) In this Chapter "order" is to be construed in accordance with section 39(6) of the Act of 2014.

GENERAL NOTE.

Chapter 14B is concerned with the privative jurisdiction of the sheriff court which, subject to two exceptions, has exclusive jurisdiction in causes up to a value of £100,000: Courts Reform (Scotland) Act 2014, s.39(1) and (2).

The exceptions are (1) family proceedings unless the only order sought is for aliment (s. 39(3)) and (2) where, in exceptional circumstances, the cause is remitted to the Court of Session, for which see s. 92(7) of the Act of 2014. (s. 39(4)). Section 39(1) of the Act of 2014 provides that the jurisdiction of the sheriff court applies where one or more of the orders of value sought does not exceed £100,000 or where the aggregate total value of all orders of value sought does not exceed £100,000. An order of value is an order for payment of money or an order determining rights in relation to property: Act of 2014, s. 39(6). Chapter 14B assists in determining the value of an order and the aggregate total value. Chapter 14 B is made under ss.39(7) and 103(1) of the Act of 2014.

Value of an order for payment of money

14B.2.—[3](1) This rule applies where the order sought is an order for payment of money.

(2) The value of the order is the sum of money sought unless the court otherwise determines.

(3) Where the order sought is for—

(a) payment in instalments; or

(b) a periodical payment, that is a payment that recurs at specified intervals or on the occurrence of specified events,

the instalments or periodical payments are added together to determine the sum of money sought.

(4) Where an award of interest is sought from the court in addition to the payment of money, that interest is not to be taken into account for the purposes of this rule.

(5) Where the party seeking the order considers that its value exceeds the value of the sum of money sought, that party must make averments stating—

(a) why it considers that to be the case;

(b) its true value, and

its value is the sum stated in those averments, unless the court otherwise determines.

GENERAL NOTE.

Rule 14B.2 sets out how to calculate the value of an order of the payment of money in relation to the privative jurisdiction of the sheriff court under s. 39 of the Courts Reform (Scotland) Act 2014.

Value of an order determining rights in relation to property

14B.3.—[4](1) This rule applies where the order sought is an order determining rights in relation to property.

---

[1] Ch. 14B and r. 14B.1 as inserted by S.S.I. 2015 No. 228 r. 2 (effective 22 September 2015).

[2] Ch. 14B and r. 14B.1 as inserted by S.S.I. 2015 No. 228 r. 2 (effective 22 September 2015).

[3] Rule 14B.2 as inserted by S.S.I. 2015 No. 228 r. 2 (effective 22 September 2015).

[4] Rule 14B.3 as inserted by S.S.I. 2015 No. 228 r. 2 (effective 22 September 2015).

(2)   The party seeking the order must make averments stating—

    (a)   the value of that order;

    (b)   why it considers that to be the value, and

its value is the sum stated in those averments, unless the court otherwise determines.

GENERAL NOTE.

14B.3.1   Rule 14B.3 requires averments in pleadings about the value of an order determining rights in relation to property. It does not set out how to calculate the value. Where the value of an order is unascertainable, r. 14B.4 applies.

Provision where the value of an order is unascertainable

14B.4   **14B.4.**—[1](1)   This rule applies where a party seeking an order considers that its value is unascertainable at the time when the order is sought.

(2)   That party must make averments stating why it considers the value to be unascertainable.

(3)   The court is to put the cause out on the By Order Roll—

    (a)   where the cause has been commenced by summons, on the first suitable court day after the expiry of the period for lodging defences under rule 18.1(2); or

    (b)   where the cause has been commenced by petition, on the first suitable court day after the expiry of the period of notice for lodging answers under rule 14.6(1).

(4)   At the hearing under paragraph (3), the parties may make submissions in relation to the value of the order and whether it is unascertainable.

(5)   Where the court determines that the value is unascertainable, its value is to be taken as exceeding £100,000.

GENERAL NOTE.

14B.4.1   Where a party considers that the value of an order is unascertainable, that party must make averments stating why: r. 14B.4. The court will put the case out By Order to determine if it is unascertainable. If the value of the order is unascertainable, it is to be treated as exceeding £100,000 (and the sheriff court does not have exclusive jurisdiction): r. 14B.4(5).

Determining the aggregate total value of orders in a cause

14B.5   **14B.5.**—[2](1)   This rule applies where more than one order is sought in a cause, including where—

    (a)   a party seeks orders against more than one other party in the same cause;

    (b)   more than one party seeks an order in the same cause, whether against one or more other parties.

(2)   The aggregate total value is determined by adding together the value of each order as determined in accordance with this Chapter.

(3)   An order that is alternative to any other order sought by the same party is to be disregarded in determining the aggregate total value.

(4)   An order sought in a counterclaim is to be disregarded in determining the aggregate total value.

GENERAL NOTE.

14B.5.1   Rule 14B.5 deals with calculating the aggregate total value of an order for the purposes of s. 39(1)(b)(ii) of the Courts Reform (Scotland) Act 2014 .

Determination by the court

14B.6   **14B.6.**—[3](1)   This rule applies where the court requires to determine the value of an order or the aggregate total value of all the orders sought.

---

[1] Rule 14B.4 as inserted by S.S.I. 2015 No. 228 r. 2 (effective 22 September 2015).
[2] Rule 14B.5 as inserted by S.S.I. 2015 No. 228 r. 2 (effective 22 September 2015).
[3] Rule 14B.6 as inserted by S.S.I. 2015 No. 228 r. 2 (effective 22 September 2015).

(2) The court is to have regard to the pleadings in the cause, including any defences or answers that have been lodged.

(3) The court may put the cause out on the By Order Roll in order that parties may make submissions where the court considers that doing so would assist it to determine the value of an order or the aggregate total value of all the orders sought.

(4) The court must put the cause out on the By Order Roll in order that parties may make submissions if it is considering making a determination that the aggregate total value of all the orders sought is less than £100,000.

GENERAL NOTE.

Rule 14B.6 states where, apart from r. 14B.4(3) (by order hearing where value of an order is unascertainable), the court may (if the court considers doing so would assist to determine value), or must (if considering making a determination that the total value is less than £100,000), have a By Order hearing to determine value.

14B.6.1

CHAPTER 15 APPLICATION BY MINUTE OR NOTE

Applications by minute

15.1.—(1) Subject to paragraph (6) and to any other provision in these Rules, this rule applies to any application to the court by minute in a cause.

(2) A minute shall—

    (a) include a crave, a statement of facts and appropriate pleas-in-law; and

    (b) be lodged in the process of the cause to which it relates.

(3) On lodging a minute, the minuter shall enrol a motion, as appropriate—

    (a) for a warrant for service of the minute on a person who has not entered the process of the cause;

    (b) where the cause is not a depending cause, for service of the minute on parties to that cause;

    (c) for intimation of the minute to any person;

    (d) to dispense with service on, or intimation to, a person; and

    (e) for an order for any answers to the minute to be lodged in process within the period of notice.

(4) A notice in Form 15.1 shall be attached to the minute to be served or intimated under paragraph (3).

(5) After the expiry of the period of notice, the court shall, on the motion of any party, after such further procedure, if any, as it thinks fit, determine the application.

(6) This rule shall not apply to—

    (a) a minute of abandonment;

    (b) a minute of amendment;

    (c) a minute of sist;

    (d) a minute of transference;

    (e) a minute of objection to a minute of transference; or

    (f)[1] a minute to dismiss a claim under rule 21A.

GENERAL NOTE.

This is a new rule intended to provide a general provision for applications by minute. Particular rules may exclude or augment the provisions of this rule.

An application in an action, which may not be made by motion, is made by minute or where the court orders that a minute regarding the subject-matter of an application be lodged within a prescribed period (e.g. variation of aliment or access: e.g. rr. 49.42(4) and 49.43(4)).

FORM OF MINUTE.

The crave, statement of facts and pleas-in-law should follow the principles applicable to the conclusions, condescendence and pleas-in-law in an action. On conclusions, see note 13.2.3. On the condescendence, see note 13.2.4. On pleas-in-law, see notes 13.2.5 and 18.1.4. The instance should be the same as in the summons. On use of metric units of measurement, see note 13.2.18.

"SERVICE".

For methods, see Chap. 16, Pt. I.

"INTIMATION".

For methods, see rr. 16.7 and 16.8. Particular rules may require a warrant for intimation.

"DEPENDING CAUSE".

A cause is depending from the time it is commenced (i.e. from the time an action is served or a first order in a petition is made) until final decree, whereas a cause is in dependence until final extract. For the meaning of commenced, see note 13.4.4 (action) or 14.6.1 (petition). For the meaning of final decree, see note 4.15.2(2). For the meaning of final extract, see note 7.1.2(2).

---

[1] R. 15.1(6)(f) inserted by S.S.I. 2008 No. 349 (effective 1st December 2008).

15.1.5   This period is determined in accordance with rule 14.6 (period of notice for lodging answers) by virtue of r. 1.3(1) (definitions of "period of notice" and "writ").

"ANSWERS".

15.1.6   For form and lodging of answers, see r. 18.3 and notes.

FEE.

15.1.7   The court fee for lodging a minute is payable on lodging by a person, other than an originating party, on first appearing, or for variation of an order in a family action. For fee, see Court of Session etc. Fees Order 1997, Table of Fees, Pt. I, B, item 2, 6 or 8 [SI 1997/688, as amended, pp. C1201 et seq.]. Certain persons are exempt from payment of fees: see 1997 Fees Order, art.5, substituted by SSI 2002/270. A fee exemption certificate must be lodged in process: see P.N. No.1 of 2002.

Where the minuter is legally represented, the fee may be debited under a credit scheme introduced on 1st April 1976 by P.N. No. 4 of 1976 to the account (if one is kept or permitted) of the agent by the court cashier, and an account will be rendered weekly by the court cashier's office to the agent for all court fees due that week for immediate settlement. Party litigants, and agents not operating the scheme, must pay (by cash, cheque or postal order) on each occasion a fee is due at the time of lodging at the counter at the General Department.

MINUTES TO WHICH THIS RULE DOES NOT APPLY.

15.1.8   The minutes listed in r. 15.1(6) have their own forms and procedures and r. 15.1 does not therefore apply. On minutes of abandonment, see Chap. 29. On minutes of amendment, see Chap. 24. On minutes of sist, see r. 31.1. On minutes of transference and minutes of objection to such a minute, see r. 31.2.

PARTY MINUTERS.

15.1.9   There are no rules as to the form of a minute to be lodged by a person seeking to be sisted as a party (a party minuter) other than a minute of sist by a person representing a deceased or incapacitated party (see r. 13.1). A variety of styles are encountered, namely, a simple minute of sist with no pleadings, a minute of sist with pleadings attached, or simply answers, each accompanied by a motion to be sisted. The appropriate form of writ will often depend on the circumstances. In some instances the form of intimation will specify the writ to be lodged. As a general rule, however, unless otherwise provided in the R.C.S. 1994, a minute should seek to be sisted stating the ground on which the person wishes to become a party. The minute should be accompanied by the appropriate writ containing the pleadings.

Applications by note

15.2   **15.2.**—(1)   Subject to paragraph (4) and to any other provision in these Rules, this rule applies to any application to the court by note in a cause.

(2)   A note shall—

(a)   include a statement of facts and a prayer; and

(b)   be lodged in the process of the cause to which it relates.

(3)   The following provisions of Chapter 14 (petitions) shall, with the necessary modifications and the modification mentioned below, apply to a note under this rule as they apply to a petition:—

rule 14.5 (first order in petitions),

rule 14.6 (period of notice for lodging answers),

rule 14.7 (intimation and service of petitions) with the substitution in paragraph (2) of that rule of the words "a notice in Form 15.2" for the words "a citation in Form 14.7",

rule 14.8 (procedure where answers lodged),

rule 14.9 (unopposed petitions).

(4)   This rule shall not apply to—

(a)   a note to the Extractor; or

(b)   a note of objection.

GENERAL NOTE.

15.2.1   This is a new rule intended to provide a general provision for applications by note. Particular rules may exclude or augment the provisions of this rule.

An application in a petition, which may not be made by motion, is made by note.

For procedure, see the rules and corresponding annotations in Chap. 14 referred to in r. 15.2(3).

FORM OF NOTE.

The Address, statement of facts and prayer should follow the principles applicable to a petition. On the Address, see note 14.4.2. On the statement of facts, see note 14.4.3. On the prayer, see note 14.4.8. On use of metric units of measurement, see note 14.4.14.

15.2.2

ANSWERS.

For form and lodging of answers to a note, see r. 18.3 and notes.

15.2.3

FEE.

The court fee for lodging a note is payable on lodging by a person, other than an originating party, on first appearing. For fee, see Court of Session etc. Fees Order 1997, Table of Fees, Pt. I, C, item 4 [SI 1997/688, as amended, pp. C 1201 et seq.]. Certain persons are exempt from payment of fees: see 1997 Fees Order, art. 5 substituted by SSI 2002/270. A fee exemption certificate must be lodged in process: see P.N. No.1 of 2002.

15.2.4

Where the noter is legally represented, the fee may be debited under a credit scheme introduced on 1st April 1976 by P.N. No. 4 of 1976 to the account (if one is kept or permitted) of the agent by the court cashier, and an account will be rendered weekly by the court cashier's office to the agent for all court fees due that week for immediate settlement. Party litigants, and agents not operating the scheme, must pay (by cash, cheque or postal order) on each occasion a fee is due at the time of lodging at the counter at the Petition Department.

NOTES TO WHICH THIS RULE DOES NOT APPLY.

The notes listed in r. 15.2(4) have their own forms and procedure and r. 15.2 does not therefore apply. On notes to the Extractor, see r. 7.1(3). On notes of objections, see r. 42.4 (note of objection to Auditor's report) and r. 61.26 (note of objection to state of funds or scheme of division in judicial factory on estate of deceased person).

15.2.5

CHAPTER 16 SERVICE, INTIMATION AND DILIGENCE

Part I – Service and Intimation

Methods and manner of service

16.1.—(1) Subject to any other provision in these Rules or any other enactment, service of a document required under these Rules on a person shall be executed—

    (a) in the case of an individual—

        (i) personally, by tendering the document and any citation or notice, as the case may be, to that individual;

        (ii) by leaving the document and any citation or notice, as the case may be, in the hands of a person, or failing which, depositing it, in a dwelling place where the person executing service, after due enquiry, has reasonable grounds for believing that that individual resides but is not available;

        (iii) by leaving the document and any citation or notice, as the case may be, in the hands of a person at, or depositing it in, a place of business where the person executing service, after due enquiry, has reasonable grounds for believing that that individual carries on business; or

        (iv) by posting the document and any citation or notice, as the case may be, to the known dwelling place of that individual;

    (b) in the case of any other person—

        (i) by leaving the document and any citation or notice, as the case may be, in the hands of an individual at, or depositing it in, the registered office, other official address or a place of business, of that other person, in such a way that it is likely to come to the attention of that other person; or

        (ii) by posting the document and any citation or notice, as the case may be, to the registered office, other official address or a place of business, of that other person.

(2) Service of a principal writ on a person whose known residence is the same as that of the party on whose behalf service is to be executed shall be executed personally.

(3) Subject to paragraph (4), where service has been executed, the party on whose behalf service has been executed shall attach to the document served and lodge in process—

    (a) a certificate of service as required by these Rules;

    (b) a copy of any notice or advertisement ordered to be published; and

    (c) a copy of any interlocutor ordering service of that document.

(4) In relation to a petition or note, where service has been executed by a petitioner or noter, he shall attach the documents required by paragraph (3)(a) and (b) to a copy of the petition or note, as the case may be, marked "Execution Copy" and certified a true copy.

Deriv. R.C.S. 1965, r. 74A(1) inserted by S.I. 1984 No. 472 and amended by S.I. 1985 No. 1600, 1986 No. 1941 and 1990 No. 705 (r. 16.1(1)), r. 74A(3) inserted by S.I. 1984 No. 472 and r. 77 (r. 16.1(3)), and r. 195(d) (r. 16.1(4))

GENERAL NOTE.

This rule, subject to any other provision in the R.C.S. 1994 or any other enactment, applies to the service of any document (including a summons, petition or note). The rule is subject, e.g. to the rules for service furth of the UK (r. 16.2) or where the address of the person to be served is not known (r. 16.5). The rules for execution of diligence are in Part II of this Chapter which apply certain of the rules for service in Part I to the execution of diligence: see r. 16.12.

Service of a summons marks the commencement of the action: Erskine, III.vi.3; *Alston v. Macdougall* (1887) 15 R. 78; *Smith v. Stewart & Co.* 1960 S.C. 329, 334 per L.P. Clyde. The cause is then in dependence: *Aitken v. Dick* (1863) 1 M. 1038, 1041 per Lords Deas and Ardmillan. A petition or note is commenced and is in dependence when the first order is granted. Service on a defender in an action (or a respondent in a petition) is often called citation. Although a cause is not in dependence until served, certain applications may be made to the court: e.g. motions before calling or first order (r. 23.8), motions where caveat lodged (r. 23.9) or motions by defender or other party before calling (r. 23.10).

SERVICE ON AN INDIVIDUAL (A NATURAL PERSON).

16.1.2   There are six methods of service on natural persons provided in r. 16.1. These are of general application, subject to any other provision in the R.C.S. 1994 or any other enactment in particular the rules for service furth of the UK and the qualifications in rr. 16.3, 16.4 and 16.5.

(1) Personal service: r. 16.1(1)(b)(i).

This may only be executed on a natural person and not a corporate or unincorporated body or firm: cf. r. 16.1(1)(b). It may only be executed in Scotland by a messenger-at-arms (or elsewhere in the UK by his equivalent: a process server) who must explain the purpose of the service to the person served: r. 16.3(1) and (6). The execution of service must be witnessed and the certificate of service signed by the witness: r. 16.3(2). The essential part of personal service is the tendering (giving or offering) of the citation or other document: Stair, IV.xxxviii.15. Hence personal service may be regarded as executed even if the document is refused (Stair, IV.xxxviii.15) or obstructed (*Busby v. Clark* (1904) 7 F. 162): if this occurs the fact should be stated in the certificate of service. The citation or other document should be delivered if possible and, if it is not possible to serve personally, another method should be attempted. Service must be personal where service is of a principal writ (defined in r. 1.3(1)) on a person living at the same address as the party on whose behalf service is executed: r. 16.1(2). Personal service may not be executed on a Sunday: Bell's *Comm.*, ii,460; *Oliphant v. Douglas* (1633) Mor. 15002; *McNiven v. Glasgow Corporation* 1920 S.C. 584.

(2) Leaving in the hands of a person in the dwelling place

where the person on whom service is to be executed resides: r. 16.1(1)(a)(ii). The person executing service (in Scotland, a messenger-at-arms: r. 16.3(1); or, elsewhere in the UK, his equivalent: r. 16.3(6)) must have reasonable grounds for believing that the person on whom service is to be executed normally resides there: r. 16.1(1)(a)(ii). A person's dwelling place is his usual place of residence: *Corstorphine v. Kasten* (1898) 1 F. 287. The name and designation of the person in whose hands the documents are left must be stated in the certificate of service: r. 16.3(5). The documents to be served must be placed in a sealed envelope: r. 16.3(3). The execution of service must be witnessed and the certificate of service signed by the witness: r. 16.3(2). It should be noticed that simply *leaving* the documents *at* the person's residence is not enough. This method of service may not be executed on a Sunday: Bell's *Comm.*, ii,460; *Oliphant v. Douglas* (1633) Mor. 15002; *McNiven v. Glasgow-Corporation* 1920 S.C. 584.

(3) Depositing in the dwelling place

where the person on whom service is to be executed resides: r. 16.1(1)(a)(ii). The person executing service (in Scotland, a messenger-at-arms: r. 16.3(1); or, elsewhere in the UK, his equivalent: r. 16.3(6)) must have reasonable grounds for believing that the person on whom service is to be executed normally resides there: r. 16.1(1)(a)(ii). A person's dwelling place is his usual place of residence: *Corstorphine v. Kasten* (1898) 1 F. 287. The execution of service must be witnessed and the certificate of service signed by the witness: r. 16.3(2). It should be noticed that depositing at (i.e. simply leaving, fixing to the outside of the dwelling or in the lockhole) is not sufficient; the documents must be placed inside the dwelling (e.g. through the letterbox or under the door): *Docherty v. Docherty* 1981 S.L.T. (Notes) 24. This method of service may not be executed on a Sunday: Bell's *Comm.*, ii,460; *Oliphant v. Douglas* (1633) Mor. 15002; *McNiven v. Glasgow Corporation* 1920 S.C. 584.

(4) Leaving in the hands of a person at a place of business

where the person on whom service is to be executed carries on business: r. 16.1(1)(a)(iii). Service by leaving in the hands of a person at the workplace of the person on whom service is to be executed is permissible, but the documents must be placed in a sealed envelope: r. 16.3(3). The name and designation of the person in whose hands the documents are left must be stated in the certificate of service: r. 16.3(5). The person executing service (in Scotland, a messenger-at-arms: r. 16.3(1); or, elsewhere in the UK, his equivalent: r. 16.3(6)) must have reasonable grounds for believing that the person on whom service is to be executed normally carries on business there: r. 16.1(1)(a)(iii). The execution of service must be witnessed and the certificate of service signed by the witness: r. 16.3(2). This method of service may not be executed on a Sunday: Bell's *Comm.*, ii,460; *Oliphant v. Douglas* (1633) Mor. 15002; *McNiven v. Glasgow Corporation* 1920 S.C. 584.

(5) Depositing in a place of business

where the person on whom service is to be executed carries on business: r. 16.1(1)(a)(iii). The person executing service (in Scotland, a messenger-at-arms: r. 16.3(1); or, elsewhere in the UK, his equivalent: r.

16.3(6)) must have reasonable grounds for believing that the person on whom service is to be executed normally carries on business there: r. 16.1(1)(a)(iii). The execution of service must be witnessed and the certificate of service signed by the witness: r. 16.3(2). It should be noticed that depositing at (i.e. simply leaving, fixing to the outside of the workplace or in the lockhole) is not sufficient; the documents must be placed inside (e.g. through the letterbox or under the door): see *Docherty v. Docherty* 1981 S.L.T. (Notes) 24. This method of service may not be executed on a Sunday: *Bell's Comm.*, ii,460; *Oliphant v. Douglas* (1633) Mor. 15002; *McNiven v. Glasgow Corporation* 1920 S.C. 584.

(6)   By post: r. 16.1(1)(a)(iv).

The detailed rules for service by post are in r. 16.4.

SERVICE ON PERSONS OTHER THAN INDIVIDUALS (NON-NATURALPERSONS).

There are three methods of service on legal persons, subject to any other provision in the R.C.S. 1994 or any other enactment and in particular the rules for service furth of the UK and the qualifications in rr. 16.3, 16.4 and 16.5.   **16.1.3**

(1)   Leaving in the hands of an individual

at the registered office or place of business, etc., of the person on whom service is to be executed: r. 16.1(1)(b)(i). Service by leaving in the hands of a person at the registered office or place of business of the person on whom service is to be executed is permissible, but the documents must be placed in a sealed envelope: r. 16.3(3). The name and designation of the person in whose hands the documents are left must be stated in the certificate of service: r. 16.3(5). The person executing service (in Scotland, a messenger-at-arms: r. 16.3(1); or, elsewhere in the UK, his equivalent: r. 16.3(6)) must have reasonable grounds for believing that the person on whom service is to be executed normally carries on business there: r. 16.1(1)(a)(iii). The execution of service must be witnessed and the certificate of service signed by the witness: r. 16.3(2). This method of service may not be executed on a Sunday: *Bell's Comm.*, ii,460; *Oliphant v. Douglas* (1633) Mor. 15002; *McNiven v. Glasgow Corporation* 1920 S.C. 584.

(2)   Depositing in the registered office or place of business, etc.,

of the person on whom service is to be executed: r. 16.1(1)(b)(i). The person executing service in Scotland must be a messenger-at-arms: r. 16.3(1); or, elsewhere in the UK, his equivalent: r. 16.3(6). The execution of service must be witnessed and the certificate of service signed by the witness: r. 16.3(2). It should be noticed that depositing at, e.g. by leaving the documents to be served under a stone on a vacant piece of ground or tied to the railings where a building once was, does not constitute a valid service. The documents must be placed in a building; if there is no building service cannot be executed. This method of service may not be executed on a Sunday: *Bell's Comm.*, ii,460; *Oliphant v. Douglas* (1633) Mor. 15002; *McNiven v. Glasgow Corporation* 1920 S.C. 584.

Section 725(1) of the Companies Act 1985 provides for service of a document on a company by leaving it at, or sending by post to, the company's registered office; and s.695 of the 1985 Act provides for service of process or any notices on an overseas company which has established a place of business in Great Britain. But r. 16.1(1)(b) of the R.C.S. 1994 is more particular, and must be followed with respect to service of documents under the R.C.S. 1994.

(3)   By post: r. 16.1(1)(b)(ii).

The detailed rules for service by post are in r. 16.4. On service on companies, see para.(2), above.

SERVICE ON MEMBERS OF THE ARMED FORCES IN MAINTENANCE PROCEEDINGS.

Where service in connection with maintenance proceedings is to be effected on a member of the armed forces, service may be made by post to the person's commanding officer. The service is of no effect if the commanding officer certifies that the defender is absent without leave or has deserted. It is also without effect if it was served in the U.K. and the defender would be required to appear in court but the commanding officer certifies that the defender is under orders for active service out of the U.K.: see Naval Forces (Enforcement of Maintenance Liabilities) Act 1947, Army Act 1955, section 153; and Air Force Act 1955, section 153).   **16.1.3A**

"CITATION OR NOTICE".

A citation in Form 13.7 must be attached to a summons when served on a defender: r. 13.7(1)(a). In the case of a petition a citation in Form 14.7 is attached to the petition served on any person: r. 14.7(2). In the case of a minute served or intimated on a person there must be attached a notice in Form 15.1; and in the case of a note, a notice in Form 15.2. Other notices may be required to be served under particular rules.   **16.1.4**

EVIDENCE OF SERVICE.

The evidence required by the court for service is (a) a certificate of service by the person executing it, (b) a copy of any notice (e.g. the London, Edinburgh or Belfast Gazette) or advertisement ordered to be served, and (c) a copy of any interlocutor ordering service: r. 16.1(3). Where a form of notice is also required to be served on a person, a copy of that notice must also be lodged. The reason for the docu-   **16.1.5** ments required in addition to the certificate of service is so that the clerk of session can check that what was served was in, referred to or complied with, the same terms of any original interlocutor ordering service, or is a form of notice in compliance with the R.C.S. 1994. In actions these documents are attached to the principal writ: r. 16.1(3). The citation and certificate of service are stitched into the principal summons for lodging for calling. Where any service is executed after calling of a summons or lodging of an execution copy of a petition or note, any citation and certificate of service are lodged as a separate step of process (on which, see r. 4.4). For petitions and notes, see note 16.1.6.

"EXECUTION COPY" OF PETITION OR NOTE.

16.1.6   In petitions and notes the documents required as evidence of service (see note 16.1.5) are attached (stitched in) to an execution copy of the principal writ: r. 16.1(4). A walling certificate is no longer required: P.N. No. 7 of 1994, para. 4.

Service furth of United Kingdom

16.2   **16.2.**—(1)   Subject to any other enactment, this rule applies to service of a document on a person on whom service is to be executed in a country furth of the United Kingdom.

(2)   Service under this rule may be executed by any of the following methods of service, if, and in a manner, permitted under a convention providing for service in that country or by the laws of that country:—

(a)   by post to the known residence, registered office or place of business, as the case may be, of the person on whom service is to be executed;

(b)[1]   through the central, or other appropriate, authority of that country, at the request of the Scottish Ministers;

(c)[2]   through a British consular office in that country, at the request of the Secretary of State for Foreign, Commonwealth and Development Affairs;

(d)   by an *huissier*, other judicial officer or competent official of that country, at the request of a messenger-at-arms, a party or his agent; or

(e)   personally by the party executing service or his authorised agent tendering the document and the citation (if any) to the person on whom service is to be executed.

(3)[3]   Where service is to be executed through a central, or other appropriate, authority at the request of the Scottish Ministers, the party executing service shall—

(a)   send a copy of the document, with a request for service by the method indicated in the request, to the Scottish Ministers; and

(b)   lodge in process a certificate signed by the authority which executed service stating that it has been, and the manner in which it was, served.

(3A)[4]   Where service is to be executed through a British consular officer at the request of the Secretary of State for Foreign, Commonwealth and Development Affairs, the party executing service shall—

(a)   send a copy of the document, with a request for service by the method indicated in the request, to the Secretary of State for Foreign, Commonwealth and Development Affairs; and

(b)   lodge in process a certificate signed by the authority which executed service stating that it has been, and the manner in which it was, served.

(4)   Where service is to be executed by an *huissier*, other judicial officer or competent official at the request of a messenger-at-arms—

---

[1] Rule 16.2(2)(b) amended by S.S.I. 2011 No.190 (effective 11th April 2011).

[2] As amended by the Transfer of Functions (Secretary of State for Foreign, Commonwealth and Development Affairs) Order 2020 (S.I. 2020 No. 942) Sched. 1(2) para. 10 (effective 30th September 2020).

[3] Rule 16.2(3) substituted by S.S.I. 2011 No.190 (effective 11th April 2011).

[4] As amended by the Transfer of Functions (Secretary of State for Foreign, Commonwealth and Development Affairs) Order 2020 (S.I. 2020 No. 942) Sched. 1(2) para. 10 (effective 30th September 2020).

(a) the messenger-at-arms shall send a copy of the document with a request for service by the method indicated in the request to the official in the country in which service is to be executed; and

(b) the party on whose behalf service has been executed shall lodge in process a certificate of the official who executed service stating that it has been, and the manner in which it was, served.

(5) Where service has been executed personally by the party executing service or his authorised agent—

(a) the execution of service shall be witnessed by one witness who shall sign the certificate of service (which shall state his name, occupation and address); and

(b) the person who executed service shall complete a certificate of service in Form 16.2.

(6) Where service is executed by a method mentioned in paragraph (2)(a) or (e), the party executing service shall lodge in process a certificate by a person qualified in the law of the country, or a duly accredited representative of the country, in which service was executed stating that the method of service used is permitted by the law of that country.

Deriv. R.C.S. 1965, r. 74B(1) (r. 16.2(2)), r. 74B(4) (r. 16.2(3)), r. 74B(5) (r. 16.2(4)) and r. 74B(6) (r. 16.2(5)), all inserted by S.I. 1986 No. 1941.

GENERAL NOTE.

This rule provides for all the methods of service available under the *Hague Convention on the Service Abroad of Judicial and Extrajudicial Documents in Civil or Commercial Matters* dated 15th November 1965 (Cmnd 3986 (1969)), and personal service, and applies to any country furth of the U.K. It is necessary, however, to check that, in any foreign country in which service is to be executed, the method to be used is permitted in that country and is one listed in r. 16.2(1) unless the method is one specifically permitted under a particular enactment (see note 16.2.2). This is particularly important in relation to postal or personal service under r. 16.2(2)(a) or (e) as there may be no intervening authority or official in the country concerned who would execute service by a permitted method; and in these two cases a certificate from a qualified person stating that the method is permitted must be lodged in process: r. 16.2(6). **16.2.1**

Consideration has to be given as to whether the person on whom service is to be executed is in (a) a Hague Convention country, (b) a Brussels or Lugano Convention country (to which Sched. 1 or 3C of the C.J.J.A. 1982 applies), (c) an EU Member State other than Denmark, (d) a country with which the U.K. has a bilateral civil procedure convention, or (e) a country with which the U.K. has no convention.

For service in Member States of the EU other than Denmark, see now r. 16.2A (service of judicial and extra judicial documents in civil or commercial matters under Council Regulation (EC) No. 1348/2000).

Guidance on service may be obtained from: Private International Law Branch, Civil Justice and International Division, Justice Department, Scottish Executive, St Andrew House, Regent Road, Edinburgh EH1 3DG, Tel. +44 (0)131-244 4826, Fax. +44 (0)131-244 4848; and the Foreign and Commonwealth Office, Treaty and Nationality Department, 1 Palace Street, London SW1E 5HE, tel. 0171-238 4575 or 4577. See also the Hague Convention website: *www.hcch.net.*

"SUBJECT TO ANY OTHER ENACTMENT".

A statute may provide for a method of service other than one listed in r. 16.2. For example, under s.12 of the State Immunity Act 1978 any writ or document to be served for instituting proceedings other than a counterclaim or an action in rem against a State is served by transmitting it through the Foreign and Commonwealth Office to the Minister of Foreign Affairs of the State concerned, and service is deemed effected when the document is received at that Ministry; time for entering appearance begins to run from two months after that date. On proceedings in respect of which the court has jurisdiction over a foreign State, see note 13.2.2(B)(2). **16.2.2**

For service in Member States of the EU other than Denmark, see now r. 16.2A (service of judicial and extra judicial documents in civil or commercial matters under Council Regulation (EC) No. 1348/2000).

SERVICE IN HAGUE CONVENTION COUNTRIES.

The *Hague Convention countries under the Hague Convention on the Service Abroad of Judicial and Extrajudicial Documents in Civil or Commercial Matters* dated 15th November 1965 (Cmnd. 3986 (1969)) are: **16.2.3**

Albania	Kuwait*
Antigua and Barbuda*	Latvia

Argentina
Armenia
Australia (and dependant territories)
Bahamas*
Barbados*
Belarus
Belgium
Belise*
Bosnia and Hertzegovina
Botswana*
Bulgaria
Canada
China
Columbia*
Croatia
Cyprus
Czech Republic
Denmark
Egypt
Estonia
Finland
France
Germany
Greece
Hungary
Hong Kong**
Iceland
India
Ireland
Israel
Italy
Japan
Korea

Lithuania
Luxembourg
Malawi*
Malta
Mexico
Moldovia*
Monaco
Montenegro
Morocco
Netherlands (and Aruba)
Norway
Pakistan*
Poland
Portugal
Romania
Russian Federation
Saint Vincent and the Grenadines*
San Marino*
Serbia
Seychelles*
Slovakia
Slovenia
Spain
Sri Lanka
Sweden
Switzerland
Former Yugoslav Republic of
Macedonia
Turkey
Ukraine
UK (and dependent territories)
USA (and Mariana Islands)
Venezuela

Note

*Countries marked with a single asterisk are not members of the Hague Organisation.
**The correct designation of Hong Kong is now "Special Administrative Region of the People's Republic of China".

Of the Member States of the European Communities, only Austria and Ireland are not Hague Convention countries.

The Hague Convention has been extended to the following U.K. dependencies:—

Anguilla
Bermuda
British Virgin Islands
Caymen Islands
Falkland Islands
Gibraltar
Guernsey

Isle of Man
Jersey
Montserrat
Pitcairn
Saint Helena
Turks and Caicos Islands

The USA dependencies are: Guam, Puerto Rico and the Virgin Islands.

On the Hague Convention countries and the methods of service acceptable in each country, see the Practical Handbook on the Operation of the Hague Convention on Service Abroad published for the Permanent Bureau of the Hague Convention on Private International Law by Maklu Uitgevers; see also Bowman & Harris on *Multilateral Treaties*; and see the Hague Convention's website: *www.hcch.net*.

The Hague Convention only applies where the address of the person on whom service is to be executed is known: Art.1. The central authorities of the requested State will help to find an address. Where the address of the person on whom service is to be executed is not known r. 16.5 will have to be resorted to for service by advertisement and decree in absence may be obtained after six months: rr. 13.4(1)(d) or 14.6(1)(d). The Hague Convention does not state what is a civil or commercial matter or whether the law of the requesting or the requested country applies. The Special Commission of April 1989 indicated that "civil or commercial matter" should be interpreted in an autonomous manner without reference exclusively to the law of the requesting or requested State or both. On the meaning of "civil and commercial matter" in the Brussels Convention in Sched.1 to the C.J.J.A. 1982, see note 13.2.12; on the meaning in the Hague Convention on the Taking of Evidence Abroad in Civil or CommercialMatters, 1970 (Cmnd. 6727 (1977)) and s.9(1) of the Evidence (Proceedings in Other Jurisdictions) Act 1975, see note 66.1.2.

Where the method of service is by transmission through the central authority (see r. 16.2(2)(b)), the forwarding (central) authority in the U.K. is the Secretary of State for Foreign and Commonwealth Affairs. The model form of request and certificate of service in the convention should be used and sent with the documents for service (all in duplicate: Art.3(2)) to The Foreign and Commonwealth Office, Treaty and Nationality Department, 1 Palace Street, London SW1E 5HE. A translation may be required: r. 16.6.

The model form of request and certificate is as follows:—

REQUEST

FOR SERVICE ABROAD OF JUDICIAL OR EXTRAJUDICIAL DOCUMENTS

Convention on the service abroad of judicial and extrajudicial documents in civil or commercial matters, signed at The Hague, 15 November 1965.

Identity and address of the applicant	Address of receiving authority

The undersigned applicant has the honour to transmit—in duplicate—the documents listed below and, in conformity with article 5 of the above-mentioned Convention, requests prompt service of one copy thereof on the addressee, i.e.,

(identity and address) ....

....

(a) in accordance with the provisions of sub-paragraph (a) of the first paragraph of article 5 of the Convention*.

(b) in accordance with the following particular method (sub-paragraph (b) of the first paragraph of article 5)*:

....

....

....

(c) by delivery to the addressee, if he accepts it voluntarily (second paragraph of article 5)*.

The authority is requested to return or to have returned to the applicant a copy of the documents—and of the annexes*—with a certificate as provided on the reverse side.

List of Documents

....

....

....

....

....

....

....

....   Done at ....

....   Date ....

....   Signature and/or stamp ....

Delete if inappropriate

Reverse of the request

CERTIFICATE

The undersigned authority has the honour to certify, in conformity with article 6 of the Convention,

1)   that the document has been served*

- the (date) ....
- at (place, street, number) ....
....
- in one of the following methods authorised by article 5—
(a)   in accordance with the provisions of sub-paragraph (a) of the first paragraph of article 5 of the Convention*.
(b)   in accordance with the following particular method*:.........
....
(c)   by delivery to the addressee, who accepted it voluntarily*.
The documents referred to in the request have been delivered to:

- (identity and description of person) ....
....
- relationship to the addressee (family, business or other):
....

2)   that the document has not been served, by reason of the following facts*:
....
....
....

In conformity with the second paragraph of article 12 of the Convention, the applicant is requested to pay or reimburse the expenses detailed in the attached statement*.

Annexes
Documents returned: ....
....
....

In appropriate cases, documents establishing the service:
....
....
....

Done at ....
Date ....

Signature and/or stamp ....

*Delete if inappropriate
SUMMARY OF THE DOCUMENT TO BE SERVED
Convention on the service abroad of judicial and extrajudicial documents in civil or commercial matters, signed at The Hague, 15 November 1965.
(article 5, fourth paragraph)
Name and address of the requesting authority: ....
....
....
Particulars of the parties*: ....
....
....
JUDICIAL DOCUMENT**
Nature and purpose of the document:...............
....
....
Nature and purpose of the proceedings and, where appropriate, the amount in dispute:
....
....
Date and place for entering appearance**: ....
....
....
Court which has given judgment**: ....
....
....
Date of judgment**: ....
Time limits stated in the document**: ....
EXTRAJUDICIAL DOCUMENT**
Nature and purpose of the document: ....
....
....
Time limits stated in the document**: ....
....
....

*If appropriate, identity and address of the person interested in the transmission of the document.
**Delete if inappropriate

SERVICE IN BRUSSELS OR LUGANO CONVENTION COUNTRIES.

Art. IV of the Annexed Protocol to the 1968 Brussels Convention in Sched.1, and Art. IV of the Protocol No. 1 to the Lugano Convention in Sched.3C, to the C.J.J.A. 1982 provide for transmission of documents in accordance with the conventions between the Member States (including the Hague Convention) and by public officials in one State directly to public officials in another State. This latter method is intended to provide for transmission by messengers-at-arms and their equivalents such as *huissiers* and is covered by r. 16.2(2)(d): see P. Jenard at pp. 40-41.

The 1968 Brussels Convention has been superseded by, now, the EC Service Regulation (EC) No. 1393/2007 for participating Member States of the EU to the Regulation: i.e. all the Member States of the E.U. except Denmark. Accordingly, the 1968 Convention applies only to Denmark, and will have to be used in relation to that country. For the EU Service Regulation, and participating Member States of the E.U., see note 16.2A.1.

The Lugano Convention has been superseded by, now, the EC Service Regulation (EC) No. 1393/2007 for participating States to the Regulation. The Lugano Convention applies now only to the following countries:

Denmark
Iceland
Norway.

The EU Regulation will apply to the Member States of the E.U. except Denmark.

For countries to which the conventions apply and the methods of service, further information can be obtained from Private International Law Branch, Civil Justice and International Division, Justice Department, Scottish Executive, St Andrew House, Regent Road, Edinburgh EH1 3DG, Tel. +44 (0)131-244 4826, Fax. +44 (0)131-244 4848; and the Foreign and Commonwealth Office, Treaty and Nationality Department, 1 Palace Street, London SW1E 5HE, tel. 0171-238 4575 or 4577; and see also Bowman & Harris on *Multilateral Treaties*.

SERVICE IN BILATERAL CONVENTION COUNTRIES.

In relation to countries with which the U.K. has bilateral civil procedure conventions and the methods of service, information can be obtained from the Foreign and Commonwealth Office, Treaty and Nationality Department, 1 Palace Street, London SW1E 5HE, tel. 0171-238 4575 or 4577. Countries with which the U.K. has bilateral conventions are listed in the Practical Handbook on the Operation of the Hague Convention on Service Abroad published for the Permanent Bureau of the Hague Convention on Private International Law by Maklu Uitgevers. Details can also be obtained from Government websites (e.g. *www.gov.uk/uk-treaties*)

The U.K. has bilateral conventions with the following countries which have been extended to Scotland:

Algeria	Lebanon
Austria	Libya
Belgium	Netherlands
Bahamas	Norway
Czechoslovakia	Poland
Denmark	Portugal
Finland	Romania
France	Spain
Germany	Sweden
Greece	Switzerland
Hungary	Turkey
Iraq	United Arab Emirates
Israel	Yugoslavia
Italy	

SERVICE BY POST: R. 16.2(2) (A).

R. 16.4 (service by post) will apply, but service must be by 1 registered post as the recorded delivery service is not available outside Great Britain, Northern Ireland, the Channel Islands and the Isle of Man: it is not available in the Republic of Ireland. Not every country permits service by post, including some Hague Convention countries. Information can be obtained from the sources mentioned in note 16.2.1.

A certificate is required that the method of service is permitted in the country where service is executed in addition to the certificate of service: r. 16.2(6). Where English is not an official language a translation

16.2.4

16.2.5

16.2.6

of the documents to be served will be required: r. 16.4(3). Such certificates may be obtained from the accredited representatives (embassies and consulates) of the countries concerned. Certificates from embassies and consulates can be cheaper and quicker to obtain than those obtained from lawyers abroad.

SERVICE THROUGH A CENTRAL AUTHORITY AT REQUEST OF THE FOREIGN OFFICE: R. 16.2(2) (B).

16.2.7   The Hague Convention model form of request and certificate of service in the convention should be used and sent with the documents for service (all in duplicate: Art.3(2)), with a letter requesting service, a summary of the documents to be served and any necessary translation certified as correct (r. 16.6) and the appropriate Foreign Office fee, to The Foreign and Commonwealth Office, Treaty and Nationality Department, 1 Palace Street, London SW1E 5HE. The certificate of service (in the model form) will be signed by the authority executing service.

SERVICE THROUGH A BRITISH CONSULAR OFFICE: R. 16.2(2) (C).

16.2.8   The documents for service, any necessary translation certified as correct (r. 16.6) and a letter requesting service are sent to The Foreign and Commonwealth Office, Treaty and Nationality Department, 1 Palace Street, London SW1E 5HE. The certificate of service is signed by the authority executing service: r. 16.2(3). This method should only be used as a method of last resort.

SERVICE BY AN HUISSIER ETC.: R. 16.2(2) (D).

16.2.9   This method may be used at the request of a messenger-at-arms, a party or his agent as mentioned in the Hague Convention. The word "agent" means solicitor or a person having a right to conduct the litigation: r. 1.3(1). On messengers-at-arms, see note 16.3.1.

    This method is surer than postal service and quicker and more reliable than transmission through the central authorities. The expression "competent official" would probably include an unofficial process server, who is permitted to serve documents in some countries. The certificate of service is signed by the official executing service: r. 16.2(4).

PERSONAL SERVICE BY PARTY OR AUTHORISED AGENT: R. 16.2(2) (E).

16.2.10   Personal service by a party or his authorised agent is not mentioned in the Hague Convention but appears in the rule because such service is permitted in some countries, the authorised agent usually being a solicitor (or his equivalent) or a notary. In this provision "authorised agent" does not mean only a solicitor, or a person having a right to conduct the litigation, in Scotland: r. 1.3(1) (definition of "agent").

    This form of service must be witnessed and the person serving completes a certificate of service in Form 16.2: r. 16.2(5). There must also be lodged a certificate that the method of service is permitted in the country in which service is executed: r. 16.2(6).

"CITATION OR NOTICE".

16.2.11   A citation in Form 13.7 must be attached to a summons when served on a defender: r. 13.7(1)(a). In the case of a petition a citation in Form 14.7 is attached to the petition served on any person: r. 14.7(2). In the case of a minute served or intimated on a person there must be attached a notice in Form 15.1; and in the case of a note, a notice in Form 15.2. Other notices may be required to be served under particular rules.

Service under the EC Service Regulation[1]

16.2A   **16.2A.**—[2](1)   In this rule—

"competent receiving agency" and "Member State" have the same meaning as in the EC Service Regulation; and

"EC Service Regulation" means Regulation (EC) No. 1393/2007 of the European Parliament and of the Council of 13th November 2007 on the service in the Member States of judicial and extrajudicial documents in civil or commercial matters (service of documents) and repealing Council Regulation (EC) No. 1348/2000, as amended from time to time.

(2)   This rule applies to service of a document under the EC Service Regulation on a person on whom service is to be executed in a Member State other than the United Kingdom.

(3)   Where a document is being served by a competent receiving authority under Article 7 of the EC Service Regulation, rule 16.6(1) (translations of documents) shall not apply.

---

[1] Heading and r. 16.2A substituted by S.S.I. 2008 No.349 (effective 13th November 2008).
[2] R. 16.2A inserted by S.S.I. 2004 No. 52 (effective 1st March, 2004) and substituted by S.S.I. 2007 No.449 (effective 25th October 2007).

(4) Where a document has been served by a competent receiving authority under Article 7 of the EC Service Regulation, the party executing service shall lodge the certificate of service mentioned in Article 10 of the EC Service Regulation.

General note.

The EC Service Regulation, Regulation (EC) No. 1393/2007, may be used for service in EU Member States except Denmark for judicial and extra-judicial documents in civil and commercial matters. See now the Service Regulation in Regulation (EC) No. 1393/2007.

16.2A.1

The Member States of the EU are—

Austria	Italy
Belgium	Latvia (from 1st May 2004)
Bulgaria (from 1st January 2007)	Lithuania (from 1st May 2004)
Croatia (from 1st July 2013)	Luxembourg
Cyprus (from 1st May 2004)	Malta (from 1st May 2004)
Czech Republic (from 1st May 2004)	Netherlands
Denmark	Poland (from 1st May 2004)
Estonia (from 1st May 2004)	Portugal
Finland	Romania (from 1st January 2007)
France	Slovakia (from 1st May 2004)
Germany	Slovenia (from 1st May 2004)
Greece	Spain
Hungary (from 1st May 2004)	Sweden
Ireland	United Kingdom

The points to note for service under this EC Service Regulation are—

1. The Regulation does not apply where the address of the person to be served is not known (art.1(2)).
2. Service is made via the transmitting agency of one Member State and the receiving agency of the Member State in which the document is to be served (art.2). The central bodies and transmitting agencies for Scotland and other EU countries can be found at *http:llec.europa.eu/justiceJiomelJudicialatlascivillhtmllds_docs_en.htm*. The central body for Scotland is: Private International Law Branch, Civil and International Division, Justice Department, St Andrew's House, Regent Road, Edinburgh, EH1 3DG, Tel: +44 (0)131 244 4826, Fax: +44(0)131 244 4848. The transmitting agencies in Scotland are Messengers-at-Arms and accredited solicitors.
3. The document to be transmitted may not have to be translated if served via the transmitting and receiving agencies; but a document not translated into an official language of the receiving Member State may be refused to be accepted by the recipient (see arts. 5 and 8).
4. Service will be by a method of the receiving Member State unless a particular form is requested which is also valid in that State (art.7).
5. A request form in the Annex to the Regulation in an official language of the receiving Member State must accompany the document (art.4(3)). For form, see below.)
6. A certificate of service in the form in the Annex to the regulation will be returned (art.10(1)).
7. Service is free except costs occasioned by use of a judicial officer or other competent person or by use of a particular method requested (art. 11).
8. Service is also permitted, unless a Member State has made a derogation—
     • by consular or diplomatic channels,
     • directly by post,
     • through a judicial officer (see r. 16.2(2)(d)).
    The form of request for service in the Annex to the Regulation should be used.

"SERVICE IS TO HE EXECUTED IN A MEMBER STATE OTHER THAN THE UNITED KINGDOM".

Notwithstanding these words in r. 16.2A(2), the EC Service Regulation method does not apply to Denmark: r. 16.2 will have to be used for service in Denmark.

16.2A.2

"SERVED BY A COMPETENT RECEIVING AUTHORITY…RULE16.6(1) (TRANSLATION OF DOCUMENTS) SHALL NOT APPLY".

One should not be confused into thinking that the document need never be translated. The form in the Annex to the EC Service Regulation accompanying the document must be in an official language of the receiving Member State if the Regulation method is used: art.4(3). The person to be served may, however refuse to accept the document if the document itself is not in an official language of the receiving Member State: art.8.

16.2A.3

Translation required by r. 16.6 will be necessary where service is by any of the other methods.

"CERTIFICATE OF SERVICE MENTIONED IN ARTICLE 10".

16.2A.4 When service has been completed a certificate of service in the form provided in the Annex to the Regulation is sent to the transmitting agency in Scotland.

Service by messenger-at-arms

16.3 **16.3.**—(1) Service by a method mentioned in rule 16.1(1)(a)(i), (ii) or (iii), or (b)(i), shall be executed by a messenger-at-arms who shall—

(a) explain the purpose of service to any person on whom he executes service;

(b) complete a citation or notice, as the case may be, and a certificate of service in Form 16.3; and

(c) send the certificate of service to the pursuer.

(2) Such service shall be witnessed by one witness who shall sign the certificate of service (which shall state his name, occupation and address).

(3)[1] Where service is executed by a method mentioned in rule 16.1(1)(a)(ii) or (iii), or (b)(i), the document and the citation or notice of intimation, as the case may be, shall be placed in an envelope (bearing the notice specified in rule 16.4(2)) and sealed by the messenger-at-arms.

(4) Subject to paragraph (4A), a messenger-at-arms shall, when he executes service of a document, have in his possession—

(a) in the case of service of a copy of a principal writ, the principal writ or a copy of it certified as correct by the agent for the party whose writ it is, and

(b) where an interlocutor has been pronounced allowing service of the document, a certified copy of that interlocutor,

which he shall show, if required, to the person on whom he executes service.

(4A)[2] Where the firm which employs the messenger-at-arms has in its possession—

(a) the principal writ or a certified copy of it, it shall be competent for the messenger-at-arms to execute service of the document without having that writ or certified copy in his possession, in which case he shall, if required to do so by the person on whom service is executed and within a reasonable time of being so required, show the principal writ or certified copy to the person;

(b) a certified copy of the interlocutor, it shall be competent for the messenger-at-arms to execute service of the document if he has in his possession a facsimile copy of the certified copy interlocutor which he shall show, if required, to the person on whom he executes service.

(5) The certificate of service required under paragraph (1) shall include the full name and designation of any person in whose hands any document and the citation or notice, as the case may be, were left.

(6)[3] In the application of this rule to service in England and Wales, reference to a messengers-at-arms shall be construed as a reference to a person entitled to serve Senior Courts writs; and in the application of this rule to service in Northern Ireland, reference to a messenger-at-arms shall be construed as a reference to a person entitled to serve Court of Judicature writs.

Deriv. R.C.S. 1965, r.74(i) (r.16.3(4)) and r.74A(4) substituted by SI 1984/472 and amended by SI 1990/705 and 1991/1157 (r.16.3(1), (2), (3), and (5))

---

[1] Rule 16.3(3) amended by S.S.I. 2010 No. 417 (effective 1st January 2011).
[2] Rule 16.3(4A) inserted by S.S.I. 2001 No. 305, r.2(2) (effective 18th September 2001).
[3] Rule 16.3(6) substituted by S.S.I. 2010 No. 205 (effective 15th June 2010).

GENERAL NOTE.

Messengers-at-arms are members of the ancient corps of Her Majesty's officers-of-arms (heralds, pursuivants, macers and messengers-at-arms): see *Stair Memorial Encyclopedia of the Laws of Scotland*, Vol. 14, paras. 1501 et seq. A messenger-at-arms is appointed by the Lord Lyon King of Arms, but his qualifications, training, examination, discipline and, to some extent, functions, are governed by the Debtors (Scotland) Act 1987 and the A.S. (Messengers-at-Arms and Sheriff Officers Rules) 1991 [SI 1991/1397]. Appointment is made on the recommendation of the Court of Session: 1987 Act, s.77(1) and the Messengers-at-Arms and Sheriff Officers Rules, r. 7. He must have a bond of caution of not less than £50,000, and a policy of professional indemnity insurance of not less than £100,000, in respect of each claim: 1991 Rules, r. 9.

A messenger-at-arms executes all warrants of the Court of Session, the High Court of Justiciary (along with others empowered to do so: Criminal Procedure (Scotland) Act 1995, s.307(1)) and the Court of the Lord Lyon. In relation to the Court of Session his functions include (a) collecting any debt constituted by decree or summary warrant; (b) executing diligence; (c) executing a citation or serving any document in a legal process; and (d) unless otherwise provided, serving notices to be served under any enactment: 1991 Rules, rr. 14(1) and 15(1). He may refuse to act if a reasonable fee is not tendered or it is not reasonably practicable for him to act: 1991 Rules, r. 14(4). Solicitors are personally liable in the first instance for the fees of a messenger-at-arms instructed by them: Maclaren on *Court of Session Practice*, p. 1115 (and see *Stirling Park & Co. v. Digby Brown & Co. 1995 S.C.L.R. 375* (sheriff officers)). A messenger-at-arms can do nothing without a legal warrant to do it and he must act in strict conformity with it. If he fails to do so he and his cautioner may be liable in reparation. For wrongful diligence the messenger-at-arms, the cautioner and the agent may be liable to the debtor: Graham Stewart on *Diligence*, p. 799.

In a sheriff court district where there is no resident messenger-at-arms, a sheriff officer authorised to practise in that district has the powers of a messenger-at-arms in regard to service of a summons, writ, citation or other proceeding, or the execution of or diligence on, any decree, warrant or order: Execution of Diligence (Scotland) Act 1926, s.1.

16.3.1

"ONE WITNESS".

S.32 of the Debtors (Scotland) Act 1838 and s.1 of the Citations (Scotland) Act 1846 provide that more than one witness is not required; hence one witness is required to the execution of service by a messenger-at-arms. He does not sign any citation, but he does sign the certificate of service: r. 16.3(2).

16.3.2

DOCUMENTS TO BE SERVED IN SEALED ENVELOPE.

The documents served must be sealed in an envelope where they are left (a) in the case of an individual by leaving it with a person at his dwelling or at his place of business, or (b) in the case of a person other than an individual, in the hands of a person at the registered or other office: r. 16.1(1)(a)(ii), (iii) or (b)(i) respectively. The certificate of service must state that person's name and designation: r. 16.3(5). The envelope must have on the face of it the notice which must appear on the envelope when service is by post (the notice which indicates what the contents are and what is to be done if they cannot be delivered to the person on whom service is to be executed: see r. 16.4(2)): r. 16.3(3).

16.3.3

"PRINCIPAL WRIT OR A COPY OF IT CERTIFIED".

The messenger-at-arms must have the principal writ (defined in r. 1.3(1)) or a copy of it in his possession (r. 16.3(4)) or in the possession of his firm (r. 16.3(4A)). The reference to "the firm which employs him" in r. 16.3(4A) is a reference to the firm of messenger-at-arms and not a reference to the agent (solicitor) instructing him or his firm.

Although the rule permits him or his firm to have a copy certified by the agent, a messenger-at-arms or his firm would not normally proceed without the principal writ because it has the Court of Session stamp on it.

16.3.4

SERVICE ELSEWHERE IN U.K.

A messenger-at-arms does not have jurisdiction outside Scotland. There is no direct equivalent officer in England and Wales or Northern Ireland. In those jurisdictions the plaintiff or his agent may effect service, and this is usually done by an inquiry agent or a county court bailiff. Process servers are only appointed in England and Wales for the purposes of civil procedure conventions with foreign countries: R.S.C. 1965, Ord. 69, r. 4.

16.3.5

"SUPREME COURT".

Under Sched. 1 to the Interpretation Act 1978, this means the Court of Appeal, High Court and Crown Court in England and Wales or the Supreme Court of Judicature in Northern Ireland.

16.3.6

Service by post

16.4

16.4.—[1](1) This rule applies to service of a document by post but is subject to rule 61.2(3) and (4) (order as respects intimation of petition for appointments of judicial factor).

(2) Service by post shall be executed by—

(a) a messenger-at-arms, or

(b) an agent,

posting a copy of the document to be served with any citation or notice, as the case may be, by registered post or the first class recorded delivery service addressed to the person on whom service is to be executed and having on the face of the envelope a notice in the following terms: "This envelope contains a citation to, or intimation from, the Court of Session. If delivery of the letter cannot be made it must be returned immediately to the Deputy Principal Clerk of Session, Court of Session, 2 Parliament Square, Edinburgh EH1 IRQ.".

(3) Where English is not an official language of the country in which service is to be executed, a translation in an official language of that country of the notice required under paragraph (2) shall appear on the face of the envelope.

(4) The person executing service of a document shall complete—

(a) a citation or notice, as the case may be; and

(b) a certificate of service in Form 16.4.

(5)[2] Where a document is served by a registered post service, a receipt of posting by the operator of that service shall be attached to the certificate of service.

(6) The date of execution of service shall be deemed to be the day after the date of posting.

(7) Subject to rule 16.11 (no objection to regularity of service or intimation), the execution of service by post shall be valid unless the person on whom service was sought to have been made proves that the envelope and its contents were not tendered or left at his address.

Deriv. R.C.S. 1965, r. 68A inserted by S.I. 1968 No. 1150, r. 74A(5) inserted by S.I. 1984 No. 472 and amended by S.I. 1991 No. 2483, and r. 74B(3)(a) (part) inserted by S.I. 1986 No. 1941 and amended by S.I. 1991 No. 2483 (r. 16.4(2)); r. 72(2) and r. 192(2), both substituted by S.I. 1986 No. 1941 (r. 16.4(6)); r. 74(a) (part) (r. 16.4(4)); r. 74A(6) (r. 16.4(2)), r. 74A(7) (r. 16.4(4)) and r. 74A(8) (r. 16.4(7)), all inserted by S.I. 1984 No. 472; and r. 74B(3)(b) (r. 16.4(4)), and r. 74B(7)(b) (r. 16.4(3)), both inserted by S.I 1986 No. 1941.

GENERAL NOTE.

16.4.1

Service by post must be to the known dwelling place of the person on whom service is to be executed, i.e. his usual place of residence: *Corstorphine v. Kasten* (1898) 1 F. 287. It is not enough to post the documents to the last known address of the person on whom service is to be executed if it is known he no longer lives there.

This rule replaces much of the Citation Amendment (Scotland) Act 1882 and ss.3, 4(1)-(4), 5 and 6 of, and Scheds 1 and 2 to, the 1882 Act are repealed by Sched.3 to the A.S. (R.C.S. 1994) 1994 [SI 1994/ 1443].

"MESSENGER-AT-ARMS".

16.4.2

See note 16.3.1.

"AGENT".

16.4.3

This means a solicitor or a person having a right to conduct the litigation: see r. 1.3(1) (definition of "agent") and note 1.3.4. "Solicitor" is defined in the C.S.A. 1988, s.51.

"CITATION OR NOTICE".

16.4.4

A citation in Form 13.7 must be attached to a summons when served on a defender: r. 13.7(1)(a). In the case of a petition a citation in Form 14.7 is attached to the petition served on any person: r. 14.7(2). In

---

[1] R. 16.4(1) amended by S.I. 1997 No. 1720 (effective 1st August 1997).
[2] R. 16.4(5) substituted by S.S.I. 2008 No. 349 (effective 1st December 2008).

the case of a minute served or intimated on a person there must be attached a notice in Form 15.1; and in the case of a note, a notice in Form 15.2. Other notices may be required to be served under particular rules.

"REGISTERED POST".

Service by registered post was introduced by the Citation Amendment (Scotland) Act 1882. Such service could be made throughout the British Isles and in many foreign countries (cf. the recorded delivery service: see note 16.4.6). The Post Office receipt of posting must be attached to the certificate of service in Form 16.4: r. 16.4(5).

16.4.5

Where the letter is returned to the Deputy Principal Clerk with the reason for failure to deliver marked on it, he intimates to the party on whose behalf service was attempted in order that re-service may be attempted or an order sought from the court: Citation Amendment (Scotland) Act 1882, s.4(5). If the court is satisfied that, in the case of a party, a letter was tendered at his proper address, it may hold the tender equal to a good citation: 1882 Act, s.4(5).

Registered post is a service no longer provided by the Post Office. It has been replaced by the Special Delivery service. The latter service is not provided for in r. 16.4; and, accordingly, the only form of postal service available under R.C.S. 1994 is first class recorded delivery.

"FIRST CLASS RECORDED DELIVERY".

The use of the recorded delivery service as an alternative to registered post was introduced by the Recorded Delivery Service Act 1962 but is only available in the United Kingdom, the Channel Islands and the Isle of Man but not the Republic of Ireland. Service by this means must be by the first class recorded delivery service. The Post Office certificate of posting must be attached to the certificate of service in Form 16.4: r. 16.4(5). Rule 16.4 does not mention the international recorded delivery service provided by the Royal Mail; accordingly this service may not be used for service abroad.

16.4.6

Where the letter is returned to the Deputy Principal Clerk with the reason for failure to deliver marked on it, he intimates to the party on whose behalf service was attempted in order that re-service may be attempted or an order sought from the court: Citation Amendment (Scotland) Act 1882, s.4(5). If the court is satisfied that, in the case of a party, a letter was tendered at his proper address, it may hold the tender equal to a good citation: 1882 Act, s.4(5).

SERVICE ON MEMBER OF HM FORCES IN NORTHERN IRELAND.

A document served on a person in HM Forces in Northern Ireland at a private address should be addressed as if that person were a private citizen and should not state on the envelope his rank and number. Where the address of that person's barracks is known the document should preferably be sent there. See P.N. 17th December 1974.

16.4.7

DATE OF EXECUTION OF SERVICE.

The date of execution of service by post is the day *after* the date of posting: r. 16.4(6). This abrogates the provisions for the date of execution in s.4(1) of the Citation Amendment (Scotland) Act 1882; and is consistent with s.7 of the Interpretation Act 1978 as applied by s.23 of that Act. Any period of notice begins to run from the end of the day after the day of posting.

16.4.8

SERVICE ON A SUNDAY.

Service by post cannot be executed on a Sunday.

16.4.9

VALIDITY OF SERVICE.

Service by post is deemed to be effected by properly addressing, pre-paying and posting a letter containing the document to be served: Interpretation Act 1978, s.7 as applied by s.23. An execution of service by post is valid unless it is proved that the letter and its contents were not tendered or left at the address of the person on whom service is to be executed: r. 16.4(7) replacing s.3 (part) of the Citation Amendment (Scotland) Act 1882. The "address" of the person on whom service is to be executed is the usual place of residence, registered office, etc., or place of business. Proof that the letter was not delivered to the address does not invalidate the service if the documents are nonetheless received: *Steuart v. Ree* (1885) 12 R. 563. If the person on whom service is to be executed appears in the process he cannot object to the irregularity of service: r. 16.11. The question of validity can only be raised, therefore, in other proceedings, e.g. suspension or reduction.

16.4.10

Proof that a letter has been posted raises a presumption that it was duly addressed and delivered; and this presumption is still applicable notwithstanding the modern postal service: *Netherfield Visual Productions v. Caledonian Land Properties Ltd* , 21st March 1996 (1996 G.W.D. 19-1107). The presentation can be rebutted by positive evidence tending to show that the letter was not delivered to the addressee or that it was delivered to someone else: *Mackenzie v. Dott* (1861) 23 D. 1310.

A pursuer who accepts delivery of a letter to a defender enclosing documents served and does not see that the defender gets them cannot claim that the service was good: *Morrison v. Vallance's Exrs* 1907 S.C. 999.

Where a postal citation is returned marked "refused", the court is entitled to regard the refusal as having been deliberate and the citation properly served: *Arthur v. SMT Sales & Service Co Ltd* 1999 S.C. 109.

Service where address of person is not known

16.5
16.5.—(1) Where the residence of the person to be served with a document is not known and cannot reasonably be ascertained or service on that person cannot be executed under rule 16.1 (methods and manner of service) or 16.2 (service furth of United Kingdom), the party who wishes to execute service may apply by motion—

    (a) for an order for service by the publication of an advertisement in a specified newspaper circulating in the area of the last known residence of that person or elsewhere; or

    (b) on special cause shown, for an order to dispense with service; and

    (c) stating the last known residence of that person and what steps have been taken to ascertain his present whereabouts.

(2) On enrolling such a motion, a copy of the document to be served shall be lodged with the Deputy Principal Clerk who shall retain it for a period of three years and from whom it may be uplifted by the person for whom it is intended.

(3) Where an interlocutor has been pronounced ordering publication of an advertisement under this rule—

    (a) the advertisement shall be in Form 16.5; and

    (b) publication of the advertisement shall have effect as if service of the document had been executed on the date of publication.

(4) Where an interlocutor has been pronounced dispensing with service under this rule—

    (a) service of the document shall be deemed to have been executed on the date of the interlocutor; and

    (b) the period of notice shall be dispensed with.

(5) A motion under paragraph (1) made before calling shall be heard in chambers.

(6) Where publication of an advertisement has been made under this rule, there shall be lodged in process—

    (a) a copy of the newspaper containing the advertisement; or

    (b) a certificate of publication by the publisher stating the date of publication and the text of the advertisement.

Deriv. R.C.S. 1965, r. 75(1) substituted by S.I. 1986 No. 1941 and amended by S.I. 1987 No. 1206 (r. 16.5(1)); r. 75(2) substituted by S.I. 1986 No. 1941 (r. 16.5(1)); r. 75(3) substituted by S.I. 1986 No. 1941 and amended by S.I. 1991 No. 2483 (r. 16.5(5)); r. 75(4) (r. 16.5(3)), and r. 75(5) (r. 16.5(6)), both substituted by S.I. 1986 No. 1941.

GENERAL NOTE.

16.5.1
Edictal citation has now been abolished and the only means of service where a person's whereabouts are unknown (as distinct from execution of diligence: cf. r. 16.12(4)) is by advertisement under r. 16.5. Steps, however, must have been taken to ascertain the address of the person on whom service is to be executed, and what those steps were and an explanation of why service cannot be executed must be stated in the motion; r. 16.5(1); in a summons (or minute) all this must be stated in the condescendence (or statement of facts); r. 13.3. In *Young v. Harper* 1970 S.C. 174, 177 Lord Fraser held that "known" (in relation to art. 1 of the A.S. 14th December 1805) did not mean known only to the pursuer but known generally to persons having business or social dealings with the defender; accordingly, some steps must be taken to find an address or else a belief that an address is not known must be based on some evidence that none is known. Service may be dispensed with on cause shown.

In the case of service by advertisement, the date of the advertisement is that date of execution of service: r. 16.5(3)(b). That day is excluded in calculating the period of notice.

"MOTION".

16.5.2
For motions, see Chap. 23.

MOTION BEFORE CALLING.

16.5.3
See r. 23.8.

LODGING OF ADVERTISEMENT OR CERTIFICATE OF PUBLICATION.

16.5.4
The newspaper containing the advertisement or the publisher's certificate of publication required under r. 16.5(6) is lodged as a production: see r. 4.5.

Translations of documents served or advertised abroad

16.6.—(1)[1] Subject to rule 16.2A (service under the Council Regulation) where English is not an official language of the country in which a document is to be served, the document shall be accompanied by a translation in an official language of that country.

16.6

(2) An advertisement authorised under rule 16.5 (service where address of person is not known) to be published in a newspaper in a country in which English is not an official language of that country shall be in an official language of that country.

(3) With any certificate of service, or advertisement under rule 16.5, in a language other than English there shall be lodged a translation in English.

(4) A translation under this rule shall be certified as correct by the translator; and the certificate shall include his full name, address and qualifications.

Deriv. R.C.S. 1965, r. 74B(4)(b) and (6)(b) (r. 16.6(3)), r. 74B(7)(a) (r. 16.6(1) and r. 74B(8) (r. 16.6(4)), all inserted by S.I. 1986 No. 1941; also amended by S.S.I. 2004 No. 52 (effective 1st March, 2004)

DISPENSING WITH TRANSLATION.

Where, for instance, the person on whom service is to be executed, in a country in which English is not an official language, is a British citizen who can be expected to speak English, the court might be persuaded to dispense with the requirement under r. 2.1 to serve a translation of the documents to be served.

16.6.1

A "SUBJECT TO RULE 16.2A".

Rule 16.2A provides for service of documents in Member States of the EU except Denmark under Council Regulation (EC) No. 1348/2000). A translation may not be required *only* where service is via the transmitting agency in Scotland (see note.16.2A.1) and the receiving agency in the Member State in which service is to be effected. It should be noted, however, that the person to be served may refused to accept a document served by this method if it is not translated into an official language of his Member State. Translations will be required where other methods of service are used.

16.6.1A

QUALIFICATION OF TRANSLATOR.

There is no particular qualification or standard of qualification required of a translator.

16.6.2

OBTAINING AND COST OF TRANSLATIONS.

The responsibility for obtaining and paying for a translation falls on the party serving the document.

In relation to simplified divorce applications under Pt XI of Chap. 49, service is made or arranged by the Deputy Principal Clerk of Session. Nonetheless, that service is made on behalf of the applicant who will be required to obtain and pay for any translation required for service abroad.

16.6.3

Intimation of documents

16.7—(1) Subject to rule 16.8 (intimation on a warrant to intimate), rule 16.9 (written intimation) and any other provision in these Rules, where intimation of a document is to be given under these Rules to any person, the intimation shall be given—

16.7

    (a) personally, by tendering the document and the notice of intimation (if any) to that person; or

    (b) by registered post or the first class recorded delivery service—

        (i) in the case of an individual, addressed to the known, or last known, dwelling place or a place of business of that individual; or

        (ii) in the case of any other person, addressed to the registered office, other official address or a place of business of that person.

(2) Where intimation has been given in accordance with paragraph (1), the party on whose behalf intimation has been given shall attach to the principal writ or lodge in process, as the case may be—

    (a) a certificate of intimation in Form 16.7;

---

[1] R. 16.6(1) amended by S.S.I. 2004 No. 52 (effective 1st March 2004).

(b)   a copy of any notice of intimation which was intimated; and

(c)   a copy of any interlocutor ordering the intimation.

GENERAL NOTE.

16.7.1   This rule and rr.16.8 and 16.9 are intended to introduce formality and distinction between the methods of intimation, heretofore impliedly permitted under the R.C.S. 1965, by rationalizing "intimation" into three categories. Intimation may be (*a*) formal intimation of a cause or document for the purposes of information (r.16.7), (*b*) intimation on a warrant to intimate to a person informing him of the existence of a cause in which he may have an interest so that he can enter the process if he wishes (r.16.8), and (*c*) intimation usually restricted to informing a party of steps taken in a process (r.16.9).

INTIMATION OF DOCUMENTS.

16.7.2   R.16.7 provides for the category of intimation whereby a cause or document is intimated to a person for the purposes primarily of information and not to enable him to enter the process or of a step taken in the process.

A certificate of intimation in Form 16.7 is stitched into the principal summons for lodging for calling or the execution copy of the petition or note for lodging after expiry of the period of notice. A separate certificate of intimation is lodged as a step of process when intimation is given after calling of the summons or the lodging of the execution copy of the petition or note. A copy of any notice of intimation required to be intimated must be attached to the certificate as well as any interlocutor ordering intimation (r. 16.7(2)): the reason for this is so that the clerk of session can check that the notice of intimation intimated is in accord with that provided for in R.C.S. 1994 and that the interlocutor intimated was in the same terms as the interlocutor in the interlocutor sheet.

There are two methods of such intimation:—

(1) Personal: r.16.7(1) (a).

This is the same as personal service; the rules of personal service apply: see note 16.1.2(1).

(2) Registered post or the first class recorded delivery service.

In the case of an individual this may be to his known or last known dwelling place (i.e. his usual place of residence: *Corstorphine v. Kasten* (1898) 1 F. 287) or his place of business. It will be noticed that in this case intimation to a last known address is permitted (cf. service: see note 16.4.1). In the case of a person other than an individual intimation may be made to the registered office, other official address or place of business as in the case of service.

Intimation on a warrant to intimate

16.8   **16.8.—**(1)[1]   Where intimation of a document is to be given to a person for whom a warrant to intimate has been obtained, the intimation shall be made in the same manner as service of a document; and the following rules shall, with the necessary modifications, apply to that intimation as they apply to service of a document:—

rule 16.1 (methods and manner of service),

rule 16.2 (service furth of United Kingdom),

rule 16.2A (service under the Council Regulation),

rule 16.3 (service by messenger-at-arms),

rule 16.4 (service by post),

rule 16.5 (service where address of person is not known),

rule 16.6 (translations of documents served or advertised abroad).

(2)   Where intimation has been given in accordance with paragraph (1), the party on whose behalf intimation has been given shall attach a copy of any notice of intimation to the certificate of intimation.

INTIMATION ON A WARRANT.

16.8.1   R.16.8 provides for the category of intimation on a warrant to intimate to a person to bring to his attention a cause in which he may have an interest so that he can enter the process if he wishes. Intimation in this case is made in the same way as service, and the rules for service apply as modified.

The certificate of intimation which must be lodged will be the certificate of service required according to the method of intimation used. The certificate of intimation in Form 16.7 is stitched into the principal summons for lodging for calling or the execution copy of the petition or note for lodging after expiry of the period of notice. A separate certificate of intimation is lodged as a step of process when intimation is

---

[1] R.16.8(1) amended by S.S.I. 2004 No. 52 (effective 1st March, 2004).

given after calling of the summons or the lodging of the execution copy of the petition or note. A copy of any notice of intimation required to be intimated must be attached to the certificate (r. 16.8(2)) as well as any interlocutor ordering intimation (r. 16.1(3) by virtue of r. 16.8(2)): the reason for this is so that the clerk of session can check that the notice of intimation intimated is in accord with that provided for in R.C.S. 1994 and that the interlocutor intimated was in the same terms as the interlocutor in the interlocutor sheet.

Written intimation

16.9. Where a provision in these Rules requires written intimation to be given to a person, that intimation may be made by first class post or other means of delivery to that person.

16.9

WRITTEN INTIMATION.

R. 16.9 provides for the category of intimation usually restricted to informing a party of a step taken in a cause, e.g. the lodging of a step of process (r.4.6(1)(a)), the enrolling of a motion (r.23.3(1)) or opposition to a motion (r.23.4(4)), or intimation by the Deputy Principal Clerk or a clerk of session of something done or a document sent to the court in a process.

16.9.1

Acceptance of service or intimation and dispensing with period of notice

16.10.—(1) An agent may accept service or intimation of a document on behalf of the person on whom service is to be executed or to whom intimation is to be given and may dispense with any period of notice.

16.10

(2) A person on whom service of a document is executed or to whom intimation of a document is given may dispense with any period of notice as respects him in relation to that document.

(3) Where a period of notice is dispensed with under paragraph (1) or (2), it shall be deemed to expire on the day on which the party on whose behalf service is executed or intimation is given receives written intimation that the period of notice has been dispensed with.

Deriv. R.C.S. 1965, r.74(b) amended by S.I. 1991 No. 2843

GENERAL NOTE.

An agent may accept service or intimation and dispense with a period of notice on his client's behalf: r. 16.10(1). A person served may himself dispense with a period of notice to which he is entitled: r. 16.10(2).

16.10.1

Acceptance of service or intimation is made by the agent for the party on whose behalf service or intimation is accepted endorsing a holograph docquet on the principal or a copy of the document served or intimated in the following terms:

"(*Place and date*). I, (*name of agent*), on behalf of and authorised by (*name of person on whom service is to be executed or to whom intimation to be given*) acknowledge to have received a service copy of the summons [*or as the case may be*]. I accept service [*or* intimation] on his [*or* her *or* its] behalf.

(*Signed*)."

If the period of notice is dispensed with the words "and dispense with the period of notice" are added after the word "service".

Where the person served with a document or who has a document intimated to him dispenses with a period of notice himself he should endorse a holograph docquet on the principal or a copy of the document served or intimated in the following terms:

"(*Place and date*). I, (*name of person served or to whom document intimated*), dispense with the period of notice in the summons [*or as the case may be*].

(*Signed*)."

On the meaning of "agent", see r. 1.3(1) (definition of "agent"). On the meaning of "period of notice", see r. 1.3(1) (definition of "period of notice") and rr.13.4 and 14.6.

WRITTEN INTIMATION OF ACCEPTANCE OR DISPENSATION.

The written intimation will usually consist of the return of the document docquetted with the holograph acceptance of service, intimation or dispensation with a period of notice, as the case may be. For methods of written intimation, see r.16.9.

16.10.2

No objection to regularity of service or intimation

16.11

16.11.—(1) A person who enters the process of a cause shall not be entitled to state any objection to the regularity of the execution of service or intimation of a document on him; and his appearance shall be deemed to remedy any defect in such service or intimation.

(2) Nothing in paragraph (1) shall preclude a person from pleading that the court has no jurisdiction.

Deriv. R.C.S. 1965, r. 82

IRREGULARITY IN SERVICE OR INTIMATION.

16.11.1

The object of citation (or service or intimation) is to bring to the knowledge of the defender (or other person) the proceedings against him in order for him to take steps to protect his interests. The phrase "no party appearing to object to regularity" in s.21 of the C.S.A. 1868 (replaced by R.C.S. 1965, r. 82 and repealed by Sched. 2 to the C.S.A. 1988) shows that if the object (of citation, service or intimation) is attained by the defender appearing, it is immaterial whether or not there were irregularities: *Corstorphine v. Kasten* (1898) 1 F. 287, 296 per Lord Adam. Irregularities may consist in citation, service or intimation in accordance with a wrong or inappropriate rule or not in accordance with any rule, and in either case the objection is to regularity: *Corstorphine*, above per Lord McLaren at p. 297; see also *Struthers v. Magistrates of Kirkintilloch* 1951 S.L.T. (Notes) 77.

It is *pars judicis* to notice that service or intimation has been irregular.

A person seeking to challenge an irregular service or intimation should seek suspension or reduction of the execution of service or intimation. An irregular service on or intimation to a person may be challenged in the process in which the irregularity occurs by a person sisted in place of the person concerned: *Morrison v. Vallance's Exrs.* 1907 S.C. 999.

In an action of reduction of a decree in absence in the sheriff court, the pursuer successfully contended that, because the defender (who had raised the sheriff court action against the pursuer) was not entitled to practise as a solicitor (having been suspended from holding a practising certificate), he was not empowered by s. 3 of the Citation Amendment (Scotland) Act 1882 Act validly to serve the initial writ on the pursuer: *McKechnie v Murray* 2016 S.C. 339 (Extra Div.). In that case, the pursuer (the defender in the sheriff court action) had not entered the process in the sheriff court action.

PLEA OF NO JURISDICTION.

16.11.2

A person who enters the process of a cause to challenge jurisdiction is not barred from challenging an irregularity of service on which the jurisdiction is based and his appearance does not remedy a defect in the service or intimation: *Dallas & Co. v. McArdle* 1949 S.C. 481 (no personal service to constitute jurisdiction). The fact that there has been an irregularity does not preclude such a person from entering the process simply to challenge the jurisdiction of the court: the C.J.J.A. 1982, Scheds. 1, 3C and 4, art. 18 and Sched. 8, r. 6(2) provide that a court does not have jurisdiction over the substance or merits of a cause where appearance is entered solely to contest jurisdiction, and this principle has been extended to all persons.

Part II – Diligence

Execution of diligence[1]

16.12

16.12.—(1) This rule applies to—

    (a) the execution of any diligence on a warrant, act or decree of the court other than—

        (i) an arrestment to which rule 16.13 (arrestment of ships and arrestment in rem of cargo on board ship) applies; or

        (ii) an arrestment to which rule 16.14(1) (arrestment in rem of cargo landed or transhipped) applies; and

    (b) diligence in execution of a writ registered for execution in the Books of Council and Session.

(2) Subject to the following paragraphs of this rule, the execution of any diligence by virtue of these Rules on a person shall be executed by a messenger-at-arms in the same manner as service of a document is permitted under rule 16.1(1)(a)(i), (ii) or (iii) or (b)(i) (methods and manner of service); and, where ap-

---

[1] Heading amended by S.I. 1994 No. 2901 (clerical error).

propriate, the following provisions of Part I (service and intimation) shall, with the necessary modifications, apply to the execution of diligence as they apply to service of a document:—

    rule 16.3(1) to (4) (service by messenger-at-arms),

    rule 16.4(2)(a), (3), (6) and (7) (service by post).

(3)   In the application under this rule, by virtue of paragraph (2), of—

   (a)   sub-paragraph (b) of paragraph (1) of rule 16.3 (completion of citation or notice and certificate of service), for the reference to Form 16.3 in that sub-paragraph, there shall be substituted a reference to the appropriate form of certificate of execution in rule 16.15 (forms for diligence); and

   (b)   sub-paragraph (b) of paragraph (4) of rule 16.4 (completion of citation or notice and certificate of service), for the reference to Form 16.4 in that sub-paragraph, there shall be substituted a reference to the appropriate form of certificate of execution in rule 16.15.

(4)   The execution of such diligence on—

   (a)   an individual who is resident furth of Scotland,

   (b)   a person who has no registered office, other official address or a place of business in Scotland,

   (c)   a person whose residence is not known and cannot reasonably be ascertained, or

   (d)   a person on whom service cannot be executed in a manner permitted under paragraph (2),

shall be executed edictally by a messenger-at-arms leaving or depositing the appropriate schedule mentioned in rule 16.15 at the office of the Extractor.

(5)   Where the execution of diligence is made edictally under paragraph (4), a copy of the schedule left at the office of the Extractor shall be sent by a messenger-at-arms by registered post or the first class recorded delivery service to the place furth of Scotland where the person on whom diligence is executed edictally resides, has his registered office, official address or place of business, as the case may be, or such last known place.

(6)   A messenger-at-arms executing diligence shall have in his possession—

   (a)   in the case of diligence on a warrant in a principal writ, the principal writ or a copy or it certified as correct by the agent for the party whose writ it is,

   (b)   in the case of diligence on a warrant in an interlocutor, a certified copy of that interlocutor, or

   (c)   in the case of diligence on an extract of an act or a decree, or a document registered in the Books of Council and Session, the extract,

which he shall show, if required, to any person on whom he executes diligence.

(7)   The party on whose behalf diligence has been executed in a cause depending before the court shall attach the certificate of execution to the document containing the warrant for diligence.

Deriv. R.C.S. 1965, r. 67 (r.16.12(2) (part)

GENERAL NOTE.

The rules which govern the execution of diligence have not been entirely clear. Pt. II of Chap. 16 is an attempt to provide a comprehensive code for the execution of diligence (*a*) following an order or warrant of the court or (*b*) on a writ registered for execution in the Books of Council and Session.

    16.12.1

In general the rules for service of documents apply to the execution of diligence. In relation to execution on a person furth of Scotland or whose whereabouts are unknown or on whom execution cannot be made, however, execution by advertisement was seen to be impractical and productive of delay, and execution by post impractical and uncertain. Accordingly, edictal execution, abolished for service of documents, has been retained (or re-introduced) for execution of diligence in these circumstances.

Special rules apply in relation to arrestment of ships and cargo: see rr. 16.13 and 16.14 respectively.

16.12.2   The Books of Council and Session were the court books of the Lords of Council and Session. There are three registers in the Books of Council and Session—the Register of Deeds and Probative Writs, the Register of Protests and the Register of Judgments. Registration for execution gives the holder a decree of registration which is in effect a decree of the Court of Session (Bell's *Comm.*, i,4; *Taylor, Petr.* 1931 S.L.T. 260, 261 per Lord Pitman) and on the warrant inserted by the Keeper of the Registers or his deputy on an extract of a registered document diligence may be executed against the debtor's moveable property under s.3 of the Writs Execution (Scotland) Act 1877 as substituted by s.87(4) of the Debtors (Scotland) Act 1987. Diligence against heritable property may be executed by inhibition on the grant of letters of inhibition (see Chap. 59) or by action of adjudication founding on the decree of registration.

Registration for execution of deeds and probative writs in the Books of Council and Session may be made of probative writs which contain a clause of consent to registration for execution (other than a regulated consumer credit agreement: Consumer Credit Act 1974, s.93A inserted by the Debtors (Scotland) Act 1987, Sch.6, para.16) where the granter of the obligation resides in Scotland or is otherwise subject to the jurisdiction of the court. A bond or obligation in favour of the Crown may be registered as if it contained a clause of registration: Exchequer Court (Scotland) Act 1856, s.38. The procedure (protesting) for enforcing bills of exchange and promissory notes, but not cheques, is contained in the Bills of Exchange Act 1882. Judgments of certain foreign courts, awards of arbiters and others under various statutory provisions may be registered in the Register of Judgments: see Chap. 62.

EXECUTION BY PERSON ACQUIRING RIGHT TO THE EXTRACT DECREE.

16.12.3   Where a person acquires a right as creditor, by assignation or confirmation as executor or otherwise, to a decree, or a document registered in the Books of Council and Session, he must apply to the Deputy Principal Clerk by letter enclosing the extract decree or document, the document establishing his right and, in the case of assignation, evidence of its intimation, for a warrant authorising execution at the instance of that creditor: Debtors (Scotland) Act 1987, s.88(2). If the warrant is granted the words "*Fiat ut petitur (Date and signature)*" are written on the extract which is then warrant for diligence at the hands of the new creditor.

"MESSENGER-AT-ARMS".

16.12.4   See note 16.3.1.

METHODS OF EXECUTION OF DILIGENCE.

16.12.5   Subject to the special provisions for arrestment of ships and cargo (for which, see rr. 16.13 and 16.14), the methods of execution of diligence (a) on a warrant, act or decree of the court or (b) in execution of a writ registered for execution in the Books of Council and Session are as follows:

1.   Execution on an individual (a natural person)—
    (a)   personally: see note 16.1.2(1);
    (b)   by leaving the execution in the hands of a person at the dwelling place of the person on whom execution is to be made: see note 16.1.2(2);
    (c)   by depositing the execution at the dwelling place of the person on whom execution is to be made: see note 16.1.2(3);
    (d)   by leaving the execution in the hands of a person at the place of business of the person on whom execution is to be made: see note 16.1.2(4);
    (e)   by depositing the execution at the place of business of the person on whom execution is to be made: see note 16.1.2(5);
    (f)   edictal execution where person on whom execution to be made is furth of Scotland or whose whereabouts are unknown or on whom execution cannot be made: see note 16.12.6.

2.   Execution on any other person (i.e. a non-natural person such as a corporate or unincorporated body or firm)—
    (a)   by leaving the execution in the hands of a person at the registered office, other official address or place of business of the person on whom execution is to be made: see note 16.1.3(1);
    (b)   by depositing the execution at the place of business of the person on whom execution is to be made: see note 16.1.3(2);
    (c)   edictal execution where person on whom execution to be made is furth of Scotland or whose whereabouts are unknown or on whom execution cannot be made: see note 16.12.6.

The certificate of execution by the messenger-at-arms will be in the appropriate Form in r. 16.15 and not Form 16.3: r. 16.12(3). R. 16.3(1) to (4) in relation to messengers-at-arms applies. The application of provisions in r. 16.4 (service by post) only arises in edictal execution: see note 16.12.5.

Subject to r. 16.13(1) (arrestment of ships and arrestment of cargo in rem) and r. 16.14(2) (arrestment of cargo on board ship), diligence may not be executed on a Sunday: Stair, III.i.37; Bell's *Comm.*, ii,460; *Oliphant v. Douglas* (1633) Mor. 15002.

EDICTAL EXECUTION OF DILIGENCE.

This procedure has been retained for execution of diligence on (a) an individual resident furth of Scotland, (b) a person having no registered office, etc., in Scotland or (c) a person on whom the diligence cannot be executed because, e.g. his address is unknown: r. 16.12(4). Execution is by a messenger-at-arms who leaves the appropriate schedule at the Office of the Extractor (as Keeper of the Register of Edictal Citations and Executions of Diligence), Parliament House, Edinburgh and sends a copy by registered letter or the first class recorded delivery service to the residence or place of business, on the last known place, of the debtor: r. 16.12(4) and (5). The recorded delivery service may be used in Great Britain, Northern Ireland, the Channel Islands and the Isle of Man but not the Republic of Ireland. R. 16.4(2)(a) (notice on envelope), (3) (translation), (6) (date of execution) and (7) (validity of execution) apply: r. 16.12(2).

16.12.6

EXECUTION OF ARRESTMENT TO FOUND JURISDICTION.

A schedule of arrestment in Form 16.15-A (or 16.15-AA in the case of arrestment of a ship to found jurisdiction) is served on the arrestee by a messenger-at-arms and a certificate of execution in Form 16.15-H (or 16.15-HH) completed: r. 16.15(1)(a). The certificate is attached to the summons: r. 16.12(7).

Arrestment to found jurisdiction may be obtained by a warrant in a summons (r. 13.6(b)). On arrestment to found jurisdiction generally, see note 13.6.1. On arrestment of ships to found jurisdiction, see note 16.13.1(1).

16.12.7

EXECUTION OF ARRESTMENT ON THE DEPENDENCE.

A schedule of arrestment in Form 16.15-B (or 16.15-BB in the case of a ship) is served on the arrestee by a messenger-at-arms and a certificate of execution in Form 16.15-H (or 16.15-H (or 16.15-J in the case of a ship) completed: r. 16.15(1)(b). The certificate is attached to the summons or other document: r. 16.12(7).

Arrestment on the dependence is a preventive diligence restraining a debtor (arrestee) from making payment of a debt or satisfying an obligation to the defender (common debtor). As a general rule, a pursuer is entitled to insert a warrant for arrestment as a right in respect of a debt due. It may be recalled or restricted with or without conditions (see r. 13.10); and the pursuer will be liable in damages only for its wrongful use where executed on a defective warrant, in an irregular manner, or with malice or without probable cause: see *Wolthekker v. Northern Agricultural Co.* (1862) 1 M. 211, 212 per L.J.-C. Inglis; *Grant v. Magistrates of Airdrie* 1939 S.C. 738, 758-9 per L.P. Normand. Arrestment on the dependence may be obtained by warrant in a summons (r. 13.6(c)(ii)), by motion after signeting in an action (r. 13.8(1)), by warrant in a counterclaim or motion thereafter (r. 25.2(2)), by motion on a third party notice (r. 26.3(2)) or by motion in a petition under s.27 of the C.J.J.A. 1982 on the dependence of foreign proceedings (on which, see, e.g. *Stancraft Securities Ltd v. McDowall* 1990 S.C. 274).

In relation to a summons, arrestment may be executed at any time after signeting and before service of the summons, and is effective provided the summons is served within 20 days of the diet of compearance or, if that date is in vacation, the next calling date: Debtors (Scotland) Act 1838, s.17. There is no equivalent to the diet of compearance in modern practice; it has been argued that its equivalent is the first day on which the summons can call at the expiry of the period of notice, but this was rejected in *Brash v. Brash* 1966 S.L.T. 157, 158 per Lord Kissen; accordingly it is sufficient if the summons is served within 20 days after service of the arrestment. Arrestment may be executed after calling at any time until the action is disposed of by a final decree. It may not be used if the action has fallen asleep (i.e. where the action has been in court for a year and a day with no interlocutor having been pronounced). An arrestment will fall if the summons is not called within a year and a day of the expiry of the period of notice: *Thorhum v. Cox* (1830) 8 S. 945. Arrestment is enforced, except in the case of an earnings arrestment, a current maintenance arrestment or a conjoined arrestment order within the meaning of Part III of the Debtors (Scotland) Act 1987 (which are subject to the provisions of that Part), by an action of furthcoming (*Lucas's Trs. v Campbell* (1894) 21 R. 1096, 1103 per Lord Kinnear) in which both the common debtor and the arrestee are called as defenders. The arrestee must be subject to the jurisdiction of the court and the debt must have been constituted by a decree.

On arrestment on the dependence generally, see further note 13.6.3.

16.12.8

EXECUTION OF ARRESTMENT OF SHIPS.

See r. 16.13.

16.12.9

EXECUTION OF ARRESTMENT OF CARGO.

See rr. 16.13 and 16.14.

16.12.10

EXECUTION OF ARRESTMENT IN EXECUTION.

A schedule of arrestment where there was arrestment on the dependence, a copy of the final decree in Form 16.16 or where there was no such arrestment and there is arrestment in execution only or arrestment on a document of debt is served by a messenger-at-arms on the arrestee and a certificate of execution in Form 16.15-H completed: r. 16.15(1)(f). In relation to an earnings arrestment, Form 30, or, in relation to a current maintenance arrestment Form 34, and a certificate of execution in Form 60, in the A.S. (Proceedings in the Sheriff Court under the Debtors (Scotland) Act 1987) 1988 [SI 1988/2013] must be used.

16.12.11

Arrestment in execution follows a decree for payment in a decree of the court or a decree of registration in the Books of Council and Session (on which, see note 16.12.2). The warrant for arrestment is implied in the words "all lawful execution on this decree (or "hereon")" inserted in the extract decree by the Extractor under r. 7.10 (or the Keeper of the Registers in a decree of registration for execution in the Books of Council and Session) by virtue of s.87(2) of the Debtors (Scotland) Act 1987 (decrees of the court) and s.3 of the Writs Execution (Scotland) Act 1877 substituted by s.87(4) of the 1987 Act (decrees of registration). Arrestment of the debtor's earnings in the hands of his employer must be by an earnings arrestment, a current maintenance arrestment to enforce current maintenance or a conjoined arrestment order to enforce payment of debts due to different creditors from the same earnings: see Part III of the 1987 Act.

Arrestment is enforced, except in the case of an earnings arrestment, a current maintenance arrestment or a conjoined arrestment order within the meaning of Part III of the 1987 Act (which are subject to the provisions of that Part), by an action of furthcoming (*Lucas's Trs. v. Campbell* (1894) 21 R. 1096, 1103 per Lord Kinnear) in which both the common debtor and the arrestee are called as defenders. The arrestee must be subject to the jurisdiction of the court and the debt must have been constituted by a decree.

On arrestment generally, see note 13.6.3.

EXECUTION OF INHIBITION.

16.12.12   A schedule of inhibition in Form 16.15-F is served on the defender or other person inhibited by a messenger-at-arms and a certificate of execution in Form 16.15-H is completed: r. 16.15(1)(h). Where inhibition is on the dependence of a cause the certificate is attached to the summons or other document containing the warrant for the diligence: r. 16.12(7).

Inhibition may be used to prevent heritable property being burdened or disposed of by the debtor (1) on the dependence of an action, (2) on a document of debt or (3) in execution of a decree. It is generally only competent in relation to debts due (*Dove v. Henderson (1865) 3 M. 339*) but in all three cases inhibition in security may be obtained in respect of future or contingent debts where there are special circumstances (for which see note 13.6.3(3)). Inhibition may only be obtained from the Court of Session. It may proceed on a warrant for inhibition on the dependence of an action in the Court of Session (r. 13.6(c)(i)), by motion after signeting in an action (r. 13.8(1)), by warrant in a counterclaim or motion thereafter (r. 25.2(2)), by motion on a third party notice (r. 26.3(2)) or by motion in a petition under s.27 of the C.J.J.A. 1982 on the dependence of foreign proceedings (on which, see, e.g. *Stancroft Securities Ltd v. McDowall* 1990 S.C. 274). In other instances (i.e. on the dependence of a sheriff court action, in execution of a Court of Session or sheriff court decree, in execution of writs and foreign judgments registered for execution in the Books of Council and Session (on which, see note 16.12.2), on a document of debt or in security of future or contingent debts other than on the dependence of a Court of Session process) inhibition is obtained by letters of inhibition: see Chap. 59.

(1) Inhibition on the dependence.

See note 13.6.2.

(2) Inhibition on a document of debt.

A document of debt is a probative writ in which the debtor binds himself to pay. A negotiable instrument such as a bill of exchange or a promissory note is a document of debt for this purpose: Stair, IV .xlii.6. Consent to registration in the Books of Council and Session is not required; but where such a document contains a clause of registration for execution, a warrant to inhibit may be obtained on the decree of registration rather than the document of debt.

(3) Inhibition in execution.

Inhibition may be obtained on a decree of the Court of Session or the sheriff court or on a decree of registration of a writ or judgment registered for execution in the Books of Council and Session.

EXECUTION OF CHARGE FOR PAYMENT.

16.12.13   A charge for payment in Form 16.15-G is served on the debtor and a certificate of execution in Form 16.15-K is completed: r. 16.15(1)(i).

The warrant in a decree of the court or a decree of registration of a writ or judgment registered for execution in the Books of Council and Session (on which, see note 16.12.2) authorises the charging of the debtor to pay a money debt within a specified period and, where the debtor fails to pay, an earnings arrestment and attachment: Debtors (Scotland) Act 1987, s.87(2)(a) (decrees of the court) and s.3 of the Writs Execution (Scotland) Act 1877 substituted by s.87(4) of the 1987 Act (decrees of registration), both Acts amended by para. 17 of Sched.3 to the Debt Arrangement and Attachment (Scotland) Act 2002. The period for payment is 14 days if the person on whom the charge is executed is in the U.K. and 28 days if he is furth of the U.K.: 1987 Act, s.90(3). A charge to enforce an obligation *ad factum praestandum* is no longer competent: 1987 Act, s.100(2).

An earnings arrestment (within the meaning of Part III of the 1987 Act) or a attachment is not competent unless a charge for payment has been served on the debtor and must be executed within two years after the date of service of the charge, a right which may be reconstituted by serving a further charge: 1987 Act, s.90 as amended by the 2002 Act, Sched.3, para. 17(10). Earnings arrestments are governed by Part III of the 1987 Act. Attachment is governed by Pt.2 of the 2002 Act. In relation to an earnings arrestment, Form 30, and a certificate of execution in Form 60, in the A.S. (Proceedings in the Sheriff Court under the Debtors (Scotland) Act 1987) 1988 [SI 1988/2013] must be used. In the case of attachment, a schedule in Form 3 and a report of attachment in Form 8 in Appendix 1 of Sched. 1 to the Act of Sederunt (Debt Arrangement and Attachment (Scotland) Act 2002) 2002 [S.S.I. 2002 No. 560] must be used.

SUSPENSION OF EXECUTION.

Execution of diligence may be prevented or suspended by suspension of the charge and diligence or by suspension of the diligence, by suspension and interdict (where real diligence has begun), or by suspension and liberation (where the debtor has been imprisoned). See further, Chap. 60. **16.12.14**

EXPENSES OF EXECUTION.

The expenses of executing diligence by an earnings arrestment schedule or a conjoined arrestment order (within the meaning of Part III of the Debtors (Scotland) Act 1987), are recoverable from the debtor by the diligence under s.93(1) of the 1987 Act. The expenses of executing a schedule of arrestment and an action of furthcoming or sale are recoverable from the debtor out of the arrested property, and the court shall grant decree in the action of furthcoming for any balance not so recovered: 1987 Act, s.93(2). The expenses incurred in executing a current maintenance arrestment (within the meaning of Part III of the 1987 Act) are recoverable by diligence other than a current maintenance arrestment: 1987 Act, s.93(6). **16.12.15**

LIABILITY FOR WRONGFUL DILIGENCE.

For wrongful diligence the messenger-at-arms, the cautioner and the agent may be liable to the debtor: Graham Stewart on *Diligence*, p. 799. The party executing diligence will be liable in damages for its wrongful use where executed on a defective warrant, in an irregular manner, or with malice or without probable cause: see *Wolthekker v. Northern Agricultural Co.* (1862) 1 M. 211, 212 per L.J.-C. Inglis; *Grant v. Magistrates of Airdrie* 1939 S.C. 738, 758-759 per L.P. Normand. Where the charge is irregularly or unwarrantably executed, an averment of "wrongful" diligence is sufficient: *Dramgate Ltd v. Tyne Dock Engineering Ltd* , 2000 S.C. 43. **16.12.16**

Arrestment of ships and arrestment in rem of cargo on board ship

16.13.—(1)   An arrestment of a ship in rem or on the dependence, or an arrestment in rem of cargo on board ship, may be executed on any day by a messenger-at-arms who shall affix the schedule of arrestment— **16.13**

  (a)   to the mainmast of the ship;

  (b)   to the single mast of the ship; or

  (c)   where there is no mast, to some prominent part of the ship.

 (2)   In the execution of an arrestment of a ship on the dependence, the messenger-at-arms shall, in addition to complying with paragraph (1), mark the initials "ER" above the place where the schedule of arrestment is fixed.

 (3)[1]   On executing an arrestment under paragraph (1), the messenger-at-arms shall deliver a copy of the schedule of arrestment and a copy of the certificate of execution of it to the master of the ship, or other person on board in charge of the ship or cargo, as the case may be, as representing the owners or demise charterers of, or parties interested in, the ship or the owners of the cargo, as the case may be.

 (4)   Where the schedule of arrestment and the copy of the certificate of execution of it cannot be delivered as required under paragraph (3)—

  (a)   the certificate of execution shall state that fact; and

  (b)   either—

   (i)   the arrestment shall be executed by serving it on the harbour master of the port where the ship lies; or

   (ii)   where there is no harbour master, or the ship is not in a harbour, the pursuer shall enrol a motion for such further order as to intimation and advertisement, if any, as may be necessary.

 (5)   A copy of the schedule of arrestment and a copy of the certificate of execution of it shall be delivered by the messenger-at-arms to the harbour master, if any, of any port where the ship lies.

---

[1] R. 16.13(3) amended by S.S.I. 2010 No. 205 (effective 15th June 2010).

(6) In this rule, "ship" has the meaning assigned in section 48(f) of the Administration of Justice Act 1956.

Deriv. R.C.S. 1965, r. 140(a) (r. 16.13(1) (part), (3) and (4))

ARRESTMENT OF SHIPS.

16.13.1

A ship is any description of vessel used in navigation not propelled by oars: r. 16.13(6) importing the definition in the Administration of Justice Act 1956, s.48(f). The phrase "used in navigation" means used in navigating the seas: *Oakes v. Monkland Iron Co.* (1884) 11 R. 579, 584 per L.J.-C. Moncreiff.

There are restrictions, for example, the Brussels Convention relating to arrest of sea-going ships, 1952: see the 1956 Act; and the *UN Convention on the Law of the Sea* 1982, Art. 28 (Cmnd 8941): see Merchant Shipping Act 1995, s.129.

(1) Arrestment of ship to found jurisdiction.

Subject to two exceptions arrestment may not be executed where the defender is domiciled in the U.K. or a Contracting State to the 1968 Brussels or the Lugano Convention: C.J.J.A. 1982, Scheds 1 and 3C, Art. 3(2), Sched.4, Art. 3 and Sched.8, r. 2(8). The exceptions are: (a) In an action of reparation arising out of the collision or manoeuvring of ships, or non-compliance with ship collision regulations under s.45 of the Administration of Justice Act 1956 the restrictions of the C.J.J.A. 1982 do not apply to defenders domiciled outside the U.K.: C.J.J.A. 1982, Scheds 1 and 3C, Art. 54 and Sched.9, para. 6. (b) In an Admiralty cause where the defender is domiciled in the U.K. or elsewhere except another Contracting State to the 1968 or Lugano Convention: C.J.J.A. 1982, Sched.5, para. 7 and Sched.9, para. 6. An Admiralty action is defined in R.C.S. 1994, r. 46.1. Arrestment of a ship to found jurisdiction is subject to the ordinary rules of arrestment of any property to found jurisdiction, and must be made in the hands of a third party: see note 13.6.1.

For a strange argument, doubted by Lord Prosser, that there can be no arrestment to found jurisdiction in Admiralty cases since the C.J.J.A. 1982, see *Ladgroup Ltd v. Euroeast Lines S.A.* 1997 S.L.T. 916.

A schedule of arrestment in Form 16.15-AA is served on the defender and a certificate of execution in Form 16.15-HH is completed: r. 16.15(1)(a). The certificate is attached to the summons or other document containing the warrant for the diligence: r. 16.12(7).

(2) Arrestment of ships in rem.

An arrestment in rem may be executed in (a) an Admiralty action in rem to enforce a maritime lien or (b) an Admiralty action in personam to enforce a non-pecuniary claim relating to the ship under s.47(2)(p)–(s) of the Administration of Justice Act 1956 by virtue of s.47(3) of that Act. An Admiralty action is defined in r. 46.1. Arrestment of a ship is a real diligence directed against the vessel itself: *Carlberg v. Borjesson* (1877) 5 R. 188, 195 per Lord Shand. There is no arrestee: *Barclay, Curle & Co. Ltd v. Sir James Laing & Sons Ltd* 1908 S.C. 82, 89 per Lord McLaren. The ship may be arrested while in the possession of the defender. Arrestment of the ship does not arrest the cargo or freight. Arrestment in rem founds jurisdiction. The ship is fixed in the place where she is at the time of the execution of the arrestment until a declarator of lien is obtained and a process of sale completed: *Carlberg*, above. The arrestment cannot be executed when the ship is on passage: *Carlberg*, above; 1956 Act, s.47(6). The expenses of arrestment are recoverable as expenses of process because they are essential to the obtaining of the decree in rem: *Hatton v. A/S Durban Hansen* 1919 S.C. 154.

(a) Arrestment in rem to enforce maritime lien. A maritime lien is a form of hypothec or security without possession over a ship, her apparel or cargo enforceable by an Admiralty action in rem in which the res is attached by the arrestment, declarator of the lien is granted and the *res* sold. Such a lien arises (i) at common law in respect of damage done by a ship, bonds of bottomry or *respondentia*, seamen's wages, salvage and (ii) by creation by statute—master's wages and disbursements (1995 Act, s.41), compensation to owners or occupiers of land for damage occasioned by shipwreck (Merchant Shipping Act 1995, s.234(5)), fees and expenses of receiver of wrecks (1995 Act, s.249(3)), remuneration for services of coastguard (1995 Act, s.250(3)(c)). Under s.47(1) of the 1956 Act arrestment in rem is only competent if the action involves a claim in s.47(2), and the statutory liens except master's wages and disbursements and rights to life and property salvage are probably excluded. A schedule in Form 16.15-C is used and a certificate of execution in Form 16.15-I is completed: r. 16.15(1)(c). The schedule is attached by a messenger-at-arms to the mainmast or other prominent part and a copy delivered to the master of the ship or person in charge whom failing the harbour master whom failing a motion for further procedure must be enrolled: r. 16.13(1), (3) and (4). This may be done on any day, including Sunday: r. 16.13(1). The certificate is attached to the summons or other document containing the warrant for the diligence: r. 16.12(7).

(b) Arrestment in rem in an Admiralty action in personam to enforce non-pecuniary claims under s.47(2)(p)–(s) of the 1956 Act by virtue of s.47(3) of that Act. These provisions relate to a dispute as to ownership or possession of or a share in a ship, between co-owners of a ship about ownership, possession, employment or earnings of that ship, the mortgage or hypothecation of or share in a ship, or the forfeiture or condemnation of a ship or goods or the restoration of the ship or goods. Arrestment may be used whether or not the ship belongs to the defender: Arrest of Ships—4, Scotland, p. 87, by I. G. Inglis (Lloyds of London, 1987). There is no declarator of lien and no sale and the arrestment simply secures implement of the decree. A schedule in Form 16.15-D is used and a certificate of execution in Form 16.15-I is completed: r. 16.15(1)(d). The schedule is attached by a messenger-at-arms to the mainmast or other prominent part and a copy delivered to the master of the ship or person in charge whom failing the harbour master whom failing a motion for further procedure must be enrolled: r. 16.13(1), (3) and (4). This may be done on any day, including Sunday: r. 16.13(1). The certificate is attached to the summons or other document containing the warrant for the diligence: r. 16.12(7).

(3) Arrestment of ship on the dependence.

A ship may be arrested on the dependence of an Admiralty action in personam (a) to enforce or secure a claim in s.47(2) of the 1956 Act by virtue of s.47(1) of that Act where the ship is the ship with which the action is concerned (and is partly owned by the defender: see e.g. *William Batey & Co. (Exports) Ltd v. Kent* 1985 S.L.T. 490, affd. 1987 S.L.T. 557) or all the shares are owned by the defender or (b) to enforce a claim in s.47(2)(p)–(s) by virtue of s.47(3)(a) of the 1956 Act if the conclusion is a pecuniary conclusion and the ship is the ship to which the conclusion relates. In *Oceaneering International AG, Ptnrs.* , 2011 S.L.T. 667 (OH), it was held that the supply of remotely operated vehicles, systems, services and personnel for an offshore intervention vessel was the supply of marine equipment and services to a ship for the operational benefit of it and fell within s.47(2)(k) and (l) of the 1956 Act. On "damage done by a ship", in s.47(2)(a) of the 1956 Act, see *Fish & Fish Ltd v. Sea Shepherd UK* , 2012 S.L.T. 156 (OH). An Admiralty action is defined in r. 46.1. It used not to be clear whether s.47(1) limits the common law right to arrest a sister ship: see e.g. *Sheaf Steamship Co. Ltd v. Compania Transmediterranea* 1930 S.C. 660; cf. Brussels Convention relating to the Arrest of Seagoing Ships, May 10, 1952, art. 3(3), *The "Banco"* [1971] P. 137 (English law) and comments in *Gatoil International Inc. v. Arkwright-Boston Manufacturers Mutual Insurance Co.* 1985 S.C.(H.L.) 1, 15 per Lord Keith of Kinkel. It has now been held in the Outer House that only one ship (the ship concerned or a sister ship) per action may be arrested on the dependence under s.47(1) of the Administration of Justice Act 1956: *Interatlantic (Namibia) (Pty) Ltd v. Okeasnki Ribolov Ltd* 1996 S.L.T. 819; reported as *The "Afala"* [1995] 2 Lloyd's Rep. 286. The action is directed against the defenders and not the ship. The expenses of the arrestment are not recoverable at common law as expenses of process because the arrestment is not essential to obtaining the decree in personam: *Black v. Jehangeer Framjee & Co.* (1887) 14 R. 678. Quaere whether they are recoverable as a debt due in a separate action or under s.93(2) of the Debtors (Scotland) Act 1987.

A schedule in Form 16.15-BB is used and a certificate of execution in Form 16.15-J is completed: r. 16.15(1)(e). The schedule is attached by a messenger-at arms to the mainmast or other prominent part, the letters "ER" chalked above and a copy of the schedule delivered to the master of the ship or person in charge whom failing the harbour master whom failing a motion for further procedure must be enrolled: r. 16.13(1)–(4). This may be done on any day, including Sunday: r. 16.13(1). The certificate is attached to the summons or other document containing the warrant for the diligence: r. 16.12(7).

WARRANT TO DISMANTLE.

An arrestment on the dependence or in rem of a ship fixes her in the place where she is found. To make sure the ship is not moved a warrant to dismantle may be sought (in the summons (r. 13.6(c)(iv)) or subsequently by motion (r. 13.8)). Dismantling should be done by a suitably qualified person (such as a marine engineer) under the supervision of the messenger-at-arms.Dismantling may be unnecessary if the ship does not have customs clearance to sail.

16.13.2

ARRESTMENT IN REM OF CARGO ON BOARD SHIP.

This arrestment may be executed in an Admiralty action (defined in r. 46.1) in rem to enforce a maritime lien (on which, see note 16.13.1(2)(a)). It temporarily detains the ship until the cargo is discharged. Where the cargo cannot be discharged the court may even loose the arrestment to enable this to be done out of the jurisdiction: *Svenska Petroleum A.B. v. H.O.R. Ltd* 1982 S.L.T. 343. It is not clear if the arrestment immobilises the ship where it is until the cargo is discharged or merely prevents the shipmaster from sailing with the cargo out of the jurisdiction. It is probable that s.47(1) of the Administration of Justice Act 1956 does not apply to such an arrestment: see e.g. *Svenska Petroleum A.B. v. H.O.R. Ltd* 1982 S.L.T. 343, 1983 S.L.T. 493 and 1986 S.L.T. 513; *West Cumberland Farmers Ltd v. Ellon Hinengo Ltd* 1988 S.C. 294.

A schedule in Form 16.15-C is used and a certificate of execution in Form 16.15-I is completed: r. 16.15(1)(c). The schedule is attached by a messenger-at-arms to the mainmast or other prominent part and a copy delivered to the master of the ship or person in charge whom failing the harbour master whom failing a motion for further procedure must be enrolled: r. 16.13(1), (3) and (4). This may be done on any day, including Sunday: r. 16.13(1). The certificate is attached to the summons or other document containing the warrant for the diligence: r. 16.12(7).

16.13.3

MOVEMENT OF ARRESTED SHIP OR CARGO.

Any person having an interest may apply by motion to move an arrested vessel or cargo. This may be to move a ship to a safe harbour (*Turner v. Galway* (1882) 19 S.L.R. 892; *The "Grey Dolphin"* 1982 S.C. 5) or to move her from a place where she is obstructing or causing loss to a third party. If a cargo is arrested but cannot be unloaded the ship is effectively immobilised: see *Svenska Petroleum A.B. v. H.O.R. Ltd* 1982 S.L.T. 343; *West Cumberland Farmers Ltd v. Director of Agriculture of Sri Lanka* 1988 S.L.T. 296. See also note 13.11.1.

16.13.4

16.13.5   R. 16.13(1) permits arrestment of a ship in rem or on the dependence, or an arrestment in rem of cargo on board ship, to be executed on any day. The common law prohibition of executing diligence on a Sunday gave rise to difficulty when the turn-round time of ships is often short and tankers and bulk-ore carriers are frequently discharged at weekends.The common law in relation to arrestment on the dependence in an Admiralty action was altered by *Nederlandse Scheepshypotheekbank v. Cam Standby* 1994 S.C.L.R. 956.

Arrestment of cargo

16.14   **16.14.**—[1](1) An arrestment of cargo on board a ship shall be executed by a messenger-at-arms who shall serve the schedule of arrestment on—

    (a)   the master of the ship;

    (b)   any other person in charge of the ship or cargo; or

    (c)   other proper arrestee.

(2)   Where the schedule of arrestment cannot be executed in accordance with paragraph (1), the arrestment may be executed as provided for in rule 16.13(4) and (5).

(3)   A person who has an interest in a ship or cargo which is the subject of an arrestment under this rule may apply by motion for a warrant authorising the movement of the ship or cargo and rule 13.11 shall apply to such a motion.

Deriv. R.C.S. 1965, r. 140(b)

16.14.1   Subject to an exception, arrestment may not be executed where the defender is domiciled in the U.K. or a Contracting State to the 1968 Brussels or the Lugano Convention: C.J.J.A. 1982, Scheds 1 and 3C, Art. 3(2), Sch.4, Art. 3 and Sch.8, r. 2(8). The exception is in an Admiralty cause where the defender is domiciled in the U.K. or elsewhere except another Contracting State to the 1968 or Lugano Convention: C.J.J.A. 1982, Sched.5, para. 7 and Sched.9, para. 6. An Admiralty action is defined in R.C.S. 1994, r. 46.1. Arrestment of a cargo to found jurisdiction is subject to the ordinary rules of arrestment of any property to found jurisdiction, and must be made in the hands of a third party: see note 13.6.1.

A schedule of arrestment in Form 16.15-A is served by a messenger-at-arms on the defender or other person inhibited and a certificate of execution in Form 16.15-H is completed: r. 16.15(1)(a). The certificate is attached to the summons or other document containing the warrant for the diligence: r. 16.12(7).

16.14.2   This arrestment may be executed in an Admiralty action (defined in r. 46.1) to enforce a maritime lien (on which, see note 16.13.1(2)(a)).

A schedule in Form 16.15-C is served by a messenger-at-arms and a certificate of execution in Form 16.15-I is completed: r. 16.15(1)(c). The certificate is attached to the summons or other document containing the warrant for the diligence: r. 16.12(7). There is no provision for this arrestment to be executed on a Sunday and the common law applies: r. 16.14(2); Stair, III.i.37; Bell's *Comm.*, ii,460; *Oliphant v. Douglas* (1633) Mor. 15002. Whether or not the cargo has been delivered to the owner, the messenger-at-arms serves the schedule on the custodian of the cargo or, where on the quay or harbour shed, on the harbour master. Where the cargo has been landed on the quay or in a harbour shed the option of serving on the custodian is still available: this is useful where, e.g. there is no harbour master.

16.14.3   Where the cargo has been or is in the course of being landed or transhipped it no longer has the character of cargo on board ship and there is no reason for treating it as liable to an Admiralty arrestment; the arrestment must be in the hands of a third party: see note 13.6.3. Where cargo is in the possession of the cargo owner on land the ordinary rules of arrestment also apply: see note 13.6.3.

A schedule in Form 16.15-B is served on the arrestee by a messenger-at-arms and a certificate of execution in Form 16.15-H is completed: r. 16.15(1)(b). The certificate is attached to the summons or other document containing the warrant for the diligence: r. 16.12(7). There is no provision for this arrestment to be executed on a Sunday and the common law applies: r. 16.14(2); Stair, III.i.37; Bell's *Comm.*, ii,460; *Oliphant v. Douglas* (1633) Mor. 15002; but cf. *Nederlandse Scheepshypotheekbank NV v. Cam Standby Ltd* 1994 S.C.L.R. 956.

---

[1] R. 16.14 substituted by S.S.I. 2010 No. 205 (effective 15th June 2010).

ARRESTMENT ON THE DEPENDENCE OF CARGO ON BOARD SHIP.

This arrestment may be used in an ordinary action or in an Admiralty action in personam. An Admiralty action is defined in r. 46.1. There must be an arrestee, e.g. a third party or the ship-master (even if he is the employee of the cargo owner) or the cargo owner himself: r. 16.14(2). **16.14.4**

A schedule in Form 16.15-B is served on the arrestee by a messenger-at-arms and a certificate of execution in Form 16.15-J is completed: r. 16.15(1)(e). The arrestment may be executed on any day, including Sunday: r. 16.14(2). The certificate is attached to the summons or other document containing the warrant for the diligence: r. 16.12(7).

MOVEMENT OF ARRESTED SHIP OR CARGO.

Any person having an interest may apply by motion to move arrested cargo. If a cargo is arrested but cannot be unloaded the ship is effectively immobilised: see *Svenska Petroleum A.B. v. H.O.R. Ltd* 1982 S.L.T. 343; *West Cumberland Farmers Ltd v. Director of Agriculture of Sri Lanka* 1988 S.L.T. 296. See also note 13.11.1. **16.14.5**

ARRESTMENT OF CARGO ON A SUNDAY.

The common law prohibition of executing diligence on a Sunday gave rise to difficulty when the turn-round time of ships is often short and tankers and bulk-ore carriers are frequently discharged at weekends. Arrestment of cargo on a Sunday is permitted: (a) in rem of cargo on board ship: r. 16.13(1); (b) on the dependence of an Admiralty action in personam, or of an ordinary action, of cargo on board ship: r. 16.14(2). **16.14.6**

Forms for diligence

16.15.—(1) In the execution of diligence, the following forms shall be used— **16.15**
  (a)[1] in the case of—
     (i) an arrestment to found jurisdiction (other than the arrestment of a ship), a schedule in Form 16.15-A and a certificate of execution in Form 16.15-H;
     (ii) an arrestment of a ship to found jurisdiction, a schedule in Form 16.15-AA and a certificate of execution in Form 16.15-HH;
  (b) subject to sub-paragraph (e), in the case of an arrestment on the dependence, a schedule in Form 16.15-B and a certificate of execution in Form 16.15-H;
  (c)[2] in the case of an arrestment in rem of a ship, cargo or other maritime res to enforce a maritime hypothec or lien, a schedule in Form 16.15-C and a certificate of execution in Form 16.15-I;
  (d) in the case of an arrestment in rem of a ship to enforce a non-pecuniary claim, a schedule in Form 16.15-D and a certificate of execution in Form 16.15-I;
  (e)[3] in the case of an arrestment on the dependence of—
     (i) a cargo on board a ship, a schedule in Form 16.15-B;
     (ii) a ship, a schedule in Form 16.15-BB, and a certificate of execution in Form 16.15-J;
  (f)[4] subject to paragraph (g), in the case of an arrestment in execution, a certificate of execution in Form 16.15-H;
  (g) in the case of an earnings arrestment, or a current maintenance arrestment, within the meaning of Part III of the Debtors (Scotland) Act 1987, a schedule in Form 30 (in respect of an earnings arrestment), or Form 34 (in respect of a current maintenance arrestment), and a certificate of execution in Form 60, in the Schedule to the Act of Sederunt (Proceedings in the Sheriff Court under the Debtors (Scotland) Act 1987) 1988;
  (h) *[Omitted by S.S.I. 2009 No. 104 (effective 22nd April 2009).]*

---

[1] R. 16.15(1)(a), (c) and (e) substituted by S.I. 1998 No.2637 (effective 1st December 1998)
[2] R. 16.15(1)(a), (c) and (e) substituted by S.I. 1998 No.2637 (effective 1st December 1998)
[3] R. 16.15(1)(a), (c) and (e) substituted by S.I. 1998 No.2637 (effective 1st December 1998)
[4] R. 16.15(f) amended by S.S.I. 2009 No. 104 (effective 22nd April 2009)

(i) in the case of the execution of a charge for payment of money, a charge in Form 16.15-G and a certificate of execution in Form 16.15-K;

(j)[1] in the case of an attachment, a schedule in form 3, and a report of attachment in form 8, in Appendix 1 of Schedule 1 to the Act of Sederunt (Debt Arrangement and Attachment (Scotland) Act 2002) 2002; and

(k)[2] in the case of an interim attachment, a schedule in Form 2a, and a report of attachment in Form 2b, in Appendix 1 of Schedule 1 to the Act of Sederunt (Debt Arrangement and Attachment (Scotland) Act 2002) 2002.

(2) Where two or more of the arrestments mentioned in paragraph (1)(a), (b), (c) and (d) are to be executed, they may be combined in one schedule of arrestment.

Deriv. R.C.S. 1965, r. 74(c), and r. 140(c) (r. 16.15(2))

FORMS FOR DILIGENCE.

16.15.1   In respect of the following forms in r. 16.15, see the notes mentioned to which the forms relate:

Form 16.15-A—see notes 16.12.7, 16.13.1(1) and 16.14.1;
Form 16.15-AA—see notes 16.12.7 and 16.13.1(1);
Form 16.15-B—see notes 16.12.8, 16.13.1(3) and 16.14.3;
Form 16.15-BB—see notes 16.12.8 and 16.13.1(3);
Form 16.15-C—see notes 16.13.1(2)(a), 16.13.3 and 16.14.2;
Form 16.15-D—see note 16.13.1(2)(b);
Form 16.15-F—see note 16.12.12;
Form 16.15-G—see note 16.12.13;
Form 16.15-H—see notes 16.12.7, 16.12.8, 16.12.11, 16.12.12, 16.13.1(1), 16.14.1 and 16.14.3;
Form 16.15-HH—see notes 16.12.7 and 16.13.1(1);
Form 16.15-I—see notes 16.13.1(2), 16.13.3 and 16.14.2;
Form 16.15-J—see notes 16.13.1(3) and 16.14.4;
Form 16.15-K—see note 16.12.13.

In respect of earnings arrestments and current maintenance arrestments within the meaning of Pt III of the Debtors (Scotland) Act 1987 the forms in the Schedule to the Act of Sederunt (Proceedings in the Sheriff Court under the Debtors (Scotland) Act 1987) 1988, and, in the case of attachment, the form in Appendix 1 of Sched. 1 to the Act of Sederunt (Debt Arrangement and Attachment (Scotland) Act 2002) 2002 [SSI 2002/560], are to be used. Proceedings following the execution of such diligence are in the sheriff court.

Form of Service of copy decree

16.16   **16.16.**[3] The copy final decree served under section 73C(2) of the Debtors (Scotland) Act 1987 shall be in Form 16.16

---

[1] R. 16.15(1)(j) substituted by S.S.I. 2002/560 No. art.4, Sched.3, para. 5 (effective 30th December 2002)

[2] R. 16.15(1)(k) inserted by S.S.I. 2008 No. 122 (effective 1st April 2008)

[3] R. 16.16 inserted by S.S.I. 2009 No. 104 (effective 22nd April 2009).

CHAPTER 17 APPEARANCE IN ACTIONS

Entering appearance

17.1.—(1)   Appearance in an action shall be entered within three days after the date on which the summons has called by the defender requesting a clerk of session in the appropriate section of the General Department to mark on the summons—

>   (a)   the names of the counsel, or other person having a right of audience, and the agent acting for him; or
>   (b)   that he appears for himself.

(2)   On entering appearance, the defender shall give written intimation to the pursuer that appearance has been entered.

(3)   On entering appearance, the defender shall have the right to borrow any production which has been lodged in process.

Deriv. R.C.S. 1965, r. 81(1) substituted by SI 1991/2483 (r. 17.1(1)), r. 81(1B) inserted by SI 1991/2483 (r. 17.1(2)) and r. 86 (r. 17.1(3))

GENERAL NOTE.

Appearance is no longer entered on the calling list but by a clerk of session on the principal summons (heretofore an informal practice). The effect of entering appearance is (a) the defender cannot challenge a defective execution of service on himself (*Corstorphine v. Kasten* (1898) 1 F. 287) and (b) the defender may borrow any productions from process (r. 17.1(3)). If the defender does not enter appearance or having done so has not lodged defences, the pursuer may obtain a decree in absence which may become a decree in foro: r. 19.1(1) and (7).

Entering appearance may be done in person at the public counter of the appropriate section of the General Department, or by post or fax (P.N. No. 4 of 1994, para. 5, or by e-mail (P.N. No. 2 of 2001). Where this is done by post, fax or e-mail details of the cause reference number, the parties, date of calling and the information required for the purposes of r. 17.1(1) must be given by 4 p.m. on the last day for entering appearance: P.N. No. 4 of 1994, para. 5(2); P.N. No. 2 of 2001, para. 2.

"WITHIN THREE DAYS".

The day on which the summons calls is not counted in calculating the period; but the third day is included in the period. Where the last day falls on a Saturday or Sunday or a public holiday on which the Office of Court is closed, appearance may be entered on the next available day: r. 1.3(7). For office hours and holidays, see note 3.1.2. For calling of summons, see r. 13.13.

"COUNSEL, OR OTHER PERSON HAVING A RIGHT OF AUDIENCE".

See r. 1.3(1) (definitions of "counsel" and "other person having a right of audience") and note 1.3.4.

"AGENT".

This means a solicitor or a person having a right to conduct the litigation: see r. 1.3(1) (definition of "agent") and note 1.3.4. "Solicitor" is defined in the C.S.A. 1988, s.51.

"WRITTEN INTIMATION".

For methods, see r. 16.9.

BORROWING PRODUCTIONS.

The defender no longer has the right to borrow the principal summons: there is no need for him to do so; and the only effect or purpose of the former right was to prevent the pursuer obtaining a decree in absence. For borrowing and returning productions, see r. 4.12.

Appearance not to imply acceptance of jurisdiction

17.2   The entering of appearance shall not imply acceptance of the jurisdiction of the court.

Deriv. R.C.S. 1965, r. 81(2) inserted by SI 1986/1941

GENERAL NOTE.

This rule was introduced by A.S. (R.C.A. No. 9) (Jurisdiction and Enforcement) 1986 [SI 1986/1941] because the C.J.J.A. 1982, Scheds 1, 3C and 4, Art. 18 and Sched.8, r. 6(2) provide that a court does not have jurisdiction over the substance or merits of a cause where appearance is entered solely to contest jurisdiction.

Defences may be lodged contesting jurisdiction only or contesting jurisdiction and defending on the merits: see r. 18.2(1). But, where the defender first admits jurisdiction and subsequently seeks to take a plea of jurisdiction, he may be taken as having consented to the jurisdiction of the court: *Clarke v. Fennoscandia Ltd (No.2)* , 10th March 2000, (2000 G.W.D. 11-377) (OH).

17.1

17.1.1

17.1.2

17.1.3

17.1.4

17.1.5

17.1.6

17.2

17.2.1

CHAPTER 18 DEFENCE AND ANSWERS

Form and lodging of defences

18.1

18.1.—(1) Defences to an action shall consist of—

(a) numbered answers corresponding to the articles of the condescendence annexed to the summons; and

(b) appropriate pleas-in-law.

(2) Subject to rule 46.6 (ship collisions and preliminary acts), defences to an action shall be lodged in process within 7 days after the date on which the summons has called, or, if the seventh day is in vacation, on the next day on which a summons may be called.

Deriv. R.C.S. 1965, r. 83(a) (r. 18.1(2)) and (b) (r. 18.1(1))

GENERAL NOTE.

18.1.1

Where defences are to be lodged, the principal must be taken to the clerk of session in the Signet Office in the General Department to be initialled by him before being presented at the section in the department in which the process of the action is lodged (see note 3.2.1 for departmental sections). Defences may be sent by post by a Court of Session account holder or if accompanied by a cheque for the court fee for lodging: P.N. No. 4 of 1994, paras 1, 2 and 8.

Litiscontestation takes place when defences are lodged and any decree thereafter is a decree *in foro contentioso*: *Gow v. Henry* (1899) 2 F. 48, 52 per Lord Young; *Argyllshire Weavers Ltd v. A. Macauley (Tweeds) Ltd* 1962 S.C. 388, 394 per Lord Hunter.

FORM OF DEFENCES.

18.1.2

"Our whole system of pleading and disposal of cases upon preliminary pleas must depend upon each party stating with candour what are the material facts upon which he relies and admitting the facts stated by his opponent which he knows to be true": *Ellon Castle Estates Co. Ltd v. Macdonald* 1975 S.L.T.(Notes) 66 per Lord Stewart.

In family actions, defences may contain conclusions: r. 49.31(2)(b)(i). On answers to condescendence, see note 18.1.3; on pleas-in-law, see note 18.1.4.

On the requirement for the use of metric units of measurement in pleadings, see note 13.2.18.

ANSWERS TO CONDESCENDENCE.

18.1.3

There should be a concise, accurate and frank response to the articles of the condescendence. Every fact should be answered. In each answer to each article, these rules should be followed: First, admit specifically all those averments which are admitted ("Admitted that *(set out the averment)*"); one should not admit a variation of the averment. An averment may be admitted subject to an explanation ("Admitted that ... under explanation that ...") where it is convenient to include it and this can be done shortly; otherwise there should be no admission and the explanation dealt with after the general denial. An admission must be read with any qualification or explanation unless disproved (*Picken v. Arundale & Co.* (1872) 10 M. 987) or irrelevant (*Robertson & Co. v. Bird & Co.* (1897) 24 R. 1076). Where all averments are admitted, "Admitted." will do. Admissions exclude the need for evidence and are conclusive in that cause against the party making them (Erskine IV.ii.33) except in consistorial actions (*Macfarlane v. Macfarlane* 1956 S.C. 472); and if deleted from the record may yet be the subject of cross-examination (*Lennox v. National Coal Board* 1955 S.C. 438).

Second (exceptionally), where facts are outwith the defender's knowledge but are believed to be true, these averments should be dealt with by "Believed to be true that *(set out averment)*": an averment that something is believed to be true is equivalent to an admission: *Scottish North Eastern Railway Co. v. Napier* (1859) 21 D. 700, 703 per L.J.-C. Inglis (the Acts of Sederunt containing this principle are no longer in force, but the principle remains). The party met by such a reply is entitled to take it that the point believed to be true is not disputed and is not one on which evidence is required: *Binnie v. Rederij Theodoro BV* 1993 S.C. 71, 86G per L.P. Hope.

Thirdly, where averments are outwith the defender's knowledge and are not admitted, these should be dealt with by "Not known and not admitted that *(set out averment)*". Where all averments are not known and not admitted, "Not known and not admitted." will do.

Fourthly, all other averments, being those which are denied, should be answered with a general denial, "Quoad ultra, denied.": this is because every averment of fact within the defender's knowledge which is not denied is deemed to be admitted: *Pegler v. Northern Agricultural Implements and Foundry Co. Ltd* (1877) 4 R. 435, 438 per L.P. Inglis; and knowledge means his state of knowledge (*Central Motor Engineering Co. v. Galbraith* 1918 S.C. 755, 756 per L.P. Strathclyde) on any matter which he does not have to make enquiries about to discover the truth (*O'Connor v. W. G. Auld & Co. (Engineering) Ltd* 1970 S.L.T.(Notes) 16). The averment "Not admitted" or "No admission is made" is similarly treated: *Ellis v. Fraser* (1840) 3 D. 264, 271 per L.P. Hope; *Clark v. Clark* 1967 S.C. 296, 305 per Lord Milligan. An averment that the defender performed all statutory duties incumbent upon him may be treated as an admission of the applicability of the statute averred by the pursuer: *McNaught v. British Railways Board* 1979 S.L.T.(Notes) 99; but such an averment will not bar the defender from subsequently taking a plea to the relevancy if the statute does not apply: *Lamont v. Monklands D.C.* 1992 S.L.T. 428; and see the discussion in *Ballantyne v. John Young & Co. (Kelvinhaugh) Ltd* 1996 S.L.T. 358. An averment that a document is "referred to for its terms" is not an admission: *Pringle v. Bremner & Stirling* (1867) 5 M. (H.L.) 55; *Ballantyne*, above (statutory duty). Where all averments are denied, "Denied." will do. A defender's unqualified denial on record of a pursuer's detailed averments on matters within the defender's knowledge could indicate a lack of candour which entitled the court to proceed on the basis that the pursuer's averments were well founded and grant decree *de plano*: *EFT Finance Ltd v. Hawkins* 1994 S.C. 34. The form "it is specifically denied that...", sometimes seen in sheriff court pleadings, is an example of bad pleading and does not conform to the rules just set out.

There then follows the defender's explanation or version of the facts. The explanation and any additional facts averred should be such as is necessary to give fair notice of the line of the defence or to provide the foundation for the substantive defence and the pleas-in-law without pleading evidence (i.e. the manner in which the facts averred will be proved): *Neilson v. Househill Coal and Iron Co.* (1842) 4 D. 1187, 1193 per L.J.-C. Hope "The beauty of the Scotch system is, that, without disclosing what is properly called evidence, you must at least state the line of the defence, and the main facts and points in the enquiry on which you rest, so that the other party shall be fully able previously to investigate the case, and be prepared for it." Law should not be pled except (a) as a matter of practice, in a reparation action the duties owed by the defender to the pursuer are pled; (b) a private Act of Parliament before 1850 (Interpretation Act 1978, s.3); and (c) foreign law if different from Scots law, otherwise it will be presumed to be the same as Scots law (*Emerald Stainless Steel Ltd v. South Side Distribution Ltd* 1982 S.C. 61), unless judicial knowledge must be taken of it (for which see Macphail on Sheriff Court Practice, paras 2-04 to 2-07).

The defender cannot normally raise issues not pled on record (*Smith v. Green* (1854) 16 D. 429) but a defence emerging in cross-examination and unforeseen may be put forward (*Bile Bean Manufacturing Co. v. Davidson* (1906) 8 F. 1181). All grounds of defence and pleas must be stated at the same time, except that of no jurisdiction (see r. 18.2). A defender may plead alternative defences: *Smart v. Bargh* 1949 S.C. 57, 61 per L.P. Cooper.

Skeletal defences—i.e. bare denials—are rarely proper or satisfactory: it is rare for a straight denial to be the whole of a defence, no alternative version of events can be put forward in evidence or cross-examination and they may result in the pursuer obtaining summary decree (see Chap. 21) or decree *de plano* at procedure roll (*Ellon Castle Estates Co. Ltd v. Macdonald* 1975 S.L.T.(Notes) 66; *Foxley v. Dunn* 1978 S.L.T.(Notes) 35; cf. *McManus v. Spiers Dick and Smith Ltd* 1989 S.L.T. 806 (circumstances where skeletal defences entitled defender to put pursuer to his proof).

A pursuer or a defender, in the pleadings, may "call" on the other to be specific or more specific about an averment or lack of one. Guidance was given by the LJ-C Inglis in *Gordon, above*, at p. 768 about the circumstances in which a call may properly be made and requires to be answered: "When a pursuer's statement is irrelevant or verging on irrelevancy, I could understand a call of this kind as a warning to call the pursuer's attention to the state of his averments, that he might have no reason afterwards to complain that he was taken by surprise, or that he understood that no greater specification was wanted." A failure to answer a call could, in certain circumstances, result in an implied admission that the other party's position is correct: see, e.g., *Marine & Offshore (Scotland) Ltd v Robert Jack* [2017] CSOH 89, para. [56].

PLEAS-IN-LAW.

18.1.4 These are distinct legal propositions applicable to the facts of the case: *J. & R. Young & Co. v. Graham* (1860) 23 D. 36 per L.J.-C. Inglis.Pleas may be divided into (1) preliminary pleas and (2) pleas on the merits (peremptory pleas). Pleas-in-law must be supported by averments.

(A) Preliminary pleas.

These are decided before the merits are decided and if sustained lead to disposal of the action without inquiry into the merits.They result in dismissal (or sist) but do not make the cause res judicata, and the pursuer may raise a fresh action: *Menzies v. Menzies* (1893) 20 R.(H.L.) 108, 110 per Lord Watson. Where such a plea is so bound up with the merits, a proof before answer may be allowed instead of disposing of the action at procedure roll. It is good practice to disclose in the plea the ground on which the plea is taken, particularly in the case of general pleas of relevancy and specification: the practice heretofore of regarding proper notice of fact or the line of evidence as essential but not notice of the point of law is defective; the practice is tempered by the possibility of being required to lodge and intimate a note of argument (see rr. 22.4 (general provision), 43.24(8) (optional procedure in certain actions of damages), 47.12(1)(d) (commercial actions) and 55.3(4)(b) (causes relating to intellectual property)). The most common pleas are as follows:

(A)(1) *"All parties not called."* This short form is normally used. The plea is that all persons whose absence from the cause will prejudice the defender in his defence or after the defence has been repelled (Maclaren on *Court of Session Practice*, p. 381; see e.g. *Arthur v. The SMT Sales & Service Co. Ltd* , 1998 S.C. 525) or whose presence is necessary to have the question at issue effectively disposed of (*Wilson v. Independent Broadcasting Authority* 1979 S.C. 351, 356 per Lord Ross) have not been called as defenders: e.g. where the party not called is a joint owner (*North British Railway Co. v. North Eastern Railway Co.* (1896) 24 R.(H.L.) 19); where a joint and several obligation has to be constituted by decree (*Neilson v. Wilson* (1890) 17 R. 608).

Prejudice to the defender may not exist where third party procedure is available: *Lang v. Ure* 1994 S.L.T. 1235. It is *pars judicis* to notice that all parties are not called: *Connell v. Ferguson* (1857) 19 D. 482, 486 per Lord Deas.

(A)(2)   *Competent and omitted.* "The present action being based on averments that (*briefly detail*) and having been omitted from that action, the present action is incompetent and the action should be dismissed [*or* the defender should be assoilzied]." The plea now seems to be regarded as a preliminary or dilatory plea: see, e.g. *Murray v. Seath* 1939 S.L.T. 348; *Cantors Properties (Scotland) Ltd v. Swears & Wells Ltd* 1978 S.C. 310. The plea should specify the grounds of objection and be supported by relevant averments.Where a defender has put forward a defence which is unsuccessful he cannot in a subsequent process challenge the prior judgment on grounds which it was competent to plead in the prior process but which he omitted to do: Maclaren on *Court of Session Practice*, p. 401; *Macdonald v. Macdonald* (1842) 1 Bell's App. 819, 829 per Lord Campbell; *Cantors Properties (Scotland) Ltd*, above; *Dickie v. Goldie* 1995 S.L.T. 780 (failure to plead compensation in prior action not a bar). It does not apply to a pursuer in a prior cause who can raise further actions based on different grounds: *Macdonald*, above. The considerations for this plea are similar to those in the plea of res judicata: *Rorie v. Rorie* 1967 S.L.T. 75, 78 per Lord Milligan. For res judicata, see (B)(5) below.

(A)(3)   *Forum non conveniens:* "The court being *forum non conveniens*, the action should be dismissed [*or* sisted]." Ss.22 and 49 of the C.J.J.A. 1982 save the application of this doctrine in relation to the jurisdiction of the court under Sch.8, but it has no application to causes to which either the 1968 or Lugano Convention applies where the defender is domiciled in another Convention country or where Sch.1 or 4, Art. 16 applies (exclusive jurisdiction). Under these conventions the doctrine of *lis pendens* applies.The doctrine of forum non conveniens applies "whenever it can be shown that the case cannot, consistently with fairness and justice, be tried in this country": *Sim v. Robinow* (1892) 19 R. 665, 666 per Lord Low; see also *Clements v. Macauley* (1866) 4 M. 583, 592 per L.J.-C. Inglis.Where the jurisdiction of the court is competently founded, the court has no discretion whether to exercise it or not: *Clements*, above; *Sim*, above, per Lord Kinnear at p. 668. Something more than mere practical inconvenience is required to sustain a plea of forum non conveniens. The proper translation of "*conveniens*" is "appropriate"; the actual convenience of the parties is not to be considered but that which is the appropriate forum for securing the ends of justice, and the decision must be taken in the light of the whole surrounding circumstances: *Societe du Gaz de Paris v. Société Anonyme de Navigation "Les Armateurs Francais"* 1926 S.C.(H.L.) 13, 18 per Lord Dunedin. The general principles were recently set out by Lord Jauncey in *Credit Chimique v. James Scott Engineering Group Ltd* 1979 S.C. 406. The initial onus is on the defender to raise and justify the plea: *De Mulder v. Jadranska Linijska (Jadrolinija)* 1989 S.L.T. 269. The mere fact that evidence of foreign law is required is not enough. It is not enough to show that the defence will have a better chance of succeeding elsewhere, as one must look to the interests of the pursuer as well as those of the defender "and the thing to be shown is not that there will be a disadvantage in that sense, but that there will be unfair disadvantage, so that justice is unlikely to be done": *Longworth v. Hope* (1865) 3 M. 1049, 1057 per Lord Deas.Once the defender has satisfied the initial onus it is for the pursuer to establish that to litigate abroad would deprive him of an advantage of such importance that it would cause injustice to deprive him of it (*De Mulder*, above) or that substantial justice could not be done in the other court (*Sokha v. Secretary of State for the Home Department* 1992 S.L.T. 1049, 1054 per Lord Prosser). In *Sokha*, above, at p. 1054A, it was observed by Lord Prosser that where the choice of jurisdiction was between competing jurisdictions within the U.K. a strong preference might be given to the forum chosen by the pursuer. For a recent example of there being another convenient forum but the difficulties in accessing the Kenyan courts and securing substantial justice meant that the plea of *forum non conveniens* could not be upheld, see *Campbell KC v. James Finlay (Kenya) Ltd*, 2023 S.L.T. 856. The plea will usually be inappropriate in causes relating to immoveables as the courts of the *lex situs* will be the only courts competent to grant decree in rem: *Foster v. Foster's Trs* 1923 S.C. 212. For a recent example of an unsuccessful plea, see *The Royal Bank of Scotland plc v. Davidson* , 2010 S.L.T. 92 (OH).

(A)(4)   *Incompetency:* "The action, being incompetent [because (state reason)], should be dismissed." The ground on which objection is taken should be specified: *Coxall v. Stewart* 1976 S.L.T. 275. This plea is an objection to the form of the summons or condescendence and is distinguished from relevancy: Maclaren on *Court of Session Practice*, p. 387. Competency and relevancy run into each other: *Coutts v. Coutts* (1866) 4 M. 802, 803 per L.P. McNeill. A party acting inconsistently with his plea may be held to have waived it: *North British Railway Co. v. Carter* (1870) 8 M. 998. It is pars judicis to notice questions of competency, and an action may be dismissed without such a plea being stated: *Hamilton v. Murray* (1830) 9 S. 143. Where there is a statutory time-limit for the raising of an action, this may raise an issue of jurisdictional competency rather than an extinctive prescription or limitation. For example, the time-limit for raising an action for financial claims arising out of cohabitation under ss.28 or 29 of the Family Law (Scotland) Act 2006 is mandatory and not an issue of prescription or limitation: *Simpson v. Downie*, 2013 S.L.T. 178, 2012 Fam. L.R. 121, para. [13] (Extra Div.).

(A)(5)   *"Lis [alibi] pendens."* This short form is usually used. If the prior cause is in another court the plea is *lis alibi pendens*. If the prior cause is in the same court the plea is lis pendens: *Levy v. Gardiner* 1965 S.L.T.(Notes) 86. The common law plea of *lis alibi pendens* does not apply where the prior action is in a foreign court: *Martin v. Stopford-Blair's Exrs* (1879) 7 R. 329, 331 per L.P. Inglis. Where the 1968 (Brussels) or Lugano Convention applies, the provisions of those conventions for *lis pendens* and related actions apply: C.J.J.A. 1982, Scheds 1 and 3C, Arts 21-23; and see note 13.2.11. Where the prior action is in a foreign country to which those conventions do not apply or another part of the U.K., the plea of forum non conveniens must be relied on to exclude jurisdiction: see para.(A)(3) above. In consistorial causes the plea of lis alibi pendens is not usually taken, the position being governed by para.9 of Sch.3 to the Domicile and Matrimonial Proceedings Act 1973 so that where proceedings are continuing in another court relating to the marriage or its validity the court may, after considering the balance of fairness, convenience and all other relevant factors, grant a sist of the Scottish cause pending the outcome of those proceedings: see, e.g. *Mitchell v. Mitchell* 1992 S.C. 372.

   (a)   The common law plea. There must be supporting averments: *Flannigan v. British Dyewood Co.* 1971 S.C. 110, 111 and 114 per Lord Fraser. There must be, when the plea is considered (*Flannigan*, above), (a) a prior action in dependence—after service of the summons and before the action is finally disposed of (including expenses) (*Aitken v. Dick* (1863) 1 M. 1038), and even if the action is asleep (*Denovan v. Cairns* (1845) 7 D. 378)—(b) in another court in Scotland (*Martin*, above) of competent jurisdiction, (c) between the same parties in the same legal capacities or interest (*Longmuir v. Longmuir* (1850) 12 D. 926; *Alston v. Alston's Trs* 1912 2 S.L.T. 22), (d) in which the same question is raised (*Wilson v. Dunlop, Bremner & Co. Ltd* 1921 1 S.L.T. 35). The plea is avoided by abandonment (*Laidlaw v. Smith* (1834) 12 S. 538; *McAuley v. Cowel* (1873) 1 R. 307) or disclaimer (*Alston*, above) of the prior cause. The plea is not available if the defender prorogates the jurisdiction (*Longmuir*, above).

   (b)   Where proceedings involving the same cause of action between the same parties are brought in the courts of different Contracting States to the 1968 Convention in Sched. 1, or the Lugano Convention in Sched. 3C, to the C.J.J.A. 1982, any court other than the court first seized of the proceedings shall at its own instance sist the proceedings until the jurisdiction of the court first seized is established: C.J.J.A. 1982, Scheds 1 and 3C, Art. 21(1). As the court has to examine jurisdiction itself (and particularly if decree in absence is sought), the court must know (ex facie of the summons) whether it has jurisdiction. Proceedings will have been brought in a court if the proceedings have commenced according to the procedural rules of that court (*Zelger v. Salinitri (No. 2)* [1984] E.C.R. 2397). In Scotland this is the date of execution of citation of the defender (Erskine, III.iv.3; *Alston v. Macdougall* (1887) 15 R. 78; *Smith v. Stewart & Co.* 1960 S.C. 329, 334 per L.P. Clyde; though in relation to the plea of forum non conveniens it has been affirmed that priority of process in terms of litiscontestation (when defences are lodged) is the normal test (*Argyllshire Weavers Ltd v. A. Macauley (Tweeds) Ltd* 1962 S.C. 388, 400 per L.P. Clyde)). The nature and factual basis of the claim must be the same. As well as the same cause of action and same parties, there must also be the same subject-matter: *Gubisch Maschinenfabrik v. Palumbo* [1987] E.C.R. 4861. Where the foreign proceedings are only for protective measures and do not concern the substantive issues, there may not be a cause of action which has arisen between the parties: *Bank of Scotland v. S.A. Banque Nationale de Paris* 1996 S.L.T. 103. Where jurisdiction of the first court is contested the second court may sist the cause before it rather than decline jurisdiction: C.J.J.A. 1982, Scheds 1 and 3C, Art. 21(2). Where the concurrent proceedings do not involve the same parties or cause of action they may yet be related actions: in the case of related actions the second court may sist the action before it (Scheds 1 and 3C, Art. 22(1)) or on the application of a party decline jurisdiction if the actions can be consolidated and there is jurisdiction over both actions in the first court (Scheds 1 and 3C, Art. 22(2)); "related actions" means actions so closely connected that it is expedient to hear and determine them together to avoid the risk of irreconcilable judgments (Scheds 1 and 3C, Art.22(3)). Where more than one court has exclusive jurisdiction any court other than the court first seized shall decline jurisdiction: Scheds 1 and 3C, Art. 23. Art. 17 (prorogation) prevails over Arts 21 and 22: Bank of Scotland, above. For the application of the 1968 or Lugano Convention in Scheds 1 and 3C to the C.J.J.A. 1982, see note 13.2.12.

(A)(6)   *No jurisdiction:* "The court having no jurisdiction [because (*state reason*)], the action should be dismissed." The short form "No jurisdiction" has been criticised: *Love v. Love* 1907 S.C. 728, 729 per Lord Dundas; cf. *Carter v. Allison* 1966 S.C. 257. For jurisdiction, see notes 13.2.7 to 13.2.14. The plea should be taken at the first opportunity; if not, and the defender first admits jurisdiction but subsequently seeks to take the plea, he may be taken as having consented to the jurisdiction of the court: *Clarke v. Fennoscandia Ltd (No.2)* , 10th March 2000, (2000 G.W.D. 11-377) (OH).

(A)(7)   *No title to sue:* "The pursuer having no title to sue [*or* no interest] to sue [because (*state reason*)], the action should be dismissed." The ground of objection must be specifically averred: *North British Railway Co. v. Brown, Gordon & Co.* (1857) 19 D. 840. A plea of no title permits the defender to contend that title fails through lack of any interest: *Agnew v. Laughlan* 1948 S.C. 656, 661 per Lord Macintosh. This plea is not appropriate where the pursuer's title is the *de quo* of the action: *Luss Estates Co. v. B.P. Oil Grangemouth Refinery Ltd* 1981 S.L.T. 97. The plea is judged as at the time the summons was served: *Swanson v. Manson* 1907 S.C. 426, 430 per L.P. Dunedin. See also, note 13.2.2(c) (title and interest).

(A)(8)   *Reference to arbitration:* "The parties having agreed to arbitration upon the subject-matter of the action, the action should be sisted pending such arbitration." This is the correct form of the plea: *Inverclyde (Mearns) Housing Society Ltd v. Lawrence Construction Co. Ltd* 1989 S.L.T. 815, 821F per Lord McCluskey. It must be established that a valid contract exists (*Ransohoff & Wissler v. Burrell* (1897) 25 R. 284) and that there is a dispute (*Mackay & Son v. Leven Police Commissioners* (1893) 20 R. 1093, 1102 per Lord Adam; *Allied Airways (Gander Dower) Ltd v. Secretary of State for Air* 1950 S.C. 249) to which the arbitration clause applies (*Crawford Brothers v. Commissioners of Northern Lighthouses* 1925 S.C.(H.L.) 22). The action is sisted rather than dismissed so that recourse can be made to the court where the arbitration breaks down, other questions arise or to enforce an arbitral award: *Hamlyn & Co. v. Talisker Distillery* (1894) 21 R.(H.L.) 21, 27 per Lord Watson.

A contract will not be interpreted as excluding the jurisdiction of the court unless by clear words or necessary implication: *Brodie v. Ker* 1952 S.C. 216, 224 (Second Div. plus three consulted judges from First Div.). For a recent example, see *Fraserburgh Harbour Commissioners v. McLaughlin and Harvey Ltd* 2022 S.C. 84 (First Div.).

The plea should be taken early in the proceedings and before the record is closed: *Halliburton Manufacturing and Services Ltd v. Bingham Blades & Partners* 1984 S.L.T. 388. Failure to observe the proper practice could constitute a very strong indication that the right had been waived and, in any event, delay in taking the plea could render that party liable for expenses abortively incurred: *Presslie v. Cochrane McGregor Group Ltd* , 1996 S.C. 289, 1996 S.L.T. 988; *La Pantofola D'Ora SpA v. Blane Leisure Ltd* , 2000 S.L.T. 105 (OH); *UBC Group Ltd v. Atholl Developments (Slackbuie) Ltd* , 2011 S.L.T. 805 (OH) (a commercial action in which there was no open or closed record, a sist for arbitration sought by the pursuer at a continued preliminary hearing was refused on the ground that the pursuer's conduct had been unequivocally that of a party intending to litigate).

(A)(9)   *Relevancy and specification:* "The pursuer's averments [in respect of (*refer to averment attacked*)] being irrelevant *et separatim* lacking in specification, the action should be dismissed [or should not be remitted to probation]." The ground on which the relevancy or specification of the pleadings is attacked ought to be specified; although a general plea is common, and the specific plea directed to exclusion of averments from probation. Where the pursuer does not offer to amend and the plea would otherwise be successful, the action will be dismissed. Where the plea is directed to the exclusion of certain averments, the action is not dismissed and the plea seeks exclusion of those averments from probation.

(a)   A plea to the relevancy is that even on the assumption that the pursuer's averments are true in fact, he cannot succeed in law in obtaining the decree he has concluded for. The onus is on the defender: *Jamieson v. Jamieson* 1952 S.C.(H.L.) 44, 50 per Lord Normand. The proper approach is to consider whether, on a fair reading and assuming them to be true, the pursuer's case is bound to fail: *Wislon v. Norwich Union Fire Insurance Society Ltd* , 6 June 1999, unreported. In deciding relevancy, the pursuer's averments are considered; but, where the pursuer admits an averment of the defender, that too will be considered: *Pringle v. Bremner and Stirling* (1867) 5 M.(H.L.) 55, 58 per Lord Chelmsford L.C. A reparation action for personal injuries will rarely be dismissed on relevancy: *Miller v. South of Scotland Electricity Board* 1958 S.C.(H.L.) 20, 33 per Lord Keith of Avonholm; cf. *Davie v. Edinburgh Corporation* 1977 S.L.T.(Notes) 5 and *Robb v. Dundee D.C.* 1980 S.L.T.(Notes) 91; *Kemp v. Secretary of State for Scotland* 1997 S.L.T. 1174. The ultimate test of relevancy is whether the material in question has a reasonably direct bearing on the subject under investigation; it being a matter of degree in each case (in which expediency has a part to play): *Strathmore Group Ltd v. Credit Lyonnais* 1994 S.L.T. 1023, 1031H per Lord Osborne. Where a case is of doubtful relevancy a proof before answer will be allowed. See further on relevancy, note 13.2.4.

(b)   A plea relating to specification is usually combined with the relevancy plea. It is to the effect that the pursuer has not given fair notice of the case the defender has to meet; the matter must be looked at broadly to ascertain whether fair notice has been given: *McMenemy v. James Dougal & Sons Ltd* 1960 S.L.T.(Notes) 84 per Lord Guest. The ultimate test is one of fairness: *Maclean v. Forestry Commission* 1970 S.L.T. 265, 272 per Lord Wheatley. In the field of criminal law it has been held that lack of fair notice can only be a justifiable complaint if it results in material prejudice: *Lockhart v. National Coal Board* 1981 S.L.T. 161, 170. The plea is available where the fact not averred is in the defender's knowledge: *Macdonald v. Glasgow Western Hospital's Board of Management* 1954 S.C. 453, 465 per L.P. Cooper. In modern practice calls are sometimes made in pleadings on a pursuer for further specification: this will alert him to a defective case (*Gordon v. Davidson* (1864) 2 M. 758, 768 per L.J.-C. Inglis) which he may improve and prevent the defender from obtaining dismissal; but if the plea is properly drafted the pursuer may be alerted anyway. A call to make an averment which the pursuer does not need to do to make his case relevant is of no effect: *Bonnor v. Balfour Kilpatrick Ltd* 1974 S.C. 223, 227 per Lord Kincraig, and 228 per L.P. Emslie. A party is not bound to answer a call (*Gordon*, above); and a call is not an averment of fact and does not amount to a denial of the pursuer's averments (*Bonnor*, above).

(A)(10)   *Time-bar (limitation of action):* "The action, not having been commenced timeously in terms of [section [17] of the Prescription and Limitation (Scotland) Act 1973, should be dismissed." An action is commenced on the date the citation is served on the defender: *Miller v. National Coal Board* 1960 S.C. 376. The period of limitation runs to midnight on the same day at the end of the limitation period: *Cavers Parish Council v. Smailholm Parish Council* 1909 S.C. 195; Bell's Prin., para. 46 (note). Section 17(2) of the 1973 Act, as substituted by s.2 of the Prescription and Limitation (Scotland) Act 1984, provides that, subject to s.17(3) (legal disability) and s. 19A, no action shall be brought unless it is commenced within three years after (a) the date on which the injuries were sustained (or where the act/omission to which the injuries were attributable was a continuing one, that date or the date on which the act/omission ceased whichever the later), or (b) the date (if later than the date in (a)) on which the pursuer became, or on which in the opinion of the court it would have been reasonably practicable for him in all the circumstances to become, aware of the facts set out in (b)(i), (ii) and (iii). All losses, past and prospective, must be brought in the one action: *Stevenson v. Pontifex* , (1887) 15 R. 125. The date on which the injuries were sustained in s.17(2)(a) means the date on which there were sustained the injuries which gave a right of action (by reason of the concurrence of *inujuria* and *damnum*). This means that there are not two dates or different dates for different injuries. See *Aitchison v. Glasgow City Council* , 2010 S.C. 411 (Five judges). This is important where a claim arises for physical abuse many years ago followed by psychological damage which is sought to be claimed later.

The limitation periods for actions of personal injuries or death in the 1973 Act are subject to the discretion of the court under s.19A of the Prescription and Limitation (Scotland) Act 1973 (inserted by s.23 of the Law Reform (Miscellaneous Provisions) (Scotland) Act 1980 and amended by the Prescription and Limitation (Scotland) Act 1984, Sched. 1, para. 8), where it is equitable to do so, to allow the pursuer to bring the action outwith the limitation period. On the underlying policy of s.19A of the 1973 Act, which was to avoid the *real* possibility of significant prejudice to the defender but the burden rests on the pursuer to prove that special circumstances exist for the discretion to be exercised in favour of the pursuer, see *AS v. Poor Sisters of Nazareth* , 2008 S.C. (H.L.) 146, 155 at paras. [23] and [25] per Lord Hope of Craighead. The court has an unfettered discretion to be exercised on all the relevant circumstances: *Donald v. Rutherford* 1984 S.L.T. 70; *Forsyth v. A. F. Stoddard & Co. Ltd* 1985 S.L.T. 51. On relevant factors, see *Carson v. Howard Doris Ltd* 1981 S.C. 278; *Donald*, above; *Forsyth*, above; *Anderson v. City of Glasgow D.C.* 1987 S.L.T. 279; and see summary in *McLaren v. Harland and Wolff Ltd* 1991 S.L.T. 85, 87 per Lord Milligan. It is relevant that the pursuer has a right of action against his legal advisors for their negligence in failing to raise the action timeously: *Donald, Forsyth*, above. An action of reparation for failing to raise an action of reparation for personal injuries is not an action of reparation for personal injuries: *McGahie v. Union of Shop Distributive & Allied Workers* 1966 S.L.T. 74. A preliminary proof may be required to determine the question of time-bar or the discretion to override it: *Donald*, above.

A plea-in-law by a defender in adjustments that an order for specific implement should be granted requiring the pursuer to perform contractual obligations was a decisive step with the intention of obtaining a judicial ruling, and it interrupted the running of the prescriptive period: *Ecclesiastical Insurance Office PLC v. Whitehouse-Grant-Christ*, 2016 S.L.T. 990 (Extra Div.).

Where there is a statutory time-limit for the raising of an action, this may raise an issue of jurisdictional competency rather than an extinctive prescription or limitation. For example, the time-limit for raising an action for financial claims arising out of cohabitation under s.28 or 29 of the Family Law (Scotland) Act 2006 is mandatory and not an issue of prescription or limitation: *Simpson v. Downie*, 2013 S.L.T. 178, 2012 Fam. L.R. 121, para. [13] (Extra Div.).

Section 18(2) of the Prescription and Limitation (Scotland) Act 1973 does not apply to suspend or interrupt a time period already in train and s. 18(3) does not apply to other stand-alone provisions in other enactments: *Warner v Scapa Flow Charters*, 2016 SLT 918 (OH) (action governed by art. 16 of the Athens Convention on Carriage of Passengers and their Luggage by Sea 1974).

(A)(11)   *Personal bar.* "The pursuer being personally barred from (*state reason*), the action should be dismissed [*or where the plea relates only to some of the averments in a specified article of condescendence*, the averments in article (*specify*) of condescendence should not be remitted to probation]." This includes acquiescence, holding out, personal bar by representation or notice, and waiver. On acquiescence, see definition in *Cairncross v. Lorimer* (1860) 3 Macq. 827, 829 per Lord Campbell L.C. On personal bar by representation, see definition in *Gatty v. Maclaine* 1921 S.C.(H.L.) 1, 7 per Lord Birkenhead L.C. On waiver, see e.g. *Armia Ltd v. Daejan Developments Ltd* 1979 S.C.(H.L.) 56. On waiver of arbitration, see *Presslie v Cochran McGregor Group Ltd*, 1996 S.C. 289 (Second Div); *La Pantofolo D'Ora SpA v Blane Leisure Ltd*, 2000 S.L.T. 105 (OH); and *UBC Group Ltd v Atholl Developments (Slackbuie) Ltd*, 2011 S.L.T. 805 (OH). This plea is usually so tied up with the merits that a proof before answer is allowed and is not disposed of at procedure roll or a preliminary proof.

(A)(12)   *Mora.* This plea is usually regarded as a peremptory plea: see (B)(3) below. Where the plea is directed to seeking proof instead of jury trial is a preliminary plea: *Hunter v. John Brown & Co.* 1961 S.C. 231. On waiver of arbitration, see *Presslie v. Cochran McGregor Group Ltd* , 1996 S.C. 289 (Second Div); *La Pantofola D'Oro SpA* , 2000 S.L.T. 105 (OH); and *UBC Group Ltd v. Atholl Developments (Slackbuie) Ltd* , 2011 S.L.T. 805 (OH).

(B)   Pleas to the merits (peremptory pleas).

These pleas are dependent on the facts and circumstances of each case. They should not simply be a negative form of the pursuer's pleas. Such a plea where successful results in absolvitor for the defender if it affects the whole cause: *Forrest v. Dunlop* (1875) 3 R. 15; cf. *Matuszczyk v. National Coal Board* 1955 S.C. 418. Such pleas include:

(B)(1)   *General pleas.* Where the facts are in dispute—e.g. "The pursuer's averments, so far as material, being unfounded in fact, the defender should be assoilzied."; "In any event the sum sued for being excessive, decree should not be pronounced as concluded for."

(B)(2)   *Compensation or set-off.* "The defender, being entitled to retain (*specify*) due to the pursuer and to set that sum off against sums due by the defender, should be assoilzied [*or* the pursuer is not entitled to decree as concluded for]." Under the Compensation Act 1592 compensation may be pleaded where one debt is to be set off against another debt of the same nature (see *Mycroft, Petr.* 1983 S.L.T. 342), the debts must be due at the same time (*Paul & Thain v. Royal Bank of Scotland* (1869) 7 M. 361; but not where one party is insolvent when there may be a balancing of accounts), both debts must be liquid (*Hamilton v. Wright* (1839) 2 D. 86; *Scottish North Eastern Railway Co. v. Napier* (1859) 21 D. 700 (a claim for damages is illiquid)) and there must be *concursus debiti et crediti* (Bell's *Comm.*, ii, 124; *Stuart v. Stuart* (1869) 7 M. 366; *Matthews v. Auld & Guild* (1874) 1 R. 1224 (not where debt due by third party to disclosed principal and debt due by agent to third party); cf. *Macgregor's Tr. v. Cox* (1883) 10 R. 1028, *National Bank of Scotland v. Dickie's Tr.* (1895) 22 R. 740). The plea must be pled before decree: 1592 Act. As a general rule the plea is excluded after decree (when separate proceedings must be raised: *Cuninghame v. Wilson*, Jan. 17, 1809, FC); but the general rule does not apply to a decree for expenses (*Fowler v. Brown* 1916 S.C. 597). On set-off in balancing accounts in bankruptcy, see McBryde on *Contract*, paras 22-75 to 22-88. On compensation and set-off in relation to the Crown, see Crown Proceedings Act 1947, s.35 as applied by s.50; and see note 25.1.7.

(B)(3)   *Mora:* "The pursuer being barred by mora, taciturnity and acquiescence from insisting in this action, the defender should be assoilzied." There must be supporting averments inferring prejudice or acquiescence because delay short of prescription is not a defence unless the defender is prejudiced or the pursuer has acquiesced: *Halley v. Watt* 1956 S.C. 370, 374 per L.P. Clyde. In *Hendrick v. Chief Constable, Strathclyde Police*, 2014 S.L.T. 382 (Extra Div.), it was confirmed that the plea might succeed without the party taking the plea demonstrating that he had suffered or would suffer prejudice if prejudice or acquiescence could be inferred from the facts and circumstances.The plea may be pleaded as a preliminary plea as a ground for proof instead of jury trial: *Hunter v. John Brown & Co.* 1961 S.C. 231.

(B)(4)   *Prescription.* Pleas based on the negative prescriptions are pleas to the merits, that is peremptory pleas: *Munro v. Tod* (1829) 7 S. 648. It is unclear whether it is *pars judicis* to take a plea of prescription in the absence of a plea (it is not *pars judicis* to do so in relation to limitation). It has been held that a party pleading prescription must have an interest to do so: *York-Buildings Co v Wauchope* (1781) Mor. 10706 aff'd (1782) 2 Pat. App. 595. Where there is a statutory time-limit for the raising of an action, this may raise an issue of jurisdictional competency rather than an extinctive prescription or limitation. For example, the time-limit for raising an action for financial claims arising out of cohabitation under ss.28 or 29 of the Family Law (Scotland) Act 2006 is mandatory and not an issue of prescription or limitation: *Simpson v. Downie*, 2013 S.L.T. 178, 2012 Fam. L.R. 121, para. [13] (Extra Div.).

(B)(5)   *"Res judicata."* This short form is used. A more detailed form may be used: see e.g. *Anderson v. Wilson* 1978 S.C. 147, 148. The plea is that the substantial merits of the cause have already been decided by a court of competent jurisdiction in an action about the same subject-matter on the same grounds between the same parties or parties having the same interest: *Esso Petroleum Co. Ltd v. Law* 1956 S.C. 33, 38 per Lord Carmont. There must have been a proper judicial determination of the merits—i.e. a decree *in foro*: see e.g. *Margrie Holdings Ltd v. City of Edinburgh D.C.* 1994 S.C. 1 (where case settled extrajudicially (in the Inner House) there is nothing decided). A decree in absence (*Esso Petroleum*, above; including one pronounced after an undefended consistorial proof: *Paterson v. Paterson* 1958 S.C. 141), unless it has become *in foro* under r. 19.1(7), or a decree of dismissal on the ground of irrelevancy without inquiry into the merits (*Gillespie v. Russel* (1859) 3 Macq. 757; *Menzies v. Menzies* (1893) 20 R.(H.L.) 108, 111 per Lord Watson), will not found the plea. The court looks at the essence and reality of the matter and enquires as to what was litigated and what was decided: *Grahame v. Secretary of State for Scotland*, 1951 S.C. 368, per Lord Cooper, LP. The law is summarised in *Durkin v. HSB Bank PLC*, 2017 S.L.T. 125 (Extra Div.), 127, at paras. [9]-[11].

The court must be a court of competent jurisdiction, which includes the sheriff court: *Murray v. Seath* 1939 S.L.T. 348; *Hynds*, above; as also a foreign court. The subject-matter of the actions must be identical: *Leith Dock Commissioners v. Miles* (1866) 4 M.(H.L.) 14, 19 per Lord Chelmsford; and see, e.g. *Dollar Land (Cumbernauld) Ltd v. CIN Properties Ltd* 1996 S.C. 331. The parties must be the same or have the same interest: *Ryan v. McBurnie* 1940 S.C. 173; an *actio popularis* decided against one member of the public is res judicata against all: *Potter v. Hamilton* (1870) 8 M. 1064; a decree in rem is res judicata against any other person litigating about the same matter: *Administrator of Austrian Property v. Von Lorang* 1926 S.C. 598, 620 per Lord Sands, approved 1927 S.C.(H.L.) 80, 88 per Viscount Haldane and p. 91 per Viscount Dunedin. The grounds of action in fact and law (the *media concludendi*) must be the same: see *Edinburgh & District Water Trs v. Clippens Oil Co.* (1899) 1 F. 859, 907 per L.P. Robertson; a new *medium concludendi* elides the plea (*Edinburgh & District Water Trs*, above; *Short's Tr. v. Chung (No. 2)* 1998 S.L.T. 200; aff'd, 1999 S.C. 471 (Extra Div.)) unless irrelevant (*Earl of Perth v. Lady Willoughby de Eresby's Trs* (1877) 5 R.(H.L.) 26) or met by the plea of competent and omitted. Whether there was identity of *media concludendi* depends on the pleadings and decision of the previous action and not antecedent rights or equities: *Edinburgh & District Water Trs*, above. As Lord Cooper, LP, said in *Grahame v. Secretary of State for Scotland,* 1951 S.C 368, 387, the court should not concentrate on the specific terms of the conclusions or the pleas in law, but look to "the essence and reality of the matter" and simply inquire – "What was litigated and what was decided?" A plea of *res noviter veniens ad notitiam* elides it: *Phosphate Sewage Co. v. Molleson* (1879) 6 R.(H.L.) 113, 117 per Lord Cairns L.C.; on *res noviter*, see *McCarroll v. McKinstery* 1924 S.C. 396, rev. in 1926 S.C.(H.L.) 1; *Maltman v. Tarmac Civil Engineering Ltd* 1967 S.C. 177; and see further note 39.1.1(5).

A decree of dismissal (without inquiry into the merits, fact or law, as on relevancy) means that the pursuer is entitled to bring a fresh action on the same grounds: see *Menzies*, above. It has been said that the word "dismiss" is used when it is open to a party to bring another action and "assoilzie" where it is not: *Stewart v. Greenock Harbour Trs* (1868) 6 M. 954, 958 per Lord Deas. See also *Waydale Ltd v. DHL Holdings (UK) Ltd.* 2000 S.C. 172 (Extra Div.) overruling Lord Hamilton at 1999 S.L.T. 631, 637C (who held that where dismissal on relevancy followed inquiry, another action on the same grounds could be excluded) and doubting *Johnston v. Standard Property Investment Co. Ltd* 1909 1 S.L.T 23. A decree after a compromise or settlement (*Young v. Young's Trs* 1957 S.C. 318) or a decree of consent (*Glasgow and South-Western Railway Co. v. Boyd & Forrest* 1918 S.C.(H.L.) 14, 26 per Lord Dunedin; *Hynds v. Hynds* 1966 S.C. 201, 202 per Lord Cameron) can found the plea. Scots law does not recognise the doctrine of issue estoppel known to English law: *Clink v. Speyside Distillery Co. Ltd* 1995 S.L.T. 1344.

There is a one-action rule in respect of damages for tangible property claims arising out of a single delictual act so that a claim for dmages for personal injury and a claim arising out of damage to property caused by the same wrong has to be in one action for reparation: *Smith v. Sabre Insurance Co Ltd,* 2013 S.L.T. 665 (Extra Div); *McSheehy v. MacMillan,* 1993 S.L.T. (Sh Ct) 10 (distinguishing between insured and uninsured patrimonial losses) was wrongly decided. Thus, if a person sues another for personal injuries and settles or succeeds, the obligation to make reparation is superseded or extinguished and he cannot thereafter sue a second time for injuries or damage which subsequently emerge caused by the same wrong even if he did not know about them. Hence in *Smith*, above, the subject matter of the present action was the same as the earlier action and the plea of res judicata was upheld.

SIGNING OF DEFENCES.

18.1.5   Only counsel, other person having a right of audience or a party litigant may sign defences: r. 4.2(4). Where counsel or other person having a right of audience sign defences they are regarded as the drawer of them and answerable for what they contain: r. 4.2(8). For the definition of "counsel" and "other person having a right of audience", see r. 1.3(1) and note 1.3.4.

"SUBJECT TO RULE 46.6".

18.1.6   Where the preliminary act procedure is followed in an action arising out of the collision of ships, the defender does not have to lodge defences until after the envelopes containing the preliminary acts have been opened: r. 46.6(10).

"WITHIN 7 DAYS".

18.1.7   The period of 14 days has been reduced to seven days because the defender has a minimum notice of the action of 21 days (the period of notice), giving him at least four weeks in which to prepare defences. The date of calling is not counted in calculating the period; but the seventh day is included in the period. When the last day falls on a Saturday or Sunday or a public holiday on which the Office of Court is closed, the defences may be lodged on the next available day: r. 1.3(7). For office hours and holidays, see note 3.1.2. Note the power of the court to relieve a party from failure to comply with a rule, under which power defences may be received late: r. 2.1(1). There is no provision for prorogating the time for lodging defences: see r. 4.9.

Defences may be lodged on any day, Monday to Friday, and not just on a sederunt day.

DAY ON WHICH A SUMMONS HAS OR MAY BE CALLED.

18.1.8   In session a summons may be called on a sederunt day (r. 13.13(3)(a)); the sederunt days are Tuesdays to Fridays (r. 10.2(1) and 10.3(1)). In vacation a summons may call on a calling day (r. 13.13(3)(b)), which will be one of the sederunt days in vacation of which notice has been given in the rolls at the beginning of the vacation that it is a calling day.

DOCUMENTS FOUNDED ON OR ADOPTED.

18.1.9   Any document founded on or adopted as incorporated in the defences must be lodged as a production when the defences are lodged: r. 27.1(1)(b). For lodging of productions, see r. 4.5.

On lodging defences, the defender must give written intimation, and send a copy of the defences, to every other party: r. 4.6(1). There must be a docquet on the back of the backing with the word "Intimated" as evidence of intimation required by r. 4.6. For methods of written intimation, see r. 16.9.

18.1.10

FEE.

The court fee for lodging defences is payable at this stage. For fee, see Court of Session etc. Fees Order 1997, Table of Fees, Pt I, B, item 2 or 6 (consistorial) [SI 1997/688, as amended, pp. C 1201 et seq.]. Certain persons are exempt from payment of fees: see 1997 Fees Order, art.5, substituted by SSI 2002/270. A fee exemption certificate must be lodged in process: see P.N. No.1 of 2002.

18.1.11

Where the defender is legally represented, the fee may be debited under the credit scheme introduced on 1st April 1976 by P.N. No. 4 of 1976 to the account (if one is kept or permitted) of the defender's agent by the court cashier, and an account will be rendered weekly by the court cashier's office to agents for all court fees due that week for immediate settlement. Party litigants, and agents not operating the scheme, must pay (by cash, cheque or postal order) at the time of lodging at the counter at the General Department.

Contesting jurisdiction

18.2.—(1) Where a defender seeks to contest the jurisdiction of the court, he may—

18.2

(a) lodge defences relating both to jurisdiction and the substantive issues of the action without submitting to the jurisdiction of the court; or

(b) lodge defences relating only to the question of jurisdiction in the first instance.

(2) Where a defender lodges defences under paragraph (1)(b) and is unsuccessful in contesting jurisdiction, the court shall allow the defender to amend his defences to defend on the substantive issues of the action within such period as the court thinks fit.

Deriv. RCS 1965, r. 83(e) inserted by SI 1986/1941

GENERAL NOTE.

Under Art. 18 of Scheds 1 (the 1968 Convention), 3C (Lugano Convention), r. 13(2) of Sched.4 (allocation of jurisdiction in U.K.), and r. 7(2) of Sched.8 (jurisdiction of Scottish courts), to the C.J.J.A. 1982, and Art. 24 of the Brussels I Regulation (Council Regulation (EC) No. 44/2001) a defender does not submit to the jurisdiction of the court by contesting jurisdiction alone or at the same time as defending on the merits: see *Elefanten Schuh v. Jacqmain* [1981] E.C.R. 1671; *Rohr v. Ossberger* [1981] E.C.R. 2431. But, where the defender first admits jurisdiction and subsequently seeks to take a plea of jurisdiction, he may be taken as having consented to the jurisdiction of the court: *Clarke v. Fennoscandia Ltd (No.2)* , 10th March 2000, (2000 G.W.D. 11-377) (OH).

18.2.1

This rule extends to all actions, whether governed by the C.J.J.A. 1982 or not.

Where a defender does enter appearance without contesting jurisdiction he will be held to have submitted to the jurisdiction unless another court has exclusive jurisdiction (under the C.J.J.A. 1982).

A defender contesting jurisdiction may not obtain an order for inspection under s. 1(1) of the Administration of Justice (Scotland) Act 1972 or other order relating to the substantive issues before the plea of no jurisdiction has been repelled (unless, of course, the court has been given the power to do so): *MT Group v. James Howden & Co. Ltd* 1993 S.L.T. 409.

Under s.27 of the C.J.J.A. 1982 the court has power to grant warrant for arrestment or inhibition where proceedings have been commenced, or interim interdict where proceedings are to be commenced, in another Brussels or Lugano Contracting State, a Brussels I Regulation State, or in England and Wales or Northern Ireland. Under s.28 of the 1982 Act, where proceedings have been or are likely to be brought in another Brussels or Lugano Contracting State, a Brussels I Regulation State, or in England and Wales or Northern Ireland in respect of a matter which is within the scope of Art. 1 of the the Brussels Regulation, the court may make an order under s.1 of the 1972 Act. S.24 of the 1982 Act provides that any power of a court in Scotland to grant protective measures pending the decision of any hearing applies to a case where the subject of the proceedings includes a question as to the jurisdiction of the court to entertain them. The court's power to grant the warrants or orders above-mentioned is extended by the Civil Jurisdiction and Judgments Act 1982 (Provisional and Protective Measures) (Scotland) Order 1997 [SI 1997/2780] as follows:— (a) anything mentioned in s.27 or 28 of the C.J.J.A. 1982 in relation to proceedings commenced otherwise than in a Brussels or Lugano Contracting State or proceedings whose subject-matter is not within the scope of the 1968 Brussels Convention; and (b) the granting of interim interdict under s.27(1)(c), or an order under s.1 of the 1972 Act by virtue of s.28, of the C.J.J.A. 1982 in relation to proceedings which are to be commenced otherwise than in a Brussels or Lugano Contracting State.

Answers

18.3   **18.3.**—(1)   This rule applies to answers lodged to a petition, counterclaim, minute or note.

(2)   Answers shall consist of—

(a)   numbered answers corresponding to the paragraphs of the statement of facts in the writ to which they apply; and

(b)   appropriate pleas-in-law.

(3)   Answers may be lodged at any time within the period of notice specified in the interlocutor calling for answers.

Deriv. R.C.S. 1965, r. 196(a) (r. 18.3(3)) and r. 196(b) (r. 18.3(2))

GENERAL NOTE.

18.3.1   Notes 18.1.2 to 18.1.5 are in general relevant to this rule.

A person should disclose his private address in his answers and not an accommodation address: *Stein v. Stein* 1936 S.C. 268.

A person entering the process of a petition or note who is not at issue with the petitioner or noter does not, as a matter of practice, lodge answers but a minute (unless he seeks for himself an order of the court): r. 15.1 (applications by minute) does not apply because the minute in this case is not an application to the court.

Answers may be lodged by post by a Court of Session account holder or if accompanied by a cheque for the court fee for lodging: P.N. No. 4 of 1994, paras. 1, 2 and 8.

FORM OF ANSWERS.

18.3.2   Notes 18.1.2 to 18.1.5 on defences are relevant to answers. Any interlocutor allowing the answers to be lodged must be written or typed above the instance of the answers. On the requirement for the use of metric units of measurement in pleadings, see note 14.4.14.

"PERIOD OF NOTICE".

18.3.3   This period is determined in accordance with rule 14.6 (period of notice for answers) by virtue of r. 1.3(1) (definitions of "period of notice" and "writ").

PROROGATION OF TIME.

18.3.4   The time for lodging answers may be prorogated: r. 4.9(2). The former rule (R.C.S. 1965, r. 21(a)) stated that cause must be shown for an extension of time. The requirement to show cause has been omitted from the rule as it did not accord with current practice. It does not follow, however, that the court may not require cause to be shown in a particular case, as prorogation is in the discretion of the court.

Application to lodge a document late must be made by motion to the court under r. 2.1(1) (relief for failure to comply with rules).

DOCUMENTS FOUNDED ON OR ADOPTED.

18.3.5   Any document founded on or adopted as incorporated in the answers must be lodged as a production when the defences are lodged: r. 27.1(1)(b). For lodging of productions, see r. 4.5.

INTIMATION TO OTHER PARTIES.

18.3.6   On lodging answers, the respondent or as the case may be, must give written intimation, and send a copy of the answers, to every other party: r. 4.6(1). There must be a docquet on the back of the backing with the word "Intimated" as evidence of intimation required by r. 4.6. For methods of written intimation, see r. 16.9.

FEE.

18.3.7   The court fee for lodging answers on first entering the cause is payable on lodging. For fee, see Court of Session etc. Fees Order 1997, Table of Fees, Pt. I, B, item 2 or C, item 4 [SI 1997/688, as amended, pp. C 1201 et seq.]. Certain persons are exempt from payment of fees: see 1997 Fees Order, art.5, substituted by SSI 2002/270. A fee exemption certificate must be lodged in process: see P.N. No.1 of 2002.

Where the party is legally represented, the fee may be debited under a credit scheme introduced on 1st April 1976 by P.N. No. 4 of 1976 to the account (if one is kept or permitted) of the agent by the court cashier, and an account will be rendered weekly by the court cashier's office to the agent for all court fees due that week for immediate settlement. Party litigants, and agents not operating the scheme, must pay (by cash, cheque or postal order) on each occasion a fee is due at the time of lodging at the counter at the appropriate department.

No fee is payable for answers lodged other than answers by a person, who is not an originating party, on first entering the cause.

CHAPTER 19 DECREES IN ABSENCE

Decrees in absence

19.1.[1](1) This rule applies to any action other than an action in which the court may not grant decree without evidence.

(2) Where a defender—

    (a) fails to enter appearance in accordance with rule 17.1(1), or

    (b) having entered appearance, fails to lodge defences in accordance with rule 18.1(2),

the pursuer may apply by motion for decree in absence against him.

(3) A motion enrolled under paragraph (2) shall specify—

    (a) the decree sought; and

    (b) where appropriate, whether expenses are sought—

        (i) as taxed by the Auditor; or

        (ii) as elected by the pursuer in accordance with paragraph (3A).

(3A) Where the pursuer elects to claim expenses comprising—

    (a) the inclusive charge set out in Part 1 of Table 1 in schedule 2 of the Act of Sederunt (Taxation of Judicial Expenses Rules) 2019; and

    (b) outlays not exceeding £471.50 (excluding value added tax), the court may grant decree for payment of such expenses without the necessity of taxation.

(4) Where a motion has been enrolled under paragraph (2), the court shall grant decree in absence in terms of all or any of the conclusions of the summons—

    (a) subject to such restrictions, if any, as may be set out in a minute appended to the summons and signed by the pursuer;

    (b) if satisfied that it has jurisdiction;

    (c) if satisfied that the rules of service have been complied with; and

    (d) where the summons was served on the defender furth of Scotland, if satisfied about service on the defender—

        (i) in a case to which the Civil Jurisdiction and Judgments Act 1982 applies, as required by Article 20(2) or (3) of the convention in Schedule 1 or 3C, or Article 20(2) of Schedule 4, to that Act, as the case may be;

        (ii) in a case in which service has been executed on the defender under the Hague Convention on the Service Abroad of Judicial and Extrajudicial Documents in Civil or Commercial Matters dated 15th November 1965, as required by Article 15 of that convention; or

        (iii) in a case in which service has been executed on the defender under a convention between the United Kingdom and the country in which service was executed, as required by the provisions of that convention.

(5) In an undefended action in which a defender is designed as resident or carrying on business furth of the United Kingdom and has no known solicitor in Scotland, the court shall, in the interlocutor granting decree in absence against him, supersede extract of that decree for such period beyond seven days as it thinks fit to allow for the number of days required in the ordinary course of post for the transmission of a

---

[1] As amended by S.S.I. 2019 No. 74 r. 4(2) (effective 29th April 2019).

letter from Edinburgh to the residence, registered office, other official address or place of business, as the case may be, of that defender and the transmission of an answer from there to Edinburgh.

(6) Where a copy of the summons has been served on the defender furth of the United Kingdom under rule 16.2 and decree in absence is pronounced against him as a result of his failure to enter appearance, a certified copy of the interlocutor granting decree shall be served on him forthwith by the pursuer.

(7) Where a decree in absence on which a charge may be made has been granted after personal service of a summons on the defender or after the defender has entered appearance, and—

    (a) the decree has not been recalled,

    (b) the decree has been extracted,

    (c) a charge on the decree has not been brought under review by suspension, and

    (d) 60 days have elapsed since the expiry of the charge,

that decree shall have effect as a decree *in foro contentioso*.

Deriv. R.C.S. 1965, r. 89(a)(part) amended by SI 1984/472 (r. 19.1(1) and (2)), r. 89(aa) inserted by SI 1984/472 (r. 19.1(4)), r. 89(6) and (c) substituted by S.I. 1986 No. 1941 (r. 19.1(5) and (6)), and r. 89(i) inserted by SI 1984/472 and amended by SI 1986/1941 (r. 19.1(7)).

GENERAL NOTE.

19.1.1 A decree in absence is not a decree *in foro contentioso* (which is res judicata between the parties unless a decree of dismissal: *Forrest v. Dunlop* (1875) 3 R. 15) until the conditions in rule 19.1(7) are met (see note 19.1.14). It must be distinguished from a decree by default which at common law is a decree obtained after defences have been lodged (i.e. litiscontestation has taken place) where a party has failed to comply with a statutory provision, a rule of court or an order of the court and irrespective of the merits of the action: cf. r. 20.1. A decree in absence does not imply an admission by the defender of the pursuer's claim: *Mackintosh v. Smith and Lowe* (1864) 2 M. 1261 per L.P. McNeill, (1865) 3 M.(H.L.) 6.

It is pointed out in Macfadyen et al in Court of Session Practice, p. K/5 para. 11, that a motion for recall may be allowed late where there has been a straightforward mistake in failing to enter appearance or lodge defences (cf. note 19.2.2). Because of this, a prudent agent for a pursuer will refrain from seeking decree in absence if aware that a defender intends to resist the claim and will intimate his intention to seek decree in absence. In *Wallace v. Kelthray Plant Ltd* , 2006 S.L.T. 428 (OH) Lady Paton did not grant decree in absence for £5 million in an action of reparation under the new Chap. 43 procedure (the summons, therefore, containing no detailed averments of how the first defender would be liable); intimation was ordered on the first defender.

CAUSES IN WHICH COURT CANNOT GRANT DECREE WITHOUT EVIDENCE.

19.1.2 Decree in absence may not be obtained where the court cannot grant decree in an action without evidence. These actions are: an action of proving the tenor (see r. 52.3), an action of divorce, separation, declarator of marriage, nullity of marriage, legitimacy, legitimation, illegitimacy, parentage or non-parentage (Civil Evidence (Scotland) Act 1988, s.8), an action of declarator of freedom and putting to silence, an action of reduction of divorce (*Acutt v. Acutt* 1935 S.C. 525), an action of declarator of death and dissolution of marriage (Presumption of Death (Scotland) Act 1977, s.2(1)). A declarator of sanity may also fall within this category although if the defenders in such an action do not have an interest to defend and do not oppose the action, then even if decree is granted after the leading of evidence it will have no value against them (e.g. *Mackintosh v. Smith and Lowe* (1864) 2 M 1261, 1264 per L.P. McNeill, followed in (1865) 3 M (H.L.) 6).

Where there are several defenders and only some enter appearance and lodge defences, decree in absence against the other defenders may be refused *in hoc statu* if it would be inequitable to grant it and prejudicial to other defenders: *Morrison v. Somerville* (1860) 22 D. 1082; *Symington, Son & Co. Ltd v. Larne Shipping Co. Ltd* 1921 2 S.L.T. 32.

DECREES IN ABSENCE AGAINST THE CROWN.

19.1.3 A decree in absence against the Crown is not operative without leave of the court after notice (intimation) to the Crown: Crown Proceedings Act 1947, s.35(2)(a) as applied by s.50; leave is applied for by motion (for which, see Chap. 23).

"FAILS TO ENTER APPEARANCE".

19.1.4 A defender must enter appearance within three days after the date on which the summons has called: r. 17.1(1).

"FAILS TO LODGE DEFENCES".

A defender must lodge defences, generally, within seven days after the date on which the summons has called: 18.1(2).

19.1.5

TIME TO PAY DIRECTIONS.

Although not entering appearance a defender may have applied for a time to pay direction under s.1(1) of the Debtors (Scotland) Act 1987 in an action against an individual including a conclusion for the payment of any principal sum of money not exceeding £10,000. If the pursuer does not object to the application by the defender he must state this in the motion for decree in absence. If he does object he must intimate the motion to the defender and state the grounds of objection in Form 44.3; the motion will require the attendance of counsel or other person having a right of audience whether or not the defender appears. See generally, r. 44.3.

19.1.6

"PURSUER MAY APPLY BY MOTION FOR DECREE".

A pursuer must now enrol a motion which will appear in the Motion Roll (unstarred where appearance is not required; starred where an explanation, and therefore appearance, is required). The undefended causes roll (created by A.S. 14th October 1868 following provision for undefended causes on the Motion Roll in s.22 of the C.S.A. 1868 which was repealed by the C.S.A. 1988, Sched. 2 and superseded by R.C.S. 1965, r. 89(a)) has been abolished as that part of R.C.S. 1965, r. 89(a) has not been re-enacted. An undefended cause slip is no longer required. For motions, see Chap. 23. Note what is required in a motion where the defender has applied for a time to pay direction: see note 19.1.6 and r. 44.3.

19.1.7

EXPENSES.

The practice applicable to defended causes is now applied to undefended actions whereby, when expenses are sought as taxed, two interlocutors will be pronounced, namely, one for the principal conclusion and the other a decerniture for the expenses. Where the election is made for the inclusive fee in Pt. I of Chapter III of the Table of Fees in r. 42.16, the sum elected to be charged is included in the interlocutor granting decree. The election is made by a minute of election attached to the summons; r. 15.1 (applications by minute) does not apply. A blank form of minute of election may be obtained from the Office of Court. The inclusive fee for which the pursuer may elect is the fee current at the date of signeting and not the fee current at the date of decree. Under r. 19.1(3)(b)(ii) the pursuer must indicate whether expenses are sought as taxed or whether an election is to be made to charge the inclusive fee.

Fees of and rules for solicitors, skilled witnesses, witnesses, shorthand writers etc., are not now dealt with in R.C.S. 1994, Part II (rules 42.8–42.16) of Chap. 42 having been revoked and replaced by a freestanding A.S., the A.S. (Taxation of Judicial Expenses Rules) 2019 [S.S.I. 2019 No. 75].

19.1.8

MINUTE OF RESTRICTION.

R. 19.1(4)(a) is originally derived from s.23 of the C.S.A. 1868 (repealed by A.S. (R.C.A. No. 8) (Miscellaneous) 1986 [SI 1986/1937] and re-enacted in R.C.S. 1965, r. 89(aa) by A.S. (R.C.A. No. 2) (Miscellaneous) 1984 [SI 1984/472]). Notwithstanding that the pursuer must enrol for the particular decree sought under r. 19.1(3)(a), including any restriction of the conclusions, he must also append a minute of restriction to the summons signed by the pursuer or his agent indicating the extent to which any conclusions are restricted (e.g. by taking a decree for less than the sum sued for). The purpose of this provision is so that the Extractor can see on the face of the summons to what the conclusions have been restricted. The minute is appended by writing it immediately after the conclusions of the summons or on a paper apart attached; r. 15.1 (applications by minute) does not apply.

Where a solicitor sues for his professional fees, those fees will be taxed before he can obtain a decree (see r. 42.7(1)(6)); a minute of restriction may be required for the taxed amount.

19.1.9

COURT MUST BE SATISFIED IT HAS JURISDICTION.

Under Art. 20(1) of Scheds. 1, 3C and Sched. 4, and r. 8 of Sched. 8, to the C.J.J.A. 1982 the court must be satisfied that it has jurisdiction in actions to which that Act applies where the defender does not enter appearance or it must declare at its own instance that it has no jurisdiction. As a general rule the court will be concerned in any action to confirm it has jurisdiction. Whether the court has jurisdiction is discoverable from the averments about jurisdiction (except prorogation unless agreed in advance) in the summons required by r. 13.2(4)(b). Notice also that under the C.J.J.A. 1982 where it appears to the court that a court in another country has exclusive jurisdiction, it must at its own instance decline jurisdiction: Art.19 of Scheds. 1, 3C and Sched. 4, and r. 7 of Sched. 8, to the C.J.J.A. 1982. The former requirement (in R.C.S. 1965, r. 89(ac)) to state the ground of jurisdiction in the motion for decree is no longer required as it is considered unnecessary because the ground (except prorogation unless agreed in advance) is stated in the summons.

19.1.10

COURT MUST BE SATISFIED ABOUT SERVICE.

This is established by the appropriate certificates of service, intimation and copies of any newspaper advertisements: see Chap. 16, Pt. I, on service.

Under Art. 20(2) of Scheds. 1, 3C and 4 to the C.J.J.A. 1982 the court must sist the cause so long as it has not been shown that the defender has been able to receive the summons in sufficient time to enable him to defend or that all necessary steps have been taken to effect service: "all necessary steps" means that all necessary approaches have been made to the competent authorities of the country in which the

19.1.11

defender is domiciled to reach him in sufficient time (Jenard report on 1968 Convention, p. 40). Art. 20 does not apply where the defender's whereabouts are unknown.

Under Art. 15 of the Hague Convention on Service Abroad (Cmnd. 3986 (1969)) (which may also be used in a country to which the 1968 or Lugano Convention applies: Art. 20(3) of Scheds. 1 and 3C to the C.J.J.A. 1982) the court must be satisfied that service was executed by a method prescribed by the internal law of the country concerned or delivered by a method provided for under the convention in sufficient time to enable the defender to defend. Decree may be granted, however, even if no certificate of service or delivery has been received where the summons was transmitted by a method under the convention, six months have elapsed since the date of transmission and no certificate has been received even though every reasonable effort has been made to obtain it: the UK has made the necessary declaration to bring this provision into effect. Art. 15 does not apply where the whereabouts of the defender are unknown: Art. 1(2). For the countries to which the Hague Convention applies, see note 16.2.3.

In relation to any other civil procedure convention with a foreign country, regard will require to be had to its terms, if any, about the court's satisfaction about service. Where there is no convention, the court will be satisfied by any form of service under r. 16.2; it may not enquire whether, or require a certificate that, the form of service used is permitted by the laws of the country concerned, leaving it to the pursuer to take care to use a method which will enable him to enforce the decree there.

Service under any convention must also be a form of service permitted under r. 16.2 unless otherwise provided in an enactment: r. 16.2(1).

SUPERSEDING EXTRACT.

19.1.12   The reason for superseding extract where the defender is designed as furth of the UK under r. 19.1(5) is to give the defender time after he has received notice of the decree under r. 19.1(6) to apply to recall the decree under r. 19.2(6) before the pursuer can extract the decree.

SERVICE OF DECREE ON DEFENDER FURTH OF UK.

19.1.13   The purpose of this rule stems from Art. 47(1) of Sched. 1 to the C.J.J.A. 1982 which requires a judgment to have been served on the defender before an order for enforcement can be obtained in cases to which that Schedule applies. The provision is extended to all decrees in absence against defenders furth of the UK.

DECREE IN ABSENCE AS DECREE IN FORO.

19.1.14   R. 19.1(7) is derived from s. 24 of the C.S.A. 1868 (repealed by A.S. (R.C.A. No. 8) (Miscellaneous) 1986 [S.I. 1986 No. 1937]) and re-enacted in R.C.S. 1965, r. 89(i) by A.S. (R.C.A. No. 2) (Miscellaneous) 1984 [SI 1984/472]). A decree is not res judicata between the parties unless *in foro contentioso* (i.e. one pronounced after defences have been lodged): *Forrest v. Dunlop* (1875) 3 R. 15.

A decree in absence in an action of removing under s.9 of the Land Tenure Reform (Scotland) Act 1974 is not challengeable in a question with onerous third parties in good faith when an extract has been recorded in the Register of Sasines: 1974 Act, s.9(7). A decree in absence after personal service of the defender cannot be challenged after his death: *Blair v. Common Agent in Sale of Kinloch* (1789) Mor. 12196.

DECREE IN ABSENCE WHERE CHARGE MAY BE MADE.

19.1.15   A charge may only be made on a decree for payment of money: Debtors (Scotland) Act 1987, s.100(2) (a charge on a decree *ad factum praestandum* is no longer competent).

"60 DAYS HAVE ELAPSED".

19.1.16   The last day of the period of charge is not counted in calculating the period.

"DECREE IN FORO CONTENTIOSO".

19.1.17   This is a decree pronounced in a cause after defences have been lodged. See note 19.1.4.

Recall of decrees in absence

19.2   **19.2.**—(1)   A decree in absence may not be reclaimed against.

(2)   A defender may, not later than—

(a)   7 days after the date of a decree in absence against him, or

(b)   the last day of the period for which extract of the decree has been superseded,

apply by motion for recall of the decree and to allow defences to be received.

(3)   Where a defender enrols a motion under paragraph (2), he shall—

(a)   at the same time lodge defences in process;

(b)   have paid the sum of £25 to the pursuer; and

(c)   lodge the receipt for that sum in process.

(4)   On compliance by the defender with paragraphs (2) and (3), the court shall recall the decree against him and allow the defences to be received; and the action shall proceed as if the defences had been lodged timeously.

(5)   Where a summons has been served on a defender furth of the United Kingdom under rule 16.2 and decree in absence has been pronounced against him as a result of his failure to enter appearance, the court may, on the motion of that defender, recall the decree and allow defences to be received if—

(a)   without fault on his part, he did not have knowledge of the summons in sufficient time to defend;

(b)   he has disclosed a prima facie defence to the action on the merits; and

(c)   the motion is enrolled within a reasonable time after he had knowledge of the decree or in any event before the expiry of one year from the date of the decree;

and, where that decree is recalled, the action shall proceed as if the defences had been lodged timeously.

(6)   On enrolling a motion under paragraph (5), the defender shall lodge defences in process.

(7)   The recall of a decree under this rule shall be without prejudice to the validity of anything already done or transacted, of any contract made or obligation incurred, or of any appointment made or power granted, in or by virtue of that decree.

Deriv. R.C.S. 1965, r. 89(ab) inserted by SI 1984/472 (r. 19.2(1)), r. 89(d) substituted by SI 1986/1941 (r. 19.2(5)), r. 89(e) and (f) (r. 19.2(2), (3) and (4)), and r. 89(j)) amended by SI 1986/1941 (r. 19.2(7))

GENERAL NOTE.

R. 19.2(1)-(4) is derived in part from s.23 of the C.S.A. 1868 (repealed by A.S. (R.C.A. No. 8) (Miscellaneous) 1986 [S.I. 1986 No. 1937]).

19.2.1

Recall under r. 19.2(4) on payment of the fee in r. 19.2(3)(b) to the pursuer is granted as a matter of course.

A defender furth of the UK has an additional opportunity to seek to recall the decree under r. 19.2(5). The basis for the procedure under r. 19.2(5) where a summons has been served on a defender furth of the UK is Art. 16 of the *Hague Convention on Service Abroad of Judicial and Extrajudicial Documents in Civil or Commercial Matters*, 1965 (Cmnd. 3986 (1969)) which is applied in r. 19.2(5) to any country furth of the UK whether or not one to which the convention applies. The UK made a declaration in relation to Scotland under Art.16 limiting the period within which application may be made for recall to one year and this is enshrined in r. 19.2(5)(c). Although such a defender has a year within which to seek recall, the decree may be extracted (under r. 7.1) by the pursuer in accordance with r. 19.1(5) and may become a decree *in foro* under r. 19.1(7). There is an identical provision to art. 16 in art. 19(4) of the Council Regulation (EC) No. 1348/2000 on Service in the Member States of Judicial and Extra Judicial Documents in Civil and Commercial Matters.

In *Bank of Scotland v. Kunkel-Griffin* , 2nd November 2004, unreported, it was argued that the lack of reference in r. 19.2(5) to the provision in the Hague Convention and the Service Regulation to "knowledge of the judgment in sufficient time to appeal" meant that the rule was deficient and deprived the defender of a second bite at the cherry. Lord Emslie considered, obiter, that r.19.2(2)-(4) might be regarded as a legitimate equivalent of the appeal envisaged and perhaps broader and more readily available. Of course, the argument overlooks the fact that r. 19.2 is concerned with recalling decrees in absence (granted for failing to lodge a notice of intention to defend or defences) from which there is no appeal. If one can rely on lack of knowledge of the summons one does not need to rely on lack of knowledge of the judgment. The provision for lack of knowledge of the judgment in order to appeal is not a provision for a second bite at the cherry, but a provision for a different situation with which this rule is not concerned.

Recall does not affect the validity of things done or transacted, or appointments made, in or by virtue of the decree: r. 19.2(7).

An interlocutor on a motion to recall a decree in absence out of time, being in respect of an incidental matter of procedure, requires leave under r. 38.3(5): *Robertson v. Robertson's Exr.* 1991 S.C. 21.

It may be possible to reduce a decree in absence in an action of reduction. In such an action it is not necessary to aver exceptional circumstances (*contra* a decree *in foro*), but the whole circumstances must be looked at: *Sinclair v. Brown* (1837) 15 S. 770, 772; *Robertson's Exr v. Robertson* 1995 S.C. 23; *Nunn v. Nunn* 1997 S.L.T. 182. The correct approach is consideration of the whole circumstances bearing upon the justice of the case: *Royal Bank of Scotland Plc v. Matheson,* 2013 S.C. 146, 157, para. [37] (Extra Div). See further, annotation 53.2.1.

"NOT LATER THAN".

19.2.2   The period has been reduced from 10 to seven days in which to seek recall. The date of the decree or the last day of the period of supersession of extract is not counted in calculating the period. Where the last day falls on a Saturday or Sunday or a public holiday on which the Office of Court is closed, the next available day is allowed: r. 1.3(7). For office hours and public holidays, see note 3.1.2.

In *Robertson v. Robertson's Trs*. 1991 S.L.T. 875 Lord Weir decided that the period within which a defender could seek to recall a decree in absence was peremptory and the general dispensing power in A.S. (Rules of Court, consolidation and amendment) 1965, para. 4 [SI 1965/321], now r. 2.1, did not apply to R.C.S. 1965, r. 89(f) (now R.C.S. 1994, r. 19.2(2)). The decision may be doubted as the discretionary dispensing power in r. 2.1 is apparently applicable to every rule and there is no reason in principle why it should not apply to r. 19.2(2) in a proper case bearing in mind the defender has recourse to reduction or suspension. Lord Weir went on to say that if the dispensing power applied the case was not a proper one for exercising the power. Cf. *Graham v. John Tullis & Son (Plastics) Ltd (No. 1)* 1992 S.L.T. 507, 509J per L.P. Hope (the power extends to the time within which anything required or authorised to be done shall or may be made or done). In *Thomson v. Omal Ltd* , 1994 S.L.T. 705, Lord MacLean, not following *Robertson*; above, on competency indicated that it could not be said that the dispensing power could never be exercised in relation to R.C.S. 1965, r. 89(f), but because that provision contained its own dispensing power the general dispensing power would only be exercised in very exceptional circumstances. In *Semple Cochrane plc v. Hughes* , 2001 S.L.T. 1121 (OH) Lord Carloway followed *Thomson*, above, but did not agree with Lord MacLean that the general dispensing power in r. 2.1 was qualified by the words "in exceptional circumstances" where there was an express dispensing power. Rule 2.1 was applied in *Little Cumbrae Estate Ltd v. Rolyat1 Ltd*, 2014 S.L.T. 1118 (OH), because there were ongoing negotiations and the pursuer did not intimate the motion for decree in absence to the defender.

In *Strain v. Byers* , 2005 S.C.L.R. 157, Lord McCluskey held (with hesitation on an unopposed motion) that the fact that the decree had been extracted, was no absolute bar to the application of r. 19.2 coupled with the discretionary power in r. 2.1. In *Little Cumbrae Estate Ltd v. Rolyat1 Ltd*, 2014 S.L.T. 1118 (OH), above, Lord Woolman took the view that r. 19.2 does not state that recall becomes incompetent at any particular point and the fact that diligence has been done is not decisive against recall (motion for recall competent because no irrevocable step had been taken for enforcement).

"MOTION".

19.2.3   For motions, see Chap. 23.

"PAID THE SUM OF £25".

19.2.4   This sum is a modest penalty to include the cost of the pursuer's agent writing to his client to inform him of the motion, booking the interlocutor and the like. These items would not normally be recoverable on a party and party taxation.

LODGING RECEIPT FOR PAYMENT OF £25.

19.2.5   It may not always be possible to lodge the receipt timeously: the pursuer or his agent may be remote from Edinburgh or it might not be possible to obtain a receipt if, e.g. the pursuer's agent has withdrawn from acting. In such circumstances the defender should include in his motion under r. 19.2(2) a motion under r. 2.1 to relieve him from the failure to comply with the requirement.

CHAPTER 20 DECREES BY DEFAULT

Decrees where party in default

20.1.—(1) Without prejudice to the power of the court to grant decree by default in other circumstances, where a party fails to attend before the Lord Ordinary on the calling of a cause—

    (a)   on the By Order Roll,

    (b)   on the Procedure Roll,

    (c)   for a proof, or

    (d)   for jury trial,

that party shall be in default.

(2) Where a pursuer is in default under paragraph (1)(a), (c) or (d), the court may grant decree by default against him with expenses.

(3) Where a pursuer is in default under paragraph (1)(b), the court may grant decree of dismissal with expenses.

(4) Where a defender is in default under paragraph (1), the court may grant decree by default against him with expenses.

(5) Where a third party is in default under paragraph (1), the court may grant decree by default against him with expenses or make such finding or order as it thinks fit.

Deriv. R.C.S. 1965, r. 94(d) amended by S.I. 1991 No. 2483 (r. 20.1(1)(b), (3) and (4)).

GENERAL NOTE.

There are now stipulated, in this rule, four circumstances in which decree by default may be granted; but this does not exclude the granting of such decree in other circumstances, a decree by default being one pronounced after defences have been lodged (i.e. litiscontestation has taken place) for failure to comply with a statute, rule of court or other enactment, or an order of the court: Maclaren on *Court of Session Practice*, p. 1094; Mackay's *Manual of Practice*, p. 310; and see e.g. *Mackenzie v. Scott* (1861) 23 D. 1201 and *Forrest v. Dunlop* (1879) 3 R. 15. For this reason the words "without prejudice to the power of the court to grant decree by default in other circumstances" appear in r. 20.1(1). The power of the court to grant decree of dismissal for failure to lodge rather than decree by default (properly so-called) should be noted: r. 22.1(3) (open record) and r. 22.3(3) (closed record). Rule 20.1 applies to any cause, not merely actions; it appears in that group of Chapters applying to all causes and expressly applies to "a cause". See further, note 20.1.5.

A decree by default at common law is a decree *in foro contentioso* (i.e. one pronounced after defences have been lodged): Courts Act 1672, art. 19; *Forrest*, above. Under this rule, however, where a pursuer is in default under paragraph (1)(a) decree of absolvitor (a decree by default) may be granted even where defences have not been lodged, and where a pursuer is in default under paragraph (1)(b) decree of dismissal (not a decree *in foro*) may be granted. A decree *in foro* (unless a decree of dismissal) is res judicata between the parties: *Forrest*, above; and see note 18.1.4(B)(5) on res judicata.

The court has a discretion to grant decree of default under r. 20.1 where an agent has intimated that he has withdrawn from acting and the party is in default by failing to appear: *Munro & Miller (Pakistan) Ltd v. Wyvern Structures Ltd* 1996 S.L.T. 135, affirmed 1997 S.C. 1. Given that typically a party is not obliged by any statutory provision or order of the court to appear at a motion roll hearing, failure to do so is unlikely to be found to be default at common law: see *Battenberg v. Dunfallandy House* 2010 S.C. 507, 514 per Extra Division.

A decree by default is distinguished from a decree in absence, the principal distinction being that the latter is not at first a decree *in foro*: see r. 19.1(7) and notes 19.1.1 and 19.1.14.

Decree is obtained by motion. For motions, see Chap. 23.

Where the court grants decree by default under r. 20.1, there is no need to supersede extract if the court wishes to give the party in default time to reclaim because, under r. 38.9, the fact that an extract has been issued does not of itself preclude review: see *Munro & Miller (Pakistan) Ltd*, above, where the superseding of extract was commented on adversely by the First Division.

WHERE PURSUER IN DEFAULT.

Where the pursuer is in default, the appropriate decree is one of 20 absolvitor and is res judicata between the parties; unless the default is failure to appear at procedure roll when decree of dismissal is granted (r. 20.1(3)) which is not res judicata and does not preclude the pursuer from raising a fresh action (*Stewart v. Greenock Harbour Trs* (1868) 6 M. 954).

A decree of dismissal (without inquiry into the merits, fact or law, as on relevancy) means that the pursuer is entitled to bring a fresh action on the same grounds: see *Menzies*, above. It has been said that the word "dismiss" is used when it is open to a party to bring another action and "assoilzie" where it is not: *Stewart*, above, at p. 958 per Lord Deas. See also *Waydale Ltd v. DHL Holdings (UK) Ltd*, 2000 S.C.

172 (Extra Div.) overruling Lord Hamilton at 1999 S.L.T. 631, 637C (who held that where dismissal on relevancy followed inquiry, another action on the same grounds could be excluded) and doubting *Johnston v. Standard Property Investment Co. Ltd* 1909 1 S.L.T. 23.

In an undefended consistorial action where decree is refused after evidence the appropriate decree is one of dismissal (*Paterson v. Paterson* 1958 S.C. 141); and it may be that, in an undefended consistorial action where a pursuer is in default under this rule, the appropriate decree should always be dismissal and not absolvitor.

Where a pursuer fails to appear at a jury trial the defender has the option of seeking decree by default under this rule or obtaining a verdict in his favour without leading evidence under r. 37.5(b).

WHERE DEFENDER IN DEFAULT.

20.1.3   Where a defender is in default, the appropriate decree is usually as concluded for (a decree of condemnator).

DECREE BY DEFAULT WHERE AGENT WITHDRAWS.

20.1.3A   Where a party's agent has intimated that he has withdrawn from acting and that party fails to attend a proof, the court has a discretion whether to grant decree by default under r. 20.1 or to ordain that party under r. 30.2 to intimate whether he intends to proceed: *Munro & Miller (Pakistan) Ltd v. Wyvern Structures Ltd* 1996 S.L.T. 135, affirmed 1997 S.C. 1. Where an agent withdraws on the morning of the proof, an order under r. 30.2 would be more appropriate.

RECLAIMING.

20.1.4   A decree by default may be reclaimed against without leave within 21 days: r. 38.3(1). The decree may be recalled on such conditions as to expenses or otherwise as the court thinks fit: r. 38.9(2). Where the decree was granted because of a failure to lodge a step of process or other document, the document must be lodged on or before the motion is enrolled for recall: r. 38.11(1). The usual condition being payment of expenses: see *Bedfordshire Loan Co. v. Russell* 1909 2 S.L.T. 481. Where the decree has not been reclaimed within that period, an action of reduction must be brought. The remedy of reduction is not available as of right, and while the court has power to award substantial justice, it will require a strong statement of facts to support an application: *Forrest v. Dunlop* (1875) 3 R. 15. (In relation to decrees by default pronounced in the sheriff court, the court has emphasised that the remedy is not available as of right, but is only available in exceptional circumstances as a means of avoiding injustice: *Adair v. Cohille & Sons*, 1926 S.C. (H.C.) 51, 56 per Viscount Dunedin; *Kirkwood v. City of Glasgow Council*, 1988 S.L.T. 430, 431 per Lord Weir (OH); *Shaw v. Performing Right Society Ltd*, 9th July 2002, unreported (OH).) A decree by default in the Inner House may be set aside by consent (*Tough v. Smith* (1832) 10 S. 619), by appeal to the House of Lords or by an action of reduction.

PETITIONS, NOTES AND MINUTES.

20.1.5   The language of paras (2)-(5) of this rule is appropriate to actions. But a party to a petition or note may still be in default under r. 20.1(1). Confirmation of this is hardly necessary, having regard to the position of the rule and the reference to "a cause", but is to be found in *Thomson v. Rush*, 26th May 2000, (2000 G.W.D. 24-9030 (OH). In such a case an equivalent decree appropriate to the circumstances will be pronounced: i.e. a decree of refusal with expenses against a petitioner or noter in default under r. 20.1 (1)(a), (c) or (d) or a decree of dismissal with expenses where the default is under r. 20. 1(1)(b); where the respondent is in default the prayer of the petition or note will usually be granted. A decree of refusal of a petition is equivalent to a decree of absolvitor: *Luxmoore v. The Red Deer Commission* 1979 S.L.T.(Notes) 53.

In the case of a minute the decree will be the same as that for an action.

CHAPTER 21 SUMMARY DECREES

Application of this Chapter

21.1. This Chapter applies to any action other than—

  (a) a family action within the meaning of rule 49.1(1);

  (b) an action of multiplepoinding;

  (c) an action of proving the tenor; or

  (d) an action under the Presumption of Death (Scotland) Act 1977.

Deriv. RCS 1965, r. 89B(1) inserted by S.I. 1984 No. 499 and amended by S.I. 1990 No. 705

GENERAL NOTE.

Certain actions are excluded from those in which summary decree may be obtained. These are: (1) Those actions for which summary decree is not appropriate (certain family actions and actions of multiplepoinding: r. 21.1(a), (b) and (c)). (2) Actions in which decree cannot be granted without evidence: actions of divorce, separation or declarator of marriage, nullity of marriage, legitimacy, legitimation, illegitimacy, parentage or non-parentage (Civil Evidence (Scotland) Act 1988, s.8; and r. 21.1(a) (which is wider than the Act because of (1) above)), an action of proving the tenor (r. 52.3) and an action under the Presumption of Death (Scotland) Act 1977 (1977 Act, s.2(1)). Although an action of damages for personal injuries or the death of a person is not excluded, it will be uncommon for summary decree to be obtained in such an action: see e.g. *McManus v. Speirs Dick and Smith Ltd* 1989 S.L.T. 806; *Ross v. British Coal Corporation* 1990 S.L.T. 854; cf. *Campbell v. Golding* 1992 S.L.T. 889 (decree granted where defender, convicted of offence relating to accident, failed to aver that the accident had occurred without fault on his part); *Frew v. Field Packaging Scotland Ltd* 1994 S.L.T. 1193; *Struthers v. British Alcan Rolled Products Ltd* 1995 S.L.T. 142.

"ACTION".

Summary decree is only obtainable in an action. An action is a cause initiated by summons: C.S.A. 1988, s.51.

Applications for summary decree

21.2.—(1) Subject to paragraphs (2) to (5) of this rule, a pursuer may, at any time after a defender has lodged defences while the action is depending before the court, apply by motion for summary decree against that defender on the ground that there is no defence to the action, or a part of it, disclosed in the defences.

  (2) In applying for summary decree, the pursuer may move the court—

  (a) to grant decree in terms of all or any of the conclusions of the summons;

  (b) to pronounce an interlocutor sustaining or repelling a plea-in-law; otic) to dispose of the whole or a part of the subject-matter of the action.

  (3) The pursuer shall—

  (a) intimate a motion under paragraph (1) by registered post or the first class recorded delivery service to every other party not less than 14 days before the motion is enrolled; and

  (b) on enrolling the motion, lodge in process—

    (i) a copy of each letter of intimation; and

    (ii)[1] a certificate of intimation by post in Form 16.4 in respect of each letter of intimation.

  (4) On a motion under paragraph (1), the court may—

  (a) if satisfied that there is no defence to the action disclosed or to any part of it to which the motion relates, grant the motion for summary decree in whole or in part, as the case may be; or

  (b) ordain any party, or a partner, director, officer or office-bearer of, any party—

    (i) to produce any relevant document or article;

    (ii) to lodge an affidavit in support of any assertion of fact made in the pleadings or at the bar.

---

[1] R. 21.3(b)(ii) substituted by S.S.I. 2008 No. 349 (effective 1st December 2008).

(5) Notwithstanding the refusal of all or a part of a motion for summary decree, a subsequent motion may be made where there has been a change of circumstances.

Deriv. RCS 1965, r. 89B(2) to (6) inserted by S.I. 1984 No. 499 (r. 21.2(1) to (5))

GENERAL NOTE.

21.2.1   Summary decree was first suggested by the principal annotator (N. Morrison Q.C.) to the Rules Council in 1979 as a means of preventing defenders delaying meeting unanswerable claims. These rules were introduced by A.S. (R.C.A. No. 3) (Summary Decree and Other Amendments) 1984 [S.I. 1984 No. 499] after consultation with the Faculty of Advocates, the Law Society and the Joint Committee of Legal Societies of Midlothian; considerable use was made of draft rules prepared by a committee of the Faculty of Advocates. Formerly it was difficult to prevent a defender with no obvious defence delaying decree against him by putting the pursuer to his proof: the record could be closed early on the Adjustment Roll; or the pursuer could seek decree *de plano* at procedure roll where skeletal defences were irrelevant (*Ellon Castle Estates Ltd v. Macdonald* 1975 S.L.T. (Notes) 66; *Foxley v. Dunn* 1978 S.L.T. (Notes) 35), but these means were inadequate. The background and application of summary decree is summarised by Lord Rodger of *Earlsferry in Henderson v. 3052775 Nova Scotia Ltd* , 2006 S.C. (H.L.) 85: See note 21.2.6 below.

In *McAlinden v. Bearsden and Milngavie D.C.* , 26th March 1985, unreported, Lord McDonald said that the procedure for summary decree is intended to deal with the situation where there is no valid stateable defence but procedural technicalities are used to delay settlement of the claim; but that it is not intended to provide opportunity on the Motion Roll for legal debate appropriate to the Procedure Roll. See also *Frimokar (UK) Ltd v. Mobile Technical Plant (International) Ltd* 1990 S.L.T. 180, 181L per Lord Caplan; *Brunswick Bowling and Billiards Corporation v. Bedrock Bowl Ltd* 1991 S.L.T. 187, 189F per Lord Allanbridge.

The distinction between the tests for summary decree and in a procedure roll debate was explained by Lord Johnston in *First Fidelity Bank, N.A. v. Hudson* , 1995 G.W.D. 28-1499, unreported. In the latter, the court is required to focus on relevancy; in the former, although relevancy arguments are permissible, the court is only required to be satisfied that there is an issue to try at all.

Summary decree does not apply to attempting to enforce an out of court settlement which is not a decree following a joint minute: *Gallacher v. Morrison & MacDonald (Paisley) Ltd.* , May 30, 2003, 2003 G.W.D. 23-670 (OH), *aff'd* on appeal, at 33-924 unreported.

Chap. 21 is permissive rather than mandatory and where issues of fact are to be investigated at proof the court should be slow to deny probation to some other aspects of fact and breach of duty in relation to the same conduct: *Frew v. Field Packaging Scotland Ltd* 1994 S.L.T. 1193 (summary decree in fact granted in relation to the statutory case).

"SUMMARY DECREE".

21.2.2   This means any of the interlocutors sought in r. 21.2(2): cf. observation in *Brunswick Bowling and Billiards Corporation v. Bedrock Bowl Ltd* 1991 S.L.T. 187 at 189F per Lord Allanbridge, although he may have overlooked the terms of R.C.S. 1965, r. 89B(3).

"AT ANY TIME AFTER A DEFENDER HAS LODGED DEFENCES".

21.2.3   Where the defender does not enter appearance or fails to lodge defences, the pursuer can obtain decree in absence: r. 19.1. Although summary decree is usually sought soon after defences have been lodged, it may be sought at any time up to final decree (see note 21.2.5). In, e.g. *Struthers v. British Alcan Rolled Products Ltd* 1995 S.L.T. 142, summary decree was sought and granted after proof before answer was allowed.

"APPLY BY MOTION".

21.2.4   For motions, see Chap. 23.

"DEPENDING".

21.2.5   A cause is depending from the time it is commenced (i.e. from the time an action is served) until final decree, whereas a cause is in dependence until final extract. For the meaning of commenced in an action, see note 13.4.4. For the meaning of final decree, see note 4.15.2(2). For the meaning of final extract, see note 7.1.2(2).

NO DEFENCE DISCLOSED.

21.2.6   The approach to be adopted is summarised by Lord Rodger of Earlsferry in *Henderson v. 3052775 Nova Scotia Ltd* , 2006 S.C. (H.L.) 85, 90, para. [19]: The judge is entitled to proceed not merely on what is said in the defences, but on the basis of any facts which can be clarified, from documents, articles and affidavits, without trespassing on the role of the proof judge in resolving factual disputes after hearing the evidence; the judge can grant summary decree if he is satisfied, first, that there is no issue raised by the defender which can be properly resolved only at proof and, secondly, that, on the facts which have been clarified in this way, the defender has no defence to all, or any part, of the action; in other words, before he grants summary decree, the judge has to be satisfied that, even if the defender succeeds in proving the substance of his defence as it has been clarified, his case must fail; so, if the judge can say no more than that the defender is unlikely to succeed at proof, summary decree will not be appropriate: it is only appropriate where the judge can properly be satisfied on the available material that the defender is bound to fail and so there is nothing of relevance to be decided in a proof.

The court is entitled to look beyond the defences to see if there is a defence. It is proper to take account of a minute of amendment: *Robinson v. Thomson* 1987 S.L.T. 120 per Lord Cullen, obiter. The court is concerned not only to test the relevancy of the defence but to see if there is a genuine defence, and the defender must be able to satisfy the court at the time of the motion that a proper defence was likely to be available: *Frimokar (UK) Ltd v. Mobile Technical Plant (International) Ltd* 1990 S.L.T. 180, 181L per Lord Caplan.

The court must be satisfied there is no defence disclosed. It has been held in the Outer House that "satisfied" means the same as in a motion for interim payment of damages under r. 43.9(3)—i.e. more than probability but less than complete certainty is required to succeed: *Watson-Towers Ltd v. McPhail* 1986 S.L.T. 617; *Robinson v. Thomson* , 6th May 1986, unreported on this point. But in *Keppie v. The Marshall Food Group Ltd* 1997 S.L.T. 305, Lord Hamilton doubted that the test was the same as for interim damages. He did so on the ground that on a motion for summary decree the court was concerned with whether a defence was disclosed and not with forecasting the outcome of a proof; the consequence of a successful motion was to exclude the relation issue from inquiry. In *P. & M. Sinclair v. The Bamber Gray Partnership* 1987 S.C. 203, 206, Lord Prosser referred to the "near certainty" required to justify summary decree. That case was applied in *Wyman-Gordon Ltd v. Proclad International Ltd* , 2006 S.L.T. 390 (OH). Summary decree is not limited to those cases where there is no defence stated at all or the stated defence is plainly irrelevant; the court is not barred from pronouncing decree simply because the defender makes unspecific assertions which, if established, would provide a defence where the defender does not offer to prove it: *Rankin v. Reid* 1987 S.L.T. 352. In *Pope v. James McHugh Contracts Ltd* , 2006 S.L.T. 386 (OH), summary decree was granted, with hesitation, where there was no defence on the merits but contributory negligence, apportionment and quantum was raised, with proof restricted to those issues.

Where there is more than one defence to the action, summary decree cannot be obtained against a defence to part of the action if there remains a defence to the whole of the action: *Brunswick Bowling and Billiards Corporation v. Bedrock Bowl Ltd* 1991 S.L.T. 187.

Summary decree is not a substitute for full procedure roll discussion: *P. & M. Sinclair*, above, per Lord Prosser at p. 207. But questions of law or fact may be dealt with in a motion for summary decree; and the court should not refuse, however, to deal with the matter on the Motion Roll merely because it involves a question of law: see e.g. *Royal Bank of Scotland plc v. Dinwoodie* 1987 S.L.T. 82. In relation to a question of law, the test is whether it admits of a clear and obvious answer in favour of the pursuer: *Mackays Stores Ltd v. City Wall (Holdings) Ltd* 1989 S.L.T. 835, 836E per Lord McCluskey.

If the defences raise questions of fact it may be difficult to be satisfied that there is no defence: *Patterson & O'Grady v. Alu-Lite Windows Ltd* , 10th September 1985, unreported. A defender may not be entitled, however, to put a pursuer to proof on a question of fact where it is apparent it is part of a tactic to delay progress of the action: *Spink & Son Ltd v. McColl* 1992 S.L.T. 470, 473D per Temp. Judge Horsburgh, Q.C.

It is permissible for the court to have regard to documents or other material not referred to in the pleadings, not agreed, or not ordered to be produced under r. 21.2(4)(b): *Spink & Son Ltd*, above. Hence, summary decree procedure is more far reaching than a procedure roll hearing where relevancy is tested only by reference to pleadings and incorporated documents: *Spink & Son Ltd*, above, per Temp. Judge Horsburgh, Q.C. at p. 472K.

In *Henderson v. 3052775 Nova Scotia Ltd* , 2006 S.L.T. 489, 492 (HL), para. [19] it was held by the House of Lords that a judge considering summary decree is entitled to proceed, not merely on what is said in the defences, but on the basis of any facts which can be clarified from documents, articles and affidavits, without trespassing on the role of the proof judge; and he can grant summary decree if satisfied that (1) there is no issue raised by the defence which can be properly resolved only at proof and (2) on the facts which have been clarified, the defender has no defence at all to all, or part, of the action: in other words, before he grants summary decree he has to be satisfied that, even if the defender succeeds in proving the substance of his defence as clarified, his case *must* fail.

"DOCUMENT OR ARTICLE".

By virtue of r. 1.3(1) "document" has an extended meaning as defined in s.9 of the Civil Evidence (Scotland) Act 1988. The word "article" should cover any other material.

21.2.7

ORDER TO PRODUCE A DOCUMENT OR LODGE AN AFFIDAVIT.

A document can be ordered to be produced only if it is known to be in existence and can be identified by the party seeking summary decree: *M. & I. Instruments v. Varsada* , 9th May 1985, unreported.

21.2.8

Affidavits enable the court to go behind the bald assertions in the pleadings to see whether there is anything to support the pleadings: *Rankin v. Reid* 1987 S.L.T. 352, 354C per Lord McCluskey. R.21.2(4)(b)(ii) clearly envisages that the court may proceed on the basis of affidavit evidence even in the face of a denial: *Ingram Coal Co. v. Nugent* 1991 S.L.T. 603.

"SUBSEQUENT MOTION ON A CHANGE OF CIRCUMSTANCES".

There may be more than one subsequent motion. A change of circumstances must involve an alteration in the pleadings or the coming to light of a document (or information) not previously available to the pursuer. On analogy with variation of periodical allowance in a divorce action, there is no "change of circumstances" where the original decision was based on a failure to put all the information then avail-

21.2.9

able to the court: *Stewart v. Stewart* 1987 S.L.T. 246.

21.2.10

An interlocutor pronounced under this rule may be reclaimed against with leave of the Lord Ordinary or vacation judge within 14 days after the date of the interlocutor on such conditions, if any, as he thinks fit: r. 38.4(1).

Leave to reclaim must be sought whether the summary decree is a final or interlocutory decision. The suggestion by Lord Coulsfield in *Maus Freres S.A. v. Hoon* , 24th November 1995, 1996 G.W.D. 10.594, that leave to reclaim is not required where the summary decree is a final interlocutor, would defeat the purpose of the rule intended by the rule's clear and unambiguous terms. Paragraph (2) of r. 38.3 which provides for reclaiming a final interlocutor without leave, is, by virtue of para.(1) of that rule, subject to r. 38.4(1) (leave to reclaim summary decree). It is submitted that Lord Coulsfield's opinion is wrong on this point. It is understood that subsequently the Inner House directed that leave was required.

Application of summary decree to counterclaims etc.

21.3

21.3.—(1) Where a defender has lodged a counterclaim—

    (a)   he may apply by motion for summary decree against the pursuer on that counterclaim on the ground that there is no defence to the counterclaim, or a part of it, disclosed in the answers to it; and

    (b)   paragraphs (2) to (5) of rule 21.2 shall, with the necessary modifications, apply to a motion by a defender under this paragraph as they apply to a motion by a pursuer under paragraph (1) of that rule.

(2) Where a defender or third party has made a claim against another defender or third party who has lodged defences or answers, as the case may be—

    (a)   he may apply by motion for summary decree against that other defender or third party on the ground that there is no defence to his claim, or a part of it, disclosed in the defences or answers, as the case may be; and

    (b)   paragraphs (2) to (5) of rule 21.2 shall, with the necessary modifications, apply to a motion by a defender or third party under this paragraph as they apply to a motion by a pursuer under paragraph (1) of that rule.

Deriv. R.C.S. 1965, r. 89B(7) (r. 21.3(1)) inserted by SI 1984/499

21.3.1

The application of the procedure for summary decree has been extended to third party pleadings as well as to counterclaims.

CHAPTER 21A DISMISSAL OF A CLAIM DUE TO DELAY

Dismissal of a Claim Due to Delay

Dismissal of a claim due to delay

21A.1.—[1](1) Any party to a claim may, while that claim is depending before the court, apply by minute for the court to dismiss the claim due to inordinate and inexcusable delay by another party or another party's agent in progressing the claim, resulting in unfairness.

(2) A minute under paragraph (1) shall—

   (a) include a statement of the grounds on which dismissal of the claim is sought; and

   (b) be lodged in the process of the action to which it relates.

(3) On lodging a minute under paragraph (2)(b), the party seeking dismissal of the claim shall enrol a motion for—

   (a) intimation of the minute on any other parties to the claim; and

   (b) an order for answers to the minute to be lodged in process within the period of 21 days from the date of intimation.

(4) On the expiry of the period referred to in paragraph (3)(b), the party seeking dismissal of the claim shall enrol a motion for further procedure.

(5) In determining an application made under this rule, the court may dismiss the claim if it appears to the court that—

   (a) there has been an inordinate and inexcusable delay on the part of any party or any party's agent in progressing the claim; and

   (b) such delay results in unfairness specific to the factual circumstances, including the procedural circumstances, of that claim.

(6) In determining whether or not to dismiss a claim under paragraph (5), the court shall take account of the procedural consequences, both for the parties and for the work of the court, of allowing the claim to proceed.

21A.1

GENERAL NOTE.

There was divergence of opinion in the Outer House, about whether the court has an inherent power to dismiss an action for want of insistence or prosecution where there has been excessive delay by a pursuer in proceeding with the action. There is no express power, as there is for summary decree sought by a pursuer against a defender who has no defence (although the principal annotator considered proposing it when summary decree was introduced). In *McKie v. MacRae* , 2006 S.L.T. (OH), Lord Glennie held that the court has an inherent power to bring a case to an end where delay has caused prejudice to a defender, or put in jeopardy the possibility of a fair trial. He disagreed with Lady Smith in *Tonner v. Reiach & Hall*, 2005 S.L.T. 936, who held that there was no such power. The Extra Div., 2008 S.C. 1, overturned Lady Smith, holding at paras. [62] and [123] that the court did have an inherent power to put an end to a pending action, though as a power of last resort. The power will be used only where the following conditions are met (paras. [130]–[138]): (1) there is inordinate and inexcusable delay; and (2) there is an element of unfairness specific to the particular factual including procedural context. In considering the procedural context, account should be taken of the procedural consequences of allowing the action to proceed for the parties and the work of the court. This last point is almost expressed as a third condition or criterion, but it cannot be because it is hardly possible to assess as such. Furthermore, it is difficult to see why the work of the court should be a consideration in striking out an action. While absolvitor is appropriate where personal bar by mora, taciturnity and acquiescence is successfully pled, the appropriate decree is dismissal as the action cannot be disposed of on the merits. The court considered that the appropriate procedure for seeking to have an action brought to an end was by minute and answers, seemingly oblivious to the fact that that procedure can be used in such a way as to cause even more delay. In *Hepburn v. Royal Alexandra NHS Trust* , 2011 S.C. 20 (First Div.), a case before Chap. 21A came into force, *Tonner*, above, was followed by a majority.

The case of *McKie*, above, must have inspired the decision to insert Chap. 21 by A.S. (R.C.S.A. No.5) (Miscellaneous) 2008 [S.S.I. 2008 No. 349]. In *Hepburn*, above, the vires of Chap. 21 was raised but not decided.

In *Abram v British International Helicopters Ltd* 2014 S.C.L.R. 95, paras. [24], [25] and [28], the

21A.1.1

---

[1] Chap. 21A and r. 21 A.1 inserted by S.S.I. 2008 No. 349 (effective 1st December 2008) and number and heading as amended by S.S.I. 2009 No. 450 (effective 25th January 2010).

Second Division gave guidance about the application of Chap. 21A. First of all the court has to determine if the criteria in r. 21A.1(5) of delay and unfairness have been made out. Secondly, if so, then the court goes on to consider the discretionary exercise of whether to dismiss the claim. The overarching principle is whether it is in the interests of justice that an action should be dismissed or allowed to proceed. The starting point for that is a recognition that the power is a draconian one of last resort (*Tonner v Reiach and Hall* 2008 S.C. 1 (Extra Div)). The power to dismiss should only be exercised if the judge is satisfied that there is "at least" a substantial risk that justice cannot be done or, put another way, that a fair trial cannot occur, if the proceedings are allowed to continue.

"CLAIM".

21A.1.2   The term "claim" is not defined. It presumably means more that summons or petition, and would include a claim made in any way, e.g., in a counterclaim, minute or note.

"MINUTE".

21A.1.3   Rule 15.1 does not apply: r. 15.1(6)(e).

"INTIMATION".

21A.1.4   For methods, see r.16.8.

CHAPTER 22 MAKING UP AND CLOSING RECORDS

Making up open record

22.1.—[1,2](1) Subject to any other provision in these rules—

    (a) where defences have been lodged, the pursuer in an action shall, within 14 days after the date on which the time for lodging defences expired or on which the defences were lodged (whichever date was the earlier); or

    (b) where in a cause a party is ordered by the court to make up an open record he shall within such period as is specified by the court,

lodge two copies of the open record in process; and on being given, in accordance with rule 22.2(1), a date for the commencement of the adjustment period and a date on which it shall close, he shall forthwith send a copy of the open record (endorsed in pursuance of that rule) to every other party.

(2) Where the pursuer, petitioner, noter or minuter, as the case may be, fails to comply with the requirements of paragraph (1), the defender or other party may apply by motion for decree of dismissal.

(3) An open record shall consist of the pleadings of the parties and the interlocutors pronounced in the cause.

Deriv. R.C.S. 1965, r. 90(1) (r. 22.1(1)), and r. 90(2) (r. 22.1(3)), both amended by S.I. 1980 No. 1144

GENERAL NOTE.

The only difference in substance between the new rule (substituted by A.S. (R.C.S.A.) (Miscellaneous) 1998 [SI 1998/890]) and the former rule is the requirement on the pursuer (or other party ordered to make up an open record) to send the copies of the record to the other parties, not within the time for lodging the two court copies in process, but "forthwith" after being given the date for the commencement of the adjustment period by the clerk of session under r. 22.2(1).

"OPEN RECORD"

The open record is an important part of the system of pleading: it is on this document that adjustments are made. In the open record in an action, the summons is set out in full, but, after each article of condescendence there is set out the relative answer in the defences of each defender in turn; after the pursuer's pleas there are set out the pleas of the defender(s). At the end there are set out the interlocutors pronounced before the open record was made up. On the front sheet of the record, below the cause reference number and the names of the parties, there are set out the names of the parties' solicitors (including any correspondents); and between that and a repetition of the instance a space is left for any interlocutor ordering the open record (there will be none for an open record made up under this rule).

The date of signeting of the summons should be included at the end of the Address in the summons in the open record print: this is all too often omitted.

An open record may be ordered under r. 14.8 in an opposed petition (or note); it may also be ordered (though rarely) in a minute and answers: the principles about form and practice of open records in actions apply in such cases. An open record may also be ordered where a closed record is opened up. The interlocutor ordering the open record in these instances will specify the period within which the open record must be sent to other parties and lodged in process. On the lodging of answers by a third party after a third party notice has been served an open record has to be lodged by the defender introducing the third party: r. 26.7(1)(a).

"SUBJECT TO ANY OTHER PROVISION".

The other provisions are: (a) r. 43.23 (no record in optional procedure); (b) r. 46.6(12) (open record in ship collision cases); (c) r. 47.4 (no open record in commercial action); (d) r. 49.33(1) (no record in family actions); (e) r. 51.4(3) (open record where objections to action of multiplepoinding); and (f) r. 51.7(1) (open record where defences lodged to condescendence of the fund *in medio* in action of multiplepoinding).

"WHERE DEFENCES HAVE BEEN LODGED".

An open record is only made up in an action where defences have been lodged. Where there is only one defender the record must be lodged within 14 days after the date defences were lodged or the date on which the time for lodging defences has expired. Where there is more than one defender and at least one of them has lodged defences the record must be lodged within 14 days after the date on which the time for lodging defences has expired. Where defences are allowed to be lodged late (under r. 2.1) no motion

22.1

22.1.1

22.1.1A

22.1.2

22.1.3

---

[1] Rule 22.1 substituted by S.I. 1998 No. 890 (effective 21st April 1998).
[2] Rule 22.1 amended by S.S.I. 2007 No. 7 r. 2(3) (effective 29th January 2007).

is required when lodging an open record incorporating late defences unless the record is also late. Where defences have been allowed to be lodged late and there is already an open record, a further open record incorporating the defences must be lodged by the pursuer (subject to any order of the court in relation to expenses occasioned by the late defences).

"WITHIN FOURTEEN DAYS".

22.1.4   The date from which the period is calculated is not counted. Where the last day falls on a Saturday or Sunday or a public holiday on which the Office of Court is closed, the next available day is allowed: r. 1.3(7). For office hours and public holidays, see note 3.1.2. Note the power of the court to relieve a party from failure to comply with a rule: r. 2.1.

"SEND".

22.1.5   This includes deliver: r. 1.3(1) (definition of "send").

"TWO COPIES OF THE OPEN RECORD".

22.1.6   One copy of the record is the process copy, the other is for the Keeper of the Rolls and is used to regulate the progress of the cause on the Adjustment Roll. The latter copy is passed to the Keeper at the close of business on a Friday.

It is advisable to take a third copy which can have the dates of the adjustment period stamped on it (see r. 22.2(1) and also note 22.1.11), which will be the same date as that stamped on the court copies.

PARTY ORDERED TO MAKE UP OPEN RECORD.

22.1.7   A party may be ordered to make up an open record in an opposed petition or note under r. 14.8, in a minute and answers or where the closed record is opened up. The period within which the record is to be sent and lodged under r. 22.1(2) may be prorogated: r. 4.9(2).

"MOTION".

22.1.8   For motions, see Chap. 23.

"DECREE OF DISMISSAL".

22.1.9   The penalty for failure of a pursuer to lodge or send the copies of the open record is dismissal of the action. This is not a decree by default (properly so-called). A decree of dismissal in an action is not res judicata between the parties and the pursuer may bring a fresh action: *Stewart v. Greenock Harbour Trs* (1868) 6 M. 954. The position is the same for a petitioner, noter or minuter.

Where the party who fails to lodge the open record is not the pursuer (or petitioner, noter or minuter) decree of dismissal is not the appropriate decree, the appropriate decree being decree *de plano* in an action or a decree granting the prayer of a petition or note, as the case may be.

Dismissal is not common for late lodging and recourse may be had to the dispensing power in r.2.1. If there is no satisfactory or reasonable explanation for the failure to lodge timeously, the dispensing power may not be exercised and dismissal may be granted: see, e.g. *Maund v. Julia Arredamenti SpA* , 9th October 2001 (OH), 2001 G.W.D. 38-1417.

"OR OTHER PARTY".

22.1.10   This would be the respondent in a petition or note.

"ON BEING GIVEN ... A DATE FOR THE COMMENCEMENT OF THE ADJUSTMENT PERIOD ... FORTHWITH SEND".

22.1.11   The pursuer (or other party ordered to make up an open record) must now send the four or more copies of the record to the other parties, not within the time for lodging the two court copies in process, but "forthwith" after being given the date for the commencement of the adjustment period by the clerk of session under r. 22.2(1).

The word "forthwith" was banished from the R.C.S. 1994 as originally enacted because it lacked enforceable precision. Unfortunately it appears to be making a comeback.

Adjustment

22.2   **22.2.**—[1](1) On an open record being lodged in process the Assistant Clerk of Session shall endorse it, and the interlocutor sheet, with a stamp so as to show the date of lodging, a date on which the adjustment period shall commence (which shall be a date determined by the Deputy Principal Clerk of Session, being ordinarily the first Wednesday which occurs at least three days after the date of lodging but which may be such later date as the Deputy Principal Clerk of Session considers appropriate) and a date on which that period shall end and the record shall close (which shall

---

[1] R. 22.2 substituted by S.I. 1998 No. 890 (effective 21st April 1998).

be the date eight weeks after that on which the adjustment period commences); but this paragraph is without prejudice to paragraph (3).

(2) During the adjustment period parties may adjust their respective pleadings and shall intimate any such adjustments to one another.

(3) At any time during the adjustment period the court may, on the motion of any party, pronounce an interlocutor—

(a) closing the record; or

(b) extending the period of adjustment to such date as the court thinks fit, on which date the record shall close.

(4)[1] On enrolling a motion under paragraph (3), a party shall make available for use of the court a copy of the open record (endorsed in pursuance of paragraph (1)) showing the adjustments, if any, as at the date of enrolment.

(5) An endorsement in pursuance of paragraph (1) may be corrected or altered by the Deputy Principal Clerk of Session at any time before the date for the time being shown in the endorsement as the date on which the record shall close.

(6) An endorsement which cannot be corrected or altered under paragraph (5) may, on cause shown, be corrected by the Lord Ordinary at any time.

Deriv. R.C.S. 1965, r. 90(3) (r. 22.2(2)), r. 90A(2)(a) and (3) (r. 22.2(3) and (4)) and r. 90A(3) (r. 22.2(3) and (4)), all inserted by S.I. 1980 No. 1144

GENERAL NOTE.

The Adjustment Roll has been abolished by A.S. (R.C.S.A.) (Miscellaneous) 1998 [S.I. 1998 No. 890]. That said, lists of causes at adjustment are being printed in the Rolls under the heading "Adjustment Roll"! (Thus already do we find practice and the rules parting company—one of the problems the R.C.S.1994 were designed to overcome.) The erroneously titled Continued Adjustment Roll is, as a consequence, also abolished: there never was any provision for such a roll, cases being properly continued on the Adjustment Roll.

The new provision in r. 22.2(1) is that the assistant clerk of session (no other clerk of session has authority apparently) will stamp the two court copies of the open record, and the interlocutor sheet, with the date of (a) lodging, (b) commencement of the adjustment period and (c) the end of the adjustment period. The pattern for the commencement of adjustment will be like this:—

22.2.1

Records lodged	Adjustment commenced	Notice in Rolls
Monday 16th	Wednesday 25th	Friday 27th
Tuesday 17th	Wednesday 25th	Friday 27th
Wednesday 18th	Wednesday 25th	Friday 27th
Thursday 19th	Wednesday 25th	Friday 27th
Friday 20th	Wednesday 25th	Friday 27th

This new provision does not apply where an open record has been lodged before 21st April 1998.

During the adjustment period when parties may adjust their respective pleadings as of right.

A defended action will always have a period of adjustment (when the open record is lodged) unless sought to be dispensed with. Any other defended cause will only have an adjustment period if an open record is ordered by the court to be made up.

A list of causes at adjustment is published in the rolls on the Wednesday on which the interlocutors appointing those causes to that roll are pronounced with a note of the date to which each case has been continued and the names of parties' agents: P.N. 27th March 1987.

"EIGHT WEEKS".

The eight-week period at adjustment includes any period in vacation. The inclusion of vacation days in calculating the period was introduced by A.S. (R.C.A. No. 5) (Miscellaneous) 1987 [S.I. 1987 No. 2160]. The adjustment period is, however, suspended during any time the cause is sisted. Once the sist is recalled time starts to run again including any period of adjustment before the sist. R.C.S. 1965, r. 90(7) which so provided in relation to a sist is not re-enacted, not because the provision no longer applies but because the obvious does not need to be stated.

22.2.2

---

[1] R. 22.2(4) amended by S.S.I. 1999 No. 109 (effective 29th October 1999).

22.2.3   The pleadings which may be adjusted in an action are the condescendence and pleas-in-law annexed to the summons, the answers and pleas-in-law in the defences, the statement of facts and pleas-in-law in a counterclaim and the answers and pleas-in-law to it and answers and pleas-in-law to a third party notice. In a petition, note or minute, the statement of facts and any pleas-in-law, and any answers and pleas, may be adjusted if a period of adjustment is allowed. The instance in a cause and the conclusions in a summons (or defences in a family action) may not be adjusted; these may only be amended: Maclaren on *Court of Session Practice*, p. 450. On amendment, see r. 24.1.

Adjustments are made by counsel or other person having a right of audience. The adjustments are written on, or typed on papers apart attached to, a copy of the open record. Each party prepares an intimation print incorporating the adjustments which is intimated to the other parties. Different colours should be used for adjustments made at different times and e date on which those adjustments were made should be marked on the back of the backing of the open record.

The court has no control over what averments are made by adjustment except in relation to scandalous and irrelevant averments: *C v. W* 1950 S.L.T. (Notes) 8 (an exception which may now be doubted). A party may radically alter his pleadings during the adjustment period and may include a case not previously pled and even a case which is pled outwith a statutory time-limit. Thus a new case may be added out with the triennium in s.17 of the Prescription and Limitation (Scotland) Act 1973 at adjustment: *Sellers v. IMI Yorkshire Imperial Ltd* 1986 S.L.T. 629. On the rules in relation to amendment, see note 24.1.2.

"MOTION".

22.2.4   For motions, see Chap. 23.

22.2.5   Formerly a record could not be closed before the end of four weeks of the adjustment period. There was no obvious reason for such a restriction which was removed when the RCS 1994 were enacted.

22.2.6   Under r. 22.2(3)(b) the adjustment period may be extended. The motion for continuation must be enrolled before the expiry of the previous period of adjustment.

Closing record

22.3   **22.3.—(1)**[1] The pursuer shall, within four weeks after the date on which the record is closed—

(a)[2]   send a copy of the closed record to the defender and to every other party; and

(b)   lodge three copies of the closed record in process,

and if there is failure to do so the defender or any other party may apply by motion for decree of dismissal.

(2)[3]   A closed record shall consist of the pleadings of the parties and the interlocutors pronounced in the action or cause (endorsed in pursuance of rule 22.2(1)).

(3)   *[Revoked by S.I. 1998 No. 890.]*

(4)   *[Revoked by S.I. 1998 No. 890.]*

(5)[4]   The pursuer shall, on lodging the copies of the closed record as required by paragraph (1)(b), enrol a motion craving the court—

(a)   where parties have agreed on further procedure, of consent—

(i)   to appoint the cause to the Procedure Roll for consideration of all the preliminary pleas of parties or such of the pleas as may be specified;

(ii)   to allow to parties a preliminary proof on specified matters or in respect of specified pleas;

(iii)   to allow to parties a proof before answer of their respective averments under reservation of such preliminary pleas as may be specified;

---

[1] R. 22.3(1) and (2) substituted for r. 22.3(1)–(4) by S.I. 1998 No. 890 (effective 21st April 1998).
[2] R. 22.3(1)(a) amended by S.S.I. 2007 No. 7 r. 2(4) (effective 29th January 2007).
[3] R. 22.3(1) and (2) substituted for r. 22.3(1)–(4) by S.I. 1998 No. 890 (effective 21st April 1998).
[4] R. 22.3(5) amended by S.I. 1998 No. 890 (effective 21st April 1998).

      (iv)   to allow a proof;

      (v)   to allow issues for jury trial; or

      (vi)   to make some other specified order; or

(b)   where parties have been unable to agree on further procedure, to appoint the cause to the By Order (Adjustment) Roll.

(6) In a cause which is one of more than one cause arising out of the same cause of action, the court may, on or after pronouncing an interlocutor ordering further procedure under paragraph (5)—

   (a)   on the motion of a party to that cause, and

   (b)   after hearing parties to all those causes,

appoint that cause or any other of those causes to be the leading cause and to sist the other causes pending the determination of the leading cause.

(7) In this rule, "pursuer" includes petitioner, noter or minuter, as the case may be.

Deriv. R.C.S. 1965, r. 91(1) and (2) (r. 22.3(1) and (2)), r. 91(3) (r. 22.3(5)), r. 91(5) (r. 22.3(3)), and r. 91(6) (r. 22.3(6)), all substituted by S.I. 1982 No. 1825

GENERAL NOTE.

With the abolition of the Adjustment Roll and the automatic closing of the record by virtue of new r. 22.2(1) substituted by A.S. (R.C.S.A.) (Miscellaneous) 1998 [S.I. 1998 No. 890], there is no need for an interlocutor closing the record as previously provided in r. 22.3(1). The A.S. accordingly removes that provision and paras (2) to (4) of r. 22.3 are now paras (1) to (2). **22.3.1**

The period for lodging a closed record has been reduced from five to four weeks.

On the closing of the record parties must discuss the future procedure in the cause with particular regard to the resolution of points at issue without recourse to a hearing on the Procedure Roll: P.N. No. 3 of 1991, para. 1(a). Whether this has been done may be taken into account by the court in dealing with expenses: P.N. No. 3 of 1991, para. 2.

"CLOSED RECORD"

A closed record is an important part of the pleading system. It is on the basis of the pleadings in this document that parties go to proof or debate. The summons is set out in full; but, after each article of condescendence (there is only one condescendence), there is set out the relative answer in the defences of each defender in turn (if more than one). After the pursuer's pleas-in-law, there are set out in turn the pleas of each defender in turn. At the end there are set out the interlocutors pronounced before the record was closed. On the front sheet of the record, below the cause reference number and the names of the parties, there are set out the names of the parties' solicitors (including any correspondents). Between that and a repetition of the instance, there is set out the interlocutor closing the record. **22.3.2**

The date of the signeting of the summons should be included at the end of the Address in the summons: this is all too often omitted.

[THE NEXT PARAGRAPH IS 22.3.4]

"THREE COPIES OF THE CLOSED RECORD".

One copy is the process copy, one is for the clerk of court and the third is for the Keeper of the Rolls (used by him in preparing the lists of causes for fixing diets). **22.3.4**

FAILURE TO SEND OR LODGE CLOSED RECORD.

The penalty for failure by a pursuer (or petitioner, noter or minuter) to lodge or send the copies of the closed record is dismissal of the cause. This is not a decree by default (properly so-called) as the pursuer may, in the case of dismissal, raise fresh proceedings: *Stewart v. Greenock Harbour Trs* (1868) 6 M. 954; *Forrest v. Dunlop* (1875) 3 R. 15. A party may seek to lodge a closed record late under r. 2.1: *Carroll v. Glasgow Corporation* 1965 S.L.T. 95. **22.3.5**

Where the party who fails to lodge the closed record is not the pursuer (or petitioner, noter or minuter), decree of dismissal is not the appropriate decree, the appropriate decree being decree *de plano* in an action or a decree granting the prayer of a petition or note, as the case may be.

"PROCEDURE ROLL".

The Procedure Roll is where preliminary pleas (e.g. objections to the instance, objections to jurisdiction, and pleas against the action itself such as competency, relevancy and specification of pleadings) are debated and disposed of, including whether inquiry is to be by proof or jury trial or whether there should be a preliminary proof if these matters are not agreed by the parties. Irrelevant averments should be excluded at procedure roll: *Inglis v. National Bank of Scotland Ltd* 1909 S.C. 1038. So, e.g. averments of facts collateral to the issue such as similar fact evidence: see *A v. B* (1895) 22 R. 402 (First Div.); *Inglis* above; *EG v. The Governors of the Fettes Trust* [2021] CSOH 128. **22.3.6**

A cause will be appointed to the Procedure Roll where parties are agreed to send it there or, where parties are not so agreed, may be sent there when the case is heard (because of the lack of agreement) at the By Order (Adjustment) Roll: r. 22.3(5). The interlocutor appointing a cause to the Procedure Roll should state on whose motion the cause has been so appointed and in relation to which plea(s)-in-law. A party who has not moved for the cause to be sent to procedure roll is not precluded from debating a plea of his at a hearing on that roll: *McIntosh v. Cockburn & Co. Ltd* 1953 S.C. 88.

On the closing of the record parties must discuss the future procedure in the cause with particular regard to the resolution of points at issue without recourse to a hearing on the Procedure Roll: P.N. No.3 of 1991, para. 1(a). Whether this has been done may be taken into account by the court in dealing with expenses: P.N. No.3 of 1991, para. 2.

An action of damages for personal injuries will rarely be dismissed on procedure roll on the ground of irrelevancy: *Miller v. South of Scotland Electricity Board* 1958 S.C.(H.L.) 20, 33 per Lord Keith of Avonholm. It is not normally appropriate (except on a point of law only), where the welfare of children is involved, to dispose of an application for an order relating to parental rights solely on the pleadings, some kind of inquiry into the facts being necessary: *O v. O* 1995 S.C. 569.

"PRELIMINARY PLEAS".

22.3.7   A preliminary plea is one which, if sustained, leads to the disposal of the whole or part of the cause without inquiry into the merits of that part of the cause: see further note 18.1.4(A).

"PRELIMINARY PROOF".

22.3.8   Since proof is defined as including a proof before answer (see r. 1.3(1)), a preliminary proof before answer may be allowed.

A preliminary proof is not usually allowed in respect of the merits of a cause but is confined to where an issue is raised in the pleadings which could bar the action from proceeding. Such cases fall into three categories: (a) cases in which there is a plea of no jurisdiction (see *McLeod v. Tancred, Arrol & Co.* (1890) 17 R. 514; *Dallas & Co. v. McArdle* 1949 S.C. 481), (b) cases of bar either in connection with the discharge of a claim or in connection with a statutory bar in the way of an action, and (c) cases which raise questions of title: *Burroughs Machines Ltd v. George Davie, Crawford & Partners* 1976 S.L.T.(Notes) 35 per Lord Grieve. A preliminary proof will not be allowed on an issue which is so bound up with the merits that they cannot be separated: *McCafferty v. McCabe* (1898) 25 R. 872; cf *A.B. v. C.D.* 1937 S.C. 408. A preliminary proof may be required to determine the question of time-bar or the discretion to override it under s.19A of the Prescription and Limitation (Scotland) Act 1973: *Donald v. Rutherford* 1984 S.L.T. 70.

PROOF BEFORE ANSWER AND PROOF.

22.3.9   Probation may be by (a) proof *prout de jure* (without restriction as to method: see (1) below), (b) proof by writ or oath only (e.g. in loan, payment of money exceeding £100 Scots, obligations of relief, gratuitous obligations and innominate contracts of unusual character)—abolished for causes commenced on or after 1st August 1995 by s.11 of the Requirements of Writing (Scotland) Act 1995, (c) proof *habili modo* (this means proof by the manner competent to each part of the case—see (2A) below), (d) proof before answer (see (2) below) or (e) jury trial (see note 28.1.8 and Chap. 37).

There is some flexibility in fixing proof diets to permit adequate time to prepare and to secure counsel of choice, but once a diet of proof is fixed different considerations arise; the sooner the other party and the court is put in the picture about a need for a discharge the more likely it is that a favourable view will be taken: *AppA UK Ltd v. Scottish Daily Mail* , 2008 S.C. 145 (First Div.) (discharge of proof two weeks before diet, because of difficulties entirely of pursuer's making, refused).

(1) Proof.

It is sometimes thought that the allowance of proof excludes consideration of questions of relevancy after the proof, but the matter is not free from doubt: cf. Mackay's *Practice of the Court of Session*, ii, 18 (although questions of law may be argued after proof, the party against whom facts are proved can no longer maintain no proof should have been allowed and facts disregarded) and *Duke of Hamilton's Trs v. Woodside Coal Co.* (1897) 24 R. 294, 296 per Lord McLaren (an interlocutor allowing parties proof of their averments leaves all questions of relevancy open to further consideration). In that case Lord McLaren said the words "before answer" were unnecessary for reserving questions of law and relevancy although the proper time for raising questions of law is when the Lord Ordinary is moved to allow a proof. Where a proof has been allowed evidence may be led which might have been excluded on the ground of irrelevance or lack of specification if such a plea had been taken: *Barr v. Bain* (1896) 23 R. 1090. Objection cannot be taken to proving an averment admitted to probation: *Scott v. Cormack Heating Engineers Ltd* 1942 S.C. 159, 162 per L.P. Normand.

(2) Proof before answer.

Proof before answer may be allowed where there is a plea to the relevancy of averments, questions of law and relevancy being reserved until the evidence has been led: *Robertson v. Murphy* (1867) 6 M. 114; *Fleming v. Eadie & Son* (1897) 25 R. 3, 5–6 per Lord Young; *Moore v. Stephen & Sons* 1954 S.C. 331, 336 per Lord Patrick. Proof before answer strictly means proof before answer as to relevancy, but not competency: *Fleming*, above; *Macvean v. Maclean* (1873) 11 M. 506 per Lord Neaves; cf. L.J.-C.

Moncreiff at p. 509 who thought it might be as to either. A proof before answer reserving a plea to competency may be allowed where evidence on the merits may be relevant to the question of competency (*Shaw v. Renton & Fisher Ltd* 1977 S.L.T.(Notes) 60) or even, in exceptional circumstances, jurisdiction (*McLeod v. Tancred, Arrol & Co.* (1890) 17 R. 514) although it would be more usual to allow a preliminary proof on issues of competency or jurisdiction (see note 28.1.5). A proof before answer may be allowed where it cannot be said in advance whether the facts averred are sufficient to support the legal conclusions or the law cannot be stated until the facts are determined: *Moore*, above, at p. 335 per L.J.-C. Thomson and p. 336 per Lord Patrick.

The allowance of a proof before answer does not authorise the admission of incompetent evidence: *Robertson*, above; and, e.g. confidentiality is not waived even if a proof before answer was of consent: *Duke of Argyll v. Duchess of Argyll* 1962 S.C.(H.L.) 88, 93–94 per Lord Reid and 97–98 per Lord Guest.

In an action of damages for personal injuries involving only two parties it should seldom be necessary to allow a proof (before answer) with all pleas standing including time-bar. The court, however, must determine whether averments relating to s.19A of the 1973 Act are relevant and, if so, if there is sufficient agreement on the material facts, adjudicate on the issue on the basis of submissions, or if there is insufficient agreement allow a preliminary proof: *Clark v. McLean* , 1994 S.C. 410.

(2A)   Proof habili modo.

As mentioned at the beginning of this note, a proof *habili modo* means that proof is allowed by the manner competent to each part of the case, e.g., where parts of the cause may be proved *prout de jure* (according to law) and other parts are restricted. The judge rules on the admissibility of evidence with respect to a restricted part at the proof: *Clark's Exrx v. Brown* 1935 S.C. 110. Objection should be taken to the competency of a particular form of evidence at the time it is adduced: *Royal Bank of Scotland plc v. Malcolm* , 16th April 1999, unreported. The judge may rule on it then or, more commonly, reserve consideration of it until the conclusion of the proof: *Gill v. Gill* 1907 S.C. 532; *Jackson v. Ogilvie's Exr* 1935 S.C. 154.

(3)   Interlocutors.

The interlocutor allowing probation will specify the nature of probation allowed.

(a)   In relation to proof (at large) the possibilities are: (i) "allows to parties a proof of their respective averments on record" where each party makes averments, enabling each to lead evidence in support of his own case; (ii) "allows the pursuer a proof of his own averments and to the defender a conjunct probation" where the defender only denies the pursuer's averments, the conjunct probation permitting him to contradict the pursuer's case; and (iii) "allows the defender a proof of his averments and to the pursuer a conjunct probation" where the defender admits the pursuer's claim but makes counter-averments.

(b)   In relation to a proof before answer the interlocutor is "allows to parties a proof before answer of their respective averments on record; appoints said proof to proceed on the day of 19 at 10 o'clock forenoon and grants diligence for citing witnesses and havers".

(c)   In relation to jury trial the interlocutor is "approves of the proposed issue [and counter-issue] No(s). [and] of process and allows them as now authenticated to be the issue [and counter-issue] for the trial of the cause; appoints the said issue [and counter-issue] to be tried by jury on.......... the.......... day of.......... 19 at 10 o'clock forenoon; authorises and appoints a jury to be summoned for that purpose in common form; grants warrant for citing witnesses and havers".

(d)   In relation to proof by writ or oath the interlocutor is "allows the cause to proceed by writ or oath of the defender; appoints said proof to proceed on.......... the.......... day of.......... 19 at 10 o'clock forenoon and grants diligence for citing the defender".

(e)   In relation to proof *habili modo* the interlocutor is "allows to parties a proof *habili modo* of their averments on record; appoints said proof to proceed on.......... the.......... day of.......... 19 at 10 o'clock forenoon and grants diligence for citing witnesses and havers".

(f)   In relation to a preliminary proof the interlocutor is "allows a preliminary proof restricted solely to (*nature of proof or averments to go to proof*); appoints said proof to proceed on.......... the.......... day of.......... 19 at 10 o'clock forenoon and grants diligence for citing witnesses and havers".

"ISSUES FOR JURY TRIAL".

Issues (and counter-issues) are the concise statements of the questions of fact to be answered by the jury: Bell's *Dictionary*. On the procedure for lodging issues, see r. 37.1.

22.3.10

PROOF OR JURY TRIAL.

Certain causes, the "enumerated causes", must be sent to jury trial unless the parties otherwise agree or special cause is shown: C.S.A. 1988, s.9(b). The statutory provision is not modified by r. 28.1: *Graham v. Paterson & Son Ltd* 1938 S.C. 119. It has been held that, where the pursuer claims provisional damages under s.12 of the Administration of Justice (Scotland) Act 1982, Parliament has by implication deprived the pursuer of jury trial: *Potter v. McCulloch* 1987 S.L.T. 308, 311L per Lord Weir, although he also

22.3.11

found special cause existed. It might be unwise, however, to rely on exclusion by implication: see note 28.1.8(B) (Special cause) and *McFadyen v. Crudens Ltd* 1972 S.L.T.(Notes) 62 per L.P. Emslie; cf. *Winchester v. Ramsay* 1966 S.C. 41 (effect of third party notice).

The court may allow jury trial in a cause other than an enumerated cause: e.g. *Fletcher v. Lord Advocate* 1923 S.C. 27; *Blount v. Watt* 1953 S.L.T.(Notes) 39. In this case the court has an unfettered discretion, although it may require a special reason (cause) to send a case which is not an enumerated cause to jury trial. According to present-day practice proof before a judge is the normal and convenient method of inquiry in actions which are not appropriated by statute to trial by jury: *Blount*, above, per Lord Guthrie at p. 40. The enumerated causes are: (a) an action of damages for personal injuries; (b) an action for libel or defamation; (c) an action founded on delinquency or quasi-delinquency where the conclusion is for damages only and expenses; and (d) an action of reduction on the ground of incapacity, essential error, or force and fear: C.S.A. 1988, s.11. The longer list in s.28 of the C.S.A. 1825 was replaced by this shorter list in the C.S.A. 1988 because none of the others had been sent to jury trial in living memory. S.49 of the C.S.A. 1850 had allowed proof on commission as an alternative in the enumerated causes except cases of libel, nuisance or damages; s.4 of the Evidence (Scotland) Act 1866 introduced the alternative of proof to jury trial where parties consented or special cause was shown (both these provisions are repealed by the C.S.A. 1988, Sch.2).

A proof may, after amendment, be recalled and the cause sent for jury trial (*Higgins v. Burton* 1968 S.L.T.(Notes) 14); and, after amendment, allowance of issues recalled and a proof allowed (*Nicol v. McIntosh* 1987 S.L.T. 104 (obiter)).

For a more detailed discussion of the question of proof or jury trial, see note 28.1.8.

BY ORDER (ADJUSTMENT) ROLL.

22.3.12   This roll generally involves a purely formal hearing where parties are not agreed as to the next step in procedure. The roll is of little value because where parties are not agreed about the next step at the hearing on this roll the cause will be sent to procedure roll. A party may not consent to the further procedure under r. 22.3(5)(a) if he seeks to have the other party lodge a note of argument for a procedure roll discussion (see r. 22.4) and that party does not agree. Should parties agree further procedure after a cause has been appointed to the By Order (Adjustment) Roll, a motion may be enrolled by any party of consent craving the court to make an order under r. 22.3(5)(a)(i)–(iv).

Where a By Order (Adjustment) Roll hearing occurs because a party has not intimated his wishes earlier and the other party would have agreed to the procedure proposed, thus obviating the need for the hearing, the court may award the expenses of that hearing to that other party.

"LEADING CAUSE".

22.3.13   It is possible to appoint one of a number of causes arising out of the same cause of action to be the leading cause and sist the others: r. 22.3(6). This procedure is infrequently used (similarly, conjunction); it is possible, administratively, to arrange for proofs of causes to be heard together. It is not essential to make the evidence in the leading cause the evidence in the other causes. The words "same cause of action" in r. 22.3(6) probably mean that the nature and factual basis of the causes must be the same.

In *Anderson v. The Braer Corporation* 1996 S.L.T. 779, Lord Gill decided that as r. 22.3(6) applies after the record has closed, he was precluded from exercising any discretion to sist a case and appoint a leading case before the record had closed. If he was wrong, he concluded that it was inappropriate to sist a number of actions and appoint leading actions, because (a) the time to decide the matter was when the issues of fact and law had been defined in the pleadings (i.e. when the record has closed), (b) it must be clear that the actions must arise out of the same cause of action, (c) there must be a clear and concise question of fact or law, and (d) the decisions in the leading action should resolve issues to reduce the time, effort and expense incurred overall, especially where there was no agreement that the decisions would be regarded as decisions of questions in other cases.

RECLAIMING.

22.3.14   An interlocutor allowing or refusing proof or proof before answer, jury trial, limiting the mode of proof or adjusting issues, may be reclaimed against without leave within 14 days of the interlocutor being pronounced: r. 38.3(4).

Although an interlocutor of the Lord Ordinary is final in the Outer House (C.S.A. 1988, s.18), a subsequent amendment of pleadings may have the result that a prior interlocutor as to the mode of inquiry can be regarded as superseded and the Lord Ordinary can consider the mode of inquiry of new without the prior interlocutor having to be reclaimed: *Bendex v. James Donaldson & Sons Ltd* 1990 S.C. 259; *Gillon v. Gillon (No. 2)* 1994 S.C. 162, 165F per L.P. Hope.

FEE.

22.3.15   A court fee is payable on lodging a closed record or when the mode of inquiry is determined. For fee, see Court of Session etc. Fees Order 1997, Table of Fees, Pt I, B, item 14 or C, item 11 [S.I. 1997 No. 688, as amended, pp. C1201 et seq.]. A court fee is also payable for fixing a proof: Court of Session etc. Fees Order 1997, Table of Fees, Pt I, B, item 15 or C, item 12. Certain persons are exempt from payment of fees: see 1997 Fees Order, art.5, substituted by S.S.I. 2002 No. 270. A fee exemption certificate must be lodged in process: see P.N. No.1 of 2002.

Where the party is legally represented, the fee may be debited under a credit scheme introduced on 1st April 1976 by P.N. No. 4 of 1976 to the account (if one is kept or permitted) of the agent by the court cashier, and an account will be rendered weekly by the court cashier's office to the agent for all court fees due that week for immediate settlement. Party litigants, and agents not operating the scheme, must pay (by cash, cheque or postal order) on each occasion a fee is due at the time of lodging at the counter at the appropriate department.

Notes of argument

22.4.—[1](1) Where a cause has been appointed to the Procedure Roll, a party seeking to have a preliminary plea sustained shall—

    (a)   lodge in process a concise note of argument consisting of numbered paragraphs stating the grounds on which he proposes to submit that the preliminary plea should be sustained,

    (b)   lodge a copy of the note with the Keeper of the Rolls, and

    (c)   send a copy of the note to every other party.

(2) The note shall be lodged and sent in accordance with paragraph (1) within 28 days after the date of the interlocutor appointing the cause to the Procedure Roll unless the court, at its own instance or on the motion of a party, orders that the note be lodged and sent within a different period.

22.4

GENERAL NOTE.

This is a new provision giving the court a discretionary power at its own instance or on the motion of a party to order a note of argument in any cause appointed to the Procedure Roll whether or not it has been on the Adjustment Roll or whether or not a record is required. An infelicitously drafted P.N. No. 4 of 1997 sought to provide a mandatory requirement for notes of argument. Furthermore, it did not indicate whether it superseded the requirement in para. 1(b) of P.N. No. 3 of 1991 to inform an opponent of the nature of the proposal argument at the earliest opportunity. The confusion and inconsistency between the rule and the P.N.s has recently been made by Lord Osborne, without reference or acknowledgement to the comments in this note up to Release 79 (January 2005) in *Fairbarn v. Vayro* , 2001 S.L.T. 1167.

This new rule sorts out the problem. It is now mandatory to lodge a note of argument in process, send a copy to the Keeper and to every other party after the interlocutor appointing the cause to the Procedure Roll. The only discretion is that the court may change the period of 28 days in which to do this: r. 22.4(2).

Special provision for notes of argument is made in the following causes: (a) commercial actions (r. 47.12(1)(d)); and (b) causes relating to intellectual property (r. 55.3(4)(b)).

A copy of the note of argument must also be sent to the Keeper of the Rolls: P.N. No. 6 of 1997.

22.4.1

"PROCEDURE ROLL".

A cause is appointed to the Procedure Roll under r. 22.3(5) (where a record is closed) or r. 14.8 (procedure where answers lodged in a petition), r. 15.1(5) (further procedure in minutes) or r. 15.2(3) (application of r. 14.8 to applications by note). A cause is so appointed where there are preliminary pleas (see note 22.3.6) to be argued. For Procedure Roll, see Chap. 28.

22.4.2

"NOTE OF ARGUMENT".

The note of argument does not require to be signed. R.15.2 (applications by note) does not apply because a note of argument is not an application to the court.

A note of argument should set out the basis of the argument including any relevant authority but need not do so in detail.

The court may order different periods for lodging the note in process and sending a copy of it to the other parties concerned (not every party will necessarily be concerned with the plea).

A note of argument lodged in process must be backed and comply with r. 4.1(3) and (4). It need not be signed. It may be lodged by post: P.N. No. 4 of 1994, paras. 1 and 8.

22.4.3

"PRELIMINARY PLEA".

See note 22.3.6.

22.4.4

"SENT".

This includes deliver: r. 1.3(1) (definition of "send").

22.4.5

"WITHIN 28 DAYS AFTER".

The date from which the period is calculated is not counted.

22.4.6

"LODGE IN PROCESS".

On lodging steps of process, see rr. 4.4-4.6.

22.4.7

---

[1] R.22.4 substituted by S.S.I. 2004 No. 331 (effective 6th August 2004).

CHAPTER 23 MOTIONS

Part 1[1] – Introduction

Interpretation of this Chapter

23.1. In this Chapter, unless the context otherwise requires, "party" includes any person entitled under these Rules to enrol a motion or to whom intimation of a motion is required to be made by these Rules or the court.

GENERAL NOTE.

Persons entitled to enrol motions are generally only parties to the cause, but there are exceptions: e.g. any person having an interest may apply by motion to the court for the loosing, restriction or recall of an arrestment or the recall of an inhibition (r. 13.10(1)) or to move arrested property (r. 13.11(1)) or a person seeking leave to be sisted as a party.

Making of motions

23.1A.—[2](1) A motion by a party may be—
- (a) made orally at the bar with leave of the court during any hearing of a cause; or
- (b) enrolled in the cause in accordance with the relevant rules.

(2) In paragraph (1)(b), the "relevant rules" are—
- (a) where paragraph (3) applies, Parts 2 and 4 of this Chapter;
- (b) where paragraph (3) does not apply, Parts 3 and 4 of this Chapter.

(3) This paragraph applies—
- (a) where the cause was initiated by summons, is proceeding in the Outer House and is not a commercial action; and
- (b) each party has provided to the Deputy Principal Clerk an email address for the purpose of transacting motion business.

(4) Subject to paragraph (5), an agent representing a party in a cause of the sort mentioned in paragraph (3)(a) must provide to the Deputy Principal Clerk an email address for the purpose of transacting motion business.

(5) An agent who does not have suitable facilities for transacting motion business by email may make a declaration in writing to that effect, which must be—
- (a) sent to the Deputy Principal Clerk; and
- (b) intimated to each of the other parties to the cause.

(6)[3] The Deputy Principal Clerk must maintain a list of the email addresses provided to him for the purpose of transacting motion business, which must be published in up-to-date form on the website of the Scottish Courts and Tribunals Service.

(7) The Deputy Principal Clerk must also include on the list maintained under paragraph (6) an email address of the court for the purpose of enrolling motions.

(8) In this rule, "transacting motion business" means—
- (a) intimating and enrolling motions;
- (b) receiving intimation of motions;
- (c) intimating consent or opposition to motions;
- (d) receiving intimation of or opposition to motions.

GENERAL NOTE.

Chapter 23 has been re-cast to take account of the new facility for motions by email in Outer House cases other than commercial actions and petitions (r. 23.1A(3)(a)). Ordinarily, except in excluded

---

[1] Chap. 23 Pt 1 heading inserted by S.S.I. 2009/387 (effective 1st February 2010).

[2] R. 23.1A inserted by S.S.I. 2009/387 (effective 1st February 2010).

[3] Rule 23.1A(6) as amended by the Courts Reform (Scotland) Act 2014 (asp 18) Pt 10 s.130(4) (effective 1 April 2015: as SSI 2015/77).

23.1

23.1.1

23.1A

23.1A.1

categories, motions *must* be made by email where a party is represented by an agent unless the agent has declared that he does not have suitable facilities. While, theoretically a technological advance, motions by email are not yet more efficient and quicker than turning up in person, and sometimes the latter is necessary in addition.

A special department deals with motions called the Court Motions Team. It may be contacted on *courtofsession.motions@scotcourts.gov.uk* or on 0131 240 6882.

P.N. No. 3 of 2009 provides guidance on the application of the procedure.

Part 2 of Chap. 23 deals with intimation and enrolment of motions by email; Pt. 3 deals with intimation and enrolment of motions by other means; and Pt. 4 applies to both.

Thus a motion may be made—

- orally at the Bar,
- by email in an Outer House action other than a commercial action (but not a petition),
- in writing in Form 23.2 by lodging it, by fax, or by post.

A motion which has to be made by email is emailed to the court only once it has been opposed or the period for opposition has elapsed without opposition (see r. 23.ID: rr. 23.1F and 23.1G).

"MADE ORALLY AT THE BAR".

23.1A.2   Motions must usually be made by email or in writing in Form 23.2 and require to be intimated where there is an opposing party. A motion made at the bar can therefore really only be made with leave of the court. Since in a defended cause intimation is required, the court is unlikely to grant leave if the opponent does not consent, although the court does have a power to dispense with intimation (see r. 23.3(3)(c) which it may exercise if there is no prejudice). An opposing party concerned in the motion may object on the ground of prejudice because the motion has not been intimated. Certain motions require a lengthy period of intimation (see, e.g. a motion one year after the last interlocutor (r. 23.3(4)) and variation of certain orders in family actions (e.g. rr. 49.40(2), 49.41(2), 49.42(2), 49.43(2) and (5))) and such a motion will rarely be heard in the absence of such intimation without consent of the opposing party concerned.

FAILURE OF SERVER.

23.1A.3   The rules make no provision for failure of an internet server. Para. 15 of P.N. No. 3 of 2009 attempts to address this by providing that the court may treat a written or faxed motion as if it had been enrolled or intimated by email. It is not competent to do this by P.N.; and such provision should be in the Rules.

EMAIL ADDRESSES.

23.1A.4   The email address of the court for motions is *courtofsession.motions@scotcourts.gov.uk*. The email addresses of agents (and any party litigants) for motions are to be found on the SCS website, *www.scotcourts.gov.uk* under New Motions Procedure on the Professional page.

Part 2[1] – Motions etc. intimated and enrolled by email

Interpretation of this Part

23.1B   **23.1B.**—[2](1)   In this Part—

"court day" means a day on which the Office of Court is open;

"court day 1" means the court day on which a motion is treated as being intimated under rule 23.1C;

"court day 3" means the second court day after court day 1;

"court day 4" means the third court day after court day 1;

"enrolling party" means the party enrolling the motion; and

"receiving party" means a party receiving intimation of the motion from the enrolling party.

(2)   In this Part, a reference to a party's address is a reference to the email address listed for that party's agent or, as the case may be, that party, in the list maintained under rule 23.1A(6); and a reference to the court's email address is a reference to the email address included on that list by virtue of rule 23.1A(7).

COURT DAYS.

23.1B.1   These are days on which the Office of Court is open: see note 3.1.2.

---

[1] Part 2 and R. 23.1B inserted by S.S.I 2009/387 (effective 1st February 2010).
[2] Part 2 and R. 23.1B inserted by S.S.I 2009/387 (effective 1st February 2010).

The day on which a motion is intimated by email by 5pm to another party is called court day 1. Opposition must be made to the enrolling party by 5pm on court day 3 (ie the day after the following day). If there is no opposition marked the enrolling party may email an unopposed motion to the court, also in Form 23.1C by 12.30pm on court day 4 (ie the day after court day 3).

EMAIL ADDRESSES.

See note 23.1A.4.

23.1B.2

Intimation of motions by email

23.1C.—[1](1) Subject to paragraph (2) and any other provision in these Rules, an enrolling party in a cause where—

23.1C

    (a)   appearance has been entered by a defender under rule 17.1(1),

    (b)   defences, a minute or answers have been lodged by a party, or

    (c)   provision is made for intimation of a motion to a party in accordance with this Part,

shall give intimation of his intention to make such enrolment, and of the terms of the motion, to every such party by sending an email in Form 23.1C to the addresses of every such party.

(2) The requirement under paragraph (1) to give intimation of a motion to a party by email shall not apply where that party—

    (a)   having entered appearance, fails to lodge defences within the period for lodging those defences;

    (b)   has not lodged answers within the period of notice for lodging those answers; or

    (c)   has withdrawn or is deemed to have withdrawn his defences, minute, note or answers, as the case may be.

(3) Subject to rule 23.1J, a motion intimated under this rule shall be intimated not later than 5 p.m. on a court day.

GENERAL NOTE.

A motion *must* be made and intimated to other parties by email in Form 23. 1C unless:

23.1C.1

- the party is not represented by a solicitor who has not made a declaration that he does not have suitable facilities for email,
- the process is a petition or a commercial action,
- appearance has not be entered by another party,
- defences, minute or answers have not been lodged timeously or they have been withdrawn.

"INTIMATION".

This is by email. It is to be made by 5pm on a court day under r. 23.1C(3). Where another rule provides another period of intimation (eg within 14 days), that rule applies and not r. 23.1C(3): r. 23.1J(1).

23.1C.2

Opposition to motions by email

23.1D.—[2](1) A receiving party shall intimate any opposition to a motion intimated under rule 23.1C by sending an email in Form 23.ID to the address of the enrolling party.

23.1D

(2) Subject to paragraph (3) and rule 23.1J, any opposition to a motion under this rule shall be intimated to the enrolling party not later than 5 p.m. on court day 3.

(3) Late opposition to a motion under this rule should be sent to the email address of the court and may only be allowed with the leave of the court, on cause shown.

"COURT DAY 3".

This is the day after the day following the intimation of the motion: r. 23.1B(1). Where another rule provides a different period of intimation, that rule applies: r. 23.1J.

23.1D.1

---

[1] R. 23.1C inserted by S.S.I. 2009/387 (effective 1st February 2010).
[2] R. 23.1D inserted by S.S.I. 2009/387 (effective 1st February 2010).

LATE OPPOSITION.

23.1D.2   Late opposition should be sent to the email address of the court and will be allowed only with leave of the court. Late opposition is difficult as an unopposed motion is granted the same day as enrolled under r. 23.1F on court day 4.

Consent to motions by email

23.1E   **23.1E.**[1]   Where a receiving party seeks to consent to a motion intimated under rule 23.1C, the receiving party may intimate such consent by sending an email confirming the consent to the address of the enrolling party.

GENERAL NOTE.

23.1E.1   There is no time-limit for consenting to a motion.

CONSENT TO SHORTENED PERIOD OF INTIMATION.

23.1E.2   It is possible to consent to a shortened period of intimation; but, if so, this should be stated in the intimation of consent: r. 23.1J(2).

Enrolling unopposed motions by email

23.1F   **23.1F.**—[2](1)   This rule applies where a motion has been intimated under rule 23.1C and no opposition has been intimated under rule 23.1D.

(2)   The motion shall be enrolled by the enrolling party not later than 12.30 p.m. on court day 4 by sending an email in Form 23.1C headed "Unopposed Motion" to the email address of the court.

(3)   Subject to paragraph (4), a motion enrolled under paragraph (2) shall be determined by the court by 5 p.m. on court day 4.

(4)   Where for any reason it is not possible for a motion enrolled under paragraph (2) to be determined by 5 p.m. on court day 4, the clerk of session shall advise the parties or their agents of that fact and shall give reasons.

(5)   A motion enrolled under paragraph (2) shall appear in the rolls.

GENERAL NOTE.

23.1F.1   The clerk of session may try to decline to deal with a motion because of some perceived irregularity or incompetency rather than putting it before a judge.

"COURT DAY 4".

23.1F.2   This is the third day after court day 1 (the day on which the motion is intimated): r. 23.1B(1). The motion must be enrolled by email by 12.30pm for it to be dealt with that day. A motion received at 12.31pm or later will be dropped.

Where there is consent, the motion may be heard earlier: r. 23.1J(4).

In the subject matter of the email the name of the case, the case reference and that the motion is unopposed must be stated.

The Court Motions Team now sends an email to advise that a motion has been received and is being processed, but no reference is given to identify the case to which the email refers!

If there is a problem with a motion or something is missing, the Team will email and, or, telephone. Usually the agent is given until 3pm to fix the problem.

DOCUMENTS AND PRODUCTIONS REFERRED TO IN MOTIONS.

23.1F.3   Any document referred to in a motion must be attached to the email in electronic form in "Word" or pdf format: P.N. No. 3 of 2009, para. 8. It may need to be scanned to be put into that format. If the document is 20 pages or fewer the court will make the necessary number of copies; what is "necessary" is not stated. If the document is more than 20 pages long, the court will print one copy and the party concerned will have to go to the General Department the next day and lodge any additional copies: P.N. No 3 of 2009, paras. 9 and 10.

In relation to productions, only the inventory need be sent by email and the court will print it off. The productions have to be lodged in process the next day: P.N. No. 3 of 2009, para. 11.

---

[1] R. 23.1E inserted by S.S.I. 2009/387 (effective 1st February 2010).
[2] R. 23.1F inserted by S.S.I. 2009/387 (effective 1st February 2010).

Direction No. 3 of 2010 makes special provision for the date and time of the hearing of motions in commercial actions (defined in r. 47.1(2)), proceedings in the Outer House in a cause under the Insolvency Act 1986 or the Company Directors Disqualification Act 1986, and s.896 (holding a meeting) and s.899 (sanction of compromise or arrangement) of the Companies Act 2006.

Any opposed motion, or a motion requiring explanation, will be put out for a hearing at a date and time convenient to the court and, where possible, to the parties. Where a motion is opposed or otherwise starred (see notes 23.2.14 and 23.2.16), the clerk of court will fix a date for the hearing and give intimation of that date to the parties. Urgent motions will be dealt with on a priority basis.

23.1F.4

Enrolling opposed motions by email

23.1G.—[1](1)   This rule applies where opposition to a motion has been intimated under rule 23.ID.

23.1G

(2)   The motion shall be enrolled by the enrolling party not later than 12.30 p.m. on court day 4 by sending an email in Form 23.1C headed "Opposed Motion", together with an attached Form 23.1D to the email address of the court.

(3)[2]   Where a motion is enrolled under paragraph (2) the motion shall be heard on the first sitting day after court day 4, or, if this is not possible, at another date and time convenient to the court and, where possible, to parties.

(4)   Where a motion is opposed under this Part, the entry in the rolls in respect of that motion shall be starred.

GENERAL NOTE.

The clerk of session may try to decline to deal with a motion because of some perceived irregularity or incompetency rather than putting it before a judge.

23.1G.1

"COURT DAY 4".

This is the third day after court day 1 (the day on which the motion is intimated): r. 23.1B(1). The motion must be enrolled by 12.30pm for it to be dealt with on the next sederunt day after that day. A motion received at 12.31pm or later will be dropped.

23.1G.2

Where there is consent, the motion may be heard earlier: r. 23.1J(4).

In the subject matter of the email the name of the case, the case reference and that the motion is opposed must be stated.

The Court Motions Team now sends an email to advise that a motion has been received and is being processed, but no reference is given to identify the case to which the email refers!

If there is a problem with a motion or something is missing, the Team will email and, or, telephone. Usually the agent is given until 3pm to fix the problem.

Issuing of interlocutor by email

23.1H.[3]   Where the court pronounces an interlocutor in respect of a motion intimated and enrolled under this Part, the clerk of session shall forthwith email a copy of the interlocutor to the addresses of the enrolling party and every receiving party.

23.1H

Other periods of intimation etc. under these Rules

23.1J.—[4](1)   Where these Rules otherwise provide for a period of intimation of—

23.1J

    (a)   a motion;

    (b)   opposition to a motion; or

    (c)   consent to a motion,

that period shall apply, notwithstanding the intimation period referred to in this Part.

(2)   Paragraph (1) applies whether or not the intimation period mentioned elsewhere in these Rules is referred to by a specific number of days.

(3)   Where—

---

[1] R. 23.1G inserted by S.S.I. 2009/387 (effective 1st February 2010).

[2] R. 23.1G(3) amended by S.S.I. 2017 No. 414 r. 3(2) (effective 1st January 2018).

[3] R. 23.1H inserted by S.S.I. 2009/387 (effective 1st February 2010).

[4] R. 23.1J inserted by S.S.I. 2009/387 (effective 1st February 2010).

(a) every receiving party in a cause consents to a shorter period of intimation; or

(b) the court shortens the period of intimation,

the enrolling party, when intimating a motion by email under rule 23.1C, may indicate that the period within which opposition to the motion is to be intimated by a receiving party is shortened accordingly; and rule 23.1D(2) shall be read accordingly.

(4) Where paragraph (3) applies, notwithstanding the time periods referred to in rule 23.1F(2), (3) and (4) and rule 23.1G(2) and (3), the motion may be enrolled by the enrolling party, or heard or otherwise determined by the court at an earlier time and date than that which is specified in those rules.

(5) Subject to paragraphs (1) and (2), where a motion is intimated under this Part after the lapse of one year from the date of the last interlocutor in the cause—

(a) in the application of rule 23.1D, the reference to court day 3 shall be read as a reference to the fourteenth court day after court day 1; and

(b) in the application of rules 23.1F and 23.1G, references to court day 4 shall be read as references to the fifteenth court day after court day 1.

GENERAL NOTE.

23.1J.1   Periods of intimation in this Chapter are subject to any period of intimation specified elsewhere in the Rules, and consent to a shortened period of intimation should be stated in the intimation of consent.

MOTIONS INTIMATED AFTER LAPSE OF ONE YEAR.

23.1J.2   Rule 23.1 J(5) makes the email motion procedure for wakening a cause that has fallen asleep consistent with r. 23.3(4).

Part 3[1] – Motions etc. intimated and enrolled by other means

Enrolment of motions

23.2   **23.2.**—(1) *[Repealed by S.S.I. 2009/387 (effective 1st February 2010).]*

(2) A motion may be enrolled—

(a) by lodging it in Form 23.2, with any document which requires to be lodged with or which accompanies the motion, at the appropriate department of the Office of Court during its normal office hours;

(b) subject to paragraph (3), by posting it in Form 23.2, with any document which requires to be lodged with or which accompanies the motion, to the appropriate department of the Office of Court; or

(c) subject to paragraph (4), by sending it by facsimile transmission in Form 23.2, with any document which requires to be lodged with or which accompanies the motion, to the appropriate department of the Office of Court.

(3) A motion may not be enrolled under paragraph (2)(b) where a fee is payable with that motion unless—

(a) the motion is enrolled by an agent who has a Court of Session account; or

(b) is accompanied by a cheque from the agent for the fee.

(4) A motion may not be enrolled under paragraph (2)(c) where—

(a) a document which requires to be lodged with, or which accompanies, the motion—

(i) is a step of process which requires to be or is signed;

(ii) is an open or closed record, reclaiming print, appeal print or appendix;

(iii) consists of more than four pages (including the backing sheet); or

(iv) does not fall within a class of documents prescribed by the Lord

---

[1] Chap. 23 Pt 3 heading inserted by S.S.I. 2009/387 (effective 1st February 2010).

President by direction as a document which may be sent by facsimile transmission in support of a motion of a category, and on such conditions, prescribed by that direction;

    (b) a fee is payable with that motion unless the motion is enrolled by an agent who has a Court of Session account; or

    (c) it falls within a category of motions prescribed by the Lord President by direction as unsuitable for enrolment by facsimile transmission.

(5) On receipt of a motion lodged, sent by post or transmitted by facsimile under paragraph (2), a clerk of session shall attach the motion to the motion sheet.

(6) A motion sent by post or facsimile transmission under paragraph (2) shall be treated as enrolled when it is received in the appropriate department of the Office of Court.

(7) *[Repealed by S.S.I. 2009/387 (effective 1st February 2010).]*

Deriv. R.C.S. 1965, r. 93(a) (r. 23.2(1)), r. 93(b) and (c) (part), r. 198 amended by SI 1978/799 and P.N. No. 8 of 1991, para. 10(3) (r. 23.2(2)), r. 93(d) (part) (r. 23.2(7)), P.N. No. 8 of 1991, para. 2 (r. 23.2(3)), and P.N. No. 8 of 1991, para. 10(2) and (5) (r. 23.2(4))

GENERAL NOTE.

A motion is the means by which the court is asked to grant some application in the cause (whether incidental or substantive) or to allow a document to be lodged.   **23.2.1**

"MOTIONS MADE ORALLY AT THE BAR".

Motions must usually be made by email or in writing in Form 23.2 and require to be intimated where there is an opposing party. A motion made at the bar can therefore really only be made with leave of the court. Since in a defended cause intimation is required, the court is unlikely to grant leave if the opponent does not consent, although the court does have a power to dispense with intimation (see r. 23.3(3)(c) which it may exercise if there is no prejudice). An opposing party concerned in the motion may object on the ground of prejudice because the motion has not been intimated. Certain motions require a lengthy period of intimation (see, e.g. a motion one year after the last interlocutor (r. 23.3(4)) and variation of certain orders in family actions (e.g. rr. 49.40(2), 49.41(2), 49.42(2), 49.43(2) and (5))) and such a motion will rarely be heard in the absence of such intimation without consent of the opposing party concerned.   **23.2.2**

ENROLLING A MOTION.

There are three methods of enrolling a motion under Pt 3: (a) lodging Form 23.2 (the motion form) at the appropriate public counter of the General or Petition Department; (b) sending Form 23.2 by post if, where a fee is payable with the motion, the party's agent has a Court of Session account (see P.N. No. 4 of 1976) or accompanied by a cheque for the fee (r. 23.2(3)); or (c) sending Form 23.2 by fax if it is not a motion to which r. 23.2(4) applies. The fax no. for the General Department is 031-225 5496; the fax no. for the Petition Department is 031-225 7233.   **23.2.3**

For the categories of cause lodged in the General Department, see r. 3.2 and notes. The causes lodged in the Petition Department are all petitions and notes in petition processes and certain references under statute (see note 3.3.1).

FORM 23.2.

Motions must be written or typed on a form in Form 23.2 whether lodged in person at the public counter of the appropriate Department, posted or faxed. The form is in three parts. In the case of a motion in a cause lodged in the General Department, all three parts must be completed where the motion is enrolled by post or fax; only Parts II and III (the latter being a motion slip) need be completed where enrolment is by lodging in person. In the case of a cause lodged in the Petition Department, Parts I and II must be completed where the motion is enrolled by post or fax; only Part II need be completed where enrolment is by lodging in person (a motion slip (Part III) is not required because, given the variety of petitions and the need for accuracy in the rolls of court, the clerks in the Petition Department have, historically, always written the motion slips and transmitted them to the Keeper of the Rolls for publication in the rolls).   **23.2.4**

For the categories of cause lodged in the General Department, see r. 3.2 and notes. The causes lodged in the Petition Department are all petitions and notes in petition processes and certain references under statute (see note 3.3.1).

Under P.N. 10th December 1986, para. 3 certain motions require reasons or explanations to be given and this information must be included in Form 23.2; a document may also be required. The document may be a writ or a production lodged with an inventory.

A motion which is expected to be starred and to require more than 10 minutes' duration on the motion roll must have the estimated duration marked on the form: P.N. No. 4 of 1996.

"AGENT".

23.2.5   This means a solicitor or a person having a right to conduct the litigation: see r. 1.3(1) (definition of "agent") and note 1.3.4. "Solicitor" is defined in the C.S.A. 1988, s.51.

"COURT OF SESSION ACCOUNT".

23.2.6   Fees may be debited under a credit scheme introduced on 1st April 1976 by P.N. No. 4 of 1976 to the account (if one is kept or permitted) of the agent by the court cashier, and an account will be rendered weekly by the court cashier's office to the agent for all court fees due that week for immediate settlement. Party litigants are not allowed to use this scheme.

DOCUMENTS LODGED WITH MOTIONS.

23.2.7   Such a document may be a writ, other step of process (a document not a production: r. 1.3(1)) or a production. Note the extended meaning of document in r. 1.3(1). A document may be lodged in person or by post (P.N. No. 4 of 1994, paras 1 and 8).

To facilitate enrolling motions by fax certain documents no longer require to be signed: see r. 4.2(9). Certain documents may not be transmitted by fax; these are: steps of process which must be signed, an open or closed record, a reclaiming or appeal print or appendix, a document of more than four pages or a document which does not fall within a class prescribed by the Lord President by direction as a document which may be faxed (for which, see note 23.2.9): r. 23.2(4).

Certain motions may require a document to be lodged. In relation to unopposed motions an indication of what documents are required for particular motions is given in P.N. 10th December 1986. Certain documents in support of certain motions may be transmitted by fax: see Direction No. 3 of 1994 and note 23.2.9. In either case the document must be lodged as a production: see r. 4.5.

"STEP OF PROCESS WHICH REQUIRES TO HE OR IS SIGNED".

23.2.8   A step of process is any document lodged in process, other than a production (r. 1.3(1)), including those listed in r. 4.4(1) and any inventory of productions. A step of process which requires to be or is signed would include, e.g. defences, answers (other than answers to a minute of amendment), a report by a reporter or a legal aid certificate. Note the documents which no longer require to be signed: r. 4.2(9), and see note 23.2.7.

DOCUMENTS OF A CLASS PRESCRIBED AS DOCUMENTS WHICH MAY BE FAXED.

23.2.9   The Lord President has made a direction under r. 23.2(4)(iv) prescribing certain productions lodged solely in support of a particular motion as documents which may be sent by fax with a faxed motion: see Direction No. 3 of 1994 (Productions which may be sent by facsimile transmission) (formerly P.N. No. 8 of 1993, para. 10(5) and Appendix C): see Section Two, 2. If the production is more than four pages long it may not be faxed by virtue of r. 23.2(4)(a)(iii). Where a production is sent by fax the principal will subsequently have to be lodged before the motion is heard (a) where the motion is opposed or (b) at the request of the court: Direction No. 3 of 1994, para. 3.

MOTIONS UNSUITABLE FOR FAX.

23.2.10   The Lord President has not yet made a direction defining a category of motions unsuitable for fax transmission.

"MOTION SHEET".

23.2.11   This is one of the steps of process (No. 3 of Process): r. 4.4. Motions lodged are attached to the motion sheet by an india tag or other suitable fixing.

"APPEARANCE".

23.2.12   Appearance may be by a party litigant, counsel or other person having a right of audience. A solicitor also has a right of audience before the vacation judge: C.S.A. 1988, s. 48(2)(a).

For the meaning of party litigant, see note 4.2.6. For definitions of "counsel" and "other person having a right of audience", see r. 1.3(1).

"ROLLS".

23.2.13   The rolls are the lists of the business of the court issued by the Keeper of the Rolls.

"STARRED".

23.2.14   A motion is starred (i.e. an asterisk is placed at the beginning of the entry in the rolls for the Motion Roll or Single Bills) (a) where the appearance of a party litigant, counsel or other person having a right of audience is required (i) because the motion is not an unopposed motion to which P.N. 10th December 1986 applies or (ii) by the court (r. 23.2(7)); or (b) the motion is opposed (r. 23.4(6)). For starred unopposed motions requiring appearance, see notes 23.2.16 (Outer House) and 23.2.17(2) (Inner House). It should be noted that P.N. 10th December 1986 does not apply to motions in causes in the Inner House, although the spirit of it in relation to consultation with practitioners before motions are dropped is followed. On motions in the Inner House, see note 23.2.17.

There is now a rule for starring motions that require an appearance of the party enrolling the motion: r. 23.15.

These are unopposed motions which do not require the appearance of a party litigant, counsel or other person having a right of audience. The categories of unopposed motions in the Outer House are defined by P.N. 10th December 1986 as (1) those which according to present practice are unstarred, (2) those of a procedural nature which hitherto have required the appearance of counsel, and (3) those which hitherto required appearance of counsel and judicial consideration. Motions in categories (1) and (2) are dealt with by a depute clerk of session and the interlocutor is signed by him (r. 4.15(3)) or if the interlocutor is seen by the judge is signed by the judge. A motion in category (3) is dealt with, and the interlocutor signed by, the judge.

23.2.15

(1) Unopposed motions unstarred according to current practice.

These are:

A sist of process, and recall of sist,
Amendment (by motion or minute),
Proof before answer,
Commission and diligence for recovery of documents,
Recovery of evidence under the Bankers' Books Evidence Act 1879,
Third party notice procedure,
Order for defences,
Intimation of withdrawal of agent,
Minute of sist applications,
Minute of transference applications,
Approval of issues,
Allowance of issues.

(2) Unopposed unstarred motions of a procedural nature.

These are those listed in Appendix I to P.N. 10th December 1986. Written reasons and explanations (examples of which are given in column 2 of the appendix) must accompany the motion.

(3) Unopposed unstarred motions which require judicial consideration.

These are those listed in Appendix II in P.N. 10th December 1986. Written reasons and explanations and any documents required (examples of which are given in column 2 of the appendix) must accompany the motion.

The lists above are not in fact exhaustive; the clerks of session should be consulted to determine which category a motion not listed falls into and what information and documentation is required.

For starred unopposed motions which hitherto required appearance, see note 23.2.16.

These motions require the appearance of a party litigant, counsel or other person having a right of audience. They fall into two categories:

23.2.16

1. *A motion for which the court requires appearance for some reason requiring explanation or justification.*
2. *Motions which hitherto have required appearance.* These are:
   Interim interdict (before and after calling),
   Perpetual interdict,
   Interim orders under the Matrimonial Homes (Family Protection) (Scotland) Act 1981,
   Intimation and service in judicial review petitions where interim orders are sought.

The P.N. 10th December 1986 does not apply to the Inner House. The vacation judge has power to dispose of motions, of a procedural nature and which do not dispose of the merits, enrolled in causes pending before the Inner House (r. 11.1(1)(c)); and the interlocutors are signed by the vacation judge and not the clerk. The following practice applies during term.

23.2.17

(1) Unopposed unstarred motions in the Inner House.

These are scrutinised by the clerk to the Division and, if he is satisfied that the relevant procedural rules have been complied with, he prepares an interlocutor for signature by the chairman of the Division. All interlocutors are signed by the chairman and never the clerk. Such motions are:

Order for grounds of appeal,
Appointment of cause to Summar Roll,

Sist of cause (reason stated in motion),

Recall of sist,

Ordaining party to intimate insistence of reclaiming motion or appeal where agent has withdrawn from acting,

Refusing reclaiming motion or appeal following above,

Motion by reclaimer/appellant to refuse reclaiming motion/appeal,

Amendment (except amendment of pleadings: P.N. 26th March 1981),

Expenses after judgment (unless starred by the court): see Notice 4th September 1997.

(2) *Unopposed starred motions in the Inner House.*

These fall into two categories:

(a) A motion for which the court requires appearance for some reason requiring explanation or justification and could relate to any of the motions listed in note 23.2.15.

(b) Motions which hitherto have required appearance. These are:

Late lodging of a document,

Ordaining a party to find caution,

Prorogation of time to find caution,

Adjustment of a writ,

Amendment of grounds of appeal previously lodged,

Relief from compliance with rule (r. 2.1),

Refusing opponent's reclaiming motion or appeal (except where consented to),

Late motion for review,

Prorogation of time to lodge document,

Discharge of diet on Summar Roll,

Interim interdict,

Interim payment or execution,

Sist of a mandatory,

Lost step of process,

Second sist for legal aid,

Modification of liability for expenses of legally aided person,

Expenses (except where consented to or unopposed: see Notice 4th September 1997 following a judgment unless starred by the court).

The lists above are not in fact exhaustive; the clerk of one of the Divisions should be consulted to determine which category a motion not listed falls into and what information and documentation is required.

DURATION OF MOTIONS.

23.2.18 Where the hearing of a motion is likely to last more than 20 minutes, the Keeper's office must be informed so that the Keeper can re-arrange other business, if necessary: Notice, 7th March 1990.

FEE.

23.2.19 The court fee for a motion will be payable. For fee, see Court of Session etc. Fees Order 1997, Table of Fees, Pt 1, B and C [S.I. 1997/688, as amended, pp. C1201 et seq.]. A party making a first appearance in a cause by enrolling a motion is liable to a fee under the 1997 Fees Order, Table of Fees, Pt 1, B, item 2 or C item 5. Certain persons are exempt from paying fees: see 1997 Order, art.5, substituted by S.S.I. 2002/270. A fee exempt certificate must be in existence in process and a fee exemption slip must be lodged certifying that there has been no change in circumstances since the certificate: see P.N. No.1 of 2002. Certain motions are exempt from fees: see Fees Order, art. 5A, inserted by S.S.I. 1999/755.

Where the party enrolling the motion is represented, the fee may be debited under the credit scheme introduced on 1st April by P.N. No.4 of 1976 to the account (if one is kept or permitted) of the party's agent by the court cashier, and an account will be rendered weekly by the court cashier's office to the agents for all court fees due that week for immediate settlement. Party litigants, and agents not operating the scheme, must pay (by cash, cheque or postal order) at the time of lodging at the counter of the appropriate department.

Intimation of motions

23.3 **23.3.—**[1](1) Subject to paragraph (2) and any other provision in these Rules, the party enrolling a motion in a cause where—

---

[1] R. 23.3 amended by S.S.I. 2009 No. 387 (effective 1st February 2010).

    (a)   appearance has been entered by a defender under rule 17.1(1),

    (b)   defences, a minute or answers have been lodged by a party, or

    (c)   provision is made for intimation of a motion to a party in accordance with this Part,

shall give written intimation of his intention to make such enrolment, and of the terms of the motion, to every such party.

    (2)   The requirement under paragraph (1) to give written intimation of a motion to a party shall not apply where that party—

    (a)   having entered appearance, fails to lodge defences within the period for lodging those defences;

    (b)   has not lodged answers within the period of notice for lodging those answers; or

    (c)   has withdrawn or is deemed to have withdrawn his defences, minute, note or answers, as the case may be.

    (3)   Such intimation shall be made so as to reach the other party not later than 12.30 p.m. on the day before enrolment, except where—

    (a)   the other party concerned in the motion consents to a shorter period of intimation;

    (b)   the period of intimation is otherwise provided in these Rules; or

    (c)   the court shortens or extends the period of intimation or dispenses with intimation.

    (4)   Where a motion is enrolled under rule 23.2 after the lapse of one year from the date of the last interlocutor in the cause, written intimation shall be given to every other party not less than 14 days before the date of enrolment.

    (5)   Where written intimation of a motion has been given under this rule, the party enrolling the motion shall state that this has been done on the motion in Form 23.2.

Deriv. R.C.S. 1965, r. 93(c) amended by S.I. 1980 No. 1144 (r. 23.3(1) and (3)), r. 93(b) (part) (r. 23.3(5)) and r. 105 (r. 23.3(4))

GENERAL NOTE.

    Intimation of a motion is not required by a pursuer of a motion made before calling of a summons or by a petitioner or noter before the interlocutor containing the first order is pronounced (for which see r. 23.8) unless expressly required by a rule. Provision is made in certain rules for intimation of a motion to a person who is not a party, e.g.: **23.3.1**

    r. 35.3, to haver, and Lord Advocate,

    r. 35.8(3), to person claiming confidentiality where confidential envelope to be opened in recovery of evidence,

    r. 49.39, to local authority of motion relating to child under care or supervision of that local authority,

    r. 49.62, to local authority where court considering committing care or supervision of child to local authority.

    Where intimation is required and has not been made the motion will be dropped by the court and will have to be re-enrolled after having been re-intimated as required under the relevant rule.

"WRITTEN INTIMATION".

    For methods, see r. 16.9. **23.3.2**

PERIOD OF INTIMATION.

    Where intimation is required, r. 23.3(3) provides that it must be made by 12.30 p.m. the day before enrolment unless (a) the other party consents, (b) the period is otherwise provided for or (c) the court shortens, extends or dispenses with the period. **23.3.3**

    For an experimental period from 25th November 1996, a motion should be intimated (subject to the exceptions in r. 23.3(3)) so that intimation reaches the other party not later than 12.30 p.m. two days before enrolment: P.N. No. 7 of 1996. The purpose of this is to enable a person opposing a motion to include in his notice of opposition a brief statement of the extent and bases of his opposition as required by that P.N.

Longer periods of intimation are required in the rules for some motions: see, e.g. a motion one year after the last interlocutor (r. 23.3(4)) and variation of certain orders in family actions (e.g. rr. 49.40(2), 49.41(2), 49.42(2), 49.43(2) and (5)). The court might shorten a period of intimation in, e.g. a motion to move arrested property (r. 13.11).

STATEMENT THAT WRITTEN INTIMATION GIVEN.

23.3.4   The date of intimation must now be inserted in Form 23.2. Where intimation is made to persons other than parties, this should be stated on Form 23.2.

WAKENING A CAUSE.

23.3.5   R.C.S. 1965, r. 105 (now R.C.S. 1994, r. 23.3(4)) superseded the former procedure for wakening a cause which had fallen asleep because no interlocutor had been pronounced within a year of the last interlocutor (for which see Maclaren on *Court of Session Practice*, p. 462). Where the address of another party is unknown application to dispense with intimation will have to be made under r. 23.3(3)(c). Where a party seeks to enrol a motion to interpone authority to a joint minute or to obtain decree in terms of a minute of tender and minute of acceptance (where these have been recently lodged), the court will look favourably on a motion to dispense with the requirement to give 14 days' intimation under r. 23.3(4).

Opposition to motions

23.4   **23.4.**—[1](1)   Where a party seeks to oppose a motion under rule 23.2, he shall—

(a)   not later than the day and time as the Lord President shall prescribe by direction for the lodging of notices of opposition to motions, lodge a notice of opposition in Form 23.4 at the appropriate department of the Office of Court during its normal office hours;

(b)   post a notice of opposition in Form 23.4 to the appropriate department of the Office of Court; or

(c)   send by facsimile transmission a notice of opposition in Form 23.4 to the appropriate department of the Office of Court.

(2)   Opposition to a motion sent by post or facsimile transmission under paragraph (1)(b) or (c) shall be treated as lodged when the notice of opposition is received in the appropriate department of the Office of Court.

(3)   On receipt of a notice of opposition lodged, sent by post or facsimile transmission under paragraph (1), a clerk of session shall attach the notice to the motion sheet.

(4)   A party who opposes a motion under this rule shall give written intimation of his opposition to every other party so as to reach such other party not later than 12.30 p.m. on the day on which the opposition is lodged or treated as lodged.

(5)   Where written intimation of opposition to a motion has been given under this rule, the party who has given such intimation shall state that this has been done on the notice of opposition in Form 23.4.

(6)   Where a motion is opposed under this rule, the entry in the rolls in respect of that motion shall be starred.

Deriv. R.C.S. 1965, r. 93(e) (part) (r. 23.4(1), (5) and (6)), and r. 93(e) (part) amended by S.I. 1980 No. 1144 (r. 23.4(4))

GENERAL NOTE.

23.4.1   If a motion is not timeously opposed and the motion is unstarred as not requiring appearance, the opportunity to oppose it may be lost. If an approach to the clerk of court is made before the Motion Roll is heard (and the interlocutor is signed), it may be possible to postpone the motion to the next (convenient) day, particularly if the opposition was eventually intimated (although out of time). If the motion is starred the opponent can ask leave of the court to be heard when the motion is heard on the Motion Roll; and this will usually be granted if there is no prejudice to the party who enrolled the motion. In either case the question of whether the opponent should pay expenses of the motion may arise.

DAY AND TIME FOR OPPOSITION TO MOTIONS PRESCRIBED BY DIRECTION.

23.4.2   The current direction is Direction No. 3 of 2009: see Directions, pp. C1501 et seq. The general rule is that a motion enrolled before 4pm on one weekday will be heard on the second sederunt day thereafter; and notice of opposition to a motion must be lodged by 12.30pm the weekday before the motion is due to

---

[1] R. 23.4 amended by S.S.I. 2009 No. 387 (effective 1st February 2010).

be heard in court: Direction No. 3 of 2009, para. 3. Where it is not possible for a motion to be heard in accordance with the timetable, the motion will be heard on a date and time convenient to the court and, where possible, the parties. Urgent motions will be dealt with on a priority basis. Where the motion is in an Inner House cause that may not be dealt with by a Lord Ordinary or the vacation judge and would be heard outwith a term or in vacation, it will be put out in the Single Bills on the earliest convenient day in the next term: Direction No. 3 of 2009. This Direction does not apply to motions by a pursuer before calling or a petitioner before the first order (r. 23.8), motions where a caveat is lodged (r. 23.9) or motions by a defender or others before calling (r. 23.10).

FORM 23.4.

Opposition to a motion must be in this form. The form is in three parts. In the case of a motion in a cause lodged in the General Department, all three parts must be completed where the motion is enrolled by post or fax; only Parts II and III (the latter being an opposition slip) need be completed where enrolment is by lodging in person. In the case of a cause lodged in the Petition Department, Parts I and II must be completed where the motion is enrolled by post or fax; only Part II need be completed where enrolment is by lodging in person (an opposition slip (Part III) is not required because, given the variety of petitions and the need for accuracy in the rolls of court, the clerks in the Petition Department have, historically, completed opposition slips and transmitted them to the Keeper of the Rolls for publication in the rolls). When a motion is opposed the opponent's agent's name is added (after a dash after the enroller's agent's name) to the entry in the Motion Roll and, if the entry was previously unstarred, an asterisk added at the beginning of the entry indicating that appearance is required at the hearing on the Motion Roll.

For the categories of cause lodged in the General Department, see r. 3.2 and notes. The causes lodged in the Petition Department are all petitions and notes in petition processes and certain references under statute (see note 3.3.1).

The expected duration of the hearing of the motion on the motion roll must be marked on the form: P.N. No. 4 of 1996.

For an experimental period from 25th November 1996, the notice of opposition in the form must include a brief statement of the extent and bases of opposition: P.N. No. 7 of 1996.

"WRITTEN INTIMATION".

For methods, see r. 16.9.

STATEMENT THAT WRITTEN INTIMATION GIVEN.

The date of intimation must now be inserted in Form 23.4.

"ROLLS".

The rolls are the lists of the business of the court issued by the Keeper of the Rolls.

"STARRED".

An asterisk is placed at the beginning of the entry in the rolls for the Motion Roll or Single Bills.

FEE.

There is currently no court fee for a party opposing a motion, except for opposition to a motion for variation of an order in a consistorial cause (for which see Court of Session etc. Fees Order 1997, Table of Fees, Pt. I, B, item 9 [S.I. 1997 No. 688, as amended, pp. C1201 et seq.]). A fee is payable for opposing a motion by a person other than an originating party making his first appearance in the process (for which see Court of Session etc. Fees Order 1997, Table of Fees, Pt. I, B, item 2 or 6, or C, item 5). A person making a first appearance in a process by enrolling a motion is liable to pay a court fee under the Court of Session etc. Fees Order 1984, Table of Fees, Pt. I, B, item 2 or C, item 5. Certain persons are exempt from payment of fees: see 1997 Fees Order, art.5, substituted by S.S.I. 2002 No. 270. A fee exemption certificate must be lodged in process: see P.N. No.1 of 2002.

Where a party is legally represented, the fee may be debited under the credit scheme introduced on 1st April 1976 by P.N. No. 4 of 1976 to the account (if one is kept or permitted) of the defender's agent by the court cashier, and an account will be rendered weekly by the court cashier's office to agents for all court fees due that week for immediate settlement. Party litigants, and agents not operating the scheme, must pay (by cash, cheque or postal order) at the time of lodging at the counter at the appropriate department.

23.4.3

23.4.4

23.4.5

23.4.6

23.4.7

23.4.8

Consent to motions

23.5.[1] Where a party seeks to consent to a motion enrolled under rule 23.2, he may—

    (a)   endorse the motion with his consent;

    (b)   post a notice of consent in Form 23.5 to the appropriate department of the Office of Court; or

23.5

---

[1] R. 23.5 amended by S.S.I. 2009 No. 387 (effective 1st February 2010).

(c)   send by facsimile transmission a notice of consent in Form 23.5 to the appropriate department of the Office of Court.

GENERAL NOTE.

23.5.1   This is a new rule required to facilitate consent to motions by post or fax.

Hearing of motions

23.6   **23.6.**—¹(1)   Subject to the rules mentioned in paragraph (2), the day of publication on the walls of the court and of the hearing of a motion enrolled under this Part on any day shall be determined in accordance with such provisions as the Lord President shall prescribe by direction.

(2)²   The rules referred to in paragraph (1) are:

rule 23.7 (motions in vacation),

rule 23.8 (motions by pursuer before calling or petitioner before first order),

rule 23.9 (motions where caveat lodged),

rule 23.10 (motions by defender or other person before calling).

(3)   A motion enrolled in a cause in the Outer House shall be heard by the Lord Ordinary.

(4)   A motion enrolled in a cause in the Inner House shall be heard in the Single Bills by a Division of the Inner House.

Deriv. R.C.S. 1965, r. 93(d) (part) (r. 23.6(1))

GENERAL NOTE.

23.6.1   Paragraphs (3) and (4) of r. 23.6 are new provisions. A motion heard by the Lord Ordinary is not always heard in the Motion Roll: i.e. motions before calling in actions and motions before first order in petitions, and certain motions on the Diet Roll in actions under the optional procedure for actions of damages.

DAY OF PUBLICATION AND HEARING OF MOTIONS PRESCRIBED BY DIRECTION.

23.6.2   The current Direction is Direction No. 3 of 2009: see Directions, pp. C1501 et seq. The general rule is that a motion enrolled before 4pm on one weekday will be heard on the second sederunt day thereafter: Direction No. 3 of 2009, para. 3.

The Direction does not apply to rr. 23.8, 23.9 and 23.10: see those rules and Direction No. 3 of 2009, para. 2.

"PUBLICATION ON THE WALLS OF THE COURT".

23.6.3   Motions in the Single Bills and the Motion Roll are published in the rolls and on the noticeboard outside the First Division courtroom (Court 1) under the courtroom and Division or Lord Ordinary before whom they are to be dealt with (if unstarred) or heard (if starred).

MOTIONS IN COURT OR IN CHAMBERS.

23.6.4   Motions are usually heard in open court. A motion may be heard in chambers in certain instances particularly where a cause has not yet called. Motions for interim interdict are sometimes heard in chambers for convenience, though the press and public are not excluded. Motions to shorten a period of notice before calling of an action or first order in petition (for which an agent has a right of audience: r. 23.14(1)) are always dealt with in chambers in term; in vacation they have been dealt with in the vacation court. Motions in proceedings under the Adoption (Scotland) Act 1978, the Solicitors (Scotland) Act 1980 and the Human Fertilisation and Embryology Act 1990 are always dealt with in chambers.

URGENT MOTIONS OUTWITH COURT OR OFFICE HOURS.

23.6.4A   The arrangements for urgent business when the offices are closed are as follows. Telephone the Court of Session (0131-225 2595). The telephone is manned at all times. On telephoning, leave a contact number. The security staff will contact a clerk who will contact you and make the necessary arrangements. At weekends in session there is a rota for stand-by judges. In vacation the vacation judge is the stand-by judge.

HEARING OF MOTIONS.

23.6.5   P.N. No. 4 of 1996 provides:—

1.   Starred motions requiring no more than 10 minutes. A Lord Ordinary naming substantive busi-

---

¹ R. 23.6 amended by S.S.I. 2009 No. 387 (effective 1st February 2010).
² R. 23.6(2) amended by S.S.I. 2017 No. 414 r. 3(3) (effective 1st January 2018).

ness (e.g. a proof) may be allocated no more than three such motions. Allowance will be made for such other number of starred motions or other interlocutory business as can be accommodated up to 10.30am.

2.   Other starred motions and those likely to take more than 10 minutes. These will be assigned to a Lord Ordinary assigned to the motion roll for that day. Such motions will be published in the rolls in groups allocated to a specific half-hour period between 10am and 1pm; those remaining will be published for disposal not before 2pm. Motions will be heard in the order printed in the rolls which the court otherwise allows.

The former provision was that where the hearing of a motion is likely to last more than 20 minutes, the Keeper's office must be informed so that the Keeper can re-arrange other business, if necessary: Notice, 7th March 1990. This notice has not, for some reason, been revoked, although it is obviously superseded by P.N. No. 4 of 1996.

MOTIONS IN COMMERCIAL ACTIONS AND CERTAIN INSOLVENCY AND COMPANY CAUSES.

Direction No. 3 of 2010 makes special provision for the date and time of the hearing of motions in commercial actions (defined in r. 47.1(2)), proceedings in the Outer House in a cause under the Insolvency Act 1986 or the Company Directors Disqualification Act 1986, and s.896 (holding a meeting) and s.899 (sanction of compromise or arrangement) of the Companies Act 2006. **23.6.5A**

Any opposed motion, or a motion requiring explanation, will be put out for a hearing at a date and time convenient to the court and, where possible, to the parties. Where a motion is opposed or otherwise starred (see notes 23.2.14 and 23.2.16), the clerk of court will fix a date for the hearing and give intimation of that date to the parties. Urgent motions will be dealt with on a priority basis.

FEE.

The court fee for a hearing of a motion on the Motion Roll or Single Bills is payable by each party for every 30 minutes or part thereof after the first 30 minutes. For fee, see Court of Session etc. Fees Order 1997, Table of Fees, Pt 1, B, item 21 or 22 [S.I. 1997 No. 688, as amended, pp. C1201 et seq.]. A motion heard out of hours (i.e. after 4.30pm and before 8.30am unless parties were ready to proceed before 4.30pm) is subject to a higher fee: Table of Fees, Pt. I, B, item 24 or C, item 23. Certain persons are exempt from payment of fees: see 1997 Fees Order, art.5 substituted by S.S.I. 2002 No. 270. A fee exemption certificate must be lodged in process: see P.N. No. 1 of 2002. **23.6.6**

Where a party is legally represented, the fee may be debited under a credit scheme introduced on 1st April 1976 by P.N. No. 4 of 1976 to the account (if one is kept or permitted) of the agent by the court cashier, and an account will be rendered weekly by the court cashier's office to the agent for all court fees due that week for immediate settlement. An agent not on the credit scheme will have an account opened for the purpose of lodging the fee: P.N. No. 2 of 1995.

A party litigant must pay (by cash, cheque or postal order) to the clerk at the end of the hearing or, if the hearing lasts more than a day, at the end of each day: P.N. No. 2 of 1995.

Part 4[1] – General provision relating to motions

Motions in vacation

23.7.—[2](1)   A motion which is to be heard by the Lord Ordinary in vacation by the vacation judge, shall not appear in the rolls. **23.7**

(2)   A party enrolling such a motion shall be informed at the time of enrolment whether or not any appearance is required.

(3)   Any such motion which is opposed in accordance with rule 23.4 shall require appearance for the party whose motion it is.

(4)   On the afternoon of the day preceding each sitting of the vacation judge there shall be published on the walls of the court a list of unopposed motions for which appearance is required followed by a list of opposed motions, each in alphabetic order.

(5)   Motions before the vacation judge shall be called for hearing in the order in which they appear in the list published under paragraph (4).

Deriv. P.N. 31st March 1970

GENERAL NOTE.

Motions before the Lord Ordinary in session outwith a term will be subject to the same procedure as motions in vacation. **23.7.1**

---

[1] Chap. 23 Pt 4 heading inserted by S.S.I. 2009 No. 387 (effective 1st February 2010).
[2] R. 23.7 amended by S.S.I. 2017 No. 414 r. 3(4) (effective 1st January 2018).

The vacation court normally sits at 10.30am, or as soon as possible thereafter, on Tuesdays to Fridays (except on public or local holidays or on a Tuesday where Monday is a public or local holiday). During the Winter (Christmas) vacation there may be only two vacation court days.Business is normally conducted in open court but may be conducted in chambers or in private. The days on which the vacation court sits are published in the rolls about four weeks before the end of the preceding term. The vacation court sits on such days and at such times as may be convenient or necessary subject to any direction of the Lord President: r. 10.5(2).

More than one judge may sit as a vacation judge if pressure of business requires it.

"ROLLS".

23.7.2   The rolls are the lists of the business of the court issued by the Keeper of the Rolls.Motions in session outwith a term or in vacation are not published in the rolls, but they are displayed on the walls of the court: r. 23.7(4).

"APPEARANCE".

23.7.3   Appearance in vacation may be by a party litigant, counsel or other person having a right of audience. A solicitor also has a right of audience before the vacation judge: C.S.A. 1988, s.48(2)(a) (substituted by the Law Reform (Miscellaneous Provisions) (Scotland) Act 1990, Sch.8, para.38).

For the meaning of party litigant, see note 4.2.6. For definitions of "counsel" and "other person having a right of audience", see r. 1.3(1).

Motions by pursuer before calling or petitioner before first order

23.8   **23.8.**—(1)   A motion enrolled by a pursuer in an action before the calling of the summons or by a petitioner before an order under rule 14.5(1)(a) (order for intimation, service and advertisement in petitions) has been made—

(a)   shall, subject to any other provision in these Rules, be brought as soon as reasonably practicable by the Keeper of the Rolls, or a clerk of session instructed by him, before the Lord Ordinary sitting in court or in chambers; and

(b)   shall not require to be published in the rolls.

(2)   On enrolling such a motion, the pursuer or petitioner, as the case may be, shall be informed whether or not appearance is required.

GENERAL NOTE.

23.8.1   A motion made under this rule is made before the calling of a summons (and before the defender is able to enter appearance) or before a respondent has been served with a petition. Accordingly, neither the defender nor the respondent has a right to appear and, if the pursuer or petitioner is seeking protective measures such as arrestment, inhibition or interdict, should not have prior warning of the motion unless (where competent) he has lodged a caveat: see r. 5.1.

"SUBJECT TO ANY OTHER PROVISION IN THESE RULES".

23.8.2   R. 23.8(1)(a) is subject to r. 23.9 under which the caveator has the right to appear.

"SITTING IN COURT OR IN CHAMBERS".

23.8.3   Motions are usually heard in open court. A motion may be heard in chambers in certain instances particularly where a cause has not yet called. Motions for interim interdict are sometimes heard in chambers for convenience, though the press and public are not excluded. Motions to shorten a period of notice before calling of an action or first order in petition (for which an agent has a right of audience: r. 23.14(1)) are always dealt with in chambers in term; in vacation they have been dealt with in the vacation court. Motions in proceedings under the Adoption (Scotland) Act 1978, the Solicitors (Scotland) Act 1980 and the Human Fertilisation and Embryology Act 1990 are always dealt with in chambers.

"ROLLS".

23.8.4   The rolls are the lists of the business of the court issued by the Keeper of the Rolls.

"APPEARANCE".

23.8.5   Appearance may be by a party litigant, counsel or other person having a right of audience. A solicitor also has a right of audience in such a motion: r. 23.14.

For the meaning of party litigant, see note 4.2.6. For definitions of "counsel" and "other person having a right of audience", see r. 1.3(1).

Motions where caveat lodged

23.9   **23.9.**   Where a motion in respect of which a caveat has been lodged is enrolled, the Keeper of the Rolls shall—

   (a)   fix a hearing of the motion before the Lord Ordinary sitting in court or in chambers as soon as reasonably practicable; and

   (b)   inform the parties concerned of the date and time of the hearing.

Deriv. R.C.S. 1965, r. 79(1) (part) and (2), and r. 236(b) amended by S.I. 1984 No. 499

GENERAL NOTE.

When a motion is enrolled in a cause ex parte for an order against which a caveat may be lodged the clerk of session in the General or Petition Department, as the case may be, checks the register of caveats to see if a caveat has been lodged. If a caveat has been lodged he informs the Keeper of the Rolls who arranges a hearing of the motion (day or night) at a time when both parties can attend. Where the motion is enrolled by a pursuer before the calling of the summons or by a petitioner before the granting of the first order, r. 23.8 will apply.

   23.9.1

If the duty clerk of session has to be contacted after 5pm, ring the Court of Session (031-225 2595), leave your name and telephone number, and the duty security guard will contact a clerk who will contact you.

For the orders against which a caveat may be lodged, see r. 5.1. For the form and lodging of caveats, see r. 5.2.

"CAVEAT".

A caveat is a document lodged in the Petition Department (r. 5.2(1)) by a person to ensure that certain orders may not be made against him without his receiving intimation of the application for the order and having an opportunity to be heard before the order may be made.

   23.9.2

"SITTING IN COURT OR IN CHAMBERS".

Motions are usually heard in open court. A motion may be heard in chambers in certain instances particularly where a cause has not yet called. Motions for interim interdict are sometimes heard in chambers for convenience, though the press and public are not excluded. Motions to shorten a period of notice before calling of an action or first order in petition (for which an agent has a right of audience: r. 23.14(1)) are always dealt with in chambers in term; in vacation they have been dealt with in the vacation court. Motions in proceedings under the Adoption (Scotland) Act 1978, the Solicitors (Scotland) Act 1980 and the Human Fertilisation and Embryology Act 1990 are always dealt with in chambers.

   23.9.3

Motions by defender or other person before calling

23.10.—(1)[1] A motion, enrolled in an action before the calling of the summons by a person other than the pursuer shall be intimated forthwith by the Deputy Principal Clerk to the pursuer.

   23.10

  (2) The Keeper of the Rolls shall—

   (a)   fix a hearing of such a motion before the Lord Ordinary sitting in court or in chambers as soon as reasonably practicable; and

   (b)   inform the parties concerned of the date and time of the hearing.

GENERAL NOTE.

This is a new rule. This rule might apply, e.g. where a defender or a person having an interest applies for recall etc. of arrestment or inhibition under r. 13.10 or for warrant to move arrested property under r. 13.11.

   23.10.1

"SITTING IN COURT OR IN CHAMBERS".

Motions are usually heard in open court. A motion may be heard in chambers in certain instances particularly where a cause has not yet called. Motions for interim interdict are sometimes heard in chambers for convenience, though the press and public are not excluded. Motions to shorten a period of notice before calling of an action (for which an agent has a right of audience: r. 23.14(1)) are always dealt with in chambers in term; in vacation they have been dealt with in the vacation court. Motions in proceedings under the Adoption (Scotland) Act 1978, the Solicitors (Scotland) Act 1980 and the Human Fertilisation and Embryology Act 1990 are always dealt with in chambers.

   23.10.2

Statutory applications by motion

23.11. Unless otherwise provided in these Rules or any other enactment, an application to the court under any other enactment in a cause depending before the court shall be made by motion.

   23.11

---

[1] R. 23.10(1) amended by S.I. 1994 No. 2901 (clerical error).

23.11.1   This is a new rule. Unless the Rules or any other enactment provide that an application to the court under an enactment (statute or statutory instrument) is to be by other means in a depending cause, it may be by motion.

A recent example would be an application under s.4(2) of the Requirements of Writing (Scotland) Act 1995 (endorsation or decree that document dated or signed at place on date on, or place at, which it bears so to be). The court might, if the motion were opposed and if the question raised were not straightforward, order the issue to be dealt with by minute and answers.

"DEPENDING".

23.11.2   A cause is depending from the time it is commenced (i.e. from the time an action is served or a first order in a petition is made) until final decree, whereas a cause is in dependence until final extract. For the meaning of commenced, see note 13.4.4 (action) or 14.6.1 (petition). For the meaning of final decree, see note 4.15.2(2). For the meaning of final extract, see note 7.1.2(2).

Expenses of motions

23.12   **23.12.**   Where a motion is called for hearing in the Motion Roll or Single Bills and is dropped, the Auditor shall, in taxing any expenses found due to the party on whose behalf the motion was enrolled, disallow the expenses occasioned by the motion unless he is satisfied that the motion was properly enrolled and properly dropped.

Deriv. R.C.S. 1965, r. 93(f)

EXPENSES OF MOTIONS.

23.12.1   Often no motion is made for expenses of a motion and the court makes no finding. In an opposed motion, a motion for expenses may well be made by the successful party. It had been thought that there should be a rule that, if expenses are not otherwise dealt with at the time of the motion, expenses are in the cause (i.e. whoever is ultimately successful in the cause and subsequently obtains a general order for the expenses of the cause gets the expenses of such a motion: *Glasgow and South-Western Railway Co. v. Magistrates of Ayr* 1911 S.C. 298) unless the court otherwise orders.

The problem with such a rule is that a motion might have to be opposed in order simply to ensure that expenses of a motion which the mover of the motion ought to pay (e.g. the allowance of a minute of amendment) are not "in the cause". The proposal has not been followed. The Auditor has no discretion where the court makes a finding of expenses in the cause: see note 42.5.2. But he does have a discretion where there is a general finding of expenses (usually at the end of a cause) to disallow a party so entitled to expenses on a matter on which he was in fact unsuccessful or he incurred expenses through his own fault: see r. 42.5(2). This discretion sufficiently covers the situation where no particular finding for expenses in respect of a motion has been made.

"PROPERLY ENROLLED AND PROPERLY DROPPED".

23.12.2   A motion which it was right to enrol but dropped because its purpose was satisfied without the court having to adjudicate on the matter is one which the Auditor will allow the expenses for.

Conditions attached to granting of motions

23.13   **23.13.**   Where the court grants a motion in whole or in part, it may do so subject to such conditions, if any, as to expenses or otherwise as it thinks fit.

GENERAL NOTE.

23.13.1   This is a new rule which states what the court may always do.

CONDITIONS AS TO EXPENSES OR OTHERWISE.

23.13.2   Apart from being found liable in expenses on losing a motion, a party might be ordered to pay expenses as a condition of being allowed to proceed with a cause. This may arise where there has been a failure or delay such that, although it is in the interests of justice that the case proceeds, it is just and equitable that the opponent should be paid before the cause proceeds: see *Colbron v. United Glass Ltd* 1965 S.L.T. 366; *McGregor v. Rooney* , 5th February 1971, Outer House, unreported; *Masinimport v. Scottish Mechanical Light Industries Ltd* , 15th May 1973, unreported. Other conditions might be caution or consignation. On caution, see note 33.1.2. On consignation, see note 33.4.3.

Appearance by solicitor for certain motions

23.14   **23.14.**—(1)   A solicitor shall have a right of audience before the court in respect of a motion which is heard in chambers under any of the following rules—

rule 23.8 (motions by pursuer before calling or petitioner before first order),

rule 23.9 (motions where caveat lodged),

rule 23.10 (motions by defender or other person before calling).

(2) *[R. 23.14(2) revoked by S.S.I. 2017 No. 414 r. 3(5) (effective 1st January 2018).]*

GENERAL NOTE.

This rule is made under s.48(2)(b) of the C.S.A. 1988 and in relation to r. 23.14(1) confirms the current practice. R. 23.14(2) provides for the right of audience of a solicitor before the Lord Ordinary in session outwith a term (a provision introduced by r. 10.4). The right of a solicitor to appear before the vacation judge is provided by s.48(2)(a) of the C.S.A. 1988 (substituted by the Law Reform (Miscellaneous Provisions) (Scotland) Act 1990, Sched.8, para. 38).

23.14.1

Starred motions

23.15.[1] Where appearance for the party who enrolled the motion is required for a motion, the entry in the rolls in respect of that motion shall be starred.

23.15

GENERAL NOTE.

For the starring of motions, and starred and unstarred motions, see notes 23.2.14, 23.2.16, and 23.2.17 (Inner House).

23.15.1

---

[1] R. 23.15 inserted by S.S.I. 2009 No. 387 (effective 1st February 2010).

CHAPTER 24 AMENDMENT OF PLEADINGS

Powers of court

24.1.—(1) In any cause the court may, at any time before final judgment, allow an amendment mentioned in paragraph (2).

(2) Paragraph (1) applies to the following amendments—

    (a) an amendment of a principal writ which may be necessary for the purpose of determining the real question in controversy between the parties, notwithstanding that in consequence of such amendment—

        (i) the sum sued for in a summons is increased or restricted; or

        (ii) a different remedy from that originally concluded for or craved is sought;

    (b) an amendment which may be necessary—

        (i) to correct or supplement the designation of a party to the cause;

        (ii) to enable a party who has sued or has been sued in his own right to sue or be sued in a representative capacity;

        (iii) to enable a party who has sued or has been sued in a representative capacity to sue or be sued in his own right or in a different representative capacity;

        (iv) to add the name of an additional pursuer, a petitioner or person whose concurrence is necessary;

        (v) where the cause has been commenced or presented in the name of the wrong person, or it is doubtful whether it has been commenced or presented in the name of the right person, to allow any other person to be sisted in substitution for, or in addition to, the original person; or

        (vi) to direct conclusions against a third party brought into an action under Chapter 26 (third party procedure);

    (c) an amendment of a condescendence, defences, answers, pleas-in-law or other pleadings which may be necessary for determining the real question in controversy between the parties; and

    (d) where it appears that all parties having an interest have not been called or that the cause has been directed against the wrong person, an amendment inserting in the instance of the principal writ an additional or substitute party and directing existing or additional conclusions or craves, averments and pleas-in-law against that party.

Deriv. R.C.S. 1965, r. 92(1) and (3) amended by SI 1967/1789

GENERAL NOTE.

The statutory origins of this Chapter are ss.20 and 29 of the C.S.A. 1868 (repealed by the C.S.A. 1988, Sched.2). Alteration of the instance of a cause or the conclusions of a summons must always be by amendment under this rule. Alteration of any other pleadings (including the prayer of a petition) may be (a) during any adjustment period allowed by the court, by adjustment without permission of the court; and (b) at any other time, by amendment under this rule.

A wide reading should be given to the terms of the rule: *Rackstraw v. Douglas* 1919 S.C. 354, 357 per L.J.-C. Scott Dickson.

Amendment is in the discretion of the court, and in exercising it the court will consider delay in seeking the amendment, any prejudice to another party, the stage at which the amendment is sought to be made and any conditions which might be imposed for allowing the amendment. In deciding whether to allow an amendment the court seeks to do justice to all the parties: see *Dryburgh v. National Coal Board* 1962 S.C. 485, 492 per Lord Guthrie. In *Link Housing Association Ltd v. Gray Aitken Partnership Ltd (erroneously cited as Gray Aitken Partnership Ltd v. Link Housing Association Ltd)* , 2007 S.C. 294, 302 para. [19] per LP Hamilton, it was held that delay will not of itself justify refusal of amendment; there must be prejudice or some other material disadvantage to the other party. It is not just to dismiss an action because of a formal pleading defect which can be put right without prejudice to the other party: *G.U.S. Property Management Ltd v. Littlewoods Mail Order Stores Ltd* 1982 S.C.(H.L.) 157, 178 per Lord Keith of Kinkel.

The court will not amend a party's pleadings at its own instance: *Lord Advocate v. Johnston* 1983 S.L.T. 290.

Amendment is a question of discretion and not competency: *Thomson v. Glasgow Corporation* 1962 S.C.(H.L.) 36; and see note 24.1.2. Accordingly, the competency of the original cause is simply one of the factors to be taken into account in exercising the discretion: *Shanks v. Central R.C.* 1988 S.L.T. 212.

The general rule is that an interlocutor of a Lord Ordinary is final (s.18 of the 1988 Act), and a Lord Ordinary cannot alter the substance of an interlocutor refusing a minute of amendment by subsequently allowing a minute of amendment in substantially the same terms even on a material change of circumstances: *Henderson v. Greater Glasgow Health Board*, 2014 S.C. 681 (extra Div) approving *Bremner v. Martin t/a George Martin Engineering* , 2006 S.L.T. 169 (OH).

AMENDMENT AFTER EXPIRY OF TIME-LIMIT.

24.1.2
"The court will not, in general, allow a pursuer by amendment to substitute the right defender for the wrong defender, or to cure a radical incompetence in his action, or to change the basis of his case if he only seeks to make such amendments after the expiry of a time limit which would have prevented him at that stage from raising fresh proceedings": *Pompa's Trs. v. Magistrates of Edinburgh* 1942 S.C. 119, 125 per L.J.-C. Cooper. This is a question of discretion not of competency: *O'Hara's Exx. v. Western Heritable Investment Co. Ltd* 1965 S.C. 97, 104 per L.J.-C. Grant; *Hynd v. West Fife Cooperative Ltd* 1980 S.L.T. 41, 42; *Sellars v. IMI Yorkshire Imperial Ltd* 1986 S.L.T. 629. In *Perth and Kinross Council v. Scottish Water Ltd*, 2015 S.L.T. 788 (OH), upheld 2017 S.C. 164 (Extra Div.) it was held that when an amendment is proposed after a time-limit has expired the court must consider the substance rather than the mere form of the amendment and consider whether any of the criteria stated by Lord Cooper in *Pompa's Trs*, applies: the substitution of an entirely different defender, or the curing of a radical and fundamental incompetence, or a change in the basis of the case.

In respect of the discretionary power to allow an action of reparation for, or in respect of death from, personal injuries to be raised out with the triennium under s.19A of the Prescription and Limitation (Scotland) Act 1973 (inserted by the Law Reform (Miscellaneous Provisions) (Scotland) Act 1980, s.23 and amended by the Prescription and Limitation (Scotland) Act 1984, Sched. 1, para. 8), the question of amendment ought to be simply one of discretion in such cases. The notion that the question may have been one of competency might have been because of the unfortunate, if not erroneous, use of the word "competency" in R.C.S. 1965, r. 92 and its predecessors and the historical test of competency of amendment by reference to the competency of raising a supplementary summons: see *Mackie v. Glasgow Corporation* 1924 S.L.T. 510.

Changing the method of formulating the case is not changing the basis or substance of it: *McPhail v. Lanarkshire C.C.* 1951 S.C. 301. The introduction of a new ground will not be excluded where the case remains about the same accident and danger: *Hynd*, above, at p. 43.

The time for considering whether such an amendment should be allowed is at a hearing of the motion to allow the pleadings to be amended in terms of the minute of amendment: *Greenhorn v. J. Smart & Co. (Contractors) Ltd* 1979 S.C. 427, 432. It may be possible to consider it at the motion to allow the minute of amendment to be received: *Sellars*, above, at p. 638A per Lord Dunpark. It is too late to challenge an amendment on the basis of time-bar or prescription once the amendment has been allowed (and the record amended), unless the interlocutor is timeously reclaimed: *Jones v. Lanarkshire Health Board* 1991 S.C. 285.

The *punctum temporis* when the case commenced for considering a new case introduced by amendment is the date when the minute of amendment is lodged and the motion to allow it to be received is intimated and enroled: *Boyle v. Glasgow Corporation* 1975 S.C. 238; but not the date of the interlocutor allowing the amendment: see *Boyle v. Glasgow Corporation* 1973 S.L.T.(Notes) 42 per Lord Dunpark; *Morrison v. Scotstoun Marine Ltd* 1979 S.L.T.(Notes) 76 per Lord Ross.

Where a time-bar plea has been included in the answers to a minute but the exclusion of the amendment has been rejected, the plea should not be printed in the amended closed record: *Gibson v. Droopy & Browns Ltd* 1989 S.L.T. 172.

So long as an action to enforce an obligation is in court a "relevant claim" is being made and the prescriptive period under s.6 of the Prescription and Limitation (Scotland) Act 1973 recommences when the action is dismissed or abandoned. Hence, where a claim in a counterclaim was deleted a relevant claim was being made until the claim was deleted, the new prescriptive period ran from the time the claim was deleted and an amendment to re-introduce the claim after five years after the original counterclaim but within one year after its deletion was made within the new prescriptive period and the claim had not prescribed; in other words, an amendment deleting a ground of claim in a pending action will trigger the running of a fresh prescriptive period for that ground of claim and allow that ground to be re-introduced by a further amendment: *G. A. Estates Ltd v. Caviapen Trs. Ltd (No. 2)* 1993 S.L.T. 1045, 1049 per Lord Coulsfield; *G. A. Estates Ltd v. Caviapen Trs. Ltd* 1993 S.L.T. 1051, 1059 per Lord McCluskey, 1061 per Lord Weir, 1065 per Lord Penrose. Where an alternative case added by amendment is based on the same obligation or is fundamentally the same as the primary case timeously pled, a party will not be prevented from pursuing it because it was added after expiry of the quinquennial prescription under s.6 of the 1973 Act: *Devos Gebroeder, N.V. v. Sunderland Sportswear Ltd* 1990 S.L.T. 473; *Safdar v. Devlin* 1995 S.L.T. 530. It should be averred that the onus of proof of the negative presumptions falls on the party alleging the affirmative: *Strathclyde R.C. v. W.A. Eairhurst and Partners* 1997 S.L.T. 658.

The words "induced to refrain" in s.6(4) of the 1973 Act include not only a conscious act of self-restraint but also doing nothing to enforce the obligation because it is being concealed: *BP Exploration Operating Co Ltd v. Chevron Shipping Co.* , 2002 S.C. (H.L.) 19.

1. Amendment at or before procedure roll will generally be allowed unless there is prejudice or delay. At procedure roll the party amending, if he does not lodge a minute of amendment at the time, ought (and should be required) to indicate what the amendment will be, for he should not have the opportunity to amend if amendment could not cure a defect or assist his case. Any such indication may be sought to be noted by the clerk of court in the Minute of Proceedings.

24.1.3

2. Amendment may be allowed when issues have, or a proof has, been allowed; *McKenna v. British Transport Commission* 1960 S.L.T.(Notes) 30; cf. *McFarquhar v. British Railways Board* 1976 S.L.T.(Notes) 102 and *Muldoon v. Carntyne Steel Castings Co. Ltd* 1965 S.L.T.(Notes) 63.

3. Amendment near to the date of the proof (or trial) may be refused as too late if it would involve the discharge of the diet or the investigation by an opponent of a new case: *Dryburgh v. National Coal Board* 1962 S.C. 485; cf. *Doig v. Randsgrove Ltd* 1980 S.L.T.(Notes) 16 (new matter could not have been reasonably ascertained earlier); *Jones v. McDermott (Scotland)* 1986 S.L.T. 551 (new case on same facts); cf. *Cork v. Greater Glasgow Health Board* 1997 S.L.T. 404 (proof discharged when amendment allowed but motion to amend record made six months later; motion refused because defender prejudiced and second proof diet would have to be discharged), but overruled on reclaiming motion reported at 1997 S.L.T. 740.

4. Amendment may be allowed during the proof or trial, and ought to be made as soon as the difficulty arises: *Lawrence v. Arrol* 1958 S.C. 348, 352 per L.P. Cooper (proof); *Rafferty v. Weir Housing Corporation Ltd* 1966 S.L.T.(Notes) 23 (jury trial); *Cameron v. Lanarkshire Health Board* 1997 S.L.T. 1040 (jury trial). The overriding consideration is fairness and the interests of justice: *Chapman v. James Dickie & Co. (Drop Forging) Ltd* 1985 S.L.T. 380 (amendment refused); cf. *Campbell v. Cordale Investment Ltd* 1985 S.L.T. 305 (amendment allowed). An adverse circumstance to allowing an amendment is where the facts were or should have been known to the party beforehand: *Thomson v. Glasgow Corporation* 1962 S.C.(H.L.) 36, 57 per Lord Macintosh. In such a case the diet may have to be discharged or witnesses recalled: see *Campbell*, above.

   Where distinct grounds of action emerge during a proof which are not raised in the pleadings, the new grounds cannot be made the basis of decision unless the appropriate amendment is made: *Black v. John Williams & Co. (Wishaw) Ltd* 1924 S.C.(H.L.) 22; *"Vitruvia" SS Co. Ltd v. Ropner Shipping Co. Ltd* 1924 S.C.(H.L.) 31; both explained in *Gunn v. John McAdam & Son Ltd* 1949 S.C. 31, 39 per L.P. Cooper. The modern rule would appear to be that where no objection is taken to evidence led introducing a new ground of action for which there is no record, amendment may not be required: *McGlone v. British Railways Board Ltd* 1966 S.C.(H.L.) 1.

   Amendment is not necessary if what is proved in evidence is merely a "variation, modification or development" of what is pled; but it is necessary if what is pled is "new, separate and distinct": *Burns v. Dixon's Iron Works Ltd* 1961 S.C. 102, 107 per L.J.-C. Thomson; see also *Cleisham v. British Transport Commission* 1964 S.C.(H.L.) 8; *O'Hanlon v. John G. Stein & Co. Ltd* 1965 S.C.(H.L.) 23, 42 per Lord Guest; *Hamilton v. John Brown & Co. (Clydebank) Ltd* 1969 S.L.T.(Notes) 19; *McIntosh v. Walker Steam Trawl Fishing Co. Ltd* 1971 S.L.T.(Notes) 75; *McCusker v. Saveheat Cavity Wall Insulation* 1987 S.L.T. 24. See also *McCluskey v. Wallace* 1998 S.C. 711 (submission of joint fault, where sole fault averred and defender pled "caused or at least materially contributed to by the fault on the part of the said child" and had a plea of contributory negligence, allowed; use of the word "*esto*" was unnecessary).

5. Amendment may be allowed before judgment itself. It may be refused on the grounds of prejudice and injustice: *Oswald v. Fairs* 1911 S.C. 257 (completely new defence raised in hearing on evidence); *McLean v. Victoria Spinning Co. Ltd* 1971 S.L.T.(Notes) 10 (lack of notice in hearing on evidence of evidence of earnings lower than they would have been before accident).

6. Amendment may be allowed on, during or after reclaiming or an appeal. This is common after debate but uncommon after evidence has been led. In the former case, if allowed the Inner House may refuse to hear argument until the judge at first instance has reconsidered the amended pleadings and the case will be remitted for that purpose: *Wallace v. Scottish Special Housing Association* 1981 S.L.T.(Notes) 60; and see r. 38.21. In the latter case, amendment to raise fresh issues of fact may not be allowed because it could unjustly prejudice the other party who might have conducted his case differently: *Thomson v. Glasgow Corporation* 1962 S.C.(H.L.) 36; *McGuffie v. Forth Valley Health Board* 1991 S.L.T. 231; cf. *Johnston v. Johnston* (1903) 5 F. 659 (allowed to aver facts not known at time of proof (*res noviter*)); *Moyes v. Burntisland Shipping Co.* 1952 S.C. 429 (allowed in exceptional circumstances to clarify existing controversy not a new one). For an example of amendment in the House of Lords, see *CIN Properties Ltd v. Dollar Land (Cumbernauld) Ltd* 1992 S.C.(H.L.) 104 (amendment to cover point not argued below allowed; no reasons given).

7. "Final judgment" means a decree which can no longer be appealed: i.e. the reclaiming days have expired without a reclaiming motion having been enrolled or, a reclaiming motion having been determined, the period within which appeal to the House of Lords has expired (three months: H.L. Directions, Direction 8.1) without an appeal or where an appeal has been made and finally determined there.

"NECESSARY FOR ... DETERMINING THE REAL QUESTION IN CONTROVERSY".

24.1.4   Where the amendment is to the conclusions, condescendence, or pleas-in-law, it must be necessary for the purpose of determining the real question in controversy between the parties: see, e.g. *Moyes v. Burntisland Shipbuilding Co.* 1952 S.C. 429 (allowed exceptionally after jury trial to clarify existing controversy). The amendment may include the introduction or elaboration of a new basis of action even if it is made after expiry of a limitation period: *O'Hara's Exx. v. Western Heritable Investment Co. Ltd* 1965 S.C. 97. Nothing in the dictum of L.J.-C. Cooper in *Pompa's Trs. v. Magistrates of Edinburgh* 1942 S.C. 119, 125 was intended to restrict the scope of what is now r. 24.1. The dictum had been interpreted erroneously, to suggest that the introduction of a new basis of action against an existing defender was incompetent: *Dryburgh v. National Coal Board* 1962 S.C. 485 and *O'Hara's Exx.* above. It is now clear that the court has complete discretion to consider an amendment to change the basis of a pursuer's case against an existing defender notwithstanding that it is made after the expiry of any limitation period: *Hynd v. West Fife Cooperative Ltd* 1980 S.L.T. 41, 42 and *Sellars v. I.M.I. Yorkshire Imperial Ltd* 1986 S.L.T. 629.

Even if the proposed amendment is necessary to determine the real question in controversy, the court must consider whether it is in the interests of justice to allow it: *Thomson v. Glasgow Corporation* 1962 S.C.(H.L.) 36, 51 per L.J.-C. Thomson. The court has a complete discretion in exercising the power of amendment: *Browns Trs. v. Hay* (1897) 24 R. 1108, per Lord McLaren. The timing of the proposed amendment and the prejudice caused to the other parties are significant factors. See also *Evans v. Northern Coasters Ltd* 1995 G.W.D. 9-515 (I.H.).

The absence of any conclusions in a summons is not a fundamental nullity where it is plain to the defender from the pleadings what the nature of the claim against him is, and amendment to add conclusions has been allowed under rr. 2.1 and 24.1(2)(a): *Wilson v. Lothian R.C.* 1995 S.L.T. 991.

"THE SUM SUED FOR IN A SUMMONS IS INCREASED".

24.1.5   This is unaffected by any statutory time-limit for bringing an action: *Mackie v. Glasgow Corporation* 1924 S.L.T. 510. Amendment may be made even after the defender has consented to decree against him: *Cowie v. Carron Co. Ltd* 1945 S.C. 280.

"A DIFFERENT REMEDY FROM THAT ORIGINALLY CONCLUDED FOR OR CRAVED".

24.1.6   See, e.g. *Summerlee Iron Co. Ltd v. Caledonian Railway Co.* 1911 S.C. 458; *Campbell v. Henderson* 1949 S.C. 172. But a petition for interdict may not be amended to become a petition for judicial review: *Sleigh v. Edinburgh D.C.* 1988 S.L.T. 253.

"ADD THE NAME OF AN ADDITIONAL PURSUER".

24.1.7   Such an amendment may be made even where the title to sue of the existing pursuer is or becomes defective: *Donaghy v. Rollo* 1964 S.C. 278. Such an amendment is subject to any statutory time-limit: see *McLean v. British Railways Board* 1966 S.L.T. 39.

A minute of sist is not required: *Stewart v. Highlands and Islands Development Board* 1991 S.L.T. 787, 790C-F per Lord MacLean.

"CAUSE ... COMMENCED ... IN THE NAME OF THE WRONG PERSON".

24.1.8   See, e.g. *Morrison v. Morrison's Exx.* 1912 S.C. 892. This may be done even if the original pursuer's title is defective: *A.C. Stewart & Partners v. Coleman* 1989 S.L.T. 430. In *Link Housing Association Ltd v. Gray Aitken Partnership Ltd* (erroneously cited as *Gray Aitken Partnership Ltd v. Link Housing Association Ltd*) , 2007 S.C. 294 (First Div.), the pursuer was not allowed to amend out with a contractual limitation period to change the name of the pursuer to that of another related company.

"DOUBTFUL ... COMMENCED ... IN THE NAME OF THE RIGHT PERSON".

24.1.9   See, e.g. *Anderson v. Balnagowan Estates Co.* 1939 S.C. 168.

"CAUSE ... DIRECTED AGAINST THE WRONG PERSON".

24.1.10   An amendment to rectify this is subject to any statutory time-limit for bringing an action. "The court will not, in general, allow a pursuer by amendment to substitute the right defender for the wrong defender, or to cure a radical incompetence in his action, or to change the basis of his case if he only seeks to make such amendments after the expiry of a time limit which would have prevented him at that stage from raising fresh proceedings": *Pompa's Trs. v. Magistrates of Edinburgh* 1942 S.C. 119, 125 per L.J.-C. Cooper. It should be noted that an amendment to insert or substitute a new defender may constitute the "bringing of an action" under s.17 or 18 of the Prescription and Limitation (Scotland) Act 1973: *Miller v. National Coal Board* 1960 S.C. 376. In *Perth and Kinross Council v Scottish Water Ltd,* 2015 S.L.T. 788 (OH), upheld 2017 S.C. 164 (Extra Div.), it was held that deleting the word "Ltd" from the instance was a correction and not a substitution.

The *punctum temporis* for determining when an action commenced against a party added by amendment is the date when the amended pleadings are served on that party: *Miller*, above, where the pursuer sought to amend to introduce a new defender after the expiry of the limitation period the proposed amendment was held to be incompetent; cf. *Pompa's Trs.*, above.

Amendment of petition for judicial review.

In a petition for judicial review there is a time-limit for an application under s. 27A(1) of the CSA 1988 of (a) three months beginning with the date on which the grounds giving rise to the application first arise or (b) such longer period as the court considers equitable in all the circumstances.

Amendment before permission granted. In *Chong Wang v Scottish Ministers* [2017] CSOH 140, Lady Stacey held that a minute of amendment after the petition was lodged and before permission to proceed was granted was not competent. The amendment was sought because the decision to be judicially reviewed had been superceded by a decision to the same effect on different grounds. Lady Stacey's decision was based on s. 27B(1) of the CSA 1988 (no proceedings may be taken unless permission granted). That appears to overlook the fact that a petition has to be presented in order to seek permission and gives an unrealistic meaning to "no proceedings may be taken". It really means "no proceedings may be proceeded with"; if that were so, why should a petition not be amended to determine the real question? Would the outcome have been different if it had not been a different decision now sought to be judicially reviewed? Why would that matter if the decision was to the same effect as the first? The comments of Lord Carloway, LP, in *MIAB v Secretary of State for the Home Department*, 2016 S.C. 871, 887, para. [63] were not referred to; the decision in *RA*, below, was distinguished on its facts.

Amendment at stage of review of permission decision. In *RA v Secretary of State for the Home Department* [2016] CSOH 182, the petitioner requested a review (under s. 27C(2) and r.58.8) of a decision to refuse permission to proceed and lodged a minute of amendment responding to the answers and raising a new matter not available at the time of lodging the petition (a tribunal decision in an analogous case). Lord Boyd of Duncansby held the minute competent under r. 24.1(2) but it was in the discretion of the court to grant it which would only be in rare and exceptional circumstances because (1) it should not be sufficient to allow it on the basis it responds to answers or to the refusal of permission, (2) the test in s.27B(2)(b) of real prospects of success had to be met (*MIAB v Secretary of State for the Home Department*, 2016 S.C. 871, 887, per Lord Carloway, obiter, at para. [64], save in exceptional circumstances), and (3) the time-limit test in s. 27A had to be met and, save in exceptional circumstances it would only be where the amendment contained matters not known at the time of lodging the petition. (It cannot be that the reference to "rare and exceptional circumstances" was intended to create a new hurdle of itself for amendment.)

24.1.11

Applications to amend

24.2.—(1) Subject to paragraph (2), a party seeking to amend shall lodge a minute of amendment in process setting out his proposed amendment and, at the same time, enrol a motion—

    (a)   to allow the minute of amendment to be received; and

    (b)   to allow—

        (i)   amendment in terms of the minute of amendment and, where appropriate, to grant an order under rule 24.3(1) or (2) (service of amended pleadings); or

        (ii)   in any other case, where the minute of amendment may require to be answered, any other party to lodge answers within a specified period or such period as the court thinks fit.

(2) Where the amendment proposed is of a minor and formal nature, the party seeking to amend may enrol a motion to allow amendment in the terms set out in the motion.

(3) Where the court has pronounced an interlocutor allowing a minute of amendment to be received and answered, then—

    (a)[1]   where answers have been lodged, unless the court otherwise orders parties may adjust the minute of amendment and answers within four weeks after the date on which answers were lodged or, where more than one set of answers have been lodged, the latest date on which answers were lodged;

    (b)   the party who has lodged the minute of amendment shall—

        (i)   where answers have been lodged, within 14 days after the expiry of the period for adjustment of the minute of amendment and answers or any continuation of it, or

        (ii)   where no answers have been lodged, within 14 days after the

24.2

---

[1] R. 24.2(3)(a) amended by S.I. 1994 No. 2901 (effective 5th December 1994).

expiry of the period for lodging answers or any prorogation of it, enrol a motion to amend the writ or other pleadings in terms of the minute of amendment and answers (if any) or for other further procedure, as the case may be.

(4) Where a party fails to enrol a motion under paragraph (3)(b), the court shall appoint the cause to be put out on the By Order Roll and, having heard parties on that roll, may—

(a) if moved to do so, allow the amendment;

(b) make such order as to further procedure as it thinks fit; and

(c) in any event, make such order in respect of expenses as it thinks fit.

(5)[1] Where a party to a cause before the Inner House enrols a motion to amend a record in terms of a minute of amendment and answers (if any), he shall at the same time enrol for an order for further procedure, and if it is reasonably practicable to do so, the party shall specify the nature of such further procedure.

Deriv. P.N. 26th March 1981 (r. 24.2(5)) and P.N. 27th March 1986 (r. 24.2(3) and (4))

GENERAL NOTE.

24.2.1   On lodging a minute of amendment, written intimation must be given of its lodging, and a copy sent, to every other party: r. 4.6(1); on methods of written intimation, see r. 16.9.

Where the amendment is of a minor or formal nature, a minute of amendment is not required. P.N. No. 2 of 2009 makes it clear that the court regards alteration of a sum sued for in a conclusion as being of such a nature.

FORM OF MINUTE OF AMENDMENT.

24.2.2   A minute of amendment is headed with the instance of the cause. There follows a preamble:

"[X] for the pursuer [*or as the case may be*] craved and hereby craves leave of the court to amend the summons [*or as the case may be*] as follows:—."

The amendments to the pleadings are then listed in numbered paragraphs. The minute ends with the words "IN RESPECT WHEREOF". The minute no longer needs to be signed: r. 4.2(9)(a). R. 15.1 (applications by minute) does not apply to a minute of amendment: r. 15.1(6)(b).

No fee is payable on a party lodging a minute of amendment.

"PERIOD OF NOTICE".

24.2.3   This period is determined in accordance with rule 14.6 (period of notice for answers) by virtue of r. 1.3(1) (definitions of "period of notice" and "writ").

FORM AND LODGING OF ANSWERS.

24.2.4   Where answers are lodged in response to a minute of amendment, there must be inserted, above the instance of the answers, the date of the interlocutor allowing answers to be lodged and the time for lodging them: r. 4.9(3) (it is no longer necessary to insert the interlocutor). After the instance there follows a preamble:

"[Y] for the defender [*or as the case may be*] craved and hereby craves leave of the court to answer the Minute of Amendment for the pursuer [*or as the case may be*] No. (*insert number*) as follows:—."

The answers are then listed in numbered paragraphs. The answers end with the words "IN RESPECT WHEREOF". The answers no longer need to be signed: r. 4.2(9)(b).

On lodging answers, written intimation must be given of their lodging, and a copy sent, to every other party: r. 4.6(1); on methods of written intimation, see r. 16.9.

No fee is payable on a party lodging answers to a minute of amendment.

"WITHIN 4 WEEKS AFTER".

24.2.5   The date from which the period is calculated is not counted.

"WITHIN 14 DAYS".

24.2.6   The date from which the period is calculated is not counted. Where the last day falls on a Saturday or Sunday or a public holiday on which the Office of Court is closed, the next available day is allowed: r. 1.3(7). For office hours and public holidays, see note 3.1.2.

---

[1] R.24.2(5) amended by S.I. 1999 No.1386 (effective 19th May 1999).

When pleadings are amended in the Inner House, it may refuse to hear argument until the judge at first instance has considered the amended pleadings: *Wallace v. Scottish Special Housing Association* 1981 S.L.T. (Notes) 60; and see r. 38.21. In that case the Second Division awarded expenses of the reclaiming motion against the party amending because that party could have enrolled a motion to allow the reclaiming motion and remit to the Lord Ordinary for reconsideration. After this case P.N. 26th March 1981 (the foundation for r. 24.2.(5)) was issued requiring a motion to amend and for an order for further procedure (which may well be for a remit to the court below).

24.2.7

Note the statutory power of the court to allow amendment of a record in an appeal under s.28 of the Sheriff Courts (Scotland) Act 1907: C.S.A. 1988, s.32(1).

BY ORDER ROLL HEARING.

No court fee is payable for a hearing on this By Order Roll.

24.2.8

Service of amended pleadings

24.3.—(1)   In an undefended action where no appearance has been entered or in an unopposed petition or note, unless the amendment is formal in character, the court shall—

24.3

(a)   order that a copy of the principal writ as amended be served on a specified person; and

(b)   allow that person to lodge defences or answers, as the case may be, within such period as the court thinks fit.

(2)   Where an amendment under rule 24.1(2)(d) (all parties not, or wrong person, called) has been made—

(a)   the court shall order that a copy of the pleadings as so amended be served by the party who made the amendment on that additional or substitute party with a notice in Form 24.3 specifying the date by which defences or answers, as the case may be, must be lodged; and

(b)   the party who made the amendment shall lodge in process—

(i)   a copy of the pleadings as amended;

(ii)   a copy of the notice mentioned in sub-paragraph (a);

(iii)   a copy of the interlocutor ordering service; and

(iv)   a certificate of service.

(3)   When paragraph (2) has been complied with, the cause as so amended shall proceed in every respect as if that party had originally been made a party to the cause.

Deriv. R.C.S. 1965, r. 92(3) (r. 24.3(1))

"UNDEFENDED ACTION WHERE NO APPEARANCE HAS BEEN ENTERED".

Where appearance has been entered, only written intimation and not service is required: see r. 4.6.

24.3.1

"SERVED".

For methods of service, see Chap. 16, Part I.

24.3.2

"ANSWERS".

See note 24.2.4.

24.3.3

"SUCH PERIOD AS THE COURT THINKS FIT".

It is usual to use the period of notice for service of a summons or petition (21 days within Europe and 42 days furth of Europe: see rr. 13.4 and 14.6), but this may be shortened or extended, and any answers must be lodged *within* that period.

24.3.4

"LODGE IN PROCESS A COPY OF THE PLEADINGS" ETC.

The documents required to be lodged under r. 24.3(2)(b) are made up as an execution copy of the pleadings (writ) and lodged as a step of process (on which, see r. 4.4).

24.3.5

FORM 24.3.

A copy of this form has to be lodged in process with the amended writ because the court must be satisfied that service has been properly executed and that all that was required to be served was served.

24.3.6

Expenses and conditions of amendment

24.4 **24.4.** The court shall find the party making an amendment liable in the expenses occasioned by the amendment unless it is shown that it is just and equitable that the expenses occasioned by the amendment should be otherwise dealt with, and may attach such other conditions as it think fit.

Deriv. R.C.S. 1965, r. 92(2)

GENERAL NOTE.

24.4.1 The general rule is that the party making an amendment pays the expenses occasioned by it (and these include the expenses of his opponent preparing answers: *Campbell v. Henderson* 1949 S.C. 172, 183). An amendment which so alters a case that what has gone before is rendered abortive will result in the party making the amendment being found liable to expenses at least from the date of the amendment: *Stevens v. Motherwell Entertainments Ltd* 1914 S.C. 957 (expenses since closed record); *Black v. John Williams & Co. (Wishaw) Ltd* 1924 S.C.(H.L.) 22, 27 (whole expenses of process to date). If amendment should have made earlier, expenses may be awarded from an earlier date than that of the amendment.

Where amendment is proposed at procedure roll, the party seeking to amend will, as a general rule, have to pay the expenses of the abortive hearing; and payment of those expenses may be made a condition precedent of that amendment: *Colbron v. United Glass Ltd* 1965 S.L.T. 366.

Payment of expenses may be made a condition precedent of further procedure: *Moves v. Burntisland Shipbuilding Co.* 1952 S.C. 429; *Colbron*, above; cf. *The Edinburgh Modern Quarry Co. Ltd v. Eagle Star Insurance Co. Ltd* 1965 S.L.T.(Notes) 91. Cases cited in McLaren on *Expenses*, pp. 6-7, are no longer followed: *Smellie v. Smellie* 1953 S.L.T.(Notes) 53, 54 per L.P. Cooper. A time limit for payment may be laid down: *Stevens*, above.

Conditions are not limited to expenses: see e.g. *Duthie Bros. & Co. v. Duthie* (1892) 19 R. 905 (pursuer to be entitled to sist further pursuers); *Morrison v Marshall Henderson & Whyte SSC* , 28 May 2003 (OH), unreported (condition that evidence of a particular witness be taken on commission).

The conditions cannot be objected to after amendment has been made: *Duthie*, above.

Effect of amendment on diligence

24.5 **24.5.** Where an amendment has been allowed, the amendment shall—

    (a) not validate diligence used on the dependence of a cause so as to prejudice the rights of creditors, of the party against whom the diligence has been executed, who are interested in defeating such diligence; and

    (b) preclude any objection to such diligence stated by a party or any person by virtue of a title acquired or in right of a debt contracted by him subsequent to the execution of such diligence.

Deriv. R.C.S. 1965, r. 92(4)

GENERAL NOTE.

24.5.1 An amendment will not make good diligence used on the dependence before amendment so as to give the pursuer a preference over other creditors: *Fischer & Co. v. Andersen* (1896) 23 R. 395. In such a case, the pursuer will have to obtain a fresh warrant for diligence on the dependence.

Applications to amend the name of a party in more than one cause

24.6 **24.6.**—[1](1) This rule applies where a party—

    (a) is a party to more than one cause depending before the court; and

    (b) wishes the pleadings in those causes to be amended to reflect a change in the party's name.

(2) A party mentioned in paragraph (1) may apply to the court for the pleadings in each of the affected causes to be amended by the substitution of the new name for the old name—

    (a) in the instance or, as the case may be, address;

    (b) in any averments or, as the case may be, statement of facts which have the sole purpose of identifying or designating that party by name.

(3) The application shall be made by motion and include—

    (a) a list of all of the affected causes;

    (b) official evidence of the change of name (for example, an extract of an

---

[1] Rule 24.6 substituted by S.S.I. 2013 No. 162 (effective June 4, 2013).

entry in the register of companies or an extract of an entry in a register held by the National Records of Scotland);

(c)   a statement that the applicant has informed all other parties in the affected causes of the applicant's intention to make the application and that the other parties have been given a reasonable opportunity to object to the amendment of the pleadings.

(4)[1] Subject to paragraph (5), the motion shall be placed before a Lord Ordinary in chambers for determination.

(5) Where any of the affected causes is in the Inner House, the application shall be placed before an Inner House judge in chambers for determination.

(6) An interlocutor pronounced under this rule shall have effect as an interlocutor in each of the affected causes.

(7) A party to any of the affected causes may apply to the court for a determination made under this rule to be reconsidered in respect of that cause.

GENERAL NOTE.

This rule facilitates amendment of the name of a party in more than one action (e.g. multiple, class actions or conjoined actions) by one motion instead of a motion in each case.   **24.6.1**

"MOTION".

For motions, see Chap. 23.   **24.6.2**

---

[1] As amended by the Act of Sederunt (Rules of the Court of Session Amendment No.7) (Miscellaneous) 2013 (SSI 2013/317) r.2 (effective December 2, 2013).

CHAPTER 25 COUNTERCLAIMS

Counterclaims

25.1.—(1) In any action other than a family action within the meaning of rule 49.1(1) or an action of multiplepoinding, a defender may lodge a counterclaim against a pursuer—

    (a)   where the counterclaim might have been made in a separate action in which it would not have been necessary to call as a defender any person other than the pursuer; and

    (b)   in respect of any matter—

        (i)   forming part, or arising out of the grounds, of the action by the pursuer;

        (ii)   the decision of which is necessary for the determination of the question in controversy between the parties; or

        (iii)   which, if the pursuer had been a person not otherwise subject to the jurisdiction of the court, might have been the subject-matter of an action against that pursuer in which jurisdiction would have arisen by reconvention.

  (2) A counterclaim may be lodged in process—

    (a)   at any time before the record is closed; or

    (b)   at any later stage, with leave of the court and subject to such conditions, if any, as to expenses or otherwise as the court thinks fit.

  (3) A counterclaim shall be headed "Counterclaim for the defender" and shall contain—

    (a)   conclusions, stated in accordance with the appropriate short style, if any, in Form 13.2-B which, if the counterclaim had been made in a separate action, would have been appropriate in the summons in that separate action;

    (b)   a statement of facts in numbered paragraphs setting out the facts on which the counterclaim is founded, incorporating by reference, if necessary, any matter contained in the defences; and

    (c)   appropriate pleas-in-law.

Deriv. R.C.S. 1965, r. 84(a) (part) and (j) (r. 25.1(1) and (2)), r. 84(a) (part) (r. 25.1(1)) and r. 84(b) (r. 25.1(3))

GENERAL NOTE.

The present power to make rules for counterclaims is in s.6(v) of the C.S.A. 1988.

Not every claim may form the basis of a counterclaim: three conditions must be satisfied—(a) the counterclaim could have formed a separate action, (b) it would not have been necessary in that separate action to call another person as defender other than the pursuer and (c) the subject-matter of the counterclaim must (i) form part of the pursuer's action, or (ii) arise out of the grounds of it, or (iii) be a matter the decision of which is necessary for the determination of the question in controversy between the parties or (iv) if the pursuer had not otherwise been subject to the jurisdiction of the court, have arisen by reconvention. The rule is not limited to claims of compensation, set-off or other pecuniary claims: e.g. interdict (*McLean v. Marwhirn Developments Ltd* 1976 S.L.T.(Notes) 47), or a decree *ad factum praestandum* (*Borthwick v. Dean Warwick Ltd* 1985 S.L.T. 269 (delivery), *MacKenzie v. MacLeod's Exr.* 1988 S.L.T. 207 (delivery)).

The rationale for counterclaim procedure is expediency; that does not justify a third party minuter entering the process to maintain a claim against the pursuer, even as assignee of the defender's claim: *Tods Murray, W.S. v. Arakin Ltd* 2000 S.L.T. 758 (OH aff'd 2001 S.C. 840, 2001 S.L.T. 1193 (Extra Div.)). In that case Lord Macfadyen in the Outer House observed (p.760F (para. 10)) that the position would be different if the minuter assumed the defender's liability to the pursuer and the pursuer consented to the substitution of the minuter for the defender.

CAUSES IN WHICH COUNTERCLAIMS EXCLUDED.

There are special rules in family actions for making claims against the pursuer in defences: see r. 49.31. A counterclaim is inappropriate in an action of multiplepoinding, the nature of the process being one by which it is decided which persons who have lodged claims are entitled to a fund held by another: see Chap. 51.

25.1.3   Jurisdiction over the person sued in a counterclaim is now governed by the C.J.J.A. 1982. Subject to the rules for consumer contracts, exclusive jurisdiction and prorogation, a person may be sued in the courts for the place in which he is domiciled or, in a counterclaim, in the court where the original claim is pending under the statutory rule for reconvention in the C.J.J.A. 1982. Where the person to be sued is domiciled furth of Scotland, jurisdiction will only be by reconvention and r. 25.1(1)(b)(iii) will apply. For jurisdiction generally, see notes 13.2.7 to 13.2.14; and for reconvention, see note 25.1.6.

"FORMING PART, OR ARISING OUT OF THE GROUNDS, OF THE ACTION".

25.1.4   Where a contract is one and indivisible a counterclaim may be made in respect of one item in answer to a claim on the whole contract; but if there is a series of transactions forming separate contracts, a counterclaim in respect of one can only be pleaded in relation to that contract: *J.W. Chafer (Scotland) Ltd v. Hope* 1963 S.L.T.(Notes) 11.

"NECESSARY FOR THE DETERMINATION OF THE QUESTION IN CONTROVERSY".

25.1.5   The question in controversy is ascertained from the whole pleadings and is wider than simply the pursuer's action: *Fulton Clyde Ltd v. J.F. McCallum & Co. Ltd* 1960 S.L.T. 253 (counterclaim for damages for breach of contract in action for payment of price); see also *Borthwick v. Dean Warwick Ltd* 1983 S.L.T. 269 (ancillary contracts).

RECONVENTION.

25.1.6   A person not otherwise subject to the jurisdiction of the court may render himself liable to its jurisdiction by litigating in it. This jurisdiction of reconvention is based solely on equity, the fundamental principle being that a party is not entitled to take the benefit of the jurisdiction of our courts, and at the same time refuse that jurisdiction in relative matters: *Thompson v. Whitehead* (1862) 24 D. 331, per L.J.-C. Inglis. At common law reconvention arises not only where the two claims arise *in eodem negotio* (arising out of the same matter), but also where they arise *ex diversis causis*, provided they are claims which can fairly be set against one another, without violating some other rule of pleading or principle of equity: *Thompson*, above, per L.J.-C. Inglis at p. 345; *MacKenzie v. MacLeod's Exr.* 1988 S.L.T. 207.

    The common law now only applies to those matters (where applicable) in Sched.9 of the C.J.J.A. 1982 which are excluded from the application of Sched.8 to that Act. The rule now is, in all matters other than those in Sched.9, that, subject to the rules of jurisdiction over consumer contracts, exclusive jurisdiction and prorogation of jurisdiction in the 1982 Act, a person may be sued, on a counterclaim arising from the same contract or facts on which the original claim was based, in the court in which the original claim is pending (and not only in the courts for the place in which he is domiciled): C.J.J.A. 1982, Sched.8, r. 2(15)(c). Where the person to be sued on the counterclaim is domiciled in a Contracting State to which the 1968 (Brussels) Convention, or the Lugano Convention, applies or is domiciled in another part of the UK, the same statutory rule applies: C.J.J.A. 1982, Sched.1 (1968 Convention), Art. 6(3); Sched.3C (Lugano Convention), Art. 6(3); Sched.4 (Inter-UK jurisdiction), Art. 6(3). Note *Spitzley v. Sommer Exploitation* [1985] E.C.R. 787 where no objection to jurisdiction was entered in relation to a counterclaim on a contract not based on the same contract and in respect of which another court had exclusive jurisdiction by virtue of an agreement; it was held by the European Court that the court hearing the counterclaim had jurisdiction by virtue of Art. 18 of the 1968 Convention (entering appearance without contesting jurisdiction).

COUNTERCLAIMS AND THE CROWN.

25.1.7   A person is not allowed to avail himself of any set-off (see *Laing v. Lord Advocate* 1973 S.L.T.(Notes) 81) or counterclaim in proceedings by the Crown (a) for recovery of taxes, duties or penalties or (b) arising out of a right or claim to repayment of taxes, duties or penalties: Crown Proceedings Act 1947, s.35(2)(b) as applied by s.'50. A person is not entitled, without leave of the court, to avail himself of any set-off or counterclaim in any proceedings by the Crown if the subject-matter does not relate to the government department on whose behalf the proceedings are brought: 1947 Act, s.35(2)(c) as applied by s.50. Similarly, the Crown may not, without leave of the court, set-off or counterclaim if the subject-matter does not relate to the government department concerned: 1947 Act, s.35(2)(d) as applied by s.50.

    In considering whether leave to the Crown should be granted, where leave may be sought, the court will balance the common law right against the statutory duty to seek leave (*Smith v. Lord Advocate* 1980 SC 227, 237 per Lord Avonside) and take into account the similarity between the nature of the claims (*Laing*, above, at p. 82 per Lord Keith).

FORM AND LODGING OF COUNTERCLAIM.

25.1.8   A counterclaim must be in a separate writ and not alternatively, as formerly, in the defences (whether as drafted or by adjustment or amendment). If a counterclaim satisfies the conditions of r. 25.1(1), the court, in general, has no discretion to refuse it if it is lodged before the record is closed. Exceptions to the general rule are—(a) counterclaims by or against the Crown (see note 25.1.7) or (b) where leave is required under the Insolvency Act 1986, s.130 (but leave is not required where set-off is for a lesser sum than that in the action: *G. & A. (Hotels) Ltd v. T.H.B. Marketing Services Ltd* 1983 S.L.T. 497).

    But the court has a discretion if the counterclaim is sought to be lodged after the record has closed: it may be refused as coming too late. It is not clear what factors the court would take into account in granting or refusing leave. The considerations may be similar to those in deciding whether to allow amendment, including delay, prejudice and the stage at which it is sought to lodge the counterclaim: see note 24.1.1. If it is sought to amend the defences in light of the counterclaim, then the circumstances in which amendment is allowed after the record has closed will apply: see r. 24.1 and notes 24.1.1-24.1.3.

On the form of pleadings and pleas-in-law, see notes 13.2.3-13.2.5.

Where a counterclaim is lodged the record (open or closed) will contain it and any answers in addition to, but separate from, the summons and defences.

On lodging a counterclaim the defender must give written intimation of its lodging, and send a copy of it, to every other party: r. 4.6(1). On methods of written intimation, see r. 16.9.

FEE.

There is no court fee for lodging a counterclaim.

25.1.9

Authority for diligence etc. on counterclaims

25.2.—[1](1) A defender who lodges a counterclaim may apply by motion for authority for diligence by—

25.2

    (a)   inhibition on the dependence of the action;

    (b)   arrestment on the dependence of the action where there is a conclusion for the payment of money;

    (c)   arrestment in rem; or

    (d)   dismantling a ship.

(2) A certified copy of an interlocutor granting a motion under paragraph (1) shall be sufficient authority for execution of the diligence.

(3) A certified copy of an interlocutor granting authority for inhibition under this rule may be registered with a certificate of execution in the Register of Inhibitions and Adjudications.

(4)[2] A notice of a certified copy of an interlocutor granting authority for inhibition under this rule may be registered in the Register of Inhibitions and Adjudications; and such registration is to have the same effect as registration of a notice of inhibition under section 155(2) of the Titles to Land Consolidation (Scotland) Act 1868.

Deriv. R.C.S. 1965, r. 84(c)

GENERAL NOTE.

On arrestment in rem or dismantling a ship, see notes 13.6A.3-13.6A.4; on arrestment on the dependence and inhibition on the dependence, see Chap. 14A.

25.2.1

"MOTION".

For motions, see Chap. 23.

25.2.2

Answers to counterclaims

25.3.—(1) Answers to a counterclaim may be lodged by a pursuer—

25.3

    (a)   where the counterclaim is lodged before the record is closed, within 14 days after the date on which the counterclaim is lodged; or

    (b)   in any other case, within the period appointed by the interlocutor allowing the counterclaim to be received.

(2) Where answers to a counterclaim have been lodged, the court may, on the motion of the pursuer or defender, allow such period for adjustment as it thinks fit.

Deriv. R.C.S. 1965, r. 84(k)

FORM AND LODGING OF ANSWERS.

For form of answers, see r. 18.3.

No court fee is payable on the lodging of answers by a party to a counterclaim.

25.3.1

---

[1] R. 25.2 substituted by S.S.I. 2003 No. 537 (effective 10th November, 2003).
[2] R. 25.2(4) substituted by S.S.I. 2009 No. 104 (effective 22nd April, 2009).

"WITHIN 14 DAYS".

25.3.2   The date from which the period is calculated is not counted. Where the last day falls on a Saturday or Sunday or a public holiday on which the Office of Court is closed, the next available day is allowed: r. 1.3(7). For office hours and public holidays, see note 3.1.2.

Effect of abandonment of action

25.4   **25.4.**—(1)   The right of a pursuer to abandon his action under rule 29.1 shall not be affected by a counterclaim; and any expenses for which the pursuer is found liable as a condition, or in consequence, of such abandonment shall not include the expenses of the counterclaim.

(2)   Notwithstanding abandonment by the pursuer, a defender may insist in his counterclaim; and the proceedings in the counterclaim shall continue in dependence as if the counterclaim were a separate action.

Deriv. R.C.S. 1965, r. 84(d) (r. 25.4(1)) and r. 84(f) (r. 25.4(2))

GENERAL NOTE.

25.4.1   On abandonment by pursuer, see r. 29.1; on abandonment by defender of counterclaim, see r. 29.2.

Proof or jury trial of counterclaims

25.5   **25.5.**—(1)   Where a proof or jury trial is allowed between parties to an action, the court may allow any counterclaim to proceed to proof or jury trial, as the case may be, before, at the same time as or after, the action as it thinks fit.

(2)   Where evidence is led in a counterclaim separately from the evidence in the action, the evidence in one cause shall, so far as competent and relevant, be evidence in the other cause.

Deriv. R.C.S. 1965, r. 84(g)

GENERAL NOTE.

25.5.1   The court may, under r. 25.5(1), allow a counterclaim to proceed before, at the same time as or after the action. The court may, of course, dismiss the action (see e.g. *Feld British Agencies Ltd v. James Pringle Ltd* 1961 S.L.T. 123), grant decree for a sum admittedly due (see e.g. *Fulton Clyde Ltd v. J. F. McCallum & Co. Ltd* 1960 S.L.T. 253) or for which there is no relevant defence stated and allow the counterclaim to proceed. Where the pursuer obtains decree it would not be usual, though not incompetent, to supersede extract.

Interlocutors in respect of counterclaims

25.6   **25.6.**—   A decree or other interlocutor which could have been pronounced in a separate action brought to enforce the conclusions stated in a counterclaim may be pronounced in respect of the counterclaim.

Deriv. R.C.S. 1965, r. 84(h)

CHAPTER 25A DEVOLUTION ISSUES

Chapter 25A[1]

Devolution Issues

Interpretation of this Chapter

25A.1[2] In this Chapter—

"Advocate General" means the Advocate General for Scotland;
"devolution issue" means a devolution issue within the meaning of—
    (a)   Schedule 6 to the Scotland Act 1998;
    (b)   Schedule 10 to the Northern Ireland Act 1998; or
    (c)   Schedule 9 to the Government of Wales Act 2006,
and any reference to Schedule 6, Schedule 10 or Schedule 9 is a reference to that Schedule to, respectively, the Scotland Act 1998, the Northern Ireland Act 1998 and the Government of Wales Act 2006;
"relevant authority" means the Advocate General and—
    (a)   in the case of a devolution issue within the meaning of Schedule 6, the Lord Advocate;
    (b)   in the case of a devolution issue within the meaning of Schedule 10, the Attorney General for Northern Ireland, and the First Minister and deputy First Minister acting jointly;
    (c)   in the case of a devolution issue within the meaning of Schedule 9, the Counsel General to the Welsh Government.

GENERAL NOTE.

Chap. 25A was inserted by A.S. (Devolution Issues Rules) 1999 [SI 1999/1345]. It makes provision for the manner and time in which a "devolution issue" (see note 25A.1.2) may be raised and dealt with.

"DEVOLUTION ISSUE".

An Act of the Scottish Parliament is not law in so far as any provision is outside the legislative competence of the Parliament: Scotland Act 1998, s.29(1). It would appear that what is intended, although not clearly expressed, is that only the provision outwith legislative competence is affected and not the whole Act. Such an intention is clearly expressed in s.6(1) of the Northern Ireland Act 1998; and there were attempts to amend the Scottish provision to make it clearer. A provision of an Act is outside legislative competence if (a) it would form part of the law of a country or territory other than Scotland or confer or remove functions exercisable otherwise than in or as regards Scotland; (b) it relates to reserved matters (see s.30 and Sched.5 to the Scotland Act 1998); (c) it is in breach of the restrictions in Sched.4 (enactments protected from modification); (d) it is incompatible with any of the Convention rights in the Human Rights Act 1998 or European Community law; or (e) it would remove the Lord Advocate from his position as head of the systems of criminal prosecution and investigation of deaths in Scotland: Scotland Act 1998, s.29(2).

The courts may be called upon to decide whether a provision in an Act is within or without the legislative competence of the Parliament. Sched.6 of the Scotland Act 1998 provides the mechanism for devolution issues raised in proceedings in Scotland, England and Wales and Northern Ireland. Similar provision is made for devolution issues with respect to Northern Ireland in Sched.10 to the Northern Ireland Act 1998, and to Wales in Sched.9 to the Government of Wales Act 2006 which may be raised in proceedings, in e.g. Scotland, including intimation of those proceedings to the other countries' law officers.

A "devolution issue" is defined in Sched. 6 to the Scotland Act 1998 as (a) a question whether an Act of the Scottish Parliament or any provision of it is within the legislative competence of the Parliament; (b) a question whether any function (purportedly or proposed to be exercised) is a function of the Scottish Ministers, the First Minister or the Lord Advocate; (c) a question whether the purported or proposed exercise of a function by a member of the Scottish Executive is or would be within devolved competence; (d) a question whether the purported or proposed exercise by a member of the Scottish Executive is or would be incompatible with any of the Convention rights or with Community law; (e) a question whether a failure to act by a member of the Scottish Executive is incompatible with any of the Convention rights or with Community law; (f) any other question about whether a function is exercisable within devolved

---

[1] Chap. 25A and r. 25A.1 invoked by S.I. 1999 No. 1345 (effective 6th May 1999).
[2] Rule 25A.1 amended by S.S.I. 2007 No. 360 (effective 10th August 2007), S.S.I. 2009 No. 323 (effective 1st October 2009) and the Wales Act 2014 (c.29) Pt 1 s.4(4)(a) (effective 17 February 2015).

competence in or as regards Scotland an any other question arising by virtue of the Scotland Act 1998 about reserved matters. Similar definitions are contained in the Northern Ireland Act 1998 and the Government of Wales Act 1998.

Under s.102 of the Scotland Act 1998 (and s.81 of the Northern Ireland Act and s.110 of the Government of Wales Act), where the court decides that an Act or a provision of an Act is not within the legislative competence of the Parliament or a member of the Scottish Executive does not have power to make, confirm or approve a provision of subordinate legislation, the court may remove or limit any retrospective effect or suspend the effect of the decision of the court.

Proceedings where devolution issue raised in principal writ

25A.2   **25A.2.**[1]   Where any summons, petition or other principal writ contains an averment or conclusion which raises a devolution issue, the principal writ shall be served on the relevant authority, unless he has initiated the proceedings.

"INDIVIDUAL ISSUE".

25A.2.1   See note 25A.1.2.

"PRINCIPAL WRIT".

25A.2.2   This means the writ by which a cause is initiated before the court: r. 1.3(1).

"SERVED".

25A.2.3   For rules of service, see Chap. 16.

Time for raising devolution issue

25A.3   **25A.3.**—[2](1)   It shall not competent for a party to any proceedings to raise a devolution issue otherwise than in the pleadings before any evidence is led, unless the court, on cause shown, otherwise determines.

(2)   Where the court determines that a devolution issue may be raised as mentioned in paragraph (1) it shall make such orders as to the procedure to be followed as appear to it to be appropriate and, in particular, it shall make such orders—

(a)   as are necessary to ensure that intimation of the devolution issue is given in writing to the relevant authority for the purposes of paragraph 5 of Schedule 6 or as the case may be paragraph 23 of Schedule 10 or paragraph 14(1) of Schedule 9; and

(b)   as to the time in which any step is to be taken by any party in the proceedings.

GENERAL NOTE.

25A.3.1   The general rule is that a devolution issue must be raised in pleadings and before any evidence is led: s.25A. 3(i). Cause will have to be shown to raise such an issue which is not in the pleadings or after evidence has begun.

No procedure is laid down for dealing with a devolution issue. A practice may develop in due course. What is apparent is that a devolution issue may not have to await a hearing on the Procedure Roll. As soon as the issue is raised in, e.g. the summons, a party may apply by motion or presumably the court may at its own instance (see the terms of r. 25A.3(2) although probably only after hearing parties on whether to do so), for the court to order the procedure to be followed.

The court has power to refer the issue to a higher court, i.e. the Outer House to the Inner House or the Inner House to the Supreme Court of the United Kingdom: Scotland Act 1998, Sched. 6, paras 7, 8 and 10.

"DEVOLUTION ISSUE".

25A.3.2   See note 25A.1.2.

"RELEVANT AUTHORITY".

25A.3.3   See definition in r. 25A.1.

---

[1] Rule 25A.2 inserted by S.I. 1999 No. 1345 (effective 6th May 1999).
[2] Rule 25A.3 inserted by S.I. 1999 No. 1345 (effective 6th May 1999) and amended by S.S.I. 2007 No. 360 (effective 10th August 2007).

Specification of devolution issue

25A.4.—[1](1) Any party raising a devolution issue shall specify—

   (a)   where he initiates the action, in the principal writ;

   (b)   where a counterclaim is lodged, in the counterclaim;

   (c)   in any other case, in the defences or answers,

the facts and circumstances and contentions of law on the basis of which it is alleged that the devolution issue arises in sufficient detail to enable the court to determine, for the purposes of paragraph 2 of Schedule 6 or, as the case may be, of Schedule 10 or Schedule 9, whether a devolution issue arises in the proceedings.

(2) Where a party wishes to raise a devolution issue after the lodging of any writ mentioned in paragraph (1), he shall do so either by adjustment or amendment so as to specify in his pleadings the matters mentioned in that paragraph.

25A.4

"DEVOLUTION ISSUE".

See note 25A.1.2.

25A.4.1

"PRINCIPAL WRIT".

This means the writ by which a cause is initiated before the court: r. 1.3(1).

25A.4.2

"PARAGRAPH 2 OF SCHEDULE 6",

Paragraph 2 of Sched. 6 to the Scotland Act (and para. 2 of Sched. 10 to the Northern Ireland Act 1998 and Sched. 8 to the Government of Wales Act 1998) provides that a devolution issue shall not be taken to arise merely because of any contention of a party which appears to the court to be frivolous or vexatious.

25A.4.3

Intimation of devolution issue

25A.5—[2](1) Intimation of a devolution issue in pursuance of paragraph 5 of Schedule 6 or, as the case may be, paragraph 23 of Schedule 10 or paragraph 14(1) of Schedule 9 shall be given to the relevant authority (unless he is a party to the proceedings or has been served with the principal writ in pursuance of rule 25A.2) in accordance with this rule.

(2) Where the devolution issue is raised in the principal writ, service of the principal writ on the relevant authority shall be treated as such intimation.

(3) In any other case, the party raising the devolution issue shall, as soon as practicable, enrol a motion craving a warrant to intimate the devolution issue to the relevant authority and on hearing the motion, where it appears to the court that a devolution issue arises, the court shall order such intimation in Form 25A.5.

(4) The intimation of a devolution issue shall specify 14 days, or such other period as the court on cause shown may specify, as the period within which a relevant authority may give notice to the Deputy Principal Clerk of his intention to take part as a party in the proceedings as mentioned in paragraph 6 of Schedule 6 or, as the case may be, paragraph 24 of Schedule 10 or paragraph 14(2) of Schedule 9.

25A.5

"DEVOLUTION ISSUE".

See note 25A.1.2.

25A.5.1

INTIMATION.

Subject to r. 16.8, for methods of intimation, see r. 16.7. Rule 16.8 deals with intimation on a warrant to intimate, such as under r. 25A.5(3).

Intimation has to be given, unless a party, to the Advocate General and the Lord Advocate under para. 5 of Sched. 6 to the Scotland Act 1998. Where a devolution issue under the Northern Ireland Act 1998 or the Government of Wales Act 1998 arises in civil proceedings in Scotland there are provisions for intimation in para. 23 of Sched. 10 and para. 14(1) of Sched. 8, respectively, to those Acts.

25A.5.2

---

[1] Rule 25A.4 inserted by S.I. 1999 No. 1345 (effective 6th May 1999) and amended by S.S.I. 2007 No. 360 (effective 10th August 2007).

[2] Rule 25A.5 inserted by S.I. 1999 No. 1345 (effective 6th May 1999) and amended by S.S.I. 2007 No. 360 (effective 10th August 2007).

"RELEVANT AUTHORITY".

25A.5.3   See definition in r. 25A.1.

"MOTION".

25A.5.4   For motions, see Chap. 23.

25A.5A   **25A.5A.**[1] Where, after determination at first instance of any proceedings in which a devolution issue has been raised, a party to those proceedings—

    (a) marks a reclaiming motion under rule 38.6; or

    (b) makes an application to the nobile officium of the court under rule 14.3,

that party shall, unless the relevant authority is already party to the proceedings, at the same time intimate the motion to, or seek leave to serve the petition on, the relevant authority together with a notice in Form 25A.5A.

"INTIMATE".

25A.5A.1   For intimation, see r. 16.7.

Response to intimation

25A.6   **25A.6**—[2](1) Where a relevant authority gives notice as mentioned in rule 25A.5(4), he shall, not later than 7 days after the date of such notice lodge a minute of his written submissions in respect of the devolution issue together with conclusions and pleas in law as appropriate.

    (1A)[3] Where a relevant authority does not take part as a party in the proceedings at first instance the court may allow him to take part as a party in any subsequent appeal, reclaiming motion or reference to a higher court.

    (2) The minute lodged in accordance with paragraph (1) shall be intimated to all other parties in the proceedings.

"NOT LATER THAN 7 DAYS AFTER".

25A.6.1   The day of the date of the notice is not counted, the period of time commencing at the beginning of the following day and ending at the close of office hours of Office of Court on the seventh day after that date.

"RELEVANT AUTHORITY".

25A.6.2   See definition in r. 25A.1

Reference of devolution issue to Inner House

25A.7   **25A.7.**—[4](1) Where a devolution issue arises in any proceedings before the Lord Ordinary, any reference of the devolution issue to the Inner House as mentioned in paragraph 7 of Schedule 6 or, as the case may be, paragraph 25 of Schedule 10 or paragraph 15 of Schedule 9 shall by means of a report in accordance with Chapter 34 of these Rules.

    (2)[5] Where, in any proceedings before the Lord Ordinary, reference of a devolution issue is made to the Inner House, the Deputy Principal Clerk shall, unless the relevant authority is already party to the proceedings, not later than seven days after the reference has been made, give notice of the reference in Form 25A.7 to the relevant authority.

GENERAL NOTE.

25A.7.1   There is a statutory power for a Lord Ordinary to refer a devolution issue to the Inner House. The procedure is that for reporting to the Inner House in Chap. 34.

---

[1] Rule 25A.5A inserted by S.S.I. 2007 No. 360 (effective 10th August 2007).
[2] R. 25A.6 inserted by S.I. 1999 No. 1345 (effective 6th May 1999).
[3] R.25A.6(1A) inserted by S.S.I. 2000 No. 66, para. 2(3) (effective 7th April 2000).
[4] R. 25A.7 inserted by S.I. 1999 No. 1345 (effective 6th May 1999) and amended by S.S.I. 2007 No. 360 (effective 10th August 2007).
[5] Rule 25A.7(2) inserted by S.S.I. 2007 No. 360 (effective 10th August 2007).

See note 25A.1.2.

Reference of devolution issue to Supreme Court

25A.8.—[1](1) Where the court—

(a) decides in accordance with paragraph 10 of Schedule 6 or, as the case may be, paragraph 28 of Schedule 10 or paragraph 18 of Schedule 9; or

(b) is required as mentioned in paragraph 33 of Schedule 6 or, as the case may be, paragraph 33 of Schedule 10 or paragraph 29 of Schedule 9, to refer a devolution issue to the Supreme Court, it shall pronounce an interlocutor giving directions to the parties about the manner and time in which the reference is to be drafted and adjusted.

(2) When the reference has been drafted at the sight of the court, the court shall make and sign the reference.

(3) The reference shall include such matter as may be required by accordance with Practice Direction 10 of the Supreme Court, and shall have annexed to it the interlocutor making the reference.

(4) Service of the reference in accordance with Practice Direction 10 of the Supreme Court may be effected by the Deputy Principal Clerk by first class recorded delivery post.

GENERAL NOTE.

Only a court of three or more judges of the Court of Session (i.e. the Inner House), and not the Lord Ordinary, may refer a devolution issue to the Supreme Court of the United Kingdom. There is also provision for appeals to the Supreme Court of the United Kingdom: see r. 25A.11.

THE REFERENCE.

The reference must set out (a) the questions referred; (b) the addresses of the parties; (c) the name and address of the person who applied for or required the reference; (d) a concise statement of the background to the matter including the facts of the case (including any findings in fact) and the main issues in the case and the contentions of the parties; (e) the relevant law including the relevant provisions of the Scotland Act 1998, and (f) the reasons why an answer to the question is considered necessary for the purpose of disposing of the proceedings: Judicial Committee (Devolution Issues) Rules Order 1999, r. 2.9(1) (S.I. 1999 No. 665).

All judgments already given in the proceedings, including copies of any interlocutors and any notes attached to such interlocutors, must be annexed to the reference: r. 2.9(2) of the above Rules.

"SERVICE OF THE REFERENCE".

Rule 2.8 of the Judicial Committee (Devolution Issues) Rules 1999 (S.I. 1999 No. 665) provides that the court lodging the reference must serve copies of it on the parties and law officer who is not already a party and who has a potential interest in the proceedings. Rule 2.8(3)(a) specifies that where the reference or appeal is from a court in Scotland the Law Officers having a potential interest will be the Lord Advocate and the Advocate General.

"DEVOLUTION ISSUE".

See note 25A.1.2.

Sist of cause on reference to Supreme Court

25A.9.—[2](1) Subject to paragraph (2), on a reference being made to the Supreme Court as mentioned in rule 25A.8, the cause shall, unless the court when making the reference otherwise orders, be sisted until the Supreme Court has determined the devolution issue.

(2) The court may recall a sist made under paragraph (1) for the purpose of making any interim order which a due regard to the interests of the parties may require.

---

[1] R. 25A.8 inserted by S.I. 1999 No. 1345 (effective 6th May 1999) and amended by S.S.I. 2007 No. 360 (effective 10th August 2007) and S.S.I. 2009 No. 323 (effective 1st October 2009).

[2] R. 25A.9 inserted by S.I. 1999 No. 1345 (effective 6th May 1999) and amended by S.S.I. 2009 No. 323 (effective 1st October 2009).

Transmission of reference

25A.10   **25A.10.**—[1](1)   The reference shall be transmitted by the Deputy Principal Clerk to the Registrar of the Supreme Court.

(2)   Unless the court otherwise directs, the reference shall not be sent to the Registrar of the Supreme Court where a reclaiming motion or an appeal against the making of the reference is pending.

(3)   For the purpose of paragraph (2), a reclaiming motion or an appeal shall be treated as pending—

(a)   until the expiry of the time for marking that reclaiming motion or appeal; or

(b)   where a reclaiming motion or an appeal has been made, until it has been determined.

Appeals to the Supreme Court

25A.11   **25A.11.**—[2](1)   Where an appeal to the Supreme Court is made—

(a)   under paragraph 12 of Schedule 6 or, as the case may be, paragraph 30 of Schedule 10 or paragraph 20 of Schedule 9; or

(b)   with leave or special leave, under paragraph 13(b) of Schedule 6 or, as the case may be, paragraph 31(b) of Schedule 10 or paragraph 21(b) of Schedule 9,

the court from whose determination the appeal is made may make such orders as it thinks fit, having regard to the interests of the parties to the cause, for the purpose of regulating the proceedings pending the determination of the appeal by the Supreme Court, including orders relating to interim possession, execution and expenses already incurred.

(2)   Where the determination of an appeal by the Supreme Court does not dispose of the whole cause, the court against whose determination the appeal was made shall order such further procedure as is necessary to enable it to dispose of the whole cause.

GENERAL NOTE.

25A.11.1   There is a right of appeal to the Supreme Court of the United Kingdom from the Inner House against a determination by it of a devolution issue with leave of the Inner House or, failing which, with special leave of the Supreme Court of the United Kingdom: 1998 Act, Sched.6, para. 13.

The word "determination" in para. 13 of Sched.6 to the 1998 Act implies the making of a decision on the merits of a devolution issue and, where no such decision has been made, an application for leave to appeal is incompetent: *C v. Miller* , 2003 S.L.T. 1402 (Extra Div.).

Orders mitigating the effect of certain decisions

25A.12   **25A.12.**—[3](1)   In any proceedings where the court is considering making an order under—

(a)   section 102 of the Scotland Act 1998;

(b)   section 81 of the Northern Ireland Act 1998; or

(c)[4]   section 153 of the Government of Wales Act 2006,

(power of the court to vary or suspend the effect of certain decisions), the court shall order intimation of the fact to be made by the Deputy Principal Clerk to every person to whom intimation is required to be given by that section.

(2)   Intimation as mentioned in paragraph (1) shall—

---

[1] R. 25A.10 inserted by S.I. 1999 No. 1345 (effective 6 May 1999) and amended by S.S.I. 2009 No. 323 (effective 1st October 2009).

[2] R. 25A.11 inserted by S.I. 1999 No. 1345 (effective 6th May 1999) and amended by S.S.I. 2007 No. 360 (effective 10th August 2007) and amended by S.S.I. 2009 No. 323 (effective 1st October 2009).

[3] Rule 25A.12 inserted by S.I. 1999 No. 1345 (effective 6th May 1999).

[4] Rule 25A.12(1)(c) substituted by S.S.I. 2007 No. 360 (effective 10th August 2007).

(a) be made forthwith in Form 25A.12 by first class recorded delivery post; and

(b) specify 7 days, or such other period as the court thinks fit, as the period within which a person may give notice of his intention to take part in the proceedings.

GENERAL NOTE.

Under s.102 of the Scotland Act 1998 (and s.81 of the Northern Ireland Act and s.110 of the Government of Wales Act), where the court decides that an Act or a provision of an Act is not within the legislative competence of the Scottish Parliament or a member of the Scottish Executive does not have power to make, confirm or approve a provision of subordinate legislation, the court may remove or limit any retrospective effect or suspend the effect of the decision of the court.

Where the court is considering whether to make such an order it must intimate that to the appropriate law officers mentioned in s.102 of the Scotland Act 1998 (or the equivalent provisions of the other Acts mentioned above, as the case may be).

25A.12.1

CHAPTER 26 THIRD PARTY PROCEDURE

Applications for third party notice

26.1.—(1)   Where, in an action, a defender claims that—

  (a)   he has in respect of the subject-matter of the action a right of contribution, relief or indemnity against any person who is not a party to the action, or

  (b)   a person whom the pursuer is not bound to call as a defender should be made a party to the action along with the defender in respect that such person is—

      (i)   solely liable, or jointly or jointly and severally liable with the defender, to the pursuer in respect of the subject-matter of the action, or

     (ii)   liable to the defender in respect of a claim arising from or in connection with the liability, if any, of the defender to the pursuer,

he may apply by motion for an order for service of a third party notice on that other person in Form 26.1-A for the purpose of convening that other person as a third party to the action.

(2)   Where—

  (a)   a pursuer against whom a counterclaim has been made, or

  (b)   a third party convened in the action,

seeks, in relation to the claim against him, to make against a person who is not a party, a claim mentioned in paragraph (1) as a claim which could be made by a defender against a third party, he shall apply by motion for an order for service of a third party notice in Form 26.1-B (notice by pursuer) or Form 26.1-C (notice by third party), as the case may be, in the same manner as a defender under that paragraph; and rules 26.2 to 26.7 shall, with the necessary modifications, apply to such a claim as they apply in relation to such a claim by a defender.

Deriv. R.C.S. 1965, r. 85(1) (preamble (part)) amended by SI 1980/1144 (r. 26.1(1)) and r. 85(1)(g) and (2) amended by SI 1980/1144 (r. 26.1(2))

GENERAL NOTE.

First introduced in R.C.S. 1934, Ch. II, r. 20(d) [S.R. & O. 1934 No. 967, third party procedure was abolished by A.S. 25th May 1937 [S.R. & O. 1937 No. 180] (about which, see 1937 S.L.T. (News) 98) and re-introduced by A.S. (R.C.A.) 1963 [SI 1963/380], and re-enacted in R.C.S. 1965, r. 85, after the introduction of contribution between joint wrongdoers by s.3 of the Law Reform (Miscellaneous Provisions) (Scotland) Act 1940.

The purpose of the rule is to enable questions arising out of one matter, including claims by a defender against a third party for contribution, relief or indemnity and liability between a defender and a third party, to be disposed of in one action, saving time and expenses: *Winchester v. Ramsay* 1966 S.C. 41, 46 per Lord Kissen; *Beedie v. Norrie* 1966 S.C. 207, 210 per L.P. Clyde; *Buchan v. Thomson* 1976 S.L.T. 42; *Nimmo's Exrs v. White's Exr.* 1976 S.L.T. 70, 71 per Lord Grieve. It enables a third party to be heard on any matter in which he has a relevant interest in relation to the case between the pursuer and defender: *Barton v. William Low & Co. Ltd* 1968 S.L.T. (Notes) 27, 28 per Lord Stott.

The rule is procedural and is not concerned with substantive right: *Findlay v. National Coal Board* 1965 S.L.T. 328, 330 per Lord Kissen; *Aitken v. Norrie* 1966 S.C. 168, 174 per L.P. Clyde.

It is an advantage to the defender to convene a third party where he has a right of contribution, relief or indemnity, or for apportionment of liability, against the third party because it saves intimating progress of the action and raising a separate action of relief (*Dorman, Long & Co. v. Harrower* (1899) 1 F. 1109, 1115 per Lord Kinnear). Where liability is either solely that of the defender or a third party, the defender may prefer not to convene the third party, thus avoiding paying expenses to the third party if he himself is found wholly liable.

The rule applies to a pursuer against whom a counterclaim is made or to a third party seeking to bring in a second third party (see, e.g. *Nicol Homeworld Contracts Ltd v. Charles Gray Builders Ltd* 1986 S.L.T. 317).

The court has a discretion whether to grant an order for service of a third party notice. In considering the question it will have regard to what would be in the interests of doing justice between the parties: *Rodgers v. James Crow & Sons Ltd* 1971 S.C. 155. That a party may lose his right to jury trial or other mode of inquiry is not a relevant factor: *Rodgers*, above. An order may be refused if there has been inordinate delay in seeking the order and the prejudice in refusing is outweighed by the prejudice to the other party in postponing the determination of the action: *Tait v. Leslie & Saddler Ltd* 1971 S.L.T.(Notes) 79; *Halbert v. British Airports Authority plc* 1996 S.L.T. 97.

26.1.2   The rule is, in all matters other than those in Sched. 9 to the C.J.J.A. 1982, that, subject to the rules of jurisdiction over consumer contracts, exclusive jurisdiction and prorogation of jurisdiction in the 1982 Act, a person maybe sued, as a third party in an action on a warranty or guarantee or in any other third party proceedings, in the court seized of the original proceedings (and not only in the courts for the place in which he is domiciled) unless solely for the purpose of removing him from the jurisdiction of a competent court: C.J.J.A. 1982, Sched. 8, r. 2(15)(b). Where the person to be sued as a third party is domiciled in a Contracting State to which the 1968 (Brussels) Convention, or the Lugano Convention, applies or is domiciled in another part of the UK, the same statutory rule applies: C.J.J.A. 1982, Sched. 1 (1968 Convention), Art. 6(2); Sched. 3C (Lugano Convention), Art. 6(2); Sched. 4 (Inter-UK jurisdiction), Art. 6(2). Jurisdiction may be invoked whatever the ground of jurisdiction in the original proceedings unless the jurisdiction of another court has been prorogated by agreement. Note *Hagen v. Zeehaghe* [1990] E.C.R. I-1845 where it was held that Art. 6 merely determines jurisdiction and is not concerned with the procedural rules for determining what third party claims the national court will admit to be heard under its own procedural rules provided the effectiveness of the convention is not impaired.

"SUBJECT-MATTER OF THE ACTION".

26.1.3   This means no more than the claim by the pursuer: *Buchan v. Thomson* 1976 S.L.T. 42, 45 per Lord Fraser.

"RIGHT OF CONTRIBUTION, RELIEF OR INDEMNITY".

26.1.4   This is the first ground on which a defender may bring in a third party. Such a right gives rise to a separate claim by the defender against the third party only, ancillary to the action between the pursuer and defender but incorporated with it in the same process. A third party may be convened by a defender after the expiry of a time-limit for the raising of the main action: see, e.g. *Findlay v. National Coal Board* 1965 S.L.T. 328. Where there are two or more pursuers, one may be convened as a third party: *Buchan v. Thomson* 1976 S.L.T. 42.

The defender must have title and interest at the time of service of the third party notice: *Cobham v. Minter* 1986 S.L.T. 336. He may have an interest although he does not have an enforceable right to recover until he has paid the pursuer: *Findlay v. National Coal Board* 1965 S.L.T. 328, 330 per Lord Kissen; *Beedie v. Norrie* 1966 S.C. 207, 210 per L.P. Clyde (cases on whether a third party could be convened with respect to a claim under s.3(2) of the Law Reform (Miscellaneous Provisions) (Scotland) Act 1940).

(1)   Right of contribution.

Technically this exists only where the defender and third party are co-obligants to the same principal: *Lanarkshire Speedway and Sports Stadium Ltd v. Gray* 1970 S.L.T.(Notes) 54. But, following *Anderson v. Anderson* 1981 S.L.T. 271, "contribution" should no longer be regarded as a term of art and third party procedure is not limited to its technical meaning: and see (2) below. Under s.3(1) of the Law Reform (Miscellaneous Provisions) (Scotland) Act 1940 persons found jointly and severally liable in damages or expenses for wrongful or negligent acts or omissions are liable inter se to contribute to those damages or expenses in such proportions as the court may deem just; but this does not affect the right of the pursuer to obtain decree against one or any of them, leaving it to him or them to recover from the others.

(2)   Right of relief.

The better view now is that "relief" here is not a term of art and is not limited to claims which would constitute an action of relief proper; and third party procedure may be used even where the defender seeks relief only in respect of part of the pursuer's claim, not just where the liability of the third party is commensurate or co-extensive with his: *Nimmo's Exrs. v. White's Exr.* 1976 S.L.T. 70; *Anderson v. Anderson* 1981 S.L.T. 271; *Nicol Homeworld Contracts Ltd v. Charles Gray Builders Ltd* 1986 S.L.T. 317. The view that the term is limited to its technical meaning (see *Lanarkshire Speedway and Sports Stadium Ltd v. Gray* 1970 S.L.T.(Notes) 54) must now be regarded as no longer the law. An action of relief proper arises generally where the pursuer and defender were under a common obligation which ought first to have been performed by the defender (*Caledonian Railway Co. v. Colt* (1860) 3 Macq. 833) and the damages claimed must be to a certain extent commensurate and must be founded on the same kind of liability (*Caledonian Railway Co.*, above; *Ovington v. McVicar* (1864) 2 M. 1066, 1073 per L.J.-C. Inglis; *Buchanan & Carswell v. Eugene Ltd* 1936 S.C. 160, 182 per Lord Murray). A defender sued in contract cannot claim a right of relief based on negligence under s.3(2) of the Law Reform (Miscellaneous Provisions) (Scotland) Act 1940 because that provision is concerned with joint wrongdoers: *National Coal Board v. Knight Bros.* 1972 S.L.T.(Notes) 24. Also, if sued for negligence, a defender cannot claim a right of relief on the ground that the third party was in breach of a duty to him because liability to make a contribution under s.3(2) of the 1940 Act arises out of a duty by the third party to the pursuer: *R. & W. Watson Ltd v. David Traill & Sons Ltd* 1972 S.L.T.(Notes) 38. Abandonment by a pursuer of an action so far as directed against a defender does not affect a claim under s.3(2) of the 1940 Act between defenders (or between a defender and a third party): *Singer v. Gray Tool Co. (Europe) Ltd* 1984 S.L.T. 149. The extinction of the obligation to contribute under s.3(2) of the 1940 Act which has subsisted for two years after the date on which the right to recover the contribution became enforceable without a relevant claim or acknowledgement should be noted: Prescription and Limitation (Scotland) Act 1973, s.8A inserted by the Prescription and Limitation (Scotland) Act 1984, s.1.

(3) Right of indemnity.

An indemnity arises where, by law or agreement, one person is liable for the liability of another. It should not be regarded as a term of art and in third party procedure is not limited to any technical meaning: and see (2) above.

THIRD PARTY SOLELY, JOINTLY OR JOINTLY AND SEVERALLY LIABLE.

This is the second ground on which the defender can bring in a third party. Under this head the defender claims the third party is (to some extent) liable to the pursuer: *Buchan v. Thomson* 1976 S.L.T. 42, 45 per Lord Fraser. The pursuer can only recover from the third party if he amends to include a claim against him: *Findlay v. National Coal Board* 1965 S.L.T. 328, 329 per Lord Kissen. If the pursuer does not make a claim against the third party or call him as a defender he cannot succeed against him: *Aitken v. Norrie* 1966 S.C. 168. The pursuer does not have to make the third party a defender (*Jack v. Glasgow Corporation* 1965 S.L.T. 227) though he may do so (*Thomson v. Greig* 1967 S.L.T.(Notes) 113). If a defender claims the third party is solely liable and the pursuer does not make a case against the third party, the latter can obtain dismissal of the defender's case against him: *Connor v. Andrew Main & Sons* 1967 S.L.T.(Notes) 71 (no claim of indemnity or joint liability). If the pursuer does not amend where joint or joint and several liability is averred and established, the court grants decree to the pursuer against the defender, finds the defender entitled to a right of relief against the third party for his proportion of the liability to the pursuer and decerns against the third party for payment to the defender for that proportion. If the defender does not pay the pursuer, the latter may sue the third party (subject to prescription and limitation).

A pursuer may not amend to add a claim against a third party after expiry of a limitation or prescriptive period (*Aitken v. Norrie* 1966 S.C. 168) unless he can invoke s.19A of the Prescription and Limitation (Scotland) Act 1973 (inserted by the Law Reform (Miscellaneous Provisions) (Scotland) Act 1980, s.23 and amended by the Prescription and Limitation (Scotland) Act 1984, Sched. 1, para. 8) (discretion to dispense with limitation period) or the time-limit runs from a date other than the date on which the injuries or death occurred. It is sufficient if the conclusions are amended before expiry of the limitation or prescriptive period: *Cross v. Noble* 1975 S.L.T.(Notes) 33. It is sufficient if the minute of amendment is allowed to be received and intimated before expiry of its limitation or prescriptive period and it is not required that the record be amended in terms of the minute of amendment: *Boyle v. Glasgow Corporation* 1975 S.C. 238, 251 per L.J.-C. Wheatley.

Joint liability means liability pro rata, each liable for his proportionate share. Joint and several liability means liability *in solidum*, each liable for the whole amount.

ARISING FROM OR IN CONNECTION WITH THE LIABILITY OF THE DEFENDER.

This is the third ground on which the defender can bring in a third party. This head was proposed by the Rules Review Group. It is wide enough to include the other two grounds in r. 26.1 (see notes 26.1.4 and 26.1.5) and anything left out by them and overcomes any doubt about the meaning of the phrase "right of contribution, relief or indemnity".

"MOTION".

For motions, see Chap. 23

JURY TRIAL.

The presence of a third party may result in the pursuer losing his right to jury trial, because the discretion in this rule supersedes the pursuer's statutory right (C.S.A. 1988, s.11) to jury trial: *Winchester v. Ramsay* 1966 S.C. 41, 45 per Lord Kissen. In deciding whether to grant an order for service of a third party notice it is not relevant to consider whether a party may lose his right to jury trial: *Rodgers v. James Crow & Sons Ltd* 1971 S.C. 155.

Averments where order for service of third party notice sought

26.2.—(1) Where a defender intends to apply by motion for an order for service of a third party notice before the closing of the record, he shall, before enrolling the motion, set out in his defences, by adjustment to those defences, or in a separate statement of facts annexed to those defences—

    (a)   averments setting out the grounds on which he maintains that the proposed third party is liable to him by contribution, relief or indemnity or should be made a party to the action; and

    (b)   appropriate pleas-in-law.

(2) Where a defender applies by motion for an order for service of a third party notice after the closing of the record, he shall, on enrolling the motion, lodge a minute of amendment containing—

26.1.5

26.1.6

26.1.7

26.1.8

26.2

(a)   averments setting out the grounds on which he maintains that the proposed third party is liable to him by contribution, relief or indemnity or should be made a party to the action, and

(b)   appropriate pleas-in-law,

unless those grounds and pleas-in-law have been set out in the defences in the closed record.

Deriv. R.C.S. 1965, r. 85(1) (preamble (part)) amended by SI 1980/1144

GENERAL NOTE.

26.2.1

If application for a third party notice is made before the record has been closed, an adjusted print of the open record (or other pleadings) should be lodged showing the averments which would justify the third party notice.

Authority for diligence etc. on third party notices

26.3

26.3.—[1](1)   A defender who applies for an order for service of a third party notice may apply by motion for authority for—

(a)   arrestment to found jurisdiction; or

(b)   diligence by—

    (i)   inhibition on the dependence of the action;

    (ii)   arrestment on the dependence of the action where there is a conclusion for the payment of money;

    (iii)   arrestment in rem; or

    (iv)   dismantling a ship.

(2)   A certified copy of an interlocutor granting a motion under paragraph (1) shall be sufficient authority for execution of the arrestment to found jurisdiction or, as the case may be, the diligence.

(3)   A certified copy of an interlocutor granting authority for inhibition under this rule may be registered with a certificate of execution in the Register of Inhibitions and Adjudications.

(4)[2]   A notice of a certified copy of an interlocutor granting authority for inhibition under this rule may be registered in the Register of Inhibitions and Adjudications; and such registration is to have the same effect as registration of a notice of inhibition under section 155(2) of the Titles to Land Consolidation (Scotland) Act 1868.

Deriv. R.C.S. 1965, r. 85(1)(b)

GENERAL NOTE.

26.3.1

For arrestment and inhibition on the dependence, see Chap. 14A. For arrestment in rem and dismantling of a ship, see notes 13.6A.3 and 13.6A.4.

"MOTION".

26.3.2

For motions, see Chap.23.

Service on third party

26.4

26.4.—(1)   A third party notice shall be served on the third party within such period as the court shall specify in the interlocutor allowing service of that notice.

(2)   Where service of a third party notice has not been made within the period specified by virtue of paragraph (1), the order for service of it shall cease to have effect; and no service of the notice may be made unless a further order for service of it has been applied for and granted.

(3)   There shall be served with a third party notice—

(a)   a copy of the pleadings (including any adjustments and amendments);

---

[1] R. 26.3 substituted by S.S.I. 2004 No. 537 (effective 10th November, 2003).

[2] R. 26.3(4) substituted by S.S.I. 2009 No. 104 (effective 22nd April 2009).

    (b)   a copy of the interlocutor allowing service of the notice; and

    (c)[1] where the pleadings have not been amended in accordance with the minute of amendment, a copy of that minute.

  (4) The defender who served the third party notice shall lodge in process—

    (a)   a copy of the third party notice; and

    (b)   a copy of the interlocutor allowing service of it; and

    (c)   a certificate of service.

Deriv. R.C.S. 1965, r. 85(1)(a)

SERVICE WITHIN THE PERIOD SPECIFIED.

The court will usually specify the period of notice for service of a summons (21 days within Europe and 42 days furth of Europe: see r. 13.4), but this may be shortened or extended, and the notice must be served *within* that period. For methods of service, see Chap. 16, Pt. I.   **26.4.1**

"COPY OF THE INTERLOCUTOR ORDERING SERVICE".

A copy of this interlocutor will have been served with the third party notice. A copy must be lodged in process with a certificate of service and a copy of the third party notice, as an execution copy, so that the clerk of session can check the copy of the interlocutor served against the interlocutor itself. The execution copy is lodged as a step of process: see r. 4.4.   **26.4.2**

Answers to third party notice

26.5.—(1) An order for service of a third party notice shall specify 28 days, or such other period as the court on cause shown may specify, as the period within which the third party may lodge answers.   **26.5**

  (2) Answers for a third party shall include—

    (a)   answers to the averments of the defender against him in the form of numbered paragraphs corresponding to the numbered articles of the condescendence annexed to the summons and incorporating, if the third party so wishes, answers to the averments of the pursuer; or

    (b)   where a separate statement of facts has been lodged by the defender under rule 26.2(1), answers to the statement of facts in the form of numbered paragraphs corresponding to the numbered paragraphs of the statement of facts; and

    (c)   appropriate pleas-in-law.

Deriv. R.C.S. 1965, r. 85(1) (preamble (part)) amended by S.I. 1980 No. 1144

FORM AND LODGING OF ANSWERS.

These are dealt with in r. 26.5(2).   **26.5.1**

FEE.

The court fee for lodging answers is payable on lodging by a person who is entering the process for the first time. For fee, see Court of Session etc. Fees Order 1984, Table of Fees, Pt. I, B, item 6 [SI 1984/256, Table as amended, pp. C1202 et seq.]. The fee may be debited under a credit scheme introduced on 1st April 1976 by P.N. No. 4 of 1976 to the account (if one is kept or permitted) of the agent by the court cashier, and an account will be rendered weekly by the court cashier's office to the agent for all court fees due that week for immediate settlement. Party litigants and agents not operating the scheme must pay cash on each occasion a fee is due at the time of lodging at the counter at the General Department.   **26.5.2**

Consequences of failure to lodge answers

26.6.—(1) Where a third party fails to lodge answers, the defender may apply by motion for such finding, order or decree against the third party as may be appropriate to give effect to the claim in the third party notice.   **26.6**

(1A)[2] Where a minute of amendment under rule 26.2(2) has been lodged, the defendants may not apply by motion under paragraph (1) unless, at or before the

---

[1] R.26.4(3) amended by S.S.I. 2001 No. 305, para. 3 (effective 18th September 2001).

[2] R.26.6(1) revoked and r. 26.6(1A) inserted by S.S.I. 2004 No. 52 (effective 1st March, 2004).

date on which he makes the application, he applies by motion to amend the pleadings in terms of the minute of amendment.

(2)   Where such a finding, order or decree is pronounced by the court, rule 19.2 (recall of decrees in absence) shall, with the necessary modifications, apply to that finding, order or decree as it applies to recall of a decree in absence by a defender.

"MOTION".

26.6.1   For motions, see Chap.23.

"PARAGRAPH (1)".

26.6.2   This presumably means para.(1) of this rule (r. 26.6).

Procedure following answers

26.7   **26.7.**—(1)   Within 14 days after the date on which answers are lodged by the third party, the defender who has served the third party notice shall—

(a)   make up an open record incorporating the pleadings of all parties;

(b)   deliver four copies of that record to every other party; and

(c)   lodge two copies of that record in process.

(2)   When an open record is lodged in process under paragraph (1), the action shall be put out on the Adjustment Roll and the court shall pronounce an interlocutor continuing the action on that roll for six weeks.

(3)   Where a proof or jury trial is necessary between parties to the action, the court may allow the action so far as directed against the third party to proceed to proof or jury trial, as the case may be, before, at the same time as or after, the action between the pursuer and the defender as the court thinks fit.

(4)   Where a third party challenges the case pled by the pursuer, he may appear at the proof or jury trial of the pursuer's case and lead evidence as if he were a defender; and such evidence, so far as competent and relevant, shall be evidence for or against the pursuer or for or against the defender, as the case may be, and shall be available to all the parties in the action.

(5)   Subject to the preceding provisions of this Chapter and unless the context otherwise requires, the other provisions of these Rules in relation to actions shall, with the necessary modifications, apply as between the defender and a third party or the pursuer and a third party, as the case may be, as they apply to the action between the pursuer and defender.

Deriv. R.C.S. 1965, r. 85(1)(c) (part) amended by S.I. 1976 No. 2197 and 1980 No. 1144 (r. 26.7(1)) and r. 85(1)(e) (r. 26.7(3) and (4))

"WITHIN 14 DAYS".

26.7.1   The date from which the period is calculated is not counted. Where the last day falls on a Saturday or Sunday or a public holiday on which the Office of Court is closed, the next available day is allowed: r. 1.3(7). For office hours and public holidays, see note 3.1.2.

"OPEN RECORD".

26.7.2   See r. 22.1(4).

ADJUSTMENT.

26.7.3   For the Adjustment Roll, see r. 22.2.

PROOF OF CLAIM AGAINST THIRD PARTY.

26.7.4   It may sometimes be appropriate to sist the action between the pursuer and defender until the determination of the dispute between the defender and third party: *Cookney v. Laverty* 1967 S.L.T. (Notes) 89.

In *Vetco Gray UK Ltd v. Slessor* , 2006 S.C. 398 (Second Div.), it was held that r. 26.7(3), though slightly differently worded than the former R.C.S. 1965, r. 85(e), did not exclude the two stages being conducted by different modes of inquiry (and pursuer not deprived of right to jury trial because of proof before answer on indemnity issue).

Third party challenging pursuer's case.

As the third party is entitled to be heard on any matter in which he has a relevant interest (*Barton v. William Low & Co. Ltd* 1968 S.L.T. (Notes) 27, 28 per Lord Stott), he may challenge the claim of the pursuer against the defender; he may adopt the pursuer's case against the defender and blame the defender (see, e.g. *Algeo v. Melville Dundas & Whitson Ltd* 1973 S.L.T. (Notes) 90).

26.7.5

Application of other rules.

R. 26.7(5) is necessary to ensure the application, where appropriate, of rules which apply to a pursuer or defender to a third party.

26.7.6

CHAPTER 26A GROUP PROCEDURE[1]

Part 1 – General Provisions

Interpretation and application of this Chapter

26A.1.—(1) In this Chapter—

"the Act" means the Civil Litigation (Expenses and Group Proceedings) (Scotland) Act 2018 ;

"group" has the meaning provided in section 20(2) of the Act;

"group member" means a person who, along with one or more other persons, expressly consents to the group proceedings to be brought on his or her behalf;

"group proceedings" has the meaning provided in section 20(1) of the Act;

"group register" is a record, in Form 26A.15, of those persons who are group members;

"representative party" has the meaning provided in section 20(2) of the Act.

(2) In rules 26A.6, 26A.7, 26A.9, 26A.11 and 26A.15 "applicant" has the meaning given in rule 26A.5(1) .

(3) This Chapter applies to group proceedings as provided for by Part 4 of the Act.

GENERAL NOTE

In 1996 the Scottish Law Commission published a report on Multi-Party Actions (Scot Law Com No 154) recommending them. This followed, inter alia, a report by a Working Party on Multi-Party Actions in 1993 on which the principal author served. The Law Commission report contained a draft Act of Sederunt introducing a Chapter 43A on Group Proceedings. The report and draft rules were never implemented.

Twenty-two years later, the Scottish Parliament passed the Civil Litigation (Expenses and Group Proceedings) (Scotland) Act 2018 introducing group proceedings, and the rules made under that Act came into effect on 31st July 2020. (The Scottish Law Commission recommendation was adopted by the Gill Review (*Report of the Scottish Civil Courts Review* 2009, Chapter 13,para. 64.)

The background and features of the Scottish Group Procedure are set out by Lord Ericht in *Bridgehouse v BMW*, 2024 S.L.T. 116 (OH). The approach of the Competition Appeals Tribunal has been to interpret the legislation for collective proceedings purposively and in accordance with the objectives of the regime (*Mastercard v Merricks* [2020] UKSC 51 at paras [2], [37], [92]; *Commercial and Interregional Card Claims I Ltd and Others v Mastercard Inc and Others* [2023] CAT 38 at para. [42]; *BT Group plc v Justin le Patourel* [2022] EWCA Civ 593 at paras. [25]-[29]). That approach should also be adopted in relation to the Scottish Group Procedure: *Bridgehouse v BMW* 2024 S.L.T. 116, para [7].

Chapter 26A applies to proceedings in which there are two or more persons each with a separate claim which raises issues that are the same or similar, or related to each other, and which may be the subject of civil proceedings: P. N. No. 2 of 2020. The actual definition is in s. 20(2) of the 2018 Act:

"A person (a "representative party") may bring group proceedings on behalf of two or more persons (a "group") each of whom has a separate claim which may be the subject of civil proceedings".

The expression "civil proceedings" probably means any proceedings which may be brought before the civil court in which the group proceedings are raised (in this instance, the Court of Session). The expression is not defined in the Act or elsewhere. Oddly, the representative party does not have to be a member of the group on whose behalf the proceedings are brought: s. 20(3)(a).

Section 20(7) allows for group proceedings to be opt-in or opt-out proceedings. Opt-in proceedings are those in which each member of the group expressly consents to them. Opt-out proceedings are those in which (a) each member is domiciled in Scotland and has not given notice that he or she does not consent or (b) is not domiciled in Scotland and has given express consent: s. 20(7) and (8). Chapter 26A makes no provision for opt-out proceedings.

Group proceedings may not be tried by jury: s. 20(10).

The procedure in Chap. 26A is as follows. First, a person must apply by motion to be appointed as a representative party. Second, thereafter, an application has to be made by motion for permission to bring group proceedings. (Could one motion by the person seeking to be a representative party contain both applications?) Third, the proceedings are commenced in relation to members of the group when, permission

---

[1] Chapter 26A inserted by S.S.I. 2020 No. 208 r. 2(5) (effective 31st July 2020).

having been granted, a group register of members of the group is served on the defender: see r. 26A.18. When a new member joins, in relation to that member it is commenced when the revised register is served.

Any person seeking to be a representative party must be authorised by the court and group proceedings may be brought only with the permission of the court: s. 20(3) and (5). Group proceedings begin by one or more persons applying to the court under s. 20(3) of the 2018 Act by motion to be a representative party. Where one person applies, the procedure is set out in r. 26A.5. Where the court receives more than one application from persons seeking to be the representative party, the procedure is set out in r. 26A.6; only one person may be a representative party: s. 20(4).

Once such a person has been authorised to be the representative party (see r. 26A.7), that person, or any other person, must then enrol a motion to seek permission to bring group proceedings: s. 20(5) and r. 26A.9.

A practice note, P.N. No. 2 of 2020, has been issued which contains a narrative version of the rules.

Counsel or solicitors having rights of audience who are principally instructed are expected to appear at all hearings. It may be appropriate for one pursuers' agent to be designated the lead agent, which it is expected would be the agent for the representative party (there can be only one: s. 20(4) of the 2018 Act). See P.N. No. 2 of 2020, paras. 6 and 7.

Disapplication of certain rules

26A.2 **26A.2.**—(1) The requirement in rule 4.1(4) (form, size, etc., of documents forming the process) for a step in process to be folded lengthwise does not apply in proceedings to which this Chapter applies.

(2) An open record is not to be made up in, and Chapter 22 (making up and closing records) does not apply to, proceedings to which this Chapter applies unless otherwise ordered by the Lord Ordinary.

(3) The following rules do not apply to proceedings to which this Chapter applies—

    (a)   rule 6.2 (fixing and allocation of diets in Outer House);

    (b)   rule 36.3 (lodging productions).

Procedure in group proceedings

26A.3 **26A.3.**—(1) Subject to the other provisions of this Chapter, the procedure in proceedings to which this Chapter applies is to be such as the Lord Ordinary is to order or direct.

(2) All proceedings in the Outer House to which this Chapter applies are to be heard or determined on such dates and at such times as are fixed by the Lord Ordinary.

(3) The fixing of a hearing for a specified date and time in proceedings to which this Chapter applies does not affect the right of any party to apply by motion at any time under these rules.

PRACTICE NOTE

26A.3.1 P. N. No. 2 of 2020 applies to group proceedings.

Arrangements will be made to ensure that group proceedings will be dealt with by the same judge and, in the case of proceedings of a transaction or dispute of a commercial or business nature, by a commercial judge nominated by the Lord President: P.N. No. 2 of 2022, para. 5.

Motions under this Chapter

26A.4 **26A.4.**—(1) Chapter 23 (motions) applies to motions under this Chapter.

(2) Motions under this Chapter may be intimated and enrolled in accordance with Part 2 of Chapter 23.

Email motions in Form 23.1C and opposition in Form 23.1D may be enrolled by emailing the completed form to gcs@scotcourts.gov.uk: P.N. No. 2 of 2020, para. 38.

26A.4.1

Part 2 – Representative Party

Application to be a representative party

26A.5.—(1) An application by a person (the "applicant") under section 20(3)(b) of the Act to be a representative party to bring group proceedings is to be made by motion, in Form 26A.5.

26A.5

(2) On a motion being enrolled under paragraph (1), the application is to be brought before a Lord Ordinary on the first available day after being made, for an order for—

(a) intimation and service of the application on the defender and such other person as the Lord Ordinary thinks fit within 7 days of the date of the order, or within such other period as the Lord Ordinary thinks fit;

(b) such advertisement as the Lord Ordinary thinks fit to take place within 7 days of the date of the order, or within such other period as the Lord Ordinary thinks fit;

(c) any person on whom the application has been served, to lodge answers and any relevant documents, if so advised, within 21 days after the date of service, or within such other period as the Lord Ordinary thinks fit.

(3) A person served with the application who intends to participate in the decision as to whether authorisation should be given must lodge answers within the period ordered for the lodging of answers.

(4) Where answers are lodged under paragraph (2)(c) a hearing must be fixed.

(5) The applicant and any person who has lodged answers must be given at least 7 days' notice of a hearing ordered under paragraph (4).

(6) Where application for permission to bring proceedings is being made under rule 26A.9(1) at the same time as an application is made under paragraph (1) then paragraphs (7) and (8) apply.

(7) The applicant must, at the same time as making the applications under this rule and rule 26A.9(1), lodge in the General Department—

(a) the summons by which it is proposed to institute proceedings;

(b) a group register in Form 26A.15; and

(c) all relevant documents in the applicant's possession which are necessary for the court to determine whether or not to give permission.

(8) The applicant must, at the same time as lodging papers in the General Department under paragraph (7), serve those papers on the defender.

(9) Evidence of service in accordance with Chapter 16 must be provided to the General Department within 14 days from the date of service.

The first step in group proceedings is that they are brought by a representative party on behalf of two or more persons having separate claims which may be the subject of civil proceedings and that person must apply to the court to be authorised to be the representative party. The person seeking to be the representative party must be the applicant. That person does not have to be a member of the group on whose behalf the proceedings are brought: 2018 Act s. 20(3)(a). While that seems odd, it allows for an ideological pursuer such as a consumer body to be a representative party provided it has standing to bring proceedings (Gill Review Chapter 13 para. 69) or for other pursuers who have neither an ideological interest nor a claim against the defenders: see comment in *Bridgehouse v BMW* 2024 S.L.T. 116 (OH), para. [40]. In that case (at para. [42], commenting on the recent appointment of retired lawyers as representative parties, Lord Ericht said that such appointments should not become the norm in Scottish Group Procedure: a policy objective of the 2018 Act is to help to broaden access to justice; insistence on appointment of an independent person rather than a group member could unduly restrict the number of group proceedings brought in Scotland and restrict, rather than broaden, access to justice.

26A.5.1

It is not suitable for a firm of solicitors acting for pursuers in group proceedings also to be the representative party as there is a potential for or appearance of conflict: *Thomsons Solicitors Scotland v. James Finlay (Kenya) Ltd* 2022 S.L.T. 731 (OH).

Where the court receives more than one application from persons seeking to be the representative party, the procedure is set out in r. 26A.6; only one person may be a representative party: s. 20(4).

Rule 26A.7 sets out matters to be considered in deciding whether the person applying is a suitable person to be authorised as the representative party.

It is preferred that the group register is lodged in electronic form in pdf format; and that data protection measures are applied: P.N. No. 2 of 2020, para. 26.

"MOTION"

26A.5.2   For motions, see Chap. 23 and r. 26A.4. The application will be treated as a motion made before calling which does not have to be (but may be) intimated: P.N. No. 2 of 2020, para. 11.

"INTIMATION AND SERVICE"

26A.5.3   For intimation and service, see Chap. 16. A schedule of service must be added to the application: P.N. No. 2 of 2020, para. 14.

The application should aver what advertisement has been undertaken so far and what further advertisement would be appropriate or if not, why not: P.N. No. 2 of 2020, para. 15. Supporting documentation should include copies of any advertisements already made.

"THE SUMMONS"

26A.5.4   On the form of summons, see r. 26A.19.

"WITHIN 7 DAYS OF", "WITHIN 21 DAYS AFTER", "WITHIN 14 DAYS FROM"

26A.5.5   The drafter of Chap. 26A has peppered the chapter with a variety of "of", "from", "after", "following" and "prior" in relation to time without regard to time-honoured phrases judicially construed.

It is not clear whether "of" is intended to be different from "from". Use of "from" is ambiguous: does it include the day from which time commences or from the termination of it? The context may indicate that it is excluded if "of" implies that the day from which time commences is included.

Within 21 days "after" is clearer: the date from which the period is calculated is not counted.

Where the last day falls on a Saturday or a Sunday or a public holiday on which the Office of Court is closed, the next available day is allowed: r. 1.3(7). For office hours and public holidays, see note 3.1.2.

"ANSWERS"

26A.5.6   See r. 18.3.

Application by more than one person to be a representative party

26A.6   **26A.6.**—(1) This rule applies where—

    (a)   more than one application made under rule 26A.5(1) is received by the court from more than one applicant in connection with the same issues (whether of fact or law) which may be subject to group proceedings; and

    (b)   the Lord Ordinary has not determined the first received application at the point a subsequent application is received.

(2) A hearing on the applications must be fixed by the court.

(3) The applicants must be given at least 7 days' notice of a hearing fixed under paragraph (2).

GENERAL NOTE

26A.6.1   Where the court receives more than one application from persons seeking to be the representative party, the procedure is set out in r. 26A.6. This is because only one person may be a representative party: 2018 Act s. 20(4).

"7 DAYS NOTICE"

26A.6.2   Seven *clear days'* notice would mean that the first and last days are excluded from the calculation. Is that what is meant?

Determination of an application by a person to be a representative party

26A.7   **26A.7.**—(1) An applicant may be authorised under section 20(3)(b) of the Act to be a representative party in group proceedings only where the applicant has satisfied the Lord Ordinary that the applicant is a suitable person who can act in that capacity should such authorisation be given.

(2)   The matters which are to be considered by the Lord Ordinary when deciding whether or not an applicant is a suitable person under paragraph (1) include—

    (a)   the special abilities and relevant expertise of the applicant;

    (b)   the applicant's own interest in the proceedings;

    (c)   whether there would be any potential benefit to the applicant, financial or otherwise, should the application be authorised;

    (d)   confirmation that the applicant is independent from the defender;

    (e)   demonstration that the applicant would act fairly and adequately in the interests of the group members as a whole, and that the applicant's own interests do not conflict with those of the group whom the applicant seeks to represent; and

    (f)   the demonstration of sufficient competence by the applicant to litigate the claims properly, including financial resources to meet any expenses awards (the details of funding arrangements do not require to be disclosed).

(3)   The Lord Ordinary may refuse an application made by an applicant seeking authorisation to be given under section 20(3)(b) of the Act where the applicant has not satisfied the Lord Ordinary that the applicant is a suitable person, in terms of paragraphs (1) and (2), to act in that capacity.

(4)   Authorisation given under paragraph (1) endures until the group proceedings finish or until permission is withdrawn.

GENERAL NOTE

26A.7.1

The court may give permission for group proceedings only if (a) all the claims raise issues of fact or law which are the same as, or similar, or related to, each other, (b) it is satisfied that the representative party has made all reasonable efforts to identify all potential members of the group and (c) in accordance with provisions made under s. 21(1): 2018 Act s. 20(6).

The provisions made under s. 21(1) include those set out in r. 26A. The applicant to be the representative party must be a suitable person who can act in that capacity and the court must consider, among any others, those listed in r. 26A.7(2).

The test for authorisation to be a representative party is that the court must be satisfied he is a suitable person who can act in that capacity should such authorisation be given (r. 26A.7.(1)), having considered the non-exclusive list of matters set out in r. 26A.7.(2): *Bridgehouse v BMW*, 2024 S.L.T. 116 (OH). Because the representative party will have the advice of counsel, the court should not expect too much or be too demanding in evaluating whether a person can properly serve as a representative party: *Bridgehouse*, at para. [44] referring to *Sondhi v Deloitte Management Services LP*, 2018 ONSC 271 at para. [42].

There is no requirement in Scotland for the court to assess the competence of the lawyers acting for the proposed representative party: *Bridgehouse*, para. [37].

Whether a representative party should have an advisory council is a matter for the court and not the defender. The costs of such a council would be contrary to the policy objective of broadening access to justice. The basis on which the Competition Appeals Tribunal considered such a council was different from that under the Scottish group procedure. See *Bridgehouse*, paras. [50]-[59].

Replacement of a representative party

26A.8

26A.8.—(1)   A representative party may apply to the court, by motion in Form 26A.8, seeking the permission of the court to authorise, in place of that party, another person as the representative party, who may or may not be a group member.

(2)   A group member may apply to the court, by motion in Form 26A.8, seeking the permission to authorise the replacement of the representative party with another person, who may or may not be a group member.

(3)   On a motion being enrolled in terms of paragraph (1) or (2), the application is to be brought before a Lord Ordinary on the first available day after being made, for an order for—

    (a)   intimation and service of the application on—

        (i)   the defender;

        (ii)   in the case of an application made under paragraph (2), the representative party;

(iii)   the group members; and

(iv)   such other person as the Lord Ordinary thinks fit,

in a manner which the Lord Ordinary thinks most appropriate in the circumstances, within 7 days of the date of the order, or within such other period as the Lord Ordinary thinks fit;

(b)   such advertisement as the Lord Ordinary thinks fit to take place within 7 days of the date of the order, or within such other period as the Lord Ordinary thinks fit;

(c)   any person on whom the application has been served, to lodge answers and any relevant documents, if so advised, within 21 days after the date of service, or within such other period as the Lord Ordinary thinks fit.

(4)   A person served with an application under this rule who intends to participate in the decision as to whether permission should be given must lodge answers within the period ordered for the lodging of answers.

(5)   Subject to paragraphs (6) and (7), the Lord Ordinary may—

(a)   where satisfied it is appropriate to do so, decide to proceed without holding a hearing;

(b)   fix a date for the hearing of the application;

(c)   require further information from the representative party, the proposed replacement representative party or the group members before making any further order.

(6)   Where—

(a)   in the case of an application made under paragraph (2), the representative party;

(b)   in the case of an application made under paragraph (1) or (2), a group member,

has lodged answers in opposition to the application then paragraph (7) applies.

(7)   A hearing on the application and the answers lodged thereto must be fixed by the court.

(8)   Where a hearing on the application is fixed by the court, it must give—

(a)   the applicant;

(b)   the defender;

(c)   the representative party;

(d)   the person who is to replace the representative party; and

(e)   the group members,

an opportunity to be heard before considering whether to grant the application or not.

(9)   Subject to paragraph (10), the Lord Ordinary may grant an application made under paragraph (2) only where it appears to the Lord Ordinary that the representative party is not able to represent the interests of the group members adequately.

(10)   No application made under paragraph (1) or (2) may be granted unless the Lord Ordinary is satisfied that—

(a)   the person who is to replace the representative party is a suitable person who can act in that capacity should such authorisation be given, having regard to the matters mentioned in rule 26A.7(2); and

(b)   the best interests of the group members are met.

(11)   Where the Lord Ordinary makes an order authorising a person to be a representative party under section 20(3)(b) of the Act in place of a person who had previously been so authorised, the newly authorised representative party must, as soon as practicable and no later than 14 days after the date on which the order is made, inform all other parties and the group members of the order.

(12) The Lord Ordinary may, when making an order under this rule, make any such order as the Lord Ordinary thinks fit.

GENERAL NOTE

Rule 26A.8 makes provision for a representative party or a group member to replace the representative party.

26A.8.1

"MOTION"

For motions, see Chap. 23 and r. 26A.4.

26A.8.2

"INTIMATION AND SERVICE"

For intimation and service, see Chap. 16.

26A.8.3

"WITHIN 7 DAYS OF", WITHIN 21 DAYS AFTER", "NO LATER THAN 14 DAYS AFTER"

The word "of" implies that the day from which time commences is included in the calculation.

Within 21 days "after" is clearer: the date from which the period is calculated is not counted. No later than 14 days after means that the day of the order is not counted.

Where the last day falls on a Saturday or a Sunday or a public holiday on which the Office of Court is closed, the next available day is allowed: r. 1.3(7). For office hours and public holidays, see note 3.1.2.

26A.8.4

Part 3 – Permission to Bring Group Proceedings

Application for permission

26A.9.—(1) An application for permission to bring group proceedings under section 20(5) of the Act is to be made by the representative party or, as the case may be, the applicant by motion, in Form 26A.9.

26A.9

(2) On a motion being enrolled in terms of paragraph (1), the application is to be brought before a Lord Ordinary on the first available day after being made, for an order for—

(a) intimation and service of the application on the defender and such other person as the Lord Ordinary thinks fit within 7 days of the date of the order, or within such other period as the Lord Ordinary thinks fit;

(b) such advertisement as the Lord Ordinary thinks fit to take place within 7 days of the date of the order, or within such other period as the Lord Ordinary thinks fit;

(c) any person on whom the application has been served, to lodge answers and any relevant documents, if so advised, within 21 days after the date of service, or within such other period as the Lord Ordinary thinks fit.

(3) The representative party or, as the case may be, the applicant must lodge in the General Department—

(a) the summons by which it is proposed to institute proceedings;

(b) a group register in Form 26A.15; and

(c) all relevant documents in their possession which are necessary for the court to determine whether or not to give permission,

at the same time as making an application for permission under paragraph (1).

(4) The representative party or, as the case may be, the applicant must, at the same time as lodging papers in the General Department under paragraph (3), serve those papers on the defender.

(5) Evidence of service in accordance with Chapter 16 must be provided to the General Department within 14 days from the date of service.

(6) A person served with the application who intends to participate in the decision as to whether permission should be given must lodge answers within the period ordered for the lodging of answers.

GENERAL NOTE

Normally, the person seeking permission will be the person appointed to be the representative party under r. 26A.5. However, it is permissible for a person seeking to be appointed the representative party to

26A.9.1

lodge an application for permission to bring the proceedings under r. 26A.9, at the same time as the application under r. 26A.5 to be appointed as the representative party: implication of r. 26A.5(6).

Rules 26A.10 to 26A.13 make further provision for that application including a right of appeal by reclaiming motion against the refusal or grant of permission.

Form 26A.9 requires, in para. 6, details of the grounds on which permission is sought. The grounds for refusing permission in r. 26A.11(5) should be addressed: P.N. No. 2 of 2020, para. 17.

"MOTION"

26A.9.2   For motions, see Chap. 23 and r. 26A.4.

"INTIMATION AND SERVICE"

26A.9.3   For intimation and service, see Chap. 16.

"WITHIN 7 DAYS OF", WITHIN 21 DAYS AFTER", WITHIN 14 DAYS FROM"

26A.9.4   It is not clear whether "of" is intended to be different from "from". Use of "from" is ambiguous: does it include the day from which time commences or from the termination of it? The context may indicate that it is excluded if "of" implies that the day from which time commences is included.

Within 21 days "after" is clearer: the date from which the period is calculated is not counted.

Where the last day falls on a Saturday or a Sunday or a public holiday on which the Office of Court is closed, the next available day is allowed: r. 1.3(7). For office hours and public holidays, see note 3.1.2.

"SAME AS, OR SIMILAR OR RELATED TO, EACH OTHER"

26A.9.5   In *Campbell v. James Finlay (Kenya) Ltd* 2022 S.L.T. 751 (First Div.), it was argued that a group doing the same kind of work was not the same, similar or related issue of fact or law. It was held that the issue of fact related to the nature of the defender's working practices and the issue of law was whether those practices amounted to negligence.

"SUMMONS"

26A.9.6   On the form of the summons, see r. 26A.19.

Application for permission: further provision

26A.10   **26A.10.**—(1) If a party seeks any of the orders mentioned in paragraph (3), that party must apply by motion.

(2) The Lord Ordinary must have regard to the need for the fair and efficient determination of the action when making any such order.

(3) The orders are—

    (a) dispensing with intimation, service or advertisement;

    (b) adjusting the period for intimation, service or advertisement;

    (c) adjusting the period for the lodging of answers and any relevant documents;

    (d) an interim order; or

    (e) a sist, on cause shown.

(4) A sist must be for no longer than 28 days, but can be renewed.

(5) The representative party must, within 7 days of the date of the interlocutor, notify the Scottish Legal Aid Board of a sist for legal aid.

"MOTION"

26A.10.1   For motions, see Chap. 23.

"WITHIN 7 DAYS OF"

26A.10.2   The word "of" implies that the day from which time commences is included in the calculation.

The permission stage

26A.11   **26A.11.**—(1) Within 14 days of the expiry of the period within which answers may be lodged the Lord Ordinary may—

    (a) if satisfied that it is appropriate to do so, make an order giving permission for group proceedings to be brought under section 20(5) of the Act without holding a hearing;

    (b) require further information from any of the parties before making any further order; or

    (c)   fix a date and time for a hearing of the application for permission and of any answers thereto.

  (2) The Keeper of the Rolls must notify—

    (a)   the representative party or, as the case may be, the applicant; and

    (b)   any person who has lodged answers,

of the date and time of any hearing fixed under paragraph (1)(c).

  (3) The parties must be given at least 7 days' notice of a hearing fixed under paragraph (1)(c).

  (4) At a hearing fixed under paragraph (1)(c), the Lord Ordinary may—

    (a)   grant the application (including the giving of permission subject to conditions or only on particular grounds); or

    (b)   refuse the application.

  (5) The circumstances in which permission to bring proceedings to which this Chapter applies may be refused by the Lord Ordinary are as follows—

    (a)   the criteria set out in section 20(6)(a) or (b) (or both (a) and (b)) of the Act have not been met;

    (b)   it has not been demonstrated that there is a prima facie case;

    (c)   it has not been demonstrated that it is a more efficient administration of justice for the claims to be brought as group proceedings rather than by separate individual proceedings;

    (d)   it has not been demonstrated that the proposed proceedings have any real prospects of success.

  (6) Where permission is refused (or permission is granted subject to conditions or only on particular grounds), the Lord Ordinary must give reasons for the decision.

"WITHIN 14 DAYS OF"

The word "of" implies that the day from which time commences is included in the calculation.   **26A.11.1**

Grant of permission

  26A.12.—(1) Where the Lord Ordinary gives permission for group proceedings to be brought the Lord Ordinary is to make an order which—   **26A.12**

    (a)   states the name and designation of the representative party;

    (b)   defines the group and the issues (whether of fact or law) which are the same as, or similar or related to, each other raised by the claims;

    (c)   requires the lodging, by the representative party, of a group register;

    (d)   specifies the procedure which must be followed for a person to be a group member;

    (e)   specifies the period of time in which claims may be brought by persons in the group proceedings;

    (f)   specifies that group members may withdraw their consent to being bound by the group proceedings;

    (g)   specifies the procedure which must be followed by a group member to withdraw their claim from the group proceedings; and

    (h)   requires such advertisement of the permission to bring group proceedings to take place—

        (i)   within 7 days of the date of the order; and

        (ii)   thereafter, within the period during which persons may opt-in to the proceedings,

    as the Lord Ordinary thinks fit.

  (2) The Lord Ordinary may, when making an order under this rule, make any such order as the Lord Ordinary thinks fit.

26A.12.1   Paragraph 18 of P.N. No. 2 of 2020 asserts that the summons must be lodged for signeting seven days after the date on which permission to bring group proceedings has been given, but there is no rule to that effect.

DEFINE THE ISSUES

26A.12.2   Under r. 26A.12(1)(b), what is required is a succinct statement of the issues in general terms. It is not necessary for the Lord Ordinary to set out the issues in detail; all that is necessary is to set out the issues which "are the same as, or similar or related to, each other" (s.20(6)(a) and r. 26A.12(1)(b)). The English practice of ascertaining common issues is of no relevance to the Scottish procedure. See *Bridgehouse v BMW*, 2024 S.L.T. 116 (OH), paras. [68]-[70].

GROUP REGISTER

26A.12.3   The group register under r.26A.12(1)(c) has two functions: (1) to record the persons who form the group (and see P.N. No. 2 of 2020, para. 9 and Form 26A.15) and (2) to establish the date of commencement of the proceedings by each individual group member (see r. 26A.18). It is not the function of the Group Register to go beyond these functions and contain detailed information or pleading about the individual circumstances of group members and their individual claims. Nor is it appropriate to make inclusion of a person in the Register conditional on that person agreeing to provide that information. See *Bridgehouse v BMW*, 2024 S.L.T. 116 (OH), paras. [75]-[79].

PROCEDURE FOR ADDING OR WITHDRAWING FROM THE GROUP

26A.12.4   See r. 26A.12(1)(d), (f) and (g) and rr. 26A.14 and 26A.15. It was indicated in *Bridgehouse v BMW*, 2024 S.L.T. 116 (OH), that the mechanisms in rr. 26A.14 and 26A.15 were proving cumbersome in practice. Following what was done in the James Finlay (Kenya) Ltd Group Proceedings, Lord Ericht dispensed with the requirements of r.26A14 insofar as a person giving consent to group proceedings required to give notice in Form 26A.14A or withdrawing consent required to give notice in Form 26A.14B. He directed that compliance with those rules was met by highlighting new members in green and highlighting in red group members who had withdrawn. In relation to r. 26A.15, changes to group membership are to be highlighted in the group register and the changes intimated to the defenders and lodged in the General Department every 28 days without the requirement to notify all group members of the changes. See para. [80].

RULE 26A.12(2): ANY OTHER ORDER AS THE COURT THINKS FIT

26A.12.5   In *Bridgehouse v BMW*, 2024 S.L.T. 116 (OH), the defenders sought an order requiring each group member to answer 35 detailed questions in a Schedule of Information, to sign it and state that they believed the facts stated to be true. Lord Ericht held that at this stage, the court was determining the summons and not the individual claims and that the focus would be on provision of information required to determine the summons; the court would not order a statement of truth as required in the very different English procedural rules (paras. [88]-[90]).

The permission stage: appeals

26A.13   **26A.13.** An appeal against the granting or refusing of permission (including the granting of permission either subject to conditions or only on particular grounds) for group proceedings to be brought is made by reclaiming motion.

"RECLAIMING MOTION"

26A.13.1   For reclaiming, see Chap. 38.
Leave to reclaim must be sought within 14 days after the decision to grant or refuse: see. r. 38.2(6).

Part 4 – Opt-in Procedure

Opt-in proceedings – notices

26A.14   **26A.14.**—(1) A person gives consent for their claim to be brought in group proceedings by sending notice to that effect to the representative party in Form 26A.14-A.

(2) A group member withdraws their consent for their claim to be brought in group proceedings by sending notice to that effect to the representative party in Form 26A.14-B.

(3) A notice under paragraph (1) or (2) may be sent either—

(a) by first class post; or

(b) where paragraph (4) applies, by email.

(4) This paragraph applies where the representative party has confirmed consent to—

(a) a prospective group member;

(b) a group member,

to receiving a notice under paragraph (1) or (2) by electronic means, and has provided an email address to such persons for that purpose.

(5) In this rule a "representative party" includes a person who has made or, as the case may be, is to make an application seeking the authorisation of the court under section 20(3)(b) of the Act to be a representative party in group proceedings.

GENERAL NOTE

Chapter 26A provides only for opt-in proceedings. Opt-out proceedings are those in which (a) each member is domiciled in Scotland and has not given notice that he or she does not consent or (b) is not domiciled in Scotland and has given express consent: s. 20(7) and (8) of the 2018 Act. **26A.14.1**

NOTICE TO BE MEMBER OF OR WITHDRAW FROM GROUP PROCEEDINGS

It was indicated in *Bridgehouse v BMW*, 2024 S.L.T. 116 (OH,, that the mechanisms in rr. 26A.14 and 26A.15 were proving cumbersome in practice. Following what was done in the James Finlay (Kenya) Ltd Group Proceedings, Lord Ericht dispensed with the requirements of r.26A14 insofar as a person giving consent to group proceedings required to give notice in Form 26A.14A or withdrawing consent required to give notice in Form 26A.14B. He directed that compliance with those rules was met by highlighting new members in green and highlighting in red group members who had withdrawn. See para. [80]. **26A.14.2**

CHANGES TO GROUP REGISTER

It was indicated in *Bridgehouse v BMW*, 2024 S.L.T. 116 (OH), that the mechanisms in rr. 26A.14 and 26A.15 were proving cumbersome in practice. Following what was done in the James Finlay (Kenya) Ltd Group Proceedings, Lord Ericht ordered that, in relation to r. 26A.15, changes to group membership are to be highlighted in the group register and the changes intimated to the defenders and lodged in the General Department every 28 days without the requirement to notify all group members of the changes. See para. [80]. **26A.14.3**

Opt-in proceedings – group register

26A.15.—(1) A group register is to be in Form 26A.15. **26A.15**

(2) Subject to paragraph (4), paragraph (3) applies where, following the lodging in the General Department and the service upon the defender of a group register under rule 26A.5(7)(b) and (8) or, as the case may be, rule 26A.9(3)(b) and (4) , the membership of the group of persons on whose behalf proceedings are to be, or have been, brought changes following either, or both—

(a) the addition into the group of a new group member;

(b) the withdrawal from the group of a group member.

(3) The representative party or, as the case may be, the applicant must—

(a) lodge in the General Department; and

(b) at the same time, serve on the defender,

a revised group register, in Form 26A.15, as soon as possible and no later than 21 days following the representative party's or, as the case may be, the applicant's receipt of any notice made under rule 26A.14.

(4) Where the Lord Ordinary grants an application made under rule 26A.16(1) or 26A.17(1) the representative party must—

(a) lodge in the General Department; and

(b) at the same time, serve on the defender,

a revised group register, in Form 26A.15, as soon as possible and no later than 21 days following the grant of the application by the Lord Ordinary.

(5) The representative party or, as the case may be, the applicant must, at the same time as lodging in the General Department and serving on the defender a revised group register, inform all group members of the changes to the membership of the group of persons.

(6) The lodging of a group register in the General Department and the service on a defender under rule 26A.5(8), 26A.9(4) or paragraph (3) or (4) of this rule, may be by first class post or by electronic means.

(7) The group register is to be considered by the court at all hearings of the proceedings.

(8) Evidence of service in accordance with Chapter 16 must be provided to the General Department within 14 days from the date of service.

GENERAL NOTE

26A.15.1   Where there is a change in the group register, a revised full register must contain details of all members of the group. For that reason, it may be more suitable for the representative party's agent to lodge the revised register in electronic form: P.N. No. 2 of 2020.

There appears to be no requirement to inform the court of what the change is.

"NO LATER THAN 21 DAYS FOLLOWING"

26A.15.2   No later than 14 days *after* means that the day of the order is not counted. What does "following" mean?

Opt-in proceedings – late application

26A.16   **26A.16.**—(1) This rules applies where, following the allowance of proof, a person sends notice under rule 26A.14(1) in Form 26A.14-A, to the representative party seeking their claim to be brought in the group proceedings.

(2) Application is to be made by the representative party by motion in Form 26A.16.

(3) On a motion being enrolled under paragraph (2), the application is to be brought before the Lord Ordinary on the first available day after being made, for an order for—

    (a) intimation and service of the application on the defender and such other person as the Lord Ordinary thinks fit within 7 days of the date of the order, or within such other period as the Lord Ordinary thinks fit;

    (b) such advertisement as the Lord Ordinary thinks fit to take place within 7 days of the date of the order, or within such other period as the Lord Ordinary thinks fit;

    (c) any person on whom the application has been served, to lodge answers and any relevant documents, if so advised, within 14 days after the date of service, or within such other period as the Lord Ordinary thinks fit.

(3) A person served with an application made under paragraph (2) who intends to participate in the decision as to whether the application should be granted must lodge answers within the period ordered for the lodging of answers.

(4) A motion enrolled under paragraph (2) is to be granted only—

    (a) after giving the defender the opportunity to be heard;

    (b) on cause shown; and

    (c) on such conditions, if any, as to the expenses or otherwise as the Lord Ordinary thinks fit.

"MOTION"

26A.16.1   For motions, see Chap. 23 and r. 26A.4.

"INTIMATION AND SERVICE"

26A.16.2   For intimation and service, see Chap. 16.

Opt-in proceedings – late withdrawal of consent for a claim to be brought in the proceedings or where, following withdrawal, there would be less than two pursuers

26A.17   **26A.17.**—(1) This rule applies where a group member sends notice under rule 26A.14(2), in Form 26A.14-B, to the representative party either (or both)—

    (a) after the commencement of any proof;

    (b) where there would, should that person's claim not be brought in the proceedings, be less than two persons having a claim in the proceedings.

(2)   Application is to be made by the representative party by motion in Form 26A.17.

(3)   On a motion being enrolled in terms of paragraph (2), the application is to be brought before the Lord Ordinary on the first available day after being made, for an order for—

(a)   intimation and service of the application on the defender and such other person as the Lord Ordinary thinks fit within 7 days of the date of the order, or within such other period as the Lord Ordinary thinks fit;

(b)   such advertisement as the Lord Ordinary thinks fit to take place within 7 days of the date of the order, or within such other period as the Lord Ordinary thinks fit;

(c)   any person on whom the application has been served, to lodge answers and any relevant documents, if so advised, within 14 days after the date of service, or within such other period as the Lord Ordinary thinks fit.

(4)   A motion enrolled under paragraph (2) is to be granted only—

(a)   after giving the defender an opportunity to be heard; and

(b)   on such conditions, if any, as to expenses or otherwise as the Lord Ordinary thinks fit.

"MOTION"

For motions, see Chap. 23 and r. 26A.4.   **26A.17.1**

"INTIMATION AND SERVICE"

For intimation and service, see Chap. 16.   **26A.17.2**

Part 5 – Commencement of Group Proceedings

Commencement of group proceedings

26A.18.—(1)   The service upon a defender of a group register under either rule   **26A.18**
26A.5(8) or rule 26A.9(4) amounts to the commencement of the proceedings in respect of those persons who are group members, and are recorded as such on the group register that is served.

(2)   The lodging with the court of a group register, in revised form, under rule 26A.15(3)(a) amounts to the commencement of the proceedings in respect of any new group member who has, following the lodging and service of the group register under either rule 26A.5(7)(b) and (8) or rule 26A.9(3)(b) or (4) , joined the group.

(3)   Paragraph (4) applies where, following an application being made by the representative party under rule 26A.16(1), the Lord Ordinary grants the application allowing a claim for a person to which rule 26A.16(1) applies to be brought in the proceedings.

(4)   The enrolment of a motion under rule 26A.16(2) in connection with an application made under rule 26A.16(1) amounts to the commencement of the proceedings in respect of a person to which rule 26A.16(1) applies.

GENERAL NOTE

Rule 26A.18 contains important provisions about when proceedings are commenced.   **26A.18.1**

Part 6 – Summonses and Defences

Summons in group proceedings actions

26A.19.—(1)   A summons in proceedings to which this Chapter applies is made   **26A.19**
in Form 13.2-AA.

(2)   A summons in proceedings to which this Chapter applies is to—

(a)   specify, in the form of conclusions, the orders sought;

(b)   identify the parties to the proceedings and the matters from which the proceedings arise;

(c)   specify any special capacity in which the representative party is bringing the proceedings or any special capacity in which the proceedings are brought against the defender;

(d)   summarise the circumstances out of which the proceedings arise; and

(e)   set out the grounds on which the action proceeds.

(3)   There is to be appended to a summons in a group proceedings action a schedule listing the documents founded on or adopted as incorporated in the summons, which is also to be lodged as an inventory of productions.

GENERAL NOTE

26A.19.1   The summons must run in the name of the person who has been granted permission to bring proceedings. That person will be the representative party appointed under r. 26A.5.

Paragraph 18 of P.N. No. 2 of 2020 asserts that the summons must be lodged for signeting seven days after the date on which permission to bring group proceedings has been given, but there is no rule to that effect.

"SUMMONS"

26A.19.2   Pleadings in traditional form are not normally required or encouraged: P.N. No. 2 of 2020, para. 19. Pleadings should be in abbreviated form, although in some actions this will not be appropriate. The overriding requirement is fair notice of the essential elements of the case. See P.N. No. 2 of 2020, para. 19.

Defences

26A.20   **26A.20.**—(1)   Defences in proceedings to which this Chapter applies are to be in the form of answers to the summons with any additional statement of facts or legal grounds on which it is intended to rely.

(2)   There is to be appended to the defences in proceedings to which this Chapter applies a schedule listing the documents founded on or adopted as incorporated in the defences, which must be lodged as an inventory of productions.

DEFENCES AND ANSWERS

26A.20.1   See Chap. 18.

Pleadings in traditional form are not normally required or encouraged: P.N. No. 2 of 2020, para. 20. It is not necessary that each averment should be admitted, not known or denied, as the case may be, so long as the extend of the dispute is identified. Documents founded on or adopted must be lodged with the defences: r. 27.1(1)(b).

Defences must be lodged within seven days after the summons has called: r. 18.1(2).

"ADDITIONAL STATEMENT OF FACTS OR LEGAL GROUNDS"

26A.20.2   This is an unusual provision and a departure from the simplicity of Scottish pleadings, that the facts and disputed facts appear in the pleadings and not in a document accompanying them, or that legal grounds are other than pleas-in-law. How and where is a pursuer to respond to an additional statement of facts or legal grounds?

COUNTERCLAIMS AND THIRD PARTY NOTICES

26A.20.3   P.N. No. 2 of 2020, para. 24 states that no counterclaim or convening of a third party may be pursued without an order from the Lord Ordinary. There is, however, no rule to that effect in relation to counterclaims. Service of a third-party notice, on the other hand, requires a motion and order from the court: r. 26.1(1). We are fast departing from the beauty of Scottish pleadings where the case is found in one document to an unfortunate position akin to pleadings in England and Wales where, to find what the case is about, one has to read several or many documents.

Part 7 – Procedure

Preliminary hearing

26A.21   **26A.21.**—(1)   An action in proceedings to which this Chapter applies is to call for a preliminary hearing within 14 days after defences have been lodged.

(2)   At the preliminary hearing, the Lord Ordinary—

(a)   is to determine whether and to what extent and in what manner further specification of the claims and defences must be provided;

(b)   may make an order in respect of any of the following matters—

(i)   detailed written pleadings to be made by a party either generally or restricted to particular claims or issues;

(ii)   a statement of facts to be made by one or more parties either generally or restricted to particular claims or issues;

(iii)   the allowing of an amendment by a party to their pleadings;

(iv)   disclosure of the identity of witnesses and the existence and nature of documents relating to the proceedings or authority to recover documents either generally or specifically;

(v)   documents constituting, evidencing or relating to the subject-matter of the proceedings or any correspondence or similar documents relating to the proceedings to be lodged in process within a specified period;

(vi)   each party to lodge in process, and send to every other party, a list of witnesses;

(vii)   reports of skilled persons or witness statements to be lodged in process;

(viii)   affidavits concerned with any of the issues in the proceedings to be lodged in process; and

(ix)   to proceed to a hearing without any further preliminary procedure either in relation to the whole, or any particular aspect or any particular claim, of the proceedings;

(c)   may fix the period within which any such order is to be complied with;

(d)   may continue the preliminary hearing to a date to be appointed by the Lord Ordinary;

(e)   may make such other order as the Lord Ordinary thinks fit for the efficient determination of the proceedings.

(3)   Where the Lord Ordinary makes an order under paragraph (2)(b)(i) or (ii) or (2)(c), the Lord Ordinary may ordain the representative party to—

(a)   make up a record; and

(b)   lodge that record in process within such period as the Lord Ordinary thinks fit.

(4)   At the conclusion of the preliminary hearing, the Lord Ordinary must, unless the Lord Ordinary has made an order under paragraph (2)(b)(ix), fix a date for a case management hearing to determine further procedure.

(5)   The date fixed under paragraph (4) for a case management hearing may be extended on cause shown by application to the court, by motion, not less than two days prior to the date fixed for the case management hearing.

(6)   In paragraph (2)(b)(i) to (iii) "party" and "parties" may, where the Lord Ordinary so orders after being addressed on the matter, include a group member, group members or a sub-set of group members.

GENERAL NOTE

26A.21.1

Parties are expected to have clear, fully formed views, or even an agreed view, about how the issues may be litigated in the most efficient way: P.N. No. 2 of 2020, para. 28.

Parties are to be in a position to lodge a document setting out concisely the issues they contend require judicial determination. This document should be lodged (although there is no requirement under r. 26A.21 to do so) by 4pm two working days before the preliminary hearing. See P.N. No. 2 of 2020, para. 32.

Continuations of preliminary hearings simply to enable information to be obtained which should have been obtained before the hearing are likely to be refused: P.N. No. 2 of 2020, para. 31.

In making orders for things to be done, the court will set "realistic" deadlines; and extensions will be granted only on reasonable cause shown: P.N. No. 2 of 2020, para. 33.

26A.21.2   Yet another document which is, may be or is not part of the plethora of "pleadings". What the purpose of this is and how it would be incorporated in any closed record ordered is not clear.

ADJUSTMENTS

26A.21.3   Adjustments will normally be restricted to clarification of a party's position in response to averments or requests for further explanation by another party. Adjustments should be on a copy of the document adjusted with the adjustments shown using track changes, strikethrough or a different font. See P.N. No. 2 of 2020, paras 29 and 23.

JOINT MEETINGS

26A.21.4   Paragraph 54 of P.N. No. 2 of 2020 asserts that the judge has power to order parties to hold a joint meeting to explore extra-judicial settlement or restriction of the issues. There is no express power in Chap. 26A, but the breadth of r. 26A.21(2)(e) would permit it.

"WITHIN 14 DAYS AFTER"

26A.21.5   The date from which the period is calculated is not counted.
      Where the last day falls on a Saturday or a Sunday or a public holiday on which the Office of Court is closed, the next available day is allowed: r. 1.3(7). For office hours and public holidays, see note 3.1.2.

Case management hearing

26A.22   **26A.22.**—(1) Not less than 14 days, or such other period as may be prescribed by the Lord Ordinary at the preliminary hearing, before the date fixed under rule 26A.21(4) for the case management hearing, each party must—

(a) lodge in process and, at the same time, send to every other party a written statement of proposals for further procedure which must state—

(i)   whether the party seeks to have the proceedings appointed to debate or to have the proceedings sent to proof on the whole or any part of it;

(ii) what the issues are which the party considers should be sent to debate or proof; and

(iii) the estimated duration of any debate or proof;

(b) where it is sought to have the proceedings appointed to proof, lodge a list of the witnesses the party proposes to cite or call to give evidence, identifying the matters to which each witness is to speak;

(c) where it is sought to have the proceedings appointed to proof, lodge the reports of any skilled persons;

(d) where it is sought to have the proceedings appointed to debate, lodge a note of argument consisting of concise numbered paragraphs stating the legal propositions on which it is proposed to submit that any preliminary plea should be sustained or repelled with reference to the principal authorities and statutory provisions to be founded on; and

(e) send a copy of any such written statement, lists, reports or note of argument, as the case may be, to every other party.

(2) At the case management hearing, the Lord Ordinary—

(a) must determine whether the group proceedings are to be appointed to debate or sent to proof on—

(i)   all or some of the claims;

(ii) all or some of the issues raised by the claims,

made in the proceedings;

(b) where the proceedings are appointed to debate or sent to proof, may order that written arguments on any question of law must be submitted;

(c) where the proceedings are sent to proof, may determine whether evidence at the proof is to be by oral evidence, the production of documents or affidavits on any issue;

(d) where the proceedings are sent to proof, may direct that parties serve on one another, and lodge in process, signed witness statements or affidavits from each witness whose evidence they intend to adduce, setting out in full the evidence which it is intended to take from that witness, and fix a timetable for the service (whether by exchange or otherwise) and lodging of such statements or affidavits as may be thought necessary;

(e) may direct that such witness statements or affidavits are to stand as evidence in chief of the witness concerned, subject to such further questioning in chief as the Lord Ordinary may allow;

(f) may determine, in the light of any witness statements, affidavits or reports produced, that proof is unnecessary on any issue;

(g) where the proceedings are sent to proof, may appoint parties to be heard at a pre-proof hearing under rule 26A.24;

(h) may direct that skilled persons hold a meeting with a view to reaching agreement and identifying areas of disagreement, and may order them thereafter to produce a joint note, to be lodged in process by one of the parties, identifying areas of agreement and disagreement, and the basis of any disagreement;

(i) without prejudice to Chapter 12 (assessors), may appoint an expert to examine, on behalf of the court, any reports of skilled persons or other evidence submitted and to report to the court within such period as the Lord Ordinary may specify;

(j) where the proceedings are sent to proof, may make an order fixing the time allowed for the examination and cross-examination of witnesses;

(k) may, on the motion of a party, direct the proceedings to be determined on the basis of written submissions, or such other material, without any oral hearing;

(l) may continue the case management hearing to a date to be appointed by the Lord Ordinary;

(m) may make an order for parties to produce a joint bundle of productions arranged in chronological order or such other order as will assist in the efficient conduct of the proof;

(n) may order and fix a date for a further case management hearing or fix a date for the hearing of any debate or proof;

(o) may make such other order as the Lord Ordinary thinks fit.

GENERAL NOTE

Parties will be expected to discuss the issues and the method of disposing of them, the steps taken to achieve extra-judicial settlement, the likelihood of it being achieved and any steps the court might take to assist in resolution: P.N. No. 2 of 2020, para. 34. **26A.22.1**

DEBATES AND PROOFS

Rule 26A.22(1)(d) provides that a party seeking a debate must lodge a note of argument stating the legal propositions on which it is sought to have a preliminary plea sustained or repelled with reference to the principal authorities. **26A.22.2**

Rule 26A.22(2)(b) provides that the Lord Ordinary may order written arguments on questions of law where proceedings are sent to debate or proof (or proof before answer). Paragraphs 42 and 44 of P.N. No. 2 of 2020 assert that each party should lodge a note of argument at least 10 days before a debate and at least 21 days before a proof.

Where a party seeks to have the proceedings appointed to debate at a case management hearing, the provisions of r. 26A.23 should be noted. That party must lodge the legal argument on which a preliminary plea should be upheld or repelled and the principal authorities. By virtue of r. 26A.22(1), this must be done not less than 14 days before the hearing (or such other date as the Lord Ordinary decides at the preliminary hearing). Under r. 26A.23(4) the Lord Ordinary may order written arguments to be submitted (unless, presumably, the judge has done so at the case management hearing under r. 26A.22(2)(b)).

JOINT MEETINGS

Paragraph 54 of P.N. No. 2 of 2020 asserts that the judge has power to order parties to hold a joint meeting to explore extra-judicial settlement or restriction of the issues. There is no express power in **26A.22.3**

Chap. 26A, but the breadth of r. 26A.22(2)(o) would permit it.

Debates

26A.23

26A.23.—(1) Where a party seeks to have the proceedings appointed to debate, the application must include—

 (a) the legal argument on which any preliminary plea is to be sustained or repelled;

 (b) the principal authorities (including statutory provisions) on which the argument is founded.

(2) Following application being made to the court under paragraph (1), before determining whether the action is to be appointed to debate the Lord Ordinary is to hear from the parties with a view to ascertaining whether agreement can be reached on the points of law in contention.

(3) The Lord Ordinary, having heard the parties, is to determine whether the action is to be appointed to debate.

(4) Where the action is appointed to debate, the Lord Ordinary may order that written arguments on any question of law are to be submitted.

(5) With the exception of rule 28.1(3)(d) which is not to apply, Chapter 28 (procedure roll), applies to a debate ordered under rule 26A.22(2)(a) as it applies to a cause appointed to the Procedure Roll.

GENERAL NOTE

26A.23.1

Rule 26A.23(4) is a repetition of r. 26A.22(2)(b).

Rule 26A.22(2)(b) provides that the Lord Ordinary may order written arguments on questions of law where proceedings are sent to debate. Paragraphs 42 and 44 of P.N. No. 2 of 2020 assert that each party should lodge a note of argument (different from written arguments?) at least 10 days before a debate. Presumably, also, these may be fuller than those submitted for consideration at the case management hearing where that party has been seeking a debate; or possibly unnecessary where that is not required. More than one authority should not be cited in support of a given proposition and, except on cause shown, no submission will be allowed and no authority allowed which is not included in the note of argument: P.N. No. 2 of 2020, paras. 45 and 46. If an argument is no longer to be insisted upon, the other party and the court should be informed as soon as practicable: P.N. No. 2 of 2020, para. 47. Under r. 26A.23(4) the Lord Ordinary may order written arguments to be submitted (unless, presumably, the judge has done so at the case management hearing under r. 26A.22(2)(b)).

Note para. 53 of P.N. No. 2 of 2020 for the identification of authorities in folders. Authorities may be lodged in electronic format.

Pre-proof hearing

26A.24

26A.24. Not less than 2 days prior to any hearing appointed under rule 26A.22(2)(g), parties must lodge in process an estimated timetable for the conduct of the proof together with a note of any issues which are to be addressed prior to the proof.

GENERAL NOTE

26A.24.1

The general purpose of a pre-proof hearing is to ascertain the state of preparedness of the parties and to review the estimated duration of the proof (or proof before answer): P.N. No. 2 of 2020, para. 55. There may also be considered any joint minute of admissions (to be lodged two days prior to the hearing), a review of productions and other documents (to be lodged two days prior to the hearing), and an up-to-date position about expert reports including any meeting between experts to reach agreement about points in common and what remains in dispute.

Not less than two days prior to the pre-proof hearing patties should lodge an estimated timetable for the conduct of the proof: P.N. No. 2 of 2020, para. 56.

Lodging of productions for proof

26A.25

26A.25.—(1) Unless an earlier date is specified by the Lord Ordinary, any document not previously lodged but required for any proof in proceedings to which this Chapter applies must be lodged as a production not less than 7 days before the date fixed for the proof.

(2) No document may be lodged as a production after the date referred to in paragraph (1), even by agreement of all parties, unless the court is satisfied that any document sought to be lodged could not with reasonable diligence have been lodged in time.

GENERAL NOTE

Rule 26A.22(2)(m) states that the Lord Ordinary *may* make an order at a case management hearing for parties to prepare a working bundle of productions arranged in chronological order or such other order as will assist in the efficient conduct of the proof. Paragraph 40 of P.N. No. 2 of 2020 states that before any proof, the pursuer should prepare a working bundle arranged chronologically or in another appropriate order without multiple copies of the same document.

Productions may be lodged in electronic format. Inventories should be lodged electronically but may require to be lodged in hard copy also. See P.N. No. 2 of 2020, para. 41.

Note that r. 36.3 (lodging of productions) does not apply: r. 26A.2(3)(b).

26A.25.1

Part 8 – Withdrawal from Group Proceedings

Withdrawal of claim from group proceedings

26A.26. The lodging with the court of a group register, in revised form, under rule 26A.15(3)(a) or (4)(a), following the withdrawal from the group of a group member, amounts to the point at which the person concerned withdraws consent for their claim to be brought in the group proceedings.

26A.26

Part 9 – Orders of the Court

Power to make orders

26A.27. At any time before final judgment, the Lord Ordinary may, at the Lord Ordinary's own instance or on the motion of any party, make such order as the Lord Ordinary thinks necessary to secure the fair and efficient determination of the proceedings.

26A.27

Effect of interlocutor given in group proceedings

26A.28.—(1) Subject to paragraph (2), an interlocutor given in group proceedings—

(a)   must describe or otherwise identify the group members who will be affected by it; and

(b)   binds all such persons, other than any person who has, as at the date of the interlocutor, withdrawn their consent to their claim being brought in the proceedings.

(2) An interlocutor given in group proceedings prior to a person joining the group as a group member binds such a person, except where the Lord Ordinary, on cause shown, orders otherwise.

26A.28

Failure to comply with rule or order of Lord Ordinary

26A.29.— Any failure by a party to comply timeously with a provision in these Rules or any order made by the Lord Ordinary in proceedings to which this Chapter applies entitles the Lord Ordinary, at his or her own instance—

(a)   to refuse to extend any period of compliance with a provision in these Rules or an order of the court;

(b)   to dismiss the action, as the case may be, in whole or in part;

(c)   to grant decree in respect of all or any of the conclusions of the summons, as the case may be; or

(d)   to make an award of expenses,

26A.29

as the Lord Ordinary thinks fit.

Part 10 – Settlement

Settlement of proceedings

26A.30   **26A.30.** The representative party must consult with the group members on the terms of any proposed settlement before any damages in connection with the proceedings may be distributed.

CHAPTER 27 DOCUMENTS FOUNDED ON OR ADOPTED IN PLEADINGS

Lodging of documents founded on or adopted

27.1.—(1) Any document founded on by a party, or adopted as incorporated, in his pleadings shall, so far as in his possession or within his control, be lodged in process as a production by him—

(a) when founded on or adopted in a summons, at the time of lodging the summons for calling;

(b) when founded on or adopted in a petition, note, application, minute, defences, counterclaim or answers, at the time of lodging that writ; and

(c) when founded on or adopted in an adjustment to any pleadings, at the time when such adjustment is intimated to any other party.

(2) Paragraph (1) shall be without prejudice to any power of the court to order the production of any document or to grant a commission and diligence for recovery of it.

27.1

Deriv. R.C.S. 1965, r. 134E inserted by S.I. 1990 No. 705

GENERAL NOTE.

This provision originated from s.3 of the C.S.A. 1825 which was formally repealed by the C.S.A. 1988, Sched. 2. R.C.S. 1965, r. 134E, which was inserted by A.S. (R.C.S.A. No. 1) (Miscellaneous) 1990 [SI 1990/705], replaced R.C.S. 1965, r. 78(d) (part) which applied to summonses only.

27.1.1

DOCUMENTS FOUNDED ON OR ADOPTED.

Documents founded on are those which are not merely evidence but on which the action is based, though only if in the party's possession or control: *Western Bank of Scotland v. Baird* (1863) 2 M. 127. For the consequences of failure to lodge a document, see r. 27.2.

27.1.2

Documents adopted as incorporated in the pleadings (*brevitatis causa*) may not necessarily be documents founded on; but by virtue of this rule, even where they are not founded on, documents which are adopted in the pleadings must now be lodged with the pleadings if in the party's possession or control. As no reference can be made to productions on procedure roll without agreement of parties, if reliance is to be placed for relevancy or specification in pleadings on documents they must be "adopted and held as repeated herein *brevitatis causa*": see *Gordon v. Davidson* (1864) 2 M. 758, 769 per L.J.-C. Inglis; *Eadie Cairns v. Programmed Maintenance Painting Ltd* 1987 S.L.T. 777, per Lord Avonside at p. 780E and Lord Jauncey at p. 783F; the *Royal Bank of Scotland Plc v. Holmes,* 1999 S.L.T. 563 (OH), 570E per Lord Macfadyen.

In *Prophit v. BBC* 1997 S.L.T. 745, Temporary Judge T. G. Coutts refused to listen to a tape recording of a programme because the issues at procedure roll had to be rested solely on the averments and the tape had not been incorporated into the pleadings. The implication is that if it had been so incorporated, the court would have listened to it.

The other party is entitled to see such documents; for any other document a commission and diligence has to be obtained unless there is agreement to disclose it: *Reavis v. Clan Line Steamers Ltd* 1926 SC 215.

In family actions marriage and birth certificates which are referred to in the pleadings must be lodged with the pleadings: see r. 49.10.

The rule does not apply to statutes, Royal proclamations, Orders in Council or other statutory instruments or European Community legislation. Judicial notice is taken of an Act of Parliament passed after 1850 (s.3 of, and Sched. 2, para. 2 to, the Interpretation Act 1978), a statutory instrument as defined by the Statutory Instruments Act 1946 (Walkers on *Evidence*, para. 198(c); *Macmillan v. McConnell* 1917 J.C. 43, 47 per L.J.-C. Scott Dickson) and European Community legislation (ss.2 and 3 of the C.J.J.A. 1982). They do not have to be produced and proved. In fact, Acts of Parliament before 1850, including pre-1707 Acts do not have to be proved: *Macmillan*, above. Should a question arise about the terms of a statute, its terms are established by a copy printed by the Queen's Printer or under authority of HMSO: Dickson on *Evidence*, para. 1105. In the case of a Scots' statute, the Record edition should be produced: Walkers on *Evidence*, para. 194(a). In case of doubt, the terms of a statutory instrument are established by an HMSO copy (Documentary Evidence Acts of 1868 and 1882) and of its date of issue by a list issued by HMSO under s.3(1) of the Statutory Instruments Act 1946. Law reports do not have to be produced and proved.

By virtue of r. 1.3(1) (definition of "document"), "document" has an extended meaning as defined in s.9 of the Civil Evidence (Scotland) Act 1988.

"LODGED IN PROCESS".

The documents are lodged as productions with an inventory of productions in accordance with r. 4.5.

27.1.3

POWER OF COURT TO ORDER PRODUCTION OR RECOVERY.

27.1.4   The court has a statutory power to order production or recovery under s.1(1) of the Administration of Justice (Scotland) Act 1972. For commission and diligence for recovery of documents, see Chap. 35.

Consequences of failure to lodge documents founded on or adopted

27.2   **27.2.** Where a party fails to lodge a document in accordance with rule 27.1(1), he may be found liable in the expenses of any order for the production or recovery of it obtained by any other party.

GENERAL NOTE.

27.2.1   Failure to lodge documents founded on or adopted as incorporated may result in expenses being awarded against that party for any order for production or recovery.

CHAPTER 28 PROCEDURE ROLL

Hearings on procedure roll

28.1.—(1) When a cause calls on the Procedure Roll and no counsel, other person having a right of audience or party attends, the Lord Ordinary may pronounce an interlocutor dismissing or refusing the cause, as the case may be, and finding no expenses due to or by any party.

(2) An interlocutor pronounced under paragraph (1) may, if reclaimed, be recalled on such conditions, if any, as to expenses or otherwise as the court thinks fit.

(3) The court, after hearing parties on the Procedure Roll, may dispose of all or any of the preliminary pleas and may—

    (a) allow parties a preliminary proof on specified matters or in respect of specified pleas;

    (b) allow parties a proof before answer of their respective averments under reservation of such preliminary pleas as may be specified;

    (c) allow a proof;

    (d) allow issues for jury trial; or

    (e) may make such other order as it thinks fit.

(4) Where a cause has been appointed to the Procedure Roll, parties may, of consent, apply by motion to withdraw the cause from that roll and for any order which might have been pronounced at the hearing of the cause on that roll.

Deriv. R.C.S. 1965, r. 94(c) amended by S.I. 1991 No. 2483 (r. 28.1(1) and (2)) and r. 94(e) (r. 28.1(4))

GENERAL NOTE.

The Procedure Roll is where preliminary pleas (e.g. objections to the instance, objections to jurisdiction, and pleas against the action itself such as competency, relevancy and specification of pleadings) are debated and disposed of, including whether inquiry is to be by proof or jury trial or whether there should be a preliminary proof if these matters are not agreed by the parties. Irrelevant averments should be excluded at procedure roll: *Inglis v. National Bank of Scotland Ltd* 1909 S.C. 1038. So, e.g., averments of facts collateral to the issue such as similar fact evidence: see *A v. B* (1895) 22 R. 402 (First Div.); *Inglis*; *EG v. The Governors of the Fettes Trust* [2021] CSOH 128.

A cause will be appointed to the Procedure Roll where parties are agreed to send it there or, where parties are not so agreed, may be sent there when the case is heard (because of the lack of agreement) at the By Order (Adjustment) Roll: r. 22.3(5). The interlocutor appointing a cause to the Procedure Roll should state on whose motion the cause has been so appointed and in relation to which plea(s)-in-law.

On the closing of the record parties must discuss the future procedure in the cause with particular regard to the resolution of points at issue without recourse to a hearing on the Procedure Roll: P.N. No. 2 of 2004, para. 2. Whether that has been done may be taken into account by the court on the question of expenses: P.N. No. 2 of 2004, para. 3.

A cause may be finally disposed of on procedure roll where the parties have renounced probation.

A party who has not moved for the cause to be sent to procedure roll is not precluded from debating a plea of his at a hearing on that roll: *Mcintosh v. Cockburn & Co. Ltd* 1953 S.C. 88.

Although a particular mode of inquiry has already been allowed, the court is not precluded from reconsidering and altering the mode of inquiry on a minute of amendment altering the pleadings: *Bendex v. James Donaldson & Sons Ltd* 1990 S.C. 259. For an example of the court refusing to allow alteration of the mode of proof after amendment, see *Johnston v. Clark* 1998 S.L.T. 139.

FIXING AND ALLOCATION OF HEARINGS ON PROCEDURE ROLL.

The Keeper of the Rolls puts out causes which are estimated to last one or two days on procedure roll in the rolls the Thursday of the week preceding the date on which the cause is to be heard, unless parties agree otherwise or they wish to arrange a fixed diet where the cause is of some length or complexity: see r. 6.2(3) and (4). The Keeper will publish in the rolls a Procedure Roll warning list two weeks before the Thursday's roll on which diets are allocated for hearing the following week. Such hearings will be put out for one day unless, in response to the warning list, the Keeper is requested to fix more than one day under r. 6.2(4) ("some length" in r. 6.2(4) means, in practice, more than one day). On fixing and allocation of diets in the Outer House, see generally r. 6.2 and note 6.2.2.

UNALLOCATED PROCEDURE ROLL HEARINGS.

A debate may not have been allocated to a particular Lord Ordinary on the first day of the diet. A representative of the agents for each party in such a case must attend the Keeper's office between 10 am and 10.20 am. The Keeper must be informed about the existence of any discussions with a view to settlement. Agents may be required to attend later at intervals during the day. See generally, Notice [i.e. P.N.], 13th June 1996.

NON-APPEARANCE AT PROCEDURE ROLL.

28.1.3   R.28.1(1) deals with the situation where no party appears or is represented. Such a decree may be recalled with or without conditions: r. 28.1(2).

The calling of a cause on procedure roll is peremptory and if any party does not appear any other party who does appear is entitled to a decree of dismissal or default, as the case may be; and such a decree may also be recalled in the same way: see Chap. 21 (decrees by default).

PRELIMINARY PLEAS.

28.1.4   A preliminary plea is one which, if sustained, leads to the disposal of the whole or part of the cause without inquiry into the merits of that part of the cause. If such a plea is sustained it results in dismissal (or sist) but does not make the cause res judicata, and the pursuer may raise a fresh action: *Menzies v. Menzies* (1893) 20 R.(H.L.) 108, 110 per Lord Watson; and see further note 18.1.4(A). Where a preliminary plea is to be argued at procedure roll the court expects the party whose plea is to be argued to inform his opponent of the nature of his proposed argument at the earliest opportunity: P.N. No. 3 of 1991. The court may, at its own instance or on the motion of a party, order a party to lodge a note of argument on a preliminary plea: r. 22.4 (general rule), r. 43.24(8) (on Diet Roll in actions for damages for personal injuries or death under optional procedure), r. 47.5(6) (on Commercial Roll in commercial causes) and r. 55.3(4)(b) (pre-proof hearing in causes relating to intellectual property).

As no reference can be made to productions on procedure roll without agreement of parties, if reliance is to be placed for relevancy or specification in pleadings on documents they must be "adopted and held as repeated herein *brevitatis causa*": see *Gordon v. Davidson* (1864) 2 M. 758, 769 per L.J.-C. Inglis; *Eadie Cairns v. Programmed Maintenance Painting Ltd* 1987 S.L.T. 777, per Lord Avonside at p. 780E and Lord Jauncey at p. 783F.

As to particular preliminary pleas, see note 18.1.4(A).

PRELIMINARY PROOF.

28.1.5   Since proof is defined as including a proof before answer (see r. 1.3(1)), a preliminary proof before answer may be allowed.

A preliminary proof is not usually allowed in respect of the merits of a case but is confined to where an issue is raised in the pleadings which could bar the action from proceeding. Such cases fall into three categories: (a) cases in which there is a plea of no jurisdiction (see *McLeod v. Tancred, Arrol & Co.* (1890) 17 R. 514; *Dallas & Co. v. McArdle* 1949 S.C. 481), (b) cases of bar either in connection with the discharge of a claim or in connection with a statutory bar in the way of an action, and (c) cases which raise questions of title: *Burroughs Machines Ltd v. George Davie, Crawford & Partners* 1976 S.L.T.(Notes) 35 per Lord Grieve. A preliminary proof will not be allowed on an issue which is so bound up with the merits that they cannot be separated: *McCafferty v. McCabe* (1898) 25 R. 872; cf *A.B. v. C.D.* 1937 S.C. 408. A preliminary proof may be required to determine the question of time-bar or the discretion to override it under s. 19A of the Prescription and Limitation (Scotland) Act 1973: *Donald v. Rutherford* 1984 S.L.T. 70.

It is doubtful whether it would ever be proper to hold a preliminary proof as to the motive of a pursuer in bringing an action: *Mullan v. Anderson (No. 2)* 1997 S.L.T. 93, 97D-F per Temp. Judge Coutts, Q.C.

PROOF BEFORE ANSWER AND PROOF.

28.1.6   Probation may be by (a) proof *prout de jure* (without restriction as to method: see (1) below), (b) proof by writ or oath only (e.g. in loan, payment of money exceeding £100 Scots, obligations of relief, gratuitous obligations and innominate contracts of unusual character)—abolished for causes commenced on or after August 1, 1995 by s.11 of the Requirements of Writing (Scotland) Act 1995, (c) proof *habili modo* (where parts of a cause may be proved *prout de jure* and other parts may be restricted, the decision being made at the proof), (d) proof before answer (see (2) below) or (e) jury trial (see note 28.1.8 and Chap. 37).

(1) Proof.

It is sometimes thought that the allowance of proof excludes consideration of questions of relevancy after the proof, but the matter is not free from doubt: cf. Mackay's *Practice of the Court of Session*, ii, 18 (although questions of law may be argued after proof, the party against whom facts are proved can no longer maintain no proof should have been allowed and facts disregarded) and *Duke of Hamilton's Trs. v. Woodside Coal Co.* (1897) 24 R. 294, 296 per Lord McLaren (an interlocutor allowing parties proof of their averments leaves all questions of relevancy open to further consideration). In that case Lord McLaren said the words "before answer" were unnecessary for reserving questions of law and relevancy although the proper time for raising questions of law is when the Lord Ordinary is moved to allow a proof. Where a proof has been allowed evidence may be led which might have been excluded on the ground of irrelevance or lack of specification if such a plea had been taken: *Barr v. Bain* (1896) 23 R. 1090. Objection cannot be taken to proving an averment admitted to probation: *Scott v. Cormack Heating Engineers Ltd* 1942 S.C. 159, 162 per L.P. Normand.

(2) Proof before answer.

Proof before answer may be allowed where there is a plea to the relevancy of averments, questions of law and relevancy being reserved until the evidence has been led: *Robertson v. Murphy* (1867) 6 M. 114; *Fleming v. Eadie & Son* (1897) 25 R. 3, 5-6 per Lord Young; *Moore v. Stephen & Sons* 1954 S.C. 331, 336 per Lord Patrick. Proof before answer strictly means proof before answer as to relevancy, but not competency: *Fleming,* above; *Macvean v. Maclean* (1873) 11 M. 506 per Lord Neaves; cf. L.J.-C. Moncreiff at p. 509 who thought it might be as to either. A proof before answer reserving a plea to competency may be allowed where evidence on the merits may be relevant to the question of competency (*Shaw v. Renton & Fisher Ltd* 1977 S.L.T.(Notes) 60) or even, in exceptional circumstances, jurisdiction (*McLeod v. Tancred, Arrol & Co.* (1890) 17 R. 514) although it would be more usual to allow a preliminary proof on issues of competency or jurisdiction (see note 28.1.5). A proof before answer may be allowed where it cannot be said in advance whether the facts averred are sufficient to support the legal conclusions or the law cannot be stated until the facts are determined: *Moore,* above, at p. 335 per L.J.-C. Thomson and p. 336 per Lord Patrick.

The allowance of a proof before answer does not authorise the admission of incompetent evidence: *Robertson,* above; and, e.g. confidentiality is not waived even if a proof before answer was of consent: *Duke of Argyll v. Duchess of Argyll* 1962 S.C.(HL) 88, 93-94 per Lord Reid and 97-98 per Lord Guest.

The Lord Ordinary who hears the proof is not bound by the views on legal questions of the judge who allowed the proof before answer: *Forbes v. Forbes Trs.* 1957 S.C. 325, 337-338 per Lord Guthrie.

(3) Interlocutors.

The interlocutor allowing probation will specify the nature of probation allowed.

(a) In relation to proof (at large) the possibilities are: (i) "allows (both) parties a proof of their respective averments" where each party makes averments, enabling each to lead evidence in support of his own case; (ii) "allows the pursuer a proof of his own averments and to the defender a conjunct probation" where the defender only denies the pursuer's averments, the conjunct probation permitting him to contradict the pursuer's case; and (iii) "allows the defender a proof of his averments and to the pursuer a conjunct probation" where the defender admits the pursuer's claim but makes counter-averments.

(b) In relation to a proof before answer the interlocutor is "allows to parties a proof before answer of their respective averments on record; appoints said proof to proceed on the day of 19 at 10 o'clock forenoon and grants diligence for citing witnesses and havers".

(c) In relation to jury trial the interlocutor is "approves of the proposed issue [and counter-issue] No(s). [and] of process and allows them as now authenticated to be the issue [and counter-issue] for the trial of the cause; appoints the said issue [and counter-issue] to be tried by jury on the day of 19 at 10 o'clock forenoon; authorises and appoints a jury to be summoned for that purpose in common form; grants warrant for citing witnesses and havers".

(d) In relation to proof by writ or oath the interlocutor is "allows the cause to proceed by writ or oath of the defender; appoints said proof to proceed on the day of 19 at 10 o'clock forenoon and grants diligence for citing the defender".

(e) In relation to proof *habili modo* the interlocutor is "allows to parties a proof *habili modo* of their averments on record; appoints said proof to proceed on the day of 19 at 10 o'clock forenoon and grants diligence for citing witnesses and havers".

(f) In relation a preliminary proof the interlocutor is "allows a preliminary proof restricted solely to (*nature of proof or averments to go to proof*); appoints said proof to proceed on the day of 19 at 10 o'clock forenoon and grants diligence for citing witnesses and havers".

ISSUES.

Issues (and counter-issues) are the concise statements of the questions of fact to be answered by the jury: Bell's *Dictionary.* On the procedure for lodging issues, see r. 37.1.

28.1.7

PROOF OR JURY TRIAL.

Certain causes, the "enumerated causes" (see (A) below), must be sent to jury trial unless the parties otherwise agree or special cause is shown (see (B) below): C.S.A. 1988, s.9(b). The statutory provision is not modified by r. 28.1: *Graham v. Paterson & Son Ltd* 1938 S.C. 119. It has been held that, where the pursuer claims provisional damages under s.12 of the Administration of Justice (Scotland) Act 1982, Parliament has by implication deprived the pursuer of jury trial: *Potter v. McCulloch* 1987 S.L.T. 308, 311L per Lord Weir, although he also found special cause existed. It might be unwise, however, to rely on exclusion by implication: see (B) below (Special cause) and *McFadyen v. Crudens Ltd* 1972 S.L.T.(Notes) 62 per L.P. Emslie; cf. *Winchester v. Ramsay* 1966 S.C. 41 (effect of third party notice).

The court may allow jury trial in a cause other than an enumerated cause: e.g. *Fletcher v. Lord Advocate* 1923 S.C. 27; *Blount v. Watt* 1953 S.L.T.(Notes) 39. In this case the court has an unfettered discretion, although it may require a special reason (cause) to send a case which is not an enumerated cause to jury

28.1.8

trial. According to present day practice proof before a judge is the normal and convenient method of inquiry in actions which are not appropriated by statute to trial by jury: *Blount*, above, per Lord Guthrie at p. 40.

In choosing proof or jury trial (whether in an enumerated cause or not) the question is essentially one of discretion, the object being to select as between the alternative methods of inquiry which type of tribunal would best secure justice between the parties: *Graham v. Associated Electrical Industries Ltd* 1968 S.L.T. 81, 82 per L.P. Clyde; *Blount*, above.

A proof may, after amendment, be recalled and the cause sent for jury trial (*Higgins v. Burton* 1968 S.L.T.(Notes) 14); and, after amendment, allowance of issues recalled and a proof allowed (*Nicol v. McIntosh* 1987 S.L.T. 104 (obiter)).

(A) The enumerated causes.

These are: (1) an action of damages for personal injuries; (2) an action for libel or defamation; (3) an action founded on delinquency or quasi-delinquency where the conclusion is for damages only and expenses; and (4) an action of reduction on the ground of incapacity, essential error, or force and fear: C.S.A. 1988, s.11. The longer list in s.28 of the C.S.A. 1825 was replaced by this shorter list in the C.S.A. 1988 because none of the others had been sent to jury trial in living memory. S.49 of the C.S.A. 1850 had allowed proof on commission as an alternative in the enumerated causes except cases of libel, nuisance or damages; s.4 of the Evidence (Scotland) Act 1866 introduced the alternative of proof to jury trial where parties consented or on special cause shown (both these provisions are repealed by the C.S.A. 1988, Sched. 2).

(1) Action of damages for personal injuries.

This phrase in s.11(a) of the C.S.A. 1988, which is a consolidating measure, was not intended to and did not change the law, from that under s.28 of the C.S.A. 1825, to exclude claims for loss of society as a result of the death of a relative: *Morris v. Drysdak* 1992 S.L.T. 186. In *McFarlane v. Thain*, 2006 S.C. 360; 2006 S.L.T. 107 (Second Div.), the Motor Insurers' Bureau was a party minuter seeking a ruling on the applicability of their liability, where it was alleged that the pursuer knew, or ought to have know, that the vehicle he was in was uninsured. The opinion was expressed at para. [21] of the judgment that the case was a hybrid case going beyond the issue of personal injuries and was, therefore, not an enumerated cause.

(2) An action for libel or defamation.

This means an action for written or oral defamation, the former being sometimes known as libel and the latter as slander. Defamation means a communication to the injured party or another of a false statement or idea which is an imputation injurious to the character or credit of the injured party: *Brownlie v. Thomson* (1859) 21 D. 480, 485 per L.J.-C. Inglis; *A.B. v. C.D.* (1904) 7 F. 22. Malice only requires to be proved where qualified privilege is claimed: *Langlands v. Leng* 1916 S.C.(H.L.) 102, 109 per Lord Shaw of Dunfermline. Other types of verbal injury are convicium, slander of title, property, or goods or business, and malicious falsehood, which require proof of malice: these are not included in the meaning of defamation.

(3) Action founded on delinquency and quasi-delinquency.

Delinquency means fault or violation of duty and these terms are, therefore, synonymous with delict and quasi-delict.

(4) Action of reduction on ground of incapacity, essential error, or force or fear.

(a) Incapacity may arise through nonage (a child under 16: Age of Legal Capacity (Scotland) Act 1991, s.1(1)(a)) or insanity or other mental incapacity (including drunkenness: Stair, I.x.13; Erskine, III.i.16; *Taylor v. Provan* (1864) 2 M. 1226). (b) Essential error: see *Stewart v. Kennedy* (1890) 17 R.(H.L.) 25; *Menzies v. Menzies* (1893) 20 R.(H.L.) 108, 142 per Lord Watson; *Woods v. Tulloch* (1893) 20 R.(H.L.) 477 per Lord Watson; *Westville Shipping Co. v. Abram Steamship Co.* 1922 S.C. 571. (c) Force and fear. A contract induced by threats or violence sufficient to overcome the fortitude of a reasonable man is void: Stair, I.ix.8; Erskine, III.i.16; but a bill of exchange is voidable (Bills of Exchange Act 1882, ss.29(2), 30(2) and 38).

(B) Special cause.

The cause must be special to the particular case and not a general cause: *Taylor v. Dumbarton Tramways Co. Ltd* 1918 S.C.(H.L.) 96, 108 per Lord Shaw of Dunfermline; *Walker v. The Pitlochry Motor Co.* 1930 S.C. 565, 575 per L.P. Clyde. It is not a "special clause" that the right to a fair trial under Art. 6 of the European Convention on Human Rights might be infringed by jury trial as that cause would apply to almost every case: *Gunn v. Newman*, 2001 S.C. 525. What constitutes special cause is within the discretion of the Lord Ordinary, and the Inner House will be slow to interfere with that discretion: *Vallery v. McAlpine & Sons* (1905) 7 F. 640; *Walker*, above; *Graham v. Paterson & Son Ltd* 1938 S.C. 119, 136 per Lord Wark; *McLellan v. Western S.M.T. Co. Ltd* 1950 S.C. 112, 116 per Lord Russell. The Inner

House will interfere, however, where the Lord Ordinary has proceeded on a consideration which is general and not special to the particular case or he has not had material before him upon which to exercise a discretion.

In *Sandison v. Graham Begg Ltd* , 2001 S.C. 821 (OH), it was decided, obiter, that it was not necessary for detailed reasons to be given by a jury before a party dissatisfied with its decision on quantum could exercise the statutory right to apply for a new trial and there was, therefore, no risk of infringing Art. 6 of the ECHR.

A plea appropriate to the special cause should be stated (*Rigley v. Remington Rand Ltd* 1964 S.L.T.(Notes) 100) supported by specific averments (*McFaull v. Campania Navigacion Sota y Anzar* 1937 S.L.T. 118, 123 per Lord Russell).

Since special cause must be special to the particular case, one case is of little guidance when considering another: *Walters v. National Coal Board* 1961 S.L.T.(Notes) 82. The cases appear to disclose that only a case which is straightforward in relation to the legal and factual issues should be sent for jury trial. Special cause has been found on the following grounds, among others:

(a) Difficult and complex questions of fact: *Robertson v. T. & H. Smith Ltd* 1962 S.C. 628; and see *Miller v. Lanarkshire Health Board* 1993 S.L.T. 453 (medical issue); *McKechnie's C.B. v. Gribben* 1996 S.L.T. 136 (post-traumatic stress, cost of administration and special needs); *Johnston v. Clark* 1997 S.L.T. 923 (interpretation of patrimonial losses); *McInnes v. Kirkforthar Brick Co. Ltd* 1998 S.L.T. 568 (medical issues; loss of employability); *McKenna v. Sharp* 1998 S.C. 297, sub. nom. McKenna v. Chief Constable Strathclyde Police 1998 S.L.T. 1161 (issues allowed as jury able to discriminate between medical opinions).

(b) A question of law in relation to which it would be difficult to give the jury an effective direction: *Caldwell v. Wright* 1970 S.C. 24, 28 per Lord Avonside; *Potter v. McCulloch* 1987 S.L.T. 308, 312C per Lord Weir; and see also *Cassidy v. Argyll and Clyde Health Board* 1997 S.L.T. 934 (difficult and delicate questions of law could arise about foreseeability); *Ireland v. Dunfermline D.C.* 1998 S.L.T. 321. But, that a legal question may arise is not generally a sufficient ground (*Gardner v. Hastie* 1928 S.L.T. 497, 499 per Lord Fleming; cf. *Sneddon v. Baxter* 1967 S.L.T.(Notes) 67) and a difficult question of statutory construction is not a sufficient ground for withholding jury trial (*Mcintosh v. Commissioners of Lochgelly* (1897) 25 R. 32; cf. *Potter*, above, in conjunction with another factor). In *McFarlane v. Thain* , 2006 S.C. 360; 2006 S.L.T. 107 (Second Div.), it was held that the phrase "ought to have known" (that the pursuer knew that the driver was uninsured) in relation to the Motor Insurers' Bureau Agreement would give rise to difficulties in charging a jury.

(c) Questions of mixed fact and law in respect of which it would be difficult to give the jury an effective direction: *Bygate v. Edinburgh Corporation* 1967 S.L.T.(Notes) 65; *Morris v. Drysdale* 1992 S.L.T. 186; *Pietryea v. Strathclyde R.C.* 1998 S.L.T. 184 (fact). Cf *Robertson v. Smith* , 2000 S.L.T. 1013 (Extra Div.) (an argument, that the decision in *Wells v. Wells* [1999] 1 A.C. 345 meant that future loss of earnings had to be quantified with greater precision and that greater precision is averment or that difficult questions of fact and law would arise, was not sustained in that case); *Morris v. Fife Council* , 2003 S.L.T. 926 (OH); aff'd 2004 S.L.T. 1139 (Extra Div.) (risk of prejudice to defenders re evidence of consequences of sexual abuse that direction could not remove). See also *Potts v. McNulty* , 2000 S.L.T. 1269 (insufficient specification about claim relating to pension).

(d) Where there are averments of doubtful relevancy: *Robertson*, above; *Walters*, above; *Englert v. Stakis p.l.c.* , 5th July 1996, unreported; *Gibson v. McAndrew Wormald & Co Ltd* 1998 S.L.T. 562; *Currie v. Strathclyde Regional Council Fire Brigade* , 1999 S.L.T. 62.

(e) Where the law applicable to the facts cannot be stated with precision until the facts are determined, as jury trial proceeds on the basis that questions of relevancy have been disposed of: *Moore v. Alexander Stephen & Sons Ltd* 1954 S.C. 331, 334 per L.-C. Thomson; and see *Miller*, above. See also *Higgins v. DHL International (UK) Ltd* , 2003 S.L.T. 1301 (pleadings under new Chap. 43 insufficient).

(f) Where there are several grounds of action: *Mackenzie v. John Smith & Sons* 1955 S.L.T.(Notes) 25.

(g) Where a third party is brought in, particularly where this could otherwise involve two different modes of inquiry: *Winchester v. Ramsay* 1966 S.C. 41; *Rodgers v. James Crow & Sons Ltd* 1971 S.C. 155. Cf *Vetco Gray UK Ltd v. Slessor* , 2006 S.C. 398 (Second Div), and note 26.7.4.

(h) Where it might be impossible for the court to identify, for the purposes of the Interest on Damages (Scotland) Act 1958 (as amended by the Act of 1971), the elements of the lump sum awarded by the jury: *Cooper v. Pat Munro (Alness) Ltd* 1972 S.L.T.(Notes) 21; cf. *McMahon v. J. & P. Coats (United Kingdom) Ltd* 1972 S.L.T.(Notes) 16, *McFadyen v. Crudens Ltd* 1972 S.L.T.(Notes) 62. Most of the difficulties may be overcome by the practice of a form of issue in which the claim is broken down into various heads of claim: *McDonald v. Glasgow Corporation* 1973 S.C. 52.

(i) Where prejudice is caused by delay in raising or proceeding with an action (*mora*): *Hunter v. John Brown & Co. Ltd* 1961 S.C. 231, 236 per L.P. Clyde and Lord Guthrie. The delay must be inordinate, that is, beyond what normally occurs: *Conetta v. Central S.M.T. Co. Ltd* 1966 S.L.T. 302, 305 per Lord Migdale. The delay may be due to some factor outside the party's control: *Conetta*, above. The party relying on delay must be prejudiced, e.g. in preparation or presentation of the case because of the dimming of the recollection of witnesses: *Hunter*, above; cf. *Davidson v. Chief Constable, Fife Police* 1995 S.L.T. 545.

 (j) Where there are difficulties for the jury in the proper assessment of damages. For example, where, in a claim for services under s.9 of the Administration of Justice Act 1982, the averments are not clear, precise and defined to an obvious basis rendering it difficult to instruct a jury as to the approach to valuing the services: *Stark v. Ford* 1995 S.L.T. 69, aff'd on appeal in Stark v. Ford (No. 2) 1996 S.L.T. 1329; *Johnston v. Clark* 1997 S.L.T. 923; *Marshall v. PLM Helicopter Ltd* 1997 S.L.T. 1039 (on "services", see *Ingham v. John G. Russell (Transport) Ltd* 1991 S.C. 201 and *O'Brien's C.B. v. British Steel plc* 1991 S.C. 315). See also *Potts v. McNulty* , 2000 S.L.T. 1269 (different multipliers to various injuries); *Forrest v. Gourlay* , 2003 S.L.T. 783 (pursuer left open a range of issues which created uncertainty and would necessitate the formulation of many directions about a multiplicity of possible situations relating to disability).

"MAY MAKE SUCH OTHER ORDER".

28.1.9 This is a catch-all provision. It would, e.g. permit the court to allow an amendment (see note 28.1.10).

AMENDMENT AT PROCEDURE ROLL.

28.1.10 Where a cause has been sent to procedure roll, an offer to amend cannot usually be resisted unless it can be said that no amendment could cure the defect. It is not just to dismiss an action because of a formal pleading defect which can be put right without prejudice to the other party: *G.U.S. Property Management Ltd v. Littlewoods Mail Order Stores Ltd* 1982 S.C.(H.L.) 157, 178 per Lord Keith of Kinkel. Nowadays the party seeking to amend at the hearing on procedure roll will usually, and ought to, be required to indicate what the proposed amendment will be if a minute of amendment is not already lodged; any such indication may be sought by any other party to be noted (by the clerk of court) in the minute of proceedings. Any other party who appears at the hearing will be entitled to the expenses of a discharge of the procedure roll hearing occasioned by leave to amend being granted.

Although it is for the party seeking to amend to move the court for leave to do so, it is not incompetent for the Lord Ordinary to put the cause out By Order *after a hearing* on the Procedure Roll expressly or impliedly reserving the right of a party to apply for leave to amend: *Kennedy v. Norwich Union Fire Insurance Society Ltd* 1993 S.C. 578; see also *Craig v. Jarvis (Scotland) Ltd* , 30th May, 1997 unreported.

On the grounds on which amendment may be allowed, see r. 24.1 and notes 24.1.1-24.1.10.

Although a particular mode of inquiry has already been allowed, the court is not precluded from reconsidering and altering the mode of inquiry on a minute of amendment altering the pleadings: *Bendex v. James Donaldson & Sons Ltd* 1990 S.C. 259. For an example of the court refusing to allow alteration of the mode of proof after amendment, see *Johnston v. Clark* 1998 S.L.T. 139.

Where amendment is proposed at procedure roll, the party seeking to amend will, as a general rule, have to pay the expenses of the abortive hearing, and payment of these expenses may be made a condition precedent of that amendment: *Colbron v. United Glass Ltd* 1965 S.L.T. 366.

"MOTION".

28.1.11 For motions, see Chap. 23.

RECLAIMING.

28.1.12 A decision on the Procedure Roll which disposes of a cause (i.e. the subject-matter), whether or not expenses are dealt with, may be reclaimed against without leave within 21 days of the interlocutor: r. 38.3(2) and (5). An interlocutor allowing or refusing proof, proof before answer, jury trial, limiting the mode of proof, or adjusting issues may be reclaimed against without leave within 14 days: r. 38.3(4).

JUDGMENT: AUTHORITIES NOT CITED BY COUNSEL ETC.

28.1.13 If, at avizandum, the Lord Ordinary discovers an authority not cited by parties which he is inclined to rely on, a new argument occurs to him or a question arises about the appropriate interlocutor, the case should be put out by order to allow parties to make further submissions: *Lees v. North East Fife D.C.* 1987 S.C. 265, 273 per L.J.-C. Ross; *Brebner v. British Coal Corporation* , 1988 S.C. 333, 340 per L.J.-C. Ross; *Kennedy v. Norwich Union Fire Insurance Society* , 1993 S.C. 578, 1994 S.L.T. 617; *Wyman-Gordon Ltd v. Proclad International Ltd* , 2011 S.C. 338 (Second Div.), 359 at paras [56]–[59]. If the only outstanding issue is the form of the interlocutor, the Lord Ordinary may give judgment expressing his conclusions but should allow parties an opportunity to address him on that point: *Libertas-Kommerz v. Johnson* 1977 S.C. 191. See generally, *Osborne v. British Coal Property* 1996 S.L.T. 736.

FEE.

28.1.14 The court fee for a hearing on the Procedure Roll is payable by each party for every 30 minutes or part thereof. For fee, see Court of Session etc. Fees Order 1997, Table of Fees, Pt I, B, item 16 or C, item 16 [S.I. 1997 No. 688, as amended, pp. C 1201 et seq.]. Certain persons are exempt from payment of fees: see 1997 Fees Order, art.5, substituted by S.S.I. 2002 No. 270. A fee exemption certificate must be lodged in process: see P.N. No. 1 of 2002.

Where a party is legally represented, the fee may be debited under a credit scheme introduced on 1st April 1976 by P.N. No. 4 of 1976 to the account (if one is kept or permitted) of the agent by the court cashier, and an account will be rendered weekly by the court cashier's office to the agent for all court fees due that week for immediate settlement. An agent not on the credit scheme will have an account opened for the purpose of lodging the fee: P.N. No. 2 of 1995. A debit slip and a copy of the court hearing time sheet will be delivered to the agent's box or sent by DX or post.

A party litigant must pay (by cash, cheque or postal order) to the clerk of court at the end of the hearing or, if the hearing lasts more than a day, at the end of each day: P.N. No. 2 of 1995. A receipt will be issued. The assistant clerk of session will acknowledge receipt of the sum received from the clerk of court on the Minute of Proceedings.

DOCUMENTS NOT PLED.

As no reference can be made to productions on procedure roll without agreement of parties, if reliance is to be placed for relevancy or specification in pleadings on documents they must be "adopted and held as repeated herein *brevitatis causa*": see *Gordon v. Davidson* (1864) 2 M. 758, 769 per L.J.-C. Inglis; *Eadie Cairns*, above per Lord Avonside at p.780E and Lord Jauncey at p.783F. The wholesale incorporation of lengthy documents, only parts of which are relevant, is generally unsatisfactory, however, and may well be held not to give the specification required: *Royal Bank of Scotland plc v. Holmes* , 1999 S.L.T. 563. In *Prophit v. BBC* , 1997 S.L.T. 745, Temporary Judge T. G. Coutts refused to listen to a tape recording of a programme because the issues at procedure roll had to be tested solely on the averments and the tape had not been incorporated into the pleadings. The implication is that if it had been so incorporated, the court would have listened to it.

28.1.15

CITATION OF AUTHORITIES.

The general rule is that when a case has been reported in Session Cases or the (English) Law Reports, it should be cited from that source: *McGowan v. Summit at Lloyds* , 2002 S.L.T. 1258, 1273 at para.[57] (Ex Div.). See also now, P.N. No. 5 of 2004. The citation of cases from reproduction of electronic formats is permitted by that P.N.

28.1.16

CHAPTER 28A NOTICES TO ADMIT AND NOTICES OF NON-ADMISSION

Notices to Admit and Notices of Non-Admission

Notices to admit and notices of non-admission

28A.1.—[1](1) At any time after the record has closed, a party may intimate to any other party a notice or notices calling on him to admit for the purposes of that cause only—

    (a)   such facts relating to an issue averred in the pleadings as may be specified in the notice;

    (b)   that a particular document lodged in process and specified in the notice is—

          (i)   an original and properly authenticated document; or

         (ii) a true copy of an original and properly authenticated document.

  (2) Where a party on whom a notice is intimated under paragraph (1)—

    (a)   does not admit a fact specified in the notice, or

    (b)   does not admit, or seeks to challenge, the authenticity of a document specified in the notice,

he shall, within 21 days after the date of intimation of the notice under paragraph (1), intimate a notice of non-admission to the party intimating the notice to him under paragraph (1) stating that he does not admit the fact or document specified.

  (3) The party intimating a notice under paragraph (1) or (2) shall lodge a copy of it in process.

  (4) The court may, at any time, allow a party to amend or withdraw an admission made by him on such conditions, if any, as it thinks fit.

  (5) A party may, at any time, withdraw in whole or in part a notice of non-admission by intimating a notice or withdrawal.

GENERAL NOTE.

Chapter 28A was inserted by A.S. (R.C.S.A. No. 4) (Miscellaneous) 1996 [SI 1996/2168]. It was formerly r. 36.6 which permitted a notice to admit to be served at any time after a proof had been allowed. The Cullen *Review of Outer House Business* of December 1995 recommended that a notice to admit should be permitted at any time after the lodging of defences. This recommendation did not find favour and the Rules Council recommended that such notices be permitted after the record has closed. This recommendation is now in the rule: see r. 28A.1(1). If and when records are abolished following the Cullen review, a further change will be required. Because the rule now is to permit such notices *before* a proof has been allowed, r. 36.6 has been taken out of Chap. 36 (proofs) and has had to be given a Chapter of its own.

The opportunity has been taken to divide r. 36.6 into two rules in Chap. 28A, r. 28A.1 providing for the procedure for notices and r. 28A.2 dealing with the consequences of failure to intimate a notice of non-admission.

Chap. 28A (formerly r. 36.6) was originally suggested by the principal annotator to the Jauncey Working Party on Patent Litigation which recommended its adoption in the intellectual property rules, and this was done in R.C.S. 1965, r. 253 as amended by A.S. (R.C.S.A. No. 7) (Patent Rules) 1991 [S.I. 1991 No. 1621] (now R.C.S. 1994, r. 55.4).

It might be thought that Chap. 28A is not necessary when the system of Scottish pleadings should result in it being clear by the time proof has been allowed what is in issue and what has to be proved. Not all relevant documentary material, however, previously in dispute by the time the proof approaches, and the authenticity of such material, or an averment, may be the subject of a general denial which would otherwise necessitate proof. It may, of course, be possible to obtain agreement by consent. The purpose of the rule is to provide an additional means to assist in reducing documentary material and averments having to be proved which in the end of the day do or did not require proof and the time taken in proving them. It is also considered that this might be a more effective way of obtaining admissions than calls in the pleadings.

The relationship of Chap. 28A to rr. 36.7 and 36.8 should be noticed. The possibility of a minute of admission by one or more parties is not affected by Chap. 28A. A deemed admission may arise, however, under r. 28A.2(1) if a notice of non-admission is intimated in response to a notice to admit. Under

---

[1] Chap. 28A and r. 28A.1 inserted by SI 1996/2168 (effective 23rd September 1996).

s.2(1)(b) of the Civil Evidence (Scotland) Act 1988 any document (including an affidavit) may be received in evidence without being spoken to by a witness as evidence not merely that it was made but as to the truth of its contents, and r. 36.8 provides the mechanism for obtaining the permission of the court to produce such evidence without being spoken to. In respect of the authenticity of a document it may also be possible to use the procedure in Chap. 28A.

FORM OF NOTICES.

28A.1.2   A notice of admission and a notice of non-admission do not require to be formal signed documents in the style of a Minute ("X for the pursuer called and hereby calls on the defender to admit:—"). It is preferred that the notice is headed (after the cross-heading "In the Court of Session") "Notice to Admit [*or* of non-admission]" with the instance of the cause.

"INTIMATE".

28A.1.3   For methods, see r. 16.7.

"WITHIN 21 DAYS".

28A.1.4   The date from which the period is calculated is not counted. Where the last day falls on a Saturday or Sunday or a public holiday on which the Office of Court is closed, the next available day is allowed: r. 1.3(7). For office hours and public holidays, see note 3.1.2.

"LODGE A COPY OF IT IN PROCESS".

28A.1.5   The copy is lodged as a step of process and not as a production: r. 1.3(1) (definition of "step of process"). On steps of process, see r. 4.4.

Consequences of failure to intimate notice of non-admission

28A.2   **28A.2.**—[1](1)   A party who fails to intimate a notice of non-admission under paragraph (2) of rule 28A.1 shall be deemed to have admitted the fact or document specified in the notice intimated to him under paragraph (1) of that rule; and such fact or document may be used in evidence at a proof if otherwise admissible in evidence, unless the court, on special cause shown, otherwise directs.

(2)   *[Revoked by S.I. 1997 No. 1050 (effective 6th April 1997).]*

(3)   A deemed admission under paragraph (1) of this rule shall not be used against the party by whom it was deemed to be made other than in the cause for the purpose for which it was deemed to be made or in favour of any person other than the party by whom the notice was given under rule 28A.1(1).

GENERAL NOTE.

28A.2.1   This rule was formerly part of r. 36.6. For the history of the rule, see note 28A.1.1.

The rule as originally enacted was not entirely satisfactory: if a fact is deemed to be admitted by virtue of r. 28A.2(1), proof is unlikely to be required and the provision for the expenses of proving it under r. 28A.2(2), is unnecessary. The latter provision has been revoked by A.C. (R.C.S.A. No. 4) (Miscellaneous) 1997 [S.I. 1997 No. 1050]. Accordingly, now failure to lodge a notice of non-admission of a fact or document results in it being deemed to be admitted. The party serving the notice to admit does not have to prove the fact or document, and there is no need for the rule to deal with expenses.

It might have been better if the rule provided, where there is a failure to lodge a notice of non-admission, (a) in relation to facts, for the expenses of proving facts set out in the notice (no deemed admission), and (b) in relation to documents, for a deemed admission of their authentication.

"INTIMATE".

28A.2.2   For methods, see r. 16.7.

"WITHIN 21 DAYS".

28A.2.3   The date from which this period is calculated is not counted. Where the last day falls on a Saturday or Sunday or a public holiday on which the Office of Court is closed, the next available day is allowed: r. 1.3(7). For office hours and public holidays, see note 3.1.2.

---

[1] R. 28A.2 inserted by S.I. 1996 No. 2168 (effective 23rd September 1996).

CHAPTER 29 ABANDONMENT

Abandonment of actions

29.1.—(1) A pursuer may abandon an action by lodging a minute of abandonment in process and—

    (a)   consenting to decree of absolvitor; or

    (b)   seeking decree of dismissal.

(2) The court shall not grant decree of dismissal under paragraph (1)(b) unless—

    (a)[1] full judicial expenses have been paid to the defender, and to any third party against whom the pursuer has directed any conclusions, within 28 days after the date of intimation of the report of the Auditor on the taxation of the account of expenses of that party; and

    (b)   where abandonment is made in a proof or jury trial, the minute of abandonment is lodged before avizandum is made in the proof or the charge to the jury by the presiding judge has begun in the jury trial, as the case may be.

(3) If the pursuer fails to pay the expenses referred to in sub-paragraph (a) of paragraph (2) to the party to whom they are due within the period specified in that sub-paragraph, that party shall be entitled to decree of absolvitor with expenses.

Deriv. R.C.S. 1965, r. 91A inserted by S.I. 1984 No. 472 (r. 29.1(b), (2) and (3)).

GENERAL NOTE.

R.C.S. 1965, r. 91A (now R.C.S. 1994, r. 29.1(1)(b) and (2)) was inserted by A.S. (R.C.A. No. 2) (Miscellaneous) 1984 [S.I. 1984 No. 472], r. 29.1(1)(b) and (2) replacing s.10 of the C.S.A. 1825 (repealed by A.S. (R.C.A. No. 8) (Miscellaneous) 1986 [S.I. 1986 No. 1937]) which was extended by s.39 of the C.S.A. 1868 (repealed by A.S. (R.C.S. 1994) 1994, Sched. 5 [S.I. 1994 No. 1443]. Abandonment at common law meant the pursuer was prepared to release the defender for all time without reservation, the defender could obtain decree of absolvitor and the court had discretion only in relation to expenses; whereas abandonment under statute (s.10 of the C.S.A. 1825 as extended by s.39 of the C.S.A. 1868 and substituted by R.C.S. 1965, r. 91A) was under reservation (of his right to raise a fresh action) involving payment of expenses with a view to obtaining dismissal: see *Esso Petroleum Co. Ltd v. Hall Russell & Co. Ltd* 1988 S.L.T. 33, 39E-I per L.P. Emslie. At common law the court had no discretion to prevent a party abandoning, he having an unfettered right to abandon subject to the conditions which the court could lawfully impose (i.e. expenses): *Lee v. Pollock's Trs* (1906) 8 F. 857, 860 per L.P. Dunedin; *Castlegreen Storage & Distributors Ltd v. Schreiber* 1982 S.L.T. 269, 271 per Lord Murray; *Esso Petroleum*, above, per L.P. Emslie.

Up to release 63 this annotation contained the statement "R.29.1(1)(a) replaced the common law and r. 29.1(1)(b) and (2) replaces R.C.S. 1965, r. 91A and the former statutory rules." Rule 91A(1) was intended by the draftsman (W. Galbraith Q.C.) to replace the common law rule of abandonment under reservation. In *Beattie v. The Royal Bank of Scotland plc* , 2003 S.L.T 564 (OH), Lord Reed held that the common law right to abandonment under reservation had not been abolished by r. 29.1 or by the former r. 91A. The distinction between abandonment under r. 29.2(1)(b) (dismissed on payment of expenses required by r. 29.1(2)) and common law abandonment under reservation is that under common law abandonment it is in the discretion of the court what, if any, expenses are to be paid as a condition of obtaining the decree of dismissal. In fact payment of expenses was the "normal" condition: *Singer v. Gray Tool Co. (Europe) Ltd* , 1984 S.L.T. 149, 150 per Emslie, L.P. In *Beattie*, resort to the common law rule was made because expenses had been agreed and not taxed as stipulated in r. 29.1(2). In *VP Packaging Ltd v. The ADF Partnership* , 2002 S.L.T. 1224 (OH) it had been held in a similar situation that as expenses had been agreed and not taxed as required by r. 29.1(2)(a) there could be no abandonment under r. 29.1(1)(b) and the pursuer must be presumed to have waived any right to ask for dismissed under that rule. In *Beattie*, Lord Reed held that if he was wrong about the continuing existence of the common law right, it would have been competent to exercise, and he would have exercised, the dispensing power under r. 2.1. He did not follow *VP Packaging* in which Lord Wheatley held that r. 2.1 could not apply where the failure to comply with r. 29.1(2)(a) was deliberate.

Abandonment may be made at any time after calling and before final decree; but the decree on abandonment and the conditions for abandonment differ depending on the time at which abandonment is sought. Abandonment may be against one or more or all other parties; it does not have to be abandonment against all parties. The pursuer cannot obtain abandonment in respect of part of the action in which the defender has obtained a (final) decree although the whole action has not been disposed of: formerly A.S. 11th July 1828, s.115.

---

[1] R.29.1(2)(a) amended by S.S.I. 2001 No. 305 (effective 18th September 2001).

Abandonment by a pursuer under r. 29.1 is of right, and is not in the discretion of the court: *Frost v. Unity Trust Bank plc* 1997 S.L.T. 1358. It should be obvious that the word "may" in the opening words of r. 29.1(1) is not conferring a discretion on the court but an option for the pursuers which he may or may not choose to take ("shall" could not be substituted because the pursuer cannot be obliged to abandon his action).

(1) Abandonment with consent to decree of absolvitor

may be obtained at any time after calling and before final decree without conditions imposed by the court (cf. common law when the court had a discretion as to dismissal or absolvitor). A decree of absolvitor is a decree *in foro* in favour of a defender on the merits which is res judicata: *Forrest v. Dunlop* (1875) 3 R. 15; on res judicata, see note 18.1.4(B)(5). When the defender moves for decree of absolvitor he may seek an order for expenses, and he would be entitled to expenses of the cause unless otherwise agreed or determined. The court has a discretion in relation to expenses: see *Esso Petroleum Co. Ltd v. Hall Russell & Co. Ltd* 1988 S.L.T. 33, 39F per L.P. Emslie.

(2) Abandonment with a decree of dismissal.

Since a decree of dismissal (which is not res judicata) enables a pursuer to raise a fresh action (*Menzies v. Menzies* (1893) 20 R.(H.L.) 108, 110 per Lord Watson), it is subject to the two conditions in r. 29.1(2). The restriction of abandonment before avizandum or the charge to the jury derives from s.39 of the C.S.A. 1868. The minute of abandonment for decree of dismissal must be accompanied by a motion for decree of dismissal and for finding the party abandoning liable in expenses as taxed. On payment of expenses, see note 29.1.4. Dismissal, carrying with it the right to bring a new action, is a remedy that has to be acquired by taking certain steps in terms of the rules. If dismissal is not available then the only appropriate course is absolvitor: *VP Packaging Ltd v. The ADF Partnership* , 29th January 2002, unreported, 2002 G.W.D. 5-144 (OH).

A decree of dismissal (without inquiry into the merits, fact or law, as on relevancy) means that the pursuer is entitled to bring a fresh action on the same grounds: see *Menzies*, above. It has been said that the word "dismiss" is used when it is open to a party to bring another action and "assoilzie" where it is not: *Stewart v. Greenock Harbour Trs* (1868) 6 M. 954, 958 per Lord Deas. See also *Waydale Ltd v. DHL Holdings (UK) Ltd* , 2000 S.C. 172 (Extra Div.) overruling Lord Hamilton at 1999 S.L.T. 631, 637C (who held that where dismissal on relevancy followed inquiry, another action on the same grounds could be excluded) and doubting *Johnston v. Standard Property Investment Co. Ltd* 1909 1 S.L.T. 23.

A solicitor should obtain a special mandate to abandon: *Urquhart v. Grigor* (1857) 19 D. 853, 855 per L.J.-C. Hope. Counsel may abandon without instructions but usually does not do so: *Batchelor v. Pattison and Mackersy* (1876) 3 R. 914, 918 per L.J.-C. Inglis.

A party might abandon at the Bar in the course of a cause without lodging a minute.

The question arises as to the meaning of "full judicial expenses" in r. 29.1(2)(a): see note 29.1.4.

MINUTE OF ABANDONMENT.

29.1.2

Rule 15.1 (form of applications by minute, etc.) does not apply: r. 15.1(6). The minute has to be signed, and accordingly a pursuer's motion for decree of dismissal and the minute of abandonment cannot be faxed to the court: see r. 23.2(4).

The minute should not include any conditions or qualifications: *Adamson, Howie & Co. v. Guild* (1868) 6 M.347, 358 per L.P. Inglis; *Stewart v. Stewart* (1906) 8 F. 769. The minute may only be signed by the counsel or other person having a right of audience responsible for the cause; it cannot be signed on his behalf.

The text of the minute under r. 29.1(1)(a) should be along the following lines:

"[X] for the pursuer stated and hereby states to the court that the pursuer abandons this cause [in so far as it relates to the [first] defender] under rule 29.1(1)(a) of the Rules of the Court of Session 1994 and consents to decree of absolvitor [in favour of the [first] defender]."

The text of the minute under r. 29.1(1)(b) should be along the following lines:

"[X] for the pursuer stated and hereby states to the court that the pursuer abandons this cause under rule 29.1(1)(b) of the Rules of the Court of Session 1994 and seeks decree of dismissal."

INTIMATION OF MINUTE OF ABANDONMENT.

29.1.3

Written intimation of the lodging of the minute must be given to every other party and a copy of it sent to every such party: r. 4.6(1). For methods of written intimation, see r. 16.9. The back of the minute must be marked "Intimated".

PAYMENT OF EXPENSES TO OBTAIN DECREE OF DISMISSAL.

29.1.4

The minute of abandonment for decree of dismissal must be accompanied by a motion to find the party abandoning liable in expenses as taxed and to appoint the defender to lodge an account of expenses within a specified period (usually four months as this is the period specified in r. 42.1(2)) and to remit that account for taxation. The pursuer must specify a period otherwise the defender could delay lodging an account indefinitely and prevent the pursuer obtaining decree of dismissal. If the defender fails to lodge an account the pursuer will no doubt have to resort to the dispensing power in r. 2.1 to dispense with the requirement to pay the expenses and obtain decree of dismissal. The court pronounces an interlocutor in those terms remitting the defender's account of expenses to the Auditor to tax and report but with no decerniture for the expenses as taxed. The object of remitting for taxation is to get a fixed sum which the pursuer has to pay: *Lee v. Pollock's Trs* (1906) 8 F. 857. When the Auditor reports a note of objection may be taken to the report in the usual way. There is, however, no award or decerniture for the expenses as taxed, but the pursuer has 28 days under r. 29.1(2)(a) to pay the expenses. If he pays he should obtain a receipt which he lodges in process and is entitled to decree of dismissal. A pursuer who agrees to settle expenses without reference to the Auditor must be presumed to have abandoned any right to ask for dismissal in terms of r. 29.1: *VP Packaging Ltd v. The ADF Partnership*, 29th January 2002, unreported, 2002 G.W.D. 5-144 (OH).

The expenses recoverable by the defender are the expenses which he could have recovered from the pursuer under a decree of absolvitor with expenses had the action not been abandoned (i.e. he is not entitled to recover expenses for procedure in which he was unsuccessful and earlier expenses awarded against him may not be recovered): *Nobel's Explosives Co. Ltd v. British Dominions General Insurance Co. Ltd* 1919 S.C. 455; *Lord Hamilton v. Glasgow Dairy Co.* 1933 S.C. 18. The pursuer is not liable for the expenses of a counterclaim as a condition or consequence of abandonment: r. 24.5.

What does "full judicial expenses" mean? Generally expenses will be awarded on a party and party basis, but may be awarded on a solicitor and client basis in appropriate circumstances: *P v. P* 1940 S.C. 389, 391 per L.J.-C. Aitchison; followed in *Lord Advocate v. ASAU JV*, 24th March 2006, 2006 G.W.D. 21-454 (OH), [2006] CSOH 50.

It has been held that r. 29.1(2)(a) does not apply to a pursuer who agrees expenses and does not submit an account for taxation: *VP Packaging Ltd v. The ADF Partnership*, 2002 S.L.T. 1224 (OH). In that case it was held that the pursuer must be presumed to have abandoned any right to ask for dismissal in terms of r. 29.1 and that the dispensing power in r. 2.1 could not apply because the agreement on expenses was deliberate. But in *Beattie v. The Royal Bank of Scotland plc*, 2002 S.L.T. 564 (OH), Lord Reed held that the dispensing power in r. 2.1 could be applied as the failure to comply with the taxation provision was an excusable cause. He observed that an agreement on expenses might be regarded as equivalent to the intimation of the auditor's report on taxation required by r. 29.1(2)(a).

Where the pursuer is legally aided there is no power for the court to modify the expenses the pursuer is liable to pay either instead of remitting to the Auditor (*Johnston v. Johnston* 1985 S.L.T. 510, 512 per Lord Cowie) or on a motion to modify under s.18(2) of the Legal Aid (Scotland) Act 1986 (*Collum v. Glasgow Corporation* 1964 S.L.T. 199 not following *Thompson v. Fairfield Shipbuilding and Engineering Co.* 1954 S.C. 354) because there is no "award" of expenses made by the court.

If the pursuer fails to pay the expenses the defender or other party to whom they are due is entitled to absolvitor: r. 29.1(3). This accords with *Ross v. Mackenzie* (1889) 16 R. 871 and *Donnelly v. Morrison* (1895) 2 S.L.T. 582. There is no discretion in the court to grant decree of dismissal: *Cobb v. Baker Oil Tools (U.K.) Ltd* 1984 S.C. 60.

Abandonment of family action.

Where a pursuer abandons a family action (as defined by r. 49.1(1)), the defender may continue with   **29.1.5**
any conclusions for custody, aliment or access in his defences: r. 49.32.

Effect of abandonment on counterclaim.

The right of a pursuer to abandon is not affected by the presence of a counterclaim, the pursuer is not   **29.1.6**
liable for any expenses of the counterclaim as a condition or consequence of abandonment and the counterclaim continues as if a separate action: r. 25.4.

Withdrawal of minute.

A minute of abandonment may be withdrawn before final decree: *Lee v. Pollock's Trs* (1906) 8 F. 857.   **29.1.7**
The minute must be withdrawn by motion. The defender may move for absolvitor which will be granted unless the pursuer shows his proceedings have been bona fide, in which case the pursuer may proceed subject to any conditions the court imposes: *Lee*, above, per L.P. Dunedin at p. 861. The pursuer will usually have to pay the expenses connected with the aborted abandonment: *Todd & Higginbotham v. Corporation of Glasgow* (1879) 16 S.L.R. 718; *Dalgleish v. Mitchell* (1886) 23 S.L.R. 552.

Application of abandonment of actions to counterclaims

29.2. Rule 29.1 shall, with the necessary modifications, apply to the abandon-   **29.2**
ment by a defender of his counterclaim as it applies to the abandonment of an action.

Deriv. RCS 1965, r. 84(e)

General note.

This rule applies r. 29.1 to counterclaims. The principles are the same.   **29.2.1**

Abandonment of petitions, minutes and notes

29.3.—(1) A petition, minute or note may be abandoned by the petitioner,   **29.3**
minuter or noter, as the case may be—

    (a)   enrolling a motion for abandonment of the cause; and

    (b)   intimating the motion to every person who lodged answers.

    (2)   The court may grant a motion under paragraph (1) subject to such conditions as to expenses or otherwise, if any, as it thinks fit.

GENERAL NOTE.

29.3.1   This new rule provides for abandonment of petitions, minutes and notes. Intimation only has to be made to those who have entered the process: r. 23.3.

    Where a petition for sequestration or liquidation is dismissed, there is an order for advertisement of the interlocutor dismissing the petition.

CHAPTER 30 WITHDRAWAL OF AGENTS

Intimation of withdrawal of agent

30.1.—[1](1) This rule applies where an agent withdraws from acting on behalf of a party.

(2) The agent must intimate withdrawal by letter to the Deputy Principal Clerk and every other party.

(3) That letter must specify the last known address of the party.

(4) Where any previously fixed hearing is to take place within 14 days from the date of the withdrawal, the agent must confirm in the letter that they have taken all reasonable steps to—

    (a) notify the party of the hearing date;

    (b) advise the party that they must attend the hearing or arrange representation at the hearing to state whether or not they intend to proceed; and

    (c) advise the party that a failure to attend or be represented at the hearing may result in the court granting decree or making another finding or order.

(5) The Deputy Principal Clerk must lodge the letter in process.

30.1

GENERAL NOTE.

This Chapter contains new rules which reflect the current practice on withdrawal of solicitors from acting.

When intimating his withdrawal the agent must disclose to every other party his former client's current address if known to him and different from that stated in the pleadings so that the procedure under r. 30.2 can be carried out: *Sime, Sullivan & Dickson's Tr. v. Adam* 1908 S.C. 32.

Leave of the court to withdraw is not required: *Scott v. Christie* (1856) 19 D. 178.

Notwithstanding that an agent has withdrawn, the court has a discretion, where a party is in default under r. 20.1 for failure to appear, to grant decree of default: *Munro & Miller (Pakistan) Ltd v. Wyvern Structures Ltd* 1996 S.L.T. 135, affirmed 1997 S.C. 1.

"AGENT".

This means a solicitor or a person having a right to conduct the litigation: see r. 1.3(1) (definition of "agent") and note 1.3.4. "Solicitor" is defined in the C.S.A. 1988, s.51.

"INTIMATE".

For methods, see r. 16.7.

"LODGED IN PROCESS".

The letter becomes a step in process.

30.1.1

30.1.2

30.1.3

30.1.4

Intimation to party whose agent has withdrawn

30.2.—(1)[2, 3] The court shall, on the motion of any other party or, where there is no other party, at its own instance, pronounce an interlocutor ordaining the party whose agent has withdrawn from acting to intimate to the Deputy Principal Clerk within 14 days (or such other period as the court, on cause shown, thinks fit) after service of the notice as required by paragraph (2) whether or not he intends to proceed, under certification that if he fails to intimate whether or not he intends to proceed, the court may grant such decree or make such order or finding as it thinks fit.

(2)[4, 5] The party who enrolled a motion under paragraph (1), or the court where there is no other party, shall forthwith serve a notice in Form 30.2 to the party whose agent has withdrawn from acting.

30.2

---

[1] R 30.1 substituted by S.S.I. 2017 No. 200 r 2(2) (effective 17th July 2017).

[2] R. 30.2(1) and (2) amended by S.I. 1996 No. 2168 (effective 23rd September 1996)

[3] R 30.2(1) amended by S.S.I. 2017 No. 200 r 2(3)(a) (effective 17th July 2017).

[4] R. 30.2(1) and (2) amended by S.I. 1996 No. 2168 (effective 23rd September 1996)

[5] R 30.2(2) amended by S.S.I. 2017 No. 200 r 2(3)(b) (effective 17th July 2017).

GENERAL NOTE.

30.2.1   On receiving intimation of withdrawal under r. 30.1(1) any other party may enrol a motion for an order under r. 30.2 ordaining the party whose agent has withdrawn to intimate whether he intends to proceed. The motion is unstarred unless a period of notice other than 14 days is sought. The notice in Form 30.2 must be served. The A.S. (R.C.S.A. No. 4) (Miscellaneous) 1996 [S.I. 1996 No. 2168] abolished the requirement to serve the interlocutor as well as the notice in order to save duplication: all that is necessary is in the notice.

For a case in which this was not done and the defender sought and was granted decree of absolvitor at a proof at which the pursuer did not appear following withdrawal of its agents from acting, see *Munro & Miller (Pakistan) Ltd v. Wyvern Structures Ltd* 1996 S.L.T. 135.

Where the whereabouts of the party on whom the notice is to be served becomes unknown, it may be necessary to serve the notice by advertisement: see r. 16.5.

"MOTION".

30.2.2   For motions, see Chap. 23.

"WITHIN 14 DAYS".

30.2.3   The date from which the period is calculated is not counted. Where the last day falls on a Saturday or Sunday or a public holiday on which the Office of Court is closed, the next available day is allowed: r. 1.3(7). For office hours and public holidays, see note 3.1.2.

"SERVE".

30.2.4   For methods, see Chap. 16, Pt I.

INTIMATION OF INTENTION BY PARTY WHOSE AGENT HAS WITHDRAWN.

30.2.5   Form 30.2 explains that the party whose agent has withdrawn must write to the Deputy Principal Clerk indicating whether he intends to proceed. If he does intend to proceed he will be informed what the next step is which is required to be done in the cause. The letter will be placed in process by the Deputy Principal Clerk. A form on which to do this is sent with Form 30.2. The language of Form 30.2 is clear and peremptory, and a cogent reason for its being disregarded would be required: *Connelly v. Lanarkshire Health Board* 1999 S.C. 364.

If the party whose agent has withdrawn intimates that he does not intend to proceed, the Deputy Principal Clerk causes the letter to be lodged in process. The other party must check the process after the period for intimation has expired. If there is no letter intimating an intention to proceed he may enrol a motion for such decree or other order as is appropriate in the circumstances.

"DECREE, ORDER OR FINDING".

30.2.6   The decree or other order will depend on the circumstances, including which party's agent has withdrawn. The decree could be *de plano*, absolvitor or dismissal or the grant or refusal of the prayer of a petition.

DECREE BY DEFAULT WHERE AGENT WITHDRAWS.

30.2.7   Where a party's agent has withdrawn from acting and that party fails to attend a proof, the court has a discretion whether to grant decree by default under r. 20.1 or to ordain that party under r. 30.2 to intimate whether he intends to proceed: *Munro & Miller (Pakistan) Ltd v. Wyvern Structures Ltd* 1996 S.L.T. 135, affirmed 1997 S.C. 1.

Consequences of failure to intimate intention to proceed

30.3   **30.3.**[1]   Where a party on whom a notice has been served under rule 30.2(2) fails to intimate to the Deputy Principal Clerk within the period specified in the notice that he intends to proceed, the court shall, on the motion of any other party where a certificate of service of the notice has been lodged in process, grant such decree, order or finding as it thinks fit.

"CERTIFICATE OF SERVICE".

30.3.1   The certificate of service signed by the person executing service (with the requisite proof of delivery where service is by post), a copy of the notice and the interlocutor served must be lodged as a step of process (not a production): r. 16.1(3). On lodging steps of process, see r. 4.1(3) and (4).

"DECREE, ORDER OR FINDING".

30.3.2   The decree or other order will depend on the circumstances including which party's agent has withdrawn. The decree could be *de plano*, absolvitor or dismissal, or the grant or refusal of the prayer of a petition and an order or finding for expenses.

---

[1] R. 30.3 amended by S.I. 1997 No. 1050 (effective 6th April 1997).

A decree of dismissal after defences have been lodged, granted when the defender failed to intimate his intention to proceed after withdrawal of his agents, is a decree *in foro* but not res judicata: *Mason v. A. & R. Robertson & Black* 1993 S.L.T. 773.

Reclaiming.

Where a decree passes against a party under r. 30.3, the decree may be reclaimed against, without leave, within 21 days after the date on which the decree was pronounced (r. 38.3(2)). Failing that, an action of reduction would have to be brought. For a recent case, see *Dundee Football Club Ltd v. Souter* , 6th December 1996, unreported (action unsuccessful).

30.3.3

CHAPTER 31 MINUTES OF SIST AND TRANSFERENCE

Minutes of sist

31.1.—(1) Where a party dies or comes under legal incapacity while a cause is in dependence, any person claiming to represent that party or his estate may apply to the court by minute to be sisted as a party to the cause.

(2) Intimation of such an application shall be made to each party.

Deriv. R.C.S. 1965, r. 106 (part)

GENERAL NOTE.

This rule deals with only two situations in which a sist of a person as a party may arise (on which see notes 31.1.2 and 31.1.3); there are others.

(1) General rule as to sist of person as party.

Any person having sufficient title and interest may apply to be sisted as a party to an action: see e.g. *Muir v. Corporation of Glasgow* 1917 2 S.L.T. 106. On title and interest, see note 13.2.2(C). It is *par judicis* to allow a person to appear whom the court considers may have an interest: *Lord Blantyre v. Lord Advocate* (1876) 13 S.L.R. 213, 214 per Lord Deas; to this end the court may order intimation to enable that person to be sisted if so advised: *Orr Ewing's Trs v. Orr Ewing* (1884) 12 R. 343. As a general rule, in petitions and notes there is no need to be sisted as a party because any person may lodge answers as the first order under r. 14.5 states. The procedure for sisting a person to a cause is the same as the procedure in r. 31.1.

(2) Sist of person as pursuer or petitioner.

This may arise on the motion of any party or the person lodging a minute of sist seeking to be sisted. Note, however, the provisions of r. 24.1(1)(b)(iv) (adding name of additional pursuer by amendment), r. 24.1(1)(d) (additional or substitute party by amendment) and r. 24.2 (applications to amend). A connected person (as defined by r. 43.1(2)) may apply by minute to be sisted to an action of damages arising out of the death of a person from personal injuries under r. 43.6. An executor may sist himself to an action of damages for personal injuries in respect of any rights transmitted to him: Damages (Scotland) Act 1976, s.2A inserted by the Damages (Scotland) Act 1993, s.4.

(3) Sist of person as defender.

This may arise on the person's own motion or the motion of a party lodging a minute of sist seeking to be sisted as a defender. If he can show title and interest he may be sisted and allowed to lodge defences: see e.g. *Macfie v. Scottish Rights of Way and Recreation Society (Ltd)* (1884) 11 R. 1094. Note, however, the provisions of r. 24.1(2)(d) (additional or substitute party) and r. 24.2 (applications to amend) to bring in a person by amendment.

(4) Transmission of interest.

The interest in the subject-matter of a cause may pass to another party other than by death or incapacity. A transferee is entitled to take the place of the party who is divested of the interest which is in the subject-matter of the action: *Waddell v. Hope* (1843) 6 D. 160; *Fearn v. Cowper* (1899) 7 S.L.T. 68 (assignee); *Mavor v. Governors of Aberdeen Educational Trust* (1902) 10 S.L.T. 156 (disponee).

SIST OF REPRESENTATIVE ON DEATH OF PARTY.

On death of a party during the dependence of a cause all procedure is suspended (including extract) and any further proceedings are null and void unless that party's representatives sist themselves or the action is transferred against them (see r. 31.2): Maclaren on *Court of Session Practice*, p. 466; *Davidson v. Robertson* (1827) 5 S. 751; *Thompson v. Crawfurd* 1979 S.L.T.(Notes) 91. The cause must be one which transmits against representatives (*Gibson v. Barbour's Reps.* (1846) 8 D. 427) although the representatives may be sisted reserving all questions as to their right to insist in the cause to be subsequently determined (*Martin's Exx. v. McGhee* 1914 S.C. 628).

Representatives may be sisted at any stage while the cause is in dependence, i.e. until final extract (see note 31.1.4): *Marquis of Douglas v. Earl of Dalhousie*, 15th November 1811, F.C.; *Gibson's Trs. v. Gibson* (1869) 7 M. 1061; *Cumming v. Stewart* 1928 S.C. 709.

R. 31.1 is procedural and does not affect the substantive rules of law in relation to time bar: see *Marshall v. Black* 1981 S.L.T. 228; and see further on time bar note 24.1.2.

SIST OF REPRESENTATIVE ON INCAPACITY OF PARTY.

Incapacity includes sequestration.

(1) Sequestration.

A bankrupt until discharged and reinvested with his estate (*Flett v. Mustard* 1936 S.C. 269) has no title to pursue actions which his trustee may and does pursue (*Dickson v. United Dominion Trusts Ltd* 1988 S.L.T. 19). Where a person is sequestrated the permanent trustee may, with the consent of any commissioners, be sisted to continue to pursue or defend a cause if he considers it would be beneficial to the estate: Bankruptcy (Scotland) Act 1985, s.39(2)(b). A bankrupt may bring and continue proceedings relating to his status or personal affairs or where he may do so by virtue of s.32(9) of the Bankruptcy (Scotland) Act 1985: see further note 13.2.2(D)(4).

A liquidator of a company being wound up may be sisted to continue to pursue or defend a cause: Insolvency Act 1986, s.165(3) (in voluntary winding up without sanction of court), or s.167(1)(b) (in winding up by the court with court's sanction), and Sched. 4, para. 4. Note also the power of an administrator or receiver to bring or defend legal proceedings as agent of the company: Insolvency Act 1986, ss.14 and 55.

(2) Incapacity.

A person of unsound mind and incapable of managing his own affairs or of giving instruction for their management has no *persona standi in judicio* (*Reid v. Reid* (1839) 1 D. 400; *Moodie v. Dempster* 1931 S.C. 553) and if a person becomes incapable during the dependence of a cause no further steps can be taken in his name and any subsequent interlocutors are null and void. Accordingly, under the old law in respect of a person aged 16 or over, a curator *bonis* would be appointed, although there may be cases where appointment of a curator *ad litem* was sufficient: *Moodie*, above. The curator *bonis* may apply to sist himself to the cause. In family actions the procedure is to appoint a curator *ad litem*: r. 49.17. A curator *bonis* is appointed to a person by presenting a petition for appointment of a curator *bonis*.

As from 1st April 2002 a curator *bonis* may no longer be appointed to a person aged 16 or over and a guardian must be appointed instead: Adults with Incapacity (Scotland) Act 2000, ss.57, 64 and 80. Where a curator *bonis* has been appointed he will become a guardian under the 2000 Act with power to manage the property and financial affairs of the adult: 2000 Act, Sch. 4, para. 1(1). He would have the power to act as the adult's legal representative. "Incapable" under the 2000 Act means incapable of asking, making decisions, communicating decisions or retaining memory of decisions by reason of mental disorder or of inability to communicate because of physical disability: 2000 Act, s. 1(6).

A person given power under an intervention order under s. 53(1) of the 2000 Act, to make decisions and give instructions in respect of an action, does not require to be sisted as a party to the action, the order being sufficient authority: *Riley v. James Beaton & Co (Plumbers) Ltd* , 2004 S.L.T. 1083 (OH).

"IN DEPENDENCE".

31.1.4   A cause is depending from the time it is commenced (i.e. from the time an action is served or a first order in a petition is made) until final decree, whereas a cause is in dependence until final extract. For the meaning of commenced, see note 13.4.4 (action) or 14.6.1 (petition). For the meaning of final decree, see note 4.15.2(2). For the meaning of final extract, see note 7.1.2(2).

"MINUTE".

31.1.5   R. 15.1 (applications by minute) does not apply to a minute of sist: r. 15.1(6)(c). The minute of sist must narrate the death and the representative's title and crave to be sisted in room and place of the deceased or incapacitated person. The minute does not require to be signed: r. 4.2(9)(c). Any documents proving title have to be lodged (e.g. an extract confirmation). A motion will have to accompany the minute seeking to have it sustained.

"INTIMATION".

31.1.6   For methods, see r. 16.7. Written intimation of the motion to allow the person to be sisted must be given: for methods, see r. 16.9.

EXPENSES.

31.1.7   A person who sists himself or is sisted as a party may not impose conditions about his liability for expenses: *Ellis v. Ellis* (1870) 8 M. 805. A person who sists himself or is sisted as an additional party but has no title to appear may be liable in expenses from the date of the minute of sist: *Hope v. Landward District Committee of Parish Council of Inveresk* (1906) 8 F. 896. A person who sists himself in place of another may be liable for all expenses: *Torbet v. Borthwick* (1849) 11 D. 694; *Ellis*, above.

FEE.

31.1.8   There is currently no fee for lodging a minute of sist.

Minutes of transference

31.2   **31.2.**—(1) Where a party dies or comes under legal incapacity while a cause is depending before the court and the provisions of rule 31.1 (minutes of sist) are not invoked, any other party may apply to the court by minute to have the cause transferred in favour of or against, as the case may be, any person who represents that party or his estate.

(1A)[1] Where—

(a) a question of liability is the subject of proceedings before the court; and

(b) the effect of any statutory transfer while the cause is depending before the court is to transfer the liability if proved to a person other than an existing party to the cause,

any party to the proceedings may apply to the court by minute to have the cause transferred in favour of or against, as the case may be, the person to whom the liability has been transferred.

(2) Where a minute of transference has been lodged in process, the court shall pronounce an interlocutor—

(a) granting warrant for service of a copy of the minute of transference, a copy of the pleadings (including any adjustments and amendments) and a copy of that interlocutor on such person; and

(b) allowing such person to lodge a minute of objection to the minute of transference within such period as the court thinks fit.

Deriv. R.C.S. 1965, r. 106 (part)

TRANSFERENCE ON DEATH OR LEGAL INCAPACITY.

Where a party dies or comes under legal incapacity and his representatives do not sist themselves under r. 31.1, another party may apply under r. 31.2 to have them sisted (on the minute of transference, see note 32.2.4). The representatives must be subject to the jurisdiction of the court, e.g. domicile: *Mackenzie v. Drummond's Exrs.* (1868) 6 M. 932.

In the case of transference sought by a party instead of a representative seeking to be sisted, the cause must be one which is depending (see note 31.2.2) before the court: *Forbes v. Clinton* (1872) 10 M. 449.

The rule is silent on what happens if there is no appearance in response to a minute of transference. If the representatives do not appear the other party may (*a*) in the case of death, take decree of constitution against a deceased defender's estate (a decree *cognitionis causa tantum*) or decree of absolvitor against a deceased pursuer; or (*b*) in the case of incapacity, a decree which has effect as a decree in absence. In the case of transference sought against a person to whom an interest has been alienated or otherwise transferred (*a*) if the transferee would be the pursuer but fails to sist himself, the action may be dismissed; or (*b*) if the transferee would be the defender but he fails to sist himself, the pursuer may amend and call the transferee as an additional defender: r. 24.1(b)(v) or (d).

31.2.1

STATUTORY TRANSFERENCE.

Rule 31.2(1A), inserted by A.S. (R.C.S.A. No.4) (Miscellaneous) 2001 [S.S.I. 2001 No. 305], applies the transference rules to, and provides for joining the new owner of an undertaking to, an action where statute has transferred the relevant liability of an undertaking to the new owner.

The word "undertaking" has not been defined. It commonly refers to water, electricity, telephone, gas and other services.

31.2.1A

"DEPENDING".

A cause is depending from the time it is commenced (i.e. from the time an action is served or a first order in a petition is made) until final decree, whereas a cause is in dependence until final extract. For the meaning of commenced, see note 13.4.4 (action) or 14.6.1 (petition). For the meaning of final decree, see note 4.15.2(2). For the meaning of final extract, see note 7.1.2(2).

31.2.2

"SERVICE".

For methods, see Chap. 16, Pt. I.

31.2.3

"MINUTE OF TRANSFERENCE".

R. 15.1 (applications by minute) does not apply to a minute of transference: r. 15.1(6)(d). The minute must narrate the death and the representative's name and title and crave warrant to serve a copy of the pleadings on him, for him to lodge a minute of objection if so advised and to transfer the cause against the representative. The minute does not require to be signed: r. 4.2(9)(d). A motion will have to accompany the minute seeking to have it sustained.

31.2.4

---

[1] R.31.2(1A) inserted by S.S.I. 2001 No. 305, para. 5 (effective 18th September 2001).

"MINUTE OF OBJECTION".

31.2.5   R. 15.1 (applications by minute) does not apply to a minute of objection: r. 15.1(6)(e). The minute will be a form similar to a note of objection. The minute does not require to be signed: r. 4.2(9)(e).

FEE.

31.2.6   There is currently no fee for lodging a minute of transference or a minute of objection to a minute of transference.

Death of party: further provisions

31.3   **31.3—**[1](1) Subject to rule 43.20 (Rights of Relatives to Damages (Mesothelioma) (Scotland) Act 2007), as soon as reasonably practicable after the death of a party, any agent who immediately prior to the death was instructed in a cause by that party shall notify the court of the death.

(2) The notification under paragraph (1) shall be by letter to the Deputy Principal Clerk and shall be accompanied by a certified copy of the death certificate relative to the deceased party.

(3) The letter shall include an estimate of the length of time required for confirmation to the deceased party's estate by an executor.

(4) On receipt of the letter, the Deputy Principal Clerk shall place it in the process and shall place the cause before a Lord Ordinary in chambers.

(5) The Lord Ordinary may, if satisfied that the party has died and after considering the estimate provided under paragraph (3), pronounce a sist in the cause for a specified period of not less than three months.

(6) A party may apply by motion for—

    (a)   recall of a sist pronounced under paragraph (5); or

    (b)   variation of the specified period referred to in paragraph (5).

(7) A motion under paragraph (6)(b) shall be granted only on cause shown.

(8) On pronouncing a sist under paragraph (5); recalling a sist under paragraph (6)(a); or, varying a specified period under paragraph (6)(b), the Lord Ordinary may make such order as regards further procedure as he thinks fit including, in the case of a personal injuries action, such variation of the timetable issued under rule 43.6 as he thinks fit.

(9) Any personal injuries action in which a sist has been pronounced under paragraph (5) and the period of sist has expired may be put out by order by the Keeper of the Rolls.

(10) In this rule, "personal injuries action" has the same meaning as in rule 43.1(2).

---

[1] Rule 31.3 inserted by S.S.I. 2007 No. 282 (effective 2nd May 2007).

CHAPTER 32 TRANSMISSION AND REMIT OF CAUSES

Remits to sheriff court

32.1

32.1.—[1](1) An application by a party under section 93 of the Act of 2014 (remit of cases from the Court of Session) (remit from court to sheriff) shall be made by motion.

(2) Where an action is remitted to a sheriff, the Deputy Principal Clerk shall, within four days after the interlocutor remitting the cause has been pronounced, transmit the process to the sheriff clerk of the sheriff court specified in the interlocutor.

(3) When transmitting a process under paragraph (2), the Deputy Principal Clerk shall—

(a) give written intimation of the transmission to the parties; and

(b) certify on the interlocutor sheet that such written intimation has been given.

(4) Failure by the Deputy Principal Clerk to comply with paragraph (3) shall not affect the validity of a remit made under paragraph (1).

Deriv. R.C.S. 1965, r. 104B inserted by S.I. 1986 No. 1955 and amended by S.I. 1987 No. 1206

GENERAL NOTE.

32.1.1

S. 14 of the Law Reform (Miscellaneous Provisions) (Scotland) Act 1985 allows the court at its own instance or on the motion of a party to remit a particular action before it to a sheriff before whom it could competently have been brought where in the opinion of the court the nature of the action makes it appropriate to do so. This provision was introduced as a corollary of the powers to transfer a cause from the sheriff to the court. The then Lord Advocate indicated a remit might be appropriate where other related proceedings are pending before the sheriff and where for reasons of efficiency and convenience of the parties it is desirable that all proceedings be dealt with by the sheriff: H.L. Debates, Vol. 467, col. 194 per Lord Mackay of Clashfern. But the fact that there is an action in the sheriff court is not determinative: *Rae v. Rae* 1991 S.L.T. 45.

The provision is there to meet the needs of particular cases and not to effect a general redistribution of work between the courts: *McIntosh v. British Railways Board (No. 1)* 1990 S.L.T. 637, 639 per L.P. Hope. Actions inappropriate to the sheriff court are not to be sent there: *McIntosh*, above. The fact that an action is small in value or simple is not, except in extreme cases (i.e. where the pursuer could not recover more than the privative limit of the sheriff court (currently £5,000)), enough to justify a remit: *McIntosh*, above, per L.P. Hope at p. 640A. Where there is concurrent jurisdiction the pursuer is not to be deprived of his choice of court on grounds which would apply generally to every case: *McIntosh*, above, per L.P. Hope at p. 640D. The court is entitled to have regard to practical and procedural advantages in adopting one forum rather than another: *McIntosh*, above, per L.P. Hope at p. 640L overruling *Hamilton v. British Coal Corporation* 1990 S.L.T. 287 and *Westcott v. James Dickie & Co. Ltd* 1991 S.L.T. 200. Section 14 of the 1985 Act is not to be used as a means for the defender to avoid being exposed to an award trivial in relation to expense unless the pursuer could not recover more than the privative amount: *McIntosh*, above, per L.P. Hope at p. 641D.

A remit has been made on the grounds of expense of defending a divorce action in the Court of Session: *Gribb v. Gribb* 1993 S.L.T. 178. A remit was refused on the grounds of procedural advantage to the pursuer because of his union's policy of pursuing all actions of reparation in the Court of Session and the availability of optional procedure: *McIntosh*, above. An early proof diet in the sheriff court is not a factor for remitting as it does not relate to "the nature of the action" of which s. 14 speaks; the efficiency of a centralised processing of personal injury cases under Chap. 43 resulting in cost saving to the pursuer or his trade union may be a factor against remitting: *Peterson v. Advocate General for Scotland*, 2007 S.L.T. 846 (O.H.) (remit refused). In *R v. Highland Council*, 2007 S.L.T 513 (O.H.), an action where the pursuer was suing for damages for failures in duties when she was a child in care, it was held that "the nature of the action" in s.14 of the 1985 Act did not include entitlement to legal aid which had been granted only for the sheriff court (the action was also novel, difficult and important; and remit refused). For recent examples of remits, see *McKay v. Lloyds TSB Mortgages Ltd*, 2004 G.W.D. 37-757, 2nd November 2004 (OH); and *Drimsynie Estate Ltd v. Ramsay*, 2006 S.L.T. 528 (OH) (action of declarator and removing).

The power in s.14 of the 1985 Act does not affect the power of the court to modify an award of expenses to one of the sheriff court scales where appropriate: *McIntosh*, above, per L.P. Hope at 641B; see e.g. *Smith v. British Railways Engineering Ltd* 1985 S.L.T. 463.

Note also remit to the sheriff court of a winding up petition under s.120(3)(a)(i) of the Insolvency Act 1986.

---

[1] Rule 32.1 as amended by S.S.I. 2015 No. 227 para. 3 (effective 22nd September 2015).

TRANSMISSION TO SHERIFF COURT.

32.1.2   Where the action could be transmitted to more than one sheriff court the action will be transmitted to the court of the pursuer's choice leaving it to the sheriff to determine under the sheriff court rules whether the action should be remitted to another sheriff court: *McIntosh v. British Railways Board (No. 1)* 1990 S.L.T. 637, 641F–G per L.P. Hope.

"WRITTEN INTIMATION".

32.1.3   For methods, see r. 16.9.

Transmissions on contingency

32.2   **32.2.**—(1)   An application under section 33 of the Act of 1988 (transmission from sheriff on ground of contingency) shall be made—

(a)   by motion at the instance of a party to the cause depending before the court; or

(b)   by minute at the instance of any other person having an interest (including a party to the cause depending before the sheriff).

(2)   A copy of the pleadings and the interlocutors in the cause depending before the sheriff, certified by the sheriff clerk, shall be lodged with any motion enrolled or any minute lodged under paragraph (1).

(3)   A decision made on an application under paragraph (1) may not be reclaimed; but where an application has been refused, a subsequent application may be made where there has been a change of circumstances.

Deriv. R.C.S. 1965, r. 104A inserted by S.I. 1984 No. 472

GENERAL NOTE.

32.2.1   R.C.S. 1965, r. 104A, inserted by A.S. (R.C.A. No. 2) (Miscellaneous) 1984 [S.I. 1984 No. 472], derived from ss.74 and 75 of the C.S.A. 1868 (s.74 being repealed by Sched. 2 to the C.S.A. 1988 and s.75 being repealed by A.S. (R.C.A. No. 8) (Miscellaneous) 1986 [S.I. 1986 No. 1937]). s.74 of the C.S.A. 1868 and R.C.S. 1965, r. 104A were in part replaced by s.33 of the C.S.A. 1988.

TRANSMISSION ON CONTINGENCY.

32.2.2   S.33 of the C.S.A. 1988 allows the Court of Session, on an application to it, to order a sheriff court cause to be transferred to the Court of Session if it is of opinion that there is contingency between the sheriff court cause and a cause depending before the Court of Session. The expression "sheriff court cause" means a cause depending before the sheriff principal or the sheriff: C.S.A. 1988, s.33(2). A cause is depending from the time it is commenced (i.e. from the time it is served) until final decree. For the meaning of commenced, see note 13.4.4 or 14.6.4. For the meaning of final decree, see note 4.15.2(2). On contingency, see note 32.2.3.

CONTINGENCY.

32.2.3   Causes may be transmitted *ob contingentiam* where a contingency exists in a cause in the Court of Session and a cause in the sheriff court. No satisfactory definition of contingency has been made. It is not very easy to define the legal term "contingency": *Liquidators of Western Bank v. Douglas* (1860) 22 D. 447, 472 per L.P. Inglis. In *Duke of Athole v. Robertson* (1869) 8 M. 304, 305, L.J.-C. Moncreiff said "I do not think there is a contingency unless a decision in one of the actions would decide the other in whole or in part".

A contingency may be said to exist (a) where the same parties dispute the same subject-matter; (b) where one action arises directly out of the other; (c) where the result of one action may affect the consequences of the other; (d) where the parties are different but the subject-matter is or may be the same and the decision in one will decide the dispute in both actions; and (e) where the parties are different but it is expedient to have the dispute decided once and for all in one action: see *Reid's Trs. v. Reid* (1873) 45 Sc. Jur. 191, sub nom. Reid v. Reid's Trs. (1893) 10 S.L.R. 168; *McFadyen v. United Alkali Co. Ltd* (1897) 4 S.L.T. 321; *Wilson v. Junor* (1907) 15 S.L.T. 182; Maclaren on *Court of Session Practice*, pp. 490 et seq.

Although the sheriff court action is transmitted the actions are not necessarily conjoined. Conjunction is in the discretion of the court and will only be appropriate if "the same issue will try both causes" but not if they are complicated or there are such shades of distinction that confusion and embarrassment may be produced: *Duke of Buccleuch v. Cowan* (1866) 4 M. 475, 480 per L.J.-C. Inglis (affd. (1876) 4 R.(H.L.) 14). The parties seeking conjunction must be connected with one another in the matters pursued for or have been aggrieved by the same act: *Boulting v. Elias* 1990 S.C. 135. There will be no conjunction if a party is prejudiced: *Gatt v. The Angus Shipping Co. Ltd* (1907) 14 S.L.T. 749. Conjunction is rarely resorted to except where different pursuers raise separate actions of damages arising out of the same circumstances: see, e.g. *Gatt*, above; *Simpson v. Imperial Chemical Industries Ltd* 1983 S.L.T. 601. An alternative arrangement is to appoint one cause to be the leading cause and to sist the others: r. 22.3(6). Another alternative is to appoint simultaneous proof (or hearing) diets.

A conjoined action may be disjoined: see, e.g. *Turner v. Tunnock's Trs.* (1864) 2 M. 509, 514.

"MOTION".

The sheriff court process number must be stated in the motion to be incorporated in the interlocutor. For motions, see Chap. 23. **32.2.4**

"MINUTE".

R. 15.1 (applications by minute) applies to a minute under this rule. **32.2.5**

"SUBSEQUENT APPLICATION".

There may be more than one subsequent application on a change of circumstances. On analogy with variation of periodical allowance in a divorce action, there is no "change of circumstances" where the original decision was based on a failure to put all the information then available to the court: *Stewart v. Stewart* 1987 S.L.T. 246. **32.2.6**

Form of remit request

32.2A.—[1](1)   A request under section 92(4) of the Act of 2014 (request for remit to the Court of Session) is made by interlocutor. **32.2A**

(2)   Within 14 days of the issuing of that interlocutor, the party seeking the remit must lodge—

    (a)   a remit request, consisting of—

        (i)   the whole pleadings and interlocutors in the cause;

        (ii)   the note of the sheriff mentioned in rule 26.2A(2) of the Ordinary Cause Rules 1993 in Schedule 1 to the Sheriff Courts (Scotland) Act 1907;

    (b)   a process in accordance with rule 4.4 (steps of process).

GENERAL NOTE.

Section 92(4) of the Courts Reform (Scotland) Act 2014 provides for the sheriff requesting the Court of Session to allow a cause to be remitted to the Court of Session if the sheriff considers that the importance or difficulty of the proceedings makes it appropriate to do so. Where such a request is made, the Court of Session may, on cause shown, allow the proceedings to be remitted: Act of 2014, s.92(5) . There are thus two bites at the cherry and two hurdles to overcome. Interestingly, while the sheriff can only make the request on the ground of importance or difficulty, the Court of Session may allow the cause to be remitted "on cause shown". **32.2A.1**

In considering whether cause has been shown to allow a cause to be remitted from the sheriff court to the Court of Session under s. 92(5) of the Courts Reform (Scotland) Act 2014, the court does not have to consider the issue in the same way as the sheriff is obliged to do under s. 92(4); remits of causes for which the sheriff court has exclusive jurisdiction should be exceptional: *B v. NHS Ayrshire and Arran*, 2016 S.L.T. 977 (OH) (pelvic mesh cases; of particular importance was the procedure available in the Court of Session under Direction No. 2 of 2015).

"WITHIN 14 DAYS".

The date from which the period is calculated is not counted. Where the last day falls on a Saturday, Sunday or a public holiday on which the Office of Court is closed, the next available day is allowed: r. 1.3(7). For office hours and public holidays, see note 3.1.2. **32.2A.2**

Determination of remit request

32.2B.—[2](1)   Where a remit request is lodged, the court is to put the request out on the By Order roll in order that the party seeking the remit and any other party to the sheriff court proceedings may make submissions about whether the proceedings should be remitted. **32.2B**

(2)   The Lord Ordinary, having heard parties, may—

    (a)   refuse the request; or

    (b)   make an order under section 92(5) of the Act of 2014 allowing the proceedings to be remitted.

(3)   The Deputy Principal Clerk must, within 4 days after the interlocutor has been pronounced under paragraph (2), send a copy of the interlocutor to the sheriff

---

[1] Rule 32.2A as inserted by S.S.I. 2015 No. 227 para. 3 (effective 22nd September 2015).
[2] Rule 32.2B as inserted by S.S.I. 2015 No. 227 para. 3 (effective 22nd September 2015).

clerk of the sheriff court specified in the interlocutor.

GENERAL NOTE.

32.2B.1   Section 92(5) of the Act of 2014 provides for the Court of Session to allow the remit "on cause shown". See further, note 32.2A.1.

Intimation of receipt of process transmitted from sheriff court

32.3   **32.3.** On receipt of a process transmitted by a sheriff clerk by virtue of an order made under any enactment to remit a cause to the court, the Deputy Principal Clerk shall—

    (a)   write the date of receipt on the interlocutor sheet of the sheriff court process; and

    (b)   give written intimation of that date to each party.

Deriv. R.C.S. 1965, r. 274 substituted by S.I. 1980 No. 1801

"ORDER MADE UNDER ANY ENACTMENT".

32.3.1   The enactments under which a cause may be remitted from the sheriff court to the Court of Session include:

(1) S.44 of the Crown Proceedings Act 1947.

Proceedings against the Crown must be remitted from the sheriff to the Court of Session if a certificate of the Lord Advocate is produced stating that the proceedings may involve an important question of law, or may be decisive of other cases, or are for other reasons more fit for trial (*sic*) in the Court of Session.

(2) S.8(3) of the Law Reform (Miscellaneous Provisions) (Scotland) Act 1966.

An appeal to the sheriff to vary or recall a decree of the Court of Session for aliment, periodical allowance, or an order under s.9 of the Conjugal Rights (Scotland) (Amendment) Act 1861, Pt II of the Matrimonial Proceedings (Children) Act 1958 or Pt II of the Guardianship Act 1973 shall be remitted to the Court of Session on the request of any other party.

(3) S.37(1)(b) of the Sheriff Courts (Scotland) Act 1971

(as amended by s.16 of the Law Reform (Miscellaneous Provisions) (Scotland) Act 1980). A cause in the sheriff court may be remitted by the sheriff principal or the sheriff on condition that (a) the value of the cause exceeds the privative limit of sheriff court jurisdiction (currently £1,500: Sheriff Courts (Scotland) Act 1907, s.7 and S.I. 1988 No. 1993), (b) application is made by a party and (c) the importance or difficulty of the cause makes it appropriate. An action should not be remitted on a ground which would justify a remit in every case of its kind but on grounds particular to the cause: *Dunbar v. Dunbar* 1912 S.C. 19, 21 per Lord Kinnear. In *Mullan v. Anderson* 1993 S.L.T. 835 a bench of five judges decided (overruling *Data Controls (Middlesbrough) Ltd v. British Railways Board* 1991 S.C. 105) that importance or difficulty were not the only factors to be taken into account. The majority held that there was a single stage determination which included consideration of the characteristics of the *fora* and the question of importance to the parties when deciding whether the importance or difficulty of the cause made it appropriate to remit; and observations in *Shaw v. Lanarkshire Health Board* 1988 S.C.L.R. 13 were disapproved.

(4) S.1(6) or 4(4) of the Presumption of Death (Scotland) Act 1977.

An action of declarator of death or an application for variation or recall of a decree in such an action in the sheriff court may be remitted by the sheriff at his own instance or on the motion of a party or on the order of the Court of Session on the motion of a party where the sheriff or the Court of Session, as the case may be, considers such remit desirable because of the importance or complexity of the matters at issue.

(5) S. 63(3) of the Bankruptcy (Scotland) Act 1985.

This provides for an application to cure defects of procedure in a sequestration to be remitted to the Court of Session by the sheriff at his own instance or on the motion of a person having an interest or by the Court of Session on an application by any such person.

(6) S. 120(3) (a) (ii) of the Insolvency Act 1986.

This provides for the Court of Session to require a petition in the sheriff court to wind up a company to be remitted to the Court of Session.

(7) S. 33 of the C.S.A. 1988.

This is transmission from the sheriff on the ground of contingency between a sheriff court cause and a cause depending in the Court of Session: see r. 32.2 and notes.

"WRITTEN INTIMATION".

For methods, see r. 16.9.

32.3.2

Lodging of process and motion for further procedure

32.4.—[1](1) Within 14 days after the date of receipt of the sheriff court process, the party who sought the remit must make up and lodge in the General Department a process incorporating the sheriff court process.

(2) Where that party has already lodged a process under rule 32.2A(b), the party must incorporate the sheriff court process in that process within the same period.

(3) When the party who sought the remit has complied with paragraph (1) or (2)—

    (a) that party must apply by motion for an order for such further procedure as that party thinks fit,

    (b) the cause is to proceed as if it had been an action in the court initiated by a summons.

(4) A motion under paragraph (3)(a) is to be disposed of by the Lord Ordinary.

Deriv. R.C.S. 1965, r. 275(2) substituted by S.I. 1982 No. 1825 (r. 32.4(1))

GENERAL NOTE.

32.4

This and the following rules in this Chapter provide the procedure for the transmission or remit of a cause from the sheriff court under any enactment. Formerly such a cause was dealt with initially in the Inner House, but this is no longer the case and such a cause is dealt with in the Outer House: r. 32.4(3).

"WITHIN 14 DAYS".

32.4.1

The date from which the period is calculated is not counted. Where the last day falls on a Saturday or Sunday or a public holiday on which the Office of Court is closed, the next available day is allowed: r. 1.3(7). For office hours and public holidays, see note 3.1.2.

"LODGE A PROCESS".

32.4.2

See rr. 4.3 and 4.4.

"MOTION".

32.4.3

For motions, see Chap. 23.

SIST OF PROCESS.

32.4.4

It will be necessary to seek a sist of process to prevent time-limits running. If legal aid has been granted in the sheriff court, an application will have to be made to the Scottish Legal Aid Board to extend the certificate to the Court of Session: a sist may be required for this to be done.

32.4.5

Reponing against failure to comply with rule 32.4

32.5.—[2](1) Where the party who sought the remit fails to comply with the requirements of rule 32.4(1), (2), or (3)(a) (lodging of process and motion for further procedure), that party may apply by motion to be reponed within 7 days after the expiry of the period specified in rule 32.4(1).

(2) Paragraph (3) applies where the failure mentioned in paragraph (1) is a failure to lodge a process under rule 32.4(1), or incorporate a process in accordance with rule 32.4(2).

(3) The party enrolling a motion under paragraph (1) must, on enrolling that motion—

    (a) lodge a process in accordance with rule 32.4(1), or, as the case may be, incorporate a process under rule 32.4(2);

32.5

---

[1] Rule 32.4 as substituted by S.S.I. 2015 No. 227 para. 3 (effective 22nd September 2015).
[2] Rule 32.5 as substituted by S.S.I. 2015 No. 227 para. 3 (effective 22nd September 2015).

(b) apply by motion for an order for such further procedure as that party thinks fit.

(4) A motion under paragraph (1) is to be granted only on cause shown and on such conditions, if any, as to expenses or otherwise as the court thinks fit.

Deriv. R.C.S. 1965, r. 275(5)(a) and (b)(i) substituted by S.I. 1982 No. 1825

"WITHIN SEVEN DAYS".

32.5.1   The date from which the period is calculated is not counted. Where the last day falls on a Saturday or Sunday or a public holiday on which the Office of Court is closed, the next available day is allowed: r. 1.3(7). For office hours and public holidays, see note 3.1.2.

"MOTION".

32.5.2   For motions, see Chap. 23.

"LODGE A PROCESS".

32.5.3   See rr. 4.3 and 4.4.

Insistence in remit by another party

32.6   **32.6.**[1] Where the party who sought the remit has failed to comply with the requirements of rule 32.4(1), (2), or (3)(a) (lodging of process and motion for further procedure), any other party to the cause may, within 7 days after the expiry of the period specified in rule 32.4(1), comply with the requirements of those paragraphs and insist in the remit.

Deriv. R.C.S. 1965, r. 275(5)(b)(ii) substituted by S.I. 1982 No. 1825

"WITHIN SEVEN DAYS".

32.6.1   The date from which the period is calculated is not counted. Where the last day falls on a Saturday or Sunday or a public holiday on which the Office of Court is closed, the next available day is allowed: r. 1.3(7). For office hours and public holidays, see note 3.1.2.

Re-transmission to sheriff clerk

32.7   **32.7.**[2] Where, on the expiry of 21 days after the date of receipt of the process referred to in rule 32.3 (intimation of receipt of process transmitted from sheriff court), no motion has been enrolled under rule 32.5(1) (reponing against failure to comply with rule 32.4) and no motion has been enrolled under rule 32.6 (insistence in remit by another party), the remit shall be deemed to be abandoned and the Deputy Principal Clerk shall—

(a) write on the interlocutor sheet the words "Re-transmitted in respect that the remit has been abandoned.";

(b) add his signature and the date; and

(c) transmit the process to the sheriff clerk.

Deriv. R.C.S. 1965, r. 275(6) substituted by S.I. 1982 No.1825

"EXPIRY OF 21 DAYS".

32.7.1   The date from which the period is calculated is not counted.

Transfer of application for forfeiture of property from the sheriff: proceeds of crime

32.8   **32.8.**—[3, 4](1) This rule applies to an application under—

(a) paragraph 10G(1)(b) of schedule 1 of the Anti-terrorism, Crime and Security Act 2001 for the forfeiture of property which has been transferred to the court by the sheriff under paragraph 10J(1) of that schedule;

---

[1] Rule 32.6 as substituted by S.S.I. 2015 No. 227 para. 3 (effective 22nd September 2015).
[2] Rule 32.7 as amended by S.S.I. 2015 No. 227 para. 3 (effective 22nd September 2015).
[3] Rule 32.8 as inserted by S.S.I. 2019 No.146 para.2 (effective 1st June 2019).
[4] Rule 32.8 as amended by S.S.I. 2019 No. 405 para.2 (effective 28th December 2019).

(b)   section 303O(1)(b) of the Proceeds of Crime Act 2002 for the forfeiture of property which has been transferred to the court by the sheriff under section 303R(1) of that Act.

(c)   article 213L(1) of the Proceeds of Crime Act 2002 (External Requests and Orders) Order 2005(a) for the forfeiture of property which has been transferred to the court by the sheriff under article 213O(1) of that Order.

(2)   Within 14 days after the date of receipt by the Scottish Ministers of written notice of the transfer from the sheriff clerk, the Scottish Ministers must apply to the court by motion for an order for further procedure.

(3)   The application is to proceed as if it had been an action initiated by petition.

(4)   On applying for an order for further procedure under paragraph (2), the Scottish Ministers must make up and lodge in the General Department a process incorporating the sheriff court process.

CHAPTER 32A TRANSFER OF CAUSES TO AND FROM THE COMPETITION APPEAL TRIBUNAL

Chapter 32A[1]

Transfer of Causes to and from the Competition Appeal Tribunal

Transfers to the Competition Appeal Tribunal

32A.1.—[2](1) An application to transfer a cause to the Competition Appeal Tribunal shall be made by motion.

(2) Where a cause is transferred to the Competition Appeal Tribunal, the Deputy Principal Clerk of Session shall, within four days after the interlocutor transferring the cause has been pronounced, transmit the process to the party on whose motion the transfer was made together with a certified copy of the interlocutor granting the motion under paragraph (1).

(3) When transmitting a process under paragraph (2), the Deputy Principal Clerk shall—

(a) give written intimation of the transmission to—
  (i) the other parties;
  (ii) the Registrar of the Competition Appeal Tribunal; and
(b) certify on the interlocutor sheet that such written intimation has been given.

(4) A failure by the Deputy Principal Clerk to comply with paragraph (3) shall not affect the validity of any transfer of a cause.

32A.1

GENERAL NOTE.

The Competition Appeal Tribunal (CAT), as it now is, was created by the Enterprise Act 2002. The new tribunal takes over the functions of the Competition Commission Appeal tribunal under the Competition Act 1998. The power to transfer to CAT from the court is provided in s. 16 of the 2002 Act. The court may transfer to CAT so much of any proceedings before it as relate to a claim to which s. 47A of the 1998 Act applies. Section 47A, inserted by s. 18 of the 2002 Act, deals with monetary claims before CAT being claims for damages, or other claims for a sum of money, which a person who has suffered loss or damage as a result of an infringement of a relevant prohibition under the 1998 Act or Art. 81 or 82 of the EC Treaty or art. 65 or 66 of the ECSC Treaty may make in civil proceedings. It is not clear what the test would be for a transfer. It is thought that CAT would be better placed as a specialist tribunal to resolve such issues.

The Lord Chancellor has power by regulation to transfer from the court to CAT so much of any proceedings that relate to an infringement issue: 2002 Act, s. 16(1).

32A.1.1

"MOTION".

For motions, see Chap.23.

32A.1.2

"WRITTEN INTIMATION".

For method, see r. 16.9.

32A.1.3

Receipt of transfers from the Competition Appeal Tribunal

32A.2.[3] On receipt of documentation in respect of a claim which has been directed to be transferred to the court by the Competition Appeal Tribunal, the Deputy Principal Clerk of Session shall—

(a) mark the first page of the documentation or, as the case may be, the interlocutor sheet, with the date of receipt; and
(b) give written intimation of that date to each party.

32A.2

---

[1] Chap.32A and r. 32A.1 inserted by S.S.I. 2004 No. 52 (effective 1st March, 2004).
[2] Chap.32A and r. 32A.1 inserted by S.S.I. 2004 No. 52 (effective 1st March, 2004).
[3] R.32A.2 inserted by S.S.I. 2004 No. 52 (effective 1st March, 2004).

General note.

32A.2.1   The Competition Appeal Tribunal, may transfer proceedings under s. 47A of the Competition Act 1998 before it to the Court of Session. On s. 47A of the 1998 Act, see note 32A.1.1.

"written intimation".

32A.2.2   For method, see r. 16.9.

Motion for further procedure and lodging of process in transfers from the Competition Appeal Tribunal

32A.3   **32A.3.**—[1](1) Within 14 days after the date of receipt of documentation referred to in rule 32A.2 (receipt of transfers from the Competition Appeal Tribunal)—

    (a)   the party at whose request the transfer was directed, or

    (b)   in proceedings in which the transfer was directed by the Tribunal at its own initiative, the party who initiated the proceedings,

shall apply by motion for an order for such further procedure as he desires; and the cause shall proceed as if it had been an action in the court initiated by summons.

    (2)   On applying by motion under paragraph (1) the party shall make up and lodge a process incorporating the documentation referred to in rule 32A.2 (receipt of transfers from the Competition Appeal Tribunal) unless the documentation includes a process previously transferred to the Competition Appeal Tribunal under rule 32A.1 (transfers to the Competition Appeal Tribunal).

    (3)   A motion under paragraph (1) shall be disposed of by the Lord Ordinary.

"Within 14 days".

32A.3.1   The date from which the period is calculated is not counted. Where the last day falls on a Saturday or Sunday or a public holiday on which the Office of Court is closed, the next available day is allowed: r. 1.3(7). For office hours and public holidays, see note 3.1.2.

"motion".

32A.3.2   For motions, see Chap.23.

"process".

32A.3.3   For rules about a process, see Chap.4.

Reponing against a failure to comply with rule 32A.3(1) or (2)

32A.4   **32A.4.**—[2](1) Where

    (a)   the party at whose request the transfer was directed; or

    (b)   in proceedings in which the transfer was directed by the Tribunal at its own initiative, the party who initiated the proceedings, fails to comply with the requirements of rule 32A.3(1) or (2) (motion for further procedure and lodging of process), he may, within seven days after the expiry of the period specified in rule 32A.3(1), apply by motion to be reponed.

    (2)   The party enrolling a motion under paragraph (1), where the failure is a failure to lodge a process under rule 32A.3, shall on enrolling the motion, lodge such a process and shall apply by motion for an order for such further procedure as he desires.

    (3)   A motion under paragraph (1) shall be granted only on cause shown and on such conditions, if any, as to expenses or otherwise as the court thinks fit.

"within seven days".

32A.4.1   The date from which the period is calculated is not counted. Where the last day falls on a Saturday or Sunday or a public holiday on which the Office of Court is closed, the next available day is allowed: r. 1.3(7). For office hours and public holidays, see note 3.1.2.

---

[1] R.32A.3 inserted by S.S.I. 2004 No. 52 (effective 1st March, 2004).
[2] R.32A.4 inserted by S.S.I. 2004 No. 52 (effective 1st March, 2004).

"MOTION".

For motions, see Chap.23.

32A.4.2

Insistence in transfer by another party

32A.5.[1] Where—

32A.5

(a) the party at whose request the transfer was directed; or

(b) in proceedings in which the transfer was directed by the Tribunal at its own initiative, the party who initiated the proceedings, has failed to comply with the requirements of paragraph (1) or (2) of rule 32A.3 (motion for further procedure and lodging of process), any other party to the proceedings may, within seven days after the expiry of the period specified in rule 32A.3(1), comply with the requirements of those paragraphs himself and insist in the transfer.

"WITHIN SEVEN DAYS".

The date from which the period is calculated is not counted. Where the last day falls on a Saturday or Sunday or a public holiday on which the Office of Court is closed, the next available day is allowed: r. 1.3(7). For office hours and public holidays, see note 3.1.2.

32A.5.1

Re-transmission to Registrar of the Competition Appeal Tribunal

32A.6.[2] Where, on the expiry of 21 days after the receipt of the documentation referred to in rule 32A.2 (intimation of the date of receipt of documentation), no motion has been enrolled under rule 32A.4 (reponing against failure to comply with rule 32A.3(1) or (2)) and no motion has been enrolled under rule 32A.5 (insistence on transfer by another party), the transfer shall be deemed to be abandoned and the Deputy Principal Clerk shall—

32A.6

(a) write on the first page of the documentation or, as the case may be, the interlocutor sheet the words "Re-transmitted in respect that transfer has been abandoned.";

(b) add his signature and the date; and

(c) transmit the documentation to the Registrar of the Competition Appeal Tribunal.

"ON THE EXPIRY OF 21 DAYS AFTER".

The first day is excluded.

32A.6.1

"MOTION".

For motions, see Chap.23.

32A.6.2

---

[1] R.32A.5 inserted by S.S.I. 2004 No. 52 (effective 1st March, 2004).
[2] R.32A.6 inserted by S.S.I. 2004 No. 52 (effective 1st March, 2004).

CHAPTER 33 CAUTION AND SECURITY

Application of this Chapter

33.1. Subject to any other provisions in these Rules, this Chapter applies to—

   (a)   any cause in which the court has power to order a person to find caution or give other security; and

   (b)   security for expenses ordered to be given under section 136 of the Representation of the People Act 1983 in an election petition.

CAUTION OR OTHER SECURITY.

"Caution" (or "cautionary") is the Scots legal term for the obligation by which a person becomes surety for another: Bell's *Dictionary*, p. 151. The English word "surety" includes the concept of caution but has a wider meaning and would include a personal surety by a person in addition to the original obligation. A bond of caution is a particular form of written surety whereby one person obligates himself for another that he will pay a certain sum or perform a certain act: Bell's *Dictionary*, p. 128. Formerly the rules permitted only surety by caution, but the new rules permit other forms of security so that surety may be given by guarantee (a difference in form rather than substance) or consignation (see note 33.4.3).

Caution or guarantee does not require the advance of money, but consignation would require the lodging of money (although consigned money would earn interest).

CIRCUMSTANCES IN WHICH CAUTION REQUIRED.

Caution may be required in the following circumstances.

(A) For expenses as a condition precedent to proceed with or defend a cause.

(1)   Common law.

This is entirely within the discretion of the court: *Will v. Sneddon, Campbell & Munro* 1931 S.C. 164; *Stevenson v. Midlothian District Council* 1983 S.C.(H.L.) 50. It should only be ordered where the interests of justice require it and may be required of a pursuer or defender: *Thom v. Andrew* (1888) 15 R. 780, 782 per Lord Young. The Lord Ordinary's discretion will only be overturned on appeal if his discretion was so unreasonable that no other judge could have pronounced it: *Stevenson*, above per L.P. Emslie at p. 52. It is usually only ordered in the situations mentioned below.

Poverty alone is not a ground for ordering caution: *Walker v. Kelty's Trustees* (1839) 1 D. 1066, 1070 per L.P. Hope; *Will*, above, at 168 per L.J-C. Alness (mere impecuniosity is not sufficient), at least in relation to individuals. A person with a statable case should not be excluded from the court unless in exceptional circumstances: *Stevenson*, above, per Lord Fraser of Tullybelton at p. 58. If he does not have a statable case he may be required to find caution, even if he is not in a financial position to provide a sum, as it would be unfair to oblige his opponent to carry on defending the action: *Rush v. Fife R.C.* 1985 S.L.T. 451.

In *McTear's Exrx v. Imperial Tobacco Ltd* 1997 S.L.T. 530, the Extra Div. considered that although impecuniosity alone was not sufficient, a wide variety of factors could be taken into account, the overriding principle being that the defender was entitled to be protected against the necessity of incurring heavy expenses where the nature of the litigation or the conduct of the pursuer was such that the interests of justice required such protection; but this was subject to what was said in *Stevenson*, above, that it would be wrong that a litigant with a statable case should be in effect excluded from the court by an order for caution unless in exceptional circumstances. In that case the court said it had to consider whether the factors advanced by the defenders were so cogent and compelling that they overcame the general principle that an impecunious litigant is entitled to advance a statable case. The court held that the Lord Ordinary's decision to refuse to order caution should be upheld.

The distinction between s.72.6(2) of the Companies Act 1985 (see (A)(2) below) and the common law is that at common law impecuniosity alone is not sufficient, there has to be something more such as prima facie poor prospects of success: see (1) above. In *Total Containment Engineering Ltd v. Total Waste Management Alliance Ltd*, [2012] CSOH 163, para. [12], Lord Hodge did not accept that the common law test was the same for companies as it was for natural persons and could see no good reason for it to more difficult to obtain caution at common law against a non-British company (the pursuer in that case) than against a British company; and caution was ordered.

In *Monarch Energy Ltd v. Powergen Retail Ltd* , 2006 S.L.T. 743 (OH), a case under s. 726(2) of the Companies Act 1985 (see (A)(2) below), it was held that the right of access to a court under Art. 6 of the ECHR, was not absolute and the requirement that a litigant should provide security for expenses had been held to be a permissible limitation, provided it pursued a legitimate aim and that there was a reasonable relationship of proportionality between the means employed and the legitimate aim sought to be achieved. In *Ewing v. Times Newspapers Ltd* , 2010 CSIH 67 (Second Div.), it was held that an order to find caution was not a breach of art. 6 of ECHR.

There is no rule that a person on legal aid may not be ordered to find caution: *Stevenson*, above. The grant of legal aid may be a change of circumstances justifying recall of an order for caution: *Forrest v. Fleming Builders Ltd,* [2013] CSOH 105.

A motion for caution to be found may be made at any time: *Mackinnon, Noter* , 5th March 1999, unreported.

There is no general rule that the court should be reluctant to adopt a step-by-step approach to caution, ordering caution up to a particular stage such as Procedure Roll: *Merrick Homes Ltd v. Duff* 1995 S.L.T. 932.

A defender would not normally be required to find caution because he is exercising his right to defend; cf. *Robertson v. McCaw* 1911 S.C. 650. The common law test is even more difficult to satisfy in the case of a defender than in the case of a pursuer because a defender is in the action only because he has been brought into it by the pursuer and is seeking to defend himself: *Balfour Beatty Ltd v. Brinmoor Ltd* 1997 S.L.T. 888, 891F, per Lord Abernethy. The court is always slow to ordain a defender to find caution for payment of any expenses that may ultimately be awarded against him, but the court is entitled in the exercise of its discretion to ordain any party, including a defender, to find caution if the circumstances are special: *Matheson v. Marsh* 1996 S.C. 25.

Caution is ordered, at common law, only in the case of bankruptcy or other exceptional circumstances:

(a) Bankruptcy of pursuer. The general rule is that where the pursuer is, or pendente lite becomes, bankrupt he must find caution; and leave to proceed without caution is only granted in exceptional circumstances: *Clarke v. Muller* (1884) 11 R. 418, 419 per L.P. Inglis. For an example of such circumstances, see *Neil v. South East Lancashire Insurance Co.* 1930 S.C. 629 where pursuer made bankrupt by defender re expenses of reclaiming and *McCue v. Scottish Daily Record & Sunday Mail Ltd* 1999 S.C. 332. Actual sequestration is not necessary: see generally *Maxwell v. Maxwell* (1847) 9 D. 797, 802–803 per Lord Jeffrey; *Clarke*, above. An admission of insolvency may be sufficient: *Maxwell*, above; cf. *Hegard v. Hegard* 1981 S.L.T. (Notes) 45 (no evidence of practical insolvency). One reason for the rule is that the bankrupt is usually seeking to recover what belongs to his estate: *Stevenson v. Midlothian B.C.* 1983 S.C.(H.L.) 50, 58 per Lord Fraser of Tullybelton. A discharged bankrupt may sue without caution for sums not recovered by his trustee: *Cooper v. Frame & Co.* (1893) 20 R. 920. A person nominally the pursuer but in substance the defender (as in suspension) is not ordinarily required to find caution: *Stephen v. Skinner* (1800) 22 D. 1122. Where a pursuer becomes bankrupt pendente lite, caution may well be ordered for past as well as future expenses: *Torbet v. Borthwick* (1849) 11 D. 694; *Mackersy v. Muir* (1850) 12 D. 1057; cf. *Maxwell*, above; *Ramedy v. Stenhouse and Grant* (1847) 10 D. 234.

(b) Bankruptcy of defender. As a general rule, caution is not ordered of a bankrupt defender as he is entitled to defend himself (*Lawrie v. Pearson* (1888) 16 R. 62; *Johnstone v. Henderson* (1906) 8 F. 689) unless he is in substance the pursuer: *Ferguson Lamont & Co.'s Trs v. Lamont* (1889) 17 R. 282—e.g. where the only dispute is a counterclaim: *Robb v. Dickson* (1901) 9 S.L.T. 224; see also Goudy on *Bankruptcy*, pp. 365–367 and Maclaren on *Court of Session Practice*, pp. 239 et seq.

(c) Other circumstances. These include: (i) Where the pursuer did not disclose her address: *Murdoch v. Young* (1909) 2 S.L.T. 450. (ii) Where a ship's master broke an arrestment on the dependence: *Meron v. Umland* (1896) 3 S.L.T. 286. (iii) Where the pursuer is a mere catspaw: *Porteous v. Pearl Life Assurance Co. Ltd* (1901) 8 S.L.T. 430, 431 per Lord Stormonth Darling; or where the pursuer is not the true *dominus litis*, (iv) Where there are exceptional circumstances: *Rush v. Fife R.C.* 1985 S.L.T. 451 (impecunious pursuer pursuing irrelevant action); *Kennedy v. Hamilton Brothers Oil and Gas Ltd* 1986 S.L.T. 110 (pursuer of admittedly no substance who had failed to satisfy two decrees).

In deciding whether to order a party to find caution, regard may be had to the nature of the claim or defence as disclosed in the pleadings, and also to whether that party is on legal aid.

It is not essential that there are averments in the pleadings or in a separate minute in support of a motion to ordain a party to find caution so long as there has been proper notice: *Hegard*, above; cf. *Nakeski-Cumming v. Gordon's J.F.* 1923 S.C. 770. An order for caution, being an incidental order, may be modified or superseded on a change of circumstances: *Whyte v. City of Perth Co-operative Society* 1932 S.C. 482. Consignation may be allowed in lieu of caution: *Morrison v. Morrison's Exx* 1912 S.C. 892; and see note 33.4.3.

(2)   S.726 of the Companies Act 1985.

A limited company pursuer to which the Companies Act applies may be required to find caution if it appears by credible testimony that there is reason to believe that the company will be unable to pay the defender's expenses: see e.g. *Dean Warwick Ltd v. Borthwick* 1981 S.L.T.(Notes) 18; *Merrick Homes Ltd v. Duff* 1996 S.L.T. 932. The common law power is unaffected: see below. The distinction between this statutory provision and the common law is that at common law impecuniosity alone is not sufficient, there has to be something more such as prime facie poor prospects of success: see (1) above. In *Total Containment Engineering Ltd v. Total Waste Management Alliance Ltd,* [2012] CSOH 163, para. [12], Lord Hodge did not accept that the common law test was the same for companies as it was for natural persons and could see no good reason for it to be more difficult to obtain caution at common law against a non-British company (the pursuer in that case) than against a British company; and caution was ordered.

In *Monarch Energy Ltd v. Powergen Retail Ltd* , 2006 S.L.T. 743 (OH), it was held that the right of access to a court under Art. 6 of the ECHR was not absolute and the requirement that a litigant should provide security for expenses had been held to be a permissible limitation, provided it pursued a legitimate aim and that there was a reasonable relationship of proportionality between the means employed and the legitimate aim sought to be achieved.

In *Centenary 6 Ltd v Caven*, 2018 S.L.T. 423 (Second Div.), the LJC and Lord Glennie disagreed (obiter) as to whether "caution" in s. 726(2) of the 1985 Act meant formal caution as understood in Scots Law or simply "security" (see paras. [33]–[35] and [118]–[121]). Since s.726(2) is an overtly Scottish provision, it is not unreasonable to assume that "caution" means caution as it is understood in Scots law; and that has been the assumption heretofore. In *Centenary 6 Ltd*, it was held that a security under s. 726(2) of the Companies Act 1985 had to be by way of caution and not the after the event (ATE) policy proffered. An ATE policy was considered and rejected as caution under s.726(2) in *Monarch Energy Ltd*.

If a liquidator sues in his own name rather than in the name of the company he should not be ordered to find caution as he has accepted responsibility for the expenses (unless it appears that he would be unable to pay): *Arch Joinery Contracts Ltd v. Arcade Building Services Ltd* 1992 S.L.T. 755. While a liquidator enjoys a special position as an officer of the court and subject to its supervision, creditors and contributories granted leave to raise an action in the name of an insolvent company are not and caution is required: *Caledonian Produce (Holdings) Ltd v. Price Waterhouse* 1993 S.C. 181.

A company which opposes a reclaiming motion or appeal as successful pursuer is not a pursuer for the purposes of s. 726(2) of the 1985 Act (*Star Fire and Burglary Insurance Co. Ltd v. Davidson & Sons* (1902) 4 F. 997); similarly, a company appearing as unsuccessful defender (*Sinclair v. Glasgow and London Contract Corporation Ltd* (1904) 6 F. 818). In *Assuranceforeningen Skuld v. International Oil Pollution Compensation Fund (No.3)* , 2000 S.L.T. 1352 (OH) Lord Gill, distinguishing *Star Fire*, above, held that *Assuranceforeningen*, formerly a pursuer in an action against the Braer Corporation and had become a claimant in the limitation fund action seeking compensation arising out of the Braer oil tanker disaster, could be ordered to find caution for expenses as it was a "pursuer" in "other legal proceedings" within s. 726(2) of the 1985 Act. Lord Gill held that one looked at the realities of the situation.

"Credible testimony" may be in the pleadings, documents, affidavits or asserted at the bar where not disputed or satisfactorily explained (*New Mining and Exploring Syndicate Ltd v. Chalmers & Hunter* 1909 S.C. 1390; *Dean Warwick Ltd v. Borthwick* 1981 S.L.T.(Notes) 18); but probably not merely an assertion at the bar on its own (*Edinburgh Modern Quarry Co. Ltd v. Eagle Star Insurance Co. Ltd* 1965 S.L.T.(Notes) 91): *Edinburgh Entertainments Ltd v. Stevenson* 1925 S.C. 848; *Dean Warwick Ltd*, above; *UK Leasing Ltd v. Bremners plc* 1990 S.L.T. 684. It may include the company's balance sheets or other documents lodged with the Registrar of Companies: *Dean Warwick Ltd*, above. Even if satisfied by that testimony the court still has a discretion whether to order caution: *Brownrigg Coal Co. Ltd v. Sneddon* 1911 S.C. 1064, per Lord Salvesen at p. 1068 and per Lord Mackenzie at p. 1069.

The power to ordain a party to find caution at common law is independent of the statutory power under s. 726(2). While the legislation makes clear that it is not possible to ordain a limited company defender to find caution for expenses in terms of s. 726(2), there is nothing there which prevents the court from ordaining such a company to find caution for expenses at common law: *Kaiser Bautechnik GmbH v. G.A. Group Ltd* 1993 S.L.T. 826; *Balfour Beatty Ltd v. Brinmoor Ltd* , 1997 S.L.T. 888, 891A per Lord Abernethy.

A motion for caution is competent where the company is a defender and has counterclaimed against the pursuer: *Atlas Hydraulic Loads Ltd v. Seaton Ltd* , 22nd April, 1997 unreported (1997 G.W.D. 15-683).

There is no general rule that the court should be reluctant to adopt a step-by-step approach to caution, ordering caution up to a particular stage such as Procedure Roll: *Merrick Homes Ltd v. Duff* 1996 S.L.T. 932.

In considering the question of additional caution, it is not relevant to consider whether the litigation was a simple one in which the approach to expenses would be straightforward (which was relevant only to whether caution should be ordered at all): *Merrick Homes Ltd*, above.

Where the company is ordered to find caution, the court should sist the cause while caution is found rather than set a time limit for doing so: *Pioneer Seafoods Ltd v. The Braer Corporation* , 21st May 1999 (OH), unreported (1999 G.W.D. 20-956). Lod Gill indicated in that case that if caution was not found in a reasonable time, the defender could move the court to recall the sist and grant decree in absolvitor.

(B) As a condition for recall of arrestment or inhibition.

Caution may be offered or required as a condition of recall of an arrestment or inhibition on the dependence. Caution is expressly referred to in r. 13.10(2). Recall of arrestment will be made on caution being found on the basis that the arrested fund, subject or value of it, or the whole debt including principal, interest and expenses to the extent of the arrested fund will be made forthcoming. Recall may be made where less than full caution is offered depending on the circumstances. If the arrested property exceeds the debt, caution should be required only to the extent of the debt. Where the sum sued for is a random sum (as in an action of damages) caution will be fixed having regard to the nature of the claim, the likely award, the amount arrested and the financial circumstances of the common debtor: see Graham Stewart on *Diligence*, pp. 202–204; see also *Henderson v. George Outram and Co. Ltd* 1993 S.L.T. 824.

Caution may be not only for the principal sum and interest but also for expenses: *McPhedron and Currie v. McCallum* (1888) 16 R. 45.

Caution will not be required where arrestment is nimious or oppressive, wrongful or where the subjects are not arrestable: see Bell's *Principles*, s. 2280 and note 13.10.5.

The principle in relation to recall of arrestment on caution is the same in relation to recall of inhibition: see, e.g. *Fisher v. Weir* 1964 S.L.T.(Notes) 99. In deciding whether a guarantee offered is an adequate alternative security to replace that held by an arrestment, the relevant comparison is between the security afforded by the proposed guarantee on the one hand and that afforded by the arrestment (and not a guarantee by an independent financial institution) on the other: *Global Marine Drilling Co. v. Triton Holdings Ltd* (No.2), 26th January 2000, (2000 G.W.D. 5-210) (OH). There is no rule that recall should normally be on the provision of a guarantee by such an institution: *Global Marine Drilling Co*, above.

Consignation may be ordered instead of caution (*Fisher*, above) or the debtor may be given the option (*McPhedron and Currie*, above). See further, note 13.10.5.

(C) In lieu of sisting a mandatory.

Caution for expenses cannot be required of foreigners seeking redress, or in the enforcement of certain foreign judgments, under certain international and European conventions. Such conventions which are adopted as part of the law of the U.K. include:

the Brussels and Lugano Conventions on jurisdiction and enforcement of judgments in civil and commercial matters, 1968, in the C.J.J.A 1982, Scheds 1 and 3C, Art. 45 (no security, bond or deposit however described shall be required of a party in one Contracting State seeking to enforce a judgment in another Contracting State on the ground that he is a foreign national or that he is not domiciled or resident in that State);

the Geneva Convention on contract for international carriage of goods by road, 1965, in the Carriage of Goods by Road Act 1956, Sch., Art. 31(5);

the Geneva Convention on carriage of passengers and luggage by road, 1956, in the Carriage of Passengers by Road Act 1974, Sch., Art. 21(5);

the Berne International Convention on Carriage by Rail, 1980, Art. 18(4): see International Transport Conventions Act, 1983, s.1.

A pursuer resident abroad is usually required to sist a mandatory, rather than provide security by caution or consignation (see (1) below). Where a convention provides that a foreign party shall not be required to find caution for expenses ("security for costs"), the question arises whether he can be required to sist a mandatory. In *General Trading Corporation v. James Mills (Montrose) Ltd* 1982 S.L.T. (Sh. Ct.) 30 it was decided in a case under the Geneva Convention on Carriage of goods by road that sisting a mandatory was not excluded. The Maxwell *Report on Jurisdiction and Enforcement* (HMSO 1980), pp. 143–144, appears to consider the requirement would not be imposed in enforcement proceedings under the 1968 Convention in Sched. 1 to the C.J.J.A. 1982 (and see *Mund & Fester v. Hatrex International Transport* [1994] E.C.R. 1-467 (a right to seizure of assets simply on the ground that judgment is to be enforced abroad in another Member State is contrary to the prohibition of discrimination in art. 6 of the EC Treaty)); and it was waived in proceedings for enforcement of judgments under the Judgments Extension Act 1868 and has been waived under the Foreign Judgments (Reciprocal Enforcement) Act 1933. Requiring a mandatory may be because providing security for payment of expenses is not the sole purpose of sisting a mandatory; it also ensures that there is someone within the jurisdiction responsible for the proper conduct of the cause (see *Lawson's Trs. v. British Linen Co.* (1874) 1 R. 1065, 1066 per L.P. Inglis). In any event, the sisting of a mandatory is in the discretion of the court (*Fellowes' Exr. v. Fellowes' Trs.* 1988 S.L.T. 730), and the provisions of a convention against security for costs must be a relevant and important consideration. The point was not raised in *Kaiser Bautechnik GmbH v. G A Group Ltd* 1993 S.L.T. 826.

(1) Circumstances in which mandatory sisted.

Subject to what is stated in the next paragraph, a pursuer or defender resident furth of Scotland (including a domiciled Scotsman) may be required to sist a mandatory to have someone in the jurisdiction responsible for the conduct of the cause: *Renfrew and Brown v. Magistrates of Glasgow* (1861) 23 D. 1003, 1005 per L.J.-C. Inglis. The matter is entirely in the discretion of the court: *Lawson's Trs.*, above. Factors to be considered in exercising the discretion are as follows: (i) impecuniosity is not in itself a sufficient ground: *Dessau v. Daish* (1897) 24 R. 976; (ii) the enforceability of a decree for expenses abroad: *Kaiser Bautechnik GmbH*, above; (iii) the applicability of a convention containing a protection against requiring security for costs; (iv) the ownership of heritable property in Scotland which is not the subject-matter of the cause and of sufficient value: *Smith v. Norval* (1828) 6 S. 852, *Caledonian and Dumbartonshire Railway Co. v. Turner* (1849) 12 D. 406, *Lawson's Trs.*, above; (v) where there has been established a prima facie case: *McLean v. McGarvey* (1908) 16 S.L.T. 174; *N.V. Ondix International v. James Landay Ltd* 1963 S.C. 270; (vi) where pursuer is suing on a protested bill of exchange: *N.V. Ondix International*, above; (vii) where he is a claimant in a multiplepoinding: *Stow's Trs. v. Salvester* (1900) 8 S.L.T. 253.

A party who is a national of and resident in another member state of the EU which is a party to the 1968 Brussels Convention on Jurisdiction and Enforcement of Judgments (see C.J.J.A. 1982, Sched. 1) should not be required to sist a mandatory: *Dieter Rossmeier v. Mounthooly Transport* 2000 S.L.T. 208 (First Div.). The reasons are that it is discrimination contrary to art.12 of the EC Treaty to require such a sist for such a national, and the convention makes relevant orders enforceable in other states which are parties to the convention. (The 1968 Convention now applies between the Member States of the EU and Denmark; between the other Member States of the EU, the relevant "convention" is the Council Regulation (EC) No. 44/2001 (the "Brussels I Regulation").) A party resident in another part of the U.K. should not be required to sist a mandatory: *Lawson's Trs*, above. The reason is that since the Judgments Extension Act 1868, relevant judgments of the court may be enforced throughout the U.K.

An assisted person resident outside Scotland may be ordered to sist a mandatory: *Herzberg v. Herzberg* 1952 S.L.T. (Sh. Ct.) 65; cf. *Harley v. Kinnear Moodie & Co. Ltd* 1964 S.L.T. 64 (order refused, it being observed that s. 2(6)(e) of the Legal Aid (Scotland) Act 1967 (now s. 18(2) of the Legal Aid (Scotland) Act 1986) only applied to expenses against an assisted person not his mandatory).

A court has a larger discretion in requiring a defender to sist a mandatory than a pursuer and will do so less usually: *Simla Bank v. Home* (1878) 8 M. 781; *N.V. Ondix International*, above. A refusal to sist a mandatory is always *in hoc statu* and a further motion may be made on a change of circumstances: *Aitkenhead v. Bunton & Co.* (1892) 19 R. 803, 804 per L.P. Robertson.

(2)   Procedure for sisting a mandatory.

The court may order a party to sist a mandatory within a specified time. Time may be prorogated: *Murray v. Murray* (1845) 7 D. 1000. The order may be recalled on a change of circumstances: *N.V. Ondix International*, above. A minute of sist must be lodged in process by the named mandatory, thereafter an interlocutor is pronounced sisting the mandatory as a party to the cause. The mandate itself is not required (*Elder v. Young & Co.* (1854) 16 D. 1003) unless demanded by the other party (*Gunn & Co. v. Couper* (1871) 10 M. 116). The court will normally accept as mandatory any person who is solvent (*Railton v. Mathews* (1844) 7 D. 105) other than another party to the cause (*Scott & Steven's Tr. v. Smith* (1851) 13 D. 854). Whether a solicitor may be mandatory for his client depends on the extent of his authority: *Knight v. Freeto* (1863) 2 M. 386. If a pursuer fails to obtemper an order to sist a mandatory, the defender is assoilzied: *Masinimport v. Scottish Mechanical Light Industries* 1972 S.L.T. (Notes) 76; if a defender fails, the pursuer is entitled to decree. Either may be reclaimed on lodging a minute of sist and also possibly a mandate: rr. 38.2(1), 38.9(1); and *Thomson v. Woodthorpe* (1863) 1 M. 635.

(3)   Liability of mandatory.

A mandatory cannot insist on his liability under the mandate being subject to conditions: *Robertson & Co. v. Exley, Dinsdale & Co.* (1833) 11 S. 320. He has general authority to take all usual steps (*Renfrew and Brown v. Magistrates of Glasgow* (1861) 23 D. 1003, 1005 per L.J.-C. Inglis) though he requires special authority to settle an action (*Thoms v. Bain* (1888) 15 R. 613). He is not liable to implement any decree, he is merely the security that it will be binding on his principal: *Thoms*, above.

(4)   Withdrawal of mandatory.

A mandatory may withdraw on lodging a minute of resignation (*Martin v. Underwood* (1827) 5 S. 783) though he remains liable for expenses prior to his withdrawal (*Chapman v. Balfour* (1875) 2 R. 291). He may be removed if he becomes insolvent: *Harker v. Dickson* (1856) 18 D. 793.

(5)   Death of mandatory.

On death the mandatory's estate is liable for expenses prior to his death: *Barclay & Ewart's Reps. v. Barclay* (1850) 12 D. 1253.

(D)   In suspension, suspension and interdict, and suspension and liberation.

See r. 60.3.

(E)   In judicial factories, by a judicial factor on his appointment.

See Judicial Factors Acts 1849, s.2, and 1889, s.6; and see r. 61.9(1).

(F)   By administrators appointed under para. 1(8) of Sched. 1 to the Proceeds of Crime (Scotland) Act 1995.

See r. 75.11.

"ANY CAUSE IN WHICH THE COURT HAS POWER".

The court is given express power in certain rules to order caution, e.g. r. 13.10(2) (recall etc. of arrestment or inhibition), r. 35.2(4) (recovery of documents etc.).

The court also has power to grant motions subject to such conditions, if any, as to expenses or otherwise as it thinks fit (r. 23.13); and this could include caution or other security.

33.1.3

The court has power under certain statutes to order caution: e.g. Judicial Factors Act 1849, s.2; Bills of Exchange Act 1882, s.100; Sale of Goods Act 1979, s.11(5); Proceeds of Crime (Scotland) Act 1995, Sched. 1, para. 1(8).

SECURITY FOR EXPENSES UNDER THE REPRESENTATION OF THE PEOPLE ACT 1983.

33.1.4   The methods of caution or security under s.136 of the Representation of the People Act 1983 are governed by r. 69.4.

Form of applications

33.2   **33.2.**—(1)   An application for an order for caution or other security, or for variation or recall of such an order, shall be made by motion.

(2)   The grounds on which such an application is made shall be set out in the motion.

"MOTION".

33.2.1   The grounds of the motion must be set out in the motion: r. 33.2(2). For motions, see Chap. 23.

Orders to find caution or other security

33.3   **33.3.**   Subject to section 726(2) of the Companies Act 1985 (order on company to find caution), an order to find caution or give other security shall specify the period within which such caution is to be found or such security given.

PERIOD WITHIN WHICH CAUTION TO BE FOUND.

33.3.1   The former rule in R.C.S. 1965, r. 200(c) in relation to judicial factors stipulated one month as the period in which caution had to be found. There is not now a fixed period, but the period fixed must be specified. The period fixed may be prorogated: r. 4.9(2).

The court must fix a reasonable time within which to find caution; failure to find caution within that time (unless prorogated) will result in decree in favour of the other party except in judicial factories (see note 61.9.3). This rule applies also to s.726 of the Companies Act 1985: *Augustinus Ltd v. Anglia Building Society* 1990 S.L.T. 298.

COMPANIES ACT 1985, s.726(2).

33.3.2   Where a limited company to which the Companies Act applies is pursuer in an action or other legal proceedings, the court may, if it appears by credible testimony that there is reason to believe the company will be unable to pay the defender's expenses if successful in his defence, order the company to find caution and sist the proceedings until caution is found: Companies Act 1985, s.726(2). The common law power is unaffected. See further, note 33.1.2(A)(2).

Methods of finding caution or giving security

33.4   **33.4.**—(1)   A person ordered—

(a)   to find caution, shall do so by obtaining a bond of caution; or

(b)   to consign a sum of money into court, shall do so by consignation under the Court of Session Consignations (Scotland) Act 1895 in the name of the Accountant of Court.

(2)   The court may approve a method of security other than one mentioned in paragraph (1), including a combination of two or more methods of security.

(3)   Subject to paragraph (4), any document by which an order to find caution or give other security is satisfied shall be lodged in process.

(4)   Where the court approves a security in the form of a deposit of a sum of money in the joint names of the agents of parties, a copy of the deposit receipt, and not the principal, shall be lodged in process.

(5)   A bond of caution or consignation receipt lodged in process shall be accompanied by a copy of it.

BONDS OF CAUTION.

33.4.1   Where caution is by bond of caution, the bond may be (a) by an insurance company authorised to conduct such business (see r. 33.5) or (b) by any person, in which case it is more likely that the sufficiency of the caution will have to be established: r. 33.7(2). In (a), there is usually a formal bond; otherwise a letter from the cautioner indicating that he will satisfy the obligation in the amount of the caution will suffice. All bonds must comply with the requirements of r. 33.6. A consignation receipt for the full amount of the caution is acceptable in place of a bond (see note 33.4.3).

Except in relation to judicial factors, a bond (or letter) must be lodged as a step of process and marked with a number of process (r. 4.4(3)) and intimated to other parties (r. 4.6). In the case of a bond other than a bond by an insurance company, it is docquetted by the Deputy Principal Clerk (or on his behalf) confirming that the bond of caution or other document is in proper form (he is no longer concerned with sufficiency, which is a matter for the parties: see r. 33.7). The bond is transmitted by the party required to lodge it to the Accountant of Court by the transmission book for safekeeping; the book is receipted and returned to the appropriate department of the Office of Court. When the bond is allowed to be uplifted, it is transmitted by the Accountant of Court's transmission book to the appropriate department of the Office of Court; the book is receipted and returned. Transmission is undertaken by the party concerned. The Accountant of Court is custodian of all bonds of caution: Judicial Factors Act 1849, s. 35. In relation to judicial factories, see r. 61.9.

In *Centenary 6 Ltd v Caven*, 2018 S.L.T. 423, it was held that a security under s. 726(2) of the Companies Act 1985 had to be by way of caution and not the after the event (ATE) policy proffered. An ATE policy was considered and rejected as caution under s.726(2) in *Monarch Energy Ltd v Powergen Retail Ltd*, 2006 S.L.T. 743 (OH).

SECURITY OTHER THAN BONDS OF CAUTION.

33.4.2

This might be a guarantee rather than a formal bond, a consignation receipt (see note 33.4.3) or a deposit receipt in joint names of parties' agents.

CONSIGNATION.

33.4.3

This may be ordered or allowed by the court: (a) in lieu of caution for expenses: *Morrison v. Morrison's Exx.* 1912 S.C. 892; (b) in lieu of sisting a mandatory: *Bell v. Strathearn & Blair* 1953 S.L.T. (Notes) 23; (c) in lieu of diligence in security; or (d) in lieu of caution in suspensions, suspension and interdict, and suspension and liberation: r. 60.2(2). Consignation is less common than caution because a party will be out of his money until the dispute is settled, although interest will be earned. Furthermore, the procedure is more complicated than for bonds of caution because, before an interlocutor allowing the consigned money to be uplifted may be granted, a certificate from the Inland Revenue under r. 8.1(1)(a) must be produced.

Under the Court of Session Consignations (Scotland) Act 1895, ss. 2 and 3, the Accountant of Court is custodian of all sums lodged by order of the court or under any Act of Parliament ("consignations").

By a Notice [i.e. P.N. No. 1 of 1996] the former procedure for consignation receipts has been abolished. Such receipts were subject to criticism because of the low rate of interest and their use, as a consequence, was rare. The low rate of interest was justified by the banks on the ground that consignation receipts were expensive to administer. The new form, a special deposit account, allows a higher rate of interest. Consignation receipts had an advantage over ordinary deposit receipts in that partial upliftment was possible. Partial upliftment will be possible from a special deposit account.

The new procedure is that where consignation is ordered, the consigned funds should be lodged in a special deposit account opened at any branch of the Royal Bank of Scotland (though the amounts will be held at the Edinburgh North Bridge Branch, 31 North Bridge, EH1 1SF, of that bank). An opening statement of account should then be sent to the Accountant of Court. The Accountant will then write to inform the Deputy Principal Clerk of Session of the consignation (this will replace the copy consignation receipt formerly lodged in process). Existing consignations will be transferred to the new account by the Accountant of Court.

The procedure under P.N. No. 1 of 2006 does not preclude the court from ordering consigned funds to be placed in some other account earning a higher rate of interest: *FM Finnieston Ltd v. Ross*, 2009 S.C. 106 (OH) (in that case the RBS special deposit account was not offering a commercial rate of interest).

Applications to uplift consigned sums will be made by motion under reference to the special deposit accounts. When a certified copy interlocutor authorising upliftment is shown to the Accountant of Court, he will draw on the account and make payment as directed by the court.

An interlocutor permitting the uplifting of the whole or a part of the sum consigned should clearly state to whom the Accountant should pay any sum ("pay to A" does not include A's solicitor) and whether interest is to be included. Such an interlocutor will not be signed by the court until a tax clearance certificate from the Inland Revenue as required under r. 8.1(1)(a) has been produced, notwithstanding that income tax on interest in the hands of a deposit taker (including an authorised institution or a municipal bank within the meaning of the Banking Act 1987) is deducted at source before payment: Income and Corporation Taxes Act 1988, s. 479. This deduction at source provision does not apply, however, where the beneficial owner of the deposit is not ordinarily resident in the UK.

COPY BONDS OF CAUTION OR CONSIGNATION RECEIPTS.

33.4.4

A copy of a bond of caution or a consignation receipt has to be lodged because the principal may not be borrowed out of process: r. 4.11(3)(g).

Cautioners and guarantors

33.5

33.5.[1] A bond of caution or other security shall be given only by a person authorised to carry on a regulated activity under section 31 of the Financial Services and Markets Act 2000.

GENERAL NOTE.

33.5.1

This is a new rule, replacing R.C.S. 1965, r. 200(e)(iv) which provided for a list of guarantee companies for the purposes of obtaining caution in judicial factories (the list was used more widely in fact). That rule arose out of s. 27 of the Judicial Factors Act 1849 which provided for the court to authorise bonds or policies of certain companies carrying on guarantee business in Scotland in relation to caution to be found by factors. This led to a list of "approved" guarantee companies imposing a burden on the Accountant of Court to investigate to satisfy himself that a company could be approved by the Lord President for the list. There is no requirement in s. 27 of the 1849 Act for the court to approve a list of companies. Regard must now be had to Arts. 59 and 60 of the EEC Treaty which allow a company from another Member State to supply services here.

The solution was to abandon the list of approved guarantee companies and to provide for companies authorised to carry on business in class 15 in Sched. 2 to the Insurance Companies Act 1982. That Act is now replaced by reference to those authorised under s. 31 of the Financial Services and Markets Act 2000.

Form of bonds of caution and other securities

33.6

33.6.—[2](1) A bond of caution shall oblige the cautioner, his heirs and executors to make payment of the sums for which he has become cautioner to the party to whom he is bound, as validly and in the same manner as the party and his heirs and successors, for whom he is cautioner, are obliged.

(2) Revoked by SSI 2004/514.

Deriv. R.C.S. 1965, r. 238(a)

GENERAL NOTE.

33.6.1

Rule 33.6(2) required a bond by an insurance company to state whether the insurance company was authorised under the Insurance Companies Act 1982. That Act was repealed by the Financial Services and Markets Act 2000.

Sufficiency of caution or security and objections

33.7

33.7.—(1) The Deputy Principal Clerk shall satisfy himself that any bond of caution or other document, lodged in process under rule 33.4(3), is in proper form.

(2) A party who is dissatisfied with the sufficiency or form of the caution or other security offered in obedience to an order of the court may apply by motion for an order under rule 33.10 (failure to find caution or give security).

GENERAL NOTE.

33.7.1

The practice has been for the Deputy Principal Clerk to satisfy himself as to the sufficiency of caution found, a matter which is really not his concern. It is for the party who is dissatisfied with the caution found by another party to raise the matter with the court and if necessary seek decree by default: r. 33.10. The Deputy Principal Clerk is concerned only with the form of the document of caution or security.

"MOTION".

33.7.2

For motions, see Chap. 23.

Juratory caution

33.8

33.8.—(1) Where a pursuer in an action with a conclusion for suspension is ordered to find caution or give other security, he may offer to do so by juratory caution.

(2) Such an offer shall be made—

    (a) at the time the order for caution or other security is made; or

---

[1] Rule 33.5 amended by SSI 2004/331 (effective 6th August 2004).

[2] R. 33.9(d)(i) substituted by SSI 2009/63, para. 3 (effective 25th February 2009) and substituted again by SSI 2010/417 (effective 1st January 2011).

(b) by enrolling a motion within the period allowed for finding caution or giving other security, as the case may be, or any prorogation of it, for the appointment of a commissioner.

(3) Where such an offer is made, the court shall—

(a) appoint a commissioner to take the deposition of the pursuer at a time and place to be fixed by the commissioner;

(b) ordain the pursuer to give notice of at least seven days of the time and place so fixed by the commissioner to every other party to the action; and

(c) where the offer has been made by motion under paragraph (2)(*b*), prorogate the time for finding caution or giving other security, as the case may be, by such period as it thinks fit.

(4) At the time and place fixed by the commissioner in accordance with paragraph (3)(a), the pursuer shall be examined as to the nature and extent of his whole estate wheresoever situated and the other parties to the action shall be entitled to cross-examine him.

(5) After his examination, the pursuer shall send to the Deputy Principal Clerk—

(a) a bond of caution;

(b) a full inventory of his whole estate;

(c) a declaration attached to the inventory, stating that he will not dilapidate or dispose of any of his property or uplift any of the debts due to him, without the authority of the court (under pain of imprisonment or being otherwise punished as being guilty of fraud) or the consent of the party entitled to the benefit of the caution until the interlocutor disposing of the subject-matter of the action has become final and, where he has been found liable to pay any sum, including expenses, 12 weeks (and any further period that the court, on the motion of any party, may grant) have passed since the interlocutor became final;

(d) the vouchers of any debts due to the pursuer;

(e) the title deeds of any heritable property belonging to the pursuer, so far as in his possession or under his control; and

(f) where required by the party entitled to the benefit of the caution—

(i) a standard security in favour of such party over any heritable property belonging to the pursuer, and

(ii) an assignation of all debts or other rights due to the pursuer,

prepared at the expense of the pursuer.

(6) Subject to rule 33.12(1) (bond of caution or consignation receipt transmitted to Accountant of Court), the Deputy Principal Clerk shall retain any documents lodged under paragraph (5) of this rule until further order of the court.

Deriv. R.C.S. 1965, r. 240

GENERAL NOTE.

Juratory caution is rare. It only arises in a suspension where offered, which is infrequent, and involves the appointment of a commissioner in a process with intimations of bankruptcy procedure.   **33.8.1**

"SUSPENSION".

Suspension is the means of preventing execution of diligence, to stop infringement of a right or to bring a decree under review: see Chap. 60.   **33.8.2**

"CAUTION OR OTHER SECURITY".

See note 33.1.1.   **33.8.3**

"MOTION".

For motions, see Chap. 23.   **33.8.4**

Insolvency or death of cautioner or guarantor

33.9

33.9. Where caution has been found by bond of caution or security has been given by guarantee and the cautioner or guarantor, as the case may be—

    (a)[1] becomes apparently insolvent within the meaning assigned by section 16 of the Bankruptcy (Scotland) Act 2016 (meaning of apparent insolvency),

    (b) calls a meeting of his creditors to consider the state of his affairs,

    (c) dies unrepresented, or

    (d) is a company and—

        (i)[2] an administration order, bank administration order, building society special administration order, winding up order, bank insolvency order or building society insolvency order has been made, or a resolution for a voluntary winding up has been passed, with respect to it,

        (ii) a receiver of all or any part of its undertaking has been appointed, or

        (iii) a voluntary arrangement (within the meaning assigned by section 1(1) of the Insolvency Act 1986) has been approved under Part I of that Act,

the party entitled to benefit from the caution or guarantee may apply by motion for a new security or further security to be given.

Deriv. R.C.S. 1965, r. 238(f)

GENERAL NOTE.

33.9.1

The party whose cautioner becomes bankrupt or insolvent, etc., or dies should apply for new caution. If he does not the other party may object to further procedure without this being done: *A.B. v. C.D.* (1836) 15 S. 158.

"APPARENT INSOLVENCY".

33.9.2

S. 7 of the Bankruptcy (Scotland) Act 1985 lists the events which give rise to the constitution of apparent insolvency.

ADMINISTRATION OR WINDING UP ORDERS OR APPOINTMENT OF RECEIVER.

33.9.3

An administration order is made under Part II of the Insolvency Act 1986, a receiver is appointed under Part III of that Act and a winding up order made under Part IV of that Act. An insurance company (a body of persons, whether incorporated or not, carrying on insurance business) whether established within or outside the UK, carrying on business in the UK may be wound up under the 1986 Act: Insurance Companies Act 1982, ss. 15, 53, 54 and 96(1).

"VOLUNTARY ARRANGEMENT".

33.9.4

The directors of a company (in respect of which an administration order is not in force) may propose under Part I of the Insolvency Act 1986 to the company and its creditors a composition in satisfaction of its debts or a scheme of arrangement of its affairs: 1986 Act, s. 1(1). The word "composition" means an arrangement whereby the creditors will not be paid in full or will have their debts postponed.

"MOTION".

33.9.5

For motions, see Chap. 23.

Failure to find caution or give security

33.10

33.10. Where a party fails to find caution or give other security (such a party being in this rule referred to as "the party in default"), any other party may apply by motion—

    (a) where the party in default is a pursuer, for decree of absolvitor; or

    (b) where the party in default is a defender or a third party, for decree by default or for such other finding or order as the court thinks fit.

---

[1] R. 33.9(a) amended by SSI 2016/312 para. 2 (effective 30th November 2016).

[2] R. 33.9(d)(i) substituted by SSI 2009/63, para. 3 (effective 25th February 2009) and substituted again by SSI 2010/417 (effective 1st January 2011).

This rule enshrines the current practice.

"MOTION".

33.10.1

For motions, see Chap. 23.

"DECREE OF ABSOLVITOR".

33.10.2

This is the decree when the court decides finally in the (defender's) favour; it is a decree in foro and is one which is res judicata between the parties: see note 20.1.1; and on res judicata, see note 18.1.4(B)(5).

"DECREE BY DEFAULT".

33.10.3

A decree by default is a decree in foro and is one which is res judicata between the parties: see note 20.1.1; and on res judicata, see note 18.1.4(B)(5).

RECLAIMING.

33.10.4

A decree by default may be reclaimed against without leave within 21 days: r. 38.2(1). The decree may be recalled on such conditions as to expenses or otherwise as the court thinks fit: r. 38.9(2). The document of caution or security must be lodged on or before the reclaiming motion is enrolled: r. 38.9(1).

33.10.5

Interlocutors authorising uplifting of consignation receipts

33.11. An interlocutor authorising a party to uplift a consignation receipt from the Accountant of Court shall state the name of the person entitled to any interest which has accrued on the sum consigned.

33.11

GENERAL NOTE.

This is a new rule which reflects existing practice.

"CONSIGNATION RECEIPT".

33.11.1

See note 33.4.3.

33.11.2

Accountant of Court

33.12.—(1) A bond of caution or a consignation receipt lodged in any process shall be transmitted by the party lodging it, after the Deputy Principal Clerk has complied with rule 33.7(1), to the Accountant of Court.

33.12

(2) A bond of caution may be uplifted from the Accountant of Court on exhibition to him of the interlocutor granting discharge.

(3) A consignation receipt may be uplifted from the Accountant of Court on exhibition to him of a certified copy of the interlocutor authorising it.

(4) The form of the book to be kept by the Accountant of Court under section 4 of the Court of Session Consignations (Scotland) Act 1895 (consignations to be entered in books kept by Accountant of Court) shall be in Form 33.12.

Deriv. R.C.S. 1965, r. 13(d) (r. 33.12(1)); P.N. 14th May 1970 (r. 33.12(2))

ACCOUNTANT OF COURT.

See note 3.1.3.

33.12.1

TRANSMISSION TO ACCOUNTANT OF COURT.

The clerk of session at the appropriate public counter of the Petition or General Department will enter particulars of the process in a transmission book. The party who lodged the document of caution or other security will take the document and the transmission book to the Accountant of Court's office. On a receipt being entered in the book by the Accountant's staff the book is taken back to the Petition or General Department.

33.12.2

UPLIFTING OF BOND OF CAUTION OR CONSIGNATION RECEIPT.

On bonds of caution, see note 33.4.1; on consignation receipts, see note 33.4.3.

33.12.3

CHAPTER 34 REPORTS TO INNER HOUSE

Report by Lord Ordinary to Inner House

34.1.—(1) The Lord Ordinary may, at any stage of a cause on intimation to the parties, report the cause or any incidental matter which arises in the course of it, to the Inner House for a ruling.

(2) The Lord Ordinary shall give effect to the ruling of a Division of the Inner House on a report to the Inner House unless the Division decides the cause or incidental matter itself or remits to the Lord Ordinary with directions to proceed in a particular way.

Deriv. R.C.S. 1965, r. 91B(1) inserted by SI 1984/472 and amended by SI 1986/1937, and r. 198A(1) inserted by SI 1986/1937

GENERAL NOTE.

This Chapter is derived from s.19 of the C.S.A. 1825 (incidental matter) and s.14 of the C.S.A. 1850 (whole cause), both replaced by R.C.S. 1965, r. 91B (and R.C.S. 1965, r. 198A) and repealed by A.S. (R.C.A. No. 8) (Miscellaneous) 1986 [SI 1986/1937].

"REPORT THE CAUSE".

Report of a whole cause (see e.g. *Borland v. Borland* 1947 S.C. 432) to the Inner House has fallen into desuetude.

"INCIDENTAL MATTER".

Any incidental matter in the course of a cause may be reported to the Inner House. Such a matter would include a point on which there is a difference of practice in the Outer House (e.g. *Johnson v. Caledonian Railway Co.* (1892) 20 R. 222) or a matter of practice about which there is doubt (e.g. *Gould v. Gould* 1966 S.C. 88).

Where the Inner House has made an order, such as for a particular mode of inquiry, which subsequently appears to be inappropriate, the proper course is for the Lord Ordinary to report the matter back to the Inner House: *Kerr v. John Brown & Co.* 1965 S.C. 144.

It is incompetent for a Lord Ordinary to remit a cause to the Inner House simpliciter, it must be done in an appropriate case by a report under this Chapter: *Alliance & Leicester Building Society v. Lindsays W.S.*, 25th July (1997 G.W.D. 36-1862).

Fixing hearings for reports

34.2.—(1) Where the Lord Ordinary reports a cause, or any incidental matter in a cause, under rule 34.1(1) to the Inner House, each party shall, within seven days after the date on which the report of the Lord Ordinary is issued, inform the Keeper of the Rolls of the estimate of counsel or other person having a right of audience of the duration of the hearing before the Inner House.

(2) If a party fails to comply with paragraph (1), the Keeper of the Rolls may put the cause out on the By Order Roll before a Division of the Inner House.

(3) Where, at any time after an estimate has been given to the Keeper of the Rolls under paragraph (1), a party's estimate of the likely length of the hearing alters materially, that party shall inform the Keeper of the Rolls of the new estimated length.

(4) On the basis of the information provided to him under this rule, the Keeper of the Rolls shall—

   (a) put the cause out for hearing before a Division of the Inner House in the Single Bills or on the Summar Roll as he thinks fit; and

   (b) give written intimation of the date of the hearing to each party.

GENERAL NOTE.

This rule sets out expressly the procedure to be followed when a report is made.

"COUNSEL OR OTHER PERSON HAVING A RIGHT OF AUDIENCE".

See r. 1.3(1) (definitions of "counsel" and "other person having a right of audience").

"WRITTEN INTIMATION".

For methods, see r. 16.9.

34.1

34.1.1

34.1.2

34.1.3

34.2

34.2.1

34.2.2

34.2.3

34.2.4   There must be lodged four copies of any document a party wishes to refer to at the hearing in the Inner House on the second sederunt day before the hearing: r. 4.7(2). This should be the responsibility of the party on whose motion the court decided to report.

BY ORDER ROLL HEARING.

34.2.5   No court fee is payable for a hearing on this By Order Roll.

Disposal of reports

34.3   **34.3.**—(1)   On considering the report of the Lord Ordinary and hearing parties, the Inner House may—

(a)   dispose of the cause or matter reported to it; or

(b)   remit to the Lord Ordinary with such directions as it thinks fit.

(2)   The decision of the Inner House on a report to it under rule 34.1(1) shall be final.

(3)   The Inner House may determine any question of expenses in respect of the matter reported to it or may reserve any such question.

(4)   An interlocutor pronounced by the Lord Ordinary in obedience to directions given under paragraph (1) shall be deemed to be an interlocutor of the Inner House.

Deriv. R.C.S. 1965, r. 91B(2), inserted by SI 1984/472 and amended by SI 1986/1937 (r. 34.3(1) to (3)), and r. 198A(2) and (3) inserted by SI 1986/1937.

DISPOSAL BY INNER HOUSE OR LORD ORDINARY.

34.3.1   Disposal by either the Inner House or remit to the Outer House may be adopted. Formerly, where the whole cause was reported the cause became an Inner House cause: *Gould v. Gould* 1966 S.C. 88.

An interlocutor of the Lord Ordinary following a report includes the words "having advised with the Lords of the First [or Second] Division".

The Lord Ordinary should not sit with the Division considering the report: *F v. F* 1945 S.C. 202, 212 per Lord Moncrieff.

CHAPTER 34A PURSUERS' OFFERS

Chapter 34A[1]

Pursuers' Offers

Interpretation of this Chapter

34A.1.[2, 3] In this Chapter—

"appropriate date" means the date by which a pursuer's offer could reasonably have been accepted;

"charges" charges for work carried out by the pursuer's solicitor, and includes any additional charge;

"pursuer's offer" means an offer by a pursuer to settle a claim against a defender made in accordance with this Chapter;

"relevant period" means the period from the appropriate date to the date of acceptance of the pursuer's offer or, as the case may be, to the date on which judgment was given, or on which the verdict was applied.

GENERAL NOTE.

Chapter 34A was first inserted by A.S. (R.C.S.A. No. 4) (Miscellaneous) 1996 [SI 1996/2168] following a recommendation of the Cullen Review of Outer House Business in December 1995. The Chapter was revoked with effect from 14th November 1996 by A.S. (R.C.S.A. No. 6) 1996 [SI 1996/2769]. The revocation does not affect offers made before it came into effect. The procedure was brought to an abrupt halt when, in *Taylor*, below, the former r. 34A.(6) provided for a "penalty" by which the pursuer on beating his own offer could be awarded a sum equal to the taxed expenses. Section 5 of the Court of Session Act 1988, it was held, did not include a power to make such a provision. Section 103 of the Courts Reform (Scotland) Act 2014 contains the current powers for making the rules of the court. Section 103(2)(k) contains an express power to make provision for "other payments such parties may be required to make in respect of their conduct relating to such proceedings". This should make a rule for payment of a sum equivalent to expenses *intra vires*.

The idea of pursuers' offers was first proposed by Lord President Hope after he discovered its existence in Canada in 1991. Research was carried out by the Lord President's Private Office and a consultation exercise carried out on proposals for its introduction. Not all those consulted were in favour, but the majority were; and the Rules Council was persuaded reluctantly to accept it. It was agreed that Chap. 34A would be in operation as an experiment for two years after which it would be reviewed. Pursuers' offers were brought to the attention of the Woolf Committee examining English procedure by the Lord President's office; the idea was taken up and adopted in Lord Woolf's interim and final reports (without acknowledgement).

Rules for such offers exist in Canada (British Columbia, New Brunswick, Nova Scotia, Ontario and Saskatchewan) and Australia (New South Wales, Queensland, South Australia and Victoria).

Chap. 34A was introduced as part of the armoury of procedures to increase early settlements. The policy behind the rules (applying to both pursuers and defenders) in the other jurisdictions mentioned was to encourage settlement and replaced the English-based rules for payment into court (where our procedure for tenders appears not to have existed). Anecdotal evidence suggests the procedure works successfully in these jurisdictions, but no statistics were available to show how significant the contribution of offers to settle to early settlements has been. In South Australia an offer to settle must be made at the end of a pre-trial conference.

The success or failure of pursuers' offers will depend on the appropriate form of sanction being imposed on a defender who, having refused to accept an offer, does not succeed at proof in achieving a lower award or in winning the case. It would be unfortunate if the procedure failed because an inappropriate sanction were chosen; and the penalty in r. 34A.6(2)(b) is not the most appropriate.

Few other jurisdictions elected for a rule for up to a 100 per cent uplift in expenses. A notable exception is British Columbia where the double costs rule applies only to tariff items covering preparation for trial, trial and proceedings after trial other than appeal, exclusive of disbursements and expenses. It may be that Chap. 34A had been revoked because of the unsatisfactory nature of r. 34A.6 which provided for a 100 per cent uplift in the whole expenses (except any additional fee). The 100 per cent uplift should be a general rule "unless the court otherwise orders" rather than a fixed 100 per cent or any figure between 0 and 100 per cent. Consideration should have been given to limiting expenses to those incurred after the offer is lodged, as with tenders.

In *Taylor v. Marshalls Food Group Ltd* (No. 2) 1998 S.C. 841 (First Div.), it was held that the provi-

---

[1] Chapter 34A inserted by S.S.I. 2017 No. 52 r. 2(2) (effective 3rd April 2017).
[2] Inserted by S.S.I. 2017 No. 52 r. 2(2) (effective 3rd April 2017).
[3] As amended by S.S.I. 2019 No. 74 r. 4(3) (effective 29th April 2019).

sion in r.34A.6, for the pursuer to be entitled on beating his own offer to a sum equal to the taxed expenses, was *ultra vires*. But all was not lost. Pursuers' offers may have experienced a form of reprieve in *Cameron v. Kvaerner Govan Ltd* 1999 S.L.T. 638. In that case the pursuer was held to be entitled to an additional fee under r.42.14(2)(g) (settling or limiting matters) where the pursuer offered to settle for a fixed sum, thus encouraging the issues to be focused, and the defender subsequently tendered that sum. Lord Bonomy said any step which might clarify the position of a party or limit the areas in dispute should be encouraged. At present it cannot be said that a pursuer's offer can be equiperated with a tender and any law and procedure applicable to tenders: *Tenbey v. Stolt Comex Seaway Ltd* , 2001 S.C. 638.

The pursuer's offer procedure is not available in respect of a challenge to a final decision taken in the Outer House, the procedure being by implication in Chap. 34A to proceedings in the Outer House: *Anderson v Imrie*, 2019 S.C. 243 (Extra Div.). It was observed that the appeal of an interlocutory decision did not prevent the lodging of a pursuer's offer while the matter was pending in the Inner House.

Pursuers' offers

34A.2

34A.2.—[1](1) A pursuer's offer may be made in any cause where the summons includes a conclusion for an order for payment of a sum or sums of money, other than an order—

    (a) which the court may not make without evidence; or

    (b) the making of which is dependent on the making of another order which the court may not make without evidence.

    (2) This Chapter has no effect as regards any other form of offer to settle.

GENERAL NOTE.

34A.2.1

For the history of this rule, see note 34A.1.1.

"CONCLUSION".

34A.2.2

On conclusions, see note 13.2.3.

ORDERS WITHOUT EVIDENCE.

34A.2.3

The court may not grant decree, e.g., in certain family actions (see Civil Evidence (Scotland) Act 1988, s.8).

"OTHER FORM OF OFFER".

34A.2.4

Chap. 34A was designed primarily with reparation actions in mind. The exclusion of other forms of offer would exclude an extra-judicial offer. It is not entirely clear why r.34A.2(2) is necessary.

The original rule (34A.2(2)(a)) required the offer to be in a particular form; now, however, no form or formality is required except that a reference is required that it is made, if it be the case, under Chap. 34A for the provisions of Chap. 34A to apply. It may be that the lack of formality makes r. 34A.2(2) thought to be necessary. A particular form might lead to less confusion or uncertainty.

Making an offer

34A.3

34A.3.—[2](1) A pursuer's offer is made by lodging in process an offer in the terms specified in rule 34A.4.

    (2) A pursuer's offer may be made at any time before—

    (a) the court makes avizandum or, if it does not make avizandum, gives judgment; or

    (b) in a jury trial, the jury retires to consider the verdict.

    (3) A pursuer's offer may be withdrawn at any time before it is accepted by lodging in process a minute of withdrawal.

GENERAL NOTE.

34A.3.1

For the history of this rule, see note 34A.1.1.

FORM OF OFFER.

34A.3.2

The original rule (34A.2(2)(a)) required the offer to be in a particular form; now, however, no form or formality is required except that a reference is required that it is made, if it be the case, under Chap. 34A, with acceptance of a sum inclusive of interest as well as taxed expenses, for the provisions of Chap. 34A to apply. These requirements are set out in r. 34A.4.

---

[1] Inserted by S.S.I. 2017 No. 52 r. 2(2) (effective 3rd April 2017).
[2] Inserted by S.S.I. 2017 No. 52 r. 2(2) (effective 3rd April 2017).

Form of offer

34A.4.[1] A pursuer's offer must—

(a) state that it is made under this Chapter;

(b) offer to accept—

    (i) a sum or sums of money, inclusive of interest to the date of the offer; and

    (ii) the taxed expenses of process; and

(c) specify the conclusion or conclusions of the summons in satisfaction of which the sum or sums and expenses referred to in paragraph (b) would be accepted.

34A.4

GENERAL NOTE.

For the history of this rule, see note 34A.1.1.

34A.4.1

THE OFFER

The original rule (34A.2(2)(a)) required the offer to be in a particular form; now, however, no form or formality is required except that a reference is required that it is made, if it be the case, under Chap. 34A, with acceptance of a sum inclusive of interest as well as taxed expenses, for the provisions of Chap. 34A to apply. The original rule did not require interest or expenses to be included.

34A.4.2

Disclosure of offers

34A.5.—[2](1) No averment of the fact that a pursuer's offer has been made may be included in any pleadings.

(2) Where a pursuer's offer has not been accepted—

(a) the court must not be informed that an offer has been made until—

    (i) the court has pronounced judgment; or

    (ii) in the case of a jury trial, the jury has returned its verdict; and

(b) a jury must not be informed that an offer has been made until it has returned its verdict.

34A.5

GENERAL NOTE.

For the history of this rule, see note 34A.1.1.

34A.5.1

Acceptance of offers

34A.6.—[3](1) A pursuer's offer may be accepted any time before—

(a) the offer is withdrawn;

(b) the court makes avizandum or, if it does not make avizandum, gives judgment; or

(c) in the case of a jury trial, the jury retires to consider its verdict.

(2) It is accepted by lodging in process an acceptance of the offer in the form of a minute of acceptance.

(3) A minute of acceptance must be unqualified other than as respects any question of contribution, indemnity or relief.

(4) On acceptance of a pursuer's offer either the pursuer or the defender may apply by motion for decree in terms of the offer and minute of acceptance.

(5) Where a pursuer's offer includes an offer to accept a sum of money in satisfaction of a conclusion for decree jointly and severally against two or more defenders, the offer is accepted only when accepted by all such defenders.

(6) However, the court may, on the motion of the pursuer, and with the consent of any defender who has lodged a minute of acceptance, grant decree in terms of the offer and minute of acceptance.

34A.6

MINUTE OF ACCEPTANCE

While the offer does not require to be in any particular form, the acceptance must be.

34A.6.1

---

[1] Inserted by S.S.I. 2017 No. 52 r. 2(2) (effective 3rd April 2017).
[2] Inserted by S.S.I. 2017 No. 52 r. 2(2) (effective 3rd April 2017).
[3] Inserted by S.S.I. 2017 No. 52 r. 2(2) (effective 3rd April 2017).

34A.6.2   For motions, see Chap. 23.

Late acceptance of offers

34A.7   **34A.7**—[1](1)   This rule applies to the determination of a motion under rule 34A.6(4) where the court is satisfied that a defender lodged a minute of acceptance after the appropriate date.

(2)   On the pursuer's motion the court must, except on cause shown—

(a)   allow interest on any sum decerned for from the date on which the pursuer's offer was made; and

(b)   find the defender liable for payment to the pursuer of a sum calculated in accordance with rule 34A.9.

(3)   Where the court is satisfied that more than one defender lodged a minute of acceptance after the appropriate date the court may find those defenders liable to contribute to payment of the sum referred to in paragraph (2)(b) in such proportions as the court thinks fit.

(4)   Where the court makes a finding under paragraph (2)(b), the pursuer may apply for decerniture for payment of the sum as so calculated no later than 21 days after the later of—

(a)   the date of the Auditor's report of the taxation of the pursuer's account of expenses; and

(b)   the date of the interlocutor disposing of a note of objection.

"NO LATER THAN 21 DAYS AFTER".

34A.7.1   There is a time limit for the pursuer to apply for decerniture.
The date on which the application is deemed to have been received by the applicant is not counted.

Non-acceptance of offers

34A.8   **34A.8**—[2](1)   This rule applies where—

(a)   a pursuer's offer has been made, and has not been withdrawn;

(b)   the offer has not been accepted;

(c)   either—

(i)   the court has pronounced judgment; or

(ii)   in the case of a jury trial, the verdict of the jury has been applied;

(d)   the judgment or verdict, in so far as relating to the conclusions of the summons specified in the pursuer's offer, is at least as favourable in money terms to the pursuer as the terms offered; and

(e)   the court is satisfied that the pursuer's offer was a genuine attempt to settle the proceedings.

(2)   For the purpose of determining if the condition specified in paragraph (1)(d) is satisfied, interest awarded in respect of the period after the lodging of the pursuer's offer is to be disregarded.

(3)   On the pursuer's motion the court must, except on cause shown, decern against the defender for payment to the pursuer of a sum calculated in accordance with rule 34A.9.

(4)   No such motion may be enrolled after the expiry of 21 days after the later of—

(a)   the date of the Auditor's report of the taxation of the pursuer's account of expenses; and

(b)   the date of the interlocutor disposing of a note of objection.

---

[1] Inserted by S.S.I. 2017 No. 52 r. 2(2) (effective 3rd April 2017).
[2] Inserted by S.S.I. 2017 No. 52 r. 2(2) (effective 3rd April 2017).

(5) Where more than one defender is found liable to the pursuer in respect of a conclusion specified in the offer, the court may find those defenders liable to contribute to payment of the sum referred to in paragraph (3) in such proportions as it thinks fit.

LIABILITY OF MORE THAN ONE DEFENDER.

Under r. 34A.8(5) the court may fix the proportion of liability to contribute between multiple defenders as it thinks fit. This does not preclude defenders agreeing the proportion, or the court not thinking it fit. **34A.8.1**

Extent of defender's liability

34A.9[1, 2] The sum that may be decerned for under rule 34A.7(2)(b) or rule 34A.8(3) is a sum corresponding to half the charges allowed on taxation of the pursuer's account of expenses, in so far as those charges are attributable to the relevant period, or in so far as they can reasonably be attributed to that period. **34A.9**

EXTENT OF EXPENSES PAYABLE.

Under the original rule (34A.6) the defender could have been liable up to a 100 per cent uplift in expenses. Under new r. 34A.9 the defender's liability on expenses is half the fees (now called charges) allowed to solicitors (including any additional fee) allowed on taxation (see r. 34A.1) of the pursuer's account of expenses from the date by which the offer could reasonably be accepted to the date of acceptance, judgment or jury verdict. The rule applies to late acceptance of offers (r.34A.7(2)(b)) and non-acceptance of offers (r. 34A.8(3)). Under those provisions the court *must* decern for that amount except on cause shown. While cause would usually be sought to be shown by a defender seeking to pay a sum less than half, the provision does not preclude a pursuer seeking more or a calculation on some other basis (an unintended consequence, no doubt). Presumably a sum less than half would be more justified for a late acceptance than for a non-acceptance. **34A.9.1**

---

[1] Inserted by S.S.I. 2017 No. 52 r. 2(2) (effective 3rd April 2017).
[2] As amended by S.S.I. 2019 No. 74 r. 4(4) (effective 29th April 2019).

(3) Where more than one defendant is found liable to the payment in respect of a conclusion specified in the offer, the court may find those defendants liable to contribute to payment of the sum referred to in paragraph (A) in such proportions as it thinks fit.

Where more than one defendant

3.4.8.1 Under r.3A.8(3) the court may fix the proportions of liability to contribute between each defendant. This does not provide guidance as to agreeing the proportion, or the court not thinking it fit.

Extent of defender's liability

3.4.9 **3A.9.**—(1) The sum that may be decerned for under rule 3A.7(2)(D) or rule 3A.8(3) is a sum corresponding to both the charges allowed on taxation of the pursuer's account of expenses, in so far as those charges are attributable to the relevant period, of in so far as the expenses can reasonably be attributed to that period.

Extent of expenses to be paid

3.4.9.1 Under the earlier rule r.3A.6, the defender could have been liable up to a 30 day time limit to the expenses. Under new r.3A.9 the defender's liability to expenses as such is now called charges allowed on taxation, including any additional fee allowed under function (a.e.A.7(A.1)) of the pursuer's account of expenses. From the date by which the offer could reasonably be accepted to the date of non-acceptance of any relative. The rule requires that acceptance of the offer 3A.7(2)(c) and non-acceptance of offers r.3A.8(3). Under these provisions the court must decern to that amount except on cause shown. While costs would usually be sought to be shown by a defender seeking to pay said in full that the provision does not preclude a pursuer seeking more or a coloutinum in some other circumstanced compensation or doubt. Presumably a sum less than that said would be more justified for a late acceptance than for non-acceptance.

Inserted by S.S.I. 2010 No.279 r.2(2) effective 3rd April 2017 r.
As amended by S.S.I. 2019 No.34 r.2(4) effective 29th April 2019.

CHAPTER 35 RECOVERY OF EVIDENCE

Application and interpretation of this Chapter

35.1.—(1) This Chapter applies to the recovery of any evidence in a cause depending before the court.

35.1

(2) In this Chapter, "the Act of 1972" means the Administration of Justice (Scotland) Act 1972.

GENERAL NOTE.

This Chapter applies to the recovery of evidence in a depending cause (on the meaning of which, see note 35.1.2). If the cause is not depending, e.g. the summons has not been served, recovery may not be sought. An application, e.g. under s.1(1) of the Administration of Justice (Scotland) Act 1972 for preservation, custody or detention of documents before a cause has been commenced would have to be by petition under Chap. 64.

35.1.1

"DEPENDING".

A cause is depending from the time it is commenced (i.e. from the time an action is served or a first order in a petition is made) until final decree, whereas a cause is in dependence until final extract. For the meaning of commenced, see note 13.4.4 (action) or 14.6.1 (petition). For the meaning of final decree, see note 4.15.2(2). For the meaning of final extract, see note 7.1.2(2).

35.1.2

Applications for commission and diligence for recovery of documents or for orders under section 1 of the Act of 1972

35.2.—(1) An application by a party for—

35.2

    (a)   a commission and diligence for the recovery of a document, or

    (b)   an order under section 1 of the Act of 1972,

shall be made by motion.

(2) At the time of enrolling a motion under paragraph (1), a specification of—

    (a)   the document or other property sought to be inspected, photographed, preserved, taken into custody, detained, produced, recovered, sampled or experimented on or with, as the case may be, or

    (b)   the matter in respect of which information is sought as to the identity of a person who might be a witness or a defender,

shall be lodged in process.

(3) A copy of the specification lodged under paragraph (2) and the motion made under paragraph (1) shall be intimated by the applicant to—

    (a)   every other party;

    (b)   in respect of an application for an order under section 1(1) of the Act of 1972, any third party haver; and

    (c)[1] where necessary—

        (i)   the Advocate General for Scotland (in a case where the document or other property sought is in the possession of either a public authority exercising functions in relation to reserved matters within the meaning of Schedule 5 to the Scotland Act 1998, or a cross-border public authority within the meaning of section 88(5) of that Act); or

        (ii)   the Lord Advocate (in any other case),

    and if there is any doubt, both.

(4) Where the Lord Ordinary grants a motion made under paragraph (1), in whole or in part, in an action before calling of the summons, he may order the applicant to find such caution or give such other security as he thinks fit.

(5) The decision of the Lord Ordinary on a motion under paragraph (1) in an action before calling of the summons shall be final and not subject to review.

---

[1] R. 35.2(3)(c) substituted by SSI 2001 No. 305, r. 6 (effective 18th September 2001).

(6)[1] The Advocate General for Scotland or the Lord Advocate or both, as appropriate, may appear at the hearing of any motion under paragraph (1).

Deriv. R.C.S. 1965, r. 95(a)(part) amended by SI 1992/88 (r. 35.2(5) and (6)), r. 95(b) (r. 35.2(1)(a), (2) and (3), r. 95A(a)(part) inserted by SI 1972/2021 and amended by SI 1992/88 (r. 35.2(5) and (6)); r. 95A(b) inserted by SI 1972/2021 (r. 35.2(1) to (4); r. 95A(d)(i) substituted by SI 1987/1206 (r. 35.2(1)(b))

General note.

35.2.1
This rule is the principal provision for obtaining an order to recover documents or for an order under s. 1 of the Administration of Justice (Scotland) Act 1972 in a depending cause (on which, see note 35.1.2). Where there is no depending cause the application is by petition under Chap. 64.

A commission and diligence to recover documents refers strictly to the common law rules for recovery of documents (on which, see note 35.2.5). The power of the court to take the depositions of havers on commission is preserved by s. 10(a) (and in relation to the Inner House, s. 38) of the C.S.A. 1988. Under s. 1 of the Act of 1972 orders may be sought (for a commission and diligence) for the inspection, photographing, preservation, custody and detention of documents and other property and for their production and recovery, the taking of samples or the carrying out of experiments or for disclosure of information about the identity of a potential witness or defender. A motion for a commission and diligence must be accompanied by a specification of the documents or property sought: r. 35.2(2); and see note 35.2.10

In relation to actions of damages for personal injuries or the death of a relative where the optional procedure has been adopted there is a procedure for automatic mandatory disclosure of documents: r. 43.25.

A commission and diligence may not be obtained to recover from the keeper of any public record original registers or deeds in his custody or processes kept by the Keeper of the Records of Scotland or an inferior court; the procedures in rr. 35.9 or 35.10 respectively must be used.

A party who has obtained possession of documents or other items under a commission and diligence at common law or under s. 1 of the 1972 Act is subject to an implied obligation or undertaking to the court not to use them or allow them to be used for any purpose other than the conduct of the actual or proposed proceedings for which there were recovered: *Iomega Corporation v. Myrica (U.K.) Ltd* 1998 S.C. 636 (I.H.). For a recent example of authority being given to use documents in one action in another, see *Duff & Phelps Ltd, Minuter*, 2022 S.L.T. 450 (OH).

"commission and diligence".

35.2.2
In granting a motion for recovery of documents the court, where appropriate, (a) appoints a commissioner with a warrant under which the commissioner may enter premises and search for the documents or property, (b) authorises a named person to photograph, inspect, take samples of, or carry out an experiment on the property, (c) grants warrant to cite a party or third party haver to appear before a commissioner to produce the document or other property or answer questions about where it is or with whom it is or has been, or (d) authorises one or more of the above either at the same time or one at a time: for execution of commissions, see r. 35.4. Where it is not possible for a commissioner to blank out commercially confidential material in excerpting from documents the court has authorised counsel, solicitors and an independent expert to inspect the documents provided they signed an undertaking about non-disclosure: *Iomega Corporation v. Myrica (U.K.) Ltd (No. 1)* 1999 S.L.T. 793.

Before a commission is executed there is an optional procedure for serving the order for recovery of a document (but not other property) on the haver to obtain voluntary production: r. 35.3.

Documents or other property recovered are not productions in the cause. They only become so if subsequently lodged as productions by a party.

The Lord Ordinary cannot sist a commission and diligence after it has been granted: *Exal Sampling Services Ltd v. Massie* 1993 S.L.T. 1220.

The court has power to impose conditions for the use of information recovered by commission and diligence, although it is not normal practice for the court to do so: *McInally v. John Wyeth & Brother Ltd* 1992 S.L.T. 344; *Union Carbide Corporation v. B.P. Chemicals Ltd* 1995 S.C. 398, 404G per L. Hope.

"document".

35.2.3
This word has been defined in the R.C.S. 1994 by reference to the inclusive definition in s. 9 of the Civil Evidence (Scotland) Act 1988: r. 1.3(1).

"other property".

35.2.4
This phrase is not defined in the R.C.S. 1994. In s. 1(1) of the Act of 1972 the phrase is defined as "including, where appropriate, land". "Property" in the Act of 1972 means corporeal property; but the court has a common law power to order inspection and video recording of things such as a process or activity: *Christie v. Arthur Bell & Sons Ltd* 1989 S.L.T. 253; and see cases there cited.

Recovery of documents (common law).

35.2.5
The purpose of a commission and diligence is to put the court in possession of documents about the issues of fact which have to be determined: *Paterson v. Paterson* 1919 1 S.L.T. 12. Hence a fishing

---

[1] R. 35.2(6) substituted by S.S.I. 2007 No. 7, r. 2(5) (effective 29th January 2007).

diligence by a party to discover material for a case not pled will not be allowed: *County Council of Fife v. Thoms* (1898) 25 R. 1097; *Earl of Morton v. Fleming* 1921 1 S.L.T. 205. A fishing diligence is one for which there is no basis in the averments or one which involves too wide a search among all the papers of the haver: *Civil Service Building Society v. MacDougall* 1988 S.C. 58, 62 per L.J.-C. Ross. Real evidence is not recoverable by this means: *Mactaggart v. MacKillop* 1938 S.L.T. 559; cf. s. 1 of the Act of 1972. Sensitive personal data belonging to a party to an action differs from classified or security sensitive information and privileged information, and cannot be withheld if relevant: *M v. A Scottish Local Authority*, 2012 S.L.T. 6 (OH). In that case the question of whether pre-notification to alleged abusers referred to in findings in fact (which were not published) in a Scottish Executive report (which was published) of the motion to open up the confidential material was raised and it was held that there was no requirement.

The suggested rule for the recovery of documents in Walker and Walker on *The Law of Evidence in Scotland*, 4th edn, at para. 21.6.2, is: "Subject to confidentiality and relevancy, a document is recoverable if it is a deed granted by or in favour of a party or his predecessor in title, or a communication sent to, or by or on behalf of, a party, or a written record kept by or on behalf of a party."; and "A document is not recoverable if it has not been communicated to or by one of the parties and if it can be used only to provide material for the examination-in-chief or in cross-examination of a witness who is not a party". No judge can be called on to produce his notebook in order for it to be ascertained what the reasons for his decision were: *Behrent v. MacKillop*, 2003 S.L.T. 1049 (OH).

The document must be relevant to the facts averred but it does not have to be admissible in evidence: *Admiralty v. Aberdeen Steam Trawling and Fishing Co. Ltd* 1909 S.C. 335, 340 per L.P. Dunedin (*de recenti* report by ship master to owner); *Black v. Bairds & Dalmellington* 1939 S.C. 472 (post-mortem medical report); *Johnston v. South of Scotland Electricity Board* 1968 S.L.T. (Notes) 7 (*de recenti* statements to third party). A commission and diligence may not be refused because averments remitted to probation are irrelevant or of doubtful relevance: *Duke of Hamilton's Trs. v. Woodside Coal Co.* (1897) 24 R. 294.

Documents prepared for the purposes or in anticipation of the litigation are as a general rule not recoverable: *Anderson v. St Andrew's Ambulance Association* 1942 S.C. 555; *Young v. National Coal Board* 1957 S.C. 99; and see note 35.2.7 on confidentiality. Precognitions obtained by the Crown for a criminal prosecution are not recoverable: see *B v. Burns*, 1993 S.C. 232; and *Strain v. Premier Custodial Group Ltd*, 2007 S.L.T. 262.

At common law a commission and diligence was not normally granted before the closed record, and was granted after the open record (but before proof was allowed) only to enable a party to make more specific averments already pled or to answer averments or calls for further specification but not to gather material for evidence in preparation for proof: *Boyle v. Glasgow Royal Infirmary and Associated Hospitals* 1969 S.C. 72, 77 per L.P. Clyde. That power has been extended, by the effect of s.1(2) of the Act of 1972, to any time from the time the cause has commenced (i.e. the action has been served or the first order in a petition has been granted): *Moore v. Greater Glasgow Health Board*, 1978 S.C. 123, 131 per Lord Cameron. On the granting of a commission and diligence after the record has closed but where the cause has been appointed to the Procedure Roll, see *Graham Builders Merchants Ltd v. The Royal Bank of Scotland plc* 1992 S.C.L.R. 402; *Bank of East Asia Ltd v. Shepherd and Wedderburn, W.S.* 1994 S.C.L.R. 526. The grounds on which the commission will be granted at any time before the record has closed are the same as in *Boyle*, above: *Moore*, above: it must be shown that the documents are necessary for the purpose of enabling a party to make more pointed or more specific what is already averred or to enable him to make adequate and specific replies to his opponent's averments; in short "what he must show is that the documents sought to be recovered are required to serve the purposes of the pleadings as those pleadings stand at the time the diligence is sought": *Moore*, above, per Lord Cameron at p. 131. S. 1(2) has not inverted the onus on the party seeking to establish that the commission and diligence should be granted: *Civil Service Building Society v. MacDougall* 1988 S.C. 58; and see note 35.2.6.

In the Cullen *Review of Outer House Business* in December 1995, it was recommended that there should be no difference between the test for recovery applied before the closing of the record and the test applied after the record has closed, subject to a proviso that the court may refuse to allow recovery where it is related to amendments in respect of which there is an unresolved dispute as to whether probation should be allowed. This is similar to the position adopted by Lord Grieve in *McGown v. Erskine* 1987 S.L.T.(Notes) 4 but not followed by the Inner House in *Moore*, above and *Civil Service Building Society*, above. No rule has been promulgated to alter the common law in the hope that the judicial climate will change.

There is a divergence of opinion about the time when recovery of documents may be allowed on the strength of averments in a minute of amendment. Some clerks and judges take the view that a commission and diligence may be granted when the minute of amendment is allowed to be received, while others take the view that the commission and diligence may only be granted when the record (or other pleadings) are amended in terms of the minute of amendment. The latter view may be based on the principle that until the record is amended the averments in the minute do not form part of the pleadings. In theory the averments might be adjusted out, the minute not insisted in or the amendment of the record not allowed (e.g. it is at the motion to amend the record that normally the issue of amendment after expiry of a limitation or prescriptive period is determined: *Greenhorn v. J. Smart & Co. (Contractors) Ltd* 1979 S.C. 427, 432). No such purist view is taken about a commission and diligence sought on the basis of adjustments prior to a record closing. It may be that a distinction is to be made between, on the one hand, a commission and diligence to enable a party to make more specific certain averments or to answer calls and, on the other hand, a commission and diligence to prepare for the proof. This distinction has been made with respect to recovery of documents sought before the record has closed (or proof allowed), the former being allowed and the latter not: see *Boyle v. Glasgow Royal Infirmary and Associated Hospitals* 1969 S.C. 72 and note 35.2.4 above.

There must be a specification of the documents sought which is intimated to every other party and, where necessary, the Lord Advocate or Advocate General (see note 35.2.14): r. 35.2(2) and (3).

ORDERS UNDER S.1 OF THE ADMINISTRATION OF JUSTICE (SCOTLAND) ACT 1972.

35.2.6   Under s.1(1) of the Act of 1972 orders may be sought (for a commission and diligence) for the inspection, photographing, preservation, custody and detention of documents and other property and for their production and recovery, the taking of samples or the carrying out of experiments (even if this involves destruction). The court may also order any person (not just a party) to disclose any information he has about the identity of any person who appears to the court to be a person who might be a witness in any existing civil proceedings: Act of 1972, s. 1(1A) inserted by the Law Reform (Miscellaneous Provisions) (Scotland) Act 1985, s. 19 (for information about possible witnesses or defenders in proceedings which are likely to be brought, see Chap. 64): for a recent unsuccessful attempt under s. 1(1A) of the Act of 1972, see *Pearson v. Educational Institute of Scotland* 1997 S.C. 245. These provisions do not affect the law and practice about privilege or witnesses and havers, confidentiality or public interest, and s. 47 of the Crown Proceedings Act 1947 (recovery of documents in possession of the Crown) applies: Act of 1972, s. 1(4). The privilege against self-incrimination cannot be claimed in respect of certain proceedings under s. 1(1) of the Act of 1972 for infringement relating to intellectual property: see note 35.2.7(6).

Section 1(1A) of the Act of 1972 cannot be used simply to get an order for the disclosure of the identity of witnesses in an action early unless there are circumstances which in justice required that the ordinary rule in P.N. No. 8 of 1994 (exchange of list of witnesses 28 days before proof) should yield in favour of early disclosure: *Boyce v. Cape Contracts Ltd* , 1998 S.L.T. 889; *Moffat v. News Group Newspapers Ltd* (O.H.) 19th June 1999, unreported (1999 G.W.D. 24-1126).

An order may be sought at any time after the cause has commenced (i.e. the action has been served or the first order in a petition has been granted) unless there is special reason why the application should not be granted: Act of 1972, s. 1(2)(a). This provision was designed to overrule the common law practice (see note 35.2.5) that a commission and diligence was rarely granted before the record was closed. In *Baxter v. Lothian Health Board* 1976 S.L.T.(Notes) 37 Lord Dunpark said that s. 1(2)(a) of the Act of 1972 meant that the common law test applied so that a person seeking an order before the closed record had to show cause why recovery should be allowed although even if a prima facie case was made out there may yet be a special reason for refusing it. In *McGown v. Erskine* 1987 S.L.T.(Notes) 4 Lord Grieve held that if it was in the interests of justice to grant the motion it should be granted unless there were special reasons for refusing it. The decision of the Inner House in *Moore v. Greater Glasgow Health Board,* 1978 S.C. 123 (in which *Baxter,* and *McGown,* above were cited but not referred to in the judgments) indicates that the former view prevails, and this was confirmed in *Civil Service Building Society v. MacDougall* 1988 S.C. 58: on *Moore,* see note 35.2.5.

In the Cullen *Review of Outer House Business* in December 1995, it was recommended that there should be no difference between the test for recovery applied before the closing of the record and the test applied after the record has closed, subject to a proviso that the court may refuse to allow recovery where it is related to amendments in respect of which there is an unresolved dispute as to whether probation should be allowed. This is similar to the position adopted by Lord Grieve in *McGown v. Erskine,* above, but not followed by the Inner House in *Moore,* above and *Civil Service Building Society,* above. No rule has been promulgated to alter the common law in the hope that the judicial climate will change.

There must be a specification of the documents or property sought which must be intimated to any third party haver as well as the other parties and, where necessary, the Lord Advocate (see note 35.2.14): r. 35.2(2) and (3).

The optional procedure for serving the order for recovery of documents to obtain voluntary production does not apply: r. 35.3(1).

A defender contesting jurisdiction may not obtain an order for inspection under s. 1 of the Act of 1972 before the plea of no jurisdiction has been repelled: *M. T. Group v. James Howden & Co. Ltd* 1993 S.L.T. 409.

MEDICAL EXAMINATION AND BLOOD TESTS.

35.2.6A   Medical examinations are usually arranged by agreement between parties in actions of damages for personal injuries. The court may order a pursuer to be medically examined in such an action: *Junner v. North British Railway Co.* (1877) 4 R. 686.

Such an examination might extend to a psychological examination as distinct from a physical one (*McLaren v. Remploy Ltd* 1996 S.L.T. 382 per Lord Macfadyen as a preliminary view) but may not extend to examination by a person without any medical or professional qualification (*Mearns v. Smedvig Ltd* 1999 S.C. 243). The court may have to consider whether an examination may be made a condition of pursuing a claim where there is a refusal to undergo it; the test is whether the refusal prevents the just determination of the cause: *Mearns,* above, at p. 249E per Lord Eassie. In *McMurray v. Safeway Stores plc* , 2000 S.L.T. 1033, Lady Paton held that the defender had to demonstrate the appropriate validation of the system of tests by a physiotherapist in a physical evaluation company; and since tests would be painful and it was questionable whether confidentiality would be maintained, the pursuer's opposition to the test was reasonable.

An order may not be made in respect of a witness, and evidence sought to be adduced which cannot be tested by the other party without obtaining a medical examination to which there is no consent will be excluded: *Davidson v. Davidson* (1860) 22 D. 749. A party cannot, at common law, be ordered to undertake an examination because if he refused he could, in theory, be imprisoned for contempt: *Whitehall v. Whitehall* 1958 S.C. 252, 258 per L.J.-C. Thomson. In practice, therefore, only an adverse inference may be drawn (*Docherty v. McGlynn* 1983 S.C. 202, 214, per Lord Cameron).

An adult may consent to a blood test; but he cannot be compelled to provide a blood sample: *Torrie v. Turner* 1990 S.L.T. 718. Under s. 6 of the Law Reform (Parent and Child) (Scotland) Act 1986 (as amended by s. 70(3) of the Law Reform (Miscellaneous Provisions) (Scotland) Act 1990) consent to a blood test or to the taking of other body fluids or tissue of a child under 16 for evidence relating to the determination of parentage in civil proceedings may be given, but cannot be compelled to be given, by his guardian or the person having custody or care and control of the child or, where the child cannot give consent, by the court. By s. 70 of the 1990 Act a party to any civil proceedings may be requested to give a sample of blood, other body fluid or tissue for analysis or to consent to the taking of such a sample from a child in relation to whom he has power to give consent, and where that party refuses or fails to do so an adverse inference may be drawn.

A curator ad litem cannot consent to the taking of blood samples from his ward: *Docherty*, above. This rule is unaffected by s. 70 of the 1990 Act: *Cameron v. Carr's curator ad litem* 1998 S.L.T.(Sh.Ct) 22.

CONFIDENTIALITY OR PRIVILEGE.

Certain communications are recognised to be confidential and privileged.

35.2.7

(1) Solicitor and client.

The general rule is that communications between solicitor and client for professional purposes are confidential and cannot be recovered. There are exceptions where fraud or other illegality is alleged against a party in relation to a transaction in which the solicitor was concerned (*Micosta S.A. v. Shetland Islands Council* 1983 S.L.T. 483), where the very existence of the solicitor and client relationship is in issue or where the communication is the subject-matter of the cause for which it is sought to be recovered (*Kid v. Bunyan* (1842) 5 D. 193) or where solicitor and client are involved in a transaction to derive benefit for a client from his knowledge of fraud by another (*Conoco (U.K.) Ltd v. The Commercial Law Practice* , 1997 S.L.T. 372). The client may waive the privilege for a series of communications but not for an isolated document in a series: *Wylie v. Wylie* 1967 S.L.T.(Notes) 9. There is no rule that there is no confidentiality in the identity of a client or that by waiving confidentiality in relation to the contents of a letter the client has waived it in relation to his identity: *Conoco (U.K.) Ltd*, above. Under s. 1 of the Evidence (Scotland) Act 1852, where a party adduces his agent (solicitor) as a witness on any matter which he could not otherwise competently be led, that party cannot object on the ground of confidentiality to any question on a matter pertinent to the issue. See also *Narden Services Ltd v Inverness Retail and Business Park Ltd*, 2008 S.C. 335, p. 338, para. [11]; Lord Reed in *R (on the application of Prudential plc) v Special Commissioner of Income Tax* [2013] 2 A.C.185, paras. 103–108 ; Lord Rodger of Earlsferry in *Three Rivers District Council v Governor and Company of the Bank of England (No.6)* [2005] 1 A.C. 610, para. 50.

In *Whitehouse v Lord Advocate*, 2019 S.L.T. 573 (OH), it was held that the privilege could extend to the Lord Advocate as client and advice from a legally qualified member of COPFS or an advocate-depute.

(2) Solicitor and solicitor.

Communications between solicitors with a view to achieving settlement of litigation are confidential and not recoverable: *Fyfe v. Miller* (1835) 13 S. 809. Stating that a communication is "without prejudice", however, will not make it privileged (*Burns v. Burns* 1964 S.L.T.(Sh.Ct.) 21); and a statement of fact is not protected from use as an admission because the words "without prejudice" have been used: *Watson-Towers Ltd v. McPhail* 1986 S.L.T. 617; *Daks Simpson Group plc v. Kuiper* , 1994 S.L.T. 689.

(3) Communications post litem motam.

Documents prepared for the purposes or in anticipation of the litigation are confidential and as a general rule are not recoverable: *Anderson v. St Andrew's Ambulance Association* 1942 S.C. 555; *Young v. National Coal Board* 1957 S.C. 99. The question of whether a report is one prepared *post litem motam* requires the court to make a judgment as to whether or not the document has been prepared in anticipation of litigation or in response to a development in litigation already raised; and it is not appropriate to take a broad brush approach to the issue based on the interests of justice or fairness: *Hepburn v. Scottish Power Plc.* 1997 S.L.T. 859. Precognitions obtained by the Crown for a criminal prosecution are not recoverable: see *B v. Burns* , 1993 S.C. 232; and *Strain v. Premier Custodial Group Ltd* , 2007 S.L.T. 262. In *Komori v. Tayside Health Board* , 2010 S.L.T. 387 (OH), an action for damages for medical negligence, the pursuer sought recovery of hospital records held by the defender in relation to an investigation into a complaint she made to the Scottish Public Services Ombudsman before she took legal action. It was held that documents in the investigation of the complaint were prepared to respond to the complaint and not with a view to preparation of the defender's case; and it could not be said that litigation was apparent, threatened, mooted, or that parties were at arms length or obviously going to be, or that the defender was investigating the accident for its own purposes.

Accordingly, reports of accidents are generally excluded. The reason is that after an accident each party must be able to investigate free from the risk of having to reveal his information to the other side: *Johnstone v. National Coal Board* 1968 S.C. 128.

(a)   An exception to this general rule is that a report by an employee, present at the time of the accident, to his employer is not confidential (it is a *de recenti* statement or a spontaneous report on a matter of fact) and may be recovered by the opponent: *Young,* above. Photographs fall into the same category as reports: *More v. Brown & Root Wimpey Highland Fabricators Ltd* 1983 S.L.T. 669 (in which the general rule and its only exception were reaffirmed). An employer's accident book is not recoverable unless an entry in it comes within the exception: *Dobbie v. Forth Ports Authority* 1974 S.C. 40. A medical report instructed for the purposes of the litigation is not recoverable: *Teece v. Ayrshire & Arran Health Board* 1990 S.L.T. 512. Reports of a receiver or liquidator on the conduct of directors prepared under s. 7(3) of the Company Directors Disqualification Act 1986 are not recoverable: *Secretary of State for Trade and Industry v. Houston* 1995 S.L.T. 196.

Reports prepared to ascertain and present facts (scientifically and objectively) rather than with an aim to litigation are, on the other hand, recoverable: *Waddington v. Buchan Poultry Products Ltd* 1961 S.L.T. 428; *Marks & Spencer Ltd v. British Gas Corporation* 1983 S.L.T. 196.

(b)   The only other exception is where an examination undertaken in anticipation or in development of a party's case destroys or materially alters the subject-matter with the result that the person in possession of the report of the examination is in a position of knowledge about the cause and circumstances of the incident which the other party is unable to acquire: *Black v. Bairds & Dalmellington* 1939 S.C. 472. A report may contain observations of the fact as well as expressions of opinion; and there may be circumstances in which an opinion as to the cause of an accident may be difficult to disentangle from observations of fact; in such a case a commissioner should be appointed to take exception from the report: *Hepburn v. Scottish Power plc.* 1997 S.L.T. 859, 864H.

Confidentiality does not cease on completion of the case for which the report was prepared: *Hunter v. Douglas Reyburn & Co. Ltd* 1993 S.L.T. 637; and see *Ward v. Marine Harvest Ltd* 1997 S.L.T. 469.

(4)   Public policy (public interest immunity).

The only situation in which a document or other property may be withheld on the ground of public policy or public interest is where the interest is a national one put forward by the Crown: *Higgins v. Burton* 1968 S.L.T.(Notes) 52. The view that the law of Scotland does not recognise the concept of public interest immunity beyond that of Crown privilege, and does not divide confidentiality into public interest immunity and private confidentiality, was confirmed in *Parks v. Tayside R.C.* 1989 S.L.T. 345, 348A–348F per Lord Sutherland. See note 35.2.8 on Crown privilege or immunity.

(5)   Spouses.

Communications between spouses are confidential and one is not a competent or compellable witness against the other (Evidence (Scotland) Act 1853, s. 3) except where the cause is concerned with their conduct towards each other, e.g. in a divorce (*MacKay v. MacKay* 1946 S.C. 78). The privilege subsists after death or divorce: Dickson on *Evidence,* para. 1660.

(6)   Self-incrimination of haver.

As a general rule a document or other property which would render the haver liable to prosecution because it is self-incriminating is privileged. There is an exception. The privilege against self-incrimination cannot be claimed in respect of proceedings under s. 1(1) of the Act of 1972 for infringement, to obtain disclosure of information about infringement, or to prevent any apprehended infringement, of intellectual property rights or passing off: Law Reform (Miscellaneous Provisions) (Scotland) Act 1985, s. 15.

(7)   Clergy, doctors and journalists.

It is sometimes said that communications to such persons are confidential. This is true in a popular but not a legal sense. Confidentiality does not appear to attach to communications to clergy. It does not attach to communications to doctors or journalists. The ordinary rule excluding recovery in relation to a medical report made in connection with the litigation would, however, apply to a doctor.

(8)   Communications made as a matter of duty.

"A communication honestly made upon any subject in which a person has an interest, social or moral, or in reference to which he has a duty, is privileged if made to a person having a corresponding interest or duty.": *James v. Baird* 1916 S.C. 510, 517 per L.P. Strathclyde. For a recent example of this type of privilege, see *Pearson v. Educational Institute of Scotland* , 1997 S.C. 245.

Waiver of confidentiality will not necessarily result from documents being referred to in open court by the party entitled to the privilege; it depends on the purpose and whether there was publication of the contents: *Barclay v. Morris* , 1998 S.C. 74. See also *Duke of Argyll v. Duchess of Argyll* , 1962 S.C.(H.L.) 88 (admission on record of specific entries in diaries not waiver of whole contents); and *Cunningham v. The Scotsman Publications Ltd* , 1987 S.C. 107.

Where confidentiality is claimed the documents or property, where practicable, are sealed in an enclosed packet and a motion has to be enrolled to have the packet opened up or such recovery allowed: r. 35.8.

On waiver, in the context of confidentiality, see *Scottish Lion Insurance Co v Goodrich Corp* 2011 S.C .534 (Extra Div.) *per* Lord Reed, para. [43] *et seq*).

CROWN PRIVILEGE OR IMMUNITY.

Commission and diligence may be granted for recovery, etc., of documents or property in the posses- **35.2.8** sion of the Crown, whether or not a party, subject to two provisos, (i) a document or property may be withheld on the ground that its disclosure would be injurious to the public interest and (ii) the existence of a document or property shall not be disclosed if in the opinion of a Minister of the Crown it would be injurious to the public interest to disclose the existence of it: Crown Proceedings Act 1947, s. 47; Act of 1972, s. 1(4). The first proviso relates to a particular document and the second to a class. The court has, however, an inherent power to overrule an objection by the Crown which is preserved by s. 47 of the 1947 Act. The test to be applied is whether the public interest in the administration of justice not being frustrated outweighs the objection: *Glasgow Corporation v. Central Land Board* 1956 S.C.(H.L.) 1 confirming the law of Scotland recognised in *Sheridan v. Peel* 1907 S.C. 577, 580 per L.P. Dunedin; *Henderson v. McGowan* 1916 S.C. 821, 826 per L.P. Strathclyde. It is based on the ground that the fair administration of justice between subject and subject and between the subject and the Crown is a public interest of a high order, and that its protection is in the care of the courts: *Glasgow Corporation*, above, per Viscount Normand at pp. 12–13. Where objection is taken to a class of documents the court can take into account not only the interests of the applicant but also the interests of the public as a whole: *Friel, Petr.* 1981 S.C. 1.

The court is bound to accept the assertion of the Crown that there is an aspect of public policy to protect: *Admiralty v. Aberdeen Steam Trawling and Fishing Co. Ltd* 1909 S.C. 335; *Friel*, above; *AB v. Glasgow and West of Scotland Blood Transfusion Service* 1993 S.L.T. 36.

Where public interest immunity is claimed in respect of the whole or part of a document, the starting point is that the redacted passages are relevant and there is no onus on the party seeking it to show why they should recover the full version; the decision on whether the document or redacted passages should be recovered is for the court to decide after balancing the competing interests of the party seeking the relevant material and of the public in maintaining the confidentiality of that material; and that cannot be done without the Lord Ordinary looking at the document: where the holder of the document objects to producing it on the ground of confidentiality, it is the duty of the judge to read it and decide whether disclosure of the contents is necessary for the fair disposal of the cause: *Somerville v. The Scottish Ministers* , 2008 S.C. (H.L.) 45, in particular Lord Rodger of Earlsferry at paras. [155]–[156]. And see *Science Research Council v. Nassé* [1980] A.C. 1028; *Air Canada v. Secretary of State for Trade (No. 2)* [1983] 2 A.C. 394.

Immunity does not apply to documents or property which do not come into the possession of a servant or agent of the Crown in the ordinary course of his official duties: *Whitehall v. Whitehall* 1957 S.C. 30. Immunity only arises where the public interest is a national one: *Higgins v. Burton* 1968 S.L.T. (Notes) 52; *Parks v. Tayside R.C.* 1989 S.L.T. 345, 348A–F per Lord Sutherland.

"MOTION".

For motions, see Chap. 23. **35.2.9**

"SPECIFICATION".

A specification consisting of numbered paragraphs or "calls" of the documents, property or informa- **35.2.10** tion sought to be recovered (or as the case may be) must be lodged with the motion to grant the order. Calls should be framed with reference to the issues of fact on which the documents etc. are supposed to have a bearing (*Paterson v. Paterson* 1919 1 S.L.T. 12) and the averments in the pleadings. The names of persons thought to be in possession of documents, property or information do not require to be stated in the specification.

Where it is sought to recover information from a document which may contain matters not relevant to the pleadings, the words "in order that excerpts may be taken therefrom at the sight of the commissioner of all entries showing or tending to show (*the information relevant to the matters averred)*" are used. It is customary to insert a final call in these terms: "Failing principals, drafts, copies or duplicates of the above or any of them".

Deletions may be required or the specification otherwise adjusted when the motion is heard. The interlocutor should record what calls or parts of calls were allowed or refused where the whole of the specification is not granted.

A specification for the recovery of documents at common law is intimated to every other party and, where necessary, the Lord Advocate or Advocate General (see note 35.2.14); a specification for an order under s. 1 of the Act of 1972 is also intimated to any third party haver: r. 35.2(3).

The specification is lodged in process as a step of process: see r. 4.4 and r. 1.3(1) (definition of "step of process"). It may be sent by post or fax with the motion: P.N. No. 4 of 1994, paras. 1, 8(2) and 9.

"HAVER".

35.2.11   A haver is a person who has (is believed to have or has had) the document or other property sought. He may be a party or anyone else ("a third party haver").

CAUTION ON APPLICATION BEFORE CALLING.

35.2.12   This is rarely required. On caution generally, see Chap. 33.

"FINAL AND NOT SUBJECT TO REVIEW".

35.2.13   The decision of the Lord Ordinary may not be reclaimed against.

INTIMATION TO AND APPEARANCE OF LORD ADVOCATE OR ADVOCATE GENERAL.

35.2.14   This must be done where recovery is sought of a document belonging to or in possession of the Crown: *Sheridan v. Peel* 1907 S.C. 577, 580 per L.P. Dunedin; *Henderson v. McGowan* 1916 S.C. 821, 825 per L.P. Strathclyde; *Whitehall v. Whitehall* 1957 S.C. 30, 42 per Lord Sorn. This used to apply also to records of an NHS hospital: *Glacken v. National Coal Board* 1951 S.C. 82; but the practice of intimating to the Lord Advocate, deriving from a P.N. in 1950, is now no longer necessary in relation to the recovery of medical records: P.N. No. 2 of 2006. Care should be taken about whether a document relates to a "reserved matter", in which case intimation is to the Advocate General; or a "developed matter", in which case intimation is to the Lord Advocate. The provision for intimation to both in case of doubt avoids a difficulty when intimation has been on the wrong law officer. When intimation has been made the back of the specification should be marked (docquetted) with the words "Intimated to Lord Advocate [*or Advocate General as the case may be*]".

The Lord Advocate may appear or be represented at any motion under this rule: r. 35.2(6). No mention is made of appearance by the Advocate General; but if he has an interest, he would hardly be denied a hearing.

CAVEATS.

35.2.15   A caveat may not be lodged against an order under s. 1 of the Act of 1972: r. 5.1(c).

BANKERS' BOOKS.

35.2.16   A commission and diligence may be sought to recover bank books although it is often possible to agree excerpts with the bank and the opponent. Certain statutory provisions should be noted.

A copy of any document purporting to be authenticated by a person responsible for making the copy shall, unless the court otherwise directs, be deemed a true copy and treated as if it were the document itself, and ss. 3–5 of the Bankers' Books Evidence Act 1879 do not apply: Civil Evidence (Scotland) Act 1988, s. 6. A document may be taken to form part of the record of a business or undertaking if certified as such by a docquet signed by a officer of the business, and a statement contained in the certified document may be received in evidence without being spoken to by a witness: 1988 Act, s. 5. The evidence of an officer of a business that a statement is not contained in the records of the business is admissible as evidence of that fact, whether or not the records have been produced, and such evidence may be given by affidavit: 1988 Act, s. 6. On receiving affidavits in evidence, see r. 36.8.

Where a bank is not a party it cannot be compelled to produce books the contents of which can be proved under the 1879 Act or the 1988 Act: 1879 Act, s. 6 as amended by the 1988 Act, s. 7(4).

S.7 of 1879 Act contains provisions for the court to order, in any legal proceedings, the inspection and taking of copies of entries in banker's books, the order being served three clear days before it is to be obtempered unless the court otherwise directs. The grounds on which, and the time at which, an order may be made are probably the same as for recovery of documents at common law or under s. 1 of the Act of 1972. "Bank" means an institution authorised under the Banking Act 1987 or a municipal bank, a building society, National Savings Bank or the Post Office: 1987 Act, s. 9.

RECLAIMING.

35.2.17   A motion for an order under r. 35.2 may be reclaimed against with leave within 14 days after the date of the interlocutor: r. 38.3(5).

CONTEMPT.

35.2.18   A party who seeks to enforce an order for recovery of documents may be met with refusal or obstruction and tempted to lodge a minute for contempt. Regard should be had to the factors mentioned in paras [31] and [32] in *Sovereign Dimensional Survey Ltd v. Cooper*, 2009 S.C. 382 (Extra Div.).

Optional procedure before executing commission and diligence

35.3.—[1](1)[2] Subject to rule 35.3A (optional procedure where there is a party litigant), this rule applies where a party has obtained a commission and diligence for the recovery of a document on an application made under rule 35.2(1)(a).

(2) Such a party may, at any time before executing the commission and diligence against a haver, serve on the haver an order in Form 35.3-A (in this rule referred to as "the order").

(3) The order and a copy of the specification referred to in rule 35.2(2), as approved by the court, shall be served on the haver or his known agent and shall be complied with by the haver in the manner and within the period specified in the order.

(4) Not later than the day after the day on which the order, and any document recovered, is received from a haver by the party who obtained the order, that party—

    (a) shall give written intimation of that fact in Form 35.3-B to the Deputy Principal Clerk and every other party; and

    (b) shall—

        (i) if the document has been sent by post, send a written receipt for the document in Form 35.3-C to the haver; or

        (ii) if the document has been delivered by hand, give a written receipt in Form 35.3-C to the person delivering the document.

(5) Where the party who has recovered any such document does not lodge in it process within 14 days of receipt of it, he shall—

    (a) forthwith give written intimation to every other party that that party may borrow, inspect or copy the document within 14 days after the date of that intimation; and

    (b) in so doing, identify the document.

(6) Where any party, who has obtained any such document under paragraph (5), wishes to lodge the document in process, he shall—

    (a) lodge the document within 14 days after receipt of it; and

    (b) at the same time, send a written receipt for the document in Form 35.3-D to the party who obtained the order.

(7) Where—

    (a) no party wishes to lodge or borrow any such document under paragraph (5), the document shall be returned to the haver by the party who obtained the order within 14 days after the expiry of the period specified in subparagraph (a) of that paragraph; or

    (b) any such document has been uplifted by another party under paragraph (5) and that party does not wish to lodge it in process, the document shall be returned to the haver by that party within 21 days after the date of receipt of it by him.

(8) Any such document lodged in process shall be returned to the haver by the party lodging it within 14 days after the expiry of any period allowed for appeal or reclaiming or, where an appeal or reclaiming motion has been marked, from the disposal of any such appeal or reclaiming motion.

---

[1] R. 35.3 substituted by S.I. 1996 No. 2168 (effective 23rd September 1996).
[2] As amended by the Act of Sederunt (Rules of the Court of Session, Ordinary Cause Rules and Summary Cause Rules Amendment) (Miscellaneous) 2014 (SSI 2014/152) r.2 (effective 7th July, 2014).

(9)   If any party fails to return any such document as provided for in paragraph (7) or (8), the haver shall be entitled to apply by motion (whether or not the cause is in dependence) for an order that the document he returned to him and for the expenses occasioned by that motion.

(10)   The party holding any such document (being the party who last issued a receipt for it) shall be responsible for its safekeeping during the period that the document is in his custody or control.

(11)   If the party who served the order is not satisfied that—

(a)   full compliance has been made with the order, or

(b)   adequate reasons for non-compliance have been given,

he may execute the commission and diligence under rule 35.4.

(12)   Where an extract from a book of any description (whether the extract is certified or not) is produced under the order, the court may, on the motion of the party who served the order, direct that that party shall be allowed to inspect the book and take copies of any entries falling within the specification.

(13)   Where any question of confidentiality arises in relation to a book directed to be inspected under paragraph (12), the inspection shall be made, and any copies shall be taken, at the sight of the commissioner appointed in the interlocutor granting the commission and diligence.

(14)   The court may, on cause shown, order the production of any book (not being a banker's book or book of public record) containing entries falling under a specification, notwithstanding the production of a certified extract from that book.

Deriv. R.C.S. 1965, r. 96(a) to (f)

OPTIONAL PROCEDURE BEFORE EXECUTING COMMISSION AND DILIGENCE.

35.3.1   The Cullen *Review of Business of the Outer House of the Court of Session* in December 1995 recommended that a procedure should be devised for documents recovered under a commission and diligence to be sent by the haver directly to the party who obtained the order rather than to the Deputy Principal Clerk of Session, and made available to all parties as soon as possible. A working group was set up to devise such a procedure, now enacted in substance by the A.S. (R.C.S.A. No. 4) (Miscellaneous) 1996 [S.I. 1996 No. 2168]. The group foresaw difficulties in the case of documents recovered where there was a party litigant in the process or in respect of which confidentiality was claimed: a separate procedure for such situations is provided in r. 35.3A.

The procedure is available for recovery of documents at common law except where one of the parties is a party litigant or confidentiality is claimed: r. 35.3(1). The order in Form 35.3 and the specification as approved by the court is served on the haver or his known agent (on which, see definition in r. 1.3(1)). The form specifies seven days as the period within which the order must be obtempered. The haver must complete the certificate in the order stating what documents are produced, that he has no such documents, that such documents are in existence but not in his possession or that he knows of the existence of no such documents. If confidentiality is claimed the documents should be put in a sealed packet: r. 35.8.

The documents and the order duly certified are sent by the haver to the party who obtained the order, who informs the Deputy Principal Clerk and every other party of their receipt. The party who recovered the documents must lodge them in process within 14 days or give written intimation to every other party that he may borrow, inspect or copy them within 14 days.

"COMMISSION AND DILIGENCE".

35.3.2   See note 35.2.2.

"DOCUMENT".

35.3.3   See note 35.2.3.

"SERVE".

35.3.4   For methods, see Chap. 16, Pt. I.

"HAVER".

35.3.5   See note 35.2.11.

"WRITTEN INTIMATION".

35.3.6   For methods, see r. 16.9.

"EXTRACT FROM A BOOK OF ANY DESCRIPTION".

The provision in r. 35.3(9) is required because there will be no commissioner who can inspect the books and make the necessary excerpts at this stage. A difficulty arises, however, in granting such a motion as a party obtaining the order may have access to material he ought not to see, and accordingly r. 35.3(10) provides for the commissioner appointed in the original interlocutor granting the commission and diligence to deal with this. **35.3.7**

"CONFIDENTIALITY".

On the meaning of confidentiality, see note 35.2.7. Where confidentiality is claimed, r.35.8 applies, the document must be put in a sealed packet and a motion must be enrolled by the party seeking to open it which is intimated to the haver concerned. **35.3.8**

PRODUCTION OF ORIGINAL BOOKS NOTWITHSTANDING PRODUCTION OF EXTRACT.

Ss. 5 and 6 of the Civil Evidence (Scotland) Act 1988 provide for production as evidence of copies of business records and other documents. The court retains a power under the optional procedure (because the originals will not normally have been inspected by the party seeking recovery or by a commissioner) to order production of the original documents. There are exceptions in relation to bankers' books and public records. **35.3.9**

In relation to bankers' books the exception was no doubt made because the Bankers' Books Evidence Act 1879 was introduced in the interests of bankers to prevent interference with their business and to facilitate the giving in evidence of information from their books. Ss. 3–5 of the 1879 Act have been superseded by rules of evidence of general application in ss. 5 and 6 of the 1988 Act. See further, note 35.2.16.

In relation to public records, see r. 35.9.

LODGE IN PROCESS.

On lodging documents recovered in process, see r. 4.5 (productions). **35.3.10**

Optional procedure where there is a party litigant

35.3A.—[1](1)[2] This rule applies where any of the parties to the action is a party litigant. **35.3A**

(2) *[As repealed by the Act of Sederunt (Rules of the Court of Session, Ordinary Cause Rules and Summary Cause Rules Amendment) (Miscellaneous) 2014 (SSI 2014/152) r.2 (effective 7th July, 2014).]*

(3) The party who has obtained a commission and diligence for the recovery of a document on an application made under rule 35.2(1)(a) may, at any time before executing it against a haver, serve on the haver an order in Form 35.3A-A (in this rule referred to as "the order").

(4) The order and a copy of the specification referred to in rule 35.2(2), as approved by the court, shall be served on the haver or his known agent and shall be complied with by the haver in the manner and within the period specified in the order.

(5) Not later than the day after the date on which the order, and any document recovered, is received from a haver by the Deputy Principal Clerk, he shall give written intimation of that fact to each party.

(6) No party, other than the party who served the order, may uplift any such document until after the expiry of 7 days after the date of intimation under paragraph (5).

(7) Where the party who served the order fails to uplift any such document within 7 days after the date of intimation under paragraph (5), the Deputy Principal Clerk shall give written intimation of that failure to every other party.

(8) Where no party has uplifted any such document within 14 days after the date of intimation under paragraph (7), the Deputy Principal Clerk shall return it to the haver who delivered it to him.

---

[1] R. 35.3A inserted by S.I. 1996 No. 2168 (effective 23rd September 1996).

[2] As amended by the Act of Sederunt (Rules of the Court of Session, Ordinary Cause Rules and Summary Cause Rules Amendment) (Miscellaneous) 2014 (SSI 2014/152) r.2 (effective 7th July, 2014).

(9)   Where a party who has uplifted any such document does not wish to lodge it, he shall return it to the Deputy Principal Clerk who shall—

(a)   give written intimation of the return of the document to every other party; and

(b)   if no other party uplifts the document within 14 days after the date of intimation, return it to the haver.

(10)   Any such document lodged in process shall be returned to the haver by the party lodging it within 14 days after the expiry of any period allowed for appeal or reclaiming or, where an appeal or reclaiming motion has been marked, from the disposal of any such appeal or reclaiming motion.

(11)   If any party fails to return any such document as provided for in paragraph (9) or (10), the haver shall be entitled to apply by motion (whether or not the cause is in dependence) for an order that the document be returned to him and for the expenses occasioned by that motion.

(12)   The party holdings any such document (being the party who last issued a receipt for it) shall be responsible for its safekeeping during the period that the document is in his custody or control.

(13)   If the party who served the order is not satisfied than—

(a)   full compliance has been made with the order, or

(b)   adequate reasons for non-compliance have been given, he may execute the commission and diligence under rule 35.4.

(14)   Where an extract from a book of any description (whether the extract is certified or not) is produced under the order, the court may, on the motion of the party who served the order, direct that that party shall be allowed to inspect the book and take copies of any entries falling within the specification.

(15)   Where any question of confidentiality arises in relation to a book directed to be inspected under paragraph (14), the inspection shall be made, and any copies shall be taken, at the sight of the commissioner appointed in the interlocutor granting the commission and diligence.

(16)   The court may, on cause shown, order the production of any book (not being a banker's book or book of public record) containing entries falling under a specification, notwithstanding the production of a certified extract from that book.

GENERAL NOTE.

35.3A.1   This rule was inserted by A.S. (R.C.S.A. No. 4) (Miscellaneous) 1996 [S.I. 1996 No. 2168] following recommendations of the Cullen *Review of Business of the Outer House of the Court of Session* in December 1995 and a working group, in relation to a new procedure for documents recovered under the optional procedure under r. 35.3 to be sent directly to the party obtaining the order rather than to the Deputy Principal Clerk. That new procedure in r. 35.3 does not apply where one of the parties is a party litigant or where confidentiality is claimed. The procedure for these exceptions is that of the former r. 35.3—i.e. the haver sends the documents to the Deputy Principal Clerk.

"CONFIDENTIALITY".

35.3A.2   On the meaning of confidentiality, see note 35.2.7. Where confidentiality is claimed, r.35.8 applies, the document must be put in a sealed packet and a motion must be enrolled by the party seeking to open it which is intimated to the haver concerned.

"DOCUMENT".

35.3A.3   See note 35.2.3.

"COMMISSION AND DILIGENCE".

35.3A.4   See note 35.2.2.

"SERVE".

35.3A.5   For methods, see Chap. 16, Pt. I.

"HAVER".

35.3A.6   See note 35.2.11.

"WRITTEN INTIMATION".

For methods, see r. 16.9.

"LODGED IN PROCESS".

See r. 4.5.

"EXTRACT FROM A BOOK OF ANY DESCRIPTION".

See note 35.3.7.

PRODUCTION OF ORIGINAL BOOKS NOTWITHSTANDING PRODUCTION OF EXTRACT.

See note 35.3.9.

35.3A.7

35.3A.8

35.3A.9

35.3A.10

Execution of commission and diligence for recovery of documents

35.4.—(1) The party who seeks to execute a commission and diligence for recovery of a document obtained on an application under rule 35.2(1)(a) shall—

35.4

(a) provide the commissioner with a copy of the specification, a copy of the pleadings (including any adjustments and amendments) and a certified copy of the interlocutor of his appointment;

(b) fix a diet for the execution of the commission in consultation with every other party;

(c) instruct the clerk and any shorthand writer; and

(d) be responsible, in the first instance, for the fees of the commissioner, his clerk and any shorthand writer.

(2) The interlocutor granting such a commission and diligence shall be sufficient authority for citing a haver to appear before the commissioner.

(3) A haver shall be cited to appear at a commission for the recovery of documents by service on him of a citation in Form 35.4-A—

(a) by registered post or the first class recorded delivery service; or

(b) personally, by messenger-at-arms.

(4) A certificate of citation of a haver—

(a) under paragraph (3)(a) shall be in Form 35.4-B; and

(b) under paragraph (3)(b) shall be in Form 35.4-C.

(5) There shall be served on the haver with the citation a copy of the specification and, where necessary for a proper understanding of the specification, a copy of the pleadings (including any adjustments and amendments).

(6) The agent for a party, or a party litigant, as the case may be, shall be personally liable, in the first instance, for the fees and expenses of a haver cited to appear at a commission for that party.

(7) The parties and the haver shall be entitled to be represented by counsel or other person having a right of audience, or an agent, at the execution of the commission.

(8) At the commission, the commissioner shall—

(a) administer the oath *de fideli administratione* to the clerk and shorthand writer appointed for the commission; and

(b) administer to the haver the oath in Form 35.4-D, or, where the haver elects to affirm, the affirmation in Form 35.4-E.

(9) The report of the execution of the commission and diligence, any document recovered and an inventory of that document, shall be sent by the commissioner to the Deputy Principal Clerk.

(10) Not later than the day after the date on which such a report, any document recovered and an inventory of that document are received by the Deputy Principal Clerk, he shall give written intimation to the parties that he has received them.

(11)   No party, other than the party who served the order, may uplift such a document until after the expiry of 7 days after the date of intimation under paragraph (10).

(12)[1]   Where the party who served the order fails to uplift such a document within 7 days after the date of intimation under paragraph (10), the Deputy Principal Clerk shall give written intimation of that failure to every other party.

(13)   Where no party has uplifted such a document within 14 days after the date of intimation under paragraph (12), the Deputy Principal Clerk shall return it to the haver.

(14)   Where a party who has uplifted such a document does not wish to lodge it, he shall return it to the Deputy Principal Clerk who shall—

(a)   give written intimation of the return of the document to every other party; and

(b)   if no other party uplifts the document within 14 days of the date of intimation, return it to the haver.

Deriv. R.C.S. 1965, r. 97

"COMMISSION AND DILIGENCE".

35.4.1   See note 35.2.2.

"DOCUMENT".

35.4.2   See note 35.2.3.

"COMMISSIONER".

35.4.3   The commissioner is appointed and named in the interlocutor granting the commission and diligence. If the original appointee has to be replaced before the commission this change may be done by the clerk of court after consultation with the judge.

The commissioner is usually a member of the Bar.

"CERTIFIED COPY OF THE INTERLOCUTOR".

35.4.4   The copy is prepared by the party and is stamped, dated, certified a true copy and signed by the clerk of session at the public counter of the appropriate department.

"INSTRUCT THE CLERK AND SHORTHAND WRITER".

35.4.5   The clerk and shorthand writer are usually the same person.

RESPONSIBILITY FOR FEES OF COMMISSIONER, CLERK AND SHORTHAND WRITER.

35.4.6   The party obtaining the commission and diligence is responsible in the first instance for the fees of the commissioner, clerk and shorthand writer and must pay them: r. 35.4(1)(d). On expenses, see note 35.4.17.

"HAVER".

35.4.7   See note 35.2.11.

SERVICE OF CITATION ON HAVER.

35.4.8   Service of the citation, specification and any pleadings is by registered or first class recorded delivery post (see r. 16.4) or personally by messenger-at-arms (see r. 16.3). A citation furth of Scotland cannot be enforced. Resort can be made to letters of request: see r. 35.15. On failure of a haver to attend a commission, see note 35.4.13.

RESPONSIBILITY FOR FEES AND EXPENSES OF HAVER.

35.4.9   The agent for the party, or the party litigant, obtaining the commission and diligence is responsible in the first instance for the fees and expenses of the haver: r. 35.4(6). The haver is entitled to an attendance fee at the commission and a fee for searching for the documents, subject to taxation, but not for copying when the call is merely to produce: *Forsyth v. Pringle Taylor & Lamond Lawson* (1906) 14 S.L.T. 658; *Mackinnon v. Guildford* (1894) 2 S.L.T. 309.

---

[1] R. 35.4(12) amended by S.I 1994 No. 2901 (minor correction).

See r. 1.3(1) (definitions of "counsel", "other person having a right of audience" and "agent") and note 1.3.4. It is suggested by Maclaren that the expense of counsel is not usually allowed at a commission for examination of a haver unless there are questions of nicety: Maclaren on *Expenses*, p. 449.

35.4.10

THE COMMISSION.

The purpose of the commission is to achieve the handing over of documents or to ascertain where they are or what has happened to them: see *Sommervell v. Sommervell* (1900) 8 S.L.T. 84. The commission is under the charge of the commissioner. The commissioner puts the clerk and shorthand writer on oath to "faithfully discharge the duties of clerk and shorthand writer at this commission" and administers the oath or affirmation to the haver: r. 35.4(8). The party seeking recovery asks questions first after any introduction by the commissioner.

35.4.11

The haver may be asked: (1) If he has the document. (2) If he has had the document in his possession at any time. (3) If he no longer has the document, (*a*) if he knows or suspects where it is and (*b*) who has or may have it. (4) If the document has or has not ever existed. (5) If the document has been destroyed. (6) If the document has been destroyed, (*a*) when and where it was destroyed and (*b*) by whom. The haver may not be asked about the merits of the cause or about the terms of a document. See generally, Maclaren on *Court of Session Practice*, p. 1079. The haver need not answer any question which may incriminate him except in respect of proceedings under s. 1(1) of the Act of 1972 for infringement, to obtain disclosure of information about infringement, or to prevent any apprehended infringement, of intellectual property rights or passing off: Law Reform (Miscellaneous Provisions) (Scotland) Act 1985, s. 15.

Whoever represents the haver and any other party at the commission may then ask questions to achieve a full and fair disclosure: *Dunlop's Trs. v. Lord Belhaven* (1852) 14 D. 825.

Objections to questions should as a general rule be dealt with by the commissioner. Where objection relates to confidentiality the proper course is to repel the objection and allow the document to be recovered subject to competency and relevancy; the document is sealed up by the commissioner and parties can argue the point before the court on a motion to open up the sealed packet. Other matters of difficulty the commissioner may prefer to leave to the court to decide, in which case he repels the objection under reservation of competency and relevancy; and the document is sealed up to await the decision of the court on a motion to open up the packet.

Where a document is produced which should be, but is not, subject to a restriction in the call for excerpting at the sight of the commissioner, it may be agreed at the commission that this in fact be done. A document subject to excerpting in a call may be agreed to be handed over in its entirety without excerpting. Where there is a call for excerpting the haver is obliged only to produce the document and not to excerpt the material himself: *Forsyth v. Pringle Taylor & Lamond Lawson* (1906) 14 S.L.T. 658. Excerpting is done by the commissioner and his clerk.

The commissioner may seek or may be given authority by the court to have the assistance of a qualified person in looking at documents and excerpting entries and to give him advice in determining what documents fall within a call: *Argyllshire Weavers Ltd v. A. Macauley (Tweeds) Ltd* 1962 S.L.T. (Notes) 96; *Santa Fe International Corporation v. Napier Shipping S.A.* 1985 S.L.T. 430.

Where a haver refuses to produce a document the commissioner has no power to order production, the commission has to be adjourned and the commissioner will usually report to the court. On the motion of the party whose commission it is, the court may, after hearing parties and the haver (see e.g. *Montgomerie v. A. B.* (1845) 7 D. 553; *Train & McIntyre Ltd v. Forbes* 1925 S.L.T. 286), order production. A failure to produce thereafter renders the haver liable to penalty for contempt of court (letters of second diligence are inappropriate: *National Exchange Co. v. Drew and Dick* (1858) 20 D. 837). An alternative is for the haver to be cited to appear at the proof to produce the document.

At the end of the diet of commission the commission may be closed or, if all the documents sought are not recovered, it may be adjourned. If there is no adjournment, although not all the documents are recovered, and the commission is closed, a further commission and diligence has to be sought from the court.

For failure of haver to appear at a commission, see note 35.4.13.

COMMISSIONS FURTH OF SCOTLAND.

Commissions may be taken outside Scotland on an interlocutor granting a commission and diligence where the foreign country does not object and the haver is willing. Where either is not the case an application will have to be made by minute for a letter of request: see r. 35.15. But note the provisions in the Hague Convention on the Taking of Evidence Abroad in Civil or Commercial Matters, 18th March 1970 (Cmnd. 6727 (1977)) for the taking of evidence by diplomatic or consular officials, or by a commissioner, and the powers of compulsion they may be able to seek: see further note 35.15.2.

35.4.12

FAILURE OF HAVER TO APPEAR AT COMMISSION.

If a haver in Scotland fails to appear at a commission in Scotland the modern practice is to adjourn the commission (the commissioner will report) and for the party whose commission it is to enrol a motion for warrant to messengers-at-arms to apprehend the haver and bring him to the adjourned diet. The historical practice of obtaining letters of second diligence (in effect having the same result) is no longer followed.

35.4.13

Where the commission in the UK is furth of Scotland, resort may be had to letters of request under the Evidence (Proceedings in Other Jurisdictions) Act 1975: see note 35.15.3. Where the commission is furth of the UK, resort may be had to the Hague Convention on the Taking of Evidence in Civil or Commercial Matters, 18th March 1970 (Cmnd. 6727 (1977)) under which powers of compulsion may be exercised under letters of request by the convention country or may be applied for by diplomatic or consular officials or a commissioner in certain convention countries: see note 35.15.2.

REPORT OF COMMISSION.

35.4.14   The report (or interim report) of a commission (adjourned or closed) includes a transcript of the deposition of the haver, the documents recovered and those sealed up, and an inventory of those documents: for form of report, see Maclaren on *Court of Session Practice*, p. 1081. The report is signed by the commissioner and sent (or delivered: r. 1.3(1) (definition of "send") to the Deputy Principal Clerk: r. 35.4(8).

UPLIFTING DOCUMENTS RECOVERED.

35.4.15   The Deputy Principal Clerk intimates to parties that he has received the report and any documents recovered; and during the first seven days after such intimation only the party whose commission it was may uplift the documents, failing which the Deputy Principal Clerk intimates that failure to every other party who have seven days after that to uplift them: r. 35.4(10) and (11). If the documents are not uplifted 14 days after that the documents are returned to the haver: r. 35.4(12).

"WRITTEN INTIMATION".

35.4.16   For methods, see r. 16.9.

EXPENSES.

35.4.17   Expenses are in the cause (i.e. expenses follow success) if the documents recovered are lodged as productions, unless some other order has been made: *Mackie & Stark v. Cruickshank* (1896) 4 S.L.T. 84. It is suggested by Maclaren that the expense of counsel is not usually allowed at a commission for examination of a haver unless there are questions of nicety: Maclaren on *Expenses*, p. 449.

Execution of orders for production or recovery of documents or other property under section 1(1) of the Act of 1972

35.5   **35.5.**—(1) An order under section 1(1) of the Act of 1972 for the production or recovery of a document or other property shall grant a commission and diligence for the production or recovery of that document or other property.

(2) Rule 35.3 (optional procedure before executing commission and diligence) and rule 35.4 (execution of commission and diligence for recovery of documents) shall apply to an order to which paragraph (1) applies as they apply to a commission and diligence for the recovery of a document.

GENERAL NOTE.

35.5.1   See rr. 35.3 and 35.4 and notes.

Execution of orders for inspection etc. of documents or other property under section 1(1) of the Act of 1972

35.6   **35.6.**—(1) An order under section 1(1) of the Act of 1972 for the inspection or photographing of a document or other property, the taking of samples or the carrying out of any experiment thereon or therewith, shall authorise and appoint a specified person to photograph, inspect, take samples of, or carry out any experiment with or on, any such document or other property, as the case may be, subject to such conditions, if any, as the court thinks fit.

(2) A certified copy of the interlocutor granting such an order shall be sufficient authority for the person specified to execute the order.

(3) When such an order is executed, the party who obtained the order shall serve on the haver a certified copy of the interlocutor granting it, a copy of the specification and, where necessary for a proper understanding of the specification, a copy of the pleadings (including any adjustments and amendments).

GENERAL NOTE.

35.6.1   The person carrying out the inspection etc. must be named in the interlocutor and a certified copy of the interlocutor, the specification and any necessary pleadings served on the haver.

Execution of orders for preservation etc. of documents or other property under section 1(1) of the Act of 1972

35.7.—(1) An order under section 1(1) of the Act of 1972 for the preservation, custody and detention of a document or other property shall grant a commission and diligence for the detention and custody of that document or other property.

(2) The party who has obtained an order under paragraph (1) shall—

(a)

provide the commissioner with a copy of the specification, a copy of the pleadings (including any adjustments and amendments) and a certified copy of the interlocutor of his appointment;

(b) be responsible for the fees of the commissioner and his clerk; and

(c) serve a copy of the order on the haver.

(3) The report of the execution of the commission and diligence, any document or other property taken by the commissioner and an inventory of such property, shall be sent by the commissioner to the Deputy Principal Clerk for the further order of the court.

GENERAL NOTE.

The commissioner appointed will be named in the interlocutor granting the commission and diligence. The interlocutor granting the order must be served on the haver:r. 35.7(2)(c).

RESPONSIBILITY FOR FEES OF COMMISSIONER AND CLERK.

See r. 35.4.6.

"FURTHER ORDER OF THE COURT".

Where a document or other property has been recovered at common law or under s. 1 of the Act of 1982 and it is subsequently sought to use it for the purposes of foreign proceedings, it is not necessary to present a petition under s. 1 of the Evidence (Proceedings in Other Jurisdictions) Act 1975 or s. 1 of the Act of 1972 as extended by s. 28 of the C.J.J.A. 1982 or by S.I. 1997 No. 2780. The application for such permission, which is in the court's power to grant, may be made in the process in which the evidence was recovered. The better practice is to proceed by minute rather than by motion. See *Iomega Corporation v. Myrica (U.K.) Ltd* 1998 S.C. 636 (First Div.).

Confidentiality

35.8.—(1) Where confidentiality is claimed for any document or other property sought to be recovered under any of the following rules, such document or other property shall, where practicable, be enclosed in a sealed packet:

rule 35.3 (optional procedure before executing commission and diligence),

[1]rule 35.3A (optional procedure where there is a party litigant),

rule 35.4 (execution of commission and diligence for recovery of documents),

rule 35.5 (execution of orders for production or recovery of documents or other property under section 1(1) of the Act of 1972),

rule 35.7 (execution of orders for preservation etc. of documents or other property under section 1(1) of the Act of 1972).

(2) A motion to have such a sealed packet opened up or such recovery allowed may be made by—

(a) the party who obtained the commission and diligence; or

(b) any other party after the date of intimation by the Deputy Principal Clerk under rule 35.3(5) or 35.4(12) (intimation of failure to uplift documents).

(3) In addition to complying with rule 23.3 (intimation of motions), the party enrolling such a motion shall intimate the terms of the motion to the person claiming confidentiality by registered post or the first class recorded delivery service.

35.7

35.7.1

35.7.2

35.7.3

35.8

---

[1] As amended by the Act of Sederunt (Rules of the Court of Session, Ordinary Cause Rules and Summary Cause Rules Amendment) (Miscellaneous) 2014 (SSI 2014/152) r.2 (effective 7th July, 2014).

(4) The person claiming confidentiality may oppose a motion made under paragraph (2).

Deriv. R.C.S. 1965, r. 98

"CONFIDENTIALITY".

35.8.1 On the meaning of confidentiality, see note 35.2.7.

"MOTION".

35.8.2 For motions, see Chap. 23. The person claiming confidentiality must have the motion to open up the packet or allow the recovery intimated to him so that he may appear and oppose it: r. 35.8(4).

OPENING THE SEALED PACKET.

35.8.3 The haver, or commissioner, seals up the documents and delivers or sends them to the DPCS who informs the parties (r. 35.3A(5)). By virtue of r. 35.3A(7), the party seeking the document has seven days (any other party has 14 days) to enrol a motion to open the sealed packet. The motion, made under r. 35.8(2), must be intimated to the haver so that he may oppose it if he wishes under r. 35.8(4).

The question of legal privilege or confidentiality will be determined (if necessary by the judge examining the documents) at such a hearing, at which all relevant parties may be represented (including the haver): see *Narden Services Ltd v. Inverness retail and Business Park Ltd* , 2008 S.C. 335 (Extra Div.); and see *McCowan v. Wright* , (1852) 15 D. 229 and *Santa Fe International Corporation v. Napier Shipping SA* , 1985 S.L.T. 430 (O.H.).

Warrants for production of original documents from public records

35.9 **35.9.**—(1) Where a party seeks to obtain from the keeper of any public record production of the original of any register or deed in his custody for the purposes of a cause, he shall apply to the court by motion.

(2) Written intimation of a motion under paragraph (1) shall be given to the keeper of the public record concerned at least two days before the motion is enrolled.

(3) Where it appears to the court that it is necessary for the ends of justice that a motion under this rule should be granted, authority shall be given to such keeper, on production of a certified copy of the interlocutor granting the motion, to produce or exhibit, as the case may be, the original register or deed to the court.

(4) The expense of the production or exhibition of such an original register or deed shall be met, in the first instance, by the party who applied by motion under paragraph (1).

Deriv. R.C.S. 1965, r. 103(a) to (c)

GENERAL NOTE.

35.9.1 The original of any register or deed in the custody of the keeper of a public record may not be recovered by commission and diligence. Extracts are usually sufficient: see Registration Act 1617, Titles to Land Consolidation (Scotland) Act 1868, s. 142 and Conveyancing and Feudal Reform (Scotland) Act 1970, s. 45 (extracts of Register of Sasines); Writs Execution (Scotland) Act 1877, s. 5 (extracts of the Books of Council and Session). If an original is required the keeper of the record will be ordered to bring it to court and one of his officials will do so, but it will remain in his custody.

"PUBLIC RECORD".

35.9.2 This term is not statutorily defined. It obviously extends to the public records kept by the Keeper of the Records of Scotland, the registers kept by the Keeper of the Registers of Scotland, the records of the Court of the Lord Lyon King of Arms, the registers of births, marriages and deaths kept by the Registrar General for Scotland, and deeds registered in sheriff court books and other sheriff court records (other than processes: for which see r. 35.10) before transfer to the Keeper of the Records (not sooner than 25 years: Public Records (Scotland) Act 1937, s. 2(1)). On the sheriff court records transferred to the Keeper of the Records, see the Preservation of Sheriff Court Records Regulations 1969, Sched. 2 [S.I. 1969 No. 1756].

This rule does not apply to processes in the custody of the Keeper of the Records (Court of Session processes after five years (r. 9.1(2)) and sheriff court processes after 25 years (see paragraph above)) or processes of inferior courts not in the custody of the Keeper of the Records. Recovery of such processes for use in another cause is governed by r. 35.10. A process of the Court of Session in the custody of the Keeper of the Records which is not a finally extracted process may be transmitted back to the court under r. 9.2 to be looked at or for something to be done in it; and r. 35.9 does not apply.

An order for production of a public record for evidence in foreign proceedings may be made under s. 1 of the Evidence (Proceedings in Other Jurisdictions) Act 1975 (formerly R.C.S. 1965, r. 103(d)).

"MOTION".

For motions, see Chap. 23. The Keeper of the Records must have two days' written intimation (see r. 16.9) of the motion.

35.9.3

EXPENSES.

Fees may be due for inspection, searches, extracts, copyings and attendance at court: see e.g. Sheriff Court Fees Order 1985 [S.I. 1985 No. 827], Act of Sederunt (Fees in the Scottish Record Office) 1990 [S.I. 1990 No. 44], Fees in the Registers of Scotland Order 1991 [S.I. 1991 No. 2093].

35.9.4

Warrants for transmission of processes

35.10.—(1) A party who seeks to lodge in process any process in the custody of the Keeper of the Records, or any process depending or which depended in any inferior court in Scotland, may apply by motion to the court for a warrant to authorise and direct the Keeper of the Records or the clerk of the inferior court, as the case may be, on production of a certified copy of the interlocutor granting the motion, to transmit that process to the Deputy Principal Clerk.

35.10

(2) A party who enrols a motion under paragraph (1) shall give written intimation of the motion to the Keeper of the Records or the clerk of the inferior court, as the case may be, at least two days before the motion is enrolled.

(3) The Deputy Principal Clerk shall grant a receipt for any process transmitted to him under an order made under paragraph (1) and lodge it in the process of the cause.

(4) No process transmitted under paragraph (1) may be borrowed.

(5) After a process transmitted under paragraph (1) ceases to be required, the Deputy Principal Clerk shall return it to the Keeper of the Records or the clerk of the inferior court, as the case may be.

Deriv. R.C.S. 1965, r. 104

GENERAL NOTE.

This rule is concerned with processes in one cause in the custody of the Keeper of the Records or an inferior court which are required as evidence in another; a commission and diligence is not competent. The rule applies to processes in the custody of the Keeper of the Records (Court of Session processes after five years (r. 9.1(2)) and sheriff court processes after 25 years (not sooner than 25 years: Public Records (Scotland) Act 1937, s.2(1))) or processes of inferior courts not in the custody of the Keeper of the Records. On the sheriff court records transferred to the Keeper of the Records, see the Preservation of Sheriff Court Records Regulations 1969, Sched. 2 [S.I. 1969 No. 1756].

35.10.1

A process of the Court of Session in the custody of the Keeper of the Records which is not a finally extracted process may be transmitted back to the court under r. 9.2 to be looked at or for something to be done in it; and r. 35.10 does not apply.

"PROCESS".

This means the documents constituting the cause.

35.10.2

"KEEPER OF THE RECORDS".

The Keeper of the Records of Scotland is appointed under the Public Registers and Records (Scotland) Act 1948. Under ss.1 and 2 of the Public Records (Scotland) Act 1937 processes of the Court of Session and the sheriff court are transferred to the custody of the Keeper after a certain passage of time (on which, see note 35.10.1).

35.10.3

"INFERIOR COURT".

This includes the Lyon Court, the sheriff court and the district court.

35.10.4

"MOTION".

For motions, see Chap. 23.

35.10.5

"WRITTEN INTIMATION".

For methods, see r. 16.9.

35.10.6

Commissions for examination of witnesses

35.11.—(1) This rule applies to a commission—

35.11

(a) to take the evidence of a witness on a ground mentioned in section 10(b) of the Act of 1988;

(b) in respect of the evidence of a witness which is in danger of being lost, to take the evidence to lie in retentis; or

(c) on special cause shown, to take the evidence of a witness on a ground other than one mentioned in sub-paragraph (a) or (b).

(2) An application by a party for a commission to examine a witness shall be made by motion; and that party shall specify in the motion the name and address of at least one proposed commissioner for approval and appointment by the court.

(2A)[1] A motion under paragraph (2) may include an application for authority to record the proceedings before the commissioner by video recorder.

(3) Where a motion under paragraph (2) is made in an action before calling of the summons—

(a) the applicant shall give written intimation of the motion to every other person named in the instance; and

(b) the decision of the Lord Ordinary shall be final and not subject to review.

(4) The interlocutor granting such a commission shall be sufficient authority for citing the witness to appear before the commissioner.

(5) A witness shall be cited to give evidence at a commission by service on him of a citation in Form 35.11-A—

(a) by registered post or the first class recorded delivery service; or

(b) personally, by a messenger-at-arms.

(6) The certificate of citation of a witness—

(a) under paragraph (5)(a) shall be in Form 35.11-B; and

(b) under paragraph (5)(b) shall be in Form 35.111-C.

(7) The agent for a party, or a party litigant, as the case may be, shall be personally liable, in the first instance, for the fees and expenses of a witness cited to appear at a commission for that party.

(8) At the commission, the commissioner shall—

(a) administer the oath *de fideli administratione* to the clerk and any shorthand writer appointed for the commission; and

(b) administer to the witness the oath in Form 35.4-D, or, where the witness elects to affirm, the affirmation in Form 35.4-E.

(9) In a cause involving the collision of ships, such an application shall be granted on condition, where necessary, that the applicant shall, at least 24 hours before the evidence is taken, lodge in process a preliminary act which the commissioner shall be entitled to open before the witness is examined.

(10) Where a commission is granted for the examination of a witness, the court may, on the motion of any party and on cause shown, dispense with interrogatories.

Deriv. R.C.S. 1965, rr. 100 and 101

GENERAL NOTE.

35.11.1
Until the middle of the 19th century proof was usually on commission, a practice virtually abolished by s.2 of the Evidence (Scotland) Act 1866. The evidence of witnesses must now usually be heard by the court at a proof or jury trial. There are three exceptions to the modern rule—evidence on commission permitted under s.10 of the C.S.A. 1988, evidence in danger of being lost to lie *in retentis* and evidence on any other ground on special cause shown. The exception in relation to evidence to lie *in retentis* is part of the existing practice of the court preserved by s.10 of the C.S.A. 1988. S.10 of the C.S.A. 1988 re-enacted the first two exceptions which were in s.2 of the 1866 Act. S.10 of the C.S.A. 1988 did not (apparently inadvertently) re-enact a proviso in s.2 of the 1866 Act which preserved the right of the court to grant a commission to take the evidence of a witness according to the existing law and practice on special cause shown or of consent of parties. Although only the proviso in relation to evidence in danger of being

---

[1] R. 35.11(2A) inserted by S.S.I. 2007 No. 282, r. 2 (effective 2nd May 2007).

lost has been preserved it could not have been intended by Parliament in a consolidating statute to deprive the court of a power to grant a commission in other circumstances in which it has even today been used to do, such as where a witness (other than perhaps a crucial witness) is going abroad. The Scottish Law Commission recommendations to the Bill (now the C.S.A. 1988) did not mention repeal of the proviso. The court's power to grant a commission in circumstances other than those referred to in s.10 of the C.S.A. 1988 is preserved in this rule by virtue of the general rule-making power in s.5 of that Act.

S.10 OF THE C.S.A. 1988.

S.10 of the C.S.A. 1988 applies to actions in the Outer House and is applied to petitions by s.25(3), and to the Inner House by s.38, of the C.S.A. 1988. There are two statutory grounds.

35.11.2

(1) Witness resident beyond the jurisdiction of the court.

A commission may be granted and executed where the foreign country does not object and the witness is willing. Where either is not the case an application will have to be made by minute for a letter of request: see r. 35.15. But note the provisions in the Hague Convention on the Taking of Evidence Abroad in Civil or Commercial Matters, 18th March 1970 (Cmnd. 6727 (1977)) for the taking of evidence by diplomatic or consular officials, or by a commissioner, and the powers of compulsion they may be able to seek: see further note 35.12.2.

A motion for such a commission may be refused if the evidence of the witness is of primary importance for the proper determination of the issue between the parties or if the party against whom the witness is to be adduced would be prejudiced by having the evidence taken on commission or non-attendance at a proof would be merely for the convenience of the witness unconnected with any duty incumbent on the witness: *Grant v. Countess of Seafield* 1926 S.C. 274.

(2) Witness unable to attend proof or jury trial by reason of age, infirmity or sickness.

(a)   *Age* The practice is to treat a person who is 70 years old or more as a person whose evidence may be taken on commission: *Wilson v. Young* (1896) 4 S.L.T. 73. A birth certificate should be produced.

(b)   *Infirmity* This means a permanent disability which prevents the witness coming to court. A medical certificate is required.

(c)   *Sickness* This is not limited to such illness as would give rise to a risk that the evidence of the witness may be lost (as that is covered by the common law exception) but includes someone whose illness is such that he cannot come to court. A medical certificate is required. If the witness is an important one the proper course might be to discharge the diet of proof or jury trial; and see *Grant*, above.

EVIDENCE TO LIE IN RETENTIS.

The only ground for taking the evidence of a witness to be retained until the proper time for using it is where evidence is in danger of being lost because a witness is aged or infirm. The matter is in the discretion of the Lord Ordinary. Thus where there were other witnesses who could provide the same evidence the application for a commission was refused: *Dudgeon v. Forbes* (1832) 10 S 810. Even the pursuer's evidence may in appropriate circumstances be taken on commission: *Anderson v. Morrison* (1905) 7 F. 561.

35.11.3

(1) Aged.

The practice is to treat a person who is 70 years old or more as aged even if hale and hearty: *Wilson v. Young* (1896) 4 S.L.T. 73. A birth certificate should be produced.

(2) Infirmity.

This means any illness or disability which gives rise to a risk or danger of the evidence of that witness being lost. A medical certificate is required.

EVIDENCE ON COMMISSION ON SPECIAL CAUSE SHOWN.

The court has for long enough been used to granting commissions to take the evidence of witnesses on grounds other than those mentioned in notes 35.11.2 and 35.11.3. Grounds have included a witness about to go abroad of necessity, e.g. pre-arranged holidays, attending a professional conference, a person in HM Forces called for duty or a merchant seaman called to his ship: see dicta in *Grant v. Countess of Seafield* 1926 S.C. 274 and Tonner, below. A commission may be allowed in the case of *penuria testium* (lack of witnesses): *Maltman's Factor v. Cook* (1867) 5 M. 1076. The court may not grant such a commission where the witness is important or an opponent would be prejudiced (in which case the diet of proof or jury trial would have to be discharged): *Grant v. Countess of Seafield* 1926 S.L.T. 213. A balance has to be struck between the importance of the witness's evidence and the loss or inconvenience which would result if the commission were not granted, and the fact that the motion is unopposed or consented to is a point to be taken into account: *Tonner v. FT Everard & Sons Ltd* 1994 S.C. 593, 599B per L.P. Hope (witness due to go on holiday and another to sit examination during proof).

35.11.4

"MOTION".

35.11.5   For motions, see Chap. 23.

"COMMISSIONER".

35.11.6   Where the commission is on interrogatories the commissioner may be a member of the Bar or, where the witness is remote from Edinburgh, a sheriff or solicitor. Where the commission is an open commission (i.e. interrogatories have been dispensed with) the commissioner will usually be a member of the Bar. Where the commission is furth of the U.K. the commissioner will usually be a member of the Bar, or a lawyer of the country concerned or even a British consular officer (who has power to administer oaths and take affidavits: Commissioners for Oaths Act 1889, s.6). The practice is to specify that "X" whom failing "Y" be nominated and appointed. A Lord Ordinary may be appointed to be the commissioner.

MOTION BEFORE CALLING OF A SUMMONS.

35.11.7   See r. 23.8.

"WRITTEN INTIMATION".

35.11.8   For methods, see r. 16.9.

CITATION OF WITNESS.

35.11.9   Citation is by registered or first class recorded delivery post (see r. 16.4) or personally by messenger-at-arms (see r. 16.3).
    Citation of a witness furth of the U.K. and Ireland cannot be enforced. In the case of citation elsewhere in the U.K. and Ireland, and on failure of a witness to appear at a commission, see note 35.11.12.
    On competence and compellability of witnesses, see note 36.2.8.

RESPONSIBILITY FOR FEES AND EXPENSES OF WITNESS.

35.11.10   The agent for the party, or the party litigant, obtaining the commission is responsible in the first instance for the fees and expenses of the haver: r. 35.11(7). For witnesses' fees, see Chap. II of the Table of Fees in r. 42.16.

THE COMMISSION.

35.11.11   The form of the commission depends on whether the commission is with or without interrogatories: see notes 35.12.5 and 35.13.5.

FAILURE OF WITNESS TO APPEAR AT COMMISSION.

35.11.12   If a witness in Scotland fails to appear at a commission in Scotland the modern practice is to adjourn the commission (the commissioner will report) and for the party whose commission it is to enrol a motion for warrant to messengers-at-arms to apprehend the witness and bring him to the adjourned diet. The historical practice of obtaining letters of second diligence (in effect having the same result) is not usually followed.
    Attendance at a commission in Scotland of a witness who resides in the U.K. furth of Scotland or in Ireland, may be enforced under the Attendance of Witnesses Act 1854 as extended by s.4 of the Evidence (Proceedings in Other Jurisdictions) Act 1975. The 1854 Act applies to Northern Ireland by virtue of the General Adaptation of Enactments (Northern Ireland) Order 1921 [SR & O. 1921/1804] and to the Republic of Ireland by virtue of the Irish Free State (Consequential Adaptation of Enactments) Order 1923 [SR & O. 1923/405] (preserved by the Ireland Act 1949). Under ss.1, 2 and 3 of the 1854 Act the court may order a warrant of citation in special form containing a notice that it is issued by special order of the court, and on proof of service and default of appearance the court may transmit a certificate to the Supreme Court in which jurisdiction the witness resides for that court to punish the witness (but he cannot otherwise be forced to go). The witness must have had tendered to him his attendance money: 1854 Act, s.4. An alternative is to apply for letters of request: see r. 35.15.
    Where the commission is furth of the U.K., resort may be had to the Hague Convention on the Taking of Evidence in Civil or Commercial Matters, 18th March 1970 (Cmnd. 6727 (1977)) under which powers of compulsion may be exercised under letters of request by the convention country or may be applied for by diplomatic or consular officials or a commissioner in certain convention countries: see note 35.15.2.

COLLISION OF SHIPS AND PRELIMINARY ACTS.

35.11.13   A preliminary act is a document setting out certain specified details where an Admiralty action of damages arising out of the collision of ships has been brought: see r. 46.6. A preliminary act may be dispensed with under r. 46.7. It may be required for the purpose of taking evidence on commission and if so must be lodged before the commission where it has not already been lodged.

"DISPENSE WITH INTERROGATORIES".

35.11.14   A commission is on interrogatories unless these are dispensed with: r. 35.11(10). On interrogatories, see note 35.12.1. Interrogatories are not a satisfactory means of obtaining evidence except for straightforward evidence or to save expense where a witness is abroad. But even if dispensation is not opposed, the party seeking the commission must show cause why a commission without interrogatories (an "open commission") is preferable to one with interrogatories: *Venter v. Scottish Legal Aid Board* (below),

153F per L.P. Hope; and Tonner, above, 598D per First Division. The court may be interested in the possible consequences for the case in the light of the various alternatives.

Interrogatories may be dispensed with, e.g. where the witness is in the U.K. (this ground was expressly mentioned in R.C.S. 1965, r. 100(c) but is not excluded because it is not now mentioned) and in *Dexter & Carpenter v. Waugh & Robertson*, 1925 S.C. 28 or where credibility and reliability of the witness is in issue (*Nicolson v. McLachlan and Brown* 1985 S.C.48 (for which interrogatories are a wholly inadequate expedient)). Where the commission is to obtain evidence to lie in retentis on the grounds of illness or age of a witness in Scotland, delay caused by the preparation of interrogatories may make them inappropriate (*McLean and Hope v. Fleming* (1867) 5 M 579, 582 per L.J.-C. Patton).

The matter is in the discretion of the Lord Ordinary: *Dexter & Carpenter v. Waugh & Robertson* 1925 S.C. 28, 32 per Lord Skerrington. *Venter v. Scottish Legal Aid Board* 1993 S.L.T. 147, 153F per L.P. Hope. In the exercise of the discretion the Lord Ordinary will consider the stage which has been reached in the action, the potential consequences of the alternative procedures which may be open and the probable course of events in the future: *Nicolson* (above), 50 per L.J-C. Wheatley.

Where the party seeking a commission without interrogatories (or any other course of action of an unusual nature or involving unusually large expenditure) is legally aided, that party should seek the prior approval of the Legal Aid Board before that course of action is proposed to the court: *Venter v. Scottish Legal Aid Board* 1993 S.L.T. 147,154D per L.P. Hope at p. 154D.

EXPENSES.

Expenses are in the cause (i.e. expenses follow success) if the evidence taken on commission is used at the proof or jury trial. If the witness is subsequently examined at the proof the expenses of the commission may not be allowed unless the expense was incurred on reasonable necessity, a question which is for the Auditor to decide: *Webster & Others v. Simpson's Motors & Others* 1967 S.L.T. 287. Where the party obtaining the commission neither calls the witness nor uses his evidence from a commission at the proof or jury trial the expense of the commission will be disallowed (*Parker v. North British Railway Co*, (1900) 8 S.L.T. 18). If neither proof nor jury trial is eventually allowed then the expenses of the commission will be disallowed unless there was a serious danger of loss of evidence (e.g. where the commission was one for evidence to lie in retentis) or the commission was obtained by a party of consent (*Gilchrist v. National Cash Register Co.*, 1929 S.C. 272, 274 per Lord Sands). **35.11.15**

Commissions on interrogatories

35.12.—(1) Where interrogatories have not been dispensed with, the party who obtained the commission to examine a witness under rule 35.11 shall lodge draft interrogatories to be adjusted at the sight of the clerk of court. **35.12**

(2) Any other party may lodge cross-interrogatories to be adjusted at the sight of the clerk of court.

(3) The interrogatories and any cross-interrogatories, when adjusted, shall be extended and returned to the clerk of court for approval.

(4) The party who has obtained the commission shall—

(a)

provide the commissioner with a copy of the pleadings (including any adjustments and amendments), the approved interrogatories and any cross-interrogatories and a certified copy of the interlocutor of his appointment;

(b) instruct the clerk; and

(c) be responsible, in the first instance, for the fee of the commissioner and his clerk.

(5) The commissioner shall, in consultation with the parties, fix a diet for the execution of the commission to examine the witness.

(6) The executed interrogatories, any document produced by the witness and an inventory of that document, shall be sent by the commissioner to the Deputy Principal Clerk.

(7) Not later than the day after the date on which the executed interrogatories, any document and an inventory of that document, are received by the Deputy Principal Clerk, he shall give written intimation to each party that he has received them.

(8) The party who obtained the commission to examine the witness shall lodge in process—

(a) the report of the commission; and

(b)   the executed interrogatories and any cross-interrogatories.

GENERAL NOTE.

35.12.1   Interrogatories are written numbered questions. They are intimated in draft form to the other parties and lodged in process. Any other party may intimate and lodge draft cross-interrogatories. These may be adjusted at the sight of the clerk of court: see note 35.12.2. Cross-interrogatories cannot be postponed until answers to the interrogatories are lodged: *Charteris v. Charteris* 1967 S.C. 33.

"ADJUSTED AT THE SIGHT OF THE CLERK OF COURT".

35.12.2   This means that the questions are checked by the clerk to see that they are relevant and relate to matters on record. If he has a doubt he consults a judge. Once adjusted the clerk adds the following docquet to the interrogatories:

"Edinburgh, *(date)*. These interrogatories consisting of this and the preceding pages adjusted at my sight.
(Signed), Depute Clerk of Session."

"COMMISSIONER".

35.12.3   See note 35.11.6.

RESPONSIBILITY FOR FEES OF COMMISSIONER AND CLERK.

35.12.4   The party obtaining the commission and diligence is responsible in the first instance for the fees of the commissioner and his clerk and must pay them: r. 35.4(1)(d). On expenses, see note 35.11.15.

THE COMMISSION.

35.12.5   The commissioner puts the clerk on oath to "faithfully discharge the duties of clerk at this commission" and administers the oath or affirmation to the witness: r. 35.11(8). He reads the questions to the witness writing down the answers to each, numbering them in accord with the numbers of the questions. He may put further questions to the witness to add to or explain an answer.
   The commissioner and the witness sign each page of the answers: *Elrick v. Elrick* 1967 S.L.T. (Notes) 68.
   Any report, the executed interrogatories and cross-interrogatories and any document produced are sent or delivered to the Deputy Principal Clerk.

COMMISSIONS FURTH OF SCOTLAND.

35.12.6   Commissions may be taken outside Scotland on an interlocutor granting a commission where the foreign country does not object and the witness is willing. Where either is not the case an application will have to be made by minute for a letter of request: see r. 35.15. But note the provisions in the Hague Convention on the Taking of Evidence Abroad in Civil or Commercial Matters, 18th March 1970 (Cmnd. 6727 (1977)) for the taking of evidence by diplomatic or consular officials, or by a commissioner, and the powers of compulsion they may be able to seek: see further note 35.15.2.

"WRITTEN INTIMATION".

35.12.7   For methods, see r. 16.9.

Commissions without interrogatories

35.13   **35.13.**—(1)   Where interrogatories have been dispensed with, the party who has obtained a commission to examine a witness under rule 35.11 shall—

(a)   provide the commissioner with a copy of the pleadings (including any adjustments and amendments) and a certified copy of the interlocutor of his appointment;

(b)   fix a diet for the execution of the commission in consultation with the commissioner and every other party;

(c)   instruct the clerk and any shorthand writer; and

(d)   be responsible, in the first instance, for the fees of the commissioner, his clerk and any shorthand writer.

(2)   All parties shall be entitled to be present and represented by counsel or other person having a right of audience, or agent, at the execution of the commission.

(3)   The report of the execution of the commission, any document produced by the witness and an inventory of that document, shall be sent by the commissioner to the Deputy Principal Clerk.

(4) Not later than the day after the date on which such a report, any document and an inventory of that document are received by the Deputy Principal Clerk, he shall give written intimation to each party that he has received them.

(5) The party who obtained the commission to examine the witness shall lodge the report in process.

GENERAL NOTE.

A commission without interrogatories is called an open commission. It is conducted according to the normal rules of evidence and procedure.

35.13.1

"COMMISSIONER".

See note 35.11.6.

35.13.2

RESPONSIBILITY FOR FEES OF COMMISSIONER AND CLERK.

See note 35.12.4.

35.13.3

"COUNSEL OR OTHER PERSON HAVING A RIGHT OF AUDIENCE, OR AN AGENT".

See r. 1.3(1) (definitions of "counsel", "other person having a right of audience" and "agent") and note 1.3.4.

35.13.4

THE COMMISSION.

The commissioner puts the clerk and shorthand writer on oath to "faithfully discharge the duties of clerk and shorthand writer at this commission" and administers the oath or affirmation to the witness: r. 35.11(8). The commission is conducted according to the normal rules of evidence with examination-in-chief, cross-examination and re-examination at which the parties may all be present or represented. The commissioner will have to rule on objections but, in cases of difficulty or on request of a party, he may allow evidence subject to competency and relevancy (on which the court will decide at the proof or jury trial).

On competence and compellability of witnesses, see note 36.2.8.

35.13.5

REPORT OF COMMISSION.

The report (or interim report) of a commission (adjourned or closed) includes a transcript of the deposition of the witness, any documents produced and an inventory of those documents: for form of report, see Maclaren on *Court of Session Practice*, p. 1052. The report is signed by the commissioner and sent (or delivered: r. 1.3(1) (definition of "send")) to the Deputy Principal Clerk: r. 35.13(3).

35.13.6

Evidence taken on commission

35.14.—(1) Subject to the following paragraphs of this rule and to all questions of relevancy and admissibility, evidence taken on commission under rule 35.12 or 35.13 may be used as evidence at any proof or jury trial of the cause.

35.14

(2) Any party may object to the use of such evidence at a proof or jury trial; and the objection shall be determined by the court.

(3) Such evidence shall not be used at a proof or jury trial if the witness becomes available to attend the diet of proof or jury trial, as the case may be.

(4) A party may use such evidence in accordance with the preceding paragraphs of this rule notwithstanding that it was obtained at the instance of another party.

Deriv. A.S. 16th February 1841, s. 17

GENERAL NOTE.

The deposition should be made expressly part of the proof. Any party may use the evidence: r. 35.14(4).

35.14.1

Evidence on commission in one action has been allowed in a subsequent action on the same circumstances where the witness had since died: *Hogg v. Frew and Another* 1951 S.L.T. 397. Quaere whether this would be allowed under the terms of r. 35.14(1).

There is no onus on the party tendering the evidence taken on commission to establish that the deponent was unavailable to attend the proof or jury trial: *Boettcher v. Carron Co* (1861) 23 D 322, 325. If the deponent is available to attend the proof or jury trial and gives evidence at that hearing, that evidence will supersede the evidence taken on commission and cannot be used to establish that he made a different statement on a previous occasion: r. 35. 14(3); and Forrests v. Low's Trs., 1907 S.C. 1240.

If the deponent does not give evidence at a proof or jury trial, it is open to the party who did not obtain the evidence on commission to use that evidence. That is the apparent purpose of r. 35.14(4).

Letters of request

35.15   **35.15.**—(1) This rule applies to an application for a letter of request to a court or tribunal outside Scotland to obtain evidence of the kind specified in paragraph (2), being evidence obtainable within the jurisdiction of that court or tribunal, for the purposes of a cause depending before the Court of Session.

(2) An application to which paragraph (1) applies may be made in relation to a request—

    (a)   for the examination of a witness,

    (b)   for the inspection, photographing, preservation, custody, detention, production or recovery of, or the taking of samples of, or the carrying out of any experiment on or with, a document or other property, as the case may be,

    (c)   for the medical examination of any person,

    (d)   for the taking and testing of samples of blood from any person, or

    (e)   for any other order for obtaining evidence,

for which an order could be obtained in the Court of Session.

(3) Such an application shall be made by minute in Form 35.15-A with a proposed letter of request in Form 35.15-B.

(4) It shall be a condition of granting a letter of request that the agent for the applicant, or a party litigant, as the case may be, shall be personally liable, in the first instance, for the whole expenses which may become due and payable in respect of the letter of request to the court or tribunal obtaining the evidence and to any witness or haver who may be examined for the purpose; and he shall consign into court such sum in respect of such expenses as the court thinks fit.

(5) Unless the court or tribunal to which a letter of request is addressed is a court or tribunal in a country or territory—

    (a)   where English is an official language, or

    (b)   in relation to which the Deputy Principal Clerk certifies that no translation is required,

then the applicant shall, before the issue of the letter of request, lodge in process a translation of that letter and any interrogatories and cross-interrogatories into the official language of that court or tribunal.

(6) The letter of request when issued, any interrogatories and cross-interrogatories adjusted as required by rule 35.12 and the translations (if any), shall be forwarded by the Deputy Principal Clerk to such person and in such manner as the Lord President may direct.

Deriv. R.C.S. 1965, r. 102 substituted by S.I. 1976 No. 283

GENERAL NOTE.

35.15.1   This rule applies to the obtaining of evidence for a depending cause in the Court of Session from a witness or haver furth of Scotland; where proceedings are contemplated, letters of request may be sought by petition. There is an international convention (the Hague Convention; on which, see note 35.15.2) which many countries have ratified and to which resort may be had to assist in obtaining such evidence (see note 35.15.2) and, within the UK, resort may be had to the Evidence (Proceedings in Other Jurisdictions) Act 1975 (see note 35.15.3). Letters of request should be used not only in the UK or a Hague Convention country but in any foreign country (whether a Hague Convention country or not) as many such countries will in fact assist. For requests to a court in a Member State of the European Union other than Denmark, see. r. 35.16.

Further information and guidance may be obtained from: Justice Department, Division II, Branch 1, Hayweight House, 23 Lauriston Street, Edinburgh EH3 9DQ, tel. 0131-229 9200; and The Foreign and Commonwealth Office, Nationality and Treaty Department, Clive House, Petty France, London SW1H 9HD, tel. 071-270 4086 or 4087.

THE HAGUE CONVENTION.

35.15.2   The Hague Convention on the Taking of Evidence Abroad in Civil or Commercial Matters, 18th March 1970 (Cmnd.6727 (1977)), provides for letters of request to convention countries seeking the assistance of the judicial authorities of the foreign country to take the evidence of a witness or haver in proceedings which are pending (or contemplated). The Contracting State may use methods of compulsion to assist in obtaining the evidence.

Under the convention two other methods are available. (1) A UK diplomatic officer or consular agent in the country in which he exercises his functions may take the evidence of a UK national in respect of proceedings in the UK and, with the consent of the convention country, a national of that country: Arts. 15 and 16. (2) A commissioner (appointed by the court) may take evidence in the territory of another Contracting State with its consent: Art. 17. The diplomatic officer, consular agent or commissioner may apply to the competent authority of the convention country for assistance to obtain evidence by compulsion if a declaration has been made to that effect: Art. 18. Only Czechoslovakia, Italy and the USA have made such a declaration.

The Hague Convention countries are:

Argentina	Mexico
Australia	Monaco
Barbados	Netherlands
Belarus	Norway
Bulgaria	Poland
Cyprus	Portugal
Czechoslovakia[1]	Russian Federation
Denmark	Singapore
Estonia	South Africa
Finland	Spain
France	Sweden
Germany	Switzerland
Greece	Turkey
Israel	Ukraine
Italy	UK (with extensions)
Latvia	USA (with extensions)
Luxembourg	Venezuala

The UK extensions are to: the Sovereign Base areas of Akrotiri and Dhekelia, the Cayman Islands, Falkland Islands and dependencies, Gibraltar, Hong Kong and the Isle of Man.

The USA extensions are to: Guam, Puerto Rico and the Virgin Islands.

On the Hague Convention countries, see the *Practical Handbook on the Operation of the Hague Convention on the Taking of Evidence Abroad* published for the Permanent Bureau of the Hague Convention on Private International Law published by Maarten Kluwers, Antwerp; *Bowman & Harris* on Multilateral Treaties published by Butterworths; and see the Hague Conventions website: *www.hcch.net.*

The Hague Convention does not state what is a civil or commercial matter. It has been held in England in a case under the Evidence (Proceedings in Other Jurisdictions) Act 1975 that the words "civil or commercial matter" have a wide meaning and include all proceedings other than criminal proceedings (a meaning broader than the same words in the C.J.J.A. 1982): *Re State of Norway's Application (Nos. 1 and 2)* [1990] 1 A.C. 723, 806F per Lord Goff of Chieveley. It was also held in that case that whether proceedings are civil is a matter of law and practice of the requesting court: per Lord Goff of Chieveley at p. 805B.

A requested court can only grant orders it can ordinarily grant. The witness or haver may be legally represented: Art. 20.

A convention country may declare that it will not execute letters of request issued for the purpose of obtaining pre-trial discovery of documents as known in Common Law countries (the UK has made such a declaration).

EVIDENCE (PROCEEDINGS IN OTHER JURISDICTIONS) ACT 1975.

This Act enabled the UK to ratify the Hague Convention on the Taking of Evidence Abroad in Civil or Commercial Matters, 1970 (Cmnd. 6727 (1977)) in 1976. An application may be made to the Court of Session for letters of request to the High Court in England and Wales or Northern Ireland for an order to obtain evidence there provided that the steps taken to obtain it are steps which could be required there: 1975 Act, ss. 1 and 2.

35.15.3

An order may not be made by the requested court which would require a person (*a*) to state what documents relevant to the proceedings to which the application relates are or have been in his possession, custody or power, or (*b*) to produce any documents other than particular documents specified in the order

---

[1] Czechoslovakia is now divided into the Czech and Slovak Republics.

as being documents appearing to the court making the order (the requested court) to be, or to be likely to be, in his possession, custody or power. In England the words "particular documents specified in the order" is given a strict construction. A compendious description of a number of documents is permitted provided that the exact document in each case is clearly indicated, and recovery will be ordered only of documents which the court is satisfied do or did exist: see *Re Westinghouse Uranium Contract* [1978] A.C. 547, 609 and 635; *Re Asbestos Insurance* [1985] 1 W.L.R. 331, 337 and 338 per Lord Fraser of Tullybelton.

"DEPENDING".

35.15.4   A cause is depending from the time it is commenced (i.e. from the time an action is served or a first order in a petition is made) until final decree, whereas a cause is in dependence until final extract. For the meaning of commenced, see note 13.4.4 (action) or 14.6.1 (petition). For the meaning of final decree, see note 4.15.2(2). For the meaning of final extract, see note 7.1.2(2).

ORDERS WHICH MAY BE OBTAINED.

35.15.5   Two conditions must be met: the order must be one which can be obtained (*a*) within the jurisdiction of the requested court and (*b*) from the Court of Session in the cause for which the letters of request are sought.

For the circumstances in which an order may be obtained in the Court of Session:

1. *Examination of witnesses.* See notes 35.11.2–35.11.4. On compellability of witnesses, see 36.2.8.
2. *Recovery of documents.* See note 35.2.5.
3. *Inspecting, photographing, etc., of documents or other property.* See note 35.2.6.
4. *Medical examinations and blood tests.* See note 35.2.6A

"APPLICATION".

35.15.6   The application is by minute in Form 35.15-A and r. 15.1 applies except as to the form. The form of letters of request (Form 35.15-B) is the style in the Hague Convention on the Taking of Evidence Abroad in Civil or Commercial Matters (Cmnd. 6727 (1977)).

The letters of request will be forwarded by the Deputy Principal Clerk to the foreign court (r. 35.15(6)), but not before consignation as required by r. 35.15(4) for the expenses of executing them (for which the agent for the applicant or the party litigant is, in the first instance, liable: r. 35.15(4)). A translation may be required.

FEE.

35.15.7   A court fee for a letter of request is payable. For fee, see Court of Session etc. Fees Order 1997, Table of Fees, Pt I, B, item 11 [S.I. 1997 No. 688, as amended, pp. C 1201 et seq.]. Certain persons are exempt from payment of fees: see 1997 Fees Order, art.5 substituted by S.S.I. 2002 No. 270. A fee exemption certificate must be lodge in process: see P.N. No. 1 of 2002.

Where the applicant is legally represented, the fee may be debited under a credit scheme introduced on 1st April 1976 by P.N. No. 4 of 1976 to the account (if one is kept or permitted) of the agent by the court cashier, and an account will be rendered weekly by the court cashier's office to the agent for all court fees due that week for immediate settlement. Party litigants, and agents not operating the scheme, must pay (by cash, cheque or postal order) on each occasion a fee is due at the time of lodging at the counter at the appropriate department.

Applications for requests that evidence be taken under the Council Regulation

35.16   **35.16.**—[1](1)   In this rule—

"the Council Regulation" means the Council Regulation (EC) No. 1206/2001 of 28 May 2001 on co-operation between the courts of the Member States in the taking of evidence in civil or commercial matters;

"Member State" has the same meaning as in Article 1(3) of the Council Regulation;

"request" means a request to which Article 1(1)(a) of the Council Regulation applies; and

"requested court" has the same meaning as in Article 2(1) of the Council Regulation.

(2)   This rule applies to an application under the Council Regulation for a request to a requested court in a Member State other than the United Kingdom for the purposes of a cause depending before the Court of Session.

---

[1] Inserted by S.S.I. 2004 No.514 (effective 30th November 2004).

(3)   An application to which paragraph (2) applies shall be made by minute in Form 35.16-A with a proposed request in form A (request for the taking of evidence) or form I (request for direct taking of evidence) set out in the Annex to the Council Regulation.

(4)   It shall be a condition of granting an application for a request that the agent for the applicant, or a party litigant, as the case may be, shall be personally liable, in the first instance, for any reimbursement required by the requested court in respect of any fees paid to experts and interpreters and the costs occasioned by the use of any requested special procedure in executing the request for evidence, or the use of requested communications technology at the performance of the taking of evidence; and that he shall consign into court any such sum as is required by the requested court as deposit or advance towards the costs of executing the request.

(5)   Unless the requested court is in a country or territory—

(a)   where English is an official language, or

(b)   in relation to which the Deputy Principal Clerk certifies that no translation is required,

then the applicant shall, before the issue of the request, lodge in process a translation of the request and any interrogatories and cross-interrogatories into the official language of that country or territory.

(6)   Where an application under this rule has been granted, the request shall be forwarded by the Deputy Principal Clerk to—

(a)   the requested court; or

(b)   the central body or competent authority designated by the other Member State to be responsible for taking decisions on requests to take evidence directly.

(7)   The Deputy Principal Clerk shall, as soon as reasonably practicable after receipt of any communication from the requested court, send written intimation of that communication to the parties.

(8)   If a request is made to take the evidence of a witness directly in another Member State, the Deputy Principal Clerk shall intimate to the witness who is to give evidence, a notice in Form 35.16-B and the witness shall return Form 35.16-C to the Deputy Principal Clerk, within 14 days after the date of intimation of the notice.

GENERAL NOTE.

Rule 35.16 was inserted by A.S. (R.C.S. A. No. 6) (Miscellaneous) 2004 [S.S.I. 2004 No. 514].   **35.16.1**

Under Council Regulation (EC) No. 1206/2001 of 28th May 2001 on co-operation between Member States of the EU in the taking of evidence in civil or commercial matters, evidence may be taken in another Member State for proceedings in Scotland. The Council Regulation does not apply to Denmark. The Hague Convention of 18th March 1970 (see note 35.15.2) applies only to 11 Member States of the EU.

"MEMBER STATE".

This means Member State of the EU other than Denmark: Council Regulation, art.1(3).   **35.16.2**

THE COUNCIL REGULATION.

There are a number of points to notice.   **35.16.3**

1.   There is no definition of civil or commercial matter. On the interpretation of this phrase under the Hague Convention, see note 35.15.2.

2.   The request may be made only for use in judicial proceedings commenced or contemplated: art.1(2).

3.   There may be direct transmission between courts.

4.   Member States draw up lists of courts competent to take evidence.

5.   The central body for Scotland for information to courts, and forwarding a request in exceptional circumstances is:- Private International Law Branch, Civil and International Division, Justice Department, St Andrew's House, Regent Road, Edinburgh EH1 3DG; tel. + 44 (0)131-244 4826; fax.+44 (0)131-244 4848.

6.   The request is made in Form A (where evidence is to be taken by the requested court) or Form I (where evidence to be taken by the requesting court) in the Annex to the Regulation, with a translation in the language of the requested court:

    (a)   in a request in Form A—

- it must be executed within 90 days in accordance with the law of the requested State or in accordance with a special procedure of the requesting State, unless incompatible with the law of the requested State: art. 10;
- if provided for by the law of the *requesting* State, the parties and their representatives may be present at the taking of evidence (art. 11) as also may representatives of the requested court (art. 12);
- a person may refuse to give evidence under the law of the requesting or requested court and on grounds in art. 14;

    (b)   a request in Form I—

- is made via the central body or competent authority;
- only if it can be done voluntarily without the need for coercive measures;
- the requested State may assign a court to take part to ensure compliance with art. 17.

"CONSIGN".

35.16.4   For consignation, see r. 33.4 and note 33.4.3.

"LODGE IN PROCESS".

35.16.5   The translation lodged under r. 35.16(5) will be lodged as a step of process (and must therefore be intimated to other parties): rr. 4.4 and 4.6.

"WRITTEN INTIMATION".

35.16.6   For methods, see r. 16.9.

"INTIMATE".

35.16.7   It may have been intended that intimation by the DPCS under r. 35.16(8) would be written intimation under r. 16.9; however, the methods under r. 16.7 have been stipulated.

FEE.

35.16.8   A court fee for a request is payable. For fee, see Court of Session etc. Fees Order 1997, Table of Fees, Pt I, B, item 11 [SI 1997/688 as amended, pp. C1201 et seq.]. Certain persons are exempt from payment of fees: see 1997 Fees Order, art.5 substituted by S.S.I. 2002 No. 270. A fee exemption certificate must be lodged in process: see P.N. No. 1 of 2002.

Where the pursuer is legally represented, the fee may be debited under a credit scheme introduced on 1st April 1976 by P.N. No. 4 of 1976 to the account (if one is kept or permitted) of the pursuer's agent by the court cashier, and an account will be rendered weekly by the court cashier's office to the agent for all court fees due that week for immediate settlement. Party litigants and agents not operating the scheme must pay (by cash, cheque or postal order) on each occasion a fee is due at the time of lodging at the counter at the General Department.

CHAPTER 35A VULNERABLE WITNESSES (SCOTLAND) ACT 2004

Vulnerable Witnesses (Scotland) Act 2004

Interpretation

35A.1.[1] In this Chapter—

"the Act of 2004" means the Vulnerable Witness (Scotland) Act 2004;

"child witness notice" has the meaning given in section 12(2) of the Act of 2004;

"review application" means an application for review of arrangements for vulnerable witnesses pursuant to section 13 of the Act of 2004;

"vulnerable witness application" has the meaning given in section 12(6) of the Act of 2004.

GENERAL NOTE.

The Vulnerable Witnesses (Scotland) Act 2004 is now fully in force. Its application to civil proceedings was fully brought into force on 1st November 2007 by the Vulnerable Witnesses (Scotland) Act (Commencement No.6, Savings and Transitional Provisions) Order 2007 [S.S.I. 2007No.447]. It applies to proceedings where the initiating writ was served on the first person to be served on or after 1st November 2007.

In the case of a child witness, the party intending to cite the child as a witness must lodge a child witness notice setting out any special measures (defined in s.18) or other measures considered most appropriate for taking the child's evidence, or that the child should give evidence without any special measure: 2004 Act, s.12(2). The court must make an order authorising the use of special measures or measures most appropriate for taking the child's evidence, or stating that the child is to give evidence without any special measure: 2004 Act, s.12(1).

In the case of any other vulnerable witness, a party intending to cite a person who is a vulnerable witness to give evidence lodges a vulnerable witness application and the court may make an order authorising the use of special measures or measures most appropriate: 2004 Act, s.12(6).

A vulnerable witness is (a) a child under 16 on the date of commencement (ie when the writ is served on the first person served: s. 11(3)) of the proceedings or (b) where the person is not a child witness, there is a significant risk that the quality of that person's evidence will be diminished by reason of mental disorder within the meaning of s. 328 of the Mental Health (Care and Treatment) (Scotland) Act 2003 or fear or distress in connection with giving evidence in the proceedings: 2004 Act, s. 11(1).

In determining whether a person other than a child witness is vulnerable the court has to take into account the factors in s. 11(2) of the 2004 Act. In addition the court must have regard to a witness's best interests and take account of any views of the witness (in the case of a child, having regard to the child's age and maturity) and, where the witness is a child, any views of the child's parents.

Special measures are (a) evidence on commission under s. 19, (b) live TV link under s. 20, (c) use of screens under s. 21, (d) use of a supporter under s. 22, (e) such other measure as Scottish Ministers may make by SSI (none so far): 2004 Act, s. 18.

Child Witness Notice

35A.2.[2] A child witness notice lodged in accordance with section 12(2) of the Act of 2004 shall be in Form 35A.2.

GENERAL NOTE.

In the case of a child witness, the party intending to cite the child as a witness must lodge a child witness notice setting out any special measures (defined in s.18) or other measures considered most appropriate for taking the child's evidence, or that the child should give evidence without any special measure: 2004 Act, s. 12(2). The court must make an order authorising the use of special measures or measures most appropriate for taking the child's evidence, or stating that the child is to give evidence without any special measure: 2004 Act, s.12(1).

"LODGED IN ACCORDANCE WITH SECTION 12(2)".

Section 12(2) does not in fact provide the mechanism for lodging. That is to be found in Chap. 4 of the R.C.S. 1994.

---

[1] Chap. 35A and r. 35A.1 inserted by S.S.I. 2007 No. 450 (effective 1st November 2007).
[2] R. 35A.2 inserted by S.S.I. 2007 No. 450 (effective 1st November 2007).

Vulnerable Witness Application

35A.3   **35A.3.**[1] A vulnerable witness application lodged in accordance with section 12(6) of the Act of 2004 shall be in Form 35A.3.

GENERAL NOTE.

35A.3.1   In the case of a vulnerable witness other than a child witness, a party intending to cite a person who is a vulnerable witness to give evidence lodges a vulnerable witness application and the court may make an order authorising the use of special measures or measures most appropriate: 2004 Act, s.12(6).

"LODGED IN ACCORDANCE WITH SECTION 12(6)".

35A.3.2   Section 12(6) does not in fact provide the mechanism for lodging. That is to be found in Chap. 4 of the R.C.S. 1994.

Intimation

35A.4   **35A.4.**—[2](1) The party lodging a child witness notice or vulnerable witness application shall intimate a copy of the child witness notice or vulnerable witness application to all the other parties to the proceedings and complete a certificate of intimation.

(2) A certificate of intimation referred to in paragraph (1) shall be in Form 35A.4 and shall be lodged with the child witness notice or vulnerable witness application.

"INTIMATE".

35A.4.1   For methods of intimation, see r. 16.7.

Procedure on lodging child witness notice or vulnerable witness application

35A.5   **35A.5.**—[3](1) On receipt of a child witness notice or vulnerable witness application, the Lord Ordinary may—

    (a) make an order under section 12(1) or (6) of the Act of 2004 without holding a hearing;

    (b) require further information from any of the parties before making any further order;

    (c) fix a date for a hearing of the child witness notice or vulnerable witness application.

(2) The Lord Ordinary may, subject to any statutory time limits, make an order altering the date of the proof or other hearing at which the child or vulnerable witness is to give evidence and make such provision for intimation of such alteration to all parties concerned as he deems appropriate.

(3) An order fixing a hearing for a child witness notice or vulnerable witness application shall be intimated by the Deputy Principal Clerk—

    (a) on the day the order is made; and

    (b) in such manner as may be prescribed by the Lord Ordinary,

to all parties to the proceedings and such other persons as are named in the order where such parties or persons are not present at the time the order is made.

"MAY ... MAKE AN ORDER ALTERING THE DATE OF THE PROOF OR OTHER HEARING".

35A.5.1   It is unthinkable that the court would alter the date of a proof without prior intimation to, or hearing, parties.

Review of arrangements for vulnerable witnesses

35A.6   **35A.6.**—[4](1) A review application shall be in Form 35A.6.

(2) Where the review application is made orally, the Lord Ordinary may dispense with the requirements of paragraph (1).

---

[1] R. 35A.3 inserted by S.S.I. 2007 No. 450 (effective 1st November 2007).
[2] R. 35A.4 inserted by S.S.I. 2007 No. 450 (effective 1st November 2007).
[3] R. 35A.5 inserted by S.S.I. 2007 No. 450 (effective 1st November 2007).
[4] R. 35A.6 inserted by S.S.I. 2007 No. 450 (effective 1st November 2007).

GENERAL NOTE.

Rule 35A.6 provides for an application by a party to review and alter arrangements at any stage for the giving of evidence by a vulnerable witness which is provided for in s. 13 of the 2004 Act.

Chap. 35A make no provision for the court reviewing the arrangements at its own motion as provided for in s. 13 (1)(b) of the 2004 Act. If the court is not seeking to review arrangements in the course of a hearing of some sort (eg. a motion or proof), it will no doubt simply put the case out by order.

35A.6.1

Intimation of review application

35A.7.—[1](1) Where a review application is lodged, the applicant shall intimate a copy of the review application to all other parties to the proceedings and complete a certificate of intimation.

35A.7

(2) A certificate of intimation referred to in paragraph (1) shall be in Form 35A.7 and shall be lodged together with the review application.

"INTIMATE".

For methods of intimation, see r. 16.7.

35A.7.1

Procedure on lodging a review application

35A.8.—[2](1) On receipt of a review application, a Lord Ordinary may—

35A.8

    (a) if he is satisfied that he may properly do so, make an order under section 13(2) of the Act of 2004 without holding a hearing or, if he is not so satisfied, make such an order after giving the parties an opportunity to be heard;

    (b) require of any of the parties further information before making any further order;

    (c) fix a date for a hearing of the review application.

(2) The Lord Ordinary may, subject to any statutory time limits, make an order altering the date of the proof or other hearing at which the child or vulnerable witness is to give evidence and make such provision for intimation of such alteration to all parties concerned as he deems appropriate.

(3) An order fixing a hearing for a review application shall be intimated by the Deputy Principal Clerk—

    (a) on the day the order is made; and

    (b) in such manner as may be prescribed by the Lord Ordinary,

to all parties to the proceedings and such other persons as are named in the order where such parties or persons are not present at the time the order is made.

"MAY ... MAKE AN ORDER ALTERING THE DATE OF THE PROOF OR OTHER HEARING".

It is unthinkable that the court would alter the date of a proof without prior intimation to, or hearing, parties.

35A.8.1

Determination of special measures

35A.9.[3] When making an order under section 12(1) or (6) or 13(2) of the Act of 2004 a Lord Ordinary may, in light thereof, make such further orders as he deems appropriate in all the circumstances.

35A.9

GENERAL NOTE.

This rule is of doubtful validity. In this age of parliamentary micro-management, ss.12 and 13 of the 2004 Act lay down exactly what the court may do.

35A.9.1

Intimation of an order under section 12(1) or (6) or 13(2)

35A.10.[4] An order under section 12(1) or (6) or 13(2) of the Act of 2004 shall be intimated by the Deputy Principal Clerk—

35A.10

---

[1] R. 35A.7 inserted by S.S.I. 2007 No. 450 (effective 1st November 2007).
[2] R. 35A.8 inserted by S.S.I. 2007 No. 450 (effective 1st November 2007).
[3] R. 35A.9 inserted by S.S.I. 2007 No. 450 (effective 1st November 2007).
[4] R. 35A.10 inserted by S.S.I. 2007 No. 450 (effective 1st November 2007).

(a)   on the day the order is made; and

(b)   in such manner as may be prescribed by the Lord Ordinary,

to all parties to the proceedings and such other persons as are named in the order where such parties or persons are not present at the time the order is made.

Taking of evidence by commissioner

35A.11   **35A.11.**—[1](1)   An interlocutor authorising the special measure of taking evidence by a commissioner shall be sufficient authority for the citing the vulnerable witness to appear before the commissioner.

(2)   A vulnerable witness shall be cited to give evidence at a commission by service on him of a citation in Form 35.11-A—

(a)   by registered post or the first class recorded delivery service; or

(b)   personally, by a messenger-at-arms.

(3)   The certificate of citation of a witness—

(a)   under paragraph 2(a) shall be in Form 35.11-B; and

(b)   under paragraph 2(b) shall be in From 35.11-C.

(4)   The agent for a party, or a party litigant, as the case may be, shall be personally liable in the first instance for the fees and expenses of a witness cited to appear at a commission for that party.

(5)   At the commission the commissioner shall—

(a)   administer the oath de fideli administratione to the clerk appointed for the commission; and

(b)   administer to the witness the oath in Form 35.4-D, or where the witness elects to affirm, the affirmation in Form 35.4-E.

(3)   Where a commission is granted as a special measure, the court may, on the motion of any party and on cause shown, dispense with interrogatories.

GENERAL NOTE.

35A.11.1   Evidence on commission is one of the special measures specified in s. 18.

This rule follows that in r. 35.11. It provides for the dispensing of interrogatories on cause shown as in r.35.11(10), on which see note 35.11.4. It was never envisaged that the commission would normally be on interrogatories (and the sheriff court rule in OCR 1993, r. 45.11(3) is the other way around—i.e., that the commission proceeds without interrogatories unless there is cause shown that it should be on interrogatories).

The commission must be video-recorded. Except with leave of the court (not the commissioner), a party may not be present in the room where it takes place but is entitled to watch and hear by suitable means: 2004 Act, s. 19(3). This, for practical reasons, means that a remote child witness suite will have to be used. Leave of the court is provided for in r. 35A.16.

Commission on interrogatories

35A.12   **35A.12.**—[2](1)   Where interrogatories have not been dispensed with, the party citing or intending to cite the vulnerable witness shall lodge draft interrogatories to be adjusted at the sight of the clerk of court.

(2)   Any other party may lodge cross-interrogatories to be adjusted at the sight of the clerk of court.

(3)   The interrogatories and cross-interrogatories, when adjusted, shall be extended and returned to the clerk of court for approval.

(4)   The party who cited the vulnerable witness shall—

(a)   provide the commissioner with a copy of the pleadings (including any adjustments and amendments), the approved interrogatories and any cross-interrogatories and a certified copy of the interlocutor of his appointment;

(b)   instruct the clerk; and

---

[1] R. 35A.11 inserted by S.S.I. 2007 No. 450 (effective 1st November 2007).
[2] R. 35A.12 inserted by S.S.I. 2007 No. 450 (effective 1st November 2007).

    (c)   be responsible in the first instance for the fee of the commissioner and his clerk.

(5)   The commissioner shall, in consultation with the parties, fix a diet for the execution of the commission to examine the witness.

GENERAL NOTE.

This rule follows the form of r. 35.12. See the notes to that rule.   **35A.12.1**

Commission without interrogatories

35A.13.—[1](1)   Where interrogatories have been dispensed with, the party citing or intending to cite the vulnerable witness shall—   **35A.13**

    (a)   provide the commissioner with a copy of the pleadings (including any adjustments and amendments) and a certified copy of the interlocutor of his appointment;

    (b)   fix a diet for the execution of the commission in consultation with the commissioner and every other party;

    (c)   instruct the clerk; and

    (d)   be responsible in the first instance for the fees of the commissioner and his clerk.

(2)   All parties shall be entitled to be represented by counsel or other person having a right of audience, or agent, at the execution of the commission.

GENERAL NOTE.

This rule follows the form of r. 35.12. See the notes to that rule.   **35A.13.1**

Lodging of video record and documents

35A.14.—[2](1)   Where evidence is taken on commission pursuant to an order made under section 12(1) or (6) or 13(2) of the Act of 2004 the commissioner shall lodge the video record of the commission and relevant documents with the Deputy Principal Clerk.   **35A.14**

(2)   Not later than the day after the date on which the video record and any documents are received by the Deputy Principal Clerk, he shall—

    (a)   note—

        (i)   the documents lodged;

        (ii)   by whom they were lodged; and

        (iii)   the date on which they were lodged, and

    (b)   give written intimation of what he has noted to all parties concerned.

Custody of video record and documents

35A.15.—[3](1)   The video record and documents referred to in rule 35A.14 shall, subject to paragraph (2), be kept in the custody of the Deputy Principal Clerk.   **35A.15**

(2)   Where the video record of the evidence of a witness is in the custody of the Deputy Principal Clerk under this rule and where intimation has been given to that effect under rule 35A.14(2), the name and address of that witness and the record of his evidence shall be treated as being in the knowledge of the parties; and no party shall be required, notwithstanding any enactment to the contrary—

    (a)   to include the name of that witness in any list of witnesses; or

    (b)   to include the record of his evidence in any list of productions.

---

[1] R. 35A.13 inserted by S.S.I. 2007 No. 450 (effective 1st November 2007).

[2] R. 35A.14 inserted by S.S.I. 2007 No. 450 (effective 1st November 2007) and as correctly numbered by S.S.I. 2009 No. 450 (effective 25th January 2010).

[3] R. 35A.15 inserted by S.S.I. 2007 No. 450 (effective 1st November 2007).

Application for leave for party to be present at the commission

35A.16

35A.16.[1]   An application for leave for a party to be present in the room where the commission proceedings are taking place shall be by motion.

GENERAL NOTE.

35A.16.1

Under s. 19(3) of the 2004 Act, except with leave of the court (not the commissioner), a party may not be present in the room where it takes place but is entitled to watch and hear by suitable means. This, for practical reasons, means that a remote child witness suite will have to be used.

---

[1] R. 35A.16 inserted by S.S.I. 2007 No. 450 (effective 1st November 2007).

CHAPTER 35B LODGING AUDIO OR AUDIO-VISUAL RECORDINGS OF CHILDREN

Lodging Audio or Audio-visual Recordings of Children

Interpretation

35B.1.[1] In this Chapter, "child" means a person under the age of 16 on the date of commencement of the proceedings and "children" shall be construed accordingly.

35B.1

Lodging an audio or audio-visual recording of a child

35B.2.—[2](1) Where a party seeks to lodge an audio or audio-visual recording of a child as a production, that party must—

35B.2

    (a) ensure that the recording is in a format that can be heard or viewed by means of equipment available in court;

    (b) place the recording together with a copy of the relevant inventory of productions in sealed envelope marked with—

        (i)   the names of the parties to the court action;

        (ii) the case reference number;

        (iii) (where available) the date and time of commencement and of termination of the recording; and

        (iv) the words "recording of a child—confidential".

(2) The sealed envelope must be lodged with the Deputy Principal Clerk.

(3) In the remainder of this Chapter a "recording of a child" means any such recording lodged under this rule.

Separate inventory of productions

35B.3.—[3](1) On each occasion that a recording of a child is lodged, a separate inventory of productions shall be lodged in process.

35B.3

(2) The Deputy Principal Clerk shall mark the date of receipt and the number of the process on the sealed envelope containing the recording.

Custody of a recording of a child

35B.4.—[4](1) A recording of a child—

35B.4

    (a) shall be kept in the custody of the Deputy Principal Clerk; and

    (b) subject to rule 35B.5, will not form a borrowable part of the process.

(2) The envelope containing the audio or audio-visual recording of a child shall only be unsealed with the authority of the court and on such conditions as the court thinks fit (which conditions may relate to listening to or viewing the recording).

Access to a recording of a child

35B.5.—[5](1) An application by a party to gain access to and to listen to or view a recording of a child may be made by motion.

35B.5

(2) The court may refuse such a motion or grant it on such conditions as the court thinks fit, including—

    (a) allowing only such persons as the court may specify to listen to or view the recording;

    (b) specifying the location where such listening or viewing is to take place;

    (c) specifying the date and time when such listening or viewing is to take place;

---

[1] Rule 35B.1 inserted by S.S.I. 2012 No. 275 r. 6(1) (effective 19th November 2012).
[2] Rule 35B.2 inserted by S.S.I. 2012 No. 275 r. 6(1) (effective 19th November 2012).
[3] Rule 35B.3 inserted by S.S.I. 2012 No. 275 r. 6(1) (effective 19th November 2012).
[4] Rule 35B.4 inserted by S.S.I. 2012 No. 275 r. 6(1) (effective 19th November 2012).
[5] Rule 35B.5 inserted by S.S.I. 2012 No. 275 r. 6(1) (effective 19th November 2012).

(d) allowing a copy of the recording to be made (in the same or different format) and arrangements for the safe-keeping and disposal of such copy;

(e) arrangements for the return of the recording and re-sealing of the envelope.

Exceptions

35B.6 **35B.6.**—[1](1) The court may, on the application of a party and on cause shown, disapply the provisions of this Chapter.

(2) An application under paragraph (1) shall be made—

(a) at the time of presenting the recording for lodging;

(b) by letter addressed to the Deputy Principal Clerk stating the grounds on which the application is made.

Application of other rules

35B.7 **35B.7.**[2] The following rules do not apply to an audio or audio-visual recording of a child—

(a) rule 4.5 (productions);

(b) rule 4.11 (documents not to be borrowed); and

(c) rule 4.12 (borrowing and returning documents).

[1] Rule 35B.6 inserted by S.S.I. 2012 No. 275 r. 6(1) (effective 19th November 2012).
[2] Rule 35B.7 inserted by S.S.I. 2012 No. 275 r. 6(1) (effective 19th November 2012).

CHAPTER 36 PROOFS

Hearing parts of proof separately

36.1.—(1) In any cause the court may—

    (a) at its own instance, or

    (b) on the motion of any party,

order that proof on liability or any other specified issue be heard separately from proof on any other issue and determine the order in which the proofs shall be heard.

(2) The court shall pronounce such interlocutor as it thinks fit at the conclusion of the first proof of any cause ordered to be heard in separate parts under paragraph (1).

Deriv. R.C.S. 1965, r. 108

GENERAL NOTE.

The restriction in R.C.S. 1965, r. 108 limiting separation of parts of a proof to an action with pecuniary conclusions and to the merits and quantum has been omitted. It is now possible to separate any issue from any other issues and hear them separately, although in practice the circumstances in which such separation is appropriate may be limited. Obvious examples are (a) separation of proof on liability and quantum and (b) preliminary proofs (on which, see note 22.3.8).

The court will not, however, use its procedures to order issues to be heard separately to assist a party to avoid the consequences of current legislation: *Dyer v. Balfour Beattie Construction (Northern) Ltd* , 10th January 1997 (1997 G.W.D. 5-178) (motion to postpone proof on quantum until changes in rules on deduction of benefits on damages awards refused).

The appropriate stage at which to apply for an order under r. 36.1 is when an order for proof is first made: *BP Exploration Operating Co. Ltd v. Chevron Shipping Co. Ltd (No.2)* , 13th November 2002, 2002 G.W.D. 37-1217 (OH).

Citation of witnesses

36.2.—(1) A witness shall be cited for a proof by service on him of a citation in Form 36.2-A—

    (a) by registered post or the first class recorded delivery service, by the agent for the party on whose behalf he is cited; or

    (b) personally, by a messenger-at-arms.

(2) A certified copy of the interlocutor allowing a proof shall be sufficient warrant to a messenger-at-arms to cite a witness on behalf of a party.

(3) A certificate of citation of a witness—

    (a) under paragraph (1)(a) shall be in Form 36.2-B; and

    (b) under paragraph (1)(b) shall be in Form 36.2-C.

(4) The agent for a party, or a party litigant, as the case may be, shall be personally liable, in the first instance, for the fees and expenses of a witness cited by him to appear at a proof.

(5) Where a party to a cause is a party litigant, he shall—

    (a) not later than 12 weeks before the diet of proof, apply to the court by motion to fix caution for the expenses of witnesses in answering a citation in such sum as the court considers reasonable having regard to the number of witnesses he proposes to cite and the period for which they may be required to attend court; and

    (b) before instructing a messenger-at-arms to cite a witness, find the caution which has been fixed.

(6) A party litigant who does not intend to cite all the witnesses referred to in his application under paragraph (5)(a) may apply by motion for variation of the amount of caution.

Deriv. R.C.S. 1965, r. 106A inserted by S.I. 1984 No. 472 (r. 36.2(2)) and r. 106B inserted by S.I. 1986 No. 1955 (r. 36.2(5))

GENERAL NOTE.

36.2.1   A witness is a person who gives evidence at a proof or jury trial for any purpose and includes a haver cited to produce a document at a proof or jury trial.

The interlocutor allowing a proof or jury trial contains the warrant to cite witnesses and havers.

For exchange of lists of witnesses, see note 36.2.9.

"CITATION".

36.2.2   Service of the citation is by registered or first class recorded delivery post (see r. 16.4) or personally by messenger-at-arms (see r. 16.3). On witnesses in custody, see note 36.2.3.

Citation of a witness furth of the U.K. and Ireland cannot be enforced. In the case of citation elsewhere in the U.K. and Ireland, and on failure of a witness to attend, see note 36.2.7.

Travelling expenses should be tendered with the citation and other arrangements made for outlays and attendance. A witness is entitled to demand his travelling expenses before answering the citation.

WITNESSES IN CUSTODY.

36.2.3   A written application should be made to the Governor of the institution in Scotland or to the Home Office, Cleland House, Page Street, London SW1P 4LN, where the prisoner is elsewhere in the U.K. The letter should give details of the case and the reason why the evidence of the witness is required because it is for the Minister responsible to be satisfied that the attendance of the prisoner is desirable in the interests of justice: Criminal Justice Act 1961, s. 29(1).

RESPONSIBILITY FOR FEES AND EXPENSES OF WITNESS.

36.2.4   The agent for the party or the party litigant who cites the witness is responsible in the first instance for the fees and expenses of the witness: r. 36.2(4). For witnesses' fees, see Ch.II of the Table of Fees in r. 42.16.

WITNESSES OF PARTY LITIGANT.

36.2.5   R.C.S. 1994, r. 36.2(5) was introduced in R.C.S. 1965, r. 106B by A.S. (R.C.A. No. 10) (Miscellaneous) 1986 [S.I. 1986 No. 1955] to deal with party litigants citing numerous witnesses from the Sovereign down. The rule does not empower the court directly to limit the number of witnesses, but simply to order the party litigant to find caution to ensure that the witness's expenses are covered. In *Scottish Ministers v. Stirton* , 26th February 2009 (OH) unreported, it was argued before Lady Stacey that even if the rule did not give the court power to prevent citation of certain witnesses, the court had power to do so as part of its inherent jurisdiction to control procedure and prevent abuse. Lady Stacey, ex tempore, ordered a minute and answers on what purpose would be served by the appearance of the witnesses sought by the defender at the proof.

The first step is for the party litigant to ask the court at least 12 weeks before the proof to fix the amount of caution he should find in respect of all the witnesses having regard to the number of witnesses he proposes to cite and the period for which they may each be required to attend court. Thereafter before any witness is cited the party litigant must find caution.

A party litigant may only cite witnesses by messenger-at-arms, he is not entitled to cite witnesses by post: r. 16.4(2).

On finding caution, see Chap. 33.

"MOTION".

36.2.6   For motions, see Chap. 23.

FAILURE OF WITNESS TO ATTEND COURT.

36.2.7   If a witness in Scotland fails to appear at a proof or jury trial the modern practice is for the party whose witness he is to enrol a motion for warrant to messengers-at-arms to apprehend the witness and bring him to the proof. The historical practice of obtaining letters of second diligence (in effect having the same result) is not usually followed, although it may be where it is known in advance that the witness will not attend. Before granting the warrant the court must be satisfied that citation has been executed; a certificate of execution must be produced.

Attendance at a proof or jury trial in the Court of Session of a witness who resides in the U.K. furth of Scotland or in Ireland, may be enforced under the Attendance of Witnesses Act 1854 as extended by s.4 of the Evidence (Proceedings in Other Jurisdictions) Act 1975. The 1854 Act applies to Northern Ireland by virtue of the General Adaptation of Enactments (Northern Ireland) Order 1921 [S.R. & O. 1921 No. 1804] and to the Republic of Ireland by virtue of the Irish Free State (Consequential Adaptation of Enactments) Order 1923 [S.R. & O. 1923 No. 405] (preserved by the Ireland Act 1949). Under ss.1, 2 and 3 of the 1854 Act the court may order a warrant of citation in special form containing a notice that it is issued by special order of the court, and on proof of service and default of appearance the court may transmit a certificate to the Supreme Court in which jurisdiction the witness resides for that court to punish the witness (but he cannot otherwise be forced to go). The witness must have had tendered to him his attendance money: 1854 Act, s.4. On the application of the 1854 Act, see "Witnesses from England in the Court of Session" by DIK MacLeod, W.S. in the *Civil Practice Bulletin*, 1996, Issue 12, p. 9. An alternative is to apply for letters of request to take his evidence in that country: see r. 35.15; and this would also apply to a witness furth of the U.K. and Ireland who cannot be compelled to attend.

The historical practice for an application under the 1854 Act needs to be brought up to date. An application should now be made by minute in an action (see r. 15.1 and note 15.1.1) or note in a petition (see r. 15.2 and note 15.2.1) in the following form. Theoretically, the application could be made by motion, but it is convenient (though not essential) to make it by minute (or note) so that the warrant of the citation issued by the court and the clerk's certificate attached the minute can be served as one document. The crave and plea in a minute (or prayer in a note) may be simply expressed. The statement of facts may be expressed thus in one paragraph:

"The Honourable Lord (*name*) has appointed a proof to take place in this cause on (*day*) the (*date*) of (*month*) (*year*). I, (*solicitor's name, designation and address*) have reason to believe that the following necessary witness for the [*pursuer or defender*] resident in England, namely, (*full name and address*) will not attend at the proof unless commanded by your Lordships in a warrant of citation in the special form referred to in section 1 of the Attendance of Witnesses Act 1854."

The warrant and certificate, which may be added at the end of the minute (leaving blanks for the court to complete) or which the court should issue, should be in the following form:

"EDINBURGH (*date to he inserted*), The Lords of Council and Session by the Honourable Lord (*name to be inserted*) one of the judges of the Court of Session, having considered the foregoing minute, hereby grant warrant for citation in this the special form used in the Court, commanding the above named witness (*full name of witness*) to attend the proof on (*day*) the (*date*) of (*month*) (*year*) and subsequent days wherever (s)he may be within the United Kingdom, to answer at the instance of the pursuer, [AB] (or the defender [CD]); and grant authority to all officers of the law to cite the said witness accordingly, in terms of the Attendance of Witnesses Act 1854.

(*signed by the judge*)

I hereby certify that this warrant of citation in the special form used in the Court of Session is issued on the special orders of the Court of Session by the Honourable Lord (*name to be inserted*), one of the judges of that Court.

2 Parliament Square

Edinburgh

(*date*)

(*signed*)

[Depute] Clerk of Session"

A citation and execution of which should be prepared by the party calling the witness in accordance with the motion forms in Forms 36.2—A and 36.2—C, modified for use under the 1854 Act, for the foreign process server to use.

COMPETENCE AND COMPELLABILITY OF WITNESSES.

(1) Heads of State.

They are probably competent but not compellable: see Macphail on *Evidence*, para. 3.04.

36.2.8

(2) Diplomatic missions etc.

See the Diplomatic Privileges Act 1964, Consular Relations Act 1968, Diplomatic and Other Privileges Act 1971 and International Organisations Act 1981.

(3) Judges.

Supreme court judges are not competent witnesses about judicial proceedings which took place before them: *Muckarsie v. Wilson* (1834) Bell's Notes to Hume, 99; *H.M. Advocate. v. Monaghan* (1844) 2 Broun 131.

(4) Bankers.

Where a bank is not a party it cannot be compelled to produce books the contents of which can be proved under the Bankers' Books Evidence Act 1879 or the Civil Evidence (Scotland) Act 1988: 1879 Act, s.6 as amended by the 1988 Act, s.7(4).

(5) Spouses.

Under s.3 of the Evidence (Scotland) Act 1853 a spouse is a competent witness, but nothing in the section renders a spouse a competent or compellable witness against the other spouse of any matter communicated by one to the other during the marriage. A spouse is not compellable to give evidence about whether marital intercourse took place at any time: Law Reform (Miscellaneous Provisions) Act 1949, s.7. In consistorial causes (or any family action perhaps) the court should have all available and relevant evidence before it and should not be deprived of it by e.g. a defender (not called as a witness by the pursuer) not calling any evidence (including his own): *Bird v. Bird* 1931 S.C. 731, 734 per L.J.-C. Alness; *White v. White* 1947 S.L.T. (Notes) 51 per L.P. Cooper.

(6) Parties.

A party is competent and compellable: Evidence (Scotland) Act 1853, s.3; Evidence Further Amendment (Scotland) Act 1874, s.1.

(7) Advocates and solicitors.

An advocate is a competent witness, even if he is conducting the case. A party's solicitor's evidence is admissible even if he is conducting the case: Evidence (Scotland) Act 1852, s.1 as amended by the 1853 Act, s.1; 1853 Act, s.2. Under s.1. of the Evidence (Scotland) Act 1852, where a party adduces his agent (solicitor) as a witness on any matter which he could not otherwise competently be led, that party cannot object on the ground of confidentiality to any question on a matter pertinent to the issue.

(8) Persons not cited as witnesses.

A person is not excluded from giving evidence because he was not cited: 1852 Act, s. 1.

(9) Person in breach of court order.

Such a person may not be compellable as a witness on proof of the breach.

EXCHANGE OF LISTS OF WITNESSES.

36.2.9   Under P.N. No. 8 of 1994, not later than 28 days before the diet fixed for a proof (or jury trial) each party must give written intimation to every other party of a list of his witnesses and lodge a copy in process. Leave is required to call a witness not on the list. This P.N. does not apply to optional procedure cases under Chap. 43, Pt V or to commercial actions under Chap. 47 for which express similar provision is made.

Lodging productions

36.3   **36.3.**—(1)   Where a proof has been allowed, all productions which are intended to be used at the proof shall be lodged in process not later than 28 days before the diet of proof.

(2)   A production which is not lodged in accordance with paragraph (1) shall not be used or put in evidence at a proof unless—

(a)   by consent of parties; or

(b)   with the leave of the court on cause shown and on such conditions, if any, as to expenses or otherwise as the court thinks fit.

Deriv. R.C.S. 1965, r. 107(part) amended by S.I. 1972 No. 2022

GENERAL NOTE.

36.3.1   Documents founded on or incorporated in the pleadings must be lodged as productions when the pleadings in which they are referred to are lodged: r. 27.1. Other productions must be lodged 28 days before the proof (r. 36.3(1)), otherwise (with one exception noted in note 36.3.2) they may not be referred to without consent of parties or leave of the court (r. 36.3(2)): On lodging productions, see r. 4.5. Consent of other parties is either orally at the Bar or by marking the back of the inventory of productions of the late production "Of consent (*date and name of solicitor*)". Productions borrowed out must be returned by 12.30pm the day before the proof: r. 36.5.

DOCUMENTS USED TO TEST CREDIBILITY.

36.3.2   A document used to test the credibility of a witness may be produced during the proof without having been previously lodged: *Paterson & Sons (Camp Coffee) v. Kit Coffee Co. Ltd* (1908) 16 S.L.T. 180. The reason is said to be because it will not be known in advance whether the witness will be adduced by the other party; and for this reason it had been thought that a document used to test the credibility of a *party* should be lodged before the proof in accordance with r. 36.3. In *Robertson v. Anderson* , 15th May 2001, unreported (OH), Lord Carloway held that there was no distinction between a party and any other witness and that a document not lodged as a production could be put to a party in cross-examination to test credibility.

A statement made by a witness otherwise than in the course of the proof is admissible as evidence in so far as it tends to reflect favourably or unfavourably on the witness's credibility: Civil Evidence (Scotland) Act 1988, s.3. There are exceptions: statements collateral to the issue, e.g. similar fact evidence (*A v. B* (1895) 22 R. 402, 404 per L.P. Robertson; *Inglis v. National Bank of Scotland Ltd* 1909 S.C. 1038 (Extra Div.); *EG v. The Governors of the Fettes Trust* [2021] CSOH 128), precognitions (see *Kerr v. H.M. Advocate* 1958 J.C. 14, 19 per L.J.-C. Thomson) and reports in accident books unless they were written by the witness (*Dobbie v. Forth Ports Authority* 1974 S.C. 40, 44 per L.J.-C. Wheatley).

Copy productions

36.4.—[1](1) A copy of every documentary production, marked with the appropriate number of process of the principal production, shall be lodged for the use of the court at a proof not later than 48 hours before the diet of proof.

(2) Each copy production consisting of more than one sheet shall be securely fastened together by the party lodging it.

GENERAL NOTE.

The provisions of r. 4.8 should be noted. A clerk of session may refuse to accept a copy for use of the court if, e.g. it is not legible.

This rule applies, obviously, only to documentary productions.

Returning borrowed documents before proof

36.5. All steps of process and productions which have been borrowed shall be returned to process before 12.30 p.m. on the day preceding the diet of proof.

Deriv. R.C.S. 1965, r. 107(part)

GENERAL NOTE.

On borrowing productions, see r. 4.12.

Notices to admit and notices of non-admission

36.6. *[Revoked by S.I. 1996 No. 2168 (effective 23rd September 1996).]*

GENERAL NOTE.

For notices to admit and notices of non-admission, see now Chap. 28A. That Chapter was inserted by the A.S. (R.C.S.A. No. 4) (Miscellaneous) 1996 [S.I. 1996 No. 2168] following a recommendation of the Cullen *Review of Outer Bouse Business* in December 1995 that such notices should be permitted before a proof was allowed. Rule 36.6 applied only where proof had been allowed. The new provisions which apply after the record has closed is not appropriate to this chapter on proofs.

Admissions by parties

36.7.—[2](1) Where a party admits—

    (a) any matter of fact whether averred in the pleadings or not;

    (b) the authenticity of any document; or

    (c) the sufficiency of a copy or extract of such a document as equivalent to the original,

which has not been admitted in the pleadings or in respect of which a notice under rule 28A.1(1) has not been intimated, a minute of admission signed by counsel or other person having a right of audience for the party making such admission, shall be lodged in process.

(2) An admission made in a minute of admission may be used in evidence at a proof if otherwise admissible in evidence.

(3) In taxing any account of expenses, the Auditor shall disallow the expenses of any evidence led on matters covered by a minute of admission, unless special cause is shown to him.

Deriv. R.C.S. 1965, r. 109

GENERAL NOTE.

A minute of admission may be by one party or, more commonly, by more than one party (a joint minute).

A (joint) minute of admission(s) is conclusive for the purposes of the action in which it is made. A joint minute of admission is a contract by which the parties accept as true the facts stated in it: *Carswell & Son v. Finlay* (1887) 24 S.L.R. 643, 645 per L.P. Inglis. A joint minute may agree facts, that a document bears to be what it is, that the facts in it are true or that it is the evidence of its author.

Parties should agree what can be agreed because, where evidence is led of a skilled witness on a matter not in issue which could have been incorporated in a joint minute, the court may refuse to note the

36.4

36.4.1

36.5

36.5.1

36.6

36.6.1

36.7

36.7.1

---

[1] Rule 36.4(1) amended by S.I. 1996 No. 2168 (effective 23rd September 1996).

[2] R. 36.7(1) amended by S.I. 1997 No. 1050 (minor correction).

witness in the Minute of Proceedings as. a skilled witness in attendance at court and direct that his fee is not chargeable against the opponent: *Ayton v. National Coal Board* 1965 S.L.T. (Notes) 24.

R. 15.1 does not apply to a minute of admission because it is not an application to the court.

"COUNSEL OR OTHER PERSON HAVING A RIGHT OF AUDIENCE".

36.7.2   See definitions of "counsel" and "other person having a right of audience" in r. 1.3(1).

"LODGED IN PROCESS".

36.7.3   The minute of admission is lodged as a step of process and not as a production: r. 1.3(1) (definition of "step of process"). On steps of process, see r. 4.4.

EXPENSES.

36.7.4   Expenses in relation to proof of matters in a minute of admission are disallowed unless special cause is shown to the Auditor: r. 36.7(3). It is not clear what the special cause might be. It might include evidence led before the minute of admission was signed.

See also note 36.7.1 on disallowance by the court of expenses of a skilled witness whose evidence is not in issue.

Lodging of certain written statements

36.8   **36.8.**[1] A party who wishes to have any written statement (including an affidavit) or report, admissible under section 2(1)(b) of the Civil Evidence (Scotland) Act 1988, received in evidence shall lodge the statement or report in process and shall intimate such lodging to the other party or parties.

GENERAL NOTE.

36.8.1   Following the passing of the Civil Evidence (Scotland) Act 1988 which abolished the (secondary) hearsay rule (s 2 of the 1988 Act), a somewhat cumbersome mechanism was provided for obtaining the permission of the court to allow any document (including an affidavit) to be received in evidence without being spoken to by a witness as evidence not merely that it was made but as to the truth of its contents: see R.C.S. 1994, r. 36.8 which in its original form was derived from R.C.S. 1965, r. 108A which was inserted by A.S. (R.C.S.A. No. 1) (Witness Statements) 1989 [S.I. 1989 No. 435], Such evidence was made admissible under s. 2(1)(b) of the 1988 Act.

In *Ebrahem v. Ebrahem* 1989 S.L.T. 808, 809J-K, Lord Capian indicated, obiter, that r. 36.8 was not suitable where the witness was speaking to critical matters in dispute and was not intended to supplant the taking of evidence by commission where that alternative was available. It would, however, be possible for the court to allow an affidavit as evidence in chief without depriving another party of having the witness called to cross-examine him. It would curtail the usefulness of r. 36.8 if affidavits could not be admitted merely because the evidence could be taken on commission. It has since been held that there is nothing in s. 2 of the 1988 Act or r. 36.8 (formerly R.C.S. 1965, r. 108A) which is restrictive or which suggests that the evidence must be undisputed: *Smith v. Alexander Baird Ltd* 1993 S.C.L.R. 563, 564D per Lord Cameron of Lochbroom. In *McVinnie v. McVinnie* 1995 S.L.T.(Sh.Ct.) 81, Sheriff Macphait, Q.C., went further and stated that a statement admissible in evidence under s. 2(1)(b) of the 1988 Act by affidavit by virtue of r. 36.8 cannot be excluded because part of the statement is disputed or because the other party claims he would be prejudiced. There is no prejudice in a party not being able to cross-examine because the court would take account of the fact that the evidence had not been subjected to cross-examination: *Smith*, above, at p. 565B; *McVinnie*, above, at p. 85F.

In *Glaser v. Glaser* 1997 S.L.T. 456, Lord Macfadyen approved *McVinnie*, above, and held that the court has no discretion to refuse an application to admit an affidavit using the procedure under r. 36.8. (It has been observed here until Release 61 that if the court is to have no discretion, there is little point in an elaborate procedure involving an application to the court, and the affidavit may as well simply be lodged and intimated to the other side.)

Rule 36.8 has been changed following *Glaser*, above. Now the statement or report is simply lodged in process, and intimated, for what it is worth: A.S. (R.C.A. No.4) (Miscellaneous) 2001 [S.S.I. 2001 No. 305]. Some questions remain unanswered, such as how is the other party to react when he has no idea what credence the court may give to the statement.

S.2(1)(b) of the 1988 Act provides that a statement made by a person otherwise than in the course of proof shall be admissible as evidence of any matter contained in the statement of which direct oral evidence by that person would be admissible. The test in s.2(1)(b) is one of admissibility and not one of competency: *T v. T*, 2001 S.C. 337 overruling *F v. Kennedy*, 1992 S.C. 28 and cases following it. A copy of a document (a statement of the signatories) is not admissible as evidence of the contents of the principal because it is not a statement made by a person otherwise than in the course of proof, as only the principal would be such a statement; and direct oral evidence of the signatories would not otherwise be admissible because, under the best evidence rule, their oral evidence would be inadmissible: *Japan Leasing (Europe) plc v. Weir's Trs (No. 2)* 1998 S.C. 543.

---

[1] R.36.8 substituted by S.S.I. 2001 No. 305, para. 7(1) (effective 18th September 2001).

As to the form of a statement lodged as an affidavit, see note 1.3.7. **36.8.2**

Where there are contradictions between affidavits, and no other evidence to support a conclusion one way or another, no conclusion can be drawn by the court: *D v. D* , 2002 S.C. 33, 37D (Extra Div.).

PROVISIONS TO WHICH THIS RULE DOES NOT APPLY.

Express provision is made in certain rules for certain evidence to be adduced without resort having to be made to this rule. These are: (a) evidence in certain undefended family actions (r. 49.28) and (b) affidavits in causes under the Adoption (Scotland) Act 1978 (r. 67.6(2)), (c) affidavits in causes under the Matrimonial Homes (Family Protection) (Scotland) Act 1981 (r. 49.71) and (d) affidavits in causes under the Human Fertilisation and Embryology Act 1990 (r. 81.6(2)). **36.8.3**

"MOTION".

For motions, see Chap. 23. **36.8.4**

LODGE IN PROCESS AS A PRODUCTION.

On lodging productions, see r. 4.5. **36.8.5**

Attendance, and lists, of witnesses

36.9.—(1) It shall be the duty of each party to ensure that his witnesses, if any, are— **36.9**

    (a) in attendance in the vicinity of the courtroom; and

    (b) available when called to give evidence.

(2) Each party shall, before his case begins, give to the macer of the court a numbered list of any witnesses of his in the order in which it is proposed to call them.

(3) No witness at a proof shall, except with leave of the court—

    (a) be present in the courtroom during the proceedings prior to the giving of his evidence; or

    (b) leave the courtroom after giving evidence.

(4) No party, other than the party citing a witness, shall have access to that witness while he is in attendance at court.

Deriv. RCS 1965, r. 111(a) to (d)

GENERAL NOTE.

Witnesses should be advised not to discuss evidence they are giving (if during an adjournment) or have given during the course of a proof. Counsel and agents may not discuss with a witness during an adjournment the evidence he is giving. **36.9.1**

WITNESSES NOT TO BE IN COURT BEFORE GIVING EVIDENCE.

The general rule is stated in r. 36.9(3); it does not apply to a party who may be present in court. Under s.3 of the Evidence (Scotland) Act 1840 the court may admit the evidence of a witness who was in court before he gave evidence if his presence was not due to culpable negligence or intent and the witness was not unduly instructed or influenced by what he heard; it does not apply to a party. **36.9.2**

Even though parties consent to a witness being in court before he gives evidence, the leave of the court must also be obtained: r. 36.9(3).

Leave is often sought and granted to allow a skilled witness to hear the evidence of an opponent's witness(es), but not usually an opponent's skilled witness, or to assist counsel during the course of the proof.

WITNESS LEAVING COURT AFTER GIVING EVIDENCE.

The purpose of the provision in r. 36.9(3) that a witness may not leave the court after giving evidence without leave of the court is that in granting leave the witness is released from his citation. **36.9.3**

UNALLOCATED PROOFS.

A proof may not have been allocated to a particular Lord Ordinary on the first day of the diet. A representative of the agents for each party in such a case must attend the Keeper's Office between 10am and 10.20am. The Keeper must be informed about the existence of any discussions with a view to settlement. Agents may be required to attend later at intervals during the day. See generally, Notice [i.e. P.N.], 13th June 1996. **36.9.4**

Administration of oath or affirmation to witnesses

36.10

36.10. The Lord Ordinary shall administer the oath to a witness in Form 36.10-A or, where the witness elects to affirm, the affirmation in Form 36.10-B.

Deriv. RCS 1965, r. 122A(2) inserted by S.I. 1984 No. 472

GENERAL NOTE.

36.10.1

The oath is usually taken by the witness raising his right hand and repeating the oath after the judge who also stands with right hand raised. It is permissible to take the oath in another form appropriate to one's religious belief; but where it is not practicable without inconvenience or delay to administer an oath in the manner appropriate to his religious belief the witness shall affirm: Oaths Act 1978, s.5(2). A person who objects to being sworn may affirm: 1978 Act, s.5(1). The fact that a person without religious belief takes an oath does not affect the validity of the oath: 1978 Act, s.4(2).

The affirmation is administered in the same way as an oath but without the judge or the witness raising his right hand.

CHILDREN AND OTHER VULNERABLE WITNESSES.

36.10.2

The oath is not usually administered to a child under the age of 12; he is admonished to tell the truth. A child between 12 and 14 is sworn or admonished at the judge's discretion; and a child over 14 is usually sworn. The competency test of ascertaining whether a child under 14 knew the difference between the truth and lies, in order to be allowed to give evidence, has been abolished by s. 24 of the Vulnerable Witnesses (Scotland) Act 2004 and came into force on 1st April 2005. That section provides (1) that the evidence of *any* witness is not inadmissible solely because the witness does not understand (a) the nature of the duty to give truthful evidence or (b) the difference between truth and lies; and (2) that the court must not, before that witness gives evidence, take any steps intended to establish whether the witness understands those matters.

Recording of evidence

36.11

36.11.—(1) Subject to any other provision in these Rules, evidence at a proof shall be recorded by—

    (a) a shorthand writer to whom the *oath de fideli administratione officii* has been administered on his appointment as a shorthand writer in the Court of Session; or

    (b) tape recording or other mechanical means approved by the Lord President.

(2) The record of the evidence at a proof shall include—

    (a) any objection taken to a question or to the line of evidence;

    (b) any submission made in relation to such an objection; and

    (c) the ruling of the court in relation to the objection and submission.

(3) A transcript of the record of the evidence shall be made only on the direction of the court; and the cost shall, in the first instance, be borne—

    (a) in an undefended cause, by the agent for the pursuer; and

    (b) in a defended cause, by the agents for the parties in equal proportions.

(4) The transcript of the record of the evidence provided for the use of the court shall be certified as a faithful record of the evidence by—

    (a) the shorthand writer or shorthand writers, if more than one, who recorded the evidence; or

    (b) where the evidence was recorded by tape recording or other mechanical means, the person who transcribed the record.

(5) The court may make such alterations to the transcript of the record of the evidence as appear to it to be necessary after hearing the parties; and, where such alterations are made, the Lord Ordinary shall authenticate the alterations.

(6) Where a transcript of the record of the evidence has been made for the use of the court, copies of it may be obtained by any party from the shorthand writer on payment of his fee.

(7) Except with leave of the court, the transcript of the record of the evidence may be borrowed from process only for the purpose of enabling a party to consider whether to reclaim against the interlocutor of the court on the proof.

(8) Where a transcript of the record of the evidence is required for the purpose of a reclaiming motion but has not been directed to be transcribed under paragraph (3), the reclaimer—

(a) may request such a transcript from the shorthand writer, or as the case may be, the cost of the transcript being borne by the agent for the reclaimer in the first instance; and

(b) shall lodge the transcript in process;

and copies of it may be obtained by any party from the shorthand writer, or as the case may be, on payment of his fee.

Deriv. RCS 1965, r. 110 (r. 36.11(2)), r. 113(a) (r. 36.11(1), (4) and (5)), r. 113(b) (r. 36.11(3) and (8)), r. 113(c) (r. 36.11(7)), and r. 113(d) (r. 36.11(6)); P.N. 2nd March 1972 (r. 36.11(2))

GENERAL NOTE.

R. 36.11 includes a reference to recording evidence by tape recording or other mechanical means as well as to recording by a shorthand writer. With effect from 1st April 1997, proofs are recorded by mechanical means: Notice (*sic*), 6th March 1997.

36.11.1

Digital recording has now been approved: PN No. 4 of 2010. There is a protocol or guidance in relation to digital recording: PN No. 3 of 2010.

THE PROOF.

For the distinction between proof, proof before answer and proof *habili modo*, see note 22.3.9. A few points are mentioned here about proofs in general.

36.11.2

(1) Proofs heard in public.

A proof is conducted in open court: see C.S.A. 1693. There are statutory exceptions: see, e.g. Adoption (Scotland) Act 1978, s. 57.

(2) Judge's rôle.

The judge's role is to see that the litigation is carried out fairly between the parties: *Thomson v. Glasgow Corporation* 1962 S.C.(H.L.) 36, 52 per L.J.-C. Thomson. He should not interrupt so as to frustrate the development of a line of examination-in-chief or cross-examination. He may question witnesses with caution (*Thomson*, above, per L.J.-C. Thomson at p. 52), usually after cross-examination to clear up an obscurity or ambiguity. If he elicits new matter, parties should be given an opportunity to question the witness again on that matter.

(3) Duties of advocates and agents.

On the duties of advocates and agents, see *Batchelor v. Pattison and Mackersy* (1876) 3 R. 914, 918 per L.P. Inglis. Lord Hope of Craighead translated what Lord Inglis, L.P., said into modern practice in *Arthur JS Hall v. Simons* , [2002] 1 A.C. 615, 725–726.

(4) Leading at proof.

The party on whom the initial onus of proof lies leads at a proof, and, unless the contrary is stated in an interlocutor before proof, that party is the pursuer. The defender may be ordained to lead where so much of the pursuer's case is admitted that the onus is transferred to him. Where each party has to rebut a presumption, who leads depends on a comparison of the strengths of the presumptions. The question of who leads is not merely dependent on where the initial onus lies but sometimes on consideration of convenience: *Macfarlane v. Macfarlane* 1947 S.L.T.(Notes) 34 per L.P. Cooper.

(5) Objections.

Objections to evidence must be made when the evidence is sought to be given, otherwise it may become part of the evidence on which reliance may be made. Evidence objected to may, however, be allowed subject to competency and relevancy, to be argued about at the end in submissions.

(6) Presence of witnesses in court.

Parties may be present in court during the examination of witnesses. The common law rule, that a witness other than a skilled witness may be excluded if he has been in court during the evidence of previous witnesses, is modified by s. 3 of the Evidence (Scotland) Act 1840. This provides that if objection is taken that a witness has been present without the permission of the court or the consent of the party objecting, the court may admit the witness if his presence was not through culpable negligence or criminal intent and he has not been unduly instructed or influenced by what took place while he was in court or that injustice will not be done by his examination.

Skilled witnesses may remain in court during the evidence of witnesses (of fact) other than the evidence of other skilled witnesses, unless of consent.

(7) Examination-in-chief.

It is the invariable practice in Scotland to ask a witness his age; this is because it may indicate the witness's capacity, maturity and understanding, and ought not to be omitted: *Meiklejohn v. Stevenson* (1870) 8 M. 890.

Leading questions (questions which suggest the answer) must not be asked which relate to the facts in issue. They may be asked about purely formal matters, matters not in dispute, matters established by other evidence or with the consent of the other party. The answer to a leading question may be regarded as of little weight: *Bishop v. Bryce*, 1910 S.C. 426, 435 per L.P. Dunedin; *McKenzie v. McKenzie*, 1943 S.C. 108, 109 per L.J.-C. Cooper. Leading questions are permitted of an hostile witness, and leave of the court is not required for this purpose: *Lowe v. Bristol Omnibus Co.*, 1934 S.C. 1; *Avery v. Cantilever Shoe Co. Ltd*, 1942 S.C. 469.

Published academic material may be put to an expert witness in evidence in chief without being produced beforehand as a production: *Roberts v. British Railways Board* 1998 S.C.L.R. 577.

(8) Cross-examination.

The order for cross-examination of a pursuer's witnesses where there is more than one defender is 1D, 2D, 3D; for cross-examination of a second defender's witnesses, it is 3D, 1D, P.

The purpose of cross-examination is to weaken or destroy the witness's version of facts and to elicit evidence favourable to the cross-examiner. Cross-examination is not limited to the evidence-in-chief.

Leading questions are permitted, though sometimes evidence not so elicited has more weight.

Nowadays, failure to cross-examine on a point does not preclude a party leading evidence to contradict that point, but such evidence will be subject to comment (*Dawson v. Dawson*, 1956 S.L.T.(Notes) 58), may be given little weight, may result in the opponent being allowed to lead evidence in replication (*Wilson v. Thomas Usher & Son Ltd*, 1934 S.C. 332, 338 per L.J.-C. Aitcheson), or may result in the witness being recalled for further cross-examination (expenses may be awarded: *Bishop*, above per L.P. Dunedin at p. 431). The modern practice was confirmed in *Bryce v. British Railways Board*, 1996 S.L.T. 1378 in which the 2nd Div held that a Lord Ordinary was entitled to have regard to evidence from a medical witness for the defender which had not been put in cross-examination to the pursuer's witness, which had not be objected to by the pursuer and on which the pursuer had not cross-examined the witness. In *Dollar Air Services Ltd v. Highland Council*, 11th July 1997, unreported (1997 G.W.D. 28-1435), Lord Marnoch, because there had been a failure to put an opposing version of an important telephone call in cross-examination of the pursuer's witness, was disinclined to make any adverse findings about that witness's credibility (in *Hobbin v. Vertical Descents Ltd* [2013] CSIH 1 (Extra Div.), para. [26], it was indicated that the problem is more commonly one of prejudice to the party whose witness has not had the chance to comment rather than credibility). In *Roberts v. John Johnston & Son*, 26th June 1998, unreported on this point, Lord Osborne, while acknowledging that a failure to put to the pursuer the defender's case of contributory negligence might not be fatal, refused to infer any failure because no challenge to the pursuer's case was made in cross-examination and no evidence in support of the defender's case was led. See also *Currie v. Clamp's Exr*Unreported 27th February 2001 (2001 G.W.D. 16-625). Where no evidence is led contradicting the pursuer's version of events, the court is entitled to draw the most favourable inferences of which the evidence is reasonably capable: *O'Donnell v. Murdoch Mackenzie & Co. Ltd*, 1967 S.C. (H.L.) 63, 71 per Lord Upjohn.

If intending to treat a witness's evidence as incredible or unreliable, the witness must be questioned about that evidence to give him the opportunity to respond to the challenge, and the evidence which contradicts him must be put to him: *Avery*, above. Similarly, where the evidence of the witness about the issues is to be contradicted, the contradictory evidence should be put to the witness: *McKenzie*, above. Where the character or honesty of the witness is questioned, there must be a basis for it in fact.

Where credibility of a witness is in issue, the witness is open to challenge in cross-examination on the truth of any statement made by him during his evidence even if it is collateral to the crucial facts (*King v. King* (1841) 4 D. 124) and even if there is no record for the questions: *Clinton v. News Group Newspapers Ltd* 1999 S.C. 367 per Lord Nimmo Smith. In *Clinton*, the pursuer stated in cross-examination that he had not had sexual relations with any woman. The defender's counsel was permitted to put to the pursuer that he had had sexual relations with another woman (not the 2nd pursuer) even though there was no record for it (nor would there have been for it was not crucial to the defender's case). Opinion was reserved as to whether the defender would be allowed to lead evidence to support the line (in fact it was lead without objection). It would surely have to follow, from the fact that the witness could be questioned as to certain facts, that evidence in support of the line would have to be allowed.

A document used to test the credibility of a witness may be produced during the proof without having been previously lodged: *Paterson & Sons (Camp Coffee) v. Kit Coffee Co. Ltd* (1908) 16 S.L.T. 180. The reason is said to be because it will not be known in advance whether the witness will be adduced by the other party; and for this reason it had been thought that a document used to test the credibility of a *party* should be lodged before the proof in accordance with r. 36.3. In *Robertson v. Anderson* 2014 S.L.T. 709, Lord Carloway held that there was no distinction between a party and any other witness, and that a document not lodged as a production could be put to a party in cross-examination to test credibility. Where a party intends to use a document as proof of an averment, he has to lodge it, in terms of the relevant rule of court, in advance of the proof or, if the statement relied on is oral, that party ought to refer to it on record.

A statement made by a witness otherwise than in the course of the proof is admissible as evidence in so far as it tends to reflect favourably or unfavourably on the witness's credibility: Civil Evidence (Scotland) Act 1988, s. 3. There are exceptions: statements collateral to the issue, e.g. similar fact evidence (*A v. B* (1895) 22 R. 402, 404, per L.P. Robertson; *Inglis v. National Bank of Scotland Ltd* 1909 S.C. 1038 (Extra Div.); *EG v. The Governors of the Fettes Trust* [2021] CSOH 128), precognitions (see *Kerr v. H.M. Advocate*, 1958 J.C. 14, 19, per L.J.-C. Thomson) and reports in accident books unless they were written by the witness (*Dobbie v. Forth Ports Authority*, 1974 S.C. 40, 44, per L.J.-C. Wheatley). Evidence of a different statement made on a previous occasion is not admissible unless a foundation has been laid in cross-examination: *Hoey v. Hoey* (1884) 11 R. 578.

(9) Re-examination.

This is restricted to matters (though it may include new facts) arising out of or relating to the points raised in cross-examination. Where re-examination is permitted on a new matter, further cross-examination will be allowed on it. Leading questions are no more allowed in re-examination than in examination-in-chief.

(10) Recall of, and additional, witnesses.

A witness who has given evidence may be recalled at the judge's instance or on the motion of a party: Evidence (Scotland) Act 1852, s. 4. The power may be exercised, e.g. where the pursuer would be prejudiced by the defender's case not being properly put in cross-examination: *Wilson v. Thomas Usher & Son* 1934 S.C. 332, 338–339 per L.J.-C. Aitchison. The court might recall a witness to clear up an ambiguity: Dickson on *Evidence*, para. 1769. Under s. 4 of the Civil Evidence (Scotland) Act 1988 and for the purposes of s. 2 (admissibility of hearsay) or s. 3 (statement as evidence as to credibility), at any time before closing submissions a person may be recalled as a witness (whether or not he was present in court after first giving evidence) or a person may be called as an additional witness (whether or not he was present in court during the proof). This would enable a party to call the maker of a statement to give evidence. In *Davies v. McGuire* 1995 S.L.T. 755 Lord Gill held that evidence of statements made by eyewitnesses to a police officer could not be allowed (in cross in this case) in advance of the evidence of the eyewitnesses, this not being warranted by s. 2 or 3 of the 1988 Act; but the police officer could be recalled under s. 4 of that Act after the eyewitnesses had given evidence.

(11) Views.

A view may be made of a place or object in relation to any matter arising at the proof at the instance of the judge or a party. The purpose of a view is to enable the judge to understand the evidence not to criticise or contradict it: *Hattie v. Leitch* (1889) 16 R. 1128. The judge, the clerk of court and representatives of the parties should be present.

(12) Hearing on evidence.

The hearing on evidence is usually heard as soon as the proof is finished, but may be postponed through lack of time or in order to obtain the notes of evidence. The party who leads at the proof speaks first (pursuer) and the other party (defender) or parties may each reply. It is in the discretion of the court to grant the pursuer a right of reply (P.N. 14th May 1970), and this is exercised where, e.g. a defender referred to authorities not mentioned by the pursuer.

The Lord Ordinary may request, or a party may proffer without a request, a written skeletal (or full) submission for the hearing on evidence.

The citation of cases from reproduction of electronic formats is permitted by P.N. No. 5 of 2004. A case reported in Session Cases must be cited from that source: P.N. No. 5 of 2004; the general rule is that when a case has been reported in Session Cases or the (English) Law Reports, it should be cited from that source: *McGowan v. Summit at Lloyds* , 2002 S.L.T. 1258, 1273 at para.[57] (Extra Div.).

(13) Judgment.

In giving his opinion, the Lord Ordinary has a duty to record all the arguments and submissions made to him and his views upon them: *Morrow v. Enterprise Sheet Metal Works (Aberdeen) Ltd* 1986 S.C. 96, 101; *Hogan v. Highland R.C.* 1995 S.C. 1, 2C, per L.J.-C. Ross. Where a decision on a fact is based on credibility, the Lord Ordinary should leave no doubt as to the grounds of decision: *Duncan v. Watson* 1940 S.C. 221, 225, per L.P. Normand.

If, at avizandum, the Lord Ordinary discovers an authority not cited by parties which he is inclined to rely on, or a new argument occurs to him or a question arises about the appropriate interlocutor, the case should be put out by order to allow parties to make further submissions: *Lees v. North East Fife D.C.* 1987 S.C. 265; *Kennedy v. Norwich Union Fire Insurance Society* , 1993 S.C. 578, 1994 S.L.T. 617; *Wyman-Gordon Ltd v. Proclad International Ltd* , 2011 S.C. 338 (Second Div.), 359 at paras [56]–[59]. If the only outstanding issue is the form of the interlocutor, the Lord Ordinary may give judgment expressing his conclusions but should allow parties an opportunity to address him on that point: *Libertas-Kommerz v. Johnson* 1977 S.C. 191. See generally, *Osborne v. British Coal Property* 1996 S.L.T. 736.

The form of opinions and neutral citation of cases is dealt with in P.N. No. 5 of 2004.

(14) The best evidence rule.

The rule is that only the best obtainable evidence is admissible: Dickson on *Evidence*, p. 195. Thus, hearsay evidence (and in particular secondary hearsay) was, with exceptions, excluded until s. 2(1) of the Civil Evidence (Scotland) Act 1988. The expression "best evidence rule" has tended to be used with reference to documentary or real evidence, the word "hearsay" to oral statements.

A procedure for admitting evidence under s. 2(1) of the 1988 Act is laid down in RCS 1994, r. 36.8 (on which see note 36.8.1). It is now up to the court to assess all the evidence which is led (including admissible hearsay) and to determine its weight: *L. v. L.* 1998 S.L.T. 672, 676H per L.P. Rodger.

(A)   (Secondary) hearsay evidence.

There were exceptions to the general common law rule excluding hearsay. The statutory rule now is that (a) evidence is not excluded solely on the ground that it is heresay and (b) a statement made by a person otherwise than in the course of the proof is admissible of any matter in it of which direct oral evidence by that person would be admissible, and (c) a fact may be proved by hearsay evidence (secondary hearsay): 1988 Act, s. 2(1). Nothing in s. 2(1) affects the rule about the admissibility of a statement as evidence that it was made (primary hearsay as distinct from secondary hearsay which goes to the truth of the statement).

A statement is admissible as evidence as to credibility whether favourable or unfavourable: 1988 Act, s. 3. But it is still the law that the hearsay evidence of what the maker of the statement said on a previous occasion may be led only after the maker of the statement has given evidence: *Davies v. McGuire* 1995 S.L.R. 755 (such evidence could not be led in advance, but the witness could be recalled after the maker of the statement had given evidence). Section 2 of the 1988 Act overrides the best evidence rule so that the fact that the maker of the statement has given oral evidence does not prevent hearsay evidence being given of what he said on another occasion: *F. v. Kennedy (No. 2)* 1993 S.L.T. 1284 (I.H.) (evidence of social workers about what children said when interviewed).

Section 2(1)(b) of the 1988 Act allows hearsay evidence of a statement to be admissible if it relates to a matter on which direct oral evidence by the maker of the statement would be admissible. It does not involve a competency test but a test of admissibility of evidence, namely, that hearsay evidence is admissible unless direct oral of the matter would be inadmissible: *T v. T*, 2001 S.C. 337 overruling *F v. Kennedy*, 1992 S.C. 28 and cases following it (e.g. *L v. L*, 1996 S.L.T. 767).

While a statement in a precognition is inadmissible, what was said by a person to a precognoscer is admissible: *Anderson v. Jas. B. Fraser & Co. Ltd* 1992 S.L.T. 1129. Similarly in *Ellison v. Inspirations East Ltd*, 2002 S.L.T. 291 (OH) evidence from a solicitor who had taken notes of a statement by a coach driver was admitted. But, where there is no precise record of what was asked and answered, evidence of the precognoscer might be of little weight: see *Cavanagh v. BP Chemicals Ltd* 1995 S.L.T. 1287.

The admissibility of hearsay evidence does not breach the right to a fair hearing under ECHR art.6(1): *Irvine v. Arco Atholl Ltd*, 2002 S.L.T 931 (OH) (infringement argued because the third party had not cited for health reasons the maker of the statement relied on by defender).

(B)   Best evidence rule (documents or real evidence).

This rule exists to prevent prejudice to one party and unfair advantage to the other party to a dispute where better evidence than that before the court exists. It does not apply to exclude evidence of a party which is no longer capable of being examined usefully; but where that is the case, that party's case will be examined with greater care and a heavier burden of proof will be imposed: *Stirling Aquatic Technology Ltd v. Farmocean AB (No. 2)* 1996 S.L.T. 456 (fish nets). For a recent example of the application of the rule, see *Peacock Group Plc, v. Railston Ltd*, 2007 S.L.T. 269 (OH).

In relation to documents, the best evidence rule requires that the contents of a document have to be proved by the document itself and not by a copy or parole evidence: *S & U Newspapers Ltd v. Gherson's Trs* 1987 S.C. 27; *Inverkip D.C. v. Carswell* 1987 S.C.L.R. 145. The rule in s. 2(1) of the 1988 Act applies to (statements in) documents other than precognitions: 1988 Act, s. 9. But a copy of a document is inadmissible unless authenticated by the maker of it under s. 6 of the 1988 Act or it is agreed by the parties. The reason for exclusion of a copy is that a copy cannot be evidence of the principal admissible under s. 2(1)(b) of the 1988 Act because it is not "a statement made by a person otherwise than in the course of the proof", a "statement" could only apply to the principal document: *Japan Leasing (Europe) plc v. Weir's (No. 2)* 1998 S.C. 543 (I.H.) (copy of hire purchase contract). In that case the court went on to say that direct oral evidence of the signatories about the contents of the document would not be admissible, apart from s. 2 of the 1988 Act, because of the best evidence rule (which states that the principal document is the best evidence). The trouble with the case of *Japan Leasing* is that it appears, on the one hand, to treat the document as the "statement" of the signatories while, on the other hand, the court excludes evidence of the signatories about what is in the document because the best evidence is not their statement but the principal document itself. Does this mean that s. 2 of the 1988 Act has abolished the best evidence rule in relation to oral statements but has not abolished the rule in relation to documents?

(15)   Corroboration.

Section 1(1) of the Civil Evidence (Scotland) Act 1988 abolishes the requirement for corroboration. There is now no rule that requires the court to scrutinise with special care the evidence of a witness simply because he made prior statements to persons not led in evidence: *L. v. L.* 1998 S.L.T. 672. Per Lord Coulsfield in that case, it was doubted that there was now any validity in the previous rule (see *McLaren v. Caldwell's Paper Mill Co. Ltd* , 1973 S.L.T. 158) that failure to lead other (corroborative) evidence which was available should lead a judge to regard such evidence with special care and attention. This case was distinguished by Lord Marnoch in *Rae v. The Chief Constable, Strathclyde Police* 1998 Rep.L.R. 63 where he said that, in relation to the weight to be attached to a single witness's evidence, the court may be disinclined to give maximum weight to uncorroborated testimony where a crucial witness is not led to substantiate a party's position.

(16) Expenses.

An extra-judicial offer, whenever made, that has not been accepted may be taken into account in considering an award of expenses: *Pearce & Co. v. Owners of SS Hans Maersk* 1935 S.C. 703 (during action by pursuer); *O'Donnell v. A.M. & G. Robertson* 1965 S.L.T. 155 (before action brought). The old practice (see *Gunn v. Hunter* (1886) 13 R. 573, 574 per LP Inglis) that, if an offer was made before litiscontestation (when defences lodged) which was repeated on record and the pursuer was awarded less, expenses were awarded to the defender; but if the offer was not repeated on record, there were no expenses due to or by, is long since dead. It is rare to find offers on record as pleadings are not regarded as the place for providing the basis for arguments about expenses: *O'Donnell*, above.

(17) Citation of authorities.

The general rule is that when a case has been reported in Session Cases or the (English) Law Reports, it should be cited from that source: *McGowan v. Summit at Lloyds*, 2002 S.L.T. 1258, 1273 at para.[57] (Ex Div.). See also now, P.N. No. 5 of 2004. The citation of cases from reproduction of electronic formats is permitted by that P.N.

(18) Fee for proof.

See note 36.11.6.

(19) Skilled witnesses.

An analysis of expert opinion evidence, expert evidence of fact, the admissibility of a skilled witness and the evidence, is to be found in *Kennedy v. Cordia (Services) LLP*, 2016 S.C. (UKSC) 59, at paras. [39]-[61].

That case stated that there are four considerations to be taken into account in considering the admissibility of a person as a skilled witness: (i) whether the proposed skilled evidence will assist the court in its task; (ii) whether the witness has the necessary knowledge and experience; (iii) whether the witness is impartial in his or her presentation and assessment of the evidence; and (iv) whether there is a reliable body of knowledge or experience to underpin the expert's evidence. All four considerations apply to opinion evidence, although, when the first consideration is applied to opinion evidence the threshold is the necessity of such evidence. The four considerations also apply to skilled evidence of fact, where the skilled witness draws on the knowledge and experience of others rather than or in addition to personal observation or its equivalent.

REPORTS OF PROOFS.

The Judicial Proceedings (Regulation of Reports) Act 1926 regulates the publishing of indecent material. S.46 of the Children and Young Persons (Scotland) Act 1937 empowers the court to direct that the identity of a child should not be disclosed. Under s. 4(2) of the Contempt of Court Act 1981 an order may be made to postpone a report of proceedings to avoid substantial risk of prejudice to the administration of justice.

36.11.3

Under s. 11 of the 1981 Act, where the court allows a name or other matter to be withheld from the public, it may prohibit publication of that name or matter in connection with the proceedings. In relation to s.11, the court has to consider first whether it has power to allow a name or matter to be withheld and second whether to exercise the power; the language of the provision made it difficult to suggest that there was an inherent power of the court to grant anonymity and there was no power to impose reporting restrictions other than where express authority could be found. But, in *BBC, Applicants*, 2013 S.L.T. 749 (First Div.), it was held that the court did have an inherent power to order a name or matter to be withheld from the public.

TRANSCRIPTS OF EVIDENCE.

These are ordered by the court either at the request of the court to assist in writing the judgment or at the request of a party (r. 36.11(3)), or requested by a party from the shorthand writers for the purposes of a reclaiming motion (r. 36.11(8)).

36.11.4

Transcripts, if ordered, are not usually available for some weeks after the proof; but daily transcripts may be ordered and obtained by arrangement with the shorthand writers at extra cost.

Although r. 36.11(7) provides for borrowing the record of the evidence to enable a party to consider whether to reclaim, a transcript of the evidence is rarely available before the expiry of the reclaiming days unless there are daily transcripts.

The court shorthand writers are William Hodge (Shorthand Writers) Ltd, 20 York Place, Edinburgh EH1 3EP (tel. 0131-556 5660).

Details of transcribers for transcripts of digital recording may be obtained from the Offices of Court: PN No. 3 of 2010.

SHORTHAND WRITER'S FEE.

36.11.5   For shorthand writer's fees, see r. 42.16, Table of Fees, Chap. IV.

FEE.

36.11.6   The court fee for a proof is payable by each party for every 30 minutes or part thereof. For fee, see Court of Session etc. Fees Order 1997, Table of Fees, Pt I, B, item 16 or C, item 16 [S.I. 1997 No. 688, as amended, pp. C 1201 et seq.]. Certain persons are exempt from payment of fees: see 1997 Fees Order, art.5 substituted by S.S.I. 2002 No. 270. A fee exemption certificate must be lodge in process: see P.N. No. 1 of 2002.

Where a party is legally represented, the fee may be debited under a credit scheme introduced on 1st April 1976 by P.N. No. 4 of 1976 to the account (if one is kept or permitted) of the agent by the court cashier, and an account will be rendered weekly by the court cashier's office to the agent for all court fees due that week for immediate settlement. An agent not on the credit scheme will have an account opened for the purpose of lodging the fee: P.N. No. 2 of 1995. A debit slip and a copy of the court hearing time sheet will be delivered to the agent's box or sent by DX or post.

A party litigant must pay (by cash, cheque or postal order) to the clerk of court at the end of the hearing or, if the proof lasts more than a day, at the end of each day: P.N. No. 2 of 1995. A receipt will be issued. The assistant clerk of session will acknowledge receipt of the sum received from the clerk of court on the Minute of Proceedings.

EXTRA-JUDICIAL SETTLEMENTS.

36.11.7   Where a case is settled there are three possible ways of bringing the cause to an end:— (a) the court is asked to grant the agreed decree at the proof and the proof is discharged, (b) a joint minute is lodged setting out the terms of settlement and a motion is enrolled for the court to interpone authority to the joint minute and for decree in terms of it (or such parts of it as the court may grant) and for discharge of the proof, or (c) a motion (usually at the bar) to discharge the proof because the cause has settled and a joint minute is subsequently lodged.

(1)   Joint minutes.

The joint minute sets out the terms of settlement. It is lodged in process (or tendered at the bar) with a motion to interpone authority to it, for decree in terms of it (or such parts of it as the court may grant decree for) and to discharge any proof diet fixed. The settlement is binding on the parties even though the court has not interponed authority to it: *McAthey v. Patriotic Investment Co Ltd* , 1910 S.C. 584. Once lodged the minute cannot be withdrawn unless the court could not grant decree in terms of it at all: *McAthey*, above (where agreement with liquidator to settle dispute on payment to pursuer thus giving a creditor a preference); or possibly in other exceptional circumstances: *Paterson v. Magistrates of St Andrews* (1880) 7 R. 712. In *Paterson* it appears there was a doubt whether the town council really had properly authorised the settlement and there is hint in Lord Ormidale's opinion that the minute could be withdrawn as not moved for and because authority had not been interponed to it by the court (Lord Young's dissenting view in *Gow v. Henry* (1899) 2 F. 48). The case of *Paterson* is not mentioned in *McAthey*. The court will grant decree in terms of the joint minute insofar as its terms are within the perimeters of the conclusions: *McAthey*, above. It is not necessary to postpone decree where the action is settled with respect to one defender in order to preserve another defender's rights of relief under s. 3 of the Law Reform (Miscellaneous Provisions) (Scotland) Act 1940: *Singer v. Gray Tool Co (Europe) Ltd* , 1984 S.L.T. 149 (First Div.). The form of a joint minute is:

"[X] for the pursuer and
[Y] for the defender stated and hereby state to the court that the parties are agreed that ..."

(2)   Disputes about settlements.

In *Dixon v. Van de Weterfing* , 17th March 2000 (OH), unreported (2000 G.W.D. 12-409), parties thought that the case was settled on the morning of the proof but the defender refused to pay because he thought he had been induced to agree by misrepresentation by the pursuer. The pursuer enrolled for decree. Lord Bonomy considered that, where the court was being asked to give effect to an agreement the terms of which were not clearly stated and acknowledged and was arguably reducible, the issue must be plainly and quickly identified in writing. He ordered the pursuer to lodge in seven days a minute setting out the facts relating to the settlement, the remedy sought and pleas and the defender to lodge answers in seven days thereafter. It might be possible to determine the matter at a subsequent hearing. If not, further procedure (amendment, debate and proof) would be necessary. There is nothing new about this procedure (see *Lawrence v. Knight* , 1972 S.C. 26 (OH)) but it is useful to be reminded of it. The procedure is at the discretion of the court. There may be circumstances, however, where the better course is for the party alleging settlement to bring an action of declarator (or specific implement): *North British Railway Co. v. Bernards Ltd* , (1900) 7 S.L.T. 329 (OH).

(3) Expenses.

Expenses "as taxed" means the expenses of process, but does not include expenses incurred before the cause was brought: *Clyde Nail Co Ltd v. A. G. Moore & Co Ltd* ,1949 S.L.T. (Notes) 43. Expenses include expenses appropriate to the case, which may include an additional fee under r. 42.14 whether or not expressly included in the terms of settlement (but not if excluded): *Marks and Spencer Ltd v. British Gas Corporation* , 1984 S.C. 86 (Second Div.); *UCB Bank plc v. Dundas & Wilson C.S.* , 1990 S.C. 377 (First Div.). Where a party wishes to reserve the right to seek modification of a liability for expenses as a legally assisted person, this should be stated in the settlement otherwise the right will be held to have been surrendered: *Boughen v. Scott* , 1983 S.L.T. (Sh. Ct.) 94; *Roy, Nicholson, Becker & Day v. Clarke* , 1984 S.L.T. (Sh. Ct.) 16.

JUDICIAL SETTLEMENTS—TENDERS.

A tender is a judicial offer because it is a formal written offer by a defender (or third party) to a pursuer (or a pursuer to a defender in a counterclaim) in the process of the cause. A tender may be made in the pleadings or, more commonly, in a separate minute of tender lodged in process. A tender may be lodged at any time from the bringing of the proceedings until final judgment. The money is not lodged in court.

36.11.8

A tender may be withdrawn by a minute of withdrawal of tender at any time before the tender is accepted. A tender may lapse, e.g. because of subsequent events: see *Macrae v. Edinburgh Street Tramway Co* , (1885) 13 R, 365 (tender sought to be accepted after referee's lower award); *Bright v. Weatherspoon* , 1940 S.C. 280 (tender accepted after reclaiming judgment of Lord Ordinary). A tender is not brought to the attention of the judge until the question of expenses is dealt with: *Avery v. Cantilever Shoe Co* , 1942 S.C. 469, 470 per L.P. Normand.

(1) Form of tender.

The form of a tender is:

"[Y] for the defender stated and hereby states to the court that, without admitting liability and under reservation of his [*or* its] whole rights and pleas, the defender tendered and hereby tenders to the pursuer the sum of (*state in words and figures*) sterling together with the taxed expenses of process to the date hereof in full of the conclusions of the summons."

A tender should be in clear and unambiguous terms. It has been said that it should be unqualified and unconditional: *Bisset v. Anderson* (1847) 10 D. 233, 234 (obiter) and *Gunn v. Marquis of Breadalbane* (1849) 11 D. 1040, 1050–1052 (obiter). But in *Ferguson v. Maclennan Salmon Co Ltd* , 1990 S.C. 45, 51, Lord McCluskey held that a tender did not have to be unqualified. The principle was that if one party made a judicial offer in clear and unambiguous terms which was open to the other party to accept, thereby ending the litigation, and the other party did not accept it, then if, after further litigation, the court made an award which benefits the non-accepting party to no greater extent than he would have benefited by accepting the offer, then, in the absence of other considerations, it is he and not the offerer who should pay for the unnecessary litigation subsequent to its date. A party cannot seek to impose conditions on another party after tender and acceptance between them: *Talbot v Babcock International Ltd*, 2014 S.L.T. 1077 (OH).

(2) Expenses.

The tender must contain an unconditional offer to pay the expenses to the date of the tender: *Little v. Burns* (1881) 9 R. 118. An exception may be where the pursuer unreasonably failed to intimate the claim before raising the action and the tender is lodged with defences: *Lees v. Gordon* 1929 S.L.T. 400 (OH). Phrases such as "such expenses as the court may award" and "such expenses as the court considers proper" should not be used: see *McKenzie v. H.D. Fraser & Sons* , 1990 S.C. 311, 321 per L.P. Hope (the dispute was whether the usual form of tender, or another, should be used when a defender wished to argue that expenses should be awarded on a sheriff court scale; the court adhered to the usual form of tender). The phrase "expenses of process" means that the court has a discretion as to the level or amount of expenses: *McKenzie*, above; see also *Gillespie v. Fitxpatrick* , 2003 S.L.T. 999 (motion for expenses on sheriff court ordinary scale granted). The expenses of process will include any additional fee awarded. See also *Martin v. Had-Fab Ltd* , 2005 S.C.L.R. 129 (defenders unsuccessfully argued that "expenses to date" entitled the court to award expenses to the date of an earlier tender). See also *Brackencroft Ltd v. Slivers Marine Ltd* , 2006 S.L.T. 85.

The pursuer has a reasonable time to consider the tender: *Wood v. Miller* 1960 S.C. 86, 98 per LJ-C Thomson. For a case where it was held that it was reasonable to accept a tender, made on the first day, on the following morning of the proof, see *Pagan v. The Miller Group Ltd* , 2002 S.C. 150 (OH). Accordingly, where the pursuer accepts the tender, expenses "to the date of tender" includes that reasonable time thereafter. Determination of this true date of the tender is very much the province of the auditor: *Smeaton v. Dundee Corporation* , 1941 S.C. 600. But where the court has all the facts, the court may determine the date: see, e.g. *Morton v. O'Donnell* , 1979 S.L.T. (Notes) 26. The pursuer's expenses will include the expenses of considering the tender: *Jack v. Black* , 1911 S.C. 691, 700 per L.P. Dunedin. For expenses where the tender is not accepted, see (5) below.

(3) Interest.

Interest may be excluded or restricted. Unless otherwise stated, in an action of damages, a tender is in full satisfaction of any claim for interest: Interest on Damages (Scotland) Act 1958, s. 1(1B). In considering whether an award is equal to or greater than the sum tendered, therefore, the court will have to take account of such part as it considers appropriate of any interest awarded under the Act. See, e.g. *Manson v. Skinner* , 2002 S.L.T. 448 in (5) below. In *Tait v. Campbell* , 2004 S.L.T. 187, it was held that the pursuer was entitled to interest at the full rate until payment (but liable for expenses from the date of the second tender) notwithstanding an unsuccessful motion for a new trial as it was only in exceptional circumstances that a pursuer should suffer a lower award as a result of the passage of time arising from the exercise of a right to such a new trial.

In any other case whether interest is included will depend on construction of the terms of the tender. The words "in full satisfaction and settlement of the claim" may not include interest: see *Carmichael v. Caledonian Railway Co* , (1868) 6 M. 671, 681, *Riddell v. Lanarkshire and Ayrshire Railway Co* , (1904) 6 F. 432 and The "Devotion II", 1979 S.C. 80, 91 per Lord Wylie.

(4) Acceptance of tender.

The form of acceptance is:

[X] for the pursuer stated and hereby states to the court that the pursuer accepted and hereby accepts the tender contained in the minute of tender, No. of Process, in full of the conclusion(s) of the summons."

A motion for decree in terms of the minutes of tender and acceptance has also to be made. The pursuer has a reasonable time to consider the tender: *Wood v. Miller* 1960 S.C. 86, 98 per LJ-C Thomson.

(5) Expenses where tender not accepted.

The general principles are these. (A) Where the pursuer beats the tender by being awarded more than the tender, he is entitled to the whole expenses of process: *Heriot v. Thomson* , (1833) 12 S. 145. (B) Where the pursuer fails to beat the tender by being awarded less or no more than the tender, the pursuer gets expenses to the date of the tender (not the date he should have accepted the tender) and the defender gets expenses from that date. Circumstances may justify another determination. Thus, although an award of damages may exceed the tender, where that excess is due to interest accrued since the date of the tender, the court may in effect treat the tender as not being beaten and award expenses to the defender from the date of the tender. Such a course of action would arise where the refusal of the tender unnecessarily prolonged the proceedings to no purpose and the excess of the award over the tender was due to the interest accrued since the date of tender: *Manson v. Skinner* , 2002 S.L.T. 448.

(6) Plurality of parties.

Where there is more than one pursuer, each having separate conclusions, there must be a tender to each pursuer: *Flanagan v. Dempster, Moore & Co* , 1928 S.C. 308 (First Div.).

A defender sued jointly and severally may alone tender to a pursuer. If for the full sum and the pursuer accepts and is paid, the pursuer may not continue his action against the other defenders. Where the averments of the defender making the tender make it prudent for the pursuer to call a second defender, the tender of expenses includes a right of the pursuer to relief from the tendering defender for any expenses awarded against the pursuer in favour of the second defender: *Clegg v. McKirdy & MacMillan* , 1932 S.C. 442, 446 (Second Div.); cf *Mitchell v. Redpath Engineering Ltd* , 1990 S.L.T. 259.

(7) Tender by one defender to pursuer and other defenders.

One of jointly and severally sued defenders may tender to the pursuer and to the other defenders that they contribute in certain proportions: see, e.g. *Houston v. British Road Services Ltd* , 1967 S.L.T. 329.

(8) Williamson tenders.

One of jointly and severally sued defenders may offer to the other defenders that he will admit liability to the pursuer if the other defenders will contribute with that defender in certain proportions: *Williamson v. McPherson* , 1951 S.C. 438. If agreed a joint tender is then made to the pursuer.

The form of a Williamson tender is:

[Y] for the first (-named) defender stated and hereby states to the court that, without prejudice to and under reservation of his whole rights and pleas, the first defender offered and hereby offers to the second defender to admit liability to make reparation to the pursuer jointly and severally with the second defender on the basis that the defenders shall be liable inter se to contribute to any damages and expenses awarded to the pursuer in the proportion of ..."

Finality of decision on sufficiency of stamp

36.12. The decision of the Lord Ordinary that a document adduced in evidence is sufficiently stamped, or does not require to be stamped, shall be final and not subject to review.

Deriv. RCS 1965, r. 264(f)

GENERAL NOTE.

Judicial notice must be taken of the omission or insufficiency of the stamp on a document subject to stamp duty: Stamp Act 1891, s. 14(1).

Under s. 14(4) of the 1891 Act an instrument in Sched. 1 to that Act executed in the U.K., or relating wherever executed to any property, or to any matter or thing or to be done, in the U.K., shall not be given in evidence or be available for any purpose whatsoever unless it be stamped in accordance with the law in force at the time it was first executed.

The duty due and a penalty may be paid at the proof to the clerk of court: 1891 Act, s. 14(1).

Death, disability, retiral, etc., of Lord Ordinary

36.13.—(1) Where the Lord Ordinary, before whom proof has been taken, in whole or in part, dies, retires or otherwise becomes unable to give judgment or to hear further proof, as the case may be, any party to the cause may apply by motion to the Inner House for directions—

   (a) that the cause shall be continued before, and shall be disposed of by, another Lord Ordinary;

   (b) that the notes of evidence already taken, as certified by the shorthand writer, shall be evidence in the cause; and

   (c) that the notes of the Lord Ordinary taken at the proof shall be made available to the Lord Ordinary before whom the cause is to be continued.

(2) On making directions under paragraph (1), the Inner House may make such other order as it thinks fit.

(3) On enrolling a motion under paragraph (1), the party enrolling it shall—

   (a) lodge in process four copies of the closed record (incorporating all interlocutors pronounced in the cause and amendments to the record allowed since the closing of the record); and

   (b) send one copy of that record to every other party.

(4) It shall not be necessary for any documents to be lodged in support of such a motion unless the court otherwise directs.

(5) The vacation judge may not hear or determine a motion under paragraph (1).

Deriv. R.C.S. 1965, r. 112 amended by S.I. 1976 No. 137

"MOTION".

For motions, see Chap. 23.

"LODGE IN PROCESS".

The closed records are lodged in process as a step of process: r. 1.3(1) (definition of "step of process"). On steps of process, see r. 4.4.

RECUSAL OF JUDGE: BIAS.

The test to be applied by a judge in considering whether to recuse himself or herself from hearing a case on the ground of bias is whether the fair-minded and informed observer, having considered the facts, would conclude that the judge was biased: see *Millar v. Dickson* , 2001 S.L.T. 988; *Porter v. Magill* , [2002] 2 A.C. 357 per Lord Hope of Craighead at para. [103]; *Helow v. Advocate General for Scotland* , 2007 S.C. 303, 323 at para. [34] (Extra Div.).

DEATH OF A LORD ORDINARY.

For an example of the procedure after the death of a Lord Ordinary, see *Christies Parks Ltd v. Scottish Water* [2016] CSOH 155, where Lord Jones died when the case was at avizandum and the case was dealt with by another Lord Ordinary on the basis of transcripts of evidence and further submissions.

CHAPTER 37 JURY TRIALS

Applications for jury trial

37.1.—(1) Within 14 days after the date of an interlocutor allowing issues in an action, the pursuer shall lodge in process the proposed issue for jury trial and a copy of it for the use of the court.

(2) Where a pursuer fails to lodge a proposed issue for jury trial under paragraph (1), he shall, unless—

    (a) the court, on cause shown, otherwise orders, or

    (b) a proposed issue is lodged by another party under paragraph (3), be held to have departed from his right to jury trial; and any other party may apply by motion for a proof.

(3) Where a pursuer fails to lodge a proposed issue under paragraph (1), any other party may, within seven days after the expiry of the period specified in that paragraph, lodge in process a proposed issue for jury trial and a copy of it.

(4) Where a proposed issue has been lodged under paragraph (1) or (3), any other party may, within seven days after the date on which the proposed issue has been lodged, lodge in process a proposed counter-issue and a copy of it.

(5) A proposed counter-issue lodged by a party under paragraph (4) may include any question of fact which is made the subject of a specific averment on record or is relevant to his pleas-in-law notwithstanding that it does not in terms meet the proposed issue.

(6) The party lodging a proposed issue under paragraph (1) or (3) shall, on the day after the date on which the period for lodging a proposed counter-issue under paragraph (4) expires, apply by motion for approval of the proposed issue.

(7) Any party who has lodged a proposed counter-issue under paragraph (4) shall, within seven days after the enrolment of a motion for approval of a proposed issue under paragraph (6), apply by motion for approval of his proposed counter-issue.

(8) Where a proposed counter-issue has been lodged, the motion for approval of a proposed issue shall be heard at the same time as the motion for approval of the proposed counter-issue.

(9) The Lord Ordinary, on granting a motion for approval of a proposed issue or proposed counter-issue, shall authenticate with his signature the proposed issue or proposed counter-issue as lodged or as adjusted.

(10) Where an issue or counter-issue has been approved by the court, the party whose issue or counter-issue it is shall lodge 18 copies of the approved issue or counter-issue for the use of the court; and such copies need not contain the authentication of the Lord Ordinary.

Deriv. R.C.S. 1965, r. 114(1) to (5) (r. 37.1(1) to (5)), r. 114(6) (r. 37.1(6) and (7)) and r. 114(7) (r. 37.1(9)), all substituted by S.I. 1982 No. 1825; P.N. 28th February 1955 (r. 37.1(10))

GENERAL NOTE.

Civil jury trial was introduced in Scotland with the Jury Court by the Jury Trials (Scotland) Act 1815, after a lengthy debate, begun perhaps by Lord Swinton in a pamphlet in 1789, as a means of dealing with the dire state into which the forms of Scottish pleading and litigation had fallen by the end of the 18th century. Furthermore the House of Lords saw in it a means of improving Scottish litigation and discouraging appeals, they being also more familiar with the English (jury) trial system. The Jury Court was abolished and the power to try causes by jury transferred to the Court of Session by the C.S.A. 1830.

Civil jury trial does not infringe art.6(1) of the ECHR (right to fair trial): *Heasman v. J M Taylor & Partners*, 2002 S.C. 326; 2002 S.L.T. 451 (Ex Div). The grounds of challenge in that case were that no meaningful guidance was given to juries on levels of solatium and the jury gave no reasons for its decision. The case was reported to the Inner House. The challenge was unsuccessful and the Extra Division held that the procedures followed were adequate to give the assurance that the jury was directed to the proper questions and the appellate procedure ensured that a party did not suffer the consequences of an unfair trial.

37.1.2   Certain causes, the "enumerated causes", must be sent to jury trial unless the parties otherwise agree or special cause is shown: C.S.A. 1988, s. 9(b). The court may allow jury trial in a cause other than an enumerated cause: e.g. *Fletcher v. Lord Advocate* 1923 S.C. 27; *Blount v. Watt* 1953 S.L.T. (Notes) 39. In this case the court has a discretion, although it may require a special reason (cause) to send a case which is not an enumerated cause to jury trial.

The enumerated causes are: (1) an action of damages for personal injuries; (2) an action for libel or defamation; (3) an action founded on delinquency or quasi-delinquency where the conclusion is for damages only and expenses; and (4) an action of reduction on the ground of incapacity, essential error, or force and fear: C.S.A. 1988, s. 11. The longer list in s. 28 of the C.S.A. 1825 was replaced by this shorter list in the C.S.A. 1988 because none of the others had been sent to jury trial in living memory. S. 49 of the C.S.A. 1850 had allowed proof on commission as an alternative in the enumerated causes except cases of libel, nuisance or damages; s. 4 of the Evidence (Scotland) Act 1866 introduced the alternative of proof to jury trial where parties consented or on special cause shown (both these provisions are repealed by the C.S.A. 1988, Sched. 2).

(1)   Action of damages for personal injuries.

This phrase in s. 11(a) of the C.S.A. 1988, which is a consolidating measure, was not intended to and did not change the law, from that under s. 28 of the C.S.A. 1825, to exclude claims for loss of society as a result of the death of a relative: *Morris v. Drysdale* 1992 S.L.T. 186.

(2)   Action for libel or defamation.

This means an action for written or oral defamation, the former being sometimes known as libel and the latter as slander. Defamation means a communication to the injured party or another of a false statement or idea which is an imputation injurious to the character or credit of the injured party: *Brownlie v. Thomson* (1859) 21 D. 480, 485 per L.J.-C. Inglis; *A.B. v. C.D.* (1904) 7 F. 22. Malice only requires to be proved where qualified privilege is claimed: *Langlands v. Leng* 1916 S.C.(H.L.) 102, 109 per Lord Shaw of Dunfermline. Other types of verbal injury are *convicium*, slander of title, property, or goods or business, and malicious falsehood, which require proof of malice: these are not included in the meaning of defamation.

(3)   Action founded on delinquency and quasi-delinquency.

Delinquency means fault or violation of duty and these terms are, therefore, synonymous with delict and quasi-delict.

(4)   Action of reduction on ground of incapacity, essential error, or force or fear.

(a) Incapacity may arise through nonage (a child under 16: Age of Legal Capacity (Scotland) Act 1991, s. 1(1)(a)) or insanity or other mental incapacity (including drunkenness: Stair, 1.x.13; Erskine, III.i.16; *Taylor v. Provan* (1864) 2 M. 1226). (*b*) Essential error: see *Stewart v. Kennedy* (1890) 17 R.(H.L.) 25; *Menzies v. Menzies* (1893) 20 R.(H.L.) 108, 142 per Lord Watson; *Woods v. Tulloch* (1893) 20 R.(H.L.) 477 per Lord Watson; *Westville Shipping Co. v. Abram Steamship Co.* 1922 S.C. 571. (*c*) Force and fear. A contract induced by threats or violence sufficient to overcome the fortitude of a reasonable man is void: Stair, I.ix.8; Erskine, III.i.16; but a bill of exchange is voidable (Bills of Exchange Act 1882, ss. 29(2), 30(2) and 38).

See note 28.1.8(B) for a discussion of special cause for disallowing jury trial.

"WITHIN 14 DAYS", "WITHIN SEVEN DAYS".

37.1.3   The date from which the period is calculated is not counted. Where the last day falls on a Saturday or Sunday or a public holiday on which the Office of Court is closed, the next available day is allowed: r. 1.3(7). For office hours and public holidays, see note 3.1.2.

"INTERLOCUTOR ALLOWING ISSUES".

37.1.4   This will be the interlocutor pronounced (*a*) after the record has closed either of consent under r. 22.3(5)(a)(v) or at the By Order (Adjustment) Roll appointed under r. 22.3(5)(b), or (*b*) after a hearing on the Procedure Roll under Chap. 28.

"PROPOSED ISSUE".

37.1.5   R.C.S. 1965, r. 115 which provided for jury trial without issues has not been re-enacted because it is thought to have fallen into desuetude, although jury trial without issues was ordered in *Ryan v. Orr* 1965 S.L.T. 12.

Issues are concise statements of questions of fact to be decided by the jury: Bell's *Dictionary*, p. 586. They are a device to simplify the jury's task: *Lawrie v. Glasgow Corporation* 1952 S.C. 361, 366 per L.J.-C. Thomson. They must be in conformity with the averments on record: *Lawrie*, above. The issues put before the jury should be as uncomplicated as is compatible with a fair representation of the rival pleas: *Taylor v. National Coal Board* 1953 S.C. 349, 354 per L.J.-C. Thomson. It is a long established practice that a jury has to answer the question of a defender's liability, and an issue should include a question as to the defender's liability: *Black v. North British Railway* , 1908 S.C. 444: *Mitchell v. Laing* , 1998 S.C. 342, 353A–C per Rodger, L.P. In a case where liability has been admitted, the answer to the question is a formality; but the jury must still give an affirmative answer by direction of the judge, the answer must be recorded by the clerk of court on the issue as being the verdict of the jury (r.37.9): *Benson v. Scottish Lion Engineering Ltd* , 2002 S.C. 228.

Issues may be general or particular. A general issue is an issue specific as to time and place but general as to other facts and where there are no separate grounds on which the case rests, and is the usual form in actions for damages for personal injuries: Maclaren on *Court of Session Practice*, p. 565; e.g. "Whether on or about (*date*) at (*place*) the pursuer was injured through the fault of the defenders to his loss, injury and damage?". A particular issue is one which includes a particular averment which the pursuer must prove in order to succeed: e.g. that the pursuer was in the employment of the defenders or that there was a negligent exercise of a statutory duty.

Several pursuers injured by the same conduct of the defender have separate conclusions and separate issues except in the case of pursuers suing for death of a relative. A pursuer suing several defenders for the same delict may have one issue against all and, if in the alternative, with the addition of the words "or one or other and which of them"; although separate issues may be necessary to distinguish different damages claimed against each: *Smith v. Taylor* (1882) 10 R. 291, 299 per L.P. Inglis. On styles for issues, see *Christie's Tutor v. Kirkwood* 1991 S.L.T. 805 (issue where contributory negligence and damages claimed against both defenders or one of them); *Hayden v. Glasgow Corporation* 1948 S.C. 143 (issue and counter-issue in personal injury action with contributory negligence); *McLean v. The Admiralty* 1960 S.C. 199 (issue in personal injury action where no contributory negligence); *Stewart v. Blythswood Shipbuilding Co. Ltd* 1951 S.L.T.(Notes) 47 (issue where existence of accident in dispute); *Cairnie v. Secretary of State for Scotland* 1966 S.L.T.(Notes) 57 (issue where there is a third party).

At the end of the issue there will be a schedule of the damages claimed. In an action of damages for personal injuries, there are separate entries in the schedule for solatium past and future, and for loss of earnings past and future: *MacDonald v. Glasgow Corporation* 1973 S.C. 52, 55 (where the style is set out). In an action of damages for the death of a relative, there are separate entries for loss of society (or its recent replacement) past and present: *McAllister v. Abram* 1981 S.L.T. 85. There should not now be a sum stated for "Damages claimed" in the schedule: *Hamilton v Ferguson Transport (Spean Bridge) Ltd,* 2012 S.C. 486, 521, para.[77] (Five Bench). Where there is more than one pursuer there are separate entries for heads of claim for each pursuer. Where more than one wrong is alleged there may be more than one schedule corresponding to the separate conclusions; there will not be more than one schedule simply because there is a common law case and a statutory case alleged in an action for personal injuries. Loss of employability may be divided into past and future loss: *Hill v. Watson* 1998 S.C. 81.

Where the pursuer received benefits to which the Social Security (Recovery of Benefits) Act 1997 applies, the issue for the pursuer will have to be framed in such a way that the jury can specify the damages it is awarding under each, if any, of the heads of compensation in column 1 of Sched. 2 to the 1997 Act. The reason is that the court, on pronouncing decree for payment of the damages, must specify the amount of compensation payment in the case of each head of compensation: 1997 Act, s.15(2). Under the 1997 Act, the person (the compensator) compensating the victim of an accident, injury or disease is liable to pay in full to the Secretary of State for Social Security the amount of the recoverable social security benefits (for which see column 2 of Sched. 2 to the 1997 Act) paid to the victim. The compensator is entitled to deduct, from certain specified heads of compensation he is to pay to the victim, the amount of the recoverable benefits (see 1997 Act, s.8). These heads, specified in column 1 of Sched. 2 to the 1997 Act, are the compensation for earnings lost, the compensation for cost of care, and the compensation for loss of mobility, during the relevant period. The compensator will then pay the sum deducted to the Secretary of State (to the CRU). The "relevant period" is the five years immediately following the date of the accident or injury or, in the case of disease, the date on which the victim first claimed a listed benefit): see 1997 Act, s.3(2) and (3). If at any time before the end of that period a compensation payment is made in final discharge of any claim, the relevant period ends on that date: 1997 Act, s.3(4)(a). The £2,500 small payments threshold has been abolished. A difficulty arises where the final decree is pronounced within the five-year relevant period: is the court required to specify the damages for a period ending on the date of payment (not then determinable) after final decree, the final discharge occurring and the relevant period ending, under s.3(4)(a) of the 1997 Act, on the date of payment; or is the date of decree to be deemed to be the date of payment? The solution has been provided by the Inner House in *Mitchell v. Laing* , 1998 S.C. 342. The court held that the intention of the legislation was that the amount of recoverable benefits to be deducted from the heads of compensation was the amount payable over the whole five-year period. Accordingly, the court in pronouncing decree would specify the damages due for the specified heads of compensation for the full five years; and the issue must, therefore, be framed in such a way that the jury can specify the damages due for earnings lost, cost of care or loss of mobility for the five years following the date of the accident or injury, or, in the case of disease, the date on which a listed benefit was first claimed.

The relevant part of the issue approved in *Mitchell*, above, was in the following terms as amended by *Hamilton v Ferguson Transport (Spean Bridge) Ltd,* 2012 S.C. 486, 521, para.[77] (Five Bench) which indicated that no sum should be stated against the heading "Damages claimed".:

Damages claimed

Past solatium £

Future solatium £

Damages claimed

Past wage loss	£
Past services by stepmother	£
(cost of care component:— £)	£
(loss of mobility component:— £)	£
Past cost of tradesmen	£
Past cost of physiotherapy	£
Past cost of medical care	£
Future cost of medical care	£
(amount to 26.7.98— £)	£
Cost of cancellation of Africa trip	£
Total damages	£

A schedule of reference for lengthy documents founded on, as in a defamation action, may be attached to an issue.

If no proposed issue is lodged and no other party lodges a proposed issue, the pursuer is deemed to have departed from his right to jury trial: r. 37.1(2). The court may, on cause shown, allow a proposed issue to be received late under r. 37.1(2)(a): see, e.g. *McGee v. Matthew Hall Ltd* , 1996 S.L.T. 399 (narrow case of agents' inadvertence). Because r. 37.1(2) contains its own provision for granting relief, the court will not exercise the dispensing power in r. 2.1 unless in extraordinary circumstances: *McGee*, above, obiter per Lord Caplan.

On counter-issues, see note 37.1.8.

"LODGE IN PROCESS".

37.1.6 The issue is lodged in process as a step of process: r. 1.3(1) (definition of "step of process"). On steps of process, see r. 4.4.

"MOTION".

37.1.7 For motions, see Chap. 23.

"COUNTER-ISSUE".

37.1.8 Counter-issues are concise statements of questions of fact to be decided by the jury: Bell's *Dictionary*, p. 586. They must be in conformity with the averments on record: *Lawrie v. Glasgow Corporation* 1952 S.C. 361, 366 per L.J.-C. Thomson. The issues put before the jury should be as uncomplicated as is compatible with a fair representation of the rival pleas: *Taylor v. National Coal Board* 1953 S.C. 349, 354 per L.J.-C. Thomson.

The circumstances in which a counter-issue may or may not be appropriate were considered by Lord Patrick in *Taylor v. National Coal Board* 1953 S.C. 349, 363–368. He made the following points:

(a) A counter-issue is not necessary where the defence is a direct negative of the pursuer's issue.

(b) A counter-issue is not allowed if it is not a counter to the pursuer's issue, because if a counter-issue is answered in the defender's favour he should get the verdict.

(c) If in a case of slander the defender wishes to prove *veritas* as a complete defence he must lodge a counter-issue but not if he merely wishes to prove circumstances in order to reduce the damages.

(d) A counter-issue should not be allowed unless the fact on which the defender founds is one which, if proved, is a complete defence.

(e) The words "notwithstanding that it does not in terms meet the proposed issue" in r. 37.1 (5) (in the same terms as those introduced in R.C.S. 1934, Chap. 11, r. 34(c)) mean that facts which the defender will have to establish to support the counter-issue which are different from the facts the pursuer will have to establish to support the issue may be contained in a counter-issue.

(f) A counter-issue of contributory negligence is viewed as, if not necessary, at least expedient for the due administration of justice: see also *Lawrie*, above; and see *Hayden v. Glasgow Corporation* 1948 S.C. 143, 146 per L.P. Cooper and *Christie's Tutor v. Kirkwood* 1991 S.L.T. 805 per Lord McCluskey for styles. The words "they have proved that" should not be added: *Gallagher v. National Coal Board* 1962 S.L.T. 160.

(g) If the pursuer's issue is to prove a breach of statutory duty and the defender has to prove that if there was such a breach it was not reasonably practicable to prevent it, the defender must have a counter-issue.

(h) A counter-issue is appropriate where it is expedient for the due administration of justice and is in the Lord Ordinary's discretion.

If, in a defamation action where the defender pleads *veritas*, the counter-issue simply mirrors the issues, it may be appropriate for the defender to lead at the proof.

On styles for counter-issues, see *Hayden*, above (counter-issue in personal injury action with contributory negligence); *Gallagher*, above (counter-issue where defender alleging impracticability of preventing breach of statutory duty); *Christie's Tutor*, above (apportionment between defenders under s.3 of the Law Reform (Miscellaneous Provisions) (Scotland) Act 1940).

APPROVAL OF ISSUES.

On lodging the proposed issue the pursuer must enrol a motion for approval of issues the day after the expiry of the period for lodging a counter-issue (seven days after proposed issue): r. 37.1(4) and (6). The court may relieve a party under r. 2.1 of his failure to move for approval of issues timeously: *Flynn v. Morris Young (Perth) Ltd* 1996 S.C. 255. The Lord Ordinary must authenticate any proposed issue and counter-issue by signing them; and an interlocutor approving issues is dealt with by the Lord Ordinary and not a clerk of session under r. 4.15. The docquet of authentication does not have to be reproduced on the copies for use of the court: P.N. 21st January 1955.

37.1.9

In approving issues the court can insist in modification of them (*Hayden v. Glasgow Corporation* 1948 S.C. 143, 145 per L.P. Cooper); and did so in *MacDonald v. Glasgow Corporation* 1973 S.C. 52 to specify separately the several heads of claim. Although a proposed issue is deficient because it lacks the essential question about liability, it does not follow that it is not a proposed issue as it may require to be, and may be, adjusted to meet the court's approval: *Benson v. Scottish Lion Engineering Ltd (No.2)* , 2002 S.C. 228 (2nd Div.).

RECLAIMING.

An interlocutor adjusting issues may be reclaimed against without leave within 14 days of the interlocutor: r. 38.3(4)(d). The issue (or counter-issue) must be lodged and a copy sent to every other party: r. 38.12.

37.1.10

FEES.

A court fee for a jury trial is payable by each party for every 30 minutes or part thereof. For fee, see Court of Session etc. Fees Order 1997, Table of Fees, Pt I, B, item 18 [SI 1997/688, as amended, pp.C1201 et seq.]. Certain persons are exempt from payment of fees: see 1997 Fees Order, art.5, substituted by S.S.I. 2002 No.270. A fee exemption certificate must be lodged in process: see P.N. No.1 of 2002.

37.1.11

Where a party is legally represented, the fee may be debited under a credit scheme introduced on 1st April 1976 by P.N. No. 4 of 1976 to the account (if one is kept or permitted) of the agent by the court cashier, and an account will be rendered weekly by the court cashier's office to the agent for all court fees due that week for immediate settlement. Agents on the credit scheme will be billed in the usual way. An agent not on the credit scheme will have an account opened for the purpose of lodging the fee: P.N. No. 2 of 1995. A debit slip and a copy of the court hearing time sheet will be delivered to the agent's box or sent by DX or post. A party litigant must pay (by cash, cheque or postal order) to the clerk of court at the end of the hearing or, if the hearing lasts more than a day, at the end of each day: P.N. No. 2 of 1995. A receipt will be issued. The assistant clerk of session will acknowledge receipt of the sum received from the clerk of court on the Minute of Proceedings.

Citation of jurors

37.2.—(1)[1] Not less than 70 days before the diet for jury trial, the pursuer shall attend at the General Department and request the issue of a jury precept.

37.2

(2)[2] Where the pursuer has failed to request the issue of a jury precept under paragraph (1), any other party may request a jury precept not less than 63 days before the diet for jury trial.

(3) A jury precept shall be in Form 37.2-A.

(4) Where a jury precept is issued, it shall be transmitted by a clerk of session to the sheriff principal of the sheriffdom of Lothian and Borders who shall cause a list of jurors to be prepared of an equal number of men and women in accordance with the precept.

(5)[3] A citation of a person to attend as a juror shall be in Form 37.2-B and shall be executed by the sheriff clerk at Edinburgh (or a depute authorised by him) by post.

---

[1] R.37.2(1) amended by S.I. 1999 No. 1386 (effective 19 May 1999) and S.S.I. 2018 No. 266 r.2(2)(a) (effective 21 September 2018: substitution has effect subject to the saving provision specified in S.S.I. 2018 No.266 r.3).

[2] R.37.2(2) amended by S.I. 1999 No. 1386 (effective 19th May 1999) and S.S.I. 2018 No. 266 r.2(2)(b) (effective 21 September 2018: substitution has effect subject to the saving provision specified in S.S.I. 2018 No.266 r.3).

[3] As amended by the S.S.I. 2015 No. 227 r.2(3) (effective 22 September 2015).

(6) Where no party requests the issue of a jury precept under paragraph (1) or (2), each party shall be held to have departed from the application for a jury trial and inquiry into the facts of the cause shall be taken by proof.

Deriv. RCS 1965, r. 117A(1) (r. 37.2(1)), r. 117A(2) (r. 37.2(4)), both substituted by S.I. 1990 No. 2118; r. 119(b) (r. 37.2(5))

"JURY PRECEPT".

37.2.1
The jurors for a jury trial must be summoned by virtue of an authority or precept signed by the Lord Ordinary or a clerk of court and issued to the sheriff principal: C.S.A. 1988, s.12. Under r. 37.2(4) the precept is transmitted to the sheriff principal of the Sheriffdom of the Lothian and Borders, and jurors are selected from the list kept by the sheriff clerk of that sheriffdom of persons living in the sheriff court districts of Edinburgh, Linlithgow and Haddington (see form of precept in Form 37.2-A).

If there is no precept the jury cannot be summoned. The pursuer's agent would have to bear the expenses of the discharge of any diet fixed: see *Center v. Duncan* 1965 S.L.T. 168.

There is a fee due for the precept: see note 37.2.3.

JURORS.

37.2.2
The sheriff clerk must cite 36 jurors of an equal number of men and women in terms of the precept in Form 37.2-A.

The general qualifications for jury service are set out in s.1 of the Law Reform (Miscellaneous Provisions) (Scotland) Act 1980, i.e. every person who is a registered parliamentary or local government elector not less than 18 nor more than 65 years old ordinarily resident in the U.K., the Channel Islands or the Isle of Man for any period of at least five years since the age of 13 and not among those listed in Pt I or II of Sched. 1. On ineligibility, disqualification and excusal from jury service, see notes to r. 37.3.

FEE.

37.2.3
The court fee for citation of a jury is payable on receipt of instructions for precept. For fee, see Court of Session etc. Fees Order 1997, Table of Fees, Pt I, B, item 12 [S.I. 1997 No. 688, as amended, pp.C1201 et seq.]. Certain persons are exempt from payment of fees: see 1997 Fees Order, art.5, substituted by S.S.I. 2002 No. 270. A fee exemption certificate must be lodged in process: see P.N. No.1 of 2002.

Where a party is legally represented, the fee may be debited under a credit scheme introduced on 1st April 1976 by P.N. No. 4 of 1976 to the account (if one is kept or permitted) of the agent by the court cashier, and an account will be rendered weekly by the court cashier's office to the agent for all court fees due that week for immediate settlement. Party litigants and agents not operating the scheme must pay (by cash, cheque or postal order) at the time at the counter at the General Department.

Ineligibility for, and excusal from, jury service

37.3
37.3.—(1) A person summoned to serve on a jury may, as soon as possible after receipt of his citation, apply in writing to the Deputy Principal Clerk to be released from his citation; and the Deputy Principal Clerk may, if he is satisfied that there are good and sufficient grounds for excusal, grant the application.

(2) The Lord Ordinary to preside at the jury trial may, at any time before the jury is empanelled, excuse any person summoned to attend as a juror from attendance if he is satisfied that there are good and sufficient grounds for doing so.

Deriv. RCS 1965, r. 119(a) and (c)

GENERAL NOTE.

37.3.1
A person may be ineligible or disqualified for, or excused as of right from, jury service under statute; or excused on application in writing to the Deputy Principal Clerk before the trial diet or by the judge at the trial. A notice is sent to persons about to be put on the register of jurors on the exemptions.

A person cited who fails to attend is liable to a fine: Law Reform (Miscellaneous Provisions) (Scotland) Act 1980, s.2.

Jurors are entitled to travelling and subsistence for attending court, whether selected for the jury or not, and for serving on the jury: Juries Act 1949, s.24 as amended by the 1980 Act, Sched. 2, para. 3; and see Jurors Allowances (Scotland) Regulations 1977 [S.I. 1977 No. 445].

INELIGIBILITY, DISQUALIFICATION AND EXCUSAL UNDER STATUTE.

37.3.2
S. 1 of and Sched. 1 to the Law Reform (Miscellaneous Provisions) (Scotland) Act 1980 reforms and restates the law on qualification and ineligibility for, and excusal from, jury service previously in some 10 statutes. Pt I of Sched. 1 to the 1980 Act lists those ineligible for jury service and Pt II lists those who are disqualified from jury service. Pt III of Sched. 1 lists those who shall be excused as of right on attending court in answer to a citation or on writing to the clerk who issued the citation (in fact the Deputy Principal Clerk): 1980 Act, s.1(2) and (3).

Under r. 37.3(1) the Deputy Principal Clerk may excuse a person from jury service before the trial diet **37.3.3**
if there are good and sufficient grounds. This is discretionary. The matter is dealt with initially by a clerk
of session in the Signet Office. Such grounds might include illness or disability, work or holiday commitments, depending on the circumstances.

EXCUSAL FROM JURY SERVICE BY LORD ORDINARY.

Under r. 37.3(2) the Lord Ordinary to preside at the trial may excuse a person from jury service if **37.3.4**
there are good and sufficient grounds. This is discretionary. Such grounds might include illness or disability, work or holiday commitments, depending on the circumstances.

Application of certain rules relating to proofs

37.4.[1] The following provisions of these Rules shall apply in relation to an ac- **37.4**
tion in which issues have been approved for jury trial as they apply to a cause in
which a proof has been allowed:—

   rule 36.2 (citation of witnesses),
   rule 36.3 (lodging productions),
   rule 36.4 (copy productions),
   rule 36.5 (returning borrowed documents before proof),
   rule 36.7 (admissions by parties),
   rule 36.8 (conditions for receiving certain written statements in evidence),
   rule 36.9 (attendance, and lists, of witnesses),
   rule 36.10 (administration of oath or affirmation to witnesses).

   Deriv. RCS 1965, r. 121, r. 122, r. 122A(2) (inserted by S.I. 1984 No. 472), and r. 123, (r. 37.4 (part))

GENERAL NOTE.

This rule simply imports rules relating to proofs which are of equal application to jury trial. **37.4.1**
The A.S. (R.C.S.A.) (Miscellaneous) 1998 [S.I. 1998 No. 890] removes the references to r. 36.6
(notices to admit and notices of non-admission), for which provision is now in Chapter 28A, and r. 36.11
(recording of evidence) for which provision is now made in r. 37.5A.

THE TRIAL.

(1) Selection of the jury.

A jury of 12 persons is selected by ballot: C.S.A. 1988, s.13(1). The selection of any juror may be **37.4.2**
challenged for an assigned reason: C.S.A. 1988, s.13(3). Such a reason might be enmity against a party or
interest in the cause. Each party may also challenge four jurors without assigning any reason: C.S.A.
1988, s. 13(3); "each party" meaning each set of pursuers and defenders: *Dobbie v. Johnston and Russell*
(1861) 23 D. 1139. It is no longer possible for a jury to be chosen of all men or all women, proviso (b) to
s.1 of the Sex Disqualification (Removal) Act 1919 having been repealed by the Statute Law (Repeals)
Act 1989, Sched. 1. Jurors are sworn in: r. 37.6.

(2) Illness of jurors.

If the presiding judge is satisfied that a juror is through illness unable to continue, or ought for any
other reason to be discharged, he may discharge the juror so long as the jury does not fall below 10
jurors: C.S.A. 1988, s.15.

(3) Opening speeches.

The main purpose is to inform the jury of the nature and character of the case and to bring to its notice
the issue to be tried, and the speech must be fairly related to the record and the issue: *Robertson v.
Federation of Icelandic Co-operative Societies* 1948 S.C. 565, 569 per L.J.-C. Thomson. It need not be
co-extensive with the pleadings, the test is one of fairness: *Greig v. Sir William Arrol & Co. Ltd* 1965
S.L.T. 242, 244 per Lord Wheatley. It offends against standards of advocacy simply to read the record:
Greig, above. The jury does not have the record. The facts should be briefly outlined and reference
should be made to all the grounds of fault averred and alleged. The jury should be told how it is sought
that the question in the issue is to be answered. Objection can be made to evidence not covered by the
opening speech: *Robertson*, above; and evidence not covered should be objected to as there may be
circumstances in which an omission to refer to part of a case might be interpreted as a departure from it.
If a party departs deliberately from part of his case he should say so at the close of his opening speech:
Greig, above, per Lord Walker at p. 245. A party may ask for clarification at the end of a vague opening

---

[1] R. 37.4 amended by S.I. 1998 No. 890 (effective 21st April 1998).

speech (and clarification of any matter should be sought whenever it arises in the course of the trial so that it is recorded in the notes): see *Jamieson v. W. Brown & Sons (Hamilton) Ltd* 1938 S.C. 456, 456 per L.J.-C. Aitchison. The jury should not be referred to authorities. If reliance is to be placed on particular authorities which it is thought necessary to bring to the judge's attention at an early stage, the authorities should be mentioned to the judge at the end of the opening speech. While a precise figure for damages may not be mentioned (because assessment of damages is for the jury), the jury may be told that the sum sued for, stated in the schedule of damages attached to the issue, is a ceiling or maximum figure. Counsel in addressing the jury are free to suggest figures that they maintained were appropriate but should not cite authority: *Hamilton v Ferguson Transport (Spean Bridge) Ltd,* 2012 S.C. 486 (Five Bench) at p.521, para.[77].

The first opening speech is by the party on whom the initial burden of proof rests (usually the pursuer): the speech is normally delivered by the junior counsel.

After the pursuer has led his evidence, if no motion is made to withdraw the case from the jury (see (7) below), an opening speech may be made for the defender (normally by junior counsel) before he leads any evidence. Again the purpose of this speech is to explain his case. Reference is made to the pursuer's case only where it is necessary to explain his own case. There should be no reasoned attack on the pursuer's case: Maclaren on *Court of Session Practice,* p. 607. Where there is a counter-issue it is undesirable not to make an opening speech: *Dellett v. Winter* 1969 S.L.T. (Notes) 27, 28 per Lord Hunter.

(4) Objections.

Notwithstanding any objection taken in the course of the trial to the opinion or direction of the judge, the trial proceeds until the jury returns a verdict (C.S.A. 1988, s. 16) or until the case is withdrawn from the jury.

(5) Views.

Any party may apply to a Lord Ordinary to view any heritable or moveable property: C.S.A. 1988, s. 14.

(6) Motion to withdraw case from jury.

Such a motion may be made, e.g. if the facts in evidence are different from the averments on record on the faith of which the issue was obtained (*Tully v. North British Railway Co.* (1907) 46 S.L.R. 715, 718 per L.P. Dunedin) or if the pursuer failed to adduce legal evidence of averments on record (*McCafferty v. Lanarkshire Tramways Co.* 1910 S.C. 797).

(7) Amendment.

This is very difficult during a jury trial: *Rafferty v. Weir Housing Corporation Ltd* 1966 S.L.T. (Notes) 23 per Lord Hunter. On amendment, see r. 24.1.

(8) Closing speeches.

First the party who led (usually the pursuer) and then the defender may address the jury on the evidence. It is permissible to state what the wage loss is and to suggest what multiplier might be applied. If reliance is to be placed on particular authorities not previously referred to, the authorities should be mentioned to the judge. Counsel in addressing the jury are free to suggest figures that they maintained were appropriate but should not cite authority: *Hamilton v Ferguson Transport (Spean Bridge) Ltd,* 2012 S.C. 486 (Five Bench) at p.521, para.[77].

(9) Judge's charge to jury.

It is the jury's function to decide the facts. The judge will direct them on the standard of proof, on whom the burden lies and the principles of law to be applied. He may explain what facts have to be established and inform them what parts of the case have to be ignored as not supported by the evidence. The jury's function is to decide not only what evidence is credible but also what weight is to be attached to the evidence. The judge will explain the issues and counter-issues. The judge may add supplementary questions to the issues: see r. 37.8. He will tell them that the verdict may be by a simple majority (C.S.A. 1988, s. 17). He may not mention precise figures for damages but should inform them that the figure in the issue is a maximum which has no bearing on what would be a proper award. On exceptions to the charge, see r. 37.7. In the absence of the jury, parties should address the judge as to the level of non-pecuniary damages that would be appropriate. In the light of those submissions, the judge would suggest to the jury a spectrum within which the award might be, but was not binding on them (per Lords Eassie and Emslie, there might be cases where it might be better to give broad possible reference points being information as to general level of contrasting or comparable awards in different fields on non-patrimonial loss). The issue will no longer contain a sum for "damages claimed". See *Hamilton v Ferguson Transport (Spean Bridge) Ltd,* 2012 S.C. 486 (Five Bench) at p.521, para.[77], 522, para.[83] and 523, para.[90].

(10) Fee for jury trial.

For court fees payable for jury trial, see note 37.1.10.

Failure of party to appear at jury trial

37.5. Where a party does not appear at the diet for jury trial, then— **37.5**

   (a) if the party appearing is the pursuer or the party on whom the burden of proof lies, he shall be entitled to lead evidence, and go to the jury for a verdict;

   (b) if the party appearing is the defender or the party on whom the burden of proof does not lie, he shall be entitled to obtain a verdict in his favour without leading evidence.

Deriv. R.C.S. 1965, r. 127

Recording of proceedings at jury trial

37.5A.—[1](1) Subject to any other provision in these Rules, proceedings at a jury trial shall be recorded by— **37.5A**

   (a) a shorthand writer to whom the oath *de fideli administratione officii* has been administered on his appointment as a shorthand writer in the Court of Session; or

   (b) tape recording or other mechanical means approved by the Lord President.

(2) In paragraph (1), "the proceedings" means the whole proceedings including, without prejudice to that generality—

   (a) discussions—

      (i)with respect to any challenge of a juror; and

      (ii)on any question arising in the course of the trial;

   (b) the decision of the Lord Ordinary on any matter referred to in subparagraph (a);

   (c) the evidence led at the trial;

   (d) the Lord Ordinary's charge to the jury;

   (e) the speeches of counsel or agents;

   (f) the verdict of the jury; and

   (g) any request for a direction to be given under rule 37.7, any hearing in relation to such a request and any direction so given.

(3) A transcript of the record of proceedings shall be made only on the direction of the court; and the cost shall, in the first instance, be borne by the agents for the parties in equal proportions.

(4) Any transcript so made shall be certified as a faithful record of proceedings—

   (a) where the recording was under sub-paragraph (a) of paragraph (1), by whoever recorded the proceedings; and

   (b) where it was under sub-paragraph (b) of that paragraph, by whoever transcribed the record.

(5) The Lord Ordinary may make such alterations to the transcript as appear to him to be necessary after hearing the parties; and, where such alterations are made, he shall authenticate the alterations.

(6) Where a transcript has been so made for the use of the court, copies of it may be obtained by any party from the transcriber on payment of his fee.

(7) Except with leave of the court, the transcript may be borrowed from process only for the purpose of enabling a party to consider whether to reclaim against the interlocutor of the court applying the verdict of the jury or whether to apply for a new trial.

---

[1] R. 37.5A inserted by S.I. 1998 No. 890 (effective 21st April 1998).

(8)   Where a transcript is required for a purpose mentioned in paragraph (7) but has not been directed to be transcribed under paragraph (3), a party—

(a)   may request such a transcript from the shorthand writer, or as the case may be, from a person who might have transcribed the recording had there been such a direction, the cost of the requested transcript being borne by the agent for the requester in the first instance; and

(b)   shall lodge the transcript in process;

and copies of it may be obtained by any party from the transcriber on payment of his fee.

GENERAL NOTE.

37.5A.1   This rule was inserted by A.S. (R.C.S.A.) (Miscellaneous) 1998 [SI 1998/890]. The purpose, and reason for a provision different from r. 36.11 (recording of evidence in proofs), is that (as in criminal jury trials) the whole of the proceedings in a civil jury trial will now be recorded.

Rule 37.5A(1) includes a reference to recording by tape recording or other mechanical means as well as to recording by a shorthand writer. With effect from 1st April 1997, jury trials are recorded by mechanical means: Notice (sic), 6th March 1997.

Digital recording has now been approved: PN No. 4 of 2010. There is a protocol or guidance in relation to digital recording: PN No. 3 of 2010.

REPORTS OF JURY TRIALS.

37.5A.2   The Judicial Proceedings (Regulation of Reports) Act 1926 regulates the publishing of indecent material. S.46 of the Children and Young Persons (Scotland) Act 1937 empowers the court to direct that the identity of a child should not be disclosed. Under s. 4(2) of the Contempt of Court Act 1981 an order may be made to postpone a report of proceedings to avoid substantial risk of prejudice to the administration of justice.

Under s. 11 of the 1981 Act, where the court allows a name or other matter to be withheld from the public, it may prohibit publication of that name or matter in connection with the proceedings. In relation to s.11, the court has to consider first whether it has power to allow a name or matter to be withheld and second whether to exercise the power; the language of the provision made it difficult to suggest that there was an inherent power of the court to grant anonymity and there was no power to impose reporting restrictions other than where express authority could be found. But, in *BBC, Applicants*, 2013 S.L.T. 749 (First Div.), it was held that the court did have an inherent power to order a name or matter to be withheld from the public.

TRANSCRIPTS OF EVIDENCE.

37.5A.3   These are ordered by the court either at the request of the court to assist in writing the judgment or at the request of a party (r. 36.11(3)), or requested by a party from the shorthand writers for the purposes of a reclaiming motion (r. 36.11(8)). Arrangements for transcription of tape recorded evidence must be made by a party personally with a contractor of his choice who will obtain the tapes from the court: Notice (sic), 6th March 1997. Details of transcribers for transcripts of digital recording may be obtained from the Offices of Court: PN No. 3 of 2010.

Transcripts, if ordered, are not usually available for some weeks after the jury trial; but daily transcripts may be ordered and obtained by arrangement with the shorthand writers at extra cost.

Although r. 36.11(7) provides for borrowing the record of the evidence to enable a party to consider whether to reclaim, a transcript of the evidence is rarely available before the expiry of the reclaiming days unless there are daily transcripts.

The court shorthand writers are William Hodge (Shorthand Writers) Ltd, 20 York Place Edinburgh EH1 3EP (tel. 0131-556 5660).

SHORTHAND WRITER'S FEE.

37.5A.4   For shorthand writer's fees, see r. 42.16, Table of Fees, Chap. IV.

FEE.

37.5A.5   The court fee for a jury trial is payable by each party for every 30 minutes or part thereof. For fee, see Court of Session etc. Fees Order 1984, Table of Fees, Pt I, B, item 17 [SI 1984/256, Table as amended, pp. C 1202 et seg.]. The fee may be debited under a credit scheme introduced on 1st April 1976 by P.N. No.4 of 1976 to the account (if one is kept or permitted) of the agent by the court cashier, and an account will be rendered weekly by the court cashier's office to the agent for all court fees due that week for immediate settlement. An agent not on the credit scheme will have an account opened for the purpose of lodging the fee: P.N. No.2 of 1995. A debit slip and a copy of the court hearing time sheet will be delivered to the agent's box or sent by DX or post.

A party litigant must pay cash to the clerk of court at the end of the hearing or, if the proof lasts more than a day, at the end of each day: P.N. No.2 of 1995. A receipt will be issued. The assistant clerk of session will acknowledge receipt of the sum received from the clerk of court on the Minute of Proceedings.

Administration of oath or affirmation to jurors

37.6.—(1) Subject to paragraph (2), the clerk of court shall administer the oath collectively to the jury in Form 37.6-A.

(2) Where a juror elects to affirm, the clerk shall administer the affirmation to that juror in Form 37.6-B.

Deriv. R.C.S. 1965, r. 122A(1) inserted by SI 1984/472

37.6

Exceptions to judge's charge

37.7.—(1) Where a party seeks to take exception to a direction on a point of law given by the Lord Ordinary in his charge to the jury or to request the Lord Ordinary to give a direction differing from or supplementary to the directions in the charge, he shall, immediately on the conclusion of the charge, so intimate to the Lord Ordinary, who shall hear counsel for the parties in the absence of the jury.

(2) The party dissatisfied with the charge to the jury shall formulate in writing the exception taken by him or the direction sought by him; and the exception or direction, as the case may be, and the judge's decision on it, shall be recorded in a note of exception under the direction of the Lord Ordinary and shall be certified by him.

(3) After the note of exception has been certified by the Lord Ordinary, he may give such further or other directions to the jury in open court as he thinks fit before the jury considers its verdict.

Deriv. R.C.S. 1965, r. 124

37.7

NOTE OF EXCEPTION(S).

A note of exception(s) is a contemporaneous record of what has taken place drawn up by counsel and signed by the judge who gave the direction to which exception is taken and/or the direction sought. It must be made at the conclusion of the charge: r. 37.7(1). It is useful to have a blank prepared in advance in case of need. It is a summary and informal procedure because exceptions are made on the spur of the moment in the heat of battle, and it is out of keeping to demand a precise meticulous exposition of the point at issue: *Robertson v. Federation of Icelandic Co-operative Societies* 1948 S.C. 565, 572 per L.J.-C. Thomson. In some cases it may be enough to object to what the judge said for the purpose of having him withdraw what he said and otiose to invite him to state the opposite, or to invite him to make a direction in certain terms and otiose to table an exception that he was silent, or it may be enough where the terms of the direction sought clearly imply the terms of the direction objected to: Robertson, above. The note should be short and explicit. For a style of a note of exception, see *McArthur v. Weir Homing Corporation Ltd* 1970 S.C. 135, 137.

Any direction sought must be a direction in law: *McDougall v. Girdwood* (1867) 5 M. 937, 941 per Lord Curriehill.

Whatever happens to the exception taken the trial proceeds to a verdict: C.S.A. 1988, s.16.

Withdrawal of a case from the jury is not a charge to the jury and the jury does not return a verdict; and a note of exceptions is not taken against a withdrawal of the case from the jury.

On applications for new trial on the ground of misdirection, the note of exceptions must be lodged: r. 39.1.

37.7.1

"IMMEDIATELY"

Intimation of an exception to a charge to the jury has to be made immediately on conclusion of the charge and there is no scope for latitude in post-Hamilton practice and non-binding guidance on damages is not a direction on a point of law: *Bridges v. Alpha Insurance A/S*, 2016 S.L.T. 859 (OH) (intimation of exception *re* range of solatium made after jury out for over an hour).

37.7.2

Further questions for jury

37.8. The Lord Ordinary may, after the evidence has been led, submit to the jury in writing along with the issue and any counter-issue such further questions as he thinks fit.

Deriv. R.C.S. 1965, r. 116(b)

37.8

GENERAL NOTE.

R.C.S. 1965, r. 128 provided for special verdicts whereby the jury could be asked to answer specific questions, to which the judge applied the law, and did not give a verdict for either party. That rule has not been re-enacted. The view has been taken that they are obsolete. The judge, however, may ask the jury additional questions under r. 37.8.

37.8.1

Verdicts

37.9

37.9. After a verdict has been returned by a jury, the verdict shall be written on the issue and dated and signed by the clerk of court.

Deriv. R.C.S. 1965, r. 125(a)

GENERAL NOTE.

37.9.1

The verdict can be by a simple majority: C.S.A. 1988, s.17(2). The verdict is not operative until applied on an application under r. 37.10.

The jury may be discharged if it has been enclosed for three hours and is unable to agree: C.S.A. 1988, s.17(2).

The jury is asked to return a verdict on the issues and not to give a verdict for a party. If the verdict on the issue is in the negative the jury is not asked to give a verdict on the counter-issue.

Withdrawal of a case from the jury is not a charge to the jury and the jury does not return a verdict.

On applications for a new trial, see r. 39.1. On applications to the Inner House on a point of law to enter a jury verdict, see r. 39.6.

Application of verdicts

37.10

37.10. Any party may, after the expiry of seven days after the date on which the verdict was written on the issue and signed, apply by motion to apply the verdict, grant decree in accordance with it and make any award in relation to expenses.

Deriv. R.C.S. 1965, r. 125(b)

GENERAL NOTE.

37.10.1

The verdict is a finding in fact and is not operative until applied on an application under r. 37.10 to apply the verdict, for judgment (including interest) and expenses. The motion is dealt with by the presiding judge. He applies the legal result of the verdict and cannot amend it: *Morgan v. Morris* (1858) 20 D.(H.L.) 18. The judge can only look at the verdict and the issues in construing the verdict: *Morgan*, above. A verdict negative of the pursuer's case but not affirmative of the defender's results in the defender being assoilzied: *Melrose v. Hastie* (1854) 17 D.(H.L.) 4. An ambiguous verdict will result in a new trial: *Morgan*, above.

On applications to the Inner House on a point of law to enter a jury verdict, see r. 39.6.

CHAPTER 37A PROCEDURAL BUSINESS IN THE INNER HOUSE

Chapter 37A[1]

Procedural Business in the Inner House

Quorum of Inner House for certain business

37A.1.—[2](1) In relation to such procedural business of the Inner House as is specified in paragraph (2), the quorum of a Division of the Inner House shall be one judge.

(2) The procedural business mentioned in paragraph (1) is such business as arises under—

- (a) a reclaiming motion, up to and including the procedural steps mentioned in rule 38.16(2);
- (b) an application for a new trial under section 29 of the Act of 1988 or to enter a jury verdict under section 31 of the Act of 1988 up to and including the procedural steps mentioned in rule 39.7(2) or, as the case may be, rule 39.9; and
- (c) an appeal from an inferior court within the meaning of rule 40.1(2)(c), up to and including the procedural steps mentioned in rule 40.14(2);
- (d)[3] an appeal to the court under Chapter 41 (appeals under statute)—
  - (i) in the case of an appeal under Part II of that Chapter (appeals by stated case etc.), up to and including the procedural steps mentioned in rule 41.21(2);
  - (ii) in the case of an appeal under Part III of that Chapter (appeals in Form 41.25), up to and including the procedural steps mentioned in rule 41.32(2).

37A.1

GENERAL NOTE.

The reform of the way Inner House business is conducted arose out of the Penrose Report on the Review of Inner House Business in 2009. The report itself followed independent research by Dr Rachel Wadia into the efficient and effective use of Inner House resources in order to "inform" the review. She produced a damning indictment of the efficiency and cost-effectiveness of Inner House business.

What is not dealt with in Chap. 37A or elsewhere is whether the decision of the procedural judge is final or open to appeal to a larger bench of the Division. Since r. 37A.1(1) states that the quorum of a Division is one judge for the purposes of procedural business, that would indicate that the decision of the procedural judge is a decision of the Division and consideration by a larger constituted Division at common law is available only on the limited grounds on which such may be done, or on appeal to the UK Supreme Court. It would have been better to state what the position is in the Rules, e.g. the decision of the procedural judge is final or there is an appeal to a bench of three or more judges with leave of the procedural judge. The limited grounds for consideration by a larger constituted Division are that the cause is one of difficulty or importance or that the Division is equally divided: C.S.A. 1988, s. 36. A larger court may be constituted to reconsider a precedent of the court. The House of Lords, in *Girvan v. Inverness Farmers Dairy* , 1998 S.C. (H.L.) 1, 21C-G per Lord Hope of Craighead, reiterated that it is not appropriate to refer matters of the practice and procedure of the Court of Session to that court (now the UK Supreme Court).

37A.1.1

"PROCEDURAL BUSINESS".

This is defined in r. 37A.1(2). In effect, this is all business up to the appointment of the reclaiming motion, motion for a new jury trial or an appeal to a hearing.

37A.1.2

APPEARANCES.

Counsel, or other persons having rights of audience, responsible for the conduct of the reclaiming motion, and authorised to take decisions on questions of substance and procedure, are expected to appear at hearings before the procedural judge: P.N. No. 1 of 2010, para. 31.

37A.1.3

---

[1] Chap. 37A and r. 37A.1 substituted by SSI 2010/30 (effective 5th April 2010).
[2] Chap. 37A and r. 37A.1 substituted by SSI 2010/30 (effective 5th April 2010).
[3] Rule 37A.1(2)(d) inserted by SSI 2011/303 (effective 27th September 2011).

Procedural judges in the Inner House

37A.2

37A.2.—[1](1)[2]   All judges of the Inner House, except the Lord President and the Lord Justice Clerk, are procedural judges before whom proceedings in the Inner House shall be brought in accordance with Chapters 38 to 41.

(2)[3]   In this rule and in Chapters 38 to 41, "procedural judge" means a judge as referred to in paragraph (1).

(3)   A Division of the Inner House comprising three or more judges may deal with a matter which would otherwise be dealt with by a procedural judge in accordance with those Chapters where the Division considers that to be appropriate; and references in those Chapters to a procedural judge shall be construed accordingly.

"PROCEDURAL JUDGE".

37A.2.1

The judge(s) nominated to be the procedural judge(s) to deal with Inner house procedural business (defined in r. 37A.1(2); and see note 37A.1.2) are the judges of the Inner House other than the Lord President and Lord Justice-Clerk.

---

[1] Rule 37A.2 substituted by SSI 2010/30 (effective 5th April 2010).
[2] Rule 37A.2(1) and (2) substituted by S.S.I. 2011 No. 303 (effective 27th September 2011).
[3] Rule 37A.2(1) and (2) substituted by S.S.I. 2011 No. 303 (effective 27th September 2011).

CHAPTER 38 RECLAIMING
Chapter 38[1]
Reclaiming

Introduction

38.1.—[2](1) This Chapter applies subject to any other provision in these Rules or any enactment.

(2) Any party to a cause who is dissatisfied with an interlocutor pronounced by—

    (a) the Lord Ordinary;

    (b) the Lord Ordinary in Exchequer Causes; or

    (c) the vacation judge,

and who seeks to submit that interlocutor to review by the Inner House shall do so by reclaiming within the reclaiming days in accordance with the provisions of this Chapter.

(3) In this Chapter, "reclaiming days" means the days within which an interlocutor may be reclaimed against.

Deriv. R.C.S. 1965, r. 153C inserted by SI 1984/472 and r. 261(a)(part)

GENERAL NOTE.

The reform of the way Inner House business is conducted arose out of the Penrose Report on the Review of Inner House Business in 2009. The report itself followed independent research by Dr Rachel Wadia into the efficient and effective use of Inner House resources in order to "inform" the review. She produced a damning indictment of the efficiency and cost-effectiveness of Inner House business.

The core of the reform is that one judge of the Inner House, the procedural judge, is responsible for the cause until it is appointed to a full hearing and there is an automatic timetable that can be sisted or varied for the progress of the cause to that point. All procedural business (defined in r. 37A.1(2)), up to the appointment of the cause to a hearing, is dealt with by a procedural judge appointed under r. 37A.2.

Regard should be had to PN No. 3 of 2011 (Causes in the Inner House).

"RECLAIMING".

Reclaiming is a power of review of an interlocutor pronounced by a Lord Ordinary exercised by the Inner House. Other powers of review of the court are suspension (see Chap. 60), reduction (see Chap. 53) and appeals from inferior courts (see Chap. 40) and under various statutes (see Chap. 41). Reclaiming is a re-hearing by three or more senior judges from a decision of a single judge derived from the days when the court was a unitary court: *Clippens Oil Co. Ltd v. Edinburgh and District Water Trs.* (1906) 8 F. 731, 750 per L.P. Dunedin. A rehearing does not mean that the evidence is heard afresh but that the cause may be reconsidered on the evidence which was led before the Lord Ordinary as well as on a point of law.

The statutory power for reclaiming is s.28 of the C.S.A. 1988.

An interlocutor reclaimed against need not be implemented except if it is an award of custody, access or aliment, in which case it must be implemented unless the court otherwise orders (r. 38.6(5)). Oddly, an interlocutor (except in relation to certain family actions: see r. 7.2) may be extracted before the days within which the interlocutor may be reclaimed against have expired (i.e. seven days: r. 7.1(1)), and, theoretically, enforced before the end of that period. The fact, however, that an interlocutor has been extracted within the reclaiming days does not of itself prevent the interlocutor being reclaimed against: r. 38.7.

It had been thought that it is incompetent for a party to reclaim against an interlocutor pronounced on his own motion: *Watson v. Russell* (1894) 21 R. 433; *McGuinness v. Bremner plc* 1988 S.L.T. 340; *Jongejan v. Jongejan* 1993 S.L.T. 595. But in *McCue v. Scottish Daily Record* 1998 S.C. 811, a court of five judges indicated that, where a party sought to reclaim against an interlocutor pronounced on his own motion in order to submit to review a prior interlocutor (as in *McGuinness v. Bremner plc* 1988 S.L.T. 340), this was not a question of competency but that the court would not normally countenance it. Accordingly, there may be circumstances in which the court would permit it.

Where an interlocutor has been pronounced "of consent", both parties may be barred from challenging it: *Anderson v. British Coal Corporation* 1992 S.L.T. 398, 400I per L.J.-C. Ross (obiter); *Jongejan*, above. But, where the Lord Ordinary has indicated that he is minded to grant an order which has been opposed and requests parties to discuss its terms, the party who opposed the order is not precluded from reclaiming against the granting of the order merely because he complied with the request to discuss it and even proposed terms to be included in it: *Osborne v. British Broadcasting Corporation* 2000 S.L.T. 150

38.1

38.1.1

38.1.2

---

[1] Chap 38 and r. 38.1 substituted by S.S.I. 2010 No. 30 (effective 5th April 2010).
[2] Chap 38 and r. 38.1 substituted by S.S.I. 2010 No. 30 (effective 5th April 2010).

(Extra Div.). Mere acquiescence in the terms of an interlocutor does not debar a party from reclaiming on a point of law: *Vetco Gray UK Ltd v. Slessor* , 2006 S.C. 398 (Second Div.).

"SUBJECT TO ANY OTHER PROVISION".

38.1.3   Certain interlocutors, by virtue of a rule to that effect, may not be reclaimed against. A statute or other enactment may state that a particular decision may not be reclaimed.

The following provisions in these Rules provide that certain interlocutors of a Lord Ordinary may not be reclaimed:

r. 4.2(5) (decision to allow party litigant to proceed with action or petition without signature),

r. 12.7(3) (decision in relation to leading evidence from one skilled witness where evidence is within the qualifications of the assessor),

r. 13.4(3)(b) (decision to shorten or extend period of notice in a summons before service),

r. 14.6(3) (decision to shorten or extend period of notice in a petition at time of first order),

r. 19.2(1) (decree in absence),

r. 35.2(5) (decision on application for recovery of evidence made before calling of summons),

r. 36.12 (decision on sufficiency of stamp duty on a document),

r. 38.5(6) (decision to grant or refuse leave to reclaim),

r. 49.79 (decree in a simplified divorce application),

r. 59.1(5) (decision on application for letters of arrestment or inhibition in which a claim under s.19 of the Family Law (Scotland) Act 1985 is made).

Some interlocutors may only be reclaimed against with leave of the Lord Ordinary: see rr. 38.2(6) and 38.3.

"PARTY"

38.1.4   In *Scottish Ministers v Mizra*, 2015 S.C. 334, 2015 S.L.T. 20, it was held (by a single judge in the Inner House), where a petition had been served, in which one party had lodged answers and after which, following an opposed hearing, the Lord Ordinary had granted a recovery order, that the other party (a company), which had not lodged answers, could not reclaim because it was not a "party" as defined in r.1.3(1). In *Firm of Barry and Susan Peart v Promontoria (Henrico) Ltd*, 2018 S.L.T. 93 (Second Div.), it was held, where interim interdicts were granted *before* service, that the defender could reclaim against them: the definition of "party" in r.1.3(1) applied "unless the context otherwise requires"; the fact that the summons had not been served meant that the context required "party" to mean something other than the definition in r. 1.3(1). Otherwise, the incompetency argument would lead to injustice and the interim interdicts (obtained *ex parte*) could not be challenged except by recall on a change of circumstances.

Reclaiming days

38.2   **38.2.**—[1,2](1) An interlocutor disposing, either by itself or taken along with a previous interlocutor, of—

(a)   the whole subject matter of the cause; or

(b)   the whole merits of the cause whether or not the question of expenses is reserved or not disposed of,

may be reclaimed against, without leave, within 21 days after the date on which the interlocutor was pronounced.

(2) Where an interlocutor which reserves or does not dispose of the question of expenses is the subject of a reclaiming motion under paragraph (1)(b), any party to the cause who seeks an order for expenses before the disposal of the reclaiming motion shall apply by motion to the Lord Ordinary for such an order within 14 days of the date of enrolment of that reclaiming motion.

(3) An interlocutor disposing of the merits of the action and making an award of provisional damages under section 12(2)(a) of the Administration of Justice Act 1982 may be reclaimed against, without leave, within 21 days after the date on which the interlocutor was pronounced.

(4) An interlocutor mentioned in paragraph (5) may be reclaimed against, without leave, within 14 days after the date on which the interlocutor was pronounced.

(5) Those interlocutors are—

---

[1] Rule 38.2 as substituted by S.S.I. 2010 No. 30 (effective 5th April 2010).
[2] Rule 38.2 as amended by S.S.I. 2016 No. 102 para.2(4) (effective 21 March 2016).

(a) an interlocutor disposing of part of the merits of a cause;

(b) an interlocutor allowing or refusing proof, proof before answer or jury trial (but, in the case of refusal, without disposing of the whole merits of the cause);

(c) an interlocutor limiting the mode of proof;

(d) an interlocutor adjusting issues for jury trial;

(e) an interlocutor granting, refusing, recalling, or refusing to recall, interim interdict or interim liberation;

(f) an interlocutor in relation to an exclusion order under section 4 of the Matrimonial Homes (Family Protection) (Scotland) Act 1981;

(g) an interlocutor granting or recalling a sist of execution or procedure;

(h) an interlocutor loosing, restricting or recalling an arrestment or recalling in whole or in part an inhibition used on the dependence of an action or refusing to loose, restrict or recall such an arrestment or inhibition;

   (i) an interlocutor granting authority to move an arrested vessel or cargo;

(j) an interlocutor deciding (other than in a summary trial) that a reference to the European Court should be made.

(6) An interlocutor (other than a decree in absence or an interlocutor mentioned in paragraph (2), (3) or (5) of this rule) may be reclaimed against, with leave, within 14 days after the date on which the interlocutor was pronounced.

Deriv. R.C.S. 1965, r. 264(a)(part) substituted by S.I. 1990 No. 705 (r. 38.2(1)), r. 134D inserted by S.I. 1984 No. 919 (r. 38.2(3)), r. 264(b) amended by S.I. 1977 No. 1621, 1980 No. 1144 and 1985 No. 1600 (r. 38.2(4) and (5)), and r. 264(c)(part) (r. 38.2(6))

Formerly R.C.S. 1994, r. 38.3

GENERAL NOTE.

There are three general time-limits in the R.C.S. 1994 for reclaiming: (1) reclaiming, without leave within 21 days, of interlocutors which dispose of the whole cause or the whole merits (r. 38.3(2) and (3)); (2) reclaiming, without leave within 14 days, of certain interlocutors which do not dispose of the whole cause (r. 38.2(4)); and (3) reclaiming, with leave within a specified period, of any other interlocutor (rr. 38.2(6) and 38.3).   **38.2.1**

The provision in r. 38.10 for allowing a reclaiming motion to proceed out of time should be noted.

The date from which the reclaiming days are calculated is, the date of the issue of the interlocutor containing the decision in question. See also note 38.2.5.

Where an ex tempore judgment is given, that date will normally be the same as the day of the ex tempore judgment; it will not be the date of issue of any subsequent written opinion: P.N. No. 2 of 1990. Similarly, where a decision is given with reasons to be given later, the relevant date will normally be the date on which the decision was given as that will be the date-of the interlocutor.

There is an exception in relation to undefended divorce actions dealt with wholly by affidavit procedure. The relevant date is the date on which the public notice of the decree appears in the rolls and not the date on which the interlocutor is signed: *Smith v. Smith* 1989 S.L.T. 668.

"SUBJECT-MATTER OF THE CAUSE".

This means that the whole merits of the cause (whether or not evidence was led) and expenses have been decided, although expenses may not have been taxed, modified or decerned for: *Baird v. Barton* (1882) 9 R. 970. Such an interlocutor may be reclaimed against without leave within 21 days of being pronounced: r. 38.2(1)(a).   **38.2.2**

In *Our Generation Ltd v Aberdeen City Council*, 2019 S.L.T. 243 (OH), the question arose whether leave was required where the pursuer's action had been dismissed but a separate mutually exclusive counterclaim was in existence. It was held that as there was no interdependency between the principal action and the counterclaim which might preclude disposal of the whole merits of the principal action, leave was not required

WHOLE MERITS OF THE CAUSE WHETHER OR NOT EXPENSES DISPOSED OF.

This provision was introduced by A.S. (R.C.S.A. No. 1) (Miscellaneous) 1990 [S.I. 1990 No. 705] following *McGuinness v.Bremner plc* 1988 S.L.T. 340. In that case it was argued that a difficulty was created by a Lord Ordinary pronouncing a decree on the merits before dealing with expenses, as leave was required to reclaim the former interlocutor and could only be reclaimed without leave when the interlocutor for expenses was pronounced thereby disposing of the whole subject-matter of the cause. Under r.   **38.2.3**

38.2(1)(b) an interlocutor disposing of the merits either by itself or along with a previous interlocutor may be reclaimed against without leave within 21 days of the interlocutor being pronounced whether or not expenses have been dealt with.

In *Robertson, Ptnr. (No. 1)* , 2010 S.L.T. 143 (First Div.), it was held that an interlocutor making no further orders after a continuation to see if further orders would be required was not dispositive as no order was made disposing of any part of the merits of the cause and the reclaiming motion was incompetent, whereas the previous interlocutor would have been reclaimable without leave under r. 38.3(2)(b) (now r. 38.2(1)(b)). If further orders had been necessary the position might have been different. The position of a party waiting to see if further orders are required and then being unable to appeal (without leave) because there are none required is somewhat strange.

Where an interlocutor which reserves expenses or does not dispose of expenses is reclaimed, a party who seeks those expenses before disposal of the reclaiming motion must apply by motion to the Lord Ordinary within 14 days of the marking of the reclaiming motion: r. 38.2(2).

"WITHOUT LEAVE".

38.2.4   The permission of the Lord Ordinary or vacation judge who made the decision is not required.

"WITHIN 21 DAYS".

38.2.5   The date from which the period is calculated is not counted. Where the last day falls on a Saturday or Sunday or a public holiday on which the Office of Court is closed, the next available day is allowed: r. 1.3(7). For office hours and public holidays, see note 3.1.2.

The 21 days are, therefore, counted from the day after the date of the interlocutor reclaimed against. Where the interlocutor to be reclaimed disposes of the merits, the start of the period is not postponed because questions of expenses are not dealt with: *Dingley v. Chief Constable, Strathclyde Police* , 6th December 1996 (IH), unreported (1996 G.W.D. 39-2250); and see Notice, 6th February 1997.

"AWARD OF PROVISIONAL DAMAGES".

38.2.6   See note 43.2.4.

"ADJUSTING ISSUES FOR JURY TRIAL".

38.2.7   See note 37.1.9.

"SIST OF EXECUTION OR PROCEDURE".

38.2.8   This applies not only to sist of execution and diligence but also sist of process which is a stoppage of procedure, and "procedure" does not relate only to the former: *Thornton v. North Star Fishing Co. Ltd* 1983 S.L.T. 530.

"LOOSING, RESTRICTING OR RECALLING AN ARRESTMENT OR RECALLING AN INHIBITION".

38.2.9   See notes 13.10.3 and 13.10.4.

"AUTHORITY TO MOVE AN ARRESTED VESSEL OR CARGO".

38.2.10   See note 13.11.1.

"REFERENCE TO THE EUROPEAN COURT".

38.2.11   See Chap. 65.

"WITHOUT LEAVE, WITHIN 14 DAYS".

38.2.12   The date from which the period is calculated is not counted.

Where the last day falls on a Saturday or Sunday or a public holiday on which the Office of Court is closed, the next available day is allowed: r. 1.3(7). For office hours and public holidays, see note 3.1.2.

"WITH LEAVE, WITHIN 14 DAYS".

38.2.13   The permission of the Lord Ordinary or vacation judge who made the decision must be sought before the interlocutor may be reclaimed against: r. 38.4(2). If the Lord Ordinary is not available another Lord Ordinary or the vacation judge may decide whether to grant leave: r. 38.4(2). In the event that such a judge continues a motion for leave until the Lord Ordinary who made the decision sought to be reclaimed is available, the days during which the motion is continued are not counted in calculating the reclaiming days: r. 38.4(4). The decision to grant or refuse leave to reclaim is final and not subject to review: r. 38.4(6).

Rule 38.2(6) which provides for reclaiming against interlocutors other than those in r. 38.2(2), (3) or (5), or decrees in absence, is subject to r. 38.3 which provides for leave in certain cases.

The reclaiming motion must be enrolled (see r. 38.5) within 14 days; accordingly care must be taken to obtain leave within such period as to leave time to mark the reclaiming motion. The date from which the period is calculated is not counted. Where a motion for leave is continued until the Lord Ordinary who made the decision is available, the days during which the motion is continued are not counted in calculating the period of the reclaiming days: r. 38.4(4).

Where, e.g. it is sought to reclaim against a decision involving the exercise of a discretion it is essential to ask the Lord Ordinary for an opinion at the earliest opportunity; this may be when leave is sought: *Hodge v. British Coal Corporation* 1992 S.L.T. 484, 486K per L.P. Hope.

Interlocutors in respect of all incidental matters of procedure except interlocutors mentioned in r. 38.3(4) require leave to reclaim: *Robertson v. Robertson's Exr.* 1991 S.C. 21. The dispensing power in r. 2.1 will not be exercised to allow, without leave, a reclaiming motion which required leave to proceed as that would frustrate the object of the rule requiring leave: *Robertson*, above.

"DECREE IN ABSENCE".

A decree in absence may not be reclaimed against, but may be recalled by the Lord Ordinary: r. 19.2.   **38.2.14**
An interlocutor on a motion to recall a decree in absence out of time, being in respect of an incidental matter of procedure, requires leave under r. 38.2(6): *Robertson v. Robertson's Exr.* 1991 S.C. 21.

Leave to reclaim etc. in certain cases

38.3.—[1,2](1) An interlocutor granting or refusing a motion for summary decree   **38.3**
may be reclaimed against only with the leave of the Lord Ordinary within 14 days after the date on which the interlocutor was pronounced.

(2) In the application of section 103(3) of the Debtors (Scotland) Act 1987 (appeals on questions of law arising from making, variation or recall of time to pay directions)—

    (a) leave to appeal shall be sought within 14 days after the date of the decision of the Lord Ordinary appealed against; and

    (b) an appeal shall be made by motion to the Inner House within 14 days after the date on which leave was granted.

(3)[3] An interlocutor, other than an interlocutor—

    (a) deciding whether to give permission (including the giving of permission either subject to conditions or only on particular grounds) for group proceedings to be brought under Chapter 26A (group procedure);

    (b) deciding whether to grant permission for the application to proceed under section 27B(1) of the Act of 198811 or an interlocutor determining the application, pronounced under Chapter 58 (applications for judicial review),

may be reclaimed against only with the leave of the Lord Ordinary within 14 days after the date on which the interlocutor was pronounced.

(4) The decision of the Lord Ordinary on a note of objection to the report of the Auditor under rule 42.4 may be reclaimed against only with the leave of the Lord Ordinary within 7 days after the date on which the decision was made.

(5) An interlocutor granting or refusing a motion under rule 47.10(1) (appointing action to be a commercial action) may be reclaimed against only with the leave of the commercial judge within 14 days after the date on which the interlocutor was pronounced.

(6) An interlocutor pronounced on the Commercial Roll, other than an interlocutor which makes such disposal as is mentioned in rule 38.2(1), may be reclaimed against only with the leave of the commercial judge within 14 days after the date on which the interlocutor was pronounced.

Deriv. R.C.S. 1965, r. 89B(8) inserted by S.I. 1984 No. 499 (r. 38.3(1)), r. 88G(3) inserted by S.I. 1988 No. 2060 (r. 38.3(2)), r. 260B(21) inserted by S.I. 1985 No. 500 (r. 38.3(3)), r. 349(7) substituted by S.I. 1983 No. 836 (r. 38.3(5))
Formerly R.C.S. 1994, r. 38.4

GENERAL NOTE.

This rule contains special provisions for reclaiming certain interlocutors with leave.   **38.3.1**

---

[1] Rule 38.3 substituted by S.S.I. 2010 No. 30 (effective 5th April 2010).
[2] Rule 38.3 as amended by S.S.I. 2015 No. 228 para.3 (effective 22 September 2015: amendment subject to saving as specified in S.S.I. 2015 No. 228 para. 4).
[3] Rule 38.3(3) substituted by S.S.I. 2020 No. 208 r.2(6) (effective 31 July 2020).

"SUMMARY DECREE".

38.3.2   See Chap. 21. The purpose of this provision is to prevent further delay by a defender who has no defence to an action reclaiming against a summary decree.

Leave to reclaim must be sought whether the summary decree is a final or interlocutory decision. The suggestion by Lord Coulsfield in *Maus Feres S.A. v. Hoon* , 24th November 1995, 1996 G.W.D. 10.594, that leave to reclaim is not required where the summary decree is a final interlocutor, would defeat the purpose of the rule intended by the rule's clear and unambiguous terms. Paragraph (1) of r. 38.2 which provides for reclaiming a final interlocutor without leave, is, by virtue of r. 38.1(1), subject to r. 38.3(1) (leave to reclaim summary decree). It is submitted that Lord Coulsfield's opinion is wrong on this point. It is understood that subsequently the Inner House directed that leave was required.

"SECTION 103(3) OF THE DEBTORS (SCOTLAND) ACT 1987".

38.3.3   An appeal may be made on a question of law with leave from the Lord Ordinary against a decision by him on an application for a time to pay direction, or variation or recall of a time to pay direction, or recall or restriction of an arrestment in respect of the debt for which decree containing a time to pay direction has been granted: 1987 Act, s. 103(3). Not only must leave be sought within 14 days but the reclaiming motion must be enrolled (see r. 38.5) within 14 days thereafter: r. 38.3(2).

"JUDICIAL REVIEW".

38.3.4   Rule 38.8(3), inserted by A.S. (R.C.S.A No. 2) (Causes in the Inner House) 2010 (S.S.I. 2010/30) and as amended by A.S. (R.C.S.A. (No.3) (Courts Reform (Scotland) Act 2014 (S.S.I. 2015/228), provides for reclaiming with leave against interlocutors in a petition for judicial review, other than one determining the application or deciding whether to grant permission. On the face of it, but for r. 38.2(6), the interlocutors excluded from the requirement of leave, could be reclaimed without leave. The intention was probably to prohibit the excluded interlocutors in r. 38.8(3) from being appealable at all until the end of the case in order to ensure speedy disposal of the petition; but that, perhaps, has not been achieved without excluding r.38.2(6).

"NOTE OF OBJECTION TO THE REPORT OF THE AUDITOR".

38.3.5   While it is competent to reclaim against the decision of the Lord Ordinary with leave within seven days (r. 38.3(4)) on a matter of expenses, such motions are not encouraged unless a point of principle is involved: *Aird v. School Board of Tarbert* 1907 S.C. 22, 24 per Lord McLaren; *Ramm v. Lothian and Borders Fire Board* 1994 S.C. 226.

On the report of the Auditor on a taxation of an account of expenses on a judicial account (or, by virtue of r. 42.7(9), on a solicitor's own account), see r. 42.3.

"WITH THE LEAVE".

38.3.6   The permission of the Lord Ordinary who made the decision must be sought before the interlocutor may be reclaimed against. If the Lord Ordinary is not available another Lord Ordinary or the vacation judge may decide whether to grant leave: r. 38.4(2). In the event that such a judge continues a motion for leave until the Lord Ordinary who made the decision sought to be reclaimed is available, the days during which the motion is continued are not counted in calculating the reclaiming days: r. 38.4(4). The decision to grant or refuse leave to reclaim is final and not subject to review: r. 38.4(6).

Where, e.g. it is sought to reclaim against a decision involving the exercise of a discretion it is essential to ask the Lord Ordinary for an opinion at the earliest opportunity; and this may be when leave is sought: *Hodge v. British Coal Corporation* 1992 S.L.T. 484, 486K per L.P. Hope.

The dispensing power in r. 2.1 will not be exercised to allow, without leave, a reclaiming motion which required leave to proceed as that would frustrate the object of the rule requiring leave: *Robertson v. Robertson's Exr.* 1991 S.C. 21.

It is not a breach of art.6(1) of the ECHR for the judge at first instance, who determined the substantive issue, to be the judge who also decides whether leave to appeal should be granted: *Umair v. Umair* , 2002 S.C. 153 (Ex Div).

"WITHIN 14 DAYS", "WITHIN 7 DAYS".

38.3.7   The reclaiming motion must be enrolled (see r. 38.5) within the period specified; accordingly care must be taken to obtain leave within such period as to leave time to mark the reclaiming motion. Where a motion for leave is continued until the Lord Ordinary who made the decision is available, the days during which the motion is continued are not counted in calculating the period of the reclaiming days: r. 38.4(4).

The date from which the period is calculated is not counted.

LEAVE TO RECLAIM DECISIONS OF THE COMMERCIAL JUDGE.

38.3.8   The commercial judge is appointed under r. 47.2. He hears a motion to transfer an ordinary action to be a commercial action on the Commercial Roll: r. 47.10(2); a decision to grant or refuse the motion may only be reclaimed against with his leave within 14 days of the interlocutor: r. 38.3(6). To assist with the principle of speedy determination of actions on the Commercial Roll (for which, see r. 47.8), an interlocutor, other than an interlocutor disposing of the whole subject-matter of the cause or the whole merits but not necessarily the expenses, pronounced in a commercial action may only be reclaimed against with leave of the commercial judge within 14 days of that interlocutor: r. 38.3(7).

On the meaning of "final interlocutor", see note 4.15.2(2).

Applications for leave to reclaim

38.4.—[1](1) An application for leave to reclaim against an interlocutor shall be made by motion.

(2) A motion under paragraph (1) shall be brought—

    (a) before the Lord Ordinary who pronounced the interlocutor;

    (b) where that Lord Ordinary is, for whatever reason, unavailable, before another Lord Ordinary; or

    (c) before the vacation judge.

(3) Where a motion under paragraph (1) is brought before a judge under paragraph (2)(b) or (c), that judge shall—

    (a) continue the motion until the Lord Ordinary who pronounced the interlocutor is available; or

    (b) where the matter is of such urgency that a continuation would not be appropriate, grant or refuse leave, as the case may be.

(4) Any period during which a motion under paragraph (1) is continued by virtue of an order under paragraph (3)(a) shall not be taken into account in calculating the reclaiming days under rule 38.2(6) (reclaiming days and leave) or rule 38.3 (leave to reclaim etc. in certain cases).

(5) In granting leave to reclaim, the Lord Ordinary may impose such conditions, if any, as he thinks fit.

(6) The decision of the Lord Ordinary or the vacation judge to grant or refuse leave to reclaim shall be final and not subject to review.

(7) Leave to reclaim against an interlocutor shall not excuse obedience to or implement of the interlocutor unless by order of the Lord Ordinary, a procedural judge or the vacation judge.

    Deriv. R.C.S. 1965, r. 264(c)(part) (r. 38.4(2), (6) and (7))
    Formerly R.C.S. 1994, r. 38.5

"MOTION".

    For motions, see Chap. 23.

"CONDITIONS".

    Conditions may be imposed in respect, e.g. of expenses, caution or consignation.

"FINAL AND NOT SUBJECT TO REVIEW".

    The decision of the Lord Ordinary may not be reclaimed against.

    While r. 38.4(6) excludes from review the decision to grant or refuse leave to appeal against an interlocutor, the interlocutor in respect of which leave was sought may be submitted to review as a prior interlocutor under r. 38.6(1) unless it is expressly or by implication a final interlocutor: *McCue v. Scottish Daily Record* 1998 S.C. 811 (court of five judges). On what is expressly or by implication a final interlocutor, see note 38.6.1(1).

LEAVE TO RECLAIM DOES NOT EXCUSE OBEDIENCE.

    The granting of leave to reclaim does not excuse obedience to or implement of an interlocutor unless the court otherwise orders: r. 38.4(7). Once the reclaiming motion is enrolled (see r. 38.5) the interlocutor need not be implemented unless it is an award of custody, access or aliment in respect of which the court has not excused obedience: see r. 38.6(5).

HUMAN RIGHTS.

    It is not a breach of art.6(1) of the ECHR for the judge at first instance, who determined the substantive issue, to be the judge who also decides whether leave to appeal should be granted: *Umair v. Umair*, 2002 S.C. 153 (Ex Div).

38.4

38.4.1

38.4.2

38.4.3

38.4.4

38.4.5

---

[1] R. 38.4 substituted by S.S.I. 2010 No. 30 (effective 5th April 2010).

TIME-LIMIT.

38.4.6   There is no time-limit for leave to reclaim under this rule (there may be time-limits under other provisions—e.g. r. 38.3(1)). If leave to reclaim is sought outwith the reclaiming days from a Lord Ordinary from his decision, it is not incompetent to seek *leave* to reclaim (unless that is outwith a time-limit); it is for the Inner House to decide in due course under r. 38.7 whether to allow a reclaiming motion, enrolled out of time, to proceed out of time: *Bank of Scotland v. Kunkel-Griffin* , [2005] CSIH 18, 15th February 2005, unreported (First Div.).

"PROCEDURAL JUDGE".

38.4.7   See Chap.37A on the meaning, jurisdiction and powers of the procedural judge.

Method of reclaiming

38.5   **38.5.**—[1](1)   A party who seeks to reclaim against an interlocutor shall mark a reclaiming motion by enrolling a motion for review in Form 38.5 before the expiry of the reclaiming days.

(2)   On enrolling a motion for review under paragraph (1), the reclaimer shall lodge a reclaiming print in the form of a record which shall contain—

(a)   the whole pleadings and interlocutors in the cause;

(b)   where the reclaiming motion is directed at the refusal of the Lord Ordinary to allow the pleadings to be amended in terms of a minute of amendment and answers, the text of such minute and answers; and

(c)   where available, the opinion of the Lord Ordinary.

(3)   A party who reclaims against an interlocutor adjusting issues for jury trial shall, on enrolling the motion for review—

(a)   lodge in process the issue or counter-issue proposed by him showing the amendment to the issues, as adjusted, sought to be made; and

(b)   send a copy of the issue or counter-issue, as the case may be, to every other party.

Deriv. R.C.S. 1965, r. 262(a) and (b) (r. 38.5(1); r.117 (r. 38.5(2))
Formerly R.C.S. 1994, r. 38.6

GENERAL NOTE.

38.5.1   When enrolling a reclaiming motion in a cause in which no opinion has yet been issued by the Lord Ordinary, his clerk should be informed that the motion has been enrolled and that an opinion is required: P.N. No. 3 of 2011, para. 9. Where a point likely to be at issue in the reclaiming motion is one which the Lord Ordinary has not dealt with in his opinion, this should be indicated in the motion sheet and his clerk informed that an opinion is required on the point: P.N. No. 3 of 2011, para. 10.

Where no opinion is available and a reclaiming motion has been enrolled, the clerk of one of the Divisions will write to the Lord Ordinary drawing his attention to the fact that no opinion has yet been lodged, that a reclaiming motion has been marked and that grounds of appeal have to be lodged by a certain date. If the opinion is not to be available by that date, the Lord Ordinary should inform his clerk who will advise the reclaimer who, in turn, may enrol for prorogation of the time to lodge grounds of appeal.

"MOTION".

38.5.2   For motions, see Chap. 23.

"LODGE A RECLAIMING PRINT".

38.5.3   The print is lodged as a step of process: r. 1.3(1) (definition of "step of process"). On lodging the principal reclaiming print when enrolling the motion for review under r. 38.5(2), six copies must be lodged for use of the court and six copies sent to every other party: r. 4.7(1).

On what must be contained in a reclaiming print, see r. 38.5(2).

FEE.

38.5.4   A court fee is payable on enrolling a reclaiming motion. For fee, see Court of Session etc. Fees Order 1997, Table of Fees, Pt I, B, item 13, or C, item 10 [S.I. 1997 No. 688, as amended, pp. C 1201 et seq.]. Certain persons are exempt from payment of fees: see 1997 Fees Order, art.5, substituted by S.S.I. 2002 No.270. A fee exemption certificate must be lodged in process: see P.N. No.1 of 2002.

Where the reclaimer is legally represented, the fee may be debited under a credit scheme introduced on 1st April 1976 by P.N. No. 4 of 1976 to the account (if one is kept or permitted) of the agent by the

---

[1] R. 38.5 substituted by S.S.I. 2010 No.30 (effective 5th April 2010).

court cashier, and an account will be rendered weekly by the court cashier's office to the agent for all court fees due that week for immediate settlement. Party litigants, and agents not operating the scheme, must pay (by cash, cheque or postal order) on each occasion a fee is due at the time of lodging at the counter at the appropriate department.

Effect of reclaiming

38.6.—[1](1) Subject to paragraph (2), a reclaiming motion shall have the effect of submitting to the review of the Inner House all previous interlocutors of the Lord Ordinary or any interlocutor of the Lord Ordinary in a motion under rule 38.2(2), not only at the instance of the party reclaiming but also at the instance of any other party who appeared in the cause, and without the necessity of any counter-reclaiming motion.

38.6

(2) Where an interlocutor, either by itself or taken along with a previous interlocutor, has disposed of the whole merits of the cause, a reclaiming motion against a subsequent interlocutor dealing with expenses shall have the effect of submitting to review only that interlocutor and any other interlocutor so far as it deals with expenses.

(3) After a reclaiming motion has been enrolled, the reclaimer shall not be at liberty to withdraw it without the consent of the other parties who have appeared in the cause; and if he does not insist on the reclaiming motion, any other party may do so in the same way as if the motion had been enrolled at his instance.

(4) An unopposed motion by a party to refuse a reclaiming motion shall be treated as if all parties consented to it.

(5)[2] Where an interlocutor contains an award of residence, contact or aliment, the marking of a reclaiming motion shall not excuse obedience to or implement of the award of residence, contact or aliment, as the case may be, unless by order of the court.

Deriv. R.C.S. 1965, r. 264(d)
Formerly R.C.S. 1994, r. 38.7

GENERAL NOTE.

As well as submitting to review the interlocutor reclaimed against, all previous interlocutors are submitted to review at the instance of either party (r. 38.6(1)) subject to two exceptions.

38.6.1

1. A prior interlocutor which is expressly or by implication a final interlocutor is not submitted to review. A prior interlocutor expressly final is one not reclaimed against within the time prescribed under the R.C.S. 1994 or another enactment: *Copeland v. Lord Wimborne* 1912 S.C. 355; *Cumptsie v. Waterston* 1933 S.C. 1. A prior interlocutor which is final by implication is one which has been acted on as the basis of subsequent proceedings: *Macaskill v. Nicol* 1943 S.C. 17, 20 per L.J.-C. Cooper; see also *Spencer v. Macmillan* 1957 S.L.T.(Notes) 32, *Campbell v. James Walker Insulation Ltd* 1988 S.L.T. 263, *Gillon v. Gillon* 1994 S.C. 162. It had been thought that a prior interlocutor was also expressly final where leave to reclaim is required and has been refused in respect of it: *Marsh v. Baxendale* 1994 S.C. 157. But in *McCue v. Scottish Daily Record* 1998 S.C. 811 a court of five judges held that this was not so. A distinction has to be drawn between, on the one hand, a rule which excludes subsequent review of an interlocutor if not reclaimed against within a specified time (e.g. final if not reclaimed against within X days: *Copeland*, above; *Cumptsie*, above) and, on the other hand, one which merely delimits the period within which an interlocutor may be reclaimed. The former is excluded from review by r. 38.6(1) but the latter is not (unless excluded by actings). Thus, while r. 38.4(6) excludes from review the interlocutor granting or refusing leave to appeal against an interlocutor, the interlocutor in respect of which leave was sought may be submitted to review as a prior interlocutor under r. 38.6(1). The decisions in *Marsh*, above, and *Mowbray v. D.C. Thomson Ltd* 1996 S.C. 197 (appeal without the necessary leave from the sheriff court held expressly final and incapable of review as a prior interlocutor under s. 29 of the Sheriff Courts (Scotland) Act 1907) are overruled.

In *McCue*, above, the court went on to say that actings after an interlocutor which may exclude review of that interlocutor was not a matter of competency but because the court considers that it should not exercise the power of review in respect of it (see pp. 820D to 821G). Thus, "acquiescence" in a prior interlocutor does not necessarily exclude review of it. In *Clark v. Greater Glasgow Health Board*, 2017 S.C. 297 (First Div.), 307, at para. [40], the statement of

---

[1] Rule 38.6 substituted by S.S.I. 2010 No. 30 (effective 5th April 2010).
[2] Rule 38.6(5) amended by S.S.I 2011 No. 303 (effective 27th September 2011).

Lord Carloway, LP, that "As a generality, so far as the procedural steps in the Outer House are concerned, this court will not normally review an interlocutor in which parties can be seen to have, in essence, acquiesced", may be too strict an interpretation of the comments in *McCue*.

Also in *McCue*, above, it was stated that, where a party sought to reclaim against an interlocutor pronounced on his own motion in order to submit to review a prior interlocutor (as in *McGuinness v. Bremner plc* 1988 S.L.T. 340), this was not a question of competency but that the court would not normally countenance it. Accordingly, there may be circumstances in which the court would permit it.

It should be noted that an interlocutor pronounced by the Lord Ordinary is final in the Outer House subject to the provisions for review (C.S.A. 1988, s. 18); an exception being an interlocutor as to the mode of proof which is superseded as a result of subsequent amendments (*Bendex v. James Donaldson & Sons Ltd* 1990 S.C. 259).

In *Prospect Healthcare (Hairmyres) Ltd v. Kier Build Ltd and Carrilion Construction Ltd* [2017] CSIH 70, 2018 S.L.T. 47, at para. [23], Lord Carloway, LP. asserted that, as a generality, it is not competent to challenge an interlocutor that has nothing to do with the merits of the interlocutor which is the subject of the reclaiming motion. He cited as authority the decision in *John Muir Trust v. Scottish Ministers*, 2017 S.C. 207 (First Div.), 223, per Lord Carloway, LP, at para. [57] where *McCue*, above, was cited as the authority. It does not appear that *McCue* is authority for such a proposition. In *Telfer v. Buccleuch Estates Ltd*, 2013 S.L.T. 899, 911, at para. [42] Lord Brodie observed, in commenting on *McCue*, "on the appeal of a final judgment, a prior interlocutor may or may not be open to review. It is not a matter of competency. It is a matter of whether the appellate court considers the interlocutor should be subject to review in all the circumstances. If it is purely procedural or otherwise seen to be final or spent it may be that it will be held not subject to review. On the other hand, if it continues to be linked to, or is directly influential in the order which is the subject of a timeous challenge then it may be subject to review."

2. Where an interlocutor, either by itself or taken with another has disposed of the merits, a reclaiming motion against a subsequent interlocutor dealing with expenses only submits for review the interlocutor dealing with expenses and any other interlocutor in so far as it deals with expenses: r. 38.6(2). To reclaim against the previous interlocutors on the merits the interlocutor dealing with the merits must be reclaimed timeously.

EFFECT OF RECLAIMING ON INTERLOCUTOR RECLAIMED AGAINST.

38.6.2
When an interlocutor is reclaimed, the effect of that appeal, from the time the reclaiming motion is marked, is to sist all execution on the decree until the reclaiming motion has been determined: *Macleay v. Macdonald* 1928 S.C. 776, 782, per Lord Anderson. The exception is that awards of custody, access (now called residence and contract respectively) or aliment are not affected by the marking of a reclaiming motion and must be complied with unless the court otherwise orders: r. 38.6(5). The court will be the court which made the order, or the vacation judge, where the application is made before (or at the time) the reclaiming motion is marked; once the reclaiming motion has been marked, the application must be made to the Inner House.

An appeal against the recall of interim interdict has the effect of suspending the operation of the recall, resulting in the interim interdict remaining in force: *Mulhern v. The Scottish Police Services Authority* , 2009 S.L.T. 353 (Extra Div.).

Execution before the marking of the appeal will not be affected unless and until the interlocutor is successfully reclaimed against or some interim order is sought from the court such as will suspend or sist the execution.

The marking of a reclaiming motion precludes extract of the interlocutors subject to review: see *Fowler v. Fowler (No. 2)* 1981 S.L.T.(Notes) 78.

INTERLOCUTORY MATTERS WHILE RECLAIMING MOTION PENDING.

38.6.3
As a general rule, when an interlocutor has been reclaimed, nothing can be done in the Outer House in the cause pending in the Inner House. There are two unreported cases which support this statement. In *Shell UK Exploration and Production Ltd v. Innes* , 31st August 1995 (First Div.), unreported, it was held that a cause cannot be in both Houses of the Court at the same time. The crucial date for deciding when the case is in the Inner House is the date of marking of the reclaiming motion (under r. 38.5): *Bonnier Media Ltd v. Smith* , 23rd August 2002, unreported (First Div.). In both cases, after a reclaiming motion had been marked against refusal to recall of interdict a minute for breach of interdict was enrolled. In fact it may be possible for the Lord Ordinary to deal with certain interlocutory matters notwithstanding the cause is in the Inner House; but he would not be able to do so where the interlocutory matter would affect, (a) the effect of an interlocutor previous to that which has been reclaimed (because under r. 38.6(1) all previous interlocutors are submitted for review), or (b) the finality of the interlocutor reclaimed against (because s. 18 of the C.S.A. 1988 provides that every interlocutor is final in the Outer House—i.e. the Lord Ordinary cannot reconsider his own decisions except where recall is permitted by law or rule). An example might be a motion for commission and diligence to recover documents or for evidence. A specific exception is now in r. 38.2(2) which allows a Lord Ordinary to deal with a question of Outer House expenses of a case reclaimed to the Inner House. The creation of this exception lends support to the truth of the statement in the first sentence.

Deriv. R.C.S. 1965, r. 262(c) (r. 38.6(1) and (3)), r. 264(a)(part) substituted by S.I. 1990 No. 705 (r. 38.6(5))

Effect of extracted interlocutor

38.7.[1] Review by the Inner House of an interlocutor shall not be prevented by reason only that extract has been issued before the expiry of the reclaiming days.

38.7

Deriv. R.C.S. 1965, r. 63B inserted by S.I. 1986 No. 1937
Formerly R.C.S. 1994, r. 38.9

"EXTRACT".

On extracts, see Chap. 7.

38.7.1

LAND TENURE REFORM (SCOTLAND) ACT 1974.

R. 38.9 is subject to s. 9(7) of the Land Tenure Reform (Scotland) Act 1974 which provides that a decree in an action of removing for breach of condition of a long lease is, in a question with third parties who have acted onerously and in good faith, to be final when the extract is recorded in the Register of Sasines.

38.7.2

SUPERSEDING EXTRACT.

Where, e.g., the court grants decree by default under r. 20.1, there is no need to supersede extract if the court wishes to give the party in default time to reclaim because, under r. 38.9, the fact that an extract has been issued does not of itself preclude review: cf. *Munro & Miller (Pakistan) Ltd v. Wynern Structures Ltd* 1996 S.L.T. 135 where the court superseded extract, though this was commented on adversely by the First Division at 1997 S.C. 1, 3C.
See also note 7.1.6.

38.7.3

Appeals treated as reclaiming motions

38.8.[2, 3] In respect of the following appeals, the rules in this Chapter shall apply to those appeals as they apply to reclaiming—

38.8

(a) an appeal from a decision of the Lord Ordinary under section 6 of and Article 37 or 41 of the convention in Schedule 1 or 3C to, the Civil Jurisdiction and Judgments Act 1982 (appeals in relation to decisions on enforcement); and

(b) an appeal from a decision of the Lord Ordinary under section 6A of the Civil Jurisdiction and Judgments Act 1982 and Article 44 and Annex IV to the Lugano Convention, as defined in rule 62.26(2) (application and interpretation of Part V of Chapter 62 of these Rules); and

(c) an appeal from a decision of the Lord Ordinary under section 103(3) of the Debtors (Scotland) Act 1987 (appeals on questions of law).

(d) an appeal from a decision of the Lord Ordinary concerning permission to proceed in petitions for judicial review under section 27D of the Act of 1988 (appeal following oral hearings).

Formerly R.C.S. 1994, r. 38.10

GENERAL NOTE.

This rule takes account of the references, in the enactments specified in the rule, to "appeal".

38.8.1

C.J.J.A. 1982, SCHED. 1 OR 3C, ART. 37 OR 41.

A decision authorising enforcement of a judgment given in another Contracting State to the 1968 (Brussels) Convention or the Lugano Convention may be appealed against to the Inner House on a point of law by the party against whom enforcement was sought: C.J.J.A. 1982, s. 6 and Sched. 1 or 3C, Arts 36 and 37. A decision refusing enforcement of such a judgment may be appealed against to the Inner House on a point of law by the applicant for enforcement: C.J.J.A. 1982, s. 6 and Sched. 1 or 3C, Arts 40 and 41. These provisions are extended to authentic instruments and court settlements: C.J.J.A. 1982, Sched. 1 or 3C, Art. 50.

38.8.2

Art. 37 of the 1968 Brussels Convention in Sched. 1 to the C.J.J.A. 1982, limiting appeals against decisions authorising enforcement of foreign judgments, has to be construed strictly and a court seized of

---

[1] R. 38.7 substituted by S.S.I. 2010 No. 30 (effective 5th April 2010).
[2] R. 38.8 substituted by S.S.I. 2010 No. 30 (effective 5th April 2010).
[3] Rule 38.3 as amended by S.S.I. 2015 No. 228 para.3 (effective 22 September 2015: amendment subject to saving as specified in S.S.I. 2015 No. 228 para. 4).

an appeal does not have power to impose or re-impose a sist: *Société D'Informatique Service Réalisation Organisation (SISRO) v. Ampersand Software BV , The Times,* 25th September 1995.

"SECTION 103(3) OF THE DEBTORS (SCOTLAND) ACT 1987".

38.8.3 An appeal may be made on a question of law with leave from the Lord Ordinary against a decision by him on an application for a time to pay direction, or variation or recall of a time to pay direction, or recall or restriction of an arrestment in respect of the debt for which decree containing a time to pay direction has been granted: 1987 Act, s. 103(3). Not only must leave be sought within 14 days but the reclaiming motion must be enrolled (see r. 38.5) within 14 days thereafter: r. 38.3(2).

Reclaiming against decree by default

38.9 **38.9.**—[1](1) Where decree by default has been granted against a party in respect of his failure to lodge a step of process or other document, a motion for review by that party of the interlocutor granting such decree shall be refused unless the document is lodged on or before the date on which the motion is enrolled.

(2) A decree by default may, if reclaimed against, be recalled on such conditions, if any, as to expenses or otherwise as the court thinks fit.

Deriv. R.C.S. 1965, r. 264(e)
Formerly R.C.S. 1994, r. 38.11

"DECREE BY DEFAULT".

38.9.1 See Chap. 20 and r. 33.10.

A decree under r. 43.9(7) is a decree by default to which r. 38.9 (reclaiming against decree by default) applies: *Moran v Freyssinet Ltd,* 2017 S.C. 188, 2015 S.L.T. 829 (Extra Div.).

RECALL OF DECREE BY DEFAULT.

38.9.2 The principles set out by Lord Reid in *Thomson v Corporation of Glasgow,* 1962 S.C. (H.L.) 36, 66, for review of a Lord Ordinary's exercise of discretion, apply: Moran v Freyssinet Ltd, 2015 S.L.T. 829 (Extra Div.)

Where the court is exercising its own discretion, whether a decree by default should be recalled under r. 38.9(2) is a matter for the discretion of the court, in the exercise of which the guiding principle is what would do justice between the parties in the particular circumstances of the case: *Hyslop v. Flaherty,* 1933 S.C. 588. In *Moran v Freyssinet Ltd,* 2017 S.C. 188, 2015 S.L.T. 829 (Extra Div.), the court considered that it should also have regard to the interests of the public and court users generally. Even where careless-ness on the part of the defender has delayed the course of the procedure of the action, the court still may be prepared to consider whether the decree should be recalled, provided that the case as pleaded discloses a substantial defence: *McKelvie v. Scottish Steel Scaffolding Co. Ltd,* 1938 S.C. 278.

In *Battenberg v. Dunfallandy House,* 2010 S.C. 507 (Extra Div.) it was held that the appellate court exercises a discretion of its own on the question of recalling a decree by default and reponing the party in default and is not confined to a review of the exercise by the judge at first instance of his discretion. *Battenberg* was distinguished in *Moran,* above, on the ground that in that case the reason for the failure of the party to appear was not known to the Lord Ordinary and the failure might have been of no consequence.

"LODGE A STEP OF PROCESS OR OTHER DOCUMENT"

38.9.3 The provision of r. 38.9(1), that failure to lodge by the date of enrolment of the motion would result in the motion to review being refused, is not mandatory, and it had to be doubted whether any procedural rule of this nature could ever be absolutely binding on a court of justice: *Shanley v. Clydesdale Bank plc* 2018 S.L.T. 572 (Second Div.). In that case the documents were lodged after that date.

Reclaiming out of time

38.10 **38.10.**—[2](1) In a case of mistake or inadvertence, a procedural judge may, on an application made in accordance with paragraph (2), allow a motion for review to be received outwith the reclaiming days and to proceed out of time on such conditions as to expenses or otherwise as the judge thinks fit.

(2) An application under paragraph (1) shall be made by motion included in the motion for review made under rule 38.5(1).

Formerly R.C.S. 1994, r. 38.12

---

[1] R. 38.9 substituted by S.S.I. 2010 No. 30 (effective 5th April 2010).
[2] R. 38.10 substituted by S.S.I. 2010 No. 30 (effective 5th April 2010).

GENERAL NOTE.

The reclaiming print will have to be lodged when enrolling the motion for review under this rule: r. 38.6. On lodging the principal reclaiming print under r. 38.6(2), six copies must be lodged for use of the court and six copies sent to every other party: r. 4.7(1).

38.10.1

The dispensing power in r. 38.5 will not be exercised so as to have the effect of avoiding the necessity for leave to appeal if this would otherwise be required: see *Robertson v. Robertson's Exr* 1991 S.C. 21.

"MISTAKE OR INADVERTENCE".

Similar considerations to those arising in the application of the dispensing power in r. 2.1 occur in applying this rule.

38.10.2

"MOTION".

For motions, see Chap. 23.

38.10.3

Urgent disposal of reclaiming motion

38.11.—[1](1) Where the reclaimer seeks urgent disposal of a reclaiming motion, he shall include in his motion under rule 38.5(1) either the words "and for urgent disposal on the Summar Roll" or the words "and for urgent disposal in the Single Bills".

38.11

(2) Where a respondent seeks urgent disposal of a reclaiming motion, he shall, within the period allowed for opposing the motion, endorse on the motion of the reclaimer under rule 38.5(1), or send by post or facsimile transmission a notice of opposition in Form 23.4 including the words "The respondent (*name*) seeks urgent disposal on the Summar Roll" or the words "The respondent (*name*) seeks urgent disposal in the Single Bills", as the case may be.

(3) The entry in the rolls in respect of the motion for urgent disposal shall be starred; and the motion shall call before a procedural judge.

(4) At the hearing of the motion, the parties shall provide the procedural judge with an assessment of the likely duration of the hearing to determine the reclaiming motion.

(5) The procedural judge may—

(a) grant the motion for urgent disposal and either appoint the reclaiming motion to the Summar Roll for a hearing or direct that the reclaiming motion be heard in the Single Bills; or

(b) refuse the motion for urgent disposal.

(6) Where the procedural judge grants the motion for urgent disposal, he may make such order as to the future timetabling of, and procedure in, the reclaiming motion as he thinks fit.

(7) Rules 38.12 to 38.16 shall apply to a reclaiming motion in respect of which the procedural judge has granted a motion for urgent disposal only to the extent that he so directs.

Formerly R.C.S. 1994, r. 38.13

GENERAL NOTE.

The original rule was proposed by the Rules Review Group to provide a formal means for seeking early disposal of urgent reclaiming motions.

38.11.1

The reclaimer, on enrolling for early disposal, must specify whether he seeks urgent disposal on the Single Bills or on the Summar Roll: r. 38.11(1). It does not follow that because early disposal is sought in the Single Bills that the court will not determine that the reclaiming motion should be disposed of on the Summar Roll: see r. 38.11(5)(a). Which Roll will be decided by the procedural judge. On Single Bills (and reclaiming motions appropriate for it), see note 38.16.4; on the Summar Roll, see note 38.16.3.

Grounds of appeal do not have to be lodged for the motion seeking early disposal. At the hearing of the motion, the court will decide when and if grounds of appeal should be lodged: r. 38.13(2).

The nature of the urgency should be included in the motion: P.N. No. 1 of 2010, para. 15.

---

[1] R. 38.11 substituted by S.S.I. 2010 No. 30 (effective 5th April 2010).

A motion for urgent disposal will be starred requiring appearance of counsel or other person having a right of audience; and the court will wish to know parties' estimate of the duration of the hearing: r. 38.11(3).

"MOTION".

38.11.2   For motions, see Chap. 23.

LODGING GROUNDS OF APPEAL.

38.11.3   The grounds of appeal are lodged as a step of process (r. 1.3(1) (definition of "step of process")), intimated, and a copy sent, to every other party (r. 4.6).

"PROCEDURAL JUDGE".

38.11.4   See Chap.37A on the meaning, jurisdiction and powers of the procedural judge.

Required application for urgent disposal of certain reclaiming motions

38.11A   **38.11A.—**[1]   Where a party reclaims against an interlocutor in relation to an order under section 11(1) of the Children (Scotland) Act 1995, the reclaimer shall seek urgent disposal of the reclaiming motion under rule 38.11(1).

Objections to the competency of reclaiming

38.12   **38.12.—**[2](1)   Any party other than the reclaimer may object to the competency of a reclaiming motion by—

    (a)   lodging in process; and

    (b)   serving on the reclaimer,

a note of objection in Form 38.12.

(2)   Where the Deputy Principal Clerk considers that a reclaiming motion may be incompetent he may (whether or not any party has lodged and served a note of objection under paragraph (1)) refer the question of competency to a procedural judge.

(3)   Where the Deputy Principal Clerk refers a question of competency, he shall intimate to the parties the grounds on which he considers that question of competency arises.

(4)   A note of objection may be lodged, and the Deputy Principal Clerk may refer a question of competency, only in the period of 14 days after the date on which the reclaiming motion was marked.

(5)   Where a note of objection is lodged, or the Deputy Principal Clerk has referred a question of competency, the Keeper of the Rolls shall—

    (a)   allocate a diet for a hearing before a procedural judge; and

    (b)   intimate the date and time of that diet to the parties.

(6)   Each party shall, within the period of 14 days after the date on which a note of objection is lodged or a question of competency is referred by the Deputy Principal Clerk—

    (a)   lodge in process; and

    (b)   serve on the other party,

a note of argument giving fair notice of the submissions which the party intends to make as to competency.

(7)   At the hearing allocated under paragraph (5), the procedural judge may—

    (a)   refuse the reclaiming motion as incompetent;

    (b)   direct that the reclaiming motion is to proceed as if the note of objection

---

[1] As inserted by the Act of Sederunt (Rules of the Court of Session Amendment No. 6) (Miscellaneous) 2013 (SSI 2013/294) r.2(1) (effective 11th November, 2013).

[2] R. 38.12 substituted by S.S.I 2010 No. 30 (effective 5th April 2010).

had not been lodged or the question not been referred, whether under reservation of the question of competency or having found the reclaiming motion to be competent; or

    (c) refer the question of competency to a bench of three or more judges;

and he may make such order as to expenses or otherwise as he thinks fit.

(8) Where a procedural judge refers a question of competency under paragraph (7)(c), the cause shall be put out for a hearing in the Single Bills before a Division of the Inner House comprising three or more judges.

(9) At the hearing in the Single Bills arranged under paragraph (8), the Inner House may—

    (a) dispose of the objection to competency;

    (b) appoint the cause to the Summar Roll for a hearing on the objection;

    (c) reserve the objection until grounds of appeal have been lodged and order such grounds to be lodged;

    (d) reserve the objection for hearing with the merits.

Deriv. R.C.S. 1965, r. 263(b) (r. 38.12(1) to (3))
Formerly R.C.S. 1994, r. 38.14

GENERAL NOTE.

Formerly competency was opposed by motion. Now it is by a note of objection. The reference by the DPCS to the procedural judge (instead of formerly to a single judge) is consistent with the new procedure for procedural judges of the Inner House to deal with procedural business of the Inner House. **38.12.1**

Formerly the decision of the single judge was final and not subject to review. There is no such provision in the new rule. There is no provision for the procedural judge to refer the case to a bench of three or more judges; but there is no right of appeal stated. Since r. 37A.1(1) states that the quorum of a Division is one judge for the purposes of procedural business, that would indicate that the decision of the procedural judge is a decision of the Division and appeal is only to a larger constituted Division on the limited grounds on which such may be done, or to the UK Supreme Court. It would have been better to state what the position is in the Rules, e.g. the decision of the procedural judge is final or there is an appeal to a bench of three or more judges with leave of the procedural judge. The limited grounds for appeal to a larger constituted Division are that the cause is one of particular difficulty or importance or the Division is equally divided: C.S.A. 1988, s.36. A larger court may be constituted to reconsider a precedent of the court.

"INCOMPETENCY".

A reclaiming motion may be opposed on being enrolled (on which, see r. 38.6) on the ground that it is incompetent. **38.12.2**

A reclaiming motion may be incompetent, e.g. because the reclaiming days have expired before the reclaiming motion was enrolled, because leave was not sought or because the interlocutor may not be reclaimed against. It had been thought that it is incompetent to reclaim against an interlocutor because it was pronounced on the motion of the party seeking to reclaim (*Watson v. Russell* (1894) 21 R. 433; *McGuinness v. Bremner plc* 1988 S.L.T. 340). But in *McCue v. Scottish Daily Record* , 5th June 1998, unreported (1998 G.W.D. 23-1153), a court of five judges indicated that, where a party sought to reclaim against an interlocutor pronounced on his own motion in order to submit to review a prior interlocutor (as in *McGuinness v. Bremner plc* 1988 S.L.T. 340), this was not a question of competency but that the court would not normally countenance it. Accordingly, there may be circumstances in which the court would permit it.

The court may take the objection itself and will not entertain an incompetent appeal even if objection is waived by the respondent: *Governors of Stricken Endowments v. Diverall* (1891) 19 R. 79.

Although a respondent has not marked a reclaiming motion as incompetent, it is still open to him to raise the matter of competency at the reclaiming motion: see *A.B. and C.D., Petrs* 1992 S.L.T. 1064.

REFERRAL OF RECLAIMING MOTION TO SINGLE JUDGE.

This provision was introduced to prevent the time of the Inner House being wasted on a reclaiming motion (particulary by party litigants) which is incompetent. It is now consistent with procedural matters being dealt with by the judge. **38.12.3**

Timetable in reclaiming motion

38.13.—[1](1) The Keeper of the Rolls shall—   **38.13**

    (a) issue a timetable in Form 38.13, calculated by reference to such periods as

---

[1] R. 38.13 substituted by S.S.I. 2010 No. 30 (effective 5th April 2010).

are specified in this Chapter and such other periods as may be specified from time to time by the Lord President, stating the date by which the parties shall comply with the procedural steps listed in paragraph (2) and the date and time of the hearing allocated in terms of subparagraph (b) of this paragraph; and

    (b)   allocate a diet for a procedural hearing in relation to the reclaiming motion, to follow on completion of the procedural steps listed in paragraph (2).

(2)   The procedural steps are—

    (a)   the lodging of grounds of appeal and answers;

    (b)   the lodging of any appendices to the reclaiming print or, as the case may be, the giving of intimation that the reclaimer does not intend to lodge any appendices;

    (c)   the lodging of notes of argument; and

    (d)   the lodging of estimates of the length of any hearing on the Summar Roll or in the Single Bills which is required to dispose of the reclaiming motion.

(3)   The Keeper of the Rolls shall take the steps mentioned in paragraph (1)—

    (a)   where no note of objection has been lodged and no question of competency has been referred by the Deputy Principal Clerk within the period mentioned in rule 38.12(4), within 7 days of the expiry of that period;

    (b)   where a procedural judge has made a direction under rule 38.12(7)(b), within 7 days after the date that direction was made; or

    (c)   where a question of competency has been referred to a bench of three or more judges and—

        (i)   an interlocutor has been pronounced sustaining the competency of the reclaiming motion under rule 38.12(9)(a) or following a Summar Roll hearing under rule 38.12(9)(b), or

        (ii)   an interlocutor has been pronounced under rule 38.12(9)(c) or (d),

within 7 days after the date of that interlocutor.

GENERAL NOTE.

38.13.1   In a similar way to timetabling in reparation actions under Chap. 43, there is an automatic timetable for reclaiming motions, including the lodging of grounds of appeal, unless an issue of competency has been raised or referred under r. 38.12. The timetable includes a date for the procedural hearing under r. 38.16 before the procedural judge to determine whether the reclaiming motion should be appointed for a hearing of the reclaiming motion in the Summary Roll or the Single Bills.

Table A to P.N. No. 3 of 2011 sets out the timetable that it is envisaged will be prescribed by the Lord President.

Under r. 38.14 there is provision for sisting the reclaiming motion or varying the timetable.

Penalties for failing to comply with the timetable are provided in r. 38.15.

"GROUNDS OF APPEAL".

38.13.2   See further, r. 38.18 and notes to that rule.

"APPENDICES".

38.13.3   An appendix contains material not in the appeal print.

"NOTES OF ARGUMENT".

38.13.4   P.N. No. 3 of 2011 states at para. 86 that a note of argument should comply with the following general principles (these are slightly different from those in P.N. No. 1 of 2010)—

    1.   A note of argument should be a concise summary of the submissions to be developed.

    2.   It should contain a numbered list of the points which the party wishes to make.

    3.   Each point should be followed by a reference to any transcript of evidence or other document on which the party wishes to rely. The note of argument should identify the relevant passage in the document in question.

    4.   A note of argument should state, in respect of each authority cited—

        (a)   the proposition of law that the authority demonstrates; and

    (b)   the parts of the authority (identified by page or paragraph references) that support the proposition.

5.   More than one authority should not be cited in support of a given proposition unless the additional citation is necessary for a proper presentation of the argument.

In *AW, as legal representative of LW v. Greater Glasgow Health Board* [2017] CSIH 58 (Second Div.), the court commented (para. [9]) on written submissions (notes of argument) as not being comprehensive and reasonably succinct, or contained in one document. It was also indicated that summaries of evidence in written submissions should be accompanied by references to the specific passages in the notes of evidence (para. [10]).

"PROCEDURAL JUDGE".

See Chap.37A on the meaning, jurisdiction and powers of the procedural judge.   **38.13.5**

Sist or variation of timetable in reclaiming motion

38.14.—[1](1) A reclaiming motion may be sisted or the timetable may be varied on the application by motion of any party.   **38.14**

(2) An application under paragraph (1) shall be—

    (a)   placed before a procedural judge; and

    (b)   granted only on special cause shown.

(3) The procedural judge before whom an application under paragraph (1) is placed may—

    (a)   determine the application;

    (b)   refer the application to a bench of three or more judges; or

    (c)   make such other order as he thinks fit to secure the expeditious disposal of the reclaiming motion.

(4)[2] Where the timetable is varied, the Keeper of the Rolls may—

    (a)   discharge the procedural hearing fixed under rule 38.13(1)(b);

    (b)   fix a date for a procedural hearing; and

    (c)   issue a revised timetable in Form 38.13.

(5)[3] Upon recall of a sist, the Keeper of the Rolls may—

    (a)   fix a date for a procedural hearing; and

    (b)   issue a revised timetable in Form 38.13.

GENERAL NOTE.

The automatic timetable for reclaiming motions may be varied or the reclaiming motion may be sisted.   **38.14.1**

Penalties for failing to comply with the timetable are provided in r. 38.15.

SIST OR VARIATION ONLY ON SPECIAL CAUSE SHOWN.

A sist or variation may be granted only on special cause shown. A motion to vary could be made, for example, because the Lord Ordinary's opinion is not yet available: see *McAdam v. Shell U.K. Ltd* , 1991 S.C. 360, 363 per L.P. Hope. P.N. No. 3 of 2011, para. 27 suggests that special cause might be shown where a party has to obtain notes of evidence, the opinion of the Lord Ordinary or legal aid.   **38.14.2**

"PROCEDURAL JUDGE".

See Chap.37A on the meaning, jurisdiction and powers of the procedural judge.   **38.14.3**

Failure to comply with timetable in reclaiming motion

38.15.—[4](1) Where a party fails to comply with the timetable, the Keeper may, whether on the motion of a party or otherwise, put the reclaiming motion out for a hearing before a procedural judge.   **38.15**

(2) At a hearing under paragraph (1), the procedural judge may—

---

[1] Rule 38.14 substituted by S.S.I. 2010 No. 30 (effective 5th April 2010).

[2] Rule 38.14(4) and (5) amended by S.S.I. 2011 No. 303 (effective 27th September 2011).

[3] Rule 38.14(4) and (5) amended by S.S.I. 2011 No. 303 (effective 27th September 2011).

[4] R. 38.15 substituted by S.S.I. 2010 No.30 (effective 5th April 2010).

> (a) in any case where the reclaimer or a respondent fails to comply with the timetable, make such order as he thinks fit to secure the expeditious disposal of the reclaiming motion;
>
> (b) in particular, where the reclaimer fails to comply with the timetable, refuse the reclaiming motion; or
>
> (c) in particular, where a sole respondent fails or all respondents fail to comply with the timetable, grant the reclaiming motion.

GENERAL NOTE.

38.15.1   This rule provides penalties for failure to comply with the timetable under r. 38.13 or as varied. Under r. 38.14 there is provision for sisting the reclaiming motion or varying the timetable.

Procedural hearing in reclaiming motion

38.16   **38.16.**—[1](1) At the procedural hearing fixed under rules 38.13(1)(b) or 38.14(4)(b) or (5)(a), the procedural judge shall ascertain, so far as reasonably practicable, the state of preparation of the parties.

(2) The procedural judge may—

> (a) appoint the reclaiming motion to the Summar Roll for a hearing and allocate a date and time for that hearing;
>
> (b) appoint the reclaiming motion to the Single Bills for a hearing and allocate a date and time for that hearing; or
>
> (c) make such other order as he thinks fit to secure the expeditious disposal of the reclaiming motion.

(3) Where this paragraph applies the procedural judge is to make an order under paragraph (2)(c) appointing the reclaiming motion to be determined in chambers without appearance unless satisfied that cause exists for making some other order.

(4) Paragraph (3) applies where—

> (a) the interlocutor reclaimed against is an interlocutor disposing of an application for a protective expenses order under Chapter 58A of these Rules; and
>
> (b) the grounds of appeal do not seek to submit to the review of the Inner House any other interlocutor, other than a subsequent interlocutor dealing with expenses.

Deriv. R.C.S. 1965, r. 294B(5)(b) inserted by S.I. 1987 No. 1206 (r. 38.16(2))
Formerly R.C.S. 1994, r. 38.17

GENERAL NOTE.

38.16.1   The timetable under r. 38.13 or as varied under r. 38.14 includes a date for the procedural hearing under r. 38.16 before the procedural judge to determine whether the reclaiming motion should be appointed for a hearing of the reclaiming motion in the Summary Roll or the Single Bills.

The primary purpose of the procedural hearing is that no case is sent for a hearing on its merits unless the procedural judge is satisfied that a hearing is necessary and that parties are prepared: PN No. 3 of 2011, para. 31. Under paras 31–34 of that PN, parties are expected to discuss the issues in the reclaiming motion and the methods of disposing of them. The procedural judge will decide the length of the hearing and when it will take place. Continued procedural hearings are to be avoided.

Under para. 90 of PN No. 3 of 2011, the reclaimer, after consultation with the respondent, should lodge a bundle of photocopies of authorities on which each party intends to rely. There should not be more than 10 authorities unless the scale of the reclaiming motion warrants more extensive citation. If there is to be citation of more than 10 authorities, this must be brought to the attention of the precedural judge in advance of the hearing and before lodging them; if not, the court may disallow the expenses of lodging more than 10 or more than allowed by the procedural judge: *Thomson v. Scottish Ministers,* 2013 S.C. 628, 633, para. [15] (Second Div.).

---

[1] R. 38.16 substituted by S.S.I. 2010 No. 30 (effective 5th April 2010) and amended by S.S.I. 2018 No. 348 (effective 10 December 2018).

SUMMAR ROLL.

As a general rule, reclaiming motions are appointed to and heard on the Summar Roll. Originally the Summar Roll was the roll for dealing with causes summarily and the Short Roll was for more complicated causes; the latter, however, has fallen into desuetude. Once appointed to the Summar Roll a diet is fixed by the Keeper of the Rolls in accordance with r. 6.3 after parties have sent him Form 6.3 duly completed.

38.16.2

SINGLE BILLS.

The Single Bills is the motion roll of the Inner House.

As a general rule reclaiming motions are not heard in the Single Bills. Reclaiming motions dealt with on the Single Bills might include an urgent reclaiming motion, an appeal clearly incompetent, a reclaiming motion in respect of recall of arrestment or inhibition or interlocutory decisions where, e.g. an imminent proof might be saved. Determination of a reclaiming motion in the Single Bills may be appropriate for a short, sharp point.

38.16.3

HEARINGS BEFORE INNER HOUSE.

A reclaiming motion will be heard by a Division of the Inner House. A Division consists of five judges, but three are a quorum: C.S.A. 1988, s. 2(2) and (4). Because of pressure of criminal business in the High Court of Justiciary and other civil business it is unusual nowadays for a Division to sit with more than three judges. The Lord President may direct three judges to sit as an Extra Division: C.S.A. 1988, s. 2(3).

Where a Division before whom a cause is pending (a) considers the cause to be one of difficulty or importance or (b) the Division is equally divided in opinion, it may appoint the cause to be reheard by such larger court as is necessary for the proper disposal of the cause: C.S.A. 1988, s. 36. A larger court may be instructed to reconsider a precedent of the court. A larger court would in the first instance be a court of five judges; a rehearing of a cause on a point which had been decided by a court of five judges would be heard by a court of seven judges and so on. It is not always necessary for the cause to be heard by the Division before it is reheard by a larger court, particularly where all parties are agreed. A larger court will be required where consideration has to be given as to whether to overturn a previous decision of a Division. Hearings before a larger court may be appropriate on questions of practice or procedure. Where the question at issue is construction of a U.K. statute the preferable course is for appeal to the UK Supreme Court see *Drummond v. I.R.C.* 1951 S.C. 482.

The general rule is that when a case has been reported in Session Cases or the (English) Law Reports, it should be cited from that source: *McGowan v. Summit at Lloyds* , 2002 S.L.T. 1258, 1273 at para.[57]. See also now, P.N. No. 5 of 2004. The citation of cases from reproduction of electronic formats is permitted by that P.N.

38.16.4

FEE.

The court fee for the hearing of a reclaiming motion on the Summar Roll is payable by each party for every 30 minutes or part thereof. For fee, see Court of Session etc. Fees Order 1997, Table of Fees, Pt I, B, item 14 or C, item 16 [S.I. 1997 No. 688, as amended, pp. C 1201 et seq.]. The fee for a reclaiming motion in the Single Bills will be under Pt I, B, item 22 or C, item 21. Certain persons are exempt from payment of fees: see 1997 Fees Order, art.5, substituted by S.S.I. 2002 No. 270. A fee exemption certificate must be lodged in process: see P.N. No.1 of 2002.

Where a party is legally represented, the fee may be debited under a credit scheme introduced on 1st April 1976 by P.N. No. 4 of 1976 to the account (if one is kept or permitted) of the agent by the court cashier, and an account will be rendered weekly by the court cashier's office to the agent for all court fees due that week for immediate settlement. An agent not on the credit scheme will have an account opened for the purpose of lodging the fee: P.N. No. 2 of 1995. A debit slip and a copy of the court hearing time sheet will be delivered to the agent's box or sent by DX or post.

A party litigant must pay cash to the clerk of court at the end of the hearing or, if the hearing lasts more than a day, at the end of each day: P.N. No. 2 of 1995. A receipt will be issued. The assistant clerk of session will acknowledge receipt of the sum received from the clerk of court on the Minute of Proceedings.

38.16.5

Amendment of pleadings in reclaiming motion

38.17.—[1](1) Where, after a reclaiming motion has been marked, any party applies by motion to have the pleadings amended in terms of a minute of amendment and answers, he shall apply for a direction as to further procedure.

(2) Where it appears that the amendment makes a material change to the pleadings, the Inner House may recall the interlocutor of the Lord Ordinary reclaimed against and remit the cause back to the Lord Ordinary for a further hearing.

38.17

Deriv. P.N. 26th March 1981
Formerly R.C.S. 1994, r. 38.21

---

[1] R. 38.17 substituted by S.S.I. 2010 No. 30 (effective 5th April 2010).

GENERAL NOTE.

38.17.1   Amendment may be allowed on, during or after reclaiming. This may occur after debate but is uncommon after evidence has been led. In the former case, if allowed, the Inner House may refuse to hear argument until the judge at first instance has reconsidered the amended pleadings and the case will be remitted for that purpose: *Wallace v. Scottish Special Housing Association* 1981 S.L.T. (Notes) 60. In the latter case, amendment to raise fresh issues of fact may not be allowed because it could unjustly prejudice the other party who might have conducted his case differently: *Thomson v. Glasgow Corporation* 1962 S.C.(H.L.) 36; *McGuffie v. Forth Valley Health Board* 1991 S.L.T. 231; cf. *Moyes v. Burntisland Shipping Co.* 1952 S.C. 429 (allowed in exceptional circumstances to clarify existing controversy not a new one).

The purpose of r. 38.17 is to give the Inner House the opportunity to consider, before the reclaiming motion is heard, whether the amendment involves a material change as requires consideration by the Lord Ordinary.

Where the amendment is sought to be made when the reclaiming motion is before the procedural judge, that is the reclaiming motion has not been appointed to the Single Bills or the Summar Roll for a hearing, it will be dealt with by the procedural judge. Where the amendment is sought to be made after the reclaiming motion has been appointed to a hearing, it will presumably be dealt with in the Single Bills.

"MOTION".

38.17.2   For motions, see Chap. 23. A motion enrolled under r. 38.17 will require appearance on behalf of the party enrolling the motion.

"PROCEDURAL JUDGE".

38.17.3   See Chap.37A on the meaning, jurisdiction and powers of the procedural judge.

Grounds of appeal in reclaiming motion

38.18   **38.18.**—[1](1)   Grounds of appeal shall consist of brief specific numbered propositions stating the grounds on which it is proposed to submit that the reclaiming motion should be granted.

(2)   On lodging grounds of appeal, the party lodging them shall—

(a)   lodge three copies of them in process; and

(b)   send a copy of them to every other party.

(3)   A party who has lodged grounds of appeal or answers to the grounds of appeal may apply by motion to amend the grounds or answers, on cause shown.

(4)   An application under paragraph (3) shall include any necessary application under rule 38.14(1) (sist or variation of timetable).

Deriv. R.C.S. 1965, r. 294B(3) inserted by S.I. 1987 No. 1206 (r. 38.18(1)), r. 294B(5)(a) inserted by S.I. 1987 No. 1206 (r. 38.18(2)), r. 294B(6) inserted by S.I. 1987 No. 1206 (r. 38.18(3))

Formerly R.C.S. 1994, r. 38.16

GENERAL NOTE.

38.18.1   The time within which grounds of appeal must be lodged is set in the timetable issued under r. 38.13.

"GROUNDS OF APPEAL".

38.18.2   These are brief specific numbered propositions (see r. 38.18(1)) for which the reclaimer contends which, if correct, should result in the reclaiming motion being granted. The authorities on which the propositions are based should be mentioned. It is not necessary to detail all the propositions or to list every authority which will be referred to at the hearing of the reclaiming motion. Where grounds of appeal do not comply with the requirement of r. 38.18(1) the reclaiming motion may be refused as being a failure to comply with the timetable: r. 38.15(1); and see note 38.18.5.

The purpose of grounds of appeal is to give notice to the parties and to the court of the grounds on which the reclaiming motion is to be argued: *Eurocopy Rentals Ltd v. Tayside Health Board* 1996 S.C. 410, 413G per L.P. Hope. The purpose of grounds of appeal is to give notice to the parties and to the court of the grounds on which the appeal is to be argued: *Eurocopy Rentals Ltd v. Tayside Health Board* , 1996 S.C. 410, 413 per L.P. Hope.

A statement that the Lord Ordinary "erred in fact and law" is insufficient as a ground of appeal to afford a proper notice of what is to be contended: *Clark v. Chief Constable, Lothian and Borders Police* 19th February 1993, unreported on this point, 1993 G.W.D. 11-759; see also *McAdam v. Shell U.K. Ltd* 1991 S.C. 360, 364 per L.P. Hope and *City of Glasgow D.C. v. Secretary of State for Scotland (No. 1)* 1993 S.L.T. 198, 204E-G per Lord Caplan.

Grounds of appeal do not have to be signed.

---

[1] R. 38.18 substituted by S.S.I. 2010 No. 30 (effective 5th April 2010).

Grounds of appeal are lodged as a step of process: see note 38.18.2.

It should be noted that the Lord Ordinary has a duty to record in his opinion all the arguments and submissions made to him and his views upon them: *Morrow v. Enterprise Sheet Metal Works (Aberdeen) Ltd* 1986 S.C. 96, 101; *Hogan v. Highland B.C.* 1995 S.C. 1. 2C per L.J.-C. Ross.

"LODGING GROUNDS OF APPEAL".

Grounds of appeal are lodged as a step of process (r. 1.3(1) (definition of "step of process")). On lodging the principal, three copies must be lodged: r. 38.18(2)(a). They may be lodged in person at the public counter of the appropriate department or sent by post (P.N. No. 4 of 1994, paras. 1 and 8).

38.18.3

Written intimation of the lodging of grounds of appeal must be given, as well as one copy sent, to every other party: rr. 4.6(1) and 38.18(2).

"LEAVE TO AMEND GROUNDS OF APPEAL".

This may be done to include additional grounds or to alter grounds already stated. It is done by motion or a minute of amendment (and a motion). Appearance will be required for such a motion. Cause must be shown for leave to be granted: r. 38.18(3).

38.18.4

On amending grounds of appeal at the hearing of the reclaiming motion, see *McInnes v. Lawrence* 1996 S.C.L.R. 169, where leave was refused on a motion at the start of an appeal because no special cause had been shown and proper notice had not been given so as to get a proper allocation of court time. See also *Eurocopy Rentals Ltd v. Tayside Health Board* 1996 S.C. 410 (motion to amend to add new grounds refused). The time for a reclaimer considering whether the grounds of appeal are adequate is before the By Order hearing under r. 6.3(9): *Noble Organisation Ltd v. Kilmarnock and Loudoun D.C.* 1993 S.L.T. 759, 761I; *Eurocopy*, above, at p. 1324J.

"FAILURE TO LODGE GROUNDS OF APPEAL".

In this rule's predecessor (r. 38.16(5)) there was specific provision for refusal of a reclaiming motion for failure to lodge grounds of appeal in accordance with the rule. A respondent could apply by motion to have a reclaiming motion refused (a) because there are no grounds of appeal lodged or (b) because the grounds lodged do not comply with the requirement for brief specific numbered propositions stating the grounds on which it was proposed to submit that the reclaiming motion should be allowed or they did not disclose such a ground. There is no such specific provision in the current rule. There is power in r. 38.15 for the procedural judge to refuse a reclaiming motion for failure to comply with the timetable. To include failure to comply with the requirement in r. 38.18(1) for specific numbered propositions stating the grounds of appeal, the court would have to hold that that failure was a failure "to comply with the timetable" to lodge grounds of appeal.

38.18.5

For an example of an appeal being refused because the grounds of appeal were inadequate under the former r. 40.14(5), see *Ferguson v. Whitbread and Co. plc* 1996 S.L.T. 659.

CIRCUMSTANCES IN WHICH INNER HOUSE WILL INTERFERE WITH DECISION OF THE LORD ORDINARY.

(1) Facts.

Review of facts will depend on examination and assessment of the evidence and rules of evidence, and credibility, reliability, weight and sufficiency. In relation to credibility, the Inner House will be reluctant to reverse findings of credibility for the reason that it is denied the advantage of the judge at first instance who saw and heard the witnesses. The court must be persuaded, and come to the clear conclusion, that the judge who had that advantage was plainly wrong: *Clarke v. Edinburgh and District Tramways Co.* 1919 S.C.(H.L.) 35, 37, per Lord Shaw of Dunfermline. Where an appellate court is disposed to come to a different conclusion, it should not do so unless it is satisfied that any advantage enjoyed by the judge at first instance could not be sufficient to explain or justify his conclusion; where the reasons given by that judge are not satisfactory or it unmistakenly so appears from the evidence, the appellate court may be satisfied he has not taken proper advantage of seeing and hearing the witnesses and the matter will be at large for the appellate court: *Thomas v. Thomas* 1947 S.C.(H.L) 45, 54, per Lord Thankerton. The phrase "plainly wrong" was explained in *Henderson v. Foxworth Investments Ltd,* 2014 S.C. (UKSC) 203, 219, paras. [62] and [67] per Lord Reed, as meaning a decision that no reasonable judge could have reached or the decision of the trial judge cannot reasonably be explained or justified. See further *McGraddie v. McGraddie* [2014] S.C. (UKSC) 12, paras. [1]-[6] per Lord Reed and the comments of Lord Hodge in *Royal Bank of Scotland Plc v Carlyle* [2015] UKSC 13, para. 22; 2015 S.C. (UKSC) 93. For a case in which the UK Supreme Court reversed the findings in fact of the courts below, see *Montgomery v. Lanarkshire Health Board,* 2015 S.C. (UKSC) 63; 2015 S.L.T. 189.

38.18.6

There has been much analysis in the Inner House since the UK Supreme Court decisions about when the appellate court may interfere with the court at first instance on matters of fact. In *AW, as legal representative of LW v. Greater Glasgow Health Board* [2017] CSIH 58 (Second Div.), it was explained, with reference to Lord Reid in *Benmax v Austin Motor Co Ltd* [1955] A.C. 370, 375 that the ability of the appellate court to interfere with the decision at first instance is greater where the challenge is to an inference that the judge has drawn than it is where the decision is based on credibility and reliability of crucial witnesses.

The court in *AW*, above, identified at least four categories of decision at first instance (para. 39).

"The first consists of decisions as to credibility, reliability and the primary facts: what the persons involved actually did or said, or what happened to them. The second consists of inferences of fact drawn from the primary facts. The third comprises the application of the law to the facts, both primary facts and inferences; such questions are frequently referred to as questions of mixed law and fact. What is involved, however, is the application of a legal norm to facts that have been found by the court. The fourth category consists of decisions on pure questions of law, that is to say, the general rules of law in the abstract."

The approach of the appellate court in that case to these is as follows (paras. 48–52).

"First, as indicated in Lord Thankerton's primary statement of principle in *Thomas*, above, an appellate court should not come to a different conclusion from the trial judge on the basis of the printed evidence unless it is satisfied that any advantage enjoyed by the trial judge through having seen and heard the witnesses could not be sufficient to explain or justify his conclusion. Nevertheless, in certain cases, 'either because the reasons given by the trial judge are not satisfactory, or because it unmistakably so appears from the evidence', an appellate court may be satisfied that the judge has not taken proper advantage of his having seen and heard the witnesses, in which case matters are at large. Secondly, an appellate court may interfere with the findings of fact made by the trial judge more readily in a case where the findings are inferences drawn from the primary facts rather than findings of primary fact based on the credibility and reliability of the witnesses ... In such cases, 'an appeal court is generally in as good a position to evaluate the evidence as the trial judge, and ought not to shrink from that task, though it ought, of course, to give weight to his opinion' ... Thirdly, it is apparent from *Henderson v Foxworth Investments Ltd* that an appellate court may interfere with the trial judge's decision on issues of fact for a range of reasons. The fact that the trial judge has gone 'plainly wrong' in the sense that his decision is one that no reasonable judge could have reached, is not the only criterion for interference with his decision. The expression 'plainly wrong' is found in the speech of Lord Macmillan in *Thomas* (at page 59), in the passage quoted above at paragraph [44]. It is plain from that passage that going 'plainly wrong' was merely a residual category; other specific grounds for interference with the trial judge on the facts included cases where it could be demonstrated on the printed evidence that he had been affected by 'material inconsistencies and inaccuracies', or where he was shown to have failed to appreciate the weight or bearing of circumstances admitted or proved ... This is recognised in *Henderson* (at paragraph 67), where the court accepts that a trial judge's decision may be interfered with on a range of grounds ... The final ground, that the appellate court is satisfied that the trial judge's decision cannot reasonably be explained or justified, is a residual category, as with Lord Macmillan's reference to the judge's having gone 'plainly wrong'. For the foregoing reasons we are of opinion that the flexible approach adopted in the earlier cases ... that has been adopted in repeated Scottish cases ... is an approach based firmly on the advantage enjoyed by the trial judge of having seen and heard the witnesses. Moreover, the formulation in *Henderson v Foxworth Investments Ltd* (at paragraphs of 62 and 67) is confined to findings of fact made by the trial judge. Those observations are ... confined to findings of primary fact – the credibility or reliability of witnesses – rather than the proper inferences to be drawn from proved facts ... the formulation in Henderson, important as it is, is concerned with findings of primary fact. An appellate court may still reassess the inferences drawn by the trial judge from proven facts. It is obvious that an appellate court may interfere with the decision of a trial judge on questions of law, including the application of legal principles to the facts of the case." See also *SSE Generation Ltd v Hochtief Solutions AG* 2018 S.L.T. 579 (First Div), *Anderson v Imrie* 2018 S.C. 328 (Extra Div); *Woodhouse v. Lochs and Glens (Transport) Ltd* 2020 S.L.T. 1203 (First Div.) and *Cameron v. Swan* 2022 S.C. 1 (First Div.).

Expert evidence is not evidence of primary facts, but is rather an expression of opinion about the analysis of those facts according to the specialist knowledge and skill of the expert; as such, it should be treated as inferential in nature, and an appellate court is fully entitled to assess such evidence and if so advised to come to a different conclusion from the judge at first instance: *Ted Jacob Engineering Group Inc v Morrison* 2019 S.C. 487 (First Div).

Where a decision on fact is based on credibility, the judge at first instance should leave no doubt as to the grounds of his decision: *Duncan v. Watson* 1940 S.C. 221, 225, per L.P. Normand. The appellate court will more readily treat the matter as at large where clear and satisfactory reasons are not given: *Morrison v. J. Kelly & Sons Ltd* 1970 S.C. 65. In *Hamilton v. Allied Domecqpic* , 2006 S.C. 221, 242, para. [84], Lord Hamilton said that the constraints on an appeal court, in relation to matters of fact, did not absolve the appeal court from reconsidering the evidence and determining whether critical findings of fact were justified.

(2) Discretion.

A discretion will not be lightly interfered with. It is not enough that the appellate court would have exercised the discretion differently. The tests have been variously described, depending to some extent on the area of law concerned. The tests may be stated as follows: (a) has there been a failure to exercise the discretion at all (*Orr Pollock & Co. (Printers) Ltd v. Mulholland* 1983 S.L.T. 558), (b) has the judge misdirected himself in law (*Forsyth v. A. F. Stoddard & Co. Ltd* 1985 S.L.T. 51), (c) has the judge misunderstood, misused or failed to balance the evidence (*Skiponian Ltd v. Barratt Developments (Scotland) Ltd* 1983 S.L.T. 313, 314), (d) has the judge taken into account an irrelevant factor (*Thomson v. Glasgow Corporation* 1962 S.C.(H.L.) 36, 66, per Lord Reid), (e) has the judge failed to take into account a relevant factor (*Thomson, above*), (f) is the decision unreasonable (*Thomson, above*), (g) is the decision unjudicial (*Thomson, above*). See also *Britton v. Central R.C.* 1986 S.L.T. 207.

ARGUMENT NOT PRESENTED TO LORD ORDINARY.

38.18.7   There is no general rule, unlike in the UK Supreme Court, that the Inner House will not entertain an argument not advanced before the Lord Ordinary; although it may be unfortunate that the argument was not so advanced (*Varney (Scotland) Ltd v. Lanark Town Council* 1974 S.C. 245, 249, per L.J.-C.

Wheatley.) It is always open to the court to consider competency which strikes at the root of the proceedings: *Wolfson v. Glasgow District Licensing Board* 1980 S.C. 136, 128, per L.J.-C. Wheatley.

There are exceptions. A fresh argument which cannot be advanced without amendment to the pleadings will generally not be heard because the court will usually wish the judge at first instance to consider the amended pleadings (if allowed: on which see note 38.21.1) and have the benefit of his opinion: see e.g. *Wallace v. Scottish Special Housing Association* 1981 S.L.T. (Notes) 60 and r. 38.17. A new argument cannot be advanced other than on evidence led unless the court has allowed that further evidence or is willing to consider a change of circumstances since the hearing before the Lord Ordinary.

FRESH EVIDENCE.

The appellate court possesses a discretionary power to allow additional proof on the ground of *res noviter veniens ad notitiam*, to be exercised as the court considers appropriate in the interests of justice, in the circumstances of the particular case, bearing in mind the need for finality in litigation, conclusiveness of proof and ensuring that each party has had a fair opportunity to investigate its case and obtain relevant evidence: *Rankin v. Jack*, 2010 S.C. 642 (Extra Div.), 642, per Lord Reed at para. [37]. The court will not, however, allow a party a second opportunity where that party or its legal advisors failed to put forward at proof evidence which was available or which would have been available if proper investigation were carried out; that non-availability at proof alone will not necessarily result in allowance of fresh evidence; and the court will consider the cogency of the proposed additional evidence, each case being fact specific: *Rankin*, above, per Lord Reed at paras. [38]-[40].

In judicial review, where there has not been a proof of facts, the appellate court, in *Scotch Whisky Association v. Lord Advocate*, 2016 S.C. 465 (First Div.), at para. [109], in looking at new material not before the Lord Ordinary, considered simply whether it was in the interests of justice to look at the material.

Where a proof is ordered in the Inner House, on a point not led before the Lord Ordinary, s. 37 of the CSA 1988 provides that it shall be taken before one of the judges of the Inner House, to whom it may be remitted. See, e.g., *Hewat v. Edinburgh Corporation*, 1944 S.C. 30.

"REMIT TO LORD ORDINARY".

It is not "normally" competent in a reclaiming motion, unlike in certain statutory appeals where that is expressly made competent, to remit to the (*Scottish Ministers v. Stirton and Anderson*, 2014 S.C. 218, 244 at para. [87] per LJ-C Carloway), or another (*MacLeod's Legal Representatives v. Highland Health Board*, 2016 S.C. 647, 704, para. [158]-[162]), Lord Ordinary to rehear the case. The Inner House can look at the transcripts of evidence, or remit for proof to a judge of the Inner House on a point not led before the Lord Ordinary (s.37 of the CSA 1988). There is precedent, however, for a remit to the Lord Ordinary: see *Mackay v. Mackay*, 1946 S.C. 78.

"WRITTEN INTIMATION".

For methods, see r. 16.9.

"MOTION".

For motions, see Chap. 23.

38.18.8

38.18.9

38.18.10

38.18.11

Lodging of appendices in reclaiming motion

38.19.—[1](1) Where, in a reclaiming motion, the reclaimer considers that it is not necessary to lodge an appendix to the reclaiming print, the reclaimer shall, by the relevant date specified in the timetable—

    (a)   give written intimation of that fact to the Deputy Principal Clerk; and

    (b)   send a copy of that intimation to each respondent.

(2) Where the reclaimer provides intimation under paragraph (1), a respondent may apply to a procedural judge, by motion, for an order requiring the reclaimer to lodge an appendix.

(3) An application under paragraph (2) shall include specification of the documents that the respondent seeks to have included in the appendix.

(4) Where an application is made under paragraph (2), a procedural judge may make an order requiring the reclaimer to lodge any appendix that the procedural judge considers necessary, within such time as the procedural judge may specify.

(5) An order under paragraph (4) may only be granted by a procedural judge after having heard parties.

(6) Paragraph (7) applies where—

38.19

---

[1] R. 38.19 substituted by S.S.I. 2010 No. 30 (effective 5th April 2010).

    (a)   a respondent seeks to submit for consideration by the court notes of evidence or documents in respect of which the reclaimer has given written intimation to the respondent that the reclaimer does not intend to include in his appendix; and

    (b)   a procedural judge has not made an order under paragraph (2) requiring the reclaimer to lodge an appendix which includes such notes of evidence or documents.

(7)   The respondent shall incorporate such notes or documents in an appendix which he shall lodge within such period as is specified by the procedural judge in disposing of the application under paragraph (4).

(8)   Where, in any reclaiming motion other than one in which intimation is given under paragraph (1)—

    (a)   the opinion of the Lord Ordinary has not been included in the reclaiming print; or

    (b)   it is sought to submit notes of evidence or documents for consideration by the court,

the reclaimer shall lodge an appendix incorporating such documents within such period as shall be specified in the timetable.

Deriv. R.C.S. 1965, r. 294A(a)(part) inserted by S.I. 1972 No. 2022, and P.N. No. 2 of 1989, para. 2(2)

GENERAL NOTE.

38.19.1   The reclaimer must lodge any appendix in accordance with the timetable under r. 38.13. If he does not intend to lodge an appendix the reclaimer must give written intimation of that to the DPCS and respondent: r. 38.19(1). The respondent may lodge an appendix if he wishes and the reclaimer does not. The procedural judge may order one. Parties should discuss and try to agree the documents to be lodged in one appendix.

Failure to lodge a required appendix is a failure to comply with the timetable under r. 38.13 and a ground for refusal of the reclaiming motion (or the granting order of the failure is by the respondent).

"PROCEDURAL JUDGE".

38.19.2   See Chap.37A on the meaning, jurisdiction and powers of the procedural judge.

Notes of evidence not extended when agreed

38.20   **38.20.**[1] Where, in a reclaiming motion, the parties are agreed that on any particular issue the interlocutor reclaimed against is not to be submitted to review, it shall not be necessary to reproduce the notes of evidence or documents relating to that issue.

Deriv. R.C.S. 1965, r. 262(d)

Single Bills

38.21   **38.21.**[2] At any hearing of a reclaiming motion in the Single Bills, the Inner House may determine the motion or make such other order as it thinks fit.

---

[1] R. 38.20 substituted by S.S.I. 2010 No. 30 (effective 5th April 2010).
[2] R. 38.21 substituted by S.S.I. 2010 No. 30 (effective 5th April 2010).

CHAPTER 39 APPLICATIONS FOR NEW TRIAL OR TO ENTER JURY VERDICTS

Applications for New Trial or to Enter Jury Verdicts

Applications for new trial

39.1.—[1](1) An application under section 29(1) of the Act of 1988 (application for new trial) shall be made to a procedural judge, by motion, within 7 days after the date on which the verdict of the jury was written on the issue and signed.

(2) A motion under paragraph (1) shall specify the grounds on which the application is made.

(3) An application under section 29(1)(a), (b) or (c) of the Act of 1988 may not be made unless—

   (a)   in the case of an application under section 29(1)(a) (misdirection of judge), the procedure in rule 37.7 (exceptions to judge's charge) has been complied with;

   (b)   in the case of an application under section 29(1)(b) (undue admission or rejection of evidence), objection was taken to the admission or rejection of evidence at the trial and recorded in the notes of evidence under the direction of the judge presiding at the trial; or

   (c)   in the case of an application under section 29(1)(c) (verdict contrary to evidence), it sets out in brief specific numbered propositions the reasons the verdict is said to be contrary to the evidence.

(4) On enrolling a motion for a new trial under paragraph (1), the party enrolling it shall lodge—

   (a)   a print of the whole pleadings and interlocutors in the cause incorporating the issues and counter-issues;

   (b)   the verdict of the jury; and

   (c)   any exception and the determination on it of the judge presiding at the trial.

(5) Rule 38.6 (effect of reclaiming) shall, with the necessary modifications, apply to an application for a new trial under section 29 of the Act of 1988 as it applies to a reclaiming motion.

Deriv. R.C.S. 1965, r. 126(a) (r. 39.1(1) to (3))

GENERAL NOTE.

The reform of the way Inner House business is conducted arose out of the *Penrose Report on the Review of Inner House Business* in 2009. The report itself followed independent research by Dr Rachel Wadia into the efficient and effective use of Inner House resources in order to "inform" the review. She produced a damning indictment of the efficiency and cost-effectiveness of Inner House business.

The core of the reform is that one judge of the Inner House, the procedural judge, is responsible for the cause until it is appointed to a full hearing and there is an automatic timetable that can be sisted or varied for the progress of the cause to that point. All procedural business (defined in r. 37A.1(2)), up to the appointment of the cause to a hearing, is dealt with by a procedural judge appointed under r. 37A.2.

Regard should be had to PN No. 3 of 2011 (Causes in the Inner House).

GROUNDS OF APPLICATION FOR NEW TRIAL.

The grounds are set out in s. 29(1) of the C.S.A. 1988. They are: (a) misdirection by the judge; (b) undue admission or rejection of evidence; (c) that the verdict is contrary to the evidence; (d) excess or inadequacy of damages; (e) *res noviter veniens ad notitiam*; or on such other ground as is essential to the justice of the cause. These are dealt with in turn below.

A motion for a new trial on any of the statutory grounds in (a) to (e) is subject to the statutory proviso that it will only be granted if it is essential to the justice of the case: *Tate v. Fischer* 1998 S.L.T. 1419. Any party seeking a new trial under s. 29 has to satisfy the overarching test demonstrating that one of the grounds (a) to (e) was made out such that it was essential to the justice of the cause that the verdict be set aside and a new trial ordered: *Sheridan v. News Group Newspapers Ltd*, 2016 S.L.T. 941 (Extra Div.).

---

[1] Chap. 39 and r. 39.1 substituted by S.S.I. 2010 No. 30 (effective 5th April 2010).

(1) Misdirection by the presiding judge.

It is not necessary to show that the jury was misled, it is sufficient to show that the misdirection was calculated to mislead: *Cleland v. Weir* (1847) 6 Bell's App. 70, 76 per Lord Cottenham, L.C. There must have been a note of exception(s) drawn up: r. 39.1(3)(a); and see r. 37.7. The fact that the court has only the note of exception and not the shorthand writer's record of the judge's charge has been criticised, and it has been suggested that the whole of the charge should be available to the appeal court: see *Douglas v. Cunningham* 1963 S.C. 564, 570 per Lord Guthrie and *McArthur v. Weir Housing Corporation Ltd* 1970 S.C. 135, 138-139 per Lord Wheatley.

(2) Undue admission or rejection of evidence.

Objection must have been taken at the time in the trial: r. 39.1(3)(b). (a) A new trial will not be allowed if the exclusion of the evidence admitted would not have led to a different verdict: C.S.A. 1988, s. 30(1). The onus of showing that the evidence adduced, but which should have been excluded, was immaterial rests on the party who adduced it: *Livingstone v. Strachan, Crerer & Jones* 1923 S.C. 794. Evidence admitted which is objectionable on the ground of surprise is a ground for allowing a new trial, but the surprise must be of such a character which the party taken by surprise could not reasonably have been expected to anticipate: *Christie's Curator ad litem v. Kirkwood* 1996 S.L.T. 1299, 1300I. (b) Where the presiding judge rejected parole evidence it must be shown that the evidence was wrongly rejected and that its admission might have led to a different result; if it can be demonstrated that, whatever that evidence, no reasonable jury would have returned a verdict for the aggrieved party there will be no new trial: *Greig v. Sir William Arrol & Co. Ltd* 1965 S.L.T. 242. If the evidence rejected is documentary evidence, a new trial may be refused if its admission would not have affected the result: C.S.A. 1988, s. 30(2).

(3) Verdict contrary to the evidence.

It is not the court's function to review the jury's verdict. The test is whether the jury came to a conclusion to which reasonable people of ordinary intelligence could have come on the whole evidence: *Keenan v. Scottish Co-operative Society Ltd* 1914 S.C. 959, 961 per Lord Johnston, approved in *Potec v. Edinburgh Corporation* 1964 S.C.(H.L.) 1, 7 per Lord Guest, in *Macarthur v. Chief Constable, Strathclyde Police* 1989 S.L.T. 517 and *Currie v. Kilmarnock and Loudoun D.C.* 1996 S.L.T. 481. A verdict will not be lightly set aside: *Robertson v. John White & Son* 1963 S.C.(H.L.) 22, 29 per Lord Guest. The verdict must be either one for which there was no evidence to support it or one flagrantly opposed to the evidence: *Magistrates of Elgin v. Robertson* (1862) 24 D. 301, 305 per Lord Wood. The verdict must be one, on the evidence, to which no jury properly directed could reasonably have come (*Robertson*, above, per Lord Guest at p. 29) or it must be a verdict which cannot from any point of view be reconciled with the evidence (*Kinnell v. Peebles* (1890) 17 R. 416, 424 per Lord McLaren). It is not enough that the court might have reached a different conclusion and disagrees with the jury's findings: *Keenan*, above. For a recent example of a verdict set aside on this ground, see *Ross v. Fife Healthcare NHS Trust* , 2000 S.C.L.R. 620 (First Div.).

(4) Excess or inadequacy of damages.

The test laid down in *Landell v. Landell* (1841) 3 D. 819, 825 to establish that damages were excessive is: "It is evidently not enough, in order to bring the damages within the description of excessive, that they are more, and even a great deal more, than the amount at which the injury sustained might have been estimated, in the opinion of the individual members of the Court to whom the application is made ... It is clear that, in order to warrant the application of the term 'excessive', the damages must be held to exceed, not what the Court might think enough, but even that latitude which, in a question of amount so very vague, any set of reasonable men could be permitted to indulge. The excess must be such as to raise on the part of the Court the moral conviction that the jury, whether from wrong intention or incapacity or some mistake, have committed gross injustice, and have given higher damages than any jury of ordinary men, fairly and without gross mistake exercising their functions, could have awarded." That this is the correct approach was confirmed by the House of Lords in *Girvan v. Inverness Farmers Dairy* , 1998 S.C. 1. A right to a fair trial under Art. 6 of the European Convention on Human Rights is not infringed by the court applying the test in *Landell*, above: *McLeod v. British Railways Board* , 2001 S.C. 534, 536-537 (First Div.).

In *Hamilton v Ferguson Transport (Spean Bridge) Ltd*, 2012 S.C. 486 (Five Bench), Lord President Hamilton at p.518, para.[70], stated the test thus: "[W]hether 'no reasonable jury' properly directed could have assessed damages at the sum or sums in question". To be "excessive" the damages awarded have to exceed the latitude which any reasonable jury could be permitted to indulge and have to raise a conviction in the court that a gross injustice had been committed (p. 31 C-D). A fairly broad approach has to be taken to the question whether the jury has committed a gross injustice or reached a palpably wrong result. The matter can be considered in two stages. First, the court can make a judicial assessment of the value of the claim, taking into account judicial and jury awards and secondly it can compare that with the award of the jury (p. 16G-17C). In comparing the awards, the 100 per cent working rule (derived from *Young v. Glasgow Tramway and Omnibus Co. (Ltd)* (1882) 10 R. 242, 245 per L.P. Inglis) can be considered in relation to solatium only; the rule has no application to other elements of an award which are capable of reasonable precision (patrimonial loss, multipliers): a relatively small departure from a judicial assessment maybe excessive in relation to patrimonial loss. The working rule is not, however, a formula; it is no more than a rule of thumb or a check which the court may use as a guide (p. 17G). It is legitimate to take into account assessments made by previous juries in the same case (p. 18A–C, H).

(5) "res noviter veniens ad notitiam" (information newly discovered).

The allowance of *res noviter* is more or less in the nature of an indulgence: *Miller v. Mac Fisheries Ltd* 1922 S.C. 157, 160 per L.P. Clyde. There may be new evidence or new fact: *Miller*, above, per L.P. Clyde at p. 162. New evidence must not be merely additional evidence of a fact originally averred and spoken to: *Miller*, above, per L.P. Clyde at p. 160. The new material must have been unknown and not available at the time of the trial to the party moving for a new trial through no fault of his: *Bannerman v. Scott* (1846) 9 D. 163, 165 per L.P. Boyle; *Miller*, above, per L.P. Clyde at p. 162; *Maltman v. Tarmac Civil Engineering Ltd* 1967 S.C. 177, 181 per L.P. Clyde. It must be material to the justice of the cause: *Miller*, above, per L.P. Clyde at p. 160. The court does not have to be convinced that the evidence certainly or probably would lead to a different verdict: *Bannerman*, above, per L.P. Boyle at p. 166; *Maltman*, above, per L.P. Clyde at p. 182. If *res nova* is of a fact, it may require amendment of the pleadings, unless it is extraneous to the pleadings, in which case a minute should be lodged recording it; if it is new evidence which does not affect the pleadings, a minute should be lodged setting out what it is and how it is to be proved: *Miller*, above, per L.P. Clyde at p. 161. Answers may be lodged to a minute of amendment or minute.

(6) "such other ground essential to the justice of the cause".

S.29(1) of the C.S.A. 1988 ends with a general catch-all provision. It depends on the circumstances what may be included in this ground. It may include evidence not presaged on record, taking the other party by surprise (*Smith v. The Anchor Line Ltd* 1961 S.L.T.(Notes) 54) or unfair conduct of the case (*Reekie v. McKinven* 1921 S.C. 733, 734–735 per L.P. Clyde). It may also include wrongful withdrawal of the case from the jury: see *Gibson v. Nimmo & Co.* (1895) 22 R. 491.

Where there are two or more defenders a verdict cannot stand against one and be set aside against any others, the whole verdict has to go: *Simpson v. Glasgow Corporation* 1916 S.C. 345.

"WITHIN 7 DAYS".

The date from which the period is calculated is not counted. Where the last day falls on a Saturday or Sunday or a public holiday on which the Office of Court is closed, the next available day is allowed: r. 1.3(7). For office hours and public holidays, see note 3.1.2.

39.1.2

Note the provision for applications out of time: r. 39.2.

"MOTION".

For motions, see Chap. 23.

39.1.3

LODGING COPIES OF DOCUMENTS.

Six copies of an appeal print of the record, the issues and the note of exceptions, and of any appendix, must be lodged when the motion for a new trial is enrolled (and four copies of any other document the day before the hearing): r. 4.7.

39.1.4

EXPENSES.

If a new trial is granted expenses are generally dealt with at the time the new trial is ordered: *McInnes v. British Transport Commission* 1961 S.C. 156; cf. *Watson v. British Transport Commission* 1961 S.C. 152, 155 per L.J.-C. Thomson.

39.1.5

FEE.

The court fee for a hearing on the Summar Roll is payable by each party for every 30 minutes or part thereof. For fee, see Court of Session etc. Fees Order 1997, Table of Fees, Pt I, B, item 17 [SI 1997/688, as amended, pp. C 1201 et seq.]. Certain persons are exempt from payment of fees: see 1997 Fees Order, art.5, substituted by SSI 2002 No.270. A fee exemption certificate must be lodged in process: see P.N. No.1 of 2002.

39.1.6

Where a party is legally represented, the fee may be debited under a credit scheme introduced on 1st April 1976 by P.N. No. 4 of 1976 to the account (if one is kept or permitted) of the agent by the court cashier, and an account will be rendered weekly by the court cashier's office to the agent for all court fees due that week for immediate settlement. An agent not on the credit scheme will have an account opened for the purpose of lodging the fee: P.N. No. 2 of 1995. A debit slip and a copy of the court hearing time sheet will be delivered to the agent's box or sent by DX or post.

A party litigant must pay (by cash, cheque or postal order) to the clerk of court at the end of the hearing or, if the hearing lasts more than a day, at the end of each day: P.N. No. 2 of 1995. A receipt will be issued. The assistant clerk of session will acknowledge receipt of the sum received from the clerk of court on the Minute of Proceedings.

"PROCEDURAL JUDGE".

See Chap.37A on the meaning, jurisdiction and powers of the procedural judge.

39.1.7

Applications for new trial: sheriff court cases

39.1A.—[1](1) An application under section 69(1) of the Act of 2014 (application for new trial) must be made to a procedural judge, by motion, within 7 days after the date on which the jury have returned their verdict.

(2) A motion under paragraph (1) must specify the grounds on which the application is made.

(3) An application under section 69(1) of the Act of 2014 may not be made unless in the case of an application specifying the ground in—

   (a) section 69(2)(a) of the Act of 2014 (misdirection by sheriff), the procedure in rule 36B.8 of the Ordinary Cause Rules (exceptions to sheriff's charge) has been complied with;

   (b) section 69(2)(b) of the Act of 2014 (undue admission or rejection of evidence), objection was taken to the admission or rejection of evidence at the trial and recorded in the notes of evidence under the direction of the sheriff presiding at the trial; or

   (c) section 69(2)(c) of the Act of 2014 (verdict contrary to evidence), it sets out in brief specific numbered propositions the reasons the verdict is said to be contrary to the evidence.

(4) On enrolling a motion for a new trial, the party enrolling it must lodge—

   (a) a print of the whole pleadings and interlocutors in the cause incorporating the issues and counter-issues;

   (b) the verdict of the jury; and

   (c) any exception and the determination on it of the sheriff presiding at the trial.

(5) In this rule—

"the Ordinary Cause Rules" means the Ordinary Cause Rules in Schedule 1 to the Sheriff Courts (Scotland) Act 1907.

GENERAL NOTE.

39.1A.1   Section 69(1) of the Act of 2014 provides for application to the Sheriff Appeal Court for a new trial. The relevance of an application to a procedural judge of the Court of Session is to cover a transitional period in relations to appeals before the coming into force of the civil jurisdiction of the Sheriff Appeal Court.

The Civil Division of the Sheriff Appeal Court was not established when the new national personal injury court was introduced in September 2015. Paragraph 4 of the A.S (Rules of the Court of Session 1994 and Sheriff Court Rules Amendment) (No. 2) (Personal Injury and Remits) 2015 [S.S.I. 2015 No. 227] introduced rr. 39.1A and 39.9A, which provide for the application to a procedural judge in the Court of Session. Paragraph 5 provides that para. 4 only has effect until section 47 of the Act of 2014 comes into force for the purposes of the Sheriff Appeal Court's civil competence and jurisdiction. Section 47 of the Act of 2014 was brought into force on 1st January 2016, along with the A.S. (Rules of the Court of Session, Sheriff Appeal Court Rules and Sheriff Court Rules Amendment) (Sheriff Appeal Court) 2015 [S.S.I. No. 419/2015] which provides for rules of court. Paragraph 18 of that instrument amends the A.S. (Rules of the Court of Session 1994 and Sheriff Court Rules Amendment) (No. 2) (Personal Injury and Remits) 2015 by substituting a new para. 5 to provide that para. 4 has effect in relation to any application made under s. 69 or 71 of the Act of 2014 before 1st January 2016.

"PROCEDURAL JUDGE".

39.1A.2   See Chap.37A on the meaning, jurisdiction and powers of the procedural judge.

MOTION.

39.1A.3   For motions, see Chap. 23.

"WITHIN 7 DAYS".

39.1A.4   The date from which the period is calculated is not counted. Where the last day falls on a Saturday, Sunday or a public holiday on which the Office of Court is closed, the next available day is allowed: r. 1.3(7). For office hours and public holidays, see note 3.1.2.

---

[1] Rule 39.1A as inserted by S.S.I. 2015 No. 227 para.4 (effective 22nd September 2015).

Applications out of time

39.2.—[1, 2](1) A procedural judge may, on an application made in accordance with paragraph (2), allow an application for a new trial under section 29(1) of the Act of 1988 or section 69(1) of the Act of 2014 to be received outwith the period specified in rule 39.1(1) or rule 39.1A(1) and to proceed out of time on such conditions as to expenses or otherwise as the procedural judge thinks fit.

(2) An application under paragraph (1) shall be made by motion included in the motion made under rule 39.1(1) or rule 39.1A.

GENERAL NOTE.

An application out of time for a new trial may only be made provided the verdict has not been applied or a motion to apply it has not been enrolled.

"MOTION".

For motions, see Chap. 23.

"LEAVE TO PROCEED OUT OF TIME".

The considerations for leave to proceed out of time may well include mistake or inadvertence and those arising in the application of the dispensing power in r. 2.1.

39.2

39.2.1

39.2.2

39.2.3

Objections to the competency of application

39.3.—[3](1)[4] Any party other than the applicant may object to the competency of an application for a new trial under section 29(1) of the Act of 1988 or section 69(1) of the Act of 2014 by—

    (a) lodging in process; and

    (b) serving on the applicant,

a note of objection in Form 39.3.

(2) A note of objection may be lodged only within the period of 7 days after the date on which the motion under rule 39.1(1) was enrolled.

(3) Where a note of objection is lodged, the Keeper of the Rolls shall—

    (a) allocate a diet for a hearing before a procedural judge; and

    (b) intimate the date and time of that diet to the parties.

(4) Each party shall, within the period of 7 days after the date on which a note of objection is lodged—

    (a) lodge in process; and

    (b) serve on the other party,

a note of argument giving fair notice of the submissions which the party intends to make as to competency.

(5) At the hearing allocated under paragraph (3), the procedural judge may—

    (a) refuse the application for a new trial as incompetent;

    (b) direct that the application for a new trial is to proceed as if the note of objection had not been lodged or the question not been referred, whether under reservation of the question of competency or having found the application to be competent; or

    (c) refer the question of competency to a bench of three or more judges;

and he may make such order as to expenses or otherwise as he thinks fit.

(6) Where a procedural judge refers a question of competency under paragraph (5)(c), the cause shall be put out for a hearing in the Single Bills before a Division of the Inner House comprising three or more judges.

39.3

---

[1] R. 39.2 substituted by S.S.I. 2010 No. 30 (effective 5th April 2010).
[2] Rule 39.2 as amended by S.S.I. 2015 No. 227 (effective 22nd September 2015).
[3] R. 39.3 substituted by S.S.I. 2010 No. 30 (effective 5th April 2010).
[4] Rule 39.3(1) as amended by S.S.I. 2015 No. 227 (effective 22nd September 2015).

(7)   At the hearing in the Single Bills arranged under paragraph (6), the Inner House may—

(a)   dispose of the objection to competency;

(b)   appoint the cause to the Summar Roll for a hearing on the objection; or

(c)   reserve the objection for hearing with the merits.

GENERAL NOTE.

39.3.1   Formerly competency was opposed by motion. Now it is by a note of objection. The reference by the DPCS to the procedural judge (instead of formerly to a single judge) is consistent with the new procedure for procedural judges of the Inner House to deal with procedural business of the Inner House.

"INCOMPETENCY".

39.3.2   An application for a new trial may be opposed on being enrolled on the ground that it is incompetent. The application may be incompetent, e.g. because the period within which the application may be made has expired.

The court may take the objection itself and will not entertain an incompetent appeal even if objection is waived by the respondent: *Governors of Strichen Endowments v. Diverall* (1891) 19 R. 79.

"PROCEDURAL JUDGE".

39.3.3   See Chap.37A on the meaning, jurisdiction and powers of the procedural judge.

Timetable in application for a new trial

39.4   **39.4.**—[1](1)   The Keeper of the Rolls shall—

(a)   issue a timetable in Form 39.4, calculated by reference to such periods as are specified in this Chapter and such other periods as may be specified from time to time by the Lord President, stating the date by which the parties shall comply with the procedural steps listed in paragraph (2) and the date and time of the hearing allocated in terms of subparagraph (b) of this paragraph; and

(b)   allocate a diet for a procedural hearing in relation to the application for a new trial, to follow on completion of the procedural steps listed in paragraph (2).

(2)   The procedural steps are—

(a)   the lodging of any appendices to the documents mentioned in rule 39.1(4) or, as the case may be, the giving of notice that the applicant does not intend to lodge any appendices;

(aa) [2]   the lodging of any appendices to the documents mentioned in rule 39.1A(4) or, as the case may be, the giving of notice that the applicant does not intend to lodge any appendices;

(b)   the lodging of any notes of argument; and

(c)   the lodging of estimates of the length of any hearing required to dispose of the application for a new trial.

(3)   The Keeper of the Rolls shall take the steps mentioned in paragraph (1)—

(a)   where no note of objection has been lodged within the period mentioned in rule 39.3(2), within 7 days of the expiry of that period;

(b)   where a procedural judge has made a direction under rule 39.3(5)(b), within 7 days after the date that direction was made; or

(c)   where a question of competency has been referred to a bench of three or more judges and—

(i)   an interlocutor has been pronounced sustaining the competency of the application for a new trial under rule 39.3(7)(a) or following a Summar Roll hearing under rule 39.3(7)(b), or

---

[1] R.39.4 inserted by S.S.I. 2010 No. 30 (effective from 5th April 2010).

[2] Rule 39.4(2)(aa) as inserted by S.S.I. 2015 No. 227 (effective 22nd September 2015).

(ii) an interlocutor has been pronounced under rule 39.3(7)(c),
within 7 days after the date of that interlocutor.

GENERAL NOTE.

In a similar way to timetabling in reparation actions under Chap. 43, there is an automatic timetable **39.4.1**
for applications for a new trial unless an issue of competency has been raised or referred under r. 39.3.
The timetable includes a date for the procedural hearing under r. 39.7 before the procedural judge to
determine whether the cause should be appointed for a hearing of the reclaiming motion in the Summary
Roll or the Single Bills.

Table B to P.N. No. 3 of 2011 sets out the timetable that it is envisaged will be prescribed by the Lord
President.

Under r. 39.5 there is provision for sisting the reclaiming motion or varying the timetable.

Penalties for failing to comply with the timetable are provided in r. 39.6.

"APPENDICES".

An appendix contains material not in the print of pleadings under r. 39.1(4). **39.4.2**

"NOTES OF ARGUMENT".

P.N. No. 3 of 2011 states at para. 86 that a note of argument should comply with the following general **39.4.3**
principles (these are slightly different from those in P.N. No. 1 of 2010)—

1.   A note of argument should be a concise summary of the submissions to be developed.
2.   It should contain a numbered list of the points which the party wishes to make.
3.   Each point should be followed by a reference to any transcript of evidence or other document
      on which the party wishes to rely. The note of argument should identify the relevant passage in
      the document in question.
4.   4. A note of argument should state, in respect of each authority cited—(a) the proposition of law
      that the authority demonstrates; and (b) the parts of the authority (identified by page or
      paragraph references) that support the proposition.
5.   More than one authority should not be cited in support of a given proposition unless the ad-
      ditional citation is necessary for a proper presentation of the argument.

Sist or variation of timetable in application for a new trial

39.5.—[1](1) An application for a new trial may be sisted or the timetable may be **39.5**
varied on the application by motion of any party.

(2) An application under paragraph (1) shall be—

(a) placed before a procedural judge; and

(b) granted only on special cause shown.

(3) The procedural judge before whom an application under paragraph (1) is
placed may—

(a) determine the application;

(b) refer the application to a bench of three or more judges; or

(c) make such other order as he thinks fit to secure the expeditious disposal of
the application.

(4)[2] Where the timetable is varied, the Keeper of the Rolls may—

(a) discharge the procedural hearing fixed under rule 39.4(1)(b);

(b) fix a date for a procedural hearing; and

(c) issue a revised timetable in Form 39.4.

(5)[3] Upon recall of a sist, the Keeper of the Rolls may—

(a) fix a date for a procedural hearing; and

(b) issue a revised timetable in Form 39.4.

GENERAL NOTE.

The automatic timetable for applications for a new trial may be varied or the cause may be sisted. **39.5.1**
Penalties for failing to comply with the timetable are provided in r. 39.6.

---

[1] Rule 39.5 inserted by S.S.I. 2010 No. 30 (effective from 5th April 2010).
[2] Rule 39.5(4) and (5) amended by S.S.I. 2011 No. 303 (effective 27th September 2011).
[3] Rule 39.5(4) and (5) amended by S.S.I. 2011 No. 303 (effective 27th September 2011).

The points made in paras. 25–29 of P.N. No. 3 of 2011 should be considered: P.N. No. 3 of 2011, para. 42.

Sist or variation only on special cause shown.

39.5.2   A sist or variation may be granted only on special cause shown. A motion to vary the timetable could be made, for example, because the Lord Ordinary's opinion is not yet available: see *McAdam v. Shell U.K. Ltd* , 1991 S.C. 360, 363 per L.P. Hope. P.N. No. 3 of 2011, para. 27 suggests that special cause might be shown where a party has to obtain notes of evidence, the opinion of the Lord Ordinary or legal aid.

"procedural judge".

See Chap.37A on the meaning, jurisdiction and powers of the procedural judge.

Failure to comply with timetable in application for a new trial

39.6   **39.6.—**[1](1) Where a party fails to comply with the timetable, the Keeper may, whether on the motion of a party or otherwise, put the application for a new trial out for a hearing before a procedural judge.

(2) At a hearing under paragraph (1), the procedural judge may—

(a) in any case where the applicant or a respondent fails to comply with the timetable, make such order as he thinks fit to secure the expeditious disposal of the application;

(b) in particular, where the applicant fails to comply with the timetable, refuse the application; or

(c) in particular, where a sole respondent fails or all respondents fail to comply with the timetable, allow the application.

General note.

39.6.1   This rule provides penalties for failure to comply with the timetable under r. 39.4 or as varied.
Under r. 39.5 there is provision for sisting the reclaiming motion or varying the timetable.

"procedural judge".

See Chap.37A on the meaning, jurisdiction and powers of the procedural judge.

Procedural hearing in application for a new trial

39.7   **39.7.—**[2](1) At the procedural hearing fixed under rules 39.4(1)(b, 39.5(4)(b) or (5)(a), the procedural judge shall ascertain, so far as reasonably practicable, the state of preparation of the parties.

(2) The procedural judge may—

(a) appoint the application to the Summar Roll for a hearing and allocate a date and time for that hearing;

(b) appoint the application to the Single Bills for a hearing and allocate a date and time for that hearing; or

(c) make such other order as he thinks fit to secure the expeditious disposal of the application.

General note.

39.7.A1   Paragraph 44 of P.N. No. 3 of 2011 applies paras. 31–34 of that P.N. The primary purpose of the procedural hearing is that no case is sent for a hearing on its merits unless the procedural judge is satisfied that a hearing is necessary and that parties are prepared: para. 31. Under paras. 31–34, parties are expected to discuss the issues in the reclaiming motion and the methods of disposing of them. The procedural judge will decide the length of the hearing and when it will take place. Continued procedural hearings are to be avoided.

Under para. 90 of P.N. No. 3 of 2011, the applicant, after consultation with the respondent, should lodge a bundle of photocopies of authorities on which each party intends to rely. There should not be more than 10 authorities unless the scale of the reclaiming motion warrants more extensive citation. If there is to be citation of more than 10 authorities, this must be brought to the attention of the procedural

---

[1] Rule 39.6 inserted by S.S.I. 2010 No. 30 (effective from 5th April 2010).
[2] Rule 39.7 inserted by S.S.I. 2010 No. 30 (effective from 5th April 2010).

judge in advance of the hearing and before lodging them; if not, the court may disallow the expenses of lodging more than 10 or more than allowed by the procedural judge: *Thomson v. Scottish Ministers*, 2013 S.C. 628, 633, para. [15] (Second Div.).

SUMMAR ROLL.

As a general rule, applications for a new trial are appointed to and heard on the Summar Roll. Originally the Summar Roll was the roll for dealing with causes summarily and the Short Roll was for more complicated causes; the latter, however, has fallen into desuetude. Once appointed to the Summar Roll a diet is fixed by the Keeper of the Rolls in accordance with r. 6.3 after parties have sent him Form 6.3 duly completed.

39.7.1

SINGLE BILLS.

The Single Bills is the motion roll of the Inner House. As a general rule, applications for a new trial are not heard in the Single Bills.

39.7.2

SPEECHES APPLICATION FOR NEW TRIAL.

At the hearing the convention is that there is only one speech for each party.

39.7.3

"PROCEDURAL JUDGE".

See Chap.37A on the meaning, jurisdiction and powers of the procedural judge.

Lodging of appendix

39.8.[1, 2] Rule 38.19 (lodging of appendices in reclaiming motions) shall, with the necessary modifications, apply to an application for a new trial under section 29(1) of the Act of 1988 or section 69(1) of the Act of 2014 as it applies to a reclaiming motion.

39.8

Formerly R.C.S. 1994, r. 39.5.

APPENDIX.

This would include the notes of evidence (so far as relevant) and other documents to be considered by the court. The appendix has to be lodged in accordance with the timetable under r. 39.4. Where the party moving for a new trial does not intend to lodge an appendix, he must inform the other party in case he wants to do so: see r. 38.19(6) and (7). Six copies of the appendix must be lodged: r. 4.7(1)(f).

39.8.1

Applications to enter jury verdict

39.9.—[3](1) An application under section 31(1) of the Act of 1988 (verdict returned subject to opinion of Inner House on point reserved) shall be made by motion to a procedural judge.

39.9

(2) On enrolling a motion under paragraph (1), the party enrolling it shall lodge in process four copies of the closed record incorporating—

(a) all interlocutors pronounced in the cause and any amendments to the record allowed;

(b) the issues and counter-issues;

(c) any exception taken during the trial and the determination on it of the judge presiding at the trial; and

(d) the verdict of the jury,

and send one copy of it to every other party.

(3) Unless the procedural judge otherwise directs, it shall not be necessary for the purposes of such a motion to print the notes of evidence, but the notes of the judge presiding at the trial may be produced at any time if required.

(4) In the case of complexity or difficulty, the procedural judge may appoint an application referred to in paragraph (1) to the Summar Roll for hearing.

Deriv. R.C.S. 1965, r. 125(c) inserted by S.I. 1984 No. 472 (r. 39.9(3))
Formerly R.C.S. 1994, r. 39.6

---

[1] Rule 39.8 inserted by S.S.I. 2010 No. 30 (effective from 5th April 2010).
[2] Rule 39.3(8) as amended by S.S.I. 2015 No. 227 (effective 22nd September 2015).
[3] Rule 39.9 inserted by S.S.I. 2010 No. 30 (effective from 5th April 2010).

GENERAL NOTE.

39.9.1   Where the presiding judge has directed the jury on a question of law (subject to the opinion of the court on the direction), a party against whom the verdict was given may apply to the Inner House to enter the verdict for him on the ground that (a) the direction was erroneous and that he was truly entitled to the verdict in whole or in part, or (b) it is necessary to set aside the verdict and order a new trial: C.S.A. 1988, s. 31(1).

"MOTION".

39.9.2   For motions, see Chap. 23.

FEE.

39.9.3   The court fee for a hearing on the Summar Roll is payable by each party for every 30 minutes or part thereof. For fee, see Court of Session etc. Fees Order 1997, Table of Fees, Pt. I, B, item 17 [SI 1997/688, as amended, pp. C 1201 et seq.]. Certain persons are exempt from payment of fees: see 1997 Fees Order, art.5, substituted by SSI 2002 No.270. A fee exemption certificate must be lodged in process: see P.N. No.1 of 2002.

Where a party is legally represented, the fee may be debited under a credit scheme introduced on 1st April 1976 by P.N. No. 4 of 1976 to the account (if one is kept or permitted) of the agent by the court cashier, and an account will be rendered weekly by the court cashier's office to the agent for all court fees due that week for immediate settlement. An agent not on the credit scheme will have an account opened for the purpose of lodging the fee: P.N. No. 2 of 1995. A debit slip and a copy of the court hearing time sheet will be delivered to the agent's box or sent by DX or post.

A party litigant must pay (by cash, cheque or postal order) to the clerk of court at the end of the hearing or, if the hearing lasts more than a day, at the end of each day: P.N. No. 2 of 1995. A receipt will be issued. The assistant clerk of session will acknowledge receipt of the sum received from the clerk of court on the Minute of Proceedings.

"PROCEDURAL JUDGE".

39.9.4   See Chap.37A on the meaning, jurisdiction and powers of the procedural judge.

Application to enter jury verdict: sheriff court cases

39.9A   **39.9A.**[1](1)   An application under section 71(2) of the Act of 2014 (verdict subject to opinion of the Court) must be made by motion to a procedural judge.

(2)   On enrolling a motion under paragraph (1), the party enrolling it must lodge in process four copies of—

    (a)   a print of the whole pleadings and interlocutors in the cause incorporating the issues and counter–issues;

    (b)   any exception taken during the trial and the determination on it of the sheriff presiding at the trial; and

    (c)   the verdict of the jury,

and send one copy of it to every other party.

(3)   Unless the procedural judge otherwise directs, it will not be necessary for the purposes of such a motion to print the notes of evidence, but the notes of the sheriff presiding at the trial may be produced at any time if required.

(4)   In the case of complexity or difficulty, the procedural judge may appoint an application referred to in paragraph (1) to the Summar Roll for hearing.

GENERAL NOTE.

39.9A.1   Section 71(2) of the Act of 2014 provides for a party against whom a jury verdict has been returned may apply to the Sheriff Appeal Court for the verdict to be entered in that party's favour. The relevance of an application to a procedural judge of the Court of Session is to cover a transitional period in relations to appeals before the coming into force of the civil jurisdiction of the Sheriff Appeal Court.

The Civil Division of the Sheriff Appeal Court was not established when the new national personal injury court was introduced in September 2015. Paragraph 4 of the A.S. (Rules of the Court of Session 1994 and Sheriff Court Rules Amendment) (No. 2) (Personal Injury and Remits) 2015 [S.S.I. 2015 No. 227] introduced rr. 39.1A and 39.9A, which provide for the application to a procedural judge in the Court of Session. Paragraph 5 provides that para. 4 only has effect until section 47 of the Courts Reform (Scotland) Act 2014 comes into force for the purposes of the Sheriff Appeal Court's civil competence and jurisdiction. Section 47 of the 2014 Act was brought into force on 1st January 2016, along with the A.S. (Rules of the Court of Session, Sheriff Appeal Court Rules and Sheriff Court Rules Amendment) (Sheriff

---

[1] Rule 39.9A as inserted by S.S.I. 2015 No. 227 (effective 22nd September 2015).

Appeal Court) 2015 [S.S.I. 2015 No. 419] which provides for rules of court. Paragraph 18 of that instrument amends the A.S. (Rules of the Court of Session 1994 and Sheriff Court Rules Amendment) (No. 2) (Personal Injury and Remits) 2015 by substituting a new para. 5 to provide that para. 4 has effect in relation to any application made under s. 69 or 71 of the 2014 Act before 1st January 2016.

"MOTION".

For motions, see Chap. 23.

39.9A.2

"PROCEDURAL JUDGE".

See Chap.37A on the meaning, jurisdiction and powers of the procedural judge.

39.9A.3

Single Bills

39.10.[1] At any hearing of an application for a new trial in the Single Bills, the Inner House may determine the application or make such other order as it thinks fit.

39.10

---

[1] Rule 39.10 inserted by S.S.I. 2010 No. 30 (effective from 5th April 2010).

CHAPTER 40 APPEALS FROM INFERIOR COURTS

Chapter 40[1]

Appeals from Inferior Courts

Application and interpretation of this Chapter

40.1.—(1) This Chapter applies to an appeal to the court from any decision pronounced by an inferior court which may be appealed to the court.

(2) In this Chapter—

  (a) "appeal process" means—

    (i) the process of the inferior court; or

    (ii) where the cause is recorded in an official book of an inferior court, a copy of the record in that book certified by the clerk of the inferior court;

  (b) "decision" includes interlocutor, judgment or other determination;

  (c)[2] "inferior court" means—

    (i) the Lyon Court;

    (ii) the Sheriff Appeal Court, in respect of an appeal under section 113(1) of the Act of 2014 or section 38(b) of the Sheriff Courts (Scotland) Act 1971;

    (iii) the sheriff principal, in respect of an appeal under section 114(1) of the Act of 2014;

  (d) any reference to leave to appeal includes permission to appeal in terms of section 113(1) of the Act of 2014.

Deriv. R.C.S. 1965, r. 267.

GENERAL NOTE.

The reform of the way Inner House business is conducted arose out of the *Penrose Report on the Review of Inner House Business* in 2009. The report itself followed independent research by Dr Rachel Wadia into the efficient and effective use of Inner House resources in order to "inform" the review. She produced a damning indictment of the efficiency and cost-effectiveness of Inner House business.

The core of the reform is that one judge of the Inner House, the procedural judge, is responsible for the appeal until it is appointed to a full hearing and there is an automatic timetable that can be sisted or varied for the progress of the appeal to that point. All procedural business (defined in r. 37A.1(2)), up to the appointment of the appeal to a hearing, is dealt with by a procedural judge appointed under r. 37A.2.

Regard should be had to P.N. No. 3 of 2011 (Causes in the Inner House).

"INFERIOR COURT".

This term is now defined. The Sheriff Appeal Court is an inferior court as is the Lyon Court (*Cunninghame v. Cunyngham* (1849) 11 D. 1139; Erskine, I.iv.32).

The A.S. (R.C.S.A. No.3) (Miscellaneous) 1996 [SI 1996/1756] removed the Employment Appeal Tribunal from the definition or inferior court. Thus appeals from the EAT will no longer be dealt with under Chap.40 but under Chap.41 Part II (appeals in Form 41.19).

The Employment Appeal Tribunal found it difficult administratively to deal with appeals to the Court of Session under this Chapter.

"THE SHERIFF APPEAL COURT".

This Chapter applies to appeals from (1) the Sheriff Appeal Court in respect of appeals under s. 113 of the Courts Reform (Scotland) Act 2014, (2) a sheriff principal under s. 114 of the 2014 Act in respect of proceedings brought before a sheriff principal under another enactment and (3) a sheriff principal under s.38(b) of the Sheriff Courts (Scotland) Act 1971 in respect of an appeal in a summary cause.

(1) *Sheriff Appeal Court.* An appeal from the Sheriff Appeal Court (SAC) to the Court of Session may only be taken with the permission of the SAC or, if the SAC refuses, the Court of Session, except as otherwise provided, restricted or excluded under any other enactment: 2014 Act, s. 113. On leave to appeal, see further, note 40.2.1.

40.1

40.1.1

40.1.2

40.1.3

---

[1] Chap. 40 and r. 40.1 substituted by S.S.I. 2010 No. 30 (effective from 5th April 2010).

[2] Rule 40.1(c) substituted by S.S.I. 2015 No. 419 (effective 1 January 2016: substitution has effect subject to savings specified in S.S.I. 2015 No. 419 r.20(4)(a)).

(2) *Sheriff Principal*. Some enactments provide for proceedings to be brought directly before a sheriff principal. An appeal may be taken to the Court of Session directly from the sheriff principal's final judgment except as otherwise provided, restricted or excluded by any other enactment: 2014 Act, s. 114.

(3) *Summary causes and simple procedure cases*. An (old) summary cause may be appealed to the sheriff principal on a point of law from a final judgment of the sheriff; and from the sheriff principal to the Court of Session if the sheriff principal certifies the cause as suitable for such an appeal: 1971 Act, s. 38. In a (new) simple procedure case, an appeal on a point of law from a decision of a sheriff's final judgment may be taken to the SAC (2014 Act, s. 82); and from there, under s.113 of the 2014 Act, to the Court of Session.

This chapter does not apply to appeals directly to the Court of Session from the sheriff or the sheriff principal under other enactments, to which Chap.41 applies.

FINAL JUDGMENT

40.1.4   Final judgment means an interlocutor which, by itself, or taken along with previous interlocutors, disposes of the subject-matter of the cause, notwithstanding that judgment may not have been pronounced on every question raised, and that the expenses found due may not have been modified, taxed or decerned for: 1907 Act, s. 3(h). If liability for expenses has not been decided the appellant will have to obtain such a decree in order to present an appeal: see *Russell v. Allan* (1877) 5 R. 22.

A prior interlocutor which is expressly or by implication a final interlocutor cannot be submitted to appeal. A prior interlocutor expressly final is one not appealed within the time prescribed: *Copeland v. Lord Wimborne*, 1912 S.C. 355; *Cumptsie v. Waterston*, 1933 S.C. 1. A prior interlocutor which is final by implication is one which has been acted on as the basis of subsequent proceedings: *Macaskill v. Nicol*, 1943 S.C. 17, 20 per L. J.-C. Cooper; see also *Spencer v. Macmillan*, 1957 S.L.T.(Notes) 32, *Campbell v. James Walker Insulation Ltd*, 1988 S.L.T. 263. It had been thought that a prior interlocutor was also expressly final where leave to appeal is required and has been refused in respect of it: *Marsh v. Baxendale*, 1994 S.C. 157. But in *McCue v. Scottish Daily Record*, 1998 S.C. 811 a court of five judges held that this was not so. A distinction has to be drawn between, on the one hand, a rule which excludes subsequent review of an interlocutor if not reclaimed against (or appealed) within a specified time (e.g. final if not reclaimed against within X days: *Copeland*, above; *Cumptsie*, above) and, on the other hand, one which merely delimits the period within which an interlocutor may be reclaimed (or appealed). The former is excluded from review by s. 29 of the 1907 Act but the latter is not (unless excluded by actings). Thus, where an interlocutor granting or refusing leave to appeal against an interlocutor excludes from review the interlocutor appealed against, the interlocutor in respect of which leave was sought may be submitted to review as a prior interlocutor under s. 29 of the 1907 Act. The decisions in *Marsh*, above, and *Mowbray v. D.C. Thomson Ltd*, 1996 S.C. 197 (appeal without the necessary leave from the sheriff court held expressly final and incapable of review as a prior interlocutor under s. 29) are overruled.

In *McCue*, above, the court went on to say that actings after an interlocutor which may exclude review of that interlocutor was not a matter of competency but because the court considers that it should not exercise the power of review in respect of it (see pp. 820D to 821G). Thus, "acquiescence" in a prior interlocutor does not necessarily exclude review of it. In *Clark v. Greater Glasgow Health Board*, 2017 S.C. 297 (First Div.), 307, at para. [40], the statement of Lord Carloway, LP, that "As a generality, so far as the procedural steps in the Outer House are concerned, this court will not normally review an interlocutor in which parties can be seen to have, in essence, acquiesced", may be too strict an interpretation of the comments in *McCue*.

Also in *McCue*, above, it was stated that, where a party sought to reclaim against an interlocutor pronounced on his own motion in order to submit to review a prior interlocutor (as in *McGuinness v. Bremner plc* 1988 S.L.T. 340), this was not a question of competency but that the court would not normally countenance it. Accordingly, there may be circumstances in which the court would permit it.

In *Prospect Healthcare (Hairmyres) Ltd v. Kier Build Ltd and Carrilion Construction Ltd* [2017] CSIH 70, 2018 S.L.T. 47, at para. [23], Lord Carloway, LP. asserted that, as a generality, it is not competent to challenge an interlocutor that has nothing to do with the merits of the interlocutor which is the subject of a reclaiming motion. He cited as authority the decision in *John Muir Trust v. Scottish Ministers*, 2017 S.C. 207 (First Div.), 223, per Lord Carloway, LP, at para. [57] where *McCue*, above, was cited as the authority. It does not appear that *McCue* is authority for such a proposition. In *Telfer v. Buccleuch Estates Ltd*, 2013 S.L.T. 899, 911, at para. [42] Lord Brodie observed, in commenting on *McCue*, "on the appeal of a final judgment, a prior interlocutor may or may not be open to review. It is not a matter of competency. It is a matter of whether the appellate court considers the interlocutor should be subject to review in all the circumstances. If it is purely procedural or otherwise seen to be final or spent it may be that it will be held not subject to review. On the other hand, if it continues to be linked to, or is directly influential in the order which is the subject of a timeous challenge then it may be subject to review."

Applications for leave to appeal from inferior court

40.2   **40.2.—**[1](1) Where leave to appeal is required, an application for such leave shall be made in the first instance to the inferior court unless the enactment allowing the appeal requires the application to be made to the court.

---

[1] R. 40.2 substituted by S.S.I. 2010 No. 30 (effective from 5th April 2010).

(2) Where—

(a) the inferior court has refused leave to appeal and such refusal is not final, or

(b) leave to appeal is required from the court and not the inferior court,

any application to the court for leave to appeal shall be made in Form 40.2 to a procedural judge.

(3) An application to the court under paragraph (2) for leave to appeal shall be lodged in the General Department—

(a) within the period prescribed by the enactment by virtue of which it is made; or

(b) where no such period is prescribed, within 14 days after the date specified in paragraph (4).

(4) The date referred to in paragraph (3)(b) is—

(a) the date on which the decision of the inferior court refusing leave to appeal was intimated to the appellant; or

(b) where the application for leave to appeal is required to be made to the court and not the inferior court—

(i) the date on which the decision of the inferior court complained of was issued; or

(ii) where the inferior court issued reasons for its decision later than the decision, the date of issue of the reasons.

(5) An application to the court for leave to appeal shall include a statement setting out the proposed grounds of appeal and the grounds on which leave to appeal is sought.

(6) There shall be lodged with an application to the court under paragraph (3)—

(a) a process in accordance with rule 4.4 (steps of process);

(b) where applicable—

(i) evidence that leave to appeal has been refused by the inferior court;

(ii) a copy of the grounds of appeal intimated to the inferior court; and

(iii) any note by the inferior court setting out the reasons for its refusal;

(c) a copy of the decision of the inferior court complained of and any reasons for that decision; and

(d) where the inferior court itself exercised an appellate function, a copy of the decision of the tribunal from which that appeal was taken and any reasons given for that decision.

Deriv. P.N. 6th November 1986 (r. 40.2(5) and (6))

GENERAL NOTE.

Some enactments require either the inferior court or the Court of Session to grant leave to appeal. Where leave may be sought from either court, r. 40.2(1) requires leave to be sought in the first instance from the inferior court. Where leave must be sought from the inferior court, application to the Court of Session for leave to appeal where the sheriff has refused leave is incompetent because the sheriff's decision is final: *Frost v. Bulman* 1995 S.C.L.R. 579.

The sole function of r. 40.2 is to lay down a procedure for applying for leave to appeal; the right to appeal to the court has to be found in the enactment providing for the inferior court's decision to be appealed against: *Bulman v. Frost* 1995 G.W.D. 17-971 (sheriffs decision to refuse leave under s. 103(1) of the Debtors (Scotland) Act 1987 is final).

It is not a breach of art.6(1) of the ECHR for the judge at first instance, who determined the substantive issue, to be the judge who also decides whether leave to appeal should be granted: *Umair v. Umair*, 2002 S.C. 153 (Ex Div.).

(1) Sheriff Appeal Court.

An appeal from the Sheriff Appeal Court (SAC) to the Court of Session may only be taken with the permission of the SAC or, if the SAC refuses, the Court of Session, except as otherwise provided, restricted or excluded under any other enactment: 2014 Act, s. 113. Permission will only be granted if—

40.2.1

(a) the appeal would raise an important point of principle or practice, or

(b) there is some other compelling reason for the Court of Session to hear the appeal: s. 113(2).

In *Politakis v. Spencely*, 2018 S.L.T. 29, the First Division said this about the test for permission to appeal:

"[20] …The purpose of the test is to restrict the scope for a second appeal (*Eba v Advocate General for Scotland*, 2012 S.C. (UKSC) 1, *per* Lord Hope of Craighead, para 48). The language used mirrors the former test for obtaining leave, from the Court of Appeal in England and Wales, to appeal from an appellate decision of a lower court (Civil Procedure Rules, r.52.13(2); see now r.52.7(2), which includes a prospects of success test).

[21] In *Uphill v BRB (Residuary) Ltd*, [2005] 1 W.L.R. 2070, the Court of Appeal considered the circumstances in which permission for a second appeal should be granted. Raising an important point of principle or practice is a reference to one which has not yet been established (*ibid* p.2074, para.18). It does not include a question of whether an established principle or practice has been correctly applied …

[22] The existence of some other compelling reason presupposes that no important point of practice or principle has been raised (*Uphill v BRB* (Residuary) (*supra*) Dyson LJ at p.2075, para.19). In *Uphill*, the court explained (*ibid*) that, when considering whether some other compelling reason existed, it was important to emphasise the "truly exceptional nature of the jurisdiction" in relation to second appeals. "Compelling" is a "very strong word", albeit that the test is there to enable the court to deal with the case justly (*ibid* at p.2076, para.23). A good starting point is a consideration of the prospects of success (*ibid* at pp.2076–2077, para.24). The test can be met if it is clear that the court hearing the first appeal reached a decision which is "plainly wrong" because, for example, "it is inconsistent with authority". Alternatively, there may be "good grounds for believing that the hearing was tainted by some procedural irregularity so as to render the first appeal unfair" (*ibid*). The court agrees with this analysis. The tests will be satisfied only where the decision in the first appeal is clearly wrong, such as where it ignores established precedent, or where there is a procedural irregularity in that appeal which demonstrates that the applicant did not have a fair hearing (*Eba v Advocate General for Scotland* (*supra*) Lord Hope at para.48)."

The SAC was criticised in *Bridging Loans Ltd v Hutton* [2018] CSIH 63 (First Div.) and *Khaliq v Gutowski* 2019 S.C. 136 (First Div.) for allowing appeals to the Court of Session in these cases which did not raise any point of principle or practice, far less an important one, or that there was a compelling reason for the court to hear the appeal.

(2) Sheriff court in appeals not under s. 113 of the Courts Reform (Scotland) Act 2014.

If leave to appeal is required from the sheriff court but not sought before the appeal is marked, the appeal will (usually) fail because once an appeal has been marked the procedure for the appeal is then regulated by the Court of Session under Chap. 40 and it is no longer competent for the sheriff court to deal with the cause: *McArthur v. McArthur's Tr.* 1997 S.L.T. 926 (Extra Div.); and see *Sheltered Housing Management Ltd v. Aitken* 1998 S.C. 150 (Extra Div.). So leave to appeal cannot be granted by the sheriff court after the appeal has been marked. But the Court of Session cannot supply the want of leave unless an application has been made to and refused by the sheriff court. A way out of this vicious circle has been found. In *DTL Gas Supplies Ltd v. Protan SRL*, 1999 S.L.T. 397 (First Div.) the Inner House (where the sheriff principal said leave was not necessary but the I.H. said it was) remitted back to the sheriff under s. 32(2) of the C.S.A. 1988 to consider whether to exercise the dispensing power and a late application for leave. The court held that s. 32(2) of the C.S.A. 1988 does not apply only to appeals properly taken under s. 28 of the 1907 Act but may also apply to an appeal marked late or for which the required leave had not been granted. *DTL Gas*, above, was distinguished in *Walker v. Tidewater Cyprus Ltd*, December 5, 2003, 2003 G.W.D. 40-1070 (First Div.) where it was held that an appellant was not entitled as a matter of course to a remit (there was a plain failure to apply for leave).

The absence of a decerniture is not decisive against the finality of an interlocutor for the purpose of determining whether leave to appeal is required. Leave to appeal is not required for an appeal from a sheriffs decision under s. 49(6) of the Bankruptcy (Scotland) Act 1985 to admit the claim of a creditor in sequestration proceedings: *Japan Leasing (Europe) plc v. Weir's Tr.* 1998 S.L.T. 224.

The Inner House of the Court of Session has power to entertain appeals to rectify an injustice occasioned by the sheriff or sheriff principal doing something which in the proper exercise of his judicial duty he was not entitled to do (this is done nowadays by judicial review or the *nobile officium*): *Lord Advocate v. Johnston*, 1982 S.L.T. 290, 293 per L.J-C Wheatley; *Gupta v. West Lothian Council*, [2012] CSIH 82 (Extra Div), para. [17](5) (obiter).

Fee.

40.2.2   There is no fee for lodging an application for leave to appeal. There will be a fee for the hearing of the motion to grant the application under r. 40.3: see note 40.3.2.

Determination of applications for leave to appeal from inferior court

40.3   **40.3.**—[1](1) An application for leave to appeal under rule 40.2 shall, without a motion being enrolled—

---

[1] Rule 40.3 substituted by S.S.I. 2011 No. 303 (effective from 27th September 2011).

    (a) during session, be brought before a procedural judge on the first available day after being made for an order for—

        (i) service of the application on the respondent and such other person as the procedural judge thinks fit within 7 days of the date of the order or such other period as the procedural judge thinks fit; and

        (ii) any person on whom the application has been served, to lodge answers, if so advised, within 14 days after the date of service or within such other period as the procedural judge thinks fit; and

    (b) during vacation, be brought before the vacation judge for such an order.

(2) An order for service under paragraph (1) shall include a requirement to intimate the application to the clerk of the inferior court.

(3) Where an application for leave to appeal is served under paragraph (1), evidence of service in accordance with Chapter 16 of these Rules shall be provided to the General Department within 14 days from the date of service.

(4) Within 14 days after expiry of the period within which answers may be lodged, the applicant may apply by motion for the application to be granted.

"GENERAL NOTE".

A challenge to the competency of consideration of permission to appeal to the Court of Session from the Sheriff Appeal Court being dealt with by a procedural judge alone was rejected in *Politakis v. Spencely*, 2018 S.L.T. 29 (First Div.). At the time of that case the rule making power in s.31A of the CSA 1988 inserted by s. 115 of the Courts Reform (Scotland) Act 2014 (single judge to determine leave or permission) had not been exercised. It has still not been exercised. The existing rule for leave to appeal being considered by a single procedural judge was made under s.5 of the CSA 1988.   **40.3.1**

MOTION

For motions, see Chap. 23.   **40.3.2**

FEE.

A court fee for the hearing of the application will be payable. Notwithstanding the terms of the Court of Session etc. Fees Order 1984, Table of Fees [SI 1984/256, Table as amended, pp. C 1202 et seq.], the fee for the application, which is heard in the Single Bills, will be the same as for a motion on the Motion Roll, namely, a fee payable by each party for every 30 minutes after the first 30 minutes under Pt I, B, item 17.   **40.3.3**

The fee may be debited under a credit scheme introduced on 1st April 1976 by P.N. No. 4 of 1976 to the account (if one is kept or permitted) of the agent by the court cashier, and an account will be rendered weekly by the court cashier's office to the agent for all court fees due that week for immediate settlement. An agent not on the credit scheme will have an account opened for the purpose of lodging the fee: P.N. No. 2 of 1995. A debit slip and a copy of the court hearing time sheet will be delivered to the agent's box or sent by DX or post.

A party litigant must pay cash to the clerk of court at the end of the hearing or, if the hearing lasts more than a day, at the end of each day: P.N. No. 2 of 1995. A receipt will be issued. The assistant clerk of session will acknowledge receipt of the sum received from the clerk of court on the Minute of Proceedings.

Time and method of appeal

40.4.—[1](1) An appeal from an inferior court shall be made—   **40.4**

    (a) within the period prescribed by the enactment by virtue of which the appeal is made; or

    (b) where no such period is prescribed, within 21 days after—

        (i) the date on which the decision appealed against was given;

        (ii) where the inferior court issued written reasons for its decision later than the decision, the date on which the written reasons were issued; or

        (iii) where leave to appeal was granted by the inferior court or applica-

---

[1] Rule 40.4 substituted by S.S.I. 2010 No. 30 (effective from 5th April 2010).

tion for leave to appeal was made to the court under rule 40.2(2), the date on which leave was granted by the inferior court or the court, as the case may be.

(2)   A party seeking to appeal from an inferior court shall mark an appeal by writing a note of appeal in Form 40.4—

    (a)   on the interlocutor sheet, minute of court or other written record containing the decision appealed against; or

    (b)   where such a decision is not available or the proceedings of the inferior court are recorded in an official book, on a separate sheet lodged with the clerk of the inferior court.

(3)   A note of appeal shall—

    (a)   be signed by the appellant or his agent;

    (b)   bear the date on which it is signed; and

    (c)   where the appellant is represented, specify the name and address of the agent who will be acting for him in the appeal.

Deriv. R.C.S. 1965, r. 268(1) substituted by S.I. 1990 No. 2118 and amended by S.I. 1991 No. 2483

GENERAL NOTE.

40.4.1   The appeal is marked in the inferior court process. In the sheriff court, O.C.R. 1993, r. 31.3(1) and (2) mirrors R.C.S. 1994, r. 40.4.

Once an appeal has been marked, the procedure governing the appeal is regulated by Chap. 40 of R.C.S. 1994; *McArthur's Tr. v. McArthur* , 1997 S.C.L.R. 252, 1997 S.L.T. 926.

EFFECT OF APPEAL.

40.4.2   The effect of marking an appeal is to sist all execution on the decree appealed against until the appeal is determined: *Macleay v. Macdonald* 1928 S.C. 776, 782 per Lord Anderson. An appeal precludes extract: *Fowler v. Fowler (No. 2)* 1981 S.L.T.(Notes) 78.

Execution before the marking of the appeal will not be affected unless and until the interlocutor is successfully reclaimed against or some interim order is sought from the court such as will suspend or sist the execution.

Once permission for an appeal has been granted, the procedure governing the appeal is regulated by r. 40.6 and the other provisions of Chap. 40: see *McArthur v. McArthur's Tr.* 1997 S.L.T. 926. The lower court is no longer competent to deal with matters relating to the appeal: but see note 40.6.2 about certain interim orders.

An appeal against the recall of interim interdict has the effect of suspending the operation of the recall, resulting in the interim interdict remaining in force: *Mulhern v. The Scottish Police Services Authority* , 2009 S.L.T. 353 (Extra Div.).

Leave to appeal out of time

40.5   **40.5.**—[1](1)   An application to allow an appeal to be received outwith the time prescribed for marking an appeal and to proceed out of time shall be included in the note of appeal.

(2)   Within 14 days after the date of receipt by the Deputy Principal Clerk of the appeal process from the clerk of the inferior court under rule 40.6(1), the appellant shall apply by motion to allow the appeal to be received outwith the time prescribed for marking an appeal and for leave to proceed out of time.

(3)   The motion enrolled in terms of paragraph (2) shall be disposed of by a procedural judge.

(4)   Where a motion under paragraph (2) is refused, the Deputy Principal Clerk shall—

    (a)   give written intimation to the clerk of the inferior court that leave to appeal out of time has been refused; and

    (b)   transmit the appeal process and note of appeal to him.

Deriv. R.C.S. 1965, r. 268(2) substituted by S.I. 1990 No. 2118

---

[1] Rule 40.5 substituted by S.S.I. 2010 No. 30 (effective from 5th April 2010).

No test is laid down for allowing an appeal out of time. The equivalent rule for allowing a reclaiming motion to be marked out of time provides that it can only be done in the case of mistake or inadvertence: see r. 38.10.

In *Simpson v. Assessor for Selkirkshire* , 1948 S.C. 270 (LVAC), at 272, Lord Jamieson said that where an Act says that appeals are to be lodged not later than a certain date, it means what it says, and if an appeal is not lodged by that time it is not a competent appeal. In *National Commercial Bank of Scotland v. Assessor for Fife* , 1963 S.C. 197, the LVAC allowed a valuation appeal out of time because it was said that the time-limit in the relevant legislation (not the same as in *Simpson*) in a schedule to the Act which the Secretary of State could and had amended by statutory instrument was directory and regulatory of procedure and not imperative. In *Collins v. Scottish Ministers* , 2004 S.L.T. 228 (First Div.) a planning appeal was held to be incompetent as out of time because of the clear sections of the Act.

In *Hume v. Nursing and Midwifery Council* , 2007 S.C. 644 (First Div.), an appeal under a statutory instrument was allowed out of time by exercise of the dispensing power under R.C.S. 1994, r.2.1. *Collins* was distinguished because of a "limited ouster clause" in the planning Act excluding validity of an Act being questioned except by the express right of appeal within a specific time and by (tortuously) treating the time-limit as subject to the procedural requirements of r. 41.20(1) which let in r. 2.1. In *Holmes v. Nursing and Midwifery Council* , 2010 S.C. 246 (Extra Div.), the court was bound by *Hume*, but considered that that case was probably wrongly decided and that the dispensing power could not be used. The court referred to *Simpson, Mucelli v Albania* , [2009] 1 W.L.R. 276 (where it was held that the court could not extend the time-limit in relation to an appeal under sections in the Extradition Act 2003 under a dispensing power of the English Civil Procedure Rules), and to *WY v. Law Society of Scotland* , 2009 S.C. 430 (Extra Div.). In the latter case a late appeal from a disciplinary tribunal under a section of the Solicitors (Scotland) Act 1980 was not competent. The court said that the *National Commercial Bank* case was not authority for the proposition that they could allow a statutory appeal lodged out of time in relation to time-limits contained in the primary sections of an Act. The reason was said to be that in the *Bank* case the time-limit was in a schedule to the Act which the Secretary of State could and had amended by statutory instrument and was directory and regulatory of procedure and not imperative. It is not at all clear why it should make any difference in principle whether the time-limit is in a section of or schedule to an Act or may be amended by statutory instrument.

The previous statement in this annotation that an appeal might be allowed out of time if the statutory time-limit was not imperative and there was not substantial prejudice was not, therefore, wrong. It may be going too far to say that the general rule is that, if the statute does not provide for allowing an appeal out of time, there may not be a late appeal. Ultimately it is a matter of statutory interpretation or construction. What can be said is that, unless the statute provides for a late appeal (either expressly or by reference to the court rules), the court has no power to exercise, in relation to the statutory time-limit, its dispensing power in relation to the application of its own rules.

Transmission of appeal process

40.6.—[1](1) Within 4 days after an appeal has been marked, the clerk of the inferior court shall—

(a) give written intimation of the appeal to every other party and certify on the interlocutor sheet, other record or separate note of appeal, as the case may be, that he has done so; and

(b) transmit—

(i) the appeal process, and

(ii) any separate note of appeal,

to the Deputy Principal Clerk.

(2) On receipt of an appeal process sent to him under paragraph (1), the Deputy Principal Clerk shall—

(a) mark the date of receipt on the interlocutor sheet, other record or separate note of appeal, as the case may be; and

(b) give written intimation of that date to the appellant.

(3) Where the clerk of the inferior court or the Deputy Principal Clerk fails to comply with a provision of this rule, the appeal shall not be invalidated; but the court may give such remedy for any disadvantage or inconvenience occasioned thereby as it thinks fit.

Deriv. R.C.S. 1965, r. 268(3) and (4) amended by S.I. 1990 No. 2118

40.5.1

40.6

---

[1] Rule 40.6 substituted by S.S.I. 2010 No. 30 (effective from 5th April 2010).

GENERAL NOTE.

40.6.1   In the sheriff court, O.C.R. 1993, r. 31.5 mirrors this rule.

Within 14 days of lodging the appeal process of the inferior court, the name and address of the appellant's agent must be given (r. 40.7(1)) and within 28 days a Court of Session process must be lodged (r. 40.7(2)).

INTERIM ORDERS.

40.6.2   Pending the making up of a Court of Session process, interim orders of possession, aliment and adjustment of rights should be sought in and regulated by the inferior court: *Cunningham v. Cunningham* 1965 S.C. 78; cf. *Macleay v. Macdonald* 1928 S.C. 776 (interim liberation sought from and granted by Court of Session).

Once permission to appeal has been granted it passes to the Court of Session, and the sheriff has no power to pronounce an interlocutor granting leave: see *McArthur v. McArthur's Tr.* 1997 S.L.T. 926 (Ex Div.).

The Deputy Principal Clerk has no power to do anything other than comply with r. 40.6(2). He does not have the right to return the process (e.g. to have leave to appeal sorted out because the sheriff has no power to grant it after the appeal has been marked). But, as Lord Prosser remarks at p. 932L, that does not mean to say there might not be other situations in which it may be proper for the DPCS to return a process for some administrative matter to be sorted out before marking the process as received. See *McArthur*, above (in that case what the DPCS should have done was bring the matter before a judge under r. 40.12(4) and (5)). In *Sheltered Housing Management Ltd v. Aitken* 1998 S.C. 150 (Ex Div.) the DPCS did so refer the matter (because the appeal was out of time and leave had not been granted). Representations were sought from the parties, but the defender indicated he was not insisting on his appeal "at this stage". The process was returned; the defender subsequently sought and was granted leave to appeal out of time by the sheriff principal and an appeal was again marked to the Court of Session. It was held that the Lord Ordinary should have refused the appeal when it was placed before him. In any event, in returning the process to the sheriff court after the defender indicated he was not insisting in his appeal, the interlocutor of the sheriff principal incompetently appealed against ceased to be reviewable and became final. Following *McArthur*, above, it was not competent for the sheriff principal to grant leave out of time after the appeal had been marked.

"WITHIN 4 DAYS".

40.6.3   The date from which the period is calculated is not counted. Where the last day falls on a Saturday or Sunday or a public holiday on which the Office of Court is closed, the next available day is allowed: r. 1.3(7). For office hours and public holidays, see note 3.1.2.

"WRITTEN INTIMATION".

40.6.4   For methods, see r. 16.9.

Procedure following transmission of appeal process

40.7   **40.7.**—[1](1)   Within 14 days after the date of receipt by the Deputy Principal Clerk of the appeal process, each party seeking to appear in the appeal shall—

    (a)   give written intimation to the Deputy Principal Clerk of, or

    (b)   state by note written on the interlocutor sheet, minute of court, or other record containing the decision appealed against, or on the separate note of appeal, as the case may be,

his name and address and that of his agent (if any).

(2)   Subject to rule 40.15(2) (appeals deemed abandoned), within 28 days after the date of receipt by the Deputy Principal Clerk of the appeal process, or the date of the interlocutor granting a motion made under rule 40.5(2) (leave to appeal out of time), whichever is the later, the appellant shall—

    (a)   lodge a process, including each part of the appeal process, in accordance with rule 4.4 (steps of process);

    (b)   lodge an appeal print in the form of a record which shall contain—

        (i)   the whole pleadings and interlocutors in the cause;

        (ii)   where the appeal is directed at the refusal of the inferior court to allow the pleadings to be amended, the text of the proposed amendment; and

---

[1] Rule 40.7 substituted by S.S.I. 2010 No. 30 (effective from 5th April 2010).

(iii)[1]   where available, the judgment of the inferior court (including in an appeal in a summary cause under the Act of Sederunt (Summary Cause Rules) 2002, the stated case of the sheriff, or in an appeal in a simple procedure case, the Decision Form and Appeal Report); and

(c)   send a copy of the appeal print, in accordance with rule 4.6(1) (intimation of steps of process).

Deriv. R.C.S. 1965, r. 269(a) amended by S.I. 1974 No. 845 and 1991 No. 2483, and P.N. 13th November 1969, para. 2 (r. 40.7(1)), r. 269(b)(part) amended by S.I. 1974 No. 845 (r. 40.7(2))

"WITHIN 14 DAYS."

The date from which the period is calculated is not counted. Where the last day falls on a Saturday or Sunday or a public holiday on which the Office of Court is closed, the next available day is allowed: r. 1.3(7). For office hours and public holidays, see note 3.1.2.   **40.7.1**

"WRITTEN INTIMATION".

For methods, see r. 16.9.   **40.7.2**

"WITHIN 28 DAYS".

Failure to lodge the process or appeal print timeously will result in the appeal being deemed to be abandoned unless the appellant is reponed: rr. 40.15(1) and 40.16. In an appropriate case the dispensing power in r. 2.1 may be applied: *X v. Dumfries and Galloway R.C.* 1994 S.C. 498.   **40.7.3**

The date from which the period is calculated is not counted. Where the last day falls on a Saturday or Sunday or a public holiday on which the Office of Court is closed, the next available day is allowed: r. 1.3(7). For office hours and public holidays, see note 3.1.2.

"APPEAL PRINT".

Six copies are required as well as the principal: r. 4.7(1). The appeal print is lodged as a step of process (r. 1.3(1) (definition of "step of process")). On lodging steps of process, see r. 4.4.   **40.7.4**

"SEND".

This includes deliver: r. 1.3(1) (definition of "send").   **40.7.5**

"IN ACCORDANCE WITH RULE 4.6 (1)".

This provision requires a copy of a step of process lodged to be sent to every other party.   **40.7.6**

FEE.

The court fee for lodging the appeal is payable on lodging the appeal process. For fee, see Court of Session etc. Fees Order 1997, Table of Fees, Pt I, B, item 2 [S.I. 1997 No. 688, as amended, pp. C 1201 et seq.]. Certain persons are exempt from payment of fees: see 1997 Fees Order, art.5, substituted by S.S.I. 2002 No. 270. A fee exemption certificate must be lodged in process: see P.N. No.1 of 2002.   **40.7.7**

Where the appellant is legally represented, the fee may be debited under a credit scheme introduced on 1st April 1976 by P.N. No. 4 of 1976 to the account (if one is kept or permitted) of the agent by the court cashier, and an account will be rendered weekly by the court cashier's office to the agent for all court fees due that week for immediate settlement. Party litigants, and agents not operating the scheme, must pay (by cash, cheque or postal order) on each occasion a fee is due at the time of lodging at the counter at the General Department.

Sist of process of appeal

40.8.—[2](1)   Within 14 days after the date of receipt by the Deputy Principal Clerk of the appeal process, the appellant may apply by motion to a procedural judge for a sist of process.   **40.8**

(2)   On enrolling a motion under rule 40.5(2) (leave to appeal out of time) or under paragraph (1) of this rule, the appellant shall lodge a motion sheet and an interlocutor sheet, if not already lodged.

(3)   Where the procedural judge grants a motion under paragraph (1), the period of 28 days mentioned in rule 40.7(2) (lodging process etc.) shall not run during any period in which the appeal is sisted.

---

[1] As amended by S.S.I. 2016 No. 315 para.2 (effective 28 November 2016).
[2] R. 40.8 substituted by S.S.I. 2010 No. 30 (effective from 5th April 2010).

(4)   The provisions of this rule are without prejudice to the power of the court to sist an appeal, as referred to in rule 40.12.

Deriv. R.C.S. 1965, r. 269(b)(part) amended by S.I. 1974 No. 845

GENERAL NOTE.

40.8.1   Where the appeal is sisted the period for lodging the process and appeal print is suspended. Once the sist is recalled the period begins to run again, including any days before the sist was granted: this interpretation was confirmed in *X v. Dumfries and Galloway R.C.* 1994 S.C. 498.

There is a power to sist under r. 40.12 (see note 40.8.4). The power to sist under r. 40.8, which has been repeated from the former Chap. 40, operates during the 14 or more days' gap between receipt by the DPCS of the appeal process from the inferior court and the issuing of the timetable under r. 40.11 for the progress of the appeal. It also has the effect of interrupting the time from running under r. 40.7(2) for the lodging of a process and an appeal print. It applies only to an appellant and postpones the cost of lodging a process and appeal print.

"MOTION".

40.8.2   For motions, see Chap. 23.

"PERIOD OF 28 DAYS MENTIONED IN R. 40.7(2)".

40.8.3   This is the period within which the appeal print must be lodged.

POWER OF SIST IN RULE 40.12.

40.8.4   There is a new power to sist an appeal to prevent the automatic timetable from running under r. 40.11. The timetable is not issued until after the expiry of 14 days after receipt by the DPCS of the appeal process from the inferior court. There is thus a gap filled by the power of sist under r. 40.8 on application by an appellant only (see note 40.8.1) which postpones the cost of lodging a process and appeal print.

"PROCEDURAL JUDGE".

40.8.5   See Chap.37A on the meaning, jurisdiction and powers of the procedural judge.

Urgent disposal of appeal

40.9   **40.9.—**[1](1)   Where the appellant seeks urgent disposal of an appeal, he shall, on lodging an appeal print under rule 40.7(2)(b), apply by motion to a procedural judge for urgent disposal of the appeal, specifying in the motion whether he seeks urgent disposal on the Summar Roll or urgent disposal in the Single Bills.

(2)   Where a respondent seeks urgent disposal of an appeal, he shall—

(a)   within the period allowed for opposing the motion, endorse on the motion of the appellant under paragraph (1), or send by post or facsimile transmission a notice of opposition in Form 23.4 including the words "The respondent (*name*) seeks urgent disposal in the Summar Roll" or the words "The respondent (*name*) seeks urgent disposal in the Single Bills", as the case may be; or

(b)   enrol a motion for urgent disposal on the Summar Roll or for urgent disposal in the Single Bills, within 7 days of the respondent intimating his name and address and that of his agent (if any) in terms of rule 40.7(1).

(3)   The entry in the rolls in respect of a motion for urgent disposal under this rule shall be starred; and the motion shall call before a procedural judge.

(4)   At the hearing of the motion, the parties shall provide the procedural judge with an assessment of the likely duration of the hearing to determine the appeal.

(5)   The procedural judge may—

(a)   grant the motion for urgent disposal and either appoint the cause to the Summar Roll for hearing or direct that the cause be heard in the Single Bills;

(b)   refuse the motion for urgent disposal.

---

[1] Rule 40.9 substituted by S.S.I. 2010 No. 30 (effective from 5th April 2010).

(6) Where the procedural judge grants the motion for urgent disposal, he may make such order as to the future timetabling of, and procedure in, the appeal as he thinks fit.

(7) Rules 40.10 to 40.14 shall apply to an appeal in respect of which the procedural judge has granted a motion for urgent disposal only to the extent that he so directs.

GENERAL NOTE.

The original rule (r. 40.11) was proposed by the Rules Review Group to provide a formal means for seeking early disposal of urgent appeals.

The appellant, on enrolling for urgent disposal, must specify whether he seeks urgent disposal in the Single Bills or on the Summar Roll: r. 40.9(1).

It does not follow that because early disposal is sought in the Single Bills that the court will not determine that the appeal should be disposed of on the Summar Roll: see r. 40.9(5)(a).

On Single Bills (and appeals appropriate for it), see note 40.14.3; on the Summar Roll, see note 40.14.2.

Grounds of appeal do not have to be lodged for the motion seeking urgent disposal. At the hearing of the motion, the court will decide when and if grounds of appeal should be lodged: r. 40.9(6).

Note also Short Notice Diets in P.N. No. 6 of 1992 under which the Keeper of the Rolls may issue peremptory diets where the hearing has been assessed as being not more than two days. A notice is published in the rolls of causes which may be subject to this procedure. At least two days' notice of a short notice diet will be given. The assessment of duration will normally be made on the basis of the estimate given in Form 6.3 where the appeal has been appointed to the Summar Roll. An appeal will not normally be considered for a short notice diet unless any appendix required has been lodged.

"MOTION".

See Chap. 23.

"STARRED".

A motion which is starred means that counsel, or other person having a right of audience, must appear.

"PROCEDURAL JUDGE".

See Chap.37A on the meaning, jurisdiction and powers of the procedural judge.

40.9.1

40.9.2

40.9.3

40.9.4

Required application for urgent disposal of appeal against certain interlocutors

40.9A.—[1] On lodging an appeal print under rule 40.7(2)(b) in respect of an appeal marked against an interlocutor of an inferior court containing an order made under section 11(1) of the Children (Scotland) Act 1995, the appellant shall seek urgent disposal of the appeal under rule 40.9(1).

40.9A

Objections to the competency of appeals

40.10.—[2](1) Any party other than the appellant may object to the competency of an appeal made under this Chapter by—

(a) lodging in process; and

(b) serving on the appellant,

a note of objection in Form 40.10.

(2)[3] Where the Deputy Principal Clerk considers that an appeal made under this Chapter may be incompetent he may (whether or not any party has lodged and served a note of objection under paragraph (1)) refer the question of competency to a procedural judge at any time within the period of 14 days after receipt by the Deputy Principal Clerk of the appeal process.

40.10

---

[1] As inserted by the Act of Sederunt (Rules of the Court of Session Amendment No. 6) (Miscellaneous) 2013 (SSI 2013/294) r.2(2) (effective from 11th November, 2010).
[2] Rule 40.10 substituted by S.S.I. 2010 No. 30 (effective from 5th April 2010).
[3] Rule 40.10(2) and (4) amended by S.S.I. 2011 No. 303 (effective 27th September 2011).

(3) Where the Deputy Principal Clerk refers a question of competency, he shall intimate to the parties the grounds on which he considers that question of competency arises.

(4)[1] A note of objection may be lodged only within 14 days after the expiry of the period specified in rule 40.7(2) (lodging process etc.).

(5) Where a note of objection is lodged, or the Deputy Principal Clerk has referred a question of competency, the Keeper of the Rolls shall—

(a) allocate a diet for a hearing before a procedural judge; and

(b) intimate the date and time of that diet to the parties.

(6) Each party shall, within the period of 14 days after the date on which a note of objection is lodged or a question of competency is referred by the Deputy Principal Clerk—

(a) lodge in process; and

(b) serve on the other party,

a note of argument giving fair notice of the submissions which the party intends to make as to competency.

(7) At the hearing allocated under paragraph (5), the procedural judge may—

(a) refuse the appeal as incompetent;

(b) direct that the appeal is to proceed as if the note of objection had not been lodged or the question not been referred, whether under reservation of the question of competency or having found the appeal to be competent; or

(c) refer the question of competency to a bench of three or more judges;

and he may make such order as to expenses or otherwise as he thinks fit.

(8) Where a procedural judge refers a question of competency under paragraph (7)(c), the cause shall be put out for a hearing in the Single Bills before a Division of the Inner House comprising three or more judges.

(9) At the hearing in the Single Bills arranged under paragraph (8), the Inner House may—

(a) dispose of the objection to competency;

(b) appoint the cause to the Summar Roll for a hearing on the objection;

(c) reserve the objection until grounds of appeal have been lodged and order such grounds to be lodged;

(d) reserve the objection for hearing with the merits.

Deriv. R.C.S. 1965, r. 270 (r. 40.10(1)) and (3))

GENERAL NOTE.

40.10.1   Formerly competency was opposed by motion. Now it is by a note of objection. The reference by the DPCS to the procedural judge (instead of formerly to a single judge) is consistent with the new procedure for procedural judges of the Inner House to deal with procedural business of the Inner House.

Formerly the decision of the single judge was final and not subject to review. There is no such provision in the new rule. There is provision for the procedural judge to refer the case to a bench of three or more judges; but there is no right of appeal stated. Since r. 37A.1(1) states that the quorum of a Division is one judge for the purposes of procedural business, that would indicate that the decision of the procedural judge is a decision of the Division and appeal is only to a larger constituted Division on the limited grounds on which such may be done, or to the UK Supreme Court. It would have been better to state what the position is in the Rules, e.g. the decision of the procedural judge is final or there is an appeal to a bench of three or more judges with leave of the procedural judge. The limited grounds for appeal to a larger constituted Division are that the cause is one of particular difficulty or importance or the Division is equally divided: C.S.A. 1988, s.36. A larger court may be constituted to reconsider a precedent of the court.

"INCOMPETENCY".

40.10.2   An appeal may be incompetent, e.g. because the days for appeal have expired before the appeal was enrolled, because leave was not sought or because the interlocutor may not be appealed. It had been

---

[1] Rule 40.10(2) and (4) amended by S.S.I. 2011 No. 303 (effective 27th September 2011).

thought that it is incompetent to reclaim against an interlocutor because it was pronounced on the motion of the party seeking to appeal (see *Watson v. Russell* (1894) 21 R. 433; *McGuinness v. Bremner plc* 1988 S.L.T. 340). But in *McCue v. Scottish Daily Record* 1998 S.C. 811, a court of five judges indicated that, where a party sought to reclaim against an interlocutor pronounced on his own motion in order to submit to review a prior interlocutor (as in *McGuinness v. Bremner plc* 1988 S.L.T. 340), this was not a question of competency but that the court would not normally countenance it. Accordingly, there may be circumstances in which the court would permit it.

When leave to appeal is required, it is not competent to seek leave out of time subsequent to having marked an (incompetent) appeal without leave: *McArthur v. McArthur's Tr.* 1997 S.L.T. 926, 1997 S.C.L.R. 252 (Extra Div.).

The court may take the objection itself and will not entertain an incompetent appeal even if objection is waived by the respondent: *Governors of Stricken Endowments v. Diverall* (1891) 19 R. 79.

Although a respondent has not marked an appeal as incompetent, it is still open to him to raise the matter of competency at the appeal: *A.B. and CD. Ptrs* 1992 S.L.T. 1064.

REFERRAL OF APPEAL TO PROCEDURAL JUDGE.

This provision was introduced in 1996 in its original form to prevent the time of the Inner House being wasted on an appeal (particularly by party litigants) which is incompetent because, e.g. it seeks to review a final interlocutor. **40.10.3**

In *Sheltered Housing Management Ltd v. Aitken* 1998 S.C. 150 (Extra Div.) the Deputy Principal Clerk, no doubt smarting after the decision in *McArthur v. McArthur's Tr.* 1997 S.L.T. 926; 1997 S.C.L.R. 252 (Extra Div.), referred an appeal because the appeal was out of time and leave had not been granted instead of returning the process to the sheriff court as had been done in *McArthur*, above. Representations were sought from the parties, but the defender indicated he was not insisting on his appeal "at this stage". The process was returned; the defender subsequently sought and was granted leave to appeal out of time by the sheriff principal and an appeal was again marked to the Court of Session. It was held that the Lord Ordinary should have refused the appeal when it was placed before him. In any event, in returning the process to the sheriff court after the defender indicated he was not insisting in his appeal, the interlocutor of the sheriff principal incompetently appealed against ceased to be reviewable and became final. Following *McArthur*, above, it was not competent for the sheriff principal to grant leave out of time after the appeal had been marked.

The procedural judge may refer the appeal to a larger bench under r. 40.10(7)(c), e.g. where the position about competency is uncertain: see *M and K, Appellants*, 23rd May 2002, 2002 G.W.D. 18–585 (OH) per Lord Hamilton.

"PROCEDURAL JUDGE".

See Chap.37A on the meaning, jurisdiction and powers of the procedural judge. **40.10.4**

Timetable in appeal from inferior court

40.11.—[1](1)[2] The Keeper of the Rolls shall— **40.11**

    (a)   issue a timetable in Form 40.11, calculated by reference to such periods as are specified in this Chapter and such other periods as may be specified from time to time by the Lord President, stating the date by which the parties shall comply with the procedural steps listed in paragraph (2) and the date and time of the hearing allocated in terms of subparagraph (b) of this paragraph; and

    (b)   allocate a diet for a procedural hearing in relation to the appeal, to follow on completion of the procedural steps listed in paragraph (2).

  (2) The procedural steps are—

    (a)   the lodging of a process in accordance with rule 40.7(2)(a);

    (b)   the lodging and sending a copy of the appeal print in accordance with rule 40.7(2)(b);

    (c)   the enrolling of any motion for a sist of process in terms of rule 40.8;

    (d)   the lodging of grounds of appeal and answers;

    (e)   the lodging of appendices to the appeal print or, as the case may be, the giving of intimation that the appellant does not intend to lodge any appendices;

    (f)   the lodging of notes of argument; and

---

[1] Rule 40.11 substituted by S.S.I. 2010 No. 30 (effective from 5th April 2010).
[2] Rule 40.11(1) amended by S.S.I. 2011 No. 303 (effective 27th September 2011).

(g) the lodging of estimates of the length of any hearing on the Summar Roll or in the Single Bills which is required to dispose of the appeal.

(3) The Keeper of the Rolls shall take the steps mentioned in paragraph (1)—

(a) where no note of objection has been lodged and no question of competency has been referred by the Deputy Principal Clerk within the period mentioned in rule 40.10(4), within 7 days of the expiry of that period;

(b) where a procedural judge has made a direction under rule 40.10(7)(b), within 7 days after the date that direction was made; or

(c) where a question of competency has been referred to a bench of three or more judges and—

(i) an interlocutor has been pronounced sustaining the competency of the appeal under rule 40.10(9)(a) or following a Summar Roll hearing under rule 40.10(9)(b), or

(ii) an interlocutor has been pronounced under rule 40.10(9)(c) or (d), within 7 days after the date of that interlocutor.

GENERAL NOTE.

40.11.1 In a similar way to timetabling in reparation actions under Chap. 43 and as in Chaps 38 and 39, there is an automatic timetable for appeals, including the lodging of grounds of appeal, unless an issue of competency has been raised or referred under r. 40.10. The timetable includes a date for the procedural hearing under r. 40.14 before the procedural judge to determine whether the appeal should be appointed for a hearing of the appeal in the Summary Roll or the Single Bills.

Table C in P.N. No. 3 of 2011 sets out the timetable that it is envisaged will be prescribed by the Lord President.

Under r. 40.12 there is provision for sisting the appeal or varying the timetable. Penalties for failing to comply with the timetable are provided in r. 40.13.

"GROUNDS OF APPEAL".

40.11.2 See further, r. 40.18 and notes to that rule.

"APPENDICES".

40.11.3 An appendix contains material not in the appeal under r. 40.7(2)(b).

"NOTES OF ARGUMENT".

40.11.4 P.N. No. 3 of 2011 states at para. 86 that a note of argument should comply with the following general principles (these are slightly different from those in P.N. No. 1 of 2010)—

1. A note of argument should be a concise summary of the submissions to be developed.

2. It should contain a numbered list of the points which the party wishes to make.

3. Each point should be followed by a reference to any transcript of evidence or other document on which the party wishes to rely. The note of argument should identify the relevant passage in the document in question.

4. A note of argument should state, in respect of each authority cited—

(a) the proposition of law that the authority demonstrates; and

(b) the parts of the authority (identified by page or paragraph references) that support the proposition.

5. More than one authority should not be cited in support of a given proposition unless the additional citation is necessary for a proper presentation of the argument.

"PROCEDURAL JUDGE".

40.11.5 See Chap.37A on the meaning, jurisdiction and powers of the procedural judge.

Sist or variation of timetable in appeal from inferior court

40.12 **40.12.**—[1](1) An appeal under this Chapter may be sisted or the timetable may be varied on the application by motion of any party.

(2) An application under paragraph (1) shall be—

(a) placed before a procedural judge; and

(b) granted only on special cause shown.

---

[1] Rule 40.12 substituted by S.S.I. 2010 No. 30 (effective from 5th April 2010).

(3) The procedural judge before whom an application under paragraph (1) is placed may—

    (a)   determine the application;

    (b)   refer the application to a bench of three or more judges; or

    (c)   make such other order as he thinks fit to secure the expeditious disposal of the appeal.

(4)[1] Where the timetable is varied, the Keeper of the Rolls may—

    (a)   discharge the procedural hearing fixed under rule 40.11(1)(b);

    (b)   fix a date for a procedural hearing; and

    (c)   issue a revised timetable in Form 40.11.

(5)[2] Upon recall of a sist, the Keeper of the Rolls may—

    (a)   fix a date for a procedural hearing; and

    (b)   issue a revised timetable in Form 40.11.

GENERAL NOTE.

The automatic timetable for appeals may be varied or the appeal may be sisted. Penalties for failing to comply with the timetable are provided in r. 40.13.

The points made in paras. 25 to 29 of P.N. No. 3 of 2011 should be considered: P.N. No. 3 of 2011, para. 42.

40.12.1

SIST OR VARIATION ONLY ON SPECIAL CAUSE SHOWN.

A sist or variation may be granted only on special cause shown. P.N. No. 1 of 2010, para. 26 suggests that special cause might be shown where a party has to obtain notes of evidence or legal aid.

40.12.2

"PROCEDURAL JUDGE".

See Chap.37A on the meaning, jurisdiction and powers of the procedural judge.

40.12.3

Failure to comply with timetable in appeal from inferior court

40.13.—[3](1) Where a party fails to comply with the timetable, the Keeper may, whether on the motion of a party or otherwise, put the appeal out for a hearing before a procedural judge.

40.13

(2) At a hearing under paragraph (1), the procedural judge may—

    (a)   in any case where the appellant or a respondent fails to comply with the timetable, make such order as he thinks fit to secure the expeditious disposal of the appeal;

    (b)   in particular, where the appellant fails to comply with the timetable, refuse the appeal; or

    (c)   in particular, where a sole respondent fails or all respondents fail to comply with the timetable, allow the appeal.

GENERAL NOTE.

This rule provides penalties for failure to comply with the timetable under r. 40.11 or as varied.

Under r. 40.12 there is provision for sisting the reclaiming motion or varying the timetable.

40.13.1

"PROCEDURAL JUDGE".

See Chap.37A on the meaning, jurisdiction and powers of the procedural judge.

40.13.2

Procedural hearing in appeal from inferior court

40.14.—[4](1) At the procedural hearing fixed under rules 40.11(1)(b), 40.12(4)(b) or (5)(a), the procedural judge shall ascertain, so far as reasonably practicable, the state of preparation of the parties.

40.14

(2) The procedural judge may—

---

[1] Rule 40.12(4) and (5) amended by S.S.I. 2011 No. 303 (effective 27th September 2011).

[2] Rule 40.12(4) and (5) amended by S.S.I. 2011 No. 303 (effective 27th September 2011).

[3] R. 40.13 substituted by S.S.I. 2010 No. 30 (effective from 5th April 2010).

[4] R. 40.14 substituted by S.S.I. 2010 No. 30 (effective from 5th April 2010).

(a) appoint the appeal to the Summar Roll for a hearing and allocate a date and time for that hearing;

(b) appoint the appeal to the Single Bills for a hearing and allocate a date and time for that hearing; or

(c) make such other order as he thinks fit to secure the expeditious disposal of the appeal.

GENERAL NOTE.

40.14.A1   Paragraph 57 of P.N. No. 3 of 2011 applies paras. 31 to 34 of that P.N. The primary purpose of the procedural hearing is that no case is sent for a hearing on its merits unless the procedural judge is satisfied that a hearing is necessary and that parties are prepared: para. 31. Under paras. 31–34, parties are expected to discuss the issues in the reclaiming motion and the methods of disposing of them. The procedural judge will decide the length of the hearing and when it will take place. Continued procedural hearings are to be avoided.

Under para. 90 of P.N. No. 3 of 2011, the applicant, after consultation with the respondent, should lodge a bundle of photocopies of authorities on which each party intends to rely. There should not be more than 10 authorities unless the scale of the reclaiming motion warrants more extensive citation. If there is to be citation of more than 10 authorities, this must be brought to the attention of the precedural judge in advance of the hearing and before lodging them; if not, the court may disallow the expenses of lodging more than 10 or more than allowed by the procedural judge: *Thomson v. Scottish Ministers*, 2013 S.C. 628 (Second Div), 633, para. [15].

SUMMAR ROLL.

40.14.1   As a general rule, appeals are appointed to and heard on the Summar Roll. Originally the Summar Roll was the roll for dealing with causes summarily and the Short Roll was for more complicated causes; the latter, however, has fallen into desuetude. Once appointed to the Summar Roll a diet is fixed by the Keeper of the Rolls in accordance with r. 6.3 after parties have sent him Form 6.3 duly completed.

SINGLE BILLS.

40.14.2   The Single Bills is the motion roll of the Inner House. As a general rule appeals are not heard in the Single Bills. Appeals dealt with on the Single Bills might include an urgent appeal, an appeal clearly incompetent or an appeal in respect of recall of arrestment or inhibition or interlocutory decisions where, e.g. an imminent proof might be saved.

HEARINGS BEFORE INNER HOUSE.

40.14.3   An appeal will be heard by a Division of the Inner House. A Division consists of four judges, but three are a quorum: C.S.A. 1988, s. 2(2) and (4). Because of pressure of criminal business in the High Court of Justiciary and other civil business it is unusual nowadays for a Division to sit with more than three judges. The Lord President may direct three judges to sit as an Extra Division: C.S.A. 1988, s. 2(3).

Where a Division before whom a cause is pending (*a*) considers the cause to be one of difficulty or importance or (*b*) the Division is equally divided in opinion, it may appoint the cause to be reheard by such larger court as is necessary for the proper disposal of the cause: C.S.A. 1988, s. 36. A larger court would in the first instance be a court of five judges; a rehearing of a cause on a point which had been decided by a court of five judges would be heard by a court of seven judges and so on. It is not always necessary for the cause to be heard by the Division before it is reheard by a larger court, particularly where all parties are agreed. A larger court will be required where consideration has to be given as to whether to overturn a previous decision of a Division. Hearings before a larger court may be appropriate on questions of practice or procedure. Where the question at issue is construction of a UK statute the preferable course is for appeal to the House of Lords: see *Drummond v. I.R.C.* 1951 S.C. 482.

The general rule is that when a case has been reported in Session Cases or the (English) Law Reports, it should be cited from that source: *McGowan v. Summit at Lloyds*, 2002 S.L.T. 1258, 1273 at para.[57] (Ex Div.). See also now P.N. No. 5 of 2004 (in respect of Session Cases).

FEE.

40.14.4   The court fee for the hearing of an appeal on the Summar Roll is payable by each party for every 30 minutes or part thereof. For fee, see Court of Session etc. Fees Order 1997, Table of Fees, Pt I, B, item 17 or C, item 17 [S.I. 1997 No. appeal heard in the Single Bills will under Pt I, B, item 22, or C, item 21. Certain persons are exempt from payment of fees: see 1997 Fees Order, art.5, substituted by S.S.I. 2002 No. 270. A fee exemption certificate must be lodged in process: see P.N. No. 1 of 2002.

Where a party is legally represented, the fee may be debited under a credit scheme introduced on 1st April 1976 by P.N. No. 4 of 1976 to the account (if one is kept or permitted) of the agent by the court cashier, and an account will be rendered weekly by the court cashier's office to the agent for all court fees due that week for immediate settlement. An agent not on the credit scheme will have an account opened for the purpose of lodging the fee: P.N. No. 2 of 1995. A debit slip and a copy of the court hearing time sheet will be delivered to the agent's box or sent by DX or post.

A party litigant must pay (by cash, cheque or postal order) to the clerk of court at the end of the hearing or, if the hearing lasts more than a day, at the end of each day: P.N. No. 2 of 1995. A receipt will be issued. The assistant clerk of session will acknowledge receipt of the sum received from the clerk of court on the Minute of Proceedings.

Remit to sheriff court, or proof or additional proof.

The powers of the court in s. 32 of the C.S.A. 1988 (to remit to the sheriff court or order proof or additional proof) should be noted. The court may order proof or additional proof: see e.g. *Pirie v. Leask* 1964 S.C. 103 (res noviter). The power is exercised only under exceptional circumstances: *Coul v. Ayrshire C.C.* 1909 S.C. 422; *Mitchell v. Sellar* 1915 S.C. 360, 361 per L.P. Strathclyde. The court may remit to the sheriff principal or sheriff: e.g. for a report on the accuracy of an interlocutor (*Whyte v. Whyte* (1895) 23 R. 320). That the power to remit was one to be exercised only in circumstances which justify this as an exceptional course of action was mentioned in *Japan Leasing (Europe) plc v. Weir's Tr (No. 2)* 1998 S.C. 543. In *DTL Gas Supplies Ltd v. Protan Srl* , 1999 S.L.T. 397 (First Div.), a remit was made under s. 32(2) of the 1988 Act for the sheriff to consider whether to exercise the dispensing power in a late application for leave to appeal. A remit was not made for this purpose in *Walker v. Tidewater Cyprus Ltd* , December 5, 2003, 2003 G.W.D. 40-1070 (First Div.) where it was held that an appellant was not entitled as a matter of course to a remit (there was a plain failure to apply for leave).

Although the court has to consider the interests of justice in considering a motion for additional proof, it will be slow to reopen a proof which has been concluded when both parties were legally represented at the proof and where judgment has been issued determining all matters ventilated at the proof: *Ralston v. Secretary of State for Scotland* 1991 S.C. 336 (dicta of L.P. Dunedin in *Coul*, above, at p. 424 applied that the court will not make an order on light grounds particularly where a party has by his own negligence failed to bring forward available evidence or where a party seeks leave to introduce new evidence to strengthen a weak point).

"procedural judge".

See Chap.37A on the meaning, jurisdiction and powers of the procedural judge.

Appeals deemed abandoned

40.15.—[1](1) If an appellant fails—

   (a) to apply by motion in accordance with rule 40.5(2) (leave to appeal out of time), or

   (b) to comply with the requirements of rule 40.7(2) (lodging process etc.),

he shall be deemed to have abandoned his appeal on the expiry of the period for marking an appeal or for complying with the requirements of rule 40.7(2), as the case may be.

(2) Where an appeal has been deemed to be abandoned by reason of paragraph (1)(b), a respondent may, within 7 days after the date on which the appeal is deemed to be abandoned, comply with the requirements of rule 40.7(2) (lodging process etc.) and thereafter insist in the appeal as if it had been marked by him; and the following provisions of this Chapter applying to an appellant shall, with the necessary modifications, apply to an appeal by a respondent under this paragraph.

(3) Where a respondent insists on an appeal under paragraph (2), the appellant shall be entitled to insist in the appeal notwithstanding that his appeal has been deemed to be abandoned.

(4) If, on the expiry of the period of 7 days after the date on which an appeal is deemed to be abandoned by virtue of paragraph (1)—

   (a) the appellant has not been reponed under rule 40.16, and

   (b) a respondent does not insist in the appeal under paragraph (2) of this rule,

the decision appealed against shall be treated in all respects as if no appeal had been marked, and the Deputy Principal Clerk shall transmit the appeal process to the clerk of the inferior court in accordance with paragraph (5) of this rule.

(5) Where an appeal process falls to be transmitted to the inferior court under paragraph (4), the Deputy Principal Clerk shall—

40.14.5

40.14.6

40.15

---

[1] R. 40.15 substituted by S.S.I. 2010 No. 30 (effective 5th April 2010).

(a) write on the interlocutor sheet, minute of court or other record containing the decision appealed against or on the separate note of appeal, as the case may be, a certificate in Form 40.15;

(b) send the appeal process to the clerk of the inferior court; and

(c) give written intimation to each party to the appeal of the date on which the appeal process was transmitted.

(6) Where an appeal is deemed to be abandoned under paragraph (1) and has been transmitted to an inferior court under paragraph (5)—

(a) a respondent in the appeal may apply by motion to that court for an award of the expenses of the abandoned appeal; and

(b) the inferior court shall on such motion grant decree for payment to that respondent of those expenses as taxed by the Auditor of the Court of Session.

Deriv. R.C.S. 1965, r. 269(b)(part) amended by S.I. 1974 No. 845 (r. 40.10(1)) and r. 272 amended by S.I. 1985 No. 1600 (r. 40.10(2) to (6))

Formerly R.C.S. 1994, r. 40.9

GENERAL NOTE.

40.15.1
If there is no motion under r. 40.16 to be reponed against a deemed abandonment, the interlocutor appealed against becomes final: *Watt Brothers & Co. v. Foyn and Ors* (1879) 7 R. 126. Notwithstanding that the interlocutor appealed against has become final, an appellant may, provided that at the time of the motion the process has not been transmitted to the clerk of the inferior court, make a motion under r. 2.1 (power of relief) for relief from any failure mentioned in r. 40.9(1): *Grieve v. Batchelor and Buckling* 1961 S.C. 12; and *X v. Dumfries and Galloway R.C.* 1994 S.C. 498.

Circumstances in which it might be possible to reduce a deemed abandonment should be noted: see *Bain v. Hugh L.S. McConnell Ltd* 1991 S.L.T. 691.

The respondent may insist in an appeal deemed abandoned. If so, the appellant may insist in his appeal although previously deemed abandoned: r. 40.15(3).

EXPENSES OF ABANDONED APPEAL.

40.15.2
The motion is made to the inferior court but any award of expenses is subject to taxation by the Auditor of the Court of Session: r. 40.9(6). The clerk of the inferior court must incorporate in the interlocutor for expenses a remit to the Auditor of the Court of Session.

Reponing against deemed abandonment

40.16
40.16.—[1](1) An appellant may, within 7 days after the date on which the appeal has been deemed to be abandoned under rule 40.15(1), apply by motion to a procedural judge to be reponed.

(2) A procedural judge may grant a motion under paragraph (1) on such conditions as to expenses or otherwise as he thinks fit.

(3) On enrolling a motion under paragraph (1), the appellant shall lodge a process (or such necessary steps of process as have not already been lodged) and an appeal print.

Deriv. R.C.S. 1965, r. 271 (r. 40.16(1) and (2))

Formerly R.C.S. 1994, r. 40.10

GENERAL NOTE.

40.16.1
If there is no motion to be reponed the interlocutor appealed against becomes final.

Circumstances in which it might be possible to reduce a deemed abandonment should be noted: see *Bain v. Hugh L.S. McConnell Ltd* 1991 S.L.T. 691.

"MOTION".

40.16.2
For motions, see Chap. 23. Appearance is required for a motion under r. 40.10.

"LODGE A PROCESS …".

40.16.3
Part of the process may have been lodged under r. 40.8(2) if a sist has been sought. The necessary steps of process at this stage are Nos. 1 to 4: see r. 4.4(1) and note 4.4.8.

---

[1] R. 40.16 substituted by S.S.I. 2010 No. 30 (effective from 5th April 2010).

"APPEAL PRINT".

On the meaning of appeal print, see r. 40.7(2)(b). Six copies are required as well as the principal: r. 4.7(1). The appeal print is lodged as a step of process (r. 1.3(1) (definition of "step of process")). On lodging steps of process, see r. 4.4.

40.16.4

GROUNDS FOR REPONING.

No test is laid down in the rule. Mistake and inadvertence are obvious factors to be considered.

40.16.5

"PROCEDURAL JUDGE".

See Chap.37A on the meaning, jurisdiction and powers of the procedural judge.

40.16.6

Amendment of pleadings in appeals

40.17.—[1](1) Where, after an appeal has been marked, any party applies by motion to have the pleadings amended in terms of a minute of amendment and answers, he shall apply for a direction as to further procedure.

40.17

(2) Where it appears that the amendment makes a material change to the pleadings, the Inner House may set aside the decision, or recall the interlocutor of the inferior court appealed against and.remit the cause back to the inferior court for a further hearing.

Deriv P.N. 26th March 1981
Formerly R.C.S. 1994, r. 40.19

GENERAL NOTE.

Amendment may be allowed on, during or after an appeal. This may occur after debate but is uncommon after evidence has been led. In the former case, if allowed the Inner House may refuse to hear argument until the judge at first instance has reconsidered the amended pleadings and the appeal will be remitted for that purpose: *Wallace v. Scottish Special Housing Association* 1981 S.L.T.(Notes) 60. In the latter case, amendment to raise fresh issues of fact may not be allowed because it could unjustly prejudice the other party who might have conducted his case differently: *Thomson v. Glasgow Corporation* 1962 S.C.(H.L.) 36; *McGuffie v. Forth Valley Health Board* 1991 S.L.T. 231; cf. *Moyes v. Burntisland Shipping Co.* 1952 S.C. 429 (allowed in exceptional circumstances to clarify existing controversy not a new one).

40.17.1

The purpose of r. 40.17 is to give the Inner House the opportunity to consider, before the appeal is heard, whether the amendment involves a material change as requires consideration by the Lord Ordinary.

"MOTION".

For motions, see Chap. 23. A motion enrolled to amend pleadings will require appearance on behalf of the party enrolling the motion.

40.17.2

Grounds of appeal

40.18.—[2](1) Grounds of appeal shall consist of brief specific numbered propositions stating the grounds on which it is proposed to submit that the appeal should be allowed.

40.18

(2) On lodging grounds of appeal, the party lodging them shall—

(a) lodge three copies of them in process; and

(b) send a copy of them to every other party.

(3) A party who has lodged grounds of appeal or answers to the grounds of appeal may apply by motion to amend the grounds or answers, on cause shown.

(4) An application under paragraph (3) shall include any necessary application under rule 40.12(1).

Deriv. R.C.S. 1965, r. 294B(3), (5) and (6) inserted by S.I. 1987 No. 1206 and amended by S.I. 1991 No. 1157

"GROUNDS OF APPEAL".

These are brief specific numbered propositions (see r. 38.16(2)) for which the appellant contends, which, if correct, should result in the appeal being granted. The authorities on which the propositions are based should be mentioned. It is not necessary to detail all the propositions or to list every authority which will be referred to at the hearing of the appeal. Where grounds of appeal do not comply with the requirement of r. 40.14(2) the appeal may be refused: r. 40.13(2); and see note 40.18.3. The purpose of

40.18.1

---

[1] R. 40.17 substituted by S.S.I. 2010 No. 30 (effective from 5th April 2010).
[2] R. 40.18 substituted by S.S.I. 2010 No. 30 (effective from 5th April 2010).

grounds of appeal is to give notice to the parties and to the court, of the grounds on which the appeal is be argued: *Eurocopy Rentals Ltd v. Tayside Health Board* 1996 S.C. 410, 413 per L.P. Hope.

A statement that the Lord Ordinary "erred in fact and law" is an insufficient ground of appeal to afford a proper notice of what is to be contended: *Clark v. Chief Constable, Lothian and Borders Police* 19th February 1993, unreported on this point (1993 G.W.D. 11-759); see also *McAdam v. Shell U.K. Ltd* 1991 S.C. 360, 364 per L.P. Hope; and *City of Glasgow D.C. v. Secretary of State for Scotland (No. 1)* 1993 S.L.T. 198, 204E-F per Lord Caplan in relation to the similarly worded r. 41.19(2)(e), that: "The purpose of the rule is obviously to ensure that the respondent will receive fair advance notice of any points to be taken on appeal."

Grounds of appeal do not have to be signed.

Grounds of appeal are lodged as a step of process; written intimation of the lodging of them must be given, as well as one copy sent, to every other party: rr. 4.6(1) and 40.18(2). They may be lodged in person at the public counter of the appropriate department or sent by post (P.N. No. 4 of 1994, paras 1 and 8).

Only the principal copy of the grounds of appeal must be lodged unless urgent disposal has been applied for (in which case three copies will have had to be lodged: r. 40.11(3)). Where the grounds of appeal are to be referred to at any hearing (on the Single Bills or the Summar Roll or otherwise) and copies have not previously been lodged for the motion for early disposal, four copies must be lodged by 12 noon on the second sederunt day before the hearing: r. 4.7(2).

"MOTION TO AMEND GROUNDS OF APPEAL".

40.18.2   This may be done to include additional grounds or to alter grounds already stated. It is done by motion or a minute of amendment (and a motion). Appearance will be required for such a motion. Cause must be shown for leave to be granted: r. 40.14(4).

On amending grounds of appeal at the hearing of the appeal, see *McInnes v. Lawrence* 1996 S.C.L.R. 169, where leave was refused on a motion made at the start of the appeal because no special cause had been shown and proper notice had not been given so as to get a proper allocation of court time; see also *Eurocopy Rentals Ltd v. Tayside Health Board* 1996 S.L.T. 1322 (motions to amend to add new grounds refused). The time for an appellant considering whether the grounds of appeal are adequate is before the By Order hearing under r. 6.3(9): *Noble Organisation Ltd v. Kilmarnock and Loudoun D.C.* 1993 S.L.T. 759, 761I, *Eurocopy*, above, at p. 1324.

"FAILURE TO LODGE GROUNDS OF APPEAL".

40.18.3   In this rule's predecessor (r. 40.14(5)) there was specific provision for refusal of a reclaiming motion for failure to lodge grounds of appeal in accordance with the rule. A respondent could apply by motion to have an appeal refused (a) because there are no grounds of appeal lodged or (b) because the grounds lodged do not comply with the requirement of paragraph (2) (i.e. they are not brief specific numbered propositions stating the grounds on which it is proposed to submit that the appeal should be allowed or they do not disclose such a ground). The court could at its own instance refuse an appeal on the same grounds.

There is no such specific provision in the current rule. There is power in r. 40.13 for the procedural judge to refuse a reclaiming motion for failure to comply with the timetable. To include failure to comply with the requirement in r. 40.18(1) for specific numbered propositions stating the grounds of appeal, the court would have to hold that that failure was a failure "to comply with the timetable" to lodge grounds of appeal.

For an example of an appeal being refused because the grounds of appeal were inadequate, see *Ferguson v. Whitbread and Co. plc* 1996 S.L.T. 659 (the courts below had "erred"); and *S v. S* , 4 July 2002, 2002 G.W.D. 24-758 (Ex Div.).

CIRCUMSTANCES IN WHICH APPELLATE COURT WILL INTERFERE WITH DECISION OF THE COURT BELOW.

(1) Facts.

40.18.4   Review of facts will depend on examination and assessment of the evidence and rules of evidence, and credibility, reliability, weight and sufficiency. In relation to credibility, the appellate court will be reluctant to reverse findings of credibility for the reason that it is denied the advantage of the judge at first instance who saw and heard the witnesses. The court must be persuaded, and come to the clear conclusion, that the judge who had that advantage was plainly wrong: *Clarke v. Edinburgh and District Tramways Co.* 1919 S.C.(H.L.) 35, 37, per Lord Shaw of Dunfermline. Where an appellate court is disposed to come to a different conclusion, it should not do so unless it is satisfied that any advantage enjoyed by the judge at first instance could not be sufficient to explain or justify his conclusion; where the reasons given by that judge are not satisfactory or it unmistakenly so appears from the evidence, the appellate court may be satisfied he has not taken proper advantage of seeing and hearing the witnesses and the matter will be at large for the appellate court: *Thomas v. Thomas* 1947 S.C.(H.L.) 45, 54, per Lord Thankerton. The phrase "plainly wrong" was explained in *Henderson v. Foxworth Investments Ltd,* 2014 S.C. (UKSC) 203, 219, paras. [62] and [67] per Lord Reed, as meaning a decision that no reasonable judge could have reached or the decision of the trial judge cannot reasonably be explained or justified. See further *McGraddie v. McGraddie* [2014] S.C. (UKSC) 12, paras. [1]-[6] per Lord Reed and the comments of Lord Hodge in *Carlyle v. Royal Bank of Scotland Plc* [2015] UKSC 13, para. 22.

There has been a disagreement between the UK Supreme Court and the Inner House about interfering with the court at first instance on matters of fact. In *AW, as legal representative of LW v. Greater Glasgow Health Board* [2017] CSIH 58 (Second Div.), it was explained, with reference to Lord Reid in *Benmax v Austin Motor Co Ltd* [1955] A.C. 370, 375 that the ability of the appellate court to interfere with the decision at first instance is greater where the challenge is to an inference that judge has drawn than it is where the decision is based on credibility and reliability of crucial witnesses. This sentiment was repeated in *SSE Generation Ltd v Hochtief Solutions AG* 2018 S.L.T. 579 (First Div). Mention was also made of the Court of Session being a unitary court with the Inner House (not being a separate appellate court as in other jurisdictions such as England) hearing reclaiming motions from Outer House judges exercising delegated functions.

Where a decision on fact is based on credibility, the judge at first instance should leave no doubt as to the grounds of his decision: *Duncan v. Watson* 1940 S.C. 221, 225, per L.P. Normand. The appellate court will more readily treat the matter as at large where clear and satisfactory reasons are not given: *Morrison v. J. Kelly & Sons Ltd* 1970 S.C. 65.

Where the Court of Session is reviewing concurrent findings as to credibility by the judge at first instance and an intermediate court of appeal (i.e. the sheriff principal or Sheriff Appeal Court), the following rules apply: (a) Concurrent findings-in-fact, depending on an assessment of credibility, ought only to be reviewed when it can be clearly demonstrated that the findings were erroneous. It is not enough that the court would have taken a different view of the facts: a concurrent finding can only be reversed where it could be demonstrated either that some cardinal fact had been overlooked, or that some altogether erroneous view had been taken of the bearing of the evidence on the case, (b) The court will reverse concurrent findings-of-fact where these do not depend upon as assessment of credibility, (c) A reluctance to reverse a concurrent finding-in-fact will not be shown where the finding is not a finding of a specific fact but is really an inference from facts specifically found. See *Brodie v. British Railways Board* 1972 S.L.T.(Notes) 37.

(2) Discretion.

A discretion will not be lightly interfered with. It is not enough that the appellate court would have exercised the discretion differently. The tests have been variously described, depending to some extent on the area of law concerned. The tests may be stated as follows: (*a*) has there been a failure to exercise the discretion at all (*Orr Pollock & Co. (Printers) Ltd v. Mulholland* 1983 S.L.T. 558), (*b*) has the judge misdirected himself in law (*Forsyth v. A. F. Stoddard & Co. Ltd* 1985 S.L.T. 51), (*c*) has the judge misunderstood, misused or failed to balance the evidence (*Skiponian Ltd v. Barratt Developments (Scotland) Ltd* 1983 S.L.T. 313, 314), (*d*) has the judge taken into account an irrelevant factor (*Thomson v. Glasgow Corporation* 1962 S.C.(H.L.) 36, 66, per Lord Reid), (*e*) has the judge failed to take into account a relevant factor (*Thomson, above*), (*f*) is the decision unreasonable (*Thomson, above*), (*g*) is the decision unjudicial (*Thomson, above*). See also *Brittan v. Central R.C.* 1986 S.L.T. 407.

40.18.5

Argument not presented to court below.

There is no general rule, unlike in the UK Supreme Court, that the appellate court will not entertain an argument not advanced before the court below; although it may be unfortunate that the argument was not so advanced (*Varney (Scotland) Ltd v. Lanark Town Council* 1974 S.C. 245, 249, per L.J.-C. Wheatley.) It is always open to the court to consider competency which strikes at the root of the proceedings: *Wolfson v. Glasgow District Licensing Board* 1980 S.C. 136, 128, per L.J.-C. Wheatley.

40.18.6

There are exceptions. A fresh argument which cannot be advanced without amendment to the pleadings will generally not be heard because the court will usually wish the judge at first instance to consider the amended pleadings (if allowed: on which see note 38.21.1) and have the benefit of his opinion: see e.g. *Wallace v. Scottish Special Housing Association* 1981 S.L.T. (Notes) 60 and r. 38.21. A new argument cannot be advanced other than an evidence led unless the court has allowed that further evidence or is willing to consider a change of circumstances since the hearing in the court below.

Lodging of appendices in appeals

40.19.—[1](1) Where, in an appeal under this Chapter, the appellant considers that it is not necessary to lodge an appendix to the appeal print, the appellant shall, by the relevant date specified in the timetable—

40.19

    (a)   give written intimation of that fact to the Deputy Principal Clerk; and

    (b)   send a copy of that intimation to each respondent.

(2) Where the appellant provides intimation under paragraph (1), a respondent may apply to a procedural judge, by motion, for an order requiring the appellant to lodge an appendix.

(3) An application under paragraph (2) shall include specification of the documents that the respondent seeks to have included in the appendix.

---

[1] R. 40.19 substituted by S.S.I. 2010 No. 30 (effective from 5th April 2010).

(4) Where an application is made under paragraph (2), a procedural judge may make an order requiring the appellant to lodge any appendix that the procedural judge considers necessary, within such time as the procedural judge may specify.

(5) An order under paragraph (4) may only be granted by a procedural judge after having heard parties.

(6) Paragraph (7) applies where—

(a) a respondent seeks to submit for consideration by the court notes of evidence or documents in respect of which the appellant has given written intimation to the respondent that the appellant does not intend to include in his appendix; and

(b) a procedural judge has not made an order under paragraph (2) requiring the appellant to lodge an appendix which includes such notes of evidence or documents.

(7) The respondent shall incorporate such notes or documents in an appendix which he shall lodge within such period as is specified by the procedural judge in disposing of the application under paragraph (4).

(8) Where, in any appeal other than one in which intimation is given under paragraph (1)—

(a) the judgment of the inferior court has not been included in the appeal print, or

(b) it is sought to submit notes of evidence or documents for consideration by the court,

the appellant shall lodge an appendix incorporating such documents within such period as shall be specified in the timetable.

Formerly R.C.S 1994, r. 40.17

GENERAL NOTE.

40.19.1   The appellant must lodge any appendix in accordance with the timetable under r. 40.11. If he does not intend to lodge an appendix, the appellant must give written intimation of that to the respondent: r. 40.19(1). Where the appellant does not intend to include in his appendix documents which the respondent wishes to be lodged, the clear implication of r. 40.19(6) is that he must given written intimation of that fact to the respondent to enable the latter to lodge an appendix. Parties should discuss and try to agree the documents to be lodged in one appendix.

If an appellant fails to lodge an appendix timeously the respondent may apply by motion to have the appeal refused: r. 40.13(2).

Where a motion for urgent disposal has been granted under r. 40.9, the interlocutor may have to make special provision for the lodging of appendices.

"APPENDIX".

40.19.2   An appendix contains material not in the appeal print under r. 40.7(2)(b).

"WRITTEN INTIMATION".

40.19.3   For methods, see r. 16.9.

"MOTION".

40.19.4   For motions, see Chap. 23.

"PROCEDURAL JUDGE".

40.19.5   See Chap.37A on the meaning, jurisdiction and powers of the procedural judge.

Notes of evidence not extended when agreed in appeals

40.20   **40.20.**[1] Where, in an appeal, the parties are agreed that on any particular issue the decision appealed against is not to be submitted to review, it shall not be necessary to reproduce the notes of evidence or documents relating to that issue.

Deriv. R.C.S. 1965, r. 262(d)

---

[1] R. 40.20 substituted by S.S.I. 2010 No. 30 (effective from 5th April 2010).

Formerly R.C.S. 1994, r. 40.18

Referral to family mediation in appeals from the Sheriff Appeal Court

40.21.[1] In an appeal from the Sheriff Appeal Court in which an order in relation to parental responsibilities or parental rights under section 11 of the Children (Scotland) Act 1995 is in issue, a procedural judge may, where he considers it appropriate to do so, refer that issue to a mediator accredited to a specified family mediation organisation.

40.21

Formerly R.C.S. 1994, r. 40.20

GENERAL NOTE.

This rule was inserted to enable the court to refer a case on appeal from the sheriff court to mediation if it so wished. Rule 40.21 is in the same terms as r. 49.23 which applies to family actions in the Court of Session and O.C.R. 1993, r. 33.22 which applies to such motions in the sheriff court.

On referral to mediation, see note 49.23.1.

40.21.1

"PROCEDURAL JUDGE".

See Chap.37A on the meaning, jurisdiction and powers of the procedural judge.

40.21.2

Use of Gaelic

40.22.—[2](1) This rule applies where an inferior court has authorised the use of Gaelic by a party.

40.22

(2) If the party wishes to address the Inner House in Gaelic at any hearing fixed under rule 40.14(2), he may'

   (a)   at any time up to and including the procedural hearing fixed under rules 40.11(1)(b), 40.12(4)(b) or (5)(a), apply by motion to the procedural judge for authority to do so; or

   (b)   at any time after the procedural hearing fixed under rules 40.11(1)(b), 40.12(4)(b) or (5)(a) and before final disposal of the appeal, apply by motion for authority to do so.

(3) Where proof has been ordered by the Inner House, if the party wishes to give oral evidence in Gaelic, he may apply by motion for authority to do so.

(4) Where the court has granted authority under paragraphs (2) or (3), an interpreter shall be provided by the court.

Formerly R.C.S. 1994, r. 40.21

GENERAL NOTE.

The Act of Court (No.1 of 2001) of the Sheriffdom of Grampian, Highlands and Islands authorites the use of Gaelic in Portree, Lochmaddy and Stornoway sheriff courts.

40.22.1

"MOTION".

For motions, see Chap.23

40.22.2

Single Bills

40.23.[3] At any hearing of an appeal from a decision pronounced by an inferior court in the Single Bills, the Inner House may determine the motion or make such other order as it thinks fit.

40.23

---

[1] R. 40.21 substituted by S.S.I. 2010 No. 30 (effective from 5th April 2010) and amended by S.S.I. 2015 No. 419 (effective 1 January 2016).

[2] R. 40.22 substituted by S.S.I. 2010 No. 30 (effective from 5th April 2010).

[3] R. 40.23 inserted by S.S.I. 2010 No. 30 (effective from 5th April 2010).

Formerly R.C.S. 1994, r.40.1s

Referral to family mediation in appeals from the Sheriff Appeal Court

40.21 In an appeal from the Sheriff Appeal Court in which an order relating to parental responsibilities or parental rights under section 11 of the Children (Scotland) Act 1995 is in issue, a procedural judge may, where he considers it appropriate to do so, refer that issue to a mediator accredited to a specified family mediation organisation.

Formerly R.C.S. 1994, r.40.20

General Note

40.21.1 This rule was inserted to enable the court to refer a case on appeal from the Sheriff Court to mediation if it is so wished. Rule 40.21 is in the same terms as r.49.23 which applies to such actions in the Court of Session and O.C.R. 1993 r.33C1 which applies to such actions in the sheriff court. On referral to mediation see note 49.23.15.

Procedural judge.

40.21.2 See Chap.37A for the meaning, jurisdiction and powers of the procedural judge.

Use of Gaelic

40.22.—(1) This rule applies where an inferior court has authorised the use of Gaelic by a party.

(2) If the party wishes to address the Inner House in Gaelic at any hearing fixed under rule 40.1(2), he may

(a) at any time up to and including the procedural hearing fixed under rules 40.11(1)(b), 40.12(1)(b) or 40.13(1)(b) or (5)(a), apply by motion to the procedural judge for authority to do so; or

(b) at any time after the procedural hearing fixed under rules 40.11(1)(b), 40.12(1)(b) or (5)(a) and before that disposal of the appeal, apply by motion for authority to do so.

(3) Where proof has been ordered by the Inner House, if the party wishes to give oral evidence in Gaelic, he may apply by motion for authority to do so.

(4) Where the court has granted authority under paragraphs (2) or (3), an interpreter shall be provided by the court.

Formerly R.C.S. 1994, r.40.21.

General Note

40.22.1 The Act of Court (No.1 of 2001) of the Vice-President of Grampian, Highlands and Islands authorises the use of Gaelic in Portree, Lochmaddy and Stornoway sheriff courts.

Motion.

40.22.2 For motions, see Chap.23.

Single Bills

40.23 At any hearing of an appeal from a decision pronounced by an inferior court in the Single Bills, the Inner House may determine the motion or make such other order as it thinks fit.

R.40.21 substituted by S.S.I. 2016 No. 39 (effective from 5th April 2016) and amended by S.S.I. 2015 No. 419 (effective 1 January 2016).

R.40.22 substituted by S.S.I. 2010 No. 30 (effective from 5th April 2010).

R.40.23 inserted by S.S.I. 2010 No.30 (effective from 5th April 2010).

CHAPTER 41 APPEALS UNDER STATUTE

Chapter 41[1]

Appeals Under Statute

Part I – General Provisions

Application and interpretation of this Chapter

41.1.—[2](1)[3] This Chapter applies to an appeal from any decision of a tribunal, unless one of the following Chapters applies—

    (a)   Chapter 38 (reclaiming);

    (b)   Chapter 39 (applications for new trial or to enter jury verdicts);

    (c)   Chapter 40 (appeals from inferior courts).

    (2) In this Chapter, unless the context otherwise requires—

> "appeal" includes stated case, case, special case (other than a special case under section 27 of the Act of 1988), reference or submission, or an application under an enactment by virtue of which a person may question the validity of a decision;

> "case" means stated case, special case (other than a special case under section 27 of the Act of 1988), reference or submission;

> "decision" includes assessment, determination, order or scheme;

> "party" means the person appearing before the tribunal against the decision of which appeal is taken or any other person who has exercised a statutory right of appeal;

> "tribunal" means court, Secretary of State, Minister (including the Scottish Ministers), Department, statutory tribunal, referee, authority or arbiter, as the case may be, against whose decision the appeal is taken.

Deriv. RCS 1965, r. 276 amended by S.I. 1972 No. 2021, and r. 290(a)(part) amended by S.I. 1973 No. 540 and 1986 No. 1955

GENERAL NOTE.

This rule is in almost identical terms to the previous rule immediately before this rule came into force (apart from the extended definition of "party").

Most statutory appeals are directed to be to the Court of Session and, following a long tradition, are dealt with in the Inner House. An enactment may, however, provide that an appeal is to be heard by the Lord Ordinary or a single judge in which case r. 41.43 (appeals to Lord Ordinary) will apply.

Appeal processes are lodged in the General Department: r. 3.2(2)(b).

Regard should be had to P.N. No. 3 of 2011 (Causes in the Inner House).

STATED CASE AND APPEALS IN FORM 41.25.

This Chapter provides two forms of appeal, stated case and appeals made in Form 41.25.

1.   Stated case procedure applies to a stated case, case, special case (other than one under s. 27 of the C.S.A. 1988: for which see Chap. 78), reference and submission. It requires the tribunal to state findings-in-fact on which its decision was based, rehearse the evidence relevant to those findings and give its reasons, these often not all being given in full at the time of the decision. The procedure is cumbersome but appropriate in such cases.

2.   Appeal under the Form 41.25 procedure is a simpler procedure involving reproducing in or appending to the appeal in Form 41.25 the decision appealed against. It is the appropriate procedure where a reasoned decision has been given by the tribunal or findings-in-fact are not required.

"DECISION".

On the meaning of "decision", see *Sheltered Housing Management Ltd. v. Jack,* where an "order" with no reasons was held to be a decision including two earlier issued "opinions".

41.1

41.1.1

41.1.2

41.1.3

---

[1] Chap. 41 substituted by S.S.I. 2011 No. 303 (effective 27th September 2011).
[2] Rule 41.1 substituted by S.S.I. 2011 No. 303 (effective 27th September 2011).
[3] Rule 41.1(1) as substituted by S.S.I. 2015 No. 419 (effective 1 January 2016).

Applications for leave to appeal

41.2

41.2.—[1](1)   Where leave to appeal is required, an application for such leave shall be made, in the first instance, to the tribunal which made the decision sought to be appealed against unless—

(a)   the enactment allowing the appeal requires the application to be made to the court; or

(b)   there are special circumstances which make it impracticable or impossible to apply to the tribunal.

(2)   An application may be made to the court for leave to appeal under paragraph (3) where—

(a)   the tribunal has refused leave to appeal and such refusal is not final, or

(b)   leave to appeal is required from the court and not the tribunal.

(3)   Any application to the court for leave to appeal shall be made in Form 40.2.

(4)   An application to the court under paragraph (3) for leave to appeal shall be lodged in the General Department—

(a)   within the period prescribed by the enactment by virtue of which it is made; or

(b)   where no such period is prescribed—

(i)   within 42 days after the date on which the decision appealed against was intimated to the appellant;

(ii)   where the tribunal issued a statement of reasons for its decision later than the decision, within 42 days after the date of intimation of that statement of reasons to the appellant.

(5)   An application to the court for leave to appeal shall include a statement setting out the proposed grounds of appeal and the grounds on which leave to appeal is sought.

(6)   There shall be lodged with an application to the court under paragraph (3)—

(a)   a process in accordance with rule 4.4 (steps of process);

(b)   where applicable—

(i)   evidence that leave to appeal has been refused by the tribunal;

(ii)   a copy of the grounds of appeal submitted to the tribunal; and

(iii)   any note by the tribunal setting out the reasons for its refusal;

(c)   a copy of the document issued by the tribunal setting out the decision complained of and any reasons for that decision; and

(d)   where the tribunal itself exercised an appellate function, a copy of the decision of the tribunal from which that appeal was taken and any reasons given for that decision.

Deriv. P.N. 6th November 1986 (41.2(4) and (5))

GENERAL NOTE.

41.2.1

This rule is in almost identical terms to the previous rule immediately before this rule came into force (apart from paras (2), (3) and (4) which are expressed in a slightly different way to the same effect).

An enactment may require either the tribunal or the Court of Session to grant leave to appeal. Where leave may be sought from either the tribunal or the court, r. 41.2(1) requires leave to be sought in the first instance from the tribunal.

TIME FOR SEEKING LEAVE.

41.2.2

Following the amendment in A.S. (R.C.S.A. No. 3) (Miscellaneous) 1996 [SI 1996/1756], the rule now is that where leave to appeal is sought from the court it must be sought within the period specified in the enactment under which it is made or, where there is no such period, within the period for lodging the appeal in the RCS 1994, i.e., within 42 days after the date specified in r. 41.2(3)(b): see e.g., *Francis v. Pertemps Recruitment Partnership Ltd*, 2012 S.C. 39 (Second Div).

---

[1] Rule 41.2 substituted by S.S.I. 2011 No. 303 (effective 27th September 2011).

It may be that when leave is sought from the court the time for lodging an appeal may be close to expiry (because of, e.g. the time taken in seeking leave from the tribunal) and the time for lodging the appeal may expire before or by the time leave is granted. To deal with this problem created by having to seek leave from the court within the same period as the time for lodging the appeal, r. 41.26(3) provides that (so long as leave is sought timeously) the period for lodging the appeal after leave is granted is extended by 7 days.

A further problem is that an appellant may be presented with a difficulty in obtaining leave from the tribunal, imperilling his ability to seek leave from the court within the 42 day period for lodging the appeal. For example, the tribunal may not have decided to refuse leave or even not been able to consider it, but the time limit for seeking leave of the court and lodge the appeal is about to expire. To meet this difficulty, r. 41.2(1)(b) provides for seeking leave of the court without first seeking leave of the tribunal where it is impracticable or impossible to do so.

Rules 41.2 and 41.26(3) do not deal with a situation where leave must be sought from a tribunal first and is refused, there being a right to apply after the refusal to the court for leave. That is, where the 42 day period, from the (substantive) decision sought to be appealed against, required by rr. 41.2 and 41.26(1)(b), has expired before leave is refused or an appeal to the court can thereafter be made. In *Hakim v. Secretary of State for the Home Department* , 2001 S.C. 789 it was held by an Extra Div, unattracted to requiring an appellant to seek judicial review or to use the dispensing power in r. 2.1, that the 42 day period runs from the date of refusal of leave. What is odd about this case is that the appellant still had eight days remaining, of the 42 day period after the date of intimation of refusal of leave, in which to lodge an application to the court for leave. No explanation was given or sought for his not doing so.

The former provisions in r. 41.2 created an unsatisfactory position, in certain circumstances giving an appellant 42 days to seek leave from the tribunal, 14 days to seek leave from the court and a further 42 days to lodge the appeal.

LEAVE TO APPEAL OUT OF TIME.

In *Simpson v. Assessor for Selkirkshire* , 1948 S.C. 270 (LVAC), at 272, Lord Jamieson said that where an Act says that appeals are to be lodged not later than a certain date, it means what it says, and if an appeal is not lodged by that time it is not a competent appeal. In *National Commercial Bank of Scotland v. Assessor for Fife* , 1963 S.C. 197, the LVAC allowed a valuation appeal out of time because it was said that the time-limit in the relevant legislation (not the same as in *Simpson*) in a schedule to the Act which the Secretary of State could and had amended by statutory instrument was directory and regulatory of procedure and not imperative. In *Collins v. Scottish Ministers* , 2004 S.L.T. 228 (First Div.) a planning appeal was held to be incompetent as out of time because of the clear sections of the Act.

In *Hume v. Nursing and Midwifery Council* , 2007 S.C. 644 (First Div.), an appeal under a statutory instrument was allowed out of time by exercise of the dispensing power under R.C.S. 1994, r. 2.1. *Collins* was distinguished because of a "limited ouster clause" in the planning Act excluding validity of an Act being questioned except by the express right of appeal within a specific time and by (tortuously) treating the time-limit as subject to the procedural requirements of r. 41.20(1) which let in r. 2.1. In *Holmes v. Nursing and Midwifery Council* , 2010 S.C. 246 (Extra Div.), the court was bound by *Hume*, but considered that that case was probably wrongly decided and that the dispensing power could not be used. The court referred to *Simpson, Mucelli v Albania* , [2009] 1 W.L.R. 276 (where it was held that the court could not extend the time-limit in relation to an appeal under sections in the Extradition Act 2003 under a dispensing power of the English Civil Procedure Rules), and to *WY v. Law Society of Scotland* , 2009 S.C. 430 (Extra Div.). In the latter case a late appeal from a disciplinary tribunal under a section of the Solicitors (Scotland) Act 1980 was not competent. The court said that the *National Commercial Bank* case was not authority for the proposition that they could allow a statutory appeal lodged out of time in relation to time-limits contained in the primary sections of an Act. The reason was said to be that in the *Bank* case the time-limit was in a schedule to the Act which the Secretary of State could and had amended by statutory instrument and was directory and regulatory of procedure and not imperative. It is not at all clear why it should make any difference in principle whether the time-limit is in a section of or schedule to an Act or may be amended by statutory instrument.

The previous statement in this annotation that an appeal might be allowed out of time if the statutory time-limit was not imperative and there was not substantial prejudice was not, therefore, wrong. It may be going too far to say that the general rule is that, if the statute does not provide for allowing an appeal out of time, there may not be a late appeal. Ultimately it is a matter of statutory interpretation or construction. What can be said is that, unless the statute provides for a late appeal (either expressly or by reference to the court rules), the court has no power to exercise, in relation to the statutory time-limit, its dispensing power in relation to the application of its own rules.

HUMAN RIGHTS.

It is not a breach of art.6(1) of the ECHR for the judge at first instance, who determined the substantive issue, to be the judge who also decides whether leave to appeal should be granted: *Umair v. Umair* , 2002 S.C. 153 (Ex Div.).

FEE.

There is no fee for lodging an application for leave to appeal.

41.2.3

41.2.3A

41.2.4

Determination of applications for leave to appeal

41.3   **41.3.**—[1](1)   An application for leave to appeal under rule 41.2 shall, without a motion being enrolled—

    (a)   during session, be brought before a procedural judge on the first available day after being made for an order for—

        (i)   service of the application on the respondent and such other person as the procedural judge thinks fit within 7 days of the date of the order or such other period as the procedural judge thinks fit; and

        (ii)   any person on whom the application has been served, to lodge answers, if so advised, within 14 days after the date of service or within such other period as the procedural judge thinks fit; and

    (b)   during vacation, be brought before the vacation judge for such an order.

  (2)   An order for service under paragraph (1) shall include a requirement to intimate the application to the clerk of the tribunal.

  (3)   Where an application for leave to appeal is served under paragraph (1), evidence of service in accordance with Chapter 16 of these Rules shall be provided to the General Department within 14 days from the date of service.

  (4)   Paragraph (5) applies where an enactment—

    (a)   provides that leave to appeal is required;

    (b)   does not prescribe a period for lodging an application for leave to appeal; and

    (c)   prescribes a period for lodging an appeal which is shorter than the period mentioned in rule 41.2(4)(b).

  (5)   A procedural judge or, as the case may be, the vacation judge may order that answers may be lodged to the application for leave to appeal within such period as he or she considers appropriate, having regard to the need for the application for leave to appeal to be dealt with before the period prescribed for lodging an appeal.

  (6)   Within 14 days after expiry of the period within which answers may be lodged, the applicant may apply by motion to a procedural judge for the application to be granted.

  (7)   Where an application for leave to appeal has been granted—

    (a)   the Deputy Principal Clerk shall send a certified copy of the interlocutor granting the application to the tribunal; and

    (b)   in an appeal by stated case, within 14 days after the date on which the certified copy of the interlocutor was sent to it, the tribunal shall state a case in accordance with rule 41.12 (preparation and issue of the case).

  (8)   Where an application for leave to appeal has been refused, the Deputy Principal Clerk shall send to the tribunal a copy of the interlocutor refusing the application.

GENERAL NOTE.

41.3.A1   This rule is similar to the former rule but provides for the procedural judge to deal with applications for leave.

    The only interpretation of r. 41.3 is that the decision to grant leave is to be made by the procedural judge alone and, in the absence of a successful challenge to the existence of the rule itself, decisions on leave to appeal are competently placed before and decided by a single procedural judge of the Inner House and obtaining leave is solely a procedural matter which could be determined by a procedural judge: *R v. Secretary of State for the Home Department,* 2013 S.L.T. 1108 (Second Div). The appellant had sought to have the interlocutor of the procedural judge held *pro non scripto*, which was something only the judge who pronounced the order could do (para. [22]). Obiter, the appellant should have challenged the interlocutor appointing the procedural hearing.

---

[1] Rule 41.3 substituted by S.S.I. 2011 No. 303 (effective 27th September 2011).

"MOTION".

For motions, see Chap. 23. A motion in the Inner House is heard in the Single Bills: r. 23.6(4). 　　**41.3.1**

"SERVICE".

For methods, see Chap. 16, Pt I. 　　**41.3.2**

"ANSWERS...WITHIN 14 DAYS OR SUCH OTHER PERIOD".

The dichotomy between paras (1)(a)(ii) and (5) should be noted. The first says answers within 14 days or such other period as the procedural judge thinks fit; the second says answers within such period as the procedural judge considers appropriate. 　　**41.3.3**

"SEND".

This includes deliver: r. 1.3(1) (definition of "send"). 　　**41.3.3A**

FEE.

A court fee for the hearing of the application will be payable by each party for every 30 minutes after the first 30 minutes or part thereof. For fee, see Court of Session etc. Fees Order 1997, Table of Fees, Pt I, item 22 [S.I. 1997 No. 688, as amended, pp.C1201 et seq.]. Certain persons are exempt from payment of fees: see 1997 Fees Order, art.5, substituted by S.S.I. 2002 No. 270. A fee exemption certificate must be lodged in process: see P.N. No. 1 of 2002. 　　**41.3.4**

Where a party is legally represented, the fee may be debited under a credit scheme introduced on 1st April 1976 by P.N. No. 4 of 1976 to the account (if one is kept or permitted) of the agent by the court cashier, and an account will be rendered weekly by the court cashier's office to the agent for all court fees due that week for immediate settlement. An agent not on the credit scheme will have an account opened for the purpose of lodging the fee: P.N. No. 2 of 1995. A debit slip and a copy of the court hearing time sheet will be delivered to the agent's box or sent by DX or post.

A party litigant must pay cash to the clerk of court at the end of the hearing or, if the hearing lasts more than a day, at the end of each day: P.N. No. 2 of 1995. A receipt will be issued. The assistant clerk of session will acknowledge receipt of the sum received from the clerk of court on the Minute of Proceedings.

"PROCEDURAL JUDGE".

See Chap.37A on the meaning, jurisdiction and powers of the procedural judge. 　　**41.3.5**

Urgent disposal of appeal

41.4.—[1](1)　Where the appellant or a respondent seeks urgent disposal of an appeal, he or she shall apply by motion for urgent disposal of the appeal, specifying in the motion whether the appellant or respondent seeks urgent disposal on the Summar Roll or urgent disposal in the Single Bills. 　　**41.4**

(2)　An application under paragraph (1) may be made—

    (a)　in an appeal under Part II of this Chapter, at any time before the expiry of the period of 14 days from the date intimation is given of the lodging of the case under rule 41.14(1)(b) (intimation of the lodging of the case in court);

    (b)　in an appeal under Part III of this Chapter, not later than three days after the expiry of the period allowed for lodging answers to the appeal.

(3)　The entry in the rolls in respect of a motion for urgent disposal under this rule shall be starred; and the motion shall call before a procedural judge.

(4)　At the hearing of the motion, the parties shall provide the procedural judge with an assessment of the likely duration of the hearing to determine the appeal.

(5)　The procedural judge may—

    (a)　grant the motion for urgent disposal and either appoint the cause to the Summar Roll for hearing or direct that the cause be heard in the Single Bills;

    (b)　refuse the motion for urgent disposal.

(6)　Where the procedural judge grants the motion for urgent disposal, he or she may make such order as to the future procedure in and, if appropriate, timetabling of, the appeal as he or she thinks fit.

---

[1] Rule 41.4 substituted by S.S.I. 2011 No. 303 (effective 27th September 2011).

(7) The following rules apply to an appeal in respect of which the procedural judge has granted a motion for urgent disposal only to the extent that he or she so directs—

    (a)   rule 41.5 (competency of appeals);

    (b)   in an appeal under Part II of this Chapter, rules 41.18 to 41.21.

    (c)   in an appeal under Part III of this Chapter, rules 41.29 to 41.32.

GENERAL NOTE.

41.4.1   This new rule is similar to r. 38.11 for urgent disposal of reclaiming motions.

"PROCEDURAL JUDGE".

41.4.2   See Chap.37A on the meaning, jurisdiction and powers of the procedural judge.

Competency of appeals

41.5   **41.5.**—[1](1) Any party other than the appellant may object to the competency of an appeal made in accordance with this Chapter by lodging in process and serving on the appellant a note of objection in Form 41.5.

(2) A note of objection referred to in paragraph (1) may be lodged—

    (a)   in an appeal dealt with under Part II of this Chapter, at any time before the expiry of the period of 14 days from the date intimation is given of the lodging of the case under rule 41.14(1)(b) (intimation of the lodging of the case in court); or

    (b)   in an appeal dealt with under Part III of this Chapter, at any time before the expiry of the period of 14 days from the date of service of the appeal under rule 41.27.

(3) Where the Deputy Principal Clerk considers that an appeal made under this Chapter may be incompetent he may refer the question of competency to a procedural judge—

    (a)   in an appeal dealt with under Part II of this Chapter, at any time within the period of 14 days from the date the case is lodged under rule 41.14; or

    (b)   in an appeal dealt with under Part III of this Chapter, at any time within the period of 14 days from the date the appeal is lodged under rule 41.26.

(4) Where the Deputy Principal Clerk refers a question of competency, he shall intimate to the parties the grounds on which he considers that question of competency arises.

(5) Where a note of objection is lodged, or the Deputy Principal Clerk refers a question of competency, the Keeper of the Rolls shall—

    (a)   allocate a diet for a hearing before a procedural judge; and

    (b)   intimate the date and time of that diet to the parties.

(6) Each party shall, within the period of 14 days after the date on which a note of objection is lodged or a question of competency is referred by the Deputy Principal Clerk, lodge in process and serve on the other party a note of argument giving fair notice of the submissions which the party intends to make as to competency.

(7) At the hearing allocated under paragraph (5), the procedural judge may—

    (a)   refuse the appeal as incompetent;

    (b)   direct that the appeal is to proceed as if the note of objection had not been lodged or the question not been referred, whether under reservation of the question of competency or having found the appeal to be competent; or

---

[1] Rule 41.5 substituted by S.S.I. 2011 No. 303 (effective 27th September 2011).

(c)   refer the question of competency to a bench of three or more judges; and the procedural judge may make such order as to expenses or otherwise as he or she thinks fit.

(8)   Where a procedural judge refers a question of competency under paragraph (7)(c), the cause shall be put out for a hearing in the Single Bills before a Division of the Inner House composed of three or more judges.

(9)   At the hearing in the Single Bills arranged under paragraph (8), the Inner House may—

(a)   dispose of the objection to competency;

(b)   appoint the cause to the Summar Roll for a hearing on the objection;

(c)   reserve the objection until grounds of appeal have been lodged and order such grounds to be lodged;

(d)   reserve the objection for hearing with the merits.

GENERAL NOTE.

This rule replaces former r. 41.3A. Any party may object to competency, not just the DPCS, and the matter is dealt with by the procedural judge. It replicates the provisions in r. 38.12 (objections to competency of reclaiming motions) and r. 40.10 (objections to competency of appeals from inferior courts) in respect of other appeals. It was introduced to prevent the time of the Inner House being wasted by incompetent appeals (particularly by party litigants).   **41.5.1**

Formerly the decision of the single judge was final and not subject to review. There is no such provision in the new rule. There is provision for the procedural judge to refer the case to a bench of three or more judges; but there is no right of appeal stated. Since r. 37A.1(1) states that the quorum of a Division is one judge for the purposes of procedural business, that would indicate that the decision of the procedural judge is a decision of the Division and appeal is only to a larger constituted Division on the limited grounds on which such may be done, or to the UK Supreme Court. It would have been better to state what the position is in the Rules, e.g. the decision of the procedural judge is final or there is an appeal to a bench of three or more judges with leave of the procedural judge. The limited grounds for appeal to a larger constituted Division are that the cause is one of particular difficulty or importance or the Division is equally divided: C.S.A. 1988, s.36. A larger court may be constituted to reconsider a precedent of the court.

"INCOMPETENT".

An appeal may be incompetent because, e.g., the appeal days have expired before the appeal was made or because the decision may not be appealed.   **41.5.2**

"FINAL AND NOT SUBJECT TO REVIEW".

The decision of the single judge may not be reclaimed against.   **41.5.3**

"PROCEDURAL JUDGE".

See Chap.37A on the meaning, jurisdiction and powers of the procedural judge.   **41.5.4**

Intimation of final interlocutor

41.6.—[1](1)   The Deputy Principal Clerk shall send to the tribunal a copy of the final interlocutor in an appeal under this Chapter.   **41.6**

This rule was previously r. 41.3B.   **41.6.A1**

"SEND".

This includes deliver: r. 1.3(1) (definition of "send").   **41.6.1**

Part II – Appeals by Stated Case etc.

Application and interpretation of this Part

41.7.—[2](1)   Subject to the provisions of the enactment providing for appeal and to Parts III to XIII, this Part shall regulate the procedure in—   **41.7**

(a)   an appeal by stated case, special case, case, reference or submission against the decision of a tribunal;

(b)   a case stated by an arbiter;

---

[1] Rule 41.6 substituted by S.S.I. 2011 No. 303 (effective 27th September 2011).
[2] Rule 41.7 substituted by S.S.I. 2011 No. 303 (effective 27th September 2011).

(c) all statutory proceedings for obtaining the opinion of the court on a question before the issue of a decision by a tribunal or by appeal against such a decision; and

(d) a case required to be stated by a tribunal referred to in subsection (1), as modified by subsection (7), of section 11 of the Tribunals and Inquiries Act 1992.

Deriv. R.C.S. 1965, r. 276 amended by S.I. 1972 No. 2021

GENERAL NOTE.

41.7.1

This rule is in the same terms as the previous r. 41.4.

Stated case procedure applies to a stated case, case, special case (other than one under s. 27 of the C.S.A. 1988: for which see Chap. 78), reference and submission. It involves the tribunal in stating findings-in-fact on which its decision was based, rehearsing the evidence relevant to those findings and giving its reasons, these often not all being given in full at the time of the decision. The procedure is cumbersome but appropriate in such cases.

Appeals to which this Part applies include the following:

1. *Stated cases.* These include—Stamp Act 1891, s. 13 (from Commissioners of Inland Revenue re assessment of duty); Taxes Management Act 1970, s. 56 (from General or Special Commissioners); Inheritance Tax Act 1984, s. 225 (from Special Commissioners); Stamp Duty Reserve Tax Regulations 1986 [S.I. 1986 No. 1711], reg.10 (from Special Commissioners); Tribunals and Inquiries Act 1992, s. 11 and Sched. 1 and Tribunals and Inquiries (Value Added Tax Tribunals) Order 1972 [S.I. 1972 No. 1210] (from VAT and Duties Tribunals); Pensions Appeal Tribunal Act 1943, ss. 6 and 13 (from PAT); Lands Tribunal Act 1949, s. 3(3) (from LT); Agricultural Marketing Act 1958, s. 12(2) (from disciplinary committee); Building (Scotland) Act 1959, s. 16(3) (from sheriff); Industrial and Provident Societies Act 1965, s. 60(9) (re disputes involving registered society); Social Work (Scotland) Act 1968, s. 50 (from sheriff from children's hearing); Administration of Justice (Scotland) Act 1972, s. 3 (from arbiter); Town and Country Planning (Scotland) Act 1972, s. 234 (from Secretary of State in determining planning permission under s. 51); Social Security Act 1973, s. 86 (from Occupational Pensions Board: by stated case by virtue of r. 41.34); Local Government (Scotland) Act 1973, s. 103(2) (on special report to Commission by Controller of Audit); Friendly Societies Act 1974, s. 78 (re certain disputes); Restrictive Practices Court Act 1976, s. 10 (from RPC); Iron and Steel Act 1982, s. 26(5)(a) (from Iron and Steel Arbitration Tribunal); Representation of the People Act 1983, s. 134(1) (from sheriffs principal who cannot agree re election of councillors) and s. 146(4) (from election court on admissibility of evidence etc.); New Roads and Street Works Act 1991, s. 158(2) (from arbiter); Social Security Administration Act 1992, ss. 18(1) and 58 (from Secretary of State: by stated case by virtue of r. 41.34); Friendly Societies Act 1992, s. 80(4) (from arbiter); Tribunal and Inquiries Act 1992, s. 11 and Sched. 1 (from various tribunals).

2. *Special cases.* These include—Compensation (Defence) Act 1939, ss. 7 and 18(2) (from Shipping Tribunal or General Tribunal); Crofters (Scotland) Act 1961, s. 4(3) (from Land Court); Rules of the Scottish Land Court 2014, r. 83 [S.I. 2014 No. 229]; Representation of the People Act 1983, s. 146(1) (from election court).

3. *References.* These include—Defamation Act 1952, s. 4(4) (re steps in fulfilment of offer of amends): see r. 54.1; Social Security Administration Act 1992, ss. 18(1) and 58 (from Secretary of State: by stated case by virtue of r. 41.34); Pension Schemes Act 1993, s. 150(7) (from Pensions Ombudsman: by stated case by virtue of r. 41.34) and s. 173(1) (from Occupational Pensions Board: by stated case by virtue of r. 41.34). Certain references are by petition and not by appeal (and are assigned to the Petition Department). These are—Railway and Canal Commission (Abolition) Act 1949, s. 1(1): by petition by virtue of r. 14.2(h); Mines (Working Facilities and Support) Act 1966, s. 4(3) (grant of right re minerals and compensation): by petition by virtue of r. 14.2(h); Defamation Act 1952, s. 4(4) (re steps in fulfilment of offer of amends where no action for defamation taken): r. 54.2.

CASE BY TRIBUNAL UNDER SECTION 11(1)OF THE TRIBUNALS AND INQUIRIES ACT 1992.

41.7.2

S.11(1) as modified by s. 11(7) of the 1992 Act provides that any party to proceedings before certain specified tribunals in Sched. 1 to the Act who is dissatisfied in point of law with a decision of the tribunal may appeal to, or require the tribunal to state a case for the opinion of, the Court of Session.

Applications for case

41.8

41.8.—[1](1) An application for a case for the opinion of the court on any question shall be made by minute setting out the question on which the case is applied for.

---

[1] Rule 41.8 substituted by S.S.I. 2011 No. 303 (effective 27th September 2011).

(2)   A minute under paragraph (1) shall be sent to the clerk of the tribunal—

(a)   where the application must be made before the issue of the decision of the tribunal, at any time before the issue of the decision;

(b)   where the application may be made after the issue of the decision of the tribunal, within the period mentioned in paragraph (3); or

(c)   where, in a cause in which a statement of the reasons for the decision was given later than the issue of the decision, the application may be made after the issue of that statement, within the period mentioned in paragraph (3).

(3)   The period referred to in paragraph (2)(b) and (c) is—

(a)   the period prescribed by the enactment under which the appeal is made; or

(b)   where no such period is prescribed, within 14 days after the issue of the decision or statement of reasons, as the case may be.

Deriv. R.C.S. 1965, r. 277(a) amended by S.I. 1982 No. 1825 (r. 41.5(1) and (2))

GENERAL NOTE.

This rule is in the same terms as former r. 41.5 immediately before this rule came into force but para. (2) is set out differently.

41.8.A1

"MINUTE".

R.15.1 (applications by minute) does not apply as the minute is not an application to the Court of Session.

41.8.1

"SENT".

This includes deliver: r. 1.3(1) (definition of "send").

41.8.2

"WITHIN 14 DAYS".

The date from which the period is calculated is not counted.

41.8.3

PERIOD FOR LODGING APPEAL.

Where the enactment under which the appeal is made does not prescribe a time-limit, r. 41.8 prescribes 14 days after the issue of the decision or reasons.

41.8.4

It should be noted that in appeals to which this part applies (stated cases), the period for appealing under r. 41.8(2)(b) is 14 days and not 42 days as in the case of appeals to which Pt III applies (see r. 41.26(1)(b)). Such a mistake was made in *City of Edinburgh Council v. Rapley* , 2000 S.C. 78.

Additional questions by other parties

41.9.—[1](1)   On receipt of an application under rule 41.8 (applications for case), the clerk of the tribunal shall send a copy of the minute to every other party.

41.9

(2)   Within 14 days after the date on which the clerk of the tribunal complied with paragraph (1), any other party may lodge with the clerk a minute setting out any additional question he or she proposes for the case; and on so doing he or she shall send a copy of it to every other party.

Deriv. R.C.S. 1965, r. 277(b)

GENERAL NOTE.

This rule is in the same terms as former r. 41.6 immediately before this rule came into force.

41.9.A1

"SEND".

This includes deliver: r. 1.3(1) (definition of "send").

41.9.1

"WITHIN 14 DAYS".

The date from which the period is calculated is not counted.

41.9.2

"MINUTE".

R.15.1 (applications by minute) does not apply as the minute is not an application to the Court of Session.

41.9.3

---

[1] Rule 41.9 substituted by S.S.I. 2011 No. 303 (effective 27th September 2011).

Consideration of application by tribunal

41.10   **41.10.**—[1](1) Within 21 days after the expiry of the period allowed for lodging a minute under rule 41.9(2) (additional questions by other parties), the tribunal shall—

(a) decide to state a case on the basis of the questions set out in the application for a case under rule 41.8(1) and any minute under rule 41.9(2);

(b) refuse to state a case on a proposed question where it is of the opinion that that question—

(i) does not arise;

(ii) does not require to be decided for the purposes of the appeal; or

(iii) is frivolous; or

(c) where the application under rule 41.8(1) is made before the facts have been ascertained and the tribunal is of the opinion that it is necessary or expedient that the facts should be ascertained before the application is disposed of, defer further consideration of the application until the facts have been ascertained by it.

(2) Where the tribunal has deferred a decision under paragraph (1)(c), it shall, within 14 days after it has ascertained the facts, decide whether to state or refuse to state a case.

(3) Where the tribunal makes a decision under paragraph (1) or (2), the clerk of the tribunal shall intimate that decision to each party.

(4) Where the tribunal has refused to state a case on any question, there shall be sent to the applicant with the intimation under paragraph (3)—

(a) a certificate specifying—

(i) the date of the decision of the tribunal; and

(ii) the reasons for refusal; and

(b) where the refusal has been made after the facts have been ascertained, a note of the proposed findings-in-fact on which the tribunal proposes to base its decision; or

(c) where the refusal has been made before the facts have been ascertained, a note of, or sufficient reference to, the averments of the parties in the appeal on which the refusal is based.

Deriv. R.C.S. 1965, r. 277(c) and (d)

GENERAL NOTE.

41.10.A1   This rule is in the same terms as former r. 41.7 immediately before this rule came into force (though the opening words of para. (1)(b) have been changed).

"WITHIN 14 DAYS".

41.10.1   The date from which the period is calculated is not counted.

"INTIMATE".

41.10.2   For methods, see r. 16.7.

"SENT".

41.10.3   This includes deliver: r. 1.3(1) (definition of "send").

"WHERE THE TRIBUNAL REFUSES TO STATE A CASE".

41.10.4   In an arbitration the arbiter has a discretion on an application to state a case to postpone further consideration of the application until the facts have been ascertained, and it is inappropriate for the court to require him to do so under s. 3 of the Administration of Justice Act 1972: *Edmond Nuttall Ltd v. Amec Projects Ltd* 1992 S.C. 133. But the arbiter's decision might be judicially reviewed: *Shanks & McEwan (Contractors) Ltd v. Mifflin Construction Ltd* 1993 S.L.T. 1124.

---

[1] Rule 41.10 substituted by S.S.I. 2011 No. 303 (effective 27th September 2011).

Procedure for ordaining tribunal to state a case

41.11.—[1](1) Where the tribunal has refused to state a case on any question, the party whose application has been refused may, within 14 days after the date on which intimation of such refusal was made under rule 41.10(3), lodge in the General Department— **41.11**

    (a)   an application by note to a procedural judge for an order to require the other party to show cause why a case should not be stated;

    (b)   the certificate and any note issued under rule 41.10(4); and

    (c)   a process in accordance with rule 4.4 (steps of process).

  (2) A note under paragraph (1)(a) shall—

    (a)   state briefly the grounds on which the application is made; and

    (b)   specify the order and any incidental order sought.

  (3) An application under paragraph (1) shall be placed before a procedural judge on the first available day after the date on which the note under paragraph (1)(a) was lodged for an order for service of the note on—

    (a)   the tribunal; and

    (b)   every other party.

  (4) After the period for lodging answers has expired, the procedural judge shall, on a motion by the noter, without hearing parties—

    (a)   appoint the note to the Summar Roll for hearing; or

    (b)   direct that the note be heard in the Single Bills.

  (5) The noter shall intimate the decision of the procedural judge on the note to the tribunal.

Deriv. R.C.S. 1965, r. 278

GENERAL NOTE.

This rule is in the same terms as former r. 41.8 except that the matter is dealt with by the procedural judge. **41.11.A1**

"REFUSED TO STATE A CASE".

A tribunal refuses to state a case where it agrees to state a case on certain questions but refuses to do so in respect of others: *John G. McGregor (Contractors) Ltd v. Grampian R.C.* 1989 S.L.T. 299. **41.11.1**

"WITHIN 14 DAYS".

The date from which the period is calculated is not counted. Where the last day falls on a Saturday or Sunday or a public holiday on which the Office of Court is closed, the next available day is allowed: r. 1.3(7). For office hours and public holidays, see note 3.1.2. **41.11.2**

"NOTE".

R. 15.2 (applications by note) applies. The grounds for the application must be briefly stated and must specify any incidental order sought (as well as an order requiring any other party to the proceedings before the tribunal to show cause why a case should not be stated): r. 41.8(1) and (2). **41.11.3**

"ORDER FOR SERVICE".

The note and the interlocutor must be served on the tribunal as well as every other party to the proceedings before the tribunal: r. 41.11(3). Where the tribunal has a clerk, the order may be served on him, otherwise it should be served on the chairman of the tribunal. **41.11.4**
For service, see Chap. 16, Pt. I.

SUMMAR ROLL.

As a general rule, appeals are appointed to and heard on the Summar Roll. The court must be satisfied that service has been executed. An execution copy of the appeal must be lodged before the motion is enrolled for a hearing. Originally the Summar Roll was the roll for dealing with causes summarily and the Short Roll was for more complicated causes; the latter, however, has fallen into desuetude. Once appointed to the Summar Roll a diet is fixed by the Keeper of the Rolls in accordance with r. 6.3 after parties have sent him Form 6.3 duly completed. **41.11.5**

---

[1] Rule 41.11 substituted by S.S.I. 2011 No. 303 (effective 27th September 2011).

41.11.6   The Single Bills is the motion roll of the Inner House. As a general rule, appeals are not heard in the Single Bills. Appeals dealt with on the Single Bills might include an urgent appeal or an appeal clearly incompetent.

"INTIMATE".

41.11.7   For methods, see r. 16.7.

"PROCEDURAL JUDGE".

41.11.8   See Chap.37A on the meaning, jurisdiction and powers of the procedural judge.

Preparation and issue of the case

41.12   **41.12.**—[1](1) Where the tribunal has decided, or is ordered under rule 41.11, to state a case, the tribunal shall, within 14 days after the date of intimation of its decision to the parties, cause the case to be prepared in Form 41.12 and copies of it to be submitted in draft to each party.

(2) The case shall—

(a) specify the relevant provision of the enactment under which it is prepared;

(b) state in numbered paragraphs the facts and the circumstances out of which the case arises, as agreed or found, or as the case may be, the decision of the tribunal and the reasons for the decision; and

(c) set out the question for answer by the court.

(3) Within 21 days after the date on which the draft case is submitted under paragraph (1), each party shall—

(a) return a copy of it to the clerk of the tribunal with a note of any amendments which he or she seeks to have made; and

(b) intimate such amendments to every other party.

(4) Within 28 days after the expiry of the period for return of the case under paragraph (3), the tribunal—

(a) shall adjust and settle the case; and

(b) may, when so doing, add such further or additional findings-in-fact and such additional questions as it thinks necessary for the disposal of the subject-matter of the case.

(5) Where the tribunal does not accept any amendment sought by a party, it shall append to the case a note of—

(a) the terms of the amendment proposed by the party and any statement by that party in support of the proposal; and

(b) its reasons for rejecting the proposed amendment.

(6) When the case has been settled by the tribunal, the case shall be authenticated by the clerk of the tribunal who shall send it to the party, or first party, who applied for it.

Deriv. R.C.S. 1965, r. 279 (r. 41.9(1)(part) and (2))

GENERAL NOTE.

41.12.A1   This rule is in the same terms as former r. 41.9 immediately before this rule came into force.

"WITHIN 14 DAYS", "WITHIN 21 DAYS", "WITHIN 28 DAYS".

41.12.1   The date from which the period is calculated is not counted.

"SEND".

41.12.2   This includes: deliver: r. 1.3(1) (definition of "send").

---

[1] Rule 41.12 substituted by S.S.I. 2011 No. 303 (effective 27th September 2011).

Intimation of intention to proceed

41.13.—[1](1) The party to whom the case has been sent under rule 41.12(6) or paragraph (3) of this rule shall, within 14 days after the date of receipt of it—

  (a) intimate to every other party a notice stating whether or not he or she intends to proceed with the case; and

  (b) send a copy of the case to every other party.

(2) Where the party to whom the case has been sent under rule 41.12(6) does not intend to proceed with it, he or she shall, on intimating that fact to every other party under paragraph (1), send the case back to the clerk of the tribunal.

(3) On receipt of the case sent back under paragraph (2), the clerk of the tribunal shall send it to any other party who had applied for a case.

Deriv. R.C.S. 1965, r. 277(h)(i) (r. 41.10(1)) and r. 277(j) (r. 41.10(2) and (3))

GENERAL NOTE.

This rule is in the same terms as former r. 41.10 immediately before this rule came into force.

"WITHIN 14 DAYS".

The date from which the period is calculated is not counted.

"INTIMATE".

For methods, see r. 16.7.

"SEND".

This includes deliver: r. 1.3(1) (definition of "send").

Lodging of case in court

41.14.—[2](1) The party who applied for the case shall, within the period mentioned in paragraph (2)—

  (a) lodge in the General Department—

    (i) the case; and

    (ii) a process in accordance with rule 4.4 (steps of process) including any productions to be referred to in the appeal;

  (b) *[Repealed by S.S.I. 2016 No. 102 (effective 21 March 2016).]*

  (c) endorse and sign a certificate on the case that the requirements of rule 4.6 (intimation of steps of process) have been complied with.

(2) The period referred to in paragraph (1) is—

  (a) the period prescribed by the enactment under or by virtue of which the appeal is brought; or

  (b) where no such period is prescribed, within 28 days after the date on which the case was received by the party from the clerk of the tribunal by virtue of rule 41.12(6) or 41.13(3), as the case may be.

Deriv. R.C.S. 1965, r. 277(h)(ii)(part) and (k)(i)(part) amended by S.I. 1984 No. 499

GENERAL NOTE.

This rule is in the same terms as former r. 41.11 immediately before this rule came into force. On lodging a case a motion must be enrolled for a hearing: r. 41.15(1).

"LODGE IN THE GENERAL DEPARTMENT".

Six copies of the case must be lodged with the principal: r. 4.7(1). Four copies of any productions must be lodged. Lodging may be done by post: P.N. No. 4 of 1994, paras. 1 and 8.

41.13

41.13.A1

41.13.1

41.13.2

41.13.3

41.14

41.14.1

41.14.2

---

[1] Rule 41.13 substituted by S.S.I. 2011 No. 303 (effective 27th September 2011).
[2] Rule 41.14 substituted by S.S.I. 2011 No. 303 (effective 27th September 2011).

41.14.3   The date from which the period is calculated is not counted. Where the last day falls on a Saturday or Sunday or a public holiday on which the Office of Court is closed, the next available day is allowed: r. 1.3(7). For office hours and public holidays, see note 3.1.2.

FEE.

41.14.4   The court fee for lodging the appeal is payable on lodging the stated case. For fee, see Court of Session etc. Fees Order 1997, Table of Fees, Pt. I, B, item 1 [[S.I. 1997 No. 688, as amended, pp. C1201 et seq.]. Certain persons are exempt from payment of fees: see 1997 Fees Order, art.5 substituted by S.S.I. 2002 No. 270. A fee exemption certificate must be lodged in process: see P.N. No. 1 of 2002.

Where the appellant is legally represented, the fee may be debited under a credit scheme introduced on 1st April 1976 by P.N. No. 4 of 1976 to the account (if one is kept or permitted) of the agent by the court cashier, and an account will be rendered weekly by the court cashier's office to the agent for all court fees due that week for immediate settlement. Party litigants, and agents not operating the scheme, must pay (by cash, cheque or postal order) on each occasion a fee is due at the time of lodging at the counter at the General Department.

Abandonment of appeal

41.15   **41.15.**—[1](1) A party shall be deemed to have abandoned his or her appeal if he or she—

　　(a) fails to comply with a requirement of rule 41.14(1) (lodging of case in court); and

　　(b) does not apply to be reponed under rule 41.16 (reponing against deemed abandonment).

(2) Where a party is deemed to have abandoned his or her appeal under paragraph (1) and another party has also applied for a case and has had no opportunity of proceeding with his or her appeal, the party deemed to have abandoned his or her appeal shall—

　　(a) intimate to that other party that his or her appeal is abandoned; and

　　(b) send the case to that other party.

(3) Where paragraph (2) applies, that other party shall be entitled to proceed in accordance with rule 41.14.

(4) In the application of rule 41.14 to a party entitled to proceed by virtue of paragraph (3) of this rule, for the words "on which the case" to "rule 41.12(6) or 41.13(3), as the case may be" in paragraph (2)(b) of that rule, substitute the words "of intimation of abandonment under rule 41.15(2)".

Deriv. R.C.S. 1965, r. 277(k)(part) (r. 41.12(1)) and r. 277(k)(ii) (r. 41.12(2))

GENERAL NOTE.

41.15.1   This rule is to exactly the same effect as former r. 41.12 immediately before this rule came into force.

If there is no motion under r. 41.16 to be reponed against a deemed abandonment, the decision appealed against becomes final. The circumstances in which it might be possible to reduce a deemed abandonment should be noted: see *Bain v. Hugh L.S. McConnell Ltd* , 1991 S.L.T. 691.

Where another party wishes to take up the appeal which has been deemed to be abandoned, he has 28 days to do so from the date on which the party whose appeal is deemed to be abandoned has intimated that fact to him: r. 41.15(4).

"INTIMATE".

41.15.2   For methods, see r. 16.7.

"SEND".

41.15.3   This includes deliver: r. 1.3(1) (definition of "send").

---

[1] Rule 41.15 substituted by S.S.I 2011 No. 303 (effective 27th September 2011).

Reponing against deemed abandonment

41.16.[1] A party may apply by motion to a procedural judge within 7 days after the expiry of the period specified in rule 41.14(2) (period for lodging of case in court), to be reponed against a failure to comply with a requirement of rule 41.14(1).

Deriv. R.C.S. 1965, r. 277(k)(i)(part)

GENERAL NOTE.

This rule is to exactly the same effect as former r. 41.13 immediately before this rule came into force except that the motion is dealt with by the procedural judge.

If there is no motion to be reponed the decision appealed against becomes final. The circumstances in which it might be possible to reduce a deemed abandonment should be noted: see *Bain v. Hugh L.S. Mc-Connell Ltd* , 1991 S.L.T. 691.

On enrolling to be reponed the appellant must lodge the stated case and a process as required by r. 41.14(1) and the six copies of the stated case as required by r. 4.7(1).

"MOTION".

For motions, see Chap. 23.

"WITHIN SEVEN DAYS".

The date from which the period is calculated is not counted. Where the last day falls on a Saturday or Sunday or a public holiday on which the Office of Court is closed, the next available day is allowed: r. 1.3(7). For office hours and public holidays, see note 3.1.2.

GROUNDS FOR REPONING.

No test is laid down in the rule. Mistake and inadvertence are obvious factors to be considered.

"PROCEDURAL JUDGE".

See Chap.37A on the meaning, jurisdiction and powers of the procedural judge.

Procedure on abandonment

41.17.—[2](1) On abandonment of the appeal by all parties entitled to proceed, the case shall be sent to the Deputy Principal Clerk.

(2) On receiving a case sent under paragraph (1), the Deputy Principal Clerk shall—

    (a) endorse the case with a certificate in Form 41.17; and

    (b) transmit the case to the clerk of the tribunal.

(3) Where a case has been transmitted under paragraph (2), the tribunal shall, on a motion being made to it to that effect—

    (a) dispose of the cause; and

    (b) where one party only has applied for a stated case, find that party liable for payment to the other party in the appeal of the expenses of the abandoned appeal as taxed by the Auditor of the Court of Session.

Deriv. R.C.S. 1965, r. 277(k)(iii)

GENERAL NOTE.

This rule is in the same terms as former r. 41.14.

"SENT".

This includes deliver: r. 1.3(1) (definition of "send"). The party last in possession of the stated case will be the party responsible for sending the case to the Deputy Principal Clerk.

EXPENSES OF ABANDONED APPEAL.

The motion is made to the tribunal but any award of expenses is subject to taxation by the Auditor of the Court of Session: r. 41.17(3). The tribunal should make a finding in relation to expenses and "remit to the Auditor of the Court of Session to tax".

This provision does not apply to appeals under the s. 51 of the Children (Scotland) Act 1995: r. 41.40(2).

41.16

41.16.1

41.16.2

41.16.3

41.16.4

41.16.5

41.17

41.17.A1

41.17.1

41.17.2

---

[1] Rule 41.16 substituted by S.S.I 2011 No. 303 (effective 27th September 2011).
[2] Rule 41.17 substituted by S.S.I. 2011 No. 303 (effective 27th September 2011).

Timetable in appeal under Part II of this Chapter

41.18 **41.18.**—[1](1) Where a case has been lodged in accordance with rule 41.14, the Keeper of the Rolls shall—

(a) issue a timetable in Form 41.29, calculated by reference to such periods as are specified in this Chapter and such other periods as may be specified from time to time by the Lord President, stating the date by which parties shall comply with the procedural steps listed in paragraph (2) and the date and time of the hearing allocated in terms of subparagraph (b) of this paragraph; and

(b) allocate a diet for a procedural hearing in relation to the appeal, to follow on completion of the procedural steps listed in paragraph (2).

(2) The procedural steps are—

(a) the lodging of any productions relating to, or appendices to, the appeal;

(b) the lodging of notes of argument; and

(c) the lodging of estimates of the length of any hearing on the Summar Roll or in the Single Bills which is required to dispose of the appeal.

(3) The Keeper shall take the steps mentioned in paragraph (1)—

(a) where no note of objection has been lodged and no question of competency has been referred by the Deputy Principal Clerk, within 7 days after expiry of the 14 day period mentioned in rule 41.5(2)(a);

(b) where a procedural judge has made a direction under rule 41.5(7)(b), within 7 days after the date that direction was made;

(c) where a question of competency has been referred to a bench of three or more judges, within 7 days after the date of the interlocutor mentioned in paragraph (4).

(4) An interlocutor referred to in paragraph (3)(c) is—

(a) an interlocutor that has been pronounced sustaining the competency of the appeal under rule 41.5(9)(a) or following a Summar Roll hearing under rule 41.5(9)(b);

(b) an interlocutor that has been pronounced under rule 41.5(9)(c) or (d).

Deriv. R.C.S. 1965, r. 280(a)

GENERAL NOTE.

41.18.1 The automatic timetabling procedure in reclaiming motions in Chap. 38 and Chap. 41, unless an issue of competency has been raised or referred under r. 41.5, has been extended to statutory appeals under Chap. 41. The timetable includes a date for the procedural hearing under r. 41.21 before the procedural judge to determine whether the reclaiming motion should be appointed for a hearing of the reclaiming motion in the Summary Roll or the Single Bills.

Table D to P.N. No. 3 of 2011 sets out the timetable that it is envisaged will be prescribed by the Lord President.

Under r. 41.19 there is provision for sisting the reclaiming motion or varying the timetable. Penalties for failing to comply with the timetable are provided in r. 38.15.

"RULES OF ARGUMENT".

41.18.2 P.N. No. 3 of 2011 states at para. 86 that a note of argument should comply with the following general principles (these are slightly different from those in P.N. No. 1 of 2010)—

1. A note of argument should be a concise summary of the submissions to be developed.

2. It should contain a numbered list of the points which the party wishes to make.

3. Each point should be followed by a reference to any transcript of evidence or other document on which the party wishes to rely. The note of argument should identify the relevant passage in the document in question.

4. A note of argument should state, in respect of each authority cited—

(a) the proposition of law that the authority demonstrates; and

---

[1] Rule 41.18 substituted by S.S.I. 2011 No. 303 (effective 27th September 2011).

(b)   the parts of the authority (identified by page or paragraph references) that support the proposition.

5.   More than one authority should not be cited in support of a given proposition unless the additional citation is necessary for a proper presentation of the argument.

SUMMAR ROLL.

As a general rule, appeals are appointed to and heard on the Summar Roll. Originally the Summar Roll was the roll for dealing with causes summarily and the Short Roll was for more complicated causes; the latter, however, has fallen into desuetude.

41.18.3

SINGLE BILLS.

The Single Bills is the motion roll of the Inner House. As a general rule, appeals are not heard in the Single Bills. Appeals dealt with on the Single Bills might include an urgent appeal or an appeal clearly incompetent.

41.18.4

Sist or variation of the timetable in appeal under Part II of this Chapter

41.19.—[1](1)   An appeal under Part II of this Chapter may be sisted or the timetable may be varied on the application by motion of any party.

41.19

(2)   An application under paragraph (1) shall be—

(a)   placed before a procedural judge; and

(b)   granted only on special cause shown.

(3)   The procedural judge before whom an application under paragraph (1) is placed may—

(a)   determine the application;

(b)   refer the application to a bench of three or more judges; or

(c)   make such other order as the procedural judge thinks fit to secure the expeditious disposal of the appeal.

(4)   Where the timetable is varied, the Keeper of the Rolls may—

(a)   discharge the procedural hearing fixed under rule 41.18(1)(b);

(b)   fix a date for a procedural hearing; and

(c)   issue a revised timetable in Form 41.29.

(5)   Upon recall of a sist, the Keeper of the Rolls may—

(a)   fix a date for a procedural hearing; and

(b)   issue a revised timetable in Form 41.29.

GENERAL NOTE.

The automatic timetable may be varied or the appeal may be sisted. Penalties for failing to comply with the timetable are provided in r. 41.20.

The points made in paras. 25 to 29 of P.N. No. 3 of 2011 should be considered: P.N. No. 3 of 2011, para. 55.

41.19.1

SIST OR VARIATION ONLY ON SPECIAL CAUSE SHOWN.

A sist or variation may be granted only on special cause shown. A motion to vary could be made, for example, because the decision is not yet available: see *McAdam v Shell UK Ltd* , 1991 S.C. 360, 363 per L.P. Hope. P.N. No. 3 of 2011, para. 27 suggests that special cause might be shown where a party has to obtain notes of evidence or legal aid.

41.19.2

"PROCEDURAL JUDGE".

See Chap.37A on the meaning, jurisdiction and powers of the procedural judge.

41.19.3

Failure to comply with timetable in appeal under Part II of this Chapter

41.20.—[2](1)   Where a party fails to comply with the timetable, the Keeper may, whether on the motion of a party or otherwise, put the appeal out for a hearing before a procedural judge.

41.20

(2)   At a hearing under paragraph (1), the procedural judge may—

---

[1] Rule 41.19 substituted by S.S.I. 2011 No. 303 (effective 27th September 2011).

[2] Rule 41.20 substituted by S.S.I. 2011 No. 303 (effective 27th September 2011).

    (a)   in any case where the appellant or a respondent fails to comply with the timetable, make such order as the procedural judge thinks fit to secure the expeditious disposal of the appeal;

    (b)   in particular, where the appellant fails to comply with the timetable, refuse the appeal; or

    (c)   in particular, where a sole respondent fails or all respondents fail to comply with the timetable, allow the appeal.

GENERAL NOTE.

41.20.1   This rule provides penalties for failure to comply with the timetable under r. 41.18. Under r. 41.19 there is provision for varying or sisting the timetable.

"PROCEDURAL JUDGE".

41.20.2   See Chap.37A on the meaning, jurisdiction and powers of the procedural judge.

Procedural hearing in appeal under Part II of this Chapter

41.21   **41.21.**—[1](1) At the procedural hearing fixed under rule 41.18(1)(b), or rule 41.19(4)(b) or (5)(a), the procedural judge shall ascertain, so far as reasonably practicable, the state of preparation of the parties.

    (2) At the procedural hearing mentioned in paragraph (1), the procedural judge may—

    (a)   appoint the appeal to the Summar Roll for a hearing and allocate a date and time for that hearing;

    (b)   appoint the appeal to the Single Bills for a hearing and allocate a date and time for that hearing; or

    (c)   make such other order as the procedural judge thinks fit to secure the expeditious disposal of the appeal.

GENERAL NOTE.

41.21.A1   Paragraph 71 of P.N. No. 3 of 2011 applies paras. 31–34 of that P.N. The primary purpose of the procedural hearing is that no case is sent for a hearing on its merits unless the procedural judge is satisfied that a hearing is necessary and that parties are prepared: para. 31. Under paras. 31–34, parties are expected to discuss the issues in the reclaiming motion and the methods of disposing of them. The procedural judge will decide the length of the hearing and when it will take place. Continued procedural hearings are to be avoided.

      Under para. 90 of P.N. No. 3 of 2011, the applicant, after consultation with the respondent, should lodge a bundle of photocopies of authorities on which each party intends to rely. There should not be more than 10 authorities unless the scale of the reclaiming motion warrants more extensive citation. If there is to be citation of more than 10 authorities, this must be brought to the attention of the procedural judge in advance of the hearing and before lodging them; if not, the court may disallow the expenses of lodging more than 10 or more than allowed by the procedural judge: *Thomson v. Scottish Ministers,* 2013 S.C. 628 (Second Div), 633, para. [15].

SUMMAR ROLL.

41.21.1   As a general rule, appeals are appointed to and heard on the Summar Roll. Originally the Summar Roll was the roll for dealing with causes summarily and the Short Roll was for more complicated causes; the latter, however, has fallen into desuetude.

SINGLE BILLS.

41.21.2   The Single Bills is the motion roll of the Inner House. As a general rule, appeals are not heard in the Single Bills. Appeals dealt with on the Single Bills might include an urgent appeal or an appeal clearly incompetent.

HEARINGS BEFORE INNER HOUSE.

41.21.3   An appeal will be heard by a Division of the Inner House. A Division consists of four judges, but three are a quorum: C.S.A. 1988, s. 2(2) and (4). Because of pressure of criminal business in the High Court of Justiciary and other civil business it is unusual nowadays for a Division to sit with more than three judges. The Lord President may direct three judges to sit as an Extra Division: C.S.A. 1988, s. 2(3).

---

[1] Rule 41.21 substituted by S.S.I. 2011 No. 303 (effective 27th September 2011).

Where a Division before whom a cause is pending (*a*) considers the cause to be one of difficulty or importance or (*b*) the Division is equally divided in opinion, it may appoint the cause to be reheard by such larger court as is necessary for the proper disposal of the cause: C.S.A. 1988, s. 36. A larger court would in the first instance be a court of five judges; a rehearing of a cause on a point which had been decided by a court of five judges would be heard by a court of seven judges and so on. It is not always necessary for the cause to be heard by the Division before it is reheard by a larger court, particularly where all parties are agreed. A larger court will be required where consideration has to be given as to whether to overturn a previous decision of a Division. Hearings before a larger court may be appropriate on questions of practice or procedure. Where the question at issue is construction of a U.K. statute the preferable course is for appeal to the House of Lords: see *Drummond v. I.R.C.* 1951 S.C. 482.

The general rule is that when a case has been reported in Session Cases or the (English) Law Reports, it should be cited from that source: *McGowan v. Summit at Lloyds* , 2002 S.L.T. 1258, 1273 at para.[57] (Ex Div.). See also now P.N. No. 5 of 2004 (in respect of Session Cases).

FEE.

The court fee for the hearing of an appeal on the Summar Roll is payable by each party for every 30 minutes or part thereof. For fee, see Court of Session etc. Fees Order 1997, Table of Fees, Pt I, B, item 17 [S.I. 1997 No. 688, as amended, pp. C1201 et seq.]. The fee for an appeal heard in the Single Bills will under Pt I, B, item 22. Certain persons are exempt from payment of fees: see 1997 Fees Order, art.5 substituted by S.S.I. 2002 No. 270. A fee exemption certificate must be lodged in process: see P.N. No. 1 of 2002.

41.21.4

Where a party is legally represented, the fee may be debited under a credit scheme introduced on 1st April 1976 by P.N. No. 4 of 1976 to the account (if one is kept or permitted) of the agent by the court cashier, and an account will be rendered weekly by the court cashier's office to the agent for all court fees due that week for immediate settlement. An agent not on the credit scheme will have an account opened for the purpose of lodging the fee: P.N. No. 2 of 1995. A debit slip and a copy of the court hearing time sheet will be delivered to the agent's box or sent by DX or post.

A party litigant must pay (by cash, cheque or postal order) to the clerk of court at the end of the hearing or, if the hearing lasts more than a day, at the end of each day: P.N. No. 2 of 1995. A receipt will be issued. The assistant clerk of session will acknowledge receipt of the sum received from the clerk of court on the Minute of Proceedings.

CIRCUMSTANCES IN WHICH APPELLATE COURT WILL INTERFERE WITH DECISION OF THE COURT BELOW.

(1) Facts.

Review of facts will depend on examination and assessment of the evidence and rules of evidence, and credibility, reliability, weight and a sufficiency. In relation to credibility, the appellate court will be reluctant to reverse findings of credibility for the reason that it is denied the advantage of the judge at first instance who saw and heard the witnesses. The court must be persuaded, and come to the clear conclusion, that the judge who had that advantage was plainly wrong: *Clarke v. Edinburgh and District Tramways Co.* 1919 S.C. (H.L.) 35, 37, per Lord Shaw of Dunfermline. Where an appellate court is disposed to come to a different conclusion, it should not do so unless it is satisfied that any advantage enjoyed by the judge at first instance could not be sufficient to explain or justify his conclusion; where the reasons given by that judge are not satisfactory or it unmistakenly so appears from the evidence, the appellate court may be satisfied he has not taken proper advantage of seeing and hearing the witnesses and the matter will be at large for the appellate court: *Thomas v. Thomas* S.C. (H.L.) 45, 54, per Lord Thankerton. The phrase "plainly wrong" was explained in *Henderson v. Foxworth Investments Ltd,* 2014 S.C. (UKSC) 203, 219, paras. [62] and [67] per Lord Reed, as meaning a decision that no reasonable judge could have reached or the decision of the trial judge cannot reasonably be explained or justified. See further *McGraddie v. McGraddie* [2014] S.C. (UKSC) 12, paras. [1]-[6] per Lord Reed and the comments of Lord Hodge in *Carlyle v. Royal Bank of Scotland Plc* [2015] UKSC 13, para. 22.

41.21.5

There has been a disagreement between the UK Supreme Court and the Inner House about interfering with the court at first instance on matters of fact. In *AW, as legal representative of LW v. Greater Glasgow Health Board* [2017] CSIH 58 (Second Div.), it was explained, with reference to Lord Reid in *Benmax v Austin Motor Co Ltd* [1955] A.C. 370, 375 that the ability of the appellate court to interfere with the decision at first instance is greater where the challenge is to an inference that judge has drawn than it is where the decision is based on credibility and reliability of crucial witnesses. This sentiment was repeated in *SSE Generation Ltd v Hochtief Solutions AG* 2018 S.L.T. 579 (First Div). Mention was also made of the Court of Session being a unitary court with the Inner House (not being a separate appellate court as in other jurisdictions such as England) hearing reclaiming motions from Outer House judges exercising delegated functions.

Where a decision on fact is based on credibility, the judge at first instance should leave no doubt as to the grounds of his decision: *Duncan v. Watson* 1940 S.C. 221, 225, per L.P. Normand. The appellate court will more readily treat the matter as at large where clear and satisfactory reasons are not given: *Morrison v. J. Kelly & Sons Ltd* 1970 S.C. 65.

The question of the Court of Session reviewing concurrent findings of credibility of the tribunal at first instance as an intermediate court of appeal will arise infrequently in statutory appeals to which Chap. 41 applies. In an appeal in which this issue does arise, see note 40.18.4.

In *Professional Standards Authority for Health and Social Care v. Nursing and Midwifery Council* 2017 S.C. 542 (Extra Div.), 549, at para. [25], it was observed that, in dealing with appeals from regulatory and disciplinary bodies, the court can interfere with the decision of the tribunal below if there is a serious flaw in the process or reasoning. Failing such a flaw, a decision should stand unless it is plainly wrong or manifestly inappropriate. This has since been followed: see, e.g. *Thomson v. Architect Registration Board* 2022 S.L.T. 762 (Second Div.).

(2) Discretion.

A discretion will not be legally interfered with. It is not enough that the appellate court would have exercised the discretion differently. The tests have been variously described, depending to some extent on the area of law concerned. The tests may be stated as follows: (a) has there been a failure to exercise the discretion at all (*Orr Pollock & Co. (Printers) Ltd v. Mulholland* 1983 S.L.T. 558), (b) has the judge misdirected himself in law (*Forsyth v. A. F. Stoddard & Co. Ltd* 1985 S.L.T. 51), (c) has the judge misunderstood, misused or failed to balance the evidence (*Skiponian Ltd v. Barratt Developments (Scotland) Ltd* 1983 S.L.T. 313, 314), (d) has the judge taken into account an irrelevant factor (*Thomson v. Glasgow Corporation* 1962 S.C. (H.L.) 36, 66 per Lord Reid), (e) has the judge failed to take into account a relevant factor (*Thomson, above*), (f) is the decision unreasonable (*Thomson, above*), (g) is the decision unjudicial (*Thomson, above*). See also *Brittan v. Central R.C.* 1986 S.L.T. 407.

ARGUMENT NOT PRESENTED TO COURT BELOW.

41.21.6   There is no general rule, unlike in the House of Lords or UK Supreme Court, that the appellate court will not entertain an argument not advanced before the court below; although it may be unfortunate that the argument was not so advanced (*Varney (Scotland) Ltd v. Lanark Town Council* 1974 S.C. 245, 249, per L.J.-C. Wheatley.) It is always open to the court to consider competency which strikes at the root of the proceedings: *Wolfson v. Glasgow District Licensing Board* 1980 S.C. 136, 128, per L.J.-C. Wheatley.

There are exceptions. A fresh argument which cannot be advanced without amendment to the pleadings will generally not be heard because the court will usually wish the tribunal at first instance to consider the amended pleadings (if allowed: on which see r. 41.22) and have the benefit of its opinion: see e.g. *Wallace v. Scottish Special Housing Association* 1981 S.L.T. (Notes) 60 and r. 38.21. A new argument cannot be advanced other than on evidence led unless the court has allowed that further evidence or is willing to consider a change of circumstances since the hearing in the court below.

"PROCEDURAL JUDGE".

41.21.7   See Chap.37A on the meaning, jurisdiction and powers of the procedural judge.

Amendment or re-statement of case

41.22   **41.22.**[1] The Inner House may, at any time before the final determination of the case—

    (a) allow the case to be amended with the consent of the parties; or

    (b) remit the case for re-statement, or further statement, in whole or in part by the tribunal.

Deriv. R.C.S. 1965, r. 280(b)(part)

GENERAL NOTE.

41.22.1   This rule is in the same terms as former r. 41.16 immediately before this rule came into force.

Remit to reporter

41.23   **41.23.**—[2](1) Where, in order to determine the case, any inquiry into matters of fact may be made, the Inner House may remit to a reporter, the Lord Ordinary or, in the case of a bench of three or more judges, one of the Inner House's own number to take evidence and to report to the court.

(2) On completion of a report made under paragraph (1), the reporter shall send his or her report and three copies of it, and a copy of it for each party, to the Deputy Principal Clerk.

(3) On receipt of such a report, the Deputy Principal Clerk shall—

    (a) cause the report to be lodged in process; and

    (b) give written intimation to each party that this has been done and that each party may uplift a copy of the report from process.

(4) After the lodging of such a report, any party may apply by motion for an order in respect of the report or for further procedure.

---

[1] Rule 41.22 substituted by S.S.I. 2011 No. 303 (effective 27th September 2011).
[2] Rule 41.23 substituted by S.S.I. 2011 No. 303 (effective 27th September 2011).

Deriv. R.C.S. 1965, r. 280(b)(part)

GENERAL NOTE.

This rule is in the same terms as former r. 41.17 immediately before this rule came into force.   **41.23.1**

Where a remit is made the solicitors for the parties will be personally liable in the first instance for the reporter's fees and outlays unless the court otherwise orders and one party will be made liable: r. 42.18.

"SEND".

This includes deliver: r. 1.3(1) (definition of "send").   **41.23.2**

"WRITTEN INTIMATION".

For methods, see r. 16.9.   **41.23.3**

"MOTION".

For motions, see Chap. 23.   **41.23.4**

Part III – Appeals in Form 41.25

Application of this Part

41.24.[1] Subject to the provisions of the enactment providing for appeal, this Part   **41.24**
applies to an appeal against a decision of a tribunal other than an appeal to which
Part II (appeals by stated case, etc.) applies.

Deriv. R.C.S. 1965, r. 290(a)(part) amended by S.I. 1973 No. 540

GENERAL NOTE.

This rule is in the same terms as former r. 41.18 immediately before this rule came into force.   **41.24.1**

Appeal under the Form 41.25 procedure is a simpler procedure than that of the stated case involving reproducing in or appending to the appeal in Form 41.25 the decision appealed against. It is the appropriate procedure where a reasoned decision has been given by the tribunal or findings-in-fact are not required: cf. notes 41.1.2 and 41.7.1 on stated case procedure.

APPEALS TO WHICH THE FORM 41.25 PROCEDURE APPLIES.

These include—Taxes Management Act 1970, ss. 53, 100B(3) and 100C(4) (appeals re penalties from   **41.24.2**
General or Special Commissioners); Inheritance Tax Act 1984, s. 222 (against determination of Commissioners of Inland Revenue), and ss. 249(3) and 251(2) (appeals re penalties from Special Commissioners); Oil Taxation Act 1975, s. 1 and Sched. 2, para. 1 (from Commissioners re penalties); Stamp Duty Reserve Tax Regulations 1986 [S.I. 1986 No. 1711], reg.8 (against determination of Commissioners of Inland Revenue); Tribunal and Inquiries Act 1992, s. 11 (from VAT Tribunals); Burial Grounds (Scotland) Act 1855, s. 10; Pharmacy Act 1954, ss. 10 and 24(2) (against directions); Therapeutic Substances Act 1956, ss. 2(4) and 6 (from suspension of licence); Teaching Council (Scotland) Act 1965, s. 12 as substituted by Standards in Scotland's Schools etc. Act 2000 (appeal against direction re registration); Fair Trading Act 1973, s. 42 (re protection of consumers from Restrictive Practices Court); Consumer Credit Act 1974, s. 41A inserted by Consumer Credit Act 2006, s. 57 (on point of law from Consumer Credit Appeals Tribunal); Control of Pollution Act 1974, s. 85 (from sheriff); Restrictive Practices Court Act 1976, s. 10(2) (from RPC in proceedings under Pt III of the Fair Trading Act 1973 (re protection of consumer); Patents Acts: 1949 Act, s. 87(3) and 1977 Act, Sched. 4 (re decision of comptroller under 1949 Act, s. 55), 1977 Act, s. 97 (from comptroller); Estate Agents Act 1979, s. 7(4) (from Secretary of State from Director General of Fair Trading re estate agency work); Education (Scotland) Act 1980, s. 112(8) as amended by the Education (Scotland) Act 1981, s. 1 and Sched. 2, para. 3 (from Council re issue of practising certificate), ss. 16 (from Council re restoration to roll) and 54 (from discipline tribunal); Public Passenger Vehicles Act 1981, s. 51 (from Secretary of State from Traffic Commissioners); Medical Act 1983, s. 40 as amended by the NHS Reform and Health Care Professionals Act 2002, s. 30 (from General Council); Dentists Act 1984, s. 29 as amended by the NHS Reform and Health Care Professionals Act 2002, s. 31 (appeal from Professional Conduct and Health Committees)); Mental Health (Scotland) Act 1984, s. 66A(1) (appeal from sheriff); Transport Act 1985, s. 117(2) and Sched. 4, para. 14(1) (from Transport Tribunal); Legal Aid (Scotland) Act 1986, s. 31(4) (re exclusion of lawyer from selection in legal aid cases); Building Societies Act 1986, s. 49(1) and (2) (from tribunal from B.S. Commission); Banking Act 1987, s. 31 (from Banking Appeal Tribunal); Copyright, Designs and Patents Act 1988, s. 152(1) (from Copyright Tribunal) and s. 251(2) (from Comptroller General re design rights); Opticians Act 1989, s. 23 as amended by the NHS Reform and Health Care Professionals Act 2002, s. 32 (from Disciplinary Committee); Human Fertilisation and Embryology Act 1990, s. 21 (re determination of licence by HFEA); Child Support Act 1991, s. 25 (from the Child Support Commissioner); Social Security Administration Act 1992, ss. 18(3) and 58 (from decisions or determinations by the Secretary of State) and 24 (from the SS Commissioner); Local Government Finance Act 1992, s. 82(4) (from valua-

---

[1] Rule 41.24 substituted by S.S.I. 2011 No. 303 (effective 27th September 2011).

tion appeal committee re council tax); Friendly Societies Act 1992, s. 61 (from tribunal re decision of Commission); Tribunal and Inquiries Act 1992, s. 11 and Sched. 1 (from various tribunals); Railways Act 1993, s. 57 (re validity of order); Pension Schemes Act 1993, s. 151(4) (from Pensions Ombudsman) and s. 173(3) (from Occupational Pensions Board); Osteopaths Act 1993, ss. 24 and 25 (against interim suspension orders, s. 29 (from Registrar), and s. 31 as amended by the NHS Reform and Health Care Professionals Act 2002, s. 33 (from Professional Conduct Committee); Chiropractors Act 1994, s. 31 as amended by the NHS Reform and Health Care Professionals Act 2002, s. 34 (from Professional Conduct Committee or appeal tribunal); Trade Marks Act 1994, s. 76(2) (from registrar); Drug Trafficking Act 1994, s. 45 (from forfeiture order by sheriff); Pensions Act 1995; s. 97(3) (from Occupational Pensions Regulatory Authority); Industrial Tribunals Act 1996, s. 37(1) (from Employment Appeal Tribunal); Architects Act 1997, s. 22 (re registration); Nurses, Midwives and Health Visitors Act 1997, s. 12 (re removal from register); Special Immigration Appeals Commission Act 1997, s. 7 (from Special Immigration Appeals Commission); Social Security Act 1998, s. 15 (with leave from Social Security Commissioner); Data Protection Act 1998, s. 49(6) (on point of law from Data Protection Tribunal); Competition Act 1998, s. 49 (on point of law from appeal tribunal); Road Traffic (NHS Charges) Act 1999, s. 9(2) (on point of law from appeal tribunal); Financial Services and Marketing Act 2000, s. 137(1) (from Financial Services and Markets tribunal); Terrorism Act 2000, s. 6(1) (from Proscribed Organisations Commission); Postal Services Act 2000, s. 36(2) (by person aggrieved); Freedom of Information (Scotland) Act 2002, s. 56 (from Scottish Information Commissioner on point of law); Proceeds of Crime Act 2002, s. 299 (from sheriff); Enterprise Act 2002, s. 114 (from Competition Appeal Tribunal); Nationality, Immigration and Asylum Act 2002, s. 103 (from Immigration Appeal tribunal); Trade Union and Labour Relations (Consolidation) Act 1992, s. 212A(7) and R.C.S. 1994, 4. 41.58(1) (appeal from ACAS scheme).

The appeals in Form 41.25 procedure also applies to applications to challenge the validity of a decision which are of the nature of an appeal (by virtue of r. 41.1). These include—Acquisition of Land (Authorisation Procedure) (Scotland) Act 1947, s. 1 and Sched. 1, para. 15 (re validity of compulsory purchase order); Housing (Scotland) Act 1966, ss. 36, 38, 43 and Sched. 2, para. 2 (re clearance orders); Ancient Monuments and Archaeological Areas Act 1979, s. 55(1) (re validity of designation orders); Wildlife and Countryside Act 1981, ss. 29, 34 and Sched. 11, para. 7 (re validity of order re areas of scientific interest), s. 36 and Sched. 12, para. 8 (re validity or order re marine nature reserves); Civil Aviation Act 1982, Sched. 7, para. 7 (re validity of orders); Telecommunications Act 1984, s. 18 (re orders of Secretary of State); Roads (Scotland) Act 1984, Sched. 2, para. 2 (re validity of orders and schemes); Films Act 1985, Sched. 2, para. 9 (from decision of Secretary of State to refuse to certify or to revoke certification for purposes of s. 72 of the Finance Act 1982); Gas Act 1986, s. 30 (re orders of Secretary of State); National Heritage (Scotland) Act 1991, Sched. 5, para. 10 (re validity of irrigation control order); Railways Act 1993, s. 57 (re validity of order); Coal Industry Act 1994, s. 33 (re validity of enforcement order); Town and Country Planning (Scotland) Act 1997, s. 238 (re validity of structure or local plan), s. 239 (re validity of other orders, etc.); Planning (Listed Buildings and Conservation Areas) (Scotland) Act 1997, s. 58 (re validity of orders etc.); Planning (Hazardous Substances) (Scotland) Act 1997, s. 20 (re validity of decisions); Petroleum Act 1998, s. 42 (decisions from the Secretary of State); Immigration and Asylum Act 1999, Sched. 5, para. 33 (appeal from Immigration Appeal tribunal); Financial Services and Markets Act 2000, s. 137(1) (appeal from Financial Services and Markets tribunal); Terrorism Act 2000, s. 6(1) (appeal from Proscribed Organisations Commission); Postal Services Act 2000, s. 36(2) (appeal by person aggrieved); Tribunals, Courts and Enforcement Act 2007, s. 13(2) (appeal from Upper Tribunal); Marine (Scotland) Act 2010, s.63A (person aggrieved questioning validity of decision).

The meaning of "aggrieved person" was considered, obiter, in *Walton v Scottish Ministers*, 2013 S.C.(UKSC) 67, per Lord Reed at para. [83] et seq. It is not limited to a person with a legal grievance; its meaning will vary according to context and one must have regard to the particular legislation and the nature of the grounds on what the appellant claims to be aggrieved; persons will ordinarily be regarded as aggrieved if they made objections or representation as part of the procedure which preceded the decision challenged, and their complaint is that the decision was not properly made, but there may be circumstances in which a person who has not participated in the process may be aggrieved; it does not include the mere busybody (someone who interferes in something in which he has no legitimate concern).

Form of appeal

41.25

41.25.—[1](1) An appeal to which this Part applies shall be made in Form 41.25.

(2) An appeal referred to in paragraph (1) shall—

    (a) specify the relevant provision of the enactment under the authority of which the appeal is brought;

    (b) specify the decision complained of, the date on which the decision was made and on which it was intimated to the appellant, and any other necessary particulars;

    (c) where the appeal is against only a part of such a decision, specify or distinguish that part;

---

[1] Rule 41.25 substituted by S.S.I. 2011 No. 303 (effective 27th September 2011).

    (d)   set out the decision appealed against or refer to the decision (a copy of which shall be appended to the appeal);

    (e)   state, in brief numbered propositions, the grounds of appeal; and

    (f)   set out in a schedule the names and addresses of the respondents in the appeal and the name and address, so far as known to the appellant, of any other person who may have an interest in the appeal.

Deriv. R.C.S. 1965, r. 290(a)(part) and (d) (r. 41.19(1)(part)) and r. 290(a)(part), (b) and (c) (r.41.19(2))

General note.

This rule is in the same terms as former r. 41.19 immediately before this rule came into force. **41.25.1**

It is not essential to repeat in the appeal the decision appealed against if a copy of it can more conveniently be appended to the appeal.

"State, in brief numbered propositions, the grounds of appeal".

"The purpose of the rule is obviously to ensure that a respondent will receive fair advance notice of **41.25.2** any points to be taken on appeal": *City of Glasgow District Council v. Secretary of State for Scotland (No. 1)* 1993 S.L.T. 198, 204E-G per Lord Caplan (bare averment that decision contrary to the principles of natural justice not enough); see also *Eurocopy Rentals Ltd v. Tayside Health Board* 1996 S.C. 410, 413G per L.P. Hope.

Lodging of appeal in court

41.26.—[1](1) Subject to paragraphs (2) and (3), the appeal shall be lodged in the **41.26** General Department—

    (a)   within the period prescribed by the enactment under which it is brought; or

    (b)   where no such period is prescribed—

        (i)   within 42 days after the date on which the decision appealed against was intimated to the appellant; or

       (ii)   where the tribunal issued a statement of reasons for its decision later than the decision, within 42 days after the date of intimation of that statement of reasons to the appellant.

    (2) Where leave to appeal to the court has been granted by the tribunal under any of the following enactments, the appeal shall be lodged in the General Department within 42 days after the date on which the decision to grant leave was intimated to the appellant—

    (a)   section 37 of the Employment Tribunals Act 1996 (appeal on a question of law from a decision or order of the Employment Appeal Tribunal with leave of the Tribunal);

    (b)   section 15 of the Social Security Act 1998 (appeal from a decision of a commissioner on a question of law with leave of a commissioner);

    (c)   section 13 of the Tribunals, Courts and Enforcement Act 2007 (appeal from decision of Upper Tribunal with leave from the Upper Tribunal).

    (3) Where an application for leave to appeal was made to the court within the period specified in paragraph (1)(b) but that period has expired before leave has been granted, the appeal may be lodged within 7 days after the date on which that leave was granted.

    (4) There shall be lodged with the appeal under paragraph (1)—

    (a)   a process in accordance with rule 4.4 (steps of process), unless an application has already been made to the court for leave to appeal;

    (b)   where appropriate, evidence that leave to appeal has been granted by the tribunal;

---

[1] Rule 41.26 substituted by S.S.I. 2011 No. 303 (effective 27th September 2011).

   (c)   the documents mentioned in rule 41.2(6)(c) and (d) (copies of decisions of tribunal) unless already lodged; and

   (d)   such other documents founded upon by the appellant so far as in his or her possession or within his or her control.

Deriv. R.C.S. 1965, r. 290(a)(part) amended by S.I. 1984 No. 499 (r. 41.20(1)(part)), and r. 290(i) inserted by S.I. 1982 No. 1825 (r. 41.20(1)(b)(ii))

GENERAL NOTE.

41.26.1
   This rule is in the same terms as former r. 41.20 immediately before this rule came into force under deletion of paras (2A) and (2B).

   Unless the statute under which the appeal is made otherwise provides, the general rule now is that the appeal must be lodged within 42 days after the date of intimation of the decision or, if later, of intimation of reasons for the decision: r. 41.26(1)(b). The meaning of the word "decision" of the relevant tribunal can sometimes cause problems: see, e.g., *Sheltered Housing Management Ltd v. Jack* , 2009 S.C. 109; 2008 S.L.T. 1058 (Extra Div.).

   Where leave to appeal is sought from the tribunal or, under r. 41.2, from the court, it must be sought (where r. 41.26(1)(b) applies) within the 42 day period for lodging the appeal.

   Where leave to appeal is sought from the court, the 42 day period may be extended by 7 days after the date on which leave was granted: r. 41.26(3). The former rule for the 42 day period for lodging an appeal to begin to run from the date of leave being granted was revoked by A.S. (R.C.S.A. No. 3) [S.I. 1996 No. 1756]. The reason for this was that the provision resulted in there being no period within which to seek leave from, e.g., the Employment Appeal Tribunal.

   There are three exceptions to the general rule provided for in r. 41.26(2). The reason is that in relation to the tribunals in the enactments mentioned, provision is made for the period within which leave to appeal must be sought from the tribunal (on which, see notes 41.26.5 and 41.26.6).

   Rules 41.2 and 41.26(2) do not deal with a situation where leave must be sought from a tribunal first and is refused, there being a right to apply after the refusal to the court for leave. That is, where the 42 day period, from the (substantive) decision sought to be appealed against, required by rr. 41.2 and 41.26(1)(b), has expired before leave is refused or an appeal to the court can thereafter be made. In *Hakim v. Secretary of State for the Home Department* , 2001 S.C. 789 it was held by an Ex Div, unattracted to requiring an appellant to seek judicial review or to use the dispensing power in r. 2.1, that the 42 day period runs from the date of refusal of leave. What is odd about this case is that the appellant still had eight days remaining, of the 42 day period after the date of intimation of refusal of leave, in which to lodge an application to the court for leave. No explanation was given or sought for his not doing so.

"APPEAL SHALL BE LODGED IN THE GENERAL DEPARTMENT".

41.26.2
   Six copies of the appeal must be lodged with the principal (r. 4.7(1)) as well as a process (r. 41.26(4)).

"WITHIN 42 DAYS".

41.26.3
   The date from which the period is calculated is not counted. Where the last day falls on a Saturday or Sunday or a public holiday on which the Office of Court is closed, the next available day is allowed: r. 1.3(7). For office hours and public holidays, see note 3.1.2.

   It should be noted that in appeals by stated case under Pt II where it is not prescribed in the enactment under which the appeal is brought the period for appealing under r. 41.8(2)(b) is 14 days (or 28 days for lodging it: r. 41.14(2)(b)) and not 42 days as in the case of appeals to which this part applies (see r. 41.26(1)(b)). Such a mistake was made in *City of Edinburgh Council v. Rapley* , 2000 S.C. 78.

FEE.

41.26.4
   The court fee for lodging the appeal is payable on lodging the stated case. For fee, see Court of Session etc. Fees Order 1997, Table of Fees, Pt I, B, item 1 [S.I. 1997 No. 688, as amended, pp.C1201 et seq.]. Certain persons are exempt from payment of fees: see 1997 Fees Order, art.5 substituted by S.S.I. 2002 No. 270. A fee exemption certificate must be lodged in process: see P.N. No. 1 of 2002.

   Where the appellant is legally represented, the fee may be debited under a credit scheme introduced on 1st April 1976 by P.N. No. 4 of 1976 to the account (if one is kept or permitted) of the agent by the court cashier, and an account will be rendered weekly by the court cashier's office to the agent for all court fees due that week for immediate settlement. Party litigants, and agents not operating the scheme, must pay (by cash, cheque or postal order) on each occasion a fee is due at the time of lodging at the counter at the General Department.

Orders for service and answers

41.27
   41.27.—[1](1) The appeal shall, without a motion being enrolled—

   (a)   during session, be brought before a procedural judge on the first available day after being lodged for an order for—

---

[1] Rule 41.27 substituted by S.S.I. 2011 No. 303 (effective 27th September 2011).

> (i) service of the appeal on the respondent and such other person as the procedural judge thinks fit within 7 days of the date of the order or such other period as the procedural judge thinks fit; and
>
> (ii) any person on whom the appeal has been served, to lodge answers, if so advised, within the period of notice; and

(b) during vacation, be brought before the vacation judge for such an order.

(2) Where an appeal is served under paragraph (1), evidence of service in accordance with Chapter 16 of these Rules shall be provided to the General Department within 14 days from the date of service.

(3) In the application of paragraph (1) to an appeal under section 9(5) of the Transport Act 1985 (appeal from a decision of the Secretary of State), the order for service under that paragraph shall include a requirement to serve the appeal on—

(a) the Secretary of State; and

(b) every person who had, or if aggrieved would have had, a right of appeal to the Secretary of State, whether or not that person has exercised that right.

(4) In the application of paragraph (1) to an appeal under section 15 of the Social Security Act 1998 (appeal from a Social Security Commissioner) or, in respect of the exercise of functions transferred from a Child Support Commissioner or a Social Security Commissioner to the Upper Tribunal, section 13 of the Tribunals, Courts and Enforcement Act 2007 (appeal from Upper Tribunal), the order for service under that paragraph shall include a requirement to serve the appeal on—

(a) the Secretary of State for Work and Pensions; and

(b) if it appears to the court that a person has been appointed by the Secretary of State to pursue a claim for benefit to which the appeal relates, that person.

(5) In the application of paragraph (1) to an appeal from a tribunal referred to in subsection (1), as modified by subsection (7), of section 11 of the Tribunals and Inquiries Act 1992, the order for service pronounced under that paragraph shall include a requirement to serve an appeal on every other party to the proceedings before the tribunal and on the clerk of the tribunal.

Deriv. R.C.S. 1965, r. 290(e) (r. 41.21(1)), r. 293(a) amended by S.I. 1972 No. 1835 (r. 41.21(2)), r. 293B(5) inserted by S.I. 1980 No. 1754 and amended by S.I. 1992 No. 2289 (r. 41.21(3)), r.292(a) amended by S.I. 1972 No. 1835 (r. 41.21(4)) and r. 293A(a) amended by S.I. 1976 No. 847 (r. 41.21(5))

General note.

This rule is in the same terms as former r. 41.21 immediately before this rule came into force subject to orders being made by the procedural judge. **41.27.1**

"service"

For methods, see Chap. 16, Pt. I. **41.27.2**

"vacation".

See note 11.1.11. **41.27.3**

"answers".

R. 18.3 does not apply. Where appropriate, the principles of answers to a condescendence apply: see r. 18.1.3. It is usual also to include pleas-in-law. The primary purpose of the answers is to respond to the contentions of the appellant. **41.27.4**

"section 9(5) of the Transport Act 1985".

This provides for an appeal on a point of law from a decision of the Secretary of State in relation to traffic regulation conditions. **41.27.5**

"section 15 of the Social Security Act 1998".

This is the general provision for appeals on a question of law, from a Social Security Commissioner, with leave of the Commissioner or, if he refuses, the court. **41.27.6**

41.27.7   Certain functions of the Child Support Commissioner and the Social Security Commissioner have been transferred to the new Upper Tribunal by the Tribunals, Courts and Enforcement Act 2007 (see s. 30). Under s. 13 of the 2007 Act there is an appeal from the Upper Tribunal to the court with the permission of the Upper Tribunal or, if it refuses, the court.

SECTION 11 OF THE TRIBUNALS AND INQUIRIES ACT 1992.

41.27.8   Section 11(1) as modified by s. 11(7) of the 1992 Act provides that any party to proceedings before certain specified tribunals in Sched. 1 to the Act who is dissatisfied in point of law with a decision of the tribunal may appeal to, or require the tribunal to state a case for the opinion of, the Court of Session.

Provision is made in s. 11(6) as modified by s. 11(7) of the 1992 Act for appeal to the Court of Session on a point of law from a decision of the Secretary of State on an appeal under s. 41 of the Consumer Credit Act 1974 from a determination of the Director General of Fair Trading in relation to licensing of credit and hire businesses by a company registered in Scotland or by any other person whose principal or prospective principal place of business in the UK is in Scotland.

"PROCEDURAL JUDGE".

41.27.9   See Chap.37A on the meaning, jurisdiction and powers of the procedural judge.

Motion for further procedure

41.28   **41.28.—**[1](1)   This rule applies—

    (a)   where no note of objection to competency has been lodged within the period mentioned in rule 41.5(2)(b) and no question of competency has been referred by the Deputy Principal Clerk within the period mentioned in rule 41.5(3)(b);

    (b)   where a procedural judge has made a direction under rule 41.5(7)(b); or

    (c)   where a question of competency has been referred to a bench of three or more judges and—

        (i)   an interlocutor has been pronounced sustaining the competency of the appeal under rule 41.5(9)(a) or following a Summar Roll hearing under rule 41.5(9)(b), or

        (ii)   an interlocutor has been pronounced under rule 41.5(9)(c) or (d).

(2)   Where no answers to the appeal have been lodged, within 14 days after expiry of the period allowed for lodging answers, the appellant shall apply by motion to a procedural judge for—

    (a)   such order for further procedure as is sought; or

    (b)   an order for a hearing.

(3)   The procedural judge shall, on a motion under paragraph (2)—

    (a)   in relation to a motion under paragraph (2)(a), make such order as he or she thinks fit; or

    (b)   in relation to a motion under paragraph (2)(b), without hearing parties—

        (i)   appoint the cause to the Summar Roll for hearing; or

        (ii)   direct that the cause be heard in the Single Bills.

GENERAL NOTE.

41.28.A1   This rule replaces former r. 41.22 and is to similar effect, namely, the appellant to enrol for further procedure within 14 days after the expiry of the period for lodging answers, save that the rule applies only where no answers are lodged. If answers are lodged the timetabling provisions in r. 41.29 will apply.

"WITHIN 14 DAYS".

41.28.1   The date from which the period is calculated is not counted. Where the last day falls on a Saturday or Sunday or a public holiday on which the Office of Court is closed, the next available day is allowed: r. 1.3(7). For office hours and public holidays, see note 3.1.2.

"MOTION".

41.28.2   For motions, see Chap. 23.

---

[1] Rule 41.28 substituted by S.S.I. 2011 No. 303 (effective 27th September 2011).

SUMMAR ROLL.

As a general rule, appeals are appointed to and heard on the Summar Roll. Originally the Summar Roll was the roll for dealing with causes summarily and the Short Roll was for more complicated causes; the latter, however, has fallen into desuetude. Once appointed to the Summar Roll a diet is fixed by the Keeper of the Rolls in accordance with r. 6.3 after parties have sent him Form 6.3 duly completed.

41.28.3

SINGLE BILLS.

The Single Bills is the motion roll of the Inner House. As a general rule, appeals are not heard in the Single Bills. Appeals dealt with on the Single Bills might include an urgent appeal or an appeal clearly incompetent.

41.28.4

HEARINGS BEFORE INNER HOUSE.

An appeal will be heard by a Division of the Inner House. A Division consists of four judges, but three are a quorum: C.S.A. 1988, s. 2(2) and (4). Because of pressure of criminal business in the High Court of Justiciary and other civil business it is unusual nowadays for a Division to sit with more than three judges. The Lord President may direct three judges to sit as an Extra Division: C.S.A. 1988, s. 2(3).

41.28.5

Where a Division before whom a cause is pending (a) considers the cause to be one of difficulty or importance or (b) the Division is equally divided in opinion, it may appoint the cause to be reheard by such larger court as is necessary for the proper disposal of the cause: C.S.A. 1988, s. 36. A larger court would in the first instance be a court of five judges; a rehearing of a cause on a point which had been decided by a court of five judges would be heard by a court of seven judges and so on. It is not always necessary for the cause to be heard by the Division before it is reheard by a larger court, particularly where all parties are agreed. A larger court will be required where consideration has to be given as to whether to overturn a previous decision of a Division. Hearings before a larger court may be appropriate on questions of practice or procedure. Where the question at issue is construction of a UK statute the preferable course is for appeal to the House of Lords: see *Drummond v. I.R.C.* 1951 S.C. 482.

FEE.

The court fee for the hearing on an appeal on the Summar Roll is payable by each party for every 30 minutes or part thereof. For fee, see Court of Session etc. Fees Order 1997, Table of Fees, Pt I, B, item 17 [SI 1997 No. 688, as amended, pp. C1201 et seq.]. The fee for an appeal heard in the Single Bills will under Pt I, B, item 22. Certain persons are exempt from payment of fees: see 1997 Fees Order, art.5 substituted by S.S.I. 2002 No. 270. A fee exemption certificate must be lodged in process: see P.N. No. 1 of 2002.

41.28.6

Where a party is legally represented, the fee may be debited under a credit scheme introduced on 1st April 1976 by P.N. No. 4 of 1976 to the account (if one is kept or permitted) of the agent by the court cashier, and an account will be rendered weekly by the court cashier's office to the agent for all court fees due that week for immediate settlement. An agent not on the credit scheme will have an account opened for the purpose of lodging the fee: P.N. No. 2 of 1995. A debit slip and a copy of the court hearing time sheet will be delivered to the agent's box or sent by DX or post.

A party litigant must pay (by cash, cheque or postal order) to the clerk of court at the end of the hearing or, if the hearing lasts more than a day, at the end of each day: P.N. No. 2 of 1995. A receipt will be issued. The assistant clerk of session will acknowledge receipt of the sum received from the clerk of court on the Minute of Proceedings.

CIRCUMSTANCES IN WHICH APPELLATE COURT WILL INTERFERE WITH DECISION OF THE COURT BELOW.

(1) Facts.

Review of facts will depend on examination and assessment of the evidence and rules of evidence, and credibility, reliability, weight and sufficiency. Issues in relation to credibility will not arise often in appeals to which this Part of Chap. 41 applies; where it does, see note 41.15.6.

41.28.7

The question of the Court of Session reviewing concurrent findings of credibility of the tribunal at first instance as an intermediate court of appeal will arise infrequently in statutory appeals to which Chap. 41 applies. In an appeal in which the issue does arise, see note 40.18.4.

(2) Discretion.

A discretion will not be legally interfered with. It is not enough that the appellate court would have exercised the discretion differently. The tests have been variously described, depending to some extent on the area of law concerned. The tests may be stated as follows: (a) has there been a failure to exercise the discretion at all (*Orr Pollock & Co. (Printers) Ltd v. Mulholland* 1983 S.L.T. 558), (b) has the judge misdirected himself in law (*Forsyth v. A.F. Stoddard & Co. Ltd* 1985 S.L.T. 51), (c) has the judge misunderstood, misused or failed to balance the evidence (*Skiponian Ltd v. Barratt Developments (Scotland) Ltd* 1983 S.L.T. 313, 314), (d) has the judge taken into account an irrelevant factor (*Thomson v. Glasgow Corporation* 1962 S.C. (H.L.) 36, 66 per Lord Reid), (e) has the judge failed to take into account a relevant factor (*Thomson, above*), (f) is the decision unreasonable (*Thomson, above*), (g) is the decision unjudicial (*Thomson, above*). See also *Brittan v. Central R.C.* 1986 S.L.T. 407.

ARGUMENT NOT PRESENTED TO COURT BELOW.

41.28.8   There is no general rule, unlike in the House of Lords or the UK Supreme Court, that the appellate court will not entertain an argument not advanced before the court below; although it may be unfortunate that the argument was not so advanced (*Varney (Scotland) Ltd v. Lanark Town Council* 1974 S.C. 245, 249 per L.J.-C. Wheatley). It is always open to the court to consider competency which strikes at the root of the proceedings: *Wolfson v. Glasgow District Licensing Board* 1980 S.C. 136, 128 per L.J.-C. Wheatley.

There are exceptions. A fresh argument which cannot be advanced without amendment to the pleadings will generally not be heard because the court will usually wish the tribunal at first instance to consider the amended pleadings and have the benefit of its opinion: see e.g. *Wallace v. Scottish Special Housing Association* 1981 S.L.T. (Notes) 60 and r. 38.17. A new argument cannot be advanced other than on evidence led unless the court has allowed that further evidence or is willing to consider a change of circumstances since the hearing in the tribunal below.

"PROCEDURAL JUDGE".

41.28.9   See Chap.37A on the meaning, jurisdiction and powers of the procedural judge.

Timetable in appeal under Part III of this Chapter

41.29   **41.29.**—[1](1) Where answers to the appeal have been lodged, the Keeper of the Rolls shall—

(a) issue a timetable in Form 41.29, calculated by reference to such periods as are specified in this Chapter and such other periods as may be specified from time to time by the Lord President, stating the date by which the parties shall comply with the procedural steps listed in paragraph (2) and the date and time of the hearing allocated in terms of subparagraph (b) of this paragraph; and

(b) allocate a diet for a procedural hearing in relation to the appeal, to follow on completion of the procedural steps listed in paragraph (2).

(2) The procedural steps are—

(a) the lodging of any productions relating to, or appendices to, the appeal;

(b) the lodging of notes of argument; and

(c) the lodging of estimates of the length of any hearing on the Summar Roll or in the Single Bills which is required to dispose of the appeal.

(3) The Keeper shall take the steps mentioned in paragraph (1) after answers have been lodged to the appeal and, in particular—

(a) where no note of objection has been lodged and no question of competency has been referred by the Deputy Principal Clerk, within 7 days of the lodging of answers to the appeal;

(b) where, after answers have been lodged to the appeal, a procedural judge has made a direction under rule 41.5(7)(b), within 7 days after the date that direction was made;

(c) where, after answers have been lodged to the appeal, a question of competency has been referred to a bench of three or more judges, within 7 days after the date of an interlocutor mentioned in paragraph (4).

(4) An interlocutor referred to in paragraph (3)(c) is—

(a) an interlocutor that has been pronounced sustaining the competency of the appeal under rule 41.5(9)(a) or following a Summar Roll hearing under rule 41.5(9)(b);

(b) an interlocutor that has been pronounced under rule 41.5(9)(c) or (d).

GENERAL NOTE.

41.29.1   In a similar way to timetabling in reparation actions under Chap. 43 and as in Chaps 38 and 40, there is an automatic timetable for appeals, including the lodging of grounds of appeal, unless an issue of competency has been raised or referred under r. 40.15. The timetable includes a date for the procedural

---

[1] Rule 41.29 substituted by S.S.I. 2011 No. 303 (effective 27th September 2011).

hearing under r. 41.29 before the procedural judge to determine whether the appeal should be appointed for a hearing of the appeal in the Summary Roll or the Single Bills.

Table C to P.N. No. 3 of 2011 sets out the timetable that it is envisaged will be prescribed by the Lord President.

Under r. 41.30 there is provision for sisting the appeal or varying the timetable. Penalties for failing to comply with the timetable are provided in r. 41.31.

"APPENDICES".

An appendix contains material not in the appeal.

41.29.2

"NOTES OF ARGUMENT".

P.N. No. 3 of 2011, para. 86, states that a note of argument should comply with the general principles (these are slightly different from those in P.N. No. 1 of 2010)—

41.29.3

1. A note of argument should be a concise summary of the submissions to be developed.
2. It should contain a numbered list of the points which the party wishes to make.
3. Each point should be followed by a reference to any transcript of evidence or other document on which the party wishes to rely. The note of argument should identify the relevant passage in the document in question.
4. A note of argument should state, in respect of each authority cited—
   (a) the proposition of law that the authority demonstrates; and
   (b) the parts of the authority (identified by page or paragraph references) that support the proposition.
5. More than one authority should not be cited in support of a given proposition unless the additional citation is necessary for a proper presentation of the argument.

Sist or variation of the timetable in appeal under Part III of this Chapter

41.30.—[1](1) An appeal under Part III of this Chapter may be sisted or the timetable may be varied on the application by motion of any party.

41.30

(2) An application under paragraph (1) shall be—
  (a) placed before a procedural judge; and
  (b) granted only on special cause shown.

(3) The procedural judge before whom an application under paragraph (1) is placed may—
  (a) determine the application;
  (b) refer the application to a bench of three or more judges; or
  (c) make such other order as the procedural judge thinks fit to secure the expeditious disposal of the appeal.

(4) Where the timetable is varied, the Keeper of the Rolls may—
  (a) discharge the procedural hearing fixed under rule 41.29(1)(b);
  (b) fix a date for a procedural hearing; and
  (c) issue a revised timetable in Form 41.29.

(5) Upon recall of a sist, the Keeper of the Rolls may—
  (a) fix a date for a procedural hearing; and
  (b) issue a revised timetable in Form 41.29.

GENERAL NOTE.

The automatic timetable may be varied or the appeal may be sisted. Penalties for failing to comply with the timetable are provided in r. 41.31.

41.30.1

The points made in paras. 25 to 29 of P.N. No. 3 of 2011 should be considered: P.N. No. 3 of 2011, para. 73.

SIST OR VARIATION ONLY ON SPECIAL CAUSE SHOWN.

A sist or variation may be granted only on special cause shown. A motion to vary could be made, for example, because the decision is not yet available: see *McAdam v Shell UK Ltd* , 1991 S.C. 360, 363 per L.P. Hope. P.N. No. 3 of 2011, para. 27 suggests that special cause might be shown where a party has to obtain notes of evidence or legal aid.

41.30.2

---

[1] Rule 41.30 substituted by S.S.I 2011 No. 303 (effective 27th September 2011).

41.30.3 "PROCEDURAL JUDGE".

See Chap.37A on the meaning, jurisdiction and powers of the procedural judge.

Failure to comply with timetable in appeal under Part III of this Chapter

41.31 **41.31.**—[1](1) Where a party fails to comply with the timetable, the Keeper may, whether on the motion of a party or otherwise, put the appeal out for a hearing before a procedural judge.

(2) At a hearing mentioned in paragraph (1), the procedural judge may—

    (a) in any case where the appellant or a respondent fails to comply with the timetable, make such order as the procedural judge thinks fit to secure the expeditious disposal of the appeal;

    (b) in particular, where the appellant fails to comply with the timetable, refuse the appeal; or

    (c) in particular, where a sole respondent fails or all respondents fail to comply with the timetable, allow the appeal.

GENERAL NOTE.

41.31.1 This rule provides penalties for failure to comply with the timetable under r. 41.29. Under r. 41.30 there is provision for varying or sisting the timetable.

"PROCEDURAL JUDGE".

41.31.2 See Chap.37A on the meaning, jurisdiction and powers of the procedural judge.

Procedural hearing in appeal under Part III of this Chapter

41.32 **41.32.**—[2](1) At the procedural hearing fixed under rule 41.29(1)(b), or rule 41.30(4)(b) or (5)(a), the procedural judge shall ascertain, so far as reasonably practicable, the state of preparation of the parties.

(2) At the procedural hearing mentioned in paragraph (1), the procedural judge may—

    (a) appoint the appeal to the Summar Roll for a hearing and allocate a date and time for that hearing;

    (b) appoint the appeal to the Single Bills for a hearing and allocate a date and time for that hearing; or

    (c) make such other order as the procedural judge thinks fit to secure the expeditious disposal of the appeal.

GENERAL NOTE.

41.32.A1 Paragraph 75 of P.N. No. 3 of 2011 applies paras. 31–34 of that P.N. The primary purpose of the procedural hearing is that no case is sent for a hearing on its merits unless the procedural judge is satisfied that a hearing is necessary and that parties are prepared: para. 31. Under paras. 31–34, parties are expected to discuss the issues in the reclaiming motion and the methods of disposing of them. The procedural judge will decide the length of the hearing and when it will take place. Continued procedural hearings are to be avoided.

Under para. 90 of P.N. No. 3 of 2011, the applicant, after consultation with the respondent, should lodge a bundle of photocopies of authorities on which each party intends to rely. There should not be more than 10 authorities unless the scale of the reclaiming motion warrants more extensive citation. If there is to be citation of more than 10 authorities, this must be brought to the attention of the procedural judge in advance of the hearing and before lodging them; if not, the court may disallow the expenses of lodging more than 10 or more than allowed by the procedural judge: *Thomson v. Scottish Ministers*, 2013 S.C. 628 (Second Div.), 633, para. [15].

SUMMAR ROLL.

41.32.1 As a general rule, appeals are appointed to and heard on the Summar Roll. Originally the Summar Roll was the roll for dealing with causes summarily and the Short Roll was for more complicated causes; the latter, however, has fallen into desuetude. Once appointed to the Summar Roll a diet is fixed by the Keeper of the Rolls in accordance with r. 6.3 after parties have sent him Form 6.3 duly completed.

---

[1] Rule 41.31 substituted by S.S.I 2011 No. 303 (effective 27th September 2011).
[2] Rule 41.32 substituted by S.S.I 2011 No. 303 (effective 27th September 2011).

Single Bills.

The Single Bills is the motion roll of the Inner House. As a general rule, appeals are not heard in the Single Bills. Appeals dealt with on the Single Bills might include an urgent appeal or an appeal clearly incompetent.

41.32.2

Hearings before Inner House.

An appeal will be heard by a Division of the Inner House. A Division consists of four judges, but three are a quorum: C.S.A. 1988, s. 2(2) and (4). Because of pressure of criminal business in the High Court of Justiciary and other civil business it is unusual nowadays for a Division to sit with more than three judges. The Lord President may direct three judges to sit as an Extra Division: C.S.A. 1988, s. 2(3).

41.32.3

Where a Division before whom a cause is pending (a) considers the cause to be one of difficulty or importance or (b) the Division is equally divided in opinion, it may appoint the cause to be reheard by such larger court as is necessary for the proper disposal of the cause: C.S.A. 1988, s. 36. A larger court would in the first instance be a court of five judges; a rehearing of a cause on a point which had been decided by a court of five judges would be heard by a court of seven judges and so on. It is not always necessary for the cause to be heard by the Division before it is reheard by a larger court, particularly where all parties are agreed. A larger court will be required where consideration has to be given as to whether to overturn a previous decision of a Division. Hearings before a larger court may be appropriate on questions of practice or procedure. Where the question at issue is construction of a UK statute the preferable course is for appeal to the House of Lords: see *Drummond v. I.R.C.* 1951 S.C. 482.

Fee.

The court fee for the hearing on an appeal on the Summar Roll is payable by each party for every 30 minutes or part thereof. For fee, see Court of Session etc. Fees Order 1997, Table of Fees, Pt I, B, item 17 [S.I. 1997 No. 688, as amended, pp. C1201 et seq.]. The fee for an appeal heard in the Single Bills will under Pt I, B, item 22. Certain persons are exempt from payment of fees: see 1997 Fees Order, art.5 substituted by S.S.I. 2002 No. 270. A fee exemption certificate must be lodged in process: see P.N. No. 1 of 2002.

41.32.4

Where a party is legally represented, the fee may be debited under a credit scheme introduced on 1st April 1976 by P.N. No. 4 of 1976 to the account (if one is kept or permitted) of the agent by the court cashier, and an account will be rendered weekly by the court cashier's office to the agent for all court fees due that week for immediate settlement. An agent not on the credit scheme will have an account opened for the purpose of lodging the fee: P.N. No. 2 of 1995. A debit slip and a copy of the court hearing time sheet will be delivered to the agent's box or sent by DX or post.

A party litigant must pay (by cash, cheque or postal order) to the clerk of court at the end of the hearing or, if the hearing lasts more than a day, at the end of each day: P.N. No. 2 of 1995. A receipt will be issued. The assistant clerk of session will acknowledge receipt of the sum received from the clerk of court on the Minute of Proceedings.

Circumstances in which Appellate Court will Interfere with Decision of the Court below.

(1) Facts.

Review of facts will depend on examination and assessment of the evidence and rules of evidence, and credibility, reliability, weight and sufficiency. Issues in relation to credibility will not arise often in appeals to which this Part of Chap. 41 applies; where it does, see note 41.15.6.

41.32.5

The question of the Court of Session reviewing concurrent findings of credibility of the tribunal at first instance as an intermediate court of appeal will arise infrequently in statutory appeals to which Chap. 41 applies. In an appeal in which the issue does arise, see note 40.18.4.

(2) Discretion.

A discretion will not be legally interfered with. It is not enough that the appellate court would have exercised the discretion differently. The tests have been variously described, depending to some extent on the area of law concerned. The tests may be stated as follows: (a) has there been a failure to exercise the discretion at all (*Orr Pollock & Co. (Printers) Ltd v. Mulholland* 1983 S.L.T. 558), (b) has the judge misdirected himself in law (*Forsyth v. A.F. Stoddard & Co. Ltd* 1985 S.L.T. 51), (c) has the judge misunderstood, misused or failed to balance the evidence (*Skiponian Ltd v. Barratt Developments (Scotland) Ltd* 1983 S.L.T. 313, 314), (d) has the judge taken into account an irrelevant factor (*Thomson v. Glasgow Corporation* 1962 S.C. (H.L.) 36, 66 per Lord Reid), (e) has the judge failed to take into account a relevant factor (Thomson, *above*), (f) is the decision unreasonable (Thomson, *above*), (g) is the decision unjudicial (Thomson, *above*). See also *Brittan v. Central R.C.* 1986 S.L.T. 407.

Argument not presented to court below.

There is no general rule, unlike in the House of Lords or the UK Supreme Court, that the appellate court will not entertain an argument not advanced before the court below; although it may be unfortunate that the argument was not so advanced (*Varney (Scotland) Ltd v. Lanark Town Council* 1974 S.C. 245, 249 per L.J.-C. Wheatley). It is always open to the court to consider competency which strikes at the root of the proceedings: *Wolfson v. Glasgow District Licensing Board* 1980 S.C. 136, 128 per L.J.-C. Wheatley.

41.32.6

There are exceptions. A fresh argument which cannot be advanced without amendment to the pleadings will generally not be heard because the court will usually wish the tribunal at first instance to consider the amended pleadings and have the benefit of its opinion: see e.g. *Wallace v. Scottish Special Housing Association* 1981 S.L.T. (Notes) 60 and r. 38.17. A new argument cannot be advanced other than on evidence led unless the court has allowed that further evidence or is willing to consider a change of circumstances since the hearing in the tribunal below.

"PROCEDURAL JUDGE".

41.32.7   See Chap.37A on the meaning, jurisdiction and powers of the procedural judge.

Part IV – Exchequer Appeals

Revenue appeals by stated case

41.33   **41.33.**—[1](1)   This rule applies to an appeal to the court as the Court of Exchequer in Scotland under—

(a)   section 13(5) of the Stamp Act 1891 (appeal from Commissioners for Her Majesty's Revenue and Customs); or

(b)   regulation 20(1) of the General Commissioners (Jurisdiction and Procedure) Regulations 1994.

(2)   In relation to appeals in respect of instruments executed before 1st October 1999, paragraph (1)(a) has effect as if the reference to section 13(5) of the Stamp Act 1891 were a reference to section 13(1) of that Act as it has effect in relation to such instruments.

(3)   Subject to paragraph (4), Part II (appeals by stated case etc.) shall apply to an appeal to which paragraph (1) applies.

(4)   The following provisions of Part II shall not apply to an appeal to which this rule applies—

rule 41.8 (applications for case),

rule 41.9 (additional questions by other parties),

rule 41.10 (consideration of application by tribunal),

rule 41.11 (procedure for ordaining tribunal to state a case),

rule 41.12 (preparation and issue of the case),

rule 41.13 (intimation of intention to proceed).

Deriv. R.C.S. 1965, r. 281(1)(part) substituted by S.I. 1976 No.1849 and amended by S.I. 1984 No. 499

GENERAL NOTE.

41.33.1   This rule is in the same terms as former r. 41.23 immediately before this rule came into force.

Stated case procedure applies in principle, but rr. 41.8–41.13 do not apply because the enactments under which the appeals are made provide for the procedure to be followed.

Only the party who was unsuccessful in the appeal to or proceedings before the Commissioners is "dissatisfied" in point of law, and there should only be one stated case even if the other party raises a point of law: *Gordon v. Inland Revenue Commissioners* 1991 S.C. 149.

"SECTION 13(5) OF THE STAMP ACT 1891".

41.33.2   A person dissatisfied with the assessment of the Commissioners of Inland Revenue (now Commissioners for Her Majesty's Revenue and Customs) may, within 30 days of notice of the decision, appeal to the Court of Session and require the Commissioners to state a case: Stamp Act 1891, s. 13(1) substituted by Sched. 12 to the Finance Act 1999. Section 13B of the 1891 Act as amended contains the procedural provisions for stating a case and lodging it for hearing.

"REGULATION 20(1) OF THE GENERAL COMMISSIONERS (JURISDICTION AND PROCEDURE) REGULATIONS 1994".

41.33.3   Reg.20(1) of the 1994 Regulations [S.I. 1994 No. 1812] provides a general provision for appeal to the Court of Session by stated case from an appeal to or proceedings before the General Commissioners under the Taxes Acts by a person dissatisfied with a decision or determination as being erroneous in point of law. The procedure is laid down in regs 20–23 of the 1994 Regulations. The application for a stated case must be made within 30 days of the determination and the case lodged (in the General Department under r. 41.14) within 30 days of receiving it.

---

[1] Rule 41.33 substituted by S.S.I 2011 No. 303 (effective 27th September 2011).

Appeals relating to certain determinations of the Commissioners for Her Majesty's Revenue and Customs

41.34.—[1](1)   This rule applies to an appeal against a determination of the Commissioners for Her Majesty's Revenue and Customs specified in a notice to the appellant under section 221 of the Inheritance Tax Act 1984 or regulation 6 of the Stamp Duty Reserve Tax Regulations 1986.

(2)   Where the court grants leave to appeal under rule 41.3(6) in an application notified to it under section 222(3) of the said Act or regulation 8(3) of the said Regulations, as the case may be, or it is agreed between the appellant and the Commissioners of Inland Revenue that the appeal is to be notified to the court, the appellant shall, within 30 days after the date on which leave to appeal is granted or, as the case may be, after the date on which the Board intimates its agreement to the appellant—

(a)   lodge a statement of facts and grounds of appeal in Form 41.25, and a process unless a process has already been lodged under rule 41.2(6) (lodging process in applications for leave to appeal), in which case the statement of facts and grounds of appeal shall be lodged in that process; and

(b)   on so doing, apply by motion for an order for service in accordance with rule 41.27 (orders for service and answers).

(3)   The appellant shall apply by motion to a procedural judge for an order for a hearing—

(a)   following the lodging of answers or on the expiry of any period of adjustment allowed, or

(b)   where no answers have been lodged, on the expiry of the period allowed for lodging answers.

(4)   A motion under paragraph (3) shall be intimated to the solicitor in Scotland to the Commissioners of Her Majesty's Revenue and Customs whether or not answers have been lodged by the Commissioners.

(5)   Rule 41.28(3)(b) shall apply to a motion under paragraph (3) of this rule as it applies to a motion under paragraph (2)(b) of that rule.

(6)   If an appellant fails to comply with any time-limit imposed by this rule, the appellant shall be deemed to have abandoned the appeal.

(7)   Where it appears to the court in an appeal under this rule that any question as to the value of land in the United Kingdom requires to be determined, the court shall remit the cause—

(a)   where the land is in Scotland, to the Lands Tribunal for Scotland,

(b)   where the land is in England and Wales, to the Upper Tribunal (Lands Chamber),

(c)   where the land is in Northern Ireland, to the Lands Tribunal for Northern Ireland,

to determine that question and remit back to a procedural judge for further procedure.

Deriv. R.C.S. 1965, r. 283(1), (2), (5) and (11) to (13) substituted by S.I. 1976 No.1849 and amended by S.I. 1990 No.705.

GENERAL NOTE.

This rule is in similar terms to former r. 41.26 immediately before this rule came into force. The appeals in this rule are made in Form 41.25.

"LODGE A STATEMENT OF FACTS AND GROUNDS OF APPEAL".

In addition to lodging the principal, six copies have to be lodged (r. 4.7(1)).

41.34

41.34.1

41.34.2

---

[1] Rule 41.34 substituted by S.S.I 2011 No.303 (effective 27th September 2011).

41.34.3

"SERVICE".

For methods, see Chap. 16, Pt I.

"MOTION".

41.34.4

For motions, see Chap. 23.

Part V[1, 2] – Appeals under Part 15 of the Children's Hearings (Scotland) Act 2011

Application of Part II to this Part

41.35

41.35.[3] Part II (appeals by stated case etc.) shall apply to an appeal to the court by stated case under sections 163, 164 or 165 of the Act of 2011 subject to the following provisions of this Part.

GENERAL NOTE.

41.35.1

This rule is in the same terms as former r. 41.28.

Section 50 of the Social Work (Scotland) Act 1968 provided for an appeal by stated case on a point of law or an irregularity from a decision of the sheriff. Section 50 of the 1968 Act has been replaced by s. 51(11) of the Children (Scotland) Act 1995 which makes provision for an appeal by stated case on a point of law, but with one variation. Under the new provision the appeal may be made to the sheriff principal or to the Court of Session. If an appeal is made to the sheriff principal, a further appeal may be made to the Court of Session with leave of the sheriff principal. Section 50 of the 1968 Act continues to apply to proceedings not concluded when that section was repealed (1st April 1997). The stated case should be confined to proper findings-in-fact and should not include extraneous comments or questions not asked for by a party: *Kennedy v. A.* 1986 S.L.T. 358; *Sloan v. B.* 1991 S.L.T. 530, 544I-545E per L.P. Hope; *Kennedy v. R's Curator ad Litem* 1992 S.C. 300, 305 per L.P. Hope.

Interpretation of this Part

41.36

41.36.[4] In this Part—

"the Act of 2011" means the Children's Hearings (Scotland) Act 2011; and

"the Principal Reporter" means the Principal Reporter appointed under paragraph 8 of Schedule 3 to the Act of 2011 or any person to whom there is delegated, under paragraph 10(1) of Schedule 3 to the Act of 2011, any function of the Principal Reporter under that Act.

GENERAL NOTE.

41.36.1

This rule is in the same terms as former r. 41.29.

Lodging of reports and statements with sheriff

41.37

41.37.—[5, 6, 7](1) Paragraph (2) applies where, on an appeal being made to the court by stated case under section 163, 164 or 165 of the Act of 2011—

    (a)   it appears to the sheriff or the Sheriff Appeal Court that any report or statement lodged under section 155(2), or report lodged under section 155(6) of that Act in the appeal to the sheriff or the Sheriff Appeal Court is relevant to any issue which is likely to arise in the stated case; and

    (b)   the report or statement has been returned to the Principal Reporter.

    (2)   The sheriff or the Sheriff Appeal Court may require the Principal Reporter to lodge the report or statement with the sheriff clerk or the Clerk of the Sheriff Appeal Court; but on the stated case being sent to the person who applied for it, the sheriff clerk or the Clerk of the Sheriff Appeal Court shall return the report or statement to the Principal Reporter.

---

[1] Part V and r. 41.35 substituted by S.S.I. 2011 No. 303 (effective 27th September 2011).
[2] Part V and r. 41.35 amended by S.S.I. 2013 No. 162 (effective 24th June 2013).
[3] Part V and r. 41.35 substituted by S.S.I. 2011 No. 303 (effective 27th September 2011).
[4] Rule 41.36 substituted by S.S.I 2013 No. 303 (effective 24th June 2013).
[5] Rule 41.37 substituted by S.S.I. 2011 No. 303 (effective 27th September 2011).
[6] Rule 41.37(1) amended by S.S.I. 2011 No. 303 (effective 24th June 2013).
[7] Rule 41.37 amended by S.S.I. 2015 No. 419 (effective 1 January 2016).

Deriv. R.C.S. 1965, r. 289A(2) and (4)(part) inserted by S.I. 1971 No. 203

GENERAL NOTE.

This rule is to the same effect as former r. 41.30 immediately before this rule came into force.   **41.37.1**

Lodging etc. of reports and statements in court

41.38.—[1](1)   Within seven days after the date on which the case is lodged under   **41.38**
rule 41.14(1), the Principal Reporter shall send to the Deputy Principal Clerk the
principal and three copies of every report or statement which he was required, under
rule 41.37, to lodge.

(2)   Neither the principal nor any copy of any such report or statement shall be
made available to any of the other parties unless the court otherwise orders.

(3)   Subject to any such order, every such report or statement shall remain in the
custody of the Deputy Principal Clerk until the appeal has been determined or
abandoned and then shall be returned by the Deputy Principal Clerk to the Principal
Reporter.

Deriv. R.C.S. 1965, r. 289A(6) and (8) inserted by S.I. 1971 No. 203

GENERAL NOTE.

This rule is to the same effect as former r. 41.31 immediately before this rule came into force.   **41.38.A1**

"WITHIN SEVEN DAYS".

The date from which the period is calculated is not counted. Where the last day falls on a Saturday or   **41.38.1**
Sunday or a public holiday on which the Office of Court is closed, the next available day is allowed: r.
1.3(7). For office hours and public holidays, see note 3.1.2.

"SEND".

This includes deliver: r. 1.3(1) (definition of "send").   **41.38.2**

Hearing in private

41.39.[2]   The court may direct that all or part of the appeal shall be heard in private.   **41.39**

Deriv. R.C.S. 1965, r. 289A(7) inserted by S.I. 1971 No. 203

GENERAL NOTE.

This rule is in the same terms as former r. 41.32 immediately before this rule came into force.   **41.39.1**

Expenses

41.40.—[3](1)   No expenses shall be awarded to or against any party in respect of   **41.40**
the appeal.

(2)   Rule 41.17(3)(b) (award of expenses in abandoned appeal) shall not apply to
an appeal to which this Part applies.

Deriv. R.C.S. 1965, r. 289A(9) inserted by S.I. 1971 No. 203

GENERAL NOTE.

This rule is in the same terms as former r. 41.33 immediately before this rule came into force.   **41.40.1**

Part VI – Appeals under the Representation of the People Act 1983

Application of this Part

41.41.[4]   This Part applies to an appeal under section 56, as applied by section 57,   **41.41**
of the Representation of the People Act 1983 (registration appeals).

Deriv. R.C.S. 1965, r. 284 (preamble) amended by S.I. 1980 No. 1144

GENERAL NOTE.

This rule is in the same terms as former r. 41.34.   **41.41.1**

---

[1] Rule 41.38 substituted by S.S.I. 2011 No.303 (effective 27th September 2011).
[2] Rule 41.39 substituted by S.S.I. 2011 No. 303 (effective 27th September 2011).
[3] Rule 41.40 substituted by S.S.I. 2011 No. 303 (effective 27th September 2011).
[4] Part VI and r. 41.41 substituted by S.S.I. 2011 No. 303 (effective 27th September 2011).

Section 56, as applied by s.57, of the Representation of the People Act 1983 provides for appeal on a point of law from a decision of the sheriff from a decision of the registration officer in relation to local government elections. Appeal is to three judges of the Court of Session appointed by A.S. (1983 Act, s.57(2)) and known as the Registration Appeal Court: see r. 41.43.

Form of appeal under this Part

41.42

41.42.[1] An appeal to which this Part applies shall be made by stated case to which Part II (appeals by stated case etc.) shall apply subject to the following provisions of this Part.

Deriv. R.C.S. 1965, r. 284 (preamble) amended by S.I. 1980 No. 1144

GENERAL NOTE.

41.42.1

This rule is in the same terms as former r. 41.35.

Registration Appeal Court

41.43

41.43.[2] In the application of Part II by virtue of this Part, references to a procedural judge shall be read as references to the Registration Appeal Court constituted under section 57(2) of the Representation of the People Act 1983.

Consolidated appeals

41.44

41.44.—(1) Where several persons have applied for a stated case and it appears to the sheriff that such applications, or any two or more of them, raise the same question of law, the sheriff may consolidate the appeals into one stated case and, where he or she does so, he or she shall—

    (a) state in the case the reasons why he has consolidated the appeals; and

    (b) name one of the appellants as the appellant.

(2) Where appeals have been consolidated under paragraph (1), the appellant named under paragraph (1)(b), on receiving the stated case from the sheriff clerk, shall send a copy of it to every other appellant on request.

Deriv. R.C.S. 1965, r. 284(a)
[1] Rule 41.44 substituted by S.S.I. 2011 No. 303 (effective 27th September 2011).

GENERAL NOTE.

41.44.1

This rule is in the same terms as former r. 41.36.

"SEND".

41.44.2

This includes deliver: r. 1.3(1) (definition of "send").

Hearing before Registration Appeal Court

41.45

41.45.—[3](1) On the stated case being lodged in accordance with rule 41.14, the appeal shall be put out for hearing before the Registration Appeal Court on the earliest available day.

(2) Rule 41.18 (timetable in appeal under Part III of this chapter) shall not apply to an appeal to which this Part applies.

Deriv. R.C.S. 1965, r. 284(b)

GENERAL NOTE.

41.45.1

This rule is in the same terms as former r. 41.37.

The Registration Appeal Court is constituted under s.57(2) of the Representation of the People Act 1983.

The judges of the court are currently Lord Pentland, Lady Paton and Lord Harrower: A.S. (Registration Appeal Court) 2021 [S.S.I. 2021/309].

---

[1] Rule 41.42 substituted by S.S.I. 2011 No. 303 (effective 27th September 2011).
[2] Rule 41.43 substituted by S.S.I. 2011 No. 303 (effective 27th September 2011).
[3] Rule 41.45 substituted by S.S.I. 2011 No. 303 (effective 27th September 2011).

Decision of Registration Appeal Court

41.46.—[1](1) The Registration Appeal Court shall, in its decision, specify any alteration or correction to be made on the register in pursuance of such decision.

(2) The Deputy Principal Clerk shall send a copy of the decision of the Registration Appeal Court to the registration officer within four days after the date of the decision.

Deriv. R.C.S. 1965, r. 284(c)

GENERAL NOTE.

This rule is in the same terms as former r. 41.38.

"SEND".

This includes deliver: r. 1.3(1) (definition of "send").

Part VII – Stated Cases under Section 11(3) of the Tribunals and Inquiries Act 1992

Case stated by tribunal at its own instance

41.47.—[2](1) A tribunal referred to in subsection (1), as modified by subsection (7), of section 11 of the Tribunals and Inquiries Act 1992 may, at its own instance, state a case for the opinion of the court on any question arising in the course of proceedings before it.

(2) Part II (appeals by stated case etc.) shall apply to a case stated under paragraph (1) subject to the following provisions of this Part.

Deriv. R.C.S. 1965, r. 291(2) (preamble)

GENERAL NOTE.

This rule is in the same terms as former r. 41.39.

Section 11(1), as modified by s. 11(7), of the Tribunals and Inquiries Act 1992 provides that any party to proceedings before certain specified tribunals in Sched. 1 to the Act who is dissatisfied in point of law with a decision of the tribunal may appeal to, or require the tribunal to state a case for the opinion of, the Court of Session.

Modifications of Part II to appeals under this Part

41.48.—[3](1) The following rules shall apply to a case to which this Part applies subject to the following provisions of this rule—

rule 41.12 (preparation and issue of the case),

rule 41.14 (lodging of case in court).

(2) For paragraph (1) of rule 41.12 substitute—

"(1) Where the tribunal decides to state a case at its own instance, it shall intimate that decision to each party.".

(3) For paragraph (6) of rule 41.12 substitute—

"(6) When the case has been settled by the tribunal, the case shall be authenticated by the clerk of the tribunal who shall—

    (a)   send a copy of the case to each party; and

    (b)   transmit to the Deputy Principal Clerk the case with a certificate endorsed on it and signed by him or her certifying that subparagraph (a) has been complied with.

(7) The Deputy Principal Clerk shall endorse the case with the date on which he received it from the clerk of the tribunal and return it to the clerk.".

(4) For rule 41.14 substitute—

41.46

41.46.1

41.46.2

41.47

41.47.1

41.48

---

[1] Rule 41.46 substituted by S.S.I. 2011 No. 303 (effective 27th September 2011).
[2] Part VII and r. 41.47 substituted by S.S.I. 2011 No. 303 (effective 27th September 2011).
[3] Rule 41.48 substituted by S.S.I. 2011 No. 303 (effective 27th September 2011).

"**41.14.** Not earlier than seven days and not later than 14 days after the date on which the case was received by the Deputy Principal Clerk, the clerk of the tribunal shall—

    (a)   lodge in the General Department—

        (i)   the case; and

        (ii) a process in accordance with rule 4.4 (steps of process) including any productions to be referred to in the appeal;

    (b)   *[Repealed by S.S.I. 2016 No. 102 (effective 21 March 2016).]*

    (c)   endorse and sign a certificate on the case that the requirements of rule 4.6 (intimation of steps of process) have been complied with."

Deriv. R.C.S. 1965, r. 291(a), (b), (c) and (d) (amended by S.I. 1985 No. 1600)

GENERAL NOTE.

41.48.1   Paragraphs (1) to (4) of this rule are in the same terms as in former r. 41.40. The modifications are necessary because the clerk of the tribunal is requested to send the case to the Deputy Principal Clerk before lodging it in the General Department within a period determined from the date it was received by the Deputy Principal Clerk.

"INTIMATE".

41.48.2   For methods, see r. 16.7.

"SEND".

41.48.3   This includes deliver: r. 1.3(1) (definition of "send").

"LODGE IN THE GENERAL DEPARTMENT".

41.48.4   Six copies of the case must be lodged with the principal: r. 4.7(1). Four copies of any productions must be lodged. Lodging may be done by post: P.N. No. 4 of 1994, paras. 1 and 8.

Part VIII – Appeals under Social Security Acts

Form of appeal under certain Social Security Acts

41.49   **41.49.**[1] A reference or appeal under any of the following provisions shall be by stated case to which Part II (appeals by stated case etc.) shall apply—

    (a)   a reference by the Pensions Ombudsman under section 150(7) of the Pension Schemes Act 1993;

    (b)   an appeal under section 151(4) of the Pension Schemes Act 1993;

    (c)   a reference by the Ombudsman for the Board of the Pension Protection Fund under section 215 of the Pensions Act 2004; and

    (d)   an appeal under section 217 of the Pensions Act 2004.

Deriv. R.C.S. 1965, r. 288(1) substituted by S.I. 1992 No. 2289

GENERAL NOTE.

41.49.1   This rule is to the same effect as former r. 41.41 immediately before this rule came into force.

PENSION SCHEMES ACT 1993 AND THE PENSIONS ACT 2004.

41.49.2   Section 150(7) of the 1993 Act provides for a reference to the Court of Session of a question of law arising from a determination in connection with a complaint or dispute investigated by the Pensions Ombudsman. Section 151(4) of the 1993 Act provides for an appeal on a point of law to the Court of Session from a determination of the Pensions Ombudsman at the instance of certain persons.

Section 173(1) of the 1993 Act provided for references to the Court of Session by the Occupational Pensions Board of questions of law and s. 173(3) of that Act provided for appeal by a person aggrieved by a determination of the Board involving a question of law which has not been referred by the Board to the court.

Section 173 of the Pension Schemes Act 1993 was repealed and replaced by s. 97 of the Pensions Act 1995 which was replaced by ss.103 and 104 of the 2004 Act. The Occupational Pensions Board was replaced by the Occupational Pensions Regulatory Authority under the 1995 Act, which was replaced by the Pensions Regulator by s. 1 of the 2001 Act. A reference may be made to the Pensions Regulator Tribunal and an appeal on a point of law may be taken to the Court of Session with leave of the tribunal or the court (but this is not dealt with under this rule): 2004 Act, s. 104. The 2004 Act created the Pensions Protection Fund ("PPF"), the Board of the PPF and the PPF Ombudsman. The PPF Ombudsman

---

[1] Rule 41.49 substituted by S.S.I. 2011 No. 303 (effective 27th September 2011).

may refer a question of law to the Court of Session under s. 215 and there is a right of appeal on a point of law to the Court of Session under s. 217 of the 2004 Act.

Modifications of Part II to appeals under this Part

41.50.—[1](1) The following rules shall apply to a case to which this Part applies subject to the following provisions of this rule—

rule 41.12 (preparation and issue of the case),

rule 41.14 (lodging of case in court).

(2) For paragraph (1) of rule 41.12 substitute—

"(1) Where the tribunal decides to state a case at its own instance, it shall intimate that decision to each party.".

(3) For paragraph (6) of rule 41.12 substitute—

"(6) When the case has been settled by the tribunal, the case shall be authenticated by the clerk of the tribunal who shall—

(a) send a copy of the case to each party; and

(b) transmit to the Deputy Principal Clerk the case with a certificate endorsed on it and signed by him or her certifying that subparagraph (a) has been complied with.

(7) The Deputy Principal Clerk shall endorse the case with the date on which he received it from the clerk of the tribunal and return it to the clerk.".

(4) For rule 41.14 substitute—

"**41.14.** Not earlier than seven days and not later than 14 days after the date on which the case was received by the Deputy Principal Clerk, the clerk of the tribunal shall—

(a) lodge in the General Department—

(i) the case; and

(ii) a process in accordance with rule 4.4 (steps of process) including any productions to be referred to in the appeal;

(b) *[Repealed by S.S.I. 2016 No. 102 (effective 21 March 2016).]*

(c) endorse and sign a certificate on the case that the requirements of rule 4.6 (intimation of steps of process) have been complied with.".

Deriv. R.C.S. 1965, r. 288(3) and (4) substituted by S.I. 1992 No. 2289

GENERAL NOTE.

Paragraphs (1) to (4) of this rule are in the same terms as former r. 41.42. The modifications are necessary because the clerk of the tribunal is required to send the case to the Deputy Principal Clerk before lodging it in the General Department within a period determined from the date it was received by the Deputy Principal Clerk.

"INTIMATE".

For methods, see r. 16.7.

"SEND".

This includes deliver: r. 1.3(1) (definition of "send").

"LODGE IN THE GENERAL DEPARTMENT".

Six copies of the case must be lodged with the principal: r. 4.7(1). Four copies of any productions must be lodged. Lodging may be done by post: P.N. No. 4 of 1994, paras 1 and 8.

Part IX – Appeals to Lord Ordinary

Application of Parts II and III to this Part

41.51.[2] Unless otherwise provided in these Rules, in an appeal to the court which is directed by these Rules or any other enactment to be made to a single judge of the

41.50

41.50.1

41.50.2

41.50.3

41.50.4

41.51

---

[1] Rule 41.50 substituted by S.S.I. 2011 No. 303 (effective 27th September 2011).

[2] Part IX and r. 41.51 substituted by S.S.I. 2011 No. 303 (effective 27th September 2011).

court, the Outer House or the Lord Ordinary, Part II (appeals by stated case etc.) or Part III (appeals in Form 41.25), as the case may be, shall apply to that appeal subject to the following modifications—

    (a)   for references to the Inner House, a procedural judge or a bench of three or more judges substitute references to the Lord Ordinary;

    (b)   for references to the Single Bills substitute references to the Motion Roll; and

    (c)   for references to the Summar Roll substitute references to a hearing.

GENERAL NOTE.

41.51.1

This rule is in the same terms as former rule 41.43 save that there are now references to the procedural judge and the bench of judges.

Although most appeals are dealt with by the Inner House, an enactment may specify that an appeal is to be dealt with by a single judge or the Lord Ordinary.

Appeals to the court under, e.g. the Patents Acts 1949 and 1977, and the Trade Marks Act 1994, are heard by the patents judge: see rr. 55.14 and 55.19 respectively. Under s. 97 of the Patents Act 1977 an appeal from the Comptroller of Patents, Designs and Trade Marks is to the Outer House in the first instance.

Appeals to be heard in Outer House

41.52

41.52.—[1](1) Subject to paragraph (4), an appeal to the court to which this Chapter applies may be remitted by the Inner House to the Outer House to be heard by the Lord Ordinary in the first instance.

    (2) An appeal may be remitted by the Inner House under paragraph (1)—

    (a)   at its own instance after hearing parties, or

    (b)   on the motion of a party.

    (3) An appeal may be remitted under paragraph (1) on a motion being enrolled at any time after answers have been lodged.

    (4)[2] Paragraphs (1) to (3) do not apply to the following appeals—

    (a)   an appeal under an enactment which specifies that the appeal is to the Inner House;

    (b)   an appeal to which Part IV of this Chapter applies (Exchequer appeals);

    (c)   an appeal to which Part V of this Chapter applies (appeals under section 51 of the Children (Scotland) Act 1995);

    (d)   an appeal to which Part VI of this Chapter applies (appeals under the Representation of the People Act 1983);

    (e)   an appeal from the Land Court;

    (f)   an appeal from the Lands Tribunal for Scotland;

   (fa)[3] an appeal from the Sheriff Appeal Court;

    (g)   *[Repealed by SSI 2011/303 (effective June 24, 2013).]*

    (h)   an appeal under paragraph 14 of Schedule 4 to the Transport Act 1985 (appeal from the Transport Tribunal);

    (i)   an appeal under section 13 of the Tribunals, Courts and Enforcement Act 2007 (appeal from Upper Tribunal);

    (j)   an appeal under section 15 of the Social Security Act 1998 (appeal from a Social Security Commissioner);

    (k)   an appeal under section 49 of the Competition Act 1998 (appeal from the Competition Commission).

---

[1] Rule 41.52 substituted by S.S.I. 2011 No. 303 (effective 27th September 2011).
[2] Rule 41.52(4) amended by S.S.I. 2014 No. 201 r.2 (effective 1 August 2014).
[3] Rule 41.52(4)(fa) inserted by S.S.I. 2015 No. 419 r. 7 (effective 1 January 2016).

This rule (apart from paras (2) and (3)) is in the same terms as former r. 41.44 immediately before this rule came into force. **41.52.1**

Public concern has been expressed about the apparent delay in hearing some statutory appeals, such as planning appeals, in the Inner House. Some statutory appeals are more akin to judicial review proceedings. In U.K. statutes, where an appeal in England and Wales is to the High Court or the Court of Appeal, the Scottish provision provides simply for the Court of Session in either case. The historical convention is that all such statutory appeals are heard in the Inner House.

Rule 41.52(1) provides for the Inner House to remit statutory appeals to which Chap. 41 applies, subject to certain exceptions, to the Outer House for a Lord Ordinary to determine in the first instance.

The exceptions are, in principle, appeals under an enactment which stipulates appeals which the Inner House wishes to retain (Exchequer and Social Work appeals); appeals from tribunals consisting of a (judicial) panel of two or more (e.g. the Lands Tribunal); and appeals under U.K. statutes which, in relation to England and Wales, specify the Court of Appeal as the appeal court.

REMIT TO OUTER HOUSE.

There is no indication in r. 41.52(1) as to the circumstances in which a remit might be appropriate. **41.52.2** Regard would be had to the principle which is behind the choice of some of the appeals listed in r. 41.52(2) as appeals which cannot be remitted. These principles are that the enactment under which the appeal is made specifies the Inner House; appeals which the Inner House wishes to retain (Exchequer and Social Work appeals); appeals from a tribunal consisting of a (judicial) panel of two or more; and appeals under U.K. statutes which, in relation to England and Wales, specify the Court of Appeal as the appeal court.

Other factors might include the fact that the appeal was a test case, or raised a point of public importance or a novel point of law on which there was no judicial authority. Another factor might be the urgency for a decision.

Reclaiming against decision of Lord Ordinary

41.53.[1] The decision of the Lord Ordinary on an appeal heard in the Outer House by virtue of rule 41.52 (appeals to be heard in Outer House) may be reclaimed against. **41.53**

GENERAL NOTE.

This rule is in the same terms as r. 41.45 immediately before this rule came into force. **41.53.1**
This rule is a consequence of r. 41.52 for the remit of certain statutory appeals of the Outer House.

Although delay in hearing appeals might be overcome by a power to remit to the Outer House, delay could be built back in by providing for a further appeal to the Inner House. Provision for a further appeal, however, is inevitable if, under a U.K. statute, a party to an appeal in England and Wales would have the opportunity to appeal from the High Court to the Court of Appeal.

Part X[2] – References and Appeals under an ACAS Arbitration Scheme

Interpretation

41.54.[3] In this Part, "an ACAS Scheme" means an arbitration scheme set out in an order under section 212A(7) of the Trade Union and Labour Relations (Consolidation) Act 1992. **41.54**

GENERAL NOTE.

This rule is in the same terms as former r. 41.55 immediately before this rule came into force. **41.54.1**

Section 212A of the Trade Union and Labour Relations (Consolidation) Act 1992 was inserted by s. 7 of the Employment Rights (Dispute Resolution) Act 1998. It provides that ACAS may prepare a scheme for arbitration in disputes involving proceedings in, or claims which could be proceedings before, an employment tribunal arising out of an (alleged) contravention of Pt X of the 1996 Act (unfair dismissal) or other enactment specified by the Secretary of State.

Such a scheme may provide, in an arbitration conducted in accordance with Scots law, for a reference on a preliminary point, or a right of appeal, to the Court of Session: 1992 Act, s.212A(7).

---

[1] Rule 41.53 substituted by S.S.I. 2011 No. 303 (effective 27th September 2011).
[2] Part X and r. 41.54 substituted by S.S.I. 2011 No. 303 (effective 27th September 2011).
[3] Part X and r. 41.54 substituted by S.S.I. 2011 No. 303 (effective 27th September 2011).

References under an ACAS Scheme

41.55

41.55.—[1](1) A reference on a preliminary point under an ACAS Scheme shall be made to a procedural judge in Form 41.55 and shall—

    (a)   state in numbered paragraphs the facts and circumstances out of which the reference arises; and

    (b)   set out the question for answer by the court.

(2) On a reference under paragraph (1) being lodged, the court shall, without a motion being enrolled for that purpose, pronounce an interlocutor for—

    (a)   service of the reference on such persons as appears necessary; and

    (b)   any person on whom the reference has been served, to lodge answers, if so advised, within such period as is specified by the court.

(3) Within 14 days after the expiry of the period allowed for the lodging of answers, the person making the reference shall apply by motion for such further procedure as that person seeks, and the court shall make such order for further procedure as it thinks fit.

GENERAL NOTE.

41.55.1

This rule is in the same terms as former r. 41.54. The questions raised in note 41.55.2, about whether the reference is a petition lodged in the Petition Department, when r. 41.54 was inserted by S.S.I. 2004 No. 331 have, surprisingly, been ignored when repeating the terms in this rule.

"REFERENCE".

41.55.2

The only initiating processes in R.C.S. 1994 are summons and petition; there are no general rules for a reference. In other cases of references to the court, the usual course is to provide for the reference to be by petition, thus attracting the general (or such general) rules for petitions as may be necessary. Since there is no initiating process known as a reference, there are no rules which can be applied to it. Are petition rules or rules for actions to apply? Is the reference lodged in the Petition or General Department (one assumes the former)?

"SERVICE".

41.55.3

See Chap. 16, Pt.1.

"ANSWERS".

41.55.4

See r. 18.3 for guidance.

"WITHIN 14 DAYS".

41.55.5

The date from which the period is calculated is not counted. Where the last day falls on a Saturday or Sunday or a public holiday on which the Office of Court is closed, the next available day is allowed: r. 1.3(7). For office hours and public holidays, see note 3.1.2.

"MOTION".

41.55.6

For motions, see Chap. 23.

Appeals

41.56

41.56.—[2](1) Subject to paragraph (2), Part III (appeals in Form 41.25) shall apply to appeals under an ACAS Scheme.

(2) An appeal under an ACAS Scheme shall be made within the time limits specified in that scheme.

GENERAL NOTE.

41.56.1

This rule is in the same terms as former r. 41.58.

---

[1] Rule 41.55 substituted by S.S.I. 2011 No. 303 (effective 27th September 2011).
[2] Rule 41.56 substituted by S.S.I. 2011 No. 303 (effective 27th September 2011).

Under s. 13 of the Tribunals, Courts and Enforcement Act 2007 there is an appeal from the Upper Tribunal to the court with the permission of the Upper Tribunal or, if it refuses, the court.

Part XI – Appeals under the Tribunals, Courts and Enforcement Act 2007

Permission to appeal against decisions of the Upper Tribunal

41.57.—[1, 2](1)   This rule applies where an application is made to the court under section 13(4) of the Tribunals, Courts and Enforcement Act 2007 for permission to appeal a decision of the Upper Tribunal which falls within section 13(7) of that Act and for which the relevant appellate court is the Court of Session.

(2)   Permission shall not be granted on the application unless the court considers that—

    (a)   the proposed appeal would raise some important point of principle; or

    (b)   there is some other compelling reason for the court to hear the appeal.

41.57

GENERAL NOTE.

Rule 41.57 was inserted by A.S. (R.C.S.A. No. 5) (Miscellaneous) 2008 (S.S.I. 2008/349) as r. 41.59. In *KP v Secretary of State for the Home Department* [2012] CSIH 38 (Extra Div), it was held that this rule (r. 41.57), which restricted the grounds on which leave to appeal to the Inner House from the Upper Tribunal (leave only if the appeal would raise an important point of principle or practice or some other compelling reason), was ultra vires. It was inserted as r. 41.57 by A.S. (R.C.S.A. No. 5) (Causes in the Inner House) 2011 (SSI 2011/303), and then revoked. This rule was revoked by A.S. (R.C.S.A. No. 3) (Miscellaneous) 2012 (S.S.I. 2012 No. 189) (effective 9th July, 2012). This prompted the passing of s.23 of the Crime and Courts Act 2013 which, by inserting s.13(6A) to the Tribunals, Courts and Enforcement Act 2007, gave the court power to introduce what is called the second appeals test (see *Eba v. Advocate General*, 2012 S.C. (UKSC) 1). The rule was then re-instated by Act of Sederunt (Rules of the Court of Session Amendment No. 5) (Miscellaneous) 2013 (S.S.I. 2013/238). Unfortunately, there was a drafting error in the primary legislation in s.23 of the 2013 Act which omitted the words "or practice" in the fist limb of the second appeals test ("some important point of principle or practice"). Hence the rule had to be amended (Act of Sederunt (Rules of the Court of Session Amendment No. 6) (Miscellaneous) 2013 (S.S.I. 2013/294)) to delete the words "or practice". It is not clear if this will make a difference in practice; but one day the legislators may get it right.

Rule 41.59 was inserted by A.S. (R.C.S.A. No. 5) (Miscellaneous) 2008 (S.S.I. 2008/349). In KP v Secretary of State for the Home Department [2012] CSIH 38 (Extra Div), it was held that this rule (r. 41.57), which restricted the grounds on which leave to appeal to the Inner House from the Upper Tribunal (leave only if hte appeal would raise an important point of principle or practice or some other compelling reason), was ultra vires. This rule was revoked by A.S. (R.C.S.A. No. 3) (Miscellaneous) 2012 (S.S.I. 2012 No. 189) (effective 9th July, 2012).

41.57.1

Part XII – Marine Licence Applications etc.

Application of this Part and modification of this Chapter for the purposes of this Part

41.58.—[3](1)   This Part applies to applications under—

    (a)   Section 63A of the Marine (Scotland) Act 2010;

    (b)   Section 73A of the Marine and Coastal Access Act 2009;

    (c)   Section 36D of the Electricity Act 1989;

    (d)   Paragraph 5B of Schedule 8 to the Electricity Act 1989.

(2)   The following provisions of Part I (general provisions) shall not apply to an application mentioned in paragraph (1)—

    (a)   rule 41.2 (applications for leave to appeal);

    (b)   rule 41.3 (determination of applications for leave to appeal);

    (c)   rule 41.5 (competency of appeals).

41.58

---

[1] Rule 41.57 substituted by S.S.I. 2011 No. 303 (effective 27th September 2011) and revoked by S.S.I. 2012 No. 189 (effective 9th July 2012).

[2] As inserted by the Act of Sederunt (Rules of the Court of Session Amendment No.5) (Miscellaneous) 2013 (SSI 2013/238) r.2 (effective 19th August 2013), amended further by the Act of Sederunt (Rules of the Court of Session Amendment No.6) (Miscellaneous) 2013 (SSI 2013/294) r.3 (effective 11th November 2013).

[3] Part XII and r.41.58 inserted by S.S.I. 2015 No. 35 (effective 26th February 2015).

(3) Part III (appeals in Form 41.25) shall apply to an application mentioned in paragraph (1), subject to the following provisions of this Part.

(4) The following provision of Part III (appeals in Form 41.25) shall not apply to an application mentioned in paragraph (1)—

    (a) rule 41.25 (form of appeal);

    (b) rule 41.26 (lodging of application in court);

    (c) rule 41.27 (orders for service and answers);

    (d) rule 41.28(1) (motion for further procedure).

GENERAL NOTE

41.58.1   All the provisions in r. 41.58(1) provide for persons aggrieved by a decision of Scottish Ministers, wishing to question the validity of the decision, to apply to the Inner House.

Form application and lodging of application in court

41.59   **41.59.**—[1](1) An application shall be made in Form 41.59.

(2) That application shall—

    (a) specify the provision of the enactment under which the application is made;

    (b) specify—

        (i) the decision complained of;

        (ii) the date on which the decision was made;

        (iii) the date on which it was intimated to the applicant; and

        (iv) any other relevant information;

    (c) where the application concerns only part of the decision, specify or distinguish that part;

    (d) have appended to it a copy of the decision;

    (e) state, in brief numbered propositions—

        (i) the grounds on which the validity of the decision is questioned; and

        (ii) why the court should grant permission; and

    (f) set out in a schedule the names and addresses of the respondents in the application and the name and address, so far as known to the applicant, of any other person who may have an interest in the application.

(3) The application shall be lodged in the General Department.

(4) There shall be lodged within the application—

    (a) a process in accordance with rule 4.4 (steps of process);

    (b) all documents founded upon by the applicant so far as in the applicant's possession or within the applicant's control.

Determination of application for permission to proceed

41.60   **41.60.**—[2](1) An application for permission shall, without a motion being enrolled—

    (a) during session, be brought before a procedural judge on the first available day after being made for an order for—

        (i) service of the application on the respondent and such other person as the procedural judge thinks fit within 7 days of the date of the order or such other period as the procedural judge thinks fit; and

        (ii) any person on whom the application has been served, to lodge answers restricted to the question of whether permission should be

---

[1] Rule 41.59 inserted by S.S.I. 2015 No. 35 (effective 26th February 2015).
[2] Rule 41.60 inserted by S.S.I. 2015 No. 35 (effective 26th February 2015).

granted, if so advised, within 14 days after the date of service or within such other period as the procedural judge thinks fit; and

(b)   during vacation, be brought before the vacation judge for such an order.

(2)   Where an application for permission is served under paragraph (1), evidence of service in accordance with Chapter 16 of these Rules shall be provided to the General Department within 14 days from the date of service.

(3)   Within 14 days after expiry of the period within which answers may be lodged, the applicant may apply by motion to the procedural judge for the application for permission to be granted.

Further procedure where the court grants permission to proceed

41.61.[1]   Where the court has granted permission for an application to proceed—   **41.61**

(a)   the court shall make an order for any person on whom the application has been served to lodge answers to the application, if so advised, within such period as the court thinks fit;

(b)   the applicant or a respondent may seek urgent disposal of the application under rule 41.4 (urgent disposal of appeal);

(c)   in rule 41.4(2)(b) (urgent disposal of appeal), rule 41.28(2) (motion for further procedure) and rule 41.29(1) (timetable in appeal under Part III), "answers" means answers lodged following an order under rule 41.61(a).

---

[1] Rule 41.61 inserted by S.S.I. 2015 No. 35 (effective 26th February 2015).

Chapter 41A

Appeals to the Supreme Court

Application of this Chapter

41A.1.[1] This Chapter applies to an application for permission to appeal to the Supreme Court under section 40(1)(a) or (3) of the Act of 1988(b).

41A.1

Applications for permission to appeal

41A.2.—[2](1) An application is made in Form 41A.2.

(2) The application must set out the proposed grounds of appeal and the basis on which permission to appeal is sought.

41A.2

Determination of applications for permission to appeal

41A.3.—[3](1) An application must, without a motion being enrolled, be brought before the Inner House on the first available day after being made for an order for—

41A.3

   (a)   service of the application on the respondent and such other person as the Inner House thinks fit within 7 days of the date of the order or such other period as is thought fit;

   (b)   any person on whom the application has been served to lodge answers, if so advised, within 14 days after the date of service or within such other period as is thought fit.

(2) Where an application is served under paragraph (1), evidence of service in accordance with Chapter 16 of these Rules is to be provided to the General Department within 14 days from the date of service.

(3) Within 14 days after expiry of the period within which answers may be lodged, the applicant may apply by motion to the Inner House for the application to be granted.

---

[1] Ch. 41A and r. 41A.1 as inserted by S.S.I. 2015 No. 228 r. 5 (effective 22nd September 2015).

[2] Rule 41A.2 as inserted by S.S.I. 2015 No. 228 r. 5 (effective 22nd September 2015).

[3] Rule 41A.3 as inserted by S.S.I. 2015 No. 228 r. 5 (effective 22nd September 2015).

CHAPTER 41B QUALIFIED ONE-WAY COSTS SHIFTING

Application and interpretation of this Chapter

41B.1.—(1) [1]This Chapter applies in civil proceedings, where either or both—

(a) an application for an award of expenses is made to the court;

(b) such an award is made by the court.

(2) Where this Chapter applies—

(a) rules 29.1(2) and (3) (abandonment of actions), 40.15(6) (appeals deemed abandoned) and 41.17(3)(b) (procedure on abandonment);

(b) any common law rule entitling a pursuer to abandon an action or an appeal, to the extent that it concerns expenses,

are disapplied.

(3) In this Chapter—

"the Act" means the Civil Litigation (Expenses and Group Proceedings) (Scotland) Act 2018;

"the applicant" has the meaning given in rule 41B.2(1), and "applicants" is construed accordingly;

"civil proceedings" means civil proceedings to which section 8 of the Act (restriction on pursuer's liability for expenses in personal injury claims) applies.

Application for an award of expenses

41B.2.—(1) Where civil proceedings have been brought by a pursuer, another party to the action ("the applicant") may make an application to the court for an award of expenses to be made against the pursuer, on one or more of the grounds specified in either or both—

(a) section 8(4)(a) to (c) of the Act;

(b) paragraph (2) of this rule.

(2) The grounds specified in this paragraph, which are exceptions to section 8(2) of the Act, are as follows—

(a) failure by the pursuer to obtain an award of damages greater than the sum offered by way of a tender lodged in process;

(b) unreasonable delay on the part of the pursuer in accepting a sum offered by way of a tender lodged in process;

(c) abandonment of the action or the appeal by the pursuer in terms of rules 29.1(1), 40.15(1) or 41.15(1), or at common law.

Award of expenses

41B.3.—(1) Subject to paragraph (2), the determination of an application made under rule 41B.2(1) is at the discretion of the court.

(2) Where, having determined an application made under rule 41B.2(1), the court makes an award of expenses against the pursuer on the ground specified in rule 41B.2(2)(a) or (b)—

(a) the pursuer's liability is not to exceed the amount of expenses the applicant has incurred after the date of the tender;

(b) the liability of the pursuer to the applicant, or applicants, who lodged the tender is to be limited to an aggregate sum, payable to all applicants (if more than one) of 75% of the amount of damages awarded to the

41B.1

41B.2

41B.3

---

[1] Ch.41B inserted by S.S.I. 2021 No.226 (effective 30th June 2021).

597

pursuer, and that sum is to be calculated without offsetting against those expenses any expenses due to the pursuer by the applicant, or applicants, before the date of the tender;

(c)   the court must order that the pursuer's liability is not to exceed the sum referred to in sub-paragraph (b), notwithstanding that any sum assessed by the Auditor of Court as payable under the tender procedure may be greater or, if modifying the expenses in terms of rule 42.5 (modification or disallowance of expenses)(a) or 42.6(1) (modification of expenses awarded against assisted persons), that such modification does not exceed that referred to in sub-paragraph (b);

(d)   where the award of expenses is in favour of more than one applicant the court, failing agreement between the applicants, is to apportion the award of expenses recoverable under the tender procedure between them.

(3)   Where, having determined an application made under rule 41B.2(1), the court makes an award of expenses against the pursuer on the ground specified in rule 41B.2(2)(c), the court may make such orders in respect of expenses, as it considers appropriate, including—

(a)   making an award of decree of dismissal dependant on payment of expenses by the pursuer within a specified period of time;

(b)   provision for the consequences of failure to comply with any conditions applied by the court.

Procedure

41B.4   **41B.4.**—(1)   An application under rule 41B.2(1)—

(a)   must be made by motion, in writing, and Chapter 23 (motions)(b) otherwise applies to motions made under this Chapter;

(b)   may be made at any stage in the case prior to the pronouncing of an interlocutor disposing of the expenses of the action or, as the case may be, the appeal.

(2)   Where an application under rule 41B.2(1) is made, the court may make such orders as it thinks fit for dealing with the application, including an order—

(a)   requiring the applicant to intimate the application to any other person;

(b)   requiring any party to lodge a written response;

(c)   requiring the lodging of any document;

(d)   fixing a hearing.

Award against legal representatives

41B.5   **41B.5.**   Section 8(2) of the Act does not prevent the court from making an award of expenses against a pursuer's legal representative in terms of section 11 (awards of expenses against legal representatives) of the Act.

CHAPTER 42 TAXATION OF ACCOUNTS, ETC.

Part I – Taxation of Accounts

Remit to the Auditor

42.1.—[1](1) Where expenses are found due to a party in any cause, the court shall—

    (a) pronounce an interlocutor finding that party entitled to expenses and, subject to rule 42.6(1) (modification of expenses awarded against assisted persons), remitting to the Auditor for taxation; and

    (b) without prejudice to rule 42.4 (objections to report of the Auditor), unless satisfied that there is special cause shown for not doing so, pronounce an interlocutor decerning against the party found liable in expenses as taxed by the Auditor.

(2)[2] Any party found entitled to expenses shall—

    (a) lodge an account of expenses in process not later than four months after the final interlocutor in which a finding in respect of expenses is made; or

    (b) lodge such account at any time with leave of the court but subject to such conditions (if any) as the court thinks fit to impose.

(2A) On lodging an account under paragraph (2)(a) or (b), any party found entitled to expenses must intimate a copy of it forthwith to the party found liable to pay those expenses.

(3) Rule 4.6(1) (intimation of steps of process) shall not apply to the lodging of an account of expenses.

Deriv. R.C.S. 1965, r. 348(1) and (2) substituted by S.I. 1983 No. 826

GENERAL NOTE.

The principle upon which the court proceeds in awarding expenses is that the cost of litigation should fall on him who has caused it, unless the circumstances justify otherwise: *Shepherd v. Elliot* (1896) 23 R. 695. Allowance of a late plea of arbitration clause does not fall within the exception to the general rule that expenses follow success: *Presslie v. Cochrane McGregor Group Ltd (No. 2)* 1997 S.C. 159. Disputed compensation cases under the Land Compensation (Scotland) Acts where an advance payment, but no tender, has been made, follow the general principle: *City of Aberdeen D.C. v. Emslie & Simpson Ltd* 1995 S.C. 264. In *Miller v Chivas Bros.* 2015 S.C. 85 (Extra Div.), 91, paras. [22] and [23], the court reiterated the general principle, indicating that the court will exercise considerable reserve in departing from it and that appeals on expenses require severely to be discouraged. One example where the principle may be departed from is where the conduct of the successful party caused or unduly extended the litigation: e.g., *Ramm v Lothian and Borders Fire Board* 1994 S.C. 226 (Second Div.) (taking time raising and exploring issues, for which there was no proper basis, which failed).

A decision on expenses in a financial provision on divorce case primarily involves the exercise of discretion, but regard will be given to, amongst other matters, (i) success on the issues in contention at proof, (ii) conduct and (iii) extra judicial offers (*Sweeney v Sweeney No 3* 2007 SC 396 ; *McCallion v McCallion* 2022 Fam LR 63). It is also relevant to consider the impact an award of expenses may have on the division of matrimonial property achieved through court orders (*Little v Little* 1990 SLT 785; *Sweeney v Sweeney No 3* at p 398). See *Foster v Foster* [2023] CSIH 44 (Extra Div.), *2024 S.C.L.R. 124*, para. [3].

The general rule that expenses follow success applies even though the whole of the sum awarded is paid to the CRU (Compensation Recovery Unit) of the DSS under the Social Security (Recovery of Benefits) Act 1997: *Gray v. Lanarkshire Health Board* 1998 S.L.T. 1378.

There are three forms of taxation—(1) party and party, (2) agent and client, client paying, and (3) agent and client, third party paying. An interlocutor awarding expenses without qualification implies taxation on a party and party basis; if expenses are to be taxed on another basis, that must be specified: *Fletcher's Trs v. Fletcher* , (1888) 15 R. 862; *Magistrates of Aberchirder v. Banff District Committee* , (1906) 8 F. 571, 573 per Lord McLaren. (1) Expenses on a party and party basis means expenses reasonable for conducting the litigation in a proper manner. Expenses are taxed on the scale in r. 42.16, unless otherwise specifically ordered (e.g. on a sheriff court scale). (2) Expenses on a solicitor and client basis without further specification will be solicitor and client, client paying: see *Milligan v. Tinnes's Trs* , 1971 S.L.T. (Notes) 64; and *Trunature Ltd v. Scotnet (1974) Ltd* , 2008 S.L.T. 653 (Second Div.). A client is liable for all expenses reasonably incurred by the agent for the protection of the client's interest, and those

---

[1] Chapter heading and r. 42.1 as amended by S.S.I. 2019 No. 74 r. 4 (effective 29th April 2019).
[2] R. 42.1(2) substituted by S.S.I. 2008 No. 123, r. 2(1) (effective 1st April 2008).

specifically authorised, even though not (otherwise) recoverable from the other party: *Mackay's Practice*, ii, 585; *Maclaren on Expenses*, p. 431. In exceptional circumstances the court may award expenses on an "agent and client" basis (*Plasticisers Ltd v. William R. Stewart & Sons (Hacklemakers) Ltd* 1973 S.L.T. 58, 63. It has been said that all the expenses incurred by the client are allowable except those unreasonably or extravagantly incurred, or unreasonable in amount, the benefit of any doubt being given to the receiving party. In no case are expenses which are not expenses of process allowable: *Milligan*, above; *Cabot Financial UK Ltd v. Weir* 2022 S.C. 117 (First Div.) (a success fee is not an expense of process). (3) Expenses on a solicitor and client, third party paying (i.e. the opposite side) is not so generous as in the case of client paying, but not as rigorous as on a party and party basis: *Maclaren on Expenses*, p. 509. The expenses are those that would be incurred by a prudent man of business: *Hood v. Gordon* , (1896) 23 R. 675, 676 per Lord Patrick. It is said to be the appropriate basis where statute authorises expenses as between agent and client (*Hood*, above) and in multiplepoindings where expenses are awarded on an agent and client basis out of the fund *in medio* (*Park v. Colvilles Ltd* , 1960 S.C. 143, 153).

Expenses common to more than one action brought on the same grounds should normally be apportioned amongst the parties liable so that each such party is only liable for a proportionate part: *Lujo Properties Ltd v. Schuh Ltd* , 2009 S.L.T. 553; an exception will be where only one defender is found liable for the debt or delict.

The taxation of accounts, whether between party and party (Chap. 42, Pt II; A.S. (Taxation of Judicial Expenses Rules) 2019 for proceedings commenced on or after 29th April 2019 [S.S.I. 2019 No. 75]), or agent and client (r. 42.7), is left almost entirely to the Auditor. The court has shown reluctance, except in exceptional circumstances, to interfere with his discretion. It is not the function of the court in reviewing an exercise of discretion to substitute its own views of the material under consideration: *Wood v. Miller* 1960 S.C. 86, 97 per L.J.-C. Thomson. In *Stuart v. Reid* [2015] CSOH 175 at para. [25], Lord Woolman summed up the roles of the court and the Auditor of Court as follows:

(a) The Auditor acts essentially as a valuer.
(b) He is expected to apply his knowledge and experience in carrying out his task of assessing a fair and reasonable fee.
(c) The court will be slow to disturb his decision if he has properly exercised his discretion.
(d) It will not substitute its own views for those of the Auditor.
(e) It will not attempt to tax an account itself.
(f) The court will, however, intervene if the Auditor did not have sufficient materials on which to proceed, or his decision is unreasonable.

The Auditor has no power to refuse or modify the expenses of proceedings ordered by the court (*Stott v. McWilliam* (1856) 18 D. 716, 719 per Lord Ivory), even when these proceedings have been held as incompetent (*Sleigh v. City of Edinburgh D.C.* 1988 S.L.T. 253); and unusually in a cause which was abandoned the petitioner was still awarded expenses (*Laing's Tr. v. Messenger* 1993 G.W.D. 12-898).

The Auditor's power in taxing an account includes not only taxing off and reducing items which appear to have been improperly charged but also to increase items that he considers as understated, not filled up, or altogether omitted: *Reeve v. Dykes* (1829) 7 S.632. The existence of an express power to address the scope of taxation in inclusive fees does not prejudice or restrict the auditor's wider discretionary powers whether to allow the insertion at taxation of sums omitted from the account: *Collie v. Tesco Stores Ltd*, 2016 S.L.T. 1213 (OH).

"WHERE EXPENSES ARE FOUND DUE".

42.1.2   The court has no power to award expenses against a person who was not a party to, or associated with, the litigation: *Meekison v. Uniroyal Engelbert Tyres Ltd* 1995 S.L.T. (Sh. Ct.) 63.

The court, when granting decree for expenses, must pronounce an interlocutor finding a party entitled to expenses and, unless satisfied that there is special cause for not doing so, it must further (a) decern against the party found liable as taxed and (b) remit the account of expenses to the Auditor to tax. It has been held that where an interlocutor refers to expenses as taxed there is no need for an express remit, that being implied in cases where it is not expressed: *Gilbert's Tr. v. Gilbert* 1988 S.L.T. 680. Special cause for postponement of an immediate for modification as the court is functus: *Stewart v. Stewart* 1989 S.L.T. 80. Since 1983, in a cause in which the person liable for the expenses is not legally aided there are usually two interlocutors at the conclusion of a cause (or wherever expenses are dealt with); one disposing of the merits and the other decerning for expenses as taxed (and when taxed, the amount of expenses authorised by the Auditor is inserted by the Extractor in the extract), the latter being the last or final interlocutor. An interlocutor awarding expenses against a non-legally-aided party has a decerniture pronounced at the time the finding of expenses is made. Where a party liable in expenses is legally aided there is no decerniture when the finding is made: a finding of liability in expenses is made with a remit to the Auditor to tax and report. A decerniture is only made thereafter after consideration of any objections or application for modification. The reason for the difference in the case of a legally aided party is that it is not competent to modify expenses after decerniture: *Gilbert's Tr.*, above.

A decerniture for expenses cannot be altered or recalled: *U.C.B. Bank plc v. Dundas & Wilson, C.S.* 1991 S.L.T. 90, 93L per L.P. Hope; and see, e.g. *Davis v. British Coal Corporation* 1993 S.L.T. 697 (further expenses sought not allowed after expenses decerned for).

Expenses may be awarded even if not concluded for: *Elliot & Stewart v. McDougall* 1956 S.L.T.(Notes) 36.

Expenses of an appeal include expenses of adjustment and preparation of stated case or appeal: *Macdonald v. Stornoway Trust* 1989 S.L.T. 87.

An award of "expenses of process as taxed" does not refer to the expenses of another process: *Rankin v. Upper Clyde Shipbuilders Ltd (in liquidation)* 1990 G.W.D. 3-139.

As reserved expenses will be carried automatically along with the expenses of the cause awarded by the final interlocutor; if it is desired that they be dealt with differently it is important that they be specifically dealt with as soon as possible after being reserved: *Bank of Scotland v. Morrison* 1911 S.C. 593.

A party may not be awarded expenses where he has no separate interest from another party which renders his appearance necessary: *Robertson v. City of Edinburgh District Licensing Board* 1994 S.C. 83.

As the general rule is that the cost of litigation falls on the party who has caused it. He cannot normally, at least in ordinary course and in the absence of some unreasonable behaviour, be liable for the expenses of a party he has not brought into the process and against whom he has directed no case. The expenses of third parties are generally only recoverable against the party who has directed a case against them: *Albert Bartlett & Sons (Airdrie) v Gilchrist & Lynn* [2010] CSIH 33 (Extra Div.), per Lord Carloway, delivering the opinion of the court, at para. [12]); *Prospect Healthcare (Hairmyres) Ltd v Kier Build Ltd (No.2)*, 2018 S.C. 569 (First Div.).

Where a party succeeded in an appeal upon a different ground from that advanced in the lower court and which emerged only in the course of the appeal no award of expenses was made: *Speyside Electronics Ltd v. The Royal Bank of Scotland plc* , 2nd Div., 10th February 1995, 1995 G.W.D. 12-629.

Where the original action was incompetent and irrelevant and a minute of amendment constituted a new action based on a different ground and seeking a different result the successful pursuer was found liable in expenses: *Manson v. Manson* , O.H., 12th January 1996, 1996 G.W.D. 11-645.

The general rule as to expenses in tenders where there are two or more defenders is that, if a pursuer convenes two or more defenders and one or more is assoilzied, the pursuer and not the unsuccessful defender pays the expenses of the successful defender: *Mitchell v. Redpath Engineering Ltd* 1990 S.L.T. 259. That case lays down the principles to be applied. There is an exception where a defender causes or induces the pursuer to convene another party. Where by tender a defender had, in effect, accepted full liability although in the defences had made a bare denial of the pursuer's averments and adopted the averments of fault against the pursuer of other defenders which required the pursuer to maintain his action against the other defenders until the lodging of the tender following upon which the pursuer lodged a minute of abandonment in respect of the other defenders, the defender was found liable in the whole expenses of the cause: *Bremner v. Press Offshore Ltd* , 1994, S.C.L.R. 772.

It is not competent to award expenses against counsel personally: see *Reid v. Edinburgh Acoustics Ltd (No. 2)* , 1995 S.L.T. 982.

An award of expenses may be made, in exceptional circumstances, against a solicitor personally: *Blyth v. Watson* 1987 S.L.T. 616; *Stewart v. Stewart* 1984 S.L.T. (Sh. Ct) 58; *L., Petitioners (No. 6)* , 1st Div., 24th October 1995, 1995 G.W.D. 39-2025 (failure to apply timeously for legal aid). For example where he acted in excess of instructions or without due regard to his duty to the court or his responsibilities to the Legal Aid Fund. But not where the solicitor acted on the advice of counsel: *Reid*, above; for a recent case in which a solicitor was found liable, see *Russell v Russell*, 2018 S.C. 130 (OH).

As a matter of practice, expenses are not ordinarily awarded against compearing parties in petitions where local authorities seek permanence orders unless there was reprehensible behaviour or an unreasonable stance taken (by the local authority): *Perth and Kinross Council, Ptnrs, 2018 S.L.T. 275*.

Reclaiming motions on expenses are discouraged by the court: *Ramm v. Lothian and Borders Fire Board* , 1994 S.C. 226.

"ACCOUNT OF EXPENSES".

42.1.3 The account should be typed on A4 size account paper with columns for figures to the left and right of the text of the items claimed; the left hand column is for the Auditor to enter figures taxed off or added. The dates of the items of work are entered in chronological order with the details of the work being succinctly stated, giving sufficient information to show the nature of the work carried out for which the charge is claimed. The outlays should be numbered to correspond with the numbers on the vouchers to be produced to support them. The account is stitched into a process backing sheet showing the names of parties (the instance) and the cause reference number. The interlocutor containing the finding to which the account relates must be reproduced on the first page of the account.

"LODGE THE ACCOUNT OF EXPENSES IN PROCESS".

42.1.4 The account of expenses is lodged as a step in process; it must be backed and have the number of process and the cause reference number marked on it: see rr. 4.1(3) and 4.4(3). It may be lodged by post: P.N. No. 4 of 1994, paras 1 and 8.

A fee is payable on lodging the account: see note 42.1.9.

THE FOUR-MONTH RULE.

42.1.5 The general rule is that an account of expenses must be lodged not later than four months after a final interlocutor (on which see note 4.15.2(2)) in which a finding in respect of expenses was made (i.e. not just the one which awards a specified sum of expenses): r. 42.1(2)(a). A "month" means a calendar month. Hence, if the final interlocutor is dated 20th October the account must be lodged by the end of 20th February; if the final interlocutor is dated 30th October, the account must be lodged by the end of 28th February (or 29th in a leap year). The time-limit does not apply to an account of expenses prepared on a finding of expenses in a final interlocutor pronounced before September 5, 1994: Interpretation Act 1978, s. 16(1) as applied by s. 23(1); and the presumption against retrospectivity.

The provision was changed (by A.S. (R.C.S. A No. 2) (Fees of Solicitors) 1995 [S.I. 1995 No. 1396]) from "within a period of 4 months" to "not later than 4 months" to avoid a notion that an account for an incidental award of expenses may be lodged only within the four month period after the *final* interlocutor.

The reason for the four month rule is so that the paying party may know the amount of his liability within a reasonable period. In *King v. Global Marine (UK) Ltd* , 2003 S.C. 269 (Second Div.), it was argued for the pursuer, seeking leave to lodge an account late, that the change of wording in r. 42.1(2)(a) from "*a* final interlocutor" to "*the* final interlocutor" made by A.S. (R.C.S.A. No.3) (Miscellaneous) 1996 [S.I. 1996 No. 1756] meant the final interlocutor (the very last in the process) on the subject of expenses pronounced in the cause. It was submitted that otherwise a series of individual accounts of expenses during the course of the litigation would have to be lodged instead of at the end. It was held that "the final interlocutor" referred to was not necessarily the final interlocutor on the subject of expenses in the process, but, in this case the final interlocutor on expenses between this pursuer in the cause and the defender. Otherwise, the unreasonable result would be that where one party settled with an award of expenses and the process continued for resolution of the other claims, that party could delay lodging an account until the end of the case. The purpose of the rule is to ensure that when a decree for expenses was granted, the party liable should receive an account of them promptly; and the change of wording is of no significance.

An application for prorogation of the period by which an account may be lodged in terms of the rule must be made within the four month period otherwise application for late lodging will require to be made under r. 42.1(2)(aa). Some solicitors resented the four-month rule and sought its abolition or a less onerous timetable. They have been to some extent successful in that r. 42.1(2)(aa) has been inserted by A.S. (R.C.S.A.) (Miscellaneous) 1998 [S.I. 1998 No. 890]. This provision allows late lodging of an account with leave of the court subject to any conditions it may impose. The provision does not state that cause has to be shown to obtain leave. It is inconceivable, however, that some cause does not have to be shown: if leave is required it may be withheld, and, therefore, a reason (cause) must be given. Formerly resort had to be made to the dispensing power, for cause, under r. 2.1. What is the perceived difference between the new provision in r. 42.1(2)(aa) and "other excusable cause" in r. 2.1? This new provision bears all the hallmarks of an unsatisfactory compromise between two opposing camps. The new provision also states that leave to lodge the account late may be granted on such conditions (if any) as the court may impose. But what conditions can the court impose (the expenses of the motion will have to be paid in any event)? In relation to the meaning of "conditions" in r. 42.1(2)(aa), it was held in *Finlayson v. British Steel plc* , 2003 S.L.T. 903 (OH) that a condition of a financial penalty could not be imposed as the court had no power to impose penalties. In *Finlayson's Guardian v. Scottish Rig Repairers* , 2006 S.L.T. 329 (OH), leave to lodge an account late was refused.

Under the original provision in r. 42.1(2)(a) special cause had to be shown for an extension of the four months. Following the new provision for late lodging introduced in r. 42.1(2)(aa) (inserted by S.I. 1998 No. 890), it made little sense to require special cause for an extension of time under r. 42.1(2)(a). The provision for late lodging on special cause shown in r. 42.1(2)(a) has been removed by A.S. (R.C.S.A. No.4) (Miscellaneous) 2001 [S.S.I. 2001 No. 305].

The law, under the former strict four-month rule, on an application under r. 2.1, appears from the following cases. In *Fane v. Murray* 1996 S.C. 51 (I.H.), late lodging was refused by the Extra Division where the delay was due to absence of the solicitor and subsequent negotiations; the case indicates a strict compliance with r. 42.1(2)(a) is required. In *Stakeman v. Brien* , 6th September 1996, unreported (1996 G.W.D. 33-1980), it was held that it was not special cause that there was no prejudice or that there was a belief that the parties would endeavour to agree a sum for expenses. Although r. 2.1 does not require the very high test of "special cause shown" the court may be less willing to exercise its discretion when specific provision has been made for extension of the period: see *Smith v. Smith (I.H.)* , 23rd June 1995, unreported; *McGee v. Matthew Hall Ltd* 1996 S.L.T. 399, 399K per Lord Caplan (a case on r. 37.1(2)(a)).

If the final substantive interlocutor of the Inner House is appealed to the House of Lords, the four-month period will not commence until that appeal has been determined.

Decerniture for expenses principally occurs in causes where the person found liable in expenses is in receipt of legal aid in which case he is entitled to apply to the court for modification: r. 42.5. If, however, the court has gone on to make a decerniture for expenses it is incompetent to apply.

A solicitor acting for an assisted person awarded expenses must (unless perhaps where both parties are legally aided and the unsuccessful party had his liability modified within the four month period) prepare (a) a party and party account of expenses and lodge it in court within the four month period and (b) the agent and client account for lodging within the Legal Aid Board. The cost of taxation may be included in the agent and client account or a supplementary account lodged with the Board.

The clerk of session in the appropriate department will check that the account is being lodged within the required period. If it is not, a motion will need to be enrolled seeking to prorogate the time for lodging under r. 42.1(2)(a), failing which enrolling a motion for leave to lodge the account late under r. 2.1.

The date from which the period is calculated is not counted. Where the last day falls on a Saturday or Sunday or a public holiday on which the Office of Court is closed, the next available day is allowed: r. 1.3(7). For office hours and public holidays, see rule 3.1.2.

In *Canon (UK) Ltd v. Craig* , 2005 G.W.D. 10-156, 2nd February 2005 (OH), it was argued that, as the principal summons had not been served though signeted, there was no process in which the defender could lodge an account. It was held that the requirement under r. 42. 1(2)(a) was met by the existence of a process in the sense of a bundle of documents with a reference number.

"FINAL INTERLOCUTOR IN WHICH A FINDING IN RESPECT OF EXPENSES IS MADE".

A "final interlocutor" is one which, by itself or along with previous interlocutors, disposes of the whole subject-matter of the cause. An interlocutor final in the Outer House by virtue of s.18 of the C.S.A. 1988 is not a "final interlocutor" in this sense (which is the sense used in this rule). In *King v. Global Marine (UK) Ltd* , 2003 S.C. 269, 272, 2003 S.L.T. 1334, 1336, para. [14] the Second Division held that a "final interlocutor" in r. 42.1(2)(a) means the final interlocutor on expenses in the claim between the parties concerned (in that case the first pursuer and the first defender) and not the final interlocutor in the process. In *Scottish Enterprise v. Archibald Russell of Denny Ltd* , 22nd August 2003, unreported (Second Div.), it was held that an interlocutor by a sheriff principal allowing a proof before answer was not a final interlocutor. In *Canon (UK) Ltd v. Craig* , 2005 G.W.D. 10-156, 2nd February 2005 (OH), it was said that "final" is not a point in time but relates to the determinative or decisive quality of the interlocutor.

In a cause in which the person liable in expenses is not legally aided, wherever expenses are dealt with there are usually two interlocutors at the conclusion of the cause: one disposing of the merits and the other decerning for expenses as taxed (the latter being the final interlocutor). Where the party liable in expenses is legally aided a finding for expenses is made with a remit to the Auditor to tax and report, but there is no decerniture for expenses until after the Auditor has reported and after consideration of any objections or an application for modification. See further, note 4.15.2(2).

The expression "finding for expenses" was changed to "finding in respect of expenses" by A.S. (R.C.S.A. No. 3) (Miscellaneous) 1996 [S.I. 1996 No. 1756]. It was thought that the former expression excluded a finding of no expenses due to or by and would mean that a party could not lodge an account of expenses in respect of an earlier interlocutor making a finding for expenses if that interlocutor was more than four months before the final interlocutor.

"INTIMATION OF COPY OF THE ACCOUNT TO THE PARTY FOUND LIABLE".

It is not necessary to intimate the account of expenses to a party not found liable to pay those expenses, hence the disapplication of r. 4.6(1): see rr. 4.1(2) and (3).

The account should be accompanied by the information required in P.N. No. 3 of 1993, paras 2.2 and 2.3.

For methods of intimation, see r. 16.7. Before 1st April 2008 the less formal written intimation under r. 16.9 was sufficient.

TRANSMISSION OF THE PROCESS TO THE AUDITOR.

Formerly this was done by the party seeking to have the account taxed. Nowadays the process is transmitted (by court messenger) from the appropriate department with the department's transmission book to the office of the Auditor. The entry in the transmission book for the cause is receipted and returned to the department from which it came.

FEE.

The Auditor's fee for lodging an account of expenses is payable on receipt of the account in the Auditor's office. For fee, see Court of Session etc. Fees Order 1984, Table of Fees, Pt III, I, 1(a) [S.I. 1984 No. 256, Table as amended, pp. C 1202 et seq.]. Lodging dues and fee fund dues must be paid to the Auditor's office. The Auditor's office issues invoices or the collection of lodging dues and fee fund dues are paid on taxation of the account. Party litigants must pay cash when lodging dues or fee fund dues are incurred.

EXPENSES AGAINST PARTY LITIGATING IN A REPRESENTATIVE CAPACITY.

The general rule is that a person who litigates in a representative capacity may still expose himself to personal liability in expenses but may be entitled to relief from the funds he holds in that capacity. In *Dyer v. Craiglaw Developments Ltd* , 29th October 1998, unreported (1998 G.W.D. 39-2015) Lord Hamilton gave guidance on the form of words to be used in the interlocutor awarding expenses to such a party:—(1) Where the award is to be against the party in his representative capacity and therefore limited to the funds he holds, the interlocutor should state that the award of expenses is against him with the expression "as" followed by his particular capacity (*Craig v. Hogg* (1896) 24 R. 6), e.g. "as liquidator". (2) Where the award is against him personally while preserving his right of relief against the funds he holds, the interlocutor should state that the award of expenses is against him without qualification, e.g. "pursuer" or as the case may be. (3) Where the award is against him personally but is intended to be unrestricted without a right of relief against the funds he holds, the interlocutor should state that the award of expenses is against him "personally" (*Kilmarnock Theatre Co. v. Buchanan* 1911 S.C. 607).

PAYMENT OF INTERIM EXPENSES.

An order for payment of interim expenses before an account has been taxed is competent: *Cameron and Waterston v Muir & Sons*. In *Martin & Co (UK) Ltd, Petrs* [2013] CSOH 25, a case in which the respondent did not appear, Lord Drummond Young held that it was necessary to show special reasons for making an interim award. This was followed in *Tods Murray WS v. Arakin Ltd* [2013] CSOH 134, by Lord Woolman. In *Kidd v. Paull & Williamson LLP* [2017] CSOH 124, a case in which the competency was accepted, Lord Tyre considered that Lord Drummond Young did not mean that such an order would

42.1.6

42.1.7

42.1.8

42.1.9

42.1.10

42.1.11

only be made in exceptional circumstances; in his opinion, it was in the discretion of the court to depart from the ordinary way (lodging an account etc.) if satisfied that there was a sufficient reason for doing so.

Diet of taxation

42.2

42.2.—[1](1) Subject to paragraph (2), the Auditor shall fix a diet of taxation on receipt of—

(a) the process of the cause;

(b) vouchers in respect of all outlays, including counsel's fees; and

(c) a letter addressed to the Auditor confirming that the items referred to in subparagraph (b) have been intimated to the party found liable in expenses.

(2) The Auditor may fix a diet of taxation notwithstanding that paragraphs (1)(b) and (c) have not been complied with.

(3) The Auditor shall intimate the diet of taxation to—

(a) the party found entitled to expenses; and

(b) the party found liable in expenses.

(4) The party found liable in expenses shall, not later than 4.00pm on the fourth business day before the diet of taxation, intimate to the Auditor and to the party found entitled to expenses, particular points of objection, specifying each item objected to and stating concisely the nature and ground of objection.

(5) Subject to paragraph (6), if the party found liable in expenses fails to intimate points of objection under paragraph (4) within the time limit set out there, the Auditor shall not take account of them at the diet of taxation.

(6) The Auditor may relieve a party from the consequences of a failure to comply with the requirement contained in paragraph (5) because of mistake, oversight or other excusable cause on such conditions, if any, as the Auditor thinks fit.

(7)[2] At the diet of taxation or within such reasonable period of time thereafter as the Auditor may allow, the party found entitled to expenses shall make available to the Auditor all documents, drafts or copies of documents sought by the Auditor and relevant to the taxation.

(8) In this rule, a "business day" means any day other than a Saturday, Sunday, or public holiday as directed by the Lord President of the Court of Session.

Deriv. R.C.S. 1965, r. 348(3) and (4) substituted by S.I. 1983 No. 826

"DIET OF TAXATION".

42.2.1

A diet of taxation is a hearing conducted by the Auditor in his Office at which the receiving and paying parties attend personally, or at which they may be represented by their respective solicitors or such other persons as the Auditor may allow.

The Auditor appoints a day and time for the taxation. The Auditor will not normally fix a diet until he has received the process, vouchers for all outlays including counsel's fees and a letter confirming that the vouchers have been intimated to the party found liable in expenses (r. 42.2(1)); but r. 42.2(2) provides that the auditor may fix a diet even though the provision for vouchers or letter or both have not been complied with. This is notified to the receiving and paying parties, who are required to attend the diet under certification that if the paying party does not appear to state any objections to the account the Auditor may proceed to tax the account forthwith.

A strict time-table for, and written specification of, the points of objection are now required: r.42.1(4) and (5). The Auditor has a similar discretion to that of the court in r.2.1 to relieve a party from the consequences of a failure to comply with these requirements (which is that the objections will not be considered: r.42.2(5)) r.42.2(6). These provisions replace para 4.1 and 4.2 of P.N. No. 3 of 1993.

At the diet the Auditor hears parties orally on the points of objections and he will usually give his decisions on these as they arise, but he may require to take time to consider them along with information given to him at the diet.

It is the duty of parties appearing at the diet to make full submissions to the Auditor to help him in reaching decisions: *Griffiths v. Kerr* 1992 S.L.T. 1024.

---

[1] Rule 42.2 substituted by S.S.I. 2011 No. 402 para. 3 (effective 1st January 2012).
[2] Rule 42.2(7) as amended by S.S.I. 2019 No. 74 r. 4 (effective 29th April 2019).

A tender of expenses prior to taxation does not entitle the paying party to the expenses of attendance at the diet of taxation even when the amount taxed is less than the amount tendered: *Gilmour's Tutor v. Renfrew C.C.* 1970 S.L.T.(Notes) 47.

Before the Auditor completes his taxation of the account he adds a charge in respect of fee fund dues: see note 42.2.5. The fee is added to the taxed account. The Auditor taxes off a sum proportionate to the amount taxed off from the account, so that the receiving party recovers only that proportion of the fee fund dues he has to pay which bears to the net amount of the account after taxation.

"INTIMATE".

For methods, see r. 16.7.

42.2.2

"ALL VOUCHERS, DOCUMENTS, DRAFTS OR COPIES OF DOCUMENTS".

At the diet the Auditor is entitled to see all necessary documentation and to receive such information as he may require to enable him to complete the taxation of the account: on documentation, see also P.N. No. 3 of 1993, para. 5. The Auditor cannot allow an outlay which has not been adequately vouched: *Goldie v. Mohr*, 18th November 1992 (1993 G.W.D. 1-40). The paying party is entitled to see receipts and vouchers in respect of all outlays claimed: formerly r. 42.16, Table of Fees, Chap. II, para. 6. All vouchers should be numbered separately and correspondingly numbered in the account: P.N. No. 3 of 1993, para. 6.

42.2.3

As far as charges for professional and skilled witnesses are concerned, the Auditor requires to see full details of the work done, the time taken to do it, and the hourly rate claimed for it. An interlocutor must have been pronounced certifying them as skilled persons: see r. 42.13A. The court may, on cause shown, allow late certification: *Mains v. Uniroyal Englebert Tyres Ltd (No. 2)* 1995 S.C. 538. The Auditor has no such discretion: *Clark v. Laddaws Ltd* 1994 S.L.T. 792.

As far as an employed witness is concerned, the Auditor requires to see satisfactory evidence of lost wages or remuneration. This information will usually take the form of a certificate from the employer on his notepaper stating the actual (net) loss sustained by the witness.

In the case of a witness who is self-employed, the Auditor will have to be satisfied that the witness has sustained a loss; therefore, the vouching must show objective information as to the amount of the actual net loss.

Claims can be made only for those witnesses who have actually given evidence or whose names have been noted in the Minute of Proceedings as having been in attendance or as having been held as concurring with a witness who has given evidence.

If an item is challenged and the necessary information is not made available to the Auditor at the diet of taxation, the Auditor may disallow it entirely. If satisfactory vouching has been exhibited before the diet of taxation to the paying party, in response to his request for it (see r. 42.16, Table of Fees, Chap. II, para. 6), the Auditor may modify or tax off completely the receiving party's fee for attendance at the taxation. If the paying party has not requested sight of a voucher in respect of any outlay charged in the account, then he will be deemed to have accepted that charge.

"4PM ON THE FOURTH BUSINESS DAY BEFORE THE DIET OF TAXATION".

The phrase in r. 42.2(1A) in its previous form (not later than 3 working days prior to the diet of taxation) was not felicitously drafted. In *Coyle v. Auditor of the Court of Session* , 2006 S.L.T. 1045 (OH), the court proceeded, after discussion, on the basis that it meant the working day of the Auditor whose office closes at 4pm (objections being lodged at 4.46pm at the end of the fourth day). It was held in a judicial review that, though technically late (on the basis that there was no gap between the end of a working day and the beginning of the next, they were at most one minute late), the Auditor had acted unreasonably in exercising his discretion (presumably that in r. 42.2(6)). No doubt as a consequence of this case, and possibly the criticism in this annotation, the wording has been changed to "4pm on the fourth business day". A "business day" is now defined in r. 42.2(8).

42.2.3A

OBJECTIONS TO ACCOUNTS.

By 4.00pm on the fourth business day before the diet the Auditor must receive a note of all outstanding points of objection to items in the account and a copy of it must also be sent to the receiving party: r.42.2(4). Where it is intended to refer to any authorities at the diet, prior notification of these should also be given both to the other party and the Auditor. The Auditor will not expect to be addressed on any points of objection not previously intimated both to him and the other party.

42.2.4

At the diet the Auditor hears parties orally on the points of objection and he will usually give his decisions on these as they arise, but he may require to take time to consider them along with information given to him at the diet. It is the duty of parties appearing at the diet to make full submissions to the Auditor to help him in reaching decisions: *Griffiths v. Kerr* 1992 S.L.T. 1024.

The Auditor may, however, at his own instance, report or reserve points of objection for consideration by the court either during the taxation or in his report at the conclusion of it.

If the Auditor sustains an objection to any extent to an item in the account, he records his decision by marking in the left-hand margin of the account the amount disallowed or abated.

Fee.

42.2.5

The fee for taxing the account is payable on issue of the Auditor's report. For fee, see Court of Session etc. Fees Order 1984, Table of Fees, Pt III, I, item 1(b) [SI 1984/256, Table as amended, pp. C 1202 et seq.]. The fee is a fixed sum for accounts under £300, and £4 for every additional £100 of the gross amount of the account lodged for taxation.

Lodging dues and fee fund dues must be paid to the Auditor's office. The Auditor's office issues invoices for the collection of lodging dues and fee fund dues are paid on taxation of the account. Party litigants must pay cash when lodging dues or fee fund dues are incurred.

Report of taxation

42.3

42.3.—(1)[1] The Auditor must—

    (a) prepare a statement of the amount of expenses as taxed;

    (b)[2] transmit the process of the cause, the taxed account and the statement to the appropriate Department of the Office of Court; and

    (c) on the day on which the documents mentioned in sub-paragraph (b) are transmitted, intimate that fact and the date of the statement to each party to whom the Auditor intimated the diet of taxation.

(2)[3] The party found entitled to expenses shall, within seven days after the date of receipt of intimation under paragraph (1)(c), exhibit the taxed account, or send a copy of it, to the party found liable to pay the expenses.

Deriv. RCS 1965, r. 349(1) substituted by SI 1983/826

"STATEMENT OF THE AMOUNT OF EXPENSES".

42.3.1

The report of the taxation, which is prepared by the Auditor, commences with a reference to each of the interlocutor(s) awarding expenses to the party covered by items contained in the taxed account, specifies the total in words and figures of the amount of the taxed account and names the party who has been found liable to pay the taxed expenses. The report which forms a step in the process is not borrowable.

"TRANSMIT THE PROCESS OF THE CAUSE, THE TAXED ACCOUNT AND THE REPORT".

42.3.2

This is done by a court messenger taking the process from the office of the Auditor with a transmission book to the department from which the process came. The entry in the transmission book for the cause is receipted and returned to the office of the Auditor.

"INTIMATE".

42.3.3

For methods, see r. 16.7.

"WITHIN SEVEN DAYS".

42.3.4

The date from which the period is calculated is not counted.

"SEND A COPY OF IT, TO THE PARTY FOUND LIABLE".

42.3.5

As the Auditor's taxations appear on only the process copy of the account the receiving party is obliged to send the taxed account, or a full copy of it, to the paying party within seven days after the date of the Auditor's report: r. 42.3(2). This gives respective parties time to decide whether to accept the taxations or take a note of objection to the report within 14 days after the date of the report (see r. 42.4(1)).

"Send" includes deliver: r. 1.3(1) (definition of "send").

MOTION FOR APPROVAL OF REPORT AND DECREE IN TERMS OF IT.

42.3.6

Where the party found liable for the expenses is not an assisted person, it is not usually necessary for the party entitled to the expenses to enrol a motion for approval of the report and for decree in terms of it because of the interlocutor containing the decerniture against the paying party for the expenses as taxed. In such a case all that is necessary is for the Extractor, when the application for an extract is made, to enter the taxed amount in the extract of the interlocutor decerning for expenses as taxed.

Where the party found liable for the expenses is legally aided, on receipt of the taxed account the receiving party may enrol a motion for approval of the report and for decree in terms of it after expiry of the days within which a party can lodge a note of objection or modification (14 days: see rr. 42.4(1) and 42.6(2)).

---

[1] As substituted by S.S.I. 2019 No. 74 r. 4 (effective 29th April 2019).

[2] Rule 42.3(1)(b) and (2) amended by S.S.I. 2011 No. 402 para. 4 (effective 1st January 2012)

[3] Rule 42.3(1)(b) and (2) amended by S.S.I. 2011 No. 402 para. 4 (effective 1st January 2012).

Objections to report of the Auditor

42.4.—[1](1)[2] Any party to a cause who has appeared or been represented at the diet of taxation may object to the Auditor's statement by lodging in process a note of objection within 14 days after the date of the statement.

(2)[3] A party lodging a note of objection shall—

(a) intimate a copy of the note and a motion under subparagraph (b) to the Auditor and to any party who appeared or was represented at the diet of taxation;

(b) apply by motion for an order allowing the note to be received; and

(c) intimate forthwith to the Auditor a copy of the interlocutor pronounced on a motion under subparagraph (b).

(2A)[4] Within 14 days after the date of receipt of intimation under paragraph (2)(c), the Auditor shall lodge a minute stating the reasons for his or her decision in relation to the items to which objection is taken in the note.

(3) After the minute of the Auditor has been lodged in process, the party who lodged the note of objection shall, in consultation with any other party wishing to be heard, arrange with the Keeper of the Rolls for a diet of hearing before the appropriate court.

(4) At the hearing on the note of objection, the court may—

(a) sustain or repel any objection in the note or remit the account of expenses to the Auditor for further consideration; and

(b) find any party liable in the expenses of the procedure on the note.

(5) *[Omitted by S.S.I. 2011 No. 402 para. 5 (effective 1st January 2012).]*

Deriv. RCS 1965, r. 349(2) substituted by SI 1992/1433 (r. 42.4(1)), r. 349(3) substituted by SI 1983/826 and amended by SI 1991/1157 (r. 42.4(2)), and r. 349(4) to (6) substituted by SI 1983/826 (r. 42.4(3) to (5))

GENERAL NOTE.

Rule 42.4 is designed to deal with objections to specific items in the auditor's report or statement. The rule does not envisage that there will be disputed questions of evidence or that there will be a challenge because of some fundamental irregularity: *Urquhart v. Ayrshire and Arran Health Board*, 2000 S.L.T. 829 (OH). "The audit is not a process in which the disappointed party ... can re-open the substantive issues which have been dealt with by the court. Nor can it be used to question the orders for expenses on the basis of which it proceeds. The only purpose of the audit is to ensure that the expenses claimed by the successful party ... in respect of the matters covered by the order for expenses, are proper and reasonable in accordance with the rules of court and established case law": *Kenneil v Scottish Legal Complaints Commission*, 2018 S.L.T. 244 per Lord Glennie.

Before taking or replying to a note of objection(s) consideration should be given to whether or not any principle is involved, since the expenses of the note of objections which may be awarded against the unsuccessful party may equal or exceed the sum in dispute. If on reflection the party, whose objection was sustained by the Auditor, no longer wishes to insist in the objection that should be intimated to the Auditor as soon as possible to minimise expense.

Parties can at any time consent in a request to the Auditor to tax an account at an agreed sum with fee fund dues in addition.

The court can only interfere with the decision of the Auditor if he misdirected himself as to the considerations which regulate his discretion (irrelevant material taken into account, relevant material not taken into account, he misunderstood or misdirected himself as to the facts or law): *Wood v. Miller* 1960 S.C. 86, 98 per LJ-C Thomson. The procedure is limited in scope and the court cannot carry out a complete rehearing of matters debated before the Auditor and substitute its own assessment; and the court's practice was not to hear oral evidence about what happened during taxation: *Tods Murray, WS v. Arakin Ltd (No.2)* 2002 S.C.L.R. 759 (OH), 764, para. [12]. See also *Shanley v. Stewart* 2019 S.L.T. 1090 (First Div.), 1095, para. [25]; *Kirkwood v. Thelem Assurances* 2022 S.L.T. 1016 (OH) (English solicitors' fees disallowed).

---

[1] Rule 42.4 amended by S.S.I. 2011 No. 402 para. 5 (effective 1st January 2012).
[2] As amended by S.S.I. 2019 No. 74 r. 4 (effective 29th April 2019).
[3] Rule 42.4 amended by S.S.I. 2011 No. 402 para. 5 (effective 1st January 2012).
[4] Rule 42.4 amended by S.S.I. 2011 No. 402 para. 5 (effective 1st January 2012).

"NOTE OF OBJECTION".

42.4.2   R. 15.2 (applications by note) does not apply to a note of objection: r. 15.2(4). The note must specify the grounds of objection and the appropriate alteration sought: *Crossan v. Caledonian Railway Co.* (1902) 5 F. 187, 190 per Lord Trayner; *Mowbray v. Kirkcaldy D.C.* , 10th December 1993 (Extra Div.), unreported, 1994 G.W.D. 3-153. The note need not be signed: r. 4.2(9)(f).

"LODGE IN PROCESS".

42.4.3   The note of objection is lodged in person or by post (P.N. No. 4 of 1994, paras 1 and 8) in process as a step of process (see rr. 4.4 and 4.6).

"WITHIN 14 DAYS".

42.4.4   It may be possible to persuade the court to exercise its dispensing power under r. 2.1 to allow late lodging of a note of objection, but mere oversight to lodge the note within the required period may not of itself be a good reason to excuse more especially as it further delays payment of expenses. In any event, if an interlocutor has been pronounced approving the Auditor's report and decerning for expenses, no note of objection may be lodged.

The date from which the period is calculated is not counted. Where the last day falls on a Saturday or Sunday or a public holiday on which the Office of Court is closed, the next available day is allowed: r. 1.3(7). For office hours and public holidays, see note 3.1.2.

"INTIMATE".

42.4.5   For methods, see r. 16.7.

"MOTION".

42.4.6   For motions, see Chap. 23.

"MINUTE".

42.4.7   R. 15.1 does not apply as the minute is not an application to the court. The minute is headed with the instance of the cause. Unless the reasons are very short the Auditor gives his reasons in an appendix.

"INTIMATE FORTHWITH TO THE AUDITOR".

42.4.8   On the meaning of "forthwith", see *Brown v. Magistrates of Bonnyrigg and Lasswade* 1936 S.C. 258, 265 per L.P. Normand (it must be construed according to the circumstances).

"ARRANGE WITH THE KEEPER OF THE ROLLS FOR A DIET".

42.4.9   Once the Auditor has lodged his minute it is the responsibility of the party who lodged the note of objections to consult immediately with any other party wishing to be heard and arrange with the Keeper of the Rolls for a diet of hearing before the appropriate court. The Keeper must be informed whether it is sought to have the diet assigned to a particular judge and, if so, the reason for it: P.N. No. 1 of 1994. As the procedure involves delay, it should be carried through with the utmost expedition since it prevents the receiving party from obtaining even the undisputed amount of expenses as taxed. Interest on expenses runs only from the date of the decree of the taxed amount: *Dalmahoy & Wood v. Magistrates of Brechin* (1859) 21 D. 210.

Although it may be necessary to have the note heard by a particular judge, it may not be necessary to delay the hearing so that counsel previously instructed can conduct it. It is always open to a party to enrol for a hearing on the note if he considers that the other party is unreasonably delaying it.

"HEARING ON THE NOTE OF OBJECTION".

42.4.10   As the Auditor is not present at the hearing on the note of objections, the party whose objection was sustained on taxation and objected to in the note should appear at the hearing in support of it, but the court will not automatically grant the note of objection if there is no contradictor. Although a note of objections has been lodged, it remains open to parties to resolve objections informally, and have the note refused or agree by joint minute with a request to the court that the Auditor give effect to the agreement reached. In the absence of any such agreement the court will hear parties on the note and the Auditor's minute. It may sustain or repel any objection or remit the account to the Auditor for further consideration.

The procedure is limited in scope and the court cannot carry out a complete rehearing of matters debated before the Auditor and substitute its own assessment; and the court's practice was not to hear oral evidence about what happened during taxation: *Tods Murray, WS v. Arakin Ltd (No.2)* , 5th April 2002, 2002 G.W.D. 13-420 (OH). The possibility of factual disputes cannot be ruled out, but the correct procedure is for the hearing to proceed by way of legal submissions and if factual issues arose it would be necessary to address at that point how to resolve them: *Tods Murray, WS*, above. On the grounds on which the court can interfere, see last paragraph of note 42.4.1.

Once the court has ruled on the note the successful party must move for the expenses of the hearing immediately thereafter and before the interlocutor dealing with it is signed. Where the Auditor has himself reported or reserved a point for the consideration of the court, the court usually makes no award of expenses.

RECLAIMING.

The decision of the Lord Ordinary on a note of objection may be reclaimed against with leave of the Lord Ordinary within seven days after the date of the decision: r. 38.4(5). Subject to r. 38.5, leave must be sought, and the reclaiming motion if leave granted must be marked, within seven days.

42.4.11

While it is competent to reclaim against the decision of the Lord Ordinary on a matter of expenses, such motions are not encouraged unless a point of principle is involved: *Aird v. School Board of Tarbert* 1907 S.C. 22, 24 per Lord McLaren; *Ramm v. Lothian and Borders Fire Board* 1994 S.C. 226; see also *Gray v. Babcock Power Ltd* 1990 S.L.T. 693, 694K-L per L.P. Hope.

Interest on expenses

42.4A.—[1](1) At any time before extract of a decree for payment of expenses as taxed by the Auditor the court may, on the application of the party to whom expenses are payable, grant decree against the party decerned against for payment of interest on the taxed expenses, or any part thereof, from a date no earlier than 28 days after the date on which the account of expenses was lodged.

42.4A

(2) Paragraph (1) is without prejudice to the court's other powers in relation to expenses.

"ON THE APPLICATION OF THE PARTY"

Presumably, the application is made by motion.

42.4A.1

"INTEREST"

On interest on judicial expenses, see note 7.7.5.

42.4A.2

The practice has been for the Extractor to add interest to the taxed expenses from the date of the Auditor's report. Rule 42.4A(1) makes provision for application for interest from a date no earlier than 28 days after the date of lodging of the account of expenses. Having regard to the saving provision in r. 42.4A(2), it is not clear whether the practice is superseded by the rule.

Modification or disallowance of expenses

42.5.—(1) In any cause where the court finds a party entitled to expenses, the court may direct that expenses shall be subject to such modification as the court thinks fit.

42.5

(2) *[Revoked by S.S.I. 2019 No. 74 r. 4 (effective 29th April 2019).]*

Deriv. R.C.S. 1965, r. 347(c) (r. 42.5(1))

"MODIFICATION".

Where the court has awarded expenses subject to modification it is the duty of the Auditor to tax the account without regard to modification and then to give effect to the modification in the final sum taxed: *McIlroy & Sons v. Tharsis Sulphur and Copper Co.* (1879) 6 R. 1119; *Arthur v. Lindsay* (1895) 22 R. 904. Where a tender specified the amount of expenses to be paid it was not considered to be a judicial tender but nevertheless when the pursuer recovered less than the sum offered he was found liable to the defender in the expenses of the cause modified to one half: *Banks v. D.R.G. plc* 1988 S.L.T. 825.

42.5.1

The general rule is that a party put to the expense of vindicating his rights is entitled to recover the expense from the person by whom it was created: *Howitt v. Alexander & Sons Ltd* 1948 S.C. 124; *William Nimmo & Co. Ltd v. Russell Construction Co. Ltd (No. 2) (2nd Div.)* 1997 S.L.T. 122. It is not incompatible with art.6 of ECHR to award expenses to a successful party: *Ackerman v. Logan's Exrs (No.2)* , November 1, 2001, 2001 G.W.D. 35-1346 (Extra Div.). While it is permissible to take into account time spent on matters on which the party awarded expenses was unsuccessful, that did not necessarily lead to any diminution of expenses: *Howitt*, above. Where a party has misjudged the correct scope and character of his claim and where the other party advanced a number of points which failed to affect their case and thereby both parties contributed to the length and expense of the proof, no expenses were found due to or by either party: *Elf Caledonia Ltd v. London Bridge Engineering Ltd (No. 2)* , 10th December 1997 (1998 G.W.D. 2-86). In *Gray v. Lanarkshire Health Board* 1998 S.L.T. 1378 Lord Abernethy modified the account of expenses by 15 per cent as a substantial part of the pursuer's case was misconceived prolonging the proof by about a day.

A pursuer who brings his action in the Court of Session may, if he receives only a trivial award in relation to the expenses, suffer modification of his account: *McIntosh v. British Railways Board (No. 1)* , 1990 S.C. 338, 1990 S.L.T. 637 (First Div.) In that case, Hope, L.P., said at p. 343: "[I]f the pleadings show that the pursuer could possibly recover more than the upper limit [of sheriff court privative jurisdiction] then the action should be regarded as appropriate to the Court of Session unless some other factor is present which shows that the nature of the particular case is such that it is appropriate for it to be dealt with in the sheriff court". The wish to have a jury trial in order to test the adequacy of the level of dam-

---

[1] As inserted by S.S.I. 2019 No. 74 r. 4 (effective 29th April 2019).

ages awarded by the courts regarded as being too low is not in itself adequate justification for selecting the Court of Session: *Smillie v. Lanarkshire Health Board*, 8th May 1996, unreported (1996 G.W.D. 22-1288). The court may award expenses limited to one of the sheriff court scales (with or without sanction of counsel) where decree is for a small amount. While the amount of any settlement or award is relevant, the proper approach is to determine whether the initial choice of forum of the Court of Session was justified in the circumstances known to the pursuer's advisers when the action was brought having regard to the high level of expenses likely to be incurred by bringing the action there, judgment on the matter being assisted by consideration of events subsequent to that date including the result of the case: *Coyle v. William Fairey Installations Ltd* 1991 S.C. 16; see also *Kinnaird v. Walter Alexander (Falkirk) Ltd*, 28th June 1995 (unreported), 1995 G.W.D. 32-1648), where the court refused to modify expenses. The size of the award is not therefore the only test: see, e.g. *Campbell v. SCA Packaging Ltd (No. 2)* 1995 G.W.D. 23-1253; *Gordon v. Strathclyde Buses Ltd* 1995 S.L.T. 1019 (case settled at less than sheriff court summary cause maximum limit. Expenses modified to sheriff court ordinary cause scale on ground that award might have been just outside sheriff court privative jurisdiction of £1,500). The saga continues of the court, on the one hand, not wishing to be troubled with reparation actions of small value, and on the other hand of awarding expenses on the Court of Session scale rather than a sheriff court scale in such actions brought under Chap. 43 procedure, on the anecdotal submissions that the Court of Session procedure is cheaper and quicker than the sheriff court procedure: see *Galbraith v. First Glasgow (No. 1) Ltd*, 2006 S.L.T. 317 (OH), and cases there cited. In *Hylands v. Glasgow City Council*, 2008 S.L.T. 988 (OH), Lord Drummond Young said, obiter, that in the ordinary case it would be appropriate to modify expenses where the award or settlement was less than the limit of privative jurisdiction of the sheriff court; but in the special circumstances of that case (summons signeted before privative jurisdiction increased from £1,500 to £5,000 but served after the increase (a tender of £2,500 being accepted)), expenses would not be modified. Special circumstances were also found in *Emerson v. The Edrington Group Ltd* 2009 S.L.T. 681 (OH) where, although the settlement was for £2,000, it was reasonable for the agents to conclude that the case would have attracted damages at a greater level than the sheriff court summary cause limit of £5,000.

Where a defender achieved a measure of success in showing that the level of support was considerably less than the pursuer had claimed in her evidence which was exposed as unreliable in regard to matters within her knowledge and documents under her control, her award of expenses was restricted to three quarters: *Bhatia v. Tribax Ltd* 1994 S.L.T. 1201.

The fact that a pursuer has claimed custody in a concurrent petition for custody and an action of divorce will not necessarily result in a refusal or modification of expenses: *Shishodia v. Shishodia (No. 3)*, 13th June 1995, unreported (1995 G.W.D. 34-1742).

The court still has power to modify where a tender offers expenses of process to date: *Neilson v. Motion* 1992 S.L.T. 124; *McKenzie v. H.D. Fraser & Sons* 1990 S.L.T. 629.

There must be an award of expenses against a party before he can seek modification of them. So, when a minute of abandonment is lodged, as no "award" of expenses falls to be made against the pursuer before or as a condition precedent of dismissal, the court has no jurisdiction to modify expenses: *Mica Insulator Co. Ltd v. Bruce Peebles & Co. Ltd* 1907 S.C. 1293; see also *Frost v. Unity Trust Bank plc* 1997 S.L.T. 1358. If the taxed amount of the expenses is not paid within a reasonable time the receiving party is entitled to enrol for absolvitor: *Collum v. Glasgow Corporation* 1964 S.L.T. 199.

Where the court proposes to restrict the expenses of a cause to the sheriff court scale and is also prepared to sanction the employment of counsel, it should be asked to specify if that includes both senior and junior counsel or solely one of them. It is competent for senior counsel to appear without junior counsel: see Resolution of the Faculty of Advocates, 4th February 1977: see 1977 S.L.T. (News) 142.

For modification of expenses against legally aided persons, see r.42.6.

The principle that expenses follow success is not applied with full rigour in divorce (or other family) actions: *Little v. Little* 1990 S.L.T. 785, 790C per L.P. Hope. For recent examples, see *Whittome v. Whittome (No. 2)* 1994 S.L.T. 130 (to wife defender); *Macdonald v. Macdonald* 1995 S.L.T. 72, 75F per Lord Caplan (60% to wife pursuer); *Adams v. Adams (No. 2)* 1997 S.L.T. 150 (husband defender awarded expenses of proof; otherwise, no expenses due to or by); *De Winton v. De Winton*, 29th November 1996, unreported (1996 G.W.D. 2-58) (no expenses due to or by).

Leave to lodge productions late may result in the party lodging them being held liable in the whole expenses of the cause to date: *Readman v. McGregor*, 15th January, 1997, unreported (1997 G.W.D. 8-302).

That a cause cannot proceed by reason of a judge's other judicial commitments does not justify any special disposal of associated expenses: *Independent Pension Trustee Ltd v. L A W Construction Co. Ltd (No. 2)*, 17th December, 1996, unreported (1997 G.W.D. 8-336).

DISALLOWANCE OF EXPENSES BY AUDITOR IN RESPECT OF A MATTER.

42.5.2   Rule 42.5(2) is a statement of the current practice. Although the court may itself award expenses against a party who has been shown to have caused unnecessary expense through failure to observe correct procedure (*Franchetti v. Franchetti* 6th July 1993, unreported), the Auditor is empowered to tax off all expenses incurred by a party unnecessarily or due to that party's own fault or where in his opinion it appears that a party has been unsuccessful in any part of a cause: *Aitken v. Classen* 1928 S.C. 628; and see *Mica Insulator Co. Ltd v. Bruce Peebles & Co. Ltd* 1907 S.C. 1293, 1300 per L.P. Dunedin.

Where the court awarded full expenses to the pursuer in a cause where the major part of the proof was taken up with matters in which the pursuer failed, the court on a reclaiming motion allowed the defender one half of his expenses: *Alvis v. Harrison* 1989 S.C. 136; see also *William Nimmo & Co. Ltd v. Russell*

Construction Ltd (No. 2) (2nd Div.) 1997 S.L.T. 122, a substantial part of pursuers' claim had been rejected and the defenders found liable in expenses, but excluding therefrom one half of the expenses incurred by the pursuer which were occasioned by the proof. See also *Whittome v. Whittome* above, where partial expenses were awarded to successful defender.

In *Elliot v. J. & C. Finney (No. 2)* 1989 S.L.T. 241, upheld in *Elliot v. J. & C. Finney* 1989 S.L.T. 605, an award of full expenses was made after a preliminary proof on a plea of time-bar in which the pursuer persuaded the court to exercise its discretion to allow the claim to proceed under section 19A of the Prescription and Limitation (Scotland) Act 1973, although the pursuer had amended just prior to the proof to bring in a point about the date of the start of the triennium on which point he failed and notwithstanding the time taken up by the evidence on the unsuccessful point. In such a case it would not be open to the Auditor to tax off expenses in respect of the unsuccessful work.

Where there is a general finding of expenses in favour of a party who was unsuccessful in an earlier part of the cause and in respect of which the court has made no finding of expenses, it may be difficult to persuade the Auditor that r. 42.5(2) applies merely because a plea was refused since that does not of itself signify lack of success in a particular branch or part of the case. It is therefore essential to bring fully to the attention of the court any special circumstances or conditions by reference to which the exercise of its discretion should be guided: *Howitt v. Alexander & Sons Ltd* 1948 S.C. 124. Similarly where the court finds expenses of any part of the cause to be expenses in the cause, the Auditor has no discretion in the matter even if it is submitted to him that the party was truly unsuccessful in that part of the cause. It is, therefore, essential to ensure that the court, when considering the question of expenses, is fully aware that by making an award of expenses "to be expenses in the cause", it is thereby removing the Auditor's discretion: *Turner v. Thomson* 1991 G.W.D. 19-1159.

Where a defender has incurred expense between the date of lodging a minute of tender and the date of the minute of acceptance of it and he wishes to recover these expenses, he must seek these prior to the decerniture for expenses following the interponing of authority by the court to the minutes of tender and acceptance; it is too late to seek these expenses thereafter, even before the Auditor: *Wilson v. Pilgrim Systems plc* 1993 S.L.T. 1252; for a contrary view, see article at 1994 S.L.T.(News) 159. In a case where the pursuer had beaten two tenders (one in the Outer House and one in the Inner House), and the Inner House reduced the award made in the Outer House—but which award still exceeded the higher sum tendered—the defender was nevertheless awarded expenses. It was held that the ordinary rule that expenses followed success applied and the defender was entitled to the expenses of the reclaiming motion irrespective of whether the award was reduced to any figure tendered; the pursuer could have made an extra-judicial offer which, while not conclusive, might have been relevant to the question whether any expenses had been incurred unnecessarily: *Morrison v. Barton* 1994 S.C. 100.

Where a pursuer was successful at procedure roll as a result of crucial late adjustments to answers to a minute of amendment based on facts known to him before the action was raised, a finding of no expenses due to or by either party was made: *McSkimming v. The Royal Bank of Scotland plc*, 4th April 1996, unreported (1996 G.W.D. 31-1881).

Even though a party at a late stage in a cause successfully pleads an arbitration clause, that party will not be liable for the whole of the antecedent expenses caused by him, because the time for dealing with expenses is when the case is determined unless the case involves an exception of the rule that expenses follow success: *Presslie v. Cochrane McGregor Group Ltd* 1997 S.C. 159.

Where there has been divided success in a procedure roll debate expenses were made expenses in the cause: *Third v. North East Ice & Storage Co. Ltd (No. 2)*, 31st October 1996, unreported (1996 G.W.D. 37-2167).

Modification of expenses awarded against assisted persons

42.6.—(1) In a cause in which the court finds an assisted person liable in expenses, the court may, on the motion of any party to the cause, instead of remitting the account of expenses of the party in whose favour the finding is made to the Auditor for taxation, determine to what extent the liability of the assisted person for such expenses shall be modified under—

    (a)   section 2(6)(e) of the Legal Aid (Scotland) Act 1967; or

    (b)   section 18(2) of the Legal Aid (Scotland) Act 1986.

(2) Where a remit is made to the Auditor for taxation in a cause in which an assisted person is found liable in expenses, an application for modification under a statutory provision mentioned in paragraph (1) may be made by motion within 14 days after the date of the report of the Auditor made under rule 42.3 (report of taxation).

Deriv. R.C.S. 1965, r. 349(8) substituted by S.I. 1983 No. 826; P.N. January 16, 1970

<small>GENERAL NOTE.</small>

A legally assisted person may apply to the court to have modified (or assessed) his liability to pay the expenses of an unassisted person in whose favour the cause has been finally determined. The court may, without the necessity of having an account of expenses taxed, proceed to modify the expenses to a fixed sum or to nil. Section 18(2) of the Legal Aid (Scotland) Act 1986 (formerly s. 2(6)(e) of the Legal Aid

42.6

42.6.1

(Scotland) Act 1967) does not require that the account of expenses be taxed before a decision can be made on the question of modification and set-off, but there has to be sufficient financial information available to enable a proper decision to be made: *McInally v. Clackmannan D.C.* 1993 S.C. 314. The 1967 Act only has application to legal aid granted under that Act.

If the court does remit an account of expenses for taxation then the assisted person may, within 14 days of the date of the Auditor's report, ask the court to modify these expenses: r. 42.6(2).

The court must have regard to all the circumstances including the means of all the parties and their conduct in connection with the dispute in determining the amount; but the assisted person's house, wearing apparel, household furniture and the tools and implements of his trade or profession are not taken into account in assessing his means: 1986 Act s. 18(3). There must be an award of expenses by the court against the legally assisted person and he must be afforded a reasonable time to pay before the defender can enrol for absolvitor: *Collum v. Glasgow Corporation* 1964 S.L.T. 199. On "having regard to all the circumstances", see *Douglas v. Cunningham* 1966 S.L.T. (Notes) 7 (Motor Insurance Bureau behind legally assisted defender). On "the means of all the parties", see *Ballantyne v. Douglas* 1953 S.C. 258; *Todd v. Todd* 1966 S.L.T. 50; *Armstrong*, below. In considering means, the court is entitled to take any damages recovered into account: *MacKenzie v. Lothian and Borders Police* 1995 S.L.T. 1332. On "conduct in connection with the dispute", see *Burns v. James McHaffie & Sons Ltd* 1965 S.L.T. 238; *O'Donnell v. A.M. & G. Robertson* 1965 S.L.T. (Notes) 32; *Armstrong*, below; *Clelland v. Clelland* 1988 S.L.T. 674; *Cullen v. Cullen*, 22nd November 1996, unreported (1997 G.W.D. 259) (modification to £20,000 where conduct reprehensible).

The general principle governing modification is indicated in *Armstrong v. Armstrong* 1970 S.C. 161, 166 by the First Division: "The figure should not be so high as to render it for practical purposes impossible for the party, with the resources available to him, to meet the liability. It equally seems clear that it was not intended that the liability should as a matter of course be fixed at a nominal sum or even at nil." The matter is one of discretion. The award to the legally aided person may be taken into account: *McInally*, above. For a recent example see *Jack v. McIntyre's Exrs*, 1999 S.L.T. 85.

Failure to mark the steps of process with the words: "Assisted Person" following issue of a legal aid certificate as required by r. 3(1) of the A.S. (Civil Legal Aid Rules) 1987 [SI 1987/492] may result in the court not only pronouncing a finding of liability for expenses against the assisted person but also a decerniture for these expenses as taxed. This point is important because, once expenses have been decerned for, it is incompetent thereafter to apply for modification of the taxed expenses under s.18(2) of the 1986 Act: *Gilbert's Tr. v. Gilbert* 1988 S.L.T. 680; *Stewart v. Stewart* 1989 S.L.T. 80. It is therefore essential that the assisted person's solicitor mark the process appropriately immediately the legal aid certificate is issued; the legal aid certificate must, however, be lodged in process first.

Where a pursuer who is an assisted person abandons his action the court has no jurisdiction to modify his liability for expenses either under the legal aid provisions or at common law because there is no "award" of expenses made by the court: *Collum*, above (not following *Thompson v. Fairfield Shipbuilding and Engineering Co* 1954 S.C. 354); *Johnston v. Johnston*, 1985 S.L.T. 510, 512 per Lord Cowie.

Where a legally-aided pursuer accepted a tender but was found liable to the defender in the latter's expenses post-tender he was able to have his liability reduced to nil: *Ross v. McDermott International Inc* 1987 G.W.D 36-1284.

Rules in relation to the making of awards of expenses against assisted persons are in r. 4 of the A.S. (Civil Legal Aid Rules) 1987 (S.I. 1987 No. 492).

A successful party, if an unassisted person, may be entitled to claim expenses against the Legal Aid Fund (*Walker v. Walker*, 1987 S.L.T. 129); but only on conclusion of the whole case (*Moss v. Penman (No. 2)*, 1994 S.L.T. 602), and only if a motion under s. 19(1) of the 1986 Act is made to the court awarding expenses: see *Fulton v. Bell* Unreported 22nd November 1996 (1997 G.W.D. 1-29). The limitation imposed by *Moss*, above, does not apply in the House of Lords: *Herd v. Clyde Helicopters Ltd*, 1997 S.L.T. 672. Expenses out of the Fund may be made only if (a) an order for expenses could otherwise be made, (b) in the case of expenses in proceedings at first instance, the proceedings were instituted by the legally assisted person and the court is satisfied that the unassisted successful party will suffer financial hardship unless the order is made, and (c) in any case, it is just and equitable in all the circumstances that the award should be paid out of public funds. For recent cases of an award being made, see *Young v. Bohannon*, 2009 S.L.T. 928 (OH) and *Ashiq v Secretary of State for the Home Department*, 2016 S.C. 297 (Extra Div.). Under s.19(3)(b), regard has to had not to the nature of the organisation seeking the order but to the effect on its finances if the order were not made: *H v. B*, 2013 S.L.T. 681 (OH). It was observed, in that case, that, where an unassisted party's sole purpose was charity, an expenses award could cause it to be materially less able to fulfil that function, that would amount to financial hardship. In considering whether it was just and equitable to make an award, it was observed that the circumstances in which legal aid was granted and whether the party seeking the award had no choice but to enter the process were relevant.

Where a defender who is an assisted person enters into a joint minute agreeing to be found liable as an assisted person, he is entitled to seek modification of his liability: *Jeffrey v. Jeffrey*, 1987 S.L.T 488.

An appeal for re-assessment of the amount of an award of expenses to which s.18(2) of the 1986 Act applies may be made on a relevant change of circumstances within one year after the date of the award: 1986 Act s.20(4) and Civil Legal Aid (Scotland) Regulations 1987 (S.I. 1987 No. 331), reg. 38. It is thought that the application may be made by motion under this rule although the cause may no longer be depending (cf. r. 23.11); otherwise the application would have to be by petition by virtue of r. 14.2(h).

Article 26 of Sched. 1 to the Child Abduction and Custody Act 1985 (Hague Convention) does not apply to expenses not normally covered by legal aid: *Matznick v. Matznick* 1998 S.L.T. 636.

It is competent to reclaim against a decision on modification of expenses awarded against an assisted person: *Cullen v. Cullen* 2000 S.C. 396 (Ct of Five Judges) overruling in part *Todd v. Todd* 1966 S.L.T. 50. But as assessment is intended to be carried out by the Lord Ordinary, in the event of a successful reclaiming motion, the re-assessment of liability should be carried out by the Lord Ordinary subject to whatever directions the Inner House considers appropriate: *Cullen*, above.

"MOTION".

For motions, see Chap. 23.

42.6.2

Taxation of solicitors' own accounts

42.7.—[1, 2](1) Subject to section 61A(1) of the Solicitors (Scotland) Act 1980, the court may remit to the Auditor the account of a solicitor to his client—

42.7

    (a) where the account is for work done in relation to a cause in the Court of Session, on the motion of the solicitor or the client; or

    (b) in an action in which the solicitor or his representative sues the client for payment of the account.

(2) A motion under paragraph (1)(a) may be enrolled notwithstanding that final decree in the cause has been extracted.

(3) The account referred to in paragraph (1) shall—

    (a) be in such form as will enable the Auditor to establish the nature and extent of the work done to which the account relates;

    (b) detail the outlays incurred by the solicitor; and

    (c) be accompanied by such supporting material as is necessary to vouch the items in the account.

(4) The Auditor shall—

    (a) fix a diet of taxation not earlier than 14 days after the date on which he receives the account; and

    (b) intimate the diet to the solicitor.

(5) On receipt of intimation of the diet of taxation from the Auditor, the solicitor shall forthwith send to his client by registered post or the first class recorded delivery service—

    (a) a copy of the account to be taxed;

    (b) a copy of the interlocutor remitting the account; and

    (c) a notice in Form 42.7 of the date, time and place of the diet of taxation.

(6) In taxing an account remitted to him under paragraph (1), the Auditor—

    (a) shall allow a sum in respect of such work and outlays as have been reasonably incurred;

    (b) shall allow, in respect of each item of work and outlay, such sum as may be fair and reasonable having regard to all the circumstances of the case;

    (c) shall, in determining whether a sum charged in respect of an item of work is fair and reasonable, take into account any of the following factors:—

        (i) the complexity of the cause and the number, difficulty or novelty of the questions raised;

        (ii) the skill, labour, and specialised knowledge and responsibility required, of the solicitor;

        (iii) the time spent on the item of work and on the cause as a whole;

        (iv) the number and importance of any documents prepared or perused;

        (v) the place and circumstances (including the degree of expedition required) in which the work of the solicitor or any part of it has been done;

---

[1] As amended by S.S.I. 2019 No. 74 r. 4 (effective 29th April 2019).
[2] Rule 42.7 amended by S.S.I. 2011 No. 402 para. 6 (effective 1st January 2012).

    (vi)   the importance of the cause or the subject-matter of it to the client;

    (vii) the amount or value of money or property involved in the cause; and

    (viii) any informal agreement relating to fees;

   (d)   shall presume (unless the contrary is demonstrated to his satisfaction) that—

    (i)   an item of work or outlay was reasonably incurred if it was incurred with the express or implied approval of the client;

    (ii)   the fee charged in respect of an item of work or outlay was reasonable if the amount of the fee or the outlay was expressly or impliedly approved by the client; and

    (iii) an item of work or outlay was not reasonably incurred, or that the fee charged in respect of an item of work or outlay was not reasonable if the item of work, outlay or fee charged, was unusual in the circumstances of the case, unless the solicitor informed the client before carrying out the item of work or incurring the outlay that it might not be allowed (or that the fee charged might not be allowed in full) in a taxation in a cause between party and party; and

   (e)   may disallow any item of work or outlay which is not vouched to his satisfaction.

  (7) The Auditor must—

   (a)   prepare a statement of the fees and outlays as taxed;

   (b)   transmit the statement and the taxed account to the appropriate Department of the Office of Court; and

   (c)   send a copy of the statement to the solicitor and the client.

  (7A) The solicitor shall, within 7 days after the date of receipt of the statement under paragraph (7)(c), exhibit the taxed account, or send a copy of it, to his or her client.

  (8) The solicitor or his client may, where he or a representative attended the diet of taxation, state any objection to the Auditor's statement; and rule 42.4 (objections to report of the Auditor) shall apply to such objection as it applies to an objection under that rule.

Deriv. R.C.S. 1965, r. 350 substituted by S.I. 1992 No. 1433

GENERAL NOTE.

42.7.1   The court is not concerned with identifying the applicability of any of the heads in r. 42.7(6) in the taxation of a solicitor's business account with his client: *Bradnock v. Liston (No. 2)* 1994 S.L.T. 1195.

As to the Auditor's general power to recognise responsibility when taxing a solicitor's business account, see *Davidson & Syme, W.S. v. Booth* 1972 S.L.T. 122.

The power of the Auditor to allow a fee for special responsibility in appropriate circumstances was not abolished by the 1992 substitution of R.C.S. 1965, r. 350 and continued in R.C.S. 1994, r. 42.7. The discretion was neither expressly nor impliedly limited by r. 42.7(6): *Tods Murray W.S., v. McNamara*, 2007 S.C. 435; 2007 S.L.T. 687 (2nd Div.).

The solicitor's account must be lodged in process before the court will remit the account to the Auditor for taxation.

A certificate of audit is not a taxation—see *Law Society of Scotland's Table of Fees for Conveyancing and General Business*, Chapter 2.1 (d)—and must not be represented to the client or a court as such: *Rollo Davidson & McFarlane v. Anderson*, 18th February, 1997, unreported (1997 G.W.D. 12-522).

Although silent on the matter, r. 42.7(1) would have limited practical effect if the court could do nothing in the process of the original action to determine liability and grant decree for expenses between a solicitor and his client once the auditor had assessed and reported on the reasonableness of the expenses, and the court had such power even though the action itself was no longer in dependence: *Stuart v. Bulger*, 2008 S.L.T. 817 (OH).

"SUBJECT TO SECTION 61A(1) OF THE SOLICITORS (SCOTLAND) ACT 1980".

42.7.2   Where a solicitor and his client have reached agreement in writing as to the solicitor's fees it is not competent for the court, in any litigation arising out of a dispute as to the amount due under the agreement, to remit the solicitor's account for taxation: 1980 Act s. 61A(1) inserted by the Law Reform (Miscellaneous Provisions) (Scotland) Act 1990 s. 36(3).

"THE ACCOUNT OF A SOLICITOR TO HIS CLIENT".

It is the client's own solicitor's account which may be lodged, and that account may include as an outlay any account incurred to other solicitors employed by the client's solicitor. The employed solicitor, who is not directly the client's solicitor, has a right to be reimbursed by the instructing (Scottish) solicitor unless the employing solicitor has expressly disclaimed liability: Solicitors (Scotland) Act 1980 s. 30.

42.7.2A

"FINAL DECREE".

This is the decree disposing of the whole subject-matter of the cause including expenses: see note 4.15.2(2).

42.7.3

"NOT EARLIER THAN 14 DAYS AFTER", "WITHIN 7 DAYS AFTER".

The date from which the period is calculated is not counted.

42.7.4

"ANY INFORMAL AGREEMENT RELATING TO FEES".

Rule 42.7(6)(c)(viii) is a new factor to be considered. It may be that there was no written agreement about fees but that an hourly rate was quoted to which the client may have acquiesced.

42.7.5

FEE.

The fee for taxing the account is payable on issue of the Auditor's report. For fee, see Court of Session etc. Fees Order 1984, Table of Fees, Pt III, I, item 1(b) [S.I. 1984 No. 256, Table as amended, pp. C 1202 et seq.]. The fee is a fixed sum for accounts under £300, and £4 for every additional £100 of the gross amount of the account lodged for taxation.

42.7.6

Lodging dues and fee fund dues must be paid to the Auditor's office. The Auditor's office issues invoices for the collection of lodging dues and fee fund dues are paid on taxation of the account. Party litigants must pay cash when lodging dues or fee fund dues are incurred.

Part II – Fees of Solicitors

[Revoked by S.S.I. 2019 No. 74 r. 4 (effective 29th April 2019; applies in respect of proceedings commenced on or after 29th April 2019).]

[THE NEXT PARAGRAPH IS 42.17]

Part III – Fees in Speculative Causes

Fees of solicitors in speculative causes

42.17.—(1) Where—

42.17

    (a) any work is undertaken by a solicitor in the conduct of a cause for a client,

    (b) the solicitor and client agree that the solicitor shall be entitled to a fee for the work only if the client is successful in the cause, and

    (c) the agreement is that the fee of the solicitor for all work in connection with the cause is to be based on an account prepared as between party and party,

the solicitor and client may agree that the fees element in that account shall be increased by a figure not exceeding 100 per cent.

(2) The client of the solicitor shall be deemed to be successful in the cause where—

    (a) the cause has been concluded by a decree which, on the merits, is to any extent in his favour;

    (b) the client has accepted a sum of money in settlement of the cause; or

    (c) the client has entered into a settlement of any other kind by which his claim in the cause has been resolved to any extent in his favour.

(3) In paragraph (1), "the fees element" means all the fees in the account of expenses of the solicitor—

    (a) for which any other party in the cause other than the client of the solicitor has been found liable as taxed or agreed between party and party;

    (b) before the deduction of any award of expenses against the client; and

    (c) excluding the sums payable to the solicitor in respect of—

615

(i)   any fees payable for copying documents and the proportion of any session fee in the Table of Fees and posts and incidental expenses under rule 42.11;

(ii)   any additional fee allowed under rule 42.14 to cover the responsibility undertaken by the solicitor in the conduct of the cause; and

(iii)   any charges by the solicitor for his outlays.

Deriv. R.C.S. 1965, r. 350A inserted by S.I. 1992 No. 1898

GENERAL NOTE.

42.17.1   Rule 42.17 (formerly R.C.S. 1965, r. 350A) arises out of s. 61A(3) of the Solicitors (Scotland) Act 1980 (inserted by s. 36(3) of the Law Reform (Miscellaneous Provisions) (Scotland) Act 1990), which provides for a solicitor and his client to agree, in relation to a litigation undertaken on a speculative basis, that in the event of success the solicitor's fee chargeable against his client may be increased by such a percentage as has been agreed. The uplift is based on the taxed or agreed expenses recovered from the paying party but excluding copyings and any additional fee allowed.

In relation to the fees of counsel a similar rule for an increase not exceeding 100 per cent is provided for in A.S. (Fees of Advocates in Speculative Actions) 1992 S.I. 1992 No. 1897.

Part IV – Remuneration of reporters

Remuneration of reporters

42.18   **42.18.**—[1](1) This rule applies where any matter in a cause is remitted by the court, at its own instance or on the motion of a party, to a reporter or other person to report to the court.

(2) The party liable to the reporter or other person for payment of that person's fee, and reimbursement of that person's outlays, is—

(a)   where the court makes the remit at its own instance, the party so ordained by the court;

(b)   where the court makes the remit on the motion of a party, that party.

(3) The solicitor for the liable party is personally liable in the first instance for payment of such fee and outlays.

(4) This rule applies subject to—

(a)   any other provision in these Rules;

(b)   any order of the court; or

(C)   any agreement between a party and that party's solicitor.

GENERAL NOTE.

Rule 42.18 makes a rule what was a practice requiring words that had to be set out in every interlocutor making the remit to the reporter.

---

[1] Part IV and r. 42.18 as inserted by S.S.I. 2019 No. 74 r. 4 (effective 29th April 2019).

Chapter 42A Case Management of Certain Personal Injuries Actions

PART IV

SPECIAL PROVISIONS IN RELATION TO PARTICULAR PROCEEDINGS

Chapter 42A[1]

Case management of certain personal injuries actions

Application and interpretation of this Chapter

42A.1.—(1) Subject to paragraph (3), this Chapter applies to actions—

    (a)   proceeding as ordinary actions by virtue of rule 43.1A (actions based on clinical negligence) or rule 43.5 (motions to dispense with timetable);

    (b)   appointed to the procedure in this Chapter under paragraph (2).

(2) The Lord Ordinary may, after considering the likely complexity of an action and being satisfied that the efficient determination of the action would be served by doing so, appoint an action to which Chapter 43 (actions of damages for, or arising from, personal injuries) applies (including actions relating to catastrophic injuries) to the procedure in this Chapter.

(3) Any party to an action may apply by motion to have the action withdrawn from the procedure in this Chapter.

(4) No motion under paragraph (3) is to be granted unless the court is satisfied that there are exceptional reasons for not following the procedure in this Chapter.

(5) In this Chapter—

"personal injuries" and "personal injuries action" have the meanings assigned to them in rule 43.1(2) (interpretation of Chapter 43);

"proof" includes jury trial.

(6) Rule 22.3 (closing record) does not apply to an action to which this Chapter relates.

GENERAL NOTE.

    Chapter 42A was inserted by A.S. (R.C.S.A. No. 3) (Miscellaneous) 2013 [S.S.I. 2013 No. 120] and applies to actions raised after May 1, 2013. It was replaced by A.S. (R.C.S. 1994 A.) (Case Management of Certain Personal Injuries Actions) 2019 [S.S.I. 2019 No. 404] and applies to actions commenced on or after March 1, 2020 [S.S.I. 2019 No. 404, para. 3(2).] The court may direct that Chap. 42A applies to an action raised before that date after giving all parties an opportunity to be heard. The purpose of the Chapter is to allow the court to identify and resolve issues that are known reasons for seeking variation of the timetable or discharge of the proof: P.N. No. 2 of 2019, para. 7. It applies to actions based on clinical negligence (see r. 43.1A) or actions in which the timetable for personal injury actions has been dispensed with (see r. 43.5) and have been appointed to the procedure in this Chapter having regard to the complexity and to its efficient determination (r. 42A.1(2)).

    P.N. No. 2 of 2019 provides guidance on the application of this Chapter. This, like other practice notes, follows the (bad) practice of paraphrasing a rule, sometimes misleadingly. Failure to comply with a requirement in the practice note may be met in expenses: para. 41.

"CLINICAL NEGLIGENCE"

    The expression "clinical negligence" is defined in r. 43.1A(9).

42A.1

42A.1.1

42A.1.2

---

[1] Chapter 42A inserted by S.S.I. 2013 No. 120 (effective 1st May 2013) and substituted by S.S.I. 2019 No. 404 (effective 1st March 2020).

Lodging of closed record etc.

42A.2   **42A.2.**—¹(1)   The pursuer must, no later than 14 days after the date on which the record is closed—

(a)   lodge three copies of the closed record in process;

(b)   at the same time, send a copy of the closed record to every other party.

(2)   A closed record is to consist of the pleadings of the parties and the interlocutors pronounced in the action.

No later than 14 days after

42A.2.1   The time expires at the end of the fourteenth day.

Send

42A.2.2   This includes deliver: r.1.3(1) (definition of "send").

Debates

42A.3   **42A.3.**—²(1)   Where a party seeks to have the action appointed to debate, then that party must—

(a)   on the lodging of the closed record in process, notify the court and the other party, or parties, that an application for a debate is to be made;

(b)   make such application to the court, by motion, not more than 1 week from the date on which the closed record is lodged in process.

(2)   The application must include—

(a)   the legal argument on which any preliminary plea should be sustained or repelled;

(b)   the principal authorities (including statutory provisions) on which the argument is founded.

(3)   Following application being made to the court under paragraph (1)(b), before determining whether the action should be appointed to debate the Lord Ordinary is to hear from the parties with a view to ascertaining whether agreement can be reached on the points of law in contention.

(4)   The Lord Ordinary, having heard the parties, is to determine whether the action should be appointed to debate.

(5)   Where the action is appointed to debate, the Lord Ordinary may order that written arguments on any question of law are to be submitted.

(6)   Where, following application made to the court under paragraph (1)(b), the court has determined that a hearing of any debate is not required then the time-frames specified in—

(a)   rule 42A.4(3);

(b)   rule 42A.5(2);

(c)   rule 42A.5(3);

(d)   rule 42A.5(4);

(d)   rule 42A.6(2),

commence from the date on which the court has made such a determination.

(7)   Where, following application made to the court under paragraph (1)(b), the cause is appointed to debate and is disposed of by the court, other than by decree of dismissal, then the time-frames specified in—

(a)   rule 42A.4(3);

---

¹ Rule 42A.2 inserted by S.S.I. 2013 No. 120 (effective 1st May 2013) and substituted by S.S.I. 2019 No. 404 (effective 1st March 2020).
² Rule 42A.3 inserted by S.S.I. 2013 No. 120 (effective 1st May 2013) and substituted by S.S.I. 2019 No. 404 (effective 1st March 2020).

    (b)   rule 42A.5(2);

    (c)   rule 42A.5(3);

    (d)   rule 42A.5(4);

    (d)   rule 42A.6(2),

commence from the date on which the court disposes of all or any of the preliminary pleas.

GENERAL NOTE

The court, having heard parties, decides whether there should be a debate: r. 42A.3(4).   **42A.3.1**

"NOT MORE THAN 1 WEEK FROM"

Use of "from" is ambiguous: does it include the day from which time commences or from the termination of it? The context may indicate that it is included.   **42A.3.2**

Fixing a case management hearing

42A.4.—[1](1) Subject to paragraph (2), the court must, as soon as practicable   **42A.4** after the closed record is lodged in process, fix a date for a case management hearing.

(2) Where a party seeks to have the action appointed to debate, the court must not fix a date for a case management hearing until such time as the court has determined such application and, as the case may be, disposed of the preliminary pleas at debate.

(3) Subject to rule 42A.3(6) and (7), the case management hearing fixed under this rule is to be not less than 16 weeks from the date on which the closed record is lodged in process.

GENERAL NOTE.

In the actions to which this rule applies, the court will be directly involved in the managing of the case instead of the automatic procedures in Chap. 43.   **42A.4.1**

The power in r.42A.4(6) may only be exercised at the time of deciding whether to send the case to proof or debate: *Logan v. Johnston* 2013 S.L.T. 971 (OH), para.[26].

"NOT LESS THAN 16 WEEKS FROM"

Use of "from" is ambiguous: does it include the day from which time commences or from the termination of it? The context ("not less than") may indicate that it is included as is the last day.   **42A.4.2**

Exchange of information by parties

42A.5.—[2](1) Where an application for debate has been made in terms of rule   **42A.5** 42A.3(1)(b), this rule is subject to rule 42A.3(6) or (7), as the case may be.

(2) The parties must, no later than 3 weeks after the date on which the closed record is lodged in process, exchange—

    (a)   reports, in draft form, from all skilled persons upon whose evidence the parties anticipate relying in the case;

    (b)   lists of witnesses (including their addresses and, where known, their occupations), in draft form;

    (c)   statements of all witnesses, who are named on the lists which are provided under sub-paragraph (b), which are available, and where any statement is not exchanged, an explanation as to why such a statement is not available;

    (d)   lists, in draft form, showing the discipline or expertise, of the skilled persons whom the parties have either instructed or intend to instruct, as the case may be, other than those already disclosed under sub-paragraph (a).

---

[1] Rule 42A.4 inserted by S.S.I. 2013 No. 120 (effective 1st May 2013) and substituted by S.S.I. 2019 No. 404 (effective 1st March 2020).

[2] Rule 42A.5 inserted by S.S.I. 2013 No. 120 (effective 1st May 2013) and substituted by S.S.I. 2019 No. 404 (effective 1st March 2020).

(3)   The parties must, no later than 7 weeks after the date on which the closed record is lodged in process—

   (a)   exchange statements of the provisional valuation of the claim, in draft form, together with any available vouching;
   (b)   exchange written statements containing proposals for further procedure for providing the information required by rule 42A.6(2)(a), in draft form;
   (c)   exchange a note of the issues which are in dispute between the parties, in draft form;
   (d)   exchange lists, in draft form, of all documentation in the possession of the parties relevant to the issues in dispute and upon which the parties intend to rely, to include—
        (i)   details of the institutions from which the parties have obtained medical records;
        (ii)   a note of the pagination of such medical records, and of any other records (such as social security, schools and social work records), including the dates which the records span;
   (e)   consider whether a meeting between skilled persons would be useful and, if so, at what stage of the action;
   (f)   make any requests for information to each other, to include—
        (i)   facilities for precognoscing witnesses;
        (ii)   statements from witnesses who are listed on the list mentioned in paragraph (2)(b) which have not yet been provided.

(4)   The pursuer must, no later than 9 weeks after the date on which the closed record is lodged in process, send to the defender—

   (a)   a joint minute, in draft form, which includes—
        (i)   all matters, including matters admitted in the pleadings;
        (ii)   a glossary of terminology (such as medical or technical terms);
        (iii)   any heads of damage;
        (iv)   a chronology of events, as an appendix to the joint minute, which are either agreed, or are considered by the pursuer capable of being agreed, by the parties;
   (b)   a paginated joint bundle, in draft form, of—
        (i)   medical records containing all the records from each institution;
        (ii)   other records (such as social security, schools and social work records),

in the possession of the pursuer which are relevant to the issues in dispute and upon which the pursuer intends to rely.

(5)   The defender must, no later than 3 weeks after the date on which the defender received the draft joint minute and the draft paginated joint bundle of records, return to the pursuer—

   (a)   the joint minute, either in unamended form or following any revisals having been made to it, as required, by the defender;
   (b)   the paginated joint bundle of records, following the addition into the bundle of any further records in the possession of the defender,

relevant to the issues in dispute and upon which the defender intends to rely.

(6)   Documents, when in draft form—

   (a)   must not be lodged with the court;
   (b)   must not be put in evidence at a proof or used in any other way, unless by consent of the parties.

GENERAL NOTE

The aim of this rule is to ensure that the court is fully informed for the case management hearing to be fully effective: P.N. No. 2 of 2019. It does not give the court power to make an order counter to the general rule that personal financial and insurance information is private; and there is no inherent power either: *N v. Astora Women's Health LLC* 2022 S.L.T. 285 (Second Div.) (an order had been sought against the defender to state whether it had assets or insurance cover to meet any liabilities in damages and expenses).

42A.5.1

"NO LATER THAN ... AFTER"

Time begins after the end of the day from which time is calculated and expires at the end of the last day.

42A.5.2

"CLOSED RECORD"

See annotation 22.3.2.

42A.5.3

WITNESS STATEMENT

A statement of a witness should contain a full and clear factual account: P.N. No. 2 of 2019, para. 9.

42A.5.4

Lodging of statements of proposals and joint minutes

42A.6.—[1](1) Where an application for debate has been made in terms of rule 42A.3(1)(b), this rule is subject to rule 42A.3(6) or (7), as the case may be.

42A.6

(2) No later than 14 weeks after the date on which the closed record is lodged in process—

    (a) the parties must lodge in process and, at the same time, send to every other party a written statement containing proposals for further procedure, which must include—

        (i) the issues for proof;

        (ii) a list of the witnesses (including their addresses and, where known, their occupations) who are intended to be called to give evidence, including the matters to which each witness is expected to speak and the time estimated for each witness;

        (iii) information as to whether any such witness is considered to be a vulnerable witness within the meaning of section 11(1) of the Vulnerable Witnesses (Scotland) Act 2004 (interpretation of Part 2 of the Act)(a) and whether any child witness notice under section 12(2) of that Act (orders authorising the use of special measures for vulnerable witnesses) or any vulnerable witness application under section 12(6) of that Act has been, or is to be, lodged in respect of that witness;

        (iv) a list of the reports of any skilled persons which have been exchanged;

        (v) a list of all relevant documents, including medical records, which have been exchanged;

        (vi) a list of the witness statements which have been exchanged, and a note of any further witness statements which have not yet been exchanged but are anticipated;

        (vii) the time estimated for proof and how that estimate was arrived at;

        (viii) information as to whether any other progress that has been made, is to be made, or could be made in advance of the proof;

        (ix) information as to whether an application has been or is to be made under rule 37.1 (applications for jury trial);

    (b) the pursuer must, after liaising with the defender, lodge in process and, at

---

[1] Rule 42A.6 as inserted by S.S.I. 2015 No. 227 (effective 22nd September 2015) and substituted by S.S.I. 2019 No. 404 (effective 1st March 2020).

the same time, send to every other party a signed joint minute setting out the matters which have been agreed between the parties;

(c) where there are matters relevant to the issues in dispute which are not included in the joint minute lodged under sub-paragraph (b), then the parties must lodge in process and, at the same time, send to every other party a written statement explaining why such matters have not been agreed by the parties.

"NO LATER THAN 14 WEEKS AFTER"

42A.6.1   Time begins after the end of the day from which time is calculated and expires at the end of the last day.

"SEND"

42A.6.2   "Send" includes deliver: r. 1.3(1).

Case management hearing

42A.7   **42A.7.**—[1](1) At the case management hearing, after considering the written statements lodged by the parties under rule 42A.6(2)(a), the Lord Ordinary is to determine whether the action should be sent to proof on the whole or any part of the action.

(2) Before making a determination under paragraph (1), the Lord Ordinary is to—

(a) hear from the parties, with a view to ascertaining—
  (i)   the matters in dispute between the parties;
  (ii) the readiness of the parties to proceed to proof;

(b) without prejudice to the generality of sub-paragraph (a), hear from the parties with a view to ascertaining—
  (i)   whether reports, in draft form, of skilled persons have been exchanged;
  (ii)   the nature and extent of the dispute between skilled persons;
  (iii) whether there are any facts that have been agreed between the parties, upon which skilled persons can comment;
  (iv)   the extent to which agreement can be reached between the parties on the relevant literature upon which skilled persons intend to rely;
  (v)   whether there has been a meeting between skilled persons, or whether such a meeting would be useful and, if so, at what stage of the action;
  (vi)   where a meeting between skilled persons has taken place, the form of the report which is to be produced following that meeting;
  (vii) whether a proof on a particular issue would allow scope for the matter to be resolved;
  (viii) whether all witness statements have been exchanged;
  (ix)   whether any party is experiencing difficulties in obtaining precognition facilities;
  (x)   whether all relevant records have been recovered and whether there is an agreed bundle of records;
  (xi)   whether there is a relevant case that is supported by evidence of skilled persons;
  (xii) if there is no evidence of skilled persons to support a relevant case, whether such evidence is necessary;

---

[1] Rule 42A.7 as inserted by S.S.I. 2019 No. 404 (effective 1st March 2020).

    (xiii)   whether there is a relevant defence to any or all of the case supported by evidence of skilled persons;

    (xiv)   if there is no evidence of skilled persons to support a relevant defence, whether such evidence is necessary;

    (xv)   whether causation of some or all of the injuries is the main area of dispute and, if so, the position of the respective skilled persons;

    (xvi)   if, following the exchange of valuations, in draft form, a significant disparity is shown, whether the parties should be asked to provide an explanation for such disparity;

    (xvii)   whether a further joint minute, other than the joint minute provided for in rule 42A.6(2)(b), has been considered;

    (xviii)   whether any of the heads of damage can be agreed;

    (ixx)   whether any orders would facilitate the resolution of the case or the narrowing of the scope of the dispute;

    (xx)   whether a pre-trial meeting should be fixed;

    (xxi)   whether amendment, other than updating, is anticipated;

    (xxii)   the time required for proof.

(3) Where the action is sent to proof, the Lord Ordinary must—

    (a)   fix a date for the hearing of the proof;

    (b)   fix a pre-proof timetable in accordance with rule 42A.8.

(4) The Lord Ordinary may fix a further case management hearing—

    (a)   on the motion of any party;

    (b)   at the Lord Ordinary's own instance.

GENERAL NOTE

The Lord Ordinary has a broad discretion at a case management hearing whether to allow a debate or appoint a proof before answer: *A v. A* [2020] CSIH 24. It was held that a decision of the Lord Ordinary would only be interfered with if it was not open to a reasonable Lord Ordinary to make.   **42A.7.1**

Rule 42A.10 gives the Lord Ordinary power, at a case management hearing, to make such orders necessary to secure the efficient determination of the action. P.N. No. 2 of 2019, para. 14, refers to the wide powers in that rule.

This rule does not give the court power to make an order counter to the general rule that personal financial and insurance information is private; and there is no inherent power either: *N v. Astora Women's Health LLC* 2022 S.L.T. 285 (Second Div.) (an order had been sought against the defender to state whether it had assets or insurance cover to meet any liabilities in damages and expenses).

Pre-proof timetable

42A.8.—[1](1) Subject to paragraph (4), the pre-proof timetable mentioned in rule 42A.7(3)(b) must contain provision for the following—   **42A.8**

    (a)   no later than 6 months before the proof—

        (i)   a date for a further case management hearing;

        (ii)   the last date for the lodging of—

            (aa)   a valuation;

            (ab)   vouchings, with the exception of those records which are included, or are to be included, in the joint bundle of productions,

        by the pursuer;

    (b)   no later than 5 months before the proof, the last date for the lodging of—

        (i)   a valuation;

        (ii)   vouchings, with the exception of those records which are included, or are to be included, in the joint bundle of productions,

        by the defender;

---

[1] Rule 42A.8 as inserted by S.S.I. 2019 No. 404 (effective 1st March 2020).

     (c)   no later than 4 months before the proof, the last date for the lodging of—

         (i)   witness lists;

        (ii)   productions, including a paginated joint bundle of productions, and a list of the contents of the paginated joint bundle of productions, in final form;

       (iii)   a core bundle of productions, and list of productions that comprise the core bundle of productions,

     by the parties;

     (d)   no later than 3 months before the proof, the last date for the pre-trial meeting;

     (e)   no later than 2 months before the proof, a date for a further case management hearing.

(2)   Rule 43.10(1), (2)(b) and (5) (pre-trial meetings)(a) applies to a pre-trial meeting held under this Chapter as it applies to a pre-trial meeting held under Chapter 43 (actions of damages for, or arising from, personal injuries).

(3)   Prior to the case management hearing mentioned in paragraph (1)(e)—

     (a)   the pursuer must lodge in process a joint minute of the pre-trial meeting in Form 43.10 (minute of pre-trial meeting);

     (b)   the parties must lodge in process any other joint minutes.

(4)   At any time the Lord Ordinary may, at the Lord Ordinary's own instance or on the motion of a party—

     (a)   fix a further case management hearing;

     (b)   vary the pre-proof timetable,

where the Lord Ordinary considers that the efficient determination of the action would be served by doing so.

JOINT AND CORE BUNDLES

42A.8.1   On joint and core bundles, and the requirements in relation to them, see P.N. No. 2 of 2019, paras. 17–28.

    A core bundle is a bundle of productions which must be lodged no later than four months before the proof: r. 42A.8(1)(c)(iii). It should contain copies of productions already lodged and which are central to the issues but should not ordinarily exceed 150 pages: P.N. No. 2 of 2019, paras. 26–27. There must also be a list of them.

    A (paginated) joint bundle of productions, including the productions, in final form must be lodged no later than four months before the proof: r. 42A.8(1)(c)(ii).

    The rule does not, but P.N. No. 2 of 2019, para. 17 does, refer to a joint bundle of records (medical, etc. records) which must also be lodged where a proof has been appointed. One might wonder what the difference is between a production and a record. One might presume, from r. 42A.5(4)(b), that a joint bundle of records consists of medical records and other records such as social security, school and social work records. All other documents will be productions.

    It should be noted that a draft joint bundle of medical and other records is required to be sent to the defender no later than nine weeks after the date on which the closed record is lodged in process: (r. 42A.5(4)(b).

    Rule 42A.8 does not refer to intimation of joint bundles, but P.N. No. 2 of 2019, para. 18 does.

Non-compliance by parties in the exchange of information

42A.9   **42A.9.—**[1](1) Where a party fails to comply with a requirement provided by any of the following rules—

     (a)   42A.5(2);

     (b)   42A.5(3)(a) to (d),

then that party may, on the motion of any other party, be ordained to appear before the court to provide an explanation as to why they failed to comply, and the court has the power to make any such order as appears appropriate in the circumstances.

---

[1] Rule 42A.9 as inserted by S.S.I. 2019 No. 404 (effective 1st March 2020).

Power to make orders

42A.10.—[1](1) Following the fixing of a case management hearing under rule 42A.7(4) or 42A.8(4)(a), or the variation of the pre-proof timetable under rule 42A.8(4)(b), the Lord Ordinary may make such orders as the Lord Ordinary thinks necessary to secure the efficient determination of the action.

(2) In particular, the Lord Ordinary may make orders to resolve any matters arising or outstanding from the written statements lodged by parties under rule 42A.6(2)(a) or the preproof timetable fixed under rule 42A.7(3)(b).

42A.10

GENERAL NOTE

This rule does not give the court power to make an order counter to the general rule that personal financial and insurance information is private; and there is no inherent power either: *N v. Astora Women's Health LLC* 2022 S.L.T. 285 (Second Div.) (an order had been sought against the defender to state whether it had assets or insurance cover to meet any liabilities in damages and expenses).

42A.10.1

---

[1] Rule 42A.10 as inserted by S.S.I. 2019 No. 404 (effective 1st March 2020).

CHAPTER 43 ACTIONS OF DAMAGES FOR, OR ARISING FROM, PERSONAL INJURIES

Chapter 43[1]

Actions of Damages For, or Arising From, Personal Injuries

Application and interpretation of this chapter

43.1.—[2,3](1)[4] Subject to paragraph (4) and rule 43.1 A (actions based on clinical negligence) this Chapter applies to a personal injuries action.

43.1

(2) In this Chapter—

"connected person" means a person, not being a party to the action, who has title to sue the defender in respect of the personal injuries from which a deceased died or in respect of his death;[5]

"personal injuries" includes any disease or impairment, whether physical or mental;

"personal injuries action" means an action of damages for, or arising from, personal injuries or death of a person from personal injuries; and

"relative" has the meaning assigned to it by section 14(1) of the Damages (Scotland) Act 2011.

(3)[6] The following rules shall not apply to an action to which this Chapter applies—

rule 4.9(2) (prorogation of time for lodging document),

rule 6.2 (fixing and allocation of diets in Outer House)

rule 13.2 (form of summonses),

rule 13.6A(1)(a) (arrestment to found jurisdiction),

rule 13.7 (service and intimation of summonses),

rule 13.13(6) (falling of instance),

rule 18.1(1)(b) (defences to include pleas-in-law),

rule 22.1 (making up open record),

rule 22.2 (adjustment),

rule 22.3 (closing record),

rule 36.3 (lodging productions).

(4)[7] This Chapter does not apply to any claim for loss of life or personal injury which falls to be dealt with as an Admiralty action within the meaning of rule 46.1 (interpretation of Chapter 46).

Deriv. R.C.S. 1965, r. 75A(2) substituted by S.I. 1984 No. 920 and amended by S.I. 1986 No. 1941 (r. 43.1(2) (part))

GENERAL NOTE.

In respect of actions commenced (on the meaning of which see notes 13.2.8(A) and 13.4.4) on or after 1st April 2003, new *obligatory* rules for all actions of reparation for personal injuries or death of a relative were introduced by A.S. (R.C.S.A. No. 2) (Personal Injuries Actions) 2002 [S.S.I. 2002 No. 570]. The former Chap. 43 still applies to actions commenced before 1st April 2003.

The old Chap. 43 had six parts, Part v. of which contained the Optional Procedure Rules introduced in 1985. The new Chap. 43 applies to all actions of damages for, or arising from, personal injuries or death

43.1.1

---

[1] Chapter 43 and r. 43.1 substituted by S.S.I. 2002 No. 570 (effective 1st April 2003) and r. 43.1(3) substituted by S.S.I. 2004 No. 291 (effective 29th June 2004).

[2] Chapter 43 and r. 43.1 substituted by S.S.I. 2002 No. 570 (effective 1st April 2003) and r. 43.1(3) substituted by S.S.I. 2004 No. 291 (effective 29th June 2004).

[3] Rule 43.1 amended by S.S.I. 2007 No. 282 (effective 2nd May 2007).

[4] Rule 43.1(1) amended and r. 43.1(4) inserted by S.S.I. 2009 No. 63 r. 5 (effective 23rd March 2009).

[5] Rule 43.1(4) amended by S.S.I. 2011 No. 288 (effective 7th July 2011).

[6] Chapter 43 and r. 43.1 substituted by S.S.I. 2002 No. 570 (effective 1st April 2003) and r. 43.1(3) substituted by S.S.I. 2004 No. 291 (effective 29th June 2004).

[7] Rule 43.1(1) amended and r. 43.1(4) inserted by S.S.I. 2009 No. 63 r. 5 (effective 23rd March 2009).

of a person from personal injuries. These rules are obligatory, that is, they apply in all such actions unless a motion is made successfully under r. 43.5, after defences have been lodged, to have the action proceed as an ordinary action. There are no distinct or discreet parts in the new chapter, and the former Parts dealing with connected persons, interim damages and further damages have been tacked on to the end of the chapter and provisions for provisional damages are subsumed into r. 43.2(2).

The new Chap. 43 has been some seven years in gestation and is considerably watered down from the detailed proposals in 1995. The story begins with the publication of the Cullen *Review of Business of the Outer House of the Court of Session* in December 1995. That review contained radical proposals for reform with 63 recommendations. The then Lord President (Hope of Craighead) accepted the recommendations and resolved to bring the reforms into effect in stages. Some of the reforms were implemented in 1996, e.g. permitting notices to admit before proof is allowed (Chap. 28A) and averments about medical treatment and lodging of medical reports (rr. 43.29–43.31 in Pt VI of old Chap. 43). The more radical proposals, including abbreviated pleadings and case management in all actions, were postponed to a later stage. That never happened. In January 1997 some judges expressed concern about case management hearings in all defended actions as just another expensive layer of procedure. The new Lord President (by this time Rodger of Earlsferry) set up a working party on Court of Session procedure under Lord Coulsfield in October 1997. The remit was to consider whether a simplified procedure eliminating unnecessary delay and expense could be devised for routine cases.

The working party produced its report in 2000 (*www.scotcourts.gov.uk/session/report/coulreport.htm*). The working party ascertained that over a three-week period, of 97 cases, 71 were routine of which 57 were personal injury cases. In personal injury and death actions, it is the case that 98.2 per cent settle before proof; one-third of those being in the week before proof. Also, apparently, such cases take on average two years to reach a conclusion. That report recommended limited reforms in relation only to personal injury reparation actions and abandoned the Cullen proposal for case management by the court. Late settlement is a cause of inconvenience to the courts, the parties and other litigants. The working party wished to replicate the circumstances that brought about late settlement at an earlier stage, including the exchange of information about quantum which could lead to settlement. The proposals were for (1) an automatic timetable triggered by the lodging of defences; (2) policing or monitoring by the court (which seemed to be limited to reminding parties what the next automatic stage is); (3) discouraging sists, and in particular the granting of sists for legal aid except on cause shown; (4) action following a failure to comply with a procedural step (limited to requiring an explanation); (5) initially, minimal pleadings; (6) automatic recovery of documents; (7) both parties to lodge a valuation of the claim; (8) a pre-trial settlement meeting between the parties; and (9) judgments within eight weeks of the conclusion of the proof. Any notion that the judiciary should be pro-active in litigation has been abandoned in favour of a principle of minimum intervention (which explains the limited policing role). Case management consists of an automatic timetable. The optional procedure rules restricting the number of experts (*contra* England & Wales) and listing witnesses is allegedly not followed, having been seen to be too restrictive. Although initially a success, by this time the Optional Procedure Rules had, apparently, fallen into disfavour as having a relatively rigid structure together with the inconsistent approach by the judges including their approach to vague pleadings. It is imagined that judges will adopt a consistent approach in relation to the new rules, which they did not do with the Optional Procedure Rules, particularly with regard to simple pleadings. As the working party recognises, however, it is not a change of rules that will produce consistency.

The proposals in the *Report of the Working Party on Court of Session Procedure* (referred to in this chapter as "the 2000 Report") were rejected by the Rules Council which endorsed the view that more than skeletal pleadings were necessary. A representative group of the working party was asked by the Lord President (now Lord Cullen) to meet again. In July 2002 the Group presented a supplementary report to the Lord President (*www.scotcourts.gov.uk/session/report/supplementary.htm*). That report endorsed the working party's approach and reiterated the need for short pleadings that excluded stylistic standard phrases and ritual incantations (which one might think were the hallmark of short pleadings!). The group considered that "pleadings should be couched in such a way as to requiring individual answers to individual averments of fact", which "discouraged general denials". This *crie de coeur* has been made in note 13.2.4 since the Annotations were first published in 1994. The Group provided illustrations of appropriate pleadings. Finally, the rules were promulgated together with a practice note (P.N. No. 2 of 2003) and new fees for solicitors in A.S. (R.C.S.A.) (Fees of Solicitors) 2003 [S.S.I. 2003 No. 194].

A users' group is to be set up to monitor the effectiveness of the new rules.

"PERSONAL INJURIES ACTION".

43.1.2   Notwithstanding the title of the chapter, Chap. 43 applies to actions in relation to death of a relative from personal injuries. The definition of "personal injuries action" includes actions of "damages for, or *arising from*, personal injuries or death of a person from personal injuries". Does this mean that an action of damages, against a solicitor arising out of his failure to raise an action of damages for personal injuries, is an action of damages *arising from* personal injuries? In *Mackenzie v. Digby Brown & Co.*, 1992 S.L.T. 891, it was held that the expression "an action of damages for personal injuries" in old r. 43.8 (about interim damages) did not include such an action. An action of that kind could, however, be said to *arise from* personal injuries, although remote and not directly. It is to be hoped that it is not a natural consequence of personal injuries that the subsequent and consequent action is not raised timeously. P.N. No. 2 of 2003 offers no guidance, indicating only that it is not intended that "actions of defamation or any *similar* actions" should be covered by Chap. 43. Insofar as it is relevant to an interpretation of the definition, the 2000 Report states in the sixth paragraph of Chap. 1 (introductory) that it devised a scheme to deal with routine reparation actions. In *Tudhope v. Finlay Park t/a Park Hutchison, Solicitors*, 2003

S.L.T. 1305 (OH), however, at the time of lodging the summons it was held, relying on *Mackenzie*, above, the Working Party Reports and P.N. No.2 of 2003, that an action for professional negligence in a personal injuries action was an action "arising from" personal injuries. But in this case at 2004 S.L.T. 783 (OH), on the defender's motion to have the case withdrawn from Chap. 43, it was held that the action was not one for personal injuries and the action was appointed to proceed as an ordinary action.

The definition of personal injuries includes "any disease or impairment whether physical or mental": r. 43.1(2). The definition in old Chap. 43 is that used in s. 10(1) of the Damages (Scotland) Act 1976 (dealing with death claims), s. 13(1) of the Administration of Justice Act 1982 (which introduced provisional damages) and s. 14(1) of the Damages (Scotland) Act 2011: i.e. "any disease or any impairment of a person's physical or mental condition". It is not clear that any difference of meaning was intended in the new definition; but it is also not clear why a slightly different definition, from that found in statutes in this area, is used.

An action for damages for harassment is not an action for personal injuries; a distinction has to be made between actions, which in a broad sense might be described as actions, of damages for personal injuries and those which fell within the narrow definition of "personal injuries" in r. 43.1(2): *G v. S*, 2006 S.L.T. 795 (OH).

Where the admiralty jurisdiction of the court is invoked, Chap. 43 does not apply, and Chap. 46 (Admiralty Actions) does: *Stephen v. Simon Mokster Shipping AS*, 2008 S.L.T. 743 (O.H.). It has been thought necessary to confirm this in r. 43.1(4).

By virtue of Direction No. 2 of 2010, Chap. 43 does not apply to an action of damages for or arising from personal injury or death through taking the drug Vioxx or Celebrex; the action must be an ordinary action and the particular procedures in that Direction apply. Furthermore, a pursuer may apply to have an action based on clinical negligence proceed, in exceptional circumstances, as an ordinary action (r. 43.1A); and any party may within 28 days of defences being lodged apply for a Chap. 43 action to proceed as an ordinary action.

"CONNECTED PERSON".

The definition in r. 43.1(2), as in old r. 43.1(2), is "a person, not being a party to the action, who has title to sue the defender in respect of the personal injuries from which a deceased died or in respect of his death. The connected persons to the deceased are thus (a) the executors, and (b) the relatives defined in Sched. 1 to the Damages (Scotland) Act 1976. In *McGibbon v. McAllister*, 2008 S.L.T. 459 (O.H.) Lord Brodie held that the partner of 16 years of the deceased's mother and de facto "stepfather" had, having regard to arts 14 and 16 of ECHR, title to sue (though on the ordinary meaning of Sched. 1 he was not a "parent").   **43.1.2A**

"RELATIVE".

The Damages (Scotland) Act 1976 has been replaced by the Damages (Scotland) Act 2011. Section 14(1) of the 2011 Act gives effect to recommendation 15 of the *Scottish Law Commission Report on Damages for Wrongful Death* (Scot. Law Com. 213) by defining the relatives entitled to claim for both patrimonial and non-patrimonial loss to include only those members of the victim's "immediate family" currently able to claim for non-patrimonial loss. The definition is in effect that in Sch. 1 to the 1976 Act.   **43.1.2B**

In relation to a death before 7th July 2011, the definition of relative is construed in accordance with art. 4 of the Damages (Scotland) Act 2011 (Commencement, Transitional Provisions and Savings) Order 2011 [SSI 2011/268]: A.S. (R.C.S. A. No. 4) (Miscellaneous) 2011 [SSI 2011/288]. In art. 4 of the 2011 Order, in relation to any death before 4th May 2006, "relative" has the meaning in Sch.1 to the 1976 Act and any reference to a person's immediate family is construed in accordance with s.10(2) of the 1976 Act.

NON-APPLICATION OF CERTAIN RULES.

For obvious reasons, certain general rules are inapplicable to the new procedure; and these are listed in r. 43.1(3). It is not entirely clear, however, why arrestment to found jurisdiction is excluded from personal injuries actions in Chap. 43. Is a pursuer to be denied the right to subject a person to the jurisdiction of the court who would not otherwise be subject to it? Since one cannot apply to have the action proceed as an ordinary action until defences have been lodged (see r. 43.5), it may be too late by then.   **43.1.3**

JURISDICTION.

For jurisdiction in delict, see note 13.2.8(A) and (B) Rule, Ground (3).   **43.1.4**

Actions based on clinical negligence

43.1A.—[1],[2](1)   This rule applies to a personal injuries action based on alleged clinical negligence.   **43.1A**

(2)   Where a pursuer intends to make an application under paragraph (3) to raise the action as an ordinary action, the pursuer must—

---

[1] Rule 43.1A inserted by S.S.I. 2007 No. 282 (effective 2nd May 2007).
[2] Rule 43.1A as substituted by S.S.I. 2015 No. 227 (effective 22nd September 2015).

    (a)   present the summons for signeting in Form 13.2–A (form of summons and backing);

    (b)   include in the summons a draft interlocutor in Form 43.1A (form of draft interlocutor granting authority to raise action based on clinical negligence as an ordinary action).

(3) At the same time as a summons which includes a draft interlocutor in Form 43.1A is presented for signeting, the pursuer must apply by motion for authority to raise the action as an ordinary action.

(4) On the making of a motion under paragraph (3), the summons will be placed before a Lord Ordinary in chambers and in the absence of the parties for consideration.

(5) On consideration of the summons, the Lord Ordinary may—

    (a)   after considering the likely complexity of the action and being satisfied that the efficient determination of the action would be served by doing so, grant authority for the cause to proceed as an ordinary action by signing the draft interlocutor in the summons; or

    (b)   fix a hearing;

(6) The Keeper of the Rolls must notify the parties of the date and time of any hearing under paragraph (5)(b).

(7) At a hearing under paragraph (5)(b), the Lord Ordinary may—

    (a)   refuse the application; or

    (b)   after considering the likely complexity of the action and being satisfied that the efficient determination of the action would be served by doing so, grant authority for the cause to proceed as an ordinary action by signing the draft interlocutor in the summons.

(8) Where the Lord Ordinary grants an application under paragraph (3) in respect of a summons—

    (a)   this Chapter does not apply to a cause commenced by that summons; but

    (b)   the following rules apply despite subparagraph (a)—

        (i)   rule 43.11 (applications for interim payments of damages);

        (ii) rule 43.12 (adjustment on final decree);

        (iii) rule 43.13 (applications for further damages).

(9) In this rule—

       "clinical negligence" means a breach of duty of care by a health care professional in connection with that person's diagnosis or the care and treatment of any person, by act or omission, while the health care professional was acting in a professional capacity; and

       "health care professional" includes—

    (a)   a registered medical practitioner;

    (b)   a registered nurse; or

    (c)   any other member of a profession regulated by a body mentioned in section 25(3) (the Professional Standards Authority for Health and Social Care) of the National Health Service Reform and Health Care Professions Act 2002.

GENERAL NOTE.

43.1A.1   By including the draft interlocutor in Form 43.1A and enrolling a motion under r.43.1A(3), a personal injury action involving clinical negligence (defined in r.43.1A(9)) may be removed from the special Chap. 43 procedure, and be treated as an ordinary action if the motion is granted for the reasons of complexity and efficient determination.

      Chapter 42A may be applied to the action: r. 42A.1(2).

"MOTION".

43.1A.2   For motions, see Chap. 23.

Form of summons

43.2.—[1](1) The summons shall be in Form 43.2-A and there shall be annexed to it a brief statement containing—

(a) averments in numbered paragraphs relating only to those facts necessary to establish the claim; and

(b) the names of every medical practitioner from whom, and every hospital or other institution in which, the pursuer or, in an action in respect of the death of a person, the deceased received treatment for the personal injuries.

(2) An application for an order under section 12(2)(a) of the Administration of Justice Act 1982 (provisional damages for personal injuries) shall be made by including in the summons a conclusion for provisional damages; and, where such an application is made, averments as to the matters referred to in paragraphs (a) and (b) of section 12(1) of that Act shall be included in the statement made under paragraph (1)(a).

(3) In paragraph (2) above "provisional damages" means the damages referred to in section 12(4)(a) of the Administration of Justice Act 1982.

(4) A summons may include—

(a) warrants for intimation in so far as permitted under these Rules; and

(b) a specification of documents in Form 43.2-B.

(5) In relation to an action to which this Chapter applies, any references to the condescendence of a summons and to articles of the condescendence shall be construed as a reference to the statement required under paragraph (1) above and numbered paragraphs of that statement.

Deriv. R.C.S. 1965, r. 134B inserted by S.I. 1984 No. 919 (r. 43.2(2)).

GENERAL NOTE.

On the introduction of the new Chap. 43 and this rule, see note 43.1.1. Rule 13.2 (form of summons) does not apply.

SUMMONS IN FORM 43.2-A.

A summons no longer has a condescendence (with articles) attached to it or pleas-in-law, but simply a statement of claim (not facts) with numbered paragraphs. It seems a pity to dispense with the word condescendence, as if a change of name will produce a change of practice. P.N. No. 3 of 2004 confirms that pleas-in-law should not be inserted in pleadings.

The new brief form of statement of claim is remarkably similar to the old optional procedure Form 43.18, a style to which the judges, according to the 2000 Report, were inconsistent in demanding adherence. P.N. No. 2 of 2003 quotes from the 2000 Report and the Supplementary Report as to what is required: "the briefest description of the events on which the claim is based together with a brief indication of the ground for alleged kindly specific reference to any statutory provision". The detail of the financial aspects of the claim will be in the statement of value of claim (see r. 43.9). The supplementary report contains three illustrations of the new style of brief pleading. It is not entirely clear how brief pleadings can be "couched in such a way as to require individual answers to particular averments of fact", as stated in the supplementary report: that requires a large number of detailed paragraphs. The requirement in r. 43.2(1)(a) to aver facts "necessary to establish the claim" should be observed with care; failure to aver sufficient facts could result in the pursuer being denied issues for jury trial: see, eg, *Higgins v. DHL International (UK) Ltd* , 2003 S.L.T. 1301 (OH) (insufficient facts pled).

Under the old optional procedure rules, it was said that the requirement of fair notice in a broad rather than a narrow technical sense is one which should be reasonably met: *McFarnon v. British Coal Corporation* , 1988 S.L.T. 242 (OH), 243B per Lord Murray; and see *Rodgers v. British Steel plc* , 1990 S.L.T. 642 (OH) where an alternative case not pled could not be advanced.

On the form of defences, see note 43.2.2A.

The following example of a statement of claim (with modifications to style of layout, grammar, syntax and punctuation) is taken from one of the illustrations in the Supplementary Report. The illustration uses letters of the alphabet; e.g. paras 1-11 below were 1A-1K. That system has not been followed here, although a hint of it as a possibility is to be found in para. 12.

STATEMENT OF CLAIM

1.   On 3rd June 1998 the pursuer was a bus assembler employed by the defender.

43.2

43.2.1

43.2.2

---

[1] R.43.2 substituted by S.S.I. 2002 No. 570 (effective 1st April, 2003).

2.   On that date, the pursuer was working on the Olympian Line fitting an anti-roll bar to a bus which consisted of a rod 5cm (2 inches) in diameter and about 304cm (10 feet) in length and of a solid metal construction.

3.   A rod was fitted across the width of the bus around 91cm (three feet) from ground height.

4.   This was not the pursuer's normal job as the employee who did the job, Thomas Ferguson, was absent for a week.

5.   The pursuer was carrying out the job in the way that he had seen Mr Ferguson doing it, and had not been otherwise trained or instructed in the job.

6.   To fit the rod, the pursuer exerted force from a crouching position on one knee placing the end of the rod onto the front of the chassis where it was bolted.

7.   The pursuer used a pinch bar held in his left hand to wedge the end of the rod in the proper place for connection to the chassis.

8.   There was no mechanical device to guide the rod to where it was fitted.

9.   The pursuer was locating the rod when the pinch bar jammed and suddenly released, and released the rod with the pinch bar hitting the pursuer on his right shin and the rod on his right knee.

10.   There was no harness provided to support the rod while being located.

11.   Following the accident the defender provided an alternative type of pinch bar and instructed operators as to the correct method of construction.

12.   The defender was in breach of the following duties of care.
       (1)   [or 12A] The defender failed to take reasonable care for the safety of the pursuer and exposed him to risk of injury by not devising a safe system of work.
       (2)   [or 12B] The defender failed to take reasonable care to provide safe and adequate plant and equipment.

13.   The defender was in breach of the following statutory duties.
       (1)   Regulation 13 of the Workplace (Health, Safety and Welfare) Regulations 1992.
       (2)   Regulation 5 of the Provisions and Use of Work Equipment Regulations 1992.
       (3)   Regulation 20 of the Provisions and Use of Work Equipment Regulations 1992.

14.   The pursuer suffered the following injuries—
       (i)   damaged anterior cruciate ligament bucket handle tear of the cartilage of the right knee; and
       (ii)   adjustment disorder with mixed anxiety and depressed mood.

15.   The pursuer was treated by—
       (i)   Dr McCreadie, Almswell Road, Kilwinning, Ayrshire (*insert for what?*); and
       (ii)   Crosshouse Hospital, Kilmarnock (*insert for what?*)

16.   The pursuer seeks damages under the following heads of claim.
       (1)   Solatium (*insert amount if known?*).
       (2)   Earnings lost till June 2000 (*insert amount if known?*).
       (3)   Earnings loss from employment he would have obtained (*insert amount if known?*).
       (4)   Future earnings loss or failing which, loss of employability on the open labour market (*insert amount if known?*).
       (5)   Cost of travelling for medical treatment (*insert amount if known?*).
       (6)   Prescription costs (*insert amount if known?*).
       (7)   Services provided by the pursuer that he can no longer perform for his parents since the year 2000 (*insert amount if known?*).
       (8)   Services that the pursuer is unable to carry out by way of home decoration, gardening and car maintenance (*insert amount if known?*).

The requirement under the old r. 43.30 in relation to averments about medical treatment is now contained in r. 43.2 (1)(b).

Whereas under the optional procedure rules it was possible for the sum awarded to be greater than the sum sued for (see first conclusion in old Form 43.18), this is not provided for in the new Chap.43. The requirement for a specific sum to be concluded for is related to jury trial.

For the rules in relation to "connected persons" to whom intimation of an action of damages for death of a person from personal injuries should be given, see rr. 43.14–43.19.

DEFENCES.

43.2.2A   Chap. 43 makes no provision for the form of defences. Accordingly, r. 18.1 applies and defences should contain pleas-in-law; but P.N. No. 3 of 2004 says they must not contain pleas-in-law. There is nothing in Chap. 43 about defences having to be brief. Blanket denials, unless there is good reason, are unacceptable: P.N. No. 1 of 2013, para. 5.

Fair notice must, however, be given of the case it is proposed to make. Accordingly, a defender cannot secure a finding of contributory negligence if some reference to it is not made in the defences: *McGowan v. W & JR Watson Ltd* , 2007 S.C. 272 (Extra Div.).

SOCIAL SECURITY (RECOVERY OF BENEFITS) ACT 1997.

43.2.3   For a discussion of this Act and its effect on payment of damages, see note 43.9.10.

"PROVISIONAL DAMAGES".

(1) General.

In old Chap. 43, the rules for provisional and further damages were in Part III. The rules for further damages are now in r. 43.13. An application for provisional damages may be made only by the injured person: Administration of Justice Act 1982, s. 12(2).

43.2.4

(2) Section 12 of the 1982 Act.

This provision sets out the circumstances in which provisional damages may be claimed: (a) there must be a risk that, at some definite or indefinite time in the future, the pursuer will, as a result of the act or omission which gave rise to the cause of action, develop some serious disease or suffer some serious deterioration of his physical or mental condition; and (b) that the defender was, at the time of the act or omission which gave rise to the cause of action, a public authority, public corporation or insured or otherwise indemnified in respect of the claim. Evidence of risk that the pursuer will, as a result of the act or omission which gave rise to the cause of action, develop some serious disease or suffer some serious deterioration in his condition, should be led and the court asked to make a finding that there is such a risk, but to assess and award damages on the assumption that the pursuer will not develop the disease or suffer the deterioration. In making the award the court may order that an application for further damages may only be made within a specified period: 1982 Act, s. 12(2).

A minute of tender and acceptance, while binding between the parties, did not bind the court to award provisional damages: *Fraser v Kitsons Insulation Contractors Ltd,* 2015 S.L.T. 753 (OH) (court ordered that pursuer might apply for further damages).

(3) Interpretation; meaning of "serious" and "future deterioration".

The word "serious" primarily qualifies the word disease or deterioration rather than the effects of the disease or deterioration, although in assessing seriousness account must be taken of effects on the pursuer's physical abilities: *White v. Inveresk Paper Co. Ltd* , 1988 S.L.T. 2 (OH), 5L per Lord Murray; *Robertson v. British Bakeries Ltd* , 1991 S.L.T. 434 (OH), 439G per Lord Osborne. It is not the case that a triggering incident causing future deterioration means that s. 12 of the 1982 Act does not apply. The question is whether the deterioration is the result of the act or omission which gave rise to the cause of action, and that could be the case notwithstanding that the deterioration is brought about by an interaction between the condition produced by the original act and a future triggering event: *Meek v. Burton's Gold Medal Biscuits Ltd* , 1989 S.L.T. 338 (OH).

(4) Social Security (Recovery of Benefits) Act 1997.

For a discussion of this Act and its effect on payment of damages, see note 43.9.10.

"WARRANTS FOR INTIMATION".

See generally, note 13.6.6. The obvious example in reparation actions is intimation to connected persons: see further, in r. 43.15.

43.2.5

DILIGENCE.

Warrants for arrestment or inhibition on the dependence must now be applied for by motion under Chap. 14A.

43.2.6

"SPECIFICATION OF DOCUMENTS".

Rule 43.2(4) provides that the summons may "include" a specification of documents. In r. 43.4(5) the specification is referred to as being annexed to the summons. It is not clear if it is really intended that the specification be part of the summons, for it would not be in accordance with normal practice to serve the summons on a haver other than a party. If the specification is part of the summons it is not a separate step of process and is not given a separate process number and will not incur a separate fee. Clearly the specification has to be served with the summons on the defender so that he has notice that the standard form of specification has been applied for and granted. It would have been better to provide for the pursuer, on lodging the summons, to apply by motion ex parte for a commission and diligence for recovery of documents on a specification containing the standard calls, which document would be supplied by the court in the order.

43.2.7

No distinction is made, as in Chap. 35, between recovery of documents by a represented party and a party litigant; indeed, Form 43.2-B assumes that the pursuer is legally represented. Following the Cullen *Review of Business of the Outer House of the Court of Session*, where the party is represented r. 35.3 provides the procedure for the haver to send the documents directly to the party's agent; but in the case of a party litigant r. 35.3A follows the old rule that documents have to be sent to the DPCS: see notes 35.3.1 and 35.3A.1. Form 43.2-B as substituted by S.S.I. 2004 No. 291 now provides for the documents to be sent to the pursuer's agent: the alternative in the old form for sending them to the Office of Court has been removed; but there is still no alternative procedure provided for where the pursuer is a party litigant as in r. 35.3A.

In any event, this is the automatic recovery of documents' procedure. Under the optional procedure (old r. 43.25), each party had to disclose documents in his possession to the other side, but documents in possession of a haver had to be sought by commission and diligence in the normal way. The new procedure is that the pursuer is entitled, on lodging the summons, to (an order for) recovery of documents in a standard specification in Form 43.2-B without prior intimation to the defender. The standard calls are for recovery of the relevant medical records, earnings and accident reports.

Unfortunately, the specification of documents is provided by the pursuer and not the court. The clerk of session will have to check the document very carefully to see that it is word for word in identical terms to Form 43.2-B.

The pursuer is not precluded from seeking recovery of these documents at a later stage or any other documents or property at common law or under s. 1 of the Administration of Justice (Scotland) Act 1972: r. 43.4(5).

For execution of the order for recovery of documents, see r. 43.4.

Service and calling of summons

43.3

43.3.—[1](1) Where a summons in an action to which this Chapter applies is to be executed, a copy of the summons which has passed the signet shall be—

    (a) served on the defender with a citation in Form 43.3 attached to it; and

    (b) intimated to any person named in a warrant for intimation.

(2) Where a summons has not called within three months and a day after the date of signeting, the instance shall fall.

(3) Where a summons cannot be served within the period of notice determined in accordance with rule 13.4 and called before the expiry of the period mentioned in paragraph (2), the court may—

    (i) on the application of the pursuer by motion; and

    (ii) on cause shown,

extend that period.

(4) An application under paragraph (3) shall be made before the expiry of the period mentioned in paragraph (2).

GENERAL NOTE.

43.3.1

On the introduction of the new Chap. 43 and this rule, see note 43.1.1. Rule 13.7 (service and intimation of summons) does not apply.

"SERVED".

43.3.2

For service, see Chap. 16. The citation on the defender is in Form 43.3 and not Form 13.7. The only difference is the second paragraph which states that the action is a claim for reparation.

"INTIMATED".

43.3.3

For methods, see r. 16.8.

"CALLED WITHIN THREE MONTHS AND A DAY".

43.3.4

The period expires at the end of the last day, three months and a day after the day of signeting (that day will not be included in the calculation). The reason for the extra day is connected to the historically "year and a day" provisions now in rr. 13.7(2) and 13.13. The general rule that the instance falls if the summons is not executed within a year and a day after signeting (r. 13.7(2)) or if the summons is not called within a year and a day after the expiry of the period of notice (r. 13.13(6)) does not apply. Instead, under r. 43.3(2), the instance falls if the summons is not *called* within *three months* and a day after signeting. Although the defender has the right of protestation under r. 13.14 if the summons is not called within seven days after the expiry of the period of notice, this rule ensures that there is no delay. Rule 43.3(3) provides for the situation where the summons cannot be served within the period of notice and called within three months and a day of signeting. On cause shown, the three-month cut-off period may be prorogued. No other situation is provided for. Having regard to the decision in *MacDonald v. Kwok*, 1999 S.L.T. 593 (OH), on which see note 13.13.9, it was argued that relief from the rigours of the rule may be sought under r. 2.1. This was done in *Jackson v. McDougall*, 2004 S.L.T. 770 (OH) and *Roberts v. Chisholm*, 2004 S.L.T. 1171 following *MacDonald*, above. *McDonald*, however, was overruled in *Brogan v. O'Rourke Ltd*, 2005 S.L.T. 29 (Extra Div.) where it was held that rr. 13.13(6) and 43.3(2) were plain and the meaning of "the instance shall fall" was perfectly understood: where the summons has not called within the specified period the instance falls and it was incompetent to apply to the court under r. 2.1. Sense having prevailed in *Brogan*, it ought to follow that *Jackson* and *Roberts*, though not referred to in *Brogan*, are no longer good law.

For calling of the summons, see r. 13.13.

---

[1] Rule 43.3 substituted by S.S.I. 2002 No. 570 (effective 1st April 2003).

FEE.

The court fee for signeting a summons is payable. For fee, see Court of Session etc. Fees Order 1997, Table of Fees, Pt I, A and B, item 1 [S.I. 1997 No. 688 as amended, pp.C1201 et seq.]. Certain persons are exempt from payment of fees: see 1997 Fees Order, art. 5 substituted by S.S.I. 2002 No. 270. A fee exemption certificate must be lodged in process: see P.N. No. 1 of 2002.

43.3.5

Where the pursuer is legally represented, the fee may be debited under a credit scheme introduced on 1st April 1976 by P.N. No. 4 of 1976 to the account (if one is kept or permitted) of the pursuer's agent by the court cashier, and an account will be rendered weekly by the court cashier's office to the agent for all court fees due that week for immediate settlement. Party litigants and agents not operating the scheme must pay (by cash, cheque or postal order) on each occasion a fee is due at the time of lodging at the counter at the General Department.

PLEURAL PLAQUES, AND ASBESTOS-RELATED CONDITIONS, CASES.

Direction No. 2 of 2012 applies to these cases following the passing of the Damages (Asbestos-related Conditions) (Scotland) Act 2009.

Cases already raised and new cases will be sisted until parties have complied with the provisions of the Direction. These include the pursuer delivering a "pursuer's pack" including a summary and evidence of employment history and medical records; the defender intimating a proposal for settlement with eight weeks; and the pursuer having four weeks to agree. If the defender does not respond to the pursuer's pack or does not propose to settle, the pursuer may enrol a motion to recall the sist and for a by order hearing before the nominated judge.

The nominated judge for these cases is Lady Clark of Calton, who will discharge the court's management functions.

Inspection and recovery of documents

43.4.—[1](1) This rule applies where the summons contains a specification of documents by virtue of rule 43.2(4)(b).

43.4

(2) Upon signet an order granting commission and diligence for the production and recovery of the documents mentioned in the specification shall be granted and the Deputy Principal Clerk of Session shall certify Form 43.2-B to that effect.

(3) An order under paragraph (2) shall be treated for all purposes as an interlocutor of the court granting commission and diligence signed by the Lord Ordinary.

(4)[2] The pursuer may serve an order under paragraph (2) and the provisions of rule 35.3 or 35.3A shall thereafter apply, subject to any necessary modifications, as if the order were an order obtained on an application made under rule 35.2(1)(a).

(5) Nothing in this rule shall affect the right of a party to apply under rule 35.2 for a commission and diligence for recovery of documents or for an order under section 1 of the Administration of Justice (Scotland) Act 1972 in respect of any document or other property not mentioned in the specification annexed to the summons.

GENERAL NOTE.

On the introduction of the new Chap. 43 and this rule, see note 43.1.1.

43.4.1

"AN ORDER GRANTING COMMISSION AND DILIGENCE".

43.4.2

Rule 43.4(2) states that an order is granted and that the DPCS certifies that it has been. The rule does not state who has granted the order. Rule 43.4(3) implies that it is not granted by a Lord Ordinary but is to be treated as if it had been. Either the DPCS, or some other clerk of session, has granted the order or r. 43.4(2) should have made it clear that an order is *deemed* to have been granted and is certified by the DPCS. It would have been better to provide for the pursuer, on lodging the summons, to apply by motion ex parte for a commission and diligence for recovery of documents on a specification containing the standard calls, which document would be supplied by the court.

For the meaning of commission and diligence, see note 35.2.2.

Form 43.2-B is a confused document. The description of the form is that it is an order, but the document itself does not state that it is an order of the court and there is no official place for the certificate of the DPCS (the certificate may be stamped on). The form itself is headed "Specification of Documents" (rather than "Order of the Court of Session", as in Form 35.3-A, or "Order for Recovery of Documents") which, in our procedure, is not the order for a commission and diligence but the document lodged that specifies the documents for which the commission and diligence is sought and accompanies the order.

---

[1] Rule 43.4 substituted by S.S.I. 2002 No. 570 (effective 1st April 2003).
[2] Rule 43.4(4) amended by S.S.I. 2011 No. 190 (effective 11th April 2011) and S.S.I. 2011 No. 288 (clerical error; effective 21st July 2011).

RULE 43.4(4).

43.4.3 The erroneous reference to r. 35.2 in r. 43.4(4) when r.43.4 was substituted by S.S.I. 2001 No. 570 has been corrected by S.S.I. 2011 No. 190. Rule 35.3A should be applied where there is a party litigant or confidentiality is claimed.

A pursuer, or any other party, is not precluded by the automatic procedure from applying for recovery of documents under Chap.35 in the normal way: r. 43.4(5).

INTIMATION AND SERVICE.

43.4.4 Intimation is not made to the Lord Advocate or the Advocate General. P.N. No. 2 of 2003 confirms this in relation to the Lord Advocate.

In relation to medical records, the order should be served on the Central Legal Office, NHS Scotland, Anderson House, Breadalbane Street, Bonnington Road, EH6 5JR: P.N. No. 2 of 2003 (for "sent" read "served").

Documents are expected to be released promptly: P.N. No. 2 of 2009.

Motions to dispense with timetable

43.5 **43.5.**—[1](1) Any party to an action may, within 28 days of the lodging of defences, by motion apply to have the action withdrawn from the procedure in this Chapter and to be appointed to proceed as an ordinary action.

(2) No motion under paragraph (1) shall be granted unless the court is satisfied that there are exceptional reasons for not following the procedure in this Chapter.

(3) In determining whether there are exceptional reasons justifying the granting of a motion made under paragraph (1), the Lord Ordinary shall have regard to—

    (a) the likely need for detailed pleadings;

    (b) the length of time required for preparation of the action; and

    (c) any other relevant circumstances.

(4) Where the court appoints the cause to proceed as an ordinary action under paragraph (1)—

    (a) the pursuer shall, within seven days, lodge an open record in terms of rule 22.1; and

    (aa)[2] on the application of a party by motion, the court may, if satisfied that it is appropriate—

        (i) ordain a party to lodge a medical report which would have been lodged under Chapter 43 had the action not been withdrawn from that procedure;

        (ii) ordain a party to lodge a statement of valuation of claim which would otherwise have been lodged under rule 43.9;

        (iii) ordain the parties to hold a pre-trial meeting which would otherwise have been held under rule 43.10, and to lodge a minute of such meeting within such period as the court deems appropriate;

    (b) rules 43.11, 43.12 and 43.13 shall apply to the action.

GENERAL NOTE.

43.5.1 On the introduction of the new Chap. 43 and this rule, see note 43.1.1.

This rule provides a "get out" for any party, once defences have been lodged, by application to have the case proceed as an ordinary action. This may be achieved only if there are "exceptional reasons": see note 43.5.5.

"WITHIN 28 DAYS".

43.5.2 The date from which the period is calculated is not counted. Where the last day falls on a Saturday or Sunday, or a public holiday on which the Office of Court is open, the next available day is allowed: r. 1.3(7). For office hours and public holidays, see note 3.1.2.

"LODGING OF DEFENCES".

43.5.3 On defences, see generally Chap.18. On lodging defences, see r. 18.1(2).

---

[1] R.43.5 substituted by S.S.I. 2002 No. 570 (effective 1st April 2003).
[2] R. 43.5(4)(aa) inserted by S.S.I. 2008 No. 349 (effective 1st December 2008).

For motions, see generally Chap.23.

The timetable in Direction No. 4 of 1994 applies subject to the following for opposed or urgent motions. Any opposed motion will be put out for hearing at a date and time convenient to the court and, where possible, the parties; urgent motions will be dealt with on a priority basis. See Direction No. 2 of 2007.

43.5.4

"EXCEPTIONAL REASONS".

An action to which Chap.43 applies may only proceed as an ordinary action if there are exceptional reasons for not allowing the procedure in Chap.43: r. 43.5(2). Guidance as to the meaning of this phrase is given in r. 43.5(3) and P.N. No. 2 of 2003. Rule 43.5(3) requires the Lord Ordinary to have regard, inter alia, to (a) the need for detailed pleadings, and (b) the length of time and required to prepare the case. The P.N. states that a transfer to the ordinary roll is likely to be granted only in cases of exceptional complexity. A motion should detail specifically all the items in para.(3) of r. 43.5: *Broadfoot's CB v. Forth Valley Acute Hospitals NHS Trust* , July 3, 2003, 2003 G.W.D. 26-729 (OH).

43.5.5

It should not be assumed that merely because an action involves professional negligence that it will automatically be appointed to proceed as an ordinary action: *Broadfoot's CB*, above.

Where a case is transferred to the ordinary roll, r. 43.5(4) provides that the rules relating to interim and further damages (rr. 43.11–43.13) continued to apply. Nothing, however, is said about rr. 43.17-43.19 relating to connected persons continuing to apply.

"WITHIN SEVEN DAYS".

The date from which the period is calculated is not counted. Where the last day falls on a Saturday or Sunday, or a public holiday on which the Office of Court is open, the next available day is allowed: r. 1.3(7). For office hours and public holidays, see note 3.1.2.

43.5.6

Allocation of diets and timetables

43.6.—[1](1) The Keeper of the Rolls shall, on the lodging of defences or, where there is more than one defender the first lodging of defences—

43.6

    (a)   allocate a diet for proof of the action;

    (b)   issue a timetable stating the date mentioned in sub-paragraph (a) and calculated by reference to periods specified from time to time by the Lord President, in accordance with which—

        (i)   an application for a third party notice under rule 26.1 may be made;

        (ii)[2]   the pursuer may serve a commission for recovery of documents under rule 43.4;

        (iii)   parties may adjust their pleadings;

        (iv)   the pursuer shall lodge a statement of valuation of claim in process;

        (v)   the pursuer shall lodge a record;

        (vi)   the defender (and any third party to the action) shall lodge a statement of valuation of claim in process;

        (vii)   the parties shall each lodge in process a list of witnesses together with any productions upon which they wish to rely; and

        (viii)   the pursuer shall lodge in process the minute of the pre-trial meeting.

(2)   A timetable issued under paragraph (1) shall be in Form 43.6 and shall be treated for all purposes as an interlocutor of the court signed by the Lord Ordinary; and so far as the timetable order is inconsistent with any provision in these rules which relates to a matter to which the timetable relates, the timetable shall prevail.

(3)[3]   Where a party fails to comply with any requirement of a timetable, the Keeper of the Rolls may put the cause out to be heard on the By Order roll.

---

[1] Rule 43.6 substituted by SSI 2002/570 (effective 1st April 2003) and amended by SSI 2007/282 (effective 2nd May 2007).

[2] Rule 43.6(1)(b)(ii) amended by SSI 2011/190 (effective 11th April 2011).

[3] As amended by the Act of Sederunt (Rules of the Court of Session, Ordinary Cause Rules and Summary Cause Rules Amendment) (Miscellaneous) 2014 (SSI 2014/152) r.2 (effective 7th July, 2014).

(4)   The pursuer shall lodge two copies of the record, which shall consist of the pleadings of the parties, in process by the date specified in the timetable and shall at the same time send one copy to the defender and any other parties.

(5)   The pursuer shall, on lodging the copies of the record as required by paragraph (4), enrol a motion craving the court—

    (a)   to allow to parties a preliminary proof on specified matters;

    (b)   to allow a proof;

    (c)   to allow issues for jury trial; or

    (d)   to make some other specified order.

(5A)[1]   The pursuer shall include in the enrolled motion under paragraph (5) his estimate of the likely duration of the preliminary proof, proof or jury trial, or any other hearing sought, and request that the diet be allocated accordingly.

(5B)[2]   If any party considers that the estimate included under paragraph (5A) is too low, he shall record upon the enrolled motion his own estimate.

(5C)[3]   Any estimate included or recorded by a party under paragraph (5A) or (5B) shall be certified in Form 43.6A by that party's solicitor or by any counsel or other person having a right of audience instructed by that party to represent him at the preliminary proof, proof, jury trial or other hearing, as the case may be.

(5D)[4]   A certificate under paragraph (5C) shall be lodged—

    (a)   where it relates to an estimate included under paragraph (5A) at the time of enrolling the motion under paragraph (5);

    (b)   where it relates to an estimate recorded under paragraph (5B) at the time of recording that estimate.

(6)   In the event that any party proposes to ask the court to make any order other than one of those specified in sub-paragraphs (b) or (c) of paragraph (5), that party shall, on enrolling or opposing (as the case may be) the pursuer's motion, specify the order to be sought and give full notice in the motion or notice of opposition, of the grounds thereof.

(7)   *[As repealed by the Act of Sederunt (Rules of the Court of Session, Ordinary Cause Rules and Summary Cause Rules Amendment) (Miscellaneous) 2014 (SSI 2014/152) r.2 (effective 7th July, 2014).]*

(8)   A production which is not lodged in accordance with paragraph (1)(b)(vii) shall not be used or put in evidence at a proof unless—

    (a)   by consent of parties; or

    (b)   with the leave of the court on cause shown and on such conditions, if any, as to expenses or otherwise as the court thinks fit.

(9)   In a cause which is one of more than one cause arising out of the same cause of action, the court may—

    (a)   on the motion of a party to that cause; and

    (b)   after hearing parties to all those causes,

appoint that cause or any other of those causes to be the leading cause and to sist the other causes pending the determination of the leading cause.

(10)   In this rule, "pursuer" includes additional pursuer, noter or minuter, as the case may be.

---

[1] Paras (5A) to (5D) of r.43.6 inserted by SSI 2007/548 (effective 7th January 2008).
[2] Paras (5A) to (5D) of r.43.6 inserted by SSI 2007/548 (effective 7th January 2008).
[3] Paras (5A) to (5D) of r.43.6 inserted by SSI 2007/548 (effective 7th January 2008).
[4] Paras (5A) to (5D) of r.43.6 inserted by SSI 2007/548 (effective 7th January 2008).

GENERAL NOTE.

On the introduction of the new Chap. 43 and this rule, see note 43.1.1. Rules 4.9(2) (prorogation of time for lodging documents), 6.2 (fixing and allocation of diets in the Outer House), 22.1 (open records), 22.2 (time for adjustment on Adjustment Roll), 22.3 (closing of record) and 36.3 (lodging of productions) do not apply.

43.6.1

This rule is crucial to the success of the scheme. A rigid timetable must be adhered to once defences have been lodged. Following the US Federal model, a date for the proof (or jury trial) is fixed when defences are lodged. The date for a proof will be about 12 months after the date on which defences are lodged. Thus parties know the date to which they have to work. The 2000 Report indicates that the working party considered that, instead of judicial case management, which it concluded would be an unnecessary and unjustified expense in most cases, there should be an automatic timetable with which parties would have to comply. Although adjustment of the timetable may be required, that should be done where possible without affecting the date allocated for proof or jury trial.

PLEURAL PLAQUES, AND ASBESTOS-RELATED CONDITIONS, CASES.

It is implied by the terms of paragraph 11 of Direction No. 2 of 2012 (which applies to cases to which the Damages (Asbestos-related Conditions) (Scotland) Act 2009 applies), that the timetable and allocation of diets will be fixed by the nominated judge under paragraph 11 of the Direction and that r. 43. 6 will not apply.

"THE KEEPER OF THE ROLLS SHALL, ON THE LODGING OF DEFENCES".

Rule 43.6(1) would appear to require that the timetable will be issued by the Keeper on the day that the defences, or the first defences, are lodged.

43.6.2

"TIMETABLE".

The period of time for the doing or completion of various stages and the proof date will all be set out in the timetable issued to the parties by the Keeper in Form 43.6. The stages include application for third party notices, execution of commission and diligence, adjustment, lodging of statements of value of claim, lodging of record, list of witnesses and productions, and minute of pre-trial meeting.

43.6.3

The Keeper will calculate these periods according to periods specified by the Lord President: r.43.6(1)(b). The rule makes no provision for publication by a P.N. The periods currently envisaged are set out in Table 1 to P.N. No. 2 of 2003.

P.N. No. 2 of 2003 stipulates that the period set out in the timetable order will be strictly insisted on. If they are not adhered to, the cause may be put out on the By Order Roll: r.43.6(3). As to the sanctions available day by order hearing, see r.43.7(2) and note 43.7.2.

"ALLOCATE A DIET FOR PROOF".

Rule 43.6(1)(a) refers to allocating a diet for proof of the action, which must mean proof or jury trial. The timetable order in Form 43.6 on the other hand refers to the diet of trial: it should be a reference to proof or jury trial.

43.6.4

Normally, four days are allocated. If four days is not appropriate, the Keeper should be contacted: P.N. No. 2 of 2003.

In *Hamilton v. Seamark Systems Ltd* , 2004 S.C. 543 (OH), it was held that as "proof" included proof before answer (see r. 1.3), and as examination of questions of law after evidence was not excluded by the new Chap. 43 procedure, there could be a proof before answer where appropriate. Lady Paton, obiter, at para. [23], indicated that there might be little difference between proof and proof before answer, as parties may make submissions about the law after proof (see note 28.1.6).

"COMMISSION FOR RECOVERY OF DOCUMENTS".

The reference in r.43.6(1)(b)(ii) to a commission should be to a commission and diligence. It refers only to the automatic or standard specification provided for in r.43.4, i.e. the one that may be included in (sic) the summons. If the pursuer has not already executed it, this must be done by the date specified in the timetable order.

43.6.5

"STATEMENT OF VALUATION OF CLAIM".

The pursuer first, and then by a later date, the defender must lodge a statement of the value of claim. On the statement of value of claim, see r.43.9.

43.6.6

"LIST OF WITNESSES TOGETHER WITH ANY PRODUCTIONS".

The 2000 Report indicates in Chap. 5 that the requirement in the old optional procedure rules for a list of witnesses had been found to be unduly restrictive. New r.43.6(1)(b)(vii), however, requires that parties must lodge a list of witnesses and any productions by the date stipulated in the timetable order. Unlike old r.43.26, there is no express provision prohibiting the calling of witnesses not on the list without leave. It may not, however, be implied that there is such a prohibition in relation to witnesses under the new provision because there is an express prohibition in relation to productions: see below in this note.

43.6.7

It should be noted that the action will be subject to P.N. No. 8 of 1994 which states in para.2 that a party may call a witness not on his list subject to such conditions, if any, as the court may impose. This is, of course, only a P.N. and not a rule. In *Quigley v. Hart Builders (Edinburgh) Ltd* , [2006] CSOH 118, 28

July 2006, unreported (O.H.), Lord Glennie allowed a new list of witnesses for the pursuer at the proof (an earlier one having been refused on a motion for discharge) on condition that the defender's expert on that list could be called to give evidence restricted to the report he had provided to the defender). In *Smith v. Greater Glasgow & Clyde NHS Health Board*, 2014 S.L.T. 137 (OH), Lord Jones held that where a party has not lodged a list of witnesses timeously and seeks to do so late, a motion must be enrolled under r. 43.8 to vary the timetable; and such a motion may be made after the date for compliance has passed or when it has been put out by order under r. 43.6(3); and special cause must be shown. Lord Jones doubted the dictum in *Quigley*, above, that it is competent for a party who has not lodged a list of witnesses could apply for a list to be received late. He observed that, where a list had been timeously lodged and a party wished to add a witness, the court had power at common law to deal with it in the interests of justice.

A production not lodged timeously under r.43.6(1)(b)(vii), on the other hand, may not be used or put in evidence unless with the consent of parties or with leave of the court on cause shown and on such conditions, if any, as the court may impose: r.43.6(8). This provision appears to prohibit the putting of documents not lodged to a witness to test credibility, on which see notes 36.3.2 and 36.11.2(8). But, since leave of the court can be obtained under r.43.6(7), it will presumably be granted for this purpose. In P.N. No. 1 of 2007 practitioners are reminded that parties are expected (in accordance with the principle of early disclosure) to lodge all expert reports within a reasonable time after receipt; failure to do so may have consequences in expenses.

On lodging such steps of process, see rr.4.4–4.6 and notes.

"PRE-TRIAL MEETING".

43.6.8   Parties must hold a joint pre-trial (sic) meeting and lodge a minute in respect of it. On pre-trial meetings, see r.43.10.

"LODGE...IN PROCESS".

43.6.9   On lodging steps of process, see rr.4.4-4.6.

LODGING OF RECORDS.

43.6.10   It should be noted that unlike a record in any other action (see r.22.3(2)), the record in an action under Chap. 43 contains only the pleadings and not any of the interlocutors.

Two copies of the record are required as one is the process copy and the other is for the use of the Keeper of the Rolls. (In other actions, three copies are required, the third being required for the clerk of court.)

Where the record is not lodged by the date in the timetable order, the case will, not may, be put out by order for an explanation. On the by order hearing and sanctions for failure to comply with the timetable order, see r.43.7.

MOTIONS FOR FURTHER PROCEDURE.

43.6.11   On the lodging of the record the pursuer must enrol a motion for a preliminary proof, a proof, issues for jury trial or some other specified order: r.43.6(6). The court expects that a proof will be sought: P.N. No. 2 of 2003. If a preliminary proof or debate is sought, or any other specified order is sought, a motion will have to be accompanied by written notice of the grounds: r.43.6(6) and P.N. No. 2 of 2003. Such a motion will not be lightly granted, and normally questions of specification of pleadings will be dealt with at the motion. Parties are expected to have discussed duration of the proceedings before enrolling a motion (and to keep it under review): P.N. No. 3 of 2007.

For motions enrolled on lodging the record under r. 43.6(5), the timetable in Direction No. 4 of 1994 applies subject to the following for opposed or urgent motions. Any opposed motion will be put out for hearing at a date and time convenient to the court and, where possible, the parties; urgent motions will be dealt with on a priority basis. See Direction No. 2 of 2007.

"MOTION".

43.6.12   For motions, see Chap. 23.

APPOINTING CAUSE TO BE THE LEADING CAUSE.

43.6.13   See note 22.3.13.

Hearings on the By Order roll

43.7   **43.7.**—[1](1) Where the Keeper of the Rolls puts a case out to be heard on the By Order roll under paragraphs (3) or (7) of rule 43.6 or paragraph (3) of rule 43.10 he shall—

(a) put the cause out to be heard not less than seven days after the date of the notice referred to in sub-paragraph (b) on the By Order roll; and

(b) give notice to the parties to the action—

---

[1] R. 43.7 substituted by SSI 2002/570 (effective 1st April 2003).

    (i)   of the date of the hearing of the cause on the By Order roll; and

    (ii) requiring the party in default to lodge in process a written explanation as to why the timetable has not been complied with and to intimate a copy to all other parties, not less than two clear working days before the date of the hearing.

(2) At a hearing on the By Order roll under any of the provisions mentioned in the foregoing paragraph, the Lord Ordinary—

    (a)   shall consider any explanation provided by the party in default;

    (b)   may award expenses against that party; and

    (c)   may make any other appropriate order, including decree of dismissal.

(3) Expenses awarded under paragraph (2)(b) shall not exceed the expenses of the process before the date of the hearing on the By Order roll.

GENERAL NOTE.

On the introduction of the new Chap. 43 and this rule, see note 43.1.1. The party in default must lodge in process a written explanation for the default: r.43.7(1)(b)(ii). The by order hearing will still take place even if the party in default has since complied: P.N. No. 2 of 2003.   **43.7.1**

SANCTIONS.

From the 2000 Report, Chap. 10, it appears that it is hoped that a state of co-operation will become the new culture and that bludgeoning parties into compliance may be counter-productive. The working party recognised that the sanction of expenses could lose its bite if parties settled and dealt with expenses as part of the settlement (although they could not directly defeat an award). The working party considered that, generally, failure to comply with a step should result in the party having to explain the failure to the court. Hence the provision for the by order hearing. In two situations the working party considered severe sanctions should be imposed: (1) failure to lodge a document or comply with a date in the timetable order, by awarding expenses of process to date against the party in default; and (2) failure to lodge a statement of value of claim, by dismissing the action (if pursuer in default) or granting decree for the amount in the claim (if defender in default). The former is dealt with in r.43.7(2) and the latter in r.43.9(7).   **43.7.2**

The sanctions in r.43.7 are (a) expenses, which are not to exceed the expenses of process to date (r. 43.7(2)(b) and (3)), and (b) any other appropriate order, including dismissal (r. 43.7(2)(c)). Expenses could be party in party, agent and client, or modified expenses. Other appropriate orders may include: payment of expenses as a condition precedent to further procedure; and liability for an additional fee. Absolvitor is not specifically excluded but may be implied by the rule being inclusive of dismissal.

"NOT LESS THAN SEVEN DAYS AFTER".

The date of notice of the date of the by order hearing is not counted.   **43.7.3**

"LODGE IN PROCESS".

The written explanation will be a step in process (r.1.3(1)). On lodging steps of process, see rr.4.4–4.6.   **43.7.4**

"NOT LESS THAN TWO CLEAR WORKING DAYS BEFORE".

The date of the hearing is not counted.   **43.7.5**

Applications for sist or for variation of timetable order

43.8.—[1](1) The action may be sisted or the timetable issued under rule 43.6 may be varied by the court on an application by any party to the action by motion.   **43.8**

(2) An application under paragraph (1)—

    (a)   shall be placed before the Lord Ordinary; and

    (b)[2] shall be granted only on cause shown.

(3) Any sist of an action shall be for a specific period.

(4) Where a timetable issued under rule 43.6 is varied under this rule, the Keeper of the Rolls shall issue a revised timetable in Form 43.6.

(5) A revised timetable issued under paragraph (4) shall have effect as if it were a timetable issued under rule 43.6 and any reference in this Chapter to any action

---

[1] R. 43.8 substituted by SSI 2002/570 (effective 1st April 2003).

[2] As amended by the Act of Sederunt (Rules of the Court of Session, Ordinary Cause Rules and Summary Cause Rules Amendment) (Miscellaneous) 2014 (SSI 2014/152) r.2 (effective 7th July, 2014).

being taken in accordance with the timetable shall be construed as a reference to its being taken in accordance with the timetable as varied under this rule.

GENERAL NOTE.

43.8.1   On the introduction of the new Chap. 43 and this rule, see note 43.1.1.

SIST.

43.8.2   Applications for sist, such as for legal aid, should be made before, or when, defences are lodged in order to avoid the need to vary the timetable order: P.N. No. 2 of 2003.

The 2000 Report, Chap. 4, suggests that sists should be discouraged and that all grants of sist should be for a fixed period. A sist for legal aid should be granted only on special cause shown. If legal aid has not already been applied for, an interlocutor granting a sist should be intimated to SLAB. Delay in applying for legal aid may result in a motion to sist being refused.

VARIATION OF TIMETABLE.

43.8.3   A motion to extend the timetable is unlikely to be granted, whereas one to accelerate the timetable (particularly where the pursuer's life expectancy is within the period of the timetable) is more likely to be favourably considered: P.N. No. 2 of 2003.

Any motion should contain full details of the grounds, including any relevant supporting medical evidence: P.N. No. 2 of 2003.

"MOTION".

43.8.4   For motions, see Chap. 23.

"SPECIAL CAUSE".

43.8.5   The motion must disclose what the special cause is: P.N. No. 1 of 2013, para. 2.

Statements of valuation of claim

43.9   **43.9.**—[1](1) Each party to an action shall make a statement of valuation of claim in Form 43.9.

(2) A statement of valuation of claim (which shall include a list of supporting documents) shall be lodged in process.

(3) Each party shall, on lodging a statement of valuation of claim—

(a)   intimate the list of documents included in the statement of valuation of claim to every other party; and

(b)   lodge each of those documents.

(4)–(5) *[Omitted by SSI 2007/282 (effective 2nd May 2007).]*

(6) Nothing in paragraph (3) shall affect—

(a)   the law relating to, or the right of a party to object to the recovery of a document on the ground of, privilege or confidentiality; or

(b)   the right of a party to apply under rule 35.2 for a commission and diligence for recovery of documents or an order under section 1 of the Administration of Justice (Scotland) Act 1972.

(7) Without prejudice to paragraph (2) of rule 43.7 (hearings on the By Order roll), where a party has failed to lodge a statement of valuation of claim in accordance with a timetable issued under paragraph (2) of rule 43.6 (allocation of diets and timetables) the court may at a hearing of the cause on the By Order roll under paragraph (3) of that rule—

(a)   where the party in default is the pursuer, dismiss the action; or

(b)   where the party in default is the defender, grant decree against the defender for an amount not exceeding the amount of the pursuer's valuation.

GENERAL NOTE.

43.9.1   On the introduction of the new Chap. 43 and this rule, see note 43.1.1.

---

[1] Rule 43.9 substituted by SSI 2002/570 (effective 1st April 2003) and amended by SSI 2007/282 (effective 2nd May 2007).

The statement of value of claim is one of the cornerstones of the scheme (confirmed in *Moran v Freyssinet Ltd*, 2016 S.C. 188, 2015 S.L.T. 829 (Extra Div.)). The 2000 Report states, in Chap. 7, that the object is to bring forward the point at which a party can see how each other party is approaching the valuation of the claim and what material supports it. There are draconian sanctions available to the court for failure to comply: see r.43.9(7) and note 43.9.9.

The practice of stating "TBC" (to be confirmed) is to cease: P.N. No. 1 of 2013, para. 3.

"STATEMENT OF VALUE OF CLAIM".

The statement must be in Form 43.9. The form has no heading or instance; but the statement should be headed up, have the court reference number and the instance in order to identify the case to which it refers. The form is a template or pro forma and may be adjusted to suit the particular case: *Logic v. Fife Council* , 16th August 2006, 2006 G.W.D. 26-585 (OH), [2006 CSOH] 127.

43.9.2

Each party must lodge a statement of valuation. According to the timetable order issued under r.43.6(1), the pursuer will do so first and the defender will do so some eight weeks later. It should be noted that under r.4.6 a copy of the statement should be sent to every other party.

In addition to lodging a statement of valuation, each party must (a) give written intimation to every other party of the list of documents that support the valuation, and (b) lodge that list in process: r.43.9(2) and (3).

P.N. No. 2 of 2003, although not a statement, or rule, of law, states (a) that the statement of valuation is not binding on a party, yet (b) can be founded on by any party.

"DOCUMENTS".

The word "document" has been defined in R.C.S. 1994 by reference to the inclusive definition in s.9 of the Civil Evidence (Scotland) Act 1988: see r.1.3(1). The documents in support of the valuation might include medical report, wage certificates, the report in respect of any special needs claim, and statements and vouching of any claim for services.

43.9.3

"LODGED IN PROCESS".

The statements of valuation of claim will be lodged as steps of process (r.1.3(1) (definition of "step of process"). On lodging a step of process, see rr.4.4–4.6).

43.9.4

"WRITTEN INTIMATION".

For methods, see r.16.9.

43.9.5

"WITHIN 14 DAYS AFTER".

The date of receipt of the list is not counted. The difficulty with calculating the date from the date of receipt, rather than the date of sending the list, is that the date of receipt is not a definitely known and instantly verifiable date.

43.9.6

INSPECTION OF DOCUMENTS.

Rule 43.9(4)–(6) has been taken from old r.43.25. Parties should agree the time and place for inspection. If a party is being unreasonable, the other party could apply to the court for an order for which failure to obtemper would constitute contempt.

43.9.7

"PRIVILEGE OR CONFIDENTIALITY".

For privilege and confidentiality, see note 35.2.7.

43.9.8

SANCTIONS.

Rule 43.9(7) follows the proposal in the 2000 Report, Chap. 10, for failure to lodge a statement of claim in accordance with the timetable order.

43.9.9

Where a party fails to lodge a statement of claim in accordance with the timetable, the court may, at the by order hearing held under r.43.7, (a) dismiss the action, if the pursuer is in default, or (b) grant decree for an amount not exceeding the pursuer's valuation, if the defender is in default: r.43.9(7). These powers may be exercised even where there is no or no adequate information or no reasonable explanation for their lack. In complex cases, where it is impracticable to provide the information, P.N. No. 2 of 2009 suggests a motion to vary the timetable. In *Moran v Freyssinet Ltd,* 2016 S.C. 188, 2015 S.L.T. 829 (Extra Div.), the Lord Ordinary's decision, to grant decree for the sum sued for (the defender having failed to lodge a statement of valuation), was upheld because of persistent failures to comply with the rules indicating a casual approach to the rules.

For the hearing on the By Order Roll, see r.43.7.

SOCIAL SECURITY (RECOVERY OF BENEFITS) ACT 1997.

Under the Social Security (Recovery of Benefits) Act 1997, the person (the compensator) compensating the victim of an accident, injury or disease is liable to pay in full to the Secretary of State for Social Security the amount of the recoverable social security benefits (for which see column 2 of Sched. 2 to the 1997 Act) paid to the victim in respect of payment of damages on or after 6th October 1997. The compensator is entitled to deduct, from certain specified heads of compensation he is to pay to the victim, the amount of the recoverable benefits (see 1997 Act, s.8). These heads, specified in column I of Sched. 2

43.9.10

to the 1997 Act, are the compensation for earnings lost, the compensation for cost of care, and the compensation for loss of mobility, during the relevant period. The compensator will then pay the sum deducted to the Secretary of State (to the CRU). The "relevant period" is the five years immediately following the date of the accident or injury or, in the case of disease, the date on which the victim first claimed a listed benefit: see 1997 Act, s.3(2) and (3). If at any time before the end of that period a compensation payment is made in final discharge of any claim, the relevant period ends on that date: 1997 Act, s.3(4)(a). The £2,500 small payments threshold has been abolished.

Where the pursuer received benefits to which the 1997 Act applies, the court, on pronouncing decree for payment of the damages, must specify the amount of compensation payment in the case of each head of compensation: 1997 Act, s. 15(2). A difficulty arises where the final decree is pronounced within the five-year relevant period: is the court required to specify the damages for a period ending on the date of payment (not then determinable) after final decree, the final discharge occurring and the relevant period ending, under s.3(4)(a) of the 1997 Act, on the date of payment; or is the date of decree to be deemed to be the date of payment? The solution has been provided by the Inner House in *Mitchell v. Laing* , 1998 S.C. 342 (First Div). The court held that the intention of the legislation was that the amount of recoverable benefits to be deducted from the heads of compensation was the amount payable over the whole five-year period. Accordingly, the court in pronouncing decree would specify the damages due for the specified heads of compensation for the full five years.

Other points raised by the 1997 Act are:

1. *Tenders.* There are five possibilities: (a) a tender in the usual form (i.e. stipulating a total or global sum); (b) a tender containing specification or a breakdown of the offer of damages for loss of earnings, and any cost of care and loss of mobility attributable to the relevant period; (c) a tender in the usual form accompanied by a back letter giving the breakdown; (d) a tender of an offer of damages stating that it is net of benefits; or (e) a tender of an offer of damages stating that it is net of benefits accompanied by a back letter giving the breakdown. All have their drawbacks. A pursuer will not wish to accept a tender in form (a) because he will not know whether the element from which the deductions are to be made may be the largest part of the offer. It may be that a tender in form (b) would satisfy all those having an interest. It has now been confirmed, in *Spence v. Wilson (No.2)* , 1998 S.L.T. 959 (OH), that a tender in form (a) is invalid and, accordingly a tender should be in form (b). For tenders generally, see 36.11.8.

2. *Contributory negligence.* This will reduce the amount of damages to the pursuer but not the amount of recoverable benefits payable by the defender to the CRU.

3. *Interest.* The 1997 Act repeals s. 103 of the Social Security (Administration) Act 1992 which provided that in assessing interest the award of damages is reduced by a sum equal to the amount of relevant benefits received. Section 81(5) of the 1992 Act has been re-enacted in s. 17 of the 1997 Act which provides that in assessing damages the amount of any listed benefits paid is to be disregarded. The question arises whether, now, in assessing interest the whole of the listed benefits received should be deducted and interest applied only to the balance or that no deduction should be made and interest applied to the gross award. There was a divergence of judicial opinion in the Outer House. In *George v. George C. Peebles & Son* , 1998 S.L.T. 685 (OH), Lord Nimmo Smith held that, since the primary purpose of an award of interest is to compensate a pursuer for being deprived of the use of money which he would have received but for the accident, it was inappropriate to leave out of account the fact that he had received benefits in place of earnings he would have received. The inference was that Parliament intended that the discretion conferred by s.1(1A) of the Interest on Damages (Scotland) Act 1958 should continue to be exercised; and interest was awarded in that case on the difference between the loss of earnings and income support received. In *Spence v. Wilson* , 1998 S.C. 433 (OH), Lord Eassie came to the opposite opinion. He held that s.103 and its statutory predecessor innovated on the preceding common law and that the repeal of s.103 and omission of a re-enactment implied a legislative intention that the receipt of benefits was to be disregarded in the assessment of interest just as in the assessment of damages (notwithstanding, it must be supposed, that there is an express provision for the latter). The issue has now been determined by the Inner House in a report from the Lord Ordinary in *Wisely v. John Fulton (Plumbers) Ltd* , 1998 S.C. 910 and confirmed by the House of Lords (2000 S.L.T. 494). It was held that, by virtue of s.17 of the 1997 Act, the court disregards any benefits received by the pursuer when working out interest and, therefore, calculates interest on the whole amount of the damages for past loss of earnings. The case of *George*, above, was wrongly decided because it is inconsistent with the scheme of the 1997 Act.

    The compensation for earnings lost during the relevant period in col. 1 of Sched. 2 to the 1997 Act, against which the compensator may set off his liability to repay the listed benefits, includes any sum of interest on damages for past loss of earnings: *Wisely*, above.

4. *The interlocutor granting decree.* Under P.N. No. 3 of 1997, parties seeking decree in an action of reparation for personal injuries (except where that decree is sought of consent, e.g. because of a joint minute) must lodge in process a schedule of damages for the purposes of s. 15(2) of the Social Security (Recovery of Benefits) Acts 1997 stating the amount of any compensation in respect of the relevant period under the heads of compensation in column 1 of Sched. 2 to the 1997 Act. It is apparent that the interlocutor subsequently pronounced will not itself specify the amounts under each head but will refer to a (or the) appended schedule which does. Clerks of session have been issuing blank schedules in the following form:

    Schedule to interlocutor of even date (*amend as necessary*)

1. Solatium—   To date:

            Future:

2. Loss of Earnings—To end of relevant period (*date*):

    Subsequent to end of relevant period:

3. Compensation for

      (1) cost of care:

          to end of relevant period (*date*):

          subsequent to end of relevant period (*date*):

      (2) loss of mobility

          to end of relevant period date:

          subsequent to end of relevant period (*date*):

4. Section 8 services:

5. Section 9 services:

6. Medical expenses:

TOTAL:

Loss of pension rights, etc.:

Less ( )% due to contributory negligence: Sum decerned for:

5. *Benefits disregarded.* Section 17 of the 1997 Act provides that, in respect of any accident, injury or disease, the amount of any listed benefits paid or likely to be paid is to be disregarded. That does not include benefits received prior to the accident: *McKenna v. Sharp* , 1998 S.C. 297 (OH), sub. nam. *McKenna v. Chief Constable Strathclyde Police* , 1998 S.L.T. 1161.

6. *Heads of compensation from which relevant benefits may be deducted.* These heads, specified in column 1 of Sched. 2 to the 1997 Act, are the compensation for earnings lost, the compensation for cost of care, and the compensation for loss of mobility, during the relevant period. In *Mitchell v. Laing* , 1998 S.C. 342 (First Div.) it was held that "loss of mobility" means damages for patrimonial loss suffered as a result of loss of mobility due to the accident, injury or disease. In *McManus' Exrx v. Babcock Energy Ltd* , 1999 S.C. 569 (OH) it was held that an award for services rendered to an injured person under s. 8 of the Administration of Justice Act 1982 was not "compensation for cost of care" and, therefore, benefits such as attendance allowance could not be deducted under s. 8 of the 1997 Act.

7. *Expenses.* The general rule that expenses follow success applies even though the whole of the sum awarded is paid to the CRU (Compensation Recovery Unit) of the DSS under the Social Security (Recovery of Benefits) Act 1997: *Gray v. Lanarkshire Health Board* , 1998 S.L.T. 1378 (OH).

Pre-trial meetings

43.10.—[1,2](1) For the purposes of this rule, a pre-trial meeting is a meeting between the parties to—

 (a) discuss settlement of the action; and

 (b) agree, so far as is possible, the matters which are not in dispute between them.

(2) A pre-trial meeting must—

 (a) be held not later than four weeks before the date assigned for the proof or trial; and

 (b) be attended by parties—

  (i) in person; or

  (ii) by means of video-conference facilities.

(3) A joint minute of a pre-trial meeting, made in Form 43.10 (minute of pre-trial meeting), must be lodged in process by the pursuer not later than three weeks before the date for the proof or trial.

43.10

---

[1] R.43.10 substituted by SSI 2002/570 (effective 1st April 2003).
[2] Rule 43.10 as substituted by S.S.I. 2015 No. 227 (effective 22nd September 2015).

(4) Where a joint minute in Form 43.10 has not been lodged in accordance with paragraph (3) and by the date specified in the timetable, the Keeper of the Rolls must put the case out to be heard on the By Order roll.

(5) If a party is not in attendance during the pre-trial meeting, the representative of such party must have access to the party or another person who has authority to commit the party in settlement of the action.

GENERAL NOTE.

43.10.1   On the introduction of the new Chap. 43 and this rule, see note 43.1.1.

Since most reparation actions go to proof (or prove before answer), it would have been better to call this a pre-proof hearing rather than to use the Anglo-American terminology of a pre-trial hearing. The word "proof" does not exclude jury trial as even in a trial there must be proof; whereas the word "trial" excludes the Scottish concept of a proof.

The Cullen *Review of the Business of the Outer House of the Court of Session* in 1995 recommended a pre-proof hearing before a judge. The 2000 Report proposed that the pre-proof hearing should simply be a meeting between the parties. It was considered, without reference to any empirical evidence, that the Cullen model added a stage that was expensive for parties and burdensome for the court. That proposal is reflected in r. 43.10. Thus the court has gone against the trend in other common law jurisdictions such as the US and England and Wales. In the US, for example, the pre-trial hearing does not have to be chaired by a judge, but there is always a facilitator (e.g. a judge or another lawyer) to chair the meeting. It is not clear how the Court of Session model will work to achieve settlements where there is no person at the meeting to facilitate, mediate or direct the settlement discussion between parties already locked in combat. All that this model is doing, rather than increase the number of settlements, is to bring forward the door-of-court-settlement process to a date some three weeks before the proof.

"PRE-TRIAL MEETING".

43.10.2   Rule 43.10(1) states that the pre-trial, or more correctly pre-proof, meeting is between parties. The 2000 Report and P.N. No. 2 of 2003 make it clear that the meeting will be conducted by the legal advisers. In fact it is not necessary that the person with authority to settle the action for a party need be present, so long as he is contactable during the meeting: r. 43.10(5). It is envisaged that the meeting could be by video conferencing. It is expected that counsel will attend the meeting, because the joint minute of the meeting must be signed by counsel (or solicitor-advocate).

Parties are expected to discuss two things: (a) settlement, and (b) in any event, agree matters not in dispute: r. 43.10(1).

From the terms of the form of joint minute of the meeting in Form 43.10, it is clear that a number of questions *must* be answered on detailed aspects of the case. They must, therefore, be discussed at the pre-proof meeting.

Parties are expected to take such steps as are necessary to comply with the spirit as well as the letter of the rule. Where a party considers that not all steps have been taken to comply with the letter and spirit of the rule, that party should not sign the joint minute: P.N. No. 1 of 2013, para. 4. Parties are encouraged to make use of the Chap. 28A procedure (notices to admit/of non-admission): para. 4.

Where there are a number of defenders and, or, third parties, a voluntary meeting before the compulsory meeting under this rule is suggested in P.N. No. 2 of 2009.

"NOT LATER THAN FOUR WEEKS BEFORE".

43.10.3   The day from which the calculation is made is not counted.

JOINT MINUTE.

43.10.4   The joint minute must be in Form 43.10. The timetable order will specify the date by which the joint minute of the pre-proof meeting must be lodged, failing which there will be a by order hearing (see note 43.10.7). That date cannot be less than three weeks before the proof date: r. 43.10(2). The joint minute must be signed by counsel or other person having a right of audience (solicitor-advocate).

Section 2 of the joint minute may assume that parties will have used the notices to admit and non-admission procedure in Chap. 28A, as the section has space for the calls made to admit certain facts and whether they were admitted or denied. It would be possible for calls to be made at the pre-proof meeting without using the Chap. 28A procedure.

It is the responsibility of the pursuer to lodge the joint minute in process: r. 43.10(2).

"LODGED IN PROCESS".

43.10.5   The joint minute will be lodged as a step of process (r. 1.3(1) (definition of "step of process"). On lodging a step of process, see rr. 4.4–4.6).

"NOT LESS THAN THREE WEEKS BEFORE".

43.10.6   The day from which the calculation is made is not counted. Where the last day falls on a Saturday or Sunday, or a public holiday on which the Office of Court is closed, the next available day is allowed: r. 1.3(7). For office hours and public holidays, see note 3.1.2.

BY ORDER ROLL.

Where the joint minute is not lodged by the date in the timetable order, there must be a by order hearing: r. 43.10(4). At that hearing the court will require an explanation and may award (a) expenses against a party, or (b) make any other order, including dismissal (if the pursuer is at fault). See further, r. 43.7.

43.10.7

Applications for interim payments of damages

43.11.—[1](1)   A pursuer may, at any time after defences have been lodged, apply by motion for an order for interim payment of damages to him by the defender or, where there are two or more of them, by any one or more of them.

43.11

(2)   The pursuer shall give written intimation of a motion under paragraph (1) to every other party not less than 14 days before the date on which the motion is enrolled.

(3)[2]   On a motion under paragraph (1), the court may ordain—

(a)   any defender who has admitted liability to the pursuer in the action; or

(b)   where the court is satisfied that, if the action proceeded to proof, the pursuer would succeed on the question of liability without any substantial finding of contributory negligence on his part, or on the part of any person in respect of whose injury or death the claim of the pursuer arises, and would obtain decree for damages, any defender who has not admitted liability to the pursuer in the action,

to make an interim payment to the pursuer of such amount as it thinks fit, not exceeding a reasonable proportion of the damages which, in the opinion of the court, are likely to be recovered by the pursuer.

(4)   Any such payment may be ordered to be made in one lump sum or otherwise as the court thinks fit.

(5)   No order shall be made against a defender under this rule unless it appears to the court that the defender is—

(a)   a person who is insured in respect of the claim of the pursuer;

(aa)[3]   a person who is not insured but in respect of whose liability the Motor Insurers' Bureau will be liable to make payment;

(b)   a public authority; or

(c)   a person whose means and resources are such as to enable him to make the interim payment.

(6)   Notwithstanding the grant or refusal of a motion for an interim payment, a subsequent motion may be made where there has been a change of circumstances.

(7)   Subject to Part IV (management of money payable to children), any interim payment shall be made to the pursuer unless the court otherwise directs.

(8)   This rule shall, with the necessary modifications, apply to a counterclaim for damages for personal injuries made by a defender.

(9)   In this rule "defender" includes a third party against whom the pursuer has a conclusion for damages.

(10)[4]   For the purposes of this rule, the reference in paragraph (5)(a) to a person who is insured in respect of the claim of a pursuer includes a reference to a person in respect of whose liability an insurer under section 151 of the Road Traffic Act 1988 will be liable to make payment.

Deriv. R.C.S. 1965, r. 89A(1)(a) to (g) (r. 43.11(1)–(8)) inserted by SI 1974/845; and R.C.S. 1994, old r. 43.8(2) (part) (r. 43.11(9))

---

[1] R. 43.11 substituted by SSI 2002/570 (effective 1st April, 2003).
[2] R. 43.11(3) inserted by SSI 2006/83 (effective 17th March 2006).
[3] R. 43.11(5)(aa) inserted by SSI 2004/331 (effective 6th August 2004).
[4] R. 43.11(10) inserted by SSI 2010/205 (effective 15th June 2010).

GENERAL NOTE.

43.11.1   Rule 43.11(1)—(8) is in the same terms as old r. 43.9, even including the reference to Part IV of old Chap. 43, which was revoked by the A.S. (R.C.S.A. No. 2) (Personal Injuries Actions) 2002 [SSI 2002/570], the rules in that Part having been revoked by SI 1996/2587!

Temp. Judge Coutts, Q.C., has suggested, in *Hogg v. Carrigan's Exr* , 2001 S.C. 542, 554D (para.[9]), that r. 43.9 (now r. 43.11) should be radically rephrased. Rule 43.9(3)(a) did not, it was suggested, indicate whether it is liability to make reparation or an admission of fault that is meant. This invitation has not so far been taken up.

An amendment has been made to r. 43.11(3) by A.S. (R.C.S.A.) (Miscellaneous) 2006 [SSI 2006/83], but not as suggested in that case. The amendment deals with a problem that the previous wording of r. 43.11(3)(b) referred to "that defender". Although r.43.11(3) has been set out slightly differently, the only change is to make "that defender" now "any defender": thus restoring the rule to its form in R.C.S. 1965, r. 89A(1); and see further note 43.11.7 for the reason for this.

WHAT DOCUMENTS MAY HE CONSIDERED?

43.11.2   It was held by Lord Allanbridge in *McCann v. Miller Insulation and Engineering Ltd* , 1986 S.L.T. 147 (OH), that, when considering the question of liability and contributory negligence, the court must look at the pleadings alone and not medical reports or other productions. But in *Stone v. Mountford* , 1995 S.L.T. 1279 (OH), Lord Johnston did not follow McCann, and held that the approach in that case did not amount to a general rule, that the discretion available to the court is wide enough to enable the court to review material before it other than the pleadings and to look at productions. It is, however, entitled, when looking at the pleadings, to consider notorious facts: *Reith v. Aberdeen Mineral Water Co.* , 1987 S.C.L.R. 689 (OH). The court may look at reports and other productions when considering quantification of the interim payment.

"MOTION".

43.11.3   For motions, see Chap. 23.

"WRITTEN INTIMATION".

43.11.4   For methods, see r. 16.9.

"SATISFIED".

43.11.5   Satisfaction is less than complete certainty but it requires more than probability or even high probability: *Douglas's C.B. v. Douglas* , 1974 S.L.T. (Notes) 67 (OH) per Lord Maxwell. It means "almost certainly": *Nelson v. Duraplex Industries Ltd* , 1975 S.L.T. (Notes) 31 (OH), 33 per Lord Grieve. This approach was accepted by counsel in *Walker v. Infabco Diving Services Ltd* , 1983 S.L.T. 633 (Extra Div.), and confirmed in *Cowie v. Atlantic Drilling Co. Ltd* , 1995 S.C. 288 (First Div.), where it was held (p. 1154H-Jper Hope, L.P.) that the pursuer has to show that it was practically certain that he would succeed on the question of liability or that he would almost certainly do so.

On the question of liability, a relevant conviction may assist the court in being satisfied: *Reid v. Planet Welding Equipment Ltd* , 1980 S.L.T. (Notes) 7 (OH). It may be difficult to be satisfied where the defender denies material averments: *Reid v. J. Smart & Co. Ltd* , 1981 S.L.T. (Notes) 20 (OH); *McCann v. Miller Insulation and Engineering Ltd* , 1986 S.L.T. 147 (OH).

Proximity of the motion for interim payment to the proof is a relevant factor, but only in exceptional circumstances would it justify making no award: *Kay v. G.P. Inveresk Corporation* , 1988 S.L.T. 711 (OH), 713E per Lord Dervaird.

"WITHOUT ANY SUBSTANTIAL FINDING OF CONTRIBUTORY NEGLIGENCE".

43.11.6   The better view is that "substantial" means a considerable amount, and does not mean of substance in the sense of not being de minimis, because the fact that the pursuer was contributorily negligent to some extent does not mean he will get nothing when damages are ultimately assessed: *Reid v. Planet Welding Equipment Ltd* , 1980 S.L.T. (Notes) 7 (OH); *McNeill v. Roche Products Ltd* , 1988 S.L.T. 705 (OH); cf *Nelson v. Duraplex Industries Ltd* , 1975 S.L.T. (Notes) 31 (OH); *Noble v. Noble* , 1979 S.L.T. (Notes) 75 (OH) and *Herron v. Kennon* , 1986 S.L.T. 260 (OH). This view was upheld in *Cowie v. Atlantic Drilling Co. Ltd* , 1995 S.C. 288 (First Div.), 294D per Hope, L.P: "substantial" means something of real importance to the assessment of the extent of the defender's liability; and the court must be satisfied that the finding of contributory negligence will not be so large as to have a material effect on the assessment of damages the pursuer is likely to recover.

In *Reid*, above, Lord Ross did not regard contributory negligence which would not exceed one-quarter or a third as substantial. In *Hogg v. Carrigan's Exr* , 2001 S.C. 542 (OH), 544F at para.[10], it was suggested that even contributory negligence of 50 per cent was not "substantial".

"WOULD OBTAIN DECREE FOR DAMAGES AGAINST ANY DEFENDER".

43.11.7   Under R.C.S. 1965, r. 89A(1), where the court was satisfied the pursuer was likely to succeed against at least one of a number of defenders, it could make an award against any one or more of the defenders from whom an interim payment was sought: *Walker v. Infabco Diving Services Ltd* , 1983 S.L.T. 633 (Extra Div.). Under R.C.S. 1994, r. 43.11(3), before amendment in 2006, interim damages could only be obtained from the defender against whom the pursuer would be likely to succeed. This was because the phrase "the defender" in the former rule was replaced by "*that* defender" in the latter rule; hence, the rule in *Walker*, above, could not apply. An amendment has been made to r. 43.11(3) by A.S. (R.C.S.A.) (Miscellaneous) 2006 [SSI 2006/83]. The amendment deals with a problem that the previous wording of r. 43.11(3)(b) referred to "that defender". Although r. 43.11(3) has been set out slightly differently, the only change is to make "that defender" now "any defender": thus restoring the rule to its form in R.C.S. 1965, r. 89A(1). Accordingly, the decision in *Walker*, can be applied.

"SUCH AMOUNT ... NOT EXCEEDING A REASONABLE PROPORTION ... LIKELY TO BE RECOVERED".

Quantification is a matter of discretion. The restraint of the words "not exceeding" provides a ceiling, and, as the limit is a proportion, a conservative and moderate approach is necessary: *Nisbet v. The Marley Roof Tile Co. Ltd* , 1988 S.L.T. 608 (OH). In *D's Parent and Guardian v. Argyll and Clyde Acute Hospitals NHS Trust* , 2003 S.L.T.511 (OH), Lord Carloway considered that 75% or more should not necessarily be seen as exceeding a "reasonable proportion", especially where a minimum figure of likely damages is accepted by the defender in a given case. In *Lennox v. Bishop* , 2005 G.W.D. 32-613, 1st July 2005 (OH), it was held that there was no justification for taking, as a starting point, the minimum award likely and then applying a conservative percentage around 30 to 40 per cent.

43.11.8

The stage which an action has reached is a relevant but not determinative consideration.

An award may be made notwithstanding: (a) that the intention is to spend the award to meet expenditure which is not a head of claim (*Thompson's C.B. v. Burnett* 1989 S.L.T. 264 (OH)); or (b) that the award may involve payment which exceeds the value of the claim for loss to date (*Nisbet*, above; *Thompson's C.B.*, above).

The pursuer does not have to show he is suffering actual hardship (*McNicol v. Buko Ltd* , 1986 S.L.T. 12 (OH), 14E per Lord McCluskey; *Curran v. H.A.T. Painters (Scotland) Ltd* , 1987 S.L.T. 98 (OH) per Lord Cullen; *McNeill v. Roche Products Ltd* , 1988 S.L.T. 705 (OH), 706H per Lord Coulsfield), although it may be a relevant factor (*McNicol*, above).

State benefits may have to be taken into account: *Curran*, above.

"LUMP SUM OR OTHERWISE".

An interim payment of damages may, where parties consent, be ordered to be paid in the form of periodical payments: Damages Act 1996, s. 2.

43.11.9

"A PERSON WHO IS INSURED...A PUBLIC AUTHORITY...A PERSON WHOSE MEANS AND RESOURCES ARE SUCH".

The basic purpose of r. 43.11(5) is that interim damages will only be made when the person liable is able to make the payment: *Gellatly v. AXA Corporate Solutions Assurance SA* 2009 S.L.T. 721 (OH). In that case the defender's insurers would be liable by virtue of s. 151 of the Road Traffic Act 1988 because the vehicle was insured though the defender driver was uninsured because she did not have the permission of the insured to drive. It was argued unsuccessfully that a motion for interim damages was incompetent because the defender driver was not insured. "[A] person whose means and resources" refers to a person who can meet the obligation to pay out of funds which are his or his to dispose of at will: *Ferguson v. McGrandles*, 1993 S.L.T. 822 (OH), 823 per Lord Penrose.

43.11.10

SUBSEQUENT MOTION ON A CHANGE OF CIRCUMSTANCES

There may be more than one subsequent motion.

In *Murphy v. Dunbia (UK) (t/a Highland Meats)* 2022 S.L. T. 1219 (OH), 1222, para. [13], Lord Lake held that, whether the earlier motion had been refused or granted, the change of circumstances would have to relate to something that bears on the issues that have to be decided such that a different outcome might be expected to result and would, therefore, have to be material and directly relevant to the key factors that must be considered in such a motion.

43.11.11

MANAGEMENT OF MONEY PAYABLE TO CHILDREN.

Where the interim payment is for the benefit of a child the court will have to consider the management of that money: see Children (Scotland) Act 1995, s. 13; and note 49.88.2 for detailed discussion.

43.11.12

SOCIAL SECURITY (RECOVERY OF BENEFITS) ACT 1997.

Under the Social Security (Recovery of Benefits) Act 1997, the person (the compensator) compensating the victim of an accident, injury or disease is liable to pay in full to the Secretary of State for Social Security the amount of the recoverable social security benefits (for which see column 2 of Sched. 2 to the 1997 Act) paid to the victim in respect of payment of damages on or after 6th October 1997. The compensator is entitled to deduct, from certain specified heads of compensation he is to pay to the victim, the amount of the recoverable benefits (see 1997 Act, s. 8). These heads, specified in column 1 of Sched. 2 to the 1997 Act, are the compensation for earnings lost, the compensation for cost of care, and the compensation for loss of mobility, during the relevant period. The compensator will then pay the sum deducted to the Secretary of State (to the CRU). The "relevant period" is the five years immediately following the date of the accident or injury or, in the case of disease, the date on which the victim first claimed a listed benefit): see 1997 Act, s. 3(2) and (3). If at any time before the end of that period a compensation payment is made in final discharge of any claim, the relevant period ends on that date: 1997 Act, s. 3(4)(a). The £2,500 small payments threshold has been abolished.

Where the pursuer received benefits to which the 1997 Act applies, the court, on pronouncing decree for payment of the interim damages, must specify the amount of compensation payment in the case of

43.11.13

each head of compensation: 1997 Act, s. 15(2). A difficulty arises where the decree is pronounced *within* the five-year relevant period: is the court required to specify the damages for a period ending on the date of payment (not then determinable) after decree, the final discharge occurring and the relevant period ending, under s. 3(4)(a) of the 1997 Act, on the date of payment; or is the date of decree to be deemed to be the date of payment? The solution has been provided by the Inner House in *Mitchell v. Laing* , 1998 S.C. 342. The court held that the intention of the legislation was that the amount of recoverable benefits to be deducted from the heads of compensation was the amount payable over the whole five-year period. Accordingly, the court in pronouncing decree would specify the damages due for the specified heads of compensation for the full five years. As at the date of interim damages, the benefits recoverable from the relevant heads of compensation are the listed benefits paid or likely to be paid during the period from the date of injury (or claim for benefit in the case of disease) to the date of payment of interim damages or the end of the five year period, whichever is earlier.

The court also held in that case that the words "loss of mobility" in column 1 of Sched. 2 to the 1997 Act mean damages for patrimonial loss suffered as a result of loss of mobility due to the accident, injury or disease.

Adjustment on final decree

43.12   **43.12.**[1] Where a defender has made an interim payment order under rule 43.11(3), the court may make such order, when final decree is pronounced, with respect to the interim payment as it thinks fit to give effect to the final liability of that defender to the pursuer; and in particular may order—

    (a)   repayment by the pursuer of any sum by which the interim payment exceeds the amount which that defender is liable to pay the pursuer; or

    (b)   payment by any other defender or a third party of any part of the interim payment which the defender who made it is entitled to recover from him by way of contribution or indemnity or in respect of any remedy or relief relating to, or connected with, the claim of the pursuer.

Deriv. R.C.S. 1965, r.89A(2) inserted by SI 1974/845; and R.C.S. 1994, old r.43.10

GENERAL NOTE.

43.12.1   Rule 43.12 is in the same terms as old r.43.10.

"MAY MAKE SUCH ORDER ... AS IT THINKS FIT".

43.12.2   That the court may make such order as it thinks fit, gives the court a wide general discretion; and the words "and in particular may order" is a clear indication that what follows are two examples of what the court may do, without prejudice to the generality.

In *Walker v. Infabco Diving Services Ltd* , 1983 S.L.T. 633 (Extra Div.), Lord Cowie observed that r.43.10(a) (now r.43.12(a)) allows the court to adjust the position whether liability to the pursuer is established or not; and r.43.10(b) (now r.43.12(b)) allows the court to adjust the position between defenders and envisages the position that one defender, against whom an order for interim payment has been made, may be assoilzied and may recover that amount from a defender against whom liability has been established.

Where a final award is made, care must be taken to ensure that interest is not applied to that portion which formed an interim award after the date on which that interim award was paid.

"FINAL DECREE".

43.12.3   This relates individually to the position of any particular defender and not simply to the last of a number of defenders whose position is considered; so, where a pursuer, who was paid interim damages by two defenders, abandoned against one of them, it was competent for that defender to recover his share from the other defender: *Mitchell v. H.A.T. Contracting Services Ltd (No. 3)* , 1993 S.L.T. 1199 (OH).

INTEREST ON REPAYMENT.

43.12.4   In *Walker v. Infabco Diving Services Ltd* , 1983 S.L.T. 633 (Extra Div.), Lord Ross observed at p.641 that interest would be due on repayment of the interim damages; but Lord Stott at p.638, and Lord Cowie at p.642, took a contrary view as the rule made no mention of interest. The fact that the rule does not specifically mention interest is not conclusive; the rule gives the court a wide discretion to make such order as it thinks fit, which could include an order relating to interest.

Applications for further damages

43.13   **43.13.**—[2](1) An application for further damages by a pursuer in respect of whom an order under section 12(2)(b) of the Administration of Justice Act 1982 has been

---

[1] Rule 43.12 substituted by S.S.I. 2002 No. 570 (effective 1st April 2003).
[2] Rule 43.13 substituted by S.S.I. 2002 No. 570 (effective 1st April 2003).

made shall be made by minute and shall include—

    (a)   a conclusion in Form 43.13-A; and

    (b)   averments in the statement of facts supporting that conclusion.

   (2) On lodging such a minute in process, the pursuer shall apply by motion for warrant to serve the minute on—

    (a)   every other party; and

    (b)   where such other party is insured or otherwise indemnified, his insurer or indemnifier, if known to the pursuer.

   (3) A notice of intimation in Form 43.13-B shall be attached to the copy of the minute served on a warrant granted on a motion under paragraph (2).

   (4) Any such party, insurer or indemnifier may lodge answers to such a minute in process within 28 days after the date of service on him.

Deriv. R.C.S. 1965, r.134C inserted by SI 1984/919; and R.C.S. 1994 old r.43.13

GENERAL NOTE.

Rule 43.13 is in the same terms as old r.43.13, save that the minute has no pleas-in-law: see r.43.13(1). **43.13.1**

'MINUTE".

For applications by minute, see r.15.1. **43.13.2**

"LODGING SUCH A MINUTE IN PROCESS".

The minute is lodged as a step of process (r. 1.3(1) (definition of "step of process")) in the process of **43.13.3**
the action to which it relates. On lodging a step of process, see rr.4.4–4.6.

"SERVE".

For methods, see Chap. 16, Pt I. **43.13.4**

EVIDENCE OF SERVICE.

See note 16.1.5. On expiry of the period of notice after service, the certificate of service must be at- **43.13.5**
tached to the minute lodged under this rule.

"ANSWERS".

See r.18.3. **43.13.6**

"WITHIN 28 DAYS".

The date from which the period is calculated is not counted. Where the last day falls on a Saturday or **43.13.7**
Sunday, or a public holiday on which the Office of Court is closed, the next available day is allowed:
r.1.3(7). For office hours and public holidays, see note 3.1.2.

SECTION 12 OF THE ADMINISTRATION OF JUSTICE ACT 1982

Section 12 of the Administration of Justice Act 1982 provides for provisional damages for personal **43.13.8**
injuries to be awarded where there is proved or admitted to be a risk that at some definite or indefinite
time in the future the injured person will, as a result of the act or omission which gave rise to the cause of
action, develop some serious disease or suffer some serious deterioration in his physical or mental
condition. Rule 43.13 provides the procedure for applying for the further damages as a result of the order
(for provisional damages and) for the right to apply for further damages under s. 12(2) of the 1982 Act .

A question has arisen in relation to further damages following a tender and acceptance which must be
unqualified, clear and unambiguous. A minute of tender and acceptance, while binding between the parties, does not bind the court to award provisional damages: *Fraser v Kitsons Insulation Contractors
Ltd,* 2015 S.L.T. 753 (OH) (court ordered that pursuer might apply for further damages). In *Talbot v
Babcock International Ltd,* 2014 S.L.T. 1077 (OH) 160, there was a tender for and acceptance of
provisional damages (which could only be made if there was an admitted or proved risk of future
damages). The pursuer, in moving for decree, sought to reserve the right to apply for further damages if
the pursuer developed certain conditions. The defender sought to impose different limiting conditions for
such an application. It was held that there was no statutory right of the defender (or the pursuer) to
impose conditions.

Actions by connected persons

43.14

43.14.—[1](1)[2] This rule applies in an action of damages in which, following the death of any person from personal injuries, damages are claimed—

(a) in respect of the injuries from which the deceased died; or

(b) in respect of the death of the deceased.

(2) The pursuer shall aver in the condescendence, as the case may be—

(a) that there are no connected persons;

(b) that there are connected persons, being persons specified in the warrant for intimation; or

(c) that there are connected persons in respect of whom intimation should be dispensed with on the ground that—

(i) the names or whereabouts of such persons are not known to, and cannot reasonably be ascertained by, the pursuer; or

(ii) such persons are unlikely to be awarded more than the sum of £200 each.

Deriv. R.C.S. 1965, r.75A(1) and (2) substituted by S.I. 1984 No. 920 and amended by S.I. 1986 No. 1941; and R.C.S. 1994, old r.43.1(1) and 43.2

GENERAL NOTE.

43.14.1

Rule 43.14 is substantially in the same terms as old rr. 43.1(1) and 43.2. Section 5 of the Damages (Scotland) Act 1976 first introduced detailed provisions for avoidance of multiplicity of actions in respect of the death of a relative requiring the pursuer to serve a notice on every person not a party who would have title to sue the defender as executor or relative of the deceased in an action based on the injuries or death. This proved cumbersome and expensive and s. 5 was repealed by s. 14(2) of the Administration of Justice Act 1982 following a report of the Scottish Law Commission (Scot. Law Com. No. 64), leaving it to the court to make appropriate provision in the rules. Such rules were made by A.S. (A.R.C. No. 5) (Intimation in Fatal Accident Cases) 1984 [S.I. 1984 No. 920].

The rules for intimation to connected persons are plainly intended to ensure that intimation is only required when it is sensible: *Henderson v. Occidental Petroleum (Caledonia) Ltd* , 1990 S.L.T. 315 (OH), 316G per Lord Prosser.

"PERSONAL INJURIES".

43.14.2

The definition is now in r. 43.1(2): see note 43.1.2.

"CONNECTED PERSON".

43.14.3

The definition in r.43.1(2), as in old r.43.1(2), is "a person, not being a party to the action, who has title to sue the defender in respect of the personal injuries from which a deceased died or in respect of his death". The connected persons to the deceased are thus (a) the executors, (b) the relatives defined in Sched. 1 to the Damages (Scotland) Act 1976 (now s. 14(1) of the Damages (Scotland) Act 2011). In *McGibbon v. McAllister* , 2008 S.L.T. 459 (O.H.) Lord Brodie held that the partner of 16 years of the deceased's mother and de facto "stepfather" had, having regard to arts. 14 and 16 of ECHR, title to sue (though on the ordinary meaning of Sched. 1 he was not a "parent").

A "relative" means only those listed formerly in Sched. 1 to the Damages (Scotland) Act 1976 as amended by s. 14(4) of the Administration of Justice Act 1982 and now in s. 14(1) of the 2011 Act. A relative as defined may sue for distress and anxiety in contemplation of the deceased suffering, grief and sorrow, loss of society and loss of support, where the deceased died in consequence of personal injuries as a result of an act or omission of another unless the liability to the deceased or his executor was excluded or discharged before his death: 2011 Act s. 4. Such a right transfers to the relative's executor (2011 Act s. 9). The deceased's claim for damages for personal injuries (except patrimonial loss after death) transmits to his executor: 2011 Act s.2.

The meaning of "child" in s. 14(1) of the 2011 Act is not age restricted but correlative of relationship: *Hunter's Executrix v. Advocate General*, 2016 S.L.T. 1287 (OH).

Civil partners, or persons in a relationship which has the same characteristics as a civil partnership (same sex relationship), are now relatives: 1976 Act, Sched. 1 as amended by the Civil Partnership Act 2004 Sched. 28, para. 42 and now s. 14(1) of the 2011 Act. *Telfer v. Killock* , 2004 S.L.T. 1291 (OH) is thus overruled.

The only sensible interpretation of s. 1(4A) of the 1976 Act (inserted by s. 35 of the Family Law (Scotland) Act 2006) is that exclusion of a person related to the deceased by affinity had effect only where there was nothing more than a relationship of affinity between the claimant and the deceased:

---

[1] Rule 43.14 substituted by S.S.I. 2002 No. 570 (effective 1st April 2003).

[2] Rule 4.3.14(1) amended by S.S.I. 2011 No. 288 (effective 7th July 2011).

Mykoliw v. Botterill , 2010 S.L.T. 1219 (OH) (married stepfather who accepted deceased as a child of his family was a "relative"). It was held that art. 8 of ECHR would be undermined where the literal construction would permit a claim by an unmarried person who had accepted the deceased as a member of the family but would exclude a person, married to the natural parent, who had accepted the child into family.

In relation to a death before 4th May 2006, "relative" has the meaning in Sch. 1 to the 1976 Act and any reference to a person's immediate family is construed in accordance with s. 10(2) of the 1976 Act: Damages (Scotland) Act 2011 (Commencement, Transitional Provisions and Savings) Order 2011 [SSI 2011/268].

INTIMATION TO CONNECTED PERSONS.

Intimation should be made to (a) the executors of the deceased, (b) members of the deceased's immediate family, and (c) remoter relatives. A relative belonging to the deceased's immediate family will probably be known and should be named and receive intimation because he or she may sue for loss of society and loss of support (unless unlikely to receive more than £200); a remoter relative may sue only for loss of actual or likely support: see note 43.14.3.

43.14.4

In the case of relatives remoter than the immediate family (for which, see Damages (Scotland) Act 1976, s.10(2) as amended by the Administration of Justice Act 1982, s.14(4)), it has been held that it is not necessary to set out the names and whereabouts of such persons, even when these are known, and no need to take any steps to ascertain names or whereabouts which are unknown. In the absence of current or specific likelihood of support, the grounds for seeking dispensation, and the reasons for granting it, do not turn on identification of the relative or the number or relationship of such relatives. It is sufficient to aver that there are persons other than the pursuer(s) having title as relatives of the deceased, that no such person was receiving, or is likely in the future to receive, support from the deceased; and that in these circumstances it is believed and averred that none of those persons is likely to be awarded more than £200: *Henderson v. Occidental Petroleum (Caledonia) Ltd* , 1990 S.L.T. 315 (OH), 316K per Lord Prosser.

43.15.—[1] Warrants for intimation in actions by connected persons

43.15

(1) Where the pursuer makes averments under rule 43.14(2)(b) (existence of connected persons), he shall insert a warrant for intimation in the summons in the following terms:—

> "Warrant to intimate to (*name and address*) as a person who is believed to have title to sue the defender in an action in respect of the personal injuries from which the late (name and last place of residence) died [or the death of the late (*name and last place of residence*)]".

(2) A notice of intimation in Form 43.15 shall be attached to the copy of the summons where intimation is given on a warrant under paragraph (1).

Deriv. R.C.S. r.75A(6) and (7) (part) substituted by S.I. 1984 No. 920 and amended by S.I. 1986 No. 1941; and R.C.S. 1994, old r.43.3

INTIMATION.

For methods, see r.16.8. For evidence of intimation, see note 16.8.1.

43.15.1

Applications to dispense with intimation in actions by connected persons

43.16.—[2](1) Where the pursuer makes averments under rule 43.14(2)(c) (dispensing with intimation to connected persons), he shall apply by motion for an order to dispense with intimation.

43.16

(2) In determining a motion under paragraph (1), the court shall have regard to—

(a) the desirability of avoiding multiplicity of actions; and

(b) the expense, inconvenience or difficulty likely to be involved in taking steps to ascertain the name or whereabouts of the connected person.

(3) Where the court is not satisfied that intimation to a connected person should be dispensed with, it may—

(a) order intimation to a connected person whose name and whereabouts are known;

---

[1] Rule 43.15 substituted by S.S.I. 2002 No. 570 (effective 1st April 2003).
[2] Rule 43.16 substituted by S.S.I. 2002 No. 570 (effective 1st April 2003).

(b) order the pursuer to take such further steps as it may specify in the interlocutor to ascertain the name or whereabouts of any connected person; and

(c) order that such advertisement be made in such manner, in such place and at such times as it may specify in the interlocutor.

Deriv. R.C.S. 1965, r. 75A(4) (r. 43.16(1)), and r. 75A(5) (r. 43.16(2) and (3), both substituted by S.I. 1984 No. 920 and amended by S.I. 1986 No. 1941; and R.C.S. 1994, old r. 43.4.

GENERAL NOTE.

43.16.1   Rule 43.16 is in the same terms as old r.43.4.

DISPENSING WITH INTIMATION.

43.16.2   Intimation should only be required on anyone beyond the immediate family (for which, see Damages (Scotland) Act 1976, s. 10(2) as amended by the Administration of Justice Act 1982, s. 14(4)) in those cases (presumably rare) in which the pursuer's agents have reason to believe that some particular relative has suffered an actual loss of support, or is for specific reasons to be regarded as someone who the deceased would have supported in the future: *Henderson v. Occidental Petroleum (Caledonia) Ltd* , 1990 S.L.T. 315 (OH), 316H per Lord Prosser. See further, notes 43.14.2 to 43.14.4.

Where a relative in respect of whom the court has dispensed with intimation becomes known, intimation may be required: r. 43.17; and see note 43.17.2.

"MOTION".

43.16.3   For motions, see Chap. 23.

Subsequent disclosure of connected persons

43.17   **43.17.**[1] Where the name or whereabouts of a person, in respect of whom the court has dispensed with intimation on a ground specified in rule 43.14(2)(c) (dispensing with intimation to connected persons), subsequently becomes known to the pursuer while the action is depending before the court, the pursuer shall apply by motion under rule 13.8(1) (warrants after signeting) for a warrant for intimation to such a person; and such intimation shall be made in accordance with rule 43.15(2).

Deriv. R.C.S. 1965, r.75A(7) (part) substituted by S.I. 1984 No. 920 and amended by S.I. 1986 No. 1941; and R.C.S. 1994, old r.43.5.

GENERAL NOTE.

43.17.1   Rule 43.17 is in the same terms as old r. 43.5.

IS INTIMATION MANDATORY?

43.17.2   Having regard to what Lord Prosser said in *Henderson v. Occidental Petroleum (Caledonia) Ltd* , 1990 S.L.T. 315 (OH), at 316H about the only persons on whom intimation ought to be required (see note 43.16.2), intimation on a relative may, notwithstanding the terms of r. 43.17, be dispensed with.

"DEPENDING"

43.17.3   A cause is depending from the time it is commenced (i.e. from the time an action is served) until final decree, whereas a cause is in dependence until final extract. For the meaning of "commenced", see note 13.4.4. For the meaning of final decree, see note 4.15.2(2). For the meaning of final extract, see note 7.1.2(2).

"MOTION".

43.17.4   For motions, see Chap. 23.

Connected persons entering the process

43.18   **43.18.**—[2](1) A connected person may apply to the court by minute in the process of the action craving leave to be sisted as an additional pursuer to the action.

(2) Any such minute shall be placed before the Lord Ordinary who may grant the minute and shall make such order as he considers appropriate, having regard to the provisions in this Chapter.

---

[1] Rule 43.17 substituted by S.S.I. 2002 No. 570 (effective 1st April 2003).
[2] Rule 43.18 substituted by S.S.I. 2002 No. 570 (effective 1st April 2003).

Deriv. R.C.S. 1965, r.75A(9) (part) substituted by S.I. 1984 No. 920 and amended by S.I. 1986 No. 1941; and R.C.S. 1994, old r.43.6(1)

GENERAL NOTE.

A connected person should join the existing action otherwise he will not be awarded expenses in any separate action raised by him: r.43.19.

43.18.1

"MINUTE".

Old r.43.6(2) required the minuter to crave leave to adopt the existing pleadings for the pursuer or set out separate pleadings. That provision has not been repeated in the new rule.
A fee will be payable for entering the process.

43.18.2

PROCEDURE ON MINUTE.

Old r.43.6(3) and (4) provided for intimation of the minute to other parties before the minute was lodged. That provision has not been repeated.

43.18.3

Failure by connected person to enter process

43.19.—[1](1)   Where a connected person to whom intimation is made—

43.19

   (a)   does not apply to be sisted as an additional pursuer to the action;

   (b)   subsequently brings a separate action against the same defender in respect of the same personal injuries or death; and

   (c)   would, apart from this rule, be awarded the expenses or part of the expenses of that action,

he shall not be awarded those expenses except on cause shown.

Deriv. R.C.S. 1965, r.75A(1) substituted by S.I. 1984 No. 920 and amended by S.I. 1986 No. 1941; and R.C.S. 1994, old r.43.7

GENERAL NOTE.

Rule 43.19(1) (there is in fact no r.43 19(2)) is in the same terms as old r.43.7.

43.19.1

It behoves a connected person to join an existing action to avoid having to pay his or her own expenses for not doing so.

Mesothelioma actions: special provisions

43.20.—[2](1)   This rule applies where liability to a relative of the pursuer may arise under section 5 of the Damages (Scotland) Act 2011 (discharge of liability to pay damages: exception for mesothelioma).

43.20

(2)   On settlement of the pursuer's claim, the pursuer may apply by motion for any or all of the following:—

   (a)   a sist for a specified period;

   (b)   discharge of the proof;

   (c)   variation of the timetable issued under rule 43.6.

(3)   Paragraphs (4) to (7) apply where a motion under paragraph (2) has been granted.

(4)   As soon as reasonably practicable after the death of the pursuer, any agent who immediately prior to the death was instructed in a cause by the deceased pursuer shall notify the court of the death.

(5)   The notification under paragraph (4) shall be by letter to the Deputy Principal Clerk and shall be accompanied by a certified copy of the death certificate relative to the deceased pursuer.

(6)   A relative of the deceased may apply by motion for the recall of the sist and for an order for further procedure.

(7)   On the expiration of the period of any sist pronounced on a motion under paragraph (2) the Keeper may put the case out to be heard on the By Order roll.

---

[1] Rule 43.19 substituted by S.S.I. 2002 No. 570 (effective 1st April 2003).
[2] Rule 43.20 inserted by S.S.I. 2007 No. 282 (effective 2nd May 2007) and substituted by S.S.I. 2011 No. 288 (effective 7th July 2011).

43.20.1   Section 5 of the Damages (Scotland) Act 2011 provides that in mesothelioma cases where liability for damages is discharged and the death and discharge occurred on or after 20th December 2006 liability arises under s. 4(1) but is limited to damages under s. 4(3)(b) (i.e. the non-patrimonial claims for distress and anxiety, grief and sorrow and loss of society).

In relation to a death before 7th July 2011, this rule is construed in accordance with art. 4 of the Damages (Scotland) Act 2011 (Commencement, Transitional Provisions and Savings) Order 2011 [SSI 2011/268]; A.S. (R.C.S.A. No. 4) (Miscellaneous) 2011 [SSSI 2011/288]. In art.4 of the 2011 Order, in relation to any death before 4th May 2006, "relative" has the meaning in Sch.1 to the 1976 Act and any reference to a person's immediate family is construed in accordance with s. 10(2) of the 1976 Act.

CHAPTER 43A ACTIONS OF HARASSMENT

Chapter 43A

Actions of Harassment

Application and interpretation of this Chapter[1]

43A.1.—(1) This Chapter applies to an action of harassment within the meaning of section 8(2) of the 1997 Act.

(2) In this Chapter—

"the 1997 Act" means the Protection from Harassment Act 1997;

"non-harassment order" means an order granted under section 8(5)(b)(ii) of the 1997 Act.

43A.1

GENERAL NOTE.

The Protection from Harassment Act 1997 was originally conceived because of the inadequacies of English criminal law to deal with harassment of women, which was given media attention in 1996. For Scotland, the Act creates a (statutory) delict of harassment. Our criminal law is already able to deal with harassment as a breach of the peace, although the 1997 Act provides for the obtaining of non-harassment orders against an offender.

The new delict of harassment occurs where there is an actual or apprehended breach of the duty not to pursue a course of conduct which amounts to harassment of another and is intended to amount to harassment or occurs in circumstances where it would appear to a reasonable person that it would amount to harassment: 1997 Act, s.8(1) and (2). "Conduct" includes speech and "harassment" includes alarm or distress. The court may award damages, grant interdict or interim interdict or a non-harassment order: 1997 Act, s.8(5). There are statutory defences of authorisation by enactment or rule of law, preventing or detecting crime, or reasonableness: 1997 Act, s.8(4).

In *Marinello v City of Edinburgh Council* , 2011 S.C. 736 (First Div.), it was held that in order to satisfy the test of relevancy averments in an action of harassment must provoke a positive response to the following three questions: (a) are the averments capable of supporting the conclusion that there was a course of conduct being pursued; (b) if so, did that course of conduct amount to harassment of the pursuer; and (c) if so, was the conduct intended to amount to harassment or did it occur in circumstances in which a reasonable person would consider it to be harassment of the pursuer?

43A.1.1

Procedure for variation or revocation of non-harassment order

43A.2. An application under section 8(7) of the 1997 Act after final decree in an action of harassment for the variation or revocation of a non-harassment order shall be made by minute in the process of the action to which the application relates.

43A.2

[1] R. 43A.2 inserted by S.I. 1997 No. 1527 (effective 16th June 1997).

GENERAL NOTE.

On the Protection from Harassment Act 1997, see note 43A.1.1.

43A.2.1

"SECTION 8(7) OF THE 1997 ACT".

Where a non-harassment order has been made under s.8(5)(b)(ii) of the 1997 Act in an action of harassment to protect a person against further harassment, either the harasser or the harassed person may apply to the court which made the order to revoke or vary the order.

43A.2.2

"MINUTE".

For applications by minute, see r. 15.1.

43A.2.3

---

[1] Chap. 43A and r. 43A.1 inserted by S.I. 1997 No. 1527 (effective 16th June 1997).

CHAPTER 44 TIME TO PAY DIRECTIONS

Application and interpretation of this Chapter

44.1.—(1) This Chapter applies to an action in which a person may apply under section 1(1) of the Debtors (Scotland) Act 1987 for a time to pay direction.

(2) In this Chapter—

"the Act of 1987" means the Debtors (Scotland) Act 1987;

"time to pay direction" means a direction made under section 1(1) of the Act of 1987.

Deriv. R.C.S. 1965, r. 88A inserted by S.I. 1988 No. 2060 (r. 44.1(2))

GENERAL NOTE.

S. 1(1) of the Act of 1987 enables the court, on an application made to it by an individual debtor, to direct that any principal sum of money decerned for in a decree (and, subject to certain conditions, any interest and expenses for which that debtor is found liable) be paid by that debtor either by instalments or as a deferred lump sum.

An application for a time to pay direction must be made before the court grants decree. The right to apply may be exercised by any individual debtor who is a party to any cause and against whom a decree for payment of a sum of money is pronounced, e.g. a pursuer held liable in a counterclaim, or a third party minuter.

Time to pay directions are competent only in actions where the principal sum of money being decerned for is less than £10,000 (exclusive of interest, whenever accruing, and expenses), or such other amount as may be prescribed in regulations made by the Lord Advocate: Act of 1987, s.1(5)(a). It is not competent for the court to make a time to pay direction where the decree contains an award of a capital sum on divorce, on the granting of a declarator of nullity of marriage, in connection with a maintenance order or in actions for payment of various rates, taxes and duties: Act of 1987, s.1(5). Although not a time to pay direction, it is possible to achieve payment of a capital sum in a divorce action by instalments.

Notice about time to pay directions

44.2.—(1) In an action in which a defender may apply to the court for a time to pay direction, the pursuer shall serve on that defender a notice in Form 44.2-A and an application in Form 44.2-B at the same time as he serves a copy of the summons, or pleadings, as amended by a minute of amendment calling him as a defender.

(2) Before serving a notice and an application under paragraph (1), the pursuer shall insert in Form 44.2-A the date by which Form 44.2-B must be returned to the court by the defender (being the date on which the period of notice expires) and shall complete Part A of Form 44.2-B.

Deriv. R.C.S. 1965, r. 88B inserted by S.I. 1988 No. 2060

GENERAL NOTE.

Form 44.2-A is a notice informing the defender of his right under the Act of 1987 to apply for a time to pay direction which must be served with the application form for a time to pay direction in Form 44.2-B.

"SERVICE".

For methods, see Chap. 16, Pt. I. The certificate of service required under r. 16.1(2) must state that Forms 44.2-A and 44.2-B have been served in a cause in which they are required.

"PERIOD OF NOTICE".

This period is determined in accordance with rule 14.6 (period of notice for answers) by virtue of r. 1.3(1) (definitions of "period of notice" and "writ").

Applications for time to pay directions where appearance not entered

44.3.—(1) Where a defender—

(a) does not enter appearance in an action,

(b) intends to apply to the court for a time to pay direction, and

(c) where appropriate, seeks recall or restriction of an arrestment,

he shall complete and send the application in Form 44.2-B to the Deputy Principal Clerk before the date specified in Form 44.2-A.

(2) On receipt of an application for a time to pay direction, the Deputy Principal Clerk shall—

44.1

44.1.1

44.2

44.2.1

44.2.2

44.2.3

44.3

(a)   cause the application to be lodged in the process to which it relates; and

(b)   give written intimation to the pursuer that he has received the application.

(3)   Where the pursuer does not object to the application by a defender for a time to pay direction or the recall or restriction of an arrestment, he may apply by motion for decree in absence stating that he does not object to the application.

(4)   Where the pursuer objects to the application by a defender for a time to pay direction or the recall or restriction of an arrestment, he shall intimate—

(a)   the motion for decree in absence, and

(b)   the grounds of objection to the application by the defender,

in Form 44.3 to the defender not less than seven days before the date on which the motion is enrolled.

(5)   On enrolling a motion for decree in absence, the pursuer shall lodge in process a copy of Form 44.3 intimated to the defender.

(6)   The defender need not appear at the hearing of the motion for decree in absence and may send to the Deputy Principal Clerk written representations in response to the grounds of objection of the pursuer.

(7)   A motion for decree in absence to which paragraph (4) applies shall require the appearance of counsel or other person having a right of audience.

Deriv. R.C.S. 1965, r. 88C inserted by S.I. 1988 No. 2060

GENERAL NOTE.

44.3.1   A defender may apply for a time to pay direction even though he admits the debt and does not enter appearance. He may also apply for the recall or restriction of an arrestment which the court may consider when making the time to pay direction: Act of 1987, s. 2(3).

"ENTER APPEARANCE".

44.3.2   A defender must enter appearance within three days after the calling of the summons if he intends to defend: r. 17.1.

"RECALL OR RESTRICTION OF ARRESTMENT".

44.3.3   The arrestment may be on the dependence of the action or in security of the debt concerned: see Act of 1987, s. 2(2). On recall of arrestment, see note 13.10.4.

"WRITTEN INTIMATION".

44.3.4   For methods, see r. 16.9.

"DECREE IN ABSENCE".

44.3.5   A decree in absence may be granted where a defender fails to enter appearance, or having entered appearance, fails to lodge defences in a cause in which the court may grant decree without evidence: r. 19.1. On decrees in absence generally, see Chap. 19.

"INTIMATE".

44.3.6   For methods, see r. 16.7.

"COUNSEL OR OTHER PERSON HAVING A RIGHT OF AUDIENCE".

44.3.7   See definitions in r. 1.3(1).

APPEALS.

44.3.8   An "appeal" against a decision of the Lord Ordinary on an application for a time to pay direction may be made on a question of law with leave of the Lord Ordinary: Act of 1987, s. 103(3). The application for leave must be made within 14 days of the decision and the reclaiming motion enrolled within the next 14 days: r. 38.4(2). Such an appeal is treated as a reclaiming motion: r. 38.10(b). The decision of the Lord Ordinary whether or not to grant leave is final: r. 38.5(6).

Applications for time to pay directions where appearance entered but defences not lodged

44.4   **44.4.**—(1)   Where a defender—

(a)   after entering appearance does not lodge defences,

(b)   intends to apply to the court for a time to pay direction, and

(c)   where appropriate, seeks recall or restriction of an arrestment, then, notwithstanding the date specified in Form 44.2-A as the date by which Form 44.2-B must be returned, he shall complete and send the application in Form 44.2-B to the court not later than the day on which defences would have had to be lodged in process.

(2) Paragraphs (2) to (7) of rule 44.3 (applications for time to pay directions where appearance not entered) shall apply to an application under this rule as they apply to an application under that rule.

Deriv. R.C.S. 1965, r. 88D inserted by S.I. 1988 No. 2060

GENERAL NOTE.

See r. 44.3 and notes.   44.4.1

LODGING DEFENCES.

Defences must be lodged in process within seven days after the calling of the summons or, if the   44.4.2
seventh day is in vacation, on the next day on which a summons may call: r. 18.1(2).

Applications for time to pay directions where defences lodged

44.5. An application for a time to pay direction by—   **44.5**

   (a)   a defender in an action in which defences have been lodged by that defender, or

   (b)   any other party,

shall be made by motion.

Deriv. R.C.S. 1965, r. 88E inserted by S.I. 1988 No. 2060

GENERAL NOTE.

Any party intending to apply for a time to pay direction in a cause after defences have been lodged   **44.5.1**
should particularly note the provisions of the Act of 1987 in relation to expenses. In the Court of Session,
expenses are not quantified when decree is granted. Where the party liable for expenses is not legally
aided the court's practice since 1983 is usually to pronounce two interlocutors, one disposing of the
merits and finding that party liable in expenses and the other decerning for expenses as taxed by the
Auditor (the sum being entered in any extract by the Extractor after taxation). Where a party liable in
expenses is legally aided there is no decerniture for expenses when the finding is made: a finding of liability is made with a remit to the Auditor to tax and report (on which, see Chap. 42). A decerniture is
only made after the Auditor has reported and any objections or an application for modification have been
determined. See further, note 4.15.2. The expenses decree in either case cannot be extracted until the
expenses have been taxed, and that extract, when it becomes available will specify the amount of the
expenses as taxed.

S. 1(3) of the Act of 1987 provides that where the court grants a decree which contains a finding as to
liability for expenses, but does not at the same time make a time to pay direction, it shall not at any time
thereafter be competent for the court to make a time to pay direction in relation to those expenses. In
order therefore to obtain a direction covering the expenses awarded against him, the debtor must apply
expressly for it before the court makes a finding as to liability for expenses. The reasoning behind this
rule is that the court should only be required to exercise its discretion to make a time to pay direction on
one occasion only during a court action for payment of a principal sum: see *Scottish Law Commission
Report on Diligence and Debtor Protection (Scot. Law Com. No. 95)* at para. 3.19.

"ANY OTHER PARTY".

This would include a pursuer in a counterclaim or a third party.   **44.5.2**

"MOTION".

The motion ought to be made at the same time as decerniture for payment is sought. For motions, see   **44.5.3**
Chap. 23.

APPEALS.

An "appeal" against a decision of the Lord Ordinary on an application for a time to pay direction may   **44.5.4**
be appealed on a question of law with leave of the Lord Ordinary: Act of 1987, s.103(3). The application
for leave must be made within 14 days of the decision and the reclaiming motion enrolled within the next
14 days: r. 38.4(2). Such an appeal is treated as a reclaiming motion: r. 38.10(b). The decision of the Lord
Ordinary whether or not to grant leave is final: r.38.5(6).

Applications for variation or recall of time to pay directions or arrestments

44.6.—(1) An application under section 3(1) of the Act of 1987 (variation or   **44.6**
recall of time to pay direction or recall or restriction of arrestment) shall be made by
motion.

    (2) The applicant shall—

      (a) in a motion under paragraph (1), state briefly the grounds on which the order is sought; and

      (b) give written intimation of the motion to the debtor or creditor, as the case may be, not less than 14 days before the date on which the motion is enrolled.

    (3) On enrolling a motion under paragraph (1), the applicant shall lodge in process—

      (a) a copy of the letter of intimation;

      (b) the Post Office receipt or certificate of posting of that letter; and

      (c) any document he intends to rely on at the hearing of the motion.

Deriv. R.C.S. 1965, r. 88F inserted by S.I. 1988 No. 2060

GENERAL NOTE.

44.6.1   Either the debtor or the creditor may apply to the court to vary or recall a time to pay direction. The court will only grant such application "if it is satisfied that it is reasonable to do so": Act of 1987, s. 3(1)(a).

      Similarly, the debtor or creditor may apply to the court for recall or restriction of any arrestment in effect in respect of the debt concerned, and the court may order variation, recall or restriction of the arrestment, subject to the fulfilment by the debtor of such conditions as it thinks fit: Act of 1987, s. 3(1)(b) and (2). Where an arrestment on the dependence was in place before the granting of a decree containing a time to pay direction, the effect of the granting of the decree is to convert the arrestment on the dependence into an arrestment in execution. The consequence of the time to pay direction being attached, however, is that no action of furthcoming or sale is competent: Act of 1987, s. 2(1)(b)(i).

      While a time to pay direction is in effect, the creditor is not entitled to seek to enforce payment of the debt by means of serving a charge or the diligences of arrestment and action of furthcoming or sale, poinding and sale, earnings arrestment or adjudication for debt: Act of 1987, s. 2(1). The creditor does however retain his entitlement to inhibit. The right of a creditor to call up a heritable security, exercise a lien or utilise any of those special diligences available to enforce a heritable debt or arrears of a ground annual is similarly not affected by the making of a time to pay direction.

      The right of the creditor to exercise the ordinary diligences available to him in respect of an unpaid debt revives where the time to pay direction is recalled, or has lapsed as a consequence of default or death on the part of the debtor: Act of 1987, s.2(5). On recall or where lapse has occurred, as described in ss. 4 and 14(2) of the Act of 1987, the creditor may proceed with diligence without returning to court for the recall of the time to pay direction.

"MOTION".

44.6.2   For motions, see Chap. 23.

"WRITTEN INTIMATION".

44.6.3   For methods, see r. 16.9.

"LODGE IN PROCESS".

44.6.4   The copy letter of intimation, the certificate of posting and any document which the applicant intends to rely on are lodged in process as productions: r. 4.5.

APPEALS.

44.6.5   An "appeal" against a decision of the Lord Ordinary on an application for variation or recall of a time to pay direction or arrestment may be made on a question of law with leave of the Lord Ordinary: Act of 1987, s. 103(3). The application for leave must be made within 14 days of the decision and the reclaiming motion enrolled within the next 14 days: r. 38.4(2). Such an appeal is treated as a reclaiming motion: r. 38.10(b). The decision of the Lord Ordinary whether or not to grant leave is final: r. 38.5(6).

Notice to debtor for payment of interest on decrees

44.7   **44.7.** Where a creditor seeks to recover interest (other than interest awarded as a specific sum) under a decree containing a time to pay direction, the notice to be served under section 1(7) of the Act of 1987 shall be served on the debtor by the creditor—

      (a) in the case of a decree containing a time to pay direction for payment by instalments, not less than 14 days before the date on which the last instalment is due to be paid; and

(b) in the case of a decree which includes a time to pay direction for payment by deferred lump sum, not less than 14 days before the date on which the lump sum is due to be paid.

Deriv. R.C.S. 1965, r. 88H inserted by S.I. 1988 No. 2060

GENERAL NOTE.

This rule applies where a creditor seeks to recover interest which was not quantified and included in the decree or which has accrued subsequent to the decree being granted. The creditor must, in terms of s. 1(7) of the Act of 1987, and within the periods specified in r. 44.7(a) and (b), serve a notice on the debtor stating that he is claiming interest and specifying the amount claimed. Unless this is done timeously, the right to recover such interest is lost: Act of 1987, s. 1(6).

As a consequence of s. 1(6) and 1(7) of the Act of 1987, the normal rule that payments made by a debtor are ascribed to interest before capital must be reversed where interest is payable under a decree subject to a time to pay direction. Where the time to pay direction is for payment by instalments, payments to account are applied to the capital sum outstanding until it has been recovered in full. Only then are payments applied to any interest which is claimed. Where the time to pay direction is for payment by deferred lump sum, the principal sum and the interest become payable together at the end of such period as was specified by the court, following intimation by the creditor to the debtor of an extract of the decree containing the time to pay application.

"SERVED".

For methods, see Chap. 16, Pt. I.

44.7.1

44.7.2

Chapter 45

Actions of Division and Sale

Remit to reporter to examine property

45.1.—(1) In an action of division and sale of heritable property, the court shall, in accordance with paragraph (2), remit to a reporter to examine the property and to report to the court—

45.1

(a) whether the property is capable of division in a manner equitable to the interests of the *pro indiviso* proprietors and, if so, how such division may be effected; and

(b) in the event that the property is to be sold—

    (i) whether the property should be sold as a whole or in lots and, if in lots, what those lots should be;

    (ii) whether the property should be exposed for sale by public roup or private bargain;

    (iii) whether the sale should be subject to any upset or minimum price and, if so, the amount;

    (iv) the manner and extent to which the property should be advertised for sale; and

    (v) any other matter which the reporter considers pertinent to a sale of the property.

(2) A remit under paragraph (1) shall be made—

(a) where the action is undefended, on the motion of the pursuer at any time after the period for lodging defences has expired;

(b) where the action is defended—

    (i) at the closing of the record, on the motion of any party to the action;

    (ii) on the court finding, after a hearing on the Procedure Roll or a proof, that the pursuer is entitled to bring and insist in the action of division and sale; or

    (iii) at such other time as the court thinks fit.

(3) On completion of a report made under paragraph (1), the reporter shall send the report, with a copy for each party, to the Deputy Principal Clerk.

(4) On receipt of such a report, the Deputy Principal Clerk shall—

(a) cause the report to be lodged in process; and

(b) give written intimation to each party that this has been done and that he may uplift a copy of the report from the process.

(5) After the lodging of such a report, any party may apply by motion for further procedure or for approval of the report.

(6) At the hearing of a motion under paragraph (5), the court may—

(a) in the event of challenge to any part of the report, order a note of objection to the report and answers to the note to be lodged within such period as the court thinks fit; or

(b) in the absence of such challenge, order that the property be divided or sold, as the case may be, in accordance with the recommendations of the reporter, subject to such modification, if any, as the court thinks fit.

(7) Where, in accordance with paragraph (6)(a), the lodging of a note of objection and answers has been ordered, the cause shall be put out on the By Order Roll

before the Lord Ordinary after the expiry of the period for lodging the note of objection and answers; and the court may make such order for further procedure as it thinks fit.

GENERAL NOTE.

45.1.1
The distinctive feature of common property, derived from the fact that each co-owner has a separate and separable interest (in a legal, rather than a physical, sense), is the absolute right of every co-owner to terminate the community at will: *Banff Magistrates v. Ruthin Castle Ltd* 1944 S.C. 36, 68 per L.J.-C. Cooper. The *pro indiviso* proprietor is entitled to have the property divided, or if division is impracticable or would operate unfairly, to have it sold and the price divided: *Morrison v. Kirk* 1912 S.C. 44, 49 per Lord Salvesen. Accordingly, the right to insist on an action of division and sale at any time cannot be affected by considerations of the financial position, present or contingent, of any pro indiviso proprietor or other equitable consideration. The proper context for equitable considerations is the working out of the remedy (i.e. division or sale, and, if sale, by what method): *Upper Crathes Fishings Ltd v. Bailey's Executors* 1991 S.L.T. 747, 750L per L.P. Hope. Personal bar is not a relevant defence to an action of division and sale, though it might be relevant to determine how the property is to be divided up as a consequence of some agreement or acting of the parties: *Riddell v. Morisetti (No. 2)* , 22 November 1996, unreported (1996 G.W.D. 40-2292). The absolute nature of this right is justified on grounds of public policy, and especially to ensure the advantageous management of such property: *Brock v. Hamilton* (1852) 19 D. 701, 703 per Lord Rutherford.

There are, however, circumstances in which the exercise of this right may be denied. For instance, it is always open to a person to deprive himself of his right to such an action by contract, or by the operation of personal bar: *Upper Crathes Fishings Ltd*, above, per L.P. Hope at p.749C-D. An action of division and sale may not lie in respect of a thing of common and indispensable use, such as a staircase or vestibule: Bell's *Prin.,*s. 1082. In relation to matrimonial homes owned in common by a husband and wife, s. 19 of the Matrimonial Homes (Family Protection) (Scotland) Act 1981 confers on the court a discretion to refuse to grant decree, postpone the granting of decree, or grant decree subject to conditions, in an action of division and sale brought by a spouse.

"HERITABLE PROPERTY".

45.1.2
The absolute entitlement of each co-owner to terminate the community by means of an action of division and sale applies to all common property, whether heritable or moveable, corporeal or incorporeal: see Bell's *Comm.*, i, 62 (references to ships) and *Robertson's Tr. v. Roberts* 1982 S.L.T. 22 (concerning a lease). This Chapter refers specifically to, and deals only with, heritable property.

"REMIT TO A REPORTER".

45.1.3
Whether the division of the property which is the subject of an action of division and sale is reasonably practicable has in the past been determined by means of proof, e.g. *Bryden v. Gibson* (1837) 15 S. 486, but in general, the question is far better decided on a remit to a person of skill and experience: *Thom v. Macbeth* (1875) 3 R. 161, 165 per Lord Gifford. R. 45.1(1) provides that in an action of division and sale of heritable property, the court *shall* remit to a reporter, the implication of which is that proof is no longer a competent means of establishing whether heritable subjects are capable of equitable division.

Where there has been a remit to a reporter, that becomes the exclusive mode of proof of the issues comprised in the remit: *Williams v. Cleveland and Highland Holdings Ltd* 1993 S.L.T. 398 at 400K-L per Lord Penrose. The interlocutor ordering the remit both defines the issues for the reporter and prescribes the procedure to be followed by him: *Williams*, above, at 401B-C. Therefore, in approaching the question of a remit to a reporter in the context of division or sale, the parties have both an opportunity and an obligation to define the issues with clarity, since it is they who have to determine the scope of the reporter's power to bind them by his decision: *Williams*, above, at 401L. It has been pointed out that the observations of Lord Penrose in *Williams*, above, were made before the promulgation of the present r. 45.1. In *Riddell v. Morisetti (No. 2)* , 22 November 1996, unreported (1996 G.W.D. 40-2292), the court declined to order the reporter to consider specified matters. Counsel in that case were asked to produce an agreed formula as to the matters to which the reporter ought to have regard, which failing the court desired further submissions.

It is open to the court to give the reporter instructions about further particular matters to which he should have regard in addition to those mentioned in r. 45.1: *Riddell v. Morisetti* , 19th January 1996, unreported.

The solicitors for the parties are personally liable for the fees and outlays of the reporter and the court will order which party is liable: r. 42.15.

"CAPABLE OF DIVISION IN A MANNER EQUITABLE TO THE INTERESTS OF THE PRO INDIVISO PROPRIETORS".

45.1.4
Only if it is established that the subjects cannot be divided in a manner equitable to the interests of the *pro indiviso* proprietors is the remedy of sale under authority of the court and division of the price available to a pursuer. It may be physically possible to divide most subjects if all considerations of expense of division and of deterioration or possible destruction of the subjects are disregarded. These considerations, however, cannot be left out of view, and it is on them that, in most cases, the answer to the question whether the subjects should be divided will depend: *Thom v. Macbeth* (1875) 3 R. 161, 165 per Lord Gifford. Sale and subsequent division of the price will be resorted to where division is not reasonably practicable without sacrificing to an appreciable extent the interests of some or all of the parties: *Thom*,

above, per L.J.-C. Moncrieff at p. 164. For instance, sale would be appropriate where division would sacrifice a considerable portion of the value of the property: *Thom*, above, per Lord Ormidale at p. 164. Factors such as the emotional attachment of parties to the subjects are not relevant considerations in assessing the feasibility of the physical division of land: *Williams v. Cleveland and Highland Holdings Ltd* 1993 S.L.T. 398 at 402H–I per Lord Penrose. A remit is necessary even in undefended actions to establish that sale is expedient and necessary: *Bryden v. Gibson* (1837) 15 S. 486, 487 per Lord Balgray.

"SALE BY PUBLIC ROUP OR PRIVATE BARGAIN".

The question of whether a sale under the authority of the court for the purpose of division should be by public roup or private bargain is essentially a practical one, in which the court is exercising an equitable jurisdiction. The aim must be to effect a sale which is fair to all parties, and the common goal of all parties is to achieve the best bargain which can be obtained in all the circumstances: *The Miller Group Ltd v. Tasker* 1993 S.L.T. 207, 208H–K per Lord Weir. Before the decision of the Inner House in *Campbells v. Murray* 1972 S.C. 310, a sale for the purpose of division was invariably effected by public roup. In *Campbells*, the court held that this practice was not in the nature of a rule of law, and that sale by private bargain, after an adequate test of the relevant market, was now more likely to lead to sale at the best price which could reasonably be obtained. Since then, private bargain has usually been the preferred method of conducting a sale under the authority of the court for the purpose of division, but there may be situations in which a sale by public roup is to be preferred: *The Miller Group Ltd*, above. In terms of the r. 45.1(1)(b)(ii), the reporter to whom the examination of the property is remitted may recommend which of the two methods is appropriate in the circumstances of the case.

It is not settled whether it is competent for the court, in the absence of agreement between the parties, to order that the subjects be disposed of by means other than public roup or sale by private bargain in the open market. In *Scrimgeour v. Scrimgeour* 1988 S.L.T. 590, Lord McCluskey was prepared, on the basis of civilian and institutional authority, in an undefended action, to grant warrant in terms of the pursuer's conclusion for the sale of the defender's one-half pro indiviso share in the former matrimonial home to the pursuer at the price fixed on an open market valuation by the reporter appointed by the court. A motion in similar terms, however, was refused in *Berry v. Berry (No. 2)* 1989 S.L.T. 292, Lord Cowie rejecting the proposition that he had a wide discretion to lay down how the subjects should be disposed of and commenting that even if he had such a discretion, he would not regard the method of sale proposed as being in the best interests of the parties, which would be properly served by obtaining the highest price for the property through sale by private treaty in the open market.

"MOTION".

For motions, see Chap. 23.

"SEND".

This includes deliver: r. 1.3(1) (definition of "send").

OBJECTIONS TO THE REPORT.

The reporter's findings are final, subject only to a remit for reconsideration, by the same reporter, if available, on the basis of articulate objections made to the report provided and on restricted grounds. Whether a further remit will be made depends on the cogency of the objections, considered in the light of the original remit, and on those objections relating to the performance by the reporter of his duty under the remit, or to some issue or principle identifiable on the face of the report: *Williams v. Cleveland and Highland Holdings Ltd* 1993 S.L.T. 398, 401J–K per Lord Penrose. It is not legitimate for a party to include in a note of objections, contentions on the approach which the reporter might have adopted in carrying out the remit, where such contentions are in substance innovations on the procedure provided for in the remit, nor to use the procedure by way of objection to present arguments which might have been presented on the making of the original remit: *Williams*, above, per Lord Penrose at p. 401D–E.

"NOTE OF OBJECTION".

R. 15.2 does not apply to the note of objection (r. 15.2(4)(b)) and the note does not have to be signed (r. 4.2(9)(f). The note is lodged as a step of process (r. 1.3(1) (definition of "step of process")). On lodging steps of process, see r. 4.4. The list may be lodged by post: P.N. No. 4 of 1994, paras. 1 and 8; and see note 4.4.10.

Division or sale of property

45.2.—(1) Where the court orders the division or sale of heritable property, it shall direct that the division or sale, as the case may be, shall be conducted under the oversight and direction of the Deputy Principal Clerk or any other fit person whom it may appoint for that purpose.

(2) The Deputy Principal Clerk or person appointed under paragraph (1), as the case may be, may report any matter of difficulty arising in the course of the division or sale to the court.

45.1.5

45.1.6

45.1.7

45.1.8

45.1.9

45.2

(3) At a hearing on a report made under paragraph (2), the court may give such directions as it thinks fit, including authority to the Deputy Principal Clerk to sign, on behalf of any proprietor, a disposition of his interest in the property.

(4) On the conclusion of a sale of property—

(a) the proceeds of the sale, under deduction of the expenses of the sale, shall be consigned into court; and

(b) the Deputy Principal Clerk or the person appointed under paragraph (1), as the case may be, shall lodge in process a report of the sale and a proposed scheme of division of the proceeds of sale.

(5) At the hearing of a motion for approval of a report of the sale of property lodged under paragraph (4) and a proposed scheme of division, the court may—

(a) approve the report and scheme of division, and direct that payment of the proceeds of sale be made in terms of the report;

(b) deal with any question as to the expenses of process or of sale; and

(c) make such other order as it thinks fit.

"AUTHORITY TO THE DEPUTY PRINCIPAL CLERK TO SIGN … A DISPOSITION".

45.2.1   This may be necessary where a defender refuses to obtemper an order to sign and deliver a disposition of the subjects: e.g. *Whyte v. Whyte* 1913 2 S.L.T. 85.

A sale under r. 45.2 is not a sale by the parties; the person appointed to carry out the sale does not act as the agent of the proprietors but as a court authorised officer who enters into missives and procures a disposition: see *Kenneil v. Kenneil* , 2006 S.L.T. 449 (OH).

"CONSIGNED INTO COURT".

45.2.2   For consignation into court, see r. 33.4(1)(b) and note 33.4.3.

"MOTION".

45.2.3   For motions, see Chap. 23.

CHAPTER 45A ACTIONS OF REMOVING

Application of this Chapter

45A.1.—[1](1) Subject to paragraph (2), this Chapter applies only to a conclusion for removing in an action of removing against a person or persons in possession of heritable property without right or title to possess the property.

(2) This Chapter shall not apply with respect to a person who has or had a title or other right to occupy the heritable property and who has been in continuous occupation since that title or right is alleged to have come to an end.

GENERAL NOTE.

Chapter 45A was inserted by A.S. (R.S.C.A. No. 4) (Miscellaneous) 1996 [SI 1996/2168]. It implements recommendations 103 to 105 in Scot. Law Com. Report No. 118 on *Recovery of Possession of Heritable Property*.

The Scottish Law Commission felt that something was needed to be done about the problem of removing unidentified and unlawful occupants (e.g. trespassers or squatters) of land or buildings against whom it is difficult to bring proceedings because a writ cannot be served on them, and to do so speedily. Procedure exists in England and Wales: C.P.R. 1998, r. 55.6.

Before Chap. 45A was inserted, resort was made, where the identity of the occupiers was known, to a petition under s. 46 of the C.S.A. 1988 for reinstatement of a possessory right to heritable property. For use of s. 46 of the C.S.A. 1988 where the names of the occupiers are not known, see note 45A.1.3.

Chapter 45A provides (a) a means of service on occupiers whose names are not known, (b) a means for such persons to enter the process, and (c) for shortening or dispensing with periods of time under the RCS 1994.

ACTIONS OF REMOVING.

The conventional wisdom is that an action of removing without any other substantive conclusion is not competent in the Court of Session, although there is no statute or rule of law excluding it: see *Scot. Law Com. report no. 118* at para. 9.1. The competency of a simple action of removing in the Court of Session was questioned but not decided by Lord Penrose in *Marco's Leisure Ltd v. Occupiers of the subjects known as the Corn Exchange, New Market Road, Edinburgh* , 25th May 1999, unreported (and no judgment) and referred to in *Oliver & Son Ltd, Petrs* , 1999 S.L.T. 1039. In *Marco's Leisure Ltd*, the motion for interim orders was dropped and in *Oliver & Son Ltd* the answer was not necessary for the decision. The matter was resolved in *Beriston Ltd v. Dumbarton Motor Boat and Sailing Club* , 2007 S.L.T. 227 (OH). It was held that the Court of Session has no jurisdiction in "pure" actions of removing or actions that do not contain a conclusion as a preliminary step towards removing; it has concurrent jurisdiction with the sheriff court where declarator is sought as a preliminary step; and it has exclusive jurisdiction where reduction is sought as a preliminary to removing. Nothing in rule 45A.1 could change the substantive law as to what was competent in the Court of Session.

It is accepted that an action with a conclusion for removing is competent if associated with another conclusion such as interdict. In relation to the difficulties with interdict associated with this procedure, see note 45A.1.3.

"CHAPTER APPLIES ONLY TO A CONCLUSION FOR REMOVING".

It is not uncommon for a pursuer to seek to reinforce a decree of removing with an interdict. In relation to interdict, however, it is not competent to obtain an interdict against unnamed persons such as "any other person having notice of said interlocutor": *Lord Advocate v. The Scotsman Publications Ltd* 1989 S.C. (H.L.) 122, 135, 147, 155 and 161 (founding on *Pattison v. Fitzgerald* (1823) 2 S. 536), approved by the Inner House and not overruled by the House of Lords. It would be inappropriate to affect the law on this point by a side wind in altering procedure in relation to removing. Accordingly r. 45A.1(1) makes it clear that Chap. 45A, which provides for effective service on unnamed persons, applies *only* with respect to a conclusion for removing.

It was explained in *Oliver & Son Ltd, Petrs* , 1999 S.L.T. 1039, by the First Div. on a report to the Inner House by Lord Penrose, that the underlying reasoning in *The Scotsman Publications*, above, and *Pattison*, above, was that it is incompetent to pronounce an interdict on persons on whom the proceedings are not served or to move for its recall. In *Oliver*, the petitioners sought an order under s. 46 of the C.S.A. 1988 to be reinstated in their possessory right to heritable property which was occupied by persons whose names were unknown to them but who could be identified as the occupiers of the petitioners' land. A first order for service was sought on the unnamed persons; those who were served would be able to enter the process and resist the making of any substantive order. The First Div. held that the persons on whom service was to be made were sufficiently identified; were it otherwise the court would be powerless to act and would be handing to those who concealed their identity a weapon to wreak injustice. It was indicated for the petitioners that messengers-at-arms would hand copies of the petition to individuals they found occupying the land and record what they had done and might photograph those on the land

45A.1

45A.1.1

45A.1.2

45A.1.3

---

[1] Chap. 45A and r. 45A.1 inserted by S.I. 1996 No. 2168 (effective 23rd September, 1996).

and the steps taken to serve the petition. Accordingly it should be possible to bring an action for removing with conclusions for interdict and interim interdict against unnamed persons and to seek service of the action on those who can be found and identified with respect to the conclusions for interdict. But it would not be possible to seek interim interdict on those unnamed persons before service.

"WITHOUT RIGHT OR TITLE TO POSSESS THE PROPERTY".

45A.1.4   The procedures in Chap. 45A are intended to be available only against persons who enter or remain in property without licence or consent such as trespassers or squatters. The purpose of r. 45A.1(2) is to exclude tenants or persons remaining after termination of a tenancy.

Service on unnamed occupiers

45A.2   **45A.2.**—[1](1)   Where the name of a person in occupation of a heritable property is not known and cannot reasonably be ascertained, the pursuer shall call that person as a defender by naming him as an "occupier".

(2)   Where the name of a person in occupation of the heritable property is not known and cannot reasonably be ascertained, the summons shall be served (whether or not it is also served on a named person), unless the court otherwise directs, by a messenger-at-arms—

    (a)   affixing a copy of the summons and a citation in Form 45A.2 addressed to "the occupiers" to the main door or other conspicuous part of the premises, and if practicable, depositing a copy of each of those documents in the premises; or

    (b)   in the case of land only, inserting stakes in the ground at conspicuous parts of the occupied land to each of which is attached a sealed transparent envelope containing a copy of the summons and a citation in Form 45A.2 addressed to "the occupiers".

(3)   Paragraphs (1), (2) and (4) of rule 16.3 (service by messenger-at-arms) shall apply to service of a summons under this rule as they apply to service by a method to which those paragraphs apply.

GENERAL NOTE.

45A.2.1   For the history of the rule, see note 45A.1.1. This rule provides the means for service on occupiers whose names are not known or cannot reasonably be ascertained.

     In *Marco's Leisure Ltd v. Occupiers of the subjects known as the Corn Exchange, New Market Road, Edinburgh* , 25th May 1999, unreported (and no judgment) and referred to in *Oliver & Son Ltd, Petrs* 1999 S.L.T. 1039, Lord Penrose questioned the vires of r. 45A.2, but did not decide the issue because the motion for interim orders was dropped. The court has power to regulate and prescribe the procedure and practice of the court under s.5(a) of the C.S.A. 1988. If the court may provide rules for service by virtue of that power, the court may make provision for service on unnamed persons.

"NOT KNOWN AND CANNOT REASONABLY BE ASCERTAINED".

45A.2.2   Steps must have been taken to ascertain the address of the person on whom service is to be executed, and what those steps were and an explanation of why service cannot be executed must be stated in the summons: r. 13.3. In *Young v. Harper* 1970 S.C. 174, 177 Lord Fraser held that "known" (in relation to art. 1 of the A.S. 14th December 1805) did not mean known only to the pursuer but known generally to persons having business or social dealings with the defender; accordingly, some steps must be taken to find an address or else a belief that an address is not known must be based on some evidence that none is known.

METHODS OF SERVICE.

45A.2.3   The two methods for service on unnamed persons are (1) in the case of buildings affecting and depositing in, or (2) in the case of land without buildings, inserting stakes in the ground with the summons and citation attached.

     Service on named persons will be in accordance with normal rules of service, on which see Chap. 16, Pt I.

---

[1] R. 45A.2 inserted by S.I. 1996 No. 2168 (effective 23rd September 1996).

The provision in r. 45A.2(2)(b) for inserting stakes in the ground in the case of land only, is designed for (a) land occupied on which there are no buildings, or (b) where there is a building but the land and not the building is occupied.

45A.2.4

Shortening or dispensing with periods of time

45A.3.[1]   Where the action is directed against a person in occupation of the heritable property *vi clam aut precario*, the pursuer may apply by motion to shorten or dispense with the period of notice or other period of time in these Rules relating to the conduct of the action or the extracting of any decree.

45A.3

GENERAL NOTE.

For the history of this rule, see note 45A.1.1.

Where a person is in possession of property *vi clam aut precario* and without right or title to process or occupy that property, the court may shorten or dispense with (a) the period of notice, or (b) any other period of time specified in the RCS 1994 relating to the action: r. 45A.3.

The power of the court under r. 7.1(4) to authorise immediate extract or to supersede extract for such period as it thinks fit should be noted.

45A.3.1

"VI CLAM AUT PRECARIO".

This phrase means by force, stealth or precarious possession.

45A.3.2

"MOTION".

For motions, see Chap. 23.

P.N. No. 3 of 2018 requires a local authority petitioning under s. 46 of the C.S.A. 1988 for removal of persons camping without authority to aver in any motion under r. 45A.3 (A) what its procedures and policies are for removal of such persons, (b) whether it has followed them and how they have been applied, and (c) why removal is required (one would expect that to be in the petition) and the reason why the period of notice requires to be shortened or dispensed with. The P.N. is confused: it relates to petitions whereas r.45A.3 is concerned with actions!

45A.3.3

Application by occupiers to become defenders

45A.4.[2]   A person not named as a defender in the summons who is in occupation of the heritable property may, within the period of notice, apply by minute to be sisted as a defender to the action.

45A.4

GENERAL NOTE.

For the history of this rule, see note 45A.1.1.

An unnamed occupier enters the process by applying by minute to be sisted as a defender: r. 45A.4. Once he identifies himself by doing so, he will become a named defender and be liable as any named defender to, e.g., interdict.

45A.4.1

"APPLY BY MINUTE TO BE SISTED".

On a minute of sist, see note 15.1.9.

45A.4.2

EXPENSES.

The question arises about obtaining expenses against unnamed occupiers.

45A.4.3

---

[1] R. 45A.3 inserted by S.I. 1996 No. 2168 (effective 23rd September 1996).
[2] R. 45A.4 inserted by S.I. 1996 No. 2168 (effective 23rd September 1996).

45A.2.4

45A.3

Shortening or dispensing with periods of time

45A.3.1 Where the action is directed against a person in occupation of the heritable property without any warrant, the pursuer may apply, by motion, to shorten or dispense with the period of notice or other period of time in these Rules relating to the conduct of the action or the extracting of any decree.

45A.3.1

45A.3.2

45A.3.3

Application by occupier to become defender

45A.4.1 A person not named as a defender in the summons who is in occupation of the heritable property may, within the period of notice, apply by minute to be sisted as a defender to the action.

45A.4.1

45A.4.2

45A.4.3

672

CHAPTER 46 ADMIRALTY ACTIONS

Chapter 46

Admiralty Actions

Interpretation of this Chapter

46.1.[1] In this Chapter—

46.1

"Admiralty action" means an action having a conclusion appropriate for the enforcement of a claim to which section 47(2) of the Administration of Justice Act 1956 applies;

"ship" has the meaning assigned in section 48(f) of that Act.

Deriv. RCS 1965, r. 135

"ADMIRALTY ACTION".

The definition of "Admiralty action" follows a proposal of the *Scottish Law Commission's Discussion Paper on Diligence on the Dependence and Admiralty Arrestments (Scot. Law Com. Discussion Paper No. 84)* to define Admiralty actions by reference to the list of claims in s.47(2) of the Administration of Justice Act 1956 being the claims in respect of which arrestments may be laid. This brings Scots law into line with English law and the theory that Admiralty jurisdiction is over ships and that the appropriate remedy lies in proceedings against the ship (see "The Scottish Court of Admiralty: A Retrospect" (1922) 34 J.R. 38). An arrestment on the dependence or in rem is different from an ordinary arrestment and is a real diligence against the ship itself: *Carlberg v. BoRjesson* (1877) 5 R. 188, 195 per Lord Shand. S.47 of the 1956 Act was enacted to enable the U.K. to ratify the *Brussels International Convention relating to the Arrest of Sea-going Ships 1952 (Cmnd. 1128 (1960))*. Contracts of *respondentia* have been added to the definition, only bottomry bonds being mentioned in s.47(2)(h) of the 1956 Act, although both are obsolete. Under the Merchant Shipping (Salvage and Pollution) Act 1994 (replaced by s.224 of the Merchant Shipping Act 1995), implementing the *London International Convention on Salvage 1989 (Cm. 1526)*, s.47(2)(c) of the 1956 Act is amended to refer to the Salvage Convention 1989 and to contracts of salvage; accordingly, any claim not covered by the Convention will not properly be salvage to which s.47(2) of the 1956 Act applies and will not be an Admiralty action.

46.1.1

S.47 of the 1956 Act does not define the jurisdiction of the Scottish courts.

The purpose of Chap. 46 is to provide for the special rules of arrestment in relation to ships and their cargo and completion of these arrestments by sale, and for the special rules for ship collision cases, salvage and the International Oil Pollution Compensation Fund.

Maritime or Admiralty actions not included in s.47(2) of the 1956 Act could proceed as commercial actions under Chap. 47. An Admiralty action mentioned in s.47(2) of the 1956 Act which relates to a dispute of a commercial nature may also proceed as a commercial action: see r. 47.1(1)(b).

"SHIP".

S.48(f) of the Administration of Justice Act 1956 defines "ship" as including any description of vessel used in navigation not propelled by oars. The meaning of "ship" or "vessel" is important in determining what subjects are arrestable by Admiralty arrestments. In a case under the Merchant Shipping Act 1854, "ship" was held to be a vessel which goes to sea, and "used in navigation" meant "used in navigating the seas": *Oakes v. Monkland Iron Co.* (1884) 11 R. 579, 583 and 584 per L.J.-C. Moncreiff. This definition is rather limiting.

46.1.2

"Ship" includes hovercraft: Hovercraft Act 1968 s. 2(1).

Note also s.87(1) of the Civil Aviation Act 1982 and the Aircraft (Wreck and Salvage) Order 1938 [S.R. & O. 1938 No. 136] which apply Admiralty jurisdiction (and arrestments) to claims for salvage of aircraft.

JURISDICTION.

S.47(2) of the Administration of Justice Act 1956 does not define the jurisdiction of the Scottish courts; but to the extent that Admiralty jurisdiction is over ships and the appropriate remedy lies in proceedings against the ship (see note 46.1.1), that provision, by listing those claims in respect of which arrestment may be laid, provides a sort of indirect definition of jurisdiction. The limits of Admiralty jurisdiction are not entirely clear.

46.1.3

Under Art. 3(g) of Sched. 4 (inter- U.K. jurisdiction) of the C.J.J.A. 1982, in relation to remuneration for salvage of cargo or freight, a person domiciled in one country may be sued in the courts of another country under the authority of which the cargo or freight was or could have been arrested. Sched. 8 (jurisdiction of Scottish courts) does not apply to Admiralty actions where jurisdiction is based on arrestment in rem or to found jurisdiction of a ship, cargo or freight: C.J.J.A. 1982, Sched. 9, para. 6.

---

[1] R. 46.1 amended by S.S.I. 2010 No.205 (effective 15th June 2010).

In actions of reparation arising out of ship collisions, close manoeuvring or non-compliance with collision regulations (but not an action in rem to enforce a collision lien), the court has jurisdiction if (a) the defender has his habitual residence or place of business within the jurisdiction; (b) the cause of action arose within the jurisdiction and either within inland waters or the limits of a port; (c) an action arising out of the same incident(s) is proceeding or has been heard or determined in the court; (d) the defender has prorogated the jurisdiction of the court; or (e) a ship in which the defender owns shares has been arrested to found jurisdiction or on the dependence within the jurisdiction: 1956 Act s. 45.

In relation to salvage, under the Merchant Shipping (Salvage and Pollution) Act 1994 (replaced by s. 224 of the Merchant Shipping Act 1995), implementing the *London International Convention on Salvage* 1989 (Cm. 1526), any claim not covered by the Convention will not properly be salvage to which s. 47(2) of the 1956 Act applies and will not be an Admiralty action. This will not affect any possible "salvage" claims based on *negotiorum gestio*. Note also s. 87(1) of the Civil Aviation Act 1982 and the Aircraft (Wreck and Salvage) Order 1938 [S.R. & O. 1938 No. 136] which apply Admiralty jurisdiction (and arrestments) to claims for salvage of aircraft.

Forms of action

46.2

46.2.—[1](1) An Admiralty action against the owners or demise charterers of, or other parties interested in, a ship or the owners of the cargo may be brought—

(a) in rem, where the conclusion of the summons is directed to recovery in respect of a maritime lien against the ship or cargo or the proceeds of it as sold under order of the court or where arrestment in rem may be made under section 47(3) of the Administration of Justice Act 1956;

(b) in personam, where the conclusion of the summons is directed to a decree in common form against the defender; or

(c) both in rem and in personam, where sub-paragraphs (a) and (b) apply.

(2) When bringing an Admiralty action, the pursuer shall insert the words "Admiralty Action in rem", "Admiralty Action in personam" or "Admiralty Action in rem and in personam", as the case may be, immediately below the words "IN THE COURT OF SESSION" where they occur above the instance, and on the backing, of the summons and any copy of it.

Deriv. R.C.S. 1965, r. 136

GENERAL NOTE

46.2.1

On Admiralty actions in rem, see r. 46.3 and notes. On Admiralty actions in personam, see r. 46.4 and notes.

Actions in rem

46.3

46.3.—[2](1) In an Admiralty action in rem—

(a) where the owners or demise charterers of, or other parties interested in, the ship or the owners of the cargo against which the action is directed are known to the pursuer, they shall be called as defenders by name;

(b) where such owners or demise charterers or other parties are unknown to the pursuer—

(i) the pursuer may call them as defenders as "the owners or demise charterers of, or other parties interested in the ship (*name and identify by its port of registry*) *[or* the owners of the cargo]"; and

(ii) the master, if known, shall also be called as a defender representing the owners or demise charterers.

(2) In an Admiralty action in rem, the ship or cargo shall be arrested in rem and a warrant for such arrestment shall be inserted in the summons in the form in Form 13.2-A.

Deriv. R.C.S. 1965, r. 137(a) and (b)

---

[1] R. 46.2 amended by S.S.I. 2010 No. 205 (effective 15th June 2010).

[2] R. 46.3(1) amended by S.S.I. 2010 No. 205 (effective 15th June 2010) and S.S.I. 2011 No. 288 (effective 21st July 2011).

An Admiralty action in rem is directed against the ship or cargo itself, as the case may be, to enforce a maritime lien. The action has conclusions for declarator that the pursuer has a maritime lien over the ship or cargo for a specified sum and interest preferable to the rights of others and for warrant to sell the ship or cargo on the lien being declared and to apply the proceeds in satisfaction of the lien: see Form 13.2-B(9). The action can only proceed on an arrestment in rem: r. 46.3(2). The arrestment in rem is an integral part of the action and should be sought in the summons when signeted. It is now possible to convert an Admiralty action in personam into an action in rem after signeting: see r. 13.8; cf. *Mill v. Fildes* 1982 S.L.T. 147 under R.C.S. 1965. The arrestment attaches the whole ship or cargo, as the case may be, the whole being subject to sale. On arrestment in rem, see further notes 46.3.2–46.3.4.

46.3.1

A maritime lien is a form of hypothec or security without possession over a ship, her apparel or cargo enforceable by an Admiralty action in rem in which the res is attached by the arrestment, declarator of the lien is granted and the res sold. Such a lien arises (i) at common law in respect of damage done by a ship, bonds of bottomry or respondentia, seamen's wages, salvage and (ii) by creation of statute—master's wages and disbursements (Merchant Shipping Act 1995 s. 41), compensation to owners or occupiers of land for damage occasioned by shipwreck (1995 Act s. 234(5)), fees and expenses of receiver of wrecks (1995 Act s. 249(3)), remuneration for services of coastguard (1995 Act s. 250(3)(c)). Under s. 47(1) of the Administration of Justice Act 1956, arrestment in rem is only competent if the action involves a claim in s. 47(2), and the statutory liens except master's wages and disbursements and rights to life and property salvage are probably excluded.

An arrestment in rem may be executed in (a) an Admiralty action in rem to enforce a maritime lien or (b) an Admiralty action in personam to enforce a nonpecuniary claim relating to the ship under s. 47(2)(p)–(s) of the Administration of Justice Act 1956 by virtue of s. 47(3) of that Act. An Admiralty action is defined in r. 46.1. Arrest- ment of a ship is a real diligence directed against the vessel itself: *Carlberg v. Borjesson* (1877) 5 R. 188, 195 per Lord Shand. There is no arrestee: *Barclay, Curle & Co. Ltd v. Sir James Laing & Sons Ltd* 1908 S.C. 82, 89 per Lord McLaren. The ship may be arrested while in the possession of the defender. Arrestment of the ship does not arrest the cargo or freight. Arrestment in rem founds jurisdiction. The ship is fixed in the place where she is at the time of the execution of the ar- restment until a declarator of lien is obtained and a process of sale com- pleted: *Carlberg*, above. The ar- restment cannot be executed when the ship is on passage: *Carlberg*, above; 1956 Act s. 47(6). The expenses of arrestment are recoverable as expenses of process because they are essential to the obtaining of the decree in rem: *Hatton v. A/S Durban Hansen* 1919 S.C. 154. Under s. 47(1) of the 1956 Act arrest- ment in rem is only competent if the action involves a claim in s. 47(2), and the statutory liens except master's wages and disbursements and rights to life and property salvage are probably excluded. On maritime liens, see note 46.3.1. Note also arrestment in rem in an Admiralty action in personam to enforce a non-pecuniary claim under s. 47(2)(p)–(s) of the 1956 Act: see note 46.4.4.

46.3.2

A schedule in Form 16.15-C is used and a certificate of execution in Form 16.15-I is completed: r. 16.15(1)(c). The schedule is attached by a messenger-at-arms to the mainmast or other prominent part and a copy delivered to the master of the ship or person in charge whom failing the harbour master whom failing a motion for further procedure must be enrolled: r. 16.13(1), (3) and (4). This may be done on any day, including Sunday: r. 16.13(1). The certificate is attached to the summons or other document contain- ing the warrant for the diligence: r. 16.12(7).

This arrestment may be executed in an Admiralty action in rem to enforce a maritime lien (on which, see note 46.3.1). It temporarily detains the ship until the cargo is discharged. Where the cargo cannot be discharged the court may even loose the arrestment to enable this to be done out of the jurisdiction: *Svenska Petroleum A.B. v. H.O.R. Ltd* 1982 S.L.T. 343. It is not clear if the arrestment immobilises the ship where it is until the cargo is discharged or merely prevents the ship-master from sailing with the cargo out of the jurisdiction. It is probable that s.47(1) of the Administration of Justice Act 1956 does not apply to such an arrestment: see e.g. *Svenska Petroleum A.B. v. H.O.R. Ltd* 1982 S.L.T. 343, 1983 S.L.T. 493 and 1986 S.L.T. 513; *West Cumberland Farmers Ltd v. Ellon Hinengo Ltd* 1988 S.L.T. 294.

46.3.3

A schedule in Form 16.15-C is used and a certificate of execution in Form 16.15-I is completed: r. 16.15(1)(c). The schedule is attached by a messenger-at-arms to the mainmast or other prominent part and a copy delivered to the master of the ship or person in charge whom failing the harbour master whom failing a motion for further procedure must be enrolled: r. 16.13(1), (3) and (4). This may be done on any day, including Sunday: r. 16.13(1). The certificate is attached to the summons or other document contain- ing the warrant for the diligence: r. 16.12(7).

This arrestment may be executed in an Admiralty action to enforce a maritime lien (on which, see note 46.3.1).

46.3.4

A schedule in Form 16.15-C is served by a messenger-at-arms and a certificate of execution in Form 16.15-I is completed: r. 16.15(1)(c). The certificate is attached to the summons or other document contain- ing the warrant for the diligence: r. 16.12(7). There is no provision for this arrestment to be executed on a Sunday and the common law applies: r. 16.14(2); Stair, III.i.37; Bell's *Comm.*, ii, 460; *Oliphant v. Douglas* (1663) Mor. 15002 (quaere whether arrestment permitted following *Nederlandse Scheepshypotheekbank v. Cam Standby* 1994 S.C.L.R. 956). Whether or not the cargo has been delivered to the owner, the messenger-at-arms serves the schedule on the custodian of the cargo or, where on the quay or harbour shed, on the harbour master. Where the cargo has been landed on the quay or in a harbour shed the option of serving on the custodian is still available: this is useful where, e.g. there is no harbour master.

WARRANT TO DISMANTLE.

46.3.5   An arrestment in rem of a ship fixes her in the place where she is found. To make sure the ship is not moved a warrant to dismantle may be sought (in the summons (r. 13.6(c)(iv)) or subsequently by motion (r. 13.8)). Dismantling should be done by a suitably qualified person (such as a marine engineer) under the supervision of the messenger-atarms. Dismantling may be unnecessary if the ship does not have customs clearance to sail.

MOVEMENT OF ARRESTED SHIP OR CARGO.

46.3.6   Any person having an interest may apply by motion to move an arrested vessel or cargo. This may be to move a ship to a safe harbour (*Turner v. Galway* (1882) 19 S.L.R. 892; *J.W.A. Upham v. Torode* 1982 S.L.T. 229, sub nom. The "Grey Dolphin" 1982 S.C. 5) or to move her from a place where she is obstructing or causing loss to a third party. If a cargo is arrested but cannot be unloaded the ship is effectively immobilised: see *Svenska Petroleum A.B. v. H.O.R. Ltd* 1982 S.L.T. 343; *West Cumberland Farmers Ltd v. Director of Agriculture of Sri Lanka* 1988 S.L.T. 296. See also note 13.11.1.

ARRESTMENT ON A SUNDAY.

46.3.7   R. 16.13(1) permits arrestment of a ship in rem, or an arrestment in rem of cargo on board ship, to be executed on any day. The common law prohibition of executing diligence on a Sunday gave rise to difficulty as the turn-round time of ships is often short and tankers and bulk-ore carriers are frequently discharged at weekends.

Actions in personam

46.4   **46.4.—**[1](1) In an Admiralty action in personam directed against the owners or demise charterers, or other parties interested in a ship, or the owners of cargo, the defenders shall, if known to the pursuer, be called as defenders by name.

(2)   In such an action, where—

(a)   the vessel is not a British ship, and

(b)   the names of the owners or demise charterers are not known to the pursuer, the master of the ship may be called as the defender representing the owners or demise charterers.

(3)   In an action to which paragraph (2) applies, any warrant to arrest to found jurisdiction shall be executed against the master of the ship in his representative capacity.

(4)   In an action to which paragraph (2) applies, any decree shall be pronounced against the master in his representative capacity.

(5)   A decree in an Admiralty action in personam may be pronounced against an owner or demise charterer of, or other party interested in, the ship or the owner of the cargo only where that owner or demise charterer or other party interested, as the case may be, has been called or added as a defender.

Deriv. R.C.S. 1965, r. 138 (r. 46.4(1) to (3)) and r. 142 (r. 46.4(4) and (5))

ADMIRALTY ACTIONS IN PERSONAM.

46.4.1   An Admiralty action in personam is an Admiralty action other than one in rem (on which, see note 46.3.1) listed in s.47(2) of the Administration of Justice Act 1956; but note arrestment in rem in an Admiralty action in personam to enforce a non-pecuniary claim under s.47(2)(p)–(s) of the 1956 Act: see note 46.4.4. An Admiralty action in personam may be a petitory action (an action for payment or performance) to enforce an obligation secured by a maritime lien but does not enforce the lien itself. The action is directed against a person and not the ship or cargo, although the master of the ship may be called as a defender if the ship is not British and the owners are not known: r. 46.4(1). Arrestment (on the dependence) is not essential. To found jurisdiction an arrestment to found jurisdiction must be executed. Arrestment attaches the share(s) of the ship owned by the defender, only the share(s) arrested being subject to sale. The whole ship is detained by the arrestment if the ship is the ship with which the action is concerned or all the shares in it are owned by the defender against whom the conclusion is directed: 1956 Act, s.47(1).

---

[1] R. 46.4 amended by S.S.I. 2010 No. 205 (effective 15th June 2010).

ARRESTMENT OF SHIP OR CARGO TO FOUND JURISDICTION.

Subject to two exceptions arrestment to found jurisdiction may not be executed where the defender is domiciled in the U.K. or a Contracting State to the 1968 Brussels, or the Lugano, Convention: C.J.J.A. 1982, Scheds 1 and 3C, Art. 3(2), Sched. 4, Art. 3 and Sched. 8, r. 2(8). The exceptions are: (a) In an action of reparation arising out of the collision or manoeuvring of ships, or non-compliance with ship collision regulations under s.45 of the Administration of Justice Act 1956, the restrictions of the C.J.J.A. 1982 do not apply to defenders domiciled outside the U.K.: C.J.J.A. 1982, Scheds 1 and 3C, Art. 54 and Sched. 9, para. 6. (b) In an Admiralty action where the defender is domiciled in the U.K. or elsewhere except another Contracting State to the 1968 Brussels, or the Lugano, Convention: C.J.J.A. 1982, Sched. 5, para. 7 and Sched. 9, para. 6. (For an argument that the 1968 Brussels Convention and Sched. 8 to the C.J.J.A. 1982 have affected and do not permit our law of arrestment to found jurisdiction, see *Ladgroup Ltd v. Euroeast Lines SA* 1997 S.L.T. 916.) Arrestment of a ship or cargo to found jurisdiction is subject to the ordinary rules of arrestment of any property to found jurisdiction, and must be made in the hands of a third party: see note 13.6.1. There are also restrictions in the *UN Convention on the Law of the Sea* 1982, Art. 28 (Cmnd 8941): see Merchant Shipping Act 1995, s. 129.

A schedule of arrestment in Form 16.15-A is served on the defender and a certificate of execution in Form 16.15-H is completed: r. 16.15(1)(a). The certificate is attached to the summons or other document containing the warrant for the diligence: r. 16.12(7).

46.4.2

ARRESTMENT OF SHIPS ON THE DEPENDENCE.

A ship may be arrested on the dependence of an Admiralty action in personam (a) to enforce or secure a claim in s.47(2) of the Administration of Justice Act 1956 by virtue of s.47(1) of that Act where the ship is the ship with which the action is concerned (and is partly owned by the defender: see e.g. *William Batey & Co. (Exports) Ltd v. Kent* 1985 S.L.T. 490, affd. 1987 S.L.T. 557) or all the shares are owned by the defender or (b) to enforce a claim in s.47(2)(p)–(s) by virtue of s.47(3)(a) of the 1956 Act if the conclusion is a pecuniary conclusion and the ship is the ship to which the conclusion relates. For a recent example on whether remotely operated vehicle equipment (with which the vessel would be deployed), systems, services and personnel supplied for a particular vessel was for the supply of goods or materials "to" a ship "for her operation" under s. 47(2)(k) of the 1956 Act or the "equipment of any ship" under s. 47(2)(l) of that Act, see *Oceaneering International AG, Ptnrs.* , 2011 S.L.T. 667 (OH). An Admiralty action is defined in r. 46.1. It is not clear whether s.47(1) limits the common law right to arrest a sister ship: see e.g. *Sheaf Steamship Co. Ltd v. Compania Transmediterranea* 1930 S.C. 660; cf. Brussels Convention relating to the Arrest of Seagoing Ships, 10th May 1952, art. 3(3), *The "Banco"* [1971] P. 137 (English law) and comments in *Gatoil International Inc. v. Arkwright-Boston Manufacturers Mutual Insurance Co.* 1985 S.C.(H.L.) 1, 15 per Lord Keith of Kinkel. The action is directed against the defenders and not the ship. The expenses of the arrestment are not recoverable at common law as expenses of process because the arrestment is not essential to obtaining the decree in personam: *Black v. Jehangeer Framjee & Co.* (1887) 14 R. 678. Quaere whether they are recoverable as a debt due in a separate action or under s.93(2) of the Debtors (Scotland) Act 1987. There are also restrictions in the *UN Convention on the Law of the Sea* 1982, Art. 28 (Cmnd 8941): see Merchant Shipping Act 1995, s. 129.

A schedule in Form 16.15-B is used and a certificate of execution in Form 16.15-J is completed: r. 16.15(1)(e). The schedule is attached by a messenger-at-arms to the mainmast or other prominent part, the letters "ER" chalked above and a copy of the schedule delivered to the master of the ship or person in charge whom failing the harbour master whom failing a motion for further procedure must be enrolled: r. 16.13(1)–(4). This may be done on any day, including Sunday: r. 16.13(1). The certificate is attached to the summons or other document containing the warrant for the diligence: r. 16.12(7).

46.4.3

ARRESTMENT IN REM IN AN ADMIRALTY ACTION IN PERSONAM.

Such an arrestment may be executed to enforce a non-pecuniary claim under s.47(2)(p)–(s) of the Administration of Justice Act 1956 by virtue of s.47(3) of that Act. These provisions relate to a dispute as to ownership or possession of or a share in a ship, between co-owners of a ship about ownership, possession, employment or earnings of that ship, the mortgage or hypothecation of or share in a ship, or the forfeiture or condemnation of a ship or goods or the restoration of the ship or goods. Arrestment may be used whether or not the ship belongs to the defender: *Arrest of Ships—4*, Scotland, p. 87, by I. G. Inglis (Lloyds of London, 1987). There is no declarator of lien and no sale and the arrestment simply secures implement of the decree. There are also restrictions in the *UN Convention on the Law of the Sea 1982, Art. 28 (Cmnd 8941)*: see Merchant Shipping Act 1995, s. 129.

A schedule in Form 16.15-D is used and a certificate of execution in Form 16.15-I is completed: r. 16.15(1)(d). The schedule is attached by a messenger-at-arms to the mainmast or other prominent part and a copy delivered to the master of the ship or person in charge whom failing the harbour master whom failing a motion for further procedure must be enrolled: r. 16.13(1), (3) and (4). This may be done on any day, including Sunday: r. 16.13(1). The certificate is attached to the summons or other document containing the warrant for the diligence: r. 16.12(7).

46.4.4

ARRESTMENT ON THE DEPENDENCE OF CARGO LANDED OR TRANSHIPPED.

Where the cargo has been or is in the course of being landed or transhipped it no longer has the character of cargo on board ship and there is no reason for treating it as liable to an Admiralty arrestment; the arrestment must be in the hands of a third party: see note 13.6.3. Where cargo is in the possession of the cargo owner on land the ordinary rules of arrestment also apply: see note 13.6.3.

46.4.5

A schedule in Form 16.15-B is served on the arrestee by a messenger-at-arms and a certificate of execution in Form 16.15-H is completed: r. 16.15(1)(b). The certificate is attached to the summons or other document containing the warrant for the diligence: r. 16.12(7). There is no provision for this arrestment to be executed on a Sunday and the common law applies: r. 16.14(2); Stair, III.i.37; Bell's *Comm.*, ii, 460; *Oliphant v. Douglas* (1633) Mor. 15002; but cf. *Nederlandse Scheepshypotheekbank NV v. CAM Standby Ltd* 1994 S.C.L.R. 956.

ARRESTMENT ON THE DEPENDENCE OF CARGO ON BOARD SHIP.

46.4.6 This arrestment may be used in an ordinary action or in an Admiralty action in personam. There must be an arrestee, e.g. a third party or the ship-master (even if he is the employee of the cargo owner) or the cargo owner himself: r. 16.14(2).

A schedule in Form 16.15—B is served on the arrestee by a messenger-at-arms and a certificate of execution in Form 16.15—J is completed: r. 16.15(1)(e). The arrestment may be executed on any day, including Sunday: r. 16.14(2). The certificate is attached to the summons or other document containing the warrant for the diligence: r. 16.12(7).

WARRANT TO DISMANTLE.

46.4.7 An arrestment on the dependence of a ship fixes her in the place where she is found. To make sure the ship is not moved a warrant to dismantle may be sought (in the summons (r. 13.6(c)(iv)) or subsequently by motion (r. 13.8)). Dismantling should be done by a suitably qualified person (such as a marine engineer) under the supervision of the messenger-at-arms. Dismantling may be unnecessary if the ship does not have customs clearance to sail.

MOVEMENT OF ARRESTED SHIP OR CARGO.

46.4.8 Any person having an interest may apply by motion to move an arrested vessel or cargo. This may be to move a ship to a safe harbour (*Turner v. Galway* (1882) 19 S.L.R. 892; *J.W.A. Upham v. Torode* 1982 S.L.T. 229 sub nom. The "Grey Dolphin" 1982 S.C. 5) or to move her from a place where she is obstructing or causing loss to a third party. If a cargo is arrested but cannot be unloaded the ship is effectively immobilised: see *Svenska Petroleum A.B. v. H.O.R. Ltd* 1982 S.L.T. 343; *West Cumberland Farmers Ltd v. Director of Agriculture of Sri Lanka* 1988 S.L.T. 296. See also note 13.11.1.

ARRESTMENT ON A SUNDAY.

46.4.9 The common law prohibition of executing diligence on a Sunday gave rise to difficulty when the turnround time of ships is often short and tankers and bulk-ore carriers are frequently discharged at weekends. Arrestment on any day, including Sunday, is permitted on the dependence of an Admiralty action in personam, or of an ordinary action, of cargo on board ship: r. 16.14(2). The common law in relation to arrestment on the dependence in an Admiralty action was altered by *Nederlandse Scheepshypotheekbank v. Cam Standby* 1994 S.C.L.R. 956 in which Lord Allanbridge permitted arrestment on a Sunday.

Sale of ship or cargo

46.5 **46.5.**—(1) This rule shall not apply to the sale of a cargo arrested on the dependence of an Admiralty action in personam.

(1A)[1] Where section 47E of the Administration of Justice Act 1956 applies, the pursuer may apply for an order for the sale of the ship by public auction or private bargain.

(1B)[2] Where the owner or demise charterer of the ship has made payment of the sum due under section 47E(2)(a) of the Administration of Justice Act 1956, or has tendered the sum due under section 47E(2)(b) of that Act and that tender has not been accepted within a reasonable time, the owner or demise charterer may apply to the court for an order declaring that the arrestment ceased to have effect from a specified date.

(2) Where, in an Admiralty action or an action of declarator and sale of a ship—

(a) the court makes a finding that the pursuer has a claim which falls to be satisfied out of an arrested ship or cargo, or

(b) a decree for a sum of money has been granted in an action in which a ship has been arrested on the dependence,

the pursuer may apply by motion for an order for the sale of that ship or a share in it, or the cargo, as the case may be, by public auction or private bargain.

---

[1] R. 46.5(1A) and (1B) inserted by S.S.I. 2010 No.205 (effective 15th June 2010).
[2] R. 46.5(1A) and (1B) inserted by S.S.I. 2010 No.205 (effective 15th June 2010).

(3)   Before making such an order, the court shall remit to a reporter for the purpose of obtaining—

(a)   an inventory of,

(b)   a valuation and recommended upset price for, and

(c)   any recommendation as to the appropriate advertisement for the sale of, the ship, share or cargo.

(4)   Where a remit is made under paragraph (3), the pursuer shall instruct the reporter within 14 days after the date of the interlocutor making the remit and be responsible, in the first instance, for payment of his fee.

(5)   On completion of a report following a remit under paragraph (3), the reporter shall send the report and a copy for each party to the Deputy Principal Clerk.

(6)   On receipt of such a report, the Deputy Principal Clerk shall—

(a)   give written intimation to each party of receipt of the report;

(b)   request the pursuer to show to him a discharge in respect of the fee for which he is responsible under paragraph (4); and

(c)   after sight of such a discharge—

   (i)   lodge the report in process;

   (ii)   give written intimation to each party that this has been done and that he may uplift a copy of the report from process; and

   (iii)   cause the action to be put out on the By Order Roll before the Lord Ordinary.

(7)   Where the court orders the sale of a ship, share or cargo, the conduct of the sale, including any advertisement of it, shall be under the direction of the Deputy Principal Clerk.

(8)   Where such a sale is the sale of a ship or a share in it, the interlocutor ordering the sale shall include a declaration that the right to transfer the ship or share to the purchaser is vested in the Deputy Principal Clerk.

(9)   Where, in such a sale, no offer to purchase the ship, share or cargo, as the case may be, has reached the upset price, the pursuer may apply by motion for authority to expose such ship, share or cargo for sale at a reduced upset price.

(10)   The proceeds of such a sale shall be consigned into court, under deduction of all dues to the date the court adjudges the ship, share or cargo to belong to the purchaser under paragraph (11)(a), payable to Her Majesty's Customs and Excise or to the port or harbour authority within the jurisdiction of which the ship or cargo lies and in respect of which such port or harbour authority has statutory power to detain the ship or cargo.

(11)   On consignation being made under paragraph (10), the court shall—

(a)   adjudge the ship, share or cargo, as the case may be, declaring the same to belong to the purchaser, freed and disburdened of all bonds, mortgages, liens, rights of retention and other incumbrances affecting it and ordering such ship, share or cargo to be delivered to the purchaser on production of a certified copy of the interlocutor pronounced under this sub-paragraph; and

(b)   order such intimation and advertisement, if any, for claims on the consigned fund as it thinks fit.

(12)   The court shall, after such hearing or inquiry as it thinks fit—

(a)   determine all questions of expenses;

(b)   rank and prefer any claimants in order of preference; and

(c)   make such other order, if any, as it thinks fit.

Deriv. R.C.S. 1965, r. 143

SALE OF SHIP OR CARGO.

46.5.1   Sale is the completion of the arrestment of a ship either in rem or on the dependence, or of cargo in rem. The sale is under r. 46.5 under the direction of the Deputy Principal Clerk. In the case of an arrestment on the dependence of an Admiralty action in personam, a separate action of declarator and sale is competent; but it is now specified in r. 46.5(2) (to clear up a doubt) that such a sale in a separate action is subject to r. 46.5. It is clear from the terms of r. 46.5(1) and (2) that r. 46.5 applies to arrestment on the dependence of an Admiralty action in personam; and see *Banque Indo Suez v. Maritime Co. Overseas Inc.* 1985 S.L.T. 517 where this seems to have been assumed.

Where the arrestment is of cargo on the dependence of an Admiralty action in personam, the appropriate process to complete the arrestment is an action of furthcoming, and r. 46.5 does not apply: r. 46.5(1).

Where the arrestment is of a ship or cargo in execution of a decree in an Admiralty action in personam, or an ordinary action for payment, the appropriate process for completion of the arrestment is an action of furthcoming.

Sale may be by public auction or private bargain: r. 46.5(2). Often the price obtained at auction is less than can be obtained by private bargain.

"MOTION".

46.5.2   For motions, see Chap. 23.

"WITHIN 14 DAYS".

46.5.3   The date from which the period is calculated is not counted.

Remit to a reporter.

[THE NEXT PARAGRAPH IS 46.5.5]

"SEND".

46.5.5   This includes deliver: r. 1.3(1) (definition of "send").

"WRITTEN INTIMATION".

46.5.6   For methods, see r. 16.9.

"CONSIGNED INTO COURT".

46.5.7   On consignation, see r. 33.4(1)(b) and note 33.4.3.

"FREED AND DISBURDENED".

46.5.8   The reasoning for freeing the ship, share or cargo, as the case may be, from all claims on its sale is explained by Lord Fleming in *The "Sierra Nevada"* (1932) 42 L1.L.Rep. 309, 310. That case was an action in rem but the reasoning is said to be equally applicable in an action in personam, and r. 46.5(11) applies to both.

Ship collisions and preliminary acts

46.6   **46.6.**—(1) Subject to rule 46.7 (applications to dispense with preliminary acts), this rule applies to an Admiralty action of damages arising out of a collision between ships at sea.

(2) An action to which this rule applies may be brought in rem, in personam or in rem and in personam.

(3) A summons in such an action shall not contain a condescendence or pleas-in-law.

(4) Where such an action is brought in personam, the conclusion of the summons shall contain sufficient detail to enable the defender to identify the date and place of, and the ships involved in, the collision.

(5) Within seven days after the summons has called, the pursuer shall lodge in process a sealed envelope containing—

    (a) a preliminary act in Form 46.6; and

    (b) a brief condescendence and appropriate pleas-in-law.

(6) Within 28 days after the preliminary act for the pursuer has been lodged under paragraph (5), the defender shall lodge in process a sealed envelope containing a preliminary act in Form 46.6.

(7) A party who lodges a preliminary act under paragraph (5) or (6) shall not send a copy of it to any other party.

(8)   On the lodging of a preliminary act by the defender under paragraph (6), a clerk of session in the General Department shall—

   (a)   open both sealed envelopes;

   (b)   mark the contents of those envelopes with appropriate numbers of process; and

   (c)   give written intimation to each party that sub-paragraphs (a) and (b) have been complied with.

(9)   On receipt of the written intimation under paragraph (8)(c), the pursuer and defender shall exchange copies of the contents of their respective envelopes.

(10)   Within 7 days after the sealed envelopes have been opened up under paragraph (8), the defender may lodge defences to the action in process and any counterclaim on which he proposes to found.

(11)   Within 7 days after a counterclaim has been lodged under paragraph (10), the pursuer may lodge answers to it in process.

(12)   Within 14 days after defences have been lodged under paragraph (10) or answers have been lodged under paragraph (11), whichever is the earlier, the pursuer shall make up an open record with a copy of each of the preliminary acts appended to it; and Chapter 22 (making up and closing records) shall, subject to paragraph (13) of this rule, apply to the action as it applies to an ordinary action.

(13)   No amendment, adjustment or alteration may be made to a preliminary act except by order of the court.

Deriv. R.C.S. 1965, r. 144

PRELIMINARY ACTS.

    The procedure for preliminary acts is an English importation of 1934 introduced there in 1855 by Dr Lushington (see *The "Inflexible"* (1856) Sw. 32, 34 n. (a)) to get a statement from the parties of the circumstances recenti facto and to prevent the defender from shaping his case to meet the pursuer's case: *The "Vortigern"* (1859) Sw. 518. "They are not merely pleading allegations. They are statements of fact made under such circumstances that they rank as formal admissions of fact binding the party making them perhaps as strongly as any admissions of fact can do. An admission of fact, as such, does not constitute an estoppel. It may be shown that it was made under mistake, and the Court may be satisfied that such was the case; but it is evidence against the party making it, its strength varying according to the conditions under which it is made. An admission under circumstances which necessitate that it must have been made after full consideration, has an evidential value far higher than a casual admission made without any opportunity of reflection or verification. The statements of fact in a preliminary act are statements which must be presumed to be made after the most careful examination and consideration. To my mind they carry such weight, from the nature of a preliminary act and from the circumstances under which it is made, that I should doubt whether otherwise than under the most special circumstances and with the special leave of the court, a party would be allowed to depart from the admissions in the preliminary act, at all events as far as evidence-in-chief is concerned": *The "Seacombe"* [1912] P. 21, 59 per Fletcher Moulton L.J; and see also *The "Channel Queen"* [1928] P. 157 and *The "Semiramis"* [1952] 2 Lloyd's Rep. 86, 93 per Willmer J.

    In *Regent Shipping Co. (Aberdeen) v. George Robb & Sons* 1940 S.N. 50, sub nom. The "Barbara Robb" (1940) 67 Ll.L.Rep. 407, 411 affd. H.L. (1941) 70 Ll.L.Rep. 227, L.P. Normand said that the statements which a preliminary act contains "are as much binding on the party who makes them as averments in the condescendence of an ordinary action, and the adverse party is entitled to found on them as judicial admissions.Great care should be taken to fill in the preliminary act intelligibly as well as candidly; and a motion to amend it should rarely be granted, since its purpose is to obtain from the parties a statement of the facts de recenti, and to prevent one party from shaping his case to meet the facts alleged by the other". In *Morrison v. Scott (The "Scottish Maid")* , 15th June 1979, unreported, Lord Grieve said that statements "made in a preliminary act have effect as formal admissions of fact (Rule of Court 144(*g*)) and, in my opinion, that means that parties must be held bound by the statements in their respective preliminary acts and cannot seek to controvert them in evidence. Where the evidence led on behalf of a party is in conflict with a statement of fact in that party's preliminary act, the latter must be preferred...Preliminary acts are intended to be final documents capable of alteration only by order of the court." It is not thought that the absence of the express provisions, (*a*) for making additions with the leave of the court where the statements required by the preliminary act are not fully set out and (*b*) that the statements have effect as formal admissions, in R.C.S. 1965, r. 144(g) from R.C.S. 1994, r. 46.6(13) is intended to alter the law.

    The requirement for preliminary acts applies even where a party is not the owner of a colliding ship. Where such is the case, however, application may be made to dispense with a preliminary act: see r. 46.7.

46.6.1

JURISDICTION.

46.6.2   In actions of reparation arising out of ship collisions, close manoeuvring or non-compliance with collision regulations (but not an action in rem to enforce a collision lien), the court has jurisdiction if (*a*) the defender has his habitual residence or place of business within the jurisdiction, (*b*) the cause of action arose within the jurisdiction and either within inland waters or the limits of a port, (*c*) an action arising out of the same incident(s) is proceeding or has been heard or determined in the court, (*d*) the defender has prorogated the jurisdiction of the court, or (*e*) a ship in which the defender owns shares has been arrested to found jurisdiction or on the dependence within the jurisdiction: 1956 Act, s.45.

"ARISING OUT OF A COLLISION BETWEEN SHIPS AT SEA".

46.6.2A   On the meaning of "collision at sea", see *The "Star of the Isles"* (1938) 61 Ll.L.Rep. 168 (Outer House) and *Baird v. Aberdeen Coal & Shipping Co. Ltd* 1975 S.L.T. (Notes) 50.

"WITHIN 7 DAYS", "WITHIN 28 DAYS".

46.6.3   The date from which the period is calculated is not counted. Where the last day falls on a Saturday or Sunday or a public holiday on which the Office of Court is closed, the next available day is allowed: r. 1.3(7). For office hours and public holidays, see note 3.1.2.

"LODGE IN PROCESS".

46.6.4   A preliminary act is lodged as a step of process (r. 1.3(1) (definition of "step of process")). On lodging steps of process, see r. 4.4. The list may be lodged by post: P.N. No.4 of 1994, paras. 1 and 8; and see note4.4.10.

"WRITTEN INTIMATION".

46.6.5   For methods, see r. 16.9.

Applications to dispense with preliminary acts

46.7   **46.7.**—(1) Within 7 days after the date on which the summons has called, any party may apply for an order to dispense with preliminary acts in an action to which rule 46.6 applies.

(2) An application under paragraph (1) shall be made by minute craving the court to dispense with preliminary acts and setting out the grounds on which the application is made.

(3) Before lodging such a minute in process, the party making the application shall intimate a copy of the minute, and the date on which it will be lodged, to every other party.

(4) Any other party may lodge in process answers to such a minute within 14 days after such a minute has been lodged.

(5) After the expiry of the period mentioned in paragraph (4), the court may, on the motion of any party, after such further procedure, if any, as it thinks fit, dispense with preliminary acts.

(6) Where the court dispenses with preliminary acts, the pursuer shall lodge a condescendence with appropriate pleas-in-law within such period as the court thinks fit; and the action shall thereafter proceed in the same way as an ordinary action.

(7) Where the court refuses to dispense with preliminary acts, it shall ordain a party or parties, as the case may be, to lodge preliminary acts under rule 46.6 within such period as it thinks fit.

(8) An interlocutor dispensing or refusing to dispense with preliminary acts shall be final and not subject to review.

Deriv. R.C.S. 1965, r. 145

GENERAL NOTE.

46.7.1   Where a party is not the owner of a colliding ship, such as the owner of a third vessel, the crew of a colliding ship or the cargo owner, that party may not be in a position to complete a preliminary act. On the exercise of the discretion to dispense with a preliminary act in England, which arises where there is no mutuality, see *The "El Oso"* (1925) 21 Ll.L.Rep. 340; *The "Carlston" and the "Balcombe"* [1926] P. 82; and see, more recently, *The "Beaverford"* [1960] 2 Lloyd's Rep. 216.

The date from which the period is calculated is not counted. Where the last day falls on a Saturday or Sunday or a public holiday on which the Office of Court is closed, the next available day is allowed: r. 1.3(7). For office hours and public holidays, see note 3.1.2.

46.7.2

"MINUTE".

For applications by minute, see r. 15.1.

46.7.3

"INTIMATE".

For methods, see r. 16.7.

46.7.4

Ship collision and salvage actions

46.8.—(1) Without prejudice to rule 36.3(1) (lodging productions for proof), in an Admiralty action arising out of a collision between ships at sea or salvage, the parties shall—

46.8

   (a) within 4 days after the interlocutor allowing proof,

   (b) within 4 days before the taking of evidence on commission, or

   (c) on or before such other date as the court, on special cause shown, shall determine,

lodge in process the documents, if any, mentioned in paragraph (2).

   (2) The documents to be lodged under paragraph (1) are—

   (a) the log books, including scrap log books, of the ships concerned;

   (b) all *de recenti* written reports in connection with the collision or salvage, as the case may be, by the masters or mates of the vessels concerned to their respective owners; and

   (c) reports of any surveys of the ship in respect of which damage or salvage is claimed.

Deriv. RCS 1965, r. 147

GENERAL NOTE.

It is usual to have an assessor sitting with the court in a ship collision case. On assessors, see Chap. 12.

46.8.1

"WITHIN 4 DAYS AFTER".

The date from which the period is calculated is not counted. Where the last day falls on a Saturday or Sunday or a public holiday on which the Office of Court is closed, the next available day is allowed: r. 1.3(7). For office hours and public holidays, see note 3.1.2.

46.8.2

"LODGE IN PROCESS".

The documents are lodged as productions. On lodging productions, see r. 4.5.

46.8.3

International Oil Pollution Compensation Fund

46.9.—[1,2](1) In this rule—

46.9

   "the Act of 1995" means the Merchant Shipping Act 1995;

   "the Fund" means the International Fund established by the Fund Convention referred to in section 172(1)(b) of the Act of 1995; and

   "the Supplementary Fund" has the meaning given in section 172(1)(f) of the Act of 1995.

   (2) In an action in respect of liability under section 153 of the Act of 1995, intimation of the action under section 177(2) of that Act to the Fund shall be given by the pursuer in accordance with paragraphs (3) and (4) of this rule.

---

[1] Rule 46.9 amended by S.I. 1996 No. 1756 (effective 5th August 1996).
[2] Rule 46.9 amended by S.S.I. 2007 No.7 (effective 29th January 2007).

(3) Where intimation is to be made under paragraph (2), the pursuer shall insert a warrant for intimation in the summons in the following terms:—"Warrant to intimate to the International Oil Pollution Compensation Fund (*address*) as a person having an interest in this action.".

(4) Intimation under paragraph (2) shall be given by a notice of intimation in Form 46.9 attached to a copy of the summons.

(5) Where the Fund or the Supplementary Fund is not a party to an action to which this rule applies, a defender may apply by motion for warrant to serve a third party notice on the Fund or the Supplementary Fund, as the case may be.

(6) Where, in an action under section 175 of the Act of 1995 (compensation from Fund for persons suffering pollution damage) or section 176A of that Act (liability of the Supplementary Fund), the court grants decree against the Fund or the Supplementary Fund, as the case may be, the clerk of court shall, within 14 days after the date of the decree, send a copy of it by first class post to the Fund or the Supplementary Fund, as the case may be.

(7) Any notice under section 176(3)(b) or section 176B(2)(b) of the Act of 1995 (notification of whether amount of claim to be reduced) by the Fund to the court shall be sent to the Deputy Principal Clerk.

(8) An application by virtue of section 176(3)(a) or section 176B(2)(a) of the Act of 1995 for leave to enforce a decree against the Fund or the Supplementary Fund, as the case may be shall be made by motion.

Deriv. RCS 1965, r. 147A inserted by S.I. 1979 No. 670

GENERAL NOTE.

46.9.1   The Merchant Shipping (Oil Pollution) Act 1971 (now Pt VI, Chap. III of the Merchant Shipping Act 1995) provides for civil liability for oil pollution caused by merchant ships. It implements the Brussels International Convention on Civil Liability for Oil Pollution Damage 1969 (Cmnd. 6183 (1975)) as amended by Protocol in 1984 (Cmnd. 9927 (1986)). By the Merchant Shipping (Salvage and Pollution) Act 1994, the U.K. implemented the amendment to this convention (the Liability Convention) by the Protocol of November 27, 1992 (now the Liability Convention of 1992 which provides for strict liability and limitation of liability for oil pollution damage caused by oil tankers): see now Pt VI, Chap. III of the 1995 Act which replaces the 1994 Act as well as the 1971 Act. Under the 1971 Act (now s.158 of the 1995 Act) the owner of a ship alleged to have incurred liability may apply to the court for limitation of that liability.

By the Act of 1974 (now Pt VI, Chap. IV of the Merchant Shipping Act 1995) the U.K. ratified the Brussels International Convention on Establishment of an International Fund for Compensation for Oil Pollution Damage 1971 (Cmnd. 7383). By the Merchant Shipping (Salvage and Pollution) Act 1994, the U.K. implemented the amendment to the convention by the Protocol of November 27, 1992 (now the Fund Convention of 1992 which changes the entry into force requirements of the 1984 protocols): see now Pt VI, Chap. IV of the 1995 Act which replaces the 1994 Act as well as the 1974 Act. Under this convention (the Fund Convention) victims of oil pollution damage unable to obtain a complete remedy from the liable shipowner under the 1971 Act (now the 1995 Act) may make a claim against the Fund: see 1995 Act, s.175. Where a claim is subsequently amended outwith that period, the test is whether the modified version of the claim is presented on a fundamentally different basis: *Assuranceforeningen Skuld v. International Oil Pollution Compensation Fund (No.2)* , 2000 S.L.T. 1348.

Section 5(3) of the 1971 Act is not intended to extinguish a claim made out of time but is merely a procedural provision regulating the making of the claim, and the court might allow further time after the appointed day has passed: *Assuranceforeningen Skuld v. International Oil Pollution Compensation Fund (No.1)* , 2000 S.L.T. 1333.

Liability under the 1971 Act and the 1974 Act does not extend to liability for economic loss of a secondary or relational kind: *Landcatch Ltd v. International Oil Pollution Compensation Fund* , 1999 S.L.T. 1208. "Damage" under the 1971 and 1974 Acts may include psychological conditions such as stress, anxiety and depression: *Black v. The Braer Corporation* 1999 S.L.T. 1401 (OH).

Section 9 of the 1971 Act (now s.162 of the 1995 Act) creates one prescriptive period of three years applicable to all claims after the claim arose: *Gray v. The Braer Corporation* , 1999 S.L.T. 141. The effect of s.9 of the 1971 Act is that a claim is extinguished on the third anniversary of its emergence: *Eunson v. The Braer Corporation* 1999 S.L.T. 1405 (OH).

The purpose of intimation to the Fund under r. 46.9 is that where the Fund is given notice of proceedings against an owner or guarantor in respect of liability under s.153 of the 1995 Act any judgment in the proceedings becomes binding on the Fund: Act of 1974, s.6(2) (now 1995 Act, s.177(2)).

The liability of the Fund may be limited under the Fund Convention. The court must notify the Fund of a judgment in proceedings under s.4 of the Act of 1974 (now s.175 of the 1995 Act) and no steps may be taken to enforce the judgment unless the court gives leave to enforce it: Act of 1974, s.4A(3)(a) inserted by the Merchant Shipping Act 1988, Sched. 4, para. 17(5) (now 1995 Act, s.176(3)(a)). Leave shall not be given until the Fund notifies the court that the amount of the claim is or is not to be reduced: Act of 1974, s.4A(3)(b) (now 1995 Act, s.176(3)(b)).

For parties to the Liability Convention, see the Merchant Shipping (Oil Pollution) (Parties to Convention) Order 1986 [S.I. 1986 No. 2225]. On parties to the Fund Convention, see the International Oil Pollution Compensation Fund (Parties to Convention) Order 1986 [S.I. 1986 No. 2223].

"INTIMATE".

For methods, see r. 16.8.   **46.9.2**

"MOTION".

For motions, see Chap. 23.   **46.9.3**

"THIRD PARTY NOTICE".

For third party procedure, see Chap. 26.   **46.9.4**

"WITHIN 14 DAYS".

The date from which the period is calculated is not counted.   **46.9.5**

"SEND".

This includes deliver: r. 1.3(1) (definition of "send").   **46.9.6**

LIMITATION ACTIONS UNDER THE MERCHANT SHIPPING (OIL POLLUTION) ACT 1971.

A limitation action is one brought by the owner of a ship to limit his liability, for damage or costs   **46.9.7**
incurred where oil is discharged or escapes from his ship, to an amount determined by the court under the Act. The court directs distribution of the amount among those making claims in the proceedings in proportion to their claims. By P.N. No. 1 of 1999, a procedure is provided in a limitation action under s.5 of the 1971 Act for advertisement for, the lodging of, objections to, and adjustment of any condescendence and claims, and for a by order hearing for further procedure. The P.N. also provides that, where a condescendence and claim is based on an existing (presumably "depending") action, all steps of process in that action become steps of process in the limitation action (how they are numbered is not explained).

One imagines, although it is not expressed, that the P.N. is intended to apply also to a limitation action brought under s.158 of the Merchant Shipping Act 1995 which repeals and re-enacts s.5 of the 1971 Act.

Chapter 47

Commercial Actions

Application and interpretation of this Chapter

47.1.—[1](1) This Chapter applies to a commercial action.

(2) In this Chapter—

"commercial action" means an action arising out of, or concerned with, any transaction or dispute of a commercial or business nature in which an election has been made under rule 47.3(1) or which has been transferred under rule 47.10;

"preliminary hearing" means a hearing under rule 47.11;

"procedural hearing" means a hearing under rule 47.12.

GENERAL NOTE.

This Chapter was substituted by A.S. (R.C.S. 1994 Amendment No. 1) (Commercial Actions) 1994 [S.I. 1994 No. 2310] replacing Chap. 47 in RCS 1994 (A.S. (R.C.S. 1994) 1994 [S.I. 1994 No. 1443]) which repealed the rules in RCS 1965 as substituted by A.S. (R.C.S.A. No. 4) (Commercial Actions) 1988 [S.I. 1988 No. 1521] as amended by A.S. (R.C.S.A. No. 5) (Miscellaneous) 1990 [S.I. 1990 No. 2118]. It follows recommendations of the Working Party on Commercial Causes (see note 47.1.2). It was not possible to include those new rules in the RCS 1994 as originally drafted because of lack of time caused by the need for consultation on the draft rules for commercial actions.

The rules in this Chapter make available for the disposal of commercial actions a procedure swifter, more flexible and with less of an emphasis on written pleadings than ordinary procedure. The procedure on the Commercial Roll enables disputes of a business or commercial nature to be dealt with as quickly as possible under the close supervision of the court: *Stirling Aquatic Technology Ltd v. Farmocean AB* 1993 S.L.T. 713, 715L per L.P. Hope. Once a case has been put in the list of commercial actions the court has all the powers it requires to secure its speedy disposal: *Jones & Bailey Contractors Ltd v. George H. Campbell & Co. (Glasgow) Ltd* 1983 S.L.T. 461, 462 per L.P. Emslie. These points made in these cases under the former Rules apply equally to the new rules. The new procedures are the answer to the perception of the business community that the court's procedures caused delay and lacked expertise.

The introduction of special rules of procedure to govern the conduct of disputes of a business or commercial nature represents an attempt by the court not only to respond to the demands of the business and commercial community for a quick and relatively straight-forward means of resolving the sort of disputes which arise in the course of business, but also to compete more effectively with other forums available (e.g. the courts of other jurisdictions, arbitrations, ADR, etc.) for the resolution of these disputes.

In the light of experience the rules may be amended.

WORKING PARTY ON COMMERCIAL CAUSES.

The rules on commercial actions as previously constituted, in 1978 by A.S. (R.C.A. No. 4) (Commercial Causes) 1978 [S.I. 1978 No. 690] and A.S. (R.C.S.A. No. 4) (Commercial Actions) 1988 [S.I. 1988 No. 1521] as amended by A.S. (R.C.S.A. No. 5 (Miscellaneous) 1990 [S.I. 1990 No. 2218], had only limited success. Only 55 cases called on the Commercial Roll in 1991. 1992 saw a slight increase (to 66) in the number of causes brought under this procedure, but there were only 50 in 1993. This low level of use is thought most unlikely to reflect the true level of commercial disputes in Scotland: Report of the Working Party on Commercial Causes, November 1993, para. 3. Accordingly, the Lord President set up a Working Party, under the chairmanship of Lord Coulsfield (a nominated commercial judge) with terms of reference to "examine the existing practice in relation to the hearing of commercial litigation in the Court of Session ... to consider any changes which may be desirable in order to improve the handling of such cases and to make this more expeditious and more convenient to litigants". After wide-ranging consultation with representatives of the commercial and legal communities, the Working Party reported in November 1993. It did not recommend radical departures from the existing scheme. It advocated that familiar procedures be adapted rather than new ones devised or imported. The recommendations, and the rules in this Chapter, are the answer to the perception of the business community that in commercial litigation the court's procedures were slow and lacking in expertise.

It will be necessary to read the rules in Chap. 47 in conjunction with P.N. No. 6 of 2004 (and subsequent P.N.s). In due course, a Guide for Practitioners will be published from time to time to keep readers up to date with the developing practice of the commercial judges. For an introductory overview of the operation of the rules for commercial actions, including a discussion of what "judicial proactivity"

47.1

47.1.1

47.1.2

---

[1] R. 47.1 substituted by S.I. 1994 No. 2310 (effective 20th September 1994).

has meant in practice, based upon analysis of 180 actions brought under the new procedure, see: Ronald Clancy, Andrew Murray and Rachel Wardia: "The New Commercial Cause Rules" in 1997 S.L.T.(News) 45, 58.

Jurisdiction.

47.1.3   For jurisdiction, see notes 13.2.8 to 13.2.15.

"Commercial Action".

47.1.4   The definition of a commercial action is in the widest terms. It will include those matters previously listed in R.C.S. 1994, r. 47.1(2) (see new P.N. No. 6 of 2004, para. 1), namely:

    (i)   the construction of a commercial or mercantile document,

    (ii)   the sale or hire purchase of goods,

    (iii) the export or import of merchandise,

    (iv) the carriage of goods by land, air or sea (other than an Admiralty action within the meaning of rule 46.1),

    (v)   insurance,

    (vi) banking,

    (vii) the provision of financial services,

    (viii) mercantile agency,

    (ix) mercantile usage or a custom of trade,

    (x)   a building, engineering or construction contract, and

    (xi) a commercial lease.

It would also include an action which would otherwise be an Admiralty action in personam which does not require the special rules in r. 46 where the identity of the ship owners is not known (P.N. No. 6 of 2004, para. 1). Any other Admiralty action could not be brought as a commercial action by election under r. 47.3, but it might be transferred to the Commercial Roll in an appropriate case under r. 47.10.

It is unlikely that a consumer contract would ordinarily be treated as a commercial action. The new procedures are not intended to resolve disputes between a commercial organisation and a lay purchaser. Such an action would probably be withdrawn from the Commercial Roll under new rule 47.9 if a motion were made to that effect. An exception would be where it could be demonstrated, for example, that the case turned on an interpretation of a standard commercial document the construction of which was important not simply in the case in question.

The phrase "any transaction or dispute of a commercial or business nature" in r. 47.1(2) is intended to be of broad scope and is habile to include an action by a trustee in sequestration for declarator of vesting of acquirenda, where the issue was one of insolvency and not of succession: *Rankin's Trs v. H.C. Somerville & Russell* , 1999 S.C. 166.

It is not competent to bring as, or incorporate into, a commercial action an application which under the R.C.S. 1994 requires to be brought by petition. So, e.g., in *Ross v. Davy* , 1996 S.C.L.R. 369, a commercial action at the instance of a liquidator against a company director and founded on that director's alleged breach of fiduciary duty, the court refused as incompetent an attempt by the liquidator to seek to add by minute of amendment an order under s. 212 of the Insolvency Act 1986, where such an application must, by virtue of r. 74.2, be brought as a petition.

Proceedings before commercial judge

47.2   **47.2.**[1] All proceedings in the Outer House in a commercial action shall be brought before a judge of the court nominated by the Lord President as a commercial judge or, where a commercial judge is not available, any other judge of the court (including the vacation judge); and "commercial judge" shall be construed accordingly.

Deriv. R.C.S. 1965, r. 149 substituted by S.I. 1988 No. 1521

General note.

47.2.1   In March 1994, L. P. Hope appointed Lord Penrose to be, in effect, a full-time commercial judge. The commercial judge has no duties as a trial judge in the High Court of Justiciary and commercial actions in the Court of Session have priority. He will be assisted by two other judges and arrangements will be made to ensure that at least one of these other two will always be available. There should always, therefore, be two commercial judges available at any time.

Under r. 10.7 the commercial judge can hear and determine a commercial action when the court is in session or in vacation. A commercial judge will be available all 52 weeks of the year. During about two weeks in April, the month of August and the Christmas and New Year vacation, only interlocutory or incidental business will normally be done: proofs and debates will not, as a general rule, be heard.

---

[1] R. 47.2 substituted by S.I. 1994 No. 2310 (effective 20th September 1994).

Steps will be taken to ensure that all appearances on the Commercial Roll of a particular action will be before the same commercial judge: P.N. No. 6 of 2004, para. 19(1).

NOMINATED JUDGES.

The current commercial judges are Lords Hodge, Malcolm and Woolman.   47.2.2

"VACATION JUDGE".

The powers of the vacation judge are limited by r. 11.1.   47.2.3

Election of procedure for commercial actions

47.3.—[1](1)   The pursuer may elect to adopt the procedure in this Chapter by   47.3
bringing an action in which there are inserted the words "Commercial Action" immediately below the words "IN THE COURT OF SESSION" where they occur above the instance, and on the backing, of the summons and any copy of it.

(2)   A summons in a commercial action shall—

    (a)   specify, in the form of conclusions, the orders sought;

    (b)   identify the parties to the action and the transaction or dispute from which the action arises;

 (ba)[2]   specify any special capacity in which the pursuer is bringing the action or any special capacity in which the action is brought against the defender;

    (c)   summarise the circumstances out of which the action arises; and

    (d)   set out the grounds on which the action proceeds.

(3)[3]   There shall be appended to a summons in a commercial action a schedule listing the documents founded on or adopted as incorporated in the summons, which should also be lodged as an inventory of productions.

Deriv. R.C.S. 1965, r. 148(3) substituted by S.I. 1988 No. 1521 (r. 47.3(1))

GENERAL NOTE.

Prior to reform in 1988, an action could proceed as a commercial cause only with the consent of the   47.3.1
other parties. Where such consent was not forthcoming, a pursuer who wished to employ commercial cause procedure required to raise an ordinary action and then enrol a motion seeking that it be placed on the list of commercial causes. It was then for that party to persuade the court that his action was one appropriate to be dealt with under commercial cause procedure. The requirement of consent was perceived to be an obstacle in the way of the success of commercial cause procedure, and so in 1988 the rules were changed to permit a pursuer to elect, at the outset, to bring an action under the procedure in this Chapter; and this provision is repeated in R.C.S. 1994, r. 47.3(1). Defenders are, however, protected from the consequences of inappropriate adoption by a pursuer of this procedure r. 47.9(1), which provides for the withdrawal of a commercial action from this procedure by the court, on the motion of any party (but not now at its own instance, strangely), where it considers that the speedy and efficient determination of the action would not be served by the cause being dealt with as a commercial action. The onus then appears to have shifted on to the defender to explain why a dispute is inappropriate to be dealt with according to the procedure under the Chapter.

"INSTANCE".

On the instance, see note 13.2.2.   47.3.2

FORM OF SUMMONS.

Underlying the procedure in this Chapter is the principle that the normal requirements of pleadings in   47.3.3
ordinary actions may be dispensed with. The nature of the dispute between the parties may determine the form of pleading adopted in a particular commercial action. R.47.3(2) is intended to indicate that a summons may be short and simple; the only formal requirements being set out in r. 47.3(2). The purpose is to identify the subject-matter of the dispute and the legal issues. Lengthy narrative is to be discouraged.

Summonses may still be drawn with the familiar three parts of conclusions, condescendence and pleas-in-law, however brief; although a summons without such formal parts as a condescendence and pleas-in-law will not be incompetent. Where only the construction of a document is sought, a pursuer may serve a summons consisting solely of conclusions specifying the document in dispute and the pursuer's preferred construction of it: P.N. No. 6 of 2004, para. 3(1).

---

[1] Rule 47.3 substituted by S.I. 1994 No. 2310 (effective 20th September 1994).

[2] Rule 47.3(2)(ba) inserted by S.S.I. 2008 No. 349 (effective 1st December 2008).

[3] Rule 47.3(3) amended by S.S.I. 2012 No. 275 r. 2(2) (effective 19th November 2012).

It should be noted, however, that while in many commercial actions, detailed written pleadings may be inappropriate generally, or appropriate only in relation to particular issues, it by no means follows that the requirements of fair notice are dispensed with. On the contrary, it is a cardinal feature of commercial action business that parties make full and frank disclosure. Sometimes, such disclosure may be in a form other than formal pleadings, but when, for instance, an allegation of fraud is made, the basis for that allegation must be set forth to the same standard of relevancy and specification as is required for such an allegation in any other proceedings: *Kaur v. Singh* 1998 S.C. 233, 237C per Lord Hamilton; *Marine & Offshore (Scotland) Ltd v Hill*, 2018 S.L.T. 239 (First Div.). If not in formal pleadings, material adequate for the purposes of fair notice and enabling the court to determine whether or not inquiry was justified must be provided: *Johnston v. WH Brown Construction (Dundee) Ltd* 2000 S.L.T. 223.

Initial pleadings are expected to be in abbreviated form: the purpose of the pleadings is to give notice of the essential elements of the case to the court and other parties: P.N. No. 6 of 2004, para. 3(1). Before a commercial action is commenced, save exceptionally, matters in dispute should have been discussed and focused in pre-litigation communications: P.N. No. 6 of 2004, para. 11(1).

For averments about identity of parties, capacity and special capacity and title to sue, see note 13.2. Any special capacity must now be stated: r. 13.2(4)(e); the express provision in the Rules was probably inspired by *Royal Insurance (UK) Ltd v. AMEC Construction Scotland Ltd*, 2008 S.C. 201 (O.H.), in which Lord Emslie at p. 216, para. [21] re-affirmed the requirement for proper disclosure in the instance of any special capacity in which a party sues or is sued.

SCHEDULE OF DOCUMENTS.

47.3.4   Documents founded on or adopted in the summons must be lodged as productions when the summons is lodged for calling: r. 27.1(1)(a). Such documents must also be listed in a schedule to the summons. Rule 47.3(3) is intended to require a party to produce the "core" or essential documents to establish a contract or transaction: P.N. No. 6 of 2004, para. 3(2).

COMMERCIAL ACTION REGISTRATION FORM.

47.3.5   A special registration form (Form CA1), copies of which are obtainable from the General Department, must be completed and signed by the pursuer when the summons is lodged for signeting: P.N. No. 6 of 2004, para. 3(3). The form identifies the parties, the nature of the case, the legal advisers, etc. The form is in duplicate: one of the copies is retained in process and the other must be attached to the copy summons served on the defender.

Disapplication of certain rules

47.4   **47.4.**—[1](1)   The requirement in rule 4.1(4) for a step of process to be folded lengthwise shall not apply in a commercial action.

(2)   An open record shall not be made up in, and Chapter 22 (making up and closing records) shall not apply to, a commercial action unless otherwise ordered by the court.

(3)[2]   The following rules shall not apply to a commercial action—

rule 6.2 (fixing and allocation of diets in Outer House),

rule 25.1(3) (form of counterclaim),

rule 25.2(1) (authority for diligence etc. on counterclaims),

rule 36.3 (lodging productions).

GENERAL NOTE.

47.4.1   The other rules of the R.C.S. 1994 apply to a commercial action to which Chap. 47 applies except in so far as specifically excluded under r. 47.4 or excluded by implication because of a provision in Chap. 47. This statement is repeated in P.N. No. 6 of 2004, para. 4.

FLAT PROCESSES.

47.4.2   R. 47.4(1) is intended to permit flat (i.e. unfolded) A4 processes and the lodging of steps of process in flat form rather than folded.

Procedure in commercial actions

47.5   **47.5.**[3]   Subject to the provisions of this Chapter, the procedure in a commercial action shall be such as the commercial judge shall order or direct.

---

[1] Rule 47.4 substituted by S.I. 1994 No. 2310 (effective 20th September 1994).
[2] Rule 47.4(3) amended by S.S.I. 2012 No. 275 r. 2(3) (effective 19th November 2012).
[3] Rule 47.5 substituted by S.I. 1994 No. 2310 (effective 20th September 1994).

Greater discretion may be exercised by the commercial judge in dealing with unopposed motions without requiring the appearance of counsel or other person having a right of audience than is the case in respect of unopposed motions on the Motion Roll (for which, see notes 23.2.15 and 23.2.16).

"WITHIN 14 DAYS".

The date from which the period is calculated is not counted. Where the last day falls on a Saturday or Sunday or a public holiday on which the Office of Court is closed, the next available day is allowed: r. 1.3(7). For office hours and public holidays, see note 3.1.2.

47.8.4

RECLAIMING.

To assist with the principle of speedy determination of actions on the Commercial Roll, an interlocutor, other than a final interlocutor, pronounced in a commercial action may only be reclaimed against with leave of the commercial judge within 14 days of that interlocutor: r. 38.4(7).

47.8.5

Withdrawal of action from Commercial Roll

47.9.—[1](1) At any time before or at the preliminary hearing, the commercial judge shall—

47.9

    (a)   on the motion of a party, withdraw a commercial action from the procedure in this Chapter and appoint it to proceed as an ordinary action where, having regard to—

        (i)   the likely need for detailed pleadings to enable justice to be done between the parties,

        (ii) the length of time required for preparation of the action, or

        (iii) any other relevant circumstances,

        he is satisfied that the speedy and efficient determination of the action would not be served by the cause being dealt with as a commercial action; and

    (b)   on the motion of a party with the consent of all other parties, withdraw a commercial action from the Commercial Roll and appoint it to proceed as an ordinary action.

(1A)[2] At any time before or at the preliminary hearing the commercial judge may, on the motion of a party, if he is satisfied that the action is not a commercial action, withdraw it from the Commercial Roll and appoint it to proceed as an ordinary action.

(2) If a motion to withdraw a commercial action from the Commercial Roll made before or renewed at a preliminary hearing is refused, no subsequent motion to withdraw the action from the Commercial Roll shall be considered except on special cause shown.

(3)[3] At any time the commercial judge may, at his own instance, after hearing the parties to the action, if he is satisfied that it is not appropriate for the action to remain on the Commercial Roll, withdraw it from the Commercial Roll and appoint it to proceed as an ordinary action.

GENERAL NOTE.

This rule provides some protection for a defender against the potentially adverse consequences for him of the election by a pursuer to adopt the procedure under this Chapter in an action ill-suited to it. A party may, at any time before or at the preliminary hearing, enrol a motion to have that action withdrawn from the Commercial Roll and, if granted, the action reverts to being an ordinary action. Commercial procedure is not limited to straightforward or simple cases and does not exclude cases involving investigation or difficulty and complicated facts: P.N. No. 6 of 2004, para. 9.

47.9.1

Originally, in r. 47.6(1) the commercial judge could, at his own instance, withdraw an action from the Commercial Roll and make it an ordinary action. When Chap. 47 was re-written in September 1994 this

---

[1] Rule 47.9 substituted by S.I. 1994 No. 2310 (effective 20th September 1994)

[2] Rule 47.9(1A) as inserted by S.S.I. 2000 No. 66, para. 2(7) (effective 7th April 2000) and substituted by S.S.I. 2014 No. 291 r. 2 (effective 8th December 2014).

[3] Rule 47.9(3) as inserted by S.S.I. 2014 No. 291 r. 2 (effective 8th December 2014).

provision was not re-enacted in r. 47.9 in order to encourage commercial actions. The rule has been changed again and r. 47.9(1A) now permits the commercial judge to withdraw an action from the Commercial Roll at his own instance.

Although the motion to withdraw must be made at or before the preliminary hearing, a subsequent motion (if the earlier motion is refused) may be made at any time; but it may be made only on special cause shown.

"MOTION".

47.9.2   For motions, see Chap. 23.

"SPEEDY AND EFFICIENT DETERMINATION OF THE ACTION".

47.9.3   The test for withdrawal of an action from the Commercial Roll is whether the commercial judge is satisfied that the "speedy and efficient determination of the action would not be served by the cause being dealt with as a commercial action": r. 47.9(1)(a). In applying that test certain factors (items (i)-(iii) in para.(1)(a)) must be considered.

Transfer of action to Commercial Roll

47.10   **47.10.**—[1](1)   In an action within the meaning of rule 47.1(2) (definition of commercial action) in which the pursuer has not made an election under rule 47.3(1), any party may apply by motion at any time to have the action appointed to be a commercial action on the Commercial Roll.

(2)   A motion enrolled under paragraph (1) shall be heard by the commercial judge.

(3)[2]   Where an interlocutor is pronounced under paragraph (1) appointing an action to be a commercial action on the Commercial Roll, the action shall immediately proceed to a preliminary hearing.

GENERAL NOTE.

47.10.1   It is not open to the court at its own instance to appoint an ordinary action to proceed as a commercial action.

"MOTION".

47.10.2   The date and time of a motion to transfer an action will be fixed by the commercial judge: r. 47.10(2). For motions generally, see Chap. 23.

RECLAIMING.

47.10.3   The former rule (in r. 47.7(3)) provided that the decision whether or not to transfer was final. The rule now is that the decision may only be reclaimed against with the leave of the commercial judge within 14 days of the date of the interlocutor: r. 38.4(6).

Preliminary hearing

47.11   **47.11.**—[3](1)   Unless a commercial action is withdrawn under rule 47.9 from the Commercial Roll then, at the preliminary hearing of a commercial action in which an election has been made under rule 47.3(1), the commercial judge—

   (a)   shall determine whether and to what extent and in what manner further specification of the claim and defences should be provided;

   (b)   may make an order in respect of any of the following matters:

      (i)   detailed written pleadings to be made by a party either generally or restricted to particular issues;

      (ii)   a statement of facts to be made by one or more parties either generally or restricted to particular issues;

      (iii) the allowing of an amendment by a party to his pleadings;

      (iv)   disclosure of the identity of witnesses and the existence and nature of documents relating to the action or authority to recover documents either generally or specifically;

---

[1] Rule 47.10 substituted by S.I. 1994 No. 2310 (effective 20th September 1994).
[2] Rule 47.10(3) substituted by S.S.I. 2012 No. 275 r. 2(6) (effective 19th November 2012).
[3] Rule 47.11 substituted by S.I. 1994 No. 2310 (effective 20th September 1994).

      (v)   documents constituting, evidencing or relating to the subject-matter of the action or any invoices, correspondence or similar documents relating to it to be lodged in process within a specified period;

     (vi)   each party to lodge in process, and send to every other party, a list of witnesses;

    (vii)   reports of skilled persons or witness statements to be lodged in process;

   (viii)   affidavits concerned with any of the issues in the action to be lodged in process; and

     (ix)   the action to proceed to a hearing without any further preliminary procedure either in relation to the whole or any particular aspect of the action;

  (c)   may fix the period within which any such order shall be complied with;

  (d)   may continue the preliminary hearing to a date to be appointed by him; and

  (e)   may make such other order as he thinks fit for the speedy determination of the action.

(2)   Where the commercial judge makes an order under paragraph 1(b)(i) or (ii) or (c), he may ordain the pursuer to—

  (a)   make up a record; and

  (b)   lodge that record in process within such period as the commercial judge thinks fit.

(3)   At the conclusion of the preliminary hearing, the court shall, unless it has made an order under rule 47.11(a)(ix) (order to proceed without a further hearing), fix a date for a procedural hearing to determine further procedure.

(4)[1]   The date fixed under paragraph (3) for a procedural hearing may be extended on cause shown by application to the court, by motion, not less than two days prior to the date fixed for the procedural hearing.

GENERAL NOTE.

   The preliminary hearing is one of the two critical hearings in the preparation of a commercial action for debate or proof; the other is the procedural hearing (for which, see r. 47.12). It is unlikely that at the preliminary hearing (which is held within 14 days after defences have been lodged: r. 47.8(2)) the action will be ready to go to debate or proof; if it is, the commercial judge may order that at once: r. 47.11(1)(b)(ix). More commonly, at this hearing there will be a discussion about what is required more clearly to identify and disclose the factual and legal issues to be decided and how long will be needed to do this. To this end further specification of pleadings, the disclosure of the identity of witnesses and documents, and the ordering of the production of documents, may be required: r. 47.11(1)(b). Time-limits will be set within which any matter required is to be done: for the consequences of failure to observe time-limits, see r. 47.16. It is likely that it will not be possible to settle all these matters at one hearing; the hearing may, therefore, be continued to another date to deal with remaining issues: r. 47.11(1)(d).

   At the (final) preliminary hearing a date will be fixed for the next critical hearing, the procedural hearing: r. 47.11(3).

47.11.1

FORM OF THE PRELIMINARY HEARING.

   The hearing will normally be conducted on the basis that the pre-action communications provisions of para. 11 of the P.N. No. 6 of 2004 have been complied with: P.N. No. 6 of 2004, para. 12(1). A continuation of a hearing brought about by a failure to comply with para. 11 may result in an adverse finding of expenses on an agent and client basis; and motions for continuations to obtain information which should have been obtained may be refused: P.N. No. 6 of 2004, para. 12(3).

   Parties should lodge before the hearing all correspondence and other documents which set out their material contentions of fact and law which show their compliance with para. 11: P.N. No. 6 of 2004, para. 12(2) (and this is supplemental to the requirement in rr. 47.3(3) and 47.6(2) for a schedule of documents).

   Parties should be in a position to lodge a document (where possible, agreed) setting out concisely the issues requiring judicial determination: P.N. No. 6 of 2004, para. 12(4).

47.11.2

---

[1] Rule 47.11(4) substituted by S.S.I. 2012 No. 275 r. 2(7) (effective 19th November 2012).

Time-limits will be expected to be achieved and extensions of time will only be granted in certain circumstances: P.N. No. 6 of 2004, para. 12(5).

It is anticipated that the hearing will be rather less formal than hearings on the motion or diet rolls. It is more likely that, at a hearing which is more in the nature of a round-table discussion, agreement can be reached on how cases proceed and what needs to be done than in the more adversarial context of a hearing in court.

The main purpose of the hearing, in achieving a speedy resolution of cases, is to reduce to a minimum the time spent in preparing cases for proof or debate, and the time spent in court on proof or debate, proving or arguing points which at the end of the day are not disputed or which turn out to be immaterial.

It is important that the counsel or other persons having rights of audience and the agents actually involved in the case are present at this hearing because the commercial judge will expect such persons to be fully informed about the case, see P.N. No. 6 of 2004, para. 19(1).

"DETAILED WRITTEN PLEADINGS", "AMENDMENT", "RECORD".

47.11.3   The detailed written pleadings necessary in an ordinary action are neither encouraged nor required, as a general rule, in a commercial action. It is unlikely, therefore, that there should be a need in most cases for further specification, amendment or a record (as a consequence of either of the former). Although in an ordinary action, if a defender raises an issue in his defences, the pursuer would require to plead an answer to it, such a rule will not normally apply in a commercial action so long as it is clear to the parties and the court at the preliminary hearing (or at the latest, the procedural hearing) what the issues are, what the position of the parties is to them and what each party is intending to establish.

Where pleadings or other documents are to be adjusted, a fresh copy of the writ must be prepared with new material shown in under-lining, side-lining, red-lining, a different type face or other means: P.N. No. 6 of 2004, para. 19(2).

RECOVERY AND DISCLOSURE OF DOCUMENTS.

47.11.4   The procedures in Chap. 35 for recovery of evidence are still available to parties. The former rule (in r. 47.8) is not explicitly re-enacted. In new r. 47.11(1)(b)(iv) and (v), for example, there are powers for parties to seek, and for the commercial judge to order at his own instance or on the motion of a party, disclosure of documents relating to the dispute. If these powers are exercised, resort to Chap. 35 may be unnecessary.

The word "document" has been defined in the R.C.S. 1994 by reference to the inclusive definition in s. 9 of the Civil Evidence (Scotland) Act 1988: r. 1.3(1).

EXCHANGE OF LISTS OF WITNESSES.

47.11.5   This may be ordered at this stage: r. 47.11(1)(b)(vi). There is a requirement to lodge and exchange such lists before the procedural hearing where a proof is sought: r. 47.12(1)(b).

The list of witnesses is lodged as a step of process (r. 1.3(1) (definition of "step of process")). On lodging steps of process, see r. 4.4. The list may be lodged by post: P.N. No. 4 of 1994, paras 1 and 8; and see note 4.4.10.

REPORTS OF SKILLED PERSONS AND WITNESS STATEMENTS.

47.11.6   These may be ordered to be lodged under r. 47.11(1)(b)(vii).

A witness statement is not the same as a precognition and should be signed.

As these documents are ordered by the court to be lodged they will be lodged as steps of process (r. 1.3(1) (definition of "step of process")) and not as productions. On lodging steps of process, see r. 4.4. The reports may be lodged by post: P.N. No. 4 of 1994, paras. 1 and 8; and see note 4.4.10.

When preparing an affidavit or witness statement following an order under r. 47.11, it is not appropriate for a solicitor to show witness statements or draft statements of other witnesses and, when proffering an initial affidavit or witness statement, the solicitor should "certify by letter to the court that the witness has not seen or been told about the evidence of others or, if he has, specify the statements which the witness has seen or been told about and the circumstances in which that has occurred": *Luminar Lava Ignite Ltd v. Mama Group plc* , 2010 S.C. 310, para. [74] (First Div.). This is consistent with the rule that it is not permitted to brief or coach a witness with a view to altering his evidence. It is not clear why the witness should not certify it in the affidavit (or the solicitor's certificate be appended to the affidavit), as the solicitor's letter could become separated from the affidavit or lost from the process.

"AFFIDAVITS".

47.11.7   As these documents are ordered by the court to be lodged they will be lodged as steps of process (r. 1.3(1) (definition of "step of process")) and not as productions. On lodging steps of process, see r. 4.4. The affidavits may be lodged by post: P.N. No. 4 of 1994, paras. 1 and 8; and see note 4.4.10.

When preparing an affidavit or witness statement following an order under r. 47.11, it is not appropriate for a solicitor to show witness statements or draft statements of other witnesses and, when proffering an initial affidavit or witness statement, the solicitor should "certify by letter to the court that the witness has not seen or been told about the evidence of others or, if he has, specify the statements which the witness has seen or been told about and the circumstances in which that has occurred": *Luminar Lava Ignite Ltd v. Mama Group plc* , 2010 S.C. 310, para. [74] (First Div.). This is consistent with the rule that it is not permitted to brief or coach a witness with a view to altering his evidence. It is not clear why the witness should not certify it in the affidavit (or the solicitor's certificate be appended to the affidavit), as the solicitor's letter could become separated from the affidavit or lost from the process.

"SPEEDY DETERMINATION".

While the speedy determination of the question in dispute between the parties may be the primary objective of the procedure under this Chapter, it may be stated as a general principle that this objective is not to be achieved at the expense of a thorough examination of the issues and the correctness and fairness of the court's eventual decision. Where it becomes apparent that speed in disposal cannot be reconciled with a thorough examination of the issues, this may indicate that it is inappropriate for the action to continue under the procedure in this Chapter.

47.11.8

FEE.

The court fee for a preliminary hearing is payable by each party for every 30 minutes or part thereof. For fee, see Court of Session etc. Fees Order 1984, Table of Fees, Pt I, B, item 16 [S.I. 1984 No. 256, Table as amended, pp. C1202 et seq.]. The fee may be debited under a credit scheme introduced on 1st April 1976 by P.N. No. 4 of 1976 to the account (if one is kept or permitted) of the agent by the court cashier, and an account will be rendered weekly by the court cashier's office to the agent for all court fees due that week for immediate settlement. An agent not on the credit scheme will have an account opened for the purpose of lodging the fee: P.N. No. 2 of 1995. A debit slip and a copy of the court hearing time sheet will be delivered to the agent's box or sent by DX or post.

47.11.9

A party litigant must pay cash to the clerk of court at the end of the hearing: P.N. No. 2 of 1995. A receipt will be issued. The assistant clerk of session will acknowledge receipt of the sum received from the clerk of court on the Minute of Proceedings.

Procedural hearing

47.12.—[1](1) Not less than 3 days, or such other period as may be prescribed by the commercial judge at the preliminary hearing, before the date fixed under rule 47.11(3) for the procedural hearing, each party shall—

    (a) lodge a written statement of his proposals for further procedure which shall state—

        (i) whether he seeks to have the commercial action appointed to debate or to have the action sent to proof on the whole or any part of it;

        (ii) what the issues are which he considers should be sent to debate or proof; and

        (iii) the estimated duration of any debate or proof;

    (b) where it is sought to have the action appointed to proof, lodge a list of the witnesses he proposes to cite or call to give evidence, identifying the matters to which each witness will speak;

    (c) where it is sought to have the action appointed to proof, lodge the reports of any skilled persons;

    (d) where it is sought to have the action appointed to debate, lodge a note of argument consisting of concise numbered paragraphs stating the legal propositions on which it is proposed to submit that any preliminary plea should be sustained or repelled with reference to the principal authorities and statutory provisions to be founded on; and

    (e) send a copy of any such written statement, lists, reports or note of argument, as the case may be, to every other party.

  (2) At the procedural hearing, the commercial judge—

    (a) shall determine whether the commercial action should be appointed to debate or sent to proof on the whole or any part of the action;

    (b) where the action is appointed to debate or sent to proof, may order that written arguments on any question of law should be submitted;

47.12

---

[1] Rule 47.12 inserted by S.I. 1994 No. 2310 (effective 20th September 1994) and substituted by S.S.I. 2012 No. 275 r. 2(8) (effective 19th November 2012).

(c)   where the action is sent to proof, may determine whether evidence at the proof should be by oral evidence, the production of documents or affidavits on any issue;

(d)   where the action is sent to proof, may direct that parties serve on one another and lodge in process signed witness statements or affidavits from each witness whose evidence they intend to adduce, setting out in full the evidence which it is intended to take from that witness, and fix a timetable for the service (whether by exchange or otherwise) and lodging of such statements or affidavits as may be thought necessary;

(e)   may direct that such witness statements or affidavits shall stand as evidence in chief of the witness concerned, subject to such further questioning in chief as the court may allow;

(f)   may determine, in the light of any witness statements, affidavits or reports produced, that proof is unnecessary on any issue;

(g)   where the action is sent to proof, may appoint parties to be heard By Order at a date prior to the proof diet;

(h)   may direct that skilled persons should meet with a view to reaching agreement and identifying areas of disagreement, and may order them thereafter to produce a joint note, to be lodged in process by one of the parties, identifying areas of agreement and disagreement, and the basis of any disagreement;

(i)   without prejudice to Chapter 12 (assessors), may appoint an expert to examine, on behalf of the court, any reports of skilled persons or other evidence submitted and to report to the court within such period as the commercial judge may specify;

(j)   where the action is sent to proof, may make an order fixing the time allowed for the examination and cross-examination of witnesses;

(k)   may, on the motion of a party, direct the cause to be determined on the basis of written submissions, or such other material, without any oral hearing;

(l)   may continue the procedural hearing to a date to be appointed by him;

(m)   may make an order for parties to produce a joint bundle of productions arranged in chronological order or such other order as will assist in the efficient conduct of the proof;

(n)   may order and fix a date for a further procedural hearing or fix a date for the hearing of any debate or proof; and

(o)   may make such other order as he thinks fit.

General note.

47.12.1   The procedural hearing is the second critical hearing held before debate or proof unless the action has been appointed to debate or proof at the preliminary hearing under r. 47.11(1)(b)(ix). If the action has not been so appointed, the procedural hearing is the hearing at which the decision is taken whether the action is to be sent to debate or proof, what issues have to be decided and the form in which either debate or proof is to be undertaken.

Parties will be expected to discuss realistically the issues involved and the methods of disposing of them; parties' positions will have been ascertained and identified and all prospects for settlement fully discussed and exhausted: P.N. No. 6 of 2004, para. 13(1).

For the procedural hearing each party must, not less than three days before the hearing, (a) lodge a statement of his proposals for further procedure stating, among other things, whether he seeks debate or proof and on what issues, and (b) lodge a note of argument for the debate or certain productions for the proof, as the case may be: r. 47.12(1). These requirements are mandatory and are necessary to enable the commercial judge to make an informed decision about the orders he will make under r. 47.12(2).

There is unlikely to be more than one procedural hearing. But note the pre-proof by order hearing: see r. 47.12(2)(g) and note 47.12.17.

FORM OF PROCEDURAL HEARING.

It is anticipated that the hearing will be rather less formal than hearings on the motion or diet rolls. It is more likely that, at a hearing which is more in the nature of a round-table discussion, agreement can be reached on how cases proceed and what needs to be done than in the more adversarial context of a hearing in court. **47.12.2**

The main purpose of the hearing, in achieving a speedy resolution of cases, is to reduce to a minimum the time spent in preparing cases for proof or debate, and the time spent in court on proof or debate, proving or arguing points which at the end of the day are not disputed or which turn out to be immaterial.

It is important that the counsel or other persons having rights of audience and the agents actually involved in the case are present at this hearing because the commercial judge will expect such persons to be fully informed about the case. See P.N. No. 6 of 2004, para. 19(1).

"NOT LESS THAN 3 DAYS BEFORE".

This is synonymous with clear days, and the day from which the period is calculated is not included. **47.12.3**

"WRITTEN STATEMENT OF HIS PROPOSALS FOR FURTHER PROCEDURE".

Parties must have a clear idea about what they want, what has to be established and what issues have to be determined. **47.12.4**

The requirements of r. 47.12(1)(a) are mandatory and are necessary to enable the commercial judge to make an informed decision about the orders he will make under r. 47.12(2).

The statement should be lodged as a step of process (r. 1.3(1) (definition of "step of process")). On lodging steps of process, see r. 4.4. The written statement may be lodged by post: P.N. No. 4 of 1994, paras. 1 and 8; and see note 4.4.10. A copy of the written statement must be sent to the other parties: r. 47.12(1)(e).

"LODGE A LIST OF WITNESSES".

The former provision was in r. 47.9(1). This must be done notwithstanding that an order to lodge a list may previously have been made and obtempered under r. 47.11(1)(b)(vi) unless the list is the same as that previously ordered and lodged. **47.12.5**

The list of witnesses is lodged as a step of process (r. 1.3(1) (definition of "step of process")). On lodging steps of process, see r. 4.4. The list may be lodged by post: P.N. No. 4 of 1994, paras. 1 and 8; and see note 4.4.10. A copy of the list must be sent to the other parties: r. 47.12(1)(e).

In *McGunnigal v. D. B. Marshall (Newbridge) Ltd* 1993 S.L.T. 769, under the optional (reparation) procedure, the defender was refused leave to lead witnesses because it had not lodged a list of witnesses.

"LODGE THE REPORTS OF ANY SKILLED PERSONS".

This means the reports of skilled persons who may give evidence. **47.12.6**

This may already have been done following an order under r. 47.11(1)(b)(vii).

Any report is lodged as a production. On lodging productions, see r. 4.5. The report may be lodged by post: P.N. No. 4 of 1994, paras. 1 and 8; and see note 4.5.5. A copy of the report must be sent to the other parties: r. 47.12(1)(e).

"LODGE A NOTE OF ARGUMENT".

This is required under r. 47.12(1) (d) where a party seeks to have a case sent to debate. The note of argument should consist of numbered paragraphs setting out briefly the legal propositions to be advanced at debate by the party lodging it, supported by citations of the principal authorities for those propositions and any statutory provisions relied on. **47.12.7**

A note of argument is lodged in process as a step of process (r. 1.3(1) (definition of "step of process")) and does not require to be signed. R.15.2 does not apply. On lodging a step of process, see r. 4.4. The note may be lodged by post: P.N. No. 4 of 1994, paras. 1 and 8; and see note 4.4.10. A copy of the note must be sent to the other parties: r. 47.12(1)(e).

"DEBATE".

See r. 47.13. **47.12.8**

It is for the court to determine whether an action should be sent to debate or proof and, unlike in an ordinary action, a party with a preliminary plea may not insight on a debate: *Highland and Universal Properties Ltd v. Safeway Properties Ltd* 1996 S.C. 424.

"PROOF".

Chap. 36 applies except that r. 47.14 (lodging productions) replaces r. 36.3. In the application of r. 36.4 (lodging copies of productions for use of the court), the requirement of P.N. No. 12 of 1994, para. 14 is that parties should agree a single paginated working bundle of productions for the judge. **47.12.9**

There is no present intention to depart from the principle of the adversarial nature of a proof.

It is for the court to determine whether an action should be sent to debate or proof and, unlike in an ordinary action, a party with a preliminary plea may not insight on a debate: *Highland and Universal Properties Ltd v. Safeway Properties Ltd* 1996 S.C. 424.

The normal form of interlocutor, allowing parties a proof [before answer] of their respective averments, may not always be appropriate in a commercial action. Because the condescendence and defences may be brief (see rr. 47.3(2) and 47.6(1)), the written statement lodged under r. 47.12(1)(a) may contain, in the statement of issues sought to be sent to proof, matters on which it is intended to lead evidence which are not spelt out in the pleadings. In such a case the interlocutor should allow a "proof [before answer] of their respective averments and of the issues set forth in the written statements lodged under rule 47.12(1) of the Rules of the Court of Session 1994". See *Highland and Universal Properties Ltd*, above, at pp. 425H–426D.

"WRITTEN ARGUMENTS".

47.12.10   These may be ordered on questions of law at debate or proof, even though a note of argument has been lodged under r. 47.12(1)(d): r. 47.12(2)(b). In *Deans v. Thus plc* , 2005 S.C.L.R. 148. 149, Lord Clarke indicated that it was not for parties to ignore such an order on the basis that their earlier note (under r. 47.12(1)(d)) was sufficient, because the purpose of the order was to ensure that a party applied his mind to what exactly was the position he wished to adopt at debate.

A written argument is lodged in process as a step of process (r. 1.3(1) (definition of "step of process")) and does not require to be signed. On lodging a step of process, see r. 4.4. The written argument may be lodged by post: P.N. No. 4 of 1994, paras. 1 and 8; and see note 4.4.10.

"AFFIDAVITS".

47.12.11   These may be ordered on any issue or in respect of any witness instead of oral evidence; r. 47.12(2)(c). It is conceivable that evidence-in-chief of a witness could be ordered in the first instance to be by affidavit, the position about cross-examination being reserved or preserved.

An affidavit is lodged in process as a step of process (r. 1.3(1) (definition of "step of process")). On lodging a step of process, see r. 4.4. The affidavit may be lodged by post: P.N. No. 4 of 1994, paras. 1 and 8; and see note 4.4.10.

When preparing an affidavit or witness statement following an order under r. 47.12, it is not appropriate for a solicitor to show witness statements or draft statements of other witnesses and, when proffering an initial affidavit or witness statement, the solicitor "should certify by letter to the court that the witness has not seen or been told about the evidence of others or, if he has, specify the statements which the witness has seen or been told about and the circumstances in which that has occurred": *Luminar Lava Ignite Ltd v. Mama group plc* , 2010 S.C. 310, para. [74] (First Div.). This is consistent with the rule that it is not permitted to brief or coach a witness with a view to altering his evidence. It is not clear why the witness should not certify it in the affidavit (or the solicitor's certificate be appended to the affidavit), as the solicitor's letter could become separated from the affidavit or lost from the process.

"CONSULTATION BETWEEN SKILLED PERSONS".

47.12.12   Consultation between experts is sometimes "ordered" by reporters in planning inquiries, and can be useful in reducing if not eliminating an area of disagreement.

"APPOINT AN EXPERT".

47.12.13   It is a novel provision to empower the court to appoint its own expert to examine reports of skilled persons or other evidence (e.g. on a matter of trade or business practice).

"REMIT TO A PERSON OF SKILL".

47.12.14   The former provision for a remit for a person of skill has been omitted from the new rule: Act of Sederunt (Rules of the Court of Session Amendment No. 5) (Miscellaneous) 2012 (SSI 2012/275).

"WRITTEN SUBMISSIONS".

47.12.15   If invited to do so by the parties, the commercial judge may determine an action in a suitable case by written submissions or other material without any oral hearing of a debate or proof.

Written submissions are lodged in process as a step of process (r. 1.3(1) (definition of "step of process")). On lodging a step of process, see r. 4.4. The written submissions may be lodged by post: P.N. No. 4 of 1994, paras. 1 and 8; and see note 4.4.10.

"DOCUMENT".

47.12.16   The word "document" has been defined in the R.C.S. 1994 by reference to the inclusive definition in s. 9 of the Civil Evidence (Scotland) Act 1988: r. 1.3(1).

PRE-PROOF BY ORDER HEARINGS.

Rule 47.12(2)(g) and P.N. No. 6 of 2004, para. 15, provides that where a proof or proof before answer is allowed there may be a pre-proof by order hearing to ascertain the parties' state of preparation and to review the estimated length of that hearing. Also there will be:— (1) Consideration of any joint minutes of admissions (to be lodged 2 days before the hearing). (2) A review of documents and productions to be relied on (to be lodged 2 days before the hearing). (3) The update position re expert reports and what consultation between experts to agree points has taken place. (4) Where there is to be a proof before answer, a statement of legal argument lodged and lists of authorities which may be relied on.

"FIXING THE TIME ALLOWED FOR EXAMINATION".

New r. 47.12(2)(j) to court may fix the time allowed for examination-in-chief and cross-examination.

"JOINT BUNDLE OF PRODUCTIONS"

Rule 47.12(2)(m) provides that the court may order parties to lodge a joint bundle of productions. In *Shanley v Clydesdale Bank plc*, 2018 S.L.T. 572 (Second Div.), the pursuer had twice failed to lodge a joint bundle, expenses had been awarded against him on an agent and client basis, an interim order for expenses was made and eventually the action was dismissed because of the pursuer's non-compliance (the failings were ultimately those of the pursuer's solicitors). It was held that a joint bundle was essentially an administrative task for which both parties bore some responsibility designed to promote efficient conduct of the proof and was not essential to a fair trial of the issues; dismissal of the action was quashed. It was said by Lord Malcolm that dismissal was available where there was a flagrant breach.

FEE.

The court fee for a procedural hearing is payable by each party for every 30 minutes or part thereof. For fee, see Court of Session etc. Fees Order 1997, Table of Fees, Pt I, B, item 16 [S.I. 1997 No. 688, as amended, pp. C1201 et seq.]. Certain persons are exempt from payment of fees: see 1997 Fees Order art.5 substituted by S.S.I. 2002 No. 270. A fee exemption certificate must be lodged in process: see P.N. No. 1 of 2002.

Where a party is legally represented, the fee may be debited under a credit scheme introduced on 1st April 1976 by P.N. No. 4 of 1976 to the account (if one is kept or permitted) of the agent by the court cashier, and an account will be rendered weekly by the court cashier's office to the agent for all court fees due that week for immediate settlement. An agent not on the credit scheme will have an account opened for the purpose of lodging the fee: P.N. No. 2 of 1995. A debit slip and a copy of the court hearing time sheet will be delivered to the agent's box or sent by DX or post.

A party litigant must pay (by cash, cheque or postal order) to the clerk of court at the end of the hearing: P.N. No. 2 of 1995. A receipt will be issued. The assistant clerk of session will acknowledge receipt of the sum received from the clerk of court on the Minute of Proceedings.

Debates

47.13.[1] Chapter 28 (procedure roll) shall apply to a debate ordered in a commercial action under rule 47.12(2)(a) as it applies to a cause appointed to the Procedure Roll.

47.13

GENERAL NOTE.

A note of argument will have been lodged under r. 47.12(1)(d).

47.13.1

Pre-proof By Order

47.13A.[2] Not less than 2 days prior to any hearing appointed under rule 47.12(2)(g) parties shall lodge in process an estimated timetable for the conduct of proof together with a note of any issues which are to be addressed prior to the proof.

47.13A

"NOT LESS THAN 2 DAYS PRIOR"

This is synonymous with clear days, and the day from which the period is calculated is not included. To be consistent with the other rules in R.C.S. 1994, the word "before" should have been used rather than "prior".

Lodging of productions for proof

47.14.—[3](1)[4] Unless an earlier date is specified by the court, any document not previously lodged required for any proof in a commercial action shall be lodged as a production not less than 7 days before the date fixed for the proof.

47.14

(2) No document may be lodged as a production after the date referred to in paragraph (1), even by agreement of all parties, unless the court is satisfied that any document sought to be lodged could not with reasonable diligence have been lodged in time.

---

[1] Rule 47.13 inserted by S.I. 1994 No. 2310 (effective 20th September 1994).
[2] Rule 47.13A inserted by S.S.I. 2012 No. 275 r. 2(9) (effective 19th November 2012).
[3] Rule 47.14 inserted by S.I. 1994 No. 2310 (effective 20th September 1994).
[4] Rule 47.14(1) amended by S.S.I. 2012 No. 275 r. 2(10) (effective 19th November 2012).

GENERAL NOTE.

47.14.1   R. 47.14 replaces r. 36.3 on lodging productions for the proof.

In relation to productions not lodged timeously, the commercial judge will not allow late lodging unless satisfied that the document could not with reasonable diligence have been lodged in time: r. 47.14(2).

In the application of r. 36.4 (lodging copies of productions for use of the court), the requirement of P.N. No. 6 of 2004, para. 16 is that parties should agree a single paginated working bundle of productions for the judge.

"DOCUMENT".

47.14.2   The word "document" has been defined in the R.C.S. 1994 by reference to the inclusive definition in s. 9 of the Civil Evidence (Scotland) Act 1988: r. 1.3(1).

"NOT LESS THAN 7 DAYS BEFORE".

47.14.3   This is synonymous with clear days, and the day from which the period is calculated is not included.

Hearings for further procedure

47.15   **47.15.**[1] At any time before final judgment, the commercial judge may, at his own instance or on the motion of any party, have a commercial action put out for hearing for further procedure; and the commercial judge may make such order as he thinks fit.

GENERAL NOTE.

47.15.1   Where a proof or proof before answer has been allowed, there may, e.g., be a pre-proof hearing: r. 47.12(2)(g) and P.N. No. 6 of 2004, para. 15.

Failure to comply with rule or order of commercial judge

47.16   **47.16.**[2] Any failure by a party to comply timeously with a provision in these Rules or any order made by the commercial judge in a commercial action shall entitle the judge, at his own instance—

    (a)   to refuse to extend any period for compliance with a provision in these Rules or an order of the court,

    (b)   to dismiss the action or counterclaim, as the case may be, in whole or in part,

    (c)   to grant decree in respect of all or any of the conclusions of the summons or counterclaim, as the case may be, or

    (d)   to make an award of expenses,

as he thinks fit.

GENERAL NOTE.

47.16.1   This rule provides the commercial judge with the sanctions open to him as the means of imposing discipline on parties in pursuit of the aim to achieve speedy determination of commercial actions.

The sanctions most likely to be frequently used are refusal to extend time-limits and awards of expenses. Where, e.g. a party fails to lodge a document within the specified period, he may have to proceed without that document or be found liable in expenses occasioned by delay. In *McGunnigal v. D. B. Marshall (Newbridge) Ltd* 1993 S.L.T. 769, under the optional (reparation) procedure, the defender was refused leave to lead witnesses because it had not lodged a list of witnesses.

---

[1] Rule 47.15 inserted by S.I. 1994 No. 2310 (effective 20th September 1994).
[2] Rule 47.16 inserted by S.I. 1994 No. 2310 (effective 20th September 1994).

Chapter 48

Exchequer Causes

Proceedings before Lord Ordinary in Exchequer Causes

48.1.—(1) Subject to Part IV of Chapter 41 (Exchequer appeals), all proceedings in an Exchequer cause shall be brought before the Lord Ordinary in Exchequer Causes.

(2) An application for the suspension of a decree, charge, threatened charge or diligence in an Exchequer cause shall be made to the Lord Ordinary in Exchequer Causes.

(3) Where another judge of the court acts in place of the Lord Ordinary in Exchequer Causes, any interlocutor pronounced by him shall state that he acted in the absence of the Lord Ordinary in Exchequer Causes.

Deriv. R.C.S. 1965, r. 153A(2) (r. 48.1(1)), and r. 153B (r. 48.1(2)), both inserted by S.I. 1984 No. 472

GENERAL NOTE.

48.1

48.1.1

Article XIX of the Treaty of Union between Scotland and England ratified by the Union with England Act 1706 and the Union with Scotland Act 1707 stipulated that there be a Court of Exchequer in Scotland after the Union for deciding questions concerning the revenues of customs and excises there. The Exchequer Court (Scotland) Act 1707 established a new Court of Exchequer in Scotland. It was to have the same power and authority within Scotland as the Court of Exchequer had in England. The procedures of the new court were also based on the English model. The Court of Exchequer in Scotland was, with the Courts of Session and Justiciary, one of the three Supreme Courts of Scotland and appeals were taken from it to the House of Lords: e.g. see *Brand v. Mackenzie* (1710) 1 Robert 8 (HL).

The jurisdiction of the Court of Exchequer in Scotland was defined as encompassing all the revenues and duties and profits appertaining to the Crown, all forfeited lands and all the remedies and means for the recovering of the same; all forfeitures and penalties due and payable in Scotland by force or virtue of any law or statute touching on or relating to the custom and excise or by force or virtue of any penal or other laws or statutes whatsoever and also all fines, issues, forfeitures or penalties arising to the Crown, and all actions, securities, prosecutions and remedies concerning the same: 1707 Act, s. 7. In essence, the purpose of the Court of Exchequer in Scotland was to receive the King's custom and other things that belonged thereto and to make reckoning and give count thereof at the King's Chequer: Clerk and Scrope, *A Historical View of the Forms and Powers of the Court of Exchequer in Scotland* (1820), p. 98.

The whole power, authority and jurisdiction of the Court of Exchequer in Scotland was transferred to and vested in the Court of Session by the Exchequer Court (Scotland) Act 1856, s. 1. That jurisdiction has been augmented by subsequent taxation legislation to include various new taxes and duties.

Any tax may be sued for and recovered from the person charged therewith in the Court of Session sitting as the Court of Exchequer as a debt due to the Crown: Taxes Management Act 1970, s. 68. Today, the core of Exchequer causes consists in actions for the recovery of central government taxes due to the Board of Inland Revenue and the various customs, excise and other duties due to the Board of Customs and Excise: Scottish Law Commission *Report on Diligence and Debtors Protection* (Scot. Law Com. No. 95), para. 7.81. The Crown, as part of its prerogative power, may insist on any cause falling within this jurisdiction which has been raised in another court (the sheriff court) being remitted to the Court of Session as the Court of Exchequer: *Sharpe v. Miller* (1861) 23 D. 1015. On remits to the court, see rr. 32.3 et seq.

The court, as the Court of Exchequer in Scotland, has three further areas of jurisdiction:—

1. It exercises an appellate function: see rr. 41.23–41.25.
2. The Lord Ordinary in Exchequer Causes, in exercise of the ministerial jurisdiction of the Court of Exchequer, has various responsibilities in relation to Crown writs. (a) Where, in the course of an application for a Crown writ, a mistake in the terms of the last Crown writ or retour or decree of service comes to light, no rectification of such mistake shall be allowed, nor shall the draft Crown writ be held as finally revised or authenticated as such, until the same have been reported to and approved of by the Lord Ordinary in Exchequer Causes: Titles to Land Consolidation (Scotland) Act 1868, ss. 66 and 67. (b) Where a note of objections is lodged, by the person applying for it, to the revisals made to a draft Crown writ, the Lord Ordinary in Exchequer Causes hears the parties and adjudicates on the objection. Where it appears to him that the objections should to any extent receive effect, he shall cause such alterations and corrections as seem to him proper to be made, and shall authenticate them with his signature: 1868 Act, ss. 75 and 76. (c) Where a note of objection is lodged by an applicant who has sought but has been refused a Crown writ for want of sufficient production of titles, the Lord Ordinary in Exchequer Causes must hear the parties and sustain or repel such objection, or pronounce such judgment or deliverance on it as seems to him just: 1868 Act, s. 77.

3.   It exercises the jurisdiction, derived from the Sovereign as pater patriae, to grant authority for taking steps in the best interests of those who are incapable of giving their authority or consent for the purpose.

In 1856, the duties previously performed by or incumbent upon the Court of Exchequer with regard to the nomination, appointment and control of tutors-dative were transferred to the Court of Session (as successor to the Court of Exchequer in exercise of the right of the Crown as *pater patriae*: Erskine, I.vii.8), involving a special procedure of summary petition to the Inner House: Exchequer Court (Scotland) Act 1856, s. 19. That provision was repealed by the C.S.A. 1988, Sched. 2 because the procedure was not used in practice and was superseded by the power of the court to appoint a factor *loco tutoris* by petition to the Outer House (see r. 14.2(a)). Such a factor, however, has no authority over the person of his ward (unlike a tutor-dative). The appointment of tutors-dative to pupil children was effectively rendered obsolete by the Age of Legal Capacity (Scotland) Act 1991: see note 61.1.2(4). The appointment of tutors-dative to adults who are mentally *incapax* is noted in two articles in the *Scots Law Times* (referring to a number of recent unreported cases): see "Revival of Tutors-Dative" 1987 S.L.T.(News) 69, and "Tutors to Adults: Developments", 1992 S.L.T.(News) 325. With the repeal of s. 19 of the 1856 Act, such an appointment was thought (and was stated in this note) to be incompetent because Parliament repealed that section in the belief that it was a substantive provision which had fallen into desetude. Ironically, by the time the recommendation of the Scottish Law Commission had been enacted (indeed before its report) the appointment of tutors-datives to mentally incapacitated adults had, as disclosed by the above articles, revived. In *Law Hospital N.H.S. Trust v. Lord Advocate* 1996 S.C. 301, it was authoritatively expressed that s. 19 of the 1856 Act was only a procedural provision and the power of the Court of Exchequer to make such appointments in exercise of its parens patriae jurisdiction remains and was transferred to the Court of Session by the unrepealed s. 1 of the Act. See further, note 14.2.11.

"LORD ORDINARY IN EXCHEQUER CAUSES".

48.1.2   A judge of the court who usually sits as a Lord Ordinary is appointed by the Lord President to act as the Lord Ordinary in Exchequer Causes, and no other judge shall so act unless and until such judge is appointed in his place; in the event of the absence or inability of the Lord Ordinary in Exchequer Causes, for whatever reason, any of his duties may be performed by any other Lord Ordinary acting in his place: C.S.A. 1988, s. 3 (as amended by the Law Reform (Miscellaneous Provisions) (Scotland) Act 1990, Sched. 4, para. 4(3)) and r. 48.1(3).

The former Lord Ordinary in Exchequer Causes was Lord Docherty. Following his elevation to the Inner House, the post is currently vacant.

An Exchequer cause may be dealt with in vacation by the Lord Ordinary in Exchequer Causes: r. 10.6. In his absence or inability an Exchequer cause may be dealt with by another Lord Ordinary (C.S.A. 1988, s. 3) or, in vacation, by the vacation judge (C.S.A. 1988, s. 3 and r. 11.1(1)(a)). Where this occurs any interlocutor begins with the words "The Lord Ordinary [*or* Vacation Judge] in room and stead of the Lord Ordinary in Exchequer Causes". Where the Lord Ordinary in Exchequer Causes is the vacation judge, an interlocutor in an Exchequer cause begins with the words "The Lord Ordinary in Exchequer Causes".

Procedure in Exchequer causes

48.2   **48.2.** An Exchequer cause commenced by summons shall proceed as an ordinary action.

Deriv. R.C.S. 1965, r. 153A(1) inserted by S.I. 1984 No. 472

GENERAL NOTE.

48.2.1   The specialities of procedure based on the procedure of the English Court of Exchequer, to which Exchequer causes were originally subject, survived the transfer of the jurisdiction of the Court of Exchequer in Scotland to the Court of Session in 1856, but the consequence of a number of twentieth-century enactments is that an Exchequer cause now follows the same procedure as an ordinary action, subject to three exceptions: (1) Exchequer causes at all times take precedence and have preference over all other causes in the court: C.S.A. 1988, s. 21. (2) All Exchequer causes brought on behalf of the Crown, or by any person alleging any ground of action against the Crown, are respectively at the instance of or directed against the Lord Advocate, except where any enactment otherwise provides: C.S.A. 1988, s. 22. Examples of enactments which do otherwise provide include s. 13 of the Stamp Act 1891 and s. 56 of the Taxes Management Act 1970. (3) In all Exchequer causes the Lord Advocate, in pleading on behalf of the Crown, has the privilege of being heard last: C.S.A. 1988, s. 23.

Because the eighteenth-century English Exchequer Court would not have entertained an action against a person who was not served within the jurisdiction, it follows that the existence of a subsisting general jurisdiction over non-residents, without personal service, cannot be asserted simply on the basis that the 1707 Act empowered the Court of Exchequer in Scotland to adjudicate on revenue matters pertaining to Scotland: *Lord Advocate v. Tursi* , 1998 S.L.T. 1035 per Lord Penrose.

The special modes of diligence, under distinctive forms of warrant, for the enforcement of Crown debts, constituted by a decree of the Court of Session sitting as the Court of Exchequer, available formerly to the Crown, were abolished by the Debtors (Scotland) Act 1987, s. 74(5). Now an Exchequer decree will contain a warrant for execution of the ordinary diligences: 1987 Act, s. 87. The Inland Revenue and H.M. Customs and Excise must proceed by way of summary warrant in the sheriff court to take advantage of summary diligence: 1987 Act, s. 74(1) and (2), Scheds 4 and 5.

In relation to counterclaims and the Crown, see note 25.1.7.

An interlocutor of the Lord Ordinary in Exchequer Causes may be reclaimed against to the Inner House in the ordinary way: see C.S.A. 1988, s. 28; and see Chap. 38. An appeal may be brought to the House of Lords against the judgment of the Inner House in an Exchequer cause as if it were a judgment of the Inner House on the whole merits of the case in an ordinary action: C.S.A. 1988, s. 24. **48.2.2**

Precedence of extracts

48.3.   The Extractor shall give priority to extracts in Exchequer causes over all other business. **48.3**

Deriv. R.C.S. 1965, r. 153E inserted by S.I. 1984 No. 472

General note.

On the Extracts Department, see r. 3.5. On the duties of the Extractor, see note 3.5.2. On extracts, see Chap. 7. **48.3.1**

Part I – General Provisions

Interpretation of this Chapter

49.1.—[1](1)   In this Chapter, "family action" means—

49.1

(a)   an action of divorce;

(b)   an action of dissolution of a civil partnership;

(c)   an action of separation of spouses or of civil partners;

(d)   an action of declarator of nullity of marriage or civil partnership;

(e)   an action of declarator of marriage;

(f)   an action of declarator of legitimacy;

(g)   an action of declarator of illegitimaChcy;

(h)   an action of declarator of parentage;

(i)   an action of declarator of non-parentage;

(j)   an action of declarator of legitimation;

(k)   an action or application for, or in respect of, an order under section 11 of the Children (Scotland) Act 1995 (court orders relating to parental responsibilities etc.) except a petition for the appointment of a judicial factor;

(l)   an action of, or application for or in respect of, aliment;

(m)   an action or application for financial provision after a divorce or annulment an in overseas country with the meaning of Part IV of the Matrimonial and Family Proceedings Act 1984;

(n)   an action or application for financial provision after a dissolution or annulment of a civil partnership in an overseas country within the meaning of section 125 of and Schedule 11 to the Civil Partnership Act 2004;

(o)   an action or application for an order under the Matrimonial Homes (Family Protection) (Scotland) Act 1981;

(p)   an action or application for an order under Chapter 3 or 4 of Part 3 of the Civil Partnership Act 2004;

(q)[2]   an application under section 28 or 29 of the Family Law (Scotland) Act 2006 (financial provision for former co-habitants).

(r)[3]   an action for declarator of recognition, or non-recognition, of a relevant foreign decree within the meaning of section 7(9) of the Domicile and Matrimonial Proceedings Act 1973.

(s)[4]   an action for declarator of recognition, or non-recognition, of a relevant foreign decree within the meaning of paragraph 1 of Schedule 1B to the Domicile and Matrimonial Proceedings Act 1973, or of a judgment to which paragraph 2(1)(b) of that Schedule refers.

(2)   In this Chapter, unless the context otherwise requires—

"the Act of 1975" means the Children Act 1975;

"the Act of 1976" means the Divorce (Scotland) Act 1976;

"the Act of 1973" means the Domicile and Matrimonial Proceedings Act 1973;

"the Act of 1981" means the Matrimonial Homes (Family Protection) (Scotland) Act 1981;

"the Act of 1985" means the Family Law (Scotland) Act 1985;

---

[1] R. 49.1 substituted by S.S.I. 2005 No. 632 (effective 8th December 2005).
[2] R. 49.1(1)(q) inserted by S.S.I. 2006 No. 206 (effective 4th May 2006).
[3] R. 49.1(1)(r) inserted by S.S.I. 2010 No. 417 (effective 1st January 2011).
[4] Rule 49.1(1)(s) inserted by S.S.I. 2014 No. 302 (effective 16th December 2014).

"the Act of 1995" means the Children (Scotland) Act 1995;

"the Act of 2004" means the Gender Recognition Act 2004;

"the CP Act of 2004" means the Civil Partnership Act 2004;

"civil partnership" has the same meaning as in section 1(1) of the CP Act of 2004;

"contact order" has the same meaning as in section 11 (2)(d) of the Act of 1995;

"corrected gender recognition certificate" means a certificate issued under section 6(4) of the Act of 2004;

"dissolution of a civil partnership" means a decree granted under section 117(2) of the CP Act of 2004;

"full gender recognition certificate" and "interim gender recognition certificate" have the same meanings as in section 25 of the Act of 2004;

"Gender Recognition Panel"[1] is to be construed in accordance with Schedule 1 to the Act of 2004;

"incapable"[2] means

    (a)   acting;

    (b)   making decisions;

    (c)   communicating decisions;

    (d)   understanding decisions; or

    (e)   retaining the memory of decisions,

but a person is not incapable by reason only of a lack of deficiency in a faculty of communication where that lack or deficiency can be made good by human or mechanical aid (whether of an interpretative nature or otherwise);

"local authority" means a council constituted under section 2 of the Local Government etc. (Scotland) Act 1994;

"mental disorder" has the same meaning as in section 328 of the Mental Health (Care and Treatment) (Scotland) Act 2003;

"action for declarator of nullity of a civil partnership" means an action for declarator that a civil partnership is void within the meaning of section 123 of the CP Act of 2004;

"order for financial provision" means, except in Parts VII and VIIA of this Chapter (financial provision after overseas divorce, dissolution of a civil partnership, or annulment of marriage or civil partnership), an order mentioned in section 8(1) of the Act of 1985;

"parental responsibilities" has the same meaning as in section 1(3) of the Act of 1995;

"parental rights" has the same meaning as in section 2(4) of the Act of 1995;

"residence order" has the same meaning as in section 11(2) of the Act of 1995;

"section 11 order" means an order under section 11 of the Act of 1995;

"action of separation of civil partners" means an action for decree under section 120 of the CP Act of 2004.

(3)   For the purposes of rule 49.2 (averments in certain family actions about other proceedings) and rule 49.3 (averments where section 11 order sought), and in relation to proceedings in another jurisdiction, Schedule 3 to the Act of 1973 (sisting of consistorial actions in Scotland) and rule 49.18A (applications for sist in actions

---

[1] Definition inserted by S.S.I. 2014 No. 302 para.2 (effective 16th December 2014).
[2] Definition inserted by S.S.I. 2017 No. 132 para.3 (effective 1 June 2017).

involving civil partnerships), proceedings are continuing at any time after they have commenced and before they are finally disposed of.

Deriv. R.C.S. 1965, r. 154(1) and (2) substituted by S.I. 1976 No. 1994 and amended by S.I. 1986 No. 1231 (r. 49.1(1) and (2))

GENERAL NOTE.

Family causes (called "family actions" and defined in r. 49.1(1)), including all applications for custody (see now "residence order"), are now initiated by summons; none is commenced by petition. The difficulty in *Hogg v. Dick* 1987 S.L.T. 716 that an application for custody could not be sought in an action of declarator of paternity should now be overcome: see rr. 49.1(1), 49.58(1) and 49.59.

49.1.1

A consistorial action, included in the family actions to which Chap. 49 applies, is an action between husband and wife involving status. An application for custody (see now a residence order) is not a consistorial action: *Hogg*, above.

"SECTION 11 ORDER".

This means an order under s. 11 of the Children (Scotland) Act 1995. Under that section the court may make an order in relation to parental responsibilities (defined in s. 1), parental rights (defined in s. 2), guardianship and administration of a child's property. Without prejudice to that generality, the court may (a) make an order depriving a person of parental responsibilities or parental rights in respect of a child under 18, (b) make an order imposing such responsibilities or rights in respect of a child under 18, (c) make a residence order in respect of a child under 16, (d) make a contact order in respect of a child under 16, (e) make a specific issue order in relation to a matter arising out of or in connection with a matter in (a) to (d), (f) grant interdict in relation to parental responsibilities, parental rights or the administration of property of a child under 18, (g) appoint a judicial factor in respect of a child under 18, or (h) appoint or remove a guardian of a child under 18.

49.1.2

CIVIL PARTNERSHIP ACT 2004.

Chap. 49 has been amended to take account of this Act, which provides for registered partnerships between people of the same sex.

49.1.3

Averments in certain family actions about other proceedings

49.2.—(1)[1] This rule applies to an action of divorce, separation, declarator of marriage, declarator of nullity of marriage, dissolution of a civil partnership, separation of civil partners or declarator of nullity of a civil partnership.

49.2

(2) In an action to which this rule applies, the pursuer shall state in the condescendence of the summons—

(a)[2] whether to his knowledge any proceedings are continuing in Scotland or in any other country in respect of the marriage or civil partnership to which the summons relates or are capable of affecting its validity or subsistence; and

(b) where such proceedings are continuing—

(i) the court, tribunal or authority before which the proceedings have been commenced;

(ii) the date of commencement;

(iii) the names of the parties;

(iv) the date, or expected date of any proof (or its equivalent), in the proceedings; and

(v)[3] such other facts as may be relevant to the question of whether or not the action in the Court of Session should be sisted under Schedule 3 to the Act of 1973, or rule 49.18A.

(3) Where—

(a) such proceedings are continuing;

(b) the action in the Court of Session is defended; and

(c) either—

---

[1] Rule 49.2(1) & (2)(a) amended by S.S.I. 2005 No. 632 (effective 8th December 2005).
[2] Rule 49.2(1) & (2)(a) amended by S.S.I. 2005 No. 632 (effective 8th December 2005).
[3] Rule 49.2(2)(b)(v) substituted by S.S.I. 2005 No. 632 (effective 8th December 2005).

(i) the summons does not contain the statement referred to in paragraph (2)(b), or

(ii)[1] the particulars mentioned in paragraph (2)(b) as set out in the summons are incomplete or incorrect,

any defences or minute, as the case may be, lodged by any person to the action shall include that statement and, where appropriate, the further or correct particulars mentioned in paragraph (2)(b).

Deriv. R.C.S. 1965, r. 157(3) substituted by S.I. 1976 No. 1994

GENERAL NOTE.

49.2.1   The Domicile and Matrimonial Proceedings Act 1973 and the Council Regulation (EC) No. 2201/2003 of 27th November 2003 (sometimes called Brussels IIA (or IIa) or Brussels II *bis*, replacing 1347/2000 of 29th May 2000) contain provisions for the jurisdiction of the court in actions of divorce, declarator of marriage, declarator of nullity of marriage and judicial separation. The 1973 Act was amended by the European Communities (Matrimonial and Parental Responsibility Jurisdiction and Judgments) (Scotland) Regulations 2005 (S.S.I. 2005 No. 42) to take account of the Council Regulation (EC) No. 1347/2000 of 29th May 2000 (Brussels II). The Council Regulation has had direct effect in the U.K. since 1st March 2001 with respect to the jurisdiction and enforcement of judgments in matrimonial matters and matters of parental responsibility for children of both spouses. The Council Regulation made provisions for common rules on jurisdiction in matrimonial proceedings to apply throughout the member states of the E.U. other than Denmark. Matrimonial matters are defined in art. 2 of the Council Regulation as divorce, separation or marriage annulment. Parental responsibility is defined in art. 2(7) as meaning all rights and duties relating to the person or property of a child including custody and access; and art. 1(2) is referred to as including also guardianship, curatorship, etc., placement in foster care and child protection. It did not apply to paternity, adoption, maintenance, trusts or succession.

The amendments to the 1973 Act made by S.S.I. 2005 No. 42, and the Council Regulation, were revoked by the Jurisdiction and Judgments (Family, Civil Partnership and Marriage (Same Sex Couples)) (EU Exit) (Scotland) (Amendment etc.) Regulations 2019 [S.S.I. 2019 No. 104] (as read with the European Union (Withdrawal) Act 2018) from 11pm on 31st December 2020 except in relation to proceedings commenced before that date. The Brussels II Regulation of 2003 no longer applies between Scotland and Member States of the EU. Jurisdiction is now what it was before 2005 in relation to Member States of the EU (the Brussels II regime never applied to Denmark) and as it still is in relation to other countries under the 1973 Act.

The jurisdiction of the court is now, therefore, as follows:

(A)   The court has jurisdiction to entertain an action for divorce or separation, including a same sex marriage, if either of the parties to the marriage (a) is domiciled in Scotland on the date when the action is begun, (b) was habitually resident in Scotland throughout the period of one year ending with that date: 1973 Act, s. 7(2A), and Sched. 1B, para. 3 (in relation to a same sex marriage).

(B)   The court has jurisdiction to entertain an action for declarator of marriage, declarator of nullity of marriage or for declarator of recognition, or non-recognition, of a relevant foreign decree (a decree of divorce, nullity or separation granted outwith the U.K., the Channel Islands and the Isle of Man), including a same sex marriage, if either of the parties to the marriage (a) is domiciled in Scotland on the date when the action is begun; (b) was habitually resident in Scotland throughout the period of one year ending with that date; or (c) died before that date and either (i) was at death domiciled in Scotland, or (ii) had been habitually resident in Scotland throughout the period of one year ending with the date of death: 1973 Act s. 7(3) and (3A) and Sched. 1B paras. 4, 5 and 6 (in relation to a same sex marriage).

(C)   The court, at any time when proceedings are pending in respect of which it has jurisdiction by virtue of the above subsections, also has jurisdiction to entertain other proceedings, in respect of the same marriage, for divorce, separation or declarator of marriage, declarator of nullity of marriage, notwithstanding that jurisdiction would not be exercisable under any of those subsections: 1973 Act 7(5).

(D)   The foregoing provisions are without prejudice to any rule of law whereby the court has jurisdiction in certain circumstances to entertain actions for separation as a matter of necessity and urgency: 1973 Act s.7(7).

On the meaning of domicile, see *Bell v. Kennedy* (1868) 6 M. (H.L.) 69 and *Udny v. Udny* (1869) 7 M. (H.L.) 89. On a recent case on domicile of choice, see *Spence v. Spence* 1995 S.L.T. 335. On the meaning of habitual residence, see *Dickson v. Dickson* 1990 S.C.L.R. 692 (1st Div), *Rellis v. Hart* 1993 S.L.T. 738; *Scullion v. Scullion* 1990 S.C.L.R. 577, 581A per Sheriff Stoddart. An action is begun when it is served on the defender: Erskine, III. vi. 3; *Alston v. Macdougall* (1887) 15 R. 78; *Smith v. Stewart & Co.* 1960 S.C. 329, 334 per L.P. Clyde; *Miller v. National Coal Board* 1960 S.C. 376.

---

[1] R. 49.2(3)(c)(ii) amended by S.I. 1994 No. 2901 (minor correction).

The 1973 Act gives the court having jurisdiction in divorce etc., jurisdiction over ancillary matters such as custody, residence and access and other orders relating to children (but not in declarator of marriage), aliment and financial provision: 1973 Act s. 10 (as modified by s. 13 of the Family Law Act 1986).

Sched. 3 to the 1973 Act contains a duty to give certain information to the court about other related proceedings in any other court. It also contains provisions for the mandatory sist of proceedings before the court in certain circumstances and for a discretionary sist in others. On the exercise of the discretionary sist, see *Mitchell v. Mitchell* 1991 S.L.T. 410. An application for a sist is made by motion: r. 49.18.

Part 3 of Chap. 5 of the Civil Partnership Act 2004 contains provisions for jurisdiction in relation to proceedings under that Act.

"CONDESCENDENCE".

See generally, note 13.2.4.

49.2.2

Averments where Section 11 order sought[1]

49.3.—(1)[2] A party to a family action, who makes an application in that action for a section 11 order in respect of a child, shall include in his pleadings—

49.3

(a)[3] where that action is an action of divorce, separation, declarator of nullity of marriage, dissolution of a civil partnership, separation of civil partners or declarator of nullity of a civil partnership averments giving particulars of any other proceedings known to him, whether in Scotland or elsewhere and whether concluded or not, which relate to the child in respect of whom the section 11 order is sought;

(b) in any other family action—

(i) the averments mentioned in sub-paragraph (a); and

(ii)[4] averments giving particulars of any proceedings known to him which are continuing, whether in Scotland or elsewhere, and which relate to the marriage or civil partnership of the parents or either of the parents of that child.

(2)[5] Where such other proceedings are continuing or have taken place and the averments of the applicant for such a section 11 order—

(a) do not contain particulars of the other proceedings, or

(b) contain particulars which are incomplete or incorrect,

any defences or minute, as the case may be, lodged by any person to the family action shall include such particulars or such further or correct particulars as are known to him.

(3) In paragraph (1)(b)(ii), "child" includes a child of the family within the meaning assigned in section 42(4) of the Family Law Act 1986.

Deriv. R.C.S. 1965, r. 170B(11) (inserted by S.I. 1988 No. 615), r. 260EA (inserted by S.I. 1988 No. 615) and the Family Law Act 1986, (r. 49.3(1))

GENERAL NOTE.

The jurisdiction of the court to entertain an application for residence, custody, care or control of a child, or contact with or access to a child (all included in the meaning of a "Part I order" under the Act) in proceedings other than divorce, nullity of marriage or judicial separation is governed by ss. 9 (habitual residence), 10 (presence of child), 12 (emergency) and 15(2) (original order granted by court) of the Family Law Act 1986. The preeminent ground in such proceedings is habitual residence, on the meaning of which see *Dickson v. Dickson* 1990 S.C.L.R. 692 (1st Div); *Rellis v. Hart* 1993 S.L.T. 738; *Scullion v. Scullion* 1990 S.C.L.R. 577, 581A per Sheriff Stoddart. The jurisdiction of the court in relation to orders relating to children in actions of divorce, nullity and judicial separation is governed by the Domicile and Matrimonial Proceedings Act 1973 (as modified by s. 13 of the 1986 Act). See note 49.2.1.

49.3.1

The Family Law Act 1986 contains provisions for avoiding conflict of jurisdiction within the U.K. in relation to Part I orders. The court in matrimonial proceedings may decline jurisdiction if it would be more appropriate for the matter to be dealt with in another court having jurisdiction: 1986 Act, s. 13(6).

---

[1] Heading and r. 49.3(1) and (2) amended by S.I. 1996 No. 2587 (effective 1st November 1996).
[2] Heading and r. 49.3(1) and (2) amended by S.I. 1996 No. 2587 (effective 1st November 1996).
[3] Rule 49.3(1)(a) & (b)(ii) amended by S.S.I. 2005 No. 632 (effective 8th December 2005).
[4] Rule 49.3(1)(a) & (b)(ii) amended by S.S.I. 2005 No. 632 (effective 8th December 2005).
[5] Heading and r. 49.3(1) and (2) amended by S.I. 1996 No. 2587 (effective 1st November 1996).

Under s. 14(2) of the 1986 Act, where, at any stage of the proceedings for a Part I order, it appears to the court (a) that proceedings with respect to matters to which the application relates are continuing outside Scotland or in another court in Scotland or (b) that it would be more appropriate for those matters to be determined in proceedings outside Scotland or in another court in Scotland and such proceedings are likely to be taken there, the court may sist the proceedings. It has been held by Lord McCluskey, in *Hill v. Hill* 1991 S.L.T. 189 and by Lord MacLean in *B v. B* 1998 S.L.T. 1245 that the principle of forum non conveniens (whether it would be more appropriate for another court to determine the matter) applies both to para.(a) and (b) of s. 14(2) of the 1986 Act.

"SECTION 11 ORDER".

49.3.2 See note 49.1.2.

Averments where identity or address of person not known

49.4 **49.4.** In a family action, where the identity or address of any person referred to in rule 49.8 as a person in respect of whom a warrant for intimation requires to be applied for is not known and cannot reasonably be ascertained, the party required to apply for the warrant shall include in his pleadings an averment of that fact and averments setting out what steps have been taken to ascertain the identity or address, as the case may be, of that person.

Deriv. R.C.S. 1965, r. 157(1) substituted by S.I. 1976 No. 1994

"NOT KNOWN".

49.4.1 The word "known" refers not to the pursuer's knowledge but to that of persons generally who had business or social dealings with the defender (*Young v. Harper* 1970 S.C. 174, 177 per Lord Fraser); accordingly the pursuer must take some steps to ascertain an address, and this is required for a motion in respect of service where the address of the defender is not known: r. 16.5(1)(c). Where the address is not known service by advertisement will be required unless dispensed with: r. 16.5. That rule applies by virtue of r. 16.8(1) which applies rules for service to persons for whom a warrant to intimate has been obtained.

Averments about maintenance orders

49.5 **49.5.** In a family action in which an order for aliment or periodical allowance is sought, or is sought to be varied or recalled, by any party, the pleadings of that party shall contain an averment stating whether and, if so, when and by whom a maintenance order (within the meaning of section 106 of the Debtors (Scotland) Act 1987) has been granted in favour of or against that party or any other person in respect of whom the order is sought.

GENERAL NOTE.

49.5.1 S.106 of the Debtors (Scotland) Act 1987 contains a convenient list of maintenance orders.

Averments where aliment sought for a child

49.6 **49.6.**—(1) In this rule—

"the Act of 1991" means the Child Support Act 1991;
"child" has the meaning assigned in section 55 of the Act of 1991;
"conclusion relating to aliment" means—

    (a)   for the purposes of paragraph (2), a conclusion for decree of aliment in relation to a child or for recall or variation of such a decree; and

    (b)   for the purposes of paragraph (3), a conclusion for decree of aliment in relation to a child or for recall or variation of such a decree or for the variation or termination of an agreement on aliment in relation to a child;

"maintenance assessment" has the meaning assigned in section 54 of the Act of 1991.

(2) A family action containing a conclusion relating to aliment to which section 8(6), (7), (8) or (10) of the Act of 1991 (top up maintenance orders) applies shall—

    (a)   include averments stating, where appropriate—

     (i)   that a maintenance assessment under section 11 of that Act is in force;

     (ii)   the date of the maintenance assessment;

     (iii) the amount and frequency of periodical payments of child support maintenance fixed by the maintenance assessment; and

     (iv) the grounds on which the sheriff retains jurisdiction under section 8(6), (7), (8) or (10) of that Act; and

  (b)   unless the court on cause shown otherwise directs, be accompanied by any document issued by the Secretary of State to the party intimating the making of the maintenance assessment referred to in sub-paragraph (a).

(3)   A family action containing a conclusion relating to aliment to which section 8(6), (7), (8) or (10) of the Act of 1991 does not apply, shall include averments stating—

  (a)   that the habitual residence of the absent parent, person with care or qualifying child, within the meaning of section 3 of that Act, is furth of the United Kingdom;

  (b)   that the child is not a child within the meaning of section 55 of that Act; or

  (c)   the grounds on which the court retains jurisdiction.

(4)   In an action for declarator of non-parentage or illegitimacy—

  (a)   the summons shall include an article of condescendence stating whether the pursuer previously has been alleged to be the parent in an application for a maintenance assessment under section 4, 6 or 7 of the Act of 1991 (applications for maintenance assessment); and

  (b)   where an allegation of paternity has been made against the pursuer, the Secretary of State shall be named as a defender in the action.

(5)   A family action involving parties in respect of whom a decision has been made in any application, review or appeal under the Act of 1991 relating to any child of those parties, shall—

  (a)   include averments stating that such a decision has been made and giving details of that decision; and

  (b)   unless the court on cause shown otherwise directs, be accompanied by any document issued by the Secretary of State to the parties intimating that decision.

GENERAL NOTE.

   Where the Child Support Agency has jurisdiction the court may nonetheless have jurisdiction to make a maintenance order including a maintenance order to top up child support maintenance and orders to meet expenses of education and training, to meet expenses attributable to a disability or where the order is to be made against a person with care of the child: Child Support Act 1991, s. 8. An order may be made where the Child Support Agency does not have jurisdiction, i.e. where the child, parent with care or absent parent is not habitually resident in the UK or the child is not a qualifying child within the meaning of s. 3 of the Act of 1991. When a statutory instrument is made to that effect, the court will retain jurisdiction to make a maintenance order where a written agreement provides for an absent parent to make periodic payments to or for the child and that agreement is not enforceable and the maintenance order made by the court is in all material respects in the same terms as that agreement. The court retained jurisdiction during the transitional period (from 5th March 1993 for an indefinite period: Child Support Act 1995 s. 18), where a maintenance provision already existed to deal with applications for variation of such provision whether under order of the court or a maintenance agreement until a child maintenance assessment is made, or to deal with a conclusion for aliment in a pending action: Child Support Act 1991 (Commencement No. 3 and Transitional Provisions) Amendment Order 1992 [S.I. 1992 No. 2644].

   A maintenance agreement for less than could be awarded under a maintenance assessment will be insecure because an application to the Child Support Agency for a maintenance assessment cannot be prevented: 1991 Act, s. 9.

49.6.1

Averments where divorce sought on ground of issue of interim gender recognition certificate

49.6A

49.6A.—[1](1) This rule applies to an action of divorce in which divorce is sought on the ground that an interim gender recognition certificate has been issued to either party.

(2) In an action to which this rule applies, the pursuer shall state in the condescendence of the summons—

    (a) where the pursuer is the party to whom the interim gender recognition certificate was issued, whether or not the Gender Recognition Panel has issued a full gender recognition certificate to the pursuer, and

    (b) where the defender is the party to whom the interim gender recognition certificate was issued, whether—

        (i) since the issue of the interim gender recognition certificate, the pursuer has made a statutory declaration consenting to the marriage continuing, and

        (ii) the Gender Recognition Panel has given the pursuer notice of the issue of a full gender recognition certificate to the defender.

Warrants for arrestment or inhibition on dependence

49.7

49.7.—(1) A warrant for inhibition or arrestment on the dependence in a family action or in respect of a claim to which section 19 of the Act of 1985 (action for aliment or claim for order for financial provision) applies shall be applied for by motion.

(2) A certified copy of the interlocutor granting warrant for diligence applied for under paragraph (1) shall be sufficient authority for execution of the diligence.

(3) A certified copy of the interlocutor containing a warrant for inhibition granted under this rule and an execution of service of it may be registered in the Register of Inhibitions and Adjudications.

(4)[2] A notice of a certified copy of the interlocutor containing a warrant for inhibition granted under this rule may be registered in the Register of Inhibitions and Adjudications; and such registration is to have the same effect as registration of a notice of inhibition under section 155(2) of the Titles to Land Consolidation (Scotland) Act 1868.

Deriv. R.C.S. 1965, r. 155A(1) inserted by S.I. 1991 No. 1157

GENERAL NOTE.

49.7.1

Section 19 of the Family Law (Scotland) Act 1985 has been repealed by the Bankruptcy and Diligence etc. (Scotland) Act 2007. The law relating to diligence on the dependence in family actions is now the same as in any other action and as provided by the 2007 Act: see Debtors (Scotland) 2007 Act 1987, ss. 15A–15M inserted by the 2007 Act; and see Chap.14A.

The previous position was as follows. In an action of aliment or a claim for financial provision in an action of divorce or declarator of nullity of marriage, which is for a future or contingent debt, warrant to arrest or inhibit may only be granted by the court (by motion: r. 49.7) on cause shown subject to any limit as to property or value (property only in inhibition), and is not limited to the common law grounds: Family Law (Scotland) Act 1985, s. 19(1). Arrestment can only be granted at common law on a claim for a future debt where there are special circumstances averred, e.g. that the defender is *vergens ad inopiam* or *in meditatione fugae* or considering putting away his funds with the intention of not implementing any decree or not fulfilling his obligations: *Symington v. Symington* (1875) 3 R. 205; *Gillanders v. Gillanders* 1966 S.C. 54; *Wilson v. Wilson* 1981 S.L.T. 101.

See further, Chap. 14A and notes.

EXECUTION OF WARRANTS FOR ARRESTMENT OR INHIBITION.

49.7.2

See Chap. 16, Pt. II.

---

[1] R. 49.6A as inserted by S.S.I. 2014 No.302 (effective 16th December 2014).
[2] R. 49.7(4) substituted by S.S.I. 2009 No. 104 (effective 22nd April 2009).

For how and when registration is effected, see note 14A.3.1.

49.7.3

Warrants for intimation in family actions

49.8.—[1](1)[2] Subject to paragraph (5) and rule 49.8A (warrants and forms for intimation to a child and for seeking a child's views), in the summons in a family action, the pursuer shall insert a warrant for intimation—

49.8

(a)[3] in an action where the address of the defender is not known to the pursuer and cannot reasonably be ascertained, to—

    (i) every child of the marriage between the parties, or child who has been accepted by both partners of a civil partnership as a child of the family, who has reached the age of 16 years, and

    (ii) one of the next-of-kin of the defender who has reached that age, unless the address of such a person is not known to the pursuer and cannot reasonably be ascertained, in the following terms:—

        "Warrant to intimate to (name and address) as a child of the marriage [or to (name and address) as a child who has been accepted by both partners of a civil partnership as a child of the family] [or to (name and address) the (relationship to defender), as one of the next-of-kin of the defender]."

(b) in an action where the pursuer alleges that the defender has committed adultery with another person, to that person, unless—

    (i) that person is not named in the summons and, if the adultery is relied on for the purposes of section 1(2)(a) of the Act of 1976 (irretrievable breakdown of marriage by reason of adultery), the summons contains an averment that his or her identity is not known to the pursuer and cannot reasonably be ascertained, or

    (ii) the pursuer alleges that the defender has been guilty of rape upon or incest with, that named person,

  in the following terms:— "Warrant to intimate to (name and address) as a person with whom the defender is alleged to have committed adultery.";

(c)[4] in an action where the defender is a person who is suffering from a mental disorder, to—

    (i) those persons mentioned in sub-paragraph (a)(i) and (ii), unless the address of such person is not known to the pursuer and cannot reasonable be ascertained;

    (ii) any person holding the office of curator bonis to the defender, if one has been appointed; and

    (iii) any person holding the office of guardian, or continuing or welfare attorney to the defender under or by virtue of the Adults with Incapacity (Scotland) Act 2000, if one has been appointed,

  in the following terms:— "Warrant to intimate to (name and address) as a child of the marriage [or to (name and address) as a child who has been accepted by both partners of a civil partnership as a child of the family], (name and address) the (relationship to the defender) as one of the next-of-kin of the defender and (name and address) guardian [or continuing [or

---

[1] As amended by S.S.I. 2019 No. 123 para.2 (effective 24th June 2019).

[2] R. 49.8(1), (3), (4) and (7) amended, and r. 49.8(8) inserted, by S.I. 1996 No. 2587 (effective 1st November 1996).

[3] R. 49.8(1)(a), (c), (e) & (k) substituted by S.S.I. 2005 No. 632 (effective 8th December 2005).

[4] R. 49.8(1)(a), (c), (e) & (k) substituted by S.S.I. 2005 No. 632 (effective 8th December 2005).

welfare] attorney] to the defender." (ii) the curator bonis to the defender, if one has been appointed, in the following terms:— "Warrant to intimate to (*name and address*) as a child of the marriage, (*name and address*) the (*relationship to defender*) as one of the next-of-kin of the defender and (*name and address*), curator bonis to the defender.";

(d) in an action relating to a marriage which was entered into under a law which permits polygamy where—

    (i) one of the decrees specified in section 2(2) of the Matrimonial Proceedings (Polygamous Marriages) Act 1972 is sought; and

    (ii) either party to the marriage in question has any spouse additional to the other party,

to any such additional spouse in the following terms:— "Warrant to intimate to (*name and address*) as an additional spouse of the pursuer *[or defender]*.";

(e)[1] in an action of divorce, separation, declarator of nullity of marriage, dissolution of a civil partnership, separation of civil partners or declarator of nullity of a civil partnership where the court may make a section 11 order in respect of a child—

    (i) who is in the care of a local authority, to that local authority in the following terms:— "Warrant to intimate to the chief executive of (name and address of local authority) as the local authority having care of (name and address of child).";

    (ii) who, being a child of one party to the marriage who has been accepted as a child of the family by the other party to the marriage or is a child of one partner in a civil partnership who has been accepted by both partners as a child of the family, and who is liable to be maintained by a third party, to that third party in the following terms:— "Warrant to intimate to (name and address) as a person liable to maintain (name and address of child).", or

    (iii) in relation to whom a third party in fact exercises care or control, to that third party in the following terms:— "Warrant to intimate to (name and address) as a person who in fact exercises care or control of (name and address of child)."

(f)[2] in an action where the pursuer concludes for a section 11 order, to any parent or guardian of the child who is not a party to the action in the following terms:— "Warrant to intimate to (*name and address*) as a parent *[or guardian]*.";

(g)[3] in an action where the pursuer concludes for a residence order in respect of a child and he is—

    (i) not a parent of that child, and

    (ii) resident in Scotland when the summons is presented for signeting, to the local authority within which area the pursuer resides in the following terms:— "Warrant to intimate to the chief executive of (*name and address of local authority*) as the local authority within which area the pursuer, not being a parent of (*name and address of child*), resides.";

---

[1] R. 49.8(1)(a), (c), (e) & (k) substituted by S.S.I. 2005 No. 632 (effective 8th December 2005).
[2] R. 49.8(1), (3), (4) and (7) amended, and r. 49.8(8) inserted, by S.I. 1996 No. 2587 (effective 1st November 1996).
[3] R. 49.8(1), (3), (4) and (7) amended, and r. 49.8(8) inserted, by S.I. 1996 No. 2587 (effective 1st November 1996).

    (i)   in an action where the pursuer makes an application for an order under section 8(1)(aa) of the Act of 1985 (transfer of property) and—

        (i)   the consent of a third party to such a transfer is necessary by virtue of an obligation, enactment or rule of law, or

        (ii)   the property is subject to a security,

to the third party or creditor, as the case may be, in the following terms:— "Warrant to intimate to (*name and address*) as a person the consent of whom is required in respect of the transfer sought [*or* as a person who is believed to be a creditor of (*name of party*) in respect of the property sought to be transferred] in the (*number*) conclusion of this summons.";

    (j)   in an action where the pursuer makes an application for an order under section 18 of the Act of 1985 (which relates to avoidance transactions), to—

        (i)   any third party in whose favour the transfer of, or transaction involving, the property is to be or was made, and

        (ii)   any other person having an interest in the transfer of, or transaction involving, the property,

in the following terms:— "Warrant to intimate to (*name and address*) as the person in whose favour the transfer of [*or* transaction involving] property referred to in the condescendence attached to this summons was made [*or* is to be made] [*or* is a person having an interest in the transfer of [*or* transaction involving] property referred to in the condescendence attached to this summons].";

    (k)[1]   in an action where the pursuer makes an application for an order under the Act of 1981—

        (i)   where he is a non-entitled partner and the entitled partner has a spouse, or civil partner, to that spouse or civil partner, or

        (ii)   where the application is under section 2(1)(e), 2(4)(a), 3(1), 3(2), 4, 7, 13, or 18 of that Act, and the entitled spouse or entitled partner is a tenant or occupies the matrimonial home by permission of a third party, to the landlord or the third party, as the case may be, in the following terms:— "Warrant to intimate to (name and address) as a person with an interest in the order sought in the (number) conclusion of this summons."

    (l)   in an action where the pursuer makes an application for an order under—

        (i)   section 8(1)(ba) of the Act of 1985 (orders under s. 12A of the Act of 1985 for pension lump sum), or

        (ii)   section 8(1)(baa) of that Act (pension sharing orders),

to the person responsible for the pension arrangement, in the following terms—"Warrant to intimate to (*name and address*) as the person responsible for the pension arrangement in respect of which an order is sought in the (*number*) conclusion of this summons.";

    (m)[2]   in an action where the pursuer makes an application for an order under Chapter 3 of Part 3 of the CP Act of 2004 where the application is under section 102(1)(e), 102(4)(a), 103(1), 103(2), 104, 107 or 112 of that Act and the entitled civil partner is a tenant or occupies the family home by permission of a third party, to the landlord or the third party, as the case

---

[1] R. 49.8(1)(a), (c), (e) & (k) substituted by S.S.I. 2005 No. 632 (effective 8th December 2005).
[2] R. 49.8(1)(m) & (3)(n) inserted by S.S.I. 2005 No. 632 (effective 8th December 2005) and substituted by S.S.I. 2006 No. 206 (effective 4th May 2006).

may be, in the following terms:— "Warrant to intimate to (*name and address*) as a person with an interest in the order sought in the (*number*) conclusion of this summons;"

(n)[1] in an action where the pursuer makes an application for an order under section 29(2) of the Act of 2006 (application by survivor for provision on intestacy) to any person having an interest in the deceased's net intestate estate, in the following terms:— "Warrant to intimate to (name and address) as a person having an interest in the deceased's net intestate estate referred to in the condescendence attached to this summons."

(2) Expressions used in—

(i) paragraph (1)(k) which are also used in the Act of 1981;

(ii) paragraph (1)(m) which are also used in the CP Act of 2004; and

(iii) paragraph (1)(n) which are also used in section 29 of the Act of 2006,

have the meanings given in those Acts, or that section, as the case may be.

(3)[2] A notice of intimation shall be attached to the copy of the summons where intimation is given on a warrant—

(a) under paragraph (1)(a) (address of defender not known), in Form 49.8-A;

(b) under paragraph (1)(b) (allegation of adultery), in Form 49.8-B;

(c) under paragraph (1)(c) (mental disorder of defender), in Form 49.8-C;

(d) under paragraph (1)(d) (polygamous marriage), in Form 49.8-D;

(e) under paragraph (1)(e)(i) or (ii) (where section 11 order may be made in respect of a child in care of local authority or accepted as a child of the marriage), in Form 49.8-E;

(f) under paragraph (1)(e)(iii) (where section 11 order may be made in respect of a child in relation to whom a third party in fact exercises care or control), in Form 49.8-F;

(g) under paragraph (1)(f) (section 11 order sought by guardian), in Form 49.8-G;

(h) under paragraph (1)(g) (residence order sought by non-parent resident in Scotland), in Form 49.8-H;

(i) [Revoked by SI 1996/2587 (effective 1st November 1996).]

(j) under paragraph (1)(i) (transfer of property), in Form 49.8-J;

(k) under paragraph (1)(j) (avoidance transactions), in Form 49.8-K;

(l) under paragraph (1)(k) (orders sought under the Act of 1981), in Form 49.8-L;

(m) under—

(i) paragraph (1)(1)(i) (orders for pension lump sums) in Form 49.8-M; and

(ii) paragraph (1)(1)(ii) (person sharing orders), in Form 49.8-MA;

(n)[3] under paragraph (1)(m) (order sought under Chapter 3 of Part 3 of the CP Act of 2004), in Form 49.8-0; and

---

[1] R. 49.8(1)(n) and r.49.8(3)(o) inserted by, and r.49.8(2) and r.49.8(3)(m) substituted by, S.S.I. 2006 No. 206 (effective 4th May 2006).

[2] R. 49.8(1), (3), (4) and (7) amended, and r. 49.8(8) inserted, by S.I. 1996 No. 2587 (effective 1st November 1996).

[3] R. 49.8(1)(m)& (3)(n) inserted by S.S.I. 2005 No. 632 (effective 8th December 2005) and substituted by S.S.I. 2006 No. 206 (effective 4th May 2006).

   (o)[1] under paragraph (1)(n)(order under section 29 of the Act of 2006), in Form 49.8-P

(4) In a family action, where the pursuer—

   (a)[2] concludes for a residence order in respect of a child;

   (b) is not a parent of the child; and

   (c) is not resident in Scotland when the summons is presented for signeting,

he shall, on presenting the summons for signeting, apply by motion for an order for intimation in Form 49.8-H to such local authority as the court thinks fit.

(5)[3] Where the address of a person mentioned in paragraph (1)(b), (d), (e), (f), (g), (i), (j), (k), (1) or (m) is not known and cannot reasonably be ascertained, the pursuer shall, immediately after the calling of the summons, apply by motion to dispense with intimation; and the court may grant that motion or make such other order as it thinks fit.

(6) Where the identity or address of a person to whom intimation of a family action is required becomes known during the course of the action, the party who would have been required to insert a warrant for intimation to that person shall apply by motion for a warrant for intimation to that person or to dispense with such intimation.

Deriv. R.C.S. 1965, r. 155(3)(a) and (4) substituted by S.I. 1976 No. 1994 (r. 49.8(1)(a)); r. 155(1) and (2) substituted by S.I. 1976 No. 1994 (r. 49.8(1)(b)); r. 155(3)(b) and (4) substituted by S.I. 1976 No. 1994 (r. 49.8(1)(c)); r. 155(5) substituted by S.I. 1976 No. 1994 (r. 49.8(1)(d)); r. 155(6) substituted by S.I. 1976 No. 1994, and r. 170B(6)(a) inserted by S.I. 1976 No. 1994 and amended by S.I. 1986 No. 1955 and S.I. 1990 No. 705, (r. 49.8(1)(e)); Children Act 1975, s. 48 amended by Law Reform (Parent and Child) (Scotland) Act 1986, Sched. 2 (r. 49.8(1)(f)); Children Act 1975, s. 49(1)(a) amended by Law Reform (Parent and Child) (Scotland) Act 1986, Sched. 1, para. 14 (r. 49.8(1)(g)); r. 170D(9) inserted by S.I. 1986 No. 1231 (r. 49.8(1)(i)); r.155(7) inserted by S.I. 1982 No. 1825, and r. 170D(4)(c) substituted by S.I. 1977 No. 1621 and amended by S.I. 1986 No. 1231 (r. 49.8(1)(j)); r. 188D(7) and (10) inserted by S.I. 1982 No. 1381 (r. 49.8(1)(k));

Children Act 1975, s. 49(1)(b) amended by Law Reform (Parent and Child) (Scotland) Act 1986, Sched. 1, para. 14 (r. 49.8(4))

"WARRANTS FOR INTIMATION".

For methods of intimation, see r. 16.8.   **49.8.1**

"MOTION".

For motions, see Chap. 23.   **49.8.3**

"SECTION 11 ORDER".

See note 49.1.2.   **49.8.4**

Warrants and forms for intimation to a child and for seeking a child's views

   49.8A.—[4](1) Subject to paragraph (2), in an action which includes a conclusion   **49.8A** for a section 11 order in respect of a child who is not a party to the action, the pursuer must—

   (a) include in the condescendence of the summons averments setting out the reasons why it is appropriate to send Form 49.8A to the child;

   (b) when the summons is presented for signeting—

      (i) apply by motion for a warrant for intimation and the seeking of the child's views in Form 49.8A, specifying the articles of condescendence in the summons which contain the reasons for the request;

---

[1] R. 49.8(1)(n) and r.49.8(3)(o) inserted by, and r.49.8(2) and r.49.8(3)(m) substituted by, S.S.I. 2006 No. 206 (effective 4th May 2006).

[2] R. 49.8(1), (3), (4) and (7) amended, and r. 49.8(8) inserted, by S.I. 1996 No. 2587 (effective 1st November 1996).

[3] R. 49.8(5) amended by S.I. 1996 No. 1756 (effective 5th August 1996) and (1)(1) substituted by S.S.I. 2000 No. 412 (effective 1st December 2000).

[4] R. 49.8A as inserted by S.S.I. 2019 No. 123 para.2 (effective 24th June 2019).

    (ii)   submit a draft Form 49.8A, showing the details that the pursuer proposes to include when the form is sent to the child.

(2) Where the pursuer considers that it would be inappropriate to send Form 49.8A to the child (for example, where the child is under 5 years of age), the pursuer must—

    (a)   when the summons is presented for signeting, apply by motion for the court to dispense with intimation and the seeking of the child's views in Form 49.8A, specifying the articles of condescendence in the summons which contain the reasons for the request;

    (b)   include in the condescendence of the summons averments setting out the reasons why it is inappropriate to send Form 49.8A to the child.

(3) The court must be satisfied that the draft Form 49.8A submitted under paragraph (1)(b) has been drafted appropriately

(4) The court may dispense with intimation and the seeking of views in Form 49.8A or make any other order it considers appropriate.

(5) An order granting warrant for intimation and the seeking of the child's views in Form 49.8A under this rule must—

    (a)   state that the Form 49.8A must be sent in accordance with rule 49.8A(6);

    (b)   be signed by the Lord Ordinary.

(6) The Form 49.8A must be sent in accordance with—

    (a)   rule 49.20 (views of the child – undefended actions), where the action is undefended;

    (b)   rule 49.20A (views of the child – section 11 order sought by pursuer only), where the action is defended and a section 11 order is sought by the pursuer only;

    (c)   rule 49.20B (views of the child – section 11 order sought by defender only), where a section 11 order is sought by the defender only; or

    (d)   rule 49.20C (views of the child – section 11 orders sought by both pursuer and defender), where a section 11 order is sought by both parties.

"CHILD WHO IS NOT A PARTY TO THE ACTION".

49.8A.1   R. 49.8A provides for a warrant to intimate to a child a family action which may affect him. This was previously provided for in r. 49.8(1)(h). Under art. 12 of the UN Convention on the Rights of the Child (Cm. 1976 (1992)), ratified by the UK on 16th December 1991, a child who is capable of forming his own views has the right to express those views freely in all matters affecting him and his views must be given due weight in accordance with his age and maturity. For this purpose the child must be given the opportunity to be heard in any judicial and administrative proceedings affecting him, either directly or through a representative or appropriate body, in a manner consistent with the procedural rules of national law. This principle is now enshrined in s. 11(7) of the Children (Scotland) Act 1995.

The child need not become a party, and may express his views by writing a letter. A form (Form 49.8A) is sent to the child. A child should be able to instruct a solicitor: Age of Legal Capacity (Scotland) Act 1991, s. 2(1)(a). The old Form 49.8-N used to provide expressly for the child to indicate if he or she wanted someone else to tell the court his or her views. The new Form 49.8A refers expressly only to filling in the form if the child wants to express views in writing. There is an unhelpful question asking if the child would like to say what he or she thinks in a different way. That is likely to be confusing to a child if it is intended to allow the child to say that he or she wants someone else to tell or wants to tell the judge in person; it does not tell the child what any of these different ways may be. It is implied in r. 49.20D that the child may wish to express views in a different way, but, since the child only receives Form 49.8A and not r. 49.20, this is not very helpful to the child.

The court cannot always know in advance whether a child is capable of forming his own views and a minimum age cannot be laid down. On the other hand a child cannot know he has the right to be heard unless he is informed of that right. There appears to be no alternative but to provide for intimation in every case while providing in r. 49.8A(4) for the court to dispense with intimation in certain circumstances (e.g. the child is a baby). There is a statutory presumption that a child of 12 or more is of sufficient age and maturity to form a view: Act of 1995, s. 11(10).

In *S v. S.* 2002 S.C. 246 (Ex Div.), sub nom. *Shields v. Shields*, 2002 S.L.T. 579, paras [10] and [11], it was observed (1) that in affording a child the opportunity to make known his views the only test is practicality; (2) how the child should be given that opportunity depends on the circumstances including the child's age, and could be (a) by intimation in Form [49.8-N] (b) by seeing the child in chambers, (c) by the views of the child being made known to the court by a person known to the child or a child psychologist; (3) if it was practicable to give the child an opportunity to express his views, the only safe course was to employ whatever method was practicable; (4) the formal process of intimation in Form [49.8-N] should not be the principal mode of complying with s. 11(7)(b) of the Children (Scotland) Act 1995 and other methods must be preferable, particularly where younger children are involved or there is risk of upsetting the child; and (5) the duty on the court to comply with s. 11(7)(b) continues until the order is made and dispensing with formal intimation does not relieve the court from complying with that continuing duty.

R. 49.3(3)–(7) provides equivalent provisions where the defender seeks a s. 11 order.

Intimation where relevant association

49.9.—(1) In a family action where the pursuer alleges an association as defined in paragraph (4) between the defender and another named person, the pursuer shall, when the summons is presented for signeting, apply by motion for an order for intimation to that person or to dispense with such intimation.

(2) In determining a motion under paragraph (1), the court may—

   (a) make such order for intimation as it thinks fit; or

   (b) dispense with intimation; and

   (c) where it dispenses with intimation, order that the name of that person be deleted from the condescendence of the summons.

(3) Where intimation is ordered under paragraph (2), a notice of intimation in Form 49.9 shall be attached to the copy of the summons to be intimated.

(4)[1] In paragraph (1), "relevant association" means sodomy, incest or any homosexual relationship, and where the family action is in relation to a civil partnership shall include any heterosexual relationship.

Deriv. R.C.S. 1965, r. 162 substituted by S.I. 1976 No. 1994

"MOTION".

For motions, see Chap. 23.

"INTIMATION".

For methods, see r. 16.8.

Productions in action of divorce or where section 11 order may be made[2]

49.10.—[3](1) There shall be lodged as a production with the principal writ when first lodged in process—

   (a) in an action of divorce—

      (i) an extract or certified copy of the relevant entry in the register of marriages; and

      (ii) where an action relies on section 1(1)(b) of the Act of 1976 (grounds of divorce: interim gender recognition certificate), the interim gender recognition certificate or a certified copy of it;

   (b) in an action of dissolution of a civil partnership—

      (i) an extract or certified copy of the relevant entry in the civil partnership register; and

      (ii) where the action relies on section 117(2)(b) of the CP Act of 2004 (grounds for dissolution of civil partnership: interim gender recognition certificate), the interim gender recognition certificate or a certified copy of it; and

   (c) in a family action in which the court may make a section 11 order, an extract or certified copy of the relevant entry in the register of births.

---

[1] R. 49.9 substituted by S.S.I. 2005 No. 632 (effective 8th December 2005).
[2] R. 49.10 substituted by S.S.I. 2005 No. 632 (effective 8th December 2005).
[3] R. 49.10 substituted by S.S.I. 2005 No. 632 (effective 8th December 2005).

(2) In the application of sub-paragraph (a) of paragraph (1) to an action of divorce, or sub-paragraph (b) of paragraph (1) in an action of dissolution of a civil partnership, where the address of the defender is not known, the documents to be lodged under those sub-paragraphs, as the case may be, shall be obtained and dated within three months before the date on which it is lodged.

Lodging productions.

49.10.1   See r. 4.5.

Execution of service on, or intimation to, local authority

49.11   **49.11.**—(1)[1] Where a local authority referred to in rule 49.8(1)(g) (residence order sought by non-parent resident in Scotland) or rule 49.8(4) (residence order sought by non-parent not resident in Scotland) is called as a defender in a summons at the time of signeting, service of the summons on that local authority shall be executed within seven days after the date of signeting.

(2) Where in a family action—

(a)   to which rule 49.8(1)(g) applies, or

(b)   in which a motion under rule 49.8(4) is required,

the local authority referred to in that provision is called as a defender in the summons at the time of signeting, a notice in Form 49.8-H shall be attached to the copy of the summons served on that local authority unless the court otherwise orders.

(3) In any family action, the court may, if it thinks fit, order intimation to a local authority, and such intimation shall be in Form 49.8-H.

1(4) Where, by virtue of paragraph (3) of this rule or rule 49.8(1)(g), 49.8(4) or 49.15(3), intimation of an application for a section 11 order is to be made to a local authority, intimation to that local authority shall be given within seven days after the date of signeting or order for intimation, as the case may be; and a notice in Form 49.8-H shall be attached to the copy of the summons intimated to that local authority.

Deriv. Children Act 1975, s. 49 amended by Law Reform (Parent and Child) (Scotland) Act 1986, Sched. 1, para. 14

General note.

49.11.1   Under s. 49 of the Children Act 1975 where the pursuer was not the parent of the child, an order for custody could be made unless, where he resided in Scotland, he had given notice within seven days of making the application to the local authority of the area in which he resided or, in any other case (i.e. he did not reside in Scotland), he gave notice within such period and to such local authority as the court directed. On receipt of the notice the local authority had to investigate and report to the court on the circumstances of the child and on the proposed arrangements for his care and upbringing.

Section 49 of the 1975 Act was repealed, but *not* replaced, by the Children (Scotland) Act 1995. A local authority is no longer required to provide such a report; but it is understood that local authorities are prepared to continue to do so. Rule 49.11 remains, therefore, but in an amended form; and the court is only able to *request* such a report.

"within seven days".

49.11.2   The date from which the period is calculated is not counted.

"residence order".

49.11.3   This replaces, but is not the whole of, what was formerly custody. It means an order regulating arrangements as to with whom or with whom during what periods a child under 16 is to live: Children (Scotland) Act 1995, s. 11(2)(c).

"section 11 order".

49.11.4   See note 49.1.2.

---

[1] R. 49.13(1)(a) substituted by S.S.I. 2005 No. 632 (effective 8th December 2005).

Notice of actions by advertisement

49.12. Where notice of a family action is given by advertisement under rule 16.5 (service where address of person is not known), the period of notice shall be 21 days from the date of publication of the advertisement unless the court otherwise orders.

49.12

Deriv. R.C.S. 1965, r. 159(2) substituted by S.I. 1986 No.1941 and amended by S.I. 1987 No. 1206

GENERAL NOTE.

The normal period of notice by advertisement is six months, which is inappropriate in family actions.

49.12.1

Service in cases of mental disorder of defender

49.13.—(1) In a family action where the defender suffers or appears to suffer from mental disorder and is resident in a hospital or other similar institution, service of the summons shall be executed in accordance with rule 16.4 (service by post) addressed to the medical officer in charge of that hospital or institution; and there shall be included with the copy of the summons—

49.13

   (a)[1]   any notice required by rule 49.14(1) (notices in certain actions of divorce or separation) or by rule 49.14A(1) (notices in certain actions of dissolution of civil partnership or separation of civil partners);

   (b)   request in Form 49.13-A requesting the medical officer to—

      (i)[2]   deliver and explain the summons, citation and any notice or form of notice of consent required under rule 49.14(1) or rule 49.14A(1); or

      (ii)   certify that such delivery or explanation would be dangerous to the health or mental condition of the defender; and

      (iii)   complete the certificate in Form 49.13-B; and

   (c)   a stamped envelope addressed for return of that certificate to the pursuer or his agent, if he has one.

(2) The medical officer referred to in paragraph (1) shall send the certificate in Form 49.13-B duly completed to the pursuer or his agent, as the case may be.

(3) The certificate mentioned in paragraph (2) shall be attached to the summons when it is lodged for calling.

(4) Where such a certificate bears that the summons has not been delivered to the defender, the court may, at any time while the action is depending—

   (a)   order such further medical inquiry, and

   (b)   make such order for further service or intimation,

as it thinks fit.

Deriv. R.C.S. 1965, r. 159(5) and (6) substituted by S.I. 1976 No. 1994

"SEND".

This includes deliver: r. 1.3(1) (definition of "send").

49.13.1

"DEPENDING".

A cause is depending from the time it is commenced (i.e. from the time an action is served) until final decree, whereas a cause is in dependence until final extract. For the meaning of commenced, see note 13.4.4. For the meaning of final decree, see note 4.15.2(2). For the meaning of final extract, see note 7.1.2(2).

49.13.2

"MENTAL DISORDER".

This is defined in r. 49.1(2) as "mental illness or mental handicap however caused or manifested". In the R.C.S. 1965, r. 15.4(3) "mental deficiency" appeared in place of mental handicap. The definition in the R.C.S. 1994 is now the same as that in s. 1 of the Mental Health (Scotland) Act 1984.

49.13.3

---

[1] R. 49.13(1)(a) substituted by S.S.I. 2005 No. 632 (effective 8th December 2005).
[2] R. 49.13(1)(b)(i) amended by S.S.I. 2005 No. 632 (effective 8th December 2005).

Notices in certain actions of divorce or separation

49.14

49.14.—(1) In the following actions of divorce or separation, there shall be attached to the copy of the summons served on the defender—

(a)[1] in an action relying on section 1(2)(d) of the Act of 1976 (no cohabitation for one year with consent of defender to decree)—

    (i) which is an action of divorce, a notice in Form 49.14-A and a form of notice of consent in Form 49.14-B;

    (ii) which is an action of separation, a notice in Form 49.14-C and a form of notice of consent in Form 49.14-D;

(b)[2] in an action relying on section 1(2)(e) of the Act of 1976 (no cohabitation for two years)—

    (i) which is an action of divorce, a notice in form 49.14-E;

    (ii) which is an action of separation, a notice in Form 49.14-F.

(c)[3] in an action relying on section 1(1)(b) of the Act of 1976 (grounds for divorce: interim gender recognition certificate), a notice in Form 49.14-G.

(2) The certificate of service of a summons in an action mentioned in paragraph (1) shall state which notice or form mentioned in paragraph (1) has been included with the summons.

Deriv. R.C.S. 1965, r. 161 substituted by S.I. 1976 No. 1994

GENERAL NOTE.

49.14.1

Where amendment is made changing the ground of divorce, the appropriate notice will have to be sent. In certain circumstances this may be dispensed with: see *Duncan v. Duncan* 1986 S.L.T. 17.

Notices in certain actions of dissolution of civil partnership or separation of civil partners

49.14A

49.14A.—(1)[4] In the following actions of dissolution of civil partnership or separation of civil partners, there shall be attached to the copy of the summons served on the defender—

(a)[5] in an action relying on section 117(3)(c) of the CP Act of 2004 (no cohabitation for one year with consent of defender to decree)—

    (i) which is an action of dissolution of a civil partnership, a notice in Form 49.14A-A and a form of notice of consent in Form 49.14A-B;

    (ii) which is an action of separation of civil partners, a notice in Form 49.14A-C and a form of notice of consent in Form 49.14A-D;

(b)[6] in an action relying on section 117(3)(d) of the CP Act of 2004 (no cohabitation for two years)—

    (i) which is an action of dissolution of a civil partnership, a notice in Form 49.14A-E;

    (ii) which is an action of separation of civil partners, a notice in Form 49.14A-F;

(c) in an action relying on section 117(2)(b) of the CP Act of 2004 (grounds of dissolution: interim gender recognition certificate), a notice in Form 49.14A-G.

---

[1] R. 49.14(1)(a) and (b) amended by S.S.I. 2006 No. 206 (effective 4th May 2006).
[2] R. 49.14(1)(a) and (b) amended by S.S.I. 2006 No. 206 (effective 4th May 2006).
[3] R. 49.14(1)(c) inserted by S.S.I. 2005 No. 19 (effective 1st April, 2005).
[4] R. 49.14A inserted by S.S.I. 2005 No. 632 (effective 8th December 2005).
[5] R. 49.14(1)(a) and (b) amended by S.S.I. 2006 No. 206 (effective 4th May 2006).
[6] R. 49.14(1)(a) and (b) amended by S.S.I. 2006 No. 206 (effective 4th May 2006).

(2) The certificate of service of a summons in an action mentioned in paragraph (1) shall state which notice or form mentioned in paragraph (1) has been included with the summons.

Orders for intimation by the court

49.15.—[1](1)[2] Except in relation to intimation to a child in Form 49.8A, in any family action, the court may, at any time—   **49.15**

    (a)   order intimation to be made to such person as it things fit;

    (b)   postpone intimation, where it considers that such postponement is appropriate and in that case, the court shall make such order in respect of postponement of intimation as it thinks fit; or

    (c)   dispense with intimation, where it considers that such dispensation is appropriate.

(3) Where a party makes an application or averment in a family action which, had it been made in a summons when presented for signeting, would have required a warrant for intimation under rule 49.8, that party shall apply by motion for a warrant for intimation or to dispense with such intimation; and rule 49.8 shall, with the necessary modifications, apply to a warrant under this paragraph as it applies to a warrant under that rule.

Deriv. R.C.S. 1965, r. 164 substituted by S.I. 1976 No. 1994 (r. 49.15(1))

"MOTION".

For motions, see Chap. 23.   **49.15.1**

"INTIMATION".

For methods, see r. 16.8.   **49.15.2**

"SECTION 11 ORDER".

See note 49.1.2.   **49.15.3**

LORD ADVOCATE.

Section 19(1) of the C.S.A. 1988 (intimation to the Lord Advocate where the court considers it necessary for the proper disposal of an action of declarator of nullity of marriage or for divorce) has been repealed by the Family Law (Scotland) Act 2006.   **49.15.4**

Interested persons entering process

49.16.—(1) A person on whom intimation has been made of a family action or an application in a family action, may apply by minute for leave to be sisted as a party and to lodge defences, answers or a minute, as the case may be—   **49.16**

    (a)   where the intimation was made on a warrant in a summons, within 7 days after the summons is lodged for calling; and

    (b)   in any other case, within the period of notice.

(2) Where the court grants a motion under paragraph (1), it shall make such order for further procedure as it thinks fit.

Deriv. R.C.S. 1965, r. 165 substituted by S.I. 1976 No. 1994

"MINUTE".

See r. 15.1. A fee will be payable on lodging a minute under this rule: see note 15.1.7.   **49.16.1**

"WITHIN 7 DAYS".

The date from which the period is calculated is not counted. Where the last day falls on a Saturday or Sunday or a public holiday on which the Office of Court is closed, the next available day is allowed: r. 1.3(7). For office hours and public holidays, see note 3.1.2.   **49.16.2**

---

[1] As amended by S.S.I. 2019 No. 123 para.2 (effective 24th June 2019).
[2] R. 49.15 amended by S.I. 1996 No. 2587 (effective 1st November 1996).

49.16.3   Section 19(1) of the C.S.A. 1988 (Lord Advocate may enter appearance as a party in any action of declarator of nullity of marriage or for divorce and lead such evidence and maintain such pleas as he thinks fit) has been repealed by the Family Law (Scotland) Act 2006.

Appointment of curators ad litem to defenders

49.17   **49.17.**[1](1)[2]   This rule applies to a family action, where it appears to the court that the defender has from a mental disorder.

(2)   In an action to which this rule applies, the court shall, after the expiry of the period for lodging defences—

    (a)   appoint a curator ad litem to the defender; and

    (b)   make an order requiring the curator ad litem to lodge in process a report, based on medical evidence, stating whether or not, in the opinion of a suitably qualified medical practitioner, the defender is incapable of instructing a solicitor to represent the defender's interests.

(3)   Within 7 days after the appointment of a curator ad litem under paragraph (2)(a), the pursuer shall send to him a copy of the summons and any defences lodged (including any adjustments and amendments).

(4)   On lodging a report under paragraph (2)(b), the curator ad litem must intimate that this has been done to—

    (a)   the pursuer; and

    (b)   the solicitor for the defender, if known.

(5)   Within 14 days after the report required under paragraph (2)(b) has been lodged, the curator ad litem must lodge in process one of the writs mentioned in paragraph (6).

(6)   The writs referred to in paragraph (5) are—

    (a)   defences to the action;

    (b)   a minute adopting defences already lodged in process; and

    (c)   a minute stating that the curator ad litem does not intend to lodge defences.

(7)   Notwithstanding that he has lodged a minute stating that he does not intend to lodge defences, a curator ad litem may appear at any stage of the action to protect the interests of the defender.

(8)   At such intervals as the curator ad litem considers reasonable having regard to the nature of the defender's mental disorder, the curator ad litem must review the defender's capacity to instruct a solicitor, in order to ascertain whether it is appropriate for the appointment to continue.

(8A)   If it appears to the curator ad litem that the defender may no longer be incapable, the curator ad litem must by motion seek the court's permission to obtain an opinion on the matter from a suitably qualified medical practitioner.

(8B)   If the motion under paragraph (8A) is granted, the curator ad litem must lodge in process a copy of the opinion as soon as possible.

(8C)   Where the opinion concludes that the defender is not incapable of instructing a solicitor, the curator *ad litem* must seek discharge from appointment by minute.

(9)   The pursuer shall be responsible, in the first instance, for payment of the fees and outlays of the curator ad litem incurred during the period from his appointment until—

    (a)   he lodges a minute stating that he does not intend to lodge defences;

    (b)   he decides to instruct the lodging of defences or a minute adopting defences already lodged; or

---

[1] R. 49.17 amended by S.S.I. 2017 No. 132 para.3 (effective 1st June 2017).
[2] R. 49.17(1) & (2)(b) inserted by S.S.I. 2005 No. 632 (effective 8th December 2005).

(c)   being satisfied after investigation that the defender is not incapable of instructing a solicitor, he is discharged.

Deriv. R.C.S. 1965, r. 167(1) substituted by S.I. 1976 No. 1994 (r. 49.17(1) to (7)); P.N. 10th February 1983 (r. 49.17(9))

GENERAL NOTE.

R. 49.17 is made under s. 11 of the Divorce (Scotland) Act 1976.   **49.17.1**

"MENTAL DISORDER".

This is defined in r. 49.1(2) as mental illness or mental handicap however caused or manifested. This   **49.17.2**
is the definition in s. 1 of the Mental Health (Scotland) Act 1984.

It will not be every mental disorder which will justify the appointment of a curator ad litem. Although it is not stated in the rule, the implication is, and the court would not normally make the appointment unless, the defender is incapable of managing his affairs or of giving instructions for their management. The practice is for the pursuer to produce medical certificates from two doctors (although with the abolition of the rule for corroboration by s. 1(1) of the Civil Evidence (Scotland) Act 1988, one should be sufficient).

On the duties of a curator ad litem, see *Finlay v. Finlay* 1962 S.L.T. (Sh.Ct.) 43. Rule 49.17(2)(b) requires a report from the curator and r. 49.17(8A) and (8C) requires the curator to keep the issue of capacity under review and to seek a discharge if the defender is no longer incapable of instructing a solicitor.

GUARDIANS.

Under s. 64(1)(c) of the Adults with Incapacity (Scotland) Act 2000, a guardian may be appointed to a   **49.17.2A**
person aged 16 or over, who is suffering from a mental disorder, with power to pursue or defend an action of nullity of marriage or divorce or separation.

"INCAPABLE".

This word is defined in r. 49.1(2).

"WITHIN 7 DAYS", "WITHIN 14 DAYS".

The date from which the period is calculated is not counted. In relation to r. 49.17(5), where the last   **49.17.3**
day falls on a Saturday or Sunday or a public holiday on which the Office of Court is closed, the next available day is allowed: r. 1.3(7). For office hours and public holidays, see note 3.1.2.

"SEND".

This includes deliver: r. 1.3(1) (definition of "send").   **49.17.4**

"SEEK HIS OWN DISCHARGE".

The curator should seek his discharge by minute: *Walls v. Walls* 1953 S.L.T. 269.   **49.17.5**

Applications for sist

49.18.   An application for a sist, or the recall of a sist, under Schedule 3 to the   **49.18**
Domicile and Matrimonial Proceedings Act 1973 shall be made by motion.

Deriv. R.C.S. 1965, r. 167(2) substituted by S.I. 1976 No. 1994

GENERAL NOTE.

Sched. 3 to the Domicile and Matrimonial Proceedings Act 1973 contains provisions for the manda-   **49.18.1**
tory sist of proceedings before the court in certain circumstances and for a discretionary sist in others. On the exercise of the discretionary sist, see *Mitchell v. Mitchell* 1991 S.L.T. 410.

"MOTION".

For motions, see Chap. 23.   **49.18.2**

Applications for sist in actions involving civil partnerships

49.18A.—[1](1)   Schedule 3 to the Act of 1973 (sisting of consistorial actions in   **49.18A**
Scotland) shall apply to actions for dissolution of civil partnerships, separation of civil partners or declarator of nullity of civil partnerships subject to the following modifications—

(a)   for "consistorial action", wherever it appears, there shall be substituted "action concerning a civil partnership";

---

[1] R. 49.18A inserted by S.S.I. 2005 No. 632 (effective 8th December 2005).

    (b)   for "divorce", wherever it appears there shall be substituted "dissolution of a civil partnership";

    (c)   for "separation", wherever it appears, there shall be substituted "separation of civil partners";

    (d)   for "declarator of nullity of marriage", wherever it appears, there shall be substituted "declarator of nullity of a civil partnership";

    (e)   for "marriage", wherever it appears, there shall be substituted "civil partnership";

    (f)   for "spouse", wherever it appears, there shall be substituted "civil partner";

    (g)   in paragraph 2 "declarator of marriage" shall be omitted;

    (h)   in paragraph 8(b) for "marriage was contracted" there shall be substituted "civil partnership was registered";

    (i)   in paragraphs 4(a), 7, and 9(4) "or in a sheriff court" shall be omitted; (j) in paragraph 8 "or in the Sheriff Court" shall be omitted;

    (k)   in paragraph 9(1) "or in a sheriff court" shall be omitted.

(2)   An application for a sist or a recall of a sist under Schedule 3 to the Act of 1973 as it applies under paragraph (1) shall be made by motion.

GENERAL NOTE.

49.18A.1   Sched. 3 to the Domicile and Matrimonial Proceedings Act 1973 contains provisions for mandatory sist of proceedings before the court in certain circumstances and for a discretionary sist in others. On the exercise of the discretionary sist, see *Mitchell v. Mitchell* , 1991 S.L.T. 410.

"MOTION".

49.18A.2   For motions, see Chap. 23.

Notices of consent to divorce, separation, dissolution of civil partnership or separation of civil partners[1]

49.19   **49.19.**—(1)[2, 3]   Where, in an action of divorce, or separation in which the facts in section 1(2)(d) of the Act of 1976, or dissolution of a civil partnership or separation of civil partners in which the facts in section 117(3)(d) of the CP Act of 2004, (no cohabitation for one year with consent of defender to decree) are relied on, the defender wishes to consent to the grant of decree—

    (a)   of divorce or separation he shall do so by giving notice in writing in Form 49.14-B (divorce) or Form 49.14-D (separation), as the case may be; or

    (b)   of dissolution of a civil partnership or separation of civil partners, he shall do so by giving notice in writing in Form 49.14A-B (dissolution) or Form 49.14A-D (separation of civil partners), as the case may be;

to the Deputy Principal Clerk.

(2)   The evidence of one witness shall be sufficient for the purpose of establishing that the signature on a notice of consent under paragraph (1) is that of the defender.

(3)[4]   In an action of divorce, separation, dissolution of a civil partnership, or separation of civil partners where the summons includes for the purposes of section 1(2)(d) of the Act of 1976, or section 117(3)(d) of the CP Act of 2004, as the case may be, an averment that the defender consents to the grant of decree, the defender may give notice by letter to the Deputy Principal Clerk stating that he has not so consented or that he withdraws any consent which he has already given.

(4)   On receipt of a letter under paragraph (3), the Deputy Principal Clerk shall—

---

[1] Heading and Rule 49.19(1) & (3) substituted by S.S.I. 2005 No. 632 (effective 8th December 2005).

[2] Heading and Rule 49.19(1) & (3) substituted by S.S.I. 2005 No. 632 (effective 8th December 2005).

[3] Rule 49.14(1)(a) and (b) amended by S.S.I. 2006 No. 206 (effective 4th May 2006).

[4] Heading and Rule 49.19(1) & (3) substituted by S.S.I. 2005 No. 632 (effective 8th December 2005).

(a) cause the letter to be lodged in process; and

(b) give written intimation of the terms of the letter to the pursuer.

(5)[1] On receipt of an intimation under paragraph (4)(b), the pursuer may, within 14 days after the date of the intimation, if none of the other facts mentioned in section 1(2) of the Act of 1976 or section 117(3) of the CP Act of 2004, as the case may be, is averred in the summons, apply by motion for the action to be sisted.

(6) If no such motion is enrolled, the pursuer shall be deemed to have abandoned the action and the action shall be dismissed.

(7) If a motion under paragraph (5) is granted and the sist is not recalled or renewed within a period of six months from the date of the interlocutor granting the sist, the pursuer shall be deemed to have abandoned the action and the action shall be dismissed.

Deriv. R.C.S. 1965, r. 166 substituted by S.I. 1976 No. 1994

"SENT".

This includes deliver: r. 1.3(1) (definition of "send").   **49.19.1**

"WITHIN 14 DAYS".

The date from which the period is calculated is not counted. Where the last day falls on a Saturday or Sunday or a public holiday on which the Office of Court is closed, the next available day is allowed: r. 1.3(7). For office hours and public holidays, see note 3.1.2.   **49.19.2**

"MOTION".

For motions, see Chap. 23.   **49.19.3**

Views of the child – undefended actions

49.20.—[2](1) This rule applies to undefended actions in which a section 11 order is sought and warrant has been granted for intimation and the seeking of the child's views in Form 49.8A.   **49.20**

(2) The pursuer must—

(a) following the expiry of the period for lodging defences, send the child the Form 49.8A that was submitted and approved under rule 49.8A (warrants and forms for intimation to a child and for seeking a child's views);

(b) lodge with the minute for decree a certificate of intimation in Form 49.8B;

(c) not send the child a copy of the summons.

(3) Except on cause shown, the court must not grant decree in the period of 28 days following the date on which the Form 49.8A was sent to the child.

GENERAL NOTE.

The former r. 49.20 is now in new r. 49.20D. New r. 49.20 is now concerned with when the Form 49.8A is to be sent to the child in an undefended action (and r. 49.20A deals with defended actions in which only the pursuer seeks a section 11 order). The Form 49.8A has to be approved (or dispensed with) by the court under r. 49.8A.   **49.20.1**

Views of the child – section 11 order sought by pursuer only

49.20A.—[3](1) This rule applies to defended actions in which only the pursuer seeks a section 11 order and warrant has been granted for intimation and the seeking of the child's views in Form 49.8A.   **49.20A**

(2) The pursuer must—

(a) no later than 14 days after defences are lodged, send the child the Form 49.8A that was submitted and approved under rule 49.8A (warrants and forms for intimation to a child and for seeking a child's views);

(b) on the same day, lodge a certificate of intimation in Form 49.8B;

---

[1] Rule 49.19(5) amended by S.S.I. 2005 No. 632 (effective 8th December 2005).
[2] As substituted by S.S.I. 2019 No. 123 para.2 (effective 24th June 2019).
[3] As inserted by S.S.I. 2019 No. 123 para.2 (effective 24th June 2019).

    (c)   not send the child a copy of the summons or the defences.

GENERAL NOTE.

49.20A.1   New r. 49.20 is concerned with when the Form 49.8A is to be sent to the child in a defended action where the pursuer seeks a section 11 order. The Form 49.8A has to be approved (or dispensed with) by the court under r. 49.8A. Rule 49.20C deals with where both pursuer and defender seek s. 11 orders.

Views of the child – section 11 order sought by defender only

49.20B   **49.20B.**—[1](1) This rule applies to defended actions in which only the defender seeks a section 11 order and warrant has been granted for intimation and the seeking of the child's views in Form 49.8A.

    (2) The defender must—

    (a)   no later than 14 days after warrant to intimate to the child is granted under rule 49.31(7) (defences in family actions), send the child the Form 49.8A that was submitted and approved under rule 49.31;

    (b)   on the same day, lodge a certificate of intimation in Form 49.8B;

    (c)   not send the child a copy of the summons or the defences.

GENERAL NOTE.

49.20B.1   New r. 49.20B is now concerned with when the Form 49.8A is to be sent to the child in defended action where the defender seeks a section 11 order. The Form 49.8A has to be approved (or dispensed with) by the court under r. 49.8A. Rule 49.20C deals with where both pursuer and defender seek s. 11 orders.

Views of the child – section 11 orders sought by both pursuer and defender

49.20C   **49.20C.**—[2](1) This rule applies to defended actions in which section 11 orders are sought by both the pursuer and the defender and warrant has been granted for intimation and the seeking of the child's views in Form 49.8A.

    (2) The pursuer must—

    (a)   no later than 14 days after defences are lodged, send the child the Form 49.8A that was submitted and approved under rule 49.8A (warrants and forms for intimation to a child and for seeking a child's views), amended so as also to narrate the section 11 order sought by the defender;

    (b)   on the same day—

        (i)   lodge a certificate of intimation in Form 49.8B;

        (ii) send the defender a copy of the Form 49.8A that was sent to the child;

    (c)   not send the child a copy of the summons or the defences.

GENERAL NOTE.

49.20C.1   New r. 49.20C is now concerned with when the Form 49.8A is to be sent to the child in defended action where both the pursuer and defender seek a section 11 order. The Form 49.8A has to be approved (or dispensed with) by the court under r. 49.8A.

Views of the child – the court's role

49.20D   **49.20D.**—[3](1) In a family action, in relation to any matter affecting a child, where that child has—

    (a)   returned a Form 49.8A to the court; or

    (b)   otherwise indicated to the court a wish to express views,

the court must not grant any order unless an opportunity has been given for the views of that child to be obtained or heard.

---

[1] As inserted by S.S.I. 2019 No. 123 para.2 (effective 24th June 2019).
[2] As inserted by S.S.I. 2019 No. 123 para.2 (effective 24th June 2019).
[3] As inserted by S.S.I. 2019 No. 123 para.2 (effective 24th June 2019).

(2)   Where the court is considering making an interim section 11 order before the views of the child have been obtained or heard, the court must consider whether, and if so how, to seek the child's views in advance of making the order.

(3)   Where a child has indicated a wish to express views, the court must order any steps to be taken that it considers appropriate to obtain or hear the views of that child.

(4)   The court must not grant an order in a family action, in relation to any matter affecting a child who has expressed views, unless the court has given due weight to the views expressed by that child, having regard to the child's age and maturity.

(5)   In any action in which a section 11 order is sought, where Form 49.8A has not been sent to the child concerned or where it has been sent but the court considers that the passage of time requires it to be sent again, the court may at any time order any party to—

    (a)   send the Form 49.8A to that child within a specified timescale;

    (b)   on the same day, lodge—

        (i)   a copy of the Form 49.8A that was sent to the child;

        (ii)   a certificate of intimation in Form 49.8C.".

GENERAL NOTE.

Paragraphs (1) to (3) of r. 49.20D were formerly r. 49.20.   **49.20D.1**

Under art. 12 of the UN Convention on the Rights of the Child (Cm. 1976 (1992)), ratified by the UK on 16th December 1991, a child who is capable of forming his own views has the right to express those views freely in all matters affecting him and his views must be given due weight in accordance with his age and maturity. For this purpose the child must be given the opportunity to be heard in any judicial and administrative proceedings affecting him, either directly or through a representative or appropriate body, in a manner consistent with the procedural rules of national law. This principle is now enshrined in s. 11(7) of the Children (Scotland) Act 1995.

The child need not become a party, and may express his views by writing a letter or be given an opportunity to express his views orally to the judge in private: a form (Form 49.8-N) is sent to the child. The formal process of intimation in Form 49.8-N should not be the principal mode of complying with s. 11(7)(b) of the Children (Scotland) Act 1995: *S v. S* , 2002 S.C. 246 (Ex Div.) sub nom. *Shields v. Shields* , 2002 S.L.T. 579 and see further, note 49.20.2. A child should be able to instruct a solicitor: Age of Legal Capacity (Scotland) Act 1991, s. 2(1)(a).

The court cannot always know in advance whether a child is capable of forming his own views and a minimum age cannot be laid down. On the other hand a child cannot know he has the right to be heard unless he is informed of that right. There appears to be no alternative but to provide for intimation in every case while providing in r. 49.8(8) for the court to dispense with intimation in certain circumstances (e.g. the child is a baby). There is a statutory presumption that a child of 12 or more is of sufficient age and maturity to form a view: Act of 1995, s. 11(10). See further, note 49.20.2.

R. 49.8(7) provides that the summons is not intimated to the child, but that a notice in Form 49.8-N is sent to him.

"ANY STEPS TO BE TAKEN AS IT CONSIDERS APPROPRIATE".

It is not clear what steps will be appropriate to ascertain the views of a child. One view is that a cura-   **49.20D.2**
tor ad litem must be appointed in every case. Sometimes a reporter (usually an officer of the court) is appointed to obtain a child's views. A person will be barred from working with children under s. 92 of the Protection of Vulnerable Groups (Scotland) Act 2007 if he or she is included in the Children's List under the Act or the equivalent lists kept under the equivalent legislation in England and Wales or Northern Ireland. Under P.N. No. 1 of 2011, para. 3, if a person is contacted by a clerk of court to ascertain if he or she is free to be appointed a reporter in a particular case, that person must inform the clerk if he or she is a barred individual.

In *S v. S* , 2002 S.C. 246 (Ex Div.), sub nom. *Shields v. Shields* , 2002 S.L.T. 579, paras [10] and [11], it was observed (1) that in affording a child the opportunity to make known his views the only test is practicality; (2) how the child should be given that opportunity depends on the circumstances including the child's age, and could be (a) by intimation in Form [49.8-N] (b) by seeing the child in chambers, (c) by the views of the child being made known to the court by a person known to the child or a child psychologist; (3) if it was practicable to give the child an opportunity to express his views, the only safe course was to employ whatever method was practicable; (4) the formal process of intimation in Form [49.8-N] should not be the principal mode of complying with s. 11(7)(b) of the Children (Scotland) Act 1995 and other methods must be preferable, particularly where younger children are involved or there is risk of upsetting the child; and (5) the duty on the court to comply with s. 11(7)(b) continues until the order is made and dispensing with formal intimation does not relieve the court from complying with that continuing duty. Rule 49.20D reflects (5).

Reports by local authorities under section 49(2) of the Act of 1975

49.21

49.21. [Revoked by SI 1996/2587 (effective 1st November 1996).]

GENERAL NOTE.

49.21.1

Reports by local authorities were required where the applicant for custody of a child was not a parent of the child under s. 49 of the Children Act 1975. Section 49 of the 1975 Act has been repealed, but not replaced, by the Children (Scotland) Act 1995. A report may still be requested: see r. 49.11 and note 49.11.1.

Child welfare reporters

49.22

49.22.—[1](1) At any stage of a family action the court may, in relation to any matter affecting a child, appoint a person (referred to in this rule as a "child welfare reporter")—

    (a) to seek the views of the child and to report any views expressed by the child to the court; or

    (b) to undertake enquiries and to report to the court.

(2) A child welfare reporter may only be appointed under paragraph (1)(b) where the court is satisfied that the appointment—

    (a) is in the best interests of the child; and

    (b) will promote the effective and expeditious determination of an issue in relation to the child.

(3) An interlocutor appointing a child welfare reporter must—

    (a) specify a date by which the report is to be submitted to the court;

    (b) include a direction as to the fees and outlays of the child welfare reporter;

    (c) where the appointment is under paragraph (1)(a), specify the issues in respect of which the child's views are to be sought and include a direction as to whether a copy of the report is to be provided to the parties under paragraph (9)(d);

    (d) where the appointment is under paragraph (1)(b), specify the enquiries to be undertaken, and the issues requiring to be addressed in the report; and

    (e) where the appointment is under paragraph (1)(b) and seeking the views of the child forms part of the enquiries to be undertaken, include a direction as to whether the views of the child should be recorded in a separate report and, if so, whether a copy of that report is to be provided to the parties under paragraph (9)(d).".

(4) An interlocutor complies with subparagraph (c) or (d) of paragraph (3) if the issues or, as the case may be, the enquiries referred to in that subparagraph are specified in an annex to the interlocutor in Form 49.22.

(5) Where the court has appointed a child welfare reporter with a view to the report being considered at an assigned hearing, the date specified in accordance with paragraph (3)(a) must be a date no less than three clear days before that hearing, excluding any day on which the Office of Court is not open, unless cause is shown for specifying a later date.

(6) On appointing a child welfare reporter, the court may also—

    (a) make such further order as may be required to facilitate the discharge of the child welfare reporter's functions;

    (b) direct that a party to the proceedings is to be responsible for providing the child welfare reporter with copies of such documents lodged in the process as may be specified; and

    (c) give the child welfare reporter directions.

---

[1] Rule 49.22 substituted by S.S.I. 2015 No. 312 (effective 26th October 2015).

(7) The direction referred to in paragraph (3)(b) must assign liability for payment of the child welfare reporter's fees and outlays in the first instance, and require that liability to be borne—

    (a)   in equal shares by—

         (i)   the pursuer;

        (ii)   any defender who has entered appearance; and

      (iii)   any other person who has been sisted as a party to the proceedings; or

    (b)   by one or more parties to the proceedings on such other basis as may be justified on cause shown.

(8) On the granting of an interlocutor appointing a child welfare reporter the Deputy Principal Clerk must—

    (a)   give the child welfare reporter—

         (i)   a certified copy of the interlocutor, and

        (ii)   sufficient information to enable the child welfare reporter to contact the solicitor for each party to the proceedings, or any party not represented by a solicitor; and

      (iii)   intimate the name and address of the child welfare reporter to any local authority to which intimation of the proceedings has been made.

(9) A child welfare reporter appointed under this rule must—

    (a)   where the appointment is under paragraph (1)(a)—

         (i)   seek the child's views on the specified issues, and

        (ii)   prepare a report for the court reporting any such views;

    (b)   where the appointment is under paragraph (1)(b)—

         (i)   undertake the specified enquiries, and

        (ii)   prepare a report for the court having regard to the specified issues;

    (c)   send the report to the Deputy Principal Clerk by the date specified;

    (d)   unless otherwise directed, send a copy of the report to each party to the proceedings by that date.

(10) A child welfare reporter may—

    (a)[1]   apply to the Deputy Principal Clerk to be given further directions by the court;

    (b)   bring to the attention of the Deputy Principal Clerk any impediment to the performance of any function arising under this rule.

(11) Where a child welfare reporter acts as referred to in paragraph (10), the court may, having heard parties, make any order or direction that could competently have been made under paragraph (6).

Deriv. R.C.S. 1965, r. 170B(14)(c), (d), (f) and (g) inserted by S.I. 1990 No. 705, and r. 260D(4), (5), (7) and (8) inserted by S.I. 1986 No. 515, (r. 49.22(1), (4) and (5)); P.N. November 13, 1969, para. 3 (r. 49.22(2)(b))

GENERAL NOTE.

    Section 11(1) of the Matrimonial Proceedings (Children) Act 1958 gives the court a power in proceedings between husband and wife to order a report from a local authority, without prejudice to its power to order a report from any other person, on the circumstances of the child and the proposed arrangements for his care and upbringing. The reporter may be required to appear and be examined and cross-examined on oath: 1958 Act s. 11(4). The reporter should not be cited as a witness unless so required: P.N. 6th June 1968.

    The court's powers under the above statutory provision is without prejudice to its power, recognised in r. 49.22(1)(b), to appoint any person to investigate and report.

49.22.1

---

[1] Rule 49.22(10)(a) amended by S.S.I. 2016 No. 102 (effective 21 March 2016).

The court is free to accept statements of fact in the report along with any other relevant facts proved in the action: *Macintyre v. Macintyre* 1962 S.L.T. (Notes) 70.

"SECTION 11 ORDER".

49.22.2   See note 49.1.2.

"SEND".

49.22.3   This includes deliver: r. 1.3(1) (definition of "send").

Appointment of local authority to report on a child

49.22A   **49.22A.—**[1](1)   This rule applies where the court appoints a local authority to investigate and report to the court on the circumstances of a child and on the proposed arrangements for the care and upbringing of the child.

(2)   The following provisions of rule 49.22 apply as if the reference to the child welfare reporter was a reference to the local authority appointed by the court—

(a)   paragraph (3)(a) and (b);

(b)   paragraph (6)(a) and (b);

(c)   paragraph (7); and

(d)   paragraph (8).

(3)   On completion of the report referred to in paragraph (1), the local authority must—

(a)   send the report to the Deputy Principal Clerk; and

(b)   unless otherwise directed by the court, send a copy of the report to each party to the proceedings.

"SEND".

49.22A.1   This includes deliver: r. 1.3(1) (definition of "send").

Referral to family mediation

49.23   **49.23.**[2, 3]   In any family action in which an order in relation to parental responsibilities or parental rights is in issue, the court may, at any stage of the action where it considers it appropriate to do so, refer that issue to a mediator accredited to a specified family mediation organisation.

Deriv. R.C.S. 1965, r. 170B(15), and r. 260D(10), both inserted by S.I. 1990 No. 705

GENERAL NOTE.

49.23.1   Mediation is concerned with helping parties resolve difficulties arising out of the breakdown of a marriage, particularly in relation to residence and contact (custody and access) of children. There are mediation services available throughout Scotland. For further information, contact Relationships Scotland, *www.relationships-scotland.org.uk*, 18 York Place, Edinburgh, EH1 3EP (tel. 0345 119 2020). The Law Society of Scotland also accredits mediators, most of whom join CALM (Comprehensive Accredited Lawyer Mediators) *www.calmscotland.co.uk* who mediate on financial matters as well. For further information, contact Law Society of Scotland, Atria One, 144 Morrison Street, Edinburgh EH3 8EX; tel. 0131 226 7411; *www.lawscot.co.uk*. The Act does not apply to the extent that the Hague Convention on Child Abduction matters are discussed: *M v M,* 2015 S.L.T. 683 (OH).

Under s. 1 of the Civil Evidence (Family Mediation) (Scotland) Act 1995, information as to what occurred during family mediation (whether or not on a referral by the court) conducted by an accredited mediator of an approved organisation is not admissible in evidence in civil proceedings. S. 1 of the 1995 Act does not apply to civil proceedings in which evidence has been given or heard (in whole or in part) at any time prior to 19th February 1996: Civil Evidence (Family Mediation) (Scotland) Act 1995 (Commencement and Transitional Provision) Order 1996. S.2 of the 1995 Act contains exceptions to the inadmissibility rule.

Family Mediation Scotland and CALM are approved organisations.

Approval of an organisation concerned with mediation is given by the Lord President and applications by organisations for approval should be made to the Scotland Office, Parliament House, Edinburgh EH1 IRQ.

---

[1] Rule 49.22A inserted by S.S.I. 2015 No. 312 (effective 26 October 2015).
[2] Rule 49.23 and heading amended by S.I. 1996 No. 1756 (effective 5th August 1996).
[3] Rule 49.23 amended by S.I. 1996 No. 2587 (effective 1st November 1996).

The requirement of consent of parties to mediation was removed by A.S. (R.C.S.A. No. 3) (Miscellaneous) 1996 [SI 1996/1756]. This brings r. 49.23 into line with the sheriff court rule (O.C.R. 1993, r. 33.22).

There are no legal requirements for consideration to be given to reconciliation between husband and wife. If the court considers there are prospects for reconciliation it may continue an action for such attempts to be made: Divorce (Scotland) Act 1976, s. 2(1). P.N. 11th March 1977 invites legal practitioners to encourage parties to seek advice and guidance from a marriage counsellor in those cases in which parties might be thought to benefit from it.

Applications for orders to disclose whereabouts of children

49.24.—(1)   An application for an order under section 33(1) of the Family Law Act 1986 (which relates to the disclosure of the whereabouts of a child) shall be made by motion.

(2)   Where the court makes an order under section 33(1) of the Family Law Act 1986, it may ordain the person against whom the order has been made to appear before it or to lodge an affidavit.

Deriv. R.C.S. 1965, r. 170B(12), and r. 260EB, both inserted by S.I. 1988 No. 615

GENERAL NOTE.

The court may order a person to disclose information about the whereabouts of a child: Family Law Act 1986, s. 33(1). Such a person may not refuse to answer on the ground of incrimination, and any answer may not be used in evidence for an offence other than perjury: 1986 Act, s. 33(2). The court has a common law power to order a person to make such a disclosure, to take evidence from such a person and to grant warrant to messengers-at-arms to search for children: *Abusaif v. Abusaif* 1984 S.L.T. 90, 91 *per* L.P. Emslie.

"MOTION".

For motions, see Chap. 23.

Applications in relation to removal of children

49.25.—(1)[1]   An application for leave under section 51(1) of the Act of 1975 (authority to remove a child from the care and possession of the applicant for a residence order) or for an order under section 35(3) of the Family Law Act 1986 (application for interdict or interim interdict prohibiting removal of child from jurisdiction)—

    (a)   by a party, shall be made by motion;

    (b)   by a person other than a party, shall be made by minute in the process of that action.

(2)   An application under section 35(3) of the Family Law Act 1986 need not be served or intimated.

(3)   An application under section 23(2) of the Child Abduction and Custody Act 1985 (declarator that removal of child from United Kingdom was unlawful) shall be made—

    (a)   in an action depending before the court—

        (i)   by a party, in the summons, defences or minute, as the case may be, or by motion; or

        (ii)   by any other person, by minute; or

    (b)   after final decree, by minute in the process of the action to which the application relates.

Deriv. R.C.S. 1965, r. 170B(13), and r. 260EC, both inserted by S.I. 1988 No. 615 (r. 49.25(1)(part)); r. 170C(2), and r. 260E(2) and (3), both inserted by S.I. 1986 No. 515 (r. 49.25(1)(part))

SECTION 51(1) OF THE ACT OF 1975.

Leave is required to remove a child from the care of the applicant for a residence order because it is an offence to remove the child without the authority of the court or an enactment: Children Act 1975, s. 51(1).

---

[1] Rule 49.25(1) amended by S.I. 1996 No. 2587 (effective 1st November 1996).

49.24

49.24.1

49.24.2

49.25

49.25.1

"RESIDENCE ORDER".

49.25.1A   This replaces, but is not the whole of, what was formerly custody. It means an order regulating arrangements as to with whom or with whom during what periods a child under 16 is to live: Children (Scotland) Act 1995, s. 11(2)(c).

SECTION 35(3) OF THE FAMILY LAW ACT 1986.

49.25.2   The court may interdict a person from removing a child, in respect of whom it has jurisdiction to make an order, from not only Scotland but from anywhere in the UK: Family Law Act 1986, s. 35(3). The court has jurisdiction other than in matrimonial proceedings to make an order as provided in ss. 9 (habitual residence), 10 (presence of child), 12 (emergency) and 15(2) (original order granted by court) of the 1986 Act. The court's jurisdiction in matrimonial proceedings (divorce, nullity or separation) is unaffected; and the court dealing with matrimonial proceedings has primacy in dealing with residence, custody, care or control of or contact with a child: 1986 Act, s. 11.

Interim interdict will be refused if there is no evidence that the child is likely to be removed furth of the UK: *Woodcock v. Woodcock* 1990 S.L.T. 848.

"MINUTE".

49.25.3   See r. 15.1.

"MOTION".

49.25.4   For motions, see Chap. 23.

Intimation to local authority before supervised contact order[1]

49.26   **49.26.**—(1)[2] Where the court, at its own instance or on the motion of a party, is considering making a contact order or an interim contact order subject to supervision by the social work department of a local authority, it shall ordain the party moving for such an order to intimate to the chief executive of that local authority (unless a party to the action and represented at the hearing at which the issue arises)—

(a) the terms of any relevant motion;

(b) the intention of the court to order that the contact order be supervised by the social work department of that local authority; and

(c) that the local authority shall, within such period as the court has determined—

   (i) notify the Keeper of the Rolls whether it intends to make representations to the court through counsel or other person having a right of audience or in writing; and

   (ii)[3] where it intends to make representations in writing, do so within that period.

(2) After receiving notice or written representations, as the case may be, under paragraph (1)(c), the Keeper of the Rolls shall put the action out on the By Order Roll before the Lord Ordinary on such a date as may be convenient, for the court to determine, after considering any representations of a local authority under paragraph (1), whether to order such supervision.

Deriv. P.N. No. 1 of 1988

"INTIMATE".

49.26.1   For methods, see r. 16.7.

"CONTACT ORDER".

49.26.2   A contact order is an order regulating the arrangements for maintaining personal relations and direct contact between a child under 16 and a person with whom he is not, or will not be, living: Children (Scotland) Act 1995, s. 11(2)(d).

---

[1] Rule 49.26(1) and heading amended by S.I. 1996 No. 2587 (effective 1 November 1996).
[2] Rule 49.26(1) and heading amended by S.I. 1996 No. 2587 (effective 1 November 1996).
[3] Rule 49.14(1)(a) and (b) amended by S.S.I. 2006 No. 206 (effective 4 May 2006).

Joint minutes

49.27.[1] Where any parties have reached agreement in relation to—

(a) a section 11 order,

(b) aliment for a child, or

(c) an order for financial provision,

a joint minute may be entered into expressing that agreement; and, subject to rule 49.20(3) (no order before views of child expressed), the court may grant decree in respect of those parts of the joint minute in relation to which it could otherwise make an order, whether or not such a decree would include a matter for which there was no conclusion or crave.

Deriv. R.C.S. 1965, r. 170B(5) inserted by S.I. 1976 No. 1994

49.27

General note.

A joint minute may record an agreement with provisions other than those mentioned in r. 47.27 and the court may interpone authority to such an agreement. But the court cannot grant decree in respect of anything in the joint minute *except* in relation to a matter listed in r. 47.27.

There are four points to note about the form of the joint minute. (1) The effect of the court interponing authority is to show that the agreement was made in the presence of the court and the court did not object to it: *Gow v. Henry* (1899) 2 F. 48, 53 per Lord Young obiter. The authority of the court is not required, however, to bind the parties to the agreement signed by or on their behalf, and there is no *locus poenitentiae* until such authority is interponed: *Gow*, above; *McAthey v. Patriotic Investment Society Ltd* 1910 1 S.L.T. 121; *Lothian v. Lothian* 1965 S.L.T. 368; *Jongejan v. Jongejan* 1993 S.L.T. 595. The fact that the joint minute is stated to be conditional "in the event of decree of divorce being pronounced" does not enable one party to resile from it: *Lothian*, above. (2) Where a joint minute requests the court to "interpone authority hereto and to grant decree in terms thereof [*or in terms of specified paragraphs*]", the subsequent decree and not the agreement regulates those provisions of the agreement in respect of which decree has been granted. (3) Where a joint minute records an agreement and requests the court to "interpone authority hereto and to make no order for aliment [or financial provision] [or to assoilzie the defender from the ... conclusion of the summons (*or as the case may be*)]", if the court grants decree accordingly, the agreement in the joint minute will regulate the position of the parties. (4) The joint minute must clearly state what the parties are requesting the court to do, i.e. to interpone authority to it, to grant decree in terms of all or some (and if so which) of its paragraphs; or, in granting decree in terms of some of it, to assoilzie any party from a particular conclusion or crave.

Even an agreement in a joint minute will be subject to the power of the court under s. 16 of the Act of 1985 to vary or set aside a term relating to periodical allowance where the agreement expressly provides for the court to do it or a term where the agreement was not fair and reasonable at the time it was made. An agreement relating to periodical allowance may also be set aside or varied which is affected by sequestration or a voluntary trust deed of one of the parties or where a maintenance assessment has been made under the Child Support Act 1991.

It should also be noted that a joint minute which is a maintenance agreement (i.e. an agreement for making or securing periodical payment of aliment to or for the benefit of a child) for less than could be awarded under a maintenance assessment will be insecure because an application to the Child Support Agency for a maintenance assessment cannot be prevented: Child Support Act 1991, s. 9. The court's power to award aliment for a child is dealt with in ss. 3 and 8 of the 1991 Act.

49.27.1

Fee.

A court fee is payable on lodging a joint minute by a party other than an originating party who makes his first appearance by signing a joint minute. For fee, see Court of Session etc. Fees Order 1997, Table of Fees, Pt. I, B, item 6 [S.I. 1997 No. 688, as amended, pp. C1201 et seq.]. Certain persons are exempt from payment of fees: see 1997 Fees Order, art. 5 substituted by S.S.I. 2002 No. 270. A fee exemption certificate must be lodged in process: see P.N. No.1 of 2002.

Where the new party is legally represented, the fee may be debited under a credit scheme introduced on 1st April 1976 by P.N. No. 4 of 1976 to the account (if one is kept or permitted) of the agent by the court cashier, and an account will be rendered weekly by the court cashier's office to the agent for all court fees due that week for immediate settlement. Party litigants, and agents not operating the scheme, must pay (by cash, cheque or postal order) on each occasion a fee is due at the time of lodging at the counter at the General Department.

49.27.2

Expenses of curator ad litem appointed to a child

49.27A.[2] Where in any family action a curator ad litem is appointed to a child, the pursuer shall be responsible, in the first instance, for payment of the fees and

49.27A

---

[1] Rule 49.27 amended by S.I. 1996 No. 2587 (effective 1st November 1996).
[2] Rule 49.27A inserted by S.I. 1999 No. 109 (effective 29 October 1999).

outlays of the curator ad litem incurred during the period from his appointment until the occurrence of any of the following events—

    (a)   the lodging of a minute by the curator stating that he does not intend to lodge defences;

    (b)   the curator instructing the lodging of defences or a minute adopting defences which are already lodged; or

    (c)   the discharge, before the occurrence of the events mentioned in subparagraphs (a) and (b), of the curator.

GENERAL NOTE.

49.27A.1   The problem that this new rule addresses is the funding of work of a curator ad litem appointed before legal aid is granted directly to a child.

    The rule was inserted by A.S. (R.C.S.A. No. 7) (Miscellaneous) 1999 [S.S.I. 1999 No. 109]. The pursuer is analagous to that for appointment of a curator ad litem to a defender in a divorce act under r. 49.17.

CURATORS AD LITEM.

49.27A.2   A curator ad litem is a person appointed by the court to act for a child, or a person under some disability, to protect the child's interests in the action. The common law power of the court to appoint a curator ad litem to a child under the age of 16 is preserved by the Age of Legal Capacity (Scotland) Act 1991, s. 1(3)(f)(ii). Normally the child's parent or guardian will act as the child's legal representative, but in a family action there may be a conflict of interest between the child and that representative. The circumstances in which a curator may be appointed include:- where there is no parent or guardian; where the action is by the legal representative against the child or the child against the legal representative; where the child brings an action and the legal representative will not act; where there is a conflict of interest between the child and the legal representative; where there is not necessarily a conflict of interest but the child's interests nonetheless require protection.

    A curator ad litem takes the oath *de fideli administratione*. The responsibilities of the curator do not extend beyond the subject of the action. They do not extend to the estate of the child. The appointment may be recalled by the court and in any event terminates with the action. The curator must exercise independent judgment. He may conduct or compromise the action and is the dominus litis (*M'Cuaig v. M'Cuaig* 1909 S.C. 355, 357 *per* L.P. Dunedin): *Dewar v. Dewar's Trs* (1906) 14 S.L.T. 238, 239 *per* Lord Dundas. In relation to remuneration and outlays, where the pursuer is not the child to whom the curator is appointed, the pursuer is, by r. 49.27A, responsible in the first instance for these expenses. Where the pursuer is the child to whom the curator is appointed, the curator (if the court has not made another party responsible) may apply to the court to direct that funds are made available from any appropriate source or he should apply for legal aid: see *L, Petr. (No. 4)* 1997 S.L.T. 44. In that case the curator was not covered by legal aid for part of his work and, because the court considered that no other party should bear the cost, the court ordered payment out of public funds. The curator is not personally responsible for expenses if not successful in the action.

Corrected gender recognition certificates

49.27B   **49.27B.**—(1)[1]   An application after final decree for a corrected gender recognition certificate under section 6 of the Act of 2004 shall be made by minute in the process of the action in which the full gender recognition certificate was issued.

    (2) Where the court issues a corrected gender recognition certificate, the Deputy Principal Clerk shall send a certified copy of the certificate to the Secretary of State.

"CORRECTED GENDER RECOGNITION CERTIFICATE".

49.27B.1   Under the Gender Recognition Act 2004 a person may apply for a gender recognition certificate on the basis of living in the other gender or having changed gender. Where the certificate was issued by the court (which would occur in divorce proceedings) and there is an error in the certificate, an application may be made to the court for a corrected certificate under s. 6.

"MINUTE".

49.27B.2   For applications by minute, see r. 15.1.

"SEND".

49.27B.3   This includes deliver: r. 1.3(1) (definition of "send").

---

[1] Rule 49.27B inserted by S.S.I. 2005 No. 193 (effective 1 April 2005).

Applications for postponement of decree under section 3A of the Act of 1976

49.27C.[1] An application under section 3A(1) (application for postponement of decree where impediment to religious marriage exists) or section 3A(4) (application for recall of postponement) of the Act of 1976 shall be made by minute in the process of the action to which the application relates.

49.27C

"MINUTE".

For applications by minute, see r. 15.1.

49.27C.1

Part II – Undefended Family Actions

Evidence in certain undefended family actions

49.28.—(1) This rule—

49.28

  (a) subject to sub-paragraph (b), applies to all family actions in which no defences have been lodged, other than a family action—

      (i)   [Revoked by S.S.I. 2019 No. 123.]

      (ii) for financial provision after an overseas divorce or annulment within the meaning of Part IV of the Matrimonial and Family Proceedings Act 1984; or

      (iii) for an order under the Act of 1981;

      (iv)[2] for financial provision after overseas proceedings to dissolve or annul a civil partnership within the meaning of Schedule 11 to the CP Act of 2004; or

      (v)[3] for an order under Chapter 3 or 4 of Part 3 of the CP Act of 2004;

      (vi)[4] for declarator of recognition, or non-recognition, of a relevant foreign decree within the meaning of section 7(9) of the Domicile and Matrimonial Proceedings Act 1973;

      (vii)[5] for declarator of recognition, or non-recognition, of a relevant foreign decree within the meaning of paragraph 1 of Schedule 1B to the Domicile and Matrimonial Proceedings Act 1973, or of a judgment to which paragraph 2(1)(b) of that Schedule refers.

  (b) applies to a family action in which a curator ad litem has been appointed under rule 49.17(2)(a) where the curator ad litem to the defender has lodged a minute intimating that he does not intend to lodge defences;

  (c) applies to any family action which proceeds at any stage as undefended where the court so directs;

  (d) applies to the merits of a family action which is undefended on the merits where the court so directs, notwithstanding that the action is defended on an ancillary matter.

(2) Unless the court otherwise directs, evidence shall be given by affidavit.

(3) Unless the court otherwise directs, evidence relating to the welfare of a child shall be given by affidavit, at least one affidavit being sworn by a person other than a parent or party to the action.

(4) Evidence in the form of a written statement bearing to be the professional opinion of a duly qualified medical practitioner, which has been signed by him and lodged in process, shall be admissible in place of parole evidence by him.

---

[1] Rule 49.27(C) inserted by S.S.I. 2006 No. 206 (effective 4 May 2006) and amended by S.S.I. 2007 No. 7 r. 9 (effective 26 February 2007).
[2] Rule 49.28(1)(a)(iv) and (v) inserted by S.S.I. 2005 No. 632 (effective 8 December 2005).
[3] Rule 49.28(1)(a)(iv) and (v) inserted by S.S.I. 2005 No. 632 (effective 8 December 2005).
[4] Rule 49.28(1)(a)(vi) inserted by S.S.I. 2010 No. 417 (effective 1 January 2011).
[5] Rule 49.28(1)(a)(vii) inserted by S.S.I. 2014 No. 302 r.2 (effective 16 December 2014).

(5)[1] Rule 36.8 (lodging of certain written statements) shall not apply in an undefended family action to which this rule applies.

Deriv. R.C.S. 1965, r. 168(1), (2), (5) and (6) substituted by S.I. 1978 No. 106 and amended by S.I. 1980 No. 1144 (r. 49.28(1) to (4))

General note.

49.28.1   In certain family actions, even if undefended, decree cannot be granted without the grounds of action being established by evidence; these are actions for divorce, separation, declarator of marriage, nullity of marriage, legitimacy, legitimation, illegitimacy, parentage or non-parentage: Civil Evidence (Scotland) Act 1988, s. 8(1) and (2). The grounds of action are not limited to the conclusion concerning status (e.g. divorce) but include a conclusion for financial provision. Except where parties are agreed, there must be evidence before the court which must be considered by the judge before an award for financial provision can be made: *Gould v. Gould* , 1966 S.C. 88; *Ali v. Ali* , 2001 S.C. 618.

In undefended family actions specified in r. 49.28(1), the evidence may be by affidavit evidence alone. Although the requirement for corroboration has been abolished by s. 1(1) of the 1988 Act, in an action of divorce, separation, declarator of marriage or nullity of marriage evidence must consist of or include evidence other than that of a party to the marriage: 1988 Act, s. 8(3).

If the court is not satisfied on the evidence, it may continue the case to enable the pursuer to adduce additional evidence: *Paterson v. Paterson* 1958 S.C. 141, 146 per L.P. Clyde.

The requirement for evidence in section 11 orders was removed by A.S. (RCS 1994 and OCR 1993 Amendment) (Views of the Child) [S.S.I. 2019 No. 123].

"section 11 order".

49.28.2   See note 49.1.2.

"affidavits".

49.28.3   On the form and requirements of an affidavit, see P.N. No. 1 of 2004. Note also the definition of an affidavit in r. 1.3(2).

"any family action which proceeds at any stage as undefended where the court so directs".

49.28.4   The court so directs in undefended divorce actions even where custody, access or aliment is sought.

Fee.

49.28.5   A court fee is payable for initial lodging of affidavits in a family action where proof by affidavit evidence has been allowed on the Procedure Roll. For fee, see Court of Session etc. Fees Order 1997, Table of Fees, Pt. I, B, item 7 [S.I. 1997 No. 688, as amended, pp. C 1201 et seq.]. Certain persons are exempt from payment of fees: see 1997 Fees Order, art. 5 substituted by SSI 2002 No. 270. A fee exemption certificate must be lodged in process: see P.N. No.1 of 2002.

Where the pursuer is legally represented, the fee may be debited under a credit scheme introduced on 1st April 1976 by P.N. No. 4 of 1976 to the account (if one is kept or permitted) of the agent by the court cashier, and an account will be rendered weekly by the court cashier's office to the agent for all court fees due that week for immediate settlement. An agent not on the credit scheme or a party litigant must pay (by cash, cheque or postal order) at the public counter of the General Department.

Procedure for decree in actions under rule 49.28

49.29   **49.29.**—(1) In an action to which rule 49.28 (evidence in certain undefended family actions) applies, if counsel or other person having a right of audience, on consideration of the available affidavits and supporting documents, is satisfied that a motion for decree may properly be made, he may, at any time after the expiry of the period for lodging defences, move the court by minute in Form 49.29-A to grant decree in terms of the conclusions of the summons or in such restricted terms as may be appropriate.

(2) On lodging such a minute in process, the pursuer shall—

(a)   lodge in process the documents specified in the schedule to the minute; and

(b)   send to the Deputy Principal Clerk, Form 49.29-B duly completed.

(3) The court may, at any time after the minute and other documents referred to in paragraph (2) have been lodged, without requiring the appearance of counsel or other person having a right of audience—

---

[1] Rule 49.28(5) amended by S.S.I. 2001 No. 305 para. 7(2) (effective 18 September 2001).

(a)   grant decree in terms of the motion for decree contained in the minute; or

(b)   put the action out on the By Order Roll before the Lord Ordinary for such further procedure, if any, including proof by parole evidence, as the court thinks fit.

(4)   Notice shall be given in the rolls of all decrees granted under paragraph (3)(a).

Deriv. R.C.S. 1965, r. 168(7) to (11) substituted by S.I. 1978 No. 106

DATE OF DECREE.

The date of the decree will be the date on which notice of the decree appears in the rolls under r. 49.29(4) and not the date on which the interlocutor was signed: *Smith v. Smith* 1989 S.L.T. 668.

49.29.1

No suspension in undefended actions of divorce or civil partnerships[1]

49.30.   A defender may not bring any proceedings for the suspension of any decree of divorce or dissolution of a civil partnership pronounced in an undefended action.

49.30

Deriv. R.C.S. 1965, r. 170A inserted by S.I. 1976 No. 1994

GENERAL NOTE.

As suspension of decree of divorce in an undefended action is not competent, such a decree can be reduced only in an action of reduction or *ope exceptiones* in another action. The Court of Session has jurisdiction to reduce any decree granted by a Scottish court whether or not jurisdiction exists independently in the action of reduction: Law Reform (Miscellaneous Provisions) (Scotland) Act 1980, s. 20. On reduction generally, see Chap. 53.

49.30.1

A defender may not reclaim a decree in an undefended family action if he has not entered appearance: rr. 38.2, 38.3 and 1.3(1) (definition of "party"). It should be noted that R.C.S. 1965, r. 169(1)(c) (power of court to allow defender not present at proof in an undefended consistorial action to reclaim) has not been re-enacted.

Part III – Defended Family Actions

Defences in family actions

49.31.—[2](1)   This rule applies where the defender in a family action seeks—

49.31

(a)   to oppose any conclusion in the summons;

(b)   to make a claim for—

    (i)   aliment;

    (ii)   an order for financial provision within the meaning of section 8(3) of the Act of 1985; or

    (iii)[3]   a section 11 order; or

(c)   an order—

    (i)   under section 16(1)(b) or (3) of the Act of 1985 (setting aside or varying agreement as to financial provision);

    (ii)   under section 18 of the Act of 1985 (which relates to avoidance transactions); or

    (iii)   under the Act of 1981; or

    (iv)[4]   under Chapter 3 or 4 of Part 3 of the CP Act of 2004

(d)   to challenge the jurisdiction of the court.

(2)   In an action to which this rule applies, the defender shall—

(a)   lodge defences to the action in process; and

(b)   make any claim or seek any order, as the case may be, referred to in paragraph (1) in those defences by setting out in those defences—

    (i)   conclusions;

---

[1] Heading and r. 49.30 amended by S.S.I. 2005 No. 632 (effective 8 December 2005).

[2] As amended by S.S.I. 2019 No. 123 para.2 (effective 24th June 2019).

[3] Rule 49.31(1)(b)(iii) amended by S.I. 1996 No. 2587 (effective 1st November 1996).

[4] Rule 49.31(1)(c)(iv) inserted by SSI 2005 No. 632 (effective 8th December 2005).

     (ii)   averments in the answers to the condescendence in support of those conclusions; and

     (iii) appropriate pleas-in-law.

(3) Subject to paragraph (4), where the defences include a conclusion for a section 11 order in respect of a child who is not a party to the action and where the summons does not include a conclusion for a section 11 order, the defender must, when the defences are lodged—

     (a) apply by motion for a warrant for intimation and the seeking of the child's views in Form 49.8A;

     (b) submit a draft Form 49.8A, showing the details that the defender proposes to include when the form is sent to the child.

(4) Where the defender considers that it would be inappropriate to send Form 49.8A to the child (for example, where the child is under 5 years of age), the defender must—

     (a) when the defences are lodged, apply by motion for the court to dispense with intimation and the seeking of the child's views in Form 49.8A, specifying which numbered paragraphs of the defences contain the reasons for the request;

     (b) include in the defences averments setting out the reasons why it is inappropriate to send Form 49.8A to the child.

(5) The court must be satisfied that the draft Form 49.8A submitted under paragraph (3)(b) has been drafted appropriately.

(6) The court may dispense with intimation and the seeking of views in Form 49.8A or make any other order that it considers appropriate.

(7) An order granting warrant for intimation and the seeking of the child's views in Form 49.8A under this rule must—

     (a) state that the Form 49.8A must be sent to the child in accordance with rule 49.20B (views of the child – section 11 order sought by defender only);

     (b) be signed by the Lord Ordinary.".

Deriv. R.C.S. 1965, r. 170B(3) and (4) inserted by S.I. 1976 No. 1994; r. 170D(2) inserted by S.I. 1976 No. 1994 and amended by S.I. 1986 No. 1231, 1990 No. 705 and 1991 No. 1157; r. 170D(4)(a) substituted by S.I. 1977 No. 1621 and amended by S.I. 1986 No. 1231; r. 170D(5) substituted by S.I. 1986 No. 1231; and r. 170D(7)(b) inserted by S.I. 1986 No. 1231

GENERAL NOTE.

49.31.1   It is not competent for a pursuer to have a conclusion craving an order on behalf of the defender: *T. v. T.* 1987 S.L.T. (Sh.Ct.) 74 (custody); *Young v. Young* 1991 G.W.D. 13-798 (financial provision). The defender must seek his own remedies.

     A defender may not counterclaim in a family action (r. 25.1(1)), and in order to avoid him having to bring a cross-action, he may exceptionally conclude for certain remedies (see r. 49.31(1)) in his defences: r. 49.31(2)(b)(i).

     Paragraphs (3) to (7) of r. 49.31 contain provisions equivalent to r. 49.8A where the defender seeks a section 11 order.

"SECTION 11 ORDER".

49.31.2   See note 49.1.2.

"DEFENCES".

49.31.3   See rr. 18.1 and 18.2.

Abandonment by pursuer

49.32   **49.32.** Notwithstanding abandonment by a pursuer, the court may allow a defender to pursue an order or claim sought in his defences; and the proceedings in relation to that order or claim shall continue in dependence as if a separate cause.

"ABANDONMENT".

49.32.1   On abandonment of actions, see Chap. 29.

A cause is depending until final decree, whereas a cause is in dependence until final extract. For the meaning of final decree, see note 4.15.2(2). For the meaning of final extract, see note 7.1.2(2).

49.32.2

Case management hearing

49.32A.—[1](1) When defences are lodged, the court must fix a date for a case management hearing.

49.32A

(2) The date fixed for the case management hearing must be not less than 4 weeks and not more than 8 weeks after the date on which defences were lodged.

(3) At the case management hearing, each party must address the court on—

  (a) any matters that are capable of agreement;

  (b) the matters that are in dispute between the parties;

  (c) any matters of potential complexity or difficulty;

  (d) any documents likely to be relevant to the matters in dispute;

  (e) any valuations that are likely to be required;

  (f) any expert evidence that is likely to be required;

  (g) whether steps require to be taken to give a child an opportunity to express views;

  (h) whether steps require to be taken to investigate any facts or circumstances relating to a child;

  (i) the estimated duration of the proof;

  (j) further procedure;

  (k) any other issues that the court considers appropriate.

(4) At the case management hearing, the court may—

  (a) order and fix a date for a further case management hearing;

  (b) order and fix a date for a pre-proof hearing not less than 6 weeks and not more than 8 weeks before the date fixed for the proof;

  (c) make such other orders as it considers appropriate for the expeditious progress of the cause.

Pre-proof hearing

49.32B.—[2](1) The purpose of a pre-proof hearing is to ascertain, so far as is reasonably practicable, whether the cause is likely to proceed to proof on the date fixed.

49.32B

(2) Where the court appoints a pre-proof hearing, the parties must provide the court with sufficient information to enable it to conduct the hearing as provided for in this rule.

(3) At the pre-proof hearing, the court must consider—

  (a) the state of preparation of the parties;

  (b) whether the proof has been fixed for an appropriate number of days;

  (c) the extent to which the parties have complied with any orders made by the court;

  (d) whether special measures will be required for the purposes of taking the evidence of any vulnerable witnesses;

  (e) whether a live link may be required.

(4) At the pre-proof hearing, the court may—

  (a) discharge the proof and fix a new date for it;

  (b) continue the pre-proof hearing;

---

[1] Rule 49.32A inserted by S.S.I. 2017 No. 242 (effective 18th September 2017).
[2] Rule 49.32B inserted by S.S.I. 2017 No. 242 (effective 18th September 2017).

(c)   order parties to lodge joint minutes, affidavits, and expert reports within such period as it considers appropriate;

(d)   direct how evidence is to be given by expert witnesses;

(e)   make an order authorising the use of special measures for the purposes of taking the evidence of any vulnerable witnesses;

(f)   make an order authorising the use of a live link;

(g)   make such other orders as it considers appropriate to secure the expeditious progress of the cause.

Adjustment and further procedure

49.33

49.33.—[1](1) Chapter 22 (making up and closing records) shall not apply to a family action.

(2) The court shall, 14 days after the date on which defences were lodged, or a minute by a person on whom intimation has been made under rule 49.8, 49.9 or 49.15 was lodged, pronounce an interlocutor allowing the parties a proof of their respective averments.

(3)[2] Notwithstanding the pronouncement of an interlocutor under paragraph (2), the parties may adjust their respective pleadings until 56 days before the diet of proof; and any such adjustments shall be written on the summons, defences or minute, as the case may be.

(4) Not earlier than 28 days after the allowance of proof, the court may, on cause shown, withdraw the allowance of proof and appoint the action to the Procedure Roll.

(5) The pursuer shall, within seven days after the end of the adjustment period under paragraph (3) or the appointment of the action to the Procedure Roll, as the case may be—

(a)   subject to rule 49.68 (procedure for minutes in causes under the Act of 1981) or rule 49.71E (procedure for minutes in causes under Chapters 3 and 4 of Part 3 of the CP Act of 2004) as the case may be, make up a copy of the adjusted pleadings in the form of a record;

(b)   send not less than three copies of the record to every other party; and

(c)   not later than 48 hours before the diet of proof or hearing on the Procedure Roll, as the case may be, lodge two copies of the record in process.

Deriv. R.C.S. 1965, r. 168A inserted by S.I. 1980 No. 1144 and amended by S.I. 1982 No. 1381 (r. 49.33(5)(part))

GENERAL NOTE.

49.33.1

R. 49.33 sets out a new procedure for defended family actions. 14 days after defences have been lodged an interlocutor is automatically pronounced allowing parties a proof, but parties are entitled to adjust their pleadings until 56 days before the diet of proof. The significance of 56 days is that that is the number of days before the diet of proof by which productions and a list of witnesses must be lodged: see r. 49.33A. An action may, however, be sent to procedure roll: r. 49.33(4).

PROCEDURE ROLL.

49.33.2

A hearing on the Procedure Roll is rare in a family action. It is not normally appropriate (except on a point of law only), where the welfare of children is involved, to dispose of an application for an order relating to parental rights solely on the pleadings, some kind of inquiry into the facts being necessary: *O. v. O.* 1994 S.C. 569.

On the Procedure Roll, see Chap. 28.

---

[1] Rule 49.33 amended by S.S.I. 2005 No. 632 (effective 8th December 2005).
[2] As amended by the Act of Sederunt (Rules of the Court of Session 1994 Amendment) (Miscellaneous) 2021 (S.S.I. 2021 No. 22) r. 2(2) (effective 22nd February 2021).

Lodging of productions and witness lists

49.33A.—[1](1) Rule 4.5 (productions) and rule 36.3 (lodging productions) do not apply to a family action.

49.33A

(2) Where a proof has been allowed in a family action—

    (a) copies of all productions which are intended to be used at the proof must be intimated to every other party not later than 56 days before the diet of proof;

    (b) an inventory of productions which are intended to be used at the proof must be intimated to every other party and lodged in process not later than 56 days before the diet of proof; and

    (c) the productions included in the inventory of productions must be lodged in process no later than 14 days before the diet of proof.

(3) A production may be intimated and lodged electronically with the permission of, and in accordance with directions given by, the judge.

(4) A production lodged in hard copy must be—

    (a) marked with a number of process with the cause reference number assigned to the principal writ; and

    (b) if consisting of more than one sheet, securely fastened together.

(5) A production which is not intimated and lodged in accordance with paragraph (2) must not be used or put in evidence at a proof without—

    (a) consent of the parties; or

    (b) leave of the court on cause shown and on such conditions, if any, as to expenses or otherwise as the court thinks fit.

(6) Not later than 56 days before the diet fixed for a proof, each party must—

    (a) give written intimation to every other party of a list containing the name, occupation (if known) and address of each person whom the party intends to call as a witness; and

    (b) lodge a copy of that list in process.

(7) A party who seeks to call as a witness a person not on the list mentioned in paragraph (6)(a) may only do so—

    (a) by consent of the parties; or

    (b) with the leave of the court on cause shown and on such conditions, if any, as to expenses or otherwise as the court think fit.

GENERAL NOTE

Rule 4.5 is the general rule about lodging an inventory of productions with a production and numbering the productions. Rule 36.3 is the general provision about lodging productions 28 days before the diet of proof.

49.33A.1

Now, in a family action, under r. 49.33A, productions (and an inventory of them) and a list of witnesses must be lodged and intimated to the other party not later than 56 days before the diet of proof. (Under r. 4.5 only a copy of the inventory of productions had to be intimated.)

"PRODUCTIONS"

The provision for not being able to use a document not lodged as a production without consent or leave of the court on cause shown (r. 49.33A(5)) is in the same terms as r. 43.6(8). On the face of it, it excludes documents put in evidence, although not lodged, to test credibility. Formerly, it has been possible to put a document to a witness, although not lodged, to test credibility: see the discussion and cases in note 36.11.2(8). One may assume that, were r. 49.33A(5) be said to exclude it, cause could readily be shown under the rule for doing so without having lodged the document previously.

49.33A.2

As for the numbering of productions, it is not clear whether P.N. No. 4 of 1994, para. 8 or the (illegal) P.N. No. 2 of 1997, para. (4) applies. The P.N. No. 2 of 1997 attempted (illegally) "for an experimental period" to set aside the provisions of the statutory instrument which contains the RCS 1994 [S.I. 1994

---

[1] Inserted by the Act of Sederunt (Rules of the Court of Session 1994 Amendment) (Miscellaneous) 2021 (S.S.I. 2021 No. 22) r. 2(3) (effective 22nd February 2021).

No. 1443]. It is not competent to set aside a statutory instrument by a practice note without there being a power to do so. P.N. No. 2 of 1997 did not, however, revoke P.N. No. 4 of 1994.

"LIST OF WITNESSES"

49.33A.3   Paragraphs (6) and (7) of r. 49.33A, which deal with the lodging of lists of witnesses and the calling of witnesses not on the list, are in the same terms as P.N. No. 8 of 1994.

"NOT LATER THAN 56 DAYS BEFORE"

49.33A.4   The date of the proof is not counted in calculating the minimum number of days.

Late appearance by defenders

49.34   **49.34.**—[1](1) In a family action, the court may, at any time while the action is depending, make an order with such conditions, if any, as it thinks fit, allowing a defender—

    (a)[2] to lodge defences to the action; or

    (b) to appear and be heard at a diet of proof although he has not lodged defences, but he shall not, in that event, be allowed to lead evidence without the pursuer's consent.

(2) Where the court makes an order under paragraph (1)(a), the pursuer may recall a witness already examined or lead other evidence whether or not he closed his proof before that order was made.

(3) Where the court makes an order under paragraph (1)(a), it must order any steps to be taken that it considers appropriate to obtain or hear the views of the child in relation to any section 11 order that may be sought by the defender.

Deriv. R.C.S. 1965, r. 169 substituted by S.I. 1976 No. 1994

GENERAL NOTE.

49.34.1   The court has a discretion to refuse to allow a defender to lodge defences or appear: see, e.g. *Watt v. Watt* 1978 S.L.T. (Notes) 55; cf. *Stirton v. Stirton* 1969 S.L.T. (Notes) 48.

While r. 49.34(1)(b) gives the court a discretion to allow a defender to appear at the proof, where the proof has in fact been heard it would probably not allow the defender a further diet of proof without him lodging defences.

The provision in R.C.S. 1965, r. 169(1)(c), by virtue of which the court could allow a defender who had not appeared at the proof to reclaim, has not been re-enacted in r. 49.34. Accordingly, only reduction is competent if the defender did not enter appearance (rr. 38.2 and 1.3(1) (definition of "party")); if the action was defended but the defender failed to appear at the proof, he would still have a right to reclaim under r. 38.3.

Rule 49.34(3) contains a provision so that what is require of a defender under r. 49.31 may be achieved.

"DEFENCES".

49.34.2   See rr. 18.1 and 18.2.

"DEPENDING".

49.34.3   A cause is depending until final decree, whereas a cause is in dependence until final extract. For the meaning of final decree, see note 4.15.2(2). For the meaning of final extract, see note 7.1.2(2).

Part IV – Applications and Orders Relating to Children in Certain Actions

Application of this Part[3]

49.35   **49.35.**[4] This Part applies to actions of divorce, separation, declarator of nullity of marriage, dissolution of a civil partnership, separation of civil partners and declarator of nullity of a civil partnership.

Deriv. R.C.S. 1965, r. 170B(1)(b) inserted by S.I. 1976 No. 1994 (r. 49.35(1))

---

[1] Rule 49.34 amended by S.S.I. 2019 No. 123 para. 2 (effective 24th June 2019).
[2] Rule 49.34 amended by S.S.I. 2007 No. 548 (effective 7th January 2008).
[3] Heading and r. 49.35 substituted by S.S.I. 2005 No. 632 (effective 8th December 2005).
[4] Heading and r. 49.35 substituted by S.S.I. 2005 No. 632 (effective 8th December 2005).

Applications in relation to parental rights in family actions other than an action of divorce, separation or declarator of nullity of marriage are dealt with in Pt. IX (rr. 49.58 to 49.63).

49.35.1

JURISDICTION.

The court having jurisdiction in an action of divorce, separation or declarator of nullity of marriage has jurisdiction in relation to orders relating to children: Domicile and Matrimonial Proceedings Act 1973 s. 10 (as modified by s. 13 of the Family Law Act).

49.35.2

Applications in actions to which this Part applies

49.36.—(1)   An application for an order mentioned in paragraph (2) shall be made—

49.36

    (a)   by a conclusion in the summons or defences, as the case may be, in an action to which this Part applies; or

    (b)   where the application is made by a person other than the pursuer or defender, by minute in that action.

(2)   The orders referred to in paragraph (1) are—

    (a)[1] an order for a section 11 order; and

    (b)   an order for aliment for a child.

"SUMMONS".

On form of summons, see r. 13.2.

49.36.1

"DEFENCES".

On form of defences, see r. 18.1.

49.36.2

"MINUTE".

On applications by minute, see r. 15.1.

49.36.3

"SECTION 11 ORDER".

See note 49.1.2.

49.36.4

Any person claiming an interest may apply for an order relating to parental rights: Children (Scotland) Act 1995, s. 11(3)(a). On the meaning of "interest" under s. 3(1) of the Law Reform (Parent and Child) (Scotland) Act 1986, see *D. v. Grampian R.C.* 1995 S.C.(H.L.) 1. In any proceedings for a section 11 order the court shall regard the welfare of the child as the paramount consideration and shall not make any order unless it would be better for the child that an order be made than that none be made and having regard to views expressed by the child: Act of 1995, s. 11(7).

A mother always has parental responsibilities and parental rights in relation to her child; a father has them only if he is married to the child's mother or was married to her at the time of or after the child's conception: Act of 1995, s. 3. The right to parental responsibilities is subject to what is in the interests of the child: Act of 1995, s.1(1).

The advantage to a very young child of being with its mother is a consideration which has to be taken into account in deciding where its best interests lie but which will yield to competing advantages which more effectively promote the welfare of the child: *Brixey v. Lynas* 1997 S.C. (H.L.) 1.

In relation to contact orders, where a person has parental rights, it is not required to aver in detail the basis on which contact is sought: *O. v. O.* 1995 S.L.T. 238. It should be noted that a parent does not have an absolute right of contact with his or her child, he or she is only entitled to contact if the court is satisfied that it is in the best interests of the child: *Porchetta v. Porchetta* 1986 S.L.T. 105; and see now the Act of 1995, s.11(7). In *Sanderson v. McManus* 1996 S.L.T. 751 the majority in the Extra Division held that (1) s. 3(2) of the Law Reform (Parent and Child) (Scotland) Act 1986 (see now s. 11(7) of the Act of 1995) sets out the only test; (2) the child's father if not married to its mother does not have parental rights; (3) there is no "right" in a parent to access; and (4) although the parent-child relationship may have intrinsic value, and the status quo should be preserved (*Brixey v. Lynas* , 1994 S.C. 606), these are not propositions of law capable of being determinative but are simply factors which may or may not be significant. Lord McCluskey, dissenting, took the view that the "traditional approach" that the link between a child and his natural parent would be conducive to the child's welfare or should be preserved unless there were strong reasons to the contrary (*Blance v. Blance* 1978 S.L.T. 74; *Brannigan v. Brannigan* 1979 S.L.T. (Notes) 73) was not altered by s. 3(2) of the 1986 Act or *Porchetta*, above. The majority opinion in *Sanderson*, above was upheld in the House of Lords in 1997 S.L.T. 629. In *White v. White* , 2001 S.C. 689, it was held that the court requires where regard to the welfare of the child as its paramount consideration and will generally consider that it is conducive to the welfare of children if the absent parents maintain personal relations and direct contact on a regular basis (see also Lord Hope of Craighead

---

[1] Rule 49.40 substituted by S.I. 1996 No. 2587 (effective 1 November 1996).

in *Sanderson*). There is, however, no legal onus on the person seeking a contact order, the court simply considers all the relevant material and decides what is conducive to the child's welfare: *White*, above, per L.P. Rodger at p.698H.

The parent having a residence order does not fulfil his or her obligations where a contact order is awarded by leaving it to the child to decide whether to go or not; that parent must encourage and persuade, although not physically coerce, the child to accept contact by the other parent: see *Blance*, above, per Lord Stewart at p. 75.

In an action of divorce, separation or nullity of marriage, the court must consider whether to make a section 11 order or a reference to the Principal Reporter; and where it is of the opinion that such action may be required, or that it is not in a position to take such action without further consideration, or that it is not desirable in the interests of the child to grant decree until it is in a position to do so, it shall postpone its decision to grant decree: Act of 1995, s. 12(1).

It is not appropriate to dispose of an appeal for parental rights solely on the pleadings: *O.*, above.

"ALIMENT".

49.36.5   See ss. 1 to 7 of the Family Law (Scotland) Act 1985.

Intimation before committal to care or supervision

49.37   **49.37.** [Revoked by S.I. 1996 No. 2587 (effective 1st November 1996).]

Care or supervision orders

49.38   **49.38.** [Revoked by S.I. 1996 No. 2587 (effective 1st November 1996).]

Intimation of certain applications to local authorities or other persons

49.39   **49.39.** [Revoked by S.I. 1996 No. 2587 (effective 1st November 1996).]

Applications in depending actions by motion

49.40   **49.40.**—(1)[1],[2] An application by a party in an action depending before the court to which this Part applies for, or for variation of, an order for—

    (a)   interim aliment for a child under the age of 18, or

    (b)   an interim residence order or an interim contact order, shall be made by motion.

(2)[3] Written intimation of a motion under paragraph (1) shall be given to every other party not less than 7 days before the date on which the motion is enrolled.

"DEPENDING".

49.40.1   A cause is depending from the time it is commenced (i.e. from the time an action is served) until final decree, whereas a cause is in dependence until final extract. For the meaning of commenced, see note 13.4.4. For the meaning of final decree, see note 4.15.2(2). For the meaning of final extract, see note 7.1.2(2).

"RESIDENCE AND CONTACT ORDERS".

49.40.2   A residence order replaces, but is not the whole of, what was formerly custody. It means an order regulating arrangements as to with whom or with whom during what periods a child under 16 is to live: Children (Scotland) Act 1995, s. 11(2)(c).

A contact order replaces access. It is an order regulating the arrangements for maintaining personal relations and direct contact between a child under 16 and a person with whom he is not, or will not be, living: Act of 1995, s. 11(2)(d).

"MOTION".

49.40.3   For motions, see Chap. 23.

---

[1] R. 49.40 substituted by S.I. 1996 No. 2587 (effective 1st November 1996).
[2] R. 49.40 amended by S.I. 1997 No. 1050 (effective 6th April 1997: insertion of "(1)").
[3] R. 49.40(2) inserted by S.I. 1997 No. 1050 (effective 6th April 1997).

Applications after decree relating to a section 11 order[1]

49.41.—[2](1)[3] An application after final decree for, or for the variation or recall of, a section 11 order shall be made by minute in the process of the action to which the application relates.

49.41

(2)[4] Where a minute has been lodged under paragraph (1), any party—

    (a)   may apply by motion for any interim order which may be made pending the determination of the application; and

    (b)   shall intimate any such motion to every other party not less than 7 days before the date on which the motion is enrolled.

GENERAL NOTE.

In relation to parental rights, a party (i.e. person in the process: r. 1.3(1)) may apply under this rule, as also may any person claiming interest: Children (Scotland) Act 1995, s.11(3)(a). On the meaning of "interest" under s.3(1) of the Law Reform (Parent and Child) (Scotland) Act 1986, see *D. v. Grampian R.C.* 1995 S.C.(H.L.) 1. The court's power is derived from s. 9(2) of the 1986 Act and s. 20(1) of the C.S.A. 1988.

49.41.1

"SECTION 11 ORDER".

A section 11 order is an order under s. 11 of the Children (Scotland) Act 1995. Under that section the court may make an order in relation to parental responsibilities (defined in s. 1), parental rights (defined in s. 2), guardianship and administration of a child's property. Without prejudice to that generality, the court may (a) make an order depriving a person of parental responsibilities or parental rights in respect of a child under 18, (b) make an order imposing such responsibilities or rights, (c) make a residence order in respect of a child under 16, (d) make a contact order in respect of a child under 16, (e) make a specific issue order in relation to the matter arising out of or in connection with a matter in (a) to (d), (f) grant interdict in relation to parental responsibilities, parental rights or the administration of property of a child under 18, (g) appoint a judicial factor in respect of a child under 18, or (h) appoint or remove a guardian of a child under 18.

49.41.2

"CONTACT ORDER".

A contact order replaces access. It is an order regulating the arrangements for maintaining personal relations and direct contact between a child under 16 and a person with whom he is not, or will not be, living: Children (Scotland) Act 1995, s. 11(2)(d).

The test for variation of a contact order is the same as in seeking a contact order and is that laid down in *Sanderson v. McManus* 1997 S.C. (H.L.) 55: *Thomson v. Thomson* , 14th June 2000, unreported, 2000 G.W.D. 23-874 (First Div.).

49.41.3

"MINUTE".

On applications by minute, see r. 15.1. Apart from the provision for a fee due by a person first entering the process, a court fee will be payable by a party on lodging a minute for variation of an order in a family action: see note 15.1.7.

49.41.3A

"MOTION".

For motions, see Chap. 23.

49.41.4

"INTIMATE".

For methods, see r. 16.7.

49.41.5

"PARTY".

See definition in r. 1.3(1).

49.41.6

Warrants for intimation to child and permission to seek views relating to section 11 order

49.42.—[5](1) Subject to paragraph (2), when lodging a minute under rule 49.41 (applications after decree relating to a section 11 order) which includes a crave after

49.42

---

[1] Rule 49.41(1) and heading amended by S.I. 1996 No. 2587 (effective 1 November 1996).
[2] As amended by S.S.I. 2019 No. 123 para.2 (effective 24th June 2019).
[3] Rule 49.41(1) and heading amended by S.I. 1996 No. 2587 (effective 1 November 1996).
[4] Rule 49.41(2) amended by S.I. 1996 No. 2587 (clerical error).
[5] As substituted by S.S.I. 2019 No. 123 para.2 (effective 24th June 2019).

final decree for, or the variation or recall of, a section 11 order in respect of a child who is not a party to the action, the minuter must—

    (a)   include in the minute a crave for a warrant for intimation and the seeking of the child's views in Form 49.8A;

    (b)   when lodging the minute, submit a draft Form 49.8A, showing the details that the minuter proposes to include when the form is sent to the child.

(2) Where the minuter considers that it would be inappropriate to send Form 49.8A to the child (for example, where the child is under 5 years of age), the minuter must include in the minute—

    (a)   a crave to dispense with intimation and the seeking of the child's views in Form 49.8A;

    (b)   averments setting out the reasons why it is inappropriate to send Form 49.8A to the child.

(3) The court must be satisfied that the draft Form 49.8A submitted under paragraph (1)(b) has been drafted appropriately.

(4) The court may dispense with intimation and the seeking of views in Form 49.8A or make any other order that it considers appropriate.

(5) An order granting warrant for intimation and the seeking of the child's views in Form 49.8A under this rule must—

    (a)   state that the Form 49.8A must be sent in accordance with rule 49.42(6);

    (b)   be signed by the Lord Ordinary.

(6) The Form 49.8A must be sent in accordance with—

    (a)   rule 49.42A (views of the child – unopposed minutes relating to a section 11 order), where the minute is unopposed;

    (b)   rule 49.42B (views of the child – craves relating to a section 11 order sought by minuter only), where the minute is opposed and a section 11 order is sought by the minuter only; or

    (c)   rule 49.42C (views of the child – craves relating to a section 11 order sought by both minuter and respondent), where a section 11 order is sought by both the minuter and the respondent.

Deriv. R.C.S. 1965, r. 170B(10) inserted by S.I. 1977 No. 1621 (r. 49.42(1) to (4))

GENERAL NOTE.

49.42.1   In relation to parental rights, a party (i.e. a person in the process: r. 1.3(1)), may apply under this rule, as also may any person claiming interest: Children (Scotland) Act 1995, s. 11 (3)(a). On the meaning of "interest" under s. 3(1) of the Law Reform (Parent and Child) (Scotland) Act 1986, see *D. v. Grampian R.C.* 1995 S.C.(H.L.) 1. The court's power is derived from s. 9(2) of the 1986 Act and s. 20(1) of the C.S.A. 1988.

       This new substituted rule provides the equivalent provisions in r. 49.8A on the minuter as on the pursuer in an action for a section 11 order where the child is not a party to the action.

[THE NEXT PARAGRAPH IS 49.42.3]

"MOTION".

49.42.3   For motions, see Chap. 23.

"NOT LESS THAN 14 DAYS BEFORE".

49.42.4   The first and last days are included in calculating the period so that there are 14 clear days.

"LODGE IN PROCESS".

49.42.5   The copy letter of intimation of the motion and certificate of posting are lodged in process as productions. On lodging productions, see r. 4.5. Productions may be lodged by post: P.N. No. 4 of 1994, paras. 1 and 8; and see note 4.5.5.

"MINUTE".

49.42.6   On applications by minute, see r. 15.1. Apart from the provision for a fee due by a person first entering the process, a court fee will be payable by a party on lodging a minute for variation of an order in a consistorial cause: see note 15.1.7.

"ANSWERS".

"ANSWERS".

See r. 18.3.   **49.42.7**

"PARTY".

See definition in r. 1.3(1).   **49.42.8**

Views of the child – unopposed minutes relating to a section 11 order

49.42A.—[1](1)   This rule applies to minutes which include a crave after final   **49.42A**
decree for, or the variation or recall of, a section 11 order in respect of which no
answers are lodged and warrant has been granted for intimation and the seeking of
the child's views in Form 49.8A.
(2)   The minuter must—
   (a)   send the child the Form 49.8A that was submitted and approved under
      rule 49.42 (warrants for intimation to child and permission to seek views
      relating to section 11 order);
   (b)   on the same day, lodge a certificate of intimation in Form 49.8B;
   (c)   not send the child a copy of the minute.
(3)   Except on cause shown, the court must not determine the minute in the period
of 28 days following the date on which the Form 49.8A was sent to the child.

GENERAL NOTE.

This rule provides rules equivalent to r. 49.20A.   **49.42A.1**

"SEND".

This includes deliver: r. 1.3(1) (definition of "send").   **49.42A.2**

Views of the child – craves relating to a section 11 order sought by minuter only

49.42B.—[2](1)   This rule applies where answers have been lodged in respect of a   **49.42B**
minute after final decree and a crave for, or the variation or recall of, a section 11
order is sought by the minuter only and warrant has been granted for intimation and
the seeking of the child's views in Form 49.8A.
(2)   The minuter must—
   (a)   no later than 14 days after answers are lodged, send the child the Form
      49.8A that was submitted and approved under rule 49.42 (warrants for
      intimation to child and permission to seek views relating to section 11
      order);
   (b)   on the same day, lodge a certificate of intimation in Form 49.8B;
   (c)   not send the child a copy of the minute or answers.

GENERAL NOTE.

This rule provides rules equivalent to r. 49.20B.   **49.42B.1**

"SEND".

This includes deliver: r. 1.3(1) (definition of "send").   **49.42B.2**

Views of the child – craves relating to a section 11 order sought by both minuter and respondent

49.42C.—[3](1)   This rule applies where answers have been lodged in respect of a   **49.42C**
minute after final decree and craves for, or the variation or recall of, a section 11
order are sought by both the minuter and the respondent and warrant has been
granted for intimation and the seeking of the child's views in Form 49.8A.

---

[1] As inserted by S.S.I. 2019 No. 123 para.2 (effective 24th June 2019).
[2] As inserted by S.S.I. 2019 No. 123 para.2 (effective 24th June 2019).
[3] As inserted by S.S.I. 2019 No. 123 para.2 (effective 24th June 2019).

(2)   The minuter must—

    (a)   no later than 14 days after answers are lodged, send the child the Form 49.8A that was submitted and approved under rule 49.42 (warrants for intimation to child and permission to seek views relating to section 11 order), amended so as also to narrate the section 11 order sought by the respondent;

    (b)   on the same day—

        (i)   lodge a certificate of intimation in Form 49.8B;

        (ii)   send the respondent a copy of the Form 49.8A that was sent to the child;

    (c)   not send the child a copy of the minute or answers.".

GENERAL NOTE.

49.42C.1   This rule provides rules equivalent to r. 49.20C.

"NO LATER THAN 14 DAYS AFTER".

49.42C.2   The time expires at the end of the 14th day.

"SEND".

49.42C.3   This includes deliver: r. 1.3(1) (definition of "send").

Applications after decree relating to aliment

49.43   **49.43.**—(1)   An application after final decree for, or for the variation or recall of, an order for aliment for a child shall be made by motion in the process of the action to which the application relates.

(2)   A motion under paragraph (1) shall—

    (a)   include a brief statement of the reasons for the order sought; and

    (b)   be intimated by registered post or the first class recorded delivery service to any person concerned or a solicitor known to be acting on behalf of that person, not less than 14 days before the date on which the motion is enrolled.

(3)   On enrolling a motion under paragraph (1), the applicant shall lodge in process—

    (a)   a copy of the letter of intimation;

    (b)   the Post Office receipt or certificate of posting of that letter; and

    (c)   written evidence of the earnings or other income of the applicant or, if not employed, written evidence of that fact.

(4)   At the hearing of a motion under paragraph (1), the court may order that the application be made by minute; and, in such a case, shall make an order for the lodging of answers to the minute in process within such period as the court thinks fit.

(5)   Where the court makes an order under paragraph (4), any party—

    (a)   may apply by motion for an interim order pending the determination of the application; and

    (b)   shall give written intimation of any such motion to every other party not less than seven days before the date on which the motion is enrolled.

Deriv. R.C.S. 1965, r. 170B(10) inserted by S.I. 1977 No. 1621

"FINAL DECREE".

49.43.1   This is the decree disposing of the whole subject-matter of the cause including expenses: see note 4.15.2(2).

"ALIMENT".

49.43.2   See ss. 1 to 7 of the Family Law (Scotland) Act 1985.

    Before an award of aliment can be varied or recalled by virtue of s. 5 of the 1985 Act the court has to be satisfied that there has been a material change of circumstances; and it is not a material change that the

original award has been made on the basis of incomplete or inaccurate information: *Walker v. Walker* 1994 S.C. 482 applying *Stewart v. Stewart* 1987 S.L.T. 246.

An obligation of aliment is owed by a husband to his wife, a wife to her husband, a father or mother to his or her child and a person to a child (other than a child who has been boarded out to him by a local or public authority or voluntary organisation) who has been accepted by him as a child of the family: Family Law (Scotland) Act 1985, s. 1(1).

The obligation subsists until the child is 18 or, if the child is undergoing education at an educational establishment or training for a profession, trade or vocation, until the age of 25; and while under 18, aliment must be claimed on the child's behalf and not by the child: Act of 1985, s. 1. Both parents owe an obligation to aliment their child: Act of 1985, s. 1(1)(c); and see, e.g. *Howarth v. Howarth* 1990 S.L.T. 289. The obligation is to provide such support as is reasonable in the circumstances, having regard to the needs and resources of the parties, their earning capacities and all the circumstances of the case (subject to s. 4(3)): Act of 1985, ss. 1(2) and 4(1). The award may be backdated: Act of 1985, s. 3(1).

The court may order a party to provide details of his or her resources or those relating to a child: Act of 1985, s. 20.

The court has a very wide discretion in awarding interim aliment (which is provided for in s. 6(2) of the Act of 1985). Interim aliment is for the relief of need. An award may be reclaimed only with leave of the Lord Ordinary (r. 38.3(5)) unless the interlocutor contains an order not requiring leave. Interim aliment is determined on the basis of gross earnings not net earnings after tax: *MacInnes v. MacInnes* 1993 S.L.T. 1108.

As a general rule aliment is paid out of post-tax income, the payer receives no allowance for it and the recipient is not taxed on it: Income and Corporation Taxes Act 1988, s. 347A (inserted by s. 36(1) of the Finance Act 1988). An exception is provided for qualifying maintenance payments (i.e. a periodic payment under a court order by a party to the marriage to a child of the family) whereby a payer receives an allowance against his income by deducting such payments from his total income equal to the married couple's allowance: 1988 Act, s. 347B. It is not now, therefore, necessary or effective to make the payment payable to a parent as guardian of the child (see formerly *Huggins v. Huggins* 1981 S.L.T. 179). The small maintenance payment regime has also gone. For a discussion of the pre—, and post—, 1988 law, see Alan Barr "*A Vintage Year for Aliment*" 1989 S.L.T.(News) 57.

Variation or recall of a decree for aliment may only be made on a material change of circumstances: Act of 1985, s. 5(1). That incomplete or incorrect information was before the court on the previous occasion is not a change of circumstances: *Walker v. Walker* 1994 S.C. 482, 486F—H obiter per 2nd Div. The making of a maintenance assessment by the C.S.A. is a material change: Act of 1985, s. 5(1A). Interim aliment may be varied or recalled: Act of 1985, s. 6(4). The court has power to order repayment of aliment where a variation or recall of an award of aliment is made and backdated (Act of 1985, s. 5(4)) but has no such power where the award is of interim aliment (*McColl v. McColl* 1993 S.C. 276).

"MOTION".

For motions, see Chap. 23. Apart from the provision for a fee due by a person first entering the process, a court fee will be payable by a party on lodging a minute for variation of an order in a consistorial cause: see note 23.2.18. | **49.43.3**

"LODGE IN PROCESS".

The copy letter of intimation of the motion and certificate of posting are lodged in process as productions. On lodging productions, see r. 4.5. Productions may be lodged by post: P.N. No. 4 of 1994, paras 1 and 8; and see note 4.5.5. | **49.43.4**

"MINUTE".

On applications by minute, see r. 15.1. Apart from the provision for a fee due by a person first entering the process, a court fee will be payable by a party on lodging a minute for variation of an order in a family action: see note 15.1.7. | **49.43.5**

"ANSWERS".

See r. 18.3. | **49.43.6**

"PARTY".

See definition in r. 1.3(1). | **49.43.7**

Applications after decree by persons over 18 years for aliment

49.44.—(1) A person— | **49.44**

    (a) to whom an obligation of aliment is owed under section 1 of the Act of 1985,

    (b) in whose favour an order for aliment while under the age of 18 years was made in an action to which this Part applies, and

    (c) who seeks, after attaining that age, an order for aliment against a person in that action against whom the order for aliment in his favour was made, shall apply by minute in the process of that action.

(2)   An application for interim aliment pending the determination of an application under paragraph (1) shall be made by motion.

(3)   Where a decree has been pronounced in an application under paragraph (1) or (2), any application for variation or recall of any such decree shall be made by motion; and rule 49.43 (applications after decree relating to aliment) shall apply to a motion under this paragraph as it applies to a motion under that rule.

GENERAL NOTE.

49.44.1   The obligation to aliment a child exists after the child is 18 years old until the age of 25 if the child is undergoing instruction at an educational establishment or training for a profession, trade or vocation: Act of 1985, s. 1(5).

See further, note 49.43.2.

"MINUTE".

49.44.2   For applications by minute, see r. 15.1.

"MOTION".

49.44.3   For motions, see Chap. 23.

Part V – Orders Relating to Financial Provision etc.

Application and interpretation of this Part

49.45   **49.45.—**   This Part applies to an action of divorce, declarator of nullity of marriage, dissolution of a civil partnership, or declarator of nullity of a civil partnership.[1]

(2)   In this Part, "incidental order" has the meaning assigned in section 14(2) of the Act of 1985.

Deriv. R.C.S. 1965, r. 170D(11) inserted by S.I. 1986 No. 1231 (r. 49.45(1))

GENERAL NOTE.

49.45.1   For aliment in family actions other than an action of divorce or declarator of nullity of marriage, see Pt. VIII (rr. 49.54 to 49.57).

Applications in actions to which this Part applies

49.46   **49.46.—**(1)   An application for an order mentioned in paragraph (2) shall be made—

    (a)   by a conclusion in the summons or defences, as the case may be, in an action to which this Part applies; or

    (b)   where the application is made by a person other than the pursuer or defender, by minute in that action.

(2)   The orders referred to in paragraph (1) are—

    (a)   an order for financial provision within the meaning of section 8(3) of the Act of 1985;

    (b)   an order under section 16(1)(b) or (3) of the Act of 1985 (setting aside or varying agreement as to financial provision);

    (c)   an order under section 18 of the Act of 1985 (which relates to avoidance transactions); and

    (d)   an order under section 13 of the Act of 1981 (transfer or vesting of tenancy of a matrimonial home).

    (e)[2]   an order under section 112 of the CP Act of 2004.

Deriv. R.C.S. 1965, r. 170D(1) and (2)(part) inserted by S.I. 1976 No. 1994 and amended by S.I. 1986 No. 1231; r. 170D(4)(a) substituted by S.I. 1977 No. 1621; r. 188D(4)(part) and (5)(part) inserted by S.I. 1982 No. 1381

---

[1] Rule 49.45(1) substituted by SSI 2005 No. 632 (effective 8th December 2005).
[2] Rule 49.46(1)(e) inserted by SSI 2005 No. 632 (effective 8th December 2005).

It is permissible to add a conclusion "For such other order as the court may consider appropriate." The reason for this is that it is not always possible to have a conclusion to meet every circumstance which may arise, particularly in relation to incidental orders relating to capital payments.

In the R.C.S. 1965, r. 156(2) expressly provided for such a conclusion but in Chap. 49 of the R.C.S. 1994 there is no convenient peg on which to have such a rule. It is not thought that a rule is a prerequisite.

The rule that expenses follow success is not irrelevant to disputes about financial provision on divorce, but should not be applied in its full rigour: *Sweeney v. Sweeney (No. 3)*, 2007 S.C. 396, 399 at para. [7] (First Div.). Thus, where parties made full disclosure and agreed valuations where possible, the just disposal may be no expenses due to or by. Where a party takes the other to proof on issues on which he is unsuccessful to the extend of the other party securing an award significantly greater than that offered, the expenses caused to the successful party may be recovered.

"SUMMONS".

On form of summons, see r. 13.2.

"DEFENCES".

On form of defences, see r. 18.1.

"MINUTE".

On applications by minute, see r. 15.1.

"ORDER FOR FINANCIAL PROVISION WITHIN THE MEANING OF SECTION 8(3) OF THE ACT OF 1985".

The orders for financial provision defined in s. 8(3) of the Act of 1985 are those listed in s. 8(1), namely, capital sum (including a pension lump sum), transfer of property, periodical allowance, a pension sharing order, and an incidental order (defined in s. 14(2)). An order must be justified by the principles set out in s. 9 and reasonable having regard to the resources of the parties: Act of 1985, s. 8(2)(a) and (b). Both conditions must be satisfied: *Latter v. Latter* 1990 S.L.T. 805, 807F per Lord Marnoch; *Wallis v. Wallis* 1993 S.C.(H.L.) 49, 56C per Lord Jauncey of Tullichettle. There are restrictions in ss. 12 and 15.

The court of first instance is entitled to take a broad and practical approach as a matter of discretion: *Little v. Little* 1990 S.L.T. 785, 786K, 787D per L.P. Hope; *Peacock v. Peacock* 1993 S.C. 88, 92C per L.J.-C. Ross; *Jacques v. Jacques* 1995 S.C. 327. The discretion of the Lord Ordinary will only be interfered with by the Inner House if it can be shown that he misdirected himself in law, failed to take into account a relevant and material factor (or took into account an irrelevant factor) or reached a result which is manifestly inequitable or plainly wrong: *Gray v. Gray* 1968 S.C. 185, 193 per Lord Guthrie; *Little*, above, per L.P. Hope at p. 786K.

One of the principles in s. 9 is that the net value (as at the relevant date: s. 10(2)) of matrimonial property (defined in s. 10(4); and see *Mitchell v. Mitchell* 1994 S.C. 601) should be shared fairly (i.e. equally or in such other proportions as are justified by special circumstances: s. 10(1)). The relevant date is the earlier of the date on which the parties ceased to cohabit or the date of service of the summons: Act of 1985, s. 10(3). There is nothing in s. 10 of the Act of 1985 which requires an unequal division whenever special circumstances are found to exist; the court must determine, first, whether an event in s. 10(6) amounted to special circumstances and, secondly, if so, whether it justifies an unequal division: *Jacques v. Jacques* 1997 S.C.(H.L.) 20. By virtue of s. 16 of the Family Law (Scotland) Act 2006, in relation to orders for the transfer of property (s. 8(1)(aa) of the 1985 Act), the valuation date is not now the relevant date but the "appropriate valuation date" (i.e. the date the parties agree, failing which the date of the order or, in exceptional cases, such other date as the court may determine).

The net value of any property for the purposes of s. 10(2) of the Act of 1985 is the price a hypothetical willing purchaser would pay and a hypothetical willing seller receive for that property on a hypothetical sale at the (relevant) date in question; it is not constituted by that price less any costs, such as capital gains tax, that the seller would incur: *Sweeney v. Sweeney*, 2004 S.C. 372, S.L.T. 125 (Extra Div.)

In assessing the net value of matrimonial property at the relevant date after deduction of debts under s. 10(2) of the 1985 Act, the incidence of any capital gains tax or other contingent tax liability hypothetically incurred at the relevant date should not be deducted from the valuation of realizable assets: *Sweeney v. Sweeney*, 2004 S.C. 372 (Extra Div.). In *Sweeney v. Sweeney (No. 2)*, 2006 S.C. 82, 90 paras. [20] and [21], it was held by the Extra Division that, although a contingent tax liability should not be brought into account by reducing the net value of the matrimonial home, it could be brought into account in determining the proportions in which matrimonial property would be shared fairly and in determining what was reasonable having regard to the parties' resources.

Nothing in the Act of 1985 justifies a division of the increase in the net value which has taken place at the time of the proof: *Wallis*, above. A change in the value of matrimonial property between the relevant date and the proof does not amount to special circumstances for the purposes of s. 10(1): *Wallis*, above, per Lord Keith of Kinkel at p. 55D (obiter); *Welsh v. Welsh* 1994 S.L.T. 828.

On the meaning and effect of s. 8(2) of the Act of 1985 (order reasonable having regard to parties' resources), see *Wallis*, above; *Welsh*, above, per Lord Osborne at p. 835L.

On payment of a capital sum out of a pension, at a present or future date, see *Bannon v. Bannon* 1993 S.L.T. 999; *McEwan v. McEwan* (Extra Div.), 29th August 1995, unreported, 1995 G.W.D. 31-1610.

49.46.1

49.46.2

49.46.3

49.46.4

49.46.5

S.12A of the Act of 1985 (inserted by s. 167(3) of the Pensions Act 1995) provides for orders for payment of pension lump sums. Under that section the court may order the trustees or managers of the pension scheme (to whom intimation must be made under r. 49.8(1)(1)) to pay a whole or part of the lump sum, when it becomes due, to the other party of the marriage. If the trustees or managers of the pension scheme do not enter the process, any order of the court would require to be intimated to them by order of the court.

A pension sharing order may be made, as from 1st December 2000, by virtue of s. 8(1)(baa) of the Act of 1985 inserted by s. 20(1) of the Welfare and Pensions Reform Act 1999. The order is one which provides that one party's shareable rights under a pension arrangement or shareable state scheme rights are made subject to pension sharing for the benefit of the other party to a specified percentage value or amount transferred to the other party: Act of 1985, s. 27(1) definition inserted by s. 20(3) of the 1999 Act. The mechanics are dealt with in Chaps.I and II of Pt.IV of the 1999 Act. The idea is to give the other spouse a pension that continues during the life of the recipient. The majority in *McDonald v McDonald*, 2015 S.L.T. 589 (Extra Div.) held that the proportion of the value of a pension referable to the marriage was what was acquired during the marriage but before the relevant date and once payment into the pension ceased the pension was not still being acquired.

A widow's (or spouse's) prospective pension rights do not form part of the matrimonial property for the purpose of division: *Dible v. Dible* 1997 S.C. 134.

"Resources" under s. 27(1) of the Act of 1985 include prospective earnings: *Cunniff v. Cunniff* 1999 S.C. 537 (Extra Div.).

Pleadings should specify which of the principles in s. 9(1) of the Act of 1985 are being relied on: *Toye v. Toye* 1991 G.W.D. 32-1922. The pleas-in-law should not merely state that the party is "entitled", but that the orders sought are "justified by the principles in s. 9 and are reasonable having regard to the resources of the parties".

In the case of an order for transfer of property, the interlocutor must contain a sufficiently detailed description of the subject to be transferred to enable the necessary conveyance to be made and to distinguish the property from other property: *Walker v. Walker* 1991 S.L.T. 157.

The principles for the award of periodical allowance are set out in s. 13 of the Act of 1985. An award may be varied or recalled on a material change of circumstances: Act of 1985, s. 13(4). That incomplete or incorrect information was before the court on the previous occasion is not a change of circumstances: *Stewart v. Stewart* 1987 S.L.T. 246.

The loss of a right to aliment on divorce, even though aliment was not enforced after the separation, would itself be a hardship brought about by the divorce rather than by the separation and an award of periodical allowance was competent under s. 9(1)(e) of the Act of 1985: *Hangan v. Hangan* 1996 S.L.T. 321.

An incidental order under s. 14(2) of the Act of 1985 must be an order in connection with a financial provision; it does not include, e.g. a provision for security for educational expenses because an order for such would be alimentary: *Macdonald v. Macdonald* 1995 S.L.T. 72, 74D per Lord Caplan. An application for an incidental order must be ancillary to a claim for financial provision: *Demarco v. Demarco* 1990 S.C.L.R. 635, 638D obiter per Lord Cameron of Lochbroom; *MacClue v. MacClue* 1994 S.C.L.R. 933, 934F per Sheriff Principal Cox, Q.C., relying on *Reynolds v. Reynolds* 1991 S.C.L.R. 175, 176 per Sheriff Simpson. There does not, however, have to be an order to which an order under s. 14(2) is incidental; but the order under s. 14(2) must be aimed at financial provision, justified by the principles in s. 9 and be reasonable having regard to the resources of the parties: *Reynolds*, above.

Read together, ss. 8, 9 and 14(2)(k) are clearly designed to give the court power to make such range of orders as the circumstances of the case require: *Foster v Foster* [2023] CSIH 35 (Extra Div.), *2023 S.C.L.R. 669, per* Lady Wise at para. [31].

The court may order a party to provide details of his or her resources: Act of 1985, s. 20.

"AN ORDER UNDER SECTION 16(1)(B)".

49.46.6   The court has power, (a) at any time after granting divorce, to set aside or vary an agreement relating to periodical allowance which expressly provided for it or (b) on granting divorce or within a specified period after that, to set aside or vary an agreement if the agreement was not fair and reasonable at the time it was entered into. In (a), the agreement must expressly state that the power is exercisable by the court: *Ellerby v. Ellerby* 1991 G.W.D. 15-936. In relation to (b), it is not possible to contract out of the right to apply to set aside or vary an agreement as to financial provision: Act of 1985, s. 16(4). In considering the issue of fairness and reasonableness, which has to be looked at in relation to the agreement as a whole, one has to look at all the circumstances; and the quality of legal advice available to a party might be a relevant factor: *Gillon v. Gillon (No. 1)* 1994 S.L.T. 978. The principles to be applied are summarised in *Gillon v. Gillon (No. 3)* 1995 S.L.T. 678.

"AN ORDER UNDER SECTION 18".

49.46.7   An application to set aside or vary a transaction or transfer involving property effected by the other party not more than five years before the claim for financial provision must be made not later than one year from the date that the claim was disposed of: Act of 1985, s. 18(1). The court must be satisfied that the transaction or transfer had the effect of or is likely to have the effect of defeating in whole or in part the claim for aliment or claim for, or for variation or recall of a decree for, financial provision: Act of 1985, s. 18(2). On the similar wording of the previous law in s. 6 of the Divorce (Scotland) Act 1976, see *Leslie v. Leslie* 1987 S.L.T. 232.

justifies a variation: *Macpherson v. Macpherson* , 1989 S.L.T. 231, 235A-B per LJ-C Ross. To discover that the information before the court when the original order was made is not a material change of circumstances: *Stewart v. Stewart* , 1987 S.L.T. 246 (OH).

There is no statutory power for the court to vary post-decree agreements. In such an agreement it is important to be clear whether the decree is superseded by the agreement, otherwise the decree could be varied. That this could occur arose in *McDonnell v. McDonnell* , 2001 S.C. 877 (Extra Div.), an unsatisfactory decision in many ways as, though it was held that the decree could be varied, the agreement was unaffected by the variation. One method adopted in post-decree agreements, to invoke the power for variation s.7(2) of the Act of 1985 over agreements on aliment, is to treat the variation of periodical allowance as (a variation of) aliment for a child (if there is one).

Applications after decree relating to agreements or avoidance transactions

49.50. An application for an order—
    (a)   under section 16(1)(a) or (3) of the Act of 1985 (setting aside or varying agreement as to financial provision), or
    (b)   under section 18 of the Act of 1985 (which relates to avoidance transactions),

made after final decree shall be made by minute in the process of the action to which the application relates.

49.50

Deriv. R.C.S. 1965, r. 170D(7)(c) inserted by S.I. 1986 No. 1231

GENERAL NOTE.

It is not possible to contract out of the right to apply for an order to set aside or vary an agreement as to financial provision: Family Law (Scotland) Act 1985, s. 16(4).

49.50.1

For applications in family actions other than an action of divorce or declarator of nullity of marriage, see r. 49.51.

On setting aside or variation of agreements (s. 16 of the Act of 1985), see note 49.46.6. On avoidance transactions, see note 49.46.7.

"FINAL DECREE".

This is the decree disposing of the whole subject-matter of the cause including expenses: see note 4.15.2(2).

49.50.2

"MINUTE".

For applications by minute, see r. 15.1.

49.50.3

Part VI – Applications Relating to Avoidance Transactions

Form of applications relating to avoidance transactions

49.51.—(1) An application for an order under section 18 of the Act of 1985 (which relates to avoidance transactions) by a party to a family action shall be made by including in the summons, defences or minute, as the case may be, appropriate conclusions, averments and pleas-in-law.

49.51

(2) An application for an order under section 18 of the Act of 1985 after final decree in a family action, shall be made by minute in the process of the action to which the application relates.

Deriv. R.C.S. 1965, r. 170D(4)(a) substituted by S.I. 1977 No. 1621 and amended by S.I. 1986 No. 1231 (r. 49.51(1)); r. 170D(7)(c) inserted by S.I 1986 No. 1231 (r. 49.51(2))

GENERAL NOTE.

An application, to set aside or vary a transaction or transfer involving property effected by the other party not more than five years before the claim for financial provision, must be made not later than one year from the date that the claim was disposed of: Act of 1985, s. 18(1). The court must be satisfied that the transaction or transfer had the effect of or is likely to have the effect of defeating in whole or in part the claim for aliment or claim for, or for variation or recall of a decree for, financial provision: Act of 1985, s. 18(2). On the similar wording of the previous law in s. 6 of the Divorce (Scotland) Act 1976, see *Leslie v. Leslie* 1987 S.L.T. 232.

49.51.1

An order does not prejudice a third party (a) who has in good faith acquired the property or any rights in relation to it for value or (b) who derives title to it or rights from any person who has done so: Act of 1985, s. 18(3).

A third party, who may be affected by an order under s. 18 of the Family Law (Scotland) Act 1985 to set aside or vary a transaction involving property, has a right to be heard: *Harris v. Harris* 1988 S.L.T. 101.

The terms of s. 18(2) are very wide and can be interpreted as permitting interdict and interim interdict which might affect third parties: *M v. M and Wards Estate Trustees Ltd* , 2009 S.L.T. 608 (OH).

For applications in actions of divorce or declarator of nullity of marriage, see r. 49.50.

"SUMMONS".

49.51.2   On form of summons, see r. 13.2.

"DEFENCES".

49.51.3   On form of defences, see r. 18.1.

"MINUTE".

49.51.4   On applications by minute, see r. 15.1.

"FINAL DECREE".

49.51.5   This is the decree disposing of the whole subject-matter of the cause including expenses: see note 4.15.2(2).

Part VII – Financial Provision after Overseas Divorce or Annulment

Interpretation of this Part

49.52   **49.52.** In this Part—

"the Act of 1984" means the Matrimonial and Family Proceedings Act 1984;

"order for financial provision" has the meaning assigned in section 30(1) of the Act of 1984;

"overseas country" has the meaning assigned in section 30(1) of the Act of 1984.

Applications for financial provision after overseas divorce or annulment

49.53   **49.53.**—(1) An application under section 28 of the Act of 1984 for an order for financial provision after a divorce or annulment in an overseas country shall be made by summons.

(2) An application for an order in an action to which paragraph (1) applies—

    (a)   made before or after final decree under—

        (i)   section 13 of the Act of 1981 (transfer of tenancy of matrimonial home),

        (ii)   section 29(4) of the Act of 1984 for interim periodical allowance, or

        (iii)   section 14(4) of the Act of 1985 (variation or recall of an incidental order), or

    (b)   made after final decree under—

        (i)   section 12(4) of the Act of 1985 (variation of date or method of payment of capital sum or date of transfer of property),

        (ii)   section 13(4) of the Act of 1985 (variation, recall, backdating or conversion of periodical allowance), or

        (iii)   section 14(4) of the Act of 1985 (variation or recall of incidental order),

shall be made by motion.

(3)[1] Rule 49.43 (applications after decree relating to aliment) shall apply to a motion under paragraph (2) of this rule as it applies to a motion under that rule.

(4)[2] An application under—

    (a)   paragraph (5) of section 12A of the Act of 1985 (recall or variation of order in respect of a pension lump sum), or

---

[1] R. 49.53(3) amended by S.I. 1996 No. 1756 (effective 5th August 1996).

[2] R. 49.53(4) inserted by S.I. 1996 No. 1756 (effective 5th August 1996 and (4)(b) amended by S.S.I. 2000 No. 412 (effective 1st December 2000).

(b)   paragraph (7) of that section (variation of order in respect of pension lump sum to substitute person responsible for the pension arrangement),

shall be made by minute in the process of the motion to which the application relates.

Deriv. R.C.S. 1965, r. 170M inserted by S.I. 1986 No. 1231

GENERAL NOTE.

The Family Law Act 1986 contains provisions for the recognition in Scotland of divorces obtained **49.53.1** elsewhere in the British Islands and furth of the British Islands. A divorce, annulment or separation by a court of civil jurisdiction (subject to two exceptions) within the British Islands (i.e. the UK, Channel Islands and Isle of Man: Interpretation Act 1978, Sched. 1) is recognised throughout the U.K. An overseas divorce (i.e. one obtained outside the British Islands) by a court or by other means is recognised if it satisfies certain conditions.

Certain ancillary orders of an overseas divorce may be enforceable here, e.g. under the Foreign Judgments (Reciprocal Enforcement) Act 1933, the Maintenance Orders (Reciprocal Enforcement) Act 1972, the C.J.J.A. 1982 or formerly the Council Regulation (E.C.) No. 2201/2003 of 27th November 2003 (new Brussels II) which replaced the Council Regulation (EC) No. 1347/2000 of 29th May 2000 (Brussels II) which applied between member states of the E.U. (except Denmark). The Council Regulation does not apply after 31st December 2020, having been revoked by the Jurisdiction and Judgments (Family, Civil Partnership and Marriage (Same Sex Couples)) (EU Exit) (Scotland) (Amendment etc.) Regulations 2019 [S.S.I. 2019 No. 104] (as read with the European Union (Withdrawal) Act 2018) except in relation to proceedings commenced before the 2019 Regulations came into force at 11pm on 31st December 2020. The Court of Session may, however, be able to make an order for financial provision following an overseas divorce under Pt. IV of the Matrimonial and Family Proceedings Act 1984. There are jurisdictional requirements including that the applicant is domiciled or habitually resident in Scotland and that the other party to the marriage is or must have been domiciled here when they last lived together or owns or is the tenant of property in Scotland which had been the matrimonial home: Act of 1984, s. 28(2).

The orders which the court may make are any one or more of the orders in s. 8(1) of the Act of 1985 (capital sum, transfer of property, periodical allowance or incidental order) or an order under s. 13 of the Act of 1981 (transfer of tenancy of matrimonial home): Act of 1984, s. 30(1). For a recent example, see *Tahir v. Tahir (No. 2)* 1995 S.L.T. 451.

"SUMMONS".

On form of summons, see r. 13.2.   **49.53.2**

"FINAL DECREE".

This is the decree disposing of the whole subject-matter of the cause including expenses: see note   **49.53.3** 4.15.2(2).

"MOTION".

For motions, see Chap. 23.   **49.53.4**

Part VIIA[1] – Financial Provision after Overseas Dissolution or Annulment of a Civil Partnership

Interpretation of this Part

49.53A.[2]   In this Part—   **49.53A**

"order for financial provision" has the meaning given in paragraph 4 of Part 4 of Schedule 11 to the CP Act of 2004;
"overseas proceedings" means proceedings in a country or territory outside the British Islands.

Applications for financial provision after overseas dissolution or annulment of civil partnership

49.53B.—(1)[3]   An application under paragraph 2 of Schedule 11 to the CP Act of   **49.53B** 2004 for an order for financial provision after a dissolution or annulment of a civil partnership in overseas proceedings shall be made by summons

(2)   An application for an order in an action to which paragraph (1) applies—

---

[1] Part VIIA and r. 49.53A inserted by S.S.I. 2005 No. 632 (effective 8th December 2005).
[2] Part VIIA and r. 49.53A inserted by S.S.I. 2005 No. 632 (effective 8th December 2005).
[3] Rule 49.53B inserted by S.S.I. 2005 No. 632 (effective 8th December 2005).

(a) made before or after final decree under—

    (i) section 112 of the CP Act of 2004 (transfer of tenancy of family home);

    (ii) paragraph 3(4) of Schedule 11 to the CP Act of 2004 (interim periodical allowance);

    (iii) section 14(4) of the Act of 1985 (variation or recall of an incidental order); or

(b) made after final decree under—

    (i) section 12(4) of the Act of 1985 (variation of date or method of payment of capital sum of date of transfer of property);

    (ii) section 13(4) of the Act of 1985 (variation, recall, backdating or conversion of periodical allowance); or

    (iii) section 14(4) of the Act of 1985 (variation or recall of incidental orders);

shall be made by motion.

(3) Rule 49.43 (applications after decree relating to aliment) shall apply to a motion under paragraph (2) of this rule as it applies to a motion under that rule.

(4) An application under—

(a) paragraph (5) of section 12A of the Act of 1985 (recall or variation of order in respect of a pension lump sum); or

(b) paragraph (7) of that section (variation of order in respect of pension lump sum to substitute person responsible for the pension arrangement);

shall be made by minute in the process of the motion to which the application relates.

General note.

49.53B.1   Chap. 3 of Pt. 5 of the Civil Partnership Act 2004 contains provisions for the recognition of overseas civil partnerships.

"summons".

49.53B.2   On the form of a summons, see r. 13.2.

"motion".

49.53B.3   For motions, see Chap. 23.

Part VIII – Actions of Aliment

Interpretation of this Part

49.54   **49.54.** In this Part, "action of aliment" means a claim for aliment under section 2(1) of the Act of 1985.

General note.

49.54.1   The court may entertain a claim for aliment (1) in an action for aliment or (2) in proceedings (a) for divorce, separation, declarator of marriage or declarator of nullity of marriage, (b) relating to orders for financial provision, (c) concerning rights and obligations relating to children, (d) concerning parentage or legitimacy and (e) of any other kind where the court considers it appropriate: Family Law (Scotland) Act 1985, s. 2(1) and (2).

A claim for interim aliment may be sought in an action of aliment: Family Law (Scotland) Act 1985, s. 6(1).

Jurisdiction.

49.54.2   The jurisdiction of the court will depend on the jurisdiction to entertain the proceedings in which the claim for aliment is made.

Jurisdiction in an action for aliment alone depends on the C.J.J.A. 1982, Sched. 8, r. 1 (defender's domicile in Scotland), r. 2(1) (personal citation), r. 2(e) as amended by the Jurisdiction and Judgments (Family) (Amendment etc.) (EU Exit) Regulations 2019 [S.I. 2019 No. 519] as amended by S.I. 2020 No. 1574 (in matters relating to maintenance, in the courts for the place where the maintenance creditor is domiciled or habitually resident), r. 2(8) (where defender not domiciled in U.K. has moveable property which has been arrested, or has immoveable property, here). Where a person is domiciled elsewhere in the U.K., jurisdiction is on the grounds of domicile of defender, contract or domicile or habitual residence of pursuer in an action relating to maintenance: C.J.J.A. 1982, Scheds. 1, 3C and 4, arts. 2 and 5(1) and (2). See further, notes 13.2.8 to 13.2.15.

Jurisdiction with respect to aliment (including variation and recall) in an action of divorce, separation, declarator of marriage or declarator of nullity of marriage will arise if the court has jurisdiction to determine that action: Domicile and Matrimonial Proceedings Act 1973 s. 10 and Sched. 2, para. 2A. C.J.J.A. 1982, Sched. 8, r. 2(e) (if the matter is ancillary to proceedings concerning the status of a person, in the court which has jurisdiction to entertain those proceedings). Jurisdiction concerning status will arise if either party is domiciled in Scotland or habitually resident for one year ending with the date when the action is begun: 1973 Act s.7.

The Council Regulation (EC) No. 2201/2003 (new Brussels II), which applied between members of the EU except Denmark, was repealed by the Jurisdiction and Judgments (Family, Civil Partnership and Marriage (Same Sex Couples)) (EU Exit) (Scotland) (Amendment etc.) Regulations 2019 [S.S.I. 2019 No. 104] (as read with the European Union (Withdrawal) Act 2018) with effect from 11pm on 31st December 2020 except in relation to proceedings already commenced. As a result, jurisdiction is as under the C.J.J.A. 1982 or the 1973 Act.

It should be noted that recognition and enforcement of maintenance orders for children by a court in a Contracting State to the 2007 Hague Convention on the International Recovery of Child Support is dealt with in the sheriff court under the International Recovery of Maintenance (Hague Convention 2007) (Scotland) Regulations 2012 [S.S.I. 2012 No. 301]. The U.K. was a member as part of the EU but joined separately on 1st January 2021.

Undefended actions of aliment

49.55.—(1) Where a motion for decree in absence is enrolled in an action of aliment, the pursuer shall, on enrolling the motion, lodge all documentary evidence of the means of the parties available to him in support of the amount of aliment sought.

(2) Where the court requires any appearance for the pursuer, the cause shall be put out for hearing on the Motion Roll.

49.55

Deriv. R.C.S. 1965, r. 170N inserted by S.I. 1986 No. 1231

"MOTION".

For motions, see Chap. 23. Wage certificates etc. may be sent by fax: Direction No. 3 of 1994.

49.55.1

"DECREE IN ABSENCE".

See Chap. 19.

49.55.2

Applications relating to aliment

49.56.—(1) An application for, or for the variation of, an order for interim aliment in an action of aliment depending before the court shall be made by motion.

49.56

(2) Written intimation of a motion under paragraph (1) shall be given not less than seven days before the date on which the motion is enrolled.

(3) An application after final decree for the variation or recall of an order for aliment in an action of aliment shall be made by motion; and rule 49.43 (applications after decree relating to aliment) shall apply to a motion under this paragraph as it applies to a motion under that rule.

(4) A person—

(a) to whom an obligation of aliment is owed under section 1 of the Act of 1985,

(b) in whose favour an order for aliment while made under the age of 18 years was made in an action of aliment, or

(c) who seeks, after attaining that age, an order for aliment against the person in that action against whom the order for aliment in his favour was made,

shall apply by minute in the process of that action.

(5) An application for interim aliment pending the determination of an application under paragraph (4) shall be made by motion.

(6) Where a decree has been pronounced in an application under paragraph (3) or (4), any application for variation or recall of any such decree shall be made by motion; and rule 49.43 (applications after decree relating to aliment) shall apply to a motion under this paragraph as it applies to a motion under that rule.

Deriv. R.C.S. 1965, r. 170P inserted by S.I. 1986 No. 1231

GENERAL NOTE.

49.56.1

An obligation of aliment is owed by a husband to his wife, a wife to her husband, a father or mother to his or her child and a person to a child (other than a child who has been boarded out to him by a local or public authority or voluntary organisation) who has been accepted by him as a child of the family: Family Law (Scotland) Act 1985, s. 1(1).

The obligation subsists until the child is 18 or, if the child is undergoing education at an educational establishment or training for a profession, trade or vocation, until the age of 25; and while under 18, aliment must be claimed on the child's behalf and not by the child: Act of 1985, s. 1. Both parents owe an obligation to aliment their child: Act of 1985, s. 1(1)(c); and see, e.g. *Howarth v. Howarth* 1990 S.L.T. 289. The obligation is to provide such support as is reasonable in the circumstances, having regard to the needs and resources of the parties, their earning capacities and all the circumstances of the case (subject to s. 4(3)): Act of 1985, s. 1(2) and 4(1). The award may be backdated: Act of 1985, s. 3(1).

The court may order a party to provide details of his or her resources or those relating to a child: Act of 1985, s. 20.

The court has a very wide discretion in awarding interim aliment (which is provided for in s. 6(2) of the Act of 1985). Interim aliment is for the relief of need. An award may be reclaimed only with leave of the Lord Ordinary (r. 38.3(5)) unless the interlocutor contains an order not requiring leave. Interim aliment is determined on the basis of gross earnings, not net earnings after tax: *MacInnes v. MacInnes* 1993 S.L.T. 1108.

As a general rule aliment is paid out of post-tax income, the payer receives no allowance for it and the recipient is not taxed on it: Income and Corporation Taxes Act 1988, s. 347A (inserted by s. 36(1) of the Finance Act 1988). An exception is provided for qualifying maintenance payments (i.e. a periodic payment under a court order by a party to the marriage to a child of the family) whereby a payer receives an allowance against his income by deducting such payments from his total income equal to the married couple's allowance: 1988 Act, s. 347B. It is not now, therefore, necessary or effective to make the payment payable to a parent as guardian of the child (see formerly *Huggins v. Huggins* 1981 S.L.T. 179). The small maintenance payment regime has also gone. For discussion of the pre-, and post-, 1988 law, see Alan Barr *"A Vintage Year for Aliment"* 1989 S.L.T.(News) 57.

The court's power to deal with aliment is now restricted. Where the Child Support Agency has jurisdiction, the court may nonetheless have jurisdiction to make a maintenance order including a maintenance order to top up child support maintenance and orders to meet expenses of education and training, to meet expenses attributable to a disability or where the order is to be made against a person with care of the child: Child Support Act 1991, s. 8. An order may be made where the Child Support Agency does not have jurisdiction, i.e. where the child, parent with care or absent parent is not habitually resident in the U.K. or the child is not a qualifying child within the meaning of s. 3 of the 1991 Act. The court retains jurisdiction (even though a child support officer has jurisdiction) to make a maintenance order where a written agreement (whether or not enforceable) provides for an absent parent to make periodic payments to or for the child and the maintenance order made by the court is in all material respects in the same terms as that agreement: Child Support (Written Agreements) (Scotland) Order 1997 [S.I. 1997 No. 2943]. The court retains jurisdiction during the transitional period (5th March 1993 to 6th April 1997), where a maintenance provision already exists, to deal with applications for variation of such provision whether under order of the court or a maintenance agreement until a child maintenance assessment is made, or to deal with a conclusion for aliment in a pending action: Child Support Act 1991 (Commencement No. 3 and Transitional Provisions) Amendment Order 1992 [S.I. 1992 No. 2644].

A maintenance agreement for less than could be awarded under a maintenance assessment will be insecure because an application to the Child Support Agency for a maintenance assessment cannot be prevented: 1991 Act, s. 9.

"MOTION".

49.56.2

For motions, see Chap. 23.

"MINUTE".

49.56.3

For applications by minute, see r. 15.1.

VARIATION OR RECALL OF ALIMENT.

49.56.4

Before an award of aliment can be varied or recalled by virtue of s. 5 of the Family Law (Scotland) Act 1985 the court has to be satisfied that there has been a material change of circumstances; and it is not a material change that the original award has been made on the basis of incomplete or inaccurate information: *Walker v. Walker* 1994 S.C. 482, 486H obiter per 2nd Div. applying *Stewart v. Stewart* 1987 S.L.T. 246. The making of a maintenance assessment by the C.S.A. is a material change: Act of 1985, s. 5(1A).

Interim aliment may be varied or recalled: Act of 1985, s. 6(4).

The court has power to order repayment of aliment where a variation or recall of an award of aliment is made and backdated (Act of 1985, s. 5(4)) but has no such power where the award is of interim aliment: *McColl v. McColl* 1993 S.C. 276.

Applications relating to agreements on aliment

49.57. An application under section 7(2) of the Act of 1985 (variation or termination of agreement on aliment) shall be made by summons or in defences in a family action, as the case may be.

Deriv. R.C.S. 1965, r. 170R inserted by SI 1096/1231

GENERAL NOTE.

A provision in an agreement which purports to exclude future liability for aliment or to restrict any right to bring an action for aliment has no effect unless it was fair and reasonable in all the circumstances at the time the agreement was made: Act of 1985, s. 7(1). If the agreement will terminate on the granting of divorce, an application for variation of the agreement in a divorce action is misconceived (*Mackenzie v. Mackenzie* 1987 S.C.L.R. 671) unless, perhaps, interim aliment is sought.

An application under s. 7(2) of the Act of 1985 may be made only in respect of an obligation created by s. 1(1) of that Act and cannot be invoked where a couple are merely cohabiting or have been divorced: *Drummond v. Drummond* 1995 S.C. 321. Variation or termination of an agreement on aliment may be made on a material change of circumstances: Act of 1985, s. 7(2). The making of a maintenance assessment in respect of a child is a material change of circumstances: Act of 1985, s. 7(2A).

The court has no power to backdate a variation: *Ellerby v. Ellerby* 1991 G.W.D. 15-936.

The power to vary an agreement relating to aliment of a child is restricted: Child Support Act 1991, s. 9(5).

JURISDICTION.

The court has jurisdiction to entertain an application under s. 7(2) of the Act of 1985 if it would have jurisdiction to entertain an action for aliment between the parties to the agreement: Act of 1985, s. 7(5).

On jurisdiction in an action for aliment, see note 49.54.2.

Part IX – Applications for Orders Under Section 11 of the Children (Scotland) Act 1995[1]

Application of this Part

49.58.[2] This Part applies to an application for a section 11 order in a family action other than in an action of divorce, separation, declarator of nullity of marriage, dissolution of a civil partnership, separation of civil partners, or declarator of nullity of a civil partnership.

Deriv. R.C.S. 1965, r. 260C(1) inserted by S.I. 1986 No. 515

GENERAL NOTE.

For applications for section 11 orders in actions of divorce, separation or declarator of nullity of marriage, see Pt. IV (rr. 49.35 to 49.42).

The Council Regulation (EC) No. 2201/2003 (new Brussels II), which applied between members of the EU except Denmark, was repealed by the Jurisdiction and Judgments (Family, Civil Partnership and Marriage (Same Sex Couples)) (EU Exit) (Scotland) (Amendment etc.) Regulations 2019 [S.S.I. 2019 No. 104] (as read with the European Union (Withdrawal) Act 2018) with effect from 11pm on 31st December 2020 except in relation to proceedings already commenced. As a result, jurisdiction is as under the 1986 Act.

JURISDICTION.

The jurisdiction of the court in a family action other than an action of divorce, separation or declarator of marriage is determined, in relation to residence, custody, care or control of a child, contact with or access to (but not guardianship of a child), by ss. 9 (habitual residence), 10 (presence of child), 12 (emergency) and 15(2) (original order granted by court) of the Family Law Act 1986 except where the Council Regulation (E.C.) No. 2201/2003 of 27th November 2003 (new Brussels II) which replaced the Council Regulation (EC) No. 1347/2000 of 29th May 2000 (Brussels II) applies (it applies between member states of the E.U.). The preeminent ground in such proceedings is habitual residence, on the meaning of which see *Dickson v. Dickson* 1990 S.C.L.R. 692 (1st Div.); *Rellis v. Hart* 1993 S.L.T. 738; *Scullion v. Scullion* 1990 S.C.L.R. 577, 581A per Sheriff Stoddart.

An order under s. 11(1) of the 1985 Act may not be made by the court where (a) the court is exercising a jurisdiction in proceedings by virtue of Art. 3 of the Council Regulation and (b) the making of such an order would contravene Art. 6 of the Council Regulation (exclusive jurisdiction of member state of habitual residence, etc., of the defender): 1995 Act, s. 11(1A). The Council Regulation applies to matrimonial matters and matters of parental responsibility for the children of both spouses. Under Art. 6,

---

[1] Cross-heading to Pt. IX substituted by S.I. 1996 No. 2587 (effective 1st November 1996).
[2] Rule 49.58 substituted by S.S.I. 2005 No. 632 (effective 8th December 2005).

a spouse, who is (a) habitually resident in the territory of a member state of the E.U. or is a national of a member state or (b) in the case of U.K. or Ireland has his domicile in that state, may be sued in another member state only in accordance with Arts 3-5 of the Council Regulation.

"SECTION 11 ORDER".

49.58.3   See note 49.1.2.

Form of applications relating to section 11 orders[1]

49.59   **49.59.**[2] Subject to any other provision in this Chapter, an application for a section 11 order shall be made—

    (a)   by a section 11 order;

    (b)   by a conclusion in the summons or defences, as the case may be, in any other family action to which this Part applies; or

    (c)   where the application is made by a person other than a party to an action mentioned in paragraph (a) or (b), by minute in that action.

"SECTION 11 ORDER".

49.59.1   See note 49.1.2.

Any person claiming an interest may apply for an order relating to parental rights: Children (Scotland) Act 1995, s. 11(3)(a). On the meaning of "interest" under s. 3(1) of the Law Reform (Parent and Child) (Scotland) Act 1986, see *D. v. Grampian R.C.* 1995 S.C.(H.L.) 1. In any proceedings for a section 11 order the court shall regard the welfare of the child as the paramount consideration and shall not make any order unless it would be better for the child that an order be made than that none be made and having regard to the views expressed by the child: Act of 1995, s. 11(7).

A mother always has parental responsibilities and parental rights in relation to her child; a father has them only if he is married to the child's mother or was married to her at the time of or after the child's conception: Act of 1995, s. 3(1). The right to parental responsibilities is subject to what is in the best interests of the child: Act of 1995, s. 1(1).

The advantage to a very young child of being with its mother is a consideration which has to be taken into account in deciding where its best interests lie but which will yield to competing advantages which more effectively promote the welfare of the child: *Brixey v. Lynas* 1997 S.C (H.L.) 1.

In relation to a contact order, where a person has parental rights, it is not required to aver in detail the basis on which contact is sought: *O. v. O.* 1995 S.L.T. 238. It should be noted that a parent does not have an absolute right to contact with his or her child. He or she is only entitled to contact if the court is satisfied that it is in the best interests of the child: *Porchetta v. Porchetta* 1986 S.L.T. 105; and see now the Act of 1995, s. 11(7). In *Sanderson v. McManus* 1996 S.L.T. 751, the majority in the Extra Division held that (1) s. 3(2) of the Law Reform (Parent and Child) (Scotland) Act 1996 (see now s. 11(7) of the Act of 1995) sets out the only test; (2) the child's father if not married to its mother does not have parental rights; (3) there is no "right" in a parent to access; and (4) although the parent-child relationship may have intrinsic value, and the status quo should be preserved (*Brixey v. Lynas* , 1994 S.C. 606), these are not propositions of law capable of being determinative but are simply factors which may or may not be significant. Lord McCluskey, dissenting, took the view that the "traditional approach" that the link between a child and his natural parent would be conducive to the child's welfare or should be preserved unless there were strong reasons to the contrary (*Blance v. Blance* 1978 S.L.T. 74; *Brannigan v. Brannigan* 1979 S.L.T. (Notes) 73) was not altered by s. 3(2) of the 1986 Act or *Porchetta*, above.) The majority opinion in *Sanderson*, above was upheld in the House of Lords in 1997 S.L.T. 629. Lord Hope of Craighead stated at p. 634E that the party who seeks the order (for contact or residence) must show on a balance of probabilities, that the welfare of the child requires that the order be made in the child's best interests. In *White v. White* , 2001 S.C. 689 it was held that the court required to have regard to the welfare of the child as its paramount consideration and will generally consider that it is conducive to the welfare of children if the absent parents maintain personal relations and direct contact on a regular basis (see also Lord Hope of Craighead in *Sanderson*, above). There is, however, no legal onus on the person seeking a contact order, the court simply considers all the relevant material and decides what is conducive to the child's welfare: *White*, above, per L.P. Rodger at p. 698H.

The parent having a residence order does not fulfil his or her obligations where a contact order is awarded by leaving it to the child to decide whether to go or not; that parent must encourage and persuade, although not physically coerce, the child to accept contact by the other parent (*Blance*, above, per Lord Stewart at p. 75).

In an action of divorce, separation or nullity of marriage the court must consider whether to make a section 11 order or a reference to the Principal Reporter; and where it is of the opinion that such action may be required, or that it is not in a position to take such action without further consideration, or that it is not desirable in the interests of the child to grant decree until it is in a position to do so, it shall postpone its decision to grant decree: Act of 1995, s. 12(1).

---

[1] R. 49.59 and heading amended by S.I. 1996 No. 2587 (effective 1st November 1996).
[2] R. 49.59 and heading amended by S.I. 1996 No. 2587 (effective 1st November 1996).

In relation to relocation cases, the court's approach is that the welfare and best interests of the child is paramount and falls to be judged without any preconceived leaning in favour of the rights and interests of others: *M v M* 2012 SLT 428, para. [9], *per* Lord Emslie. In *Donaldson v Donaldson* 2014 Fam LR 126, para. [27], Lady Smith held that it is no part of our law that a judge requires to regard any particular factor as having greater weight than any other. *Cf* England, where the reasonable plan of a parent with sole primary care of a child, including the effect of the refusal of an application to relocate by that parent, is regarded as a material factor (*Payne v Payne* [2001] 2 WLR 1826).

It is not appropriate to dispose of an appeal for parental rights solely on the pleadings: O., above.

"SUMMONS".

On form of summons, see r. 13.2.

49.59.2

"DEFENCES".

On form of defences, see r. 18.1.

49.59.3

"MINUTE".

On applications by minute, see r. 15.1.

49.59.4

Defenders in actions for a section 11 order

49.60.[1] In an action for a section 11 order, the pursuer shall call as a defender—

49.60

- (a) the parents or other parent of the child in respect of whom the order is sought;
- (b) any guardian of the child;
- (c) any person who has treated the child as a child of his family;
- (d) any person who in fact exercises care or control in respect of the child; and
- (e) Revoked by S.I. 1998/890.

GENERAL NOTE.

Rule 49.60(e), which provided for calling the Lord Advocate as a defender where there was no one in the other paragraphs to call, was revoked by A.S. (R.C.S.A.) (Miscellaneous) 1998 [SI 1998/890]. Paragraph (e) had been inserted at the suggestion of the Rules Review Group in case there was no one else to call as a defender. Such a situation was rather remote. It had been thought such an event might arise, e.g. where a sole surviving parent required a formal order for immigration purposes. The court might subsequently require intimation to the local authority in whose area the child resides.

49.60.1

"SECTION 11 ORDER".

See note 49.1.2.

49.60.2

Applications relating to interim orders in depending actions

49.61.—(1)[2] An application, in an action depending before the court to which this Part applies, for, or for the variation or recall of, an interim residence order or an interim contact order shall be made by motion.

49.61

(2) Written intimation of a motion under paragraph (1) shall be given not less than 7 days before the date on which the motion is enrolled.

Deriv. P.N. 13th November 1969, para. 1 (r. 49.61(2))

"DEPENDING".

A cause is depending until final decree, whereas a cause is in dependence until final extract. For the meaning of final decree, see note 4.15.2(2). For the meaning of final extract, see note 7.1.2(2).

49.61.1

RESIDENCE AND CONTACT ORDERS.

A residence order replaces, but is not the whole of, what was formerly custody. It means an order regulating arrangements as to with whom or with whom during what periods a child under 16 is to live: Children (Scotland) Act 1995, s. 11(2)(c).

49.61.2

A contact order replaces access. It is an order regulating the arrangements for maintaining personal relations and direct contact between a child under 16 and a person with whom he is not, or will not be, living: Act of 1995, s. 11(2)(d).

---

[1] Rule 49.60 amended by S.I. 1996 No. 2587 (effective 1st November 1996).
[2] Rule 49.61(1) amended by S.I. 1996 No. 2587 (effective 1st November 1996).

"MOTION".

49.61.3   For motions, see Chap. 23.

"WRITTEN INTIMATION".

49.61.4   For methods, see r. 16.9.

"NOT LESS THAN 7 DAYS BEFORE".

49.61.5   The first and last days are included in calculating the period so that there are seven clear days.

Care and supervision by local authorities

49.62   **49.62.**   Revoked by S.I. 1996 No. 2587 (effective 1st November 1996).

Applications after decree

49.63   **49.63.**—[1](1)[2]   An application after final decree for the variation or recall of a section 11 order shall be made by minute in the process of the action to which it relates.

(2)   Where a minute has been lodged under paragraph (1), any party—

    (a)   may apply by motion for an interim order pending the determination of the application; and

    (b)   shall intimate such a motion to every other party not less than seven days before the date on which the motion is enrolled.

(3)   Rules 49.42 (warrants for intimation to child and permission to seek views relating to section 11 order) to 49.42C (views of the child – craves relating to a section 11 order sought by both minuter and respondent) apply (with the necessary modifications) to the seeking of the child's views in relation to a minute lodged in accordance with this rule.".

Deriv. R.C.S. 1965, r. 260E(1)(b) inserted by S.I. 1986 No. 515

"SECTION 11 ORDER".

49.63.1   See note 49.1.2.

"MINUTE".

49.63.2   For applications by minute, see r. 15.1.

"MOTION".

49.63.3   For motions, see Chap. 23.

Part X – Causes under the Matrimonial Homes (Family Protection) (Scotland) Act 1981

Interpretation of this Part

49.64   **49.64.**   Unless the context otherwise requires, words and expressions used in this Part which are also used in the Act of 1981 have the same meaning as in that Act.

Deriv. R.C.S. 1965, r. 188D(1)(c) inserted by S.I. 1982 No. 1281

Form of applications under the Act of 1981

49.65   **49.65.**   Subject to any other provision in this Chapter, an application for an order under the Act of 1981 shall be made—

    (a)   by an action for such an order;

    (b)   by a conclusion in the summons or in defences, as the case may be, in any other family action; or

    (c)   where the application is made by a person other than a party to an action mentioned in paragraph (a) or (b), by minute in that action.

Deriv. R.C.S. 1965, r. 188D(2), (4)(b) and (5) inserted by S.I. 1982 No. 1381

---

[1] As amended by S.S.I. 2019 No. 123 para. 2 (effective 24th June 2019).
[2] Rule 49.63(1) and (3) amended by S.I. 1996 No. 2587 (effective 1st November 1996).

"SUMMONS".

On form of summons, see r. 13.2.   **49.65.1**

"DEFENCES".

On form of defences, see r. 18.1.   **49.65.2**

"MINUTE".

On applications by minute, see r. 15.1.   **49.65.3**

JURISDICTION.

The jurisdiction of the court depends on the proceedings in which the application under the Act of   **49.65.4**
1981 is brought. The court may make an order under the Act of 1981 as an ancillary order by virtue of s.
14(2) of the Family Law (Scotland) Act 1985 in an action of divorce. The jurisdiction of the court to
entertain either of those proceedings is found in s. 7 of the Domicile and Matrimonial Proceedings Act
1973. The Council Regulation (EC) No. 2201/2003 (new Brussels II), which applied between member
states of the EU except Denmark, was repealed by the Jurisdiction and Judgments (Family, Civil Partnership and Marriage (Same Sex Couples)) (EU Exit) (Scotland) (Amendment etc.) Regulations 2019 [S.S.I.
2019 No. 104] (as read with the European Union (Withdrawal) Act 2018) with effect from 11pm on 31st
December 2020 except in relation to proceedings already commenced. As a result, jurisdiction is as under
the 1985 Act.
   Jurisdiction in an action for an order under the Act of 1981 only, will be determined by the C.J.J.A.
1982. The Scottish courts have, amongst other grounds, exclusive jurisdiction in proceedings which have
as their object, rights in rem in or tenancies of immoveable property: Scheds 1, 3C and 4, Art. 16(1) and
Sched. 8, r. 4(1)(a).

Defenders in causes under the Act of 1981

49.66.   The applicant for an order under the Act of 1981 shall call as a defender—   **49.66**

   (a)   where he is seeking an order as a spouse, the other spouse;
   (b)   where he is a third party making an application under section 7(1)
         (dispensing with consent of non-entitled spouse to a dealing), or section
         8(1) (payment from non-entitled spouse in respect of loan), of the Act of
         1981, both spouses;
   (c)   where the application is made under section 18 of the Act of 1981 (oc-
         cupancy rights of cohabiting couples), or is one to which that section ap-
         plies, the other partner; and
   (d)[1] where the application is made under section 18A of the Act of 1981 (ap-
         plication for domestic interdict), the other partner.

Deriv. R.C.S. 1965, r. 188D(7)(a) and (b) inserted by S.I. 1982 No. 1381

"NON-ENTITLED SPOUSE".

The "entitled spouse" is the spouse entitled, or permitted by a third party, to occupy a matrimonial   **49.66.1**
home (defined in s. 22 of the Act of 1981) and the other spouse who is not so entitled or permitted is the
"non-entitled spouse"; and the non-entitled spouse has a right to enter into and occupy or to continue to
occupy the matrimonial home with any child of the family: 1981 Act, s. 1(1).

"OCCUPANCY RIGHTS OF COHABITING COUPLES".

If a man and a woman are living together as man and wife, or two persons of the same sex living   **49.66.2**
together as civil partners, in a house which one of them (the "entitled partner") is entitled, or permitted by
a third party, to occupy and the other (the "non-entitled partner") is not so entitled or permitted, the court
may grant occupancy rights to the non-entitled partner for a period not exceeding six months (or extend
such period for a further period not exceeding six months): Act of 1981, s. 18(1).

Applications by motion under the Act of 1981

49.67.—(1)   An application under any of the following provisions of the Act of   **49.67**
1981 shall be made by motion—

   (a)   section 3(4) (interim order for regulation of rights of occupancy etc.);
   (b)   section 4(6) (interim order suspending occupancy rights);
   (c)   section 5 (variation and recall of orders regulating occupancy rights and
         of exclusion order);

---

[1] Rule 49.66(d) inserted by S.S.I. 2006 No. 206 (effective 4th May 2006).

    (d)   Rule 49.67(1) (d) omitted by S.S.I. 2006 No. 206 (effective 4th May 2006)

    (e)   Rule 49.67(1)(e) omitted by S.S.I. 2006 No. 206 (effective 4th May 2006)

    (f)   the proviso to section 18(1) (extension of period of occupancy rights).

(2) Written intimation of a motion under paragraph (1) shall be given not less than 7 days before the date on which the motion is enrolled—

    (a)   to the other spouse or partner, as the case may be;

    (b)   where the motion is under paragraph (1)(a), (b), (c) or (f) and the entitled spouse or partner is a tenant or occupies the matrimonial home by the permission of a third party, to the landlord or third party, as the case may be; and

    (c)   to any other person to whom intimation of the application was or is to be made by virtue of rule 49.8(1)(k) (warrant for intimation to certain persons in actions for orders under the Act of 1981) or 49.15 (orders for intimation by the court).

Deriv. R.C.S. 1965, r. 188D(3) (r. 49.67(1)), and r. 188D(7) and (9) (r. 49.67(2)), both inserted by S.I. 1982 No. 1381

"MOTION".

49.67.1   For motions, see Chap. 23.

Section 3(4) of the Act of 1981.

49.67.2   An entitled or non-entitled spouse (see s. 1(1)) may apply for an order declaring, enforcing, restricting, regulating or protecting occupancy rights in the matrimonial home (see s. 22): Act of 1981, s. 3(1). On such an application the court may make such interim order as is necessary or expedient in relation to the residence of either spouse in the home, their personal effects or the furniture and plenishings: Act of 1981, s. 3(4).

Section 4(6) of the Act of 1981.

49.67.3   A spouse (or partner of a cohabiting couple), whether entitled, non-entitled (see s. 1(1) or where both spouses are entitled, or permitted by a third party, to occupy a matrimonial home (see s. 22), may, whether in occupation or not, apply for an exclusion order suspending the occupancy rights of the other spouse in the home: Act of 1981, s. 4(1). Pending the making of an exclusion order the court may make an interim order suspending the occupancy rights of the non-applicant spouse including summary ejection and interdict: Act of 1981, s. 4(6).

The test for the grant of an interim order is the same as that for an exclusion order (for which see s. 4(2)): *Brown v. Brown* 1985 S.L.T. 376.

An interim order may only be made if the non-applicant spouse has been given an opportunity to be heard Act of 1981, s. 4(6) proviso.

Affidavits, permitted under r. 49.71, may be required so that relevant evidence is before the court. The Lord Ordinary may interview the parties (*Bell v. Bell* 1983 S.L.T. 224; *Smith v. Smith* 1983 S.L.T. 275) or refer to a custody report (*Ward v. Ward* 1983 S.L.T. 472).

As an interim order is in the discretion of the Lord Ordinary, a decision may be successfully reclaimed against only if he erred in law or his decision was unwarranted (i.e. so unreasonable no other judge would have reached it): *Brown*, above; *McCafferty v. McCafferty* 1986 S.L.T. 650.

Section 5 of the Act of 1981.

49.67.4   An order regulating occupancy rights (see s. 3) in the matrimonial home, or an exclusion order (see s. 4), may be varied or recalled under s. 5 of the Act of 1981. Such an order will, in any event, cease to have effect on the termination of the marriage, on the entitled spouse ceasing to be entitled or, where both are entitled or permitted, on both ceasing so to be: Act of 1981, s. 5(1).

Section 15 of the Act of 1981.

49.67.5   A power of arrest must be attached to (a) a matrimonial interdict which is ancillary to an exclusion order or an interim exclusion order (on which see s. 4 of the Act of 1981 and note 49.67.3), or (b) any other matrimonial interdict where the non-applicant spouse (or partner of a cohabiting couple) has had the opportunity of being heard by the court unless in all the circumstances such a power is unnecessary: Act of 1981, s. 15(1). A "matrimonial interdict" means an interdict or interim interdict which restrains or prohibits the conduct of one spouse against the other spouse or a child of the family or prohibits a spouse from entering or remaining in or in the vicinity of the matrimonial home: Act of 1981, s. 14(2). On the form of words for a non-molestation interdict, see *Murdoch v. Murdoch* 1973 S.L.T. (Notes) 13 in which the court said it would have to be satisfied that the pursuer, unless interdict is granted, is likely to be exposed, without adequate protection, to conduct by the defender which will put her at risk or in fear, alarm or distress.

A copy of (*a*) the application for interdict, (*b*) the interlocutor granting interdict and the power of arrest attached and (*c*) a certificate of service of the interdict must be intimated, after service of it, to the chief constable of the police area in which the matrimonial home is situated and, if the applicant spouse resides in another area, to the chief constable of that police area: Act of 1981, s. 15(4). For certificates of execution of such intimation, see r. 49.70.

A power of arrest under s. 15 of the Act of 1981 may not be imposed if the non-applicant spouse (or partner of a cohabiting couple) would be subject to a power of arrest under that Act and the Protection from Abuse (Scotland) Act 2001: Act of 1981, s. 15(1A) inserted by s. 6 of the 2001 Act.

For applications for a power of arrest in interdicts for protection from abuse, see Chap. 85.

"WRITTEN INTIMATION".

For methods, see r. 16.9.

49.67.6

"NOT LESS THAN 7 DAYS BEFORE".

The first and last days are included in calculating the period so that there are seven clear days.

49.67.7

Procedure for minutes

49.68. Where an application is made by minute under rule 49.65(c) (form of application under the Act of 1981 by a person other than a party) and answers to that minute are lodged, the minute and answers shall not be included with the other pleadings in the action in any record, but shall be made up separately in the form of a record; and rule 49.33(5)(b) and (c) (lodging etc. of records) shall apply to that record as it applies to a record under that rule.

49.68

Deriv. R.C.S. 1965, r. 188D(6) inserted by S.I. 1982 No. 1381

Sist of actions to enforce occupancy rights

49.69. Unless the court otherwise directs, the sist of an action by virtue of section 7(4) of the Act of 1981 (where action raised by non-entitled spouse to enforce occupancy rights) shall apply only to such part of the action as relates to the enforcement of occupancy rights by a non-entitled spouse.

49.69

Deriv. R.C.S. 1965, r. 188D(11) inserted by S.I. 1982 No. 1381

GENERAL NOTE.

As a general rule the exercise of occupancy rights by a non-entitled spouse is protected against any dealing (e.g. sale or lease) of the entitled spouse relating to the matrimonial home without consent of the non-entitled spouse: Matrimonial Homes (Family Protection) (Scotland) Act 1981, s. 6. The court can dispense with that consent on an application to it under s. 7 of the Act of 1981. Where such an application has been made and the non-entitled spouse has brought an action to enforce occupancy rights, that action or that part of it which relates to the claim for occupancy rights can be sisted pending the proceedings in the application: Act of 1981, s. 7(4).

49.69.1

Certificates of execution of delivery of documents to chief constable

49.70.— [Revoked by S.S.I. 2006 No. 206 (effective 4th May 2006).]

49.70

Evidence in causes under the Act of 1981

49.71—(1) For the purposes of proof in any application for an order under the Act of 1981, evidence by affidavit shall be admissible in place of parole evidence.

49.71

(2) Rule 36.8 (conditions for receiving certain written statements in evidence) shall not apply in a cause to which paragraph (1) of this rule applies.

Deriv. R.C.S. 1965, r. 188D(15) inserted by S.I. 1982 No. 1381

GENERAL NOTE.

The reference in R.C.S. 1965, r. 188D(15) to evidence by affidavit not being insufficient by reason only that it is not supported by parole evidence has been omitted as unnecessary; see also s. 1 of the Civil Evidence (Scotland) Act 1988.

49.71.1

"AFFIDAVIT".

49.71.2   Note meaning in r. 1.3(1).

Part XA[1] – Causes Under Chapters 3 and 4 of Part 3 of the Civil Partnership Act 2004

Interpretation of this Part

49.71A   **49.71A.**—(1)[2] In this Part, unless the context otherwise requires, words and expressions used in this Part which are also used in Chapters 3 and 4 of Part 3 of the CP Act of 2004 have the meaning given in those Chapters.

GENERAL NOTE.

49.71A.1   Pt. XA contains rules similar to those in Pt. X for proceedings under the Matrimonial Homes (Family Protection) (Scotland) Act 1981.

Forms of applications under Chapters 3 and 4 of Part 3 of the Act of 2004

49.71B   **49.71B.**[3] Subject to any other provision in this Chapter, an application for an order under Chapter 3 or 4 of Part 3 of the CP Act of 2004 shall be made—

(a) by an action for such an order;

(b) by a conclusion in the summons or in defences, as the case may be, in any other family action; or

(c) where the application is made by a person other than a party to an action mentioned in paragraph (a) or (b), by minute in that action.

"SUMMONS".

49.71B.1   On form of summons, see r. 13.2.

"DEFENCES".

49.71B.2   On form of defences, see r. 18.1.

"MINUTE".

49.71B.3   On applications by minute, see r. 15.1.

Defenders in causes under Chapters 3 and 4 of Part 3 of the CP Act of 2004

49.71C   **49.71C.**[4] The applicant for an order under Chapter 3 or 4 of Part 3 of the CP Act of 2004 shall call as a defender—

(a) where he is seeking an order as a civil partner, the other civil partner; and

(b) where he is a third party making an application under section 107(1) (dispensing with the consent of non-entitled partner to a dealing), or section 108(1) (payment from non-entitled partner in respect of loan) of the CP Act of 2004, both partners.

Applications by motion under Chapters 3 and 4 of the CP Act of 2004

49.71D   **49.71D.**—[5](1)-(2) Rule 49.71D omitted by SSI 2006/206 (effective 4th May 2006)

Procedure for minutes

49.71E   **49.71E.**[6] Where an application is made by minute under rule 49.71B(c) (form of application under Chapter 3 or 4 of Part 3 of the CP Act of 2004) by a person other than a party and answers to that minute are lodged, the minute and answers shall not be included with the other pleadings in the action in any record, but shall be made

---

[1] Part XA and r. 49.71A inserted by S.S.I. 2005 No. 632 (effective 8th December 2005).
[2] Part XA and r. 49.71A inserted by S.S.I. 2005 No. 632 (effective 8th December 2005).
[3] Rule 49.71B inserted by S.S.I. 2005 No. 632 (effective 8th December 2005).
[4] Rule 49.71C inserted by S.S.I. 2005 No. 632 (effective 8th December 2005).
[5] Rule 49.71E inserted by S.S.I. 2005 No. 632 (effective 8th December 2005).
[6] Rule 49.71E inserted by S.S.I. 2005 No. 632 (effective 8th December 2005).

up separately in the form of a record; and rule 49.33(5)(b) and (c) (lodging etc. of records) shall apply to that record as it applies to a record under that rule.

Sist of actions to enforce occupancy rights

49.71F.[1]   Unless the court otherwise directs, the sist of an action by virtue of section 107(4) of the CP Act 2004 (where the action raised by non-entitled partner to enforce occupancy rights) shall apply only to such part of the action as relates to the enforcement of occupancy rights by a non-entitled partner.

49.71F

Certificates of execution of delivery to the chief constable

49.71G.[2](1)-(2)   Rule 49.71G revoked by S.S.I. 2006 No. 206 (effective 4th May 2006)

49.71G

Evidence in causes under Chapter 3 or 4 of Part 3 of the Act of 2004

49.71H.—[3](1)   For the purposes of proof in any application for an order under Chapter 3 or 4 of the CP Act of 2004, evidence by affidavit shall be admissible in place of parole evidence.

49.71H

(2)   Rule 36.8 (conditions for receiving certain written statements in evidence) shall not apply in a cause to which paragraph (1) of this rule applies.

"AFFIDAVIT".

Note the meaning of affidavit in r. 1.3(1); and see note 1.3.7 on affidavits.

49.71H.1

Part XI – Simplified Divorce Applications

Application and interpretation of, and directions under, this Part

49.72.—(1)   This Part applies to an application for divorce by a party to a marriage made in the manner prescribed in rule 49.73 (form of applications for simplified divorce) if, but only if—

49.72

(a)[4, 5]   that party relies on the facts set out in section 1(2)(d) (no cohabitation for one year with consent of defender to decree), section 1(2)(e) (no cohabitation for two years) or section (1)(1)(b) (issue of interim gender recognition certificate), of the Act of 1976;

(b)   in an application under section 1(2)(d) of the Act of 1976, the other party consents to decree of divorce being granted;

(c)   no other proceedings are pending in any court which could have the effect of bringing the marriage to an end;

(d)   there are no children of the marriage under the age of 16 years;

(e)   neither party to the marriage applies for an order for financial provision on divorce;

(f)   neither party to the marriage suffers from mental disorder; and

(g)[6]   neither party to the marriage applies for postponement of decree under section 3A of the Act of 1976 (postponement of decree where impediment to religious marriage exists).

(2)   If an application ceases to be one to which this Part applies at any time before final decree, it shall be deemed to be abandoned and shall be dismissed.

(3)   In this Part, "simplified divorce application" means an application mentioned in paragraph (1).

---

[1] Rule 49.71F inserted by S.S.I. 2005 No. 632 (effective 8th December 2005).
[2] Rule 49.71H inserted by S.S.I. 2005 No. 632 (effective 8th December 2005)
[3] Rule 49.71H inserted by S.S.I. 2005 No. 632 (effective 8th December 2005)
[4] R. 49.72(1)(a) amended by S.S.I. 2005 No. 632 (effective 8th December 2005).
[5] R. 49.72(1)(a) amended by S.S.I. 2006 No. 206 (effective 4th May 2006).
[6] R. 49.72(1)(g) inserted by S.S.I. 2006 No. 206 (effective 4th May 2006) and substituted by S.S.I. 2007 No. 7, r. 2 (effective 26th February 2007).

(4) The Principal Clerk shall give directions in relation to the administrative procedures to be followed on the lodging of a simplified divorce application for—

(a) the registration and service of such an application,

(b) having it brought before the court for consideration,

(c) in the event of decree of divorce being granted, for notification to the parties, and

(d) connected purposes,

and such directions shall have effect subject to the provisions of this Part.

Deriv. R.C.S. 1965, r. 170E inserted by S.I. 1982 No. 1679 (r. 49.72(1) to (3)); and r. 170H(1) inserted by S.I. 1982 No. 1679 (r. 49.72(4))

General note.

49.72.1   Simplified (or "do-it-yourself) divorce procedure was introduced by A.S. (R.C.A. No. 6) (Simplified Divorce Procedure) 1982 [S.I. 1982 No. 1679].

"final decree".

49.72.2   This is the decree disposing of the whole subject-matter of the cause including expenses: see note 4.15.2(2).

Directions by the Principal Clerk.

49.72.3   There are none.

Form of applications for simplified divorce

49.73   **49.73.**—(1)[1] A simplified divorce application in which the facts set out in section 1(2)(d) of the Act of 1976 (no cohabitation for one year with consent of defender to decree) are relied on shall be made in Form 49.73-A and shall only be of effect if—

(a) it is signed by the applicant; and

(b) the form of consent in Part 2 of Form 49.73-A is signed by the party to the marriage giving consent.

(2)[2] A simplified divorce application in which the facts set out in section 1(2)(e) of the Act of 1976 (no cohabitation for two years) are relied on shall be made in Form 49.73-B and shall only be of effect if it is signed by the applicant.

(3)[3] A simplified divorce application in which the facts set out in section 1(1)(b) of the Act of 1976(grounds of divorce: interim gender recognition certificate) are relied on shall be made in Form 49.73-C and shall only be of effect if signed by the applicant.

Deriv. R.C.S. 1965, r. 170F inserted by S.I. 1982 No. 1679

Lodging and registration of simplified divorce applications

49.74   **49.74.**—(1) The applicant shall send a simplified divorce application to the Deputy Principal Clerk with—

(a)[4] an extract or certified copy of the marriage certificate;

(b)[5] the appropriate fee; and

(c)[6] an application under section 1(1)(b) of the Act of 1976, the interim gender recognition certificate or a certified copy.

---

[1] Rule 49.73(1) and (2) amended by S.S.I. 2006 No. 206 (effective 4th May 2006).

[2] Rule 49.73(1) and (2) amended by S.S.I. 2006 No. 206 (effective 4th May 2006).

[3] Rule 49.73(3) inserted by S.S.I. 2005 No. 632 (effective 8th December 2005).

[4] Rule 49.74(1)(a) & (b) amended and r. 49.74(1)(c) inserted by S.S.I. 2005 No. 632 (effective 8th December 2005).

[5] Rule 49.74(1)(a) & (b) amended and r. 49.74(1)(c) inserted by S.S.I. 2005 No. 632 (effective 8th December 2005).

[6] Rule 49.74(1)(a) & (b) amended and r. 49.74(1)(c) inserted by S.S.I. 2005 No. 632 (effective 8th December 2005).

(2) Subject to the following rules of this Part, a simplified divorce application shall, on being registered in accordance with any directions made under rule 49.72(4), be treated as a summons in an action of divorce which has commenced.

Deriv. R.C.S. 1965, r. 170G inserted by S.I. 1982 No. 1679 (r. 49.74(1)); and r. 170H(2) inserted by S.I. 1982 No. 1679 (r. 49.74(2))

Fee.

A fee is payable by the applicant. For fee, see Court of Session etc. Fees Order 1997, Table of Fees, Pt. I, B, item 4 [S.I. 1997 No. 688, as amended, pp.C1201 et seq.]. Certain persons are exempt from payment of fees; see 1997 Fees Order, art. 5 substituted by S.S.I. 2002 No. 270.

49.74.1

Warrants for service or intimation of simplified divorce applications

49.75.—(1) On registration of a simplified divorce application where the address of the other party to the marriage is known, a clerk of session shall grant warrant for service of the application.

49.75

(2)[1,2] On registration of an application in which the facts set out in section 1(2)(e) of the Act of 1976 (no cohabitation for two years) or section 1(1)(b) of the Act of 1976 (grounds of divorce: interim gender recognition certificate) are relied on where the address of the other party to the marriage is not known to the applicant and cannot reasonably be ascertained—

(a) the Deputy Principal Clerk shall grant warrant for intimation of the application to—

(i) every child of the marriage, and

(ii) one of the next of kin of the other party who has reached the age of 16 years,

unless the address of such person is not known and cannot reasonably be ascertained; and

(b) the application shall thereafter be placed before the Lord Ordinary for such order under rule 16.5 (service where address of person is not known) as he thinks fit.

(3) A warrant granted under paragraph (1) or (2)(a) shall be sufficient authority for such service and intimation.

Deriv. R.C.S. 1965, r. 170I(1) inserted by S.I. 1982 No. 1679 (r. 49.75(1)), and r. 170I(3) inserted by S.I. 1982 No. 1679 and amended by S.S.I. 2006 No. 206 (r. 49.75(2))

Execution of service or intimation of simplified divorce applications

49.76.—(1) Subject to the following paragraphs, service or intimation of a simplified divorce application on a warrant granted under rule 49.75 on any person whose address is known to the applicant shall be made—

49.76

(a) by the Deputy Principal Clerk by post in accordance with rule 16.4 (service by post); or

(b) by a messenger-at-arms.

(2) In the application of Part I of Chapter 16 (service and intimation) to service or intimation under this rule, the following provisions of that Part of that Chapter shall not apply:—

rule 16.1(3) (which relates to a party lodging a certificate of service in process),

rule 16.3(1)(73) (form of citation and certificate of service by messenger-at-arms),

rule 16.4(2)(b) (service by post by agent),

rule 16.4(4) (form of citation in service by post).

---

[1] Rule 49.75(2) amended by S.S.I. 2005 No. 632 (effective 8th December 2005).
[2] Rule 49.75(2) amended by S.S.I. 2006 No. 206 (effective 4th May 2006).

(3)[1,2]   In the case of service of a simplified divorce application on the other party to the marriage under paragraph (1), the person executing service shall complete a citation in Form 49.76-A (no cohabitation for one year with consent to divorce) Form 49.76-B (no cohabitation for two years) or Form 49.76-BA (interim gender recognition certificate), as the case may be.

(4)   In the case of intimation of a simplified divorce application on a person under paragraph (1), the person giving intimation shall complete a notice of intimation in Form 49.76-C.

(5)   A certificate of service or intimation in Form 49.76-D (certificate by Deputy Principal Clerk) or Form 49.76-E (certificate by messenger-at-arms), as the case may be, shall be—

(a)   completed by the person executing service or giving intimation;

(b)   in the case of a certificate completed by a messenger-at-arms, sent to the Deputy Principal Clerk; and

(c)   attached to the application by the Deputy Principal Clerk.

Opposition to simplified divorce applications

49.77   **49.77.**—(1)   Any person on whom service or intimation of a simplified divorce application has been made may give notice by letter sent to the Deputy Principal Clerk within the period of notice that he challenges the jurisdiction of the court or opposes the grant of decree of divorce and giving the reasons for his opposition to the application.

(2)   Where opposition to a simplified divorce application is made under paragraph (1), the court shall dismiss the application unless it is satisfied that the reasons given for the opposition are frivolous.

(3)   The Deputy Principal Clerk shall give written intimation of the decision under paragraph (2) to the applicant and the respondent.

(4)   The sending of a letter under paragraph (1) shall not imply acceptance of the jurisdiction of the court.

Deriv. R.C.S. 1965, r. 170J inserted by S.I. 1982 No. 1679

"FRIVOLOUS".

49.77.1   Reasons which do not amount in law to a defence are frivolous.

Evidence in simplified divorce applications

49.78   **49.78.**—(1)   Parole evidence shall not be given in a simplified divorce application.

(2)   Rule 36.8 (conditions for receiving certain written statements in evidence) shall not apply in a simplified divorce application.

No reclaiming in simplified divorce applications

49.79   **49.79.**   A decree pronounced in a simplified divorce application may not be reclaimed against.

GENERAL NOTE.

49.79.1   To set aside a decree pronounced in a simplified divorce action, an action of reduction would have to be brought. On actions of reduction, see Chap. 53.

Applications after decree in simplified divorce applications

49.80   **49.80.**—(1)   Any application to the court after decree of divorce has been granted in a simplified divorce application which could have been made if it had been an action of divorce shall be made by minute.

---

[1] Rule 49.76(3) amended by S.S.I. 2005 No. 632 (effective 8th December 2005).
[2] Rule 49.76(3) amended by SSI 2006/206 (effective 4th May 2006).

(2) On lodging a minute under paragraph (1), the minuter shall lodge a process.

Deriv. R.C.S. 1965, r. 170L inserted by S.I. 1982 No. 1679

"MINUTE".

For applications by minute, see r. 15.1.

49.80.1

Part XIA[1] – Simplified Applications for Dissolution of Civil Partnerships

Application and interpretation of, and directions under, this Part

49.80A.—[2](1)   In this Part—

49.80A

"child of the family" has the meaning given in section 12(4)(b) of the Act of 1995;[3]

"simplified dissolution application" means an application mentioned in paragraph (2).

(2)   This Part applies to an application for dissolution of a civil partnership by a party to a civil partnership made in the manner prescribed in rule 49.80B (form of application for simplified dissolution of a civil partnership) if, but only if—

(a)[4]   that party relies on the facts set out in section 117(3)(c) (no cohabitation for one year with consent of defender to decree), section 117(3)(d) (no cohabitation for two years), or section 117(2)(b) (issue of a gender recognition certificate) of the CP Act of 2004,

(b)   in an application under section 117(3)(c) of the CP Act of 2004, the other party consents to a decree of dissolution being granted;

(c)   no other proceedings are pending in any court which could have the effect of bringing the civil partnership to an end;

(d)   there are no children of the family under the age of 16 years;

(e)   neither party to the civil partnership applies for an order for financial provision on dissolution of the civil partnership; and

(f)   neither party to the civil partnership suffers from a mental disorder.

(3)   If an application ceases to be one to which this Part applies at any time before final decree, it shall be deemed to be abandoned and shall be dismissed.

(4)   The Principal Clerk shall give directions in relation to the administrative procedures to be followed on the lodging of a simplified dissolution application for—

(a)   the registration and service of such an application;

(b)   having it brought before the court for consideration;

(c)   in the event of decree of dissolution of the civil partnership being granted, for notification to the parties; and

(d)   connected purposes;

and such directions shall have effect subject to the provisions of this Part.

GENERAL NOTE.

Pt. XIA contains provisions similar to simplified divorce applications under Pt. XI.

49.80A.1

"FINAL DECREE".

This is the decree disposing of the whole subject-matter of the cause including expenses: see note 4.15.2(2).

49.80A.2

DIRECTIONS BY THE PRINCIPAL CLERK.

There are none.

49.80A.3

---

[1] Part XIA and r. 49.80A inserted by S.S.I. 2005 No. 632 (effective 8th December 2005).

[2] Part XIA and r. 49.80A inserted by S.S.I. 2005 No. 632 (effective 8th December 2005).

[3] Rule 49.80A(1) and (2)(a) amended by S.S.I. 2006 No. 206 (effective 4th May 2006).

[4] Rule 49.80A(1) and (2)(a) amended by S.S.I. 2006 No. 206 (effective 4th May 2006).

Form of application for simplified dissolution of a civil partnership

49.80B   **49.80B.**—[1](1)[2] A simplified dissolution application in which the facts set out in section 117(3)(c) of the CP Act of 2004 (no cohabitation for one year with consent of defender to decree) are relied on shall be made in Form 49.80B-A and shall only be of effect if—

    (a)   it is signed by the applicant; and

    (b)   the form of consent in Part 2 of Form 49.80B-A is signed by the party to the civil partnership giving consent.

    (2)[3] A simplified dissolution application in which the facts set out in section 117(3)(d) of the CP Act of 2004 (no cohabitation for two years) are relied on shall be made in Form 49.80B-B and shall only be of effect if signed by the applicant.

    (3) A simplified dissolution application in which the facts set out in section 117(2)(b) of the CP Act of 2004 (issue of interim gender recognition certificate) are relied on shall be made in Form 49.80B-C and shall only be of effect if signed by the applicant.

Lodging and registration of simplified dissolution applications

49.80C   **49.80C.**—[4](1) The applicant shall send a simplified dissolution application to the Deputy Principal Clerk with—

    (a)   an extract or certified copy of the certificate of civil partnership;

    (b)   the appropriate fee; and

    (c)   in an application under section 117(2)(b) of the CP Act of 2004, the interim gender recognition certificate or a certified copy.

    (2) Subject to the following rules of this Part, a simplified dissolution application shall, on being registered in accordance with any directions made under rule 49.80A(4), be treated as a summons in an action of dissolution of a civil partnership which has commenced.

Fee.

49.80C.1   A fee is payable by the applicant. For fee, see Court of Session, etc. Fees Order 1997, Table of Fees, Pt. I, B, [SI 1997/688, as amended, pp C1201 et seq.] Certain persons are exempt from payment of fees: see 1997 Fees Order, art. 5 substituted by S.S.I. 2002 No. 270.

Warrants for service or intimation of simplified dissolution applications

49.80D   **49.80D.**—[5](1) On registration of a simplified dissolution application where the address of the other party to the civil partnership is known, a clerk of session shall grant warrant for service of the application.

    (2)[6] On registration of an application in which the facts set out in section 117(3)(d) (no cohabitation for two years) or section 117(2)(b) (issue of interim gender recognition certificate) of the Act of 2004 are relied on where the address of the other party to the civil partnership is not known to the applicant and cannot reasonably be ascertained—

    (a)   the Deputy Principal Clerk shall grant warrant for intimation of the application to—

        (i)   every child of the family, and

        (ii)   one of the next-of-kin of the other party who has reached the age

---

[1] Rule 49.80B inserted by S.S.I. 2005 No. 632 (effective 8th December 2005).

[2] Rule 49.80B(1) and (2) amended by S.S.I. 2006 No. 206 (effective 4th May 2006).

[3] Rule 49.80B(1) and (2) amended by S.S.I. 2006 No. 206 (effective 4th May 2006).

[4] Rule 49.80C inserted by S.S.I. 2005 No. 632 (effective 8th December 2005).

[5] Rule 49.80D inserted by S.S.I. 2005 No. 632 (effective 8th December 2005).

[6] Rule 49.80D(2) amended by S.S.I. 2006 No. 206 (effective 4th May 2006).

of 16 years,

unless the address of such person is not known an cannot reasonably be ascertained; and

(b) the application shall thereafter be placed before the Lord Ordinary for such order under rule 16.5 (service where address of person is not known) as he thinks fit.

(3) A warrant granted under paragraph (1) or (2)(a) shall be sufficient authority for such service and intimation.

Execution of service or intimation of simplified dissolution application

49.80E.—[1](1) Subject to the following paragraphs, service or intimation of a simplified dissolution application on a warrant granted under rule 49.80D on any person whose address is known to the applicant shall be made—

    (a) by the Deputy Principal Clerk by post in accordance with rule 16.4 (service by post); or

    (b) by a messenger-at-arms.

(2) In the application of Part I of Chapter 16 (service and intimations) to service and intimation under this rule, the following provisions of that Part of that Chapter shall not apply:—

rule 16.1(3) (which relates to party lodging a certificate of service in process),

rule 16.3(1)(b) (form of citation and certificate of service by messenger-at-arms),

rule 16.4(2)(b) (service by post by agent),

rule 16.4(4) (form of citation in service by post).

(3)[2] In the case of service of a simplified dissolution application on the other party to the civil partnership under paragraph (1), the person executing service shall complete a citation in Form 49.80E-A (no cohabitation for one year with consent to divorce), Form 49.80E-B (no cohabitation for two years), or Form 49.80E-C (interim gender recognition certificate) as the case may be.

(4) In the case of intimation of a simplified dissolution application on a person under paragraph (1) the person giving intimation shall complete a notice of intimation in Form 49.80E-D.

(5) A certificate of service or intimation in Form 49.80E-E (certificate by Deputy Principal Clerk) or Form 49.80E-F (certificate by messenger-at-arms), as the case may be, shall be—

    (a) completed by the person executing service or giving intimation;

    (b) in the case of a certificate completed by a messenger-at-arms, sent to the Deputy Principal Clerk; and

    (c) attached to the application by the Deputy Principal Clerk.

49.80E

Opposition to simplified dissolution application

49.80F.—[3](1) Any person on whom service or intimation of a simplified dissolution application has been made may give notice by letter sent to the Deputy Principal Clerk within the period of notice that he challenges the jurisdiction of the court or opposes the grant of the decree of dissolution and giving the reasons for his opposition to the application.

(2) Where opposition to a simplified dissolution application is made under paragraph (1), the court shall dismiss the application unless it is satisfied that the reasons given for the opposition are frivolous.

49.80F

---

[1] Rule 49.80E inserted by S.S.I. 2005 No. 632 (effective 8th December 2005).
[2] Rule 49.80E(3) amended by S.S.I. 2006 No. 206 (effective 4th May 2006).
[3] Rule 49.80F inserted by S.S.I. 2005 No. 632 (effective 8th December 2005).

(3) The Deputy Principal Clerk shall give written intimation of the decision under paragraph (2) to the applicant and the respondent.

(4) The sending of a letter under paragraph (1) shall not imply acceptance of jurisdiction of the court.

"FRIVOLOUS".

49.80F.1 Reasons which do not amount in law to a defence are frivolous.

Evidence in simplified dissolution applications

49.80G **49.80G.**—[1](1) Parole evidence shall not be given in a simplified dissolution application.

(2) Rule 36.8 (conditions for receiving certain written statements in evidence) shall not apply in a simplified dissolution application.

No reclaiming in simplified dissolution applications

49.80H **49.80H.**[2] A decree pronounced in a simplified dissolution application may not be reclaimed against.

GENERAL NOTE.

49.80H.1 To set aside a decree pronounced in a simplified dissolution application, an action of reduction would have to be brought. On actions of reduction, see Chap. 53.

Applications after decree in simplified dissolution applications

49.80I **49.80I.**—[3](1) Any application to the court after decree of dissolution has been granted in a simplifed dissolution application which could not have been made if it had been an action of dissolution of a civil partnership shall be made by minute.

(2) On lodging a minute under paragraph (1), the minuter shall lodge a process.

"MINUTE".

49.80I.1 For applications by minute, see r. 15.1.

Part XII – Child Support Act 1991

Interpretation of this Part

49.81 **49.81.**[4] In this Part—

"the Act of 1991" means the Child Support Act 1991;
"child" has the meaning assigned in section 55 of the Act of 1991;
"maintenance assessment" has the meaning assigned in section 54 of the Act of 1991.

GENERAL NOTE.

49.81.1 On averments required in a family action where aliment is sought for a child, see r. 49.6. For jurisdiction of the court in relation to aliment which may be affected by the Child Support Act 1991, see note 49.6.1.

Restriction of expenses

49.82 **49.82.** Where the Secretary of State is called as a defender in an action for declarator of non-parentage or illegitimacy, and the Secretary of State does not defend the action, no expenses shall be awarded against the Secretary of State.

GENERAL NOTE.

49.82.1 The Secretary of State may be made a defender to an action of declarator of non-parentage or illegitimacy: Child Support Act, s. 28; and r. 49.6(4)(b) provides that where an allegation of paternity is made against the pursuer the Secretary of State must be called as a defender. Such an action is brought

---

[1] Rule 49.80G inserted by S.S.I. 2005 No. 632 (effective 8th December 2005).
[2] Rule 49.80H inserted by S.S.I. 2005 No. 632 (effective 8th December 2005).
[3] Rule 49.80I inserted by S.S.I. 2005 No. 632 (effective 8th December 2005).
[4] R. 49.81 amended by SI 1996/1756 (minor correction).

under s. 7 of the Law Reform (Parent and Child) (Scotland) Act 1986. The Secretary of State is likely only to defend where the mother of the child does not defend and where there are strong grounds; accordingly expenses may not be recovered from him if he does not defend.

Effect of maintenance assessments

49.83. The Deputy Principal Clerk shall, on receiving notification that a maintenance assessment has been made, cancelled or has ceased to have effect so as to affect an order of a kind prescribed for the purposes of section 10 of the Act of 1991, endorse on the interlocutor sheet relating to that order a certificate in Form 49.83-A or 49.83-B, as the case may be.

49.83

GENERAL NOTE.

A court order for aliment may cease to have effect when a maintenance assessment is made which supersedes it. Form 49.83-A applies where a maintenance assessment has been made, and Form 49.83-B applies where it is cancelled or ceases to have effect. Extracts may also be affected: see r. 49.84.

49.83.1

Effect of maintenance assessments on extracts relating to aliment

49.84.—(1) Where an order relating to aliment is affected by a maintenance assessment, any extract of that order issued by the Extractor shall be endorsed with a certificate in Form 49.84-A.

49.84

(2) Where an order relating to aliment has ceased to have effect on the making of a maintenance assessment, and that maintenance assessment is later cancelled or ceases to have effect, any extract of that order issued by the Extractor shall be endorsed also with a certificate in Form 49.84-B.

GENERAL NOTE.

A court order for aliment may cease to have effect when a maintenance assessment is made which supersedes it. Where an extract of the order which is affected by a maintenance assessment is issued the certificate in Form 49.84—A will be endorsed on it. A certificate in Form 49.84-B will be endorsed on the extract when the maintenance assessment is cancelled or ceases to have effect. These certificates can only be endorsed on the extract if the extract happens to be sought after one of the foregoing events has occurred.

49.84.1

Part XIII[1] – Referrals to Principal Reporter

Application and interpretation of this Part

49.85.—[2](1) This Part applies where the court, in a family action, refers a matter to the Principal Reporter under section 54 of the Act of 1995 (reference to the Principal Reporter by court).

49.85

(2) In this Part, "Principal Reporter" has the meaning assigned in section 93(1) of the Act of 1995.

Intimation to Principal Reporter

49.86.[3] Where a matter is referred by the court to the Principal Reporter under section 54 of the Act of 1995, the clerk of court shall give written intimation of the interlocutor making the reference to the Principal Reporter; and that intimation shall specify which of the conditions in section 52(2)(a) to (h), (j), (k) or (1) of that Act it appears to the court have been satisfied.

49.86

"SECTION 54 OF THE ACT OF 1995".

In an action of divorce, judicial separation, or for declarator of marriage, nullity of marriage, percentage or non-percentage, or proceedings relating to parental responsibilities or parental rights, the court may refer a child (see s. 93(2)(b)) to the Principal Reporter if any of the conditions in s. 52(2)(a) to (h), (j), (k) or (1) are satisfied: Children (Scotland) Act 1995, s. 54. Those conditions relate to the circumstances in which compulsory measures of supervision may be required.

49.86.1

---

[1] Pt. XIII and r. 49.85 inserted by S.I. 1996 No. 2587 (effective 1st November 1996).
[2] Pt. XIII and r. 49.85 inserted by S.I. 1996 No. 2587 (effective 1st November 1996).
[3] R. 49.86 inserted by S.I. 1996 No. 2587 (effective 1st November 1996).

49.86.2   For methods, see r. 16.9.

Intimation of decision by Principal Reporter

49.87   **49.87.—**[1](1) Where a matter has been referred by the court to the Principal Reporter under section 54 of the Act of 1995 and the Principal Reporter, having made such investigation as he thinks appropriate and having reached the view that compulsory measures of supervision are necessary, arranges a children's hearing under section 69 of that Act (continuation or disposal of referral by children's hearing), the Principal Reporter shall give written intimation to the court which referred the matter to him of—

    (a) the decision to arrange such children's hearing;

    (b) where there is no appeal made against the decision of that children's hearing once the period for appeal has expired, the outcome of the children's hearing; and

    (c) where such an appeal has been made, that an appeal has been made and, once determined, the outcome of that appeal.

    (2) Where a matter has been referred by the court to the Principal Reporter under section 54 of the Act of 1995 and the Principal Reporter, having made such investigation as he thinks appropriate and having considered whether compulsory measures of supervision are necessary, decides not to arrange a children's hearing under section 69 of that Act, the Principal Reporter shall give written intimation of that decision to the court which referred the matter to him.

"SECTION 54 OF THE ACT OF 1995".

49.87.1   See note 49.86.1.

"WRITTEN INTIMATION".

49.87.2   For methods, see r. 16.9.

Part XIV[2] – Management of Money Payable to Children

Application under section 11(1) (d) of the Act of 1995 following order under section 13 of that Act[3]

49.88   **49.88.**[4] Where the court has made an order under section 13 of the Act of 1995 (awards of damages to children), an application by a person for an order by virtue of section 11(1)(d) of that Act (administration of child's property) may be made by minute in the process of the cause in which the order under section 13 of that Act was made.

GENERAL NOTE.

49.88.1   Part IV of Chap. 43 has been revoked by the A.S. (R.C.S.A. No. 5) (Family Actions and Miscellaneous) 1996 [S.I. 1996 No. 2587] because s. 13 of the Children (Scotland) Act 1995 contains the substantive provisions for the management of money payable to children in any court proceedings.

    S.13 of the 1995 Act implements the recommendations of the Scottish Law Commission *Report on Family Law*, para. 4.6 [Scot. Law Com. No. 135]. Advice that rr. 43.14 to 43.17 implemented these recommendations and were more flexible in rules than in primary legislation was not accepted.

    The only rule which survives in the R.C.S. 1994 is a rule for administration now in r. 49.88 which replaces r. 43.17 (subsequent orders).

"SECTION 13 OF THE ACT OF 1995".

49.88.2   The side-note to s. 13 of the Children (Scotland) Act 1995 states that the section deals with awards of damages payable to children. In fact its terms are very wide and extend to where any "sum of money

---

[1] R. 49.87 inserted by S.I. 1996 No. 2587 (effective 1st November 1996).
[2] Pt. XIV and r. 49.88 inserted by S.I. 1996 No. 2587 (effective 1st November 1996).
[3] Heading to r. 49.88 inserted by S.I. 1997 No. 1050.
[4] Pt. XIV and r. 49.88 inserted by S.I. 1996 No. 2587 (effective 1st November 1996).

becomes payable to, or for the benefit of, a child under the age of sixteen years". It applies in any court proceedings. An extra-judicial settlement after an action or other proceedings have been brought would arise in court proceedings and would be covered by s. 13. In *S v. Argyll and Clyde Acute Hospitals NHS Trust* , 2009 S.L.T. 1016(OH), Lord Brodie doubted that he had jurisdiction where the damages had been *paid*, but went on to describe the purpose of s. 13 as being to safeguard a number of interests: to allow a defender to obtain a discharge, to relieve a pursuer of a responsibility that he or she might not want to undertake, and to provide that monies received as damages are put into the hands of a person best suited to administer them for the benefit of the child.

The court may make such order relating to the payment and management of that sum as it thinks fit: 1995 Act, s. 13(1).

Without prejudice to that generality, the court may—

(a) appoint a judicial factor to invest, apply or otherwise deal with the money for the benefit of the child;

(b) order the money to be paid to the sheriff clerk or the Accountant of Court, or to a parent or guardian of the child, to be invested, applied or otherwise dealt with under directions of the court for the benefit of the child; or

(c) order the money to be paid directly to the child.

A receipt by such a person is a sufficient discharge of the obligation to make payment.

Some guidance on the appropriateness of the alternative orders is needed. No criterion is laid down in the Act. In *I v. Argyll and Clyde Health Board* , 2003 S.L.T. 231 (OH), reference is made to a report by the Accountant of Court in which comments are made on some of the merits and the demerits of appointing a factor or the Accountant of Court. In that case Lord Carloway observed that, especially where there is no criticism or suspicion about the ability of parents to look after their child's funds, there is no obligation on a defender to raise s. 13 of the 1995 Act with the court. The court's power was described as a wide discretionary power.

(1) Judicial factor.

Where the sum is very large the appointment of a judicial factor may be appropriate, but not otherwise because the costs of appointment and administration are substantial: there have to be paid annually the caution premium, the factor's commission and the statutory fees payable to the Accountant of Court including the audit fee (in the case of damages, the award could attempt to take account of these). The audit fee includes a fee currently of 17.5 per cent of the factor's commission: see Court of Session etc. Fees Order 1984, Table of Fees, Pt. II, item 3 [SI 1984/256, Table as amended, pp. C 1202 et seq.]. The running cost depends on the amount of capital, the level of activity and the demands on the time of the factor. It might be thought that a judicial factory was not appropriate for sums less than £50,000. A judicial factor is subject to the Judicial Factors Act 1849, the Judicial Factors (Scotland) Act 1889, the Trusts (Scotland) Acts 1921 and 1961 and the Trustee Investments Act 1961. He is subject to the supervision of the Accountant of Court. He must find caution.

On judicial factors, see further Chap. 61.

(2) Sheriff clerk.

In this case the expense of a judicial factor or the Accountant of Court is avoided. There is no charge for administration by the sheriff clerk. Money paid to the sheriff clerk passes out of the control of the court to that of the sheriff court unless an order is subsequently sought under r. 49.88 to make a change. The Ordinary Cause Rules 1993 in Sched. 1 to the Sheriff Courts (Scotland) Act 1907 were substituted for the previous rules by A.S. (Sheriff Court Ordinary Cause Rules) 1993 [SI 1993/1956]. Management of money paid to the sheriff clerk is dealt with in O.C.R. 1993, r. 36.17 (in Pt. IV of Chap. 36). Money has to be invested in accordance with the Trustee Investments Act 1961: O.C.R. 1993, r. 36.17(4).

(3) Accountant of Court.

The Accountant might be appropriately appointed in cases where the sum is less than £50,000 (see note 43.16.2) but more than £5,000 or where the amount of administration is likely to be less than that which would justify a factor. £50,000, however should not be regarded as an upper limit. A lower limit of £5,000 is intended to cover those cases where the money is not so substantial as to justify being invested but should rather be placed in a bank account as the transactions in relation to it are likely to be few. As there is no statutory provision for the Accountant to be paid, the interlocutor appointing him should find him entitled to the expenses and outlays incurred. The costs of administration would be less than that of a judicial factory: that would be no caution premium, no inventory or audit fees (see note 43.16.2) and the overall cost saving could be 25 per cent or more compared to the costs of a judicial factory.

(4) Guardian.

A guardian normally includes the child's parents as one of their parental rights, any person on application to the court may be appointed a guardian and a parent may appoint any person to be the child's guardian: Law Reform (Parent and Child) (Scotland) Act 1986, ss. 2–4 and 8 as amended by the Age of Legal Capacity (Scotland) Act 1991, Sched. 1.

A guardian is a trustee subject to the Trusts (Scotland) Acts 1921 and 1961 and the Trustee Investments Act 1961. It might be thought that sums of up to £20,000 could be administered by a guardian (or £5,000 where there was concern about the ability of the guardian to handle the money): see *Report on Family Law*, Scot. Law Com. No. 135, para. 4.17.

The court might require a guardian to take the advice of a (named) person, such as a solicitor.

In *IC v. Argyll and Clyde Health Board*, above, Lord Carloway observed that it may be prudent in the case of even reliable and trustworthy parents, who are appointed to be paid and to manage the award, to attach some form of reporting requirement at least where the sum is very large and on which the child may be largely dependent in later life. In that case, on the recommendation of the Accountant of Court, Lord Carloway attached the following conditions to the payment of the funds to the parents: (i) confirmation to the Accountant of investment of funds in accordance with disclosed advice; (ii) lodging with the Accountant a voucher of the level of initial investment; (iii) the funds to be held in the parents' joint names for the child; (iv) withdrawals in excess of 2.5 per cent of capital to require the Accountant's approval; (v) all revenue spent to be for the benefit of the child; and (vi) an annual report to the Accountant of the level of funds and expenditure.

(5) Payment direct to child.

Payment of only small sums may be appropriate, having regard particularly to the restrictions on transactions under the Age of Legal Capacity (Scotland) Act 1991.

A decree for payment will arise on an award of damages, interim damages or provisional damages. A payment arising on decree of absolvitor would occur where there is an extra-judicial settlement: see, e.g. *Scott v. Occidental Petroleum (Caledonia) Ltd* 1990 S.C.L.R. 278.

Damages awarded for future necessary services under s. 3 of the Administration of Justice Act 1982 (substituted by the Law Reform (Miscellaneous Provisions) (Scotland) Act 1990, s. 69(1)) would appear to be for the child's benefit and subject to s. 13 of the Act of 1995.

CURATOR AD LITEM.

49.88.3   Where a curator ad litem has been appointed to the child, he should prepare a report detailing the arrangements for the payment and management of the money: *Riddoch v. Occidental Petroleum (Caledonia) Ltd* 1991 S.L.T. 721, 722L per Lord McCluskey.

"MINUTE".

49.88.4   For applications by minute, see r. 15.1.

Part XV[1] – Management of Child's Property by Virtue of Section 9(5)(A) or 11(2)(G) of the Act of 1995

Directions

49.89   **49.89.**[2] In making an appointment under section 9(5)(a) or 11(2)(g) of the Act of 1995, or when it receives a report under the said section 11(2)(g), the court may give such directions as it thinks fit regarding the management of the property concerned, and it may from time to time, on the application of a judicial factor so appointed, of the Accountant of Court or of any other person having an interest, give further such directions.

[THE NEXT PARAGRAPH IS 49.89.2]

SECTION 9(5) (A) OF THE CHILDREN (SCOTLAND) ACT 1995.

49.89.2   Subject to section 13 of the Act of 1995 (court awards of money to children), where property is owned by or due to a child, is held by a person other than a parent or guardian, would otherwise require to be transferred to a parent with parental responsibilities, or to a guardian, for administration for the child (unless appointed a trustee under a trust deed to administer the property for the child) and (1) the person holding the property is a trustee or executor, then (a) if the value of the property exceeds £20,000, he shall, (b) if the value of the property is not less than £5,000 and does not exceed £20,000, he may, or (2) the person holding the property is not a trustee or executor, he may, apply to the Accountant of Court for directions: Act of 1995, s. 9(1), (2) and (3). When such an application is made to the Accountant of Court, he may, among other things, apply to the Court for the appointment of a judicial factor: Act of 1995, s. 9(5)(a).

---

[1] Pt. XV and r. 49.89 inserted by S.I. 1997 No. 1720 (effective 1st August, 1997); heading inserted by S.S.I. 2004 No. 52 (effective 1st March, 2004).
[2] Pt. XV and r. 49.89 inserted by S.I. 1997 No. 1720 (effective 1st August, 1997); heading inserted by S.S.I. 2004 No. 52 (effective 1st March, 2004).

Section 11(1) of the Act of 1995 empowers the court to make an order in any proceedings for the administration of a child's property (subject to the jurisdictional rules in s. 14(1) and (2)). The court may appoint a judicial factor or remit the matter to the Accountant of Court to report on suitable arrangements: Act of 1995, s. 11(2)(g).

49.89.3

"application".

Strictly, by virtue of r. 14.2(h), an application under r. 49.89 is by petition to the Outer House. This is clearly not intended (possibly because the current draftsman may not be familiar with the structure of the Rules). There is no reason why such an application may not be by motion or minute, where there is a depending process in which it could be made.

49.89.4

Part XVA[1] – Application by Survivor for Provision on Intestacy

49.90.—[2](1) The applicant for an order under section 29(2) of the Act of 2006 (application by survivor for provision on intestacy) shall call the deceased's executor as a defender.

49.90

(2) An application under section 29(9) of the Act of 2006 for variation of the date or method of payment of the capital sum shall be made by minute in the process of the action to which the application relates.

(3) Words and expressions used in this Part shall have the same meaning as in section 29 of the Act of 2006.

General note.

Where two people are living together as man and wife, or as civil partners, and one dies intestate, the survivor may apply for payment of a capital sum out of the deceased's net intestate estate, or for the transfer of property: Act of 2006, s. 29.

49.90.1

"minute".

For applications by minute, see r. 15.1.

49.90.2

Part XVI[3] – Action for Declarator of Recognition or Non-recognition of a Foreign Decree

Action for declarator in relation to certain foreign decrees

49.91.—[4](1)[5] This rule applies to an action for declarator of recognition, or non-recognition, of a decree of divorce, nullity or separation granted outwith the United Kingdom, the Channel Islands or the Isle of Man.

49.91

(2) In an action to which this rule applies, the pursuer shall state in the condescendence of the summons—

  (a) the court, tribunal or other authority which granted the decree;

  (b) the date of the decree of divorce, annulment or separation to which the action relates;

  (c) the date and place of the marriage to which the decree of divorce, nullity or separation relates;

  (d) the basis on which the court has jurisdiction to entertain the action;

  (e) whether to the pursuer's knowledge any other proceedings whether in Scotland or in any other country are continuing in respect of the marriage to which the action relates or are capable of affecting its validity or subsistence; and

  (f) where such proceedings are continuing—

---

[1] Part XVA and r. 49.90 inserted by S.S.I. 2006 No. 206 (effective 4th May 2006).
[2] Part XVA and r. 49.90 inserted by S.S.I. 2006 No. 206 (effective 4th May 2006).
[3] Pt XVI and r. 49.91 inserted by S.S.I. 2010 No. 417 (effective 1st January 2011).
[4] Pt XVI and r. 49.91 inserted by S.S.I. 2010 No. 417 (effective 1st January 2011).
[5] As substituted by the Act of Sederunt (Rules of the Court of Session 1994 and Sheriff Court Rules Amendment) (Miscellaneous) 2021 (S.S.I. 2021 No. 75) r. 2(2) (effective 1st March 2021).

    (i)   the court, tribunal or authority before which the proceedings have been commenced;

    (ii)   the date of commencement;

    (iii) the names of the parties; and

    (iv) the date, or expected date of any proof (or its equivalent), in the proceedings.

(3)   Where—

  (a)   such proceedings are continuing;

  (b)   the action in the Court of Session is defended; and

  (c)   either—

    (i)   the summons does not contain the statement referred to in paragraph (2)(e), or

    (ii)   the particulars mentioned in paragraph (2)(f) as set out in the summons are incomplete or incorrect,

any defences or minute, as the case may be, lodged by any person to the action shall include that statement and, where appropriate, the further or correct particulars mentioned in paragraph (2)(f).

(4) Unless the court otherwise directs, a declarator of recognition, or non-recognition, of a decree under this rule shall not be granted without there being produced with the summons—

  (a)   the decree in question or a certified copy of the decree;

  (b)   the marriage extract or equivalent document to which the action relates.

(5) Where a document produced under paragraph (4)(a) or (b) is not in English it shall, unless the court otherwise directs, be accompanied by a translation certified by a notary public or authenticated by affidavit.

(6) For the purposes of this rule, proceedings are continuing at any time after they have commenced and before they are finally disposed of.

JURISDICTION.

49.91.1   The court's jurisdiction to entertain an action for declarator of recognition or non-recognition of a foreign decree is determined by s. 7(3A) of the Domicile and Matrimonial Proceedings Act 1973 inserted by s. 37(2) of the Family Law (Scotland) Act 2006 and brought into force by S.S.I. 2006 No. 212. Within the EU (except Denmark), jurisdiction is determined by the Council Regulation (EC) 2201/2003. For other foreign decrees jurisdiction exists if the action is (a) an excluded action (i.e. no EU court has jurisdiction under the Council regulation and defender not an EU national (other than U.K. or Ireland) or domiciled in Ireland) or one of the parties died before the action began and (b) one of the parties is domiciled in Scotland when the action began or died before that date and at the time of death was domiciled in Scotland or was habitually resident in Scotland throughout the year ending with the death.

Chapter 50

Causes Under the Presumption of Death (Scotland) Act 1977

Interpretation of this Chapter

50.1. In this Chapter—

50.1

"the Act of 1977" means the Presumption of Death (Scotland) Act 1977;

"action of declarator" means an action under section 1(1) of the Act of 1977;

"missing person" has the meaning assigned in section 1(1) of the Act of 1977.

Deriv. RCS 1965, r. 188B(1) inserted by S.I. 1978 No. 161

GENERAL NOTE.

A question as to whether a person has died may be dealt with (a) in an action of declarator of death under the Act of 1977; or (b) incidentally to some other process (*Bruce v. Smith* (1871) 10 M. 130 (action of multiplepoinding); *Secretary of State for Scotland v. Sutherland* 1944 S.C. 79 (application for state pension)).

50.1.1

A natural person is presumed to live for 80 to 100 years: Stair, IV.xlv.17; Bankton, II.vi.31. Anyone who requires to prove that a person has died has to overcome this presumption on a balance of probabilities: Act of 1977, s. 2(1) and (3).

"MISSING PERSON".

This is a person who is thought to have died or has not been known to be alive for a period of at least seven years: Act of 1977, s. 1(1).

50.1.2

JURISDICTION.

The court has jurisdiction where (a) the pursuer is the spouse of the missing person and is domiciled in Scotland at the date of raising the action or was habitually resident in Scotland throughout the period of one year ending in that date, or (b) in any other case the missing person was domiciled in Scotland on the date on which he was last known to be alive or had been habitually resident there throughout the period of one year ending with that date: Act of 1977, s. 1(3).

50.1.3

THE PURSUER.

The pursuer may be any person having an interest: Act of 1977, s. 1(1); e.g. spouse, beneficiary in succession, factor loco absentis, etc. The Lord Advocate may be a pursuer: Act of 1977, ss. 1(1) and 17.

50.1.4

Parties to, and service and intimation of, actions of declarator

50.2.—(1) The missing person shall be called as the defender in an action of declarator and service on that person shall be by advertisement in such newspaper or other publication as the court thinks fit of such of the facts relating to the missing person and set out in the summons as the court may specify.

50.2

(2)[1] The period of notice where service is executed in accordance with paragraph (1) rule shall be 21 days from the date of publication of the advertisement unless the court otherwise orders.

(3) Revoked by SI 1999/1386 (effective 19th May 1999).

(4) Subject to paragraph (6), in the summons in an action of declarator, the pursuer shall insert a warrant for intimation to—

    (a) the missing person's—

        (i)[2] spouse or civil partner, and

        (ii) children or, if he has no children, nearest relative known to the pursuer,

    (b) any person, including any insurance company, who so far as known to the pursuer, has any interest in the action, and

    (c) the Lord Advocate,

---

[1] Rule 50.2(1) and (2) amended by S.I. 1999 No. 1386 (effective 19th May 1999).

[2] Rule 50.2(4)(a)(i) amended by S.S.I. 2005 No. 632 (effective 8th December 2005).

in the following terms:— "Warrant for intimation to (*name and address*) as [husband *or* wife, child or nearest relative] [a person having an interest in the presumed death] of (*name and last known address of the missing person*) and to the Lord Advocate.".

(5)   A notice of intimation in Form 50.2-B shall be attached to the copy of the summons where intimation is given on a warrant under paragraph (4).

(6)   The court may, on the motion of the pursuer, dispense with intimation on a person mentioned in paragraph (4)(a) or (b).

(7)   Notwithstanding the reference in subsection (5) of section 1 of the Act of 1977 (person interested in seeking determination or appointment not sought by pursuer) to lodging a minute, an application under that subsection shall be made by lodging defences containing a conclusion for the determination or appointment sought, averments in the answers to the condescendence in support of that conclusion and an appropriate plea-in-law.

(8)   On lodging defences under paragraph (7), the defender shall, as well as complying with rule 4.6 (intimation of steps of process)—

  (a)   send a copy of the defences by registered post or the first class recorded delivery service to each person to whom intimation of the action has been made under paragraph (4); and

  (b)[1] lodge in process a certificate of intimation of those defences by post in Form 16.4.

Deriv. RCS 1965, r. 188B(3) and (4)(part) (r. 50.2(4)), r. 188B(4)(part) and (5) (r. 50.2(5)), and r. 188B(6) (r. 50.2(6)), all inserted by S.I. 1978 No. 161

SERVICE BY ADVERTISEMENT.

50.2.1   As by definition the current address of the missing person will not be known service of the summons has to be executed by advertisement: r. 50.2(1).

Advertisement is no longer in Form 16.5 because the references in r. 50.2 to Form 16.5 (service by advertisement) were revoked by A.S. (R.C.S.A. No. 5) (Miscellaneous) 1999 [S.I. 1999 No. 1386]. The reason is simply that the rule now provides that the advertisement must contain such facts relating to the missing person set out in the summons as the court may specify. Nonetheless the form or style of the advertisement should, apart from this and the 21 day period of notice, comply with that in Form 16.5. The motion for service by advertisement should set out the averred facts about the missing person that the pursuer considers might be included in the advertisement, or the motion should be accompanied by a draft advertisement containing such averred facts, for approval by the court.

The new procedure for the first service by advertisement rolls into one the former two-stage process whereby, if no defences were lodged after the first advertisement, a second advertisement containing facts relating to the missing person was required (r. 50.3(1)). Rule 50.3(1) is accordingly revoked.

"PERIOD OF NOTICE".

50.2.2   The period of notice in an action of declarator of death is 21 days from the date of publication of the advertisement: r. 50.2(2). This contrasts with the general provision of six months: r. 13.4(1)(d). An application to shorten or extend the period of notice may be made by motion: r. 13.4(2).

INTIMATION.

50.2.3   The warrant should be inserted in the summons after the address and charge, and before the conclusions: r. 13.2 and Form 32.2.A. For methods of service, see r. 16.8.

DEFENCES.

50.2.4   See rr. 18.1 and 18.2.

LODGE IN PROCESS THE CERTIFICATE OF POSTING.

50.2.5   The certificate of posting and a copy of the notice of intimation in Form 50.2-B must be lodged as productions. On lodging productions, see r. 4.5.

Further advertisement and procedure

50.3   **50.3.**—(1)   Revoked by S.I. 1999/1386 (effective 19th May 1999).

---

[1] Rule 50.2(8)(b) substituted by S.S.I. 2008 No. 349 (effective 1st December 2008).

(2)   At any time before the determination of the action, the court may, at its own instance or on the motion of a party, make such order for further advertisement as it thinks fit.

General note.

Rule 50.3(1)(derived from RCS 1965, r. 188B (7) inserted by S.I. 1978 No. 161) provided for advertisement containing facts relating to the missing person where no defences were lodged within the period of notice. The new procedure for the first service by advertisement rolls into one the former two-stage process whereby, if no defences were lodged after the first advertisement, a second advertisement containing facts relating to the missing person was required (r. 50.3(1)). Rule 50.3(1) is accordingly revoked. But, because the effect of a decree is that the missing person is deemed to be dead for all civil law purposes (Act of 1977, s. 3(1)), an additional safeguard remains in r. 50.3(2) for further advertisement if required.

"MOTION".

For motions, see Chap. 23.

Applications for proof

50.4.   In an action of declarator where no defences have been lodged, the pursuer shall, after such further advertisement as may be ordered under rule 50.3, apply by motion for an order for a proof.

"MOTION".

For motions, see Chap. 23.

Proof.

See generally, Chap. 36.

Any person (including the Secretary of State for Social Services) who possesses information relating to the survival or death of the missing person and who is aware that an action of declarator has been raised or an application for a variation order made, must disclose that information by letter to the Principal Clerk: Act of 1977, s. 9(1). The usual rules on inadmissibility on grounds of privilege or confidentiality apply: Act of 1977, s. 9(2). A statement purporting to be an instrument made or issued by or on behalf of any Minister of the Crown containing facts relating to an action of declarator or application for a variation order is sufficient evidence of the facts stated therein: Act of 1977 s. 9(3). The reporting of the action by the press is not restricted by the Judicial Proceedings (Regulation of Reports) Act 1926 (which prohibits the printing or publishing in relation to any judicial proceedings, any indecent matter the publication of which would be calculated to injure public morals): Act of 1977, s. 14; the missing person is decreed to be dead for all civil law purposes.

Effect of decree.

The decree takes effect on the expiry of the time for reclaiming with no reclaiming motion having been marked or on the withdrawal or refusal of a reclaiming motion; the missing person is deemed to be dead for all civil law purposes: Act of 1977, s. 3(1). The time for reclaiming is 21 days after the date on which the interlocutor granting decree was pronounced: r. 38.3(2).

The missing person is automatically deprived of any rights from the expiry of the reclaiming days after the granting of decree: Act of 1977, s. 3(1). Even if the missing person re-appears and obtains a recall or variation of the decree under s. 4 of the Act of 1977, he is not per se entitled to recover his former property: Act of 1977, s. 5(1).

Intimation to Registrar General.

Where the court has granted decree of declarator of death or pronounced a variation order and the reclaiming days have expired with no reclaiming motion having been marked or the reclaiming motion has been refused, the clerk of court must notify the prescribed particulars in connection with such decree or order to the Registrar General for Births, Marriages and Deaths for Scotland: Act of 1977, s. 12(1). The prescribed particulars in so far as known are (a) the date of decree or variation order; (b) the full name, last known usual residence and last known occupation of the deceased; (c) the date of birth or age of the deceased; (d) the time and date of death as determined by the court; (e) the marital status of the deceased at the date of death and if married the name and address of the surviving spouse; (f) the full name and address of the pursuer in the action or applicant in the application and his or her relationship (if any) to the deceased; and (g) the name and address of the agent for said pursuer or applicant: Registration of Presumed Deaths (Prescription of Particulars) (Scotland) Regulations 1978 [S.I. 1978 No. 160], Reg. 3. There is a form of Notice of import of decree or order for variation or recall of declarator of death which the clerk completes.

	50.3.1
	50.3.2
	50.4
	50.4.1
	50.4.2
	50.4.3
	50.4.4

Applications for variation or recall of decrees

50.5

50.5.—(1) An application under section 4(1) of the Act of 1977 (variation or recall of decree) shall be made by minute in the process of the action to which the application relates.

(2) On the lodging of such a minute, the minuter shall apply by motion for an order—

(a) for service on the missing person, where his whereabouts have become known;

(b) for intimation to those persons mentioned in rule 50.2(4) or to dispense with intimation to a person mentioned in rule 50.2(4)(a) or (b); and

(c) for any answers to the minute to be lodged in process within such period as the court thinks fit.

(3) An application under section 4(3) of the Act of 1977 (person interested seeking determination or appointment not sought by applicant for variation order) shall be made by lodging answers containing a crave for the determination or appointment sought.

(4)[1] A person lodging answers containing a crave under paragraph (3) shall, as well as sending a copy of the answers to the minuter—

(a) send a copy of the answers by registered post or the first class recorded delivery service to each person on whom service or intimation of the minute was ordered; and

(b)[2] lodge in process a certificate of intimation of those answers by post in Form 16.4.

Deriv. R.C.S. 1965, r. 188B(2), (3), (5) and (6) inserted by S.I. 1978 No. 161 (r. 50.5(1) and (2))

GENERAL NOTE.

50.5.1

A variation order is an order varying or recalling a decree in an action of declarator of death: Act of 1977, s. 4(1). The variation order may vary or recall the decree in any matter which could have been dealt with in the original decree except in relation to any property acquired as a result of the original decree: Act of 1977, ss. 4(2) and 1(1). A variation order may not revive a marriage: Act of 1977, s. 4(5).

If following an application made no later than five years after the date of the original decree the court pronounces a variation order, the court may make such further order in relation to any property rights acquired as a result of the original decree as it considers fair and reasonable in all the circumstances: Act of 1977, s. 5(2) and (4). Such further order may not affect the entitlement to any income accruing between the date of the decree and the variation order: Act of 1977, s. 5(2). The further order may be craved in the minute for the variation order.

Any person having an interest may apply: Act of 1977, s. 4(1). This includes the Lord Advocate for the public interest: Act of 1977, s. 17.

JURISDICTION.

50.5.2

The court has jurisdiction where:

1. it granted the decree of declarator of death which is sought to be varied or recalled: Act of 1977, s. 4(1); or

2. the sheriff or the court itself remits an application under s. 4(1) of the Act of 1977 to the court due to the importance or complexity of the matters at issue: Act of 1977, s. 4(4); and see rr. 50.5 and 32.3.

"MINUTE".

50.5.3

See r. 15.1. The minute may include a crave for a further order in relation to property under s. 5(2) of the Act of 1977.

"MOTION".

50.5.4

For motions, see Chap. 23.

---

[1] R. 50.5(4) amended by S.I. 1994 No. 2901 (minor correction).
[2] R. 50.5(4)(b) substituted by S.S.I. 2008 No. 349 (effective 1st December 2008).

"SERVICE".

For methods, see Chap. 16.   **50.5.5**

"INTIMATION".

For methods, see r. 16.8.   **50.5.6**

"ANSWERS".

See r. 18.3.   **50.5.7**

PROOF.

See note 50.4.2.   **50.5.8**

INTIMATION TO REGISTRAR GENERAL.

See note 50.4.4.   **50.5.9**

Applications for remit from sheriff court

50.6.—(1)   An application by a person for a direction under section 1(6) or 4(4)   **50.6**
of the Act of 1977 (remit of action or application to the court) shall be made by
petition.

(2)   An action of declarator or an application which is remitted to the court under
section 1(6) or 4(4) of the Act of 1977 shall proceed in the Outer House as if it were
an action brought or an application made, as the case may be, in that court.

Deriv. R.C.S. 1965, r. 188B(8) and (9) inserted by S.I. 1978 No. 161

GENERAL NOTE.

An application to the court for a remit of an application or action from the sheriff to the court may be   **50.6.1**
made by any party to the application or action: Act of 1977, ss. 1(6) and 4(4).

"PETITION".

For petitions generally, see Chap. 14.   **50.6.2**
An application to the court for a remit of an application or action from the sheriff to the court may be
made by any party to the application or action: Act of 1977, ss. 1(6) and 4(4).

FURTHER PROCEDURE.

Where the petition is granted, for further procedure see rr. 32.3 et seq.   **50.6.3**

Appointment of judicial factors

50.7.—(1)   Rule 61.6 (documents relating to judicial factories for Accountant of   **50.7**
Court) shall apply to an application for the appointment of a judicial factor under
section 2(2)(c) or section 4(2) of the Act of 1977 as it applies to a petition for the appointment of a judicial factor.

(2)   Where, in an action of declarator or an application under section 4(1) of the
Act of 1977 (variation or recall of decree), a judicial factor on the estate of the missing person is appointed, the process shall forthwith be transmitted to, and retained
by, the Petition Department; and the judicial factory shall proceed as if the judicial
factor had been appointed in a petition for that purpose.

(3)   In the application of rule 50.5 (applications for variation or recall of decrees)
to an application under section 4(1) of the Act of 1977 in a cause transmitted to the
Petition Department under paragraph (2), for references to a minute there shall be
substituted references to a note.

GENERAL NOTE.

On judicial factories generally, see Chap. 61.   **50.7.1**

Chapter 51

Actions of Multiplepoinding

Application of this Chapter

51.1. This Chapter applies to an action of multiplepoinding. **51.1**

GENERAL NOTE.

The purpose of an action of multiplepoinding is to enable a person, pursued by different pursuers upon distinct rights, to cite all persons in a single process, so that he may be liable only in once and single payment and performance and free from subsequent claims: Stair, IV.xvi.3. It is an action by which property, whether heritable or moveable, claimed by different parties is brought into court either by the holder of the property or by one of the claimants, in order that the true ownership of, or respective rights to, the property can be determined. Accordingly, "a process of multiplepoinding implies all powers necessary for determining the rights of the parties...the effect being such as to authorise the court to discuss incidentally all such points arising in the course of it, as are necessary for extricating the rights of the parties": More's Notes to Stair, ccclxxviii-ccclxxix. It has been described as a "congeries of actions" in which, as a general rule, "all deeds and decrees founded on by one claimant may be set aside by other claimants ope exceptionis without the necessity of a substantive action of reduction": *Jarvie's Trs. v. Bannatyne* 1927 S.C. 34, 36 per Lord Fleming. Sometimes thought cumbersome and slow, a multiplepoinding has been (unfairly) described as a process in which, if there is anything left in the fund *in medio* at the conclusion of the action, some step of procedure has been omitted. Examples of issues which have been tried in an action of multiplepoinding include: reduction ope exceptionis of a decree in absence (*Jarvie's Trs.*, above); looking beyond the terms of a decree and to examine its media concludendi (*Thomson & Co. v. Friese-Greene's Tr.* 1944 S.C. 336); the existence or validity of a marriage (*Dean's J.F. v. Deans* 1912 S.C. 441); legitimacy (*Brook's Exx. v. James* 1970 S.C. 147, affd. 1971 S.C. (H.L.) 77); presumption of death (*Tait's Factor v. Meikle* (1890) 17 R. 1182: the court may sist the cause to enable a separate process for the declarator of death to be presented (*Clark's Exr. v. Clark* 1953 S.L.T. (Notes) 58), as was done in *Shepherd's Trs. v. Brown* (1902) 9 S.L.T. 487); the effect of the passing of an Act of Parliament on a bequest (*McClement's Trs. v. Lord Advocate* 1949 S.L.T. (Notes) 59) or whether the fund *in medio* (or part of it) fell to be regarded as heritable or moveable in a question of succession (*Cowan's Trs. v. Cowan* (1887) 14 R. 670). It is competent, though unusual, to set up a claim by one claimant in a multiplepoinding by reference to the oath of a competing claimant: *Farquhar v. Farquhar* (1886) 13 R. 596.

An action of multiplepoinding may involve a succession of separate actions to determine (1) objections to the raising of the action (usually by taking a plea to the competency), (2) the extent and identity of the fund *in medio* and (3) the claims of the respective claimants in a competition on that fund. Each of these distinct stages, if necessary (because an objection has been made), proceeds as an ordinary action, complete with a condescendence, defences and open record.

JURISDICTION.

R. 2(9) of Sched. 8 to the C.J.J.A. 1982, relating to "proceedings ... to assert, declare or determine proprietary or possessory rights ... in or over moveable property ... in the courts for the place where the property is situated", is sufficiently broad to encompass an action of multiplepoinding. If the fund *in medio* is comprised of or includes immoveable property situated in Scotland, r. 4(1)(a) of Sched. 8 to the C.J.J.A. 1982 will also confer jurisdiction on the court, even if the defender's domicile is outwith the UK: C.J.J.A. 1982, Sched. 8, r. 2(8)(d). Further, it will be sufficient to establish jurisdiction in a multiplepoinding if at least one of the defenders is domiciled in Scotland: C.J.J.A. 1982, Sched. 8, r. 2(15)(a).

The existence of the fund *in medio* in Scotland is sufficient to found jurisdiction and supersedes the necessity of arrestment to found jurisdiction: *Miller v. Ure* (1838) 16 S. 1204.

51.1.1
51.1.2

Parties to actions of multiplepoinding

51.2.—(1) An action of multiplepoinding may be brought by any person holding, or having an interest in, or claim on, the fund *in medio*, in his own name. **51.2**

(2) The pursuer shall call as defenders to such an action—

    (a) all persons so far as known to him as having an interest in the fund *in medio*; and

    (b) where he is not the holder of the fund, the holder of that fund.

Deriv. R.C.S. 1965, r. 175 substituted by S.I. 1986 No. 1941

"ACTION OF MULTIPLEPOINDING".

See note 51.1.1. **51.2.1**

"ANY PERSON HOLDING ... THE FUND".

51.2.2   The holder of the property in dispute (the "fund *in medio*") is always known as the pursuer. If the holder of the fund raises the action, he is known as the "pursuer and real raiser". If someone other than the holder of the fund raises the action (the "real raiser"), the holder is known as the "pursuer and nominal raiser".

"IN HIS OWN NAME".

51.2.3   The person who raises an action of multiplepoinding, regardless of whether or not he is the holder of the property in dispute (the "fund *in medio*"), is known as the "real raiser". The real raiser, if he holds the fund *in medio*, is also the pursuer. If he is not the pursuer (i.e. the holder of the fund) he is known as the "defender and real raiser". The real raiser should always conclude for distribution of the fund *in medio* among the claimants found entitled thereto: see the style in Form 13.2-B. If the real raiser is also the holder, he may also conclude for his exoneration and discharge. If the action is raised by someone other than the holder of the fund, the holder may, at a later stage, apply for his exoneration and discharge: see, e.g. r. 51.10 (consignation of fund into court after approval of the condescendence of the fund *in medio*) and r. 51.15 (consignation and exoneration at the conclusion of the multiplepoinding). Other conclusions in an action brought by the holder of the fund *in medio* may include: that he should be found liable only in once and single payment (or consignation) of the fund for the behoof of the persons who may have right thereto; that all claimants and others pretending right to the fund ought to produce their respective grounds of debt or other interest in the fund, and dispute their preference; and for his expenses out of the fund (on which see note 51.1.3): see Mackay's *Manual of Court of Session Practice*, ii.117-118.

A judicial factor may not competently obtain his exoneration and discharge in the course of a multiplepoinding, although he may competently raise such an action if competing claims are made on the estate under his charge: *Campbell v. Grant* (1890) 8 M. 988. Others holding funds in a fiduciary capacity, such as trustees and executors, may seek their exoneration and discharge in the course of an action of multiplepoinding only in limited circumstances: see note 51.4.1(4).

"HAVING AN INTEREST IN, OR CLAIM ON".

51.2.4   As the purpose of a multiplepoinding is to free the holder from a multitude of claims in respect of the fund *in medio*, all persons who have made or are believed entitled to make a claim should be called as defenders. Persons not called may be allowed to lodge a claim at a later stage than they would otherwise would be: *Morgan v. Morris* (1856) 18 D. 797; affd. sub. nom. *Young v. Morris* (1858) 20 D.(H.L.) 12. This is the justification for the provisions for advertisement inviting objections to the action (r. 51.5) and claims on the fund (r. 51.8). The holder of the fund may also make a claim on the fund. When the holder of the fund is the real raiser, he does so in the condescendence of the fund. If the holder is not the real raiser, he states his claim in his objections to the action itself (stated in his defences, in terms of r. 51.4(1)) or in a separate condescendence of the fund (r. 51.3(2)(a)).

"PURSUER".

51.2.5   For an action raised by a person falling within the terms of r. 51.2(2)(b), the reference to the pursuer in the beginning of r. 51.2(2) should be read as a reference to the pursuer as nominal raiser. Otherwise, the person holding the fund and raising the action is known as the "pursuer and real raiser".

"DEFENDERS".

51.2.6   In an action of multiplepoinding, the holder of the fund is always the pursuer. All persons having an interest in the fund should be called as defenders, of which there must be at least two. On the requirement of double distress generally, see note 51.4.1(4).

"FUND IN MEDIO".

51.2.7   The property in dispute, whatever form it takes, is known as the "fund *in medio*". The fund *in medio* may be comprised of heritable property (e.g. *Edinburgh Merchant Maidens Hospital v. Greig's Exrs.* (1902) 12 S.L.T. 317; *Boyd's Trs. v. Boyd* (1906) 13 S.L.T. 878; the statement in Bell's Comm., ii ,276 and Mackay's *Practice of the Court of Session*, ii. p. 113 to the contrary are incorrect), moveable property (including determination of right to title deeds: *Baillie v. Baillie* (1830) 8 S. 318) or a combination of heritable and moveable (*Logan v. Byres* (1895) 2 S.L.T. 455). In the course of a multiplepoinding the court may have to decide whether the fund *in medio* falls to be regarded as heritable or moveable, e.g. in determining rights of succession to the property comprising that fund: *Cowan v. Cowan* (1887) 14 R. 670. Rights *in spe* cannot alone form the fund *in medio* (*Provan v. Provan* (1840) 23 D. 298), although an unascertained amount may (*Highland Railway Co. v. British Linen Co.* (1901) 38 S.L.R. 584). The fund *in medio* should only include what is the subject-matter of the dispute and no other property: *McNab v. Waddell* (1894) 21 R. 827; *MacGillvray's Trs. v. Dallas* (1905) 7 F. 733. The court may dismiss such an action as incompetent (*McNab*, above) or allow the holder to amend the condescendence of the fund (*MacGillvray's Trs.*, above). Where the holder loses title to property in the fund *in medio* (i.e. by reduction of that title in a separate action) before the action of multiplepoinding is concluded, that property to which the holder no longer has valid title should be excluded from the condescendence of the fund: *Dunn's Trs. v. Barstow* (1870) 9 M. 281.

EFFECT OF RAISING ACTION.

Bell noted in his *Commentaries* (ii ,276), that because of its effect on diligence, an action of multiplepoinding was also known as "suspension of double poinding". He further stated that the effect of raising the action was to render the fund litigious, i.e. to prevent the holder from granting any voluntary conveyance of the fund while the action of multiplepoinding was in dependence: Bell's, Comm., ii,278. It has been stated that the raising of an action of multiplepoinding does not sist all diligence against the fund, but any creditor who appears as a claimant could not proceed with diligence: Graham Stewart on *Diligence*, pp. 136-137. The point is not free from doubt. In *Ferguson v. Bothwell* (1882) 9 R. 786, a poinding creditor proceeded with diligence notwithstanding being cited as a defender in the multiplepoinding raised by his debtor. In that case the court observed that the proper course for the debtor would have been to raise his own action of suspension of the diligence. **51.2.8**

Condescendence of fund in medio

51.3.—(1) Where the pursuer is the holder of the fund *in medio*, he shall include a detailed statement of the fund in the condescendence annexed to the summons. **51.3**

(2) Where the pursuer is not the holder of the fund *in medio*, the holder shall, unless he has lodged defences in accordance with rule 51.4 (objections to actions of multiplepoinding), lodge in process a condescendence of the fund *in medio*, stating—

(a)   any claim or lien which he may profess to have on that fund, and

(b)   all persons so far as known to him as having an interest in the fund, within seven days after the date on which the summons has called.

Deriv. R.C.S. 1965, r. 176 substituted by S.I. 1986 No. 1941

"WHERE THE PURSUER IS THE HOLDER OF THE FUND".

The pursuer is the real raiser. **51.3.1**

"WHERE THE PURSUER IS NOT THE HOLDER ... ".

The real raiser is not the "pursuer", in the sense of being the holder of the fund. In such an action the holder of the fund is designed as the "pursuer and nominal raiser" and the real raiser is himself one of the defenders and is designed as "defender and real raiser". **51.3.2**

"DETAILED STATEMENT OF THE FUND".

It should be sufficient to identify the property comprising the fund: see, e.g. the style in Green's *Encyclopaedia of Styles*, vol. 7, p. 105 (No. 74). **51.3.3**

"CONDESCENDENCE OF THE FUND IN MEDIO".

The purpose of the condescendence of the fund, annexed to the summons by the pursuer and real raiser (under r. 51.3(1)) or lodged in process where the holder is not the real raiser (under r. 51.3(2)), is to enable the court to establish the extent, if any, of the fund *in medio*. This is an essential prior step to determining the rights of the respective claimants thereto. There must be a condescendence: *Carmichael v. Todd* (1853) 15 D. 473 (real raiser criticised by the court for, inter alia, failing to have a condescendence of the fund). **51.3.4**

"LODGED DEFENCES".

The holder of the fund may object to the action of multiplepoinding and does so by lodging defences in accordance with r. 51.4(1). **51.3.5**

"CLAIM OR LIEN".

The holder may have a claim upon, or a lien over, the fund *in medio* (or that part of the fund in his possession). A holder's failure to assert a claim at this stage, i.e. in objections to the action itself, may not bar the claim, if the claim is stateable by way of retention or compensation, when objections to the condescendence of the fund are determined: *Ramsay's J.F. v. British Linen Bank* 1912 S.C. 206, 208. Trustees holding a fund for administration are obliged to lodge a claim, as trustees, for the whole fund for the purpose of administration: *Hall's Trs. v. McDonald* (1892) 19 R. 567, 577 per Lord Kinnear. **51.3.6**

"SUMMONS".

See Chap. 13. **51.3.7**

"HAS CALLED".

On calling of a summons, see r. 13.13. **51.3.8**

Objections to actions of multiplepoinding

51.4

51.4.—(1) Any objection to an action of multiplepoinding on any ground shall be made by lodging defences.

(2) Where the holder of a fund *in medio* lodges defences under paragraph (1), he shall, notwithstanding his objection to the action, disclose all persons so far as known to him and reasonably ascertainable who have an interest in that fund.

(3) On defences being lodged under paragraph (1), the pursuer shall comply with rule 22.1 (making up open records); and the action shall proceed for the purpose of determining the objection stated in the defences as an ordinary action.

(4) Where the holder of the fund *in medio* has lodged defences, the court shall, on determining those defences without dismissing the action, ordain the holder of the fund to lodge a condescendence of the fund *in medio* stating any claim or lien which he may profess to have on that fund, within such period as it thinks fit.

Deriv. R.C.S. 1965, r. 176(b)(part) amended by S.I. 1986 No. 1941 (r. 51.4(1)(part), (2) and (4)), r. 177(a) amended by S.I. 1986 No. 1941 (r. 51.4(1)(part)), and r. 177(b) (r. 51.4(3))

"OBJECTION ... ON ANY GROUND".

51.4.1

An objection to an action of multiplepoinding must be dealt with before all other questions: *Connell v. Ferguson* (1861) 23 D. 683, 686 per Lord Neaves; *Clark v. Campbell* (1873) 1 R. 281 (e.g. before determining whether a foreign-domiciled real raiser was required to sist a mandatory). The following objections have been taken:

(1) No jurisdiction.

The situation of any part of the fund *in medio* in Scotland is sufficient to confer jurisdiction on the court: see note 51.1.2. Accordingly, the court has jurisdiction over a foreign-domiciled defender in an action of multiplepoinding, but that does not otherwise make that person subject to the jurisdiction of the court in another action brought by a third party: *Bell v. Stewart* (1852) 14 D. 837.

(2) Forum non conveniens.

See, e.g. *Okell v. Foden* (1884) 11 R. 906.

(3) No fund in medio.

It is a valid objection to the competency of an action of multiplepoinding that there is no fund: see, e.g. *Provan v. Provan* (1840) 23 D. 298 (where the Lord Ordinary raised the question of competency on this ground at his own instance); but see *Crombie v. Crombie's Trs.* (1830) 8 S. 745, which is to the contrary effect. This defence is peculiar to the pursuer and nominal raiser: MacLaren on *Court of Session Practice*, p. 660. An objection that the real raiser is not entitled to the fund is not an objection to the competency of the action, but one which affects the merits: *Greenshield's Trs. v. Greenshield* 1915 2 S.L.T. 189.

(4) No double distress.

In its original form, multiplepoinding (or "double poinding" in Stair's usage (Stair, IV.xvi.1) required double distress in the technical sense of double diligence. In his proposed style, Stair referred to multiple arrestments or poindings, from which the name of this action is presumably derived: Stair, IV.xvi.7. The nineteenth century saw some modification of this prerequisite for double diligence, as long as there was a double claim on the fund: "it is still however necessary to the validity of the action that there should be a true case of double claim to one fund or property on separate and hostile grounds, not a mere ostensible case got up in order to try a question of debt or obligation between two individuals, the proper mode of trying which is a direct action": *Russel v. Johnston* (1859) 21 D. 886, 887 per Lord Kinloch, quoted with approval by Lord Johnston in *Glen's Trs. v. Miller* 1911 S.C. 1178, 1185. If a direct action is available to the claimant, an action of multiplepoinding will be incompetent. So, e.g. an action of multiplepoinding has been held incompetent to determine a dispute between debtor and creditor (*Clark v. Campbell* (1873) 1 R. 281), between cedent and assignee (*Russel*, above), between trustees and beneficiaries (*Robb's Trs. v. Robb* (1880) 7 R. 1049), to determine whether the real raiser was entitled to legitim (*Scott's J.F. v. Richardson* (1905) 13 S.L.T. 537) and where it was used in lieu of an action of count and reckoning (*Carmichael v. Todd* (1853) 15 D. 473, 476 per Lord Cuninghame; *Park v. Mackersy* (1843) 5 D. 482; cf. *National Providential Institute v. Mcleod* 1915 2 S.L.T. 329 (in which an originally competent action of multiplepoinding became, because of the withdrawal of other claims, a direct action of count and reckoning)). A distinction, however, falls to be drawn between an action raised by a claimant and one raised by the holder of the fund: *Russel*, above. In the latter case, greater latitude is allowed. The holder of the fund "is entitled to be relieved by means of an action of multiplepoinding ... and accordingly it is sufficient justification of the institution of the action, and is the criteria of its competency, that the claims intimated make it impossible for the depositary to pay to one of the parties without running the risk of an action at the instance of the other.": *Winchester v. Blakey* (1890) 17 R. 1046, 1050 per Lord MacLaren. The rationale is that a holder "can never raise a direct action, and is not bound to remain a depositary till the day of his death": *Winchester*, above. Accordingly, it is sufficient if there are competing claims which the holder of the fund is unable to meet: *Winchester*, above. So, e.g. actions of multiplepoinding which would otherwise have been dismissed as incompetent, because only raising an issue between two claimants triable by direct action, were nonetheless allowed when raised by the holders: *Royal Bank of Scotland v. Price* (1893) 20 R. 290; *Commercial Bank of Scotland v. Muir* (1897) 25 R. 219.

Resort to an action of multiplepoinding should not be made by trustees, executors and those who hold monies on behalf of others simply as a means to determine disputes in relation to those monies where there is no genuine double distress. So, e.g. an action of multiplepoinding raised by trustees was refused where the only dispute was between a beneficiary and a creditor on the estate (*Glen's Trs. v. Miller* 1911 S.C. 1178; cf. *Ogilvie's Trs. v. Chevalier* (1874) 1 R. 693 (in which a multiplepoinding by testamentary trustees was only reluctantly allowed where the only dispute was between the sole beneficiary and her creditor)) or where a solicitor was called upon to pay over the estate to the confirmed executor and another party claimed right to those funds (*Adam Cochran & Co. v. Conn* 1989 S.L.T. (Sh. Ct.) 27). An attempt to use an action of multiplepoinding in this way may be an abuse of process: *Ogilvie's Trs.*, above. Nor should executors or trustees resort to a multiplepoinding in order to obtain exoneration and discharge where there is no difficulty obtaining this extrajudicially: *Mackenzie's Trs. v. Gray* (1895) 2 S.L.T. 422. It has been held competent, however, for those holding monies in a fiduciary capacity, such as trustees and executors, to raise an action of multiplepoinding to obtain their exoneration and discharge if those in whose power it is to grant this refuse to do so (*Fraser's Exr. v. Wallace's Trs.* (1893) 20 R. 374, 379 per Lord MacLaren; *Mackenzie's Trs. v. Sutherland* (1894) 22 R. 233, 237 per Lord Kinnear), are otherwise unable to grant sufficient exoneration (*Davidson v. Ewen* (1895) 3 S.L.T. 162) or because of doubts as to the construction of testamentary bequests it is unclear who is entitled to the fund and able to give valid discharge (*McClement's Trs. v. Lord Advocate* 1949 S.L.T. (Notes) 59).

A judicial factor may not competently obtain his exoneration and discharge in the course of an action of multiplepoinding. A judicial factor is appointed by the court in the exercise of its *nobile officium* and his ultimate discharge is likewise granted in exercise of those powers: *Campbell v. Grant* (1869) 7 M. 227, 233 per Lord Deas, (1870) 8 M. 988.

(5) All parties not called.

See, e.g. *Connell v. Ferguson* (1861) 23 D. 683.

(6) Irregular statement of facts.

For an unusual case in which objection was taken to the statement of facts by the defender and real raiser, see *Carmichael v. Todd* (1853) 15 D. 473, in which the single beneficiary under a trust deed raised an action of multiplepoinding in the name of the judicial factor appointed to manage the estate after the death of all the testamentary trustees. The real raiser proceeded to make detailed allegations of misconduct against the judicial factor. The court dismissed the multiplepoinding as both incompetent, there being no double distress, and irregular, in that the statement of facts contained averments which the nominal raiser, in whose name the action had been raised, was bound to deny.

"AN ORDINARY ACTION".

The action proceeds as an ordinary action for the purpose of determining the objections to the raising of the action of multiplepoinding stated in the defences. An open record is made up. This is only one of several records within an action of multiplepoinding, the others concerning the ascertainment of the fund *in medio*, if objections are taken to the condescendence of the fund (as opposed to the action itself) and, thirdly, the competition (if any) of the claimants on the fund.

"HOLDER ... LODGES DEFENCES".

These may be preliminary (e.g. because there is no double distress or no fund) or substantive. **51.4.3**

"LODGE A CONDESCENDENCE OF THE FUND".

If the holder is the real raiser, he will have annexed a condescendence of the fund to the summons. Where, however, he is only the nominal raiser, he should lodge a condescendence of the fund in terms of r. 51.3(2). Alternatively, the holder may, under this rule (r. 51.4(4)), be ordained to lodge a condescendence, once the objections to the action have been determined by the court. On the condescendence of the fund, see note 51.3.4. **51.4.4**

"FOR THE PURPOSE OF DETERMINING THE OBJECTION".

This only determines objections to the action. The court may, by separate causes each with its own record, have to determine objections to the condescendence of the fund *in medio* and, finally, to determine the respective rights of the claimants to that fund. **51.4.5**

Advertisement for objections to condescendence and claims

51.5.—(1) The pursuer may— **51.5**

(a) after the expiry of the period for lodging defences without defences having been lodged, or

(b) where defences have been lodged, after those defences have been repelled and, where an order is made under rule 51.4(4), the condescendence of the fund has been lodged,

apply by motion for the orders mentioned in paragraph (2).

(2) The orders referred to in paragraph (1) are—

(a) the ordaining of any objection to the condescendence of the fund *in medio* and claims on the fund to be lodged within such period as the court thinks fit; and

(b) advertisement of the call for any objection and claims in such newspapers or other publications and for such number of insertions as the court thinks fit.

(3) An advertisement ordered under paragraph (1) shall be in Form 51.5.

Deriv. R.C.S. 1965, r. 182(a) (r. 51.5(1) and (2)(a)).

"EXPIRY OF THE PERIOD FOR LODGING DEFENCES".

51.5.1   This will be seven days after the date on which the summons has called or, if the seventh day falls in vacation, the next day on which a summons may be called: r. 18.1(2).

"MOTION".

51.5.2   For motions, see Chap. 23.

"ADVERTISEMENT".

51.5.3   The purpose of intimating the raising of an action of multiplepoinding is to ensure that all persons entitled to make a claim have an opportunity to do so. It has been stated to be "an essential prerequisite to any judgment in [a] competition": *Connell v. Ferguson* (1861) 23 D. 683, 687 per Lord Neaves. Failure to make an order for claims would render a decree of preference "ineffectual or unsafe as an exoneration of the nominal raisers, if no such interlocutor allowing claims should ever have been pronounced": *Connell*, above. The court may at its own instance order advertisement or other intimation: see r. 51.9, and *Connell*, above. The newspaper containing the advertisement or the publisher's certificate of publication required under r. 51.9(a) is lodged as a production: see r. 4.5.

Form of objection to condescendence and claims

51.6   **51.6.**—(1) An objection to a condescendence of the fund *in medio* shall be made by lodging defences.

(2) A claim on the fund *in medio* shall be made in the form of a condescendence, claim and appropriate pleas-in-law.

(3) On lodging a condescendence and claim, a claimant shall lodge his ground of debt and all other documents supporting his claim.

(4) Where a person intends to—

(a) object to the condescendence on the fund *in medio*, and

(b) make a claim on the fund,

he shall lodge defences and a separate condescendence and claim.

Deriv. R.C.S. 1965. r. 180

"AN OBJECTION TO A CONDESCENDENCE OF THE FUND".

51.6.1   The condescendence of the fund *in medio* will have been lodged by the holder under r. 51.3(1) or (2) or under r. 51.4(4). If objections are stated to the condescendence of the fund *in medio*, the adjudication of those objections forms a separate cause within the multiplepoinding. A separate record is made up. The objections must be stated in defences (see r. 51.6(1)) as a separate statement of facts on which the objections are based, pleas-in-law are annexed to the condescendence and are signed by counsel or other person having a right of audience (see definition in r. 1.3(1)). The most common objection is that there is some property or monies which should be excluded from the condescendence of the fund: see, e.g. *Walker's Tr. v. Walker* (1878) 5 R. 678; *Donaldson's Trs. v. Beattie* 1914 1 S.L.T. 170. Objections, however, that clearly undisputed property has been included in the condescendence of the fund *in medio* appear to be treated as raising questions as to the competency of the action (e.g. *McNab v. Waddell* (1894) 21 R. 827), rather than stated at this stage. Objection to the condescendence of the fund should not be combined with objections (if any) to the competency of the action itself. The court will have dealt with objections to the latter under r. 51.4. In *Walker's Trs.*, above, the court allowed objections to the condescendence of the fund *in medio* to be made, notwithstanding that it had already pronounced an interlocutor finding the holder and real raiser liable only in once and single payment.

"CONDESCENDENCE".

A claimant's condescendence should give the factual basis on which his claim is founded. A condescendence by a claimant (under r. 51.1(2)) should not be confused with the holder's condescendence of the fund *in medio* (although the holder should state his own claim (if any) in the condescendence of the fund). A claimant's condescendence is in the same form as the condescendence in other actions (on which, see note 13.2.4), but must conclude with a separate short claim (on which, see note 51.6.3).

51.6.2

"CLAIM".

The claim is a short sentence in which the claimant claims to be ranked and preferred to the whole (or a specified portion) of the fund *in medio*. If a condescendence does not contain a claim, the claimant cannot be preferred to the fund *in medio*: *Connell v. Ferguson* (1861) 23 D. 683, 686 per Lord Neaves. A holder's claim may include a right of retention or compensation. Notice of such a claim should be given as early as possible in the process: *Ramsay's J.F. v. British Linen Bank* 1912 S.C. 206, 208.

In some circumstances, by what is known as a "riding claim", a person may claim to be ranked on the fund *in medio* by virtue of his debtor's claim in the multiplepoinding. However, the debtor's claim, through which the creditor is asserting a riding claim, must be a direct one and not, e.g. through the debtor's debtor: *Gill's Trs. v. Patrick* (1889) 16 R. 403. A riding claim must be constituted (*Royal Bank of Scotland v. Stevenson* (1849) 12 D. 250) and liquid (*Home's Trs. v. Ralston's Trs.* (1834) 12 S. 727; *Wilson v. Young* (1851) 13 D. 1366). The riding claim must be lodged before decree for payment is pronounced in favour of the original claimant (i.e. the debtor): *Anglo-Foreign Banking Co.* (1879) 16 S.L.R. 731. A riding claim has been described as a surrogatum of arrestment or assignation to prevent the fund being taken out of court: *Royal Bank of Scotland*, above, per Lord Jeffrey at p. 252. It would appear competent, though no reported decision has been found, for more than one riding claim to be ranked on a principal claim, compelling a separate competition in respect of those several riding claims on the principal claimant's share of the fund: Thomson & Middleton, *Manual of Court of Session Practice*, p. 124. The court has refused a riding claim where, after consideration of the *media concludendi* of the decree on which the riding claim was based, it was regarded as an attempt to obtain a preference: *Thomson & Co. v. Friese-Greene's Tr.* 1944 S.C. 336.

51.6.3

"PLEAS-IN-LAW".

The plea is that the claimant is entitled to be ranked and preferred to the fund *in medio* in terms of his claim. On pleas-in-law generally, see note 18.1.4.

51.6.4

"GROUND OF DEBT AND ALL OTHER DOCUMENTS".

Any document of debt founded on or adopted in the defences must be lodged as a production when the defences are lodged: r. 27.1(1)(b). For lodging productions, see r. 4.5.

51.6.5

"DEFENCES AND A SEPARATE CONDESCENDENCE AND CLAIM".

That is, an objection to the condescendence of the fund, separate from objections to the action itself. On claims, see note 51.6.3.

51.6.6

Procedure following call for objections

51.7.—(1) Where defences are lodged under rule 51.6 (form of objection to condescendence and claims), an open record shall be made up on the condescendence and such objection, and the pursuer shall comply with rule 22.1 (making up open records); and the cause shall proceed for the purposes of determining the objection as an ordinary action.

51.7

(2) No order shall be pronounced in relation to any claims on the fund *in medio* until any defences under rule 51.6 have been disposed of and the condescendence of the fund *in medio* approved.

(3) Where the court disposes of defences, or where no defences have been lodged under rule 51.6, the court shall—

(a) approve the condescendence of the fund *in medio*, subject to such alteration as it may make in disposing of any objection;

(b) find the pursuer, or where he is not the holder of the fund, the holder, liable only in once and single payment;

(c) make such further order, if any, for claims as it thinks fit.

Deriv. R.C.S. 1965, r. 182(c) (r. 51.7(1)) and r. 179(part) amended by S.I. 1986 No. 1941 (r. 51.7(3))

"OBJECTION TO CONDESCENDENCE".

See note 51.6.1.

51.7.1

"AS AN ORDINARY ACTION".

51.7.2   This is the second of several separate causes in the course of a multiplepoinding. The purpose is to adjudicate on the objections (if any) to the fund, in order to ascertain its extent.

"APPROVE THE CONDESCENDENCE OF THE FUND IN MEDIO".

51.7.3   This is a final interlocutor, which may be reclaimed without leave: *School Board of Harris v. Davidson* (1881) 9 R. 375; *Walker's Tr. v. Walker* (1878) 5 R. 678.

"ONCE AND SINGLE PAYMENT".

51.7.4   The purpose of finding the holder liable "only in once and single payment", once the objections (if any) are determined and the fund is approved, is to enable the holder to make payment (usually by consigning the fund into court) and effectively drop out of the action (unless the holder also wishes to assert a claim to the fund): see, e.g. r. 51.10. The court does not always require consignation: *British Linen Co. v. Breadalbane's Trs.* (1836) 15 S. 356.

Advertisement of dependence of actions

51.8   **51.8.**   The court may, at its own instance or on the motion of a party, at any time order—

    (a)   such advertisement of the dependence of the action as it thinks fit; and

    (b)   intimation of the dependence of the action to any person not called as a defender.

Deriv. R.C.S. 1965, r. 178(part) amended by S.I. 1986 No. 1941

"ADVERTISEMENT".

51.8.1   See note 51.5.3.

"DEPENDENCE OF THE ACTION".

51.8.2   A cause is depending from the time it is commenced (i. e. from the time an action is served) until final decree, whereas a cause is in dependence until final extract. For the meaning of commenced, see note 13.4.4. For the meaning of final decree, see note 4.15.2(2). For the meaning of final extract, see note 7.1.2(2).

Evidence of advertisement and intimation

51.9   **51.9.**   Where the court orders advertisement or intimation under this Chapter, the party required to make such advertisement or intimation shall lodge in process, as the case may be—

    (a)   a copy of the newspaper or other publication containing the advertisement or a certificate of publication by the publisher stating the date of publication and the text of the advertisement; or

    (b)   the certificate of intimation.

Deriv. R.C.S. 1965, r. 178(part) amended by S.I. 1986 No. 1941

"ADVERTISEMENT".

51.9.1   See note 51.5.3.

"INTIMATION".

51.9.2   For methods, see rr. 16.7 and 16.8.

Consignation of fund and discharge of holder

51.10   **51.10.**—(1)   On approval of the condescendence of the fund *in medio*, the holder of the fund may apply by motion for—

    (a)   a finding that he is entitled to his expenses out of the fund; and

    (b)   authority to consign the fund into court, after deduction of his expenses as taxed by the Auditor.

(2)   Where consignation is made by virtue of an authority under paragraph (1)(b), the holder of the fund may apply by motion for his exoneration and discharge.

"APPROVAL OF THE CONDESCENDENCE OF THE FUND IN MEDIO".

51.10.1   The court's approval of the fund is essential, as the interlocutor determines the amount for which the holder is liable to account. An interlocutor approving of the fund becomes final if not reclaimed against before the expiry of the period for so doing.

For motions, see Chap. 23.

51.10.2

"EXPENSES OUT OF THE FUND".

If the holder of the fund is not the real raiser (i.e. he is the nominal raiser), he will be entitled to the expenses of the condescendence of the fund out of that fund. If the holder is the real raiser and the action was justified, he will generally be entitled to expenses *primo loco* out of the fund. If trustees raise an action of multiplepoinding which is subsequently found to be unjustified, they may be found personally liable in expenses: *Mackenzie's Trs. v. Sutherland (1894)* 22 R. 233; *Paterson's Trs. v. Paterson* (1897) 7 S.L.T. 134; cf. *Gill's Trs. v. Miller* 1911 S.C. 1178.

51.10.3

"CONSIGNATION".

The amount consigned is the balance in the hands of the holder after deduction of the holder's taxed expenses (if any). The form of the fund, or a part of it, may make consignation difficult. In one case, where part of the fund was a bond and disposition in security, the court ordered the holder to execute and lodge in process an assignation of the bond in favour of the successful claimant: *Currie's Trs. v. Bothwell* 1954 S.L.T.(Sh.Ct) 87. On consignation generally, see note 33.4.3. The court may require an agent of the holder to consign the fund, reserving all claims by the agent: *Long v. Downie* (1872) 9 S.L.R. 308.

51.10.4

"EXONERATION AND DISCHARGE".

The effect is to take the holder out of the action and to free him from all future claims by any person: see, e.g. *Farquhar v. Farquhar* (1896) 13 R. 596. Exoneration and discharge is not normally granted until consignation of the fund *in medio* has been effected to the satisfaction of the court.

51.10.5

Claims not timeously lodged

51.11.—(1) A claimant who fails to lodge his claim within the period specified in the order under rule 51.5(2)(a) (order for any objections and for claims) may apply by motion to have his claim received.

(2) The court may allow such a claim to be received on such conditions as to expenses, if any, as it thinks fit.

Deriv. R.C.S. 1965, r. 181

51.11

"FAILS TO LODGE HIS CLAIM WITHIN THE PERIOD SPECIFIED".

It has been observed that "the process of multiplepoinding admits ... of a very great latitude in the lodging of claims, both by those who have been called as defenders and by those who have not. Claims are constantly received long after the prescribed time for lodging them has expired": *Landale v. Wilson* (1900) 2 F. 1047, 1048-1049 per Lord Stormonth-Darling. It is a matter for the court's discretion whether to allow a late claim: *Young v. Morris* (1858) 20 D.(H.L.) 12. Once a decree of ranking and preference has been pronounced the fund is no longer *in medio* and the late claimant cannot demand of right to lodge a claim: *Young*, above. A fortiori, the court will not entertain a late claim where the decree of ranking and preference has been substantially implemented and the fund paid away: *Stodart v. Bell* (1860) 22 D. 1092. Generally, a late claim will be allowed, unless an interlocutor pronounced on a ranking and preference of the claimant's respective claims has become final: *Landale*, above; *Ramsay's J.F. v. British Linen Bank* 1911 S.C. 832. If the interlocutor is final, the Lord Ordinary is functus (*Ramsay's J.F.*, above; *Terrell v. Kerr* (1900) 2 F. 1055) and it is beyond the competence of the Lord Ordinary to review that interlocutor (*Duncan's Factor v. Duncan* (1874) 1 R. 964, 965 per Lord Gifford). Nor is it within the power of a Lord Ordinary to allow a late claim, where the Inner House had pronounced decree of ranking and preference and thereafter remitted the cause to the Lord Ordinary to carry its judgment into effect: *Landale*, above. In the absence of a decree of preference being final, the Inner House may recall *in hoc statu* the interlocutor of the Lord Ordinary and, subject to payment of expenses, allow a late claim to be lodged. Leave to lodge a late claim has been allowed in relation to a person who was called as a defender but who had never appeared (*Binnie's Trs. v. Henry's Trs.* (1883) 10 R. 1075), a person who had entered appearance but had never lodged a claim (*Jaffe v. Carruthers* (1860) 22 D. 936), a person who had lodged, and then before the closing of the record withdrew, an earlier claim (*Binnie's Trs.*, above) and a fresh claim by an unsuccessful claimant after judgment on a new ground (*Dymond v. Scott* (1877) 5 R. 196). The court may be more disposed to allow a late claim by a person who was never called in the multiplepoinding: compare the court's treatment of the first and second groups of late claimants in *Morgan v. Morris* (1856) 18D. 797. The Inner House has permitted, at the bar in a reclaiming motion, amendment of a claim by the holder of the fund: *Hall's Trs. v. McDonald* (1892) 19 R. 567. In an unusual case a claim was rejected as too late, coming as it did after the expiry of the reclaiming days for the decree of ranking and preference (*Ramsay's J.F.*, above), but was subsequently allowed to be stated by way of plea of compensation or retention in the objections to the condescendence of the fund: *Ramsay's J.F v. British Linen Bank* 1912 S.C. 206. Greater latitude, however, is allowed in respect of the late lodging of a riding claim (on which see note 51.6.3) because such a claim would not disturb the existing decree of ranking and preference, but simply substitute the creditor with a riding claim in place of the successful claimant: see, e.g. *Scottish Life Assurance Co. Ltd v. John Donald Ltd* (1902) 9 S.L.T. 348; *Ramsay's J.F. v. British Linen Bank* 1911 S.C. 832, 834 per Lord Mackenzie, 1912 S.C. 206, 210 per Lord Salvesen. It is too late to lodge a riding claim once a decree for payment in favour of the claimant has

51.11.1

been made: *Anglo-Foreign Banking Co.* (1879) 16 S.L.R. 731.

"MOTION".

51.11.2 For motions, see Chap. 23.

"SUCH CONDITIONS AS TO EXPENSES ... AS IT THINKS FIT".

51.11.3 The court may order payment of a proportion of the successful claimant's expenses, usually in the same proportion as the late claimant is likely to benefit from the successful claimant's efforts: e.g. one-half (*Morgan v. Morris* (1856) 18 D. 797), one-quarter (*Cowan's Trs. v. Cowan* (1887) 14 R. 670), one-third (*National Bank of Scotland v. City Commercial Restaurant* (1901) 9 S.L.T. 211). If the person seeking leave to lodge a late claim fails to meet the condition (i.e. payment of expenses), his application for leave will be refused: *Morgan v. Morris*, above, 818-819; affd. sub nom. *Young v. Morris* (1858) 20 D.(H.L.) 12.

Procedure following approval of fund in medio

51.12 **51.12.**—(1) After the condescendence of the fund *in medio* has been approved, and it appears that there is no competition, the court may, on the motion of any claimant, rank and prefer the parties who have lodged claims.

(2) After the condescendence of the fund *in medio* has been approved and where there is competition—

(a) any party may apply by motion for an order to print a record in the competition and, on such an order being made, an open record shall be made up on the condescendences and claims and the pursuer shall comply with rule 22.1 (making up open records); and the action shall proceed for the purpose of determining the competition as an ordinary action; and

(b) during the period of adjustment, a claimant may adjust his condescendence to state any objection to any other claim.

(3) When pronouncing any decree of ranking on the fund *in medio*, the court may determine any question of expenses; and, where it finds any party entitled to expenses out of the fund *in medio*, notwithstanding rule 42.1(1)(b) (decerniture for expenses as taxed) it shall not at the same time decern for payment of those expenses.

Deriv. R.C.S. 1965, r. 183(part) (r. 51.12(1)) and r. 185 (r. 51.12(2))

"CONDESCENDENCE OF THE FUND IN MEDIO ... HAS BEEN APPROVED".

51.12.1 See note 51.7.4.

"COMPETITION".

51.12.2 A competition arises where the claims exceed the value of the fund or are competing in respect of a particular part of the fund. If there is no competition, the Lord Ordinary gives effect to the claimants' respective claims by a decree of ranking and preference (on which, see note 51.12.3). Thereafter, a decree of payment is pronounced: see, e.g. *Morgan v. Morris* (1856) 18 D. 797. If there is a competition, this forms a separate cause within the multiplepoinding. Again, a decree of ranking and preference will follow, once the claimants' respective claims have been allowed or repelled.

"RANK AND PREFER THE PARTIES WHO HAVE LODGED CLAIMS".

51.12.3 If there is no competition, the parties may agree in a joint minute to a ranking of their respective claims, though this is not necessary. The court may refuse a joint minute purporting to agree a scheme of division which is not in accordance with the claimants' respective entitlements in terms of the decree of ranking and preference: *Tennent's J.F. v. Tennent* 1956 S.L.T.(Notes) 39. A decree of ranking and preference may be granted without proof: *Union Bank v. Gracie* (1887) 25 S.L.R. 61. The court may refuse to pronounce a decree of ranking and preference, notwithstanding that there is no competition, if it appears *ex facie* of a claimant's claim that he has no right to that part of the fund to which he lays claim: *Clark's Exr. v. Clark* 1953 S.L.T. (Notes) 58. The court has refused to pronounce a decree of ranking and preference, except for "aught yet seen" (on which, see note 51.13.2), where the existence of claimants was not known and had not been excluded (i.e. by a separate declarator of presumption of death): *Kerr's Trs.* (1894) 2 S.L.T. 10. A decree of ranking and preference in favour of one party, by its nature, excludes every other party: *Duncan's Factor v. Duncan* (1874) 1 R. 964, 968 per L.P. Inglis. Once final, a decree of ranking and preference can only be brought under review by a person called as a defender in the multiplepoinding in which the decree was pronounced, by an action of reduction: *Stodart v. Bell* (1860) 22 D. 1092, 1093 per Lord Cowan.

"MOTION".

51.12.4 For motions, see Chap. 23.

"AS AN ORDINARY ACTION".

This is another of several potential separate causes in the course of a multiplepoinding. The purpose is to adjudicate on the claimants' respective claims, which are either repelled or allowed, to the fund itself.

51.12.5

"TO STATE ANY OBJECTIONS TO ANY OTHER CLAIM".

It is competent for a claimant to challenge the ground of any other claimant's claim, including a decree which may be irregular (*Fischer & Co. v. Anderson* (1896) 23 R. 395) or otherwise incompetent (*Dickson & Walker v. Mitchell & Co.* 1910 S.C. 139).

51.12.6

Decrees for payment

51.13.—(1) No decree for payment out of the fund *in medio*, whether consigned into court or not, following an order for ranking (whether for aught yet seen or otherwise) shall be made until—

51.13

    (a)[1] all accounts of expenses found payable out of the fund *in medio* have been taxed and the report of the Auditor on those accounts has been approved; and

    (b) the certificate referred to in rule 8.1(1)(b) (Inland Revenue certificate of taxes or duties paid) has been lodged.

(2) Where the fund *in medio* has been consigned into court, any decree for payment out of the fund shall include—

    (a) warrant to the bank, on production of a certified copy of the interlocutor granting decree, to pay to each party the sums for which he has been ranked; and

    (b) warrant to the Accountant of Court, on production of a certified copy of the interlocutor granting decree, to endorse and deliver the consignation receipt to the bank in order that the payments may be made.

Deriv. R.C.S. 1965, r. 183(part)

"DECREE FOR PAYMENT".

An interlocutor ranking and preferring the successful claimants in terms of their claims may include, or be followed by, an order for payment or transfer of the fund *in medio* to the claimants preferred. The interlocutor ranking and preferring the claimants determines the merits, while the decree for payment (or warrant for payment from consigned funds) is the mechanism for giving effect to the order for ranking and preference. Once decerniture for payment has been made, the holder is secure against any further claims at the instance of persons called in that action: Erskine, IV.iii.23; Mackay's *Manual of Court of Session Practice*, ii.118.

51.13.1

"FOR AUGHT YET SEEN".

A decree of ranking and preference "for aught yet seen" may be granted notwithstanding the possibility that other claimants may subsequently emerge with a preferable title to the fund *in medio*: *Clark's Exr. v. Clark* 1953 S.L.T. (Notes) 58. The wording "for aught yet seen" imports a qualification of that decree of ranking and preference. A decree for aught yet seen has been held conclusive against persons cited, and who neither appeared in the original action of multiplepoinding nor reclaimed against the decree of preference: Mackay's *Manual of Court of Session Practice*, ii.110. Compare the position of persons not called (but who should have been): *Johnston v. Elder* (1832) 10 S. 195.

51.13.2

"INLAND REVENUE CERTIFICATE".

The purpose of this rule is to provide a safeguard for the Inland Revenue by preventing any payment out of the fund *in medio* until the court has been satisfied that all government duties have been paid. If unauthorised payments have been made out of the fund, the court may not grant the holder of the fund exoneration and discharge: *Simpson's Trs. v. Fox* 1954 S.L.T. (Notes) 12. In *Simpson's Trs.*, in which per incuriam payment had been made to beneficiaries (in whose favour an order of ranking and preference had been made), the court granted exoneration and discharge after the certificates had been lodged. See Chap. 8 generally for taxes on funds in the control of the court.

51.13.3

"CONSIGNED INTO COURT".

On consignation into court, see notes 51.10.4 and 33.4.3.

51.13.4

---

[1] R. 51.13(1)(a) amended by S.I. 1994 No. 2901 (minor correction).

"CERTIFIED COPY OF THE INTERLOCUTOR".

51.13.5

A copy of the interlocutor is typed by the agent and presented to the clerk of session at the appropriate section of the General Department or at the Petition Department. The clerk checks it, certifies it as a true copy and stamps it with the court stamp.

Reclaiming by claimant against ranking for aught yet seen

51.14

51.14.—(1) A claimant who has failed to lodge his claim on the fund *in medio* before a ranking for aught yet seen, may reclaim against the interlocutor making such ranking at any time while the action is depending.

(2) The Division of the Inner House before which a motion for review of an interlocutor is brought under paragraph (1) may recall that interlocutor and remit the cause to the Lord Ordinary to receive the claim on such conditions as to expenses, if any, as it thinks fit.

Deriv. R.C.S. 1965, r. 184

"FOR AUGHT YET SEEN".

51.14.1

See note 51.13.2.

"DEPENDING".

51.14.2

A cause is depending from the time it is commenced (i.e. from the time an action is served) until final decree, whereas a cause is in dependence until final extract. For the meaning of commenced, see note 13.4.4. For the meaning of final decree, see note 4.15.2(2). For the meaning of final extract, see note 7.1.2(2).

"SUCH CONDITIONS AS TO EXPENSES ... AS IT THINKS FIT".

51.14.3

In an unusual case, no condition as to expenses was imposed where the person seeking leave to lodge a late claim after decree of preference had been pronounced ought (as an arresting creditor) to have been called as a defender in the action: *Johnston v. Elder* (1832) 10 S. 195.

Exoneration of holder where no consignation

51.15

51.15. Where the holder of the fund *in medio* has not been exonerated and discharged, he may—

    (a)   following a decree for payment,

    (b)   on production of the receipts of the persons entitled to payment under that decree, and

    (c)   on consignation of any balance of the fund remaining,

apply by motion for his exoneration and discharge.

"DECREE FOR PAYMENT".

51.15.1

See note 51.13.1.

"MOTION".

51.15.2

For motions, see Chap. 23.

Chapter 52

Actions of Proving the Tenor

Parties to action of proving the tenor

52.1. In an action of proving the tenor, the pursuer shall call as a defender—   **52.1**

(a) any person having an interest in the document to be proved; or

(b) where only the pursuer has such an interest, the Lord Advocate as representing the public interest.

Deriv. R.C.S. 1965, r. 186

GENERAL NOTE.

An action to prove the tenor is an action to obtain an order containing the tenor (i.e. terms or content)   **52.1.1** of any part of a lost or destroyed document. The order has the same effect as the original document would have had. The action is declaratory in effect but it is not a species of action of declarator: *Dunbar & Co. v. Scottish County Investment Co. Ltd* 1920 S.C. 210, 213 per L.J.-C. Scott Dickson. The document the tenor of which is sought to be proved must have been lost or destroyed erroneously. Generally, a document (e.g. a testamentary writing) which has been destroyed legitimately for the purpose of revocation may not be the subject of an action to prove the tenor (see e.g. *Bonthrone v. Ireland* (1883) 10 R. 779). Occasionally the court may grant the order containing the tenor of the document but under reservation of any question of its validity at the date of granting: *Falconer v. Stephen* (1849) 11 D. 1338.

NECESSITY FOR THE ACTION.

The action is necessary where a person requires the principal of the lost or destroyed document to   **52.1.2** establish a title to sue (*Shaw v. Shaw's Trs.* (1876) 3 R. 813) or where the document is the subject-matter of an action (*Dow v. Dow* (1848) 10 D. 1465 (action of nullity of testamentary writing)).

The action is unnecessary where the lost or destroyed document is merely a part of the evidence in a cause: *Young v. Thomson* 1909 S.C. 529; *Maxwell v. Reid* (1863) 1 M. 932. It is equally unnecessary where it is founded on by a defender or a respondent as part of a defence: *Drummond v. Thomson's Trs.* (1834) 7 W. & S. 564, 572 per Lord Brougham. Where a party to a cause has destroyed the document on which the other party (usually pursuer or petitioner) founds, he cannot plead that the other party must raise an action to prove the tenor of that document: *Seton v. Paterson* (1766) 5 Brown's Supp. 924; *Ross v. Fisher* (1833) 11 S. 467.

The person who requires the document may also overcome the need for an action to prove its tenor by agreeing its terms in a joint minute of agreement for the purposes of a proposed litigation with the other likely party. Following the widespread use of photocopying machines this may be a possible solution. Where, however, there is no other party (e.g. in a petition for appointment as an executor-dative) an action of proving the tenor may still be required to establish title to sue on the basis of the lost document.

JURISDICTION.

The applicability of the C.J.J.A. 1982 depends to some extent on the subject-matter of the document   **52.1.3** sought to be proved. Thus:

1. *In a jurisdictional issue between states party to the 1968 or Lugano Convention*, these conventions do not apply to matters relating to status or legal capacity of natural persons, wills and succession, bankruptcy, etc., social security and arbitration (C.J.J.A. 1982, Scheds. 1 and 3C, Art. 1).

2. *In a jurisdictional issue between U.K. legal systems*. Sched. 4 to the C.J.J.A. 1982 would appear to apply.

3. *In a jurisdictional issue between Scotland and any other legal system not mentioned in (1) and (2) above* because an action of proving the tenor involves an exercise of the *nobile officium* (see below), Sched. 8 to the C.J.J.A. 1982 does not apply: C.J.J.A. 1982, s. 22(3). The common law, therefore, does apply.

Jurisdiction at common law rests with the *nobile officium* of the court: *Dunbar & Co. v. Scottish County Investment Co.* 1920 S.C. 210, 217 per Lord Salvesen. Until the A.S. 20th March 1907, after the action had been raised in the Outer House, the Lord Ordinary made avizandum in the cause to the Inner House where the proof was heard and the interlocutor on the merits pronounced. Since 1907 the exercise of the *nobile officium* has been delegated to the Outer House. An action of proving the tenor is not a species of action of declarator and accordingly the sheriff does not have jurisdiction: *Dunbar & Co.*, above.

THE PURSUER.

Any person with a prima facie interest in the lost or destroyed document may be a pursuer: *Winchester*   **52.1.4** *v. Smith* (1863) 1 M. 685, 692 per Lord Deas. This may include a signatory of the document, an assignee of the signatory, a representative of a deceased signatory or a grantee of a unilaterally signed recorded document (*Brown v. Orr* (1872) 10 M. 397).

52.1.5   Every person having an interest should be called as a defender: r. 52.1(a). Where the pursuer alone has an interest he should call the Lord Advocate as representing the public interest: r. 52.1(b).

Lodging of supporting evidence

52.2   **52.2.** On lodging the summons for signeting, supporting documentary evidence of the tenor of the document to be proved in an action of proving the tenor, so far as in the possession or control of the pursuer, shall be lodged in process.

Deriv. RCS 1965, r. 187

SUMMONS.

52.2.1   For form of summons, see r. 13.2. In the conclusions, apart from the statutory requirements of r. 13.2(2) and Form 13.2-B(6), there should be a conclusion for expenses against the defender "in the event of a defender appearing to oppose the action".

In the condescendence the pursuer should aver:

1.   *The terms of the document.* These should be narrated in the conclusions. It may be sufficient only to incorporate the terms in the condescendence by reference to the conclusion.

2.   *Existence of adminicles.* These are any writs which tend to establish the contents of the document sought to be proved. They may include drafts (*McLeod v. Leslie* (1865) 3 M. 840) or informal copies (e.g. photocopies) or correspondence (Erskine, IV.i.55). Where the document lost or destroyed is one where copies, drafts or other written evidence of the contents may reasonably be expected to exist, the pursuer must produce and aver such an adminicle: Erskine, IV.i.55; *Winton & Co. v. Thomson & Co.* (1862) 24 D. 1094. An example of such a document is a formal document prepared by a law agent: *Graham v. McFarlane* (1847) 10 D. 45 (deed of entail). Where the document is not one where an adminicle would reasonably be expected (e.g. where a law agent was not involved) then an adminicle need not be averred: *Winton & Co.*, above; *Lithgow v. Murray* (1680) Mor. 15799; *A. v. B.* (1749) Mor. 15823. Adminicles, in so far as in the possession or control of the pursuer, should be lodged in process at the signeting of the summons: rr. 52.2 and 27.1;

3.   *The casus amissionis.* This is the circumstance of the loss or destruction of the document. There are two types of casus amissionis for which different levels of specification are required—

(a)   *Special casus amissionis.* Where the document to be proved is one which may be destroyed for the purpose of revocation or termination (e.g. a personal bond, bill of exchange, or a writing with testamentary effect), the pursuer must aver the particular circumstances of loss or destruction: Erskine, IV.i.54; *Winchester v. Smith* (1863) 1 M. 685, 689 per L.P. McNeill, Lords Curriehill and Ardmillan (mutual will); *Smith v. Ferguson* (1882) 9 R. 866, 879 per Lord Shand (ante-nuptial marriage contract). Averments that a testator ordered a testamentary writing to be destroyed (*Bonthrone v. Ireland* (1883) 10 R. 779), that a testator destroyed it while of unsound mind (*Laing v. Bruce* (1838) 1 D. 59) or that the testator's mental health was deteriorating (*Lander v. Briggs* , 1999 S.C. 453), have been held to be sufficient for a proof: cf. *Smith v. Ferguson* (1882) 9 R. 866 (casus amissionis insufficiently averred).

(b)   *General casus amissionis.* Where the document lost or destroyed was intended to remain constantly with the grantee or is one which requires a contrary document to be extinguished, the pursuer need only aver bare loss or destruction casu fortuito (an accident): Erskine, IV.i.54; *Winton & Co. v. Thomson & Co.* (1862) 24 D. 1094 (composition agreement).

Where any casus amissionis is that the document has been lost the pursuer must aver the steps taken in search of the document: *Walker v. Brock* (1852) 14 D. 362; *McKean* (1857) 19 D. 448. The summons should be signed by an agent or a party litigant with leave of the court: r. 4.2.

LODGING OF DOCUMENTARY EVIDENCE.

52.2.2   See r. 4.5.

Proof in undefended actions

52.3   **52.3.—[1](1)** In an action of proving the tenor in which no defences have been lodged, evidence shall be given by affidavit unless the court otherwise directs.

(2) In an action to which paragraph (1) applies, if counsel or other person having a right of audience, on consideration of the available affidavits and supporting documents, is satisfied that a motion for decree may properly be made, he or she may move the court by minute in Form 52.3 to grant decree in terms of the summons.

---

[1] R. 52.3 substituted by S.S.I. 2009 No. 63, r. 6 (effective 23rd March 2009).

(3)   The court may, on consideration of the minute, affidavits and any other supporting documents, without requiring appearance—

    (a)   grant decree in terms of the minute; or

    (b)   put the action out by order for further procedure, if any, including proof by parole evidence, as the court thinks fit.

Deriv. R.C.S. 1965, r. 188

PROOF.

Proof formerly was by parole evidence. Now it is by affidavit evidence.   **52.3.1**

Proof in an action of proving the tenor must cover (1) the tenor of the document; and (2) the casus amissionis: *Bonthrone v. Ireland* (1883) 10 R. 779, 786 per Lord Craighill.

1.   The terms of the document may be proved by the adminicles alone if they are in a formal writing (or if part of the records of a business or undertaking are docquetted by an officer of that business or undertaking: Civil Evidence (Scotland) Act 1988, s.5): *Graham v. McFarlane* (1847) 10 D. 45, 49 per Lord Jeffrey. Usually a combination of the adminicles and oral evidence is sufficient. Where oral evidence alone is relied on it must be specific about the terms of the document and not merely about the general effect of the document: *Rannie v. Ogg* (1891) 18 R. 903, 910 per Lord Kinnear.

2.   The casus amissionis may be proved by any competent and admissible evidence. It is usually necessary to prove that the casus amissionis did not affect the validity of the document: *Bonthrone, above.* Exceptionally, however, the court may hold the tenor of the document proved under reservation of the question of its validity: *Falconer v. Stephen* (1849) 11 D. 1338.

"MOTION".

For motions, see Chap. 23.   **52.3.2**

CHAPTER 53 ACTIONS OF REDUCTION

Chapter 53

Actions of Reduction

Conclusions for suspension etc.

53.1. In an action where real or personal diligence may proceed on a document sought to be reduced in the action, the pursuer may include in the summons, in relation to that diligence, such conclusions for suspension, interdict, and liberation as circumstances may require.

"REAL OR PERSONAL DILIGENCE".

Diligence is the procedure by which a creditor attaches the property of his debtor, with the object of forcing his debtor either to appear in court to answer an action at the instance of the creditor (e.g. an arrestment to found jurisdiction), to find security for implement of the judgment which may be pronounced against him in such an action (e.g. arrestment on the dependence, inhibition) or to implement a judgment already obtained against the debtor: Graham Stewart on *Diligence*, p. 1. Real diligences are the means of enforcing rights which a creditor already possesses, and include real poinding (also known as poinding of the ground), sequestration for rent, mails and duties and real adjudication. Personal diligences are the methods for obtaining rights which the creditor does not yet possess and include arrestment, inhibition, poinding and adjudication.

"SUSPENSION, INTERDICT, AND LIBERATION".

On these remedies, see Chap. 60.

PREVENTIVE DILIGENCE

In an action of reduction, the preventive diligence in security is the registration of a notice of litigiosity in the Register of Inhibitions and Adjudications: Titles to Land Consolidation (Scotland) Act 1868, s. 159. Inhibition on the dependence cannot be used in an action of reduction or declarator: *Stafford v. McLaurin* (1875) 3 R. 148. Where an action of reduction is raised to enforce an inhibition the pursuer is obliged as soon as reasonably practicable after signeting to register a notice of litigiosity: 1868 Act, s.159A.

Intimation to clerk of inferior court or tribunal

53.2.—[1](1) In an action in which reduction of a decree, order, decision or warrant of whatever nature of an inferior court or tribunal is concluded for, intimation of the action shall be made to the clerk of that court or tribunal.

(2) In an action to which paragraph (1) applies, the pursuer shall insert a warrant for intimation in the summons in the following terms:— "Warrant to the (*designation of the clerk of the relevant court or tribunal*) being the court [*or* tribunal] in which the decree [*or as the case may be*] was granted [*or* made] which is sought to be reduced in this action.".

(3) A notice of intimation in Form 53.2 shall be attached to the copy of the summons where intimation is given on a warrant under paragraph (2).

(4) An interlocutor granting reduction in an action to which paragraph (1) applies shall include a direction to the clerk of court to send a copy of the interlocutor to the clerk of the inferior court or tribunal to whom intimation of the action was made.

(5) Where such an interlocutor is reclaimed against or appealed to the Supreme Court, the reclaimer or appellant, as the case may be, shall give written intimation of that fact to the clerk of the inferior court or tribunal forthwith after the reclaiming motion has been marked or the notice of appeal to the Supreme Court has been filed, as the case may be.

---

[1] R. 53.2 amended by S.S.I. 2010 No. 205 (effective 15th June 2010).

(6)   The interlocutor disposing of such a reclaiming motion or giving effect to the judgment of the Supreme Court, shall include a direction to the clerk of court to send a copy of that interlocutor to the clerk of the inferior court or tribunal to whom intimation of the action was made.

General note.

53.2.1

The Court of Session has exclusive, inherent power to reduce its own decrees as well as the decrees of inferior courts: *Doherty v. Norwich Union Fire Insurance Society Ltd* 1975 S.L.T. 41, 43 per Lord Robertson. In these circumstances reduction is a mode of review, and decree, if granted, is given in exercise of the court's supervisory jurisdiction.

The relationship between applications to the court for reduction and judicial review should be noted. Judicial review has not superseded actions of reduction. The reference to the "supervisory jurisdiction of the court" in r. 58.1(1) (applications for judicial review) must be construed as excluding procedures for which specific provision is made elsewhere in the RCS 1994 and is confined to the type of jurisdiction described in *West v. Secretary of State for Scotland* 1992 S.C. 385: *Bell v. Fiddes* , 1996 S.L.T. 51, 52H, per Lord Marnoch (disapproving the statement made in this note before release 38 that reduction as a mode of review in exercise of the supervisory jurisdiction was superseded by Chap. 58). In that case it was held that judicial review for reduction of a decree in absence in the sheriff court and interim interdict against enforcement was incompetent and reduction should be sought in an action of reduction.

On reduction of sheriff court decrees, note *Johnstone & Clark (Engineers) v. Lockhart* 1995 S.L.T. 440.

The courts commonly observe that reduction is an equitable remedy and, where other means for review of a decree are available and either utilised or the person seeking reduction has failed to utilise such means, then reduction may not be granted. In *Bain v. Hugh L. S. McConnell Ltd* 1991 S.L.T. 691 (Second Div.), 695J, LJ-C Ross said that it is well established that a decree may be reduced in exceptional circumstances if reduction is necessary to produce substantial justice. It was, he said, incorrect to read the dictum of Viscount Dunedin in *Adair v. Colville & Sons* 1926 S.C. (H.L.) 51, 56, as meaning that reduction will never be competent whether other means of review are prescribed. While it has been said that it is not possible to define the cases in which reduction is competent, Lord Stuart, in *Sharif v Moughal* [2023] CSOH 42, para. [13] set out a number of other relevant propositions which the authorities disclosed: (a) where it is necessary to achieve substantial justice or avoid a miscarriage of justice; (b) cases turns on their own individual facts and circumstances and little is to be gained from extensive citation of other cases save as to highlight points of principle or broader propositions; (c) Reduction of a decree *in foro* is only available in exceptional circumstances; (d) reduction is a question of judicial discretion; (e) the existence of, or failure to use, an alternative remedy is not necessarily a bar to reduction; (f) the court should be reluctant to foreclose a substantive defence where this has not been heard; (g) it might be a good ground for reduction where a party intentionally kept back from the court a fact that materially undermined their entitlement to the orders sought.

In relation to an attempt to reduce an award of sequestration, see *Arthur v. S.M.T. Sales and Service Co. Ltd*, 1999 S.C. 109 (First Div.). In that case, the court held that a delay of 12 years on the part of the pursuer in seeking reduction of his sequestration was fatal.

On the test applicable and the averments required for reduction of a decree in absence, see *Robertson's Exr v. Robertson* 1995 S.C. 23 and the subsequent application of that case in *Nunn v. Nunn*, 1997 S.L.T. 182. While the party seeking to reduce a decree in absence is not required to aver "exceptional circumstances" justifying the order sought, as is required in an action for reduction of a decree in foro, the party seeking reduction must aver that in the whole circumstances of the case the decree in absence was not justified in fact and in law: "It is plain that the whole circumstances include the failure of the party seeking reduction to avail himself of other remedies, the delays and the consequences and any other special circumstances bearing upon the justice of the case" (*Robertson's Exr*, above, at p. 30B); see also *Royal Bank of Scotland Plc v. Matheson*, 2013 S.C. 146 (Extra Div). In *Jandoo v Jandoo* 2018 S.L.T. 531 (OH), para. [14], Lord Woolman sought to draw three propositions from *Robertson* and *Nunn* (a) a court decree is not to be lightly set aside, (b) there is no precise test, (c) the pursuer must show that (i) the decree ought not to have been granted on the merits, (ii) there is a reasonable explanation why he did not enter the proceedings, (iii) the whole circumstances of the individual case justify reduction. In *Fawaz v Fawaz* [2024] CSOH 7, para. [22], Lord Richardson added that it was clear from *Robertson* that the "whole circumstances" include any failure by the pursuer to avail himself of other remedies and his delays in doing so (at 30B-D); and from *Nunn*, the importance of a pursuer, providing a full and candid account of the whole circumstances which are relied upon to justify reduction (184D-E). One important factor to which the court will have regard is a candid explanation of how the decree in absence came to be granted without any opposition: *Nunn*, above, at 184D-184E.

For important observations on the sufficiency of averments of interest to sue, see *Lennox v. Scottish Branch of the British Show Jumping Association*, 1997 S.L.T. 353 and *Cameron v. Lightheart*, 1995 S.C. 341.

It should be noted that the availability of reduction is not restricted to writings but is available to reduce illegal acts: *Lennox*, above.

An action of reduction is within the court's privative jurisdiction and may be brought as a principal action, with or without other conclusions, or stated by way of exception (see r. 53.8) without the necessity of raising a separate action.

The Court of Session has jurisdiction to reduce any decree granted by a Scottish court whether or not jurisdiction exists independently in the action of reduction: Law Reform (Miscellaneous Provisions) (Scotland) Act 1980, s.20.

53.2.2

"INTIMATION".

For methods, see r. 16.8. For evidence of intimation, see note 16.8.1.

53.2.3

"SEND".

This includes deliver: r. 1.3(1) (definition of "send").

53.2.4

"WRITTEN INTIMATION".

For methods, see r. 16.9.

53.2.5

Objection by defenders to production

53.3.—(1) Where a defender objects to satisfying a conclusion for production of a document sought to be reduced in an action, he shall state in his defences—

53.3

    (a) his grounds of objection; and

    (b) any defence on the merits of the action.

(2) Where a defender objects to satisfying such a conclusion, he shall not be required to satisfy production at the time of lodging his defences.

(3) Where the court repels or reserves an objection to satisfying a conclusion for production, it shall, in the interlocutor repelling or reserving such objection, ordain the defender to satisfy production within such period as it thinks fit.

(4) Where—

    (a) the defender obtempers an order made under paragraph (3), he shall, on lodging in process any such document as is in his possession or within his control, apply by motion to hold production either satisfied or satisfied in respect of the document lodged, as the case may be; or

    (b) the defender fails to obtemper an order made under paragraph (3), the pursuer may apply by motion for decree by default.

Deriv. RCS 1965, r. 171 (r. 53.3(1)) and r. 173(part) (r. 53.3(4))

"PRODUCTION"

The pursuer should conclude for production of the deeds or other writings to be reduced, unless they are in his own possession. A defender may only be called upon to produce documents which are in his possession or within his control, e.g. documents held on his behalf by an agent: *Elder v. Smith* (1829) 7 S. 656. The court will usually order production under reservation of the defenders' pleas to the relevancy and competency of the pursuer's action, including a plea of all parties not called (*Officers of State v. Magistrates of Brechin* (1827) 5 S. 672): see, e.g. *Cochran v. Dunlop* (1872) 9 SLR. 597; *Fraser v. Macleay* (1882) 9 R. 1036; cf. *Earl of Perth v. Lady Willoughby de Eresby's Trs.* (1869) 7 M. 642. Prescriptive possession is no defence to a conclusion for production in an action for reduction of a heritable title: *Earl of Perth*, above. A defender should not lodge documents or writings which truly belong to third parties: see, e.g. *Mackintosh v. Arkley* (1868) 6 M.(HL) 141, 143 per L.J.-C. Inglis.

53.3.1

The proper evidence to be produced in reduction of a decree, those decrees being in publica custodia, is an extract: *Miller & Son v. Oliver & Boyd* (1901) 9 S.L.T. 287, 287 per Lord Pearson. In *Miller* the arbiter refused to allow the decree arbitral to be lodged until his fees had been paid. The pursuers declined to pay those fees and the court held that the onus of production of a decree arbitral under reduction was on the defenders. It is not competent to bring a decree under review by reduction until it has been extracted (*Scouler v. M'Laughlan* (1864) 2 M. 955, 959 per Lord Mackenzie), although reduction of an unextracted decree may be permitted in special circumstances (*Scouler*, above, per L.P. McNeill at p. 962). Where an extract of the decree sought to be reduced is available or can be obtained, it is lodged by the pursuer when the summons is signeted.

If the deed under reduction has been registered in the Books of Council and Session, it is sufficient to satisfy production for the defender to lodge a note of the date of its being so registered: Mackay's *Practice of the Court of Session*, p. 160.

If the defender fails to satisfy production the pursuer may move for decree contra non product a (*Miller & Son*, above; *Elder v. Smith* (1829) 7 S. 656), the effect of which is that the deed challenged is held to be void. The interlocutor pronounced in such a case would include the words "hold production satisfied and that for non-production".

"DEFENCES".

53.3.2   For defences, see Chap. 18.

"DOCUMENT".

53.3.3   This is wide enough to encompass reduction of decrees, whether in foro or otherwise, in exercise of the court's supervisory jurisdiction, or of any other deed or writing in exercise of the court's ordinary jurisdiction. It is not competent, however, to reduce a decree of adoption: *J. and J. v. C's Tutor* 1948 S.C. 642, 643 per L.P. Cooper. See also the definition of "document" in r. 1.3(1).

"OBJECTION".

53.3.4   The court appears reluctant to uphold a defender's objection to production, the duty to do so generally being on the defender, even where it is within the power of either party to obtain the document to be reduced. See, e.g. *Miller & Son v. Oliver & Boyd* (1901) 9 S.L.T. 287.
    In *Fraser v. Macleay* (1882) 9 R. 1036 the court repelled the defender's objection to producing a second document, where the objection was that the pursuers would only have title to reduce the second document if they successfully reduced the first of which production was sought.

"LODGE IN PROCESS".

53.3.5   For lodging productions, see r. 4.5.

"MOTION".

53.3.6   For motions, see Chap. 23.

"DECREE BY DEFAULT".

53.3.7   For decrees by default, see Chap. 20.

PREVENTIVE DILIGENCE.

53.3.8   In an action of reduction, the preventive diligence in security is the registration of a notice of litigiosity in the Register of Inhibitions and Adjudications: Titles to Land Consolidation (Scotland) Act 1868, s. 159. Inhibition on the dependence cannot be used in an action of reduction or declarator: *Stafford v. McLaurin* (1875) 3 R. 148.

Production by defenders where no objection

53.4   **53.4.**—(1) Where a defender does not state an objection against satisfying a conclusion for production of a document sought to be reduced, he shall—

    (a)   on lodging his defences, lodge in process any such document as is in his possession or within his control; and

    (b)   apply by motion to hold production either satisfied or satisfied in respect of the document lodged.

  (2) Where a defender—

    (a)   does not state an objection against satisfying a conclusion for production, and

    (b)   fails to comply with paragraph (1)(a),

the pursuer may apply by motion for decree by default.

    Deriv. RCS 1965, r. 172 (r. 53.4(1)) and r. 173 (part) (r. 53.4(2))

"OBJECTION".

53.4.1   See note 53.3.4.

"CONCLUSION FOR PRODUCTION".

53.4.2   See note 53.3.1.

"DEFENCES".

53.4.3   For defences, see Chap. 18.

"MOTION".

53.4.4   For motions, see Chap. 23.

"DECREE BY DEFAULT".

53.4.5   For decrees by default, see Chap. 20.

Pursuers to satisfy production

53.5.—(1) Where a document, in respect of which reduction is concluded for, is in the possession or the control of the pursuer, he shall lodge it in process on lodging the summons for calling.

(2) The court may, at any stage of an action, ordain the pursuer to satisfy a conclusion for production of a document sought to be reduced.

(3) The pursuer shall, on lodging a document under paragraph (1) or (2), apply by motion to hold production satisfied.

(4) Where a pursuer fails to obtemper an order made under paragraph (2), the defender may apply by motion for dismissal of the action.

53.5

"LODGE IN PROCESS".

For lodging productions, see r. 4.5.

53.5.1

CALLING OF SUMMONS.

For calling of the summons, see r. 13.13.

53.5.2

"MOTION".

For motions, see Chap. 23.

53.5.3

"PRODUCTION".

See note 53.3.1.

53.5.4

Joint minutes for reduction

53.6. In an action in which a conclusion for production has not been satisfied and parties enter into a joint minute in terms of which decree of reduction is to be pronounced—

(a) the document to be reduced shall be lodged in process with the joint minute; and

(b) the terms of the joint minute shall be such as to enable the court, when interponing authority to it, to hold production satisfied.

53.6

"PRODUCTION".

See note 53.3.1.

53.6.1

Production satisfied by copies

53.7. The court may, with the consent of the parties, hold production satisfied by a copy of the document sought to be reduced.

Deriv. R.C.S. 1965, r. 173(part)

53.7

GENERAL NOTE.

See, e.g. *Law v. Law's Trs.* (1903) 11 S.L.T. 155 (production of copy disposition allowed where original under reduction had already been delivered by defender to his disponee); and *Site Preparations Ltd v. Buchan Development Co Ltd,*1983 S.L.T. 317.

53.7.1

"PRODUCTION".

See note 53.3.1.

53.7.2

Challenge of deeds or writings ope exceptionis

53.8. Where, in an action, a deed or other writing is founded on by a party, any objection to it may be stated by way of exception, unless the court considers that the objection would be more conveniently disposed of in a separate action of reduction.

Deriv. R.C.S. 1965, r. 174

53.8

GENERAL NOTE.

The pursuer must have fair notice of any plea of reduction ope exceptionis (by force of exception): *Oswald v. Fairs* 1911 S.C. 257. A decree may be reduced ope exceptionis: *Thomson's Trs. v. Muir* (1867) 6 M. 145. For an example of the court's refusal to allow the plea, see *Duke of Argyll v. Muir* 1910 S.C. 96.

Hitherto, it had been thought that reduction *ope exceptionis* did not result in decree of reduction but merely that the document was set aside as between the parties. In *Easter Motor Co Ltd v. Grassick* 2022

53.8.1

S.C. 100 (First Div.), 111–114, at paras. [48]–[64]) it was observed, *obiter*, that the correct way to deal with a successful challenge to validity of a document *ope exceptionis* is to grant decree of reduction. It might be wise to include a conclusion for reduction.

A defender may challenge the validity of the decision of an adjudicator (a creature created by the Housing Grants, Construction and Regeneration Act 1996) ope exceptiones in his defences and is not obliged to petition for judicial review as he is not in effect making an application to the court for the exercise of its supervisory jurisdiction by doing so: *Vaughan Engineering Ltd v. Hinkins & Frewin Ltd* , 2003 S.L.T. 428 (OH). An argument in that case, that the defender could not seek reduction in a separate *action* but would have to proceed by petition for judicial review and therefore could not plead by way of exception under r. 53.8, was rejected.

CHAPTER 54 APPLICATION UNDER THE DEFAMATION ACT 1996

Chapter 54

Applications under the Defamation Act 1996

Form of application to court where proceedings have been taken

54.1.—[1](1) An application to the court under section 3 of the Defamation Act 1996 (which relates to offers to make amends) where proceedings for defamation have been taken shall be by minute lodged in the process of those proceedings.

(2) A minute lodged under paragraph (1) shall set out—

    (a) the questions to be determined by the court; and

    (b) the contentions of the minuter,

and shall have appended to it a copy of the offer to make amends.

Deriv. R.C.S. 1965, r. 188A(a)(part) inserted by S.I. 1966 No. 868

GENERAL NOTE.

Sections 2 to 4 of the Defamation Act 1996 provide for the defence of an offer to make amends before a defence is served in any proceedings or before a summons has even been served or lodged. These provisions replace the statutory defence of unintentional defamation in s. 4 of the Defamation Act 1952 which was little used.

The offer must include an offer to make a suitable correction and apology. It must also include an offer to pay such compensation (if any) as may be agreed by the parties (s. 2(4)(c) of the 1996 Act) or determined by the court (s. 3(5) of the 1996 Act).

The 1996 Act and the rules do not lay down any time-limit for the pursuer to respond to the offer. It is not clear if the defender should be able to impose a limit. One would expect a defender to make an offer open for acceptance within a specified period and s. 4(1) of the 1996 Act clearly envisages that an offer may be withdrawn. In *Moore v. The Scottish Daily Record and Sunday Mail Ltd* , 2007 S.L.T. 217 (OH) it was held that in order to rely on the s. 4(2) defence a defender is obliged to maintain an offer of amends duly made and *which has not been withdrawn*. The offer may, therefore, be accepted at any time; and the defender (or the court) cannot impose a time limit for its acceptance. The length of time in accepting it may be met in expenses.

Where an offer to make amends is not withdrawn it may be relied on as a defence; but where it is, the defender may not rely on any other defence: 1996 Act, s. 4(2) and (4). The offer may be relied on in mitigation of damages whether or not it was relied on as a defence: 1996 Act, s. 4(5).

Form of application to court where proceedings have not been taken

54.2[2] An application to the court under the said section 3 where proceedings for defamation have not been taken shall be by petition presented in the Outer House.

Deriv. R.C.S. 1965, r. 188A(a)(part) and (b) inserted by S.I. 1966 No. 868

GENERAL NOTE.

See generally, note 54.1.1 on offer of amends.

Where an offer of amends is accepted any question about the steps to be taken in fulfilment of the offer are, in default of agreement, to be referred to the court whose decision is final. Where no action has been commenced the reference is made to the court by petition: r. 54.2.

An application may be made to the court by petition, where there is no action, by the aggrieved person to seek an order for expenses reasonably incurred or to be incurred in consequence of the publication.

"PETITION".

A petition is presented in the Outer House: r. 54.2. The petition must be in Form 14.4 in the official printed form: rr. 4.1 and 14.4. The petition must be signed by counsel or other person having a right of audience: r. 4.2; and see r. 1.3(1) (definition of "counsel" and "other person having a right of audience") and note 1.3.4.

The petitioner must lodge the petition with the required steps of process (r. 4.4). A fee is payable on lodging the petition: see note 14.5.10.

On petitions generally, see Chap. 14.

---

[1] Rule 54.1 substituted by S.S.I. 2001 No. 93 (effective 1st April 2001).
[2] Rule 54.2 substituted by S.S.I. 2001 No. 93 (effective 1st April 2001).

Chapter 54

Applications under the Defamation Act 1996

Form of application to court where proceedings have been taken

54.1—(1) An application to the court under section 3 of the Defamation Act 1996 (which relates to offers to make amends) where proceedings for defamation have been taken shall be by originating lodged in the process of those proceedings.

(2) A minute lodged under paragraph (1) shall set out—

(a) the questions to be determined by the court; and

(b) the consequences of the minute;

and shall have appended to it a copy of the offer to make amends.

Deriv. R.C.S. 1965, r. 188.4 (added/inserted by S.I. 1996 No. 468.

54.1.1 Sections 2 to 4 of the Defamation Act 1996 provide for the defence of an offer to make amends before a defence is served in any proceedings or where a summons has even been served at Lodged. These provisions relate to the making defence of unqualified defamation in ... 4 of the Defamation Act 1996 where was introduced.

The offer must include an offer to make a suitable correction and apology; it must also include to pay compensation, or any ... as may be agreed by the parties ... 2.1(4)(c) of the 1996 Act) or determined by the court (s. 3(5) of the Act).

The 1996 Act sets the rules on not only how any time limit for the pursuer to respond to the offer but also if the pursuer should be given time to make it. The would-be pursuer a defender is made an offer open for acceptance within a specified period (rule s. 3(2) of the 1996 Act clearly envisages that a defender may be told that in order to rely on the s. 3(2) defence a defender is obliged to maintain an offer of amends duly made and was never withdrawn. The offer may thereafter be accepted at any time; and the defender or the court cannot impose a time limit for its acceptance. The length of time in accepting it may be a consideration in the expenses.

Where an offer to make amends is not withdrawn it may be relied on as a defence but thereafter the defender may not rely on any other solution to the Act, s. 4(2) ... s. 4 but offer may be relied on in mitigation of damages whether or not it was relied on as a defence (see 1996 Act, s. 4(5)).

Form of application to court where proceedings have not been taken

54.2 An application to the court under the said section 3 where proceedings for defamation have not been taken shall be by petition presented in the Outer House.

Deriv. R.C.S. 1965, r. 188.4 (part) (as part/rule) (as inserted by S.I. 1996 No. 468.

54.2.1 See generally note 54.1.1 on offer of amends.

Where an offer of amends is accepted any question about the steps to be taken in fulfilment of the offer is, in default of agreement, to be referred to the court, whose decision is final. When no action has been commenced the forum is to be made is the court by petition: r.54.2.

An application may be made to the court by petition where there is no action by the aggrieved person (i) seeking an order for expenses reasonably incurred or to be incurred in consequence of the publication in question.

54.2.2 A petition as presented in the Outer House (r. 54.2). The petition must be authentic and be put into the official prescribed form in 14.4 and rule. The petition must be signed by the pursuer or other person having a title or authority (rule 4.2) and see r. 13(1) (a minute) of "counsel" and "other person having a right of audience") and note 4.2.4.

The petition must lodge the petition which the required steps of procedure (r. 4.4). A fee is payable on the petition: see note 14.2.10.

On petitions generally see Chap. 14.

Rule 54.1 substituted by S.S.I. 2001 No. 93 (effective 1st April 2001).
Note 54.2 amended by S.S.I. 2001 No. ... (effective as 1st April 2001).

CHAPTER 55 CAUSES RELATING TO INTELLECTUAL PROPERTY

Chapter 55

Causes Relating to Intellectual Property

Application and interpretation of this Chapter

55.1.—[1,2](1)   This Chapter applies to any cause—

    (a)   under the Patents Act 1949;

    (b)   under the Registered Designs Act 1949;

    (c)   under the Defence Contracts Act 1958;

    (d)   under the Patents Act 1977;

    (e)   under the Copyright, Designs and Patents Act 1988;

    (f)   under the Trade Marks Act 1994;

    (g)   under the Olympics Association Right (Infringement Proceedings) Regulations 1995;

    (h)   for the determination of a question relating to a patent under the inherent jurisdiction of the court; or

    (i)   involving a claim for passing off.

(2)   In this Chapter—

"the Act of 1949" means the Patents Act 1949;

"the Act of 1977" means the Patents Act 1977;

"the Comptroller" means the Comptroller-General of Patents, Designs and Trade Marks;

"the Copyright Act of 1988" means the Copyright, Designs and Patents Act 1988;

"existing patent" means a patent mentioned in section 127(2)(a) or (c) of the Act of 1977;

"intellectual property cause" means a cause to which this Chapter applies and, except where the context otherwise requires, "cause" means an intellectual property cause;

"intellectual property judge" means a judge nominated as such in accordance with rule 55.2 and, except where the context otherwise requires, "judge" means an intellectual property judge or such other judge before whom proceedings are brought in accordance with rule 55.2;

"the Journal" means the journal published in accordance with rules made under section 123(6) of the Act of 1977;

"patent" means an existing patent or a patent under the Act of 1977;

"patentee" has the meaning assigned to it in section 101(1) of the Act of 1949.

"preliminary hearing" means a hearing under rule 55.2E;

"procedural hearing" means a hearing under rule 55.3.

Deriv. RCS 1965, r. 250 substituted by S.I. 1991 No. 1621

GENERAL NOTE.

The Registered Designs Act 1949 as amended is set out in Sched. 4 to the Act of 1988.

The Patents Act 1949 continues to apply to patents before the Act of 1977. The Act of 1977 was passed following the *Banks Report on the British Patent System* (Cmnd. 4407 (1970)). It was intended to permit ratification of the Patents Co-operation Treaty 1970 (Cmnd. 7340), the European Patent Convention 1973 (Cmnd. 8510 (1982)) and the Community Patent Convention 1975 (Cmnd. 6553).

55.1

55.1.1

---

[1] Rule 55.1(1) amended by S.I. 1996 No. 1756 (effective 5th August 1996).

[2] Rule 55.1 amended by S.S.I. 2012 No. 275 r. 3(12) (effective 19th November 2012).

55.1.2

Under the Art. 24(4) of the Council Regulation (EU) 1215/2012 (Brussels I Regulation) (Recast)) and Art. 22(4) of the 2007 Lugano Convention, in proceedings concerning the registration or validity of patents, trade marks, designs, or other similar rights required to be deposited or registered, the courts of the Contracting State, in which the deposit or registration has been applied for, has taken place or is under the terms of an international convention deemed to have taken place, have exclusive jurisdiction: The Regulation and the Convention do not apply in Scots Law from 11pm on 31st December 2020 except in proceedings commenced before that date: Civil Jurisdiction and Judgments (Amendment) (EU Exit) Regulations 2019 [S.I. 2019 No. 479] except in relation to proceedings not concluded before 11pm on 31st December 2020.

There is no similar rule in Sched. 4 (inter-U.K. jurisdiction) or Sched. 8 (jurisdiction of Scottish courts) of the C.J.J.A. 1982. The ordinary non-exclusive rules of jurisdiction will apply: see notes 13.2.8–13.2.15.

Proceedings before intellectual property judge

55.2

55.2.[1] All proceedings in the Outer House in a cause to which this Chapter applies shall be brought before a judge of the court nominated by the Lord President as the intellectual property judge or, where the intellectual property judge is not available, any other judge of the court (including the vacation judge).

Deriv. RCS 1965, r. 251 substituted by S.I. 1991 No. 1621

"INTELLECTUAL PROPERTY JUDGE".

55.2.1

In order to ensure that intellectual property causes will be heard by a judge with knowledge of and expertise in what is a specialised area of the law, intellectual property causes are, where possible, brought before the judge nominated by the Lord President as the patents judge.

The intellectual property judge is currently Lord Glennie.

"VACATION JUDGE".

55.2.2

The powers of the vacation judge are limited by r. 11.1.

Requirement for marking

55.2A

55.2A.[2] In a cause to which this Chapter applies, initiated—

    (a) by summons, the pursuer shall, before presenting the summons to the General Department for signeting;

    (b) by petition, the petitioner shall, before lodging the petition in the Petition Department,

mark it distinctly in red, both on the first page and on the backing, with the words "Intellectual Property Cause"; and thereafter every step of process in the cause shall be so marked by the person lodging it.

Disapplication of certain rules

55.2B

55.2B.—[3](1) The requirement in rule 4.1(4) for a step of process to be folded lengthwise does not apply in a cause to which this Chapter applies.

(2) An open record shall not be made up in, and Chapter 22 (making up and closing records) shall not apply to, an intellectual property cause initiated by summons unless otherwise ordered by a judge.

(3) The following rules shall not apply to an intellectual property cause—

rule 6.2 (fixing and allocation of diets in Outer House),

rule 14.8 (procedure where answers lodged),

rule 25.1(3) (form of counterclaim),

rule 25.2(1) (authority for diligence etc. on counterclaims),

rule 36.3 (lodging productions).

---

[1] Rule 55.2 amended by S.I. 1999 No. 1785 (effective 12th July 1999).
[2] Rule 55.2A inserted by S.I. 1999 No. 1785 (effective 12th July 1999).
[3] Rule 55.2B to r. 55.3A substituted for r. 55.3 by S.S.I. 2012 No. 275 r. 3(3) (effective 19th November 2012).

Procedure in intellectual property causes

55.2C.—[1](1) Subject to the other provisions of this Chapter, the procedure in an intellectual property cause shall be such as the judge shall order or direct.

(2) All proceedings in an intellectual property cause shall, in the Outer House, be heard and determined on such dates and at such times as shall be fixed by the judge.

(3) The fixing of a hearing for a specified date in an intellectual property cause shall not affect the right of any party to apply by motion at any time under these Rules.

55.2C

Pleadings in intellectual property causes

55.2D.—[2](1) In an intellectual property cause, the following paragraphs apply without prejudice to any specific requirements laid down elsewhere in this Chapter.

(2) A summons in such a cause shall—
- (a) specify, in the form of conclusions, the orders sought;
- (b) identify the parties to the action and the transaction or dispute from which the action arises;
- (c) specify any special capacity in which the pursuer is bringing the action or any special capacity in which the action is brought against the defender;
- (d) summarise the circumstances out of which the action arises; and
- (e) set out the grounds on which the action proceeds.

(3) A petition in such a cause shall specify, in the prayer of the petition, the orders sought and shall provide the same information as is specified in paragraph (2)(b) to (e) of this rule in relation to a summons.

(4) Defences (to a summons) and answers (to a petition) shall be in the form of answers to the summons or petition (as the case may be) with any additional statement of facts or legal grounds on which the defender or respondent intends to rely.

(5)[3] A party seeking to lodge a counterclaim or serve a third party motion shall apply by motion to do so.

(6) The judge shall, on a motion to lodge a counterclaim or to serve a third party notice, make such order and give such directions as he thinks fit with regard to—
- (a) the time within which a counterclaim may be lodged or a third party notice served and any answers lodged;
- (b) where the motion is made before the preliminary hearing, a date for the preliminary hearing if it is to be a date other than the date referred to in rule 55.2E(1);
- (c) any application for a warrant to use any form of diligence which would have been permitted under rule 14A.2 (application for interim diligence) had the warrant been sought in a summons in a separate action.

(7) Paragraph (2) of this rule shall apply to the form of a counterclaim as it applies to a summons.

(8) There shall be appended to any pleadings referred to in this rule a schedule listing the documents founded on or adopted as incorporated therein, which should also be lodged as an inventory of productions.

55.2D

---

[1] Rule 55.2B to r. 55.3A substituted for r. 55.3 by S.S.I. 2012 No. 275 r. 3(3) (effective 19th November 2012).

[2] Rule 55.2B to r. 55.3A substituted for r. 55.3 by S.S.I. 2012 No. 275 r. 3(3) (effective 19th November 2012).

[3] Rule 55.2D(5) as amended by S.S.I. 2013 No. 120 (effective May 1, 2013).

Preliminary hearings

55.2E   **55.2E.**—[1](1) An intellectual property cause shall call for a preliminary hearing within 14 days after defences or answers (as the case may be) have been lodged.

(2)   At the preliminary hearing, the judge—

    (a)   shall determine whether, to what extent and in what manner further specification of the claim and defences or answers should be provided;

    (b)   may—

       (i)   order a party to make detailed written pleadings, either generally or in relation to particular issues;

       (ii)   order one or more parties to make a statement of facts, either generally or in relation to particular issues;

       (iii)   allow a party to make an amendment to his pleadings;

       (iv)   order disclosure of the identity of witnesses and the existence and nature of documents relating to the cause or authority to recover documents, either generally or in relation to specific matters;

       (v)   order any party to lodge in process within a specified period documents constituting, evidencing or relating to the subject-matter of the cause or any invoices, correspondence or similar documents relating to it;

       (vi)   order each party to lodge in process, and send to every other party, a list of witnesses;

       (vii)   order any party to lodge in process reports of skilled persons or witness statements;

       (viii)   order any party to lodge in process affidavits relating to any of the issues in the cause;

       (ix)   except as provided for elsewhere in these Rules, order the cause to proceed to a hearing without any further preliminary procedure either in relation to the whole or any particular aspect of the cause;

    (c)   may fix the period within which any order under subparagraph (b) shall be complied with;

    (d)   may continue the preliminary hearing to a date to be appointed by him; and

    (e)   may make such other order as he thinks fit for the speedy determination of the cause.

(3)   In an intellectual property cause the judge may ordain the pursuer to—

    (a)   make up a record; and

    (b)   lodge that record in process within such period as he thinks fit.

(4)   At the conclusion of the preliminary hearing, the judge shall, unless he has made an order under paragraph (2)(b)(ix) (order to proceed without a further hearing), fix a date for a procedural hearing to determine further procedure.

(5)   The date fixed under paragraph (4) for a procedural hearing may be extended on cause shown by application to the court, by motion, not less than two days prior to the date fixed for the procedural hearing.

"WITHIN 14 DAYS AFTER".

55.2E.1   The date from which the period is calculated is not counted.

---

[1] Rule 55.2B to r. 55.3A substituted for r. 55.3 by S.S.I. 2012 No. 275 r. 3(3) (effective 19th November 2012).

Procedural hearings

55.3.—[1](1) In an intellectual property cause, not less than 3 days, or such other period as may be prescribed by the judge at the preliminary hearing, before the date fixed under rule 55.2E(4) for the procedural hearing, each party shall lodge in process and send to every other party—

55.3

(a)   a written statement of his proposals for further procedure which shall state—

    (i)   whether he seeks to have any issue of law or fact (including validity, infringement, an application for amendment of a patent under section 75 of the Act of 1977, damages or other remedies sought) to be determined separately from any other issue;

    (ii)   whether he seeks to have the cause appointed to debate or to have the cause sent to proof on the whole or any part of it;

    (iii)   what the issues are which he considers should be sent to debate or proof; and

    (iv)   the estimated duration of any debate or proof;

(b)   where it is sought to have the cause appointed to proof, a list of the witness which the party proposes to cite or call to give evidence, identifying the matters to which each witness will speak;

(c)   where it is sought to have the cause appointed to proof, the reports of any skilled persons he proposes to call to give evidence;

(d)   where it is sought to have the cause appointed to debate, a note of argument consisting of concise numbered paragraphs stating the legal propositions on which it is proposed to submit that any preliminary plea should be sustained or repelled, with reference to the principal authorities and statutory provisions to be founded on; and

(e)   where it is sought to have any particular order made at a procedural hearing, a note giving written intimation of the order sought and the reason for seeking it.

(2)   At the procedural hearing, the judge—

(a)   shall determine whether to direct that any issue of law or fact (including validity, infringement, an application for amendment of a patent under section 75 of the Act of 1977, damages or other remedies sought) should be determined separately from any other issue;

(b)   shall determine whether the cause should be appointed to debate or to proof on the whole or any part of it;

(c)   shall determine whether to remit to the Patent Office for a Report and what the terms of the remit should be;

(d)   where the cause is appointed to debate, or is sent to proof, may order that written arguments on any question of law should be submitted;

(e)   where the cause is sent to proof, may determine whether evidence at the proof should be by oral evidence, the production of documents or affidavits on any issue;

(f)   where the cause is sent to proof, may direct that parties serve on one another and lodge in process signed witness statements or affidavits from each witness whose evidence they intend to adduce, setting out in full the evidence which it is intended to take from that witness, and fix a timetable

---

[1] Rule 55.2B to r. 55.3A substituted for r. 55.3 by S.S.I. 2012 No. 275 r. 3(3) (effective 19th November 2012).

for the service (whether by exchange or otherwise) and lodging of such statements or affidavits as may be thought necessary;

(g) may direct that such witness statements or affidavits shall stand as evidence in chief of the witness concerned, subject to such further questioning in chief as the judge may allow;

(h) where the cause is sent to proof, may appoint parties to be heard By Order at a date prior to the proof date;

(i) may make an order regulating the making of any experiment, inspection, test or report;

(j) may make an order restricting the number or disciplines of expert witnesses to be called by each party;

(k) may direct that skilled persons should meet with a view to reaching agreement and identifying areas of disagreement, and may order them thereafter to produce a joint note, to be lodged in process by one of the parties, identifying areas of agreement and disagreement, and the basis of any disagreement;

(l) may determine, in the light of any witness statements, affidavits or reports produced, that proof is unnecessary on any issue;

(m) without prejudice to Chapter 12 (assessors), may appoint an expert to examine, on behalf of the court, any reports of skilled persons or other evidence submitted and to report to the court within such period as the judge may specify;

(n) may remit an issue to a person of skill appointed by the court;

(o) may fix a date by which, notwithstanding rule 36.3 (lodging productions for proofs) any documents intended to be relied on by a party shall be lodged in process or, if more appropriate, be intimated to all other parties with a view to those documents being lodged in process as part of an agreed bundle of documents;

(p) may make an order for parties to produce a joint bundle of productions arranged in chronological order or such other order as will assist in the efficient conduct of the proof;

(q) may fix a date by which a notice under rule 55.4 (notice to admit and notices of non-admission) shall be served;

(r) where the cause is sent to proof, may make an order fixing the time allowed for the examination and cross-examination of witnesses;

(s) may, on the motion of a party, direct the cause to be determined on the basis of written submissions, or such other material, without any oral hearing;

(t) may continue the procedural hearing to a date to be appointed by the judge;

(u) may order and fix a date for a further procedural hearing or fix a date for the hearing of any debate or proof; and

(v) may make such other order as the judge thinks fit.

(3) Chapter 28 (procedure roll) shall apply to a debate ordered in an intellectual property cause under this rule as it applies to a cause appointed to the Procedure Roll.

Deriv. RCS 1965, r. 252 substituted by S.I. 1991 No. 1621

General note.

55.3.1   R. 55.3 was originally introduced by A.S. (R.C.S.A. No. 7) (Patent Rules) 1991 [S.I. 1991 No. 1621] following a recommendation of the Working Party on the White Paper on Intellectual Property and Innovation (Patent Litigation) chaired by Lord Jauncey. The concept of a pre-proof hearing was recommended in the *Banks Report on the British Patent System* 1970 (Cmnd. 4407). The Working Party considered the pre-proof hearing to be of very considerable importance. The idea is that the judge takes a firm grip of the case at a very early stage, to focus the main issues, reduce the amount of evidence required and indicate the areas in which he requires assistance on technical matters. The Working Party envisaged that the pre-proof hearing might involve more than one stage. It was thought that the success of the procedure would depend on the same judge hearing the proof as the pre-proof hearing.

The *Cullen Report on the Business of the Outer House* (1995) accepted a suggestion that r. 55.3 should be extended to all causes to which this Chapter applies. This reform was introduced by the A.S. (R.C.S.A. No. 3) (Miscellaneous) 1996 [S.I. 1996 No. 1756]. Formerly, r. 55.3 applied only to causes under the Patent Act of 1949 or 1977.

The title "pre-proof hearing" was changed to the "procedural hearing" by A.S.(R.C.S.A. No.6) 1999 (S.I. 1999/1785). The main purpose of the A.S. was to provide greater flexibility in fixing a date for the procedural hearing.

"NOT LESS THAN 3 DAYS".

This is synonymous with clear days, and the day from which the period is calculated is not included.   **55.3.2**

"NOTE OF ARGUMENT".

A concise note of argument and a note of argument in reply may be ordered where a cause is sent to the Procedure Roll for debate. Each should consist of numbered paragraphs setting out briefly the legal propositions to be advanced at debate by the party lodging it, supported by citations of the principal authorities for those propositions and any statutory provisions relied on.   **55.3.3**

A note of argument is lodged in process as a step of process (r. 1.3(1) (definition of "step of process")) and does not require to be signed. R. 15.2 does not apply. On lodging a step of process, see r. 4.4. The note may be lodged by post: P.N. No. 4 of 1994, paras 1 and 8; and see note 4.4.10.

PATENT OFFICE REPORT.

This would be a technical report dealing with, e.g. obviousness. Views on its usefulness vary.   **55.3.4**

JOINT NOTE OF EXPERTS.

It can be advantageous in reducing the length of a proof to obtain, if possible, a joint or agreed report by expert witnesses on the general scientific principles applicable to the case.   **55.3.5**

EXCHANGE OF EXPERT REPORTS ETC.

The view held by some that exchange of reports lengthens cross-examination is not encountered in practice in England.   **55.3.6**

PAGINATED INVENTORY OF PRODUCTIONS.

To reduce the duplication of documentary material by both sides, agents may be required to get together to agree one set of paginated productions.   **55.3.7**

"MAY MAKE SUCH OTHER ORDER".

The court may wish to consider, for example, whether a reading guide should be prepared by the parties in consultation with each other. The guide should indicate the documents the judge should read before the proof and in what order and an up-to-date list of the principal issues to be resolved. Another consideration might be (although this may be too early a stage to contemplate it) to consider the requirement of written skeletal submissions for the hearing of evidence at the end of the proof.   **55.3.8**

"WRITTEN INTIMATION".

For methods, see r. 16.9.   **55.3.9**

Pre-proof By Order

55.3A.[1] Not less than two days prior to any hearing appointed under rule 55.3(2)(h) parties shall lodge in process an estimated timetable for the conduct of the proof together with a note of any issues which are to be addressed prior to the proof.   **55.3A**

"NOT LESS THAN 2 DAYS PRIOR"

This is synonymous with clear days, and the day from which the period is calculated is not included. To be consistent with the other rules in R.C.S. 1994, the word "before" should have been used rather than "prior".   **55.3A.1**

---

[1] Rule 55.2B to r. 55.3A substituted for r. 55.3 by S.S.I. 2012 No. 275 r. 3(3) (effective 19th November 2012).

Notices to admit and notices of non-admission

55.4

55.4.—(1)[1] In an intellectual property cause, at any time after defences or answers have been lodged but not later than such date as has been fixed by the court at a procedural hearing, a party may intimate to any other party to the cause a notice or notices calling on him to admit for the purposes of that cause only—

  (a) such facts relating to an issue averred in the pleadings as may be specified in the notice;

  (b) that a particular document lodged in process and specified in the notice is—

      (i)   an original and properly authenticated document;

      (ii) a true copy of an original and properly authenticated document; or

      (iii) correct in the particular respects specified in the notice.

(2) Where a party on whom a notice has been served under paragraph (1)—

  (a) does not admit any of the facts specified in the notice, or

  (b) does not admit, or seeks to challenge, the authenticity or correctness of any document specified in the notice,

he shall, within 28 days after the date of intimation of the notice under paragraph (1), intimate a notice of non-admission to the party intimating the notice to him under paragraph (1) stating that he does not admit the fact or document specified.

(3) A party who fails to serve a notice of non-admission under paragraph (2) shall be deemed to have admitted the matters specified in the notice intimated to him under paragraph (1); and such matters may be used in evidence at a proof if otherwise admissible in evidence unless the court, on special cause shown, otherwise directs.

(4) A party who fails to intimate a notice of non-admission under paragraph (2) within 28 days after the notice to admit intimated to him under paragraph (1) shall be liable to the party intimating the notice to admit for the expenses of proving the matters specified in that notice unless the court otherwise directs.

(5) The party intimating a notice under paragraph (1) or (2) shall lodge a copy of it in process.

(6) A deemed admission under paragraph (3) shall not be used against the party by whom it was deemed to be made other than in the cause for the purpose of which it was deemed to be made or in favour of any person other than the party by whom the notice was given under paragraph (1).

(7) The court may, at any time, allow a party to amend or withdraw an admission made by him on such conditions, if any, as it thinks fit.

Deriv. RCS 1965, r. 253 substituted by S.I. 1991 No. 1621

GENERAL NOTE.

55.4.1

  The Jauncey Working Party on Patent Litigation recommended adoption of this rule, and this was done in RCS 1965, r. 253 as amended by A.S. (R.C.S.A. No. 7) (Patent Rules) 1991 [S.I. 1991 No. 1621] (now RCS 1994, r. 55.4).

  It might be thought that r. 55.4 is not necessary when the system of Scottish pleadings should result in it being clear by the time proof has been allowed what is in issue and what has to be proved. Not all relevant documentary material, however, previously in dispute will be in dispute by the time the proof approaches, and the authenticity of such material, or an averment, may be the subject of a general denial which would otherwise necessitate proof. It may, of course, be possible to obtain agreement by consent. The purpose of the rule is to provide an additional means to assist in reducing documentary material and averments having to be proved which at the end of the day do or did not require proof and the time taken in proving them. It is also considered that this might be a more effective way of obtaining admissions than calls in the pleadings. It also provides a penalty by imposing the burden of expenses on the party who has caused unnecessary proof.

---

[1] R. 55.4(1) amended by S.I. 1999 No. 1785 (effective 12th June 1999) and substituted by S.S.I. 2012 No. 275 r. 3(4) (effective 19th November 2012).

The relationship of this rule to rr. 36.7 and 36.8 should be noticed. The possibility of a minute of admission by one or more parties is not affected by r. 55.4. A deemed admission may arise, however, under r. 55.4(3) if a notice of non-admission is not intimated in response to a notice to admit. Under s.2(1)(b) of the Civil Evidence (Scotland) Act 1988 any document (including an affidavit) may be received in evidence without being spoken to by a witness as evidence not merely that it was made but as to the truth of its contents, and r. 36.8 provides the mechanism for obtaining the permission of the court to produce such evidence without being spoken to. In respect of the authenticity of a document it may also be possible to use the procedure in r. 55.4.

"INTIMATED".

For methods, see r. 16.7.

55.4.2

"WITHIN 28 DAYS".

The date from which the period is calculated is not counted.

55.4.3

"LODGE A COPY OF IT IN PROCESS".

The copy is lodged as a step of process and not as a production: r. 1.3(1) (definition of "step of process"). On steps of process, see r. 4.4.

55.4.4

Applications for leave to amend specifications

55.5.—(1) A patentee or the proprietor of a patent intending to apply to the court under section 30 of the Act of 1949 or section 75 of the Act of 1977 (which provide for leave to amend specification) shall give notice of his intention to the Comptroller and at the same time deliver to him a form of advertisement—

55.5

    (a)   identifying the proceedings depending before the court in which it is intended to apply for such leave;

    (b)   giving particulars of the amendment sought;

    (c)   stating the address of the applicant for service within the United Kingdom; and

    (d)   stating that any person intending to oppose the amendment who is not a party to the proceedings must, within 28 days after the appearance of the advertisement, give written notice of that intention to the applicant and to the Deputy Principal Clerk.

(2) On receipt of a form of advertisement under paragraph (1), the Comptroller shall cause the advertisement to be inserted once in the Journal.

(3) A person who gives notice of intention to oppose the amendment in accordance with the advertisement shall be entitled to be heard on the application subject to any order of the court as to expenses.

(4) Within 35 days after the appearance of the advertisement, the applicant shall make his application under section 30 of the Act of 1949 or section 75 of the Act of 1977, as the case may be, by motion intimated, with a copy of the specification certified by the Comptroller and showing in coloured ink the amendment sought, to—

    (a)   the Comptroller;

    (b)   every other party; and

    (c)   any person who has intimated his intention to oppose the amendment.

(5) On enrolling a motion under paragraph (4), the applicant shall lodge in process—

    (a)   a copy of the Journal containing the advertisement referred to in paragraph (2); or

    (b)   a certificate of publication by the publisher stating the date of publication and the text of the advertisement.

(6) At the hearing of a motion under paragraph (4)—

    (a)   where there is no opposition to the amendment sought, the court may—

        (i)   grant the application; or

        (ii) make such order for further procedure as it thinks fit; or

(b) where there is opposition to the amendment sought, the court shall ordain the applicant to lodge a minute setting out the grounds of his application within such period as the court thinks fit, and allow any party or person opposing the amendment to lodge answers to the minute in process within a specified period.

(7) Within seven days after the expiry of the time for lodging answers under paragraph (6)(b), the applicant shall apply by motion for an order for further procedure.

(8) On a motion under paragraph (7), the court may—

(a) grant the application;

(b) determine whether the motion shall be heard at the same time as the hearing of the cause depending before the court relating to the patent in question or at a different time;

(c) determine the manner in which evidence shall be given and, if the evidence is to be given by affidavit, the period within which affidavits must be lodged; or

(d) make such other order for further procedure as it thinks fit.

(9) Where the court allows the specification to be amended, the applicant shall forthwith—

(a) lodge with the Comptroller a certified copy of the interlocutor; and

(b) if so required by the court or the Comptroller, leave at the Patent Office a new specification and drawings as amended, prepared in compliance with the Act of 1949 or the Act of 1977, as the case may be, and any rules made under either of those Acts.

(10) On receiving the certified copy interlocutor under paragraph (9), the Comptroller shall cause it to be inserted at least once in the Journal.

Deriv. R.C.S. 1965, r. 254 substituted by S.I. 1991 No. 1621

General note.

55.5.1   Where the validity of a patent is put in issue the court may allow the proprietor of the patent to amend the specification. The Comptroller has a similar power.

"within 35 days", "within seven days".

55.5.2   The date from which the period is calculated is not counted. Where the last day falls on a Saturday or Sunday or a public holiday on which the Office of Court is closed, the next available day is allowed: r. 1.3(7). For office hours and public holidays, see note 3.1.2.

"motion".

55.5.3   For motions, see Chap. 23.

Hearings for further procedure

55.5A   **55.5A.**[1] At any time before final judgment, the intellectual property judge may, at his own instance or on the motion of any party, have an intellectual property cause put out for hearing for further procedure; and the intellectual property judge may make such order as he thinks fit.

Failure to comply with rule or order of intellectual property judge

55.5B   **55.5B.**—[2] Any failure by a party to comply timeously with a provision in these Rules or any order made by the intellectual property judge in an intellectual property cause shall entitle the judge, at his own instance—

---

[1] Rule 55.5B inserted by SSI 2012/275 r.3(5) (effective November 19, 2012) and renumbered as r.55.5A by SSI 2013/120 (effective May 1, 2013)..

[2] Rule 55.5B inserted by SSI 2012/275 r.3(5) (effective November 19, 2012) and renumbered as r.55.5B by SSI 2013/120 (effective May 1, 2013).

(a) to refuse to extend any period for compliance with a provision in these Rules or an order of the court;

(b) to dismiss the cause or counterclaim, as the case may be, in whole or in part;

(c) to grant decree in respect of all or any of the orders sought; or

(d) to make an award of expenses, as he thinks fit.

Applications for revocation of patents

55.6.—(1) Subject to paragraph (2), an application under section 72 of the Act of 1977 (revocation of a patent) shall be made by petition.

(2)[1] Where a cause is depending before the court between the same parties in relation to the patent in question, such an application may be made by counterclaim in that cause in accordance with rule 55.2D (pleadings in intellectual property causes).

Deriv. R.C.S. 1965, r. 255 substituted by S.I. 1991 No. 1621

GENERAL NOTE.

S.72 of the Act of 1977 specifies the grounds on which a patent may be revoked by the court. The Comptroller has a similar power.

Note also r. 55.8 on challenges to the validity of a patent in proceedings for revocation.

In England, U.K. and European patents are given a "purposive" construction as set out in *Catnic Components v. Hill & Smith* [1982] R.P.C. 237 (H.L.).

"PETITION".

A petition is presented in the Outer House: r. 14.2(h). The petition must be in Form 14.4 in the official printed form: rr. 4.1 and 14.4. The petition must be signed by counsel or other person having a right of audience: r. 4.2; and see r. 1.3(1) (definition of "counsel" and "other person having a right of audience") and note 1.3.4.

The petitioner must lodge the petition with the required steps of process (r. 4.4). A fee is payable on lodging the petition: see note 14.5.10.

On petitions generally, see Chap. 14.

"DEPENDING".

A cause is depending from the time it is commenced (i.e. from the time an action is served) until final decree, whereas a cause is in dependence until final extract. For the meaning of commenced, see note 13.4.4. For the meaning of final decree, see note 4.15.2(2). For the meaning of final extract, see note 7.1.2(2).

Proceedings for infringement

55.7.—(1) In any cause in which it is alleged that a patent has been infringed, the person alleging infringement must aver in the petition or summons, as the case may be, particulars of the infringement relied on, showing which of the claims in the specification of the patent are alleged to have been infringed and giving at least one instance of each type of infringement alleged.

(2) Where, as a defence to such an allegation, it is averred that—

(a) at the time of the infringement there was in force a contract or licence relating to the patent made by or with the consent of the person alleging the infringement, and

(b) containing a condition or term void by virtue of section 44 of the Act of 1977,

the person stating that defence must aver particulars of the date of, and the parties to, each such contract or licence and particulars of each such condition or term.

Deriv. R.C.S. 1965, r. 256 substituted by S.I. 1991 No. 1621

GENERAL NOTE.

Under s. 61 of the Act of 1977 proceedings for infringement of a patent may be brought in the Court of Session or referred to the Comptroller by agreement. The court may grant (*a*) interdict, (*b*) delivery or

55.6

55.6.1

55.6.2

55.6.3

55.7

55.7.1

---

[1] Rule 55.6(2) substituted by S.S.I. 2012 No. 275 r. 3(6) (effective 19th November 2012).

destruction, (c) damages, (d) an account of profits or (e) declarator of validity and infringement. The Comptroller may only grant an order in (c) or (e).

A conclusion for infringement should refer to the claims in the specification: *Ygnis S.A. v. McFarlane Bros. (Heat) Ltd* 1969 S.L.T. (Notes) 77.

A patentee's claim has to explain his monopoly in terms which a man, reasonably competent in the art, could understand so as to enable him to work out for himself precisely what the forbidden area was for the purposes of deciding both what activities would constitute infringement and whether the patent itself was invalidated by prior art. *Smoothysigns v. Metro Products (Accessories and Leisure) Ltd , The Times,* 4th August 1995.

Objections to validity of patent

55.8 **55.8.**—(1) A person who—

    (a) brings an action under section 32 of the Act of 1949 or presents a petition under section 72 of the Act of 1977 for revocation of a patent, or

    (b) being a party to an action relating to a patent—

        (i) challenges the validity of the patent, or

        (ii) applies by counterclaim in the action for revocation of the patent,

shall aver the grounds on which the validity of the patent is challenged.

(2) Where the grounds in respect of which averments are required under paragraph (1) include—

    (a) want of novelty, or

    (b) want of any inventive step,

the averments shall include the matters mentioned in paragraph (3).

(3) The matters referred to in paragraph (2) are—

    (a) the manner, time and place of every prior publication or use relied on; and

    (b) where prior use is alleged—

        (i) specification of the name of every person alleged to have made such use;

        (ii) an averment as to whether such use is alleged to have continued until the priority date of the claim in question or of the invention, as the case may be, and, if not, the earliest and latest date on which such use is alleged to have taken place;

        (iii) a description accompanied, if necessary, by drawings sufficient to identify such use; and

        (iv) if such use relates to machinery or apparatus, an averment as to whether the machinery or apparatus is in existence and where it can be inspected.

(4) Where, in the case of an existing patent—

    (a) one of the grounds on which the validity of the patent is challenged is that the invention, so far as claimed in any claim of the complete specification, is not useful, and

    (b) it is intended, in connection with that ground, to rely on the fact that an example of the invention which is the subject of any such claim cannot be made to work, either at all or as described in the specification,

the averments shall specify that fact and identify each such claim and shall include particulars of each such example, specifying the respects in which it is alleged that it does not work or does not work as described.

Deriv. R.C.S. 1965, r. 257 substituted by S.I. 1991 No. 1621

GENERAL NOTE.

55.8.1 A patent may only be granted if it is new, involves an inventive step, is capable of industrial application and is not excluded by subsection (2) or (3): Act of 1977, s. 1(1).

"NOVELTY".

55.8.2 The applicant for a patent must not have disclosed details of his invention by, e.g. publishing an article or demonstrating it other than at an international exhibition: Act of 1977, s. 2; cf. *Quantel Ltd v.*

Spaceworld Microsystems Ltd [1990] R.P.C. 83. An invention is not new if it does not form part of the state of the art: Act of 1977, s. 2(1). State of the art includes all material available to the public (Act of 1977, s. 2(2)) or matter contained in a prior application (Act of 1977, s. 2(3)). The test is whether a person of ordinary knowledge of the subject would be able to replicate the invention from study of its alleged progenitor: *Hill v. Evans* (1862) 31 L.J.Ch. 457.

"INVENTIVE STEP".

An invention shall be taken to involve an inventive step if it is not obvious to a person skilled in the art, having regard to any matter which forms part of the state of the art which is matter available to the public: Act of 1977, s. 3.

55.8.3

The criteria for deciding whether or not the claimed invention involves an inventive step is wholly objective and requires a qualitative not a quantitative test: *Mölnycke A.B. v. Proctor & Gamble (No. 5)* [1994] R.P.C. 49.

Determination of question or application where Comptroller declines to deal with it

55.9. Where the Comptroller—

55.9

   (a)   declines to deal with a question under the following sections of the Act of 1977:—

      (i)   section 8 (entitlement to patents etc.),

      (ii)   section 12 (entitlement to foreign and convention patents),

      (iii)   section 37 (right to patent after grant), or

      (iv)   section 61(3) (infringement of patent),

   (b)   declines to deal with an application under section 40 of that Act (compensation of employees for certain inventions), or

   (c)   issues a certificate under section 72(7) of that Act (revocation of patent should be determined by the court),

any person entitled to do so may, within 28 days after the decision of the Comptroller, apply by petition to have the question or application, as the case may be, determined by the court.

Deriv. R.C.S. 1965, r. 257A substituted by S.I. 1991 No. 1621

"PETITION".

A petition is presented in the Outer House: r. 14.2(h). The petition must be in Form 14.4 in the official printed form: rr. 4.1 and 4.4. The petition must be signed by counsel or other person having a right of audience: r. 4.2; and see r. 1.3(1) (definition of "counsel" and "other person having a right of audience") and note 1.3.4.

55.9.1

The petitioner must lodge the petition with the required steps of process (r. 4.4). A fee is payable on lodging the petition: see note 14.5.10.

On petitions generally, see Chap. 14.

Applications by employees for compensation under section 40 of the Act of 1977

55.10.—(1) An application under section 40(1) or (2) of the Act of 1977 (compensation of employees for certain inventions) shall be made by summons commenced within the period which begins when the relevant patent is granted and which expires one year after it has ceased to have effect.

55.10

(2) Where a patent has ceased to have effect by reason of a failure to pay any renewal fee within the period prescribed for the payment of that fee and an application is made to the Comptroller under section 28 of the Act of 1977 (restoration of lapsed patent), the period within which the application by summons is to be made shall—

   (a)   if restoration is ordered, continue as if the patent has remained continuously in effect; or

   (b)   if restoration is refused, be treated as if expiring one year after the patent ceased to have effect or six months after the refusal, whichever is the later.

Deriv. R.C.S. 1965, r. 257B substituted by S.I. 1991 No. 1621

55.10.1
An employee may be compensated for an invention he made belonging to his employer which is of outstanding benefit to the employer, and compensation is determined under s. 41: Act of 1977, s. 40. Whether the invention belongs to the employer is determined by s. 39 of the Act of 1977.

"SUMMONS".

55.10.2
See Chap. 13.

Proceedings for determination of certain disputes

55.11
55.11. A reference or application under any of the following provisions shall be made by petition:—

    (a) a reference under—

        (i) section 48 of the Act of 1949 or section 58 of the Act of 1977 (which provide for disputes as to Crown use);

        (ii) paragraph 3 of Schedule 1 to the Registered Designs Act 1949 (disputes as to Crown use);

        (iii) section 4 of the Defence Contracts Act 1958 (payments for use and determination of disputes);

        (iv) section 251(1) (design right matters), or section 252(1) (disputes as to Crown use), of the Act of 1988; and

    (b) an application under section 45(3) of the Act of 1977 (variation of certain contracts).

Deriv. RCS 1965, r. 257C substituted by S.I. 1991 No. 1621

"PETITION".

55.11.1
A petition is presented in the Outer House: r. 14.2(h). The petition must be in Form 14.4 in the official printed form: rr. 4.1 and 14.4. The petition must be signed by counsel or other person having a right of audience: r. 4.2; and see r. 1.3(1) (definition of "counsel" and "other person having a right of audience") and note 1.3.4.

The petitioner must lodge the petition with the required steps of process (r. 4.4). A fee is payable on lodging the petition: see note 14.5.10.

On petitions generally, see Chap. 14.

Applications for rectification of Register of Designs or Patents

55.12
55.12.—(1) Subject to paragraph (2), an application under section 20(1) of the Registered Designs Act 1949 (rectification of Register of Designs) or section 34(1) of the Act of 1977 (rectification of Register of Patents) shall be made by petition.

(2)[1] Where a cause for infringement of a patent is depending before the court, an application mentioned in paragraph (1) may be made by counterclaim in that cause in accordance with rule 55.2D (pleadings in intellectual property causes).

(3) In an application under section 34(1) of the Act of 1977, the applicant shall intimate the application to the Comptroller, who may lodge answers in process and be heard on the application.

Deriv. RCS 1965, r. 257D substituted by S.I. 1991 No. 1621

"PETITION".

55.12.1
A petition is presented in the Outer House: r.14.2(h). The petition must be in Form 14.4 in the official printed form: rr. 4.1 and 14.4. The petition must be signed by counsel or other person having a right of audience: r. 4.2; and see r. 1.3(1) (definition of "counsel" and "other person having a right of audience") and note 1.3.4.

The petitioner must lodge the petition with the required steps of process (r. 4.4). A fee is payable on lodging the petition: see note 14.5.10.

On petitions generally, see Chap. 14.

"INTIMATE".

55.12.2
For methods, see r. 16.7.

---

[1] Rule 55.12(2) substituted by S.S.I. 2012 No. 275 r. 3(7) (effective 19th November 2012).

See r. 18.3.

55.12.3

Counterclaim for rectification of Register of Designs

55.13.—[1](1) Where, in any cause, an infringement of a registered design is alleged, the party against whom the allegation is made may—

    (a)   put in issue the validity of the registration of that design;

    (b)   counterclaim for an order that the Register of Designs be rectified by cancelling or varying the registration; or

    (c)   put in issue such validity and make such a counterclaim.

  (2) A party to any such cause who counterclaims for an order that the Register of Designs be rectified shall intimate to the Comptroller a copy of the counterclaim; and the Comptroller may, or (if ordered to do so by the court) shall, lodge answers in process and be heard in any such cause.

  (3) Such a counterclaim shall be made in accordance with rule 55.2D (pleadings in intellectual property causes).

Deriv. RCS 1965, r. 257E substituted by S.I. 1991 No. 1621

GENERAL NOTE.

For infringement of copyright of a registered design, see Pt I of the Act of 1988.

"INTIMATE".

For methods, see r. 16.7.

55.13

55.13.1

55.13.2

Appeals and references from Comptroller

55.14.—(1)[2],[3] Subject to the following paragraphs of this rule, an appeal under the Act of 1949, the Act of 1977 or the Copyright Act of 1988 from a decision of, or a reference under the Copyright Act of 1988 from, the Comptroller shall be heard in the Outer House by the intellectual property judge.

  (2)[4],[5] In the application of Part III of Chapter 41 (appeals in Form 41.25) by virtue of rule 41.51 (appeals to Lord Ordinary) to an appeal or a reference made in paragraph (1) of this rule—

    (a)   for references to the Inner House there shall be substituted references to the intellectual property judge; and

    (b)   the following paragraphs of this rule shall apply.

  (3)[6][7] Subject to paragraph (4), an appeal or a reference shall be lodged in the General Department—

    (a)   in the case of a decision on a matter of procedure, within 14 days after the date of the decision appealed against; and

    (b)   in any other case, within six weeks after the date of the decision appealed against or the decision referring the proceedings to the court, as the case may be.

  (4) Except with the leave of the court, no appeal under this rule shall be entertained unless it has been lodged within the period specified in paragraph (3) or within such further period as the Comptroller may allow on an application made to him before the expiry of that period.

55.14

---

[1] Rule 55.13 amended by S.S.I. 2012 No. 275 r. 3(8) (effective 19th November 2012).
[2] Rule 55.14(1) to (3) amended by S.I. 1994 No. 2901 (effective 5th December 1994).
[3] Rule 55.14(1) and (2)(a) amended by S.I. 1999 No. 1785 (effective 12th July 1999).
[4] Rule 55.14 (1) to (3) amended by S.I. 1994 No. 2901 (effective 5th December 1994).
[5] Rule 55.14(2) and (6) amended by S.S.I. 2011 No. 385 para. 6 (effective 28th November 2011).
[6] Rule 55.14 (1) to (3) amended by S.I. 1994 No. 2901 (effective 5th December 1994).
[7] Rule 55.14(2) and (6) amended by S.S.I. 2011 No. 385 para. 6 (effective 28th November 2011).

(5) Any determination by the Comptroller that a decision is on a matter of procedure shall be treated as being itself a decision on a matter of procedure.

(6)[1] In the application of paragraph (1) of rule 41.27 (orders for service and answers), the order under that paragraph shall include a requirement to—

(a) intimate the appeal to the Comptroller; and

(b) serve the appeal on every other party to the proceedings before the Comptroller.

(7) On receiving intimation of the appeal, the Comptroller shall forthwith transmit to the Deputy Principal Clerk all the papers relating to the matter which is the subject of the appeal.

(8) A respondent who, not having appealed from the decision of the Comptroller, wishes to contend at the hearing of the appeal that the decision or the grounds of the decision should be varied shall—

(a) specify the grounds of that contention in his answers; and

(b) intimate those answers to the Comptroller and to every other party to the proceedings before the Comptroller.

(9) Intimation of the date of the hearing of the appeal shall be made to the Comptroller by the appellant not less than seven days before that date, unless the court otherwise directs.

(10) An appeal under this rule shall be a re-hearing and the evidence led on appeal shall be the same as that led before the Comptroller; and, except with the leave of the court, no further evidence shall be led.

Deriv. RCS 1965, r. 257F substituted by S.I. 1991 No. 1621

GENERAL NOTE.

55.14.1   R. 41.43 provides for appeals to the Outer House or a single judge under any enactment. S. 97 of the Act of 1977 provides for appeal from the Comptroller to the Outer House.

"WITHIN 14 DAYS".

55.14.2   The date from which the period is calculated is not counted. Where the last day falls on a Saturday or Sunday or a public holiday on which the Office of Court is closed, the next available day is allowed: r. 1.3(7). For office hours and public holidays, see note 3.1.2.

"INTIMATE"; "INTIMATION".

55.14.3   For methods, see r. 16.7.

Intimation to Comptroller of reclaiming motion

55.15   **55.15.** The marking of a reclaiming motion from a decision of the patents judge on an appeal from a decision of the Comptroller shall be intimated by the reclaimer to the Comptroller as well as to the other parties to the appeal.

Deriv. RCS 1965, r. 257G substituted by S.I. 1991 No. 1621

"INTIMATED".

55.15.1   For methods, see r. 16.7.

Communication of information to European Patent Office

55.16   **55.16.**—(1) The court may authorise the communication to the European Patent Office or the competent authority of any country which is a party to the European Patent Convention of any such information in the records of the court as the court thinks fit.

(2) An application for such information shall be made by letter addressed to the Deputy Principal Clerk.

(3) Before complying with an application for the disclosure of information under paragraph (1), any person appearing to be affected by the application shall be given

---

[1] Rule 55.14(2) and (6) amended by S.S.I. 2011 No. 385 para. 6 (effective 28th November 2011).

the opportunity of making representations to the patents judge in chambers on the question whether the information should be disclosed; and the decision of the patents judge shall be final and not subject to review.

(4)   In this rule, "the European Patent Convention" has the meaning assigned in section 130(1) and (6) of the Act of 1977.

Deriv. RCS 1965, r. 257H substituted by S.I. 1991 No. 1621

GENERAL NOTE.

The *European Patents Convention* 1973 (Cmnd. 8510 (1982)) established the concept of a single European patent which may be issued by the European Patent Office valid in all or specified Contracting States. **55.16.1**

"FINAL AND NOT SUBJECT TO REVIEW".

The decision of the Lord Ordinary may not be reclaimed against. **55.16.2**

Intimation and service of certain statutory applications for orders for disposal of infringing matter[1]

55.17.[2],[3]   An application under section 114, 204 or 231 of the Copyright Act of 1988 (which provide for orders for disposal in respect of infringement of copyright, rights in performances and design rights), section 19 of the Trade Marks Act 1994 (order as to disposal of infringing goods, material or articles) or regulation 5 of the Olympics Association Right (Infringement Proceedings) Regulations 1995 (order as to disposal of infringing goods, materials or articles etc.), shall be made— **55.17**

(a)   in a cause depending before the court, by motion; or

(b)   where there is no depending cause, by petition; and

the applicant shall intimate the motion to, or serve the petition on, as the case may be, all persons, so far as known to the applicant or reasonably ascertainable, having an interest in the copy, article, recording or other thing which is the subject of the application, including any person in whose favour an order could be made in respect of the copy, article, recording or other thing under any of the said sections of the Copyright Act of 1988, section 19 of the said Act of 1994 or regulation 5 of the said Regulations.

Deriv. RCS 1965, r. 257I substituted by S.I. 1991 No. 1621

"DEPENDING".

A cause is depending from the time it is commenced (i.e. from the time an action is served or a first order in a petition is made) until final decree, whereas a cause is in dependence until final extract. For the meaning of commenced, see note 13.4.4 (action) or 14.6.1 (petition). For the meaning of final decree, see note 4.15.2(2). For the meaning of final extract, see note 7.1.2(2). **55.17.1**

"MOTION".

For motions, see Chap. 23. **55.17.2**

"PETITION".

A petition is presented in the Outer House: r. 14.2(h). The petition must be in Form 14.4 in the official printed form: rr. 4.1 and 14.4. The petition must be signed by counsel or other person having a right of audience: r. 4.2; and see r. 1.3(1) (definition of "counsel" and "other person having a right of audience") and note 1.3.4. **55.17.3**

The petitioner must lodge the petition with the required steps of process (r. 4.4). A fee is payable on lodging the petition: see note 14.5.10.

On petitions generally, see Chap. 14.

"INTIMATE".

For methods, see r. 16.7. **55.17.4**

---

[1] Rule 55.17 and heading amended by S.I 1996 No. 1756 (effective 5th August 1996).
[2] Rule 55.17 amended by S.I. 1994 No. 2901 (effective 5th December 1994).
[3] Rule 55.17 and heading amended by S.I. 1996 No. 1756 (effective 5th August 1996).

"service".

55.17.5   For methods, see Chap. 16, Pt I.

Olympics Association Right (Infringement Proceedings) Regulations 1995 [S.I. 1995 No. 3325].

55.17.6   The Olympics Association right consists of rights and remedies conferred by the Olympic Symbol etc. (Protection) Act 1995 similar to a registered trade mark. Under the 1995 Regulations the proprietor of the right (the British Olympics Association) may apply to the court for an order for delivery up of infringing goods, materials or articles. Where any such items have been delivered up an application may be made under reg. 5 for disposal.

Applications for leave to proceed

55.18   **55.18.**—(1)   Where leave of the court is required under the Copyright Act of 1988 before an action may proceed, the pursuer shall apply by motion for leave to proceed before the summons is signeted.

(2)   A motion under paragraph (1) shall be heard in chambers.

(3)   Where such leave is granted, a copy of the interlocutor allowing leave shall be attached to the copy of the summons served on the defender.

Deriv. RCS 1965, r. 257J substituted by S.I. 1991 No. 1621

"motion".

55.18.1   For motions, see Chap. 23.

Appeals and references under the Trade Marks Act 1994

55.19   **55.19.**—[1](1)   Subject to the following paragraphs of this rule, an appeal or reference under section 76 of the Trade Marks Act 1994 (appeal from registrar or reference from appointed person) shall be heard in the Outer House by the patents judge.

(2)[2]   In the application of Part III of Chapter 41 (appeals in Form 41.25) by virtue of rule 41.51 (appeals to Lord Ordinary) to an appeal or reference under paragraph (1) of this rule—

(a)   for references to the Inner House there shall be substituted references to the patents judge; and

(b)   the following paragraphs of this rule shall apply.

(3)   Subject to paragraph (4), an appeal or reference shall be lodged in the General Department—

(a)   in the case of a decision on a matter of procedure, within 14 days after the date of the decision appealed against; and

(b)   in any other case, within 6 weeks after the date of the decision appealed against or the decision referring the proceedings to the court, as the case may be.

(4)   Except with the leave of the court, no appeal or reference under this rule shall be entertained unless it has been lodged within the period specified in paragraph (3) or within such further period as the Comptroller may allow on an application made to him before the expiry of that period.

(5)   Any determination by the Comptroller that a decision is on a matter of procedure shall be treated as being itself a decision on a matter of procedure.

(6)[3]   In the application of paragraph (1) of rule 41.27 (orders for service and answers), the order under that paragraph shall include a requirement to—

(a)   intimate the appeal to the Comptroller; and

(b)   serve the appeal on every other party to the proceedings before the Comptroller.

---

[1] Rule 55.19 inserted by S.I. 1994 No. 2901 (effective 5th December 1994).
[2] Rule 55.19(2) and (6) amended by S.S.I. 2011 No. 385 para. 6 (effective 28th November 2011).
[3] Rule 55.19(2) and (6) amended by S.S.I. 2011 No. 385 para. 6 (effective 28th November 2011).

(7) On receiving intimation of the appeal, the Comptroller shall forthwith transmit to the Deputy Principal Clerk all the papers relating to the matter which is the subject of the appeal.

(8) A respondent who, not having appealed from the decision of the Comptroller, wishes to contend at the hearing of the appeal that the decision or the grounds of the decision should be varied shall—

(a) specify the grounds of that contention in his answers;

(b) intimate those answers to the Comptroller and to every other party to the proceedings before the Comptroller.

(9) Intimation of the date of the hearing of the appeal shall be made to the Comptroller by the appellant not less than 7 days before that date, unless the court otherwise directs.

(10) An appeal under this rule shall be a re-hearing and the evidence led on appeal shall be the same as that led before the Comptroller; and, except with the leave of the court, no further evidence shall be led.

General note.

R. 41.51 provides for appeals to the Outer House or a single judge under any enactment.   **55.19.1**

"within 14 days".

The date from which the period is calculated is not counted. Where the last day falls on a Saturday or Sunday or a public holiday on which the Office of Court is closed, the next available day is allowed: r. 1.3(7). For office hours and public holidays, see note 3.1.2.   **55.19.2**

"intimate"; Intimation".

For methods, see r. 16.7.   **55.19.3**

CHAPTER 56A JUDGMENTS OF THE SUPREME COURT

Applications to apply judgments of the Supreme Court

56A.1.—[1](1) An application to apply a judgment of the Supreme Court in a cause shall be made by motion in the Single Bills.

(2) On enrolling a motion under paragraph (1), a party shall lodge four copies of the Supreme Court judgment in process.

GENERAL NOTE.

A.S. (R.C.S.A. No. 4) (Miscellaneous) 2010 [S.S.I. 2010 No. 205] has "substituted" Chap. 56 with Chap. 56A! No satisfactory explanation has been given for not substituting Chap. 56 with a new Chap. 56 rather than adding (not "substituting") Chap. 56A.

Where the UK Supreme Court affirms the decision of the Court of Session and there is nothing else to be done in the cause (i.e. the subject-matter of the cause is disposed of), the Court of Session decree can be extracted and it is not necessary to apply to the court to apply the UK Supreme Court judgment: *Peters v. Magistrates of Greenock* (1893) 20 R. 924.

A judgment of the UK Supreme Court may have to be put into a form to allow extract of a decree to carry the judgment into effect, e.g. where the decision of the Court of Session is reversed. A motion to apply the judgment will be required. In such a case, where the Court of Session is simply giving effect to the judgment of the UK Supreme Court, it is acting in a ministerial or administrative capacity and cannot add to or alter the judgment of the House of Lords: *Maclachlan's Trs v. Yuill's Trs* 1939 S.C. 500; *Grant v. Sun Shipping Co. Ltd* 1949 S.C. 19.

Where the judgment of the U.K. Supreme Court does not exhaust the whole cause (because, e.g. it was an interlocutory judgment), an appropriate interlocutor of the Court of Session will have to be pronounced for further procedure. A motion to apply the judgment will be required.

A petition to apply a judgment of the House of Lords or U.K. Supreme Court is no longer required.

"MOTION".

For motions, see Chap. 23.

APPEALS TO THE U.K. SUPREME COURT.

Section 40 of the CSA 1988, as substituted by s. 117 of the Courts Reform (Scotland) Act 2014, provides for appeal from a *decision* (not "judgment") of the Inner House. The section is subject to any other enactment which restricts or excludes an appeal from the Court of Session, a special case which excludes it or any right of appeal arising apart from that section: s.40(8) and (9). There is no appeal from a Lord Ordinary to the U.K. Supreme Court: s. 40(5). For appeals from the Sheriff Appeal Court or a sheriff principal, see note 56A.1.4.

(A) Certain decisions may only be appealed (a) with the permission of the Inner House, or (b) if the Inner House has refused permission, with the permission of the UK Supreme Court. The decisions are: (a) a decision constituting final judgment in any proceedings, (b) a decision in an exchequer cause, (c) a decision on an application under s. 29 of the CSA 1988 to grant or refuse a new jury trial in any proceedings, (d) any other decision in any proceedings if (i) there is a difference of opinion among the judges making the decision or (ii) the decision is one sustaining a preliminary defence and dismissing the proceedings.

(B) An appeal may be taken against any other decision of the Inner House in any proceedings, but only with leave of the Inner House.

The expression "*final judgment*", in relation to any proceedings, means a decision which, by itself or taken along with prior decisions in the proceedings, disposes of the subject matter of the proceedings on its merits, even though judgment may not have been pronounced on every question raised or expenses found due may not have been modified, taxed or decerned for. The expression "*preliminary defence*", in relation to any proceedings, means a defence that does not relate to the merits of the proceedings. See s. 40(10).

The only ground on which the Inner House or the Supreme Court may grant permission for an appeal under s. 40 is if the Inner House or the Supreme Court considers that the appeal raises an arguable point of law of general public importance which ought to be considered by the Supreme Court at that time: CSA 1988, s.40A(3).

Under the old law, leave might not be granted unless there is a novel point of law, a point of law on which there is a conflict of judicial authority or a point of law of public importance: see also *Costain Building and Civil Engineering Ltd v. Scottish Rugby Union plc* 1993 S.C. 650, 663H per L.P. Hope. Leave may be refused where the question raised is one purely of Scottish procedure and practice (*McIntosh v. British Railways Board* 1990 S.C. 339) or against an interim order (*Ferguson v. Maclennan Salmon Co. Ltd* 1990 S.L.T. 658). The House of Lords has reiterated the point that it is not appropriate to refer matters of the procedure and practice of the Court of Session for decision by the House of Lords:

---

[1] Chap. 56A and R. 56A.1 substituted for Chap. 56 and R. 56.1 by S.S.I. 2010 No. 205 (effective 15th June 2010).

Girvan v. Inverness Farmers Dairy 1998 S.C. (H.L.) 1, 21C-G per Lord Hope of Craighead. As a general rule, at the interlocutor stage it is not the court's function to resolve difficult questions of law which call for detailed and mature reflection; and the fact that a matter of public importance was raised was not a relevant consideration in determining whether to grant leave: *Houston v. BBC* 1995 S.C. 433 (First Div. refused leave against interim interdict). Leave will not usually be granted to enable a party to advance an argument not previously put forward: *Strathclyde R.C. v. Gallagher* 1995 S.C. 241.

The U.K. Supreme Court will not usually hear a new argument not made in the courts below: *British Oxygen Co. Ltd v. South West Scotland Electricity Board* 1956 S.C.(H.L.) 112, 119–120 per Lord Normand. It may do so where justice requires, e.g., where the point would have to be decided in a later case or there is no other means of having the point decided: *British Oxygen Co. Ltd*, above; *Stonehaven Magistrates v. Kincardinshire C.C.* 1940 S.C.(H.L.) 56; *CIN Properties Ltd v. Dollar Land (Cumbernauld) Ltd* 1992 S.C.(H.L.) 104.

Where the U.K. Supreme Court is reviewing concurrent findings as to credibility by the judge at first instance and the appellate court, the following rules apply: (a) concurrent findings-in-fact, depending on the assessment of credibility, ought only to be reviewed when it can be clearly demonstrated that the findings were erroneous. It is not enough that the court would have taken a different view of the facts: a concurrent finding can only be reversed where it could be demonstrated either that some cardinal fact had been overlooked, or that some altogether erroneous view had been taken of the hearing of the evidence on the case. (b) The court will reverse concurrent findings-of-fact where these do not depend upon an assessment of credibility. (c) A reluctance to reverse a concurrent finding-in-fact will not be shown where the finding is not a finding of specific fact but is really an inference from facts specifically found. See *Brodie v. British Railways Board* 1972 S.L.T.(Notes) 37.

Procedure in the U.K. Supreme Court is governed by the Supreme Court Rules 2009 (S.I. 2009/1603) and practice directions issued by the President of the Court.

APPEALS TO HOUSE OF LORDS FROM SHERIFF COURT.

56A.1.4   Under s. 32(5) of the C.S.A. 1988, an appeal to the U.K. Supreme Court from the Inner House in an appeal from the Sheriff Appeal Court under s. 113 of the Courts Reform (Scotland) Act 2014 or a sheriff principal under s. 114 of that Act is appealable only on matters of law. The U.K. Supreme Court cannot embark on an examination of the evidence in the sheriff court but is restricted to genuine questions of law: *Laing v. Scottish Grain Distillers* 1992 S.C.(H.L.) 64, 69 per Lord Jauncey of Tullichettle and cases there cited; see also *Martinez v. Grampian Health Board* 1996 S.C.(H.L.) 1, 50-F per Lord Jauncey of Tullichettle.

INTERIM POSSESSION, EXECUTION AND EXPENSES.

56A.1.5   Under s.41(1) of the C.S.A. 1988, the Inner House may regulate all matters relating to interim possession, execution and expenses pending appeal to the U.K. Supreme Court. "Interim possession" has been held to include orders relating to custody of a child: *Brixey v. Lynas (No. 2)* 1996 S.L.T. 651.

SUPREME COURT.

56A.1.6   The term "Supreme Court" is not defined in R.C.S. 1994, the C.S.A. 1988 or the Interpretation Act 1978. It is intended to refer to the Supreme Court of the United Kingdom created by s. 23 of the Constitutional Reform Act 2005.

CHAPTER 57 ADMISSION OF ADVOCATES

Chapter 57

Admission of Advocates

Form of petition for admission as advocate

57.1. A petition by a person for admission to the public office of advocate shall be in such form as the Lord President shall, in consultation with the Dean of the Faculty of Advocates, determine.

GENERAL NOTE.

The petition for admission as an Advocate is in a special form and the ordinary rules for petitions do not apply. The petition form is obtainable from the Faculty of Advocates on applying to become an intrant of the Faculty of Advocates, and the petition is presented on the intrant's behalf by the Faculty.

An Advocate is not called to the Bar, he or she is admitted to the Faculty of Advocates and passes advocate after making, before a Lord Ordinary in a ceremony in open court, a declaration of allegiance to the Sovereign (or where allegiance is not owed, because, e.g. the person concerned is a foreign national not permitted to owe allegiance to a sovereign of another country, a declaration to faithfully discharge the office of advocate). The Advocate signs a parchment recording the declaration, the Lord Ordinary signs an interlocutor in the petition for an act of admission by the Lords of Council and Session, which is duly recorded in the Books of Sederunt.

57.1.1

Disapplication of rules in relation to petitions

57.2. The following provisions of these Rules shall not apply to a petition by a person for admission to the public office of advocate:—

rule 4.1 (form, size, etc., of documents forming the process),

rule 4.3 (lodging of processes), and

Chapter 14 (petitions).

57.2

Admission as advocate

57.3.— *[Revoked by the Act of Sederunt (Regulation of Advocates) 2011 (S.S.I. 2011 No. 312) para.2(4) (effective 27th September 2011).]*

57.3

Deriv. R.C.S. 1965, r. 351 substituted by S.I. 1968 No. 1016 (r. 57.3(2))

GENERAL NOTE.

On presentation of the petition, the Lord President signs an interlocutor in the petition remitting to the Faculty of Advocates. The qualifications, entry and training requirements are regulated by the Faculty of Advocates and are set out in Regulations as to Intrants approved by the court. Further information can be obtained from The Clerk of Faculty, Faculty of Advocates, Advocates' Library, Parliament House, Edinburgh EH1 1RF.

57.3.1

CHAPTER 58 JUDICIAL REVIEW

Chapter 58[1]

Judicial Review

Application of this Chapter

58.1.—(1) This Chapter applies to an application to the supervisory jurisdiction of the court.

(2) Such an application must be made by petition for judicial review.

(3) The following rules do not apply to a petition for judicial review—

- (a) rule 14.4 (form of petitions);
- (b) rule 14.5 (first order in petitions);
- (c) rule 14.8 (procedure where answers lodged);
- (d) rule 14.9 (unopposed petitions);
- (e) rule 14.10 (disposals in petitions).

58.1

GENERAL NOTE

The new Chap. 58, substituted by A.S. (R.C.S.A. (No.3) (Courts Reform (Scotland) Act 2014 [S.S.I. 2015/228], and its rules apply to petitions for judicial review commenced on or after 22nd September 2015. A cause is commenced when it is served, that is on the date of citation.

58.1.1

The substantial change in the new Chap. 58 is the requirement for leave to apply for judicial review (the "permission stage" in the modern jargon) required under s.27B of the Act of 1988 inserted by s. 89 of the Courts Reform (Scotland) Act 2014. There is also a statutory time-limit for seeking judicial review: see notes 58.1.3 and 58.3.4.

The special procedure in this Chapter is derived from R.C.S. 1965, r. 260B inserted by A.S. (R.C.A. No. 2) (Judicial Review) 1985 [S.I. 1985 No. 500]. This A.S. was made following a recommendation of the Dunpark Working Party on Procedure for Judicial Review of Administrative Action. The Working Party itself was set up by L.P. Emslie following remarks made by Lord Fraser of Tullybelton in *Brown v. Hamilton D.C.* 1983 S.C.(H.L.) 1, 49. Lord Fraser of Tullybelton contrasted the cumbersome ordinary action procedure then used in Scotland for judicial review, with the speedy and cheap prerogative order procedure used in England since 1973. The remarks of Lord Fraser of Tullybelton about speed and cost are reflected in the judicial review procedure. Accordingly the rules should be interpreted and applied with these elements in mind.

THE SUPERVISORY JURISDICTION OF THE COURT.

This Chapter provides procedure for all applications to the supervisory jurisdiction of the Court of Session for the judicial review of certain types of conduct of certain natural and non-natural persons and the pronouncement of an order relating to the status of such conduct. The scope of this Chapter is limited by the extent of the court's supervisory jurisdiction. The rules in this Chapter do not change the substantive law regarding the extent of the court's supervisory jurisdiction or the extent of its jurisdiction: *West v. Secretary of State for Scotland* 1992 S.C. 385, 404 per L.P. Hope.

58.1.2

The "supervisory jurisdiction of the court" excludes procedures for which specific provision is made elsewhere in the R.C.S. 1994 (e.g. reduction in Chap. 53 or suspension in Chap. 60) where the jurisdiction which is the subject of review is not of a kind as defined in *West*, above: *Bell v. Fiddes* 1996 S.L.T. 51, 52H per Lord Marnoch; *Saunders, Ptnr*, 1999 S.C. 564 (OH) (petition dismissed because reduction of sheriff court decrees was dealt with under r.53.2). In *West*, the court set out three propositions in trying to define the supervisory jurisdiction and stated that it involves a tripartite relationship. In *Gray v Braid Logistics (UK) Ltd*, 2015 S.C. 222 (Extra Div.), the court observed that the jurisdiction may be seen as a development of the nobile officium and generally applies only where there is no other remedy (the case concerned an employment dispute).

A question has arisen as to whether age assessment decisions by local authorities, as they have a duty to accommodate a "child" under s. 25 of the Children (Scotland) Act 1995 (under which other conditions also require to be met), are properly the subject of judicial review or action of declarator. The question has arisen in cases of asylum seekers claiming to be children, the question of age assessment being referred by the immigration authorities to the local authority. Reliance has been placed on an English decision on English procedure in the UKSC, *R (on the application of A) v. Croydon London Borough Council* [2009] 1 W.L.R. 2557, that the challenge to such a decision has to be dealt with by judicial review. Apart from the fact that an English decision on English procedure is no authority as to the law of Scotland, that case did not decide that these decisions had to be challenged by judicial review. In England there is no procedure for an action of declarator; if the decision has to be challenged, it could only be by judicial review. The problem in that case was whether the court could only look at the age assessment of a person as a child on *Wednesbury* principles or could determine that issue itself as a question of fact; the

---

[1] Chapter 58 as substituted by S.S.I. 2015 No. 228 (effective 22nd September 2015).

UKSC decided that whether a person was a child for the purposes of the Children Act 1989 was a question of fact which the court could decide even though, as Lady Hale pointed out, judicial review was not well suited to determine disputed questions of fact (but it was the only process available in English law). It cannot reasonably be argued that an action of declarator of age in Scotland is incompetent; and in *U v. Glasgow City Council*, 2017 S.L.T. 1109 (OH) (an action of declarator), Lord Woolman correctly held that it was competent in this situation. Lord Woolman considered, obiter, that judicial review was also competent, was the more appropriate procedure to use and recommended its use. In *L v Angus Council*, 2012 S.L.T. 304 (OH) (a petition for judicial review), Lord Stewart held that judicial review was incompetent. Questions that arise are whether (1) in Scots judicial review disputed questions of fact can be determined and (2) judicial review is the more appropriate procedure. The answer may depend on the purpose of the litigation. In the case of asylum seekers, determination of age is but a first step. Lord Woolman does not answer the first question. In answering the second question in the affirmative, he relies on a passage of Lord Hope of Craighead in *Ruddy v. Chief Constable, Strathclyde Police*, 2013 S.C. (UKSC) 126, 136, para. [32], which is in fact concerned with the competency of an action containing two distinct claims, and not therefore in point. He suggests that an advantage of judicial review is that it would not require individuals to raise two actions to obtain a final determination about their age. This justification is not clear because (a) once there is a declarator of age in an action it is of universal effect and there is no need for that issue to be decided again and (b) if the petitioner is the asylum seeker challenging the assessment that he is not a child there will be no other decision to review judicially. There is an increasingly common and erroneous practice of citing English cases as authority for principles or propositions of Scots Law without any regard for the different principles or bases on which they depend.

TIME LIMIT

58.1.3   Section 27A(1) of the Act of 1988, inserted by s. 89 of the Courts Reform (Scotland) Act 2014, provides that an application to the supervisory jurisdiction must be made before the end of three months beginning with the date on which the grounds giving rise to the application first arise or such longer period as the court considers equitable having regard to the circumstances. This was the recommendation in Chap. 12 of the Civil Courts Review. Section 27A(1) does not apply if, by virtue of any enactment, application is to be made in less than three months.

In *Odubajo v. Secretary of State for the Home Department* 2020 S.L.T. 103 (OH) 106 at para. [18], Lord Ericht held that the three-month time limit under s.27A(1)(a) of the 1988 Act ("the date on which the grounds giving rise to the application first arise") begins to run on the date on which the (challengeable) decision is made, but if the decision is not received until a later date that can be taken into account in considering whether to extend the time under s. 27A(1)(b) (the time limit was extended). In *Lauchlan and O'Neill v. Scottish Ministers* 2022 S.C. 125 (Second Div.), the court took the same view and went on to hold that the fact that there was an ongoing complaint did not prevent the commencement of the time-bar provision where it was acknowledged that the complaint procedure did not oust the jurisdiction of the court or provide an alternative remedy.

At common law, a petition may be refused because of inordinate delay in seeking judicial review, on the ground of *mora*, taciturnity and acquiescence: *Atherton v. Strathclyde R.C.* 1995 S.L.T. 557.

DISAPPLICATION OF RULES

58.1.4   Special rules apply to petitions for judicial review and, accordingly, the rules mentioned in r. 58.1(3) do not apply.

Interpretation

58.2   **58.2.** In this Chapter—

"the 2007 Act" means the Tribunals, Courts and Enforcement Act 2007;

"application to the supervisory jurisdiction of the court" includes an application made under section 45(b) (specific performance of a statutory duty) of the Act of 1988;

"oral hearing" means an oral hearing to determine whether to grant permission under sections 27B or 27C of the Act of 1988;

"permission" means permission for an application to the supervisory jurisdiction of the court to proceed, as required by section 27B(1) of the Act of 1988;

"procedural hearing" means a hearing fixed under rule 58.11(1)(b);

"substantive hearing" means a hearing fixed under rule 58.11(1)(a).

GENERAL NOTE

58.2.1   In *Vince v. Prime Minister* 2020 S.C. 78 (OH), it was held that, although r. 58.2 referred to an application under s. 45(b) of the C.S.A. 1988 being included in the term "application to the supervisory jurisdiction of the court", the wording of s. 45(b) gave the petitioner the right to raise proceedings under that section by way of summary petition.

The petition

58.3.—(1) A petition may not be lodged in respect of an application if that application could be made by appeal or review under or by virtue of any enactment.

(2) For the purposes of calculating the time limit under section 27A of the Act of 1988, an application is made when a petition is lodged.

(3) A petition for judicial review is made in Form 58.3.

(4) A petition must—

   (a)   have lodged with it all relevant documents in the petitioner's possession or control;

   (b)   have appended to it a schedule specifying—

       (i)   any documents which the petition founds on that are not in the petitioner's possession or control; and

       (ii)   the person who has possession or control over those documents;

   (c)   where the decision, act or omission in question and the basis of the challenge is not apparent from the documents lodged, have lodged with it an affidavit stating the terms of that decision, act or omission and the basis of the challenge;

   (d)[1]   identify which documents are necessary to determine—

       (i)   whether to grant permission;

       (ii)   whether to extend the time limit under section 27A of the Act of 1988.

(5)[2] Where the petitioner seeks an extension to the time limit under section 27A of the Act of 1988, this must be stated in the petition.

GENERAL NOTE.

An application to the supervisory jurisdiction of the court may only be made by a petition for judicial review. It follows that any cause which is based on the exercise of the supervisory jurisdiction (in the sense of jurisdiction as described in *West v. Secretary of State for Scotland* 1992 S.C. 385) which before 1985 could be brought by action or petition must now be brought by petition for judicial review: r. 58.3(1). In *West*, the court set out three propositions in trying to define the supervisory jurisdiction and stated that it involves a tripartite relationship. In *Gray v Braid Logistics (UK) Ltd*,2015 S.C. 222 (Extra Div.), the court observed that the jurisdiction may be seen as a development of the nobile officium and generally applies only where there is no other remedy (the case concerned an employment dispute).

An application may not be made for judicial review where the remedy may be sought by appeal or review or under any enactment: r. 58.3(2). It does not apply, e.g. to applications under para. 15 of Sched. 1 to the Acquisition of Land (Authorisation Procedure) (Scotland) Act 1947 (validity of compulsory purchase order), s.232 (validity of structure plans) and s.233 (validity of other orders, decisions and directions) of the Town and Country Planning (Scotland) Act 1972 or para. 2 of Sched. 2 to the Roads (Scotland) Act 1984 (validity of orders). See further note 58.3.3.

In a judicial review in relation to immigration or asylum status of an individual, a pre-proceedings letter should be sent to the UK Border Agency at least 14 days before commencing proceedings: P.N. No. 1 of 2012, paras. 2–6.

The court may order the specific performance of any statutory duty, under such conditions and penalties in the event of the order not being implemented as seems proper: C.S.A. 1988, s. 45(b). Only this provision is specifically included in r. 58.3(1), the implication being that s. 45(a) of the C.S.A. 1988 (restoration of possession of property of which one has been violently or fraudulently deprived) is not included because it was thought not to be appropriate for judicial review. The remedies in s. 45 of the C.S.A. 1988 are not available against the Crown: Crown Proceedings Act 1947, s. 21(1) (declarator available instead); see, e.g. *Davidson v. Scottish Ministers* , 2002 S.C. 205 (Extra Div.).

The precise terms of the order sought under s. 45(b) of the C.S.A. 1988 must be stated: *Carlton Hotel Co. v. Lord Advocate* 1921 S.C. 237. The remedy under this provision used not to be precluded because an alternative remedy was available: *T. Docherty Ltd v. Burgh of Monifieth* 1971 S.L.T. 13. It would appear, because such a remedy must be sought by judicial review and no remedy of appeal or review be available (r. 58.3), that the availability of this remedy is restricted.

58.3

58.3.1

---

[1] Rule 58.3(4)(d) inserted by S.S.I. 2017 No. 200 r. 2(4) (effective 17th July 2017).
[2] Rule 58.3(5) inserted by S.S.I. 2017 No. 200 r. 2(5) (effective 17th July 2017).

58.3.2   The petition is presented in the Outer House: r. 14.2(e). The petition must be in Form 58.6: r. 58.6(1). The petition must be in the official printed form: r. 4.1. The petition must be signed by counsel or other person having a right of audience: r. 4.2; and see r. 1.3(1) (definition of "counsel" and "other person having a right of audience") and note 1.3.4.

The petitioner must lodge the petition with the required steps of process (r. 4.4). A fee is payable on lodging the petition: see note 14.5.10.

On petitions generally, see Chap. 14.

The form of petition (see r. 58.6 and Form 58.6) provides for an abbreviated style of pleading. In *Somerville v. The Scottish Ministers* , 2008 S.C. (H.L.) 45, 69 at para. [65], Lord Hope of Craighead commented as follows on the requirements of a petition. The degree of precision and detail in written pleading traditionally looked for in other forms of action is not looked for in petitions for judicial review. The core requirements are that the factual history is set out succinctly and the issues of law should be clearly identified. The aim is to focus the issues so that the court can reach a decision upon them, in the interests of sound administration and in the public interest, as soon as possible.

Paragraph 8 of the petition should address the question why permission to proceed should be granted: PN No. 3 of 2017, para. 9.

COMPETENCY AND RELEVANCY OF THE PETITION.

58.3.3   The extent of the supervisory jurisdiction is limited by—(1) the type of person whose conduct may be reviewed; (2) the type of conduct which may be reviewed; and (3) the availability of any other statutory remedy to the petitioner. These matters affect the competency of a petition. In addition the petitioner must show title and interest to sue: this affects the relevancy of a petition. The principles by reference to which the competency of applications for judicial review is to be determined are set out in *West v. Secretary of State for Scotland* 1992 S.C. 385, 412–413 per L.P. Hope.

(A)   Persons whose conduct may be reviewed.

These are persons to whom a "jurisdiction" has been delegated or entrusted by statute, agreement, or other instrument: *West*, above per L.P. Hope at p. 412. In *West*, above, L.P. Hope at p. 413 said, "Contractual rights and obligations, such as those between employer and employee, are not as such amenable to judicial review. The cases in which the exercise of the supervisory jurisdiction is appropriate involve a tripartite relationship, between the person or body to whom the jurisdiction, power or authority has been delegated or entrusted, the person or body by whom it has been delegated or entrusted and the person or persons in respect of or for whose benefit that jurisdiction, power or authority is to be exercised.". The need for a tripartite relationship to exist has been doubted as inflexible: *Naik v. University of Stirling* 1994 S.L.T. 449, 451L–A *per* Lord Maclean; and see comments of Lord Prosser in *Joobeen v. University of Stirling* 1995 S.L.T. 120, 122F–K. A tripartite relationship is not formed when one of two parties to a relationship delegates a decision to an employee or agent: *Fraser v. Professional Golfers Association* 1999 S.C.L.R. 1032 (OH). In *Crocket v. Tantallon Golf Club* 2005 S.L.T. (OH), para. [40], Lord Reed indicated that the concept of a tripartite relationship should not be applied inflexibly. In that case, in holding that the petition was competent, it was held that there was no distinction between a decision taken by the council of a club and a decision taken by a general meeting of members; the essence of the supervisory jurisdiction was described in para. [37].

A person to whom a jurisdiction has been delegated may be a natural or non-natural person. For a recent example of a debate about who was the "decision maker" to be called as respondent, see *Thomson v. Chief Constable of Grampian Police* , 2001 S.C. 443.

There are a number of persons who have been recognised to have a jurisdiction and whose conduct in the exercise of that jurisdiction has been judicially reviewed.

(1)   Inferior civil courts and tribunals.

It has been stated in numerous cases that the decisions of inferior civil courts and tribunals are reviewable (but note r. 58.3(2)). These have included—

(a)   Church courts and office bearers: see, e.g. *Earl of Kinnoul v. Presbytery of Auchterarder* (1838) 16 S. 661 (aff'd (1839) Mac. & Rob. 220); *McMillan v. Free Church* (1861) 23 D. 1314; *Peake v. Association of English Episcopalians* (1884) 22 S.L.R. 3; *Moffat v. Kirk Session of Canonbie* 1936 S.C. 209; *Macdonald v. Burns* 1940 S.C. 376. The court has no jurisdiction, however, with respect to the exclusive jurisdiction of the courts of the Church of Scotland to legislate and adjudicate in relation to "all matters of doctrine, worship, government and discipline in the Church" including the determination of all questions covering the membership and office in the Church, the constitution and membership of its courts, the mode of election of its office bearers, and the definition of the boundaries of the spheres of labour of its ministers and other office bearers: *Logan v. Presbytery of Dumbarton* 1995 S.L.T. 1229; *Ballantyne v. Presbytery of Wigtown* 1936 S.C. 625.

(b)   Lyon Court: see *Macrae's Trs. v. Lord Lyon* 1927 S.L.T. 285.

(c)   Sheriff court in civil matters: see, e.g. *Murchie v. Fairbairn* (1863) 1 M. 800; *Maclachlan v. Rutherford* (1854) 16 D. 937; *Mackenzie v. Munro* (1894) 22 R. 45; *Mathewson v. Yeaman* (1900) 2 F. 873; *Adair v. Colville & Sons* 1926 S.C.(H.L.) 51; *Lothian R.C. v. Lord Advocate* 1993 S.C.L.R. 565 (fatal accident inquiry); cf. *Riverford Finance v. Kelly* 1991 S.L.T. 300, and *Bain v. Hugh L.S.*

McConnell Ltd 1991 S.L.T. 691. In *Gupta's Tr. v. Gupta* , 1996 S.C. 82, Lord Morrison at p. 84F said it was questionable whether ultra vires actings of a sheriff in making an order he had no power or right to pronounce, could be challenged only by judicial review. Where the R.C.S. 1994 provide specific procedures (e.g. reduction in Chap. 53 or suspension in Chap. 60) and the jurisdiction which is the subject of review is not of a kind as defined in *West*, above, a petition for judicial review is not competent: *Bell v. Fiddes* 1996 S.L.T. 51, 52H per Lord Marnoch. In *Ingle v. Ingle's Tr* 1997 S.L.T. 160, the point was not argued but parties appeared to accept that such a petition was competent. In *Saunders v. Royal Insurance plc* , 1999 S.C. 564, 2000 S.L.T. 597 Lord MacLean held that since rule 53.2 provided for reduction of a sheriff court decree, a petition for judicial review was incompetent and it was irrelevant that the case also fell within the principles of *West*, above. In *Glasgow City Council, Ptrs* , 2004 S.L.T. 61, Lord Menzies disapproved of *Saunders*, did not follow it, distinguished *Bell*, and held judicial review was competent of a sheriff's refusal of a summary application against a decision of an education authority's appeal committee. In relation to "administrative" decisions of this kind by a sheriff from which there is no appeal, Lord Menzies' approach would seem correct. If the decision is in a criminal matter the High Court of Justiciary may exercise its supervisory jurisdiction: *Reynolds v. Christie* 1988 S.L.T. 68. The exercise by the Secretary of State of a power to refer a criminal case to the High Court of Justiciary under s.263 of the Criminal Procedure (Scotland) Act 1995 is reviewable by the Court of Session: *McDonald v. Secretary of State for Scotland* 1996 S.L.T. 16.

(d) Justice of the peace in civil matters: see *Stakis plc v. Boyd* 1989 S.C.L.R. 290.

(e) District licensing boards. A decision of a licensing board which is not appealable under the Licensing (Scotland) Act 1976 is reviewable: see, e.g. *Main v. City of Glasgow District Licensing Board* 1987 S.L.T. 305; *Tait v. City of Glasgow District Licensing Board* 1987 S.L.T. 340; *Argyll Arms (McManus) Ltd v. Lorn, Mid-Argyll etc., Licensing Board* 1988 S.L.T. 290; *J. & J. (Inns) Ltd v. Angus District Licensing Board* 1992 S.L.T. 931; *Brechin Golf and Squash Club v. Angus District Licensing Board* 1993 S.L.T. 547.

(f) Valuation Appeal Committee: see, e.g. *I.C.I. plc v. Central Region Valuation Appeal Committee* 1988 S.L.T. 106.

(g) Reporter to the Secretary of State for Scotland. This is a reporter who determines an appeal to the Secretary of State under, e.g. the Town and Country Planning (Scotland) Act 1997: see, e.g. *City of Aberdeen D.C. v. Hickman* 1993 S.C.L.R. 488.

(h) Upper Tribunal. This is the tribunal constituted by the Tribunals, Courts and Enforcement Act 2007. In *Eba v Advocate General* [2011] UKSC 29 and *R (Cart) v The Upper Tribunal* [2011] UKSC 28, the UK Supreme Court held that unappealable decisions of the Upper Tribunal were subject to the supervisory jurisdiction of the Court of Session. Adopting the second-tier appeals criteria, such decisions could be subject to judicial review if some important point of principle or practice was raised or there was some other compelling reason for the court to hear the case. The UK Supreme Court thus upheld the Inner House but for different reasons in *Eba v Advocate General*, 2011 S.C. 70 (First Div.) in which the Inner House observed that a decision of the Upper Tribunal in exercise of its judicial review jurisdiction transferred to it from the Court of Session might not be amenable to judicial review in the Court of Session. Lord Hope considered, obiter, that the same test ought to apply to unappealable decisions of (other) Scottish tribunals.

(2) Arbiters.

All questions relating to the arbitration, whether about the composition or jurisdiction of an arbitral tribunal, including a single arbitrator (arbiter), is no longer subject to judicial review but is governed by the Arbitration (Scotland) Act 2010 and the Scottish Arbitration Rules contained in the 2010 Act (*Arbitration Application No.3 of 2011*, 2012 S.L.T. 150).

(3) Local authorities.

A local authority has a general jurisdiction to do anything to facilitate or be conducive or incidental to the carrying out of its functions: Local Government (Scotland) Act 1973, s.69(1). In addition to this a local authority exercises other particular functions as education authority, valuation authority, council tax authority, planning authority, public authority, fire authority, etc. The core of a local authority's jurisdiction is conferred by the Local Government (Scotland) Act 1973. Additional jurisdiction is conferred by individual statutes applicable to specific areas (e.g. Social Work etc. (Scotland) Act 1968). Local authorities, like government ministers, exercise, inter alia, an executive function and a legislative function. Both of these functions may involve the exercise of a jurisdiction which has to be exercised intra vires and is reviewable: see, e.g. *Nicol v. Magistrates of Aberdeen* (1870) 9 M. 306; *Caledonian Railway Co. v. Glasgow Corporation* (1905) 7 F. 1020; *Moss' Empires v. Assessor for Glasgow* 1917 S.C.(H.L.) 1; *Walker v. Strathclyde R.C.* 1986 S.C. 1; *Tarmac Econowaste Ltd v. Assessor for Lothian Region* 1991 S.L.T. 77.

(3A) Scottish Parliament.

The Scottish Parliament is the creature of statute and derives its' powers from statute and, unless otherwise excluded, the courts are the final authority in the interpretation of the governing legislation of the Parliament: *Whaley v. Lord Watson of Invergowrie* 2000 S.C. 340 (First Div.) The court may grant a declarator but may not grant interdict, reduction, specific implement or any like order: Scotland Act 1998, s.40(3). It may not grant an order against a member of the Parliament if its effect would be to give relief against the Parliament prohibited by s.40(3): 1998 Act, s.40(4).

(4)   The Crown and ministers.

A minister may act on behalf of the Crown using the prerogative power or a power delegated by statute.

(a)   *Prerogative power.* This is the remaining part of the sovereign's power which has not been delegated to Parliament by statute, and which is exercised by ministers at their discretion. The type of power which is a prerogative power and its rationale for so being has been explained as follows: "Prerogative powers such as those relating to the making of treaties, the defence of the realm, the prerogative of mercy, the grant of honours, the dissolution of Parliament, and the appointment of ministers, as well as others, are not, I think susceptible to judicial review because their nature and subject-matter is such as not to be amenable to the judicial powers. The courts are not the place wherein to determine whether a treaty should be concluded, or the armed forces disposed in a particular manner and Parliament dissolved on one date or another.": *Council of Civil Service Unions v. Minister for the Civil Service* [1985] A.C. 374, 418B per Lord Roskill. A new prerogative power cannot now be created (*B.B.C. v. Johns* [1965] Ch. 32) but an existing power may be modified by statute (*Attorney-General v. De Keyser's Royal Hotel* [1920] A.C. 508; *Burmah Oil Ltd v. Lord Advocate* 1964 S.C.(H.L.) 117). The predominant view is that a decision based solely on a prerogative power is not reviewable in England: *Chandler v. Director of Public Prosecutions* [1964] A.C. 763; *Blackburn v. Attorney General* [1971] 1 W.L.R. 1037. It is thought that this is also the Scottish position: see, e.g. *McCormick v. Lord Advocate* 1953 S.C. 396; *Gibson v. Lord Advocate* 1975 S.C. 136, 143 per Lord Keith.

(b)   *Delegated (statutory) power.* This is power given to a minister by statute. A decision using such a power is reviewable; see, e.g. re delegated legislation, *Air 2000 v. Secretary of State for Scotland (No. 2)* 1990 S.L.T. 335, *Singh v. Secretary of State for the Home Department* 1990 S.L.T. 300; and re delegated executive decision, *Lakin v. Secretary of State for Scotland* 1988 S.L.T. 780, *London and Clydeside Estates Ltd v. Secretary of State for Scotland* 1987 S.L.T. 459, *Ryrie (Blingery) Wick v. Secretary of State for Scotland* 1988 S.L.T. 806, *Johnston v. Secretary of State for Scotland* 1992 S.L.T. 387 and *Mensah v. Secretary of State for the Home Department* 1992 S.L.T. 177.

(5)   Trustees of public trusts.

The trustees must have a "jurisdiction" delegated to them either by statute or by private instrument: *West v. Secretary of State for Scotland* 1992 S.C. 385, 412-413 per L.P. Hope. It is suggested that for the trustees to have such a jurisdiction, the trust must have a public purpose: see, e.g. *Magistrates of Perth v. Trustees of the Road from Queensferry to Perth* (1756) Kilkerron's Notes, Brown's Suppl., Vol. 5, 318; *D. & J. Nicol v. Dundee Harbour Trs.* 1915 S.C.(H.L.) 7.

(6)   Other statutory and non-statutory bodies.

The body must be an administrative body to which a "jurisdiction" has been delegated: *West*, above, per L.P. Hope at pp. 412-413. It is suggested that such a body to which an administrative jurisdiction has been delegated by statute or private instrument must have some public or quasi-judicial function. Thus corporate bodies with purely private functions, e.g. banks, manufacturing companies, retailing companies, etc., would not be covered. On the other hand corporate bodies with public functions, e.g. regulatory organisations (commonly referred to as "quangos" (quasi-autonomous non-governmental organisations)) would be covered. Each body must be considered on its own facts. The following have been held to exercise a jurisdiction which is reviewable—

(a)   Financial services regulatory organisation: *Bank of Scotland v. Investment Management Regulatory Organisations Ltd* 1989 S.C. 107.

(b)   Scottish Legal Aid Board: see, e.g. *K. v. Scottish Legal Aid Board* 1989 S.L.T. 617; *Venter v. Scottish Legal Aid Board* 1993 S.L.T. 147.

(c)   Criminal Injuries Compensation Board: *Gray v. Criminal Injuries Compensation Board* 1993 S.L.T. 28.

(d)   Public broadcasting authorities: see, e.g. *Wilson v. Independent Broadcasting Authority* 1979 S.C. 351; and *Wilson v. Independent Broadcasting Authority (No. 2)* 1988 S.L.T. 276.

(e)   Agricultural Marketing Boards: see, e.g. *Barrs v. British Wool Marketing Board* 1957 S.C. 72.

(f)   Forestry Commissioners: *Kincardine and Deeside D.C. v. Forestry Commissioners* 1992 S.L.T. 1180.

(g)   Harbour and airport authorities: see, e.g. *Air Ecosse Ltd v. Civil Aviation Authority* 1987 S.L.T. 751; *Peterhead Towage Services Ltd v. Peterhead Bay Authority* 1992 S.L.T. 593.

(h)   Monopoly public industries: *British Oxygen Company Ltd v. South of Scotland Electricity Board* 1956 S.C.(H.L.) 112.

(i)   Housing Benefit Review Boards: *Macleod v. Banff and Buchan Housing Benefit Review Board* 1988 S.L.T. 753.

(j)   The Keeper of the Registers of Scotland: *Short's Tr. v. The Keeper of the Registers* 1994 S.C. 122, aff'd 1996 S.C.(H.L.) 14; *Millar & Bryce Ltd v. Keeper of the Registers of Scotland* 1997 S.L.T. 1000.

(k)   The Scottish Football Association: *St Johnstone Football Club v. Scottish Football Association Ltd* 1965 S.L.T. 171.

(l)   Universities: *Naik v. University of Stirling* 1994 S.L.T. 449; *Carlton v. Glasgow Caledonian University* 1994 S.L.T. 549.

(m)   Rail authorities: *Highland R.C. v. British Railway Board* 1996 S.L.T. 274.

(n)   Chief Constable: *Looney v. Chief Constable Strathclyde Police* 1997 S.C.L.R. 367; *Thomson v. Chief Constable of Grampian Police* 2001 S.C. 443 (police pension regulations).

(o)   Political parties: *Brown v. Executive Committee of Edinburgh Labour Party* 1995 S.L.T. 985.

(p)   Housing associations: *Boyle v. Castlemilk East Housing Co-operative Ltd* 1998 S.L.T. 56.

(q)   Adjudicators (creatures in construction contracts by virtue of the Housing Grants, Construction and Regeneration Act 1996): They are equiperated with arbiters. See *Ballast Plc v. The Burrell Company (Construction Management) Ltd* 2001 S.L.T. 1039 (OH), *Homer Burgess Ltd v. Chirex (Annan) Ltd* 2000 S.L.T. 277 (OH) and *SL Timber Systems Ltd v. Carillion Construction Ltd* 2002 S.L.T. 997 (OH).

There is some doubt whether the decision of a club which is owned by its members involves the exercise of a jurisdiction for the purposes of judicial review: see *Graham v. Ladeside of Kilbirnie Bowling Club* 1990 S.C. 365.

(B)   The type of conduct which may be reviewed.

The conduct must involve the exercise of a jurisdiction: *West v. Secretary of State for Scotland* 1992 S.C. 385, 412 per L.P. Hope. Where the decision is simply to enter into a contract which could be entered into by private persons, the decision is not reviewable: *West*, above. On a "decision" which was not reviewable, see *Maguire v. Secretary of State for Scotland*, 9th March 1994 (1994 G.W.D. 17-1044). Suspension from duties of a chief executive could not be judicially reviewed because the true nature of the dispute was contractual: *Blair v. Lochaber B.C.* 1995 S.L.T. 407. In *WM Fotheringham & Son v. The British Limousin Cattle Society Ltd*, 6th August 2002, unreported (OH), it was held that the true nature of the dispute was an action of reparation for breach of s. 18 of the Competition Act 1998 by abuse of a dominant position and not a challenge of the validity of bye-laws which caused the loss.

The jurisdiction of the court is not, however, limited to something identifiable as a "decision"; it includes, for example, acts, omissions and statements denying the alleged rights are subject to review, the wider basis of the jurisdiction being recognised by the terms of r. 58.6(4): *Elmsford Ltd v. City of Glasgow Council (No.2)* , 2001 S.C. 267 (declaration of rights of access over strip of land where local authority by its acts, omissions and statements over a period of time denying alleged rights).

(C)   The availability of any other statutory remedy.

The supervisory jurisdiction is residuary to the court's appellate jurisdiction. The petitioner must have had no other statutory remedy available to him or have exhausted any such remedy: r. 58.3(1); e.g., *D, Ptnr*, 2011 S.L.T. 101 (OH) (competent to review sheriff's decision to refuse legal aid in children's referral). Often there exist special statutory appeal procedures from a person's exercise of a jurisdiction. If these exist, then, subject to exceptional circumstances, the aggrieved person may not apply to the supervisory jurisdiction for judicial review: see, e.g. *Crawford v. Lennox* (1852) 14 D. 1029; *Maclachlan v. Rutherford* (1854) 16 D. 937; *Philp v. Reid* 1927 S.C. 224; *British Railways Board v. Glasgow Corporation* 1976 S.C. 224; *Simpson v. Inland Revenue Commissioners* 1992 S.L.T. 1069; *Sangha v. Secretary of State for Home Department* 1997 S.L.T. 545 (faulty advice by agent or lay adviser not exceptional circumstances). Exceptional circumstances may include where the decision-maker breached his statutory duty to inform the aggrieved person of the right of appeal under statute: *Moss' Empires v. Assessor for Glasgow* 1917 S.C.(H.L.) 1. See also discussion of s. 45(b) of the C.S.A. 1988 in note 58.3.4.

Where a remedy is available under another specific procedure in the Rules, a petition for judicial review may be refused as incompetent: see note 58.1.2.

(D)   Title and interest to sue or standing.

In *AXA General Insurance Co Ltd v Lord Advocate*, 2012 S.C. (UKSC) 122, it was held that the private law rule that title and interest had to be shown has no place in applications to the court's supervisory jurisdiction. The correct approach, as held in *AXA General Insurance*, above, is based on a concept of interests rather than a concept of rights, and a party has to show "standing" based upon a sufficient interest: *AXA General Insurance*, above, paras.F [62] and [170]. See further comments on standing in *Walton v. Scottish Ministers*, 2013 S.C. (UKSC) 67, per Lord Reed, p.90 paras [89] et seq, and Lord Hope of Craighead, p.103, para. [151] et seq.

The old law was as follows.

The petitioner must have title and interest to sue, otherwise the petition will be irrelevant. There is no comprehensive definition of what amounts to title and interest in relation to the exercise of a jurisdiction which is complained of. It has been said that the petitioner "must be a party (using the word in its widest sense) to some legal relationship which gives him some right which the person against whom he raised the action either infringes or denies": *D. & J. Nicol v Dundee Harbour Trs* 1915 S.C.(H.L.) 7, 12 per

Lord Dunedin; see also, e.g. *Simpson v. Edinburgh Corporation* 1960 S.C. 313. A commercial interest per se does not give title or interest to sue: *Bondway Properties Ltd v. City of Edinburgh Council* 1999 S.L.T. 127.

A council tax payer has a clear title and interest to see local authority accounts as a "person interested" under s. 101(1) of the Local Government (Scotland) Act 1973, and his motive for doing so is irrelevant: *Stirrat v. City of Edinburgh Council* 1999 S.L.T. 274.

The petitioner must have title and interest at or about the time of the presentation of the petition and not at some point in the future: *Shaw v. Strathclyde R.C.* 1988 S.L.T. 313; see also *Air 2000 v. Secretary of State for Scotland (No. 2)* 1990 S.L.T. 335. The petitioner may become personally barred from proceeding by judicial review: see (F) below.

(E)   Grounds of review under supervisory jurisdiction.

Where the petition is competent the court will, in exercise of its supervisory jurisdiction, review the decision to see whether it is defective thereby entitling the petitioner to the remedy which he seeks. There is no substantial difference between English law and Scots law on the grounds of defectiveness: *West v. Secretary of State for Scotland* 1992 S.C. 385, 413 per L.P. Hope. Accordingly English cases may be referred to. There are a number of grounds of defectiveness, for which see Council of *Civil Service Unions v. The Minister for the Civil Service* [1985] A.C. 374 per Lord Diplock and 414F et seq. per Lord Roskill.

(F)   Mora, taciturnity and acquiescence.

A petitioner may become personally barred from pursuing a judicial review because, e.g. of delay or silence indicating acquiescence: *Hanlon v. Traffic Commissioner* 1988 S.L.T. 802 (petition 10 months after decision); *Ingle v. Ingle's Tr.* 1997 S.L.T. 160 (acquiescence in decision of sheriff over four years earlier); and see *McIntosh v. Aberdeenshire Council* 1999 S.L.T. 93 (obiter); *Devine v. McPherson*, 2002 S.L.T. 213 (delay of seven months for judicial review of planning decision inferred acquiescence in its validity). See also *Hendrick v. Chief Constable, Stathclyde Police*, 2014 S.L.T. 382 (Extra Div) (22 months).

TIME LIMIT.

58.3.4   Section 27A(1) of the Act of 1988, inserted by s. 89 of the Courts Reform (Scotland) Act 2014, provides that an application to the supervisory jurisdiction must be made before the end of three months beginning with the date on which the grounds giving rise to the application first arise or such longer period as the court considers equitable having regard to the circumstances. This was recommendation in Chap. 12 of the Civil Courts Review. Section 27A(1) does not apply if, by virtue of any enactment, application is to be made in less than three months.

FORM OF PETITION.

58.3.5   The petition must be in Form 58.6: r. 58.6(1). The petition must be signed by counsel or other person having a right of audience: r. 4.2(3); and see r. 1.3(1) (definition of "counsel" and "other person having a right of audience") and note 1.3.4.

The form of petition (see r. 58.6 and Form 58.6) provides for an abbreviated style of pleading. In *Somerville v. The Scottish Ministers*, 2008 S.C. (H.L.) 45, 69 at para. [65], Lord Hope of Craighead commented as follows on the requirements of a petition. The degree of precision and detail in written pleading traditionally looked for in other forms of action is not looked for in petitions for judicial review. The core requirements are that the factual history is set out succinctly and the issues of law should be clearly identified. The aim is to focus the issues so that the court can reach a decision upon them, in the interests of sound administration and in the public interest, as soon as possible.

Where the petition is in respect of a decision of an adjudicator appointed under s. 12 of the Immigration Act 1971, the Home Secretary should be called as respondent and the adjudicator should receive intimation as a person having an interest: P.N. No. 1 of 1992.

"ALL RELEVANT DOCUMENTS IN THE PETITIONER'S POSSESSION".

58.3.6   The general rule is that where any party founds on, or incorporates, a document in his pleadings he must, so far as the document is in his possession or within his control, lodge it in process with those pleadings: r. 27.1(1). R. 58.6(2) extends the general rule by requiring all relevant documents to be lodged whether or not the petitioner founds on or incorporates them in his pleadings.

The proper evidence to be produced in reduction of a decree, those decrees being *in publica custodia*, is an extract: *Miller & Son v. Oliver & Boyd* (1901) 9 S.L.T. 287, 287 per Lord Pearson. In *Miller* the arbiter refused to allow the decree arbitral to be lodged until his fees had been paid. The pursuers declined to pay those fees and the court held that the onus of production of a decree arbitral under reduction was on the defenders. It is not competent to bring a decree under review by reduction until it has been extracted (*Scouler v. McLaughlan* (1864) 2 M. 955, 959 per Lord Mackenzie), although reduction of an unextracted decree may be permitted in special circumstances (*Scouler*, above, per L.P. McNeill at p. 962). Where an extract of the decree sought to be reduced is available or can be obtained, it is lodged by the pursuer when the summons is signeted.

SCHEDULE OF DOCUMENTS.

The purpose of the schedule of documents is to let the judge know the identity and location of any document which the petitioner founds on but is outwith his possession or control. The document may be located (a) in the hands of any party named as respondent in the petition or (b) in the hands of any other person.

Where the document is in the hands of the respondent, the petitioner may (a) at any time before or after the presentation of the petition apply for an order under s. 1 of the Administration of Justice (Scotland) Act 1972 (see Chaps. 35 and 64); or (b) at the first hearing make a motion for the production of the document under r. 58.9(2)(b)(vii) (see, e.g. *Kelly, Petr.* 1985 S.C. 333). When the document is in the hands of a person who has not appeared in the petition the petitioner may only apply for an order under the Administration of Justice (Scotland) Act 1972.

AFFIDAVITS.

Affidavits are extensively used in judicial review procedure in place of oral evidence. Once again the reasoning behind this is to provide speed and flexibility. The deponent of the affidavit does not need to be the petitioner. The deponent should be a person who has direct knowledge of the conduct sought to be reviewed.

The affidavit should be in the form of a statement of evidence written in the first person. The affidavit should contain evidence in support of, and expanding, the averments in the petition. It should be sworn and signed by the deponent before any person who may competently take an oath. Such a person may include a notary public (including one who has ceased to be a solicitor), a justice of the peace, a sheriff, or any judge. The person taking the oath should also sign the affidavit. Witnesses to an affidavit are unnecessary. And see definition of affidavit in r. 1.3(1).

PROTECTIVE EXPENSES ORDERS

An applicant for judicial review may seek a protective expenses order. This is an order which regulates the liability for expenses in the proceedings (including as to the future) of all or any of the parties to them, with the overall aim of ensuring that proceedings are not prohibitively expensive for the applicant. See further, Chap. 58A.

The petition: intimation and service

58.4.—(1) When a petition is lodged, the Lord Ordinary must make an order specifying—

    (a)   such intimation, service and advertisement as may be necessary;

    (b)[1] the period in which any respondent or interested party who intends to participate in the decision whether permission should be granted must, if so advised, lodge answers and any relevant documents (see rule 58.6(1));

    (c)[2] the period in which any respondent or interested party who only intends to contest the petition if permission is granted must, if so advised, give notice of that intention (see rule 58.6(2)).

    (2) That order must, except where the Lord Ordinary orders otherwise, require—

    (a)   intimation, service and advertisement to take place within 7 days from the date of the order;

    (b)   the lodging of answers and relevant documents to take place within 21 days from the date of service;

    (c)   notification of intention to contest to take place within 21 days from the date of service.

    (3) If a party seeks any of the things in paragraph (5), that party must apply by motion.

    (4) The Lord Ordinary must have regard to the need for the speedy determination of the petition when ordering any of the things in paragraph (5).

    (5) Those things are—

    (a)   dispensing with intimation, service or advertisement;

    (b)   adjusting the period for intimation, service or advertisement;

    (c)   adjusting the period for intimation of intention to contest and the lodging of answers and any relevant documents;

---

[1] Rule 58.4(1)(b) amended by S.S.I. 2017 No. 200 r. 2(6)(a) (effective 17th July 2017).
[2] Rule 58.4(1)(c) amended by S.S.I. 2017 No. 200 r. 2(6)(a) (effective 17th July 2017).

    (d)   *[Revoked by the Act of Sederunt (Rules of the Court of Session 1994 Amendment) (Withdrawal of Agents and Judicial Review) 2017 (S.S.I. 2017 No. 200) r. 2(6)(b) (effective 17th July 2017).]*

    (e)   urgent consideration of the petition;

    (f)   a discretionary transfer to the Upper Tribunal under section 20(1)(b) of the 2007 Act;

    (g)   an interim order; or

    (h)   a sist for legal aid.

    (6)   Where a party seeks urgent consideration of the petition, the motion must set out—

    (a)   the need for urgency,

    (b)   the timescale sought for the court to consider permission, and

    (c)   the date by which the substantive hearing should take place.

    (7)[1]   A sist for legal aid must be for no longer than two months, but can be renewed on cause shown.

    (8)   The clerk of court must notify the Scottish Legal Aid Board of a sist for legal aid.

GENERAL NOTE.

58.4.1   Under the former r. 58.7 (first order), the Lord Ordinary could refuse to grant a first order. That, now, is not possible because the Lord Ordinary must make an order for service and intimation under r. 58.4(1). Whether to allow the petition to proceed is postponed to the permission stage, which is within 14 days of the expiry of the period for lodging answers, under r. 58.7.

    It used to be possible to have consideration of a petition and to dispose of at the first order stage: see *Sokha v. Secretary of State for the Home Department*, 1992 S.L.T. 1049; *Butt v Secretary of State for the Home Department unreported 15th March 1995*. The test was laid down in EY v. Secretary of State for the Home Department, 2011 S.C. 388 (Extra Div).

    On lodging the petition, it is scrutinised and registered by a clerk of session in the Petition Department. A motion is enrolled by the petitioner for a first order and any interim orders. The clerk will ascertain if any caveat (on which, see Chap. 5) has been lodged on behalf of a respondent. The existence or otherwise of a caveat will be docquetted on the backing of the petition by the clerk. If there is a caveat, a copy of it will be placed with the process. The process is taken by a clerk of session from the Petition Department to the Keeper of the Rolls. If a caveat has been lodged in respect of an order which the petitioner seeks in the first order, intimation of the petition and of the hearing for the first order will be given to the respondent or his agent by a clerk in the office of the Keeper of the Rolls. A record of the intimation will be marked in the Motion Sheet. The Keeper will arrange for the motion for the first order to be heard by a nominated judge. The process is then taken to the nominated judge's clerk. At the arranged time the cause will be called. On the first order being pronounced, the period of notice is noted by the clerk of court in the Minute of Proceedings.

    In relation to judicial review of unappealable decisions refusing leave to appeal, the Court of Session must limit the use of its powers to cases in which the error of law raises either: (a) some important point of principle or practice which is an issue of general importance and not confined to the petitioner's own facts and circumstances; or (b) some other compelling reason (such as decisions that are perverse or plainly wrong or where, due to some procedural irregularity, the petitioner has not had a fair hearing): *SA v. Secretary of State for the Home Department*, 2014 S.C. 1, 11, para. [35] (Second Div) applying *Eba v. Advocate General*, 2012 S.C. (UKSC) 1, 16, paras. [48] and [49]. The petition must aver a specific error and either the important point of principle or practice or the other compelling reason; it must cry out for consideration and not just be potentially arguable.

    In relation to judicial review of decisions relating to immigration or asylum cases from the Upper Tribunal, the court will ordinarily order: (a) service on the Advocate General, within 7 days; (b) the respondent to lodge answers within four weeks of service; and (c) fix a date for a procedural first hearing: P.N. No. 1 of 2012, para. 8. At the procedural first hearing the Lord Ordinary will consider the pleadings and issues, parties' preparedness, likely duration of the first hearing and exercise the powers in r. 58.9 (first hearing). In practice, the question of whether the *Eba* (second appeals) test is met is determined at the procedural first hearing. The procedural first hearing would now be the permission stage.

"IS LODGED".

58.4.2   A petition is lodged when it is presented and accepted by the Petition Department: In *Tor Corporate AS v. Simopec Group Star Petroleum Corporation Ltd* , 2008 S.C. 303 (Extra Div.) it was held that a peti-

---

[1] As amended by the Act of Sederunt (Rules of the Court of Session 1994 Amendment) (Miscellaneous) 2021 (S.S.I. 2021 No. 22) r. 2(4) (effective 22nd February 2021).

tion is presented or lodged on the date it is accepted in the Petition Dept. (with the necessary process and fee (unless there is an account arrangement)) and not handed back or stated as not being accepted as being lodged, and not when it is later date-stamped and registered. It is important, therefore, for evidential purposes that the clerk of session at least date-stamps if not registers a petition when presented.

"INTIMATION, SERVICE AND ADVERTISEMENT".

See Chap. 16.

58.4.3

"ANSWERS".

For form, see r. 18.3 and notes.

58.4.4

The answers should give notice of the argument against the order sought in the petition: see comments in *Blair v. Lochaber DC*, 1995 S.L.T. 407, 408D per Lord Clyde. Having regard to the consideration at the permission stage of whether to allow the application to proceed (which may be dealt with without an oral hearing), if permission is to be opposed, the answers may have to contain what amounts to a submission on that issue (or the submission could be better attached as a schedule or appendix to the answers to the petition itself.

The answers should address the matter of whether permission to proceed should be given: PN No. 3 of 2017, para. 11.

"WITHIN 7 (OR 21) DAYS".

The date from which the period is calculated is not counted. Where the last day falls on Saturday or Sunday or a public holiday on which the Office of Court is closed, the next available day is allowed: r. 13(7). For office hours and public holidays, see note 3.1.2.

58.4.5

"MOTION".

For motions, see Chap.23.

58.4.6

"INTERIM ORDER".

This includes interim interdict, interim suspension, interim liberation, and any interim order which the court may make and relates to the merits of the petition. In this context it does not include an order for the production of documents: *Kelly, Petr.*, 1985 S.C. 333; cf. r. 58.9(2)(b)(vii). A caveat may be lodged against any interim order sought in a petition for judicial review: r. 5.1(c).

58.4.7

TRANSFER TO UPPER TRIBUNAL.

When enrolling for a first order, if the petitioner considers it appropriate for the judicial review to be transferred to the Upper Tribunal under s. 20(1)(b) of the Tribunals, Courts and Enforcement Act 2007, that should be indicated in the motion: P.N. No. 3 of 2008, para. 3 and now r. 58.4(3) and (5)(f). If there has not been a hearing to determine that question, and the respondent wishes to apply for transfer, he should intimate to the petitioner after service on him of the petition. Thereafter any party may enrol for transfer. See P.N. No. 3 of 2008 and now r. 58.5(2).

58.4.8

Proceedings which may be transferred to the Upper Tribunal are, under s. 20(1)(b) of the 2007 Act, those to which Conditions 1, 3 and 4 in s. 20 are met—i.e. the application for judicial review does not seek anything other than an exercise of the supervisory jurisdiction of the court, the subject matter of the application is not a devolved matter, and it does not call into question decisions made under certain enactments in s. 20(4). There are certain applications for judicial review that must be transferred to the Upper Tribunal; and see r. 58.5(1).

The Lord Ordinary has a discretionary power which he can exercise at his own motion to transfer an application in which those conditions are met: see r. 58.5(4).

The 2007 Act provides a new judicial structure for a host of UK tribunals with a First-tier Tribunal and an Upper Tribunal (dealing with appeals from the First-tier and judicial review transferred from the courts).

On transfers to the Upper Tribunal, see r. 58.5.

PROTECTIVE EXPENSES ORDER.

An applicant for judicial review may seek a protective expenses order. This is an order which regulates the liability for expenses in the proceedings (including as to the future) of all or any of the parties to them, with the overall aim of ensuring that proceedings are not prohibitively expensive for the applicant. See further, Chap. 58A.

58.4.9

The petition: transfers to the Upper Tribunal

58.5.—(1) If the conditions in section 20(1)(a) of the 2007 Act are met, instead of determining permission under rule 58.7, the Lord Ordinary must make an order transferring the application to the Upper Tribunal.

58.5

(2) If paragraph (3) applies, the Lord Ordinary may make an order transferring the application to the Upper Tribunal—

    (a)   instead of determining permission under rule 58.7;

(b)   after determining permission; or

(c)   at any subsequent hearing.

(3)   This paragraph applies if—

(a)   the conditions in section 20(1)(b) of the 2007 Act are met, and

(b)   the Lord Ordinary is satisfied that it is in all the circumstances appropriate to transfer the application.

(4)   The Lord Ordinary may make an order under paragraph (2) whether or not such an order was sought in the petition or was sought by motion by any party to the proceedings, but if no such order was sought, the parties must be heard before making an order.

(5)   Where the Lord Ordinary makes an order transferring the application to the Upper Tribunal under paragraph (1) or (2), an order may be made in respect of any expenses incurred by the parties up to that point.

MANDATORY TRANSFER TO UPPER TRIBUNAL.

58.5.1   Certain applications for judicial review must be transferred to the Upper Tribunal under s. 20(1)(a) of the Tribunals, Courts and Enforcement Act 2007. These are those in which, under s. 20(1)(a), Conditions 1, 2 and 4 are met—i.e. the application for judicial review does not seek anything other than an exercise of the supervisory jurisdiction of the court, the application falls within a class specified by act of sederunt made with the consent of the Lord Chancellor, and it does not call into question decisions made under certain enactments in s. 20(4). The A.S. (Transfer of Judicial Review Applications from the Court of Session) 2008 [S.S.I. 2008 No. 357] specifies the class of application as an application which challenges a procedural decision of a procedural ruling of the First-tier Tribunal established under s. 3(1) of the Tribunals, Courts and Enforcement Act 2007.

The 2007 Act provides a new judicial structure for a host of UK tribunals with a First-tier Tribunal and an Upper Tribunal (dealing with appeals from the First-tier and judicial review transferred from the courts).

DISCRETIONARY TRANSFER TO UPPER TRIBUNAL.

58.5.2   Parties may not have sought to transfer an application for judicial review to the Upper Tribunal in an appropriate case at the time that the petition was presented. The Lord Ordinary has a discretionary power to transfer a case at his own motion to the Upper Tribunal where, under s. 20(1)(b) of the Tribunals, Courts and Enforcement Act 2007, Conditions 1, 3 and 4 of s. 20 are met. These are that the application for judicial review does not seek anything other than an exercise of the supervisory jurisdiction of the court, the subject matter of the application is not a devolved matter, and it does not call into question decisions made under certain enactments in s. 20(4).

The 2007 Act provides a new judicial structure for a host of UK tribunals with a First-tier Tribunal and an Upper Tribunal (dealing with appeals from the First-tier and judicial review transferred from the courts).

The petition: participation in the permission stage and intention to contest

58.6   **58.6.**—(1)   A person served with the petition who intends to participate in the decision whether permission should be granted must lodge answers within the period ordered for the lodging of answers.

(2)   A person served with the petition who—

(a)   does not intend to participate in the decision whether permission should be granted; but

(b)   does intend to contest the petition if permission is granted,

must notify the court and the petitioner of that intention, within the period ordered for notification. That person may not participate in the decision whether permission should be granted.

(3)   A person served with the petition who—

(a)   does not lodge answers within the period ordered for the lodging of answers; and

(b)   does not notify the court of an intention to contest the petition if permission is granted, within the period ordered for notification,

may not participate in the decision whether permission should be granted or contest the petition, unless the Lord Ordinary or the Inner House (as the case may be) orders otherwise.

Once a petition is served, it goes to the "permission stage". A person served with a petition wishing to be heard at the permission stage, whether in support or opposition to permission, must lodge answers (though the court may allow it without answers: r. 58.6(1) and (3)).

There may be an issue of "standing" or sufficient interest to be dealt with: see further, note 58.3.3(D).

A notice to contest the petition if permission is granted should be in the form in Appendix 1 to PN No. 3 of 2017 (see para. 15).

58.6.1

ANSWERS.

The answers should give notice of the argument against the order sought in the petition: see comments in *Blair v. Lochaber DC*, 1995 S.L.T. 407, 408D per Lord Clyde. Having regard to the consideration at the permission stage of whether to allow the application to proceed (which may be dealt with without an oral hearing), if permission is to be opposed, the answers may have to contain what amounts to a submission on that issue (or the submission could be better attached as a schedule or appendix to the answers to the petition itself.

The answers should address the matter of whether permission to proceed should be given: PN No. 3 of 2017, para. 11.

58.6.2

The permission stage

58.7.—(1)[1] Within 14 days from the end of the period for lodging answers the Lord Ordinary must—

58.7

    (a)   decide whether to—

        (i)   grant permission (including permission subject to conditions or only on particular grounds);

        (ii) grant an extension to the time limit under section 27A of the 1988 Act; or

    (b)   order an oral hearing (for the purpose of making those decisions) to take place within 14 days.

(1A)[2] The petitioner, respondent and any other person who has lodged answers to the petition must be given at least 2 days' notice of the oral hearing.

(2) Where permission is refused (or permission is granted subject to conditions or only on particular grounds) without an oral hearing, the Lord Ordinary must give reasons for the decision.

(3)[3] Where an extension to the time limit under section 27A of the Act of 1988 is refused without an oral hearing, the Lord Ordinary must give reasons for the decision.

GENERAL NOTE.

The permission stage is a consequence of the introduction in s. 27B of the Act of 1988, inserted by s. 89 of the Courts Reform (Scotland) Act 2014, of a requirement of leave to apply (the "permission stage" in the modern jargon) for the application to proceed. Paragraph 12 of P.N. No. 3 of 2017 indicates that, where the judge is considering refusing permission, an oral hearing will "ordinarily" be ordered.

58.7.1

By this stage, the Lord Ordinary will have the petition and any answers lodged. The court may grant or refuse permission without an oral hearing (s. 27B(5) of the Act of 1988); but, where it refuses, or grants permission subject to conditions or on limited grounds, reasons must be given (r. 58.7(2)). Permission may be granted subject to conditions or on limited grounds: s. 27B(4) of the Act of 1988.

Where the court refuses permission or grants permission with conditions or on limited grounds *without an oral hearing*, the applicant for permission may, within seven days, request a *review*. The review is heard *at an oral hearing* before a different Lord Ordinary from the one who refused permission. If granted, there is *an oral hearing* before a different Lord Ordinary from the one who refused permission (it could, therefore, be the judge who granted the request for review). See CSA 1988, s. 27C.

Where permission is refused or permission is granted with conditions or on limited grounds at the hearing for permission, or at a review, *after an oral hearing*, the applicant for permission may, within seven days, *appeal* against the decision. See CSA 1988, s. 27D. The appeal is by reclaiming: RCS 1994, r. 58.10.

---

[1] Rule 58.7(1)(a) and (b) substituted by S.S.I. 2017 No. 200 r. 2(7)(a) (effective 17th July 2017).
[2] Rule 58.7(1A) inserted by S.S.I. 2017 No. 200 r. 2(7)(b) (effective 17th July 2017).
[3] Rule 58.7(3) inserted by S.S.I. 2017 No. 200 r. 2(7)(c) (effective 17th July 2017).

There is no right of appeal by the applicant where there is a refusal to grant a request for review of a decision as s. 28 (general right of appeal) of the CSA 1988 is disapplied; but it will be at an oral hearing. There is a right of appeal by the applicant against a refusal to grant permission at a review under s. 27D.

Where permission is refused or permission is granted with conditions or on limited grounds without an oral hearing, the Lord Ordinary must give reasons: r. 58.7(2).

In *Burns v Lord Advocate* 2019 S.L.T. 337 (OH), there was a challenge to the compatibility with ECHR of the provisions for a decision without an oral hearing with no right of appeal against a refusal of permission. Lady Carmichael decided that the provisions did not impair the essence of the right of access to the court. Art. 6 did not require a right of appeal, there was a right of review by another LO; and the provisions represented a proportionate limitation on the right of access to the court. In *Dinsmore v. The Scottish Ministers* [2019] CSOH 18, para. [19], Lord Docherty took the view that, having regard to para. 12 of P.N. No. 3 of 2017, oral hearings should be the norm where the court is minded to refuse permission. He doubted that it was anticipated or intended that there should not be an oral hearing, which he understood to be in the majority of cases where permission was refused. At the reclaiming motion in *Burns*, above, *sub. nom. Prior v Scottish Ministers* 2020 S.C. 528 (First Div.), at pp. 544 *et seq.*, paras. [53]–[60], the court held that there was no breach of the Convention.

The Lord Ordinary will ordinarily order an oral hearing if considering refusing permission: PN No. 3 of 2017, para. 12.

Test for permission.

58.7.2   Section 27B(2) of the Act of 1988 provides that, except in relation to judicial review of unappealable decisions of the Upper tribunal for Scotland, permission may be granted only if the court is satisfied that (a) the applicant has sufficient interest in the subject matter ("standing") and (b) the application has real prospects of success. Following what Lord Drummond Young said in *Carroll v Scottish Borders Council*, 2014 SLT 659, Lady Wolffe held in *O v. Secretary of State for the Home Department* 2016 S.L.T. 545 (OH), at paras. [36] to [38], that the test of "real prospects of success" in s. 27B(2)(b) of the 1988 Act was a fairly low hurdle: in Chambers Dictionary "real" is defined as "actually existing; not counterfeit or assumed; genuine". It may be considered to be the opposite of "fanciful" ... these words are not applied in a vacuum. They are applied having regard to the nature and seriousness of the issue to be argued. It may not be irrelevant to note that the introduction of the test is coupled with the introduction of a time-limit ..., and with the consequence that cases for judicial review might not be as fully presented as hitherto when there was more time in which to investigate and prepare a case. Further, in the application of the test, especially upon a brief consideration of the papers, care should be taken that the better prepared case is not equiparated with the stronger argument. In any event, the test of real prospect of success is, in my view, one which should be flexible in its application having regard to all of the relevant factors."

In the Inner House, in *Wightman v Advocate General* 2018 S.C. 388 (First Div.), para. [9], it was held that a "real prospect" was less than probable success but the prospect must be real, it must have substance.

On "sufficient interest" of the applicant, see note 58.3.3(D) (Title and interest to sue or standing).

In relation to judicial review of unappealable decisions of the Upper Tribunal for Scotland under section 46 of the Tribunals (Scotland) Act 2014, the court may grant permission only if (a) the applicant has sufficient interest, (b) the application has real prospects of success and (c) the application either (i) raises an important point of principle or practice or (ii) there is some other compelling reason for allowing the application to proceed: s. 27B(3) of the Act of 1988. This is the second appeals test in *Eba v. Secretary of State for the Home Department*, 2012 S.C. (UKSC) 1, 16, paras. [48] and [49]. In *SA v. Secretary of State for the Home Department*, 2014 S.C. 1, 11, (Second Div.), paras. [43] and [44], the court stated that the court's role is one of gatekeeper or a sifting one. The petition must aver a specific error on the part of the Upper tribunal in refusing leave and the important point of principle or practice not yet established or the other compelling reason why an appeal should be allowed to proceed. The test is a stringent one designed to allow review only in rare and exceptional cases to ensure that no compelling injustice occurs; it must cry out for consideration and not be just potentially arguable.

In *Eba*, above at para. [48], Lord Hope of Craighead said that the underlying concept of "some important point of principle or practice" was the idea that the issue would require to be one of general importance and not one confined to the petitioner's own facts and circumstances; and "some other compelling reason" would include circumstances where it was clear that the decision was perverse or plainly wrong or where due to some procedural irregularity the petitioner had not had a fair hearing at all.

The court applies the *Eba* test in judicial review of unappealable decisions of the UK Upper tribunal.

Grant of permission.

58.7.3   Following the grant of permission, the Lord Ordinary may make orders for further procedure under r. 58.11(2). The Keeper of the Rolls must fix the dates for the procedural and substantive hearings: r. 58.11(1).

Appeal, reclaiming or review.

58.7.4   Where the court refuses permission or grants permission with conditions or on limited grounds *without an oral hearing*, the applicant for permission may, within seven days, request a *review*. The review is heard *at an oral hearing* before a different Lord Ordinary from the one who refused permission. If granted, there is *an oral hearing* before a different Lord Ordinary from the one who refused permission (it could, therefore, be the judge who granted the request for review). See CSA 1988, s. 27C. For the procedure in a request for a review, see r. 58.8.

Where permission is refused or permission is granted with conditions or on limited grounds at the hearing for permission, or at a review, *after an oral hearing*, the applicant for permission may, within seven days, *appeal* against the decision. See CSA 1988, s. 27D. The appeal is by reclaiming: RCS 1994, r. 58.10.

There is no right of appeal by the applicant where there is a refusal to *grant a request* for review of a decision as s. 28 (general right of appeal) of the CSA 1988 is disapplied. There is a right of appeal by the applicant against a *refusal to grant permission at a review* under s. 27D.

Where a request for a review of a refusal or grant with conditions or limited grounds is refused, the Lord Ordinary is expected, however, to give reasons even though there is no provision requiring it: see *Prior v. Scottish Ministers* 2020 S.C. 528 (First Div.), 544, para. [49].

Where permission has been granted, a respondent who has opposed it, could, it would appear, seek to reclaim under r. 38.2(6). That rule provides for reclaiming with leave within 14 days for interlocutors other than those mentioned in the rest of r. 38.3. Rule 38.8(3), inserted by A.S. (R.C.S.A No. 2) (Causes in the Inner House) 2010 [S.S.I. 2010/30] and as amended by A.S. (R.C.S.A. (No.3) (Courts Reform (Scotland) Act 2014 [S.S.I. 2015/228], provides for reclaiming with leave against interlocutors in a petition for judicial review, other than one determining the application or deciding whether to grant permission. On the face of it, but for r. 38.2(6), the interlocutors excluded from the requirement of leave, could be reclaimed without leave. The intention was probably to prohibit the excluded interlocutors in r. 38.8(3) from being appealable at all until the end of the case in order to ensure speedy disposal of the petition; but that, perhaps, has not been achieved without excluding r.38.2(6).

PROTECTIVE EXPENSES ORDERS.

An applicant for judicial review may seek a protective expenses order. This is an order which regulates the liability for expenses in the proceedings (including as to the future) of all or any of the parties to them, with the overall aim of ensuring that proceedings are not prohibitively expensive for the applicant. See further, Chap. 58A. **58.7.5**

FEE.

The court fee for an oral hearing is payable by each party for every 30 minutes or part thereof. For fee, see, Table of Fees, Pt. I, C, Table as amended, pp. C 1202 et seq.]. The fee may be debited under a credit scheme introduced on 1st April 1976 by P.N. No. 4 of 1976 to the account (if one is kept or permitted) of the agent by the court cashier, and an account will be rendered weekly by the court cashier's office to the agent for all court fees due that week for immediate settlement. An agent not on the credit scheme will have an account opened for the purpose of lodging the fee: P.N. No. 2 of 1995. A debit slip and a copy of the court hearing time sheet will be delivered to the agent's box or sent by DX or post. **58.7.6**

A party litigant must pay cash to the clerk of court at the end of the hearing or, if the hearing lasts more than a day, at the end of each day: P.N. No. 2 of 1995. A receipt will be issued. The assistant clerk of session will acknowledge receipt of the sum received from the clerk of court on the minute of proceedings.

AMENDMENT OF PETITION BEFORE PERMISSION GRANTED.

In *Chong Wang v Scottish Ministers* [2017] CSOH 140, Lady Stacey held that a minute of amendment after the petition was lodged and before permission to proceed was granted was not competent. The amendment was sought because the decision to be judicially reviewed had been superceded by a decision to the same effect on different grounds. Lady Stacey's decision was based on s. 27B(1) of the CSA 1988 (no proceedings may be taken unless permission granted). That appears to overlook the fact that a petition has to be presented in order to seek permission and gives an unrealistic meaning to "no proceedings may be taken". It really means "no proceedings may be proceeded with"; if that were so, why should a petition not be amended to determine the real question? Would the outcome have been different if it had not been a different decision now sought to be judicially reviewed? Why would that matter if the decision was to the same effect as the first? The comments of Lord Carloway, LP, in *MIAB v Secretary of State for the Home Department*, 2016 S.C. 871, 887, para. [63] were not referred to; and the decision in RA, below, was distinguished on its facts. **58.7.7**

In *RA v Secretary of State for the Home Department* [2016] CSOH 182, the petitioner requested a review (under s. 27C(2) and r.58.8) of a decision to refuse permission to proceed and lodged a minute of amendment responding to the answers and raising a new matter not available at the time of lodging the petition (a tribunal decision in an analogous case). Lord Boyd of Duncansby held the minute competent under r. 24.1(2): see note 58.8.2 below.

"TIME LIMIT".

Rule 58.7(1)(a)(ii) provides that whether to grant an extension to the time limit of three months from the date of the decision under s. 27A of the CSA 1988 (this is presumably the Act referred to as the 1988 Act) for making an application for judicial review must be considered at the permission stage. It was observed in *Philp v. Highland Council* 2022 S.L.T. 514, (Extra Div.) 519 at para. [20], that the provision envisages that the issue of time-bar (that is whether the application is out of time) should be considered at the permission stage. **58.7.8**

The permission stage: requesting an oral hearing

58.8

58.8.—(1)[1] A request to review a decision made without an oral hearing, under section 27C(2) of the Act of 1988, is made in Form 58.8.

(2) Where a request is granted, the oral hearing must take place within 7 days.

(3) The petitioner, respondent and any other person who has lodged answers to the petition must be given at least 2 days' notice of the oral hearing.

GENERAL NOTE.

58.8.1

Section 27C of the Act of 1988 provides for a review of a refusal of permission or the grant of permission subject to conditions or on limited grounds which has been made without an oral hearing. The review must be considered by a different judge: s. 27C(4) of the Act of 1988.

AMENDMENTS AT STAGE OF REVIEW.

58.8.2

In *RA v Secretary of State for the Home Department* [2016] CSOH 182, the petitioner requested a review (under s. 27C(2) and r. 58.8) of a decision to refuse permission to proceed and lodged a minute of amendment responding to the answers and raising a new matter not available at the time of lodging the petition (a tribunal decision in an analogous case). Lord Boyd of Duncansby held the minute competent under r. 24.1(2) but it was in the discretion of the court to grant it which would only be in rare and exceptional circumstances because (1) it should not be sufficient to allow it on the basis it responds to answers or to the refusal of permission, (2) the test in s.27B(2)(b) of real prospects of success had to be met (*MIAB v Secretary of State for the Home Department*, 2016 S.C. 871, 887, per Lord Carloway, LP, obiter, at para. [64], save in exceptional circumstances), and (3) the time-limit test in s. 27A had to be met and, save in exceptional circumstances, it would only be where the amendment contained matters not known at the time of lodging the petition. (It cannot be that the reference to "rare and exceptional circumstances" was intended to create a new hurdle of itself for amendment.)

The permission stage: oral hearing

58.9

58.9.—(1) Except on cause shown, an oral hearing must not exceed 30 minutes.

(2) Where permission is refused (or permission is granted subject to conditions or only on particular grounds) at an oral hearing, the Lord Ordinary must give reasons for the decision.

GENERAL NOTE.

58.9.1

This oral hearing includes a review by a different judge of a decision made without an oral hearing refusing permission or granting permission subject to conditions or on limited grounds under s. 27C of the Act of 1988.

LENGTH OF HEARING.

58.9.2

The oral hearing is not to exceed 30 minutes: r. 58.9(1). This suggests that it is not intended that the hearing ever deals with the substantive issue in the application. It is half the time mentioned in *SA v. Secretary of State for the Home Department*, 2014 S.C. 1, 14 (Second Div.), para. [44] as the time for the procedural first hearing on judicial review of an unappealable decision of the Upper Tribunal.

GRANT OF PERMISSION.

58.9.3

Following the grant of permission, the Lord Ordinary may make orders for further procedure under r. 58.11(2). The Keeper of the Rolls must fix the dates for the procedural and substantive hearings: r. 58.11(1).

APPEAL OR RECLAIMING.

58.9.4

Where there has been an oral hearing, there is a right of appeal to the applicant under s. 27D of the Act of 1988 against a refusal of permission or a grant of permission subject to conditions or on limited grounds. The appeal is by reclaiming: r.58.10.

Where permission has been granted, a respondent who has opposed it, could, it would appear, seek to reclaim under r. 38.2(6). That rule provides for reclaiming with leave within 14 days for interlocutors other than those mentioned in the rest of r. 38.3. Rule 38.8(3), inserted by A.S. (R.C.S.A No. 2) (Causes in the Inner House) 2010 [S.S.I. 2010/30] and as amended by A.S. (R.C.S.A. (No.3) (Courts Reform (Scotland) Act 2014 [S.S.I. 2015/228], provides for reclaiming with leave against interlocutors in a petition for judicial review, other than one determining the application or deciding whether to grant permission. On the face of it, but for r. 38.2(6), the interlocutors excluded from the requirement of leave, could be reclaimed without leave. The intention was probably to prohibit the excluded interlocutors in r. 38.8(3) from being appealable at all until the end of the case in order to ensure speedy disposal of the petition; but that, perhaps, has not been achieved without excluding r. 38.2(6).

---

[1] Rule 58.8(1) amended by S.S.I. 2017 No. 200 r. 2(8) (effective 17th July 2017).

FEE.

The court fee for a review hearing is payable by each party for every 30 minutes or part thereof. For fee, see, Table of Fees, Pt. I, C, Table as amended, pp. C 1202 et seq.]. The fee may be debited under a credit scheme introduced on 1st April 1976 by P.N. No. 4 of 1976 to the account (if one is kept or permitted) of the agent by the court cashier, and an account will be rendered weekly by the court cashier's office to the agent for all court fees due that week for immediate settlement. An agent not on the credit scheme will have an account opened for the purpose of lodging the fee: P.N. No. 2 of 1995. A debit slip and a copy of the court hearing time sheet will be delivered to the agent's box or sent by DX or post.

A party litigant must pay cash to the clerk of court at the end of the hearing or, if the hearing lasts more than a day, at the end of each day: P.N. No. 2 of 1995. A receipt will be issued. The assistant clerk of session will acknowledge receipt of the sum received from the clerk of court on the minute of proceedings.

The permission stage: appeal to the Inner House

58.10. An appeal under section 27D(2) of the Act of 1988 (appeals following oral hearings) is made by reclaiming motion (see rule 38.8(d)).

GENERAL NOTE.

Under s. 27D(2) of the Act of 1988 the person making the application can "appeal" within seven days against the decision, refusing permission or granting permission subject to conditions or on limited grounds, made after an oral hearing.

This rule provides that the appeal is by reclaiming motion. This rule is really an annotation, because r. 38.8(d) already provides for appeal under s. 27D(2) to be by reclaiming motion.

The permission stage: where permission is granted

58.11.—(1) When permission is granted, the Keeper of the Rolls must, in consultation with the Lord Ordinary, fix—

(a) a date for the substantive hearing, which must be no later than 12 weeks from the date on which permission is granted, except where the Lord Ordinary is satisfied that a longer period is necessary; and

(b) a date for the procedural hearing (unless the Lord Ordinary is satisfied that a procedural hearing is unnecessary), which must be no later than 6 weeks from the date on which permission is granted, except where the Lord Ordinary is satisfied that a longer period is necessary.

(1A)[1] Where all parties email the Keeper of the Rolls to confirm that they are ready to proceed to the substantive hearing at least 3 days before the procedural hearing, the Lord Ordinary may order the procedural hearing to be cancelled.

(2) When permission is granted, the Lord Ordinary must make such orders for further procedure as are appropriate for the speedy determination of the petition and in particular may order—

(a) service of the petition, answers and relevant documents, on a person not specified in the order made under rule 58.4;

(b) service of the decision granting permission and the date of the hearing on a person specified in the order made under rule 58.4 who lodged answers;

(c) service of the decision granting permission and the date of the hearing on a person specified in the order made under rule 58.4 who did not lodge answers but who did notify the court of an intention to contest the petition;

(d) answers and any relevant documents to be lodged by a party who notified the court of an intention to contest the petition, within such period as may be specified;

(e) adjustment of the pleadings within such period as may be specified;

(f) relevant documents to be marked up to indicate the parts the party intends to rely on;

---

[1] Rule 58.11(1A) inserted by S.S.I. 2017 No. 200 r. 2(9) (effective 17th July 2017).

(g) authorities to be lodged by a certain date, and to be marked up to indicate the parts the party intends to rely on;

(h) notes of argument to be lodged by a certain date;

(i) statements of issues to be lodged by a certain date;

(j) facts founded on by a party at the hearing to be supported by evidence on affidavit to be lodged within such period as may be specified;

(k) parties to write to the court to confirm whether they are ready to proceed to the substantive hearing by a certain date.

(3) Except where the Lord Ordinary orders otherwise, any intimation, service and advertisement must be ordered to take place within 7 days of the date of the interlocutor.

ANSWERS.

58.11.1   See r. 18.3.

INTIMATION, SERVICE AND ADVERTISEMENT.

58.11.2   For methods, see Chap. 16.

DOCUMENTS OR AUTHORITIES.

58.11.3   In *M v Secretary of State for the Home Department* 2016 S.L.T. 280 (OH), Lady Wolffe gave guidance that, where an order is made for a bundle of documents or authorities, a joint bundle should be produced.

The procedural hearing

58.12   **58.12.**—(1) At the procedural hearing the Lord Ordinary must ascertain whether—

(a) the parties have complied with any order made under rule 58.11(2); and

(b) the parties are ready to proceed to the substantive hearing.

(2) At the procedural hearing the Lord Ordinary may make such order for further procedure as is appropriate for the speedy determination of the petition and in particular may make any of the orders listed in rule 58.11(2).

GENERAL NOTE.

58.12.1   At the former first hearing under old r. 58.9(2)(a), it was possible to determine the petition. No such provision is made at the procedural hearing under new r. 58.12. The purpose of the rule is to make sure that parties are ready for the substantive hearing.

In *M v Secretary of State for the Home Department* 2016 S.L.T. 280 (OH), Lady Wolffe gave guidance that the items ordered to be lodged under r. 58.11(2) at the permission stage should be lodged in advance of the hearing (not the morning of the hearing); counsel principally instructed should appear at the procedural hearing.

FEE.

58.12.2   The court fee for a hearing is payable by each party for every 30 minutes or part thereof. For fee, see, Table of Fees, Pt. I, C, Table as amended, pp. C 1202 et seq.]. The fee may be debited under a credit scheme introduced on 1st April 1976 by P.N. No. 4 of 1976 to the account (if one is kept or permitted) of the agent by the court cashier, and an account will be rendered weekly by the court cashier's office to the agent for all court fees due that week for immediate settlement. An agent not on the credit scheme will have an account opened for the purpose of lodging the fee: P.N. No. 2 of 1995. A debit slip and a copy of the court hearing time sheet will be delivered to the agent's box or sent by DX or post.

A party litigant must pay cash to the clerk of court at the end of the hearing or, if the hearing lasts more than a day, at the end of each day: P.N. No. 2 of 1995. A receipt will be issued. The assistant clerk of session will acknowledge receipt of the sum received from the clerk of court on the minute of proceedings.

The substantive hearing

58.13   **58.13.**—(1) At the substantive hearing the Lord Ordinary must hear the parties.

(2) In exercising the supervisory jurisdiction on a petition for judicial review, the Lord Ordinary may—

(a) grant or refuse any part of the petition, with or without conditions;

(b) make any order that could be made if sought in any action or petition including, in particular, an interim order or any order listed in paragraph (3) (whether or not such an order was sought in the petition).

(3) Those orders are—

   (a) reduction;

   (b) declarator;

   (c) suspension;

   (d) interdict;

   (e) implement;

   (f) restitution; and

   (g) payment (whether of damages or otherwise).

GENERAL NOTE.

After the permission stage, the next hearing at which the petition can be determined is at the substantive hearing under r. 58.13. **58.13.1**

An appeal to the Inner House from a relevant Upper Tribunal decision (under s. 46 of the Tribunals (Scotland) Act 2014 or s. 11 of the Tribunals, Courts and Enforcement Act 2007) under s. 27D of the CSA 1988 will be a rehearing; it is not necessary to find that the Lord Ordinary has made an error of or law or fact: *PA v. Secretary of State for the Home Department* 2020 S.C. 515 (First Div.), 525 at para. [33].

POWERS OF COURT.

The court, if it holds that the decision is defective or that there is an apprehended wrong, may grant such order in relation to the decision as it thinks fit: r. 58. This rule re-states the common law position. Once a petition has been presented the court has, except where the cause is directed against the Crown, complete discretion in dealing with the decision on review. It may pronounce an order at its own instance. **58.13.2**

The orders include—

1. *Reduction.* The court may reduce the decision and remit for the decision-maker to reconsider: *McCormick v. Subscription Services Ltd* 1994 G.W.D. 40-2336.

2. Declarator.

3. *Interdict (including interim interdict).* This remedy is not available in a cause against the Crown, though a declaratory order may be available instead: Crown Proceedings Act 1947, s. 21. In the House of Lords, in *Davidson v. The Scottish Ministers*, 2006 S.L.T. 110, it was held that the reference to "civil proceedings" in s. 21 is to be read as not including proceedings for judicial review in respect of the Crown. The bar to certain remedies in s. 21 does not apply, therefore, in judicial review of acts or omissions of the Crown (and *McDonald v. Secretary of State for Scotland*, 1994 S.C. 234 (Second Div.) correctly decided for the wrong reasons). Where a petitioner seeks judicial review of the Crown's conduct as ultra vires of E.C. law, he may be able to obtain interdict against the Crown: *R. v. Secretary of State for Transport, ex parte Factortame Ltd* [1990] 2 A.C. 85 and *R. v. Secretary of State for Transport, ex parte Factortame Ltd (No. 2)* [1991] E.C.R. I-3905; see also Chap. 60.

4. *Suspension.* Particular contractual decisions are not open to challenge by judicial review, and suspension of such decisions will not be granted: *Millar & Bryce Ltd v. Keeper of the Registers of Scotland,* 1997 S.L.T. 1000. Interim suspension is not so distinct from interdict or specific performance as to escape the prohibition in s. 21(1)(a) of the 1947 Act: *Ralston v. The Scottish Ministers*, 2004 S.L.T. 1263 (OH). On suspension generally, see Chap. 60.

5. *Specific implement or specific performance of a statutory duty.* Specific implement is a common law remedy. Specific performance of a statutory duty is available under s. 45(b) of the C.S.A. 1988 (formerly C.S.A. 1868, s. 91). Neither of these remedies is available against the Crown, although a declarator may be available instead: Crown Proceedings Act 1947, s. 21(1). See also note 58.3.4.

6. *Delivery or restoration of possession of violently or fraudulently deprived real or personal property.* Delivery is a common law remedy. Restoration of possession of violently or fraudulently deprived real or personal property is available under s. 45(a) of the C.S.A. 1988 (formerly C.S.A. 1868, s. 91). Neither of these remedies is available against the Crown, although a declarator may be available instead: Crown Proceedings Act 1947, s. 21(1). The remedy under s. 45(a) of the C.S.A. 1988 is not specifically included in r. 58.3(1) and by implication may be excluded from being sought by means of judicial review: see also note 58.3.4.

7. *Damages.* See, e.g. *Mallon v. Monklands D.C.,* 1986 S.L.T. 347. If a petitioner wishes to claim damages, it is desirable that he should claim for and quantify these at the presentation for the petition: see *Shetland Line (1984) Ltd v. Secretary of State for Scotland,* 1996 S.L.T. 653, 658 I per Lord Johnston.

THE DECISION TO BE REVIEWED.

The supervising jurisdiction of the court is not limited to decisions: *Elmsford Ltd v. City of Glasgow Council (No.2)* , 2001 S.C. 267; and see note 58.3.3(B) above. **58.13.3**

FEE

58.13.4   The court fee for a hearing is payable by each party for every 30 minutes or part thereof. For fee, see, Table of Fees, Pt. I, C, Table as amended, pp. C 1202 et seq.]. The fee may be debited under a credit scheme introduced on 1st April 1976 by P.N. No. 4 of 1976 to the account (if one is kept or permitted) of the agent by the court cashier, and an account will be rendered weekly by the court cashier's office to the agent for all court fees due that week for immediate settlement. An agent not on the credit scheme will have an account opened for the purpose of lodging the fee: P.N. No. 2 of 1995. A debit slip and a copy of the court hearing time sheet will be delivered to the agent's box or sent by DX or post. A party litigant must pay cash to the clerk of court at the end of the hearing or, if the hearing lasts more than a day, at the end of each day: P.N. No. 2 of 1995. A receipt will be issued. The assistant clerk of session will acknowledge receipt of the sum received from the clerk of court on the minute of proceedings.

Additional parties

58.14   **58.14.**—(1)   This rule applies to a person who—

    (a)   was not specified in an order made under rules 58.4(1), 58.11(2) or 58.12(2) as a person who should be served with the petition; and

    (b)   is directly affected by an issue raised in the petition.

(2)   That person may apply by motion for leave to enter the process.

(3)   If the motion is granted, the Lord Ordinary or Inner House (as the case may be) must make such orders as are considered appropriate to enable that person to participate in the proceedings.

MOTION

58.14.1   For motions, see Chap. 23.

Transfers to judicial review procedure

58.15   **58.15.**—(1)   The Lord Ordinary may order that a cause raised as an action should proceed as a petition for judicial review, if satisfied that—

    (a)   it should proceed in that way; and

    (b)   the requirements of section 27B(2) or (3) (as the case may be) of the Act of 1988 are met.

(4)   If the Lord Ordinary orders that an action should proceed as a petition for judicial review, it must proceed under rule 58.11 (as if permission had been granted) and the Lord Ordinary must also order—

    (a)   the petitioner to prepare a minute stating—

      (i)   the act, decision or omission to be reviewed;

      (ii)   the remedies which the petitioner seeks; and

      (iii)   the legal grounds of challenge;

      and to intimate the minute and lodge it in process within 7 days;

    (b)   the respondent to lodge and intimate answers to that minute within 14 days thereafter.

(5)   That minute and answers, together with the earlier pleadings, thereafter comprise the pleadings in the proceedings, subject to such further adjustment or amendment as the Lord Ordinary may authorise.

GENERAL NOTE.

58.15.1   This rule allows for a petition for an ordinary action to be converted to proceed as a petition for judicial review (and r. 58.16 allows for a petition for judicial review to be converted to an ordinary action).
    The original rule, r. 58.12 inserted by A.S. (R.C.S.A. No. 5) (Miscellaneous) 2012 [S.S.I. 2012 No. 275], was no doubt influenced by, and resolves one problem in, the discussions in *Ruddy v. Chief Constable, Strathclyde Police,* 2011 S.C. 527, and *Docherty v Scottish Ministers,* 2012 S.C. 150, about whether a claim should be raised as an action or by petition.

MINUTE.

58.15.2   For form of minutes, see r. 15.1.

ANSWERS.

58.15.3   For form of answers, see r. 18.3.

Intimate.

For methods, see r. 16.7

Transfers from judicial review procedure

58.16.—(1) The Lord Ordinary may order that a cause raised as a petition for judicial review should proceed as an ordinary action, if satisfied that it should proceed in that way.

(2) If the Lord Ordinary orders that a petition for judicial review should proceed as an ordinary action, it is withdrawn from the procedure under this Chapter and the Lord Ordinary must order—

    (a)   the pursuer to prepare a minute containing conclusions and pleas in law;

    (b)   the defender to prepare a minute containing pleas in law;

and that those minutes must be lodged in process within 7 days.

(3) Those minutes, together with the earlier pleadings, thereafter comprise the pleadings in the proceedings, subject to such further adjustment or amendment as the Lord Ordinary may authorise.

58.16

General note.

This rule allows for a petition for judicial review to be converted to an ordinary action (and r. 58.15 allows for an action to be converted to a petition for judicial review).

The original rule, r. 58.12 inserted by A.S. (R.C.S.A. No. 5) (Miscellaneous) 2012 [S.S.I. 2012 No. 275], was no doubt influenced by, and resolves one problem in, the discussions in *Ruddy v. Chief Constable, Strathclyde Police,* 2011 S.C. 527, and *Docherty v Scottish Ministers,* 2012 S.C. 150, about whether a claim should be raised as an action or by petition.

58.16.1

Minute.

For form of minutes, see r. 15.1.

58.16.2

Answers.

For form of answers, see r. 18.3.

58.16.3

Intimate.

For methods, see r. 16.7

58.16.4

Public interest intervention

58.17.—(1) This rule applies to a person who—

    (a)   was not specified in an order made under rules 58.4(1), 58.11(2) or 58.12(2) as a person who should be served with the petition; and

    (b)   is not directly affected by any issue raised in the petition.

(2) That person may apply by application for leave to intervene—

    (a)   in the decision whether to grant permission;

    (b)   in a petition which has been granted permission; or

    (c)   in an appeal in connection with a petition for judicial review.

(3) In rules 58.18 to 58.20, "court" means the Lord Ordinary or the Inner House, as the case may be.

58.17

General note.

Rules 58.17 to 58.20 provide for a person or organisation to intervene in a judicial review and make submissions on the ground that the cause raises a matter of public interest (on which see r. 58.19(4)). Leave is required to intervene: r. 58.19(1).

58.17.1

Public interest intervention: the minute of intervention

58.18.—(1) An application for leave to intervene is made by minute of intervention in Form 58.18.

(2) The minute of intervention must set out—

    (a)   the name and description of the applicant;

58.18

> (b) a brief statement of the issue in the proceedings which the applicant wishes to address and the applicant's reasons for believing that this issue raises a matter of public interest; and
>
> (c) a brief statement of the propositions to be advanced by the applicant and the applicant's reasons for believing that they are relevant to the proceedings and that they will assist the court.
>
> (3) The applicant must—
>
> (a) send a copy of the minute to all parties; and
>
> (b) lodge the minute, certifying on it that it has been sent to all parties.

MINUTE OF INTERVENTION.

58.18.1   Form 58.18 must be used. Once leave is granted, a submission must also be lodged in writing or, exceptionally, may be made orally: r. 58.20(4)(b).

SEND.

58.18.2   "Send" includes deliver: see r.1.3(1).

Public interest intervention: the decision of the court

58.19   **58.19.**—(1) The court may, in an application for leave to intervene—

> (a) refuse leave without a hearing;
>
> (b) grant leave without a hearing (unless a hearing is requested); or
>
> (c) refuse or grant leave after a hearing.
>
> (2) A hearing may be held if one of the parties lodges a request for a hearing—
>
> (a) in an application to intervene where the court has not yet granted permission, within 2 days from the date that the minute of intervention was lodged; or
>
> (b) in any other case, within 14 days from the date that the minute of intervention was lodged.
>
> (3) At a hearing, the parties may address the court on whether the intervention will unduly delay or otherwise prejudice the rights of the parties, including their potential liability for expenses.
>
> (4) The court may grant leave only if it is satisfied that—
>
> (a) the proceedings raise a matter of public interest;
>
> (b) the issue in the proceedings which the applicant wishes to address raises a matter of public interest;
>
> (c) the propositions to be advanced by the applicant are relevant to the proceedings and are likely to assist the court; and
>
> (d) the intervention will not unduly delay or otherwise prejudice the rights of the parties, including their potential liability for expenses.
>
> (5) The court may, when granting leave, impose such terms and conditions as it considers desirable in the interests of justice, including making provision in respect of additional expenses incurred by the parties as a result of the intervention.
>
> (6) The clerk of court must give written intimation of a grant or refusal of leave to the applicant and all parties.

GENERAL NOTE.

58.19.1   Leave to intervene is required: r. 58.19(1). The decision to grant or refuse leave may be made with or without a hearing, but a hearing may be requested by one of the parties (which includes the intervener: meaning of "party" and "writ" in r. 1.3(1)). The conditions of r. 58.19(4) must be met for leave to be granted.

PUBLIC INTEREST.

58.19.2   There must be a public interest raised in the proceedings and in the issue the intervener wishes to raise. The phrase "public interest" is not defined.

APPLICANT.

In r. 58.19(4) the reference to the "applicant" must mean the intervener.   **58.19.3**

"WRITTEN INTIMATION".

For methods, see r. 16.9.   **58.19.4**

Public interest intervention: form of intervention

58.20.—(1)   An intervention is by written submission.   **58.20**

(2)   The written submission (including appendices) must not exceed 5000 words.

(3)   The applicant must lodge the written submission and send a copy of it to all parties by such time as the court may direct.

(4)   The court may, in exceptional circumstances—

   (a)   allow a longer written submission;

   (b)   allow an oral submission.

GENERAL NOTE.

Normally the intervener must lodge a written submission. It must be not more than 5,000 words un-   **58.20.1**
less, in exceptional circumstances, longer is permitted under r. 58.20(4)(a). Exceptionally, an oral submission may be permitted: r. 58.20(4)(b).

CHAPTER 58A PROTECTIVE EXPENSES ORDERS IN ENVIRONMENTAL APPEALS AND JUDICIAL REVIEWS

Chapter 58A

Protective Expenses Orders in Environmental Appeals and Judicial Reviews

Application and interpretation of this Chapter

58A.1.—[1,2](1) This Chapter applies to applications for protective expenses orders in—

(a) an appeal under section 56 of the Freedom of Information (Scotland) Act 2002 as modified by regulation 17 of the Environmental Information (Scotland) Regulations 2004;

(b) relevant proceedings which include a challenge to a decision, act or omission which is subject to, or said to be subject to, the provisions of Article 6 of the Aarhus Convention;

(c) relevant proceedings which include a challenge to an act or omission on the grounds that it contravenes the law relating to the environment.

(2) In this Chapter—

"the Aarhus Convention" means the United Nations Economic Commission for Europe Convention on Access to Information, Public Participation in Decision-Making and Access to Justice in Environmental Matters done at Aarhus, Denmark on 25th June 1998;

"protective expenses order" means an order which regulates the liability for expenses in the proceedings, including as to the future, of all or any of the parties to them;

"the public" and "the public concerned" have the meanings given by Article 2 of the Aarhus Convention;

"relevant proceedings" means—

(a) applications to the supervisory jurisdiction of the court, including applications under section 45(b) (specific performance of a statutory duty) of the Act of 1988;

(b) appeals under statute.

(3) Proceedings are to be considered prohibitively expensive for the purpose of this Chapter if the costs and expenses likely to be incurred by the applicant for a protective expenses order—

(a) exceed the financial means of the applicant; or

(b) are objectively unreasonable having regard to—

(i) the situation of the parties;

(ii) whether the applicant has reasonable prospects of success;

(iii) the importance of what is at stake for the applicant;

(iv) the importance of what is at stake for the environment;

(v) the complexity of the relevant law and procedure; and

(vi) whether the case is frivolous.

(4) The costs and expenses mentioned in paragraph (3) are—

(a) the costs incurred by the applicant in conducting the proceedings; and

(b) the expenses for which the applicant would be liable if the applicant was found liable for the taxed expenses of process, without modification.

---

[1] Ch. 58A and r. 58A.1 inserted by S.S.I. 2013 No. 81 (effective 25 March 2013).
[2] Rule 58A.1 substituted by S.S.I. 2018 No. 348 (effective 10 December 2018).

GENERAL NOTE.

58A.1.1 Chapter 58A provides for protective expenses orders in implementation of the EU Directive 2011/92/EU on the assessment of the effects of certain public and private projects on the environment and the Directive 2008/1/EC of the European Parliament and of the Council concerning integrated pollution prevention and control. Chapter 58A should be interpreted in the light of the European Directive and case law in the ECJ: *Carroll v. Scottish Borders Council*, 2014 S.L.T. 659 (OH) per Lord Drummond Young at para. [8]. *R (on the application of Edwards) v Environment Agency [2013]* C.M.L.R. 18, [2013] 1 W.L.R. 2914, the decision of the ECJ set out a number of principles arising out of the previous European Directive. See that case in the UK Supreme Court at [2013] UKSC 78; [2014] 1 WLR 55.

An application for a protective expenses order is competent at common law and the principles to be applied in considering whether to grant an order are set out in *R (on the application of Corner House Research) v Secretary of State for trade and Industry* [2005] 1 W.L.R. 2600 2624, para. 74: *Hillhead Community Council v City of Glasgow Council*, 2015 S.L.T. 239 (OH).

PROTECTIVE EXPENSES ORDERS.

58A.1.2 The availability of such orders at common law was confirmed by Lord Glennie in *McArthur v. Lord Advocate*, 2006 S.L.T. 170 (OH) (a petition for judicial review of decisions of the Lord Advocate under the Fatal Accidents and Sudden Deaths Inquiry (Scotland) Act 1976), which set out the criteria required to be satisfied before a court can make an order; these are:

(f) the issues raised are of general public importance;

(g) the public interest requires that the issues should be resolved;

(h) the applicant should have no private interest in the outcome of the case;

(i) having regard to the financial resources of the applicant and the respondent and to the amount of expenses that are likely to be involved, it is fair and just to make the order;

(j) if the order is not made, the applicant would probably discontinue the proceedings and will be acting reasonably in doing so.

In *McGinty v. Scottish Ministers*, 2014 S.C. 81, an Extra Division upheld a decision of Lady Dorrian (exercising the common law power before Chap. 58A).

In considering whether proceedings are prohibitively expensive, the court must apply a subjective and an objective test: *Gibson v Scottish Ministers*, 2016 S.C. 454, 2016 S.L.T. 319 (Extra Div.), 300, para. [52] (referring to the case of *Edwards*, for which, see note 58.1.1; Lord Carnwath deals with several factors relevant to these tests in that case at paras. 23 and 24 in [2014] 1 W.L.R. 55).

Appeals relating to requests for environmental information

58A.2 **58A.2.**—[1, 2](1) This rule applies to an application for a protective expenses order in proceedings mentioned in rule 58A.1(1)(a).

(2) Where the person who requested the environmental information is a party to the appeal, that person may apply for a protective expenses order.

(3) The application must be made, except on cause shown—

(a) where the applicant is the appellant, no later than is reasonably practicable after the applicant becomes aware that the appeal is defended;

(b) where the applicant is the respondent, no later than the expiry of the period allowed for the lodging of answers.

(4) Where the court is satisfied that the proceedings are prohibitively expensive, it must make a protective expenses order.

GENERAL NOTE.

58A.2.1 The decision in *Carroll v. Scottish Borders Council*, 2014 S.L.T. 659 (OH) provides useful guidance on applications for protective expenses orders. Lord Drummond Young identified four features important in determining whether a protective expenses order should be made. These are—

(1) The applicant must establish that the proceedings fall within the scope of Chap. 58A.

(2) The applicant must demonstrate a sufficient interest in the proceedings.

(3) The order cannot be made if there are no real prospects of success of the proceedings, i.e. there is an arguable case, something more than a remote prospect of success.

(4) The court must consider the financial resources of the applicant and the likely expense of the proceedings; whether the proceedings would be prohibitively expensive is to be viewed objectively.

The financial resources of the applicant should be set out in a production and not the petition in order to maintain confidentiality.

---

[1] Rule 58A.2 inserted by S.S.I. 2013 No. 81 (effective 25th March 2013).
[2] Rule 58A.2 substituted by S.S.I. 2018 No. 348 (effective 10 December 2018).

Public participation in decisions on specific environmental activities

58A.3.—[1,2](1) This rule applies to an application for a protective expenses order in proceedings mentioned in rule 58A.1(1)(b).

58A.3

(2) An application for a protective expenses order may be made by the petitioner or the appellant.

(3) The application must be made, except on cause shown, no later than is reasonably practicable after the applicant becomes aware that the petition or appeal is defended.

(4) The court must make a protective expenses order where it is satisfied that—

    (a) the applicant is a member of the public concerned;

    (b) the applicant has a sufficient interest in the subject matter of the proceedings; and

    (c) the proceedings are prohibitively expensive.

GENERAL NOTE.

In *Carroll v. Scottish Borders Council*, 2014 S.L.T. 659 (OH), Lord Drummond Young commented on the documents to be lodged under r. 58A.3(4)(b) in support of an application.

58A.3.1

"MOTION".

For motions, see Chap. 23.

58A.3.2

Contravention of the law relating to the environment

58A.4.—[3,4](1) This rule applies to an application for a protective expenses order in proceedings mentioned in rule 58A.1(1)(c).

58A.4

(2) An application for a protective expenses order may be made by the petitioner or the appellant.

(3) The application must be made, except on cause shown, no later than is reasonably practicable after the applicant becomes aware that the petition or appeal is defended.

(4) The court must make a protective expenses order where it is satisfied that—

    (a) the applicant is a member of the public; and

    (b) the proceedings are prohibitively expensive.

CAP ON PROTECTIVE EXPENSES ORDER.

Under r. 58A.4(1) the applicant's liability under a protective expenses order is limited to £5,000. There is no cap on a protective expenses order where the common law power may be exercised: see *McGinty v Scottish Ministers*, 2014 S.C. 81 (Extra Division),

58A.4.1

Applications for protective expenses orders

58A.5.—[5,6](1) A protective expenses order is applied for by motion.

58A.5

(2) Intimation of the motion and of the documents mentioned in paragraph (3) must be given to every other party not less than 14 days before the date of enrolment.

(3) The applicant must lodge with the motion—

    (a) a statement setting out—

        (i) the grounds for seeking the order;

        (ii) the terms on which the applicant is represented;

        (iii) an estimate of the expenses that the applicant will incur in relation to the proceedings;

---

[1] Rule 58A.3 inserted by SSI 2013/81 (effective March 25, 2013).
[2] Rule 58A.3 substituted by S.S.I. 2018 No. 348 (effective 10 December 2018).
[3] Rule 58A.4 inserted by S.S.I. 2013 No. 81 (effective 25 March 2013).
[4] Rule 58A.4 substituted by S.S.I. 2018 No. 348 (effective 10 December 2018).
[5] Rule 58A.5 inserted by S.S.I. 2013 No. 81 (effective March 25, 2013).
[6] Rule 58A.5 substituted by S.S.I. 2018 No. 348 (effective 10 December 2018).

> > (iv) an estimate of the expenses of each other party for which the applicant may be liable in relation to the proceedings; and
> >
> > (v) in the case of an application for liability in expenses to be limited to an amount lower or, as the case may be, higher than a sum mentioned in rule 58A.7(1), the grounds on which the lower or higher amount is applied for; and
>
> (b) any documents or other materials on which the applicant seeks to rely.
>
> (4) A party opposing an application for a protective expenses order must lodge with the notice of opposition—
>
> > (a) a statement setting out the grounds for opposing the application; and
> >
> > (b) any documents or other materials on which the party seeks to rely.

GENERAL NOTE.

58A.5.1   The former erroneous reference in r. 58A.5(1) to r. 58A.3(1) instead of r. 58A.4(1) was noticed in *Carroll v. Scottish Borders Council*, 2014 S.L.T. 659 (OH). It was corrected by A.S. (R.C.S., O.C.R, and S.C.R. Amendment) (Miscellaneous) 2014 [S.S.I. 2014/152].

Determination of applications

58A.6   **58A.6.**—[1](1) Unless the Lord Ordinary or, as the case may be, the procedural judge otherwise directs—

> (a) an application for a protective expenses order is to be determined in chambers without appearance;
>
> (b) the motion is not to be starred; and
>
> (c) rule 23.4(6) (opposition to motions) is disapplied.

(2) Unless granting an unopposed application, the Lord Ordinary or, as the case may be, the procedural judge must give brief reasons in writing.

Terms of protective expenses orders

58A.7   **58A.7.**—[2](1) A protective expenses order must—

> (a) limit the applicant's liability in expenses to the respondent to the sum of £5,000, or such other sum as may be justified on cause shown; and
>
> (b) limit the respondent's liability in expenses to the applicant to the sum of £30,000, or such other sum as may be justified on cause shown.

(2) Where the applicant is the respondent in proceedings mentioned in rule 58A.1(1)(a)—

> (a) paragraph (1)(a) applies as if the reference to the applicant's liability in expenses to the respondent was a reference to the applicant's liability in expenses to the appellant; and
>
> (b) paragraph (1)(b) applies as if the reference to the respondent's liability in expenses to the applicant was a reference to the appellant's liability in expenses to the applicant.

(3) In paragraph (1), "the respondent" means—

> (a) all parties that lodge answers in an application to the supervisory jurisdiction of the court; and
>
> (b) all respondents in an appeal under statute.

Expenses protection in reclaiming motions

58A.8   **58A.8.**—[3](1) Paragraph (2) applies where—

> (a) the court has made a protective expenses order in relation to proceedings in the Outer House; and

---

[1] Rule 58A.6 inserted by S.S.I. 2018 No. 348 (effective 10 December 2018).
[2] Rule 58A.7 inserted by S.S.I. 2018 No. 348 (effective 10 December 2018).
[3] Rule 58A.8 inserted by S.S.I. 2018 No. 348 (effective 10 December 2018).

 (b) a decision of the Lord Ordinary is reclaimed at the instance of a party whose liability in expenses is limited in accordance with rule 58A.7(1)(b).

(2) Subject to any review of the protective expenses order by the Inner House, the limits on the parties' liability in expenses set by the order include liability for expenses occasioned by the reclaiming motion.

(3) Paragraphs (4) and (5) apply for the purposes of any other reclaiming motion from a decision of the Lord Ordinary in proceedings mentioned in rule 58A.1(1)(b) or (c).

(4) A party who would have been entitled to apply for a protective expenses order in the Outer House proceedings (whether or not the party did so apply) may apply for a protective expenses order in relation to the reclaiming motion in which event rule 58A.3(4) or, as the case may be, rule 58A.4(4) applies to the application.

(5) The application must be made, except on cause shown, no later than is reasonably practicable after the reclaiming motion has been marked.

Expenses of application

58A.9.—[1](1) Paragraph (2) applies where, in proceedings in which an application for a protective expenses order has been refused— **58A.9**

 (a) the applicant is found liable for payment of expenses; and

 (b) the expenses for which the applicant has been found liable comprise or include the expenses occasioned by the application.

(2) On the motion of the applicant the court must, other than on exceptional cause shown, limit the applicant's total liability in expenses, in so far as occasioned by the application, to the sum of £500.

---

[1] Rule 58A.9 inserted by S.S.I. 2018 No. 348 (effective 10 December 2018).

(b) a decision of the Land Ordinance was confirmed of the Issuance of a party whose liability in expenses is limited in accordance with rule 58A.4(1) by

(2) Subject to any review of the projected expenses order by the Inner House the limits on the parties' liability in expenses set by an order include liability for expenses occasioned by the concluding motion.

(2) Paragraphs (4) and (5) apply for the purposes of any other reclaiming motion from a decision of the Lord Ordinary in proceedings mentioned in rule 58A.1(1) by or to —

(2) A party who would have been entitled to apply for a protective expenses order in the Outer House proceedings (whether or not the party did so apply) may apply for a protective expenses order in relation to the reclaiming motion or which event rule 58A.3(3) or (4) the case may be rule 58A.4(4) applies to the application.

(5) The application must be made, except on cause shown, no later than a reasonably practicable after the reclaiming motion has been marked.

Expenses of application

58A.6.—(1) Paragraph (2) applies where, in proceedings in which an application for a protective expenses order has been made —

(a) the applicant is found liable for the payment of expenses; and
(b) the expenses for which the applicant has been found liable comprise or include the expenses occasioned by the application.

(2) On the motion of the applicant the court must, other than on exceptional cause shown, limit the applicant's total liability in expenses in so far as occasioned by the application to the sum of £5,000.

Rule 58A.6 inserted by SSI 2018/83. See footnote 19 (continued on).

870

Chapter 59

Applications for Letters

Applications for letters of arrestment or inhibition

59.1.—[1](1) An application for letters of arrestment may be made, as the case may be, in—

   (a) Form 59.1-A (arrestment);

 (b)–(f) *[Omitted by S.S.I. 2009 No. 104 (effective 22nd April 2009).]*

   (2)[2] An application under paragraph (1) shall be presented to the Deputy Principal Clerk together with any relevant supporting documents.

   (3)[3],[4] If the Deputy Principal Clerk is satisfied that the applicant for such letters is entitled to a warrant for arrestment—

   (a) he shall sign and date the warrant in such an application; and

   (b) the application shall be signeted;

and such signeted application and warrant shall constitute letters of arrestment, as the case may be.

   (4)[5],[6] If the Deputy Principal Clerk refuses to sign and date such warrant, the application shall, on request, be placed before the Lord Ordinary; and the decision of the Lord Ordinary shall be final and not subject to review.

   (4A)–(4B) *[Omitted by S.S.I. 2009 No. 104 (effective 22nd April 2009).]*

   (5) An application for letters of arrestment on the dependence of an action to which a claim under section 19 of the Family Law (Scotland) Act 1985 applies shall be placed before the Lord Ordinary; and the decision of the Lord Ordinary shall be final and not subject to review.

   Deriv. R.C.S. 1965, r. 68J(1) (r. 59.1(2)), r. 68J(2) (r. 59.1(4)), and r. 68J(3) (r. 59.1(5)), all inserted by S.I. 1991 No. 2483

GENERAL NOTE.

   Modern forms of applications for letters of arrestment or inhibition were provided by the R.C.S. 1994, r. 59.1 when introduced. The form of inhibition in Sched. QQ to the Titles to Land Consolidation (Scotland) Act 1868 has been repealed and replaced by the forms in r. 59.1(1).

   There is one document constituting the application and letters, the documents being the letters of arrestment or inhibition, as the case may be, on the warrant being granted and the application signeted.

   On arrestment on the dependence, see note 14A.2.7. On arrestment in execution, see note 16.12.11. On execution of letters of arrestment, see r. 16.12 and note 16.12.11. On inhibition on the dependence, see note 14A.2.8. On inhibition in execution, see note 16.12.12.

LETTERS OF INHIBITION.

   Letters of inhibition are now incompetent, having been rendered so by the Bankruptcy and Diligence etc (Scotland) Act 2007. They were required for inhibition (a) on the dependence of a sheriff court action, (b) in execution of a Court of Session or sheriff court decree, (c) in execution of writs and foreign judgments registered for execution in the Books of Council and Session, (d) in execution on a document of debt, and (e) in security of future or contingent debts other than on the dependence of a Court of Session process.

   By virtue of the 2007 Act, inhibition on the dependence may be sought in the sheriff court, inhibition in execution is now an authorised diligence on an extract decree, and inhibition in execution is competent to enforce documents of debt such as foreign judgments registered in the Books of Council and Session or specific implement of an obligation to convey heritable property or a real right in security.

59.1

59.1.1

59.1.2

---

[1] Rule 59.1 amended by S.S.I. 2009 No.104 (effective 22nd April 2009).

[2] Rule 59.1(2) amended by S.I. 1997 No. 1050 (effective 6th April, 1997).

[3] Rule 59.1(3) and (4) amended by S.I. 1998 No. 890 (effective 21st April, 1998).

[4] Rule 59.1(3), (4), (4A) and (4B) amended by S.S.I. 2004 No. 537 (effective 10th November, 2003).

[5] Rule 59.1(1)(f) inserted, and r. 59.1(4) amended, by S.S.I. 1999 No. 109 (effective 29th October, 1999).

[6] Rule 59.1(3), (4), (4A) and (4B) amended by S.S.I. 2004 No. 537 (effective 10th November, 2003).

"FINAL AND NOT SUBJECT TO REVIEW".

59.1.3   The decision of the Lord Ordinary may not be reclaimed against.

FEE.

59.1.4   The court fee for an application for letters is payable for the fiat. For fee, see Court of Session etc. Fees Order 1997, Table of Fees, Pt. I, C, item 7 [SI 1997/688, as amended, pp. C1201 et seq.]. Certain persons are exempt from payment of fees: see 1997 Fees Order, art. 5 substituted by SSI 2002/270. A fee exemption certificate must be lodged in process: see P.N. No.1 of 2002.

Where the applicant is legally represented, the fee may be debited under a credit scheme introduced on 1st April 1976 by P.N. No. 4 of 1976 to the account (if one is kept or permitted) of the agent by the court cashier, and an account will be rendered weekly by the court cashier's office to the agent for all court fees due that week for immediate settlement. Party litigants, and agents not operating the scheme, must pay (by cash, cheque or postal order) on each occasion a fee is due at the time of lodging at the counter at the General Department.

CHAPTER 60 APPLICATIONS FOR SUSPENSION, SUSPENSION AND INTERDICT, AND SUSPENSION AND LIBERATION

Chapter 60

Applications for Suspension, Suspension and Interdict, and Suspension and Liberation

Application of this Chapter

60.1. Subject to rule 53.1 (conclusions for suspension etc., in action of reduction), this Chapter applies to an application for suspension, suspension and interdict, or suspension and liberation.

GENERAL NOTE.

This Chapter provides special rules for applications for (1) suspension; (2) suspension and interdict; and (3) suspension and liberation. Strictly, a petition for interdict alone (historically a heresy but now not uncommon) is not subject to the special rules in this Chapter; although in practice it probably would be.

(1) Suspension.

The remedy of suspension is an ancient one. Originally a process of suspension was directed solely against any person who had obtained a decree or had obtained letters for charging or letters of caption (for civil imprisonment) or had carried out a poinding *simpliciter*, poinding of the ground or an adjudication: Stair, IV.lii.8. By the eighteenth century the scope of the remedy had expanded and Erskine described it thus: "Anywhere there is no decree there may be a suspension, though not in the strict acceptance of that word, for suspension is a process authorized by law for putting a stop not only to the execution of iniquitous decrees but to all encroachments either on property or possessions and in general to every unlawful proceeding": Erskine, IV.iii.20.

The purpose of suspension is thus to stop unlawful conduct (including execution of a decree) either temporarily or permanently. A suspension, however, has only retrospective effect. In this it is akin to arrestment. Suspension is also akin to reduction but differs in that (a) a decree of suspension cannot itself be suspended, and (b) a person seeking suspension may obtain an interim order: see Stair IV.lii.3 and 4. Often a suspension may be sought as a temporary measure preceding an action of reduction: e.g. *McCarroll v. McKinstery* 1923 S.C. 94 (suspension of charge leading to reduction of the execution of charge and underlying decree).

Suspension is thus used (1) to sist diligence and proceedings and (2) to review a decree in absence or a decree of an inferior court. Suspension of a charge following a decree merely suspends diligence whereas suspension as a mode of review challenges the decree: Mackay's Practice, 610-611; *Macdonald v. Denoon*, 1928 S.L.T. 439. In *Ali v. Ali*, 2001 S.C. 618, 622 (paras 8-11), an Extra Div. expressed the view, without deciding the issue, that in modern times the usual practice for seeking review of a decree, having obtained sist of diligence by suspension, is to bring an action of reduction. (Suspension may, of course, be sought in an action of reduction: r. 53.1.) It has also been held that reduction is the appropriate remedy where it is sought to set aside a decree on the ground of fraud or on a ground extrinsic to the case: *Smith v. Kirkwood* (1897) 24 R. 872. (There was some doubt expressed in *Smith* as to the competency of suspension of a final decree of an inferior court after the C.S.A. 1868 regarding review.) It should be noted that s. 35 of the C.S.A. 1988 recognises the suspension of sheriff court decrees. Suspension of a decree is limited. It is excluded where (a) review by appeal is competent (Mackay's Practice, ii, pp.482-3); (b) the party seeking suspension has been unsuccessful on appeal on the merits or by default (*Lamb v. Thompson* (1901) 4 F. 88, 92 per Lord Moncreiff; (c) the decree has been implemented (Mackay's Practice, ii, p.483); (d) the decree is one of absolvitor *in foro* (*McGregor v. Lord Strathallan*, (1862) 24 D. 1006); (e) the decree is for a sum within the privative jurisdiction of the sheriff court (*Brown & Critchley Ltd v. Decorative Art Journals Ltd*, 1922 S.C. 192); (f) the decree is that of the Court of Session: *McCarroll v. McKinstery* , 1923 S.C. 94. Suspension of a decree in absence before extract is in effect superseded by reponing in the sheriff court. As to reduction, see note 53.2.1.

The test of relevancy for suspension permanently of a sheriff court decree is the same as would be applicable in an action of reduction of that decree: *Ali*, above. On that test, see note 53.2.1.

Until 1933 suspension was obtainable by a note of suspension presented to the Lord Ordinary on the Bills sitting in the Bill Chamber. Since 1933, when the Bill Chamber was abolished, suspension may be obtained either by petition (*simpliciter*) or petition for judicial review (see Chap. 58). In many older cases suspension is used as a remedy to review the decisions of inferior courts or tribunals: see, e.g. *Manson v. Smith* (1871) 9 M. 492; *McCarroll*, above; and see note 60.6.1. It is also available as a remedy to review a decree in absence of the Court of Session: C.S.A. 1988, s. 34. An interim order of suspension may be obtained: see r. 14.5 and note 14.5.8. Suspension, including interim suspension, may be obtained through a conclusion ancillary to other conclusions in an action: *Gilmont Transport Services Ltd v. Renfrew District Council* 1982 S.L.T. 290.

Where the court has granted a decree of suspension, including interim suspension, it may not be appropriate for the court to ordain the respondent *ad factum praestandum* (to perform a certain act) under s. 46 of the C.S.A. 1988: *Maersk Co. Ltd v. National Union of Seamen* 1988 S.L.T. 828, 831 per Lord Cullen.

(2) Suspension and interdict.

Suspension merely affects past and not future conduct. Accordingly, where a person wishes also to prohibit future conduct he must include a crave for interdict in the prayer of the petition. Where interdict, alone or with suspension, is sought, procedure is usually by way of petition. It is nevertheless competent to conclude solely for interdict in an action: *Dunn v. Hamilton* (1837) 15 S. 853, (1838) 3 S. & M. 356 (HL); and *Exchange Telegraph Co. v. White* 1961 S.L.T. 104. Where interdict is sought with other remedies, such as damages or declarator, procedure is usually by way of action.

Interdict prohibits reasonably apprehended future breaches of duty by the respondent or defender to the petitioner or pursuer: *Inverurie Magistrates v. Sorrie* 1956 S.C. 175. Interdict is a preventive remedy prohibiting action which is threatened or continuing and looks to the future not the past; its purpose is not to compel a defender (or respondent) to restore parties to the position they were in previously, although that might be its indirect effect, but to preserve the status quo: *Church Commissioners for England v. Abbey National plc* 1994 S.C. 651 approving *Grosvenor Developments (Scotland) plc v. Argyll Stores Ltd* 1987 S.L.T. 738; and see *Retail Parks Investments v. Royal Bank of Scotland plc* 1996 S.L.T. 1156. Hence, "positive" interdicts so-called are not granted; in *Hampden Park Ltd v. Dow*, 13th July 2001 (OH), unreported, Lord Drummond Young set out a three stage approach to determining whether an interdict was truly a negative order. Section 46 (reinstating petitioner in possessory right or granting specific relief) and s. 47(2) (interim possession) of the C.S.A. 1988 enable the court to make interim orders to restore a party to the position he was in prior to the wrongful act (*Church Commissioners for England*, above (and see the cases cited at p. 965); see *Scottish Power Generation Ltd v. British Generation (UK) Ltd*, 2002 S.C. 517 (Extra Div) for the steps to be taken by the court in determining whether to grant an order under s. 47(2)) and an order may be made under s. 46 of the C.S.A. 1988 for reinstatement before a final hearing to dispose of the petition (*Maersk Co. Ltd v. National Union of Seamen* 1988 S.L.T. 828, 831G per Lord Cullen; *Five Oaks Properties Ltd v. Granite House Ltd* 1994 S.C.L.R. 740). (On the other hand, a party to a contract is generally entitled to specific implement (the decree for which passes the test of precision, specification, definition and notice) of a contractual obligation subject to the residual discretion of the court to refuse it in exceptional circumstances where cogent reasons exist as where to grant it would be inconvenient and unjust or it would cause exceptional hardship. For the most recent statement of the law, see *Highland and Universal Ltd v. Safeway Properties Ltd* 2000 S.C. 297 (First Div.)). The court always retains an equitable discretion to refuse a permanent decree of interdict: *Wm. Grant & Sons. Ltd v. Glen Catrine Bonded Warehouse Ltd.* , 2001 S.L.T. 1419, 1437 per Rodger, L.P.

An interim order of interdict may be obtained: see note 60.3.2.

The remedy of interdict is not available in civil proceedings against the Crown, though a declaratory order may be available instead: Crown Proceedings Act 1947, s. 21; and see *McDonald v. Secretary of State for Scotland* 1994 S.C. 234 on "civil proceedings against the Crown". But note that in *Davidson v. The Scottish Ministers* , 2006 S.C. (H.L.) 41; 2006 S.L.T. 110, the House of Lords held that the bar in s. 21 did not apply to judicial review as that was not "civil proceedings". In *Beggs v. The Scottish Ministers* , 2005 S.L.T. 305 (First Div.), it was held that s. 21 did not make it incompetent to find the respondents in contempt of court by reason of a breach of an undertaking to the court. In *Beggs*, it was also decided that the proceedings against the respondents were not against the Crown. The question whether the Scottish Ministers were the Crown was reserved in *Davidson*. Interdict may, however, be available where it is reasonably apprehended that the Crown will be in breach of E.C. law: see *R. v. Secretary of State for Transport, ex parte Factortame Ltd* [1990] 2 A.C. 85 and *R. v. Secretary of State for Transport, ex parte Factortame Ltd (No. 2)* [1991] 1 A.C. 603.

The remedy of interdict is not available against the Scottish Parliament, but the court may, instead, make a declarator: Scotland Act 1998, s. 40(3).

An interdict may apply to future conduct outwith Scotland: *Barratt International Resorts Ltd v. Martin* 1994 S.L.T. 434, 437L per Lord Sutherland. For enforcement of such an interdict under the C.J.J.A. 1982, see rr. 62.40 and 62.42.

On the factors to be considered in determining whether to grant interdict in contractual cases (e.g. of landlord and tenant), see *Church Commissioners for England v. Nationwide Anglia Building Society* 1994 S.L.T. 897, 899A-D per Lord Clyde.

Where a court is considering whether to grant (interim) interdict which might affect freedom of expression under ECHR, the court has to be satisfied not only that there is a prima facie case and that the balance of convenience favours granting the order but also that on a final determination the petitioner would be likely to succeed: Human Rights Act 1998, s. 12; *Dickson Minto WS v. Bonnier Media Ltd* , 2002 S.L.T. 776.

On interdict to prohibit pursuing action abroad, see *Shell U.K. Exploration and Production Ltd v. Innes* 1995 S.L.T. 807. In *FMC Corporation v. Russell* 1999 S.L.T. 99, Lord Bonomy reviewed the authorities when considering the issues to be determined in deciding whether there is a prima facie case for interim interdict for pursuing an action abroad. There must be a prima facie case that Scotland is the natural forum and that pursuing the proceedings in the foreign court is vexatious or oppressive.

In a petition for interim interdict under s. 27 of the C.J.J.A. 1982 the court may, in the exercise of comity, grant an order similar to the foreign order even though it would not have been able to do so in

Scottish proceedings provided that there was a prima facie case according to the jurisprudence of the originating jurisdiction: *G. v. Caledonian Newspapers Ltd* 1995 S.L.T. 559.

Interdict may not be granted to circumvent those provisions of the C.J.J.A. 1982 which exclude the court from interfering with a judgment made elsewhere which is to be registered in Scotland: *Clarke v. Fennoscandia Ltd* 1998 S.C. 464; and see *Clarke v. Fennoscandia Ltd (No. 3)* , 2005 S.L.T. 511 (Second Div.).

The court will only interfere in the proceedings of a voluntary association in extraordinary circumstances: *Brown v. Executive Committee of the Edinburgh District Labour Party* 1995 S.L.T. 985 (court interfered where there was an apprehension of denial of natural justice).

(3) Suspension and liberation.

Where a person who is imprisoned, following the granting of a warrant to apprehend after a breach of a civil decree, wishes to be released before the expiry of his period of imprisonment, his remedy is to apply to the court for (a) suspension of any unlawful step of procedure which led to imprisonment and liberation from his place of imprisonment; or (b) liberation *simpliciter* where he has been imprisoned after refusal to comply with a decree *ad factum praestandum* and while in prison he has either complied with the decree or no longer wilfully refuses to comply (Law Reform (Miscellaneous Provisions) (Scotland) Act 1940, s. 1(1)(ii)).

Suspension and liberation may also be sought be a person who has been detained by an immigration officer pending either a decision on leave to enter the U.K. or following directions for removal from the U.K.: see *Sokha v. Secretary of State for the Home Department* 1992 S.L.T. 1049.

Where a person seeks a suspension and liberation, the application will usually seek to review the exercise of a jurisdiction of a court or public official. Accordingly the application will usually require to be made in a petition for judicial review: see *West v. Secretary of State for Scotland* 1992 S.L.T. 636, 645J per L.P. Hope; and r. 58.4. An order for interim liberation may be obtained: C.S.A. 1988, s. 47(1). For grounds for civil imprisonment, see note 60.3.4. For grounds for suspension and liberation, see Maclaren on *Bill Chamber Practice*, p. 76.

Forms of applications

60.2.—(1) An application to which this Chapter applies shall be made by petition.

(2) It shall not be necessary in any such petition to make an offer of caution or consignation.

Deriv. R.C.S. 1965, r. 234 (part)

"PETITION".

A petition is presented in the Outer House: r. 14.2(f). The petition must be in Form 14.4 in the approved printed form: rr. 4.1 and 14.4. The petition must be signed by counsel or other person having a right of audience, or an agent: r. 4.2(3); and see r. 1.3(1) (definition of "counsel", "other person having a right of audience" and "agent") and note 1.3.4.

The petitioner must lodge the petition with the required steps of process (r. 4.4) and any documents founded on or adopted (r. 27.1(1)). A fee is payable on lodging the petition: see note 14.5.10.

On petitions generally, see Chap. 14.

CAUTION.

Caution from the petitioner is no longer ordered as a general rule in suspension and interdict unless there is a question of the petitioner's solvency or if the respondent might have a substantial damages claim in the event of the interim interdict proving wrongous: *Wright v. Thomson* 1974 S.L.T.(Notes) 15 per Lord Maxwell. For procedure for finding caution, see Chap. 33.

First order

60.3. Where the interlocutor ordering intimation, service or advertisement contains an interim suspension of execution, interim interdict or interim liberation, subject to the finding of caution or the giving of other security or any other conditions, the petition shall not be intimated, served or advertised until such condition has been met.

Deriv. R.C.S. 1965, r. 236(d) (part)

INTIMATION, SERVICE OR ADVERTISEMENT.

See r. 14.7; and for methods of service and intimation, see Chap. 16, Pt I.

INTERIM INTERDICT.

Where a petition or summons contains a crave or conclusion for interdict or liberation the court may, on the motion of any party, grant interim interdict or interim liberation: C.S.A. 1988, s.47(1). The motion may be made at any time after the presentation of the petition or signeting of the summons: *National*

60.2

60.2.1

60.2.2

60.3

60.3.1

60.3.2

Cash Register Co. Ltd v. Kinnear 1948 S.L.T.(Notes) 83. No special crave or conclusion for the interim order is required, although this is usually inserted: *National Cash Register Co. Ltd*, above. When the court considers a motion for interim interdict it first considers whether the petitioner or pursuer has made out a prima facie case, and if he has, it then considers whether the balance of convenience favours the petitioner or pursuer: *W.A.C. Ltd v. Whillock* 1989 S.C. 397, 410 per L.J.-C. Ross.

A motion for interim interdict is often made and dealt with in the absence of the person against whom the order is sought. Exceptions are:

(a)   Where that person has lodged a caveat (see Chap. 5).

(b)   Where that person has already entered the process.

(c)   Section 221(1) of the Trade Union and Labour Relations (Consolidation) Act 1992. This provides that where an application for interdict is made ex parte and the respondent (or defender) claims or would be likely to claim that he acted in furtherance of a trade dispute, the court will not grant interdict unless satisfied that all reasonable steps have been taken to secure that notice of the application and an opportunity of being heard has been given to the respondent.

(1) Prima facie case.

The petitioner or pursuer must show that his case as averred and amplified by submissions, taken on the basis of all available information, gives him a reasonable prospect of success: *W.A.C. Ltd*, above. The court is not at this stage concerned to arrive at definite conclusions on the legal issues: *W.A.C. Ltd*, above, Where a motion for recall of interim interdict would determine the cause and balance of convenience is not an issue, the motion should be dealt with on the Procedure Roll: *Zehmoon Ltd v. Akinbrook Investment Developments Ltd* 1988 S.L.T. 146, 174C per Lord Clyde. The correct test where no injury or delict has yet been committed is to consider whether the interdictor is in reasonable apprehension that a serious delict or injury will be, or is likely to be, committed against him by the defender or respondent: *Allseas UK Ltd v. Greenpeace Ltd*, 2001 S.C. 844 (OH).

(2) Balance of convenience.

The petitioner or pursuer must show that the inconvenience to him in not obtaining the interim interdict outweighs the inconvenience to the respondent or defender in obtaining interim interdict. The following is a list of factors (in no particular order of importance) which have been considered:

(a)   Irreparable nature of apprehended wrong: *Baird v. Monkland Iron and Steel Co.* (1862) 24 D. 1418, 1425 per L.J.-C. Inglis (flooding of petitioner's coal mines); *Pease v. Pease* 1967 S.C. 112 (marriage); *McGuinness v. Renfrewshire Upper District Committee* 1907 S.C. 1117 (discharge of sewage); *British Coal Corporation v. South of Scotland Electricity Board* 1988 S.L.T. 446 (catastrophic effect on pursuer's market); *Secretary of State for Scotland v. Highland Council* 1998 S.L.T. 222 (demolition of listed building); *Allied Domeq Spirits and Wine Ltd v. Murray McDavid Ltd* 1999 S.L.T. 157 (low likelihood of damage to pursuer's businesses).

(b)   Offering of caution, other security or undertaking by the respondent or defender: *Forth Yacht Marina Ltd v. Forth Road Bridge Joint Board* 1984 S.L.T. 177 (undertaking to reduce nuisance); *Highland Distilleries Co. plc v. Speymalt Whisky Distributors Ltd* 1985 S.L.T. 85 (undertaking to keep accounts); *Knox v. Paterson* (1861) 23 D. 1263 (offer of caution); *Bernard v. Bernard* (1893) 1 S.L.T. 29 (undertaking to keep accounts); *Waste Systems International Inc. v. Eurocare Environmental Services Ltd* 1999 S.L.T. 198 (undertaking to keep accounts).

(c)   Degree of likelihood of ultimate success: *Toynar Ltd v. Whitbread & Co. plc* 1988 S.L.T. 433, 434C-D per Second Div.

(d)   Financial effect of interim interdict on respondent or defender: *Orkney Seafoods Ltd, Petrs* 1991 S.L.T. 891 (minor change of name for newly established company); *Dash Ltd v. Philip King Tailoring Ltd* 1989 S.L.T. 39 (minor effect from change of name of new business); *Steiner v. Breslin* 1979 S.L.T.(Notes) 34 (major financial hardship); *Salon Services (Hairdressing Supplies) Ltd v. Direct Salon Services Ltd* 1988 S.L.T. 414 (whole savings threatened); *Waste System International Inc*, above (cessation of whole business).

(e)   Ease of quantification of putative damages: *Conoco Speciality Products (Inc.) v. Merpro Montassa Ltd (No. 1)* 1991 S.L.T. 222 (damages for loss of monopoly patent right market); *Dash Ltd v. Philip King Tailoring Ltd* 1989 S.L.T. 39 (damages for passing off); *C R Smith Glaziers (Dunfermline) Ltd v. Greenan* 1993 S.L.T. 1221, 1224G per L.J.-C. Ross (damages for breach of employee's restrictive covenant).

(f)   Adequacy of putative damages: *William E. Selkin Ltd v. Proven Products Ltd* 1992 S.L.T. 983 (damages for infringement of patent).

(g)   Safety implications: *Shell U.K. Ltd v. McGillivray* 1991 S.L.T. 667, 672I-L per Lord Cameron of Lochbroom; *Waste Systems International Inc*, above (disposal of hazardous medical waste).

(h)   Public interest: *Scottish Milk Marketing Board v. Paris* 1935 S.C. 287 (preservation of statutory public monopoly); *Forth Yacht Marina Ltd*, above (maintenance of public bridge); *Johnston v. Dumfriesshire Road Trustees* (1867) 5 M. 1127 (construction of public bridge); *Waste Systems International Inc*, above (operation of hazardous material waste-disposal factories).

(i)   Undue delay in making motion: *William Grant & Sons Ltd v. William Cadenhead Ltd* 1985 S.L.T. 291.

(3) Undertaking or caution by respondent or defender.

An undertaking may be recorded in the interlocutor or in the minute of proceedings. Breach of an undertaking does not per se entitle the aggrieved party to obtain an order for the party in breach to appear at the bar of the court: *Stirling Shipping Co. Ltd v. National Union of Seamen* 1988 S.L.T. 832, 834K-L per Lord Cullen. The breach may, however, be contempt of court: *Graham v. Robert Younger Ltd* 1955 J.C. 28; and see *Cordiner, Petr* 1973 S.L.T. 125. For procedure for finding caution, see Chap. 33.

(4) Wrongous interdict.

Interim interdict is obtained *periculo petentis* (at the risk of the person seeking it): *Fife v. Orr* (1895) 23 R. 8. Where a party obtains interim interdict which is then to any extent recalled as unjustified, that party may be sued by the person interdicted for wrongous interdict and be found liable in damages: *Fife*, above; *Clippens Oil Co. Ltd v. Edinburgh and District Water Trustees* (1906) 8 F. 731.

(5) Duration of interdict.

Interim interdict lasts from the time it is granted until it is recalled or made perpetual. An order of interim interdict may be superseded: *Phonographic Performance Ltd v. McKenzie* 1982 S.L.T. 272. Interim interdict may be recalled on a reclaiming motion, on a motion to the Lord Ordinary for recall, or on the determination of the crave or conclusion for interdict. The interim interdict may be recalled in part: *Steiner v. Breslin* 1979 S.L.T.(Notes) 34. In any event, subject to reclaiming, the interim interdict will cease on final determination by the Lord Ordinary when it is either made perpetual or recalled. If there is an appeal from the final determination the interim interdict ceases on determination of the appeal: *Clippens Oil Co. Ltd*, above per L.P. Dunedin at pp. 749-751.

(6) Operation of interdict.

Although an interim interdict is valid from when it is granted, it only becomes operative when the respondent or defender becomes sufficiently aware of its contents: *Clark v. Stirling* (1839) 1 D. 955. This would apply even in the absence of service, although service is usually made. Knowledge of the interdict by the respondent's agent may raise a presumption of knowledge by the respondent: *Henderson v. Maclellan* (1874) 1 R. 920, 923 per L.P. Inglis. Awareness by the respondent of the terms of an interim interdict does not per se make him aware of the terms of a perpetual interdict even if in identical terms: *Stewart v. Stallard* 1995 S.C.L.R. 167. Interdict cannot affect unnamed persons (e.g. "any other person having notice of the interlocutor"): *Lord Advocate v. The Scotsman Publications Ltd* 1989 S.C.(H.L.) 122; and *Pattison v. Fitzgerald* (1823) 2 S. 536. It was explained in *Oliver & Son Ltd Ptrs.* 1999 S.L.T. 1039, by the First Div. on a report to the Inner House by Lord Penrose, that the underlying reasoning in *The Scotsman Publications*, above, and *Pattison*, above, was that it is incompetent to pronounce an interdict on persons on whom the proceedings are not served or to move for its recall. In *Oliver*, the petitioners sought an order under s.46 of the C.S.A. 1988 to be reinstated in their possessory right to heritable property which was occupied by persons whose names were unknown to them but who could be identified as the occupiers of the petitioners' land. A first order for service was sought on the unnamed persons those who were served would be able to enter the process and resist the making of any substantive order. The First Div. held that the persons on whom service was to be made were sufficiently identified were it otherwise the court would be powerless to act and would be handing to those who concealed their identity a weapon to wreak injustice. It was indicated for the petitioners that messengers-at-arms would hand copies of the petition to individuals they found occupying the land and record what they had done and might photograph those on the land and the steps taken to serve the petition. Accordingly it should be possible to bring an action for removing with conclusions for interdict and interim interdict against unnamed persons and to seek service of the action on those who can be found and identified with respect to the conclusions for interdict. But it would not be possible to seek interim interdict on those unnamed persons before service. Where interim interdict is granted on condition that the pursuer finds caution it becomes operative only on the finding of caution: *Wilson v. Gilchrist* (1900) 2 F. 391; and see Chap. 33. Where the interim interdict is the first order in a petition process, the court will also automatically pronounce an order for intimation and service of the petition: r. 14.5(1). Service by registered letter tendered at the respondent's or defender's address but refused may amount to a good citation: Citation Amendment (Scotland) Act 1882, s.4(5); *Matheson v. Fraser* 1911 2 S.L.T. 493.

BREACH OF INTERDICT.

60.3.3

Breach of interim interdict in a depending cause (whether action or petition) is dealt with by minute in that process: C.S.A. 1988, s.47(1). Breach of perpetual interdict is dealt with by petition and complaint. A cause is depending until final decree, whereas a cause is in dependence until final extract. For the meaning of final decree, see note 4.15.2(2). For the meaning of final extract, see note 7.1.2(2).

The petition (or minute) must have the concurrence of the Lord Advocate as public prosecutor because of its quasi-criminal character: *Gribben v. Gribben* 1976 S.L.T. 266. That concurrence is not required for breach of any other kind of court order: *Panel on Takeovers and Mergers v. King*, 2018 S.L.T. 1205 (OH). In the case of a matrimonial interdict against molestation, the docquet is a means of informing the court that no criminal proceedings are being pursued against the alleged offender, avoiding double jeopardy. The Lord Advocate's concurrence is written on the principal petition (or minute), usually by one of his deputes. The concurrence is obtained by sending the principal of the writ to the Lord Advocate at the Lord Advocate's Chambers, Crown Office, 25 Chambers Street, Edinburgh, EH1 1LA. It is not necessary to intimate to the Lord Advocate all adjustment or amendments to the pleadings if these are averments which are part of the same course of conduct averred: *Byrne v. Ross* 1992 S.C. 498. Proceedings for breach of interdict are civil proceedings to which s.1(1) of the Civil Evidence (Scotland) Act 1988 (rule requiring corroboration abolished) applies: *Byrne*, above.

Care must be taken to name and design the respondent correctly as a material error will invalidate the petition: *Overseas League v. Taylor* 1951 S.C. 105; cf. *Anderson v. Stoddart* 1923 S.C. 755 (immaterial error). As breach of interdict constitutes a contempt of court which might lead to punishment, it is necessary in the interests of fairness that the alleged contempt is clearly and distinctly averred, and the proceedings for contempt should be confined to the averments: *Byrne*, above.

(1) Jurisdiction.

If the court has jurisdiction to grant the interdict it will have jurisdiction to deal with a breach unless jurisdiction has been lost. The court has jurisdiction under Sched. 8 to the C.J.J.A. 1982 (jurisdiction of Scottish courts), r. 1 (domicile) and r. 2(j); (interdict where wrong to be committed). See also jurisdiction under Sched. 1 (1968 Convention), Sched. 3C (Lugano Convention) and Sched. 4 (inter-U.K. jurisdiction), Art. 5(3) (jurisdiction in delict) and Art. 24 (protective measures), and s. 24(2) (protective measures where jurisdiction doubtful) and s. 27 (protective measures), and the Brussels I Regulation (Council Regulation (EC) No.44/2001).

(2) Procedure by minute.

On the form of the minute, see r. 15.1. The minute docqueted with the Lord Advocate's concurrence is lodged and a motion enrolled for the minute to be received and to ordain the party in breach (the respondent, defender or as the case may be) to appear at the bar and to explain the alleged breach. The motion will be intimated in the usual way (see r. 23.3) to that party's agent or, if be has not entered the process, to that party himself by letter. At the motion, if the respondent denies the breach, an interlocutor will be pronounced ordaining him to lodge answers within a specified time; thereafter the procedure will be that for a minute and answers. If the breach is admitted, he will be dealt with there and then if he is personally present; if not, but he is represented or there is no appearance, an interlocutor will be pronounced ordaining him to appear on a particular date (usually a week later). A certified copy of that interlocutor must be served on the respondent, personally in the case of a natural person: on personal service, see note 16.1.2(1). At the second hearing the clerk may request the presence of police officers if this is thought to be necessary. If found to be in breach the respondent may be admonished, fined or imprisoned (on which, see note 60.3.4). Where the respondent is not a natural person, it may appear by one of its office-bearers to explain the breach or be represented by counsel or other person having a right of audience. If the respondent does not appear, and he is a natural person, an interlocutor will be pronounced granting warrant to messengers-at-arms and other officers of the law to apprehend him, granting warrant to Governors of H.M. Prisons to receive and detain him pending his appearance in court, and execution of the interlocutor to proceed on a certified copy of the interlocutor. The messenger-at-arms will inform the petitioner's agent once the respondent has been apprehended.

(3) Procedure by petition and complaint.

This is an Outer House petition: r. 14.2(d). The concurrence of the Lord Advocate must be docqueted on the principal petition before it is presented. The petition proceeds in the usual way for a petition with a first order being obtained for intimation and service. If no answers are lodged, the petitioner can enrol a motion to ordain the respondent to appear at the bar and to explain the alleged breach of interdict. The procedure thereafter is the same as that of a minute for breach of interim interdict. If answers are lodged the procedure will be similar to that for a minute and answers.

CIVIL IMPRISONMENT.

60.3.4   This is available in three circumstances.

1.   Contempt of court in a civil cause.
2.   As a remedy for breach of interdict: see note 14.2.6.
3.   As a diligence for the enforcement of—
    (a)   Failure to pay a fine for contempt of court in a civil proceeding: Debtors (Scotland) Act 1880, s. 4 as amended by the Debtors (Scotland) Act 1987, Sched. 6, para. 8;
    (b)   Failure to comply with an order under s. 45 of the C.S.A. 1988: 1880 Act, s. 4 as amended by the 1987 Act, Sched. 6, para. 8;
    (c)   Failure to pay any sum decerned for aliment: 1880 Act, s. 4; and
    (d)   Failure to comply with a decree *ad factum praestandum* (for the performance of a certain act): 1880 Act, s. 4 and the Law Reform (Miscellaneous Provisions) (Scotland) Act 1940, s. 1. A decree of registration obtained following default on an obligation *ad factum praestandum* in a document registered in the Books of Council and Session or in the sheriff court books is not per se enforceable by imprisonment: 1987 Act, s. 100(1). It is unclear whether an order under s. 45 of the C.S.A. 1988 is a decree *ad factum praestandum* for the purposes of the Law Reform (Miscellaneous Provisions) (Scotland) Act 1940, s. 1(1)(ii).

"finding of caution or granting of other security".

See Chap. 33 for procedure.   **60.3.5**

Further petition following refusal by default

60.4. Where a petition for suspension, suspension and interdict, or suspension   **60.4**
and liberation has been refused—

    (a)   for failure by the petitioner to—

        (i)   find caution or give other security, or to consign money into court, or

        (ii)   comply with any other condition imposed by the court under rule 60.3 (first order), or

    (b)   on any other ground other than on the merits,

the petitioner may, having paid any expenses in which he was found liable, present another petition for suspension, suspension and interdict, or suspension and liberation, as the case may be.

    Deriv. R.C.S. 1965, r. 243

Appointing petition to Adjustment Roll

60.5.—(1) Any party may, within seven days after any answers have been   **60.5**
lodged, apply by motion for an order appointing the petition and answers to the Adjustment Roll.

(2) Where the court grants a motion under paragraph (1), the petitioner shall, within 14 days after the interlocutor granting the motion—

    (a)   send at least four copies of the petition and answers in the form of an open record to the respondent; and

    (b)   lodge two copies of the record in process;

and thereafter the cause shall proceed as an action.

    Deriv. R.C.S. 1965, r. 247

General note.

Traditionally, a party who seeks interdict alone presents a petition although an action concluding   **60.5.1**
solely for interdict has been held to be competent: *Dunn v. Hamilton* (1837) 15 S. 853, (1838) 3 S. & M.
356 (H.L.); *Exchange Telegraph Co. v. White* 1961 S.L.T. 104. Where other remedies connected with
interdict such as reduction are also sought, an action should be raised. In any event, a petition presented
under this Chapter which is opposed proceeds as an action.

"within seven days", "within 14 days".

The date from which the period is calculated is not counted. Where the last day falls on a Saturday or   **60.5.2**
Sunday or a public holiday on which the Office of Court is closed, the next available day is allowed: r.
1.3(7). For office hours and public holidays, see note 3.1.2.

"motion".

For motions, see Chap. 23.   **60.5.3**

"open record".

This consists of the pleadings of the parties and the interlocutors so far pronounced: r. 22.1(4); and see   **60.5.4**
note 22.1.1. Where the petitioner fails to comply with r. 60.5(2) the respondent may apply by motion to
have the petition refused: see note 22.1.9.

"send".

This includes deliver: r. 1.3(1) (definition of "send").   **60.5.5**

"lodge two copies of the open record in process".

The open records are lodged as steps of process (r. 1.3(1) (definition of "step of process")). On lodg-   **60.5.6**
ing steps of process, see r. 4.4. The list may be lodged by post: P.N. No. 4 of 1994, paras. 1 and 8; and see
note 4.4.10.

One copy of the record is the process copy, the other is for the Keeper of the Rolls and is used to
regulate the progress of the cause on the Adjustment Roll.

Suspension of decree of inferior court or tribunal

60.6

60.6.—(1) This rule applies to a petition for the suspension of a decree, order, decision or warrant of whatever nature of an inferior court or tribunal.

(2) The petition shall be served on the clerk of the inferior court or tribunal to which the petition relates.

(3) The Lord Ordinary may pronounce an interlocutor ordering production to the court of any part of the proceedings in the inferior court or tribunal within such period as he thinks fit.

(4) On an interlocutor being pronounced under paragraph (1), the petitioner shall exhibit to the clerk of the inferior court or tribunal a certified copy of the interlocutor; and that clerk shall transmit the documents ordered to be produced to the Deputy Principal Clerk.

(5) Where the petitioner fails to comply with the requirement on him under paragraph (4), the petition shall be refused.

(6) An interlocutor granting suspension shall include a direction to the clerk of court to send a copy of the interlocutor by post to the clerk of the inferior court or tribunal on whom service was executed under paragraph (2).

(7) Where an interlocutor granting suspension is reclaimed against, the reclaimer shall give written intimation of that fact to the clerk of the inferior court or tribunal as soon as possible after the reclaiming motion has been marked.

(8) The interlocutor disposing of such a reclaiming motion shall include a direction to the clerk of court to send a copy of that interlocutor to the clerk of the inferior court or tribunal on whom service was executed under paragraph (2).

Deriv. R.C.S. 1965, r. 242(a)

GENERAL NOTE.

60.6.1

It had been thought that it was unclear whether it was competent to present an ordinary petition for suspension of a decree, order or decision of an inferior court or tribunal following the introduction of applications for judicial review as the means of the court exercising its supervisory jurisdiction. It has now been held that the reference to the "supervisory jurisdiction of the court" in r. 58.1(1) (applications for judicial review) must be construed as excluding procedures for which specific provision is made elsewhere in the R.C.S. 1994 and as confined to the type of jurisdiction described in *West v. Secretary of State for Scotland* 1992 S.C. 385: *Bell v. Fiddes* 1996 S.L.T. 51, 52H per Lord Marnoch. In that case it was held that judicial review for reduction of a decree in absence in the sheriff court and interim interdict against enforcement was incompetent and reduction should be sought in an action of reduction.

It is not competent to suspend an unextracted decree: *Turner v. Gray* (1824) 3 S.235. It is not competent to suspend a decree of absolvitor or a decree for expenses arising to any extent from it: *McGregor v. Lord Strathallan* (1862) 24 D. 1006, 1009 per L.J.-C. Inglis. The court may not suspend a sheriff court decree where its value (exclusive of interest) brings it within the sheriff's privative jurisdiction (currently £1,500: Sheriff Courts (Scotland) Act 1907, s.7 as amended by the Sheriff Courts (Scotland) Act 1971 (Privative Jurisdiction and Summary Cause) Order 1988 [SI 1988/1993]): *Brown and Critchley Ltd v. The Decorative Art Journals Co. Ltd* 1922 S.C. 192; such a suspension must be brought before the sheriff (Sheriff Courts (Scotland) Act 1907, s.5(5) and A.S. (Summary Suspension) 1993 [SI 1993/3128]).

"SERVED".

60.6.2

For methods, see Chap. 16, Pt I.

INTERLOCUTOR ORDERING PRODUCTION.

60.6.3

This may be pronounced on the motion of any party or by the court at its own instance.

RECLAIMING.

60.6.4

See Chap. 38.

"WRITTEN INTIMATION".

60.6.5

For methods, see r. 16.9.

Interlocutor refusing suspension after proof

60.7

60.7. Where the Lord Ordinary, after a proof, refuses a petition for suspension of a decree or decision of an inferior court or tribunal, he shall specify in his interlocutor the relevant facts of the case which he finds to be established and the points of law which he has applied to such facts.

Deriv. R.C.S. 1965, r. 242(b)

Chapter 61

Judicial Factors

Part I – General Provisions

Application and interpretation of this Chapter

61.1.—(1) This Chapter applies to an application for the appointment of a
judicial factor, and to a judicial factor appointed by the court.

(2) In this Chapter, unless the context otherwise requires—

> "the Act of 1849" means the Judicial Factors Act 1849;
>
> "the Act of 1995" means the Children (Scotland) Act 1995;[1]
>
> "judicial factor" includes a curator bonis, a factor *loco absentis*, a factor on
> trust or other estates, and a guardian.

Deriv. R.C.S. 1965, r. 199 (r. 61.1(2))

GENERAL NOTE.

This Chapter provides rules for the appointment and subsequent conduct of judicial factors appointed
by the court. It applies, subject to any other specific provisions in the R.C.S. 1994, to all judicial factors
of whatever type. Until the mid-nineteenth century there was a division between (a) judicial factors appointed to manage the estates of natural persons under a legal incapacity (e.g. curators bonis (to a minor
or an incapax), factors *loco tutoris*, factors *loco absentis*); and (b) judicial factors appointed to ingather
and distribute the estates of legally capable persons, natural and non-natural, due to insolvency or other
financial or administrative difficulties. This was reflected in the application of different Acts of Sederunt
to these different types of factor. Both types of factor could only be appointed by application to the nobile
officium of the Inner House. By the C.S.A 1857 this jurisdiction was delegated to the Outer House where,
but for minor exceptions, it remains. Following the Judicial Factors (Scotland) Act 1880, the sheriff court
was given power to appoint some types of factor and, after s.14 of the Law Reform (Miscellaneous
Provisions) Act 1980, the sheriff court has concurrent jurisdiction. The fact that the application is still
technically to the *nobile officium* is reflected in judicial dicta to the effect that the remedy is only available in absolute deadlock (e.g. between parties, shareholders, co-owners) and no other legal remedy is
available.

The first statute to cover judicial factors was the Judicial Factors Act 1849 (the "Act of 1849";
originally referred to as the Pupils Protection (Scotland) Act 1849 which indicates its original purpose to
supervise, inter alia, factors managing the estates of pupils and minors). S.1 of the Act of 1849 defined
judicial factor as "factor *loco absentis*, and curator bonis". This definition and the scope of the Act of
1849 was extended to all types of judicial factor by s.6 of the Judicial Factors (Scotland) Act 1889. With
effect from 1st April 2002, the words "and curator bonis" in s.1 of the 1849 Act were repealed and no
longer form part of that definition: Adults with Incapacity (Scotland) Act 2000, Sched. 6.

The rules in this Chapter have been made under the powers in s.5 of the C.S.A. 1988, s.40 of the Act
of 1849 and s.21 of the 1889 Act (see A.S. (R.C.S. 1994) 1994, Sched. 1 [SI 1994/1443]). Accordingly,
following the Interpretation Act 1978, s.11, unless the context otherwise requires, words and expressions
used in this Chapter which are also used in the C.S.A. 1988, the Act of 1849 or the 1889 Act have the
same meaning as in those Acts, as the case may be.

JUDICIAL FACTOR.

There is no precise definition of a judicial factor. This is a result of the historical origin of judicial factors, who may be appointed by, inter alia, the exercise of the *nobile officium* of the court in a number of
different situations for a number of different purposes. Irons on *Judicial Factors* (1908) described a
judicial factor as "an officer appointed by the Court, to whose care, custody and management under its
supervision, are committed estates and interests which are without capable administration, or are the
subject of litigation, in order that such estates or interests may ... be preserved for [the beneficiaries']
behoof and of all having interest therein".

It has also been said that "there is no limit to the circumstances under which the Court ... may appoint
a judicial factor provided that the appointment is necessary to protect against loss or injustice which cannot in the circumstances be prevented by allowing the ordinary legal remedies to take their course":
Leslie's Judicial Factor 1925 S.C. 464, 469 per L.P. Clyde. For an example of a case where an appointment was not competent, see *Institute of Chartered Accountants in Scotland v. Kay*, 2001 S.L.T. 1449
(appointment over estate of unfit CA recalled as petitioners had no interest in his estate).

Nevertheless there are a number of generally recognised types of judicial factor according to the
reasons for appointment. These may be listed as follows:

61.1

61.1.1

61.1.2

---

[1] Definition inserted by S.I. 1997 No. 1720 (effective 1st August 1997).

1. *Curator bonis.* The power to appoint a curator bonis was abolished by the Adults with Incapacity (Scotland) Act 2000 from 1st April 2002. Latterly there was only one type of curator bonis, namely a curator bonis to an incapax. The appointment was made where a disabled person was incapable of managing his affairs and no-one wished to be appointed tutor-at-law (under the Curators Act 1585: see note 14.2.11) or tutor-dative (under the common law: see note 14.2.11). This included inability to supervise properly an attorney: *Fraser v. Paterson* 1987 S.L.T. 562. Physical disability may (e.g. *Blaikie* (1827) 5 S. 268) or may not (e.g. *Kirkpatrick* (1853) 15 D. 734) render a disabled person incapax. The petitioner could be any person having an interest in the estate of the incapax, including the incapax himself (e.g. *Mark* (1845) 7 D. 882; *A.B., Petr.* (1908) 16 S.L.T. 557). In particular a local authority (regional or islands council) or the Mental Welfare Commission could, in certain circumstances, present a petition: Mental Heath (Scotland) Act 1984, ss. 92 and 93. The appointment of a curator bonis supersedes the functions of any attorney previously appointed by the incapax: *Dick* (1901) 9 S.L.T. 177; *Fraser*, above.

    The appointment of a tutor-at-law or tutor-dative, except in so far as it provides otherwise, supersedes the appointment of a curator bonis and brings it to an end: *Young v. Rose* (1839) 1D 1242; and *Dick v. Douglas* 1924 S.C. 787. For a conflict between a person wishing to be appointed a tutor-at-law and a curator bonis, see *Britton v. Britton's Curator Bonis* 1996 S.C. 178.

    General Guidance Notes for Curator Bonis have been issued by the Office of the Accountant of Court following the 2000 Act.

    As from 1st April 2002 a curator bonis may not be appointed to a person with incapacity aged 16 or over, but can be if the person is under 16: Adults with Incapacity (Scotland) Act 2000, s. 80. Where a person already has a curator bonis, the curator becomes a guardian under the 2000 Act with power over the property and financial affairs of the adult: 2000 Act, Sched. 4, para. 1(1). Where the person is under 16, the curator becomes the guardian upon the child's 16th birthday: 2000 Act, Sched. 4, para. 1(2). [The effect of repeals, by Sched. 6 to the 2000 Act, to the Judicial Factors Acts is that even curators to children are not subject to the Judicial Factors Acts.] Applications for appointment of guardianship orders are to the sheriff. A tutor-dative or tutor-at-law may also not be appointed to person aged 16 or over: 2000 Act, s. 80.

    Guardians are subject to the controls in the 2000 Act.

    The *Hague Convention on the International Protection of Adults* of 13th January 2000, was ratified by Scotland on 4th November 2003.

2. *Factor loco absentis.* The appointment is made where a person has left Scotland leaving nobody to manage his affairs here. Following improvements in transport and communication a court will be more reluctant to make the appointment than it once was. An appointment will be inappropriate when there is evidence that the absent person has died or no evidence that he has been alive for the previous seven years. In that situation an action of declarator of death should be raised; and on decree being pronounced an application may be made to appoint an executor. The petitioner may be any person having an interest in the estate of the absent person, including a relative (e.g. *Dobson* (1903) 11 S.L.T. 44) or a creditor (*Lunan v. Macdonald* 1927 S.L.T. 661).

3. *Factor on trust estate.* The appointment may be made in a number of situations where no other remedy is available. Generally these occur when there is nobody to manage the trust estate (e.g. no surviving trustee, death of sine qua non trustee, or lack of quorum). If the difficulty lies with the trust purposes the remedy is a petition for their variation (see Chap. 63, Pt. I). A factor is appropriate if there is a problem with the trustee as such. Other examples include, trustees' indefinite absence from Scotland (*Nisbet* (1835) 13 S. 384; *Dean* (1852) 15 D. 17), conflict of interest between trustee qua trustee and qua individual or between trustees to two antagonistic trusts (*Thomson v. Dalrymple* (1865) 3 M. 336; *Henderson v. Henderson* (1893) 20 R. 536), deadlock in management, trustees' malverisation of office, etc.; see also Irons on *Judicial Factors*, pp. 12 and 13 and Walker on *Judicial Factors* (1974), pp. 28 et seq.

4. *Management of child's property* Guardians to a child in all circumstances are now provided for by legislation. They are no longer judicial factors.

    From 1 November 1996 all guardians of persons under the age of 16 years are appointed under the Children (Scotland) Act 1995. Guardianship of a child is therefore a statutory office under that legislation and no judicial factor (whether a factor *loco tutoris* or curator bonis) is required.

    A parent or guardian has a duty to act as a child's representative in the administration of the child's property (Children (Scotland) Act 1995, ss. 1(1)(d) and 7(5)). The duty is to administer the child's property as a reasonable and prudent person would do for his or her own property (Children (Scotland) Act 1995, s. 10(1)). However, there can arise situations where the child's interests may make it inappropriate for the parent or guardian to administer the child's property. In those circumstances a judicial factor may be appointed to administer the property. The appointment may arise in two ways: (1) A judicial factor may be appointed to administer the child's property by petition at the instance of the parent or guardian, any person "claiming an interest" or by the court on its own initiative: Children (Scotland) Act 1995, s. 11(1), (2)(g), (3)(a) and (b) and r. 61.2. (2) Alternatively, if the property is a sum of money payable to a person under the age of 16 years, who became entitled as a result of an action of court proceedings, a factor may be appointed by the court in question to manage it. See r. 49.88 and (10) below. The duties of the factor are however limited to the management of the sum of money which has become payable to the child. They do not extend to the child in any other way.

A guardian may be appointed (or removed) or a judicial factor appointed (or removed) to manage a child's property under s. 11(1), (2)(g) and (3) of the Children (Scotland) Act 1995.

5. *Factor on estate of deceased person without executor.* See r. 61.16 and note 61.16.1 for appointment under s. 11A of 1889 Act. An appointment may also be made at common law: see Irons on *Judicial Factors*, pp. 143 et seq.

6. *Factor on partnership estate.* The appointment may be made (a) before the dissolution of the partnership or (b) as part of or following the dissolution of the partnership.

   (a) Appointment before dissolution of the partnership. The court may appoint a judicial factor where the surviving partners are unfit through health or from breach of duty to carry on the partnership: *Dickie v. Mitchell* (1874) 1 R. 1030, 1033 per L.P. Inglis. Generally, however, this will be in exceptional circumstances where dissolution or common law sequestration of the partnership is not appropriate: *Dickie*, above.

   (b) Appointment as part of or following dissolution of the partnership. For circumstances constituting dissolution, see the Partnership Act 1890, ss. 32–35. Following dissolution the surviving former partner or partners are expected to gather in the assets of the partnership, pay off its liabilities, and distribute the surplus to each other according to their entitlement: 1890 Act, s. 39; *Gow v. Schultze* (1877) 4 R. 928. Where a former partner fails to carry out his duties under s. 39 of the 1890 Act, thereby prejudicing the assets of the partnership, any other former partner may present a petition for the appointment of a judicial factor and for sequestration of the partnership estate: 1890 Act, s. 39; *Dickie*, above; *Allan v. Gronmeyer* (1891) 18 R. 784; *Carabine v. Carabine* 1949 S.C. 521. The effect of the sequestration order is to transfer control of the partnership assets from the possessor to the judicial factor. Often an interim judicial factor is appointed: see, e.g. *McCulloch v. McCulloch* 1953 S.C. 189.

7. *Factor on company estate.* The appointment may be made, at common law, following illegal or dishonest conduct by the directors (*Fraser, Petr.* 1971 S.L.T. 146) or following voting deadlock between shareholders (*McGuiness v. Black* 1990 S.C. 21, 24 per Lord McCluskey). The aim of the appointment is to preserve the assets of the company. The common law power overlaps with the statutory provisions allowing remedies to a minority shareholder in the event of prejudice under the Companies Act 1985, s. 459. The petitioner may be a shareholder or anybody with a sufficient interest.

   Often the circumstances require appointment of an interim judicial factor: *Fraser*, above; *McGuiness*, above. Special powers (e.g. the same as those of a receiver) may be sought in the petition: *McGuiness*, above. Averments must be made in the petition stating the reasons why an interim appointment should be made.

   The appointment may be made under various private Acts for more limited purposes of clearing secured creditors' debts: see, e.g. *Greenock Harbour Trs. v. Judicial Factor of Greenock Harbour Trust* 1910 S.C.(H.L.) 32.

   The appointment may be made under s. 41 of the Solicitors (Scotland) Act 1980 to an incorporated solicitors' practice where the practice has failed to comply with the Solicitors (Scotland) Accounts Rules: see (8) below. The same rules as for an individual solicitor apply.

8. *Factor on solicitor's estate.* The appointment may be made where the Council of the Law Society of Scotland is satisfied (a) that the solicitor has breached the accounts rules; and (b) in connection with his practice, (i) his liabilities exceed his assets, (ii) it is not reasonably practicable to ascertain definitely from his books, accounts and other documents whether his liabilities exceed his assets or (iii) there is reasonable ground for apprehending that a claim on the guarantee fund may arise: Solicitors (Scotland) Act 1980, s. 41.

   The purpose of the appointment is to ensure the proper application of the funds in the solicitor's estate with a view to settling the solicitor's liabilities: *Council of the Law Society of Scotland v. McKinnie (No. 2)* 1995 S.C. 94, 111C per Lord Penrose and 115G-116B per L.P. Hope.

   The petitioner is the Council of the Law Society: 1980 Act, s. 41. The petition must be to the Inner House: r. 14.3(b). Before any order is pronounced in the petition the solicitor must have the opportunity to be heard: 1980 Act, s. 41.

   Special rules apply to the conduct of the judicial factor in addition to his normal duties: 1980 Act, s. 42; and see *Ross v. Gordon's Judicial Factor* 1973 S.L.T. (Notes) 91 and *Scottish Council of the Pontifical Society of St Peter Apostle for Native Clergy v. McGregor's Judicial Factor* 1974 S.C. 106. Any estate administered by the judicial factor does not vest in a trustee in sequestration who is appointed subsequently to the judicial factor: *Council of the Law Society of Scotland v. McKinnie* 1993 S.L.T. 238.

9. *Factor on common property.* The appointment may be made where the common owners of property owned by them *pro indiviso* disagree over any act of management or dealing in relation to the property which they do not wish to sell: *Mackintosh* (1849) 11 D. 1029; *Bailey v. Scott* (1860) 22 D. 1105. The court will only appoint a judicial factor where there is deadlock and no other way out, e.g. agreement on (non-judicial) factor: *Allan* (1898) 6 S.L.T. 152.

10. *Factor on money payable to a child in an action.* The appointment of such a factor (known as a factor on damages) may be made by the court in any action in which a sum of money becomes payable by virtue of a decree or an extra-judicial settlement to or for the benefit of the child in an action of for the payment of a sum of money: r.49.88. The order may be made by the court at

its own instance: Children (Scotland) Act 1995, s.13(1). The title of s. 13 refers to "actions of damages" but the power to appoint a factor or make other orders to safeguard the money relates to all claims of money in a litigation. Once the money has been paid an order cannot be made under s. 13.

11. *Factor pending litigation.* The appointment is made to secure the management of heritable or moveable property which is in dispute. Often the appointment is only an interim one. It may be made where the party not in possession contests the peaceful right to possess of the party in possession: see, e.g. *Russell* (1847) 9 D. 989. Where the party in possession has a strong prima facie right to possess, it will not usually be appropriate to appoint a judicial factor pending the outcome of an action concerning the property: *Campbell v. Campbell* (1864) 2 M.(H.L.) 41, 45 per Lord Westbury L.C. Where nobody is in possession (e.g. on death of owner occupier), the court will appoint a factor where each claimant presents a stateable case for his claim leading to a competition: *Pringle Pattison's Curator Bonis* (1898) 5 S.L.T. 400.

JURISDICTION.

61.1.3   This lies with the *nobile officium* of the Court of Session exercised, with two exceptions, by the Outer House: r. 14.2(a). An application for a factor to a solicitor's estate or to the estate of an incorporated practice of solicitors is to the Inner House: r. 14.3(b). An application for a guardian to a child is by action: Age of Legal Capacity (Scotland) Act 1991, s.5(2).

FACTOR'S FEES AND OUTLAY.

61.1.4   The fees and outlays of a judicial factor are a prior claim over all other competing claims on the factory estate: *Council the Law Society of Scotland v. McKinnie* 1995 S.C. 94.

Application for appointment of judicial factor

61.2   **61.2.**—[1](1) An application for the appointment of a judicial factor shall be made by petition.

(2) An application under section 9(5)(a) of the Act of 1995 (application by Accountant of Court for appointment of judicial factor to administer certain property of a child) shall be made by petition in Form 61.2; and Chapter 14 shall not apply as respects any such petition.

(3) A petition in Form 61.2 shall, after being lodged in the Petition Department and recorded in the Petitions Register but without appearing in the Motion Roll, be presented to the Lord Ordinary in court or in chambers; and he may—

(a) forthwith make the appointment sought; or

(b) make an order—

(i) for such intimation, service and advertisement of the petition as he considers appropriate; and

(ii) for a hearing, on such date as he may specify, as respects the petition.

(4) Without prejudice to the generality of paragraph (3)(b)(i), any order under that paragraph as to intimation may specify that rule 16.4 shall not apply and that the Accountant of Court shall make intimation by post in such manner as the Lord Ordinary thinks fit.

"PETITION".

61.2.1   The petition may be presented by anyone with an interest in the estate. This may include the incapax himself where he is aware that he may soon be unable to manage his affairs: *A.B., Petr.* (1908) 16 S.L.T. 557.

The petition is, subject to exceptions (see note 61.1.3), presented in the Outer House: r. 14.2(a). For form of petitions see r. 14.4. The petition must be signed by counsel or other person having a right of audience: r. 4.2(3); and see r. 1.3(1) (definition of "counsel" and "other person having a right of audience") and note 1.3.4. A fee is payable on lodging the petition and process: see note 14.5.10.

For petitions generally, see Chap. 14. For applications under s.9(5)(a) of the Act of 1995, see note 61.2.4.

ELIGIBILITY TO BE JUDICIAL FACTOR.

61.2.2   In general any natural person of full legal capacity is eligible. A non-natural person is ineligible: *Brogan, Petr.* 1986 S.L.T. 420. A bankrupt (*Miller* (1849) 12 D. 941), or a person having an ineligible

---

[1] R.61.2 substituted by S.I. 1997 No. 1720 (effective 1st August 1997).

adverse interest (*Leslie* (1908) 12 S.L.T. 359), is ineligible.

Only one factor may be appointed to each estate: *Sloan, Petr.* (1844) 7 D. 227.

INTERIM JUDICIAL FACTOR.

An interim judicial factor may be appointed in a situation of urgency where the intimation of the peti- **61.2.3**
tion and the lodging of answers would cause prejudicial delay: see *McGuiness v. Black* 1990 S.C. 21;
Irons on *Judicial Factors*, Chap. XIV. An interim judicial factor must be specifically craved for in the
prayer of the petition: *McGuiness*, above. The special reasons of urgency should be averred where the appointment of an interim factor is sought immediately: *Cuthbertson v. Gibson* (1887) 14 R. 736.

A motion for the appointment of an interim judicial factor may be enrolled at any time after the
presentation of the petition. If the motion is enrolled before the first order it may be heard ex parte (i.e.
without intimation) unless any person with an interest had lodged a caveat: rr. 23.8 and 23.9. The
interlocutor appointing an interim judicial factor should contain, inter alia, an express direction to the
factor to report to the Accountant of Court so long as his appointment is interim (normally at intervals of
not less than one month): *McCulloch v. McCulloch* 1953 S.C. 189, 192 per L.P. Cooper (in which such an
appointment was described as an extremely rare remedy).

The person to whose estate a factor is sought to be appointed ought to be given the opportunity of being heard on the motion for appointment of an interim judicial factor unless there is reason to suppose
that such intimation is likely to place the estate in jeopardy: *Institute of Chartered Accountants in Scotland
v. Kay* 2001 S.L.T. 1449, 1451L per Lord Carloway.

The court may restrict the power of the interim judicial factor, e.g. by prohibiting the sale of certain
assets in the estate of a dissolved partnership: *Hunter v. Hunter*, 1999 S.C. 1, 3C per Lord Osborne.

An interim judicial factor must still find caution in the usual way and is restricted in what he can do
until he does so: see notes 61.9.1 et seq.

APPLICATIONS UNDER SECTION 9(5)(A) OF THE CHILDREN (SCOTLAND) ACT 1995.

Subject to s.13 of the Act of 1995 (court awards of money to children), where property is owned by or **61.2.4**
due to a child, is held by a person other than a parent or guardian, would otherwise require to be
transferred to a parent with parental responsibilities, or to a guardian, for administration for the child (unless appointed a trustee under a trust deed to administer the property for the child) and (1) the person
holding the property is a trustee or executor, then (a) if the value of the property exceeds £20,000, he
shall, (b) if the value is not less than £5,000 and does not exceed £20,000, he may, or (2) the person holding the property is not a trustee or executor, he may, apply to the Accountant of Court for directions: Act
of 1995, s.9(1), (2) and (3). Where such an application is made to the Accountant of Court, he may,
among other things, apply to the court for the appointment of a judicial factor: Act of 1995, s.9(5)(a).

An application under s.9(5)(a) of the Act of 1995 may be signed only by the Accountant of Court (r.
4.2(3)(cc)) and must be in Form 61.2 (r. 61.2(2)). A process is not required: r. 4.3. The rules of service by
post in r. 16.4 do not apply: r. 61.2(4).

Crave to dispense with service on incapax

61.3. Where, in a petition for the appointment of a curator bonis to an incapax, **61.3**
dispensation of service on the incapax is craved on the ground that such service
would be injurious to the health of the incapax, two medical certificates to that effect shall be lodged in process.

GENERAL NOTE.

If it is sought to dispense with service on an incapax, this should be craved in the prayer of the petition **61.3.1**
and supported by averments: r. 14.4(6).

A motion to grant the dispensation of service must be enrolled and sought at the time of the first order:
r. 14.5(2).

It should be noted that injury to health is not the only ground for dispensing with personal service.
Personal service on an incapax in a remote part of Scotland may be deferred with due regard to cost in
relation to the moveable estate of the incapax: *Robertson, Petr.* 1978 S.L.T. (Notes) 39.

"TWO MEDICAL CERTIFICATES".

The examination of the incapax must be done separately by each of the two medical examiners. **61.3.2**
Notwithstanding s.1 of the Civil Evidence (Scotland) Act 1988 (rule requiring corroboration abolished),
a certificate from each of two doctors is required primarily because two medical recommendations are
required for the admission and detention of a patient under the Mental Health (Scotland) Act 1984.

Formerly the certificates had to be adopted as holograph, if not holograph and signed. Since the coming into force of the Requirements of Writing (Scotland) Act 1995 on 1st August 1995, which abolished
the privilege of documents adopted as holograph, the practice of the court is as follows. A certificate will
be accepted which is signed by the certifying doctor provided it is on headed notepaper with details of the
doctor's professional practice and address; it need not be witnessed. Such a certificate frequently bears to
be on soul and conscience, although this is not necessary following P.N. 6th June 1968 (soul and
conscience medical certificates).

The certificates, which normally contain the words "having seen and examined (name of incapax)", must not pre-date the presentation of the petition by more than 30 days.

"LODGED IN PROCESS".

61.3.3 The medical certificates are lodged as productions. On lodging productions, see r. 4.5.

Incidental applications

61.4 **61.4.** Unless otherwise provided in this Chapter, an incidental application to the court in a petition for the appointment of a judicial factor shall be made by note.

"UNLESS OTHERWISE PROVIDED IN THIS CHAPTER".

61.4.1 See, e.g. applications by letter to the Accountant of Court for authority to encroach on capital (r. 61.13) and applications for consent to do an act outwith the purpose of the factory (r. 61.14).

"NOTE".

61.4.2 For applications by note, see r. 15.2.

Intimation and service

61.5 **61.5.**—[1](1) The order for intimation and service under rule 14.5 (first order in petitions) in a petition or note relating to a judicial factory shall include a requirement for intimation to the Accountant of Court (except where the petition is in Form 61.2) by first class recorded delivery post of the petition or note, as the case may be, and any production lodged with the petition or note.

(2) The Lord Ordinary may order publication of an advertisement of the petition in Form 61.5-A in the case of a petition for the appointment of a judicial factor or in Form 61.5-B in the case of a petition for the discharge of a judicial factor.

(3) Where publication of an advertisement has been made under paragraph (2), there shall be lodged in process—

    (a) a copy of the newspaper or other publication containing the advertisement; or

    (b) a certificate of publication by the publisher stating the date of publication and the text of the advertisement.

(4)[2] After a petition for the appointment of a judicial factor is lodged in the Petition Department, the Clerk of Session in that department may (wether or not any order is made, or is competent, under rule 14.5(1)(a)) provide any interested party with details of the petition.

"INTIMATION AND SERVICE".

61.5.1 For intimation and service generally, see r. 14.7 and Chap. 16, Pt I.

"ADVERTISEMENT".

61.5.2 The advertisement may be in one or more or both of a national or local newspaper of the area where persons likely to be interested in the estate may be situated.

"LODGED IN PROCESS".

61.5.3 The copy of the newspaper or other publication containing the advertisement (or the certificate required under r. 61.5(3)(b)) is lodged as a production. On lodging productions, see r. 4.5.

Documents for Accountant of Court

61.6 **61.6.**—(1) A person who lodges any document in a cause relating to a judicial factory (other than a petition for appointment of a judicial factor) shall send a copy of that document to the Accountant of Court.

---

[1] R.61.5(4) inserted by S.I. 1997 No. 1720 (effective 1st August 1997).
[2] R.61.5(1) amended by S.I. 1997 No. 1720 (effective 1st August 1997).

(2)   The clerk of session in the Petition Department shall transmit to the Accountant of Court any part of a process in a cause relating to a judicial factory as the Accountant of Court may request unless such part of the process is, at the time of request, required by the court.

Deriv. R.C.S. 1965, r. 200(a) (r. 61.6(1)) and r. 200(b) (r. 61.6(2))

"SEND".

This includes deliver: r. 1.3(1) (definition of "send").   **61.6.1**

ACCOUNTANT OF COURT.

The Accountant of Court is appointed under s.1 of the Judicial Factors (Scotland) Act 1889. He has,   **61.6.2**
inter alia, the duty to superintend the conduct of all judicial factors whether appointed in the Court of
Session or sheriff court: Act of 1849, s.10; 1889 Act, s.6. He has numerous duties under the various Acts
and subordinate legislation on judicial factors. He may report any misconduct or breach of duty by a factor to the Lord Ordinary for disposal: Act of 1849, s.20. His address is 2 Parliament Square, Edinburgh
EH1 1RQ; tel. 0131-554 2422; fax 0131-554 3632; DX ED311.

Accountant of Court to send information on prior application

61.7.   The Accountant of Court, on receiving intimation of a petition for the ap-   **61.7**
pointment of a judicial factor, shall report any information he may possess which he
considers may be of use to the court in disposing of the petition.

GENERAL NOTE.

The Accountant of Court may for example have comments on the eligibility or suitability of the   **61.7.1**
proposed judicial factor.

Transmission of process to Accountant of Court to find caution

61.8.   The clerk of session in the Petition Department shall, on the appointment   **61.8**
of the judicial factor being made by the court, transmit the process of the petition to
the Accountant of Court for the fixing and finding of caution.

Deriv. R.C.S. 1965, r. 200(e)(preamble)

Finding caution

61.9.—(1)   The appointment of a person as a judicial factor shall be subject to   **61.9**
his finding caution; and the interlocutor appointing a judicial factor shall ordain him
to find caution.

(2)   The court may, on cause shown, on a motion made before the expiry of the
period for finding caution specified by virtue of rule 33.3 (orders to find caution or
other security), allow further time for finding caution.

(3)   The Accountant of Court shall, on receiving the process in a petition for the
appointment of a judicial factor transmitted to him under rule 61.8, fix the caution to
be found by the judicial factor.

(4)   Where the Accountant of Court considers that any caution fixed by the court
under section 27 of the Act of 1849 (amount of caution limited by court), should be
increased—

(a)   the Accountant of Court may increase the amount unless the judicial factor requires him to report to the court;

(b)   where the judicial factor requires him to report to the court, the Accountant of Court shall do so; and

(c)   on the report mentioned in sub-paragraph (b) being received, the cause
shall be put out on the By Order Roll before the Lord Ordinary to
determine the amount of caution.

(5)   A bond of caution or other security offered by a judicial factor shall be
delivered to the Accountant of Court; and rule 33.4(3) (lodging of bond of caution in
process) and rule 33.7(1) (Deputy Principal Clerk to satisfy himself that bond of
caution or other security is in proper form) shall not apply.

(6)   Except in relation to paragraph (7), where caution has been found to the satisfaction of the Accountant of Court, he shall endorse and sign, on the interlocutor sheet of the process appointing the judicial factor, a certificate stating that caution has been found, the amount of caution and the date of the certificate.

(7)   During the subsistence of a judicial factory, the Accountant of Court may, at any time—

(a)   require the judicial factor to increase the amount of, or find new or additional, caution; or

(b)   authorise the judicial factor to reduce the amount of existing caution.

Deriv. R.C.S. 1965, r. 200(c)(part) (r. 61.9(2)), r. 200(d) (r. 61.9(5)), r. 200(e)(i)(part) (r. 61.9(3)), r. 200(e)(ii)(part) (r. 61.9(4)), and r. 200(e)(i)(part) (r. 61.9(6)); and r. 200(e)(iii) amended by S.I. 1985 No. 1600 (r. 61.9(7))

GENERAL NOTE.

61.9.1   The present practice is for the court, in the interlocutor appointing a judicial factor, to state that the factor may not obtain the official certified copy of the interlocutor appointing him until he has found caution; it does not usually order him to find caution. He must, however, find caution for his intromissions with and management of the estate: Act of 1849, s. 2.

A judicial factor may not, except in exceptional circumstances, enter on the duties of his office until after caution has been found and received as sufficient: Act of 1849, s. 2; *Donaldson v. Kennedy* (1833) 11 S. 740; see also note 61.11.1.

CAUTION.

61.9.2   For the meaning of caution, see note 33.1.1. Usually caution will be in the form of a bond of caution (r. 33.4(1)(a)), or it may be any other method of security approved by the court (r. 33.4(2)). Where caution is by bond of caution the bond may be by (a) an insurance company authorised to conduct such business (see r. 33.5); or (b) any other person, in which case the court must satisfy itself as to the sufficiency of the caution. The form of all bonds must comply with r. 37.6. A bond must be sent to the Accountant of Court (together with a copy): r. 61.9(5).

The Accountant then satisfies himself as to the caution offered. On being satisfied the Accountant will sign and endorse on the interlocutor sheet of the process a certificate that caution has been found and the amount: r. 61.9(6). The Accountant of Court will then transmit the process back to the Petition Department to enable an official certified copy of the interlocutor of appointment to be issued to the factor. The Accountant of Court will, however, retain the principal bond of caution as custodian: Act of 1849, s. 35.

Caution should be sought without delay, and agreement should be reached between the petitioner and the nominated factor before the petition is presented as to whose is the responsibility for arranging caution: P.N. No. 2 of 1994.

PERIOD FOR FINDING CAUTION.

61.9.3   The former rule in R.C.S. 1965 r. 200(c) which stipulated a period of one month has not been re-enacted. There is not now a fixed period, but a period must be specified in the interlocutor appointing the factor: Act of 1849, s. 2. The period may be extended if a motion is made before its expiry: r. 61.9(2). Failure to find caution within the period specified will result in the appointment falling: Act of 1849, s. 2. In this case a motion must be enrolled for re-appointment. Such a motion requires appearance, and will be granted only on cause shown. Caution should, however, be sought without delay: P.N. No. 2 of 1994.

"MOTION".

61.9.4   For motions, see Chap. 23.

AMOUNT OF CAUTION.

61.9.5   S. 27 of the Act of 1849 enables the court to limit the amount of caution to a specified sum less than the value of the estate. Where the Accountant of Court wishes to increase the amount of caution (which he has power to do), the judicial factor may insist on the matter being decided by the court: r. 61.9(4). The former requirement in R.C.S. 1965, r. 200(e)(ii) that, where the question of the increase is referred to the court, the amount fixed by the court must not be less than two-thirds of the value of the moveable and other realisable estate has not been re-enacted; although the fraction still provides a useful rule of thumb.

DEATH OR INSOLVENCY OF CAUTIONER.

61.9.6   The factor must intimate in writing the death or insolvency of the cautioner to the Accountant of Court: Act of 1849, s. 11. The Accountant of Court will then give notice in writing to the factor requiring new caution to be found: Act of 1849, s. 11. A new cautioner may be liable for the loss resulting from misconduct by the factor before the granting of new caution: *Grant* (1828) 6 S. 982; *Wallace's Factor v. McKissock* (1898) 28 R. 642.

BOND OF CAUTION FOR CURATOR BONIS.

In addition to the usual requirements (see note 61.9.2), a bond of caution for a curator bonis to a person suffering from mental disorder within the meaning of the Mental Health (Scotland) Act 1984 must contain a consent to the registration of the bond for execution in the Books of Council and Session: Act of 1849, s. 26. Before it is sent to the Accountant of Court it must be sent to the Keeper of the Registers for registration for execution: Act of 1849, s. 26. See also Irons on *Judicial Factors*, pp. 469 and 470.

61.9.7

Issue of official certified copy interlocutor

61.10. An official certified copy of the interlocutor appointing a judicial factor shall not be issued by a clerk of session without a certificate having been endorsed on the interlocutor sheet in accordance with rule 61.9(6).

61.10

Deriv. R.C.S. 1965, r. 200(e)(i)(part) amended by S.I. 1967 No. 487

OFFICIAL CERTIFIED COPY INTERLOCUTOR.

This is issued by the Petition Department on application being made to it: r. 7.11; see also note 7.11.1.

61.10.1

Judicial factor's title to act

61.11. A judicial factor shall not be entitled to act until he has received the official certified copy of the interlocutor appointing him.

61.11

CAPACITY TO ACT.

In general a judicial factor is not entitled to act until he has received the official certified copy interlocutor ("CCI") appointing him: Act of 1849, s. 2; and r. 61.11.

61.11.1

He may, however, act immediately on appointment to preserve the estate in a situation of urgent necessity: *Calver v. Howard Baker & Co.* (1894) 22 R. 1 (raising of court action). He cannot, however, actively intromit with estate property until he has the CCI: *Donaldson v. Kennedy* (1833) 11 S. 740.

TITLE OF JUDICIAL FACTOR.

The effect of the issue of the official CCI of appointment is to assign to the factor all funds, property and effects situated or invested in any part of the British dominions, including Scotland, belonging to the estate: Judicial Factors (Scotland) Act 1889, s.13; and see *Council of the Law Society of Scotland v. McKinnie* 1995 S.C.L.R. 53, 71F per Lord Penrose.

61.11.2

STAMP DUTY.

As the official CCI is a "conveyance" it is liable to the fixed duty of 50p payable by the judicial factor: Stamp Act 1891, s.1 and Sched. The Inland Revenue allows timeous stamping within 30 days of issue after which time penalty duty must be paid.

61.11.3

Remission or modification of penal interest

61.12. The Accountant of Court may, if satisfied that the circumstances justify it, remit or modify any interest incurred by a judicial factor under section 5(1) of the Act of 1849 (interest incurred for failure by factor to lodge money in bank etc.).

61.12

Deriv. R.C.S. 1965, r. 200(g)

SECTION 5(1) OF THE ACT OF 1849.

S.5(1) of the Act of 1849 provides, inter alia, that where a judicial factor has left more than £500 of money in his hands for over 10 days he shall be charged penalty interest at the rate of 20 per cent a year on the excess over £500 held for every day over 10 days. It also provides that unless the factor has kept such money from innocent causes, he shall be dismissed by the Accountant of Court and have no claim for commission.

61.12.1

Applications to encroach on capital

61.13.—(1) Where the income from the estate of a ward is insufficient for the maintenance of the ward, the judicial factor may apply to the Accountant of Court for his consent to encroach on the capital of the estate for the purpose of maintaining the ward.

61.13

(2) An application under paragraph (1) shall be made by letter and shall be supported by such information as the Accountant of Court may require.

(3)[1] On receipt of such an application, the Accountant of Court—

---

[1] R.61.13(3) substituted by S.I. 1997 No. 1720 (effective 1st August 1997).

   (a)   may, if the proposed encroachment does not exceed 5% of the capital value of the estate as that the date when application is first made under paragraph (1), consent to the application subject to such conditions as he thinks fit to impose; and

   (b)   if he is unable, or declines, to consent under sub-paragraph (a), shall—

       (i)   ordain the judicial factor to intimate, in accordance with paragraphs (5) and (6), the making of the application; or

       (ii)   ordain him to apply by note to the Lord Ordinary for special powers.

   (4)   A person to whom intimation is given in accordance with paragraphs (5) and (6) may object to the application by—

   (a)   lodging an objection in writing with the Accountant of Court; and

   (b)   sending a copy of his objection to the judicial factor within 28 days after the date on which intimation was given to him.

   (5)[1]   The persons to whom intimation under paragraph (3)(b)(i) is to be given are—

   (a)   any cautioner of the judicial factor;

   (b)   any petitioner for the appointment of the judicial factor (other than a petitioner using Form 61.2);

   (c)   the ward, unless the circumstances of the ward are such as would warrant dispensing with service on him of a petition for the appointment of a judicial factor on his estate;

   (d)   the persons on whom the petition for appointment of the judicial factor was served and whose whereabouts are known to the judicial factor; and

   (e)   all other persons who have an interest in the estate and whose identity and whereabouts are known to the judicial factor.

   (6)[2]   The intimation under paragraph (3)(b)(i) shall include—

   (a)   a copy of the letter of application; and

   (b)   a notice setting out—

       (i)   the right of the person receiving the notice to object to the application in the manner provided in paragraph (4); and

       (ii)   that, in the absence of any such objection, the Accountant of Court may consent to the application.

   (7)[3]   The judicial factor shall, on giving intimation under paragraph (3)(b)(i), send to the Accountant of Court a certificate of intimation in Form 16.7 with a copy of the notice sent attached to it; and rule 16.7(2) (attaching certificate of intimation to principal writ or lodging it in process) shall not apply.

   (8)   Where no objections have been lodged under paragraph (4), the Accountant of Court may, on the expiry of the period for lodging objections—

   (a)   consent to the application subject to such conditions as he thinks fit; or (b) require the judicial factor to apply to the court for special powers.

   (9)   Where any objection has been lodged under paragraph (4), the judicial factor shall, on expiry of the period for lodging objections, apply to the court for special powers.

Deriv. R.C.S. 1965, r. 200B inserted by S.I. 1990 No. 705

---

[1] R.61.13(5), (6) and (7) amended by S.I. 1997 No. 1720 (effective 1st August 1997).
[2] R.61.13(5), (6) and (7) amended by S.I. 1997 No. 1720 (effective 1st August 1997).
[3] R.61.13(5), (6) and (7) amended by S.I. 1997 No. 1720 (effective 1st August 1997).

GENERAL NOTE.

This rule will apply largely to curators bonis and guardians to a child. Other factors will not have a ward. The purpose of this rule is to provide an expedited procedure which avoids the need to obtain special powers. The predecessor to R.C.S. 1994, r. 61.13 was R.C.S. 1965, r. 200B which was introduced to provide a formal procedure (in relation to what was done in practice) for application to the Accountant of Court by a curator for authority to encroach on the capital of his ward's estate in certain circumstances instead of the curator having to petition the court for special powers. That a rule should be provided was suggested by the Second Division in *Broadfoot's Curator Bonis* 1989 S.C. 90, 101. In that case it was held (1) that a curator did not have power to encroach on the capital of the ward's estate at his own hand, (2) that the Accountant of Court could authorise encroachment where (a) the estate was sufficient to meet his ward's requirements during the ward's life or (b) in the case of small estates, exhaustion of the estate would result in greater income from state funds, and (3) that in all other circumstances the curator had to apply to the court for special powers.

61.13.1

APPLICATIONS FOR SPECIAL POWERS.

If the judicial factor is nevertheless required by the Accountant of Court to obtain special powers he must apply for these by note: see r. 61.15.

61.13.2

INTIMATION BY JUDICIAL FACTOR.

For methods, see r. 16.7.

61.13.3

"SENDING", "SEND".

This includes deliver: r. 1.3(1) (definition of "send").

61.13.4

CAUTIONER.

A judicial factor who is a guardian of a person under 16 years of age may not have a cautioner as he is not bound to find caution: Act of 1849, s.25(2) inserted by the Law Reform (Parent and Child) (Scotland) Act 1986, Sched. 1, para. 1.

61.13.5

"DATE ON WHICH INTIMATION GIVEN".

Where intimation is by post the date of intimation is the day after the date of posting: r. 16.4(9). Where intimation is by any other method the date of intimation is the date of execution.

61.13.6

Applications under section 2(3) of the Trusts (Scotland) Act 1961

61.14.—(1) An application under section 2(3) of the Trusts (Scotland) Act 1961 to the Accountant of Court for his consent to the doing of an act to which that section applies shall be made by letter and shall be supported by such information as the Accountant of Court may require.

61.14

(2) Any person to whom intimation requires to be given in accordance with paragraph (3) may object to the application by lodging any objection with the Accountant of Court, and sending a copy of it to the judicial factor, within 28 days after the date on which the intimation was given.

(3) On the date on which he makes the application referred to in paragraph (1), the judicial factor shall intimate the application to—

    (a)   any cautioner of the judicial factor;

    (b)[1] any person who petitioned for the judicial factor to be appointed (except where the petition was in Form 61.2);

    (c)   the ward, unless the circumstances of the ward are such that would warrant dispensing with service on him of a petition for the appointment of a judicial factor on his estate;

    (d)   the persons upon whom the application for appointment of the judicial factor was served and whose whereabouts are known to the judicial factor; and

    (e)   all other persons who have an interest in the estate and whose identity and whereabouts are known to the judicial factor.

(4) The intimation to be given under paragraph (3) shall include—

    (a)   a copy of the letter of application, and

---

[1] R.61.14(3)(b) substituted by S.I. 1997 No. 1720 (effective 1st August 1997).

(b) a notice setting out—

    (i) the right of the person receiving the notice to object to the application in the manner provided in paragraph (2); and

    (ii) that, in the absence of any such objection, the Accountant of Court may consent to the application.

(5) The judicial factor shall, on giving intimation under paragraph (3), send to the Accountant of Court a certificate of intimation in Form 16.7 with a copy of the notice required under paragraph (4) attached to it; and rule 16.7(2) (attaching certificate of intimation to principal writ or lodging it in process) shall not apply.

Deriv. R.C.S. 1965, r. 200A inserted by S.I. 1980 No. 1803

GENERAL NOTE.

61.14.1   Where a judicial factor thinks it expedient to do an act described in paras (a) to (ee) of s.4 of the Trusts (Scotland) Act 1921 but feels that the act may be at variance with the terms of his appointment or the purposes of the judicial factory, he may apply to the Accountant of Court for the consent of the Accountant of Court to the doing of the Act: Trusts (Scotland) Act 1961, s.2(3). This rule does not cover consenting to encroachment on capital which is to be expended on the maintenance of a ward: *Broadfoot's Curator Bonis* 1989 S.C. 90, 100 per L.J.-C. Ross; for power to encroach on the capital of the estate of a ward application must be made to the Accountant of Court in an appropriate case (see r. 61.13) or for special powers under r. 61.15.

INTIMATION BY JUDICIAL FACTOR.

61.14.2   For methods, see r. 16.7.

"SENDING", "SEND".

61.14.3   This includes deliver: r. 1.3(1) (definition of "send").

"DATE ON WHICH INTIMATION GIVEN".

61.14.4   Where intimation is by post the date of intimation is the day after the date of posting: r. 16.4(9). Where intimation is by any other method the date of intimation is the date of execution.

CAUTIONER.

61.14.5   A judicial factor who is a guardian of a person under 16 years of age may not have a cautioner as he is not bound to find caution: Act of 1849, s.25(2) inserted by the Law Reform (Parent and Child) (Scotland) Act 1986, Sched. 1, para. 1.

Applications for special powers or authority under section 5 of the Trusts (Scotland) Act 1921

61.15   **61.15.**—(1) This rule applies to an application by a judicial factor—

(a) for special powers at common law or under section 7 of the Act of 1849; or

(b) under section 5 of the Trusts (Scotland) Act 1921 (application for authority to do an act at variance with terms or purposes of the judicial factory).

(2) An application may be made—

(a) in the petition for the appointment of the judicial factor; or

(b) by note in the process of that petition.

(3) Before making an application, the judicial factor shall apply to the Accountant of Court for an opinion by lodging with him a report explaining why the special powers or authority are necessary and concluding with a statement of the precise powers he seeks.

(4) The Accountant of Court shall, after making any necessary inquiry, send his written opinion to the judicial factor.

(5) The judicial factor shall lodge in process his report to, and the opinion of, the Accountant of Court.

(6) The judicial factor shall send to the Accountant of Court a copy of the interlocutor disposing of the application within two days after the date of the interlocutor.

(7)   An application by a judicial factor for special powers under this rule shall not be made before he has received an official certified copy of the interlocutor appointing him.

(8)   An application by a judicial factor in respect of special powers sought in the petition for his appointment shall be made by him by motion.

GENERAL NOTE.

A judicial factor is appointed to take charge of an estate for a specific purpose. The purpose will differ depending on the nature of the estate and any ward. In most factories the main purpose will be to conserve the value of the estate. In some factories, e.g. on a bankruptcy estate or estate of a solicitor, distribution of all or part of the estate will be a purpose.

61.15.1

At common law a judicial factor has power to do anything reasonable to fulfil the purpose of the factory (usually to conserve the estate): see Irons on *Judicial Factors*, pp. 49 et seq.; Walker on *Judicial Factors*, Chap. XIII.

In addition a judicial factor has the powers, so far as exercisable by a factor, listed in s.4(1) of the Trusts (Scotland) Act 1921, provided they are not at variance with the terms or purposes of the factory. Where a factor wishes to exercise a power under s.4(1) of the 1921 Act he should also obtain the prior consent of the Accountant of Court to ensure that the subsequent transaction has the benefit of s.2(1) of the Trusts (Scotland) Act 1961 (making the transaction unchallengeable on the ground of ultra vires). A factor also has the power and duties of a trustee under the 1961 Act and the Trustee Investments Act 1961: see Trusts (Scotland) Act 1961, s.6, and Trustee Investments Act 1961, s.17(5).

A judicial factor has no powers other than these. In particular he does not have any additional power in a trust deed of a trust estate to which he is appointed: *Carmichael's Judicial Factor* 1971 S.L.T. 336. If a judicial factor wishes further powers, known as "special powers" then he must apply to the court for them: see note 61.15.2.

A curator bonis is in the same category as an agent appointed by a capax to manage his affairs, rather than that of a trustee under a deed; his powers are not, therefore, less than that of his ward's, and his duty is to manage the estate for the benefit of the ward: *D's Curator Bonis* , 1998 S.L.T. 2, 3L per Lord Nimmo Smith. This dictum must be read as subject to the rules regarding encroachment on capital of the ward: see note 61.13.1.

SPECIAL POWERS.

There is no fixed list of acts for which a factor requires special powers. Where a factor is in any doubt whether a proposed act is within the terms and purposes of the judicial factory he should seek a special power to do it: *Marquess of Lothian's Curator Bonis* 1927 S.C. 579. An act which may not require special power in one factory may require special power in another factory due to the difference in the estates: contrast *Marquess of Lothian's Curator Bonis*, above, with *Barclay* 1962 S.C. 594 (power to sell heritage). Acts which have required special powers have included granting heritable security (*Maconochie, Noter* (1857) 19 D. 366), compromising a litigation (*Tennent's Judicial Factor v. Tennent* 1954 S.C. 215), retention of shares in a private limited company in face of the duties under the Trustee Investments Act 1961 (*Fraser v. Paterson (No. 2)* 1988 S.L.T. 124) and donating heritable property for the purpose of inheritance tax planning (*D's Curator Bonis, Noter* 1998 S.L.T. 2).

61.15.2

Special powers may be granted retrospectively: *Blair's Curator Bonis, Petr* 1921 1 S.L.T. 248; *Hamilton's Tutors* 1924 S.C. 364.

Special power to encroach on the capital of the estate of a ward where the estate is insufficient for the ward's maintenance may be sought from the Accountant of Court under r. 61.13.

For guidance on the granting of special powers to a curator bonis to make gifts of substantial parts of the ward's estate for inheritance tax planning, see *D's Curator Bonis, Noter* 1998 S.L.T. 2.

In *Bell's C.B., Noter* 1998 S.C. 365 it was held competent for a curator bonis to be given power to enter into a structured settlement of his ward's reparation action for personal injuries, involving the purchase of an annuity. Guidance must be provided to show that the proposed insurance arrangements are satisfactory. A guardian appointed under the Adults with Incapacity (Scotland) Act 2000 could be given that express power by the sheriff under s. 64(1) of that Act.

JURISDICTION.

The court has jurisdiction to grant special powers:

61.15.3

(a)   under the *nobile officium* of the Inner House: *Tennent's Judicial Factor v. Tennent* 1954 S.C. 215;

(b)   formerly under s. 7 of the Act of 1849; and

(c)   in respect of some acts under s. 5 of the Trusts (Scotland) Act 1921.

Where a statutory application would encompass a common law application, the statutory application should be followed: *Tennent's Judicial Factor*, above, per L.P. Cooper at p. 225.

With effect from 1st April 2002, the definition of the term "judicial factor" appearing in s. 1 of the 1849 Act ceased to extend curators bonis: Adults with Incapacity (Scotland) Act 2000, Sched. 6. The reference in s. 7 of the 1849 Act to "factor" thus excludes "curator bonis". On 1st April 2002, any person holding office as curator bonis to an adult became guardian of that adult with power to manage the property or financial affairs of that adult: 2000 Act, Sched. 4, para. 1(1).

For a recent example of the exercise of the power under s. 5 of the 1921 Act, see *Inverclyde Council v. Dunlop*, 2005 S.L.T. 967 (Second Div.).

"PETITION".

61.15.4   See note 61.2.1. If special powers are sought immediately the specific power sought must be craved in the prayer and supported by averments. The power sought must be for a specific act and not general in nature: *Carmichael's Judicial Factor* 1971 S.L.T. 336.

"NOTE".

61.15.5   For applications by note, see r. 15.2.

"SEND".

61.15.6   This includes deliver: r. 1.3(1) (definition of "send").

"LODGE IN PROCESS HIS REPORT".

61.15.7   The report of the judicial factor to the Accountant of Court for special powers and the Accountant's opinion on it must be lodged in process as steps of process (r. 1.3(1) (definition of "step of process")). On lodging steps of process, see r. 4.4. They may be lodged by post: P.N. No. 4 of 1994, paras 1 and 8; and see note 4.4.10.

"MOTION".

61.15.8   For motions, see Chap. 23.

Part II – Applications under Section 11A of the Judicial Factors (Scotland) Act 1889

Application of this Part

61.16   **61.16.** This Part applies to a petition under section 11A of the Judicial Factors (Scotland) Act 1889 (appointment of a judicial factor on estate of person deceased).

Deriv. R.C.S. 1965, r. 201(preamble) substituted by S.I. 1986 No. 514

GENERAL NOTE.

61.16.1   A judicial factor appointed to the estate of a deceased person is akin to a trustee in a sequestration or an executor creditor. The appointment is made where it appears that the deceased died intestate and nobody wishes to be executor-dative or a named executor refuses to be confirmed: Judicial Factors (Scotland) Act 1889, s. 11A(1) inserted by the Bankruptcy (Scotland) Act 1985, Sched. 7, para. 4. The appointment may also be made where an executor has to resign due to conflict of interest: see *Murray's Judicial Factor v. Thomas Murray & Sons (Ice Merchants) Ltd* 1992 S.C. 435. The petitioner may be a creditor or anyone with an interest in the estate of the deceased (e.g. a beneficiary or his representative).

Once appointed the duty of the judicial factor is to ingather the estate and then to distribute it to those entitled according to the proper order of ranking and succession.

Form of applications under section 11A of the Judicial Factors (Scotland) Act 1889

61.17   **61.17.** A petition to which this Part applies shall include averments stating—

(a)   the name, last known address and date of death of the deceased person;

(b)   the reasons for the appointment being necessary;

(c)   the interest of the petitioner, including—

(i)   if a creditor, the nature and amount of the debt, how constituted, vouched or established, or

(ii)   if a person having an interest in the succession to the estate, the nature of that interest;

(d)   details of the estate of the deceased person so far as known to the petitioner including heritable and moveable property, any stock in trade, interests in any business or partnership, debts owed to or by the deceased and any other relevant facts;

(e)   the names and addresses of all persons known to the petitioner as having an interest in the estate either as creditors or in the succession to the estate, and the nature of the interest in each case; and

(f) the name, designation and address of the person nominated to be the judicial factor.

Deriv. R.C.S. 1965, r. 201(a) amended by S.I. 1986 No. 514

"PETITION".

The application is by petition: Judicial Factors (Scotland) Act 1889, s. 11A(1). The petition is presented in the Outer House: r. 14.2(h). The petition must be in Form 14.4 in the official printed form: rr. 4.1 and 14.4. The petition must be signed by counsel or other person having a right of audience: r. 4.2; and see r. 1.3(1) (definition of "counsel" and "other person having a right of audience") and note 1.3.4.

The petitioner must lodge the petition with the required steps of process (r. 4.4) and any documents founded on or adopted (r. 27.1(1)). A fee is payable on lodging the petition: see note 14.5.10.

On petitions generally, see Chap. 14.

61.17.1

Intimation and service of section 11A petition

61.18. The order for intimation and service under rule 14.5 (first order in petitions) in a petition under this Part shall include a requirement for—

(a) a notice of the petition in the Edinburgh Gazette in Form 61.18; and

(b) service of the petition on such persons named in the petition as personal representatives of the deceased who are not parties to the petition.

Deriv. R.C.S. 1965, r. 201(b)(part)

61.18

"INTIMATION AND SERVICE".

See r. 14.7; and see Chap. 16, Pt. I.

ADVERTISEMENT IN THE EDINBURGH GAZETTE.

61.18.1

The Edinburgh Gazette is published weekly by HMSO. Notices for advertisement should be sent to: HMSO Scotland, 71 Lothian Road, Edinburgh EH3 9AZ; tel: 031-228 4964; fax: 031-229 2734.

61.18.2

Interim appointment

61.19. The court may make an interim appointment of a judicial factor in a petition to which this Part applies when the petition is presented or at any time thereafter.

Deriv. R.C.S. 1965, r. 201(c)(part)

61.19

INTERIM JUDICIAL FACTOR.

An interim judicial factor may be appointed in a situation of urgency where the intimation of the petition and lodging of answers would cause prejudicial delay to the estate. The special reasons of urgency should be averred in the petition if the interim factor is sought immediately: *Cuthbertson v. Gibson* (1887) 14 R. 776; see also note 61.2.3.

61.19.1

Notice calling for claims

61.20.—(1) In order to ascertain the claims on the estate, the judicial factor shall, within 14 days after he has received the official certified copy of the interlocutor appointing him, place a notice in the Edinburgh Gazette, and in such other newspaper as he thinks fit, in Form 61.20.

(2) The judicial factor shall lodge in process—

(a) a copy of each newspaper containing the notice under paragraph (1); or

(b) a certificate of publication by the publisher of each such newspaper stating the date of publication and text of the notice.

(3) The period within which a creditor shall intimate a claim on the estate to the judicial factor shall be four months from the date of publication of the notice under paragraph (1).

Deriv. R.C.S. 1965, r. 201(d) amended by S.I. 1967 No. 487

61.20

NOTICE IN THE EDINBURGH GAZETTE.

The Edinburgh Gazette is published weekly by HMSO. Notices for advertisement should be sent to: HMSO Scotland, 71 Lothian Road, Edinburgh EH3 9AZ; tel: 031-228 4964; fax: 031-229 2734.

"LODGE IN PROCESS".

61.20.1

The copy of the newspaper or publisher's certificate is lodged in process as a production. On lodging productions, see r. 4.5.

61.20.2

Claims

61.21   **61.21.**—(1) The judicial factor shall examine the claims of creditors in order to ascertain whether the debts are properly due from the estate of the deceased, and may—

(a)   call for further evidence in support of the claims;

(b)   if he thinks fit, require a creditor to constitute such claim by decree in a competent court in an action in which the judicial factor shall be called as a defender.

(2) For the purpose of ranking and payment of creditors, the date of the appointment of the judicial factor shall be deemed to be equivalent to the date of sequestration.

Deriv. R.C.S. 1965, r. 201(e).

"DATE OF APPOINTMENT OF JUDICIAL FACTOR".

61.21.1   This will be the date of the interlocutor appointing the judicial factor rather than the date of the official certified copy interlocutor.

"DATE OF SEQUESTRATION".

61.21.2   For the meaning of this, see s. 12(4) of the Bankruptcy (Scotland) Act 1985 substituted by s. 4(5) of the Bankruptcy (Scotland) Act 1993. The date is significant because it determines whether diligence on a debt has given it a preferred ranking. For the purposes of ranking and payment of creditors, a judicial factor acts as a trustee in sequestration.

SECTION 51 OF THE BANKRUPTCY (SCOTLAND) ACT 1985.

61.21.3   An order of priority for the unsecured debts of the creditors is provided in s. 51 of the Bankruptcy (Scotland) Act 1985. Unsecured debts rank after secured debts.

Custody and inspection of inventory of estate, etc.

61.22   **61.22.** There shall remain in the possession of the Accountant of Court and be open to inspection, within his office, by any creditor or person in the succession of the deceased—

(a)   the inventory of estate, when adjusted and approved by the Accountant of Court and signed by him and the judicial factor;

(b)   any report of the state of debts; and

(c)   all subsequent accounts submitted by the judicial factor to the Accountant of Court.

Deriv. R.C.S. 1965, r. 201(f)(part) amended by S.I. 1967 No. 487

INVENTORY OF ESTATE.

61.22.1   The judicial factor must lodge an inventory of the estate to which he has been appointed with the Accountant of Court within six months of the lodging of his bond of caution: Act of 1849, s. 3.

COPIES OF DOCUMENTS.

61.22.2   The Accountant of Court may issue signed copies of any document lodged with him which shall have the same effect as originals: Act of 1849, s. 36.

FEES FOR INSPECTION AND COPIES.

61.22.3   There is a fee for examining the inventory of the estate and a fee for copying (and any searching). For fees, see Court of Session etc. Fees Order 1984, Table of Fees, Pt. II, H, item 2 and Pt. IV, J, items 3 and 4 [S.I. 1984 No. 256, Table as amended, pp. C1202 et seq.].

Administration, deathbed and funeral expenses

61.23   **61.23.**—(1) Out of the first funds realised by him, the judicial factor shall reserve sufficient funds to defray the estimated costs of his administration including the legal expenses of the judicial factory.

(2)[1] On the expiry of the period for lodging claims, the judicial factor shall be entitled to pay out of such funds, with the prior approval of the Accountant of Court,

---

[1] R. 61.23(2) amended by SSI 2016/312 para. 2 (effective 30th November 2016).

those debts listed in paragraphs (a) to (e) of section 129(1) of the Bankruptcy (Scotland) Act 2016 (priority in distribution).

Deriv. R.C.S. 1965, r. 201(n).

RESERVE FUND FOR ADMINISTRATION EXPENSES.

On the initial disposal of the assets of the estate, the factor must set aside part of the funds thereby realised to form a reserve fund to meet the estimated costs of administration of the factor: r. 61.23(1). **61.23.1**

"EXPIRY OF THE PERIOD FOR LODGING CLAIMS".

This occurs on a date four months after the last publication of the notice calling for claims in the Edinburgh Gazette and/or another newspaper: r. 61.20(3). **61.23.2**

"SUCH FUNDS".

These are the reserve fund created by the judicial factor under r. 61.23(1). **61.23.3**

"DEBTS LISTED IN PARAGRAPHS (A) TO (E) OF SECTION 51(1) OF THE BANKRUPTCY (SCOTLAND) ACT 1985".

These include outlays and remuneration of an interim factor (1985 Act, s. 51(1)(a)), outlays and remuneration of the permanent factor (1985 Act, s. 51(1)(b)), reasonable deathbed and funeral expenses (1985 Act, s. 51(1)(c)), reasonable expenses of the petitioner for the factor (1985 Act, s. 51(1)(d)) and preferred debts (excluding any interest accrued thereon to the date of appointment) (1985 Act, s. 51(1)(e)). **61.23.4**

Preferred debts include (a) debts to Inland Revenue and Customs and Excise; (b) Class 1, 2 or 4 National Insurance contributions; pension contributions under Schedule 3 to the Social Security Pensions Act 1975; and (c) debts to employees, including employees' remuneration not exceeding £800: Bankruptcy (Scotland) Act 1985, s. 51(2) and Sched. 3.

Procedure where there are creditors

61.24.—(1) Where claims are lodged, the judicial factor shall— **61.24**

    (a)   where funds remain available for division after payment of the claims referred to in rule 61.23(2), prepare a state of funds and scheme of division amongst the creditors; or

    (b)   where no such funds remain after payment of those claims, prepare a state of funds only.

(2) The judicial factor shall—

    (a)   lodge with the Accountant of Court—

        (i)   the state of funds and any scheme of division,

        (ii)   all relevant writings and documents; and

    (b)   provide the Accountant of Court with such explanations as he may require.

(3) The Accountant of Court shall prepare a written report on the state of funds and any scheme of division containing such observations as he thinks fit for consideration by the court.

(4) The Accountant of Court shall issue the report under paragraph (3) to the judicial factor.

Deriv. R.C.S. 1965, r. 201(g)(part).

GENERAL NOTE.

Rr. 61.24 to 61.28 apply where creditors have lodged claims within the four month period of notice. R. 61.29 applies where no creditor has lodged a claim. **61.24.1**

Notice to creditors

61.25.—(1) As soon as the report of the Accountant of Court under rule 61.24(3) has been issued, the judicial factor shall— **61.25**

    (a)   lodge in process that report, the state of funds and any scheme of division;

    (b)   send to each person who has lodged with him a claim on the estate of the deceased a notice by first class post, or, if that person is furth of Europe, by air mail, stating—

        (i)   that the state of funds and scheme of division or state of funds only, as the case may be, and a report have been lodged in court; and

(ii)   the amount for which the creditor has been ranked and whether his claim is to be paid in full or by a dividend and the amount of it; or

(iii)   that his claim has been rejected; or

(iv)   that no funds are available for division;

(c)   place a notice in Form 61.25 in the Edinburgh Gazette; and

(d)   if—

(i)   any person, other than a person who has lodged a claim with him, is stated in the application or in the books, deed of settlement, or other papers of the deceased, to be a creditor of the estate or has an interest in the estate, or

(ii)   he has reason to believe that any other person is either a creditor of the estate or has an interest in the estate,

give notice to such person, by first class post or, if that person is furth of Europe, by air mail, that no dividend is allotted to him in the scheme of division.

(2)   Any creditor or person having an interest in the succession to the deceased's estate shall be entitled to examine—

(a)   the state of funds and any scheme of division lodged in process; and

(b)   the claims and supporting vouchers or evidence lodged with the judicial factor.

Deriv. R.C.S. 1965, r. 201(h) (r. 61.25(1)) and r. 201(j)(part) (r. 61.25(2))

"LODGE IN PROCESS".

61.25.1   The report, etc., is lodged in process as a step of process (r. 1.3(1) (definition of "step of process")). On lodging steps of process, see r. 4.4. They may be lodged by post: P.N. No. 4 of 1994, paras. 1 and 8; and see note 4.4.10.

"SEND".

61.25.2   This includes deliver: r. 1.3(1) (definition of "send").

"EACH PERSON WHO HAS LODGED WITH HIM A CLAIM".

61.25.3   This includes creditors and beneficiaries with rights of succession.

EDINBURGH GAZETTE.

61.25.4   The Edinburgh Gazette is published weekly by HMSO. Notices for advertisement should be sent to: HMSO Scotland, 71 Lothian Road, Edinburgh EH3 9AZ; tel: 031-228 4964; fax: 031-229 2734.

Approval of state of funds or scheme of division

61.26   **61.26.**—(1)   Any creditor or person having an interest in the succession to the estate of the deceased who is dissatisfied with the state of funds or any scheme of division may lodge in process a note of objection within 28 days after the date of the notice given under rule 61.25(1)(b) and, until the expiry of that period, the court shall not approve the state of funds and any scheme of division.

(2)   Where a note of objection under paragraph (1) is lodged, the court shall dispose of the note after hearing any objector and the judicial factor and making such investigations as it thinks fit.

(3)   If any objection is sustained to any extent, the necessary alterations shall be made to the state of funds and any scheme of division, and shall be approved by the court.

(4)   Where no note of objection is lodged, the court shall approve the state of funds and any scheme of division.

Deriv. R.C.S. 1965, r. 201(f)(part) (r. 61.26(1)) and r. 201(k) (r. 61.26(2) and (3))

"LODGE IN PROCESS".

61.26.1   The note of objection is lodged in process as a step of process (r. 1.3(1) (definition of "step of process")). On lodging steps of process, see r. 4.4. The note may be lodged by post: P.N. No. 4 of 1994, paras. 1 and 8; and see note 4.4.10.

The note does not have to be signed: r. 4.2(9)(f). R. 15.2 (applications by note) does not apply: r. 15.2(4)(b).

61.26.2

Payment following approval of scheme of division

61.27. After the court has approved a scheme of division, the judicial factor shall pay, deliver or convey to the parties the sums or other property to which they are entitled under the scheme.

61.27

Deriv. R.C.S. 1965, r. 201(l).

Partial division on first scheme of division

61.28.—(1) Where, in the opinion of the judicial factor, a partial division of funds among the creditors who have claimed may be made with safety in the interests of all concerned, the judicial factor may, with the approval of the Accountant of Court, prepare a state of funds and first scheme of division as soon as possible after the period for lodging claims has expired.

61.28

(2) The following provisions of this Part shall apply to a state of funds and first scheme of division prepared under paragraph (1) of this rule as they apply to a state of funds and scheme of division prepared under rule 61.24(1)(a):—

rule 61.24(2) (lodging of state of funds etc. with Accountant of Court),

rule 61.24(3) (report by Accountant of Court on state of funds),

rule 61.25 (notice to creditors),

rule 61.26 (approval of state of funds or scheme of division), subject to paragraph (3) of this rule.

(3) Subject to paragraph (4), the court may, not earlier than six months after the death of the deceased, approve the first scheme of division and, where it so approves, the judicial factor shall pay, deliver or convey to the parties the sums or other property to which they are entitled under the first scheme.

(4) Out of the funds there shall be retained and deposited in an institution authorised under the Banking Act 1987 or other appropriate institution a sufficient sum to meet—

    (a)   the amount of the claims of creditors whose debts have not at that time been admitted by the judicial factor, or whose debts are future or contingent; and

    (b)   the full amount of such debts as are claimed as preferable but the priority of which is not admitted by the judicial factor.

Deriv. R.C.S. 1965, r. 201(m).

This occurs on a date four months after the last publication of the notice calling for claims in the Edinburgh Gazette or another newspapers: r. 61.20(3).

61.28.1

This is a body corporate or partnership formed under the law of any part of the E.C. or a savings bank which has been authorised by the Bank of England to accept a deposit in the course of carrying on a deposit-taking business for the purposes of the Banking Act 1987: Banking Act 1987, ss. 9, 104 and 106.

61.28.2

This includes, e.g. the National Savings Bank, or a building society incorporated (or deemed to be incorporated) under the Building Societies Act 1986; cf. Act of 1849, s. 5(1).

61.28.3

Procedure where no creditors

61.29. Where, on the expiry of the period for lodging claims, no creditor has lodged a claim, the judicial factor shall not lodge a state of funds but shall prepare a report with regard to the disposal of the surplus estate in accordance with rule 61.30.

61.29

Deriv. R.C.S. 1965, r. 201(g)(part).

Disposal of surplus estate

61.30

61.30.—(1) Where, after payment of the creditors, there is a surplus, the judicial factor shall lodge with the Accountant of Court a statement of—

    (a)   the amount of the surplus;

    (b)   the parties claiming that surplus and their respective grounds of claim; and

    (c)   those parties who, in the opinion of the judicial factor, are entitled to the surplus and the reasons for his opinion.

(2) The Accountant of Court shall prepare a written opinion on the statement of the judicial factor lodged under paragraph (1) and issue that opinion to the judicial factor.

(3) On receipt of the opinion of the Accountant of Court under paragraph (2), the judicial factor shall—

    (a)   lodge in process that opinion and the statement prepared under paragraph (1); and

    (b)   give notice to each party claiming an interest or apparently entitled to any part of the estate, by first class post or, if that person is furth of Europe, by air mail, that—

        (i)   the statement of the judicial factor and the opinion of the Accountant of Court have been lodged in process; and

        (ii)   should any such party wish to lodge any objection to the statement, he shall lodge a note of objection with the Deputy Principal Clerk within 28 days after the date of the posting of the notice by the judicial factor.

(4) On expiry of the period for lodging objections under paragraph (3)(b)(ii), the court, on considering the statement, opinion, and any note of objection and, after such procedure as it thinks fit, shall—

    (a)   determine which parties are entitled to the surplus estate and direct the judicial factor to make payment accordingly; or

    (b)   if the court considers that it is desirable that the judicial factor should continue to administer the surplus estate, direct the judicial factor to do so.

Deriv. R.C.S. 1965, r. 201(o)

"LODGE IN PROCESS".

61.30.1

The opinion of the Accountant of Court and the statement prepared under r. 61.30(1) by the judicial factor are lodged in process as steps of process (r. 1.3(1) (definition of "step of process")). On lodging steps of process, see r. 4.4. They may be lodged by post: P.N. No. 4 of 1994, paras. 1 and 8; and see note 4.4.10.

"NOTE OF OBJECTION".

61.30.2

The note does not have to be signed: r. 4.2(9)(f). R. 15.2 (applications by note) does not apply: r. 15.2(4)(b).

"WITHIN 28 DAYS".

61.30.3

The date from which the period is calculated is not counted. Where the last day falls on a Saturday or Sunday or a public holiday on which the Office of Court is closed, the next available day is allowed: r. 1.3(7). For office hours and public holidays, see note 3.1.2.

Part III – Discharge of Judicial Factors

Applications for discharge to Accountant of Court

61.31

61.31.—(1) This rule applies to a judicial factor appointed as a—

    (a)   curator bonis;

    (b)   guardian;

    (c)   Factor *loco absentis*; or

(d)   commissary factor.

(2)   Where a judicial factory is terminated by reason of the recovery, death or coming of age of the ward, or by reason of the exhaustion of the estate, the judicial factor, or where he has died, his representative, may apply to the Accountant of Court for a certificate of discharge.

(3)   The judicial factor shall intimate a notice in Form 61.31 of an application under paragraph (2) to—

(a)   the cautioner; and

(b)   any person having an interest in the estate of the ward.

(4)   Any person to whom intimation has been given under paragraph (3) may make written representations relating to the application to the Accountant of Court within 21 days after the date of such intimation.

(5)   On the expiry of the period specified in paragraph (4), the Accountant of Court shall, after considering the application and representations made, send to—

(a)   the factor,

(b)   the Deputy Principal Clerk, and

(c)   any person who has made representations,

a copy of his decision to issue or refuse to issue a certificate of discharge and a note of his reasons for making that decision.

(6)   The Accountant of Court—

(a)   shall not sign a certificate of discharge until the time for lodging an appeal under rule 61.32 has expired; and

(b)   shall, on issuing a certificate of discharge, give written intimation of the issue of the certificate to the Deputy Principal Clerk.

(7)   The issue of a certificate of discharge shall be sufficient authority for the judicial factor to uplift his bond of caution.

Deriv. R.C.S. 1965, r. 201Z (r. 61.31(1)), r. 201AA (r. 61.31(2)), r. 201BB(1) (r. 61.31(3)), r. 201CC (r. 61.31(4)), r. 201DD (r. 61.31(5)) and r. 201EE (r. 61.31(6) and (7)), all inserted by S.I. 1991 No. 1915

GENERAL NOTE.

Generally a judicial factor must, at the termination of his office, present a petition to the court for his discharge: Act of 1849, s.34. The purpose of this rule is to avoid the necessity for certain types of judicial factor to present separate petitions to the court for discharge. The power to make this rule is in S.34A of the Act of 1849, which permits the court to make provision for the discharge of factors in cases where the judicial factory is terminated by reason of the recovery, death or coming of age of the ward, or by reason of the exhaustion of the estate (on which see note 61.31.2A). This rule applies only to judicial factors appointed as curators bonis, guardians, factors *loco absentis*, or commissary factors: r. 61.31(1).

61.31.1

Where an application for discharge is made under this rule it will be unnecessary for the factor to petition for recall of his appointment.

FORM OF APPLICATION.

The application is by letter. The letter should be addressed to: The Accountant of Court, Parliament House, Parliament Square, Edinburgh EH1 1RF; tel. 0131-554 2422; fax 0131-554 3632; DX ED311.

61.31.2

"BY REASON OF EXHAUSTION OF THE ESTATE".

The power to provide for an application to the Accountant of Court for a discharge is, and this phrase appears, in S.34A of the 1849 Act. In some cases the estate will be constructively exhausted: e.g. where the expenses of the factory exceed the interest on the capital, where the capital is rapidly disappearing in nursing home fees, or where the cost of the factory or the petition for discharge will use up what little is left of the estate. It is thought that in cases where a factory is exhausted in the sense that its assets will not cover its future liabilities, then administrative discharge is available. The Notes for the Guidance of Curators prepared by the Accountant of Court (see *P.H. Book*, Vol. 5, M 301) refer to situations where the "estate is substantially exhausted" (p. 11) on the death of a curator. It is thought that administrative discharge may be sought in similar cases of constructive exhaustion, even where the curator has not died.

61.31.2A

"INTIMATE".

For methods, see r. 16.7.

61.31.3

"WITHIN 21 DAYS".

The date from which the period is calculated is not counted.

61.31.4

"SEND".

61.31.5   This includes deliver: r. 1.3(1) (definition of "send").

GROUNDS OF TERMINATION OF FACTORY.

61.31.6   In relation to termination of a factory by means of recovery of the ward, the question has arisen as to the sufficiency of evidence. Either the common law rule of corroboration does not apply to the Accountant of Court (who acts in an administrative capacity) or, if an application under r. 61.31 is a civil proceeding, the rule has been abolished by s.1 of the Civil Evidence (Scotland) Act 1988. It is understood that the Accountant of Court may be satisfied on the evidence from one source.

Appeals against decisions under rule 61.31

61.32   **61.32.**—(1)   The judicial factor, or any person who has made representations under rule 61.31(4), may, within 14 days after intimation of a decision to him under rule 61.31(5), appeal to the Lord Ordinary against the determination of the Accountant of Court.

(2)   An appeal under paragraph (1) shall be—

(a)   made by letter to the Deputy Principal Clerk containing a statement of the grounds of appeal; and

(b)   intimated to the Accountant of Court.

(3)   On receipt of an appeal under paragraph (1), the Deputy Principal Clerk shall place the appeal before the Lord Ordinary in chambers for determination.

(4)   On disposing of such an appeal, the Lord Ordinary may—

(a)   direct the Accountant of Court to sign the certificate of discharge;

(b)   ordain the judicial factor to lodge a petition for his discharge; or

(c)   make such other order as he thinks fit.

(5)   The decision of the Lord Ordinary on an appeal to him under paragraph (1) shall be final and not subject to review.

Deriv. R.C.S. 1965, r. 201FF inserted by S.I. 1991 No. 1915

"WITHIN 14 DAYS".

61.32.1   The date from which the period is calculated is not counted. Where the last day falls on a Saturday or Sunday or a public holiday on which the Office of Court is closed, the next available day is allowed: r. 1.3(7). For office hours and public holidays, see note 3.1.2.

"LETTER TO THE DEPUTY PRINCIPAL CLERK".

61.32.2   The address and telephone number, etc., of the Deputy Principal Clerk are: The Deputy Principal Clerk of Session, Court of Session, 2 Parliament Square, Edinburgh EH1 1RQ; tel. 0131-225 2595; fax 0131-225 8213; DX ED306.

"FINAL AND NOT SUBJECT TO REVIEW".

61.32.3   The decision of the Lord Ordinary may not be reclaimed against.

Applications for discharge to court

61.33   **61.33.**—(1)   Where a judicial factor, other than one to whom rule 61.31 (applications for discharge to Accountant of Court) applies, seeks his discharge, he, or where he has died, his representative, shall apply to the court by petition for his discharge.

(2)   The order for intimation and service under rule 14.5 (first order in petitions) in a petition for discharge of a judicial factor appointed under section 11A of the Judicial Factors (Scotland) Act 1889 shall include a requirement for—

(a)   a notice of the petition in the Edinburgh Gazette in Form 61.33; and

(b)   service on the cautioner and on the personal representatives of the deceased person in respect of whom the appointment was made.

(3)   The court shall remit a petition under paragraph (1) to the Accountant of Court to report to the court on the petition.

Deriv. R.C.S. 1965, r. 201(p)

GENERAL NOTE.

61.33.1   A judicial factor, other than a curator bonis, guardian, factor *loco absentis* or commissary factor, requires to apply to the court for his discharge: Act of 1849, s. 34.

The most frequent reasons for a petition for discharge are death of the person in respect of whose estate the appointment was made, all monies having been disbursed, and death or retiral of the factor. In the latter case it is common practice to crave in the petition for the appointment of a new factor. The new factor will normally be appointed at the time when the remit is made under r. 61.33(3) to the Accountant of Court to report on the intromissions of the deceased or retiring factor. In some cases it may be appropriate to seek an appointment of an interim factor pending the full appointment: see note 61.2.3.

"PETITION"

A petition is presented in the Outer House: r. 14.2(h). The petition must be in Form 14.4 in the official printed form: rr. 4.1 and 14.4. The petition must be signed by counsel or other person having a right of audience: r. 4.2; and see r. 1.3(1) (definition of "counsel" and "other person having a right of audience") and note 1.3.4.

The petitioner must lodge the petition with the required steps of process (r. 4.4) and any documents founded on or adopted (r. 27.1(1)). A fee is payable on lodging the petition: see note 14.5.10.

On petitions generally, see Chap. 14.

EDINBURGH GAZETTE.

The *Edinburgh Gazette* is published weekly by HMSO. Notices for advertisement should be sent to: HMSO Scotland, 71 Lothian Road, Edinburgh EH3 9AZ; tel. 0131-228 4964; fax 0131-229 2734.

"SERVICE".

For methods, see Chap. 16, Pt. I.

REMIT TO ACCOUNTANT OF COURT.

After intimation and service of the petition an execution copy of the petition must be lodged in process: see r. 16.1(4) and note 16.1.6. A motion should then be enrolled for the remit to the Accountant of Court "to inquire into and report to the court on the factor's [*or* curator's] intromissions with the factory [*or* curatory] estate with a view to discharge". On the motion being granted the process is transmitted by the Petition Department to the Accountant of Court.

On completion of the Accountant's report, it is lodged in process and the process returned to the Petition Department by the Accountant of Court's office. The petitioner may then enrol a motion in respect of the report (if favourable) to grant the prayer of the petition for discharge. The interlocutor pronounced "exoners and discharges the factor [*or* curator] and grants authority for delivery of his bond of caution".

61.33.2

61.33.3

61.33.4

61.33.5

PART V OTHER PROCEEDINGS IN RELATION TO STATUTORY APPLICATIONS: CHAPTER 62 RECOGNITION AND ENFORCEMENT OF JUDGMENTS UNDER THE CIVIL JURISDICTION AND JUDGMENTS ACT 1982, COUNCIL REGULATION (EC) NO. 44/2001 OF 22ND DECEMBER 2001, THE CONVENTION ON CHOICE OF COURT AGREEMENTS OF 30TH JUNE 2005 OR THE LUGANO CONVENTION OF 30TH OCTOBER 2007

PART V[1]

OTHER PROCEEDINGS IN RELATION TO STATUTORY APPLICATIONS

Chapter 62

Recognition, Registration and Enforcement of Foreign Judgments, etc

Part I – General Provisions

Disapplication of certain rules to this Chapter

62.1.—[2] Subject to Part XIII the following rules shall not apply to a petition or application under this Chapter:

14.5 (first order in petitions),

14.6 (period of notice for lodging answers),

14.7 (intimation and service of petitions),

14.9 (unopposed petitions).

GENERAL NOTE.

The recognition and enforcement of judgments or awards from outwith Scotland should ideally be a speedy and inexpensive process. The merits of the judgment or award will already have been decided. Essentially the involvement of the Scottish court should be to check that it has jurisdiction under the relevant statutory provisions under which the application for enforcement is made. The jurisdiction provisions of the C.J.J.A. 1982 do not apply to an application for the recognition and enforcement of a judgment from a non-contracting state: *Owens Bank Ltd v. Bracco* [1994] 2 W.L.R. 759. For the meaning of "contracting state", see note 62.36.3.

The rules in Chap. 62 provide for enforcement to be by petition dealt with ex parte with any submission which may be required being dealt with in chambers. The procedures for service of the cause on the judgment debtor vary in detail but the general approach is for the debtor to receive notice only after the court has determined the application. After receiving notice of the cause and any determination, a debtor who wishes to object to enforcement must either comply with a specified statutory procedure or present a petition for suspension and interdict.

Certificate of currency conversion

62.2.—[3](1) Subject to paragraph (4), where the sum payable under a judgment, award, recommendation or determination to be registered in accordance with a provision of this Chapter is expressed in a currency other than sterling, the petitioner or applicant, as the case may be, before applying to the Keeper of the Registers for registration of such a document, shall lodge in the Petition Department—

    (a)   a certified statement of the rate of exchange prevailing at—

        (i)   the date of the judgment, award, recommendation or determination,

        (ii)   the date on which the certified statement is lodged, or

        (iii)   a date within three days before the date on which the certified statement is lodged,

    and of the sterling equivalent, at that rate, of the principal sum, interest and expenses contained in the judgment, award, recommendation or determination, as the case may be; and

---

[1] Heading as amended by S.S.I. 2019 No. 85 r. 2 (effective 28th March 2019).

[2] Rule 62.1 amended by S.S.I 2006 No. 199 (effective 6th April 2006).

[3] Rule 62.2 amended and r. 62.2(4) inserted by S.S.I. 2010 No. 205 (effective 15th June 2010).

(b)   a certificate of currency conversion in Form 62.2.

(2)   The certified statement required under paragraph (1) shall be by an official in the Bank of England or an institution authorised under the Banking Act 1987.

(3)   On receipt of the documents specified in paragraph (1), the clerk of session shall, if satisfied with the terms of those documents, sign and date the certificate of currency conversion.

(4)[1]   This rule does not apply in relation to an application for registration of a judgment, court settlement or authentic instrument on uncontested claims certified as a European Enforcement Order under the Regulation, as defined in rule 62.81(1).

Deriv. P.N. No. 7 of 1988

GENERAL NOTE.

62.2.1   R. 62.2 is a new rule which applies to the recognition and enforcement of any non-Scottish judgment or award which is expressed in a currency other than sterling. It replaces the fragmented and unclear position under the R.C.S. 1965.

"CERTIFIED STATEMENT OF THE RATE OF EXCHANGE".

62.2.2   The petitioner or applicant should obtain from an official in the Bank of England or an institution authorised under the Banking Act 1987 (see note 62.2.3) a certified statement of the rate of exchange prevailing at the date of conversion from the foreign currency into sterling: r. 62.2(1)(a). The petitioner should obtain the statement before applying to the Keeper of the Registers for registration of the judgment: r. 62.2(1).

"INSTITUTION AUTHORISED UNDER THE BANKING ACT 1987".

62.2.3   This is any corporate body, whenever incorporated, any UK partnership or Scottish savings bank established under the Savings Bank (Scotland) Act 1819 which has been authorised by the Bank of England to carry on a deposit-taking business: Banking Act 1987, s. 106. In practice this will include most UK banks, but not building societies.

DATE OF CONVERSION.

62.2.4   When the petitioner or applicant requests a bank for a certified statement of the rate of exchange he may request for the rate to be at any one of three dates of conversion, namely (1) the date of the judgment or award; (2) the date the statement is issued provided that later that day he lodges the statement and certificate of currency conversion with the Petition Department; or (3) any date within three days before the date when he lodges those items with the Petition Department.

It follows that where the petitioner or applicant does not wish to have the date of the judgment or award as the date of conversion, he must within three days of the date of conversion in the statement lodge with the Petition Department the certified statement together with the certificate of currency conversion. If the petitioner or applicant fails to meet this deadline, he must obtain a fresh certified statement of the rate of exchange.

CERTIFICATE OF CURRENCY CONVERSION.

62.2.5   This should be in Form 62.2 and lodged completed but unsigned by the petitioner or applicant together with the certified statement of the rate of exchange with the Petition Department within any applicable time limit: r. 62.2(1).

Where the documents lodged are in order the clerk of session in the Petition Department will sign and date the certificate of currency conversion and return it to the petitioner or applicant: r. 62.2(3).

On receipt of the signed certificate of conversion the petitioner or applicant will be entitled to apply to the Keeper of the Registers for registration of the judgment or award.

Translation of document lodged

62.3   **62.3.—**   Where a judgment, award, or other document lodged with a petition or application to which this Chapter applies is in a language other than English, there shall be produced with the petition a translation into English certified as correct by the translator; and the certificate shall include his full name, address and qualification.

Deriv. R.C.S. 1965, r. 249E(2)(a)(v) inserted by S.I. 1986 No. 1941

---

[1] Rule 62.2 amended and r. 62.2(4) inserted by S.S.I. 2010 No. 205 (effective 15th June 2010).

General note.

A translation of any judgment or award not in English should be lodged with the petition: r. 62.3. The translation should bear the certificate required by r. 62.3.

Electronic signing and transmission of documents

62.3A.—[1](1) This rule applies in relation to a document which is to be given to, or issued by, the Keeper of the Registers under this Chapter.

(2) In this rule—

"document" includes a copy of a document;

"electronic signature" is to be construed in accordance with section 7(2) of the Electronic Communications Act 2000 (electronic signatures and related certificates), but includes a version of an electronic signature which is produced on a paper document;

"the Keeper of the Registers' website" means the website maintained by, or on behalf of, the Keeper of the Registers with the domain name ros.gov.uk.

(3) An electronic signature fulfils any requirement (however expressed) that the document be signed.

(4) The document may be—

(a) given to the Keeper of the Registers by transmitting it to the Keeper of the Registers electronically;

(b) issued to a person by the Keeper of the Registers by—

(i) transmitting it to the person electronically;

(ii) transmitting it (electronically or otherwise) to a solicitor engaged to act on the person's behalf in relation to the document.

(5) For the purposes of paragraph (4)(a), the document may be transmitted by a means (and in a form) which is specified on the Keeper of the Registers' website as being acceptable for those purposes.

(6) For the purposes of paragraph (4)(b)—

(a) electronic transmission of a document by the Keeper of the Registers to another person ("the recipient") must be effected in a way that the recipient has indicated to the Keeper of the Registers that the recipient is willing to receive the document;

(b) the recipient's indication of willingness to receive a document in a particular way may be—

(i) specific to the document in question or generally applicable to documents of that kind;

(ii) expressed specifically to the Keeper of the Registers or generally (for example, on a website);

(iii) inferred from the recipient having previously been willing to receive documents from the Keeper of the Registers in that way and not having indicated unwillingness to do so again;

(c) the Keeper of the Registers' uploading of a document to an electronic

---

[1](1) As inserted by S.S.I. 2022 No. 277 r. 2 (effective 1st October 2022).

storage system from which the recipient is able to download the document may constitute electronic transmission of the document from the Keeper of the Registers to the recipient.

Part II – Registration and Enforcement under the Administration of Justice Act 1920 and the Foreign Judgments (Reciprocal Enforcement) Act 1933

Application and interpretation of this Part

62.4

62.4.—(1)   This Part applies to an application to the court under the Administration of Justice Act 1920 or the Foreign Judgments (Reciprocal Enforcement) Act 1933.

(2)   In this Part—

"the Act of 1920" means the Administration of Justice Act 1920;

"the Act of 1933" means the Foreign Judgments (Reciprocal Enforcement) Act 1933.

GENERAL NOTE.

62.4.1

Until Pt. II of the Act of 1920 only judgments from other UK jurisdictions could be enforced in Scotland by registration. Registration was under the Judgments Extension Act 1868 or (in the sheriff court) the Inferior Courts Judgments Extension Act 1882. Where a person wished to enforce any non-UK judgment in Scotland he required to raise a common law action for a decree conform. The common law action is still required to enforce a judgment where none of the provisions of Chap. 62 apply. In practice, the common law action still covers judgments from most countries. For a discussion of the common law action, see Anton on *Private International Law*, 2nd ed., pp. 220 et seq. and Graham Stewart on *Diligence*, pp. 430 et seq. Where there is a statutory procedure for recognition and enforcement of judgments, the use of the common law action is prohibited or discouraged through the exclusion of recovery of expenses of enforcement: see the Act of 1920, s. 9(5); the Act of 1933, s. 6; and the C.J.J.A. 1982, s. 18(8).

Part II of the Act of 1920 followed the Sumner *Report on the Conduct of Legal Proceedings between Parties in this Country and Parties Abroad and the Enforcement of Judgments and Awards* 1919 (Cmd. 251). The aim of the report was to examine the feasibility of giving the judgment of a supreme court in any part of the British Empire equal validity in any other part, merely on compliance with formalities along the lines of the intra-UK Act of 1868. Accordingly decisions under the Act of 1868 may to some extent be used in considering the provisions of the Act of 1920.

The Act of 1933 was passed to provide a parallel requirement for countries outwith the British Empire with which the UK concluded bilateral conventions on recognition and enforcement of certain judgments of certain courts. At the same time the Act of 1920 was restricted to those territories already covered by it (see note 62.5.3) and the Act of 1933 was put forward as the UK model for any future bilateral conventions for reciprocal recognition and enforcement of judgments.

DEFINITIONS IN THE ACT OF 1920.

62.4.2

Part II of this Chapter is made under s. 11 of the Act of 1920 in relation to proceedings under that Act: A.S. (R.C.S. 1994) 1994, Sched. 1 [S.I. 1994 No. 1443]. Accordingly a word or expression used in Pt. II which is also used in the Act of 1920 has the meaning given in that Act unless the contrary intention appears: Interpretation Act 1978, s. 11. The following are definitions used in both Pt. II of the Act of 1920 and Pt. II of this Chapter:

(1)   *"judgment"*. This is any judgment or order given or made by a court in civil proceedings whereby a sum of money is made payable: Act of 1920, s. 12(1). It includes an award in proceedings or an arbitration if, in the place where the award was made, it became enforceable in the same way as a judgment of a court: Act of 1920, s. 12(1). A judgment reducing or annulling an assignation is not per se a judgment whereby a sum of money is made payable: *Platt v. Platt* 1958 S.C. 95. A decree for a sum of money obtained by the registration of a probative writ for execution is a judgment for this purpose: *Taylor, Petr.* 1931 S.L.T. 260. A judgment has to be a decision of some description: *Ivory, Petr.* , 2006 S.L.T. 758 (OH).

(2)   *"judgment creditor"*. This is the person who obtained the judgment or award and includes the successors and assignees of that person: Act of 1920, s. 12(1).

(3)   *"judgment debtor"*. This is the person against whom the judgment or award was given and includes any person against whom the judgment or award is enforceable in the place where it was given: Act of 1920, s. 12(1).

(4)   *"original court"*. This is the court (or arbiter) which gave the judgment or award: Act of 1920, s. 12(1).

DEFINITIONS IN THE ACT OF 1933.

62.4.3

Part II of this Chapter is made under s. 12(b) of the Act of 1933 in relation to proceedings under that Act: A.S. (R.C.S. 1994) 1994, Sched. 1 [S.I. 1994 No. 1443]. Accordingly a word or expression used in

Pt. II which is also used in the Act of 1933 has the meaning given in that Act unless the contrary intention appears: Interpretation Act 1978, s. 11. The following are definitions used in both the Act of 1933 and Pt. II of this Chapter:

(1) *"appeal"*. This includes any proceeding by way of discharging or setting aside a judgment or an application for a new trial or a stay of execution: Act of 1933, s. 11(1).

(2) *"court"*. This includes a tribunal, but not in relation to the enforcement of an arbitral award in the country of origin: Act of 1933, s. 11(1).

(3) *"judgment"*. This is a judgment or order given or made by a court in any civil proceedings, or a judgment or order given or made by a court in any criminal proceedings, for the payment of a sum of money in respect of compensation or damages to an injured party: Act of 1933, s. 11(1). The 1933 Act does not apply to a judgment given in proceedings which are founded on a judgment of a court in (yet) another country and having as their object enforcement of that judgment: Act of 1933, s. 1(2A). Subject to ss. 1(5) and 6 of the Act of 1933 an award in an arbitration is treated as a judgment if, in the place where the award was made, it became enforceable in the same way as a judgment of a court: Act of 1933, s. 10A inserted by the C.J.J.A. 1982, Sched. 10, para. 4. A judgment reducing or annulling an assignation is not per se a judgment whereby a sum of money is made payable: *Platt v. Platt* 1958 S.C. 95. A judgment includes a decree for a sum of money obtained by the registration of a probative writ for execution: *Taylor, Petr.* 1931 S.L.T. 260. A judgment has to be a decision of some description: *Ivory, Petr.*, 2006 S.L.T. 758 (OH).

(4) *"judgment creditor"*, *"judgment debtor"* and *"original court"*. These have the same meaning as in the Act of 1920: see note 62.4.2.

Applications for registration under the Act of 1920 or 1933

62.5.—(1) An application under section 9 of the Act of 1920 (enforcement in United Kingdom of judgments obtained in superior courts in other British Dominions etc.) shall be made by petition.

(2) An application under section 2 of the Act of 1933 (application for registration of a foreign judgment) shall be made by petition.

62.5

Deriv. R.C.S. 1965, r. 248(a)(part) (r. 62.5(1)) and r. 249.1 (r. 62.5(2))

JURISDICTION UNDER THE ACT OF 1920.

The court has jurisdiction for an application under s. 9 of the Act of 1920 where—

62.5.1

(a) the application is made within 12 months after the date of the judgment to be enforced, or such longer period as the court may allow;

(b) the application is in respect of a "judgment" as defined in s. 12(1) of the Act of 1920 (see note 62.4.2) from a superior court (Act of 1920, s. 3(1));

(c) Part II of the Act of 1920 applies to the judgment (see note 62.5.3); and

(d) jurisdiction is not otherwise excluded: Act of 1920, s. 9(1); and see note 62.5.4.

TIME-LIMIT UNDER S.9 OF THE ACT OF 1920.

The court has a discretion to allow an application to be made after the expiry of the 12-month period after the date of the judgment to be enforced: Act of 1920, s.9(1).

62.5.2

APPLICABILITY OF PT II OF THE ACT OF 1920.

Part II of the Act of 1920 applies to a judgment of a superior court in (1) any part of H.M. Dominions outside the United Kingdom, or (2) any territory under H.M. protection or for which a government of any Dominion exercises a mandate, to which Pt II of the Act has been applied by Order in Council: Act of 1920, ss.9(1), 13 and 14.

62.5.3

Part II of the Act of 1920 may not now be extended to any territory to which it did not apply on 10th November 1933: Act of 1933, s.7(1) and the Reciprocal Enforcement of Judgments (General Application to His Majesty's Dominions, etc.) Order 1933 [S.R. & O. 1933 No. 1073]. In addition Pt II of the Act of 1920 may be disapplied from any territory to which it previously applied by the extension of the Act of 1933 to that territory by Order in Council: Act of 1933, s.7(2). Where this happens transitional provisions apply: Administration of Justice Act 1956, s.51.

The countries and territories to which Pt II of the Act of 1920 applies are listed in the Reciprocal Enforcement of Judgments (Administration of Justice Act 1920, Part II) (Consolidation) Order 1984 [S.I. 1984 No. 129] as amended by the Reciprocal Enforcement of Judgments (Administration of Justice Act 1920, Part II) (Amendment) Order 1985 [S.I. 1985 No. 1994], the Reciprocal Enforcement of Judgments (Australia) Order 1994 [S.I. 1994 No. 1901] and the Reciprocal Enforcement of Judgments (Administration of Justice Act 1920, Pt II) (Amendment) Order 1997 [S.I. 1997 No. 2601]. They are:

Anguilla

Antigua and Barbuda

Mauritius

Montserrat

Bahamas	Newfoundland
Barbados	New Zealand
Belize	Nigeria
Bermuda	Territory of Norfolk Island
Botswana	Papua New Guinea
British Indian Ocean Territory	St Christopher and Nevis
British Virgin Islands	St Helena
Cayman Islands	St Lucia
Christmas Island	St Vincent and the Grenadines
Cocos (Keeling) Islands	Saskatchewan
Republic of Cyprus	Seychelles
Dominica	Sierra Leone
Falkland Islands	Singapore
Fiji	Soloman Islands
The Gambia	Sovereign Base Area of Akrotíri and
Ghana	Dhekelia in Cyprus
Grenada	Sri Lanka
Guyana	Swaziland
Jamaica	Tanzania
Kenya	Trinidad and Tobago
Kiribati	Turks and Caicos Islands
Lesotho	Tuvalu
Malawi	Uganda
Malaysia	Zambia
Malta	Zimbabwe

EXCLUSION OF JURISDICTION UNDER THE ACT OF 1920.

62.5.4   S.9(2) of the Act of 1920 excludes the jurisdiction of the court where—

(a)   the original court acted without jurisdiction;

(b)   the judgment debtor did not carry on business or was not resident within the jurisdiction of the original court and did not voluntarily appear or otherwise submit to that court's jurisdiction;

(c)   the judgment debtor was ordinarily resident or carried on business within or agreed to submit to the jurisdiction of the original court but was not served in the process of the original court and did not appear;

(d)   the judgment was obtained by fraud: see *Owens Bank Ltd v. Bracco* [1992] 2 A.C. 444, 480 et seq. per Lord Bridge of Harwich;

(e)   the judgment debtor satisfies the court that either an appeal is pending or that he is entitled and intends to appeal against the judgment; or

(f)   the judgment was in respect of a course of action which for reasons of public policy or for some other reason could not have been entertained by the court (e.g. the judgment included penalty damages).

JURISDICTION UNDER THE ACT OF 1933.

62.5.5   The court has jurisdiction under s.2 of the Act of 1933 where—

(a)   the application is made within six years of—

(i)   the date of the judgment; or

(ii)   where the judgment has been appealed against, the date of the last judgment given in the appeal;

(b)   the application is in respect of a "judgment" as defined in s.11(1) as extended by s.10A of the Act of 1933 (see note 62.4.3);

(c)   the Act of 1933 applies to the judgment (see note 62.5.7); and

(d)   jurisdiction is not otherwise excluded (see note 62.5.8).

TIME-LIMIT UNDER S.2 OF THE ACT OF 1933.

62.5.6   The six-year time-limit for the presentation of a petition is imposed under s.2 of the Act of 1933. Accordingly there is no scope for the use of the dispensing power under r. 2.1.

APPLICABILITY OF THE ACT OF 1933.

The Act of 1933 has been applied to judgments in two ways, (1) by reference to the court of the territory where the judgment was given and (2) by reference to the subject-matter of the judgment.

(1) Territorial applicability.

The Act of 1933 applies to judgments or any class of judgments given by a recognised court of a foreign country or any part of H.M. Dominions (including mandated territories) to which the Act has been extended by Order in Council: Act of 1933, ss.1(1) and 7(2) and (3).

The Act of 1933 has been extended to the recognised courts (specified in the relevant Order in Council) of the following countries:

Country (S.R. & O. S.I. or S.S.I.)

Australia (1994 No. 1901)	France (metropolitan) (1936 No. 609)
Austria (1962 No. 1339)	Germany (including former G.D.R.) (1961 No. 1199)
Belgium (1936) No. 1169)	
Canada:	Guernsey (1973 No. 610)
Federal Court (1987 N. 468)	India (states and territories listed) (1958 No. 425)
British Columbia (1987 No. 468)	
Manitoba (1987 No. 468)	Isle of Man (1973 No. 611)
New Brunswick (1987 No. 468)	Israel (1971 No. 1039)
Nova Scotia (1987 No. 468)	Italy (1973 No. 1894)
Ontario (1987 No. 468)	Jersey (1973 No. 612)
Yukon Territory (1987 No. 2211)	Netherlands (1969 No. 1063)
Prince Edward Island (1988 No. 1304)	Netherlands Antilles (1977 No. 2149)
Saskatchewan (1988 No. 1853)	Norway (1962 No. 636 amended S.S.I. 2020 No. 371)
Northwest Territories (1989 No. 987)	Pakistan (1958 No. 141)
Newfoundland (1991 No. 1724)	Suriname (1981 No. 735)
	Tonga (1980 No. 1523)

Where any Order in Council made before 1st January 1987 specifies a court of a country to be a "superior court", then it is to be treated as a recognised court for the purposes of s.1 of the Act of 1933: Act of 1933, s.1(5).

The above extensions of the Act cover only a judgment of a recognised court which is—

(a)   given at first instance;

(b)   either final or conclusive between the judgment debtor and the judgment creditor or requires the former to make an interim payment to the latter (notwithstanding that it may still be subject to appeal);

(c)   requires payment of a sum of money, not being a sum payable in respect of taxes, or other charges of a like nature or in respect of a fine or other penalty: see *S.A. Consortium General Textiles v. Sun and Sand Ltd* [1978] Q.B. 279;

(d)   given after the Order in Council which made the court which gave it (a "recognised court") had come into force;

(e)   not regarded as a judgment of the recognised court just for the purposes of enforcement and which was given or made in another country; or

(f)   not given by the recognised court in proceedings founded on a judgment of a court in another country and having as their object enforcement of that judgment: Act of 1933, s.1(2), (2A) and (3).

(2) Applicability related to subject-matter.

The Act of 1933 (subject to variation) applies to judgments of a certain subject-matter to which it has been applied by the following Acts:

Carriage of Goods by Road Act 1965, ss.4 and 11(2) in respect of any judgment given by a court or tribunal of a party to the 1950 Geneva Convention on the Contract for the International Carriage of Goods by Road ("the C.M.R. Convention") in proceedings arising out of carriage under the Convention;

Nuclear Installations Act 1965, s.17(4) in respect of any judgment of any foreign country which is certified by the Secretary of State to be a judgment which is enforceable under the 1960 Paris Convention on Third Party Liability in the Field of Nuclear Energy (as amended) (*Cmnd. 2514*) in a country bound by that Convention;

Carriage of Passengers by Road Act 1974, s.5: not yet in force;

Civil Aviation (Eurocontrol) Act 1983, s.1 in respect of any determination made by a relevant authority in a state designated by Order in Council as a party to the 1981 Multilateral Agreement relating to Route Charges, to enforce a sum due to Eurocontrol in respect of air navigation charges;

International Transport Conventions Act 1983, s.6 in respect of a judgment pronounced by the court of a state designated by Order in Council as a member state of the 1980 Berne Convention Concerning International Carriage by Rail to enforce a claim pronounced under the Convention;

Merchant Shipping Act 1995, s.166(4) in respect of any judgment given by a court in a country in respect of which the *Brussels International Convention on Civil Liability for Oil Pollution Damage* 1992 (formerly 1969 and 1984 (Cmnd. 6183)) is in force, to enforce a claim for the discharge or escape of persistent oil from a ship (the Convention is in force in many major shipping countries including the UK, Bahamas, Panama, Liberia: see Merchant Shipping (Oil Pollution) (Parties to Convention) Order 1986 [S.I. 1986 No. 2225]);

Merchant Shipping Act 1995, s.177(4) and (5) in respect of any judgment given by a court in a country in respect of which the *Brussels International Convention on the Establishment of an International Fund for Cooperation for Oil Pollution Damage* 1992 (formerly 1971) is in force, to enforce a claim for liability for pollution damage.

EXCLUSION OF JURISDICTION UNDER THE ACT OF 1933.

62.5.8 The jurisdiction of the court is excluded under the Act of 1933 where—

(a) the judgment has at the time of the application been wholly satisfied (Act of 1933, s.2(1)(a));

(b) the judgment could not be enforced by execution at the date of the application in the country of the original court: Act of 1933, s.2(1)(b), and see *S.A. Consortium General Textiles v. Sun and Sand Ltd* [1978] Q.B. 279, 300 per Goff L.J.); or

(c) the Act of 1933 has been superseded by the 1968 Brussels or 1988 Lugano Convention (C.J.J.A. 1982, s.9(1) and Scheds. 1 and 3C, Art. 1).

"PETITION".

62.5.9 A petition is presented in the Outer House: r. 14.2(h). The petition must be in Form 14.4 in the approved printed form: rr. 4.1 and 14.4. The petition may be signed by the petitioner, counsel or other person having a right of audience, or an agent: r. 4.2(3)(d); and see r. 1.3(1) (definition of "counsel", "other person having a right of audience" and "agent") and note 1.3.4.

The petitioner must lodge the petition with the required steps of process (r. 4.4) and any documents founded on or adopted (r. 27.1(1)). A fee is payable on lodging the petition: see note 14.5.10.

On petitions generally, see Chap. 14.

Supporting documents

62.6 **62.6.**—(1) There shall be produced with the petition for registration referred to in rule 62.5 an affidavit—

(a) referring to the judgment or a certified copy of the judgment issued by the original court and authenticated by its seal; and

(b) stating—

(i) the full name, title, trade or business and the usual or last known place of residence or business of the judgment creditor and the judgment debtor respectively;

(ii) that the petitioner is entitled to have the judgment registered under the Act of 1920 or the Act of 1933, as the case may be;

(iii) where the judgment is in respect of several matters, only some of which may be registered, those in respect of which the petitioner seeks registration;

(iv) the amount of the interest, if any, which under the law of the country of the original court has become due under the judgment up to the date of the affidavit;

(v) the amount of the judgment which is unsatisfied;

    (vi)   that at the date of presentation of the petition the judgment may be enforced by execution in the country of the original court;

    (vii)   that if the judgment were registered, the registration would not be, or be liable to be, set aside under section 4 of the Act of 1933; and

    (viii)   that the judgment is not a judgment to which section 5 of the Protection of Trading Interests Act 1980 (restriction on enforcement of certain overseas judgments) applies.

(2) There shall be produced with a petition referred to in rule 62.5 such other evidence with respect to the matters referred to in sub-paragraphs (b)(iv) and (b)(vi) of paragraph (1) as may be required having regard to the provisions of an order in Council made under section 1 of the Act of 1933 (power to extend the Act of 1933 to the country of the original court).

Deriv. R.C.S. 1965, r. 248(a)(part), and r. 249.2 amended by S.I. 1980 No. 891

PRODUCTIONS.

The petitioner must produce with the petition (a) a certified copy of the judgment issued by the original court and authenticated by its seal (r. 27.1); (b) if necessary, a translation of any document lodged (r. 62.3); (c) an affidavit (r. 62.6(1)); and (d) if necessary, documents certifying the amount of interest which has become due under the judgment to the date of the affidavit and that at the date of the presentation of the petition the judgment may be enforced by execution in the country of the original court (r. 62.6(2)). **62.6.1**

AFFIDAVIT.

The affidavit should be in the form of a statement of evidence written in the first person. The affidavit should contain the evidence of the deponent in support of the averments in the petition. In particular the affidavit should deal with the matters listed in r. 62.6(1). **62.6.2**

An affidavit should be sworn and signed by the deponent before any person who may competently take an oath, whether in Scotland or in any other country. In Scotland such a person may include a notary public, justice of the peace, sheriff, or any judge. The person taking the oath should also sign the affidavit. Where the affidavit is not in English a duly certified translation should also be lodged.

See also the definition of affidavit in r. 1.3(1).

SETTING ASIDE OF REGISTRATION.

For circumstances where a judgment registered under the Act of 1933 may be set aside, see note 62.10.1. **62.6.3**

PROTECTION OF TRADING INTERESTS ACT 1980, s.5.

This prohibits the recovery of any sum under the Act of 1920 or 1933 or at common law, in a judgment for multiple damages: Protection of Trading Interests Act 1980, s.5(1) and (2). A judgment for multiple damages is defined as a judgment for an amount arrived at by doubling, trebling, or otherwise multiplying a sum assessed as compensation for the loss or damage sustained by the person in whose favour the judgment is given: 1980 Act, s.5(3). Even the compensatory part of such a judgment may not be recovered. The Secretary of State also has powers under s.5(4) of the 1980 Act to extend the prohibitions to any judgment based on any rule of law appearing to him to be designed to restrain, distort, restrict or promote business competition: 1980 Act, s.5(2)(a) and (4). To date this power has not been exercised. **62.6.4**

Warrant for registration under the Act of 1920 or 1933

62.7.—(1) The court shall, on being satisfied that the petition complies with the requirements of the Act of 1920 or the Act of 1933, as the case may be, pronounce an interlocutor granting warrant for the registration of the judgment. **62.7**

(2) The interlocutor under paragraph (1) shall specify a date by which the judgment debtor may apply to the court to set aside the registration; and in fixing such date, regard shall be had to the place of residence of the judgment debtor.

(3) In fixing the date under paragraph (2), the court shall have regard, in the case of a judgment debtor furth of Scotland, to the periods for superseding extract of a decree in absence in rule 19.1(5).

Deriv. R.C.S. 1965, r. 248(b) amended by SI 1980/891 and r. 249.5(1) (r. 62.7(1)); and r. 248(c) and r. 249.5(2) and (3) (r. 62.7(2) and(3))

General note.

62.7.1   In Scotland a foreign judgment is enforced under statute by the court granting a warrant for the judgment to be registered in the register of judgments of the Books of Council and Session (or sheriff court books in the case of certain maintenance judgments) for execution. On registration, the foreign judgment becomes a Scottish decree of registration and may be enforced by any diligence or sequestration or liquidation. Registration for execution gives the holder a decree of registration which is in effect a decree of the Court of Session (Bell's *Comm., i,4; Taylor, Petr.* 1931 S.L.T. 260, 261 per Lord Pitman), and, on the warrant inserted by the Keeper of the Registers or his deputy on an extract of a registered document, diligence may be executed against the debtor's moveable property under s.3 of the Writs Execution (Scotland) Act 1877 as substituted by s.87(4) of the Debtors (Scotland) Act 1987. Diligence against heritable property may be executed by inhibition on the grant of letters of inhibition (see Chap. 59) or by action of adjudication founding on the decree of registration.

Although analytically distinct, recognition and enforcement are closely linked, and, if it would not be competent to pronounce declarators that a judgment was not enforceable, it would not be competent to pronounce declarators that they were not capable of being recognised: *Clarke v. Fennoscandia Ltd* , 2008 S.C. (H.L.) 122.

Period for setting aside registration under the Act of 1933.

62.7.2   Under s.4 of the Act of 1933 the judgment debtor may apply to the court for the setting aside of any registration which has taken place. The judgment creditor may not proceed to any step of execution until the expiry of the period for an application under s.4 of the Act of 1933 or if an application has been made within that period until the determination of the application.

Accordingly, the interlocutor granting warrant for registration must specify the date when the period for such an application expires: r. 62.7(1). In determining the period and date the court must have regard to the residence of the judgment debtor and, if he resides furth of Scotland, have regard to the periods for superseding extract of a decree of absence: r. 62.7(1) and (2). These are the number of days required in the ordinary course of post for the transmission of a letter from Edinburgh to the residence, registered office, other official address or place of business, as the case may be, of that defender and the transmission of an answer from there to Edinburgh being more than seven days: r. 19.1(5).

Expenses of petition and registration procedure.

62.7.3   The reasonable costs of and incidental to the registration procedure (including the obtaining of a certified copy judgment and the petition proceedings) are recoverable as if they were sums contained in the judgment being enforced: Act of 1920, s.9(3)(c); Act of 1933, s.2(6). The interlocutor granting the warrant for registration should provide for the awarding of expenses in relation to the petition procedure.

Registration of judgments under the Act of 1920 or 1933

62.8   **62.8.**—(1)   Where the court pronounces an interlocutor under rule 62.7(1) granting warrant for registration, the Deputy Principal Clerk shall enter details of the judgment in a register of judgments under the Act of 1920 or the Act of 1933, as the case may be, kept in the Petition Department.

(2)   On presentation by the petitioner to the Keeper of the Registers of—

(a)   a certified copy of the interlocutor under rule 62.7(1) granting warrant for registration,

(b)   the judgment or a certified copy of the judgment and any translation of it, and

(c)[1]   any certificate of currency conversion under rule 62.2(1)(b),

they shall be registered in the register of judgments of the Books of Council and Session.

(3)   An extract of a registered judgment with a warrant for execution shall not be issued by the Keeper of the Registers until the certificate mentioned in rule 62.10(3) is produced to him.

Deriv. R.C.S. 1965, r. 249.6 (r. 62.8(1)); and r. 248(d), and r. 249.7, both amended by SI 1986/1941 (r. 62.8(2) and (3))

"Keeper of the Registers".

62.8.1   This is the Keeper of the Registers of Scotland: r. 1.3(1). The Register of Judgments is at Meadowbank House, 153 London Road, Edinburgh EH8 7AU; tel. 0131-659 6111; fax 0131-459 1221; DX ED300.

---

[1] R. 62.8(2)(c) amended by SI 1996/2168 (minor correction).

"CERTIFIED COPY OF THE INTERLOCUTOR".

A copy of the interlocutor is typed by the agent and presented to the clerk of session in the Petition Department. The clerk checks it, certifies it as a true copy and stamps it with the court stamp. A fee is payable.

62.8.2

"CERTIFIED COPY OF THE JUDGMENT".

The copy of the judgment should be authenticated with the seal of the original court.

62.8.3

"TRANSLATION".

See r. 62.3.

62.8.4

"CERTIFICATE OF CURRENCY CONVERSION".

This should be obtained from the clerk of session in the Petition Department duly signed by him: r. 62.2(3); and see notes 62.2.4 and 62.2.5.

62.8.5

REGISTRATION FEE.

A fee will be payable to the Keeper of the Registers for registration and any extract: see the Fees in the Registers of Scotland Order 1991 [SI 1991/2093].

62.8.6

CERTIFICATE OF CONFIRMATION OF REGISTRATION.

Where the court either receives no application by the judgment debtor to set aside the registration within the period stated in the interlocutor or refuses such an application, the Deputy Principal Clerk may, at the request of the petitioner, issue a certificate certifying this: r. 62.10(3). The petitioner has to produce this certificate to the Keeper of the Registers before he can obtain an extract of the registered judgment and proceed to execution: r. 62.8(3).

62.8.7

Service on judgment debtor

62.9.— On registration of a judgment under rule 62.8(2), the petitioner shall serve a notice of the registration on the judgment debtor in Form 62.9.

62.9

Deriv. R.C.S. 1965, r. 248(e) amended by SI 1986/1941 and r. 249.8

GENERAL NOTE.

The purpose of service on the judgment debtor is to enable him to apply under s.9(4)(b) of the Act of 1920 or s.4 of the Act of 1933 to set aside the registration or, in the case of registration under the Act of 1920, to present a petition for suspension and interdict.

62.9.1

"SERVE".

For methods, see Chap. 16, Pt. I.

62.9.2

"JUDGMENT DEBTOR".

See note 62.4.2.

62.9.3

Application to set aside registration under the Act of 1920 or 1933

62.10.—(1) An application by a judgment debtor to set aside the registration of a judgment shall be made by note and supported by affidavit and any documentary evidence.

62.10

(2) In relation to such an application, the court may order such inquiry as it thinks fit.

(3) Where no such application is made by the date specified in the interlocutor pronounced under rule 62.7(2) or where the application has been made and refused, the Deputy Principal Clerk shall, at the request of the petitioner, issue a certificate to that effect.

(4) Subject to paragraph (5), where such an application is granted, a certificate to that effect issued by the Deputy Principal Clerk shall be sufficient warrant to the Keeper of the Registers to cancel the registration and return the judgment to the petitioner.

(5) Where the court makes an order under section 5(3) of the Act of 1933 (judgment ordered to be registered for balance payable), it shall pronounce an interlocutor—

(a) recalling the warrant for registration granted under rule 62.7; and

917

(b)   granting warrant for registration of the judgment in respect of the balance remaining payable at the date of the original petition for registration.

Deriv. R.C.S. 1965, r. 249.9 (r. 62.10(1) and (2)), r. 248(f)(part) and r. 249.11 (r. 62.10(3)) and r.248(g) (r. 62.10(4)).

GENERAL NOTE.

62.10.1   Following registration under Pt. II of the Act of 1920, the court may set aside the registration of a judgment on such terms as it thinks fit: Act of 1920, s.9(4)(b). Following registration under the Act of 1933, the court—

(a)   shall set aside the registration if it is satisfied—

    (i)   that the judgment is not a "judgment" under the Act and so was registered in contravention of the Act;

    (ii)   that the courts of the country of the original court had no jurisdiction in the circumstances of the case (see note 62.10.2);

    (iii)   that the judgment debtor, being the defender in the proceedings in the original court, did not (notwithstanding that process may have been duly served on him in accordance with the law of the country of the original court) receive notice of those proceedings in sufficient time to enable him to defend the proceedings and did not appear;

    (iv)   that the judgment was obtained by fraud: see *Owens Bank Ltd v. Bracco* [1992] 2 A.C. 444, 480 et seq. per Lord Bridge of Harwich;

    (v)   that the enforcement of the judgment would be contrary to public policy in this country; or

    (vi)   that the rights under the judgment were not vested in the person by whom the application for registration was made (Act of 1933, s. 4(1)(a)); or

(b)   may set aside the registration if it is satisfied that the matter in dispute in the proceedings in the original court had, previously to those proceedings, been the subject of a final and conclusive judgment of a court having jurisdiction in the matter (Act of 1933, s. 4(1)(b)); or

(c)   may, if the applicant satisfies it that either an appeal is pending or that he is entitled and intends to appeal, set aside the registration or adjourn the application to set aside until the expiry of a period which appears to the court to be reasonably sufficient for the applicant to have the appeal disposed of on such terms as it thinks just (Act of 1933, s. 5(1); and see *S.A. Consortium General Textiles v. Sun and Sand Ltd* [1978] Q.B. 279, 306 per Goff, L.J.).

JURISDICTION OF THE COURTS OF THE COUNTRY OF THE ORIGINAL COURT.

62.10.2   Where the courts have had no jurisdiction the registration of the judgment may be set aside: Act of 1933, s. 4(1)(a)(ii). These courts are deemed to have jurisdiction if paragraphs (a) to (c) in s. 4(2) of the Act of 1933 apply. In relation to paragraph (a), see *Société Co-operative Sidmetal v. Titan International Ltd* [1966] 1 Q.B. 828 (re submission to the jurisdiction) and *S.A. Consortium General Textiles v. Sun and Sand Ltd* [1978] Q.B. 279 (re prorogation agreement under s. 4(1)(a)(iii)).

Application for enforcement abroad under the Act of 1920 or 1933

62.11   **62.11.**—(1) An application under section 10 of the Act of 1920 or the Act of 1933, as the case may be, for a certified copy of a judgment pronounced by the court shall be made by letter to the Deputy Principal Clerk.

(2) On receipt of such an application, the Deputy Principal Clerk shall issue under the seal of the court a copy of the judgment certified by him in Form 62.11.

(3) Where such an application is made under section 10 of the Act of 1933, the Deputy Principal Clerk shall issue with the certified copy of the judgment a further certificate under the seal of the court signed by him containing the details, and having appended the documents, mentioned in paragraph (4).

(4) A certificate under paragraph (3) shall—

(a)   state—

    (i)   the manner in which the principal writ or counterclaim was served on the judgment debtor;

    (ii)   whether or not the judgment debtor entered appearance or lodged answers in the process of the cause;

    (iii)   any objection made to the jurisdiction;

    (iv)   that the time limit for appeal has expired and that no appeal has been taken, or that an appeal was taken but was refused; and

   (v) such other particulars as may be required by the foreign court which may enable execution of the judgment; and

 (b) number, identify and have appended to it a copy of—

   (i) the principal writ or counterclaim showing the manner in which such writ was served on the judgment debtor;

   (ii) the pleadings, if any, in the cause resulting in the judgment; and

   (iii) a copy of the opinion, if any, of the judge or judges who issued the judgment.

 (5) Where necessary, the applicant shall provide the copies of the documents mentioned in paragraph (4).

Deriv. R.C.S. 1965, r. 248(h) and r. 249.13

GENERAL NOTE.

Recognition and enforcement of judgments is almost invariably done on a reciprocal basis. Accordingly this rule provides for the obtaining of a certified copy of a judgment together with an additional certificate of particulars for the purpose of enforcement abroad under either the Act of 1920 or the Act of 1933. **62.11.1**

"JUDGMENT".

For definition, see notes 62.4.2 (Act of 1920) and 62.4.3 (Act of 1933). The Act of 1920 allows only judgments obtained in the Court of Session to be enforced abroad: Act of 1920, s. 10(1)(a). This includes a decree obtained by the registration of a document of debt in the Books of Council and Session: *Taylor, Petr.* 1931 S.L.T. 260. **62.11.2**

The Act of 1933 allows any judgment given by a court or tribunal in the UK under which a sum of money is payable, not being a sum payable in respect of taxes or other charges of a like nature or in respect of a fine or other penalty, to be enforced abroad: Act of 1933, s. 10(2). Presumably this will include sums awarded in sheriff court decrees, or industrial tribunal decisions, and compensation orders under s. 58(1) of the Criminal Justice (Scotland) Act 1980, amongst others. R. 62.11, however, applies only to judgments pronounced by the Court of Session: r. 62.11.

"LETTER TO THE DEPUTY PRINCIPAL CLERK".

The address and telephone number, etc., of the Deputy Principal Clerk are: The Deputy Principal Clerk of Session, Court of Session, 2 Parliament Square, Edinburgh EH1 1RQ; tel. 031-225 2595; fax 031-225 8213; DX ED306. **62.11.3**

Part III – Registration of Awards under the Arbitration (International Investment Disputes) Act 1966

Application and interpretation of this Part

 62.12.—(1) This Part applies to the registration of awards under the Arbitration (International Investment Disputes) Act 1966. **62.12**

 (2) In this Part—

  "the Act of 1966" means the Arbitration (International Investment Disputes) Act 1966;

  "award" has the meaning assigned to it in section 1(7) of the Act of 1966;

  "the Convention" means the Convention mentioned in section 1(1) of the Act of 1966.

Deriv. R.C.S. 1965, r. 249A.1 inserted by S.I. 1971 No. 1809 (r. 62.12(2))

GENERAL NOTE.

Part III of this Chapter provides rules for the recognition and enforcement in Scotland of awards made by the International Centre for Settlement of Investment Disputes. The International Centre acts under the 1965 Washington Convention on the Settlement of Investment Disputes Between States and Nationals of Other States. The Arbitration (International Investment Disputes) Act 1966 was passed, inter alia, to allow for recognition and enforcement in the UK of awards made by the International Centre. **62.12.1**

Part III of this Chapter has been made under s. 7 of the Act of 1966: A.S. (R.C.S. 1994) 1994, Sched. 1 [S.I. 1994 No. 1443]. Accordingly a word or expression used in Pt. III which is also used in the Act of 1966 has the meaning given in that Act unless the contrary intention appears: Interpretation Act 1978, s. 11.

"AWARD".

62.12.2   This includes any decision interpreting, revising, or annulling an award being a decision under the Convention and any decision as to costs which under the Convention is to form part of the award: Act of 1966, s. 1(7)(a).

"THE CONVENTION".

62.12.3   This is the Convention on the Settlement of Investment Disputes Between States and Nationals of Other States opened for signature in Washington on 18th March 1965, set out in the Schedule to the Act of 1966.

Applications for registration under the Act of 1966

62.13   **62.13.**—(1)   An application for recognition or enforcement of an award under Article 54 of the Convention shall be made by petition.

(2)   There shall be produced with such a petition an affidavit—

    (a)   exhibiting a copy of the award certified under the Convention; and

    (b)   stating—

        (i)   the full name, title, trade or business and the usual or the last known place of residence or, where appropriate, of the business of the petitioner and of the party against whom the award was made;

        (ii)   that the petitioner is entitled to have the award registered under the Act of 1966;

        (iii)   the amount of the award which is unsatisfied;

        (iv)   whether the enforcement of the award has been sisted (provisionally or otherwise) under the Convention and whether any, and if so what, application has been made under the Convention which, if granted, might result in a sist of enforcement of the award.

Deriv. R.C.S. 1965, r. 249A.2 and 3 inserted by S.I. 1971 No. 1809

"PETITION".

62.13.1   A petition is presented in the Outer House: r. 14.2(h). The petition must be in Form 14.4 in the official printed form: rr. 4.1 and 14.4. The petition may be signed by the petitioner, counsel or other person having a right of audience, or an agent: r. 4.2(3)(d); and see r. 1.3(1) (definition of "counsel", "other person having a right of audience" and "agent") and note 1.3.4.

The petitioner must lodge the petition with the required steps of process (r. 4.4) and any documents founded on or adopted (r. 27.1(1)). A fee is payable on lodging the petition: see note 14.5.10.

On petitions generally, see Chap. 14.

PRODUCTIONS.

62.13.2   The petitioner must produce with the petition (a) a copy of the award under the Convention certified by the Secretary-General of the International Centre (Act of 1966, Sched., Art. 54(2); and r. 17.1); (b) an affidavit (r. 62.13(2)); and (c) if necessary, a translation of any document lodged (r. 62.3).

AFFIDAVIT.

62.13.3   The affidavit should be in the form of a statement of evidence written in the first person. The affidavit should contain the evidence of the deponent in support of the averments in the petition. In particular the affidavit should deal with the matters listed in r. 62.6(1).

An affidavit should be sworn and signed by the deponent before any person who may competently take an oath, whether in Scotland or in any other country. In Scotland such a person may include a notary public, justice of the peace, sheriff, or any judge. The person taking the oath should also sign the affidavit. Where the affidavit is not in English a duly certified translation should also be lodged.

See also the definition of affidavit in r. 1.3(1).

Warrant for registration under the Act of 1966

62.14   **62.14.**—   The court shall, subject to rule 62.17 (sist of enforcement), on being satisfied that the petition complies with the requirements of the Act of 1966, pronounce an interlocutor granting warrant for the registration of the award.

Deriv. R.C.S. 1965, r. 249A.5 inserted by S.I. 1971 No. 1809

Registration under the Act of 1966

62.15.—(1) Where the court pronounces an interlocutor under rule 62.14 granting warrant for registration, the Deputy Principal Clerk shall enter details of the interlocutor and the award in a register of awards under the Act of 1966.

(2) On presentation by the petitioner to the Keeper of the Registers of—

(a) a certified copy of the interlocutor under rule 62.14,

(b) a certified copy of the award and any translation of it; and

(c)[1] any certificate of currency conversion under rule 62.2(1)(b),

they shall be registered in the register of judgments of the Books of Council and Session.

(3) An extract of the registered award with warrant for execution shall not be issued by the Keeper of the Registers until a certificate of service under rule 62.16 is produced to him.

Deriv. R.C.S. 1965, r. 249A.6 (r. 62.15(1)), and r. 249A.7(3)(part) (r. 62.15(3)), both inserted by S.I.1971 No. 1809

"KEEPER OF THE REGISTERS".

This is the Keeper of the Registers of Scotland: r. 1.3(1). The Register of Judgments is at Meadowbank House, 153 London Road, Edinburgh EH8 7AU; tel. 031-659 6111; fax 031-459 1221; DX ED300.

"CERTIFIED COPY OF THE INTERLOCUTOR".

A copy of the interlocutor is typed by the agent and presented to the clerk of session in the Petition Department. The clerk checks it, certifies it as a true copy and stamps it with the court stamp.
A fee is payable.

"CERTIFIED COPY OF THE AWARD".

The copy of the award should be certified by the Secretary-General of the International Centre for Settlement of Investment Disputes: Act of 1966, Sched., Art. 54(2).

"TRANSLATION".

See r. 62.3.

"CERTIFICATE OF CURRENCY CONVERSION".

In obtaining this, notwithstanding the provisions of r. 62.2(1), the date of conversion in the certified statement should be the date of the award: Act of 1966, s. 1(3).
The certificate should be obtained from the clerk of session and should be signed by him: r. 62.2(3); and see notes 62.2.4 and 62.2.5.

REGISTRATION FEE.

A fee will be payable to the Keeper of the Registers for registration and any extract: see the Fees in the Registers of Scotland Order 1991 [S.I. 1991 No. 2093].

Service on party against whom award made

62.16.— On registration under rule 62.15, the petitioner shall forthwith serve a notice of the registration on the party against whom the award was made in Form 62.16.

Deriv. R.C.S. 1965, r. 249A.7(1) and (2) inserted by S.I. 1971 No. 1809

"SERVE".

For methods of service, see Chap. 16, Pt. I.

Sist of enforcement under the Act of 1966

62.17.—(1) Where it appears to the court that—

(a) the enforcement of the award has been sisted (whether provisionally or otherwise) under the Convention, or

(b) any application has been made under the Convention which, if granted, might result in a sist of the enforcement of the award,

62.15

62.15.1

62.15.2

62.15.3

62.15.4

62.15.5

62.15.6

62.16

62.16.1

62.17

---

[1] R. 62.15(2)(c) amended by S.I. 1996 No. 2168 (minor correction).

the court shall, or in the case referred to in sub-paragraph (b) may, sist the petition for such time as it thinks fit.

(2)   Where the court has granted a warrant for registration under rule 62.14, the party against whom the award was made may apply to the court for suspension or interdict of execution of the award.

(3)   An application under paragraph (2) shall—

(a)   be made on ground (a) or (b) of paragraph (1);

(b)   notwithstanding rule 60.2 (form of applications for suspension), be made by note in the process of the petition under rule 62.13; and

(c)   be accompanied by an affidavit stating the relevant facts.

Deriv. R.C.S. 1965, r. 249A.8 and 9 inserted by S.I. 1971 No. 1809

"SUSPENSION OR INTERDICT".

62.17.1   See Chap. 60.

"NOTE".

62.17.2   For applications by note, see r. 15.2.

Part IV[1] – EU Judgments

Interpretation of this Part

62.18   62.18.—(1)[2]   In this Part—

"EU judgment" means any decision, judgment or order which is enforceable under or in accordance with—

(a)[3]   Article 280 or 299 of the Treaty on the Functioning of the European Union,

(b)   Article 18, 159 or 164 of the Euratom Treaty,

(c)   Article 44 or 92 of the E.C.S.C. Treaty, or

(d)[4]   Article 82 of Regulation 40/94 of December 20, 1993 (regulation of the Council of the European Union: on the community trade mark).

"Euratom inspection order" means an order made by or in the exercise of the functions of the President of the European Court or by the Commission of the European Communities under Article 81 of the Euratom Treaty;

"European Court" means the Court of Justice of the European Communities;

"order for enforcement" means an order by or under the authority of the Secretary of State that the EU judgment to which it is appended is to be registered for enforcement in the United Kingdom.

(2)[5]   In paragraph (1), the expressions "Euratom Treaty" and "E.C.S.C. Treaty" have the meanings assigned respectively in Schedule 1 to the European Communities Act 1972.

(3)[6]   In paragraph (1), "the Treaty on the Functioning of the European Union" means the treaty referred to in section 1(2)(s) of the European Communities Act 1972.

Deriv. R.C.S. 1965, r. 296F inserted by SI 1972/1982

---

[1] Part IV and r. 62.18(1) amended by S.S.I. 2011 No. 288 (effective 21st July 2011).

[2] Part IV and r. 62.18(1) amended by S.S.I. 2011 No. 288 (effective 21st July 2011).

[3] Rule 62.18(1)(a) and (2) amended and (3) inserted by S.S.I. 2012 No. 275 r. 7(1) (effective 19th November 2012).

[4] Rule 62.1.8(1)(d) inserted by S.I. 1998 No. 2637 (effective 1st December 1998).

[5] Rule 62.18(1)(a) and (2) amended and (3) inserted by S.S.I. 2012 No. 275 r. 7(1) (effective 19th November 2012).

[6] Rule 62.18(1)(a) and (2) amended and (3) inserted by S.S.I. 2012 No. 275 r. 7(1) (effective 19th November 2012).

GENERAL NOTE.

Part IV of this Chapter provides rules for the enforcement of (a) decisions of the Council and Commission of the E.C. which impose pecuniary obligations on persons other than States or (b) orders made by the President of the European Court or the Commission under Art. 81 of the Euratom Treaty.

The term "European Economic Community" in the E.E.C. Treaty was replaced by the term "European Community" by Art.G(1) of Title II of the Treaty on European Union (Maastricht): see European Communities Act 1972, s. 1(2)(k) as amended by the European Communities (Amendment) Act 1993, s. 1(1). That in turn was changed to the "European Union" by the Treaty of Lisbon amending the Treaty on European Union and the Treaty Establishing the European Community signed at Lisbon on 13th December 2007. Hence the references in the rest of this Part to "EU".

The reference to Art. 82 of Regulation 40/94 may be found in the Official Journal (of the E.U.) 1994, 11/1.

Register of EU judgments

62.19.—[1] A register shall be kept by the Deputy Principal Clerk for the purpose of registering—

    (a)   any EU judgment to which the Secretary of State has attached an order for enforcement;

    (b)   any Euratom inspection order; or

    (c)   any order of the European Court that enforcement of a registered EU judgment shall be suspended.

Deriv. R.C.S. 1965, r. 296G inserted by SI 1972/1982

Applications for registration of EU judgments

62.20.—[2](1) An application for registration of an EU judgment or Euratom inspection order shall be made by petition.

(2) Where the application is for registration of an EU judgment under which a sum of money is payable, the petition shall set out—

    (a)   the name, trade or business and the usual or last known place of residence or business of the judgment debtor, so far as known to the petitioner; and

    (b)   the amount of the judgment which remains unsatisfied.

(3) There shall be produced with a petition referred to in paragraph (1) the EU judgment and the order for its enforcement or the Euratom inspection order, as the case may be, or a copy of it.

Deriv. R.C.S. 1965, r. 296H(i)(part) (r. 62.20(1)), r. 296H(iii)(a) and (b) (r. 62.20(2)), and r. 296H(ii)(part) (r. 62.20(3)), all inserted by SI 1972/1982

"PETITION".

A petition is presented in the Outer House: r. 14.2(h). The petition must be in Form 14.4 in the official printed form: rr. 4.1 and 14.4. The petition may be signed by the petitioner, counsel or other person having a right of audience, or an agent: r. 4.2; and see r. 1.3(1) (definition of "counsel", "other person having a right of audience" and "agent") and note 1.3.4.

The petitioner must lodge the petition with the required steps of process (r. 4.4) and any documents founded on or adopted (r. 27.1(1)). A fee is payable on lodging the petition: see note 14.5.10.

On petitions generally, see Chap. 14.

Warrant for registration of EU judgments

62.21.—[3](1) On an application being made under rule 62.20, the court shall direct that any Euratom inspection order or any EU judgment which has appended to it an order for enforcement shall be entered in the register kept under rule 62.19 and—

    (a)   in respect of an EU judgment, subject to paragraph (2), pronounce an interlocutor granting warrant for registration of the judgment in the Books of Council and Session; or

62.18.1

62.19

62.20

62.20.1

62.21

---

[1] Rule 62.19 amended by S.S.I. 2011 No. 288 (effective 21st July 2011).
[2] Rule 62.20 amended by S.S.I. 2011 No. 288 (effective 21st July 2011).
[3] Rule 62.21 amended by S.S.I. 2011 No. 288 (effective 21st July 2011).

(b)   in respect of a Euratom inspection order, pronounce such interlocutor as is necessary for the purpose of ensuring that effect is given to that order.

(2)   Where it appears that an EU judgment under which a sum of money is payable has been partly satisfied at the date of the application under rule 62.20, warrant for registration in the Books of Council and Session shall be granted only in respect of the balance remaining payable at that date.

Deriv. R.C.S. 1965, r. 296H(i)(part) (r. 62.21(1)) inserted by SI 1972/1982

Registration of EU judgments

62.22

62.22.—[1](1)   On presentation by the petitioner to the Keeper of the Registers of—

(a)   a certified copy of an interlocutor pronounced under rule 62.21(1)(a),

(b)   the EU judgment or a certified copy of it and any translation of it, and

(c)[2]   any certificate of currency conversion under rule 62.2(1)(b), they shall immediately be registered in the register of judgments of the Books of Council and Session.

(2)   On registration under paragraph (1), the Keeper of the Registers shall issue an extract of the registered EU judgment with a warrant for execution.

"KEEPER OF THE REGISTERS".

62.22.1

This is the Keeper of the Registers of Scotland: r. 1.3(1). The Register of Judgments is at Meadowbank House, 153 London Road, Edinburgh EH8 7AU; tel. 0131-659 6111; fax 0131-459 1221; DX ED300.

"CERTIFIED COPY OF THE INTERLOCUTOR".

62.22.2

A copy of the interlocutor is typed by the agent and presented to the clerk of session in the Petition Department. The clerk checks it, certifies it as a true copy and stamps it with the court stamp.
A fee is payable.

"TRANSLATION".

62.22.3

See r. 62.3.

"CERTIFICATE OF CURRENCY CONVERSION".

62.22.4

The certificate should be obtained from the clerk of session in the Petition Department and should be signed by him: r. 62.2(3); and see notes 62.2.4 and 62.2.5.

REGISTRATION FEE.

62.22.5

A fee will be payable to the Keeper of the Registers for registration and any extract: see the Fees in the Registers of Scotland Order 1991 [SI 1991/2093].

Service on judgment debtor of EU judgment

62.23

62.23.—[3]   On an interlocutor being pronounced under rule 62.21(1)(a), the petitioner shall forthwith serve a copy of it on the person against whom the EU judgment was given or the Euratom inspection order was made, as the case may be.

Deriv. R.C.S. 1965, r. 296H(iv)(part) inserted by S.I. 1972 No. 1982

"SERVE".

62.23.1

For methods of service, see Chap. 16, Pt. I.

Variation or cancellation of registration

62.24

62.24.—[4](1)   An application for the variation or cancellation of any registration shall be made by note in the process of the petition under rule 62.20(1).

---

[1] Rule 62.22 amended by S.S.I. 2011 No. 288 (effective 21st July 2011).
[2] Rule 62.22(1)(c) amended by S.I. 1996 No. 2168 (effective 23rd September 1996).
[3] Rule 62.23 amended by S.S.I. 2011 No. 288 (effective 21st July 2011).
[4] Rule 62.24 amended by S.S.I. 2011 No. 288 (effective 21st July 2011).

(2)   Where the court grants an application under paragraph (1), it may direct that the entry in the register kept under rule 62.19, and, in the case of variation of an EU judgment, the entry in the Books of Council and Session, shall be varied as sought by the noter.

Deriv. R.C.S. 1965, r. 296J inserted by S.I. 1972 No. 1982

"NOTE".

For applications by note, see r. 15.2.

62.24.1

Suspension of enforcement of EU judgments

62.25.—[1](1)   An order of the European Court that enforcement of a registered EU judgment be suspended—

    (a)   shall—

        (i)   on production of the order to the Court of Session, and

        (ii)   on application made by note,

      be registered forthwith, and

    (b)   shall be of the same effect as if the order had been an order made by the Court of Session on the date of its registration suspending the execution of the judgment for the same period and on the same conditions as are stated in the order of the European Court.

(2)   No steps to enforce the judgment mentioned in paragraph (1) shall be taken while such an order of the European Court remains in force.

Deriv. R.C.S. 1965, r. 296K inserted by S.I. 1972 No. 1982

62.25

GENERAL NOTE.

Enforcement of a community judgment enforceable under Art. 192 of the E.C. Treaty may be suspended only by a judgment of the European Court: E.C. Treaty, Art. 192. Rule 62.25 provides for (a) the procedure to enforce a European Court order suspending a community judgment; and (b) the effect of a European Court order suspending a community judgment.

62.25.1

Part V[2] – Recognition and Enforcement of Judgments under the Civil Jurisdiction and Judgments Act 1982 or under the Lugano Convention of 30th October 2007

Application and interpretation of this Part

62.26.—[3, 4, 5, 6, 7](1)   This Part applies to the recognition and enforcement of a judgment under the Act of 1982, the Council Regulation, the 2005 Hague Convention or the Lugano Convention.

(2)   Unless the context otherwise requires, in this Part—

    "the Act of 1982" means the Civil Jurisdiction and Judgments Act 1982;

    "Contracting State" has the meaning assigned in section 1(3) of the Act of 1982;

    "the Council Regulation" means Council Regulation (EC) No. 44/2001 of 22nd December 2000 on jurisdiction and the recognition and enforcement of judgments in civil and commercial matters and as applied by the Agreement of 19th October 2005 between the European Community and the Kingdom of Denmark on jurisdiction and the recognition and enforcement of judgments in civil and commercial matters;

62.26

---

[1] Rule 62.25 amended by S.S.I. 2011 No. 288 (effective 21st July 2011).
[2] Part V and r. 62.26 substituted by S.S.I. 2004 No. 52 (effective 1st March 2004).
[3] Part V and r. 62.26 amended by S.S.I. 2004 No. 52 (effective 1st March 2004).
[4] Rule 62.26 amended by S.S.I. 2009 No. 450 r. 2 (effective 1st January 2010).
[5] Part V heading and r. 62.26 as amended by S.S.I. 2015 No. 26 r. 2 (effective 7th February 2015).
[6] Rule 62.26 as amended by S.S.I. 2019 No. 85 r. 2 (effective 28th March 2019).
[7] Part V and r. 62.26 as amended by S.S.I. 2020 No. 440 r. 2(3) (effective IP completion day, 31st December 2020 subject to savings specified in S.S.I. 2020 No. 440 r. 5).

"the 2005 Hague Convention" means the Convention on Choice of Court Agreements concluded on 30th June 2005 at the Hague;

"judgment" includes an authentic instrument or court settlement.;

"the Lugano Convention" means the Convention on jurisdiction and the recognition and enforcement of judgments in civil and commercial matters, between the European Community and the Republic of Iceland, the Kingdom of Norway, the Swiss Confederation and the Kingdom of Denmark and signed by the European Community on 30th October 2007;[1]

"Member State" has the same meaning as Member State in the Council Regulation.

Deriv. R.C.S. 1965, r. 249D(1)(part) (r. 62.26(2)) inserted by S.I. 1986 No. 1941

General note.

62.26.1   Many foreign judgments are now enforced in Scotland under the C.J.J.A. 1982. The C.J.J.A. 1982 did two things in the field of recognition and enforcement, namely (1) replaced the Judgments Extension Act 1868 or (in the sheriff court) the Inferior Courts Judgments Extension Act 1882 in relation to reciprocal recognition and enforcement of judgments between different U.K. jurisdictions; and (2) provided a new regime for the reciprocal recognition and enforcement of judgments between the U.K. and other member States of the E.C. The latter regime uses the 1968 Brussels Convention as amended by the 1971 Protocol and the 1978, 1982, and 1989 Accession Conventions with regard to the other member States of the E.C. (see note 62.26.2). The C.J.J.A. 1982 was amended on each occasion a new state acceded to the 1968 Convention to include a reference to the new state. Following the 1989 Accession Convention to admit Spain and Portugal some additional textual changes were made to the 1968 Convention. These were brought into force in the U.K. by the Civil Jurisdiction and Judgments Act 1982 (Amendment) Order 1990 [S.I. 1990 No. 2591] on 1st December 1991.

The major amendment to the C.J.J.A. 1982 was made by the C.J.J.A. 1991 which came into force on 1st May 1992. This introduced a requirement for reciprocal recognition and enforcement parallel to the 1968 Brussels Convention built on the almost identically worded 1988 Lugano Convention between the U.K. and the member States of the European Free Trade Association (EFTA). As states leave EFTA and join the E.C. they will have to accede to the 1968 Brussels Convention: C.J.J.A. 1982, Sched. 1, Art. 63. To fill their absence the 1988 Lugano Convention envisaged the accession to it of non-EFTA States, perhaps from Eastern Europe: C.J.J.A. 1982, Sched. 3C, Art. 62(1)(b) (see note 62.26.3). The 1988 Lugano Convention was replaced by the 2007 Lugano Convention. Schedule 3C to the C.J.J.A. 1982, which contained the 1988 Convention, has been repealed and the 2007 Convention does not feature in the C.J.J.A. 1982. The signatories to that Convention are the European Community, Denmark and Norway from 1st January 2010, Switzerland from 1st January 2011 and Iceland from 1st May 2011. It served as a parallel to the Council Regulation (see below).

The Council Regulation (EC) No. 44/2001 (Brussels 1 Regulation) really superseded the 1968 Brussels Convention which applied between the pre-2004 EU states and territories and other signatories.

In addition the C.J.J.A. 1982 provided that Her Majesty could by Order in Council, apply the terms of the 1968 Brussels Convention for the regulation of jurisdiction and the recognition and enforcement of judgments between the U.K., the Isle of Man, any Channel Island, and any U.K. colony. C.J.J.A. 1982, s. 39. Her Majesty has used this power to regulate the jurisdiction and enforcement of judgments between the U.K. and Gibraltar (apply Arts 1–54, 57 and 65 of the Convention): Civil Jurisdiction and Judgments Act 1980 (Gibraltar) Order 1997 (S.I. 1997 No. 2602).

Pt. V. and r. 62.26 were replaced by A.S. (R.C.S.A. (Miscellaneous) 2004 [S.S.I. 2004 No. 52]. The purpose of the A.S. was to include in Pt. V. of Chap. 62 references to the Council Regulation (EC) No. 44/2001 on jurisdiction and the recognition and enforcement of judgments in civil and commercial matters between Member States of the EU (the Brussels I Regulation). Under that regime a judgment is enforceable on completion of the formalities in art. 53 and registration; refusal of recognition is further restricted. Following the coming into force of Brussels I (Recast) Regulation (EU) No. 1215/2012, the Council Regulation (E.C.) No. 44/2001 (Brussels I Regulation) no longer applied. One of the consequences of Brussels I Regulation (Recast), which applied to proceedings instituted on or after 10th January 2015, was that it was no longer necessary for the holder of a European judgment to register it here before being able to enforce it here. It was for the party who wishes recognition or enforcement to be refused who must apply to the court. Recognition and enforcement of judgments under the Brussels I Regulation (Recast) are now dealt with in Pt. VA of this chapter.

The position before Brexit (31st December 2020) was that (1) in relation to a judgment in an EU country, one looked to the Brussels 1 Regulation (Recast) - implemented by Denmark on 1st June 2013; (2) in relation to Iceland, Norway and Switzerland, one looked to the 2007 Lugano Convention; (3) in relation other countries one looked to the Administration of Justice Act 1920 or the Foreign Judgments (Reciprocal Enforcement) Act 1933. Failing those, one would have to turn to the common law and raise an action for decree conform.

---

[1] Rule 62.26 amended by S.S.I. 2009 No. 450 r. 2 (effective 1st January 2010).

The position is now as follows:

(1) In relation to proceedings not concluded before 11pm on 31st December 2020, EU law will continue to apply: Civil Jurisdiction and Judgments (Amendment) (EU Exit) Regulations 2019 [S.I. 2019 No. 479].

(2) As the U.K. has left the EU, in relation to the recognition and enforcement of judgments issued in legal proceedings begun after the end of the transition period (on or after 11pm on 31st December 2020) in countries in the EU, one will fall back on other law.

(3) Where there is a contract between a party in the U.K. and a party in another contracting state, there may be a choice of law agreement to which the 2005 Hague Convention on Choice of Court Agreements applies: see C.J.J.A. 1982, Sched. 3F inserted by the Private International Law (Implementation of Agreements) Act 2020 in force from 31st December 2020. There is a disagreement between the EU and the U.K. as to whether the 2005 Hague Convention applies to agreements on or after 1st January 2021 (EU position) or on or after 1st October 2015 when the U.K. acceded to the Convention as an EU state (U.K. position).

(4) Otherwise, former bi-lateral conventions or agreements for enforcement of judgments (by registration) under the Act of 1933 may apply (see note 62.5.7). That statutory instruments enforcing such conventions revive may be seen in the Reciprocal Enforcement of Foreign Judgments (Norway) Amendment) (Scotland) Order 2020 [S.S.I. 2020 No. 371] amending the 1961 agreement between Norway and the U.K. (see S.I. 1962 No. 636). Few former EU and Lugano countries, however, are covered by the Act of 1933.

(5) The U.K. has applied to join the 2007 Lugano Convention, having now left the EU. That convention applies between the EU member states, Iceland, Norway and Switzerland. Denmark joined separately on 24th September 2009 (it had not signed up to the Brussels I Regulation (Recast) at that time).

(6) Recognition and enforcement of judgments in relation to parental responsibility and protection of children under 18 is governed by Sched. 3D of the C.J.J.A. 1982 inserted by the Private International Law (Implementation of Agreements) Act 2020, in force from 31st December 2020.

(7) There may be special statutory rules about recognition and enforcement, such as in the Family Law Act 1986.

(8) Recognition and enforcement of maintenance orders for children by a court in a Contracting State to the 2007 Hague Convention on the International Recovery of Child Support is dealt with in the sheriff court under the International Recovery of Maintenance (Hague Convention 2007) (Scotland) Regulations 2012 [S.S.I. 2012 No. 301]. The U.K. was a member as part of the EU but joined separately on 1st January 2021.

(9) Raising an action at common law for decree conform. An official extract of the foreign judgment is produced, with a translation into English, where necessary, authenticated by an affidavit before a notary public. The onus is then on the defender to challenge it. The grounds of defence are limited to – the foreign court lacked jurisdiction; there was irregularity in the foreign proceedings; the foreign proceedings were penal or revenue decisions; the foreign judgment was not final; the foreign judgment is unenforceable by virtue of s. 5 of the Protection of Trading Interests Act 1980 (see, e.g., *Service Temps Inc v. MacLeod* 2014 S.L.T. 375 (OH); [2013] CSOH 162) or s. 32 of the C.J.J.A. 1982.

Commencement date of Convention.

Under Art. 54 of the 1968 and Lugano Conventions, in order to maintain reciprocity, it is provided that the conventions apply to a judgment the proceedings for which were instituted, or an authentic instrument which was drawn up or registered, after the relevant convention came into force in both the state of origin and the state of destination of the judgment. An exception to this is when the judgment was given after the Convention had come into force on proceedings started before the date of operation but was founded in jurisdictional rules which accorded either with the relevant convention or were contained in a separate convention between the two states: C.J.J.A. 1982, Scheds 1 and 3C, Art. 54.

Accordingly it is important to know the date when the relevant convention came first into force in *both* the U.K. *and* the other contracting state.

Further information on the dates when the convention came into force in other states may be obtained from the Treaty Records Section, Foreign and Commonwealth Office, Room CL 505, Clive House, Petty France, London SW1H 9HD; tel. 0171-270 4079; see also the Government website *www.gov.uk/uk-treaties.*

62.26.2

Definitions in the Act of 1982.

Part v. of this Chapter has been made under s. 48 of the C.J.J.A. 1982 (rr. 62.28 and 62.40 are made under s. 12 of the C.J.J.A. 1982). Accordingly a word or expression used in Pt. v. which is also used in the C.J.J.A. 1982 has the meaning given in that Act unless the contrary intention appears: Interpretation Act 1978, s. 11.

62.26.3

Disapplication of certain rules to this Part

62.27

62.27.—[1] The following provisions shall not apply to an application under this Part in addition to those rules mentioned in rule 62.1:—

rule 4.1(1) (printed form for petition),

rule 14.4 (form of petitions).

GENERAL NOTE.

62.27.1

The official printed form of petition does not have to be used where a petition is required under this Part of Chap. 62. Special forms of petition are provided in Forms 62.28 and 62.38 for petitions under the rules to which they relate.

The new rule is in identical terms to the old rule.

Enforcement of judgments, authentic instruments or court settlements from another Contracting State, Member State or State bound by the Lugano Convention[2]

62.28

62.28.—[3, 4, 5, 6, 7](1) An application under—

(a) section 4 of, and Article 31 (enforcement of judgment from another Contracting State) or Article 50 (enforcement of authentic instrument or court settlement from another Contracting State) of the Convention in Schedule 1 to, the Act of 1982;

(b) Article 38 (enforcement of judgment from Member State), Article 57 (enforcement of authentic instrument from another Member State) or Article 58 (enforcement of court settlement from another Member State) of the Council Regulation;

(ba) section 4B of the Act of 1982 (registration and enforcement of judgments under the 2005 Hague Convention); or

(c) Article 38 (enforcement of judgment from another State bound by the Lugano Convention), Article 57 (enforcement of authentic instrument from another State bound by the Lugano Convention) or Article 58 (enforcement of court settlement from another State bound by the Lugano Convention) of the Lugano Convention,

shall be made by petition in Form 62.28.

(2) Subject to paragraphs (3), (3AA) and (3AB), there must be produced with the petition—

(a) an authentic copy of the judgment to be registered;

(b) a document which establishes that, according to the law of the country in which the judgment has been given, the judgment is enforceable and has been served;

(c) where judgment has been given in absence (that is to say, in default of appearance), the original or a certified copy of the document which establishes that the party against whom judgment was given in absence was served with the document initiating the proceedings or with an equivalent document;

(d) where applicable, a document showing that the applicant is in receipt of legal aid in the country in which the judgment was given;

---

[1] Rule 62.27 substituted by S.S.I. 2004 No. 52 (effective 1st March, 2004).
[2] Heading and r. 62.28 amended by S.S.I. 2009 No. 450 (effective 1st January 2010).
[3] Rule 62.28 substituted by S.S.I. 2004 No. 52 (effective 1st March 2004).
[4] Heading and Rule 62.28 amended by S.S.I. 2009 No. 450 (effective 1st January 2010).
[5] As amended by S.S.I. 2015 No. 26 para.2 (effective 7th February 2015).
[6] Rule 62.28 as amended by S.S.I. 2019 No. 85 r. 2 (effective 28th March 2019).
[7] Rule 62.28 as amended by S.S.I. 2020 No. 440 r. 2(4) (effective IP completion day, 31st December 2020).

   (e) an affidavit stating—

      (i) whether the judgment provides for the payment of a sum of money;

     (ii) whether interest is recoverable on the judgment under the law of the country in which judgment was given and, if so, the rate of interest, the date from which interest is due and the date on which interest ceases to accrue;

    (iii) an address within the jurisdiction of the court for service on or intimation to the petitioner;

    (iv) the usual or last known place of residence or business of the person against whom the judgment was given;

    (v) the grounds on which the petitioner is entitled to enforce the judgment; and

    (vi) the part of the judgment which is unsatisfied.

  (3) Paragraph (2)(b) and (d) do not apply to a petition under Article 38 (enforcement of judgment from another Member State), Article 57 (enforcement of authentic instrument from another Member State) or Article 58 (enforcement of settlement from another Member State) of the Council Regulation but there must be produced with such a petition a certificate under Article 54 (standard form of certificate of judgment), Article 57 (standard form of certificate of authentic instrument) or Article 58 (standard form of certificate of court settlement) of the Council Regulation.

  (3AA) For applications to which paragraph (1)(ba) applies, in addition to the information specified in paragraph (2), the following must be produced with the petition—

   (a) the exclusive choice of court agreement, a certified copy thereof, or other evidence of its existence; and

   (b) in the case referred to in Article 12 (judicial settlements) of the 2005 Hague Convention, a certificate of a court of the State of origin that the judicial settlement or a part of it is enforceable in the same manner as a judgment in the State of origin.

  (3AB) An application for recognition or enforcement may be accompanied by a certificate issued by a court (including an officer of the court) of the State of origin under Article 13(3) of the 2005 Hague Convention.

  (3A) Paragraph (2)(b) and (d) shall not apply to a petition under Article 38 (enforcement of judgment from another State bound by the Lugano Convention), Article 57 (enforcement of authentic instrument from another State bound by the Lugano Convention) or Article 58 (enforcement of court settlement from another State bound by the Lugano Convention) of the Lugano Convention but there shall be produced with such a petition a certificate under Article 54 (standard form of certificate of judgment), Article 57 (standard form of certificate of authentic instrument) or Article 58 (standard form of certificate of court settlement) of the Lugano Convention.

  (4) Where the petitioner does not produce a document required under paragraph (2)(a) to (d), (3), (3AA), (3AB) or (3A), the court may—

   (a) fix a period within which that document is to be lodged;

   (b) accept an equivalent document; or

   (c) dispense with the requirement to produce the document.

  Deriv. R.C.S. 1965, r. 249E(1)(a) (r. 62.28(1)), and r. 249E(2) and (3) (r. 62.28(2) and (3)), both inserted by S.I. 1986 No. 1941.

Jurisdiction.

  The 1968 Brussels Convention in Sched. 1 to the C.J.J.A. 1982 was replaced within the EU by the Council Regulation No 44/2001 (Brussels I Regulation) which in turn was replaced by the Council Regulation No. 1215/2012 (Brussels I Regulation (Recast)). Schedule I to the C.J.J.A. 1982, the two

62.28.1

Council Regulations and the 2007 Lugano Convention were repealed or revoked by the Civil Jurisdiction and Judgments (Amendment) (EU Exit) Regulations 2019 [S.I. 2019 No. 479] except in relation to proceedings not concluded before 11pm on 31st December 2020. The U.K. has applied to join the 2007 Lugano Convention as an independent State.

The court has jurisdiction for an application under Art. 31 of the 1968 Brussels Convention or in Sched. 1 to the C.J.J.A. 1982 where—

(a) the application is in respect of a judgment, authentic instrument or court settlement;

(b) the relevant convention was in force in both the state of origin and the state addressed at the time the proceedings leading to the judgment were instituted or the authentic instrument was drawn up or registered, or the judgment was given after the relevant convention came into force in both states in proceedings instituted before the coming into force which were based on jurisdictional rules which accorded with the relevant convention or with a bilateral Convention between the state of origin and the state addressed (C.J.J.A. 1982, Sched. 1, Art. 54).

(c) the subject-matter of the judgment, authentic instrument, or court settlement is covered by the relevant convention (see C.J.J.A. 1982, Sched. 1, Art. 1); and

(d) jurisdiction is not otherwise excluded (see note 62.28.2).

EXCLUSION OF JURISDICTION.

62.28.2   The jurisdiction of the court will be excluded where it cannot recognise the judgment because:—

(a) Recognition would be contrary to public policy in the U.K. (C.J.J.A. 1982, Sched. 1, Arts. 27(1) and 34). Art. 27(1), which will only be applied in exceptional circumstances when no other ground under Art. 27 was available (*Hoffman v. Kreig* [1988] E.C.R. 645), is concerned with substantive matters and not the procedural requirements for the application for recognition: *Artic Fish Sales Co. Ltd v. Adam (No. 2)* 1996 S.L.T. 970, 973I. For a recent example, where the public policy exception was argued unsuccessfully on the ground that there had been a breach of art. 6(1) of ECHR in French proceedings (which it was held there had not been), see *SA Marie Brizzard et Roger International v. William Grant & Sons Ltd (No.2)* , 2002 S.L.T. 1365 (OH). Under art. 34(1) of the Council Regulation the public policy ground is restricted to cases *manifestly* contrary to public policy.

(b) Where given in default of appearance, the defender had not been served with the document instituting the proceedings or with an equivalent document in sufficient time to enable him to arrange for his defence (C.J.J.A. 1982, Sched. 1 Arts. 27(2) and 34): see, e.g. *Artic Fish Sales Co. Ltd (No. 2)*, above and *Selco Ltd v. Mercier* 1996 S.L.T. 1247. Under art. 45(1)(b) of the Brussels I (recast) Regulation the exclusion of recognition will not apply where the defender failed to commence proceedings to challenge the judgment in default when it was possible for him to do so.

(c) It is irreconcilable with a judgment between the same parties given in the U.K. (C.J.J.A. 1982, Sched. 1 , Arts. 27(3) and 34). A court settlement (which is essentially contractual) is not a judgment for the purposes of Art. 27(3): *Solo Kleinmotoren v. Boch* [1994] E.C.R. I-2237. In Scotland, where the court grants decree in terms of part or all of a joint minute settling an action, that decree *is* a judgment.

(d) The adjudicating court has answered a preliminary question concerning an excluded matter in Art. 1(1) (relating to the subject-matter scope of the convention) in a way inconsistent with Scots international private law (C.J.J.A. 1982, Sched. 1 , Arts. 27(4) and 34). This ground does not appear in the Brussels I Regulation (Recast).

(e) It is irreconcilable with a prior non-contracting Member state judgment which involves the same cause of action, is between the same parties, and which is entitled to be recognised in the U.K. (C.J.J.A. 1982, Sched. 1 , Arts. 27(5) and 34). This ground under art. 45(1)(d) of the Brussels I Regulation (Recast) is the same.

(f) It conflicts with the particular jurisdictional provisions in Arts. 7–16 of the relevant convention (C.J.J.A. 1982, Sched. 1 , Arts. 28 and 34); and see Art. 45(1)(e) of the Brussels I (recast) regulation.

(g) It is against a person who was not domiciled in the state of origin of the judgment and an Order in Council has designated a provision in a treaty (permitted by Art. 59) between the U.K. and a non-contracting state to allow the U.K. not to recognise judgments given in a Contracting State against a defender domiciled or habitually resident in the non-contracting state in question (C.J.J.A. 1982, s. 9(2) and Sched. 1 , Arts. 28, 34 and 59; and see the Reciprocal Enforcement of Judgments (Canada) Order 1987 [S.I. 1987 No. 468] as amended by the Reciprocal Enforcement of Judgments (Canada) (Amendment) Order 1987 [S.I. 1987 No. 2211]).

(h) The 1968 Brussels and 1988 Lugano Conventions do not apply to proceedings for the enforcement of judgments given in non-contracting States: *Owens Bank Ltd v. Bracco* , [1994] E.C.R. 1-117; and see *Clarke v. Fennoscandia Ltd* , 2004 S.C. 197, 209 at para. [32] per Lord Kingarth.

"PETITION".

62.28.3   A petition is presented in the Outer House: r. 14.2(h). The petition must be in Form 62.28 but does not have to be in the official printed form (see r. 62.27). The petition may be signed by the petitioner, counsel or other person having a right of audience, or an agent: r. 4.2(3)(d); and see r. 1.3(1) (definition of "counsel", "other person having a right of audience", and "agent") and note 1.3.4.

The petitioner must lodge the petition with the required steps of process (r. 4.4) and any documents founded on or adopted (r. 27.1(1)). A fee is payable on lodging the petition: see note 14.5.10.

On petitions generally, see Chap. 14.

Under R.C.S. 1965, r. 249E(1)(a) a simple form of application was provided for instead of a formal petition in the official printed form, the purpose being to enable an application to be made from anywhere in the E.C. In practice, as a process is required, it is unlikely that an application would be made directly from abroad; the official printed form is, however, not required in case an application is made from abroad, but it may be used.

PRODUCTIONS. UNDER THE BRUSSELS AND LUGANO CONVENTIONS:

The petitioner must produce with the petition (a) an authentic copy of the judgment, authentic instrument or court settlement which meets the conditions of C.J.J.A. 1982, s. 11 (C.J.J.A. 1982, s. 11 and Scheds 1 and 3C, Art. 46(1), and r. 62.28(2)(a)); (b) a document which establishes that according to the law of the country of origin the judgment is enforceable and has been served (C.J.J.A. 1982, Scheds 1 and 3C, Art. 47(1) and r. 62.28(2)(b)); (c) where judgment has been given in absence, the original or a certified copy of the document which establishes that the defender in the judgment was served with the document initiating proceedings against him or an equivalent document (C.J.J.A. 1982, Scheds 1 and 3C, Art. 46(2); and r. 68.28(2)(c) and see *Artic Fish Sales Co. Ltd v. Adam (No. 2)* 1996 S.L.T. 970); (d) where applicable, a document showing that the applicant is in receipt of legal aid in the country of origin (C.J.J.A. 1982, Scheds 1 and 3C, Art. 47(2); and r. 62.28(2)(d)); (e) an affidavit (r. 62.28(2)(e)); and (f) a translation of any document lodged (r. 62.3). **62.28.4**

CONDITIONS FOR AUTHENTICATION OF JUDGMENT ETC.

These are that the copy judgment (a) bears the seal of the court which gave it, or (b) is certified by any person in his capacity as a judge or officer of that court to be a true copy of a judgment given by that court: C.J.J.A. 1982, s. 11. **62.28.5**

"SERVED WITH THE DOCUMENT INITIATING THE PROCEEDINGS".

Art. 27(2) of Sched. 1 of the C.J.J.A. 1982 and Art. 34(2) of the Council Regulation provide that where judgment is given in default of appearance, the judgment shall not be recognised if the defender was not duly served with the document which instituted the proceedings or in sufficient time to enable him to arrange for his defence. In *Selco Ltd v. Mercier* 1996 S.L.T. 1247 (where registration was recalled because the writ had not been served at the defender's domicile as required by the Belgian Civil Code), Lord Coulsfield opined that if there had been proper service, one month between service and the date of judgment would not have been unreasonable. **62.28.6**

LEGAL AID.

Where a petitioner has benefited from complete or partial legal aid or exemption from costs or expenses in the state of origin, he is entitled to the most favourable legal aid or the most extensive exemption from costs and expenses provided for under Scots law: C.J.J.A. 1982, Sched. 1, Art. 44. **62.28.7**

AFFIDAVIT.

The affidavit should be in the form of a statement of evidence written in the first person by the deponent. It should contain the evidence of the deponent in support of the averments in the petition. In particular the affidavit should deal with the matters listed in r. 62.28(2)(e). **62.28.8**

An affidavit should be sworn and signed by the deponent before any person who may competently take an oath, whether in Scotland or in any other country. In Scotland such a person may include a notary public, justice of the peace, sheriff or any judge. The person taking the oath should also sign the affidavit. Where the affidavit is not in English a duly certified translation should also be lodged.

See also the definition of affidavit in r. 1.3(1).

INTEREST ON THE JUDGMENT.

Where the judgment provides for the payment of money and the law of the country where it was given provides for interest to be paid on the judgment from a specified date, the rate of interest and the date from which it is due shall be registered with the judgment. Once registered any interest will be in accordance with the registered particulars: C.J.J.A. 1982, s. 7. **62.28.9**

Protective measures and interim interdict

62.29

62.29.—[1,2](1) On lodging a petition, the petitioner may, at any time until the expiry of the period for lodging an appeal referred to in rule 62.34 or 62.34A or its disposal, apply by motion for a warrant for the execution of protective measures.

(2) On lodging such a petition, the petitioner may, at any time until the expiry of the period for lodging an appeal mentioned in rule 62.34 or 62.34A or its disposal, apply by motion for an interim interdict.

"PROTECTIVE MEASURES".

62.29.1

These are nowhere defined in the 1968 Brussels Convention or the 1988 Lugano Convention or the Council Regulation but are taken to refer to steps taken by the petitioning creditor to prevent the debtor from disposing of assets against which he may wish to enforce the judgment and which are available under the law of the country in which the protective measure is sought. Section 27 of the C.J.J.A. 1982 provides for the protective measures (arrestment, inhibition and interim interdict) which may be applied for to protect a foreign judgment, instrument or settlement in the absence of substantive proceedings in Scotland.

A litigant may apply to the court for protective measures (1) during the dependence of any action in another contracting state to which the relevant convention applies (C.J.J.A. 1982, s. 27 (on which see *Stancroft Securities Ltd v. McDowall* 1990 S.C. 274) and Sched. 1, Art. 24; or (2) after a judgment has been given in such an action and the litigant has applied under Art. 31 of the relevant convention for enforcement of the judgment (r. 62.29). Art. 31 of the Lugano Convention or the Council Regulation allow for application for protective measures.

The power of the court to grant warrant for arrestment, inhibition or interim interdict under r. 27 of the C.J.J.A. 1982 is extended by the Civil Jurisdiction and Judgments Act 1982 (Provisional and Protective Measures) (Scotland) Order 1997 [S.I. 1997 No.2780] to proceeding commenced otherwise than in a Brussels or Lugano Contrasting State or to proceeding whose subject-matter is not within the scope of the 1968 Brussels Convention.

Where a petitioner has obtained an interlocutor granting warrant for the registration of the judgment, he will be entitled to proceed to execute protective measures as of right: C.J.J.A. 1982, Scheds 1 and 3C, Art. 39; r. 62.30(1)(b); *Capelloni and Aquilini v. Pelkmans* [1985] E.C.R. 3147, 3160.

In particular, protective measures will include arrestment on the dependence, inhibition on the dependence, interim interdict, arrestment of a ship on the dependence (*Clipper Shipping Co. Ltd v. San Vincente Partners* 1989 S.L.T. 204) and possibly arrestment in rem or arrestment of cargo on board ship: see C.J.J.A. 1982, s. 27 and notes 13.6.2 et seq. For an English example, see *Republic of Haiti v. Duvalier* [1990] 1 Q.B. 202.

INTERIM INTERDICT.

62.29.2

Until the court grants warrant for, inter alia, the registration of a prohibitory judgment, the usual rules for obtaining interim interdict apply: see note 60.3.2. Once the court has granted a warrant for the registration of such a judgment (see r. 62.30), standing the decision in *Capelloni and Aquilini v. Pelkmans* [1985] E.C.R. 3147, it is suggested that the petitioner may proceed directly to execute the interdict by serving the interlocutor on the person affected.

"MOTION".

62.29.3

For motions, see Chap. 23.

Warrant for registration under the Act of 1982, the Council Regulation, the 2005 Hague Convention or the Lugano Convention[3]

62.30

62.30.—[4,5,6,7,8](1) The court shall, on being satisfied that the petition complies with the requirements of the Act of 1982, the Council Regulation, the 2005 Hague Convention or the Lugano Convention, pronounce an interlocutor—

(a) granting warrant for the registration of the judgment;

---

[1] Rule 62.29 substituted by S.S.I. 2004 No. 52 (effective 1st March 2004).
[2] Rule 62.29 as amended by S.S.I. 2020 No. 440 r. 2(5) (effective IP completion day, 31st December 2020).
[3] Heading and r. 62.30 amended by S.S.I. 2009 No. 450 (effective 1st January 2010).
[4] Rule 62.30 substituted by S.S.I. 2004 No. 52 (effective 1st March 2004).
[5] Heading and Rule 62.30 amended by S.S.I. 2009 No. 450 (effective 1st January 2010).
[6] As amended by S.S.I. 2015 No. 26 para. 2 (effective 7th February 2015).
[7] As amended by S.S.I. 2019 No. 85 r. 2 (effective 28th March 2019).
[8] Rule 62.30 as amended by S.S.I. 2020 No. 440 r. 2(6) (effective IP completion day, 31st December 2020).

(b) granting warrant for the execution of protective measures; and

(c) where necessary, granting decree in accordance with Scots law.

(2) The interlocutor pronounced under paragraph (1) shall specify—

(a) the period within which an appeal mentioned in rule 62.34 or 62.34A against the interlocutor may be made; and

(b) that the petitioner—

(i) may register the judgment under rule 62.32; and

(ii) may not proceed to execution until the expiry of the period for lodging such an appeal or its disposal.

Deriv. R.C.S. 1965, r. 249G(1) and (2) inserted by S.I. 1986 No. 1941

DETERMINATION OF THE PETITION.

The petition must be determined ex parte without delay (1968 Brussels Convention C.J.J.A. 1982, Sched. 1, Art. 34. Usually this will be done in chambers. **62.30.1**

"COMPLIES WITH THE REQUIREMENTS OF THE ACT OF 1982 OR THE COUNCIL REGULATION".

See notes 62.28.1 and 68.28.2. **62.30.2**

WARRANT FOR REGISTRATION.

The warrant will be for registration in the register of judgments of the Books of Council and Session **62.30.3** for execution. On registration the foreign judgment becomes a Scottish decree of registration and may be enforced by any Scottish diligence or sequestration or liquidation: C.J.J.A. 1982, s. 4(3) (1968 Brussels Convention). Registration for execution gives the holder a decree of registration which is in effect a decree of the Court of Session (Bell's Comm., i,4; *Taylor, Petr.* 1931 S.L.T. 260, 261 per Lord Pitman); and, on the warrant inserted by the Keeper of the Registers or his deputy on an extract of a registered document, diligence may be executed against the debtor's moveable property under s. 3 of the Writs Execution (Scotland) Act 1877 as substituted by s. 87(4) of the Debtors (Scotland) Act 1987. Diligence against heritable property may be executed by inhibition on the grant of letters of inhibition (see Chap. 59) or by action of adjudication founding on the decree of registration.

DECREE IN ACCORDANCE WITH SCOTS LAW.

This would be pronounced where the form of the foreign judgment is not suitable for a Scottish decree **62.30.4** of registration (e.g. in a foreign decree of interdict or where *ad factum praestandum*).

EXPENSES OF PETITION AND REGISTRATION PROCEDURE.

The reasonable costs or expenses of the registration (and presumably petition) procedure are recover- **62.30.5** able as if they were contained in the judgment being enforced: C.J.J.A. 1982, s. 4(2) (1968 Brussels Convention). The interlocutor granting the warrant or decree accordingly should provide for the award- ing of expenses in relation to the petition procedure.

PERIOD FOR MARKING APPEAL.

Where the appeal is by the judgment debtor it is (a) one month from the date of service under r. 62.33, **62.30.6** or (b) two months from the date of service under r. 62.33 where he is domiciled in another Contracting State to the 1968 Brussels Convention (C.J.J.A. 1982, Sched. 1 , Art. 36; and r. 62.34(1)). The appropri- ate period should be specified in the interlocutor granting the warrant or decree: r. 60.30(2)(a).

Where the appeal is by the petitioner, see note 62.34.2.

EXECUTION PENDING MARKING OR DISPOSAL OF APPEAL.

An interlocutor granting warrant for registration or decree will specify, inter alia, that the petitioner **62.30.7** may not proceed to execution until the expiry of the period for lodging such an appeal or its disposal: r. 60.30(2)(b). Execution presumably begins with the execution of diligence or the presentation of a peti- tion for sequestration or liquidation. It is unclear whether service of a charge for payment is a step in execution, rather than a preliminary step. In relation to interdict and obligations *ad factum praestandum* execution begins presumably with the service of the interlocutor: on interim interdict, see note 60.3.2.

In any event during the appeal period the petitioner is automatically entitled to execute protective measures (but no other enforcement) if he has not already done so: C.J.J.A. 1982, Scheds. 1 and 3C, Art. 39 (1968 Brussels and Lugano Conventions); and see note 62.29.1.

Intimation to petitioner

62.31.—[1] Where the court pronounces an interlocutor under rule 62.30(1) grant- **62.31** ing warrant for registration, the Deputy Principal Clerk shall intimate such interlocu-

---

[1] Rule 62.31 substituted by S.S.I. 2004 No. 52 (effective 1 March 2004).

tor to the petitioner by sending to his address for service in Scotland a certified copy of the interlocutor by registered post or the first class recorded delivery service.

Deriv. R.C.S. 1965, r. 249H inserted by S.I. 1986 No. 1941

General note.

62.31.1   The substituted r. 62.31 is in the same terms as its predecessor.

Registration under the Act of 1982, the Council Regulation, the 2005 Hague Convention or the Lugano Convention

62.32   **62.32.**—[1, 2, 3, 4](1)   Where the court pronounces an interlocutor under rule 62.30(1) granting warrant for registration, the Deputy Principal Clerk shall enter the judgment in a register of judgments, authentic instruments and court settlements under the Act of 1982, the Council Regulation, the 2005 Hague Convention and the Lugano Convention kept in the Petition Department.

(2)   On presentation by the petitioner to the Keeper of the Registers of—

(a)   a certified copy of the interlocutor under rule 62.30(1) granting warrant for registration;

(b)   an authentic copy of the judgment and any translation of it; and

(c)   any certificate of currency conversion under rule 62.2(1)(b),

they shall be registered in the register of judgments of the Books of Council and Session.

(3)   On registration under paragraph (2), the Keeper of the Registers shall issue an extract of the registered judgment with a warrant for execution.

Deriv. R.C.S. 1965, r. 249K inserted by S.I. 1986 No. 1941

"Keeper of the Registers".

62.32.1   This is the Keeper of the Registers of Scotland: r. 1.3(1). The Register of Judgments is at Meadowbank House, 153 London Road, Edinburgh EH8 7AU; tel. 0131-659 6111; fax 0131-459 1221; DX ED300.

"certified copy of the interlocutor".

62.32.2   A copy of the interlocutor is typed by the agent and presented to the clerk of session in the Petition Department. The clerk checks it, certifies it as a true copy and stamps it with the court stamp.

A fee is payable.

"authentic copy of the judgment".

62.32.3   See note 62.28.5.

"translation".

62.32.4   See r. 62.3.

"certificate of currency conversion".

62.32.5   The certificate should be obtained from the clerk of session in the Petition Department and should be signed by him: r. 62.2(3) and see note 62.2.5.

Registration fee.

62.32.6   A fee will be payable to the Keeper of the Registers for registration and any extract: see the Fees in the Registers of Scotland Order 1991 [S.I. 1991 No. 2093].

---

[1] Heading and r. 62.32 amended by S.S.I. 2009 No. 450 (effective 1st January 2010).
[2] As amended by S.S.I. 2015 No. 26 para.2 (effective 7th February 2015).
[3] As amended by S.S.I. 2019 No. 85 r. 2 (effective 28th March 2019).
[4] Rule 62.32 as amended by S.S.I. 2020 No. 440 r. 2(7) (effective IP completion day, 31st December 2020).

Service of warrant for registration under the Act of 1982, the Council Regulation, the 2005 Hague Convention or the Lugano Convention

62.33.—[1, 2, 3, 4, 5] The petitioner shall serve a copy of the interlocutor granting warrant for registration of a judgment and a notice in Form 62.33 on the person liable under the judgment.

62.33

Deriv. R.C.S. 1965, r. 249J(1) inserted by S.I. 1996 No. 1941.

GENERAL NOTE.

The substituted r. 62.33 is in the same terms as its predecessor.

62.33.1

"SERVE".

For methods of service, see Chap. 16, Pt. I.

62.33.2

Appeals under the Act of 1982, the Council Regulation or the Lugano Convention

62.34.—[6, 7, 8, 9, 10](1) An appeal under Article 37 of the convention in Schedule 1 to the Act of 1982 (appeal against granting of warrant for registration), an appeal under Article 43 (appeals by either party) of the Council Regulation or an appeal under Article 43 (appeals by either party) of the Lugano Convention against the granting of a warrant for registration shall be made by motion—

62.34

    (a)   to the Lord Ordinary; and

    (b)   within one month of service under rule 62.33 (service of warrant for registration under the Act of 1982, the Council Regulation or the Lugano Convention) or within two months of such service where service was executed on a person domiciled in another Contracting State or, as the case may be, Member State or State bound by the Lugano Convention.

(2) An appeal under Article 40 of the convention in Schedule 1 to the Act of 1982 (appeal against refusal to grant warrant for registration), an appeal under Article 43 (appeals by either party) of the Council Regulation or an appeal under Article 43 (appeals by either party) of the Lugano Convention against a refusal to grant warrant for registration shall be made by motion—

    (a)   to the Lord Ordinary; and

    (b)   within one month of the interlocutor pronounced under rule 62.30(1) (warrant for registration under the Act of 1982, the Council Regulation or the Lugano Convention).

(3) Where the respondent in any such appeal is domiciled furth of the United Kingdom—

    (a)   in relation to an appeal under paragraph (1), intimation of the motion shall be made to the address for service of the respondent in Scotland; and

    (b)   in relation to an appeal under paragraph (2), intimation of the motion shall be made in accordance with rule 16.2 (service furth of United Kingdom) or rule 16.5 (service where address of person is not known, as the case may be).

---

[1] Rule 62.33 substituted by S.S.I. 2004 No. 52 (effective 1st March 2004).
[2] As amended by S.S.I. 2015 No. 26 para. 2 (effective 7th February 2015).
[3] As amended by S.S.I. 2019 No. 85 r. 2 (effective 28th March 2019).
[4] Heading amended by S.S.I. 2009 No. 450 (effective 1st January 2010).
[5] Rule 62.33 as amended by S.S.I. 2020 No. 440 r. 2(8) (effective IP completion day, 31st December 2020).
[6] Rule 62.34 substituted by S.S.I. 2004 No. 52 (effective 1st March 2004).
[7] Heading and r. 62.34 substituted by S.S.I. 2009 No. 450 (effective 1st January 2010).
[8] As amended by S.S.I. 2015 No. 26 para. 2 (effective 7th February 2015).
[9] As amended by S.S.I. 2019 No. 85 r. 2 (effective 28th March 2019).
[10] Heading and r. 62.34 substituted by S.S.I. 2009 No. 450 (effective 1st January 2010).

(4) Where an appeal under paragraph (1) is successful, the court shall, on the motion of the appellant, pronounce an interlocutor recalling any protective measure or interim interdict.

GENERAL NOTE.

62.34.1

Under Art. 37 or 40 of the 1968 Brussels or 1988 Lugano Convention, there is a two-stage appeal process. The first stage is (with the exception of maintenance judgments) in the Outer House. The second stage is a right of appeal to the Inner House: C.J.J.A. 1982, s. 6(1)(b) and Sched. 1, Art. 37(2) in relation to the 1968 Brussels and Lugano Conventions. Rules 62.34 and 62.35 provide the procedural framework. Art. 37 of the 1968 Brussels Convention in Sched. 1 of the C.J.J.A. 1982, limiting appeals against decisions authorising endorsement of foreign judgments, has to be construed strictly and a court seized of an appeal does not have power to impose or re-impose a sist: *Société D'Informatique Service Réalisation Organisation (SISRO) v. Ampersand Software BV* , [1996] Q.B. 127 (ECJ). Art. 44 of the Council Regulation would no doubt be similarly interpreted.

Under R.C.S. 1965, r. 249K appeals had to be in the appeal form in Form 42 because the application for registration was not a petition and there were no formal requirements for a process (although in practice one was lodged). Now that applications for registration are made by petition, the appeal to the Lord Ordinary can readily be made by motion in the petition process.

TIME-LIMITS.

62.34.2

Where the prospective appellant is the judgment debtor the time-limits are imposed under Art. 36 of the 1968 Brussels and Lugano Conventions and art. 43(5) of the Council Regulation: see note 62.30.6. No extension of time may be granted on account of distance: C.J.J.A. 1982, Scheds 1 and 3C, Art. 36 (Brussels and Lugano Conventions). Accordingly there is no scope for the use of the dispensing power in r. 2.1 to relieve a party from a failure to comply with a time-limit.

Where the prospective appellant is the petitioning creditor, the time-limit is one month from the date of the interlocutor refusing warrant or decree: r. 62.34(2)(a); this is not imposed under either convention or the Council Regulation.

Art. 37(2) of the 1968 Brussels and Lugano Conventions which provides for the second appeal on a point of law (to the Inner House), is restrictively interpreted and the words "judgment given on the appeal" cannot be extended to enable an appeal to be lodged against a judgment other than that given on the first appeal: *Brennero v. Wendel* [1984] E.C.R. 3971; *Van Dalfsen v. Van Loon and Berendsen* [1991] E.C.R. I-4743. A decision to sist enforcement under Art. 38, by the court on the first appeal under Art. 37(1), may not be contested on the second appeal under Art. 37(2) as it does not constitute a judgment given on the appeal under Art. 37(1); and this is so whether or not the sist is granted in the same interlocutor as the judgment on the appeal under Art. 37(1).

In deciding whether to grant a sist of enforcement proceedings under Art. 38 of the Brussels and Lugano Conventions, the court may take into account only such submissions as the appellant was unable to make before the court of the state in which the original judgment was given: *Van Dalfsen*, above.

"MOTION".

62.34.3

For motions, see Chap. 23. Note the special rules on intimation in r. 62.34(3).

"DOMICILED".

62.34.4

This is determined under ss. 41–45 of the C.J.J.A. 1982 in relation to the 1968 Brussels and Lugano Conventions, and in paras. 9–12 of Sched. 1 to the Civil Jurisdiction and Judgments Order 2001 in relation to the Council Regulation. See also note 13.2.6.

THE APPEAL.

62.34.5

In *Artic Fish Sales Co. Ltd v. Adam (No. 1)* 1996 S.L.T. 968, 969L Lord Cameron of Lochbroom considered, without deciding the point, that, if there was a fundamental flaw in the documentation produced under r. 62.28(2), the court could recall the original interlocutor or require the proper document to be produced (or otherwise) as provided in r. 62.28(3).

In *Artic Fish Sales*, above, Lord Cameron of Lochbroom held that where the appellant wished to place evidence before the court which contradicted the petitioner's case, the court could not proceed on *ex parte* statements but would require evidence (whether by affidavit or otherwise). In that case, the appellant was disputing having had notice of the foreign proceedings in respect of which enforcement of a decree was being sought.

In an appeal under Art. 37 of the 1968 Brussels Convention, the court is not limited to the grounds of challenge in Arts 27 and 28, and an appeal may be on the ground that the proper formalities were not observed in presenting the appeal: *Artic Fish Sales Co. Ltd (No. 1)*, above.

Appeals under section 6B(1) of the Act of 1982 (appeals in relation to registration of judgments under the 2005 Hague Convention)

62.34A.—[1](1) An appeal under section 6B(1) of the Act of 1982 (appeals in relation to registration of judgments under the 2005 Hague Convention) is to be made by motion—

    (a) to the Lord Ordinary; and

    (b) within one month of service under rule 62.33 (service of warrant for registration under the Act of 1982, the Council Regulation, the 2005 Hague Convention or the Lugano Convention) or within two months of such service where service was executed on a person domiciled in another Contracting State or, as the case may be, State bound by the 2005 Hague Convention or the Lugano Convention.

(2) Where the respondent in any such appeal is domiciled furth of the United Kingdom—

    (a) where that respondent has an address for service in Scotland, intimation of the motion must be made to that address for service; and

    (b) in any other case, intimation of the motion must be made in accordance with rule 16.2 (service furth of United Kingdom) or, as the case may be, rule 16.5 (service where address of person is not known).

(3) Where an appeal under paragraph (1) is successful, the court must, on the motion of the appellant, pronounce an interlocutor recalling any protective measure or interim interdict.

Deriv. R.C.S. 1965, r. 249K inserted by S.I. 1986 No. 1941.

62.34A

Reclaiming under the Act of 1982, the Council Regulation, the 2005 Hague Convention or the Lugano Convention

62.35.—[2, 3, 4, 5, 6](1) Any party dissatisfied with the interlocutor of the Lord Ordinary in any appeal mentioned in rule 62.34 (appeals under the Act of 1982, the Council Regulation or the Lugano Convention) or rule 62.34A (appeals under section 6B(1) of the Act of 1982) may reclaim on a point of law against that interlocutor.

(2) Where a reclaiming motion under paragraph (1) against the registration of a judgment is successful, the court shall, on the motion of the appellant, pronounce an interlocutor recalling any protective measure or interim interdict.

Deriv. R.C.S. 1965, r. 249 inserted by S.I. 1986 No. 1941

RECLAIMING.

See, in general, Chap. 38. The interlocutor pronounced by the Lord Ordinary under r. 62.34 disposes of the subject-matter of the cause and may be reclaimed against, without leave, within 21 days after its date: r. 38.3(2). This is now judicially confirmed by *Selco Ltd v. Mercier (No. 2)*, 1997 S.L.T. 687.

"POINT OF LAW".

These words are used in Arts 37 and 41 of the 1968 Brussels or 1988 Lugano Convention. Accordingly it is appropriate to have regard to the tools of interpretation listed in s. 3 of the C.J.J.A. 1982 if any doubt arises whether a matter is a "point of law".

62.35

62.35.1

62.35.2

---

[1] Rule 62.34A inserted by S.S.I. 2020 No. 440 r. 2(9) (effective IP completion day, 31st December 2020).

[2] Rule 62.35 substituted by S.S.I. 2004 No. 52 (effective 1st March 2004).

[3] As amended by S.S.I. 2015 No. 26 para. 2 (effective 7th February 2015).

[4] As amended by S.S.I. 2019 No. 85 r. 2 (effective 28th March 2019).

[5] Heading and r. 62.35 substituted by S.S.I. 2009 No. 450 (effective 1st January 2010).

[6] Rule 62.35 as amended by S.S.I. 2020 No. 440 r. 2(10) (effective IP completion day, 31st December 2020).

Recognition of judgments from another Contracting State, Member State or State bound by the Lugano Convention

62.36

62.36.—[1, 2, 3, 4, 5, 6](1) For the purposes of Article 26 of the convention in Schedule 1 to the Act of 1982, Article 33 of the Council Regulation (recognition of judgment), section 4B of the Act of 1982 (registration and enforcement of judgments under the 2005 Hague Convention) or Article 33 of the Lugano Convention (recognition of judgment), an interlocutor pronounced under rule 62.30(1) (warrant for registration under the Act of 1982, the Council Regulation, the 2005 Hague Convention or the Lugano Convention) shall imply recognition of the judgment so dealt with.

(2) In an application under Article 26(2) of the convention in Schedule 1 to the Act of 1982 (application for recognition of a judgment) or Article 33(2) of the Lugano Convention (application for recognition of a judgment), Article 33(2) of the Council Regulation (application for recognition of a judgment), rules 62.26 to 62.35 shall apply to such an application as they apply to an application under Article 31 of the convention in Schedule 1 to the Act of 1982, subject to the following provisions—

(a) it shall not be necessary to produce any documents required by rule 62.28(2)(b) and (d); and

(b) rule 62.32 shall not apply.

Deriv. R.C.S. 1965 r. 249M inserted by S.I. 1986 No. 1941

JURISDICTION.

62.36.1

The court has jurisdiction where the petitioner has raised the recognition of the judgment sought to be recognised as the principal issue in a dispute: C.J.J.A. 1982, Scheds 1 and 3C, Art. 26 (in relation to the 1968 Brussels and Lugano Conventions). Where proceedings before the court depend on the determination of an incidental question of recognition the court has jurisdiction: C.J.J.A. 1982, Sched. 1 and 3C, Art. 26.

Enforcement of judgments from another part of the United Kingdom in Scotland (money provisions)

62.37

62.37.—[7](1) An application under paragraph 5 of Schedule 6 to the Act of 1982 (application for registration in the Court of Session of a certificate in relation to a money provision in a judgment from another part of the United Kingdom) shall be made by presenting to the Keeper of the Registers—

(a) a certificate under paragraph 4(1) of Schedule 6 to the Act of 1982; and

(b) any certificate of currency conversion under rule 62.2(1)(b).

(2) On presentation of the certificate mentioned in paragraph (1)(a), the Keeper of the Registers shall—

(a) register the certificate in the register of judgments of the Books of Council and Session; and

(b) issue an extract of the certificate with a warrant for execution.

(3) An application under—

(a) paragraph 9 of Schedule 6 to the Act of 1982 (application to sist proceedings for enforcement of a certificate registered under paragraph (2) of this rule); or

---

[1] Rule 62.36 substituted by S.S.I. 2004 No. 52 (effective 1st March 2004).

[2] Heading and Rule 62.36 substituted by S.S.I. 2009 No. 450 (effective 1st January 2010).

[3] As amended by S.S.I. 2015 No. 26 para. 2 (effective 7th February 2015).

[4] As amended by S.S.I. 2019 No. 85 r. 2 (effective 28th March 2019).

[5] Heading and r. 62.36 substituted by S.S.I. 2009 No. 450 (effective 1st January 2010).

[6] Rule 62.36 as amended by S.S.I. 2020 No. 440 r. 2(11) (effective IP completion day, 31st December 2020).

[7] Rule 62.37 substituted by S.S.I. 2004 No. 52 (effective 1st March 2004).

(b)   paragraph 10 of Schedule 6 to the Act of 1982 (application for reduction of registration),

shall be made by petition.

Deriv. R.C.S. 1965, r. 249P(2), (3) and (4) inserted by S.I. 1986 No. 1941.

General note.

The substituted r. 62.37 is in the same terms as its predecessor (as amended by S.I. 1996 No. 2168).   **62.37.1**

Jurisdiction.

The Keeper of the Registers of Scotland, as "the proper officer" of the court under para. 5 of Sched. 6   **62.37.2**
to the C.J.J.A. 1982, has jurisdiction to register a certificate under that paragraph where (a) it is presented within six months of the date of its issue, and (b) it is in respect of a "judgment": see note 62.26.3; and C.J.J.A. 1982, s. 18(2).

A person who has obtained an English judgment cannot be interdicted from enforcing it under Sched. 6, para. 5 of the C.J.J.A. 1982 on the ground that the judgment was defective in its merits: *Clarke v. Fennoscandia Ltd* 1998 S.C. 464.

"Keeper of the Registers".

This is the Keeper of the Registers of Scotland: r. 1.3(1). The Register of Judgments is at Meadowbank   **62.37.3**
House, 153 London Road, Edinburgh EH8 7AU; tel. 0131-659 6111; fax 0131-459 1221; DX ED300.

Certificate of money provision in judgment to be registered.

The applicant should obtain this from the "proper officer" of the English, Welsh, or Northern Irish   **62.37.4**
court where the judgment was given or entered or in whose books it was registered: C.J.J.A. 1982, Sched. 6, para. 2. In this context "judgment" has a limited meaning: see note 62.26.3; and C.J.J.A. 1982, s. 18(2).

"certificate of currency conversion".

This should, if necessary, be obtained from the clerk of session in the Petition Department duly signed   **62.37.5**
by him: r. 62.2(3) and see notes 62.2.4 and 62.2.5.

Registration fee.

A fee will be payable to the Keeper of the Registers for registration and any extract: see the Fees in the   **62.37.6**
Registers of Scotland Order 1991 [S.I. 1991 No. 2093].

Costs and expenses of registration procedure.

The reasonable costs or expenses of and incidental to the obtaining of the certificate of the money   **62.37.7**
provision in a judgment and its registration shall be recoverable as if they were costs and expenses contained in the original judgment: C.J.J.A. 1982, Sched. 6, para. 7.

Interest.

See C.J.J.A. 1982, Sched. 6, para. 8.   **62.37.8**

Enforcement of judgments from another part of the United Kingdom in Scotland (non-money provisions)

62.38.—[1](1)   An application under paragraph 5 of Schedule 7 to the Act of 1982   **62.38**
(application for registration in the Court of Session of a non-money provision in a judgment from another part of the United Kingdom) shall be made by petition in Form 62.38.

(2)   There shall be produced with the petition under paragraph (1)—

(a)   a certified copy of the judgment of the original court; and

(b)   a certificate under paragraph 4(1)(b) of Schedule 7 to the Act of 1982.

(3)   The petition under paragraph (1) shall be heard by the Lord Ordinary in chambers and shall not require any appearance for the applicant unless the court so requires.

(4)   The court shall, on being satisfied that the petition complies with the requirements of section 18 of, and Schedule 7 to, the Act of 1982, pronounce an interlocutor—

(a)   granting warrant for the registration of the judgment; and

---

[1] Rule 62.38 substituted by S.S.I. 2004 No. 52 (effective 1st March 2004).

(b)   where necessary, granting decree in accordance with Scots law.

(5)   Where the court pronounces an interlocutor under paragraph (4), rule 62.32 shall apply to the registration of a judgment under this rule as it applies to the registration of a judgment under that rule.

(6)   An application under—

(a)   paragraph 8 of Schedule 7 to the Act of 1982 (application to sist proceedings for enforcement of a judgment registered under paragraph (5) of this rule); or

(b)   paragraph 9 of Schedule 7 to the Act of 1982 (application to reduce the registration under paragraph (5) of this rule),

shall be made by petition.

Deriv. R.C.S. 1965, r. 249Q(4) to (9) inserted by S.I. 1986 No. 1941.

GENERAL NOTE.

62.38.1   The substituted r. 62.38 is in the same terms as its predecessor.

A decree of registration is not generally a suitable method to enforce a judgment which is not for the payment of money. Accordingly r. 62.38 requires an application to the court by petition.

PETITION UNDER C.J.J.A. 1982, SCHED. 7, PARA. 5.

62.38.2   A petition is presented in the Outer House: r. 14.2(h). The petition must be in Form 62.38 but does not have to be in the official printed form (see r. 62.27). The petition may be signed by the petitioner, counsel or other person having a right of audience, or an agent: r. 4.2; and see r. 1.3(1) (definition of "counsel", "other person having a right of audience", and "agent") and note 1.3.4.

The petitioner must lodge the petition with the required steps of process (r. 4.4) and any documents founded on or adopted (r. 27.1(1)). A fee is payable on lodging the petition: see note 14.5.10.

On petitions generally, see Chap. 14.

PRODUCTIONS.

62.38.3   The petitioner must produce with the petition (1) a certified copy of the judgment obtained from the "proper officer" of the original court (C.J.J.A. 1982, Sched. 7, para. 5(3)(a); and r. 62.38(a)); and (2) a certificate under para. 4(1)(b) of Sched. 7 to the C.J.J.A. 1982.

"CERTIFICATE UNDER PARAGRAPH 4(1)(H)".

62.38.4   This certifies that the period for making an appeal against the judgment has expired with no appeal having been made or that any appeal has been finally disposed of: C.J.J.A. 1982, Sched. 7, para. 3.

WARRANT FOR REGISTRATION.

62.38.5   The warrant will be for registration in the register of judgments of the Books of Council and Session for execution. On registration the foreign judgment becomes a Scottish decree of registration and may be enforced by any Scottish diligence or sequestration or liquidation: C.J.J.A. 1982, s. 4(3). Registration for execution gives the holder a decree of registration which is in effect a decree of the Court of Session (Bell's Comm., i,4; *Taylor, Petr.* 1931 S.L.T. 260, 261 per Lord Pitman); and, on the warrant inserted by the Keeper of the Registers or his deputy on an extract of a registered document, diligence may be executed against the debtor's moveable property under s. 3 of the Writs Execution (Scotland) Act 1877 as substituted by s. 87(4) of the Debtors (Scotland) Act 1987. Diligence against heritable property may be executed by inhibition on the grant of letters of inhibition (see Chap. 59) or by action of adjudication founding on the decree of registration.

DECREE IN ACCORDANCE WITH SCOTS LAW.

62.38.6   This would be pronounced where the form of the foreign judgment is not suitable for a Scottish decree of registration (e.g. in a foreign decree of interdict or where *ad factum praestandum*).

COSTS AND EXPENSES OF REGISTRATION PROCEDURE.

62.38.7   The reasonable costs or expenses of and incidental to the obtaining of the certified copy judgment, the certificate under para. 4(1)(b) of Sched. 7 to the C.J.J.A. 1982 and the petition and any registration procedure are recoverable as if they were costs and expenses incidental to registration of a money provision in a judgment: C.J.J.A. 1982, Sched. 7, para. 7(1).

Any costs and expenses recovered shall bear interest from the "date of registration" of the judgment as in accordance with Scots law: C.J.J.A. 1982, Sched. 7, para. 7(2).

Petition under C.J.J.A. 1982, Sched. 7, para. 8 or 9.

A petition is presented in the Outer House: r. 14.2(h). The petition need not be in the official printed form: r. 62.27. The petition may be signed by the petitioner, counsel or other person having a right of audience, or an agent: r. 4.2; and see r. 1.3(1) (definition of "counsel", "other person having a right of audience" and "agent") and note 1.3.4.

62.38.8

The petitioner must lodge the petition with the required steps of process (r. 4.4) and any documents founded on or adopted (r. 27.1(1)). A fee is payable on lodging the petition: see note 14.5.10.

On petitions generally, see Chap. 14.

Cancellation of registration under the Act of 1982, the Council Regulation, the 2005 Hague Convention or the Lugano Convention

62.39.—[1, 2, 3, 4, 5, 6] Where—

62.39

(a) an interlocutor under rule 62.30(1) (warrant for registration under the Act of 1982, the Council Regulation, the 2005 Hague Convention or the Lugano Convention) is recalled and registration under rule 62.32 (registration under the Act of 1982, the Council Regulation, the 2005 Hague Convention or the Lugano Convention) is ordered to be cancelled after an appeal under Article 37 of the convention in Schedule 1 to the Act of 1982, an appeal under Article 43 of the Council Regulation, an appeal under section 6B of the Act of 1982 (appeals in relation to registration of judgments under the 2005 Hague Convention) or an appeal under Article 43 of the Lugano Convention; or

(b) registration under rule 62.37(2) (registration of judgments from another part of the United Kingdom in Scotland (money provisions)) or rule 62.38(5) (registration of judgments from another part of the United Kingdom in Scotland (non-money provisions)) is reduced,

a certificate to that effect by the Deputy Principal Clerk shall be sufficient warrant to the Keeper of the Registers to cancel the registration and return the judgment, certificate or other documents to the person who applied for registration.

Deriv. R.C.S. 1965, r. 249R inserted by S.I. 1986 No. 1941.

Enforcement in another Contracting State or Member State of Court of Session judgments etc.

62.40.—[7, 8, 9, 10, 11, 12](1) Subject to paragraph (2ZA), where a person seeks to apply under section 12 of the Act of 1982 for recognition or enforcement in another Contracting State of a judgment given by the court or a court settlement in the court, he shall apply by letter to the Deputy Principal Clerk for—

62.40

(a) a certificate in Form 62.40-A;

(b) a certified copy of the judgment; and

---

[1] Rule 62.39 substituted by S.S.I. 2004 No. 52 (effective 1st March 2004).

[2] Heading and r. 62.39 substituted by S.S.I. 2009 No. 450 (effective 1st January 2010).

[3] As amended by S.S.I. 2015 No. 26 para. 2 (effective 7th February 2015).

[4] As amended by S.S.I. 2019 No. 85 r. 2 (effective 28th March 2019).

[5] Heading and r. 62.39 substituted by S.S.I. 2009 No. 450 (effective 1st January 2010).

[6] Rule 62.39 as amended by S.S.I. 2020 No. 440 r. 2(12) (effective IP completion day, 31st December 2020).

[7] Rule 62.40 substituted by S.S.I. 2004 No. 52 (effective 1st March 2004).

[8] Heading substituted and r. 62.40(2A) and (5A) inserted by S.S.I. 2009 No. 450 (effective 1st January 2010).

[9] As amended by S.S.I. 2015 No. 26 para. 2 (effective 7th February 2015).

[10] As amended by S.S.I. 2019 No. 85 r. 2 (effective 28th March 2019).

[11] Heading substituted and r. 62.40(2A) and (5A) inserted by S.S.I. 2009 No. 450 (effective 1st January 2010).

[12] Rule 62.40 as amended by S.S.I. 2020 No. 440 r. 2(13)(a) (effective IP completion day, 31st December 2020).

(c)   if required, a certified copy of the opinion of the court.

(2)   Where a person seeks to apply under Chapter III of the Council Regulation for recognition or enforcement in another Member State of a judgment given by the court, the person must apply by letter to the Deputy Principal Clerk for—

    (a)   a certificate under Article 54 of the Council Regulation;

    (b)   a certified copy of the judgment; and

    (c)   if required, a certified copy of the opinion of the court.

(2ZA)[1]   Where a person seeks to apply under Chapter III of the 2005 Hague Convention for recognition or enforcement in another Contracting State of a judgment given by the court, that person must apply by letter to the Deputy Principal Clerk for—

    (a)   a certificate under Article 13(3) of the 2005 Hague Convention;

    (b)   a certified copy of the judgment; and

    (c)   if required, a certified copy of the opinion of the court.

(2A)[2]   Where a person seeks to apply under Title III of the Lugano Convention for recognition or enforcement in another State bound by the Lugano Convention of a judgment given by the court, he shall apply by letter to the Deputy Principal Clerk for—

    (a)   a certificate under Article 54 of the Lugano Convention;

    (b)   a certified copy of the judgment; and

    (c)   if required, a certified copy of the opinion of the court.

(3)[3]   The Deputy Principal Clerk shall not issue a certificate under paragraph (1)(a), (2)(a), (2ZA)(a) or (2A)(a) unless there is produced to him an execution of service of the judgment on the person on whom it is sought to be enforced.

(4)   Where a person seeks to apply under Article 50 of the convention in Schedule 1 to the Act of 1982 for enforcement of an authentic instru-ment or court settlement registered for execution in the Books of Council and Session, he shall apply by letter to the Keeper of the Registers for—

    (a)   a certificate in Form 62.40-B or; and

    (b)   an extract of the authentic instrument or court settlement.

(5)   Where a person seeks to apply under Article 57 or 58 of the Council Regulation for enforcement in another Member State of an authentic instrument or court settlement registered for execution in the Books of Council and Session, the person must apply by letter to the Keeper of the Registers for—

    (a)   a certificate under Article 57 or 58 of the Council Regulation; and

    (b)   an extract of the authentic instrument or court settlement.

(5ZA)[4]   Where a person seeks to apply under Article 12 of the 2005 Hague Convention for enforcement in another Contacting State of a court settlement registered for execution in the Books of Council and Session, that person must apply by letter to the Keeper of the Registers for—

    (a)   a certificate under Article 13(1)(e) of the 2005 Hague Convention; and

    (b)   an extract of the court settlement.

---

[1] Inserted by S.S.I. 2020 No. 440 r. 2(13)(b) (effective 31st December subject to savings specified in S.S.I. 2020 No. 440 r. 5).

[2] Heading substituted and r. 62.40(2A) and (5A) inserted by S.S.I. 2009 No. 450 (effective 1st January 2010).

[3] As amended by S.S.I. 2020 No. 440 r. 2(13)(c) (effective 31st December subject to savings specified in S.S.I. 2020 No. 440 r. 5).

[4] Inserted by S.S.I. 2020 No. 440 r. 2(13)(d) (effective 31st December subject to savings specified in S.S.I. 2020 No. 440 r. 5).

(5A)[1] Where a person seeks to apply under Article 57 or 58 of the Lugano Convention for enforcement in another State bound by the Lugano Convention of an authentic instrument or court settlement registered for execution in the Books of Council and Session, he shall apply by letter to the Keeper of the Registers for—

    (a)   a certificate under Article 57 or 58 of the Lugano Convention; and

    (b)   an extract of the authentic instrument or court settlement.

(6)[2] The Keeper of the Registers shall not issue a certificate under paragraph (4), (5), (5ZA) unless there is produced to him an affidavit verifying that enforcement has not been suspended and that the time available for enforcement has not expired.

Deriv. R.C.S. 1965, r. 249N inserted by S.I. 1986 No. 1941.

"LETTER TO THE DEPUTY PRINCIPAL CLERK".

The address and telephone number, etc., of the Deputy Principal Clerk are: The Deputy Principal Clerk of Session, Court of Session, 2 Parliament Square, Edinburgh EH1 1RQ; tel. 031-225 2595; fax 031-225 8213; DX ED306.

62.40.1

"LETTER TO THE KEEPER OF THE REGISTERS".

The address of the Keeper of the Registers is: Meadowbank House, 153 London Road, Edinburgh EH8 7AU; tel. 0131-659 6111; fax 0131-459 1221; DX ED300.

60.40.2

AFFIDAVIT.

The affidavit should be in the form of a statement of evidence written in the first person. The affidavit should contain the evidence of the deponent in support of the application. In particular the affidavit should deal with the matters mentioned in r. 62.40(4).

60.40.3

An affidavit should be sworn and signed by the deponent before any person who may competently take an oath, whether in Scotland or in any other country. In Scotland such a person may include a notary public, justice of the peace, sheriff, or any judge. The person taking the oath should also sign the affidavit. Where the affidavit is not in English a duly certified translation should also be lodged.

See also, definition of affidavit in r. 1.3(1).

Enforcement in another part of the United Kingdom of Court of Session judgments or documents registered for execution (money provisions)

62.41.—[3](1) Where a person seeks to apply under Schedule 6 to the Act of 1982 for enforcement in another part of the United Kingdom of a money provision in a judgment given by the court, he shall apply by letter to the Deputy Principal Clerk for a certificate in Form 62.41 A.

62.41

(2) The Deputy Principal Clerk shall not issue a certificate under paragraph (1) unless there is produced to him an affidavit stating—

    (a)   the sum or aggregate of sums including interest and expenses payable and unsatisfied;

    (b)   that the time for making an appeal against such judgment has expired or such appeal has been finally determined;

    (c)   that enforcement of the judgment has not been suspended and the time available for its enforcement has not expired; and

    (d)   the address of the party entitled to enforce, and the usual or last known address of the party liable to execution on, the judgment.

(3) Where a person seeks to apply under Schedule 6 to the Act of 1982 for enforcement in another part of the United Kingdom of a document registered for execution in the Books of Council and Session, he shall apply by letter to the Keeper of the Registers for—

    (a)   a certificate in Form 62.41-B; and

---

[1] Heading substituted and r. 62.40(2A) and (5A) inserted by S.S.I. 2009 No. 450 (effective 1st January 2010).

[2] As amended by S.S.I. 2020 No. 440 r. 2(13)(e) (effective 31st December subject to savings specified in S.S.I. 2020 No. 440 r. 5).

[3] Rule 62.41 substituted by S.S.I. 2004 No. 52 (effective 1st March 2004).

(b)   an extract of the document.

(4)   The Keeper of the Registers shall not issue a certificate under paragraph (3) unless there is produced to him an affidavit which includes the statements required under paragraph (2)(a), (c) and (d).

Deriv. R.C.S. 1965, r.249P(1) and (2) inserted by S.I. 1986 No. 1941.

GENERAL NOTE:

62.41.1   The substituted r. 62.41 is in the same terms as its predecessor (as amended by S.I. 1996 No. 1756).

"LETTER TO THE DEPUTY PRINCIPAL CLERK".

62.41.2   The address and telephone number, etc., of the Deputy Principal Clerk are: The Deputy Principal Clerk of Session, Court of Session, 2 Parliament Square, Edinburgh EH1 1RQ; tel. 0131-225 2595; fax 0131-225 8213; DX ED306.

AFFIDAVIT.

62.41.3   The affidavit should be in the form of a statement of evidence written in the first person. The affidavit should contain the evidence of the deponent in support of the application. In particular the affidavit should deal with the matters listed in r. 62.41(2).

An affidavit should be sworn and signed by the deponent before any person who may competently take an oath, whether in Scotland or in any other country. In Scotland such a person may include a notary public, justice of the peace, sheriff, or any judge. The person taking the oath should also sign the affidavit. Where the affidavit is not in English a duly certified translation should also be lodged.

See also, definition of affidavit in r. 1.3(1).

"LETTER TO THE KEEPER OF THE REGISTERS".

62.41.4   The address of the Keeper of the Registers is: Meadowbank House, 153 London Road, Edinburgh EH8 7AU; tel. 0131-659 6111; fax 0131-459 1221; DX ED300.

Enforcement in another part of the United Kingdom of Court of Session judgments or documents registered for execution (non-money provisions)

62.42   **62.42.**—[1](1)   Where a person seeks to apply under Schedule 7 to the Act of 1982 for enforcement in another part of the United Kingdom of a non-money provision in a judgment of the court, he shall apply by letter to the Deputy Principal Clerk for—

(a)   a certificate in Form 62.42-A; and

(b)   a certified copy of such judgment.

(2)   The Deputy Principal Clerk shall not issue a certificate under paragraph (1) unless there is produced to him an affidavit stating—

(a)   that the time for making an appeal against such judgment has expired or such appeal has been finally determined; and

(b)   the address of the party entitled to enforce, and the usual or last known address of the party liable to execution on, the judgment or registered document.

(3)   Where the Deputy Principal Clerk issues a certificate in Form 62.42-A, he shall attach it to the certified copy judgment.

(4)   Where a person seeks to apply under Schedule 7 to the Act of 1982 for enforcement in another part of the United Kingdom of a non-money provision in a document registered for execution in the Books of Council and Session, he shall apply by letter to the Keeper of the Registers for—

(a)   a certificate in Form 62.42-B; and

(b)   an extract of the document.

(5)   The Keeper of the Registers shall not issue a certificate under paragraph (4) unless there is produced to him an affidavit referred to in paragraph (2).

(6)   Where the Keeper of the Registers issues a certificate in Form 62.42-B, he shall attach it to the extract of the document.

Deriv. R.C.S. 1965, r.249O(1) to (3) inserted by S.I. 1986 No. 1941

---

[1] Rule 62.42 substituted by S.S.I. 2004 No. 52 (effective 1st March 2004).

GENERAL NOTE.

The substituted r.62.42 is in the same terms as its predecessor.

62.42.1

"LETTER TO THE DEPUTY PRINCIPAL CLERK".

The address and telephone number, etc., of the Deputy Principal Clerk are: The Deputy Principal Clerk of Session, Court of Session, 2 Parliament Square, Edinburgh EH1 1RQ; tel. 0131-225 2595; fax 0131-225 8213; DX ED306.

62.42.2

AFFIDAVIT.

The affidavit should be in the form of a statement of evidence written in the first person. The affidavit should contain the evidence of the deponent in support of the application. In particular the affidavit should deal with the matters listed in r. 62.42(2).

62.42.3

An affidavit should be sworn and signed by the deponent before any person who may competently take an oath, whether in Scotland or in any other country. In Scotland such a person may include a notary public, justice of the peace, sheriff, or any judge. The person taking the oath should also sign the affidavit. Where the affidavit is not in English a duly certified translation should also be lodged.

See also definition of affidavit in r. 1.3(1).

"LETTER TO THE KEEPER OF THE REGISTERS".

The address of the Keeper of the Registers is: Meadowbank House, 153 London Road, Edinburgh EH8 7AU; tel. 0131-659 6111; fax 0131459 1221; DX ED300.

62.42.4

Part VA – Recognition and Enforcement of Judgments under Regulation (EU) No. 1215/2012 of the European Parliament and of the Council of 12th December 2012 on Jurisdiction and the Recognition and Enforcement of Judgments in Civil Matters (Recast)

Application and interpretation of this Part

62.42A.—[1](1)   This Part applies to the recognition and enforcement of a judgment under the Brussels I (recast) Regulation.

62.42A

(2)   In this Part, "adaptation order" means an order for the adaptation of a measure or order which is contained in a foreign judgment but is unknown under the law of Scotland, pursuant to Article 54 of the Brussels I (recast) Regulation; "authentic settlement" has the meaning given by Article 2(c) of the Brussels I (recast) Regulation; "the Brussels I (recast) Regulation" means Regulation (EU) No. 1215/2012 of the European Parliament and of the Council of 12th December 2012 on jurisdiction and the recognition and enforcement of judgments in civil and commercial matters (recast) as amended from time to time and as applied by the Agreement of 19th October 2005 between the European Community and the Kingdom of Denmark on jurisdiction and the recognition and enforcement of judgments in civil and commercial matters; "court settlement" has the meaning given by Article 2(b) of the Brussels I (recast) Regulation; "judgment" has the meaning given by Article 2(a) of the Brussels I (recast) Regulation.

GENERAL NOTE.

The Recognition and Enforcement of Judgments under Regulation (EU) No. 1215/2012 of the European Parliament and of the Council of 12 December 2012 on Jurisdiction and the Recognition and Enforcement of Judgments in Civil Matters (Recast), the Brussels I Regulation (Recast), replaced the Council Regulation (E.C.) No. 44/2001, the Brussels I Regulation. The latter is dealt with in Pt. V of this chapter.

62.42A.1

Brussels I (Recast) applies to judgments in proceedings instituted on or after 10th January 2015. Although Brussels I (Recast) replaces Brussels I, the latter still has effect to proceedings instituted before 10th January 2015: Art. 66. An important difference between Brussels I and Brussels I Regulation (Recast) is that it is no longer necessary to register a judgment of a European court; it is enforceable without registration. It is for the party who wishes recognition or enforcement to be refused who must apply to the court: Arts. 45 to 51.

A problem emerged when it was discovered that Pt.VA of RCS 1994 took no account of the fact that there will still be cases of proceedings instituted before the coming into force of Brussels I Regulation (Recast) on 10th January 2015 to which Brussels I, and not Brussels I (Recast), will continue to apply.

---

[1] Part VA and r.62.42A as inserted by S.S.I. 2015 No. 26 para.2 (effective 7th February 2015).

That problem came to the court in *Drika Bvba & Ors v Giles*, 2018 S.L.T. 823 (First Div) in which the respondent argued that there was now no provision for registration of such cases; the Lord Ordinary dismissed the application for registration with the result that the Belgium judgment could not be enforced. A possible solution was seeking decree conform at common law, but that was held not competent because it was superseded by the 1933 Act and the Brussels regime). The solution adopted by the court was to hold the petition for registration competent because, since the procedure for registration had been (erroneously) repealed, the special rules of Chap. 62 did not apply and the petition therefore proceeded as an ordinary petition under Chap. 14.

Disapplication of certain rules to this Part

62.42B

62.42B.—[1](1)   Rules 4.1(1) (printed form for petition) and 14.4 (form of petitions) do not apply to an application under this Part.

Form of applications

62.42C

62.42C.—[2](1)   An application under the following provisions of the Brussels I (recast) Regulation is to be made by petition in Form 62.42C-A—

    (a)   Article 36(2) (decision that there are no grounds for refusal of recognition as referred to in Article 45);

    (b)   Article 45(1) (refusal of recognition of judgment);

    (c)   Article 46 (refusal of enforcement of judgment);

    (d)   Article 58(1) (refusal of enforcement of authentic instrument);

    (e)   Article 59 (refusal of enforcement of court settlement).

(2)   An application for an adaptation order is to be made by petition in Form 62.42C-B.

(3)   A challenge under Article 54 (2) of the Brussels I (recast) Regulation to the adaptation of a measure or order without an adaptation order is to be made by petition in Form 62.42C-C.

"PETITION"

62.42C.1

A petition is presented to the Outer House: r.14.2(h). The petition must be in Form 14.4 in the official printed form: rr.4.1 and 14.4. The petition must be signed by counsel or other person having a right of audience: r.4.2; and see r.1.3(1) (definition of "counsel" and "other person having a right of audience") and note 1.3.4.

Part VI – Registration under the Merchant Shipping (Liner Conferences) Act 1982

Application and interpretation of this Part

62.43

62.43.—(1)   This Part applies to an application under section 9 of the Merchant Shipping (Liner Conferences) Act 1982 (recognition and enforcement of recommendations, etc., of conciliators).

(2)   In this Part, "the Liner Conferences Act" means the Merchant Shipping (Liner Conferences) Act 1982.

GENERAL NOTE.

62.43.1

The Merchant Shipping (Liner Conferences) Act 1982 was passed to give certain parts of the 1979 Geneva Convention on a Code of Conduct for Liner Conferences the force of law in the UK. The Liner Conference Code provides machinery for the settlement of disputes relating to the application or operation of its provisions between shipping lines, shippers' organisations or representatives, and liner conferences. That machinery involves the use of conciliation by which conciliators make recommendations which bind the parties to the dispute. Part VI of this Chapter is thus concerned principally with the enforcement of the recommendations of the conciliators in Scotland. It also enables the enforcement of ancillary determination of costs of conciliation and awards of costs for vexatious and frivolous proceedings.

DEFINITIONS IN THE LINER CONFERENCES ACT.

62.43.2

The rules in Pt. VI of this Chapter are made under s. 9(5) of the Liner Conferences Act. Accordingly a word or expression used in Pt. VI which is also used in the Liner Conferences Act has the meaning given in that Act unless the contrary intention appears: Interpretation Act 1978, s. 11.

---

[1] Rule 62.42B as inserted by S.S.I. 2015 No. 26 para.2 (effective 7th February 2015).
[2] Rule 62.42C as inserted by S.S.I. 2015 No. 26 para.2 (effective 7th February 2015).

The word "conference" (including "liner conference") means a group of two or more vessel-operating carriers which provides unilateral liner services for the carriage of cargo on a particular route or routes within specified geographical limits and which has an agreement or arrangement whatever its nature within the framework of which they operate under uniform or common freight rates and any other agreed condition with respect to the provisions of liner services: Liner Conferences Act, s. 14(1) and Sched., Chap. 1.

Applications for registration under the Liner Conferences Act

62.44.—(1) An application under—

62.44

(a) section 9(1)(b) of the Liner Conferences Act (application for registration for enforcement of a recommendation, determination or award), or

(b) section 9(3) of that Act (application for registration for enforcement of a determination of costs),

shall be made by petition.

(2) A petition under section 9(1)(b) of the Liner Conferences Act shall include averments in relation to—

(a) the reasons for the petition; and

(b) where appropriate, the limited extent to which the recommendation is enforceable under section 9(2) of that Act.

(3) There shall be produced with the petition—

(a) a certified copy of the recommendation, the reasons for the recommendation and the record of settlement;

(b) a copy of the acceptance of the recommendation by the parties on whom it is binding.

(4) There shall be produced with a petition under section 9(3) of the Liner Conferences Act a certified copy of the determination of costs.

Deriv. RCS 1965, r. 249B(1) to (4) inserted by S.I. 1986 No. 799

JURISDICTION UNDER THE LINER CONFERENCES ACT.

The court has jurisdiction for an application under s.9(1)(b) of the Liner Conferences Act where—

62.44.1

(a) the application is in respect of a recommendation of conciliators which has become binding as between two or more parties under Art. 37 of the Code in the Schedule to the Act; and

(b) the recommendation is unaffected by any matter in Art. 39, para. 2(a) to (d) of the Code (disability, fraud, coercion, public policy or composition or procedure of the conciliators).

The court may have jurisdiction in respect of some parts of the recommendation but not others provided the court is satisfied the parts may be severed: Liner Conferences Act, s.9(2) and Sched., Art. 39(3).

"PETITION".

A petition is presented in the Outer House: r. 14.2(h). The petition must be in Form 14.4 in the official printed form: rr. 4.1 and 14.4. The petition may be signed by the petitioner, counsel or other person having a right of audience, or an agent: r. 4.2; and see r. 1.3(1) (definition of "counsel", "other person having a right of audience" and "agent") and note 1.3.4.

62.44.2

The petitioner must lodge the petition with the required steps of process (r. 4.4) and any documents founded on or adopted (r. 27.1(1)). A fee is payable on lodging the petition: see note 14.5.10.

On petitions generally, see Chap. 14.

CERTIFIED COPY OF RECOMMENDATION AND REASONS.

There should be included the reasons of the conciliators: Liner Conferences Act, Sched., Art. 36. Ideally, there should be included the matters listed in r. 11 of the Model Rules annexed to the Schedule to the Liner Conferences Act. A certified copy recommendation, determination or award, if necessary, should be obtained from the Registrar based at the U.N. Office in Geneva: Liner Conferences Act, Sched., Art. 46(2)(d).

62.44.3

"RECORD OF SETTLEMENT".

This document is drawn up and signed by the conciliators when their recommendation has been accepted by the parties. On signature of the record of settlement the recommendation becomes binding, and thus enforceable: Liner Conferences Act, Sched., Art. 37(4).

62.44.4

Warrant for registration under the Liner Conferences Act

62.45

62.45. The court, on being satisfied that the recommendation, determination or award may be registered, shall pronounce an interlocutor granting warrant for registration of the recommendation, determination or award, as the case may be.

Deriv. RCS 1965, r. 249C(1) inserted by S.I. 1986 No. 799

GENERAL NOTE.

62.45.1

In Scotland a foreign judgment is enforced under statute by the court granting a warrant for the judgment to be registered in the register of judgments of the Books of Council and Session for execution. On registration, the foreign judgment becomes a Scottish decree of registration and may be enforced by any diligence or sequestration or liquidation. Registration for execution gives the holder a decree of registration which is in effect a decree of the Court of Session (Bell's *Comm.*, i,4; *Taylor, Petr.* 1931 S.L.T. 260, 261 per Lord Pitman); and, on the warrant inserted by the Keeper of the Registers or his deputy on an extract of a registered document, diligence may be executed against the debtor's moveable property under s.3 of the Writs Execution (Scotland) Act 1877 as substituted by s.87(4) of the Debtors (Scotland) Act 1987. Diligence against heritable property may be executed by inhibition on the grant of letters of inhibition (see Chap. 59) or by action of adjudication founding on the decree of registration.

EXPENSES OF PETITIONS AND REGISTRATION PROCEDURE.

62.45.2

The reasonable costs of and incidental to the registration procedure are recoverable as if they were sums recoverable under the recommendation, determination or award, except that they carry interest, as they would if they were an amount of costs or expenses made by the court on the date of registration: Liner Conferences Act, s.9(7).

Registration under the Liner Conferences Act

62.46

62.46.—(1) Where the court pronounces an interlocutor under rule 62.45 granting warrant for registration—

(a) the Deputy Principal Clerk shall enter the warrant in the register of recommendations, determinations and awards to be registered under section 9 of the Liner Conferences Act; and

(b) the petitioner shall serve a copy of the interlocutor containing such warrant on the party against whom the recommendation, determination or award may be enforced.

(2) On presentation by the petitioner to the Keeper of the Registers of—

(a) a certified copy of the interlocutor under rule 62.45 granting warrant for registration,

(b) a certified copy of the recommendation, determination or award to be registered and any translation of it, and

(c)[1] where necessary, a certificate of currency conversion under rule 62.2(1)(b), they shall be registered in the register of judgments of the Books of Council and Session.

(3) On registration under paragraph (2), the Keeper of the Registers shall issue an extract of the registered recommendation, determination or award, as the case may be, with a warrant for execution.

Deriv. RCS 1965, r. 249C(2) and (3) inserted by S.I. 1986 No. 799

"SERVE".

62.46.1

For methods of service, see Chap. 16, Pt I.

"CERTIFIED COPY OF THE INTERLOCUTOR".

62.46.2

A copy of the interlocutor is typed by the agent and presented to the clerk of session in the Petition Department. The clerk checks it, certifies it as a true copy and stamps it with the court stamp.

A fee is payable.

"KEEPER OF THE REGISTERS".

62.46.3

This is the Keeper of the Registers of Scotland: r. 1.3(1). The Register of Judgments is at Meadowbank House, 153 London Road, Edinburgh EH8 7AU; tel. 0131-659 6111; fax 0131-459 1221; DX ED300.

---

[1] Rule 62.46(2)(c) amended by S.I. 1996 No. 2168 (minor correction).

CERTIFIED COPY OF THE RECOMMENDATION ETC.

See note 62.44.3.

62.46.4

"TRANSLATION".

See r. 62.3.

62.46.5

"CERTIFICATE OF CURRENCY CONVERSION".

The certificate should be obtained from the clerk of session in the Petition Department and should be signed by him: r. 62.2(3) and see note 62.2.5.

62.46.6

REGISTRATION FEE.

A fee will be payable to the Keeper of the Registers for registration and any extract: see the Fees in the Registers of Scotland Order 1991 [S.I. 1991 No. 2093].

62.46.7

Part VII – Reciprocal Enforcement of Orders in Relation to Confiscation of Proceeds of Crime and to Forfeiture of Property used in Crime[1]

Interpretation of this Part

62.47.[2] In this Part—

62.47

"the Act of 1989" means the Prevention of Terrorism (Temporary Provisions) Act 1989;

"the Act of 1995" means the Proceeds of Crime (Scotland) Act 1995;

"the Act of 2000" means the Terrorism Act 2000;

"money order" means an order for the payment of money;

"non-money order" means an order which is not a money-order;

"the Order of 1995" means the Prevention of Terrorism (Temporary Provisions) Act 1989 (Enforcement of External Orders) Order 1995;

"the Order of 1999" means the Criminal Justice (International Co-operation) Act 1990 (Enforcement of Overseas Forfeiture Orders) (Scotland) Order 1999;

"the Overseas Forfeiture Order of 2005" means the Criminal Justice (International Co-operation) Act 1990 (Enforcement of Overseas Forfeiture Orders) (Scotland) Order 2005;

"the POCA Order of 2005" means the Proceeds of Crime Act 2002 (External Requests and Orders) Order 2005;

"relevant enactment" means the Act of 1989, the Act of 1995, the Order of 1995, the Order of 1999, the Overseas Forfeiture Order of 2005 or the POCA Order of 2005, as the case may be.

Deriv. RCS 1965, r. 249S(1) inserted by S.I. 1987 No. 12 and amended by S.I. 1990 No. 705 and 1991 No. 1183

GENERAL NOTE.

Part VII of this Chapter is made under s. 36(1) of the Act of 1995, and originally para. 19 of Sched. 4 to the Prevention of Terrorism (Temporary Provisions) Act 1989 (now replaced by para. 27 of Sched. 4 to the Terrorism Act 2000). Accordingly, a word or expression used in Pt. VII which is also used in those Acts has the meaning respectively given in those Acts unless the contrary intention appears: Interpretation Act 1978, s. 11.

62.47.1

Applications for registration under the relevant enactment

62.48.—[3](1) An application to which this rule applies shall be made by petition.

62.48

(2)[4, 5] This rule applies to an application under any of the following provisions:—

---

[1] Heading to Pt. II amended by S.I. 1999 No. 1220 (effective 1st May 1999).

[2] Rule 62.47 amended by S.I. 1996 No. 1756 (effective 5th August 1996) and S.I. 1999 No. 1220 (effective 1st May 1999) and S.I. 1996 No. 2168 (effective 23rd September 1996) and S.I. 2001 No.494 (effective 22nd December 2001) and by S.S.I. 2005 No. 663 (effective 31st December 2005).

[3] Rule 62.48(2) and heading amended by S.I. 1996 No. 1756 (effective 5th August 1996).

[4] Rule 62.48(2) and heading amended by S.I. 1996 No. 1756 (effective 5th August 1996).

(a)   paragraph 19(2) of Schedule 4 to the Act of 1989 (application for registration of an England and Wales order, Northern Ireland order or Islands order);

(b)   section 36(1) of the Act of 1995 (application for registration of an order to which section 35 of the Act of 1995 applies);

(c)   section 41(1) of the Act of 1995 (application for registration of external confiscation order);

(d)   article 15(1) of the Order of 1995 (application for registration of external forfeiture order in relation to terrorism);

(e)   article 16(1) of the Order of 1995 (application for registration of external restraint order);.

(f)[1]   article 5(1) of the Order of 1999 (application for registration of external forfeiture order other than in relation to terrorism).

(g)[2]   paragraph 27(3) of Schedule 4 to the Act of 2000 (application for registration of an England and Wales order, Northern Ireland order or Islands order);

(h)[3]   article 13(1) of the Overseas Forfeiture Order of 2005 (applications to give effect to external forfeiture orders);

(i)[4]   article 66(1) of the POCA Order of 2005 (applications to give effect to external orders).

(3) There shall be produced with a petition under paragraph (1) a certified copy of the order which is sought to be registered.

Deriv. RCS 1965, r. 249T(1) substituted by S.I. 1991 No. 1157, r. 249T(1A) inserted by S.I. 1991 No. 1157 and amended by S.I. 1991 No. 1183, and r. 249T(2) inserted by S.I. 1987 No. 12

GENERAL NOTE.

62.48.1   Part VII of this Chapter provides rules for the enforcement in Scotland under the Acts of 1988, 1989, 1995, 2000 (replacing the 1989 Act), and the Orders of 1995 and 1999 listed in r. 62.47 of various orders made in England and Wales or Northern Ireland under the Drug Trafficking Act 1994, Pt. VI of the Act of 1988, the Act of 1989 (now replaced by the Act of 2000), and external orders under the Order of 1995 and overseas forfeiture orders under the Order of 1999. The orders are listed in each section which gives the court jurisdiction to deal with an application.

Warrant for registration under the relevant enactment

62.49   **62.49.**[5, 6] The court shall, on being satisfied that the application complies with the requirements of the relevant enactment, as the case may be—

(a)   pronounce an interlocutor granting warrant for execution of a non-money order; or

(b)   pronounce an interlocutor granting warrant for the registration of a money order.

Deriv. RCS 1965, r. 249U(1) inserted by S.I. 1987 No. 12 and amended by S.I. 1990 No. 705 and 1991 No. 1183

Registration under the relevant enactment

62.50   **62.50.**—[7](1)[8] Where the court pronounces an interlocutor under rule 62.49, the Deputy Principal Clerk shall enter the order in the register for the registration of orders under the relevant enactment.

---

[5] Rule 62.48(2) amended by S.I. 1996 No. 2168 (effective 23rd September 1996).
[1] Rule 62.48(2)(d) amended and (2)(f) inserted, by S.I. 1999 No. 1220 (effective 1st May 1999).
[2] Rule 62.48(2)(d) amended and (2)(f) inserted, by S.I. 1999 No. 1220 (effective 1st May 1999).
[3] Rule 62.48(2)(h) & (i) inserted by S.S.I. 2005 No. 663 (effective 31st December 2005).
[4] Rule 62.48(2)(h) & (i) inserted by S.S.I. 2005 No. 663 (effective 31st December 2005).
[5] Rule 62.49 and heading amended by S.I. 1996 No. 1756 (effective 5th August 1996).
[6] Rule 62.49 and heading amended by S.I. 1996 No. 1756 (effective 5th August 1996).
[7] Rule 62.50(1) and heading amended by S.I. 1996 No. 1756 (effective 5th August 1996).
[8] Rule 62.50(1) and heading amended by S.I. 1996 No. 1756 (effective 5th August 1996).

(2)   On presentation by the petitioner to the Keeper of the Registers of—

(a)   a certified copy of the interlocutor pronounced under rule 62.49(b), and

(b)   a certified copy of the order to be registered,

they shall be registered in the register of judgments of the Books of Council and Session.

(3)   On registration under paragraph (2), the Keeper of the Registers shall issue an extract of the registered order with a warrant for execution.

Deriv. RCS 1965, r. 249U(2) inserted by S.I. 1987 No. 12 and amended by S.I. 1990 No. 705 and 1991 No. 1183, and r. 249U(3) inserted by S.I. 1987 No. 12

"KEEPER OF THE REGISTERS".

This is the Keeper of the Registers of Scotland: r. 1.3(1). The Register of Judgments is at Meadowbank House, 153 London Road, Edinburgh EH8 7AU; tel. 0131-659 6111; fax 0131-459 1221; DX ED300.   **62.50.1**

"CERTIFIED COPY OF THE INTERLOCUTOR".

A copy of the interlocutor is typed by the agent and presented to the clerk of session in the Petition Department. The clerk checks it, certifies it as a true copy and stamps it with the court stamp.   **62.50.2**
A fee is payable.

REGISTRATION FEE.

A fee will be payable to the Keeper of the Registers for registration and any extract: see the Fees in the Registers of Scotland Order 1991 [S.I. 1991 No. 2093].   **62.50.3**

Service of warrant for registration under the relevant enactment

62.51.[1]   The petitioner shall serve a copy of the interlocutor, pronounced under rule 62.49 granting warrant for registration, and a notice in Form 62.51 on the person against whom the order may be enforced.   **62.51**

Deriv. RCS 1965, r. 249V inserted by S.I. 1987 No. 12 and amended by S.I. 1991 No. 1183

"SERVE".

For methods of service, see Chap. 16, Pt. I.   **62.51.1**

Further provisions as respects warrant for registration

62.51A.[2]   Where an interlocutor granting warrant for the registration of an external confiscation order is pronounced and the order falls to be remitted for enforcement to the Sheriff of Lothian and Borders at Edinburgh, the Deputy Principal Clerk shall send a certified copy of the interlocutor, within four days after it is pronounced, to the sheriff clerk at Edinburgh.   **62.51A**

"EXTERNAL CONFISCATION ORDER".

An external confiscation order is an order, made by a court in a county designated by an Order in Council, for recovering payments or other reward or property or other economic advantage received, in connection with certain offences or drug trafficking, or the value of such payments, property, reward or economic advantage: Proceeds of Crime (Scotland) Act 1995, s. 40(2). Registration is by virtue of s. 41(1) of the Act of 1995.   **62.51A.1**

Suspension of enforcement under the Act of 1995

62.52.—[3](1)[4]   Where an order under section 36(1) of the Act of 1995 has been registered under rule 62.50, the court may, on the application of the person against whom the order may be enforced, if satisfied that an application has been made to the court which made the order to have it set aside or quashed—   **62.52**

(a)   suspend enforcement of the order; and

---

[1] Heading of r. 62.51 amended by S.I. 1996 No. 1756 (effective 5th August 1996).
[2] Rule 62.51A inserted by S.I. 1999 No. 1220 (effective 1st May 1999).
[3] Rule 62.52(1) and heading amended by S.I. 1996 No. 1756 (effective 5th August 1996) and S.I. 1996 No. 2168 (effective 23rd September 1996).
[4] Rule 62.52(1) and heading amended by S.I. 1996 No. 1756 (effective 5th August 1996) and S.I. 1996 No. 2168 (effective 23rd September 1996).

(b)   sist any proceedings for enforcement of the order.

(2)   Notwithstanding rule 60.2 (form of applications for suspension), an application under paragraph (1) shall be made by note in the process in the petition under rule 62.48(1).

Deriv. R.C.S. 1965, r. 249W inserted by S.I. 1987 No. 12 and amended by S.I. 1990 No. 705

"NOTE".

62.52.1   For applications by note, see r. 15.2.

Modification and cancellation of registration under the Act of 1989 or 1995 or 2000

62.53   **62.53.**—[1,2](1)[3,4]   An application to modify or cancel the registration of an order under the Act of 1989 or 1995 or 2000 registered under rule 62.50 shall be made—

(a)   by the petitioner, by motion; or

(b)   by any other interested party, by note.

(2)   There shall be produced with the application under paragraph (1) a certified copy of any order which modifies or revokes the registered order or which causes the order to cease to have effect.

(3)[5]   The court shall, on being satisfied—

(a)   that the registered order has been modified, revoked or has ceased to have effect, or

(b)   that the registration of an external confiscation order should be cancelled in terms of section 41(3) of the Act of 1995,

pronounce an interlocutor so modifying or cancelling the registration, as the case may be, and grant warrant for the registration of a certified copy of the interlocutor in the register of judgments of the Books of Council and Session.

(4)   Where the court pronounces an interlocutor under paragraph (3), the Deputy Principal Clerk shall modify or cancel the registration in the register kept under rule 62.50(1) in accordance with that interlocutor.

Deriv. R.C.S. 1965, r. 249X inserted by S.I. 1987 No. 12 and amended by S.I. 1991 No. 1157.

"MOTION".

62.53.1   For motions, see Chap. 23.

"NOTE".

62.53.2   For applications by note, see r. 15.2.

Incidental applications

62.54   **62.54.**—[6](1)   Any of the following applications shall be made in the prayer of the petition under rule 62.48(1) to which it relates or, if the prayer of that petition has been granted, by motion in the process of that petition:—

(a)   an application under section 32(1) of the Act of 1995 for a warrant for inhibition;

(b)   an application under section 33(1) of the Act of 1995 (warrant for arrestment);

(c)   an application under paragraph 16(1) (warrant for inhibition), or paragraph

---

[1] Rule 62.53(1) and (3) and heading amended by S.I. 1996 No. 1756 (effective 5th August 1996).

[2] Rule 62.53(1) and heading amended by S.I. 1996 No. 2168 (effective 23rd September 1996) and S.S.I. 2001 No. 494 (effective 22nd December 2001).

[3] Rule 62.53(1) and (3) and heading amended by S.I. 1996 No. 1756 (effective 5th August 1996).

[4] Rule 62.53(1) and heading amended by S.I. 1996 No. 2168 (effective 23rd September 1996) and S.S.I. 2001 No. 494 (effective 22nd December 2001).

[5] Rule 62.53(1) and (3) and heading amended by S.I. 1996 No. 1756 (effective 5th August 1996).

[6] Rule 62.54 substituted by S.I. 1996 No. 2168 (effective 23rd September 1996).

16A(1) (warrant for arrestment), of Schedule 4 to the Act of 1989 as applied by paragraph 19(5) of that Schedule or by article 18 of the Order of 1995, as the case may be.

(2) Either of the following applications shall be made in the prayer of the petition under rule 62.48(1) to which it relates or, if the prayer of the petition has been granted, by note in the process of that petition:—

(a) an application under sub-paragraph (4) of paragraph 19 of Schedule 4 to the Act of 1989 for an order in implementation of an England and Wales, Northern Ireland or Islands forfeiture order registered in the Court of Session under that paragraph;

(b) an application under article 17 of the Order of 1995 for an order in implementation of an external forfeiture order registered in the Court of Session under article 15(1) of that Order.

(3) Where the court makes an order by virtue of paragraph 19(4) of Schedule 4 to the Act of 1989 or article 17 of the Order of 1995 appointing an administrator, rules 76.24 to 76.26 (which relate to the duties of an administrator) shall apply to an administrator appointed by virtue of that paragraph or article as they apply to an order in implementation of a forfeiture order.

Deriv. R.C.S. 1965, r. 249Y inserted by S.I. 1987 No. 12 and amended by SI. 1990 No. 705 and 1991 No. 1183

"MOTION".

For motions, see Chap. 23.   **62.54.1**

INHIBITION AND ARRESTMENT.

On inhibition on the dependence, see note 13.6.2. On arrestment on the dependence, see note 13.6.3.   **62.54.2**
Applications to recall lease or restrict an arrestment or inhibition under the following enactments are by motion by virtue of r. 23.11:—

(a) with respect to inhibition—s. 32(1)(a) and (5) of the Act of 1995; para. 16(2)(a) and (6)(a) of Sched. 4 to the Act of 1989 as applied by para. 19(5) of Sched. 4 (in relation to restraint orders elsewhere in UK registered in the Court of Session) or as applied by art. 18 of the Order of 1995 (in relation to external restraint orders of a designated country registered in the Court of Session);

(b) with respect to arrestment—s. 33(2) and (4) of the Act of 1995; para. 16A(2) and (4) of Sched. 4 to the Act of 1989 as applied by para. 19(5) of Sched. 4 (in relation to relevant orders elsewhere in UK registered in the Court of Session) or as applied by art. 18 of the Order of 1995 (in relation to external restraint orders of a designated country registered in the Court of Session).

"NOTE".

For applications by note, see r. 15.2.   **62.54.3**

Cancellation of registration or variation of property under the Overseas Forfeiture Order of 2005 or the POCA Order of 2005

62.54A.—[1](1) An application under article 16(3) of the Overseas Forfeiture   **62.54A**
Order of 2005 (application for cancellation of registration or variation of property) or article 69(3) of the POCA Order of 2005 (application for cancellation of registration or variation of property) shall be made—

(a) by the Lord Advocate, by motion; or
(b) by any other interested party, by note.

(2) There shall be produced with an application under paragraph (1), a certified copy of any order which modifies or revokes the registered order or which causes the registered order to cease to have effect.

---

[1] Rule 62.54A inserted by S.S.I. 2005 No. 663 (effective 31st December 2005).

(3)   The court shall, on pronouncing an interlocutor granting an application under paragraph (1), grant warrant for the registration of a certified copy of the interlocutor in the register of judgments of the Books of Council and Session.

(4)   Where the court pronounces an interlocutor granting an application under paragraph (1), the Deputy Principal Clerk shall cancel or, as the case may be, vary the registration in the register kept under rule 62.50(1) in accordance with that interlocutor.

Registration under the POCA Order in Council of 2005: further provision

62.54B

62.54B.—[1](1)   Rule 62.2 (certificate of currency conversion) shall not apply to an application under article 66(1) of the POCA Order of 2005 (application to give effect to external orders).

(2)   An application under article 72(4) (payment within a specified period) or article 72(6) (extension of specified period) of the POCA Order of 2005 shall be made by motion in the process relating to the granting of the application under article 66(1) of the POCA Order of 2005.

(3)   The Deputy Principal Clerk shall send to the sheriff clerk appointed under article 69(1)(c) of the POCA Order of 2005 a certified copy of the interlocutor granting warrant for registration under rule 62.49 and of any subsequent interlocutor granting an application under—

(a)   rule 62.54A(1) (application for cancellation of registration or variation of property);

(b)   paragraph (3) of this rule (payment within specified period and extension of specified period);

(c)   rule 76.28(1)(i) (enforcement administrators); or

(d)   rule 76.28(3)(i) (recall and variation of order appointing administrator),

in respect of the registered order.

Part VIII – Registration of Awards under the Multilateral Investment Guarantee Agency Act 1988

Registration of awards under the Multilateral Investment Guarantee Agency Act 1988

62.55

62.55.   Part III shall, with the necessary modifications, apply to an award under Article 4 of Annex II to the convention referred to in section 1(1) of the Multilateral Investment Guarantee Agency Act 1988 as it applies to an award under the convention mentioned in section 1(1) of the Arbitration (International Investment Disputes) Act 1966.

Deriv. R.C.S. 1965, r. 249AA inserted by S.I. 1990 No. 705

GENERAL NOTE.

62.55.1

Part VIII of this Chapter is made under s. 7(e) of the Multilateral Investment Guarantee Agency Act 1988.

Under the Convention establishing the Multilateral Investment Guarantee Agency (Cm. 150 (1987)), disputes between the Agency and a member under Art. 57 may be settled by arbitration under Annex II to the convention. An award may be registered on application to the court under s.4, as applied by s.7, of the 1988 Act.

---

[1] Rule 62.54B inserted by S.S.I. 2005 No. 663 (effective 31st December 2005).

The convention is intended to promote private sector investment in developing countries by providing insurance for investors against certain kinds of non-commercial risks.

Part IX[1] – Enforcement of Arbitral Awards under the New York Convention on the Recognition and Enforcement of Foreign Arbitral Awards

Interpretation and application of this Part

62.56.—[2](1) In this Part—

  "the 2010 Act" means the Arbitration (Scotland) Act 2010;

  "the Convention" means the New York Convention on the Recognition and Enforcement of Foreign Arbitral Awards;

  "Convention award" means an award made in pursuance of a written arbitration agreement in a territory of a state (other than the United Kingdom) which is a party to the Convention.

 (2) This Part applies to an application under section 19 of the 2010 Act (recognition and enforcement of New York Convention awards).

62.56

GENERAL NOTE.

  Part IX of this Chapter provides for recognition and enforcement of non-UK awards under the 1958 New York Convention for the Recognition and Enforcement of Foreign Arbitral Awards by means of the flexible petition procedure in place of the former procedure by ordinary action. The 1958 Convention is an international treaty under which the State parties to the Convention agreed under certain conditions to recognise and allow the enforcement of arbitral awards seated in other State parties. Since 1975 the United Kingdom has been party to the Convention. There are now 148 States which are parties to the New York Convention. A copy of the Convention and further details on states that are party to the Convention can be obtained via the UNCITRAL website at *www.uncitral.org*. An arbitral award made in the territory of a State other than the United Kingdom which is party to the Convention and which was made pursuant to a written agreement or clause submitting the dispute to arbitration is known in Chap. 100 of the R.C.S. 1994 as a "Convention award".

  The New York Convention was originally implemented by the Arbitration Act 1975. The 1975 Act, in so far as it applied to Scotland, was repealed by the Arbitration (Scotland) Act 2010 and the opportunity was taken to reform the method of enforcement of a Convention award. Unfortunately the rules on enforcement of Convention awards were not put into one place. Thus the petitions under Part IX of Chap. 62 are also covered by Chap. 100 apart from rr. 100.5 and 100.7 as well as the general rules on petitions which have not been excluded by r. 104.

62.56.1

Applications for enforcement of a Convention award

62.57.—[3](1) An application for enforcement of a Convention award under section 19(2) of the 2010 Act shall be made by petition or, where there are proceedings depending before the court under the 2010 Act in relation to the same arbitration process, by note in the process of the petition.

 (2) There shall be produced with such a petition or note—

  (a) the duly authenticated original award or a certified copy of it;

  (b) the original agreement referred to in article II of the Convention or a certified copy of it;

  (c) a translation of any award or agreement which is in a language other than English, certified by an official or sworn translator or by a diplomatic or consular agent;

  (d) an affidavit stating—

   (i) the full name, title, trade or business and the usual or last known place of residence or, where appropriate, of the business of the petitioner or noter and the party against whom the Convention award was made;

   (ii) the amount of the Convention award which is unsatisfied; and

62.57

---

[1] Part IX and r. 62.56 substituted by S.S.I. 2010 No. 205 (effective 7th June 2010).
[2] Part IX and r. 62.56 substituted by S.S.I. 2010 No. 205 (effective 7th June 2010).
[3] Rule 62.57 substituted by S.S.I. 2010 No. 205 (effective 7th June 2010).

(iii) that the Convention award has become binding on the parties and has not been set aside or suspended by a court of the country which, or under the law of which, the award was made.

Deriv. R.C.S. 1965, r. 249AB inserted by SI 1991/2213

GENERAL NOTE.

62.57.1 The basic rule is that all applications for enforcement of Convention awards are to be made by petition.

"PETITION OR NOTE".

62.57.2 The basic form of application for enforcement is in the form of a petition. However in the unlikely event that there is a petition which is still "depending" before the court which relates to the same arbitration process, the application must be by note. A petition is depending before the court from the time that the court makes its first order in the petition process. It ceases to be depending when the "final decree" is made. For the meaning of final decree, see note 4.15.2(2). A final decree requires the determination of liability for expenses of the petition process, although the expenses have yet to be quantified.

"PETITION".

62.57.3 A petition is presented in the Outer House: r. 14.2(h). The petition must be in Form 14.4 in the official printed form: rr. 4.1 and 14.4. The petition may be signed by the petitioner, counsel or other person having a right of audience, or an agent: r. 4.2; and see r. 1.3(1) (definition of "counsel", "other person having a right of audience" and "agent") and note 1.3.4.

The petitioner must lodge the petition with the required steps of process (r. 4.4) and any documents founded on or adopted (r. 27.1(1)). A fee is payable on lodging the petition: see note 14.5.10.

On petitions generally, see Chap. 14.

"NOTE".

62.57.4 For procedure by note, see r. 15.2 but it must be remembered that rr. 14.5, 14.6, and 14.8 do not apply to applications (whether in the form of a note or petition) under r. 62.57: rr. 100.4 and 62.1.

PRODUCTIONS.

62.57.5 The petitioner must produce with the petition (1) the items listed in r. 62.57(2); and (2) any other document founded on or adopted into the petition.

The duly authenticated original award (or a duly certified copy of it), the original arbitration agreement (or a duly certified copy of it), and a translation of any award or agreement which is not in English (certified by an official or sworn translator or by a diplomatic or consular agent) must all be produced in terms of section 21 of the 2010 Act regardless of the requirements of rr. 62.57(1) (a) to (c). This is because these productions are necessary in terms of art. IV of the New York Convention itself.

"DULY AUTHENTICATED ORIGINAL" OR "CERTIFIED COPY".

62.57.6 The purpose of art. IV of the Convention was to ensure that the court of the state of enforcement was presented with a genuine award and a genuine arbitration agreement. Internationally the courts of different countries have taken different views on what they require by way of a "duly authenticated original award" or a "duly certified copy" of the award. Some countries' courts have required authentication and certification that is valid under the country of the seat of the arbitration instead of or as well as authentication and certification under their domestic law.

Countries have also taken differing views on whether an award whose authenticity is not challenged by the respondent but which is neither an authenticated original nor a "duly certified" copy can be accepted under art. IV. For a commentary on section 21 and the nature of the productions required, see F. Davidson, H.R. Dundas and D. Bartos Arbitration (Scotland) Act 2010 (Edinburgh: W.Green 2010, pp.80-82). There is no international consensus on whose certificate suffices for "certification" of a copy document for the purpose of registration. It has been held that certification by members of the arbitral tribunal would suffice (*Bergesen v Joseph Muller Corp.* 710 F.2d 928, 934; (1984) IX YCA 487, 494 (United States); and *Inter-Arab Investment Guarantee Corp. v. Banque Arabe et Internationale d'Investissements* Journ. Trib. 116 (1997): 319; (1997) XXII YCA 643, 657 - 658 (Belgium), but that does not exclude the possibility of others providing valid certification as has occurred in relation to registration in other countries.

As under Scots rules of international private law, matters of evidence and procedure are governed by the lex fori, namely Scots law, it is suggested that a copy award should be seen as "duly certified" if it complies with Scots domestic law, as set out in section 6 of the Civil Evidence (Scotland) Act 1988. That would also be consistent with art. III of the Convention which obliges state parties to enforce Convention awards in accordance with their rules of procedure. Given the terms of r. 62.58 which only caters for certified copy awards, it may be prudent for a petitioner to proceed down the certification route rather than that of "authentication" of an original. That would also avoid any argument over what is required for "authentication" of an original document.

With regard to the arbitration agreement it is sufficient that an unauthenticated original is produced, or that a duly certified copy is produced. The observations in relation to due certification apply equally to arbitration agreements.

"Translation".

The requirements of r. 62.57(2)(c) echo section 21(2) of the 2010 Act and paragraph 2 of article IV of the Convention. There is no requirement under any of those provisions that the certifier (whether he be an official or sworn translator or a diplomatic or consular agent) be the translator of the text. That is evident from diplomatic or consular agents being given a power to certify. It is sufficient for the person making the certification to certify that he is satisfied that the translation is an accurate and fair translation of the original document. Where the certifier is a translator, for him to become "sworn" it is sufficient for him to swear an affidavit that the translation is accurate and fair. For what is required by way of affidavit, see note 62.57.8.

62.57.7

Where the certifier is a diplomatic or consular agent, it would be sufficient for him to be of the United Kingdom. It is unclear whether a diplomatic or consular agent of, for example the country of the seat of the arbitral tribunal would suffice. It may depend on circumstances and in particular whether the diplomatic or consular agent can be taken to be familiar with both the language of the award or agreement and English. A Convention award or arbitration agreement need not be in an official language of the country in which the arbitration was seated.

In addition to the requirements of r. 62.57 and s. 21(2), r. 62.3 requires a certification by the translator together with his full, name, address and qualification. It is suggested that these additional requirements are not necessary where the certification is to be carried out by an appropriate diplomatic or consular agent.

Affidavit.

The affidavit should be in the form of a statement of evidence in the first person. It should contain the evidence of the deponent in support of the averments in the petition. In particular it should cover the matters set out in r. 62.57(2)(d).

62.57.8

An affidavit should be sworn and signed by the deponent before any person who may competently take an oath, whether in Scotland or in any other country. In Scotland such a person may include a notary public, justice of the peace, sheriff, or any judge. The person taking the oath should also sign the affidavit. Where the affidavit is not in English a duly certified translation should also be lodged.

See also definition of affidavit in r. 1.3(1).

Registration of Convention award

62.58.—[1](1)   The court, on being satisfied that the Convention award may be registered, shall grant warrant for registration.

62.58

(2)   Where the court pronounces an interlocutor under paragraph (1), the Deputy Principal Clerk shall enter the Convention award in a register of Convention awards.

(3)   Where the Keeper of the Registers receives from the petitioner or noter the documents referred to in paragraph (4), he or she shall register them in the register of judgments of the Books of Council and Session.

(4)   The documents are—

    (a)   a certified copy of the interlocutor of the warrant of registration,

    (b)   a certified copy of the Convention award to be registered, and any translation of it, and

    (c)   any certificate of currency conversion under rule 62.2(1)(b).

(5)   An extract of a registered Convention award with warrant for execution shall not be issued by the Keeper of the Registers until a certificate of service under rule 62.59 (service on party against whom Convention award made) is produced to him or her.

Deriv. R.C.S. 1965, r. 249AC inserted by S.I. 1991 No. 2213

"Warrant for registration".

The warrant will be for registration in the register of judgments of the Books of Council and Session for execution. On registration the Convention award will become a Scottish decree of registration which is in effect a decree of the Court of Session (Bell's Comm., i.4; Taylor, Petr, 1931 S.L.T. 260, 261 per Lord Pitman). The warrant inserted by the Keeper of the Registers or his deputy on an extract of the registered Convention award enables the holder to enforce the award against the debtor's moveable property under s. 3 of the Writs Execution (Scotland) Act 1877, as substituted by s. 87(4) of the Debtors (Scotland) Act 1987. The holder may enforce the Convention award against the debtor's heritable (immoveable) property by inhibition on the grant of letters of inhibition (see Chap. 59) and by action of adjudication founding on the decree of registration.

62.58.1

---

[1] Rule 62.58 substituted by S.S.I 2010 No. 205 (effective 7th June 2010).

"KEEPER OF THE REGISTERS".

62.58.2 This is the Keeper of the Registers of Scotland: r. 1.3(1). The Register of Judgments is at Meadowbank House, 153 London Road, Edinburgh EH8 7AU; tel. 0131-659 6111; fax 0131-459 1221; DX ED300.

"CERTIFIED COPY OF THE INTERLOCUTOR".

62.58.3 A copy of the interlocutor is typed by the agent and presented to the clerk of session in the Petition Department. The clerk checks it, certifies it as a true copy and stamps it with the court stamp.
A fee is payable.

62.58.4 *"certified copy of the Convention award"*.This was probably intended to be a reference back to the certified copy of the award which must be produced along with the petition, although perhaps through oversight, no mention of a duly authenticated original award is made in the rule. In principle in the unlikely event that the duly authenticated original is produced, then that should suffice for the purposes of r. 62.58(3), and relief should be sought under r. 2.1. (See generally note 62.57.6).

"TRANSLATION".

62.58.5 See r. 62.3 and 62.57.7.

"CERTIFICATE OF CURRENCY CONVERSION".

62.58.6 The certificate should be obtained from the clerk of session in the Petition Department and should be signed by him: r. 62.2(3) and see note 62.2.5.

REGISTRATION FEE.

62.58.7 A fee will be payable to the Keeper of the Registers for registration and any extract: see the Fees in the Registers of Scotland Order 1995 [S.I. 1995 No. 1945].

"CERTIFICATE OF SERVICE".

62.58.8 See the notes to r. 62.59 and the notes to the rules relating to service in Chapter 16.

Service on party against whom Convention award made

62.59 **62.59.**[1] On registration under rule 62.58, the petitioner or noter shall forthwith serve a notice of registration on the party against whom the Convention award was made in Form 62.59.

"SERVE".

62.59.1 For methods of service, see Chap. 16, Pt. I.
This will be the first formal notice of the application to the respondent: see note 62.1.1.

Application for refusal of recognition or enforcement of a Convention award

62.60 **62.60.**—[2](1) An application under article V of the Convention (request by party against whom Convention award made for refusal of recognition or enforcement) shall be made by note.

(2) A note referred to in paragraph (1) may crave—

(a) suspension or interdict of any past or future steps in the execution of the Convention award, including registration or enforcement of the award; and

(b) recall of the interlocutor pronounced under rule 62.58(1) (registration under the Convention).

(3) The note shall be supported by affidavit and any relevant documentary evidence.

(4)[3] Where any interlocutor pronounced under rule 62.58(1) is recalled, a certificate to that effect issued by the Deputy Principal Clerk shall be sufficient warrant to the Keeper of the Registers to cancel the registration and return the documents registered to the petitioner or noter on whose application the interlocutor under that rule was pronounced.

---

[1] Rule 62.59 substituted by S.S.I. 2010 No. 205 (effective 7th June 2010).
[2] Rule 62.60 substituted by S.S.I. 2010 No. 205 (effective 7th June 2010).
[3] Rule 62.60(4) amended by S.S.I. 2011 No. 288 (effective 21st July 2011).

GENERAL NOTE.

The reference in this rule to an "application" under art. V of the Convention is slightly misleading. Article V of the Convention provides that recognition and enforcement of a Convention award may be refused, at the request of the party against whom it is invoked, only if that party furnishes to the competent authority where the recognition and enforcement is sought proof of any one of five matters lettered (a) to (d). These are the grounds of refusal of recognition and enforcement set out in section 20(2) and (3) of the 2010 Act. The reason for the reference in art. V to a "request" being required was to indicate that these grounds of refusal could not be raised by the court *ex proprio motu*.

The true purpose of this rule is to provide a statutory route in the Rules of Court for the respondent to challenge the enforcement of a Convention award. As explained in the note to r. 62.1, petitions or notes under the various enforcement provisions in Chapter 62 are not generally served on the respondent to allow him to oppose by way of lodging answers. But for r. 62.60 the respondent would have been required to challenge enforcement by means of the common law procedure of a petition for suspension of the registration and interdict of future enforcement. Instead r. 62.60 provides for the respondent to have an opportunity of challenging the enforcement by means of a note in the process of the original petition. The application is therefore free-standing under r. 62.60 and not an application under the 2010 Act (or art. V of the Convention).

62.60.1

"NOTE".

For applications by note, see r. 15.2.

The craves may include but are not restricted to those in paragraph (2) of r. 62.60. The Note will require to contain averments directed to the applicable grounds for refusal of enforcement set out in s. 20 of the 2010 Act. For a commentary on section 20 and the nature of the grounds in question, see F. Davidson, H.R. Dundas and D. Bartos Arbitration (Scotland) Act 2010 (Edinburgh: W.Green 2010, pp.59–78).

It would seem plain that the note must be served on the petitioner but due to oversight, the exclusion of the automatic service provisions in rr. 14.5, and 14.6 by virtue of r. 62.1 has itself not been excluded. The practical effect of this is that the noter will have to enrol a motion for intimation and service causing additional delay and expense. For motions, generally, see Chap. 23.

62.60.2

"AFFIDAVIT".

See note 62.57.6.

The affidavit should be in the form of a statement of evidence in the first person. It should contain the evidence of the deponent in support of the averments in the petition. In particular it should cover the matters set out in r. 62.57(2)(d).

62.60.3

PRODUCTIONS.

The noter must produce with the note all relevant documentary evidence relied on whether or not founded on or adopted into the note.

62.60.4

INTERIM INTERDICT, SIST AND SECURITY.

Article VI of the Convention provides that if an application for the setting aside or suspension of the Convention award has been made to a competent authority of the country in which or under whose laws it was made, the authority before which the award is sought to be relied upon may, if it considers it proper, adjourn the decision on the enforcement of the order. Section 20(6) of the 2010 Act echoes that provision. In addition given that the Convention award will in all likelihood already have been registered in the Books of Council and Session, it is suggested that the court has a common law power to give effect to art. VI of the Convention by granting interim suspension of any past step in the execution of the award or interim interdict of any future step of diligence or sequestration or liquidation. The noter will require to enrol a motion for any sist or interim interdict that he seeks. See also the notes to r. 60.1.

For his part the petitioner may move the court under section 20(6)(b) of the 2010 Act to order the noter to give suitable security. For a commentary on the test to be applied see F. Davidson, H.R. Dundas and D. Bartos Arbitration (Scotland) Act 2010 (Edinburgh: W.Green 2010, pp.79-80). See Chapter 33 in relation to the procedure for obtaining and the forms of security which can be provided.

For motions see Chapter 23.

62.60.5

FURTHER PROCEDURE.

62.60.6   See r. 15.2.

Part X[1] – Recognition, Registration and Enforcement of Miscellaneous Decisions

Application and interpretation of this Part

62.61   **62.61**—[2](1)   This Part applies to the recognition, registration or enforcement, as the case may be, of an award, decision, judgment or order under any of the following instruments:—

(a)   Article 34.1 (enforcement of arbitral award) of the procedural rules on conciliation and arbitration of contracts financed by the European Development Fund;

(b)   Article 20 of the United Nations (International Tribunal) (Former Yugoslavia) Order 1996 (enforcement of orders for the preservation or restitution of property).

(c)[3]   Article 20 of the United Nations (International Tribunal) (Rwanda) Order 1996 (enforcement of orders for the preservation or restitution of property).

(2)   In this Part—

"decision" includes award, judgment or order;

"relevant instrument" means an instrument mentioned in paragraph (1).

GENERAL NOTE.

62.61.1   Part X was devised as a general provision for the growing number of obscure decisions of bodies which may require registration and enforcement in Scotland. The rules in this Part (based on Pt III) are of general application and apply where appropriate to decisions listed in r. 62.61(1). The idea is that, to save adding new Parts to Chap. 62 where the general rules are sufficient, subsequent appropriate enactments or other instruments containing provisions for registration and enforcement of decisions can be inserted in r. 62.61(1). Had the principal annotator thought of this idea when drafting the original Chap. 62, he would have inserted Pts III and VIII at least into this miscellaneous Part.

ARTICLE 34.1 OF EDF CONTRACTS.

62.61.2   Under Art. 233 of the Lomé Convention of 15th December 1989 (Cmnd. 1999 UKTS 47 (1992)) the European Development Fund may be used to finance projects and programmes in those African, Caribbean and Pacific (ACP) states which are parties to the Convention. Art. 307 provides for disputes between an ACP state and a contractor, supplier or provider of services during the performance of a trans-national contract financed by the Fund to be settled by arbitration in accordance with procedural rules adopted by decisions of the Council of Ministers. The procedural rules mentioned in r. 62.61(1)(a) are Annex V of Decision No. 3/90 of the ACP/EEC Council of Ministers of 29th March 1990 (O.J. L-382 of 31st December 1990).

ARTICLE 20 OF THE FORMER YUGOSLAVIA ORDER, AND THE RWANDA ORDER.

62.61.3   The United Nations (International Tribunal) (Former Yugoslavia) Order 1996 (S.I. 1996 No. 716) enables the U.K. to co-operate with the International Tribunal for the Prosecution of Persons Responsible for Serious Violations of International Humanitarian Law Committed in the Territory of the Former Yugoslavia since 1991 established by the UN Security Council Resolution 827 (1993) in the investigation and prosecution of persons before the tribunal. Article 20 provides for registration and enforcement of orders for the preservation or restitution of property.

A similar provision is made in Art. 20 of the United Nations (International Tribunal) (Rwanda) Order 1996 (S.I. 1996 No. 1296) in respect of genocide in that country following the UN Security Council Resolution 955 (1994).

Applications under this Part

62.62   **62.62.**—[4](1)   An application for recognition, registration or enforcement, as the case may be, of a decision under a relevant instrument shall be made by petition.

(2)   There shall be produced with such a petition an affidavit—

---

[1] Part X and r. 62.61 inserted by S.I. 1996 No. 2168 (effective 23rd September 1996).
[2] Part X and r. 62.61 inserted by S.I. 1996 No. 2168 (effective 23rd September 1996).
[3] Rule 62.61(1)(c) inserted by S.S.I. 2001 No. 305 para. 14 (effective 18th September 2001).
[4] Rule 62.62 inserted by S.I. 1996 No. 2168 (effective 23rd September 1996).

    (a) exhibiting a copy of the decision certified under the relevant instrument; and

    (b) stating—

       (i) the full name, title, trade or business and the usual or the last known place of residence or, where appropriate, of business of the petitioner and of the party against whom the decision was made;

      (ii) that the petitioner is entitled to have the decision recognised, registered or enforced, as the case may be, under the relevant instrument;

     (iii) the extent to which the decision is unsatisfied; and

     (iv) whether the enforcement of the decision has been sisted (provisionally or otherwise) under the relevant instrument and whether any, and if so what, application has been made under the relevant instrument which, if granted, might result in a sist of enforcement of the decision.

GENERAL NOTE.

For the history of this rule, see note 62.62.1.   **62.62.1**

"PETITION".

A petition is presented in the Outer House: r. 14.2(h). The petition must be in Form 14.4 in the official **62.62.2**
printed form: rr. 4.1 and 14.4. The petition may be signed by the petitioner, counsel or other person having a right of audience, or an agent: r. 4.2(3)(d); and see r. 13(1) (definition of "counsel", "other person having a right of audience" and "agent") and note 1.3.4.

The petitioner must lodge the petition with the required steps of process (r. 4.4) and any documents founded on or adopted (r. 27.1(1)). A fee is payable on lodging the petition: see note 14.5.10.

On petitions generally, see Chap. 14.

PRODUCTIONS.

The petitioner must produce with the petition the relevant documents. On lodging productions, see r. **62.62.3**
4.5.

AFFIDAVIT.

The affidavit should be in the form of a statement of evidence written in the first person. The affidavit **62.62.4**
should contain the evidence of the deponent in support of the averments in the petition. In particular the affidavit should deal with the matters listed in r. 62.62(2).

An affidavit should be sworn and signed by the deponent before any person who may competently take an oath, whether in Scotland or in any other country. In Scotland such a person may include a notary public, justice of the peace, sheriff, or any judge. The person taking the oath should also sign the affidavit. Where the affidavit is not in English a duly certified translation should also be lodged.

See also the definition of affidavit in r. 1.3(1).

Recognition, or warrant for registration or for enforcement under this Part

62.63.[1] The court shall, on being satisfied that the petition complies with the **62.63**
requirements of the relevant instrument, pronounce an interlocutor recognising or granting warrant for the registration or enforcement of the decision, as the case may be.

GENERAL NOTE.

For the history of this rule, see note 62.61.1.   **62.63.1**

Registration for enforcement under this Part

62.64.—[2](1) Where the court pronounces an interlocutor under rule 62.63 grant- **62.64**
ing warrant for registration or enforcement, as the case may be, the Deputy Principal Clerk shall enter details of the interlocutor and the decision in a register of decisions under this Part.

---

[1] Rule 62.63 inserted by S.I. 1996 No. 2168 (effective 23rd September 1996).
[2] Rule 62.64 inserted by S.I. 1996 No. 2168 (effective 23rd September 1996).

(2) On presentation by the petitioner to the Keeper of the Registers of—

(a) a certified copy of the interlocutor under rule 62.63,

(b) a certified copy of the decision and any translation of it, and

(c) any certificate of currency conversion under rule 62.2(1)(b),

they shall be registered in the register of judgments of the Books of Council and Session.

(3) An extract of a registered decision with warrant for execution shall not be issued by the Keeper of the Registers until a certificate of service under rule 62.65 is produced to him.

GENERAL NOTE.

62.64.1   For this history of this rule, see note 62.61.1.

"KEEPER OF THE REGISTERS".

62.64.2   This is the Keeper of the Registers of Scotland: r. 1.3(1). The Register of Judgments is at Meadowbank House, 153 London Road, Edinburgh EH8 7AU; tel. 0131-659 6111; fax 0131-459 1221; DX ED300.

"CERTIFIED COPY OF THE INTERLOCUTOR".

62.64.3   A copy of the interlocutor is typed by the agent and presented to the clerk of session in the Petition Department. The clerk checks it, certifies it as a true copy and stamps it with the court stamp.

A fee is payable.

"TRANSLATION".

62.64.4   See r. 62.3.

"CERTIFICATE OF CURRENCY CONVERSION".

62.64.5   In obtaining this, notwithstanding the provisions of r. 62.2(1), the date of conversion in the certified statement may be regarded by the relevant instrument to be the date of the decision.

The certificate should be obtained from the clerk of session and should be signed by him: r. 62.2(3); and see notes 62.2.4 and 62.2.5.

REGISTRATION FEE.

62.64.6   A fee will be payable to the Keeper of the Registers for registration and any extract: see the Fees in the Registers of Scotland Order 1991 [S.I. 1995 No. 1945].

Service on party against whom award made

62.65   **62.65.**[1]   On registration under rule 62.64, the petitioner shall forthwith serve a notice of the registration on the party against whom the decision was made in Form 62.65.

GENERAL NOTE.

62.65.1   For the history of this rule, see note 62.61.1.

"SERVE".

62.65.2   For methods of service, see Chap. 16, Pt. I.

Sist of enforcement under this Part

62.66   **62.66.**—[2](1)   Where it appears to the court that—

(a) the enforcement of the decision has been sisted (whether provisionally or otherwise) under the relevant instrument, or

(b) any application has been made under the relevant instrument which, if granted, might result in a sist of the enforcement of the award,

the court shall, or in the case referred to in sub-paragraph (b) may, sist the petition for such period as it thinks fit.

---

[1] Rule 62.65 inserted by S.I. 1996 No. 2168 (effective 23rd September 1996).
[2] Rule 62.66 inserted by S.I. 1996 No. 2168 (effective 23rd September 1996).

(2) Where the court has granted a warrant for registration under rule 62.63, the party against whom the decision was made may apply to the court for suspension or interdict of execution of the award.

(3) An application under paragraph (2) shall—

(a) be made on ground (a) or (b) of paragraph (1);

(b) notwithstanding rule 60.2 (form of applications for suspension), be made by note in the process of the petition under rule 62.62; and

(c) be accompanied by an affidavit stating the relevant facts.

GENERAL NOTE.

For the history of this rule, see note. 62.66.1   **62.66.1**
The relevant instrument may not provide for a sist, in which case this rule would not apply.

"SUSPENSION OR INTERDICT".

See Chap. 60.   **62.66.2**

"NOTE".

For applications by note, see r. 15.2.   **62.66.3**

EDF CONTRACTS.

There is no provision in the procedural rules on arbitration of contracts financed by the European   **62.66.4**
Development Fund (see r. 62.61(1)(a) and note 62.61.2) for sist of enforcement.

Part XI[1] – Registration and Enforcement of Judgments under Council Regulation (E.C.) No. 2201/2003 of 27th November 2003

Application and interpretation of this Part

62.67.—[2](1) This Part applies to the registration and enforcement of a judgment   **62.67**
under the Council Regulation.

(2) In this Part, unless the context otherwise requires—

"the Council Regulation" means Council Regulation (E.C.) No. 2201/2003 of 27th November 2003 on jurisdiction and the recognition and enforcement of judgments in matrimonial matters and matters of parental responsibility;

"judgment" includes an authentic instrument or enforceable agreement; and

"Member State" has the same meaning as in Article 2(3) of the Council Regulation.

GENERAL NOTE.

The Council Regulation No. 2201/2003 (new Brussels II) replaces Council Regulation No 1347/2000   **62.67.1**
(for which there was no special provision in the RCS 1994). It deals with jurisdiction as well as recognition and enforcement of judgments in matrimonial matters and matters of parental responsibility.

The new Council Regulation has effect from 1st March 2005. Proceedings started under C.R. No. 1347/2000 may continue under that Regulation.

Matrimonial matters and matters of parental responsibility with which the new Council Regulation is concerned are defined in art. 1 as (a) divorce, legal separation, annulment; (b) attribution, exercise, delegation, restriction or termination of parental responsibility (which includes custody, access, guardianship, curatorship and similar institutions, designation and functions of a person or body over a child's person or property or representing or assisting a child, placement in a foster family or institution, and protection of a child's property). It does *not* cover establishing or contesting a parent-child relationship, adoption or freeing for or revocation of adoption, names, emancipation, maintenance, trusts or succession, or measures as a result of criminal offences by a child.

The term "child" is not defined in the Regulation.

The Regulation applies to Member States of the E.U. except Denmark.

Chapter III of the Regulation (arts. 21-52) deals with recognition and enforcement. A judgment in a Member State will be recognised without special procedure, but application may be made for a decision

---

[1] Part XI and r. 62.67 inserted by S.S.I. 2005 No. 135 (effective 2nd March 2005).
[2] Part XI and r. 62.67 inserted by S.S.I. 2005 No. 135 (effective 2nd March 2005).

of a court in another Member State to be or not to be recognised: art. 21. A decision in relation to parental responsibility must be registered for enforcement in the UK, which is by petition: art. 28(2) and RCS 1994, r. 62.69.

Disapplication of certain rules to this Part

62.68   **62.68.**[1] The following rules shall not apply to an application under this Part:—

4.1(1) (printed form for petition),

14.4 (form of petitions),

14.5 (first order in petitions),

14.6 (period of notice for lodging answers),

14.7 (intimation and service of petitions), 14.9 (unopposed petitions).

Enforcement of judgments from another Member State

62.69   **62.69.**—[2](1) An application under Article 28 of the Council Regulation (enforceable judgments) shall be made by petition in Form 62.69.

  (2) There shall be produced with the petition—

    (a) an authentic copy of the judgment to be registered;

    (b) a certificate under Article 39 of the Council Regulation (standard forms of certificate);

    (c) where judgment has been given in absence (that is to say, in default of appearance)—

      (i) the original or a certified copy of the document which establishes that the party against whom judgment was given in absence was served with the document initiating proceedings or with an equivalent; or

      (ii) a document indicating that the party against whom the judgment was given in absence has accepted the judgment unequivocally;

    (d) where applicable, a document showing that the applicant is in receipt of legal aid in the country in which the judgment was given;

    (e) an affidavit stating—

      (i) an address within the jurisdiction of the court for service on or intimation to the petitioner;

      (ii) the name and address of the petitioner and his interest in the judgment;

      (iii) the name and date of birth of each child in respect of whom the judgment was made, the present whereabouts or suspected whereabouts of that child and the name of any person with whom he is alleged to be;

      (iv) the name and address of any other person with an interest in the judgment;

      (v) whether the judgment is already registered and, if so, where it is registered;

      (vi) details of any order known to the petitioner which affects a child in respect of whom the judgment was made and fulfils the conditions necessary for its recognition in Scotland.

  (3) Where the petitioner does not produce a document required by paragraph (2)(b) to (e), the court may—

    (a) fix a period within which that document is to be lodged;

    (b) accept an equivalent document; or

    (c) dispense with the requirement to produce the document.

---

[1] Rule 62.68 inserted by S.S.I. 2005 No. 135 (effective 2nd March 2005).

[2] Rule 62.69 inserted by S.S.I. 2005 No. 135 (effective 2nd March 2005).

GENERAL NOTE.

The only judgments to which art. 28 applies are those relating to parental responsibility. In the UK, such judgments from another Member State must be registered for enforcement before they can be enforced: art. 28(2). Registration is by petition: r. 62.69.

On the meaning of parental responsibility, see Art. 1 of the Regulation and note 62.67.1.

An address of the applicant for service in Scotland must be given or a representative ad litem appointed: art. 30(2).

62.69.1

"PETITION".

A petition is presented to the Outer House: r. 14.2(h). The petition must be in Form 62.9 in the official printed form (r. 4.1). The petition must be signed by counsel or other person having a right of audience: r. 4.2; and see r. 1.3(1) (definition of "counsel" and "other person having a right of audience") and note 1.3.4.

The petitioner must lodge the petition with the required steps of process (r. 4.4). A fee is payable on lodging the petition: see note 14.5.10.

On petitions generally, see Chap. 14.

62.69.2

PRODUCTIONS.

The documents referred to in r. 62.69(2)(a)-(c) are those required by art. 30(3). On productions and the lodging of them, see r. 4.5 and note 4.5.2.

62.69.3

"AFFIDAVIT".

The affidavit should be in the form of a statement of evidence written in the first person. The affidavit should contain the evidence of the deponent in support of the averments in the petition. In particular, the affidavit should deal with the matters listed in r. 62.69(2)(e).

An affidavit should be sworn and signed by the deponent before any person who may competently take an oath, whether in Scotland or any other country. In Scotland, such a person may include a notary public, justice of the peace, sheriff, or any judge. Where the affidavit is not in English, a duly certified translation should also be lodged.

See also the definition of affidavit in r. 1.3(1).

62.69.4

TRANSLATIONS OF JUDGMENTS.

A translation of a judgment not in English must be lodged with the petition with a certificate by the translator: r. 62.3.

62.69.5

Warrant for registration under the Council Regulation

62.70.—[1](1) The court shall, on being satisfied that the petition complies with the requirements of the Council Regulation, pronounce an interlocutor—

62.70

    (a)   granting warrant for the registration of the judgment; and

    (b)   where necessary, granting decree in accordance with Scots law.

  (2)   The interlocutor pronounced under paragraph (1) shall specify—

    (a)   the period within which an appeal mentioned in rule 62.74 (appeals under the Council Regulation) against the interlocutor may be made; and

    (b)   that the petitioner—

        (i)   may register the judgment under rule 62.72 (registration under the Council Regulation); and

        (ii)   may not proceed to execution until the expiry of the period for lodging such appeal or its disposal.

WARRANT FOR REGISTRATION.

The warrant will be for registration in the register of judgments in the Petition Department and in the Books of Council and Session for execution: see r. 67.72.

62.70.1

DECREE IN ACCORDANCE WITH SCOTS LAW.

This would be pronounced where the form of the foreign judgment is not suitable for a Scottish decree of registration.

62.70.2

PERIOD FOR MARKING APPEAL.

The period, for appeal by either party, is set out in r. 62.74(1).

62.70.3

---

[1] Rule 62.70 inserted by S.S.I 2005/135 (effective 2nd March 2005).

Intimation to the petitioner

62.71

62.71.[1] Where the court pronounces an interlocutor under rule 62.70(1) the Deputy Principal Clerk shall intimate such interlocutor to the petitioner by sending to his address for service in Scotland a certified copy of the interlocutor by registered post or the first class recorded delivery service.

Registration under the Council Regulation

62.72

62.72.—[2](1) Where the court pronounces an interlocutor under rule 62.70(1) granting warrant for registration, the Deputy Principal Clerk shall enter the judgment in the register of judgments, authentic instruments and court settlements kept in the Petition Department.

(2) On presentation by the petitioner to the Keeper of the Registers of—

(a) a certified copy of the interlocutor under rule 62.70(1) granting warrant for registration,

(b) an authentic copy of the judgment and any translation of it, and

(c) any certificate of currency conversion under rule 62.2(1)(b) for any order concerning costs and expenses of proceedings under the Council Regulation;

they shall be registered in the register of judgments of the Books of Council and Session.

(3) On registration under paragraph (2), the Keeper of the Registers of Scotland shall issue an extract of the registered document with a warrant for execution.

KEEPER OF THE REGISTERS.

62.72.1

This is the Keeper of the Registers of Scotland: r. 1.3(1). The address of the Keeper of the Registers is Meadowbank House, 153 London Road, Edinburgh EH8 7AU; tel. 0131-659 6111; fax 0131-459 1221; DX ED300.

"CERTIFIED COPY INTERLOCUTOR".

62.72.2

A copy of the interlocutor is typed by the agent and presented to the clerk of session in the Petition Department. The clerk checks it, certifies it as a true copy and stamps it with the court stamp.

"TRANSLATION".

62.72.3

A translation of a judgment not in English will have been lodged with the petition with a certificate by the translator: r. 62.3.

"CERTIFICATE OF CURRENCY CONVERSION".

62.72.4

The certificate should be obtained from the clerk of session and should be signed by him: r. 62.2(3); and see notes 62.2.4 and 62.2.5.

REGISTRATION FEE.

62.72.5

A fee will be payable to the Keeper of the Registers for registration and any extract: see the Fees in the Registers of Scotland Order 1995 [S.I. 1995 No. 1945].

"WARRANT FOR EXECUTION".

62.72.6

Registration for execution gives the holder a decree of registration which is in effect a decree of the Court of Session: Bell's *Comm.*, I, 4; *Taylor, Petr.* , 1931 S.L.T. 260, 261 per Lord Pitman); and, on the warrant inserted by the Keeper of the Registers or his deputy on an extract of a registered document, diligence may be executed against the debtor's moveable property under s. 3 of the Writs Execution (Scotland) Act 1877 as substituted by s. 87(4) of the Debtors (Scotland) Act 1987. Diligence against heritable property may be executed by inhibition on the grant of letters of inhibition (see Chap. 59) or by action of adjudication founding on the decree of registration.

---

[1] Rule 62.71 inserted by S.S.I. 2005 No. 135 (effective 2nd March 2005).
[2] Rule 62.72 inserted by S.S.I. 2005 No. 135 (effective 2nd March 2005).

Service of warrant for registration under the Council Regulation

62.73.[1] The petitioner shall serve a copy of the interlocutor under rule 62.70(1) granting warrant for registration of a judgment and notice in Form 62.73 on the person against whom enforcement is sought.

62.73

SERVICE.

For methods, see Chap. 16, Pt. I.

62.73.1

Appeals under the Council Regulation

62.74.—[2](1) An appeal under Article 33 (appeals against the enforcement decision) of the Council Regulation shall be made by motion—

62.74

    (a)   to the Lord Ordinary; and

    (b)   where the appeal is against the granting of warrant for registration under rule 62.70(1) within one month of service under rule 62.73 (service of warrant for registration under the Council Regulation) or within two months of such service where service was executed on a person domiciled in another Member State.

    (2) Where the respondent in any such appeal is domiciled furth of the United Kingdom—

    (a)   in relation to an appeal against the granting of warrant for registration under rule 62.70(1), intimation of the motion shall be made to the address for service of the respondent in Scotland;

    (b)   in relation to an appeal against a refusal to grant warrant for registration under rule 62.70(1), intimation of the motion shall be made in accordance with rule 16.2 (service furth of United Kingdom) or rule 16.5 (service where address of the person is not known), as the case may be.

GENERAL NOTE.

Art. 33 of the Council Regulation No. 2201/2003 provides for an appeal against a decision on the application for a declaration of enforceability under arts. 28 and 29.

The first appeal under the RCS 1994 is to the Lord Ordinary: r. 62.74(1)(a). There is a further appeal by reclaiming to the Inner House against the decision of the Lord Ordinary under r. 62.75.

An appeal against a declaration of enforceability must be lodged within one month (or two months if habitual residence is in another Member State) of service of the declaration of enforceability: art. 33(5). The declaration of enforceability referred to will be the interlocutor pronounced under r. 62.70.

62.74.1

Reclaiming under the Council Regulation

62.75.[3] Any party dissatisfied with the interlocutor of the Lord Ordinary in any appeal mentioned in rule 62.74 (appeals under the Council Regulation) may reclaim on a point of law against that interlocutor.

62.75

"RECLAIM".

For reclaiming, see Chap. 38.

The right of appeal under art. 33 of the Council Regulation No 2201/2003 is dealt with in r. 62.74. Reclaiming under r. 62.75 represents a further right of appeal. Do art. 33, and the time limits in art. 33(5), apply to reclaiming?

62.75.1

Recognition of judgments from another Member State

62.76.—[4](1) For the purpose of Article 21 of the Council Regulation (recognition of a judgment), an interlocutor pronounced under rule 62.70(1) (warrant for registration under the Council Regulation) shall imply recognition of the judgment so dealt with.

62.76

---

[1] Rule 62.73 inserted by S.S.I. 2005 No. 135 (effective 2nd March 2005).
[2] Rule 62.74 inserted by S.S.I. 2005 No. 135 (effective 2nd March 2005).
[3] Rule 62.75 inserted by S.S.I. 2005 No. 135 (effective 2nd March 2005).
[4] Rule 62.76 inserted by S.S.I. 2005 No. 135 (effective 2nd March 2005).

(2)   In an application under Article 21(3) of the Council Regulation for recognition of a judgment, rules 62.67 to 62.75 shall apply to such an application as they apply to an application under Article 28 of the Council Regulation (declarator of enforceability).

(3)   In an application under Article 21(3) of the Council Regulation for non-recognition of a judgment, the rules under this part shall apply to such an application as they apply to an application under Article 28 of the Council Regulation (declarator of enforceability) subject to the following provisions—

(a)   where the application relies on grounds under Article 22(b) or 23(c) of the Council Regulation (judgment given in default of appearance) for the judgment not to be recognised, it shall not be necessary to produce documents required by rule 62.69(2)(c) (document establishing service or acceptance of judgment); and

(b)[1]   rule 62.69(2)(b) (certificate under Article 39 of the Council Regulation) shall not apply.

GENERAL NOTE.

62.76.1   Under art. 21(1) of the Council Regulation No. 2201/2003, a judgement in a Member State is to be recognised without any special procedure being required. Notwithstanding that, an interested party may apply to a court for a decision that a judgment be, or not be, recognised: art. 21(3). For a judgment relating to parental responsibility to be enforced, however, it must be registered for enforcement, for which an application to the court is required: arts. 28 and 29 and R.C.S. 1994, r. 62.69.

Rule 62.76 states that a warrant for registration for enforcement under r. 62.70 (in respect of an application under r. 62.69) implies recognition for the purposes of art. 21. This no doubt refers to, and dispenses with the need for, an application for recognition under art. 21(3); although, of course, by virtue of art. 21(1) the judgment must automatically be recognised (while not automatically enforceable).

APPLICATIONS FOR RECOGNITION OR NON-RECOGNITION OF A JUDGMENT.

62.76.2   Since a judgment to which the Council Regulation No. 2201/2003 given in another Member State must be recognised, one might wonder why it would be necessary to apply for recognition as distinct from non-recognition. One situation, perhaps, would be where it is necessary to "convert" the foreign judgment into an equivalent decree known to Scots law.

Cancellation of registration under the Council Regulation

62.77   **62.77.**[2]   Where an interlocutor under rule 62.70(1) (warrant for registration under the Council Regulation) is recalled and registration under rule 62.72(2) (registration under the Council Regulation) is ordered to be cancelled after an appeal under Article 33 of the Council Regulation (appeal against decision on enforceability) a certificate to that effect by the Deputy Principal Clerk shall be sufficient warrant to the Keeper of the Registers to cancel the registration and return the judgment, certificate or other documents to the person who applied for registration.

Recognition and Enforcement in another Member State of Court of Session judgments etc.

62.78   **62.78.**—[3,][4](1)   Where a person seeks to apply under the Council Regulation for recognition or enforcement in another Member State of a judgment given by the court, he shall apply by letter to the Deputy Principal Clerk for—

(a)   a certificate under Article 39 of the Council Regulation (certificates concerning judgments in matrimonial matters or on matters of parental responsibility);

(b)   a certified copy of the judgment; and

(c)   if required, a certified copy of the opinion of the court.

---

[1] Rule 62.76(3)(b) substituted by S.S.I. 2010 No. 417 (effective 1st January 2011).
[2] Rule 62.77 inserted by S.S.I. 2005 No. 135 (effective 2nd March 2005).
[3] Rule 62.78 inserted by S.S.I. 2005 No. 135 (effective 2nd March 2005).
[4] Rule 62.78 amended by S.S.I. 2016 No. 242 (effective 3rd October 2016).

(2) If the application is for a certificate concerning a judgment on parental responsibility, the Deputy Principal Clerk shall not issue a certificate under paragraph (1)(a) above unless there is produced to him an execution of service of the judgment on the person against whom it is sought to be enforced.

(3) Where a judgment granting rights of access delivered by the Court of Session acquires a cross-border character after the judgment has been delivered and a party seeks to enforce the judgment in another Member State, he shall apply by letter to the Deputy Principal Clerk for—

(a) a certificate under Article 41 of the Council Regulation (certificate concerning rights of access); and

(b) a certified copy of the judgment.

"LETTER TO THE DEPUTY PRINCIPAL CLERK".

The address and telephone number, etc., are: The Deputy Principal Clerk of Session, Court of Session, 2 Parliament Square, Edinburgh EH1 1RQ; tel. + 44 (0)131- 225 2595; fax +44 (0)131 225 8213; DX ED306.   **62.78.1**

"CERTIFICATE UNDER ARTICLE 39".

This is a document which gives basic details of the case.   **62.78.2**

"CROSS-BORDER CHARACTER".

The English version of art. 41(3) refers to the situation of rights of access acquiring a cross-border character after judgment has been issued. A certificate under art. 41 will be issued at the request of a party. (If the case involves a "cross-border situation" at the time of the judgment, the certificate will be issued automatically.)   **62.78.3**

"CERTIFICATE UNDER ARTICLE 41".

This is a document which gives basic details of the case.   **62.78.4**

Rectification of certificates under Articles 41 and 42 of the Council Regulation

62.79.[1] Where a party seeks rectification of a certificate issued under Article 41 or 42 of the Council Regulation (certificate concerning rights of access or return of a child) he shall apply by letter to the Deputy Principal Clerk stating the details of the certificate that are to be rectified.   **62.79**

GENERAL NOTE.

Rectification of certificates is provided for in art. 43 of the Council Regulation 2201/2003.   **62.79.1**

"LETTER TO THE DEPUTY PRINCIPAL CLERK".

The address and telephone number, etc., are: The Deputy Principal Clerk of Session, Court of Session, 2 Parliament Square, Edinburgh EH1 1RQ; tel. +44 (0)131- 225 2595; fax +44 (0)131 225 8213; DX ED306.   **62.79.2**

Practical arrangements for the exercise of rights of access

62.80.—[2](1) An application by a party having an enforceable judgment granting a right of access, that has been certified under Article 41 of the Council Regulation or registered for enforcement, seeking an order making practical arrangements for organising the exercise of rights of access under Article 48 of the Council Regulation, shall be made by petition.   **62.80**

(2) There shall be produced with the petition—

(a) an authentic copy of the judgment;

(b) any certificate under Article 41 of the Council Regulation;

(c) any extract of the registered judgment with a warrant for execution; and

(d) where applicable, a document showing that the applicant is in receipt of legal aid in the country where the judgment was given.

---

[1] Rule 62.79 inserted by S.S.I. 2005 No. 135 (effective 2nd March 2005).

[2] Rule 62.80 inserted by S.S.I. 2005 No. 135 (effective 2nd March 2005).

GENERAL NOTE.

62.80.1
Art. 48 of the Council Regulation No. 2201/2003 provides for practical arrangements for organising rights of access to be made by the courts in the country for enforcement where they have not, or not sufficiently, been made in the original judgment.

"PETITION".

62.80.2
A petition is presented to the Outer House: r. 14.2(h). The petition must be in Form 86.3 in the official printed form (r. 4.1). The petition must be signed by counsel or other person having a right of audience: r. 4.2; and see r. 1.3(1) (definition of "counsel" and "other person having a right of audience") and note 1.3.4.

The petitioner must lodge the petition with the required steps of process (r. 4.4). A fee is payable on lodging the petition: see note 14.5.10.

On petitions generally, see Chap. 14

PRODUCTIONS.

62.80.3
The documents referred to in r. 62.69(2)(a)-(c) are those required by art. 30(3). On productions and the lodging of them, see r. 4.5 and note 4.5.2.

Part XII[1] – European Enforcement Orders

Interpretation and application of this Part

62.81
62.81.—[2](1) In this Part—

> "the Regulation" means Regulation (EC) No. 805/2004 of the European Parliament and of the Council of 21 April 2004 creating a European Enforcement Order for uncontested claims;
>
> "Council Regulation (EC) No. 44/2001[3]" means Council Regulation (EC) No. 44/2001 of 22 December 2000 on jurisdiction and the recognition and enforcement of judgments in civil and commercial matters as amended from time to time to time and as applied by the Agreement of 19th October 2005 between the European Community and the Kingdom of Denmark on jurisdiction and the recognition and enforcement of judgments in civil and commercial matters;
>
> "authentic instrument" has the same meaning as in Article 4(3) of the Regulation;
>
> "court settlement" means a settlement where the debtor has expressly agreed to a claim within the meaning of Article 4(2) of the Regulation by admission or by means of a settlement which has been approved by a court or concluded before a court in the course of proceedings; and
>
> "judgment" has the same meaning as in Article 4(1) of the Regulation;
>
> "Member State of origin" has the same meaning as in Article 4(4) of the Regulation.

(3) This Part applies to judgments, court settlements and authentic instruments on uncontested claims certified as European Enforcement Orders under the Regulation.

(4) Subject to rule 62.84 (certification of authentic instrument), rule 62.87 (rectification or withdrawal of certificate), rule 62.88(1) (application for registration), and rule 62.88(3) (application for refusal, stay or limitation of enforcement), an application shall be made to the Deputy Principal Clerk by letter.

(5) Rule 62.1 shall not apply to a petition under rule 62.88(3) of this Part (application for refusal, stay or limitation of enforcement).

---

[1] Part XII and r. 62.81 inserted by S.S.I. 2005 No. 521 (effective 21st October 2005).
[2] Part XII and r. 62.81 inserted by S.S.I. 2005 No. 521 (effective 21st October 2005).
[3] Rule 62.81(1) amended by S.S.I. 2007 No. 350 (effective 1st July 2007) and by S.S.I. 2010 No. 205 (effective 15th June 2010).

GENERAL NOTE.

The EU Regulation (EC) No. 805/2004 of 21st April 2004 provides for orders in uncontested claims made in one Member State to be enforced in another Member State. It does not apply, however, to Denmark.

It applies in civil and commercial matters except those relating to—

- revenue, customs, administrative matters or liability of the State in the exercise of State authority;
- status or legal capacity of natural persons, rights in property arising out of matrimonial relationship, wills and succession;
- bankruptcy, winding up of companies or other legal persons, judicial arrangements, compositions etc;
- social security;
- arbitration.

A claim is uncontested if—

- the debtor expressly agreed by admission or by a settlement approved by a court or concluded before a court in course of proceedings;
- the debtor has never objected to it, incompliance with relevant procedural requirements in the course of court proceedings;
- the debtor has not appeared or been represented at a court hearing regarding the claim after having initially objected to the claim in the course of the court proceedings, provided that it amounts to tacit admission of the claim or facts alleged by the creditor;
- the debtor has expressly agreed to it in an authentic instrument.

Certification of decree in absence or decree by default

62.82.—[1](1) An application for certification under Article 6(1) (judgment on uncontested claim) or Article 8 (partial European Enforcement Order) of the Regulation shall be accompanied by an affidavit—

- (a) verifying that the judgment was of an uncontested claim within the meaning of Article 3(1)(b) or (c) of the Regulation and that the court proceedings met the requirements set out in Chapter III of the Regulation (minimum standards for uncontested claims procedures);
- (b) providing the information required by the form of certificate in Annex I to the Regulation (European Enforcement Order—judgment);
- (c) verifying that the judgment is enforceable in Scotland, and does not conflict with the rules of jurisdiction laid down in Articles 3 and 6 of Chapter II of Council Regulation (EC) No. 44/2001; and
- (d) stating that where the debtor was a consumer and the judgment related to a contract concluded by the debtor for a purpose outside his trade or profession the judgment was given in the Member State of the debtors domicile within the meaning of Article 59 of Council Regulation (EC) No. 44/2001.

(2) The Deputy Principal Clerk shall not issue a certificate under paragraph (1) unless there is produced to him an execution of service of the judgment on the person against whom it is sought to be enforced.

"AFFIDAVIT".

On affidavits, see r. 1.3(2) and note 1.3.7.

Certification of court settlement

62.83.[2] An application for certification under Article 24 of the Regulation (court settlement) shall be accompanied by an affidavit—

- (a) verifying that the debtor admitted the claim or entered into a settlement

---

[1] Rule 62.82 inserted by S.S.I. 2005 No. 521 (effective 21st October 2005).
[2] Rule 62.83 inserted by S.S.I. 2005 No. 521 (effective 21st October 2005).

that was approved by the court or concluded before the court in the course of proceedings and is enforceable in Scotland;

    (b) verifying that the settlement concerned a claim within the meaning of Article 4(2) of the Regulation (payment of money); and

    (c) providing the information required by the form of certificate in Annex II to the Regulation (European Enforcement Order—court settlement).

"AFFIDAVIT".

62.83.1   On affidavits, see r. 1.3(2) and note 1.3.7.

Certification of authentic instrument

62.84   **62.84.**[1] An application for certification under Article 25(1) of the Regulation (authentic instrument) shall be by letter to the Keeper of the Registers and shall be accompanied by an affidavit—

    (a) verifying that the authentic instrument concerns a claim within the meaning of Article 4(2) of the Regulation (payment of money);

    (b) verifying that the authentic instrument is enforceable in Scotland; and

    (c) providing the information required by the form of certificate in Annex III to the Regulation (European Enforcement Order— authentic instrument).

KEEPER OF THE REGISTERS.

62.84.1   This is the Keeper of the Registers of Scotland: r. 1.3(1). The address of the Keeper of the Registers is Meadowbank House, 153 London Road, Edinburgh EH8 7AU; tel. 0131-659 6111; fax 0131-459 1221; DX ED300.

"AFFIDAVIT".

62.84.2   On affidavits, see r. 1.3(2) and note 1.3.7.

Certificate of lack or limitation of enforceability

62.85   **62.85.**[2] An application for certification under Article 6(2) of the Regulation (lack or limitation of enforceability) shall be accompanied by an affidavit—

    (a) stating the date on which the judgment, court settlement or authentic instrument was certified as a European Enforcement Order; and

    (b) providing the information required by the form of certificate in Annex IV to the Regulation (certificate of lack or limitation of enforceability).

"AFFIDAVIT".

62.85.1   On affidavits, see r. 1.3(2) and note 1.3.7.

Replacement certificate

62.86   **62.86.**[3] An application under Article 6(3) of the Regulation (replacement certificate) shall be accompanied by an affidavit providing the information required by the form of certificate in Annex v. to the Regulation (European Enforcement Order—replacement certificate following a challenge).

"AFFIDAVIT".

62.86.1   On affidavits, see r. 1.3(2) and note 1.3.7.

Rectification or withdrawal of certificate

62.87   **62.87.**[4] An application under Article 10(1) of the Regulation (rectification or withdrawal of European Enforcement Order certificate) shall be made in the form

---

[1] Rule 62.84 inserted by S.S.I. 2005 No. 521 (effective 21st October 2005).
[2] Rule 62.85 inserted by S.S.I. 2005 No. 521 (effective 21st October 2005).
[3] Rule 62.86 inserted by S.S.I. 2005 No. 521 (effective 21st October 2005).
[4] Rule 62.87 inserted by S.S.I. 2005 No. 521 (effective 21st October 2005).

set out in Annex VI to the Regulation and, subject to rule 62.1 (disapplication of certain rules in Chapter 14 to this Chapter), shall be treated as a petition.

"PETITION".

On petitions, see Chap. 14.

62.87.1

Registration for enforcement

62.88.—[1](1) An application for registration for enforcement of a judgment, court settlement or authentic instrument certified as a European Enforcement Order shall be made by presenting to the Keeper of the Registers—

62.88

    (a)   a certificate under Article 20(2)(b) of the Regulation (European Enforcement Order certificate);

    (b)   a copy of the judgment, court settlement, or authentic instrument in accordance with Article 20(2)(a) of the Regulation (enforcement procedure);

    (c)   where the certificate under Article 20(2)(b) is in a language other than English, a translation of the certificate into English certified as correct by the translator and stating the full name, address and qualification of the translator; and

    (d)[2] where the European Enforcement Order is expressed in a currency other than sterling, a certificate issued by a competent authority of a Member State of origin of the sterling equivalent of—

        (i)   the principal sum,

        (ii) interest, and

        (iii) expenses,

contained in the judgment, court settlement or authentic instrument, as the case may be, at the rate of exchange prevailing at a date specified under the law of the Member State of origin for obtaining currency conversion in judicial matters.

    (2) On presentation of the documents mentioned in sub-paragraphs (a) to (d) of paragraph (1) the Keeper of the Registers shall—

    (a)   register the certificate in the register of judgments of the Books of Council and Session; and

    (b)   issue an extract of the certificate with a warrant for execution.

    (3) An application under—

    (a)   Article 21 of the Regulation (refusal of enforcement); or

    (b)   Article 23 of the Regulation (stay or limitation of enforcement), shall be made by petition.

"KEEPER OF THE REGISTERS".

See note 62.84.1.

62.88.1

"PETITION".

A petition is presented to the Outer House: r. 14.2(h). The petition must be in Form 86.3 in the official printed form (r. 4.1). The petition must be signed by counsel or other person having a right of audience: r. 4.2; and see r. 1.3(1) (definition of "counsel" and "other person having a right of audience") and note 1.3.4.

62.88.2

The petitioner must lodge the petition with the required steps of process (r. 4.4). A fee is payable on lodging the petition: see note 14.5.10.

On petitions generally, see Chap. 14.

---

[1] Rule 62.88 inserted by S.S.I. 2005 No. 521 (effective 21st October 2005).
[2] Rule 62.88(4) substituted by S.S.I. 2010 No. 205 (effective 15th June 2010).

Refusal, stay or limitation of enforcement

62.89 **62.89.**[1] An interlocutor certified by the Deputy Principal Clerk shall be sufficient warrant to the Keeper of the Registers—

(a) where enforcement is refused under rule 62.88(3)(a), to cancel the registration of the certificate of the European Enforcement Order and return the judgment, certificate or other documents to the person who sought registration; or

(b) where enforcement is stayed or limited under rule 62.88(3)(b), to—

    (i) register the interlocutor in the register of judgements of the Books of Council and Session; and

    (ii) issue an extract of the interlocutor.

Part XIII[2] – Uncitral Model Law on Cross-Border Insolvency

Application and interpretation of this Part

62.90 **62.90.**—[3](1) This Part applies to applications under the Model Law and applications under the Scottish Provisions.

(2) In this Part—

"application for an interim remedy" means an application under article 19 of the Model Law for an interim remedy by a foreign representative;

"former representative" means a foreign representative who has died or who for any other reason has ceased to be the foreign representative in the foreign proceeding in relation to the debtor;

"main proceeding" means proceedings opened in accordance with Article 3(1) of the EC Insolvency Regulation and falling within the definition of insolvency proceedings in Article 2(a) of the EC Insolvency Regulation;

"the Model Law" means the UNCITRAL Model Law on Cross-Border Insolvency as set out in Schedule 1 to the Cross-Border Insolvency Regulations 2006;

"modification or termination order" means an order by the court pursuant to its powers under the Model Law modifying or terminating recognition of a foreign proceeding, the restraint, sist and suspension referred to in article 20(1) of the Model Law or any part of it or any remedy granted under article 19 or 21 of the Model Law;

"recognition application" means an application by a foreign representative in accordance with article 15 of the Model Law for an order recognising the foreign proceeding in which he has been appointed;

"recognition order" means an order by the court recognising a proceeding as a foreign main proceeding or a foreign non-main proceeding, as appropriate;

"review application" means an application to the court for a modification or termination order;

"the Scottish Provisions" are the provisions of Schedule 3 to the Cross-Border Insolvency Regulations 2006; and

words and phrases defined in the Model Law have the same meaning when used in this Part.

---

[1] Rule 62.88 inserted by S.S.I. 2005 No. 521 (effective 21st October 2005).
[2] Part XIII and r. 62.90 inserted by S.S.I. 2006 No. 199 (effective 6th April 2006).
[3] Part XIII and r. 62.90 inserted by S.S.I. 2006 No. 199 (effective 6th April 2006).

(3)[1] References in this Part to a debtor who is of interest to the Financial Conduct Authority or the Prudential Regulation Authority are references to a debtor who—

    (a)   is, or has been, an authorised person within the meaning of section 31 of the Financial Services and Markets Act 2000 (authorised persons);

    (b)   is, or has been, an appointed representative within the meaning of section 39 (exemption of appointed representatives) of that Act; or

    (c)   is carrying on, or has carried on, a regulated activity in contravention of the general prohibition.

(4) In paragraph (3) "the general prohibition" has the meaning given by section 19 of the Financial Services and Markets Act 2000 and the reference to "regulated activity" shall be construed in accordance with—

    (a)   section 22 of that Act (classes of regulated activity and categories of investment);

    (b)   any relevant order under that section; and

    (c)   Schedule 2 to that Act (regulated activities).

GENERAL NOTE.

The UNCITRAL Model Law on Cross-Border Insolvency is set out in Sched. 1 to the Cross-Border Insolvency Regulations 2006 [S.I. 2006 No. 1030].

62.90.1

General

62.91.—[2](1) Rule 62.1 (disapplication of certain rules to Chapter 62) shall not apply to an application to which this Part relates.

62.91

(2) Unless otherwise specified in this Part, an application under the Model Law or the Scottish Provisions shall be made by petition.

(3) For the purposes of the application of rule 14.5(1) (first order for intimation, service and advertisement) to a petition under this Part, where necessary, the petitioner shall seek an order for service of the petition on:—

    (a)   the foreign representative;

    (b)   the debtor;

    (c)   any British insolvency officeholder acting in relation to the debtor;

    (d)   any person appointed an administrative receiver of the debtor or as a receiver or manager of the property of the debtor in Scotland;

    (e)[3]   any member State insolvency practitioner who has been appointed in main proceedings in relation to the debtor;

    (f)   any foreign representative who has been appointed in any other foreign proceeding regarding the debtor;

    (g)   if there is pending in Scotland a petition for the winding up or sequestration of the debtor, the petitioner in those proceedings;

    (h)   any person who is or may be entitled to appoint an administrator of the debtor under paragraph 14 of Schedule B1 to the Insolvency Act 1986 (appointment of administrator by holder of qualifying floating charge); and

    (i)[4]   the Financial Conduct Authority or the Prudential Regulation Authority if the debtor is a debtor who is of interest to that Authority.

(4) On the making of—

---

[1] As amended by the Financial Services Act 2012 (Consequential Amendments and Transitional Provisions) Order 2013 (SI 2013/472) Sch.2 para.10 (effective 1st April 2013).

[2] Rule 62.91 inserted by S.S.I. 2006 No. 199 (effective 6th April 2006).

[3] Rule 62.91(3)(e) amended by S.S.I. 2017 No. 202 r. 3(2) (effective 26th June 2017: amendment has effect subject to savings specified in S.S.I. 2017 No. 202 r. 6).

[4] As amended by the Financial Services Act 2012 (Consequential Amendments and Transitional Provisions) Order 2013 (SI 2013/472) Sch. 2 para.10 (effective 1st April 2013).

   (a) a recognition order;

   (b) an order granting an interim remedy under article 19 of the Model Law;

   (c) an order granting a remedy under article 21 of the Model Law;

   (d) an order confirming the status of a replacement foreign representative; or

   (e) a modification or termination order,

the Deputy Principal Clerk shall send a certified copy of the interlocutor to the foreign representative.

"PETITION".

62.91.1   A petition is presented to the Outer House: r.14.2(h). The petition must be in Form 86.3 in the official printed form (r.4.1). The petition must be signed by counsel or other person having a right of audience: r.4.2; and see r.1.3(1) (definition of "counsel" and "other person having a right of audience") and note 1.3.4.

    The petitioner must lodge the petition with the required steps of process (r.4.4). A fee is payable on lodging the petition: see note 14.5.10.

    On petitions generally, see Chap. 14.

"SEND".

62.91.2   This includes deliver: r. 1.3(1) (definition of "send").

Recognition application

62.92   **62.92.**—[1](1) A petition containing a recognition application shall include averments as to—

   (a) the name of the applicant and his address for service in Scotland;

   (b) the name of the debtor in respect of which the foreign proceeding is taking place;

   (c) the name or names in which the debtor carries on business in the country where the foreign proceeding is taking place and in this country, if other than the name given under sub-paragraph (b);

   (d) the principal or last known place of business of the debtor in Great Britain (if any) and, in the case of an individual, his last known place of residence in Great Britain, (if any);

   (e)[2] any registered number allocated to the debtor under the Companies Act 2006;

   (f) the foreign proceeding in respect of which recognition is applied for, including the country in which it is taking place and the nature of the proceeding;

   (g) whether the foreign proceeding is a proceeding within the meaning of article 2(i) of the Model Law;

   (h) whether the applicant is a foreign representative within the meaning of article 2(j) of the Model Law;

   (i) the address of the debtor's centre of main interests and, if different, the address of its registered office or habitual residence as appropriate;

   (j) if the debtor does not have its centre of main interests in the country where the foreign proceeding is taking place, whether the debtor has an establishment within the meaning of article 2(e) of the Model Law in that country, and if so, its address.

  (2) There shall be lodged with the petition—

   (a) an affidavit sworn by the foreign representative as to the matters averred under paragraph (1);

   (b) the evidence and statement required under article 15(2) and (3) respectively of the Model Law;

[1] Rule 62.92 inserted by S.S.I. 2006 No. 199 (effective 6th April 2006).
[2] Rule 62.92(1)(e) substituted by S.S.I. 2009 No. 450 (effective 1st January 2010).

(c)   any other evidence which in the opinion of the applicant will assist the court in deciding whether the proceeding in respect of which the application is made is a foreign proceeding within the meaning of article 2(i) of the Model Law and whether the applicant is a foreign representative within the meaning of article 2(j) of the Model Law; and

(d)   evidence that the debtor has its centre of main interests or an establishment, as the case may be, within the country where the foreign proceeding is taking place.

(3)   The affidavit to be lodged under paragraph (2)(a) shall state whether, in the opinion of the applicant, the EC Insolvency Regulation applies to any of the proceedings identified in accordance with article 15(3) of the Model Law and, if so, whether those proceedings are main proceedings, secondary proceedings or territorial proceedings.

(4)   Any subsequent information required to be given to the court by the foreign representative under article 18 of the Model Law shall be given by amendment of the petition.

"LODGED".

See rr. 4.4 and 4.5.   **62.92.1**

"AFFIDAVIT".

See r. 1.3(2) and note 1.3.7.   **62.92.2**

Application for interim remedy

62.93.—[1](1)   An application for an interim remedy shall be made by note in   **62.93**
process.

(2)   There shall be lodged with the note an affidavit sworn by the foreign representative stating—

(a)   the grounds on which it is proposed that the interim remedy applied for should be granted;

(b)   the details of any proceeding under British insolvency law taking place in relation to the debtor;

(c)   whether to the foreign representative's knowledge, an administrative receiver or receiver or manager of the debtor's property is acting in relation to the debtor;

(d)   an estimate of the assets of the debtor in Scotland in respect of which the remedy is applied for;

(e)   all other matters that would in the opinion of the foreign representative assist the court in deciding whether or not to grant the remedy applied for, including whether, to the best of the knowledge and belief of the foreign representative, the interests of the debtor's creditors (including any secured creditors or parties to hire-purchase agreements) and any other interested parties, including if appropriate the debtor, are adequately protected; and

(f)   whether to the best of the foreign representative's knowledge and belief, the grant of any of the remedy applied for would interfere with the administration of the foreign main proceeding.

"NOTE".

See r. 15.2.   **62.93.1**

---

[1] Rule 62.93 inserted by S.S.I. 2006 No. 199 (effective 6th April 2006).

"affidavit".

62.93.2   See r. 1.3(2) and note 1.3.7.

Application for remedy

62.94   **62.94.**—[1](1) An application under article 21 of the Model Law for a remedy shall be made by note in process.

(2) There shall be lodged with the note an affidavit sworn by the foreign representative stating—

    (a)   the grounds on which it is proposed that the remedy applied for should be granted;

    (b)   an estimate of the value of the assets of the debtor in Scotland in respect of which the remedy is requested;

    (c)   in the case of an application by a foreign representative who is or believes that he is a representative of a foreign non-main proceeding, the reasons why the applicant believes that the remedy relates to assets that, under the law of Great Britain, should be administered in the foreign non-main proceeding or concerns information required in that proceeding; and

    (d)   all other matters that would in the opinion of the foreign representative assist the court in deciding whether or not it is appropriate to grant the remedy requested, including whether, to the best of the knowledge and belief of the foreign representative, the interests of the debtor's creditors (including any secured creditors or parties to hire-purchase agreements) and any other interested parties, including if appropriate the debtor, are adequately protected.

"note".

62.94.1   See r. 15.2.

"lodged".

62.94.2   See rr. 4.4 and 4.5.

"affidavit".

62.94.3   See r. 1.3(2) and note 1.3.7.

Application for confirmation of status of replacement foreign representative

62.95   **62.95.**—[2](1) An application under paragraph 2(3) of the Scottish Provisions for an order confirming the status of a replacement foreign representative shall be made by note in process.

(2) The note shall include averments as to—

    (a)   the name of the replacement foreign representative and his address for service within Scotland;

    (b)   the circumstances in which the former foreign representative ceased to be foreign representative in the foreign proceeding in relation to the debtor (including the date on which he ceased to be the foreign representative);

    (c)   his own appointment as replacement foreign representative in the foreign proceeding (including the date of that appointment).

(3) There shall be lodged with the note—

    (a)   an affidavit sworn by the foreign representative as to the matters averred under paragraph (2);

    (b)   a certificate from the foreign court affirming—

---

[1] Rule 62.94 inserted by S.S.I. 2006 No. 199 (effective 6th April 2006).
[2] Rule 62.95 inserted by S.S.I. 2006 No. 199 (effective 6th April 2006).

      (i)   the cessation of the appointment of the former foreign representa-tive as foreign representative, and

      (ii) the appointment of the applicant as the foreign representative in the foreign proceeding, or

(c)   in the absence of such a certificate, any other evidence acceptable to the court of the matters referred to in sub-paragraph (a).

"note".

See r. 15.2.   **62.95.1**

"lodged".

See rr. 4.4 and 4.5.   **62.95.2**

"affidavit".

See r. 1.3(2) and note 1.3.7.   **62.95.3**

Review application

62.96.—[1](1) A review application shall be made by note in process.   **62.96**

(2) There shall be lodged with the note an affidavit sworn by the applicant as to—

(a)   the grounds on which it is proposed that the remedy applied for should be granted; and

(b)   all other matters that would in the opinion of the applicant assist the court in deciding whether or not it is appropriate to grant the remedy requested, including whether, to the best of the knowledge and belief of the applicant, the interests of the debtor's creditors (including any secured creditors or parties to hire-purchase agreements) and any other interested parties, including if appropriate the debtor, are adequately protected.

"note".

See r. 15.2.   **62.96.1**

"lodged".

See rr. 4.4 and 4.5.   **62.96.2**

"affidavit".

See r. 1.3(2) and note 1.3.7.   **62.96.3**

Part XIV[2] – Parental Responsibility and Measures for the Protection of Children

Application and interpretation of this Part

62.97.—[3](1) This Part applies to the registration and enforcement of a measure   **62.97** under Article 24 or Article 26 of the 1996 Convention.

(2) In this Part—

"the 1996 Convention" means the Convention on Jurisdiction, Applicable Law, Recognition, Enforcement and Co-operation in respect of Parental Responsi-bility and Measures for the Protection of Children, signed at The Hague on 19th October 1996;

"Contracting State" means a state party to the 1996 Convention.

General note.

The Parental Responsibility and Measures for the Protection of Children (International Obligations)   **62.97.1** (Scotland) Regulations 2010 [S.S.I. 2010 No. 213] implements in Scotland the 1996 Hague Convention on Jurisdiction, Applicable Law, Recognition, Enforcement and Co-operation in respect of Parental

---

[1] Rule 62.96 inserted by S.S.I. 2006 No. 199 (effective 6th April 2006).
[2] Part XIV and r. 62.97 inserted by S.S.I. 2011 No. 190 (effective 1st November 2012).
[3] Part XIV and r. 62.97 inserted by S.S.I. 2011 No. 190 (effective 1st November 2012).

Responsibility and Measures for the Protection of Children. For example, temporary measures ordered by a judge under the 1980 Convention on International Child Abduction can be made more effective by those orders being made enforceable until the authorities in which the child is to be returned are able to put in place any necessary protection measures.

The 2010 Regulations and r. 67.97 come into force on the date that the 1996 Convention enters into force in the U.K. which date will be notified in the Edinburgh and London Gazettes.

Enforcement, recognition or non-recognition of measures from a Contracting State

62.98

62.98.—[1](1)   An application—

(a)   under Article 24 of the 1996 Convention for recognition or non-recognition of a measure taken in a Contracting State other than the United Kingdom; or

(b)   under Article 26 of the 1996 Convention for enforcement of a measure taken in a Contracting State other than the United Kingdom,

shall be made by petition in Form 62.98.

(2)   The petition shall include averments on the matters outlined at Article 23(2) of the 1996 Convention (grounds for refusal of recognition).

(3)   There shall be produced with the petition an authentic copy of any judgment or other document which outlines the measure to be registered.

(4)   The court shall, on being satisfied that the petition complies with the requirements of the 1996 Convention, pronounce an interlocutor—

(a)   granting warrant for the registration of the measure; and

(b)   where necessary, granting decree in accordance with Scots law.

(5)   The interlocutor pronounced under paragraph (4) shall specify that the petitioner may register the measure under rule 62.100 (registration under the 1996 Convention).

"PETITION".

62.98.1

A petition is presented to the Outer House: r. 14.2(h). The petition must be in Form 14.4 in the official printed form: rr. 4.1 and 14.4. The petition must be signed by counsel or other person having a right of audience: r. 4.2; and see r. 1.3(1) (definition of "counsel" and "other person having a right of audience") and note 1.3.4.

The petitioner must lodge the petition with the required steps of process: r. 4.4. A fee is payable on lodging the petition: see note 14.5.10.

On petitions generally, see Chap. 14.

Intimation to the petitioner

62.99

62.99.—[2]   Where the court pronounces an interlocutor under rule 62.98(4) the Deputy Principal Clerk shall intimate such interlocutor to the petitioner, by sending to his address for service in Scotland a certified copy of the interlocutor by registered post or the first class recorded delivery service.

Registration under the 1996 Convention

62.100

62.100.—[3](1)   Where the court pronounces an interlocutor under rule 62.98(4) granting warrant for registration, the Deputy Principal Clerk shall enter the measure in the register of judgments, authentic instruments and court settlements kept in the Petition Department.

(2)   On presentation by the petitioner to the Keeper of the Registers of—

(a)   a certified copy of the interlocutor under rule 62.98(4) granting warrant for registration,

(b)   an authentic copy of any judgment or other document which outlines the measure to be registered and any translation of such a document,

---

[1] Rule 62.98 inserted by S.S.I. 2011 No. 190 (effective 1st November 2012).
[2] Rule 62.99 inserted by S.S.I. 2011 No. 190 (effective 1st November 2012).
[3] Rule 62.100 inserted by S.S.I. 2011 No. 190 (effective 1st November 2012).

they shall be registered in the register of judgments in the Books of Council and Session.

(3) On registration under paragraph (2), the Keeper of the Registers shall issue an extract of the registered document with a warrant for execution.

Service of warrant for registration under the 1996 Convention

62.101.—[1] The petitioner shall serve a copy of the interlocutor under rule 62.98(4) granting warrant for registration of a judgment and notice in Form 62.101 on the person against whom enforcement is sought.

"SERVE".

For service, see Chap. 16.

62.101

62.101.1

PART XV

ELECTRONIC SIGNING AND TRANSMISSION OF CERTAIN DOCUMENTS

Electronic signing and transmission of certain documents

62.102.— [Inserted by the Coronavirus (Scotland) (No. 2) Act 2020 (asp 10) Sched. 4(3) para. 4(2) (effective 27th May 2020) which expired on 31st March 2022.]

62.102

---

[1] Rule 62.101 inserted by S.S.I. 2011 No. 190 (effective 1st November 2012).

CHAPTER 63 APPLICATIONS RELATING TO TRUSTS

Chapter 63

Applications Relating to Trusts

Part I – Variation or Revocation of Trusts

Interpretation of this Part

63.1. In this Part, "the Act of 1961" means the Trusts (Scotland) Act 1961.

63.1

Form of petitions under section 1(4) of the Act of 1961

63.2. In a petition under section 1(4) of the Act of 1961 (petition to vary or revoke purposes of an alimentary trust), it shall not be necessary to aver the amount or details of the income of an alimentary beneficiary from all sources.

63.2

Deriv. R.C.S. 1965, r. 260(d)

PETITION UNDER S. 1(4) OF THE ACT OF 1961.

A petition under s. 1(4) of the Act of 1961 is for the authorisation by the court of an arrangement varying or revoking a trust purpose entitling a beneficiary to an alimentary liferent or alimentary income from the trust estate: Act of 1961, s.1(4).

63.2.1

The petition may be presented by a beneficiary or trustee under the trust: Act of 1961, s. 1(4). "Beneficiary" for the purposes of s. 1 of the Act of 1961 includes any person having, directly or indirectly, an interest, whether vested or contingent, under the trust: Act of 1961, s. 1(6). This may include the beneficiary under a trust set up by the beneficiary of another trust the purposes or powers of which are sought to be varied: *Countess of Lauderdale, Petr.* 1962 S.C. 302. It does not include a remote contingent beneficiary whose interest is negligible: *Phillips and Others, Petrs* 1964 S.C. 141; *Morris, Petr.* 1985 S.L.T. 252.

For cases on the meaning of "alimentary" for the purposes of s. 1(4) of the Act of 1961: see *Strange and Another, Petrs* 1966 S.L.T. 59; *Pearson and Others, Petrs* 1968 S.L.T. 46; *Sutherland and Others, Petrs* 1968 S.L.T. 252. For necessity of the petition, see note 63.3.5.

FORM OF PETITION.

See in general note 63.3.6. In a petition under s. 1(4) of the Act of 1961 it is unnecessary to aver the amount or details of the income of an alimentary beneficiary: r. 63.2. It is sufficient for the income to be vouched by the documents lodged in the petition process: *Robertson and Others, Petrs.* 1962 S.C. 196, 203 per L.P. Clyde. An actuarial report on the apportionment of the trust fund between an alimentary liferenter and a prospective fiar should be produced: *Gibson's Trustee, Petr.* 1962 S.C. 204.

63.2.2

Service on certain persons

63.3. In a petition under section 1 of the Act of 1961 (petition for variation or revocation of trust purposes or extension of trustees' powers), the order under rule 14.5 (first order in petitions)—

63.3

(a) shall include a requirement for the petition to be served—

    (i) where the trust deed is registered in a register kept by the Keeper of the Registers or the Keeper of the Records, on the relevant Keeper; or

    (ii) where the trust deed is registered in a sheriff court book, on the sheriff clerk who keeps the relevant sheriff court book; and

(b) may include a requirement for the petition to be served on a truster or settlor or any other person who has contributed or is liable to contribute to the trust estate which may be affected by the petition.

Deriv. R.C.S. 1965, r. 260(c) and (e)

GENERAL NOTE.

At common law the purposes of a private trust could only be changed where all of the beneficiaries and potential beneficiaries were identified, fully *capax*, and in complete agreement with the proposed changes. If this happened they could direct the trustee to administer the property accordingly. This very rigid system caused difficulties with the implementation of long standing trust purposes which were affected by frequent changes in taxation law and levels, and inflation.

63.3.1

Following the Variation of Trusts Act 1958, which allowed variation of trust purposes in England and Wales, the *Law Reform Committee in Scotland in its Ninth Report* (Cmnd. 1102 (1960)) recommended the introduction of similar legislation in Scotland. In particular the report recommended the creation of a right for the trustees or any one or more of the beneficiaries to present a petition to the Outer House of the court, for approval on behalf of any unidentified, incapable, or unborn beneficiaries of an arrangement varying the purposes of the trust. The committee also recommended that the powers of the trustees could be varied in the same way. The result of the committee's recommendations was s.1(1) of the Act of 1961.

The committee also recommended changes which led to s.1(4) of the Act of 1961: see note 63.2.1.

JURISDICTION.

63.3.2   The grounds of jurisdiction for a petition under s.1(1) or s.1(4) of the Act of 1961 are largely similar.

(1)   Petition under s.1(1) of the Act of 1961.

In view of the nature of the petition it does not appear to involve any person "being sued" or to be in substance a proceeding in which a decree against any person is sought. Accordingly the C.J.J.A. 1982 would appear not to apply: C.J.J.A. 1982, Scheds 1 and 3C, Art. 3 and 4; Sched. 4, Arts 2 and 3; ss.20(1), 21(1)(b) and Sched. 9, para. 13. In addition a petition may be outwith the subject-matter scope of the C.J.J.A. 1982: C.J.J.A. 1982, Scheds 1 and 3C, Art. 1; ss.17(1) and 21(1)(a).

As the C.J.J.A. 1982 does not apply, the common law applies. At common law, the court has jurisdiction over all types of applications relating to Scottish trusts: *Clarke's Trs., Petrs.* 1966 S.L.T. 249, 251 per L.P. Clyde.

The test to decide whether a trust is Scottish is not wholly clear. It is clear that if (1) a trust was constituted in Scotland in a Scottish form, and (2) the trustees were at the time of its constitution domiciled (in the common law sense) in Scotland, the trust is Scottish: *Brockie and Another, Petrs.* (1875) 2 R. 923; *Ashburton v. Escombe* (1892) 20 R. 187, 196 per Lord Kinnear; and *Clarke's Trs.*, above. It is unclear what the position would be if only one of these requirements was fulfilled. If a trust deed declares that the trustees are to have the powers and immunities of trustees under Scots law, or some of the initial trustees are domiciled in Scotland, or the trust purposes are to be fulfilled in Scotland, these features will point towards the trust being a Scottish trust: see *Orr Ewing's Trs. v. Orr Ewing* (1885) 13 R.(H.L.) 1, 23 per Lord Watson; *Betts Brown Trust Fund Trs., Petrs.* 1968 S.C. 170.

With regard to non-Scottish trusts, at common law the court has jurisdiction (a) in an action against trustees provided they are resident, or administer trust property, in Scotland (see *Orr Ewing's Trs.*, above, per Lord Watson at p. 26); and (b) in any other application where the court is satisfied that the remedy sought is in conformity with the law of the trust (*Allan's Trs., Petrs.* (1897) 24 R. 238, 718; *Lipton's Trs., Petrs.* 1943 S.C. 521, 527 per L.J.-C. Cooper; *Bateman, Petr.* 1972 S.L.T.(Notes) 78; cf. *Hall and Others, Petrs.* (1869) 7 M. 667, and *Brockie*, above). The jurisdiction in relation to (b) has been described as an auxiliary jurisdiction of the court; and a request for its exercise will, where practicable, be sympathetically considered: *Lipton's Trs.*, above, per L.J.-C. Cooper at p. 525. The court may nevertheless refuse jurisdiction on the ground of forum non conveniens: see *Orr Ewing's Trs.*, above, per Lord Watson at pp. 26 et seq.

It is suggested that the court has jurisdiction for a petition under s.1(1) of the Act of 1961 in respect of a non-Scottish trust where the remedy sought would be approved by the courts of the law of the trust.

(2)   Petition under s.1(4) of the Act of 1961.

The grounds of jurisdiction will be the same as for a petition under s.1(1) of the Act of 1961: see (1) above.

CHOICE OF LAW.

63.3.3   Where the court has jurisdiction and the petition relates to a trust created voluntarily and evidenced in writing the court must apply the governing law of the trust as determined under Arts 6 and 7 of the Schedule to the Recognition of Trusts Act 1987: Act of 1987, Sched., Art. 6.

Effectively this means that in the exceptional situations where a "Scottish trust" was governed by a foreign law, the court could only grant the remedies sought in s.1(1) and (4) of the Act of 1961 if the courts in the country of the governing law would have been able to grant similar remedies. In that situation the court might well decline jurisdiction on grounds of forum non conveniens: see similar cases discussed by Lord Watson in *Orr Ewing's Trs. v. Orr Ewing* (1885) 13 R.(H.L.) 1, 26 et seq.

PETITION UNDER S.1(1) OF THE ACT OF 1961.

63.3.4   This is a petition for approval by the court on behalf of (a) any beneficiary who because of legal incapacity is incapable of assenting, (b) any person who may become one of the beneficiaries at a future date or event being a person of a specified description or member of a specified class provided that if he had become a beneficiary on the date of the presentation of the petition he would not have been capable of assenting, or (c) any person unborn, of an arrangement varying or revoking all or any of the trust purposes or enlarging the power of the trustees of managing and administering the trust estate: Act of 1961, s.1(1). The petition may be presented by a trustee or beneficiary. The jurisdiction of the court is, essentially, a curatorial function on behalf of beneficiaries unborn or not sui juris in granting consent (or not) on their behalf. The following issues have arisen:

    1.   *"Beneficiary"*. This includes any person having directly or indirectly an interest whether vested or contingent under the trust: Act of 1961, s.1(6). This may include the beneficiary under a trust set up by a beneficiary of another trust the purposes or powers of which are sought to be varied: *Countess of Lauderdale, Petr.* 1962 S.C. 302. It does not include a remote contingent beneficiary

whose interest is negligible: *Phillips and Others, Petrs.* 1964 S.C. 141; *Morris, Petr.* 1985 S.L.T. 252.

2. *Legal incapacity of beneficiary.* A person who is over the age of 16 years and under the age of 18 years is legally incapable of assenting for the purpose of s.1(1): Act of 1961, s.1(2).

3. *Contingent beneficiary.* The category in s.1(1)(b) of the Act of 1961 refers to a contingent beneficiary who is more than one contingency away from being a direct beneficiary: see (in relation to an almost identical English provision) *Knocker v. Youle* [1986] 2 All E.R. 914, 917 per Warner J.

4. *Trust purposes.* The arrangement may provide for the setting up of a new trust: *Aikman, Petr.* 1968 S.L.T. 137.

5. *Trustees' powers.* The arrangement may propose the extension of the powers of the trustees beyond those permitted by the trust deed or the Trustee Investments Act 1961: *Henderson, Petr.* 1981 S.L.T.(Notes) 40. It may include a power to assume new trustees (provided they are suitable having regard to the nature of the trust): see *Ommanney, Petr.* 1966 S.L.T.(Notes) 13.

NECESSITY FOR PETITION UNDER s.1(4) OF THE ACT OF 1961.

Unless there is an alimentary beneficiary the petition may be dismissed as being unnecessary: see *Strange and Another, Petrs.* 1966 S.L.T. 59; *Pearson and Others, Petrs.* 1968 S.L.T. 46. Where the alimentary purpose is contingent and revocable (e.g. where it is in a marriage contract trust and the alimented spouse has not begun to benefit) the petition may be dismissed as being unnecessary: *Findlay's Petrs.* 1962 S.C. 210. **63.3.5**

FORM OF PETITION UNDER s.1(1) OR (4) OF THE ACT OF 1961.

The petition is presented in the Inner House: r. 14.3(g). The petition must be in Form 14.4 in the official printed form: rr. 4.1 and 14.4. The petition must be signed by counsel or other person having a right of audience: r. 4.2(3); and see r. 1.3(1) (definition of "counsel" and "other person having a right of audience") and note 1.3.4. **63.3.6**

The petitioner must lodge the petition with the required steps of process (r. 4.4), and any documents founded on or adopted (r. 27.1(1)) including detailed and accurate documents as evidence in support of the petition: *Young's Trs., Petrs.* 1962 S.C. 293. A fee is payable on lodging the petition: see note 14.5.10.

On petitions generally, see Chap. 14.

The crave in the prayer should follow the express wording of the statute: *Robertson and Others, Petrs.* 1962 S.C. 196, 203 per L.P. Clyde. Any proposed arrangement should be set out in a scheme annexed to the petition, which may, if necessary, be thereafter registered in the Books of Council and Session or sheriff court books for preservation: *Colville, Petr.* 1962 S.C. 185, 195 per L.P. Clyde; *Gibson's Tr., Petr.* 1962 S.C. 204, 209 per L.P. Clyde. The proposed trust purposes or trustees' powers should be set out in full in the arrangement in an appendix to the petition and not merely incorporated by reference to another deed: *Nimmo and Another, Petrs.* 1972 S.L.T.(Notes) 68.

The petition must set forth the effect of the proposed arrangement on persons on whose behalf the court's approval is sought.

For specialities in relation to a petition under s.1(4) of the Act of 1961, see note 63.2.2.

SERVICE.

The petition on being lodged shall, without a motion being enrolled, appear in the rolls for the day after lodging in the Single Bills for an order for service: r. 14.5(1). The petition should be served on any interested party. This will include any trustee or beneficiary who is not a petitioner but may exclude a remote contingent beneficiary: *Phillips and Others, Petrs.* 1964 S.C. 141; *Morris, Petr.* 1985 S.L.T. 252. Where there are a number of contingent beneficiaries at the date of the lodging of the petition, the petition should be served on those who would become vested if the direct beneficiary died on that date: *Buchan, Petr.* 1964 S.L.T. 51. Where an interested party is a child the petition should be served on his parent or guardian. For whether a father has parental rights, see note 67.24.6. Where the purpose sought to be varied is testamentary and revocable (e.g. where a testamentary trustee is still alive) service on a beneficiary under the purpose is unnecessary: *Evetts v. Galbraith's Trs.* 1970 S.C. 211. **63.3.7**

Where the trust deed has been registered in a register (e.g. the Books of Council and Session or General Register of Sasines) kept by the Keeper of the Registers or Keeper of the Records, the petition should be served on the relevant keeper: r. 63.3(a)(i). The same applies to registering in the sheriff court books and the sheriff clerk who keeps those books: r. 63.3(a)(ii).

The petition may also be served on a trustee or any other person who has contributed to the trust estate which may be affected by the petition: r. 63.3(b).

For methods of service, see Chap. 16, Pt I.

"KEEPER OF THE REGISTERS".

This is the Keeper of the Registers of Scotland: r. 1.3(1). The address for service on the Keeper of the Registers is: Meadowbank House, 153 London Road, Edinburgh EH8 7AU. **63.3.8**

"KEEPER OF THE RECORDS".

This is the Keeper of the Records of Scotland: r. 1.3(1). The address for service on the Keeper of the Records is: Scottish Record Office, HM General Register House, Edinburgh EH1 3YY. **63.3.9**

CURATOR AD LITEM.

63.3.10   Where there are several beneficiaries whose interests do not conflict, the same curator ad litem may be appointed to represent all those beneficiaries. Where any person with an interest (including one on whose behalf approval is sought) is incapax for whatever cause or where a beneficiary is as yet unborn, the court will always in its first order appoint a curator ad litem to represent that person in the petition proceedings: *Tulloch's Trs., Petrs.* 1962 S.C. 245. The court's power to appoint a curator ad litem arises at common law by virtue of the undisputed power to regulate its own practice and procedure, the court performing the "duty it owes to all helpless persons brought to its cognisance" (*Drummond's Trs v. Peel's Trs* 1929 S.C. 484, per L.P. Clyde). In view of s.1(2) of the Act of 1961 (see note 63.3.4(2), the court would appoint a curator ad litem to a 16 to 18 year old person in a petition under s.1(1) of the Act of 1961: this position is preserved by s.1(3)(f) of the Age of Legal Capacity (Scotland) Act 1991. Despite the appointment, the petition will still be served on the person's parents, guardian or curator bonis.

Where a curator ad litem is sought to be appointed the motion for the first order will be starred, requiring appearance.

A curator ad litem is appointed, usually an advocate, from lists kept by the clerks to the two Divisions. It is not usually necessary for an advocate to take the oath *de fideli administratione* on each appointment. The petitioner's agent will inform the curator ad litem that he has been appointed and of the details of the process, and should provide the curator with a copy of the interlocutor appointing him. The curator ad litem will have to decide whether to oppose the petition by lodging answers or consent to the petition by lodging a minute of consent.

THE CURATOR'S DUTIES.

The court does not adhere to strict rules of evidence; if essential facts are disputed, enquiry is by remit (or even a proof, but that is rare) and documents produced which are accepted or not disputed may be accepted by the court without proof: *Colville, Ptnr* 1962 S.C. 185, 192 per L.P. Clyde. A curator's task should not, therefore, be underestimated.

It is the duty of the curator to exercise an independent judgment, by advising the ward where he is capable of concurring, and by acting for him where he is not, according to the true interest of the ward: *MacKay's Manual of Practice*, p. 150.

In *Drummond's Trs*, above, L.P. Clyde at pp. 496–498 stated that the court committed to the curator the duty of getting in touch with his ward and making such enquiry as to his ward's position as the court could not itself make; he must not independently; his professional responsibility is a guarantee of the purity and independence with which his duty to the ward and the court is performed; as a judicial officer as well as guardian of the ward's interests, if he found himself in difficulty, he can always report to the court. In relation to the equivalent procedure in England, Brightman, J, in *In re Whittall* [1973] 1 W.L.R. 1027, said that the guardian had the duty, under proper legal advice, to apprise himself fully of the notice of the application, of the existing beneficial interest of the infant, and of the manner in which that interest is proposed to be affected, and to inform the solicitor whom he has retained of the course he considers in the light of legal advice should be taken.

One of the first matters the curator will have to consider is whether he should be separately represented and advised in order to perform his duties. Where there are no disputed facts, and provided there are separate counsel to represent the conflicting interests, it is competent for the same agent to instruct them all: *Robertson, Petrs* 1962 S.C. 196, 203 per L.P. Clyde. Where facts are or may be in dispute, the curator should instruct separate agents to act on his behalf: it might be better to err on the side of caution if in doubt and instruct separate agents. The curator will generally wish to take the advice of counsel before determining how he should proceed; and the trustees must find the funds out of the trust to enable him to take the opinion of counsel: *Smith v. Smith's Tr.* 1900 S.L.T. 226. There may be circumstances in which the curator requires other expert advice, e.g. to assess material evidence: see "Variation of Trust Purposes" by Michael Bruce (now Lord Marnoch) in 1967 S.L.T.(News) 193.

The court may approve a scheme which positively benefits the person on whose behalf approval is sought or where the variation puts the person in question in no worse position than before: *Colville, Ptnr*, above, per L.P. Clyde at p. 194. The test will be whether, on a balance of probabilities, the arrangement not be prejudicial in the circumstances most likely to occur: Elliot in *Wilson & Duncan on Trusts, Trustees and Executors* at para. 13–31. It may be possible to eliminate the risk of potential prejudice by insurance (see e.g. *Robertson, Petrs*, above) or by a retained fund (cf. *Lobnitz* 1966 S.L.T.(Notes) 81): for a useful discussion, see *Stair Memorial Encyclopedia*, Vol. 24, para. 80. The court may approve an arrangement where the interests of the beneficiaries are remote and defeasible.

Where the curator is not satisfied that what is proposed is not prejudicial to his ward, the usual practice is for the counsel instructed on his behalf to raise his concerns with counsel for the petitioners. If the matter is not resolved to the curator's satisfaction, or there is a dispute of fact which he considers should be brought to the court, the curator will instruct answers to be lodged to the petition. Where the curator is satisfied that there is no prejudice he will instruct a minute of consent. On the form of such a minute, see note 63.3.12.

The curator is entitled to remuneration and should render a note of his fee to the petitioners agents.

REPRESENTATION.

63.3.11   Where no facts in the petition are disputed the parties may be represented by the same agent provided that they are represented by different counsel: *Robertson and Others, Petrs.* 1962 S.C. 196.

MINUTE OF CONSENT.

Where a person who has had the petition served on him does not wish to lodge answers opposing it, he should lodge a minute to that effect and appear at the hearing to ensure that he does not suffer prejudice from any amendment to the petition which may be made at the hearing: *Findlay's Petrs.* 1962 S.C. 210, 214 per L.P. Clyde. Where the court amends the arrangement the minute of consent will have to be altered to show consent to the amendment.

63.3.12

A minute of consent should be in the following form:

"X for the Minuter, — and hereby states to the court that the Minuter, having examined the terms of the Arrangement [as amended] in the appendix to the petition, and having been separately advised, considers that the Arrangement [as so amended] would not be prejudicial to the interests of his ward, and consents to approval [and authorisation (*if this petition has been presented also under section 1(4) of the Trusts (Scotland) Act 1961 concerning remuneration of an alimentary liferent)*] being granted to the Arrangement [as amended].
IN RESPECT WHEREOF
(*signed by counsel*)"

No fee is payable on lodging such a minute. R. 15.1 does not apply because the minute is not an application to the court.

OBJECTION TO THE PETITION.

The first order calls for answers. It has been known for minutes to be lodged; but obedience to the interlocutor would require answers.

63.3.13

SUMMAR ROLL.

After the expiry of the period of notice, the lodging of the execution copy of the petition (containing all executions) and the lodging of minutes of consent, and any answers, the petitioner should enrol a motion to appoint the cause to the Summar Roll. For fixing and allocation of the diet on the Summar Roll, see r. 6.3 and notes.

63.3.14

GRANTING OF THE PETITION.

Where the court grants the prayer of the petition the chairman of the court will sign a docquet attached to the arrangement in the form—

63.3.15

"Edinburgh, (*date*). The foregoing arrangement is signed and authenticated relative to the interlocutor of this date."

Where the arrangement requires to be registered in the Books of Council and Session or sheriff court books, the agent for the petitioner should (a) apply to the Petition Department for an official certified copy of the interlocutor granting the prayer (see r. 7.11); (b) make up and certify a copy of the docquetted arrangement; (c) send these two items to the Inland Revenue with a remittance for stamp duty; and on return (d) stitch the two items together and send them to the Keeper of the Registers at Meadowbank House, 153 London Road, Edinburgh EH8 7AU (DX ED300), or the sheriff clerk who keeps the relevant sheriff court books, for registration.

At the same time the clerk of session in the Petition Department will send a letter confirming the variation to the appropriate keeper.

AMENDMENT OF INTERLOCUTOR OR ARRANGEMENT.

An amendment of an interlocutor or an approved arrangement, which is not related to a mistake, clerical error, or omission in it is incompetent: *Hutchison* 1965 S.C. 240; *Bailey and Another, Petrs.* 1969 S.L.T. (Notes) 70. This is particularly important where an arrangement requires an insurance policy to be obtained by a certain date and it is not obtained in time. In that situation a fresh petition must be sought: see *Hutchison*, above.

63.3.16

Part II – Petitions by Trustees for Directions

Application of this Part

63.4.[1] This Part applies to an application for which provision is to be made by virtue of section 6(vi) of the Act of 1988[2] (provision to enable trustees under any trust deed to obtain direction of the court).

63.4

Deriv. R.C.S. 1965, r. 232

---

[1] Rule 63.4 amended by S.S.I. 2006 No. 83 (effective 17th March 2006).
[2] Section 6 of the Act of 1988 is repealed by the Courts Reform (Scotland) Act 2014 (asp 18) Sched. 5(7) para. 30(3) (effective 1st April 2015: repeal has effect as S.S.I. 2015 No. 77 subject to saving specified in S.S.I. 2015 No. 77 art. 7) .

GENERAL NOTE.

63.4.1

Part II of this Chapter was made under s.6(vi) of the C.S.A. 1988 which enables the court, with a view to securing that causes coming before it may be determined with as little delay as possible and to the simplification of procedure and reduction of expense, to provide by A.S. for enabling trustees under any trust deed to obtain the directions of the court on certain questions or the exercise of any of their powers or duties. This provision replaced the identically worded s.17(vi) of the Administration of Justice (Scotland) Act 1933. Section 6 of the C.S.A. 1988 (allocation of business etc by act of sederunt) was repealed by the Courts Reform (Scotland) Act 2014 but subordinate legislation made under it (e.g. Part II of Chap. 63) was saved by Courts Reform (Scotland) Act 2014 (Commencement No. 2 Transitional and Savings Provisions) Order 2015 (see note 2 below). In *abrdn (SLSPS Pension Trustee Co Ltd, Ptnr*, 2023 S.L.T. 791 (Extra Div.), para [26], the court suggested that the anomaly be rectified by restoration of a statutory power.

The purpose of the provision was to enable the court to make rules for the summary disposal of urgent requests by trustees acting under a trust deed for disposal of the issues listed.

The procedure has been infrequently used since the 1930s following a number of cases which restricted its scope. A petition for directions is competent where (1) the question raised is (a) one mentioned in s.6(vi) of the C.S.A. 1988 and (b) requires immediate decision by the trustees; (2) at the hearing all parties are represented who would have had to be represented if the question had been submitted in a competent special case; and (3) the pleadings must afford a satisfactory basis for answering the question put: *Peel's Trs. v. Drummond* 1936 S.C. 787, 794 per L.P. Normand. The phrase "requires immediate decision" means that there should be a live issue rather than an academic or speculative one, which affects or may be expected in the reasonably near future to affect the investment, distribution or administration of the trust estate: *Taylor, Ptnr,* 2000 S.L.T. 1223, 1225B (First Div.). A petition for directions cannot be resorted to at will in preference to a special case. The procedure, being a summary procedure, ought to be resorted to where justified by some emergency or where a more formal procedure is inefficacious or incompetent: *Henderson's Trs. v. Henderson* 1938 S.C. 461, 464 per L.P. Normand. Complex questions of law or where the facts are disputed may be better dealt with in a special case or other procedure (e.g. action or multiplepoinding): *Andrew's Trs. v. Maddeford* 1935 S.C. 857, 864–865 per L.P. Normand; *Henderson's Trs.*, above.

"ANY TRUST DEED"; "TRUSTEES".

63.4.2

Although s.6(vi) of the C.S.A. 1988, as did s.17(vi) of the Administration of Justice (Scotland) Act 1933, gives the court power to make rules for applications for directions by trustees under any "trust deed", that term is not defined. R.C.S. 1965, r. 232 defined "trust deed" by reference to the definition in s.2 of the Trusts (Scotland) Act 1921 without power to do so, and no attempt is made to define it, without a power to do so, in this Part of this Chapter of the R.C.S. 1994. It is not clear whether Parliament intended the remedy to apply to all trustees, and it is not available to trustees in a trust arising merely by operation of law.

In *Chisholm, Ptnrs.* , 2006 S.L.T. 394 (First Div), it was held that "trustees" in s. 6(vi) of the 1988 Act, could be read as including executors nominate, and the deed by which they were nominated, together with the associated testamentary writing and confirmation, could be regarded as a "trust deed". In *Cobb and Gemmell, Ptnrs*, 2023 S.L.T. 1284 (Extra Div.), para. [10], it was held that "trustees" did not include persons who have been nominated to act as executors but who have not yet been confirmed.

Form and service of application

63.5

63.5.—(1)   An application to which rule 63.4 applies shall be made by petition.

(2)[1]   Subject to rule 63.6A (executors of underwriting members of Lloyd's of London), the petition shall set out the question on which the direction of the court is sought and may include, in an appendix, any relevant documents.

(3)   The court may, in any order made under rule 14.5 (first order in petitions) or in any subsequent order, include a requirement to serve the petition on creditors, beneficiaries or other persons interested in the subject-matter of the petition.

Deriv. R.C.S. 1965, r. 233(a) (r. 63.5(1) and (2)) and r. 233(b) (r. 63.5(3))

"PETITION".

63.5.1

The petition may be presented by a trustee appointed under a trust deed: C.S.A. 1988, s.6(vi); and see note 63.4.2.

The petition is presented to the Inner House: r. 14.3(e). The petition must be in Form 14.4 in the official printed form: rr. 4.1 and 14.4. The petition must be signed by counsel or other person having a right of audience: r. 4.2(3); and see r. 1.3(1) (definition of "counsel" and "other person having a right of audience") and note 1.3.4.

---

[1] Rule 63.5 (2) amended by S.S.I. 2006 No. 83 (effective 17th March 2006).

The petitioner must lodge the petition with the required steps of process (r. 4.4) and any documents founded on or adopted (r. 27.1(1)). A fee is payable on lodging the petition: see note 14.5.10. On petitions generally, see Chap. 14.

The averments should set out, inter alia, (a) the facts of the matter which give rise to the questions on which directions are sought (*Henderson's Trs. v. Henderson* 1938 S.C. 461, 464 per L.P. Normand); (b) the immediacy or emergency which requires the question to be resolved by a petition for directions (*Andrew's Trs. v. Maddeford* 1935 S.C. 857, 864 per L.P. Normand; and *Henderson's Trs.*, above, per L.P. Normand at p. 464); and (c) that all persons with an interest in the trust agree with the facts as averred in the petition (*Andrew's Trs.*, above). The crave in the prayer should set out the question on which the direction of the court is sought: r. 63.5(2). The question should not be one where all persons interested are agreed on the answer: *Henderson's Trs.*, above; and see also *Grant's Trs. v. Hunter* 1938 S.C. 501.

JURISDICTION.

See in general note 63.3.2. In *Clarke's Trs.* 1966 S.L.T. 249 trustees petitioned for directions on whether the court would have jurisdiction to present petitions under s.1 of the Act of 1961.

63.5.2

"SERVE".

The petition will usually be served on persons interested in the subject-matter in the usual way: see r. 14.5. In some situations it may be dealt with ex parte or with a reduced period of notice. For methods of service, see Chap. 16, Pt. I.

63.5.3

Determination of petition

63.6.—(1)[1] Subject to rule 63.6A (executors of underwriting members of Lloyd's of London), the petition shall be disposed of at a hearing on the Summar Roll.

63.6

(2) At the hearing on the Summar Roll, the court may order inquiry by—
    (a) proof,
    (b) remit to a reporter, or
    (c) affidavit,
as it thinks fit.

Deriv. R.C.S. 1965, r. 233(c)

SUMMAR ROLL.

After the expiry of the period of notice (if any) the agent for the petitioner should enrol a motion to appoint the cause to the Summar Roll. For fixing and allocation of the diet on the Summar Roll, see r. 6.3 and notes.

63.6.1

Where the direction sought is on a comparatively simple question of investment, distribution, administration or a power or duty of trustees, only the petitioners need be represented. Otherwise every person who would have an interest if the direction was sought in a special case should be represented at the hearing on the Summar Roll: *Peel's Trs. v. Drummond* 1936 S.C. 786, 794 per L.P. Normand.

"PROOF".

See Chap. 36.

63.6.2

"REMIT TO A REPORTER".

The terms of the remit should be in the interlocutor ordering the remit: see *Williams v. Cleveland and Highland Holdings Ltd* 1993 S.L.T. 398, 401B–C per Lord Penrose. Where there is a remit to a reporter the report becomes the exclusive mode of proof of the issues compiled in the remit: see *Williams*, above, per Lord Penrose at p. 400L. It is not appropriate to lodge answers to the report: *Scotstown Moor Children's Camp* 1948 S.C. 630. Objections to the report may be made by lodging a note of objections.

63.6.3

The duties of the reporter are similar to those of a reporter appointed in a petition concerning a public trust: see note 63.12.3.

The agents for the parties are personally liable for the fees and outlays of the reporter and the petitioner's agent will usually be made responsible: r. 42.15.

"AFFIDAVIT".

The affidavit should be in the form of a statement of evidence written in the first person. The affidavit should contain the evidence of the deponent in support of the averments in the petition.

63.6.4

An affidavit should be sworn and signed by the deponent before any person who may competently take an oath, whether in Scotland or in any other country. In Scotland such a person may include a notary public, justice of the peace, sheriff, or any judge. The person taking the oath should also sign the affidavit. Where the affidavit is not in English a duly certified translation should also be lodged.

---

[1] Rule 63.6(1) amended by S.S.I. 2006 No. 83 (effective 17th March 2006).

See also the definition of affidavit in r. 1.3(1).

Executors of underwriting members of Lloyd's of London

63.6A

63.6A.—[1](1) This rule applies to a petition under this Part for directions as to the distribution of, or the administration of any trust relating to, the estate of a deceased underwriting member of Lloyd's of London, where—

    (a)   all liabilities of the estate in respect of syndicates of which the deceased was a member have been reinsured (whether directly or indirectly) or are otherwise the subject of indemnity; and

    (b)   the only reason for the executor delaying distribution of the estate is the possibility of personal liability to creditors of Lloyd's of London.

(2) The petition shall—

    (a)   state that this rule applies; and

    (b)   contain averments as to the matters mentioned in paragraph (1).

(3) There shall be lodged with the petition all affidavits and other documents available to the petitioner in respect of the matters mentioned in paragraph (1).

(4) If, on the expiry of the period of notice, no answers have been lodged—

    (a)   the petitioner shall apply by motion for a remit to a reporter approved by the court for that purpose; and

    (b)   where a report has been lodged in process by the reporter, the petitioner may apply by motion for an order granting the prayer of the petition.

(5) Where answers have been lodged—

    (a)   the parties may adjust the petition and answers within 28 days after the date on which the answers were lodged ("the adjustment period") and shall intimate such adjustments to one another;

    (b)   within 14 days after the expiry of the adjustment period, the petitioner shall apply by motion for such further procedure as may be specified in the motion.

(6) Where the petitioner fails to comply with the requirements of paragraph (5), a respondent may apply by motion for decree of dismissal.

GENERAL NOTE.

63.6A.1   Guidance on the application of this rule is to be found in P.N. No. 1 of 2006. In *Chisholm, Ptnrs* , 2006 S.L.T. 394 (First Div.), the court identified the issues that would normally be sufficient in a remit to a reporter. These are repeated in P.N. No.1 of 2006. In *Hutchison's Exrs, Ptnrs*,. 2022 S.L.T. 1374 (Extra Div.), following developments in 2007 and 2009 (see paras. [4] and [5]), it was suggested (para. [12]) that consideration should be given to an amended P.N and re-iterated what was said in *Lyell of Kinnordy's Exrs., Ptnrs.*, 2023 S.L.T. 181 (Extra Div.), para. [14].

"AFFIDAVIT".

63.6A.2   On affidavits, see notes 63.6.4 and 1.3.7.

Part III – Public Trusts

Application and interpretation of this Part

63.7

63.7.—(1) This Part applies to—

    (a)   an application to the *nobile officium* of the court for approval of a cy près scheme in relation to a public trust; or

    (b)   an application to the court under—

        (i)   Part VI of the Education (Scotland) Act 1980 (reorganisation of endowments); or

        (ii)   Part I of the Law Reform (Miscellaneous Provisions) (Scotland) Act 1990 (charities and reorganisation of public trusts).

---

[1] Rule 63.6(A) amended by S.S.I. 2006 No. 83 (effective 17th March 2006).

(2)   In this Part, "the Act of 1990" means the Law Reform (Miscellaneous Provisions) (Scotland) Act 1990.

Deriv. R.C.S. 1965, r. 233A inserted by S.I. 1992 No. 1533 (r. 63.7(2))

APPLICATION FOR APPROVAL OF A CY PRÈS SCHEME FOR A PUBLIC TRUST.

This is an application to the *nobile officium* of the court for approval of a scheme varying the purposes **63.7.1**
of a public trust, which have failed because (a) no means have been provided to effect the public purpose,
(b) the truster's directions cannot be carried out but there is a general charitable intention or (c) there is a
bequest to a particular public object but that object has failed after the bequest has taken effect, to approximate to those purposes: see *Gibson's Trs.* 1933 S.C. 190.

A public trust includes, but is not restricted to, charitable trusts, and the cy près jurisdiction applies to
all public trusts: *Anderson's Trs. v. Scott* 1914 S.C. 942. A public trust is a trust for the benefit of the
public; whereas a private trust is for the benefit of a third party. A public trust is valid even though it is not
charitable. Only charitable trusts, however, attract the favourable income tax regime: *Commissioners for
the Special Purposes of Income Tax v. Pemsel* [1891] A.C. 531; *Inland Revenue v. Glasgow Police
Athletic Association* 1953 S.C. (H.L.) 13.

APPLICATION UNDER PT. VI OF THE EDUCATION (SCOTLAND) ACT 1980.

There are six types of application, namely:—   **63.7.2**

1.   For the giving of effect to a draft scheme for the future government and management of any
     university, theological or less than 20 years old educational endowment or of a Carnegie Trust:
     Education (Scotland) Act 1980, s. 105(4A) (as inserted by the Education (Scotland) Act 1981,
     Sched. 6, para. 4(g)) and s. 122(2); see, e.g. *University of Glasgow, Petrs.* 1991 S.L.T. 604.
2.   By a governing body for the giving of effect to a draft scheme for the future government or
     management of an educational endowment which is at least 20 years old: 1980 Act, s. 105(4C)
     (as inserted by the 1981 Act, Sched. 6, para. 4(g)) and s. 122(1) and (2).
3.   By a governing body for the giving of effect to a draft scheme for the future government or
     management of a non-educational endowment: 1980 Act, s. 108 as amended by the 1981 Act,
     Sched. 6, para. 7(a).
4.   By the Lord Advocate for the giving of effect to a draft scheme for the future government or
     management of a non-educational endowment; 1980 Act, s. 108A renumbered and amended by
     the 1981 Act, Sched. 6, para. 7(b).
5.   For amendment or substitution of a scheme made by an education authority for the future
     government or management of an educational endowment which is at least 20 years old: 1980
     Act, s. 112(7) (as substituted by the 1981 Act, Sched. 6, para. 11(i)) and s. 122(1) and (2).
6.   By the Lord Advocate for summarily compelling governing bodies of certain educational
     endowments to give effect to a provisional order or scheme made under Part VI of the Act of
     1980 or its predecessors: 1980 Act, s. 120(1) as amended by the 1981 Act, Sched. 6, para. 18.

APPLICATIONS UNDER PT. I OF THE ACT OF 1990.

These applications include: **63.7.3**

1.   An application by the Lord Advocate in relation to the management or misconduct in the
     administration of a charitable body: see Act of 1990, s. 7.
2.   An application by trustees of a public trust for approval of a scheme for the reorganisation of
     trust purposes: see Act of 1990, s. 9; see, e.g. *Mining Institute of Scotland Benevolent Fund
     Trs., Petrs.* 1994 S.L.T. 785.

Proceedings before nominated judge

63.8.   Subject to rule 63.9 (referral to Inner House), all proceedings in an ap-   **63.8**
plication to which this Part applies shall be brought before a judge of the court
nominated for that purpose by the Lord President or, where the nominated judge is
not available, any other judge of the court (including the vacation judge); and, in
this Part, "Lord Ordinary" shall be construed accordingly.

Deriv. RCS 1965, r. 233C inserted by S.I. 1992 No. 1533

NOMINATED JUDGE.

The nominated judge is Lord Drummond Young.   **63.8.1**

Remit to Inner House

63.9.   The Lord Ordinary, if he thinks fit, may at any time remit a petition to   **63.9**
which this Part applies to the Inner House to be determined by a Division of the Inner House.

GENERAL NOTE.

63.9.1   This is a new rule to enable the Lord Ordinary to refer a petition to which this rule applies to the Inner House (which formerly dealt with such petitions).

Form of applications

63.10   **63.10.**—(1) Subject to the following paragraphs of this rule, an application to which this Part applies shall be made by petition.

(2) An application for an order in a petition to which this Part applies which is in dependence shall be made by motion.

(3) At the hearing of a motion under paragraph (2), the court may order that the application be made by note; and, in such a case, shall make an order for the lodging of answers to the note in process within such period as the court thinks fit.

(4)[1] Intimation to the court by the Scottish Ministers under section 1(6) or 5(13) of the Act of 1990 (interdict until intimation to court) shall be made by motion for recall of the interlocutor.

Deriv. RCS 1965, r. 233B(1) (r. 63.10(1)), r. 233B(2) (r. 63.10(2)), and r. 233H(1) (r. 63.10(4)), all inserted by S.I. 1992 No. 1533

"PETITION".

63.10.1   The petition is presented to the Outer House: r. 14.2(c)(iii) and (h). The petition must be in Form 14.4 in the official printed form: rr. 4.1 and 14.4. The petition must be signed by counsel or other person having a right of audience: r. 4.2(3); and see r. 1.3(1) (definition of "counsel" and "other person having a right of audience") and note 1.3.4.

The petitioner must lodge the petition with the required steps of process (r. 4.4) and any documents founded on or adopted (r. 27.1(1)). A fee is payable on lodging the petition: see note 14.5.10. On petitions generally, see Chap. 14.

The crave in the prayer should follow the express wording of the statutory provision founded on. Any proposed scheme should be set out in an appendix annexed to the petition. The proposed trust purposes or trustees' powers and duties should be set out in full in the scheme in the appendix.

In a petition under s. 9 of the Act of 1990 the application should be framed with particular reference to the conditions there set out and which have to be satisfied before the court can approve the scheme: *Mining Institute of Scotland Benevolent Fund Trs., Petrs.* 1994 S.L.T. 785.

JURISDICTION.

63.10.2   The grounds of jurisdiction depend principally on the type of petition.

(1) Petitions for the approval of a cy près scheme.

Jurisdiction is under the *nobile officium* but is otherwise akin to that in a petition under s. 1(1) of the Trusts (Scotland) Act 1961: see note 63.3.2(1). In addition, standing that the petition is to the *nobile officium*, Sched. 8 to the C.J.J.A. 1982 is disapplied: C.J.J.A. 1982, s. 22(3).

The petition is not a process for resolving preliminary matters such as whether the trust exists or whether there is uncertainty of gift or absence of charitable intention: *Church of Scotland Trust v. O'Donoghue* 1951 S.C. 85.

(2) Petition under Pt. VI of the Education (Scotland) Act 1980.

Part VI of the Act of 1980 relates to "endowments". An "endowment" is any property heritable or moveable dedicated to charitable purposes: 1980 Act, s. 122(1). There is no specific reference to an endowment having to be a trust let alone a Scottish trust. Nevertheless in practice most endowments will be held in Scottish trusts.

Where the petition is directed against a person, jurisdiction will be based on the C.J.J.A. 1982 except where its subject-matter is outwith the scope of the C.J.J.A. 1982: see notes 13.2.8 to 13.2.14.

Where the petition is not directed against a person the position will be akin to that in a petition under s. 1(1) of the Trusts (Scotland) Act 1961 and the common law will apply: see note 63.3.2(1).

(3) Petition under Pt. I of the Act of 1990.

With regard to a petition under s. 7 of the Act of 1990, in most instances the order sought will be directed against a person. Accordingly the C.J.J.A. 1982 will usually apply.

With regard to a petition under s. 9 of the Act of 1990, the position will be akin to that in a petition under s. 1(1) of the Trusts (Scotland) Act 1961 and the common law will apply: see note 63.2.2.

---

[1] R. 63.10(4) amended by S.I. 1999 No. 1386 (effective 1st July 1999).

"IN DEPENDENCE".

A cause is depending from the time it is commenced (i.e. from the time a first order in a petition is made) until final decree, whereas a cause is in dependence until final extract. For the meaning of commenced, see note 14.6.1. For the meaning of final decree, see note 4.15.2(2). For the meaning of final extract, see note 7.1.2(2).

63.10.3

"MOTION".

For motions, see Chap. 23.

63.10.4

"NOTE".

For applications by note, see r. 15.2.

63.10.5

"ANSWERS".

For form and procedure, see r. 18.3.

63.10.6

"SCOTTISH MINISTERS".

This expression means, collectively, the members of the Scottish Executive, i.e. the First Minister, the Ministers appointed by him under s. 47, the Lord Advocate and the Solicitor General for Scotland: Scotland Act 1998, s. 44(2). Sections 1(6) and 5(13) of the Act of 1990 refer to the Lord Advocate, but his functions in relation to charities under Pt. I of the Act of 1990 were transferred to the Secretary of State by the Transfer of Functions (Lord Advocate and Secretary of State) Order 1999 [S.I. 1999 No. 678] on 19th May 1999. The Lord Advocate now exercises only those functions he had immediately before he ceased to be a Minister of the Crown: Scotland Act 1998, s. 54. He ceased to be a Minister of the Crown and became a member of the Scottish Executive on 20th May 1999: The Scotland Act 1998 (Commencement) Order 1998 [S.I. 1998 No. 3178]. Accordingly the Lord Advocate does not exercise any functions in relation to charities under Pt I of the Act of 1990. Those functions were transferred from the Secretary of State to the Scottish Ministers by s.53(2)(c) of the Scotland Act 1998 which came into force on 1st July 1999 (The Scotland Act (Commencement) Order [S.I. 1998 No. 3178], art. 3). Oddly, Pt I of the Act of 1990 has not been amended.

63.10.7

Service on interested persons

63.11. A petition to which this Part applies shall be served on all persons who may have an interest in the subject-matter of the petition.

63.11

Deriv. RCS 1965, r. 233D inserted by S.I. 1992 No. 1533

"SERVED".

For methods of service, see Chap. 16, Pt I.

63.11.1

Procedure where no answers lodged

63.12.—(1) If, on the expiry of the period of notice, no answers have been lodged, the petitioner may apply by motion for an order granting the prayer of the petition.

63.12

(2) On a motion under paragraph (1), the Lord Ordinary may, before determining that motion—

    (a) remit to a reporter to inquire into, and report on, the petition and any scheme appended to it;

    (b) order the petitioner to lodge evidence by affidavit or documentary evidence;

    (c) order a further hearing; or

    (d) make such other order as he thinks fit.

Deriv. R.C.S. 1965, r. 233E inserted by S.I. 1992 No. 1533

"PERIOD OF NOTICE".

This is the period within which answers may be lodged: see r. 1.3(1) (definition of "period of notice") and r. 14.6.

63.12.1

"MOTION".

For motions, see Chap. 23.

63.12.2

"REMIT TO A REPORTER".

This is the most common method used by the court in determining the facts of a petition relating to a public trust. A motion will usually be made for such an appointment by the petitioner on the expiry of the period of notice and before applying for the prayer of the petition to be granted; in some circumstances

63.12.3

(generally exceptional) a reporter may not be necessary. An advocate is usually appointed. The terms of the remit should be in the interlocutor ordering the remit: see *Williams v. Cleveland and Highland Holdings Ltd* 1993 S.L.T. 398, 401B–C per Lord Penrose. Where there is a remit to a reporter the report becomes the exclusive mode of proof of the issues compiled in the remit: see *Williams*, above, per Lord Penrose at p. 400L. It is not appropriate to lodge answers to the report: *Scotstown Moor Children's Camp* 1948 S.C. 630. Objections to the report may be made by lodging a note of objections. In most cases, points raised by the reporter can be dealt with at the bar on the motion to grant the prayer.

The duties of the reporter are invariably specified in the interlocutor of appointment as being to "inquire into and report on the facts and circumstances" of the petition. This means more than simply perusing and commenting on the petition and draft scheme. The reporter must ascertain whether the facts averred are correct and whether the scheme is justified (or too broad or too narrow) by the facts established; to do this he must carry out a full investigation himself. The reporter is not acting as counsel, advising the petitioner(s). The reporter will invariably find it essential to visit the petitioner(s) or a representative (such as the trust's chairman, treasurer, secretary) or all of them to establish the facts and discuss the scheme. Depending on the circumstances, the reporter may wish to speak to those involved in financial arrangements, to see accounts, records and other documents. In preparing the report, the reporter should comment on the scheme, recommending any drafting improvements, or changes to the scheme in the light of the investigations, including whether the scheme should be more restricted or widened (in the latter case the question whether further service or intimation is required will have to be considered). The process will have to be examined to ascertain whether intimation and service has been properly made, all persons whom the reporter has identified as having an interest have been appropriately notified, whether any advertisement has been made and the advertisements gave proper notice, whether any answers or other communication in response to the petition have been lodged and whether the period of notice has expired.

The agents for the parties are personally liable for the reporter's fees and outlays; and the petitioner's agent will usually be responsible: r. 42.15.

"AFFIDAVIT".

63.12.4
The affidavit should be in the form of a statement of evidence written in the first person. The affidavit should contain the evidence of the deponent in support of the averments in the petition.

An affidavit should be sworn and signed by the deponent before any person who may competently take an oath, whether in Scotland or in any other country. In Scotland such a person may include a notary public, justice of the peace, sheriff, or any judge. The person taking the oath should also sign the affidavit. Where the affidavit is not in English a duly certified translation should also be lodged.

See also the definition of affidavit in r. 1.3(1).

Procedure where answers lodged

63.13
63.13.—(1) Where answers are lodged in a petition, the parties may adjust the petition and answers during the period of 28 days from the date on which answers are lodged or from the expiry of the period of notice, whichever is the later.

(2) Within 14 days after the expiry of the period allowed for adjustment under paragraph (1), the petitioner shall enrol a motion for an order for such further procedure as he shall specify.

(3) On a motion under paragraph (2), the Lord Ordinary shall make such order as he thinks fit for the further procedure of the petition; and, in particular—

(a) may—

(i) remit to a reporter to inquire into, and report on, the petition and any scheme appended to it;

(ii) order a party to lodge evidence by affidavit or documentary evidence; and

(b) then, or thereafter, shall appoint the cause to a hearing.

(4) At a hearing appointed under paragraph (3)(b), the Lord Ordinary shall—

(a) determine the petition; or

(b) make such order for further procedure as he thinks fit.

(5) If at any stage answers are withdrawn, the petition shall proceed as if answers had not been lodged.

Deriv. R.C.S. 1965, r. 233F inserted by S.I. 1992 No. 1533

ADJUSTMENT OF PLEADINGS.

63.13.1
See note 22.2.3.

"PERIOD OF NOTICE".

This is the period within which answers may be lodged: see r. 1.3(1) (definition of "period of notice") and r. 14.6.

63.13.2

"MOTION".

For motions, see Chap. 23.

63.13.3

Where answers to the petition relate to a preliminary matter (e.g. whether a trust exists or whether there is uncertainty of gift or absence of charitable intention), the petitioner should enrol a motion to sist the cause pending resolution of the matter in another process: *Church of Scotland Trust v. O'Donoghue* 1951 S.C. 85.

"REMIT TO A REPORTER."

See note 63.12.4.

63.13.4

"EVIDENCE BY AFFIDAVIT".

The affidavit should be in the form of a statement of evidence written in the first person. The affidavit should contain the evidence of the deponent in support of the averments in the petition.

63.13.5

An affidavit should be sworn and signed by the deponent before any person who may competently take an oath, whether in Scotland or in any other country. In Scotland such a person may include a notary public, justice of the peace, sheriff, or any judge. The person taking the oath should also sign the affidavit. Where the affidavit is not in English a duly certified translation should also be lodged.

See also the definition of affidavit in r. 1.3(1).

"HEARING".

The hearing is fixed once the report has been lodged: r. 63.13(3). Usually it will involve the making of submissions on the pleadings and productions without the leading of evidence.

63.13.6

Warrants for registration

63.14. An interlocutor approving a cy près scheme or a scheme for the variation or reorganisation of a public trust shall contain a warrant for the registration of an official certified copy of the interlocutor, and a copy of the scheme certified by the agent to the petitioner, in the Books of Council and Session or the books of a specified sheriff court.

63.14

Deriv. R.C.S. 1965, r. 233G inserted by S.I. 1992 No. 1533

GRANTING OF THE PETITION.

Where the court grants the prayer of a petition for the approval of a cy près scheme or for the variation or reorganisation of a public trust under the Education (Scotland) Act 1980 or the Act of 1990, the Lord Ordinary will sign a docquet attached to the scheme in the form—

63.14.1

"Edinburgh, *(date)*. The foregoing arrangement is signed and authenticated relative to the interlocutor of this date."

The interlocutor will contain a warrant for the registration of an official certified copy of it with a copy of the scheme, certified by the agent to the petitioner in the Books of Council and Session or the books of a specified sheriff court: r. 63.14.

On the interlocutor granting the prayer of the petition being pronounced the agent for the petitioner should (a) apply to the Petition Department for an official certified copy of the interlocutor (see r. 7.11); (b) make up and certify a copy of the docquetted scheme; and (c) stitch the two items together and send them to the Keeper of the Registers at Meadowbank House, 153 London Road, Edinburgh EH8 7AU (DX ED300) or the sheriff clerk who keeps the relevant sheriff court for registration.

At the same time the clerk of session in the Petition Department will send a letter confirming the variation to the appropriate keeper.

Advertisement of court orders

63.15. An order made under paragraph (a) or (g) of section 7(4) of the Act of 1990 (interim interdict or interdict of body holding itself out as a charity etc.) shall, unless the court otherwise directs, be advertised forthwith in one or more newspapers as the court shall direct for ensuring that it comes to the notice of persons dealing with a non-recognised body within the meaning of section 2(2) of that Act.

63.15

Deriv. R.C.S. 1965, r. 233I inserted by S.I. 1992 No. 1533

Narrants for registration

63.13 An interlocutor approving a new scheme or a scheme for the variation or reorganisation of a public trust shall contain a warrant for the registration of an official certified copy of the interlocutor, and a copy of the scheme certified by the agent to the petitioner, in the Books of Council and Session or the books of a special first sheriff court.

Advertisement of court orders

63.15 An order made under paragraph (a) or (b) of section 7(e) of the Act of 1990 (interim interdict or interdict of body holding) shall out and shall, unless the court otherwise directs, be advertised forthwith in one or more newspapers as the court shall direct for ensuring that it comes to the notice of persons dealing with a non-recognised body within the meaning of section 2(2) of that Act.

Chapter 64[1]

Applications under Section 1 of the Administration of Justice (Scotland) Act 1972

Application of this Chapter

64.1.[2] This Chapter applies to an application for an order under section 1 of the
Administration of Justice (Scotland) Act 1972 made where a cause is not depending
before the court in which the application may be made.

64.1

GENERAL NOTE.

This Chapter was replaced by A.S. (R.C.S.A. No.4) (Applications under section 1 of the Administration of Justice (Scotland) Act 1972) 2000 (SSI 2000/3190). The new rules were introduced to make the
procedure for applications under s. 1 of 1972 Act (known as "dawn raids") comply with Art. 8 of the
European Convention of Human Rights. These rules introduce safeguards present in Anton Piller orders
in England which were commented on by the European Court of Human Rights in *Chappell v. United
Kingdom* (1998) 12 E.H.R.R. 1 as necessary safeguards. One safeguard was that an order would not be
made unless the court was satisfied that (a) there was a very strong prima facie case, (b) the actual or
potential damage to the petitioner was very serious and (c) there was clear evidence that the respondent
had incriminating material in his possession and that there was a real possibility that he might destroy it if
forewarned. The second safeguard relates to the manner of execution of the order which must ensure
proportionality between the rights of the petitioner to recover property and the rights of the respondent in
respect for his private life. In *Thorntons Investment Holdings Ltd & Ors v. Roy Matheson & Ors*, 2024
S.C. 36 (OH); 2023 S.L.T. 985, paras. [44] and [45], it was stated that material recovered is not to be put
into the possession of the petitioner or the petitioner's agents without the consent of the haver or by order
of the court. The court, therefore, placed trust in the petitioner and agent, and the commissioner, to
respect that basic principle; and the commissioner ought not, therefore, routinely to show material to the
petitioner's solicitor; it is limited to providing the commissioner with more specialist knowledge to assist
in determining whether an item fell within description of material subject to the s. 1 order. Any knowledge
gained should be regarded as subject to a duty of confidence to the person originally in possession of the
item. A more robust attitude to the attendance of IT specialists to assist the commissioner may need to be
developed.

64.1.1

Rule 64.1 is in the same terms as the previous rule.

This Chapter applies to the recovery of documents and other property under s. 1 of the Administration
of Justice (Scotland) Act 1972 where there is no depending cause (on the meaning of which, see note
64.1.2). Where there is a depending cause the application may be made by motion in that cause under r.
35.2.

The Act of 1972 is concerned with recovery and production of evidence for use in litigation in
Scotland; recovery and production of evidence for use in foreign civil proceedings (following a letter of
request) is regulated by Chap. 66. Where, however, documents or other items have been recovered by a
commission and diligence at common law under s. 1 of the Act of 1972, the court may, on an application
to it in the process of the cause in which that recovery was made, permit those documents or other items
to be used for those proceedings in Scotland or elsewhere. It is not necessary, where there is such a
process, to bring fresh proceedings under s. 1 of the Act of 1972 or the Evidence (Proceedings in Other
Jurisdictions) Act 1975: *Iomega Corporation v. Myrica (UK) Ltd* 1998 S.C. 636 (First Div.) overruling
Dailey Petroleum Services Corporation v. Pioneer Oil Tools Ltd 1994 S.L.T. 757.

In relation to the application of s. 1 of the 1972 Act to proceedings by virtue of s. 28 of the C.I.J.A.
1982, see note 64.1.7.

A party who has obtained possession of documents or other items under a commission and diligence
at common law or under s. 1 of the Act of 1972 is subject to an implied obligation or undertaking to the
court not to use them or allow them to be used for any purpose other than the conduct of the actual or
proposed proceedings for which they were recovered: *Iomega Corporation*, above.

On retrospective permission and future collateral use, see *Iomega*, above, at pp.646C-D, 654D-F; and
Thorntons, above, at paras. [52] and [56].

"DEPENDING".

A cause is depending from the time it is commenced (i.e. from the time an action is served or a first
order in a petition is made) until final decree, whereas a cause is in dependence until final extract. For the
meaning of commenced, see note 13.4.4 (actions) and note 14.6.1 (petitions). For the meaning of final
decree, see note 4.15.2(2). For the meaning of final extract, see note 7.12.2(2).

64.1.2

---

[1] Chapter 64 and r. 64.1 substituted by S.S.I. 2000 No. 319 (effective from 2nd October 2000).
[2] Chapter 64 and r. 64.1 substituted by S.S.I. 2000 No. 319 (effective from 2nd October 2000).

Orders under s. 1 of the Administration of Justice (Scotland) Act 1972.

64.1.3   Under s. 1(1) of the Act of 1972 orders may be sought (for commission and diligence) for the inspection, photographing, preservation, custody and detention of documents and other property (including land) which appear to be property as to which any question may relevantly arise in civil proceedings which are likely to be brought, and for their production and recovery, the taking of samples or the carrying out of experiments.

The court may also order any person (not just a party) to disclose any information he has about the identity of any person who appears to the court to be a person who might be a witness or defender in any civil proceedings which are likely to be brought: Act of 1972, s. 1(1A) inserted by the Law Reform (Miscellaneous Provisions) (Scotland) Act 1985, s. 19. For a recent unsuccessful attempt under s. 1(1A) of the Act of 1972, see *Pearson v. Educational Institute of Scotland* 1997 S.C. 245 (Second Div.). In Pearson, it was confirmed that the test for an application under s. 1(1A) of the 1972 Act is that (1) the proceedings are likely to be brought and (2) in relation to those proceedings the petitioner has a prima facie, intelligible and stateable case. In order to determine whether such a case exists, it is neither necessary nor appropriate to subject the pursuer's pleadings to a detailed examination: *Harwood v. Jackson* , 2003 S.L.T. 1026 (OH), 1029H, para. [8]. Section 1(1A) of the Act of 1972 does not extend beyond Scotland; and the Scottish courts had no jurisdiction over the respondents, a company incorporated in Massachusetts) and the court could not make an order under s.1(1A): *Clark v. TripAdvisor LLC*, 2015 S.C. 368 2015 S.L.T. 59 (Extra Div). The proper course would be letters of request under r. 35.15 or to seek to recover the information in proceedings in Massachusetts.

The order under s. 1 of the Act of 1972 may only be made where civil proceedings are likely to be brought. It is not enough that proceedings are merely a possibility but would be rendered likely on the basis of the documents recovered: *Colquhoun, Petr* 1990 S.L.T. 43, 44L per Lord Prosser. There need not be full averments of fact which would make an action relevant: *Friel, Petr* 1981 S.C. 1. There must be adequate averments about the substance of and basis for the case proposed to be made before the order is granted: *Dominion Technology Ltd v. Gardner Cryogenics Ltd (No. 1)* 1983 S.L.T. 828, 832C per Lord Cullen. "Civil proceedings" has a general wide meaning, applying to proceedings of a civil character irrespective of the court or tribunal and includes arbitration: *Anderson v. Gibb* 1983 S.L.T. 726. "Property" means corporeal property; but the court has a common law power to order inspection and video recording of things such as a process or activity: *Christie v. Arthur Bell & Sons Ltd* 1989 S.L.T. 253; and see cases there cited.

These provisions do not affect the law and practice about privilege of witnesses and havers, confidentiality or public interest, and s. 47 of the Crown Proceedings Act 1947 (recovery of documents in possession of the Crown) applies: Act of 1972, s. 1(4). The privilege against self-incrimination cannot be claimed in respect of certain proceedings under s. 1(1) of the Act of 1972 for infringement, to obtain disclosure of information about infringement relating to intellectual property: see note 64.1.4(6). On confidentiality, see note 61.1.4.

The same considerations for determining whether an order should be granted as in a depending cause and as set out in *Moore v. Greater Glasgow Health Board* 1978 S.C. 123 apply: *Thorne v. Strathclyde R.C.* 1984 S.L.T. 161. These are that it must be shown that the documents are necessary for the purpose of enabling a party to make more pointed or more specific what is already averred or to enable him to make adequate and specific replies to his opponent's averments, in short "what he must show is that the documents sought to be recovered are required to serve the purposes of the pleadings as those pleadings stand at the time the diligence is sought": see *Moore*, above, per Lord Cameron at p.131. there must be a prima facie case: *Smith, Petr* 1985 S.L.T. 461.

On seeking redelivery of documents and property, see note 64.13.1.

On ex parte applications, see note 64.5.2.

CAVEATS.

64.1.4   A caveat may not be lodged in respect of an order under s.1 of the Act of 1972.

SECTION 28 OF THE C.J.J.A. 1982.

64.1.5   When any proceedings have been brought, or are likely to be brought, in a 2005 Hague Convention State (one which is party to the 2005 Hague Convention on Choice of Law Agreements) or in England and Wales or Northern Ireland in respect of any matter within the scope of Art. 1 of the Regulation, the Court of Session has the like power to make an order under s.1 of the Administration of Justice (Scotland) Act 1972 as if the proceedings had been or were likely to be brought, in that court: C.J.J.A. 1982 s.28. The court's power to grant an order under s.1 of the 1972 Act is extended by the Civil Jurisdiction and Judgements Act 1982 (Provisional and Protective Measures) (Scotland) Order 1977 [S.I. 1997 No. 2780] as follows: (a) anything mentioned in s.28 of the C.J.J.A. 1982 in relation to proceedings commenced otherwise than in a 2005 Hague Convention State or proceedings whose subject matter is not within the scope of the 2005 Hague Convention as determined by Arts. 1 and 2 of the Convention. and (b) the granting of an order under s.1 of the 1972 Act by virtue of s.28, of the C.J.J.A. 1982 in relation to proceedings which are to be commenced otherwise than in a 2005 Hague Contracting State. In *Liffe Administration and Management v. The Scottish Ministers* , 2004 S.L.T. 2 it was held that proceedings under a Complaints Ombudsman Scheme under the Financial Services and Markets Act 2000 were concerned with an administrative rather than a civil or commercial matter to which the 1968 Convention would apply and s.28 of the C.J.J.A. 1982 (when s. 28 applied to the 1968 Convention) did not, therefore, apply and the petition under s.1 of the 1972 Act was incompetent.

The application of s. 28 of the C.J.J.A. 1982 to the 1968 Brussels and Lugano Conventions, and the Council Regulations (Brussels I Regulation and Brussels I Regulation (Recast), and the references to them in the 1977 Order, were repealed and revoked by the Civil Jurisdiction and Judgments (Amendment) (EU Exit) Regulations 2019/479 except in relation to proceedings not concluded before 11pm on 31st December 2020.

Guidance has been given by the Inner House in *Union Carbide Corporation v. B.P. Chemicals Ltd* 1995 S.C. 398 on how the power in s. 28 should be exercised. (1) Section 28 of the 1972 Act is partly based on Art.24 of the Conventions above and, as only an order under s. 1 of the 1972 Act for preservation and detention as opposed to production and recovery would be "provisional" or "protective" in nature, s. 28 of the C.J.J.A. 1982 goes beyond the requirements of the Convention by allowing the court to make an order for production and recovery of information for use in foreign litigation. (2) Although the remedies available are the remedies under the law of Scotland whether available in the foreign jurisdiction or not, the question whether the Scots or a similar remedy is available in the foreign jurisdiction is an important factor to which regard must be had by the Scottish courts in determining whether to exercise the power to assist the foreign proceedings. (3) Where a party to proceedings in another country claims that an order should be made under s. 28 of the C.J.J.A. 1982 to enable him to satisfy a rule of that country, it is the rule and practice of that country that the court has to consider in order to decide what order is a reasonably necessary. (4) The court must ask itself whether it will be consistent with the ends of justice for the power in s. 28 to be exercised and, if so, on what terms; and an order should be refused if vexatious or oppressive. (5) There is a distinction between (a) cases where the party against whom the s. 28 order is sought is the same party as that against whom the proceedings in the other jurisdiction have been brought, and (b) cases where the proceedings have not yet been brought or the party is a stranger to those proceedings. In (a) the court must be careful not to be drawn into a situation where it is where it is persuaded to grant a discretionary remedy which the foreign court possessed of a similar power would not provide in the same circumstances. (6) The court has power to attach conditions to the use of information recovered by commission and diligence, although it is not normal practice for the court to do so.

Where a document or other property has been recovered by petition under s. 1 of the Act of 1972 and recovery or production of it is sought for civil proceedings in any foreign country, a separate petition need not be presented under the Evidence (Proceedings in Other Jurisdictions) Act 1975: *Iomega Corporation v. Myrica (UK) Ltd*, 1998 S.C. 636 overruling *Dailey Petroleum Services Corporation v. Pioneer Oil Tools Ltd* 1994 S.L.T. 757. The application may be made in the petition under s. 1 of the Act of 1972 because the documents or property are held until further order of the court. The better procedure is to proceed by note rather than motion: *Iomega Corporation*, above. See also Chap. 66.

In relation to the rest of the U.K. and Brussels or Lugano Convention Contracting States, or Brussels I Regulation States, there is an overlap of the 1975 Act and s. 28 of the C.J.J.A. 1982.

CONTEMPT

A party who seeks to enforce an order for recovery of documents may be met with refusal or obstruction and tempted to lodge a minute for contempt. Regard should be had to the factors mentioned in paras. [31] and [32] in *Sovereign Dimensional Survey Ltd v. Cooper*, 2009 S.C. 382 (Extra Div.). **64.1.6**

Form and content of application

64.2.[1](1)   An application to which this Chapter applies shall be made by petition. **64.2**

(2)[2]   The statement of facts shall set out—

   (a)   a list of documents and other property (in this Chapter and in Form 64.6 referred to as the "listed items") which the petitioner wishes to be made the subject of the order;

   (b)   the address of the premises within which the petitioner believes the listed items are to be found;

   (c)   the facts which give rise to the petitioner's belief that were the order not to be granted the listed items or any of them would cease to be available for the purposes of the said section 1.

Deriv. RCS 1965, r. 95A(c) (part) inserted by S.I. 1972 No. 2021 and r. 95A(d)(ii) substituted by S.I. 1987 No. 1206.

GENERAL NOTE.

See note 64.1.1. The provision in this Chapter for applications where there is no depending cause by petition is an exercise of the power in s. 1(3) of the Act of 1972. **64.2.1**

"PETITION".

A petition is presented in the Outer House: r. 14.2 (h). The petition must be in Form 14.4 in the official printed form: rr. 4.1 and 14.4. The petition must be signed by counsel or other person having a right of **64.2.2**

---

[1] Rule 64.2 substituted by S.S.I. 2000 No. 319 (effective from 2nd October 2000).
[2] Rule 64.2(2)(a) amended by S.S.I. 2004 No. 52 (effective 1st March 2004).

audience: r. 4.2; and see r. 1.3(1) (definitions of "counsel" and "other person having right of audience"), and note 1.3.4.

The petitioner must lodge the petition with the required steps of process (r. 4.4). A fee is payable on lodging the petition: see note 14.5.10.

On petitions generally, see Chap. 14.

Accompanying documents

64.3

64.3.[1] The petitioner shall lodge with the application—

    (a) an affidavit supporting the averments in the petition;

    (b) an undertaking by the petitioner that he—

        (i) will comply with any order of the court as to payment of compensation if it is subsequently discovered that the order, or the implementation of the order, has caused loss to the respondent or, where the haver is not the respondent, to the haver; and

        (ii) will bring within a reasonable time of the execution of the order any proceedings which he decides to bring; and

        (iii) will not, without leave of the court, use any information, documents or other property obtained as a result of the order, except for the purpose of any proceedings which he decides to bring and to which the order relates.

GENERAL NOTE.

64.3.1   See note 64.1.1.

"AFFIDAVIT".

64.3.2   The affidavit should be in the form of a statement written in the first person. The affidavit should contain the evidence of the deponent in support of the averments in the petition.

An affidavit should be sworn and signed by the deponent before any person who may competently take an oath, whether in Scotland or in any other country. In Scotland such a person may include a notary public, justice of the peace, sheriff, or any judge. The person taking the oath should also sign the affidavit. Where the affidavit is not in English a duly certified translation should also be lodged.

See also the definition of affidavit in r. 1.3(1).

Modification of undertakings

64.4

64.4.[2] The court may, on cause shown, modify, by addition, deletion or substitution, the undertaking mentioned in rule 64.3(b).

GENERAL NOTE.

64.4.1   See note 64.1.1.

Intimation and service of application

64.5

64.5.[3](1) Before granting the application, the court may order such intimation and service of the petition to be given or executed, as the case may be, as it thinks fit.

(2) Any person receiving intimation or service of the petition by virtue of an order under paragraph (1) may appear and oppose the application.

GENERAL NOTE.

64.5.1   See note 64.1.1.

This rule is in the same terms as the former r. 64.3.

Petitions are not usually intimated and served in the normal way before the order sought under s. 1 of the Act of 1972 is granted because most applications are ex parte applications (on which, see note 64.2.3). The court may order service on the third party haver as in intimation of a motion under s. 1 of the Act of 1972 (see r. 35.2(3)) and on the Lord Advocate (see note 64.3.3).

---

[1] Rule 64.3 substituted by S.S.I. 2000 No. 319 (effective 2nd October 2000).
[2] Rule 64.5 substituted by S.S.I. 2000 No. 319 (effective 2nd October 2000).
[3] R. 64.5 inserted by S.S.I. 2000 No. 319 (effective 2nd October, 2000).

EX PARTE APPLICATIONS.

The court may grant the application ex parte and the respondent can only object to it after the event.

An application may be granted ex parte where (a) the documents are essential to the petitioner's case and (b) are at risk of destruction or concealment: *The British Phonographic Industry Ltd v. Cohen, Cohen, Kelly, Cohen & Cohen Ltd*, 1983 S.L.T. 137.

Where the order is sought ex parte a motion is enrolled for intimation, service and the order sought. If granted the court pronounces an interlocutor ordering intimation on the walls of the court, grants warrant for service, appoints a commissioner (usually a Q.C.), authorises recovery and orders the commissioner to transmit the documents, etc., with an inventory, to the Deputy Principal Clerk "to await the further orders of the court". Once recovered, a further order may be sought (if craved in the prayer) for inspection or the carrying out of experiments, etc., and thereafter returned to the Deputy Principal Clerk (a period of time sometimes being specified). An interesting discourse on s. 1 of the Act of 1972, and obtaining such an order ex parte, is in *Sovereign Dimensional Survey Ltd v Cooper*, 2009 S.C. 382 (Extra Div).

64.5.2

SERVICE ON LORD ADVOCATE.

This must be done where recovery is sought of a document belonging to or in possession of the Crown: *Sheridan v. Peel*, 1907 S.C. 821, 825 per L.P. Strathclyde; *Whitehall v. Whitehall*, 1957 S.C. 30, 42 per Lord Sorn. This applies also to records of an NHS hospital: *Glacken v. National Coal Board*, 1951 S.C. 82.

64.5.3

Form of order

64.6.[1] An order made under this Chapter shall be in Form 64.6.

64.6

GENERAL NOTE.

See note 64.1.1.

In *Sovereign Dimensional Survey Ltd v. Cooper*, 2009 S.C. 382 (Extra Div.), doubt was cast, obiter, as to the competency of Grant (2) and Orders (4) and (5) in Form 64.6. In that case the pursuer alleged contempt of court by the respondent and haver in not complying with those orders ((d) and (e) in that case), but the item concerned was subsequently produced.

64.6.1

"FORM".

On forms, see note 1.4.1.

64.6.2

Caution and other security

64.7.[2] On granting, in whole or in part, the application the court may order the petitioner to find such caution or other security as it thinks fit.

64.7

Deriv. RCS 1965, R. 95A(C) (part) inserted by SI 1972/2021[3]

GENERAL NOTE.

See note 64.1.1.

This rule is in the same terms as the former r. 64.4.

The ordering of caution or other security is rare. But, e.g. where the haver has a right of lien over them, the petitioner may only recover them by consignation in respect of the debt due: *You v. Ogilvie & Co.*, 1985 S.L.T. 91.

64.7.1

Execution of order

64.8.[4] The order of the court shall be served by the Commissioner in person and it shall be accompanied by the affidavit referred to in rule 64.3(a).

64.8

GENERAL NOTE.

See note 64.1.1.

64.8.1

"SERVED".

For personal service, see r. 16.1. Rule 64.8 does not indicate on whom service is to be made or how. By reading the rule with r. 64.9(a), it is clear that personal service under r. 16.1(1)(a)(i) is intended.

64.8.2

---

[1] Rule 64.6 inserted by S.S.I. 2000 No. 319 (effective 2nd October, 2000) and amended by S.S.I. 2004 No. 52 (effective 1st March, 2004).
[2] Chap. 64 and r. 64.7 inserted by S.S.I. 2000 No. 319 (effective 2nd October 2000).
[3] Chap. 64 and r. 64.7 inserted by S.S.I. 2000 No. 319 (effective 2nd October 2000).
[4] R. 64.8 inserted by S.S.I. 2000 No. 319 (effective 2nd October, 2000).

COMMISSION AND DILIGENCE.

64.8.3

If the prayer is granted an interlocutor will be pronounced granting a commission and diligence. The court, where appropriate and sought, (a) appoints a commissioner with a warrant under which the commissioner may enter premises and search for the documents or property, (b) authorises a named person to photograph, inspect, take samples of, or carry out an experiment on the property, (c) grants warrant to cite a haver to appear before a commissioner to produce the document or other property or answer questions about where it is or with whom it is or has been, or (d) authorises one or more of the above either at the same time or one at a time. Were it is not possible for a commissioner to blank out commercially confidential material in excerpting from documents, the court has authorised counsel, solicitors and an independent expert to inspect the documents provided they signed an undertaking about disclosure: *Iomega Corporation v. Myrica (UK) Ltd (No.1)* , 1999 S.L.T. 793

The court has power to impose conditions for the use of information recovered by commission and diligence, although it is normal practice for the court to do so: *McInally v. John Wyeth & Brother Ltd* , 1992 S.L.T. 344; *Union Carbide Corporation v. B.P. Chemicals Ltd* , 1995 S.C. 398, 404G per L.P. Hope.

The interlocutor should indicate which of the powers in rr. 35.5, 35.6 or 35.7 should apply. Note ex parte applications in note 64.5.2.

Care must be taken in identifying correctly in the interlocutor and by the commissioner the place to be searched. Where documents are recovered erroneously at a wrong place (and therefore unlawfully) the court cannot subsequently make them competently recovered: *Dominion Technology Ltd v. Gardner Cryogenics Ltd (No.2)* , 1993 S.L.T. 832.

Duties of commissioner

64.9

64.9.[1] The Commissioner appointed by the court shall, on executing the order—

    (a)[2]   give to the haver a copy of the notice in Form 64.9;

    (b)   explain to the haver—

        (i)   the meaning and effect of the order;

        (ii)   that he may be entitled to claim that some or all of the listed items are confidential or privileged;

    (c)[3]   inform the haver of his right to seek legal advice and to ask the court to vary or discharge the order;

    (d)   enter the premises and take all reasonable steps to fulfil the terms of the order;

    (e)   where the order has authorised the recovery of any of the listed items, prepare an inventory of all the listed items to be recovered before recovering them;

    (f)   send any recovered listed items to the Deputy Principal Clerk of Session to await the further order of the court.

GENERAL NOTE.

64.9.1

See note 64.1.1.

"SEND".

64.9.2

This includes deliver: see r. 1.3(1).

Confidentiality

64.10

64.10.—[4](1) Where confidentiality is claimed for any listed item, that listed item shall, where practicable, be enclosed in a sealed envelope.

(2) A motion to have such a sealed envelope opened may be made by the party who obtained the order and he shall intimate the terms of the motion, by registered post or first class delivery, to the person claiming confidentiality.

(3) A person claiming confidentiality may oppose a motion made under paragraph (2).

---

[1] Rule 64.9 inserted by S.S.I. 2000 No. 319 (effective 2nd October, 2000).
[2] Rule 64.9(a) amended by S.S.I. 2004 No. 52 (effective 1st March, 2004).
[3] Rule 64.9(c) amended by S.S.I. 2011 No. 190 (effective 11th April 2011).
[4] Rule 64.10 inserted by S.S.I. 2000 No. 319 (effective 2nd October 2000).

General note.

See note 64.1.1.

64.10.1

"MOTION".

For motions, see Chap. 23.

64.10.2

Confidentiality or privilege.

Certain communications are recognised to be confidential and privileged.

64.10.3

(1) Solicitor and client.

The general rule is that communications between solicitor and client for professional purposes are confidential and cannot be recovered. There are exceptions where fraud or other illegality is alleged against a party in relation to a transaction in which the solicitor was concerned (*Micosta S.A. v. Shetland I.C.* , 1983 S.L.T. 483), where the very existence of the solicitor and client relationship is in issue or where the communication is the subject-matter of the cause for which it is sought to be recovered (*Kid v. Bunyan* (1842) 5 D. 193). See further, under the fraud exception, *Conoco (U.K.) Ltd v. The Commercial Law Practice* , 1996 S.C.L.R. 446, 1997 S.L.T. 372, for an order against solicitors for disclosure of the identity of their client who was in possession of information relating to a fraud on the petitioners. The client may waive the privilege for a series of communications but not for an isolated document in a series: *Wylie v. Wylie* , 1967 S.L.T. (Notes) 9.

(2) Solicitor and solicitor.

Communications between solicitors with a view to achieving settlement of litigation are confidential an d not recoverable: *Fyfe v. Miller* (1835) 13 S. 809. Stating that a communication is "without prejudice", however, will not make it privileged (*Burns v. Burns* , 1964 S.L.T. (Sh.Ct) 21); and a statement of fact is not protected from use as an admission because the words "without prejudice" have been used: *Watson-Towers Ltd v. McPhail* , 1986 S.L.T. 617; *Daks Simpson Group plc v. Kuiper* , 1994 S.L.T. 689.

(3) Communications post litem motam.

Documents prepared for the purposes or in anticipation o the litigation are confidential and as a general rule are not recoverable: *Anderson v. St Andrew's Ambulance Association* , 1942 S.C. 99. Accordingly, reports of accidents are generally excluded. The reason is that after an accident each party must be able to investigate free from the risk of having to reveal his information to the other side: *Johnstone v. National Coal Board* , 1968 S.C. 128. The only exception to this general rule is that a report by an employee present at the time of the accident to his employer is not confidential (it is a de recenti statement) and may be recovered by the opponent: *Young*, above. Photographs fall into the same category as reports: *More v. Brown & Root Wimpey Highland Fabricators Ltd* , 1983 S.L.T. 669 (in which the general rule and its only exception was reaffirmed). An employer's accident book is not recoverable unless the entry in it comes within the exception: *Dobbie v. Forth Ports Authority* , 1974 S.C. 40. A medical report instructed for the purposes of the litigation is not recoverable: *Teece v. Ayrshire & Arran Health Board* 1990 S.L.T. 512. Confidentiality does not cease on completion if the case fir which the report was prepared: *Hunter v. Douglas Reyburn & Co. Ltd* 1993 S.L.T. 637.

(4) Public policy (public interest immunity).

The only situation in which a document or other property may be withheld on the ground of public policy or public interest is where the interest is a national one put forward by the Crown: *Higgins v. Burton* 1986 S.L.T. (Notes) 52. The view that the law of Scotland does not recognise the concept of public interest immunity beyond that of Crown privilege, and does not divide confidentiality into public interest immunity and private confidentiality, was confirmed in *Parks v. Tayside R.C.* 1989 S.L.T. 345, 348a-348F per Lord Sutherland. See note 64.1.5 on Crown privilege or immunity.

(5) Spouses.

Communications between spouses are confidential and one is not a competent or compellable witness against the other (Evidence (Scotland) Act 1853, s. 3) except where the cause is concerned with their conduct towards each other, e.g. in a divorce (*MacKay v. MacKay* 1946 S.C. 78). The privilege subsists after death or divorce: *Dickson on Evidence*, para. 1660.

(6) Self-incrimination of haver.

As a general rule a document or other property which would render the haver liable to prosecution because it is self-incriminating is privileged. There is an exception. The privilege against self-incrimination cannot be claimed in respect of proceedings under s. 1(1) of the Act of 1972 for infringement, to obtain disclosure of information about infringement or to prevent any apprehended infringement of intellectual property rights or passing off: Law Reform (Miscellaneous Provisions) (Scotland) Act 19875, s. 15.

(7)   Clergy, doctors and journalists.

It is sometimes said that communications to such persons are confidential. This is true in a popular but not a legal sense. Confidentiality does not appear to attach much to communications to clergy. It does not attach to communications to doctors or journalists. The ordinary rule excluding recovery in relation to a medical report made in connection with the litigation would, however, apply to a doctor.

(8)   Communications as a matter of duty.

"A communication honestly made upon any subject in which a person has an interest, social or moral, or in reference to which he has a duty, is privileged if made to a person having a corresponding interest or duty": *James v. Baird* 1916 S.C. 510, 517 per L.P. Strathclyde. For a recent example of this type of privilege , see *Paterson v. Education Institution of Scotland* , 1997 S.C. 245.

Waiver of confidentiality will not necessarily result from documents being referred to in open court by the party entitled to the privilege; it depends on the purpose and whether there was publication of the contents: *Barclay v. Morris* 1998 S,C, 74. See also *Duke of Argyll v. Duchess of Argyll* 1962 S.C. (H.L.) 88 (admission on record of specific entries in diaries not waver of whole contents); and *Cunningham v. The Scotsman Publication Ltd* 1987 S.C. 107.

CROWN PRIVILEGE OR IMMUNITY.

64.10.4   Commission and diligence may be granted for recovery etc. of documents or property in possession of the Crown whether or not a party subject to two provisos, (i) a document or property may be withheld on the ground that its disclosure would be injurious to the public interest and (ii) the existence of a document or property shall not be disclosed if in the opinion of a Minister of the Crown it would be injurious to the public interest to disclose the existence of it; Crown Proceedings Act 1947, s. 1(4). The first proviso relates to a particular document and the second to a class. The court has, however, an inherent power to overrule an objection by the Crown which is preserved by s. 47 of the 1947 Act. The test to be applied is whether the public interest in the administration of justice not being frustrated outweighs the objection: *Glasgow Corporation v. Central Land Board* 1956 S.C. (H.L.) 1 confirming the law of Scotland recognised in *Sheridan v. Peel* 1907 S.C. 577, 580 per L.P. Dunedin; *Henderson v. McGowan* 1916 S.C. 821, 826 per L.P. Strathclyde. It is based on the ground that the fair administration of justice between subject and subject and between the subject and the Crown is a public interest of a high order, and that its protection is in the care of the courts: *Glasgow Corporation*, above, per Viscount Normand at pp. 12–13. Where objection is taken to a class of documents the court can take into account not only the interests of the applicant but also the interests of the public as a whole: *Friel, Petr* 1981 S.C. 1.

The court is bound to accept the assertion of the Crown that there is an aspect of public policy to protect: *Admiralty v. Aberdeen Steam Trawling and Fishing Co. Ltd* 1909 S.C. 335; *Friel*, above; *A.B. v. Glasgow and West of Scotland Blood Transfusion Service* 1993 S.L.T. 36.

The court may inspect the document in deciding whether it should be reproduced or to decide whether parts of it which are relevant might be produced: *Science Research Council v. Nasse* [1980] A.C. 1028; *Air Canada v. Secretary of State for Trade (No. 2)* [1986] 2 A.C. 394.

In order to persuade the court even to inspect the documents the party seeking recovery ought at least to satisfy the court that they are very likely to contain material which would give substantial support to his contention on an issue which arises in the case and that without them he might be deprived of the means of proper presentation of his case: *Air Canada*, above, per Lord Fraser of Tullybelton at p.435.

Immunity does not apply to documents or property which do not come into the possession of a servant or agent of the Crown in the ordinary course of his official duties: *Whitehall v. Whitehall* 1957 S.C. 30. Immunity only arises where the public interest is a national one: *Higgins v. Burton* 1968 S.L.T. (Notes) 52; *Parks v. Tayside R.C.* 1989 S.L.T. 345, 345A per Lord Sutherland.

Restrictions on service

64.11   **64.11.**[1](1)   Except on cause shown, the order may be served on Monday to Friday only, between the hours of 9am and 5pm only.

(2)   The order shall not be served at the same time as a search warrant granted in the course of a criminal investigation.

(3)   The Commissioner may be accompanied only by—

   (a)   any person whom he considers necessary to assist him to execute the order;

   (b)   such representatives of the petitioner as are named in the order, and if it is likely that the premises will be occupied by an unaccompanied female and the Commissioner is not herself female, one of the people accompanying the Commissioner shall be female.

---

[1] Rule 64.11 inserted by SSI 2000/319 (effective from 2nd October 2000).

(4)   If it appears to the Commissioner when he comes to serve the order that the premises are occupied by an unaccompanied female and the Commissioner is neither female nor accompanied by a female, the Commissioner shall not enter the premises.

General note.

See note 64.1.1.

64.11.1

Right of haver to consult

64.12.—[1](1)   The haver may seek legal or other professional advice of his choice.

(2)   Where the purpose of seeking this advice is to help the haver to decide whether to ask the court to vary or discharge the order, the haver may ask the Commissioner to delay starting the search for up to 2 hours or such other longer period as the Commissioner may permit.

(3)   Where the haver is seeking advice under this rule, he or she must—

    (a)   inform the Commissioner and the petitioner's agent of that fact;

    (b)   not disturb or remove any listed items;

    (c)   permit the Commissioner to enter the premises, but not to start the search.

General note.

See note 64.1.1.

64.12

64.12.1

Return of documents etc. to haver

64.13.[2]   The Deputy Principal Clerk of Session shall return the recovered listed items to the haver if the petitioner has taken no further action within 8 weeks of the date on which they are sent to him under rule 64.9(f).

General note.

See note 64.1.1.

64.13

64.13.1

This rule deals with a problem referred to in note 64.2.3 to the previous Chap. 64 (which last appeared in Release 53). In view In the view of the large number of recoveries kept by the Deputy Principal Clerk in respect of which no further action was taken, it was thought that the court might have to consider either (a) inserting in a interlocutor granting a commission and diligence a time-limit after the expiry of which the documents will be returned to the haver or (b) putting out petitions on the By Order Roll to ascertain whether the property may be returned. The haver could enter the process by lodging answers (or perhaps by motion) to recover his property, although in doing so he would be liable in the first instance to a court fee for entering the process. In *Olsen v. Forrest Estate Ltd* , 14th June 1994, unreported (1994 G.W.D. 24-1472), a motion by the havers to have documents returned was refused on the ground that the court would not be generally order return, except in exceptional circumstances, before the determination of the petition. This decision overlooked the point made above that a number of such petitions are not concluded but no further action is taken in the process after the recoveries are lodged with the Deputy Principal Clerk.

Where it can be summarily and conclusively shown that the basis on which an order for recovery of documents and property, under s. 1 of the Act of 1972 has been obtained, is false, the court can order redelivery: *Olsen*, above; *Iomega Corporation Petr* , 14th August 1994, unreported.

---

[1] Rule 64.12 inserted by S.S.I. 2000 No. 319 (effective 2nd October 2000) and substituted by S.S.I. 2011 No. 190 (effective 11th April 2011).

[2] Rule 64.13 inserted by S.S.I. 2000 No. 319 (effective from 2nd October 2000).

Chapter 65

References to the European Court of Justice

Interpretation of this Chapter

65.1.—(1) In this Chapter—

"appeal" includes an application for leave to appeal;

"the European Court" means the Court of Justice of the European Communities;

"reference" means a reference to the European Court for—

    (a)[1,2] a preliminary ruling under Article 267 of the Treaty on the Functioning of the European Union, Article 150 of the Euratom Treaty, or Article 41 of the E.C.S.C. Treaty;

    (b) a preliminary ruling on the interpretation of the Conventions, mentioned in Article 1 of Schedule 2 to the Civil Jurisdiction and Judgments Act 1982, under Article 3 of that Schedule; or

    (c) a preliminary ruling on the interpretation of the instruments, mentioned in Article 1 of Schedule 3 to the Contracts (Applicable Law) Act 1990, under Article 2 of that Schedule.

(2)[3] The expressions "Euratom Treaty" and "E.C.S.C. Treaty" have the meanings assigned respectively in Schedule 1 to the European Communities Act 1972.

(3)[4] In paragraph (1), "the Treaty on the Functioning of the European Union" means the treaty referred to in section 1(2)(s) of the European Communities Act 1972.

Deriv. RCS 1965, r. 296A inserted by SI 1972/1981

GENERAL NOTE.

The term "European Economic Community" in the E.E.C. Treaty was replaced by the term "European Community" by Art.G(1) of Title II of the Treaty on European Union (Maastricht): see European Communities Act 1972, s. 1(2)(k) as amended by the European Communities (Amendment) Act 1993, s. 1(1).

The E.C. Commission has expressed its willingness to respond to formal requests by national courts for advice and information about the application of Arts 85 and 86 (which relate to competition law) of the E.C. (formerly E.E.C.) Treaty: see Notice on co-operation between national courts and the Commission in applying Articles 85 and 86 of the E.E.C. Treaty, Official Journal [1993] c. 39/6. The court could write directly after hearing parties, or the court could request a party (or parties jointly) to write (no doubt in terms approved by the court) to the Commission for particular advice or information. The Commission could be invited to appear and make representations. No express provision is made, or required, in the RCS 1994 for this procedure.

Applications for reference

65.2. A reference may be made by the court at its own instance or on the motion of a party.

Deriv. RCS 1965, r. 296B inserted by S.I. 1972 No. 1981
[1] Rule 65.2 amended by S.I. 1999 No. 1281 (effective 1st May 1999)

GENERAL NOTE.

Where the decision of the court is one against which there is no judicial remedy under the national law (i.e. no right of appeal in the proceedings in question), the court is bound to bring before the European Court for a preliminary ruling a question of Community law arising in the proceedings pending before it:

---

[1] Rule 65.1 amended by SI 1999/1281 (effective 1st May 1999).
[2] Rule 65.1 (1)(a) and (2) amended and (3) inserted by S.S.I. 2012 No. 275 r. 7(1) (effective 19th November 2012).
[3] Rule 65.1 (1)(a) and (2) amended and (3) inserted by S.S.I. 2012 No. 275 r. 7(1) (effective 19th November 2012).
[4] Rule 65.1 (1)(a) and (2) amended and (3) inserted by S.S.I. 2012 No. 275 r. 7(1) (effective 19th November 2012).

65.1

65.1.1

65.2

65.2.1

E.E.C. Treaty, Art. 234(3) (177(3) before the Treaty of Amsterdam). The duty to refer does not arise (a) in respect of an interlocutory decision against which there is no appeal if the question of Community law may be reviewed at a later stage of the case (*Hoffmann-La Roche v. Centrafarm Vertreihsgesellschaft* [1977] E.C.R. 957) or (b) where a previous decision of the European Court is directly in point or where the correct application of Community law is obvious to all national courts (*CILFIT Srl. v. Ministry of Health* [1982] E.C.R. 3415).

A judge at first instance or the Inner House (at first instance, in a reclaiming motion or an appeal) has a discretion to request a preliminary ruling under Art. 177(2) (now Art. 234(2)) of the E.E.C. Treaty where a decision on a question of Community law is necessary to enable judgment to be given. The exercise of the discretion is itself subject to review.

The test in both cases is whether the decision on a question of Community law is necessary to decide the dispute: *CILFIT Srl.*, above. The court may decide the question itself if the point is free from doubt and obvious to all national courts: *CILFIT Srl.*, above.

A reference may be made at any time, though it is probably not appropriate before the closing of the record: *Prince v. Secretary of State for Scotland* 1985 S.C. 8.

The provisions for preliminary rulings under Art. 3 of Sched. 2 to the C.J.J.A. 1982 and Art. 2 of Sched. 3 to the Contracts (Applicable Law) Act 1990 are to similar effect. The 1990 Act implements the Rome Convention on the Law Applicable to Contractual Obligations 1980 made to achieve unification of rules of international private law in relation to contractual obligations within the E.C.

[1] The form for the reference is now provided for in r. 65.3.

"MOTION".

65.2.2 For motions, see Chap. 23.

Preparation of case for reference

65.3 **65.3.**—(1) Where the court decides that a reference shall be made, it shall pronounce an interlocutor giving directions to the parties about the manner and time in which the reference is to be drafted and adjusted.

(1A)[1] Except in so far as the court may otherwise direct, a reference shall be prepared in accordance with Form 65.3.

(1B)[2] In preparing a reference, the parties shall have regard to guidance issued by the European Court of Justice.

(2)[3] When the reference has been drafted and any adjustments required by the court have been made, the court shall make and sign the reference.

(3) A certified copy of the interlocutor making the reference shall be annexed to the reference.

"ADJUSTMENT REQUIRED BY THE COURT".

65.3.1 The reference is checked by the clerk of court in the first instance to see that it is in conformity with any requirement of the interlocutor allowing the reference and the ground on which the reference was allowed. If he has a doubt he consults the judge. Adjustments may be required by the court. Once adjusted the clerk may add the following docquet to the reference:

"Edinburgh, (*date*). This reference consisting of this and the preceding pages adjusted at my sight.

(*Signed*), Depute Clerk of Session."

GUIDANCE FROM THE ECJ.

65.3.2 The European Court of Justice (of the European Communities) has issued guidance on the making of a reference. This should be consulted when preparing the reference in Form 65.3. The guidance was reproduced in an Annex to the Rules in the amendment to r. 65.3 in S.I. 1999 No. 1281 which inserted para (1B), but, because the guidance is updated and may change from time to time, was sensibly removed in the amendment in 2005 substituting a new para (1B). The guidance referred to can be found in an information note published by the Court of Justice of the European Communities at: *www.curia.europa.eu/jcms/jcms/Jo2-7031* or at *http://eur-lex.europa.eu/LexUriServ/LexUriServ.do?uri = OJ:C.:2009:297: 0001:0006:EN:PDF*

---

[1] Rule 65.3(1A) inserted by S.I. 1999 No. 1281 (effective 1st May 1999).
[2] Rule 65.3(1B) inserted by S.I. 1999 No. 1281 and substituted by S.I. 1999 No. 1281 (effective 21st October, 2005).
[3] R. 65.3(2) amended by S.I. 1999 No. 1281 (effective 1st May 1999).

Sist of cause

65.4.—(1) Subject to paragraph (2), on a reference being made, the cause shall, unless the court when making such a reference otherwise orders, be sisted until the European Court has given a preliminary ruling on the question referred to it.

(2) The court may recall a sist made under paragraph (1) for the purpose of making an interim order which a due regard to the interests of the parties may require.

Deriv. RCS 1965, r. 296C inserted by S.I. 1972 No. 1981

65.4

Transmission of reference

65.5.—(1) Subject to paragraph (2), a copy of the reference, certified by the Deputy Principal Clerk, shall be transmitted by him to the Registrar of the European Court.

(2) Unless the court otherwise directs, a copy of the reference shall not be sent to the Registrar of the European Court where a reclaiming motion or appeal against the making of the reference is pending.

(3) For the purpose of paragraph (2), a reclaiming motion or an appeal shall be treated as pending—

(a) until the expiry of the time for marking that reclaiming motion or appeal; or

(b) where a reclaiming motion or an appeal has been made, until it has been determined.

Deriv. RCS 1965, r. 296D inserted by S.I. 1972 No. 1981

65.5

GENERAL NOTE.

When the reference is received by the Registrar of the European Court in Luxembourg it is translated into all the official languages of the court, the order of the Court of Session for the reference is served on the parties to the action, the Member States and Community institutions, all of whom may lodge written observations within two months of service. After expiry of the time to lodge observations the judge rapporteur prepares and presents a preliminary report; the Advocate-General writes an opinion. There follows a hearing at which parties can present oral argument.

For procedure generally before the European Court, see Rules of Procedure of the Court of Justice published by the court.

65.5.1

RECLAIMING OR APPEAL.

The period within which a cause may be reclaimed or appealed is determined by the enactment under which the reclaiming motion or appeal is made. Subject to any other enactment, under the RCS 1994, the time for reclaiming is determined by rr. 38.3 and 38.4 and the time for appeal determined by r. 40.4 (appeals from inferior courts), rr. 41.5 and 41.11 (appeals by stated case etc.) or r. 41.20 (appeals in Form 41.19). "Appeal" includes appeal to the House of Lords, which must be made within three months of the date on which the order appealed from was made: House of Lords Directions, Direction 8.1.

65.5.2

CHAPTER 66 APPLICATIONS UNDER THE EVIDENCE (PROCEEDINGS IN OTHER JURISDICTIONS) ACT 1975

Chapter 66

Applications under the Evidence (Proceedings in Other Jurisdictions) Act 1975

Interpretation of this Chapter

66.1. In this Chapter—

66.1

"the Act of 1975" means the Evidence (Proceedings in Other Jurisdictions) Act 1975;

"civil proceedings" has the meaning assigned in section 9(1) of the Act of 1975;

"requesting court" has the meaning assigned in section 9(1) of the Act of 1975.

GENERAL NOTE.

R.C.S. 1965, r. 102A, from which this Chapter is derived, was introduced following the enactment of the Evidence (Proceedings in Other Jurisdictions) Act 1975. Until this Act the taking of evidence of a witness or haver resident in Scotland for the purpose of proceedings in a foreign court or tribunal was regulated by the Evidence by Commission Acts 1859 and 1885 (for requests by a court in another of H.M. Dominions (including England and Wales and Ireland)) and the Foreign Tribunals Evidence Act 1856 (for requests by a court in any "foreign country"; and extended to criminal proceedings by s.24 of the Extradition Act 1870). The Act of 1975 repealed the 1856, 1859 and 1885 Acts and s.24 of the 1870 Act, and replaced these with a new unified regime for civil and criminal proceedings. The Criminal Justice (International Co-operation) Act 1990, however, replaced the Act of 1975 in respect of criminal proceedings. The Act of 1975 also enabled the U.K. to ratify the Hague Convention on the Taking of Evidence Abroad in Civil or Commercial Matters, 1970 (Cmnd. 6727 (1977)) in 1976. The Central Authority in Scotland for receipt of letters of request under the Convention is the Scottish Government Justice Directorate, Central Authority & International Law Team, St Andrews House (GW15), Regent Road, Edinburgh EH1 3DG.

66.1.1

A letter of request may be made directly to the court and not necessarily via the Central Authority. In *Liv Golf Inc v. R&A Trust Company (No. 1) Ltd* 2023 S.C. 305 (First Div.),. 2023 S.L.T. 401, the petitioner lodged a letter of request from the US District Court for Northern California seeking an order for the respondent to produce certain document under the 1975 Act in proceedings by the petitioner against PGA Tour Inc. The court asked to be addressed on the competency of a direct application to the court rather than through the Central Authority designated under the Hague Convention 1970. Section 1 of the 1975 Act does not prohibit, and Art. 27 of the Hague Convention allows for, requests by means other than the Central Authority. The Lord Advocate raised no objection on behalf of the Central Authority and the court held that it could not impose a requirement that the request pass through the Central Authority.

The Act of 1975, however, is broader than the convention in that it allows letters of request from any country and not just the parties to the convention; it also applies to courts within the U.K. Under s.6 of the Act of 1975, the Act may be applied to international proceedings. By Order in Council the Act of 1975 was extended to proceedings before the Court of Justice of the European Communities: Evidence (European Court) Order 1976 [S.I. 1976 No. 428]. With regard to U.K. dependencies the Act, as modified, applies to the Cayman Islands (S.I. 1978 No. 1600), the Falkland Islands and Dependencies (S.I. 1978 No. 1891), the Sovereign base areas of Akrotiri and Dhekelia (S.I. 1978 No. 1920), the Isle of Man (S.I. 1979 No. 1711), Guernsey (S.I. 1980 No. 1956), Jersey (S.I. 1983 No. 1700), Anguilla (S.I. 1986 No. 218), and the Turks and Caicos Islands (S.I. 1987 No. 1266).

This Chapter is made under s.1(3) of the Administration of Justice (Scotland) Act 1972 as well as under s.5 of the C.S.A. 1988.

"CIVIL PROCEEDINGS".

This means, in relation to the requesting court, proceedings in any civil or commercial matter: Act of 1975, s.9(1). It has been held in England that the words "civil or commercial matter" have a wide meaning and include all proceedings other than criminal proceedings (a meaning broader than the same words in the C.J.J.A. 1982): *Re State of Norway's Application (Nos 1 and 2)* [1990] 1 A.C. 723, 806F per Lord Goff of Chieveley. It was also held in that case that whether proceedings are civil is a matter of law and practice of the requesting court: per Lord Goff of Chieveley at p. 805 B.

66.1.2

"REQUESTING COURT".

This means the court or tribunal making the request: Act of 1975, ss.1(a) and 9(1).

66.1.3

Disapplication of certain rules to this Chapter

66.2. The following rules shall not apply to an application to which this Chapter applies:—

66.2

rule 14.5 (first order in petitions),

rule 14.6 (period of notice for lodging answers),

rule 14.7 (intimation and service of petitions),

rule 14.9 (unopposed petitions).

EX PARTE APPLICATION.

66.2.1   An application under the Act is made *ex parte* without any requirement for intimation, service or answers. This is to enable the evidence to be obtained speedily. If a witness or haver against whom an order has been made and intimated under r. 66.4 objects to it, he must apply to the court by note to have it varied or recalled: r. 66.5. Accordingly, the rules in Chap. 14 mentioned in this rule are disapplied.

Form of applications under the Act of 1975

66.3   **66.3.**—(1)   An application under section 1 of the Act of 1975 (application for assistance in obtaining evidence for foreign civil proceedings) shall be made by petition.

(2)   *[Revoked by S.I. 1998 No. 2637.]*

(3)   Where the letter of request is in a language other than English, there shall be produced with the petition a translation into English certified as correct by the translator; and the certificate shall include his full name, address and qualifications.

Deriv. R.C.S. 1965, r. 102A(2) inserted by S.I. 1976 No. 283 and amended by S.I. 1982 No. 1825 (r. 66.3(1))

APPLICATIONS UNDER S.1 OF THE ACT OF 1975.

66.3.1   All applications under the Act of 1975 are made under s.1 which relates only to evidence for civil proceedings, its application formerly by s.5 (now repealed) to criminal proceedings (furth of the U.K.) being replaced by the Criminal Justice (International Co-operation) Act 1990.

The application may be made by any court furth of Scotland including a court elsewhere in the U.K.

"PETITION".

66.3.2   The petition is presented in the Inner House: r. 14.3(f). The vacation judge may not determine the petition though he may make an incidental order: r. 11.1(c). For the form of the petition see r. 14.4. The petition must be signed by counsel or other person having a right of audience: r. 4.2(3); and see r. 1.3(1) (definitions of "counsel" and "other person having a right of audience") and note 1.3.4.

Where the application relates to oral evidence, the petition should include averments—(a) referring to the request giving rise to the application; (b) that the requesting court requires oral evidence for use in a trial or proof of fact in civil proceedings before it (*Lord Advocate, Petr.* 1993 S.C. 638); and (c) to satisfy the court that if a similar situation arose in civil proceedings before it, the court could grant a commission for the examination of a witness (Act of 1975, s.2(3)). The prayer of the petition should contain a crave for the appointment of a commissioner.

Where the application relates to real or documentary evidence, the petition should include averments—(a) similar to (a) and (b) above; and (b) to satisfy the court that if a similar situation arose in civil proceedings before it, the court could order recovery, inspection, preservation, etc., of the material sought (Act of 1975, s.2(3)). The prayer of the petition should include craves corresponding to the order sought (see, e.g. note 64.2.3). It is suggested that one of the craves may, for convenience, refer to a schedule (akin to a specification of documents) listing the real or documentary evidence sought to be recovered.

EVIDENCE IS TO BE OBTAINED FOR CIVIL PROCEEDINGS.

66.3.3   The meaning of the word "evidence" in the Act of 1975 was discussed inconclusively in *In re Westinghouse Uranium Contract* [1978] A.C. 547. Lord Diplock, with whom Lord Keith of Kinkel agreed, considered (pp. 633–634) that evidence might be obtained by an applicant to ascertain whether there existed admissible evidence to support his case or to contradict his opponent's case if that was permitted by the system of the requesting court, the only limit to fishing discovery (diligence) being in s.2 of the Act of 1975 (see note 66.3.7). Viscount Dilhorne thought (p. 619) the Act was limited to direct evidence for use at the trial (proof); and see Lord Fraser of Tullybelton at pp. 641–645. In *Lord Advocate, Petr* 1993 S.C. 638, a letter of request for the dual purpose of trial testimony and deposition testimony was allowed to the extent of trial testimony and the sheriff principal was directed to allow a legal representative of the witness to attend to object to questions on the ground of competency or relevancy. The Inner House has approved Viscount Dilhorne's views in *In re Westinghouse Uranium Contract*, above: *Lord Advocate, Petr* 1998 S.C. 87, 94H per Extra Div.; and see *First American Corporation v. Sheikh Zayed Al-Nahyan* [1998] 4 All E.R. 437 (CA).

"REQUESTING COURT".

66.3.4   See note 66.1.3.

CERTIFICATE ABOUT THE PROCEEDINGS.

Formerly, r. 66.3(2) required a certificate that the application was made by virtue of a request for evidence for the purpose of civil proceedings commenced or contemplated before the foreign court. This requirement was revoked by A.S. (R.C.S.A. No. 2) (Miscellaneous) 1998 [S.I. 1998 No. 2637] as an unnecessary formality which was in excess of the requirements of the 1970 Hague Convention (see note 66.1.1).

66.3.5

"CIVIL PROCEEDINGS".

See note 66.1.2.

66.3.6

ORDERS WHICH MAY BE OBTAINED.

Section 2 of the Act of 1975 specifies the scope of an order under it. The order must (a) give effect to the request in the application by providing for the obtaining of the evidence requested, and (b) require a person specified to take such steps as the court considers appropriate for the obtaining of the evidence requested. In giving effect to the request the court cannot make an order which it could not normally make in relation to domestic proceedings before it (Act of 1975, s.2(3); and see *Lord Advocate, Petr* 1993 S.C. 638 and *Lord Advocate, Petr* 1998 S.C. 87), or which would require a person to state what relevant documents are in his possession or to produce documents not specified in the order (Act of 1975 s.2(4)).

66.3.7

The restriction of the Act of 1975 in s.4 of the Protection of Trading Interests Act 1980 should be noted. Where the order provides for the obtaining of oral evidence, the order should narrate that the evidence is "for the purpose of trial testimony only": *Lord Advocate, Petr* 1993 S.C. 638, 641H.

The court can order a commission for the taking of evidence from a witness. It can also order recovery of documents from a haver at common law (see note 35.2.5) or under s.1 of the Administration of Justice (Scotland) Act 1972 (see note 35.2.6) or inspection, preservation, etc., under s.1 of the 1972 Act. An order for production of a public record for evidence in foreign proceedings may be made. In relation to medical examinations, see restriction in s.2 of the Age of Legal Capacity (Scotland) Act 1991. In relation to the taking of blood or other samples, see powers in s.6 of the Law Reform (Parent and Child) (Scotland) Act 1986 and s.70 of the Law Reform (Miscellaneous Provisions) (Scotland) Act 1990; and see note 35.15.5(4).

In relation to public records and entries in public registers, extracts should be sufficient. Writs in the Books of Council and Session may not be given out without the authority of the court: Writs Registration (Scotland) Act 1868; by the Writs Execution (Scotland) Act 1877, extracts are equivalent. The court is reluctant to allow original records out of the country: see *Kennedy* (1880) 7 R. 1129. Where the court does so, it may require the document to remain in the custody of an official of the public register: *Campbell's Trs* 1934 S.C. 8.

COMMISSIONER.

Where the application is made by the Lord Advocate on behalf of the Secretary of State for Foreign and Commonwealth Affairs who has received a letter of request from a foreign government official, the commissioner should be the sheriff principal or sheriff of the sheriffdom in whose jurisdiction the witness or haver resides: *Lord Advocate, Petr* 1909 S.C. 199; and see, e.g. *Lord Advocate v. Sheriffs* 1978 S.C. 56 and *Lord Advocate, Petr* 1993 S.C. 638. Where the application is made by an agent of a party to foreign proceedings or a representative of a foreign country directly and not the Lord Advocate, the court will appoint any commissioner it thinks fit in the normal way for a commission but not a sheriff: *Baron de Bildt, Petr* (1905) 7 F. 899.

66.3.8

THE COMMISSION.

The commission ought to be conducted in the same way as a commission to take the evidence of a witness under Chap. 35 (see notes 35.12.5 (on interrogatories) and 35.13.5 (without interrogatories)). In *Lord Advocate, Petr* 1994 S.L.T. 852, the court considered it was taking an unusual step, which would not normally be ordered as a matter of course, by directing the sheriff principal to allow a legal representative of the witness (as distinct presumably from the lawyer for the party whose witness he would be) to attend to object to questions on the ground of competency or relevancy.

66.3.8A

IDENTITY OF WITNESS OR HAVER.

Where the applicant wishes to examine unknown representatives of a company or similar legal persona or partnership the names of which the applicant does not know, there is no need to identify the individuals by their names in the petition and the court will ordain the company to name them: *Lord Advocate, Petr* 1925 S.C. 568.

66.3.9

Intimation of order and citation

66.4.—(1) Where the court pronounces an interlocutor making an order under section 2(1) of the Act of 1975, the petitioner shall—

    (a)   intimate a certified copy of that interlocutor to any witness or haver named in the interlocutor; and

    (b)   cite such witness or haver to give evidence.

66.4

(2) Rule 35.4(3) and (4) (citation of haver to commission) and rule 35.11(5) and (6) (citation of witness to commission) shall, with the necessary modifications, apply to the citation of a haver or witness, as the case may be, under this rule.

EXPENSES OF WITNESS OR HAVER.

66.4.1   A witness or haver who is cited following an order under s.1 of the Act of 1975 is entitled to payment of expenses for attendance: s.2(5) of the Act of 1975. The solicitor for the petitioner will be responsible for the expenses. Where the application is not made by the Lord Advocate caution may be required for these expenses.

INTIMATION.

66.4.2   For methods, see r. 16.7.

CERTIFIED COPY INTERLOCUTOR.

66.4.3   The applicant should prepare a copy for certification by the clerk of session.

CITATION OF WITNESS OR HAVER.

66.4.4   This should be done at the same time as intimation.

Variation or recall of orders

66.5   **66.5.** A witness or haver who has received intimation and citation under rule 66.4 may apply to the court by motion to have the order under section 2(1) of the Act of 1975 varied or recalled.

Deriv. RCS 1965, r. 102A(5) inserted by S.I. 1990 No. 705

"MOTION".

66.5.1   For motions, see Chap. 23. The special provisions where a witness or haver claims he is not compellable should be noted: see r. 66.6.

For an example of variation of an order, see *Lord Advocate, Petr* 1993 S.C. 638.

Procedure where witness claims he is not compellable

66.6   **66.6.**—(1) Where a witness or haver who has received intimation and citation under rule 66.4—

    (a)   claims that he is not a compellable witness or haver by virtue of section 3(1)(b) of the Act of 1975, and

    (b)   is required to give evidence,

the court or any commissioner appointed by the court shall take the evidence and record it in a document separate from the record of any other evidence; and that document shall be kept by the Deputy Principal Clerk.

(2) Where evidence is taken under paragraph (1) of this rule, the court or the commissioner, as the case may be, shall certify the grounds of the claim made under section 3(1)(b) of the Act of 1975.

(3) On certification under paragraph (2), the Deputy Principal Clerk shall send the certificate to the requesting court with a request to it to determine the claim.

(4) On receipt of the determination from the requesting court, the Deputy Principal Clerk shall—

    (a)   give written intimation of the determination to the witness or haver who made the claim; and

    (b)   in accordance with the determination, send the document in which the evidence is recorded to, as the case may be—

        (i)   the requesting court, or

        (ii)   where the claim is upheld, the witness or haver.

Deriv. R.C.S. 1965, r. 102A(3)inserted by S.I. 1976 No. 283

COMPELLABILITY.

66.6.1   A witness or haver may claim he is not compellable in relation to oral or documentary evidence which he is ordered to give or produce (a) where he would be able to do so in Scottish civil proceedings (Act of 1975, s. 3(1)); (b) where he would be able to do so in the country of the requesting court (Act of 1975, s. 3(2)); or (c) where the evidence would be prejudicial to UK security, in respect of which a certificate by or on behalf of the Secretary of State is conclusive (Act of 1975, s. 3(3)). In respect of proceedings in the country of the requesting court the question of non-compellability should be supported by a statement in the request or conceded by the applicant for the order: Act of 1975, s. 3(2). Where the claim of non-compellability is not so supported the witness or haver may be required to give evidence (Act of 1975, s. 3(2)) in which case the procedure in this rule is followed.

Where a witness fails or refuses to attend, the modern practice is to enrol a motion for warrant to messengers-at-arms to apprehend the witness. The historical practice of obtaining letters of second diligence (in effect having the same result) is not usually followed, although it may be where it is known in advance that the witness will not attend. Before granting the warrant the court must be satisfied that citation has been executed; a certificate of execution must be produced.

On compellability of witnesses, see note 36.2.8.

At common law in England the court may refuse to give effect to letters of request where it would be prejudicial to the Sovereignty of the UK: *In re Westinghouse Uranium Contract* [1978] A.C. 547.

Where the evidence is taken by a commissioner he will have to send or deliver the record of the evidence to the Deputy Principal Clerk.

"REQUESTING COURT".

See note 66.1.3. **66.6.2**

"WRITTEN INTIMATION".

For methods, see r. 16.9. **66.6.3**

Applications for evidence for proceedings under the European Patent Convention

66.7. Where the court makes an order under section 1 of the Act of 1975 as applied by section 92(1) of the Patents Act 1977, an officer of the European Patent Office may apply by motion— **66.7**

(a) to examine any witness; or

(b) to request the court or commissioner, as the case may be, to put specified questions to any witness.

Deriv. R.C.S. 1965, r. 102A(4) inserted by S.I. 1978 No. 955

EUROPEAN PATENT OFFICE.

The European Patent Office was established under Convention on the Grant of European Patents (Cmnd. 8510 (1982)). By virtue of s. 92(1) of the Patents Act 1977, ss. 1 to 3 of the Act of 1975 apply to proceedings before a relevant convention court under the convention. **66.7.1**

"MOTION".

For motions, see Chap. 23. **66.7.2**

On behalf of the Secretary of State at an Exclusive Act of 1975 ... step. In respect of proceedings in the Contract of the restrictive court the quasi-court and non-compellability should be supported by a statement in the request or concluded by the applicant for the order. Act of 1975, s. 1(2). Where the claim of contractual liability is not so supported the witness or never may be required to give evidence (Act of 1975, s. 2(2)) in which case the procedure in this rule is followed.

Where a witness claims or refuses to attend the modern practice is to grant a motion for warrant to impress the witness to appear and the witness. The historical practice of obtaining letters of request otherwise in effect having the same result is not usually followed although it may be shown on evidence that the witness will not attend. Before terminating without the court must be satisfied that either has been exhausted a certificate of exemption must be produced.

At common law in England the court may refuse to give effect to letters of request where it would be prejudicial to the Sovereignty of the UK, see Rio Tinto Zinc v Westinghouse Cannot (1978) A.C. 547.

Where the evidence is taken by a commissioner he will have to send or deliver the record of the evidence to the Deputy Principal Clerk.

Note:

See note cC.13

Note in this chapter

66.2

For method, see r. 1b.9

66.3

Applications for evidence for proceedings under the European Patent Convention

66.7 Where the court makes an order under section 1 of the 1975 Act as applied by section 92(1) of the Patents Act 1977, an officer of the European Patent Office may apply by motion—

66.7

(a) to examine any witness, or

(b) to request the court or commissioner, as the case may be, to put specified questions to any witness.

Note: R.S.C. 1965, r. 70A(4) (inserted by S.I. 1978, no. 755.

European Patent Office

The European Patent Office was established under Convention on the Grant of European Patents

66.7.1

(Cmnd. 8510 (1982)). By virtue of s. 92(1) of the Patents Act 1977, s. 1 and 2 of the Act of 1975 apply to proceedings before the relevant convention court under the convention.

Note:

For method see Chap. 75.

66.7.2

CHAPTER 67 APPLICATIONS UNDER THE ADOPTION AND CHILDREN (SCOTLAND) ACT 2007

Chapter 67[1]

Applications Under the Adoption and Children (Scotland) Act 2007

Part 1 – General

Application and interpretation

67.1.—[2](1) In this Chapter—

    "the 1995 Act" means the Children (Scotland) Act 1995;

    "the 2002 Act" means the Adoption and Children Act 2002;

    "the 2007 Act" means the Adoption and Children (Scotland) Act 2007;

    "the 2009 Regulations" means the Adoptions with a Foreign Element(Scotland) Regulations 2009;

    "adoption agency" means—

        (a) a local authority;

        (b) a registered adoption service within the meaning of section 2(3) of the 2007 Act;

        (c) an adoption agency within the meaning of section 2(1) of the 2002 Act (adoption agencies in England and Wales); or

        (d) an adoption agency within the meaning of article 3 of the Adoption (Northern Ireland) Order 1987;

    "Her Majesty's Forces" means the regular forces as defined in section 374 of the Armed Forces Act 2006;

    "Principal Reporter" has the same meaning as in section 93(1) of the 1995 Act;

    "Registrar General" means the Registrar General of Births, Deaths and Marriages for Scotland.

Deriv. R.C.S. 1965, r. 219(1) substituted by S.S.I. 1984 No. 997 (r. 67.1(2))

GENERAL NOTE.

The provisions of this Chapter are made under the Adoption and Children (Scotland) Act 2007 (as well as under s. 5 of the C.S.A. 1988). Accordingly, words and expressions used in this Chapter which are used in the 2007 Act have the same meaning as in that Act unless the contrary intention appears: Interpretation Act 1978, s.11. Definitions in the Act of 1978 are in s. 119 of that Act and include "adoption agency", "adoption order", "Convention adoption order", "local authority", "child", "guardian" and "adoption society".

These new rules came into force on 28th September 2009. The Adoption (Scotland) Act 1978 and the rules in the old Chap. 67 continue to apply to certain proceedings not determined by that date, e.g., adoption or freeing for adoption applications: see Adoption and Children (Scotland) Act 2007 (Commencement No. 4, Transitional and Savings Provisions) Order 2009 (S.S.I. 2009 No. 267) and A.S. (R.C.S. A. No. 7 (Adoption and Children (Scotland) Act 2007) 2009) para. 3 (S.S.I. 2009 No. 283). There was an error or gap in the 2009 Order in that the transitional provisions did not provide for the case where a freeing order had been applied for before the appointed day but the application had not been granted until after that date. A decision to read the transitional provision (art. 17(1)) as if it did, so that the child should be treated as if subject to a permanence order, was upheld in *O v. Aberdeen City Council,* 2012 S.C. 60 (Second Div).

The Adoption (Scotland) Act 1978 is repealed except Pt. IV (status of adopted children).

Disapplication of certain rules to this Chapter

67.2.[3] Unless otherwise provided in this Chapter, the following rules shall not apply to a petition or note to which this Chapter applies—

    rule 14.5 (first order in petitions);

    rule 14.6 (period of notice for lodging answers);

---

[1] Chap. 67 and r. 67.1 substituted by S.S.I. 2009 No. 283 (effective 28th September 2009).

[2] Chap. 67 and r. 67.1 substituted by S.S.I. 2009 No. 283 (effective 28th September 2009).

[3] R. 67.2 substituted by S.S.I. 2009 No. 283 (effective 28th September 2009).

rule 14.7 (intimation and service of petitions);

rule 14.8 (procedure where answers lodged);

rule 14.9 (unopposed petitions).

GENERAL NOTE.

67.2.1   The paramount consideration in an adoption order is the need to safeguard and promote the welfare of the child throughout the child's life: 2007 Act, s. 14(2). The rules therefore provide an expedited procedure to which certain ordinary petition rules (listed in this rule) do not apply. On the need to avoid delay in adoption petitions, see *Lothian R.C. v. A.* 1992 S.L.T. 858, 861F per L.P. Hope.

Confidentiality of documents in process

67.3   **67.3.—**[1](1) Unless the court otherwise directs, in any cause to which this Chapter applies all documents lodged in process, including the reports by the curator ad litem and reporting officer—

(a)   are to be available only to the court, the curator ad litem, the reporting officer and the parties; and

(b)   shall be treated as confidential by any persons involved in, or a party to, the proceedings and by the clerk of court.

(2)   The reporting officer and the curator ad litem—

(a)   must treat all information obtained in the exercise of their duties as confidential; and

(b)   must not disclose any such information to any person unless disclosure of such information is necessary for the purpose of their duties.

Deriv. R.C.S. 1965, r. 230(6) substituted by S.I. 1984 No. 997

GENERAL NOTE.

67.3.1   Confidentiality is necessary to ensure that a person is not reluctant to provide relevant information. All documents in process are confidential, not just the various reports. The court may order non-disclosure of a document to a person, even a party where appropriate.

INSPECTION AND BORROWING OF DOCUMENTS.

67.3.2   Writs (defined in r. 1.3(1)) and certain documents may not be borrowed from process, although a person interested (such as those mentioned in r. 67.3) may inspect them: r. 4.11. A party who is an individual may be given access (i.e. allowed to inspect) to a document: r. 67.3(2).

Selection of reporting officer or curator ad litem

67.4   **67.4.**[2] Where the court appoints a reporting officer or a curator ad litem under this Chapter and there is an established panel of persons from whom the appointment may be made, the reporting officer or curator ad litem shall be selected from that panel unless the court considers that it would be appropriate to appoint a person who is not on the panel.

Deriv. R.C.S. 1965, r. 230(8) substituted by S.I. 1984 No. 997

GENERAL NOTE.

67.4.1   The court is not obliged to appoint a curator ad litem or a reporting officer from the panel established under the Curators ad Litem and Reporting Officers (Panels) (Scotland) Regulations 2001 [S.I. 2001 No. 477], if it considers it appropriate to appoint someone not on the panel .

S. 108 of the 2007 Act specifies the general duties of the curator ad litem as being to safeguard the interests of the child in the proceedings, and of the reporting officer as being to witness agreements to adoption and to perform such other duties as may be prescribed by rules. On the appointment of a reporting officer, see r. 67.11 (adoption etc.) and 67.29(1) (permanence orders); on the duties of a reporting officer, see r. 67.12 (adoption etc.) and 67.38(1) (permanence orders). On the appointment of a curator ad litem, see r. 67.11(1) (adoption etc.) and 67.29(1) (permanence orders); on the duties of a curator ad litem, see r. 67.12(2) (adoption etc.) for Convention adoption order and 67.38(2) (permanence orders).

The court may appoint the same person to be both reporting officer and curator ad litem: 2007 Act, s. 108(2).

---

[1] Rule 67.3 substituted by S.S.I. 2009 No. 283 (effective 28th September 2009).
[2] Rule 67.4 substituted by S.S.I. 2009 No. 283 (effective 28th September 2009).

A local authority is required to establish a panel for its own area after consultation with the sheriff principal for the area of suitably qualified and experienced persons under the Curators ad Litem and Reporting Officers (Panels) (Scotland) Regulations 2001 [S.I. 2001 No. 477]. Panels may include social workers, solicitors and advocates. There are restrictions on the appointment from a panel of a person employed by an adoption agency in certain circumstances.

67.4.2

The expenses of a reporting officer or curator ad litem appointed in a particular case from the panel are paid for by the local authority: 2001 Regulations, reg. 10. Local authorities have laid down their own scales. Where additional fees or expenses are claimed these may be met by the local authority; but if not, the balance could be claimed from the petitioner on an order for expenses being obtained from the sheriff under r. 67.7.

A person appointed to the panel takes the oath *de fideli administratione* on his appointment to the panel.

PERSONS NOT ON THE PANEL.

The court may, where it considers it appropriate, appoint a person to be reporting officer or curator ad litem who is not on the panel of the local authority established under the Curators ad litem and Reporting Officers (Panels) (Scotland) Regulations 2001 [S.I. 2001 No. 477]. Where this happens the local authority will not pay the fee of the person appointed, and the fee will usually be the responsibility of the petitioner. The court may make any order it thinks fit in relation to expenses including those of a reporting officer or curator ad litem: r. 67.7.

67.4.3

There are restrictions on the appointment of a person employed by an adoption agency in certain circumstances: 2007 Act, s. 108(3).

A person not on the panel appointed to be a curator ad litem must take the oath *de fideli administratione* on his appointment.

Orders for evidence

67.5.—[1](1) In a cause to which this Chapter applies, the court may, before determining the cause, order—

67.5

(a)   production of further documents (including affidavits);

(b)   parole evidence.

(2) A party may apply by motion for the evidence of a person to be received in evidence by affidavit; and the court may make such order as it thinks fit.

Deriv. R.C.S. 1965, r. 230(5) substituted by S.I. 1984 No. 997 (r. 67.6(1)) and r. 230D (part) inserted by S.I. 1978 No. 1373 (r. 67.6(2))

"AFFIDAVITS".

The affidavit should be in the form of a statement of evidence written in the first person. The affidavit should contain evidence in support of, and expanding on, the averments in the petition. It should be sworn and signed by the deponent before any person who may competently take an oath. Such a person includes a notary public, a justice of the peace, a sheriff, or any judge. The person taking the oath should also sign the affidavit. Witnesses to the affidavit are unnecessary. And see definition of affidavit in r. 1.3(1).

67.5.1

Intimation to Principal Reporter

67.6.[2] Where, under section 54(1) of the 1995 Act (question arising as to whether compulsory measures of supervision are necessary) a matter is referred to the Principal Reporter—

67.6

(a)   the interlocutor making the reference shall specify which of the conditions referred to in that subsection it appears to the court has been satisfied; and

(b)   the clerk of court shall give written intimation of that interlocutor forthwith to the Principal Reporter.

"WRITTEN INTIMATION".

For methods, see r. 16.7. The draftsman's error of "intimation" instead of "written intimation" has been corrected.

67.6.1

---

[1] Rule 67.5 substituted by S.S.I. 2009 No. 283 (effective 28th September 2009).
[2] Rule 67.6 substituted by S.S.I. 2009 No. 283 (effective 28th September 2009) and amended by S.S.I. 2011 No. 288 (effective 21st July 2011).

Expenses

67.7 67.7.[1] In a cause to which this Chapter applies, the court may make such order as to expenses, including the expenses of a reporting officer, a curator ad litem, or any other person who attended a hearing, as it thinks fit.

Deriv. R.C.S. 1965, r. 230(7) substituted by S.I. 1984 No. 997

General note.

67.7.1 In relation to the expenses of a reporting officer and curator ad litem, note that the fees of such persons appointed from a panel established under the Curators ad Litem and Reporting Officers (Panels) (Scotland) Regulations 2001 [S.I. 2001 No. 477] are paid for by the local authority; but not if the person appointed is not on the panel, in which case the petitioner will normally be responsible for the fee.

Part 2 – Adoption Orders

Application for adoption order

67.8 67.8.—[2](1) An application for an adoption order under section 29 (adoption by certain couples) or 30 (adoption by one person) of the 2007 Act is to be made by petition in Form 67.8-A.

(2) An application for an order vesting parental responsibilities and parental rights relating to a child under section 59(1) of the 2007 Act (preliminary order where child to be adopted abroad) is to be made by petition in Form 67.8-B.

(3) The following documents must be lodged in process along with a petition under paragraph (1) or (2)—

    (a) an extract of the entry in the Register of Births relating to the child who is the subject of the application;

    (b) in the case of an application under section 29 of the 2007 Act by a relevant couple who are married to each other, an extract or a certified copy of the entry in the Register of Marriages relating to their marriage;

    (c) in the case of an application under section 29 of the 2007 Act by a relevant couple who are civil partners of each other, an extract or a certified copy of the entry in the Register of Civil Partners relating to their civil partnership;

    (d) any report by the local authority required by section 19(2) (investigation by local authority on receipt of notice of intention to apply for adoption order) of the 2007 Act, if available;

    (e) any report by an adoption agency required by section 17 (report on the suitability of the applicants and other matters) of the 2007 Act, if available;

    (f) where appropriate, an extract of the order freeing the child for adoption;

    (g) where appropriate, an extract of the permanence order made in respect of the child under section 80 of the 2007 Act;

    (h) where appropriate, the consent under section 19(1) (placing children with parental consent: England and Wales) of the 2002 Act of each parent or guardian to the child being placed for adoption, in the form prescribed under section 52(7) of that Act, if available;

    (i) where appropriate, the consent under section 20(1) (advance consent to adoption: England and Wales) of the 2002 Act of each parent or guardian to the making of a future adoption order, in the form prescribed under section 52(7) of that Act, if available;

    (j) any notice given under section 20(4) (notice that information about ap-

---

[1] R. 67.7 substituted by S.S.I. 2009 No. 283 (effective 28th September 2009).
[2] R. 67.8 substituted by S.S.I. 2009 No. 283 (effective 28th September 2009).

plication for adoption order not required: England and Wales) of the 2002 Act by a parent or guardian of the child to an adoption agency, if available;

(k) a certified copy of any placement order made under section 21(1) (placement orders: England and Wales) of the 2002 Act, if available; and

(l) any other document founded upon by the petitioner in support of the terms of the petition.

(4) A report by a local authority under section 19(2) or an adoption agency under section 17 of the 2007 Act must be in numbered paragraphs and include the following matters:—

(a) information about how the needs of the child came to the notice of the authority or agency;

(b) the family circumstances of the child;

(c) where the child was placed for adoption by an adoption agency, a description of the physical and mental health of the child, (including any special needs) and his emotional, behavioural and educational development;

(d) an account of the discussion with the parents or guardians of the child and, if appropriate, with the child about their wishes and the alternatives to adoption;

(e) the position of other relatives or persons likely to be involved;

(f) an account of any search for a parent or guardian who cannot be found;

(g) information about the mutual suitability of the petitioner and the child for the relationship created by adoption and the ability of the petitioner to bring up the child including an assessment of the personality of the petitioner and, where appropriate, that of the child;

(h) particulars of all members of the household of the petitioner and their relationship to the petitioner;

(i) a description of the accommodation in the home of the petitioner;

(j) in a petition by one only one member of a relevant couple within the meaning of section 29(3) of the 2007 Act, why the other member of that couple has not joined in the application;

(k) whether the petitioner understands the nature and effect of an adoption order and in particular that the order, if made, will make the petitioner responsible for the maintenance and upbringing of the child;

(l) whether the means and standing of the petitioner are such as to enable him to maintain and bring up the child suitably;

(m) whether the child has any right or interest in property and, if so, what right or interest;

(n) whether any payment or other reward in consideration of the adoption, other than an approved adoption allowance, has been received or agreed upon;

(o) what insurance has been offered on the life of the child;

(p) the religious persuasion, racial origin and cultural and linguistic background of the child and of the petitioner;

(q) considerations arising from the difference in age between the petitioner and the child if this is more or less than the normal difference in age between parents and children;

(r) whether adoption is likely to safeguard and promote the welfare of the child throughout his life;

(s) whether the child is subject to a supervision requirement and, if so, what steps have been taken to comply with section 73(4)(c), (5) and (13) (duration and review of supervision requirement) of the 1995 Act;

(t)   where paragraph (5) applies, the information mentioned in paragraph (6);

(u)   whether there has been a contravention of section 75 of the 2007 Act in relation to the child;

(v)   whether there has been a failure to comply with section 76(2) of the 2007 Act in relation to the child;

(w)   any other matters relevant to the operation of section 14 of the 2007 Act in relation to the application;

(x)   where appropriate, information about whether—

    (i)   in an application under section 29(1) of the 2007 Act, the petitioners are a relevant couple within the meaning of section 29(3)(c) or (d) of the 2007 Act;

    (ii)   in an application under section 30(1) of the 2007 Act, the petitioner is a member of a relevant couple within the meaning of section 29(3)(c) or (d) of the 2007 Act;

(y)   in the case of a petition under paragraph (2) to which regulation 50 of the 2009 Regulations applies, the details referred to in paragraph (7); and

(z)   any other information which may be of assistance to the court.

(5) This paragraph applies where—

(a)   the child was placed for adoption under section 19(1) (placement with parental consent: England and Wales) of the 2002 Act;

(b)   the child was placed for adoption under a placement order made under section 21(1) (placement orders: England and Wales) of the 2002 Act; or

(c)   each parent or guardian has consented under section 20(1) (advance consent to adoption: England and Wales) of the 2002 Act to the making of a future adoption order.

(6) The information referred to in paragraph (4)(t) is any available information about whether—

(a)   any placement order has been revoked;

(b)   any of the consents referred to in section 31(8) or (9) of the 2007 Act have at any time been withdrawn;

(c)   a parent or guardian of the child wishes to seek leave to oppose the petition; and

(d)   there has been any change of circumstances since the consent of the parent or guardian was given or, as the case may be, the order under section 21(1) (placement orders: England and Wales) of the 2002 Act was made.

(7) The details mentioned in paragraph (4)(y) are—

(a)   details of any reviews carried out under regulation 10 of the Adoption Agencies (Scotland) Regulations 2009; and

(b)   details of any visits carried out under regulation 25(1)(a) of those Regulations.

(8) If a report mentioned in paragraph (3)(d) or (e) is unavailable to be lodged along with the petition, the court shall pronounce an interlocutor requiring the adoption agency or local authority concerned to prepare and lodge such a report in court within 2 weeks from the date of the interlocutor, or within such other period as the court in its discretion may allow.

(9) If any of the documents required to be lodged in process under paragraph (3)(f), (g), (h), (i), (j) or (k) is unavailable to be lodged by reason of its being in the possession of an adoption agency, the court shall pronounce an interlocutor requiring the agency to lodge the document within 4 weeks from the date of the interlocutor, or within such other period as the court in its discretion may allow.

Deriv. R.C.S. 1965, r. 222(7) and (8) substituted by S.S.I. 1984 No. 997

General note.

A person who wishes to adopt a child who has not been placed with him for adoption must, at least three months before the date of the adoption, give notice to the local authority in whose area he has his home of his intention to apply for the adoption order: 2007 Act, s. 18. It might be sensible to give notice before the petition is presented. The reason for this requirement is that where the child has been placed for adoption the adoption agency will be in a position to report whereas if the child has not been so placed the agency might not yet have become involved. The local authority must investigate and submit a report to the court: 2007 Act, s. 18.

Where the child has been placed for adoption the adoption agency (a local authority or registered adoption service or adoption agency in England or Wales or Northern Ireland: 2007 Act, s. 119) which placed the child will provide a report under s. 17 of the 2007 Act dealing with the matters mentioned in that section and r. 67.8(4). On style of reports, see McNeill on *Adoption of Children in Scotland*, 2nd ed., p. 203.

An application for an adoption order is made under s. 29 (by a couple) or 30 (by one person) of the 2007 Act. Adoption extinguishes the parental rights and duties of a parent or guardian (not being one of the adopters) in whom those rights were vested before the order and vests them in the adopters: 2007 Act, ss. 28(1) and 35(2): a person over 18 may be adopted if the application is made when the person is under 18: 2007 Act, s. 28(4).

Where more than one child is sought to be adopted there should be a separate petition for each child. The two petitions can be heard together and the evidence in one can be ordered to be evidence in the other: see, e.g. *F. v. F.* 1991 S.L.T. 357.

An adopter must have attained the age of 21 years, and adoption may be sought by a couple (whether married or not) neither of whom is the child's parent), or (in certain circumstances) by one person, domiciled in the British Islands (i.e. the UK, the Channel Islands or the Isle of Man): 2007 Act, ss. 29(2) and 30.

Where a petitioner is a parent, step-parent or relative of the child, or the child was placed with the petitioner by an adoption agency, the child must be at least 19 weeks old and have had his home with (one of) the petitioner(s) during the preceding 13 weeks when the adoption order is made; in any other case the child must be at least 12 months old and have had his home with (one of) the petitioner(s) during the preceding 12 months: 2007 Act, s. 15.

An adoption order may not be made in respect of a child of 12 years of age or more without his consent unless the court is satisfied he is incapable of giving his consent: 2007 Act, s. 32.

Each parent or guardian of the child must consent or that consent must be dispensed with: 2007 Act, s. 31. (1) The grounds on which consent may be dispensed with are set out in s.31(3):

(a)   that the parent or guardian is dead;
(b)   that the parent or guardian cannot be found or is incapable of giving consent;
(c)   that subsection (4) (unable to discharge/exercise parental responsibilities/rights and likely to continue to be unable to do so) or (5) (by virtue of a permanence order, parent has no parental responsibilities/rights and it is unlikely that those will be imposed or given); and
(d)   that, where neither subsection (4) or (5) applies, the welfare of the child otherwise requires the consent to be dispensed with. The application and meaning of s.31(3)(d) were explained in *S v. L*, 2013 S.C. (UKSC) 20, per Lord Reed at paras. [30] to [37].

In reaching any decision relating to the adoption of a child the court or adoption agency staff shall have regard to all the circumstances, paramount consideration being given to the need to safeguard and promote the welfare of the child throughout his life; and so far as practicable the child's wishes should be ascertained and due consideration given to them: 2007 Act, s. 14.

Where a child is to be adopted abroad, additional rules apply (new r. 67.9) and a preliminary order may be sought (2007 Act, s. 59 and new r. 67.8(2)).

"search for parent or guardian who cannot he found" (r. 67.8(4)(f)).

Section 16(1) and (2)(a) of the Act of 1978 provides that the agreement of a parent or guardian to an adoption may be dispensed with on the ground that he cannot be found. This means that all reasonable steps have to be taken to find him or her; and, if even only one reasonable step has been omitted, it cannot be said that that person could not be found: *S v. M* 1999 S.C. 388 (Extra Div).

Jurisdiction.

The court has jurisdiction where the child is in Scotland or not in Scotland when the application for the adoption order is made: 2007 Act, s. 118.

"petition".

A petition for an adoption order is presented in the Outer House: r. 14.2(h). The petition must be in Form 67.8-A in the official printed form: rr. 4.1 and 14.4. The petition must be signed by counsel or other person having a right of audience: r. 4.2; and see r. 1.3(1) (definitions of "counsel" and "other person having a right of audience") and note 1.3.4. The petitioner must lodge the petition with the required steps of process (r. 4.4) and the productions required by r. 67.8(3) and any others (including those founded on or

67.8.1

67.8.2

67.8.3

67.8.4

adopted (r. 27.1)) with an inventory of productions (r. 4.5). Other productions which should be lodged include any consent of the child under s. 12(8), or agreement of a parent or guardian to the adoption under s. 16(1)(b), of the Act of 1978.

A fee is payable on lodging the petition: see note 14.5.10.

Additional requirements where child to be adopted abroad

67.9

67.9.—[1](1) The additional requirements in this Rule apply to a petitioner in an application for an order under section 59 of the 2007 Act.

(2) In the case of an application to which regulation 7 of the 2009 Regulations applies, the petitioner must lodge along with the petition—

   (a) the confirmation required under regulation 7(3)(a)(i) of the 2009 Regulations;

   (b) copies of the confirmations to the adoption agency referred to in regulations 7(3)(b)(i), (iii) and (iv) of the 2009 Regulations;

   (c) a copy of the report mentioned in regulation 7(3)(b)(ii) of the 2009 Regulations;

   (d) a copy of the confirmation to the adoption agency referred to in regulation 7(3)(c) or (d), as the case may be, of the 2009 Regulations; and

   (e) the documents mentioned in regulation 8 of those Regulations.

(3) In the case of an application to which regulation 50 of the 2009 Regulations applies, the petitioner must lodge along with the petition the reports, confirmations and other documents or, where appropriate, copies thereof, referred to in regulation 50(3)(a) to (d), (f) and (g) of those Regulations.

(4) Where appropriate the petitioner must also lodge in process a translation into English of any document referred to in paragraph (2) or (3) together with the certificate referred to in paragraph (5).

(5) The certificate mentioned in paragraph (4) is a certificate by the translator—

   (a) certifying that the translation is in conformity with the original document; and

   (b) giving the full name, address, and qualifications of the translator.

(6) The petitioner must adduce evidence of the law of adoption in the country or territory in which it is intended to adopt the child.

(7) The evidence of the law of adoption required under paragraph (6) may be in the form of an affidavit by a person who is conversant with that law and who—

   (a) practices or has practised law in that country or territory; or

   (b) is a duly accredited representative of the government of that country or territory in the United Kingdom.

General note.

67.9.1

A person may obtain an order granting him the parental rights and duties relating to a child whom he wishes to adopt under the law of a country outside the British Islands (UK, Channel Islands or the Isle of Man). A Convention adoption order is made where a child habitually resident in one Contracting State is being adopted in another under the Hague Convention on Protection of Children and Co-operation in respect of Interventory Adoption: see Pt. IV of this Chapter.

The child must be at least 32 weeks old and have had his home with the prospective adopter during the 10 weeks preceding the application: 2007 Act, s. 59(4).

The Adoptions with a Foreign Element (Scotland) Regulations 2009 [S.S.I. 2009 No. 182] apply where the adoption is not in a Convention adoption country.

"Petition".

67.9.2

A petition for a section 59 order is presented in the Outer House: r. 14.2(h). The petition must be in Form 67.8-B in the official printed form: rr. 4.1 and 14.4. The petition must be signed by counsel or other person having a right of audience: r. 4.2; and see r. 1.3(1) (definitions of "counsel" and "other person having a right of audience"), and note 1.3.4.

---

[1] Rule 67.9 substituted by S.S.I. 2009 No. 283 (effective 28th September 2009).

The petitioner must lodge the petition with the required steps of process (r. 4.4) and the productions required by r. 67.8(3) and any others (including those founded on or adopted (r. 27.1)) with an inventory of productions (r. 4.5). Other productions which should be lodged include a copy of any interlocutor freeing the child for adoption and any consent of the child under s. 12(8), or agreement of a parent or guardian to the adoption under s. 16(1)(b), of the Act of 1978.

A fee is payable on lodging the petition: see note 14.5.10.

"AFFIDAVIT".

On affidavits, see r. 1.3(2).

67.9.3

Protection of identity of petitioner

67.10.—[1](1)   When any person who proposes to apply under rule 67.8 wishes to prevent his identity being disclosed to any person whose consent to the order is required, he may, before presenting the petition, apply by letter to the Deputy Principal Clerk for a serial number to be assigned to him for all purposes connected with the petition.

67.10

(2)   On receipt of an application under paragraph (1), the Deputy Principal Clerk shall—

    (a)   assign a serial number to the applicant; and

    (b)   enter a note of the number opposite the name of the applicant in a register of serial numbers.

(3)   The contents of the register of serial numbers and the names of the persons to whom each number relates shall be treated as confidential by the Deputy Principal Clerk and disclosed only to the court.

(4)   Where a serial number has been assigned to an applicant under paragraph (2) any form of consent to an adoption order or order under section 59 of the 2007 Act—

    (a)   must refer to the applicant by means of the serial number assigned to him;

    (b)   must not contain the name and designation of the applicant; and

    (c)   must specify the year in which the serial number was assigned.

Deriv. R.C.S. 1965, r. 222(3) substituted by S.I. 1984 No. 997

GENERAL NOTE.

An application for a serial number to prevent disclosure of the identity of the petitioner to a parent or guardian whose consent is required will only arise if the child has not been freed for adoption.

The letter should be addressed to the Deputy Principal Clerk of Session, Court of Session, 2 Parliament Square, Edinburgh EH1 1RQ.

67.10.1

Appointment of curator ad litem and reporting officer

67.11.—[2](1)   The court shall, on the presentation of a petition under rule 67.8 appoint a curator ad litem and reporting officer.

67.11

(2)   But, subject to paragraph (3), the court shall not appoint a reporting officer where one or more of the following applies—

    (a)   an order freeing the child for adoption has been made;

    (b)   a permanence order with provision granting authority for the child to be adopted has been granted under section 80 of the 2007 Act;

    (c)   the petition is founded on one or other or both of section 31(8) (advance consent to adopt) or (9) (placement of child: England and Wales) of the 2007 Act.

(3)   Notwithstanding paragraph (2), a reporting officer shall be appointed—

    (a)   in any case in which the petition is founded on the condition in section 31(2) of the 2007 Act, whether or not it is also founded on section 31(8) or (9) of that Act; or

---

[1] Rule 67.10 substituted by S.S.I. 2009 No. 283 (effective 28th September 2009).

[2] Rule 67.11 substituted by S.S.I. 2009 No. 283 (effective 28th September 2009).

(b)   where the child who is the subject of the application is aged 12 or over, for the purpose of witnessing that child's consent, where that consent is to be executed in Scotland.

(4)   The same person may be appointed as curator ad litem and reporting officer in the same petition, if the court considers that doing so is appropriate in the circumstances.

(5)   A person may, before presenting the petition, apply by letter to the Deputy Principal Clerk for the appointment of a reporting officer.

(6)   An application under paragraph (5) shall—

(a)   set out the reasons for which the appointment is sought;

(b)   not require to be intimated to any person;

(c)   be accompanied by an interlocutor sheet; and

(d)   be placed by the Deputy Principal Clerk before the Lord Ordinary for his decision.

(6)[1]   The Deputy Principal Clerk shall give written intimation of the appointment of a curator ad litem and reporting officer under paragraph (1) or (5) to the petitioner and to the person or persons appointed.

(7)   The decision of the Lord Ordinary on an application under paragraph (5) shall be final and not subject to review.

(8)   The letter and the interlocutor sheet in an application under paragraph (5) shall be kept in the Petition Department and subsequently placed in the process of the petition.

APPOINTMENT OF REPORTING OFFICER AND CURATOR AD LITEM.

67.11.1   A curator ad litem must be appointed. A reporter may not always be appointed (see r. 67.11(2) and (3)). The court will usually appoint a person from a panel established by the local authority under the Curators ad Litem and Reporting Officers (Panels) (Scotland) Regulations 2001 [S.S.I. 2001 No. 477], but may appoint someone not on the panel where appropriate. Subject to certain restrictions in relation to persons employed by the adoption agency, the court may appoint the same person to be both reporting officer and curator ad litem: 2007 Act, s. 108(3) and r. 67.11(4).

Appointment of a reporting officer may be sought before the petition is presented, e.g. where a parent or guardian whose agreement is required is going abroad: r. 67.11(5)–(7).

The general duties of a reporting officer are to witness agreements to adoption and to perform such other duties as may be prescribed by ,rules: Act of 1978, s. 58(1). The general duty of the curator ad litem is to safeguard the interests of the child: Act of 1978, s. 58(1); and see r. 67.24.

"INTIMATE".

67.11.2   Rule 16.7 applies although it should have been written intimation under r. 16.9.

"FINAL AND NOT SUBJECT TO REVIEW".

67.11.3   The decision of the Lord Ordinary may not be reclaimed against.

"WRITTEN INTIMATION".

67.11.4   For methods, see r. 16.9.

Duties of reporting officer and curator ad litem

67.12   **67.12.**—[2](1)   The other duties of a reporting officer appointed under this Part, other than under rule 67.11(3)(b), which are prescribed for the purposes of section 108(1)(b) of the 2007 Act are—

(a)   to ascertain the whereabouts of all persons whose consent to the making of an adoption order or order under section 59 of the 2007 Act in respect of the child is required;

(b)   to ascertain whether there is any person other than those mentioned in the petition upon whom notice of the petition should be served;

---

[1] Rule 67.11(6) amended by S.S.I. 2011 No. 288 (effective 21st July 2011).
[2] Rule 67.12 substituted by S.S.I. 2009 No. 283 (effective 28th September 2009).

   (c)   in the case of each person who is not a petitioner and whose consent to the making of an adoption order or order under section 59 of the 2007 Act is required or may be dispensed with—

        (i)   to ascertain whether that person understands the effect of the adoption order or order under section 59 of the 2007 Act;

       (ii)   to ascertain whether alternatives to adoption have been discussed with that person;

      (iii)   to confirm that that person understands that he may withdraw his consent at any time before an order is made;

      (iv)   to ascertain whether that person suffers or appears to suffer from a mental disorder within the meaning of section 328 of the Mental Health (Care and Treatment) (Scotland) Act 2003;

   (d)   to report in writing on the matters mentioned in subparagraphs (a) to (c) to the court within 4 weeks from the date of the interlocutor appointing the reporting officer, or within such other period as the court may allow.

(2)   References in paragraph (1) to "consent" are to consent within the meaning of section 31(2)(a) or 32(1) of the 2007 Act, as the case may be.

(3)   A curator ad litem appointed under this Part must—

   (a)   have regard to safeguarding the interests of the child as his paramount duty;

   (b)   inquire, so far as he considers necessary, into the facts and circumstances averred in the petition and in the report mentioned in rule 67.8(4);

   (c)   obtain particulars of accommodation in the home of the petitioner and the condition of the home;

   (d)   obtain particulars of all members of the household of the petitioner and their relationship to the petitioner;

   (e)   in the case of a petition by only one member of a relevant couple within the meaning of section 29(3) of the 2007 Act, ascertain the reason of the other member of the couple for not joining the application;

   (f)   ascertain whether the means and status of the petitioner are sufficient to enable him to maintain and bring up the child suitably;

   (g)   ascertain what rights or interests in property the child has;

   (h)   establish that the petitioner understands the nature and effect of an adoption order and in particular that the making of the order will render him responsible for the maintenance and upbringing of the child;

   (i)   where appropriate, ascertain when the mother of the child ceased to have the care and possession of the child and to whom care and possession was then transferred;

   (j)   ascertain whether any payment or other reward in consideration of the adoption has been given or agreed upon;

   (k)   ascertain whether the child is subject to a supervision requirement under section 70 of the 1995 Act;

   (l)   ascertain whether the life of the child has been insured and if so for what sum;

   (m)   ascertain whether it may be in the interests of the welfare of the child that the court should make the adoption order or order under section 59 of the 2007 Act subject to particular terms and conditions or require the petitioner to make special provision for the child and, if so, what provision;

   (n)   where the petitioner is not ordinarily resident in the United Kingdom, establish whether a report has been obtained on the home and living conditions of the petitioner from a suitable agency in the country in which he is ordinarily resident;

(o) establish the reasons of the petitioner for wishing to adopt the child;

(p) establish the religious persuasion, racial origin and cultural and linguistic background of the child and of the petitioner;

(q) assess the considerations which might arise where the difference in age as between the petitioner and the child is greater or less than the normal difference in age between parents and their children;

(r) consider such other matters, including the personality of the petitioner and, where appropriate, that of the child, which might affect the suitability of the petitioner and the child for the relationship created by adoption and affect the ability of the petitioner to bring up the child;

(s) ascertain whether it would be better for the child that the court should make the order than it should not make the order;

(t) ascertain whether the adoption is likely to safeguard and promote the welfare of the child throughout his life; and

(u) ascertain from the child whether he wishes to express a view and, where a child indicates his wish to express a view, ascertain that view.

(4) Subject to paragraph (5) the curator ad litem must report in writing on the matters mentioned in paragraph (3) to the court within 4 weeks from the date of the interlocutor appointing the curator, or within such other period as the court in its discretion may allow.

(5) Subject to any order made by the court under rule 67.16(1)(a), the views of the child ascertained in terms of paragraph (3)(u) may, if the curator ad litem considers appropriate, be conveyed to the court orally.

GENERAL NOTE.

67.12.1   The duties of the reporting officer are mainly concerned with ensuring that all consents have been obtained and that those consenting understand the effect. The duties of the curator ad litem are to provide the court with evidence of the history of the child, his parents, the current situation and prospects of the adopters. The curator ad litem's function is to carry out an inquiry into all the enumerated matters on behalf of the court. It is not his function to express an opinion on matters of law: *T, Petr.* ,1997 S.L.T. 724, 731C per L.P. Hope.

"GUARDIAN".

67.12.2   This is defined in s. 119(1) of the Act of 1978 and means a person appointed by deed, a will or by the court to be a guardian.

CONSENT BY A PARENT OR GUARDIAN.

67.12.3   Each parent or guardian must agree to the adoption unless his or her consent is dispensed with on certain grounds: 2007 Act, s. 31. Section 31 of the 2007 Act is not incompatible with art.8 of the ECHR:*S v L*, 2012 S.L.T. 961 (UKSC).

CONSENT OF A CHILD.

67.12.4   An adoption order cannot be made without the consent of a child who has reached the age of 12 years unless the court is satisfied he is incapable of giving consent: 2007 Act, s. 32.

"PAYMENT OR REWARD PROHIBITED IN CONSIDERATION OF THE ADOPTION".

67.12.5   It is unlawful to make or receive a payment or reward for the adoption of a child, any agreement or consent in that connection, the transfer of the care and possession of a child with a view to adoption of the child or the making of any arrangement for the child's adoption; and a person who does so is liable on summary conviction to a fine or imprisonment: 2007 Act, s. 72.

LODGING OF REPORTS ETC.

67.12.6   A report by the reporting officer and any agreements, and any report of a curator ad litem, are, on receipt of them by the Deputy Principal Clerk, lodged in process as a step in process: r. 1.3(1) (definition of "step of process").

Consents

67.13.—[1](1) The consent of a parent or guardian to an order required by section 31(2)(a) of the 2007 Act is to be in Form 67.13-A.

(2) The consent of the child required by section 32(1) of the 2007 Act is to be in Form 67.13-B.

(3) A form of consent mentioned in paragraph (1) or (2) must be witnessed—

    (a) where it is executed in Scotland, by the reporting officer appointed under rule 67.11;

    (b) where it is executed outwith Scotland but within the United Kingdom, by a justice of the peace or a commissioner for oaths; or

    (c) where it is executed outwith the United Kingdom—

        (i) if the person who executes the form is serving in Her Majesty's forces, by an officer holding a commission in any of those forces; or

        (ii) in any other case, by a British diplomatic or consular official or any person authorised to administer an oath or affirmation under the law of the place where the consent is executed.

Deriv. R.C.S.1965, r. 220(4) (r. 67.5(2)(b)), r. 222(9)(a) (r. 67.5(I)(a) and (b)), r. 222(9)(b) (r. 67.5(2)(a)) and r. 230(1) (r. 67.5(3)), all substituted by S.I. 1984 No. 997

67.13

GENERAL NOTE.

Where the agreement or consent is executed in Scotland it should be witnessed by the reporting officer: r. 67.13(3)(a). Where the agreement or consent is executed outside Scotland it should be witnessed in accordance with r. 67.13(3)(b) or (c). By virtue of s. 81 of the Solicitors Act 1974 every solicitor who holds a practising certificate in England and Wales has the power of a commissioner for oaths under the Commissioners for Oaths Acts 1889 and 1891. The power was extended to public notaries (members of the Incorporated Company of Scriveners) within their jurisdiction by s. 65 of the Administration of Justice Act 1985. Under s. 113 of the Courts and Legal Services Act 1990, the power was extended to authorised persons and general notaries in England and Wales. An "authorised person" is an authorised advocate or litigator other than a solicitor, or a member of a body prescribed by the Lord Chancellor. From 1st August 1995 legal executives who are fellows of the Institute of Legal Executives may act as commissioners for oaths in England and Wales.

Every such solicitor, notary or authorised person has the right to use the title "Commissioner for Oaths" and should use that title (although a solicitor may accidentally omit to do so).

An agreement or consent witnessed in accordance with the forms by virtue of r. 67.13 is sufficient evidence without further proof of signature of the person by whom it was executed: 2007 Act, s. 111(1).

67.13.1

Intimation and hearing of adoption petition

67.14.—[2](1) On the lodging of a petition under rule 67.8—

    (a) the Deputy Principal Clerk shall cause the petition to be put on the By Order Roll before the Lord Ordinary not less than 6 and not more than 8 weeks thereafter;

    (b) in the case of a petition under rule 67.8(1), the petitioner or, where a serial number has been assigned under rule 67.10, the Deputy Principal Clerk shall intimate a copy of the petition along with a notice of intimation in Form 67.14-A to—

        (i) every person who can be found and whose consent to the making of the order is required to be given or dispensed with under the 2007 Act;

        (ii) if no such person can be found, a relative of the child within the meaning of section 119(1) of the 2007 Act, unless the address of such a relative is not known to the petitioner and cannot reasonably be ascertained;

67.14

---

[1] Rule 67.13 substituted by S.S.I. 2009 No. 283 (effective 28th September 2009).
[2] Rule 67.14 substituted by S.S.I. 2009 No. 283 (effective 28th September 2009).

        (iii)   every person who has consented to the making of the order under section 20 of the 2002 Act (and has not withdrawn the consent) unless the person has given a notice under subsection (4)(a) of that section which has effect; and

        (iv)   every person who, if leave were given under section 31(12) of the 2007 Act, would be entitled to oppose the making of the order;

  (c)   in the case of a petition under rule 67.8(2), the petitioner or, where a serial number has been assigned under rule 67.10, the Deputy Principal Clerk shall intimate a copy of the petition along with a notice of intimation in Form 67.14-A to every person who can be found and whose consent to the making of the order would be required if the application were for an adoption order (other than a Convention adoption order);

  (d)   in the case of a petition under rule 67.8(1) the petitioner or, where a serial number has been assigned under rule 67.10, the Deputy Principal Clerk shall intimate a copy of the petition along with a notice of intimation in Form 67.14-B to the father of the child if he does not have, and has never had, parental responsibilities or parental rights in relation to the child and if he can be found;

  (e)[1]   the Deputy Principal Clerk shall give written intimation of the date of the hearing on the By Order Roll to the curator ad litem and to any reporting officer appointed by the court under rule 67.11.

  (2) A notice of intimation under paragraph (1)(b) or (c) must state—

  (a)   that an application for adoption has been made;

  (b)   the date on which, and place where, the By Order hearing will be held;

  (c)   the fact that the person is entitled to be heard on the application;

  (d)   the fact that, unless the person wishes, or the court requires, the person need not attend the hearing.

  (3) A notice of intimation under paragraph (1)(d) must state the matters mentioned in paragraph (2)(a) and (b).

"INTIMATION", "INTIMATE".

67.14.1   For methods, see r. 16.7.

"WRITTEN INTIMATION".

67.14.2   For methods, see r. 16.9.

Order for intimation

67.15   **67.15.**[2] In any petition for an adoption order or order under section 59 of the 2007 Act, the court may at any time order intimation to be made in such terms as it considers appropriate on any person who in its opinion ought to be given notice of the application.

Procedure where child wishes to express a view

67.16   **67.16.**—[3](1) Where a child has indicated his wish to express his views the court, without prejudice to rule 67.12(3)(u)—

  (a)   may order such procedural steps to be taken as he considers appropriate to ascertain the views of that child; and

  (b)   must not make an order under this Part unless an opportunity has been given for the views of that child to be obtained or heard.

---

[1] Rule 67.14(1)(e) amended by S.S.I. 2011 No. 288 (effective 21st July 2011).
[2] R. 67.15 substituted by S.S.I. 2009 No. 283 (effective 28th September 2009).
[3] R. 67.16 substituted by S.S.I. 2009 No. 283 (effective 28th September 2009).

(2) Where the views of the child, whether under this rule or under rule 67.12, have been recorded in writing, the court may direct that such a written record is to—

    (a) be sealed in an envelope marked "Views of the child — confidential";

    (b) be available to the court only;

    (c) not be opened by any other person; and

    (d) not form a borrowable part of process.

Hearing on By Order Roll

67.17.—[1](1) At the hearing on the By Order Roll appointed under rule 67.14 the court shall—
67.17

    (a) if no party indicates his intention to oppose the petition, dispose of the cause or make such other order as it considers appropriate;

    (b) in any other case—

        (i) ascertain from the parties the anticipated length of any proof that may be required;

        (ii) fix a diet of proof not less than 12 and not more than 16 weeks after the date of the hearing on the By Order Roll unless, on cause shown, a longer period is appropriate;

        (iii) give such directions as to the preparation for the proof as he considers appropriate;

        (iv) order answers and any other documents to be lodged within 21 days of the date of the hearing on the By Order Roll or such other period as it considers appropriate;

(2) Paragraph (1)(b)(ii) shall not require a proof to be held when the court is in vacation unless the court otherwise directs.

(3) At the hearing on the By Order Roll the court may—

    (a) if it is not satisfied that the facts stated in the petition are supported by the documents lodged with it or by the reports of the curator ad litem and reporting officer, order the production of further documents;

    (b) where it considers it appropriate to do so, fix a pre-proof hearing not less than 2 and not more than 6 weeks before the diet of proof; and

    (c) make such other order as it considers appropriate for the expeditious progress of the case.

PRIVACY OF HEARINGS.

Any hearing in an adoption petition is heard in private unless the court otherwise directs: 2007 Act, s. 109.
67.17.1

The court may otherwise direct, e.g. to enable a person to appear as amicus curiae: *Strathclyde R.C. Petrs* , 1996 S.L.T. (Sh. Ct.) 65.

MULTIPLE ADOPTIONS.

Where the court is presented with two petitions for adoption—each should be heard separately and the court should issue separate interlocutors in each petition: *A.B. v. C.B.* 1985 S.L.T. 514, 561. per L.J.-C Wheatley. In practice, the petitions of siblings are by agreement often heard together and the evidence in one treated as evidence in the other petition.
67.17.2

CONTACT ORDERS.

The making of an adoption order is no longer on bar with the making of a contact order under s.11 of the Children (Scotland) Act 1995; 2007 Act, s. 107.
67.17.3

FEE.

The court fee for a proof is payable by each party for every 30 minutes or part thereof. For fee, see Court of Session etc. Fees Order 1984, Table of Fees, Pt. I, C, item 17 (or as appropriate) [S.I. 1984 No. 256. Table as amended, pp. C1202 et seq.]. The fee may be debited under a credit scheme introduced on 1st April 1976 by P.N. No.4 of 1976 to the account (if one is kept or permitted) of the agent by the court
67.17.4

---

[1] R. 67.17 substituted by S.S.I. 2009 No. 283 (effective 28th September 2009).

cashier, and an account will be rendered weekly by the court cashier's office to the agent for all court fees due that week for immediate settlement. An agent not on the credit scheme will have an account opened for the purpose of lodging the fee: P.N. No. 2 of 1995. A debit slip and a copy of the court hearing time sheet will be delivered to the agent's box or sent by DX or post.

A party litigant must pay cash to the clerk of court at the end of the hearing or, if the hearing lasts more than a day, at the end of each day: P.N. No. 2 of 1995. A receipt will be issued. The assistant clerk of session will acknowledge receipt of the sum received from the clerk of court on the Minute of Proceedings.

Pre-proof hearing

67.18

67.18—[1](1) If the court appoints a pre-proof hearing under rule 67.17(3), the parties must provide the court with sufficient information to enable it to conduct the hearing as provided for in this rule.

(2) At the pre-proof hearing the court must ascertain, so far as is reasonably practicable, whether the cause is likely to proceed to proof on the date fixed for that purpose.

(3) For the purposes of paragraph (2), the court must consider—

    (a) the state of preparation of the parties;

    (b) the extent to which the parties have complied with any orders made by the court under rule 67.17.

(4) At the pre-proof hearing the court may—

    (a) discharge the proof and fix a new date for such proof;

    (b) adjourn the pre-proof hearing;

    (c) order the lodging of joint minutes of agreement, affidavits, expert reports and any other documents within such period as it considers appropriate;

    (d) make such other order as it thinks fit to secure the expeditious progress of the cause.

Communication to the Registrar General

67.19

67.19.[2] The communication to the Registrar General of an adoption order required to be made by the clerk of court under paragraph 4(1) of Schedule 1 to the 2007 Act is to be made by sending a certified copy of the order to the Registrar General in a sealed envelope marked "Confidential".

Deriv. R.C.S. 1965, r. 229 substituted by S.I. 1984 No. 997

REGISTRAR GENERAL FOR SCOTLAND.

67.19.1

This is the Registrar General of Births, Marriages and Deaths for Scotland: 2007 Act, s. 57(1). He maintains the Adopted Children Register in which the adoption order is registered: 2007 Act, Sched. 1, paras 1 and 4.

The address is: New Register House, West Register Street, Edinburgh EHI 3YT; tel. 031-334 0380; fax 031-314 4400.

"SENDING".

67.19.2

This includes deliver: r. 1.3(1) (definition of "send").

Adoption orders

67.20

. **67.20**—[3](1) An adoption order granted by the court must specify the name and address of the adoption agency, if any, which has taken part in the arrangements for placing the child in the care of the petitioner.

(2) No extract of an adoption order is to be issued except by order of the court on an application to it—

    (a) where there is a petition for the adoption order or order under section 59 of the 2007 Act, as the case may be, depending before the court, by motion; or

---

[1] R. 67.18 substituted by S.S.I. 2009 No. 283 (effective 28th September 2009).
[2] R. 67.19 substituted by S.S.I. 2009 No. 283 (effective 28th September 2009).
[3] R. 67.20 substituted by S.S.I. 2009 No. 283 (effective 28th September 2009).

(b)   where there is no such petition depending before the court, by petition.

Final procedure

67.21—[1](1) Immediately after the communication is made under rule 67.19 or immediately upon a extract of the order being issued under rule 67.20 the clerk of court or the Extractor, as the case may be, shall—

67.21

    (a)   place the whole process in an envelope bearing only—
        (i)   the name of the petitioner;
        (ii)   the full name of the child to whom the process relates; and
        (iii) the date of the order; and
    (b)   seal the envelope and mark it "confidential".

(2) The envelope referred to in paragraph (1) is not to be unsealed by the clerk of court or any other person having control of the records of the court, and the process is not to be made accessible to any person for one hundred years after the date of the granting of the order, except—

    (a)   to an adopted child who has attained the age of 16 and to whose adoption the process refers;
    (b)   to the Deputy Principal Clerk, on an application being made to him by an adoption agency, and with the consent of the adopted person for the purpose only of ascertaining the name of the agency, if any, responsible for the placement of that person and informing the applicant of that name;
    (c)   to a person on an application made by petition presented by him to the court setting forth the reason for which access to the process is required;
    (d)   to a court, public authority or administrative board (whether in the United Kingdom or not) having power to authorise an adoption, on petition to it by the court requesting that information be made available from the process for the purpose of discharging its duties in considering an application for adoption and specifying the precise reason for which access to the process is required;
    (e)   to a person who is authorised by the Scottish Ministers to obtain information for the purposes of such research as is intended to improve the working of adoption law and practice.

(3) The clerk of court must—

    (a)   where the court also makes an order under section 36(2) (revocation of supervision requirement) of the 2007 Act, intimate that order to the Principal Reporter; and
    (b)   where appropriate, intimate the making of an adoption order or order under section 59 of the 2007 Act to the court by which—
        (i)   an order freeing the child for adoption was made; or
        (ii)   a permanence order with provision granting authority for the child to be adopted was made.

GENERAL NOTE.

The purpose of r. 67.21 is to maintain confidentiality of the process and of an adoption order or a section 59 order in respect of a child during his lifetime. R. 67.32 also applies to Convention adoption orders: r. 67.26.

67.21.1

After five years a process is transmitted from the Court of Session to the Keeper of the Records: r. 9.1.

REGISTRAR GENERAL FOR SCOTLAND.

See note 67.30.1.

67.21.2

---

[1] R. 67.21 substituted by S.S.I. 2009 No. 283 (effective 28th September 2009).

Amendment of adoption order

67.22

67.22.—[1](1)   An application under paragraph 7 of Schedule 1 to the 2007 Act (amendment of orders and rectification of registers) shall be made by petition.

(2)   The court may order the petitioner to intimate the petition to such persons as it considers appropriate.

(3)   Subject to paragraph (4), rule 67.2 (disapplication of certain rules to this Chapter) shall not apply to an application mentioned in paragraph (1).

(4)   An application mentioned in paragraph (1) shall not be intimated on the walls of court or advertised.

GENERAL NOTE.

67.22.1

An application by the adopter or adopted child to amend an adoption order in respect of a new name given to the adopted child must be made within one year of the order:2007 Act, Sched. 1, para. (7)(2). The court may amend an adoption order by correcting any errors in its particulars, or to revoke a direction for the marking of an entry in the register of births or the Adopted Children Register, at any time: 2007 Act, Sched. 1, para. 7(1).

JURISDICTION.

67.22.2

The court has jurisdiction only if it made the adoption order sought to be amended or revoked: 2007 Act, Sched. 1, para. 7.

"PETITION".

67.22.3

A petition is presented in the Outer House: r. 14.2(h). The petition must be in 67.29.3

Form 14.4 in the official printed form: n. 4.1 and 14.4. The petition must be signed by counsel or other person having a right of audience: r. 4.2; and see r. 1.3(1) (definitions of "counsel" and "other person having a right of audience") and note 1.3.4.

A fee is payable on lodging the petition: see note 14.5.10.

The ordinary petition rules apply to a petition under r. 67.22 except that it is not intimated on the walls of court or advertised: r. 67.22(3) or (4).

Applications under sections 20 to 24 of the 2007 Act

67.23

67.23.—[2](1)   An application under section 20(2) (leave to remove child placed for adoption with consent), 21(3) (leave to remove child where notice of intention to adopt given), 22(3) (leave to remove child where application for adoption order pending), 23(3) (leave to remove child looked after by local authority), 24(1) (return of child removed in breach of certain conditions) or 24(2) (order directing person not to remove child) of the 2007 Act shall be made—

(a)   if there is pending in respect of the child an application for an adoption order, by note in the process of that application; or

(b)   in any other case, by petition.

(2)   Subject to paragraph (3), rule 67.2 (disapplication of certain rules to this Chapter) shall not apply to a petition under paragraph (1)(b).

(3)   A petition under paragraph (1)(b) shall not be intimated on the walls of court or advertised.

SECTION 20(2) OF THE 2007 ACT.

67.23.1

Where a child has been placed by an adoption agency with a person with a view to being adopted and the consent of the parent or guardian has been obtained to that placement, the parent or guardian may not remove the child against the will of the person with whom the child has his home except with leave of either the adoption agency or the court: 2007 Act, s. 20(2). It is, an offence for such a person to remove the child: 2007 Act, s. 20(3).

SECTION 24 OF THE 2007 ACT.

67.23.2

An application by a person, from whose care a child has been removed in breach of s. 24(1) of the 2007 Act or who has reasonable grounds for suspecting another person is intending to remove the child, may be made to the court for an order to return the child or to prohibit the removal of the child, as the case may be (2007 Act, s. 24(2)).

---

[1] R. 67.22 substituted by S.S.I. 2009 No. 283 (effective 28th September 2009).

[2] R. 67.23 substituted by S.S.I. 2009 No.283 (effective 28th September 2009).

SECTIONS 21 AND 22 OF THE 2007 ACT.

While a petition for an adoption order in respect of a child made by a person with whom the child has had his home for five years is pending or notice of intention to adopt has been given, no person is entitled to remove the child from his care without leave of the court, consent of the adopters, the child is arrested or removal is authorised by an enactment.

67.23.3

SECTION 23 OF THE 2007 ACT.

There are restrictions imposed on a local authority removing a child from a person who has had care of the child for five years other than in accordance with s.25 or 26 or with leave of the court.

67.23.4

LEAVE UNDER THE 2007 ACT.

Leave of the court is normally required to remove a child from a prospective adopter's care. Where a child has been placed for adoption the adoption agency cannot give notice of an intention not to allow the child to remain with the person with whom the child has been placed without leave of the court: 2007 Act, s. 25.

67.23.5

"NOTE".

For form of note, see r. 15.2 and notes. A fee is payable, by a person not already a party to the cause first entering the process, on lodging a note: see note 15.2.4. The note does not have to be intimated on the walls of court or advertised: r. 67.28(4).

67.23.6

"PETITION".

A petition is presented in the Outer House: r. 14.2(h). The petition must be in Form 14.4 in the official printed form: rr. 4.1 and 14.4. The petition must be signed by counsel or other person having a right of audience: r. 4.2; and see r. 1.3(1) (definitions of "counsel" and "other person having a right of audience") and note 1.3.4.

67.23.7

A fee is payable on lodging the petition: see note 14.5.10.

The ordinary petition rules apply to a petition under r. 67.23 except that it is not intimated on the walls of court or advertised: r. 67.23(2) and (3).

PRIVACY OF HEARINGS.

Any hearing in an application under s. 24 of the 2007 Act is heard in private unless the court otherwise directs: 2007 Act, s. 109.

67.23.8

Part 3 – Convention Adoption Orders

Interpretation

67.24.[1] In this Part, unless the context otherwise requires—

67.24

"Central Authority" means the Scottish Executive;

"the Convention" means the Convention on Protection of Children and Co-operation in respect of Intercountry Adoption, concluded at the Hague on 29th May 1993;

"Convention adoption order" means an adoption which, by virtue of regulation 53(2) of the 2009 Regulations, is made as a Convention adoption order;

"Convention country" means any country or territory in which the Convention is in force.

GENERAL NOTE.

A Convention adoption order is made where a child habitually resident in one Contracting State (State of origin) has been, or is being, or is to be moved to another Contracting State (receiving State) either after adoption in the State of origin by spouses or a person habitually resident in the receiving State, or for the purposes of such adoption in the receiving State or State of origin: the Hague Convention on Protection of Children and Cooperation in respect of Intercountry Adoption, 29th May 1993, signed by the UK on 12th January 1994, art. 2. The Convention has been brought into effect in the UK by the Adoption (Intercountry Aspects) Act 1999.

67.24.1

This convention replaces the Hague Convention on the Jurisdiction, Applicable Law and Recognition of Decrees Relating to Adoptions, November 15, 1965 (Cmnd. 7342) which was ratified only by Austria, Switzerland and the UK.

An "overseas adoption" is an adoption of a description in regulations made by Scottish Ministers under the law of a country outwith the British Islands (defined in s. 119) which is not a Convention

---

[1] R. 67.24 substituted by S.S.I. 2009 No. 283 (effective 28th September 2009).

adoption: 2007 Act, s. 67. The current regulations, which stipulate the countries, are the Adoption Recognition of Overseas Adoption (Scotland) Regulations 2013 [SSI 2013/310] .

At common law, recognition and registration of a foreign adoption order (other than an overseas adoption as defined in s.67 of the 2007 Act or a Convention adoption) may be obtained in Scotland if the following tests are met: (1) was the adoption obtained lawfully in the foreign country, (2) did the concept of adoption in that jurisdiction conform with the Scottish concept and (3) was there any public policy consideration that should mitigate against recognition: *Brown, Ptnrs*, 2015 S.L.T. 378 (OH).

Application for a Convention adoption order

67.25

67.25.—[1](1) An application for a Convention adoption order is to be made by petition in Form 67.25.

(2) The following documents must be lodged in process along with a petition under paragraph (1)—

   (a) a certificate, register extract, or other proof of date of birth relating to the child who is the subject of the application, issued or authenticated by the applicable Convention country authority;

   (b) in the case of a joint petition by a married couple, a certificate, register extract or other proof of their marriage, issued or authenticated by the applicable Convention country authority;

   (c) in the case of a joint petition by a couple who are civil partners of each other, a certificate, register extract or other proof of their civil partnership, issued or authenticated by the applicable Convention country authority;

   (d) any report by the local authority required by section 19(2) (investigation by local authority on receipt of notice of intention to apply for adoption order) of the 2007 Act, if available;

   (e) any report by an adoption agency, being a Scottish accredited body, required by section 17 (report on the suitability of the applicants and other matters) of the 2007 Act, if available;

   (f) where appropriate, an extract of the order freeing the child for adoption;

   (g) where appropriate, an extract of the permanence order made in respect of the child under section 80 of the 2007 Act;

   (h) in the case of a petition to which the provisions of Chapter 1 of Part 3 of the 2009 Regulations apply—

      (i) copies of the Article 16 Information and the Agreement under Article 17(c) of the Convention referred to in regulation 34(c) of those Regulations; and

      (ii) the confirmation referred to in regulation 34(d) of those Regulations;

   (i) in the case of a petition to which the provisions of Chapter 2 of Part 3 of the 2009 Regulations apply—

      (i) copies of the Article 16 Report and the Agreement under Article 17(c) of the Convention referred to in regulation 51(c) of those Regulations; and

      (ii) the confirmation referred to in regulation 51(d) of those Regulations;

   (j) any other document founded on by the petitioner in support of the petition;

   (k) where appropriate, a translation into English of any document referred to in subparagraphs (a) to (j), together with the certificate referred to in paragraph (3).

---

[1] R. 67.25 substituted by S.S.I. 2009 No. 283 (effective 28th September 2009).

(3) The certificate mentioned in paragraph (2)(k) is a certificate by the translator—

    (a)   certifying that the translation is in conformity with the original document; and

    (b)   giving the full name, address and qualifications of the translator.

(4) A report by a local authority under section 19(2), or an adoption agency under section 17 of the 2007 Act must be in numbered paragraphs and include the following matters:—

    (a)   a description of the petitioner's background, including his family history, medical history, his social environment, his reasons for wishing to adopt, his eligibility and suitability to adopt, and in particular his suitability for a Convention adoption order;

    (b)   a description of the child's background, including his family history, his medical history and that of his family, his social environment, his physical and mental health (including any special needs), and his emotional, behavioural and educational development;

    (c)   information about the mutual suitability of the petitioner and the child for the relationship created by adoption, and the ability of the petitioner to bring up the child, including an assessment of the personalities of the petitioner and of the child;

    (d)   particulars of all the members of the household of the petitioner, and their relationship to the petitioner;

    (e)   a description of the accommodation in the home of the petitioner;

    (f)   in a petition by only one member of a relevant couple within the meaning of section 29(3) of the 2007 Act, why the other member of that couple has not joined in the application;

    (g)   whether the petitioner understands the nature and effect of an adoption order and in particular that the order, if made, will make the petitioner responsible for the maintenance and upbringing of the child;

    (h)   whether the means and standing of the petitioner are such as to enable him to maintain and bring up the child suitably;

    (i)   whether the child has any right or interest in property and, if so, what right or interest;

    (j)   whether any payment or other reward in consideration of the proposed adoption, other than an approved adoption allowance has been received or agreed;

    (k)   what insurance has been offered on the life of the child;

    (l)   the religious persuasion, racial origin, and cultural and linguistic background of the child and of the petitioner;

    (m)   considerations arising from the difference in age between the petitioner and the child if this is more or less than the normal difference between parents and children;

    (n)   whether adoption is likely to safeguard and promote the welfare of the child throughout his life;

    (o)   whether the child is subject to a supervision requirement under section 70 of the 1995 Act and, if so, what steps have been taken to comply with section 73(4)(c), (5) and (13) (duration and review of supervision requirement) of that Act;

    (p)   whether there has been a contravention of section 75 of the 2007 Act in relation to the child;

    (q)   whether there has been a failure to comply with section 76(2) of the 2007 Act in relation to the child;

(r) any other matters relevant to the operation of section 14 of the 2007 Act in relation to the application;

(s) where appropriate, information about whether—

    (i) in an application under section 29(1) of the 2007 Act, the petitioners are a relevant couple within the meaning of section 29(3)(c) or (d) of the 2007 Act

    (ii) in an application under section 30(1) of the 2007 Act, the petitioner is a member of a relevant couple within the meaning of section 29(3)(c) or (d) of the 2007 Act;

(t) in the case of a petition to which the provisions of Chapter 1 of Part 3 of the 2009 Regulations apply, the confirmation, the date and the details referred to respectively in regulation 33(a), (b) and (c) of those Regulations;

(u) any other information which may be of assistance to the court.

(5) If no report mentioned in paragraph (2)(d) or (e) is available to be lodged with the petition, the court shall pronounce an interlocutor requiring the local authority or adoption agency to prepare and lodge such a report in court within 2 weeks from the date of the interlocutor, or within such other period as the court in its discretion may allow.

"PETITION".

67.25.1

A petition for a Convention adoption order is presented in the Outer House: r. 142(h). The petition must be in Form 67.25 in the official printed form: rr. 4.1 and 14.4. The petition must be signed by counsel or other person having a right of audience: r. 4.2; and see r. 1.3(1) (definitions of "counsel" and "other person having a right of audience") and note 1.3.4.

The petitioner must lodge the petition with the required steps of process (r. 4.4) and the productions required by r. 67.25(2) and any others (including those founded on or adopted (r. 27.1)) with an inventory of productions (r. 4.5).

A fee is payable on lodging the petition: see note 14.5.10.

Application of Part 2 to this Part

67.26

67.26.[1] Rules 67.11 to 67.23 (other than paragraph (3)(n) of rule 67.12) of Part 2 are to apply to an application under this Part, so far as they are not inconsistent with this Part, except that—

(a) rule 67.11 (appointment of curator ad litem) and reporting officer) is to be read as if—

    (i) in paragraph (1), for "rule 67.8" there were substituted "rule 67.25";

    (ii) in paragraph (1) "and reporting officer" were omitted; and

    (iii) for paragraphs (2) and (3) there were substituted—

        "(2) Subject to paragraph (3), the court must not appoint a reporting officer.

        (3) A reporting officer must be appointed where the child who is the subject of the application is aged 12 or over, for the purposing of witnessing that child's consent where that consent is executed in Scotland.";

(b) rule 67.14 (intimation and hearing of adoption petition) is to be read as if—

    (i) in paragraph (1), for "rule 67.8" there were substituted "rule 67.25";

    (ii) for paragraph (1)(b) there were substituted—

        "(b) the petitioner must intimate a copy of the petition along with a notice of intimation in Form 67.14-A to—

---

[1] R. 67.26 substituted by S.S.I. 2009 No. 283 (effective 28th September 2009).

(i)   the curator ad litem and reporting officer;

(ii)   any person or body who has care or possession of the child; and

(iii)   any local authority or adoption agency that
has prepared a report under section 17 or
19(2) of the 2007 Act.";

(iii)   paragraph 1(c) and (d) were omitted.

(c)   rule 67.19 (communication to the Registrar General) is to be read as if for
it there were substituted—

"Communication to the Registrar General and the Central Authority

67.19.—(1)   The making of a Convention adoption order is to be
intimated in accordance with this rule to the Registrar General and
the Central Authority by the clerk of court.

(2)   A certified copy of the order making a Convention adoption
order must be sent to the Registrar General and the Central Authority
in a sealed envelope marked "Confidential".".

Annulment etc. of overseas adoptions

67.27.—[1](1)   This rule applies to an application for—   **67.27**

(a)   an order under section 68 (annulment and recognition) of the 2007 Act;
and

(b)   a decision under section 68(2)(b) of the 2007 Act.

(2)   Where the adopted person is under the age of 18 years on the date of the
making of an application to which this rule applies, the court shall appoint a curator
ad litem with the duties mentioned in rule 67.12(3).

(3)   On the court granting an application to which this rule applies, the Deputy
Principal Clerk shall send a notice of the order to the Registrar General specifying—

(a)   the date of the adoption;

(b)   the name and address of the authority which granted the adoption;

(c)   the names of the adopter or adopters and of the adopted person as given in
that petition;

(d)   the country in which the petition was granted;

(e)   the country of which the adopted person is a national; and

(f)   the country in which the adopted person was born.

GENERAL NOTE.

The Court of Session has power to annul a Convention adoption order on the ground that it is contrary   **67.27.1**
to public policy: 2007 Act, s. 68.

"PETITION".

A petition is presented in the Outer House: r. 14.2(h). The petition must be in Form 14.4 in the official   **67.27.2**
printed form: rr. 4.1 and 14.4. The petition must be signed by counsel or other person having a right of
audience: r. 4.2; and see r. 1.3(1) (definition of "counsel" and "other person having a right of audience")
and note 1.3.4.

The petitioner must lodge the petition with the required steps of process (r. 4.4).

A fee is payable on lodging the petition: see note 14.5.10.

---

[1] R. 67.27 substituted by S.S.I. 2009 No. 283 (effective 28th September 2009).

"SEND".

67.27.3   Send includes deliver: r. 1.3(1).

Part 4 – Permanence Orders

Application for permanence order

67.28   **67.28**—[1](1) An application for a permanence order under section 80 of the 2007 Act is to be made by petition in Form 67.28.

(2) The following documents must be lodged in process along with a petition under paragraph (1)—

(a) an extract of the entry in the Register of Births relating to the child who is the subject of the application;

(b) a report by the petitioner in numbered paragraphs which deals with the following matters—

    (i) how the needs of the child came to the notice of the petitioner;

    (ii) any relevant family circumstances of the child;

    (iii) a description of the physical and mental health of the child (including any special needs) and his emotional, behavioural and educational development;

    (iv) an account of the discussion by the petitioner with the parents or guardians of the child and, if appropriate, with the child about their wishes and the alternatives to a permanence order;

    (v) where appropriate, whether the father of the child has been given notice and provided with the prescribed information under section 105(2) of the 2007 Act;

    (vi) the knowledge of the petitioner of the position of other relatives or persons likely to be involved;

    (vii) an account of the search by the petitioner for any parent or guardian who cannot be found;

    (viii) the arrangements of the petitioner to care for the child after the making of a permanence order (including the arrangements for contact between the child and any other person);

    (ix) the child's religious persuasion, racial origin and cultural and linguistic background;

    (x) the likely effect on the child of the making of a permanence order;

    (xi) whether there is a person who has the right mentioned in section 2(1)(a) of the 1995 Act to have the child living with the person or otherwise to regulate the child's residence and, where there is such a person, evidence that the child's residence with the person is or is likely to be seriously detrimental to the welfare of the child;

    (xii) whether the child is or has been married or a civil partner;

    (xiii) in the case of a petition containing a request that the order include provision granting authority for the child to be adopted, the matters mentioned in paragraph (3);

    (xiv) in the case of a petition in respect of a child who is aged 12 or over, whether the child consents to the making of the order or is incapable of doing so;

    (xv) whether the child is subject to a supervision requirement under section 70 of the 1995 Act;

---

[1] R. 67.28 substituted by S.S.I. 2009 No. 283 (effective 28th September 2009).

(xvi) any other information which may be of assistance to the court having regard, in particular, to sections 83 (if appropriate) and 84 of the 2007 Act;

(c) any other document founded upon by the petitioner in support of the terms of the petition.

(3) The matters referred to in paragraph (2)(xiii) are—

(a) whether the child has been, or is likely to be, placed for adoption;

(b) whether each parent or guardian of the child understands what the effect of making an adoption order would be and consents to the making of such an order in relation to the child, or the grounds on which such consent should be dispensed with.

(4) If the report mentioned in paragraph (2)(b) is unavailable to be lodged with the petition, the court shall pronounce an interlocutor requiring the petitioner to prepare and lodge such a report within 2 weeks of the date of the interlocutor, or within such other period as the court in its discretion may allow.

GENERAL NOTE.

While abolishing freeing for adoption and parental rights and responsibilities orders under s. 86 of the Children (Scotland) Act 1995, the 2007 Act creates a new flexible order, called a permanence order, to allow a local authority to secure long-term care for a child according to its needs. The provisions are in ss. 84–104 of the 2007 Act. There is a mandatory provision for the vesting of parental rights and responsibilities in the local authority and a number of ancillary provisions which can be included in the order according to the child's needs: 2007 Act, ss. 80–82. There is provision for the inclusion in the order of authority for the child to be adopted and for dispensing with the consent of a parent or guardian. The grounds for dispensation are the same as for adoption, i.e. (1) where the parent or guardian has parental rights or responsibilities, that person is unable satisfactorily to discharge them and is likely to continue to be unable to do so, or (2) where the parent or guardian has, by virtue of a permanence order that does not include authority for the adoption of the child, no parental rights and responsibilities in relation to that child and is unlikely to be given to them.

Section 84(5) of the Adoption and Children (Scotland) Act 2007 sets out a threshold test which has to be addressed first and, unless satisfied, no permanence order can be made: *R v. Stirling Council*, 2016 S.L.T. 689 (Extra Div.); *West Lothian Council v. B*, 2017 S.L.T. 319 (UKSC).

67.28.1

JURISDICTION.

The Court of Session has jurisdiction concurrent with the sheriff court where the child is in Scotland and exclusive jurisdiction where the child is not in Scotland and the petition seeks authority for adoption of the child: 2007 Act, s. 11.

67.28.2

"PETITION".

A petition is presented to the Outer House: r. 14.2(h). The petition must be in Form 67.28 in the official printed form (r. 4.1). The petition must be signed by counsel or other person having a right of audience: r. 4.2; and see r. 1.3(1) (definition of "counsel" and "other person having a right of audience") and note 1.3.4.

The petitioner must lodge the petition with the required steps of process (r. 4.4). A fee is payable on lodging the petition: see note 14.5.10.

On petitions generally, see Chap. 14.

67.28.3

EXPENSES.

As a matter of practice, expenses are not ordinarily awarded against compearing parties in petitions where local authorities seek permanence orders unless there was reprehensible behaviour or an unreasonable stance taken (by the local authority): *Perth and Kinross Council, Ptnrs, 2018 S.L.T. 275*.

67.28.4

Appointment of curator ad litem and reporting officer

67.29.—[1](1) The court must, on the lodging of a petition under rule 67.28 appoint a curator ad litem and reporting officer.

(2) Subject to paragraph (3), the court must not appoint a reporting officer where the petition does not request that the order include provision granting authority for the child to be adopted.

67.29

---

[1] R. 67.29 substituted by S.S.I. 2009 No. 283 (effective 28th September 2009).

(3)   Notwithstanding paragraph (2), a reporting officer must be appointed where the child who is the subject of the application is aged 12 or over for the purpose of witnessing that child's consent where that consent is to be executed in Scotland.

(4)   The same person may be appointed as curator ad litem and reporting officer in the same petition if the court considers that doing so is appropriate in the circumstances

(5)   A person may, before presenting the petition, apply by letter to the Deputy Principal Clerk for the appointment of a reporting officer.

(6)   An application under paragraph (4) shall—

(a)   set out the reasons for which the appointment is sought;

(b)   not require to be intimated to any person;

(c)   be accompanied by an interlocutor sheet; and

(d)   be placed by the Deputy Principal Clerk before the Lord Ordinary for his decision.

(7)   The Deputy Principal Clerk shall intimate the appointment of a curator ad litem and reporting officer under paragraph (1) or (5) to the petitioner and to the person or persons appointed.

(8)   The decision of the Lord Ordinary on an application under paragraph (5) shall be final and not subject to review.

(9)   The letter and the interlocutor sheet in an application under paragraph (5) shall be kept in the Petition Department and subsequently placed in the process of the petition.

GENERAL NOTE.

67.29.1   A curator ad litem is always appointed. Notwithstanding the mandatory terms of r. 67.28(1), a reporting officer does not always have to be appointed where the petition does not include a request for authority for the child to be adopted.

"INTIMATE".

67.29.2   Although the reference takes one to r. 16.7, written intimation under r. 16.9 was probably intended.

"FINAL AND NOT SUBJECT TO REVIEW".

67.29.3   The decision of the Lord Ordinary may not be reclaimed against.

Intimation of application

67.30   **67.30.**—[1](1)   On the lodging of a petition under rule 67.28—

(a)   the Deputy Principal Clerk must cause the petition to be put on the By Order Roll before the Lord Ordinary not less than 6 and not more than 8 weeks thereafter;

(b)   where the petition does not contain a request that the order include provision granting authority for the child to be adopted, the petitioner must intimate a copy of the petition along with a notice of intimation in Form 67.30-A to—

(i)   any person who has parental responsibilities or parental rights in relation to the child; and

(ii)   any person who claims to have an interest;

(c)   where the petition contains such a request—

(i)   the petitioner must intimate a copy of the petition along with a notice of intimation in Form 67.30-A to the persons mentioned in paragraph (2); and

(ii)   the petitioner must intimate a copy of the petition along with a notice of intimation in Form 67.30-B to the father of the child if he

---

[1] R. 67.30 substituted by S.S.I. 2009 No. 283 (effective 28th September 2009).

does not have, and never has had, parental responsibilities and parental rights in relation to the child;

    (d)   the Deputy Principal Clerk must intimate the date of the hearing on the By Order Roll to the curator ad litem and to any reporting officer appointed under rule 67.29;

    (e)   the court may order the petitioner to intimate the application to such other person as it considers appropriate.

  (2) The persons referred to in paragraph (1)(c)(i) are—

    (a)   every person who can be found and whose consent to the making of the order is required to be given or dispensed with under the 2007 Act;

    (b)   if no such person can be found, a relative of the child within the meaning of section 119(1) of the 2007 Act unless the address of such a relative is not known to the petitioner and cannot reasonably be ascertained.

  (3) A notice of intimation under paragraph (1)(c)(i) must include the following matters:—

    (a)   that an application for a permanence order containing a request that the order include provision granting authority for the child to be adopted has been made;

    (b)   the date on which and place where the By Order hearing will be held;

    (c)   the fact that the person is entitled to be heard on the application;

    (d)   the fact that, unless the person wishes, or the court requires, the person need not attend the hearing.

  (4) A notice of intimation under paragraph (1)(c)(ii) must include the matters mentioned in paragraphs (3)(a) and (b).

"INTIMATE".

For methods, see r. 16.7.

           67.30.1

Hearing on the By Order Roll

67.31.—[1](1) At the By Order hearing appointed under rule 67.30 the court must—

           67.31

    (a)   if no party indicates his intention to oppose the petition, dispose of the cause or make such other order as it considers appropriate; or

    (b)   in any other case—

        (i)   ascertain from the parties the anticipated length of any proof that may be required;

       (ii)   fix a diet of proof not less than 12 and not more than 16 weeks after the date of the hearing on the By Order Roll unless, on cause shown, a longer period is appropriate;

      (iii)   give such directions as to the preparation for the proof as it considers appropriate;

      (iv)   order answers and any other documents to be lodged within 21 days of the date of the hearing on the By Order Roll or such other period as it considers appropriate.

  (2) Paragraph (1)(b)(ii) shall not require a proof to be held when the court is in vacation unless the court otherwise directs.

  (3) At the By Order hearing the court may—

    (a)   if it is not satisfied that the facts stated in the petition are supported by the documents lodged with it or by the reports of the curator ad litem and reporting officer, order the production of further documents; and

---

[1] R. 67.31 substituted by S.S.I. 2009 No. 283 (effective 28th September 2009).

(b)　where it considers it appropriate to do so, fix a pre-proof hearing not less than 2 and not more than 6 weeks before the diet of proof;

(c)　make such other order as it considers appropriate for the expeditious progress of the case.

Pre-proof hearing

67.32　**67.32—**[1](1)　If the court appoints a pre-proof hearing under rule 67.31, the parties must provide the court with sufficient information to enable it to conduct the hearing as provided for in this rule.

(2)　At the pre-proof hearing the court must ascertain, so far as is reasonably practicable, whether the cause is likely to proceed to proof on the date fixed for that purpose and, in particular, the court must consider—

(a)　the state of preparation of the parties;

(b)　the extent to which the parties have complied with any orders made by the court under rule 67.31.

(3)　At the pre-proof hearing the court may—

(a)　discharge the proof and fix a new date for such proof;

(b)　adjourn the pre-proof hearing;

(c)　order the lodging of joint minutes of agreement, affidavits and expert reports within such period as it considers appropriate;

(d)　make such other order as it considers appropriate to secure the expeditious progress of the cause.

Final procedure

67.33　**67.33.—**[2](1)　Where a permanence order has been granted, the Deputy Principal Clerk must—

(a)　after the expiry of 14 days from the date of, or date of confirmation of, the order without an appeal having been taken, issue an extract of the order to the petitioner;

(b)　where the court has also made an order under section 89(2) (revocation of supervision requirement) of the 2007 Act, intimate the making of that order to the Principal Reporter.

(2)　Where the permanence order includes provision granting authority for the child to be adopted, the Deputy Principal Clerk must, after complying with paragraph (1), seal the process in an envelope marked "Confidential".

(3)　The envelope referred to in paragraph (2) must not be unsealed by the clerk of court or any other person having control of the records of that or any court, and the process shall not be made accessible to any person for one hundred years after the date of the granting of the order except—

(a)　to the person to whom the permanence order relates once he has attained the age of 16 years;

(b)　to the Deputy Principal Clerk, on an application made to him by an adoption agency, with the consent of the person to whom the process relates, for the purpose only of ascertaining the name of the agency, if any, responsible for the placement of that person and informing the applicant of that name;

(c)　to a person, on an application made by him to the court setting forth the reasons for which access to the process is required;

(d)　to a court, public authority or administrative board (whether in the United

---

[1] R. 67.32 substituted by S.S.I. 2009 No. 283 (effective 28th September 2009).
[2] R. 67.33 substituted by S.S.I. 2009 No. 283 (effective 28th September 2009).

Kingdom or not) having power to authorise an adoption, on petition by it to the court which granted the original order requesting that information be made available from the process for the purpose of discharging its duties in considering an application for adoption and specifying the precise reasons for which access to the process is required; or

(e) to a person who is authorised by the Scottish Ministers to obtain information from the process for the purpose of such research as is intended to improve the working of adoption law and practice.

Variation of ancillary provisions in order

67.34—[1](1) An application under section 92(2) of the 2007 Act (application for variation of ancillary provisions) is to be made by note.

(2) A note under paragraph (1) must contain—

(a) the name and address of the applicant;

(b) the applicant's relationship to and interest in the child;

(c) the name and address of the local authority on whose application the permanence order was granted;

(d) details of the original application;

(e) details of any other person affected by the order;

(f) the grounds on which variation is sought;

(g) details of whether the child is subject to a supervision requirement under section 70 of the 1995 Act;

(h) details of the order sought by the applicant.

(3) On presentation of a note under paragraph (1) the court must—

(a) order the applicant to intimate the note to—

(i) the petitioner in the original application, where it is not the applicant;

(ii) any other person affected by the order; and

(iii) such other persons as the court considers appropriate; and

(b) appoint a curator ad litem.

(4) Any person to whom intimation is given under paragraph (2) may, within 14 days after the date on which intimation is made, lodge answers to the note.

(5) Where answers have been lodged under paragraph (4) the court must order a hearing to be fixed.

(6) Where no answers have been lodged under paragraph (4) the court may order a hearing to be fixed.

(7) Where the court orders a hearing to be fixed under paragraph (5) or (6) it may also order a pre-proof hearing to be fixed not less than 2 and not more than 6 weeks before the hearing.

(8) Rule 67.32 is to apply, with any necessary modifications, to any pre-proof hearing fixed under paragraph (7).

(9) The court shall order the applicant to intimate any hearing fixed under paragraph (5), (6) or (7) to the petitioner in the original application, where it is not the applicant, to any other person affected by the order and to such other persons as the court considers appropriate.

GENERAL NOTE.

A permanence order may only be varied if it contains ancillary provisions (i.e. any of those mentioned in s. 82 of the 2007 Act) because it is only ancillary provisions that may be varied: 2007 Act, s. 92(1) and (2). A person other than the local authority must obtain leave of the court to seek a variation: 2007 Act, s. 94(4).

67.34

67.34.1

---

[1] R. 67.34 substituted by S.S.I. 2009 No. 283 (effective 28th September 2009).

67.34.2   "NOTE".

Rule 15.2 will apply. The note will be lodged in the process of the petition for the permanence order.

"INTIMATE".

67.34.3   For methods, see r. 16.7.

Amendment of order to grant authority for child to be adopted

67.35   **67.35.**—[1](1) An application under section 93(2) (amendment of order to include provision granting authority for child to be adopted) of the 2007 Act is to be made by note.

(2) A note under paragraph (1) must contain—

    (a) the name and address of the applicant;

    (b) details of the original application;

    (c) details of the following matters—

        (i) whether the child has been, or is likely to be, placed for adoption;

        (ii) whether each parent or guardian of the child understands what the effect of making an adoption order would be and consents to the making of such an order in relation to the child, or the grounds on which such consent should be dispensed with;

        (iii) the child's religious persuasion, racial origin and cultural and linguistic background;

        (iv) whether the child is subject to a supervision requirement under section 70 of the 1995 Act;

        (v) the likely effect on the child of the making of the order.

(3) On the lodging of a note under paragraph (1)—

    (a) the Deputy Principal Clerk must cause the note to be put on the By Order Roll before the Lord Ordinary not less than 6 and not more than 8 weeks after the date of lodging the application;

    (b) the applicant must intimate a copy of the note along with a notice of intimation in Form 67.35-A to every person who can be found and whose consent to the making of the order is required to be given or dispensed with under the 2007 Act;

    (c) the applicant must intimate a copy of the note along with a notice of intimation in Form 67.35-B to the father of the child if he does not have, and never has had, parental responsibilities in relation to the child;

    (d) the court may order the applicant to intimate the note to such other persons as it considers appropriate;

    (e) the court must appoint a curator ad litem and reporting officer and the same person may be appointed as curator ad litem and reporting officer if the court considers that doing so is appropriate in the circumstances.

(4) A notice of intimation under paragraph (3)(b) must state the following matters:—

    (a) that an application has been made;

    (b) the date on which, and place where, the By Order hearing will be heard;

    (c) the fact that the person is entitled to be heard on the application;

    (d) the fact that, unless the person wishes, or the court requires, the person need not attend the hearing.

(5) A notice of intimation under paragraph (3)(c) must state the matters mentioned in paragraph (4)(a) and (b).

---

[1] R. 67.35 substituted by S.S.I. 2009 No. 283 (effective 28th September 2009).

(6) Rules 67.31 to 67.33 are to apply, with any necessary modifications, to an application under this rule and they apply to an application under rule 67.28

GENERAL NOTE.

Where a permanence order does not contain authority for the adoption of a child, the local authority may apply to amend the order to include such authority: 2007 Act, s. 93.

67.35.1

"NOTE".

Rule 15.2 will apply. The note will be lodged in the process of the petition for the permanence order.

67.35.2

"INTIMATE".

For methods, see r. 16.7.

67.35.3

Revocation

67.36.—[1](1) An application under section 98(1) (revocation of a permanence order) of the 2007 Act shall be made by note.

67.36

(2) A note under paragraph (1) must contain—
  (a) the name and address of the applicant;
  (b) the applicant's relationship to and interest in the child;
  (c) the name and address of the local authority on whose application the permanence order was granted;
  (d) details of the original application;
  (e) details of any other person affected by the order;
  (f) the grounds on which revocation is sought;
  (g) details of whether the child is subject to a supervision requirement under section 70 of the 1995 Act;
  (h) details of the order sought by the applicant;
  (i) detailed proposals for the future welfare of the child.

(3) On the lodging of a note under paragraph (1), the court must—
  (a) order the applicant to intimate the note to—
    (i) the petitioner in the original application, where it is not the applicant;
    (ii) any other person affected by the order; and
    (iii) such other persons as he considers appropriate; and
  (b) appoint a curator ad litem.

(4) Any person to whom intimation has been given under paragraph (3) may, within 14 days after the date on which intimation is made, lodge answers to the note.

(5) Where answers have been lodged under paragraph (4), the court must order a hearing to be fixed.

(6) Where no answers have been lodged under paragraph (4) the court may—
  (a) order the relevant local authority to submit a report to him;
  (b) order a hearing to be fixed;
  (c) order both such a report and such a hearing.

(7) Where the court orders a hearing to be fixed under paragraph (5) or (6) it may also order a pre-proof hearing to be fixed not less than 2 and not more than 6 weeks before the hearing.

(8) Rule 67.32 is to apply, with any necessary modifications, to any pre-proof hearing fixed under paragraph (7).

---

[1] R. 67.36 substituted by S.S.I. 2009 No. 283 (effective 28th September 2009).

(9) The court shall order the applicant to intimate any hearing fixed under paragraph (5), (6) or (7) to the petitioner in the original application, where it is not the applicant, to any other person affected by the order and to such other persons as the court considers appropriate.

(10) An order made in respect of an application under paragraph (1) may specify the person—

(a) on whom parental responsibilities are imposed in consequence of the making of the order; and

(b) to whom parental rights are given in consequence of the making of the order.

GENERAL NOTE.

67.36.1   Any person other than a local authority must obtain leave of the court to apply for revocation: 2007 Act, s. 98(2)(b). Where the court revokes a permanence order, it must consider whether to make an order under s.11 of the Children (Scotland) Act 1995.

"NOTE".

67.36.2   Rule 15.2 will apply. The note will be lodged in the process of the petition for the permanence order.

"INTIMATE".

67.36.3   For methods, see r. 16.7.

Protection of address of child

67.37   **67.37**—[1](1) Where an applicant under this Part wishes to prevent the address of the child being disclosed to any person whose consent to the making of an order is required, the applicant may apply to the Deputy Principal Clerk for a serial number to be assigned for that purpose.

(2) On receipt of an application under paragraph (1) the Deputy Principal Clerk must—

(a) assign a serial number in respect of the child's address; and

(b) enter a note of the number opposite the child's address in a register of serial numbers.

(3) The contents of the register of serial numbers and the addresses of the children to whom each number relates shall be treated as confidential by the sheriff clerk and are not to be disclosed to any person other than the sheriff.

(4) Where a serial number has been assigned under paragraph (2), any form of consent to a permanence order—

(a) must refer to the child's address by means of the serial number assigned to it; and

(b) must specify the year in which and the court by which the serial number was assigned.

Duties of reporting officer and curator ad litem

67.38   **67.38.**—[2](1) The other duties of a reporting officer appointed under this Part, other than under rule 67.29(3), which are prescribed for the purposes of section 108(1)(b) of the 2007 Act are—

(a) to ascertain the whereabouts of all persons whose consent to the making of an adoption order in respect of the child is required;

(b) to ascertain whether there is any person other than those mentioned in the petition upon whom notice of the petition should be served;

(c) in the case of each person whose consent to the making of an adoption order is required or may be dispensed with—

---

[1] R. 67.37 substituted by S.S.I. 2009 No. 283 (effective 28th September 2009).
[2] R. 67.38 substituted by S.S.I. 2009 No. 283 (effective 28th September 2009).

(i) to ascertain whether that person understands what the effect of making an adoption order would be;

(ii) to ascertain whether alternatives to adoption have been discussed with that person;

(iii) to confirm that that person understands that he may withdraw his consent at any time before an order is made;

(d) to confirm that each parent or guardian of the child who can be found is aware that he may apply to the court for—

(i) variation of the ancillary provisions in the permanence order under section 92 of the 2007 Act; and

(ii) revocation of a permanence order under section 98 of the 2007 Act, and of the appropriate procedure for these applications.

(e) to report in writing on the matters mentioned in subparagraphs (a) to (d) to the court within 4 weeks from date of interlocutor appointing the reporting officer, or within such other period as the court may allow.

(2) References in paragraph (1) to "consent" are to consent within the meaning of section 83(1)(c), 84(1) or 93(3) of the 2007 Act as the case may be.

(3) A curator *ad litem* appointed under this Part must—

(a) have regard to safeguarding the interests of the child as his paramount duty;

(b) inquire, so far as he considers necessary into the facts and circumstances stated in the petition or minute, as the case may be, and in any report lodged under rule 31(2)(b);

(c) where appropriate, establish the child's religious persuasion, racial origin and cultural and linguistic background;

(d) where appropriate, establish whether the order is likely to safeguard and promote the welfare of the child throughout childhood;

(e) ascertain whether the child is subject to a supervision requirement under section 70 of the 1995 Act;

(f) ascertain from the child whether he wishes to express a view and, where the child indicates his wish to express a view, ascertain that view;

(g) ascertain the likely effect on the child of the making of the order;

(h) where appropriate, ascertain whether it would be better for the child that the order be made than that it should not be made;

(i) where appropriate, ascertain whether it would be better for the child if the court were to grant authority for the child to be adopted than if it were not to grant such authority;

(j) where appropriate, ascertain whether the child has been, or is likely to be, placed for adoption.

(4) Subject to paragraph (5) the curator *ad litem* must report in writing on the matters mentioned in paragraph (3) to the court within 4 weeks from the date of the interlocutor appointing the curator, or within such other period as the court may allow.

(5) Subject to any order made by the court under rule 67.40 the views of the child ascertained in terms of paragraph (3)(f) may, if the curator *ad litem* considers appropriate, be conveyed to the court orally.

Consents

67.39.—[1](1) The consent of a parent or guardian required by section 83(1)(c) or 93(3) of the 2007 Act is to be in Form 67.39-A.

67.39

---

[1] R. 67.39 substituted by S.S.I. 2009 No. 283 (effective 28th September 2009).

(2) The consent of the child required under section 84(1) of the 2007 Act is to be in Form 67.39-B.

(3) A form of consent mentioned in paragraph (1) or (2) must be witnessed—

(a) where it is executed in Scotland, by the reporting officer appointed under this Part;

(b) where it is executed outwith Scotland but within the United Kingdom, by a justice of the peace or commissioner for oaths; or

(c) where it is executed outwith the United Kingdom—

(i) if the person who executes the form is serving in Her Majesty's forces, by an officer holding a commission in any of those forces; or

(ii) in any other case, by a British diplomatic or consular official or any person authorised to administer an oath or affirmation under the law of the place where the consent is executed.

Procedure where child wishes to express a view

67.40   **67.40.**—[1](1) Where a child has indicated his wish to express his views the court, without prejudice to rule 67.38(3)(f)—

(a) may order such procedural steps to be taken as it considers appropriate to ascertain the views of that child; and

(b) must not make an order under this Part unless an opportunity has been given for the views of that child to be obtained or heard.

(2) Where the views of a child, whether obtained under this rule or under rule 67.38(2)(f), have been recorded in writing, the court may direct that such a written record is to—

(a) be sealed in a envelope marked "Views of the child - confidential";

(b) be available to the court only;

(c) not be opened by any other person; and

(d) not form a borrowable part of the process.

Procedure where leave of court required

67.41   **67.41.**—[2](1) Where leave of the court is required under section 94(4) or 98(2)(b) of the 2007 Act before an application for variation or revocation of a permanence order may be made, the applicant must lodge along with the note a motion stating the grounds upon which leave is sought.

(2) A motion under paragraph (1) shall not be served or intimated unless the court otherwise directs.

(3) The court may hear the applicant on the motion and may grant or refuse it or make such other order in relation to it as it considers appropriate prior to determination.

(4) Where such motion is granted, a copy of the interlocutor shall be intimated along with the note of application.

Intimation to Principal Reporter

67.42   **67.42.**[3] Where an application under this Part is made in respect of a child whose case has been referred to a children's hearing or who is subject to a supervision requirement under the 1995 Act, the Deputy Principal Clerk shall intimate the fact that the application has been made to the Principal Reporter.

---

[1] R. 67.40 substituted by S.S.I. 2009 No. 283 (effective 28th September 2009).
[2] R. 67.41 substituted by S.S.I. 2009 No. 283 (effective 28th September 2009).
[3] R. 67.42 substituted by S.S.I. 2009 No. 283 (effective 28th September 2009).

Report of children's hearing

67.43.—[1](1) On receipt of a report from a children's hearing under section 95(2) of the 2007 Act the Deputy Principal Clerk shall—

    (a) lodge the report in the process of the application; and

    (b) send a copy of the report together with a notice in Form 67.43-A to—

        (i) the parties to the application;

        (ii) any relevant person in relation to the child within the meaning given by section 93(2) of the 1995 Act; and

        (iii) such other person as the court considers appropriate.

(2) Any person who receives notice under paragraph (1)(b) and who wishes to oppose the proposals of the children's hearing must lodge a form of response in Form 67.43-B within 7 days of the date notice was given.

(3) Thereafter the court shall consider the report and any form of response lodged under paragraph (2) and decide whether to refer the child's case to the Principal Reporter as mentioned in section 96(3) of the 2007 Act.

(4) Where the court decides to refer the child's case to the Principal Reporter as mentioned in section 96(3) of the 2007 Act, the court shall pronounce an order to this effect which shall narrate in terms that the court is referring the child's case to the Principal Reporter as mentioned in that provision.

(5) Where the court decides not to refer the child's case to the Principal Reporter, it may nevertheless make such other order it considers appropriate for the expeditious progress of the case.

(6) In order to assist it to decide what to do under paragraph (3), the court may order the holding of a hearing.

(7) If the court so decides, it shall fix a date for the hearing which shall be not more than 7 days after the date of the order.

(8) The Deputy Principal Clerk of Session shall intimate any hearing under paragraph (6) to—

    (a) the parties to the application;

    (b) any person who lodged a form of response under paragraph (2);

    (c) any relevant person in relation to the child within the meaning given by section 93(2) of the 1995 Act; and

    (d) such other person as the court considers appropriate.

(9) The court may allow a continuation of a hearing under paragraph (6) on two occasions only, each for a period not exceeding 14 days.

(10) After the court has made its decision under paragraph (3), the Deputy Principal Clerk of Session shall send a notice in Form 67.43-C to the Principal Reporter.

GENERAL NOTE.

Where an application for a permanence order or variation of it is made and has not been determined, and a children's hearing proposes to make a supervision order, it must prepare a report for the court: 2007 Act, s. 95.

Interim orders

67.44.—[2](1) An application for an interim order under section 97 of the 2007 Act is to be made by motion.

GENERAL NOTE.

An interim order may be made in an application for a permanence order or a variation of it: 2007 Act, s. 97. What is meant is an interim permanence order or interim variation, as the case may be. Where the

67.43

67.43.1

67.44

67.44.1

---

[1] R. 67.43 substituted by S.S.I. 2009 No. 283 (effective 28th September 2009).
[2] R. 67.44 substituted by S.S.I. 2009 No. 283 (effective 28th September 2009).

child is subject to a supervision order and the court is satisfied that compulsory measures of care would no longer be necessary, the court, on making an interim order, must make an order providing that the supervision requirement ceases to have effect: 2007 Act, s. 97(3) and (4).

CHAPTER 68 APPLICATIONS UNDER THE SOLICITORS (SCOTLAND) ACT 1980

Chapter 68

Applications under the Solicitors (Scotland) Act 1980

Application and interpretation of this Chapter

68.1.—(1) This Chapter applies to an application or appeal under the Solicitors (Scotland) Act 1980.

(2) In this Chapter—

"the Act of 1980" means the Solicitors (Scotland) Act 1980;

"the Council" means the Council of the Law Society of Scotland;

"the Discipline Tribunal" means the tribunal constituted under section 50 of the Act of 1980.

68.1

Applications and appeals under the Act of 1980

68.2.—(1) Except in the case of an application under paragraph 20 of Schedule 4 to the Act of 1980 (which shall be made by letter to the Deputy Principal Clerk), an application or appeal under the Act of 1980 shall be made by petition.

(2) An appeal under any of the following provisions of the Act of 1980 shall specify the date on which the decision appealed against was intimated to the petitioner:—

(a) section 16(2) (appeal in respect of issue of practising certificate);

(b) section 39A(8) (appeal against withdrawal of practising certificate);

(c) section 40(3) (appeal against decision to withdraw practising certificate or to refuse to terminate suspension);

(d) section 54(1) (appeal against decision of tribunal relating to discipline); and

(e) paragraph 3 of Schedule 2 (appeal in respect of restoration to roll of solicitors).

(3) An application under paragraph 5(4) of Schedule 3 to the Act of 1980 (application for order for return of documents) shall specify the date on which the notice was served on the petitioner.

(4) An application under section 54(2) of the Act of 1980 (application to vary or quash direction of the tribunal) shall specify the date on which the decision containing the direction or order was intimated to the petitioner.

Deriv. R.C.S. 1965, r. 2 substituted by SI 1992/1422

68.2

"PETITION".

The petition is presented to the Inner House: r. 14.3(b); and see r. 68.4(1). The provisions for the lodging of documents in causes in the Inner House in r. 4.7 should be noted.

On petitions generally, see Chap. 14.

68.2.1

SCH. 4, PARA. 20 OF THE ACT OF 1980.

The Discipline Tribunal constituted under the Act of 1980 may make an award of expenses to or by the complainer or respondent. The person in whose favour an award is made may apply to the court (on production of a certificate from the clerk to the tribunal that there is no appeal or the appeal was dismissed or withdrawn) for a warrant authorising recovery of those expenses: Act of 1980, Sch. 4, para. 20.

By virtue of the amendment to r. 68.2(1) by A.S. (R.C.S.A. No. 4) (Miscellaneous) 1997 [SI 1997/1050], that application is made by letter to the DPCS and not by petition.

The letter, a narrative of the findings of the tribunal, and the certificate are passed to the clerk of one of the Divisions of the Inner House. If all is in order an interlocutor is pronounced granting warrant for all lawful execution; accordingly, an extract is not required in order to do diligence. On the meaning of "all lawful execution", see note 7.10.2.

68.2.1A

SECTION 16(2) OF THE ACT OF 1980.

An appeal against a decision of the Council to refuse to issue a practising certificate must be made within 14 days of notification of the decision: Act of 1980, s. 16(2).

68.2.2

68.2.3 An appeal against a decision of the Council to withdraw a practising certificate where the solicitor has issued an account for professional fees and outlays which is grossly excessive must be made within 21 days of receiving written notice of the decision: Act of 1980, s. 39A(8).

SECTION 40(3) OF THE ACT OF 1980.

68.2.4 An appeal against a decision of the Council to withdraw a practising certificate or to refuse to terminate a suspension from practice for failure to comply with account rules etc. must be made within 21 days after receiving written notice of the decision: Act of 1980, s. 40(3).

SECTION 54 OF THE ACT OF 1980.

68.2.5 A person aggrieved by a decision of the Discipline Tribunal may appeal within 21 days of the date on which the decision was intimated to him: Act of 1980, s. 54(1). Where the tribunal has directed its decision to take effect on the date of intimation, application can be made within 21 days to vary or quash that direction: Act of 1980, s. 54(2).

Applications for admission as notary public

68.3 **68.3.**—(1) An application under section 57(2) of the Act of 1980 (application for admission as notary public) shall be made by either the Council on behalf of named persons seeking appointment as notaries public or the person seeking appointment as a notary public.

(2) The Council shall—

(a) nominate authorised representatives to administer the oath of the office of notary public;

(b) issue all commissions as notary public;

(c) keep the register of notaries public; and

(d) on request by a notary public, and on payment of such reasonable fee as the Council may impose, supply him with a duly certified and docquetted protocol book of ninety one folios.

Deriv. R.C.S. 1965, r. 3 substituted by SI 1992/1422

GENERAL NOTE.

68.3.1 The petition for admission as a notary (an Inner House petition: r. 14.3(b)) may be made by the Council on behalf of a number of applicants or by the applicant. The petition may be combined with a petition to be admitted as a solicitor (also an Inner House petition: r. 14.3(b)). The provisions for lodging documents in causes in the Inner House in r. 4.7 should be noted.

FEE.

68.3.2 The court fee for lodging the petition is payable on lodging. Where there is a combined petition for admission as a solicitor and notary, the fee for each is payable. For fee, see Court of Session etc. Fees Order 1997, Table of Fees, Pt. I, C, item 3 and 4 [S.I. 1997 No. 688, as amended, pp. C1201 et seq.].

Intimation and service in causes under this Chapter

68.4 **68.4.**—(1) A petition to which this Chapter applies shall be brought before a Division of the Inner House in chambers, and the Division may, without hearing parties and subject to the following paragraphs, make such order for intimation and service as it thinks fit.

(2) In a cause under any of the following provisions of the Act of 1980, the court shall order service of the petition on the Council:—

(a) section 16(1) (application following refusal of practising certificate to body corporate);

(b) section 19(8) (appeal in respect of decision of Council in relation to suspension);

(c) section 39A(8) (appeal against withdrawal of practising certificate);

(d) section 40(3) (appeal against decision to withdraw practising certificate or to refuse to terminate suspension); and

(e) paragraph 5(4) of Schedule 3 (application for order for return of documents).

(3) In an appeal under section 54(1) (appeal against decision of tribunal relating to discipline), or in an application under section 54(2) (application to vary or quash direction of the tribunal), of the Act of 1980, the court shall—

    (a) order service on the Discipline Tribunal and the Law Society of Scotland; and

    (b) ordain the Discipline Tribunal to lodge in process within the period for lodging answers—

        (i) the decision of the Discipline Tribunal in respect of which the appeal or application is made; and

        (ii) if available, the notes of evidence adduced before the Discipline Tribunal.

(4) In an application under any of the following provisions of the Act of 1980, the court shall order service of the petition on the respondent:—

    (a) section 41 (application for appointment of judicial factor);

    (b) paragraph 5(1) of Schedule 3 (application for order to produce documents); and

    (c) paragraph 12 of Schedule 4 (petition to cite witnesses for recovery of evidence).

(5) In an application under section 55(3) of the Act of 1980 (application for restoration to roll of solicitors), the court shall order service on the Discipline Tribunal and the Council.

Deriv. R.C.S. 1965, r. 4 substituted by S.I. 1992 No. 1422

General note.

Petitions under this Chapter are usually dealt with by the First Division. Hearings in chambers are also in private.   **68.4.1**

"INTIMATION AND SERVICE".

No order is normally sought in the prayer, enrolled for or made by the court in a petition for admission as a notary or solicitor. See r. 14.7 and notes and Chap. 16, Pt. I. Intimation is not usually made on the walls of the court except in petitions for admission.   **68.4.2**

Procedure after order for intimation and service

68.5. The court shall, after an order for intimation and service under rule 68.4, proceed on the petition summarily in such manner as it thinks fit.   **68.5**

Deriv. R.C.S. 1965, r. 5 substituted by S.I. 1992 No. 1422

General note.

Petitions are usually appointed to the Summar Roll.   **68.5.1**

Appeals under section 54(1) of the Act of 1980

68.6. In an appeal under section 54(1) of the Act of 1980 (appeal against decision of tribunal relating to discipline)—   **68.6**

    (a) the court may substitute any other punishment for that imposed by the decision appealed against, or make any order in relation to it which it thinks fit;

    (b) where the petitioner is a person or one of the persons who complained of the alleged professional misconduct of the solicitor, the court may order that person to give security for expenses (including the cost of extending the notes of evidence adduced before the Discipline Tribunal) as a condition of proceeding with the petition.

Deriv. R.C.S. 1965, r. 6 substituted by S.I. 1992 No. 1422

General note.

It requires a very strong case before the court will interfere with an order (i.e. "sentence") of the tribunal following a finding of professional misconduct: *MacColl v. Council of the Law Society of Scotland* 1987 S.L.T. 524, 528G per L.P. Emslie.   **68.6.1**

EXPENSES.

68.6.2   Where a solicitor is guilty of professional misconduct, the court may find him liable in any expenses involved in the proceedings before the court: Act of 1980, s. 55(1)(e).

Remits for further inquiry

68.7   **68.7.**—(1) In an application or appeal under the Act of 1980, the court may remit to any person to make further inquiry into the facts, or to take further evidence and to report to the court.

(2) On completion of a report made under paragraph (1), the person to whom the remit was made shall send his report and three copies of it, and a copy of it for each party, to the Deputy Principal Clerk.

(3) On receipt of such a report, the Deputy Principal Clerk shall—

(a) cause the report to be lodged in process; and

(b) give written intimation to each party that this has been done and that he may uplift a copy of the report from process.

(4) After the lodging of such a report, any party may apply by motion for an order in respect of the report or for further procedure.

Deriv. R.C.S. 1965, r. 7 substituted by S.I. 1992 No. 1422

GENERAL NOTE.

68.7.1   The solicitors for the parties are personally responsible for the fees of a reporter and the solicitor for one party will be liable: r. 42.15.

"SEND".

68.7.2   This includes deliver: r. 1.3(1) (definition of "send").

"WRITTEN INTIMATION".

68.7.3   For methods, see r. 16.9.

"MOTION".

68.7.4   For motions, see Chap. 23.

Chapter 69

Election Petitions

Interpretation of this Chapter

69.1.[1,2] In this Chapter—   **69.1**

"the Act of 1983" means the Representation of the People Act 1983;

"the 2004 Regulations" means the European Parliamentary Elections Regulations 2004;

"election court" has the meaning assigned in section 123 of the Act of 1983;

"election petition" means a petition presented under—

(a) section 121 of the Act of 1983 (whether or not the petition also includes any application under section 167 of the Act of 1983);

(b) section 121 of the Act of 1983 as applied and modified by article 82 of and Schedule 6 to the Scottish Parliament (Elections etc.) Order 2015 (whether or not the petition also includes any application under section 167 of the Act of 1983, as so applied and modified); or

(c) regulation 89 of the European Parliamentary Elections Regulations 2004 (whether or not the petition also includes any application under regulation 108 of those Regulations).

"region" means a region for the purposes of the Scotland Act 1998; and any reference in this Chapter to a constituency shall be construed as a reference to a constituency for the purposes of the said Act of 1998 where it is used in relation to a Scottish parliamentary election;

"Scottish parliamentary election" means an election for membership of the Scottish Parliament.

GENERAL NOTE.

This Chapter is concerned with Parliamentary (including Scottish Parliamentary) election petitions   **69.1.1**
and European parliamentary election petitions (see note 69.1.3).

The Scottish Parliament (Election etc.) Order 1999 (S.I. 1999/787) amended Chap. 69 so as to extend it to Scottish Parliamentary elections. The Order made provision for the conduct of elections and return of members to the Scottish Parliament established by the Scotland Act 1998. The current Order, which made a further amendment, is the 2010 Order (S.I. 2010/2999). The definition of "election petition" amended by these Orders is replaced by the definition in A.S. (R.C.S.A. No. 6) (Miscellaneous) 2011 (S.S.I. 2011/385).

Rules 69.2 to 69.4, 69.8, 69.9, 69.18 to 69.20 and 69.25 are made under provisions in the Representation of the People Act 1983: see A.S. (R.C.S. 1994) 1994, Sched. 1 (S.I. 1994 No. 1443).

"ELECTION COURT".

A Parliamentary, Scottish Parliament or European parliamentary election petition is tried by two   **69.1.2**
judges on the rota for the trial of such petitions: Act of 1983, s. 123(1). The judges are nominated by the Lord President: C.S.A. 1988, s. 44. The judges on the rota for the remainder of 2012 and 2013 are Lord Eassie and Lady Paton.

The election court has the same powers as a judge of the Court of Session presiding at a civil jury trial: Act of 1983, s. 123(2).

"ELECTION PETITION".

This is a petition relating to a Parliamentary or Scottish Parliament election or, by virtue of now the   **69.1.3**
European Assembly Elections Regulations 2004 [S.I. 2004 No. 293], a European parliamentary election.

---

[1] Rule 69.1 amended by S.I. 1999 No. 787 (effective 11th March 1999), S.I. 2007 No. 937 (effective 15th March 2007), S.I. 2010 No. 2999 (effective 30th December 2010) and S.S.I. 2011 No. 385 (effective 28th November 2011).

[2] Rule 69.1 amended by S.S.I. 2015 No. 425 Pt 5 art.92 (effective 16 December 2015 and shall have no effect for the purposes of any election for which the date of poll is on or before 4 April 2016).

Form of election petitions

69.2

69.2.—(1) An election petition shall be in Form 69.2.

(2) Such a petition shall—

(a) specify the name, designation and address of—

(i) each petitioner, and

(ii)[1] each person referred to as, or deemed to be, the respondent by virtue of section 121(2) of the Act of 1983 or regulation 89(2) of the 2004 Regulations, as the case may be; and

(b) set out in numbered paragraphs—

(i)[2] the title of the petitioner under section 121(1) of the Act of 1983 or regulation 89(1) of the 2004 Regulations to present the petition;

(ii) the proceedings at, and the result of, the election; and

(iii) the facts relied on in support of the prayer of the petition.

Deriv. RCS 1965, r. 298 amended by S.I. 1979 No. 516 and 1985 No. 1426

GENERAL NOTE.

69.2.1

The petition must be presented within 21 days after the return made to the Clerk of the Crown in Chancery: Act of 1983, s. 122(1).

"PETITION".

69.2.2

The petition must be in Form 69.2 and comply with the requirements for the paper used: r. 4.1. It must be signed by the petitioner: Act of 1983, s. 121(3).

The petitioner must lodge a process with the petition: r. 69.3. A fee is payable on lodging the petition: see note 69.3.4.

TITLE TO PRESENT PETITION.

69.2.3

A person who voted or had the right to vote, a person claiming to have had a right to be elected at the election or a person alleging himself to have been a candidate at the election may present an election petition: Act of 1983, s. 121(1).

Presentation of petition

69.3

69.3. The election petition shall be lodged in the Petition Department with—

(a) a process;

(b) six copies of the petition; and

(c) a letter signed by or on behalf of the petitioner—

(i) giving the name and address of a solicitor whom he authorises to act on his behalf or stating that he acts for himself, as the case may be; and

(ii) specifying an address within Scotland at which notices addressed to him may be delivered.

Deriv. RCS 1965, r. 297(a) amended by S.I. 1979 No. 516 and r. 299(a) amended by S.I. 1991 No. 2483

GENERAL NOTE.

69.3.1

The petition must be presented within 21 days after the return made to the Clerk of the Crown in Chancery: Act of 1983, s. 122(1).

"LODGED IN THE PETITION DEPARTMENT".

69.3.2

The petition may be lodged by post: P.N. No. 4 of 1994, paras 1, 6 and 8.

"PROCESS".

69.3.3

For the steps of process to be lodged with the petition, see r. 4.4.

---

[1] Rule 69.2(2)(a)(ii) and (2)(b)(i) amended by S.S.I. 2011 No. 385 para. 2 (effective 28th November 2011).

[2] Rule 69.2(2)(a)(ii) and (2)(b)(i) amended by S.S.I. 2011 No. 385 para. 2 (effective 28th November 2011).

FEE.

The court fee for the petition is payable on lodging. For fee, see Court of Session etc. Fees Order 1997, Table of Fees, Pt. I, E, item 1 [S.I. 1997 No. 688, as amended, pp. C1201 et seq.]. Certain persons are exempt from payment of fees: see 1997 Fees Order, art. 5 substituted by S.S.I. 2002 No. 270. A fee exemption certificate must be lodged in process: see P.N. No.1 of 2002.

69.3.4

Where the petitioner is legally represented, the fee may be debited under a credit scheme introduced on 1st April 1976 by P.N. No. 4 of 1976 to the account (if one is kept or permitted) of the agent by the court cashier, and an account will be rendered weekly by the court cashier's office to the agent for all court fees due that week for immediate settlement. Party litigants, and agents not operating the scheme, must pay (by cash, cheque or postal order) on each occasion a fee is due at the time of lodging at the counter at the Petition Department.

Security for expenses

69.4.—(1) On presentation of an election petition, the petitioner shall apply by motion for—

69.4

   (a) an order for intimation and service of the petition within such period as the court thinks fit after the giving of security,

   (b)[1] for an order for the respondent to lodge any objections in writing under section 136(4) of the Act of 1983 or regulation 94(4) of the 2004 Regulations (objections to form of security) within such period as the court thinks fit, and

   (c) the fixing of the amount of security for expenses;

and the petition shall be placed forthwith before the Lord Ordinary or the vacation judge, in court or in chambers, who shall fix the security to be given.

(2) A motion under paragraph (1) shall not be intimated to any person.

(3)[2] Where the security to be given by the petitioner under section 136 of the Act of 1983 or regulation 94 of the 2004 Regulations is given in whole or in part by bond of caution, the bond shall be in Form 69.4.

Deriv. RCS 1965, r. 299A inserted by S.I. 1985 No. 1426 (r. 69.4(1)) and r. 300 amended by S.I. 1985 No. 1426 (r. 69.4(3))

"INTIMATION AND SERVICE".

On intimation and service of petitions generally, see r. 14.7. Note the provisions of r. 69.5.

69.4.1

"SECURITY FOR EXPENSES".

The security for expenses is a sum not exceeding £5,000: Act of 1983, s. 136(2) as amended by the Representation of the People Act 1985, Sched. 4, para. 48.

69.4.2

On finding and lodging caution, see Chap. 33.

Service and intimation of election petition

69.5.—[3, 4](1) On serving the election petition on the respondent under subsection (3) of section 136 of the Act of 1983 or regulation 94(3) of the 2004 Regulations, the petitioner shall intimate a copy of each of the documents mentioned in that subsection to—

69.5

   (a) the Lord Advocate; and

   (b) the Advocate General for Scotland.

(2)[5] The notice of presentation of the petition mentioned in section 136(3) of the Act of 1983 or regulation 94(3) of the 2004 Regulations shall be in Form 69.5.

---

[1] Rule 69.4(1)(b) and (3) amended by S.S.I. S.S.I. 2011 No. 385 para. 2 para. 2 (effective 28th November 2011).

[2] Rule 69.4(1)(b) and (3) amended by S.S.I. S.S.I. 2011 No. 385 para. 2 para. 2 (effective 28th November 2011).

[3] R. 69.5(1) amended by S.I. 1999 No. 1386 (effective 19th May 1999).

[4] Rule 69.5(1),(2) and (3) amended by S.S.I. 2011 No. 385 para. 2 (effective 28th November 2011).

[5] Rule 69.5(1),(2) and (3) amended by S.S.I. 2011 No. 385 para. 2 (effective 28th November 2011).

(3)[1] Within five days after serving the petition under section 136 of the Act of 1983 or regulation 94 of the 2004 Regulations, the petitioner shall lodge in process an execution copy of the election petition containing the certificate of service and a copy of the notice mentioned in that subsection which was served on the respondent.

(4)[2] Where the court makes an order for intimation and service of an election petition, the Deputy Principal Clerk shall send a copy of the petition to the Electoral Commission.

Deriv. RCS 1965, r. 303 amended by S.I. 1985 No. 1426

GENERAL NOTE.

69.5.1   An election petition no longer has to be served within five days after presentation: Act of 1983, s.136(3) as amended by the Representation of the People Act 1985, Sched. 4, para. 48. As all the periods specified in the Act of 1983, and in this Chapter, for the doing of something in relation to an election petition are short, it is unlikely that the court would stipulate a period of notice of 21 days as in an ordinary petition.

DOCUMENTS TO BE SERVED WITH ELECTION PETITION.

69.5.2   These are the notice of presentation of the petition in Form 69.5 and the notice of the amount of caution: Act of 1983, s.136(3).

"EXECUTION COPY".

69.5.3   The documents required as evidence of service (see note 16.1.5) are attached (stitched in) to an execution copy of the principal writ: r. 16.1(4). A walling certificate is not required: P.N. No. 7 of 1994, para. 4.

Objection to form of security

69.6   **69.6.—**(1)[3] Where the respondent makes an objection under section 136(4) of the Act of 1983or regulation 94(4) of the 2004 Regulations (objection to form of security), he shall—

(a)   set out in writing the grounds of the objection;

(b)   lodge the objection in process; and

(c)   intimate a copy of the objection to the petitioner.

(2)   As soon as possible after the lodging of an objection under paragraph (1), the Keeper of the Rolls shall—

(a)   fix a diet for a hearing on the objections before one of the judges on the rota for the trial of election petitions or the vacation judge; and

(b)   give written intimation of the time and place of the diet to the parties.

(3)   The period within which the petitioner may, under section 136(7) of the Act of 1983 or regulation 94(6) of the 2004 Regulations, remove the objection shall be such period from the date of the decision on the objection as the court thinks fit.

Deriv. RCS 1965, r. 304(b) (r. 69.6(1)(a) and (b)), r. 304(c) (r. 69.6(1)(c)), r. 305 (r. 69.6(2)) and r. 306(c)(part) (r. 69.6(3))

GENERAL NOTE.

69.6.1   No form of objection is prescribed. It does not have to comply with r. 15.2. The document itself must comply with the requirements for paper used: r. 4.1.

"INTIMATE".

69.6.2   For methods, see r. 16.7.

"WRITTEN INTIMATION".

69.6.3   For methods, see r. 16.9.

---

[1] Rule 69.5(1),(2) and (3) amended by S.S.I. 2011 No. 385 para. 2 (effective 28th November 2011).
[2] R. 69.5(4) inserted by S.S.I. 2009 No. 450 (effective 25th January 2010).
[3] Rule 69.6(1) and (3) amended by S.S.I. 2011 No. 385 para. 2 (effective 28th November 2011).

Consequences of failure to give security etc.

69.7. If no security is given, or an objection to a security is allowed and not removed, the respondent may apply by motion to have the prayer of the petition refused.

69.7

GENERAL NOTE.

If no security is given or objection to it is allowed and not removed, no further proceedings shall be had on the petition: Act of 1983, s.136(8).

69.7.1

"MOTION".

For motions, see Chap. 23. See also rr. 69.29 and 69.30 on intimation of motions in an election petition.

69.7.2

List of election petitions

69.8.—(1) In preparing the list of election petitions in terms of section 138(1) of the Act of 1983, the Deputy Principal Clerk shall insert the names of the solicitors, if any, acting for the petitioner and respondent, and the addresses, if any, to which any notices may be sent.

69.8

(2) The list of election petitions may be inspected in the Petition Department at any time during its normal office hours.

Deriv. RCS 1965, r. 307 amended by S.I. 1979 No. 516 and 1985 No. 1426

Time and place of trial

69.9.—(1) The time and place of the trial of an election petition shall be fixed by the Keeper of the Rolls, who shall give written intimation of the date of the trial by post to—

69.9

   (a)   the parties;
   (b)   the Lord Advocate;
  (ba)[1] the Advocate General of Scotland;
   (c)[2] the returning officer for the relevant constituency or, as the case may be, region; and
   (d)   the House of Commons shorthand writer.

(2)[3] On receipt of intimation given under paragraph (1), the returning officer shall forthwith publish the date of the diet of trial in the constituency or, as the case may be, region to which it relates.

Deriv. RCS 1965, r. 308 amended by S.I. 1979 No. 516 and 1985 No. 1426

GENERAL NOTE.

The trial is in open court without a jury: Act of 1983, s.139(1). It may be held anywhere in Scotland. Notice of the trial diet must be given at least 14 days before: Act of 1983, s.139(1).

69.9.1

At the end of the trial the judges report to the Speaker of the House of Commons in the case of a Parliamentary election (Act of 1983, s.144(2)) and to the Secretary of State in the case of a European election.

"WRITTEN INTIMATION".

For methods, see r. 16.9.

69.9.2

Postponement of trial

69.10.—(1) The election court or any of the judges on the rota for the trial of election petitions, may, at its or his own instance or on the motion of a party, postpone the trial of a petition to such day as may be specified.

69.10

---

[1] R. 69.9(2)(ba) inserted by S.I. 1999 No. 1386 (effective 19th May 1999).
[2] R. 69.19(2)(c) amended by S.I. 1999 No. 787 (effective 11th March 1999).
[3] R. 69.19(2)(c) amended by S.I. 1999 No. 787 (effective 11th March 1999).

(2)[1] Written intimation of such postponement shall be given by the Keeper of the Rolls to the returning officer who shall forthwith publish the postponement and its new date in the constituency or, as the case may be, region.

Deriv. RCS 1965, r. 312

"WRITTEN INTIMATION".

69.10.1   For methods, see r. 16.9.

Procedure where seat claimed

69.11   **69.11.**—(1) Where a petitioner claims the seat for an unsuccessful candidate, alleging that he had a majority of lawful votes, the party complaining of, and the party defending, the return, not less than six days before the date of the trial, shall each—

(a)   lodge in process a list of the voters intended to be objected to, and of the objections to each voter; and

(b)[2] intimate a copy of that list to—

(i)   every other party;

(ii)   the Lord Advocate; and

(iii)   the Advocate General for Scotland.

(2) No evidence shall be allowed to be given against any vote or in support of any objection which is not specified in the list, except by leave of the election court or, on a motion heard before the date of the trial, of any of the judges on the rota for the trial of election petitions, on such terms as to amendment of the list, postponement of the trial and payment of expenses as may be ordered.

Deriv. RCS 1965, r. 310 amended by S.I. 1985 No. 1426

"NOT LESS THAN SIX DAYS BEFORE".

69.11.1   There must be six clear days.

"LODGE IN PROCESS".

69.11.2   The list is lodged as a step of process (r. 1.3(1) (definition of "step of process")). On lodging steps of process, see r. 4.4. The list may be lodged by post: P.N. No. 4 of 1994, paras 1 and 8; and see note 4.4.10.

"INTIMATE".

69.11.3   For methods, see r. 16.7.

Evidence under section 139(5) of the Act of 1983

69.12   **69.12.**—(1)[3] Where the respondent intends to give evidence permitted under section 139(5) of the Act of 1983 or regulation 96(4) of the 2004 Regulations (evidence to prove person not duly elected), he shall, not less than six days before the date of the trial—

(a)   lodge in process a list of the objections to the election on which he intends to rely; and

(b)[4] intimate a copy of that list to—

(i)   every other party;

(ii)   the Lord Advocate; and

(iii)   the Advocate General for Scotland.

(2) No evidence shall be allowed to be given on behalf of the respondent in support of any objection to the return not specified in the list, except with leave of the election court or, on a motion heard before the date of the trial, of any of the judges on the rota for the trial of election petitions, on such terms as to amendment of the list, postponement of the trial and payment of expenses as may be ordered.

---

[1] R. 69.10(2) amended by S.I. 1996 No. 787 (effective 11th March 1999).
[2] R. 69.11(1)(b) amended by S.I. 1999 No. 1386 (effective 19th May 1999).
[3] Rule 69.12(1) amended by S.S.I. 2011 No. 385 para. 2 (effective 28th November 2011).
[4] Rule 69.12(1)(b) amended by S.I. 1999 No. 1386 (effective 19th May 1999).

Deriv. RCS 1965, r. 311 amended by S.I. 1985 No. 1426

"NOT LESS THAN SIX DAYS BEFORE".

There must be six clear days.   **69.12.1**

"LODGE IN PROCESS".

The list is lodged as a step of process (r. 1.3(1) (definition of "step of process")). On lodging steps of   **69.12.2**
process, see r. 4.4. The list may be lodged by post: P.N. No. 4 of 1994, paras 1 and 8; and see note 4.4.10.

"INTIMATE".

For methods, see r. 16.7.   **69.12.3**

Lodging of statement of evidence to be led

69.13.—(1) Subject to paragraph (2), any party shall, not less than six days   **69.13**
before the date of the trial, lodge in process a statement of the matters on which he
intends to lead evidence.

(2)[1] Before lodging such a statement in process, the party proposing to lodge it
shall intimate a copy of the statement to—

   (a)   every other party;
   (b)   the Lord Advocate; and
   (c)   the Advocate General for Scotland.

Deriv. RCS 1965, r. 313 amended by S.I. 1985 No. 1426

"NOT LESS THAN SIX DAYS BEFORE".

There must be six clear days.   **69.13.1**

"INTIMATE".

For methods, see r. 16.7.   **69.13.2**

Evidence at trial

69.14.—(1) No evidence shall be led at the trial of an election petition other   **69.14**
than matters contained in—

   (a)   the list lodged under rule 69.11 (procedure where seat claimed) or 69.12
         (evidence under section 139(5) of the Act of 1983),
   (b)   the statement lodged under rule 69.13 (statement of evidence to be led), or
   (c)   matters which have been sufficiently set out in the petition,

except with the leave of the election court or one of the judges on the rota for the
trial of election petitions, on such conditions as to postponement of the trial, payment of expenses or otherwise, as may be ordered.

(2) The admissibility of any evidence sought to be led on the matters referred to
in paragraph (1) shall be within the discretion of the election court.

Deriv. RCS 1965, r. 314

Warrant to cite witnesses

69.15. The warrant for the citation of a witness to the trial of an election petition   **69.15**
shall be granted on the motion of any party and shall be in Form 69.15.

Deriv. RCS 1965, r. 315

GENERAL NOTE.

A judge of the election court may require any person who appears to him to have been concerned in   **69.15.1**
the election to appear as a witness and be examined by the court: Act of 1983, s.140(2) and (3).

Witnesses cannot object to a question at the trial on the ground of incrimination or privilege, but the
answer is not admissible in criminal proceedings except perjury: Act of 1983, s.141.

"MOTION".

For motions, see Chap. 23. See also rr. 69.29 and 69.30 on intimation of motions in election petitions.   **69.15.2**

---

[1] R. 69.13(2) amended by S.I. 1999 No. 1386 (effective 19th May 1999).

Clerk of court at trial

69.16

69.16. At an election court held for the trial of an election petition, a clerk of session nominated by the Principal Clerk and appointed by the court shall discharge the duties of clerk of court of the election court.

Deriv. RCS 1965, r. 317 amended by S.I. 1979 No. 516

Expenses of witnesses

69.17

69.17.—[1](1) The prescribed officer for the purposes of section 143(1) of the Act of 1983 or regulation 99(1) of the 2004 Regulations shall be the clerk of session appointed to act as clerk of court under rule 69.16.

(2) The expenses of a witness permitted under section 143(1) of the Act of 1983 or regulation 99(1) of the 2004 Regulations shall be ascertained by the clerk of court.

(3) The expenses allowed under section 143(1) of the Act of 1983 or regulation 99(1) of the 2004 Regulations shall, in the first instance, be paid by the party adducing that witness.

Deriv. RCS 1965, r. 316

GENERAL NOTE.

69.17.1

The reasonable expenses of a person appearing to give evidence on the scale for civil actions before the Court of Session (see r. 42.16, Table of Fees, Chap. II) maybe allowed by a certificate of the election court or the prescribed officer (the clerk of the election court): Act of 1983, s.143(1).

The expenses of a witness called by the court under s.140(2) of the Act of 1983 are part of the expenses of providing the election court: Act of 1983, s.143(2).

Applications for special case

69.18

69.18.[2] An application under section 146(1) of the Act of 1983 or regulation 101(1) of the 2004 Regulations for a special case, shall be made by motion to the Inner House or the vacation judge.

Deriv. RCS 1965, r. 318(1) amended by S.I. 1985 No. 426

GENERAL NOTE.

69.18.1

If it appears that the case raised by the petition can be conveniently stated as a special case, this may be ordered: Act of 1983, s.146(1). The procedure in Chap. 41, Pt II will apply.

"MOTION".

69.18.2

For motions, see Chap. 23. See also rr. 69.29 and 69.30 on intimation of motions in election petitions.

Applications for leave to withdraw election petitions

69.19

69.19.—(1)[3] A notice of intention to withdraw an election petition under section 147(2) of the Act of 1983 or regulation 102(2) of the 2004 Regulations shall be in Form 69.19-A.

(2) A copy of such notice shall be intimated by the petitioners to—

   (a)   the respondent;

   (b)   the Lord Advocate;

   (ba)[4]   the Advocate General for Scotland;

   (c)[5]   the returning officer for the relevant constituency or, as the case may be, region; and

   (d)   the Deputy Principal Clerk.

(3) On receipt of a notice under paragraph (2), the returning officer shall publish it in the constituency to which it relates.

---

[1] Rule 69.17 amended by S.S.I. 2011 No. 385 para. 2 (effective 28th November 2011).
[2] Rule 69.18 amended by S.S.I. 2011 No. 385 para. 2 (effective 28th November 2011).
[3] Rule 69.19(1) amended by S.S.I. 2011 No. 385 para. 2 (effective 28th November 2011).
[4] R. 69.19(2)(ba) inserted by S.I. 1999 No. 1386 (effective 19th May 1999).
[5] R. 69.19(2)(c) amended by S.I. 1999 No. 787 (effective 11th March 1999).

(4) An application for leave to withdraw an election petition shall—

    (a) be in Form 69.19-B;

    (b) state the ground on which the application to withdraw is made;

    (c) be signed by the person making the application and by the consenters, if any, or by their respective solicitors; and

    (d) be lodged in the process of the election petition.

Deriv. RCS 1965, r. 320 amended by S.I. 1985 No. 1426 (r. 69.19(1), (2) and (3)), and r. 321 (r. 69.19(4))

GENERAL NOTE.

If there is more than one petitioner, all must consent: Act of 1983, s.147(3). The petitioner is liable to the respondent for expenses: Act of 1983, s.147(4).   **69.19.1**

An agreement, terms or an undertaking to withdraw a petition in consideration of payment, or of the seat being vacated at any time or of the withdrawal of another election petition, is an offence: Act of 1983, s.149.

"INTIMATED".

For methods, see r. 16.7.   **69.19.2**

"LEAVE TO WITHDRAW".

Affidavits are required from all parties and their solicitors and the election agent, unless on cause   **69.19.3**
shown an affidavit is dispensed with (Act of 1983, s.148(1)), that no agreement, terms or undertaking has been given for withdrawal: Act of 1983, s.148(2).

The election court reports to the Speaker of the House of Commons in the case of a Parliamentary election (Act of 1983, s.151) or the Secretary of State in the case of a European election.

"LODGED IN THE PROCESS".

The application for leave is lodged as a step of process (r. 1.3(1) (definition of "step of process")). On   **69.19.4**
lodging steps of process, see r. 4.4. The list may be lodged by post: P.N. No. 4 of 1994, paras 1 and 8; and see note 4.4.10.

Applications to be substituted as petitioner on withdrawal

69.20.—(1) A person who seeks to apply under section 150(1) of the Act of   **69.20**
1983 to be substituted as a petitioner, shall, within five days after the date on which
the notice of intention to withdraw has been given under section 147(2) of the Act of
1983 and rule 69.19 (applications for leave to withdraw election petitions), give
notice in writing signed by him or on his behalf to the Deputy Principal Clerk of his
intention to apply, at the hearing of the application for leave to withdraw, to be
substituted as the petitioner.

(2) A copy of the notice given under paragraph (1) shall be intimated by the applicant to—

    (a) the respondent;

    (b) the Lord Advocate;

    (ba)[1] the Advocate General for Scotland; and

    (c) the returning officer for the relevant constituency.

(3) Any informality in such a notice shall not defeat an application to be
substituted as the petitioner if it is made at the hearing of the application to withdraw,
subject to such order as to postponement of that hearing and expenses as the election court thinks fit.

Deriv. RCS 1965, r. 322

"INTIMATED".

For methods, see r. 16.7.   **69.20.1**

Hearing of applications for leave to withdraw

69.21.—(1) Subject to paragraph (2), the time and place for hearing an applica-   **69.21**
tion for leave to withdraw an election petition shall be fixed by one of the judges on

---

[1] R. 69.2(2)(ba) inserted by S.I. 1999 No. 1386 (effective 19th May 1999).

the rota for the trial of election petitions or by the vacation judge, who shall hear and determine the application unless he considers that the application should be determined by the Inner House.

(2)   The time fixed under paragraph (1) shall not be earlier than seven days after the expiry of the period specified in rule 69.20.

(3)   The Keeper of the Rolls shall give written intimation of the diet fixed under paragraph (1) to—

(a)   the petitioner;

(b)   the respondent;

(c)   the Lord Advocate;

(ca)[1]   the Advocate General for Scotland;

(d)   the returning officer for the relevant constituency; and

(e)   to any person who has given notice under rule 69.20 of his intention to apply to be substituted as the petitioner.

Deriv. RCS 1965, r. 324

"NOT EARLIER THAN SEVEN DAYS AFTER".

69.21.1   There must be seven clear days.

"WRITTEN INTIMATION".

69.21.2   For methods, see r. 16.9.

Security of substituted petitioner

69.22   **69.22.**—(1)   The period within which security shall be given on behalf of a substituted petitioner before he proceeds with the petition shall be five days after the order of substitution.

(2)   The substituted petitioner shall lodge the letter referred to in rule 69.3(c) (name and address of solicitor, etc.) within five days after the order of substitution.

Deriv. RCS 1965, r. 323

GENERAL NOTE.

69.22.1   Where there has been an agreement, terms or an undertaking to withdraw a petition in consideration of payment, or of the seat being vacated at any time or of the withdrawal of another election petition, the election court may order the original security to be the security for the substituted petitioner: Act of 1983, s.150(2).

Death of petitioner

69.23   **69.23.**—(1)   In the event of the death of the petitioner or the surviving petitioner, the notice for the purpose of section 152(3) of the Act of 1983 (notice of abatement of petition by death) shall be intimated in Form 69.23 by the solicitor acting for the petitioner, the respondent, the returning officer or any other person interested to whose knowledge the death of the petitioner shall come, to, as the case may be—

(a)   the respondent;

(b)[2]   the Lord Advocate;

(ba)[3]   the Advocate General for Scotland;

(c)   the returning officer for the relevant constituency or, as the case may be, region; and

(d)   the Deputy Principal Clerk.

---

[1] R. 69(21)(3)(ca) inserted by S.I. 1999 No. 1386 (effective 19th May 1999).

[2] R. 69.23(1)(c) and (2) amended by S.I. 1999 No. 787 (effective 11th March 1999).

[3] R. 69.23(1)(ba) inserted by S.I. 1999 No. 1386 (effective 19th May 1999).

(2)[1] The returning officer shall, on receipt of such a notice, or, where he is giving notice under paragraph (1), on intimating such notice to those persons mentioned in that paragraph, publish the notice in the constituency or, as the case may be, region to which it relates.

Deriv. RCS 1965, r. 325 amended by S.I. 1985 No. 1426

General note.

Abatement occurs on the death of a sole petitioner or of the survivor of several petitioners: Act of 1983, s.152(1).

"intimated".

For methods, see r. 16.7.

69.23.1

69.23.2

Applications to be substituted on death of petitioner

69.24.—(1) An application to be substituted as a petitioner on the death of the petitioner or surviving petitioner shall be made by motion within five days after the publication of the notice.

  (2) A motion under paragraph (1) shall be intimated to—
    (a) the respondent;
    (b) the Lord Advocate;
  (ba)[2] the Advocate General for Scotland; and
    (c)[3] the returning officer for the relevant constituency or, as the case may be, region where he is not a respondent.

Deriv. RCS 1965, r. 326

"motion".

For motions, see Chap. 23. See also rr. 69.29 and 69.30 on intimation of motions in election petitions.

"intimated".

For methods, see r. 16.7.

69.24

69.24.1

69.24.2

Notice that respondent does not oppose

69.25.—(1) A notice, for the purposes of section 153(1) of the Act of 1983, by a respondent other than a returning officer, that he does not intend to oppose an election petition shall be—
    (a) signed by him; and
    (b) lodged in process not less than six days before the date of the trial.
  (2) Where a respondent lodges a notice under paragraph (1), he shall forthwith intimate a copy of it to—
    (a) the petitioner;
    (b) any other respondent;
    (c) the Lord Advocate;
  (ca)[4] the Advocate General for Scotland; and
    (d) the returning officer for the relevant constituency.
  (3) On receipt of a notice under paragraph (1), the returning officer shall publish it in the constituency to which it relates.

Deriv. RCS 1965, r. 327 amended by S.I. 1985 No. 1426

"lodged in process".

The notice that a respondent does not oppose the petition is lodged as a step of process (r. 1.3(1) (definition of "step of process")). On lodging steps of process, see r. 4.4. The list may be lodged by post: P.N. No. 4 of 1994, paras 1 and 8; and see note 4.4.10.

69.25

69.25.1

---

[1] R. 69.23(1)(c) and (2) amended by S.I. 1999 No. 787 (effective 11th March 1999).
[2] R. 69.24(2)(ba) inserted by S.I. 1999 No. 1386 (effective 19th May 1999).
[3] R. 69.24(2)(c) amended by S.I. 1999 No. 787 (effective 11th March 1999).
[4] R. 69.25(2)(ca) inserted by S.I. 1999 No. 1386 (effective 19th May 1999).

69.25.2   There must be six clear days.

Death[1], peerage or resignation of respondent

69.26   **69.26.**—(1)   Where, for the purposes of section 153(1) of the Act of 1983—

    (a)   a respondent other than a returning officer dies,

    (b)   in the case of a parliamentary election, a respondent other than a returning officer is summoned to Parliament as a Peer of Great Britain,

    (c)   a respondent other than a returning officer has vacated his seat following a resolution by the House of Commons, or

    (d)[2]   a respondent resigns or otherwise ceases to be a Member of the Scottish Parliament,

the agent for the respondent shall give notice of that fact in the constituency to which the election petition relates.

    (2)   Such a notice shall be published in at least one newspaper circulating in the constituency, and by intimating a copy of the notice, signed by him to—

    (a)   the petitioner;

    (b)   any other respondent;

    (c)   the Lord Advocate;

    (ca)[3]   the Advocate General for Scotland;

    (d)   the returning officer for the relevant constituency; and

    (e)   the Deputy Principal Clerk.

Deriv. RCS 1965, r. 328 amended by S.I. 1979 No. 516 and 1985 No. 1426

GENERAL NOTE.

69.26.1   A judge of the election court reports to the Speaker of the House of Commons in the case of a Parliamentary election (Act of 1983, s.153(4)) or the Secretary of State in the case of a European election.

"INTIMATING".

69.26.2   For methods, see r. 16.7.

Applications to be admitted as respondent

69.27   **69.27.**   The period of time within which a person may apply to be admitted as a respondent under section 153 of the Act of 1983 shall be—

    (a)   five days after the notice is intimated under rule 69.25 (notice that respondent does not oppose);

    (b)[4]   10 days after the notice is intimated under rule 69.26 (death, peerage or resignation of respondent); or

    (c)   such other period as the court thinks fit.

Deriv. RCS 1965, r. 329 amended by S.I. 1985 No. 1426

Expenses in election petitions

69.28   **69.28.**[5]   Where any expenses are awarded by the election court in the course of proceedings under the Act of 1983 or the 2004 Regulations, such an award shall be deemed equivalent to a finding of expenses in the Court of Session.

Deriv. RCS 1965, r. 330

Motions in election petitions

69.29   **69.29.**—(1)   Subject to any other provision in this Chapter or the Act of 1983, all applications shall be dealt with by motion.

---

[1] Heading and r. 69.26(1) amended by S.I 1999 No. 787 (effective 11th March 1999).
[2] Heading and r. 69.26(1) amended by S.I 1999 No. 787 (effective 11th March 1999).
[3] R. 69.26(2)(ca) inserted by S.I. 1999 No. 1386 (effective 19th May 1999).
[4] R. 69.27(b) amended by S.I. 1999 No. 787 (effective 11th March 1999).
[5] Rule 69.28 amended by S.S.I. 2011 No. 385 para. 2 (effective 28th November 2011).

(2) Subject to the provisions of this Chapter, Chapter 23 (motions) shall apply to a motion in an election petition.

(3) A motion in an election petition shall be intimated to—

(a) the Lord Advocate;

(aa)[1] the Advocate General for Scotland; and

(b)[2] the returning officer for the relevant constituency or, as the case may be, region.

Deriv. RCS 1965, r. 309 (r. 69.29(1))

Intimation to Lord Advocate

69.30. All applications to the court in an election petition other than a motion under rule 69.4(1) (security for expenses) shall be intimated to—

(a) the Lord Advocate; and

(b) the Advocate General for Scotland;

and the Lord Advocate and the Advocate General for Scotland shall be entitled to appear or be represented at the hearing of that application.

69.30

Evidence of publication by returning officer

69.31.—(1) Where a returning officer publishes a notice in accordance with a provision in this Chapter or an order of the election court, he shall forthwith send to the Deputy Principal Clerk a letter—

(a) certifying that the appropriate notice has been published; and

(b) detailing the manner in which the publication has been made.

(2) Where publication has been made by inserting a notice in a newspaper or other publication, the letter under paragraph (1) shall be accompanied by—

(a) a copy of the newspaper or other publication containing the notice; or

(b) a certificate of publication by the publisher stating the date of publication and the text of the notice.

69.31

---

[1] R. 69.29(3)(aa) inserted by S.I. 1999 No. 1386 (effective 19th May 1999).
[2] R. 69.29(3)(b) amended by S.I. 1999 No. 787 (effective 11th March 1999).

Chapter 70

Applications under the Child Abduction and Custody Act 1985

Part I – General Provisions

Interpretation of this Chapter

70.1.[1, 2] In this Chapter— **70.1**

"the Act of 1985" means the Child Abduction and Custody Act 1985;

"the European Convention" means the convention defined in section 12(1) of the Act of 1985 and as set out in Schedule 2 to the Act of 1985;

"the Hague Convention" means the convention defined in section 1(1) of the Act of 1985 and as set out in Schedule 1 to the Act of 1985;

"relevant authority" means—

(a) in the United Kingdom, a sheriff court, the Sheriff Appeal Court, a children's hearing within the meaning of the Children's Hearings (Scotland) Act 2011, the High Court, a county court or magistrates' court in England and Wales, the High Court, a county court or magistrates' court in Northern Ireland, or the Secretary of State, as the case may be; or

(b) in a relevant territory, the appropriate authority or court within that territory;

"relevant territory" means a territory outside the United Kingdom to which the Act of 1985 extends by virtue of an Order in Council made under section 28(1) of that Act or in relation to which provision is made by an Order in Council under section 28(2) of that Act.

Deriv. R.C.S. 1965, r. 260H(2) inserted by S.I. 1986 No. 1955

GENERAL NOTE.

Pts. I and II of this Chapter are made under s. 10 of the Act of 1985 as well as under s. 5 of the C.S.A. **70.1.1** 1988. Parts I and III are made under s. 24 of the Act of 1985 as well as s. 5 of the C.S.A. 1988: see A.S. (R.C.S. 1994) 1994, Sched. 1 [S.I. 1994 No. 1443]. Unless the context otherwise requires, words and expressions used in this Chapter which are also used in the Act of 1985 have the same meaning as in that Act.

"RELEVANT TERRITORY".

Under s. 28(1) of the Act of 1985 any provisions of the Act may be extended to the British Islands and **70.1.2** colonies by an Order in Council. No such Order in Council has been made.

S.28(2) of the Act of 1985 has effect only in the UK and provides that for the purpose of the law of the UK certain things done in the British Islands or colonies in respect of which an Order in Council has been made have the same effect as if done in the UK. S.28(2) would apply whether the relevant territory enacted its own legislation to give effect to the Hague or European Conventions. So far only the Isle of Man has enacted its own legislation and the only Order in Council is in respect of the Isle of Man under s. 28(2) of the Act.

The Child Abduction and Custody Act 1985 (Isle of Man) Order 1994 [S.I. 1994 No. 2799] provides that references in the Act of 1985 to orders made, proceedings brought or other things done under the Hague and European conventions in the UK have effect as if made, brought or done, as the case may be, in the Isle of Man. The Isle of Man has enacted its own legislation to give effect to the Hague and European Conventions, the Child Custody Act 1987. The "appropriate court" in the Isle of Man is the High Court of Justice of the Isle of Man.

The Child Abduction and Custody (Falkland Islands) Order 1996 [S.I. 1996 No. 3156] applies, as modified by the Order, ss. 15, 24A, 25(1) and (2), 26, 27 and Scheds. 1 to 3 of the Act of 1985 to the Falklands Islands.

---

[1] Rule 70.1 amended by S.I. 1996 No. 1756 (effective 5 August 1996).
[2] Rule 70.1 amended by S.S.I. 2015 No. 419 para.7(8) (effective 1st January 2016).

Translations of documents

70.2 **70.2.** Where any document lodged in process in a cause to which this Chapter applies is in a language other than English, there shall be lodged with that document a translation into English certified as correct by the translator; and the certificate shall include his full name, address and qualifications.

Deriv. R.C.S. 1965, r. 260J(6), and r. 260K(9), both inserted by S.I. 1986 No. 1955

Applications for certified copy or extract

70.3 **70.3.**—(1) An application for a certified copy or extract of a decree or any other interlocutor relating to a child, in respect of whom the applicant wishes to apply under the Hague Convention or the European Convention in another Contracting State, shall be made by letter to the Deputy Principal Clerk.

(2) A certified copy or extract issued on an application under paragraph (1) shall be supplied free of charge.

Deriv. R.C.S. 1965, r. 260L(1)

Disclosure of information

70.4 **70.4.** Where the court pronounces an interlocutor under section 24A of the Act of 1985 (order to a person to disclose information to the court as to a child's whereabouts), it may order that person to appear before it or to lodge an affidavit.

Deriv. R.C.S. 1965, r. 260L(2)

GENERAL NOTE.

70.4.1 S. 24A of the Act of 1985 was inserted by s. 67(4) of the Family Law Act 1986. A person is not excused from complying with an order to disclose information on the ground of incrimination of that person or his or her spouse, but a statement or admission is not admissible in evidence in criminal proceedings for an offence except perjury: Act of 1985, s. 24A(2).

The court has always had power to take whatever action was necessary to make an interlocutor effective including ordering the hearing of evidence from any witness who may have information which would assist in the recovery of a child: *Abusaif v. Abusaif* 1984 S.L.T. 90, 91 per L.P. Emslie.

Part II – International Child Abduction (The Hague Convention)

Form of applications under this Part

70.5 **70.5.**—(1)[1, 2] Subject to rule 70.16 (warrant for intimation on a child), an application for the return of a child under the Hague Convention shall be made by petition and—

   (a)   shall include averments in relation to—

       (i)   the identity of the petitioner and the person alleged to have removed or retained the child;

      (ii)   the identity of the child and his date of birth;

     (iii)   the whereabouts or suspected whereabouts of the child;

     (iv)   the date on which the child is alleged to have been wrongfully removed or retained;

      (v)   the grounds on which the petition is based; and

     (vi)   any civil cause in dependence before any other court or authority in respect of the child, or any proceedings mentioned in section 9 of the Act of 1985 relating to the merits of the rights of custody of the child in or before a relevant authority;

   (b)   there shall be produced with the petition and lodged as a production a certified or authorised copy of any relevant decision or agreement; and

---

[1] Rule 70.5(1), (2) and (3) amended by S.I. 1996 No. 1756 (effective 5th August 1996).
[2] Rule 70(5)(1) amended by S.S.I. 2005 No. 135 (effective 2nd March 2005).

(c)[1] there shall be lodged with the petition the evidence by affidavits of any witnesses and any documentary evidence, whether originals or copies initially, in support of the petition.

(2)[2,3] An application for organising or protecting rights of access granted by any court of a contracting party to the Hague Convention, or for securing respect for the conditions to which the exercise of such rights of access is subject shall be made by petition and—

    (a)   shall include averments in relation to—

        (i)   the identity of the petitioner;

        (ii)   the identity of the child and his date of birth;

        (iii)   the parents or guardians of the child;

        (iv)   the whereabouts of the child;

        (v)   the factual and legal grounds on which access is sought; and

        (vi)   any civil cause in dependence before any other court or authority in respect of the child, or any proceedings mentioned in section 9 of the Act of 1985 relating to the merits of the rights of custody of the child in or before a relevant authority;

    (b)[4]   there shall be produced with the petition and lodged as a production a certified copy of any relevant decision or agreement; and

    (c)[5]   there shall be lodged with the petition the evidence by affidavits of any witnesses and any documentary evidence, whether originals or copies initially, in support of the petition.

(3)[6] An application under section 8 of the Act of 1985 (application for declarator that removal or retention of child was wrongful) shall be made by petition and—

    (a)   shall include averments in relation to—

        (i)   the identity of the petitioner and of the person who is alleged to have removed or retained the child;

        (ii)   the identity of the child and his date of birth;

        (iii)   the whereabouts or suspected whereabouts of the child;

        (iv)   the date on which the child is alleged to have been wrongfully removed or retained;

        (v)   the proceedings which gave custody to the petitioner; and

        (vi)   the proceedings under the Hague Convention in relation to which the petition is necessary;

    (b)   there shall be produced with the petition any relevant document; and

    (c)[7]   there shall be lodged with the petition the evidence by affidavits of any witnesses and any documentary evidence, whether originals or copies initially, in support of the petition.

Deriv. R.C.S. 1965, r. 260J(1) inserted by S.I. 1986 No. 1955 and amended by S.I. 1991 No. 1157 (r. 70.5(1)); and r. 260J(2) and (3) inserted by S.I. 1986 No. 1955 (r. 70.5(2) and (3))

General note.

The U.K. has ratified the Hague Convention on the *Civil Aspects of International Child Abduction 1980* (Cmnd. 8155 (1982)). The convention is implemented by the Act of 1985 and is set out in Sched. 1 to that Act.

70.5.1

---

[1] Rule 70.5(1), (2) and (3) amended by S.I. 1996 No. 1756 (effective 5th August 1996).
[2] Rule 70.5(1), (2) and (3) amended by S.I. 1996 No. 1756 (effective 5th August 1996).
[3] Rule 70.5(2) amended by S.S.I. 2001 No. 305 para. 15 (effective 18th September 2001).
[4] Rule 70.5(2)(b) amended by S.I. 1994 No. 2901 (effective 5th December 1994).
[5] Rule 70.5(1), (2) and (3) amended by S.I. 1996 No. 1756 (effective 5th August 1996).
[6] Rule 70.5(1), (2) and (3) amended by S.I. 1996 No. 1756 (effective 5th August 1996).
[7] Rule 70.5(1), (2) and (3) amended by S.I. 1996 No. 1756 (effective 5th August 1996).

The convention applies to rights of custody which arise by operation of law, a judicial or administrative decision, or by agreement having legal effect: Act of 1985, Sched. 1, Art. 3. It also applies to rights of access. It applies to a child under the age of 16 years: Act of 1985, Sched. 1, Art. 4.

The intention of the convention is the immediate and summary return of an abducted child to the requesting country: *MacMillan v. MacMillan* 1989 S.C. 53, 60. Its provisions are intended as provisions supportive of existing rights: *Donofrio v. Burrell* , 2000 S.L.T. 1051, 1057H per Lord Prosser.

"SUBJECT TO RULE 70.16".

70.5.1A   The Council Regulation (E,C,) No. 2201/2203 of 27th November 2003 concerning jurisdiction and enforcement of judgments in matrimonial matters and matters of parental responsibility (new Brussels II) applies between Member States of the E.U except Denmark. Where an application is made under the Hague Convention to which Pt. II of Chap. 70 applies, and the child is habitually resident in a Member State of the E.U., certain requirements of the Council Regulation apply where that child has been removed to or retained in another Member State. These include: (a) the child must be given an opportunity to be heard unless inappropriate because of his age or immaturity, (b) the court deals with the case in six weeks, (c) the court cannot refuse to return the child under art. 13(b) of the Hague Convention (see 1985 Act, Sched. 1, Art 13(b) (grave risk)) if adequate arrangements have been made to secure protection on return, and (d) the court cannot refuse to return the child unless the person requesting return has been given an opportunity to be heard: art. 11 of the Council Regulation.

It should be noted that the Council Regulation does not itself provide a regime for child abduction. A Member State retains its own jurisdiction while a child is habitually resident there until the child acquires an habitual residence in another Member State: art. 10. If the Hague Convention is applicable, that vehicle will be used subject to the Council Regulation requirements.

"PETITION".

70.5.2   A petition is presented in the Outer House: r. 14.2(h). The petition must be in Form 14.4 in the official printed form: rr. 4.1 and 14.4. The petition must be signed by counsel or other person having a right of audience: r. 4.2; and see r. 1.3(1) (definition of "counsel" and "other person having a right of audience") and note 1.3.4.

The petitioner must lodge the petition with the required steps of process (r. 4.4). A fee is payable on lodging the petition: see note 14.5.10.

On petitions generally, see Chap. 14.

HAGUE CONVENTION COUNTRY.

70.5.3   A Contracting State to which the Hague Convention applies between it and the U.K. and the dates on which the convention came into force between them are specified in Orders in Council: Act of 1985, s. 2.

The countries to which the convention currently applies are listed in the Child Abduction and Custody (Parties to Conventions) Order 1986 [S.I. 1986 No. 1159], Sched. 1 as substituted by the Child Abduction and Custody (Parties to Conventions) (Amendment) Order 2023 [S.I. 2023 No. 1084]. The countries (with the dates of coming into force in brackets) are as follows:—

Albania (1st July 2016)

Andorra (1st July 2016)

Argentina (1st June 1991)

Armenia (1st July 2016)

Australia (Australian States and mainland Territories—1st January 1987)

Austria (1st October 1988)

The Bahamas (1st January 1994)

Belarus (1st September 2003)

Belgium (1st May 1999)

Belize (1st October 1989)

Bosnia and Herzegovina (7th April 1992)

Brazil (1st March 2005)

Bulgaria (1st May 2009)

Burkina Faso (1st August 1992)

Canada:

Ontario (1st August 1986)

Greece (1st June 1993)

Honduras (1st March 1994)

Hungary (1st September 1986)

Iceland (1st November 1996)

Republic of Ireland (1st October 1991)

Israel (1st December 1991)

Italy (1st May 1995)

Jamaica (1st November 2023)

Japan (1st April 2014)

Kazakhstan (1st April 2017)

Republic of Korea (1st April 2017)

Latvia (1st October 2003)

Lithuania (1st March 2005)

Luxembourg (1st January 1987)

Macedonia (1st December 1991)

New Brunswick (1st August 1986)

British Columbia (1st August 1986)

Manitoba (1st August 1986)

Nova Scotia (1st August 1986)

Newfoundland and Labrador (1st August 1986)

Prince Edward Island (1st August 1986)

Quebec (1st August 1986)

Yukon Territory (1st August 1986)

Saskatchewan (1st November 1986)

Alberta (1st February 1987)

Northwest Territories (1st April 1988)

Nunavut (1st January 2001)

Chile (1st May 1994)

China:

Hong Kong Special Administrative Region

(1st September 1997)

Macau Special Administrative Region

(1st March 1999)

Colombia (1st March 1996)

Costa Rica (1st May 2009)

Croatia (1st December 1991)

Cyprus (1st February 1995)

Czech Republic (1st March 1998)

Denmark (1st July 1991)

Dominican Republic (21st February 2020)

Ecuador (1st April 1992)

El Salvador (1st June 1992)

Estonia (1st October 2003)

Fiji (1st October 2003)

Finland (1st August 1994)

France (1st August 1986)

Georgia (1st October 1997)

Germany (1st December 1990)

Malta (1st March 2002)

Mauritius (1st June 1993)

Mexico (1st September 1991)

Monaco (1st February 1993)

Montenegro (1st December 1991)

Morocco (1st July 2016)

Netherlands (1st September 1990)

New Zealand (1st August 1991)

Norway (1st April 1989)

Panama (1st May 1994)

Peru (1st October 2003)

Poland (1st November 1992)

Portugal (1st August 1986)

Romania (1st February 1993)

Russian Federation (1st July 2016)

St Kitts and Nevis (1st August 1994)

San Marino (1st June 2011)

Serbia and Montenegro (1st December 1991)

Seychelles (1st July 2016)

Slovakia (1st February 2001)

Slovenia (1st June 1994)

South Africa (1st October 1997)

Spain (1st September 1987)

Sweden (1st June 1989)

Switzerland (1st August 1986)

Turkey (1st August 2001)

Turkmenistan (1st March 1998)

Ukraine (1st June 2011)

United States (1st July 1988)

Uruguay (1st October 2003)

Uzbekistan (1st October 2003)

Venezuala (1st January 1997)

Zimbabwe (1st July 1995)

The Act and the convention do not apply to a removal or retention of a child committed before the convention comes into force in relation to a particular country: *Kilgour v. Kilgour* 1987 S.C. 55. "Retention" means an initial act not a continuing retention, so that it would not apply to retaining a child after the convention came into force who was removed before it came into force: *Kilgour*, above.

The common law applies in respect of a country to which the convention does not apply: see note 70.5.5.

APPLICATION FOR THE RETURN OF A CHILD.

The removal or retention of a child is wrongful where it is in breach of custody rights of a person under the law of the country in which the child was habitually resident before the removal or retention and those rights were exercised at the time of the removal or retention: Act of 1985, Sched. 1, Art. 3. Removal and retention are mutually exclusive concepts, and removal or retention does not mean removal or retention out of the care of the parent having custody rights but removal or retention out of the jurisdiction of the courts of the state of a child's habitual residence: *In re H (Minors) (Abduction: Custody Rights)* [1991] 2 A.C. 476, 500 per Lord Brandon of Oakbrook; and see *Findlay v. Findlay* 1994 S.L.T.

70.5.4

709. A right of access is not within the meaning of "rights of custody" in Art. 3: *Pirrie v. Sawacki* 1997 S.C.L.R. 59. Following the coming into force of the Children (Scotland) Act 1995, a parent not having a residence order but who has, or has not lost, parental rights (other than merely a right of contact) will have a right of custody order under Art. 3. Note the provisions in s. 2 of the 1995 Act about wrongful removal from the U.K. of a child habitually resident in Scotland.

The general policy of the Hague Convention, which the court has to bear in mind, is to achieve the return forthwith of children wrongfully rendered or retained to the State of their habitual residence which State would normally become the jurisdiction in which questions of custody and access would be determined: *Singh v. Singh* 1998 S.C. 68.

It is not a pre-condition of an application under s. 8 of the Act of 1985 to have the removal of a child declared wrongful that a request must have been made under Art. 15 of the Hague Convention by the judicial or administrative authority of a contracting state: *A.J. v. F.J.* [2005] CSIH 36, 29th April 2005, 2005 G.W.D. 15-251 (Second Div.).

An habitual residence is one enjoyed voluntarily with a settled intention that it should continue for some time; in the case of a child this will be chosen by his parents and it was thought that, where his parents separate, cannot be changed by one parent without the consent of the other: *Dickson v. Dickson* 1990 S.C.L.R. 692, 703B per L.P. Hope; and see *Zenel v. Haddow* 1993 S.C. 612, 616F (where the authorities are referred to by Lord Marnoch), *Findlay v. Findlay (No. 2)* 1995 S.L.T. 492.

In *AR v RN,* 2015 S.C. (UKSC) 129, it was held that habitual residence was a question of fact requiring an evaluation of all the relevant facts, focusing on the situation of the child, the purposes and intentions of the parents being merely one of the relevant factors; it was necessary to assess the degree of integration of the child into a social and family environment in the country in question.

There is no minimum period necessary in order to establish the acquisition of a new habitual residence: *Cameron v. Cameron* 1996 S.C. 17. In that case the opinion was expressed that a person can have only one habitual residence at any one time. The word "settled" as an element of habitual residence relates to one's purpose in living where one does and not to settlement in the sense of permanent or long-term residence, because habitual residence might be only for a limited period: *Moran v. Moran* , 1997 S.L.T. 541.

"Custody rights" are those which arise by operation of law, a judicial or administrative decision, or by agreement having legal effect: Act of 1985, Sched. 1, Art. 3; and see, e.g. *McKiver v. McKiver* 1995 S.L.T. 790. They include rights of contact by virtue of the fact that s. 2(3) and (6) of the Children (Scotland) Act 1995 confers on the contact parent the right to grant or withhold consent to the child's removal from the UK: *A.J. v. F.J.*, above.

The expression "rights relating to the care of the person of the child" in Art. 5 (custody rights) does not include the rights of a parent with access rights when the child is not in that parent's actual care: *Seroka v. Bellah* 1995 S.L.T. 204. In that case Lord Prosser at p. 210I-L doubted whether a court having power to deal with custody could be said to have rights of custody: cf England in *B v. B* [1993] Fam. 32.

A wrongful removal or retention in breach of custody rights means less than full legal determination of custody rights and whether they have been breached, and the requirements of Art. 3 of Sched. 1 may be satisfied where removal is not challenged or seriously challenged as wrongful or if the removal was prima facie wrongful: *Perrin v. Perrin* 1994 S.C. 45. A court acquires rights of custody when an application for custody and access is made to it, and removal of a child from the jurisdiction of such a court is a breach of the custody right of that court even though only access had by then been dealt with: *O v. O* , 2002 S.C. 430 (OH).

Subject to Art. 13, a child must be returned forthwith if a period of less than one year has elapsed from the date of the wrongful removal or retention; and the child must also be returned after a year has elapsed unless the child is settled in its new environment: Act of 1985, Sched. 1, Art. 12. Where the lapse of time after the expiry of one year is short, the quality of evidence relied on to establish settlement has to be good: *Perrin*, above, at p. 51F. The concept of settlement appears to have two elements, a physical element relating to a community and an environment and an emotional element denoting security and stability: *Perrin*, above, at p. 51H. On the issue of settlement, the proper question is not just a balancing exercise between the interests of the child and the requirement of the convention but whether the child was so settled in the new environment that the court would be justified in disregarding an otherwise mandatory requirement to have the child returned: *Soucie v. Soucie* 1995 S.L.T. 414.

The court is not bound to return a child if the respondent establishes (a) that the person having care of the child was not actually exercising the custody rights or consented or acquiesced in the removal or retention, or (b) there is a grave risk that the child's return would expose the child to physical or psychological harm or otherwise place the child in an intolerable situation: Act of 1985, Sched. 1, Art. 13. Only in the clearest of cases should the court exercise this discretion: *Taylor v. Ford* 1993 S.L.T. 654, 658B per Temp. Judge Horsburgh, Q.C.

In relation to ground (a), consent to removal of a child does not require to be connected in time to the actual removal: *Zenel v. Haddow* 1993 S.C. 612, 624G-A per Lord Allanbridge, and 628H per Lord Mayfield; Lord Morton of Shuna, dissenting at p. 629F-B, was of the opinion that the consent must relate to the particular act of removal. A person does not cease to exercise custody rights simply because he or she is in hospital: *S v. S* , 2003 S.L.T. 344; or ill: *A.J. v. F.J.*, above. The onus is on the parent who asserts consent to removal to prove that it was: *T v. T* , 2003 S.L.T. 1316 (First Div.).

In relation to ground (b), the approach to grave risk is set out by the UK Supreme Court in the case of In *re E (Children)* [2012] 1 AC 144, paras. 32-36, and as applied in Scotland by the Inner House in *AD v SD* 2023 SLT 439 (Extra Div.): (1) The burden of proof lies with the person opposing return of the child (it being rarely appropriate to hear oral evidence of the allegations. (2) The risk must be grave; "real" is not enough, "grave" characterising the risk rather than the harm. (3) The words "physical or psychological harm" are not qualified but gain colour from the alternative "or otherwise placed in an intolerable situation"; "intolerable" when applied to a child means 'a situation which this particular child in these particular circumstances should not be expected to tolerate' and this can be exposure to the harmful effects of seeing and hearing the physical or psychological abuse of a parent. (4) Art.13(b) is looking to the future: the situation as it would be if the child were to be returned; the situation which the child will face on return depends crucially on the protective measures which can be put in place to secure that the child will not be called upon to face an intolerable situation when she gets home; if the risk is serious enough, the court is not only concerned with the child's immediate future, because the need for effective protection may persist. (5) Where allegations of domestic abuse are made, the court should first ask whether, if they are true, there would be grave risk the child would be exposed to physical or psychological harm or otherwise placed in an intolerable situation. If so, the court must ask how the child can be protected against the risk. (6) What is in the best interests of the child is a primary consideration. In *Neulinger and Shuruk v Switzerland* [2011] 1 FLR 122 (ECtHR) it was said that the best interests have two aspects: to be reunited with their parents as soon as possible, so that one does not gain an unfair advantage over the other through the passage of time; and to be brought up in a "sound environment", in which they are not at risk of harm. The Hague Convention is designed to strike a fair balance between those two interests. If it is correctly applied, it is most unlikely that there will be any breach of article 8 or other Convention rights unless other factors supervene. *Neulinger* does not require a departure from the normal summary process, provided that the decision is not arbitrary or mechanical. In *In re E*, the mother's principal argument in resisting return was that the risk to her own mental health (adjustment disorder) was such that, as she is and has always been the children's primary carer, there was a grave risk that they would be placed in an intolerable situation unless there are real and effective protective measures in place. The practice of the judge reaching a decision on grave risk and then continuing matters (by a procedural or By Order hearing) until any protective orders are in place was noted with approval, although any procedural route that appears to disadvantage one side by detailing how the other party can make their case stronger would be discouraged. The earlier Scottish cases will have to be read in light of the above: see, e.g., *MacMillan v MacMillan* 1989 S.C. 53 (Extra Div.), *Cameron v Cameron (No. 2)* 1997 S.L.T. 206 (OH) and *M, Ptnr*, 2007 S.L.T. 433 (OH). The duty to take into account the social background of the child does not mean that there has to be a social background report: *Viola v. Viola* 1988 S.L.T. 7.

The court may also refuse to order the return of the child if the child objects to being returned and has attained an age and degree of understanding at which it is appropriate to take account of his views: Act of 1985, Sched. 1, Art. 13; the word "objects" is not to be construed narrowly: *Urness v. Minto* 1994 S.C. 249 (preference to remain in Scotland was objection to return to USA). In *Cameron*, above, it was held that, though the eldest child was articulate and confident, there was no basis for attributing to her a maturity greater than her seven years and she had not therefore attained the age or degree of maturity at which her views would be taken into account. The factors of objection and maturity do not merely open the door to an exercise of the court's discretion but are themselves factors to be taken into account in exercising that discretion; and also the court has to bear in mind the general policy of the convention: *Singh v. Singh* 1998 S.C. 68. There are difficulties in interviewing a child on this issue, and some of the difficulties and points to be covered are dealt with in *W v. W*, 2003 S.L.T. 1253, 1259A-G, paras. [29]–[31] (First Div.); cf *M, Ptnr*, 2005 S.L.T. 2 (OH).

On settlement cases (where the child is settled in the new environment) and child objection cases, see *In re M*, [2008] 1 AC 1288 as the leading authority: *C v N* 2018 S.L.T. 673 (Extra Div.).

The country to which the child has been taken cannot decide on the merits of the rights of custody until it has been determined that the child is not to be returned or the application under the convention is not lodged within a reasonable time: Act of 1985, Sched. 1, Art. 16.

COMMON LAW.

The common law applies where the Hague Convention does not. A decree for custody of a court furth | **70.5.5**
of the U.K. will be recognised here if made by the court of the country where the child was habitually resident: Family Law Act 1986, s. 26. The foreign order will, however, only be given grave consideration and will not be automatically or blindly enforced, the court treating the child's welfare as the first and paramount consideration: see *Campins v. Campins* 1979 S.L.T.(Notes) 41; *Sinclair v. Sinclair* 1988 S.L.T. 87. In England the principles of the Hague Convention are applied in a non-Convention case provided that the courts of the country of the child's habitual residence apply principles acceptable to the English courts: *Re S (Minors) (Abduction)* [1994] 1 F.L.R. 297.

A decree for custody of a court in the U.K. furth of Scotland will be recognised and have effect in Scotland if the court had jurisdiction to make it, and it can be enforced here if registered in the Court of Session: Family Law Act 1986, ss. 25 and 27; and see Chap. 71 for registration and enforcement of such decrees.

"CERTIFIED OR AUTHORISED COPY OF ANY RELEVANT DECISION".

A decision of a judicial or administrative authority furth of the U.K. may be proved by an authenticated | **70.5.6**
copy: Act of 1985, s. 7.

"RELEVANT AUTHORITY".

See r. 70.1. | **70.5.7**

"EVIDENCE OF WITNESSES BY AFFIDAVITS AND ANY DOCUMENTARY EVIDENCE".

70.5.8   This is a new provision introduced by A.S. (R.C.S.A. No. 3) (Miscellaneous) 1996 [S.I. 1996 No. 1756] to expedite the determination of such cases (on which, see further note 70.6.20).

The rule is that the affidavits and documentary evidence must be lodged with the petition: r. 70.5(2)(c) and (3)(c). There may be circumstances in which it is not possible to lodge these documents with the petition, e.g. where the petition has to be lodged as a matter of urgency for the purpose of seeking an interim order. In such a case the court should be asked to dispense with the requirement to lodge the documents with the petition under r. 2.1. The court should, however, fix a period within which such documents must be lodged thereafter.

An affidavit should be in the form of a statement of evidence written in the first person. The affidavit should contain evidence in support of, and expanding on, the averments in the pleadings. It should be sworn or affirmed and signed by the deponent before any person who may competently take an oath. Such a person includes a notary, a justice of the peace, a sheriff or any judge (or in England a commissioner for oaths (includes any barrister or solicitor)). The person taking the oath or affirmation should also sign the affidavit. Witnesses are unnecessary. And see the definition of affidavit in r. 1.3(1).

Affidavits are lodged as steps of process and may be lodged by post: P.N. No. 4 of 1994, paras 1 and 8; and see note 4.4.10. They must also be served, with any documentary evidence, with the petition on the party to whom the petition is served: r. 70.6(2).

Where there are contradictions between affidavits, and no other evidence to support a conclusion on way or the other, no conclusion can be drawn by the court: *D v. D* , 2002 S.C. 33, 37D (Extra Div.).

In relation to children, it should be noted that in giving oral evidence a child under 12 is admonished to tell the truth, a child between 12 and 14 is sworn or admonished at the judge's discretion and a child over 14 is usually sworn. A child under the age of 14 should not normally swear an affidavit for two reasons: first, he is too young to be sworn (and the judge has no means of assessing the matter himself); and secondly, if the proceedings relate to him, his views should be ascertained in some other way (e.g. the appointment of a curator ad litem) so as to avoid the child being forced to take sides by one of the parties in a dispute about him. The court may have to ascertain the views of the child for the purposes of Art. 13(2) of Sched. 1 to the Act of 1985 (child objecting to being returned).

APPLICATIONS WITH RESPECT TO ACCESS TO A CHILD.

70.5.9   Questions of access may arise "under" the Hague Convention, although there may be some application that may be so different from the original order as to be essentially a new one, the convention no longer being in point: see *Donofrio v. Burrell* , 2000 S.L.T. 1051 (Extra Div.). Doubts expressed in *Donofrio* about the use of the phrase "application for access to a child under the Hague Convention" formerly used in r. 70.5(2) have been addressed by substituting words used in Art. 21 of the Convention: A.S. (R.C.A. No. 4) (Miscellaneous) 2001 [S.S.I. 2001 No. 305].

It has been suggested in *Donofrio*, per Lord Prosser at p. 1057J, that the need for the special provisions for applications for access under r. 70.5(2) should be reconsidered. The convention is concerned with urgent action to maintain the status quo on a short-term basis. Applications for access do not call for unusual expedition. The convention does not force a party to invoke it. Furthermore, r. 70.5(2) creates a procedure different from that in Chap. 49 for dealing with applications for access and is unhelpful to the satisfactory conduct of such applications. Lord Prosser's request was not taken up in A.S. (R.C.S.A. No.4) (Miscellaneous) 2001 [S.S.I. 2001 No. 305].

Period of notice, service of causes and hearings under this Part[1]

70.6   **70.6.**—(1)   Subject to rule 14.6(2), the period of notice for lodging answers to a petition to which rule 70.5 applies shall be four days.

(2)[2, 3]   Subject to rule 70.16 (intimation of notice on child), such a petition, and a copy of any affidavit and documentary evidence lodged with it, shall be served on—

(a)   the person alleged to have brought the child into the United Kingdom;

(b)   the person with whom the child is presumed to be;

(c)   any parent or guardian of the child if he or she is within the United Kingdom, or a relevant territory and not otherwise a party;

(d)[4]   the chief executive of the local authority, and for the area in which the child resides and the Principal Reporter; and

(e)   any other person who may have an interest in the child.

---

[1] Rule 70.6(2) and (3) and heading amended by S.I. 1996 No. 1756 (effective 5 August 1996).
[2] Rule 70.6(2) and (3) and heading amended by S.I. 1996 No. 1756 (effective 5 August 1996).
[3] Rule 70(6)(2) and r. 70(6)(5) amended by S.S.I 2005 No. 135 (effective 2 March 2005).
[4] Rule 70.6(2)(d) amended by S.I. 1998 No. 890 (effective 21 April 1998).

(3)[1] The first order under rule 14.5 (first order in petitions) in a petition to which rule 70.5 applies shall specify a date within seven days after the expiry of the period of notice for a first hearing to determine the further progress of the petition.

(4)[2] A respondent shall lodge in process, and send a copy to the petitioner of, the evidence by affidavits of any witnesses and any documentary evidence, whether originals or copies initially, in support of his answers to the petition at least 3 days before the first hearing fixed under paragraph (3).

(5)[3,4] Subject to rule 70.17 (views of the child), at the first hearing fixed under paragraph (3), the court—

(a) shall determine to what extent, if any, further evidence by affidavit is required, by whom and in regard to what matters, and by what date any such affidavit should be lodged;

(b) may, on special cause shown, direct that a particular matter should be the subject of oral evidence in lieu of further, or in addition to, affidavit evidence; and

(c) may, if no further evidence is required, determine the petition at the first hearing or, if further evidence is required, shall give directions as to the period within which a second hearing shall be held to determine the petition.

Deriv. R.C.S. 1965, r. 260J(4) inserted by S.I. 1986 No. 1955, and r. 260J(5) inserted by S.I. 1986 No. 1955 and amended by S.I. 1991 No. 1157 (r. 70.6(1) and (2))

"SERVED".

For service, see Chap. 16, Pt. I.

70.6.1

"SUBJECT TO RIDE 70.16" AND "SUBJECT TO RULE 70.17".

Where a child habitually resident in a Member State of the E.U. has been removed to or retained in another Member State, the requirements of the Council Regulation No. 2201/2003 about giving the child an opportunity to be heard will apply: see art. 11 of the Council Regulation and note 70.5.1A. Intimation is required on the child unless inappropriate (see r. 70.16) and a form sent for the child to complete if he wishes (r. 70.17).

70.6.1A

FIRST AND SECOND HEARINGS.

R. 70.6(3) is designed to achieve expedition. Art. 11(1) of the Hague Convention requires expedition. If the court has not reached a decision within six weeks of the commencement of the proceedings a request may be made for a statement of reasons for the delay: Act of 1985, Sched. 1, Art. 11(2). The Court of Session has been criticised for the length of time it takes to make decisions (rarely within the six weeks) and for its inability to accept the concept of affidavit evidence.

70.6.2

A new procedure has, therefore, been introduced by A.S. (R.C.S.A. No. 3) (Miscellaneous) 1996 [S.I. 1996 No. 1756] following recommendations of the Cullen Report on the Business of the Outer House (1995). Affidavits must be lodged by the petitioner with the petition (r. 705(2)(c) or (3)(c)) and by the respondent with his answers (r. 70.6(4)). At a first hearing under r. 70.6(5), the court will determine, at its own instance or at the request of a party, whether and to what extent any further affidavit evidence is required or whether oral evidence is necessary in lieu of further, or in addition to, affidavit evidence. If further oral evidence is required at the second hearing, the interlocutor appointing that hearing must grant warrant for the citation of witnesses.

The court may determine the petition at the first hearing if it considers it has enough material before it to reach a decision. Parties must be prepared for that eventuality.

Where a second hearing is ordered, the court must, in giving directions for that hearing under r. 70.6(5)(c), fix a period to comply (if possible) with the six weeks deadline in Art. 11(2).

In England, it has been held that proceedings under the Hague Convention are summary in nature, that there was no right to give oral evidence and that there was a danger if oral evidence were generally admitted it would become impossible to deal with such cases expeditiously: *Re A.F. (A Minor) (Abduction)* [1992] 1 F.C.R. 269. In that case it was decided that oral evidence should be used sparingly; where the issue had to be decided on disputed non-oral evidence, the judge had to see if there was extraneous evidence in support of one side; evidence had to be compelling before the judge was entitled to reject

---

[1] Rule 70.6(2) and (3) and heading amended by S.I. 1996 No. 1756 (effective 5 August 1996).
[2] Rule 70.6(4) and (5) inserted by S.I. 1996 No. 1756 (effective 5 August 1996).
[3] Rule 70.6(4) and (5) inserted by S.I. 1996 No. 1756 (effective 5 August 1996).
[4] Rule 70(6)(2) and r. 70(6)(5) amended by S.S.I. 2005 No. 135 (effective 2 March 2005).

sworn evidence of a deponent or, alternatively, the evidence in the affidavit might be so inherently improbable that he was entitled to reject it; and if there were no grounds for rejecting the written evidence of either side, the applicant would have failed to establish his case.

"EVIDENCE OF WITNESSES BY AFFIDAVITS AND ANY DOCUMENTARY EVIDENCE".

70.6.2A This is a new provision introduced by A.S. (R.C.S.A. No. 3) (Miscellaneous) 1996 [S.I. 1996 No. 1756] to expedite the determination of such cases (on which, see note 70.6.2).

On affidavits, see note 70.5.8.

FEE.

70.6.3 The court fee for each of the hearings to determine further procedure and the full hearing is payable by each party for every 30 minutes or part thereof. For fee, see Court of Session 1997, Table of Fees, Pt. I, C, item 18 [S.I. 1997 No. 688, as amended, pp. C 1201 et seq.]. Certain persons are exempt from payment of fees: see 1997 Fees Order, art. 5 substituted by S.S.I. 2002 No. 270. A fee exemption certificate must be lodged in process: see P.N. No. 1 of 2002.

Where the petitioner is legally represented, the fee may be debited under a credit scheme introduced on 1st April 1976 by P.N. No. 4 of 1976 to the account (if one is kept or permitted) of the agent by the court cashier, and an account will be rendered weekly by the court cashier's office to the agent for all court fees due that week for immediate settlement. An agent not on the credit scheme will have an account opened for the purpose of lodging the fee: P.N. No. 2 of 1995. A debit slip and a copy of the court hearing time sheet will be delivered to the agent's box or sent by DX or post.

A party litigant must pay (by cash, cheque or postal order) to the clerk of court at the end of the hearing or, if the hearing lasts more than a day, at the end of each day: P.N. No. 2 of 1995. A receipt will be issued. The assistant clerk of session will acknowledge receipt of the sum received from the clerk of court on the Minute of Proceedings.

The Act does not apply to the extent that the Hague Convention on Child Abduction matters are discussed: *M v M*, 2015 S.L.T. 683 (OH).

"RELEVANT TERRITORY".

70.6.4 See r. 70.1 and note 70.1.2.

Notice of other proceedings

70.7 **70.7.**—(1) Where a petition is presented under paragraph (1) of rule 70.5 and there are proceedings mentioned in section 9 of the Act of 1985 relating to the merits of the rights of custody of the child depending in or before a relevant authority, the court shall give written intimation of the petition and, in due course of the outcome of the petition, to that relevant authority.

(2) Where the court receives a notice equivalent to that under paragraph (1) from a relevant authority, all proceedings in any cause mentioned in section 9 of the Act of 1985 relating to the merits of the rights of custody of the child shall be sisted by the court until the dismissal of the proceedings in that other court under the Hague Convention; and the Deputy Principal Clerk shall give written intimation to each party of the sist and of any such dismissal.

Deriv. R.C.S. 1965, r. 260J(7) and (8) inserted by S.I. 1986 No. 1955

GENERAL NOTE.

70.7.1 A decision on the merits of rights of custody (as defined by s. 9 of the Act of 1985) cannot be taken in the country to which the child has been wrongfully taken until it has been decided that the child is not to be returned or the application for return of the child is not lodged within a reasonable time: Act of 1985, Sched. 1, Art. 16.

"WRITTEN INTIMATION".

70.7.2 For methods, see r. 16.9.

Transfer of causes

70.8 **70.8.**—(1)[1] At any stage of a cause mentioned in paragraph (1) of rule 70.5, the court may, at its own instance or on the motion of any party, pronounce an interlocutor transmitting the cause to the High Court in England and Wales or Northern Ireland, or the appropriate court of a relevant territory, as the case may be.

---

[1] R. 70.8(1), (2)(a) and (4) amended by S.I. 1996 No. 1756 (effective 5th August 1996).

(2)   Where a cause is transferred under paragraph (1), the Deputy Principal Clerk shall—

    (a)[1] transmit the process to the appropriate officer of the High Court in England and Wales or Northern Ireland, or the appropriate court of a relevant territory, as the case may be;

    (b) give written intimation of such transfer to each party; and

    (c) certify on the interlocutor sheet that such written intimation has been given.

(3)   Where a cause is transferred under paragraph (1), the question of expenses shall not be determined by the court, but shall be at the discretion of the court to which the cause is transferred.

(4)[2]   Where such a cause is transferred to the court from the High Court in England and Wales or Northern Ireland, or the appropriate court of a relevant territory—

    (a) the Deputy Principal Clerk shall, on receipt of the order transferring the cause and any documents in the cause, give written intimation to each party of the transfer;

    (b) the cause shall be deemed to have been commenced by petition; and

    (c)[3] the Deputy Principal Clerk shall, within two sitting days of the receipt of it, cause it to be put out on the By Order Roll before the Lord Ordinary.

Deriv. R.C.S. 1965, r. 260J(9) to (12) inserted by S.I. 1986 No. 1955

GENERAL NOTE.

Transfer of an application will arise if the child has moved from Scotland to another jurisdiction in the U.K. (or was never here) or from another jurisdiction in the U.K. to Scotland and saves time and the expense of raising fresh proceedings.   **70.8.1**

"WRITTEN INTIMATION".

For methods, see r. 16.9.   **70.8.2**

"RELEVANT TERRITORY".

See r. 70.1 and note 70.1.2.   **70.8.3**

Part III – Recognition and Enforcement of Custody Decisions (The European Convention)

Form of applications under this Part

70.9.—(1)   An application under any of the following provisions shall be made by petition:—   **70.9**

    (a) section 15 of the Act of 1985 (application to declare a decree for custody not to be recognised);

    (b) section 16 of the Act of 1985 (application for registration of custody decision); and

    (c) section 18 of the Act of 1985 (application for enforcement of custody decision).

(2)   An application under section 17(4) of the Act of 1985 (application for variation or revocation of registered decision), shall be made by note in the process of the petition for registration.

(3)   An application under section 23(2) of the Act of 1985 (application in custody proceedings for declarator that removal of a child was unlawful), shall be made—

---

[1] R. 70.8(1), (2)(a) and (4) amended by S.I. 1996 No. 1756 (effective 5th August 1996).
[2] R. 70.8(1), (2)(a) and (4) amended by S.I. 1996 No. 1756 (effective 5th August 1996).
[3] R. 70.8(4)(c) amended by S.S.I. 2017 No. 414 r. 3(2) (effective 1st January 2018).

    (a) by minute in the process of a cause depending before the court commenced by summons; or

    (b) by note in the process of a cause depending before the court commenced by petition.

  (4)[1] In an application mentioned in this rule—

    (a) the petition, minute or note, as the case may be, shall include averments in relation to—

        (i) the identity of the petitioner, minuter or noter, as the case may be, and his interest in the cause;

        (ii) the identity of the child and his date of birth;

        (iii) the parents or guardians of the child;

        (iv) the order which is required to be registered, enforced, declared unlawful, declared not recognised, varied or revoked, as the case may be;

        (v) the whereabouts or suspected whereabouts of the child; and

        (vi) any civil cause in dependence before any other court or authority in respect of the child, or any proceedings specified in section 20(2) of the Act of 1985 in dependence in or before a relevant authority;

    (b) there shall be produced with the petition, minute or note, as the case may be—

        (i) a certified or authorised copy of any decision to be registered or enforced;

        (ii) where a decision to be registered was given in the absence of the person against whom the decision was made or in the absence of his legal representative, a document which establishes (subject to Article 9(1)(a) of the European Convention) that that person was duly served with the document which instituted the original proceedings;

        (iii) a certificate or affidavit to the effect that any decision to be registered is enforceable in accordance with the law of the State in which the decision was made; and

        (iv) any other relevant document; and

    (c) there shall be lodged with the petition, minute or note, as the case may be, the evidence by affidavits of any witnesses and any documentary evidence, whether originals or copies initially, in support of the petition, minute or note.

Deriv. R.C.S. 1965, r. 260K(1)–(5) inserted by S.I. 1986 No. 1955

GENERAL NOTE.

70.9.1   The Act of 1985 implements the European Convention on the Recognition and Enforcement of Decisions Concerning Custody of Children 1980 (Cmnd. 8281 (1981)). The convention is set out in Sched. 2 to the Act.

    A decision concerning custody means a decision in so far as it relates to the care of the person of a child including the right to decide on the place of his residence or access to him: Act of 1985, Sched. 2, Art. 1(c). The convention applies to a child under the age of 16 years: Act of 1985, Sched. 2, Art. 1(a).

    A decision relating to custody given in a Contracting State shall be recognised and enforceable in another Contracting State (Act of 1985, Sched. 2, Art. 7), but it is not enforceable in Scotland unless it has been registered in the Court of Session (Act of 1985, ss. 15 and 16).

JURISDICTION.

70.9.1A   The jurisdiction of the court to deal with applications under the European Convention used to be subject to the rule that in relations between member states of the E.U. the Council Regulation (EC) No.

---

[1] R. 70.9(4) amended by S.I. 1996 No. 1756 (effective 5th August 1996).

2201/2003 of 27th November 2003 concerning jurisdiction and enforcement of judgments in matrimonial matters and matters of parental responsibility (new Brussels II- sometimes called Brussels IIA (or IIa) or Brussels II bis) takes precedence: Act of 1985, s. 12(3) amended by the European Community (Matrimonial and Parental Responsibility Jurisdiction and Judgments (Scotland) Regulations 2005 [S.S.I. 2005 No. 42]; and art. 60 of the Council Regulation. This replaces Council Regulation 1347/2000 of 29th May 2000 (Brussels II) and the 1985 Act s. 12(3) as inserted by S.S.I. 2000 No. 36. The primary ground under the Council Regulation 2201/2003 for a Member State to make decisions about parental responsibilities is habitual residence of the child in that Member State at the time the court in that state is seized of the matter: Art. 8, but see Arts. 9, 10 and 12.

Council Regulation (EC) No. 2201/2003 was revoked by the Jurisdiction and Judgments (Family, Civil Partnership and Marriage (Same Sex Couples) (EU Exit) (Scotland) (Amendment etc.) Regulations 2019 [S.S.I. 2019 No. 104] (as read with the European Union (Withdrawal) Act 2018) except in relation to proceedings commenced before 11pm on 31st December 2020.

For recognition and enforcement of decisions relating to parental responsibility (including custody and access) under the Council Regulation No 2001/2003, see Chap. 62, Pt. XI, rr. 62.67–62.80.

"PETITION".

A petition is presented in the Outer House: r. 14.2(h). The petition must be in Form 14.4 in the official printed form: rr. 4.1 and 14.4. The petition must be signed by counsel or other person having a right of audience: r. 4.2; and see r. 1.3(1) (definition of "counsel" and "other person having a right of audience") and note 1.3.4.

70.9.2

The petitioner must lodge the petition with the required steps of process (r. 4.4). A fee is payable on lodging the petition: see note 14.5.10.

On petitions generally, see Chap. 14.

EUROPEAN CONVENTION COUNTRY.

A Contracting State to which the European Convention applies between it and the U.K. and the dates on which the convention came into force between them are specified in Orders in Council: Act of 1985, s. 13.

70.9.3

The countries to which the convention currently applies are listed in the Child Abduction and Custody (Parties to Conventions) Order 1986 [S.I. 1986 No. 1159], Sched. 2 as substituted by the Child Abduction and Custody (Parties to Conventions) (Amendment) Order 2017 [S.I. 2017 No. 775]. The countries (with the dates of coming into force in brackets) are as follows:—

Andorra (1st July 2011)

Austria (1st August 1986)	Iceland (1st November 1996)
Belgium (1st August 1986)	Republic of Ireland (1st October 1991)
Bulgaria (1st October 2003)	Italy (1st June 1995)
Cyprus (1st October 1986)	Latvia (1st August 2002)
Czech Republic (1st July 2000)	Liechtenstein (1st August 1997)
Denmark (1st August 1991)	Lithuania (1st May 2003)
Estonia (1st September 2001)	Luxembourg (1st August 1986)
Finland (1st August 1994)	Macedonia (1st March 2003)
France (1st August 1986)	Malta (1st February 2000)
Germany (1st February 1991)	Moldova (1st May 2004)
Greece (1st July 1993)	Montenegro (6th June 2006)
Hungary (1st June 2004)	Netherlands (1st September 1990)
Norway (1st May 1989)	Slovakia (1st September 2001)
Poland (1st March 1996)[1]	Spain (1st August 1986)
Portugal (1st August 1986)	Sweden (1st July 1989)
Romania (1st September 2004)	Switzerland (1st August 1986)
Serbia (1st May 2002)	Turkey (1st June 2000)
	Ukraine (1st November 2008)

---

[1] Poland appeared in Sched. 2 to the 1986 Order by virtue of the Child Abduction and Custody (Parties to Conventions) (Amendment) Order 1996 [S.I. 1996 No. 269] on the European Convention coming into force as between that country and the U.K. on 1st March 1996, but was omitted in error from the amendment orders S.I. 1996 Nos. 2595 and 2874. It reappeared in S.I. 1997 No. 1747.

RECOGNITION AND ENFORCEMENT OF CUSTODY ORDERS.

70.9.4   A custody order of a Contracting State will be recognised unless declared not recognised by the court on an application to it: Act of 1985, s. 15(2). To be enforced here the foreign order must be registered in the Court of Session: Act of 1985, s. 15(2). An application for enforcement must be granted unless a ground in s. 16(4) is established: these are (a) the grounds specified in Sched. 2, Art. 9 or 10 (see, e.g. *Campins-Coll, Petr.* 1988 S.C. 305), (b) the decision is not enforceable in the Contracting State and is not a decision to which Art. 12 (no enforceable decision there when child removed) applies, or (c) an application under Pt. I of the Act of 1985 (international child abduction under the Hague Convention) is pending.

"MINUTE".

70.9.5   For applications by minute, see r. 15.1.

"NOTE".

70.9.6   For applications by note, see r. 15.2.

"DEPENDING", "IN DEPENDENCE".

70.9.7   A cause is depending from the time it is commenced (i.e. from the time an action is served or a first order in a petition is made) until final decree, whereas a cause is in dependence until final extract. For the meaning of commenced, see note 13.4.4 (action) or 14.6.1 (petition). For the meaning of final decree, see note 4.15.2(2). For the meaning of final extract, see note 7.1.2(2).

"RELEVANT AUTHORITY".

70.9.8   See r. 70.1.

"EVIDENCE OF WITNESSES BY AFFIDAVITS AND ANY DOCUMENTARY EVIDENCE".

70.9.9   This is a new provision introduced by A.S. (R.C.S.A. No. 3) (Miscellaneous) 1996 [S.I. 1996 No. 1756] to expedite the determination of such cases (on which see further note 70.6.20).

The rule is that the affidavits and documentary evidence must be lodged with the petition: r. 70.9(4)(c). There may be circumstances in which it is not possible to lodge these documents with the petition, e.g. where the petition has to be lodged as a matter of urgency for the purpose of seeking an interim order. In such a case the court should be asked to dispense with the requirement to lodge the documents with the petition under r. 2.1. The court should, however, fix a period within which such documents must be lodged thereafter.

An affidavit should be in the form of a statement of evidence written in the first person. The affidavit should contain evidence in support of, and expanding on, the averments in the pleadings. It should be sworn or affirmed and signed by the deponent before any person who may competently take an oath. Such a person includes a notary, a justice of the peace, a sheriff or any judge (or in England a commissioner for oaths (includes, any barrister or solicitor). The person taking the oath or affirmation should also sign the affidavit. Witnesses are unnecessary. And see the definition of affidavit in r. 1.3(1).

Affidavits are lodged as step of process and may be lodged by post: P.N. No. 4 of 1994, paras. 1 and 8; and see note 4.4.10. They must also be served, with any documentary evidence, with the petition on the party to whom the petition is served: r. 70.6(2).

In relation to children, it should be noted that in giving oral evidence a child under 12 is admonished to tell the truth, a child between 12 and 14 is sworn or admonished at the judge's discretion and a child over 14 is usually sworn. A child under the age of 14 should not normally swear an affidavit for two reasons: first, he is too young to be sworn and the judge has no means of assessing the matter himself; and secondly, if the proceedings relate to him, his views should be ascertained in some other way (e.g. the appointment of a curator ad litem) so as to avoid the child being forced to take sides by one of the parties in a dispute about him. The court may have to obtain the child's views in relation to an application under s. 16 of the Act of 1985 (registration of decisions) by virtue of Art. 15(1)(a) of Sched. 2 to that Act.

Period of notice, service of causes and hearings under this Part[1]

70.10   **70.10.**—(1) Subject to rule 14.6(2), the period of notice for lodging answers in a petition to which rule 70.9 applies shall be four days.

(2)[2] Such a petition, and a copy of any affidavit and documentary evidence lodged with it, shall be served on—

    (a) the person alleged to have brought the child into, or removed the child from, the United Kingdom, or a relevant territory, as the case may be;

    (b) the person with whom the child is presumed to be in the United Kingdom or a relevant territory;

---

[1] R. 70.9(2) and (3) and heading amended by S.I. 1996 No. 1756 (effective 5th August 1996).
[2] R. 70.9(2) and (3) and heading amended by S.I. 1996 No. 1756 (effective 5th August 1996).

    (c)   the mother and father of the child if he or she is within the United Kingdom, or a relevant territory, and not otherwise a party;

    (d)[1] the chief executive of the local authority, and for the area in which the child resides and the Principal Reporter; and (e) any other person who may have an interest in the child.

(3)[2] The first order under rule 14.5 (first order in petitions) in a petition to which rule 70.9 applies shall specify a date within seven days after the expiry of the period of notice for a first hearing to determine the further progress of the petition.

(4)[3] A respondent shall lodge in process, and send a copy to the petitioner of, the evidence by affidavits of any witnesses and any documentary evidence, whether originals or copies initially, in support of his answers to the petition to which rule 70.9 applies at least 3 days before the first hearing fixed under paragraph (3).

(5) At the first hearing fixed under paragraph (3), the court—

    (a)   shall determine to what extent, if any, further evidence by affidavit is required, by whom and in regard to what matters, and by what date any such affidavit should be lodged;

    (b)   may, on special cause shown, direct that a particular matter should be the subject of oral evidence in lieu of further, or in addition to, affidavit evidence; and

    (c)   may, if no further evidence is required, determine the petition at the first hearing or, if further evidence is required, shall give directions as to the period within which a second hearing shall be held to determine the petition.

Deriv. R.C.S. 1965, r. 260K(6) inserted by S.I. 1986 No. 1955 (r. 70.10(1)); and r. 260K(8) inserted by S.I. 1986/1955 and amended by S.I. 1991 No. 1157 (r. 70.10(2))

"SERVED".

For service, see Chap. 16, Pt I.

FIRST AND SECOND HEARINGS.

R. 70.10(3) is designed to achieve expedition in relation to applications under ss. 15, 16 and 18 of the Act of 1985 (which relate to recognition and enforcement of European custody decisions). The Court of Session has been criticised for the length of time it takes to make decisions and for its inability to accept the concept of affidavit evidence.

A new procedure has, therefore, been introduced by A.S. (R.C.S.A. No. 3) (Miscellaneous) 1996 [S.I. 1996 No. 1756] following recommendations of the Cullen Report on the Business of the Outer House (1995). Affidavits must be lodged by the petitioner with the petition (r. 70 5(2)(c) or (3)(c)) and by the respondent with his answers (r. 70.6(4)). At a first hearing under r. 70.6(5), the court will determine, at its own instance or at the request of a party, whether and to what extent any further affidavit evidence is required or whether oral evidence is necessary in lieu of further, or in addition to, affidavit evidence. If further oral evidence is required at the second hearing, the interlocutor appointing that hearing must grant warrant for the citation of witnesses.

This court may determine the petition at the first hearing if it considers it has enough material before it to reach a decision. Parties must be prepared for that eventuality.

In England, it has been held that proceedings under the Hague Convention are summary in nature, that there was no right to give oral evidence and that there was a danger if oral evidence were generally admitted it would become impossible to deal with such cases expeditiously: *Re A.F. (A Minor) (Abduction)* [1992] 1 F.C.R. 269. In that case it was decided that oral evidence should be used sparingly; where the issue had to be decided on disputed non-oral evidence, the judge had to see if there was extraneous evidence in support of one side; evidence had to be compelling before the judge was entitled to reject sworn evidence of a deponent or, alternatively, the evidence in the affidavit might be so inherently improbable that he was entitled to reject it; and if there were no grounds for rejecting the written evidence of either side, the applicant would have failed to establish his case.

70.10.1

70.10.2

---

[1] R. 70.10(2)(d) amended by S.I. 1998 No. 890 (effective 21st April 1998).
[2] R. 70.9(2) and (3) and heading amended by S.I. 1996 No. 1756 (effective 5th August 1996).
[3] R. 70.9(4) and (5) inserted by S.I. 1996 No. 1756 (effective 5th August 1996).

"EVIDENCE OF WITNESSES BY AFFIDAVITS AND ANY DOCUMENTARY EVIDENCE".

70.10.2A   This is a new provision introduced by A.S. (R.C.S.A. No. 3) (Miscellaneous) 1996 [S.I. 1996 No. 1756] to expedite the determination of such cases (on which, see note 70.10.2). On affidavits, see note 70.9.9.

FEE.

70.10.3   The court fee for each of the hearings to determine further procedure and the full hearing is payable by each party for every 30 minutes or part thereof. For fee, see Court of Session etc. Fees Order 1997, Table of Fees, Pt I, C, item 18 [S.I. 1997 No. 688, as amended, pp. C1201 et seq.]. Certain persons are exempt from payment of fees: see 1997 Fees Order, art.5 substituted by S.S.I. 2002 No. 270. A fee exemption certificate must be lodged in process: see P.N. No.1 of 2002.

Where the petitioner is legally represented, the fee may be debited under a credit scheme introduced on 1st April 1976 by P.N. No. 4 of 1976 to the account (if one is kept or permitted) of the agent by the court cashier, and an account will be rendered weekly by the court cashier's office to the agent for all court fees due that week for immediate settlement. An agent not on the credit scheme will have an account opened for the purpose of lodging the fee: P.N. No. 2 of 1995. A debit slip and a copy of the court hearing time sheet will be delivered to the agent's box or sent by DX or post.

A party litigant must pay (by cash, cheque or postal order) to the clerk of court at the end of the hearing or, if the hearing lasts more than a day, at the end of each day: P.N. No. 2 of 1995. A receipt will be issued. The assistant clerk of session will acknowledge receipt of the sum received from the clerk of court on the Minute of Proceedings.

"RELEVANT TERRITORY".

70.10.4   See r. 70.1 and note 70.1.2.

Registration

70.11   **70.11.** Where the court pronounces an interlocutor ordering registration under section 16 of the Act of 1985, the Deputy Principal Clerk shall record that interlocutor in a register of decisions pronounced under that Act.

Deriv. R.C.S. 1965, r. 260K(10) inserted by S.I. 1986 No. 1955

Other proceedings

70.12   **70.12.**—(1) Where a petition is presented under section 16 (application for registration and enforcement of custody decision), or section 18 (application for enforcement of a custody decision), of the Act of 1985 and there are proceedings mentioned in section 20(2) of that Act depending or such proceedings are commenced after the petition has been presented—

   (a)   the petitioner shall inform the court by including averments or lodging an affidavit, as the case may be, to that effect containing a concise statement of the nature of those proceedings; and

   (b)   the court shall give written intimation of the petition and, in due course of the outcome of the petition, to the relevant authority.

(2)[1] Where the court receives a notice equivalent to that under paragraph (1)(b) from the High Court in England and Wales or Northern Ireland, or the appropriate court of a relevant territory, the Deputy Principal Clerk shall give written intimation to each party to any cause which is one mentioned in section 20(2) of the Act of 1985.

Deriv. R.C.S. 1965, r. 260K(11) and (12) inserted by S.I. 1986 No. 1955

GENERAL NOTE.

70.12.1   Proceedings mentioned in s. 20(2) of the Act of 1985 which are pending may not be determined after an application has been made for registration of a custody decision (other than a decision relating to rights of access), or such a decision is registered, and the decision was made before the proceedings which are pending unless the application for registration has been refused: Act of 1985, s. 20(1).

"DEPENDING".

70.12.2   A cause is depending from the time it is commenced (i.e. from the time an action is served or a first order in a petition is made) until final decree, whereas a cause is in dependence until final extract. For the meaning of commenced, see note 13.4.4 (action) or 14.6.1 (petition). For the meaning of final decree, see

---

[1] R. 70.12(2) amended by S.I. 1996 No. 1756 (effective 5th August 1996)

note 4.15.2(2). For the meaning of final extract, see note 7.1.2(2).

"WRITTEN INTIMATION".

For methods, see r. 16.9.

70.12.3

"RELEVANT TERRITORY".

See r. 70.1 and note 70.1.2.

70.12.4

Transfers

70.13.—(1)[1] At any stage of a cause mentioned in rule 70.9, the court may, at its own instance or on the motion of any party, pronounce an interlocutor transferring the cause to the High Court in England and Wales or Northern Ireland, or the appropriate court of a relevant territory, as the case may be.

70.13

(2)   Where a cause is transferred under paragraph (1), the Deputy Principal Clerk shall forthwith—

(a)[2]   transmit the process to the appropriate officer of the High Court in England and Wales or Northern Ireland, or the appropriate court of a relevant territory, as the case may be;

(b)   give written intimation of such transfer to each party; and

(c)   certify on the interlocutor sheet that such written intimation has been given.

(3)   Where a cause is transferred under paragraph (1), the question of expenses shall not be determined by the court, but shall be at the discretion of the court to which the case is transferred.

(4)[3]   Where such a cause is transferred to the court from the High Court in England and Wales or Northern Ireland, or the appropriate court of a relevant territory—

(a)   the Deputy Principal Clerk shall, on receipt of the order transferring the cause and any papers in the cause, give written intimation to the parties of the transfer;

(b)   the cause shall be deemed to have been commenced by petition; and

(c)   the Deputy Principal Clerk shall, within two days of the receipt of it, cause it to be put out on the By Order Roll before the Lord Ordinary.

Deriv. R.C.S. 1965, r. 260K(13) to (16) inserted by S.I. 1986 No. 1955

GENERAL NOTE.

Transfer of an application will arise if the child has moved from Scotland to another jurisdiction in the U.K. (or was never here) or from another jurisdiction in the U.K. to Scotland and saves time and the expense of raising fresh proceedings.

70.13.1

"WRITTEN INTIMATION".

For methods, see r. 16.9.

70.13.2

"RELEVANT TERRITORY".

See r. 70.1 and note 70.1.2.

70.13.3

Variation and revocation of registered decision

70.14.—(1)   Where a decision registered under section 16 of the Act of 1985 is varied or revoked by an authority in the Contracting State in which the decision was made, the court shall—

70.14

(a)   on cancelling the registration of a decision which it has been notified has been revoked, give written intimation of that cancellation to—

---

[1] Rules 70.13(1), (2)(a) and (4) amended by S.I. 1996 No. 1756 (effective 5th August 1996).
[2] Rules 70.13(1), (2)(a) and (4) amended by S.I. 1996 No. 1756 (effective 5th August 1996).
[3] Rules 70.13(1), (2)(a) and (4) amended by S.I. 1996 No. 1756 (effective 5th August 1996).

(i) the person appearing to the court to have actual custody of the child;

(ii) the petitioner in the petition for registration; and

(iii) any other party to that petition; and

(b) on being notified of the variation of a decision, give written intimation to—

(i) the person having custody in fact of the child; and

(ii) any party to the petition for registration of the decision, of the variation.

(2) Any person to whom intimation of a variation has been given under paragraph (1)(b) may apply by note for the purpose of making representations before the registration is varied.

(3) An application under section 17(4) of the Act of 1985 (application to cancel or vary registration) shall be made by note.

Deriv. R.C.S. 1965, r. 260(17) and (18) inserted by S.I. 1986 No. 1955

"WRITTEN INTIMATION".

70.14.1   For methods, see r. 16.9.

"NOTE".

70.14.2   For applications by note, see r. 15.2.

Part IV[1] – Applications under the Hague Convention where the Council Regulation Applies

Application and interpretation of this Part

70.15   **70.15—**[2](1) This Part applies to petitions under rule 70.5(1) (applications for the return of a child) under the Hague Convention where the Council Regulation (E.C.) No. 2201/2003 of 27th November 2003 on jurisdiction and the recognition and enforcement of judgments in matrimonial matters and matters of parental responsibility applies.

(2) In this Part—

"the Council Regulation" means Council Regulation (E.C.) No. 2201/2003 of 27th November 2003 concerning jurisdiction and the recognition and enforcement of judgments in matrimonial matters and matters of parental responsibility;

"central authority" means a central authority designated under Article 53 of the Council Regulation;

"the Hague Convention" means the Convention defined in section 1(1) of the Child Abduction and Custody Act 1985(b) and as set out in Schedule 1 to that Act;

"Member State" has the same meaning as in Article 2(3) of the Council Regulation;

"wrongful removal or retention" has the same meaning as in Article 2(11) of the Council Regulation.

GENERAL NOTE.

70.15.1   Council Regulation (EC) No. 2201/2003 was revoked by the Jurisdiction and Judgments (Family, Civil Partnership and Marriage (Same Sex Couples)) (EU Exit) (Scotland) (Amendment etc.) Regula-

---

[1] Part IV and r. 70.15 inserted by S.S.I. 2005 No. 135 (effective 2nd March 2005). Part IIA renumbered as Pt. IV by S.S.I. 2005 No. 268 (effective 7th June 2005).
[2] Part IV and r. 70.15 inserted by S.S.I. 2005 No. 135 (effective 2nd March 2005). Part IIA renumbered as Pt. IV by S.S.I. 2005 No. 268 (effective 7th June 2005).

tions 2019 [S.S.I. 2019 No. 104] (as read with the European Union (Withdrawal) Act 2018) except in relation to proceedings commenced before 11pm on 31st December 2020.

Article 61 of the Council Regulation 2201/2003 (new Brussels II — sometimes called Brussels IIA (or IIa) or Brussels II bis) provided that the Council Regulation applies in addition to the Hague Convention of 25th October 1980, in an application to which the Hague Convention applies, where the child has his habitually residence on the territory of a Member State.

The Council Regulation (E.C.) No. 2201/2203 of 27th November 2003 concerning jurisdiction and enforcement of judgments in matrimonial matters and matters of parental responsibility (new Brussels II) applies between Member States of the E.U except Denmark. Where an application is made under the Hague Convention to which Pt. II of Chap. 70 applies, and the child is habitually resident in a Member State of the E.U., certain requirements of the Council Regulation apply where that child has been removed to or retained in another Member State. These include: (a) the child must be given an opportunity to be heard unless inappropriate because of his age or immaturity, (b) the court deals with the case in six weeks, (c) the court cannot refuse to return the child under art. 13(b) of the Hague Convention (see 1985 Act, Sched. 1, Art. 13(b) (grave risk)) if adequate arrangements have been made to secure protection on return, and (d) the court cannot refuse to return the child unless the person requesting return has been given an opportunity to be heard: art. 11 of the Council Regulation.

It should be noted that the Council Regulation does not itself provide a regime for child abduction. A Member State retains its own jurisdiction while a child is habitually resident there until the child acquires an habitual residence in another Member State: art. 10. If the Hague Convention is applicable, that vehicle will be used subject to the Council Regulation requirements.

An interim or provisional custody order does not constitute a "judgment on custody" for the purposes of art. 10(b)(iv) of Regulation 2201/2003 (Brussels II bis): *G v G*, 2012 S.L.T. 2 (the effect of a Latvian interim order authorising a child's residence in Scotland did not terminate the habitual residence of the child in the home state (Latvia) transferring jurisdiction to the other state (Scotland) and the retention of the child in Scotland was not wrongful under the Hague Convention and Brussels II bis).

Warrants and forms for intimation to a child and for seeking a child's views

70.16.—[1](1) Subject to paragraph (2), in a petition under rule 70.5(1) (form of applications under this Part) where the Council Regulation applies, the petitioner must—

70.16

   (a)   include in the prayer of the petition a crave for a warrant for intimation and the seeking of the child's views in Form 49.8A;

   (b)   include in the statement of facts in the petition averments setting out the reasons why it is appropriate to send Form 49.8A to the child;

   (c)   when presenting the petition for first orders, submit a draft Form 49.8A, showing the details that the petitioner proposes to include when the form is sent to the child.

(2) Where the petitioner considers that it would be inappropriate to send Form 49.8A to the child (for example, where the child is under 5 years of age), the petitioner must —

   (a)   include in the prayer of the petition a crave to dispense with intimation and the seeking of the child's views in Form 49.8A;

   (b)   include in the statement of facts in the petition averments setting out the reasons why it is inappropriate to send Form 49.8A to the child.

(3) The court must be satisfied that the draft Form 49.8A submitted under paragraph (1)(c) has been drafted appropriately.

(4) The court may dispense with intimation and the seeking of views in Form 49.8A or make any other order that it considers appropriate.

(5) An order granting warrant for intimation and the seeking of the child's views in Form 49.8A under this rule must be signed by the Lord Ordinary.

(6) Where the court orders intimation and the seeking of the child's views in Form 49.8A, the petitioner must—

   (a)   send Form 49.8A to the child as soon as possible;

   (b)   on the same day, lodge—

      (i)   a copy of the Form 49.8A that was sent to the child;

---

[1] As substituted by S.S.I. 2019 No. 123 para.2 (effective 24th June 2019).

(ii)   a certificate of intimation in Form 49.8B;

(c)   not send the child a copy of the petition.".

GENERAL NOTE.

70.16.1   The new procedure is that the content of the Form 49.8A must be approved (or dispensed with) by the court.

The old Form 49.8-N used to provide expressly for the child to indicate if he or she wanted someone else to tell the court his or her views. The new Form 49.8A refers expressly only to filling in the form if the child wants to express views in writing. There is an unhelpful question asking if the child would like to say what he or she thinks in a different way. That is likely to be confusing to a child if it is intended to allow the child to say that he or she wants someone else to tell or wants to tell the judge in person; it does not tell the child what any of these different ways may be. It is implied in r. 70.17 that the child may wish to express views in a different way, but, since the child only receives Form 49.8A and not r. 49.20, this is not very helpful to the child.

"WHERE THE COUNCIL REGULATION APPLIES".

70.16.2   See note 70.15.1.

INTIMATION ON A WARRANT TO INTIMATE.

70.16.3   For methods, see Chap. 16, r. 16.8.

"MOTION".

70.16.4   For motions, see Chap. 23.

Views of child

70.17   **70.17.**—[1](1)   In an application under rule 70.5(1) (application for the return of a child) where the Council Regulation applies and the child has—

(a)   returned Form 49.8-N (form of notice of intimation to a child), Form 49.8A or

(b)   otherwise indicated to the court a wish to express views on a matter affecting him,

the court shall not grant any order unless an opportunity has been given for the views of that child to be obtained or heard.

(2)   Where a child has indicated his wish to express his views, the court shall order such steps to be taken as it considers appropriate to ascertain the views of that child.

(3)   The court shall not grant an order in a petition under rule 70.5(1) (return of a child) affecting a child who has indicated his wish to express his views, unless due weight has been given by the court to the views expressed by that child, having regard to his age and maturity.

"WHERE THE COUNCIL REGULATION APPLIES".

70.17.1   See note 70.15.1.

VIEWS OF THE CHILD.

70.17.2   The child may express views in the form 49.8-N or intimate that he would like someone else to do so for him.

STEPS TO ASCERTAIN VIEWS OF CHILD.

70.17.3   The court may, e.g., appoint someone (e.g. a curator ad litem or a reporter) to take the child's views.

Continuations

70.18   **70.18.**[2]   In an application under rule 70.5(1) (application for the return of the child), where the Council Regulation applies, the court may allow a continuation of

---

[1] As amended by S.S.I. 2019 No. 123 para.2 (effective 24th June 2019).
[2] Rule 70.18 inserted by S.S.I. 2005 No. 135 (effective 2nd March 2005).

the hearing for a period not exceeding 7 days or to the first suitable court date thereafter but any further continuations shall only be allowed on special cause shown.

Recording of hearings under Article 12 of the Hague Convention

70.19.—[1](1) Any hearing on an application for the return of a child under rule 70.5(1) and Article 12 of the Hague Convention, where the Council Regulation applies, shall be recorded by—

    (a)   a shorthand writer to whom the oath de fidelis administratione officii has been administered on his appointment as a shorthand writer in the Court of Session; or

    (b)   tape recording or other mechanical means approved by the Lord President.

  (2) The record of the hearing shall include—

    (a)   any objection taken to a question or to the line of evidence;

    (b)   any submission made in relation to such an objection; and

    (c)   the ruling of the court in relation to the objection and submission.

  (3) A transcript of the record of the hearing shall be made only where an order is made under Article 13 of the Hague Convention refusing to order the return of a child in an application where the Council Regulation applies.

  (4) The transcript of the record of the hearing shall be certified as a faithful record of the hearing by—

    (a)   the shorthand writer or shorthand writers, if more than one, who recorded the hearing; or

    (b)   where the hearing was recorded by tape recording or other mechanical means, the person who transcribed the record.

  (5) The court may make such alterations to the transcript of the record of the hearing as appear to it to be necessary after hearing parties; and, where such alterations are made, the Lord Ordinary shall authenticate the alterations.

70.19

"WHERE THE COUNCIL REGULATION APPLIES".

See note 70.15.1.

70.19.1

EVIDENCE AT A HEARING.

    The Hague Convention and r. 70.6 do not envisage that oral evidence will necessarily be required: see note 70.6.2. Art. 11(6) of the Council Regulation 2201/2003 requires a transcript of the hearing to be sent to the court where the child is habitually resident where the court dealing with the application for return of the child makes an order for nonreturn under art. 13 of the Hague Convention (in Sched. 1 to the 1985 Act). The requirement is not limited to cases where there is evidence. There is no requirement for a transcript to be sent where the court orders return of the child.

70.19.2

Order under Article 13 of the Hague Convention

70.20.[2] Where an order is made under Article 13 of the Hague Convention refusing to order the return of a child in an application under rule 70.5(1) where the Council Regulation applies, the Deputy Principal Clerk shall transmit a copy of the order and a transcript of the proceedings to the central authority of the Member State where the child was habitually resident immediately before the wrongful removal or retention.

70.20

GENERAL NOTE.

See note 70.19.2.

70.20.1

---

[1] Rule 70.19 inserted by S.S.I. 2005 No. 135 (effective 2nd March 2005) and amended by S.S.I. 2006 No. 83 (effective 17th March 2006).
[2] Rule 70.20 inserted by S.S.I. 2005 No. 135 (effective 2nd March 2005).

CHAPTER 71 REGISTRATION AND ENFORCEMENT OF PART I ORDERS UNDER THE FAMILY LAW ACT 1986

Chapter 71

Registration and Enforcement of Part I Orders under the Family Law Act 1986[1]

Interpretation of this Chapter

71.1.[2] In this Chapter—

71.1

"the Act of 1986" means the Family Law Act 1986;

"appropriate court" means the High Court in England and Wales or the High Court in Northern Ireland or, in relation to a specified dependent territory, the corresponding court in that territory, as the case may be;

"Part I order" has the meaning assigned in section 32 of the Act of 1986;[3]

"proper officer" means the Secretary of the principal registry of the Family Division of the High Court in England and Wales or the Master (care and protection) of the High Court in Northern Ireland or, in relation to a specified dependent territory, the corresponding officer of the appropriate court in that territory, as the case may be;

"register" means the Part I orders register kept under rule 71.2;[4]

"specified dependent territory" means a dependent territory specified in an Order in Council made under section 43 of the Act of 1986.

Deriv. R.C.S. 1965, r. 260P(1) inserted by S.I. 1988 No. 615

GENERAL NOTE.

The Act of 1986 gives effect to the recommendations of the English and Scottish Law Commissions in their joint report on Custody of Children—Jurisdiction and Enforcement within the United Kingdom (Scot. Law Com. No. 91).

71.1.1

Part I of the Act of 1986 lays down jurisdictional rules for making what were formerly called custody orders (and are now referred to as Part I orders which include custody, access, residence and contact orders) in the UK. In general, a court has jurisdiction to make a Part I order other than in matrimonial proceedings (divorce, nullity or separation: Act of 1986, s. 18(1)) if the child is habitually resident in its jurisdiction, is present there and not habitually resident elsewhere in the UK, or in an emergency. The question of habitual residence is one of fact and not legal right: *Rellis v. Hart* 1993 S.L.T. 738.

Under Ch.V of Pt I of the Act of 1986, a Part I order made by a court in any part of the UK with respect to a child under the age of 16 years shall be recognised (except in relation to a provision as to the means of enforcement) in any other part of the UK as having the same effect as if it had been made in that other part as if the court in that other part had had jurisdiction to make it: Act of 1986, s. 25(1). The order is enforceable in that other part of the UK if registered there under s. 27 of the Act: Act of 1986, s. 25(3). Chap. 71 of the R.C.S. 1994 provides for registration of Court of Session Part I orders elsewhere in the UK (rr. 71.3 and 71.4) and registration and enforcement of Part I orders made elsewhere in the UK in Scotland (rr. 71.5 and 71.7), and for cancellation and variation of registered Part I orders (r. 71.6).

The Act of 1986 has not, apparently, affected the limited protective jurisdiction of the Court of Session to refuse to give effect to a custody order of a foreign court which the Court of Session may always exercise if it is satisfied that enforcement of the foreign decree would result in physical or moral injury to the child: *Woodcock v. Woodcock* 1990 S.C. 266, 273.

"SPECIFIED DEPENDENT TERRITORY".

The only Order in Council specifying a dependent territory is the Family Law Act 1986 (Dependent Territories) Order 1991 [S.I 1991 No. 1723]. The only dependent territory specified is the Isle of Man.

71.1.2

Part I orders register

71.2.—(1)[5] The Deputy Principal Clerk shall maintain a register to be called the Part I orders register for the purposes of Chapter V of Part I of the Act of 1986.

71.2

---

[1] Chap. heading and r. 71.1 amended by S.I. 1997 No. 795 (effective 1st April 1997).
[2] Chap. heading and r. 71.1 amended by S.I. 1997 No. 795 (effective 1st April 1997).
[3] Chap. heading and r. 71.1 amended by S.I. 1997 No. 795 (effective 1st April 1997).
[4] Chap. heading and r. 71.1 amended by S.I. 1997 No. 795 (effective 1st April 1997).
[5] R. 71.2(1) and (2) and heading amended by S.I. 1997 No. 795 (effective 1st April 1997).

(2)[1] In Part I of the register there shall be recorded applications for registration of a Part I order in another part of the United Kingdom; and in Part II of the register there shall be recorded Part I orders registered for enforcement in Scotland.

(3) The register may be inspected by—

(a) the person who applied for registration; and

(b) any other person who satisfies the Deputy Principal Clerk that he has an interest to do so.

Deriv. R.C.S. 1965, r.260Q inserted by S.I 1988 No. 615 and amended by S.I. 1991 No. 2483 (r.71.2(1) and (2)), and r.260X(3) inserted by S.I. 1988 No. 615 (r.71.2(3)).

Applications for registration of Part I orders in another court[2]

71.3

71.3.—(1)[3] An application under section 27 of the Act of 1986 to register a Part I order made by the Court of Session in an appropriate court shall be made by letter to the Deputy Principal Clerk.

(2)[4] An application under paragraph (1) shall be accompanied by—

(a) a copy of the letter of application;

(b) an affidavit by the applicant;

(c) a copy of that affidavit;

(d) a certified copy of the interlocutor of the Part I order;

(e) a certified copy of the interlocutor of any variation which is in force in respect of the Part I order; and

(f) any other document relevant to the application and a copy of it.

(3) An affidavit required under this rule shall set out—

(a) the name and address of the applicant and his right under the Part I order;

(b) the name and date of birth of the child in respect of whom the Part I order was made, the present whereabouts or suspected whereabouts of the child and the name of any person with whom he is alleged to be;

(c) the name and address of any other person who has an interest in the Part I order;

(d) whether the custody order is to be registered in England and Wales, Northern Ireland or a specified dependent territory, and the court in which it is to be registered;

(e) whether the Part I order is in force;

(f) whether the Part I order is already registered and, if so, where it is registered; and

(g) details of any order known to the applicant which affects the child and is in force in the jurisdiction in which the Part I order is to be registered.

(4)[5] Where the Deputy Principal Clerk refuses to send an application under this rule to the appropriate court on the ground that the Part I order is no longer in force, he shall give written intimation to the applicant; and the applicant shall have the right to have the application brought before the Lord Ordinary for determination.

(5)[6] The Deputy Principal Clerk shall retain the letter of application under this rule and any documents which accompany it and which are not transmitted to the appropriate court under section 27(3) of the Act of 1986.

Deriv. R.C.S. 1965, r. 260R inserted by S.I. 1988 No. 615 and amended by S.I. 1990 No. 2118 and 1991 No. 2483

---

[1] R. 71.2(1) and (2) and heading amended by S.I. 1997 No. 795 (effective 1st April 1997).

[2] R. 71.3(1)–(4) and heading amended by S.I. 1997 No. 795 (effective 1st April 1997).

[3] R. 71.3(1)–(4) and heading amended by S.I. 1997 No. 795 (effective 1st April 1997).

[4] R. 71.3(1)–(4) and heading amended by S.I. 1997 No. 795 (effective 1st April 1997).

[5] R. 71.3(1)–(4) and heading amended by S.I. 1997 No. 795 (effective 1st April 1997).

[6] R. 71.3(1)–(4) and heading amended by S.I. 1997 No. 795 (effective 1st April 1997).

S.27 of the Act of 1986 provides for applications for registration of Part I orders of the Court of Session in another part of the UK, and r. 71.3 is made under that section (A.S. (R.C.S. 1994) 1994, Sched. 1 [S.I. 1994 No. 1443]).

Unless the Deputy Principal Clerk considers that the Part I order of the Court of Session is no longer in force he shall, on receiving the application, send to the appropriate court in which it is to be registered, a certified copy of the order, particulars of any variation of it, a copy of the application and any accompanying documents: Act of 1986, s.27(3). On receiving these documents, the appropriate court shall register the order: Act of 1986, s.27(4).

71.3.1

"Part I order".

For meaning, see ss.1(1) and 32 of the Act of 1986.

71.3.2

Transmission of applications for registration

71.4.—(1)[1] Where the Deputy Principal Clerk is satisfied that the Part I order is in force, he shall send the documents mentioned in section 27(3) of the Act of 1986 to the proper officer of the court in which the Part I order is to be registered.

71.4

(2)[2] For the purposes of section 27(3)(b) of the Act of 1986, the prescribed particulars of any variation which is in force in respect of a Part I order shall be a certified copy of the interlocutor of any such variation.

(3)[3] On sending an application under paragraph (1), the Deputy Principal Clerk shall make an entry in Part I of the register recording the date and particulars of the application and the Part I order.

(4)[4] On receiving notification from a proper officer of an appropriate court that the Part I order has been registered in that court under section 27(4) of the Act of 1986, the Deputy Principal Clerk shall record the date of registration in Part I of the register.

Deriv. R.C.S. 1965, r. 260S inserted by S.I. 1988 No. 615

General note.

S. 27 of the Act of 1986 provides for registration elsewhere in the UK of Part I orders made by the Court of Session.

71.4.1

"Part I order".

For meaning, see ss.1(1) and 32 of the Act of 1986.

71.4.2

Registration of Part I orders from another court[5]

71.5.—(1) The prescribed officer under section 27(4) of the Act of 1986 shall be the Deputy Principal Clerk.

71.5

(2)[6] Where the Deputy Principal Clerk receives a certified copy of a Part I order from a court for registration under section 27(4) of the Act of 1986, he shall enter the following particulars in Part II of the register:—

   (a)   the name and address of the applicant and his interest under the Part I order;

   (b)   a brief description of the nature of the Part I order, its date and the court which made it; and

   (c)   the name and whereabouts or suspected whereabouts of the child who is the subject of the Part I order, his date of birth and the date on which he will attain the age of 16 years.

---

[1] R. 71.4(1)–(4) amended by S.I. 1997 No. 795 (effective 1st April 1997).
[2] R. 71.4(1)–(4) amended by S.I. 1997 No. 795 (effective 1st April 1997).
[3] R. 71.4(1)–(4) amended by S.I. 1997 No. 795 (effective 1st April 1997).
[4] R. 71.4(1)–(4) amended by S.I. 1997 No. 795 (effective 1st April 1997).
[5] R. 71.5(2)–(4) and heading amended by S.I. 1997 No. 795 (effective 1st April 1997).
[6] R. 71.5(2)–(4) and heading amended by S.I. 1997 No. 795 (effective 1st April 1997).

(3)[1] On registering the Part I order, the Deputy Principal Clerk shall—

    (a)   retain the application and the documents which accompanied it; and

    (b)   give written intimation to—

        (i)   the court from which he received the application, and

        (ii) the applicant who applied for registration, that the Part I order has been registered.

(4)[2] Where the Deputy Principal Clerk gives written intimation to an applicant under paragraph (3), he shall state the date when the registration of the Part I order will automatically cease to have effect on the child attaining the age of 16 years.

Deriv. R.C.S. 1965, r. 260T inserted by S.I. 1988 No. 615 and amended by S.I. 1990 No. 2118

GENERAL NOTE.

71.5.1   S.27 of the Act of 1986 provides for registration of Part I orders made by a court elsewhere in the UK in Scotland (in the Court of Session).

On receiving a certified copy of the Part I order, particulars of any variation of it, a copy of the application and any accompanying documents, the Deputy Principal Clerk shall register the order: Act of 1986, s.27(4).

Once registered, the order can be enforced (excluding provisions as to the means of enforcement) under s.29 of the Act of 1986: see r. 71.7.

"WRITTEN INTIMATION".

71.5.2   For methods, see r. 16.9.

"PART I ORDER".

71.5.3   For meaning, see ss.1(1) and 32 of the Act of 1986.

Cancellation or variation of registered Part I orders[3]

71.6   **71.6.**—(1)[4] Where the Court of Session revokes, recalls or varies a Part I order which it has made, the Deputy Principal Clerk, on being informed by the party who applied for the revocation, recall or variation that the Part I order has been registered in an appropriate court, shall—

    (a)   send a certified copy of the interlocutor of the revocation, recall or variation, as the case may be, to the proper officer of the court in which the Part I order is registered;

    (b)   record the transmission of the certified copy of that interlocutor in Part I of the register; and

    (c)   record the revocation, recall or variation, as the case may be, in Part I of the register.

(2)[5] On receiving notification from the proper officer of the court in which the Part I order is registered that he has amended his record, the Deputy Principal Clerk shall record the fact that the amendment has been made in Part II of the register.

(3)[6] Where the Deputy Principal Clerk receives a certified copy of an order which revokes, recalls or varies a Part I order registered in the Court of Session from an appropriate court, he shall—

    (a)   note the change and its date in Part II of the register; and

    (b)   give written intimation to—

        (i)   the court from which he received the certified copy of the order which revokes, recalls or varies, as the case may be, the Part I order,

---

[1] R. 71.5(2)–(4) and heading amended by S.I. 1997 No. 795 (effective 1st April 1997).
[2] R. 71.5(2)–(4) and heading amended by S.I. 1997 No. 795 (effective 1st April 1997).
[3] R. 71.6(1)–(5) and heading amended by S.I. 1997 No. 795 (effective 1st April 1997).
[4] R. 71.6(1)–(5) and heading amended by S.I. 1997 No. 795 (effective 1st April 1997).
[5] R. 71.6(1)–(5) and heading amended by S.I. 1997 No. 795 (effective 1st April 1997).
[6] R. 71.6(1)–(5) and heading amended by S.I. 1997 No. 795 (effective 1st April 1997).

(ii)   the person who applied for registration of the Part I order, and

(iii)   the person, if different, who applied for the revocation, recall or variation, as the case may be, of the Part I order,

that he has amended the register.

(4)[1]   An application to the Court of Session under section 28(2) of the Act of 1986 to cancel all or a part of the registration of a Part I order which it has registered shall be made by petition and shall be served on—

(a)   the person who applied for registration, if he is not the petitioner; and

(b)   any other interested person.

(5)[2]   Where, under section 28(2) of the Act of 1986, the court cancels all or a part of the registration of a Part I order which it has registered, the Deputy Principal Clerk shall—

(a)   note the cancellation and its date in Part II of the register; and

(b)   give written intimation to—

(i)   the court which made the Part I order;

(ii)   the person who applied for registration; and

(iii)   the person, if different, who applied for cancellation of the Part I order.

Deriv. R.C.S. 1965, r. 260U inserted by S.I. 1988 No. 615 and amended by S.I. 1990 No. 2118

GENERAL NOTE.

A Part I order may be revoked, recalled or varied by a court in the country in which it was originally made (not necessarily the court which made the order). Where the Court of Session makes such an order, notice must be given to the appropriate court where the order is registered: Act of 1986, s.28(1); and r. 71.6(1) to (3) is made under that subsection (A.S. (R.C.S. 1994) 1994, Sched. 1 [S.I. 1994 No. 1443]).

The Court of Session can cancel or vary a Part I order registered with it where the order has ceased to have effect in the part of the U.K. where it was made, other than by revocation, recall or variation (e.g. superseded by a later order by any U.K. court having jurisdiction), or as the result of an order in proceedings furth of the U.K.: Act of 1986, s.28(2). The application is made by petition: r. 71.6(4).

71.6.1

"WRITTEN INTIMATION".

For methods, see r. 16.9.

71.6.2

"PETITION".

A petition is presented in the Outer House: r. 14.2(h). The petition must be in Form 14.4 in the official printed form: rr. 4.1 and 14.4. The petition must be signed by counsel or other person having a right of audience: r. 4.2; and see r. 1.3(1) (definition of "counsel" and "other person having a right of audience") and note 1.3.4.

The petitioner must lodge the petition with the required steps of process (r. 4.4). A fee is payable on lodging the petition: see note 14.5.10.

On petitions generally, see Chap. 14.

71.6.3

"SERVED".

For methods of service, see Chap. 16, Pt I.

71.6.4

"PART I ORDER".

For meaning, see ss. 1(1) and 32 of the Act of 1986.

71.6.5

Enforcement of registered Part I orders in Scotland[3]

71.7.—(1)[4]   An application under section 29(1) of the Act of 1986 to enforce a Part I order registered in the Court of Session shall be made by petition.

(2)   Where the petitioner in an application under paragraph (1) is not the person who applied for registration of the Part I order, the petition shall be served on that person.

71.7

---

[1] R. 71.6(1)–(5) and heading amended by S.I. 1997 No. 795 (effective 1st April 1997).
[2] R. 71.6(1)–(5) and heading amended by S.I. 1997 No. 795 (effective 1st April 1997).
[3] R. 71.7(1) and heading amended by S.I. 1997 No. 795 (effective 1st April 1997).
[4] R. 71.7(1) and heading amended by S.I. 1997 No. 795 (effective 1st April 1997).

Deriv. R.C.S. 1965, r. 260V inserted by S.I. 1988 No. 615

General note.

71.7.1   Once registered in the Court of Session a custody order from another part of the U.K. may be enforced (excluding provisions as to the means of enforcement) under s.29 of the Act of 1986: i.e. the court can exercise powers it would have had if it had made the custody order itself. The court can also make interim orders pending determination of the application for enforcement.

The court should not normally make an order for enforcement without giving the respondent an opportunity to be heard: *Woodcock v. Woodcock* 1990 S.C. 267.

The provisions for sist of enforcement proceedings in s.30 of the Act of 1986 should be noted: see r. 71.8. There are also provisions for dismissal of enforcement proceedings in s.31 of the Act of 1986 (and see r. 71.8).

"petition".

71.7.2   A petition is presented in the Outer House: r. 14.2(h). The petition must be in Form 14.4 in the official printed form: rr. 4.1 and 14.4. The petition must be signed by counsel or other person having a right of audience: r. 4.2; and see r. 1.3(1) (definition of "counsel" and "other person having a right of audience") and note 1.3.4.

The petitioner must lodge the petition with the required steps of process (r. 4.4). A fee is payable on lodging the petition: see note 14.5.10.

On petitions generally, see Chap. 14.

"served".

71.7.3   For methods of service, see Chap. 16, Pt I.

"part I order".

71.7.4   For meaning, see ss.1(1) and 32 of the Act of 1986.

Application to sist or refuse enforcement proceedings

71.8   **71.8.**—(1)[1]   An application under section 30(1) of the Act of 1986 to sist enforcement proceedings, or under section 31(1) or (2), of the Act of 1986 to dismiss a petition for enforcement of a Part I order, shall be made by lodging answers at any time in the process of the petition for enforcement; and the answers shall be served on every other party and, if he is not a party, the applicant for registration of the Part I order.

(2)   An application under section 30(3) of the Act of 1986 (recall of sist of enforcement proceedings) shall be made by motion.

(3)   Where the court pronounces an interlocutor under section 30(2) or (3) or section 31(3) of the Act of 1986, the Deputy Principal Clerk shall—

(a)   make an entry in Part II of the register noting the terms of the interlocutor and the date; and

(b)   give written intimation to—

(i)   the person who applied for registration where he was not a party to the application under section 30(1) or section 31(1) or (2) of the Act of 1986; and

(ii)   the court from which the application for registration was received, of the terms of the interlocutor.

Deriv. R.C.S. 1965, r. 260W inserted by S.I. 1988 No. 615

General note.

71.8.1   The court may sist enforcement proceedings on application by any person having an interest on the ground that he has taken or intends to take other proceedings in the U.K. or elsewhere as a result of which the order may cease to have effect or have a different effect; and the court may recall the sist where there has been unreasonable delay in prosecuting those other proceedings or those proceedings have been concluded and the registered order remains in force: Act of 1986, s.30.

The intention of s.30 of the Act of 1986 is not to provide an open-ended observation to sist enforcement proceedings simply on the criteria relevant to an application for interim custody; the main issue to

---

[1] R. 71.8(1) amended by S.I. 1997 No. 795 (effective 1st April 1997).

be considered is whether special circumstances have been established which are sufficient to justify a failure to comply with the primary purpose of the legislation (to ensure enforcement of the original order): *Cook v. Blackley* 1997 S.C.45.

Enforcement proceedings may be dismissed on the application of a person having an interest on the ground that the custody order has ceased to have effect in the part of the U.K. where it was made or as a result of proceedings furth of the U.K.: Act of 1986, s.31.

"ANSWERS".

For form and procedure, see r. 18.3.   **71.8.2**

"MOTION".

For motions, see Chap. 23.   **71.8.3**

"PART I ORDER".

For meaning, see ss.1(1) and 32 of the Act of 1986.   **71.8.4**

Orders for disclosure of information

71.9. Where the court makes an order under section 33(1) of the Act of 1986   **71.9**
(order on person to disclose information as to child's whereabouts), it may ordain the person against whom the order was made to appear before it or to lodge an affidavit.

Deriv. R.C.S. 1965, r. 260X(1) inserted by S.I. 1988 No. 615

GENERAL NOTE.

The court has always had power to take whatever action was necessary to make an interlocutor effec-   **71.9.1**
tive including ordering the hearing of evidence from any witness who may have information which would assist in the recovery of a child: *Abusaif v. Abusaif* 1984 S.L.T. 90, 91 per L.P. Emslie.

The statutory provision in s. 33 of the Act of 1986 confirms the common law power including the power to order disclosure whether the order was made by a U.K. court or a court furth of the U.K. A person is not excused from complying with an order to disclose information on the ground of incrimination of that person or his or her spouse, but a statement or admission is not admissible in evidence in criminal proceedings for an offence except perjury: Act of 1986, s. 33(2).

Applications for interdict under section 35 (3) of the Act of 1986

71.10. An application by a person mentioned in section 35(4)(b) or (c) of the   **71.10**
Act of 1986 for interdict or interim interdict under section 35(3) of the Act of 1986 (prohibition of removal of child from United Kingdom) shall be made—

(a) by note in the process of a petition depending before the court to which this Chapter applies; or

(b) where there is no such depending process, by petition.

Deriv. R.C.S. 1965, r. 260X(2) inserted by S.I. 1988 No. 615

GENERAL NOTE.

Persons who may apply for interdict to restrict the removal of a child from the jurisdiction of the court   **71.10.1**
are a guardian or a person who wishes to obtain custody or care of the child: Act of 1986, s. 35(4)(b) and (c) as amended by the Age of Legal Capacity (Scotland) Act 1991, Sched. 1, para. 47.

"NOTE".

For applications by note, see r. 15.2.   **71.10.2**

"PETITION".

A petition is presented in the Outer House: r. 14.2(h). The petition must be in Form 14.4 in the official   **71.10.3**
printed form: rr. 4.1 and 14.4. The petition must be signed by counsel or other person having a right of audience: r. 4.2; and see r. 1.3(1) (definition of "counsel" and "other person having a right of audience") and note 1.3.4.

The petitioner must lodge the petition with the required steps of process (r. 4.4). A fee is payable on lodging the petition: see note 14.5.10.

On petitions generally, see Chap. 14.

"THE EC REGULATION"

means Council Regulation (EC) 1346/2000 of 29th May 2000 on insolvency proceedings.   **71.10.4**

CHAPTER 72 BANKRUPTCY (SCOTLAND) ACT 2016
Chapter 72[1]

Bankruptcy (Scotland) Act 2016

Interpretation of this Chapter

72.1.—[2](1) In this Chapter, references to a section are to sections of the Bankruptcy (Scotland) Act 2016

(2) Unless the context otherwise requires, words and expressions used in this Chapter which are also used in the Bankruptcy (Scotland) Act 2016 have the same meaning as in that Act.

72.1

GENERAL NOTE.

The Act of 1985 repealed, subject to some minor re-enactments, the Bankruptcy (Scotland) Act 1913 and largely gave effect to the proposals of the *Scottish Law Commission Report on Bankruptcy and Related Aspects of Insolvency* (Scot. Law Com. No. 68). The main changes effected by the Act of 1985 include: the introduction of an interim trustee who, as well as a permanent trustee, must be appointed in every case; the debtor may obtain an automatic discharge after the expiry of three years from the date of sequestration; the introduction of the "protected trust deed"; the introduction of a modified procedure, and payment of the trustee's remuneration and outlays from public funds, in cases where the debtor's assets are likely to be insufficient to pay a dividend ("small asset" cases); and the introduction of power conferred on the sheriff to cure defects in procedure. The effect of this last change has been to reduce the number of petitions to the *nobile officium* arising out of the bankruptcy process.

72.1.1

The Bankruptcy (Scotland) Act 2016 consolidates the Bankruptcy (Scotland) Act 1985 and the Bankruptcy (Scotland) Act 1993, the Bankruptcy and Diligence etc. (Scotland) Act 2007 and a number of other related enactments. It came into force on 30th November 2016: Bankruptcy (Scotland) Act 2016 (Commencement) Regulations [S.S.I. No. 2016 No. 294].

Sequestration is now competent only in the sheriff court: Act of 1985, ss. 9, 15–17 as amended by s. 16 of the Bankruptcy and Diligence etc. (Scotland) Act 2007. The former rules continue to apply to sequestrations before 1st April 2008.

Determination etc. under section 66: appeals and referrals

72.2.—[3](1) This rule applies to a petition containing—

(a) an appeal under section 68(4) (as read with section 68(6)(a)); or

(b) a referral for a direction under section 68(5) (as read with section 68(6)(a)).

(2) The petition must include a list of the sequestrations to which the petition relates.

(3) Where the court allows an appeal under section 68(4)—

(a) the Accountant in Bankruptcy must intimate a certified copy of the interlocutor of the court to the persons specified in section 67(2); and

(b) the court may make such orders as it thinks fit for the intimation and advertisement of its decision.

72.2

Deriv. R.C.S. 1965, r. 189(a)(vii) amended by S.I. 1986 No. 514

GENERAL NOTE.

Under s. 68(6) of the 2016 Act an appeal against a determination or appointment under s. 66 or a determination under s. 67(4) of the 2016 Act by the Accountant in Bankruptcy where it relates to two or more sequestrations in different sheriffdoms must be made by a single petition to the Court of Session. Section 66 is concerned with replacement of a trustee acting in two or more sequestrations and s. 67(4) is concerned with the outlays and remuneration of the former trustee.

72.2.1

"PETITION".

A petition is presented in the Outer House: r. 14.2(h). The petition must be in Form 14.4 in the official printed form: rr. 4.1 and 14.4. The petition may be signed by the petitioner for his own sequestration, counsel or other person having a right of audience, or an agent: r. 4.2; and see r. 1.3(1) (definition of "counsel", "other person having a right of audience" and "agent") and note 1.3.4.

72.2.2

---

[1] Chap. 72 and r. 72.1 substituted by S.S.I. 2016 No. 312 (effective 30th November 2016).
[2] Chap. 72 and r. 72.1 substituted by S.S.I. 2016 No. 312 (effective 30th November 2016).
[3] R. 72.2 substituted by S.S.I. 2016 No. 312 (effective 30th November 2016).

The petitioner must lodge the petition with the required steps of process (r. 4.4). A fee is payable on lodging the petition: see note 14.5.10.

On petitions generally, see Chap. 14.

Remit of application under section 211(1)

72.3

72.3.—[1](1) An application under section 211(5)(b) (application for a direction to remit an application under section 211(1)) is to be made by petition.

(2) A copy of the application under section 211(1) (application to sheriff to cure defects in procedure) certified by the sheriff clerk must be lodged with any application under section 211(5)(b).

(3) Where the court has determined an application under section 211(5)(b), the applicant must intimate a certified copy of the interlocutor of the court forthwith to—

    (a) the sheriff clerk; and

    (b) the Accountant in Bankruptcy.

(4) Where the court grants an application under section 211(5)(b), the sheriff clerk must, on receipt of the certified copy of the interlocutor of the court, transmit the application under section 211(1), and those parts of the sequestration process in the custody of the sheriff clerk, to the Deputy Principal Clerk.

(5) Where the court has determined the matters raised by the application under section 211(1)—

    (a) the applicant under section 211(5)(b) must intimate a certified copy of the interlocutor of the court forthwith to—

        (i) the sheriff clerk; and

        (ii) the Accountant in Bankruptcy; and

    (b) the Deputy Principal Clerk must transmit the parts of process transmitted under paragraph (4) to the sheriff clerk.

DIRECTION TO REMIT AN APPLICATION UNDER s.211(5)(B).

72.3.1

Section 63 of the 1985 Act is now s. 211 of the 2016 Act.

Any person "having an interest" may apply to the court to have an application under s.63(1) of the Act of 1985 relating to a sequestration depending before the sheriff court remitted to the Court of Session: Act of 1985, s.63(3)(b). A person having an interest may apply to the sheriff court in which the sequestration is depending for remit, or the sheriff may at his own instance remit, to the court: Act of 1985, s.63(3)(a).

The power conferred on a sheriff by s.63(1) of the Act of 1985 to cure defects in procedure (by waiving a failure to comply with any requirement of the Act or any regulations made thereunder or by making an order to enable a thing to be done) should obviate the need for a separate petition to the *nobile officium*, as was necessary before April 1, 1986. The objective of s.63 is "to prevent the sensible progress of a sequestration from being hampered by irregularities which are purely technical when equitable considerations require otherwise": *Pattison v. Halliday* 1991 S.L.T. 645, 648 per Lord Caplan. There are, however, limits on the powers exercisable under s.63(1). A sheriff cannot, in the purported exercise of the power under s.63(1), pronounce an ultra vires order: *Accountant in Bankruptcy v. Allans of Gillock Ltd* 1991 S.L.T. 765 (attempt to alter the effective date of sequestration). Accordingly, it may be necessary to remit to the Court of Session.

Examples of the exercise of the power under s.63(1) of the Act of 1985 include: waiving the failure to seek separate sequestrations in respect of the separate estates of a partnership and its individual partners (*Royal Bank of Scotland v. J. & J. Messenger* 1991 S.L.T. 492); waiving the failure to produce the original, instead of a photostat copy, of the sheriff clerk's certificate that a charge was displayed on the walls of court for the days of charge (*Waverley Vintners Ltd v. Matthews* 1991 G.W.D. 19-1130); allowing a trustee's non-timeous application under s.54 of the Act of 1985 to defer the debtor's discharge and ordering interim deferment (*Pattison*, above) although the court has also refused to exercise the power to defer a trustee's similar application in *Whittaker's Tr. v. Whittaker* 1993 G.W.D. 30-1857 (prejudice to debtor, who was pursuing a claim for solatium, outweighed possible prejudice to her creditors).

Rather than seek waiver of failures to comply with statutory obligations over prolonged periods such as accounting periods under r. 7.3 of the Insolvency Rules 1986 and s.13 of the Act of 1985, liquidators

---

[1] R. 72.3 substituted by S.S.I. 2016 No. 312 (effective 30th November 2016).

have been encouraged to apply to the court in advance to fix the length of an accounting period: *Burton, Liquidator of Ben Line Steamers Ltd* [2008] CSOH 75, para. [14]; *Burton, Liquidator of Callanish Ltd* [2012] CSOH 167, para. [7].

Petitions to the *nobile officium* may still be appropriate where, for example, through an unforeseen circumstance a person is denied a remedy afforded by the Act: *Wright v. Tennent Caledonian Breweries Ltd*, 1991 S.L.T. 823 (debtor unable to petition for recall within the 10 week time limit prescribed by the Act, as sequestration itself had only been awarded after the expiry of that period); cf. *Brown v. Middlemas of Kelso Ltd*, 1994 S.L.T. 1352.

"PETITION".

A petition is presented in the Outer House: r. 14.2(h). The petition must be in Form 14.4 in the official printed form: rr. 4.1 and 14.4. The petition must be signed by counsel or other person having a right of audience: r. 4.2; and see r. 1.3(1) (definition of "counsel" and "other person having a right of audience") and note 1.3.4.

The petitioner must lodge the petition with the required steps of process (r. 4.4). A fee is payable on lodging the petition: see note 14.5.10.

On petitions generally, see Chap. 14.

"INTIMATE".

For methods, see r. 16.7.

TRANSFER BACK TO SHERIFF COURT.

Once the court has determined an application the sequestration will be remitted back to the sheriff court. In *Pattison v. Halliday* 1991 S.L.T. 645 the court, after waiving the trustee's failure to apply timeously for deferment of the debtor's discharge under s.63 of the Act of 1985, remitted the sequestration back to the sheriff court to determine the application for deferment.

72.3.2

72.3.3

72.3.4

CHAPTER 73 RECTIFICATION OF DOCUMENTS

Chapter 73

Rectification of Documents

Application of this Chapter

73.1. This Chapter applies to an application under section 8 of the Law Reform (Miscellaneous Provisions) (Scotland) Act 1985 (rectification of defectively expressed documents).

73.1

GENERAL NOTE.

S.8 of the Law Reform (Miscellaneous Provisions) (Scotland) Act 1985 introduced a remedy not previously available where the expression of an agreement or other document is defective. Formerly, if the defect were patent it might be corrected by a favourable construction; but if latent, decree of reduction would have had to be sought: see *North British Insurance Co. v. Tunnock and Fraser* (1864) 3 M. 1; *Anderson v. Lambie* 1954 S.C.(HL) 43, 61 per Lord Reid; *Hudson v. St John* 1977 S.C. 255; cf. *Krupp v. Menzies* 1907 S.C. 903. s.8 of the 1985 Act makes no distinction between patent and latent defects and modifies the rule that parole evidence could not be led to contradict express terms of a written document: *Huewind Ltd v. Clydesdale Bank plc* 1995 S.L.T. 392.

73.1.1

S.8 of the 1985 Act implements the recommendations of the *Scottish Law Commission's Report on Rectification of Contractual and Other Documents* (Scot. Law Com. No. 79).

RECTIFICATION OF DOCUMENTS.

By s.8 of the Law Reform (Miscellaneous Provisions) (Scotland) Act 1985 a document, other than one of a testamentary nature, (a) intended to express or give effect to an agreement which fails to express accurately the common intention of the parties when made or (b) intended to create, transfer, vary or renounce a right which fails to express accurately the intention of the grantor when executed, may be rectified in any manner to give effect to the intention. Any document which would otherwise fall within (a) or (b) above and is defective as a consequence of the defect in the original document may also be rectified by the court at its own instance or on application to it. Proceedings for rectification are not by definition adversarial, a petitioner is not seeking a right against another but asking the court to provide a remedy which only the court can provide; and a petitioner cannot, for example, erect a case on a plea of personal bar: *Bank of Scotland v. Brunswick Developments* (1987) Ltd 1997 S.C. 226, 231B and 232I per L.P. Rodger. The remedy is discretionary: *Norwich Union Life Insurance Society v. Tanap Investments VK Ltd (in liquidation) (No. 3)* 1998 S.C.L.R. 627.

73.1.2

On what the court has to be satisfied for a case, and what must be averred to make the case relevant, under s.8(1)(a) of the 1985 Act, see *Shaw v. William Grant (Minerals) Ltd* 1989 S.L.T. 121; see also *Huewind Ltd v. Clydesdale Bank plc* 1995 S.L.T. 392. It is essential to aver that there is an antecedent agreement from which the parties' common intention can be inferred: *George Thompson Services Ltd v. Moore* 1993 S.L.T. 634.

The phrase "express accurately" covers a range of inaccuracies from errors of expression to errors of omission: *Bank of Scotland v. Graham's Tr.* 1992 S.C. 79, 88 per L.P. Hope. Ground (b) in s.8 of the 1985 Act extends to a mistake relating to the identity of the grantor of a document: *Bank of Scotland v. Brunswick Developments* (1987) Ltd 1995 S.C. 272. The grantor is the person who executed it if he is not the same person as that in whose name it was executed; it is the intention of the person who signs the document at the date it is executed which is in issue when rectification is sought: *Bank of Scotland v. Brunswick Developments*, above per L.P. Hope at p. 278G. For some doubts on the meaning of "grantor" given in that case, see observations of L.P. Rodger and Lord Marnoch in the sequel to that case reported in 1997 S.C. 226, 232C and 236I. In *Norwich Union Life Insurance Society v. Tanap Investments VK Ltd (in liquidation) (No. 3)* 1998 S.C.L.R. 627, the court rejected as too narrow an attempt to limit the application of ss.8 and 9 by reference to a class of error (document failed totally to reflect prior agreement). The court further observed that where parties joined issue on the facts that it would only be in the clearest case that the court could say in advance of proof that the scale or scope and character of amendments proposed went beyond the discretionary power of the court. Rectification might be justified where a document fails to adopt what might by then have become the only way of giving effect to an initial agreement expressed in broad terms: *Norwich Union Life Insurance Society v. Tanap Investments VK Ltd (in liquidation) (No.2)* 2000 S.L.T. 819, 2000 S.C. 515 (Extra Div.).

The phrase "common intention" does not simply mean a shared intention that certain words regardless of their meaning should be inserted into a contract, but that there should be a common intention as to the subject-matter of the agreement and its intended impact on the contract: *Belhaven Brewery Co. v. Swift* 1996 S.L.T.(Sh.Ct) 127, 131L–132A, per Sheriff Principal Nicholson, Q.C.

A document may only be rectified where the court is satisfied (a) that the interests of a person, who has acted or refrained from acting in reliance on the terms of the document or on the title sheet of an interest in the Land Register, would not be adversely affected to a material extent or (b) that that person has consented: 1985 Act, s.9. A party who has obtained a decree of rectification relating to an interest in land on the Land Register may, in order to implement that decree, have to apply to the Keeper of the

Register for rectification under s.9 of the Land Registration (Scotland) Act 1979 as do those who hold a decree of reduction affecting a registered interest: *Short's Tr. v. Keeper of the Registers of Scotland* 1994 S.C. 122, aff'd 1996 S.C.(HL) 14.

Section 8(1)(b) of the Law Reform (Miscellaneous Provisions) (Scotland) Act 1985 cannot be used to change a deed of appointment, validly creating the intended legal right, so as to delay its effect in order to take account of a separate legal rule of which the granter was unaware at the time (which gave a tax advantage): *Nickson's T/ees, Ptnrs*, 2016 S.L.T. 1039 (OH).

It is doubtful whether a document can be rectified vis-a-vis one party but not another: *Belhaven Brewery Co.*, above, at p. 132E.

It is not incompetent to seek an order for rectification which is an alternative to, but inconsistent with, the primary remedy sought in the same action: *Norwich Union Life Insurance Society v. Tanap Investments VK Ltd (in liquidation) (No. 1)* 1998 S.L.T. 623.

The standard of proof is on a balance of probabilities: *Rehman v. Ahmad* 1993 S.L.T. 741 distinguishing *Anderson v. Lambie* 1954 S.C.(HL) 43 (see p. 62 per Lord Reid and p. 69 per Lord Keith of Avonholm). But the presumption that a written document embodies the agreement of the parties is a strong one, and the observations in *Anderson*, above, are pertinent: *Rehman*, above, per Lord Penrose at p. 746C.

JURISDICTION.

73.1.3   The court may have jurisdiction by virtue of para. 13 of Sched. 9 to the C.J.J.A. 1982 (proceedings where no decree sought against a person) or, e.g. under r. 1 (domicile), r. 2(2) (contract), r. 2(9) (declarator of rights), r. 3 (consumer contracts), r. 4(1)(c) (exclusive jurisdiction re public registers), r. 5 (prorogation) of Sched. 8 to the C.J.J.A. 1982 (jurisdiction of Scottish courts), or on the equivalent grounds in Sched. 1 or 3C to the C.J.J.A. 1982. On jurisdiction generally, see notes 13.2.6 to 13.2.15.

PREVENTIVE DILIGENCE.

73.1.4   In a cause with a prayer or conclusion for rectification there is the possibility of preventive diligence in security by means of registration of a notice of the prayer or conclusion: Conveyancing (Scotland) Act 1924, s.44(2) (as amended by the Law Reform (Miscellaneous Provisions) (Scotland) Act 1985, Sched. 2, para. 6).

Form of applications

73.2   **73.2.**—(1) Subject to paragraph (2), an application to which this Chapter applies shall be made by petition.

(2)[1] An application to which this Chapter applies may be made—

(a)[2] in an action to which Chapter 47 (commercial actions) applies, by summons or by a conclusion ancillary to other conclusions in the summons or in a counterclaim; or

(b)[3] in any other action, by a conclusion in a summons or in a counterclaim.

Deriv. RCS 1965, r. 189(xxxi) inserted by S.I. 1987 No. 2160

GENERAL NOTE.

73.2.1   R. 73.2(1) restates the general rule that any applications to the court under any enactment which is not in a depending cause shall be made by petition to the Outer House: r. 14.2(h). The purpose of this Chapter and this rule is also to allow an application under s. 8 of the Law Reform (Miscellaneous Provisions) (Scotland) Act 1985 to be made by a conclusion ancillary to other conclusions in a summons or in a counterclaim. The converse, seeking declarator in a petition for rectification, is not competent: *Renyana-Stah Anstalt v. MacGregor*, 2001 S.L.T. 1247 (OH).

On rectification, see notes to r. 73.1.

"PETITION".

73.2.2   A petition under this Chapter is presented to the Outer House: r. 14.2(h). The petition must be in Form 14.4 in the official printed form: rr. 4.1 and 14.4. The petition must be signed by counsel or other person having a right of audience: r. 4.2; and see r. 1.3(1) (definition of "counsel" and "other person having a right of audience") and note 1.3.4.

The petitioner must lodge the petition with the required steps of process (r. 4.4). A fee is payable on lodging the petition: see note 14.5.10.

On petitions generally, see Chap. 14.

---

[1] Rule 73.2(2) amended by S.I 1994 No. 2310 (effective 20th September 1994)
[2] Rule 73.2(2)(a) and (b) as amended by S.S.I. 2000 No. 66 para. 2(8) (effective 7th April 2000).
[3] Rule 73.2(2)(a) and (b) as amended by S.S.I. 2000 No. 66 para. 2(8) (effective 7th April 2000).

A dispute as to the terms of an agreement may arise in a wide variety of litigation. A pursuer in an action concerning the terms of a written agreement may seek rectification of the agreement as part of the same process.

73.2.3

Where rectification is sought in a dispute to which the definition of commercial action in r. 47.1(2) would apply, that remedy may be sought by bringing an action by summons which is a commercial action either for that remedy alone or as ancillary to other remedies sought: r. 73.2(2)(a). This provision enables a (commercial) action to be brought for rectification alone, as otherwise the remedy would have to be sought by petition.

It is not incompetent to conclude for rectification of a document as a conclusion alternative to a principal conclusion of declarator that a document has a specific effect: *Norwich Union Life Insurance Society v. Tanap Investments VK Ltd (in liquidation) (No. 1)* 1998 S.L.T. 623.

For actions generally, see Chap. 13.

Counterclaims.

A defender may seek rectification of a deed in a counterclaim by virtue of, and subject to the conditions of, r. 25.1(1). In *Euan Wallace & Partners v. Westscot Homes plc* 2000 S.L.T. 327, 331F–G Lord Macfadyen noted that there was believed to be some doubt as to whether rectification could be sought in a counterclaim and expressed the opinion (without reference to the first sentence of this note) that the effect of r. 73.2(2)(a) read with r. 25.1(1)(a) was that it was competent. Inspite of both these comments it was somehow thought necessary to spell it out in an amendment to r. 73.2(2) by A.S. (R.C.S.A.) (Miscellaneous) 2000 [S.S.I. 2000 No. 66]. Apparently neither Lord Macfadyen nor the annotation to this rule is regarded as sufficiently authoritative.

73.2.4

CHAPTER 74 COMPANIES

Part I – General Provisions

Application and interpretation of this Chapter

74.1.—[1](1)   This Chapter applies to causes under—

(a)[2]   the Insolvency Act 1986; and

(b)   the Company Directors Disqualification Act 1986; and

(c)[3]   Chapter 3 of Part 3 of the Energy Act 2004; and

(d)[4]   Parts 2 or 3 of the Banking Act 2009; and

(e)[5]   Chapter 5 of Part 2 of the Energy Act 2011; and

(f)[6]   Part 4 of the Postal Services Act 2011; and

(g)[7]   the Payment and Electronic Money Institution Insolvency Regulations 2021.

(2)[8]   In this Chapter—

"the Act of 1986" means the Insolvency Act 1986;

"the Act of 2004" means the Energy Act 2004[9];

"the Act of 2009" means the Banking Act 2009[10];

"the Act of 2011" means the Energy Act 2011[11];

"the Act of 2020" means the Corporate Insolvency and Governance Act 2020[12];

"the Bank Administration Rules" means the Bank Administration (Scotland) Rules 2009;[13]

"the Bank Insolvency Rules" means the Bank Insolvency (Scotland) Rules 2009;[14]

"the Insolvency Rules" means the Insolvency (Scotland) Rules 1986;

"the Insolvency (CVAA) Rules" means the Insolvency (Scotland) (Company Voluntary Arrangements and Administration) Rules 2018;[15]

"the Insolvency (RWU) Rules" means the Insolvency (Scotland) (Receivership and Winding up) Rules 2018;

"the Insolvency (CVAA) Rules" means the Insolvency (Scotland) (Company Voluntary Arrangements and Administration) Rules 2018;[16]

---

[1] Rule 74.1 as amended by S.S.I. 2020 No. 440 (effective IP completion day, 31st December 2020).

[2] Rule 74.1(1)(a) amended by S.I. 1996 No. 1756 (effective 5th August 1996).

[3] Rule 74.1(1)(c) and definitions inserted by S.S.I. 2006 No. 83 (effective 17th March 2006).

[4] Rule 74.1(1)(d) and definitions inserted and r. 74.1(3) amended by S.S.I. 2009 No. 63 r. 3 (effective 25th February 2009).

[5] Rule 74.1(1)(e) inserted by S.S.I. 2013 No. 162 (effective 4th June 2013).

[6] Rule 74.1(1)(f) inserted by S.S.I. 2016 No. 318 (effective 16th November 2016).

[7] As inserted by the Act of Sederunt (Rules of the Court of Session 1994 Amendment) (Payment and Electronic Money Institution Special Administration) 2024 S.S.I. 2024 No. 75 r. 2(3) (effective 12th April 2024).

[8] Rule 74.1(2) amended by S.S.I. 2003 No. 385 (effective 15th September 2003) and substituted by S.S.I. 2007 No. 449 (effective 25th October 2007).

[9] Rule 74.1(1)(c) and definitions inserted by S.S.I. 2006 No. 83 (effective 17th March 2006).

[10] Rule 74.1(1)(d) and definitions inserted and r. 74.1(3) amended by S.S.I. 2009 No. 63 r. 3 (effective 25th February 2009).

[11] Definition inserted by S.S.I. 2013 No. 162 (effective 4th June 2013).

[12] Definition inserted by S.S.I. 2020 No. 208 r.2(2) (effective 1st July 2020).

[13] Rule 74.1(1)(d) and definitions inserted and r. 74.1(3) amended by S.S.I. 2009 No. 63 r. 3 (effective 25th February 2009).

[14] Rule 74.1(1)(d) and definitions inserted and r. 74.1(3) amended by S.S.I. 2009 No. 63 r. 3 (effective 25th February 2009).

[15] Definition inserted by S.S.I. 2019 No. 81 (effective 6 April 2019).

[16] Definition inserted by S.S.I. 2019 No. 81 (effective 6 April 2019).

"the Investment Bank Regulations" means the Investment Bank Special Administration Regulations 2011;[1]

"the Investment Bank Rules" means the Investment Bank Special Administration (Scotland) Rules 2011;[2]

"the Energy Administration Rules" means the Energy Administration (Scotland) Rules 2006;[3]

"the 2013 Rules" means the Energy Supply Company Administration (Scotland) Rules 2013[4];

"the Council Regulation" means Regulation (EU) 2015/848 of the European Parliament and of the Council of 20th May 2015 on insolvency proceedings, as amended from time to time[5];

"centre of main interests" has the same meaning as in the Council Regulation;

"establishment" has the same meaning as in Article 2(10) of the Council Regulation;[6]

"Member State" means a Member State of the European Community that has adopted the Council Regulation;

"non GB company" shall have the meaning assigned in section 171 of the Act of 2004;[7]

"the Postal Act" means the Postal Services Act 2011[8];

"the Postal Administration Rules" means the Postal Administration (Scotland) Rules 2016[9];

"registered office"[10] means—

    (i)   the place specified in the statement of the company delivered to the registrar of companies under section 9 of the Companies Act 2006 as the intended place of its registered office on incorporation, or

   (ii)   where notice has been given by the company to the registrar of companies under section 87 of the Companies Act 2006 of a change of registered office, the place specified in the last such notice;

(3)[11, 12, 13, 14, 15] Unless the context otherwise requires, words and expressions used in this Chapter which are also used in the Act of 1986, Chapter 3 of Part 3 of the Act of 2004, Parts 2 or 3 of the Act of 2009, Chapter 5 of Part 2 of the Act of 2011, Part 4 of the Postal Act, the Insolvency Rules, the Insolvency (CVAA) Rules, the Insolvency (RWU) Rules, the Bank Insolvency Rules, the Bank Administration

---

[1] Definition inserted by S.S.I. 2011 No. 385 para. 3 (effective 14th November 2011).

[2] Definition inserted by S.S.I. 2011 No. 385 para. 3 (effective 14th November 2011).

[3] Rule 74.1(1)(c) and definitions inserted by S.S.I. 2006 No. 83 (effective 17th March 2006).

[4] Definition inserted by S.S.I. 2013 No. 162 (effective 4th June 2013).

[5] Definition substituted by S.S.I. 2017 No. 202 r. 3(3)(a) (effective 26th June 2017: substitution has effect subject to savings specified in S.S.I. 2017 No. 202 r. 6).

[6] Definition amended by S.S.I. 2017 No. 202 r. 3(3)(b) (effective 26th June 2017: amendment has effect subject to savings specified in S.S.I. 2017 No. 202 r. 6).

[7] Rule 74.1(1)(c) and definitions inserted by S.S.I. 2006 No. 83 (effective 17th March 2006).

[8] Definition inserted by S.S.I. 2016 No. 318 (effective 16 November 2016).

[9] Definition inserted by S.S.I. 2016 No. 318 (effective 16 November 2016).

[10] Definition substituted by S.S.I. 2009 No. 450 (effective 25th January 2010).

[11] Rule 74.1(3) substituted by S.S.I. 2006 No. 83 (effective 17 March 2006).

[12] Rule 74.1(1)(d) and definitions inserted and r. 74.1(3) amended by S.S.I. 2009 No. 63 r. 3 (effective 25th February 2009).

[13] Rule 74.1(3) amended by S.S.I. 2013 No. 162 (effective 4 June 2013).

[14] Rule 74.1(3) amended by S.S.I. 2016 No. 318 (effective 16 November 2016).

[15] Rule 74.1(3) amended by S.S.I. 2019 No. 81 (effective 6 April 2019).

Rules, the Energy Administration Rules, the 2013 rules or the Postal Administration Rules have the same meaning as in those Acts or Rules, as the case may be.

Deriv. R.C.S. 1965, r. 202(1) (part) and (2) substituted by S.I. 1986 No. 2298 (r. 74.1(2) and (3))

Co-operation between courts.

s. 426(1) of the Act of 1986 provides that an order made by a court in any part of the UK in exercise of its jurisdiction in relation to insolvency law shall be enforced in any other part of the UK. S.426(2) provides that nothing in subsection (1) requires a court to enforce any such order in relation to property in that other part of the UK. No statutory provision is made for the means of enforcement. The order would be enforced by a petition to the insolvency judge for an appropriate order to enforce it.

74.1.1

S. 426(4) of the Act of 1986 provides that courts having jurisdiction in relation to insolvency law in the UK shall assist courts having corresponding jurisdiction in any other part of the UK or any relevant country or territory. For this purpose a request may be made to a court by any other such court to apply the insolvency law applicable by either court: Act of 1986, s. 426(5). A request is made by petition by a party to the proceedings before that court.

Orders have been made by statutory instrument in respect of a "relevant country or territory" in s. 426 of the Act of 1986. These are the Co-operation of Insolvency Courts (Designation of Relevant Countries and Territories Order 1986 [S.I. 1986 No. 2123] and the Co-operation of Insolvency Courts (Designation of Relevant Countries) Order 1996 [S.I. 1996 No. 253] and the Co-operation of Insolvency Courts (Designation of Relevant Country) Order 1998 [S.I. 1998/2766]. The countries and territories are listed below (unless otherwise specified in brackets the relevant S.I. is that of 1986):

Anguilla	Hong Kong
Australia	Republic of Ireland
The Bahamas	Malaysia (S.I. 1996 No. 253)
Bermuda	Montserrat
Botswana	New Zealand
Brunei Darussalam (S.I. 1998 No. 2766)	St Helena
Canada	South Africa (S.I. 1996 No. 253)
Cayman Islands	Turks and Caicos Islands
Falkland Islands	Tuvalu
Gibraltar	Virgin Islands

Proceedings before insolvency judge

74.2.[1, 2, 3](1)   All proceedings in the Outer House in a cause under or by virtue of the an enactment mentioned in paragraph (2) shall be brought before a judge of the court nominated by the Lord President as the insolvency judge or, where the insolvency judge is not available, any other judge of the court (including the vacation judge): and "insolvency judge" shall be construed accordingly.

74.2

(2)   The enactments referred to in paragraph (1) are—

(a)   the Act of 1986;

(b)   the Company Directors Disqualification Act 1986;

(c)   Chapter 3 of Part 3 of the Act of 2004;

(d)   Part 2 or 3 of the Act of 2009;

(e)   Part 4 of the Postal Act;

(f)   the Payment and Electronic Money Institution Insolvency Regulations 2021.

Deriv. R.C.S. 1965, r. 202(1) (part) substituted by S.I. 1986 No. 2298 and r. 218Q(2) (part) inserted by S.I. 1986 No. 2298

---

[1] Rule 74.2 substituted by S.S.I. 2006 No. 83 (effective 17th March 2006) and by S.S.I. 2009 No. 63 r. 3 (effective 25th February 2009).

[2] Rule 74.2 amended by S.S.I. 2016 No. 318 (effective 16th November 2016).

[3] As amended by the Act of Sederunt (Rules of the Court of Session 1994 Amendment) (Payment and Electronic Money Institution Special Administration) 2024 S.S.I. 2024 No. 75 r. 2(4) (effective 12th April 2024).

"INSOLVENCY JUDGE".

74.2.1   The insolvency judge is appointed in part by virtue of s. 121(1) of the Act of 1986 which provides for the court by A.S. to provide for proceedings for winding up to be heard by one of the Lords Ordinary.

The current insolvency judges are Lords Clark, Ericht, Braid and Harrower.

"VACATION JUDGE".

74.2.2   The powers of the vacation judge are limited by r. 11.1.

Notices and reports, etc., sent to the court

74.3   **74.3.**[1, 2, 3, 4](1)   Where, under an enactment mentioned in paragraph (2)—

(a)   notice of a fact is to be given to the court,

(b)   a report is to be made, or sent, to the court, or

(c)   any other document is to be sent to the court,

it shall be sent to the Deputy Principal Clerk who shall cause it to be lodged in the process to which it relates.

(2)   The enactments referred to in paragraph (1) are—

(a)   the Act of 1986;

(b)   the Act of 2004;

(c)   the Act of 2009;

(d)   the Act of 2011;

(e)   the Postal Act;

(f)   the Insolvency Rules;

(g)   the Insolvency (CVAA) Rules;

(h)   the Insolvency (RWU) Rules;

(i)   the Bank Insolvency Rules;

(j)   the Bank Administration Rules;

(k)   the Energy Administration Rules;

(l)   the 2013 Rules;

(m)   the Postal Administration Rules;

(n)   the Payment and Electronic Money Institution Insolvency Regulations 2021;

(o)   the Payment and Electronic Money Institution Insolvency (Scotland) Rules 2022.

Deriv. R.C.S. 1965, r. 218S inserted by S.I. 1986 No. 2298

"REPORT".

74.3.1   A report may be lodged to assist the court in deciding, inter alia, whether the appointment of an administrator is expedient (see Insolvency Rules r. 2.2) or whether a petition for the reduction of capital under s. 135 of the Companies Act 1985 should be granted. A report may be lodged by an inspector appointed to investigate a company's officers under Pt. XIV of the 1985 Act, or by a nominee for the purposes of a voluntary arrangement under Pt. I of the Act of 1986.

"SENT".

74.3.2   This includes deliver: r. 1.3(1) (definition of "send").

"DOCUMENT".

74.3.3   This may include, e.g. minutes of a meeting of members or directors (which are prima facie evidence that the meeting was duly held and convened and that the proceedings recorded took place: 1985 Act s.

---

[1] Rule 74.3 substituted by S.S.I. 2006 No. 83 (effective 17th March 2006) and amended by S.S.I. 2009 No. 63 r. 3 (effective 25th February 2009).

[2] Rule 74.3 amended by the S.S.I. 2013 No. 162 r. 5(2) (effective 4th June 2013).

[3] Rule 74.3 amended by S.S.I. 2016 No. 318 (effective 16th November 2016).

[4] As amended by the Act of Sederunt (Rules of the Court of Session 1994 Amendment) (Payment and Electronic Money Institution Special Administration) 2024 S.S.I. 2024 No. 75 r. 2(5) (effective 12th April 2024).

382(4)). See also the probative effect, accorded by s. 5(1) of the Civil Evidence (Scotland) Act 1988, to all memoranda, articles and minutes of meetings, if duly docqueted with a certificate by an officer (usually the secretary) of the company.

Replacement office-holders and liquidators: block transfer orders

74.3A.—[1](1)   This rule applies to an application under—

   (a)   rule 4.2(1) of the Insolvency (CVAA) Rules (application for a block transfer order);

   (b)   rule 6.2(1) of the Insolvency (RWU) Rules (application for block transfer order); and

   (c)   both of those rules.

(2)   An application mentioned in paragraph (1) must be made by petition.

(3)   Paragraph (4) applies where an application includes the name of one or more sheriff court petition.

(4)   The Deputy Principal Clerk must notify the sheriff clerk of every sheriff court listed in the application that an application has been made.

(5)   Where the court grants an application, it may order the replacement office-holder or the replacement liquidator, as the case may be, to be appointed in any or all of the cases listed in the application.

(6)   Where the court pronounces an interlocutor granting a block transfer order—

   (a)   the Deputy Principal Clerk must send a certified copy of that interlocutor to the replacement office-holder or, as the case may be, the replacement liquidator;

   (b)   the court may direct that a copy of the interlocutor is—

      (i)   to be put in the process of every Court of Session petition where the replacement office-holder or, as the case may be, the replacement liquidator has been appointed;

      (ii)   to be sent to the sheriff clerk to be put in the process of every sheriff court petition where the replacement office-holder or, as the case may be, the replacement liquidator has been appointed; and

   (c)   the court may make such orders as it thinks fit for the intimation and advertisement of the appointment of the replacement office-holder or, as the case may be, the replacement liquidator.

(7)   In this rule the *"office-holder"* means a supervisor, nominee or administrator.

Decision making

74.3B.—[2, 3](1)   An application—

   (a)   for an order under rule 5.12(1) of the Insolvency (CVAA) Rules or rule 8.12(1) of the Insolvency (RWU) Rules (notice of decision procedure by advertisement only);

   (b)   for directions under rule 8.18(4) of the Insolvency (RWU) Rules (application for directions about decision procedure);

   (c)[4]   for a direction under rules 5.22 or 5.22A of the Insolvency (CVAA) Rules or rule 8.23 of the Insolvency (RWU) Rules (adjournment by chair);

   (d)   for a direction under rule 5.33(3)(b) or 5.40(3)(b) of the Insolvency

74.3A

74.3B

---

[1] Rule 74.3A inserted by S.S.I. 2019 No. 81 (effective 6th April 2019).
[2] Rule 74.3B inserted by S.S.I. 2019 No. 81 (effective 6th April 2019).
[3] Rule 74.3B amended by S.S.I. 2020 No. 198 (effective 1st July 2020).
[4] As amended by the Act of Sederunt (Rules of the Court of Session 1994 and Sheriff Court Company Insolvency Rules Amendment) (Insolvency) 2021 (S.S.I. 2021 No. 324) art. 2(2) (effective 1st October 2021).

(CVAA) Rules or rule 8.36(3)(b) or 8.44(3)(b) of the Insolvency (RWU) Rules (direction as to validity of meeting with excluded person present);

(e)   for directions under rule 5.35(9) or 5.42(9) of the Insolvency (CVAA) Rules or rule 8.38(9) or 8.46(9) of the Insolvency (RWU) Rules (application to court for directions about action of appropriate person),

must be made by petition or, where a previous application or appeal to the court in relation to any moratorium, company voluntary arrangement, liquidation, administration or receivership of the company has been made, by note in the process of that petition.

(2) An appeal under rule 5.32 of the Insolvency (CVAA) Rules or rule 8.35 of the Insolvency (RWU) Rules (appeals against decisions about creditors' voting rights and majorities) must be made by petition or, where a previous application or appeal to the court in relation to any moratorium, company voluntary arrangement, liquidation, administration or receivership of the company has been made, by note in the process of that petition.

Moratoriums—general

74.3C **74.3C.**—[1](1) A moratorium to be obtained by lodging the relevant documents in court must be—

(a)   lodged in the Petition Department;

(b)   marked by the clerk of session receiving them with the time and date on which they are lodged and a certified copy of them so marked provided to the directors.

(2) An application to the court for a moratorium must be made—

(a)   where the eligible company is subject to an outstanding winding-up petition, by note in the process of that petition; or

(b)   in all other cases, by petition.

(3) Where the court grants an application mentioned in paragraphs (2), (6)(c) or (d), the Deputy Principal Clerk must provide forthwith a certified copy of the interlocutor to the applicant.

(4) An extension of a moratorium under section A10 (extension by directors without creditor consent) or A11 (extension by directors with creditor consent) of the Act of 1986, to be obtained by lodging the documents mentioned in section A10(1) or A11(1), respectively, and a notice of extension, must be—

(a)   lodged in the Petition Department;

(b)   marked by the clerk of session receiving them with the time and date on which they are lodged and a certified copy of them so marked provided to the directors.

(5) Termination of a moratorium by the monitor under section A38(1) (termination of moratorium by monitor) of the Act of 1986, to be obtained by lodging the notice mentioned in that subsection and copy notice mentioned in rule 1A.20(2)(a)(i) of the Insolvency (CVAA) Rules (notice bringing the moratorium to an end (section A28)), must be—

(a)   lodged in the Petition Department;

(b)   marked by the clerk of session receiving them with the time and date on which they are lodged and a certified copy of them so marked provided to the monitor.

(6) Paragraph (7) applies to an application to the court under—

---

[1] Rules 74.3C, 74.3CA substituted for r. 74.3C by the Act of Sederunt (Rules of the Court of Session 1994 and Sheriff Court Company Insolvency Rules Amendment) (Insolvency) 2021 (S.S.I. 2021 No. 324) art. 2(3) (effective 1st October 2021).

(a) section A13(1) (extension by court on application of directors);
(b) section A21(1) (restrictions on enforcement and legal proceedings);
(c) section A31(1) (disposal of charged property free from charge);
(d) section A32(1) (disposal of hire-purchase property);
(e) section A37 (application by monitor for directions);
(f) section A39(1) or (2) (replacement of monitor or appointment of additional monitor);
(g) section A42(1) (challenge to monitor's actions);
(h) rules under section A43(1) (challenges to monitor remuneration in insolvency proceedings);
(i) section A44(1) (challenge to directors' actions),

of the Act of 1986.

(7) Where this paragraph applies, an application to the court must be made—

(a) where the eligible company is subject to an outstanding winding-up petition, by note in the process of that petition;
(b) where the application for the moratorium was made by petition, by note in the process of that petition; or
(c) in all other cases, by petition.

(8) An application to the court under section A13(1) of the Act of 1986 must be marked by the clerk of session receiving it with the time and date on which it is lodged and a certified copy of the application so marked provided to the directors.

GENERAL NOTE

Moratoriums were introduced in the Act of 1986 by the Corporate Insolvency and Governance Act 2020 to help U.K. companies and similar entities by easing the burden on businesses and helping them avoid insolvency during the period of economic uncertainty caused by the Covid-19 pandemic. They are to allow companies breathing space to explore options for rescue whilst supplies are protected, to provide restructuring options free from creditor action and to suspend temporarily parts of insolvency law to support directors to continue to trade through the emergency without the threat of personal liability and to protect companies from aggressive creditor action. See the Explanatory Notes to the 2020 Act.

A moratorium, for example, will allow a company, without the need for an insolvency procedure, to enter into a voluntary scheme of arrangement (CVA) under Pt. 1 of the Act of 1986 (which does not affect the rights of secured creditors without their consent), a scheme of arrangement under Pt. 26 of the Companies Act 2006 (in which classes of creditors must vote in favour of it—75% by value and a majority by number of each class) or a restructuring under the new Pt. 26A of the 2006 Act (which, for example, can bind classes of creditors even though they have not voted in favour of it). As with a scheme of arrangement, a restructuring has to be approved by the court which has discretion whether to sanction it (see s. A4(5) of the Act of 1986).

There are restrictions on petitions to wind up a company during a moratorium. See Sched. 10 to the 2020 Act.

A moratorium is sought from the court, lasts initially for 20 business days but may be extended before coming to an end (see s. A9 of the Act of 1986), is available to "eligible" companies (see s. A2 and Sched. ZA1) and is overseen by an insolvency practitioner (called a "monitor"; see s. A7(2)).

"NOTE"

See r. 15.2.

"PETITION"

See Chap. 14. The petition will be presented in the Outer House: r. 14.2(h).

Moratoriums—service

74.3CA.[1] Unless the court otherwise directs, the order under rule 14.5 (first order in petitions), or rule 15.2(3) (applications by note), for intimation, service and advertisement must include a requirement to serve the petition or, as the case may be, note—

74.3C.1

74.3C.2

74.3C.3

74.3CA

---

[1] Rules 74.3C, 74.3CA substituted for r. 74.3C by the Act of Sederunt (Rules of the Court of Session 1994 and Sheriff Court Company Insolvency Rules Amendment) (Insolvency) 2021 (S.S.I. 2021 No. 324) art.2(3) (effective 1st October 2021).

(a) on the company and the monitor, where the application is made under section A21(1) or A42(1);

(b) on the holder of the security interest and the monitor, where the application is made under section A31(1);

(c) on the owner of the property and the monitor, where the application is made under section A32(1);

(d) on the company, where the application is made under section A37;

(e) on the monitor where the application is made by the directors, or on the directors where the application is made by the monitor, under section A39(1) or (2);

(f) on the directors and the monitor, where the application is made under section A43(1) or A44(1),

of the Act of 1986.

GENERAL NOTE

74.3CA.1 Section A21 of the 1986 Act deals with restrictions on irritancy, enforcement of security, repossession of goods, and legal process. Section 42 deals with challenges to a monitor's actions. Section 31 deals with applications to the court by a company for permission to dispose of property subject to a security interest, and s. A32 deals with applications to dispose of goods subject to a hire-purchase agreement. Section A37 deals with applications by a monitor for directions and s. A39 deals with the replacement of a monitor, or appointment of an additional monitor. Sections 43 and 44 deal with challenges to a monitor's remuneration in insolvency proceedings and challenges to directors' actions respectively.

"INTIMATION, SERVICE"

74.3CA.2 See Chap. 16.

Moratoriums—regulated companies

74.3D **74.3D.**[1] An application under any of the following sections of the Act of 1986 in relation to a regulated company is to be intimated to the appropriate regulator (as those persons are defined in section A49(13) of that Act (regulated companies: modifications to this Part))—

(a) section A31(1);

(b) section A32(1);

(c) section A39(1);

(d) section A42(1);

(e) section A44(1).

GENERAL NOTE

74.3D.1 During a moratorium, a regulated company may, with the permission of the court, dispose of property subject to a security interest as if it were not subject to the security interest, or dispose of goods subject to a hire purchase agreement: see Act of 1986, ss. A31 and A32. The court may replace a monitor or appoint an additional monitor: s. A39. Certain persons may challenge a monitor's actions: s. A42. A creditor or member of a regulated company may apply to the court to challenge the directors' actions: s. A44.

In these cases, the proceedings must be intimated to the appropriate regulator as specified in s. A49(13) of the Act of 1986. A "regulated company" is defined in that subsection.

"INTIMATED"

74.3D.2 See r. 16.7.

Moratoriums—challenge to monitor's remuneration

74.3E **74.3E.**[2] [3]An application to the court under rule 1A.24 of the Insolvency (CVAA) Rules (challenges to monitor's remuneration in subsequent insolvency proceedings) must be made—

---

[1] Rule 74.3D inserted by S.S.I. 2020 No. 198 r. 2(4) (effective 1st July 2020).

[2] Rule 74.3E inserted by S.S.I. 2020 No. 198 r. 2(4) (effective 1st July 2020).

[3] As amended by the Act of Sederunt (Rules of the Court of Session 1994 and Sheriff Court Company Insolvency Rules Amendment) (Insolvency) 2021 (S.S.I. 2021 No. 324) art.2(4) (effective 1st October 2021).

(a)　where the company is in administration or being wound-up by the court, by note in the process of those insolvency proceedings; or

(b)　in all other cases, by petition.

GENERAL NOTE

An administrator or liquidator of a company may apply to the court on the ground that the remuneration charged by the monitor in relation to a prior moratorium was excessive: Insolvency (Scotland) (Company Voluntary Arrangement and Administration) Rules 2018 [S.S.I. 2018 No. 1082] r. 1A.24.

74.3E.1

"NOTE"

See r. 15.2.

74.3E.2

"PETITION"

See Chap. 14. The petition will be presented in the Outer House: r. 14.2(h).

74.3E.3

Part II – Company Voluntary Arrangements

Lodging of nominee's report (company not in liquidation etc.)

74.4.—(1)[1]　This rule applies where the company is not being wound up by the court and is not in administration.

74.4

(2)　A report of a nominee submitted to the court under section 2(2) of the Act of 1986 (procedure where nominee is not the liquidator or administrator) shall be—

(a)　lodged, with a covering letter, in the Petition Department;

(b)　marked by the clerk of session receiving it with the date on which it is received; and

(c)　placed before the insolvency judge for consideration of any direction which he may make under section 3(1) of that Act (which relates to the summoning of meetings).

(3)　An application by a nominee to extend the time within which he may submit his report under section 2(2) of the Act of 1986 shall be made by letter addressed to the Deputy Principal Clerk who shall—

(a)　place the letter before the insolvency judge for determination;

(b)　intimate that determination by a written reply; and

(c)　attach the letter, and a copy of the reply, to the nominee's report when it is subsequently lodged.

Deriv. R.C.S. 1965, r. 203(1) to (5) substituted by S.I. 1986 No. 2298

GENERAL note.

Voluntary arrangements were introduced by Part I of the Act of 1986 as a simplified alternative to the cumbersome procedure for schemes of arrangement prescribed in s. 425 of the Companies Act 1985 but which would nonetheless be binding on the company's creditors. The purpose of proceeding by way of a voluntary arrangement is to enable an insolvent or near insolvent company to involve an independent person, who must be an insolvency practitioner, to convene a meeting of the company's creditors for the purpose of approving "a composition in satisfaction of [the company's] debts or a scheme of arrangement of its affairs": Act of 1986, s. 1(1). The proposal for a voluntary arrangement may be made by the directors of a company to which an administrator or liquidator has not been appointed: Act of 1986, s. 1(1). It is probably sufficient for this purpose that the proposal is made by a resolution of the board of directors (by analogy with *Re Equiticorp International plc* [1989] B.C.L.C. 597 (concerning the presentation of a petition for administration)) rather than by all of the directors (*Re Instrumentation Electrical Services Ltd* [1988] B.C.L.C. 550). A proposal for a voluntary arrangement may also be made by an administrator or a liquidator where an administration order is in force or where the company is being wound up: Act of 1986, s. 1(3); see r. 74.5 and note 74.5.1.

74.4.1

Directors proposing a voluntary arrangement must give notice of the proposal to a "nominee", who must also be given a copy of the proposal and a statement of the company's affairs: Act of 1986, s. 2(3). The nominee must be an insolvency practitioner: Act of 1986, s. 1(2). If the nominee agrees to act, he must docquet the notice and return it to the company forthwith: Insolvency Rules, r. 1.4. The purpose of supplying the prescribed information is to enable an independent person to form a view, on the basis of sufficient information, as to the feasibility of the proposal. The Insolvency Rules prescribe what information must be contained in the proposal (r. 1.3) and statement of affairs (r. 1.5). The nominee has powers to

---

[1] Rule 74.4(1) amended by S.S.I. 2003 No. 385 (effective 15th September 2003).

require the directors to give him certain additional information or to give him access to the company's accounts and records: Insolvency Rules, r. 1.6. It is on the basis of this information that the nominee makes his report to the court, which must be made within 28 days of notice of the proposal (or such longer period as the court may allow): Act of 1986, s. 2(2). In his report the nominee states whether meetings of the company and its creditors should be summoned to consider the proposal and, if such meetings should be summoned, the proposed dates, times and places of those meetings: Act of 1986, s. 2(2). Where the nominee is of the view that meetings should be summoned, the nominee shall (unless the court otherwise directs) summon those meetings on the specified dates and at the specified times and places: Act of 1986, s. 3(1). The Insolvency Rules prescribe the persons to whom notice of the meetings must be given (in the case of creditors' meetings, this requires notice to be given to all creditors specified in the statement of affairs and all other creditors of whose claims and addresses the nominee is aware: Act of 1986, s. 3(2)) as well as the contents of those notices (which must include a copy of the proposal and a copy of the statement of affairs or a summary thereof): Insolvency Rules, r. 1.9.

Lodging of nominee's report (company in liquidation etc.)

74.5

74.5.—(1)[1] This rule applies where the company is being wound up by the court or is in administration.

(2) In this rule, "process" means the process of the petition under section 9 (petition for administration order), or section 124 (petition to wind up a company), of the Act of 1986, as the case may be.

(3) A report of a nominee submitted to the court under section 2(2) of the Act of 1986 (procedure where nominee is not the liquidator or administrator) shall be—

  (a) lodged in process; and

  (b) placed before the insolvency judge for consideration of any direction which he may make under section 3(1) of that Act.

(4) An application by a nominee to extend the time within which he may submit his report under section 2(2) of the Act of 1986 shall be made by letter addressed to the Deputy Principal Clerk who shall—

  (a) place the letter before the insolvency judge for determination;

  (b) intimate that determination by a written reply; and

  (c) lodge the letter, and a copy of the reply, in the process of the petition to which it relates.

Deriv. R.C.S. 1965, r. 204(1) to (5) substituted by S.I. 1986 No. 2298

General note.

74.5.1

For an explanation of the purpose of a voluntary arrangement and the role of the nominee, see note 74.4.1. A proposal for a voluntary arrangement may also be made by an administrator or liquidator, as the case may be, where an administration order is in force in respect of the company or where the company is being wound up: Act of 1986, s. 1(3). Where the proposal is made by the administrator or liquidator, and where the administrator or liquidator is himself to act as nominee, no report is made to the court by him. The nominee, however, is still required to summon the meetings and to send out the prescribed notices to the prescribed persons. In addition, the proposal by the directors must also contain a list of the names and addresses of the company's preferential creditors, together with details of their claims. Where a proposal for a voluntary arrangement is made by an administrator or liquidator, but another insolvency practitioner is to act as nominee, the administrator or liquidator must give notice to the intended nominee, and must provide him with the same prescribed information (i.e. the proposal and statement of affairs) as is required of directors: Insolvency Rules, r. 1.12.

"lodged in process", "lodge the letter, and a copy of the reply, in the process".

74.5.2

The report of the nominee, and any application by him to extend the time for lodging it, are lodged in process as steps of process (r. 1.3(1) (definition of "step of process")). On lodging steps of process, see r. 4.4. The documents may be lodged by post: P.N. No. 4 of 1994, paras. 1 and 8; and see note 4.4.10.

Inspection of nominee's report

74.6

74.6. A person who states in a letter addressed to the Deputy Principal Clerk that he is a creditor, member or director of the company or his agent, may, on payment of the appropriate fee, inspect the nominee's report lodged under rule 74.4(2) (company not in liquidation etc.) or 74.5(3) (company in liquidation etc.), as the case may be.

Deriv. R.C.S. 1965, r. 203(6) and r. 204(6) substituted by S.I. 1986 No. 2298

---

[1] Rule 74.5(1) amended by S.S.I. 2003 No. 385 (effective 15th September 2003).

For an explanation of the contents of the nominee's report, and the purpose for which the nominee is appointed, see note 74.4.1.

74.6.1

FEE.

No fee is laid down in the Court of Session Fees etc. Order 1984 [S.I. 1984 No. 256, Table substituted by S.I. 1993 No. 427].

74.6.2

Report of meetings and decisions to approve arrangement

74.7.[1] The report of the result of a meeting to be sent to the court under section 4(6) and a decision of the company's creditors to be reported to the court under section 4(6A)(a) of the Act of 1986 shall be sent to the Deputy Principal Clerk who shall lodge it—

74.7

(a) in a case to which rule 74.4 (lodging of nominee's report (company not in liquidation etc.)) applies, with the nominee's report lodged under that rule; or

(b) in a case to which rule 74.5 (lodging of nominee's report (company in liquidation etc.)) applies, in process as defined by paragraph (2) of that rule.

Deriv. R.C.S. 1965, r. 206 substituted by S.I. 1986 No. 2298

GENERAL NOTE.

The report of the meetings to consider the voluntary arrangement summoned under s. 3 of the Act of 1986 is sent to the court. If the company is in liquidation or subject to an administration order, the court has to decide what to do with the winding up or the administration order: Act of 1986, s. 5.

74.7.1

The meetings of the creditors of the company and of the company are summoned by the nominee (Act of 1986, s. 3(1) or, where the administrator or liquidator himself acts as nominee, by that person (s. 3(2) of that Act). The purpose of the meetings is to decide whether to accept the proposed voluntary arrangement (with or without modifications): Act of 1986, s. 4(1). A meeting cannot approve any proposal or modification which adversely affects the rights of secured or preferential creditors without first securing the concurrence of the affected creditor: Act of 1986, s. 4(3) and (4). Meetings are conducted in accordance with the Insolvency Rules: s. 4(5). Within four days of the conclusion of each of the creditors' and company's meetings the chairman of the meeting is required to lodge in court a report of the results of the meeting to the court. He must also give notice of the results of the meeting to all persons who received notice of the meeting. It should be noted that, subject to a challenge under s. 6 of the Act of 1986, the court has itself no involvement in relation to the approval of the arrangement. The approval by each of the meetings of the proposed voluntary arrangement with the same modifications or without modifications takes effect as if made by the company at the creditors' meeting and binds every person who, in accordance with the insolvency rules, had notice of and was entitled to vote at the meeting: Act of 1986, s. 5. The approval of the arrangement may be challenged on the basis of some material irregularity or as being unfairly prejudicial to the interest of a creditor, member or contributory of the company: Act of 1986, s. 6(1). Any challenge, however, must be brought within 28 days of the day on which each report was lodged with the court: Act of 1986, s. 6(3).

"SENT".

This includes deliver: r. 1.3(1) (definition of "send").

74.7.2

Notice of termination or implementation of arrangement

74.8.[2] A notice and copy of the supervisor's report to be lodged with the court under rule 2.43(3) of the Insolvency (CVAA) Rules (termination or full implementation of CVA) must be sent to the Deputy Principal Clerk who must lodge it—

74.8

(a) in a case to which rule 74.4 (lodging of nominee's report (company not in liquidation etc.)) 5 applies, with the nominee's report lodged under that rule; or

(b) in a case to which rule 74.5 (lodging of nominee's report (company in liquidation etc.)) applies, in process as defined by paragraph (2) of that rule.

---

[1] Rule 74.7 amended by S.S.I. 2019 No. 81 (effective 6 April 2019)
[2] Rule 74.8 substituted by S.S.I. 2019 No. 81 (effective 6 April 2019)

Deriv. R.C.S. 1965, r. 207 substituted by S.I. 1986 No. 2298

74.8.1 The supervisor of the voluntary arrangement (see Act of 1986, s. 7(2)) must send a copy of the abstracts of receipts and payments at least once every 12 months to the court: Insolvency Rules, r. 1.21. The court may dispense with the requirement to send copies to members of the company (Insolvency Rules, r. 1.21(2) and (5)(a)) or to vary the dates on which the obligation arises (Insolvency Rules, r. 1.21(5)(b)).

The person responsible for carrying out the voluntary arrangement, once it takes effect, is known as the supervisor (Act of 1986, s. 7(2)) and is normally the nominee.

"SENT".

74.8.2 This includes deliver: r. 1.3(1) (definition of "send").

Form of other applications

74.9 **74.9.**—[1](1) An application to which this rule applies shall be made—

(a)[2] where the company is not being wound up by the court and is not in administration, by petition; or

(b)[3] where the company is being wound up by the court or is in administration, by note in the process to which it relates.

(1A)[4] In the case of a bank, an application to which this rule applies shall be made—

(a) where the bank is not subject to a bank insolvency order and is not in bank administration, by petition; or

(b) where the bank is subject to a bank insolvency order by the court or is in bank administration, by note in the process to which it relates.

(2) This rule applies to an application under—

(a) section 2(4) of the Act of 1986 (for the replacement of a nominee);

(b) section 6 of that Act (to challenge a decision made in relation to an arrangement);

(c) section 7(3) of that Act (to challenge the actings of a supervisor);

(d) section 7(4)(a) of that Act (by a supervisor for directions);

(e) section 7(5) of that Act (for the appointment of a supervisor);

(f) rule 2.40(10) of the Insolvency (CVAA) Rules (to dispense with delivery of reports or summaries);

(g) *[Omitted by S.S.I. 2019 No. 81 (effective 6 April 2019)].*

(h) any other provision in the Act of 1986 or the Insolvency (CVAA) Rules relating to company voluntary arrangements not mentioned in this Part; or

(i)[5] any provision in the Act of 1986, as applied by the Act of 2009, relating to voluntary arrangements.

Deriv. R.C.S. 1965, r. 205, and r. 208, both substituted by S.I. 1986 No. 2298

74.9.1 While part of the purpose of introducing voluntary arrangements was to keep the expense and formality of the court's role to a minimum, provision is made in the Act of 1986 and in the Insolvency Rules for application to be made by the court. Where there is no administration order in force in relation to the company or where the company is not being wound up, such an application must be made by petition. Where, however, one of those insolvency regimes is in place, any application must be made by note in that existing process.

The Act of 1986 provides for two circumstances where application may be made to the court prior to the taking effect of a voluntary arrangement. The first is under s. 2(4) of the Act of 1986 to replace a nominee who has failed to submit the initial report relating to the suitability and viability of the proposed

---

[1] Rule 74.9 amended by S.S.I. 2019 No. 81 (effective 6 April 2019)

[2] R. 74.9(1)(a) and (b) amended by S.S.I. 2003 No. 385 (effective 15th September 2003).

[3] R. 74.9(1)(a) and (b) amended by S.S.I. 2003 No. 385 (effective 15th September 2003).

[4] R. 74.9(1A) and r. 74.9(2)(i) inserted by S.S.I. 2009 No. 63, r. 3 (effective 25th February 2009).

[5] Rule 74.9(1A) and r. 74.9(2)(i) inserted by S.S.I. 2009 No. 63, r. 3 (effective 25th February 2009).

arrangement. The second is a challenge to the approval of any scheme, which must be brought within 28 days of the lodging in court of the report of the chairman of the meeting (as required by s. 4(6)): Act of 1986, s. 6(3). The grounds of challenge are that there has been some material irregularity at or in relation to either of the creditors' or company's meetings or that the arrangement approved at such meetings unfairly prejudices the interest of a creditor, member or contributory of the company: Act of 1986, s. 6(1).

Once an arrangement has taken effect, applications may be made by a supervisor (for directions under s. 7(4)(a) of the Act of 1986), for the appointment of a supervisor (under s. 7(5)) or in relation to the act-ings of a supervisor (s. 7(3)). The supervisor, who usually acted as the nominee prior to the approval of the arrangement, is the person responsible for carrying out the voluntary arrangement: Act of 1986, s. 7(2).

"A BANK".

Special provisions for failing banks were introduced after the banking crisis in 2007. Temporary measures were followed by the Banking Act 2009. A bank is defined in s. 2 of the 2009 Act.

74.9.1A

"PETITION".

A petition is presented in the Outer House: r. 14.2(h). The petition must be in Form 14.4 in the official printed form: rr. 4.1 and 14.4. The petition must be signed by counsel or other person having a right of audience: r. 4.2; and see r. 1.3(1) (definition of "counsel" and "other person having a right of audience") and note 1.3.4.

74.9.2

The petitioner must lodge the petition with the required steps of process (r. 4.4) and any documents founded on or adopted (r. 27.1(1)). A fee is payable on lodging the petition: see note 14.5.10.

On petitions generally, see Chap. 14.

"NOTE".

For applications by note, see r. 15.2.

74.9.3

Part III – Administration Procedure[1]

Form of petition in administration procedure

74.10.—[2, 3](1)[4] In this Part, "the petition" means a petition under section 9 of, or section 8 of and Schedule B1 to, the Act of 1986 (petition for administration order), or section 156 of the Act of 2004 (petition for energy administration order), or sec-tion 70 of the Postal Act (applications for postal administration orders).

74.10

(2) The petition shall include averments in relation to—

  (a) the petitioner and the capacity in which he presents the petition, if other than the company;

  (b) whether it is believed that the company is, or is likely to become, unable to pay its debts and the grounds of that belief;

  (c)[5, 6] in the case of a petition under the Act of 1986, how the making of that order will achieve—

    (i) any of the purposes specified in section 8(3) of the Act of 1986; or

    (ii) an objective specified in paragraph 3 of Schedule B1 to the Act of 1986;

  (d) the company's financial position specifying, so far as known, assets and liabilities, including contingent and prospective liabilities;

  (e)[7] any security known or believed to be held by creditors of the company,

---

[1] Pt. III heading amended by S.S.I. 2003 No. 385 (effective 15th September 2003).

[2] Rule 74.10 amended by S.S.I. 2016 No. 318 r. 2 (effective 16 November 2016).

[3] Rule 74.10 as amended by S.S.I. 2020 No. 440 r. 2(15) (effective IP completion day, 31st December 2020).

[4] Rule 74.10(1), (2)(c), (e), (f), (g), (h), (i), (j) amended by S.S.I. 2006 No. 83 (effective 17th March 2006).

[5] Rule 74.10(2)(c), (g), (h), (i) and heading amended by, and r. 74.10(2)(j) inserted by, S.S.I. 2003 No. 385 (effective 15th September 2003).

[6] Rule 74.10(1), (2)(c), (e), (f), (g), (h), (i), (j) amended by S.S.I. 2006 No. 83 (effective 17th March 2006).

[7] Rule 74.10(1), (2)(c), (e), (f), (g), (h), (i), (j) amended by S.S.I. 2006 No. 83 (effective 17th March 2006).

whether in any case the security confers power on the holder to appoint a receiver or an administrator, and whether a receiver or an administrator, as the case may be, has been appointed;

(f)[1] so far as known to the petitioner, whether any steps have been taken for the winding up of the company;

(g)[2, 3] other matters which, in the opinion of the petitioner, will assist the court in deciding whether to grant an order in respect of an administration or or an energy administration or a postal administration, as the case may be;

(h)[4] *[Omitted by S.S.I. 2006 No. 83 (effective 17th March 2006)].*

(i)[5, 6] the name and address of the person proposed to be appointed, and his qualification to act, as administrator or energy administrator or postal administrator, as the case may be; and

(j) in the case of a petition under the Act of 1986, averments stating, in so far as it is within the petitioner's knowledge—

   (i) whether or not the centre of main interests of the company is situated within the United Kingdom or in a Member State;

   (ii) where the centre of main interests of the company is situated in a Member State, whether or not the company possesses an establishment in the United Kingdom;

   (iii) whether there are insolvency proceedings elsewhere in respect of the company;

(k)[7] whether the Secretary of State has certified the case as one in which he considers it would be appropriate for him to petition under section 124A of the Act of 1986 (petition for winding up on grounds of public interest);

(l)[8] so far as known to the petitioner in a petition for an energy administration order or a postal administration order, as the case may be, whether any steps have been taken for an administration order under Schedule B1 to the Act of 1986;

(m)[9] whether a protected energy company in a petition for an energy administration order is a non GB company.

(n) whether a universal service provider (within the meaning of section 65(1) of the Postal Act) in a petition for a postal administration order is a foreign company.

(3) *[Omitted by S.S.I. 2006 No. 83 (effective 17th March 2006).]*

Deriv. R.C.S. 1965, r. 209(1), (3) and (4) substituted by S.I. 1986 No. 2298

General note.

74.10.1   A petition for an administration under the Act of 1986 order may be presented by a company, its directors or creditors (Act of 1986, s. 9(1)) and may be granted, where the company is or is likely to become unable to pay its debts, in order to achieve the survival of the company, the approval of a voluntary ar-

---

[1] Rule 74.10(2)(f) amended by S.I. 1994 No. 2901 (minor correction).

[2] Rule 74.10(2)(c) (g), (h), (i) and heading amended by, and r. 74.10(2)(j) inserted by, S.S.I. 2003 No. 385 (effective 15th September 2003).

[3] Rule 74.10(1), (2)(c), (e), (f), (g), (h), (i), (j) amended by S.S.I. 2006 No. 83 (effective 17th March 2006).

[4] Rule 74.10(2)(c) (g), (h), (i) and heading amended by, and r. 74.10(2)(j) inserted by, S.S.I. 2003 No. 385 (effective 15th September 2003).

[5] Rule 74.10(2)(c) (g), (h), (i) and heading amended by, and r. 74.10(2)(j) inserted by, S.S.I. 2003 No. 385 (effective 15th September 2003).

[6] Rule 74.10(1), (2)(c), (e), (f), (g), (h), (i), (j) amended by S.S.I. 2006 No. 83 (effective 17th March 2006).

[7] Rule 74.10(2), (k), (l) and (m) inserted by S.S.I. 2006 No. 83 (effective 17th March 2006).

[8] Rule 74.10(2), (k), (l) and (m) inserted by S.S.I. 2006 No. 83 (effective 17th March 2006).

[9] Rule 74.10(2), (k), (l) and (m) inserted by S.S.I. 2006 No. 83 (effective 17th March 2006).

rangement, the sanctioning of a compromise or arrangement or a more advantageous realisation of the company's assets than would be effected on a winding up: Act of 1986, s. 8. Certain others may petition where the company is authorised to carry on business under the Financial Services Act 1986 (s. 28 or 33(1)(b)), or the Bank of England may petition in relation to a company under the Banking Act 1987: Act of 1986, s. 9(1). An interim order under s. 9(4) or (5) of the Act of 1986 is not an administration order under s. 8: *Secretary of State for Trade and Industry v. Palmer* 1994 S.C. 707.

A petition by the directors should be supported by a resolution of the directors: *In re Equiticorp International plc* [1989] 1 W.L.R. 1010.

The court must be satisfied that there is a real prospect rather than probability of the purpose of the order being achieved: *In re Harris Simons Construction Ltd* [1989] 1 W.L.R. 368; *Re Rowbotham Baxter Ltd* [1990] B.C.L.C. 397.

The presentation of a petition for an administration order on ex parte statements at short notice, when the court does not have the advantage of adversarial argument to draw its attention to points weighing for or against the ground of the petition, has been discouraged in England: *Re Rowbotham Baxter Ltd*, above, approved in *Cornhill Insurance plc v. Cornhill Financial Services Ltd* [1992] B.C.C. 818, 856F-H per Dillon L.J.

It is not appropriate when considering approval of the scheme to carry out an examination of the forecasts or assumptions on which the administrator and his advisors reached their conclusions on the validity of the scheme: *Re Olympia & York Canary Wharf Holdings Ltd* [1993] B.C.C. 866.

The petition freezes the position of creditors. On being granted any petition for winding up is dismissed (Act of 1986, s. 11(1)(a)) and an administrative receiver must vacate office (Act of 1986, s. 11(1)(b)). No proceedings may be commenced except with consent of the administrator or with leave of the court. On the granting of leave, see the guidance laid down in *In re Atlantic Computer Systems plc (No. 1)* [1992] Chap. 505; and see, e.g. *Scottish Exhibition Centre Ltd v. Mirestop Ltd* 1993 S.L.T. 1034. On the meaning of "proceedings", see *Air Ecosse Ltd v. Civil Aviation Authority* 1987 S.C. 285 (application for air route licences does not constitute proceedings), *In re Barrow Borough Transport Ltd* [1990] Chap. 227 (application for extension of time to register a charge not proceedings), *Carr v. British International Helicopters Ltd* [1993] B.C.C. 855 (redundant employee's application to industrial tribunal was "proceedings", but it would only be in rare circumstances that the administrator's consent would be required) and *Scottish Exhibition Centre Ltd v. Mirestop (in Administration)* 1996 S.L.T. 8 (service of notice of irritancy on appointment of interim administrators by landlords did not constitute "other legal process" and leave of the court not, therefore, required). *In Re Olympia & York Canary Wharf Ltd* [1993] B.C.C. 154, 157D, Millet J. stated that "legal process", used in s. 11(3)(d) of the Act of 1986, means a process which requires the assistance of the court and does not extend to the service of a contractual notice, whether or not the service of such a notice is a precondition to the bringing of legal proceedings. Millet J. refused to follow Harman J. in *Exchange Travel Ltd v. Triton Property plc* [1991] B.C.C. 341.

Differences in the law of landlord's remedies between Scotland and England may lead to leave being required in one jurisdiction where it is not required in the other. In *Exchange Travel Ltd*, above peaceful re-entry by a landlord was held to be enforcing a security requiring leave under s. 11(3)(d) of the Act of 1986. Irritancy is not, in Scotland, regarded as a security and, therefore, leave under that provision would not be required (and was not sought in *Scottish Exhibition Centre Ltd*, above).

The requirements of the Insolvency Rules should be noted.

JURISDICTION.

The court having jurisdiction is the court having jurisdiction to wind up the company: Act of 1986, s. 251 and the Companies Act 1985, s. 744; Company Directors Disqualification Act 1986, s. 2(2). The C.J.J.A. 1982 does not apply: C.J.J.A. 1982, Scheds. 1 and 3C, Art. 1 (1968 Brussels and Lugano Conventions) Sched. 5, para. 1 (inter-UK jurisdiction) and Sched. 9, para. 4 (jurisdiction of Scottish courts). **74.10.2**

"PETITION".

A petition is presented in the Outer House: r. 14.2(h). The petition must be in Form 14.4 in the official printed form: rr. 4.1 and 14.4. The petition must be signed by counsel or other person having a right of audience: r. 4.2; and see r. 1.3(1) (definition of "counsel" and "other person having a right of audience") and note 1.3.4. **74.10.3**

The petitioner must lodge the petition with the required steps of process (r. 4.4) and any documents founded on or adopted (r. 27.1(1)). A fee is payable on lodging the petition: see note 14.5.10.

On petitions generally, see Chap. 14.

INTERIM ADMINISTRATOR.

The court may appoint an interim administrator until the petition is determined. It is not necessary to specify his powers under the Act of 1986. The interim administrator must be an insolvency practitioner and the petition should state that the proposed interim administrator is such. Averments in support of the application for an interim administrator should be included in the petition. Only an individual may be an insolvency practitioner, and he must have the requisite authorisation and have in force caution for the proper performance of his duties: Act of 1986, s. 390; and see the Insolvency Practitioners Regulations 1986 [S.I. 1986 No. 1995] as amended. It is not necessary for the insolvency practitioner to lodge his bond of caution in process before taking up his appointment and the court will not nowadays order this to be done. **74.10.4**

REMOVAL OF ADMINISTRATOR

74.10.5   The procedure for an application to removal of an administrator (Act of 1986, Sched. B1, para. 88) will be note in the petition for his appointment.

In *Sportsdirect.com Retail Ltd v Administrators of Goals Soccer Centres Plc* 2023 S.L.T. 1247, Lord Braid referred to *Re Fox Street Village Ltd (in admin)* [2020] EWHC 2541 (Ch), para. [61]–[64] as providing a useful summary of how to exercise the discretion to remove.

Interim orders

74.10A   **74.10A.**—[1, 2](1)[3]   On making an interim order under paragraph 13(1)(d) of Schedule B1 to the Act of 1986 or section 157(1)(d) of the Act of 2004 or section 71(1)(d) of the Postal Act the Lord Ordinary shall fix a hearing on the By Order Roll for a date after the expiry of the period of notice mentioned in rule 14.6 (period of notice for lodging answers).

(2)   At the hearing under paragraph (1) the Lord Ordinary shall make such order as to further procedure as he thinks fit.

GENERAL NOTE.

74.10A.1   Sched. B1 to the Insolvency Act 1986, inserted by the Enterprise Act 2002, makes provision for administration. One of the things the court may do on an application for an administration order is make an interim order under para. 13(1)(d) of Sched. B1. An interim order may, in particular, restrict the exercise of a power by a director or the company or confer discretion on the court or an insolvency practitioner.

Notice of petition

74.11   **74.11.**   Where—

(a)   *[Omitted by S.S.I. 2019 No. 81 (effective 6th April 2019)]*

(b)   *[Omitted by S.S.I. 2019 No. 81 (effective 6th April 2019)]*

or,

(c)[4, 5]   the petition and a notice are to be served on a person mentioned in section 156(2)(a) to (c) of the Act of 2004 (notice of application for energy administration order), rule 5(1) of the Energy Administration Rules or rule 6(1) of the 2013 Rules; or

(d)[6]   the petition and a notice are to be served on a person mentioned in section 70(2)(a) to (c) of the Postal Act (applications for postal administration orders) or Rule 7 of the Postal Administration (Scotland) Rules.

Deriv. R.C.S. 1965, r. 210 substituted by S.I. 1986 No. 2298

Report of proposals of administrator

74.12   **74.12.**—(1)   A report of the meeting to approve the proposals of the administrator to be sent to the court under section 24(4) of the Act of 1986 shall be sent to the Deputy Principal Clerk of Session, who shall—

(a)   cause it to be lodged in the process of the petition to which it relates; and

(b)   give written intimation to the parties of the receipt and lodging of the report.

(2)   Where a report under section 24(4) of the Act of 1986 discloses that the meeting has declined to approve the proposals of the administrator, the Keeper of the Rolls shall put the cause out on the By Order Roll for determination by the insolvency judge for any order he may make under section 24(5) of that Act.

Deriv. R.C.S. 1965, r. 212 substituted by S.I. 1986 No. 2298

---

[1] Rule 74.10A inserted by S.S.I. 2005 No. 268 (effective 7th June, 2005).
[2] Rule 74.10A(1) amended by S.S.I. 2006 No. 83 (effective 17th March 2006).
[3] Rule 74.10A amended by S.S.I. 2016 No. 318 r. 2 (effective 16th November 2016).
[4] Rule 74.11(c) inserted by S.S.I. 2006 No. 83 (effective 17th March 2006).
[5] As amended by the S.S.I. 2013 No. 162 r. 5(2) (effective 4th June, 2013).
[6] Rule 74.11 inserted by S.S.I. 2016 No. 318 r. 2 (effective 16th November 2016).

Where the meeting of creditors declines to approve the administrator's proposals for achieving the object of the administration order, the court may discharge the order or make any other order: Act of 1986, s. 24(5).

74.12.1

"SENT".

This includes deliver: r. 1.3(1) (definition of "send").

74.12.2

Report of administrator's proposals: Schedule B1 to the Act of 1986

74.13.—[1](1) Paragraph (2) shall apply where a report under paragraphs 53(2) or 54(6) of Schedule B1 to the Act of 1986 discloses a failure to approve, or to approve a revision of, an administrator's proposals.

(2) The Deputy Principal Clerk shall fix a hearing for determination by the insolvency judge of any order that may be made under paragraph 55(2) of Schedule B1 to the Act of 1986.

74.13

Deriv. R.C.S. 1965, r. 213 substituted by S.I. 1986 No. 2298

A copy of the abstract of receipts and payments of the administrator must be sent to the court within two months after six months from the date of his appointment and every six months thereafter, and two months after he ceases to be administrator: Insolvency Rules, r. 2.17. The two-month period may be extended by the court: Insolvency Rules, r. 2.17(2); and see r. 74.14.

74.13.1

"SENT".

This includes deliver: r. 1.3(1) (definition of "send").

74.13.2

Time and date of lodging in an administration, energy administration or postal administration

74.14.—[2, 3, 4](1) The time and date of lodging of a notice or document relating to an administration under the Act of 1986 or the Insolvency (CVAA) Rules, or an energy administration under the Act of 2004 or the Energy Administration Rules or a postal administration under the Postal Act or the Postal Administration Rules, shall be noted by the Deputy Principal Clerk upon the notice or document.

74.14

(2) Subject to any provision in the Insolvency (CVAA) Rules or the Energy Administration Rules or the Postal Administration Rules, as the case may be—

    (a) where the time of lodging of a notice or document cannot be ascertained by the Deputy Principal Clerk, the notice or document shall be deemed to be lodged at 10 a.m. on the date of lodging; and

    (b) where a notice or document under paragraph (1) is delivered on any day other than a business day, the date of lodging shall be the first business day after such delivery.

Deriv. R.C.S. 1965, r. 211(2) substituted by S.I. 1986 No. 2298

Applications during an administration, energy administration or postal administration

74.15.[5, 6, 7] An application or appeal under any provision of the Act of 1986, the Insolvency (CVAA) Rules, the Act of 2004, the Postal Act or the Energy Administration Rules or the Postal Administration Rules during an administration, energy administration or postal administration, as the case may be, shall be—

74.15

---

[1] Rule 74.13 substituted by S.S.I. 2003 No. 385 (effective 15th September 2003).
[2] R. 74.14 substituted by S.S.I. 2006 No. 83 (effective 17th March 2006).
[3] Rule 74.14 amended by S.S.I. 2016 No. 318 r. 2 (effective 16th November 2016).
[4] Rule 74.14 amended by S.S.I. 2019 No. 81 (effective 6th April 2019).
[5] Rule 74.15 substituted by S.S.I. 2006 No. 83 (effective 17th March 2006).
[6] Rule 74.14 amended by S.S.I. 2016 No. 318 r. 2 (effective 16th November 2016).
[7] Rule 74.14 amended by S.S.I. 2019 No. 81 (effective 6th April 2019).

(a) where no previous application or appeal has been made, by petition; or

(b) where a petition for an order in respect of an administration, or energy administration or postal administration, as the case may be, has been lodged, by note in the process of that petition.

Deriv. R.C.S. 1965, r. 211(1) substituted by S.I. 1986 No. 2298 (r. 74.15(1)) and r. 211(3) and (4) inserted by S.I. 1991 No. 1157 (r. 74.15(3) and (4))

APPLICATIONS FOR DIRECTIONS.

74.15.1   On an application for directions by an administrator under s. 15(2) of the Act of 1986, see *Re Maxwell Communications plc (No. 3)* [1993] B.C.C. 369.

DISCHARGE OF ADMINISTRATOR.

74.15.2   On a successful application to postpone release of an administrator, see *Re Sibec Developments Ltd* [1993] B.C.C. 148; *Re Exchange Travel (Holdings) Ltd* [1992] B.C.C. 954; and see *Re Olympia & York Canary Wharf Holdings Ltd* [1993] B.C.C. 866.

"NOTE".

74.15.3   For applications by note, see 4.15.2.

"APPLICATION".

74.15.4   An application under r. 74.15 means an application related to the supervision of, and incidental to, the administration, such as those mentioned in the pre-existing rule, and does not apply to proceedings by administrators under ss. 242 and 243 of the 1986 Act: *Joint Administrators of Prestonpans (Trading) Ltd, Petitioners*, 2013 S.L.T. 138 (OH).

Application for administration by a bank liquidator

74.15A   **74.15A.**[1] An application by a bank liquidator for an administration order under section 114 of the Act of 2009 shall be made by note in the existing process of the bank insolvency petition.

GENERAL NOTE.

74.15A.1   Special provisions for failing banks were introduced after the banking crisis in 2007. Temporary measures were followed by the Banking Act 2009. A bank is defined in s. 2 of the 2009 Act.

When a bank fails, a bank insolvency order instead of ordinary liquidation may be obtained by the Bank of England, the FSA or the Secretary of State. Where a liquidator has been appointed he may, inter alia, apply for an administration order if he thinks that administration would achieve a better result for the creditors than bank insolvency: 2009 Act, s. 114.

Part IV – Receivers

Interpretation of this Part

74.16   **74.16.** In this Part, "the petition" means a petition under section 54(1) of the Act of 1986 (petition to appoint a receiver).

Petition to appoint a receiver

74.17   **74.17** The petition shall include averments in relation to—

(a) any floating charge and the property over which it is secured;

(b)[2] so far as known to the petitioner, whether any application for an order in respect of an administration has been made, or an administrator has been appointed in respect of the company;

(c) other matters which, in the opinion of the petitioner, will assist the court in deciding whether to appoint a receiver; and

(d) the name and address of the person proposed to be appointed, and his qualification to act, as receiver.

Deriv. R.C.S. 1965, r. 214(3) substituted by S.I. 1986 No. 2298

---

[1] R. 74.15A inserted by S.S.I. 2009 No. 63, r. 3 (effective 25th February 2009).
[2] R. 74.17(b) amended by S.S.I. 2003 No. 385 (effective 15th September 2003).

GENERAL NOTE.

74.17.1

The holder of a floating charge over all or part of the property of a company may apply to the court to appoint a receiver or, where the charge attaches to the whole or substantially the whole of the company's property, an administrative receiver, of such property as is subject to the charge on the occurrence of an event under the charge which entitles the holder to make the appointment or where the court is satisfied that the position of the holder would be prejudiced if the appointment were not made or on a ground specified in s. 52(1)(a)-(c) (Act of 1986, s. 52(2)): Act of 1986, ss. 51(2) and 251. Appointments by the court are not common because the floating charge holder can appoint a receiver without a court order on the occurrence of an event which under the charge entitled him to do so or an event in s. 52(1)(a)–(d): Act of 1986, s. 52(1).

The words in s. 462(1) of the Companies Act 1985, "property and undertaking" of a company, over which it may grant a floating charge, are unqualified and are intended to allow the widest scope for the creation of floating charges. Accordingly, a floating charge which has crystallised (e.g. on the appointment of a receiver) attached to and created a priority over heritable subjects in respect of which the company had granted and delivered a disposition but which had not been recorded by the disponee by the date of the crystallisation: *Sharp v. Thomson* 1995 S.C. 455.

JURISDICTION.

74.17.2

The court having jurisdiction is the court having jurisdiction to wind up the company: Act of 1986, s. 251 and the Companies Act 1985, s. 744. The C.J.J.A. 1982 does not apply: C.J.J.A. 1982, Scheds 1 and 3C, Art. 1 (1968 Brussels and Lugano Conventions), Sched. 5, para. 1 (inter-UK jurisdiction) and Sched. 9, para. 4 (jurisdiction of Scottish courts).

"PETITION".

74.17.3

A petition is presented in the Outer House: r. 14.2(h). The petition must be in Form 14.4 in the official printed form: rr. 4.1 and 14.4. The petition must be signed by counsel or other person having a right of audience: r. 4.2; and see r. 1.3(1) (definition of "counsel" and "other person having a right of audience") and note 1.3.4.

The petitioner must lodge the petition with the required steps of process (r. 4.4) and any documents founded on or adopted (r. 27.1(1)). A fee is payable on lodging the petition: see note 14.5.10.

On petitions generally, see Chap. 14.

RECEIVER.

74.17.4

The receiver must be an insolvency practitioner: Act of 1986, s. 230(4). The petition should state that the proposed receiver is such. Only an individual may be an insolvency practitioner, and he must have the requisite authorisation and have in force caution for the proper performance of his duties: Act of 1986, s. 390; and see the Insolvency Practitioners Regulations 1986 [S.I. 1986 No. 1995] as amended. It is not necessary for the insolvency practitioner to lodge his bond of caution in process before taking up his appointment and the court will not nowadays order this to be done.

Intimation, service and advertisement under this Part

74.18.—(1) Unless the court otherwise directs, the order under rule 14.5 (first order in petitions) for intimation, service and advertisement of the petition shall include a requirement—

    (a) to serve the petition—

        (i) on the company; and

        (ii) where an application for an administration order has been presented, on that applicant and any respondent to that application; and

    (b) to advertise the petition forthwith—

        (i) once in the Edinburgh Gazette; and

        (ii) once in one or more of such newspapers as the court shall direct.

  (2) Subject to rule 14.6(2) (application to shorten or extend the period of notice), the period of notice for lodging answers to the petition shall be eight days.

  (3) An advertisement under paragraph (1) shall include—

    (a) the name and address of the petitioner;

    (b) the name and address of the agent for the petitioner;

    (c) the date on which the petition was presented;

    (d) the nature of the order sought;

    (e) the period of notice for lodging answers; and

74.18

(f) a statement that any person who intends to appear in the petition must lodge answers within the period of notice.

Deriv. R.C.S. 1965, r. 215(1), (2) and (6) to (8) substituted by S.I. 1986 No. 2298

"INTIMATION AND SERVICE".

74.18.1   See generally, r. 14.7.

"SERVE".

74.18.2   For methods, see Chap. 16, Pt. I.

"ANSWERS".

74.18.3   See r. 18.3.

Form of other applications and appeals

74.19   **74.19.**—[1](1)   An application under—

(a) section 61(1) of the Act of 1986 (by a receiver for authority to dispose of property or an interest in property),

(b) section 62 of that Act (for removal of a receiver),

(c) section 63(1) of that Act (by a receiver for directions),

(d) section 69(1) of that Act (to enforce the receiver's duty to make returns etc.), or

(e) any other provision of that Act or the Insolvency (RWU) Rules relating to receivers not mentioned in this Part,

shall, where the court has appointed the receiver, be made by note or, in any other case, by petition.

(2)   An appeal against a decision of a receiver as to expenses of making a statement of affairs and statutory declaration or a statement of concurrence under rule 2.10(2) of the Insolvency (RWU) Rules (statement of affairs: expenses) shall, where the receiver was appointed by the court, be made by note or in any other case, by petition.

(3)   An application by a receiver—

(a) under section 67(1) or (2) of the Act of 1986 (to extend the time for sending a report),

(b) under rule 2.16(3) of the Insolvency (RWU) Rules (to extend the time for sending a summary of receipts and payments),

shall, where the court has appointed the receiver, be made by motion or, in any other case, by petition.

Deriv. R.C.S. 1965, r. 216 substituted by S.I. 1986 No. 2298

APPLICATIONS BY RECEIVER FOR DIRECTIONS.

74.19.1   For recent examples of applications by receivers for directions, see *Scottish & Newcastle plc, Petrs*, 1994 S.L.T. 1140 (whether certain heritable subjects remained the property of the company at the date of the appointment of the receiver notwithstanding the omission to register an instrument of alteration or a memorandum of satisfaction under ss. 466 and 419, respectively, of the Companies Act 1985 and for declarator that the receiver was a receiver and not an administrative receiver); *McKillop v. Tayside R.C.* 1994 S.C.L.R. 746 (whether receiver personally liable for local authority rates); *Turner v. Inland Revenue Commissioners* 1994 S.L.T. 811 (whether Inland Revenue entitled to set off sums due to the company against ordinary debts rather than pro rata against ordinary and preferential debts due by the company to the Inland Revenue); *Powdrill v. Watson, Re Leyland DAF Ltd, Re Ferranti International plc* [1995] 2 All E.R. 65 (H.L.) (whether administrative receivers had "adopted" employees' contracts of employment for the purposes of s. 44(1)(b) of the Act of 1986).

The court has a discretion under s. 63(1) of the Act of 1986 whether or not to give the directions sought: *McKillop*, above. In *Jamieson & Ors, Petrs*, 1997 S.C. 195 (Extra Div.), unreported, the court declined to give a direction under s. 63(1) of 1986 Act. In that case, in anticipation of a large number of claims against receivers by employees whose contracts had been adopted subsequent to the appointment of a receiver, a number of insolvency practitioners sought a direction from the court compelling any such claimants to follow a specified procedure.

---

[1] Rule 74.19 amended by S.S.I. 2019 No. 81 (effective 6th April 2019).

"PETITION".

A petition is presented in the Outer House: r. 14.2(h). The petition must be in Form 14.4 in the official printed form: rr. 4.1 and 14.4. The petition must be signed by counsel or other person having a right of audience: r. 4.2; and see r. 1.3(1) (definition of "counsel" and "other person having a right of audience") and note 1.3.4.

The petitioner must lodge the petition with the required steps of process (r. 4.4) and any documents founded on or adopted (r. 27.1(1)). A fee is payable on lodging the petition: see note 14.5.10.

On petitions generally, see Chap. 14.

74.19.2

"NOTE".

For applications by note, see r. 15.2.

74.19.3

Part V – Winding Up of Companies

Interpretation of this Part

74.20. In this Part, "the petition" means a petition under section 124 of the Act of 1986 (petition to wind up a company).

74.20

Application to disapply restrictions on winding-up petitions

74.20A.[1] An application under paragraph 1(9) of schedule 10 of the Act of 2020 (restriction on winding-up petitions) must be made by petition.

74.20A

GENERAL NOTE

Paragraph 1(9) of the 2020 Act allows for a creditor to apply to the court for an order that certain conditions in relation to the restriction on a winding-up petition should not apply.

74.20A.1

"PETITION"

See Chap. 14. The petition will be presented in the Outer House: r. 14.2(h).

74.20A.2

Petition to wind up a company

74.21.—[2](1) The petition shall include averments in relation to—

74.21

    (a)   the petitioner, if other than the company, and his title to present the petition;

    (b)   in respect of the company—

        (i)   its current and any previous registered name;

        (ii)   the address of its registered office, and any previous such address within six months immediately before the presentation of the petition so far as known to the petitioner;

        (iii)   a statement of the nature of its business and objects, the amount of its capital (nominal and issued) indicating what part is called up, paid up or credited as paid up, and the amount of the assets of the company so far as known to the petitioner;

        (iiia)[3]   confirmation that it is not the subject of a moratorium;

        (iv)   whether or not the centre of main interests of the company is situated within the United Kingdom or in a Member State;

        (v)   where the centre of main interests of the company is situated in a Member State, whether or not the company possesses an establishment in the United Kingdom;

    (c)   whether, to the knowledge of the petitioner, a receiver has been appointed

---

[1] As inserted by the Act of Sederunt (Rules of the Court of Session 1994 and Sheriff Court Company Insolvency Rules Amendment) (Insolvency) 2021 (S.S.I. 2021 No. 324) art.2(5) (effective 29th September 2021).

[2] Rule 74.21 as amended by S.S.I. 2020 No. 440 r. 2(16) (effective IP completion day, 31st December 2020).

[3] Rule 74.21(1)(iiia) inserted by S.S.I. 2020 No. 198 r. 2(5) (effective 1st July 2020).

in respect of any part of the property of the company or a liquidator has been appointed for the voluntary winding up of the company;

(d) the grounds on which the petition proceeds; and

(e) the name and address of the person proposed to be appointed, and his qualification to act, as interim liquidator.

(f)[1] whether there are insolvency proceedings elsewhere in respect of the company.

Deriv. R.C.S. 1965, r. 217(3) substituted by SI 1986/2298

GENERAL NOTE.

74.21.1 An application to wind up a company may be made by the company, its directors, a creditor or contributory, or the Secretary of State in certain circumstances: Act of 1986, s. 124. It may also be applied for by an administrative receiver: Act of 1986, Sched. 2, para. 21.

A contributory presenting a petition for the winding up of a company must demonstrate interest as well as complying with the relevant statutory qualifications: *O'Conner v. Atlantis Fisheries Ltd* , 27th January 1998, unreported (1998 G.W.D. 8-359).

JURISDICTION.

74.21.2 The Court of Session has jurisdiction to wind up a company registered in Scotland: Act of 1986, s. 120(1). The sheriff court has concurrent jurisdiction where the share capital paid up or credited does not exceed £120,000. The C.J.J.A. 1982 does not apply: C.J.J.A. 1982, Scheds 1 and 3C, Art. 1, Sch.5, para.1 and Sch.9, para.4.

The court has power to wind up an unregistered company under s. 221 of the 1986 Act if it has a principal place of business in Scotland. For recent examples of a foreign company being wound up by the court, see *HSBC, Ptnr.*, 2010 S.L.T. 281 (OH) (the three core requirements in English law adopted); *Kingston Park House Ltd v. Granton Commercial Industrial Properties Ltd* [2022] CSIH 59 (First Div.).

"PETITION".

74.21.3 A petition is presented in the Outer House: r. 14.2(h). The petition must be in Form 14.4 in the official printed form: rr. 4.1 and 14.4. The petition must be signed by counsel or other person having a right of audience: r. 4.2; and see r. 1.3(1) (definition of "counsel" and "other person having a right of audience") and note 1.3.4.

The petitioner must lodge the petition with the required steps of process (r. 4.4) and any documents founded on or adopted (r. 27.1(1)). A fee is payable on lodging the petition: see note 14.5.10.

On petitions generally, see Chap. 14.

"GROUNDS ON WHICH THE PETITION PROCEEDS".

74.21.4 The various grounds are set out in s.122 of the Act of 1986. The Secretary of State may petition on grounds of public interest: Act of 1986, s.124A inserted by the Companies Act 1989, s.60(3). For a recent example of a successful petition at the instance of the Secretary of State on the ground of it being just and equitable in the public interest to wind up a company, see *Secretary of State for Trade and Industry v. Hasta International Ltd* 1998 S.L.T. 73 (pyramid selling constituting an illegal lottery).

WINDING UP A COMPANY UNDER S.$122(1)(F)$ (COMPANY UNABLE TO PAY ITS DEBTS).

74.21.4A A petition on this ground presented by a creditor in respect of a debt which is due and unpaid will not normally be allowed to proceed if the existence of the petitioning creditor's alleged debt is bona fide disputed by the company on reasonable and substantial grounds: see *MAC Plant Services Ltd v. Contract Lifting Services (Scotland) Ltd* , 2009 S.C. 125 (OH). A petition for winding up is not a legitimate means of seeking to enforce payment of a debt which is bona fide in dispute: *Stonegate Securities Ltd v. Gregory* [1980] 1 Ch. 576, 579, per Buckley, L.J. It would be open to the court to sist the petition to enable the petitioner to constitute the debt in a separate process. A creditor petitioning to wind up a company on the ground that it is just and equitable to do so (under s.122(1)(g)) will also require to establish that he is a creditor, either actual, contingent or prospective, of the company within the meaning of s.124 of the Act of 1986. If there is a bona fide dispute as to whether the petitioner is a creditor and has locus standi to present the petition, this issue would normally be dealt with by the court before enquiry into the merits of the application: *Rocks v. Brae Hotel (Shetland) Ltd* 1997 S.L.T. 474.

WINDING UP A COMPANY UNDER S.$122(1)(G)$ (JUST AND EQUITABLE).

74.21.4B The remedy is one of last resort. The court must carry out a three-stage analysis, asking: (a) Is the petitioner entitled to some relief? (b) If so, would the winding-up be just and equitable if there was no other remedy available? (c) If so, has the petitioner unreasonably failed to pursue some other available remedy instead of seeking winding-up? There are certain grounds on which a just and equitable order may be granted that are well-recognised: (i) loss of substratum, where a company formed to carry on a

---

[1] Rule 74.21(1)(f) inserted by S.S.I. 2007 No. 449 (effective 25th October 2007).

particular business abandons it for another; (ii) an irretrievable breakdown in confidence and trust between members of a corporate quasi-partnership; (iii) deadlock; (iv) lack of probity in the conduct of the company's affairs (see *Loch v John Blackwood Ltd* [1924] AC 783, 788 per Lord Shaw of Dunfermline). See *Chu v Lau* [2020] UKPC 24.

As a general rule, a shareholder seeking a winding up order must be able to establish that the company is solvent and that there will be a surplus remaining for distribution after payment of the company's debts and the costs and expenses of the liquidation, and a shareholder will not therefore be permitted to petition for the winding up of an insolvent company: *Fulham Football Club (1987) Ltd v Richards* [2012] Ch 333 at [54] and [55].

A creditor petitioning to wind up a company on the ground that it is just and equitable to do so does not need to have demanded payment before the petition is presented: *Macdonald v. North of Scotland Bank* 1942 S.C. 369, 375 per L.J.-C. Cooper.

"INTERIM LIQUIDATOR".

An interim liquidator is appointed by the court on the making of the winding-up order and he holds office until the liquidator is appointed: Act of 1986, s. 138. He must be an insolvency practitioner and the petition must state that he is one. Normally the provisional liquidator is appointed interim liquidator. **74.21.5**

"PROVISIONAL LIQUIDATOR".

See r. 74.25 on an application for a provisional liquidator. The averments required are set out in r. 74.25(2). He must be an insolvency practitioner, and it must be stated in the petition that he is one. There must be averments in support of the application in the petition. The provisional liquidator may be appointed before the winding-up order: Act of 1986, s.135(2). The application is usually made in the winding-up petition. **74.21.6**

Cause must be shown for the appointment of a provisional liquidator: *Levy v. Napier*, 1962 S.C. 468; *Teague, Petr*, 1985 S.L.T. 469. Appearance at a motion for such an appointment will be required.

"MAIN OR TERRITORIAL PROCEEDINGS".

By virtue of EU Council Regulation 1346 of 2000, which came into force on 31st May 2002, jurisdiction for winding up of a company depends on where the company's centre of main interests is. Such proceedings are "main proceedings" and are recognised throughout the EU except Denmark. If the company's centre of main interests is in another Member State, insolvency proceedings may only take place here if the company has an establishment here and is restricted to the assets here (territorial proceedings). Where those proceedings are sought to be raised before the main proceedings are raised elsewhere in the EU, they may be raised in certain specified circumstances. Where those proceedings are sought to be raised after the main proceedings, any winding up here will be secondary proceedings. The centre of administration on a regular basis is the centre of main interests and the place of the registered office is presumed to be the centre of main interests. See generally, art. 3 of the Council Regulation. **74.21.6A**

A Scottish liquidation may be an "ancillary winding up" to a winding up in another jurisdiction, and the rules of procedure may be modified to achieve the objectives of the ancillary winding up: *Morris, Noter, Liquidator of Bank of Credit and Commerce International SA*, 2008 S.C. 111 (O.H.).

INSOLVENCY PRACTITIONER.

Only an individual may be an insolvency practitioner; he must have the required authorisation and have in force caution for the proper performance of his duties: Act of 1986, s.390(1), (2) and (3); and see the Insolvency Practitioners Regulations 1986 [SI 1986/1995]. It is not necessary for an insolvency practitioner to lodge his bond of caution in process before taking up his appointment and the court will not nowadays order this to be done. **74.21.7**

DATE OF PRESENTATION OF PETITION.

This is the date of presentation in the Petition Department. A winding up commences at the date of presentation of the petition: Act of 1986, s.129(2). The presentation interrupts the running of the prescriptive periods (Prescription and Limitations (Scotland) Act 1973, s.9) and is important in considering gratuitous alienations or unfair preferences: Act of 1986, ss.242 and 243. The date of the interlocutor granting the winding-up order is, however, the relevant date in considering the effect of the winding up on diligence: Act of 1986, s.185. **74.21.8**

Intimation, service and advertisement under this Part

74.22.—(A1) [Revoked by the Act of Sederunt (Rules of the Court of Session 1994 and Sheriff Court Company Insolvency Rules Amendment) (Insolvency) 2021 (SSI 2021/324) art.2(6) (effective 29 September 2021).] **74.22**

(1) Unless the court otherwise directs, the order under rule 14.5 (first order in petitions) for intimation, service and advertisement of the petition shall include a requirement—

    (a) to serve the petition—

        (i) where the petitioner is not the company, on the company;

(ii)　where the company is being wound up voluntarily and a liquidator has been appointed, on the liquidator; and

(iii)　where a receiver or administrator has been appointed, on the receiver or administrator, as the case may be;

(b)　where the company is an authorised institution or former authorised institution within the meaning assigned in section 106(1) of the Banking Act 1987 and the petitioner is not the Bank of England, to serve the petition on the Bank of England; and

(c)　to advertise the petition forthwith—

(i)　once in the Edinburgh Gazette; and

(ii)　once in one or more of such newspapers as the court shall direct.

(2)　Subject to rule 14.6(2) (application to shorten or extend the period of notice), the period of notice for lodging answers to the petition shall be eight days.

(3)　An advertisement under paragraph (1) shall include—

(a)　the name and address of the petitioner and, where the petitioner is the company, its registered office;

(b)　the name and address of the agent for the petitioner;

(c)　the date on which the petition was presented;

(d)　the nature of the order sought;

(e)　where a provisional liquidator has been appointed by the court, his name, address and the date of his appointment;

(f)　the period of notice for lodging answers; and

(g)　a statement that any person who intends to appear in the petition must lodge answers within the period of notice.

Deriv. R.C.S. 1965, r. 218(2) and (6)–(8) substituted by SI 1986/2298

GENERAL NOTE.

74.22.1　　A caveat may have been lodged against a winding-up petition. If so the caveator will be notified by the Keeper of the Rolls and a hearing arranged for the motion for the first order at which appearance will be required and the caveator may be heard. On caveats, and procedure where caveats are lodged, see Chap. 5.

"INTIMATION AND SERVICE".

74.22.2　　See r. 14.7. On methods of service, see Chap. 16, Pt I.

"ADVERTISED".

74.22.3　　The advertisement in a newspaper or notice in the Gazettes should be headed with the cause reference number followed by a heading containing the name of the company.

"PERIOD OF NOTICE".

74.22.4　　See r. 14.6.

"PROVISIONAL LIQUIDATOR".

74.22.5　　Cause must be shown for the appointment of a provisional liquidator: *Levy v. Napier* 1962 S.C. 468; *Teague, Petr* 1985 S.L.T. 469. Appearance at a motion for such an appointment will be required.
　　See further notes 74.21.6 and 74.21.7.

LODGING EXECUTION COPY OF PETITION.

74.22.6　　After intimation, service and advertisement, the period of notice having expired, the execution copy of the petition (see r. 16.1(4) and note 16.1.6) must be lodged in process before further procedure is permitted.

Remits from one court to another

74.23　　**74.23.**—(1)　An application under section 120(3)(a)(i) of the Act of 1986 (application for remit of petition to a sheriff court) shall be made by motion.

(2)　An application under—

(a)　section 120(3)(a)(ii) of the Act of 1986 (application for remit of petition from a sheriff court to the court), or

(b)   section 120(3)(b) of that Act (application for remit of petition from one sheriff court to another),

shall be made by petition.

Deriv. R.C.S. 1965, r. 218B inserted by S.I. 1986 No. 2298

GENERAL NOTE.

The court may, if it thinks it expedient having regard to the amount of the company's assets, remit a winding-up petition to the sheriff court or require a petition presented in the sheriff court to be remitted to the Court of Session or another sheriff court: Act of 1986, s. 120(3)(a).

74.23.1

"MOTION".

For motions, see Chap. 23.

74.23.2

"PETITION".

A petition is presented in the Outer House: r. 14.2(h). The petition must be in Form 14.4 in the official printed form: rr. 4.1 and 14.4. The petition must be signed by counsel or other person having a right of audience: r. 4.2; and see r. 1.3(1) (definition of "counsel" and "other person having a right of audience") and note 1.3.4.

The petitioner must lodge the petition with the required steps of process (r. 4.4). A fee is payable on lodging the petition: see note 14.5.10.

On petitions generally, see Chap. 14.

74.23.3

Substitution of creditor or contributory for petitioner

74.24.—[1](1)   Where a petitioner in the petition—

74.24

(a)   is subsequently found not entitled to present the petition,

(b)   fails to make intimation, service and advertisement as directed by the court,

(c)   moves or consents to withdraw the petition or to allow it to be dismissed or refused,

(d)   fails to appear when the petition is called for hearing, or

(e)   appears, but does not move for an order in terms of the prayer of the petition,

the court may, on such terms as it thinks fit, sist as petitioner in place of the original petitioner any creditor or contributory who, in the opinion of the court, is entitled to present the petition.

(2)   An application by a creditor or a contributory to be sisted under paragraph (1)—

(a)   may be made at any time before the petition is dismissed or refused, and

(b)   shall be made by note;

and, if necessary, the court may continue the petition for a specified period to allow a note to be presented.

Deriv. R.C.S. 1965, r. 218C inserted by S.I. 1986 No. 2298

GENERAL NOTE.

A creditor may be a contingent or prospective creditor: Act of 1986, s. 124(1). A "contingent creditor" means a creditor in respect of a debt which may become due, and a "prospective creditor" means a creditor in respect of a debt which will become due.

A contributory (on the meaning of which, see s. 79 of the Act of 1986) may only be a petitioner, except where the number of members falls below two, if some of the shares in respect of which he is a contributory were originally allotted to him or have been held by him and registered in his name for at least six months during the 18 months before the commencement of the winding up or devolved to him on the death of the previous holder: Act of 1986, s. 124(2).

In the circumstances specified in r. 74.24(1), a creditor or contributory may be sisted in room of an original petitioner.

74.24.1

"NOTE".

For applications by note, see r. 15.2.

74.24.2

---

[1] Rule 74.24 as amended by S.S.I. 2020 No. 440 (effective IP completion day, 31st December 2020).

Provisional liquidator

74.25

74.25.—[1,2](1) An application to appoint a provisional liquidator under section 135 of the Act of 1986 may be made—

    (a) by the petitioner, in the prayer of the petition or, if made after the petition has been presented, by note; or

    (b)[3,4] by a creditor or contributory of the company, the company or its directors, the Secretary of State, or a person entitled under any enactment to present a petition, by note.

(2) The application mentioned in paragraph (1) shall include averments in relation to—

    (a) the grounds for the appointment of the provisional liquidator;

    (b) the name and address of the person proposed to be appointed, and his qualification to act, as provisional liquidator; and

    (c) whether, to the knowledge of the applicant, an administrator has been appointed to the company or a receiver has been appointed in respect of any part of its property or a liquidator has been appointed voluntarily to wind it up.

(3) Where the court decides to appoint a provisional liquidator—

    (a) it shall pronounce an interlocutor making the appointment and specifying the functions to be carried out by him in relation to the affairs of the company; and

    (b) it must direct the Deputy Principal Clerk to send forthwith a certified copy of such interlocutor to the person appointed.

(4) *[Omitted by S.S.I. 2019 No. 81 (effective 6th April 2019)]*

(5) An application for the discharge of a provisional liquidator shall be made by note.

Deriv. R.C.S. 1965, r. 218E inserted by S.I. 1986 No. 2298

GENERAL NOTE.

74.25.1

An application for a provisional liquidator is usually made in the winding-up petition; if not, it is made by note: see r. 74.25(1).

The averments required are set out in r. 74.25(2). The provisional liquidator must be an insolvency practitioner, and it must be stated in the petition that he is one. Only an individual may be an insolvency practitioner; he must have the required authorisation and have in force caution for the proper performance of his duties: Act of 1986, s. 390(1), (2) and (3); and see the Insolvency Practitioners Regulations 1986 [S.I. 1986 No. 1995]. It is not necessary for an insolvency practitioner to lodge his bond of caution in process before taking up his appointment and the court will not nowadays order this to be done.

The provisional liquidator may be appointed before the winding-up order: Act of 1986, s. 135(2).

Cause must be shown for the appointment of a provisional liquidator: *Levy v. Napier* 1962 S.C. 468; *Teague, Petr.* 1985 S.L.T. 469. Appearance at a motion for such an appointment will be required.

The purpose of seeking appointment of a provisional liquidator is for him to take custody of, and preserve, the assets of the company between the time of his appointment and the appointment of the liquidator. The public interest in a thorough investigation of the company's affairs, especially of a company carrying on investment business, may justify the appointment of a provisional liquidator notwithstanding that it might be cheaper to proceed with a members' voluntary winding up already under way: *Securities Investment Board v. Lancashire and Yorkshire Portfolio Management Ltd* [1992] B.C.C. 381. For an unsuccessful attempt to appoint an additional provisional liquidator, see *Re Bank of Credit and Commerce International S.A.* [1992] B.C.C. 83.

Where the company is not the petitioner it will only get notice of an application to appoint a provisional liquidator in a petition to wind it up if it has lodged a caveat. On caveats, see Chap. 5.

---

[1] Rule 74.25 amended by S.S.I. 2019 No. 81 (effective 6th April 2019).

[2] Rule 74.25 as amended by S.S.I. 2020 No. 440 r. 2(18) (effective IP completion day, 31st December 2020).

[3] Rule 74.25(1)(b) amended by S.S.I. 2003 No. 385 (effective 15th September 2003).

[4] Rule 74.25(1)(b) amended by S.S.I. 2017 No. 202 r. 3(5) (effective 26th June 2017: amendment has effect subject to savings specified in S.S.I. 2017 No. 202 r. 6).

On appointment, as well as the notifications to be made by him under r. 74.25(4), the provisional liquidator must notify the Registrar of Companies, the company and any receiver: Insolvency Rules, r. 4.2(1).

In relation to the remuneration and expenses of a provisional liquidator, the words "Without prejudice to any order of the court as to expenses" in r. 4.5(3) of the Insolvency Rules recognise the discretion of the court to order that the remuneration and expenses might form part of the expenses of the case and to order which party was to bear that cost: *Graham v. John Tullis & Son (Plastics) Ltd* 1991 S.C. 302.

"CONTRIBUTORY".

A contributory is, generally, a registered member or shareholder of the company. It has been held **74.25.1A** competent for the trustee on the sequestrated estate of a bankrupt member to be able to petition for the winding up of the company, notwithstanding that the trustee has not taken steps to register himself as the holder of the bankrupt's shareholding: *Cumming's Tr. v. Glenrinnes Farms Ltd* 1993 S.L.T. 904.

POWERS OF PROVISIONAL LIQUIDATOR.

These may be restricted (s. 135(5) of the Act of 1986) and are usually limited in the first instance to **74.25.2** those in Pt. II of Sched. 4 (power to bring or defend any action or other legal proceedings and to carry on the business of the company as may be necessary for its beneficial winding up): Act of 1986, Sched. 4, paras. 4 and 5.

"NOTE".

For applications by note, see r. 15.2. **74.25.3**

INTIMATION IN EDINBURGH GAZETTE AND NEWSPAPERS.

The advertisement in a newspaper or notice in the *Gazette* should be headed with the cause reference **74.25.4** number followed by a heading containing the name of the company.

The provisional liquidator must advertise his appointment without delay, as this is an obligation imposed on him as an officer of the court. In *International Factors v. Ves Voltech Electronic Services Ltd* 1994 S.L.T. (Sh. Ct.) 40, Sheriff Principal Hay disapproved of the practice of provisional liquidators in delaying, in some cases, to advertise their appointment. While there may be sound commercial reasons making advertisement inappropriate, the provisional liquidator must apply to the court immediately for dispensation of this requirement.

DISCHARGE OF PROVISIONAL LIQUIDATOR.

The provisional liquidator may be removed from office only by order of the court: Act of 1986, s. **74.25.5** 172(2). He may be removed, e.g. if he fails to maintain his caution: Insolvency Rules, r. 4.4(1).

If a decision to remove him is reclaimed, the provisional liquidator remains in office until the reclaiming motion is determined: *Levy* 1963 S.C. 46.

Appointment of a liquidator

74.26.—(1) Where the court pronounces an interlocutor appointing a liquida- **74.26** tor—

    (a)   the Deputy Principal Clerk shall send a certified copy of that interlocutor to the liquidator;

    (b)[1] the court may, for the purposes of rules 4.22(4)(b), 5.21(4)(b)(ii) and 5.26(4)(b)(ii) of the Insolvency (RWU) Rules (liquidator to give notice of appointment), give such direction as it thinks fit as to advertisement of such appointment.

(2) An application to appoint a liquidator under section 139(4) of the Act of 1986 shall be made by note.

Deriv. R.C.S. 1965, r. 218D, and r. 218H, both inserted by S.I. 1986 No. 2298

GENERAL NOTE.

For most purposes the winding up dates from presentation of the petition for winding up: Act of 1986, **74.26.1** s. 129(2).

When a winding-up order is made the court appoints an interim liquidator who summons separate meetings of creditors and contributories to choose a liquidator: Act of 1986, s. 138(1) to (4).

The court may appoint a liquidator (a) where no liquidator is appointed by the meetings of creditors and contributories (Act of 1986, s. 138(5)); (b) where different persons are nominated by the creditors and contributories, on the application of the contributories within seven days of the creditors' nomination (Act of 1986, s. 139(4)); (c) on the discharge of an administration order (Act of 1986, s. 140(1)); or (d)

---

[1] Rule 74.26 amended by S.S.I. 2019 No. 81 (effective 6 April 2019).

where a winding-up order is made at a time when there is a supervisor of a voluntary arrangement, in which case the court may appoint the supervisor (Act of 1986, s. 140(2)).

The liquidator has the powers in Sched. 4 to the Act of 1986. A liquidator requires the sanction of the court or of the liquidation committee for the exercise of powers enumerated in Pts I and II of that Schedule: Act of 1986, s. 167(1). No such sanction is required for the exercise of the powers set out in Pt. III of that Schedule. A sale of the company's heritage is an example of one of the powers exercisable without sanction: *Duff v. Armour* 1990 G.W.D. 22-1212. While the power to bring or defend actions and other legal proceedings requires sanction, being a power within Pt. II of the Schedule, the requirement for sanction only applies to actions and proceedings brought in the name and on behalf of the company (i.e. where the company must be a party). This does not preclude actions by the liquidator alone, e.g. under s. 242 of the Act of 1986 (challenging gratuitous alienations, as in *Dyer v. Hyslop* 1994 S.C.L.R. 171 or in *Thomson v. M.B. Trustees Ltd* 1994 G.W.D. 32-1894) or under s. 243 of the Act of 1986 (challenging unfair preferences, as in *Nicoll v. Steelpress (Supplies) Ltd* 1993 S.L.T. 533), although such actions may in fact run in the name of both the liquidator and the company (e.g. challenging a gratuitous alienation, as in *Lafferty Construction Ltd v. McComhe* 1994 S.L.T. 858). It is thought that a liquidator's failure to obtain prior sanction will not invalidate the proceedings brought but may expose the liquidator to personal liability in expenses: *Dublin City Distillery (Great Brunswick Street, Dublin) v. Doherty* [1914] A.C. 823; *Dyer*, above. A liquidator's liability in expenses against him "as liquidator" is limited to the available funds of the company: *Dyer v. Craiglaw Developments Ltd* , 29th October 1998, unreported.

The liquidator may seek the directions of the court: *Liquidator of Upper Clyde Shipbuilders Ltd* 1975 S.L.T. 39 per Lord Grieve.

"SEND".

74.26.2   This includes deliver: r. 1.3(1) (definition of "send").

"NOTE".

74.26.3   For applications by note, see r. 15.2.

Applications and appeals in relation to a statement of affairs or accounts

74.27   **74.27.**—[1](1)   An application under section 131(5) of the Act of 1986 for—

    (a)   release from an obligation imposed under section 131(1) or (2) of that Act, or

    (b)   an extension of time for the submission of a statement of affairs, shall be made by note.

(2)   A note under paragraph (1) shall be served on the liquidator or provisional liquidator, as the case may be, who may lodge—

    (a)   answers to the note; or

    (b)   a report on any matters which he considers should be drawn to the attention of the court.

(3)   Where the liquidator or provisional liquidator lodges a report under paragraph (2), he shall forthwith send a copy of it to the noter.

(4)   Where the liquidator or the provisional liquidator does not appear at any hearing on the note, a certified copy of the interlocutor disposing of the note shall be sent to him forthwith by the noter.

(5)   An appeal under—

    (a)   rule 5.15(6) of the Insolvency (RWU) Rules (appeal against refusal by liquidator of allowances towards expenses of preparing statement of affairs);

    (b)   rule 5.15(6) as applied by rule 5.17(4) of the Insolvency (RWU) Rules (appeal against refusal by liquidator of allowances towards expenses of preparing accounts),

must be made by note.

(6)   A note under paragraph (5) must be served on the liquidator or provisional liquidator, as the case may be.

Deriv. R.C.S. 1965, r. 218F inserted by S.I. 1986 No. 2298

---

[1] Rule 74.27 amended by S.S.I. 2019 No. 81 (effective 6 April 2019).

GENERAL NOTE.

The liquidator or provisional liquidator may require officers of the company or others who are or were connected with the company to prepare a statement of affairs of the company: Act of 1986, s. 131(1). He may release a person from the obligation to do so, or extend the time for doing so; but if the (provisional) liquidator refuses to exercise either power the court may exercise it: Act of 1986, s. 131(5).

An application may be made to the court against the liquidator's refusal to grant an allowance to a person required to prepare a statement of affairs who cannot prepare it himself: Insolvency Rules, r. 4.9(6).

"NOTE".

For applications by note, see r. 15.2.

"ANSWERS".

For form and procedure, see r. 18.3.

"SEND".

This includes deliver: r. 1.3(1) (definition of "send").

74.27.1

74.27.2

74.27.3

74.27.4

Appeals against adjudication of claims

74.28.—[1](1)[2] An appeal under rule 7.19(5) of the Insolvency (RWU) Rules (adjudication of claims) by a creditor or any member or contributory of the company against a decision of the liquidator shall be made by note in process or, in a voluntary winding up where no previous application or appeal to the court has been made, by petition.

(2)   A note under paragraph (1) shall be served on the liquidator.

(3)   On such a note or petition being served on him, the liquidator shall send the claim in question, and a copy of his adjudication, forthwith to the Deputy Principal Clerk who shall cause them to be lodged in process.

(4)   After the note or petition has been disposed of, the Deputy Principal Clerk shall return the claim and the adjudication to the liquidator with a copy of the interlocutor disposing of the note or petition.

Deriv. R.C.S. 1965, r. 218G inserted by S.I. 1986 No. 2298

74.28

GENERAL NOTE.

At the beginning of every meeting of creditors the liquidator has to accept or reject each creditor's claim in so far as it relates to voting at a meeting: Bankruptcy (Scotland) Act 1985, s. 49(1). When funds are available for payment of dividends in respect of an accounting period the liquidator must accept or reject each creditor's claim to be entitled to a dividend: 1985 Act, s. 49(2). A creditor dissatisfied with a decision on a claim to vote may appeal to the court within two weeks of the decision, or on a claim to entitlement to a dividend not later than two weeks before the end of the accounting period: 1985 Act, s. 49(6).

Where the liquidator rejects a claim for damages the proper course is to bring an ordinary action rather than to appeal the liquidator's decision: *Crawford v. McCulloch* 1909 S.C. 1063; *Knoll Spinning Co. Ltd v. Brown* 1977 S.C. 291.

"NOTE".

For applications by note, see r. 15.2.

"SEND".

This includes deliver: r. 1.3(1) (definition of "send").

74.28.1

74.28.2

74.28.3

Appeals against valuation of debts

74.28A.—[3](1) An appeal under rule 7.23(4) of the Insolvency (RWU) Rules (appeal against valuation of debt by liquidator) against a valuation under paragraph (2)(a) of that rule must be made by note or, in a voluntary winding up where no previous application or appeal to the court has been made, by petition.

74.28A

---

[1] Rule 74.28 amended by S.S.I. 2019 No. 81 (effective 6 April 2019).
[2] Rule 74.28 amended by the Act of Sederunt (Rules of the Court of Session and Sheriff Court Company Insolvency Rules Amendment) (Miscellaneous) 2014 (SSI 2014/119) r.2 (effective 7th July, 2014).
[3] Rule 74.28A as inserted by S.S.I. 2019 No. 81 (effective 6th April 2019).

(2)   A note under paragraph (1) must be served on the liquidator.

Removal of liquidator

74.29
74.29.—[1](1)   An application by a creditor of the company for an order—

(a)   under section 171(3)(b) of the Act of 1986 (order directing the summoning of a meeting to replace the liquidator);

(b)   under section 171(3A)(b) of that Act (order directing the instigation of qualifying decision procedure); or

(c)   under section 172 of that Act (order for removal of a liquidator),

must be made by note.

(2)   Where the court orders the removal of a liquidator, the Deputy Principal Clerk must send two copies of the interlocutor to the former liquidator.

Deriv. R.C.S. 1965, r. 218J inserted by S.I. 1986 No. 2298

General note.

74.29.1
A liquidator may be removed from office by the court or a general meeting of creditors: Act of 1986, s. 172(2); Insolvency Rules, rr. 4.23 and 4.26. A provisional liquidator may only be removed by the court: Act of 1985, s. 172(2).

In *Geddes, Petr.* , 2006 S.L.T. 664, Lord Drummond Young held that the procedures contemplated by rules 4.28 and 4.29 of the Insolvency (Scotland) Rules 1986 for a liquidator seeking to be removed and replaced were unsatisfactory, and the procedure adopted in English cases such as *Re. Equity Nominees Ltd* , [2002] BCC 84, could competently be followed where the court had statutory power to remove a liquidator and a common law power to appoint a replacement.

"NOTE".

74.29.2
For applications by note, see r. 15.2.

Appeals and applications in relation to outlays and remuneration of liquidator

74.30
74.30.—[2](1)   An appeal by a liquidator, any creditor or any contributory under rule 7.12(1) of the Insolvency (RWU) Rules (appeal against fixing of outlays and remuneration: creditors' voluntary winding up and winding up by the court) must be made by note or, in a voluntary winding up where no previous application or appeal to the court has been made, by petition.

(2)   An application—

(a)   by a liquidator under rule 7.14 of the Insolvency (RWU) Rules (recourse to the court: creditors' voluntary winding up and winding up by the court); or

(b)   by a creditor of the company under rule 7.15 of the Insolvency (RWU) Rules (creditors' claim that remuneration is excessive: creditors' voluntary winding up and winding up by the court),

must be made by note or, in a voluntary winding up where no previous application or appeal to the court has been made, by petition.

(3)   A note under—

(a)   paragraph (1) where the appeal is by a creditor or contributory;

(b)   paragraph (2)(b),

must be served on the liquidator.

Deriv. R.C.S. 1965, r. 218K inserted by S.I. 1986 No. 2298

General note.

74.30.1
The liquidator may make a claim to the liquidation committee for outlays and remuneration: Act of 1986, s. 172(6); Insolvency Rules, r. 4.28(3). He may request an increase of the remuneration fixed by resolution of the creditors: Insolvency Rules, r. 4.28(4).

An application by a creditor to reduce the remuneration must be by one or more creditors representing at least 25 per cent by value of creditors: Insolvency Rules, r. 4.35.

---

[1] Rule 74.29 as substituted by S.S.I. 2019 No. 81 (effective 6th April 2019).
[2] Rule 74.30 as substituted by S.S.I. 2019 No. 81 (effective 6th April 2019).

Where there is no liquidation committee the practice, which has no statutory basis, has been for the court to remit to a reporter to audit the accounts of the liquidator and report his views to the court and to remit the question of remuneration to the Auditor if Court for him to report on a suitable figure. Where, however, there is no realistic prospect of any party other than the secured creditor having an interest in the outcome of the liquidation, the unsecured creditors are unwilling to form a liquidation committee and the level of outlays and remuneration sought do not give rise to obvious concern, the court may not consider it necessary to remit: *Dempster, Ptnr.* , 2011 S.C. 243 (OH); and see r. 4.68 of the Insolvency (Scotland) Rules 1986 applying s. 53 of the Bankruptcy (Scotland) Act 1985.

In *Re Quantum Distribution (UK) Ltd (In Liquidation)*, 2013 S.L.T. 211 (OH), a court reporter criticised a liquidator and raised concerns about his conduct of the liquidation including negotiations of a settlement between the petitioning creditor and the company's parent company in which a solicitor acted for the liquidator and the creditor. The Auditor of the Court of Session stated that he was unable to report the suitable remuneration for the liquidator (who then convened a creditors' meeting which appointed a liquidation committee which approved his fees). Lord Hodge held that it was the duty of the liquidator and the solicitor to bring the reporter's concerns to the attention of the court. The solicitor and the liquidator had failed to distinguish between the interests of the petitioning creditor and the interests of the creditors as a whole.

In *Liquidator of Equal Exchange Trading Ltd, Noter, 2019 S.L.T. 710 (OH)*, it was held that (1) a reporter's remit under the Insolvency Rules, rr. 4.5(2)(a) and 4.32(8) was to consider whether work was reasonable undertaken and might report to the court that work had been unnecessary or inappropriate; (2) it was for the reporter to consider issues of technical difficulty and complexity faced by the liquidator, and to advise the court using his experience and expertise that the appropriate level of staff seniority had been applied to the various tasks; (3) the reporter was entitled to raise with the court wider concerns regarding the conduct of the liquidation; (4) the court would expect certain matters to be reported as concerns, which, if not reported, would render the court unable to fix a liquidator's remuneration; (5) a liquidator had to be able to exercise his judgment and discretion, and the ambit of the reporter's remit was not such that mere disagreements between reporter and liquidator in respect of a liquidator's course of action should be raised as concerns.

"NOTE".

For applications by note, see r. 15.2.

74.30.2

Applications under section 176A of the Act of 1986

74.30A.—[1](1) An application by a liquidator, administrator or receiver under section 176A of the Act of 1986 shall be—

(a) where there is no existing process in relation to any liquidation, administration or receivership, by petition; or

(b) where a process exists in relation to any liquidation, administration or receivership, by note in that process.

(2) The Deputy Principal Clerk shall—

(a) after the lodging of any petition or note fix a hearing for the insolvency judge to consider an application under paragraph (1); and

(b) give notice of the hearing fixed under paragraph (2)(a) to the petitioner or noter.

(3) The petitioner or noter shall not be required to give notice to any person of the hearing fixed under paragraph (2)(a), unless the insolvency judge directs otherwise.

74.30A

GENERAL NOTE.

The requirements of r.74.30A(1A) are taken from r. 7.13A of the Insolvency Rules 1986 but were omitted when those Rules were replaced by the Insolvency (Scotland) (Receivership and Winding Up) Rules 2018 [SSI 2018 No. 347].

74.30A.1

Application to appoint a special manager

74.31.—(1) An application under section 177 of the Act of 1986 (application for the appointment of a special manager) shall be made by note.

(2)[2] A bond of caution together with a certificate as to the adequacy of the caution by the noter under rule 3.19(4), 4.38(4) or 5.42(4) of the Insolvency (RWU) Rules (caution) must be sent to the Petition Department by the noter.

74.31

---

[1] Rule 74.30A inserted by S.S.I. 2003 No. 385 (effective 15th September 2003).
[2] Rule 74.31(2) as substituted by S.S.I. 2019 No. 81 (effective 6 April 2019).

(3) After the Deputy Principal Clerk has satisfied himself as to the sufficiency of caution under rule 33.7(1) of these Rules, the clerk of session shall issue to the person appointed to be special manager a certified copy of the interlocutor appointing him.

(4) A special manager may, before the expiry of the period for finding caution, apply to the insolvency judge for an extension of that period.

Deriv. R.C.S. 1965, r. 218L(1) and (3) to (5) inserted by S.I. 1986 No. 2298

GENERAL NOTE.

74.31.1   Where a provisional liquidator is appointed or a company is in liquidation, the court may appoint a special manager of a part or the whole of the business or property of the company: Act of 1986, s. 177. The application must be supported by a report setting out the reasons for the appointment and the estimated value of the assets concerned: Insolvency Rules, r. 4.69(1) and (2).

The order of the court appointing the special manager must specify the period of appointment, whether for a specified period, until the occurrence of an event or until further order of the court: Insolvency Rules, r. 4.69(3).

A special manager must find caution: Act of 1986, s. 177(5)(a); Insolvency Rules, r. 4.70.

"NOTE".

74.31.2   For applications by note, see r. 15.2.

Determinations of accounting periods

74.31A   **74.31A.**—[1] An application for a determination of the court under rule 7.31(2)(c)(ii) of the Insolvency (RWU) Rules (determination of accounting period by the court) must be made by the liquidator by note or, in a voluntary winding up where no previous application or appeal to the court has been made, by petition.

Specific applications—voluntary winding up

74.31B   **74.31B.**—[2] An application to the court for—

(a) the appointment or removal and appointment of a liquidator under section 108 of the Act of 1986 (appointment or removal of liquidator by the court);

(b) sanction under section 110(3)(b) of the Act of 1986 (sanction for payment of compensation to liquidator);

(c) sanction under section 114(2) of the Act of 1986 (sanction for directors to exercise power);

(d) an order under rule 3.5(6) or 4.23(7) of the Insolvency (RWU) Rules (order of court to change liquidator's default date of release);

(e) authorisation under rule 3.15(4) or 4.33(4) of the Insolvency (RWU) Rules (realisation of the company's heritable property);

(f) approval under rule 4.7(5) of the Insolvency (RWU) Rules (approval for payment to liquidator of expenses of statement of affairs),

must be made by petition or, where a previous application to the court in relation to a voluntary winding up has been made, by note in the process of that petition.

Other applications—voluntary winding up

74.31C   **74.31C.**—[3] An application under the Act of 1986 or any subordinate legislation made under that Act in relation to a voluntary winding up not mentioned in this Part must be—

(a) where no previous application to the court in relation to a voluntary winding up has been made, by petition; or

(b) where a petition for such an application has been lodged, by note in the process of that petition.

---

[1] Rule 74.31A as inserted by S.S.I. 2019 No. 81 (effective 6 April 2019).
[2] Rule 74.31B as inserted by S.S.I. 2019 No. 81 (effective 6 April 2019).
[3] Rule 74.31C as inserted by S.S.I. 2019 No. 81 (effective 6 April 2019).

Other applications—winding up by the court

74.32.—[1](1) An application under the Act of 1986 or any subordinate legislation made under that Act, or Part VII of the Companies Act 1989, in relation to a winding up by the court not mentioned in this Part shall—

(a) if made by a party to the petition, be made by motion; or

(b) in any other case, be made by note.

(2) At the hearing of a motion under paragraph (1)(a), the court may order that the application be made by note; and, in such a case, shall make an order for the lodging of answers to the note in process within such period as it thinks fit.

Deriv. R.C.S. 1965, r. 218M inserted by S.I. 1986 No. 2298 and amended by S.I. 1991 No. 1157

"MOTION".

For motions, see Chap. 23.

"NOTE".

For applications by note, see r. 15.2.

There are a large number of applications arising out of or incidental to a liquidation which may be made by the liquidator or by other persons and for which these Rules make no separate provision. Examples are noted in the following paragraphs.

Once a winding up order has been pronounced or a provisional liquidator has been appointed, leave of the court is required under s. 130 of the Act of 1986 to proceed with or commence an action against a company. For an example of a successful note by a creditor for leave to raise proceedings against a company in liquidation, see: *Canon (Scotland) Business Machines Ltd v. G.A. Business Systems Ltd (in liquidation)* 1993 S.L.T. 387.

S. 212 of the Insolvency Act 1986 makes provision for a summary procedure against a delinquent director or officer of the company. The purpose of bringing an application under s. 212 is to examine into the conduct of any person who is or has been an officer of the company, or who has acted as liquidator, administrator, or administrative receiver of the company, or who has been concerned or taken part in the promotion, formation or management of a company, and who has misapplied, retained or become accountable for the company's money or other property or who has been guilty of misfeasance or breach of duty in relation to the company. After examination, the court may compel the person in respect of whom the application was made to repay, restore or account for the money or property (with interest at such rate as the court thinks just), or to contribute such sum to the company's assets by way of compensation as the court thinks just. An application may be made by a liquidator, official receiver, or by any creditor or contributory of the company. For an example of a successful application, and observations of the Lord President (Hope) on pleadings appropriate to such an application, see *Blin v. Johnstone* 1988 S.C. 63. An application under s. 212 should not be used as a means to gather information, for which separate provision is made in ss. 236 and 237 of the Act of 1986: *Gray v. Davidson* 1991 S.L.T. (Sh. Ct.) 61. Further observations on the summary nature of an application under this section may be found in the note of Sheriff Kelbie in *Datastor Technology Ltd v. Boston*, 28th April 1994 (reported in part in the commentary to *Ross v. Davy* 1996 S.C.L.R. 369).

The liquidator, too, may apply by note, for example, to seek an order that the winding up of the company proceed jointly with the sequestration of the estates of one of the company's directors (*Taylor, Noter* 1993 S.L.T. 375) or for exoneration and discharge (although there is no express statutory provision for this) during the course of a winding up which was continuing (*Brown v. Dickson* 1995 S.L.T. 354).

Replacement liquidators: block transfer orders

74.32A. *[Omitted by S.S.I. 2019 No. 81 (effective 6 April 2019)]*

GENERAL NOTE.

A block transfer order occurs where it is sought to transfer some or all of the cases in which the outgoing liquidator holds office to one or more replacement liquidators.

---

[1](1) Rule 74.32 as amended by S.S.I. 2019 No. 81 (effective 6 April 2019).

Approval of the voluntary winding up of a bank or building society[1]

74.32B

74.32B.—[2](1)[3]   An application for the prior approval of a resolution for voluntary winding up of a bank under section 84 of the Act of 1986 or voluntary winding up of a building society under section 88 of the Building Societies Act 1986 shall be made to the Deputy Principal Clerk by letter.

(2)   An application under paragraph (1) shall be marked as having been made on the date on which the letter is received by the court.

(3)   The letter shall be placed before the insolvency judge forthwith for consideration.

(4)   The court shall approve such a resolution by pronouncing an interlocutor to that effect.

Part VI – Disqualification of Company Directors

Applications in relation to disqualification orders or undertakings

74.33

74.33.[4, 5]   An application—

(a)   under section 3(2) of the Company Directors Disqualification Act 1986 (for disqualification for persistent breaches of companies legislation),

(aa)   under section 5A of that Act (for disqualification for certain convictions abroad);

(b)   under section 6(1) of that Act (to disqualify unfit directors of insolvent companies),

(c)   under section 8 of that Act (for disqualification of unfit director after investigation of a company),

(ca)[6]   under section 8A of that Act(variation or cessation of disqualification undertaking),

(cb)   under section 8ZB of that Act (for disqualification of person instructing unfit director of insolvent company);

(cc)   under section 8ZD of that Act (for order disqualifying person instructing unfit director: other cases);

(d)   under section 11(1) of that Act (for leave by an undischarged bankrupt to be concerned in a company),

(da)   under section 15A of that Act (for compensation orders);

(db)   under section 15C of that Act (for variation and revocation of compensation undertakings);

(e)   for leave under that Act, or

(f)   by the Secretary of State under rule 3(2) of the Insolvent Companies (Reports on Conduct of Directors) (Scotland) Rules 2016 (application for order directing compliance with requirements to furnish information etc.)

shall be made by petition.

Deriv. R.C.S. 1965, r. 218N(1) inserted by S.I. 1986 No. 2298

GENERAL NOTE.

74.33.1

A person may be disqualified on a number of grounds from being a director, liquidator, administrator, receiver, manager or in any way concerned with the promotion, formation or management of a company for a specified period without the leave of the court: Company Directors Disqualification Act 1986, s. 1(1). The Act of 1986 was intended for the protection of the public and was not a purely penal statute: *Re*

---

[1] R. 74.32B(1) and heading amended by S.S.I. 2009 No. 135 (effective 29th March 2009).
[2] R. 74.32B inserted by S.S.I. 2009 No. 63, r. 3 (effective 25th February 2009).
[3] R. 74.32B(1) and heading amended by S.S.I. 2009 No. 135 (effective 29th March 2009).
[4] R. 74.33 amended by S.S.I. 2005 No. 521 (effective 21st October 2005).
[5] Rule 74.33 amended by S.S.I. 2016 No. 384 (effective 24th December 2016).
[6] R. 74.33(ca) inserted by S.S.I. 2005 No. 521 (effective 21st October, 2005).

Jaymar Management [1990] B.C.C. 303. The provisions of the Act of 1986 fall to be construed accordingly: *Secretary of State for Trade and Industry v. Lovat* 1996 S.L.T. 124.

(A) Grounds for disqualification.

The grounds for disqualification fall into three categories: (1) disqualification for misconduct in connection with a company, (2) disqualification for unfitness and (3) other reasons for disqualification. Specific grounds in category (1) include cases where the person against whom an order is sought (a) has been convicted of an indictable offence in connection with the company (s.2 of the 1986 Act); (b) has committed persistent breaches of the companies legislation relating to the filing of returns, accounts, notices or other documents at Companies House (ss.3 and 5 of the 1986 Act); and (c) has participated in fraudulent trading (s.458 of the Companies Act 1985) or other fraud or breach of duty as a director which comes to light in the course of a winding up (s.4 of the 1986 Act). The fact that the person concerned has been or may be made criminally liable for his actings as a director does not preclude the making of an order for disqualification: s.1(4) of the 1986 Act. Category (2) relates generally to cases where, by reason of a person's conduct as a director, he shows himself to be unfit to be concerned with the management of a company. In all cases where it falls to a court to determine whether a person is unfit, the court shall have regard to the matters in Pt I of Sch.1 to the 1986 Act and, where the company of which the person concerned was a director has become insolvent, the court shall also have regard to the matters in Part II of Sch.1. The court has taken into account the conduct of a person after he ceased to be a director: *Re Godwin Warren Control Systems plc* [1992] B.C.C. 557. Included in category (3) are cases (a) where the person concerned was an undischarged bankrupt while acting as a director (s.11 of the 1986 Act) and (b) where the court makes a declaration under s.213 (wrongful trading) or s.214 (fraudulent trading) of the Insolvency Act 1986 that a person is liable to make a contribution to a company's assets it may also, whether or not application for such an order has been made, make an order for disqualification: s.10 of the 1986 Act.

Where the ground is conduct which makes a person unfit to be concerned in the management of a company and he is or has been a director of an insolvent company, the court must disqualify: 1986 Act, s.6. Only the Secretary of State may make an application under s.6: 1986 Act, s.7(1)(a); and see *Re NP Engineering and Security Products Ltd* [1995] 2 B.C.L.C. 585 (action brought by official receiver incompetent).

In exceptional circumstances an English court has stayed proceedings for disqualification where medical evidence established that it would be hazardous and difficult for the respondent director to embark on a trial lasting several weeks and where the director gave an undertaking not to act as a director or be concerned with the management of a company without leave of the court: *Re Homes Assured Corp. plc* [1996] B.C.C. 297.

To be unfit the director must be guilty of a serious failure to perform the duties of a director attendant on the privilege of trading through a company with limited liability: *Re Bath Glass Ltd* [1988] B.C.L.C. 329. A "breach of commercial morality" is one of several judicial formulations of unfitness.It is not a prerequisite to a finding of unfitness that the person concerned benefited from his misconduct: *Re Stanford Services Ltd* [1987] B.C.L.C. 607. A "marked degree of incompetence", even in the absence of dishonesty, will justify an order for disqualification: In *re Sevenoaks Stationers (Retail) Ltd* [1991] Ch. 164. In *In re Continental Assurance Co. of London*, *The Times,* 2nd July 1996, it was held that a failure to read the company's accounts and to appreciate that loans lacking any commercial justification had been made to the detriment of the company's creditors constituted "gross incompetence" to justify an order. A person does not escape liability by reason of his reliance on other directors to manage the financial affairs of the company: *Re City Investment Centres Ltd* [1992] B.C.L.C. 956. Each director has a responsibility to ensure proper control of the company's finances is maintained notwithstanding that one of their number has been appointed to have particular responsibility for the company's financial affairs: *Secretary of State for Trade and Industry v. Brown* 1995 S.L.T. 550. Directors who take advantage of limited liability must conduct their companies with due regard for the ordinary standards of commercial morality. They must observe the safeguards laid down by Parliament for the benefit of others who have dealings with their companies, including the proper maintenance, preparation and filing of books and accounts: *Re Swift Ltd, Secretary of State for Trade and Industry v. Ettinger* [1993] B.C.C. 312. A blatant disregard by a director for important aspects of accountability, such as complying with the requirements of the Companies Act 1985 for lodging of accounts, will itself be sufficient to attract a disqualification order: *Secretary of State for Trade and Industry v. Ettinger,* above; a dispute with the company's auditors over their fees did not justify such a failure: *Re Ward Sherrad Ltd* [1996] B.C.C. 418. Actings which are indicative of breaches of commercial probity on the part of a director include drawing a salary inappropriate for a company in distress, receiving a remuneration package out of proportion to the company's trading success and financial health, or taking unwarranted risks with creditors' money and trading at the expense of monies due to the Crown: *Synthetic Technology Ltd* [1993] B.C.C. 549. Unfitness involves questions of fact: *Secretary of State for Trade and Industry v. Queen* 1998 S.L.T. 735 (Ex. Div.).

Under s.7(3) of the Rehabilitation of Offenders Act 1974, a court may have regard to a spent conviction in considering whether a person is unfit to be a director of a company. The provisions of s.4(3) of the 1974 Act (excluding consideration or disclosure of spent convictions) do not apply to a judicial authority: *Secretary of State for Trade and Industry v. Queen* 1998 S.L.T. 735 (Ex. Div.).

(B)   Time limit for application.

Except with leave of the court, an application to the court for an order under s.6 of the 1986 Act shall not be made after the end of two years beginning with the date on which the company became insolvent: 1986 Act, s.7(2). A company is deemed, for the purposes of calculating the start of the two year period, to have become insolvent (a) when the company goes into liquidation at a time when its liabilities exceeds it assets, (b) when an administration order is made in relation to the company or (c) when an administrative receiver of the company is appointed: 1986 Act, s.6(2). In the case of a voluntary winding up, the winding up commences on the date the resolution to wind up the company was passed: s.129(1) of the Insolvency Act 1986. A winding up by the court commences on the date the petition is presented to the court: s. 129(2) of that Act. For the purposes of calculating the two year period within which a disqualification order must be sought, an administration order means an order under s.8 of the Insolvency Act 1986 and not an interim order under s.9 of that Act: *Secretary of State for Trade and Industry v. Palmer* 1994 S.C. 707. The date of the appointment of a receiver by the holder of a floating charge, from which the two year period begins to run, is the date on which the receiver receives the instrument of appointment: Insolvency Act 1986, s.53(6)(a). The receiver's docquet on that instrument of appointment is conclusive as to the date of his appointment: *Secretary of State for Trade and Industry v. Houston* 1994 S.L.T. 775, construing s.53(6) of the Insolvency Act 1986. In the case of an appointment of a receiver by the court, under s.51(2) of that Act, the two year period runs from the date of the presentation of the petition. Where there is more than one event triggering the deemed insolvency of the company, it would appear to be the case that the two year period runs from the date of the earlier event: *Official Receiver v. Nixon , The Times,* 16th December 1990. The date of the application for a disqualification order, for the purposes of determining whether that application is timeous, is the date of the presentation of the petition, not the subsequent date of the service on the respondent of that petition: *Secretary of State for Trade and Industry v. Normand* 1994 S.L.T. 1249, following *Secretary of State for Trade and Industry v. Josolyne* 1990 S.L.T.(Sh.Ct.) 48.

In considering whether to grant the Secretary of State leave to apply for a disqualification order outwith the two year statutory period under s.7(2) of the 1986 Act, the court will have regard to (a) the length of the delay (including the delay within the two year time limit for commencing proceedings), (b) the reason for the delay, (c) the strength of the case against the director, and (d) the degree of prejudice caused to the director by the delay: *Re Probe Data Systems Ltd (No.3), Secretary of State for Trade and Industry v. Desai* [1992] B.C.L.C. 405, 416 per Scott L.J. Leave is likely to be refused where no good explanation is adduced by the Secretary of State for the delay in bringing proceedings: *Secretary of State for Trade and Industry v. Morral* [1996] B.C.C. 299. However, the adequacy of any explanation does not itself constitute a threshold test in respect of the granting of leave, but is one of the factors to be considered in the light of all the circumstances: *Secretary of State for Trade and Industry v. Davies , The Times,* 7th June 1996.

The requirement in s.16 of the 1986 Act to give not less than 10 days' notice to the person against whom a disqualification order is to be sought is directory, not mandatory; and, accordingly, an application for an order for which less than 10 days' notice had been given was not incompetent: *Secretary of State for Trade and Industry v. Lovat* 1997 S.L.T. 124; *Secretary of State for Trade and Industry v. Langridge* [1991] Ch. 402.

(C)   Period of disqualification.

Following its predilection for guidelines, the Court of Appeal in England has issued guidelines for periods of disqualification under s.6: *In re Sevenoaks Stationers (Retail) Ltd* [1991] Ch. 164. The Scottish courts have adopted and applied the guidelines in that case: see, e.g. *Secretary of State for Trade and Industry v. Marshall* 1994 G.W.D. 19-1151; *Secretary of State for Trade and Industry v. Aitken* 1994 G.W.D. 19-1152; *Secretary of State for Trade and Industry v. Brown* 1995 S.L.T. 550; *Secretary of State for Trade and Industry v. Palfreman* 1995 S.L.T. 156; *Secretary of State for Trade and Industry v. Henderson* 1995 G.W.D. 21-1159. When considering whether and for how long to make a disqualification order a court is entitled to look at specific instances of misconduct: *Secretary of State for Trade and Industry v. McTigue , The Times,* 10th July 1996. For the purpose of fixing an appropriate period under s.6, no consideration is to be given by the court to the period between the failure of the company and the making of any order: *Secretary of State for Trade and Industry v. Arif The Times,* 25th March 1996.

(D)   Procedure.

The court may be satisfied without evidence in an unopposed application. In cases where a respondent has entered the process only to contest the length, not the making of, any disqualification order, it is not uncommon for the parties to agree the relevant facts by joint minute, e.g. as was done in *Secretary of State for Trade and Industry v. Brown*, above. Affidavits sworn by accountants but containing mainly hearsay, advocacy and submissions rather than expert opinion have been struck out as irrelevant and oppressive: *Re Oakfame Construction Ltd* [1996] B.C.C. 67.

The court may order the director subject to proceedings under s. 6 of the 1986 Act to pay part or all of the costs or expenses of the Secretary of State: *Re Pamstock Ltd* [1996] B.C.C. 341 (order for director to pay one-half of Secretary of State's costs, where every possible matter for complaint had been put forward, without real regard for circumstances or merits of the complaint, and which lengthened the hearing).

(E) Leave to continue to be concerned with the company.

The person who has been, or is being, disqualified, however, may apply to the court for leave to be a director, administrator, liquidator of the company, or a receiver or manager of the company's property, or otherwise concerned with the company: s. 1(1) of the 1986 Act. In considering whether or not to grant leave the court will have regard to the public interest in securing adequate protection from any real risk of bad management and whether there is a need for leave to be granted in the interests of the company: *Re Cargo Agency Ltd* [1992] B.C.C. 388. For an example of the court disqualifying a person from being a director under s. 6 of the 1986 Act but, at the same time, granting leave for him to remain a director of another company, see *Secretary of State for Trade and Industry v. Brown* 1995 S.L.T. 550. The court may, as a condition of granting such leave, impose conditions such as requiring the appointment of an independent director to the board of the company in respect of which leave to be a director is being granted: *Secretary of State for Trade and Industry v. Palfreman*, above.

(F) Jurisdiction.

The court having jurisdiction in an application under s. 6 of the 1986 Act is, in the case of a company being wound up by the court, or a company in relation to which an administration order is in force, the court by which the winding-up order was made or by which the administration order was made: s. 6(3)(a) and (c) of the 1986 Act. In relation to a company being wound up voluntarily, application for a disqualification order may be made to any court having jurisdiction to wind up the company: s. 6(3)(b) of the 1986 Act. In any other case, the court to which application may be made includes the Court of Session. The date of the application for a disqualification order is the relevant date for determining jurisdiction. Where, therefore, a winding-up order was pronounced by a court subsequent to the appointment of a receiver, it is the court which has pronounced the winding up which had jurisdiction (*Secretary of State for Trade and Industry v. Burnett* , 1998 S.L.T. 63, notwithstanding that another court (i.e. the Court of Session) would have had jurisdiction on the basis of s. 6(3)(d) prior to the pronouncement of the winding-up order, or would have had concurrent jurisdiction in a winding up by the court. On jurisdiction in a winding up by the court, see 74.21.2.

APPLICATIONS FOR LEAVE.

A person disqualified may seek leave of the court to do something from which he is disqualified: Company Directors Disqualification Act 1986, ss. 1(1) and 17. **74.33.2**

For a recent example of the grant of leave to a person to remain as director of two companies associated with a third insolvent company in respect of which that person was being disqualified, see *Secretary of State for Trade and Industry v. Palfreman* 1995 S.L.T. 156.

The phrase "leave of the court" has been interpreted in England as empowering the court to grant leave on conditions providing adequate protection from the danger legislated against. With some hesitation, but for reasons of comity in the application of a UK statute, Lord Johnston followed this interpretation in *Palfreman*, above. Typically, these conditions may require, for a person seeking to be appointed or to remain as a director, the appointment of an independent director or requirements ensuring financial accountability, or both. In Palfreman, above, the court imposed the condition that an independent director be appointed to the two companies of which the court granted leave to the respondent to remain as a director. In *Re Chatmore Ltd* [1990] B.C.L.C. 673, the court imposed the condition that the board of the company on which the disqualified person was to be granted leave to remain as a director was to hold monthly board meetings attended by the company's auditors.

For an example of the court's refusal of leave, see *Re Cargo Agency Ltd* [1992] B.C.L.C. 686.

An application for leave is required where the person disqualified wishes to act as a director of another company. There must be a real need in the interests of the company for leave to be granted: *Secretary of State for Trade and Industry v. Brown* 1995 S.L.T. 550 following *Re Cargo Agency Ltd*, above. In addition, if leave is to be granted, steps must be taken to ensure the adequate protection of the public from the risk of bad management. Such steps can include the management of the company's accounts on a day-to-day basis, management by or the appointment of independent directors to the board of the company, or the transfer of a balancing shareholding to one or more of the independent directors: see, e.g. *Secretary of State for Trade and Industry v. Brown*, above (leave for director to continue to be director of one company as there was no real risk of bad management of that company and his expertise was of great materiality to it).

"PETITION".

A petition is presented in the Outer House: r. 14.2(h). The petition must be in Form 14.4 in the official printed form: rr. 4.1 and 14.4. The petition must be signed by counsel or other person having a right of audience: r. 4.2; and see r. 1.3(1) (definition of "counsel" and "other person having a right of audience") and note 1.3.4. **74.33.3**

The petitioner must lodge the petition with the required steps of process (r. 4.4) and any documents founded on or adopted (r. 27.1(1)). A fee is payable on lodging the petition: see note 14.5.10.

On petitions generally, see Chap. 14.

Intimation, service and advertisement under this Part

74.34.—(1) Rule 74.22, except paragraphs (1)(c) and (2) of that rule, shall apply to the intimation, service and advertisement of a petition referred to in rule 74.33 (applications in relation to disqualification orders) as it applies to a petition under that rule.

(2)[1] A petition presented under rule 74.33 shall be intimated—

(a) to the Secretary of State for Business, Enterprise and Regulatory Reform; or

(b) where a petition is presented under rule 74.33(ca) and the disqualification undertaking was given under section 9B of the Company Directors Disqualification Act 1986 (competition undertaking), to the Office of Fair Trading or any specified regulator which has accepted the undertaking, as the case may be;

unless the petition is presented by that person or body.

Deriv. R.C.S. 1965, r. 218N(3) substituted by S.I. 1990 No. 705

GENERAL NOTE.

The applicant for a disqualification order must give not less than 10 days' notice of intention to apply for the order to the person against whom the order is sought: Company Directors Disqualification Act 1986, s. 16(1).

Part VII[2] – Bank Insolvency Procedure

Petition for bank insolvency

74.35.—[3](1) An application for a bank insolvency order under section 95 of the Act of 2009 shall be made by petition.

(2) A petition under paragraph (1) shall include averments in relation to—

(a) the name and address of the person to be appointed as the bank liquidator, and his qualification to act;

(b) the current name and any other trading names of the bank;

(c) the address of the bank's registered office, and any previous such address within six months immediately before the presentation of the petition so far as known to the petitioner;

(d) a home address for each director of the bank;

(e) a statement of the amount of the bank's capital (nominal and issued) indicating what part is called up, paid up or credited as paid up, and the amount of the assets of the bank so far as known to the petitioner;

(f) whether, to the knowledge of the petitioner, a bank administrator has been appointed in respect of the bank or a supervisor has been appointed in respect of the bank under a voluntary arrangement under Part 1 of the Act of 1986; and

(g) the grounds on which the petition proceeds.

GENERAL NOTE.

Special provisions for failing banks were introduced after the banking crisis in 2007. Temporary measures were followed by the Banking Act 2009. A bank is defined in s. 2 of the 2009 Act.

When a bank fails, a bank insolvency order instead of ordinary liquidation may be obtained by the Bank of England, the FSA or the Secretary of State on certain grounds: 2009 Act, s.95. The idea is to provide an orderly winding up of a bank and for compensation to affected claimants or transfer of their accounts to another bank.

---

[1] R. 74.34(2) substituted by S.S.I. 2005 No. 521 (effective 21st October, 2005) and by S.S.I. 2007 No. 449 (effective 25th October 2007).

[2] Part VII and r. 74.35 inserted by S.S.I. 2009 No. 63, r. 3 (effective 25th February 2009).

[3] Part VII and r. 74.35 inserted by S.S.I. 2009 No. 63, r. 3 (effective 25th February 2009).

A petition is presented to the Outer House: r. 14.2(h). The petition must be in Form 14.4 in the official printed form: rr.4.1 and 14.4. The petition must be signed by counsel or other person having a right of audience: r.4.2; and see r.1.3(1) (definition of "counsel" and "other person having a right of audience") and note 1.3.4.

The petitioner must lodge the petition with the required steps of process: r.4.4. A fee is payable on lodging the petition: see note 14.5.10.

On petitions generally, see Chap. 14.

74.35.2

Intimation, service and advertisement under this Part

74.36.—[1](1) Unless the court otherwise directs, the order under rule 14.5 (first order in petitions) for intimation, service and advertisement of a petition referred to in rule 74.35 shall include—

74.36

   (a) a requirement to serve two copies of the petition—

      (i) on the bank and each director of the bank;

     (ii) on the Bank of England, if it is not the petitioner;

   (iii)[2] on the Financial Conduct Authority, if it is not the petitioner;

    (iv) on the Secretary of State, if he is not the petitioner;

     (v) on the proposed bank liquidator;

    (vi) on the Financial Services Compensation Scheme;

   (vii) on any person who has given notice to the Financial Services Authority in respect of the bank under section 120 of the Act of 2009;

  (viii) if there is in force for the bank a voluntary arrangement under Part 1 of the Act of 1986, the supervisor of that arrangement; and

    (ix) where a bank administrator has been appointed in relation to the bank, on that bank administrator;

   (b) a requirement to advertise the petition forthwith—

      (i) once in the Edinburgh Gazette; and

     (ii) once in one or more of such newspapers as the court shall direct; and

   (c) the time and date fixed by the court for the hearing of the petition.

(2) In fixing the time and date for the hearing of the petition mentioned in paragraph (1)(c) the court shall ensure that the date and time is as soon as reasonably practicable, having regard to the need to give the directors of the bank a reasonable opportunity to attend.

(3) Unless the court otherwise directs, where the petition is served under paragraph (1), one copy of the petition shall be sent electronically as soon as practicable to each of the persons named in the order and the other copy shall be served on those persons in accordance with Chapter 16 of these Rules.

(4) Any answers to the petition must be lodged 24 hours before the date fixed by the court under this rule and a copy of the answers must be served on the petitioner before that date.

(5) An advertisement under paragraph (1) shall include—

   (a) the identity of the petitioner;

   (b) the name and address of the agent for the petitioner;

   (c) the date on which the petition was presented;

   (d) where a provisional bank liquidator has been appointed by the court, his name, address and the date of his appointment; and

---

[1] Rule 74.36 inserted by S.S.I. 2009 No. 63, r. 3 (effective 25th February 2009).

[2] Rule 74.36 amended by the Financial Services Act 2012 (Consequential Amendments and Transitional Provisions) Order 2013 (SI 2013/472) Sch.2 para.10 (effective 1st April, 2013).

(e) a statement that any person who intends to appear in the petition must lodge answers no later than 24 hours prior to the date set down for a hearing in terms of paragraph (1)(c).

"INTIMATION, SERVICE AND ADVERTISEMENT".

74.36.1   See Chap. 16.

"ANSWERS".

74.36.2   See r. 18.3.

Provisional bank liquidator

74.37   **74.37.**—[1](1) An application to appoint a provisional bank liquidator under section 135 of the Act of 1986, as that provision is applied and modified by section 103 of the Act of 2009, may be made—

(a) by the petitioner, in the prayer of the petition or, if made after the petition has been presented, by note; or

(b) by any other person entitled to make an application under section 95 of the Act of 2009, by note.

(2) The application mentioned in paragraph (1) shall include averments in relation to—

(a) the grounds for appointment of the provisional bank liquidator;

(b) the name and address of the person proposed to be appointed, and his qualification to act, as provisional bank liquidator; and

(c) confirmation that the person to be appointed has consented to act as provisional bank liquidator.

(3) Where the court decides to appoint a provisional bank liquidator—

(a) it shall pronounce an interlocutor making the appointment and specifying the functions to be carried out by him in relation to the affairs of the bank; and

(b) the applicant shall forthwith send a certified copy of such interlocutor to the person appointed and to such other persons as are specified under rule 12 of the Bank Insolvency Rules (order of appointment of provisional bank liquidator).

(4) On receiving a certified copy of an interlocutor pronounced under paragraph (3), the provisional bank liquidator shall intimate his appointment forthwith—

(a) once in the Edinburgh Gazette; and

(b) once in one or more such newspapers as the court has directed.

(5) An application for the discharge of a provisional bank liquidator shall be made by note.

GENERAL NOTE.

74.37.1   On provisional liquidators generally, see note 74.25.1.

INTIMATION IN EDINBURGH GAZETTE AND NEWSPAPERS.

74.37.2   See note 74.25.4.

Applications and appeals in relation to a statement of affairs

74.38   **74.38.**—[2](1) An application under section 131(5) of the Act of 1986, as applied and modified by section 103 of the Act of 2009, for—

(a) release from an obligation imposed under section 131(1) or (2) of the Act of 1986, as so applied and modified; or

(b) an extension of time for the submission of a statement of affairs,

---

[1] Rule 74.37 inserted by S.S.I. 2009 No. 63, r. 3 (effective 25th February 2009).
[2] R. 74.38 inserted by S.S.I 2009 No. 63, r. 3 (effective 25th February 2009).

shall be made by note.

(2) A note under paragraph (1) shall be served on the bank liquidator or provisional bank liquidator, as the case may be, who may lodge—

(a) answers to the note; or

(b) a report on any matters which he considers should be drawn to the attention of the court.

(3) Where the bank liquidator or provisional bank liquidator lodges a report under paragraph (2), he shall forthwith send a copy of it to the noter.

(4) Where the bank liquidator or provisional bank liquidator does not appear at any hearing on the note, a certified copy of the interlocutor disposing of the note shall be sent to him forthwith by the noter.

(5) Where a certified copy of the interlocutor is sent to the bank liquidator or provisional bank liquidator in accordance with paragraph (4), the noter shall forthwith provide notice of that fact to the court.

(6) An appeal under rule 4.9(6) of the Insolvency Rules (appeal against refusal by liquidator of allowance towards expenses of preparing statement of affairs), as applied by rule 19 of the Bank Insolvency Rules, shall be made by note.

GENERAL NOTE.

See note 74.27.1.

74.38.1

Appeals against adjudication of claims

74.39. *[Omitted by S.S.I. 2016 No. 312 (effective 30th November 2016).]*

74.39

"NOTE".

For applications by note, see r.15.2.

74.39.1

Removal of bank liquidator

74.40.[1] An application for an order under section 108 of the Act of 2009 (removal of bank liquidator by the court) shall be made by note.

74.40

GENERAL NOTE.

An application to remove a bank liquidator may be made by the liquidation committee, the FSA or the Bank of England.

74.40.1

"NOTE".

For applications by note, see r.15.2.

74.40.2

Application in relation to remuneration of bank liquidator

74.41.—[2](1) An application—

74.41

(a) by a bank liquidator under rule 4.34 of the Insolvency Rules (application to increase remuneration), as that rule is applied by rule 47 of the Bank Insolvency Rules; or

(b) by a creditor of the bank under rule 4.35 of the Insolvency Rules (application to reduce liquidator's remuneration), as that rule is applied by rule 48 of the Bank Insolvency Rules,

shall be made by note.

"NOTE".

For applications by note, see r.15.2.

74.41.1

---

[1] R. 74.40 inserted by S.S.I. 2009 No. 63, r. 3 (effective 25th February 2009).
[2] R. 74.41 inserted by S.S.I. 2009 No. 63, r. 3 (effective 25th February 2009).

Applications under section 176A of the Act of 1986

74.42

74.42.—[1](1) An application by a bank liquidator or bank administrator under section 176A of the Act of 1986 (share of assets for unsecured creditors), as applied and modified by section 103 of the Act of 2009, shall be made by note in the existing bank liquidation or bank administration process.

(2) The Deputy Principal Clerk shall—

(a) after the lodging of any note fix a hearing for the insolvency judge to consider an application under paragraph (1); and

(b) give notice of the hearing fixed under paragraph (2)(a) to the noter.

(3) The noter shall not be required to give notice to any person of the hearing fixed under paragraph (2)(a), unless the insolvency judge directs otherwise.

GENERAL NOTE.

74.42.1

Section 176A of the 1986 Act was inserted by the Enterprise Act 2002. It is designed to re-distribute company assets whereby a prescribed part of a company's net property is available for uninsured debtors and is not distributable to proprietors of a floating charge unless the court, on a application to it, orders otherwise.

Applications to appoint a special manager

74.43

74.43.—[2](1) An application under section 177 of the Act of 1986 (application for the appointment of a special manager), as applied and modified by section 103 of the Act of 2009, shall be made by note.

(2) A bond of caution certified by the noter under rule 4.70(4) of the Insolvency Rules, as that rule is applied by rule 82 of the Bank Insolvency Rules, shall be sent to the Petition Department by the noter.

(3) After the Deputy Principal Clerk has satisfied himself as to the sufficiency of caution under rule 33.7(1) of these Rules, the clerk of session shall issue to the person appointed to be special manager a certified copy of the interlocutor appointing him.

(4) A special manager may, before the expiry of the period for finding caution, apply to the insolvency judge for an extension of that period.

"SPECIAL MANAGER".

74.43.1

See note 74.31.1.

"NOTE".

74.43.2

For applications by note, see r.15.2.

Other applications

74.44

74.44.—[3](1) An application under the Act of 1986 as applied by the Act of 2009, under the Act of 2009 or under any subordinate legislation made under those Acts, in relation to a bank insolvency not mentioned in this Part shall—

(a) if made by a party to the petition, be made by motion; or

(b) in any other case, be made by note.

(2) At the hearing of a motion under paragraph (1)(a), the court may order that the application be made by note; and, in such a case, shall make an order for the lodging of answers to the note in process within such period as it thinks fit.

"PETITION".

74.44.1

A petition is presented to the Outer House: r.14.2(h). The petition must be in Form 14.4 in the official printed form: rr.4.1 and 14.4. The petition must be signed by counsel or other person having a right of audience: r.4.2; and see r.1.3(1) (definition of "counsel" and "other person having a right of audience") and note 1.3.4.

---

[1] Rule 74.42 inserted by S.S.I. 2009 No. 63, r. 3 (effective 25th February 2009).
[2] Rule 74.43 inserted by S.S.I. 2009 No. 63, r. 3 (effective 25th February 2009).
[3] Rule 74.44 inserted by S.S.I. 2009 No. 63, r. 3 (effective 25th February 2009).

The petitioner must lodge the petition with the required steps of process: r.4.4. A fee is payable on lodging the petition: see note 14.5.10.

On petitions generally, see Chap. 14.

"NOTE".

For applications by note, see r.15.2.

74.44.2

Part VIII[1] – Bank Administration Procedure

Petition for bank administration

74.45.—[2](1) An application by the Bank of England for a bank administration order under section 142 of the Act of 2009 shall be made by petition.

74.45

(2) A petition under paragraph (1) shall include averments on the following matters—

(a) the name and address of the person to be appointed as the bank administrator, and his qualification to act;

(b) confirmation that the conditions for applying for a bank administration order, set out in section 143 of the Act of 2009, are met in respect of the bank;

(c) the bank's current financial position to the best of the Bank of England's knowledge and belief, including actual, contingent and prospective assets and liabilities;

(d) any security which the Bank of England knows or believes to be held by the creditors of the bank;

(e) whether any security confers power to appoint an administrator under paragraph 14 of Schedule B1 to the Act of 1986 (holder of qualifying floating charge) or a receiver of the whole (or substantially the whole) of the bank's property, and whether such an administrator or receiver has been appointed;

(f) any insolvency proceedings which have been instituted in respect of the bank, including any process notified to the Financial Services Authority under section 120 of the Act of 2009;

(g) details of any property transfer instrument which the Bank of England has made or intends to make under section 11(2)(b) or 12(2) of the Act of 2009 in respect of the bank;

(h) where the property transfer instrument has not yet been made, an explanation of what effect it is likely to have on the bank's financial position;

(i) how the making of a bank administration order will achieve the objectives specified in section 137 of the Act of 2009;

(j) how functions are to be apportioned where more than one person is to be appointed as bank administrator and, in particular, whether functions are to be exercisable jointly or individually; and

(k) other matters which the Bank of England considers will assist the court in deciding whether to grant a bank administration order.

GENERAL NOTE.

Only the Bank of England may make an application for a bank administration order. A provisional bank administrator may be appointed under s. 136 of the Insolvency Act 1986 by virtue of s. 145 of the 2009 Act. See notes to r. 74.25 on provisional liquidators.

74.45.1

---

[1] Part VIII and r. 74.45 inserted by S.S.I. 2009 No. 63, r. 3 (effective 25th February 2009).
[2] Part VIII and r. 74.45 inserted by S.S.I. 2009 No. 63, r. 3 (effective 25th February 2009).

74.45.2   A petition is presented to the Outer House: r.14.2(h). The petition must be in Form 14.4 in the official printed form: rr.4.1 and 14.4. The petition must be signed by counsel or other person having a right of audience: r.4.2; and see r.1.3(1) (definition of "counsel" and "other person having a right of audience") and note 1.3.4.

The petitioner must lodge the petition with the required steps of process: r.4.4. A fee is payable on lodging the petition: see note 14.5.10.

On petitions generally, see Chap. 14.

Hearing of petition

74.46   **74.46.**—[1](1) Where a petition is lodged under rule 74.45, the court shall fix a time and date for the hearing of the petition and in doing so shall ensure that the date and time is as soon as is reasonably practicable, having regard to the need to give the directors of the bank a reasonable opportunity to attend.

(2) At the hearing of a petition, each of the following may appear or be represented—

    (a)   the Bank of England;

    (b)[2] the Financial Conduct Authority;

    (ba)[3] the Prudential Regulation Authority;

    (c)   the bank;

    (d)   any director of the bank;

    (e)   any person nominated for appointment as bank administrator of the bank;

    (f)   any person who holds a qualifying floating charge for the purposes of paragraph 14 of Schedule B1 to the Act of 1986; and

    (g)   with the permission of the court, any other person who appears to have an interest.

Provisional bank administrator

74.47   **74.47.**—[4](1) An application to appoint a provisional bank administrator under section 135 of the Act of 1986, as that provision is applied and modified by section 145 of the Act of 2009, may be made by the Bank of England in the prayer of the petition or, if made after the petition has been presented, by note.

(2) The application mentioned in paragraph (1) shall include averments on the following matters—

    (a)   the grounds for appointment of the provisional bank administrator;

    (b)   the name and address of the person proposed to be appointed, and his qualification to act, as provisional bank administrator;

    (c)   confirmation that the person to be appointed has consented to act as provisional bank administrator; and

    (d)   the Bank of England's estimate of the value of the assets in respect of which the provisional bank administrator is entitled to be appointed.

(3) An order appointing any provisional bank administrator shall specify the functions to be carried out in relation to the bank's affairs and how those functions are to be apportioned where more than one person is to be appointed as provisional bank administrator and, in particular, shall specify whether functions are to be exercisable jointly or individually.

(4) Where the court decides to appoint a provisional bank administrator—

---

[1] Rule 74.46 inserted by S.S.I 2009 No. 63, r. 3 (effective 25th February 2009).

[2] Rule 74.46 amended by the Financial Services Act 2012 (Consequential Amendments and Transitional Provisions) Order 2013 (SI 2013/472) Sch.2 para.10 (effective 1st April, 2013).

[3] Rule 74.46 inserted by the Financial Services Act 2012 (Consequential Amendments and Transitional Provisions) Order 2013 (SI 2013/472) Sch.2 para.10 (effective 1st April, 2013).

[4] Rule 74.47 inserted by S.S.I. 2009 No. 63, para. 3 (effective 25th February 2009).

(a) it shall pronounce an interlocutor making the appointment and specifying the functions to be carried out by him in relation to the affairs of the bank; and

(b)[1] it shall forthwith send a certified copy of the interlocutor to the person appointed.

(5) On receiving a certified copy of an interlocutor pronounced under paragraph (4)(a), the provisional bank administrator shall intimate his appointment forthwith—

(a) once in the Edinburgh Gazette; and

(b) once in one or more such newspapers as the court has directed.

(6) An application for the discharge of a provisional bank administrator shall be made by note.

Report of bank administrator's proposals: Schedule B1 to the Act of 1986

74.48.—[2](1) Paragraph (2) shall apply where a report under paragraphs 53(2) or 54(6) of Schedule B1 to the Act of 1986 (report at conclusion of creditors' meeting), as those provisions are applied and modified by section 145 of the Act of 2009, discloses a failure to approve, or to approve a revision of, a bank administrator's proposals. **74.48**

(2) The Deputy Principal Clerk shall fix a hearing for determination by the insolvency judge of any order that may be made under paragraph 55(2) of Schedule B1 to the Act of 1986, as that provision is applied and modified by section 145 of the Act of 2009.

Time and date of lodging in a bank administration

74.49.—[3](1) The time and date of lodging of a notice or document relating to a bank administration under— **74.49**

(a) the Act of 2009;

(b) the Act of 1986, as applied by the Act of 2009;

(c) the Bank Administration Rules; or

(d) the Insolvency Rules, as applied by the Bank Administration Rules, shall be noted by the Deputy Principal Clerk upon the notice or document.

(2) Subject to any provision of the Bank Administration Rules, or the Insolvency Rules as applied by the Bank Administration Rules—

(a) where the time of lodging of a notice or document cannot be ascertained by the Deputy Principal Clerk, the notice or document shall be deemed to have been lodged at 10 a.m. on the date of lodging; and

(b) where a notice or document under paragraph (1) is delivered on any day other than a business day but is not lodged on that day, the date of lodging shall be the first business day after such delivery.

Applications during a bank administration

74.50.[4] An application or appeal under any provision of the Act of 1986 as applied by the Act of 2009, the Insolvency Rules as applied by the Bank Administration Rules, the Act of 2009 or the Bank Administration Rules, during a bank administration shall be— **74.50**

(a) where no previous application or appeal has been made, by petition; or

---

[1] Rule 74.47(4)(b) amended by S.S.I. 2010 No. 417 (effective 1st January 2011).
[2] Rule 74.48 inserted by S.S.I. 2009 No. 63, para. 3 (effective 25th February 2009).
[3] Rule 74.49 inserted by S.S.I. 2009 No. 63, para. 3 (effective 25th February 2009) and amended by S.S.I. 2009 No. 135 (effective 29th March 2009).
[4] Rule 74.50 inserted by S.S.I. 2009 No. 63, para. 3 (effective 25th February 2009).

(b) where a petition for an order in respect of a bank administration has been lodged, by note in the process of that petition.

Part IX[1] – Building Society Special Adminstration Procedure

Application of rules to building society special administration

74.51   **74.51.**—[2](1) Subject to paragraph (3), Part VIII of this Chapter applies to an application mentioned in paragraph (2) as it applies to an application for a bank administration order.

(2) An application referred to in paragraph (1) is an application for a building society special administration order under the Act of 2009, as that Act is applied and modified by section 90C of the Building Societies Act 1986 and the Building Societies (Insolvency and Special Administration) Order 2009.

(3) In the application of Part VIII of this Chapter under paragraph (1)—

(a) references to the Bank Administration Rules shall be read as references to the Building Society Special Administration (Scotland) Rules 2009;

(b) references to a rule in the Bank Administration Rules shall be read as references to the corresponding rule in the Building Society Special Administration (Scotland) Rules 2009;

(c)[3] references to the Act of 2009 shall be read as references to the Act of 2009, as applied and modified by sections 84 and 90C of the Building Societies Act 1986 and the Building Societies (Insolvency and Special Administration) Order 2009; and references to specific provisions in the Act of 2009 shall be read accordingly;

(d) references to "bank" shall be read as references to "building society";

(e) references to "bank administration" shall be read as references to "building society special administration";

(f) references to "bank administration order" shall be read as references to "building society special administration order";

(g) references to "bank administrator" shall be read as references to "building society special administrator";

(h) in rule 74.45(2)(e) (averments on power to appoint administrator or receiver), the words "an administrator under paragraph 14 of Schedule B1 to the Act of 1986 (holder of qualifying floating charge) or" and "an administrator or" shall be omitted;

(i) in rule 74.45(2)(f) (averments on insolvency proceedings), for "section 120 of the Act of 2009" substitute "section 90D of the Building Societies Act 1986"; and

(j) in rule 74.46(2) (representation at hearing of petition), subparagraph (f) shall be omitted.

(4)[4] The following rules shall, with the necessary modifications, apply in relation to building society special administration procedure as they apply in relation to bank administration procedure—

rule 74.1 (application and interpretation of Chapter 74),

rule 74.2 (proceedings before insolvency judge),

rule 74.3 (notices and reports etc. sent to the court),

rule 74.9 (form of applications).

---

[1] Part IX and r. 74.51 inserted by S.S.I. 2009 No. 135 (effective 29th March 2009).

[2] Part IX and r. 74.51 inserted by S.S.I. 2009 No. 135 (effective 29th March 2009).

[3] Rule 74.51(3)(c) and (4) amended by S.S.I. 2010 No. 417 (effective 1st January 2011).

[4] Rule 74.51(3)(c) and (4) amended by S.S.I. 2010 No. 417 (effective 1st January 2011).

GENERAL NOTE.

Provisions of the 2009 Act may be applied, subject to modification, to building societies. Section 90C of the Building Societies Act 1986 inserted by S.I. 2009/805 is such a modifying provision of application.

Part X[1] – Building Society Insolvency Procedure

Application of rules to building society insolvency

74.52.—[2](1) Subject to paragraph (3), Part VII of this Chapter applies to an application mentioned in paragraph (2) as it applies to an application for a bank insolvency order.

(2) An application referred to in paragraph (1) is an application for a building society insolvency order under the Act of 2009, as that Act is applied and modified by section 90C of the Building Societies Act 1986 and the Building Societies (Insolvency and Special Administration) Order 2009.

(3) In the application of Part VII of this Chapter under paragraph (1)—

    (a) references to the Bank Insolvency Rules shall be read as references to the Building Society Insolvency (Scotland) Rules 2010;

    (b) references to a rule in the Bank Insolvency Rules shall be read as references to the corresponding rule in the Building Society Insolvency (Scotland) Rules 2010;

    (c) references to the Act of 2009 shall be read as references to the Act of 2009, as applied and modified by section 90C of the Building Societies Act 1986 and the Building Societies (Insolvency and Special Administration) Order 2009; and references to specific provisions in the Act of 2009 shall be read accordingly;

    (d) references to any Part or provision of the Act of 1986 that is not applied by Part 2 of the Act of 2009 shall be read as references to that Part or provision as applied and modified by section 90A of, and Schedule 15A to, the Building Societies Act 1986;

    (e) references to "bank" shall be read as references to "building society";

    (f) references to "bank administration" shall be read as references to "building society special administration";

    (g) references to "bank administrator" shall be read as references to "building society special administrator";

    (h) references to "bank insolvency order" shall be read as references to "building society insolvency order";

    (i) references to "bank liquidator" shall be read as references to "building society liquidator";

    (j) rule 74.36(1)(a)(iv) (intimation, service and advertisement) shall be disregarded; and

---

[1] Part X and r. 74.52 inserted by S.S.I 2010 No. 417 (effective 1st January 2011).
[2] Part X and r. 74.52 inserted by S.S.I 2010 No. 417 (effective 1st January 2011).

(k) in rule 74.36(1)(a)(vii), the reference to "section 120 of the Act of 2009" shall be read as a reference to "section 90D of the Building Societies Act 1986".

Part XI[1] – Investment Bank Special Administration Procedure

Interpretation and application of other rules

74.53.—[2](1) Unless the context otherwise requires, words and expressions used in this Part which are also used in the Investment Bank Rules have the same meaning as in those Rules.

(2) The following rules shall, with the necessary modifications, apply in relation to an application mentioned in rule 74.54 as they apply in relation to bank insolvency procedure or bank administration procedure—

rule 5.1A (further restriction as to caveats),

rule 33.9 (insolvency or death of cautioner or grantor),

rule 74.1 (application and interpretation of Chapter 74),

rule 74.2 (proceedings before insolvency judge),

rule 74.3 (notices and reports, etc., sent to the court),

ule 74.9 (form of other applications).

GENERAL NOTE.

The Regulations provide a special administration regime for investment bankers (defined in s. 232 of the Banking Act 2009). The Rules set out the procedure for the investment bank special administration process under the Regulations which require a court order with the appointment of an administrator.

The Regulations are the Investment Bank Special Administration Regulations 2011 (S.I. 2011/245). The Rules are the Investment Bank Special Administration (Scotland) Rules 2011 (S.I. 2011/2262).

Application for special administration order, special administration (bank insolvency) order and special administration (bank administration) order

74.54.—[3](1) An application for any of the following orders shall be made by petition—

(a) a special administration order under regulation 5 of the Investment Bank Regulations;

(b) a special administration (bank insolvency) order under section 95 of the Act of 2009, as applied by Schedule 1 to the Investment Bank Regulations;

(c) a special administration (bank administration) order under section 142 of the Act of 2009, as applied by Schedule 2 to the Investment Bank Regulations.

(2) A petition referred to in paragraph (1) shall include averments on the following matters—

(a) the name and address of the person whom it is proposed should be appointed as administrator and his or her qualification to act;

(b) the grounds upon which the petition is made, and the reasons why the petitioner considers that those grounds are satisfied;

(c) in the case of an application for a special administration (bank administration) order, confirmation that the conditions for applying for such an order, as set out in section 143 of the Act of 2009, as applied by paragraph 6 of Schedule 2 to the Investment Bank Regulations) are met in respect of the investment bank;

74.53

74.53.1

74.54

---

[1] Part XI and r. 74.53 inserted by S.S.I. 2011 No. 385 para. 3 (effective 14th November 2011).
[2] Part XI and r. 74.53 inserted by S.S.I. 2011 No. 385 para. 3 (effective 14th November 2011).
[3] Rule 74.54 inserted by S.S.I. 2011 No. 385 para. 3 (effective 14th November 2011).

   (d)   to the best of the petitioner's knowledge and belief, the investment bank's current financial position, including actual, contingent and prospective assets and liabilities;

   (e)   any security known or believed to be held by the creditors of the investment bank;

   (f)   in the case of an application for a special administration (bank administration) order, details of the property transfer instrument which the Bank of England has made or intends to make in respect of the investment bank;

   (g)   in the case of an application for a special administration (bank administration) order, where the property transfer instrument has not yet been made, an explanation of what effect the instrument is likely to have on the investment bank's financial position;

   (h)   to the best of the petitioner's knowledge and belief, the amount of any client assets held by the investment bank;

   (i)   how functions are to be apportioned where more than one person is to be appointed as administrator and, in particular, whether functions are to be exercised jointly or by any or all the persons appointed;

   (j)   any other matters which the petitioner considers will assist the court in deciding whether to make a special administration order, a special administration (bank administration) order or a special administration (bank insolvency) order; and

   (k)[1]   any insolvency proceedings which have been instituted in respect of the investment bank, including any process notified to the Financial Conduct Authority or the Prudential Regulation Authority under section 120 of the Act of 2009, as applied by paragraph 7 of Schedule 1 to the Investment Bank Regulations.

  (3) Averments referred to in paragraph (2)(b) shall refer to one or more of the grounds set out in regulation 6 of the Investment Bank Regulations or section 96 or section 143 of the Act of 2009, as the case may be.

"PETITION".

A petition is presented to the Outer House: r.14.2(h). The petition must be in Form 14.4 in the official printed form: rr.4.1 and 14.4. The petition must be signed by counsel or other person having a right of audience: r.4.2; and see r.1.3(1) (definition of "counsel" and "other person having a right of audience") and note 1.3.4.

74.54.1

Intimation, service and advertisement under this Part

74.55.—[2](1) Unless the court otherwise directs, the order under rule 14.5 (first order in petitions) for intimation, service and advertisement of the petition shall include a requirement—

74.55

   (a)   where the investment bank is not the petitioner or one of the petitioners, to serve the petition on the investment bank;

   (b)   to advertise the petition immediately—

       (i)   once in the Edinburgh Gazette; and

      (ii)   once in one or more such newspapers as the court shall direct.

  (2) Subject to rule 14.6(2) (application to shorten or extend the period of notice), the period of notice for lodging answers to the petition shall be eight days.

  (3) An advertisement under paragraph (1) shall include—

---

[1] Rule 74.54 amended by the Financial Services Act 2012 (Consequential Amendments and Transitional Provisions) Order 2013 (SI 2013/472) Sch.2 para.10 (effective 1st April, 2013).

[2] Rule 74.55 inserted by S.S.I. 2011 No. 385 para. 3 (effective 14th November 2011).

(a) the name and address of the petitioner and, where the petitioner is the investment bank, its registered office;

(b) the name and address of the agent for the petitioner;

(c) the date on which the petition was presented;

(d) the nature of the order sought;

(e) where a person has been appointed by the court under section 135 of the Act of 1986, as applied by paragraph 8 of Schedule 1 or paragraph 6 of Schedule 2 to the Investment Bank Regulations, his or her name and address and the date of his or her appointment;

(f) the period of notice for lodging answers;

(g) a statement that any person who intends to appear in the petition must lodge answers within the period of notice.

"ANSWERS".

74.55.1   For the form and lodging of answers, see r. 18.3 and notes.

Person appointed under section 135 of the Act of 1986, as applied

74.56   **74.56.**—[1](1) An application to appoint a person under section 135 of the Act of 1986, as applied by paragraph 8 of Schedule 1 or paragraph 6 of Schedule 2 to the Investment Bank Regulations, may be made in the prayer of the petition referred to in rule 74.54 or, if made after the petition has been presented, by note.

(2) The application mentioned in paragraph (1) shall include averments on the following matters—

(a) the grounds upon which it is proposed that the person should be appointed;

(b) the name and address of the person whom it is proposed should be appointed;

(c) confirmation that the person whom it is proposed should be appointed has consented to that appointment;

(d) confirmation that the person whom it is proposed should be appointed is qualified to act as a person under section 135 of the Act of 1986, as relevantly applied;

(e) whether to the applicant's knowledge there has been proposed or is in force for the investment bank a company voluntary arrangement under Part 1 of the Act of 1986;

(f) the applicant's estimate of the value of the assets in respect of which the person is to be appointed;

(g) the functions the applicant wishes to be carried out by the person to be appointed in relation to the investment bank's affairs.

(3) An order appointing any person as referred to in paragraph (1) shall specify the functions to be carried out in relation to the investment bank's affairs and how those functions are to be apportioned where more than one person is to be so appointed and, in particular, shall specify whether functions are to be exercised jointly or by any or all the persons appointed.

(4) Where the court decides to appoint a person as referred to in paragraph (1)—

(a) it shall pronounce an interlocutor making the appointment and specifying the functions to be carried out by the appointed person in relation to the affairs of the investment bank; and

(b) it shall forthwith send a copy of the interlocutor to the person appointed.

(5) On receiving a certified copy of an interlocutor pronounced under paragraph (4)(a), the person appointed shall intimate his appointment forthwith—

---

[1] Rule 74.56 inserted by S.S.I. 2011 No. 385 para. 3 (effective 14th November 2011).

(a)   once in the Edinburgh Gazette; and

(b)   once in one or more such newspapers as the court has directed.

(6)   An application for the discharge of a person appointed in accordance with this rule shall be made by note.

"NOTE".

For the form and lodging of notes, see r. 15.2 and notes.   **74.56.1**

Report of administrator's proposals: Schedule B1 to the Act of 1986

74.57.—¹(1)   Paragraph (2) shall apply where a report under paragraphs 53(2) or   **74.57**
54(6) of Schedule B1 to the Act of 1986 (report at conclusion of creditors' meeting), as those provisions are applied and modified by regulation 15 of, or paragraphs 10(4) or 11(8) of Schedule 2 to, the Investment Bank Regulations, discloses a failure to approve, or to approve a revision of, an administrator's proposals.

(2)   The Deputy Principal Clerk shall fix a hearing for determination by the insolvency judge of any order that may be made under paragraph 55(2) of Schedule B1 to the Act of 1986, as that provision is applied and modified by regulation 15 of the Investment Bank Regulations or by section 145 of the Act of 2009 and paragraph 6 of Schedule 2 to the Investment Bank Regulations.

Time and date of lodging in special administration etc.

74.58.—²(1)   The time and date of lodging of a notice or document relating to a   **74.58**
special administration, special administration (bank insolvency) or special administration (bank administration) shall be noted by the Deputy Principal Clerk upon the notice or document.

(2)   Subject to any provision in the Investment Bank Rules—

(a)   where the time of lodging of a notice or document cannot be ascertained by the Deputy Principal Clerk, the notice or document shall be deemed to have been lodged at 10 a.m. on the date of lodging;

(b)   where a notice or document under paragraph (1) is delivered on any day other than a business day but is not lodged on that day, the date of lodging shall be the first business day after such delivery.

Appeals against adjudication of claims

74.59.—³(1)⁴   An appeal under section 127(5) of the Bankruptcy (Scotland) Act   **74.59**
2016, as applied by rule 127 of the Investment Bank Rules (appeal by a creditor or contributory of the investment bank against a decision of the administrator) shall be made by note.

(2)   A note under paragraph (1) shall be served on the administrator.

(3)   On such a note being served on the administrator, the administrator shall send the claim in question, and a copy of his or her adjudication, forthwith to the Deputy Principal Clerk who shall cause them to be lodged in process.

(4)   After the note has been disposed of, the Deputy Principal Clerk shall return the claim and the adjudication to the administrator with a copy of the interlocutor disposing of the note.

"NOTE".

For the form and lodging of notes, see r. 15.2 and notes.   **74.59.1**

---

¹ Rule 74.57 inserted by S.S.I. 2011 No. 385 para. 3 (effective 14th November 2011).
² Rule 74.58 inserted by S.S.I. 2011 No. 385 para. 3 (effective 14th November 2011).
³ Rule 74.59 inserted by S.S.I. 2011 No. 385 para. 3 (effective 14th November 2011).
⁴ Rule 74.59(1) amended by S.S.I. 2016 No. 312 para. 2 (effective 30th November 2016).

Applications under section 176A of the Act of 1986

74.60   **74.60.**—[1](1) An application by an administrator under section 176A of the Act of 1986 (share of assets for unsecured creditors), as applied by Table 2 in regulation 15 of, or paragraph 6 of Schedule 2 to, the Investment Bank Regulations, shall be made by note in the existing special administration process.

(2) The Deputy Principal Clerk shall—

(a) after the lodging of any note fix a hearing for the insolvency judge to consider an application under paragraph (1); and

(b) give notice of the hearing fixed under paragraph (2)(a) to the noter.

(3) The noter shall not be required to give notice to any person of the hearing fixed under paragraph (2)(a), unless the insolvency judge directs otherwise.

"NOTE".

74.60.1   For the form and lodging of notes, see r. 15.2 and notes.

Applications during a special administration etc.

74.61   **74.61.**—[2](1) An application or appeal under any provision of the Act 1986 as applied by the Act of 2009, the Investment Bank Regulations or the Investment Bank Rules during a special administration, special administration (bank insolvency) or special administration (bank administration) shall be made—

(a) where no previous application or appeal has been made, by petition; or

(b) where a petition for an order in respect of a special administration, special administration (bank insolvency) or special administration (bank administration) has been lodged, by note in the process of that petition.

PART XII[3]

PAYMENT AND ELECTRONIC MONEY INSTITUTIONS SPECIAL ADMINISTRATION PROCEDURE

Interpretation of this Part

74.62   **74.62.** In this Part—

"2021 Regulations" means the Payment and Electronic Money Institution Insolvency Regulations 2021;

"2022 Rules" means the Payment and Electronic Money Institution Insolvency (Scotland) Rules 2022;

"cause to which this Part applies" means a cause under—

(a) the 2021 Regulations;

(b) the 2022 Rules;

(c) any other enactment applied (with or without modification) by virtue of the 2021 Regulations;

"special administration order" means a special administration order under regulation 7 of the 2021 Regulations (special administration order).

"THE 2021 REGULATIONS"

74.62.1   The Payment and Electronic Money Institution Insolvency Regulations 2021 are made under the Banking Act 2009.

"SPECIAL ADMINISTRATION ORDER"

74.62.2   A special administration order under reg. 7 of the 2021 Regulations is an order appointing an insolvency practitioner as the administrator of an institution (in effect an authorised or small electronic

---

[1] Rule 74.60 inserted by S.S.I. 2011 No. 385 para. 3 (effective 14th November 2011).
[2] Rule 74.61 inserted by S.S.I. 2011 No. 385 para. 3 (effective 14th November 2011).
[3] As inserted by the Act of Sederunt (Rules of the Court of Session 1994 Amendment) (Payment and Electronic Money Institution Special Administration) 2024 S.S.I. 2024 No. 75 r. 2(6), Sched. 1 (effective 12th April 2024).

money institution which carries on electronic money and payment services in the UK).

Application and interpretation of other rules

74.63.—(1) In this Chapter, besides this Part, only the following provisions apply to a cause to which this Part applies—

  (a) Part I (general provisions);

  (b) rule 74.13 (report of administrator's proposals: schedule B1 to the Act of 1986).

(2) In relation to a cause to which this Part applies, a reference in these Rules to an enactment that is applied (with or without modification) by virtue of the 2021 Regulations is to be read as a reference to that enactment as so applied.

74.63

Application for special administration order

74.64.—(1) An application for a special administration order under regulation 8 of the 2021 Regulations (application for order) is to be made by petition.

(2) A petition referred to in paragraph (1) must include (in addition to the information required by rule 6 of the 2022 Rules (content of application)) averments on the following matters—

  (a) the reasons why the petitioner considers the grounds stated in accordance with rule 6(h) of the 2022 Rules to be satisfied;

  (b) to the best of the petitioner's knowledge and belief, the financial position of the institution in respect of which the order is sought (including actual, contingent and prospective assets and liabilities);

  (c) any security the petitioner knows, or believes, is held by the creditors of the institution;

  (d) to the best of the petitioner's knowledge and belief, the amount of any relevant funds held by the institution;

  (e) how functions are to be apportioned where more than one person is to be appointed as administrator and, in particular, whether functions are to be exercised jointly or by any or all of the persons appointed;

  (f) any other matter that the petitioner considers it will assist the court to be aware of in deciding whether to make a special administration order.

(3) In paragraph (2)(d), "relevant funds" is to be construed in accordance with regulation 6 of the 2021 Regulations (definitions).

74.64

GENERAL NOTE

An application for a special administration order may be made by the institution, the directors or a creditor, a contributor, the Secretary of State or the FCA: 2021 Regulations, reg. 8. If the FCA is not an applicant, it is entitled to be heard on the application.

74.64.1

"PETITION"

See Chap. 14. The petition will be presented in the Outer House: r. 14.2(h) and come before the insolvency judge: r. 74.2.

74.64.2

"RULE 6 OF THE 2022 RULES"

The Payment and Electronic Money Institution Insolvency (Scotland) Rules 2022are made under the Insolvency Act 1986.

An application for a special administration order must state (a) the full name and registered number of the institution, (b) any other trading names of the institution, (c)the institution's date of incorporation, (d) the institution's nominal capital and the amount of capital paid up, (e) the address of the institution's registered office, (f) an email address for the institution, (g) the identity of the person (or persons) nominated for appointment as administrator, and (h) which of the grounds in regulation 9(1) of the 2021 Regulations the applicant is relying on in making the application.

The grounds on which an application may be made are (A) that the institution is, or is likely to become, unable to pay its debts, (B) that it is fair to put it into special administration, and (C) that it is expedient in the public interest to put it into special administration. The Secretary of State may only apply in grounds (B) or (C). See the 2021 Regulations, reg. 9.

74.64.3

The court must be satisfied that the grounds are made out. The administrator has the objectives of (1) to ensure the return of relevant funds, (2) to ensure timely engagement with payment system operators and (3) either to rescue the institution as a going concern or to wind it up in the best interests of the creditors: 2021 Regulations, reg. 12.

Advertisement of petition under rule 74.64(1)

74.65 **74.65.**—(1) Unless the court otherwise directs, the order under rule 14.5 (first order in petitions) for intimation, service and advertisement of a petition under rule 74.64 (application for special administration order) must include a requirement to advertise the petition immediately—

    (a) once in the Edinburgh Gazette;

    (b) once in one or more such newspapers as the court directs.

(2) An advertisement under paragraph (1) must include—

    (a) the name and address of the petitioner and, where the petitioner is the institution in respect of which a special administration order is sought, its registered office;

    (b) the name and address of the agent for the petitioner;

    (c) the date on which the petition was presented;

    (d) the nature of the order sought;

    (e) the period of notice for lodging answers;

    (f) a statement that any person who intends to appear in the petition must lodge answers within the period of notice.

(3) This rule is without prejudice to the requirements for service in rule 9 of the 2022 Rules (service of application).

Period of notice for lodging answers to petition under rule 74.64(1)

74.66 **74.66.** Subject to rule 14.6(2) (period of notice for lodging answers), the period of notice for lodging answers to a petition under rule 74.64(1) (application for special administration order) is 8 days.

Time and date of lodging

74.67 **74.67.**—(1) The time and date of lodging a document in a cause to which this Part applies is to be noted by the Deputy Principal Clerk upon the document.

(2) Subject to any provision of the 2022 Rules—

    (a) where the time of lodging the document cannot be ascertained by the Deputy Principal Clerk, the document is to be deemed to have been lodged at 10 a.m. on the date of lodging;

    (b) where the document is delivered on a day other than a business day, but is not lodged on that day, the date of lodging is to be deemed to be the first business day after its delivery.

(3) For the avoidance of doubt, in this rule "document" includes notice.

Appeal against adjudication of claim

74.68 **74.68.**—(1) An appeal under rule 119(5) of the 2022 Rules (adjudication of claims) is to be made by note.

(2) The note is to be served on the administrator.

(3) On being served with the note, the administrator must send to the Deputy Principal Clerk, without delay—

    (a) the claim in question;

    (b) the administrator's adjudication in relation to it.

(4) The Deputy Principal Clerk, on receiving the documents sent in accordance with paragraph (3), must cause them to be lodged in process.

(5) After the note has been disposed of, the Deputy Principal Clerk must return the documents sent in accordance with paragraph (3) to the administrator with a copy of the interlocutor disposing of the note.

"RULE 119(5) OF THE 2022 RULES"

Any member of the institution or any creditor may, if dissatisfied with the acceptance or rejection of any claim (in whole or in part) by the administrator or, in relation to such acceptance or rejection, with a decision in respect of any matter requiring to be recorded under para. (4)(a) or (4)(b) of r. 119, appeal to the court not later than 14 days before the end of the accounting period, and the applicant must give notice of the application to the FCA.
74.68.1

"NOTE"

See r. 15.2.
74.68.2

Application under section 176A of the Act of 1986

74.69.—(1)   An application under section 176A1 of the Act of 1986 (share of assets for unsecured creditors) by an administrator appointed under regulation 7 of the 2021 Regulations, is to be made by note.
74.69

(2)   After the lodging of the note, the Deputy Principal Clerk must—

(a)   fix a hearing for the insolvency judge to consider the application;

(b)   give notice of the hearing to the noter.

(3)   The noter is not required to give notice of the hearing to another person, unless the insolvency judge directs otherwise.

"SECTION 176A OF THE ACT OF 1986"

This section applies where is a floating charge. The administrator makes a prescribed part of the institution's net property available for the satisfaction of unsecured debts. (The administrator must not distribute that part to the proprietor of a floating charge except in so far as it exceeds the amount required for the satisfaction of unsecured debts.)
74.69.1

"NOTE"

See r. 15.2.
74.69.2

Form of other applications and appeals

74.70.—(1)   An application or appeal to the court under an enactment mentioned in paragraph (2) is to be made—
74.70

(a)   by note in the process of the petition to which it relates; or

(b)   if there is no such petition, by petition.

(2)   The enactments referred to in paragraph (1) are—

(a)   a provision of the 2021 Regulations, except regulation 8 (application for order) (*see* rule 74.64);

(b)   a provision of the 2022 Rules, except rule 119(5) (adjudication of claims) (*see* rule 74.68);

(c)   any other enactment applied (with or without modification) by virtue of the 2021 Regulations, except section 176A of the Act of 1986 (*see* rule 74.69).

"NOTE"

See r. 15.2.
74.70.1

"PETITION"

See Chap. 14. The petition will be presented in the Outer House: r. 14.2(h); and come before the insolvency judge: r. 74.2.
74.70.2

[THE NEXT PARAGRAPH IS 74A.1]

"RULE 11.9(5) OF THE 2021 RULES."

74.68.1 "Any member of the institution of any creditor may, if dissatisfied with the acceptance or rejection of any claim (in whole or in part) by the administrator or, in a matter, non-acceptance or rejection, with a decision in respect of any matter required to be recorded under para... (a) or (b) of rule 11.9, appeal to the court not more than 14 days before the end of the accounting period, and the applicant must give notice of the application to the PCA.

"NOTE."

74.68.2 Sec. 152

Application under section 176A of the Act of 1988

74.69.—(1) An application under section 176A.1 of the Act of 1988 relating to assets for unsecured creditor(s) by an administrator appointed under regulation 7 of the 2021 Regulations, is to be made by note.

(2) After the lodging of the note, the Deputy Principal Clerk must—
  (a) fix a hearing for the insolvency judge to consider the application;
  (b) give notice of the hearing to the noter.

(3) The noter is not required to give notice of the hearing to another person, unless the insolvency judge directs otherwise.

"SECTION 176A OF THE ACT OF 1988."

74.69.1 This section applies where is a floating charge. The administrator must make a prescribed part of the debtor's net property available for the satisfaction of unsecured debts. (2) The administrator must not distribute that part to the proprietor of a floating charge except in so far as it exceeds the amount required to satisfy satisfaction of unsecured debts.

"NOTE."

74.69.2 Sec. 152

Form of other applications and appeals

74.70.—(1) An application or appeal to the court under an enactment mentioned in paragraph (2) is to be made—
  (a) as note in the process of the petition to which it relates; or
  (b) if there is no such petition, by petition.

(2) The enactments referred to in paragraph (1) are—
  (a) a provision of the 2021 Regulations, except regulation 8 (application for order) (see rule 74.61);
  (b) a provision of the 2021 Rules, except rule 11.9(5) (adjudication of claims) (see rule 74.68);
  (c) any other enactment applied (with or without modification) by virtue of the 2021 Regulations, except section 176A of the Act of 1988 (see rule 74.69).

"NOTE."

74.70.1 Sec. 152

"PETITION."

74.70.2 See Chap. 9.3. The petition will be presented at the Qutet... House... r. 14.20 and ceases to have effect, apart from... p. 42.

[THE NEXT PARAGRAPH IS 74.74.]

CHAPTER 74A ORDERS AGAINST INSOLVENCY PRACTITIONERS AND RECOGNISED PROFESSIONAL BODIES

Chapter 74A[1]

Orders Against Insolvency Practitioners and Recognised Professional Bodies

Application and interpretation of this Chapter

74A.1.—(1) This Chapter applies to applications under the Insolvency Act 1986 for orders against persons who act as insolvency practitioners and against recognised professional bodies.

(2) In this Chapter—

"the Act of 1986" means the Insolvency Act 1986;

"act as insolvency practitioner" has the same meaning as in section 388 of the Act of 1986;

"recognised professional body" has the same meaning as in section 391 of the Act of 1986.

74A.1

GENERAL NOTE.

Under s. 391P of the Act of 1986, the Secretary of State may apply to the court for a direct sanctions order to be made against a person if it appears to the Secretary of State that it would be in the public interest for the order to be made. Conditions in s. 391Q must be met and in deciding whether the conditions are met, the court must have regard to the extent to which the relevant recognised professional body has taken action against the person in respect of the failure mentioned in condition 1, and that action is sufficient to address the failure.

Under s. 391T of the Act of 1986, if at any time it appears to the Secretary of State that a recognised professional body has failed to comply with a requirement imposed on it by or by virtue of that Part, or any other person has failed to comply with a requirement imposed on the person by virtue of s. 391S, the Secretary of State may make an application to the court. The court may order the body or person to take such steps as the court considers will secure that the requirement is complied with.

74A.1.1

Applications

74A.2.—(1) An application—

(a) under section 391P of the Act of 1986 (application for, and power to make, direct sanctions order against a person acting as an insolvency practitioner); or

(b) under section 391T of the Act of 1986 (compliance order against a recognised professional body),

is made by petition.

74A.2

"PETITION".

A petition under this Chapter is presented to the Outer House: r. 14.2(h). The petition must be in Form 14.4 in the official printed form: rr. 4.1 and 14.4. The petition must be signed by counsel or other person having a right of audience: r. 4.2; and see r. 1.3(1) (definition of "counsel" and "other person have a right of audience") and note 1.3.4.

The petitioner must lodge the petition with the required step of process (r. 4.4). A fee is payable on lodging the petition: see note 14.5.10.

On petitions generally, see Chap. 14.

74A.2.1

---

[1] Chapter 74A as inserted by S.S.I. 2016 No. 384 para. 2 (effective 24th December 2016).

Chapter 75

Applications Relating to Financial Services[1]

Part I – Applications under the Financial Services Act 1986

Application and interpretation of this Part[2]

75.1.—[3](1) This Part applies to an application, under the Financial Services Act 1986, mentioned in rule 75.2.

(2) In this Part—

"the Act of 1986" means the Financial Services Act 1986.

"designated agency" has the meaning assigned in section 114(3) of the Act of 1986.

Deriv. R.C.S. 1965, r. 260M inserted by S.I. 1987 No. 2160 (r. 75.1(2))

"DESIGNATED AGENCY".

A number of the functions of the Secretary of State have been transferred to the Securities and Investments Board Ltd (currently the only designated agency): see the Financial Services Act 1986 (Delegation) Order 1987 [S.I. 1987 No. 942], the Financial Services Act 1986 (Delegation) (No.2) Order 1988 [S.I. 1988 No. 738], the Financial Services Act 1986 (Delegation) Order 1991 [S.I. 1991 No. 200] and the Financial Services Act 1986 (Delegation) (No.2) Order 1991 [S.I. 1991 No. 1256].

Form of applications under the Act of 1986

75.2.—(1) An application under any of the following provisions of the Act of 1986 shall be made by petition:—

    (a) sections 6, 61, 71(1), 91(4), 104(4), 131(8) and 184(8) (applications by Secretary of State or designated agency for interdict or restitution);

    (b) sections 12, 20, 37(8) and 39(8) (applications by Secretary of State or designated agency for compliance orders);

    (c) section 93 (applications by Secretary of State or designated agency to remove or replace a manager or trustee or to wind up a unit trust scheme); and

    (d) Schedule 11—

        (i) paragraph 6(1) (applications by the Friendly Societies Commission for compliance orders);

        (ii) paragraph 7(4) (applications by recognised self regulating organisations to set aside a direction);

        (iii) paragraph 22 (applications by the Friendly Societies Commission for interdict or to remedy a contravention); and

        (iv) paragraph 23(1) so far as it modifies section 61 as applied by section 71(1) (applications by the Friendly Societies Commission for interdict or restitution).

(2) Certification by inspectors or the court by virtue of section 94(3), or under section 178(1), of the Act of 1986 shall be made by petition.

Deriv. R.C.S. 1965, r. 260N(1) and (2) inserted by S.I. 1987 No. 2160

"PETITION".

A petition under this Chapter is presented to the Outer House: r. 14.2(h). The petition must be in Form 14.4 in the official printed form: rr. 4.1 and 14.4. The petition must be signed by counsel or other person having a right of audience: r. 4.2; and see r. 1.3(1) (definition of "counsel" and "other person having a right of audience") and note 1.3.4.

---

[1] Chap. heading, and r. 75.1 and heading, amended by S.I. 1996 No. 1756 (effective 5th August 1996).
[2] Chap. heading, and r. 75.1 and heading, amended by S.I. 1996 No. 1756 (effective 5th August 1996).
[3] Chap. heading, and r. 75.1 and heading, amended by S.I. 1996 No. 1756 (effective 5th August 1996).

The petitioner must lodge the petition with the required steps of process (r. 4.4). A fee is payable on lodging the petition: see note 14.5.10.

On petitions generally, see Chap. 14.

Intimation and service

75.3   **75.3.** An order under any of the following provisions of the Act of 1986 shall only be made following intimation and service of the petition to the person against whom the order is to be made:—

(a)   section 6 (interdict and restitution orders);

(b)   section 61 (interdict and restitution orders);

(c)   section 71(1) (orders in respect of breach of prohibition or requirement);

(d)   section 91(4) (orders in respect of contravention of a direction);

(e)   section 104(4) (orders in respect of contravention of a requirement);

(f)   section 131(8) (orders in respect of contravention of restrictions on promotion of contracts of insurance);

(g)   section 184(8) (orders in respect of contravention of notice of restriction of investment or insurance business); and

(h)   paragraph 22 of Schedule 11 (interdict of regulated friendly society).

Deriv. R.C.S. 1965, r. 260N(3) inserted by S.I. 1987 No. 2160

"INTIMATION AND SERVICE".

75.3.1   See r. 14.7 and Chap. 16, Pt. I.

Questions relating to interpretation of rules or regulations

75.4   **75.4.** Where a question of the interpretation of any of the rules or regulations referred to in section 61(1)(a) of the Act of 1986 arises in a petition under this rule, the Secretary of State, a designated agency, or any person referred to in section 61(1)(a)(iv) of that Act, and not already a party in the cause, shall be given the opportunity to make representations to the court by lodging answers to the petition.

Deriv. R.C.S. 1965, r. 260N(4) inserted by S.I. 1986 No. 2160

"ANSWERS".

75.4.1   On form and procedure for answers, see r. 18.3.

Part II[1] – Applications under the Uncertificated Securities Regulations 1995

Interpretation of this Part

75.5   **75.5.**[2] In this Part—

"operator" has the meaning assigned in regulation 3(1) of the Regulations of 1995;

"the Regulations of 1995" means the Uncertificated Securities Regulations 1995.

GENERAL NOTE.

75.5.1   Part II of this Chapter (inserted by A.S. (R.C.S.A. No. 3) (Miscellaneous) 1996 (S.I. 1996 No. 1756) extends and adapts the provisions of Pt. I to applications under the Uncertificated Securities Regulations 1995 (S.I. 1995/3272). The regulations provide a paperless system of share transfer replacing share certificates with a computer-loaded system. This system replaces the unsuccessful TAURUS system, and it is expected that CREST will apply for approval as an operator.

"OPERATOR".

75.5.2   The powers of the Treasury under the Regulations of 1995 have been delegated to the Securities and Investments Board. No person has yet been approved as operator, though applications for approval have been received.

---

[1] Pt. II and r. 75.5 inserted by S.I. 1996 No. 1756 (effective 5th August 1996).
[2] Pt. II and r. 75.5 inserted by S.I. 1996 No. 1756 (effective 5th August 1996).

Form of applications under the Regulations of 1995

75.6.[1] An application under regulation 8 (application by Secretary of State for compliance order), or regulation 9 (application by Secretary of State for interdict or restitution), of the Regulations of 1995 shall be made by petition.

"PETITION".

A petition under this Chapter is presented to the Outer House: r. 14.2(h). The petition must be in the Form 14.4 in the official printed form: rr. 4.1 and 14.4. The petition must be signed by counsel or other person having a right of audience: r. 4.2; and see r. 1.3(1) (definition of "counsel" and "other person having a right of audience) and note 1.3.4.

The petitioner must lodge the petition with the required steps of process (r. 4.4). A fee is payable on lodging the petition: see note 14.5.10.

On petitions generally, see Chap. 14.

Intimation and service

75.7.[2] An order under regulation 9 of the Regulations of 1995 shall only be made following intimation and service of the petition—

    (a)   on the person against whom the order is to be made; and

    (b)   on the operator.

"INTIMATION AND SERVICE".

See r. 14.7 and Chap. 16, Pt. I.

Questions relating to interpretation of rules of an operator

75.8.[3] Where a question of the interpretation of any of the rules of an operator referred to in regulation 9(1)(a) of the Regulations of 1995 arises in a petition under this rule, the Secretary of State and the operator, if not already parties, shall be given the opportunity to make representations to the court by lodging answers to the petition.

"ANSWERS".

On form and procedure for answers, see r. 18.3.

75.6

75.6.1

75.7

75.7.1

75.8

75.8.1

---

[1] R. 75.6 inserted by S.I. 1996 No. 1756 (effective 5th August 1996).
[2] R. 75.7 inserted by S.I. 1996 No. 1756 (effective 5th August 1996).
[3] R. 75.8 inserted by S.I. 1996 No. 1756 (effective 5th August 1996).

CHAPTER 76 CAUSES IN RELATION TO CONFISCATION OF PROCEEDS OF CRIME

Chapter 76

Causes in Relation to Confiscation of Proceeds of Crime

Part I[1] – Causes under the Proceeds of Crime (Scotland) Act 1995

Interpretation of this Chapter

76.A1.[2] In this Chapter—

> "the 2014 Regulations" means the Criminal Justice and Data Protection (Protocol No. 36) Regulations 2014; and
>
> "domestic restraint order" and "specified information" have the meanings given by paragraph 1 of schedule 1 to the 2014 Regulations.

76.A1

Interpretation of this Part

76.1.[3] In this Part—

> "the Act of 1995" means the Proceeds of Crime (Scotland) Act 1995;
>
> "administrator" means the person appointed under paragraph 1(1) of Schedule 1 to the Act of 1995;
>
> "restraint order" has the meaning assigned in section 49(1) of the Act of 1995.

76.1

Deriv. R.C.S. 1965, r. 201C inserted by S.I. 1990 No. 705

"RESTRAINT ORDER".

This means an order interdicting the person in respect of whom it is made from dealing with his realisable property, or that person and any person named in the order who appears to have received from that person an implicative gift (see s. 6 of the Act of 1995) from dealing with their own, or the other's, realisable property, whenever that property was acquired and whether described in the order or not: Act of 1995 (c. 43), s. 28.

76.1.1

Disapplication of certain rules to this Part

76.2. The following rules shall not apply to a petition or note mentioned in this Part:—

rule 14.5 (first order in petitions),

rule 14.6(1) (period of notice for lodging answers),

rule 14.7 (intimation and service of petitions),

rule 14.9 (unopposed petitions).

76.2

Applications for restraint orders

76.3.—(1)[4] An application under section 28(1) of the Act of 1995 (application for restraint order) shall be made by petition.

76.3

(2) Where the court pronounces an interlocutor making a restraint order, the Lord Advocate shall serve a certified copy of that interlocutor on every person named in the interlocutor as restrained by the order.

(3)[5] Where the application is made under the said section as applied by article 4 of the Confiscation of the Proceeds of Crime (Designated Countries and Territories) (Scotland) Order 1999 (application in relation to certain external confiscation orders etc.) or by article 4 of the Criminal Justice (International Co-operation) Act 1990 (Enforcement of Overseas Forfeiture Orders) (Scotland) Order 1999 (application in relation to certain external forfeiture orders etc.), there shall be appended to the peti-

---

[1] Part I heading amended by S.I. 1996 No. 2168 (consolidating enactment).
[2] R.76.A1 inserted by S.S.I. 2016 No. 319 para.2 (effective 12 December 2016).
[3] Part I heading and r. 76.1 amended by S.I. 1996 No. 2168 (consolidating enactment).
[4] R. 76.3(1) amended by S.I. 1996 No. 2168 (consolidating enactment).
[5] R. 76.3(3) and (4) inserted by S.I. 1999 No. 1220 (effective 1st May 1999).

tion a certificate in conformity with paragraph (b) of subsection (3) of the section as so applied by the article in question; but that certificate, as so appended, shall not include a statement of information or belief with the sources and grounds thereof if the prayer includes an application for a direction under that paragraph.

(4)[1] Where the court grants the prayer of the petition in an application such as is mentioned in paragraph (3) but declines to make such direction as is so mentioned, the petitioner shall forthwith lodge in process, as an addendum to the certificate which was appended to the petition, a statement of information or belief with the sources and grounds thereof.

(5)[2] An application by the prosecutor for a certificate under paragraph 2 of schedule 1 to the 2014 Regulations (domestic restraint orders: certification) must—

(a)   contain the specified information; and

(b)   set out why the prosecutor considers that the property to which the application relates has been used or is likely to be used for the purposes of an offence or is the proceeds of an offence.

(6)[3] Where the court makes a certificate it must—

(a)   do so in the form annexed to Council Framework Decision 2003/577/JHA of 22 July 2003 on the execution in the European Union of orders freezing property or evidence; and

(b)   provide in the domestic restraint order for notice to be given in accordance with paragraph 2(4) of schedule 1 to the 2014 Regulations.

Deriv. RCS 1965, r. 201E(1) (r. 76.3(1)), and r. 201F(2) (r. 76.3(2)), both inserted by S.I. 1990 No. 705

General note.

76.3.1   A restraint order may be applied for by the prosecutor where "proceedings have been instituted" (defined in s.49(6)) for an offence to which Part I of the Act applies (any offence "which has been prosecuted" subject to one exception), the proceedings have not been concluded and either a confiscation order has been made or it appears that in the event of conviction there are reasonable grounds for thinking that a confiscation order may be made: Act of 1995, s.29(1). The apparent dichotomy between proceedings which have been instituted and an offence which has been prosecuted, which would frustrate the intentions of Parliament, has been resolved by adopting a workable interpretation where the intention of Parliament was that a restraint order might be pronounced immediately following the institution of proceedings: *Carnègie v. McKechnie* 1999 S.L.T. 536. Accordingly, a petition may be presented at any time after a suspect has had a petition charging him intimated to him or a complaint served on him even where no indictment has yet been served: *Carnegie* 1999 S.L.T. 536, above.

A restraint order may interdict any named person from dealing with his realisable property, or that or another named person who has received a gift from that person or an implicative gift from dealing with their own or that other's realisable property; or interdict any named person from dealing with any property which is or is liable to be the subject of a suspended forfeiture order: Act of 1995, s.28(1). On gifts, see ss.5 and 6 of the Act of 1995; and on suspended forfeiture orders, see s.21 of the Act of 1995.

Section 28 of the Act of 1995 is modified by Sched. 3 to the Confiscation of the Proceeds of Crime (Designated Countries and Territories) (Scotland) Order 1999 [SI 1999/673] and by Sched. 3 to the Criminal Justice (International Co-operation) Act 1990 (Enforcement of Overseas Forfeiture Orders) (Scotland) Order 1999 [S.I. 1999 No. 675]. For the purposes of these orders (see art. 4 of each Order), s.28(3)(b) of the Act of 1995, as modified, requires a restraint order to be supported by a certificate giving certain particulars (including grounds for believing that an external confiscation order may be made in proceedings instituted or to be instituted in the designated country) and that it may, unless the court directs, a statement of information or belief with the sources and grounds thereof.

"petition".

76.3.2   A petition is presented in the Outer House: r. 14.2(h). The petition must be in Form 14.4 in the official printed form: rr. 4.1 and 14.4. The petition must be signed by counsel or other person having a right of audience: r. 4.2; and see r. 1.3(1) (definition of "counsel" and "other person having a right of audience") and note 1.3.4.

---

[1] R. 76.3(3) and (4) inserted by S.I. 1999 No. 1220 (effective 1st May 1999).
[2] R.76.3(5) inserted by S.S.I. 2016 No. 319 para.2 (effective 12 December 2016)
[3] R.76.3(6) inserted by S.S.I. 2016 No. 319 para.2 (effective 12 December 2016)

The petitioner must lodge the petition with the required steps of process (r. 4.4). A fee is payable on lodging the petition: see note 14.5.10.

On petitions generally, see Chap. 14.

"CERTIFIED COPY OF THAT INTERLOCUTOR".

A copy of the interlocutor must be prepared (handwritten or typed) by the party. It is checked by the clerk of session at the appropriate department, certified a true copy and stamped with the court stamp. A fee is payable: see Court of Session Fees etc. Order 1997, Table of Fees, Pt IV, J, item 2 (S.I. 1997 No. 688, as amended, pp. C 1201 et seq.). Certain persons are exempt from payment of fees: see 1997 Fees Order, art.5 substituted by S.S.I. 2002 No. 270. A fee exemption certificate must be lodged in process: see P.N. No.1 of 2002.

76.3.3

Applications in relation to protective measures

76.4.—[1](1) An application under any of the following provisions of the Act of 1995 shall be made by note in the process containing the interlocutor making the restraint order to which the application relates:—

76.4

(a) section 29(4) or (5) (recall of restraint order in relation to realisable property);

(b) section 30(3) or (4) (recall of restraint order in relation to forfeitable property);

(c) section 31(1) (variation or recall of restraint order);

(d) section 32(5) (recall or restriction of inhibition);

(e) section 33(4) (recall or restriction of arrestment).

(2) In respect of an application by note under paragraph (1) by a person having an interest for an order under section 31(1)(b) of the Act of 1995—

(a) the note shall be lodged in process within 21 days after service of the restraint order on that person; and

(b) subject to rule 14.6(2) (application to shorten or extend the period of notice), the period of notice for lodging answers to the note shall be 14 days.

(3)[2] An application under section 31(1)(a) of the Act of 1995 to extend a restraint order shall not be intimated, served or advertised before the application is granted.

(4)[3] An application by the Lord Advocate under section 32(1) or 33(1) of the Act of 1995 by the Lord Advocate for warrant for arrestment or inhibition may be made—

(a) in the prayer of the petition under section 28(1) of that Act; or

(b) if made after the petition has been presented, by motion which shall not be intimated.

(5) An application under section 32(1)(a) (recall, loosing or restriction of inhibition), or section 33(2) (recall, loosing or restriction of arrestment) of the Act of 1995 to loose, restrict or recall an arrestment or to recall an inhibition shall be made by motion.

(6) An application under section 28(8) of the Act of 1995 (interdict) may be made—

(a)[4] in the prayer of the petition under section 28(1) of that Act; or (b) if made after the petition has been presented, by note in the process of that petition.

(7) An application by note under paragraph (6)(b) shall not be intimated, served or advertised before the application is granted.

---

[1] R. 76.4 amended by S.I. 1996 No. 2168 (consolidating enactment).

[2] R. 76.4(3), (4) and (6)(a) amended by S.I. 1999 No. 1220 (effective 1st May 1999).

[3] R. 76.4(3), (4) and (6)(a) amended by S.I. 1999 No. 1220 (effective 1st May 1999).

[4] R. 76.4(3), (4) and (6)(a) amended by S.I. 1999 No. 1220 (effective 1st May 1999).

(7A)[1] Where the court, having pronounced an interlocutor making a restraint order, interdicts a person not subject to that order from dealing with the property affected by it while it is in force, the Lord Advocate shall so intimate to that person.

(8) Where the court pronounces an interlocutor granting an application mentioned in paragraph (3) or (4), the Lord Advocate shall serve a certified copy of that interlocutor on the persons affected by it.

(9) At the time at which he complies with section 31 (6) of the Act of 1995 (informing of persons interdicted in relation to a restraint order that the order is recalled), the clerk of court (or as the case may be the Deputy Principal Clerk) shall record in the process when and how the person in question was so informed.

Deriv. RCS 1965, r. 201G(1) (r. 76.4(1)), r. 201F(2) (r. 76.4(2)), r. 201G(4) (r. 76.4(3)), r. 201G(5) (r. 76.4(4)), and r. 201G(6) (r. 76.4(6)), all inserted by S.I. 1990 No. 705

"NOTE".

76.4.1 For applications by note, see r. 15.2.

"WITHIN 21 DAYS".

76.4.2 The date from which the period is calculated is not counted. Where the last day falls on a Saturday or Sunday or a public holiday on which the Office of Court is closed, the next available day is allowed: r. 1.3(7). For office hours and public holidays, see note 3.1.2.

"ANSWERS".

76.4.3 For form and procedure, see r. 18.3.

"MOTION".

76.4.4 For motions, see Chap. 23.

"CERTIFIED COPY OF THAT INTERLOCUTOR".

76.4.5 A copy of the interlocutor must be prepared (handwritten or typed) by the party. It is checked by the clerk of session at the appropriate department, certified a true copy and stamped with the court stamp. A fee is payable: see Court of Session Fees etc. Order 1984, Table of Fees, Pt IV, J, item 2 (S.I. 1984 No. 256, Table as amended, pp. C 1202 etseq.).

Applications for compensation

76.5 76.5.[2] An application under section 17 (compensation) of the Act of 1995 shall be made by petition.

Deriv. RCS 1965, r. 201G(7) inserted by S.I. 1990 No. 705

SECTION 17 OF THE ACT OF 1995.

76.5.1 Compensation may be payable to a person who held realisable property (including a person to whom an implicative gift was made by the person in respect of whom a confiscation order was made) and who suffered substantial loss and damage as a result of the exercise of powers under Pt I of the Act of 1995: Act of 1995, s.17.

"PETITION".

76.5.2 A petition is presented in the Outer House: r.14.2(h). The petition must be in Form 14.4 in the official printed form: rr.4.1 and 14.4. The petition must be signed by counsel or other person having a right of audience: r.4.2.; and see r.1.3(1). (definition of "counsel" and "other person having a right of audience") and note 1.3.4.

The petitioner must lodge the petition with the required steps of process (r.4.4.). A fee is payable on lodging the petition: see note 14.5.10.

On petitions generally, see Chap. 14.

Applications for disclosure of information by government departments

76.6 76.6.[3] An application under section 20 of the Act of 1995 (disclosure of information held by government departments) may be made—

(a) by petition;

---

[1] R. 76.4(7A) and (9) inserted by S.I. 1999 No. 1220 (effective 1st May 1999).
[2] R. 76.5 and heading amending by S.I. 1996 No. 2168 (consolidating enactment).
[3] R.76.6 amended by S.I. 1996 No. 2168 (consolidating enactment).

(b)   where there is a restraint order in force, by note in the process of the petition for that restraint order; or

(c)   where an administrator has been appointed, by note in the process of the petition to appoint him.

Deriv. R.C.S. 1965, r.201G(8) inserted by S.I. 1990 No. 705

GENERAL NOTE.

The court may, on the application of the Lord Advocate, order material in possession of an authorised government department to be produced to the court which would facilitate the powers of the court in relation to restraint orders, the appointment of an administrator etc., or the realisation of property: Act of 1995, s.20. The court may order disclosure to other persons, e.g. the administrator.   **76.6.1**

"PETITION".

A petition is presented in the Outer House: r.14.2(h). The petition must be in Form 14.4 in the official printed form: rr.4.1 and 14.4. The petition must be signed by counsel or "other person having a right of audience: r.4.2.; and see r.1.3(1). (definition of "counsel" and "other person having a right of audience") and note 1.3.4.   **76.6.2**

The petitioner must lodge the petition with the required steps of process (r.4.4.). A fee is payable on lodging the petition: see note 14.5.10.

On petitions generally, see Chap. 14.

"NOTE".

For applications by note, see r.15.2.   **76.6.3**

Applications for appointment of administrators

76.7.—[1](1)   An application under paragraph 1(1) of Schedule 1 to the Act of 1995 (appointment of administrators) shall be made—   **76.7**

(a)   where a restraint order has been made, by note in the process of the petition for that restraint order; or

(b)   in any other case, by petition.

(2)   The notification to be made by the clerk of court under paragraph 1(3)(a) of Schedule 1 to the Act of 1995 shall be made by intimation of a certified copy of the interlocutor to the person required to give possession of property to an administrator.

Deriv. R.C.S. 1965, r.201H inserted by S.I. 1990 No. 705

GENERAL NOTE.

An administrator may be appointed to manage property affected by a restraint order or to realise property where a confiscation order has been made, and the court may require a person having possession of the property to give it up to the administrator: Act of 1995, Sch. 1, para.1(1). The functions of the administrator are set out in para.2(1) of Sch.1 to the Act of 1995.   **76.7.1**

"NOTIFICATION BY THE CLERK OF COURT".

This is notification to persons concerned of a requirement to give up property to the administrator.   **76.7.2**

"NOTE".

For applications by note, see r.15.2.   **76.7.3**

"PETITION".

A petition is presented in the Outer House: r.14.2(h). The petition must be in Form 14.4 in the official printed form: rr.4.1 and 14.4. The petition must be signed by counsel or other person having a right of audience: r.4.2.; and see r.1.3(1). (definition of "counsel" and "other person having a right of audience") and note 1.3.4.   **76.7.4**

The petitioner must lodge the petition with the required steps of process (r.4.4.). A fee is payable on lodging the petition: see note 14.5.10. On petitions generally, see Chap. 14.

"CERTIFIED COPY OF THE INTERLOCUTOR".

A copy of the interlocutor must be prepared (handwritten or typed) by the party. It is checked by the clerk of session at the appropriate department, certified a true copy and stamped with the court stamp. A fee is payable: see Court of Session Fees etc. Order 1984, Table of Fees, Pt IV, J, item 2 (S.I. 1984 No. 256, Table as amended, pp. C 1202 et sea.).   **76.7.5**

---

[1] R.76.7 amended by S.I. 1996 No. 2168 (consolidating enactment).

Incidental applications in an administration

76.8

76.8.—[1](1) An application under any of the following provisions of Schedule 1 to the Act of 1995 shall be made by note in the process of the petition for appointment of the administrator:—

(a) paragraph 1(1) with respect to an application after appointment of an administrator to require a person to give property to him;

(b) paragraph 1(4) (making or altering a requirement or removal of administrator);

(c) paragraph 1(5) (appointment of new administrator on death, resignation or removal of administrator);

(d) paragraph 2(1)(n) (directions as to functions of administrator); and

(e) paragraph 4 (directions for application of proceeds).

(2) An application under any of the following provisions of Schedule 1 to the Act of 1995 shall be made in the prayer of the petition for appointment of an administrator under paragraph 1 of that Schedule or, if made after the petition has been presented, by note in that process:—

(a)[2] paragraph 2(1)(o) (special powers of administrator);

(b) paragraph 2(3) (vesting of property in administrator); and

(c)[3] paragraph 12 (orders to facilitate the realisation of property).

Deriv. R.C.S. 1965, r.201J inserted by S.I. 1990 No. 705

"NOTE".

76.8.1

For applications by note, see r.15.2.

Requirements where order to facilitate realisation of property considered

76.9

76.9.[4] Where the court considers making an order under paragraph 12(1) of Schedule 1 to the Act of 1995 (order to facilitate the realisation of property)—

(a) the court shall fix a date for a hearing on the Motion Roll in the first instance; and

(b) the petitioner or noter, as the case may be, shall serve a notice in Form 76.9 on any person who has an interest in the property.

Deriv. R.C.S. 1965, r.201K(2) inserted by S.I. 1990 No. 705

Documents for Accountant of Court

76.10

76.10.—(1) A person who has lodged any document in the process of an application for the appointment of an administrator shall forthwith send a copy of that document to the Accountant of Court.

(2) The clerk of session in the Petition Department shall transmit to the Accountant of Court any part of the process as the Accountant of Court may request in relation to an administration which is in dependence before the court unless such part of the process is, at the time of request, required by the court.

Deriv. R.C.S. 1965, r. 201L inserted by S.I. 1990 No. 705

GENERAL NOTE.

76.10.1

The Accountant of Court is responsible for supervising administrators appointed under para. 5 of Sched. 1 of the Act of 1995.

"SEND".

76.10.2

This includes deliver: r. 1.3(1) (definition of "send").

---

[1] R.76.8 amended by S.I. 1996 No. 2168 (consolidating enactment).
[2] R.76.8(2)(a) amended by S.I. 1994 No. 2901 (minor correction).
[3] R.76.8(2)(c) amended by S.I. 1998 No. 890 (effective 21st April, 1998).
[4] R.76.9 amended by S.I. 1996 No. 2168 (consolidating enactment).

"IN DEPENDENCE".

A cause is depending from the time it is commenced (i.e. from the time an action is served or a first order in a petition is made) until final decree, whereas a cause is in dependence until final extract. For the meaning of commenced, see note 14.6.1. For the meaning of final decree, see note 4.15.2(2). For the meaning of final extract, see note 7.1.2(2).

76.10.3

Procedure for finding caution

76.11.—(1) Rule 61.9 (finding caution in judicial factories), except paragraph (4), shall, with the necessary modifications, apply to the finding of caution by an administrator under this Part as it applies to the finding of caution by a judicial factor.

76.11

(2) A certified copy of the interlocutor appointing an administrator shall not be issued by a clerk of session until the Accountant of Court has given written intimation to the Petition Department that caution has been found or other security given.

Deriv. R.C.S. 1965, r. 201M inserted by SI 1990/705 (r. 76.11(2))

GENERAL NOTE.

It is for the Accountant of Court to impose any conditions as to caution as he thinks fit: Act of 1995, Sched. 1, para. 1(8). The procedure for finding caution is the same as that for a judicial factor under r. 61.9.

76.11.1

"WRITTEN INTIMATION".

For methods, see r. 16.9.

76.11.2

Administrator's title to act

76.12. An administrator shall not be entitled to act until he has obtained a certified copy of the interlocutor appointing him.

76.12

Duties of administrator

76.13.—(1) The administrator shall, as soon as possible, but within three months after the date of his appointment, lodge with the Accountant of Court—

76.13

   (a)   an inventory of the property in respect of which he has been appointed;

   (b)   all vouchers, securities, and other documents which are in his possession; and

   (c)   a statement of that property which he has in his possession or intends to realise.

(2) An administrator shall maintain accounts of his intromissions with the property in his charge and shall, subject to paragraph (3)—

   (a)   within six months after the date of his appointment, and

   (b)   at six monthly intervals after the first account during the subsistence of his appointment,

lodge with the Accountant of Court an account of his intromissions in such form, with such supporting vouchers and other documents, as the Accountant of Court may require.

(3) The Accountant of Court may waive the lodging of an account where the administrator certifies that there have been no intromissions during a particular accounting period.

Deriv. R.C.S. 1965, r. 201N inserted by S.I. 1990 No. 705

State of funds and scheme of division

76.14.—(1) The administrator shall—

76.14

   (a)[1]   where there are funds available for division, prepare a state of funds after application of sums in accordance with paragraph 4(2) of Schedule 1 to the Act of 1995 and a scheme of division amongst those who held property

---

[1] R. 76.14(1)(a) and (3)(c) amended by S.I. 1996 No. 2168 (consolidating enactment).

which has been realised under that Act and lodge them and all relevant documents with the Accountant of Court; or (b) where there are no funds available for division, prepare a state of funds only and lodge it with the Accountant of Court, and give to the Accountant of Court such explanations as he shall require.

(2)   The Accountant of Court shall—

(a)   make a written report on the state of funds and any scheme of division including such observations as he considers appropriate for consideration by the Lord Ordinary; and

(b)   return the state of funds and any scheme of division to the administrator with his report.

(3)   The administrator shall, on receiving the report of the Accountant of Court—

(a)   lodge in process the report, the state of funds and any scheme of division;

(b)   intimate a copy of it to the Lord Advocate; and

(c)[1]   intimate to each person who held property which has been realised under the Act of 1995 a notice stating—

(i)   that the state of funds and scheme of division or the state of funds only, as the case may be, and the report of the Accountant of Court, have been lodged in process;

(ii)   the amount for which that person has been ranked, and whether he is to be paid in full, or by a dividend, and the amount of it, or that no funds are available for payment.

Deriv. R.C.S. 1965, r. 201P inserted by S.I. 1990 No. 705

"LODGE IN PROCESS".

76.14.1 The report is lodged as a step of process (r. 1.3(1) (definition of "step of process")). On lodging steps of process, see r. 4.4. The list may be lodged by post: P.N. No. 4 of 1994, paras. 1 and 8; and see note 4.4.10.

"INTIMATE".

76.14.2 For methods, see r. 16.7.

Objections to scheme of division

76.15 **76.15.**—(1)[2]   A person wishing to be heard by the court in relation to the distribution of property under paragraph 4(3) of Schedule 1 to the Act of 1995 shall lodge a note of objection in the process to which the scheme of division relates within 21 days of the date of the notice intimated under rule 76.14(3)(c).

(2)   After the period for lodging a note of objection has expired and no note of objection has been lodged, the administrator may apply by motion for approval of the scheme of division and state of funds, or the state of funds only, as the case may be.

(3)   After the period for lodging a note of objection has expired and a note of objection has been lodged, the Lord Ordinary shall dispose of such objection after hearing any objector and the administrator and making such inquiry as he thinks fit.

(4)   If any objection is sustained to any extent, the necessary alterations shall be made to the state of funds and any scheme of division and shall be approved by the Lord Ordinary.

Deriv. R.C.S. 1965, r. 201Q inserted by S.I. 1990 No. 705

"NOTE OF OBJECTION".

76.15.1 A note of objection does not have to be signed: r. 4.2(9)(f). R. 15.2 (applications by note) does not apply: r. 15.2(4)(b).

---

[1] R. 76.14(1)(a) and (3)(c) amended by S.I. 1996 No. 2168 (consolidating enactment).
[2] R. 76.15(1) amended by S.I. 1996 No. 2168 (consolidating enactment).

For motions, see Chap. 23.   76.15.2

Application for discharge of administrator

76.16.—(1) Where the scheme of division is approved by the court and the   **76.16**
administrator has paid, delivered or conveyed to the persons entitled the sums or
receipts allocated to them in the scheme, the administrator may apply for his
discharge.

(2)[1] An application for discharge of the administrator shall be made by note in
the process of the application under paragraph 1(1) Schedule 1 to the Act of 1995.

"note".

For applications by note, see r. 15.2.   76.16.1

Appeals against determination of outlays and remuneration

76.17.—(1)[2] An appeal under paragraph 6(2) of Schedule 1 to the Act of 1995   **76.17**
(appeal against a determination by the Accountant of Court), shall be made by note
in the process in which the administrator was appointed.

(2) Where a note is lodged under paragraph (1), the Keeper of the Rolls shall put
the cause out on the By Order Roll on the first available day for a hearing before the
Lord Ordinary.

Deriv. R.C.S. 1965, r. 201R inserted by S.I. 1990 No. 705

General note.

An appeal under para. 6(2) of Sched. 1 to the Act of 1995 is an appeal in relation to an audit of the   76.17.1
administrator's accounts by the Accountant of Court.

"note".

For applications by note, see r. 15.2.   76.17.2

Remits from High Court of Justiciary

76.18.   Revoked by S.I. 1996 No. 2168.   **76.18**

Part II – Applications under the Prevention of Terrorism (Temporary Provisions)
Act 1989 or the Order of 1995[3]

Application and interpretation of this Part

76.19.[4, 5] In this Part—   **76.19**

"the Act of 1989" means the Prevention of Terrorism (Temporary Provisions)
Act 1989;
"administrator" shall be construed in accordance with paragraph 11(1)(b) of
Schedule 4 to the Act of 1989;
"the Order of 1995" means the Prevention of Terrorism (Temporary Provisions) Act 1989 (Enforcement of External Orders) Order 1995;
"restraint order" means an order made under paragraph 13(1) of Schedule 4 to
the Act of 1989.

Deriv. R.C.S. 1965, r. 201S inserted by S.I. 1991 No. 1183

General note.

This Part deals with applications to the court where a forfeiture order has been made under s.13 of the   76.19.1
1989 Act or could be made by a court in Scotland, or where the procurator fiscal proposes to apply for
such an order. In relation to applications for restraint orders and incidental applications in respect of

---

[1] R. 76.16(2) amended by S.I. 1996 No. 2168 (consolidating enactment)
[2] R. 76.17 amended by S.I. 1996 No. 2168 (consolidating enactment).
[3] Pt. II heading and r. 76.19 amended by S.I. 1996 No. 2168 (effective September 23, 1996).
[4] Pt. II heading and r. 76.19 amended by S.I. 1996 No. 2168 (effective September 23, 1996).
[5] R. 76.19 amended by S.I. 1994 No. 2901 (clerical error).

which an external forfeiture order or an order elsewhere in the U.K. has been made or in respect of which such an order could be made, see r. 62.54. An external forfeiture order is an order made in a country or territory designated under art. 3 of, and specified in Sched. 2 to, the Prevention of Terrorism (Temporary Provisions) Act 1989 (Enforcement of External Orders) 1995 (S.I. 1995 No. 760).

The Act of 1989 has been replaced by the Terrorism Act 2000. The relevant provisions of that Act came fully into force on 15th February 2001: Terrorism Act 2000 (Commencement No.3) Order 2001 [S.I. 2001 No. 421]. Accordingly, in relation to forfeiture and restraint orders made after that date, Chap.84 will apply.

"RESTRAINT ORDER".

76.19.2   The Court of Session may prohibit any person specified in the order from dealing in any property in respect of which a forfeiture order has been made or could be made in proceedings for, or where the procurator fiscal proposes to apply for a warrant to arrest and commit a person suspected of, an offence under Pt. III of the Act of 1989 (financial assistance for terrorism): Act of 1989, Sched. 4, para. 13(1).

Disapplication of certain rules to this Part

76.20   **76.20.** The following rules shall not apply to a petition or note mentioned in this Part:—

rule 14.5(1) (first order in petitions),

rule 14.6(1) (period of notice for lodging answers),

rule 14.7(1) (intimation and service of petitions),

rule 14.9(1) (unopposed petitions).

Applications for restraint orders

76.21   **76.21.**—(1) An application under paragraph 14(1) of Schedule 4 to the Act of 1989 (restraint order) shall be made by petition.

(2) Where the court pronounces an interlocutor making a restraint order, the Lord Advocate shall serve a certified copy of that interlocutor on every person named in the interlocutor as restrained by the order.

Deriv. R.C.S. 1965, r. 201T(1) (r. 76.21(1)), and r. 201U(1) (r. 76.21(2)), both inserted by S.I. 1991 No. 1183

GENERAL NOTE.

76.21.1   Application for a restraint order is made by the Lord Advocate and may be applied for ex parte in chambers (and presumably in private): Act of 1989, Sched. 4, para. 14(1).

"PETITION".

76.21.2   A petition is presented in the Outer House: r. 14.2(h). The petition must be in Form 14.4 in the official printed form: rr. 4.1 and 14.4. The petition must be signed by counsel or other person having a right of audience: r. 4.2; and see r. 1.3(1) (definition of "counsel" and "other person having a right of audience") and note 1.3.4.

The petitioner must lodge the petition with the required steps of process (r. 4.4). A fee is payable on lodging the petition: see note 14.5.10.

On petitions generally, see Chap. 14.

"CERTIFIED COPY OF THAT INTERLOCUTOR".

76.21.3   A copy of the interlocutor must be prepared (handwritten or typed) by the party. It is checked by the clerk of session at the appropriate department, certified a true copy and stamped with the court stamp. A fee is payable: see Court of Session Fees etc. Order 1984, Table of Fees, Pt. IV, J, item 2 (S.I. 1984 No. 256, Table as amended, pp. C 1202 et seq).

Applications in relation to protective measures

76.22   **76.22.**—(1) An application under any of the following provisions of Schedule 4 to the Act of 1989 shall be made by note in the process containing the interlocutor making the restraint order to which the application relates—

(a) paragraph 13(4) (discharge of a restraint order);

(b) paragraph 14(2) (variation or recall of restraint order); and

(c) paragraph 14(3) (recall of restraint order).

(2)[1] Subject to rule 14.6(2) (application to shorten or extend the period of notice), the period of notice for lodging answers to a note under paragraph (1)(b) of this rule by any person affected by a restraint order shall be 14 days.

(3)[2] An application under paragraph 16(1) of Schedule 4 to the Act of 1989 (warrant for inhibition), or 16A(1) (warrant for arrestment), may be made—

    (a)   in the prayer of the petition under paragraph 13(1) of Schedule 4 to the Act of 1989; or

    (b)   if made after the petition has been presented, by motion which shall not be intimated.

(4)[3] Any of the following applications under Schedule 4 to the Act of 1989 shall be made by motion—

    (a)   an application to recall, loose or restrict an inhibition under paragraph 16(2)(a);

    (b)   an application under paragraph 16(6)(a) (recall or restriction of inhibition);

    (c)   an application to recall, loose or restrict an arrestment under paragraph 16A(2); or

    (d)   an application under paragraph 16A(4) (recall or restriction of arrestment).

Deriv. R.C.S. 1965, r. 201V(1) to (4) inserted by S.I. 1991 No. 1183

"PERIOD OF NOTICE".

On period of notice generally, see r. 14.6.

76.22.1

"NOTE".

For applications by note, see r. 15.2.

76.22.2

"MOTION".

For motions, see Chap. 23.

76.22.3

Applications for compensation

76.23. An application under paragraph 17(1) of Schedule 4 to the Act of 1989 (compensation) shall be made by petition.

76.23

Deriv. R.C.S. 1965, r. 201V(5) inserted by S.I. 1991 No. 1183

GENERAL NOTE.

Compensation may be payable to a person who had an interest in property which was the subject of a forfeiture or restraint order where there was serious default on the part of a person in the investigation or prosecution of the offence concerned and the applicant has suffered loss in consequence of anything done in relation to the property: Act of 1989, Sched. 4, para. 17(1) and (3).

76.23.1

"PETITION".

A petition is presented in the Outer House: r. 14.2(h). The petition must be in Form 14.4 in the official printed form: rr. 4.1 and 14.4. The petition must be signed by counsel or other person having a right of audience: r. 4.2; and see r. 1.3(1) (definition of "counsel" and "other erson having a right of audience") and note 1.3.4.

76.23.2

The petitioner must lodge the petition with the required steps of process (r. 4.4). A fee is payable on lodging the petition: see note 14.5.10.

On petitions generally, see Chap. 14.

Powers and duties of administrator

76.24.—(1) Subject to any condition or exception specified by the court, an administrator appointed under paragraph 11(1)(b) of Schedule 4 to the Act of 1989—

76.24

    (a)   may take possession of the property in respect of which he has been appointed and of any document which—

---

[1] R. 76.22(2) amended by S.I. 1996 No. 2168 (minor correction).

[2] R. 76.22(3) and (4) amended by S.I. 1996 No. 2168 (consolidating enactment).

[3] R. 76.22(3) and (4) amended by S.I. 1996 No. 2168 (consolidating enactment).

        (i)   is in the possession or control of the person in whom the property is vested; and

        (ii) relates to the property;

(b)   may have access to, and copy, any document relating to the property and not in such possession or control as is mentioned in subparagraph (a);

(c)   may bring, defend or continue any legal proceedings relating to the property;

(d)   may borrow money in so far as it is necessary to do so to safeguard the property and may for the purposes of such borrowing create a security over any part of the property;

(e)   may, if the administrator considers that to do so would be beneficial for the management and the realisation of theproperty, enter into any contract, or execute any deed, with respect to the property;

(f)   may effect or maintain insurance policies with respect to the property;

(g)   may, where the person in whom the property is vested has not completed title to any of the property, complete title to it: provided that completion of title in the name of the person in whom the property is vested shall not validate by accretion any unperfected right in favour of any person other than the administrator;

(h)   may sell (but not to himself or an associate of his) the property and redeem any obligation secured on that property;

(i)   may discharge any of his functions through agents or employees: provided that the administrator shall be personally liable to meet the fees and expenses of any such agents or employees out of such remuneration as is payable to the administrator by virtue of paragraph 12(2) and (3) of Schedule 4 to the Act of 1989;

(j)   may take such professional advice as he considers necessary for the proper discharge of his functions;

(k)   may at any time apply to the court for directions with respect to the exercise of his powers and duties;

(l)   may exercise any power conferred on him by the court whether such power was conferred at the time of his appointment or on his subsequent application to the court; and

(m) may do anything incidental to the above powers and duties.

(2) Subject to the proviso to sub-paragraph (g) of paragraph (1)—

(a)   a person dealing with an administrator in good faith and for value shall not require to determine whether the administrator is acting within the powers mentioned in that sub-paragraph; and

(b)   the validity of any title shall not be challengeable by reason only of the administrator having acted outwith those powers.

(3) The exercise of a power mentioned in any of sub-paragraphs (c) to (h) of paragraph (1) shall be in the name of the person in whom the property is vested.

Deriv. R.C.S. 1965, r. 201W inserted by S.I. 1991 No. 1183

GENERAL NOTE.

76.24.1   A criminal court may make a forfeiture order under s. 13(2), (3) or (4) of the Act of 1989 where a person is guilty of an offence under s. 9, 10 or 11 of that Act (financial assistance for terrorism). Where that court does so it may make an order appointing an administrator to take possession of property to which the forfeiture order applies: Act of 1989, Sched. 4, para. 11. R. 76.24 is made under Sched. 4, para. 11(2).

     An administrator is subject to the supervision of the Accountant of Court: Act of 1989, Sched. 4, para. 12(3).

     There is no provision, as there is in para. 1 (8) of Sched. 1 to the Act of 1995, for the finding of caution.

Duties of administrator in relation to accounts

76.25.—(1) The administrator shall, as soon as possible, but within three months after the date of his appointment, lodge with the Accountant of Court—

   (a)   an inventory of the property in respect of which he has been appointed;

   (b)   all land certificates, title deeds, vouchers and other documents which relate to that property and are in his possession; and

   (c)   a statement of the property which he has in his possession or intends to realise.

   (2)   An administrator shall maintain accounts of his intromissions with the property in his charge and shall—

   (a)   lodge an account of his intromissions with the Accountant of Court in such form as the Accountant of Court may require—

      (i)   six months after the date of his appointment; and

      (ii)   at six monthly intervals after the first account during the subsistence of his appointment, unless the Accountant of Court agrees to waive the lodging of an account where the administrator certifies that there have been no intromissions during a particular accounting period; and

   (b)   lodge, with the account of his intromissions, all such supporting vouchers and other documents as the Accountant of Court may require.

Deriv. R.C.S. 1965, r. 201X inserted by S.I. 1991 No. 1183

Money received by administrator

76.26.—(1) Subject to paragraph (2), any money received by an administrator in the exercise of his powers and duties shall be deposited by him in an appropriate bank or institution, in the name of the person in whom the property is vested.

   (2)   The administrator may, at any time, retain in his hands a sum of money not exceeding £200.

   (3)   In paragraph (1), "appropriate bank or institution" means the Bank of England, an institution authorised under the Banking Act 1987 or a person for the time being specified in Schedule 2 to that Act.

Deriv. R.C.S. 1965, r. 201Y inserted by S.I. 1991 No. 1183

Part III – Applications under the Proceeds of Crime Act 2002, the Overseas Forfeiture Order of 2005 and the POCA Orders of 2005 and 2013

Interpretation and application of this Part

76.27.—[1,2,3](1) In this Part—

   (a)   "the Act of 2002" means the Proceeds of Crime Act 2002;

   (b)   "the Overseas Forfeiture Order of 2005" means the Criminal Justice (International Co-operation) Act 1990 (Enforcement of Overseas Forfeiture Orders) Order 2005;

   (c)   "the POCA Order of 2005" means the Proceeds of Crime Act 2002 (External Requests and Orders) Order 2005;

   (ca)   "the POCA Order of 2013" means the Proceeds of Crime Act 2002 (External Investigations) Order 2013;

76.25

76.26

76.27

---

[1] Part III and r. 76.27 inserted by S.S.I. 2003 No. 222 (effective 28th March 2003, heading to Pt. III and r. 76.27 substituted by S.S.I. 2005 No. 663 (effective 31st December 2005).

[2] Part III and r. 76.27 inserted by S.S.I. 2003 No. 222 (effective 28th March 2003, heading to Pt. III and r. 76.27 substituted by S.S.I. 2005 No. 663 (effective 31st December 2005).

[3] Heading to Part III and r.76.27 as amended by S.S.I. 2019 No. 405 para.2 (effective 28th December 2019).

    (d)   "external order" has the meaning given in section 447(2) of the Act of 2002;

    (da)[1] "interim freezing order" has the meaning given in section 396J(3) of the Act of 2002;

    (db)[2] "unexplained wealth order" has the meaning given in section 396A(3) of the Act of 2002;

    (e)   references to an administrator are to an administrator appointed under section 125(1) or 128(3) of the Act of 2002, article 10(1) or 18(2) of the Overseas Forfeiture Order of 2005 or article 63(1) or 73(2) of the POCA Order of 2005.

(2)   This Part applies to applications under—

    (a)   Parts 3 and 5 of the Act of 2002;

    (b)[3] Part 8 of the Act of 2002 in relation to property that is the subject of a civil recovery investigation or an interim freezing order or an unexplained wealth order;

    (c)   the Overseas Forfeiture Order of 2005 except article 13 (application to give effect to external forfeiture orders) and article 16 (registration of external orders);

    (d)   Parts 3, 4B and 5 of the POCA Order of 2005 except article 66 (application to give effect to external orders) and article 69 (registration of external orders).

    (e)   articles 46A (unexplained wealth orders) to 46R (compensation) of the POCA Order of 2013.

GENERAL NOTE.

76.27.1   The Proceeds of Crime Act 2002 provides newprocedures for the confiscation (in criminal proceedings) and civil recovery of the proceeds of crime. Civil recovery under Pt. 5 of the Act of 2002 may be pursued by the Scottish Ministers (via the Civil Recovery Unit (CRU)), generally after any criminal procedure has been used (whether or not successful). Under s.244 of the Act of 2002 proceedings may be taken against any person who the CRU thinks holds recoverable property and the proceedings may be served on anyone the CRU thinks holds any associated property (as defined in s.245): see r.76.36 for procedure. An interim administration order may be applied for to detain, obtain custody of or preserve property and to appoint an interim administrator. The order prohibits any person to whose property the order applies from dealing with the property. A recovery order under s.266 may subsequently be made, in respect of property the court is satisfied is recoverable property, vesting the property in the trustee for civil recovery. Where the CRU is making civil recovery investigations, it may seek a disclosure order requiring any person to provide specified information or documents or answer questions relevant to the investigation: see r.76.37 for procedure.

    Proceedings under Pt 5 of the 2002 Act do not involve a criminal penalty in the sense in art. 7(1) of ECHR: The *Scottish Minister v. McGuffie* , 2006 S.L.T. 1166 (Extra Div.). In *Scottish Ministers v. Doig* , 2009 S.C. 474 (Extra Div.) it was held that rights under art. 6(2) of ECHR were not infringed when the Scottish Ministers sought a recovery order in respect of money of the third respondent because of his allegedly "unlawful conduct" (concerned in supply of drugs for which he had been acquitted). Recovery proceedings are not criminal proceedings, and a finding of unlawful conduct although it might constitute a criminal offence did not offend art. 6(2).

    The court cannot competently make an appointment of an interim administrator or any other officer in an assumed name albeit it might authorise him to use an assumed name: *Scottish Ministers v. Stirton*, 2013 S.L.T. 1141 (Second Div) disapproving dicta in *Scottish Ministers v. Stirton*, 2006 S.L.T. 306.

    In relation to a criminal investigation of an offence, there may be civil proceedings for restraint orders interdicting any person from dealing with any realizable property where it is believed that the alleged offender has benefited from his criminal conduct and there is evidence not available at the time of the confiscation order that the amount of that benefit exceeds the amount confiscated: see r.76.28 for procedure.

---

[1] Rule 76.27 (1)(da) inserted by S.S.I. 2019 No. 146 para.2 (effective 1st June 2019).
[2] Rule 76.27 (1)(db) inserted by S.S.I. 2019 No. 146 para.2 (effective 1st June 2019).
[3] Rule 76.27 (2)(b) amended by S.S.I. 2019 No. 146 para.2 (effective 1st June 2019).

Part 3 is concerned with confiscation through the criminal process (confiscation orders under s.92) and restraint orders (under s.120) to interdict dealing with realizable property, together with administration of it, through a civil process as an adjunct to criminal investigation or proceedings. Part 5 is concerned with civil recovery of the proceeds of crime. Part 8 deals with investigations, and so far as the Court of Session is concerned, this means disclosure orders.

76.27.2

Restraint and administration orders

76.28.—[1](1)   An application under the following provisions shall be made by petition:—

76.28

    (a)   section 121(1) of the Act of 2002 (restraint orders);

    (b)   section 125(1) of the Act of 2002 (management administrators);

    (c)   section 128(2) of the Act of 2002 (enforcement administrators);

    (d)   article 6(1) of the Overseas Forfeiture Order of 2005 (restraint orders);

    (e)   article 10(1) of the Overseas Forfeiture Order of 2005 (management administrators);

    (f)   article 18(2) of the Overseas Forfeiture Order of 2005 (enforcement administrators);

    (g)   article 59(1) of the POCA Order of 2005 (restraint orders);

    (h)   article 63(1) of the POCA Order of 2005 (management administrators);

    (i)   article 73(2) of the POCA Order of 2005 (enforcement administrators).

    (j)[2]   paragraph 4 of schedule 1 of the 2014 Regulations (sending overseas restraint orders to the court); and

    (k)[3]   paragraph 9 of schedule 1 to the 2014 Regulations (sending overseas confiscation orders to the court).

(2)   An application under the following provisions shall be made by note in process:—

    (a)   section 121(5) of the Act of 2002 (recall and variation of restraint orders);

    (b)   section 134(2) of the Act of 2002 (protection of persons affected);

    (c)   section 140(1)(b) of the Act of 2002 (variation or discharge of confiscation orders);

    (d)   article 6(4) of the Overseas Forfeiture Order of 2005 (recall or variation of restraint orders);

    (e)   article 22(2) of the Overseas Forfeiture Order of 2005 (protection of persons affected);

    (f)   article 59(4) (recall or variation of restraint orders) of the POCA Order of 2005;

    (g)   article 81(2) (protection of persons affected) of the POCA Order of 2005;

    (h)[4]   paragraph 2 of schedule 1 of the 2014 Regulations (domestic restraint orders: certification).

(3)   An application under the following provisions shall be made by motion—

    (a)   section 123(1) and (7) of the Act of 2002 (inhibition of property affected by restraint order);

    (b)   section 124(1) and (6) of the Act of 2002 (arrestment of property affected by restraint order);

    (c)   section 135(1) of the Act of 2002 (recall and variation of order appointing administrator);

---

[1] Rule 76.28 inserted by S.S.I. 2003 N0. 222 (effective 28th March 2003), amended by S.S.I. 2004 No. 331 and substituted by S.S.I. 2005 No. 663 (effective 31st December 2005).
[2] R.76.28(1)(j) inserted by S.S.I. 2016 No. 319 para.2 (effective 12 December 2016)
[3] R.76.28(1)(k) inserted by S.S.I. 2016 No. 319 para.2 (effective 12 December 2016)
[4] R.76.28(2)(h) inserted by S.S.I. 2016 No. 319 para.2 (effective 12 December 2016)

    (d)   article 8(1) and (7) of the Overseas Forfeiture Order of 2005 (inhibition of property affected by restraint order);

    (e)   article 9(1) and (6) of the Overseas Forfeiture Order of 2005 (arrestment of property affected by restraint order);

    (f)   article 23(1) of the Overseas Forfeiture Order of 2005 (recall and variation of order appointing administrator);

    (g)   article 61(1) and (7) of the POCA Order of 2005 (inhibition of property affected by restraint order);

    (h)   article 62(1) and (6) of the POCA Order of 2005 (arrestment of property affected by restraint order;

    (i)   article 82(1) of the POCA Order of 2005 (recall and variation of order appointing administrator).

    (j)[1]   paragraph 6(4) of schedule 1 of the 2014 Regulations (application to cancel registration of overseas restraint order or to vary the property to which it applies); and

    (k)[2]   paragraph 11(4) of schedule 1 to the 2014 Regulations (application to cancel registration of overseas confiscation order or to vary the property to which it applies).

  (4)   Before granting an application under the following provisions, the court may dispense with, postpone or order intimation to be made to such persons as it thinks fit:—

    (a)   section 121(1) of the Act of 2002 (restraint orders);

    (b)   section 123(1) of the Act of 2002 (inhibition of property affected by restraint order);

    (c)   section 124(1) of the Act of 2002 (arrestment of property affected by restraint order);

    (d)   article 6(1) of the Overseas Forfeiture Order in Council of 2005 (restraint orders);

    (e)   article 8(1) of the Overseas Forfeiture Order of 2005 (inhibition of property affected by restraint order);

    (f)   article 9(1) of the Overseas Forfeiture Order of 2005 (arrestment of property affected by restraint order);

    (g)   article 59(1) of the POCA Order of 2005 (restraint orders);

    (h)   article 61(1) of the POCA Order of 2005 (inhibition of property affected by restraint order); and

    (i)   article 62(1) of the POCA Order of 2005 (arrestment of property affected by restraint order).

GENERAL NOTE.

76.28.1   A restraint order interdicting a person from dealing with any realizable property under s.120 of the Act of 2002 may be sought in support of (criminal) confiscation proceedings. The order may be recalled or varied. Inhibition and arrestment may be sought; management administrators may be appointed to manage the property and subsequently an enforcement administrator may be appointed.

    A restraint order is a temporary measure, to prevent dissipation of assets by a respondent, until the court is in a position to make, if satisfied, a confiscation or forfeiture order. A restraint order ought, from the moment it is granted ex parte, to contain a proviso for reasonable living expenses, unless good reason is shown why this should not be done; it is generally appropriate to set a limit on the amount; it covers payment of ordinary debts as they fall due; it should be policed by appropriate arrangements as referred to (but not specified) by Lord Hamilton in *Hansen v. H.M. Advocate* , [2005] HCJAC 33, para. [12], 4th March 2005; and while the court cannot, under s. 120(3)(a) of the Act of 2002, allow the respondent to pay his legal expenses of defending the criminal case, the court may allow him to incur legal expenses in connection with the restraint order: *H.M. Advocate v. M* , 2005 S.L.T. 203 (OH), per Lord Glennie.

---

[1] R.76.28(3)(j) inserted by S.S.I. 2016 No. 319 para.2 (effective 12 December 2016)
[2] R.76.28(3)(k) inserted by S.S.I. 2016 No. 319 para.2 (effective 12 December 2016)

"petition".

A petition is presented in the Outer House: r.14.2(h). The petition must be in Form 14.4 in the official printed form: rr.4.1 and 14.4. The petition must be signed by counsel or other person having a right of audience: r.4.2; and see r.1.3(1) (definition of "counsel" and "other person having a right of audience") and note 1.3.4.

The petitioner must lodge the petition with the required steps of process (r.4.4). A fee is payable on lodging the petition: see note 14.5.10.

On petitions generally, see Chap. 14.

76.28.2

"note".

For applications by note, see r.15.2.

76.28.3

"motion".

For motions, see Chap. 23.

76.28.4

"intimation".

For methods, see r.16.8.

76.28.5

Documents for Accountant of Court

76.29.—[1](1) A person who has lodged any document in the process of an application for the appointment of an administrator shall forthwith send a copy of that document to the Accountant of Court.

(2) The clerk of session in the Petition department shall transmit to the Accountant of Court any part of the process as the Accountant of Court may request in relation to an administration which is in dependence before the court unless such part of the process is, at the time of request, required by the court.

76.29

General note.

The Accountant of Court has to be sent documents relating to the administrator because he supervises the administrator. An administrator may not exercise certain powers without the consent of the Accountant of Court: Act of 2002, Sched. 3, para. 4.

76.29.1

"process".

For the process, see Chap. 4.

76.29.2

"send".

This includes deliver: r. 1.3(1).

76.29.3

Procedure for fixing and finding caution

76.30.—[2](1) Rule 61.9 (finding caution in judicial factories) shall, with the necessary modifications, apply to the finding of caution by an administrator under this Part as it applies to the finding of caution by a judicial factor.

(2) A certified copy of the interlocutor appointing an administrator shall not be issued by a clerk of session until the Accountant of Court has given written intimation to the Petition Department that caution has been found or other security given.

76.30

General note.

One of the dangers of applying another rule in this way is that it is not always clear what the modifications should be. Rule 61.9(2) applies r. 33.3 (further time for caution), but an administrator to whom r. 76.30 applies will seek any further time to pay under r. 76.31(2).

76.30.1

"caution".

On the meaning of caution, see note 33.1.1.

Usually caution will be in the form of a bond of caution (r. 33.4(1)(a)), or it may be any other method of security approved by the court (r. 33.4(2)). Where caution is by bond of caution the bond may be by (a) an insurance company authorized to conduct such business (see r. 33.5); or (b) any other person, in which

76.30.2

---

[1] Rule 76.29 inserted by SSI 2003/222 (effective 28th March, 2003) and as amended by SSI 2004/331 (effective 6th August 2004).
[2] Rule 76.30 inserted by SSI 2003/222 (effective 28th March, 2003) and as amended by SSI 2004/331 (effective 6th August 2004).

case the court must satisfy itself as to the sufficiency of the caution. The form of all bonds must comply with r. 37.6. A bond of caution must be sent to the Accountant of Court (together with a copy): r. 61.9(5). See further, note 61.9.2.

"CERTIFIED COPY INTERLOCUTOR".

76.30.3   A CCI is a copy of the interlocutor prepared by the party seeking the CCI, stamped and signed by a clerk of session in the General Department.

"WRITTEN INTIMATION".

76.30.4   For methods, see r. 16.9.

Time for finding caution

76.31   **76.31.**—[1](1)   Where the time within which caution is to be found is not stipulated in the interlocutor appointing the administrator, the time allowed for finding caution shall be, subject to paragraph (2) of this rule, limited to one calendar month from the date of the interlocutor.

(2)   The court may, on application made before the expiry of the period for finding caution, and, on cause shown, allow further time for finding caution.

GENERAL NOTE.

76.31.1   Although r.76.30 applies r. 61.9 for finding caution, r. 61.9(2), which deals with the period for finding caution (which is in the discretion of the court) and with further time to pay, clearly does not apply here. Rule 76.31 applies instead.

Administrator's title to act

76.32   **76.32.**[2]   An administrator shall not be entitled to act until he has obtained a certified copy of the interlocutor appointing him.

Accounts

76.33   **76.33.**—[3](1)   An administrator shall maintain accounts of his intromissions with the property in his charge and shall, subject to paragraph (2)—

(a)   within six months after the date of his appointment; and

(b)   at six monthly intervals after the first account during the subsistence of his appointment,

lodge with the Accountant of Court an account of his intromissions in such form, with such supporting vouchers and other documents, as the Accountant of Court may require.

(2)   The Accountant of Court may waive the lodging of an account where the administrator certifies that there have been no intromissions during a particular accounting period.

Application for discharge of administrator

76.34   **76.34.**[4]   An application to the court for the discharge of an administrator shall be made by minute in the process of the application in which the administrator was appointed.

"MINUTE".

76.34.1   For applications by minute, see r. 15.1.

---

[1] Rule 76.31 inserted by SSI 2003/222 (effective 28th March, 2003) and as amended by SSI 2004/331 (effective 6th August 2004).

[2] Rule 76.32 inserted by SSI 2003/222 (effective 28th March, 2003) and as amended by SSI 2004/331 (effective 6th August 2004).

[3] Rule 76.33 inserted by SSI 2003/222 (effective 28th March, 2003) and as amended by SSI 2004/331 (effective 6th August 2004).

[4] Rule 76.34 inserted by SSI 2003/222 (effective 28th March, 2003) and amended by SSI 2004/331 (effective 6th August 2004).

Appeals against determination of outlays and remuneration

76.35.—[1](1)[2] An appeal under—

    (a)   paragraph 9(1) of Schedule 3 to the Act of 2002 (appeal against a determination by the Accountant of Court);

    (b)   paragraph 9(1) of Schedule 1 to the Overseas Forfeiture Order of 2005 (appeal against a determination by the Accountant of Court); or

    (c)   paragraph 9(1) of Schedule 1 to the POCA Order of 2005 (appeal against a determination by the Accountant of Court),

shall be made by note in the process in which the administrator was appointed.

    (2)   Where a note is lodged under paragraph (1), the Keeper of the Rolls shall put the cause out on the By Order Roll on the first available day for a hearing before the Lord Ordinary.

76.35

GENERAL NOTE.

An administrator may appeal against the determination of the Accountant of Court as to remuneration and expenses not later than two weeks after the issuing of the determination: Act of 2002, Sched. 3, para. 9(1).

"NOTE".

For applications by note, see r. 15.2.

76.35.1

76.35.2

Civil Recovery Proceedings

Applications

76.36.—[3, 4](1)   An application for a recovery order under section 244(1) of the Act of 2002 (proceedings for recovery orders in Scotland) or article 144(1) of the POCA Order of 2005 (proceedings for a recovery order pursuant to the registration of an external order) shall be made by petition.

    (2)   There shall be produced with a petition in respect of an application under article 144 of the POCA Order of 2005 a copy of the external order which is sought to be registered.

    (3)   Where the court grants an application under article 144 of the POCA Order of 2005 the Deputy Principal Clerk shall enter the external order in the register of orders under the POCA Order of 2005.

    (4)   An application for a prohibitory property order under section 255A(1) of the Act of 2002 or article 161(1) of the POCA Order of 2005 or for an interim administration order under section 256(1) of the Act of 2002 or article 67(1) of the POCA Order of 2005 or a prohibition order under article 141ZD(1) of the POCA Order of 2005 shall be made—

    (a)   if the application is made before the enforcement authority has commenced proceedings for a recovery order, by petition; or

    (b)   if it is made after the enforcement authority has commenced such proceedings, by note in process.

    (5)   An application under the following provisions shall be made by note in process:—

    (a)   section 260(1) of the Act of 2002 (supervision of interim administrator);

    (b)   section 283(1) of the Act of 2002 (compensation);

76.36

---

[1] Rule 76.35 inserted by SSI 2003/222 (effective March 28, 2003) and amended by SSI 2004/331 (effective 6th August 2004).

[2] Rule 76.35(1) substituted by SSI 2005/663 (effective 31st December 2005).

[3] Rule 76.36 inserted by SSI 2003/222 (effective 28th March, 2003), amended by SSI 2004/331 and substituted by SSI 2005/663 (effective 31st December 2005).

[4] R.76.27 as amended by S.S.I. 2019 No. 405 para.2 (effective 28th December 2019).

(c) article 171(1) of the POCA Order of 2005 (supervision of interim administrator); and

(d) article 141ZJ(2) or article 141ZJ(2) orarticle 194(1) of the POCA Order of 2005 (compensation);

(e)[1] section 255G of the Proceeds of Crime Act 2002 (receivers in connection with prohibitory property orders) if the application is made after the application for a prohibitory property order;

(f) article 141ZHA of the POCA Order of 2005 (receivers in connection with prohibition orders)(g) if the application is made after the application for a prohibition order under article 141ZC of that Order;

(g) article 166A of the POCA Order of 2005 (receivers in connection with prohibitory property orders) if the application is made after the application for a prohibitory property order under article 161 of that Order.

(6) An application under the following provisions shall be made by motion:—

(a) section 255E(1) and (6) of the Act of 2002 (arrestment of property affected by prohibitory property order);

(b) section 255F(1) and (6) of the Act of 2002 (inhibition of property affected by prohibitory property order);

(c) section 258(1) and (7) of the Act of 2002 (inhibition of property affected by interim administration order);

(d) section 265(1) and (7) of the Act of 2002 (arrestment of property affected by interim administration order);

(e) article 165(1) and (6) of the POCA Order of 2005 (arrestment of property affected by prohibitory property order);

(f) article 166(1) and (6) of the POCA Order of 2005 (inhibition of property affected by prohibitory property order);

(g) article 169(1) and (7) of the POCA Order of 2005 (inhibition of property affected by interim administration order); and

(h) article 176(1) and (7) of the POCA Order of 2005 (arrestment of property affected by interim administration order).

(i)[2] article 141ZD(2) of the POCA Order of 2005 (variation and recall of prohibition order);

(j)[3] article 141ZH(1) and (6)(a) of the POCA Order of 2005 (inhibition of property affected by prohibition order);

(k)[4] article 141ZI(1) and (6) of the POCA Order of 2005 (arrestment of property affected by prohibition order).

(7) An application under the following provisions shall be made by motion by any party having an interest:—

(a) sections 255B(1) and 260(3) of the Act of 2002 (variation and recall of order);

(b) articles 162(1) and 171(3) of the POCA Order of 2005 (variation and recall of order);

---

[1] R.76.36(5)(e) inserted by S.S.I. 2016 No. 319 para.2 (effective 12 December 2016)

[2] As inserted by the Act of Sederunt (Rules of the Court of Session Amendment No.6) (Miscellaneous) 2013 (SSI 2013/294) r.4 (effective 11th November, 2013).

[3] As inserted by the Act of Sederunt (Rules of the Court of Session Amendment No.6) (Miscellaneous) 2013 (SSI 2013/294) r.4 (effective 11th November, 2013).

[4] As inserted by the Act of Sederunt (Rules of the Court of Session Amendment No.6) (Miscellaneous) 2013 (SSI 2013/294) r.4 (effective 11th November, 2013).

(c)[1]   section 255I of the Proceeds of Crime Act 2002 (supervision of PPO receiver and variations);

(d)   article 141ZHC of the POCA Order of 2005 (supervision of receiver and variations);

(e)   article 166C of the POCA Order of 2005 (supervision of PPO receiver and variations).

(8)   At the hearing of a motion under paragraph (7) the court may order that the application be made by note; and, in such a case, shall make an order for the lodging of answers to the note in process within such period as the court thinks fit.

(9)   Before granting an application under the following provisions, the court may dispense with, postpone or order intimation to be made to such persons as it thinks fit:—

(a)   section 255E(1) and (6) of the Act of 2002;

(b)   section 255F(1) and (6) of the Act of 2002;

(c)   section 258(1) and (7) of the Act of 2002;

(d)   section 265 (1) and (7) of the Act of 2002;

(da)[2]   section 396I of the Act of 2002;

(e)   article 165(1) and (6) of the POCA Order of 2005;

(f)   article 166(1) and (6) of the POCA Order of 2005;

(g)   article 169(1) and (7) of the POCA Order of 2005; and

(h)   article 176(1) and (7) of the POCA Order of 2005.

(i)[3]   article 141ZH(1) and (6)(a) of the POCA Order of 2005;

(j)[4]   article 141ZI(1) and (6) of the POCA Order of 2005.

Applications for a recovery order – heritable property

76.36A.   [5]   **76.36A**

GENERAL NOTE.

Once (criminal) confiscation proceedings have been concluded, abandoned or not commenced, there may be civil proceedings for the recovery by a recovery order of recoverable property in the Court of Session: Act of 2002, s. 244(1). When a recovery order is made it vests the property in the trustee for civil recovery: Act of 2002, s. 266. Property obtained through unlawful conduct (defined in s. 241) is recoverable property: Act of 2002, s. 304. Such property which has been disposed of may be followed into the hands of a person who has acquired it. Property which represents the original recoverable property is also recoverable property (s. 305(1)), property obtained in place of the recoverable property is recoverable property (s. 305(2)) and property which represents original recoverable property may be followed into the hands of a person who has acquired it (s. 305(3)). Accrued profits are recoverable property: Act of 2002, s. 307. There are exemptions: Act of 2002, ss. 308 and 309. Property may be inhibited (s. 258) or arrested (s. 265).

It was held in *The Scottish Ministers v. McGuffie* , 2006 S.L.T. 401 (OH) that recovery of assets under Pt. 5 of the Act of 2002 was not a criminal penalty within the meaning of Art. 7 of the ECHR. In *Scottish Ministers v. Doig* , 2009 S.C. 474 (Extra Div.) it was held that rights under art. 6(2) of ECHR were not infringed when the Scottish Ministers sought a recovery order in respect of money of the third respondent because of his allegedly "unlawful conduct" (concerned in supply of drugs for which he had been acquitted). Recovery proceedings are not criminal proceedings, and a finding of unlawful conduct although it might constitute a criminal offence did not offend art. 6(2).

The court cannot competently make an appointment of an interim administrator or any other officer in an assumed name albeit it might authorise him to use an assumed name: *Scottish Ministers v. Stirton*, 2013 S.L.T. 1141 (Second Div) disapproving dicta in *Scottish Ministers v. Stirton*, 2006 S.L.T. 306.

76.36.1

---

[1] R.76.36(7)(c) inserted by S.S.I. 2016 No. 319 para.2 (effective 12 December 2016)

[2] R.76.36(9)(da) inserted by S.S.I. 2019 No. 146 para.2 (effective 1 June 2019).

[3] As inserted by the Act of Sederunt (Rules of the Court of Session Amendment No.6) (Miscellaneous) 2013 (SSI 2013/294) r.4 (effective 11th November, 2013).

[4] As inserted by the Act of Sederunt (Rules of the Court of Session Amendment No.6) (Miscellaneous) 2013 (SSI 2013/294) r.4 (effective 11th November, 2013).

[5] R.76.36A omitted by S.S.I. 2019 No. 405 para.2 (effective 28th December 2019).

"PETITION".

76.36.2   A petition is presented in the Outer House: r. 14.2(h). The petition must be in Form 14.4 in the official printed form: rr. 4.1 and 14.4. The petition must be signed by counsel or other person having a right of audience: r. 4.2; and see r. 1.3(1) (definition of "counsel" and "other person having a right of audience") and note 1.3.4.

The petitioner must lodge the petition with the required steps of process (r. 4.4). A fee is payable on lodging the petition: see note 14.5.10.

On petitions generally, see Chap. 14.

INTERIM RECOVERY ORDER.

76.36.3   No mention is made in r. 76.36 of an application for an interim recovery order under s. 246 of the 2002 Act. Such an application is for the detention, custody or preservation of property and for the appointment of an interim receiver to secure the property. Such an application may be made without notice to anyone if it would prejudice a recovery order.

An application for an interim recovery order may be made in the petition for a recovery order. It is perhaps unlikely that an application would be made after a petition for a recovery order as "notice" would by then have been given; but if it were necessary, it is not clear whether the application would be by note or motion. The normal petition practice would be by note.

"NOTE".

76.36.4   For applications by note, see r. 15.2.

"MOTION".

76.36.5   For motions, see Chap. 23.

"INTIMATION".

76.36.6   For intimation, see rr. 16.7 and 16.8.

Civil Recovery Investigations

Disclosure orders

76.37   **76.37.**—[1](1)[2]   An application under section 391(1) of the Act of 2002 or article 50 of the Proceeds of Crime Act 2002 (External Investigations) Order 2013 (disclosure orders) shall be by petition.

(2)   Before the court grants an application referred to in paragraph (1), the court may dispense with, postpone or order intimation to be made to such persons as it thinks fit.

(3)[3,4]   An application under section 396(4) of the Act of 2002 or article 55(2) of the Proceeds of Crime Act 2002 (External Investigations) Order 2013 (supplementary) shall be by motion.

(4)[5]   Rule 4.11 (documents not to be borrowed) shall not apply to an application under section 391 of the Act of 2002.

(5)[6]   When an application is made under section 391 of the Act of 2002—

   (a)   the process shall be marked "Restricted Access";

   (b)   only the petitioner may borrow or inspect documents lodged in process.

---

[1] Rule 76.37 inserted by S.S.I. 2003 No. 222 (effective 28th March, 2003) and amended by S.S.I. 2004 No. 331 (effective 6th August 2004).

[2] As amended by the Act of Sederunt (Rules of the Court of Session Amendment No.6) (Miscellaneous) 2013 (SSI 2013/294) r.5 (effective 11th November, 2013).

[3] As amended by the Act of Sederunt (Rules of the Court of Session Amendment No.6) (Miscellaneous) 2013 (SSI 2013/294) r.5 (effective 11th November, 2013).

[4] As amended by the Act of Sederunt (Rules of the Court of Session Amendment No.7) (Miscellaneous) 2013 (SSI 2013/317) r.3 (effective 2nd December, 2013).

[5] Rule 76.37(1) amended and (4)–(9) inserted by S.S.I. 2012 No. 275 r. 5(1) (effective 19th November 2012).

[6] Rule 76.37(1) amended and (4)–(9) inserted by S.S.I. 2012 No. 275 r. 5(1) (effective 19th November 2012).

(6)[1] The restrictions referred to in paragraph (5) shall apply for a period of 5 years from the date of the application.

(7)[2] The petitioner may apply to the court by motion for extension of that 5 year period.

(8)[3] Any person affected by a disclosure order may apply to the court by motion to have the restrictions mentioned in paragraph (5) varied.

(9)[4] A motion under paragraph (7) or (8) shall be granted only on cause shown.

General note.

In a (criminal) confiscation investigation, the Lord Advocate, or in a civil recovery investigation the Scottish Ministers (the CRU), may apply to the Court of Session for a disclosure order. The application must state that the person specified in the application is subject to a confiscation investigation or that property specified in the application is subject to a civil recovery investigation.

A disclosure order may be sought authorizing notice in writing to a person requiring that person to answer questions, provide specified information, or produce documents, or documents of a description, specified in the notice, relevant to the investigation.

Such orders will usually be sought after other powers, such as production orders, have been tried. It may be necessary to consider whether convention rights under ECHR are affected.

76.37.1

"PETITION".

A petition is presented in the Outer House: r. 14.2(h). The petition must be in Form 14.4 in the official printed form: rr. 4.1 and 14.4. The petition must be signed by counsel or other person having a right of audience: r. 4.2; and see r. 1.3(1) (definition of "counsel" and "other person having a right of audience") and note 1.3.4.

The petitioner must lodge the petition with the required steps of process (r. 4.4). A fee is payable on lodging the petition: see note 14.5.10.

On petitions generally, see Chap. 14.

76.37.2

"INTIMATION".

For intimation, see rr. 16.7 and 16.8.

76.37.3

"MOTION".

For motions, see Chap. 23.

76.37.4

Evidence overseas

76.37A[5, 6] An application under section 282D(4) of the Act of 2002 (evidence overseas: interim receiver or interim administrator) shall be made by note in process.

76.37A

"NOTE".

For applications by note, see r.15.2.

76.37A.1

Unexplained wealth orders and interim freezing orders

76.37B.—[7, 8](1) An application under the following provisions must be made by petition—

76.37B

---

[1] Rule 76.37(1) amended and (4)–(9) inserted by S.S.I. 2012 No. 275 r. 5(1) (effective 19th November 2012).

[2] Rule 76.37(1) amended and (4)–(9) inserted by S.S.I. 2012 No. 275 r. 5(1) (effective 19th November 2012).

[3] Rule 76.37(1) amended and (4)–(9) inserted by S.S.I. 2012 No. 275 r. 5(1) (effective 19th November 2012).

[4] Rule 76.37(1) amended and (4)–(9) inserted by S.S.I. 2012 No. 275 r. 5(1) (effective 19th November 2012).

[5] As inserted by the Act of Sederunt (Rules of the Court of Session Amendment No. 4) (Miscellaneous) 2013 (SSI 2013/162) r.6 (effective 4th June, 2013).

[6] As amended by the Act of Sederunt (Rules of the Court of Session Amendment No.6) (Miscellaneous) 2013 (SSI 2013/294) r.5 (effective 11th November, 2013).

[7] Rule 76.37B inserted by S.S.I. 2019 No. 146 para.2 (effective 1st June 2019).

[8] Rule 76.37B amended by S.S.I. 2019 No. 405 para.2 (effective 28th December 2019).

(za)[1] section 396DA of the Act of 2002 (extension of period for making determination where interim freezing order has been made);

  (a) section 396A of the Act of 2002 (unexplained wealth orders);

  (b) section 396J of the Act of 2002 (application for interim freezing order) but only if the application is made at the same time as an application for an unexplained wealth order.

  (c) article 46A of the POCA Order of 2013 (unexplained wealth orders);

  (d) article 46I of the POCA Order of 2013 (unexplained wealth order: application for interim freezing order) but only if the application is made at the same time as an application under article 46A of that Order.

(2) An application under the following provisions must be made by note in process—

  (a) section 396I of the Act of 2002 (supplementary);

  (b) section 396J of the Act of 2002 (application for interim freezing order) but only if the application is made after the court has made an unexplained wealth order;

  (c) section 396K of the Act of 2002 (variation and recall of interim freezing order);

  (d) section 396S of the Act of 2002 (compensation).

  (e) article 46H of the POCA Order of 2013 (supplementary);

  (f) article 46I of the POCA Order of 2013 but only if the application is made after the court has made an order under article 46A of that Order;

  (g) article 46J of the POCA Order of 2013 (variation and discharge of interim freezing order);

  (h) article 46R of the POCA Order of 2013 (compensation).

(3) An application under the following provisions must be made by motion—

  (a) section 396N of the Act of 2002 (arrestment of property affected by interim freezing order);

  (b) section 396O of the Act of 2002 (inhibition of property affected by interim freezing order) but only if the application is made after the court has made an interim freezing order;

  (c) section 396R of the Act of 2002 (supervision of section 396P receiver and variations);

  (d) article 46M of the POCA Order of 2013 (arrestment of property affected by interim freezing order);

  (e) article 46N of the POCA Order of 2013 (inhibition of property affected by interim freezing order) but only if the application is made after the court has made an order under article 46I of that Order;

  (f) article 46Q (supervision of article 46O receiver and variations).

(4) An application under the following provisions may be made by petition, if made at the same time as an application for an interim freezing order or, if made at any time afterwards, by note in process—

  (a) section 396Q of the Act of 2002 (powers of receivers appointed under section 396P);

  (b) section 396P of the Act of 2002 (receivers in connection with interim freezing orders).

---

[1] As inserted by Act of Sederunt (Rules of the Court of Session 1994 and Sheriff Appeal Court Rules Amendment) (Miscellaneous) 2022 (SSI 2022/135) para.(2).

(4A) An application under the following provisions may be made by petition, if made at the same time as an application for an order under article 46I of the POCA Order of 2013 or, if made at any time afterwards, by note in process—

(a) article 46P of the POCA Order of 2013 (powers of receivers appointed under article 46O);

(b) article 46O of the POCA Order of 2013 (receivers in connection with interim freezing orders).

(5) At the hearing of a motion under paragraph (3) the court may order that the application be made by note; and, in such a case, must make an order for the lodging of answers to the note in process within such period as the court thinks fit.

Co-operation

Co-operation

76.38.—[1](1) In this rule "the Order of 2002" means the Proceeds of Crime Act 2002 (Enforcement in different parts of the United Kingdom) Order 2002.

(2) An application for registration under paragraph 11 of the Order of 2002 shall be by petition.

(3) Before the court grants an application referred to in paragraph (2), the court may dispense with, postpone or order intimation to be made to such persons as it thinks fit

(4) Where the Court makes an order under paragraph 11 of the Order of 2002, the Deputy Principal Clerk of Session shall—

(a) register the order; and

(b) send a copy of the order to any person affected by it.

(5) An order referred to in the foregoing paragraph shall be final and shall not be subject to review.

76.38

GENERAL NOTE.

An English, Welsh or Northern Ireland receivership order or restraint order under the 2002 Act may be registered under art. 11 of the Proceeds of Crime Act 2002 (Enforcement in different parts of the United Kingdom) Order 2002 for the purpose of enforcement.

Where an application is made, the Court of Session must direct that the order is registered in the Court of Session. The court may make such order as is appropriate to ensure that the "foreign" order is effective or to assist a receiver to exercise his functions.

In r. 76.38, the reference to "paragraph 11" of the Order of 2002 should be a reference to "article 11" (Orders in Council have articles and not paragraphs).

76.38.1

"PETITION".

A petition is presented in the Outer House: r. 14.2(h). The petition must be in Form 14.4 in the official printed form: rr. 4.1 and 14.4. The petition must be signed by counsel or other person having a right of audience: r. 4.2; and see r. 1.3(1) (definition of "counsel" and "other person having a right of audience") and note 1.3.4.

The petitioner must lodge the petition with the required steps of process (r. 4.4). A fee is payable on lodging the petition: see note 14.5.10.

On petitions generally, see Chap. 14.

76.38.2

"INTIMATION".

For intimation, see rr. 16.7 and 16.8.

76.38.3

"SEND".

This includes deliver: see r. 1.3(1).

76.38.4

"FINAL AND SHALL NOT BE SUBJECT TO REVIEW".

This means that the decision may not be reclaimed against.

76.38.5

---

[1] Rule 76.38 inserted by S.S.I. 2003 No. 222 (effective 28th March, 2003) and amended by S.S.I. 2004 No. 331 (effective 6th August 2004).

CHAPTER 76A SERIOUS CRIME PREVENTION ORDERS[1]

Interpretation of this Chapter

76A.1.[2]   In this Chapter—

"the 2007 Act" means the Serious Crime Act 2007

"person who is the subject of a serious crime prevention order" is to be construed in accordance with section 1(6) of the 2007 Act;

"serious crime prevention order" has the meaning given by section 1(5) of the 2007 Act [6]; and

"subject" means the person who is the subject of a serious crime prevention order.

76A.1

Serious Crime Prevention Orders: petitions

76A.2.—[3](1)   An application under section 8(aa) of the 2007 Act [7] (limited class of applicants for making of orders) is to be made by petition.

76A.2

(2)   The following rules shall not apply to the petition—

rule 14.5(2)(a) (dispensing with intimation, service or advertisement;

rule 14.6 (period of notice for lodging answers);

rule 14.7 (intimation and service of petitions);

rule 14.8 (procedure where answers lodged); and

rule 14.9 (unopposed petitions).

(3)   When a petition is lodged, the court must—

   (a)   order service of the petition within 7 days on the person who is the proposed subject;

   (b)   specify a period not exceeding 21 days for lodging answers; and

   (c)   appoint a hearing on the petition.

(4)   The petition is to identify any person (other than the person who is the proposed subject) in respect of whom the order sought may be likely to have a significant adverse effect or (as the case may be) state that there is no such person known to the petitioner.

(5)   If the subject is not personally present or represented at the hearing at which a serious crime prevention order is made, the petitioner must serve a copy of the order on the subject.

Third party representations

76A.3.—[4](1)   Paragraphs (2) and (3) of this rule apply where a person is identified under rule 76A.2(4).

76A.3

(2)   The court must order the petitioner to intimate the application to any such person within 7 days.

(3)   An application by a person identified by the petitioner under rule 76A.2(4) to make representations under section 9 of the 2007 Act [8] is made by motion within 14 days from the date of intimation under paragraph (2).

(4)   The court may consider a motion by a person, whether identified by the petitioner under rule 76A.2(4) or otherwise, to make representations under section 9 of the 2007 Act without a hearing unless the third party requests a hearing or it seems to the court appropriate to fix a hearing.

---

[1] Chapter 76A inserted by SSI 2016/319 r.2(6) (effective 12 December 2016).
[2] Rule 76A.1 inserted by SSI 2016/319 r.2(6) (effective 12 December 2016).
[3] Rule 76A.1 inserted by SSI 2016/319 r.2(6) (effective 12 December 2016).
[4] Rule 76A.3 inserted by SSI 2016/319 r.2(6) (effective 12 December 2016).

(5)   If the court grants an application to make representations under section 9 of the 2007 Act the court must—

    (a)   specify the manner in which representations are to be made; and

    (b)   intimate to the third party the date of any hearing fixed under rule 76A.2(3)(c).

Variation or discharge of a serious crime prevention order

76A.4

76A.4.—[1](1)   An application to vary or discharge a serious crime prevention order is to be made by minute in the process containing the interlocutor making the serious crime prevention order to which the application relates.

(2)   An application under paragraph (1) is to identify any person (other than the person who is the proposed subject of the order) in respect of whom the variation or discharge may be likely to have a significant adverse effect or (as the case may be) state that there is no such person known to the applicant.

(3)   If the subject is not personally present or represented at the hearing at which the order is varied or discharged, the applicant must serve a copy of the varied order or, as the case may be, the interlocutor discharging the order, on the subject.

---

[1] Rule 76A.3 inserted by SSI 2016/319 r.2(6) (effective 12 December 2016).

Chapter 77

Summary Trials

Application of this Chapter

77.1. This Chapter applies to a petition under section 26 of the Act of 1988 (summary trials).

77.1

GENERAL NOTE.

First introduced in R.C.S. 1934, Chap. IV, r. 40 (A.S. Rules of Court [S.I. 1934 No. 772]), summary trial procedure was originally authorised by s. 10 of the A.J.A. 1933 and re-enacted in s. 26 of the C.S.A. 1988. The purpose of a summary trial is to provide a procedure for the speedy determination of a dispute by a particular Lord Ordinary where parties agree the questions of fact or law to be determined. The procedure provides a process of arbitration without having to pay for the services of the appointed arbiter. Unfortunately, the procedure has been infrequently used. The reasons for this are believed to include (*a*) that the procedure may be held in public or be reported in the law reports and (*b*) that there is no right of appeal. In fact r. 77.4(3) provides for hearings in chambers (and presumably in private), and even in ordinary arbitrations a right of appeal may be restricted under s. 3 of the Administration of Justice (Scotland) Act 1972 or, if arbitration is adopted under the UNCITRAL Model Law on International Commercial Arbitration, the award may only be set aside on very limited grounds of form and validity but not on the merits (see Law Reform (Miscellaneous Provisions) (Scotland) Act 1990, s. 66 and Sched. 7, Art. 34). A difficulty with the procedure is, where the dispute is one of law only, getting parties to agree the facts to be included in the petition. Equally, where parties disagree on certain facts it may be difficult for parties to delineate disputed facts expressly. Furthermore, while contracts may provide for arbitration they rarely provide for summary trial.

The summary trial process has advantages over arbitration in providing a quick cheap form of adjudication by a judge of parties' choice. It is expressly provided in s. 26(3) of the C.S.A. 1988 that a summary trial shall be disposed of with as little delay as possible and where the parties agreed on the facts, must be begun to be heard within six weeks of the interlocutor appointing a hearing: r. 77.4:(3):(a).

The only limit to the use of the summary trial is that it cannot be used to decide a dispute or question which affects the status of any person: C.S.A. 1988, s. 26(4); and see note 77.7.2.

A depending action may be transferred to summary trial procedure: C.S.A. 1988. s. 26(2) and r. 77.11.

77.1.1

JURISDICTION.

Since parties must agree to summary trial, jurisdiction will be prorogated, except in those cases where, under the C.J.J.A. 1982, another court has jurisdiction under Arts. 12 (agreement on jurisdiction in insurance matters), 15 (agreement on jurisdiction in consumer contracts) or 16 (exclusive jurisdiction) in Scheds. 1 and 3C, Arts. 15 and 16 of Sched. 4 (inter-UK jurisdiction), or r. 4 (exclusive jurisdiction) of Sched. 8 (jurisdiction of Scottish Courts). On prorogation, see C.J.J.A. 1982, Scheds. 1, 3C and 4, Art. 17 and Sched. 8, r. 5. See notes 13.2.7 to 13.2.15.

77.1.2

Disapplication of certain rules to this Chapter

77.2. The following rules shall not apply to a petition under this Chapter:—
14.5 (first order in petitions),
14.6 (period of notice for lodging answers),
14.7 (intimation and service of petitions),
14.8 (procedure where answers lodged),
14.9 (unopposed petitions).

77.2

GENERAL NOTE.

The procedure in an ordinary petition does not apply to a summary trial which is presented by all parties by agreement.

77.2.1

Form of petition

77.3. A petition for a summary trial shall contain—
  (a) a concise narrative in numbered paragraphs of the facts or circumstances in relation to which the dispute or question arises;
  (b) where the parties are agreed on the facts—
      (i) a statement to that effect; and
      (ii) a note of the questions which have arisen between them;
  (c) where the parties are not agreed on the facts—

77.3

     (i)   a statement to that effect;

    (ii)   specification of the facts which are in dispute; and

   (iii)   a note of any further questions which may arise when the dispute of fact has been determined, or a reservation of such questions; and

    (d)   a prayer that the dispute or question be referred to a particular Lord Ordinary for his determination.

Deriv. R.C.S. 1965. r. 231(a) and (b)

FORM OF PETITION.

77.3.1   The general provisions in r. 14.3 apply, subject to the special rules in r. 77.3. Parties should be styled "First Party", "Second Party", etc. The petition should be signed by counsel or other person having a right of audience for each party. r. 4.2(3).

    For actions transferred to summary trial procedure, see r. 77.11

"DISPUTE OR QUESTION".

77.3.2   This is any dispute or question, regardless of value, including the minimum limit for a pecuniary action in the Court of Session (currently £1,500: Sheriff Courts (Scotland) Act 1907, s. 7 amended by the Sheriff Courts (Scotland) Act 1971 (Privative Jurisdiction and Summary Cause) Order 1988 [S.I. 1988 No. 1993]), which does not affect the status of any person: C.S.A. 1988 s. 26(4). On disputes or questions which affect the status of persons, see note 77.7.2.

Presentation to Lord Ordinary

77.4   **77.4.**—(1) The petition shall be placed before the Lord Ordinary named in the petition on the earliest available day but, subject to paragraph (2), within seven days after the date of presentation of the petition.

    (2)[1] Where the last day of the period specified in paragraph (1) falls in vacation without the petition having been brought before the Lord Ordinary, the petition shall be placed before the Lord Ordinary on the first sitting day after that vacation.

    (3) On the petition being placed before the Lord Ordinary, he shall—

    (a)   where it appears that the parties are agreed on the facts, appoint the cause to be heard before him, in court or in chambers, on a date within six weeks (excluding days in vacation) after the date of the interlocutor appointing the hearing;

    (b)   where it appears that the parties are not agreed on the facts, appoint a proof to be taken before him in court or in chambers.

    (4) The Lord Ordinary may take any hearing or proof, or any continuation of such hearing or proof, during session or vacation.

Deriv. R.C.S. 1965, r. 231(d)(part) substituted by SI 1967/387 (r. 77.4(1)). r. 231(d)(part) substituted by SI 1967/387 (r. 77.4(2)), r. 231(c) substituted by SI 1976/387 (r. 77.4(3)), and r. 231(f) (r. 77.4(4))

VACATION OR RECESS.

77.4.1   See note 11.1.2. The Lord Ordinary may only begin to consider the petition on a sederunt day during session: r. 77.4(2). The first consideration of the petition will usually be a motion by the parties on presentation of the petition for hearing or proof. A hearing or proof may be begun or continued in session, vacation or recess: r. 77.4(4).

HEARING OR PROOF.

77.4.2   The hearing or proof may be in open court or in chambers: r. 77.4(3); and see e.g. *McGeachy v. Standard Life Assurance Co.* 1972 S.C. 145. Where the parties are agreed on the facts, the hearing must begin within six weeks (excluding vacation) after the date of the interlocutor appointing the hearing: r. 77.4(3)(a). In such a case, because of any difficulty in ensuring the availability of the nominated judge, parties should consult the Keeper of the Rolls before presenting the petition to discuss a date for the hearing and check the availability of the judge.

    A hearing is appointed where the parties are agreed on the facts; a proof where they are not: r. 77.4(3). Procedure is determined by the parties with consent of the judge or by him if the parties are not agreed. Evidence at a proof is not recorded unless agreed to be: r. 77.6. On the distinction between hearings and proofs, see note 14.8.6. On proofs generally, see Chap. 36.

---

[1] R. 77.4(2) amended by S.S.I. 2017 No. 414 r. 3(6) (effective 1st January 2018).

Procedure in summary trials

77.5. Subject to any other provision in this Chapter, the petition shall follow such procedure as the parties may, with the consent of the Lord Ordinary, agree, or, failing such agreement, as the Lord Ordinary shall direct.

Deriv. R.C.S. 1965, r. 231(j)

77.5

GENERAL NOTE.

Before presenting a petition for a summary trial parties should try to agree how the petition will proceed.

77.5.1

Recording of evidence at proof

77.6. The evidence led at a proof allowed under rule 77.4(3)(6) shall not be recorded, unless the parties so agree.

Deriv. R.C.S. 1965, r. 231(g)

77.6

RECORDING OF EVIDENCE.

If parties are agreed that evidence led should be recorded the general rule on recording of evidence applies: see r. 36.11.

77.6.1

Reports to Inner House

77.7.—(1) If at any stage of the cause it appears to the Lord Ordinary that the determination of the petition may affect the status of any person, the Lord Ordinary shall report the matter to the Inner House in accordance with Chapter 34.

(2) On receiving a report under paragraph (1), the Lord President may appoint the parties to show cause before a Division of the Inner House why the petition should proceed under section 26 of the Act of 1988; and the Inner House shall, after hearing parties and subject to any conditions as it thinks fit, direct that the petition shall proceed or refuse the prayer of the petition.

Deriv. R.C.S. 1965, r. 231(h)

77.7

GENERAL NOTE.

R. 77.7 is without prejudice to Chap. 34 which provides that a Lord Ordinary may at any stage report a cause on any incidental matter arising out of it to the Inner House for a ruling: r. 34.1(1). In a summary trial if there is a question whether the determination of the petition may affect the status of any person the Lord Ordinary must report the matter to the Inner House: r. 77.7(1). The decision of the Inner House on the question raised in the report is final: r. 34.3(2). If the petition would clearly affect status, the Lord Ordinary need not report the matter and shall refuse the petition.

77.7.1

"STATUS OF ANY PERSON".

S. 26(4) of the C.S.A. 1988 provides that summary trial procedure applies to any dispute or question not affecting the status of any person which might competently be the subject of any cause in the Outer House. Status means political status such as citizenship or nationality; or civil status such as marriage, legitimacy (present or past), parentage, domicile, separation, adoption, bankruptcy or liquidation. Apart from the above (except adoption), R.C.S. 1965, r. 231(o) (amended by r. 81.13 by A.S. (R.C.A. No. 3) (Presumption of Death) 1978 [S.I. 1978 No. 161]) provided that a question affecting status for the purposes of s. 10 of the A.J.A. 1933 (repealed and re-enacted in s. 26(4) of the C.S.A. 1988) included a question which could be the subject of or might depend on the decision in actions for aliment not depending on contractual obligation, for custody of children or actions which raised questions of capacity of a person; although these actions do not per se raise questions of status. There is, however, no power in the C.S.A. 1988 to state in the rules what is included in the meaning of "status of any person", and R.C.S. 1965, r. 231(o) has not, therefore, been re-enacted. The word "person" includes a corporate or unincorporated body: Interpretation Act 1978, Sched. 1.

77.7.2

Disposal of petitions

77.8. Any decision of the Lord Ordinary shall be given effect to in an interlocutor and he may—

(a) pronounce any interlocutor which he thinks fit to enable his decision to be carried into effect; and

(b) dispose of all questions of expenses.

Deriv. R.C.S. 1965. r. 231(h)

77.8

Finality of interlocutors

77.9   **77.9.** An interlocutor of the Lord Ordinary shall be final, binding only on the parties to the petition, and shall not be subject to review.

Deriv. R.C.S. 1965, r. 231(1)

FINALITY OF INTERLOCUTORS.

77.9.1   No interlocutor in a summary trial pronounced by the Lord Ordinary may be reclaimed: r. 77.9. An interlocutor pronounced by the Inner House on a report is also final and not appealable to the House of Lords: r. 34.3(2).

Transfer to another Lord Ordinary

77.10   **77.10.**—(1) In the event of the death, disability or absence of the Lord Ordinary before the petition has been determined, the petitioners may lodge a joint minute in Form 77.10 in process for the cause to be referred to another Lord Ordinary named in that minute.

(2) On such a minute being lodged in process, the cause shall be transferred to the Lord Ordinary named in that minute who shall take up the procedure at the point which had been reached by his predecessor.

(3) The Lord Ordinary to whom the cause is transferred under paragraph (2) may re-hear the evidence of any witness heard by his predecessor.

Deriv. R.C.S. 1965, r. 231(m)

"LODGE IN PROCESS".

77.10.1   The joint minute is lodged as a step of process (r. 1.3(1) (definition of "step of process")). On lodging steps of process, see r. 4.4. The list may be lodged by post: P.N. No. 4 of 1994, paras. 1 and 8; and see note 4.4.10.

RE-HEARING OF EVIDENCE.

77.10.2   This will be necessary if the parties are not using a shorthand writer to record the evidence. R. 77.6 on the recording of evidence should be noted.

Agreement to adopt summary trial procedure in action in dependence

77.11   **77.11.**—(1) Where the parties to an action propose to adopt summary trial procedure by virtue of section 26(2) of the Act of 1988 (agreement to adopt summary trial procedure in action in dependence), they shall lodge in the process of the action a joint minute in Form 77.11.

(2) On such a joint minute being lodged in process, the Lord Ordinary shall pronounce an interlocutor directing that the action shall proceed as a summary trial.

(3) On an interlocutor being pronounced under paragraph (2), rules 77.3 to 77.10 shall, with the necessary modifications and the following modifications, apply to the further procedure in the action:—

(a)   subject to sub-paragraph (b) of this paragraph, in rule 77.4, for the word "petition" there shall be substituted the words "record or other pleading"; and

(b)   in rule 77.4(1), for the words "date of presentation of the petition" there shall be substituted the words "date of the interlocutor pronounced under rule 77.11(2)".

Deriv. R.C.S. 1965, r. 231(n)

GENERAL NOTE.

77.11.1   S. 26(2) of the C.S.A. 1988 allows an action not affecting the status of any person to be transferred to summary trial procedure. This provision is rarely used.

An action affecting the status of any person may not be transferred to summary trial procedure: C.S.A. 1988, s. 26(2). For what affects status, see note 77.7.2.

"ACTION IN DEPENDENCE".

77.11.2   An action means a cause initiated by summons: C.S.A. 1988, s. 51. An action is depending from the time it is commenced (i.e. from the time it is served) until final decree, whereas an action is in dependence until final extract. For the meaning of "commenced", see note 13.4.4. For the meaning of final decree, see note 4.15.2(2). For the meaning of final extract, see note 7.1.2(2). S. 26(2) of the C.S.A. 1988 probably should refer to a "depending" action.

CHAPTER 78 SPECIAL CASES UNDER SECTION 27 OF COURT OF SESSION ACT 1988

Chapter 78

Special Cases under Section 27 of Court of Session Act 1988

Application of this Chapter

78.1. This Chapter applies to a special case under section 27 of the Act of 1988.   **78.1**

GENERAL NOTE.

The special case introduced by s.63 of the C.S.A. 1868 (now s.27 of the C.S.A. 1988) is neither a summons nor a petition.   **78.1.1**

A special case is a contract binding on the parties to a certain statement of facts: *Aytoun v. Aytoun* 1939 S.C. 162

Where (*a*) any persons interested personally or in a fiduciary or official capacity, (*b*) in a decision of a question of law, (*c*) are agreed on the facts, and (*d*) are in dispute only on the law applicable to those facts, they may, without raising proceedings, or at any stage of any proceedings, present a special case to the Inner House for an opinion or judgment: C.S.A. 1988, s.27(1). The case must be signed by counsel. Parties may exclude appeal to the House of Lords.

After the instance, the case consists of four parts—the statement of who the parties are (called first party, second party, etc.), the statement of agreed facts, the contentions for each party, and the questions of law for the opinion or judgment of the Inner House.

All persons interested should be parties: *Mackie's Trs. v. Martins* (1875) 2 R. 621. They must have a patrimonial interest in the subject-matter: *Aberdeen Varieties Ltd v. James F. Donald (Aberdeen Cinemas) Ltd* 1940 S.C.(H.L.) 52. Agreement on the facts, including foreign law, is essential: see e.g. *Campbell's Trs. v. Campbell* (1903) 5 F. 366, 373 per Lord Kinnear. It is not essential, but it may be convenient, that the question(s) of law are in such form as can be answered yes or no. The question of law must be one which could be raised in another formal process (e.g. an action of declarator): *Ramsbotham v. Scottish American Investment Co. Ltd* (1891) 18 R. 558; *Turner's Trs. v. Turner* 1943 S.C. 389. The question of law must not be premature, hypothetical or academic: *Aberdeen Varieties Ltd*, above, per Viscount Simon L.C., at p. 54; *Turner's Trs.*, above. If the question of law is one which can competently be tried in the sheriff court, a special case can only be presented to the Inner House if the value of the subject-matter exceeds the privative limit of the sheriff court (currently £1,500: Sheriff Courts (Scotland) Act 1907, s.7 and SI 1988/1993): *Bruce* (1889) 17 R. 276. There must be a contradictor: *Mackinnon's Trs. v. McNeill* (1897) 24 R. 981; *Turner's Trs.*, above. A party may, however, be entitled to an answer to a particular question (in his favour) if other parties do not present an argument against: *Shetland Salmon Farmers v. Crown Estate Commissioners* 1991 S.L.T. 166 (but *Turner's Trs.*, above, was not cited).

Lodging and hearing of special case

78.2.—(1) A special case shall be lodged with a process in the General Department.   **78.2**

(2) A special case shall, without appearance, be put out for hearing in the Summar Roll before the Inner House.

Deriv. R.C.S. 1965, r. 265(a) (r. 78.2(1)) and r. 265(b) (r. 78.2(2))

"SPECIAL CASE LODGED WITH A PROCESS".

The special case should comply with the requirements for size and quality of paper, etc., in r. 4.1. For the essential documents for a process, see r. 4.4.   **78.2.1**

SUMMAR ROLL.

Once appointed to the Summar Roll a diet is fixed by the Keeper of the Rolls in accordance with r. 6.3 after parties have sent him Form 6.3 duly completed. The case will be heard by a Division of the Inner House, usually consisting of three judges rather than four nowadays.   **78.2.2**

In case of difficulty, importance or equal division of the Division of the Inner House hearing the special case, a larger court may hear the case: C.S.A. 1988, s.27(2).

FEE.

The court fee for each party (up to a maximum fee) is payable on lodging the special case. For fee, see Court of Session etc. Fees Order 1997, Table of Fees, Pt I, B, item 8 [SI 1997/688, as amended, pp. C 1201 et seq.]. Certain persons are exempt from payment of fees: see 1997 Fees Order, art.5 substituted by SSI 2002/270. A fee exemption certificate must be lodged in process: see P.N. No.1 of 2002.   **78.2.3**

Where a party is legally represented, the fee may be debited under a credit scheme introduced on 1st April 1976 by P.N. No. 4 of 1976 to the account (if one is kept or permitted) of the agent by the court cashier, and an account will be rendered weekly by the court cashier's office to the agent for all court fees due that week for immediate settlement. Party litigants and agents not operating the scheme must pay (by cash, cheque or postal order) on each occasion a fee is due at the time of lodging at the counter at the General Department.

The court fee for the hearing on the Summar Roll is payable by each party for every 30 minutes or part thereof. For fee, see Court of Session etc. Fees Order 1984, Table of Fees, Pt I, B, item 14 [SI 1984/256, Table as amended, pp. C 1202 et seq.]. The fee may be debited under a credit scheme introduced on 1st April 1976 by P.N. No. 4 of 1976 to the account (if one is kept or permitted) of the agent by the court cashier, and an account will be rendered weekly by the court cashier's office to the agent for all court fees due that week for immediate settlement. An agent not on the credit scheme will have an account opened for the purpose of lodging the fee: P.N. No. 2 of 1995. A debit slip and a copy of the court hearing time sheet will be delivered to the agent's box or sent by DX or post.

A party litigant must pay cash to the clerk of court at the end of the hearing or, if the hearing lasts more than a day, at the end of each day: P.N. No. 2 of 1995. A receipt will be issued. The assistant clerk of session will acknowledge receipt of the sum received from the clerk of court on the Minute of Proceedings.

Amendment of case

78.3   **78.3.**—(1)   A special case may be amended by consent of the parties.

(2)   Where parties seek to amend a special case, any one of them may apply by motion for leave to amend of consent.

Deriv. R.C.S. 1965, r. 265(c) inserted by SI 1984/472

Appointment of curator ad litem to party incapax

78.4   **78.4.**—(1)   Where a party to a special case is *incapax* by reason of nonage, insanity or otherwise, it shall be the duty of the other parties (which duty may be performed by any of them), on the lodging of the special case under rule 78.2(1), to apply by motion for the appointment of a curator *ad litem* to such *incapax*.

(2)   A curator *ad litem* appointed under paragraph (1) shall be given all necessary information and facilities by the other parties to enable him to perform his duties.

(3)   Where a curator *ad litem* is satisfied that the special case is fully and accurately stated in relation to the interests of the *incapax*, he may sign it as curator *ad litem*.

(4)   Where a curator *ad litem* is not given all necessary information and facilities by the other parties, or is not satisfied that the special case is fully and accurately stated in relation to the interest of the *incapax*, he shall report the position to the Inner House which may then recall his appointment and dispose of the special case as it thinks fit.

(5)   An award of expenses—

(a)   may not be made against a curator *ad litem*; and

(b)   may be made in favour of a curator *ad litem* as the court thinks fit.

Deriv. R.C.S. 1965, r. 266

GENERAL NOTE.

78.4.1   The court may refuse to appoint a curator *ad litem* if the interest of the person concerned is adequately represented by another party: *Macdonald's Trs. v. Medhurst* 1915 S.C. 879 (mental illness). But in *Aytoun v. Aytoun* 1939 S.C. 162 (a case involving nonage), the appointment was insisted on because the special case would not be binding on a child.

"MOTION".

78.4.2   For motions, see Chap. 23.

CHAPTER 79 APPLICATIONS UNDER THE ACCESS TO HEALTH RECORDS ACT 1990

Chapter 79

Applications under the Access to Health Records Act 1990

Application and interpretation of this Chapter

79.1.—(1) This Chapter applies to an application under section 8(1) of the Access to Health Records Act 1990 (application for order for holder of health record to comply with requirement of the Act).

(2) In this Chapter—

"the Act of 1990" means the Access to Health Records Act 1990;

"the Regulations" means the Access to Health Records (Steps to Secure Compliance and Complaints Procedures) (Scotland) Regulations 1991;

"complaint" means a written notice of complaint under regulation 3 or 4 of the Regulations;

"report" means a report under regulation 6 of the Regulations.

Deriv. R.C.S. 1965, r. 260Y(1) and (2) inserted by SI 1991/2652

GENERAL NOTE.

Under the Data Protection Act 1984 (now the Data Protection Act 1998) patients are entitled to access to computerised health records. Under the Act of 1990 they are entitled to access to written health records (but not to information to which the 1984 Act applies).

A patient's right of access to health records is not unrestricted. Access may be denied if it is in the patient's best interests to do so, e.g. because disclosure would be detrimental to the patient's health: Act of 1990, s. 3(2); and see, in England, *R. v. Mid Glamorgan Family Health Services Authority ex parte Martin* [1995] 1 All E.R. 356.

Form of applications, etc.

79.2.—(1) An application under section 8(1) of the Act of 1990 shall be made by petition.

(2) A petition under paragraph (1) shall state those steps prescribed in the Regulations which have been taken to secure compliance with the Act of 1990.

(3) On presentation of the petition, there shall be lodged in process as productions—

(a) a copy of the application under section 3 (access to health record) or section 6 (correction of inaccurate health record), as the case may be, of the Act of 1990;

(b) a copy of the complaint; and

(c) if applicable, a copy of the report.

Deriv. R.C.S. 1965, r. 260Y(3) and (5) inserted by SI 1991/2652 (r. 79.2(1) and (3))

GENERAL NOTE.

This rule is made in part under s. 8(1) of the Act of 1990. Where the holder of a health record has failed to comply with a requirement of the Act of 1990 and the applicant has taken all steps to secure compliance as may be prescribed by regulations, the court may order the holder of the record to comply with the requirement: Act of 1990, s. 8(1) and (2).

The requirements include a requirement that the patient (or certain others on his behalf) may inspect the record and have it explained on application by him (Act of 1990, s. 3) and to have a correction made to it on application by him (Act of 1990, s. 6). The steps to be taken by the applicant are to apply to the holder in writing to see the record or have it corrected, as the case may be, and to have made a complaint under the Regulations that the holder of the record has failed to comply to which he has received a reply or to which there has been no response within three months from the date of the complaint: 1991 Regulations, reg. 2.

The court may see the record; but, pending determination of the application to the court, the applicant may not see it: Act of 1990, s. 8(4).

"PETITION".

79.2.2   A petition is presented in the Outer House: r. 14.2(h). The petition must be in Form 14.4 in the official printed form: rr. 4.1 and 14.4. The petition must be signed by counsel or other person having a right of audience: r. 4.2; and see r. 1.3(1) (definition of "counsel" and "other person having a right of audience") and note 1.3.4.

The petitioner must lodge the petition with the required steps of process (r. 4.4). A fee is payable on lodging the petition: see note 14.5.10.

On petitions generally, see Chap. 14.

"LODGED IN PROCESS AS PRODUCTIONS".

79.2.3   See r. 4.5.

"A COPY OF THE APPLICATION".

79.2.4   The application to the holder of the health record must be in writing: Act of 1990, s. 11.

"COMPLAINT".

79.2.5   Written notice of the complaint must be given to the appropriate Health Board within three months of the application to the holder: 1991 Regulations, regs 3(2) and 5.

"COPY OF THE REPORT".

79.2.6   The holder of the health record is supposed to report to the applicant his response to the complaint within three months from the date of the complaint. A copy will only be available if he has reported.

Time-limit for applications

79.3   **79.3.**   An application under section 8(1) of the Act of 1990 may not be made unless the petition is presented—

(a)   where the applicant has received a report, within one year of the date after the report; or

(b)   where the applicant has not received a report, within 18 months after the date of the complaint.

Deriv. R.C.S. 1965, r. 260Y(4) inserted by SI 1991/2652

"WITHIN ONE YEAR", "WITHIN 18 MONTHS".

79.3.1   The date from which the period is calculated is not counted. Where the last day falls on a Saturday or Sunday or a public holiday on which the Office of Court is closed, the next available day is allowed: r. 1.3(7). For office hours and public holidays, see note 3.1.2.

CHAPTER 80 APPLICATIONS IN RESPECT OF QUALIFIED CONVEYANCERS AND EXECUTRY PRACTITIONERS

Chapter 80

Applications in Respect of Qualified Conveyancers and Executry Practitioners

Application and interpretation of this Chapter

80.1.—(1) This Chapter applies to an application made under the Law Reform (Miscellaneous Provisions) (Scotland) Act 1990 in respect of a qualified conveyancer or executry practitioner.

(2) In this Chapter, "the Act of 1990" means the Law Reform (Miscellaneous Provisions) (Scotland) Act 1990.

(3) The expressions "the Board", "executry practitioner" and "qualified conveyancer" have the meanings assigned respectively in section 23 of the Act of 1990.

GENERAL NOTE.

In 1992 the Scottish Conveyancing and Executry Services Board, set up under s. 16 of the Act of 1990 to regulate the provision of conveyancing and executry services by persons other than solicitors or unqualified persons under s. 32(2) of the Solicitors (Scotland) Act 1980, was suspended. The reason was that the Government considered it was unlikely that the housing market would generate many opportunities for qualified conveyancers in the short term: see 1992 S.L.T. (News) 283. The Board did not grant any applications before it was suspended.

The Board's suspension was lifted, and it opened for registration of qualifying conveyancers and executry practitioners, in early 1997.

Applications and appeals in respect of qualified conveyancers and executry practitioners

80.2.—(1) Subject to paragraph (4), an application under any of the following provisions of the Act of 1990 shall be made by petition—

   (a) section 17(6) (application following refusal to register as qualified conveyancer);

   (b) section 18(7) (application following refusal to register as executry practitioner);

   (c) section 20(7) (application for order to require practitioner to comply with direction);

   (d) section 20(11)(b) (application following review of certain decisions of Board following misconduct etc.);

   (e) section 21(5) (application following direction relating to assets);

   (f) section 21(7) (application to secure compliance with direction);

   (g) section 21(10) (application by the Board for interdict); and

   (h) paragraph 20 of Schedule 1 (application for order to produce documents).

(2) An application under section 17(6), 18(7) or 20(11)(b) of the Act of 1990 shall state the date on which the outcome of the review was intimated to the petitioner.

(3) An application under section 21(5) of the Act of 1990 shall state the date on which the direction was received by the petitioner.

(4) An application for leave under section 21(10) of the Act of 1990 shall be made by motion.

"PETITION".

A petition is presented in the Outer House: r. 15.2(h). The petition must be in Form 14.4 in the official printed form: rr.4.1 and 14.4. The petition must be signed by counsel or other person having a right of audience: r.4.2; and see r.1.3(1) (definition of "counsel" and "other person having a right of audience") and note 1.3.4.

The petitioner must lodge the petition with the required steps of process (r.4.4). A fee is payable on lodging the petition: see note 14.5.10.

On petitions generally, see Chap. 14.

"motion".

80.2.2 For motions, see Chap. 23.
Deriv. R.C.S. 1965, r. 9 substituted by S.I. 1992 No. 1422

Intimation and service in petitions under this Chapter

80.3 **80.3.**—(1) A petition to which this Chapter applies shall be brought before a Division of the Inner House in chambers, and the Division may, without hearing parties and subject to the following paragraphs, make such order for intimation and service as it thinks fit.

(2) In an application under any of the following provisions of the Act of 1990, the court shall order service of the petition on the Board—

(a) section 17(6) (application in respect of review of refusal to register as qualified conveyancer);

(b) section 18(7) (application following review of refusal to register as executry practitioner);

(c) section 20(11)(b) (application following review of certain decisions of the Board following misconduct etc.); and

(d) section 21(5) (application following direction relating to assets).

(3) In an application under any of the following provisions of the Act of 1990, the court shall order service of the petition on the executry practitioner or qualified conveyancer, as the case may be—

(a) section 20(7) (application for order to require practitioner to comply with directions);

(b) section 21(7) (application to secure compliance with direction); and

(c) paragraph 20 of Schedule 1 (application for order to produce documents).

(4) In an application under section 21(10) of the Act of 1990 (application by the Board for interdict), the court shall order service of the petition on the executry or qualified practitioner, as the case may be, and on the bank, building society or other deposit holder.

Deriv. R.C.S. 1965, r. 10 substituted by S.I. 1992 No. 1422

"intimation".

80.3.1 On intimation, see r. 16.8.

"service".

80.3.2 On service, see Chap. 16.

Procedure after order for intimation and service

80.4 **80.4.** The court shall, after an order for intimation and service under rule 80.3, proceed on the petition summarily in such manner as it thinks fit.
Deriv. R.C.S. 1965, r. 11 substituted by S.I. 1992 No. 1422

Remit for further inquiry in petitions under this Chapter

80.5 **80.5.**—(1) In a petition to which this Chapter applies, the court may remit to any person to make further inquiry into the facts, or to take further evidence and to report to the court.

(2) On completion of a report made under paragraph (1), the person to whom the remit was made shall send his report and three copies of it, and a copy of it for each party, to the Deputy Principal Clerk.

(3) On receipt of such a report, the Deputy Principal Clerk shall—

(a) cause the report to be lodged in process; and

(b) give written intimation to each party that this has been done and that he may uplift a copy of the report from process.

(4) After the lodging of such a report, any party may apply by motion for an order in respect of the report or for further procedure.

Deriv. R.C.S. 1965, r. 11B substituted by S.I. 1992 No. 1422 (r. 80.5(1))

"WRITTEN INTIMATION".

For methods, see r. 16.9.

80.5.1

CHAPTER 81 APPLICATIONS FOR PARENTAL ORDERS UNDER THE HUMAN FERTILISATION AND EMBRYOLOGY ACT 1990

Chapter 81

Applications for Parental Orders under the Human Fertilisation and Embryology Act 1990

Application and interpretation of this Chapter

81.1. *[Revoked by S.S.I. 2010 No. 136 (effective 6th April 2010).]* 81.1

GENERAL NOTE.

The 1990 Act was repealed by the Human Fertilisation and Embryology Act 2008. Section 30 of the 1990 Act, which provided for parental orders, was replaced by s. 54 of the 2008 Act. Chapter 81 is, therefore, repealed. Rules for s. 54 of the 2008 Act are now in Chap. 97. 81.1.1

Disapplication of certain rules to this Chapter

81.2. *[Revoked by S.S.I. 2010 No. 136 (effective 6th April 2010).]* 81.2

Confidentiality of documents in process

81.3. *[Revoked by S.S.I. 2010 No. 136 (effective 6th April 2010).]* 81.3

Selection of reporting officer or curator ad litem

81.4. *[Revoked by S.S.I. 2010 No. 136 (effective 6th April 2010).]* 81.4

Form of agreements to parental order

81.5. *[Revoked by S.S.I. 2010 No. 136 (effective 6th April 2010).]* 81.5

Orders for evidence

81.6. *[Revoked by S.S.I. 2010 No. 136 (effective 6th April 2010).]* 81.6

Expenses

81.7. *[Revoked by S.S.I. 2010 No. 136 (effective 6th April 2010).]* 81.7

Protection of identity of petitioners

81.8. *[Revoked by S.S.I. 2010 No. 136 (effective 6th April 2010).]* 81.8

Applications for parental order

81.9. *[Revoked by S.S.I. 2010 No. 136 (effective 6th April 2010).]* 81.9

Appointment of reporting officer and curator ad litem

81.10. *[Revoked by S.S.I. 2010 No. 136 (effective 6th April 2010).]* 81.10

Duties of reporting officer and curator ad litem

81.11. *[Revoked by S.S.I. 2010 No. 136 (effective 6th April 2010).]* 81.11

Hearing

81.12. *[Revoked by S.S.I. 2010 No. 136 (effective 6th April 2010).]* 81.12

Supervision by or committal to care of local authority

81.13. *[Revoked by SI 1997/854.]* 81.13

Applications for return, removal or prohibition of removal of child

81.14. *[Revoked by S.S.I. 2010 No. 136 (effective 6th April 2010).]* 81.14

Applications to amend, or revoke a direction in, a parental order

81.15. *[Revoked by S.S.I. 2010 No. 136 (effective 6th April 2010).]* 81.15

Registration of certified copy interlocutor

81.16. *[Revoked by S.S.I. 2010 No. 136 (effective 6th April 2010).]* 81.16

Extract of order

81.17   **81.17.** *[Revoked by S.S.I. 2010 No. 136 (effective 6th April 2010).]*

Procedure after intimation to Registrar General or issue of extract

81.18   **81.18.** *[Revoked by S.S.I. 2010 No. 136 (effective 6th April 2010).]*

CHAPTER 82 THE HUMAN RIGHTS ACT 1998

Chapter 82

The Human Rights Act 1998

Application and interpretation

82.1—[1](1) This Chapter deals with various matters relating to the Human Rights Act 1998.

(2) In this Chapter—

"the 1998 Act" means the Human Rights Act 1998;

"declaration of incompatibility" has the meaning given by section 4 of the 1998 Act.

GENERAL NOTE.

This Chapter deals with two matters arising out of the Human Rights Act 1998, which came into force on 2nd October 2000. The first is concerned with evidence of judgments (r. 82.2) and the second is concerned with declarations of incompatibility (rr. 82.3 and 82.4).

Evidence of judgments etc

82.2—[2](1) Evidence of any judgment, decision, declaration or opinion of which account has to be taken by the court under section 2 of the 1998 Act shall be given by reference to any authoritative and complete report of the said judgment, decision, declaration or opinion and may be given in any manner.

(2) Evidence given in accordance with paragraph (1) shall be sufficient evidence of that judgment, decision, declaration or opinion.

GENERAL NOTE.

This rule is concerned with the citation of judgments, decisions and opinions of the European Court of Human Rights, the European Commission of Human Rights and the Committee of Ministers.

Section 2 of the 1998 Act provides that the court must take account the decisions of the above bodies insofar as relevant. For some reason it has been thought to be necessary to provide for authorised citation of such decisions. Rule 82.2 provides for citation of authoritative and complete reports, but does not indicate what is authoritative or how purported authorisation is established. Presumably a report in a law report series such as E.H.R.R. hardly requires authorisation. A copy of a judgment stamped with a certificate of the judgment of the body concerned will not doubt be regarded as prima facie authoritative.

Declaration of incompatibility

82.3—[3](1)[4] Where in any proceedings a party seeks a declaration of incompatibility or the court is considering whether to make such a declaration at its own instance—

    (a)   notice in Form 82.3-A shall be given as soon as reasonably practicable to such persons as the Lord President may from time to time direct—

        (i)   by the party seeking the declaration; or

        (ii)   by the clerk of court,

        as the case may be, provided that there shall be no requirement to give such notice to a party or to the representative of a party; and

    (b)   where notice is given by the party seeking the declaration, the party shall lodge a certificate of notification in process.

(2) Where any—

    (a)   Minister of the Crown (or person nominated by him);

    (b)   member of the Scottish Executive;

    (c)   Northern Ireland Minister;

---

[1] Chap. 82 and r.82.1 inserted by S.S.I. 2000 No. 316 (effective from 2nd October 2000).
[2] R.82.2 inserted by S.S.I. 2000 No. 316 (effective from 2nd October 2000).
[3] R. 82.3 inserted by S.S.I. 2000 No. 316 (effective 2nd October 2000).
[4] R. 82.3(1) substituted by S.S.I. 2006 No. 83 (effective 17th March 2006).

(d) Northern Ireland department,

wishes to be joined as a party to proceedings in relation to which the Crown is entitled to receive notice under section 5 of the 1998 Act he or, as the case may be, it shall serve notice in Form 82.3-B to that effect on the Deputy Principal Clerk of Session and shall serve a copy of the notice on all other parties to the proceedings.

GENERAL NOTE.

82.3.1 This rule provides for the giving of notice under s. 5 of the 1998 Act. Where the court is considering whether to make a declaration of incompatibility, the Crown is entitled to notice of it: 1998 Act, s. 5(1). Where s. 5(1) applies, any of those "agents of the Crown" listed in r. 82.3(2) (which repeats the list in s. 5(2) of the 1998 Act) is entitled to be joined as a party: 1998 Act, s. 5(2).

Notice should be given to the Crown as early in the proceedings as possible: see *R v. A (No. 2)* [2001] 2 W.L.R. 1562 (HL); *Gunn v. Newman* , 2001 S.L.T. 776, 779G.

The purpose of intervention under s. 5(2) of the 1998 Act is not confined simply to arguing whether the court should make a declarator, but enables the Crown to address the court on the objects and purposes of the legislation in question and on any other matters which may be relevant: *R v. A (No. 2)*, above, per Lord Hope of Craighead.

"DECLARATION OF INCOMPATIBILITY".

82.3.2 A declaration (sic) of incompatibility may be made (a) under s.4(2) of the 1998 Act where a provision of primary legislation is incompatible with a Convention right or (b) under s. 4(4) of the 1998 Act where a provision of subordinate legislation is incompatible with a Convention right and the primary legislation under which it is made prevents removal of the incompatibility. "Primary legislation" means Acts of the U.K. Parliament, Orders in Council and U.K. statutory instruments bringing them into force or amending them: 1998 Act, s. 21(1).

Such a declarator does not affect the validity, operation or enforcement of the provision declared incompatible and is not binding on the parties: 1998 Act, s. 4(6).

A "Convention right" means a right in the European Convention of Human Rights mentioned in s. 1(1) of the 1998 Act.

"AS THE LORD PRESIDENT MAY FROM TIME TO TIME DIRECT".

82.3.3 The current direction is No. 1 of 2005. Notice is to be given to the Solicitor to the Advocate-General and the Solicitor to the Scottish Executive.

"SERVE".

82.3.4 For service, see Chap. 16.

82.4 **82.4[1]** Within 14 days after the date of service of the notice under rule 82.3(2), the person serving the notice shall lodge a minute in the proceedings in Form 82.4 and shall serve a copy of that minute on all other parties to the proceedings.

"WITHIN 14 DAYS".

82.4.1 The date from which the period is calculated is not counted. Where the last day falls on Saturday or Sunday or a public holiday on which the Office of Court is closed, the next available day is allowed: r. 13(7). For office hours and public holidays, see note 3.1.2.

"SERVE".

82.4.2 For service, see Chap. 16.

82.5 **82.5 [2]** The court may fix a diet for a hearing on the question of incompatibility as a separate hearing from any other hearing in the proceedings and may sist the proceedings if it considers it necessary to do so while the question of incompatibility is being determined.

---

[1] R. 82.4 inserted by S.S.I. 2000 No. 316 (effective 2nd October 2000).
[2] Rule 82.5 inserted by S.S.I. 2000 No. S (effective 2nd October 2000).

CHAPTER 83 APPLICATIONS FOR PURPOSES OF INVESTIGATIONS ORDERED PURSUANT TO ARTICLE 14 OF REGULATION 17 OF THE COUNCIL OF EUROPEAN COMMUNITIES

[Chapter 83 revoked by S.S.I. 2005 No. 193, effective April 1, 2005.]

CHAPTER 84 APPLICATION UNDER THE TERRORISM ACT 2000

Chapter 84[1]

Application under the Terrorism Act 2000

Interpretation of this Chapter

84.1[2] In this Chapter—   84.1

"the Act of 2000" means the Terrorism Act 2000;

"administrator" shall be construed in accordance with paragraph 16(1)(b) of Schedule 4 to the Act of 2000; and

"restraint order" means an order under paragraph 18(1) of Schedule 4 to the Act of 2000.

GENERAL NOTE.

This Chapter deals with applications to the court where a forfeiture order has been made by a criminal court under s. 23 of the Act of 2000 or could be made by a court in Scotland, or where the procurator fiscal proposes to apply for such an order. In relation to applications for restraint orders and incidental applications in respect of which an external forfeiture order has been made or in respect of which such an order could be made, see r. 62.54. An external forfeiture order is an order made in a country or territory designated under art. 3 of, and specified in Sched. 2 to the Prevention of Terrorism (Temporary Provisions) Act 1989 (Enforcement of External Orders) 1995 [S.I. 1995 No.760].   84.1.1

The Act of 2000, the relevant provisions of which came fully into force on 15th February 2001 by virtue of the Terrorism Act 2000 (commencement No.3) Order 2001 [S.I. 2001 No.421] replaces the provisions in the Prevention of Terrorism (temporary Provisions) Act 1989.

"RESTRAINT ORDER".

The Court of Session may prohibit any person specified in the order from dealing with any property in respect of which a forfeiture order has been made or could be made in proceedings for an offence under ss. 15 to 18 of the Act of 2000.   84.1.2

FORM OF APPLICATION.

An application to the court for a restrain order under para. 18(1) of Sched. 4 to the Act of 2000 will be by petition to the Outer House: r. 14.2(h). The petition must be in Form 14.4 in the official printed form: rr. 4.1 and 14.4. The petition must be signed by counsel or other person having a right of audience: r. 4.2; and see r. 1.3(1) (definition of "counsel" and "other person having a right of audience") and note 1.3.4.   84.1.3

The petitioner must lodge the petition with the required steps of process: r. 4.4. A fee is payable on lodging the petition: see note 14.5.10. On petitions generally, see Chap. 14.

Unlike the provisions of Pt. II of Chap76 (applications under the Prevention of Terrorism (Temporary Provisions) Act 1989, there has been no disapplication of rr. 14.5 to 14.9 in Chap. 84.

Power and duties of administrator

84.2—[3](1) Subject to any condition or exception specified by the court, an administrator appointed under paragraph 16(1)(b) of Schedule 4 to the Act of 2000—   84.2

(a) may take possession of the property in respect of which he has been appointed and of any document which—

    (i) is in the possession or control of the person in whom the property is vested; and

    (ii) relates to the property;

(b) may have access to, and copy, any document relating to the property and not in such possession or control as is mentioned in subparagraph (a);

(c) may bring, defend or continue any legal proceedings relating to the property;

(d) may borrow money in so far as it is necessary to do so to safeguard the property and may for the purposes of such borrowing create a security over any part of the property;

---

[1] Chap. 84 and r. 84.1 inserted by S.S.I. 2001 No. 494 (effective 22nd December 2001).
[2] Chap. 84 and r. 84.1 inserted by S.S.I. 2001 No. 494 (effective 22nd December 2001).
[3] R. 84.2 inserted by S.S.I. 2001 No. 494 (effective 22nd December 2001).

(e) may, if the administrator considers that to do so would be beneficial for the management and the realisation of the property, enter into any contract, or execute any deed, with respect to the property;

(f) may effect or maintain insurance policies with respect to the property;

(g) may, where the person in whom the property is vested has not completed title to any of the property, complete title to it: provided that completion of title in the name of the person in whom the property is vested shall not validate by accretion any unperfected right in favour of any person other than the administrator;

(h) may sell (but not to himself or an associate of his) the property and redeem any obligation secured on that property;

(i) may discharge any of his functions through agents or employees: provided that the administrator shall be personally liable to meet the fees and expenses of any such agents or employees out of such remuneration as is payable to the administrator by virtue of paragraph 17(2) of Schedule 4 to the Act of 2000;

(j) may take such professional advice as he considers necessary for the proper discharge of his functions;

(k) may at any time apply to the court for directions with respect to the exercise of his powers and duties;

(l) may exercise any power conferred on him by the court whether such power was conferred at the time of his appointment or on his subsequent application to the court; and

(m) may do anything incidental to the above powers and duties.

(2) Subject to the proviso to sub-paragraph (g) of paragraph (1)—

(a) a person dealing with an administrator in good faith and for value shall not require to determine whether the administrator is acting within the powers mentioned in that sub-paragraph; and

(b) the validity of any title shall not be challengeable by reason only of the administrator having acted outwith those powers.

(3) The exercise of a power mentioned in any of sub-paragraphs (c) to (h) of paragraph (1) shall be in the name of the person in whom the property is vested.

GENERAL NOTE.

84.2.1   A criminal court may make a forfeiture order under s. 23 of the Act of 2000 where a person is guilty of an offence under ss. 15 to 18 of that Act (financial assistance for terrorism). Where that court does so it may make an order appointing an administrator to take possession of property to which the forfeiture order applies: Act of 2000, Sched. 4, para 16(1)(b). Rule 84.2 is made under para. 17(1) of Sched. 4 which gives the Court of Session power to provide for the powers and duties of an administrator.

An administrator is subject to the supervision of the Accountant of Court: Act of 2000, Sched. 4, para. 17(3).

There is no provision, as there is in para. 1 (8) of Sched. 1 to the Act of 1995, for the finding of caution.

Applications for variation or recall of restraint order

84.3   **84.3**—[1](1)   An application under paragraph 19(2) (recall or variation of restraint order) of Schedule 4 to the Act of 2000 shall be made by note in the process containing the interlocutor making the restraint order to which the application relates.

(2)   Subject to rule 14.6(2) (application to shorten or extend the period of notice), the period of notice for lodging answers to a note under paragraph (1) of this rule by any person affected by a restraint order shall be 14 days.

---

[1] R. 84.3 inserted by S.S.I. 2001 No. 494 (effective 22nd December 2001).

"NOTE".

For applications by note, see r. 15.2.

84.3.1

"PERIOD OF NOTICE".

On period of notice generally, see r. 14.6.

84.3.2

CHAPTER 85 APPLICATIONS UNDER THE PROTECTION FROM ABUSE (SCOTLAND) ACT 2001

Chapter 85[1]

Applications under the Protection From Abuse (Scotland) Act 2001

Interpretation and application of this Chapter

85.1.—[2](1) In this Chapter—

85.1

"the Act of 2001" means the Protection from Abuse (Scotland) Act 2001;
"documents" includes documents in electronic form; and
"interdict" includes interim interdict.
"incoming protection measure" has the meaning given by rule 106.1 (mutual recognition of protection measures: interpretation);

(2) This Chapter does not apply to an application—

(a) under section 1(2) of the Act of 2001 to attach a power of arrest to an incoming protection measure; or

(b) under section 2(3) or 2(7) of the Act of 2001 relating to a power of arrest attached to an incoming protection measure.

GENERAL NOTE.

The Protection from Abuse (Scotland) Act 2001 extends the scope of the law on protection that began with the Matrimonial Homes (Family Protection) (Scotland) Act 1981. That Act applies only to married couples or a man and a woman cohabiting as man and wife; and is concerned with occupancy rights in the matrimonial home. The Act of 2001 follows a report in 2000 on a Proposal for a Protection from Abuse Bill (JH/00/R9 SP Paper 221). What the Act of 2001 does is simply allow for a power of arrest to be attached to interdicts.

85.1.1

The Act of 2001 allows any natural person, who is applying for or who has applied for an interdict for protection from abuse, to apply for a power of arrest to be attached to the interdict or interim interdict.

"ABUSE".

Abuse is defined in s. 7 of the Act of 2001 as including "violence, harassment, threatening conduct, and any other conduct giving rise, or likely to give rise, to physical or mental injury, fear, alarm or distress"; and "conduct" includes speech or presence in a specified place or area.

85.1.2

"DOCUMENTS".

The word "document" has been defined in R.C.S. 1994 by reference to the inclusive definition in s. 9 of the Civil Evidence (Scotland) Act 1988: see r. 1.3(1). The word includes documents in electronic form: Act of 2001, s. 7.

85.1.3

"INTERDICT".

References to interdict in this chapter include interim interdict. In the Act of 2001, interdict also includes interim interdict: Act of 2001, s. 7.

85.1.4

Interdict prohibits reasonably apprehended future breaches of duty by one person to another: *Inverurie Magistrates v. Sorrie*, 1956 S.C. 175.

On interdict, see further note 60.1.1(2). On interim interdict, see further note 60.3.2.

Attachment of power of arrest to interdict

85.2.—[3](1) An application under section 1(1) of the 2001 Act (application for attachment of power of arrest to interdict)—

85.2

(a) shall be made by a conclusion of the summons, the prayer of the petition, the defences, answers or counterclaim in which the interdict to which it relates is applied for, or, if made after the application for interdict, by motion in the process of the action in which the interdict was sought; and

---

[1] Chapter 85 and r. 85.1 inserted by S.S.I. 2002 No. 514 (effective 1st December 2002).

[2] Chapter 85 and r. 85.1 inserted by S.S.I. 2002 No. 514 (effective 1st December 2002) and amended by S.I. 2014 No. 371 (effective 11th January 2015).

[3] Rule 85.2 inserted by S.S.I. 2002 No. 514 (effective 1st December 2002).

(b)   shall be intimated to the person against whom the interdict is sought or obtained.

(2)[1] Where the court attaches a power of arrest under section 1(2) or (1A) of the Act of 2001 (order attaching power of arrest) the following documents shall be served along with the power of arrest in accordance with section 2(1) of the Act of 2001 (documents to be served along with power of arrest)—

(a)   a copy of the application for interdict;

(b)   a copy of the interlocutor granting interdict; and

(c)   where the application to attach a power of arrest was made after the interdict was granted, a copy of the certificate of service of the interdict.

(3) After the power of arrest has been served, the following documents shall be delivered by the person who obtained the power to the chief constable in accordance with section 3(1) of the Act of 2001 (notification to the police)—

(a)   a copy of the application for interdict;

(b)   a copy of the interlocutor granting interdict;

(c)   a copy of the certificate of service of the interdict; and

(d)   where the application to attach a power of arrest was made after the interdict was granted—

    (i)   a copy of the application for the power of arrest;

    (ii)   a copy of the interlocutor granting it; and

    (iii)   a copy of the certificate of service of the power of arrest and the documents that required to be served along with it in accordance with section 2(1) of the Act of 2001.

(e)[2]   where a determination has previously been made in respect of such interdict under section 3(1) of the Domestic Abuse (Scotland) Act 2011, a copy of the interlocutor making the determination.

GENERAL NOTE.

85.2.1   The power to attach a power of arrest is given in s. 1(1) of the Act of 2001. The power may be attached to an interdict from abuse granted in any proceedings.

"CONCLUSION OF THE SUMMONS".

85.2.2   On conclusions, see r. 13.2(2) and note 13.2.3.

"PRAYER OF THE PETITION".

85.2.3   See r. 14.4(2)(b) and note 14.4.8, and Chap. 60.

"DEFENCES"; "ANSWERS".

85.2.4   See Chap. 18. With the exception of defences in family actions (see r. 49.31(2)), defences and answers do not have conclusions in which an interdict can be applied for.

"COUNTERCLAIM".

85.2.5   See Chap. 25. The power of arrest will be a conclusion in the counterclaim.

"MOTION".

85.2.6   See Chap. 23.

"INTIMATED".

85.2.7   The reference to intimation in r. 85.2(1)(b) is otiose. The application for a power of arrest will be intimated by being included in the writ, minute of amendment or motion which itself requires service or intimation.

---

[1] Rule 85.2(2) amended by S.S.I. 2006 No. 206 (effective 4th May 2006).
[2] Rule 85.2(3)(e) inserted by S.S.I. 2011 No. 288 (effective 21st July 2011).

The power to attach a power of arrest is given in s. 1(1) of the Act of 2001. It must be applied for; and **85.2.8**
the person applying must be a natural person: Act of 2001, s. 7. The court cannot attach a power of arrest
to an interdict unless—

(a) the interdicted person has been given an opportunity to be heard (thus it cannot be granted on an
ex parte application for interim interdict);

(b) the interdicted person would not also be subject to a power of arrest under the Matrimonial
Homes (Family Protection) (Scotland) Act 1981; and

(c) the power is necessary to protect the applicant from *a* risk of abuse in breach of *that* interdict
(the provision does not specify a *substantial* risk).

In relation to (c) above, regard must be had to art. 5 of the ECHR (right to liberty) and art. 8 (right to
private life).

The power of arrest must be for a specified period not exceeding three years, though that may be
extended: Act of 2001, ss. 1(3) and 2(3).

Having the power of arrest attached to an interdict means that a constable may arrest the interdicted
person without warrant if the constable: (a) has reasonable grounds to suspect that person of being in
breach of the interdict; and (b) considers that there would be a risk of abuse or further abuse if not
arrested: Act of 2001, s. 4(1).

Section 4 of the Act of 2001 lays down what must happen on arrest and what the arrestee must be told.

SERVICE OF POWER OF ARREST.

A power of arrest has effect only when it has been served on the interdicted person along with such **85.2.9**
documents as may be prescribed: Act of 2001, s. 2(1). Rule 85.2(2) prescribes the additional documents
to be served as a copy of: (a) the application for the interdict; (b) the interlocutor granting it; and (c)
where the power of arrest was applied for after the interdict (in most cases in fact, following an interim
interdict), the certificate of service of the interdict.

For service, see Chap. 16. For certificate of service, see r. 161(3) and note 16.1.5.

NOTIFICATION TO POLICE.

Under s. 3(1) of the Act of 2001, the interdictor must notify the chief constable of the police area in **85.2.10**
which the interdict has effect (that may be more than one police area) by delivering the prescribed documents to him. Rule 85.2(3) prescribes these documents as a copy of: (a) the application for interdict; (b)
the interlocutor granting it; (c) the certificate of service; and (d) if separate, the power of arrest, the
interlocutor granting it and the certificate of its service.

The power of arrest has effect whether or not the chief constable is notified by receipt of these
documents: Act of 2001, s. 2(1). If the police are not aware of the power of arrest of course, they cannot
act; but they may be aware of it independently of the s. 3 notification.

Extension or recall of power of arrest

85.3.—[1](1)   An application under section 2(3) (extension of duration of power of **85.3**
arrest) or section 2(7) (recall of power of arrest) of the Act of 2001 shall be made by
minute in the process of the action in which the power of arrest was attached.

(2)   Where the court extends the duration of, or recalls, a power of arrest, the
person who obtained the extension or recall must deliver a copy of the interlocutor
granting the extension or recall in accordance with section 3(1) of the Act of 2001.

GENERAL NOTE.

A power of arrest ceases to have effect: (a) on the date it expires; (b) when recalled; or (c) when the **85.3.1**
interdict is varied or recalled: Act of 2001, s. 2(2).

The power may be extended if (i) the interdicted person has had an opportunity to be heard and (ii) the
extension is necessary to protect the interdicter from a risk of abuse in breach of that interdict: Act of
2001, s. 2(3). There may be more than one extension: Act of 2001, s. 2(6). An extension has effect only
when served on the interdicted person: Act of 2001, s. 2(5)(b).

The power of arrest must be recalled on application of the interdictor or interdicted person if it is no
longer necessary to protect the interdictor from abuse in breach of the interdict: Act of 2001, s. 2(7).

On extension of the power, the notification procedure under s. 3 of the Act of 2001 must be followed:
r. 85.3(2) which in turn brings in r. 85.2(3) (notification to police). With regard to notification to the
police on recall, see r. 85.4.

Rule 85.3 provides that the procedure for applications for extension or recall of the power of arrest is
by minute.

---

[1] R. 85.3 inserted by S.S.I. 2002 No. 514 (effective 1st December 2002).

"MINUTE".

85.3.2   The procedure for extension or recall of a power of arrest is by minute in the process of the cause in which it was obtained: r. 85.3(2).

For procedure by minute, see r. 15.1.

Documents to be delivered to chief constable in relation to recall or variation of interdict

85.4   **85.4.**[1]   Where an interdict to which a power of arrest has been attached under section 1(2) of the Act of 2001 is varied or recalled, the person who obtained the variation or recall must deliver a copy of the interlocutor varying or recalling the interdict in accordance with section 3(1) of that Act.

GENERAL NOTE.

85.4.1   Where a power of arrest is varied or recalled on an application under s. 2 of the Act of 2001, the interdictor must follow the notification procedure under s. 3(1), which in turn brings in the provisions of r. 85.2(3) specifying what documents must be notified to the chief constable.

Certificate of delivery of documents to chief constable

85.5   **85.5.**[2]   Where a person is required to comply with section 3(1) of the Act of 2001, he shall, after such compliance, lodge in process a certificate of delivery in Form 85.5.

"LODGE IN PROCESS A CERTIFICATE OF DELIVERY".

85.5.1   The certificate of delivery is lodged in process as a step of process (r. 1.3(1) (definition of "step of process")). On lodging a step of process, see rr. 4.4–4.6.

Form 85.5, the form of certificate, simply certifies that the documents to be delivered to the chief constable (see r. 85.2(3)) have been delivered.

---

[1] Rule 85.4 inserted by S.S.I. 2002 No. 514 (effective 1st December 2002).
[2] Rule 85.5 inserted by S.S.I. 2002 No. 514 (effective 1st December 2002) and amended by S.S.I. 2014 No. 371 (effective 11th January 2015).

CHAPTER 85A DOMESTIC ABUSE INTERDICTS

Chapter 85A[1]

Domestic Abuse Interdicts

Interpretation and application of this Chapter

85A.1.—[2](1) In this Chapter—

"the 2011 Act" means the Domestic Abuse (Scotland) Act 2011; and

"incoming protection measure" has the meaning given by rule 106.1 (mutual recognition of protection measures: interpretation);

"interdict" includes interim interdict.

(2) This Chapter applies to an application for a determination under section 3(1) of the 2011 Act that an interdict is a domestic abuse interdict.

(3) This Chapter does not apply to an application for a determination under section 3(1) of the 2011 Act that an incoming protection measure is a domestic abuse interdict.

Applications for determination that an interdict is a domestic abuse interdict

85A.2.—[3](1) An application made before the interdict is obtained must be made by a conclusion of the summons, the prayer of the petition, the defences, answers or counterclaim in which the interdict is sought.

(2) An application made after the interdict is obtained must be—

    (a) made by motion in process; and

    (b) intimated to the person against whom the interdict was obtained.

(3) In respect of a determination of an application under paragraph (2), the following documents must be served along with the interlocutor in accordance with section 3(4) of the 2011 Act—

    (a) a copy of the application for interdict;

    (b) a copy of the interlocutor granting interdict; and

    (c) a copy of the certificate of service of the interdict.

(4) Paragraph (5) applies where, in respect of the same interdict—

    (a) a power of arrest under section 1 of the Protection from Abuse (Scotland) Act 2001 is in effect; and

    (b) a determination under section 3(1) of the 2011 Act is made.

(5) As soon as possible after the determination has been served under section 3(4) of the 2011 Act, the documents specified in paragraph (6) must be sent by the person who obtained the determination to such chief constable as the court sees fit.

(6) The documents are—

    (a) a copy of the application for interdict;

    (b) a copy of the interlocutor granting interdict;

    (c) a copy of the certificate of service of the interdict; and

    (d) where the application for a determination was made after the interdict was granted—

        (i) a copy of the application for the determination;

        (ii) a copy of the interlocutor granting it; and

        (iii) a copy of the certificate of service of the determination.

---

[1] Chap. 85A and r. 85A.1 inserted by S.S.I. 2011 No. 288 (effective 21st July 2011).

[2] Chap. 85A and r. 85A.1 inserted by S.S.I. 2011 No. 288 (effective 21st July 2011) and amended by S.S.I. 2014 No. 371 (effective 11th January 2015).

[3] Rule 85A.2 inserted by S.S.I. 2011 No. 288 (effective 21st July 2011).

(7) Where paragraph (5) applies and the determination is recalled under section 3(5) of the 2011 Act, the court must appoint a person to send a copy of the interlocutor recalling the determination to such chief constable as the court sees fit.

(8) Where a person is required by virtue of this Chapter to send documents to a chief constable, such person must, after such compliance, lodge in process a certificate of sending documents in Form 85A.2.

GENERAL NOTE.

85A.2.1   Section 3 of the Domestic Abuse (Scotland) Act 2011 provides that a person who applies for or has obtained an interdict or interim interdict may apply to the court for a determination that the interdict is a domestic abuse interdict. The court must be satisfied that the interdict is for the protection of the applicant against a person who is or was the applicant's spouse, civil partner or living with the applicant as if husband and wife or civil partners, or in an intimate personal relationship with the applicant. The phrase "domestic abuse" is not defined but if the interdict is for the applicant's protection and the person interdicted falls into one of the above categories, it will be a domestic abuse interdict.

Before making the determination the applicant must give the person against whom the determination is sought an opportunity to make representations to the court.

It is an offence to breach a domestic abuse interdict where a power of arrest is attached under s.1(1A) or 2 of the Protection from Abuse (Scotland) Act 2001.

"MOTION".

85A.2.2   See Chap.23.

"INTIMATED".

85A.2.3   For methods, see r.16.7.

CHAPTER 86 APPLICATIONS UNDER SECTION 28, 28A, 62, 62A, 63, 65G OR 65H OF THE COMPETITION ACT 1998

Chapter 86[1]

Applications under Section 28, 28A, 62, 62A, 63, 65G or 65H of the Competition Act 1998

Application and interpretation of this Chapter

86.1.—[2](1) This Chapter applies to applications for warrants under section 28, 28A, 62, 62A, 63, 65G or 65H of the Competition Act 1998.

(2) In this Chapter, "the Act of 1998" means the Competition Act 1998.

(3) Words and expressions used in this Chapter and in the Act of 1998 shall have the meanings given in the Act of 1998.

GENERAL NOTE.

Under the sections of the Competition Act 1998 mentioned in r. 86.1, the Office of Fair Trading may seek a warrant to enter premises to look for documents in relation to investigations.

Sections 28A, 62A, 65G and 65H were inserted in the 1998 Act by the Competition Act 1998 and Other Enactments (Amendment) Regulations 2004 [S.I. 2004 No. 1261].

Disapplication of certain rules to this Chapter

86.2.[3] The following rules shall not apply to a petition to which this Chapter applies—

rule 4.3 (lodging of processes),

rule 4.4 (steps of process),

rule 4.5(1)(b) (copy inventory of productions to be sent to other parties),

rule 4.6 (intimation of steps of process),

rule 4.11 (documents not to be borrowed),

rule 4.12 (borrowing and returning documents),

rule 14.4 (form of petitions),

rule 14.5 (first order in petitions),

rule 14.6 (period of notice for lodging answers),

rule 14.7 (intimation and service of petitions),

rule 14.8 (procedure where answers lodged),

rule 14.9 (unopposed petitions).

Applications for warrants

86.3.—[4](1) An application for a warrant under section 28, 28A, 62, 62A, 63, 65G or 65H of the Act of 1998 shall be made by petition in Form 86.3.

(2) The petition shall state—

(a) the address or other identification of the premises which are intended to be the subject of the warrant;

(b) the name of the occupier of those premises;

(c) the section of the Act of 1998 under which the application is being made;

(d) the subject matter of the investigation to which the application relates;

(e) a statement of the grounds for the application; and

(f) a prayer indicating the warrant sought.

(3) There shall be lodged with the petition—

(a) a draft warrant;

(b) a signed witness statement in support of the application;

86.1

86.1.1

86.2

86.3

---

[1] Chap. 86 and r. 86.1 inserted by S.S.I. 2004 No. 331 (effective 6th August 2004).
[2] Chap. 86 and r. 86.1 inserted by S.S.I. 2004 No. 331 (effective 6th August 2004).
[3] Rule 86.2 inserted by S.S.I. 2004 No. 331 (effective 6th August 2004).
[4] Rule 86.3 inserted by S.S.I. 2004 No. 331 (effective 6th August 2004).

(c)   the written authorisation of the OFT containing the name of the officer who it is intended will be the named officer;

(d)   in the case of an application under section 62, 62A or 63 of the Act of 1998, the written authorisations of the European Commission containing the names of any of its officials and other persons authorised by it for any of the purposes set out in section 62(10), 62A(12) or 63(10) of the Act of 1998 as applicable who it is intended will accompany the named officer in executing the warrant; and

(e)   the written authorisation of the OFT containing the names of any other person who it is intended will accompany the named officer in executing the warrant.

(4) On lodging the petition, the petitioner shall provide the Deputy Principal Clerk with the draft warrant in electronic form compatible with the software used by the court.

(5) The petition and any documents lodged, sent or retained under these Rules in connection with the petition shall be treated as confidential and open only to the court unless the Lord Ordinary otherwise directs.

"PETITION".

86.3.1

A petition under this Chapter is presented to the Outer House: r. 14.2(h). The petition must be in Form 86.3 in the official printed form (r. 4.1). The petition must be signed by counsel or other person having a right of audience: r. 4.2; and see r. 1.3(1) (definition of "counsel" and "other person having a right of audience") and note 1.3.4.

The petitioner must lodge the petition with the required steps of process (r. 4.4). A fee is payable on lodging the petition: see note 14.5.10.

On petitions generally, see Chap. 14.

Hearing of petition

86.4

86.4.—[1](1) On the lodging of the petition, the Keeper of the Rolls shall appoint the petition to a hearing to determine the petition.

(2) The petition shall be heard and determined in private unless the Lord Ordinary otherwise directs.

Form of warrants

86.5

86.5.—[2](1) A warrant issued under section 28, 28A, 62, 62A, 63, 65G or 65H of the Act of 1998 shall indicate—

(a)   the address or other identification of the premises subject to the warrant;

(b)   the names of the named officer and any other persons authorised by the warrant to accompany the named officer in executing the warrant;

(c)   the date on which the warrant was issued; and

(d)   that the warrant continues in force until the end of the period of one month beginning with the day on which it is issued.

(2) Subject to paragraph (3), a warrant issued under section 28, 28A, 62, 62A, 63, 65G or 65H of the Act of 1998 may be borrowed by the petitioner.

(3) The petitioner shall give a receipt for any warrant borrowed under paragraph (2) and shall return the warrant to the Deputy Principal Clerk by the end of the period of one month referred to in paragraph (1)(d).

(4) Where a warrant is borrowed under paragraph (2), a certified copy of a warrant issued under section 28, 28A, 62, 62A, 63, 65G or 65H of the Act of 1998 shall be retained by the Deputy Principal Clerk.

---

[1] Rule 86.4 inserted by S.S.I. 2004 No. 331 (effective 6th August 2004).
[2] Rule 86.5 inserted by S.S.I. 2004 No. 331 (effective 6th August 2004).

Service of copy petition and interlocutor

86.6.[1] Within 7 days after the date of first execution of a warrant which has been issued by the court under section 28, 28A, 62, 62A, 63, 65G or 65H of the Act of 1998, the petitioner shall serve on the occupier of the premises which are the subject of the warrant and such other persons as may be specified by the court in the interlocutor granting the prayer of the petition—

    (a)   a copy of the petition; and

    (b)   a certified copy of the interlocutor granting the prayer of the petition.

"WITHIN 7 DAYS AFTER".

The date from which the period is calculated is not counted.

"SERVE".

For methods, see Chap. 16, Pt. I.

"CERTIFIED COPY OF THE INTERLOCUTOR".

A certified copy interlocutor (a CCI) is obtained by a party presenting a copy of the interlocutor to a clerk of session at the relevant department. The clerk certifies and stamps it with the court stamp.

---

[1] Rule 86.6 inserted by S.S.I. 2004 No. 331 (effective 6th August 2004).

Interpretation of this Chapter

86A.1.[1]   In this Chapter—

"the 1998 Act" means the Competition Act 1998(c);

"competition authority" has the meaning given by paragraph 3(1) of schedule 8A of the 1998 Act;

"competition proceedings" has the meaning given by paragraph 2(4) of schedule 8A of the 1998 Act;

"the Directive" means Directive 2014/104/EU of the European Parliament and of the Council of 26 November 2014 on certain rules governing actions for damages under national law for infringements of the competition law provisions of the Member States and of the European Union as amended from time to time; and

"investigation materials" has the meaning given by paragraph 3(3) of schedule 8A of the 1998 Act.

Recovery of evidence

86A.2.—[2](1)   This rule applies where a party in competition proceedings makes an application under rule 35.2(1) for—

(a)   a commission and diligence for the recovery of a document; or

(b)   an order under section 1 of the Administration of Justice (Scotland) Act 1972.

(2)   The applicant must intimate a copy of the motion made under rule 35.2(1) and the specification lodged under rule 35.2(2) to the Advocate General for Scotland.

(3)   An application in relation to a document or other evidence that is in the possession of a competition authority must contain a statement that there is no person, other than the competition authority, reasonably able to provide the document or evidence sought.

(4)   An application in relation to the investigation materials of a competition authority must contain a statement that the investigation to which those materials relate has closed.

(5)   In deciding whether to grant an application made under this rule, the court must take into account Article 5(3), and, where the document or other evidence sought is in the possession of a competition authority, Article 6(4), of the Directive.

GENERAL NOTE

Under art. 5(3) of the Directive, Member States must ensure that national courts limit the disclosure of evidence to that which is proportionate. In determining whether any disclosure requested by a party is proportionate, national courts shall consider the legitimate interests of all parties and third parties concerned. They shall, in particular, consider: (a) the extent to which the claim or defence is supported by available facts and evidence justifying the request to disclose evidence; (b) the scope and cost of disclosure, especially for any third parties concerned, including preventing non-specific searches for information which is unlikely to be of relevance for the parties in the procedure; (c) whether the evidence the disclosure of which is sought contains confidential information, especially concerning any third parties, and what arrangements are in place for protecting such confidential information.

Article 6(4) of the Directive provides that, when assessing, in accordance with art. 5(3), the proportionality of an order to disclose information, national courts shall, in addition, consider the following: (a) whether the request has been formulated specifically with regard to the nature, subject matter or contents of documents submitted to a competition authority or held in the file thereof, rather than by a non-specific application concerning documents submitted to a competition authority; (b) whether

---

[1] Chapter 86A and R.86A.1 as inserted by S.S.I. 2017 No. 130 para.2 (effective 26 May 2017).
[2] Rule 86A.2 as inserted by S.S.I. 2017 No. 130 para.2 (effective 26 May 2017).

the party requesting disclosure is doing so in relation to an action for damages before a national court; and (c) in relation to paragraphs 5 and 10, or upon request of a competition authority pursuant to paragraph 11, the need to safeguard the effectiveness of the public enforcement of competition law.

"INTIMATE".

For intimation, see r. 16.7

Applications in relation to alleged cartel leniency statement or settlement submission

86A.3　**86A.3.**—[1](1)　An application by a party under—

    (a)　paragraph 4(7) of schedule 8A of the 1998 Act for a determination by the court as to whether information is a cartel leniency statement; or

    (b)　paragraph 5(3) of schedule 8A of the 1998 Act for a determination by the court as to whether a document is a settlement submission,

must be made by motion.

    (2)　A party enrolling a motion under paragraph (1) must intimate that motion to—

    (a)　the Advocate General for Scotland; and

    (b)　the author (where known) of the document or information in question.

    (3)　The hearing of a motion enrolled under paragraph (1) must be held in private and only the persons mentioned in paragraph (2)(a) and (b) may appear at that hearing.

"MOTION".

86A.3.1　For motions, see Chap. 23

"INTIMATE".

86A.3.2　For intimation, see r. 16.7.

---

[1] Rule 86A.3 as inserted by S.S.I. 2017 No. 130 para.2 (effective 26 May 2017).

CHAPTER 87 CAUSES RELATING TO ARTICLES 101 AND 102 OF THE TREATY ON THE FUNCTIONING OF EUROPEAN UNION

Intimation of actions to the Office of Fair Trading

87.1.—[1,2](1) In this rule—

 "the Treaty" means the Treaty on the Functioning of the European Union, as referred to in section 1(2)(s) of the European Communities Act 1972;

 "the OFT" means the Office of Fair Trading.

(2) In an action where an issue under Article 101 or 102 of the Treaty is raised:—

 (a) by the pursuer or petitioner in the summons or petition;

 (b) by the defender or respondent in the defences or answers; or

 (c) by any party in the pleadings;

intimation of the action shall be given to the OFT by the party raising the issue, by a notice of intimation in Form 87.1.

(3) Where the issue under Article 101 or 102 of the Treaty is raised in the summons or petition, a warrant for intimation shall be inserted in the summons or petition in the following terms: "Warrant to intimate to the Office of Fair Trading".

(4) Where the issue under Article 101 or 102 of the Treaty is raised in defences, answers or in any other part of the pleadings, the party raising the issue shall apply by motion for an order for intimation to the OFT.

(5) A certified copy of an interlocutor granting a motion under paragraph (4) shall be sufficient authority for the party to intimate by notice in Form 87.1.

(6) The notice of intimation shall be served on the OFT within such period as the court shall specify in the interlocutor allowing intimation.

(7) There shall be attached to the notice of intimation—

 (a) a copy of the pleadings (including any adjustments and amendments);

 (b) a copy of the interlocutor allowing intimation of the notice; and

 (c) where the pleadings have not been amended in accordance with a minute of amendment, a copy of that minute.

GENERAL NOTE.

Chap. 87 was inserted by A.S. (R.C.S.A. No. 6 (Miscellaneous) 2004 [S.S.I. 2004 No.514].

                        87.1.1

"ARTICLE 81 OR 82".

Art. 81 relates to the prohibition of agreements affecting trade between Member States which prevent, restrict or distort competition.   **87.1.2**

Art. 82 relates to abuse of a dominant position with the common market.

OFFICE OF FAIR TRADING (OFT).

Intimation is required to the OFT because the Director General of Fair Trading has responsibilities in relation to competition laws.   **87.1.3**

"INTIMATION".

The method of intimation will be that provided for in r. 16.8.   **87.1.4**

"MOTION".

For motions, see Chap. 23.   **87.1.5**

---

[1] Chap. 87 and r. 87.1 inserted by S.S.I. 2004 No. 514 (effective 30th November 2004).

[2] Chap. 87 and r. 87.1 amended by S.S.I. 2012 No. 275 r. 7 (effective 19th November 2012).

Intimation of actions to the Office of Fair Trading

87.1.—(1) In this rule—

the "Treaty" means the Treaty on the Functioning of the European Union, as referred to in section 1(2)(s) of the European Communities Act 1972;

the OFT means the Office of Fair Trading.

(2) In an action where an issue under Article 101 or 102 of the Treaty is raised—

(a) by the pursuer or petitioner in the summons or petition;

(b) by the defender or respondent in the defences or answers; or

(c) by any party in the pleadings,

intimation of the action shall be given to the OFT by the party raising the issue by a notice of intimation in Form 87.1.

(3) Where the issue under Article 101 or 102 of the Treaty is raised in the summons or petition, a warrant for intimation shall be inserted in the summons or petition in the following terms: "Warrant to intimate to the Office of Fair Trading".

(4) Where the issue under Article 101 or 102 of the Treaty is raised in defences, answers or in any other part of the pleadings, the party raising the issue shall apply by motion for an order for intimation to the OFT.

(5) A certified copy of an interlocutor granting a motion under paragraph (4) shall be sufficient authority for the party to intimate by notice in Form 87.1.

(6) The notice of intimation shall be served on the OFT within such period as the court shall specify in the interlocutor allowing the intimation.

(7) There shall be attached to the notice of intimation—

(a) a copy of the pleadings (including any adjustments and amendments);

(b) a copy of the interlocutor allowing intimation of the notice; and

(c) where the pleadings have not been amended in accordance with a minute of amendment, a copy of that minute.

Deriviations

87.1.1 Chap.87 introduced by A.S. (R.C.S.A.) (No. 6 and con.etc.) 2004 [S.I. 2004 No. 514] ...

Paragraph (1) at r.2.

87.1.2 Art. 81 relates to the prohibition of agreements affecting trade between Member States which prevent, restrict or distort competition.

Art. 82 relates to abuse of a dominant position within the common market.

Office of Fair Trading (OFT)

87.1.3 Intimation is required to the OFT because the Director General of Fair Trading has responsibilities in relation to competition law.

Intimation.

87.1.4 The method of intimation will be that provided for in r.16.8

Form.

87.1.5 Intimation is in Form 87.1.

Chap. 91 and 87.1 inserted by S.S.I. 2004 No. 514 (effective 8th November 2004).
Chap. 87 and r.87.1 amended by S.I. 2012 No. 2759 ... (effective 19th November 2012).

CHAPTER 88 CIVIL MATTERS INVOLVING PARENTAL RESPONSIBILITIES UNDER THE COUNCIL REGULATION

Interpretation

88.1.[1,2] In this Chapter—

"the Council Regulation" means Council Regulation (E.C.) No. 2201/2003 of 27th November 2003 concerning jurisdiction and the recognition and enforcement of judgments in matrimonial matters and matters of parental responsibility;

"foreign court" means a court in a Member State other than the United Kingdom[3]

"parental responsibility" has the same meaning as in Article 2(7) of the Council Regulation;

"Member State" has the same meaning as in Article 2(3) of the Council Regulation.

GENERAL NOTE.

The Council Regulation No. 2201/2003 (new Brussels II) replaces Council Regulation No 1347/2000 (for which there was no special provision in the RCS 1994). It deals with jurisdiction as well as recognition and enforcement of judgments in matrimonial matters and matters of parental responsibility.

Matrimonial matters and matters of parental responsibility with which the new Council Regulation is concerned are defined in art. 1 as (a) divorce, legal separation, annulment; and (b) attribution, exercise, delegation, restriction or termination of parental responsibility (which includes custody, access, guardianship, curatorship and similar institutions, designation and functions of a person or body over a child's person or property or representing or assisting a child, placement in a foster family or institution, and protection of a child's property).

The term "child" is not defined in the Regulation.

The Regulation applies to Member States of the E.U. except Denmark.

The primary ground of jurisdiction is habitual residence. Art. 15 of the Council Regulation provides that a court having jurisdiction in a case of parental responsibilities may, if it considers that a court of another Member State with which a child has a particular connection would be better placed to hear the case, request a court of that other Member State to assume jurisdiction.

Transfer of cases involving matters of parental responsibility

88.2.[4] Where the court receives a request under Article 15(1) (request for transfer to court better placed to hear the case) or an application under Article 15(2)(c) (application for transfer of case involving parental responsibilities to foreign court) of the Council Regulation, the request or application, as the case may be, shall—

(a) contain a detailed statement on the particular connection the child is considered to have with either Scotland or the Member State of the foreign court;

(b) contain the full name, designation and address of all the parties to the action involving parental responsibilities, including any Scottish agent instructed to represent any of the parties;

(c) in the case of a request under Article 15(1), be accompanied by any order of the foreign court confirming that at least one of the parties has accepted the request;

(d) be accompanied by any other documents considered by the foreign court to be relevant to the action involving parental responsibilities including any papers forming part of the process in the foreign court.

---

[1] Chap. 88 and r. 88.1 inserted by S.S.I. 2005 No. 135 (effective 2nd March 2005).
[2] Rule 88.1 amended (definition of "requesting court" omitted) by S.S.I. 2006 No. 83 (effective 17th March 2006).
[3] Rule 88.1 definition inserted by S.S.I. 2006 No. 83 (effective 17th March 2006).
[4] Rule 88.2 inserted by S.S.I. 2005 No. 135 (effective 2nd March 2005) and substituted by by S.S.I. 2006 No. 83 (effective 17th March 2006).

General note.

88.2.1   Art. 15(1) of the Council Regulation provides that a court having jurisdiction in a case of parental responsibilities may, if it considers that a court of another Member State with which a child has a particular connection would be better placed to hear the case, request a court of that other Member State to assume jurisdiction.

The request is made directly by one court to another under art. 15(1)(b). A request by a court in another Member State to the Court of Session will be dealt with by the Deputy Principal Clerk under Chap. 88. A time limit may be set by the requesting court. It should be noted that a court in another Member State may invite parties to make a request to the other court to assume jurisdiction: such a case is not dealt with under Chap. 88. One assumes that a petition or action, as appropriate, will be initiated in respect of the particular parental responsibility.

Under art. 15(2)(a) or (c) a party or a court in one Member State with which a child has a particular connection may apply to the court in another Member State exercising jurisdiction. This is in effect an application to request the latter court to decline jurisdiction.

Transfers where proceedings ongoing in the sheriff court

88.3   **88.3.**—[1, 2](1)   Where an application under Article 15(2)(c) of the Council Regulation (application for transfer of case involving parental responsibilities to foreign court) is received and states that proceedings involving the same parties and matters involving parental responsibility are ongoing in a sheriff court, the Deputy Principal Clerk shall, within four days after the application is received, transmit the application to the sheriff clerk of the sheriff court specified in the application.

(2)   When transmitting an application under paragraph (1) the Deputy Principal Clerk shall give written intimation of the transmission to—

(a)   the parties; and

(b)   to the foreign court.

(3)   Failure by the Deputy Principal Clerk to comply with paragraph (2) shall not affect the validity of a transfer under paragraph (1).

General note.

88.3.1   The application to decline jurisdiction arises out of art. 15(2)(a) or (c) of the Council Regulation. Under art. 15(2)(a) or (c) a party or a court in one Member State with which a child has a particular connection may apply to the court in another Member State exercising jurisdiction.

"written intimation".

88.3.2   For methods, see r. 16.9.

Translations of documents

88.4   **88.4.**[3]   Where any document received under rule 88.2 (transfer of cases involving matters of parental responsibility) is in a language other than English, there shall be lodged with that document a translation into English certified as correct by the translator; and the certificate shall include his full name, address and qualifications.

Requests to accept transfer from a court in another Member State

88.5   **88.5.**—[4](1)   A request to the court to accept jurisdiction of an action involving parental responsibilities under rule 88.2 (request to transfer a case) shall be lodged with a summons in Form 13.2-A(a).

(2)   When the summons lodged under paragraph (1) is signetted the pursuer shall request the Keeper of the Rolls to allocate a hearing within 14 days of the signetting, to determine whether the court will accept jurisdiction in the action.

(3)   On allocation of the date of the hearing the pursuer shall serve a copy of the summons on the defender and at the same time intimate the date and time of the

---

[1] Rule 88.3 inserted by S.S.I. 2005 No. 135 (effective 2nd March 2005).
[2] Rule 88.3 amended by S.S.I. 2006 No. 83 (effective 17th March 2006).
[3] Rule 88.4 inserted by S.S.I. 2005 No. 135 (effective 2nd March 2005).
[4] Rule 88.5 inserted by S.S.I. 2005 No. 135 (effective 2nd March 2005).

hearing on the defender by serving on him a notice in Form 88.5 (form of notice of intimation of a hearing to determine jurisdiction), not less than 7 days before the date of the hearing.

(4)   The pursuer shall lodge a certificate of intimation in Form 16.2 (certificate of intimation furth of United Kingdom), 16.3 (certificate of service by messenger-at-arms) or 16.4 (certificate of service by post), as appropriate, at least 2 days before the date of the hearing.

(5)[1]   Where the court orders that it will accept jurisdiction of an action after a hearing under paragraph (2) the Deputy Principal Clerk shall, within seven days, send a copy of the interlocutor to the foreign court.

General note.

This rule is badly drafted. It cannot be intended to apply where it is the foreign court making the request to the Court of Session to accept jurisdiction. A foreign court can hardly be expected to lodge a summons in the Court of Session as well as making a request under r. 88.2. It can only be intended to apply where the foreign court has invited the parties to request the Court of Session to accept jurisdiction under art. 15(1)(a) of the Council Regulation. Rule 88.5, however, refers to a request under r. 88.2; but the only request under that rule is a request by a court of another Member State under art. 15(1)(b) and not a party under art. 15(1)(a).

88.5.1

"summons".

See Chap. 13.

88.5.2

"serve".

On service, see Chap. 16, Pt. I.

88.5.3

"intimate".

For methods, see r. 16.7.

88.5.4

Application for transfer of case involving parental responsibilities to foreign court[2]

88.6.[3, 4]   Where an application under Article 15(2)(c) of the Council Regulation (application for transfer of case involving parental responsibilities to foreign court) is received the Deputy Principal Clerk shall—

88.6

    (a)   on receipt of the application and any accompanying documents, give written intimation of the application to each party to the action and to any Scottish agents identified in the application as being instructed to represent any of the parties; and

    (b)[5]   within two sitting days of receipt of the application, cause it to be put out on the By Order Roll before the Lord Ordinary.

General note.

The application to decline jurisdiction arises out of art. 15(2)(a) or (c) of the Council Regulation. Under art. 15(2)(a) or (c) a party or a court in one Member State with which a child has a particular connection may apply to the court in another Member State exercising jurisdiction.

88.6.1

Placement of child in another Member State

88.7.—[6](1)   Where the court requires to obtain the consent of a competent authority in another Member State to the placement of a child under Article 56 of the Council Regulation it shall send a request in Form 88.7 and any other documents it

88.7

---

[1] Rule 88.5(5) amended by S.S.I. 2006 No. 83 (effective 17th March 2006).
[2] Rule 88.6 and heading amended by S.S.I. 2006 No. 83 (effective 17th March 2006).
[3] Rule 88.6 inserted by S.S.I. 2005 No. 135 (effective 2nd March 2005).
[4] Rule 88.6 and heading amended by S.S.I. 2006 No. 83 (effective 17th March 2006).
[5] R. 88.6(b) amended by S.S.I. 2017 No. 414 r. 3(2) (effective 1st January 2018).
[6] Rule 88.7 inserted by S.S.I. 2006 No. 83 (effective 17th March 2006).

considers to be relevant to the Scottish central authority for transmission to the central authority in the other Member State.

(2) In this rule "central authority" means an authority designated under Article 53 of the Council Regulation.

CHAPTER 89 TERRORISM PREVENTION AND INVESTIGATION MEASURES

Chapter 89[1]

Terrorism Prevention and Investigation Measures

Interpretation and application of this Chapter

89.1.—[2](1) In this Chapter—

"the Act of 2011" means the Terrorism Prevention and Investigation Measures Act 2011;

"Advocate General" means the Advocate General for Scotland;

"affected person" means an individual on whom the Secretary of State has imposed, or is proposing to impose, measures by means of a TPIM notice;

"appeal proceedings" means proceedings in the Inner House on an appeal relating to TPIM proceedings;

"legal representative" is to be construed in accordance with paragraph 4(4)(b) of Schedule 4 to the Act of 2011;

"measures" means terrorism prevention and investigation measures (which has the same meaning as in section 2 of the Act of 2011);

"relevant party" means any party to the TPIM proceedings or appeal proceedings other than the Secretary of State;

"special advocate" means a person appointed under paragraph 10(1) of Schedule 4 to the Act of 2011;

"TPIM notice" has the same meaning as in section 2(1) of the Act of 2011; and

"TPIM proceedings" has the same meaning as in section 30(1) of the Act of 2011.

(2) This Chapter applies to TPIM proceedings and appeal proceedings.

GENERAL NOTE.

The Terrorism Prevention and Investigation Measures Act 2011 replaces the Prevention of Terrorism Act 2005, and control orders are abolished. In their place under the 2011 Act the Secretary of State may by notice (a TPIM notice) impose specified terrorism prevention and investigation measures on an individual where certain conditions are met in s. 3 if the individual is or has been involved in terrorism-related activity (defined in s. 4). A notice lasts for one year and may be extended for another year (s. 5).

The Secretary of State has to apply to the court for permission to impose measures (s. 6). The court must give directions at that hearing for a further hearing (a directions hearing) for the individual to be heard and at that hearing give directions for a review hearing (s. 8). There is special provision for urgent cases (s. 7 and Sch. 2) whereby the Secretary of State must refer the imposition of measures to the court to determine whether his decisions were flawed.

TPIM orders and imposed measures: petitions

89.2.—[3](1) The following shall be made by lodging a petition with the Deputy Principal Clerk—

(a)   an application made under section 6(1)(b) of the Act of 2011 for permission to impose measures on an individual;

(b)   a reference under paragraph 3(1) of Schedule 2 to the Act of 2011.

(2) The following rules shall not apply to the petition:—

---

[1] Chap. 89 and r. 89.1 inserted by S.S.I. 2005 No. 153 (effective 16th March 2005) and substituted by S.S.I. 2011 No. 441 para. 2(2) (effective 21st December 2011: substitution has effect subject to S.S.I. 2011 No. 441 para. 2(3)).

[2] Chap. 89 and r. 89.1 inserted by S.S.I. 2005 No. 153 (effective 16th March 2005) and substituted by S.S.I. 2011 No. 441 para. 2(2) (effective 21st December 2011: substitution has effect subject to S.S.I. 2011 No. 441 para. 2(3)).

[3] Rule 89.2 inserted by S.S.I. 2005 No. 153 (effective 16th March 2005) and substituted by S.S.I. 2011 No. 441 para. 2(2) (effective 21st December 2011: substitution has effect subject to S.S.I. 2011 No. 441 para. 2(3)).

rule 4.3 (lodging of processes),

rule 4.4 (steps of process),

rule 4.5(1)(b) (copy inventory of productions to be sent to other parties),

rule 4.6 (intimation of steps of process),

rule 4.11 (documents not to be borrowed),

rule 4.12 (borrowing and returning documents),

rule 14.5 (first order in petitions),

rule 14.6 (period of notice for lodging answers),

rule 14.7 (intimation and service of petitions),

rule 14.8 (procedure where answers lodged),

rule 14.9 (unopposed petitions).

(3) Subject to rule 89.7 (permission not to disclose relevant material etc.), a petition referred to in paragraph (1)(a) shall include, in numbered paragraphs, statements of reasons—

    (a)   to support the application; and

    (b)   for imposing each of the measures under the proposed TPIM notice.

(4) Subject to rule 89.7, a petition referred to in paragraph (1)(b) shall include, in numbered paragraphs, statements of reasons—

    (a)   to support the making of the TPIM notice; and

    (b)   for imposing each of the measures contained in that notice.

(5) Subject to rule 89.7, the following documents shall be lodged with the petition—

    (a)   the productions of the Secretary of State;

    (b)   in the case of an application under section 6(1)(b) of the Act of 2011 for permission to impose measures on an individual, a draft of the proposed TPIM notice; and

    (c)   in the case of a reference under paragraph 3(1) of Schedule 2 to the Act of 2011, a copy of the TPIM notice.

"APPLICATION MADE UNDER SECTION 6(1)(B) OF THE ACT OF 2011".

89.2.1   The Secretary of State has to have the permission of the court to impose a TPIM notice unless the order contains a statement that the urgency of the case required the order to be made without permission: Act of 2011, s. 6.

On the meaning of a non-derogating control order, see note 89.1.1.

"A REFERENCE UNDER PARAGRAPH 3(1) OF SCHEDULE 2 TO THE ACT OF 2011".

89.2.2   Where the Secretary of State imposes a TPIM notice as a matter of urgency without the permission of the court, he must immediately refer the order to the court to consider if the order was obviously flawed: Act of 2011, s. 7 and Sch. 2. The court must consider the reference within seven days of the making of the order: Act of 2005, Sch. 2, para. 3(3).

On the meaning of a TPIM notice, see note 89.1.1.

"PETITION".

89.2.3   A petition is presented to the Outer House: r. 14.2(h). The petition must be in Form 86.3 in the official printed form (r. 4.1). The petition must be signed by counsel or other person having a right of audience: r. 4.2; and see r. 1.3(1) (definition of "counsel" and "other person having a right of audience") and note 1.3.4.

The petitioner must lodge the petition with the required steps of process (r. 4.4). A fee is payable on lodging the petition: see note 14.5.10.

On petitions generally, see Chap. 14.

PRODUCTIONS.

89.2.4   On productions and the lodging of them, see r. 4.5 and note 4.5.2.

"SERVED".

89.2.5   On service, see Chap. 16, Pt. I.

Initial diets

89.3.—[1](1)   On receipt of a petition under rule 89.2 (TPIM notices and imposed measures: petitions), the Deputy Principal Clerk shall allocate an initial diet for the court's consideration to begin.

89.3

(2)   The Deputy Principal Clerk shall notify the date and time of an initial diet to the Secretary of State and, unless the Lord Ordinary orders otherwise, the affected person, any legal representative of the affected person and any special advocate.

(3)   The affected person shall, not later than the date of the initial diet, lodge with the Deputy Principal Clerk and serve on the Secretary of State a copy of any answers and productions that are to be founded upon by the affected person at the initial diet.

(4)   Where a special advocate is appointed for the purposes of the initial diet, he or she shall lodge with the Deputy Principal Clerk and serve on the Secretary of State a copy of any answers that are to be founded upon by the special advocate at the initial diet.

(5)   At the initial diet, the parties present shall state their proposals for further procedure in respect of any directions hearing under section 8 of the Act of 2011 and any subsequent review hearing under section 9 of the Act of 2011.

(6)   An interlocutor of the Lord Ordinary giving directions for a directions hearing under section 8 of the Act of 2011 shall include such order for further procedure as he or she thinks fit, subject to the requirements set out in section 8 of the Act of 2011.

(7)   An interlocutor of the Lord Ordinary giving directions for a review hearing under section 9 of the Act of 2011 shall include such order for further procedure as he or she thinks fit, subject to the requirements set out in section 9 of the Act of 2011.

(8)   Where an initial diet has been held in the absence of the affected person the Deputy Principal Clerk shall serve a copy of the interlocutor of the Lord Ordinary on that person.

GENERAL NOTE.

On application to the court by the Secretary of State, for permission to impose a TPIM notice or on a reference under Sch. 2 derogating control order, there must first be an initial hearing. The initial hearing may be held in the absence of the individual in question, without his having had notice of the application and without his having had the opportunity to make any representations to the court: Act of 2011, s. 6 or Sch. 2, para. 3. If the court gives permission for a TPIM notice under s. 6 or confirms one under Sch. 2 at that stage, it must give directions for the holding of a full hearing to determine whether to confirm the order: Act of 2005, s. 4(1)(b).

89.3.1

"INITIAL DIET".

Rule 89.3 overlooks the fact that at this hearing the court may give permission for a TPIM notice under s.6 or may confirm an urgent TPIM notice under Sch.2 and may do so without the individual concerned being present, receiving notice of the application or being able to make representations: Act of 2011, s.6 and Sch.2, para.3.

A directions hearing is only ordered if the court gives permission for a TPIM notice or confirms an urgent TPIM notice.

A directions hearing must be held, unless the court otherwise directs, within seven days of the TPIM notice being served on the individual or on which the court confirms an urgent TPIM notice.

Rule 89.3(7) overlooks the fact that a review hearing, to be heard as soon as practicable, is fixed at the directions hearing: Act of 2011, s.8(4).

89.3.2

"SERVE".

On service, see Chap. 16, Pt. I.

89.3.3

---

[1] Rule 89.3 inserted by S.S.I. 2005 No. 153 (effective 16th March 2005) and substituted by S.S.I. 2011 No. 441 para. 2(2) (effective 21st December 2011: substitution has effect subject to S.S.I. 2011 No. 441 para. 2(3)).

Appeals relating to terrorism prevention and investigation measures

89.4

89.4.—[1](1) Subject to paragraphs (2) and (3) and to the modifications set out in rule 41.51 (application of Parts II and III to Part IX of Chapter 41), Part III of Chapter 41 (appeals in Form 41.25) applies to appeals under section 16 of the Act of 2011.

(2) An appeal under section 16 of the Act of 2011 shall be lodged with the Deputy Principal Clerk and served on the Secretary of State within 28 days after the date on which the affected person received notice of—

    (a) the decision by the Secretary of State to extend or revive a TPIM notice;

    (b) the decision of the Secretary of State to vary measures specified in a TPIM notice without the consent of the affected person;

    (c) the decision of the Secretary of State on an application for the variation of measures specified in a TPIM notice;

    (d) the decision of the Secretary of State on an application for the revocation of the TPIM notice; or

    (e) the decision of the Secretary of State on an application for permission for the purposes of measures specified in a TPIM notice.

(3) In a case where the Secretary of State has failed to determine an application for the revocation of the TPIM notice, for the variation of measures specified in such a notice, or for permission in connection with a measure specified in such a notice, any appeal under section 16 of the Act of 2011 shall be lodged—

    (a) not earlier than 28 days; and

    (b) not later than 42 days,

after the date on which the application was made.

GENERAL NOTE.

89.4.1

If the Secretary of State extends a TPIM notice or revives it the individual may appeal against it to the court or in relation to any decision of the Secretary of State in relation to variation, revocation or permission, on a question of law: Act of 2011, s.16.

"28 DAYS AFTER", "42 DAYS AFTER".

89.4.2

The day from which the calculation is made is not included. Where the last day falls on a Saturday or Sunday or a public holiday on which the Office of Court is closed, the next available day is allowed: r. 1.3(7). For office hours and public holidays, see note 3.1.2.

Appointment of special advocates

89.5

89.5.—[2](1) Subject to paragraph (2), the Secretary of State shall give notice to the Advocate General, upon—

    (a) making any application or reference under the Act of 2011;

    (b) making any motion in respect of TPIM proceedings or appeal proceedings; or

    (c) being served with a note of appeal, reclaiming motion or other application in respect of TPIM proceedings or appeal proceedings.

(2) Paragraph (1) applies unless—

    (a) the Secretary of State does not intend to—

        (i) oppose the appeal, reclaiming motion or other application; or

        (ii) make an application under rule 89.7 (permission not to disclose relevant material etc.); or

---

[1] Rule 89.4 inserted by S.S.I. 2005 No. 153 (effective 16th March 2005) and substituted by S.S.I. 2011 No. 441 para. 2(2) (effective 21st December 2011: substitution has effect subject to S.S.I. 2011 No. 441 para. 2(3)).

[2] Rule 89.5 inserted by S.S.I. 2005 No. 153 (effective 16th March 2005) and substituted by S.S.I. 2011 No. 441 para. 2(2) (effective 21st December 2011: substitution has effect subject to S.S.I. 2011 No. 441 para. 2(3)).

   (b)   a special advocate has already been appointed to represent the interests of the affected person in the proceedings.

(3)   Where notice is given to the Advocate General under paragraph (1), the Advocate General may appoint a special advocate to represent the interests of the affected person in the proceedings.

(4)   Where there are any TPIM proceedings or appeal proceedings but no special advocate has been appointed, the affected person or the Secretary of State may at any time request the Advocate General to appoint a special advocate.

(5)   On the appointment of any special advocate, the Advocate General shall intimate the name of the special advocate to the Deputy Principal Clerk in writing.

(6)   The special advocate may address the court in any TPIM proceedings or appeal proceedings from which the affected person (and any legal representative of the affected person) is excluded.

"SPECIAL ADVOCATE".

Under para. 10 of Schedule 4 to the Act of 2011, a special advocate may be appointed by the Advocate General to represent the interests of a relevant party in any proceedings from which the party and any legal representative are excluded. **89.5.1**

Special advocates: further provisions

89.6.—[1](1)   A special advocate upon whom material has been served under rule 89.7(7)(a) shall not communicate about the TPIM proceedings or appeal proceedings or any matter connected with such proceedings except in accordance with this rule or with the authority of the court. **89.6**

(2)   The special advocate may, without the authority of the court, communicate about the TPIM proceedings or appeal proceedings with—

   (a)   the court;

   (b)   the Secretary of State, or any person acting for the Secretary of State;

   (c)   the Advocate General, or any person acting for the Advocate General;

   (d)   any other person, except for the relevant party or his or her legal representative, with whom it is necessary for administrative purposes for the special advocate to communicate about matters not connected with the substance of the proceedings.

(3)   The special advocate may apply by motion for authority to communicate with any relevant party to the proceedings or his or her legal representative or with any other person about the proceedings or a matter connected to the proceedings.

(4)   A notice of any opposition to a motion under paragraph (3) shall be intimated to the special advocate and the relevant party.

(5)   The relevant party shall not communicate with a special advocate upon whom material has been served under rule 89.7(7) other than through a legal representative in writing.

(6)   The special advocate may, without the authority of the court, send a written acknowledgement of receipt of a communication under paragraph (5).

GENERAL NOTE.

On "special advocate", see note 89.6.1. **89.6.1**

"MOTION".

On motions, see Chap. 23. **89.6.2**

---

[1] Rule 89.6 inserted by S.S.I. 2005 No. 153 (effective 16th March 2005) and substituted by S.S.I. 2011 No. 441 para. 2(2) (effective 21st December 2011: substitution has effect subject to S.S.I. 2011 No. 441 para. 2(3)).

Special representatives: further provisions

89.6A

89.6A. *[Chapter 89 substituted for a new Chapter 89 consisting of rules 89.1–89.10 by S.S.I. 2011 No. 441 para. 2(2) (effective 21st December 2011: substitution has effect subject to S.S.I. 2011 No. 441 para. 2(3)).]*

Permission not to disclose relevant material etc.

89.7

89.7.—[1](1) In this rule, "relevant material" means—

    (a)   material on which the Secretary of State relies; and

    (b)   material which adversely affects the Secretary of State's case; and

    (c)   material which supports the case of another party to the proceedings.

(2) Subject to paragraph (3), the Secretary of State shall lodge all relevant material as productions.

(3) The Secretary of State may apply by motion for permission not to disclose relevant material.

(4) The Secretary of State shall not be required to disclose to the affected person any relevant material which is the subject of an application under paragraph (3).

(5) Subject to paragraph (6), the Secretary of State shall not rely upon any relevant material which is the subject of an application under paragraph (3) unless a special advocate has been appointed.

(6) Paragraph (5) does not apply in respect of an initial diet where the Court has ordered the Deputy Principal Clerk not to notify the affected person of the date and time of the initial diet.

(7) Where the Secretary of State makes an application under paragraph (3) and a special advocate has been appointed, the Secretary of State shall lodge with the Deputy Principal Clerk and serve on the special advocate—

    (a)   the relevant material;

    (b)   a statement of the reasons for the application for permission not to disclose the relevant material; and

    (c)   if and to the extent that it is possible to do so without disclosing information contrary to the public interest, a summary of the relevant material which can be served on the affected person.

(8) On the making of an application under paragraph (3), the court shall, unless paragraph (9) applies, direct the Deputy Principal Clerk to allocate a diet for a hearing of the application and the Deputy Principal Clerk shall intimate the date and time in writing to the Secretary of State and to any special advocate appointed under rule 89.5.

(9) This paragraph applies where—

    (a)   the special advocate gives notice that he or she does not oppose an application under paragraph (3);

    (b)   the court has previously considered an application by the Secretary of State for prohibition of disclosure of the same or substantially the same matters, and is satisfied that it would be just to prohibit disclosure without a hearing; or

    (c)   the Secretary of State and the special advocate consent to the court deciding the issue without a hearing.

(10) An application under paragraph (3) shall be considered in the absence of the affected person and his or her legal representative.

---

[1] Rule 89.7 inserted by S.S.I. 2005 No. 153 (effective 16th March 2005) and substituted by S.S.I. 2011 No. 441 para. 2(2) (effective 21st December 2011: substitution has effect subject to S.S.I. 2011 No. 441 para. 2(3)).

(11) The Court must grant the application under paragraph (3) where it considers that the disclosure of the material would be contrary to the public interest.

(12) On granting an application under paragraph (3), the court shall order the Secretary of State to serve upon every relevant party (and their legal representatives) a copy of the summary lodged under paragraph (7)(c) unless the court considers that the summary contains information or other material the disclosure of which would be contrary to the public interest.

(13) Paragraph (14) applies where the court—

(a) does not grant permission to the Secretary of State to withhold relevant material; or

(b) requires the Secretary of State to provide a relevant party to the proceedings with a summary of relevant material that is withheld.

(14) In a case where the Secretary of State elects not disclose the relevant material or (as the case may be) not to provide the summary—

(a) if the court considers that the relevant material or anything that is required to be summarised might adversely affect the Secretary of State's case or support the case of a relevant party to the proceedings, the court may direct that the Secretary of State is not to rely on such points in the proceedings or is to make such concessions or take such other steps as the court may specify; or

(b) in any other case, the court shall ensure that the Secretary of State does not rely in the proceedings on the material or (as the case may be) on what is required to be summarised.

GENERAL NOTE.

Rule 89.7 provides for applications by the Secretary of State for permission not to disclose relevant material. That rule does not indicate what power the court is exercising or what test it should apply. Rules 89.7 is made under para. 4 of Schedule 4 to the 2011 Act. Para. 4(1)(c) provides that rules of court must secure that the court is required to give permission for material not to be disclosed where it considers that the disclosure of the material would be contrary to the public interest. Rule 89.7(12), however, does provide that that is the test for granting permission not to disclose material

89.7.1

PRODUCTIONS.

On productions and the lodging of them, see r. 4.5 and note 4.5.2.

89.7.2

"MOTION".

For motions, see Chap. 23.

89.7.3

"SPECIAL ADVOCATE".

See note 89.6.1.

89.7.4

Anonymity

89.8.—[1](1) The Secretary of State or the affected person may apply for an order requiring anonymity for the affected person—

89.8

(a) in TPIM proceedings or appeal proceedings, by motion;

(b) where there are no TPIM proceedings or appeal proceedings, by lodging a petition with the Deputy Principal Clerk.

(2) The reference in this rule to an order requiring anonymity for the affected person is to be construed in accordance with paragraph 6(3) of Schedule 4 to the Act of 2011.

---

[1] Rule 89.8 inserted by S.S.I. 2005 No. 153 (effective 16th March 2005) and substituted by S.S.I. 2011 No. 441 para. 2(2) (effective 21st December 2011: substitution has effect subject to S.S.I. 2011 No. 441 para. 2(3)).

GENERAL NOTE.

89.8.1   Para. 6 of Schedule 4 to the Act of 2011 gives the court power to make rules for anonymity for an individual in respect of whom a TPIM notice is sought.

Exclusion from diets or hearings etc.

89.9   **89.9.**—[1](1) If the court considers it necessary for the affected person and his or her legal representative, or any other relevant party, to be excluded from a diet or hearing or part of a diet or hearing to secure that information is not disclosed contrary to the public interest, it shall—

(a)   make an order in that respect; and

(b)   conduct the diet or hearing, or that part of it from which the affected person and his or her legal representative or other relevant party are excluded, in private.

(2) The court may otherwise order a diet or hearing to be conducted in private if it thinks fit.

(3) When the court issues an opinion in any proceedings to which this Chapter applies, the court may withhold any or part of its reasons if and to the extent that it is not possible to give reasons without disclosing information contrary to the public interest.

(4) Where an opinion of the court does not include the full reasons for its decision—

(a)   the court shall prepare a separate opinion including those reasons; and

(b)   the Deputy Principal Clerk shall serve that separate opinion on the Secretary of State and the special advocate.

GENERAL NOTE.

89.9.1   There is provision in s.6 for the hearing to give permission, and in Sch.2 for the confirmation of an urgent TPIM notice, to be heard in the absence of the individual. There is general provision in Sch.4, para.2 of the Act of 2011 for exclusions from proceedings.

"SERVE".

89.9.2   For service, see Chap. 16, Pt I.

Recording of TPIM and appeal proceedings

89.10   **89.10.**—[2](1) TPIM proceedings and appeal proceedings shall be recorded.

(2) The record of proceedings shall include—

(a)   any objection to a question or line of evidence;

(b)   any submission made in relation to such an objection; and

(c)   the ruling of the court in relation to the objection and submission.

(3) Any transcript of the record of the proceedings shall only be made on the direction of the court and shall be subject to such order as to the cost of the transcript as the court thinks fit.

(4) The court may make such alterations to a transcript of the record of the proceedings as appear to it to be necessary after hearing the parties; and where such alterations are made, the court shall authenticate the alterations.

---

[1] Rule 89.9 inserted by S.S.I. 2005 No. 153 (effective 16th March 2005) and substituted by S.S.I. 2011 No. 441 para. 2(2) (effective 21st December 2011: substitution has effect subject to S.S.I. 2011 No. 441 para. 2(3)).

[2] Rule 89.10 inserted by S.S.I. 2005 No. 153 (effective 16th March 2005) and substituted by S.S.I. 2011 No. 441 para. 2(2) (effective 21st December 2011: substitution has effect subject to S.S.I. 2011 No. 441 para. 2(3)).

Chapter 90[1]

Freedom Of Information

Applications

90.1.—[2](1) In this rule—

"the Act of 2000" means the Freedom of Information Act 2000; and
"the Act of 2002" means the Freedom of Information (Scotland) Act 2002.

(2) An application under section 54(3) of the Act of 2000 or section 53(3) of the Act of 2002 for the court to deal with a public authority as if it had committed a contempt of court shall be by petition.

(3) There shall be attached to a petition mentioned in paragraph (2)—

    (a) where the application is under the Act of 2000, a certificate under section 54(1) of that Act (certificate by Information Commissioner of failure to comply with notice);

    (b) where the application is under the Act of 2002, a certificate under section 53(1) of that Act (certificate by Scottish Information Commissioner of failure to comply with notice).

FREEDOM OF INFORMATION ACT 2000.

Under s. 50 of the Act of 2000 a person may apply to the Information Commissioner (formerly the Data Protection Commissioner) for a decision as to whether a request for information to a public authority (defined in s. 3(1)) has been dealt with in accordance with Pt. I of the Act of 2000. When he has dealt with the application he may serve a decision notice (s. 50(3)). In dealing with the application the Commissioner may require information from the public authority by serving an information notice on it (s. 51); and if the Commissioner is satisfied that a public authority has failed to comply with a requirement of Pt. I, he may serve an enforcement notice on it (s. 52).

If a public authority fails to comply with a decision notice, information notice or enforcement notice, the Commissioner may certify in writing to the court that the public authority has failed to comply with the notice and the court may inquire into the matter: Act of 2000, s. 54.

FREEDOM OF INFORMATION (SCOTLAND) ACT 2002.

Under s. 47 of the Act of 20002 a person dissatisfied, with a notice by a Scottish public authority on an application for review of its actions and decisions on a request for information or with the failure to give such a notice, may apply to the Scottish Information Commissioner for a decision as to whether a request for information to a public authority (defined in s. 3(1)) has been dealt with in accordance with Pt. I of the Act of 2002. When he has dealt with the application he may serve a decision notice (s. 49(5)). In dealing with the application the Commissioner may require information from the public authority by serving an information notice on it (s. 50); and if the Commissioner is satisfied that a public authority has failed to comply with a requirement of Pt. I, he may serve an enforcement notice on it (s. 51).

If a public authority fails to comply with a decision notice, information notice or enforcement notice, the Commissioner may certify in writing to the court that the public authority has failed to comply with the notice and the court may inquire into the matter: Act of 2000, s. 53.

"APPLICATION UNDER S. 54(3) OF THE ACT OF 2000 OR SECTION 53(3) OF THE ACT OF 2002".

Neither provision in fact provides for an application to the court. These provisions provide for an inquiry by the court on the Commissioner certifying to the court that there has been a failure to comply (see further notes 90.1.1 and 90.1.2). There is no known procedure in our courts for certifying to the court in this way. One is hardly surprised that the UK Parliament is ignorant of our civil procedure, but one would be entitled to expect that the Scottish Parliament should inform itself of that fact.

In effect what has to be done, and what r. 90.1(2) is striving to achieve, is that the certification is brought to the court's attention by petition. The rule is silent as to who presents the petition: it is presumably the Commissioner.

90.1

90.1.1

90.1.2

90.1.3

---

[1] Chap. 90 and r. 90.1 inserted by S.S.I. 2005 No. 193 (effective 1st April, 2005).
[2] Chap. 90 and r. 90.1 inserted by S.S.I. 2005 No. 193 (effective 1st April, 2005).

"PETITION".

90.1.4   A petition is presented to the Outer House: r. 14.2(h). The petition must be in Form 86.3 in the official printed form (r. 4.1). The petition must be signed by counsel or other person having a right of audience: r. 4.2; and see r. 1.3(1) (definition of "counsel" and "other person having a right of audience") and note 1.3.4.

The petitioner must lodge the petition with the required steps of process (r. 4.4). A fee is payable on lodging the petition: see note 14.5.10.

On petitions generally, see Chap. 14.

Chapter 91[1]

Gender Recognition Act 2004

Interpretation of this Chapter

91.1.[2] In this Chapter—

91.1

"the Act of 2004" means the Gender Recognition Act 2004;

"full gender recognition certificate" has same meaning as in section 25 of the Act of 2004; and

"Gender Recognition Panel" is to be construed in accordance with Schedule 1 to the Act of 2004.

REFERENCE UNDER SECTION 8 OF THE GENDER RECOGNITION ACT 2004.

If the Secretary of State considers that the grant of an application under s. 1(1) (for a gender recognition certificate), 5(1) (issue of a full gender recognition certificate by a court) or 6(1) (corrected certificate) of the Act of 2004 has been secured by fraud, he may refer the case to the Court of Session.

91.1.1

"PETITION".

A petition is presented to the Outer House: r. 14.2(h). The petition must be in Form 86.3 in the official printed form (r. 4.1). The petition must be signed by counsel or other person having a right of audience: r. 4.2; and see r. 1.3(1) (definition of "counsel" and "other person having a right of audience") and note 1.3.4.

91.1.2

The petitioner must lodge the petition with the required steps of process (r. 4.4). A fee is payable on lodging the petition: see note 14.5.10.

On petitions generally, see Chap. 14.

References by Secretary of State

91.2.—[3](1) A reference by the Secretary of State under section 8(5) of the Act of 2004 shall be made by petition.

91.2

(2) Where the court quashes a decision by the Gender Recognition Panel to grant an application for a gender recognition certificate under section 1(1) or section 5(2), the Deputy Principal Clerk shall send a certified copy of the interlocutor to the Registrar General for Scotland.

Applications to quash decisions

91.3.—[4](1) An application under section 8(5B) of the Act of 2004 shall be made by petition.

91.3

(2) Where, on an application under section 8(5B) of the Act of 2004, the court quashes a decision to issue a gender recognition certificate, the Deputy Principal Clerk shall send a certified copy of the interlocutor to—

(a) the Registrar General for Scotland, and

(b) the Gender Recognition Panel.

---

[1] Chapter 91 and r. 91.1 inserted by S.S.I. 2005 No. 193 (effective 1st April 2005).
[2] Chapter 91 and r. 91.1 inserted by S.S.I. 2005 No. 193 (effective 1st April 2005).
[3] Rule 91.2 inserted by S.S.I. 2005 No. 193 (effective 1st April 2005).
[4] Rule 91.3 inserted by S.S.I. 2014 No. 302 (effective 16th December 2014).

Interpretation of this Chapter

91.1. In this Chapter—

"the Act of 2004" means the Gender Recognition Act 2004;

"full gender recognition certificate" has the same meaning as in section 25 of the Act of 2004; and

"Gender Recognition Panel" is to be construed in accordance with Schedule 1 to the Act of 2004.

References to a Gender Recognition Act 2004

91.1.1 If the Secretary of State considers that the conditions in paragraph s. 4(1) (i)-(e) (gender recognition certificate), 5(1)(e) or a full gender recognition certificate) or a full certificate) of the Act of 2004 has been satisfied by grant, he may refer the case to the Court of Session.

91.1.2 Section 9 proceeded to the Outer House, r. 14.2(b). The petition must be in form 86.3 in the ordinary printed form r. 4.7.1 The petition must be signed in person in any person having a right of audience r. 4.2 and see r. 2.2(1) (definition of "counsel" and "other person having a right of audience") and note. 1.3.1 The petitioner must lodge the petition with the required steps of process r. 4.6(2). A fee is payable on lodging the petition, see note 14.5.10. Competition generally, see Chap. 14.

References by Secretary of State

91.2.—(1) A reference by the Secretary of State under section 8(5) of the Act of 2004 shall be made by petition.

(2) Where the court disposes a decision by the Gender Recognition Panel to grant an application for a gender recognition certificate under section 1(1) of section 3(1), the Deputy Principal Clerk shall send a certified copy of the interlocutor to the Registrar General for Scotland.

Applications to quash decisions

91.3.—(1) An application under section 8(5H) of the Act of 2004 shall be made by petition.

(2) Where, on an application under section 8(SP) of the Act of 2004, the court finishes a decision to issue a gender recognition certificate, the Deputy Principal Clerk shall send a certified copy of the interlocutor to—

(a) the Registrar General for Scotland, and

(b) the Gender Recognition Panel.

Chap. 91 and 91.1 inserted by S.S.I. 2005 No. 191 effective 18 April 2005.
Chapter 91 para. 91.1 inserted by S.S.I. 2005 No. 195 effective 18 April 2005.
para. 91 inserted by S.S.I. 2005 No. 195 effective 18 April 2005.
Rule 91.3 amended by S.S.I. 2013 No. 302 effective 30th December 2014.

CHAPTER 92 INQUIRIES ACT 2005

Chapter 92[1]

Inquiries Act 2005

Applications

92.1.—[2](1)   In this rule "the Act of 2005" means the Inquiries Act 2005.

(2)   An application under section 36(2) of the Act of 2005 for the court to make such order by way of enforcement, or otherwise as it could make if the matter had arisen in proceedings before the court, shall be by petition.

(3)   There shall be attached to a petition mentioned in paragraph (2) a certificate under section 36(1) of the Act of 2005 (certificate by chairman of inquiry or Minister).

GENERAL NOTE.

The Inquiries Act 2005 is supposed to provide a complete statutory framework for public inquiries about matters of public concern set up by government ministers. It repeals the Tribunals of Inquiries (Evidence) Act 1921.

Restrictions on attendance or disclosure of evidence or documents may be imposed by the chairman (s. 19); and a person may be required to attend by the chairman (s. 21). Under s. 36 of the Act of 2005 the chairman or the Minister may certify to the court that a person has failed to comply or threatens to do so.

"APPLICATION UNDER SECTION 36(2)OF THE ACT OF 2005".

This provision does not in fact provides for an application to the court. It provides for an inquiry by the court on the chairman or Minister certifying to the court that there has been a failure to comply or a threat not to do so (see further notes 92.1.1). There is no known procedure in our courts for certifying to the court in this way.

In effect what has to be done, and what r. 92.1(2) is striving to achieve, is that the certification is brought to the court's attention by petition. The rule is silent as to who presents the petition: it is presumably the chairman of the inquiry or the Minister.

"PETITION".

A petition is presented to the Outer House: r. 14.2(h). The petition must be in Form 86.3 in the official printed form (r. 4.1). The petition must be signed by counsel or other person having a right of audience: r. 4.2; and see r. 1.3(1) (definition of "counsel" and "other person having a right of audience") and note 1.3.4.

The petitioner must lodge the petition with the required steps of process (r. 4.4). A fee is payable on lodging the petition: see note 14.5.10.

On petitions generally, see Chap. 14.

92.1

92.1.1

92.1.2

92.1.3

---

[1] Chapter 92 and r. 92.1 inserted by S.S.I. 2005 No. 521 (effective 21st October 2005).
[2] Chapter 92 and r. 92.1 inserted by S.S.I. 2005 No. 521 (effective 21st October 2005).

CHAPTER 93 LIVE LINKS

Chapter 93

Live Links

[Chap. 93 revoked by S.S.I. 2023 No. 168 para.2 (effective 3 July 2023) subject to transitional provisions in S.S.I. 2023 No. 168 para.4.] **93.1**

CHAPTER 94 INTERVENTIONS BY THE COMMISSIONS FOR EQUALITY AND HUMAN RIGHTS

Chapter 94[1]

Interventions by the Commissions for Equality and Human Rights

Interpretation

94.1.[2] In this Chapter, "the CEHR" means the Commission for Equality and Human Rights.

94.1

Intervention by the CEHR in proceedings

94.2.—[3](1) The CEHR may apply to the court for leave to intervene in proceedings in accordance with this Chapter.

94.2

(2) An application under paragraph (1) above may be made in relation to any proceedings (including a petition for judicial review or an appeal in connection with such a petition).

(3) This Chapter is without prejudice to—

   (a) rule 58.8 (application by compearing party to enter process of a judicial review); and

   (b) any other entitlement of the CEHR, by virtue of having title and interest in relation to the subject matter of any proceedings by virtue of section 30(2) of the Equality Act 2006 or any other enactment, to seek to be sisted as a party in those proceedings.

(4) Nothing in this Chapter shall affect the power of the court to make such other direction as it considers appropriate in the interests of justice.

(5) Any decision of the court in proceedings under this Chapter shall be final and not subject to review.

GENERAL NOTE.

The right of the CEHR to intervene in any proceedings is by virtue of s. 30 of the Equality Act 2006.

94.2.1

Application to intervene

94.3.—[4](1) An application for leave to intervene shall be by way of a minute of intervention in Form 94.3, and the CEHR shall—

94.3

   (a) send a copy of it to all the parties; and

   (b) lodge it in process, certifying that sub-paragraph (a) above has been complied with.

(2) A minute of intervention shall set out briefly—

   (a) the CEHR's reasons for believing that the proceedings are relevant to a matter in connection with which the CEHR has a function;

   (b) the issue in the proceedings which the CEHR wishes to address; and

   (c) the propositions to be advanced by the CEHR and the CEHR's reasons for believing that they are relevant to the proceedings and that they will assist the court.

(3) The court may—

   (a) refuse leave without a hearing;

   (b) grant leave without a hearing unless a hearing is requested under paragraph (4) below; or

   (c) refuse or grant leave after such a hearing.

---

[1] Chapter 94 and r. 94.1 inserted by S.S.I. 2007 No. 449 (effective 25th October 2007).
[2] Chapter 94 and r. 94.1 inserted by S.S.I. 2007 No. 449 (effective 25th October 2007).
[3] Rule 94.2 inserted by S.S.I. 2007 No. 449 (effective 25th October 2007).
[4] Rule 94.3 inserted by S.S.I. 2007 No. 449 (effective 25th October 2007).

(4)   A hearing, at which the applicant and the parties may address the court on the matters referred to in paragraph (5)(c) below, may be held if, within 14 days of the minute of intervention being lodged, any of the parties lodges a request for a hearing.

(5)   Any diet in pursuance of paragraph (4) shall be fixed by the Keeper of the Rolls who shall give written intimation of the diet to the CEHR and all the parties.

(6)   The court may grant leave only if satisfied that—

(a)   the proceedings are relevant to a matter in connection with which the CEHR has a function;

(b)   the propositions to be advanced by the CEHR are relevant to the proceedings and are likely to assist the court; and

(c)   the intervention will not unduly delay or otherwise prejudice the rights of the parties, including their potential liability for expenses.

(7)   In granting leave, the court may impose such terms and conditions as it considers desirable in the interests of justice, including making provision in respect of any additional expenses incurred by the parties as a result of the intervention.

(8)   The clerk of court shall give written intimation of a grant or refusal of leave to the CEHR and all the parties.

"SEND".

94.3.1   "Send" includes deliver: see r. 1.3(1).

"LODGE".

94.3.2   On intimation of steps of process, see r. 4.6. Rule 94.3(1)(a) requires a copy to be sent to every other party. One wonders if the draftsman is familiar with the Rules: r.4.6(1)(b) already provides that a copy of every step of process lodged must be sent to every other party; there is no need for r. 94.3(1)(a).

Form of intervention

94.4   **94.4.—**[1](1)   An intervention shall be by way of a written submission which (including any appendices) does not exceed 5000 words.

(2)   The CEHR shall lodge the submission and send a copy of it to all the parties by such time as the court may direct.

(3)   The court may in exceptional circumstances—

(a)   allow a longer written submission to be made;

(b)   direct that an oral submission is to be made.

(4)   Any diet in pursuance of paragraph (3)(b) shall be fixed by the Keeper of the Rolls who shall give written intimation of the diet to the CEHR and all the parties.

---

[1] Rule 94.4 inserted by S.I. 2007 No. 449 (effective 25th October 2007).

CHAPTER 95 SCOTTISH COMMISSION FOR HUMAN RIGHTS

Chapter 95[1]

Scottish Commission for Human Rights

Interpretation

95.1.[2] In this Chapter—

95.1

"the Act of 2006" means the Scottish Commission for Human Rights Act 2006; and

"the SCHR" means the Scottish Commission for Human Rights.

GENERAL NOTE.

The Scottish Commission for Human Rights Act 2006 creates a body with a duty to promote human rights (s. 2) with powers to provide information, education and guidance (s. 3), to monitor law, policies and practices (s. 4), and to co-operate with others (s. 5). It has no power to assist anyone in legal proceedings (s. 6), but it may, with leave, or at the invitation, of the court intervene in proceedings to make a submission on an issue arising in them relating to its general duty and raising a matter of public interest (s. 14). It may conduct inquiries into policies and practices of public authorities (s. 8).

95.1.1

Reports to the Court of Session under schedules 2 and 3 to the Act of 2006

95.2. [Revoked by the Act of Sederunt (Rules of the Court of Session 1994 Amendment) (Miscellaneous) (No.2) 2021 (SSI 2021/434) art.2(3) (effective 1 January 2022).]

95.2

REPORTS TO THE COURT UNDER SCHEDS. 2 AND 3.

Where a person to which notice has been given to give evidence at an inquiry held by the Commission and refuses or fails with reasonable excuse to comply etc. (Act of 2006, Sched. 2, para. 4(3) and (4)), or where a person obstructs the Commission entering, inspecting or interviewing a person in connection with an inquiry (Sched. 3, para. 3), the Commission may report the matter to the court to enforce the notice etc, or deal with the matter as a contempt.

95.2.1

Application to intervene

95.3.—[3](1) An application for leave to intervene under section 14(2)(a) of the Act of 2006 shall be by way of a minute of intervention in Form 95.3, and the SCHR shall—

95.3

(a) send a copy of it to all the parties; and

(b) lodge it in process, certifying that sub paragraph (a) above has been complied with.

(2) In granting leave, the court may impose such terms and conditions as it considers desirable in the interests of justice, including making provision in respect of any additional expenses incurred by the parties as a result of the intervention.

(3) Any decision of the court in proceedings under this Chapter shall be final and not subject to review.

(4) The clerk of court shall give written intimation of a grant or refusal of leave to the SCHR and all the parties.

GENERAL NOTE.

While the Commission does not have power to assist a litigant (s. 6), it may apply to the court for leave to intervene in proceedings (except proceedings relating to a children's hearing) for the purpose of making a submission on an issue arising in the proceedings: Act of 2006, s. 14. The issue must be relevant to the general duty of the Commission to promote human rights (s. 2) and raise a matter of public interest.

95.3.1

Save in exceptional circumstances the submission must be in writing and of no more than 5,000 words: r. 95.5.

---

[1] Chapter 95 and r. 95.1 inserted by S.S.I. 2008 No. 123 (effective from 1st April 2008).
[2] Chapter 95 and r. 95.1 inserted by S.S.I. 2008 No. 123 (effective from 1st April 2008).
[3] R. 95.3 inserted by S.S.I. 2008 No. 123 (effective from 1st April 2008).

"SEND".

95.3.2   Send includes deliver: see r. 1.3(1).

"LODGE".

95.3.3   On intimation of steps of process, see r. 4.6. As with r. 94.3(1)(a), it appears that the draftsman is not familiar with r. 4.6(1)(b) which provides that a copy of every step of process lodged must be sent to every other party. There is no need for r. 95.3(1)(a).

"WRITTEN INTIMATION".

95.3.4   For methods of written intimation, see r. 16.9.

Invitation to intervene

95.4   **95.4.**—[1](1)   An invitation to intervene under section 14(2)(b) of the Act of 2006 shall be in Form 95.4, and the clerk of court shall send a copy of it to the SCHR and all the parties.

(2)   An invitation under paragraph (2) shall be accompanied by—

(a)   a copy of the pleadings in the proceedings; and

(b)   such other documents relating to that proceedings as the court thinks relevant.

(3)   In issuing an invitation under section 14(2)(b) of the Act of 2006, the court may impose such terms and conditions as it considers desirable in the interests of justice, including making provision in respect of any additional expenses incurred by the parties as a result of the intervention.

GENERAL NOTE.

95.4.1   The court may invite the Commission to intervene in proceedings (except proceedings relating to a children's hearing) for the purpose of making a submission on an issue arising in the proceedings: Act of 2006, s. 14. The issue must be relevant to the general duty of the Commission to promote human rights (s. 2) and raise a matter of public interest.

Save in exceptional circumstances the submission must be in writing and of no more than 5,000 words: r. 95.5.

Form of intervention

95.5   **95.5.**—[2](1)   An intervention shall be by way of a written submission which (including any appendices) does not exceed 5000 words.

(2)   The SCHR shall lodge the submission and send a copy of it to all the parties by such time as the court may direct.

(3)   The court may in exceptional circumstances—

(a)   allow a longer written submission to be made;

(b)   direct that an oral submission is to be made.

(4)   Any diet in pursuance of paragraph (3)(b) shall be fixed by the Keeper of the Rolls who shall give written intimation of the diet to the SCHR and all the parties."

"LODGE".

95.5.1   On intimation of steps of process, see r. 4.6. As with r. 94.3(1)(a), it appears that the draftsman is not familiar with r. 4.6(1)(b) which provides that a copy of every step of process lodged must be sent to every other party. There is no need for r. 95.3(1)(a).

"SEND".

95.5.2   Send includes deliver: see r. 1.3(1).

---

[1] R. 95.4 inserted by S.S.I. 2008 No. 123 (effective from 1st April 2008).
[2] R. 95.5 inserted by S.S.I. 2008 No. 123 (effective from 1st April 2008).

CHAPTER 96 COUNTER-TERRORISM ACT 2008—FINANCIAL RESTRICTIONS PROCEEDINGS

Chapter 96[1,2]

Financial Restrictions Proceedings and Sanctions Proceedings

Interpretation and application of this Chapter

96.1.—[3,4](1)   In this Chapter—

"the 2008 Act" means the Counter-Terrorism Act 2008;

"the 2018 Act" means the Sanctions and Anti-Money Laundering Act 2018;

"appropriate minister" means

    (a)   in relation to sanctions proceedings in respect of a decision of the Secretary of State, the Secretary of State; or

    (b)   in relation to financial restrictions proceedings, or to sanctions proceedings in respect of a decision of the Treasury, the Treasury;

"financial restrictions decision" means a decision mentioned in section 63(1) of the 2008 Act;

"financial restrictions proceedings" means proceedings in the Court of Session on an application under section 63(2) of the 2008 Act or on a claim arising from any matter to which such an application relates;

"sanctions decision" means, a decision mentioned in section 38(1) of the 2018 Act;

"sanctions decision proceedings" means proceedings in the Court of Session on an application under section 38(2) of the 2018 Act;

"special advocate" means, in relation to financial restrictions proceedings or sanctions decision proceedings, a person who is appointed under section 68 of the 2008 Act to represent the interests of a party to those proceedings.

(2)   In this Chapter—

    (a)   references to a party to the proceedings do not include the appropriate minister;

    (b)   references to a party's legal representative do not include a person appointed as a special advocate.

(3)   This Chapter applies to a reclaiming motion in financial restrictions proceedings or sanctions decision proceedings as well as to financial restrictions proceedings or sanctions decision proceedings at first instance.

GENERAL NOTE.

This chapter is concerned only with financial restriction proceedings under s. 63 of the 2008 Act or a sanctions decision under s. 38 of the 2018 Act.

Application to set aside a financial restrictions decision or sanctions decision

96.2.—[5,6](1)   An application under section 63(2) of the 2008 Act to set aside a financial restrictions decision or under section 38(2) of the 2018 Act to set aside a sanctions decision shall be made by lodging a petition with the Deputy Principal Clerk.

96.1

96.1.1

96.2

---

[1] Chap. 96 and r. 96.1 inserted by S.S.I. 2008 No. 401 (effective from 4th December 2008).
[2] As amended by S.S.I. 2019 No. 72 r. 2 (effective 29th March 2019).
[3] Chap. 96 and r. 96.1 inserted by S.S.I. 2008 No. 401 (effective from 4th December 2008).
[4] Heading and r. 96.1 as amended by S.S.I. 2019 No. 72 r. 2 (effective 29th March 2019).
[5] R. 96.2 inserted by S.S.I. 2008 No. 401 (effective from 4th December 2008).
[6] As amended by S.S.I. 2019 No. 72 r. 2 (effective 29th March 2019).

(2) The petition shall include, in numbered paragraphs, statements of reasons setting out—

(a) the details of the financial restrictions decision or sanctions decision; and

(b) the grounds on which the petitioner seeks to set aside that decision.

(3) There shall be lodged with the petition—

(a) a copy of the financial restrictions decision or sanctions decision;

(b) all relevant documents in the petitioner's possession and within the petitioner's control.

GENERAL NOTE.

96.2.1

Section 63 of the 2008 Act provides for an application to the court to set aside a financial restrictions decision of the Treasury in connection with any of its functions in relation to UN terrorism orders, freezing orders under Pt. 2 of the Anti-terrorism, Crime and Security Act 2001 or Sched. 7 (except orders under para. 8 or 28(6)) to the 2008 Act (terrorist financing, money laundering and certain other activities: financial restrictions).

Section 38 of the Sanctions and Anti-Money Laundering Act 2018 provides for an application to the court to set aside a sanctions decision made under the Sanctions and Anti-Money Laundering Act 2018.

In determining whether to set aside a decision, the court must apply the principles applicable in judicial review and may make such order as it could in judicial review: 2008 Act, s. 63(3) and (4); 2018 Act s. 38(3) and (4). The court may quash the relevant order: 2008 Act, s. 63(5). The power applies retrospectively, whether the decision of the Treasury was made before or after the commencement of s. 63.

"PETITION".

96.2.2

A petition is presented in the Outer House: r. 14.2(h). The petition must be in Form 14.4 in the official printed form: rr. 4.1 and 14.4. The petition must be signed by counsel or other person having a right of audience: r. 4.2; and see r. 1.3(1) (definition of "counsel" and "other person having a right of audience") and note 1.3.4.

The petitioner must lodge the petition with the required steps of process (r. 4.4). A fee is payable on lodging the petition: see note 14.5.10.

On petitions generally, see Chap. 14.

Lodging of process

96.3

96.3.[1, 2] A process lodged under rule 4.3 in financial restrictions proceedings or sanctions decision proceedings shall be lodged with the Deputy Principal Clerk.

"MOTION".

96.3.1

For motions, see Chap.23.

Disclosure

96.4

96.4.—[3, 4](1) Subject to rule 96.5, the appropriate minister shall disclose to every other party in financial restrictions proceedings or sanctions decision proceedings—

(a) material on which they rely;

(b) material which adversely affects their case; and

(c) material which supports the case of a party to the proceedings.

(2) The Treasury shall disclose the material on being served with a petition or summons in financial restrictions proceedings or, when the material comes to the Treasury's notice after such service, as soon as practicable after that.

---

[1] R. 96.3 inserted by S.S.I. 2008 No. 401

[2] As amended by S.S.I. 2019 No. 72 r. 2 (effective 29th March 2019).

[3] R. 96.4 inserted by S.S.I. 2008 No. 401 (effective from 4th December 2008).

[4] As amended by S.S.I. 2019 No. 72 r. 2 (effective 29th March 2019).

Applications for permission not to disclose material

96.5.—[1, 2](1)   This rule applies to an application by the appropriate minister in financial restrictions proceedings or sanctions decision proceedings for permission not to disclose material otherwise than to the court and any special advocate.

(2)   The following shall not apply to the application—

rule 4.5(1)(b) (copy inventory of productions to be sent to other parties),

rule 4.6 (intimation of steps of process),

rule 4.11 (documents not to be borrowed),

Chapter 23 (motions).

(3)   The application shall be made by motion to the Deputy Principal Clerk.

(4)   The motion shall be intimated to any special advocate.

(5)   The Treasury shall not rely upon any material which the court has granted permission not to be disclosed on an application unless a special advocate has been appointed under section 68 of the 2008 Act.

(6)   At the same time as making the application the Treasury shall—

(a)   lodge with the Deputy Principal Clerk; and

(b)   serve on any special advocate,

the documents mentioned in paragraph (7) but such documents shall not be intimated to the petitioner or pursuer or any other party to the proceedings.

(7)   Those documents are—

(a)   the material;

(b)   a statement of the reasons for the application for permission not to disclose the material; and

(c)   a draft summary of the material.

(8)   The draft summary mentioned in paragraph (7)(c) shall be prepared with rule 96.7 in mind.

(9)   Where the special advocate intends to oppose an application he shall lodge notice of opposition within 14 days of the date of service by the Treasury under paragraph (6).

(10)   Where the special advocate does not intend to oppose an application he shall give notice to the court within 14 days of the date of service by the Treasury under paragraph (6).

(11)   Documents lodged in relation to an application shall be kept separately from the process by the Deputy Principal Clerk.

(12)   Documents lodged in relation to an application shall not be borrowed or inspected by any party other than by a legal representative of the Treasury or by any special advocate.

96.5

"INTIMATED".

For methods, see r. 16.8.

96.5.1

"SERVE".

For methods, see rr. 16.1 to 16.6.

96.5.2

Hearing on applications for permission not to disclose material

96.6.—[3, 4](1)   On the making of an application under rule 96.5, the Deputy Principal Clerk shall, unless paragraph (2) applies—

(a)   allocate a diet for a hearing of such an application; and

96.6

---

[1] R. 96.5 inserted by S.S.I. 2008 No. 401 (effective from 4th December 2008).
[2] As amended by S.S.I. 2019 No. 72 r. 2 (effective 29th March 2019).
[3] R. 96.6 inserted by S.S.I. 2008 No. 401 (effective from 4th December 2008).
[4] As amended by S.S.I. 2019 No. 72 r. 2 (effective 29th March 2019).

   (b)   intimate that date and time in writing to—

        (i)   the appropriate minister; and

        (ii)   any special advocate.

  (2) This paragraph applies where—

   (a)   the special advocate has given notice that he does not oppose the application;

   (b)   the court has previously considered an application by the appropriate minister for prohibition of disclosure of the same or substantially the same matters, and is satisfied that it would be just to prohibit disclosure without a hearing; or

   (c)   the appropriate minister and the special advocate have consented to the court deciding the issue without a hearing.

  (3) Where paragraph (2) applies, the Deputy Principal Clerk shall place the application before the court in chambers, and it shall determine whether to—

   (a)   decide the application without a hearing; or

   (b)   hear the appropriate minister and any special advocate.

  (4) A hearing on the application shall take place in the absence of every party to the proceedings and every party's legal representative, in private.

  (5) The court shall grant the application where it considers that the disclosure of the material would be contrary to the public interest.

Summary of material

96.7

96.7.—[1,2](1) On granting an application made under rule 96.5, the court must consider ordering the appropriate minister to serve upon every party a summary of the material.

  (2) The court is required to ensure that any such summary does not contain material the disclosure of which would be contrary to the public interest.

  (3) Where the court is of the view that such a summary should be provided it shall consider the draft summary mentioned in rule 96.5(7)(c).

  (4) Having done so, the court may—

   (a)   order the appropriate minister to serve a copy of the summary on every party and every party's representative; or

   (b)   order the appropriate minister to lodge with the Deputy Principal Clerk within a specified time period a revised summary with such changes as the court directs.

  (5) Where paragraph (4)(b) applies, the court shall—

   (a)   consider that revised summary and make any further revisals that it considers necessary; and

   (b)   order the appropriate minister to serve a copy of the summary as revised by the court on every party to the proceedings and every party's legal representative.

Election by appropriate mminister not to disclose material or to provide summary

96.8

96.8.—[3,4](1)[5] Paragraphs (2) and (3) apply where, in relation to an application made under rule 96.5—

   (a)   the appropriate minister does not receive the court's permission to with-

---

[1] R. 96.7 inserted by S.S.I. 2008 No. 401 (effective from 4th December 2008).

[2] As amended by S.S.I. 2019 No. 72 r. 2 (effective 29th March 2019).

[3] R. 96.8 inserted by S.S.I. 2008 No. 401 (effective from 4th December 2008).

[4] As amended by S.S.I. 2019 No. 72 r. 2 (effective 29th March 2019).

[5] R. 96.8(1) amended by S.S.I. 2009 No. 450 (effective 25th January 2010).

hold material, but elects not to disclose it; or

(b) the appropriate minister is required to provide a party to the proceedings with a summary of material that is withheld, but elects not to provide the summary.

(2) The appropriate minister shall, within 7 days, notify the Deputy Principal Clerk of that matter in writing.

(3) The court shall—

(a) if it considers that the material or anything that is required to be summarised might adversely affect the appropriate minister's case or support the case of a party to the proceedings, in relation to a matter under consideration by the court, order that the appropriate minister shall not rely on such points in their case, or shall make such concessions or take such other steps as the court may specify;

(b) in any other case, ensure that the appropriate minister does not rely in the proceedings on the material or (as the case may be) on what is required to be summarised.

Appointment of special advocates

96.9.—[1,2](1) Subject to paragraphs (2) and (3), the appropriate minister shall, upon—

96.9

(a) being served with any application;

(b) making any motion;

(c) a reclaiming motion being intimated or on intimating a reclaiming motion; or

(d) being served with or serving any other application,

in financial restrictions proceedings or sanctions decision proceedings or give notice of that matter to the Advocate General for Scotland, so that he may consider whether to appoint a special advocate to represent the interests of any party to the proceedings.

(2) Paragraph (1) applies only where there is at least one party to the proceedings in respect of whom a special advocate has not been appointed under section 68 of the 2008 Act to represent their interests in the proceedings.

(3) Paragraph (1) does not apply where the appropriate minister does not intend to—

(a) oppose the application concerned; or

(b) make an application under rule 96.5.

(4) Any party may at any time request the Advocate General to appoint a special advocate to represent the interests of a party in financial restrictions proceedings or sanctions decision proceedings.

(5) On the appointment of any special advocate, the Advocate General shall intimate the name of the special advocate to the Deputy Principal Clerk in writing.

(6) The special advocate may address the court in any financial restrictions proceedings or sanctions decision proceedings from which the petitioner or pursuer is excluded.

---

[1] R. 96.9 inserted by S.S.I. 2008 No. 401 (effective from 4th December 2008) and amended by S.S.I. 2009 No. 63, r. 7 (effective 23rd March 2009).
[2] As amended by S.S.I. 2019 No. 72 r. 2 (effective 29th March 2019).

Special advocates: communication about proceedings

96.10

96.10.—[1, 2](1) A special advocate shall not communicate about the proceedings or any matter connected with the proceedings except in accordance with this rule.

(2) The special advocate may, without the authority of the court, communicate with—

(a) the court;

(b)[3] the appropriate minister or its legal representative;

(c) the Advocate General for Scotland or any person acting for him;

(d) any other person, except the petitioner or pursuer or his legal representative or any other party to the proceedings, with whom it is necessary for administrative purposes for him to communicate about matters not connected with the substance of the proceedings.

(3) The special advocate may apply by motion for authority to communicate with the petitioner or pursuer or his legal representative or with any other person.

(4) The motion shall be intimated to the appropriate minister only.

(5) A notice of opposition to the motion shall be intimated by the appropriate minister—

(a) to the special advocate only; and

(b) within 7 days of intimation of the motion.

(6)[4] Where the appropriate minister opposes the motion, the court shall fix a hearing.

(7) The hearing shall take place in the absence of every party to the proceedings and every party's legal representative, in private.

(8) The petitioner or pursuer or any other party to the proceedings shall not communicate with the special advocate upon whom material has been served under rule 96.5(6) other than through a legal representative in writing.

(9) The special advocate may, without the authority of the court, send a written acknowledgement of receipt of a communication under paragraph (8).

Exclusion from hearings

96.11

96.11.—[5, 6](1) If the court considers it necessary for the petitioner or pursuer and his legal representative, or any other party to the proceedings, to be excluded from any hearing in relation to financial restrictions proceedings or sanctions decision proceedings or any part of such a hearing to secure that information is not disclosed contrary to the public interest, it shall—

(a) make an order in that respect; and

(b) conduct that hearing, or that part of it from which the petitioner or pursuer and his legal representative, or any other party to the proceedings, are excluded, in private.

(2) The court may otherwise order any hearing in relation to financial restrictions proceedings or sanctions decision proceedings to be conducted in private if it thinks fit.

(3) Where the court considers it necessary under this rule to exclude any party to the proceedings from any hearing or part of a hearing it shall make such order as it

---

[1] R. 96.10 inserted by S.S.I. 2008 No. 401 (effective from 4th December 2008).

[2] As amended by S.S.I. 2019 No. 72 r. 2 (effective 29th March 2019).

[3] R. 96.10(2)(b) and (6) amended by S.S.I. 2009 No. 450 (effective 25th January 2010).

[4] R. 96.10(2)(b) and (6) amended by S.S.I. 2009 No. 450 (effective 25th January 2010).

[5] R. 96.11 inserted by SI 2008/401 (effective from 4th December 2008).

[6] As amended by S.S.I. 2019 No. 72 r. 2 (effective 29th March 2019).

considers appropriate in relation to access to the process or inspection of documents, or in relation to any other matter, to secure that information is not disclosed contrary to the public interest.

Opinions of the court

96.12.—[1,2](1)   When the court issues an opinion in financial restrictions proceedings or sanctions decision proceedings, the court may withhold any or part of its reasons if and to the extent that it is not possible to give reasons without disclosing information contrary to the public interest.

(2)   Where an opinion of the court does not include the full reasons for its decision—

   (a)   the court shall prepare a separate opinion including those reasons; and

   (b)   the Deputy Principal Clerk shall serve that separate opinion on the Treasury and the special advocate.

"SERVE".

It should be noted that the DPCS has to "serve" the opinion and not just "send" it.

Recording of financial restrictions proceedings or sanctions decision proceedings

96.13.—[3,4](1)   Financial restrictions proceedings or sanctions decision proceedings shall be recorded by—

   (a)   a shorthand writer to whom the oath *de fideli administratione officii* has been administered on his appointment as a shorthand writer in the Court of Session; or

   (b)   tape recording or other mechanical means approved by the Lord President.

(2)   The record of the proceedings shall include—

   (a)   any objection to a question or line of evidence;

   (b)   any submission made in relation to such an objection; and

   (c)   the ruling of the court in relation to the objection and submission.

(3)   A transcript of the record of the proceedings shall only be made on the direction of the court and shall be subject to such order as to the cost of the transcript as the court thinks fit.

(4)   The transcript of the record of the proceedings shall be certified as a faithful record of the proceedings by—

   (a)   the shorthand writer or shorthand writers, if more than one, who recorded the evidence; or

   (b)   where the evidence was recorded by tape recording or other mechanical means, the person who transcribed the record.

(5)   The court may make such alterations to the transcript of the record of the proceedings as appear to it to be necessary after hearing the parties; and where such alterations are made, the court shall authenticate the alterations.

96.12

96.12.1

96.13

---

[1] R. 96.12 inserted by S.S.I. 2008 No. 401 (effective from 4th December 2008).
[2] As amended by S.S.I. 2019 No. 72 r. 2 (effective 29th March 2019).
[3] R. 96.13 inserted by S.S.I. 2008 No. 401 (effective from 4th December 2008).
[4] As amended by S.S.I. 2019 No. 72 r. 2 (effective 29th March 2019).

considers appropriate in relation to access to the process, re-imposition of decon trials, or in relation to any other matter, to secure that information is not disclosed contrary to the public interest.

(Opinions of the court)

98.12.—(1) When the court issues an opinion in financial restrictions proceedings or sanctions decision proceedings, the court may withhold any or part of its reasons if and to the extent that it is not possible to give reasons without disclosing information contrary to the public interest.

(2) Where an opinion of the court does not include the full reasons for its decision—

(a) the court shall prepare a separate opinion including those reasons; and

(b) the Deputy Principal Clerk shall serve that separate opinion on the Treasury and the special advocate.

98.12.1 It should be noted that the DPCS has to serve the opinion and not just send it.

Recording of financial restrictions proceedings or sanctions decision proceedings

98.13.—(1) Financial restrictions proceedings or sanctions decision proceedings shall be recorded by—

(a) a shorthand writer to whom the oath de fideli administratione officii has been administered on his appointment as a shorthand writer in the Court of Session; or

(b) tape recording or other mechanical means approved by the Lord President.

(2) This record of the proceedings shall include—

(a) any objection to a question or line of evidence;

(b) any submission made in relation to such an objection; and

(c) the ruling of the court in relation to the objection and submission.

(3) A transcript of the record of the proceedings shall only be made on the direction of the court and shall be subject to such orders as to the cost of the transcript as the court thinks fit.

(4) The transcript of the record of the proceedings shall be certified as a faithful record of the proceedings by—

(a) the shorthand writer or shorthand writer, if more than one, who recorded the evidence; or

(b) where the evidence was recorded by tape recording or other mechanical means, the person who transcribed the record.

(5) The court may make such alterations to the transcript of the record of the proceedings as appear to it to be necessary after hearing the parties; and where such alterations are made, the court shall authenticate the alterations.

98.12 inserted by S.S.I. 2009/450, r.2 (effective from 1st December 2009).
As amended by S.S.I. 2019/452, r.2 (effective 10th May 2019).
98.13 inserted by S.S.I. 2009/450, r.2 (effective from 4th December 2009).
As amended by S.S.I. 2019/38, r.2 (effective 29th March 2019).

CHAPTER 97 APPLICATIONS FOR PARENTAL ORDERS UNDER THE HUMAN FERTILISATION AND EMBRYOLOGY ACT 2008

Chapter 97[1]

Applications for Parental Orders under the Human Fertilisation and Embryology Act 2008

Application and interpretation

97.1.—[2, 3](1) This Chapter applies to applications for parental orders under section 54 or 54A of the Human Fertilisation and Embryology Act 2008.

(2) In this Chapter, unless the context otherwise requires—

"the 2007 Act" means the Adoption and Children (Scotland) Act 2007;

"the 2008 Act" means the Human Fertilisation and Embryology Act 2008;

"Her Majesty's Forces" means the regular forces as defined in section 374 of the Armed Forces Act 2006;

"parental order" means an order under section 54 or 54A of the 2008 Act;

"Registrar General" means the Registrar General of Births, Deaths and Marriages for Scotland; and

"the Regulations" means the Human Fertilisation and Embryology (Parental Orders) Regulations 2010.

97.1

Disapplication of certain rules

97.2.[4] Unless otherwise provided in this Chapter, the following rules do not apply to a petition or note:—

rule 14.5 (first order in petitions);

rule 14.6(1)(d) (period of notice for lodging answers where service by advertisement);

rule 14.7 (intimation and service of petitions); rule 14.8 (procedure where answers lodged);

rule 14.9 (unopposed petitions).

97.2

Application for a parental order

97.3.—[5](1) An application for a parental order is to be made by petition in Form 97.3.

(2) The following documents must be lodged in process along with the petition—

    (a) an extract or a certified copy of any entry in the Register of Births relating to the child who is the subject of the application;

    (b) extracts or certified copies of any entries in the Register of Births relating to the birth of each of the petitioners;

    (c) in the case of an application under section 54(2)(a) of the 2008 Act, an extract or a certified copy of the entry in the Register of Marriages relating to the marriage of the petitioners;

    (d) in the case of an application under section 54(2)(b) of the 2008 Act, an extract or a certified copy of the entry in the Register of Civil Partnerships relating to the civil partnership of the petitioners; and

97.3

---

[1] Chap. 97 and r. 97.1 inserted by S.S.I. 2010 No. 136 (effective 6th April 2010).
[2] Chap. 97 and r. 97.1 inserted by S.S.I. 2010 No. 136 (effective 6th April 2010).
[3] Rule 97.1 amended by S.S.I. 2019 No. 147 para. 2 (effective 24th May 2019).
[4] Rule 97.2 inserted by S.S.I. 2010 No. 136 (effective 6th April 2010).
[5] Rule 97.3 inserted by S.S.I. 2010 No. 136 (effective 6th April 2010).

(e) any other document founded on by the petitioners in support of the terms
of the petition.

GENERAL NOTE.

97.3.1   An application for a parental order is made under s. 54 of the 2008 Act which replaced s. 30 of the Human Fertilisation and Embryology Act 1990.

The application is made by two people for an order providing for a child to be treated in law as the child of the applicants.

"PETITION".

97.3.2   A petition is presented to the Outer House: r. 14.2(h). The petition must be in Form 14.4 in the official printed form: rr. 4.1 and 14.4. The petition must be signed by counsel or other person having a right of audience: r. 4.2; and see r. 1.3(1) (definition of "counsel" and "other person having a right of audience") and note 1.3.4.

The petitioner must lodge the petition with the required steps of process: r. 4.4. A fee is payable on lodging the petition: see note 14.5.10.

On petitions generally, see Chap. 14.

Confidentiality of documents in process

97.4   **97.4.**—[1](1) Unless the court otherwise directs, all documents lodged in process (including the reports by the curator *ad litem* and reporting officer)—

(a) are to be available only to the court, the curator *ad litem*, the reporting officer and the parties; and

(b) must be treated as confidential by any persons involved in, or a party to, the proceedings and by the clerk of court.

(2) The curator *ad litem* and reporting officer—

(a) must treat all information obtained in the exercise of their duties as confidential; and

(b) must not disclose any such information to any person unless disclosure of such information is necessary for the purpose of their duties.

Orders for evidence

97.5   **97.5.**—[2](1) The court may, before determining the cause, order—

(a) production of further documents (including affidavits); or

(b) parole evidence.

(2) A party may apply by motion for the evidence of a person to be received in evidence by affidavit; and the court may make such order as it thinks fit.

Expenses

97.6   **97.6.**[3] The court may make such order as to expenses, including the expenses of a reporting officer, a curator ad litem, or any other person who attended a hearing, as it thinks fit.

Protection of identity of petitioners

97.7   **97.7.**—[4, 5](1) Where persons who propose to apply for a parental order wish to prevent their identities being disclosed to any person whose agreement to the parental order is required, they may, before presenting the petition, apply by letter to the Deputy Principal Clerk for a serial number to be assigned to them for all purposes connected with the petition.

(2) On receipt of an application under paragraph (1), the Deputy Principal Clerk must—

---

[1] Rule 97.4 inserted by S.S.I. 2010 No. 136 (effective 6th April 2010).
[2] Rule 97.5 inserted by S.S.I. 2010 No. 136 (effective 6th April 2010).
[3] Rule 97.6 inserted by S.S.I. 2010 No. 136 (effective 6th April 2010).
[4] Rule 97.7 inserted by S.S.I. 2010 No. 136 (effective 6th April 2010).
[5] Rule 97.7 amended by S.S.I. 2019 No. 147 para. 2 (effective 24th May 2019).

(a)   assign a serial number to the applicants; and

(b)   enter a note of the number opposite the names of the applicants in a register of serial numbers.

(3)   The contents of the register of serial numbers and the names of the persons to whom each number relates must be treated as confidential by the Deputy Principal Clerk and disclosed only to the court.

(4)   Where a serial number has been assigned under paragraph (2)(a), any form of agreement to a parental order under section 54(6) or 54A(5) of the 2008 Act—

(a)   must refer to the petitioners by means of the serial number assigned to them;

(b)   must not contain the names and designation of the petitioners; and

(c)   must specify the year in which the serial number was assigned.

Appointment of curator ad litem and reporting officer

97.8.—[1](1)   The court must, on the presentation of a petition under rule 97.3, appoint a curator *ad litem* and reporting officer.

97.8

(2)   The same person may be appointed as curator *ad litem* and reporting officer in the same petition, if the court considers that doing so is appropriate in the circumstances.

(3)   Where the court appoints a reporting officer and a curator *ad litem*, and there is an established panel of persons from whom the appointment may be made, the reporting officer and curator *ad item* must be selected from that panel unless the court considers that it would be appropriate to appoint a person who is not on the panel.

(4)   A person may, before presenting the petition, apply by letter to the Deputy Principal Clerk for the appointment of a reporting officer.

(5)   An application under paragraph (4) does not require to be intimated to any person, but must—

(a)   set out the reasons for which the appointment is sought;

(b)   be accompanied by an interlocutor sheet; and

(c)   be placed by the Deputy Principal Clerk before the Lord Ordinary for his or her decision.

(6)   The Deputy Principal Clerk must intimate the appointment of a curator *ad litem* and reporting officer under paragraph (1) or (4) to the petitioners and to the person or persons appointed.

(7)   The decision of the Lord Ordinary on an application under paragraph (4) is final and not subject to review.

(8)   The letter and the interlocutor sheet in an application under paragraph (4) must be kept in the Petition Department and subsequently placed in the process of the petition.

Duties of a reporting officer and curator ad litem

97.9.—[2, 3](1)[4]   The other duties of a reporting officer appointed under rule 97.8 prescribed for the purposes of section 108(1)(b) of the 2007 Act as modified and applied in relation to applications for parental orders by regulation 4 of, and Schedule 3 to the Regulations (rules: appointment of curators ad litem and reporting officers) are—

97.9

---

[1] Rule 97.8 inserted by S.S.I. 2010 No. 136 (effective 6th April 2010).
[2] Rule 97.9 inserted by S.S.I. 2010 No. 136 (effective 6th April 2010).
[3] Rule 97.9 amended by S.S.I. 2019 No. 147 para. 2 (effective 24th May 2019).
[4] Rule 97.9(1) amended by S.S.I. 2010 No. 136 (effective 15th June 2010).

(a) to ascertain the whereabouts of all persons whose agreement to the making of a parental order in respect of the child is required;

(b) to ascertain whether there is any person other than those mentioned in the petition upon whom notice of the petition should be served;

(c) in the case of each person who is not a petitioner and whose agreement to the making of a parental order is required under section 54(6) or 54A(5) of the 2008 Act—

    (i) to ascertain whether that person understands the effect of the parental order;

    (ii) to ascertain whether alternatives to a parental order have been discussed with that person;

    (iii) to confirm that that person understands that he or she may withdraw his or her agreement at any time before an order is made;

    (iv) to ascertain whether that person suffers or appears to suffer from a mental disorder within the meaning of section 328 of the Mental Health (Care and Treatment) (Scotland) Act 2003;

(d) to ascertain whether the conditions in subsections (2) to (8A) of section 54 or subsections (2) to (8) of section 54A of the 2008 Act have been satisfied;

(e) to draw to the attention of the court any matter which may be of assistance; and

(f) to report in writing on the matters mentioned in subparagraphs (a) to (e) to the court within 4 weeks from the date of the interlocutor appointing the reporting officer, or within such other period as the court may allow.

(2) A curator *ad litem* appointed under rule 97.8(1) must—

(a) have regard to safeguarding the interests of the child as his or her paramount duty;

(b) enquire, so far as he or she considers necessary, into the facts and circumstances averred in the petition;

(c) establish that the petitioners understand the nature and effect of a parental order and in particular that the making of the order will render them responsible for the maintenance and upbringing of the child;

(d) ascertain whether any money or other benefit which is prohibited by section 54(8) or 54A(7) of the 2008 Act (prohibition on gift or receipt of money or other benefit) has been received or agreed upon;

(e) ascertain whether it may be in the interests of the welfare of the child that the court should make the parental order subject to particular terms and conditions or require the petitioners to make special provision for the child and, if so, what provision;

(f) ascertain whether it would be better for the child that the court should make the order than it should not make the order;

(g) ascertain whether the proposed parental order is likely to safeguard and promote the welfare of the child throughout the child's life; and

(h) ascertain from the child whether he or she wishes to express a view and, where a child indicates his or her wish to express a view, ascertain that view.

(3) Subject to paragraph (4), the curator *ad litem* must report in writing on the matters mentioned in paragraph (2) to the court within 4 weeks from the date of the interlocutor appointing the curator, or within such other period as the court in its discretion may allow.

(4) Subject to any order made by the court under rule 97.11(1), the views of the child ascertained in terms of paragraph (2)(h) may, if the curator *ad litem* considers appropriate, be conveyed to the court orally.

(5) The reporting officer must, on completion of his or her report in terms of paragraph (1), in addition send to the Deputy Principal Clerk—

    (a) a copy of his or her report for each party; and

    (b) any agreement for the purposes of section 54(6) or 54A(5) of the 2008 Act.

(6) The curator ad litem must, on completion of his or her report in terms of paragraph (3), in addition send a copy of it for each party to the Deputy Principal Clerk.

Agreement

97.10.—[1,2](1) The agreement of a person required by section 54(6) or 54A(5) of the 2008 Act is to be in Form 97.10.

97.10

(2)[3] The form of agreement mentioned in paragraph (1) must be witnessed—

    (a) where it is executed in Scotland, by the reporting officer appointed under rule 97.8;

    (b) where it is executed outwith Scotland but within the United Kingdom, by a justice of the peace or commissioner for oaths; or

    (c) where it is executed outwith the United Kingdom—

        (i) if the person who executes the form is serving in Her Majesty's Forces, by an officer holding a commission in those forces; or

        (ii) in any other case, by a British diplomatic or consular official or any person authorised to administer an oath or affirmation under the law of the place where the agreement is executed.

Procedure where child wishes to express a view

97.11.—[4,5](1) Where a child to whom section 54(11) or 54A(11) of the 2008 Act applies indicates his or her wish to express a view, the court, without prejudice to rule 97.9(2)(h)—

97.11

    (a) may order such procedural steps to be taken as the court considers appropriate to ascertain the views of that child; and

    (b) must not make a parental order unless an opportunity has been given for the views of that child to be obtained or heard.

(2) Where the views of the child, whether under this rule or under rule 97.9(2)(h) have been recorded in writing, the court may direct that such a written record is to—

    (a) be sealed in an envelope marked "Views of the child - confidential";

    (b) be available to the court only;

    (c) not be opened by any other person; and

    (d) not form a borrowable part of process.

Hearing

97.12.—[6](1) On receipt of the reports referred to in rule 97.9, the Deputy Principal Clerk shall—

97.12

    (a) cause the reports and any other documents to be lodged in process;

---

[1] Rule 97.10 inserted by S.S.I. 2010 No. 136 (effective 6th April 2010).
[2] Rule 97.10 amended by S.S.I. 2019 No. 147 para. 2 (effective 24th May 2019).
[3] Rule 97.10(2)(a) amended by S.S.I. 2010 No. 205 (effective 15th June 2010).
[4] Rule 97.11 inserted by S.S.I. 2010 No. 136 (effective 6th April 2010).
[5] Rule 97.11 amended by S.S.I. 2019 No. 147 para. 2 (effective 24th May 2019).
[6] Rule 97.12 inserted by S.S.I. 2010 No. 136 (effective 6th April 2010).

(b)   give written intimation to each party of the lodging of those documents and make them available to each party; and

(c)   within 7 days thereafter, cause—

    (i)   the petition to be put out on the By Order Roll before the Lord Ordinary; and

    (ii)   written intimation of the date of the hearing on the By Order Roll to be given to each party.

(2)   At the hearing on the By Order Roll, the court—

(a)   must pronounce an interlocutor appointing the petition to a hearing to determine the petition; and

(b)   may, in such interlocutor—

    (i)   order any person whose agreement is required to attend such hearing;

    (ii)   order intimation of the date of the hearing to any person not mentioned in paragraph 3(a), (b) or (c); and

    (iii)   order the reporting officer or curator ad litem to perform additional duties to assist the court in determining the petition.

(3)   The petitioners or, where a serial number has been assigned under rule 97.7(1) the Deputy Principal Clerk, must intimate a copy of the petition along with a notice of intimation in Form 97.12 to—

(a)   every person whose whereabouts are known to them and whose agreement is required;

(b)[1]   the reporting officer appointed under rule 97.8;

(c)   the curator *ad litem* appointed under rule 97.8(1); and

(d)   any person on whom intimation has been ordered under paragraph (2)(b)(ii).

(4)   At the hearing ordered under paragraph (2)(a)—

(a)   the petitioners, the reporting officer and the curator ad litem must, if required by the court, appear and may be represented;

(b)   any person required by the court to attend the hearing must appear and may be represented; and

(c)   any person to whom intimation was made under paragraph (3)(a) or (d) may appear or be represented.

Applications under sections 22 and 24 of the 2007 Act

97.13   **97.13.**[2]   An application under section 22(3) (restrictions on removal: application for parental order pending), section 24(1) (return of child removed in breach of certain provisions) or section 24(2) (order directing person not to remove child) of the 2007 Act all as modified and applied in relation to applications for parental orders by regulation 4 of, and Schedule 3 to, the Regulations, is to be made by note in the process of the petition for a parental order to which it relates.

Amendment of parental order

97.14   **97.14.**—[3](1)   An application under paragraph 7 of Schedule 1 to the 2007 Act, as modified and applied in relation to parental orders by regulation 4 of, Schedule 3 to, the Regulations (amendment of orders and rectification of registers), is to be made by petition.

---

[1] Rule 97.12(3)(b) amended by S.S.I. 2010 No. 205 (effective 15th June 2010).
[2] Rule 97.13 inserted by S.S.I. 2010 No. 136 (effective 6th April 2010).
[3] Rule 97.14 inserted by S.S.I. 2010 No. 136 (effective 6th April 2010).

(2)   The court may order the petitioners to intimate the petition to such persons as it considers appropriate.

(3)   Subject to paragraph (4), rule 97.2 does not apply to an application mentioned in paragraph (1).

(4)   An application mentioned in paragraph (1) shall not be intimated on the walls of the court or advertised.

Communication to the Registrar General

97.15.[1]   The communication to the Registrar General of a parental order required to be made by the clerk of court under paragraph 4(1) of Schedule 1 to the 2007 Act, as modified and applied in relation to parental orders by regulation 4 of, and Schedule 3 to, the Regulations (registration of parental orders), is to be made by sending a certified copy of the order to the Registrar General in a sealed envelope marked "Confidential".

97.15

Extract of order

97.16.[2]   An extract of a parental order must not be issued except by order of the court on an application to it—

97.16

(a)   where there is a petition for the parental order depending before the court, by motion in that process; or

(b)   where there is no such petition depending before the court, by petition.

Final procedure

97.17.—[3](1)   Immediately after the communication is made under rule 97.15 or immediately upon an extract of the order being issued under rule 97.16 the clerk of court or the Extractor, as the case may be, must—

97.17

(a)   place the whole process in an envelope bearing only—

(i)   the name of the petitioners;

(ii)   the full name of the child to whom the process relates; and

(iii)   the date of the order; and (b) seal the envelope and mark it "confidential".

(2)   The envelope referred to in paragraph (1) is not to be unsealed by the clerk of court or any other person having control of the records of the court, and the process is not to be made accessible to any person for one hundred years after the date for the granting of the order, except—

(a)   to the person who is the subject of the parental order after he or she has reached the age of 16 years;

(b)   to a person on an application made by petition presented by him or her to the court setting forth the reason for which access to the process is required.".

---

[1] Rule 97.15 inserted by S.S.I. 2010 No. 136 (effective 6th April 2010).
[2] Rule 97.16 inserted by S.S.I. 2010 No. 136 (effective 6th April 2010).
[3] Rule 97.17 inserted by S.S.I. 2010 No. 136 (effective 6th April 2010).

Chapter 98[1]

Coroners and Justice Act 2009

Applications

98.1.—[2](1)   An application under section 166(5) of the Coroners and Justice Act 2009 for the court to determine that an exploitation proceeds order is to cease to have effect or to reduce the recoverable amount by such amount (if any) as it considers just and reasonable shall be made by motion.

98.1

GENERAL NOTE.

An exploitation proceeds order may be made on application (by petition) under s. 155 of the Coroners and Justice Act 2009 by an enforcement authority (in Scotland, the Scottish Ministers). The court may make the order if satisfied on the balance of probabilities that a person is a qualifying offender (see s. 156) and has obtained exploitation proceeds from a relevant offence (see s. 159). The order requires the respondent to pay a recoverable amount in respect of exploitation proceeds obtained by the respondent from a relevant offence to the enforcement authority that applied for the order. These provisions are concerned with recovery of the proceeds or profits derived by an offender from exploitation of material (such as memoirs) relating to the offence in which the respondent took part.

98.1.1

Under s. 166(5) the respondent may apply to the court to determine that the order is to cease to have effect or to reduce the recoverable amount.

"MOTION".

See Chap. 23.

98.1.2

---

[1] Chap. 98 and r. 98.1 inserted by S.S.I. 2010 No. 136 (effective 6th April 2010).
[2] Chap. 98 and r. 98.1 inserted by S.S.I. 2010 No. 136 (effective 6th April 2010).

Chapter 99[1]

Energy Act 2008—Interdicts

Applications for interdict against unknown persons

99.1.—[2](1) Paragraph (2) applies to applications for interdict under sections 12 or 26 of the Energy Act 2008.

(2) Interdict may be granted against a person whose identity is unknown to the applicant and "the respondent" is the person against whom interdict is sought.

(3) Paragraphs (4) to (8) apply where an interdict is sought against such a person.

(4) An application for interdict under this Chapter is to be made by petition.

(5) The statement of facts must include averments stating—

   (a) that the applicant has been unable to ascertain the respondent's identity within the time reasonably available to the applicant;

   (b) the steps taken by the applicant to ascertain the respondent's identity;

   (c) a description of the respondent and, where relevant, the means by which the respondent is described in the petition;

   (d) that the description of the respondent is the best the applicant is able to provide.

(6) The court shall order the taking of such steps to make the respondent aware of the application as the court considers appropriate in the circumstances, having regard to the importance of the respondent being so aware; and the taking of such steps will constitute service.

(7) Such steps may include—

   (a) service in accordance with Part I of Chapter 16 (service and intimation);

   (b) intimation to a person;

   (c) publication in a newspaper;

   (d) publication using electronic means; or

   (e) affixing relevant documentation prominently in a particular place or on a particular structure, vehicle or vessel.

(8) The applicant must lodge in process such documentary evidence as may be ordered by the court to show that those steps have been carried out.

99.1

GENERAL NOTE.

The Secretary of State may apply for an interdict under s. 12 of the Energy Act 2008 to restrain an actual or apprehended breach of s. 2(1) of the 2008 Act (an activity in relation to importation or storage of combustible gas without a licence).

The Scottish Ministers may apply for an interdict under s. 12 of the Energy Act 2008 to restrain an actual or apprehended breach of s. 17(1) of the 2008 Act (an activity in relation to storage of carbon dioxide without a licence).

99.1.1

"PETITION".

A petition is presented to the Outer House: r. 14.2(h). The petition must be in Form 14.4 in the official printed form: rr. 4.1 and 14.4. The petition must be signed by counsel or other person having a right of audience: r. 4.2; and see r. 1.3(1) (definition of "counsel" and "other person having a right of audience") and note 1.3.4.

The petitioner must lodge the petition with the required steps of process: r. 4.4. A fee is payable on lodging the petition: see note 14.5.10.

On petitions generally, see Chap. 14.

99.1.2

---

[1] Chap. 99 and r. 99.1 inserted by S.S.I. 2010 No. 205 (effective 15th June 2010).
[2] Chap. 99 and r. 99.1 inserted by S.S.I. 2010 No. 205 (effective 15th June 2010).

Interpretation and application

100.1.—[1](1)   In this Chapter—

"the 2010 Act" means the Arbitration (Scotland) Act 2010;

"Convention award" means an award made in pursuance of a written arbitration agreement in a territory of a state (other than the United Kingdom) which is a party to the New York Convention on the Recognition and Enforcement of Foreign Arbitral Awards;

"Scottish Arbitration Rules" means the Scottish Arbitration Rules set out in schedule 1 to the 2010 Act;

"tribunal" means a sole arbitrator or panel of arbitrators.

(2)   Subject to paragraph (3), this Chapter applies to applications and appeals made under the 2010 Act (including applications and appeals made under the Scottish Arbitration Rules).

(3)   Rules 100.5 and 100.7 do not apply to an application under section 19(2) of the 2010 for enforcement of a Convention award.

GENERAL NOTE.

This Chapter provides rules for the making of applications under the Arbitration (Scotland) Act 2010 which came into force on 7th June 2010 in relation to all arbitrations begun on or after that date except for referrals to arbitration under statute (Arbitration (Scotland) Act 2010 (Commencement No. 1 and Transitional Provisions) Order 2010, arts. 2(2) and 3(1)(b) [S.S.I. 2010 No. 195]). The 2010 Act, and this Chapter, do not apply to causes relating to arbitrations begun before 7th June 2010 nor to causes relating to arbitration (whether or not begun before that date) raised or depending before the court before 7th June 2010 (2010 Order, art. 3(1)(b)). Such causes are governed by other provisions of the R.C.S. 1994 (e.g. Chap. 58 relating to judicial review) or other enactments or by the common law applicable to procedure or by a mixture of these.

The 2010 Act established a statutory code for arbitration in Scotland influenced by the UNCITRAL Model Law on International Commercial Arbitration. The 2010 Act is noteworthy for having main provisions which form part of Scots law in general in relation to both Scottish and foreign arbitrations and awards and an equally important Sch. 1 which contains a body of statutory rules which are known as the Scottish Arbitration Rules and apply only to Scottish-seated arbitrations. A Scottish seated arbitration is where the lex arbitri or law governing the arbitral procedure is Scots law. Most of the Scottish Arbitration Rules are default rules in the sense that parties can agree to opt out of or modify them: see 2010 Act, s. 9. Some such Rules however, and in particular the provisions enabling appeals on the grounds of lack of jurisdiction and serious irregularity are mandatory. Both the Scottish Arbitration Rules and the main provisions of the 2010 Act provide for appeals and applications of various types to be made to the court and these are discussed below.

Given that Chap. 100 was not enacted with the use of powers given by the 2010 Act, it follows that the definitions in the Act do not necessarily apply to the words used in the Chapter.

In *Arbitration Appeal (No. 4 of 2020)*, 2021 S.L.T. 1105 (OH), 1111 at para. [17], Lord Clark held that, in order for the terms of the arbitration agreement to be inconsistent with or disapply the right to seek leave for a legal error appeal, it is necessary to have sufficiently clear wording. While no express reference to s. 9 of the 2010 Act or r. 69 of the Scottish Arbitration Rules is required, the language must be sufficiently clear to indicate that a right to appeal has been agreed to be excluded or waived. The expression "final and binding" has been used in very many arbitration agreements over many years, including those entered into well before the 2010 Act. The meaning of that phrase is that the award is final and binding in the sense that it resolves the issues raised in the arbitration and this results in the principle of *res judicata* being applicable to those issues. The wording is therefore not of itself inconsistent with a right to appeal or seek leave to appeal in terms of the Scottish Arbitration Rules and it does not exclude or waive any such rights.

APPLICATIONS ANCILLARY TO ONGOING ARBITRATION.

One of the principal aims of arbitration is to allow a dispute to be resolved by an arbitrator or arbitrators in a prompt and cost-effective manner which allows for a flexibility of procedure not allowed for by the normal process of litigation in a court.

The Scottish Arbitration Rules give arbitrators extensive powers of case management to allow the dispute to be resolved in a prompt, cost-effective and fair manner. It is a founding principle of the 2010 Act that the court should not intervene in an arbitration except as provided by the Act itself: 2010 Act, s. 1. However, notwithstanding the powers given to the arbitrator by the parties and the Scottish Arbitration

---

[1] Chapter 100 and r. 100.1 inserted by S.S.I. 2010 No. 205 (effective 7th June 2010).

Rules (contained in Sched. 1 to the 2010 Act), no arbitrator has power over third parties such as witnesses who are not parties or havers of documents. Nor can an arbitrator enforce an interim order that he makes. It is also self-evident that arbitrators cannot appoint themselves or have the final say as to the fees and expenses that are due to them.

For all of these reasons it is necessary for the parties to be able to go to the court to allow it to exercise its powers to assist the arbitration. In response to this need the 2010 Act provides for parties to an arbitration to make a number of applications to the court in connection with the ongoing arbitration or issues relating to expenses arising out of it. Thus a party can apply to the court under the following provisions of the Scottish Arbitration Rules:

Rule 7(6) (appointment of arbitrator)

Rule 12 (removal of arbitrator)

Rule 13 (dismissal of arbitrator)

Rule 15(2) (authorisation of resignation of arbitrator)

Rule 16(1) (orders as to fees, expenses and liability consequent on cessation of arbitrator's tenure)

Rule 43 (variation of time limits set by parties)

Rule 45 (attendance of witnesses and disclosure of documentary and other material evidence)

Rule 46 (orders as to appointment of safeguarder, securing amounts in dispute, diligence on the dependence, or interim diligence, interdict or interim interdict, or recovery of evidence under s. 1 of the Administration of Justice (Scotland) Act 1972)

Rule 56(2) (issue of award pending resolution of dispute over arbitrator's fees e.t.c.)

Rule 58(3) (extension of time to seek correction of award)

APPEALS AND THE SUPERVISORY ROLE OF THE COURT

100.1.3   Aside from the court having a role supporting the arbitration, it also has a supervisory role. This is to ensure the quality of the decision-making procedure used by an arbitrator, and to a limited extent the quality of any award (formerly known as a decree arbitral) made by the arbitrator. Again, this has been recognised internationally and in Scotland over many years. Until the 2010 Act, the supervisory role was exercised by the court by means of its common law supervisory jurisdiction over inferior tribunals. Until the 2010 Act, the supervisory jurisdiction could be exercised as part of a number of different procedures. A party to an arbitration could raise an ordinary action of reduction of the award or interdict of an apprehended or ongoing step of procedure or specific implement of a failure to act. From 1985 the ordinary action seeking these remedies was replaced by a petition for judicial review under what is now Chap. 58 of the R.C.S. 1994: see notes 58.1.1 and 58.1.2. Alternatively, a party could at any time until the issue of the final award ask the arbitrator under s.3 of the Administration of Justice (Scotland) Act 1972 to state a case to the Inner House asking it to give a binding opinion on any question of law which had arisen. Finally, if an award was issued and the successful party raised an action seeking implement of the award, for example through seeking an order for payment, the unsuccessful party could seek to invoke the court's supervisory jurisdiction with the result that the award would be reduced by way of exception (*ope exceptionis*): see r. 53.8 and note 53.8.1.

Following the 2010 Act these common law methods of challenge to the arbitral procedure and any award following thereon are no longer competent (2010 Act, s.13). Nor is the stated case procedure competent (2010 Act, Sched. 2). In their place the 2010 Act has provided a comprehensive code in the Scottish Arbitration Rules for the making of challenges to arbitral procedure and awards. It has also provided more limited powers to allow parties to obtain the binding decision of the court on certain issues. This code allows for the challenging of awards by means of appeals and the obtaining of binding opinions by means of references. In one limited respect, namely a challenge as to the jurisdiction of the arbitrator is it competent to make the challenge in defence to proceedings for enforcement of the award: 2010 Act, s.13(1) and (2)). Where the party making such a jurisdictional challenge has participated in the arbitration, it is implicit that the challenge in defence will only be heard if the party has made it previously to the arbitrator: 2010 Act, Sched.1, r. 76(1) and (2).

THREE TYPES OF APPEAL

100.1.4   Appeals are available to a party in respect of the lack of jurisdiction of the arbitrator to make an award or serious irregularity of the arbitrator and in limited cases in respect of an error of law by the arbitrator. The meaning of "serious irregularity" is defined in the 2010 Act: 2010 Act, Sched.1, r. 68(2) and see the commentary thereon in F. Davidson, H.R. Dundas and D. Bartos *Arbitration (Scotland) Act 2010* (Edinburgh: W.Green 2010, pp.295-303).

Challenges to an award for lack of jurisdiction or serious irregularity stand in contrast to challenges to an award in relation to the decision on merits of the dispute. In an arbitration the parties have entrusted the decision on the merits of their dispute to the arbitrator or arbitrators. It follows that any challenge in respect of the merits should be narrowly circumscribed. Indeed under the 2010 Act the parties are free to decide that there should be no appeal on the merits at all (2010 Act, s.9). For a description of or that there should be no reference to the court for a binding opinion on a point of law (2010 Act, s.9). Any agreement that the old stated case procedure should be disapplied is deemed to be an exclusion of an appeal on the merits and an exclusion of a reference for a binding opinion on a question of law. If the parties have not excluded challenges in respect of the merits, the 2010 Act in any event circumscribes challenges on the merits to errors on a point of Scots law where the parties agree to the making of such a challenge or court has first granted leave to appeal: 2010 Act, Sched. 1, rr. 69(1) and 70(2).

A party can appeal to the court and make applications to the court incidental to the appeal under the following Scottish Arbitration Rules (contained in Sched. 1 to the 2010 Act):

Rule 21(1) (appeal against arbitrator's separate decision on jurisdiction)
Rule 67 (appeal against award on merits on basis of lack of jurisdiction)
Rule 68 (appeal against award on basis of serious irregularity)
Rule 69 (appeal against award on the basis of error of law)
Rule 70 (application for leave to appeal under Rule 69)
Rule 71(8) (application for order requiring arbitrator to state reasons)
Rule 71(10) (order for security for expenses pending appeal/application for leave)
Rule 71(12) (order for security for sum due under award pending appeal/application for leave)

During the course of the arbitration a party can, in certain limited circumstances, apply to the court for a binding decision on the question of the arbitrator's jurisdiction or on point of Scots law under the following Scottish Arbitration Rules (contained in schedule 1 to the 2010 Act) :

Rule 22 (court's decision as to jurisdiction)
Rule 41 (court's decision as to point of Scots law).

For further details of the grounds on which appeals and applications to the court for a binding decision can be made see the commentary thereon in F. Davidson, H.R. Dundas and D. Bartos, *Arbitration (Scotland) Act 2010* (Edinburgh: W.Green 2010, pp.154-155; and 210-212).

The final role of the court in relation to arbitration relates to enforcement of an arbitral award (decree arbitral). The 2010 Act provides for the enforcement of both Scottish-seated arbitral awards and other awards all of which can be seen as foreign awards. A party can seek enforcement under the following provisions of the 2010 Act:

s.12 (enforcement of Scottish and non New York Convention foreign awards)
s.19 (enforcement of New York Convention awards).

ENFORCEMENT OF CONVENTION AWARDS

Since 1975 the United Kingdom has been party to the 1958 New York Convention for the Recognition and Enforcement of Foreign Arbitral Awards. This is an international treaty under which the state parties to the Convention agreed under certain conditions to recognise and allow the enforcement of arbitral awards seated in other state parties. There are now 148 states which are parties to the New York Convention. A copy of the Convention and further details on states that are party to the Convention can be obtained via the UNCITRAL website at www.uncitral.org. An arbitral award made in the territory of a state other than the United Kingdom which is party to the Convention and which was made pursuant to a written agreement or clause submitting the dispute to arbitration is known in Chap. 100 as a "Convention award".   **100.1.5**

The New York Convention was originally implemented by the Arbitration Act 1975 under which a party seeking recognition or enforcement of Convention award required to raise an ordinary action seeking payment under or other implement of the award. The 1975 Act, in so far as it applied to Scotland, was repealed by the 2010 Act and the opportunity was taken to reform the method of enforcement of a Convention award. Unfortunately the rules on enforcement of Convention awards were not put into one place. Thus the rules are to be found in rr. 100.2, 100.3, 100.4 and 100.9 but also in rr. 62.56 to 62.60. Rules 100.5 and 100.7 do not apply to an application to enforce a Convention award.

Proceedings before a nominated judge

100.2.[1] All proceedings in the Outer House in a cause to which this Chapter applies shall be brought before a judge of the court nominated by the Lord President as an arbitration judge or, where no such judge is available, any other judge of the court (including the vacation judge).   **100.2**

NOMINATED JUDGE.

The nominated judges are Lords Menzies, Hodge, Glennie and Malcolm: P.N. No. 4 of 2011.   **100.2.1**

Procedure in causes under the 2010 Act

100.3.[2] Subject to the provisions of the Scottish Arbitration Rules and this Chapter, the procedure in a cause under the Scottish Arbitration Rules shall be such as the judge dealing with the cause shall determine.   **100.3**

---

[1] Rule 100.2 inserted by S.S.I. 2010 No. 205 (effective 7th June 2010).
[2] Rule 100.3 inserted by S.S.I. 2010 No. 205 (effective 7th June 2010).

GENERAL NOTE.

This rule applies to applications or appeals under the Scottish Arbitration Rules and not under the main body of the 2010 Act. Therefore it does not apply to petitions to enforce awards or to other applications which are covered by the main body of the 2010 Act. It is unclear why the rule does not cover such applications.

Rule 100.3 gives the judge a discretion to decide on the procedure in the application or appeal consistent with the interests of justice. The intent is that the procedure is as flexible as possible (*Arbitration Application No. 3 of 2011*, 2012 S.L.T. 150, para. [9]).

Rule 100.3 must be read with the subsequent rules 100.4 and 100.5. Rule 100.5 provides that an application or appeal under the Act (except for the enforcement of a Convention award) is to be made by petition unless a petition is already depending before the court in relation to the same arbitration process. Rule 100.4 excludes the application of the standard rules which require an automatic first order for intimation, service or advertisement of the petition to be made upon its presentation to the court, the lodging of answers by a respondent and upon the lodging of answers the making of a motion by the petitioner to move the court for further procedure. Petition procedure is inherently flexible and it is unclear why these standard rules have been excluded.

Disapplication of certain rules

100.4 **100.4.**[1] The following rules shall not apply to a cause under this Part—

rule 6.2 (fixing and allocation of diets in Outer House);

rule 14.5 (first order in petitions);

rule 14.6 (period of notice for lodging answers);

rule 14.8 (procedure where answers lodged).

GENERAL NOTE.

This rule applies to all applications or appeals under the 2010 Act whether or not under the Scottish Arbitration Rules. See note 100.3.1.

Application or appeal under the 2010 Act

100.5 **100.5.**—[2](1) Subject to paragraph (2), an application or appeal under the 2010 Act shall be made by petition.

(2) If proceedings are depending before the court under paragraph (1) in relation to the same arbitration process, an application under the 2010 Act shall be made by note in the process of the petition.

(3) Upon lodging a petition or note under paragraph (1) or (2), the petitioner or noter must enrol a motion for intimation and service of the petition or note and the court may make such order as is appropriate in the circumstances of the case.

(4) The court may make an order for intimation and service of the petition or note at the address of a party's agent or other person acting for that party in the arbitration process and the service will be effective if carried out in accordance with that order.

(5) Upon expiry of any period of notice following intimation and service of the petition or note, the petitioner or noter shall enrol a motion for further procedure and the court may make such order as is appropriate in the circumstances of the case, including, where appropriate, an order disposing of the petition or note.

GENERAL NOTE.

Rule 100.5 does not apply to applications for the enforcement of a Convention award. Instead, r.62.57 provides that such an application is to be made by petition, or in certain cases by note and in relation to such applications the reader is referred to r. 62.57.

The basic rule is that all applications or appeals under the 2010 Act are to be made by petition. There is no distinction between applications or appeals. Despite the terms of r. 100.5, however, r. 100.8 provides that an application for leave to appeal under r. 70(1) to (6) of the Scottish Arbitration Rules (SAR) is to be by motion in the petition or note forming the actual appeal under r. 69 of the SAR which is to be presented before leave has been granted. See note 100.8.2.

---

[1] Rule 100.4 inserted by S.S.I. 2010 No. 205 (effective 7th June 2010).
[2] Rule 100.5 inserted by S.S.I. 2010 No. 205 (effective 7th June 2010).

PETITION OR NOTE.

As noted the basic form of application or appeal is in the form of a petition. However where there is a petition which is still "depending" before the court which relates to the same arbitration process, the application must be by note. A petition is depending before the court from the time that the court makes its first order in the petition process. It ceases to be depending when the final decree is made. For the meaning of final decree, see note 4.15.2(2). A final decree requires the determination of liability for expenses of the petition process, although the expenses have yet to be quantified.

"PETITION".

A petition is presented to the Outer House: r. 14.2(h). The petition must be in Form 14.4 in the official printed form: rr. 4.1 and 14.4. The petition must be signed by counsel or other person having a right of audience: r. 4.2; and see r. 1.3(1) (definition of "counsel" and "other person having a right of audience") and note 1.3.4. Aside from compliance with r.14.4, the petition if it is a referral to the Outer House under rr.22 and 41 of the Scottish Arbitration Rules, or an appeal under r.67, 68, or 69 of those Rules, must comply with r.100.8 of R.C.S. 1994.

100.5.3

The petitioner must lodge the petition with the required steps of process: r. 4.4. A fee is payable on lodging.

On petitions generally, see Chap. 14 but it must be remembered that rr.14.5, 14.6 and 14.8 do not apply to petitions under the 2010 Act.

"NOTE".

For procedure by note, see r. 15.2; but it must be remembered that rr.14.5, 14.6 and 14.8 do not apply to notes under the 2010 Act.

100.5.4

MOTION FOR INTIMATION AND SERVICE.

Given that a petitioner or noter must at the outset lodge a motion for intimation and service, it is unclear why the presumed automatic intimation and service provisions of r. 14.5 has been disapplied to petitions and notes under the 2010 Act. There may be situations where intimation and service may be inappropriate. In such a situation under r. 14.5 the petitioner or noter would have enrolled a motion with the court for dispensation with intimation and service. Under r. 100.5(3) the petitioner and noter is put to the needless trouble and expense of having to enrol a motion for intimation and service and if necessary seek dispensation with that very requirement.

The clue to the disapplication of r. 14.5 is to be found in the observations in *Arbitration Application No. 3 of 2011*, 2012 S.L.T. 150 in para. [15]. That was a legal error appeal. Such appeals usually require to be made with leave but r. 100.8 requires a petition or note to be lodged before leave has been obtained and while a motion for leave still remains to be determined. For that reason it was not thought appropriate for answers to be ordered while the appeal remained prima facie incompetent because of the absence of leave and the motion for leave had not yet been disposed of: See notes 100.8.1 to 100.8.3 below.

INTIMATION AND SERVICE TO PARTY'S AGENT OR REPRESENTATIVE.

Normally intimation and service must be made to a party unless the party's agent (solicitor) has authority to accept intimation and service. Where there is an ongoing arbitration, its conduct may be in the hands of a party's solicitor or an unqualified representative who will have the party's mandate to do so. Given that many applications under the 2010 Act will be in relation to ongoing arbitrations (before the final award), and in order to expedite matters, the court has a power to order intimation and service to the party's solicitor or other representative acting in the arbitration process.

The position may be different once a final award has been issued and there is no longer an ongoing arbitral process.

MOTION FOR FURTHER PROCEDURE

For motions, generally, see Chap. 23. The purpose of intimation and service is to allow the intimation of opposition to the petition or note. In a standard process the order for intimation and service requires intimation of opposition to be made through the lodging of answers and the petitioner or noter then seeks an order for further procedure (rr. 14.6 and 14.8). Even though rr. 14.6 and 14.8 are disapplied this is what is contemplated in r. 100.5: *Arbitration Application No.3 of 2011*, 2012 S.L.T. 150, para. [10]. The further procedure sought will depend on the nature of the application or appeal, whether answers have been lodged, and if so the nature of the opposition expressed in the answers.

Thus where there are no disputed facts the further procedure may take the form of a hearing which is a debate. If there are disputed facts then further adjustment of petition and answers may be required either generally or restricted to the specific factual issue which is in dispute, with the fixing of a hearing thereafter. The court can order witness statements or affidavits to be produced: *Arbitration Application No.3 of 2011*, 2012 S.L.T. 150, above, para.[10]. Ultimately it can order a hearing to take place in the form of a proof. See the note to r. 14.8.

Application for attendance of witnesses or disclosure of evidence

100.6

100.6.[1] In relation to a petition or note lodged under rule 45 of the Scottish Arbitration Rules (court's power to order attendance of witnesses and disclosure of evidence), intimation and service of the petition or note is not required.

GENERAL NOTE.

The purpose of r. 100.6 is unclear and its effect bizarre. Rule 45 of the Scottish Arbitration Rules (SAR) allows a party or an arbitrator to apply to the court for an order requiring any person (a) to attend a hearing for the purposes of giving evidence in the arbitration or (b) to disclose documents or other material evidence to the arbitrator or arbitrators. Rule 45 of the SAR also makes it clear that the court is not to order any person to give any evidence or to disclose anything which the person would be entitled to refuse to give or disclose in civil proceedings. This exception is presumably directed at issues of confidential privilege: see notes 35.2.7 and 35.2.8

If a party seeks the attendance of a witness, then r. 45 of the SAR contemplates that objection may be taken to the witness being ordered to attend on the grounds that the evidence sought to be obtained from him is privileged and confidential. In addition objection may be taken on the grounds of the irrelevance of the evidence. Given the scope for such objections it is quite unclear why there should be a rule stating that intimation and service, presumably to either to the other party or to the witness, is not required. Perhaps r. 100.6 is based on the old common law under which a party could, after an arbiter had certified that there was good reason to do so, apply to the court for a warrant to cite the witness to attend to give evidence. Rule 45 of the SAR, however, represents a departure from the common law in that it involves an order with the potential sanction of a contempt of court being made on the witness to attend rather than a warrant being given to a party to enable citation. Failure to comply with a citation may result in arrest but is not prima facie a contempt of court.

The position is even more unsatisfactory in relation to the recovery of documents. Clearly objection can be taken to the disclosure of documents on the grounds of privilege and confidentiality and immateriality (e.g. fishing for evidence). How, if intimation is not required, is a party or a haver to be given an opportunity to object to a proposed order?

Averments in petitions and notes under the 2010 Act

100.7

100.7.—[2](1) The petitioner or noter must set out in the petition or note the facts and circumstances on which the petition or note is founded and the relief claimed.

(2) In particular, any—

    (a) application under rule 22 (referral of point of jurisdiction) or rule 41 (referral of point of law) of the Scottish Arbitration Rules, or

    (b) appeal under rule 67(1) (jurisdictional appeal), rule 68(1) (serious irregularity appeal) or rule 69(1) (legal error appeal) of the Scottish Arbitration Rules,

should, so far as is necessary, identify the matters referred to in paragraph (3).

(3) The following matters should be identified—

    (a) the parties to the cause and the arbitration from which the cause arises;

    (b) the relevant rule of the Scottish Arbitration Rules or other provision of the 2010 Act under which the petition or note has been lodged;

    (c) any special capacity in which the petitioner or noter is acting or any special capacity in which any other party to the proceedings is acting;

    (d) a summary of the circumstances out of which the application or appeal arises;

    (e) the grounds on which the application or appeal proceeds;

    (f) in the case of an appeal under rule 67(1), whether the appellant seeks the variation or the setting aside of an award (or part of it);

    (g) in the case of an appeal under rule 69(1), whether the appeal is made with the agreement of the parties to the arbitration;

    (h) any relevant requirements of the Scottish Arbitration Rules which have been met.

---

[1] Rule 100.6 inserted by S.S.I. 2010 No. 205 (effective 7th June 2010).
[2] Rule 100.7 inserted by S.S.I. 2010 No. 205 (effective 7th June 2010).

General note.

Rule 100.7 can be seen as applicable to referrals under rr. 22 and 41 of the Scottish Arbitration Rules and to appeals under rr. 67, 68 and 69 of those Rules. For some reason it is not applied expressly to an appeal under Rule 21, but it is suggested that its additional requirements for petitions or notes should be followed for such an appeal also. Rule 100.7(1) merely re-states the generality of rr. 14.4(2)(a) and 15.2(2) which apply to all petitions and notes respectively and its purpose is unclear.

The provisions of r. 14.4 (for petitions) and r. 15.2 (for notes) should be followed in addition to the provisions of r. 100.7. Subject to the terms of those rules it should not be necessary to set everything out at length in the petition or note: *Arbitration Application No.3 of 2011*, 2012 S.L.T. 150, para. [9]. As was observed in the last mentioned case, the basis of the challenge, placed (so far as relevant) in the context of the underlying dispute and what has happened in the arbitration should be set out as simply as possible since by the time that an appeal comes to be made the underlying dispute will usually be very familiar to all of the parties. Cross reference to the award should be made: *Arbitration Application No.3 of 2011*, 2012 S.L.T. 150, above, para. [11].

Appeals against arbitral award on ground of legal error

100.8.—[1](1)   In addition to complying with rule 100.5(3) and (5), upon lodging a petition or note under rule 69 of the Scottish Arbitration Rules (legal error appeal), the petitioner or noter shall at the same time—

    (a)   except in a case where an appeal is made with the agreement of the parties, enrol a motion for leave to appeal; and

    (b)   lodge any documents that the petitioner or noter intends to rely on in the application for leave (if applicable) and in the appeal.

  (2)   A motion for leave to appeal under paragraph (1) shall—

    (a)   identify the point of law concerned; and

    (b)   set out the grounds that are relied on for the giving of leave.

  (3)   Within 14 days of service of the petition or note, or such other time as the court may allow, a respondent may lodge and intimate to all other parties grounds of opposition, including any evidence to be relied upon in opposition to the application for leave.

  (4)   The application for leave to appeal shall be dealt with without a hearing unless the court considers that a hearing is required.

  (5)   Where the court considers that a hearing is required, it may give such further directions as it considers necessary.

  (6)[2]   Rule 41.2 (applications for leave to appeal), rule 41.3 (determination of applications for leave to appeal) and rule 41.5 (competency of appeals) do not apply to an application for leave to appeal under this rule.

100.8

General note.

Unless the parties agree, a legal error appeal under r. 69 of the Scottish Arbitration Rules may only be made with the leave of the court (Scottish Arbitration Rules, r. 70(2)(b)). Rule 100.8 of R.C.S. 1994, however, contemplates an appeal being made without the leave of the court but with the appellant applying for leave by way of a motion at the same time as lodging the petition or note accompanied by documents to be relied on in the application for leave. Therefore a motion is required to be made on the basis of a prima facie incompetent petition or note with the granting of the motion for leave curing the incompetency but a refusal of the motion leaving the petition or note incompetent.

It is unclear why the ordinary leave to appeal procedure in rr. 41.2 and 42.3 as applied to the Outer House by r. 41.51 (formerly r.41.44) was not applied to applications for leave. If the reason was speed then it has been achieved through an unusual procedure.

Motion for leave.

Rule 70(4) of the Scottish Arbitration Rules (SAR) requires the motion to identify the point of law on which it is said that the arbitrator or arbitrators have erred and to state why leave should be granted. The reasons for granting leave should be tied to the requirements of r. 70(3) of the SAR. For further details of the requirements in r. 70(3) of the SAR, see the commentary thereon in F. Davidson, H.R. Dundas and D. Bartos, *Arbitration (Scotland) Act 2010* (Edinburgh: W.Green 2010), pp.308–310).

---

[1] Rule 100.8 inserted by S.S.I. 2010 No. 205 (effective 7th June 2010).

[2] Rule 100.8(6) amended by S.S.I. 2011 No. 385 para. 6 (effective 28th November 2011).

For motions under r. 100.8, see Pts 3 and 4 of Ch. 23. However, given that there is no provision for intimation of the motion to be made in accordance with Pt 4 of Ch.23 the intimation provisions of that Part do not apply to a motion for leave. The motion for leave should therefore seek an order for intimation and service on the respondent with a standard time of 14 days to lodge grounds of opposition and evidence in support thereof: see r. 100.8(3). If the time is to be less than 14 days, then the motion should give reasons. For further procedure see Pt 4 of Ch. 23.

The interlocutor for intimation and service of the motion should require the petitioner to lodge in process the certificate of service on the respondent within a specified period of time: *Arbitration Application No.3 of 2011*, 2012 S.L.T. 150, para. [16]).

GROUNDS OF OPPOSITION.

Following intimation and service in ordinary petition and note procedure the respondent is given an opportunity to lodge answers to the petition or note. It is not intended, however, that this be the case for legal error appeals: *Arbitration Application No. 3 of 2011*,2012 S.L.T. 150, para. [15]. Instead the respondent is given an opportunity to lodge and intimate "grounds of opposition" and "evidence to be relied upon" in opposition to the motion for leave. The grounds of opposition are to the motion rather than to the appeal itself: *Arbitration Application No. 3 of 2011*, 2012 S.L.T. 150, above, paras. [15] and [16].

DETERMINATION OF MOTION.

The general rule is that a motion is to be determined without a hearing unless the Lord Ordinary is satisfied that a hearing is required (2010 Act, Sched. 1, r. 70(5); and r. 100.8(4) of R.C.S. 1994). It has been suggested that once the period for intimation of opposition has expired agents should intimate this to the court to allow the motion to be dealt with as expeditiously as possible. In *Arbitration Application No. 3 of 2011*, 2012 S.L.T. 150, at para. [16] per Lord Glennie, it was explained that:

"[A] system has been initiated for ensuring that motions for leave are dealt with promptly after the expiry of the time for lodging grounds of opposition. The process will be marked in the petition department with a note to the effect that, upon the lodging of grounds of opposition, the process is to be passed to the commercial clerks to place before an arbitration judge at the earliest opportunity for a decision on the application for leave."

FURTHER PROCEDURE.

If the Lord Ordinary grants leave, it is for the Lord Ordinary to make the next order for procedure in relation to the appeal: r. 100.3. This may entail the fixing of a By Order hearing at which parties can address the court on a timetable to be fixed for notes of argument or any further procedure necessary for the determination of the petition or note forming the legal error appeal itself.

Anonymity in legal proceedings

100.9

100.9.—[1](1) Where a petition or note is lodged under the 2010 Act, any application to the court under section 15 of the 2010 Act (anonymity in legal proceedings) shall be made not later than the hearing of a motion for further procedure under rule 100.5(5).

(2) Until an application under section 15 of the 2010 Act has been determined or, where no such application has been made, the time at which a motion for further procedure is made under rule 100.5(5) and, thereafter, if the court grants an order under section 15 of the 2010 Act—

(a) the petition or note shall not be available for inspection, except by court staff and the parties;

(b) the petition or note shall be referred to publicly, including in the rolls of court, as "Arbitration Application" or "Arbitration Appeal" (as the case may be) and by reference to a number and the year in which it was lodged;

(c) the court proceedings shall be heard in private.

(3) Unless the court grants an order under section 15 of the 2010 Act, all applications and appeals made under the 2010 Act shall be heard in public.

GENERAL NOTE.

One of the innovative aspects of the 2010 Act was the introduction of a duty in the Scottish Arbitration Rules (which the parties may agree to exclude) on the arbitrators and the parties not to disclose any information relating to the dispute, the arbitral proceedings, and any award which is not and has never been in the public domain (2010 Act, Sched. 1, r. 26) and see the commentary thereon in F. Davidson, H.R. Dundas and D. Bartos, *Arbitration (Scotland) Act 2010* (Edinburgh: W.Green 2010, pp.166-173).

---

[1] Rule 100.9 inserted by S.S.I. 2010 No. 205 (effective 7th June 2010).

Information relating to the dispute includes the identity of the parties. This is seen keeping the arbitration confidential which is one of the perceived benefits of arbitration. Whilst there are a number of exceptions to the duty of non-disclosure (including the necessity to comply with any rule of the R.C.S. 1994 for petitions and notes) it was felt that the an option for further protection to prevent information about the dispute and parties reaching the public domain was desirable.

That option was expressed in s. 15 of the 2010 Act which allows any party to civil proceedings relating to an arbitration to apply to the court for an order prohibiting the disclosure of the identity of a party to the arbitration in any report of the proceedings. Civil proceedings are not restricted to applications or appeals under the Act and could potentially include an ordinary action which has been sisted for the dispute to be resolved by arbitration.

FORM OF THE APPLICATION.

Neither the Act, nor surprisingly r. 100.9 specifies the form that the application under s. 15 of the 2010 Act should take. Given that the application is to be made by a party to civil proceedings to anonymise a party in a report of those proceedings, one would expect that the application would be by motion in those proceedings pursuant to r. 23.11. Unfortunately that is contrary to r. 100.5 which seems an unfortunate drafting error. Until that error is cured it would appear that most applications under s. 15 require to be made by note in those civil proceedings.

TIMING OF THE APPLICATION.

The application must be made no later than the hearing of a motion for further procedure under r. 100.5(5). There may of course not be a hearing on such a motion, and in legal error appeals where leave is refused, there may not even be such a motion. The court has however indicated that regardless of the making of an application, it will not publish decisions on the grant or refusal of leave unless they raise issues of law or practice. Nevertheless it is prudent for the application for anonymisation to be made no later than the motion for the first order in the petition or note. If no such application is made then in the unusual case of a hearing on an application for leave, it will be heard in private: r. 100.9(2)(c).

Rule 100.9(2) contains an attempt to provide provisional anonymisation pending the determination of an application or the expiry of the period for the making of the motion, whichever is the later. The effect of interim anonymisation is equated to permanent anonymisation for which see below.

EFFECT OF ORDER UNDER S. 15.

An order under s. 15 of the 2010 Act prohibits the disclosure of the identity of a party to the arbitration in any report of the proceedings. This is given practical effect by r. 100.9(2). The cases of *Arbitration Application No. 3 of 2011*, 2012 S.L.T. 150 and *Arbitration Application No. 2 of 2011* [2011] CSOH 186; [2011] Hous.L.R. 72 are examples of the effect.

Applications for enforcement of a tribunal's award under the 2010 Act

100.10.—[1](1) A petition or note under section 12 of the 2010 Act for enforce-   **100.10**
ment of a tribunal's award shall—

    (a)   identify the parties to the cause and the arbitration process from which the cause arises;

    (b)   specify that the award is not currently the subject of—

        (i)   an appeal under Part 8 of the Scottish Arbitration Rules (challenging awards);

       (ii)   any arbitral process of appeal or review; or

     (iii)   a process of correction under rule 58 of the Scottish Arbitration Rules; and

    (c)   specify the basis on which the tribunal had jurisdiction to make the award.

    (2) There shall be produced with such a petition or note—

    (a)   the original tribunal's award or a certified copy of it; and

    (b)   the documents founded upon or adopted as incorporated in the petition or note.

GENERAL NOTE.

This rule deals with an application under s. 12 of the 2010 Act seeking an order that an award may be enforced as if it were an extract registered decree bearing a warrant for execution granted by the court. It does not apply to Convention awards for which separate provision is made in s. 19 of the Act and rr. 62.56 to 62.60 of the R.C.S. 1994. The enforcement procedure under s. 12 of the 2010 Act and r. 100.10 of the R.C.S. 1994 is quicker than that for Convention awards in that upon the granting of the s. 12 application there is no need for the deeming decree to be registered in the Books of Council and Session.

---

[1] Rule 100.10 inserted by S.S.I. 2010 No. 205 (effective 7th June 2010).

The provisions of rr. 14.4 (for petitions) and 15.2 (for notes) should be followed in addition to the provisions of r. 100.10.

Applications for enforcement of a tribunal's award under the 2010 Act

100.10.—(1) A petition or note under section 12 of the 2010 Act for enforcement of a tribunal's award shall—

   (a) identify the parties to the cause and the arbitration process from which the cause arises;

   (b) specify that the award is not currently the subject of—

      (i) an appeal under Part 8 of the Scottish Arbitration Rules (errors of law in awards);

      (ii) any arbitral process of appeal or review; or

      (iii) a process of correction under rule 58 of the Scottish Arbitration Rules; and

   (c) specify the basis on which the tribunal had jurisdiction to make the award.

(2) There shall be produced with such a petition or note—

   (a) the original arbitral award or a certified copy of it; and

   (b) the document founded upon or adopted as incorporated in the petition or note.

CHAPTER 101 TERRORIST ASSET-FREEZING

[Revoked by the Act of Sederunt (Rules of the Court of Session 1994 Amendment) (Sanctions and Anti-Money Laundering) 2019 (S.S.I. 2019 No. 72) r. 3(A1) (effective 29 March 2019 subject to savings specified in S.S.I. 2019 No. 72 r. 4(1)).]

The rules in this chapter have effect only in relation to proceedings commenced but not concluded before 29th March 2019. See now, sanctions decision proceedings under the Sanctions and Anti-Money Laundering Act 2018 in Chap. 96.

101.1

CHAPTER 102 REPORTING RESTRICTIONS

Chapter 102[1]

Reporting Restrictions

Interpretation and application of this Chapter

102.1.—[2](1) This Chapter applies to orders which restrict the reporting of proceedings.

(2) In this Chapter, "interested person" means a person—

   (a) who has asked to see any order made by the court which restricts the reporting of proceedings, including an interim order; and

   (b) whose name is included on a list kept by the Lord President for the purposes of this Chapter.

102.1

Application for an order

102.1A.—[3](1) A party to the proceedings may apply to the court for an order under this Chapter to restrict the reporting of the proceedings.

(2) An application for an order under this Chapter must be made by motion and be accompanied by Form 102.1A.

Interim orders

102.2.—[4, 5](1) Where the court is considering making an order, it must first make an interim order.

(2) The clerk of court shall immediately send a copy of the interim order to any interested person.

(3) The court shall specify in the interim order why it is considering making an order.

102.2

GENERAL NOTE.

Under s. 4(1) of the Contempt of Court Act 1981 a person is not guilty of contempt under the strict liability rule in respect of a fair and accurate report of legal proceedings in public, published contemporaneously and in good faith. Under s. 4(2), where it appears to be necessary for avoiding a substantial risk of prejudice to the administration of justice, or in any other proceedings pending or imminent, the court may order that publication of any report of the proceedings or any part of them be postponed for such period as the court thinks necessary for that purpose.

Such an order is published on the Scottish Court Service website (*www.scotcourts.gov.uk*), the judiciary website (*www.scotland-judiciary.org.uk*) and to persons on the list kept by the Lord President (e.g. certain print and broadcasting media). This is so that a person aggrieved by the terms of the order can object by applying to the court to vary or revoke the order under r. 102.3.

102.2.1

PROCEDURE FOR CONTEMPT.

Where an alleged contempt is directed at the a member of the court personally, or in the case of any other contempt that it would be inappropriate for that court to deal with, the procedure is laid down in A.S. (Contempt of Court in Civil Proceedings) 2011 (SSI 2011/388). Otherwise, the contempt may be dealt with by the court ordering the contemnor to appear before the court; if admitted the contempt can be dealt with there and then; if denied, there would have to be a minute and answers procedure for proof of the contempt. The penalties for contempt are to be found in s. 15 of the Contempt of Court Act 1981.

102.2.2

---

[1] Chapter 102 and r. 102.1 inserted by S.S.I. 2011 No. 385 para. 4 (effective 28th November 2011) and substituted by S.S.I. 2015 No. 85 para. 2 (effective 1st April 2015).

[2] Chapter 102 and r. 102.1 inserted by S.S.I. 2011 No. 385 para. 4 (effective 28th November 2011) and substituted by S.S.I. 2015 No. 85 para. 2 (effective 1st April 2015).

[3] Inserted by 2023 S.S.I. 2023 No. 196 r. 2(2) (effective 2nd October 2023).

[4] Rule 102.2 inserted by S.S.I. 2011 No. 385 para. 4 (effective 28th November 2011) and substituted by S.S.I. 2015 No. 85 para. 2 (effective 1st April 2015).

[5] Rule 102.2 amended by S.S.I. 2020 No. 28 para. 2 (effective 2nd March 2020).

Representations

102.3

102.3.—[1,2](1) *[Omitted by S.S.I. 2020 No. 28 para. 2(2)(b) (effective 2 March 2020)]*

(2) An interested person who would be directly affected by the making of an order shall have an opportunity to make representations to the court before an order is made.

(3) Representations shall—

(a) be made by note in process;

(b) where an urgent hearing is sought, include reasons explaining why an urgent hearing is necessary;

(c) be lodged no later than 2 days after the interim order is sent to interested persons in accordance with rule 102.2(2).

(4) On representations being made—

(a) the court shall appoint a date for a hearing—

(i) on the first suitable court day thereafter; or

(ii) where the court is satisfied that an urgent hearing is necessary, at such earlier date and time as the court may determine;

(b) the clerk of court shall—

(i) notify the date and time of the hearing to the parties to the proceedings and the person who has made representations; and

(ii) send a copy of the representations to the parties to the proceedings.

(5) Where no interested person makes representations in accordance with rule 102.3(2), the clerk of court shall put the interim order before the court in chambers in order that the court may resume consideration of whether to make an order.

(6) Where the court, having resumed consideration under rule 102.3(5), makes no order, it shall recall the interim order.

(7) Where the court recalls an interim order, the clerk of court shall immediately notify any interested person.

APPLICATION TO VARY OR REVOKE ORDER BY PERSON AGGRIEVED.

102.3.1

Under r.102.3 a procedure is now laid down for a person aggrieved, usually a media organisation, to apply to the court to vary or revoke the order under s.4(2) of the 1981 Act to postpone publication. The application should be heard within 48 hours, and if practicable before the judge(s) who made the order: r.102.3(4).

"NOTE".

102.3.2

The application by note is made in the process of the cause to which the order relates. For the form and procedure by note, see r.15.2.

"WRITTEN INTIMATION".

102.3.3

For methods, see r.16.9.

Notification of reporting restrictions

102.4

102.4.—[3] Where the court makes an order, the clerk of court shall immediately—

(a) send a copy of the order to any interested person;

(b) arrange for the publication of the making of the order on the Scottish Court Service website.

---

[1] Rule 102.3 inserted by S.S.I. 2011 No. 385 para. 4 (effective 28th November 2011) and substituted by S.S.I. 2015 No. 85 para. 2 (effective 1st April 2015).

[2] Rule 102.3 amended by S.S.I. 2020 No. 28 para. 2 (effective 2nd March 2020).

[3] Rule 102.3 inserted by S.S.I. 2015 No. 85 para. 2 (effective 1st April 2015).

Applications for variation or revocation

102.5.—[1](1) A person aggrieved by an order may apply to the court for its variation or revocation.

(2) An application shall be made by note in process.

(3) On an application being made—

    (a) the court shall appoint the application for a hearing;

    (b) the clerk of court shall—

        (i) notify the date and time of the hearing to the parties to the proceedings and the applicant;

        (ii) send a copy of the application to the parties to the proceedings.

(4) The hearing shall, so far as reasonably practicable, be before the judge or judges who made the order.

102.5

---

[1] Rule 102.3 inserted by S.S.I. 2015 No. 85 para. 2 (effective 1st April 2015).

Applications for variation or revocation

102.5—(1) A person aggrieved by an order may apply to the court for its variation or revocation.

(2) An application shall be made by note in process.

(3) On an application being made—

(a) the court shall appoint the application for a hearing;

(b) the clerk of court shall—

(i) notify the date and time of the hearing to the parties to the proceedings and the applicant.

(ii) send a copy of the application to the parties to the proceedings.

(4) The hearing shall, so far as reasonably practicable, be before the judge or judges who made the order.

102.5

Rule 102.5 inserted by S.S.I. 2013 No. 85 para 2 (effective 1st April 2013)

CHAPTER 103 FORCED MARRIAGE

Chapter 103[1]

Forced Marriage

Interpretation of this Chapter

103.1.[2] In this Chapter, "the 2011 Act" means the Forced Marriage etc. (Protection and Jurisdiction) (Scotland) Act 2011.

103.1

GENERAL NOTE.

The Forced Marriage etc. (Protection and Jurisdiction) (Scotland) Act 2011 provides for protecting persons from being forced into marriage without their free and full consent and for protecting persons who have been forced into marriage without such consent.

103.1.1

The Court of Session or the sheriff may make a forced marriage protection order in relation to such a person under s. 1 of the 2011 Act. The court may make a forced marriage protection order without an application being made to it in civil proceedings before it where the court considers such an order should be made to protect a person (whether or not a party) and a person who would be a party to proceedings for such an order (other than the protected person) is a party to civil proceedings in which the order is considered: 2011 Act, s. 4. The court may also make an interim forced marriage protection order ex parte: 2011 Act, s. 5.

Applications for a forced marriage protection order

103.2.—[3](1) An application for a forced marriage protection order under the 2011 Act shall be made by petition.

103.2

(2) Where leave of the court is required under section 3(2) of the 2011 Act to make an application for a forced marriage protection order, the person seeking such an order shall apply by motion for leave to make the application at the time when the petition is presented to the Petition Department.

(3) A motion under paragraph (2) shall be heard in chambers.

(4) Where such leave is granted, a copy of the interlocutor allowing leave shall be attached to the copy of the petition served on the respondent.

GENERAL NOTE.

An application for a forced marriage protection order may be made by the person seeking to be protected, a relevant third party (i.e. a local authority, the Lord Advocate or a person specified by Scottish Ministers by order), or any other person only with leave of the court: 2011 Act, s.3.

103.2.1

The circumstances in which the order may be made are, oddly, divided between ss.1(2) and 3(3) and (4) including regard having to be had to all the circumstances (repeated twice). The contents of an order are dealt with in s.2.

LEAVE REQUIRED UNDER S.3(2) OF THE 2011 ACT.

Leave of the court to apply for a forced marriage protection order is required for a person other than the person seeking protection or a relevant third party (see note 103.2.1 above). Such a person must apply by motion.

103.2.2

"PETITION".

A petition is presented to the Outer House: r. 14.2(h). The petition must be in Form 14.4 in the official printed form: rr.4.1 and 14.4. The petition must be signed by counsel or other person having a right of audience: r. 4.2; and see r. 1.3(1) (definition of "counsel" and "other person having a right of audience") and note 1.3.4.

103.2.3

The petitioner must lodge the petition with the required steps of process: r. 4.4. A fee is payable on lodging the petition: see note 14.5.10.

On petitions generally, see Chap. 14.

"MOTION".

For motions, see Chap. 23.

103.2.4

---

[1] Chapter 103 and r. 103.1 inserted by S.S.I. 2011 No. 385 para. 5 (effective 28th November 2011).
[2] Chapter 103 and r. 103.1 inserted by S.S.I. 2011 No. 385 para. 5 (effective 28th November 2011).
[3] Rule 103.2 inserted by S.S.I. 2011 No. 385 para. 5 (effective 28th November 2011).

Applications for variation, recall or extension of a forced marriage protection order

103.3

103.3.—[1](1) An application for variation, recall or extension of a forced marriage protection order under the 2011 Act shall be made by note.

(2) Where leave of the court is required under section 7(1)(d) or 8(3)(d) of the 2011 Act before an application for variation, or recall or extension of a forced marriage protection order may be made, the applicant must lodge along with the note a motion stating the grounds upon which leave is sought.

(3) A motion under paragraph (2) shall not be served or intimated unless the court otherwise directs.

(4) The court may hear the applicant on the motion and may grant or refuse it or make such other order in relation to it as it considers appropriate prior to the determination.

(5) Where such a motion is granted, a copy of the interlocutor shall be intimated along with the note of application.

GENERAL NOTE.

103.3.1

An application for variation or recall, or extension, of a forced marriage protection order may be made by any person who was or would have been a party to the proceedings for the order, the protected person, a person affected by the order, or, with leave of the court, any other person: 2011 Act, s. 7 (variation or recall) and 8 (extension).

"NOTE".

103.3.2

The application is made by note. For form and procedure, see r. 15.2.

LEAVE REQUIRED UNDER s. 7(1)(D) OR 8(3)(D) OF THE 2011 ACT.

103.3.3

Leave of the court to apply for variation, recall or extension of a forced marriage protection order is required for a person other than a person who was or would have been a party to the proceedings for the order, the protected person or a person affected by the order. Such a person must apply by motion.

"MOTION".

103.3.4

For motions, see Chap. 23.

---

[1] Rule 103.3 inserted by S.S.I. 2011 No. 385 para. 5 (effective 28th November 2011).

Chapter 104

Justice and Security Act

Interpretation and application of this Chapter[1]

104.1.—(1) In this Chapter—

"the Act of 2013" means the Justice and Security Act 2013;

"Advocate General" means the Advocate General for Scotland;

"closed material application" means an application of the kind mentioned in section 8(1)(a) of the Act of 2013;

"legal representative" is to be construed in accordance with section 14(1) of the Act of 2013;

"relevant civil proceedings" is to be construed in accordance with section 14(1) of the Act of 2013;

"relevant person" is to be construed in accordance with section 14(1) of the Act of 2013;

"section 6 proceedings" is to be construed in accordance with section 14(1) of the Act of 2013;

"sensitive material" is to be construed in accordance with section 14(1) of the Act of 2013;

"special advocate" means a person appointed under section 9(1) of the Act of 2013;

"specially represented party" means a party whose interests a special advocate represents.

(2) This Chapter applies to closed material proceedings under Part 2 of the Act of 2013.

Potential disclosure: notification to Secretary of State[2]

104.2.—(1) This rule applies where the Secretary of State is not a party to relevant civil proceedings and a declaration under section 6 of the Act of 2013 has not been applied for or made.

(2) Where it appears to a party that they may be required to disclose material which might be damaging to the interests of national security the party shall notify the court in writing.

(3) Where the court has been notified in accordance with paragraph (2), or it appears to the court that a party may be required to disclose material which might be damaging to the interests of national security, the court shall—

(a) notify the Secretary of State in writing;

(b) order that the material is not to be disclosed.

(4) Within 14 days of being notified in accordance with paragraph (3) the Secretary of State shall respond in writing to the court—

(a) confirming that the Secretary of State intends to apply for a declaration under section 6 of the Act;

(b) confirming that the Secretary of State does not intend to apply for such a declaration; or

(c) requesting further time to consider whether to apply for such a declaration.

104.1

104.2

---

[1] As inserted by the Act of Sederunt (Rules of the Court of Session Amendment No.5) (Miscellaneous) 2013 (SSI 2013/238) r.3 (effective August 19, 2013).

[2] As inserted by the Act of Sederunt (Rules of the Court of Session Amendment No.5) (Miscellaneous) 2013 (SSI 2013/238) r.3 (effective August 19, 2013).

(5)   The court may make such orders as it thinks necessary pending the Secretary of State's response.

GENERAL NOTE.

104.2.1   Section 6 of the Justice and Security Act 2013 provides that a court hearing a civil case, on the application of a party, the Secretary of State or of its own motion may make a declaration that the case is one in which closed material procedure may be used; that is, where one of the parties would be required to disclose material during proceedings which would be damaging to the interests of national security in which the degree of harm to those interests if the material is disclosed would be likely to outweigh the public interest in the fair and open administration of justice and a fair determination of the proceedings is not possible by any other means. The procedure involves the non-Government parties to leave the courtroom while the sensitive material is heard; the interests of such parties are represented by security cleared lawyers (special advocates: see rr. 104.11–104.13).

104.2.2   For a recent case, see *CF v. Security Service* [2013] EWHC 3402 (QB).

104.2.3   Rule 104.2 deals with the procedure where the Secretary of State is not a party and a declaration (that the proceedings are proceedings in which a disclosed material application may be made) has not been applied for or made; r. 104.3 deals with procedure where the Secretary of State is a party.

Closed material declaration: applications[1]

104.3   **104.3.**—(1)   An application under the following provisions of the Act of 2013 shall be made by lodging a note in process with the Deputy Principal Clerk—

   (a)   section 6(2)(a) (declaration permitting closed material applications in proceedings);

   (b)   section 7(4)(a) (review and revocation of declaration under section 6).

(2)   The note shall include, in numbered paragraphs, statements of reasons in support of the application.

(3)   Where, in relation to an application under section 6(2)(a) of the Act of 2013, the applicant is the Secretary of State, the note shall include the Secretary of State's reasons for not making, or not advising another person to make, a claim for public interest immunity in relation to the material in question.

(4)   An application mentioned in paragraph (1)(a) shall be intimated to those persons mentioned in paragraph (6) no later than 14 days before the application is made.

(5)   An application mentioned in paragraph (1)(b) shall be intimated to those parties mentioned in paragraph (6) no later than 28 days before the application is made.

(6)   An application shall be intimated to—

   (a)   the Deputy Principal Clerk;

   (b)   the parties to the proceedings;

   (c)   where the Secretary of State is not a party to the proceedings, the Secretary of State;

   (d)   where a special advocate has been appointed, the special advocate.

(7)   The court may vary the period of notice mentioned in paragraph (4) or (5) on cause shown.

GENERAL NOTE.

104.3.1   Rule 104.3 deals with the procedure where the Secretary of State is a party, or a party or the court seeks to make a declaration that the proceedings are proceedings in which a disclosed material application may be made; or where it is sought by the Secretary of State, a party or the court (which must keep the matter under review) seeks to review or revoke the declaration.

"NOTE".

104.3.2   For applications by note, see r. 15.2.

---

[1] As inserted by the Act of Sederunt (Rules of the Court of Session Amendment No.5) (Miscellaneous) 2013 (SSI 2013/238) r.3 (effective August 19, 2013).

Initial diets[1]

104.4.—(1) On receipt of an application under rule 104.3(1) (closed material declaration: applications), or where directed to do so by the court acting of its own motion under section 6(2)(b) or 7(4)(b) of the Act of 2013, the Deputy Principal Clerk shall allocate an initial diet for the court's consideration to begin.

(2) The Deputy Principal Clerk shall, unless the court otherwise directs, notify the time and date of the initial diet to those parties mentioned in rule 104.3(6)(b) to (d).

(3) Where the court is acting of its own motion the notification mentioned in paragraph (2) shall be on a period of notice of 28 days.

(4) Parties shall, no later than the date of the initial diet, lodge with the Deputy Principal Clerk any answers or, as the case may be, written submissions that are to be founded upon at the initial diet.

(5) Where the application is unopposed the court may determine the application in chambers.

(6) At the initial diet parties shall state their proposals for further procedure and the court shall make such orders for further procedure as it thinks fit.

(7) The court may discharge the initial diet and make such orders for further procedure as it thinks fit.

104.4

Hearing on applications[2]

104.5.—(1)[3] Where the court has fixed a hearing on the application under rule 104.4(6) or (7), the Deputy Principal Clerk shall, unless the court otherwise directs, notify the time and date to those parties mentioned in rule 104.3(4)(b) to (d).

(2) The hearing shall take place in the absence of the specially represented party and the specially represented party's legal representatives.

(3) Within seven days of the application being determined, the applicant shall serve a copy of the interlocutor on the parties to the proceedings.

104.5

Evidence[4]

104.6. Subject to the provisions of the Act of 2013—

(a) where the court hears any evidence it shall do so in accordance with existing law and practice as to the taking of evidence in civil proceedings in Scotland; and

(b) Chapter 35 (recovery of evidence)$_2$ continues to apply.

104.6

Formal review of declaration[5]

104.7.—(1) For the purposes of section 7(3) of the Act of 2013 a formal review shall take place after the court has fixed a hearing to determine the merits of the proceedings.

(2) Where paragraph (1) applies the court shall proceed as mentioned in rule 104.4 (initial diets).

104.7

---

[1] As inserted by the Act of Sederunt (Rules of the Court of Session Amendment No.5) (Miscellaneous) 2013 (SSI 2013/238) r.3 (effective August 19, 2013).

[2] As inserted by the Act of Sederunt (Rules of the Court of Session Amendment No.5) (Miscellaneous) 2013 (SSI 2013/238) r.3 (effective August 19, 2013).

[3] As amended by the Act of Sederunt (Rules of the Court of Session Amendment No.7) (Miscellaneous) 2013 (SSI 2013/317) r.4 (effective 2nd December, 2013).

[4] As inserted by the Act of Sederunt (Rules of the Court of Session Amendment No.5) (Miscellaneous) 2013 (SSI 2013/238) r.3 (effective August 19, 2013).

[5] As inserted by the Act of Sederunt (Rules of the Court of Session Amendment No.5) (Miscellaneous) 2013 (SSI 2013/238) r.3 (effective August 19, 2013).

Closed material procedure: application[1]

104.8

104.8.—(1) This rule applies where there is a declaration under section 6 of the Act of 2013.

(2) The relevant person may apply to the court for permission not to disclose sensitive material otherwise than to—

    (a) the court;

    (b) any person appointed as a special advocate;

    (c) where the Secretary of State is not the relevant person but is a party to the proceedings, the Secretary of State.

(3) The application shall be made by lodging a note in process with the Deputy Principal Clerk.

(4) The note shall include, in numbered paragraphs, statements of reasons in support of the application and the sensitive material in question.

(5) A copy of the note in process shall be served only on the special advocate and, where the Secretary of State is not the relevant person, the Secretary of State.

(6) The relevant person may at any time amend or supplement material lodged under this rule, but only with the agreement of the special advocate or the permission of the court.

(7) The relevant person may not rely on sensitive material at a hearing unless a special advocate has been appointed to represent the interests of the specially represented party.

(8) Documents lodged in relation to an application shall be kept separately from the process by the Deputy Principal Clerk.

(9) Documents lodged in relation to an application shall not be borrowed or inspected by any party other than by a legal representative of the Secretary of State or by any special advocate.

(10) The following shall not apply to the application—

    (a) rule 4.5(1)(b) (copy of inventory of productions to be sent to other parties);

    (b) rule 4.6 (intimation of steps of process);

    (c) rule 4.11 (documents not to be borrowed).

"NOTE".

104.8.1   For applications by note, see r.15.2.

Consideration of closed material procedure application or objection to special advocate's communication[2]

104.9

104.9.—(1) This rule applies where—

    (a) the relevant person has applied under rule 104.8 (closed material procedure: application); or

    (b) the Secretary of State has objected under rule 104.13(6) (special advocate: communicating about proceedings) to a proposed communication by the special advocate.

(2) The court shall fix a hearing for the relevant party, the Secretary of State and the special advocate to make representations.

(3) The court may determine an application or objection in chambers where—

    (a) the special advocate gives notice that he or she does not challenge the application or objection;

---

[1] As inserted by the Act of Sederunt (Rules of the Court of Session Amendment No.5) (Miscellaneous) 2013 (SSI 2013/238) r.3 (effective August 19, 2013).

[2] As inserted by the Act of Sederunt (Rules of the Court of Session Amendment No.5) (Miscellaneous) 2013 (SSI 2013/238) r.3 (effective August 19, 2013).

(b)   the court has previously, in determining the application for a declaration under section 6 of the Act of 2013, found that the first condition in that section is met in relation to the same or substantially the same material and is satisfied that it would be just to give permission without a hearing;

(c)   the court has previously considered—

    (i)   an application under rule 104.8 for permission to withhold the same or substantially the same material; or

    (ii)   an objection under rule 104.13(6) to the same or substantially the same proposed communication;

   and is satisfied that it would be just to give permission or uphold the objection without a hearing; or

(d)   the relevant person, the Secretary of State and the special advocate consent to the court deciding the case without a hearing.

(4) Where the special advocate does not challenge the application or the objection, he or she must give notice of that fact to the court, the relevant person and the Secretary of State no later than—

(a)   14 days after being notified in accordance with rule 104.8(5), or

(b)   such other period as the court may direct.

(5) Where the court fixes a hearing under this rule, the relevant person, the Secretary of State and the special advocate shall, before the hearing, lodge with the Deputy Principal Clerk a joint minute identifying the issues which cannot be agreed between them.

(6) A hearing under this rule shall take place in the absence of the specially represented party and the specially represented party's legal representatives.

(7) Where the court has, in determining an application for a declaration under section 6 of the Act of 2013, found that the first condition in that section is met in relation to any material, it may give permission to withhold that material without a hearing in relation to that material.

Closed material procedure: non-disclosure of sensitive material etc.[1]

104.10.—(1) Where the court gives permission to the relevant person not to disclose sensitive material, the court must—

  104.10

(a)   consider whether to direct the relevant person to serve a summary of that material on the specially represented party and the specially represented party's legal representative; but

(b)   ensure that any such summary does not contain information or other material the disclosure of which would be damaging to the interests of national security.

(2) If the court is satisfied that the relevant person does not intend to rely on sensitive material, and that that material does not adversely affect the relevant person's case or support the case of another party to the proceedings, the court may direct that the relevant person must not rely in the proceedings on that material, without first requiring the relevant person to serve a summary of that material on the specially represented party and the specially represented party's legal representative.

(3) Where the court has not given permission to the relevant person not to disclose sensitive material to, or has directed the relevant person to serve a summary of that material on, the specially represented party and the specially represented party's legal representative—

---

[1] As inserted by the Act of Sederunt (Rules of the Court of Session Amendment No.5) (Miscellaneous) 2013 (SSI 2013/238) r.3 (effective August 19, 2013).

    (a)   the relevant person shall not be required to serve that material or summary; but

    (b)   if the relevant person does not do so, at a hearing the court may—

        (i)   if it considers that the material or anything that is required to be summarised might be of assistance to the specially represented party in relation to a matter under consideration by the court, direct that the matter is withdrawn from its consideration or that the relevant person makes such concessions or takes such other steps as the court may direct; and

        (ii)   in any other case, direct that the relevant person must not rely in the proceedings on that material or, as the case may be, on what is required to be summarised.

(4)   The court must give permission to the relevant person not to disclose sensitive material where it considers that disclosure of that material would be damaging to the interests of national security.

Appointment of special advocate[1]

104.11

    104.11.—(1) Where the Secretary of State has given or received notification of an application under rule 104.3(1) (closed material declaration: applications) he or she shall give notice of the proceedings to the Advocate General (who, under section 9(1) of the Act of 2013, has the power to appoint a special advocate).

(2)   Paragraph (1) applies unless a special advocate has already been appointed and that special advocate is not prevented from communicating with the specially represented party by virtue of rule 104.13.

(3)   Where a special advocate has not been appointed any party or, as the case may be, the Secretary of State may request that the Advocate General appoint a special advocate.

(4)   On the appointment of any special advocate, the Advocate General shall intimate the name of the special advocate to the Deputy Principal Clerk in writing.

Functions of a special advocate[2]

104.12

    104.12. The functions of a special advocate are to represent the interests of a specially represented party by—

    (a)   making submissions to the court at any hearing or part of a hearing from which the specially represented party and the specially represented party's legal representatives are excluded;

    (b)   leading evidence and cross-examining witnesses at any such hearing, or part of a hearing;

    (c)   making written submissions to the court.

Special advocate: communicating about proceedings[3]

104.13

    104.13.—(1) The special advocate may communicate with the specially represented party or the specially represented party's legal representative at any time before a relevant person serves sensitive material on the special advocate.

(2)   After the relevant person serves sensitive material on the special advocate, the special advocate shall not communicate with any person about any matter connected with the proceedings, except in accordance with paragraph (3) or with a

---

[1] As inserted by the Act of Sederunt (Rules of the Court of Session Amendment No.5) (Miscellaneous) 2013 (SSI 2013/238) r.3 (effective August 19, 2013).

[2] As inserted by the Act of Sederunt (Rules of the Court of Session Amendment No.5) (Miscellaneous) 2013 (SSI 2013/238) r.3 (effective August 19, 2013).

[3] As inserted by the Act of Sederunt (Rules of the Court of Session Amendment No.5) (Miscellaneous) 2013 (SSI 2013/238) r.3 (effective August 19, 2013).

direction of the court pursuant to a request under paragraph (4).

(3) The special advocate may, without directions from the court, communicate about the proceedings with—

(a) the court;

(b) the relevant person (where this is not the Secretary of State);

(c) the Secretary of State or any person acting for the Secretary of State;

(d) the Advocate General or any person acting for the Advocate General; or

(e) any other person, except the specially represented party or the specially represented party's legal representative, with whom it is necessary for administrative purposes for the special advocate to communicate about matters not connected with the substance of the proceedings.

(4) The special advocate may request directions from the court authorising the special advocate to communicate with the specially represented party or the specially represented party's legal representative or with any other person.

(5) Where the special advocate makes a request for directions under paragraph (4) the court must notify the relevant person and (where the relevant person is not the Secretary of State) the Secretary of State of the request, and of the content of the proposed communication and the form in which it is proposed to be made.

(6) The relevant person or the Secretary of State shall, within a period specified by the court, lodge with the court and serve on the special advocate notice of any objection which the relevant person or the Secretary of State has to the proposed communication or to the form in which it is proposed to be made.

(7) Paragraph (2) does not prohibit the specially represented party from communicating with the special advocate after the relevant person has served material on the special advocate but—

(a) the specially represented party may only communicate with the special advocate through the specially represented party's legal representative in writing; and

(b) the special advocate must not reply to the communication other than in accordance with directions of the court, except that the special advocate may without such directions send a written acknowledgment of receipt to the specially represented party's legal representative.

Opinions of the court[1]

104.14.—(1) Where the court issues an opinion in any proceedings to which this Chapter applies, it may withhold any or part of its reasons if and to the extent that it would not be possible to give those reasons without disclosing information which would be damaging to the interests of national security.

104.14

(2) Where an opinion of the court does not include the full reasons for its decision—

(a) the court shall prepare a separate opinion including those reasons; and

(b) the Deputy Principal Clerk shall serve that separate opinion on the relevant person, the Secretary of State (where not the relevant person) and the special advocate.

---

[1] As inserted by the Act of Sederunt (Rules of the Court of Session Amendment No.5) (Miscellaneous) 2013 (SSI 2013/238) r.3 (effective August 19, 2013).

Participation of Secretary of State[1]

104.15

104.15.—(1) Where the court makes a declaration under section 6 of the Act of 2013 and the Secretary of State is not already a party to the relevant civil proceedings, the court shall sist the Secretary of State as a party to the proceedings.

(2) Paragraph (1) does not apply where the Secretary of State has informed the court in writing that he or she does not wish to be sisted as a party to the proceedings.

Hearings in private[2]

104.16

104.16.—(1) Unless otherwise provided for in this Chapter, if the court considers it necessary for any party and that party's legal representative to be excluded from any hearing or part of a hearing in order to secure that information is not disclosed where disclosure would be damaging to the interests of national security, it must—

(a) direct accordingly; and

(b) conduct the hearing, or that part of it from which that party and that party's legal representative are excluded, in private but attended by a special advocate to represent the interests of the excluded party.

(2) The court may conduct a hearing or part of a hearing in private for any other good reason.

(3) In this rule "hearing" includes initial diet.

---

[1] As inserted by the Act of Sederunt (Rules of the Court of Session Amendment No.5) (Miscellaneous) 2013 (SSI 2013/238) r.3 (effective August 19, 2013).
[2] As inserted by the Act of Sederunt (Rules of the Court of Session Amendment No.5) (Miscellaneous) 2013 (SSI 2013/238) r.3 (effective August 19, 2013).

CHAPTER 105 LAND REGISTRATION ETC.

Interpretation of this Chapter

105.1.[1]   In this Chapter—

"the 2012 Act" means the Land Registration etc. (Scotland) Act 2012;
"plot of land" has the meaning given by section 3(4) and (5) of the 2012 Act;
"proprietor" has the meaning given by section 113(1) of the 2012 Act.

105.1

Applications under Part 6 of the 2012 Act

105.2.[2](1)   An application under section 67(2) (warrant to place a caveat) of the 2012 Act shall be made by motion.

105.2

(2)   The motion shall—

  (a)   identify, by reference to section 67(1) of the 2012 Act, the type of civil proceedings constituted by the cause;

  (b)   in respect of each plot of land, contain—

    (i)   a description of the registered plot of land;

    (ii)   the title number; and

    (iii)   the name and address of the proprietor;

  (c)   where the caveat is to apply only to part of a plot of land, be accompanied by a plan indicating the part so affected.

(3)   An application under the following provisions of the 2012 Act shall be made by motion—

  (a)   section 69(1) (renewal of caveat);

  (b)   section 70(1) (restriction of caveat);

  (c)   section 71(1) (recall of caveat).

GENERAL NOTE.

In civil proceedings (a) for the reduction of a registered deed on the ground that it is voidable or (b) which could result in a determination that the Land Register is inaccurate or (c) for an order which would be registrable under s. 8A of the Law Reform (Miscellaneous Provisions) (Scotland) Act 1985 (register of order for rectification), a party may, at any time while the proceedings are in dependence, apply for warrant to place a caveat in the title sheet of a plot of land to which the proceedings relate: Land Registration etc. (Scotland) Act 2012. The purpose is to warn third parties about the existence of a title dispute. If a title sheet is subsequently adversely rectified, a person could not claim, where there is a caveat, that he was unaware of the litigation.

A caveat may be renewed (s. 69), restricted (s. 70) or recalled (s. 71).

105.2.1

"MOTION".

For motions, see Chap. 23.

105.2.2

Form of orders under Part 6 of the 2012 Act

105.3.[3](1)   An order under section 67(3) or 69(2) of the 2012 Act shall be in Form 105.3-A.

105.3

(2)   An order under section 70(2) of the 2012 Act shall be in Form 105.3-B.

(3)   An order under section 71(2) of the 2012 Act shall be in Form 105.3-C.

Effect of warrant to place or renew caveat

105.4.[4]   A certified copy of the order in Form 105.3-A may be registered in the Registers of Inhibitions and Adjudications.

105.4

---

[1] Chapter 105 and r. 105.1 as inserted by S.S.I. 2014 No. 291 r. 2(5) (effective 8th December 2014).
[2] Rule 105.2 as inserted by S.S.I. 2014 No. 291 r. 2(5) (effective 8th December 2014).
[3] Rule 105.3 as inserted by S.S.I. 2014 No. 291 r. 2(5) (effective 8th December 2014).
[4] Rule 105.4 as inserted by S.S.I. 2014 No. 291 r. 2(5) (effective 8th December 2014).

105.4.1   A copy of the interlocutor is certified by a clerk of session and stamped with the court stamp.

Form of decree of reduction

105.5   **105.5.**[1]   Where a deed mentioned in section 46A(2) of the Conveyancing (Scotland) Act 1924 is reduced, the decree of reduction shall be in Form 105.5.

Form of order for rectification of a document

105.6   **105.6.**[2]   An order for rectification under section 8 of the Law Reform (Miscellaneous Provisions) (Scotland) Act 1985 in respect of a document which has been registered in the Land Register of Scotland shall be in Form 105.6.

---

[1] Rule 105.5 as inserted by S.S.I. 2014 No. 291 r. 2(5) (effective 8th December 2014).
[2] Rule 105.6 as inserted by S.S.I. 2014 No. 291 r. 2(5) (effective 8th December 2014).

CHAPTER 106 MUTUAL RECOGNITION OF PROTECTION MEASURES IN CIVIL MATTERS

Interpretation

106.1.[1,2] In this Chapter—

"incoming protection measure" means a protection measure that has been ordered in a participating Member State;

"MRP Regulation" has the meaning given by Article 3(5A) of the Regulation;

"participating Member State" has the meaning given by Article 3(5) of the Regulation;

"person causing the risk" has the meaning given by Article 3(3) of the Regulation;

"protected person" has the meaning given by Article 3(2) of the Regulation;

"protection measure" has the meaning given by Article 3(1) of the Regulation;

"registered post service" has the meaning given by section 125(1) of the Postal Services Act 2000;

"the Regulation" means Regulation (EU) No. 606/2013 of the European Parliament and of the Council of 12 June 2013 on mutual recognition of protection measures in civil matters.

106.1

Form of application for Article 5 certificate

106.2.[3] [Revoked by S.S.I. 2022 No. 329 para.2 (effective 1 December 2022).]

106.2

Issue of Article 5 certificate

106.3.[4] [Revoked by S.S.I. 2022 No. 329 para.2 (effective 1 December 2022).]

106.3

Conditions for issue of Article 5 certificate

106.4.[5](1) [Revoked by S.S.I. 2022 No. 329 para.2 (effective 1 December 2022).]

106.4

Notice of issue of Article 5 certificate

106.5.—[6](1) [Revoked by S.S.I. 2022 No. 329 para.2 (effective 1 December 2022).]

106.5

Effect of variation of order

106.6.[7]— [Revoked by S.S.I. 2022 No. 329 para.2 (effective 1 December 2022).]

106.6

Application for rectification or withdrawal of Article 5 certificate

106.7.—[8](1) [Revoked by S.S.I. 2022 No. 329 para.2 (effective 1 December 2022).]

106.7

---

[1] Chapter 106 and r. 106.1 inserted by S.S.I. 2014 No. 371 r. 2(6) (effective 11 January 2015).
[2] Rule 106.1 as amended by S.S.I. 2022 No. 329 para.2 (effective 1 December 2022).
[3] Rule 106.2 inserted by S.S.I. 2014 No. 371 r. 2(6) (effective 11 January 2015).
[4] Rule 106.3 inserted by S.S.I. 2014 No. 371 r. 2(6) (effective 11 January 2015).
[5] Rule 106.4 inserted by S.S.I. 2014 No. 371 r. 2(6) (effective 11 January 2015).
[6] Rule 106.5 inserted by S.S.I. 2014 No. 371 r. 2(6) (effective 11 January 2015).
[7] Rule 106.6 inserted by S.S.I. 2014 No. 371 r. 2(6) (effective 11 January 2015).
[8] Rule 106.7 inserted by S.S.I. 2014 No. 371 r. 2(6) (effective 11 January 2015).

Issue of Article 14 certificate

106.8   **106.8.**—[1](1)   [Revoked by S.S.I. 2022 No. 329 para.2 (effective 1 December 2022).]

Form of applications relating to incoming protection measures

106.9   **106.9.**—[2](1)   The following applications shall be made by petition—

(a)   an application for the adjustment of the factual elements of an incoming protection measure under Article 11 of the Regulation;

(b)   an application to refuse the recognition and, where applicable, the enforcement of an incoming protection measure under Article 13 of the Regulation;

(c)   a submission under Article 14(2) of the Regulation to suspend or withdraw the effects of the recognition and, where applicable, the enforcement of an incoming protection measure;

(d)   an application under section 1(1) of the Protection from Abuse (Scotland) Act 2001 for a power of arrest to be attached to an incoming protection measure;

(e)   an application under section 3(1) of the Domestic Abuse (Scotland) Act 2011 for a determination that an incoming protection measure is a domestic abuse interdict.

(2)   Where a process exists in relation to an incoming protection measure, an application mentioned in paragraph (1) shall be made by note in that process.

Adjustment of incoming protection measure

106.10   **106.10.**—[3](1)   This rule applies for the purpose of an application under Article 11 of the Regulation to adjust the factual elements of an incoming protection measure.

(2)   Unless the court considers that a hearing is required, the court may—

(a)   dispense with intimation of the application; and

(b)   determine the application without a hearing.

(3)   Where necessary, the court may grant decree in accordance with Scots law.

(4)   The Deputy Principal Clerk shall give the person causing the risk notice of the adjustment of the protection measure in accordance with paragraphs (5) to (7).

(5)   Where the address of the person causing the risk is known, notice shall be given by sending that person—

(a)   a notice in Form 106.10-A;

(b)   a copy of the interlocutor adjusting the factual elements of the protection measure.

(6)   Where the address of the person causing the risk is outwith the United Kingdom, the Deputy Principal Clerk shall send the documents mentioned in paragraph (5) by a registered post service.

(7)   Where the address of the person causing the risk is not known, notice shall be given by displaying on the walls of court a notice in Form 106.10-B.

(8)   Paragraph (9) applies where—

(a)   the court has dispensed with intimation to the person causing the risk of an application for the adjustment of the factual elements of an incoming protection measure under Article 11 of the Regulation; and

---

[1] Rule 106.8 inserted by S.S.I. 2014 No. 371 r. 2(6) (effective 11 January 2015).
[2] Rule 106.9 inserted by S.S.I. 2014 No. 371 r. 2(6) (effective 11 January 2015).
[3] Rule 106.10 inserted by S.S.I. 2014 No. 371 r. 2(6) (effective 11th January 2015).

(b) the person causing the risk reclaims against the interlocutor adjusting the incoming protection measure.

(9) Rule 38.2(1) (reclaiming days)(c) applies as if there was substituted for the reference to the date on which the interlocutor was pronounced, a reference to the date on which notice was given under paragraph (4).

Attachment of power of arrest to incoming protection measure

106.11.—[1,2](1) In this rule, "the Act of 2001" means theProtection from Abuse (Scotland) Act 2001.

(2) Where the court attaches a power of arrest to an incoming protection measure under section 1(2) of the Act of 2001, the following documents shall be served along with the power of arrest in accordance with section 2(1)—

   (a) a copy of the protection measure;

   (b) a copy of the Article 5 certificate issued by the issuing authority of a participating Member State in accordance with Article 5 of the MRP Regulation; and

   (c) a copy of any interlocutor adjusting the factual elements of the protection measure.

(3) After the power of arrest has been served, the following documents shall be delivered by the protected person to the chief constable of the Police Service of Scotland in accordance with section 3(1)—

   (a) a copy of the protection measure;

   (b) a copy of the Article 5 certificate issued by the issuing authority of a participating Member State in accordance with Article 5 of the MRP Regulation;

   (c) a copy of any interlocutor adjusting the factual elements of the protection measure;

   (d) a copy of the application for the power of arrest;

   (e) a copy of the interlocutor attaching the power of arrest;

   (f) a copy of the certificate of service of the power of arrest and the documents that required to be served along with it in accordance with section 2(1) of the Act of 2001; and

   (g) where a determination has previously been made in respect of the protection measure under section 3(1) of the Domestic Abuse (Scotland) Act 2011, a copy of the interlocutor making the determination.

(4) An application under the following provisions of the Act of 2001 shall be made by note in the process of the petition in which the power of arrest was attached—

   (a) section 2(3) (extension of power of arrest);

   (b) section 2(7) (recall of power of arrest).

(5) Where the court extends the duration of, or recalls a power of arrest, the person who obtained the extension, or the recall as the case may be, shall deliver a copy of the interlocutor granting the extension or the recall in accordance with section 3(1) of the Act of 2001.

(6) Where the court pronounces an interlocutor granting an application mentioned in rule 106.9(1)(a) to (c) in respect of an incoming protection measure to

106.11

---

[1] Rule 106.11 inserted by S.S.I. 2014 No. 371 r. 2(6) (effective 11th January 2015).
[2] Rule 106.11 as amended by S.S.I. 2022 No. 329 para. 2 (effective 1st December 2022).

which a power of arrest is attached, the applicant shall deliver a copy of that interlocutor to the chief constable of the Police Service of Scotland in accordance with section 3(1) of the Act of 2001.

(7)   Where a person is required to comply with section 3(1) of the Act of 2001, that person shall, after complying with that section, lodge in process a certificate of delivery in Form 106.11.

Determination that incoming protection measure is a domestic abuse interdict

106.12

106.12.—[1](1)   This rule applies where the court makes a determination that an incoming protection measure is a domestic abuse interdict.

(2)   A protected person who serves under section 3(4) of the Domestic Abuse (Scotland) Act 2011 a copy of an interlocutor containing a determination under section 3(1) shall lodge in process a certificate of service.

(3)   Paragraph (4) applies where, in respect of an incoming protection measure—

(a)   a power of arrest under section 1 of the Protection from Abuse (Scotland) Act 2001 is in effect; and

(b)   a determination is made.

(4)   Where such a determination is made, the person who obtained the determination shall send to the chief constable of the Police Service of Scotland a copy of the interlocutor containing the determination and the certificate of service.

(5)   Where a person is required by virtue of this rule to send documents to the chief constable of the Police Service of Scotland, that person must, after such compliance, lodge in process a certificate of sending in Form 106.12.

---

[1] Rule 106.12 inserted by S.S.I. 2014 No. 371 r. 2(6) (effective 11th January 2015).

CHAPTER 107 COUNTER-TERRORISM AND SECURITY ACT 2015—TEMPORARY EXCLUSION ORDERS

Interpretation and application of this Chapter

107.1.—[1](1)   In this Chapter—

107.1

"the 2015 Act" means the Counter-Terrorism and Security Act 2015;

"Advocate General" means the Advocate General for Scotland;

"affected person" means an individual on whom the Secretary of State has imposed, or is proposing to impose, a TEO;

"appeal proceedings" means proceedings in the Inner House on an appeal relating to TEO proceedings;

"legal representative" is to be construed in accordance with paragraph 4(4)(b) of schedule 3 of the 2015 Act;

"relevant party" means any party to the TEO proceedings or appeal proceedings other than the Secretary of State;

"special advocate" means a person appointed under paragraph 10(1) of schedule 3 of the 2015 Act;

"TEO" means a temporary exclusion order as defined by section 2(1) of the 2015 Act; and

"TEO proceedings" has the same meaning as in paragraph 1 of schedule 3 of the 2015 Act.

(2)   This Chapter applies in relation to TEO proceedings and appeal proceedings.

GENERAL NOTE.

The explanatory notes to the Bill indicated that the Bill was to make provisions in six main areas. First, it would strengthen powers to place temporary restrictions on travel where a person is suspected of involvement in terrorism. Second, it would enhance existing Terrorism Prevention and Investigation Measures to monitor and control the actions of individuals in the UK who pose a threat. Third, it would enhance law enforcement agencies' ability to investigate terrorism and serious crime by extending the retention of relevant communications data to include data that will help to identify who is responsible for sending a communication on the internet or accessing an internet communications service. Fourth, it would strengthen security arrangements in relation to the border and to aviation, maritime and rail transport. Fifth, it would reduce the risk of people being drawn into terrorism, by enhancing the programmes that combat the underlying ideology which supports terrorism through improved engagement from partner organisations and consistency of delivery. Sixth, it would amend existing terrorism legislation to clarify the law in relation to both insurance payments made in response to terrorist demands and the power to examine goods under the Terrorism Act 2000.

107.1.1

TEO petitions

107.2.—[2](1)   The following must be made by lodging a petition with the Deputy Principal Clerk—

107.2

(a)   an application made under section 3(1)(b) of the 2015 Act for permission to impose a TEO on an individual;

(b)   a reference made under paragraph 3(1) of schedule 2 of the 2015 Act;

(c)   a review made under section 11(2) of the 2015 Act.

(2)   The following rules do not apply to the petition—

(a)   rule 4.3 (lodging of processes);

(b)   rule 4.4 (steps of process);

(c)   rule 4.5(1)(b) (copy inventory of productions to be sent to other parties);

(d)   rule 4.6 (intimation of steps of process);

(e)   rule 4.11 (documents not to be borrowed);

(f)   rule 4.12 (borrowing and returning documents);

---

[1] Chapter 107 and r.107.1 as inserted by S.S.I. 2017 No. 26 r. 2(2) (effective 14th February 2017).
[2] Rule 107.2 as inserted by S.S.I. 2017 No. 26 r. 2(2) (effective 14th February 2017).

    (g)   rule 14.5 (first order in petitions);

    (h)   rule 14.6 (period of notice for lodging answers);

    (i)   rule 14.7 (intimation and service of petitions);

    (j)   rule 14.8 (procedure where answers lodged); and

    (k)   rule 14.9 (unopposed petitions).

(3)   Subject to rule 107.6 (permission not to disclose relevant material etc.)—

    (a)   a petition referred to in paragraph (1)(a) must include, in numbered paragraphs, statements of reasons to support the application;

    (b)   a petition referred to in paragraph (1)(b) must include, in numbered paragraphs, statements of reasons for imposing the TEO; and

    (c)   a petition referred to in paragraph (1)(c) must include, in numbered paragraphs, statements of reasons setting out—

        (i)   the details of each decision which it is sought to review;

        (ii)   details of how the affected person is affected by the decision; and

        (iii)   the grounds on which the affected person seeks to review the decision.

(4)   Subject to rule 107.6, the following documents must be lodged with the petition—

    (a)   in the case of a petition under paragraph (1)(a), the productions of the Secretary of State; and

    (b)   in the case of a petition under paragraph (1)(b), the productions of the Secretary of State and a copy of the TEO.

(5)   Subject to rule 107.6, the following documents must be lodged with a petition under paragraph (1)(c)—

    (a)   the productions of the affected person in support of the application;

    (b)   a copy of the notice under section 4 of the 2015 Act of the imposition of the TEO; and

    (c)   where relevant, any notice under section 9 of the 2015 Act imposing any or all of the permitted obligations.

"PETITION"

107.2.1   A petition under this Chapter is presented to the Outer House: r. 14.2(h). The petition must be in Form 14.4 in the official printed form: rr. 4.1 and 14.4. The petition must be signed by counsel or other person having a right of audience: r. 4.2; and see r. 1.3(1) (definition of "counsel" and "other person have a right of audience") and note 1.3.4.

    The petitioner must lodge the petition with the required step of process (r. 4.4). A fee is payable on lodging the petition: see note 14.5.10.

    On petitions generally, see Chap. 14.

Initial diets

107.3   **107.3.—**[1](1)   On receipt of a petition under rule 107.2, the Deputy Principal Clerk must allocate an initial diet for the court's consideration to begin.

(2)   The Deputy Principal Clerk must notify the date and time of an initial diet to the Secretary of State and, unless the Lord Ordinary orders otherwise, the affected person, any legal representative of the affected person and any special advocate.

(3)   The affected person must, not later than the date of the initial diet, lodge with the Deputy Principal Clerk and serve on the Secretary of State a copy of any answers and productions that are to be founded upon by the affected person at the initial diet.

---

[1] Rule 107.3 as inserted by S.S.I. 2017 No. 26 r. 2(2) (effective 14th February 2017).

(4)   Where a special advocate is appointed for the purposes of the initial diet, the special advocate must lodge with the Deputy Principal Clerk and serve on the Secretary of State a copy of any answers that are to be founded upon by the special advocate at the initial diet.

(5)   At the initial diet, the parties present must state their proposals for further procedure in respect of the petition and the interlocutor of the court must include such order for further procedure as the court thinks fit.

(6)   Where an initial diet has been held in the absence of the affected person the Deputy Principal Clerk must serve a copy of the interlocutor of the court on that person.

"SERVE"

See Chap. 16.   107.3.1

Appointment of special advocates

107.4.—[1](1)   Subject to paragraph (2), the Secretary of State must give notice to   **107.4**
the Advocate General upon—

- (a)   making any application or reference under section 3(1)(b) or paragraph 3(1) of schedule 2 of the 2015 Act respectively;
- (b)   making any motion in respect of TEO proceedings or appeal proceedings;
- (c)   being served with an application for review under section 11(2) of the 2015 Act; or
- (d)   being served with a note of appeal, reclaiming motion or other application in respect of TEO proceedings or appeal proceedings.

(2)   Paragraph (1) applies unless—

- (a)   the Secretary of State does not intend to—
  - (i)   oppose the appeal, reclaiming motion or other application; or
  - (ii)   make an application under rule 107.6(3); or
- (b)   a special advocate has already been appointed to represent the interest of the affected person in the proceedings.

(3)   Where notice is given to the Advocate General under paragraph (1), the Advocate General may appoint a special advocate to represent the interests of the affected person in the proceedings.

(4)   Where there are any TEO proceedings or appeal proceedings but no special advocate has been appointed, the affected person or the Secretary of State may at any time request the Advocate General to appoint a special advocate.

(5)   On the appointment of any special advocate, the Advocate General must intimate the name of the special advocate to the Deputy Principal Clerk in writing.

(6)   The special advocate may address the court in any TEO proceedings or appeal proceedings from which the affected person (and any legal representative of the affected person) is excluded.

Special advocates: further provision

107.5.—[2](1)   A special advocate upon whom material has been served under   **107.5**
rule 107.6(7)(a) must not communicate about the TEO proceedings or appeal proceedings or any matter connected with such proceedings except in accordance with this rule or with the authority of the court.

(2)   The special advocate may, without the authority of the court, communicate about the TEO proceedings or appeal proceedings with—

---

[1] Rule 107.4 as inserted by S.S.I. 2017 No. 26 r. 2(2) (effective 14th February 2017).
[2] Rule 107.5 as inserted by S.S.I. 2017 No. 26 r. 2(2) (effective 14th February 2017).

(a) the court;

(b) the Secretary of State or any person acting for the Secretary of State;

(c) the Advocate General or any person acting for the Advocate General;

(d) any other person, except for the relevant party or his or her legal representative, with whom it is necessary for administrative purposes for the special advocate to communicate about matters not connected with the substance of the proceedings.

(3) The special advocate may apply by motion for authority to communicate with any relevant party to the proceedings or his or her legal representative or with any other person about the proceedings or a matter connected to the proceedings.

(4) A notice of any opposition to a motion under paragraph (3) must be intimated to the special advocate and the relevant party.

(5) The relevant party must not communicate with a special advocate upon whom material has been served under rule 107.6(7) other than in writing and through a legal representative.

(6) The special advocate may, without the authority of the court, send a written acknowledgement of receipt of a communication under paragraph (5).

Permission not to disclose relevant material etc.

107.6 **107.6.**—[1](1) In this rule, "relevant material" means—

(a) material on which the Secretary of State relies;

(b) material which adversely affects the Secretary of State's case; and

(c) material which supports the case of another party to the proceedings.

(2) Subject to paragraph (3), the Secretary State must lodge all relevant material as productions.

(3) The Secretary of State may apply by motion for permission not to disclose relevant material.

(4) The Secretary of State is not required to disclose to the affected person any relevant material which is the subject of an application under paragraph (3).

(5) Subject to paragraph (6), the Secretary of State must not rely upon any relevant material which is the subject of an application under paragraph (3) unless a special advocate has been appointed.

(6) Paragraph (5) does not apply in respect of an initial diet where the court has ordered the Deputy Principal Clerk not to notify the affected person of the date and time of the initial diet.

(7) Where the Secretary of State makes an application under paragraph (3) and a special advocate has been appointed, the Secretary of State must lodge with the Deputy Principal Clerk and serve on the special advocate—

(a) the relevant material;

(b) a statement of the reasons for the application for permission not to disclose the relevant material; and

(c) if and to the extent that it is possible to do so without disclosing information contrary to the public interest, a summary of the relevant material which can be served on the affected person.

(8) On the making of an application under paragraph (3), the court must, unless paragraph (9) applies, direct the Deputy Principal Clerk to allocate a diet for a hearing of the application and the Deputy Principal Clerk must intimate the date and time in writing to the Secretary of State and to any special advocate appointed under rule 107.4.

---

[1] Rule 107.6 as inserted by S.S.I. 2017 No. 26 r. 2(2) (effective 14th February 2017).

(9)   This paragraph applies where—

    (a)   the special advocate gives notice that he or she does not oppose an application under paragraph (3);

    (b)   the court has previously considered an application by the Secretary of State for prohibition of disclosure of the same or substantially the same matters, and is satisfied that it would be just to prohibit disclosure without a hearing; or

    (c)   the Secretary of State and the special advocate consent to the court deciding the issue without a hearing.

(10)   An application under paragraph (3) must be considered in the absence of the affected person and his or her legal representative.

(11)   The court must grant the application under paragraph (3) where it considers that the disclosure of the material would be contrary to the public interest.

(12)   On granting an application under paragraph (3), the court must order the Secretary of State to serve upon every relevant party (and their legal representatives) a copy of the summary lodged under paragraph (7)(c) unless the court considers that the summary contains information or other material the disclosure of which would be contrary to the public interest.

(13)   Paragraph (14) applies where the court—

    (a)   does not grant permission to the Secretary of State to withhold relevant material; or

    (b)   requires the Secretary of State to provide a relevant party to the proceedings with a summary of relevant material that is withheld.

(14)   In a case where the Secretary of State elects not to disclose the relevant material or (as the case may be) not to provide the summary—

    (a)   if the court considers that the relevant material or anything that is required to be summarised might adversely affect the Secretary of State's case or support the case of a relevant party to the proceedings, the court may direct that the Secretary of State is not to rely on such points in the proceedings or is to make such concessions or take such other steps as the court may specify; or

    (b)   in any other case, the court must ensure that the Secretary of State does not rely in the proceedings on the material or (as the case may be) on what is required to be summarised.

Anonymity

107.7.—[1](1)   The Secretary of State or the affected person may apply for an order requiring anonymity for the affected person—

    (a)   in TEO proceedings or appeal proceedings, by motion;

    (b)   where there are no TEO proceedings or appeal proceedings, by lodging a petition with the Deputy Principal Clerk.

(2)   The reference in this rule to an order requiring anonymity for the affected person is to be construed in accordance with paragraph 6(3) of schedule 3 of the 2015 Act.

"MOTION"

For motions, see Chap. 23.

107.7

107.7.1

---

[1] Rule 107.7 as inserted by S.S.I. 2017 No. 26 r. 2(2) (effective 14th February 2017).

Exclusion from diets or hearings etc.

107.8

107.8.—[1](1) If the court considers it necessary for the affected person and his or her legal representative, or any other relevant party, to be excluded from a diet or hearing or part of a diet or hearing to secure that information is not disclosed contrary to the public interest, it must—

    (a)   make an order in that respect; and

    (b)   conduct the diet or hearing, or that part of it from which the affected person and his or her legal representative or other relevant party are excluded, in private.

(2) The court may otherwise order a diet or hearing to be conducted in private if it thinks fit.

(3) When the court issues an opinion in any proceedings to which this Chapter applies, the court may withhold any or part of its reasons if and to the extent that it is not possible to give reasons without disclosing information contrary to the public interest.

(4) Where an opinion of the court does not include the full reasons for its decision—

    (a)   the court must prepare a separate opinion including those reasons; and

    (b)   the Deputy Principal Clerk must serve that separate opinion on the Secretary of State and the special advocate.

Recording of TEO and appeal proceedings

107.9

107.9.—[2](1) TEO proceedings and appeal proceedings must be recorded.

(2) The record of proceedings must include—

    (a)   any objection to a question or line of evidence;

    (b)   any submission made in relation to such an objection; and

    (c)   the ruling of the court in relation to the objection and submission.

(3) Any transcript of the record of the proceedings must only be made on the direction of the court and must be subject to such order as to the cost of the transcript as the court thinks fit.

(4) The court may make such alterations to a transcript of the record of the proceedings as appear to it to be necessary after hearing the parties; and where such alterations are made, the court must authenticate the alterations.

---

[1] Rule 107.8 as inserted by S.S.I. 2017 No. 26 r. 2(2) (effective 14th February 2017).
[2] Rule 107.9 as inserted by S.S.I. 2017 No. 26 r. 2(2) (effective 14th February 2017).

CHAPTER 108 CHALLENGES TO VALIDITY OF EU INSTRUMENTS (EU EXIT)

Interpretation and application

108.1

108.1.—[1](1)   In this Chapter—

"the 2019 Regulations" means the Challenges to Validity of EU Instruments (EU Exit) Regulations 2019;

"EU instrument" has the meaning provided in schedule 1 of the Interpretation Act 1978;

"TFEU" means the Treaty on the Functioning of the European Union including the Protocols thereto;

"the proceedings" means any proceedings to which regulation 3 of the 2019 Regulations applies;

"the relevant U.K. authorities" has the meaning provided by regulation 2 of the 2019 Regulations.

(2)   This Chapter applies to challenges to the validity of an EU instrument, as provided for by regulation 3 of the 2019 Regulations.

Declarations from the court that an EU instrument was invalid – notices

108.2

108.2.[2]   Where a party to the proceedings seeks a declaration from the court that an EU instrument was invalid on any of the grounds set out in the second paragraph of Article 263 TFEU as it has effect immediately before IP completion day, or the court is considering whether to make such a declaration at its own instance in the proceedings—

   (a)   notice in Form 108.2-A is to be given to the relevant UK authorities no later than 21 days, or such other period as the court may direct, before the date on which the declaration is to be made—

      (i)   by the party seeking the declaration; or

      (ii)   by the clerk of court,

      as the case may be; and

   (b)   where notice is given by the party seeking the declaration, the party must lodge a certificate of notification in process.

GENERAL NOTE.

108.2.1

Regulation 4(1) of the 2019 Regulations [S.I. 2019/673] provides that in any proceedings to which regulation 3 applies, where the court or tribunal finds an EU instrument invalid on any of the grounds set out in the second paragraph of art.263 TFEU, it may declare it void. A declaration made under paragraph (1) has the same effect as if the EU Instrument had been declared void by the European Court under Article 264 TFEU in a case decided before IP completion day. The court or tribunal may, if it considers this necessary, state which of the effects of the EU instrument which it has declared void shall be considered as definitive.

The grounds in the second paragraph of art.263 of the Treaty on the Functioning of the European Union are: lack of competence; infringement of an essential procedural requirement; infringement of the Treaties or of any rule of law relating to their application; or misuse of powers.

The grounds in the second paragraph of art.263 of the Treaty on the Functioning of the European Union are: lack of competence; infringement of an essential procedural requirement; infringement of the Treaties or of any rule of law relating to their application; or misuse of powers.

Regulation 3(1) of the 2019 Regulations provides that para.1(1) of Sch.1 to the European Union (Withdrawal) Act 2018 does not apply in relation to a challenge to retained EU law where—(a) the challenge is on the basis that, immediately before IP completion day, an EU instrument was invalid on any of the grounds set out in the second paragraph of art.263 TFEU as it has effect immediately before IP

---

[1] Inserted by S.S.I. 2019 No. 328 art.2(2) (effective 31st December 2020).
[2] Inserted by S.S.I. 2019 No. 328 art.2(2) as amended by S.S.I. 2020 No. 472 art.2 (effective 31st December 2020).

completion day; and (b) the challenge relates to proceedings begun, but not finally decided, in a court or tribunal in the United Kingdom before IP completion day. Paragraph 1 of Schedule 1 to the 2018 Act provides: (1) There is no right in domestic law on or after IP completion day to challenge any retained EU law on the basis that, immediately before IP completion day, an EU instrument was invalid. (2) Sub-paragraph (1) does not apply so far as—(a) the European Court has decided before IP completion day that the instrument is invalid, or (b) the challenge is of a kind described, or provided for, in regulations made by a Minister of the Crown. (3) Regulations under sub-para.(2)(b) may (among other things) provide for a challenge which would otherwise have been against an EU institution to be against a public authority in the United Kingdom.

"IP COMPLETION DAY"

108.2.2   "IP completion day" means the implementation period completion day, that is the ending of the 11-month period from 31st January 2020 (31st December 2020 at 11pm) during which the U.K. remained subject to EU rules: European Union (Withdrawal Agreement) Act 2020 s. 39(1).

108.3   **108.3.**[1]   Where any of the relevant U.K. authorities wish to be joined as a party to the proceedings they must serve notice in Form 108.3-A to that effect on the Deputy Principal Clerk of Session and must serve a copy of the notice on all other parties in the proceedings.

"SERVE"

108.3.1   For methods, see Chap. 16.

---

[1] Inserted by S.S.I. 2019 No. 328 art.2(2) (effective 31st December 2020).

CHAPTER 109 CARE HOMES: EMERGENCY INTERVENTION ORDERS

Chapter 109

Care Homes: Emergency Intervention Orders

Interpretation and application of this Chapter

109.1.—[1](1)   In this Chapter—

"the 2010 Act" means the Public Services Reform (Scotland) Act 2010 as modified by paragraph 17 (emergency intervention orders) of schedule 1 of the
Coronavirus (Scotland) (No.2) Act 2020;

"emergency intervention order" has the meaning given by section 65A(2) (care
homes: emergency intervention orders) of the 2010 Act;

(2)   This Chapter applies in relation to applications made under section 65A of
the 2010 Act.

Applications under section 65A of the 2010 Act

109.2.—[2](1)   An application for an emergency intervention order under section
65A(1) of the 2010 Act must be made by petition.

(2)   An interim order under section 65A(3) of the 2010 Act must be sought by
prayer in the petition for the emergency intervention order.

(3)   An application under section 65A(13) of the 2010 Act for variation, extension or revocation of an emergency intervention order must be made by note in the
process for the emergency intervention order to which it relates.

(4)   An application under section 65A(14) of the 2010 Act for variation or recall
of an interim order granted under section 65A(3) of that Act must be made by motion.

GENERAL NOTE

Chapter 3 of Part 5 of the Public Services Reform (Scotland) Act 2010 provides for care services, and
a person who seeks to provide them must register with Social Care and Social Work Improvement
Scotland (SCSWIS). Under s. 65A of the Act the Scottish Ministers may apply to the court for an
emergency intervention order in respect of a care home service. Such an order to authorise the Scottish
Ministers to nominate a person as a nominated officer to enter the accommodation specified, direct and
control the provision of the care home service there and do anything that the nominated officer considers
necessary to ensure that the service is provided to an appropriate standard, and to require the registered
provider to comply with any direction of that officer in relation to that provision.

The Scottish Ministers may exercise the powers available under such an order before making such an
application for a reason relating to coronavirus but must apply to the court for the order within 24 hours
of exercise of the powers: s. 65A(5) and (6).

"PETITION"

For petitions, see Chap. 14.
A petition under this rule is made in the Outer House: r. 14.2(h).

"MOTION"

For motions, see Chap. 23.

---

[1] Inserted by S.S.I. 2020 No. 166 r. 2(2) (effective 2nd June 2020).
[2] Inserted by S.S.I. 2020 No. 166 r. 2(2) (effective 2nd June 2020).

APPENDIX

Forms

Rule 1.4

Form 5.2

Rule 5.2(1)

Rule 5.2(1)   FORM 5.2

Form of caveat

CAVEAT

for

[A.B.] (*designation and address**)

Should any application be made to the court for (*specify the nature of the application(s) to which the caveat is to apply*) against .... [*or* by [C.D.] (*designation and address*)], it is requested that intimation be made to the undernoted before any order is pronounced.

                 (*Signed*)
                 [A.B.]
                 [*or* Solicitor [*or* Agent for [A.B.]]

Caveator's telephone number
(only when caveat not lodged by a solicitor) ....

Particulars of solicitor or person having a right to conduct the litigation.

    Name ....

    Address ....

    Tel. No. ....

    Reference ....

Out of hours contacts

    Name and telephone number **1** ....

    Name and telephone number **2** ....

*Where appropriate state whether the caveat is lodged in an individual capacity, a specified representative capacity (*e.g.* as trustee of a named trust) or both such capacities. Where appropriate, state also the nature of the caveator's interest (*e.g.* shareholder; debenture holder).

Form 6.2

C1.2A.2   Rule 6.2(7A)

Rule 6.2(7A)   [1] FORM 6.2

Form of certificate of likely duration of diet

I, (*name and designation*), hereby certify that the likely duration of the *(insert name of diet)* is (*state estimated duration*).

(*Signed*)

Counsel [*or* Solicitor Advocate] for the Pursuer [*or* Defender]

(*Print name*)

---

[1] Form 6.2 inserted by S.S.I. 2007 No. 548 (effective 7th January 2008).

Form 6.3

C1.2A.3   Rule 6.3(7)
Form of certificate of likely duration of summar roll hearing
[Omitted by S.S.I. 2010 No. 30 (effective 5 April 2010).]

Form 7.1

C1.2A.4   Rule 7.1(3)

Rule 7.1(3)   [1] FORM 7.1

Form of application to Extractor for extract of a decree

EXTRACT NUMBER:

IN THE COURT OF SESSION

NOTE TO EXTRACTOR

A. Full name of case ....
Pursuer

against

....
Defender

Case number ....

Date and nature of interlocutor to be extracted ....

....

N.B. Where there is more than one interlocutor of a given date please be specific or alternatively produce a copy

Firm requesting extract ....

Signature of requesting solicitor ....

Date of request ....

B. (To be completed by Extracts Department)

Date sent to typing ....

Date returned ....

Date sent for amendment ....

Date returned ....

Date of extract ....

Date issued ....

Signature for receipt of process ....

Date of receipt ....

_____

[1] Form 7.1 amended by S.I. 1996 No. 1756 (effective 5th August 1996).

Form 7.6

Rule 7.6

C1.2A.5

Rule 7.6 [1] **FORM 7.6**

Form of statement of accumulated sum to be lodged with application for extract of decree of adjudication

IN THE COURT OF SESSION

STATEMENT OF ACCUMULATED SUM

in the cause

[A.B.] (*designation and address*)

Pursuer

against

[C.D.] (*designation and address*)

Defender

Amount of principal sum contained in decree dated	£
Interest thereon from to (days)	£
Penalty	£
Expenses of process (of action of constitution)	£
Dues of Extract	£
Total accumulated sum	£

(*Signed*)

(*Name of firm*)

[Solicitor for pursuer *or as the case may be*]
(*Address*)

_____

[1] Form 7.6 amended by S.I. 1997 No. 1050 (minor amendment effective 6th April 1997).

Form 12.A-A

C1.2A.6   Rule 12A.1(4)

Rule 12A.1(4)   [1] FORM 12.A-A

Application by party litigant for lay support

PART 1: to be completed by the party litigant

Cause ref:

Name and designation of pursuer:

Name and designation of defender(s):

Name and address of proposed named individual who is to support you:

Is the named individual related to you? If so, please state the relationship.

Does the named individual have relevant experience (e.g. acted as authorised lay representative in the sheriff court, acted as a McKenzie Friend in England and Wales, legal qualification, experience as a lay adviser on legal matters)? If so, please briefly describe that experience.

(*Signed*)

[Name of applicant]
[Date]

PART 2: to be completed by the prospective named individual

I confirm the information above.

I declare that:
    (a) I have no financial interest in the outcome of the case **or** I have the following financial interest in it:*
    (b) I am not receiving remuneration from the litigant, directly or indirectly, for my assistance and will not receive any such remuneration;
    (c) I accept that documents and information are provided to me by the litigant on a confidential basis and undertake to keep them confidential.

* *delete as appropriate*

(*Signed*)

[Name]
[Date]

---

[1] Form 12.A-A inserted by S.S.I. 2010 No. 205 (effective 7th June 2010).

Form 12B.2

Rule 12B.2(2)(a)

Application by party litigant for lay representation

PART 1: to be completed by the party litigant

Cause Ref:

Name and designation of pursuer (*or* petitioner *or* appellant):

Name and designation of defender(s) (*or* respondent(s)):

Name and address of proposed named individual who is to represent you:

State any relationship that the named individual has to you:

Does the named individual have any relevant experience? (e.g. acted as authorised lay representative in the Court of Session or sheriff court or in any other jurisdiction, or possesses a legal qualification)? If so, please briefly describe that experience:

Identify hearing(s) in respect of which permission for lay representation is sought:

(*Signed*)

[Name of applicant]

[Date]

PART 2: to be completed by the prospective lay representative

I confirm the information above.

I declare that:

(a) *I have no financial interest in the outcome of the case *or* I have the following financial interest in it:

(b) I am not receiving remuneration or other reward directly or indirectly from the litigant for my assistance and will not receive directly or indirectly such remuneration or other reward from the litigant.

(c) I accept that documents and information are provided to me by the litigant on a confidential basis and I undertake to keep them confidential.

(d) *I declare that I have no previous convictions *or* I have the following convictions: (*list convictions*).

(e) *I declare that I have not been declared a vexatious litigant under the Vexatious Actions (Scotland) Act 1898 *or* I was declared a vexatious litigant under the Vexatious Actions (Scotland) Act 1898 on (*insert date*).

*delete as appropriate

(*Signed*)

[Name]

[Date]

Form 13.2-A

C1.2A.8   Rule 13.2(1)

Rule 13.2(1)   [1] FORM 13.2–A

Form of summons and backing
(*First page*)

[*Insert the Royal Arms
in Scotland*]

(*This space will contain the
cause reference number
assigned to the summons on
being presented for signeting
and registration*)

IN THE COURT OF SESSION

SUMMONS

in the cause

[A.B.] (*designation, statement of any special capacity in which the pursuer is suing,
and address*), Pursuer

against

[C.D.] (*designation, statement of any special capacity in which the defender is being sued,
and address*), Defender

Elizabeth II, by the Grace of God, of the United Kingdom of Great Britain and Northern
Ireland and of Her other Realms and Territories, Queen, Head of the Commonwealth,
Defender of the Faith, to [C.D.].

By this summons, the pursuer craves the Lords of our Council and Session to pronounce a
decree against you in terms of the conclusions appended to this summons. If you have any good
reason why such decree should not be pronounced, you must enter appearance at the Office of
Court, Court of Session, 2 Parliament Square, Edinburgh EH1 1RQ, within three days after the
date of the calling of the summons in court. The summons shall not call in court earlier than [21]
days after the date of service on you of this summons. Be warned that, if appearance is not
entered on your behalf, the pursuer may obtain decree against you in your absence.

This summons is warrant for intimation to (*name and address and reason for intimation as set out
in the rule of the Rules of the Court of Session 1994 requiring intimation*).

Given under our Signet at Edinburgh on (*date*)

(*Signed*)

(*Name and address of or agent for pursuer*)

APPENDIX

Warrant for diligence

This summons is warrant for [arrestment to found jurisdiction] [arrestment *in rem* of (*details of ship or cargo*)] [dismantling (*details of ship*)].

(*Signed*)

Lord

Date: (*date*)

(*Next page—back of first page and following pages*)

(*State the conclusions, followed by the condescendence and pleas-in-law.*)

(*Backing of summons*)

(*This space will contain the cause reference number assigned to the summons on being presented for signeting and registration*)

IN THE COURT OF SESSION

Summons

in the cause

[A.B.],   Pursuer

against

[C.D.],   Defender

Action of (*nature of action as in the appropriate heading, if any, of the forms of conclusion shown in Form 13.2–B*).

(*Name of firm of agent for pursuer*)

---

[1] Form 13.2–A amended by S.I. 1994 No. 2901, S.S.I. 2004 No. 537, S.S.I. 2008 No. 122 and S.S.I. 2008 No. 349.

Form 13.2-AA[1]

C1.2A.9   Rule 13.2(1A)

Form of Summons and backing – actions subject to Chapter 26A Procedure
(Group Procedure)

(This space will contain the cause reference number assigned to the summons on being presented for signeting and registration)

IN THE COURT OF SESSION

SUMMONS

in the cause

[A.B.], Representative Party (*full name, designation and address*)

Representative Party for Pursuers

against

[C.D.] (*designation, statement of any special capacity in which the defender[s] is [are] being sued, and address*)

Defender[s]

Elizabeth II, by the Grace of God, of the United Kingdom of Great Britain and Northern Ireland and of Her other Realms and Territories, Queen, Head of the Commonwealth, Defender of the Faith, to [C.D.].

By this summons, the court having authorised [A.B.] to be a representative party in group proceedings and having granted permission to [A.B.] to bring the proceedings, the representative party for the pursuers craves the Lords of our Council and Session to pronounce a decree against you in terms of the conclusions appended to this summons. If you have any good reason why such decree should not be pronounced, you must enter appearance at the Office of Court, Court of Session, 2 Parliament Square, Edinburgh EH1 1RQ, within three days after the date of the calling of the summons in court. The summons shall not call in court earlier than [21] days after the date of service on you of this summons.

Be warned that, if appearance is not entered on your behalf, the representative party for the pursuers may obtain decree against you in your absence.

---

[1] Form 13.2-AA as inserted by SSI 2020/208 r.2(7)(a) Sch.1 (effective 31 July 2020).

This summons is warrant for intimation to (*name and address and reason for intimation as set out in the rule of the Rules of the Court of Session 1994 requiring intimation*).

Given under our Signet at Edinburgh on (*date*)

(*Signed*)

(*Name and address of agent for representative party*)

Warrant for diligence

This summons is warrant for [arrestment to found jurisdiction] [arrestment *in rem* (*details of ship or cargo*)] [dismantling (*details of ship*)].

(*Signed*)

Lord/Lady

Date: (*date*)

(*Next page – back of first page and following pages*)
(*State the conclusions, followed by the condescendence and pleas-in-law.*)

(*Backing of summons*)

This space will contain the cause reference number assigned to the summons on being presented for signeting and registration)

IN THE COURT OF SESSION

Summons

in the cause

[A.B.], Representative Party for Pursuers

against

[C.D.], Defender[*s*]

Action of (*nature of action as in the appropriate heading, if any, of the forms of conclusion shown in Form 13.2-B*).

(*Name of firm of agent for Representative Party for Pursuers*)

Form 13.2-B

Principal forms of conclusion   C1.2A.9.1

1. *Action for payment.* For payment to the pursuer by the defender [jointly and severally, or severally, *or otherwise as may be appropriate*] of the sum of (*amount in words and figures*) with interest at the rate of .... per cent a year from (*date*) until payment.

2. *Action of damages.* For payment to the pursuer by the defender of the sum of (*amount in words and figures*) with interest at the rate of .... per cent a year from (*date*) until payment.

3. *Action of reduction.* For production and reduction of (*specify deed to be set aside*).

4. *Action of declarator.* For declarator (*state declarator sought*).

5. *Action of count, reckoning and payment.* For count and reckoning with the pursuer for the defender's intromissions with (*describe fund or estate*) and for payment to the pursuer by the defender of the balance found due to him, or otherwise of the sum of (*amount in words and figures*).

6. *Action of proving the tenor.* For declarator that (*describe the lost deed*) was of the tenor following (*set out the terms of the lost deed*), and that the decree to be pronounced herein shall be equivalent to the original deed.

7. *Action of multiplepoinding and exoneration.* For distribution of (*describe the fund in medio*) among the claimants found entitled to it, and exoneration of (*name of the holder of the fund*).

8. *Action of furthcoming.* For payment to the pursuer by the arrestee of:-
    (a) the sum of (*amount in words and figures*); or
    (b) whichever is the lesser of:-
        (i) such sum as may be owing by the arrestee to (*name of debtor*) and has been arrested in his hands by the pursuer; and
        (ii) such sum as shall satisfy the pursuer in (*specify principal sum due and interest, in terms of the decree constituting the debt or otherwise, and expenses of the action in which that decree was obtained*).

    or
    For delivery to the pursuer or to such person as the court may appoint of the moveables belonging to or owing by the arrestee to (*name of the common debtor*) and arrested in his hands by the pursuer; and for warrant for the sale of such moveables under such conditions as may be directed; and for furthcoming and payment to the pursuer of the proceeds thereof, or at least of so much thereof as shall satisfy the pursuer in (i) the payment of the expenses of and incidental to the sale, and (ii) (*specify principal sum due and interest, in terms of the decree constituting the debt or otherwise, and expenses of the action in which that decree was obtained*).

9. *Admiralty action in rem.* For declarator that the pursuer has a lien over the (*name of ship*) for the sum of .... in respect of (*state the basis of the lien, as e.g. the collision – giving date*); and for declarator that the lien of the pursuer to the extent of the sum (*amount in words and figures*) of .... with interest at .... per cent a year from (*date*) to (*date*) is preferable to the right of all others having or pretending to have rights in the said ship and for warrant to sell the (*name of ship*) on the lien being declared, and to apply the proceeds in satisfaction of the lien in or towards payment of the said sum of .... and interest.

10. *Action of declarator of marriage.* For declarator that the pursuer and defender were lawfully married to one another by (*specify mode in which marriage was contracted, e.g.,* (a) interchange of consent *de praesenti* (*time and place*), (b) cohabitation by habit and repute (*time and place*) *or* (c) promise (*time*) *subsequente copula* at (*time and place*)).

11. *Action of declarator of nullity of marriage.* For declarator that a pretended marriage between the pursuer and defender at (*place*) and (*date*) is null by

reason of (*specify ground of nullity, e.g.* (a) the pursuer's or defender's impotency, (b) the parties being within the forbidden degrees, (c) the defender being married to someone else, (d) nonage of one of the parties, *or* (e) insanity of one of the parties at the date of the marriage).

12. *Action of declarator of nullity of (non-)parentage.* For declarator that (*name and address*) is [*or* was] [not] the son [*or* daughter] of (*name and address*).

13. *Action of separation.* For separation of the defender from the pursuer on the ground of [the adultery of the defender] [the behaviour of the defender] [the desertion of the defender and non-cohabitation during a period of two years or more] [non-cohabitation for a period of two years or more and the defender's consent to the granting of decree of separation] [non-cohabitation for a period of five years or more].

14. *Action of divorce.* For divorce of the defender from the pursuer in respect that the marriage has broken down irretrievably by reason of [the adultery of the defender] [the behaviour of the defender] [the desertion of the defender and non-cohabitation during a period of two years or more] [non-cohabitation for two years or more and the defender's consent to decree of divorce] [non-cohabitation for five years or more].

15. *Conclusion for capital sum and periodical allowance.* For payment by the defender to the pursuer of (1) a capital sum of (*amount in words and figures*) with interest at the rate of per cent a year from the date of decree to follow hereon until payment; and (2) a periodical allowance of (*amount in words and figures*) per week [or month] payable until the date three years after the date of decree to follow hereon [*or* until the remarriage or death of the pursuer, if sooner, *or as the case may be*].

16. [*Omitted by* SSI 2014/302 r.4 (*effective 16th December 2014*).]

17. *Conclusion for custody of children.* For custody of (*name of child or children*), the child[ren] of the marriage under the age of sixteen years; and for payment by the defender to the pursuer of (*amount in words and figures*) as aliment for each [*or* the] child while in the custody of the pursuer and under the age of eighteen years.

18. *Action for salvage.* For payment to the pursuer by the defender of the sum of (*amount in words and figures*) for salvage services performed by the pursuer to the vessel (*name of ship*) on (*date*) or for such an amount of salvage as to the court may seem just [*or in the case of a summons for apportionment*), for payment to the pursuer of an equitable proportion of the sum of (*amount in words and figures*)]. (*Refer to any agreement under which the total amount of the salvage award was fixed.*)

19. *Action of implement.* For decree ordaining the defender (*specify the order craved and such alternative conclusions as may be appropriate*).

20. *Adjudication for debt.* For adjudication of the heritable property of the defender, that is to say, All and Whole (*insert conveyancing description of subjects*) from the defender to the pursuer; and that for payment to the pursuer of the principal sum, interest and expenses of process and extract [*or as the case may be*] contained in a decree (*detail particulars of decree in pursuer's favour*); According as the same shall extend when accumulated at the date of decree to follow hereon and of the interest of the accumulated sum at the rate of per cent a year during the non-redemption of the said heritable property, and the expenses of the infeftment to follow on the decree of adjudication with interest .... at the rate of per cent a year from the date of disbursing the

same during the non-redemption.

[*Or in the case of heritable securities.* For adjudication of a [standard security] [bond and disposition in security] (*describe the security*) and of the subjects contained in the [standard security] [bond], that is to say, All and Whole (*insert conveyancing description of subjects*) from the defender to the pursuer for payment of (*describe debts*), during the non-redemption of the said lands and others].

21. *Adjudication in implement.* For adjudication from the defender of All and Whole (*insert conveyancing description of subjects*) and all rights of the defender therein and the rents thereof from and after (*date of entry under missives*) in implement of missives of sale dated .... between the defender and the pursuer and for declarator that the said lands and others belong to the pursuer and his heirs and assignees; and for decree ordaining the defender to free and relieve the said lands and others of all burdens and incumbrances affecting them, of all feuduties, and public and other burdens affecting the said lands at and preceding the pursuer's term of entry, or otherwise for payment of the sum of (*amount in words and figures*) or such sum as may be required for that purpose.

22. *Declarator and division or sale.* For declarator that the pursuer is entitled to insist in an action of division of sale of All and Whole (*insert conveyancing description of subjects*); and for division of those subjects between the pursuer and the defender, or if division of those subjects is found to be impracticable or inexpedient for declarator that those subjects should be sold and the proceeds divided between the pursuer and the defender, and for warrant to sell accordingly; and for allocation of the expenses of the sale and of this process between the pursuer and the defender.

23. *Maills and duties under Heritable Securities Act 1894.* For declarator that the pursuer has right to the rents, maills and duties of the subjects and others specified in the bond and disposition in security for ...., granted by .... in favour of .... dated and recorded in the .... register or at least so much of those rents, maills and duties as will satisfy and pay the pursuer the principal sum of (*amount in words and figures*), with interest at the rate of .... per cent a year from the .... day of .... until payment together with £.......... liquidate penalty and termly failures, all as specified and contained in the said bond and disposition in security dated and recorded as aforesaid.

24. *Poinding of the ground.*

    (a) *Against debtor in possession.* For warrant to poind and distrain all moveable goods and effects poindable or distrainable belonging to the defender which are or shall happen to be on the ground of the lands and others described and contained in the [standard security] [bond and disposition in security] [*or where the action proceeds on a real burden,* the disposition or other writ by which it is constituted] aftermentioned, that is to say, All and Whole (*insert conveyancing description of subjects*): And for payment thereof to the pursuer of the amount of the principal sum of (*amount in words and figures*) together with £.......... liquidate penalty and termly failures, with interest on said principal sum from (*date*) until payment and in all time coming during the non-redemption conform to [standard security] [bond and disposition in security] dated .... and [recorded in the Division of the General Register of Sasines applicable to the county of ....] [registered in the Land Register] both days of .... granted by the defender in favour of the pursuer [*or where the pursuer is not the original security holder,* in favour of .... and to which the pursuer has now right in virtue of (*describe title*)].

(b) *Against debtor and tenants.* For warrant to poind and distrain all moveable goods and effects poindable or distrainable of the defender [C.D.] principal debtor, [and of the defender[s] [E.F.] [and G.H.] his tenant[s] or possessor[s] of the lands and others aftermentioned which are or shall happen to be on the grounds of those lands and others described and contained in the [standard security] [bond and disposition in security] aftermentioned, that is to say, All and Whole (*insert description of subjects sufficient to identify them*) but in so far as relates to the said tenants and possessors to the amount only of the respective rents due or that may become due by them and for payment thereof to the pursuer to the amount of the principal sum of (*amount in words and figures*)with £ liquidate penalty and termly failures specified and contained in the bond and disposition in security dated .... and [recorded in the Division of the General Register of Sasines applicable to the county of ....] [registered in the Land Register] the .... [both days] of .... granted by the defender [C.D.] in favour of the pursuer, with interest from the term of .... and in all time coming during the non-redemption.

Form 13.7[1]

C1.2A.10   Rule 13.7(1)

Form of citation of defender

CITATION

Date: (*date of posting or other method of service*)

To: (*name and address of defender*)

IN HER MAJESTY'S NAME AND AUTHORITY, I, (*name of agent*), solicitor [*or person having a right to conduct the litigation*], for (*name of pursuer*) [*or (name of lead pursuer, if any, in proceedings to which Chapter 26A applies)*], [*or (name of messenger-at-arms*), messenger-at-arms], serve the attached summons on you.

The summons contains a claim made by (*name of pursuer*)) [*or (name of lead pursuer, if any, in proceedings to which Chapter 26A applies)*] against you in the Court of Session, Edinburgh.

If you intend to deny the claim you must: (1) enter appearance at the Office of Court, Court of Session, 2 Parliament Square, Edinburgh EH1 1RQ within three days after the date on which the summons calls in court;   and (2) subsequently lodge defences within seven days after the date on which the summons calls in court as required by the Rules of the Court of Session 1994.   The summons will not call in court earlier than [21] days after the date of service on you of the summons.   The date of service is the date stated at the top of this citation unless service has been by post in which case the date of service is the day after that date.

If you do not enter appearance and lodge defences the court may make an order against you.

IF YOU ARE UNCERTAIN ABOUT THE EFFECT OF THIS CITATION, you should consult a solicitor, Citizens Advice Bureau or other local advice agency or adviser immediately.

(Signed)

Messenger-at-arms
[*or* Solicitor [*or* Agent] for pursuer]
(*Address*)

---

[1] Form 13.7 as amended by SSI 2020/208 r.2(7)(b) (effective 31 July 2020).

Form 13.12

Rule 13.12(1)

Rule 13.12(1)   [1] FORM 13.12

Form of notice of intimation to person holding a heritable security in an action relating to heritable property

Date: (*date of posting or other method of intimation*)

To: (*name and address of security holder*)

TAKE NOTICE

(*Name and address of pursuer*) has brought an action against (*name and address of defender*). The action relates to heritable property over which you are believed to hold a heritable security. A copy of the summons in the action is attached.

You may apply to the court by minute for leave to lodge defences in the action. You must do so at the Office of Court, Court of Session, 2 Parliament Square, Edinburgh EH1 1RQ within [21] days after the date of intimation to you of the summons [*or if the warrant for intimation is executed before calling of the summons*, within [7] days after the summons calls in court. The summons will not call in court earlier than [21] days after the date of intimation to you of the summons]. The date of intimation is the date stated at the top of this notice unless intimation has been made by post in which case the date of intimation is the day after that date.

IF YOU ARE UNCERTAIN ABOUT THE EFFECT OF THIS NOTICE, you should consult a solicitor, Citizens Advice Bureau or other local advice agency or adviser immediately.

         (*Signed*)

         Messenger-at-arms
         [*or* Solicitor [*or* Agent] for pursuer]
         (*Address*)

---

[1] Form 13.12 amended by S.I. 1994 No. 2901 (minor correction).

Form 14.4

Rule 14.4(1)

Rule 14.4(1)   [1] FORM 14.4

Form of petition

[*Insert the Royal Arms in Scotland*] 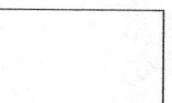 (*This space will contain the cause reference number assigned to the petition on being lodged*)

UNTO THE RIGHT HONOURABLE THE LORDS OF COUNCIL AND SESSION

The Petition of [A.B.] (*name, designation and address of petitioner and statement of any special capacity in which the petitioner is presenting the petition*)

HUMBLY SHEWETH:—

1. That (*here set out in this and following numbered paragraphs the facts and circumstances which form the grounds of petition*).

MAY IT THEREFORE please your Lordships
to (insert prayer)

According to Justice, etc.

(*Signed*)

(*Backing of petition*)

(*This space will contain the cause reference number assigned to the petition on being lodged*)

The Petition
of

[A.B.]
for

(*here describe shortly the nature or object of the petition*).

(*Name of firm of agent for petitioner*)

---

[1] Form 14.4 amended by S.I. 1994 No. 2901 and S.S.I. 2008 No. 349.

Form 14.7

Rule 14.7(2)

Rule 14.7(2)   Form 14.7

Form of citation in petition

CITATION

Date: (*date of posting or other method of service*)

To: (*name and address of person on whom petition served*)

IN HER MAJESTY'S NAME AND AUTHORITY, and in the name and authority of Lord (*name*), I, (*name of agent*), solicitor [*or* person having a right to conduct the litigation], for (*name of pursuer*) [*or* (*name of messenger-at-arms*), messenger-at-arms], serve the attached petition and interlocutor of the court on you.

The interlocutor requires you, if so advised, to lodge answers to the petition.

If you intend to lodge answers to the petition you must lodge them at the Office of Court, Court of Session, 2 Parliament Square, Edinburgh EH1 1RQ within [21] days after the date of service on you of the petition. The date of service is the date stated at the top of this citation unless service has been by post in which case the date of service is the day after that date.

Release 99: November 2008

IF YOU ARE UNCERTAIN ABOUT THE EFFECT OF THIS CITATION, you should consult a solicitor, Citizens Advice Bureau or other local advice agency or adviser immediately.

(*Signed*)

Messenger-at-arms
[*or* Solicitor [*or* Agent] for petitioner]
(*Address*)

Form 14A.2

C1.2A.14   Rule 14A.2(2)

Rule 14A.2(2)   ¹FORM 14A.2

Statement to accompany application for interim diligence

DEBTORS (SCOTLAND) ACT 1987 Section 15D

[*or* DEBT ARRANGEMENT AND ATTACHMENT (SCOTLAND) ACT 2002 Section 9C]

in the cause (Cause Reference No.   )

[A.B.] (*designation and address*)

Pursuer [*or* Petitioner]

against

[C.D.] (*designation and address*)

Defender [*or* Respondent]

STATEMENT

1. The applicant is the pursuer [*or* petitioner] [*or* defender] [*or* respondent] in the action by [A.B] (*design*) against [C.D.] (*design*).
2. [The following persons have an interest (*specify names and addresses*).]
3. The application [is *or* is not] seeking the grant under [section 15E(1) *or* 9D(1)] of the [1987 Act *or* 2002 Act] of [warrant for diligence *or* interim attachment] in advance of a hearing on the application.
4. [*Here provide such other information as may be prescribed by regulations made by the Scottish Ministers under section 15D(2)(d) of the 1987 Act or section 9C(2)(d) of the 2002 Act*]

....   (*Signed*)

Solicitor [*or* Agent] for A.B. [*or* C.D.] (*include full designation*)

_____

¹Form 14A.2 inserted by S.S.I. 2008 No. 122 (effective 1st April 2008).

Form 15.1

C1.2A.15   Rule 15.1(4)

Rule 15.1(4)   FORM 15.1

Form of notice of minute

Date: (*date of posting or other method of service or intimation*)

To: (*name and address*)

TAKE NOTICE

(*Name of minuter*) has lodged the attached Minute in the process of an action in the Court of Session in which (*name*) is the pursuer and (*name*) is the defender. By virtue of an order of [Lord (*name*) in] the Court of Session dated (*date*) you may lodge answers at the Office of Court, Court of Session, 2 Parliament Square, Edinburgh EH1 1RQ within [21] days after the date of service on [*or* intimation to] you of the Minute. The date of service or intimation is the date stated at the top of this notice unless service or intimation has been by post in which case the date of service or intimation is the day after that date.

IF YOU ARE UNCERTAIN ABOUT THE EFFECT OF THIS NOTICE, you should consult a solicitor, Citizens Advice Bureau or other local advice agency or adviser immediately.

(*Signed*)

Messenger-at-arms
[*or* Solicitor [*or* Agent] for minuter]
(*Address*)

Form 15.2

Rule 15.2(3)   **C1.2A.16**

Rule 15.2(3)   FORM 15.2

Form of notice of Note

Date: (*date of posting or other method of service or intimation*)

To: (*name and address*)

TAKE NOTICE

(*Name of noter*) has lodged the attached Note in the process of a petition in the Court of Session in which (*name*) is the petitioner [and (*name*) is the respondent]. By virtue of an order of [Lord (*name*) in] the Court of Session dated (*date*) you may lodge answers to the Note at the Office of Court, Court of Session, 2 Parliament Square, Edinburgh EH1 1RQ within [21] days after the date of service on [*or* intimation to] you of the Note. The date of service or intimation is the date stated at the top of this notice unless service or intimation has been by post in which case the date of service or intimation is the day after that date.

IF YOU ARE UNCERTAIN ABOUT THE EFFECT OF THIS NOTICE, you should consult a solicitor, Citizens Advice Bureau or other local advice agency or adviser immediately.

(*Signed*)

Messenger-at-arms
[*or* Solicitor [*or* Agent] for noter]
(*Address*)

Form 16.2

C1.2A.17   Rule 16.2(5)(b)

Rule 16.2(5)(b)   FORM 16.2

Form of certificate of personal service or intimation on a warrant on person furth of United Kingdom

CERTIFICATE OF PERSONAL SERVICE [*OR* INTIMATION] FURTH OF UNITED KINGDOM

I, (*name*) pursuer [*or* authorised agent of the pursuer], certify that I served [*or* intimated] this summons [or other document (*specify*) on [*or* to] (*name of defender or other person on whom served or to whom intimated*) by (*state method of service*) at (*place and country*), being a method of service [*or* intimation] permitted in that country, on (*date*).

I did this in the presence of (*name, occupation and address of witness*).

> (*Signed*)
>
> Pursuer [*or* Authorised agent of pursuer]
> (*Address*)
>
> (*Signed*)
> Witness

Form 16.3

C1.2A.18   Rule 16.3(1)(b)

Rule 16.3(1)(b)   FORM 16.3

Form of certificate of service or intimation on a warrant by messenger-at-arms

CERTIFICATE OF SERVICE [*OR* INTIMATION]

I, (*name*) Messenger-at-Arms, certify that I served [*or* intimated] this summons [*or other document (specify)*] [and a citation] [*or* and a notice of intimation] on [*or* to] (*name of defender or other person on whom served or to whom intimated*)—

* by leaving it and a citation [*or* notice] with (*name of defender or other person*) at (*place*) at (*time*) on (*date*).
* by leaving it and a citation [*or* notice] with (*name and occupation of person with whom left*) at (*place*) on (*date*). (*Specify that enquiry made and that reasonable grounds exist for believing that the person on whom service is to be made or to whom intimation is to be given resides at the place but is not available.*)
* by depositing it and a citation [*or* notice] in (*place*) on (*date*). (*Specify that enquiry made and that reasonable grounds exist for believing that the person on whom service is to be made or to whom intimation is to be given resides at the place but is not available.*)
* by leaving it and a citation [*or* notice] with (*name and occupation of person with whom left*) at (*place of business*) on (*date*). (*Specify that enquiry made and that reasonable grounds exist for believing that the person on whom service is to be made or to whom intimation is to be given carries on business at the place.*)
* by depositing it and a citation [*or* notice] at (*place of business*) on (*date*). (*Specify that*

Form 16.4

Rule 16.4(4)(b)

Rule 16.4(4)(b) [1] FORM 16.4

Form of certificate of service, or intimation on a warrant, by post

CERTIFICATE OF SERVICE [*OR* INTIMATION] BY POST

I, (*name and designation*), certify that I served [*or* intimated] this summons (*or other document* (*specify*)) on [*or* to] (*name of defender or other person on whom served*) [*where applicable*, by first class recorded delivery] by posting a copy of it with a citation [*or* notice] attached, to that person between (*time*) and (*time*) on (*date*) at (*name of post office*) post office in a registered envelope [*or* recorded delivery envelope] addressed as follows:— (*address*).

(*Signed*)

Solicitor [*or* Agent] for pursuer [*or* other party]
[*or* Messenger-at-Arms]
(*Address*)

---

[1] Form 16.4 amended by S.S.I. 2008 No. 349 (effective 1st December 2008).

Form 16.5

Rule 16.5(3)(a)

Rule 16.5(3)(a) [1] FORM 16.5

Form of citation by advertisement

IN THE COURT OF SESSION

in the cause

[A.B.] (*designation and address*)

Pursuer

against

[C.D.]

Defender

An action has been brought in the Court of Session, Edinburgh, [Scotland,] by [A.B.], pursuer. [A.B.] calls as a defender [C.D.] whose last known address was (*address*). If [C.D.] wishes to challenge the jurisdiction of the court or to defend the action, he [*or* she [*or* it] [*or* they]] should contact the Deputy Principal Clerk of Session, Court of Session, Parliament Square, Edinburgh EH1 1RQ (Telephone 031–225 2595) immediately and in any event by not later than six months from the date of publication of this advertisement.

(*Signed*)

Solicitor [*or* Agent] for pursuer
(*Address*)

---

[1] Form 16.5 amended by S.I. 1998 No. 890.

Form 16.7

C1.2A.21 Rule 16.7(2)(a)

[1] Form 16.5 amended by S.I. 1998 No. 890.

Rule 16.7(2)(a)   [1] FORM 16.7

Form of certificate of intimation of a document

I, (*name and designation*), certify that I intimated (*specify document*) to (*name of person to whom intimation made*) [with a copy of the interlocutor of Lord (*name*) dated (*date*) a copy of which is attached] on (*date*).

         (*Signed*)

         Solicitor [*or* Agent] for pursuer
         [*or as the case may be*]
         (*Address*)

[1] Form 16.7 amended by S.I. 1996 No. 2168 (minor correction).

Form 16.15-A

C1.2A.22 Rule 16.15(1)(a)

       Rule 16.15(1)(a)   [1] FORM 16.15–A

Form of schedule of arrestment to found jurisdiction

SCHEDULE OF ARRESTMENT TO FOUND JURISDICTION

Date: (*date of execution*)

Time: (*time arrestment executed*)

To: (*name and address of arrestee*)

IN HER MAJESTY'S NAME AND AUTHORITY, I, (*name*), Messenger-at-Arms, by virtue of a summons containing a warrant for arrestment to found jurisdiction, at the instance of (*name and address of pursuer*) against (*name and address of defender*) and signeted on (*date*), arrest to found jurisdiction against (*name of defender*) in your hands: (i) the sum of (*amount*), more or less, due by you to (*name of defender*) or to any other person on his [*or* her] [*or* its] [*or* their] behalf; and (ii) all moveable subjects in your hands and belonging or pertaining to (*name of defender*).

This I do in the presence of (*name, occupation and address of witness*).

(*Signed*)

Messenger-at-Arms
(*Address*)

NOTE

(*Do not use this note where arrestment to found jurisdiction is combined with arrestment on the dependence in one schedule.*)

This schedule arrests in your hands debts due by you to the defender mentioned in the schedule and goods and other moveables held by you on his behalf. It does so solely for the purpose of establishing the jurisdiction of the Court of Session over the defender.

IF YOU ARE UNCERTAIN ABOUT THE EFFECT OF THIS DOCUMENT, you should consult a solicitor, Citizens Advice Bureau or other local advice agency or adviser immediately.

---

[1] Form 16.15–A substituted by S.I. 1998 No. 2637 (effective 1st December 1998).

Form 16.15-AA

C1.2A.23 Rule 16.15(1)(a)(ii)

Rule 16.15(1)(a)(ii) [1] FORM 16.15–AA

Form of schedule of arrestment of ship to found jurisdiction

SCHEDULE OF ARRESTMENT OF SHIP TO FOUND JURISDICTION

Date: (*date of execution*)

Time: (*time arrestment executed*)

IN HER MAJESTY'S NAME AND AUTHORITY, I, (*name*), Messenger-at-Arms, by virtue of a summons containing a warrant for arrestment to found jurisdiction, at the instance of (*name and address of pursuer*) against (*name and address of defender*) and signeted on (*date*), arrest to found jurisdiction against (*name of defender*) the ship (*name*) presently lying in (*describe location*) and belonging to the defender.

This I do in the presence of (*name, occupation and address of witness*).

(*Signed*)

Messenger-at-Arms
(*Address*)

NOTE

You should consult your legal adviser about the effect of this arrestment.

(The name, address and twenty-four hour contact telephone number of the agent for the party on whose behalf the arrestment was executed are to be inserted here.)

(*Name of agent*)

(*Address*)

(*Telephone number*).

---

[1] Form 16.15–AA inserted by S.I. 1998 No. 2367 (effective 1st December 1998).

Form 16.15-B

Rule 16.15(1)(b) and (e)

Rule 16.15(1)(b) and (e)   ¹ FORM 16.15-B

Form of schedule of arrestment on the dependence

SCHEDULE OF ARRESTMENT ON THE DEPENDENCE

Date: (*date of execution*)

Time: (*time arrestment executed*)

To: (*name and address of arrestee*)

IN HER MAJESTY'S NAME AND AUTHORITY, I, (*name*), Messenger-at-Arms, by virtue of—

*   a summons containing a warrant for arrestment on the dependence of the action at the instance of (*name and address of pursuer*) against (*name and address of defender*) signeted on (*date*),

*   a counterclaim containing a warrant which has been granted for arrestment on the dependence of the claim by (*name and address of creditor*) against (*name and address of debtor*) and dated (*date of warrant*),

*   an order of [Lord (*name*) in] the Court of Session dated (*date of order*) granting warrant [for arrestment on the dependence of the action raised at the instance of (*name and address of pursuer*) against (*name and address of defender*)] [*or* for arrestment on the dependence of the claim in the counterclaim [*or* third party notice] by (*name and address of creditor*) against (*name and address of debtor*) [*or* to arrest in the petition of (*name and address of petitioner*) against (*name and address of respondent*)],

arrest in your hands (i) the sum of (*amount*), in excess of the Protected Minimum Balance, where applicable (see Note), more or less, due by you to (*defender's name*) [*or name and address of common debtor if common debtor is not the defender*] or to any other person on his [*or* her] [*or its*] [*or* their] behalf; and (ii) all moveable things in your hands belonging or pertaining to the said (*name of common debtor*), to remain in your hands under arrestment until they are made forthcoming to (*name of pursuer*) [*or name and address of creditor if he is not the pursuer*] or until further order of the court.

This I do in the presence of (*name, occupation and address of witness*).

(*Signed*)

Messenger-at-Arms
(*Address*)

NOTE

This schedule arrests in your hands (i) debts due by you to (*name of common debtor*); and (ii) goods and other moveables held by you for him. **You should not pay any debts to him or hand over any goods or other moveables to him without taking legal advice.**

This schedule may be used to arrest a ship or cargo. If it is, you should consult your legal adviser about the effect of it.

The Protected Minimum Balance is the sum referred to in section 73F(4) of the Debtors (Scotland) Act 1987. This sum is currently set at [*insert current sum*]. The Protected Minimum Balance applies where the arrestment attaches funds standing to the credit of a debtor in an account held by a bank or other financial institution and the debtor is an individual. The Protected Minimum Balance does not apply where the account is held in the name of a company, a limited liability partnership or an unincorporated association or where the amount is operated by the debtor as a trading account.

Under section 73G of the Debtors (Scotland) Act 1987 you must also, within the period of 3 weeks beginning with the day on which the arrestment is executed, disclose to the creditor the nature and value of the funds and/or moveable property which have been attached. This disclosure must be in the form set out in Schedule 8 to the Diligence (Scotland) Regulations 2009. Failure to comply may lead to a financial penalty under section 73G of the Debtors (Scotland) Act 1987 and may also be dealt with as a contempt of court. You must, at the same time, send a copy of the disclosure to the debtor and to any person known to you who owns (or claims to own) attached property, or to whom attached funds are (or are claimed to be) due, solely or in common with the debtor.

IF YOU ARE UNCERTAIN ABOUT THE EFFECT OF THIS DOCUMENT, you should consult a solicitor, Citizens Advice Bureau or other local advice agency or adviser immediately.

*Delete where not applicable.

---

[1] Form 16.15–B substituted by S.I. 1998 No. 2637 (effective 1st December 1998) and S.S.I. 2009 No. 104 (effective 22nd April 2009).

Form 16.15-BB

Rule 16.15(1)(e)(ii)

Rule 16.15(1)(e)(ii)   [1] FORM 16.15–BB

Form of schedule of arrestment of ship on the dependence

SCHEDULE OF ARRESTMENT OF SHIP ON THE DEPENDENCE

Date: *(date of execution)*

Time: *(time arrestment executed)*

IN HER MAJESTY'S NAME AND AUTHORITY, I, *(name)*, Messenger-at-Arms, by virtue of—

* a summons containing a warrant for arrestment on the dependence of the action at the instance of *(name and address of pursuer)* against *(name and address of defender)* signeted on *(date)*,

* a counterclaim containing a warrant which has been granted for arrestment on the dependence of the claim by *(name and address of creditor)* against *(name and address of debtor)* and dated *(date of warrant)*,

* an order of [Lord *(name)* in] the Court of Session dated *(date of order)* granting warrant [for arrestment on the dependence of the action raised at the instance of *(name and address of pursuer)* against *(name and address of defender)*] [or for arrestment on the dependence of the claim in the counterclaim [or third party notice] by *(name and address of creditor)* against *(name and address of debtor)* [or to arrest in the petition of *(name and address of petitioner)* against *(name and address of respondent)*],

arrest the ship *(name of ship)* presently lying in *(describe current location e.g. the port of X)* to remain in that *(more precisely if required)* under arrestment on the dependence of the action [*or* claim] until further order of the court.

This I do in the presence of *(name, occupation and address of witness)*.

                        (Signed)

                        Messenger-at-Arms
                        (Address)

NOTE

You should consult your legal adviser about the effect of this arrestment.

(The name, address and twenty-four hour contact telephone number of the agent for the party on whose behalf the arrestment was executed are to be inserted here.)

(Name of agent)

(Address)

(Telephone number),

*Delete where not applicable.

---

[1] Form 16.15–BB inserted by S.I. 1998 No. 2637 (effective 1st December 1998).

Form 16.15-C

C1.2A.26   Rule 16.15(1)(c)

Rule 16.15(1)(c)   [1] FORM 16.15–C

Form of schedule of arrestment in rem of ship, cargo or other maritime res to enforce maritime hypothec or lien

SCHEDULE OF ARRESTMENT *IN REM* IN ADMIRALTY ACTION *IN REM*

Date: (*date of execution*)

Time: (*time arrestment executed*)

To: (*name and address of arrestee*)

IN HER MAJESTY'S NAME AND AUTHORITY, I, (*name*), Messenger-at-Arms, by virtue of a summons containing a warrant for arrestment *in rem* of the ship (*name of ship*) [*or* cargo (*describe*)] [*or other maritime res (describe)*)] in an Admiralty action *in rem* at the instance of (*name and address of pursuer*) against (*name and address of defender*) and signeted on (*date*), arrest the ship (*name*) presently lying in (*describe current location e.g. the port of X*) with her float, boats, furniture, appurtenances and apparelling [*or* cargo] [*or other maritime res*] (*describe location*)], to remain in that (*specify more precisely if required*) under arrestment *in rem* until they are sold or until this arrestment is recalled or other order of the court.

This I do in the presence of (*name, occupation and address of witness*).

(*Signed*)

Messenger-at-Arms
(*Address*)

NOTE

You should consult your legal adviser about the effect of this arrestment.

(The name, address and twenty-four hour contact telephone number of the agent for the party on whose behalf the arrestment was executed are to be inserted here.)

(*Name of agent*)

(*Address*)

(*Telephone number*)

---

[1] Form 16.15–C substituted by S.I. 1998 No. 2637 (effective 1st December 1998).

Form 16.15-D

Rule 16.15(1)(d)

Rule 16.15(1)(d)   [1] FORM 16.15–D

Form of schedule of arrestment in rem of ship to enforce non-pecuniary claim

SCHEDULE OF ARRESTMENT *IN REM* OF SHIP UNDER THE ADMINISTRATION
OF JUSTICE ACT 1956, SECTION 47(3)(b)

Date: (*date of execution*)

Time: (*time arrestment executed*)

IN HER MAJESTY'S NAME AND AUTHORITY, I, (*name*), Messenger-at-Arms, by virtue
of—

* an order of Lord (*name*) in the Court of Session dated (*date of order*) granting warrant
  for arrestment *in rem* under section 47(3)(b) of the Administration of Justice Act 1956
  of the ship (*name of ship*) in an action,

* a summons containing a warrant for arrestment *in rem* under section 47(3)(b) of the
  Administration of Justice Act 1956 of the ship (*name of ship*).

at the instance of (*name and address of pursuer*) against (*name and address of defender*)
and signeted on (*date*), arrest the [ship] [*or* vessel] (*name*) presently lying in (*describe
current location e.g. the port of X*) with her float, boats, furniture, appurtenances and

apparelling to remain in that place (*specify more precisely if required*) under arrestment
in rem until this arrestment is recalled or other order of the court.

This I do in the presence of (*name, occupation and address of witness*).

(*Signed*)

Messenger-at-Arms
(*Address*)

NOTE

You should consult your legal adviser about the effect of this arrestment.

(The name, address and twenty-four hour contact telephone number of the agent for the
party on whose behalf the arrestment was executed are to be inserted here.)

(*Name of agent*)

(*Address*)

(*Telephone number*)

*Delete where not applicable.

---

[1] Form 16.15–D substituted by S.I. 1998 No. 2637 (effective 1st December 1998).

FORM 16.15-E

C1.2A.28   Rule 16.15(1)(f)

Rule 16.15(1)(f)   Form 16.15–E

Form of schedule of arrestment in execution

[*Omitted by S.S.I. 2009 No. 104 (effective 22nd April 2009).*]

Form 16.15-F

C1.2A.29   Rule 16.15(1)(h)

Rule 16.15(1)(h)   Form 16.15–F

Form of schedule of inhibition

[*Omitted by S.S.I. 2009 No. 104 (effective 22nd April 2009).*]

Form 16.15-G[1]

C1.2A.30   Rule 16.15(1)(i)
Form of charge for payment of money
CHARGE FOR PAYMENT OF MONEY

[A.B.] (*designation and address*)

Pursuer

against

[C.D.] (*designation and address*)

Defender

Date: (*date of execution*)

To: (*name and address of debtor*)

On (*date*) a decree against you was granted in the Court of Session for payment of a sum of money in the above action [*or give details of other document upon which charge proceeds such as a document registered for execution in the Books of Council and Session*].

The decree [*or warrant for execution of the document mentioned above*] was extracted on (*date*).

IN HER MAJESTY'S NAME AND AUTHORITY, I, (*name*), Messenger-at-Arms, by virtue of the extract decree, charge you to pay the total sum due as set out below [together with any further interest] within 14 [*or* 28] days after the date of this charge to (*name and address of person to whom payment to be made*).

If you do not pay this sum within 14 [*or* 28] days you are liable to have further action taken against you including arrestment of your earnings and the attachment and auction of articles belonging to you without further notice. If you have total debts amounting to £3,000 or more, you are also liable to be sequestrated (declared bankrupt).

---

[1] As amended by S.S.I. 2016 No. 242 (effective 3rd October 2016).

This charge is executed on you today by me by (*state method of execution*) in the presence of (*name, occupation and address of witness*).

> (*Signed*)
> Messenger-at-Arms
> (*Address*)
> (*Signed*)
> Witness

The sum now due by you is:–

	Principal sum	£
	Interest to date*	£
	Expenses	£
TOTAL OF ABOVE		£
Less paid to account		£
SUB TOTAL		£
Agent's fee		£
Expenses of messenger-at-arms:-		
	Charge fee	£
	Travelling	£
	Witness fee	£
	Other outlays in connection with service of charge (*specify*)	£
TOTAL SUM DUE		£

* Note. Interest on the principal sum will continue to run until the date of payment.

IF YOU ARE UNCERTAIN ABOUT THE EFFECT OF THIS DOCUMENT, you should consult a solicitor, Citizens Advice Bureau or other local advice agency or adviser immediately.

Form 16.15-H

Rule 16.15(1)

C1.2A.31

Rule 16.15(1) [1] FORM 16.15–H

Form of certificate of execution of arrestment or inhibition

CERTIFICATE OF EXECUTION

I, (*name*), Messenger-at-Arms, certify that I executed (*specify the kind of arrestment, whether on the dependence of an action, counterclaim or third party notice, whether on the authority of an interlocutor (specify), on letters of arrestment or in execution of a decree (specify)*), [obtained] at the instance of (*name and address of party arresting*) against (*name and address of common debtor*) on (*name of person on whom executed*)—

* by leaving the schedule of [arrestment] with (*name of defender or other person*) at (*place*) on (*date*).

* by leaving the schedule of [arrestment] with (*name and occupation of person with whom left*) at (*place*) on (*date*). (*Specify that enquiry made and that reasonable grounds exist for believing that the person on whom service is to be made resides at the place but is not available.*)

* by depositing the schedule of [arrestment] in (*place*) on (*date*). (*Specify that enquiry made and that reasonable grounds exist for believing that the person on whom service is to be made resides at the place but is not available.*)

* by leaving the schedule of [arrestment] with (*name and occupation of person with whom left*) at (*place of business*) on (*date*). (*Specify that enquiry made and that reasonable grounds exist for believing that the person on whom service is to be made carries on business at the place.*)

* by depositing the schedule of [arrestment] at (*place of business*) on (*date*). (*Specify that enquiry made and that reasonable grounds exist for believing that the person on whom service is to be made carries on business at the place.*)

* by leaving the schedule of [arrestment] at (*registered office or place of business*) on (*date*), in the hands of (*name of person*).

* by leaving [*or* depositing] the schedule of [arrestment] at (*registered office, official address or place of business*) on (*date*) in such a way that it was likely to come to the attention of (*name of defender or other person on whom served*). (*Specify how left.*)

* edictally by leaving the schedule of [arrestment] with (*name and occupation of person with whom left*) at the office of the Extractor of the Court of Session, Parliament Square, Edinburgh on (*date*) and sending a copy of the schedule by registered post [*or* first class recorded delivery service] to (*name and address of residence, registered office, official address or place of business or such last known place*) on (*date*).

I did this in the presence of (*name, occupation and address of witness*).

(*Signed*)

Messenger-at-Arms
(*Address*)

(*Signed*)

Witness

*Delete where not applicable.

---

[1] Form 16.15–H amended by S.S.I 2009 No. 104 (effective 22nd April 2009).

Form 16.15-HH

C1.2A.32   Rule 16.15(1)(a)(ii)

Rule 16.15(1)(a)(ii)   [1] FORM 16.15–HH

Form of certificate of arrestment of ship to found jurisdiction

CERTIFICATE OF EXECUTION OF ARRESTMENT OF SHIP TO FOUND JURISDICTION

I, (*name*), Messenger-at-Arms, certify that I, by virtue of a summons containing a warrant for arrestment to found jurisdiction, executed an arrestment of the ship (*name*) at the instance of (*name and address of pursuer*) against (*name and address of defender*) by affixing the schedule of arrestment to the mainmast [*or as the case may be*] of the ship (*name*) and marked the initials ER above that affixed schedule at (*place*) on (*date*).

I did this in the presence of (*name, occupation and address of witness*).

(*Signed*)

Messenger-at-Arms
(*Address*)

(*Signed*)

Witness

---

[1] Form 16.15–HH inserted by SI 1998/2637 (effective 1st December 1998).

Form 16.15-I

Rule 16.15(1)(c) and (d)

Rule 16.15(1)(c) and (d)   Form 16.15–I

Form of certificate of execution of arrestment of ship or cargo in rem

CERTIFICATE OF EXECUTION OF ARRESTMENT OF SHIP [*OR* CARGO] *IN REM*

I, (*name*), Messenger-at-Arms, certify that I executed an arrestment *in rem* of the ship [*or* vessel] (*name*) [*or* cargo (*describe*)] by virtue of a summons [*or* interlocutor of Lord (*name*) dated (*date*)] at the instance of (*name and address of pursuer*) against (*name and address of defender*) by affixing the schedule of arrestment to the mainmast [*or as the case may be*] of the ship [*or* vessel] [*or in the case of cargo landed or transhipped* on (*name*) as custodian for the time being of the cargo [*or* as harbourmaster of the harbour where the cargo lies]] [and delivering a copy of the schedule of arrestment and of this certificate to (*name*) the master of the ship [*or as the case may be*] at (*place*) on (*date*).
I did this in the presence of (*name, occupation and address of witness*).

(*Signed*)

Messenger-at-Arms
(*Address*)

(*Signed*)

Witness

Form 16.15-J

Rule 16.15(1)(e)

Rule 16.15(1)(e)   Form 16.15–J

Form of certificate of execution of arrestment of ship or cargo on the dependence

CERTIFICATE OF EXECUTION OF ARRESTMENT OF SHIP [*OR* CARGO] ON THE DEPENDENCE

I, (*name*), Messenger-at-Arms, certify that I executed an arrestment on the dependence of the ship [*or* vessel] (*name*) [*or* cargo (*describe*)] by virtue of a summons [*or* counterclaim] [*or* interlocutor of Lord (*name*) dated (*date*)] at the instance of (*name and address of pursuer*) against (*name and address of defender*) by affixing the schedule of arrestment to the mainmast [*or as the case may be*] of the ship [*or* vessel] (*name*) and marked the initials ER above the same [*or* by (*state method of service*)] at (*place*) on (*date*).

I did this in the presence of (*name, occupation and address of witness*).

(*Signed*)

Messenger-at-Arms
(*Address*)

(*Signed*)

Witness

Form 16.15-K

C1.2A.35   Rule 16.15(1)(i)

Rule 16.15(1)(i)   FORM 16.15–K

Form of certificate of execution of charge for payment

CERTIFICATE OF EXECUTION OF CHARGE FOR PAYMENT

Date: (date of service)

I, (name), Messenger-at-Arms, certify that, by virtue of the attached extract of a decree of the Court of Session at the instance of [A.B.] against [C.D.] [or of a document registered for execution in the Books of Council and Session], I charged [C.D.] to pay the sum[s] of money, principal, interest and expenses stated in the extract [or to implement and perform the obligation[s] stated in the extract] [or both to pay the sum[s] of money, principal, interest and expenses] [add where there are other debtors in the extract, so far as incumbent upon him] to [A.B.] within [   ] days after the date of the charge.

I did this—

*   by leaving the charge and a copy of the extract decree [*or* document registered for execution in the Books of Council and Session] with (*name of person charged*) at (*place*) on (*date*).

*   by leaving the charge and a copy of the extract decree [*or* document registered for execution in the Books of Council and Session] with (*name and occupation of person with whom left*) at (*place*) on (*date*). (*Specify that enquiry made and that reasonable grounds exist for believing that the person charged resides at the place but is not available.*)

*   by depositing the charge and a copy of the extract decree [*or* document registered for execution in the Books of Council and Session] in (*place*) and (*date*). (*Specify that enquiry made and that reasonable grounds exist for believing that the person charged resides at the place but is not available.*)

*   by leaving the charge and a copy of the extract decree [*or* document registered for execution in the Books of Council and Session] with (*name and designation of person with whom left*) at (*place of business*) on (*date*). (*Specify that enquiry made and that reasonable grounds exist for believing that the person charged carries on business at the place.*)

*   by depositing the charge and a copy of the extract decree [*or* document registered for execution in the Books of Council and Session] at (*place of business*) on (*date*). (*Specify that enquiry made and that reasonable grounds exist for believing that the person charged carries on business at the place.*)

*   by leaving the charge and a copy of the extract decree [*or* document registered for execution in the Books of Council and Session] at (*registered office or place of business*) on (*date*) in the hands of (*name of person*).

*   by leaving [*or* depositing] the charge and a copy of the extract decree [*or* document registered for execution in the Books of Council and Session] at (*registered office, official address or place of business*) on (*date*) in such a way that it was likely to come to the attention of (*name of person charged*). (*Specify how left.*)

I did this in the presence of (*name, occupation and address of witness*).

(Signed)

Messenger-at-Arms
(*Address*)

(*Signed*)

Witness

*Delete where not applicable.

Form 16.16

C1.2A.36   Rule 16.16

Rule 16.16   FORM 16.16

Form of Service of copy final decree under section 73C of the Debtors (Scotland) Act 1987

1.   Date   (*date of service*)

       To (*name and address of arrestee*)

2.   On (*date*) the court granted decree against (*name of debtor*) for payment of £ (*insert sum*) to (*insert name of creditor*). A copy of the final decree is attached.

3.   An arrestment on the dependence of this action attaching funds in your hands was executed on (*insert date*).

4.   You are now required to release to the creditor, on the expiry of 14 weeks beginning with this date (or earlier where a mandate authorises you to do so) the lowest of—

       (a)   the sum attached by the arrestment;

       (b)   the sum due by you to the debtor; or

       (c)   the sum of £ (*insert sum*), which is the sum calculated in accordance with section 73K(c) of the Debtors (Scotland) Act 1987.

5.   This must be done unless:

       (a)   an application is made under section 73M(1) of the Debtors (Scotland) Act 1987;

       (b)   the debtor applies to the sheriff under section 73Q(2) of that Act;

       (c)   an action of multiplepoinding is raised in relation to the funds attached by the arrestment; or

       (d)   the arrestment is recalled, restricted or otherwise ceases to have effect.

(*Signed*)   Date ....

Creditor

[*or* Solicitor for Creditor]

IF YOU ARE UNCERTAIN ABOUT THE EFFECT OF THIS DOCUMENT, you should consult a solicitor, Citizens Advice Bureau or other local advice agency or adviser immediately

---

[1] Form 16.16 inserted by S.S.I. 2009 No. 104 (effective 22nd April 2009).

Form 23.1C

Rules 23.1C(1), 23.1F(2) and 23.1G(2)

Rules 23.1C(1), 23.1F(2) and 23.1G(2) [1]FORM 23.1C

Form of motion by email

Unopposed motion/Opposed motion* (*Delete where not applicable)

To: (*court email address specified by Deputy Principal Clerk*)

1.   Case name:

2.   Court case number:

3.   Is the case in court in the next 7 days?:

4.   Agents/party enrolling motion:

      Reference:

      Telephone number:

      Email address:

5.   Enrolling motion on behalf of:

6.   Motion (in brief terms):

7.   Submissions in support of motion (if required):

8.   Date of enrolment of motion:

9.   Intimation made to:

      Provided email address(es):

      Additional email address(es) of fee-earner or other person(s) dealing with the case on behalf of a receiving party (if applicable):

10.   Date intimations sent:

11.   Opposition must be intimated to opponent not later than 5 p.m. on: (*date*)

12.   Is motion opposed/unopposed?:

13.   Has consent to the motion been provided?:

14.   Document(s) intimated and lodged with motion:

---

[1] Form 23.1C inserted by S.S.I. 2009 No. 387 (effective 1st December 2009).

Form 23.ID

C1.2A.38   Rules 23.1D(1) and 23.1G(2)

Rules 23.1D(1) and 23.1G(2)   [1]FORM 23.1D

Form of opposition to motion by email

TO BE INTIMATED TO THE ENROLLING PARTY

1.   Case name:

2.   Court case number:

3.   Date of intimation of motion:

4.   Date of intimation of opposition to motion:

5.   Agents/party opposing motion:

> Reference:

> Telephone number:

> Email address:

6.   Opposing motion on behalf of:

7.   Grounds of opposition:

8.   Estimated duration of motion roll hearing:

---

[1] Form. 23.1D inserted by S.S.I. 2009 No. 387 (effective 1st December 2009).

Form 23.2

C1.2A.39   Rule 23.2(2)

Rule 23.2(2)   FORM 23.2

Form of motion

PART I

Sheet 1 of ....sheets

(To be completed where motion enrolled by post or fax only)

Form of motion

Name of pursuer/petitioner ....

Name of first defender/respondent ....

Name and nature of petition (*e.g.* John Smith's curatory) ....
....

Court case number .... Date of last interlocutor ....

Is case due in court during the next seven days?   Yes/No*

(If Yes, state reason)

Form 23.4

Rule 23.4(1)

Rule 23.4(1)　　　　　　　　　　FORM 23.4

Form of opposition to motion

PART I　　　　　　　　　　　　　　　　　　　　Sheet 1 of ....sheets

(To be completed where motion opposed by
post or fax only)

Name of pursuer/petitioner* ....

Name of first defender/respondent* ....

Name of firm notifying opposition ....

PART II

Agent for .... Ref No. ....

Rutland Exchange No. .... Town ....

Tel. No. .... FAX No. ....

Date of notice of opposition ....

Date opposition intimated ....

Nature and effective date of enrolment of motion to be opposed ....
....

* Delete as appropriate.

PART II

OPPOSITION SLIP–General Department only

Name of case .... v. ....

Name of firm ....

† *e.g.* John Smith v. John Brown.

Form 23.5

C1.2A.41   Rule 23.5

Rule 23.5   FORM 23.5

Form of consent to motion

Sheet 1 of .... sheets

Name of pursuer/petitioner* ....

Name of first defender/respondent* ....

Name of firm notifying consent ....

Agent for .... Ref No. ....

Rutland Exchange No. ....Town ....

Tel. No. ....FAX No. ....

Date of notice of consent ....

Date consent intimated ....

Nature and effective date of enrolment of motion consented to ....

....

* Delete as appropriate.

Form 24.3

Rule 24.3(2)

Rule 24.3(2)   FORM 24.3

Form of notice to additional or substitute party

Date: (*date of posting or other method of service*)

To: (*name and address of party*)

TAKE NOTICE

(*Name and address of pursuer*) has raised an action against (*name and address of defender*) in the Court of Session, Edinburgh. By order of the court, dated (*date*), your name has been added [*or* substituted] as a party to the action. A copy of the summons [*or other principal writ or record*] in the action, as amended, is attached. If you intend to deny the claim made in the summons [*or as the case may be*] you must lodge defences [*or* answers] at the Office of Court, Court of Session, 2 Parliament Square, Edinburgh EH1 1RQ within [21] days after the date of service on you of the summons. The date of service is the date stated at the top of this notice unless service has been by post in which case the date of service is the date after that date.

If you do not lodge defences [*or* answers], the court may make an order against you.

IF YOU ARE UNCERTAIN ABOUT THE EFFECT OF THIS NOTICE, you should consult a solicitor, Citizens Advice Bureau or other local advice agency or adviser immediately.

           (*Signed*)

           Messenger-at-Arms
           [*or* Solicitor [*or* Agent] for pursuer]
           (*Address*)

Form 25A.5

C1.2A.43 Rule 25A.5

Rule 25A.5 [1] Form 25A.5

Form of intimation to a relevant authority of a devolution issue raised in civil proceedings

To: (*name and address of relevant authority*)

1. You are given notice that an action has been raised in the Court of Session which includes a conclusion or prayer in respect of a devolution issue. A copy of the pleadings in the case (*as adjusted*) is enclosed.

2. If you wish to take part as a party to the proceedings in so far as they relate to a devolution issue you must lodge with the Deputy Principal Clerk of Session, Court of Session, 2 Parliament Square, Edinburgh EH1 1RQ a notice in writing stating that you intend to take part as a party in the proceedings. The notice must be lodged within 14 days of (*insert date on which intimation was given*).

Date (*insert date*)

(*Signed*)

Solicitor for
Pursuer/Defender/Petitioner/Respondent

_____
[1] Form 25A.5 inserted by S.I. 1999 No. 1345.

Form 25A.5A

C1.2A.44 Rule 25A.5A

Rule 25A.5A [1] Form 25A.5A

Form of notice to a relevant authority of reclaiming motion [*or* application to the *nobile officium* of the court] in proceedings in which a devolution issue has been raised

To: (*name and address of relevant authority*)

You are given notice that a reclaiming motion has been marked in proceedings in which a devolution issue has been raised [*or* first orders for service and/or delivery have been obtained in a petition to the *nobile officium* of the court relating to proceedings in which a devolution issue has been raised]. A copy of the reclaiming motion [*or* petition] is enclosed.

(Signed)

Solicitor for Appellant

(*add designation and business address*)

_____
[1] Form 25A.5A inserted by S.S.I. 2007 No. 360 (effective 10th August 2007).

Form 25A.7

Rule 25A.7(2)

Rule 25A.7(2) ¹ Form 25A.7

Form of notice to a relevant authority of the reference of a devolution issue to the Inner House

To: *(name and address of relevant authority)*

You are given notice that in an action raised in the Court of Session the court has referred a devolution issue to the Inner House under paragraph 7 of Schedule 6 to the Scotland Act 1998 [*or* paragraph 25 of Schedule 10 to the Northern Ireland Act 1998] [*or* paragraph 15 of Schedule 9 to the Government of Wales Act 2006]. A copy of the relevant report is enclosed.

(Signed)

Deputy Principal Clerk of Session

---

¹ Form 25A.7 inserted by S.S.I. 2007 No. 360 (effective 10th August 2007).

Form 25A.12

Rule 25A.12

Rule 25A.12 ¹ FORM 25A.12

Form of intimation to a relevant authority that the court is considering making an order under [section 102 of the Scotland Act 1998/section 81 of the Northern Ireland Act 1998/ section 153 of the Government of Wales Act 2006]

To: *(name and address of relevant authority)*

1. You are given notice that in an action raised in the Court of Session, the court has decided [that an Act/provision of an Act of the Scottish Parliament is not within the legislative competence of the Parliament] [a member of the Scottish Executive does not have the power to make, confirm or approve a provision of subordinate legislation he has purported to make, confirm or approve]. A copy of the relevant opinion/interlocutor is enclosed.

2. The court is considering whether to make an order [removing or limiting the retrospective effect of the decision/suspending the effect of the decision to allow the defect to be corrected].

3. If you wish to take part as a party to the proceedings so far as they relate to the making of the order mentioned in paragraph 2 you must lodge with the Deputy Principal Clerk of Session, Court of Session, 2 Parliament Square, Edinburgh EH1 1RQ a notice in writing stating that you intend to take part as a party in the proceedings. The notice must be lodged within 7 days of *(date on which intimation was given)*.

Date *(insert date)*

(Signed)

Deputy Principal Clerk of Session.

---

¹ Form 25A.12 inserted by S.I. 1999 No. 1345 and amended by S.S.I. 2007 No. 360 (effective 10th August 2007).

Form 26.1-A

C1.2A.47   Rule 26.1(1)

Rule 26.1(1)   [1] FORM 26.1–A

Form of third party notice

THIRD PARTY NOTICE

in the cause

[A.B.] *(designation and address)*, Pursuer

and

[C.D.] *(designation and address)*, Defender

and

[E.F.] *(designation and address)*, Third Party

Date: *(date of posting or other method of service)*

To: *(name and address of [E.F.])*

TAKE NOTICE

(*Name and address of pursuer*), pursuer, has raised an action against (*name and address of defender*), defender, in the Court of Session, Edinburgh. In the action the pursuer claims from the defender (*amount*) as damages for (*short explanation of basis of claim*) [*or as the case may be*]. A copy of the summons and defence [*or* record] in the action is attached.

The defender admits [*or* denies] liability to the pursuer. The defender claims that [if he is liable to the pursuer] you are obliged to relieve him [partially] of his liability. He claims this because (*short explanation of basis of right of contribution, relief or indemnity*). This is explained more fully in the attached defences [*or* record].

or

The defender denies liability for the claim made by the pursuer. He states that you alone [*or* you along with *names and addresses*] are liable to the pursuer for that claim. This is explained more fully in the attached defences [*or* record].

or

The defender denies liability for the claim made by the pursuer [*or* admits liability in part for the claim made by the pursuer, but disputes the amount of that claim]. He maintains, however, that if he is liable to the pursuers [for any amount], you are jointly liable [*or* jointly and severally liable] with him to the pursuer. This is explained more fully in the attached defences [*or* record].

(*or otherwise as the case may be*)

Accordingly, on (*date*) [Lord (*name*) in] the Court of Session ordered this notice to be served on you. If you dispute the claim by the pursuer against the defender, or the defender's claim against you, you must lodge answers at the Office of Court, 2 Parliament Square, Edinburgh EH1 1RQ. You must do so within [21] days after the date of service on you of this notice. The date of service is the date stated at the top of this notice unless service has been by post in which case the date of service is the day after that date.

If you do not lodge answers, the court may make an order against you.

IF YOU ARE UNCERTAIN ABOUT THE EFFECT OF THIS NOTICE, you should consult a solicitor, Citizens Advice Bureau or other local advice agency or adviser immediately.

(*Signed*)

Messenger-at-Arms
[*or* Solicitor [*or* Agent] for defender]
(*Address*)

---

[1] Form 26.1–A amended by S.I. 1994 No. 2901 (clerical error).

Form 26.1-B

C1.2A.48   Rule 26.1(2)

Rule 26.1(2)   FORM 26.1–B

Form of third party notice by pursuer

THIRD PARTY NOTICE BY PURSUER

in the cause

[A.B.] (*designation and address*), Pursuer

and

[C.D.] (*designation and address*), Defender

and

[E.F.] (*designation and address*), Third Party

Date: (*date of posting or other method of service*)

To: (*name and address of* [E.F.])

TAKE NOTICE

(*Name and address of pursuer*), pursuer, has raised an action against (*name and address of defender*), defender, in the Court of Session, Edinburgh. In the action the pursuer claims from the defender (*amount*) as damages for (*short explanation of basis of claim*) [*or as the case may be*]. The defender has made a counterclaim against the pursuer for (*amount*) as damages for (*short explanation of basis of counterclaim*) [*or as the case may be*]. A copy of the answers, defences and counterclaim [*or record*] in the action is attached.

The pursuer admits [*or* denies] liability to the defender for the counterclaim. However, the pursuer claims that [if he is liable to the defender] you are obliged to relieve him [partially] of his liability. He claims this because (*short explanation of basis of right of contribution, relief or indemnity*). This is explained more fully in the attached defences [*or record*].

[*or otherwise as the case may be*]

Accordingly, on (*date*) [Lord (*name*) in] the Court of Session ordered this notice to be served on you. If you dispute the defender's claim against the pursuer, or the pursuer's claim against you, you must lodge answers at the Office of Court, 2 Parliament Square, Edinburgh EH1 1RQ. You must do so within [21] days after the date of service on you of this notice. The date of service is the date stated at the top of this notice unless service has been by post in which case the date of service is the day after that date.

If you do not lodge answers, the court may make an order against you.

IF YOU ARE UNCERTAIN ABOUT THE EFFECT OF THIS NOTICE, you should consult a solicitor, Citizens Advice Bureau or other local advice agency or adviser immediately.

(*Signed*)

Messenger-at-Arms
[*or* Solicitor [*or* Agent] for pursuer]
(*Address*)

Form of third party notice by third party

THIRD PARTY NOTICE BY THIRD PARTY

in the cause

[A.B.] (*designation and address*), Pursuer

and

[C.D.] (*designation and address*), Defender

and

[E.F.] (*designation and address*), Third Party

Date: (*date of posting or other method of service*)

To: (*name and address of* [*E.F.*])

TAKE NOTICE

(*Name and address of pursuer*), pursuer, has raised an action against (*name and address of defender*), defender, in the Court of Session, Edinburgh. In the action the pursuer claims from the defender (*amount*) as damages for (*short explanation of basis of claim*) [*or as the case may be*]. The defender has made a counterclaim against the pursuer for (*amount*) as damages for (*short explanation of basis of counterclaim*) [*or as the case may be*].

The defender [*or pursuer*] claims that [E.F.] is obliged to relieve him [partially] of his liability (if any) to the pursuer [*or the defender*] [*or as the case may be*]. [E.F.] admits [*or denies*] liability to do so. [E.F.], however, claims that [if he is liable to the defender [*or the pursuer*] you are obliged to relieve him [partially] of his liability. He claims this because (*short explanation of basis of right of contribution, relief or indemnity*) [*or as the case may be*].

This is explained more fully in the attached answers, defences [and counterclaim] and answers [*or record*].

Accordingly, on (*date*) [Lord (*name*) in] the Court of Session ordered this notice to be served on you. If you dispute the claim of the pursuer against the defender [*or the counterclaim of the defender against the pursuer*] [*or* [E.F.'s] liability to relieve [*or as the case may be*] the defender [*or the pursuer*]] [*or* [E.F.'s] claim against you], you must lodge answers at the Office of Court, 2 Parliament Square, Edinburgh EH1 1RQ. You must do so within [21] days after the date of service on you of this notice. The date of service is the date stated at the top of this notice unless service has been by post in which case the date of service is the day after that date.

If you do not lodge answers, the court may make an order against you.

IF YOU ARE UNCERTAIN ABOUT THE EFFECT OF THIS NOTICE, you should consult a solicitor, Citizens Advice Bureau or other local advice agency or adviser immediately.

(*Signed*)

Messenger-at-Arms
[*or* Solicitor [*or* Agent] for pursuer]
(*Address*)

Form 26A.5[1]

C1.2A.49.1   Rule 26A.5(1)

Form of application under section 20(3)(b) of the Civil Litigation (Expenses and Group Proceedings) (Scotland) Act 2018 seeking authorisation to be a representative party

UNTO THE RIGHT HONOURABLE THE LORDS OF COUNCIL AND SESSION

IN THE COURT OF SESSION

APPLICATION

for

AUTHORISATION TO BE A REPRESENTATIVE PARTY

under section 20(3)(b) of the Civil Litigation (Expenses and Group Proceedings) (Scotland) Act 2018

by

[A.B.], [Representative Party] (*full name, designation and address*)

Applicant

HUMBLY SHEWETH:-

1.   The applicant, (*insert full name, designation and address of the applicant*), applies under section 20(3)(b) of the Civil Litigation (Expenses and Group Proceedings) (Scotland) Act 2018 ("the Act") for authorisation by the court to be a representative party to bring group proceedings on behalf of (*insert details, in brief, of the group of two or more persons*), each of whom has a separate claim which may be the subject of civil proceedings.

2.   The applicant [*is a member of the group of persons on whose behalf proceedings are to be brought*] [*is not a member of the group of persons on whose behalf proceedings are to be brought*]. [(*In the event that the applicant is not a member of the group on whose behalf proceedings are to be brought*) The applicant is (*insert the capacity in which the applicant is applying to be a representative party*).]

3.   A description of the group of persons on whose behalf proceedings are to be brought is as follows:—

(*insert a full and detailed description of the group of persons on whose behalf group proceedings are to be brought*).

---

[1] Form 26A.5 inserted by SSI 2020/208 r.2(7)(c)(i), Sch.1 (effective 31 July 2020).

4.   The steps taken by the applicant to identify and notify all potential members of the group about the group proceedings are as follows:—

(insert a statement setting out all the efforts made by the applicant to identify and notify all potential members of the group about the proceedings).

5.   The applicant is [*an appropriate person who*] [*a body which*] can fairly and adequately represent the interests of the group, should authorisation under section 20(3)(b) of the Act be given by the court for the following reasons:—

(insert a full and detailed note to include the following:—

the special abilities and relevant expertise of the applicant;

the applicant's own interest in the proceedings;

whether there would be any potential benefit to the applicant, financial or otherwise, should the application be authorised;

confirmation that the applicant is independent from the defender;

a demonstration that the applicant would act fairly and adequately in the interests of the group members as a whole, and that the applicant's own interests do not conflict with those of the group whom the applicant seeks to represent;

a demonstration of sufficient competence by the applicant, including financial resources, to litigate the claims properly, and to meet any expenses awards (the details of funding arrangements do not require to be disclosed)).

6.   The applicant [*has*] [*has not*] previously applied to the court for such authorisation relating, to any extent, to the same matter. [(*Where any such previous application has been made, insert details (including, in particular, the outcome of such application*).]

MAY IT THEREFORE please your
Lordships to make an order authorising
[A.B.] to be a Representative Party

According to Justice, etc.

(*Signed*)

Applicant

[*or* Solicitor [*or* Agent] for [Applicant]]

(*Date*)

Form 26A.8[1]

C1.2A.49.2 Rule 26A.8(1) or (2)

Form of application under section 20(3)(b) of the Civil Litigation (Expenses and Group Proceedings) (Scotland) Act 2018 seeking the replacement of a representative party

UNTO THE RIGHT HONOURABLE THE LORDS OF COUNCIL AND SESSION

IN THE COURT OF SESSION

APPLICATION

in the cause (Cause Reference No.   )

for

REPLACEMENT OF A REPRESENTATIVE PARTY

under section 20(3)(b) of the Civil Litigation (Expenses and Group Proceedings) (Scotland) Act 2018

by

[A.B.], [Representative Party] [Group Member] (*full name, designation and address*)

Applicant

HUMBLY SHEWETH:-

1.　　　　The applicant, (*insert full name, designation and address of the applicant*), was authorised by the court to be a representative party to bring group proceedings on behalf of (*insert details, in brief, of the group of two or more persons*), each of whom has a separate claim which may be the subject of civil proceedings, on (*insert date*). The applicant applies, under section 20(3)(b) of the Civil Litigation (Expenses and Group Proceedings) (Scotland) Act 2018 ("the Act"), seeking the authority of the court to withdraw as the representative party in those group proceedings and be replaced with another person ("Person A") (*insert full name, designation and address of Person A*).

or

---

[1] Form 26A.8 inserted by SSI 2020/208 r.2(7)(c)(ii), Sch.1 (effective 31 July 2020).

The representative party, (*insert full name, designation and address of the representative party*), was authorised by the court to be a representative party to bring group proceedings on behalf of (*insert details, in brief, of the group of two or more persons*), each of whom has a separate claim which may be the subject of civil proceedings, on (*insert date*). The applicant, (*insert full name, designation and address of the applicant*), applies under section 20(3)(b) of the Civil Litigation (Expenses and Group Proceedings) (Scotland) Act 2018 ("the Act"), for authorisation by the court to appoint Person A (*insert full name, designation and address of Person A*) as a representative party to bring group proceedings on behalf of (*insert details, in brief, of the group of two or more persons*) in place of the representative party.

2. Person A (*insert full name*) [*is a member of the group of persons on whose behalf proceedings are to be brought [have been brought]] [is not a member of the group of persons on whose behalf proceedings are to be brought [have been brought]]. [(In the event that Person A is not a member of the group on whose behalf proceedings are to be brought or have been brought) Person A is (insert the capacity in which Person A may be, or is applying to be, a representative party).*]

3. The applicant can no longer act as the representative party in the group proceedings and, accordingly, seeks the authorisation of the court to withdraw and be replaced as the representative party by Person A for the following reasons:—

    (*insert detailed reasons as to why the applicant can no longer act as the representative party in the group proceedings*).

    or

    The applicant seeks the authority of the court to appoint Person A to bring the group proceedings in place of the representative party (*insert full name of the representative party*) for the following reasons:—

    (*insert detailed reasons as to why the court should authorise the replacement of the representative party with Person A*).

4. Person A (*insert full name*) is a suitable [*person who*] [*body which*] can act in the capacity of representative person should such authorisation be given, having regard to the matters mentioned in rule 26A.7(2), for the following reasons:—

    (*insert a full and detailed note to include the following:—*

    the special abilities and relevant expertise of Person A;

    Person A's own interest in the proceedings;

    whether there would be any potential benefit to Person A, financial or otherwise, should the application be authorised;

confirmation that Person A is independent from the defender;

a demonstration that Person A would act fairly and adequately in the interests of the group members as a whole, and that Person A's own interests do not conflict with those of the group whom Person A seeks to represent;

a demonstration of sufficient competence by Person A, including financial resources, to litigate the claims properly, and to meet any expenses awards (the details of funding arrangements do not require to be disclosed)).

5.   Person A (*insert full name*) [*has*] [*has not*] previously applied to the court for such authorisation relating, to any extent, to the same matter. [*Where any such previous application has been made, insert details (including, in particular, the outcome of such application)*].

MAY IT THEREFORE please your Lordships to make an order authorising [Person A] to be a Representative Party

According to Justice, etc.

(*Signed*)

Representative Party [Applicant]

[*or* Solicitor [*or* Agent] for Representative Party [Applicant (*insert full name*)]]

(*Date*)

Form 26A.9[1]

Rule 26A.9(1)

Form of application under section 20(5) of the Civil Litigation (Expenses and Group Proceedings) (Scotland) Act 2018 for permission for group proceedings to be brought

UNTO THE RIGHT HONOURABLE THE LORDS OF COUNCIL AND SESSION

IN THE COURT OF SESSION

APPLICATION

for

PERMISSION FOR GROUP PROCEEDINGS TO BE BROUGHT

under section 20(5) of the Civil Litigation (Expenses and Group Proceedings) (Scotland) Act 2018

by

[A.B.], [*Representative Party*] (*full name, designation and address*)

Applicant

against

[C.D.] (*full name[s], designation(s) and address[es]*)

Defender[s]

1. [A.B.], [*Representative Party*], (*insert full name, designation and address of the applicant*) applies for permission for group proceedings (within the meaning given in section 20(1) of the Civil Litigation (Expenses and Group Proceedings) (Scotland) Act 2018 ("the Act")) to be brought on behalf of (*insert details, in brief, of the group of two or more persons*), each of whom has a separate claim which may be the subject of civil proceedings.

2. The applicant [*has applied for authorisation by the court to be a representative party (within the meaning of section 20(2) of the Act)*] [*is a representative party (within the meaning of section 20(2) of the Act)*].

3. The applicant [*is a member of the group of persons on whose behalf proceedings are to be brought*] [*is not a member of the group of persons on whose behalf proceedings are to be brought*]. [(*In the event that the applicant is not a member of the group on whose behalf proceedings are to be brought*) The applicant is (*insert the capacity in which the applicant is applying to be a representative party*).]

4. [The lead pursuer, if any, in the group proceedings is (*insert full name, designation and address of the lead pursuer, if there is one*).]

---

[1] Form 26A.9 inserted by SSI 2020/208 r.2(7)(c)(iii), Sch.1 (effective 31 July 2020).

5.   The defender[s] in the group proceedings is [*are*] (*insert full name[s] and address[es] of the defender[s]*).

6.   The grounds on which the applicant seeks permission for group proceedings to be brought are as follows:—

(set out the grounds in numbered paragraphs, to include the information set out below:—

confirmation that all the claims made in the proceedings raise issues (whether of fact or law) that are the same as, or similar or related to, each other, and provide a detailed summary of the issues;

the steps taken by the applicant to identify and notify all potential members of the group about the proceedings;

demonstration that there is a prima facie case;

demonstration that it is a more efficient administration of justice for the claims to be brought as group proceedings rather than as separate individual proceedings;

demonstration that the proposed proceedings have any real prospects of success;

the number and nature of any proceedings relating to the same matter as the application for permission which have already been raised, if applicable, failing which confirmation that no such proceedings have been raised;

the number of parties, including the number of group members, that are likely to be involved in the proceedings;

the aggregate total value of the claims;

confirmation as to whether there are any matters that distinguish smaller groups of claims within the wider group and, if so, a note of such matters.).

8.   A list of persons who have consented to being members of the group on whose behalf group proceedings are proposed to be brought is attached (*attach a list of persons who have consented to being members of the group on whose behalf group proceedings are proposed to be brought*).

                                        (*Signed*)

                                        Solicitor [*or* Agent] for [A.B.],
                                        Applicant [Representative Party]

                                        (*Date*)

Form 26A.14-A[1]

Rule 26A.14(1)

Group proceedings under section 20(7)(a) of the Civil Litigation (Expenses and Group Proceedings) (Scotland) Act 2018 – Opt-in proceedings – Form of notice of consent for a person's claim to be brought in group proceedings

This Form is to be completed by you for the purpose of providing express consent for your claim, which may be the subject of civil proceedings, to be brought in group proceedings (within the meaning of section 20(1) of the Civil Litigation (Expenses and Group Proceedings) (Scotland) Act 2018 ("the Act")) under section 20(7)(a) of the Act.

Before your claim can be brought in the group proceedings the completed Form must be sent to your Representative Party (within the meaning of section 20(2) of the Act), or to the person who has submitted, or is to submit, an application for such authorisation to the court under section 20(3)(b) of the Act, as the case may be.

You may send this Form to your Representative Party (or, as the case may be, the person who has submitted, or is to submit, an application for such authorisation to the court) either by posting the notice or, where your representative party (or, as the case may be, that person) has confirmed that they accept e-mail service, by using electronic means.

Name (*provide your full name and designation*):

Address (*provide your full address, including postcode*):

Date of birth (*provide your date of birth*):

Contact telephone number (*provide your contact telephone number*):

E-mail address (*provide your email address*):

Lead pursuer (if any) in the group proceedings is

(*insert full name, designation and address of the lead pursuer (if any and if known)*):

Defender[s] in the group proceedings is [are]

(*insert full name[s] and address[es] of the defender[s] (if known)*):

Claim:

(*provide a full and detailed summary of your claim to include all such information which shows that you satisfy the eligibility criteria to be a member of the group on whose behalf group proceedings are to be, or have been, brought, such as:—*

any reference numbers/individual identifiers (for example, washing machine serial number and model number, NHS number or airline flight number etc.);

---

[1] Form 26A.14-A inserted by SSI 2020/208 r.2(7)(c)(iv), Sch.1 (effective 31 July 2020).

the date of purchase, date of your injury or operation (as the case may be) etc.;

evidence in support of your claim must be provided.).

I confirm that I am aware that by providing my express consent for my claim to be brought in group proceedings that I will be bound by interlocutors pronounced by the court in the proceedings, should the court grant permission for the bringing of the proceedings. I confirm that I am aware that this could include interlocutors pronounced by the court in the proceedings prior to my joining the group.

I, hereby, provide my express consent to [*insert the name and address of your Representative Party, or the person who has sought, or is to seek, such authority of the court*] to bring the group proceedings on my behalf.

[I confirm that no other civil proceedings are ongoing in respect of my claim, nor have I settled my claim judicially or non-judicially.]

I consent to the sharing of the information provided within this notice by [*insert the name and address of your Representative Party, or the person who has sought, or is to seek, such authority of the court*] with the Court of Session.

I consent to the sharing of my information which may be recorded in the Group Register (my name, address, date of birth and any additional information relevant to my claim) with the defender in accordance with Chapter 26A of the Rules of the Court of Session.

The further sharing of the information provided within this notice, or any such other personal data in connection with my claim, by [*insert the name and address of your Representative Party, or the person who has sought, or is to seek, such authority of the court*] may only be done with my express consent.

(*Signed*)

Pursuer

[*or* Solicitor [*or* Agent] for [Pursuer]]

(*Date*)

Form 26A.14-B[1]

Rule 26A.14(2)

Group proceedings under section 20(7)(a) of the Civil Litigation (Expenses and Group Proceedings) (Scotland) Act 2018 – Opt-in proceedings – Notice withdrawing consent for a person's claim to be brought in group proceedings

This Form is to be completed by you if you are a member of a group of persons on whose behalf group proceedings (within the meaning of section 20(1) of the Civil Litigation (Expenses and Group Proceedings) (Scotland) Act 2018 ("the Act")) are to be, or have been, brought and you no longer consent for your claim to be brought in the proceedings under section 20(7)(a) of the Act.

The completed Form must be sent to your Representative Party (within the meaning of section 20(2) of the Act), or to the person who has submitted, or is to submit, an application for such authorisation to the court under section 20(3)(b) of the Act, before your claim is no longer brought in the group proceedings.

You may send this Form to your Representative Party (or, as the case may be, the person who has submitted, or is to submit, an application for such authorisation to the court) either by posting the notice or, where your Representative Party (or, as the case may be, that person) has confirmed that they accept e-mail service, by using electronic means.

Name (*provide your full name and designation*):

Address (*provide your full address, including postcode*):

Date of birth (*provide your date of birth*):

Contact telephone number (*provide your contact telephone number*):

E-mail address (*provide your email address*):

Lead pursuer (if any) in the group proceedings is

(*insert full name, designation and address of the pursuer (if any and if known)*):

Defender[s] in the group proceedings is [*are*]

(*insert full name[s] and address[es] of the defender[s] (if known)*):

Claim:

(*provide a full and detailed summary of your claim and the date on which you provided your express consent to your Representative Party to bring proceedings on your behalf*)

I, hereby, withdraw my consent which I had given to [*insert the name and address of your Representative Party, or the person who has sought, or is to seek, such authority of the court*] for my claim to be brought in the group proceedings on my behalf.

---

[1] Form 26A.14-B inserted by SSI 2020/208 r.2(7)(c)(v), Sch.1 (effective 31 July 2020).

I consent to the information provided within this notice to be shared by [*insert the name and address of your Representative Party, or the person who has sought, or is to seek, such authority of the court*] with the Court of Session.

I acknowledge that by withdrawing my consent for my claim to be brought in the group proceedings on my behalf the defender is to be advised of my withdrawal from the proceedings by the service of a revised Group Register in accordance with Chapter 26A of the Rules of the Court of Session.

The further sharing of the information provided within this notice, or any such other personal data in connection with my claim, by [*insert the name and address of your Representative Party, or the person who has sought, or is to seek, such authority of the court*] may only be done with my express consent.

(*Signed*)

Pursuer

[*or* Solicitor [*or* Agent] for [Pursuer]]

(*Date*)

Form 26A.15[1]

Rule 26A.15(1)

Group proceedings under section 20(7)(a) of the Civil Litigation (Expenses and Group Proceedings) (Scotland) Act 2018 – Opt-in proceedings – the Group Register

Received the .... day of .... 20 ....

(Date of receipt of this register)

.... *(signed)*

Depute Clerk of Session

[in the cause (Cause Reference No.   )]

IN THE COURT OF SESSION

GROUP PROCEEDINGS [TO BE BROUGHT] [*or* BROUGHT]

under Part 4 of the Civil Litigation (Expenses and Group Proceedings) (Scotland) Act 2018

by

[A.B.], [Representative Party] (full name, designation and address)

[Representative Party for Pursuers]

[*or* Applicant seeking authorisation of the court under section 20(3)(b) of the Civil Litigation (Expenses and Group Proceedings) (Scotland) Act 2018 for Pursuers]

against

[C.D.] *(full name(s), designation(s) and address(es))*

Defender[s]

I, [A.B.] (*insert full name, designation and address of the Representative Party or as the case may be, the person who has applied for authorisation by the court under section 20(3)(b) of the Civil Litigation (Expenses and Group Proceedings) (Scotland) Act 2018 to be a Representative Party*), [Representative Party], [*is to bring*] [*has brought*] group proceedings on behalf of (*insert details, in brief, of the group of two or more persons*), each of whom has a separate claim which may be the subject of civil proceedings.

I, hereby, provide the court with a list of all those persons who, as of [*insert the date of lodging this group register with the court and service upon the defender*], expressly consent to be members of the group on whose behalf group proceedings [*are to be*] [*have been*] brought.

---

[1] Form 26A.15 inserted by SSI 2020/208 r.2(7)(c)(vi), Sch.1 (effective 31 July 2020).

I certify that there are no other civil proceedings ongoing as of [*insert the date of lodging this group register with the court and service upon the defender*], and that no claims have been settled judicially or non-judicially, in respect of the issues raised in the claims (whether of fact or law) of the persons listed below in this Form.

I certify that the group proceedings are brought within the statutory limitation period in respect of the claims of the persons listed below in this Form.

I certify that the Court of Session is the appropriate forum for the group proceedings to be brought in respect of the claims of the persons listed in this Form.

Name:	Address:	Date of birth:	Additional info — e.g. reference or serial no.:
1.			
2.			
3.			
4.			
5.			
6.			
7.			
8.			
9.			
10.			
etc.			
...			

(*Signed*)

Solicitor [*or* Agent] for [Representative Party] [*or* Applicant seeking authorisation of the court under section 20(3)(b) of the Civil Litigation (Expenses and Group Proceedings) (Scotland) Act 2018]

(*Date*)

Form 26A.16[1]

C1.2A.49.6A   Rule 26A.16(2)

Group proceedings under section 20(7)(a) of the Civil Litigation (Expenses and Group Proceedings) (Scotland) Act 2018 – Opt-in proceedings – Late application

UNTO THE RIGHT HONOURABLE THE LORDS OF COUNCIL AND SESSION

in the cause (Cause Reference No.   )

The application of [A.B.] *(full name, designation and address)*, Representative Party, on behalf of [E.F.] *(full name, designation and address)* for their claim to be brought in the group proceedings, although late

IN THE COURT OF SESSION

GROUP PROCEEDINGS BROUGHT

under Part 4 of the Civil Litigation (Expenses and Group Proceedings) (Scotland) Act 2018

by

[A.B.] *(full name, designation and address)*, Representative Party, on behalf of [E.F.] *(full name, designation and address)*

Representative Party for Pursuers

against

[C.D.] *(full name[s], designation[s] and address[es])*

Defender[s]

HUMBLY SHEWETH:-

1.   I, [A.B.] *(insert full name, designation and address)*, Representative Party, have brought group proceedings on behalf of *(insert details, in brief, of the group of two or more persons)*, each of whom has a separate claim which may be the subject of civil proceedings.

2.   A proof was allowed in the group proceedings on *(insert date on which proof was allowed)*.

---

[1] Form 26A.16 inserted by SSI 2020/208 r.2(7)(c)(vii), Sch.1 (effective 31 July 2020).

3.   I, [A.B.] (*insert full name*), Representative Party, received notice in Form 26A.14-A from [E.F.] (*insert full name, designation and address*) on (*insert date*). [A.B.], (*insert full name*), Representative Party, applies to the court on behalf of [E.F.] (*insert full name*) seeking authorisation for [E.F.]'s (*insert full name*) claim to be brought in the group proceedings, although late.

4.   The reason[s] why [E.F.] (*insert full name*) did not opt into the group proceedings before the allowance of proof in the proceedings is [are] as follows:—

(insert reason[s], in full as to why no application to opt-in to the group proceedings was made by E.F. before now and provide arguments, in full, as to why it is reasonable for E.F. to be authorised by the court to be a group member in the proceedings despite the late stage in the proceedings of this application.).

5.   I, [A.B.] (*insert full name*), Representative Party, certify that no claims have been settled judicially or non-judicially, in respect of [E.F.]'s (*insert full name*) claim (whether of fact or law).

6.   I, [A.B.] (*insert full name*), certify that the group proceedings are brought within the statutory limitation period in respect of [E.F.]'s (*insert full name*) claim.

7.   I, [A.B.] (*insert full name*), certify that the Court of Session is the appropriate forum for [E.F.]'s (*insert full name*) claim to be brought in the group proceedings.

                    MAY IT THEREFORE please your Lordships to make an order authorising [E.F.] to be a group member in the group proceedings

                    According to Justice, etc.

                    (*Signed*)

                    Solicitor [*or* Agent] for Representative Party

                    (*Date*)

Form 26A.17[1]

C1.2A.49.7   Rule 26A.17(2)

Group proceedings under section 20(7)(a) of the Civil Litigation (Expenses and Group Proceedings) (Scotland) Act 2018 – Opt-in proceedings – Withdrawal of consent for a claim to be brought in group proceedings

IN THE COURT OF SESSION

GROUP PROCEEDINGS BROUGHT

in the cause (Cause Reference No.   )

under Part 4 of the Civil Litigation (Expenses and Group Proceedings) (Scotland) Act 2018

by

[A.B.] (*full name, designation and address*)

Representative Party for Pursuers

against

[C.D.] (*full name[s], designation[s] and address[es]*)

Defender[s]

1.   I, [A.B.] (*insert full name, designation and address*), Representative Party, have brought group proceedings on behalf of (*insert details, in brief, of the group of two or more persons*), each of whom has a separate claim which may be the subject of civil proceedings.

2.   I, [A.B.], (*insert full name, designation and address*), Representative Party, received notice in Form 26A.14-B from [E.F.] (*insert full name[s], designation[s] and address[es]*) withdrawing their consent for their claim[s] to be brought in the group proceedings on (*insert date*).

3.   [The proof in the group proceedings commenced on (*insert date*). This application is made following the commencement of a proof in the proceedings.]

[*and/or* In the event that the court were to grant this application there would be less than two persons having a claim in the proceedings.]

---

[1] Form 26A.17 inserted by SSI 2020/208 r.2(7)(c)(viii), Sch.1 (effective 31 July 2020).

4. The reason[s] why [E.F.] (*insert full name*) seeks to withdraw from the group proceedings [following the commencement of proof in the proceedings] [*and/or* which, in the event that the court were to grant this application would result in there being less than two persons having a claim in the proceedings] is [*are*] as follows:—

    (*insert reason[s] in full as to either (or both):—*

    why no application to withdraw from the group proceedings was made by E.F. before now and provide arguments, in full, as to why it is reasonable for E.F. to withdraw from the proceedings despite the late stage in the proceedings of this application;

    why it is reasonable for E.F. to withdraw from the group proceedings despite the fact that should the application be approved by the court it would result in there being less than two persons having claims in the proceedings.).

6   The court is invited to consider this application, after representations being given by [C.D.] (*insert full name[s], designation[s] and address[es]*), the defender[s]).

                                        (*Signed*)

                                        Solicitor [*or* Agent] for Representative Party

                                        (*Date*)

Form 30.2

C1.2A.50   Rule 30.2(2)

Form 30.2

Form of notice of intimation to party whose agent has withdrawn

Cause Reference No.   (*insert reference*)

IN THE COURT OF SESSION

in the cause

[A.B.] (*designation and address*)

Pursuer [*or* Petitioner]

against

[C.D.] (*designation and address*)

Defender [*or* Respondent]

Date: (*date of posting or other method of service*)

To: (*name and address of party whose agent has withdrawn*)

TAKE NOTICE

The court has been informed that your solicitor [*or* agent] has withdrawn from acting on your behalf in this case.

In accordance with the interlocutor pronounced by [Lord (*name*) in] the Court of Session on (*date*) you must inform the Deputy Principal Clerk of Session within 14 days after the service of this notice whether you intend to insist in your action [*or* defences *or as the case may be*]. The date of service is the date stated at the top of this notice unless service has been by post in which case the date of service is the day after that date.

You should contact the Deputy Principal Clerk immediately to inform him what you intend to do. You must write to him at the Court of Session, 2 Parliament Square, Edinburgh EH1 1RQ quoting the name of the cause and the cause reference number at the top of this notice. You should also use the form attached to this notice.

If you do not write to the Deputy Principal Clerk and inform him what you intend to do the court may make an order or a finding or both against you as mentioned in the interlocutor referred to above.

IF YOU ARE UNCERTAIN ABOUT THE EFFECT OF THIS NOTICE, you should consult a solicitor, Citizens Advice Bureau or other local advice agency or adviser immediately.

(Signed)

Solicitor [or Agent]

(Address)

(Form to be sent with Form 30.2)

Cause Reference No.

IN THE COURT OF SESSION

in the cause

[A.B.] *(designation and address)*

Pursuer [*or* Petitioner]

against

[C.D.] *(designation and address)*

Defender [*or* Respondent]

To the Deputy Principal Clerk of Session

* I am insisting * in the above cause/* in my defences to the above cause/* in my answers to the above cause.   My new solicitor's name and address is:-

 * I am NOT insisting in the above cause/* in my defences to the above cause/* in my answers to the above cause.

(Signed)

Pursuer*/Petitioner*/Defender/ Respondent*

* Delete whatever is not applicable

This form is to be returned to the Deputy Principal Clerk of Session, 2 Parliament Square, Edinburgh EH1 1RQ.

Form 33.12

C1.2A.51   Rule 33.12(4)

Rule 33.12(4)   FORM 33.12

Form of book to be kept by the Accountant of Court under section 4 of the Court of Session Consignations (Scotland) Act 1895

No.	Date of Consignation.	By whom and Cause in which Consignation made.	Office mark.	Bank.	Date of Lodging in Bank.	Sum Consigned.	Deposits withdrawn from Bank.			Date of Payment.	Signature of Persons receiving Payment.	Date of Warrant.
							Principal.	Interest.	Total.			

Form 35.3-A

Rule 35.3(1)

Rule 35.3(1) [1] FORM 35.3–A

Form of order of court and certificate in optional procedure for recovery of documents

ORDER BY THE COURT OF SESSION

In the Cause (Cause Reference No.   )

in which

[A.B.] (*designation and address*)

Pursuer [*or* Petitioner]

against

[C.D.] (*designation and address*)

Defender [*or* Respondent]

Date: (*date of posting or other method of service*)

To: (*name and address of party or parties or named third party haver, from whom the documents are sought to be recovered*)

1. You are hereby required to produce to the agent for the Pursuer [*or as the case may be*], (*name and address of agents*) **within seven days** of the service on you of this Order—

    (a) this Order which must be produced intact;

    (b) the certificate below duly dated and signed by you; and

    (c) all documents in your possession falling within the enclosed specification and a list or inventory of such documents signed by you relating to this Order and your certificate.

2. Subject to note (1) below, you may produce these documents either by sending them by registered post or by the first class recorded delivery service or registered postal packet, or by hand to the address above.

(*Signature and business address of the*
agent for the party in whose favour
commission and diligence has been granted.)

NOTES

    (1) If you claim that any of the documents produced by you are **confidential**, you must still produce such documents but may place them in a separate sealed packet by themselves, marked "confidential". In that event they should NOT be sent to the address above, they must be delivered or sent by post as above provided to the **Deputy Principal Clerk of Session, 2 Parliament Square, Edinburgh, EH1 1RQ.**

(2) The documents will be considered by the parties to the action and they may or may not be lodged in the court process. A written receipt will be given or sent to you by the party recovering the documents, who may thereafter allow them to be inspected by the other parties. The party in whose possession the documents are will be responsible for their safekeeping.

(3) Parties are obliged by rules of court to return the documents to you when their purpose with the documents is finished. If they do not do so, you will be entitled to apply to the court, under rule 35.3(9) of the Rules of the Court of Session 1994, for an order to have this done and you may apply for an award of the expenses incurred in doing so. Further information about this can be obtained from the General Department, Court of Session, 2 Parliament Square, Edinburgh EH1 1RQ (Tel. 0131–225 2595).

Certificate

(*Date*)

I hereby certify with reference to the above order of the Court of Session in the cause (*cause reference number*) and the enclosed specification of documents, served on me and marked respectively X and Y:—

(1) That the documents which are produced and which are listed in the enclosed inventory signed by me and marked Z, are all the documents in my possession falling within the specification.

or

That I have no documents in my possession falling within the specification.

(2) That, to the best of my knowledge and belief, there are in existence other documents falling within the specification, but not in my possession. These documents are as follows:— (*describe them by reference to the descriptions of documents in the specification*). They were last seen by me on or about (*date*), at (*place*), in the hands of (*name and address of the person*).

or

That I know of the existence of no documents in the possession of any person, other than myself, which fall within the specification.

(*Signed*)

(*Name and address*)

---

[1] Form 35.3 substituted by S.I. 1996 No. 2168.

Form 35.3-B

Rule 35.3(4)(a)

Rule 35.3(4)(a)
[1] Form 35.3–B

Form of intimation to Deputy Principal Clerk of Session and other parties of documents recovered under optional procedure

In the Cause (Cause Reference No.   )

[A.B.] (*designation and address*)

Pursuer [*or* Petitioner]

against

[C.D.] (*designation and address*)

Defender [*or* Respondent]

The undernoted document[s] was [were] recovered from (*name, and address of haver*) on (*date of receipt*) under order of the court dated (*date of interlocutor authorising commission and diligence*) in so far as it relates to the specification of documents No.   of Process.

Document[s] received:— (*identify each*).

(*Signature, name and business address of the agent for the party in whose favour commission and diligence has been granted*)

Date:

[1] Form 35.3–B inserted by S.I. 1996 No. 2168.

Form 35.3-C

C1.2A.54 Rule 35J(4)(b)

Rule 35.3(4)(b) [1] FORM 35.3–C

Form of receipt to haver for documents recovered under optional procedure

In the Cause (Cause Reference No.   )

[A.B.] (*designation and address*)

Pursuer [*or* Petitioner]

against

[C.D.] (*designation and address*)

Defender [*or* Respondent]

The document[s] noted below, being recovered by order of the Court of Session dated (*date of interlocutor authorising commission and diligence*) in so far as it relates to the specification of documents No.   of Process, have been recovered from (*name and address of haver*).

Document[s] received:— (*identify each*).

(Signature, name and business address of the agent for the party in whose favour commission and diligence has been granted)

Date:
_____

_____

[1] Form 35.3–C inserted by S.I. 1996 No. 2168.

Form of receipt to haver for documents recovered under optional procedure

Form 35.3-D

Rule 35J(6)(b)

Rule 35.3(6)(b)   [1] FORM 35.3–D

Form of receipt from party other than party who originally recovered documents under optional procedure

In the Cause (Cause Reference No.   )

[A.B.] *(designation and address)*

Pursuer [*or* Petitioner]

against

[C.D.] *(designation and address)*

Defender [*or* Respondent]

I acknowledge receipt of the undernoted document[s] received from you and recovered under order of the Court of Session dated *(date of interlocutor authorising commission and diligence).*

Documents received:— *(identify each).*

(Signature, name and business address of the agent for the party receiving documents)

Date:

_____

[1] Form 35.3–D inserted by S.I. 1996 No. 2168.

Form 35.3A-A

C1.2A.56   Rule 35.3A(3)

Form 35.3A-A

**Form of order of court and certificate in optional procedure for recovery of documents –
party litigant cases**

ORDER BY THE COURT OF SESSION

In the Cause (Cause Reference No.)

in which

[A.B.] (*designation and address*)

Pursuer [*or* Petitioner]

against

[C.D.] (*designation and address*)

Defender [*or* Respondent]

Date: (*date of posting or other method of service*)

To: (*name and address of party or parties or named third party haver, from whom the documents
are sought to be recovered*)

You are hereby required to produce to the Deputy Principal Clerk of Session, 2 Parliament
Square, Edinburgh EH1 1RQ **within seven days** of the date of service on you of this Order –

(a) this Order which must be produced intact;
(b) the certificate below duly dated and signed by you;   and
(c) all documents in your possession falling within the enclosed specification and a list or
inventory of such documents signed by you relating to this Order and your
certificate.

You may produce these documents either by lodging them at the Office of the Court of Session
at the address below or by sending them by registered post or by the first class recorded delivery
service or registered postal packet, addressed to the **Deputy Principal Clerk of Session, 2
Parliament Square, Edinburgh, EH1 1RQ**.

(*Signature, name and business address of the agent
for the party in whose favour commission and
diligence has been granted.*)

NOTES

(1) If you claim that any of the documents produced by you are **confidential**, you must still produce such documents but may place them in a separate sealed packet by themselves, marked "confidential".

(2) The documents will be considered by the parties to the action and they may or may not be lodged in the court process. If they are not so lodged they will be returned to you by the Deputy Principal Clerk. The party in whose possession the documents are will be responsible for their safekeeping.

(3) Parties are obliged by rules of court to return the documents to you when their purpose with the documents is finished. If they do not do so, you will be entitled to apply to the court, under rule 35.3A(11) of the Rules of the Court of Session 1994 for an order to have this done and you may apply for an award of the expenses incurred in doing so. Further information about this can be obtained from the General Department, Court of Session, 2 Parliament Square, Edinburgh EH1 1RQ (Tel. 0131-225 2595).

Certificate

(Date)

I hereby certify with reference to the above order of the Court of Session in the cause *(cause reference number)* and the enclosed specification of documents, served on me and marked respectively X and Y:-

> (1) That the documents which are produced and which are listed in the enclosed inventory signed by me and marked Z, are all the documents in my possession falling within the specification.

or

That I have no documents in my possession falling within the specification.

> (2) That, to the best of my knowledge and belief, there are in existence other documents falling within the specification, but not in my possession. These documents are as follows:- *(describe them by reference to the descriptions of documents in the specification)*. They were last seen by me on or about *(date)*, at *(place)*, in the hands of *(name and address of the person)*.

or

That I know of the existence of no documents in the possession of any person, other than myself, which fall within the specification.

(Signed)

(Name and address)

Form 35.4-A

C1.2A.57   Rule 35.4(3)

Rule 35.4(3)   [1] FORM 35.4-A

Form of citation of haver to commission for recovery of documents

CITATION OF HAVER

Date: (*date of posting or other method of service*)

To: (*name and address of haver*)

(*Name and address of pursuer*) has raised an action against (*name and address of defender*) [*or* has presented a petition] in the Court of Session, Edinburgh. In the cause, (*name of party seeking to execute commission and diligence*) applied for a commission and diligence for the recovery of documents described in the attached specification. [A copy of the pleadings in the action is also attached.] On (*date of order*) [Lord (*name*) in] the Court of Session granted the application. The commission has been fixed before (*name of commissioner*) for (*date*) at (*time*). It will take place at (*place*).

By virtue of the order mentioned above, I hereby require you to attend the commission and to produce all documents which are in your possession and which fall within the specification and, if you are aware of any other documents within the specification, to declare where they may be.

IF YOU DO NOT ATTEND, A WARRANT MAY BE GRANTED FOR YOUR ARREST.

IF YOU ARE UNCERTAIN ABOUT THE EFFECT OF THIS NOTICE, you should consult a solicitor, Citizens Advice Bureau or other local advice agency or adviser immediately.

                                                     (*Signed*)

                                                     Messenger-at-Arms
                                                     [*or* Solicitor [*or* Agent] for (*name of party seeking to execute commission and diligence*)]
                                                     (*Address*)

---

[1] Form 35.4–A amended by S.I. 1994 No. 2901 (minor correction).

Form 35.4-B

C1.2A.58   Rule 35.4(4)

Rule 35.4(4)   FORM 35.4–B

Form of certificate of citation of haver to appear at commission

CERTIFICATE OF CITATION OF HAVER

I, (*name and designation*), certify that I cited (*name of haver*) to appear at a commission for the recovery of documents by posting a citation in Form 35.4–A to him [*or* her] between (*time*) and (*time*) on (*date*) at (*name of post office*) post office in a registered envelope [*or* recorded delivery envelope] addressed as follows:— (*address*). The post office receipt [*or* certificate of posting] is attached to this certificate.

(*Signed*)

Messenger-at-Arms
[*or* Solicitor [*or* Agent] for pursuer
[*or other party*]]
(*Address*)

Form 35.4-C

Rule 35.4(4)(b)

Rule 35.4(4)(b)   FORM 35.4–C

Form of certificate of citation of haver personally to appear at commission

CERTIFICATE OF CITATION PERSONALLY

I, (*name*), Messenger-at-Arms, certify that, on the authority of the interlocutor of the Court of Session (*date*), I cited (*name of haver*) to appear at the commission for the recovery of documents personally by leaving the citation in Form 35.4–A with him [*or* her] at (*place*) on (*date*).

I did this in the presence of (*name, occupation and address of witness*).

(*Signed*)

Messenger-at-Arms
(*Address*)

(*Signed*)

Witness

Form 35.4-D

Rule 35.4(8)(b) and 35.11(8)(b)

Rule 35.4(8)(b) and 35.11(8)(b)   FORM 35.4–D

Form of oath for haver or witness at commission

I swear by Almighty God that I will tell the truth, the whole truth and nothing but the truth.

Form 35.4-E

C1.2A.61   Rule 35.4(8)(b) and 35.11(8)(b)

Rule 35.4(8)(b) and 35.11(8)(b)   FORM 35.4–E

Form of affirmation for haver or witness at commission

I solemnly, sincerely and truly declare and affirm that I will tell the truth, the whole truth and nothing but the truth.

Form 35.11-A

C1.2A.62   Rule 35.11(5)

Rule 35.11(5)   FORM 35.11–A

Form of citation of witness to commission to take his evidence

CITATION OF WITNESS

Date: *(date of posting or other method of service)*

To: *(name and address of witness)*

(Name and address of pursuer or as the case may be) has raised an action against *(name and address of defender)* [*or* has presented a petition] in the Court of Session, Edinburgh. In the

cause, *(name of party seeking to execute commission to take the evidence of the witness)* applied for a commission to take your evidence. On *(date of order)* [Lord *(name)* in] the Court of Session granted the application. The commission has been fixed before *(name of commissioner)* for *(date)* at *(time)*. It will take place at *(place)*.

By virtue of the order mentioned above, I hereby require you to attend the commission to give evidence.

IF YOU DO NOT ATTEND, A WARRANT MAY BE GRANTED FOR YOUR ARREST.

(Signed)

Messenger-at-Arms
[*or* Solicitor [*or* Agent] for *(name of party seeking to execute commission)*]
(Address)

Form 35.11-B

Rule 35.11(6)(a)

Rule 35.11(6)(a)   FORM 35.11–B

Form of certificate of citation of witness to appear at commission

CERTIFICATE OF CITATION OF WITNESS

I, (*name and designation*), certify that I cited (*name of witness*) to appear to give evidence at a commission by posting a citation in Form 35.11–A to him [*or* her] between (*time*) and (*time*) on (*date*) at (*name of post office*) post office in a registered envelope [*or* recorded delivery envelope] addressed as follows:— (*address*). The post office receipt [*or* certificate of posting] is attached to this certificate.

(*Signed*)

Messenger-at-Arms
[*or* Solicitor [*or* Agent] for pursuer
[*or other party*]]
(*Address*)

Form 35.11-C

Rule 35.11(6)(b)

Rule 35.11(6)(b)   FORM 35.11–C

Form of certificate of citation of witness personally at commission to give evidence

CERTIFICATE OF CITATION PERSONALLY

I, (*name*), Messenger-at-Arms, certify that, on the authority of the interlocutor of the Court of Session (*date*), I cited (*name of witness*) to appear to give evidence at a commission personally by leaving the citation in Form 35.11–A with him [*or* her] at (*place*) on (*date*).

I did this in the presence of (*name, occupation and address of witness*).

(*Signed*)

Messenger-at-Arms
(*Address*)

(*Signed*)

Witness

Form 35.15-A

C1.2A.65   Rule 35.15(3)

Rule 35.15(3)   [1] FORM 35.15–A

Form of minute for letter of request

IN THE COURT OF SESSION

MINUTE

for

[A.B.] (*designation and address*)

in the cause [*or* in the petition of]

[A.B.] (*designation and address*), Pursuer [*or* Petitioner]

against

[C.D.] (*designation and address*), Defender [*or* Respondent]

(*Name of counsel or other person having a right of audience*) for the Minuter states to the court that the evidence specified in the proposed letter of request lodged with this Minute is required for the purpose of this cause and prays the court to issue a letter of request in terms of the proposed letter of request to (*specify the court or tribunal having power to obtain evidence*) to obtain the evidence so specified.

(*Signed by counsel or other person having a right of audience*)

_____

[1] Form 35.15–A amended by S.I. 1997 No. 1050 (minor amendment, effective 6th April 1997).

Form 35.15-B

Rule 35.15(3)

Rule 35.15(3)   FORM 35.15–B

Form of letter of request

(Items to be included in all letters of request)

1. Sender   *(identity & address)* ....
....
....

2. Central authority of the   *(identity & address)* ....
....

3. Person to whom the executed request is   *(identity & address)* ....
   to be returned   ....
....

4. The undersigned applicant has the
   honour to submit the following request:

5. a. Requesting judicial authority   *(identity & address)* ....
....
....

   b. To the competent authority   *(the requested State)* ....
....

6. Names and addresses of the parties and
   their representatives

   a. Pursuer   ....
....

   b. Defender   ....
....

   c. Other parties   ....
....

7. Nature and purpose of the proceedings   ....
   and summary of the facts   ....
....

8. Evidence to be obtained or other judicial act to be performed   ....

(Items to be completed where applicable)

9. Identity and address of any person to be examined   ....

10. Questions to be put to the persons to be examined or statement of the subject matter about which they are to be examined   [*or see attached list*] ....

11. Documents or other property to be inspected   (*specify whether it is to be produced, copied, valued, etc.*) ....

12. Any requirement that the evidence be given on oath or affirmation and any special form be used   (*in the event that the evidence cannot be taken in the manner requested, specify whether it is to be taken in such manner as provided by local law for the formal taking of evidence*) ....

13. Special methods or procedure to be followed   ....

14. Request for notification of the time and place for the execution of the request and identity and address of any person to be notified   ....

15. Request for attendance or participation of judicial personnel of the requesting authority at the execution of the letter of request   ....

16. Specification of privilege or duty to refuse to give evidence under the law of the State of origin   ....

17. The fees and expenses incurred will be borne by   (*identity & address*) ....

(Items to be included in all letters of request)

18. Date of request, signature and seal of the requesting authority   ....

Form 35.16-A

Rule 35.16(3)

Rule 35.16(3) [1] FORM 35.16–A

Form of minute for request to take evidence

IN THE COURT OF SESSION

MINUTE

for

[A.B.] (*or* [C.D.]) (*designation and address*)

in the cause [*or* in the petition of]

[A.B.] (*designation and address*), Pursuer [*or* Petitioner]

against

[C.D.] (*designation and address*), Defender [*or* Respondent]

(*Name of counsel or other person having a right of audience*) for the Minuter states to the court that the evidence specified in the proposed request lodged with this Minute is required for the purpose of this cause and prays the court to issue a request in terms of the proposed request to (*specify the court or tribunal having power to obtain evidence*) to obtain the evidence so specified.

(*Signed by counsel or other person having a right of audience*)

Form 35.16-B

Rule 35.16(8)

Rule 35.16(8) FORM 35.16–B

Form of notice to person in another Member State of intention to seek to take direct evidence

Date: (*date of posting or other method of intimation*)

To: (*name and address of person to give evidence*)

You are a witness for the pursuer [*or* petitioner] [*or* defender] [*or* respondent] in the case raised by [*or* to be raised by] (*name*) against (*name*).

The pursuer [*or* petitioner] [*or* defender] [*or* respondent] has requested that evidence be taken directly from you by means of (*specify the communications technology to be used*) from the (*name of the requested court*) to the Court of Session.

This evidence can only be taken directly from you if you agree to give evidence in this way. If you do not agree to give evidence directly the pursuer [*or* petitioner] [*or* defender] [*or* respondent] may apply for a request to have evidence taken from you in (*name of requested court*) without the means of (*specify the communications technology*).

Please return the enclosed response form to the Deputy Principal Clerk of Session within 14 days after the date of this notice stated at the top of this notice.

Form 35.16-C

C1.2A.69 Rule 35.16(8)

Rule 35.16(8) FORM 35.16–C

Form of response form to be completed and returned to requesting court by witness

WITNESS RESPONSE FORM

To: Deputy Principal Clerk of Session, Court of Session, Parliament House, Edinburgh, EH1 1RQ

From: (*name to be printed by person serving the notice*)

Date: (*date*)

I, (*name and address of witness to be completed by person serving the notice*), have received the notice seeking my agreement to have evidence taken directly from me as a witness for the pursuer [*or* petitioner] [*or* defender] [*or* respondent] in the Court of Session case raised by (*or to be raised by*) (*name of pursuer or petitioner*) against (*name of defender or respondent*) at (*person sending notice to specify the court*) by means of (*person serving notice to specify communications technology to be used*).

I confirm that I agree to voluntarily attend at (*person sending notice to specify the court*) to have evidence taken directly from me in this case.*

I confirm that I do not agree to voluntarily attend at (*person sending notice to specify the court*) to have evidence taken directly from me in this case.*

(**Please delete as appropriate*)

(*Signature of witness*)

---

[1] Inserted by SSI 2004/514, Art.2(8) (effective November 30, 2004).

Form 35A.2[1]

C1.2A.70 Rule 35A.2
Form of child witness notice

---

[1] Form 35A.2 as amended by SSI 2015/283 r.2(2) (effective 1 September 2015).

VULNERABLE WITNESSES (SCOTLAND) ACT 2004 Section 12

Received the ....day of ....20............

(Date of receipt of this notice)

.................(*signed*)

Depute Clerk of Session

In the Cause (Cause Reference No.   )

[A.B.] (*designation and address*)

Pursuer [*or* Petitioner]

against

[C.D.] (*designation and address*)

Defender [*or* Respondent]

CHILD WITNESS NOTICE

1. The applicant is the pursuer [*or* petitioner] [*or* defender] [*or* respondent] in the action by [A.B] (*design*) against [C.D.] (*design*).

2. The applicant has cited [*or* intends to cite] [E.F.] (*date of birth*) as a witness.

3. [E.F.] is a child witness under section 11 of the Vulnerable Witnesses (Scotland) Act 2004 [and was under the age of eighteen on the date of the commencement of proceedings].

4. The applicant considers that the following special measure[s] is [are] the most appropriate for the purpose of taking the evidence of [E.F.] [*or* that [E.F.] should give evidence without the benefit of any special measure]:–

(*delete as appropriate and specify any special measure(s) sought*).

5. [The reason[s] this [these] special measure[s] is [are] considered the most appropriate is [are] as follows:–

(*here specify the reason(s) for the special measures(s) sought*)].

OR

[The reason[s] it is considered that [E.F.] should give evidence without the benefit of any special measure is [are]-

(*here explain why it is felt that no special measures are required*)].

6. [E.F.] and the parent[s] of [*or* [person[s] with parental responsibility for] [E.F.] has [have] expressed the following view[s] on the special measure[s] that is [are] considered most appropriate [*or* the appropriateness of [E.F.] giving evidence without the benefit of any special measure]:–

(*delete as appropriate and set out the view(s) expressed and how they were obtained*).

7. Other information considered relevant to this application is as follows:–

(*here set out any other information relevant to the child witness notice*).

8. The applicant asks the court to—

(a)   consider this child witness notice;

(b)   make an order authorising the special measure[s] sought; [*or*

(c)   make an order authorising the giving of evidence by [E.F.] without the benefit of special measures.]

(*delete as appropriate*)

....(*Signed*)

Solicitor [*or* Agent] for A.B. [*or* C.D.] (*include full designation*)

NOTE: This form should be suitably adapted where section 16 of the Act of 2004 applies.

Form 35A.3

C1.2A.71   Rule 35A.3

Rule 35A.3   [1] FORM 35A.3

Form of vulnerable witness application

VULNERABLE WITNESSES (SCOTLAND) ACT 2004 Section 12

Received the ....day of ....20............
(Date of receipt of this notice)
.................(signed)
Depute Clerk of Session

In the Cause (Cause Reference No.   )
[A.B.] (*designation and address*)

Pursuer [*or* Petitioner]

against
[C.D.] (*designation and address*)

Defender [*or* Respondent]

VULNERABLE WITNESS APPLICATION

1. The applicant is the pursuer [*or* petitioner] [*or* defender] [*or* respondent] in the action by [A.B] (*design*) against [C.D.] (*design*).

2. The applicant has cited [*or* intends to cite] [E.F.] (*date of birth*) as a witness.
3. The applicant considers that [E.F.] is a vulnerable witness under section 11(1)(b) of the Vulnerable Witnesses (Scotland) Act 2004 for the following reasons:–

(*here specify reasons witness is considered to be a vulnerable witness*).

4. The applicant considers that the following special measure[s] is [are] the most appropriate for the purpose of taking the evidence of [E.F.]:–

(*specify any special measure(s) sought*).

5. The reason[s] this [these] special measure[s] is [are] considered the most appropriate is [are] as follows:–

(*here specify the reason(s) for the special measures(s) sought*).

6. [E.F.] has expressed the following view[s] on the special measure[s] that is [are] considered most appropriate:–

(*set out the views expressed and how they were obtained*).

7. Other information considered relevant to this application is as follows:–

(*here set out any other information relevant to the vulnerable witness application*).

8. The applicant asks the court to–
   (a) consider this vulnerable witness application;
   (b) make an order authorising the special measure[s] sought.

....(*Signed*)

Solicitor [*or* Agent] for A.B. [*or* C.D.]
(*include full designation*)

NOTE: This form should be suitably adapted where section 16 of the Act of 2004 applies.

―――――――――
[1] Inserted by S.S.I. 2007 No. 450 (effective 1st November 2007).

Form 35A.4

Rule 35A.4(1)

Rule 35A.4(1)   [1]FORM 35A.4

Form of certificate of intimation

VULNERABLE WITNESSES (SCOTLAND) ACT 2004 Section 12
CERTIFICATE OF INTIMATION

Cause Reference No.

I, *(name and designation)* certify that I intimated the child witness notice [*or* vulnerable witness application] relating to *(insert name of witness)* to *(insert names of parties or solicitors for parties, as appropriate)* by *(insert method of intimation)* on *(insert date of intimation)*.
Date: ....

......................*(Signed)*
Solicitor [*or* Agent]
(include full business designation)

---

[1] Inserted by S.S.I. 2007 No. 450 (effective 1st November 2007).

Form 35A.6

C1.2A.73 Rule 35A.6

Rule 35A.6 [1]FORM 35A.6

Form of application for review

VULNERABLE WITNESSES (SCOTLAND) ACT 2004 Section 13

Received the ....day of ....20...........
(Date of receipt of this notice)
.................(*signed*)
Depute Clerk of Session

In the Cause (Cause Reference No.   )
[A.B.] (*designation and address*)

Pursuer [*or* Petitioner]

against
[C.D.] (*designation and address*)

Defender [*or* Respondent]

APPLICATION FOR REVIEW OF ARRANGEMENTS FOR VULNERABLE WITNESS

1. The applicant is the pursuer [*or* petitioner] [*or* defender] [*or* respondent] in the action by [A.B.] (*design*) against [C.D.] (*design*).

2. A proof [*or* hearing] is fixed for (*date*) at (*time*).

3. [E.F.] is a witness who is to give evidence at, or for the purposes of, the proof [*or* hearing]. [E.F.] is a child witness [*or* vulnerable witness] under section 11 of the Vulnerable Witnesses (Scotland) Act 2004.

4. The current arrangements for taking the evidence of [E.F.] are (*here specify current arrangements*).

5. The current arrangements should be reviewed as (*here specify reasons for review*).

6. [E.F.] [and the parent[s] of [*or* person[s] with parental responsibility for] [E.F.]] has [have] expressed the following view[s] on [the special measure[s] that is [are] considered most appropriate] [*or* the appropriateness of [E.F.] giving evidence without the benefit of any special measure]:–

   (*delete as appropriate and set out the view(s) expressed and how they were obtained*).

7. The applicant seeks (*here specify the order sought*).

(*Signed*)
Solicitor [*or* Agent] for A.B. [*or* C.D.] (*include full designation*)

NOTE: This form should be suitably adapted where section 16 of the Act of 2004 applies.

---

[1] Inserted by S.S.I. 2007 No. 450 (effective 1st November 2007).

Form 35A.7

Rule 35A.7(2)

Rule 35A.7(2)   [1]FORM 35A.7

Form of certificate of intimation

VULNERABLE WITNESSES (SCOTLAND) ACT 2004 Section 13
CERTIFICATE OF INTIMATION

Cause Reference No.

I, (*name and designation*) certify that I intimated the review application relating to (*insert name of witness*) to (*insert names of parties or solicitors for parties, as appropriate*) by (*insert method of intimation*) on (*insert date of intimation*).

Date: ....

.....................(*Signed*)
Solicitor [*or* Agent]
(*include full business designation*)

———

[1] Inserted by S.S.I. 2007 No. 450 (effective 1st November 2007).

Form 36.2-A

Rule 36.2(1)

Rule 36.2(1)   [1] FORM 36.2–A

Form of citation of witness to proof or jury trial

(*date*)

CITATION TO COURT OF SESSION

To [A.B.] (*design*)

(*Name*) who is pursuing /defending a case against (*name*) [*or* is a (*specify*) in the case of (*name*) against (*name*) [*or* has presented a petition] in the Court of Session and has asked you to be a witness. You must attend the Court of Session, Parliament Square, Edinburgh on (*insert date*) at (*insert time*) for that purpose, [and bring with you (*specify documents*)].

If you

- would like to know more about being a witness
- are a child under 16
- think you may be a vulnerable witness within the meaning of section 11(1) of the Vulnerable Witness (Scotland) Act 2004 (that is someone the court considers may be less able to give their evidence due to mental disorder or fear or distress connected to giving your evidence at the court hearing)

you should contact (*specify the solicitor acting for the party or the party litigant citing the witness*) for further information.

If you are a vulnerable witness, then you should be able to use a special measure (such measures include the use of a screen, a live TV link or supporter, or a commissioner) to help you give evidence.

Failure to attend

It is very important that you attend court and you should note that failure to do so may result in a warrant being granted for your arrest.

If you have any questions about anything in this citation, please contact (*specify the solicitor acting for the party or the party litigant citing the witness*) **for further information.**

(*Signed*)

Messenger-at-Arms

[*or* Solicitor [*or* Agent] for (*name of party citing witness*)]
(*Address*)

Please read the notes attached and bring this citation with you when you come to the court.

NOTES

1. What must I do?

The attached document requires you to appear as a witness in the case mentioned in it.

It obliges you to attend at the Court of Session at the time and on the date mentioned. The hearing will start on that date and may continue on the following days. Because it is difficult to estimate how long it will take to hear the evidence of other witnesses, you cannot be given a precise time when you will be called to give evidence. The solicitor for the party who has called you as a witness may, however, be able to arrange to give you some indication of when you are likely to be required.

You should not bring a child under the age of 14 years with you to court unless he or she is to give evidence. You should make arrangements to have the child looked after while you are at the court.

2. Where is the court?

The Court of Session is behind St. Giles Cathedral, High Street, Edinburgh. Parking in central Edinburgh can be very difficult. If you are coming by car you should allow plenty of time to find a parking space.

3. What do I do when I get to court?

When you arrive at the Court of Session, you should enter by the main door, Door 11. You should inform the receptionist of the name of the case. You will be told where you should go. There are signs throughout the building indicating the routes and various courts and other facilities.

You should wait there until you are contacted by the solicitor for the party who cited you.

4. How long will I have to wait?

It is not possible to say how long you will require to wait before being asked to give evidence. The representative of the party who cited you will keep you advised of the situation; but you should note that you may have to stay all day. You may wish to bring a newspaper or magazine to read while you wait.

The court usually sits between 10am and 4pm, rising for lunch normally between 1pm and 2pm. There are occasions, however, when the court may sit after 4pm or may rise later for lunch, in order, for example, to complete an important part of the evidence. You will be advised when you may go for lunch and when you must return.

5. What facilities are available?

The court's restaurant is open between 9am and 3pm, and provides light refreshments as well as lunches. You should speak to the solicitor who cited you about arrangements for going to the restaurant. You should not go to the restaurant without telling the representative of the party who cited you.

There are toilets in witness rooms and other locations throughout the building. If there is not a toilet in your immediate vicinity, a security guard will direct you to the nearest one.

6. What will happen when I am called to give evidence?

A court officer (the macer) will call you into court when you are to give evidence. You will give evidence from a witness box near the front of the courtroom. The judge will ask you to repeat the oath. If you wish to affirm instead of taking the oath, it is a good idea to tell the macer or the solicitor for the party who has called you in advance.

You will be asked questions by the advocate representing the party who has called you as a witness. Then the advocate or advocates for the other party or parties may ask you questions. Finally, the first advocate will have an opportunity to ask you further questions.

You must answer all the questions truthfully and honestly to the best of your ability.

A witness normally gives evidence standing in the witness box. If you find it difficult to stand for a long period, you should ask if you may sit down.

7. Who will be in court?

The judge will be seated on the bench. The clerk of court sits at a table below the judge. The advocates will be sitting facing the judge, and solicitors, parties and their representatives will be sitting behind the advocates. The Press and members of the public may also be in court. If the case is tried by jury, there will be twelve jurors sitting in a jury box opposite you.

8. Will I be compensated?

You do not get paid for giving evidence. You are entitled to some payment for out-of-pocket travelling and subsistence expenses. You should keep any receipts for these expenses and give them to the representative of the party who has called you. If you lose earnings, or need to pay someone else to do your job, you can be paid some compensation, subject to certain limits. These payments are the responsibility of the party who has called you as a witness and his representative. It is *not* the responsibility of the court.

9. If I wish to complain, how do I do so?

There are leaflets available at the reception desk at the entrance which contain the complaints procedures in relation to the services provided by (1) court staff, (2) solicitors and (3) the legal profession generally. If you have a complaint, please bring it to the attention of the appropriate person referred to in the leaflet.

---

[1] Substituted by S.S.I. 2007 No. 450 (effective 1st November 2007).

Form 36.2-B

C1.2A.76   Rule 36.2(3)(a)

Rule 36.2(3)(*a*)   FORM 36.2–B

Form of certificate of citation of witness to appear at proof or jury trial

CERTIFICATE OF CITATION OF WITNESS

I, (*name and designation*), certify that I cited (*name of witness*) to appear at the proof [*or* jury trial] on (*date*) by posting a citation in Form 36.2–A to him [*or* her] between (*time*) and (*time*) on (*date*) at (*name of post office*) post office in a registered envelope [*or* recorded delivery envelope] addressed as follows:—(*address*). The post office receipt [*or* certificate of posting] is attached to this certificate.

(*Signed*)

Messenger-at-Arms
[*or* Solicitor [*or* Agent] for pursuer
[*or other party*]]
(*Address*)

Form 36.2-C

C1.2A.77   Rule 36.2(3)(b)

Rule 36.2(3)(b)   [1] FORM 36.2–C

Form of certificate of citation of witness personally at proof or jury trial
CERTIFICATE OF CITATION PERSONALLY

I, (*name*), Messenger-at-Arms, certify that, on the authority of the interlocutor of the Court of Session (*date*), I cited (*name of witness*) to appear at the proof [*or* jury trial] on (*date*) personally by leaving the citation in Form 36.2–A with him [*or* her] at (*place*) on (*date*).

(*Signed*)

Messenger-at-Arms
(*Address*)

---

[1] Form 36.2–C substituted by S.S.I. 2011 No. 190 (effective 11th April 2011).

Form 36.10-A

C1.2A.78   Rule 36.10

Rule 36.10   FORM 36.10–A

Form of oath for witness

I swear by Almighty God that I will tell the truth, the whole truth and nothing but the truth.

Form 36.10-B

Rule 36.10

Rule 36.10   FORM 36.10–B

Form of affirmation for witness

I solemnly, sincerely and truly declare and affirm that I will tell the truth, the whole truth and nothing but the truth.

Form 37.2-A[1]

C1.2A.80   Rule 37.2(3)

Form of jury precept

JURY PRECEPT

———

THE RIGHT HONOURABLE THE LORDS OF COUNCIL AND SESSION

To the Sheriff Principal and Sheriffs of Lothian and Borders, and to the sheriff clerk, Edinburgh or his deputes:

YOU are hereby authorised and required in terms of the statutes relating to the summoning of jurors to attach hereto a list of fifty names and addresses of equal numbers of men and women, qualified to serve as jurors, living within the sheriff court districts of Edinburgh and Livingston,

and YOU the said sheriff clerk or your depute shall cite the jurors to compear within the Parliament House at Edinburgh on the   day of   at ten o'clock forenoon, with continuation of days, to try the matters at issue in the cause

then to be tried in the Court of Session;

And YOU the said sheriff clerk or your depute shall return the List, with a certificate under your hand of the citation of the jurors, to the Deputy Principal Clerk of Session, 2 Parliament Square, Edinburgh EH1 1RQ, on or before the   day of

Assistant Clerk of Session
(*Date*)

TO   The SHERIFF PRINCIPAL and
Sheriffs of Lothian and Borders

and

The SHERIFF CLERK, Edinburgh

---

[1] As amended by S.S.I. 2016 No. 384 para.2 (effective 24 December 2016).

Form 37.2-B

Rule 37.2(5)[1]

C1.2A.81

[Form of citation of juror]

COURT OF SESSION JUROR'S CITATION

Citation Number: *Date:*

To: *Time:*

                       Place:

Name of case:

You are cited to attend personally on the date and at the time and place stated above, and on such succeeding days as may be necessary to serve, if required, as a juror. If you fail to attend, you will be liable to the penalty prescribed by Law.

Sheriff Clerk Depute

Please read the enclosed leaflets carefully BEFORE attending court for selection.

Expenses: Claims for loss of earnings and/or expenses should be made at the end of your jury service. You will be provided with an envelope for return of the completed form, and payment will be made by crossed cheque to your home address, seven to ten days from receipt of the claim.

YOU MUST BRING THIS CITATION WITH YOU TO COURT

If you wish to apply for exemption or excusal from jury service, please complete this form and return it as soon as possible to: **Deputy Principal Clerk of Session, Court of Session, 2 Parliament Square, Edinburgh EH1 1RQ.**

DECLARATION: *Please state why you are applying for exemption or excusal from jury service:*

[   ] **Age:**   I am .... years of age. My date of birth is ....

[   ] **Occupation:**   I am employed as .... and
                      therefore statutorily exempt from service.

[   ] **Medical Condition:**   I am medically unfit for jury service and enclose a medical certificate from
                           my doctor.

[   ] **Special Reason:**   ....

N.B. *Should you be excused from jury service on this occasion, a further juror's citation may be sent out to you within twelve months.*

I declare that the foregoing information is correct and acknowledge that I may be asked for proof of any statement made above.

Signature .... Date ....

If you have any queries telephone **0131 225 2595.** *Please quote citation number and date of attendance.*

Unfortunately there are no facilities for car parking at or near the court.

---

[1] Form 37.2-B as amended by SSI 2005 No. 193 (effective 1 April 2005).

CERTIFICATE OF LOSS OF EARNINGS OR PAYMENT TO SUBSTITUTE/ CHILDMINDER

(OR LOSS OF NATIONAL INSURANCE BENEFIT)

I certify that for each day M ....
is required by the Court for Jury Service a *deduction/charge of £ .... per day
(............. hours @ .... per hour) will be made from his/her* (earnings/
benefit/service supplied)

Name and Address of Employer/Substitute/Childminder or Local Office where benefit is
received

....

Date .... Signature ....

OFFICIAL USE ONLY
*(delete as applicable)

	Allowed		No. of days	Total	
	£	p		£	p
TRAVELLING					
By public transport					
(a) Say whether rail, bus &c					
(b) Daily return fare £					
In own car, &c					
(a) Car, m/cycle &c ...... Engine capacity .... c.c.					
(b) Daily mileage (round trip)					
(c) Could you have travelled by public transport? *YES/NO					
If YES, indicate how much time was saved by using your own vehicle.					
SUBSISTENCE					
On the days on which the court has NOT provided meals for you, have you necessarily incurred expenses on subsistence? *YES/NO					
If YES, give number of hours, including travelling time you were away from your home or place of business. (If you attended Court on more than one day, show the number of hours for each day)					
LOSS OF EARNINGS (only refundable if certified above)					
Will you suffer any loss of earnings as a result of your attendance for jury service? *YES/NO					
If YES, please state					
(a) your occupation					
(b) daily or hourly rate (or equivalent) £					
(c) number of days and half-days lost					
Have you paid any person to act as a substitute for you during your attendance for jury service (e.g. at your place of employment, or to look after your children &c)? *YES/NO					

If YES, please state
    (a) capacity in which paid substitute employed ....
    (b) his/her daily or hourly rate £ ....
    (c) number of days and half-days paid substitute
         employed ....

I DECLARE that to the best of my knowledge and belief the particulars in the foregoing claim are correct

.... Signature of Claimant

TOTALS

	FOR OFFICIAL USE ONLY		RECEIVED the sum of
	CERTIFIED CORRECT		£ ....
	AUTHORISED FOR PAYMENT		(Signature) ....
	DATE		(Date) ....

Form 37.6-A

Rule 37.6(1)

C1.2A.82

Rule 37.6(1)   FORM 37.6–A

Form of oath for jurors

The jurors shall raise their right hands and the clerk of court shall ask them:—

"Do you swear by Almighty God that you will well and truly try the issue and give a true verdict according to the evidence?"

The jurors shall reply:

"I do".

Form 37.6-B

Rule 37.6(2)

C1.2A.83

Rule 37.6(2)   FORM 37.6–B

Form of affirmation for jurors

The juror shall repeat after the clerk of court:—

"I solemnly, sincerely and truly declare and affirm that I will well and truly try the issue and give a true verdict according to the evidence".

Form 38.5

Rule 38.5(1)

C1.2A.84

Rule 38.5(1)   [1] FORM 38.5

Form of reclaiming motion to be written on Form 23.2

On behalf of the pursuer [*or as the case may be*], for review by the Inner House of the interlocutor of (*date*) of the Lord Ordinary.

---

[1] Form 38.5 inserted by S.S.I. 2010 No. 30 (effective 5th April 2010).

Form 38.12

C1.2A.85   Rule 38.12(1)

Rule 38.12(1)   [1] FORM 38.12

Form of note of objection to competency of reclaiming

(Cause Reference number)

IN THE COURT OF SESSION

NOTE OF OBJECTION TO COMPETENCY OF RECLAIMING

[A.B.]

Pursuer [*or* Petitioner]

against

[C.D.]

Defender [*or* Respondent]

To the Deputy Principal Clerk of Session

(*Name of reclaimer*), pursuer [*or* petitioner *or* defender *or* respondent] and reclaimer, has marked a reclaiming motion in the above cause. (*Name of objecting party*), [*where applicable*: pursuer *or* petitioner *or* defender and] respondent, objects to the competency of the reclaiming motion on the following grounds:

(*set out the grounds in brief numbered paragraphs*)

Date (*insert date*)

(Signed)

Solicitor for Pursuer/Petitioner/Defender/Respondent

(Address)

---

[1] Form 38.12 inserted by S.S.I. 2010 No. 30 (effective 5th April 2010).

Form 38.13

Rule 38.13(1)(a)

C1.2A.86

Rule 38.13(1)(a) ¹ FORM 38.13

Form of timetable in reclaiming motion

(Cause Reference number)

IN THE COURT OF SESSION

TIMETABLE IN RECLAIMING MOTION

[A.B.]

Pursuer [*or* Petitioner]

against

[C.D.]

Defender [*or* Respondent]

This timetable has effect as if it were an interlocutor of the court signed by the procedural judge. [*Where applicable:* This is a revised timetable issued under rule 38.14(4)(c) [*or* rule 38.14(5)(b)] which replaces the timetable issued on (*date*).]

1. The diet for a procedural hearing in relation to this reclaiming motion, which will follow on from the procedural steps listed in paragraphs 2 to 7 below, will take place on (*date and time*).

2. The reclaimer shall lodge grounds of appeal in the reclaiming motion, under rule 38.18(1) and (2), not later than (*date*).

3. Any answers to grounds of appeal or cross-appeal lodged under rule 38.18(1) and (2) shall be lodged not later than (*date*).

4. Subject to the terms of any order made by a procedural judge under rule 38.19(2), any appendices to the reclaiming print shall be lodged not later than (*date*).

5. Any written intimation by the reclaimer under rule 38.19(1) that he does not intend to lodge any appendices to the reclaiming print shall be provided by (*date*).

6. Not later than (*date*) parties shall lodge notes of argument in the reclaiming motion.

7. Not later than (*date*) parties shall lodge estimates of the length of any hearing required to dispose of the reclaiming motion.

(*Date*)

---

¹ Form 38.13 inserted by S.S.I. 2010 No. 30 (effective 5th April 2010) and substituted by S.S.I. 2011 No. 303 (effective 27th September 2011).

Form 39.3[1]

C1.2A.87   Rule 39.3(1)

Form of note of objection to competency of application for a new trial

(Cause Reference number)

IN THE COURT OF SESSION

NOTE OF OBJECTION TO COMPETENCY OF APPLICATION

[A.B.]

Applicant

against

[C.D.]

Respondent

To the Deputy Principal Clerk of Session

(*Name of applicant*), applicant has made an application for a new trial under section 29(1) of the Court of Session Act 1988 [*or* section 69(1) of the Courts Reform (Scotland) Act 2014] in the above cause. (*Name of objecting party*), respondent, objects to the competency of the application on the following grounds:

(*set out the grounds in brief numbered paragraphs*)

Date (*insert date*)

(*Signed*)

Solicitor for Respondent

(*Address*)

---

[1] Form 39.3 as amended by SSI 2015/227 r.4(3)(a) (effective 22 September 2015).

Form 39.4

Rule 39.4(1)

[1] FORM 39.4

Rule 39.4(1)

Form of timetable in application for a new trial

(Cause Reference number)

IN THE COURT OF SESSION

TIMETABLE IN APPLICATION FOR A NEW TRIAL

[A.B.]

Applicant

against

[C.D.]

Respondent

This timetable has effect as if it were an interlocutor of the court signed by the procedural judge. [*Where applicable*: This is a revised timetable issued under rule 39.5(4)(c) [*or* rule 38.5(5)(b)] which replaces the timetable issued on (*date*).]

1.   The diet for a procedural hearing in relation to this application, which will follow on from the procedural steps listed in paragraphs 2 to 5 below, will take place on (*date and time*).

2.   Subject to the terms of any order made by a procedural judge under rule 38.19(2), any appendices to the documents mentioned in rule 39.1(4) [*or* rule 39.1A(4)] shall be lodged not later than (*date*).

3.   Any written intimation by the applicant that he does not intend to lodge any appendices to the documents mentioned in rule 39.1(4) [*or* rule 39.1A(4)] shall be provided by (*date*).

4.   Not later than (*date*) parties shall lodge notes of argument in the application.

5.   Not later than (*date*) parties shall lodge estimates of the length of any hearing required to dispose of the application.

(*Date*)

NOTE
[1] As amended by S.S.I. 2015 No. 227 (effective 22nd September 2015).

Form 40.2[1, 2, 3]

C1.2A.89   *Form of application for leave to appeal*

IN THE COURT OF SESSION

APPLICATION

for

LEAVE TO APPEAL

under (*specify provision of enactment under which application is made*)

by

[A.B.] (*designation and address*)

Applicant

against

Decision of [*or* Refusal of leave to appeal]

(*name of court or tribunal*)

1. That on (*date*) the (*name of court or tribunal*) refused the application of the applicant for leave to appeal to the Court of Session against its decision of (*date*) refusing [*or* decided] (*briefly describe decision*). A copy of the decision of the (*name of court or tribunal*) [and of the decision refusing leave to appeal] is [*or* are] produced with this application.

2. That the reasons given by the (*name of court or tribunal*) for refusing leave to appeal are (*specify*) [*or* are set out in the copy of its decision produced with this application].

3. That the reasons given by the (*name of court or tribunal*) for its decision (*date*) against which leave to appeal is sought are (*specify*) [*or* are set out in the copy of the decision produced with this application].

4. (*in an appeal from an inferior court other than the Sheriff Appeal Court*)

That the grounds on which the applicant seeks leave to appeal to the Court of Session are as follows:- (*set out the grounds in numbered paragraphs.*)

[*or*

4. (*in an appeal from the Sheriff Appeal Court*)

---

[1] As amended by S.S.I. 2016 No. 102 (effective 21 March 2016).
[2] As amended by S.S.I. 2016 No. 384 para.2 (effective 24 December 2016).
[3] Form 40.2 para.4 as substituted by SSI 2017/4 (effective 7 February 2017).

That the grounds on which the applicant seeks leave to appeal to the Court of Session are as follows:-

The appeal raises an important point of principle or practice (*briefly state the reasons*)

[*or*

The appeal does not raise an important point of principle or practice but there is some other compelling reason for the Court of Session to hear the appeal because (*briefly state the reasons*).]]

5. That the grounds on which the applicant seeks to appeal against the decision of the (*name of court or tribunal*) of (*date*) are as follows:-(*set out the grounds in numbered sub-paragraphs*).

6. That this application is made under (*specify provision of enactment*) and rule 40.2(2) [*or* 41.2(3)] of the Rules of the Court of Session 1994.

IN RESPECT WHEREOF

(*Signed*)

Applicant

[*or* Solicitor [*or* Agent] for applicant]

Form 40.4

Rule 40.4(2)

C1.2A.90

Rule 40.4(2)   [1] FORM 40.4

Form of marking appeal from inferior court

The pursuer [*or* defender *or as the case may be*] appeals to the Court of Session.

(*Signed*)

Pursuer [*or as the case may be*]
[*or* Solicitor [*or* Agent] for pursuer
[*or as the case may be*]]. Appellant

---

[1] Form 40.4 amended by S.I. 1996 No. 2587 (rule reference).

Form 40.10

C1.2A.91   Rule 40.10(1)

Rule 40.10(1)   [1] FORM 40.10

Form of note of objection to competency of appeal from inferior court

(Cause Reference number)

IN THE COURT OF SESSION

NOTE OF OBJECTION TO COMPETENCY OF APPEAL

[A.B.]

Appellant

against

[C.D.]

Respondent

To the Deputy Principal Clerk of Session

(*Name of appellant*), appellant has marked an appeal from an inferior court in the above cause. (*Name of objecting party*), respondent, objects to the competency of the appeal on the following grounds:

(*set out the grounds in brief numbered paragraphs*)

Date (*insert date*)

(*Signed*)

Solicitor for Respondent

(*Address*)

---

[1] Form 40.10 inserted by S.S.I. 2010 No. 30 (effective 5th April 2010).

Form 40.11

Rule 40.11(1)(a)

Rule 40.11(1)(a) [1] FORM 40.11

Form of timetable in appeal from inferior court

(Cause Reference number)

IN THE COURT OF SESSION

TIMETABLE IN APPEAL

[A.B.]

Appellant

against

[C.D.]

Respondent

This timetable has effect as if it were an interlocutor of the court signed by the procedural judge. [*Where applicable*: This is a revised timetable issued under rule 40.12(4)(c) [*or* rule 40.12(5)(b)] which replaces the timetable issued on (*date*).]

1. The diet for a procedural hearing in relation to this appeal, which will follow on from the procedural steps listed in paragraphs 2 to 10 below, will take place on (*date and time*).

2. The appellant shall lodge a process under rule 40.7(2)(a) not later than (*date*).

3. The appellant shall send copies of the appeal print under rule 40.7(2)(b) not later than (*date*).

4. Any motion by the appellant to sist the process of the appeal under rule 40.8(1) shall be lodged not later than (*date*).

5. Grounds of appeal under rule 40.18(1) shall be lodged not later than (*date*).

6. Any answers to grounds of appeal or cross-appeal lodged under rule 40.18(1) shall be lodged not later than (*date*).

7. Subject to the terms of any order made by a procedural judge under rule 40.19(2), any appendices to the appeal print shall be lodged not later than (*date*).

8. Any written intimation by the appellant under rule 40.19(1) that he does not intend to lodge any appendices to the appeal print shall be provided by (*date*).

9. Not later than (*date*) parties shall lodge notes of argument in the appeal.

10. Not later than (*date*) parties shall lodge estimates of the length of any hearing on the Summar Roll or in the Single Bills which is required to dispose of the appeal.

(*Date*)

---

[1] Form 40.11 inserted by S.S.I. 2010 No. 30 (effective 5th April 2010) and substituted by S.S.I. 2011 No. 303 (effective 27th September 2011).

Form 40.15

C1.2A.93   Rule 40.15(5)(a)

Rule 40.15(5)(a)   ¹ FORM 40.15

Form of certification by Deputy Principal Clerk on retransmitting abandoned appeal

(*Date*) Retransmitted in respect of the abandonment of the appeal.

(*Signed*)

Deputy Principal Clerk of Session

---

¹ Form 40.15 inserted by S.S.I. 2010 No. 30 (effective 5th April 2010).

Form 41.5

C1.2A.94   Rule 41.5(1)

Rule 41.5(1)   ¹ FORM 41.5

Form of note of objection to competency of appeal under statute

(Cause Reference number)

IN THE COURT OF SESSION

NOTE OF OBJECTION TO COMPETENCY OF APPEAL

[A.B.]

Appellant

against

[C.D.]

Respondent

To the Deputy Principal Clerk of Session

(*Name of appellant*), appellant has marked an appeal under (*insert statutory provision under which the appeal is brought*) in the above cause. (*Name of objecting party*), respondent, objects to the competency of the appeal on the following grounds:

(*set out the grounds in brief numbered paragraphs*)

Date (*insert date*)

(*Signed*)

Solicitor for Respondent

(*Address*)

---

¹ As inserted by S.S.I. 2011 No. 303 (effective 27ᵗʰ September 2011).

Form 41.9

Rule 41.9(1)

Rule 41.9(1)   FORM 41.9

Form of case in appeal under statute to the Court of Session

CASE

for

OPINION OF THE COURT OF SESSION

under

(*State provision in enactment under which appeal is made*)

appeal by

[A.B.] (*designation and address*)

Appellant

against

[C.D.] (*designation and address*)

Respondent

I [*or* We] found the following facts admitted or proved:—

(*Set out in numbered paragraphs the facts admitted or proved*)

NOTE

(*Set out the basis on which the tribunal found the facts admitted or proved and the reasoning of the decision appealed against*)

The question(s) of law for the opinion of the court is [*or* are]:—

(*Set out the questions in numbered paragraphs*)

This case stated by [*me*]

(*Signed*)

(*Name*)

APPENDIX

(*Here append any documents referred to in the case necessary for the understanding of the case.*)

Form 41.12

C1.2A.96   Rule 41.12(1)

Rule 41.12(1)   [1] FORM 41.12

Form of case in appeal under statute to the Court of Session

CASE

for

OPINION OF THE COURT OF SESSION

under

(*state provision in enactment under which appeal is made*)

[A.B.] (*designation and address*)

Appellant

against

[C.D.] (*designation and address*)

Respondent

I [*or* We] found the following facts admitted or proved:—

(*Set out in numbered paragraphs the facts admitted or proved*)

NOTE

(*Set out the basis on which the tribunal found the facts admitted or proved and the reasoning of the decision appealed against*)

The question(s) of law for the opinion of the court is [*or are*]:—

(*Set out the questions in numbered paragraphs*)

This case stated by [*me*]

(*Signed*)

(*Name*)

APPENDIX

(*Here append any documents referred to in the case necessary for the understanding of the case*)

––––––––––

[1] As inserted by S.S.I. 2011 No. 303 (effective 27th September 2011).

Form 41.17

Rule 41.17(2)

C1.2A.97

Rule 41.17(2) [1] FORM 41.17

Form of certification by Deputy Principal Clerk on retransmitting abandoned appeal

(*Date*). Retransmitted in respect of the abandonment of the appeal.

(*Signed*)

Deputy Principal Clerk of Session

_____

[1] As inserted by S.S.I. 2011 No. 303 (effective 27th September 2011).

Form 41.25

Rule 41.25(1)

C1.2A.98

Rule 41.25(1) [1] FORM 41.25

Form of appeal in appeal under statute to the Court of Session

APPEAL

to

THE COURT OF SESSION

under

(*state provision in enactment under which appeal is made*)

[A.B.] (*designation and address*)

Appellant

against

A decision [*or as the case may be*] of (*name of tribunal*) dated (*date*) communicated to the appellant on (*date*)

The decision [*or as the case may be*] of (*name of tribunal*) dated (*date*) is in the following terms [*or where a lengthy or reasoned decision is appealed against*, is appended to this appeal].

The appellant appeals against the forgoing decision [*or as the case may be*] on the following grounds.

GROUNDS OF APPEAL

(*State the grounds of appeal in numbered paragraphs*)

The question(s) of law for the opinion of the court is [or are]:—

(*Set out the questions in numbered paragraphs*)

(*Signed*)

Appellant

[*or* Solicitor [*or* Agent] for appellant]

(Here set out lengthy or reasoned decision appealed against)

___

[1] As inserted by S.S.I. 2011 No. 303 (effective 27th September 2011).

Form 41.29

C1.2A.99   Rule 41.18(1)(a)

Rule 41.29(1)(a)

Rule 41.18(1)(a)
Rule 41.29(1)(a)   [1] FORM 41.29

Form of timetable in appeal under statute

(Cause Reference number)

IN THE COURT OF SESSION

TIMETABLE IN APPEAL

[A.B.]

Appellant

against

[C.D.]

Respondent

This timetable has effect as if it were an interlocutor of the court signed by the procedural judge.
[*Where applicable*: This is a revised timetable issued under rule 41.30(4)(c) [*or* rule 41.30(5)(b) *or*
rule 41.19(4)(c) *or* rule 41.19(5)(b)] which replaces the timetable issued on (*date*).]

1. The diet for a procedural hearing in relation to this appeal, which will follow on from the
   procedural steps listed in paragraphs 2 to 4 below, will take place on (*date and time*).
2. Any productions or appendices to the appeal shall be lodged not later than (*date*).
3. Not later than (*date*) parties shall lodge notes of argument in the appeal.
4. Not later than (*date*) parties shall lodge estimates of the length of any hearing on the
   Summar Roll or in the Single Bills which is required to dispose of the appeal.

(*Date*)

___

[1] As inserted by S.S.I. 2011 No. 303 (effective 27th September 2011).

Form 41.52C

C1.2A.99.1   *[Omitted by S.S.I. 2016 No. 102 (effective 21 March 2016).]*

[THE NEXT PARAGRAPH IS C1.2A.100]

Form 41.55

C1.2A.100   Rule 41.55
Form of reference on a preliminary point under an ACAS Scheme

Rule 41.55   [1] FORM 41.55

Form of reference on a preliminary point under an ACAS Scheme

UNTO THE RIGHT HONOURABLE

THE LORDS OF COUNCIL AND SESSION

REFERENCE ON A PRELIMINARY POINT

Under

(*specify the ACAS Scheme under which the reference is being made*)

by

[A.B.] (*address*)

Arbitrator in the case of

[C.D.] (*address*) against [E.F.] (*address*)

[or by

[C.D.] (*address*) and [E.F.] (*address*) parties in a case in which [A.B.] (*address*) is the arbitrator]

(*Here state in numbered paragraphs the facts and circumstances out of which the reference arises and set out the question for answer by the court*)

---

[1] As inserted by S.S.I. 2011 No. 303 (effective 27th September 2011).

Form 41.59[1]

Form of application for Marine Licence Applications etc.

C1.2A.100.1

Application

to

THE COURT OF SESSION

under

(state provision in enactment under which application is made)

[A.B.] *(designation and address)*

Applicant

against

A decision of the Scottish Ministers dated *(date)* communicated to the applicant on *(date)*

The decision dated *(date)* is appended to this application.

The application against the foregoing decision is on the following grounds.

GROUNDS

(State the grounds for the application in numbered paragraphs)

1.   The grounds on which the validity of the decision is questioned are *(state the grounds)*

2.   The court should grant permission for the application to proceed because *(state the reasons)*.

(signed)

Applicant

[*or* Solicitor [*or* Agent] for Applicant]

---

[1] Form 41.59 as inserted by S.S.I. 2015 No. 35 (effective 26th February 2015).

Form 41A.2[1]

Form of application for permission to appeal to the Supreme Court

IN THE COURT OF SESSION

APPLICATION

for

PERMISSION TO APPEAL TO THE SUPREME COURT

under section 40 of the Court of Session Act 1988

by

[A.B.] (*designation and address*)

Applicant

against

A decision of the Inner House

1. On (*date*) the Inner House (*briefly describe decision in respect of which permission to appeal to Supreme Court is sought*).

GROUNDS OF APPEAL

2. (*Set out the ground(s) in numbered paragraphs.*)

PERMISSION TO APPEAL

3. The appeal raises an arguable point of law of general public importance which ought to be considered by the Supreme Court at this time because (*state the reasons*).

IN RESPECT WHEREOF

(*Signed*)

Applicant

[*or* Solicitor [*or* Agent] for applicant]

---

[1] As amended by S.S.I. 2016 No. 102 (effective 21 March 2016).

Form 42.7

C1.2A.102   Rule 42.7(5)(c)

Rule 42.7(5)(*c*)   FORM 42.7

Form of notice to client intimating diet of taxation of solicitors' account

To: (*name and address*)

Date: (*date of posting*)

(*Name of solicitors*), Applicant v. [C.D.], respondent

Cause reference number:

1. We enclose a copy of the solicitors' account in respect of which we seek payment.

2. The court has, in terms of the enclosed interlocutor, remitted the account to the Auditor of the Court of Session for taxation (assessment).

3. The taxation hearing will take place at the office of the Auditor of the Court of Session, Parliament House, 2 Parliament Square, Edinburgh on (*date and time*).

4. If you wish to object to any part of the account you must appear or be represented at the taxation hearing.

5. You will lose any right to object to the account if you do not appear or are not represented at the taxation hearing.

(*Signed*)

Solicitor
(*Address*)

IF YOU ARE UNCERTAIN ABOUT THE EFFECT OF THIS NOTICE, you should consult a solicitor, Citizens Advice Bureau or other local advice agency or adviser immediately.

Form 43.1A[1]

C1.2A.103   Rule43.1A(1)
         Rule 43.1A(2)
         Form of draft interlocutor granting authority to raise action based on clinical negligence as an ordinary action

---

[1] Form 43.1A as substituted by S.S.I. 2015 No. 227 Sch.1 (effective 22nd September 2015).

[*To be inserted on the first page of the summons*]

Authority

The Lord Ordinary, having considered the application of the pursuer [and having heard counsel thereon], and being satisfied, considering the likely complexity of the action, that the efficient determination of the action would be served by doing so, grants authority for the cause to proceed as an ordinary action.

(*Signed*)

Lord/Lady

Date: (*date*)

Form 43.2-A

[1] FORM 43.2–A   C1.2A.104

Form of summons and backing in personal injuries action

[*Insert the Royal Arms in Scotland*]

(*This space will contain the cause reference number assigned to the summons on being presented for signeting and registration*)

IN THE COURT OF SESSION

SUMMONS

(Personal injuries action)

[A.B.] (*designation, statement of any special capacity in which the pursuer is suing, and address*), Pursuer

against

[C.D.] (*designation, statement of any special capacity in which the defender is being sued, and address*), Defender

Elizabeth II, by the Grace of God, of the United Kingdom of Great Britain and Northern Ireland and of Her other Realms and Territories, Queen, Head of the Commonwealth, Defender of the Faith, to [C.D.].

By this summons, the pursuer craves the Lords of our Council and Session to pronounce a decree against you in terms of the conclusions appended to this summons. If you have any good reason why such decree should not be pronounced, you must enter appearance at the Office of Court, Court of Session, 2 Parliament Square, Edinburgh EH1 1RQ, within three days after the date of the calling of the summons in court. The summons shall not call in court earlier than (*enter period of notice*) days after it has been served on you. **Be warned that, if appearance is not entered on your behalf, the pursuer may obtain decree against you in your absence.**

This summons is warrant for intimation to (*name and address and reason for intimation as set out in the rule of the Rules of the Court of Session 1994 requiring intimation*).

Given under our Signet at Edinburgh on (*date*).

(*Signed*)

(*Name and address of or agent for pursuer*)

[*Back of first page*]

CONCLUSIONS

FIRST. For payment by the defender to the pursuer of the sum of (*amount of sum in words and figures*).

SECOND. [*enter only if a claim for provisional damages is sought in terms of rule 43.2(2)*] For payment by the defender to the pursuer of (*enter amount in words and figures*) of provisional damages.

THIRD. For the expenses of the action

STATEMENT OF CLAIM

1. The pursuer is (*state designation, address, occupation and date of birth of pursuer*). [*In an action arising out of the death of a relative state designation of the deceased and relation to the pursuer*].

2. The defender is (*state designation, address and occupation of defender*).

3. The court has jurisdiction to hear this claim against the defender because (*state briefly ground of jurisdiction*).

4. (*State briefly the facts necessary to establish the claim*).

5. (*State briefly the personal injuries suffered and the heads of claim. Give names and addresses of medical practitioners and hospitals or other institutions in which the person injured received treatment*).

6. (*State whether claim based on fault at common law or breach of statutory duty; if breach of statutory duty, state provision of enactment*).

IN RESPECT WHEREOF

(*Signed*)

Solicitor [or Agent] for the pursuer
(*address and solicitor/agent's reference number*)

(*Backing of summons*)

(*This space will contain the cause reference number assigned to the summons on being presented for signeting and registration*)

---

[1] Form 43.2–A substituted by S.S.I. 2004 No. 291 (effective 29th June 2004) and amended by S.S.I. 2008 No. 349.

Form 43.2 B

Form of order of court for recovery of documents in personal injuries action

IN THE COURT OF SESSION

In the Cause (Cause Reference No.)

SPECIFICATION OF DOCUMENTS

[A.B.] (*designation and address*)

Pursuer

against

[C.D.] (*designation and address*)

Defender

Date: (*date of posting or other method of service*)

To: (*name and address of party or parties from whom the following documents are sought to be recovered*)

You are hereby required to produce to the agent for the pursuer within seven days of the service on you of this Order:—

[*Insert such of the following calls as are required.*]

1. All books, medical records, reports, charts, X-rays, notes and other documents of (*specify the name of each medical practitioner or general practitioner practice named in summons in accordance with rule 43.2(1)(b)*), and relating to the pursuer [*or, as the case may be*, the deceased], in order that excerpts may be taken therefrom at the sight of the Commissioner of all entries showing or tending to show the nature, extent and cause of the pursuer's [*or, as the case may be*, the deceased's] injuries when he intended his doctor on or after (*specify date*) and the treatment received by him since that date.

2. All books, medical records, reports, charts, X-rays, notes and other documents of (*specify, in separate calls, the name of each hospital or other institution named in summons in accordance with rule 43.2(1)(b)*), and relating to the pursuer [*or, as the case may be*, the deceased], in order that excerpts may be taken therefrom at the sight of the Commissioner of all entries showing or tending to show the nature, extent and cause of all injuries from which the pursuer [*or, as the case may be*, the deceased] was suffering when he was admitted to that institution on or about (*specify date*), the treatment received by him since that date and his certificate of discharge, if any.

3. The medical records and capability assessments held by the defender's occupational health department relating to the pursuer [*or, as the case may be*, the deceased], except insofar as prepared for or in contemplation of litigation, in order that excerpts may be taken therefrom at the sight of the Commissioner of all entries showing or tending to show the nature and extent of any injuries, symptoms and condition from which the pursuer [*or as the case may be*, the deceased] was suffering and the nature of any assessment and diagnosis made thereof on or subsequent to (*specify date*).

4. All wage books, cash books, wage sheets, computer records and other earnings information relating to the pursuer (*or, as the case may be*, the deceased) (N.I. Number (*specify number*)) held by or on behalf of (*specify employer*), for the period (*specify dates commencing not earlier than 26 weeks prior to the date of the accident or the first date of relevant absence, as the case may be*) in order that excerpts may be taken therefrom at the sight of the Commissioner of all entries showing or tending to show:—
   (a) the pursuer's [*or, as the case may be*, the deceased's] earnings, both gross and net of income tax and employee National Insurance Contributions, over the said period;

(b) the period or periods of the pursuer's [*or, as the case may be*, the deceased's] absence from employment over the said period and the reason for absence;

(c) details of any increases in the rate paid over the period (*specify dates*) and the dates on which any such increases took effect;

(d) the effective date of, the reasons for and the terms (including any terms relative to any pension entitlement) of the termination of the pursuer's [*or, as the case may be*, the deceased's] employment;

(e) the nature and extent of contributions (if any) to any occupational pension scheme made by the pursuer [*or, as the case may be*, the deceased] and his employer;

(f) the pursuer's present entitlement (if any) to occupational pension and the manner in which said entitlement is calculated.

5. All accident reports, memoranda or other written communications made to the defender or anyone on his behalf by an employee of the defender who was present at or about the time at which the pursuer [*or, as the case may be*, the deceased] sustained the injuries in respect of which the summons in this cause was issued and relevant to the matters contained in the statement of claim.

6. Any risk assessment current at the time of the accident referred to in the summons or at the time of the circumstances referred to in the summons giving rise to the cause of action (as the case may be) undertaken by or on behalf of the defender for the purpose of regulation 3 of the Management of Health and Safety at Work Regulations 1992 and subsequently regulation 3 of the Management of Health and Safety at Work Regulations 1999 [*or* (*specify the regulations or other legislative provision under which the risk assessment is required*)] in order that excerpts may be taken therefrom at the sight of the Commissioner of all entries relating to the risks posed to workers [*or* (*specify the matters set out in the statement of claim to which the risk assessment relates*)].

7. Failing principals, drafts, copies or duplicates of the above or any of them.

(*Signature, name and business address of the agent for the pursuer.*)

NOTES

(1) The documents recovered will be considered by the parties to the action and they may or may not be lodged in the court process. A written receipt will be given or sent to you by the pursuer, who may thereafter allow them to be inspected by the other parties. The party in whose possession the documents are will be responsible for their safekeeping.

(2) Parties are obliged by the rules of court to return the documents to you when their purpose with the documents is finished. If they do not, you will be entitled to apply to the court, under rule 35.3(9) of the Rules of the Court of Session 1994, for an order to have this done and you may apply for an award of expenses incurred in doing so. Further information about this can be obtained from the General Department, Court of Session, 2 Parliament Square, Edinburgh EH1 1RQ (Tel. 0131-225-2595).

(3) If you claim that any of the documents produced by you are **confidential**, you must still produce such documents but may place them in a separate sealed packet by themselves, marked "CONFIDENTIAL". In that event they must be delivered or sent by post to the **Deputy Principal Clerk of Session, 2 Parliament Square, Edinburgh, EH1 1RQ**. Any party who wishes to open the sealed packet must apply to the court by motion. A party who makes such an application must intimate the motion to you.

(4) Subject to paragraph (3) above, you may produce these documents by sending them by registered post or by the first class recorded delivery service or registered postal packet, or by hand to (*name and address of the agent for the pursuer*).

CERTIFICATE

(*Date*)

I hereby certify with reference to the above order of the Court of Session in the cause (*cause reference number*) and the enclosed specification of documents, served on me and market respectively X and Y:—

Release 90: March 2007

(1) That the documents which are produced and which are listed in the enclosed inventory signed by me and marked Z, are all the documents in my possession falling within the specification,

or

That I have no documents in my possession falling within the specification.

(2) That, to the best of my knowledge and belief, there are in existence other documents falling within the specification, but not in my possession. These documents are as follows:— (*describe them by reference to the descriptions of documents in the specification*). They were last seen by me on or about (*date*), at (*place*), in the hands of (*name and address of the person*),

or

That I know of the existence of no documents in the possession of any person, other than myself, which fall within the specification.

(Signed)

(Name and address)

---

[1] Form 43.2–B substituted by S.S.I. 2004 No. 291 (effective 29th June 2004) and amended by S.S.I. 2007 No. 282 (effective 2nd May 2007).

Form 43.3

[1] FORM 43.3

Form of citation of defender

CITATION

Date: *(date of posting or other method of service)*

To: [C.D.] *(address of defender)*

IN HER MAJESTY'S NAME AND AUTHORITY, I, *(name of agent)*, solicitor [or person having a right to conduct the litigation), for *(name of pursuer)* [or *(name of messenger-at-arms)*, Messenger-at arms], serve the attached summons on you.

The summons contains a claim for reparation for personal injuries [or for reparation arising from the death of *(name of the deceased)* from personal injuries] made by *(name of pursuer)* against you in the Court of Session, Edinburgh.

If you intend to deny this claim you must: (1) enter appearance at the Office of Court, Court of Session, 2 Parliament Square, EDINBURGH, EH1 1RQ, within three days after (the date on which the summons calls in court); and (2) subsequently lodge defences within seven days after *(the date on which the summons calls in court)*. The summons will not call in court earlier than *(enter period of notice)* days after it has been served on you. The date of service is the date stated at the top of this citation unless service has been by post in which case the date of service is the day after that date.

If you do not enter appearance and lodge defences, the court may make an order against you.

IF YOU ARE UNCERTAIN ABOUT THE EFFECT OF THIS NOTICE, you should consult a solicitor, Citizens Advice Bureau or other local advice agency or adviser immediately.

(Signed)

Messenger-at-Arms
[*or* Solicitor [*or* Agent] for pursuer(s)]
(Address)

---

[1] Form 43.3 substituted by S.S.I. 2002 No. 570 (effective 1st April 2003).

Form 43.6

[1] FORM 43.6

Form of timetable order

IN THE COURT OF SESSION

TIMETABLE ORDER

In the cause

[A.B.]

Pursuer

against

[C.D.]

Defender

This order has effect as if it were an interlocutor of the court signed by the Lord Ordinary.

1. The diet allocated for the trial of this action will begin on (*date*). Subject to any variation under rule 43.7, this order requires the parties to undertake the conduct of this action within the periods specified in paragraphs 2 to 9 below.

2. Any motion under rule 26.1 (third party notice) shall be made by (date).

3. Where the pursuer has obtained a commission and diligence for the recovery of documents by virtue of rule 43.4, the pursuer shall serve an order under rule 35.3 not later than (date).

4. The pursuer shall lodge a statement of valuation of claim under rule 43.8(2) not later than (date).

5. For the purposes of rule 43.6(1)(b)(iii), the adjustment period shall end on (date).

6. The pursuer shall lodge a record no later than (date).

7. The defender [and any third party convened in the action] shall lodge a statement of valuation of claim under rule 43.9(2) not later than (date).

8. Not later than (date) parties shall lodge list of witnesses and productions.

9. Not later than (date) the pursuer shall lodge a pre-trial minute under rule 43.10(2).

---

[1] Form 43.6 inserted by S.S.I. 2002 No. 570 (effective 1st April 2003).

Form 43.6A

Rule 43.6(5C)

Rule 43.6(5C)　　　　　　　[1] FORM 43.6A

Form of certificate of likely duration of diet

I, (*name and designation*), hereby certify that the likely duration of the (*insert name of diet*) is (*state estimated duration*).

(*Signed*)

Solicitor [*or* Counsel] [*or* Solicitor Advocate] for the Pursuer [*or* Defender]."

(*Print name*)

---

[1] Form 43.6A inserted by S.S.I. 2007 No. 548 (effective 7th January 2008).

Form 43.9

C1.2A.109

Form of Statement of Valuation of Claim

Head of claim	Components	Valuation
Solatium	Past	£x
	Future	£x
Interest on past *solatium*	Percentage applied to past solatium State percentage rate	£x
Past wage loss	Date from which wage loss claimed	£x
	(....)	
	Date to which wage loss Claimed	
	(....)	
	Rate of net wage loss (per week, per month or per annum)	
Interest on past wage loss	Percentage applied to past wage loss (*State percentage rate*)	£x
Future wage loss	Multiplier	£x
	(....)	
	Multiplicand (showing how calculated)	
	Discount factor applied (if appropriate)	
	Or specify any other method of calculation	
Past services	Date from which services claimed	
	(....)	
	Date to which services claimed	
	(....)	
	Nature of services	
	(....)	
	Person by whom services provided	
	(....)	
	Hours per week services provided	
	(....)	

1444

Head of claim	Components	Valuation
	Net hourly rate claimed (....) Total amount claimed (....) Interest	£x
Future loss of capacity to provide personal services	Multiplier (....) Multiplicand (showing how calculated	£x
Needs and other expenses	One off Multiplier (....) Multiplicand Interest	£x £x
Any other heads as appropriate (specify)		

---

[1] Form 43.9 inserted by S.S.I. 2002 No. 570 (effective 1st April 2003) and amended by S.S.I. 2007 No. 282 (effective 2nd May 2007).

Form 43.10[1]

C1.2A.110   Minute of Pre-Trial Meeting

IN THE COURT OF SESSION

Joint Minute of Pre-Trial Meeting

in the cause

[A.B.], Pursuer

against

[C.D.], Defender

[G.H.] for the pursuer and

[I.J.] for the defenders hereby state to the court:-

(1)   That the pre-trial meeting was held in this case at (*place*) [*or* by video-conference] on (*date*).

(2)   That the following persons were present:-

(*State names and designations of persons attending meeting*).

(2A)   That the following persons were available to provide instructions by telephone:-

(*State names and designations of persons available to provide instructions by telephone*);

(3)   That the persons present discussed settlement of the action.

(4)   That the following questions were addressed:-

Section 1

		Yes	No
1.	Is the diet of proof or trial still required?		
2.	If the answer to question 1 is "yes", does the defender admit liability? (If "no", complete section 2.)		

---

[1] Form 43.10 as amended by SSI 2015/227 r.6(4)(b) (effective 22 September 2015).

	If yes, does the defender plead contributory negligence? If yes, is the degree of contributory negligence agreed? If yes, state % degree of fault attributed to the pursuer;		
3.	If the answer to question 1 is "yes", is the quantum of damages agreed? (If "no", complete section 3.)		

Section 2

[To be inserted only if the proof or trial is still required.]

It is estimated that the hearing will last   days.

N.B. If the estimate differs from the number of days previously allocated for the proof or trial then this should be brought to the attention of the Keeper. This may affect prioritisation of the case.

During the course of the pre-trial meeting, the pursuer called on the defender to agree certain facts, questions of law and matters of evidence.

Those calls, and the defender's responses, are as follows:

Call	Response	
	Admitted	Denied
1.		
2.		
3.		
4.		

During the course of the pre-trial meeting, the defender called on the pursuer to agree certain facts, questions of law and matters of evidence.

Those calls, and the pursuer's responses, are as follows:-

Call	Response	
	Admitted	Denied
1.		
2.		
3.		
4.		

Section 3

Quantum of Damages

Please indicate where agreement has been reached on an element of damages.

Head of Claim	Components	Not Agreed	Agreed At
Solatium	Past		
	Future		
Interest on past *solatium*	Percentage applied to past *solatium* (*State percentage*)		
Past wage loss	Date from which wage loss claimed		
	Date to which wage loss claimed		
	Rate of net wage loss (per week, per month or per annum)		
Interest on past wage loss			
Future wage loss	Multiplier		
	Multiplicand (showing how calculated)		
Past services	Date from which services claimed		
	Date to which services claimed		

	Hours per week services provided Net hourly rate claimed		
Past personal services			
Interest on past necessary services			
Future necessary services	Multiplier Multiplicand (showing how calculated)		
Future personal services	Multiplier Multiplicand (showing how calculated)		
Needs and other expenses	Multiplier Multiplicand (showing how calculated)		
Any other heads as appropriate (specify)			

IN RESPECT WHEREOF

(Signed by counsel/solicitor advocate for each party)

Form 43.12

[*Form 43.12 revoked by S.S.I. 2002 No. 570 (effective 1st April 2003).*]   **C1.2A.111**

Form 43.13-A[1]

Form of conclusion for application for an award of further damages   **C1.2A.112**
    For payment to the pursuer by the defender of the sum (*amount in words and figures*) as further damages.

---

[1] Form 43.13-A substituted by S.S.I. 2002 No. 570 (effective 1st April 2003).

Form 43.13-B

C1.2A.113

[1] Form 43.13–B

Form of notice of application for further damages

Date: (*date of posting or other method of service*)

To: (*name and address of persons on whom served*)

TAKE NOTICE

(Pursuer's name and address), pursuer, raised an action against (defender's name and address), defender, in the Court of Session.

In the action, [Lord (name)] in the Court of Session on (date) made an award of provisional damages in favour of the pursuer against you [or (party's name)]. [The court specified that the pursuer may apply for an award of further damages at any time before (date).] The pursuer has applied by minute for an award of further damages against you [or (party's name)]. A copy of the minute is [and the summons in the action are] attached. You may lodge answers to the minute within [21] days after the date of service on you of the minute at the Office of Court, Court of Session, 2 Parliament Square, Edinburgh EH1 1RQ. The date of service is the date stated at the top of this notice unless service has been made by post in which case the date of service is the day after that date.

IF YOU ARE UNCERTAIN ABOUT THE EFFECT OF THIS NOTICE, you should consult a solicitor, Citizens Advice Bureau or other local advice agency or adviser immediately.

(*Signed*)

Messenger-at-Arms
[*or* Solicitor [*or* Agent] for pursuer]
(*Address*)

---

[1] Form 43.13–B substituted by S.S.I. 2002 No. 570 (effective 1st April 2003).

Form 43.15

[1] FORM 43.15

Form of notice of intimation to connected person in an action for damages

Date: (*date of posting or other method of intimation*)

To: (*name and address of connected person*)

TAKE NOTICE

(*Names and addresses of all pursuers*) have raised an action against (*names and addresses of all defenders*) in the Court of Session, Edinburgh. The action relates to the death of (*name and last address of deceased*) [or the personal injuries from which (*name and last address of deceased*) died].

You are believed to have a right to sue arising from his [or her] death. If this is the case, you are entitled to be added as an additional pursuer in the action. A copy of the summons in the action is attached.

You may apply to the court to be added as a pursuer after the date of intimation to you of the summons [or if the warrant for intimation is executed at the same time as citation of the defender, within seven days after the date on which the summons calls in the court. The summons may not call in Court earlier than (*enter period of notice*) days after the date of intimation to you of the summons. The date of intimation is the date stated at the top of this notice unless intimation has been made by post in which case the date of intimation is the day after that date.

If you do not apply to be added as an additional pursuer and subsequently bring a separate action, under rule 43.20 of the Rules of the Court of Session 1994 you may not be awarded the expenses of that action in the event of your being successful.

[It is proposed to apply to the court for authority to dispense with intimation to the person(s) mentioned in paragraph (number of paragraph) of the statement attached to the summons. The whereabouts of such person(s) are not known. If you know of that person (or any of those persons], you should inform the Deputy Principal Clerk of Session, Court of Session, Parliament Square, Edinburgh EH1 1RQ (Telephone 0131-225-2595)].

IF YOU ARE UNCERTAIN ABOUT THE EFFECT OF THIS NOTICE, you should consult a solicitor, Citizens Advice Bureau or other local advice agency or adviser immediately.

(*Signed*)

Messenger-at-Arms
[*or* Solicitor [*or* Agent] for pursuer(s)]
(*Address*)

---

[1] Form 43.15 inserted by S.S.I. 2002 No. 570 (effective 1st April 2003).

Form 44.2-A

C1.2A.115   Rule 44.2(1)

Form 44.2-A

Form of notice to debtor under the Debtors (Scotland) Act 1987 about time to pay directions

(Cause Reference number)

IN THE COURT OF SESSION

in the cause

[A.B.] *(designation and address)*

Pursuer

against

[C.D.] *(designation and address)*

Defender

To: *(name of defender to whom notice is directed)*

YOUR RIGHTS UNDER THE DEBTORS (SCOTLAND) ACT 1987

The purpose of this notice is to advise you of your rights under the Debtors (Scotland) Act 1987.

The Act gives you a right to apply to the court for a "time to pay direction" directing that any sum of money you are ordered to pay to the pursuer (which may include interest and court expenses) shall be by instalments or deferred lump sum (that is by one total payment by a specified date).

In addition, when making a time to pay direction the court may recall or restrict an arrestment made in connection with the action or debt (*e.g.* your bank account may have been arrested freezing the money in it).

If you admit that the sum claimed by the pursuer is due but you wish to apply for a time to pay direction you should read on. If you do not admit the sum claimed by the pursuer is due, DO NOT complete the attached application but consult a solicitor IMMEDIATELY about defending the action.

HOW TO APPLY FOR A TIME TO PAY DIRECTION WHEN CLAIM ADMITTED AND YOU DO NOT WANT TO DEFEND THE ACTION

1. Attached to this notice is an application for a time to pay direction and for recall or restriction of an arrestment, if appropriate. If you want to make an application you should complete and lodge the completed application with the court on or before the date given below. No court fee is payable when lodging the application.

2. Before completing the application please read carefully the notes attached to this notice. In the event of difficulty you may contact the General Department in the Office of Court of the Court of Session, 2 Parliament Square, Edinburgh EH1 1RQ (Telephone 0131-225-2595).

3. The date by which you must return the application form is (*insert date*).

HOW TO COMPLETE THE APPLICATION FOR A TIME TO PAY DIRECTION

PLEASE WRITE IN INK USING BLOCK CAPITALS

PART A of the application will have been completed in advance by the pursuer and gives details of the pursuer and you as the defender.

PART B. If you wish to offer instalments enter the amount and tick the appropriate box at B3(1).

If you wish to offer to pay the full sum due in one deferred payment enter the date at which you offer to pay at B3(2).

PART C. You should give full details of your financial position in the appropriate boxes.

PART D. If you wish the court, when making the time to pay direction, to recall or restrict an arrestment made in connection with the action then enter the appropriate details about what has been arrested and the place and date of the arrestment at D5, and attach the Schedule of Arrestment (*i.e.* the formal document which told you of the arrestment of your assets) or a copy of it. You should then complete D6 by deleting the words which do not apply.

Sign the application where indicated and send to the court. Retain the copy summons and this notice as you may need them at a later stage. You should ensure that your application arrives at the court before the date specified in paragraph 3 of the application for a time to pay direction.

WHAT WILL HAPPEN NEXT

If the pursuer does not accept your offer a hearing will be fixed and the pursuer will advise you in writing of the date and time.

If the pursuer accepts your offer, then a copy of the court order for payment (called an extract decree) will be served on you by the pursuer advising when payment of instalments should commence or by what date payment is to be made and to whom payments should be sent.

IF YOU ARE UNCERTAIN ABOUT THE EFFECT OF THIS NOTICE, you should consult a solicitor, Citizens Advice Bureau or other local advice agency or adviser immediately.

Form 44.2-B

C1.2A.116   Rules 44.2(1), 44.3(1) and 44.4(1)[1]

Form of application for a time to pay direction

(*Cause reference number*)

IN THE COURT OF SESSION

APPLICATION FOR A TIME TO PAY DIRECTION

Under the Debtors (Scotland) Act 1987

by

PART A*   ....
....

*This section must be completed by pursuer before service

In an action raised by

....

Pursuer(s)

This application must be sent to the court on or before

_____

PART B

1. I am the defender in the action brought by the above named pursuer[s].
2. I admit the claim and apply to the court for a time to pay direction.
3. I offer (1) To pay by instalments of £ ....

*Tick one box only. Delete whichever is not appropriate

EACH... WEEK * FORTNIGHT * MONTH

or   (2) To pay the sum ordered in one payment by

(*Insert date*)   .... 19..........

_____

PART C
*Tick one box only

4. My financial position is as follows:-

_____

[1] Form 44.2-B as amended by SI 1994 No. 2901 (minor correction).

My outgoings are: My income is:

Weekly* Fortnightly* Monthly* Weekly* Fortnightly* Monthly*

Rent/House purchase loan £		Wages/Pensions £		
Heating £		Social Security £		
Food £		Other (specify) £		
HP, etc £				
Other £				
Total £		Total £		

Here list all capital, if any (e.g. value of house, amount in bank/building society accounts, shares or other investments):

Here list any outstanding debts:

PART D
*Delete if not applicable

5. *I seek to have recalled or restricted an arrestment of which the details are as follows (Please state, and attach Schedule of Arrestment or a copy):-

6. This application is made under the Debtors (Scotland) Act 1987. Therefore I ask the court:

	(a)	To make a time to pay direction; and
	*(b)	To recall the above arrestment; or

*Delete if not applicable, State the restriction wanted

	*(c)	To restrict the above arrestment:-
		(state the restriction sought)

Signed ....
    Defender

Date ....19........

This application should be sent to the Deputy Principal Clerk of Session, Court of Session, 2 Parliament Square, Edinburgh EH1 1RQ.

Form 44.3

C1.2A.117   Rule 44.3(4)

Rule 44.3(4)   [1] FORM 44.3

Form of notice of application for decree and objection to application for time to pay direction made by defender

(*Cause reference number*)

IN THE COURT OF SESSION

SUMMONS

[A.B.] (*designation and address*)

Pursuer

against

[C.D.] (*designation and address*)

Defender

To: (*name of defender to whom notice is directed*)

THIS NOTICE tells you that the pursuer—

(*a*) intends to apply for decree against you; and
(*b*) objects to all or part of your application for a time to pay direction.

I,   , the solicitor for the pursuer give you notice:—

(1) That on (*date of proposed enrolment of motion*) I shall enrol the following motion in the above action against you and that this will come before the court on (*date and time*):—

(*insert terms of motion*)

(2) That the pursuer objects to the application which you have made for—

a time to pay direction,*
recall or restriction of an arrestment made against you,*

and will ask the court not to grant your application for the following reasons—

(set out reasons in numbered paragraphs)

You have the right to attend the hearing on *(date motion will come before the court)* and make any further points in answer to the pursuer's objections.

If you do not wish to attend court, you may reply to the pursuer's objections to your application in a letter addressed to the Deputy Principal Clerk of Session, 2 Parliament Square, Edinburgh EH1 1RQ. This letter must reach him by *(insert date before the day on which the motion will come before the court)*. The court will consider this letter at the hearing of the pursuer's motion and objection.

If you do not attend court and you wish to know the outcome of the hearing before you receive formal notice of the decree you should contact the General Department of the Court of Session, 2 Parliament Square, Edinburgh EH1 1RQ (Telephone: 031–225 2595).

IF YOU ARE UNCERTAIN ABOUT THE EFFECT OF THIS NOTICE, you should consult a solicitor, Citizens Advice Bureau or other local advice agency or adviser immediately.

(Signed)

Solicitor for pursuer

Date   19

* Delete whichever is not applicable.

---

[1] Form 44.3 amended by S.I. 1994 No. 2901 (minor corrections).

Form 45A.2

C1.2A.118   Rule 45A.2(2)

Rule 45A.2(2)   [1] FORM 45A.2

Form of citation of unnamed occupiers

IN THE COURT OF SESSION

in the cause

[A.B.] (*designation and address*)

Pursuer

against

The occupier[s] of (*address*)

Defender[s]

An action has been brought in the Court of Session, Edinburgh, by [A.B.], pursuer. [A.B.] calls as a defender the occupier[s] of the property at (*address*). If the occupier[s] [*or* any of them] wish[es] to challenge the jurisdiction of the court or to defend the action, he [*or* she [*or* it] [*or* they]] should contact the Deputy Principal Clerk of Session, Court of Session, Parliament Square, Edinburgh EH1 1RQ (Telephone 0131 225 2595) immediately and in any event by (*date on which period of notice expires*).

(*Signed*)

Solicitor [*or* Agent] for pursuer
(*Address*)

---

[1] Form 45A.2 inserted by S.I. 1996 No. 2168.

Form 46.6

Rule 46.6(5) and (6)

Rule 46.6(5) and (6)   FORM 46.6

Form of preliminary act in ship collision action

In the action in which

is Pursuer

and

is Defender

Preliminary Act

for

Pursuer [*or* Defender]

Preliminary Act

for

Pursuer [*or* Defender]

(1) (*State the names of the vessels which came into collision, their ports of registry, and the names of their masters.*)

(2) (*State the date and time of the collision.*)

(3) (*State the place of the collision.*)

(4) (*State the direction and force of the wind.*)
(5) (*State the state of the weather.*)

(6) (*State the state, direction and force of the tidal or other current.*)

(7) (*State the magnetic course steered and speed through the water of the vessel when the other vessel was first seen or immediately before any measures were taken with reference to her presence, whichever was the earlier.*)

(8) (*State the lights (if any) carried by the vessel.*)

(9) (*State the distance and bearing of the other vessel if and when her echo was first observed by radar.*)

(10) (*State the distance, bearing and approximate heading of the other vessel when first seen.*)

(11) (*State what light or combination of lights (if any) of the other vessel when first seen.*)

(12) (*State what other lights or combinations of lights (if any) of the other vessel were subsequently seen, before the collision, and when.*)

(13) (*State what alterations (if any) were made to the course and speed of the vessel after the earlier of the two times referred to in paragraph (7) up to the time of the collision, and when, and what measures (if any), other than alterations of course and speed, were taken to avoid the collision and when.*)

(14) (*State the parts of each vessel which first came into contact and the approximate angle between the two vessels at the moment of contact.*)

(15) (*State what sound signals (if any) were given, and when.*)

(16) (*State what sound signals (if any) were heard from the other vessel and when.*)

(*Dated*)

(*Signed by counsel or Agent*)

Form 46.9

C1.2A.120   Rule 46.9(4)

Rule 46.9(4)   FORM 46.9

Intimation to the International Oil Pollution Compensation Fund

Date: (*date of posting or other method of intimation*)

To: The International Oil Pollution Compensation Fund
        (*address*)

TAKE NOTICE

(*Pursuer's name and address*), pursuer, has brought an action against (*defender's name and address*), defender, in the Court of Session, Edinburgh. A copy of the summons in the action is attached. In the action the court may make an order which is binding on you.

You may apply to the court by minute for leave to lodge defences to the action. You must do so at the Office of Court, Court of Session, 2 Parliament Square, Edinburgh EH1 1RQ within 21 days after the date of intimation to you of the summons [*or if the warrant for intimation is executed before calling of the summons*, within seven days after the summons calls in court. The summons will not call in court earlier than [21] days after the date of intimation to you of the summons]. The date of intimation is the date stated at the top of this notice unless intimation has been made by post in which case the date of intimation is the day after the date.

(*Signed*)

Messenger-at-Arms
[*or* Solicitor [*or* Agent] for pursuer]
(*Address*)

Form 49.8.8-A

Rule 49.8(3)(a)

Rule 49.8(3)(a)   [1] FORM 49.8–A

Form of notice of intimation to children and next of kin in family action where address of defender is not known

Date: (*date of posting or other method of intimation*)

To: (*name and address as in warrant for intimation*)

TAKE NOTICE

(*Pursuer's name and address*), pursuer, has brought an action against (*name of defender*), defender, your father [*or* mother, *or* brother *or other relative as the case may be*] in the Court of Session, Edinburgh. A copy of the summons in the action is attached. The address of (*name of defender*) is not known. If you know of his [*or* her] present address you should immediately inform the Deputy Principal Clerk of Session, 2 Parliament Square, Edinburgh EH1 1RQ (Telephone: 031–225 2595).

In any event you may apply to the court by minute for leave to become a party to the action. You must do so at the Office of Court, Court of Session, 2 Parliament Square, Edinburgh EH1 1RQ within [21] days after the date of intimation to you of the summons [*or if the warrant for intimation is executed before calling of the summons*, within seven days after the summons calls in court. The summons will not call in court earlier than [21] days after the date of intimation to you of the summons]. The date of intimation is the date stated at the top of this notice unless intimation has been made by post in which case the date of intimation is the day after that date.

IF YOU ARE UNCERTAIN ABOUT THE EFFECT OF THIS NOTICE, you should consult a solicitor, Citizens Advice Bureau or other local advice agency or adviser immediately.

(*Signed*)

Messenger-at-Arms
[*or* Solicitor [*or* Agent] for pursuer]
(*Address*)

---

[1] Form 49.8–A amended by S.I. 1994 No. 2901 (minor correction).

Form 49.8-B

C1.2A.122   Rule 49.8(3)(ft)

Rule 49.8(3)(b)   [1] FORM 49.8–B

Form of notice of intimation to person with whom defender is alleged to have committed adultery

Date: (*date of posting or other method of intimation*)

To: (*name and address as in warrant for intimation*)

TAKE NOTICE

(*Pursuer's name and address*), pursuer, has brought an action against (*defender's name and address*), defender, in the Court of Session, Edinburgh. A copy of the summons in the action is attached. It contains an allegation that the defender has committed adultery with you.

You may apply to the court by minute for leave to become a party to the action. You must do so at the Office of Court, Court of Session, 2 Parliament Square, Edinburgh EH1 1RQ within [21] days after the date of intimation to you of the summons [*or if the warrant for intimation is executed before calling of the summons*, within seven days after the summons calls in court. The summons will not call in court earlier than [21] days after the date of intimation to you of the summons]. The date of intimation is the date stated at the top of this notice unless intimation has been made by post in which case the date of intimation is the day after that date.

IF YOU ARE UNCERTAIN ABOUT THE EFFECT OF THIS NOTICE, you should consult a solicitor, Citizens Advice Bureau or other local advice agency or adviser immediately.

(*Signed*)

Messenger-at-Arms
[*or* Solicitor [*or* Agent] for pursuer]
(*Address*)

_____

[1] Form 49.8–B amended by S.I. 1994 No. 2901 (minor correction).

Form 49.8-C

Rule 49.8(3)(c)

C1.2A.123

Rule 49.8(3)(c)   [1] Form 49.8–C

Form of notice of intimation to relatives and curator *bonis* in family action where defender suffers from mental disorder

Date: (*date of posting or other method of intimation*)

To: (*name and address as in warrant*)

TAKE NOTICE

(*Pursuer's name and address*), pursuer, has brought an action against (*defender's name and address*), defender, your father [*or* mother, *or* brother *or other relative as the case may be or* ward] in the Court of Session, Edinburgh. A copy of the summons in the action is attached.

You may apply to the court by minute for leave to become a party to the action. You must do so at the Office of Court, Court of Session, 2 Parliament Square, Edinburgh EH1 1RQ within [21] days after the date of intimation to you of the summons [*or if the warrant for intimation is executed before calling of the summons*, within seven days after the summons calls in court. The summons will not call in court earlier than [21] days after the date of intimation to you of the summons]. The date of intimation is the date stated at the top of this notice unless intimation has been made by post in which case the date of intimation is the day after that date.

IF YOU ARE UNCERTAIN ABOUT THE EFFECT OF THIS NOTICE, you should consult a solicitor, Citizens Advice Bureau or other local advice agency or adviser immediately.

(*Signed*)

Messenger-at-Arms
[*or* Solicitor [*or* Agent] for pursuer]
(*Address*)

_____

[1] Form 49.8–C amended by S.I. 1994 No. 2901 (minor correction).

Form 49.8-D

Rule 49.8(3)(d)

C1.2A.124

Rule 49.8(3)(d)   [1] Form 49.8–D

Form of notice of intimation to additional spouse of either party in proceedings relating to polygamous marriage

Date: (*date of posting or other method of intimation*)

To: (*name and address as in warrant for intimation*)

TAKE NOTICE

(*Pursuer's name and address*), pursuer, has brought an action against (*defender's name and address*), defender, in the Court of Session, Edinburgh. A copy of the summons in the action is attached. (*Party's name*) is believed to be your spouse.

You may apply to the court by minute for leave to become a party to the action. You must do so at the Office of Court, Court of Session, 2 Parliament Square, Edinburgh EH1 1RQ within [21] days after the date of intimation to you of the summons [*or if the warrant for intimation is executed before calling of the summons*, within seven days after the summons calls in court. The summons will not call in court earlier than [21] days after the date of intimation to you of the summons]. The date of intimation is the date stated at the top of this notice unless intimation has been made by post in which case the date of intimation is the day after that date.

IF YOU ARE UNCERTAIN ABOUT THE EFFECT OF THIS NOTICE, you should consult a solicitor, Citizens Advice Bureau or other local advice agency or adviser immediately.

(*Signed*)

Messenger-at-Arms
[*or* Solicitor [*or* Agent] for pursuer]
(*Address*)

---

[1] Form 49.8–D amended by S.I. 1994 No. 2901 (minor correction).

Form 49.8-E

C1.2A.125   Rule 49.8(3)(e)

Rule 49.8(3)(e)   [1] FORM 49.8–E

Form of notice to local authority or other person who may be liable to maintain a child

Date: (*date of posting or other method of intimation*)

To: (*name and address as in warrant for intimation*)

TAKE NOTICE

(*Pursuer's name and address*), pursuer, has brought an action against (*defender's name and address*), defender, in the Court of Session, Edinburgh. The pursuer seeks an order under section 11 of the Children (Scotland) Act 1995 in respect of (*child's name and address*), a child in your care [*or* liable to be maintained by you]. A copy of the summons in the action is attached.

You may apply to the court by minute to become a party to the action. You must do so at the Office of Court, Court of Session, 2 Parliament Square, Edinburgh EH1 1RQ within [21] days after the date of intimation to you of the summons [*or if the warrant for intimation is executed before calling of the summons*, within seven days after the summons calls in court. The summons will not call in court earlier than [21] days after the date of intimation to you of the summons]. The date of intimation is the date stated at the top of this notice unless intimation has been made by post in which case the date of intimation is the day after that date.

IF YOU ARE UNCERTAIN ABOUT THE EFFECT OF THIS NOTICE, you should consult a solicitor, Citizens Advice Bureau or other local advice agency or adviser immediately.

(*Signed*)

Messenger-at-Arms
[*or* Solicitor [*or* Agent] for pursuer]
(*Address*)

---

[1] Form 49.8–E amended by S.I. 1994 No. 2901 (minor correction) and S.I. 1996 No. 2587.

Form 49.8-F

Rule 49.8(3)(f)

Rule 49.8(3)(f) [1] FORM 49.8–F

Form of notice of intimation to person who in fact exercises care or control

Date: (*date of posting or other method of intimation*)

To: (*name and address as in warrant for intimation*)

TAKE NOTICE

(*Pursuer's name and address*), pursuer, has brought an action against (*defender's name and address*), defender, in the Court of Session, Edinburgh. The pursuer seeks an order under section 11 of the Children (Scotland) Act 1995 in respect of (*child's name and address*), a child at present in your care or control. A copy of the summons in the action is attached.

You may apply to the court by minute to become a party to the action. You must do so at the Office of Court, Court of Session, 2 Parliament Square, Edinburgh EH1 1RQ within [21] days after the date of intimation to you of the summons [*or if the warrant for intimation is executed before calling of the summons*, within seven days after the summons calls in court. The summons will not call in court earlier than [21] days after the date of intimation to you of the summons]. The date of intimation is the date stated at the top of this notice unless intimation has been made by post in which case the date of intimation is the day after that date.

IF YOU ARE UNCERTAIN ABOUT THE EFFECT OF THIS NOTICE, you should consult a solicitor, Citizens Advice Bureau or other local advice agency or adviser immediately.

(*Signed*)

Messenger-at-Arms
[*or* Solicitor [*or* Agent] for pursuer]
(*Address*)

---

[1] Form 49.8–F amended by S.I. 1994 No. 2901 (minor correction) and S.I. 1996 No. 2587.

Form 49.8-G

C1.2A.127   Rule 49.8(3)(g)

Rule 49.8(3)(g)   [1] FORM 49.8–G

Form of notice of intimation to parent or guardian in family action for a section 11 order

Date: (*date of posting or other method of intimation*)

To: (*name and address as in warrant for intimation*)

TAKE NOTICE

(*Pursuer's name and address*), pursuer, has brought an action against (*defender's name and address*), defender, in the Court of Session, Edinburgh. The pursuer is seeking a section 11 order in respect of the child (*child's name and address*). A copy of the summons in the action is attached.

If you wish to oppose this action, and oppose the granting to the pursuer of a section 11 order in respect of the child, you may apply to the court by minute to become a party to the action. You must do so at the Office of Court, Court of Session, 2 Parliament Square, Edinburgh EH1 1RQ within [21] days after the date of intimation to you of the summons [*or if the warrant for intimation is executed before calling of the summons*, within 7 days after the summons calls in court. The summons will not call in court earlier than [21] days after the date of intimation to you of the summons]. The date of intimation is the date stated at the top of this notice unless intimation has been made by post in which case the date of intimation is the day after that date.

IF YOU ARE UNCERTAIN ABOUT THE EFFECT OF THIS NOTICE, you should consult a solicitor, Citizens Advice Bureau or other local advice agency or adviser immediately.

                                        (*Signed*)

                                        Messenger-at-Arms
                                        [*or* Solicitor [*or* Agent] for pursuer]
                                        (*Address*)

_____
[1] Form 49.8–G substituted by S.I. 1996 No. 2587.

Form 49.8-H

C1.2A.128   Rules 49.8(3)(h), 49.8(4) and 49.11

Rules 49.8(3)(h), 49.8(4) and 49.11   [1] FORM 49.8–H

Form of notice of intimation to local authority in family action by non-parent for a residence order in respect of a child

Date: (*date of posting or other method of intimation*)

To: (*name and address as in warrant for intimation*)

TAKE NOTICE

(*Pursuer's name and address*), pursuer, has brought an action against (*defender's name and address*), defender, in the Court of Session, Edinburgh. The pursuer is seeking a residence order in respect of the child (*name and address of child*). A copy of the summons in the action is attached.

You are requested to submit to the court a report on all the circumstances of the child and on the proposed arrangements for the care and upbringing of the child without delay. On completion of the report please send it, with a copy for each party, to the Deputy Principal Clerk of Session, Court of Session, 2 Parliament Square, Edinburgh EH1 1RQ.

(*Signed*)

Messenger-at-Arms
[*or* Solicitor [*or* Agent] for pursuer]
(*Address*)

On completion of the report please send it, with a copy for each party, to the Deputy Principal Clerk of Session, Court of Session, 2 Parliament Square, Edinburgh EH1 1RQ.

(*Signed*)

Messenger-at-Arms
[*or* Solicitor [*or* Agent] for pursuer]
(*Address*)

----

[1] Form 49.8–H substituted by S.I. 1996 No. 2587.

Form 49.8-J

C1.2A.129   Rule 49.8(3)(j)

Rule 49.8(3)(j)   ¹ FORM 49.8–J

Form of notice of intimation to person whose consent is necessary or has an interest as heritable creditor in the transfer of property

Date: (*date of posting or other method of intimation*)

To: (*name and address as in warrant for intimation*)

TAKE NOTICE

(*Pursuer's name and address*), pursuer, has brought an action against (*defender's name and address*), defender, in the Court of Session, Edinburgh. A copy of the summons in the action is attached. The pursuer has applied for an order under section 8 of the Family Law (Scotland) Act 1985 to have the ownership of the property at (*address of property*) transferred to his [*or* her] name. [Your consent is necessary for the proposed transfer.]

You may apply to the court by minute to become a party to the action. You must do so at the Office of Court, Court of Session, 2 Parliament Square, Edinburgh EH1 1RQ within [21] days after the date of intimation to you of the summons [*or if the warrant for intimation is executed before calling of the summons*, within seven days after the summons calls in court. The summons will not call in court earlier than [21] days after the date of intimation to you of the summons]. The date of intimation is the date stated at the top of this notice unless intimation has been made by post in which case the date of intimation is the day after that date.

IF YOU ARE UNCERTAIN ABOUT THE EFFECT OF THIS NOTICE, you should consult a solicitor, Citizens Advice Bureau or other local advice agency or adviser immediately.

(*Signed*)

Messenger-at-Arms
[*or* Solicitor [*or* Agent] for pursuer]
(*Address*)

----

¹ Form 49.8–J amended by S.I. 1994 No. 2901 (minor correction).

Form 49.8-K

Rule 49.8(3)(k)

Rule 49.8(3)(*k*)   [1] FORM 49.8–K

Form of notice of intimation to third party transferee or other person having an interest in the transfer of property

Date: (*date of posting or other method of intimation*)

To: (*name and address as in warrant for intimation*)

TAKE NOTICE

(*Pursuer's name and address*), pursuer, has brought an action against (*defender's name and address*), defender, in the Court of Session, Edinburgh. A copy of the summons in the action is attached. The pursuer has applied for an order under section 18 of the Family Law (Scotland) Act 1985 affecting your property at (*address*).

You may apply to the court by minute to become a party to the action. You must do so at the Office of Court, Court of Session, 2 Parliament Square, Edinburgh EH1 1RQ within [21] days after the date of intimation to you of the summons [*or if the warrant for intimation is executed before calling of the summons*, within seven days after the summons calls in court. The summons will not call in court earlier than [21] days after the date of intimation to you of the summons]. The date of intimation is the date stated at the top of this notice unless intimation has been made by post in which case the date of intimation is the day after that date.

IF YOU ARE UNCERTAIN ABOUT THE EFFECT OF THIS NOTICE, you should consult a solicitor, Citizens Advice Bureau or other local advice agency or adviser immediately.

       (*Signed*)

       Messenger-at-Arms
       [*or* Solicitor [*or* Agent] for pursuer]
       (*Address*)

---

[1] Form 49.8–K amended by S.I. 1994 No. 2901 (minor correction).

Form 49.8-L

C1.2A.131   Rule 49.8(3)(l)

Rule 49.8(3)(*l*)   [1] FORM 49.8–L

Form of notice of intimation to third party or other person having an interest in an application under the Matrimonial Homes (Family Protection) (Scotland) Act 1981

Date: (*date of posting or other method of intimation*)

To: (*name and address as in warrant for intimation*)

TAKE NOTICE

(*Pursuer's name and address*), pursuer, has brought an action against (*defender's name and address*), defender, in the Court of Session, Edinburgh. A copy of the summons in the action is attached. In the action, the court may make an order affecting occupancy rights in property at (*address of property*) in which you have an interest.

You may apply to the court by minute to become a party to the action. You must do so at the Office of Court, Court of Session, 2 Parliament Square, Edinburgh EH1 1RQ within [21] days after the date of intimation to you of the summons [*or if the warrant for intimation is executed before calling of the summons*, within seven days after the summons calls in court. The summons will not call in court earlier than [21] days after the date of intimation to you of the summons]. The date of intimation is the date stated at the top of this notice unless intimation has been made by post in which case the date of intimation is the day after that date.

IF YOU ARE UNCERTAIN ABOUT THE EFFECT OF THIS NOTICE, you should consult a solicitor, Citizens Advice Bureau or other local advice agency or adviser immediately.

(*Signed*)

Messenger-at-Arms
[*or* Solicitor [*or* Agent] for pursuer]
(*Address*)

_____

[1] Form 49.8–L amended by S.I. 1994 No. 2901 (minor correction).

Form 49.8-M

Rule 49.8(3)(m)

Rule 49.8(3)(m)   [1] FORM 49.8–M

Form of notice of intimation to person responsible for pension arrangement in relation to order for payment in respect of pension lump sum under section 12A of the Family Law (Scotland) Act 1985

Date: (*date of posting or other method of intimation*)

To: (*name and address as in warrant for intimation*)

TAKE NOTICE

(*Pursuer's name and address*), pursuer, has brought an action against (*defender's name and address*), defender, in the Court of Session, Edinburgh. A copy of the summons in the action is attached. The pursuer has applied for an order under section 8 of the Family Law (Scotland) Act 1985 for a capital sum in circumstances where the matrimonial [*or* family] property includes rights in a pension arrangement under which a lump sum is payable. The relevant pension arrangement is (*give details, including number, if known*).

You may apply to the court by minute to become a party to the action. You must do so at the Office of Court, Court of Session, 2 Parliament Square, Edinburgh EH1 1RQ within [21] days after the date of intimation to you of the summons [*or if the warrant for intimation is executed before calling of the summons*, within seven days after the summons calls in court. The summons will not call in court earlier than [21] days after the date of intimation to you of the summons]. The date of intimation is the date stated at the top of this notice unless intimation has been made by post in which case the date of intimation is the day after that date.

IF YOU ARE UNCERTAIN ABOUT THE EFFECT OF THIS NOTICE, you should consult a solicitor, Citizens Advice Bureau or other local advice agency or adviser immediately.

(*Signed*)

Messenger-at-Arms
[*or* Solicitor [*or* Agent] for pursuer]
(*Address*)

---

[1] Form 49.8–M inserted by S.I. 1996 No. 1756 (effective 5th August 1996) and amended by S.S.I. 2005 No. 632 (effective 8th December 2005).

Form 49.8-MA

C1.2A.133   Rule 49.8(3)(m)

Rule 49.8(3)(m)   [1] FORM 49.8–MA

Form of notice of intimation to person responsible for pension arrangement in relation to application for pension sharing order under section 8(1)(baa) of the Family Law (Scotland) Act 1985

Date: (*date of posting or other method of intimation*).

To: (*name and address as in warrant for intimation*).

TAKE NOTICE

(*Pursuer's name and address*), pursuer, has brought an action against (*defender's name and address*), defender, in the Court of Session, Edinburgh. A copy of the summons in the action is attached. The pursuer has applied for a pension sharing order under section 8(1)(baa) of the Family Law (Scotland) Act 1985. The relevant pension arrangement is (*insert details, including number, if known*).

You may apply to the court by minute to become a party to the action. You must do so at the Office of Court, Court of Session, 2 Parliament Square, Edinburgh EH1 1RQ within [21] days after the date of intimation to you of the summons [*or if the warrant for intimation is executed before calling of the summons,* within seven days after the summons calls in court. The summons will not call in court earlier than [21] days after the date of intimation to you of the summons]. The date of intimation is the date stated at the top of this notice unless intimation has been made by post in which case the date of intimation is the day after that date.

IF YOU ARE UNCERTAIN ABOUT THE EFFECT OF THIS NOTICE, you should consult a solicitor, Citizens Advice Bureau or other local advice agency or adviser immediately.

(*Signed*)

Messenger-at-Arms
[*or* Solicitor [*or* Agent] for pursuer]
(*Address*)

_____

[1] Form 49.8-MA inserted by S.S.I. 2000 No. 412 (effective 1st December 2000).

Form 49.8-N

C1.2A.134   [*Revoked by S.S.I. 2019 No. 123 para.2 (effective 24th June 2019).*]

Form 49.8-O

Rule 49.8(3)(m)

FORM 49.8-O

Rule 49.8(3)(m)

Form of notice of intimation to third party or person having an interest in an application under Chapter 3 or 4 of Part 3 of the Civil Partnership Act 2004

Date: (*date of posting or other method of intimation*)

To: (*name and address as in warrant for intimation*)

TAKE NOTICE

(*Pursuer's name and address*), pursuer, has brought an action against (*defender's name and address*), defender, in the Court of Session, Edinburgh. A copy of the summons in the action is attached. In the action, the court may make an order affecting occupancy rights in property at (*address of property*) in which you have an interest.

You may apply to the court by minute to become a party to the action. You must do so at the Office of Court, Court of Session, 2 Parliament Square, Edinburgh EH1 1RQ within [21] days after the date of intimation to you of the summons [*or if the warrant for intimation is executed before the calling of the summons*, within seven days after the summons calls in court. The summons will not call in court earlier than [21] days after the date of intimation to you of the summons]. The date of intimation is the date situated at the top of this notice unless intimation has been made by post in which case the date of intimation is the day after that date.

IF YOU ARE UNCERTAIN ABOUT THE EFFECT OF THIS NOTICE, you should consult a solicitor, Citizens Advice Bureau or other local advice agency or adviser immediately.

(*Signed*)

Messenger-at-Arms

[*or* Solicitor [*or* Agent] for pursuer]

(*Address*)

---

[1] Form 49.8–O inserted by S.S.I. 2005 No. 632 (effective 8th December 2005).

Form 49.8-P

C1.2A.136 Rule 49.8(3)(o)

Rule 49.8(3)(o) FORM 49.8–P

Form of intimation for financial provision on intestacy under section 29(2) of the Family Law (Scotland) Act 2006

Date: *(date of posting or other method of intimation)*

To: *(name and address as in warrant for intimation)*

(Pursuer's name and address), pursuer, has brought an action against *(defender's name and address)*, defender, in the Court of Session, Edinburgh. A copy of the summons in the action is attached. The pursuer is seeking an order for financial provision on intestacy under section 29(2) of the Family Law (Scotland) Act 2006.

You may apply by minute to become a party to the action. You must do so at the Office of Court, Court of Session, 2 Parliament Square, Edinburgh, EH1 1RQ within [21] days after the date of intimation to you of the summons [*or if the warrant for intimation is executed before the calling of the summons*, within seven days after the summons calls in court. The summons will not call in court earlier than [21] days after the date of intimation to you of the summons]. The date of intimation is the date situation at the top of this notice unless intimation has been made by post in which case the date of intimation is the day after that date.

IF YOU ARE UNCERTAIN ABOUT THE EFFECT OF THIS NOTICE, you should consult a solicitor, Citizens Advice Bureau or other local advice agency or adviser immediately.

(Signed)

Messenger-at-Arms

[*or* Solicitor [*or* Agent] for pursuer]

(Address)

---

[2] Form 49.8–P inserted by S.S.I. 2006 No. 206 (effective 4th May 2006).

APPENDIX

Form 49.8A[1]

Rule 49.8A

C1.2A.136.1

Court of Session | Ref: *[insert case reference]* | Form 49.8A

Name
Address Line 1
Address Line 2
City
Postcode

Dear *[insert child's first name]*

You have been sent this letter because the judge will need to make a decision about you. The judge is a person who makes important decisions for children and families. *[Insert short summary of the section 11 order(s) sought, using child-friendly language.]* The judge has to decide about that.

The judge wants to know what you think about that. You have a right to tell the judge what you think, but you do not have to tell the judge what you think if you do not want to. What you think is very important, and it will help the judge to make a decision about what is best for you. Sometimes this might be different from what you would like to happen.

If you want to tell the judge what you think, you can use the **What I Think** form sent with this letter. You can write or draw anything you like. There is no right or wrong answer. Please send the form back to the judge when you have filled it in. We have sent you an envelope, which should already have a stamp on it. Just put the form in the envelope and put the envelope in a post box **within 2 weeks, or as soon as you can.**

The judge might not tell anyone exactly what you have written or said, but the judge has to think about this and say in court what you would like to happen.

If you are not sure what to do, you can show this letter to someone you trust. If you want to know more about what will happen next, you might get free help from a lawyer or from these places that can help children:

 The Scottish Child Law Centre – the free phone number is 0800 328 8970 or 0300 3301421 (from a mobile) and the website is www.sclc.org.uk

Clan Childlaw – the free phone number is 0808 129 0522 and the website is www.clanchildlaw.org

If there's anything you are worried or upset about and you don't know what to do, you can speak to someone at ChildLine who will listen and help you. You can phone ChildLine free on 0800 1111.

If what you think changes, you can contact a lawyer or call the phone numbers for the Scottish Child Law Centre or Clan Childlaw.

From
the Clerk of Court (the person who helps the judge)

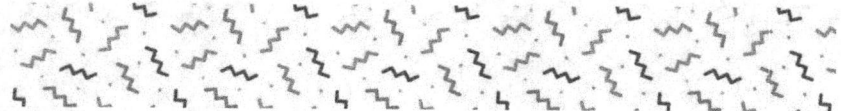

---

[1] As inserted by S.S.I. 2019 No. 123 para. 2 (effective 24th June 2019).

Court of Session | Ref: [insert case reference] | Form 49.8A

What I Think

Name:

How do you feel just now about [insert short summary of the section 11 order(s) sought, using child-friendly language]?

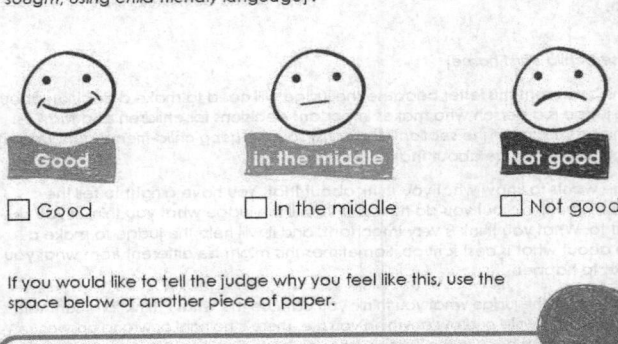

☐ Good   ☐ In the middle   ☐ Not good

If you would like to tell the judge why you feel like this, use the space below or another piece of paper.

_____

_____

_____

_____

_____

_____

Use another piece of paper if you need more space.

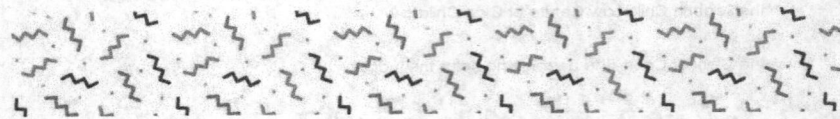

Court of Session | Ref: [insert case reference] | Form 49.8A

Is there anything else you would like to happen?

Would you like to say what you think in a different way?

Yes

No

☐ Yes   ☐ No

What different way would you like to say what you think?

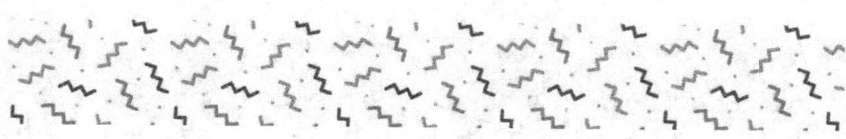

Court of Session | Ref: *[insert case reference]* | Form 49.8A

In the letter with this form, there are Freephone numbers for the Scottish Child Law Centre and Clan Childlaw, if you want some other ideas.

If someone has helped you with this **What I Think** form, please write their name and how you know them here:

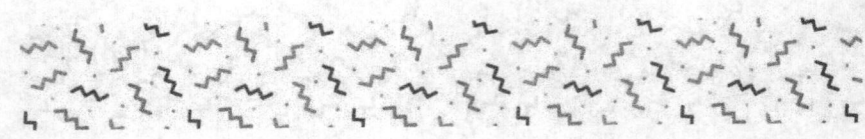

The judge will think about what you have said. It will help the judge to decide what happens next.

You can put this **What I Think** form in the envelope and send it back to the judge **within 2 weeks, or as soon as you can.** The envelope should already have a stamp on it.

Thank you.

Form 49.8B[1]

Rules 49.20(2)(b), 49.20A(2)(b), 49.20B(2)(b), 49.20C(2)(b)(i), 49.42A(2)(b), 49.42B(2)(b), 49.42C(2)(b)(i) and 70.16(6)(b)(ii)

C1.2A.136.2   Form of certificate of intimation of Form 49.8A

CERTIFICATE OF INTIMATION OF FORM 49.8A

Court Ref. No. (*insert*)

---

[1] As inserted by S.S.I. 2019 No. 123 para. 2 (effective 24th June 2019).

I certify that intimation of the Form 49.8A that was submitted to the court under *(rule 49.8A(1)(b)(ii), rule 49.31(3)(b), rule 49.42(1)(b) or rule 70.16(1)(c))* was made to *(insert name(s) of child(ren))* by *(specify whether first class, second class, recorded delivery service etc.)* post to *(insert address)* on *(insert date)*.

[*Where, in approving the draft Form 49.8A as provided for in rule 49.8A(3), 49.31(5), 49.42(3) or 70.16(3), the court has requested an amendment to the draft Form 49.8A that was submitted,* The Form 49.8A was amended in accordance with the court's request.]

[*Where the pursuer or minuter has amended the draft Form 49.8A so as to narrate the section 11 order sought by the defender or respondent,* The Form 49.8A was *(further)* amended as appropriate so as also to narrate the section 11 order sought by the *(defender or respondent).*]

Date *(insert date)*

(Signed)

Solicitor for the *(pursuer/defender/minuter/respondent)*

(add designation and business address)

or

(Pursuer/Defender/Minuter/Respondent)

Form 49.8C[1]

Rule 49.20D(5)(b)(ii)

Form of certificate of intimation of Form 49.8A (where ordered under rule 49.20D)   **C1.2A.136.3**

CERTIFICATE OF INTIMATION OF FORM 49.8A

Court Ref. No. *(insert)*

I certify that intimation of the Form 49.8A, a copy of which is attached to this certificate in accordance with rule 49.20D(5)(b)(i) was made to *(insert name(s) of child(ren))* by *(specify whether first class, second class, recorded delivery service, etc.)* post to *(insert address)* on *(insert date)*.

Date *(insert date)*

(Signed)

Solicitor for the *(pursuer/defender/minuter/respondent)*

(add designation and business address)

or

(Pursuer/Defender/Minuter/Respondent)

---

[1] As inserted by S.S.I. 2019 No. 123 para.2 (effective 24th June 2019).

Form 49.9

C1.2A.137   Rule 49.9(3)

Rule 49.9(3)   [1] FORM 49.9

Form of notice of intimation to person with whom a relevant association is alleged to have occurred

Date: (*date of posting or other method of intimation*)

To: (*name and address as in warrant for intimation*)

TAKE NOTICE

(*Pursuer's name and address*), pursuer, has brought an action against (*defender's name and address*), defender, in the Court of Session, Edinburgh. A copy of the summons in the action is attached. (*Defender's name*) is alleged to have had a relevant association with you as mentioned in the summons.

You may apply to the court by minute to become a party to the action in order to dispute the truth of the allegations made about you. You must do so at the Office of Court, Court of Session, 2 Parliament Square, Edinburgh EH1 1RQ within [21] days after the date of intimation to you of the summons [*or if the warrant for intimation is executed before calling of the summons, within seven days after the summons calls in court. The summons will not call in court earlier than [21] days after the date of intimation to you of the summons*]. The date of intimation is the date stated at the top of this notice unless intimation has been made by post in which case the date of intimation is the day after that date.

IF YOU ARE UNCERTAIN ABOUT THE EFFECT OF THIS NOTICE, you should consult a solicitor, Citizens Advice Bureau or other local advice agency or adviser immediately.

(*Signed*)

Messenger-at-Arms
[*or* Solicitor [*or* Agent] for pursuer]
(*Address*)

─────────
[1] Form 49.9 amended by S.I. 1994 No. 2901 (minor correction).

Form 49.13-A

C1.2A.138   Rule 49.13(1)(b)

Rule 49.13(1)(b)   FORM 49.13–A

Form of request for medical officer of hospital or similar institution

Date: (*date of posting or other method of intimation*)

To: (*name and address*)

TAKE NOTICE

(*Pursuer's name and address*), pursuer, has brought an action against (*defender's name and address*), defender, in the Court of Session, Edinburgh. A copy of the summons in the action and citation [and a notice [and form of consent] under rule 49.14(1) [*or* rule 49.14A(1)] of the Rules of the Court of Session 1994] are attached.

Please deliver it personally to (*name of defender*) and explain the content or meaning of it to him [*or* her] unless you are satisfied that an explanation would be dangerous to his [*or* her] health. If you are so satisfied you must certify that this is the case and give your reasons on the attached certificate. Thereafter please complete the attached certificate and return it to me in the enclosed stamped addressed envelope.

(*Signed*)

Messenger-at-Arms
[*or* Solicitor [*or* Agent] for pursuer]
(*Address*)

---

[1] Form 49.13–A amended by S.S.I. 2005 No. 632 (effective 8th December 2005).

Form 49.13-B

Rule 49.13(1)(b)(iii) and (2)

C1.2A.139

Rule 49.13(1)(b)(iii) and (2)   [1] FORM 49.13–B

Form of certificate by medical officer or hospital or similar institution

IN THE COURT OF SESSION

†(*Cause reference number*)

in the cause

†[A.B.] (*designation and address*)

Pursuer

against

†[C.D.] (*designation and address*)

Defender

I, (*name of medical officer*), hereby certify as follows:—

1. I have received a copy summons in the action of (*pursuer's name*) against (*defender's name*). The defender is under my care at (*address*).

*2. On (*date*) I personally delivered the copy summons to the defender and explained to him [*or* her] its contents.

*2. I have not delivered the copy summons to the defender nor have I explained its contents. My reasons are:—

Signature ....
Name ....
Address ....
....
....
Date ....

†To be completed by or on behalf of the pursuer.
*Medical officer to delete as appropriate.

---

[1] Form 49.13–B amended by S.I. 1997 No. 1050 (minor amendment, effective 6th April 1997).

Form 49.14-A

C1.2A.140   Rule 49.14(1)(a)(i)

Rule 49.14(1)(a)(i)   [1] FORM 49.14–A

Form of notice to defender where it is stated that he consents to decree of divorce

Date: (*date of posting or other method of service*)

To: (*name and address of defender in summons*)

TAKE NOTICE

(*Pursuer's name and address*), pursuer, has brought an action against you in the Court of Session, Edinburgh. The pursuer seeks divorce from you. A copy of the summons in the action is attached.

1. The summons states that you consent to a decree of divorce. If you do consent your husband [*or* wife] will obtain a decree of divorce if he shows that you have not cohabited with him [*or* her] at any time during a continuous period of one year after marriage and immediately before this action.

2. If your husband [*or* wife] obtains a decree of divorce, the consequences may be as follows:—
   (a) you may lose your rights of inheritance in your wife's [*or* husband's] property;

(b) you may lose the right to any pensions which depends on the marriage continuing or on your being left as a widow (the State widow's pension will not be payable to you when your husband dies);

(c) apart from these consequences there may be others depending on your particular circumstances.

3. If you consent to the grant of decree of divorce, you are still entitled to apply to the court:—

(a) to make financial or other provision for you by making an order under the Family Law (Scotland) Act 1985;

(b) to make an order under section 11 of the Children (Scotland) Act 1995 or for maintenance in respect of any child of the marriage, or any child accepted as such, who is under 16 years of age.

In order to make such an application you must lodge defences to the action seeking any such order. If you wish to do this you should consult a solicitor.

4. If after considering the above you wish to consent to decree of divorce, you should complete and sign the attached notice of consent form, and send it to:—

The Deputy Principal Clerk of Session
2 Parliament Square
Edinburgh EH1 1RQ

You may do so within [21] days after the date of service on you of the summons [or *if service is executed before calling of the summons*, within seven days after the summons calls in court. The summons will not call in court earlier than [21] days after the date of service on you of the summons]. The date of service is the date stated at the top of this notice unless service has been made by post in which case the date of service is the day after that date.

5. If after consent you wish to withdraw your consent, you must immediately inform the Deputy Principal Clerk of Session at the above address in writing. Please state the name of the court action in your letter.

IF YOU ARE UNCERTAIN ABOUT THE EFFECT OF THIS NOTICE, you should consult a solicitor, Citizens Advice Bureau or other local advice agency or adviser immediately.

(*Signed*)

Messenger-at-Arms
[*or* Solicitor [*or* Agent] for pursuer]
(*Address*)

---

[1] Form 49.14–A amended by S.I. 1994 No. 2901 (minor correction), S.I. 1996 No. 2587 and S.S.I. 2006 No. 206 (effective 4th May 2006).

Form 49.14-B

C1.2A.141 Rules 49.14(1)(a)(i) and 49.19(1)

Rules 49.14(1)(a)(i) and 49.19(1) FORM 49.14–B

Form of notice of consent in action of divorce under section 1(2)(d) of the Divorce (Scotland) Act 1976

NOTICE OF CONSENT TO DIVORCE

I have received a copy of the summons in the court action raised against me by (*pursuer's name and address*).

I understand that it states that I consent to the granting of decree of divorce in this action.

I have considered the consequences of my consent.

I consent to the granting of decree of divorce in this action.

Signature ....

Name (in Block Capitals) ....

Address ....

....

....

Date ....

Signature of Witness ....

Name (in Block Capitals) ....

Address ....

....

....

Occupation ....

Form 49.14-C

Rule 49.14(1)(a)(ii)

Rule 49.14(1)(a)(ii) [1] FORM 49.14–C

Form of notice to defender where it is stated that he consents to decree of separation

Date: (*date of posting or other method of service*)

To: (*name and address of defender in summons*)

TAKE NOTICE

(*Pursuer's name and address*), pursuer, has brought an action against you, defender, in the Court of Session, Edinburgh. The pursuer seeks separation from you. A copy of the summons in the action is attached.

1. The summons states that you consent to the grant of a decree of separation. If you consent your husband [*or* wife] will obtain a decree of separation if he shows that you have not cohabited with him [*or* her] at any time during a continuous period of one year after marriage and immediately before this action.

2. If your husband obtains a decree of separation, the consequences may be as follows:—
   (a) you will be obliged to live apart from your husband [*or* wife] but the marriage will continue to exist;
   [(b) your husband will continue to have a legal obligation to support you and his children;]
   [(b) *or* (c)] apart from the above there may be other consequences applicable to you depending on your particular circumstances.

3. If you consent to the grant of a decree of separation, you are still entitled to apply to the court:—
   (a) for an order under section 11 of the Children (Scotland) Act 1995 for maintenance in respect of any child of the marriage, or any child accepted as such, who is under 16 years of age.
   (b) for payment of aliment by your husband [*or* wife] to you.

In order to make such an application you must lodge defences to the action seeking any such order. If you wish to do this you should consult a solicitor.

4. If after considering the above you wish to consent to decree, please complete the attached notice of consent form, and send it to:—

> The Deputy Principal Clerk of Session
> 2 Parliament Square
> Edinburgh EH1 1RQ

You may do so at the Office of Court, Court of Session, 2 Parliament Square, Edinburgh EH1 1RQ within [21] days after the date of service on you of the summons [*or if service is executed before calling of the summons*, within seven days after the summons calls in court. The summons will not call in court earlier than [21] days after the date of service on you of the summons]. The date of service is the date stated at the top of this notice unless service has been made by post in which case the date of service is the day after that date.

5. If after consent you wish to withdraw your consent, you must immediately inform the Deputy Principal Clerk of Session at the above address in writing. Please state the name of the court action in your letter.

IF YOU ARE UNCERTAIN ABOUT THE EFFECT OF THIS NOTICE, you should consult a solicitor, Citizens Advice Bureau or other local advice agency or adviser immediately.

> (*Signed*)
>
> Messenger-at-Arms
> [*or* Solicitor [*or* Agent] for pursuer]
> (*Address*)

---

[1] Form 49.14–C amended by S.I. 1994 No. 2901 (minor correction), S.I. 1996 No. 2587 and S.S.I. 2006 No. 206 (effective 4th May 2006).

Form 49.14-D

C1.2A.143 Rules 49.14(1)(a)(ii) and 49.19(1)

Rules 49.14(1)(a)(ii) and 49.19(1)   Form 49.14–D

Form of notice of consent in action of separation under section 1(2)(d) of the Divorce (Scotland) Act 1976

NOTICE OF CONSENT TO SEPARATION

I have received a copy of the summons in the court action raised against me by (*pursuer's name and address*).

I understand that it states that I consent to the granting of decree of separation in this action.

I have considered the consequences of my consent.

I consent to the granting of decree of separation in this action.

Signature ....

Name (in Block Capitals) ....

Address ....

....

....

Date ....

Signature of Witness ....

Name (in Block Capitals) ....

Address ....

....

....

Occupation ....

Form 49.14-E

Rule 49.14(1)(b)(i)

Rule 49.14(1)(b)(i)   [1] FORM 49.14–E

Form of notice to defender in an action of divorce where it is stated there has been two years non-cohabitation

Date: (*date of posting or other method of service*)

To: (*name and address of defender in summons*)

TAKE NOTICE

(*Pursuer's name and address*), pursuer, has brought an action against you, defender, in the Court of Session, Edinburgh. The pursuer seeks divorce from you. A copy of the summons in the action is attached.

1. The summons states that you have not cohabited with the pursuer at any time during a continuous period of two years after marriage and immediately before this action. If the pursuer establishes this as a fact the pursuer will obtain a decree of divorce.

2. If the pursuer obtains a decree of divorce, the consequences may be as follows:—
   (a) you may lose your rights of inheritance in your wife's [*or* husband's] property;
   (b) you may lose the right to any pensions which depends on the marriage continuing or on your being left as a widow (the State widow's pension will not be payable to you when your husband dies);
   (c) apart from these consequences there may be others depending on your particular circumstances.

3. If you consent to the grant of decree of divorce, you are nevertheless entitled to apply to the court:—
   (a) to make financial or other provision for you by making an order under the Family Law (Scotland) Act 1985;
   (b) to make an order under section 11 of the Children (Scotland) Act 1995 for maintenance in respect of any child of the marriage, or any child accepted as such, who is under 16 years of age.

In order to make such an application you must lodge defences to the action seeking any such order. If you wish to do this you should consult a solicitor.

If you lodge defences, you may do so at the Office of Court, Court of Session, 2 Parliament Square, Edinburgh EH1 1RQ within [21] days after the date of service on you of the summons [*or if service is executed before calling of the summons*, within seven days after the summons calls in court. The summons will not call in court earlier than [21] days after the date of service on you of the summons]. The date of service is the date stated at the top of this notice unless service has been made by post in which case the date of service is the day after that date.

IF YOU ARE UNCERTAIN ABOUT THE EFFECT OF THIS NOTICE, you should consult a solicitor, Citizens Advice Bureau or other local advice agency or adviser immediately.

          (*Signed*)

          Messenger-at-Arms
          [*or* Solicitor [*or* Agent] for pursuer]
          (*Address*)

---

[1] Form 49.14–E amended by S.I. 1994 No. 2901 (minor correction), S.I. 1996 No. 2587 and S.S.I. 2006 No. 206 (effective 4th May 2006).

Form 49.14-F

C1.2A.145   Rule 49.14(1)(b)(ii)

Rule 49.14(1)(b)(ii)   [1] FORM 49.14–F

Form of notice to defender in an action of separation where it is stated there has been two years non-cohabitation

Date: *(date of posting or other method of service)*

To: *(name and address of defender in summons)*

TAKE NOTICE

(Pursuer's name and address), pursuer, has raised an action against you, defender, in the Court of Session, Edinburgh. The pursuer seeks separation from you. A copy of the summons in the action is attached.

1. The summons states that you have not cohabited with the pursuer at any time during a continuous period of two years after marriage and immediately before this action. If the pursuer establishes this as a fact and the court is satisfied that there are justified grounds for the decree, the pursuer will obtain a decree of separation.

2. If the pursuer obtains a decree of separation, the consequences may be as follows:—
    (a) you may be obliged to live apart from your husband [*or* wife] but the marriage will continue to exist;
    [(b) your husband will continue to have a legal obligation to support you and his children;]
    [(b) *or* (c)] apart from the above there may be other consequences applicable to you depending on your particular circumstances.

3. If you consent to the granting of a decree of separation, you are still entitled to apply to the court:—
    [(a)] for an order under section 11 of the Children (Scotland) Act 1995 for maintenance in respect of any child of the marriage, or any child accepted as such, who is under 16 years of age;
    [(b)] for payment of aliment by your husband [*or* wife] to you].

4. In order to make such an application you must lodge defences to the action. If you wish to do this you should consult a solicitor.

If you lodge defences, you must do so at the Office of Court, Court of Session, 2 Parliament Square, Edinburgh EH1 1RQ within [21] days after the date of service on you of the summons [*or if service is executed before calling of the summons*, within seven days after the summons calls in court. The summons will not call in court earlier than [21] days after the date of service on you of the summons]. The date of service is the date stated at the top of this notice unless service has been made by post in which case the date of service is the day after that date.

IF YOU ARE UNCERTAIN ABOUT THE EFFECT OF THIS NOTICE, you should consult a solicitor, Citizens Advice Bureau or other local advice agency or adviser immediately.

(Signed)

Messenger-at-Arms
[*or* Solicitor [*or* Agent] for pursuer]
(Address)

---

[1] Form 49.14–F amended by S.I. 1994 No. 2901 (minor correction), S.I. 1996 No. 2587 and S.S.I. 2006 No. 206 (effective 4th May 2006).

Form 49.14-G

Rule 49.14(1)(c)

Rule 49.14(1)(c) [1] FORM 49.14–G

Form of notice to defender in action of divorce where an interim gender recognition certificate has been issued

Date: (*date of posting or other method of service*)

To: (*name and address of defender in summons*)

TAKE NOTICE

(*Pursuer's name and address*), pursuer, has raised an action against you, defender, in the Court of Session, Edinburgh. The pursuer seeks divorce from you. A copy of the summons in the action is attached.

1. The summons states that an interim gender recognition certificate has been issued to you

[*or* the pursuer]. If the pursuer establishes this as a matter of fact the pursuer will obtain a decree of divorce.

2. If the pursuer obtains a decree of divorce, the consequences may be as follows—
    (a) you may lose your rights of inheritance in your wife's [*or* husband's] property;
    (b) you may lose the right to any pensions which depend on the marriage continuing or on you being left a widow;
    (c) apart from these consequences there may be others depending on your particular circumstances.

3. If the pursuer is entitled to a decree of divorce, you are nevertheless entitled to apply to the court—
    (a) to make financial or other provision for you by making an order under the Family Law (Scotland) Act 1985;
    (b) to make an order under section 11 of the Children (Scotland) Act 1995 for maintenance in respect of any child of the marriage, or any child accepted as such, who is under 16 years of age.

In order to make such an application you must lodge defences to the action seeking any such order. If you wish to do this you should consult a solicitor.

If you lodge defences, you may do so at the Office of Court, Court of Session, 2 Parliament Square, Edinburgh EH1 1RQ within [21] days after the date of service on you of the summons [*or if service is executed before calling of the summons*, within seven days after the summons calls in court. The summons will not call in court earlier than [21] days after the date of service on you of the summons]. The date of service is the date stated at the top of this notice unless service has been made by post in which case the date of service is the day after that date.

IF YOU ARE UNCERTAIN ABOUT THE EFFECT OF THIS NOTICE, you should consult a solicitor, Citizens Advice Bureau or other local advice agency or adviser immediately.

        (*Signed*)
        Messenger-at-Arms
        [*or* Solicitor [*or* Agent] for pursuer]
        (*Address*)

---

[1] Form 49.14–G inserted by S.S.I. 2005 No. 193 (effective 1st April, 2005).

Form 49.14A-A

Form of notice to defender where it is stated that he consents to decree of dissolution of civil partnership

Date: (*date of posting or other method of service*)

To: (*name and address of defender in summons*)

TAKE NOTICE

(*Pursuer's name and address*), pursuer, has brought an action against you in the Court of Session, Edinburgh. The pursuer seeks dissolution of your civil partnership. A copy of the summons in the action is attached.

1. The summons states that you consent to a decree of dissolution of your civil partnership. If you do consent your civil partner will obtain a decree of dissolution of your civil partnership if he shows that you have not cohabited with him [*or* her] at any time during a continuous period of two years after the registration of your civil partnership and immediately before this action.

2. If the pursuer obtains a decree of dissolution of your civil partnership, the consequences may be as follows:-
   (a) you may lose your rights of inheritance in your civil partner's property;
   (b) you may lose the right to any pensions which depends on the civil partnership continuing or on your civil partner dying;
   (c) apart from these consequences there may be others depending on your particular circumstances.

3. If you consent to the grant of decree of dissolution of your civil partnership, you are still entitled to apply to the court:-
   (a) to make financial or other provision for you by making an order under the Family Law (Scotland) Act 1985;
   (b) to make an order under section 11 of the Children (Scotland) Act 1995 or for maintenance in respect of any child of the family, or any child accepted as such, who is under 16 years of age.

   In order to make such an application you must lodge defences to the action seeking any such order. If you wish to do this you should consult a solicitor.

   If after considering the above you wish to consent to decree of divorce, you should complete and sign the attached notice of consent form, and send it to:-

   The Deputy Principal Clerk of Session
   2 Parliament Square
   Edinburgh EH1 1RQ

   You may do so within [21] days after the date of service on you of the summons [*or if service is executed before calling of the summons*, within seven days after the summons calls in court. The summons will not call in court earlier than [21] days after the date of service on you of the summons]. The date of service s the date stated at the top of this notice unless service has been made by post in which case the date of service is the day after that date.

4. If after consent you wish to withdraw your consent, you must immediately inform the Deputy Principal Clerk of Session at the above address in writing. Please state the name of the court action in your letter.

IF YOU ARE UNCERTAIN ABOUT THE EFFECT OF THIS NOTICE, you should consult a solicitor, Citizens Advice Bureau or other local advice agency or adviser immediately.

(*Signed*)
Messenger-at-Arms
[*or* Solicitor [*or* Agent] for pursuer]
(*Address*)

Form 49.14A-A inserted by S.S.I. 2005 No. 632 (effective 8th December 2005).

Form 49.14A-B

Rule 49.14A(1)(i)

[1] FORM 49.14A–B

Rule 49.14A(1)(i)

C1.2A.148

Form of notice of consent in action of dissolution of a civil partnership under section 117(3)(c) of the Civil Partnership Act 2004

NOTICE OF CONSENT TO DISSOLUTION OF CIVIL PARTNERSHIP

I have received a copy of the summons in the court action raised against me by (*pursuer's name and address*).

I understand that it states that I consent to the granting of decree of dissolution of my civil partnership in this action.

I consent to the granting of decree of dissolution of my civil partnership in this action.

Signature ....

Name (in Block Capitals) ....

Address ....

....

....

Date ....

Signature of Witness ....

Name (in Block Capitals) ....

Address ....

....

....

....

Occupation ....

---

[1] Form 49.14A–B inserted by S.S.I. 2005 No. 632 (effective 8th December 2005).

Form 49.14A-C

Form of notice to defender where it is stated that he consents to decree of separation of civil partners   C1.2A.149

Date: (*date of posting or other method of service*)

To: (*name and address of defender in summons*)

(*Pursuer's name and address*), pursuer has brought an action against you in the Court of Session, Edinburgh. The pursuer seeks separation from you. A copy of the summons in the action is attached.

1. The summons states that you consent to the grant of a decree of separation. If you consent your civil partner will obtain a decree of separation if he [*or* she] shows that you have not cohabited with him [*or* her] at any time during a continuous period of two years after the registration of your civil partnership and immediately before this action.

2. If the pursuer obtains a decree of separation, the consequences may be as follows:-
   (a) you will be obliged to live apart from your civil partnership will continue to exist;
   (b) your civil partner will continue to have a legal obligation to support you and any children of the family;]
   (c) apart from the above there may be other consequences applicable to you depending on your particular circumstances.

3. If you consent to the grant of a decree of separation, you are still entitled to apply to the court:-
   (a) for an order under section 11 of the Children (Scotland) Act 1995 for maintenance in respect of any child of the family, or any child accepted as such, who is under 16 years of age.
   (b) for payment of aliment by your civil partner to you.
   In order to make such an application you must lodge defences to the action seeking any such order. If you wish to do this you should consult a solicitor.

4. If after considering the above you wish to consent to a decree, please complete the attached notice of consent form, and send it to:-
   The Deputy Principal Clerk of Session
   2 Parliament Square
   Edinburgh EH1 1RQ
   You may do so within [21] days after the date of service on you of the summons [*or if service is executed before calling of the summons,* within seven days after the summons calls in court. The summons will not call in court earlier than [21] days after the date of service on you of the summons]. The date of service is the date stated at the top of this notice unless service has been made by post in which case the date of service is the day after that date.
   If after consent you wish to withdraw your consent, you must immediately inform the Deputy Principal Clerk of Session at the above address in writing. Please state the name of the court action in your letter.

IF YOU ARE UNCERTAIN ABOUT THE EFFECT OF THIS NOTICE, you should consult a solicitor, Citizens Advice Bureau or other local advice agency or adviser immediately.

(*Signed*)
Messenger-at-Arms
[*or* Solicitor [*or* Agent] for pursuer]
(*Address*)

Form 49.14A-C as inserted by S.S.I. 2005 No. 632 (effective 8th December 2005).

Form 49.14A-D

Rule 49.14A(1)(a)(ii)

[1] FORM 49.14A–D

Rule 49.14A(1)(a)(ii)

Form of notice of consent in action of separation of civil partners under section 117(3)(c) of the Civil Partnership Act 2004

NOTICE OF CONSENT TO SEPARATION OF CIVIL PARTNERS

I have received a copy of the summons in the court action raised against me by (*pursuer's name and address*).

I understand that it states that I consent to the granting of decree of dissolution of my civil partnership in this action.

I consent to the granting of decree of dissolution of my civil partnership in this action.

Signature ....

Name (in Block Capitals) ....

Address ....

....

....

Date ....

Signature of Witness ....

Name (in Block Capitals) ....

Address ....

....

....

Occupation ....

[1] Form 49.14A-D inserted by S.S.I. 2005 No. 632 (effective 8th December 2005).

Form 49.14A-E

Form of notice to defender in an action of dissolution of civil partnership under section 117(3)(d) of the Civil Partnership Act 2004

Date: (*date of posting or other method of service*)

To: (*name and address of defender in summons*)

TAKE NOTICE

(*Pursuer's name and address*), pursuer, has brought an action against you in the Court of Session, Edinburgh. The pursuer seeks dissolution of your civil partnership. A copy of the summons in the action is attached.

1. The summons states that you have not cohabited with the pursuer at any time during a continuous period of five years after the registration of your civil partnership and immediately before this action. If the pursuer establishes this as a fact the pursuer will obtain a decree of dissolution of your civil partnership unless in the opinion of the court the grant of decree would result in grave financial hardship to you.

2. If the pursuer obtains a decree of dissolution of your civil partnership, the consequences may be as follows:-
    (a) you may lose your rights of inheritance in your civil partner's property:
    (b) you may lose the right to any pensions which depends on the civil partnership continuing or on your civil partner dying;
    (c) apart from these consequences there may be others depending on your particular circumstances.

3. If you consent to the grant of decree of dissolution of your civil partnership, you are nevertheless entitled to apply to the court:-
    (a) to make financial or other provision for you by making an order under the Family Law (Scotland) Act 1985;
    (b) to make an order under section 11 of the Children (Scotland) Act 1995 for maintenance in respect of any child of the family, or any child accepted as such, who is under 16 years of age.

In order to make such an application you must lodge defences to the action seeking any such order. If you wish to do this you should you should consult a solicitor.

If you lodge defences, you may do so at the Office of Court, Court of Session, 2 Parliament Square, Edinburgh EH1 1RQ within [21] days after the date of service on you of the summons [*or if service is executed before calling of the summons,* within seven days after the summons calls in court. The summons will not call in court earlier than [21] days after the date of service on you of the summons]. The date of service is the date stated at the top of this notice unless service has been made by post in which case the date of service is the day after that date.

IF YOU ARE UNCERTAIN ABOUT THE EFFECT OF THIS NOTICE, you should consult a solicitor, Citizens Advice Bureau or other local advice agency or adviser immediately.

> (*Signed*)
> Messenger-at-Arms
> [*or* Solicitor [*or* Agent] for pursuer]
> (*Address*)

Form 49.14A-E as inserted by S.S.I. 2005 No. 632 (effective 8th December 2005).

Form 49.14A-F

C1.2A.152   *Form of notice to defender in an action of separation of civil partners on grounds under section 117(3)(d) of the Civil Partnership Act 2004*

Date: (*date of posting or other method of service*)

To: (*name and address of defender in summons*)

(*Pursuer's name and address*), pursuer, has brought an action against you in the Court of Session, Edinburgh. The pursuer seeks separation from you. A copy of the summons in the action is attached.

1. The summons states that you have not cohabited with the pursuer at any time during a continuous period of five years after the registration of your civil partnership and immediately before this action. If the pursuer establishes this as a fact and the court is satisfied that there are justified grounds for the decree, the pursuer will obtain a decree of separation.

2. If the pursuer obtains a decree of separation, the consequences may be as follows:-

   (a) you may be obliged to live apart from your civil partner but the civil partnership will continue to exist;

   (b) your civil partner may continue to have a legal obligation to support you and any children of the family;

   (c) apart from the above there may be other consequences applicable to you depending on your particular circumstances.

3. If you consent to the granting of a decree of separation, you are still entitled to apply to the court:-

   (a) for an order under section 11 of the Children (Scotland) Act 1995 for maintenance in respect of any child of the family, or any child accepted as such, who is under 16 years of age;

   (b) for payment of aliment by your civil partner to you.

4. In order to make such an application you must lodge defences to the action. If you wish to do this you should consult a solicitor.

If you lodge defences, you must do so at the Office of Court, Court of Session, 2 Parliament Square, Edinburgh EH1 1RQ within [21] days after the date of service on you of the summons [*or if service is executed before calling of the summons,* within seven days after the summons calls in court. The summons will not call in court earlier than [21] days after the date of service on you of the summons]. The date of service is the date stated at the top of this notice unless service has been made by post in which case the date of service is the day after that date.

IF YOU ARE UNCERTAIN ABOUT THE EFFECT OF THIS NOTICE, you should consult a solicitor, Citizens Advice Bureau or other local advice agency or adviser immediately.

          (*Signed*)

          Messenger-at-Arms

          [*or* Solicitor [*or* Agent] for pursuer]

          (*Address*)

Form 49.14A-F as inserted by S.S.I. 2005 No. 632 (effective 8th December 2005).

Form 49.14A-G

Form of notice to defender in action of dissolution of civil partnership on grounds **C1.2A.153**
under section 117(2)(b) of the Civil Partnership Act 2004

Date: (*date of posting or other method of service*)

To: (*name and address of defender in summons*)

(*Pursuer's name and address*), pursuer, has raised an action against you in the Court of Session, Edinburgh. The pursuer seeks dissolution of your civil partnership. A copy of the summons in the action is attached.

1. The summons states that an interim gender recognition certificate has been issued to you [*or* your civil partner] after the date of registration of your civil

partnership. If the pursuer establishes this as a fact the pursuer will obtain a decree of dissolution of your civil partnership.

2.   If the pursuer obtains a decree of dissolution of your civil partnership, the consequences may be as follows:-

    (a)   you may lose your rights of inheritance in your civil partner's property

    (b)   you may lose the right to any pensions which depend on the civil partnership continuing or on your civil partner dying;

    (c)   apart from these consequences there may be others depending on your particular circumstances.

3.   If you consent to the grant of decree of the dissolution of your civil partnership, you are still entitled to apply to the court:-

    (a)   to make financial or other provision for you by making an order under the Family Law (Scotland) Act 1985;

    (b)   to make an order under section 11 of the Children (Scotland) Act 1995 for maintenance in respect of any child of the family, or any child accepted as such, who is under 16 years of age;

In order to make such an application you must lodge defences to the action. If you wish to do this you should consult a solicitor.

If you lodge defences, you must do so at the Office of Court, Court of Session, 2 Parliament Square, Edinburgh EH1 1RQ within [21] days after the date of service on you of the summons [*or if service is executed before calling of the summons, within seven days after the summons calls in court. The summons will not call in court earlier than* [21] *days after the date of service on you of the summons*]. The date of service is the date stated at the top of this notice unless service has been made by post in which case the date of service is the day after that date.

IF YOU ARE UNCERTAIN ABOUT THE EFFECT OF THIS NOTICE, you should consult a solicitor, Citizens Advice Bureau or other local advice agency or adviser immediately.

                              (*Signed*)

                              Messenger-at-Arms

                              [*or* Solicitor [*or* Agent] for pursuer]

                              (*Address*)

Form 49.14A-G as inserted by S.S.I. 2005 No. 632 (effective 8th December 2005).

Form 49.22[1]

C1.2A.154   Form of annex to interlocutor appointing a child welfare reporter

    ☐   Appointment of Child Welfare Reporter under rule 49.22(1)(a).
            Where this box is ticked the Child Welfare Reporter is required to seek the views of the child [or children] on the issue(s) specified in Part 1 below.

    ☐   Appointment of Child Welfare Reporter under rule 49.22(1)(b).
            Where this box is ticked the Child Welfare Reporter is required to carry out the enquiries specified in Part 2 below, and to address the issue(s) specified in Part 3 below.

---

[1] As inserted by S.S.I. 2015 No. 312 para.2 (effective 26 October 2015) and amended by S.S.I. 2019 No. 123 para.2(15) (effective 24 June 2019).

PART 1

> Issue(s) in respect of which views of the child [or children] are to be sought
> [*specify*]

Is a copy of the report to be provided to the parties under rule 49.22(9)(d)?
□Yes
□No

PART 2

Enquiries to be undertaken—

□   Seek views of child
□   Visit home of [*specify*]
□   Visit nursery / school / child minder / other [*specify*]
□   Interview mother / father
□   Interview other family members [*specify*]
□   Interview child minder / nanny
□   Interview teacher / head teacher
□   Interview child's health visitor / GP / other health professional [*specify*]
□   Interview a party's GP / other health professional [*specify*]
□   Interview social worker [*specify*]
□   Interview domestic abuse case worker [*specify*]
□   Interview other persons [*specify*]
□   Obtain criminal conviction certificate under section 112 of the Police Act 1997 in respect of [*specify party*]
□   Observe contact [*specify*]
□   Observe child in home environment pre/post contact [*specify*]
□   Obtain record of parties' attendance from contact centre
□   Other [*specify*]

PART 3

> Issues to be addressed in report [*specify*]

Where the views of the child form part of the enquiries to be undertaken, should the views of the child be recorded in a separate report?
□Yes
□No

If yes, is a copy of that report to be provided to the parties under rule 49.22(9)(d)?
□Yes
□No

Form 49.29-A

C1.2A.154.1   Rule 49.29(1)

Rule 49.29(1)   [1] FORM 49.29–A

Form of minute for decree in undefended family action

(*Name of counsel*) for the pursuer having considered the evidence contained in the affidavits and the other documents as specified in the attached schedule and being satisfied that on this evidence a motion for decree in terms of the conclusions of the summons [*or in such restricted terms as may be appropriate*] may properly be made, moves the court accordingly.

IN RESPECT WHEREOF

(*Signature of counsel or other person having a right of audience*)

SCHEDULE
(*list of numbered documents*)

———

[1] Form 49.29–A amended by S.I. 1994 No. 2901.

Form 49.29-B

C1.2A.155   Rule 49.29(2)(b)

Rule 49.29(2)(b)   FORM 49.29–B

Form of official card to be completed when decree sought in undefended family action

C	UNDEFENDED FAMILY ACTION DECREE SLIP (Use Block Capitals Only)	FOR COURT USE ONLY DISPOSAL
	PURSUER .... (Christian names or forenames and surname only)	LORD .... DATE.......
	v	DATE......
	DEFENDER .... (Christian names or forenames and surname only)	DATE......
	COUNSEL .... (or other person having a right of audience)	DATE......
	SOLICITOR	DATE......

Form 49.70

C1.2A.156   Rule 49.70(1) and (2) and 49.71G(1)
[Omitted by S.S.I. 2006 No. 206 (effective 4 May 2006)]

Form 49.73-A[1,2]

Under the Divorce (Scotland) Act 1976, Section 1(2)(d)   **C1.2A.157**
Simplified Procedure
Court of Session
General Department
Parliament House
Edinburgh EH1 1RQ
Tel: 0131 240 6741

APPLICATION FOR DIVORCE (WITH CONSENT OF OTHER PARTY TO THE MARRIAGE)

SPOUSES HAVING LIVED APART FOR AT LEAST ONE YEAR

Before completing this form, you should have read the leaflet entitled "Do it yourself Divorce", which explains the circumstances in which divorce may be sought by that method. If simplified procedure appears to suit your circumstances, you may use this form to apply for divorce.

Below you will find directions designed to assist you with your application.

Please follow them carefully. In the event of difficulty, you may contact the Court's General Department at the above address or any Citizens Advice Bureau.

Directions for making Applications

WRITE IN INK, USING BLOCK CAPITALS

Application (Part 1)	1. Complete and sign Part 1 of the Form (pages 3-7), paying particular attention to the notes opposite each section.
Consent of Spouse (Part 2)	2. When you have filled in Part 1 of the form, send the form to your spouse for completion of the consent at Part 2 (page 9).
	NOTE: If your spouse does NOT complete and sign the form of consent, your application cannot proceed further under the simplified procedure. In that event, if you still wish to obtain a divorce, you should consult a solicitor.
Affidavit (Part 3)	3. When the application has been returned to you with the Consent (Part 2) duly completed and signed, you should then take the form to a Justice of the Peace, Notary Public, Commissioner for Oaths or other duly authorised person so that your affidavit in Part 3 (page 10) may be completed and sworn.
Returning completed Application Form to Court	4. When directions 1-3 above have all been carried out, your application is now ready to be sent to the court at the above address. With it you must enclose:
	(i) Your marriage certificate (the document headed "Extract of an entry in a Register of Marriages"), which will be returned to you in due course, and
	(ii) Either a cheque or postal order for the court fee, crossed and made payable to "Scottish Court Service"

---

[1] As amended by S.S.I. 2017 No. 132 para.2 (effective 1 June 2017).
[2] As amended by S.S.I. 2021 No. 75 r. 2(3)(a) (effective 1st March 2021).

or a completed form SP15 claiming exemption from the Court fee.

5. Receipt of your application will be promptly acknowledged. Should you wish to withdraw the application for any reason, please contact the Court of Session immediately.

THE NOTES ON THIS AND THE FOLLOWING PAGES ARE DESIGNED TO ASSIST YOU.

PLEASE READ THEM CAREFULLY BEFORE COMPLETING EACH SECTION OF THE FORM.

Notes on Sections 1 and 2 opposite

(i)   The names entered in Sections 1 and 2 opposite should be those shown on your marriage certificate. If you are known by another name which does not appear on that certificate, please write that name in brackets.

(ii) Home addresses should be given where these are known. The Court is required by law to serve a copy of this application on your spouse.

Notes on Section 3 opposite

"Domiciled" means that the person concerned regards Scotland as his/her permanent home and intends to live permanently in Scotland in the foreseeable future.

PART I

WRITE IN INK USING BLOCK CAPITALS

1. NAME AND ADDRESS OF APPLICANT

Surname...............   *Other name(s) in full*...............

Present Address   ....

....

                                Daytime telephone number (if any)

....

                                ....

2. NAME AND ADDRESS OF HUSBAND/WIFE

Surname...............   *Other name(s) in full*...............

Present Address   ....

....

                                Daytime telephone number (if any)

....

....

3. JURISDICTION

Please indicate with a tick (✔) in the appropriate box or boxes which of the following apply:

(i)   I am domiciled in Scotland on the date I signed this application ☐

(ii)   My spouse is domiciled in Scotland on the date I signed this ☐
application

(iii)   I was habitually resident in Scotland throughout the period of ☐
one year ending with the date I signed this application

(iv)   My spouse was habitually resident in Scotland throughout the ☐
period of one year ending with the date I signed this application

AND

Notes on Section 4 opposite

You will be able to obtain these details from your marriage certificate (extract entry in the register of marriages) which must accompany this application form, when you send it to the court.

A photocopy of the marriage certificate will NOT be accepted. If you cannot find the original, you should apply for an official copy to:

National Records of Scotland, Registration Section, New Register House, Edinburgh EH1 3YT, or the office where the marriage was registered,

stating both spouses' full names, and the date and place of the marriage.

(Note that the Registrar will charge a fee for this service.)

Notes of Section 5 opposite

You and your spouse must have lived apart from each other for a continuous period of at least one year after the date of your marriage and immediately before the date of this application.

This minimum period of one year's separation is extended if you and your spouse have lived together again for *not more than six months in all* during that one year period. For example, if you lived together for three months in total during the one year period, then you should not complete this application until one year and three months have elapsed from the date of your original separation.

Notes on Section 6 opposite

Is there a reasonable chance that you can still settle the differences with your spouse and resume normal married life?

Are you satisfied that there is now no possibility of the marriage succeeding?

Notes on Section 7 opposite

If your spouse is not prepared to sign the form of consent at Part 2 of this application, you will not obtain a divorce by this method.

(iii) No court of a Contracting state has jurisdiction under the ☐
Council Regulation.

4. DETAILS OF PRESENT MARRIAGE

Place of marriage ....
(Registration District)
Date of marriage: Day   ....   Month .... Year
....

5. PERIOD OF SEPARATION

(i) Please state the date on which you Day   Month
ceased to live with your spouse. (If
more than 1½ years,

Year
....

just give the month and year.)

(ii) Have you lived with your   YES ☐   NO ☐
spouse since that date? (*Tick
box which applies*)

(iii) If yes, for how long in total did you live together before finally ....
separating again?

months

6. RECONCILIATION

Is there any reasonable prospect of reconcili-   YES ☐   NO ☐
ation with your spouse? (*Tick box which ap-
plies*)

Do you consider that the marriage has broken   YES ☐   NO ☐
down irretrievably? (*Tick box which applies*)

7. CONSENT

Does your spouse consent to a divorce being   YES ☐   NO ☐
granted? (*Tick box which applies*)

8. MENTAL DISORDER

As far as you are aware, does your spouse   YES ☐   NO ☐
have any mental disorder? (whether mental
illness, personality disorder or learning disability)

(*Tick box which applies*)

(If yes, give details)

Note on Section 9 opposite

"Children of the marriage" includes any adopted children and/or children accepted into the family.

Notes on Section 11 opposite

No claim can be made in this form of divorce application for payment to you of a
periodical allowance (i.e. regular payment of money weekly, monthly etc for your
maintenance) or a capital sum (i.e. lump sum). If you wish to make such a claim,
you should consult a solicitor.

NOTE: While it may be possible to obtain an order for periodical allowance after
divorce, the right to payment of a capital sum is lost once decree of divorce is
granted.

No application can be made in this form of divorce application for postponement
of decree under section 3A of the Divorce (Scotland) Act 1976. On an application
under that section, the court may postpone the grant of decree of divorce if it is
satisfied that:

(a)   the applicant is prevented from entering into a religious marriage by virtue
of a requirement of that religion of that marriage; and

(b)   the other party can act so as to remove or enable or contribute to the removal
of, the impediment which prevents that marriage.

As at 26th February 2007 "religious marriage" for the purposes of section 3A of the Divorce (Scotland) Act 1976 means a marriage solemnised by a celebrant of any Hebrew congregation (i.e. a Jewish marriage) (S.S.I. 2006/253).

If you wish to make such an application you should consult a solicitor or Citizens' Advice Bureau.

9. CHILDREN

Are there any children of the marriage under the age of 16? (*Tick box which applies*)   YES ☐   NO ☐

10. OTHER COURT ACTIONS

Are you aware of any court actions currently proceeding in any country (including Scotland) which may affect your marriage? (*Tick box which applies*)   YES ☐   NO ☐

(If yes, give details)

11. DECLARATION AND REQUEST FOR DIVORCE

I confirm that the facts stated in Sections 1 – 10 above apply to my marriage.

I do NOT ask the Court to make any financial awards in connection with this application.

I do NOT ask the court to postpone the grant of decree under section 3A of the Divorce (Scotland) Act 1976.

I request the Court to grant decree of divorce from my spouse.

(Date)   (Signature of applicant)   ....
....

IMPORTANT — Part 1 MUST be completed, signed and dated before sending the application form to your spouse.

NOTES ON COMPLETING PART 2 OPPOSITE (PAGE 9)

1. Read over carefully PART 1 (pages 3–7) of this application, which has already been completed by your spouse.

2. *Financial Provisions* Please note that in Section 11 of Part 1, the Applicant states that he/she does NOT claim any financial awards by way of periodical allowance or capital sum. You also are required to state (items (c) and (d) opposite) that you make no claim upon the Applicant for payment of a periodical allowance or capital sum.

    Note: While it may be possible to obtain an order for *periodical allowance* after divorce, the right to payment of a *capital sum* is lost once decree of divorce is granted.

2A. *Postponement of decree* Please note that no application can be made in this form of divorce application for postponement of decree under section 3A of the Divorce (Scotland) Act 1976. On an application under that section, the court may postpone the grant of decree of divorce if it is satisfied that:

    (a) the applicant is prevented from entering into a religious marriage by virtue of a requirement of the religion of that marriage; and

    (b) the other party can act so as to remove or enable or contribute to the removal of, the impediment which prevents that marriage.

As at 26th February 2007 "religious marriage" for the purposes of section 3A of the Divorce (Scotland) Act 1976 means a marriage solemnised by a celebrant of any Hebrew congregation (i.e. a Jewish marriage) (S.S.I. 2006/ 253).

In Section 11 of Part I, the Applicant states that he/she does not apply for postponement of decree under section 3A of the Divorce (Scotland) Act 1976. You are also required to state (item (f) opposite) that you make no such application.

3.   *Warning* Divorce may result in the loss to you of property rights (e.g. the right to succeed to the Applicant's estate on his/her death) or the right, where appropriate, to a widow's pension.

(If you are in doubt about signing this form of consent, you should consult a solicitor.)

NOTICE TO CONSENTING SPOUSE PART 2

CONSENT TO APPLICATION FOR DIVORCE (SPOUSE HAVING LIVED APART FOR AT LEAST ONE YEAR)

In Part 1 of the enclosed application form your spouse is applying for divorce on the ground that the marriage has broken down irretrievably because you and he (or she) have lived apart for at least one year and you consent to the divorce being granted.

Such consent must be given formally in writing at Part 2 of the application form. BEFORE completing that part, you are requested to read it over carefully so that you understand the effect of consenting to divorce. Thereafter if you wish to consent:

(a)   check the details given by the Applicant at Part 1 of the form to ensure that they are correct to the best of your knowledge;

(b)   complete Part 2 (Consent by Applicant's spouse to divorce) by entering your name an address at the appropriate place and adding your signature and the date; and

(c)   return the whole application form to your spouse at the address given in Part 1.

Once your spouse has completed the remainder of the form and has submitted it to the court, a copy of the whole application (including your consent) will later by served upon you formally by the court.

In the event of the divorce being granted, you will automatically be sent a copy of the extract decree. (Should you change your address before receiving the copy extract decree, please notify the court immediately.)

If you do NOT wish to consent, please return the application form, with Part 2 uncompleted, to your spouse and advise him or her of your decision.

The court will NOT grant a divorce on this application if Part 2 of the form is not completed by you.

Court of Session

General Department

Parliament House

Edinburgh EH1 1RQ

Tel: 0131 240 6741

PART 2

CONSENT BY APPLICANT'S SPOUSE TO DIVORCE

NOTE:

Before completing this Part of the form, please read Part 1 and the notes opposite (page 8).

I ....

(Full names, in *BLOCK* letters, of Applicant's spouse)

residing at

....

(Address, also in *BLOCK* letters)

HEREBY STATE THAT

a.　I have read Part 1 of this application;

b.　The Applicant has lived apart from me for a continuous period of 1 year immediately preceding the date of the application (Section 11 of Part 1);

c.　I do not ask the court to make any order for payment to me by the Applicant of a periodical allowance (i.e. a regular payment of money weekly or monthly, etc for maintenance),

d.　I do not ask the court to make any order for payment to me by the Applicant of a capital sum (i.e. a lump sum payment);

e.　I understand that divorce may result in the loss to me of property rights;

f.　I do not ask the court to postpone the grant of decree under section 3A of the Divorce (Scotland) Act 1976; and

g.　*I CONSENT TO DECREE OF DIVORCE BEING GRANTED IN RESPECT OF THIS APPLICATION.*

(Date)　　　　　　　　　　　　.........　　　　　　　　　　　　(Signature)

NOTE: You may withdraw your consent, even after giving it, at any time before divorce is granted by the court. Should you wish to do so, you must immediately advise:

Court of Session

General Department

Parliament House

Edinburgh EH1 1RQ

Tel: 0131 240 6741

PART 3

APPLICANT'S AFFIDAVIT

To be completed only after Parts 1 and 2 have been signed and dated.

I,(*insert Applicant's full name*) ....

residing at (*insert Applicant's present home address*)

Town...............

Country...............

SWEAR that to the best of my knowledge and belief:

　　　　(1) the facts stated in Part 1 of this Application are true; and

　　　　(2) the signature in Part 2 of this Application is that of my husband/wife.

Signature of applicant　　　　...............

To be completed by Justice of the　SWORN at (*place*)...............

Peace, Notary Public, or Com-

missioner for Oaths

　　　　　　　　　　this ....

before me (*full name*) ....

(*full address*) ....

....

....

Signature   ....

*Justice of the Peace/*Notary Public/
*Commissioner for Oaths

* Delete where not applicable

Form 49.73A as amended by S.S.I. 2014 No. 302 (effective 16th December 2014).

Form 49.73-B[1, 2]

C1.2A.158   *Under the Divorce (Scotland) Act 1976, Section 1(2)(e)*

Simplified Procedure

Court of Session

General Department

Edinburgh EH1 1RQ

Tel: 240 6741

APPLICATION FOR DIVORCE

SPOUSES HAVING LIVED APART FOR AT LEAST 2 YEARS

Before completing this form, you should have read the leaflet entitled "Do it yourself Divorce", which explains the circumstances in which a divorce may be sought by that method. If the simplified procedure appears to suit your circumstances, you may use this form to apply for divorce.

Below you will find directions designed to assist you with your application.

Please follow them carefully. In the event of difficulty, you may contact Court's General Department at the above address or Citizens Advice Bureau.

Directions for making Application

WRITE IN INK, USING BLOCK CAPITALS

Application (*Part 1*)	1. Complete and sign Part1 of the form (pages 3–7), paying particular attention to the notes opposite each section.
Affidavit (*Part 2*)	2. When you have completed Part 1, you should take the form to a Justice of the Peace, Notary Public, Commissioner for Oaths or other duly authorised person so that your affidavit in Part2 (page8) can be completed and sworn.
Returning Completed Application Form to Court	3. When directions 1 and 2 above have been carried out, your application is now ready to be sent to court at the above address. With it you must enclose:
	(i) Your marriage certificate (the document headed "Extract of an entry in a Register of Marriages"), which will be returned to you in due course. Check the notes on page 2 to see if you also need to obtain a letter from the General Register Office stating that there is no record that your spouse has divorced you; and

[1] As amended by S.S.I. 2017 No. 132 para.2 (effective 1 June 2017).
[2] As amended by S.S.I. 2021 No. 75 r. 2(3)(b) (effective 1st March 2021).

(ii) Either a cheque or postal order for the court fee, crossed and made payable to "Scottish Court and Tribunal Service", or a completed form SP15 claiming exemption from the Court fee.

4. Receipt of your application will be promptly acknowledged. Should you wish to withdraw the application for any reason, please contact the Court of Session immediately.

THE NOTES ON THIS AND THE FOLLOWING PAGES ARE DESIGNED TO ASSIST YOU. PLEASE READ THEM CAREFULLY BEFORE COMPLETING EACH SECTION OF THE FORM.

Notes on Sections 1 and 2 opposite

(i)   The names entered in Sections 1 and 2 opposite must be those on your marriage certificate. If you are known by another name which does not appear on that certificate, please write that name in brackets.

(ii) Home addresses should be given where these are known. The Court is required by law to serve a copy of this application on your spouse.

Note on Section 3 opposite

If the address of your spouse is NOT known or cannot reasonably be ascertained, please enter "not known" in this section; you must take all reasonable steps to find out where your spouse is living and state on a separate sheet what steps you have taken and attach it to this form. Then proceed to section 4.

N.B. The statement must be signed.

Notes of Section 4 opposite

In the event that the address of your spouse is unknown to you, the Court is required by law to intimate a copy of this application to:

(i)   ONE of the next-of-kin of your spouse. ("Next-of-kin" does not include yourself or any children of the marriage for the purposes of this application. Children of the marriage includes any adopted children, and/or children accepted into the family.)

(ii) ALL children of your marriage aged 16 years or over, whether or not they live with you.

When entering the details of the next-of-kin, if any, please state his or her relationship to your spouse (i.e. "mother", "father", "brother", "sister", etc).

If you do no know the identity or whereabouts of any of the next-of-kin of your spouse, or the whereabouts of any of the children of your marriage, please enter "not known" where appropriate.

LETTER FROM NATIONAL RECORDS OF SCOTLAND. If you do not know the address of your spouse and you were married in Scotland, you must obtain a letter from the National Records of Scotland stating that there is no record that your spouse has divorced you. The letter must be issued not more than one month before the date of posting this application to the court. If you require to obtain a letter you should apply to:

National Records of Scotland, Registration Branch, New Register House, Edinburgh, EH1 3YT,

stating both spouses' full names, the date and place of your marriage and requesting that a search be made to confirm that there is no record that your spouse has divorced you. (Note - a fee will be charged for this service.)

The requirement to obtain a letter from the General Register Office does not apply if you were married outwith Scotland.

PART 1
WRITE IN INK USING BLOCK CAPITALS
1. NAME AND ADDRESS OF APPLICANT

Surname...............   *Other name(s)*...............
Present Address ....   in full ....

....
....
....   Daytime telephone number (if
                               any)

....
....

2. NAME OF SPOUSE

Surname...............   *Other name(s)*...............

....

3. ADDRESS OF SPOUSE (if the address of your spouse is not known, please
enter "not known" in this section and proceed to section 4)

Present Address

....
                              Daytime telephone number (if
                               any)
....

4. Only complete this section if you do not know the present address of your
spouse
    NEXT-OF-KIN

Name

....

Address ....
Relationship to your spouse

....

....
....

CHILDREN OF THE MARRIAGE

Names and dates of birth   Address
....
....
....
....
....
....

If sufficient space is not available here to list all the children of the marriage, please continue on separate sheet and attach to this form

Note on Section 5 opposite

"Domiciled" means that the person concerned opposite regards Scotland and his/her permanent home and intended to live permanently in Scotland in the foreseeable future.

Notes on Section 6 opposite

You will be able to obtain these details from your marriage certificate (extract entry in a register of marriages) which must accompany this application form, when you send it to the Court.

A photocopy of the marriage certificate will NOT be accepted

Notes on Section 7 opposite

You and your spouse must have lived apart from each other for a continuous period of at least 2 years after the date of your marriage and immediately before the date of this application.

This minimum period of 2 years separation is extended if you and your spouse have lived together again for *NOT MORE THAN 6 MONTHS IN ALL* during that 2 year period. For example, if you lived together for 3 months in total during the 2 year period, then you should not complete this application until 2 years and 3 months have elapsed from the date of your original separation.

5. JURISDICTION

Please indicate with a tick (✔) in the appropriate box or boxes which of the following apply:

(i)   I am domiciled in Scotland on the date I signed this application ☐

(ii)   My spouse is domiciled in Scotland on the date I signed this ☐
        application

(iii)   I was habitually resident in Scotland throughout the period of ☐
        one year ending with the date I signed this application

(iv)   My spouse was habitually resident in Scotland throughout the ☐
        period of one year ending with the date I signed this application

6. DETAILS OF PRESENT MARRIAGE

Place of marriage ....
(Registration District)

Date of marriage: Day .... Month .... Year ....

7. PERIOD OF SEPARATION

(i)   Please state the date on which you
        ceased to live with your spouse. (If
        more than 2½ years, just give the
        month and year)   Day ....   Month ....
Year   ....

(ii)   Have you lived with your spouse since   YES ☐   NO ☐
        that date? (*tick box which applies*)

(iii)   If yes, for how long in total did you live together before finally separating again?

Months

Notes on Section 8 opposite

Is there a reasonable chance that you can still settle the differences with your spouse and resume normal married life?

Are you satisfied that there is now no possibility of the marriage succeeding?

Note on Section 10 opposite

"Children of the marriage" includes any adopted children and/or children accepted into the family.

Notes on Section 12 opposite

No claim can be made I this form of divorce application for payment to you of a periodical allowance (i.e. regular payment of money weekly, monthly etc for your maintenance) or a capital sum (i.e. lump sum). If you wish to make such a claim, you should consult a solicitor.

NOTE: While it may be possible to obtain an order for periodical allowance after divorce, the right to payment of a capital sum is lost once decree of divorce is granted.

No application can be made in this form of divorce application for postponement of decree under section 3A of the Divorce (Scotland) Act 1976. On an application under that section, the court may postpone the grant of decree of divorce if it is satisfied that:

(a) the applicant is prevented from entering into a religious marriage by virtue of a requirement of that religion of that marriage; and

(b) the other party can act so as to remove or enable or contribute to the removal of, the impediment which prevents that marriage.

As at 26th February 2007 "religious marriage" for the purposes of section 3A of the Divorce (Scotland) Act 1976 means a marriage solemnised by a celebrant of any Hebrew congregation (i.e. a Jewish marriage) (S.S.I. 2006/253).

If you wish to make such an application you should consult a solicitor or Citizens' Advice Bureau.

8. RECONCILIATION

Is there any reasonable prospect of reconciliation with your spouse? (*Tick box which applies*)	YES	☐	NO	☐
Do you consider that the marriage has broken down irretrievably?	YES	☐	NO	☐

9. MENTAL DISORDER

As far as you are aware does your spouse have any mental disorder? (whether mental illness, personality disorder or learning disability) (*Tick box which applies*)	YES	☐	NO	☐

(If yes, give details below)

10. CHILDREN

Are there any children of the marriage under the age of 16? (*Tick box which applies*)	YES	☐	NO	☐

11. OTHER COURT ACTIONS

Are you aware of any court actions currently   YES   ☐   NO   ☐
proceeding in any country (including
Scotland) which may affect your marriage:
(*Tick box which applies*)
(If yes, give details)

12. DECLARATION AND REQUEST FOR DIVORCE

I confirm that the facts stated in Sections 1 – 11 above apply to my marriage.

I do *NOT* ask the Court to make any financial award in connection with this application.

I do NOT ask the court to postpone the grant of decree under section 3A of the Divorce (Scotland) Act 1976.

I request the Court to grant decree of divorce from my spouse.

(Date)   (Signature of
                                                                          applicant)

....

....

PART 2
APPLICANT'S AFFIDAVIT
To be completed only after Part 1 has been signed and dated

I (*insert Applicant's full name*)

....

residing at (*insert Applicant's present home address*)

Town...............

Country...............

SWEAR that to the best of my knowledge and belief the facts stated in Part 1 of this Application are true.

Signature of applicant

....

To be completed by Justice of the   SWORN at (*place*)
....

Peace, Notary Public, or Commissioner for Oaths

this ....day of ....20.........

before me (*full name*) ....

(*full address*)

....

....

Signature

....

*Justice of the Peace/*Notary Public/*Commissioner for Oaths
*Delete where not applicable

Form 49.73B as amended by S.S.I. 2014 No. 302 (effective 16th December 2014).

Form 49.73-C[1, 2]

C1.2A.159 *Under the Divorce (Scotland) Act 1976, Section 1(1)(b)*
Simplified Procedure
Court of Session
General Department
Parliament House
Edinburgh EH1 1RQ
Tel: 0131 240 6741
APPLICATION FOR DIVORCE
ISSUE OF INTERIM GENDER RECOGNITION CERTIFICATE
Before completing this form, you should have read the leaflet entitled "Do it yourself Divorce", which explains the circumstances in which a divorce may be sought by this method. If the simplified procedure appears to suit your circumstances, you may use this form to apply for divorce.

Below you will find directions designed to assist you with your application. Please follow them carefully. In the event of difficulty, you may contact Court's General Department at the above address or any Citizen's Advice Bureau.

Directions for making Application
WRITE IN INK, USING BLOCK CAPITALS

Application	1. Complete and sign Part 1 of the form (pages 3-7), paying particular attention to the notes opposite each section.
(Part 1)	
Affidavit	2. When you have completed Part 1, you should take the form to a Justice of the Peace, Notary Public, Commissioner for Oaths or other duly authorised person so that your affidavit in Part 2 (page 8) can be completed and sworn.
Returning Completed Application Form to Court	3. When directions 1 and 2 above have been carried out, your application is now ready to be sent to the court. With it you must enclose:-

(i) your marriage certificate (the document headed "Extract of an entry in a Register of Marriages"), which will be returned to you in due course. Check the notes on page 2 to see if you also need to obtain a letter from the National Records of Scotland stating that there is no record that your spouse has divorced you;

(ii) either a cheque or postal order in respect of the court fee, crossed and made payable to "Scottish Court and Tribunal Service", or a completed form SP15, claiming exemption from the court fee;

(iii) the interim gender recognition certificate or a certified copy of it.

4. Receipt of your application will be promptly acknowledged. Should you wish to withdraw the application for any reason, please contact the Court of Session immediately.

THE NOTES ON THIS AND THE FOLLOWING PAGES ARE DESIGNED TO

---

[1] As amended by S.S.I. 2017 No. 132 para.2 (effective 1 June 2017).
[2] As amended by S.S.I. 2021 No. 75 r. 2(3)(c) (effective 1st March 2021).

ASSIST YOU. PLEASE READ THEM CAREFULLY BEFORE COMPLETING EACH SECTION OF THE FORM.

Notes on Sections 1 and 2 opposite

(i) The names entered in Sections 1 and 2 opposite must be those on your marriage certificate. If you are known by another name which does not appear on that certificate, please write that name in brackets.

(ii) Home addresses should be given where these are known. The court is required by law to serve a copy of this application on your spouse.

Note on Section 3 opposite

If the address of your spouse is NOT known or cannot reasonably be ascertained, please enter "not known" in this section; you must take all reasonable steps to find out where your spouse is living and state on a separate sheet what steps you have taken and attach it to this form then proceed to section 4.

N.B. The statement must be signed.

Notes of Section 4 opposite

In the event that the address of your spouse is unknown to you, the court is required by law to intimate a copy of this application to:

(i) ONE of the next-of-kin of your spouse. ("Next-of-kin" does not include yourself or any children of the marriage for the purposes of this application. Children of the marriage includes any adopted children, and/or children accepted into the family.)

(ii) ALL children of your marriage aged 16 years or over, whether or not they live with you.

When entering the details of the next-of-kin, if any, please state his or her relationship to your spouse (i.e. "mother", "father", "brother", "sister", etc).

If you do no know the identity or whereabouts of any of the next-of-kin of your spouse, or the whereabouts of any of the children of your marriage, please enter "not known" where appropriate.

LETTER FROM NATIONAL RECORDS OF SCOTLAND. If you do not know the address of your spouse and you were married in Scotland, you must obtain a letter from the National Records of Scotland stating that there is no record that your spouse has divorced you. The letter must be issued not more than one month before the date of posting this application to the Court. If you require to obtain a letter you should apply to:

National Records of Scotland, Registration Branch, New Register House, Edinburgh, EH1 3YT,

stating both spouses' full names, the date and place of your marriage and requesting that a search be made to confirm that there is no record that your spouse has divorced you. (Note - a fee will be charged for this service.)

The requirement to obtain a letter from National Records of Scotland does not apply if you were married outwith Scotland.

PART 1

WRITE IN INK USING BLOCK CAPITALS

1. NAME AND ADDRESS OF APPLICANT

Surname..............   *Other name(s)*..............

Present Address   in full

....

....
....

Daytime telephone number (if any)

....
....

2. NAME OF SPOUSE

Surname...............   Other name(s)...............

....

3. ADDRESS OF SPOUSE (if the address of your spouse is not known, please enter "not known" in this section and proceed to section 4)

Present Address

....
....

Daytime telephone number (if any)

....
....

4. Only complete this section if you do not know the present address of your spouse

NEXT-OF-KIN

Name

....

Address...............

Relationship to your spouse

....
....
....

CHILDREN OF THE MARRIAGE

Names and dates of birth   Address

....
....
....
....
....
....
....
....

If sufficient space is not available here to list all the children of the marriage, please continue on separate sheet and attach to this form

Note on Section 5 opposite

"Domiciled" means that the person concerned regards Scotland and his/her permanent home and intends to live permanently in Scotland in the foreseeable future.

Notes on Section 6 opposite

You will be able to obtain these details from your marriage certificate, which must accompany this application form when you send it to the court.

A photocopy of the marriage certificate will NOT be accepted. If you cannot find the original, you should apply for an official copy to:

> General Register Office (Scotland), Registration Section, New Register House, Edinburgh EH1 3YT
>> in writing, or by e-mailing the form at
>> *http://www.gro-scotland.gov.uk/contacts/contact-form.html* or
>> the office where the marriage was registered,

stating both husband's and wife's full names, and date and place of marriage. (Note that the Registrar will charge a fee for this service.)

5. JURISDICTION

Please indicate with a tick (✔) in the appropriate box or boxes which of the following apply:

(i)	I am domiciled in Scotland on the date I signed this application	☐
(ii)	My spouse is domiciled in Scotland on the date I signed this application	☐
(iii)	I was habitually resident in Scotland throughout the period of one year ending with the date I signed this application	☐
(iv)	My spouse was habitually resident in Scotland throughout the period of one year ending with the date I signed this application	☐

6. DETAILS OF PRESENT MARRIAGE

Place of marriage   ....
(Registration
District)
Date of marriage: Day ....   Month ....   Year ....

Notes on Section 7 opposite

You will be able to obtain the details required at (ii) from the interim gender recognition certificate which must accompany this application form, when you send it to the Court.

A photocopy of the interim gender recognition certificate will NOT be accepted.

If the principal interim gender recognition certificate is not available, a copy certified by the Gender Recognition Panel should be lodged instead. This can be obtained from the Gender Recognition Panel at PO Box 6987, Leicester, LE1 6ZX, or at *http://www.grp.gov.uk*

Note on Section 9 opposite

"Children of the marriage" includes any adopted children and/or children accepted into the family.

Notes on Section 11 opposite

No claim can be made in this form of divorce application for payment to you of a periodical allowance (i.e. regular payment of money weekly, monthly etc for your maintenance) or a capital sum (i.e. lump sum). If you wish to make such a claim, you should consult a solicitor.

NOTE: While it may be possible to obtain an order for periodical allowance after divorce, the right to payment of a capital sum is lost once decree of divorce is granted.

No application can be made in this form of divorce application for postponement of decree under section 3A of the Divorce (Scotland) Act 1976. On an application under that section, the court may postpone the grant of decree of divorce if it is satisfied that:

(a)　the applicant is prevented from entering into a religious marriage by virtue of a requirement of that religion of that marriage; and

(b)　the other party can act so as to remove or enable or contribute to the removal of, the impediment which prevents that marriage.

As at 26th February 2007 "religious marriage" for the purposes of section 3A of the Divorce (Scotland) Act 1976 means a marriage solemnised by a celebrant of any Hebrew congregation (i.e. a Jewish marriage) (S.S.I. 2006/253).

If you wish to make such an application you should consult a solicitor or Citizens' Advice Bureau.

7. DETAILS OF ISSUE OF INTERIM GENDER RECOGNITION CERTIFICATE

(i)　Please state whether the interim gender recognition certificate has been issued to you or your spouse ....

(ii)　Please state the date the interim gender recognition certificate was is- Day ....　　Month ....　Year ....
sued

Please answer the following question *only* if the interim gender recognition certificate was issued to you-

(iii)　Has the Gender Recognition Panel issued you with a full

YES　☐　　　　　　　　　　NO　☐

gender recognition certificate?

Please answer the following question *only* if the interim gender recognition certificate was issued to your spouse-

(iv)　Since the date referred to in question (ii), have you made a YES statutory declaration consenting to the marriage continuing?

YES　☐　　　　　　　　　　NO　☐

8. MENTAL DISORDER

As far as you are aware does your spouse have any mental disorder (whether mental illness, personality disorder or learning disability) (*Tick box which applies*)
(If yes, give details below)

YES　☐　　　　　　　　　　NO　☐

9. CHILDREN

Are there any children of the marriage under the age of 16?)
(*Tick box which applies*)

YES　☐　　　　　　　　　　NO　☐

10. OTHER COURT ACTIONS

Are you aware of any court actions currently proceeding in any country (including YES ☐ NO ☐ Scotland) which may affect your marriage
(*Tick box which applies*)
(If yes, give details)

11. DECLARATION AND REQUEST FOR DIVORCE

I confirm that the facts stated in Sections 1 – 10 above apply to my marriage.

I do *NOT* ask the Court to make any financial award in connection with this application.

I do not ask the court to postpone the grant of decree under section 3A of the Divorce (Scotland) Act 1976.

I request the Court to grant decree of divorce from my spouse.

(Date)   (Signature of
                                                                              applicant)

....

....

PART 2
SPC
APPLICANT'S AFFIDAVIT
To be completed by the Applicant only after Part 1 has been signed and dated

I, (*insert Applicant's full name*)

....

residing at (*insert Applicant's present*

....

home address)

            Town

....

            Country..................

SWEAR that to the best of my knowledge and belief the facts stated in Part 1 of this Application are true.

Signature of applicant

....

To be completed by Justice of the   SWORN at (*place*)

....

Peace, Notary Public, or Commissioner for   this .... day of
Oaths

..........20..........

                                                         before me (*full name*)

....

                                                         (*full address*)

....

....

....

Signature

....

*Justice of the Peace/*Notary Public/*Commissioner for Oaths

*Delete where not applicable

Form 49.73C as amended by S.S.I. 2014 No. 302 (effective 16th December 2014).

Form 49.76-A

C1.2A.159A
Form of citation in simplified divorce application under section 1(2)(d) of the Divorce (Scotland) Act 1976

CITATION

Date: (*Date of posting or other method of service*)

TO: ....
 ....
 ....

APPLICATION FOR DIVORCE (WITH CONSENT OF OTHER PARTY TO THE MARRIAGE), SPOUSES HAVING LIVED APART FOR AT LEAST ONE YEAR

You are hereby served with an application by your spouse which asks the court to grant a decree of divorce.

If you wish to oppose the granting of such a decree, you should put your reasons in writing and send your letter to the address shown below. Your letter must reach the court by (*insert date on which period of notice expires*).

(*Signed*)
Deputy Principal Clerk of Session
[*or* authorised clerk of session]
[*or* Messenger-at-Arms
(*Address*)]

IMPORTANT NOTE. If you wish to exercise your right to claim a financial award, or if you wish to apply for postponement of decree under section 3A of the Divorce (Scotland) Act 1976 (postponement of decree of divorce where impediment to religious remarriage exists), you should immediately advise the court that you oppose the application for that reason, and thereafter consult a solicitor.

Court of Session
General Department
Parliament House
Edinburgh EH1 1RQ
Tel: 0131-240 6741
Form 49.76A as amended by S.S.I. 2014 No. 302 (effective 16th December 2014).

Form 49.76-B

C1.2A.160
Form of citation in simplified divorce application under section 1(2)(e) of the Divorce (Scotland) Act 1976

CITATION

Date: (*Date of posting or other method of service*)

TO: ....
 ....

....

APPLICATION FOR DIVORCE, SPOUSES HAVING LIVED APART FOR AT LEAST TWO YEARS

Your spouse has applied to the court for divorce on the ground that the marriage has broken down irretrievably because you and (s)he have lived apart for a period of at least two years.

A copy of the application is hereby served on you.

1. Please note:-
    (a) that the court may not make a financial award under this procedure and that your spouse is making no claim against you for payment of a periodical allowance (i.e. regular payment of money weekly, monthly, etc., for his [*or* her] maintenance) or a capital sum (i.e. lump sum);
    (b) that no application may be made under this procedure for postponement of decree under section 3A of the Divorce (Scotland) Act 1976 (postponement of decree where impediment to religious remarriage exists).
2. Divorce may result in the loss to you of property rights (e.g. the right to succeed to the applicant's estate on his/her death) or the right, where appropriate, to a widow's pension.
3. If you wish to oppose the granting of a divorce, you should put your reasons in writing and send your letter to the address shown below. Your letter must reach the court by (*insert date on which period of time expires*).
4. In the event of the divorce being granted, you will be sent a copy of the extract decree. (Should you change your address before receiving the copy extract decree, please notify the court immediately.)

(*Signed*)
Deputy Principal Clerk of Session
[*or* authorised clerk of session]
[*or* Messenger-at-Arms
(*Address*)]

IMPORTANT NOTE. If you wish to exercise your right to claim a financial award, or if you wish to apply for postponement of decree under section 3A of the Divorce (Scotland) Act 1976 (postponement of decree of divorce where impediment to religious remarriage exists), you should immediately advise the court that you oppose the application for that reason, and thereafter consult a solicitor.

Court of Session
General Department
Parliament House
Edinburgh EH1 1RQ
Tel: 0131-240 6741
Form 49.76B as amended by S.S.I. 2014 No. 302 (effective 16th December 2014).

Form 49.76-BA

Form of citation in simplified divorce application under section 1(1)(b) of the C1.2A.161
Divorce (Scotland) Act 1976
CITATION
Date: (*Date of posting or other method of service*)

TO: ....
....
....

APPLICATION FOR DIVORCE, INTERIM GENDER RECOGNITION CERTIFI-CATE ISSUED TO SPOUSE AFTER MARRAIGE

Your spouse has applied to the court for divorce on the ground that an interim gender recognition certificate has been issued to you or your spouse after your marriage.

A copy of the application is hereby served on you.

1. Please note that the court may not make a financial award under this procedure and that your spouse is making no claim against you for payment of a periodical allowance (i.e. regular payment of money weekly, monthly, etc., for his [*or* her] maintenance) or a capital sum (i.e. lump sum);

2. Dissolution of your marriage may result in the loss to you of property rights (e.g. the right to succeed to the applicant's estate on his/her death) or the right, where appropriate, to a pension.

2A Please note that no application may be made under this procedure for postpone-ment of decree under section 3A of the Divorce (Scotland) Act 1976 (postpone-ment of decree where impediment to religious remarriage exists).

3. If you wish to oppose the granting of a divorce, you should put your reasons in writing and send your letter to the address shown below. Your letter must reach the court by (*insert date on which period of time expires*).

4. In the event of the divorce being granted, you will be sent a copy of the extract decree. (Should you change your address before receiving the copy extract decree, please notify the court immediately.)

(*Signed*)
Deputy Principal Clerk of Session
[*or* authorised clerk of session]
[*or* Messenger-at-Arms
(*Address*)]

IMPORTANT NOTE. If you wish to exercise your right to claim a financial award, or if you wish to apply for postponement of decree under section 3A of the Divorce (Scotland) Act 1976 (postponement of decree of divorce where impediment to religious remarriage exists), you should immediately advise the court that you op-pose the application for that reason, and thereafter consult a solicitor.

Court of Session
Divorce Section (SP)
Parliament House
Edinburgh EH1 1RQ
Tel: 0131-225-2595
Form 49.76BA as amended by S.S.I. 2014 No. 302 (effective 16th December 2014).

Form 49.76-C

C1.2A.162   *Form of intimation to child or next of kin in simplified divorce application under section 1(2)(e) or 1(b) of the Divorce (Scotland) Act 1976*

CITATION

Date: (*Date of posting or other method of intimation*)

TO:　　..............

　　　　..............

　　　　..............

APPLICATION FOR DIVORCE, SPOUSES HAVING LIVED APART FOR AT LEAST TWO YEARS OR ISSUE OF INTERIM GENDER RECOGNITION CERTIFI- CATE AFTER REGISTRATION OF THE CIVIL PARTNERSHIP

..........(Applicant)　　　　　v　　　..........(Respondent)

TAKE NOTICE

1. In the above application, a copy of which is enclosed, the applicant has indicated that you are the (*state relationship*) of (*name of respondent*) whose present address is not known to the applicant.

2. Should you know the present address of your (*state relationship*) or how he [*or* she] may be contacted, you are requested to give this information at once in writing to:-

    Court of Session
    General Department (SP)
    Parliament House
    Edinburgh EH1 1RQ
    Tel: 0131 240 6741

    This will enable the court to inform the respondent that the application has been made.

3. If you are unable to provide the above information, and/or you wish for your own interest to oppose the application for divorce, you should write to the above address by (*insert date on which period of time expires*).

　　　　　　　　　　　　　　(*Signed*)
　　　　　　　　　　　　　　Deputy Principal Clerk of Session
　　　　　　　　　　　　　　[*or* authorised clerk of session]
　　　　　　　　　　　　　　[*or* Messenger-at-Arms
　　　　　　　　　　　　　　(*Address*)]

Form 49.76C as amended by S.S.I. 2014 No. 302 (effective 16th December 2014).

APPENDIX

Form 49.76-D

C1.2A.164   Rule 49.76(5)

Rule 49.76(5)   FORM 49.76–D

Form of certificate of service of simplified divorce application

CERTIFICATE OF SERVICE [*or* INTIMATION]

I, (*name*), Deputy Principal Clerk of Session [*or clerk of session authorised by him*], certify that I served [*or* intimated] this simplified divorce application by (*name of applicant*) on [*or* to] (*name of person on whom service executed or to whom intimation given*) by posting it with a citation [*or* notice of intimation] in Form (*number of form*) to that person between (*time*) and (*time*) or (*date*) at (*name of post office*) in a registered envelope [*or* recorded delivery envelope] addressed as follows:— (*address*). The Post Office receipt [*or* certificate of posting] is attached to this certificate.

(*Signed*)

Deputy Principal Clerk of Session
[*or* authorised clerk of session]
[*or* Messenger-at-Arms
(*Address*)]

(*Signed*)

Witness]

Form 49.76-E

Rule 49.76(5)

Rule 49.76(5)　　　　　Form 49.76–E

Form of certificate of service of simplified divorce application by messenger-at-arms

CERTIFICATE OF SERVICE [*OR* INTIMATION]

I, (*name*), Messenger-at-Arms, certify that I served [*or* intimated] this simplified divorce application [and a notice of intimation] on [*or* to] (*name of person on whom served or to whom intimated*)—

* by leaving it and a citation [*or* notice] with (*name of person*) at (*place*) at (*time*) or (*date*).

* by leaving it and a citation [*or* notice] with (*name and occupation of person with whom left*) at (*place*) on (*date*). (*Specify that enquiry made and that reasonable grounds exist for believing that the person on whom service is to be made or to whom intimation is to be given resides at the place but is not available.*)

* by depositing it and a citation [*or* notice] in (*place*) on (*date*). (*Specify that enquiry made and that reasonable grounds exist for believing that the person on whom service is to be made or to whom intimation is to be given resides at the place but is not available.*)

* by leaving it and a citation [*or* notice] with (*name and occupation of person with whom left*) at (*place of business*) on (*date*). (*Specify that enquiry made and that reasonable grounds exist for believing that the person on whom service is to be made or to whom intimation is to be given carries on business at the place.*)

* by depositing it and a citation [*or* notice] at (*place of business*) on (*date*). (*Specify that enquiry made and that reasonable grounds exist for believing that the person on whom service is to be made or to whom intimation is to be given carries on business at the place.*)

* by leaving it and a citation [*or* notice] at (*registered office or place of business*) on (*date*), in the hands of (*name of person*).

* by leaving [*or* depositing] it and a citation [*or* notice] at (*registered office, official address or place of business*) on (*date*) in such a way that it was likely to come to the attention of (*name of person on whom served or to whom intimated*). (*Specify how left.*)

I did this in the presence of (*name, occupation and address of witness*).

　　　　　　　　　　　　　　(*Signed*)

　　　　　　　　　　　　　　Messenger-at-Arms
　　　　　　　　　　　　　　(*Address*)]

　　　　　　　　　　　　　　(*Signed*)

　　　　　　　　　　　　　　Witness

* Delete where not applicable.

Form 49.80B-A (SPD)[1, 2]

C1.2A.166   Rule 49.80B(1)

**Form of simplified dissolution of civil partnership application under
Section 117(3)(c) of the Civil Partnership Act 2004**

Court of Session
General Department
Parliament House
Edinburgh EH1 1RQ

Tel: 0131 240 6741

**APPLICATION FOR DISSOLUTION OF A CIVIL PARTNERSHIP WITH CONSENT OF
OTHER PARTY TO THE CIVIL PARTNERSHIP (CIVIL PARTNERS HAVING LIVED
APART FOR AT LEAST ONE YEAR)**

Before completing this form, you should have read the leaflet entitled "Do it yourself Dissolution",
which explains the circumstances in which a dissolution of a civil partnership may be sought by
this method. If simplified procedure appears to suit your circumstances, you may use this form to
apply for dissolution of your civil partnership.

Below you will find directions designed to assist you with your application.

Please follow them carefully. In the event of difficulty, you may contact the Court's General
Department at the above address or any Citizen's Advice Bureau.

Directions for making Application

WRITE IN INK, USING BLOCK CAPITALS

Application (Part 1)	1. Complete and sign Part 1 of the form (pages 3-7), paying particular attention to the notes opposite each section.
Consent of civil partner (Part 2)	2. When you have filled in Part 1 of the form, send the form to your civil partner for completion of the consent at Part 2 (page 9).

**NOTE: If your civil partner does NOT complete and sign the form of consent, your
application cannot proceed further under the simplified procedure. In that event, if you still
wish to obtain a dissolution of your civil partnership, you should consult a solicitor.**

Affidavit (Part 3)	3. When the application has been returned to you with the Consent (Part 2) duly completed and signed, you should take the form to a Justice of the Peace, Notary Public, Commissioner for Oaths or other duly authorised person so that your affidavit in Part 3 (page 10) may be completed and sworn.
Returning completed Application Form to Court	4. When directions 1-3 above have all been carried out, your application is now ready to be sent to the Court. With it you must enclose:

    (i)   an extract of the registration of your civil partnership in the civil partnership register
(the document headed "Extract of an entry in the Register of Civil Partnerships", which will
be returned to you in due course, or an equivalent document, and

    (ii)   either a cheque or postal order in respect of the court fee, crossed and made payable to
"Scottish Court and Tribunal Service", or a completed form SP15 claiming exemption from
the Court fee.

    5. Receipt of your application will be promptly acknowledged. Should you wish to withdraw
the application for any reason, please contact the Court immediately.

---

[1] As amended by S.S.I. 2017 No. 132 para.2 (effective 1 June 2017).
[2] As amended by S.S.I. 2021 No. 75 r. 2(3)(d) (effective 1st March 2021).

**THE NOTES ON THIS AND THE FOLLOWING PAGES ARE DESIGNED TO ASSIST YOU.
PLEASE READ THEM CAREFULLY BEFORE COMPLETING EACH SECTION OF THE FORM.**

Notes on Sections 1 and 2 opposite

(i)   The names entered in Sections 1 and 2 opposite must be those shown on your extract of registration of civil partnership. If you are known by another name which does not appear on that extract, please write the name in brackets.

(ii) The surname given for a female partner must be her maiden name. Any names from previous marriages should be entered in the space for other names.

(iii) Home address should be given where these are known. The Court is required by law to serve a copy of this application on your civil partner.

Notes on Section 3 opposite

"Domiciled" means that the person concerned at Item (i) or (ii) opposite regards Scotland as his/her permanent home and intends to live permanently in Scotland in the foreseeable future.

WRITE IN INK USING BLOCK CAPITALS
1. NAME AND ADDRESS OF APPLICANT

Surname   Other name(s) in full

Present Address

                                 Daytime telephone number (if any)

2. NAME AND ADDRESS OF CIVIL PARTNER

Surname _____   Other name(s) in full _____

Present Address _____

_____

Daytime telephone number (if any)

_____

3. JURISDICTION

Please indicate with a tick (✔) in the appropriate box or boxes which of the following apply:

PART A

(i)   I am domiciled in Scotland on the date I signed this application   ☐

(ii)   My civil partner is domiciled in Scotland on the date I signed   ☐
       this application

(iii) I was habitually resident in Scotland throughout the period of   ☐
       one year ending with the date I signed this application

(iv)   My civil partner was habitually resident in Scotland   ☐
       throughout the period of one year ending with the date I signed
       this application

If you have ticked one of the boxes in Part A, you do not have to complete Part B. You should complete Part B if you have not ticked any of the boxes in Part A.

PART B

(i)   My civil partner and I are registered as civil partners of each   ☐
       other in Scotland

AND

(ii)   No court has, or is recognised as having, jurisdiction   ☐

AND

(iii) It is in the interests of justice for the Court of Session to as-   ☐
       sume jurisdiction in the case
       (Please give reasons below)

Notes on Section 4 opposite

You will be able to obtain these details from your extract of registration of civil partnership which must accompany this application form, when you send it to the Court.

A photocopy of the extract of registration of civil partnership will NOT be accepted. If you cannot find the original, you should apply for an officila copy to:

National Records of Scotland, Registration Section, New Register House, Edinburgh EH1 3YT, or the office where the civil partnership was registered,

stating both civil partner's full names, and the date and place of registration of the civil partnership.

(Note that the Registrar will charge a fee for this service.)

Notes of Section 5 opposite

You and your civil partner must have lived apart from each other for a continuous period of at least one year after the date of the registration of your civil partnership and immediately before the date of this application.

This minimum period of one year's separation is extended if you and your civil partner have lived together again for *not more than six months in all* during that year period. For example, if you lived together for three months in total during the one year period, then you should not complete this application until one year and three months have elapsed from the date of your original separation.

Notes on Section 6 opposite

Is there a reasonable chance that you can still settle the differences with your civil partner and resume a normal family life?

Are you satisfied that there is now no possibility of the civil partnership succeeding?

Notes on Section 7 opposite

If your civil partner is not prepared to sign the form of consent at Part 2 of this application, you will not obtain a dissolution of your civil partnership by this method.

PART 1 (continued)

PART C

(i)   My civil partner and I are registered civil partners of each other in Scotland

AND

(ii) No court has, or is recognised as having, jurisdiction under regulations made under Section 219 of the Civil Partnership Act 2004

AND

(iii) It is in the interests of justice for the Court of Session to assume jurisdiction in the case. (Please give reasons below)

4. DETAILS OF PRESENT CIVIL PARTNERSHIP

Place of Registration of Civil Partnership _____ (Registration District)

Date of Registration of Civil Partnership: Day _____ Month _____ Year _____

5. PERIOD OF SEPARATION

(i)   Please state the date on which you ceased to live with your civil partner. (If more than 1 year, just give the month and year.)

Day _____   Month _____   Year _____

(ii) Have you lived with your civil partner since that date? (*Tick box which applies*)   YES [   ]   NO [   ]

(iii) If yes, for how long in total did you live together before finally separating again? _____ months

6. RECONCILIATION

Is there any reasonable prospect of reconciliation with your civil partner? (*Tick box which applies*)   YES [   ]   NO [   ]

Do you consider that the civil partnership has broken down irretrievably? (*Tick box which applies*)   YES [   ]   NO [   ]

7. CONSENT

Does your civil partner consent to a dissolution of the civil partnership being granted? (*Tick box which applies*)   YES [   ]   NO [   ]

Note on Section 9 opposite

Children of the marriage includes children accepted into the family.

Notes on Section 11 opposite

No claim can be made in this form of dissolution application for payment to you of a periodical allowance (*i.e.* regular payment of money, weekly, monthly, etc., for your maintenance) or a capital sum (*i.e.* lump sum). If you wish to make such a claim, you should consult a solicitor.

NOTE: While it may be possible to obtain an order for periodical allowance after dissolution of a civil partnership, the right to payment of a capital sum is lost once decree of dissolution is granted.

PART 1 (continued)

---

8. MENTAL DISORDER

As far as you are aware, does your civil partner have any
mental disorder? (whether mental illness, personality
disorder or learning disability)
(*Tick box which applies*)

YES ☐   NO ☐

(If yes, give details)

---

9. CHILDREN

Are there any children of the family under the age of 16?
(*Tick box which applies*)

YES ☐   NO ☐

---

10. OTHER COURT ACTIONS

Are you aware of any court actions currently proceeding
in any country (including Scotland) which may affect your
civil partnership? (*Tick box which applies*)

YES ☐   NO ☐

(If yes, give details)

---

11. REQUEST FOR DISSOLUTION OF THE CIVIL PARTNERSHIP AND DISCLAIMER OF FINANCIAL PROVISION

I confirm that the facts stated in Sections 1 – 10 above apply to my civil partnership.

I do **NOT** ask the Court to make any financial awards in connection with this application.

I request the Court to grant decree of dissolution of my civil partnership.

(Date) _____   (Signature of applicant) _____

IMPORTANT

Part 1 MUST be completed, signed and dated before sending the application form to your civil partner.
NOTES ON COMPLETING PART 2 OPPOSITE (PAGE 9)

1. Read over carefully PART 1 (pages 3-7) of this application, which has already been completed by your civil partner.

2. **Financial Provisions**

Please note that in Section 11 of Part 1, the Applicant states that he/she does NOT claim any financial awards by way of periodical allowance or capital sum. You also are required to state (items (c) and (d) opposite) that you make no claim upon the Applicant for payment of a periodical allowance or capital sum.

Note: While it may be possible to obtain an order for periodical allowance after dissolution of a civil partnership, the right to payment of a capital sum is lost once decree of dissolution is granted.

3. **Warning**

Dissolution of your civil partnership may result in the loss to you of property rights (e.g. the right to succeed to the Applicant's estate on his/her death) or the right, where appropriate, to a pension.

(If you are in doubt about signing this form of consent, you should consult a solicitor.)

Once your civil partner has completed the remainder of the form and has submitted it to the Court, a copy of the whole application (including your consent) will later by served upon you formally by the Court.

In the event of the dissolution of the civil partnership being granted, you will automatically be sent a copy of the extract decree. (Should you change your address before receiving the copy extract decree, please notify the Court immediately.)

If you do NOT wish to consent, please return the application form, with Part 2 uncompleted, to your civil partner and advise him or her of your decision.

The Court will NOT grant a dissolution of the civil partnership on this application if Part 2 of the form is not completed by you.

PART 2

CONSENT BY APPLICANT'S CIVIL PARTNER TO DISSOLUTION OF CIVIL PARTNERSHIP

NOTE: Before completing this part of the form, please read the notes opposite (page 8).

I _____

(Full names, in **BLOCK** letters, of Applicant's civil partner)

residing at

_____

(Address, also in **BLOCK** letters)

HEREBY STATE THAT

    (a) I have read Part 1 of this application;

    (b) the Applicant has lived apart from me for a continuous period of 1 year immediately preceding the date of the application;

    (c) I do not ask the Court to make any order for payment to me by the Applicant of a periodical allowance (*i.e.* a regular payment of money weekly or monthly, etc., for maintenance);

    (d) I do not ask the Court to make any order for payment to me by the Applicant of a capital sum (*i.e.* a lump sum payment);

    (e) I understand that dissolution of my civil partnership may result in the loss to me of property rights; and

    (f) **I CONSENT TO DECREE OF DISSOLUTION BEING GRANTED IN RESPECT OF THIS APPLICATION.**

(Date) _____   (Signature) _____

NOTE: You may withdraw your consent, even after giving it, at any time before dissolution of the civil partnership is granted by the Court. Should you wish to do so, you must immediately advise:

The Court of Session
General Department
Parliament House
Edinburgh EH1 1RQ

Tel: 0131 240 6741

PART 3

APPLICANT'S AFFIDAVIT

To be completed only after Parts 1 and 2 have been signed and dated.

I, (insert Applicant's full name) _____

residing at (insert Applicant's present _____
home address)

Town _____

Country _____

SWEAR that to the best of my knowledge and belief:

(1) the facts stated in Part 1 of this Application are true; and

(2) the signature in Part 2 of this Application is that of my civil partner.

Signature of applicant _____

To be completed by Justice of the Peace,   SWORN at (insert place) _____
Notary Public, or Commissioner for
Oaths   this _____ day off _____ 20____

before me (insert full name) _____

(insert full address) _____

Signature _____

*Justice of the Peace/*Notary Public/*Commissioner for Oaths

* Delete where not applicable

Form 49.80B-B (SPE)[1, 2]

Rule 49.80B(2)   **C1.2A.167**

Form of simplified dissolution of civil partnership application under Section 117(3)(d) of the Civil Partnership Act 2004

Court of Session

General Department

---

[1] As amended by S.S.I. 2017 No. 132 para.2 (effective 1 June 2017).
[2] As amended by S.S.I. 2021 No. 75 r. 2(3)(e) (effective 1st March 2021).

Parliament House
Edinburgh EH1 1RQ
Tel: 0131 240 6741

APPLICATION FOR DISSOLUTION OF A CIVIL PARTNERSHIP
(CIVIL PARTNERS HAVING LIVED APART FOR AT LEAST TWO YEARS)

Before completing this form, you should have read the leaflet entitled "Do it yourself dissolution", which explains the circumstances in which a dissolution of a civil partnership may be sought by this method. If simplified procedure appears to suit your circumstances, you may use this form to apply for dissolution of your civil partnership.

Below you will find directions designed to assist you with your application.

Please follow them carefully. In the event of difficulty, you may contact the Court's General Department at the above address or any Citizen's Advice Bureau.

Directions for making Application

WRITE IN INK, USING BLOCK CAPITALS

Application (Part 1)

1. Complete and sign Part 1 of the form (pages 3-7), paying particular attention to the notes opposite each section.

Affidavit (Part 2)

2. When you have completed Part 1 of the form, you should take the form to a Justice of the Peace, Notary Public, Commissioner for Oaths or other duly authorised person so that your affidavit in Part 2 (page 8) can be completed and sworn.

Returning Completed Application Form to Court

3. When directions 1 and 2 above have been carried out, your application is now ready to be sent to the court. With it you must enclose:
    (i)   an extract of the registration of your civil partnership in the civil partnership register (the document headed "Extract of an entry in the Register of Civil Partnerships", which will be returned to you in due course) or an equivalent document. Check the Notes on page 2 to see if you also need to obtain a letter from National Records of Scotland stating that there is no record of your civil partner having dissolved the civil partnership; and
    (ii) Either a cheque or postal order in respect of the court fee, crossed and made payable to "Scottish Court and Tribunal Service", or a completed form SP15 claiming exemption from the Court fee.

4. Receipt of your application will be promptly acknowledged. Should you wish to withdraw the application for any reason, please contact the Court immediately.

THE NOTES ON THIS AND THE FOLLOWING PAGES ARE DESIGNED TO ASSIST YOU.

PLEASE READ THEM ACREFULLY BEFORE COMPLETING EACH SECTION OF THE FORM.

Notes on Sections 1 and 2 opposite

(i)   The names entered in sections 1 and 2 opposite must be those shown on your extract of the registration of civil partnership. If you are known by another name which does not appear on that extract, please write that name in brackets.

(ii)   The surname given for a female partner must be her maiden name. Any names from previous marriages should be entered in the space for other names.

(iii)   Home address should be given where these are known. The Court is required by law to serve a copy of this application on your civil partner.

Note on Section 3 opposite

If the address of your civil partner is NOT known or cannot reasonably be ascertained, please enter "not known" in this section; you must take all reasonable steps to find out where your civil partner is living and state on a separate sheet what steps you have taken and attach it to this form, then proceed to section 4.

N.B. The statement must be signed.

Notes of Section 4 oppposite

In the event that the address of your civil partner is unknown to you, the Court is required by law to intimate a copy of this application to:

(i)   ONE of the next-of-kin of your civil partner. ("Next-of-kin" does not include yourself or any children of the family for the purposes of this application.)

(ii)   All children of the family aged 16 years or over, whether or not they live with you. ("Children of the family" includes any adopted children, and/or children accepted into the family).

When entering the details of next-of-kin, if any, please state his and her relationship to your civil partner (i.e. "mother", "father", "brother", "sister", etc).

If you do not know the identity or whereabouts of any of the next-of-kin of your civil partner, or the whereabouts of any of the children of the family, please enter "not known" where appropriate.

LETTER FROM NATIONAL RECORDS OF SCOTLAND. If you do not know the address of your civil partner and your civil partnership was registered in Scotland, you must obatin a letter from the National Records of Scotland stating that there is no record that your civil partner has had the civil partnership dissolved. The letter must be issued not more than one month before the date of posting this application to the court. If you require to obtain a letter you should apply to:

National Records of Scotland, Registration Branch, New Register House, Edinburgh EH1 3YT,

stating both civil partners' full names, the date and place of registration of your civil partnership and requesting that a search be made to confirm that there is no record that your civil partner has had the civil partnership dissolved. (Note - a fee will be charged for this service.)

The requirement to obtain a letter from the National Records of Scotland does not apply if your civil partnership was registered outwith Scotland.

PART 1

WRITE IN INK USING BLOCK CAPITALS

1. NAME AND ADDRESS OF APPLICANT

Surname _____ Other name(s) _____

Present Address _____ in full

_____

_____ Daytime telephone number (if any)

2. NAME OF CIVIL PARTNER

Surname _____ Other name(s) _____

_____

3. ADDRESS OF CIVIL PARTNER (if the address of your civil partner is not known, please enter "not known" in this section and proceed to section 4)

Present Address _____

_____ Daytime telephone number (if any)

4. Only complete this section if you do not know the present address of your civil partner

NEXT-OF-KIN

Name _____

Address _____

Relationship to your civil partner _____

CHILDREN OF THE FAMILY

Names and dates of birth

Address _____

_____

_____

If sufficient space is not available here to list all the children of the family, please continue on separate sheet and attach to this form

Note on Section 5 opposite

"Domiciled" means that the person concerned at Item (i) or (iii) opposite regards Scotland and his/her permanent home and intends to live permanently in Scotland in the foreseeable future.

Notes on Section 6 opposite

You will be able to obtain these details from the extract of the registration of your civil partnership (Extract of an entry in the register of civil partnerships) which must accompany this application form, when you send it to the Court.

A photocopy of the civil partnership registration certificate will NOT be accepted. If you cannot find the original, you should apply for an official copy to:

> General Register Office (Scotland), Registration Section, New Register House, Edinburgh EH1 3YT or the office where the civil partnership was registered, in writing,

> or by e-mailing the form at http://www.gro-scotland.gov.uk/contacts/contact-form.html or

stating both civil partner's full names, and date and place of registration of civil partnership.

(Note that the Registrar will charge a fee for this service.)

Notes on Section 7 opposite

You and your civil partner must have lived apart from each other for a continuous period of at least 2 years after the date of registration of your civil partnership and immediately before the date of this application. This minimum period of 2 years separation is extended if you and your civil partner have lived together again for **not more than 6 months in all** during that 2 year period. For example, you lived together for 3 months in total during the 2 year period, then you should not complete this application until 2 years and 3 months have elapsed from the date of your original separation.

5. JURISDICTION

Please indicate with a tick ($\checkmark$) in the appropriate box or boxes which of the following apply:

PART A

(i)   I am domiciled in Scotland on the date I signed this application ☐

1537

(ii)   My civil partner is domiciled in Scotland on the date I signed   ☐
this application

(iii)   I was habitually resident in Scotland throughout the period of   ☐
one year ending with the date I signed this application

(iv)   My civil partner was habitually resident in Scotland   ☐
throughout the period of one year ending with the date I signed
this application

*If you have ticked one of the boxes in Part A, you do not have to complete Part B.
You should complete Part B if you have not ticked any of the boxes in Part A.*

PART B

(i)   My civil partner and I are registered as civil partners of each   ☐
other in Scotland

AND

(ii)   No court has, or is recognised as having, jurisdiction   ☐

AND

(iii)   It is in the interests of justice for the Court of Session to as-   ☐
sume jurisdiction in the case

(Please give reasons below)

6. DETAILS OF PRESENT CIVIL PARTNERSHIP

Place of registration of Civil Partnership .... (Registration District)
Date of registration of Civil Partnership Day .... Month .... Year ....

PERIOD OF SEPARATION

(i) Please state the date on which ypu ceased to live with your civil partner. (If
more than 2½ years, just give the month and year)

                             Day ....   Month ....   Year ....

(ii) Have you lived with ypur civil partner since   YES ☐   NO ☐
that date? (*Tick box which applies*)

(iii) If yes, for how long did you live together   ....
before finally separating again?   months

Notes on Section 8 opposite

Is there a reasonable chance that you can still settle the differences with your civil partner and resume normally family life?

Are you satisfied that there is now no possibility of the civil partnership succeeding?

Note on Section 10 opposite

'Children of the family' includes any children accepted into the family.

Notes on Section 12 opposite

No claim can be made in this form of dissolution application for payment to you of a periodical allowance (i.e. regular payment of money, weekly, monthly, etc., for your maintenance) or a capital sum (i.e. lump sum). If you wish to make such a claim, you should consult a solicitor.

NOTE: While it may be possible to obtain an order for periodical allowance after dissolution of your civil partnership, the right to payment of a capital sum is lost once decree of dissolution is granted.

8. RECONCILIATION

Is there any reasonable prospect of reconciliation with your civil partner? (*Tick box which applies*)   YES ☐   NO ☐

Do you consider that the civil partnership has broken down irretrievably? (*Tick box which applies*)   YES ☐   NO ☐

9. MENTAL DISORDER

As far as you are aware does your civil partner have any mental disorder? (whether mental illness, personality disorder or learning disability) (*Tick box which applies*)   YES ☐   NO ☐

(If yes, give details below)

10. CHILDREN

Are there any children of the family under the age of 16? (*Tick box which applies*)   YES ☐   NO ☐

11. OTHER COURT ACTIONS

Are you aware of any court actions currently proceeding in any country (including Scotland) which may affect your civil partnership? (*Tick box which applies*)   YES ☐   NO ☐

(If yes, give details)

12. DECLARATION AND REQUEST FOR DISSOLUTION OF CIVIL PARTNERSHIP

I confirm that the facts stated in Sections 1-11 above apply to my civil partnership.

I do **NOT** ask the Court to make any financial award in connection with this application.

I request the Court to grant decree of dissolution from my civil partnership.

(Date) _____   (Signature of applicant) _____

PART 2

APPLICANT'S AFFIDAVIT

To be completed only after Part 1 has been signed and dated

I, (insert Applicant's full name) _____

residing at (insert Applicant's present
home address) _____

Town _____

Country _____

SWEAR that to the best of my knowledge and belief the facts stated in Part 1 of this Application are true.

Signature of applicant _____

To be completed by Justice of the Peace, Notary Public, or Commissioner for Oaths	SWORN at (*place*) _____ this _____ day of _____ 20____ before me (*full name*) _____ (*full address*) _____ _____ _____ _____ _____

Signature _____

*Justice of the Peace/*Notary Public/*Commissioner for Oaths

*Delete where not applicable

Form 49.80B-C (SPF)[1,2]

C1.2A.168   Rule 49.80B(3)

Form of simplified dissolution of civil partnership application under Section 117(3)(d) of the Civil Partnership Act 2004

Court of Session
General Department
Parliament House
Edinburgh EH1 1RQ
Tel: 0131 240 6741

APPLICATION FOR DISSOLUTION OF A CIVIL PARTNERSHIP (INTERIM GENDER RECOGNITION CERTIFICATE ISSUED TO ONE OF THE CIVIL PARTNERS AFTER THE REGISTRATION OF THE CIVIL PARTNERSHIP)

Before completing this form, you should have read the leaflet entitled "Do it yourself dissolution", which explains the circumstances in which a dissolution of a civil partnership may be sought by this method. If simplified procedure appears to suit your circumstances, you may use this form to apply for dissolution of your civil partnership.

Below you will find directions designed to assist you with your application.

Please follow them carefully. In the event of difficulty, you may contact the Court's General Department at the above address or any Citizen's Advice Bureau.

Directions for making Application

WRITE IN INK, USING BLOCK CAPITALS

Application (Part 1)

1.   Complete and sign Part 1 of the form (pages 3-7), paying particular attention to the notes opposite each section.

Affidavit (Part 2)

2.   When you have completed Part 1, you should then take the form to a Justice of the Peace, Notary Public, Commissioner for Oaths or other duly authorised person so that your affidavit at Part 2 (page 8) may be completed and sworn.

Returning Completed Application Form to Court

3.   When directions 1 and 2 above have been carried out, your application is now ready to be sent to the court. With it you must enclose:

    (i)   an extract of the registration of your civil partnership in the civil partnership register (the document headed "Extract of an entry in the Register of Civil Partnerships", which will be returned to you in due course, or an equivalent document. Check the Notes on page 2 to see if you also need to obtain a letter from National Records of Scotland stating that there is no record of your civil partner having dissolved the civil partnership;

    (ii)   the interim gender recognition certificate or a certified copy of it; and

    (iii)   either a cheque or postal order in respect of the court fee, crossed and made payable to "Scottish Court and Tribunal Service", or completed form SP15 claiming exemption from the Court fee..

---

[1] As amended by S.S.I. 2017 No. 132 para.2 (effective 1 June 2017).
[2] As amended by S.S.I. 2021 No. 75 r. 2(3)(f) (effective 1st March 2021).

4.   Receipt of your application will be promptly acknowledged. Should you wish to withdraw the application for any reason, please contact the Court immediately.

THE NOTES ON THIS AND THE FOLLOWING PAGES ARE DESIGNED TO ASSIST YOU.

PLEASE READ THEM A CREFULLY BEFORE COMPLETING EACH SECTION OF THE FORM.

Notes on Sections 1 and 2 opposite

(i)   The names entered in sections 1 and 2 opposite must be those shown on your extract of registration of civil partnership. If you are known by another name which does not appear on that extract, please write the name in brackets.

(ii) The surname given for a female partner must be her maiden name. Any names from previous marriages should be entered in the space for other names.

(iii) Home address should be given where these are known. The Court is required by law to serve a copy of this application on your civil partner.

Note on Section 3 opposite

If the address of your civil partner is NOT known or cannot reasonably be ascertained, please enter "not known" in this section; you must take all reasonable steps to find out where your civil partner is living and state on a separate sheet what steps you have taken and attach it to this form, then proceed to section 4.

N.B. The statement must be signed.

Notes of Section 4 oppposite

In the event that the address of your civil partner is unknown to you, the Court is required by law to intimate a copy of this application to:

(i)   ONE of the next-of-kin of your civil partner. ("Next-of-kin" does not include yourself or any children of the family for the purposes of this application.)

(ii) All children of the family aged 16 years or over, whether or not they live with you. ("Children of the family" includes any adopted children, and or children accepted into the family).

When entering the details of next-of-kin, if any, please state his and her relationship to your civil partner (i.e. "mother", "father", "brother", "sister", etc).

If you do not know the identity or whereabouts of any of the next-of-kin of your civil partner, or the whereabouts of any of the children of the family, please enter "not known" where appropriate.

LETTER FROM National Records of Scotland: If you do not know the address of your civil partner and your civil partnership was registered in Scotland, you must obatin a letter from the National Records of Scotland stating that there is no record that your civil partner has had the civil partnership dissolved. The letter must be issued not more than one month before the date of posting this application to the court. If you require to obtain a letter you should apply to:

National Records of Scotland, Registration Branch, New Register House, Edinburgh EH1 3YT,

stating both civil partners' full names, the date and place of your registration of your civil partnership and requesting that a search be made to confirm that there is no record that your civil partner has had the civil partnership dissolved. (Note - a fee will be charged for this service.)

The requirement to obtain a letter from the National Records of Scotland does not apply if your civil partnership was registered outwith Scotland.

PART 1

WRITE IN INK USING BLOCK CAPITALS

1. NAME AND ADDRESS OF APPLICANT

Surname _____

Other name(s) in full _____

Present Address _____

_____

Daytime telephone number (if any) _____

2. NAME OF CIVIL PARTNER

Surname _____

Other name(s) in full _____

3. ADDRESS OF CIVIL PARTNER (if the address of your civil partner is not known, please enter "not known" in this section and proceed to section 4)

Present Address _____

_____

_____

Daytime telephone number (if any) _____

4. Only complete this section if you do not know the present address of your civil partner

NEXT-OF-KIN

Name _____

Address _____

Relationship to your civil partner _____

CHILDREN OF THE FAMILY

Names and dates of birth

Addresses

If sufficient space is not available here to list all the children of the family, please continue on a separate sheet and attach to this form.

Notes on Section 5 opposite

"Domiciled" means that the person concerned at Item (i) or (iii) opposite regards Scotland as his/her permanent home and intends to live permanently in Scotland in the foreseeable future.

Notes on Section 6 opposite

You will be able to obtain these details from the extract of registration of your civil partnership (Extract of an entry in the register of civil partnerships) which must accompany this application form, when you send it to the Court.

A photocopy of the civil partnership registration certificate will NOT be accepted. If you cannot find the original, you should apply for an official copy to:

General Register Office (Scotland), Registration Section, New Register House, Edinburgh EH1 3YT or the office where the civil partnership was registered, in writing,

or by e-mailing the form at http://www.gro-scotland.gov.uk/contacts/contact-form.html

stating both civil partner's full names, and the date and place of registration of the civil partnership.

(Note that the Registrar will charge a fee for this service.)

PART 1 (continued)

5. JURISDICTION

Please indicate with a tick (✔) in the appropriate box or boxes which of the following apply:

PART A

(i)   I am domiciled in Scotland on the date I signed this application ☐

(ii)   My civil partner is domiciled in Scotland on the date I signed ☐
        this application

(iii)   I was habitually resident in Scotland throughout the period of ☐
        one year ending with the date I signed this application

(iv)   My civil partner was habitually resident in Scotland ☐
        throughout the period of one year ending with the date I signed
        this application

*If you have ticked one of the boxes in Part A, you do not have to complete Part B.
You should complete Part B if you have not ticked any of the boxes in Part A.*

PART B

(i)   My civil partner and I are registered as civil partners of each   ☐
        other in Scotland

AND

(ii)   No court has, or is recognised as having, jurisdiction   ☐

AND

(iii)   It is in the interests of justice for the Court of Session to as-   ☐
        sume jurisdiction in the case
        (Please give reasons below)

6. DETAILS OF PRESENT CIVIL PARTNERSHIP

Place of Rregistration of Civil Partnership .... (Registration District)
Date of Registration of Civil Partnership: Day .... Month .... Year ....

Notes on Section 7 opposite

You will be able to obtain the details required at (ii) from the interim gender recognition certificate which must accompany this application form, when you send it to the Court.

A photocopy of the interim gender recognition certificate will NOT be accepted.

If the principal interim gender recognition certificate is not available, a copy certified by the Gender Recognition Panel should be lodged instead. This can be obtained from the Gender Recognition Panel at PO Box 6987, Leicester, LE1 6ZX, or at http://www.grp.gov.uk

Note on Section 9 opposite

Children of the marriage includes children accepted into the family.

Notes on Section 11 opposite

No claim can be made in this form of dissolution application for payment to you of a periodical allowance (*i.e.* regular payment of money, weekly, monthly, etc., for your maintenance) or a capital sum (*i.e.* lump sum). If you wish to make such a claim, you should consult a solicitor.

NOTE: While it may be possible to obtain an order for periodical allowance after dissolution of your civil partnership, the right to payment of a capital sum is lost once decree of dissolution is granted.

PART 1 (continued)

7. DETAILS OF ISSUE OF INTERIM GENDER RECOGNITION CERTIFICATE

(i)   Please state whether the interim gender recognition certificate has been issued to you
or your civil partner   _____

(ii) Please state the date the interim gender
recognition certificate was issued   Day _____ Month _____ Year _____

---

8. MENTAL DISORDER

As far as you are aware, does your civil partner have any
mental disorder? (whether mental illness, personality
disorder or learning disability) (*Tick box which applies*)   YES ☐   NO ☐

(If yes, give details)

---

9. CHILDREN

Are there any children of the family under the age of 16?   YES ☐   NO ☐
(*Tick box which applies*)

---

10. OTHER COURT ACTIONS

Are you aware of any court actions currently proceeding
in any country (including Scotland) which may affect your
civil partnership? (*Tick box which applies*)   YES ☐   NO ☐

(If yes, give details)

---

11. DECLARATION AND REQUEST FOR DISSOLUTION OF CIVIL PARTNERSHIP

I confirm that the facts stated in Sections 1 – 10 above apply to my civil partnership.

I do not ask the Court to make any financial awards in connection with this application.

I request the Court to grant decree of dissolution from my civil partnership.

(Date) _____   (Signature of applicant) _____

APPENDIX

PART 2

APPLICANT'S AFFIDAVIT

To be completed only after Part 1 has been signed and dated.

I, (insert Applicant's full name) _____

residing at (insert Applicant's present
home address) _____

Town _____

Country _____

SWEAR that to the best of my knowledge and belief the facts stated in Part 1 of this Application are true.

Signature of applicant _____

To be completed by Justice of the Peace,   SWORN at (*insert place*) _____
Notary Public, or Commissioner for
Oaths   this _____ day off _____ 20____

before me (*insert full name*) _____

(*insert full address*) _____

_____

_____

Signature _____

*Justice of the Peace/*Notary Public/*Commissioner for Oaths

* Delete as appropriate

1549

Form 49.80E-A

C1.2A.169   Rule 49.80E(3)

Rule 49.80E(3)   [1] FORM 49.80E–A

Form of citation in simplified dissolution of civil partnership application under section 117(3)(c) of the Civil Partnership Act 2004

CITATION

Date: (*Date of posting or other method of service*)

To: ....

       ....

       ....

APPLICATION FOR DISSOLUTION OF A CIVIL PARTNERSHIP (WITH CONSENT OF OTHER PARTY TO THE CIVIL PARTNERSHIP) CIVIL PARTNERS HAVING LIVED APART FOR AT LEAST ONE YEARS

You are barely served with an application by your civil partner which asks the court to grant a decree of dissolution of your civil partnership.

If you wish to oppose the granting of such a decree, you should put your reasons in writing and send your letter to the address shown below. Your letter must reach the court by (*insert date on which period of notice expires*).

(*Signed*)

Deputy Principal Clerk of Session

[*or* authorised clerk of session]

[*or* Messenger-at-Arms]

(*Address*)

IMPORTANT NOTE. If you wish to exercise your right to claim a financial award you should immediately advise the court that you oppose the application for that reason, and thereafter consult a solicitor.

Court of Session
Extracts Department (SP)
Parliament House
Edinburgh EH1 1RQ
Tel: 0131–225–2595

---

[1] Form 49.80E-A inserted by S.S.I. 2005 No. 632 (effective 8th December 2005) and S.S.I. 2006 No. 206 (effective 4th May 2006).

Form 49.80E-B

Rule 49.80E(3)[1]

Form of citation in simplified dissolution of civil partnership application under section 117(3)(d) of the Civil Partnership Act 2004

CITATION

Date: *(date of posting or other method of intimation)*

To: ....
       ....
       ....

APPLICATION FOR DISSOLUTION OF A CIVIL PARTNERSHIP. CIVIL PARTNERS HAVING LIVED APART FOR AT LEAST TWO YEARS

Your civil partner has applied to the court for a decree of dissolution of your civil partnership on the ground your civil partnership has broken down irretrievably because you and (s)he have lived apart for a period of at least two years.

A copy of the application is hereby served on you.

1.   Please note –

    (a)   that the court may not make a financial award under this procedure and that your civil partner is making no claim against you for payment of a periodical allowance (*ie* regular payment of money weekly, monthly etc for *his* or *her*) maintenance or a capital sum (*i.e.* lump sum);

2.   Dissolution of your civil partnership may result in the loss to you of property rights (*e.g.* the right to succeed to the applicant's estate on his/her death) or the right, where appropriate, to a pension.

3.   If you wish to oppose the granting of such a dissolution of your civil partnership, you should put your reasons in writing and send your letter to the address shown below. Your letter must reach the court by (*insert date on which period of notice expires*).

4.   In the event of the dissolution of your civil partnership being granted, you will be sent a copy of the extract decree. (Should you change your address before receiving the copy extract decree please notify the court immediately).

                    (Signed)

                    Deputy Principal Clerk of Session

                    [*or* authorised Clerk of Session]

                    [*or* Messenger-at-Arms]

                    (Address)

IMPORTANT NOTE: If you wish to exercise your right to claim a financial award you should immediately advise the court that you oppose the application for that reason, and thereafter consult a solicitor.

Court of Session
Extracts Department (SP)
Parliament House
Edinburgh
EH1 1RQ
Tel: 0131-225-2595

---

[1] Form 49.80E-B inserted by SSI 2005 No. 632 (effective 8th December 2005) and SSI 2006 No. 206 (effective 4th May 2006).

Form 49.80E-C

C1.2A.171   Rule 49.80E(3)[1]

Form of citation in simplified dissolution of civil partnership application under section 117(2)(b) of the Civil Partnership Act 2004

CITATION

Date: *(date of posting or other method of intimation)*

To: ....

....

....

APPLICATION FOR DISSOLUTION OF A CIVIL PARTNERSHIP. INTERIM GENDER RECOGNITION CERTIFICATE ISSUED TO ONE OF THE CIVIL PARTNERS AFTER REGISTRATION OF THE CIVIL PARTNERSHIP

Your civil partner has applied to the court for a decree of dissolution of your civil partnership on the ground that an interim gender recognition certificate has been issued to you on your civil partner after your civil partnership was registered.

A copy of the application is hereby served on you.

1.   Please note that the court may not make a financial award under this procedure and that your civil partner is making no claim against you for payment of a periodical allowance (*i.e.* regular payment of money weekly, monthly etc for *his* [or *her*] maintenance or a capital sum (*i.e.* lump sum);

2.   Dissolution of your civil partnership may result in the loss to you of property rights (*e.g.* the right to succeed to the applicant's estate on his/her death) or the right, where appropriate, to a pension.

3.   If you wish to oppose the granting of such a dissolution of your civil partnership, you should put your reasons in writing and send your letter to the address shown below. Your letter must reach the court by (*insert date on which period of notice expires*).

4.   In the event of the dissolution of your civil partnership being granted, you will be sent a copy of the extract decree. (Should you change your address before receiving the copy extract decree please notify the court immediately).

(Signed)

Deputy Principal Clerk of Session

[*or* authorised Clerk of Session]

[*or* Messenger-at-Arms]

(Address)

IMPORTANT NOTE: If you wish to exercise your right to claim a financial award you should immediately advise the court that you oppose the application for that reason, and thereafter consult a solicitor.

Court of Session
Extracts Department (SP)
Parliament House
Edinburgh
EH1 1RQ
Tel: 0131 225 2595

---

[1] Form 49.80E-C inserted by SSI 2005 No. 632 (effective 8th December 2005).

Form 49.80E-D

Rule 49.8E(4)

Rule 49.8E(4)   [1] FORM 49.80E–D

Form of intimation to child or next-of-kin in simplified dissolution of civil partnership application under section 117(3)(d) or 117(2)(b) of the Civil Partnership Act 2004

CITATION

Date: (*Date of posting or other method of service*)

To: ....

....

....

APPLICATION FOR DISSOLUTION OF A CIVIL PARTNERSHIP. CIVIL PARTNERS HAVING LIVED APART FOR AT LEAST TWO YEARS OR ISSUE OF INTERIM GENDER RECOGNITION CERTIFICATE AFTER REGISTRATION OF THE CIVIL PARTNERSHIP

....(Applicant) v .... (Respondent)

TAKE NOTICE

1. In the above application, a copy of which is enclosed, the applicant has indicated that you are the (*state relationship*) of (*name of respondent*) whose present address is not known to the applicant.

2. Should you know the present address of your (*state relationship*) or how he [*or* she] may be contacted, you are requested to give this information at once in writing to—

Court of Session
Extracts Department (SP)
Parliament House
Edinburgh EH1 1RQ
Tel: 0131–225–2595

This will enable the court to inform the respondent that the application has been made.

3. If you are unable to provide the above information, and/or you wish for your own interest to oppose the application for dissolution of the civil partnership, you should write to the above address by (*insert date on which period of time expires*).

(*Signed*)

Deputy Principal Clerk of Session

[*or* authorised clerk of session]

[*or* Messenger-at-Arms]

(*Address*)

---

[1] Form 49.80E–D inserted by SSI 2005/632 (effective 8th December 2005) and S.S.I. 2006 No. 206 (effective 4th May 2006).

Form 49.80E-E

C1.2A.173   Rule 49.780E(5)

Rule 49.780E(5)   [1] FORM 49.80E–E

Form of certificate of service of simplified dissolution application

CERTIFICATE OF SERVICE [*or* INTIMATION]

I, (*name*), Deputy Principal Clerk of Session [*or clerk of session authorised by him*], certify that I served [*or* intimated] this simplified dissolution application by (*name of applicant*) on [*or* to] (*name of person on whom service executed or to whom intimation given*) by posting it with a citation [*or* notice of intimation] in Form (*number of form*) to that person between (*time*) and (*time*) on (*date*) at (*name of post office*) in a registered envelope [*or* recorded delivery envelope] address as follows:-(*address*). The Post Office receipt [*or* certificate of posting] is attached to this certificate.

(*Signed*)

Deputy Principal Clerk of Session

[*or* authorised clerk of session]

[*or* Messenger-at-Arms]

(*Address*)

(*Signed*)

Witness

––––––––––

[1] Form 49.80E–E inserted by SSI 2005/632 (effective 8th December 2005).

Form 49.80E-F

Rule 49.780E(5)

Rule 49.780E(5)   [1] FORM 49.80E–F

Form of certificate of service of simplified dissolution application by messenger-at-arms

CERTIFICATE OF SERVICE [*or* INTIMATION]

I, (*name*), Messenger-at-Arms, certify that I served [*or* intimated] this simplified dissolution application [and notice of intimation] on [*or* to] (*name of person on whom served or to whom intimated*)—

- by leaving it and a citation [*or* notice] with (*name of person*) at (*place*) at (*time*) on (*date*).
- by leaving it and a citation [*or* notice] with (*name and occupation of person with whom left*) at (*place*) on (*date*). (*Specify that enquiry made and that reasonable grounds exist for believing that the person on whom service is to be made or to whom intimation is to be given resident the place but is not available*).
- by depositing it and a citation [*or* notice] in (*place*) on (*date*). (*Specify that enquiry made and that reasonable grounds exist for believing that the person on whom service is to be made or to whom intimation is to be given resident the place but is not available*).
- by leaving it and a citation [*or* notice] with (*name and occupation of person with whom left*) at (*place of business*) on (*date*). (*Specify that enquiry made and that reasonable grounds exist for believing that the person on whom service is to be made or to whom intimation is to be given resident the place but is not available*).
- by depositing it and a citation [*or* notice] at (*place of business*) on (*date*). (*Specify that enquiry made and that reasonable grounds exist for believing that the person on whom service is to be made or to whom intimation is to be given resident the place but is not available*).
- by leaving it and a citation [*or* notice] at (*registered office or place of business*) on (*date*), in the hands of (*name of person*).

- by leaving [*or* depositing] it and a citation [*or* notice] at (*registered office, official address or place of business*) on (*date*), in such a way as it was likely to come to the attention of (*name of person on whom served or to whom intimated*). (*Specify how left*).

I did this in the presence of (*name, occupation and address of witness*).

(*Signed*)

Messenger-at-Arms

(*Address*)

(*Signed*)

Witness

---

[1] Form 49.80E–F inserted by SSI 2005/632 (effective 8th December 2005).

Form 49.83-A

C1.2A.175   Rule 49.83

Rule 49.83   FORM 49.83–A

Form of certificate relating to the making of a maintenance assessment under the Child Support Act 1991

I, Deputy Principal Clerk of Session, certify that notification has been received from the Secretary of State under section 10 of the Child Support Act 1991 of the making of a maintenance assessment under that Act which supersedes the decree [*or* order] granted on (*date*) in relation to aliment for (*name(s) of child(ren)*) with effect from (*date*).

(*Signed*)

Deputy Principal Clerk of Session

Date:

Form 49.83-B

C1.2A.176   Rule 49.83

Rule 49.83   FORM 49.83–B

Form of certificate relating to the cancellation or ceasing to have effect of a maintenance assessment under the Child Support Act 1991

I, Deputy Principal Clerk of Session, certify that notification has been received from the Secretary of State under section 10 of the Child Support Act 1991 that the maintenance assessment made on (*date*) has been cancelled [*or* ceased to have effect] on (*date*).

(*Signed*)

Deputy Principal Clerk of Session

Date:

Form 49.84-A

C1.2A.177   Rule 49.84(1)

Rule 49.84(1)   FORM 49.84–A

Form of certificate endorsed on extract order for aliment affected by maintenance assessment

A maintenance assessment having been made under the Child Support Act 1991 on (*date*), this order, in so far as it relates to the making or securing of periodical payments to or for the benefit of (*name(s) of child(ren)*), ceases to have effect from (*date two days after the date on which the maintenance assessment was made*).

Form 49.84-B

Rule 49.84(2)

Rule 49.84(2)   FORM 49.84–B

Form of certificate endorsed on extract order for aliment on maintenance assessment being cancelled or ceasing to have effect

The jurisdiction of the child support officer under the Child Support Act 1991 having terminated on (*date*), this order, in so far as it relates to (*name(s) of child(ren)*), again shall have effect as from (*date of termination of child support officer's jurisdiction*).

Form 50.2-A

Rule 50.2(3)

Rule 50.2(3)   [1] FORM 50.2–A

Form of citation by advertisement on action of declarator of death under section 1(1) of the Presumption of Death (Scotland) Act 1977

IN THE COURT OF SESSION

in the cause

[A.B.] (*designation and address*)

Pursuer

against

[C.D.]

Defender

An action has been brought in the Court of Session, Edinburgh, by [A.B.], pursuer, to declare that [C.D.], defender, whose last known address was (*address*), is dead. Any person having an interest may apply to the court by minute to defend the action or to seek an order under section 2 of the Presumption of Death (Scotland) Act 1977. If you wish to apply to the court you must do so by (*date on which period of notice expires*) at the Office of Court, Court of Session, 2 Parliament Square, Edinburgh EH1 1RQ.

(*Signed*)

Solicitor [*or* Agent] for pursuer
(*Address*)

Form 50.2-B

C1.2A.180   Rule 50.2(5)

Rule 50.2(5)   [1] Form 50.2–B

Form of notice of intimation in an action of declarator of death under section 1(1) of the Presumption of Death (Scotland) Act 1977

Date: *(date of posting or other method of intimation)*

To: *(name and address as in warrant for intimation)*

An action has been brought in the Court of Session, Edinburgh requesting the court to declare that *(name and last known address of missing person)* is dead. A copy of the summons is attached.

You may apply to the court by minute for leave to state defences to the action or to seek a determination or appointment under section 2 of the Presumption of Death (Scotland) Act 1977 which is not sought by the pursuer. You must do so at the Office of Court, Court of Session, 2 Parliament Square, Edinburgh EH1 1RQ within [21] days after the date of intimation to you of the summons [*or if the warrant for intimation is executed before calling of the summons*, within seven days after the summons calls in court. The summons will not call in court earlier than [21] days after the date of intimation to you of the summons). The date of intimation is the date stated at the top of this notice unless intimation has been made by post in which case the date of intimation is the day after that date.

If you do not wish to lodge defences to this action but you have information which you consider may be of value to the court in this matter, you may write to the court with any such information by addressing your correspondence to the Deputy Principal Clerk of Session, 2 Parliament Square, Edinburgh EH1 1RQ.

IF YOU ARE UNCERTAIN ABOUT THE EFFECT OF THIS NOTICE, you should consult a solicitor, Citizens Advice Bureau or other local advice agency or adviser immediately.

(Signed)

Messenger-at-Arms
[*or* Solicitor [*or* Agent]
for pursuer]
(Address)

---

[1] Form 50.2–B amended by SI 1994/2901 (minor correction).

Form 51.5

Rule 51.5(3)

Rule 51.5(3)   FORM 51.5

Form of advertisement for objections and claims in action of multiplepoinding

IN THE COURT OF SESSION

in the cause

[A.B.] (*designation and address*)

Pursuer and Real [*or* Nominal] Raiser

against

[C.D.] (*designation and address*)
and Others

Defenders

An action of multiplepoinding has been brought in the Court of Session, Edinburgh by [A.B.], pursuer, in respect of (*briefly describe nature of the fund in medio*). On (*date*) Lord (*name*) ordered advertisement for objections and claims.Any person who wishes to object to the condescendence of the fund must do so by lodging defences, and any person who wishes to make a claim on the fund must do so by lodging a condescendence and claim, by (*date on which period of notice expires*) at the Office of Court, Court Session, 2 Parliament Square, Edinburgh EH1 1RQ.

(*Signed*)

[Solicitor [*or* Agent] for pursuer]
(*Address*)

Form 52.3

Rule 52.3

Rule 52.3   FORM 52.3

Form of minute for decree in undefended action of proving the tenor

(*Name of counsel*)   for the pursuer having considered the evidence contained in the affidavits and the other documents as specified in the attached schedule and being satisfied that on this evidence a motion for decree in terms of the conclusions of the summons [*or in such restricted terms as may be appropriate*] may properly be made, moves the court accordingly.

IN RESPECT WHEREOF

(*Signature of counsel or other person having a right of audience*)

SCHEDULE
(*list of numbered documents*)

---

[1] Form 52.3 inserted by S.S.I. 2009 No. 63, r. 6 (effective March 23rd 2009).

Form 53.2

C1.2A.183   Rule 53.2

Rule 53.2(3)   FORM 53.2

Form of notice of intimation to clerk of inferior court or tribunal in action of reduction

Date: (*date of posting or other method of intimation*)

To: (*designation of clerk of court or tribunal in warrant for intimation*)

TAKE NOTICE

(*Pursuer's name and address*), pursuer, has brought an action in the Court of Session, Edinburgh against (*name and address of defender*), defender, seeking reduction of (*specify document*) pronounced by you. A copy of the summons is attached.

                                        (*Signed*)

                                        Messenger-at-Arms
                                        [*or* Solicitor [*or* Agent] for pursuer]
                                        (*Address*)

[1]Form 58.3

Form of Petition for Judicial Review

C1.2A.184   Rule 58.3(3)

UNTO THE RIGHT HONOURABLE
THE LORDS OF COUNCIL AND SESSION
PETITION
of

[A.B.] (*designation and address*)

for

Judicial review of (*state briefly matter sought to be reviewed*) by [C.D.]

HUMBLY SHEWETH:—

1.   That the petitioner is as designed in the instance. The respondent[s] is [*or* are] as designed in Part 1 of the Schedule for Service. [The persons specified in Part 2 of the Schedule for Service may have an interest.] The petitioner has standing. (*State the standing of the petitioner.*)

2.   That the date on which the grounds giving rise to the petition first arose was (*date*).

3.   That on that date the respondent (*specify act, decision or omission to be reviewed*).

4.   That the petitioner seeks (*state remedies sought*). The petitioner craves the court to pronounce such further orders (including an order for expenses) as may seem to the court to be just and reasonable in all the circumstances of the case.

---

[1] Form 58.3 as substituted by S.S.I. 2015 No. 228 r. 3 (effective 22nd September 2015) and as amended by S.S.I. 2017 No. 200 r. 2(10) (effective 17th July 2017) and S.S.I. 2019 No. 293 r. 2 (effective 16th October 2019).

5. That the petitioner challenges the decision [*or* act *or* omission] of the respondent on the following ground(s).

6. (*State briefly (in numbered paragraphs) facts in support of the ground(s) of challenge.*)

7. (*State briefly (in numbered paragraphs) the legal argument with reference to enactments or authority.*)

PERMISSION TO PROCEED

8. That the petitioner satisfies section 27B(2) (requirement for permission) of the Court of Session Act 1988. (*State briefly (in numbered paragraphs) how the petitioner can demonstrate a sufficient interest in the subject matter of the petition and why the petition has a real prospect of success*). [*or*

8. That the petitioner satisfies section 27B(3) (requirement for permission: second appeals test) of the Court of Session Act 1988. (*State briefly (in numbered paragraphs) how the petitioner can (a) demonstrate a sufficient interest in the subject matter of the petition, (b) why the petition has a real prospect of success, and (c) either why the petition raises an important point of principle or practice or why there is some other compelling reason for allowing the petition to proceed*).]

(*where an extension to the time limit under section 27A of the Act of 1988 is sought*)

[8A. That the Court should allow this petition despite it being made after the period of 3 months beginning with the date set out in paragraph 2 because (*state why the Court should consider it equitable, having regard to all the circumstances, to allow this petition*).]

8B. That the following documents are necessary for the determination of permission [and extension to the time limit]:

(*set out, in a numbered list, the documents required to be identified by rule 58.3(4)(d)*).

TRANSFERS TO THE UPPER TRIBUNAL

9. That the petition is not subject to a mandatory or discretionary transfer to the Upper Tribunal. [*or*

9. That the petition is subject to a discretionary transfer to the Upper Tribunal under section 20(1)(b) of the Tribunals, Courts and Enforcement Act 2007] [*or*

9. That the petition is subject to a mandatory transfer to the Upper Tribunal under section 20(1)(a) of the Tribunals, Courts and Enforcement Act 2007.]

PLEA(S)-IN-LAW

(*Specify pleas-in-law relating to each ground of challenge and remedy sought*)
According to Justice etc.

(*Signed by counsel or other person having a right of audience or, under 4.2(3)(ca), agent*)

SCHEDULE FOR SERVICE

PART 1: RESPONDENT(S)

(*State the name and designation of the respondent(s) and whether service is sought in common form or by advertisement.*)

PART 2: INTERESTED PERSON(S)

(*State the name and designation of any interested person(s) and whether service is sought in common form or by advertisement.*)

SCHEDULE OF DOCUMENTS
(Specify any documents founded on under rule 58.3(4)(b))

Form 58.8[1]

C1.2A.184.1

Form of Request for Review

Rule 58.8(1)

IN THE COURT OF SESSION

PETITION

Of

[A.B.] (designation and address)

For

Judicial review of *(state briefly matter sought to be reviewed)* by [C.D.]

I request a review of the decision of the Lord Ordinary made on *(date)*.

(Signed by counsel or other person having a right of audience)

---

[1] Form 58.8 as inserted by S.S.I. 2015 No. 228 r. 3 (effective 22nd September 2015).

Form 58.8A

C1.2A.185

[1] FORM 58.8A

Form of Minute of Intervention

APPLICATION

for

LEAVE TO INTERVENE

in the

PUBLIC INTEREST

in the cause

[A.B.] (*designation and address*)

Petitioner [*or* Appellant]

Against

[C.D.] (*designation and address*)

Defender] *or* Respondent]

[*Here set out briefly:*
   (a) *the name and description of the applicant;*
   (b) *any issue in the proceedings which the applicant wishes to address and the applicant's reasons for believing that any such issue raises a matter of public interest;*
   (c) *the propositions to be advanced by the applicant and the applicant's reasons for believing that they are relevant to the proceedings and that they will assist the Court.*]

---

[1] Form 58.8A inserted by S.S.I. 2000 No. 317 (as 58.8) and renumbered as 58.8A by S.S.I. 2004 No. 52.

Form 58.18[1]

Form of Minute of Intervention
Rule 58.18(1)

C1.2A.185.1

---

[1] Form 58.18 as inserted by S.S.I. 2015 No. 228 r. 3 (effective 22nd September 2015).

APPLICATION

For

LEAVE TO INTERVENE

in the

PUBLIC INTEREST

in the

PETITION

Of

[A.B.] (*designation and address*)

for

Judicial review of (*state briefly matter sought to be reviewed*) by [C.D.]

(*Here set out briefly:*

(a) *the name and description of the applicant;*

(b) *any issue in the proceedings which the applicant wishes to address and the applicant's reasons for believing that any such issue raises a matter of public interest;*

(c) *the propositions to be advanced by the applicant and the applicant's reasons for believing that they are relevant to the proceedings and that they will assist the Court.*)

Form 59.1-A

C1.2A.186   Rule 59.1(1)(a)

Rule 59.1(1)(a)   FORM 59.1–A

Form of letters of arrestment

IN THE COURT OF SESSION

Application of (*applicant's name*) for Letters of Arrestment

My Lords of Council and Session—

1. In a (*describe deed*) dated (*date*), (*common debtor's name, designation and address*) bound himself [*or herself or themselves or itself*] to pay to (*applicant's name, designation and address*) (1) (*amount of principal sum in words and figures*) and (2) interest on that amount at (*rate*) from (*date*) until payment [*or as the case may be*]. These amounts [*or amount in words and figures*] remain(s) unpaid.

2. The (*short reference to deed*) was registered for execution in your Lordships' Books of Council and Session on (*date*). An extract of it is produced with this application [*or as the case may be*].

3. The applicant, therefore, requests your Lordships to grant warrant to arrest the sum of (*amount*) more or less due and all moveable things in the hands of any person who is debtor to or has the moveable things of (*name, designation and address of common debtor*) in his possession.

According to Justice etc.

(*Signed*)

Solicitor [*or* Agent] for applicant
(*Address*)

Warrant to arrest granted in accordance with the above application.

Date:

(*Signed*)

Depute [*or* Assistant] Clerk of Session
(*Signet*)

Form 59.1-B

Rule 59.1(1)(b)

C1.2A.187

Rule 59.1(1)(b)　　　　　　　FORM 59.1–B

Form of letters of inhibition where decree granted or foreign judgment registered for execution

[*Revoked by S.S.I. 2009 No. 104 (effective 22nd April 2009).*]

Form 59.1-C

Rule 59.1(1)(c)

C1.2A.188

Rule 59.1(1)(c)　　　　　　　FORM 59.1–C

Form of letters of inhibition on deed registered for execution

[*Revoked by S.S.I. 2009 No. 104 (effective 22nd April 2009).*]

Form 59.1-D

Rule 59.1(1)(d)

C1.2A.189

Rule 59.1(1)(d)　　　　　　　FORM 59.1–D

Form of letters of inhibition on dependence of action in sheriff court

[*Revoked by S.S.I. 2009 No. 104 (effective 22nd April 2009).*]

Form 59.1-E

C1.2A.190 Rule 59.1(1)(e)

Rule 59.1(1)(e)   FORM 59.1–E

Form of letters of inhibition in respect of future or contingent debt

[Revoked by S.S.I. 2009 No. 104 (effective 22nd April 2009).]

Form 59.1-F

C1.2A.191 Rule 59.1(1)(f)

Rule 59(1)(f)   FORM 59.1–F

Form of letters of inhibition on contract for transfer of heritable property

[Revoked by S.S.I. 2009 No. 104 (effective 22nd April 2009).]

Form 61.2

C1.2A.192 Rule 61.2(2)

Rule 61.2(2)   [1] FORM 61.2

Form of petition under section 9(5)(a) of the Act of 1995 for appointment of a judicial factor

UNTO THE RIGHT HONOURABLE THE LORDS OF COUNCIL AND SESSION

PETITION

of

The Accountant of Court

Under section 9(5)(a) of the Children (Scotland) Act 1995 for the appointment of a judicial factor to [C.D.] *(name of child as in birth certificate)*

HUMBLY SHEWETH:—

1. That an application has been made to the petitioner under section 9(2) or (3) of the Children (Scotland) Act 1995 for a direction as to the administration of the property of [C.D.] [*name and address of child*].

2. That [C.D.] [*name of child*] was born on [*date of birth of child*].

3. That the property is of the following description [*description of property*].

4. That the propertyís value is not less than [*minimum value of property*].

5. That the property is for the time being held by [*name, address and designation of person holding property owned by or due to the child*].

6. That for the following reason[s] the appointment of a judicial factor is more appropriate than the making of a direction under paragraph (b) or (c) of section 9(5) of the Children (Scotland) Act 1995; that is to say [*statement of reason[s]*].

MAY IT THEREFORE please your Lordships to appoint (*name and address of proposed judicial factor*), or such other person as the court shall think proper, to be judicial factor to [*name and address of child*] to administer, in terms of section 9(5)(a) of the Children (Scotland) Act 1995, the property owned by or due to the child, as described at paragraph 4 above.

According to Justice etc.

(*Signed*)

Accountant of Court

---

[1] Form 61.2 inserted by S.I. 1997 No. 1720.

Form 61.5–A

C1.2A.193   Rule 61.5(2)

Rule 61.5(2)   FORM 61.5–A

Form of advertisement of petition for appointment of judicial factor

(*Cause reference number*)

PETITION FOR APPOINTMENT OF CURATOR *BONIS* [or other judicial factor] TO
[C.D.]

NOTICE is hereby given to all persons having an interest that application has been made to the Court of Session by [A.B.] (*designation and address*) for the appointment of [E.F.] (*designation and address*) as curator *bonis* [*or other judicial factor*] to [C.D.] (*last known address*).

Any person having an interest may lodge answers to the petition. Answers must be lodged at the Office of Court, Court of Session, 2 Parliament Square, Edinburgh EH1 1RQ within [21] days after the date of this notice.

(*Name*)

Judicial Factor to [C.D.]
[*or* Solicitor [*or* Agent] for petitioner]
(*Address*)

Form 61.5-B

Rule 61.5(2)

Rule 61.5(2)   FORM 61.5–B

Form of advertisement of petition for discharge of judicial factor

(*Cause reference number*)

PETITION FOR DISCHARGE OF CURATOR *BONIS* [or other judicial factor] TO [C.D.]

NOTICE is hereby given to all persons having an interest that application has been made to the Court of Session by [E.F.] (*designation and address*) as curator *bonis* [*or other judical factor*] to [C.D.] (*last known address*) for discharge from his office [*or otherwise as the case may be*].

Any person having an interest may lodge answers to the petition. Answers must be lodged at the Office of Court, Court of Session, 2 Parliament Square, Edinburgh EH1 1RQ within [21] days after the date of this notice.

(*Name*)

Judicial Factor to [C.D.]
[*or* Solicitor [*or* Agent] for petitioner]
(*Address*)

Form 61.18

C1.2A.195   Rule 61.18(a)

Rule 61.18(a)   Form 61.18

Form of notice in the Edinburgh Gazette of application for appointment of judicial factor on estate of deceased person

(*Cause reference number*)

PETITION FOR APPOINTMENT OF JUDICIAL FACTOR ON THE ESTATE OF [C.D.]

To the creditors of any persons interested in the estate of the deceased (*name and last known address*).

NOTICE is hereby given that:—

1. An application under section 11A of the Judicial Factors (Scotland) Act 1889 has been presented to the Court of Session by [A.B.] (*address*), a creditor [*or* creditors] of the deceased [*or* having an interest in the succession of the deceased], the deceased having left no settlement appointing trustees or other parties having power to manage his estate [*or* the trustees under the deceased's settlement having refused to act], for the appointment of a judicial factor to the estate of the deceased (*name*).

2. Any person having an interest in the estate of the deceased may lodge answers to the petition. Answers must be lodged at the Office of Court, Court of Session, 2 Parliament Square, Edinburgh EH1 1RQ within [21] days after the date of this notice [*or otherwise in terms of the first order*].

                              (*Name*)

                              Petitioner
                              [*or* Solicitor [*or* Agent] for the petitioner]
                              (*Address*)

Form 61.20

Rule 61.20(1)

Rule 61.20(1)   FORM 61.20

Form of notice in the Edinburgh Gazette and appropriate newspaper calling for claims

(*Cause reference number*)

JUDICIAL FACTORY ON THE ESTATE OF [C.D.]

To the creditors and other persons interested in the estate of the deceased (*name and last known address*).

NOTICE is hereby given that [E.F.] (*designation and address*), having been appointed by the Court of Session on (*date of appointment*) as judicial factor on the estate of the deceased [C.D.] under section 11A of the Judicial Factors (Scotland) Act 1889, requires all the lawful creditors of the deceased [C.D.] and other persons interested in his estate, to lodge with the judicial factor, within four months after the date of this notice—

    (*a*)   a statement of their claims as creditors of the deceased, or as otherwise interested in his estate, and

    (*b*)   vouchers or other written evidence as they may have to found on in support of their claims,

so that the claims may be considered and reported on by the judicial factor.

                                (*Name*)

                                Judicial factor
                                [*or* Solicitor [*or* Agent] for the judicial factor]
                                (*Address*)

Form 61.25

Rule 61.25(1)(c)

Rule 61.25(1)(c)   FORM 61.25

Form of notice in the Edinburgh Gazette on lodging statement of funds and schemes of division

(*Cause reference number*)

JUDICIAL FACTORY ON THE ESTATE OF [C.D.]

To the creditors of and persons interested in the succession to the estate of the deceased (*name and last known address*).

NOTICE is hereby given by [E.F.] (*designation and address*), judicial factor on the estate of the deceased [C.D.], that he has prepared and lodged in the Court of Session a state of funds and [first] scheme of division of the estate, to be considered and approved by the court.

                                (*Name*)

                                Judicial factor
                                [*or* Solicitor [*or* Agent] for the judicial factor]
                                (*Address*)

Form 61.31

C1.2A.198   Rule 61.31(2)

Rule 61.31(2)   [1] FORM 61.31

Form of notice where application for discharge is made to Accountant of Court

Date: (*insert date of posting or other method of intimation*)

To: (*name and address of cautioner or person with interest*)

TAKE NOTICE that A.B. (*address*) curator *bonis* [*or other judicial factor*] to [*or on the estate of*] C.D. (*address*) has applied to the Accountant of Court for a certificate of discharge.

The audited accounts of the judicial factory are available for inspection at the office of the Accountant of Court, 2 Parliament Square, Edinburgh EH1 1RQ.

Representations relating to the application must be made in writing and lodged with the Accountant of Court within [21] days after the date of intimation to you of this notice. The date of intimation is the date stated at the top of this notice unless intimation was given by post in which case the date of intimation is the day after that date.

IF YOU ARE UNCERTAIN ABOUT THE EFFECT OF THIS NOTICE, you should consult a solicitor, Citizens Advice Bureau or other local advice agency or adviser immediately.

                                        (*Signed*)

                                        Curator *bonis* to [C.D.]
                                        (*or* Solicitor [*or* Agent] for [E.F.]
                                        Curator *bonis* to [C.D.]]

———————

[1] Form 61.31 amended by S.I. 1994 No. 2901 (minor correction).

Form 61.33

Rule 61.33(2)(a)

Rule 61.33(2)(a)   **FORM 61.33**

Form of notice in the Edinburgh Gazette of application for appointment of judicial factor on estate of deceased person

(Cause reference number)

PETITION FOR DISCHARGE OF JUDICIAL FACTOR ON THE ESTATE OF [C.D.]

To the creditors of and other persons interested in the succession to the estate of the deceased *(name and last known address)*.

NOTICE is hereby given that [E.F.] *(address)*, judicial factor on the estate of the deceased [C.D.], has presented a petition to the Court of Session for discharge from the office of judicial factor.

Any person having an interest may lodge answers to the petition. Answers must be lodged at the Office of Court, Court of Session, 2 Parliament Square, Edinburgh EH1 1RQ within [21] days after the date of this notice [*or otherwise in terms of the first order in the petition for discharge*].

(Name)

Judicial factor
[*or* Solicitor [*or* Agent] for petitioner]
(Address)

Form 62.2

Rule 62.2(1)(b)

Rule 62.2(1)(b)   **FORM 62.2**

Form of certificate of currency conversion

IN THE COURT OF SESSION

in the

Application of

(name, designation and address of applicant(s))

under the Civil Jurisdiction and Judgments Act 1982 for   registration of a judgment [*or other document*] of the *(name of court)* of *(date of judgment)* in the cause *(name of pursuer)* against *(name of defender)*.

In a terms of a certificate dated at *(place)* on *(date)* the sterling equivalent of *(a)* the principal sum is (£ . p); *(b)* the interest thereon is (£ . p); and *(c)* the expenses is (£ . p) at the rate of exchange prevailing at that date.

Date:

(Signed)

Depute [*or* Assistant] Clerk of Session

Form 62.9

C1.2A.201   Rule 62.9

Rule 62.9   [1] FORM 62.9

Form of notice to judgment debtor of registration of judgment under the Administration of Justice Act 1920 or the Foreign Judgments (Reciprocal Enforcement) Act 1933

IN THE COURT OF SESSION

in the PETITION of

[A.B.] (*designation and address*)

Petitioner

for

Registration of a judgment of (*name of court*)
dated (*date*)

under

section 9 of the Administration of Justice Act 1920
[*or* section 2 of the Foreign Judgments (Reciprocal Enforcement) Act 1933]

Date: (*date of posting or other method of service*)

To: (*name of judgment debtor*)

TAKE NOTICE

That a judgment (*give details*) has been registered in the register of judgments of the Books of Council and Session on (*date*) on the application of the petitioner in the above petition.

If you intend to apply to the court to have the judgment set aside you must do so by note on or before (*insert date court has fixed under R.C.S. 1994, r. 62.7(2)*). You must lodge the note in the process of the above petition in the Petition Department, Court of Session, 2 Parliament Square, Edinburgh EH1 1RQ.

IF YOU ARE UNCERTAIN ABOUT THE EFFECT OF THIS NOTICE you should consult a solicitor, Citizens Advice Bureau or other local advice agency or adviser immediately.

(*Signed*)

Messenger-at-Arms
[*or* Solicitor [*or* Agent] for petitioner]
(*Address*)

––––––––––

[1] Form 62.9 amended by S.I. 1994 No. 2901 (minor correction).

Form 62.11

C1.2A.202   Rule 62.11(2)

Rule 62.11(2)   FORM 62.11

Form of certificate to be appended to copy of judgment certified under section 10 of the Administration of Justice Act 1920 or the Foreign Judgments (Reciprocal Enforcement) Act 1933

I, Deputy Principal Clerk of Session, certify that the foregoing extract decree is a true copy of a judgment obtained in the Court of Session. This certificate is issued in accordance with section 10 of the Administration of Justice Act 1920 [*or* Foreign Judgments (Reciprocal Enforcement) Act 1933] and in obedience to an interlocutor of Lord (*name*) dated (*date*).

Date:

(*Signed*)

Deputy Principal Clerk of Session
(*Stamp*)

Form 62.16

Rule 62.16

C1.2A.203

Rule 62.16   FORM 62.16

Form of notice of registration of award under the Arbitration (International Investments Disputes) Act 1966

REGISTRATION OF AWARD UNDER THE ARBITRATION (INTERNATIONAL INVESTMENTS DISPUTES) ACT 1966

Date: (*date of posting or other method of service*)

To: (*name and address of person on whom service executed*)

TAKE NOTICE

That on (*date*) [Lord (*name*) in] the Court of Session, Edinburgh granted warrant for the registration of (*identify award to be registered*) on the application of (*name and address of petitioner*).

The above award was registered in the Books of Council and Session on (*date*) for execution (enforcement). An application will be made to the Keeper of the Registers of Scotland for an extract of the registered award with warrant for execution.

(*Signed*)

Messenger-at-Arms
[*or* Solicitor [*or* Agent] for petitioner]
(*Address*)

Form 62.28[1, 2, 3, 4]

Form of petition for registration of a judgment under section 4 of the Civil Jurisdiction and Judgments Act 1982 or under Article 38, Article 57 or Article 58 of the Council Regulation or the Lugano Convention

C1.2A.204.1

UNTO THE RIGHT HONOURABLE THE LORDS OF COUNCIL AND SESSION

PETITION

of

[A.B.] (designation and address)

---

[1] Form 62.28 as substituted by S.S.I. 2015 No. 26 Sch.1 Pt 1 (effective 7 February 2015).
[2] Form 62.28 as amended by S.S.I. 2014 No. 302 (effective 16th December 2014).
[3] Form 62.28 as amended by S.S.I. 2019 No. 85 r.4(a) (effective 28th March 2019).
[4] Form 62.28 as amended by S.S.I. 2020 No. 440 (effective IP completion day, 31st December 2020).

under the Civil Jurisdiction and Judgments Act 1982 [or under the Convention on Choice of Court Agreements concluded on 30th June 2005 at the Hague] [or under Council Regulation (EC) No. 44/2001 of 22nd December 2000 on jurisdiction and the recognition and enforcement of judgments in civil or commercial matters or under the Lugano Convention

for registration of
a judgment [or authentic instrument or court settlement [of the (name of court)]
dated the..........day of
HUMBLY SHEWETH:—

1. That this petition is presented by (name) to register a judgment [or authentic instrument or court settlement] [of the (name of court) of (date of judgment)].
2. That in the cause in which the judgment [or as the case may be] was pronounced, [A.B.] was pursuer [or defender or (as the case may be)] and [C.D.] was defender [or pursuer or as the case may be].
3. That the petitioner is a party having an interest to enforce the judgment [or as the case may be] because (state reasons).
4. That this petition is supported by the affidavit of (name of deponent) and the documents produced with it.
5. That the petitioner seeks warrant to register the judgment [or as the case may be] [and for decree in terms thereof] [and for decree to be pronounced in the following or such other terms as to the court may seem proper:— (state terms in which decree is to be pronounced in accordance with Scots law)].
6. That the petitioner seeks the authority of the court to execute the protective measure[s] of (state measures), for the following reasons (state reasons).
7. That this petition is made under section 4 of, and under Article 31 [or 50] of the Convention in Schedule 1 to, the Civil Jurisdiction and Judgments Act 1982 [or under section 4B of the Civil Jurisdiction and Judgments Act 1982] [or under Article 38 [or 57 or 58] of Council Regulation (EC) No. 44/2001 of 22nd December 2000 on jurisdiction and the recognition and enforcement of judgments in civil or commercial matters [or under Article 38 [or 57 or 58] of the Convention on jurisdiction and the recognition and enforcement of judgments in civil and commercial matters, signed by the European Community on 30th October 2007] and rule 62.28 of the Rules of the Court of Session 1994.

According to Justice etc.
(Signed)
Petitioner
[or Solicitor [or Agent] for petitioner]
(Address of solicitor or agent)
[or counsel or other person having a right of audience]

Form 62.33[1, 2, 3]

Rule 62.33

---

[1] Form 62.33 as substituted by S.S.I. 2015 No. 26 Sch.1 Pt 1 (effective 7th February 2015).
[2] Form 62.33 as amended by S.S.I. 2019 No. 85 r.4(b) (effective 28th March 2019).
[3] Form 62.33 as amended by S.S.I. 2014 No. 302 (effective 16th December 2014).

Form of notice of decree and warrant for registration of a judgment under section **C1.2A.204.**
4 of the Civil Jurisdiction and Judgments Act 1982 or under Article 38, Article 57 or
Article 58 of the Council Regulation or the Lugano Convention

IN THE COURT OF SESSION

in the

PETITION

of

[A.B.] (designation and address)

under section 4 of the Civil Jurisdiction and Judgments Act 1982 [or under Article
38 [or 57 or 58] of Council Regulation (EC) No. 44/2001 of 22nd December 2000
on jurisdiction and the recognition and enforcement of judgments in civil or commercial matters or the Lugano Convention on jurisdiction and the recognition and
enforcement of judgments in civil and commercial matters signed by the European
Community on 30th October 2007]

Date: (date of posting or other method of service)

To: (name of person against whom judgment was given and decree and warrant
granted).

TAKE NOTICE

That an interlocutor dated the..........day of.........., a certified copy of which is attached, was pronounced at the Court of Session granting decree and warrant for
registration of the judgment [or as the case may be] [of the (name of court)] dated
the..........day of.........., for (state briefly the terms of the judgment).

You have the right to appeal to a Lord Ordinary in the Outer House of the Court
of Session, Parliament Square, Edinburgh EH1 1RQ against the interlocutor granting decree and warrant for registration within one month [or two months as the case
may be] after the date of service of this notice upon you. The date of service is the
date stated at the top of this notice unless service has been executed by post in
which case the notice of service is the day after that date.

An appeal must be by motion enrolled in the process of the petition.

The registered judgment and decree of the Court of Session may not be enforced
in Scotland until the expiry of the period within which you may appeal and any appeal has been disposed of.

Intimation of an appeal should be made to the petitioner, [A.B.], at the following
address for service in Scotland:- (address).

(Signed)

Messenger-at-Arms

[or Petitioner [or Solicitor] [or Agent] for petitioner]

(Address)

Form 62.38

C1.2A.206   Rule 62.38(1)

Rule 62.38(1)   FORM 62.38

Form of petition for registration of a judgment under paragraph 5 of Schedule 7 to the Civil Jurisdiction and Judgments Act 1982

UNTO THE RIGHT HONOURABLE THE LORDS OF COUNCIL AND SESSION

PETITION

of

[A.B.] *(designation and address)*

under the Civil Jurisdiction and Judgments Act 1982

for registration of

a judgment of the *(name of court)*

dated the   day of

HUMBLY SHEWETH:—

1. That this petition is presented by *(name)* to register a judgment [*or decision or other order*] of the *(name of court)* of *(date of judgment)*.

2. That in the cause in which the judgment [*or decision or other order*] was pronounced [A.B.] was plaintiff [*or defendant or as the case may be*] and [C.D.] was defendant [*or plaintiff or as the case may be*].

3. That the petitioner is a party having an interest to enforce the judgment [*or decision or other order*] because *(state reasons)*.

4. That the petitioner believes and avers that the usual [*or last known*] address of the *(state party liable in execution)* is *(state address)*.

5. That the petitioner seeks warrant to register the judgment [and for decree in terms thereof] [and for decree to be pronounced in the following or such other terms as to the court may seem proper:— *(state terms in which decree is to be pronounced in accordance with Scots law)*].

6. That this petition is made under paragraph 5(1) of Schedule 7 to the Civil Jurisdiction and

Judgments Act 1982 and rule 62.38 of the Rules of the Court of Session 1994.

According to Justice etc.

(*Signed*)

Petitioner
[*or* Solicitor [*or* Agent] for petitioner]
(*Address of solicitor or agent*)

[*or counsel or other person having a right of audience*]

Form 62.40 A

Rule 62.40(1)(a)

C1.2A.207

Rule 62.40(1)(*a*)   [1] FORM 62.40–A

Form of certificate under section 12 of the Civil Jurisdiction and Judgments Act 1982 of a judgment given by the court or a court settlement

IN THE COURT OF SESSION

CERTIFICATE

under the Civil Jurisdiction and Judgments Act 1982

in the cause

[*or* in the petition of]

[A.B.] (*designation and address*)

Pursuer [*or* Petitioner]

against

[C.D.] (*designation and address*)

Defender [*or* Respondent]

I,   , a Deputy Principal Clerk of the Court Session, do hereby certify—

1. That the summons [*or* petition], brought [*or* presented] by the pursuer [*or* petitioner] [A.B.] was executed by citation of the defender [C.D.] served on him [*or* was served on the respondent [C.D.]] on the   day of   by (*state method of service*).

2. That in the summons [*or* petition] the pursuer, sought [payment of the sum of £   in respect of (*state briefly the nature of the claim*)] [and (*state other conclusions of the summons or orders sought in the prayer of petition*)].

3. [That the defender [C.D.] entered appearance on the   day of   ] [and lodged defences on the   day of   [*or* That the defender [C.D.] did not enter appearance].

4. That the pursuer [*or* petitioner] obtained decree [*or other order*] against the defender [*or* respondent] in the Court of Session for [payment of the sum of £   ] [*or state briefly the terms of the interlocutor or opinion of the court*] [and *state briefly other conclusions of the summons or orders sought in the prayer of the petition granted*] with the expenses of the cause in the sum of £   , all in terms of the certified copy interlocutor [and joint minute] attached.

5. That [no] objection to the jurisdiction of the court has been made [on the grounds that   ].

6. That the decree [in terms of the joint minute] includes interest at the rate of   per cent a year on the total of the sum of £   and expenses of £   from the   day of   until payment.

7. That the interlocutor containing the decree [*or other order or settlement*] has been served on the defender.

8. That the time for reclaiming (appealing) against the interlocutor has expired [and no reclaiming motion (appeal) has been enrolled within that time] [*or* and a reclaiming motion (appeal) having been enrolled within that time, has [not] been finally disposed of].

9. That enforcement of the decree has not for the time being been suspended and the time available for its enforcement has not expired.

10. That the whole pleadings of the parties are contained in the Closed Record [*or* summons *or* petition], a copy of which is attached.

11. That this certificate is issued under section 12 of the Civil Jurisdiction and Judgments Act 1982 and rule 62.40(1) of the Rules of the Court of Session 1994.

Dated the   day of

(*Signed*)

Deputy Principal Clerk of Session

---

[1] Form 62.40–A amended by S.I. 1994 No. 2901 (clerical error) and S.I. 1997 No. 1050 (minor amendment, effective 6th April 1997).

Form 62.40-B

Rule 62.40(3)

Rule 62.40(3) FORM 62.40–B

Form of certificate by Keeper of the Registers of writ registered for execution in the Books of Council and Session for registration under Article 50 of Schedule 1 or 3C to the Civil Jurisdiction and Judgments Act 1982

REGISTERS OF SCOTLAND

CERTIFICATE

under the Civil Jurisdiction and Judgments Act 1982

of

Deed [*or other writ*]

between

[A.B.] (*address*)

and

[C.D.] (*address*)

registered for execution in the Books of Council and Session

I, , the Keeper of the Registers of Scotland, and as such, Keeper of the Register of Deeds, Bonds, Protests, Judgments and other writs registered for execution in the Books of Council and Session, do hereby certify—

1. That [A.B.] registered in the Books of Council and Session on the day of for execution against [C.D.] a (*describe writ and state terms of writ for which enforcement is to be sought*).

2. That the extract of the deed [*or other writ*] attached hereto is a true copy of the deed [*or other writ*] registered for execution by [A.B.].

[3. That the deed [*or other writ*] carries interest at the rate of per cent a year from the day of until payment].

[4. That enforcement of the deed] [*or other writ*] has not for the time being been suspended and that the time available for its enforcement has not expired.

5. That the certificate is issued under Article 50 of Schedule 1 [*or 3C*] to the Civil Jurisdiction and Judgments Act 1982 and rule 62.40(3) of the Rules of the Court of Session 1994.

Dated the day of

(*Signed*)

Keeper of the Registers of Scotland

Form 62.41-A

C1.2A.209   Rule 62.41(1)

Rule 62.41(1)   [1] FORM 62.41–A

Form of certificate of money provisions in an interlocutor for registration under Schedule 6 to the Civil Jurisdiction and Judgments Act 1982

IN THE COURT OF SESSION

CERTIFICATE

under the Civil Jurisdiction and Judgments Act 1982

in the cause

[*or* in the petition of]

[A.B.] (*designation and address*)

Pursuer [*or* Petitioner]

against

[C.D.] (*designation and address*)

Defender [*or* Respondent]

I,   , a Deputy Principal Clerk of the Court Session, do hereby certify—

1. That the pursuer A.B. obtained decree [*or other order*] against the defender [C.D.] on the   day of   in the Court of Session for payment of the sum of £   in respect of (*state briefly the nature of the claim and terms of the interlocutor*) with the sum of £   as expenses.

2. That the interlocutor granting decree [*or other order*] was obtained on the grounds (*state grounds briefly*).

3. That the decree [*or other order*] carries interest at the rate of   per cent a year on the total of the sum of £   and expenses of £   from the   day of   until payment.

4. That the time for reclaiming (appealing) against the interlocutor has expired [and no reclaiming motion (appeal) has been enrolled within that time] [and a reclaiming motion (appeal) having been enrolled within that time, has been finally disposed of].

5. That enforcement of the decree [*or other order*] has not for the time being been suspended and the time available for its enforcement has not expired.

Dated the   day of   .

(*Signed*)

Deputy Principal Clerk of Session

Form 62.41-B

Rule 62.41(3)

Rule 62.41(3)   FORM 62.41–B

**Form of certificate by Keeper of the Registers of money provisions in a writ registered for
execution in the Books of Council and Session for registration under Schedule 6 to the Civil
Jurisdiction and Judgments Act 1982**

REGISTERS OF SCOTLAND

CERTIFICATE

under the Civil Jurisdiction and Judgments Act 1982

of

Deed [*or other writ*]

between

[A.B.] (*address*)

and

[C.D.] (*address*)

registered for execution in the Books of Council and Session

I,   , the Keeper of the Registers of Scotland, and as such, Keeper of the
Register of Deeds, Bonds, Protests, Judgments and other writs registered for execution in the
Books of Council and Session, do hereby certify—

1. That [A.B.] registered in the Books of Council and Session on the   day
of   for execution against [C.D.] a (*describe writ and state terms of money provision
in writ for which enforcement is to be sought*).

2. That the money provision in the deed [*or other writ*] carries interest at the rate of   per
cent a year from the   day of   until payment.

3. That enforcement of the deed [*or other writ*] has not for the time being been suspended and
that the time available for its enforcement has not expired.

4. That this certificate is issued under paragraph 4(1) of Schedule 6 to the Civil Jurisdiction and
Judgments Act 1982 and rule 62.41(3) of the Rules of the Court of Session 1994.

Dated the   day of

(*Signed*)

Keeper of the Registers of Scotland

Form 62.42-A

C1.2A.211   Rule 62.42(1)

Rule 62.42(1)   [1] FORM 62.42–A

Form of certificate of non-money provisions in an interlocutor for registration under Schedule 7 to the Civil Jurisdiction and Judgments Act 1982

IN THE COURT OF SESSION

CERTIFICATE

under the Civil Jurisdiction and Judgments Act 1982

in the cause

[*or* in the PETITION of]

[A.B.] (*designation and address*)

Pursuer [*or* Petitioner]

against

[C.D.] (*designation and address*)

Defender [*or* Respondent]

I,   , a Deputy Principal Clerk of the Court Session, do hereby certify—

1. That the copy of the interlocutor attached hereto is a true copy of the decree [*or other order*] obtained in the Court of Session [and that the copy of the opinion of the court attached hereto is a true copy thereof] and is issued in accordance with section 18 of the Civil Jurisdiction and Judgments Act 1982.

2. That the time for reclaiming (appealing) against the interlocutor has expired [and no reclaiming motion (appeal) has been enrolled within that time] [and a reclaiming motion (appeal) having been enrolled within that time has been finally disposed of].

3. That enforcement of the decree [*or other order*] has not for the time being been suspended and the time available for its enforcement has not expired.

4. That this certificate is issued under paragraph 4(1)(b) of Schedule 7 to the Civil Jurisdiction and Judgments Act 1982 and rule 62.42(1) of the Rules of the Court of Session 1994.

Dated the   day of   .

(*Signed*)

Deputy Principal Clerk of Session

---

[1] Form 62.42–A amended by S.I. 1994 No. 2901 (clerical error) and S.I. 1997 No. 1050 (minor amendment, effective 6th April 1997).

Form 62.42-B

Rule 62.42(4)

Rule 62.42(4)   FORM 62.42–B

Form of certificate by Keeper of the Registers of non-money provisions in a writ registered for execution in the Books of Council and Session for registration under Schedule 7 to the Civil Jurisdiction and Judgments Act 1982

REGISTERS OF SCOTLAND

CERTIFICATE

under the Civil Jurisdiction and Judgments Act 1982

of

Deed [*or other writ*]

between

[A.B.] (*address*)

and

[C.D.] (*address*)

registered for execution in the Books of Council and Session

I,   , the Keeper of the Registers of Scotland, and as such, Keeper of the Register of Deeds, Bonds, Protests, Judgments and other writs registered for execution in the Books of Council and Session, do hereby certify—

1. That the extract of the deed [*or other writ*] attached hereto is a true copy of the deed [*or other writ*] registered for execution by [A.B.] and is issued in accordance with section 18 of the Civil Jurisdiction and Judgments Act 1982.

2. That enforcement of the deed [*or other writ*] has not for the time being been suspended and that the time available for its enforcement has not expired.

3. That this certificate is issued under paragraph 4(1)(b) of Schedule 7 to the Civil Jurisdiction and Judgments Act 1982 and rule 62.42(4) of the Rules of the Court of Session 1994.

Dated the   day of

(*Signed*)

Keeper of the Registers of Scotland

Form 62.42C-A[1]

Form of petition under Articles 36(2), 45(1), 46, 58(1) or 59 of the Brussels I (recast) Regulation

C1.2A.212.1   Rule 62.42C(1)

UNTO THE RIGHT HONOURABLE THE LORDS OF COUNCIL AND SESSION

PETITION

of

[A.B.] (designation and address)

under Regulation (E.U.) 1215/2012 of the European Parliament and of the Council of 12th December 2012 on jurisdiction and the recognition and enforcement of judgments in civil matters (recast)

for

a decision under Article 36(2) that there are no grounds for refusal of recognition

[or refusal of recognition of a judgment under Article 45(1)]

[or refusal of enforcement of a judgment under Article 46]

[or refusal of enforcement of an authentic instrument under Article 58(1)]

[or refusal of enforcement of a court settlement under Article 59]

HUMBLY SHEWETH:

1.   That this petition is presented by (name) for (specify nature of petition, including the Article of the Brussels I (recast) Regulation under which it is brought) in respect of a judgment [or authentic instrument] [or court settlement] [of the (name of court)] of (date of judgment etc.).

2.   That in the cause in which the judgment [or authentic instrument] [or court settlement] was pronounced, [A.B.] was defender [or pursuer (or as the case may be)] and [C.D.] was pursuer [or defender (or as the case may be)].

3.   That the petitioner has an interest to seek a decision that there are no grounds for refusal of recognition [or to seek refusal of recognition [or enforcement]] because: (specify reasons).

4.   That the petitioner seeks a decision that there are no grounds for refusal of recognition [or seeks refusal of recognition [or enforcement]] because: (specify reasons).

According to Justice etc.

(Signed)
Petitioner

[or Solicitor [or Agent] for petitioner]
(address of solicitor or agent)

[or counsel or other person having a right of audience]

---

[1] Form 62.42C-A as inserted by S.S.I. 2015 No. 26 (effective 7th February 2015).

Form 62.42C-B[1]

Form of petition for an adaptation order under Article 54(1) of the Brussels I (recast) Regulation
Rule 62.42C(2)

UNTO THE RIGHT HONOURABLE THE LORDS OF COUNCIL AND SESSION

PETITION

of

[A.B.] (designation and address)

under Regulation (E.U.) 1215/2012 of the European Parliament and of the Council of 12th December 2012 on jurisdiction and the recognition and enforcement of judgments in civil matters (recast)

for

an adaptation order

HUMBLY SHEWETH:

1.   That this petition is presented by (name) for an adaptation order in respect of a judgment [or authentic instrument] [or court settlement] [of the (name of court) of (date of judgment etc.).

2.   That in the cause in which the judgment [or authentic instrument] [or court settlement] was pronounced, [A.B.] was pursuer [or defender (or as the case may be)] and [C.D.] was defender [or pursuer (or as the case may be)].

3.   That the judgment [or authentic instrument] [or court settlement] contains the following measure or order which is not known to the law of Scotland: (specify measure or order and its nature and effect).

4.   That the petitioner seeks an adaptation order in respect of that measure or order, and for decree to be pronounced in the following terms, or such other terms as to the court seem proper: (specify terms in which the measure or order is to be adapted, and decree pronounced in accordance with Scots law).

According to Justice etc.

(Signed)
Petitioner

[or Solicitor [or Agent] for petitioner]
(address of solicitor or agent)

[or counsel or other person having a right of audience]

---

[1] Form 62.42C-B as inserted by S.S.I. 2015 No. 26 (effective 7th February 2015).

Form 62.42C-C[1]

Form of petition for a challenge to the adaptation of a measure or order under Article 54 of the Brussels I (recast) Regulation

C1.2A.212.4   Rule 62.42C(3)

UNTO THE RIGHT HONOURABLE THE LORDS OF COUNCIL AND SESSION

PETITION

of

[A.B.] (designation and address)

under Regulation (E.U.) 1215/2012 of the European Parliament and of the Council of 12th December 2012 on jurisdiction and the recognition and enforcement of judgments in civil matters (recast)

challenging the adaptation of a measure or order which is not known to the law of Scotland

HUMBLY SHEWETH:

1.   That this petition is presented by (name) to challenge the adaptation of a measure or order contained in a judgment [or authentic instrument] [or court settlement] [of the (name of court) of (date of judgment etc.).

2.   That in the cause in which the judgment [or authentic instrument] [or court settlement] was pronounced, [A.B.] was pursuer [or defender (or as the case may be)] and [C.D.] was defender [or pursuer (or as the case may be)].

3.   That the measure or order in question is in the following terms: (specify measure or order and its nature and effect).

4.   That the measure or order was adapted as follows: (specify the circumstances of the adaptation, including the authority by whom it was adapted, the nature of the adaptation and the date of the adaptation).

5.   That the petitioner challenges the adaptation of the measure or order because: (specify reasons).

6.   That the petitioner considers that the measure or order should not be adapted, and seeks to have the adaptation set aside.

[or 6.   That the petitioner seeks an adaptation order in respect of the measure or order, and for decree to be pronounced in the following terms, or such other terms as the court seem proper: (specify terms in which the measure or order is to be adapted, and decree pronounced in accordance with Scots law).

According to Justice etc.

(Signed)
Petitioner

[or Solicitor [or Agent] for petitioner]
(address of solicitor or agent)

[or counsel or other person having a right of audience]

---

[1] Form 62.42C-C as inserted by S.S.I. 2015 No. 26 (effective 7th February 2015).

Form 62.51

Rule 62.51

Form of notice of decree and warrant for registration of an order under the Criminal Justice (Scotland) Act 1987, the Criminal Justice Act 1988 or the Prevention of Terrorism (Temporary Provisions) Act 1989

IN THE COURT OF SESSION

in the

PETITION of

[A.B.] (*designation and address*)

under section 28 [or 30A] of the Criminal

Justice (Scotland) Act 1987

[*or* section 90 of the Criminal Justice Act 1988]

[*or* paragraph 19(2) of Schedule 4 to the Prevention of Terrorism (Temporary Provisions) Act 1989]

for

registration of an order of

(*name of court*)

Dated the   day of |

To: (*name of person against whom the order was made and decree and warrant for registration granted*)

TAKE NOTICE

An interlocutor dated the   day of , a certified copy of which is attached, was pronounced in the Court of Session granting decree and warrant for registration in the Court of Session [and for registration in the Register of Judgments of the Books of Council and Session] of the order of the (*name of court*) dated the   day of   that (*briefly describe order*).

The order was registered in the Court of Session on (*date*).

[The order was registered in the Register of Judgments of the Books of Council and Session on (*date*) and an extract of the registered order and decree with warrant for execution has been issued by the Keeper of the Registers. Diligence in execution of the order may now be taken against you to enforce the order.]

Dated this   day of

(*Signed*)

Messenger-at-Arms
[*or* Petitioner[[*or* Solicitor
[*or* Agent] for petitioner]
(*Address*)

Form 62.59

C1.2A.214   Rule 62.59

Rule 62.59   [1] FORM 62.59

Form of notice of registration of award under the New York Convention on the Recognition and Enforcement of Foreign Arbitral Awards

REGISTRATION OF AWARD UNDER THE NEW YORK CONVENTION ON THE RECOGNITION AND ENFORCEMENT OF FOREIGN ARBITRAL AWARDS

Date: (*date of posting or other method of service*)

To: (*name and address of person on whom service executed*)

TAKE NOTICE

That on (*date*) [Lord/Lady (*name*) in] the Court of Session, Edinburgh, granted warrant for the registration of (*identify award to be registered*) on the application of (*name and address of petitioner or noter*).

The above award was registered in the Books of Council and Session on (*date*) for execution (enforcement). An application will be made to the Keeper of the Registers of Scotland for an extract of the registered award with warrant for execution.

(*Signed*)

Messenger-at-Arms
[*or* Solicitor [*or* Agent] for petitioner or noter]
(*Address*)

---

[1] Form 62.59 inserted by S.S.I. 2010 No. 205 (effective 7th June 2010).

Form 62.65

Rule 62.65

Rule 62.65

[1] FORM 62.65

Form of notice of registration of decision under a relevant instrument

REGISTRATION OF A DECISION (*or as the case may be*) UNDER THE
(*specify the relevant instrument*)

Date: (*date of posting or other method of service*)

To: (*name and address of person on whom service executed*)

TAKE NOTICE

That on (*date*) [Lord (*name*) in] the Court of Session, Edinburgh granted warrant for the registration of (*identify decision to be registered*) on the application of (*name and address of petitioner*).

The above award was registered in the Books of Council and Session on (*date*) for execution (i.e. enforcement). An application will be made to the Keeper of the Registers of Scotland for an extract of the registered award with warrant for execution.

(*Signed*)

Solicitor [*or* Agent] for petitioner
(*Address*)

---

[1] Form 62.65 inserted by S.I. 1996 No. 2168.

Form 62.69

C1.2A.216 Rule 62.69(1)

Rule 62.69(1)   [1] FORM 62.69

Form of petition for enforcement of a judgment under Article 28 of the Council Regulation

UNTO THE RIGHT HONOURABLE THE LORDS OF COUNCIL AND SESSION

PETITION

of

[A.B.] (*designation and address*)

under Council Regulation (E.C.) No. 2201/2003 of 27th November 2003 on jurisdiction and the recognition and enforcement of judgments in matrimonial matters and matters of parental responsibility

for registration of

a judgment [*or* authentic instrument *or* enforceable agreement][of the (*name of court*)]

dated the   day of

HUMBLY SHEWETH:—

1. That this petition is presented by [A.B.] to register a judgment [*or* (*as the case may be*)][of the (*name of court*)] of (*date of judgment or as the case may be*).

2. That in the cause in which the judgment [*or* (*as the case may be*)] was pronounced, [A.B.] was pursuer [*or* defender *or* (*as the case may be*)] and [C.D.] was defender [*or* pursuer *or* (*as the case may be*)].

3. That the petitioner is a party having an interest to enforce the judgment [*or* (*as the case may be*)] because (*state reasons*).

4. That this petition is supported by the affidavit of (*name of deponent*) and the documents produced with it.

5. That the petitioner seeks warrants to register the judgment [*or* (*as the case may be*)] [and for decree in terms thereof] [*or* and for decree to be pronounced in the following or such other terms as to the court seem proper:—(*state terms in which decree is to be pronounced in accordance with Scots law*)].

6. That the petition is made under Article 28 of the Council Regulation (E.C.) No. 2201/2003 of 27th November 2003 on jurisdiction and the recognition and enforcement of judgments in matrimonial matters and matters of parental responsibility and rule 62.69 of the Rules of the Court of Session 1994 [*or* (*as the case may be*)].

According to Justice etc.

(*Signed*)

Petitioner

[*or* Solicitor [*or* Agent] for petitioner]

[*Address of solicitor or agent*]

[*or* counsel or other person having a right of audience].

------

[1] Form 62.69 inserted by S.S.I. 2005 No. 135 (effective 8th December 2005).

Form 62.73

Rule 62.73

Rule 62.73   [1] FORM 62.73

**Form of notice of decree and warrant for registration of a judgment under Article 28
of the Council Regulation**

IN THE COURT OF SESSION

in the

PETITION of

[A.B.] (*designation and address*)

under Council Regulation (E.C.) No. 2201/2003 of 27th November 2003 on jurisdiction and the
recognition and enforcement of judgments in matrimonial matters and matters of parental
responsibility

for registration of

a judgment [*or* authentic instrument *or* enforceable agreement][of the (*name of court*)]

dated the   day of

Date: (*date of posting or other method of service*)

To: (*name of person against whom judgment was given and decree and warrant granted*)

TAKE NOTICE

That an interlocutor dated the   day of   , a certified copy of which is attached, was
pronounced at the Court of Session granting decree and warrant for registration of the
judgment [*or* (*as the case may be*)] [of the (*name of court*) dated the   day of   , for (*state
briefly the terms of the judgment*).

You have the right to appeal to a Lord Ordinary in the Outer House of the Court of Session,
Parliament Square, Edinburgh, EH1 1RQ against the interlocutor granting decree and warrant
for registration within one month [*or* two months (*as the case may be*)] after the date of service
of this notice upon you. The date of service is the date stated at the top of this notice unless
service has been executed by post in which case the date of service is the day after that date.

An appeal must be by motion enrolled in the process of the petition.

The registered judgment and decree of the Court of Session may not be enforced in Scotland
until the expiry of the period within which you may appeal and any appeal has been disposed of.

Intimation of an appeal should be made to the petitioner, [A.B.], at the following address for
service in Scotland:—(*specify address*)

(*Signed*)

Messenger-at-Arms

[*or* Petitioner [*or* Solicitor [*or* Agent] for Petitioner]] (*Address*)

---

[1] Form 62.73 inserted by S.S.I. 2005 No. 135, para.3 (effective 2nd March 2005).

Form 62.98

C1.2A.218   Rule 62.98(1)

Rule 62.98(1)   [1] FORM 62.98

Form of petition under Article 24 [or 26] of the 1996 Convention

UNTO THE RIGHT HONOURABLE THE LORDS OF COUNCIL AND SESSION

PETITION

of

[A.B.] (*designation and address*)

under the Convention on Jurisdiction, Applicable Law, Recognition, Enforcement and Co-operation in respect of Parental Responsibility and Measures for the Protection of Children, signed at The Hague on 19th October 1996

for registration of

a measure of the (*name of judicial or administrative authority of Contracting State*)

dated the   day of

HUMBLY SHEWETH:—

1. That this petition is presented by [A.B.] to register a measure of the (*name of judicial or administrative authority of Contracting State*).

2. That the petitioner is a party or person having an interest to enforce the measure because (*state reasons*).

3. That the petitioner seeks warrant to register the measure [and for decree to be pronounced in the following or such other terms as to the court seem proper: — (*state terms in which decree is to be pronounced in accordance with Scots law*)].

4. That the petition is made under Article 24 [*or* Article 26] of the Convention on Jurisdiction, Applicable Law, Recognition, Enforcement and Co-operation in respect of Parental Responsibility and Measures for the Protection of Children, signed at The Hague on 19th October 1996 and rule 62.98 of the Rules of the Court of Session 1994 [or (*as the case may be*)].

5. That the following grounds for refusal of recognition as set out in Article 23(2) of the said Convention apply: (*list which of the grounds mentioned in Article 23(2) apply*)

[or

That there are no grounds for refusal of recognition having regard to Article 23(2) of the said Convention.]

According to Justice etc.

(*Signed*)
Petitioner

[or Solicitor [*or* Agent] for petitioner]
[*Address of solicitor or agent*]
[or counsel *or* other person having a right
of audience]

---

[1] Form 62.98 inserted by S.S.I. 2011 No. 190 (effective 11th April 2011).

Form 62.101

C1.2A.219   Rule 62.101

Rule 62.101   [1] FORM 62.101

**Form of notice of decree and warrant for registration of a measure under Article 24
[or Article 26] of the 1996 Convention**

IN THE COURT OF SESSION

in the

PETITION of

[A.B.] *(designation and address)*

under the Convention on Jurisdiction, Applicable Law, Recognition, Enforcement and Co-operation in respect of Parental Responsibility and Measures for the Protection of Children, signed at The Hague on 19th October 1996

for registration of

a measure of the *(name of judicial or administrative authority of Contracting State)*

dated the   day of

Date: *(date of posting or other method of service)*

To: *(name of person against whom measure is sought to be enforced)*

TAKE NOTICE

That an interlocutor dated the   day of   , a certified copy of which is attached, was

pronounced at the Court of Session granting decree and warrant for registration of the measure of the *(name of judicial or administrative authority of Contracting State)* dated the day of   , for *(state briefly the terms of the measure)*.

(Signed)

Messenger-at-Arms

[*or* Petitioner [*or* Agent] for Petitioner]]
(Address)

---

[1] Form 62.101 inserted by S.S.I. 2011 No. 190 (effective 11th April 2011).

Form 64.6

Rule 64.6

Rule 64.6 [1] FORM 64.6

Form of order of court in procedure for recovery of documents under Chapter 64

ORDER BY THE COURT OF SESSION

In the Petition

of

[A.B.] (*designation and address*)

Petitioner

against

[C.D.] (*designation and address*)

Respondent

Date: (*date of interlocutor*)

To: (*name and address of party or parties or named third party haver, from whom the documents and other property are sought to be recovered*)

THE COURT having heard Counsel and being satisfied that it is appropriate to make an order under section 1 of the Administration of Justice (Scotland) Act 1972:

APPOINTS the Petition to be intimated on the walls of the court in common form and to be served upon the person(s) named and designed in the Petition;

APPOINTS (*name and designation of Commissioner*) to be Commissioner of the court;

GRANTS commission and diligence;

ORDERS the Commissioner to explain to the haver on executing the order—
    (1) the meaning and effect of the order;
    (2) that the haver may be entitled to claim that certain of the documents and other property are confidential or privileged;
    (3) that the haver has a right to seek legal or other professional advice of his choice and to apply to vary or discharge the order;
and to give the haver a copy of the Notice in Form 64.9 of the Rules of Court.

GRANTS warrant to and authorises the said Commissioner, whether the haver has allowed entry or not—
    (1) to enter, between the hours of 9am and 5pm on Monday to Friday, (*or where the court has found cause shown under rule 64.11(1), otherwise specify the time*) the premises at (*address of premises*) and any other place in Scotland owned or occupied by the haver at which it appears to the Commissioner that any of the items set out in the statement of facts in the application to the court (the "listed items") may be located;
    (2) to search for and take all other steps which the Commissioner considers necessary to take possession of or preserve (*specify the listed items*);

(3) to take possession of and to preserve all or any of the listed items and to consign them with the Deputy Principal Clerk of Session to be held by him pending the further orders of the court;

and for that purpose,

ORDERS the haver or his servants or agents to allow the Commissioner, any person whom the Commissioner considers necessary to assist him, and the Petitioner's representatives to enter the premises named in the order and to allow them—

(1) to search for the listed items and take such other steps as the Commissioner considers it reasonable to take to execute the order;

(2) (*if appropriate*) to provide access to information stored on any computer owned or used by him by supplying or providing the means to overcome any and all security mechanisms inhibiting access thereto;

(3) to remain in the premises until such time as the search is complete, including allowing them to continue the search on subsequent days if necessary;

(4) to inform the Commissioner immediately of the whereabouts of the listed items;

(5) to provide the Commissioner with a list of the names and addresses of everyone to whom he has given any of the listed items;

and not to destroy, conceal or tamper with any of the listed items except in accordance with the terms of this order;

FURTHER AUTHORISES (*specify the representatives*) to be the sole representatives of the Petitioner to accompany the Commissioner for the purpose of identification of the said documents and other property.

SCHEDULE TO THE ORDER OF THE COURT

Undertakings given by the Petitioner

The petitioner has given the following undertakings—

1. That he will comply with any order of the court as to payment of compensation if it is subsequently discovered that the order, or the implementation of the order, has caused loss to the respondent or, where the respondent is not the haver, to the haver.

2. That he will bring within a reasonable time of the execution of the order any proceedings which he decides to bring.

3. That he will not, without leave of the court, use any information, documents or other property obtained as a result of the order, except for the purpose of any proceedings which he decides to bring and to which the order relates.

(*or as modified under rule 64.4*)

----

[1] Form 64.6 inserted by S.S.I. 2000 No. 319 as 64.-A, renumbered by S.S.I. 2004 No. 52, substituted by S.S.I. 2011 No. 190 (effective 11th April 2011) and amended by S.S.I. 2011 No. 288 (effective 21st July 2011).

Form 64.9

Rule 64.9

Rule 64.9   [1] FORM 64.9

Notice to accompany order of the court when served by Commissioner

IMPORTANT

NOTICE TO PERSON ON WHOM THIS ORDER IS SERVED

1. This order orders you to allow the person appointed and named in the order as Commissioner to enter your premises to search for, examine and remove or copy the items mentioned in the order.

2. It also allows entry to the premises to any person appointed and named in the order as a representative of the person who has been granted the order and to any person accompanying the Commissioner to assist him.

3. No-one else is given authority to enter the premises.

4. You should read the order immediately.

5. You have the right to seek legal or other professional advice of your choice and you are advised to do so as soon as possible.

6. Consultation under paragraph 5 will not prevent the Commissioner from entering your premises for the purposes mentioned in paragraph 1 but if the purpose of your seeking advice is to help you to decide if you should ask the court to vary or discharge the order you are entitled to ask the Commissioner to delay searching the premises for up to 2 hours or such other longer period as the Commissioner may permit.

7. The Commissioner is obliged to explain the meaning and effect of the order to you.

8. He is also obliged to explain to you that you are entitled to claim that the items, or some of them, are protected as confidential or privileged.

9. You are entitled to ask the court to vary or discharge the order provided that—
> you take steps to do so at once; and
> you allow the Commissioner, any person appointed as a representative of the person who has been granted the order and any person accompanying the Commissioner to assist him, to enter the premises meantime.

10. The Commissioner and the persons mentioned as representatives or assistants have a right to enter the premises even if you refuse to allow them to do so, unless—
> you are female and alone in the premises and there is no female with the Commissioner (where the Commissioner is not herself female), in which case they have no right to enter the premises;
> the Commissioner serves the order before 9am or after 5pm on a weekday or at any time on a Saturday or Sunday (except where the court has specifically allowed this, which will be stated in the order);
in which cases you should refuse to allow entry.

11. You are entitled to insist that there is no-one (*or* no-one other than X) present who could gain commercially from anything which might be read or seen on your premises.

12. You are required to hand over to the Commissioner any of the items mentioned in the order which are in your possession.

13. You may be found liable for contempt of court if you refuse to comply with the order.

---

[1] Form 64.9 inserted by S.S.I. 2000 No. 319 as 64.-B, renumbered by S.S.I. 2000 No. 52 and substituted by S.S.I. 2011 No. 190 (effective 11th April 2011).

Form 65.3

Rule 65.3(1A)

Rule 65.3(1A) [1,2] FORM 65.3

Form of reference to the European Court

REQUEST

for

PRELIMINARY RULING

of

THE COURT OF JUSTICE OF THE EUROPEAN COMMUNITIES

from

THE COURT OF SESSION IN SCOTLAND

in the cause

[A.B.] *(designation and address)*

Pursuer [*or* Petitioner *or* Appellant]

against

[C.D.] *(designation and address)*

Defender [*or* Respondent]

[Here set out a clear and succinct statement of the case giving rise to the request for the ruling of the European Court in order to enable the European Court to consider and understand the issues of Community law raised and to enable governments of Member States and other interested parties to submit observations. The statement of the case should include:
  (a) particulars of the parties;
  (b) the history of the dispute between the parties;
  (c) the history of the proceedings;
  (d) the relevant facts as agreed by the parties or found by the court or, failing such agreement or finding, the contentions of the parties on such facts;
  (e) the nature of the issues of law and fact between the parties;
  (f) the Scots law, so far as is relevant;
  (g) the Treaty provisions or other acts, instruments or rules of Community law concerned; and
  (h) an explanation of why the reference is being made.]
The preliminary ruling of the Court of Justice of the European Communities is accordingly requested on the following questions:

1, 2, *etc.* *[Here set out the questions on which the ruling is sought, identifying the Treaty provisions or other acts, instruments or rules of Community law concerned.]*
  Dated the   day of   19 .".

NOTES

[1] Form 65.3 inserted by S.I. 1999 No. 1281.
[2] Annex to Form 65.3 omitted by S.S.I. 2005 No. 521 (effective 21st October, 2005).

Form 67.8—A

C1.2A.223   Rule 67.8(1)

APPLICATION FOR AN ADOPTION ORDER UNDER SECTION 29 OR 30 OF THE ADOPTION AND CHILDREN (SCOTLAND) ACT 2007 UNTO THE RIGHT HONOURABLE THE LORDS OF COUNCIL AND SESSION

Petition of

[A.B.] ....

(full name of first petitioner)

....

(insert any previous surname(s))

*delete as appropriate

*and

[C.D.] ....

(full name of second petitioner)

....

(insert any previous surname(s))

....

(insert address)

[*or* serial number where allocated]

....

for authority to adopt the child

....

(insert full name of child as shown on birth certificate)

who was born on ....

(insert child's date of birth)

....

(insert child's present address)

HUMBLY SHEWETH

A   *The child*

1.   The child is (insert age of child) years of age, having been born on the .... day of .... at

....

(insert place of birth)

2.   The child is *male/*female.

3.   The child is not and never has been married or a civil partner.

4.   The child's natural mother is ....

....

(insert full name and address)

5.   The child's natural father is ....

....

(insert full name and address)

6.   The child's natural father has*/does not have* parental responsibilities and rights.

7.   *The child has the following guardians:

....

(insert name(s) and address(es)

8. The child is of British/or ....nationality.

9. The child has not been the subject of an adoption order or of a petition for an adoption order *except that ....

(insert details of any previous order or application).

10. *The child is entitled to the following property, namely:

....

11. The following person/people is/are liable to contribute to the support of the child

....

(insert name(s) and address(es))

12. The consent (*insert name*) to the making of the adoption order should be dispensed with on the ground(s) that ....

(*give details*)

B. *The petitioner(s) and arrangements for the child*

1. *The first/second/both petitioner(s) is/are domiciled in a part of the British Islands.

2. *The petitioner(s) reside(s) in a part of the British Islands and has/have been habitually resident there or elsewhere in the British Islands for at least one year prior to the date of this application.

3. The occupation(s) of the petitioner(s) is/are ....

4. *The petitioners are married or are civil partners and reside together/apart.

5. *The petitioners are unmarried and are not civil partners but are living together as if married to each other in an enduring family relationship.

6. *The petitioner is a single person living on his/her own.

7. *The petitioner is married to/a civil partner of/living in an enduring family relationship with the natural mother/father of the child.

8. *The petitioner is married/a civil partner/living in an enduring family relationship but seeks to adopt the child on his/her own and the child is not the child of the petitioner's partner.

9. The petitioner(s) is/are (*respectively) .... (and) .... years of age.

10. The petitioner(s) has/have resident with him/her/them the following persons, namely:

....

11. The child was received into the home of the petitioner(s) on ....

.... (insert date)

12. The child has continuously had his or her home with the petitioner(s) since the date shown in 11 above.

13. *Arrangements for placing the child in the care of the petitioner(s) were made by ....

(insert full name and address of agency or authority or person making such arrangement)

and therefore notification in terms of section 18 of the Adoption and Children (Scotland) Act 2007 is not required.

14. *The petitioner(s) notified

....

(insert name of local authority notified) under section 18 of the Adoption and Children (Scotland) Act 2007 of his/her/their intention to apply for an adoption order in relation to the child on

....

(insert date of notification)

15. No reward or payment has been given or received by the petitioner(s) for or in consideration of the adoption of the child or the giving of consent to the making of an adoption order.

16. *A permanence order under section 80 of the Adoption and Children (Scotland) Act 2007, with authority for the child to be adopted was made on .... (insert date)

at .... (insert the name of the court)

17. *There is no permanence order with authority for adoption in relation to the child.

18. *An order freeing the child for adoption was made

on .... (insert date)

at .... (insert the name of the court)

19. *The child has been placed for adoption by an adoption agency within the meaning of section 2(1) (adoption agencies in England and Wales) of the Adoption and Children Act 2002 with the petitioner(s) and the child was placed for adoption [*under section 19(1) (placing the children with parental consent: England and Wales) of that Act with the consent of each parent or guardian and the consent of the mother was

	given when the child was at least six weeks old] [*under an order made under section 21(1) (placement orders: England and Wales) of that Act and the child was at least six weeks old when that order was made].
20.	*Each parent or guardian of the child has consented under section 20(1) (advance consent to adoption: England and Wales) of the Adoption and Children Act 2002 and has not withdrawn that consent.
21.	*By notice under section 20(4)(a) (notice that information about application for adoption order not required: England and Wales) of the Adoption and Children Act 2002 (*name of parent or guardian*) [and (*name of parent or guardian*)] stated that he [*or* she *or* they] did not wish to be informed of any application for an adoption order and that statement has not been withdrawn.

C *Undertaking by the petitioner(s)*

The petitioner(s) is/are prepared to undertake, if any order is made on this petition, to make for the said child the following provisions, namely —

D *Welfare of the child*

The making of an adoption order would satisfy the need to safeguard and promote the welfare of the child throughout the child's life for the following reasons —

*E *Productions accompanying the petition*

The following documents are lodged along with this application:

(i)	extract birth certificate relating to the child.
(ii)	*extract marriage certificate relating to the petitioner(s). (Note: this need be lodged only in the case of a joint application by spouses or where the application is by one spouse.)
(iii)	*extract certificate of civil partnership relating to the petitioner(s). (Note: this only needs be lodged in the case of a joint application by civil partners or where the application is by one civil partner.)
(iv)	*consent to the adoption by the child's natural mother.
(v)	*consent to the adoption by the child's natural father.
(vi)	*consent to the adoption by the child's guardian.
(vii)	*consent to the adoption by the child.
(viii)	*extract of the permanence order with authority for adoption.
(ix)	*extract of the order freeing the child for

adoption.

(x)   *acknowledgement by local authority of letter by petitioner(s) intimating intention to apply for adoption order.

(xi)   *report by the adoption agency in terms of section 17(2) of the Adoption and Children (Scotland) Act 2007.

(xii)   *report by the local authority in terms of section 19(2) of the Adoption and Children (Scotland) Act 2007.

(xiii)   *any other document not referred to above.
(list documents)

MAY IT THEREFORE please your Lordships:

(1)   to grant warrant for intimation of the petition on the natural parent(s) of the child, where their whereabouts are known, and on such other persons, if any, as the court may think proper;

(2)   to appoint a curator ad litem and, if necessary, a reporting officer and direct them to report;

(3)   thereafter, to make an adoption order in favour of the petitioner(s) under section 28 of the Adoption and Children (Scotland) Act 2007 on such terms and conditions (if any) as the court may think fit;

(4)   to direct the Registrar General for Scotland to make an entry regarding the order in the Adopted Children Register in the form prescribed by him, giving ....

(insert name) as the forename(s), and the surname of the petitioner(s) or (insert another proposed surname) as the surname of .... in the form;

(5)   further, upon proof to the satisfaction of the court in the course of the proceedings to follow hereon, that ....

(insert name of child) was born on the .... day of .... in the year ....

and is identical with the child named ....

(insert full name of child from original birth certificate)

to whom an entry numbered .... in the Resister of Births for the Registration District of ....

Relates, to direct the said Registrar General to cause such birth entry to be marked with the word ?Adopted? and to include the abovementioned date of birth in the entry recording the adoption in the manner indicated in the Schedule to the said Act; and

(6) to pronounce such other or further orders or directions upon such matters, including the expenses of this petition, as the court may think fit.

....

Signature [or Agent] for first petitioner [Address]

....

Signature [or Agent] for second petitioner [Address]

....

[or counsel or the person having a right of audience]

Form 67.8B

Rule 67.8(2)   C1.2A.224

APPLICATION FOR AN ORDER UNDER SECTION 59(1) OF THE ADOPTION AND CHILDREN (SCOTLAND) ACT 2007
UNTO THE RIGHT HONOURABLE THE LORDS OF COUNCIL AND SESSION

Petition of

[A.B.] .... (full name of first petitioner)

.... (insert any previous surname(s))

*delete as appropriate *and

[C.D.] .... (full name of second petitioner)

.... (insert any previous surname(s))

.... (insert address)

[*or* serial number where allocated]

....

for an order under section 59 of the Adoption and Children (Scotland) Act 2007 vesting in *him/her/them the parental responsibilities and parental rights relating to the child

....

(insert full name of child as shown on birth certificate)

who was born on .... (insert child's date of birth)

.... (insert child's present address)

HUMBLY SHEWETH:

A *The child*

1. The child is (insert age of child) years of age, having been born on the .... day of .... at

....

insert place of birth)

2. The child is *male/*female.

3. The child is not and never has been married or a civil partner.

4. The child's natural mother is ....

....
(insert full name and address)

5. The child's natural father is ....

....
(insert full name and address)

6. The child's natural father has*/does not have* parental responsibilities and rights.

7. *The child has the following guardians:

....
(insert name(s) and address(es))

8. The child is of British/or ....nationality.

9. The child has not been the subject of an adoption order or of a petition for an adoption order *except that ....
(insert details of any previous order or application).

10. *The child is entitled to the following property, namely:

....

11. The following person/people is/are liable to contribute to the support of the child

....
insert name(s) and address(es))

12. The consent (insert name) to the making of the order under section 59 of the Adoption and Children (Scotland) Act 2007 should be dispensed with on the ground(s) that ....
(give details)

B. *The petitioner(s) and arrangements for the child*

1. *The first/second/both petitioner(s) is/are domiciled in ....

2. *The petitioner(s) is/are habitually resident at ....

3. The occupation(s) of the petitioner(s) is/are ....

4. *The petitioners are married or are civil partners and reside together/apart.

5. *The petitioners are unmarried and are not civil partners but are living together as if married to each other in an enduring family relationship.

6. *The petitioner is a single person living on his/her own.

7. *The petitioner is married to/a civil partner of/living in an enduring family relationship with the natural mother/father of the child.

8. *The petitioner is married/a civil partner/living

in an enduring family relationship but seeks to adopt the child on his/her own and the child is not the child of the petitioner's partner.

9.   The petitioner(s) is/are (*respectively) .... (and) .... years of age.

10.   The petitioner(s) has/have resident with him/her/them the following persons, namely:

....

11.   The child was received into the home of the petitioner(s) on ....

.... (insert date)

12.   The child has continuously had his or her home with the petitioner(s) since the date shown in 11 above.

13.   *Arrangements for placing the child in the care of the petitioner(s) were made by ....

(insert full name and address of agency or authority or person making such arrangement) and therefore notification in terms of section 18 of the Adoption and Children (Scotland) Act 2007 is not required.

14.   *The petitioner(s) notified ....

(insert name of local authority notified) under section 18 of the Adoption and Children (Scotland) Act 2007 of his/her/their intention to apply for an order under section 59 of the Adoption and Children (Scotland) Act 2007 in relation to the child on

....

(insert date of notification)

15.   No reward or payment has been given or received by the petitioner(s) for or in consideration of the adoption of the child or the giving of consent to the making of an adoption order.

16.   *A permanence order under section 80 of the Adoption and Children (Scotland) Act 2007, with authority for the child to be adopted was made on .... (insert date)

at .... (insert the name of the court)

17.   *There is no permanence order with authority for adoption in relation to the child.

18.   *An order freeing the child for adoption was made

on .... (insert date)

at .... (insert the name of the court)

19.   *The child has been placed for adoption by an adoption agency within the meaning of section

2(1) (adoption agencies in England and Wales) of the Adoption and Children Act 2002 with the petitioner(s) and the child was placed for adoption [*under section 19(1) (placing the children with parental consent: England and Wales) of that Act with the consent of each parent or guardian and the consent of the mother was given when the child was at least six weeks old] [*under an order made under section 21(1) (placement orders: England and Wales) of that Act and the child was at least six weeks old when that order was made].

20.   *Each parent or guardian of the child has consented under section 20(1) (advance consent to adoption: England and Wales) of the Adoption and Children Act 2002 and has not withdrawn that consent.

21.   *By notice under section 20(4)(a) (notice that information about application for adoption order not required: England and Wales) of the Adoption and Children Act 2002 (*name of parent or guardian*) [and (*name of parent or guardian*)] stated that he [*or* she *or* they] did not wish to be informed of any application for an adoption order and that statement has not been withdrawn.

C   *Undertaking by the petitioner(s)*

The petitioner(s) is/are prepared to undertake, if any order is made on this petition, to make for the said child the following provisions, namely —

D   *Welfare of the child*

The making of an order under section 59 of the Adoption and Children (Scotland) Act 2007 would satisfy the need to safeguard and promote the welfare of the child throughout the child's life for the following reasons —

*E   *Productions accompanying the petition*

The following documents are lodged along with this application:

(i)   extract birth certificate relating to the child.

(ii)   *extract marriage certificate relating to the petitioner(s). (Note: this need be lodged only in the case of a joint application by spouses or where the application is by one spouse.)

(iii)   *extract certificate of civil partnership relating to the petitioner(s). (Note: this only needs be lodged in the case of a joint application by civil partners or where the application is by one civil partner.)

(iv)   *consent to the adoption by the child's natural mother.

(v)	*consent to the adoption by the child's natural father.
(vi)	*consent to the adoption by the child's guardian.
(vii)	*consent to the adoption by the child.
(viii)	*extract of the permanence order with authority for adoption.
(ix)	*extract of the order freeing the child for adoption.
(x)	*acknowledgement by local authority of letter by petitioner(s) intimating intention to apply for order under section 59 of the Adoption and Children (Scotland) Act 2007.
(xi)	*report by the adoption agency in terms of section 17(2) of the Adoption and Children (Scotland) Act 2007.
(xii)	*report by the local authority in terms of section 19(2) of the Adoption and Children (Scotland) Act 2007.
(xiii)	*the confirmation required under regulation 7(3)(a)(i) of the Adoptions with a Foreign Element (Scotland) Regulations 2009;
(xiv)	*copies of the confirmations referred to in regulation 7(3)(b)(i), (iii) and (iv) of the Adoptions with a Foreign Element (Scotland) Regulations 2009;
(xv)	*copy of the report mentioned in regulation 7(3)(b)(ii) of the Adoptions with a Foreign Element (Scotland) Regulations 2009;
(xvi)	*copy of the confirmation referred to in regulation 7(3)(c) (*or* 7(3)(d) of the Adoptions with a Foreign Element (Scotland) Regulations 2009;
(xvii)	*the reports, confirmations and other documents mentioned in regulation 8 of the Adoptions with a Foreign Element (Scotland) Regulations 2009 (list documents);
(xviii)	*the documents referred to in regulation 50(3)(a) to (d), (f) and (g) of the Adoption with a Foreign Element (Scotland) Regulations 2008 (list documents);
(xix)	*any other document not referred to above. (*list documents*)

MAY IT THEREFORE please your Lordships:

(1)	to grant warrant for intimation of the petition on the natural parent(s) of the child, where their whereabouts are known, and on such other persons, if any, as the court may think proper;

(2)   to appoint a curator ad litem and, if necessary, a reporting officer to the child and direct them to report;

(3)   thereafter, to make an order under section 59 of the Adoption and Children (Scotland) Act 2007 vesting in the petitioners the parental responsibilities and parental rights to the child on such terms and conditions (if any) as the court may think fit;

(4)   to authorise removal of the child for the purpose of adoption under the laws of (insert name of country) ....

(5)   to pronounce such other or further orders or directions upon such matters, including the expenses of this petition, as the court may think fit.

....

Solicitor [or Agent] for the first petitioner [Address]

....

Solicitor [or Agent] for the second petitioner [Address]

....

[or counsel or other person having a right of audience]

Form 67.13-A

C1.2A.225   Rule 67.13(1)

Rule 67.13(1)   [1] FORM 67.13–A

FORM OF CONSENT OF PARENT OR GUARDIAN UNDER SECTION 31(2)(a) OF THE ADOPTION AND CHILDREN (SCOTLAND) ACT 2007

*delete as appropriate

In the petition relating to the adoption of ....

(insert the full name of the child as it is given in the birth certificate)

*to which petition the court has assigned the serial number ....

(insert serial number)

I *(name and address)* ....

confirm that I am the mother/father/guardian of the child. I fully understand that the effect of the making of an adoption order in respect of the child will be to [*extinguish all the parental responsibilities and parental rights which I have at present in respect of the child] *or* [*share with the petitioner all the parental responsibilities and parental rights which I have at present in respect of the child]. I consent to the making of such an order.

I have signed this consent at *(place of signing)* on the ....

day of ....Two thousand and ....
(signature)

This consent was signed in the presence of:-
(signature of witness)

[Full name of witness]

Address

NOTE
[1] As inserted by S.S.I. 2009 No. 283 (effective 28th September 2009).

Form 67.13-B

Rule 67.13(2)

Rule 67.13(2) [1] FORM 67.13–B

FORM OF CONSENT OF CHILD UNDER SECTION 32(1) OF THE ADOPTION AND CHILDREN (SCOTLAND) ACT 2007

In the petition relating to the adoption of ....

(*insert the full name of the child as it is given in the birth certificate*)

I (*full name of child*) confirm that I understand the nature and effect of the adoption order for which the petitioner(s) has/have applied in respect of me. I consent to the making of such an order.

I have signed this consent at (*place of signing*) on the ....

day of ....Two thousand and ....
(*signature*)

This consent was signed in the presence of:-
(*signature of witness*)

[Full name of witness]

Address

NOTE
[1] As inserted by S.S.I. 2009 No. 283 (effective 28th September 2009).

Form 67.14-A

C1.2A.227   Rule 67.14(1)(b) and (c)

Rule 67.14(1)(b) and (c)   [1] FORM 67.14–A

NOTICE OF INTIMATION OF APPLICATION FOR ADOPTION ORDER [*or ORDER UNDER SECTION 59(1) OF THE ADOPTION AND CHILDREN (SCOTLAND) ACT 2007]

To: *(full name and address of person to whom this intimation is to be sent)*

1.   YOU ARE GIVEN NOTICE THAT in this petition the petitioner(s) is/are applying for [*an adoption order under section 28 of] [*an order under section 59(1) of] the Adoption and Children (Scotland) Act 2007 in relation to the child *(insert name of child)*.

2.   A COPY OF THE PETITION is attached to this notice.

3.   IF YOU WISH to oppose the application you must lodge a form of response in Form 8 before the expiry of the period of notice specified in the form of response. A copy of the form is attached.

4.   A hearing on the By Order Roll has been fixed for *(insert date and time)* at the Court of Session, Parliament Square, Edinburgh.

4.   IF YOU WISH TO OPPOSE the application you must attend, or be represented at the hearing.

5.   You are entitled to be heard on the application. You do not need to attend the hearing unless you do wish to be heard by the court or you are required by the court to attend.

Date *(insert date)*

[Petitioner *or* solicitor to the petitioner *or* Deputy Principal Clerk of Session]

[Address]

If you do not attend, or are not represented at, the By Order the court may make the order applied for.

IF YOU ARE UNCERTAIN WHAT ACTION TO TAKE, you should consult a solicitor.

YOU MAY BE ENTITLED TO LEGAL AID depending on your financial circumstances and you can get information about legal aid from a solicitor.

YOU MAY ALSO OBTAIN ADVICE FROM ANY CITIZENS ADVICE BUREAU OR OTHER ADVICE AGENCY.

NOTE
[1] As inserted by S.S.I 2009 No. 283 (effective 28th September 2009).

Form 67.14-B

Rule 67.14(1)(d)

Rule 67.14(1)(d) [1] FORM 67.14–B

NOTICE OF INTIMATION OF APPLICATION FOR ADOPTION ORDER TO FATHER OF CHILD WITHOUT PARENTAL RESPONSIBILITIES AND RIGHTS

To: (*full name and address of person to whom this intimation is to be sent*)

1. YOU ARE GIVEN NOTICE THAT in this petition the petitioner(s) is/are applying for an adoption order under section 28 of the Adoption and Children (Scotland) Act 2007 in relation to the child (*insert name of child*).

2. A COPY OF THE PETITION is attached to this notice.

3. A hearing on the By Order Roll has been fixed for (*insert date and time*) at the Court of Session, Parliament Square, Edinburgh.

Date (*insert date*)

[Petitioner *or* solicitor to the petitioner *or* Deputy Principal Clerk of Session]

[Address]

IF YOU ARE UNCERTAIN WHAT ACTION TO TAKE, you should consult a solicitor.

YOU MAY BE ENTITLED TO LEGAL AID depending on your financial circumstances and you can get information about legal aid from a solicitor.

YOU MAY ALSO OBTAIN ADVICE FROM ANY CITIZENS ADVICE BUREAU OR OTHER ADVICE AGENCY.

NOTE
[1] As inserted by S.S.I. 2009 No. 283 (effective 28th September 2009).

Form 67.25

Rule 67.25

Application for an convention adoption order under regulation 53 of the Adoption with Foreign Element (Scotland) Regulations 2009

> *Petition of*
> [A.B.] .... (full name of first petitioner)
> .... (insert any previous surname(s))

*delete as appropriate

> *and
>
> [C.D.] .... (full name of second petitioner)
> .... (insert any previous surname(s))
> .... (insert address)
> [*or* serial number where allocated]
> ....
> for authority to adopt the child
> ....
> (insert full name of child as shown on birth certificate)
> who was born on .... (insert child's date of birth)
> who resides at .... (insert child's present address)
> HUMBLY SHEWETH:
> A   *The child*

1. The child is (insert age of child) years of age, having been born on the .... day of .... at ....
(insert place of birth)

2. The child is *male/*female.

3. The child is not and never has been married or a civil partner.

4. The child's natural mother is ....
....
(insert full name and address)

5. The child's natural father is ....
....
(insert full name and address)

6. The child's natural father has*/does not have* parental responsibilities and rights.

7. *The child has the following guardians:
....
(insert name(s) and address(es)

8. The child is of British/or (name other Convention country) nationality.

9. *The child has his/her habitual residence in the British Islands/ (name other Convention country).

10. The child has not been the subject of an adoption order or of a petition for an adoption order *except that ....
(insert details of any previous order or application).

11. *The child is entitled to the following property, namely:
....

12. The following person/people is/are liable to contribute to the support of the child
....
(insert name(s) and address(es))

B. *The petitioner(s) and arrangements for the child*

1. The petitioner(s) is/are [a] United Kingdom/ (name other Convention country) national(s).

2. *The first/second/both petitioner(s) is/are domiciled in a part of the British Islands/(name other Convention country).

3. *The petitioner(s) is/are habitually resident in the British Islands/ (name other Convention country).

4. The occupation(s) of the petitioner(s) is/are ....

5. *The petitioners are married or are civil

partners and reside together/apart.

6.   *The petitioners are unmarried and are not civil partners but are living together as if married to each other in an enduring family relationship.

7.   *The petitioner is a single person living on his/her own.

8.   *The petitioner is married to/a civil partner of/living in an enduring family relationship with the natural mother/father of the child.

9.   *The petitioner is married/a civil partner/living in an enduring family relationship but seeks to adopt the child on his/her own and the child is not the child of the petitioner's partner.

10.   The petitioner(s) is/are (*respectively) .... (and) .... years of age.

11.   The petitioner(s) has/have resident with him/her/them the following persons, namely:

....

12.   The child was received into the home of the petitioner(s) on ....

.... (insert date)

13.   The child has continuously had his or her home with the petitioner(s) since the date shown in 11 above.

14.   *Arrangements for placing the child in the care of the petitioner(s) were made by ....

(insert full name and address of agency or authority or person making such arrangement)

and therefore notification in terms of section 18 of the Adoption and Children (Scotland) Act 2007 is not required.

15.   *The petitioner(s) notified ....

(insert name of local authority notified) under section 18 of the Adoption and Children (Scotland) Act 2007 of his/her/their intention to apply for an adoption order in relation to the child on

....

(insert date of notification)

16.   No reward or payment has been given or received by the petitioner(s) for or in consideration of the adoption of the child or the giving of consent to the making of an adoption order.

17.   *A permanence order under section 80 of the Adoption and Children (Scotland) Act 2007, with authority for the child to be adopted was

made on .... (insert date) at ....
(insert the name of the court)

18.   *There is no permanence order with authority for adoption in relation to the child.

19.   *An order freeing the child for adoption was made on .... (insert date) at ....
(insert the name of the court)

20.   *All persons, institutions and authorities whose consent to the adoption of the child in (*name Convention country*) is required, have freely given such consent in writing.

21.   *All persons who have consented to the adoption of the child have been duly informed about the effect of such consent and have been counselled as necessary.

22.   *The petitioner(s) has/have had such counselling as is necessary in respect of the adoption of the child.

23.   The child is, or will be after adoption by the petitioner(s), authorised to enter and reside permanently in the United Kingdom/(*name other Convention country*).

C   *Undertaking by the petitioner(s)*

The petitioner(s) is/are prepared to undertake, if any order is made on this petition, to make for the said child the following provisions, namely –

*D   *Productions accompanying the petition*

The following documents are lodged along with this application:

(i)   extract birth certificate/(*name equivalent document*) relating to the child.

(ii)   *extract marriage certificate/(name equivalent document of other Convention country) relating to the petitioner(s). (Note: this need be lodged only in the case of a joint application by spouses or where the application is by one spouse.)

(iii)   *extract certificate of civil partnership/(name equivalent document of other Convention country) relating to the petitioner(s). (Note: this only needs be lodged in the case of a joint application by civil partners or where the application is by one civil partner.)

(iv)   *extract of the permanence order with authority for adoption.

(v)   *extract of the order freeing the child for adoption.

(vi)   *report by the adoption agency in terms of section 17(2) of the Adoption and Children (Scotland) Act 2007.

(vii)	*report by the local authority in terms of section 19(2) of the Adoption and Children (Scotland) Act 2007.
(viii)	*copies of the Article 16 information and agreement under Article 17(c) of the Convention referred to in regulation 34(c) of the Adoptions with a Foreign Element (Scotland) Regulations 2009.
(ix)	*the confirmation referred to in regulation 34(d) of those Regulations.
(x)	*copies of the Article 16 Report and agreement under Article 17 of the Convention referred to in regulation 51(c) of those Regulations.
(xi)	*the confirmation referred to in regulation 51(d) of those Regulations.
(xii)	*any other document not referred to above (for example, a translation certificate).

(*list any other documents not referred to above*)

The petitioner(s) crave(s) the court

(1)	to grant warrant for intimation of the petition on the natural parent(s) of the child, where their whereabouts are known, and on such other persons, if any, as the court may think proper;
(2)	to appoint a curator ad litem and, if necessary, a reporting officer and direct them to report;
(3)	thereafter, to make an Convention adoption order in favour of the petitioner(s) on such terms and conditions (if any) as the court may think fit;
(4)	to direct the Registrar General for Scotland to make an entry marked "Convention adoption order" regarding the order in the Adopted Children Register in the form prescribed by him, giving .... (insert name) as the forename(s), and the surname of the petitioner(s) or (insert another proposed surname) as the surname of .... in the form;
(5)	further, upon proof to the satisfaction of the court in the course of the proceedings to follow hereon, that .... (insert name of child) was born on the .... day of .... in the year .... and is identical with the child named .... (insert full name of child from original birth certificate) to whom an entry numbered .... in the Resister of Births for the Registration District of .... Relates, to direct the said Registrar General to cause such birth entry to be marked with the word "Adopted"

and to include the abovementioned date of birth in the entry recording the adoption in the manner indicated in the Schedule to the said Act; and

(6) to pronounce such other or further orders or directions upon such matters, including the expenses of this petition, as the court may think fit.

....

Signature of first petitioner

....

Signature of second petitioner

....

Signature of solicitor with designation and address

Form 67.28

Rule 67.28

Rule 67.28 | Form 67.28

APPLICATION FOR A PERMANENCE ORDER UNDER SECTION 80 OF THE ADOPTION AND CHILDREN (SCOTLAND) ACT 2007

UNTO THE RIGHT HONOURABLE THE LORDS OF COUNCIL AND SESSION

Petition of

[A.B.] ....
(designation of local authority)

....
(insert full name of child as shown on birth certificate)

who was born on .... (insert child's date of birth)

....(insert child's present address)

[*or* serial number where allocated]

(insert the name(s) of the parent(s) or guardian(s)) ....

on the ground that ....

HUMBLY SHEWETH:

*delete as appropriate

1.   The child is (*insert age of child*) years of age, having been born on the .... day of ....at ....(insert place of birth)

2.   The child is *male/*female.

3.   The child is not and never has been married or a civil partner.

4.   The child's natural mother is ....

        (insert full name and address)

5.   The child's natural father is ....

        (insert full name and address)

6.   The child's natural father has*/does not have* parental responsibilities and rights.

7.   *The child has the following guardians: ....
        (insert name(s) and address(es))

8.   *The child has been/is likely to be placed for adoption ....
        (give details).

9.   *The child's case was referred to the Children's Hearing on .... (*date*).

Arrangements for the child

10.   *There is no person who has the right to have the child with him or otherwise to regulate the child's residence under section 2(1)(a) of the Children (Scotland) Act 1995.

11.   *The following person(s) have the right to have the child living with him/her/them or otherwise to regulate the child's residence:

        (insert name(s) of person(s))

        but the child's residence with that/those person(s) is likely to be seriously detrimental to the welfare of the child for the following reason(s) (give details).

The following documents are lodged with this application:

(i)   extract birth certificate in relation to the child;

(ii)   *consent of [*name and address*] to the making of an adoption order;

(iii)   *consent of the child dated ....;

(iv)   *local authority report dated ....

The petitioner craves the court to make a permanence order under section 80 of the Adoption and Children (Scotland) Act 2007, in relation to the child including the mandatory provision *and to include the following ancillary provisions (*insert ancillary provisions sought in terms of section 82 of the Adoption and Children (Scotland) Act 2007*)
*and to include that order provision granting authority for the child to be adopted
*and to dispense with the consent of ....

Signed ....
[designation]

Date

NOTE
[1] As inserted by S.S.I. 2009 No. 283 (effective 28th September 2009).

Form 67.30 A

C1.2A.231   Rule 60.30(1)(b) and (c)(i)

Rule 60.30(1)(b) and (c)(i)   [1] FORM 67.30–A

NOTICE OF INTIMATION OF APPLICATION FOR PERMANENCE ORDER UNDER SECTION 80(1) OF THE ADOPTION AND CHILDREN (SCOTLAND) ACT 2007

To: (*full name and address of person to whom this intimation is to be sent*)

1.   YOU ARE GIVEN NOTICE THAT in this petition the petitioner is applying for a permanence order under section 80(1) of the Adoption and Children (Scotland) Act 2007 in relation to the child (*insert name of child*) [*including provision granting authority for the child to be adopted].   ***delete as appropriate**

2.   A COPY OF THE PETITION is attached to this notice.

3.   A hearing on the By Order Roll has been fixed for (*insert date and time*) at the Court of Session, Parliament Square, Edinburgh.

4.   **IF YOU WISH to oppose the application, you must attend or be represented at the By Order hearing.

5.   You are entitled to be heard on the application. You do not need to attend the hearing unless you do wish to be heard by the court or you are required by the court to attend.

Date (*insert date*)

[Petitioner *or* solicitor to the petitioner *or* Deputy Principal Clerk of Session]

[Address]

**If you do not attend, or are not represented at, the By Order hearing the court may make the order applied for.

IF YOU ARE UNCERTAIN WHAT ACTION TO TAKE, you should consult a solicitor.

YOU MAY BE ENTITLED TO LEGAL AID depending on your financial circumstances and you can get information about legal aid from a solicitor.

YOU MAY ALSO OBTAIN ADVICE FROM ANY CITIZENS ADVICE BUREAU OR OTHER ADVICE AGENCY.

NOTE
[1] As inserted by S.S.I. 2009 No. 283 (effective 28th September 2009).

Form 67.30 B

Rule 67.30(1)(c)(ii)

Rule 67.30(1)(c)(ii) [1] FORM 67.30–B

NOTICE OF INTIMATION OF APPLICATION FOR PERMANENCE ORDER UNDER SECTION 80(1) OF THE ADOPTION AND CHILDREN (SCOTLAND) ACT 2007 TO FATHER OF CHILD WITHOUT PARENTAL RESPONSIBILITIES AND RIGHTS

To: (*full name and address of person to whom this intimation is to be sent*)

1.   YOU ARE GIVEN NOTICE THAT in this petition the petitioner(s) is/are applying for a permanence order under section 28 of the Adoption and Children (Scotland) Act

2007 in relation to the child (*insert name of child*) including provision granting authority for the child to be adopted.

2.   A COPY OF THE PETITION is attached to this notice.

3.   A hearing on the By Order Roll has been fixed for (*insert date and time*) at the Court of Session, Parliament Square, Edinburgh.

Date (*insert date*)

[Petitioner *or* solicitor to the petitioner *or* Deputy Principal Clerk of Session]

[Address]

IF YOU ARE UNCERTAIN WHAT ACTION TO TAKE, you should consult a solicitor.

YOU MAY BE ENTITLED TO LEGAL AID depending on your financial circumstances and you can get information about legal aid from a solicitor.

YOU MAY ALSO OBTAIN ADVICE FROM ANY CITIZENS ADVICE BUREAU OR OTHER ADVICE AGENCY.

NOTE
[1] As inserted by S.S.I. 2009 No. 283 (effective 28th September 2009).

Form 67.35 A

C1.2A.233 Rule 67.35(3)(b)

Rule 67.35(3)(b) [1] FORM 67.35–A

NOTICE OF INTIMATION OF APPLICATION FOR AMENDMENT OF PERMANENCE ORDER TO INCLUDE PROVISION GRANTING AUTHORITY FOR THE CHILD TO BE ADOPTED

To: (*full name and address of person to whom this intimation is to be sent*)

1. YOU ARE GIVEN NOTICE THAT in this note the noter is applying for amendment of the permanence order in relation to the child (*insert name of child*) to include provision granting authority for the child to be adopted under section 93 of the Adoption and Children (Scotland) Act 2007.

2. A COPY OF THE NOTE is attached to this notice.

3. A hearing on the By Order Roll has been fixed for (*insert date and time*) at the Court of Session, Parliament Square, Edinburgh.

4. IF YOU WISH to oppose the application you must attend or be represented at that hearing.

5. You are entitled to be heard on the application. You do not need to attend the hearing unless you do wish to be heard by the court or you are required by the court to attend.

Date (*insert date*)

[Noter *or* solicitor to the noter]

[Address]

If you do not attend, or are not represented at, the hearing the court may make the order applied for.

IF YOU ARE UNCERTAIN WHAT ACTION TO TAKE, you should consult a solicitor.

YOU MAY BE ENTITLED TO LEGAL AID depending on your financial circumstances and you can get information about legal aid from a solicitor.

YOU MAY ALSO OBTAIN ADVICE FROM ANY CITIZENS ADVICE BUREAU OR OTHER ADVICE AGENCY.

NOTE
[1] As inserted by S.S.I. 2009 No. 283 (effective 28th September 2009).

Form 67.35 B

Rule 67.35(3)(c)

C1.2A.234

Rule 67.35(3)(c)   [1] FORM 67.35–B

NOTICE OF INTIMATION OF APPLICATION FOR AMENDMENT OF PERMANENCE ORDER TO INCLUDE PROVISION GRANTING AUTHORITY FOR THE CHILD TO BE ADOPTED TO FATHER OF CHILD WITHOUT PARENTAL RESPONSIBILITIES AND RIGHTS

To: (*full name and address of person to whom this intimation is to be sent*)

1.   YOU ARE GIVEN NOTICE THAT in this note the noter is applying for amendment of the permanence order in relation to the child (*insert name of child*) to include provision granting authority for the child to be adopted under section 93 of the Adoption and Children (Scotland) Act 2007.

2.   A COPY OF THE NOTE is attached to this notice.

3.   A hearing has been fixed for (*insert date and time*) at the Court of Session, Parliament Square, Edinburgh.

Date (*insert date*)

[Noter *or* solicitor to the noter]

NOTE
[1] As inserted by S.S.I. 2009 No. 283 (effective 28th September 2009).

Form 67.39 A

C1.2A.235   Rule 67.39(1)

Rule 67.39(1)   [1] FORM 67.39–A

**FORM OF CONSENT OF PARENT OR GUARDIAN UNDER SECTION 83(1)(c) [or 93(3)]
OF THE ADOPTION AND CHILDREN (SCOTLAND) ACT 2007**

In the petition for permanence order in relation to the child

(insert the full name of the child as it is given in the birth certificate)

including provision granting authority for the child to be adopted

*to which petition the court has assigned the serial number ....   ***delete as**
(insert serial number)   **appropri-
                                                                                                          ate**

I *(name and address)*   ....

confirm that I am the mother/father/guardian of the child. I fully understand that the effect of
the making of an adoption order in respect of the child will be to [*extinguish all the parental
responsibilities and parental rights which I have at present in respect of the child]. I consent
generally and unconditionally to the making of an adoption order in relation to the child. I have
signed this consent at *(place of signing)* on the .... day of .... Two thousand
and ....

(signature)

This consent was signed in the presence of:-

(signature of reporting officer)

[Full name of reporting officer]

Address

NOTE
[1] As inserted by S.S.I. 2009 No. 283 (effective 28th September 2009).

Form 67.39 B

Rule 67.39(2)

Rule 67.39(2) [1] FORM 67.39–B

FORM OF CONSENT OF CHILD UNDER SECTION 84(1) OF THE ADOPTION AND CHILDREN (SCOTLAND) ACT 2007

In the petition of ....

(insert name and address of petitioner)

I *(full name of child)* confirm that I understand the nature and effect of the permanence order for which the petitioner has applied in respect of me. I consent to the making of such an order

I have signed this consent at *(place of signing)* on the ....day of ....
Two thousand and ....

(signature)

This consent was signed in the presence of:-

(signature of reporting officer)

[Full name of reporting officer]

Address

NOTE
[1] As inserted by S.S.I. 2009 No. 283 (effective 28th September 2009).

Form 67.43 A

C1.2A.237   Rule 67.43(1)(b)

Rule 67.43(1)(b)   [1] FORM 67.43–A

NOTICE OF REPORT FROM CHILDREN'S HEARING UNDER SECTION 95 OF THE ADOPTION AND CHILDREN (SCOTLAND) ACT 2007

Sheriff Court .... 20 ....

To: (*full name and address of person to whom this notice is sent*)

....

CHILD IN RESPECT OF WHOM APPLICATION FOR PERMANENCE ORDER/ VARIATION OF PERMANENCE ORDER HAS BEEN MADE:

(*give full name and date of birth*)

1.   YOU ARE GIVEN NOTICE THAT a children's hearing has made a report to the sheriff under section 95(2) of the Adoption and Children (Scotland) Act 2007.

2.   A COPY OF THE REPORT is attached to this notice.

3.   IF YOU WISH to oppose the proposals in the report you must lodge a form of response in Form 67.43-B within 7 days of the date of this notice. A copy of the form is attached.

Date (insert date)

[Deputy Principal Clerk of Session]

IF YOU ARE UNCERTAIN WHAT ACTION TO TAKE, you should consult a solicitor.

YOU MAY ALSO OBTAIN ADVICE FROM ANY CITIZENS ADVICE BUREAU OR OTHER ADVICE AGENCY.

NOTE
[1] As inserted by S.S.I. 2009 No. 283 (effective 28th September 2009).

Form 67.43 B

C1.2A.238   Rule 67.43(2)

Rule 67.43(2)   [1] FORM 67.43–B

NOTICE OF RESPONSE TO REPORT FROM CHILDREN'S HEARING UNDER SECTION 95 OF THE ADOPTION AND CHILDREN (SCOTLAND) ACT 2007

(Date) .... 20 ....

(insert place and date)
(insert designation and address)

CHILD IN RESPECT OF WHOM APPLICATION FOR PERMANENCE ORDER/ VARIATION OF PERMANENCE ORDER HAS BEEN MADE:

(give full name and date of birth)

The respondent wishes to oppose the proposals in respect of the child set out in the report of the children's hearing for the following reasons:

(insert here reasons for opposing the proposals set out in the report)

Date *(insert date)*

[name and designation]

NOTE
[1] As inserted by S.S.I. 2009 No. 283 (effective 28th September 2009).

Form 67.43 C

Rule 67.43(10)

C1.2A.239

Rule 67.43(10)   [1] FORM 67.43–C

FORM OF NOTICE OF COURT'S DECISION FOLLOWING RECEIPT OF A REPORT FROM CHILDREN'S HEARING UNDER SECTION 95 OF THE ADOPTION AND CHILDREN (SCOTLAND) ACT 2007

(Date) .... 20 ....

APPLICATION FOR A PERMANENCE ORDER/VARIATION OF PERMANENCE ORDER IN RESPECT OF *[insert name of child]*.

*The Court of Session has considered the report from the children's hearing under section 95(2) of the Adoption and Children (Scotland) Act 2007 and has decided to refer the child's case to the Principal Reporter as mentioned in section 96(3) of that Act. A copy of the court's order is attached.

*The Court of Session has considered the report from the children's hearing under section 95(2) of the Adoption and Children (Scotland) Act 2007 and has decided not to refer the child's case to the Principal Reporter as mentioned in section 96(3) of that Act. Accordingly in terms of section 96(2) of that Act a supervision requirement in respect of the child may not be made, or modified under paragraph (c) or (d) of section 73(9) of the Children (Scotland) Act 1995, until the above application has been determined (or as the case may be, withdrawn or abandoned).

Delete as appropriate

Deputy Principal Clerk of Session

Date *(insert date)*

NOTE
[1] As inserted by S.S.I. 2009 No. 283 (effective 28th September 2009).

Form 69.2

C1.2A.240 Rule 69.2(1)

Rule 69.2(1)   [1] FORM 69.2

Form of election petition

IN THE ELECTION COURT

PETITION

under the Representation of the People Act 1983 [*or* the European Parliamentary Elections Regulations 2004]

[A.B.] [and [C.D.]] (*designation and address*)

Petitioner[s]

against

[E.F.] (*designation and address*), as the member whose election or return is complained of

First Respondent

[E.F.] (*designation and address*), the returning officer

Second Respondent

in respect of

The election for (place) held on day of

HUMBLY SHEWETH:—

1. That the [first named] petitioner voted [*or* had a right to vote, *as the case may be*] as an elector at the above election [*or* claims to have had a right to be elected or returned at the above election, *or* was a candidate at the above election, *as the case may be*]. The second named petitioner (*here state in like manner the right of each petitioner*).

2. That the election was held on the day of , when [A.B.] and [C.D.] (*name them*) were candidates, and the returning officer has returned [A.B.] (*name*) as being duly elected.

3. That (*state the facts on which the petitioners rely on in this and following numbered paragraphs*).

[4.] That the petition is presented under the Representation of the People Act 1983 [*or* the European Parliamentary Elections Regulations 2004] and rule 69.2 of the Rules of the Court of Session 1994.

MAY IT THEREFORE please the court to determine that [E.F.] was not duly elected or returned, and that the election was void [*or* that [A.B.] [*or* C.D.] was duly elected, and ought to have been returned, *or as the case may be*].

According to Justice etc.

(*Signed*)

---

[1] Form 69.2 substituted by S.S.I. 2011 No. 385.

Form 69.4

Rule 69.4(3)

C1.2A.241

Rule 69.4(3)   [1] FORM 69.4

Form of bond of caution in election petition

BOND OF CAUTION

Representation of the People Act 1983

We, [I.J.] and [K.L.] (*names and designations*), considering that a petition has been presented by [A.B.], complaining of an undue return (*or* undue election *as the case may be*) of [E.F.] as a member to serve in Parliament for the constituency of   [*or* representative to the European Parliament for (*name of constituency*) *or* Member of the Scottish Parliament for (*name of constituency or region*)] on the   day of   , and that by section 136 of the Representation of the People Act 1983, it is provided that security for the payment of all costs, charges, and expenses that may become payable by the petitioner in terms of the Act, shall, on presentation of such petition, be given on behalf of the petitioners, to the amount of £   ; and that by rule 69.4(3) of the Rules of the Court of Session 1994 for the trial of election petitions, under the Act, it is prescribed that the security so to be given on behalf of the petitioners may be by lodging a bond of caution, in terms of the Act; and seeing that we, the said parties, are willing to grant such bond, therefore we, the said parties, as cautioners, sureties, and full debtors for and with [A.B.], petitioner, do hereby bind and oblige ourselves conjunctly and severally, and our respective heirs, executors, and successors whomsoever, that [A.B.], petitioner, shall make payment of all costs, charges, and expenses that may become payable by him to any person or persons, by virtue of any decree to be pronounced in the petition; and that to the amount of £   sterling, with one-fifth part more of liquidate penalty in case of failure; and we consent to the registration hereof for execution. IN WITNESS WHEREOF, etc.

---

[1] Form 69.4 amended by S.I. 1999 No. 787.

Form 69.5

C1.2A.242   Rule 69.5(2)

Rule 69.5(2)   [1] FORM 69.5

Form of notice of the presentation of an election petition and of the nature of the proposed security

Representation of the People Act 1983

Date: (*insert date of posting or other method of intimation*)

To: (*name and address*)

TAKE NOTICE

(1) That, under the Representation of the People Act 1983 and rule 69.3 of the Rules of the Court of Session 1994, a petition has been presented to the Court of Session, Edinburgh touching the election of a Member of Parliament [*or* representative to the European Parliament *or* Member of the Scottish Parliament] for the (*place*), of which petition the foregoing is a full copy, and that you are named therein as a respondent.

(2) That the security which has been given in terms of section 136 of the above Act is in the form of a bond of caution to the amount of £   granted by [A.B.] and [C.D.] (*names, designations and addresses*) *or* by consignation of £   in the Bank of   . If you desire to object to the above bond of caution in terms of section 136(4) of the above Act, you may do so within [14] days of the date of this notice by lodging the objection in writing in the Petition Department, Court of Session, 2 Parliament Square, Edinburgh EH1 1RQ and sending or delivering a full copy of it to me at the following address (*address*).

(*Signed*)

Petitioner
[*or* Solicitor [*or* Agent] for petitioner]
(*Address*)

---

[1] Form 69.5 amended by S.I. 1999 No. 787.

Form 69.15

Rule 69.15

Rule 69.15   [1] FORM 69.15

Form of warrant to cite witnesses in election petition

Representation of the People Act 1983

(place and date)

Having considered the motion for the petitioner [*or* respondent], grants warrant to all officers of the law for citing   (*name them*), to attend the Election Court, for the trial of the election petition to be held at   within (*name court-house*) on the   day of   , at   o'clock forenoon [*or* forthwith, *as the case may be*], to be severally examined as witnesses in the petition, and to attend the Election Court until their examination shall have been completed.

(Signed)

Judge of the Election Court

---

[1] Form number amended by S.I. 1994 No. 2901 (clerical error).

Form 69.19-A

Rule 69.19(1)

Rule 69.19(1)   [1] FORM 69.19–A

Form of notice of intention to withdraw election petition

Representation of the People Act 1983 *or* the European Parliamentary Elections Regulations 2004

In the Election Petition for   in which   is petitioner and   is respondent.

Date: (*insert date of posting or other method of intimation*)

To: (*name and address*)

TAKE NOTICE

(1) That the above petitioner has, on the   day of   , lodged at the office of the Deputy Principal Clerk of Session notice of application to withdraw his petition, of which the following is a copy:— (*Set it out*)

(2) That under section 150 of the Representation of the People Act 1983 and rule 69.20 of the Rules of the Court of Session 1994, any person who might have been a petitioner, in respect of the election, may, within five days after publication of this Notice give notice in writing, signed by him or on his behalf, to the said Deputy Principal Clerk of Session, 2 Parliament Square, Edinburgh EH1 1RQ, of his intention to apply at the hearing to be substituted for the petitioner.

(*Signed*)

Petitioner
[*or* Solicitor [*or* Agent] for petitioner]
(*Address*)

----

[1] Form 69.19–A amended by S.S.I. 2011 No. 385.

Form 69.19-B

Rule 69.19(4)

Rule 69.19(4)   [1] FORM 69.19–B

Form of application for leave to withdraw election petition

Representation of the People Act 1983

Parliamentary [*or* European
Parliament[1] *or* Scottish Parliament] constituency [*or* region] of

IN THE ELECTION COURT

APPLICATION TO WITHDRAW

by

[A.B.] [and [C.D.]] (*designation and addresses*)

Petitioner[s]

in the PETITION of

[A.B.] [and [C.D.]] (*designation and addresses*)

Petitioner

against

[E.F.] (*designation and address*)

First Respondent

[G.H.] (*designation and address*)

Second Respondent

The petitioner [A.B.], with the consent of the petitioner [C.D.], applies for leave to withdraw his petition on the following grounds: (*state grounds in numbered paragraphs*), and prays that a day may be appointed for hearing his application.
Dated the   day of

> (*To be signed by the applicant and con-*
> *senter, if any, or their respective solicitors,*
> *who shall each append to their signatures a*
> *statement of whether they sign as or on*
> *behalf of an applicant or a consenter.*)

-----

[1] Form 69.19–B amended by S.I. 1999 No. 787.

Form 69.23

C1.2A.246   Rule 69.23(1)

Rule 69.23(1)   FORM 69.23

Form of notice of abatement of petition by death of petitioner

Representation of the People Act 1983

Constituency of

The election for (*place*) held on   day of

The election petition presented by [A.B. [and [C.D.]] (*designations and addresses*) against [E.F.] (*designation and address*), the member whose election or action is complained of, has been abated by the death of [A.B.] the [surviving] petitioner.

Any person who might have been a petitioner in respect of this election may apply by motion in the Election Court, Court of Session, 2 Parliament Square, Edinburgh EH1 1RQ within [14] days after the date of this notice to be substituted as a petitioner.

Date (*insert date*):

(*Signed*)

Form 72.4

C1.2A.247   *[Omitted by S.S.I. 2016 No. 312 (effective 30th November 2016).]*

Form 76.9

C1.2A.248   Rule 76.9

Rule 76.9   [1,2]FORM 76.9

Form of notice to person with interest in property subject to an application for an order under paragraph 12 of Schedule 1 to the Proceeds of Crime (Scotland) Act 1995

(*Cause reference number*)

IN THE COURT OF SESSION

in the

PETITION [*or* NOTE]

of

[A.B.] (*designation and address*)

for an order under paragraph 12 of Schedule 1 to the Proceeds of Crime (Scotland) Act 1995 in respect of the estates of [C.D.] (*address*)

Date: (*date of posting or other method of service*)

To: (*name and address of person on whom notice is to be served*)

This Notice—
  (a) gives you warning that an application has been made to the Court of Session for an order which may affect your interest in property; and
  (b) informs you that you have an opportunity to appear and make representations to the court before the application is determined.

TAKE NOTICE

1. That on (*date*) in the High Court of Justiciary at (*place*) a confiscation order was made under section 1 of the Proceeds of Crime (Scotland) Act 1995 in respect of [C.D.] (*address*).

2. That on (*date*) the administrator appointed under paragraph 1(1)(a) of Schedule 1 to the Act of 1995 on (*date*) was empowered to realise property belonging to [C.D.].

or

2. That on (*date*) the administrator was appointed under paragraph 1(1)(b) of Schedule 1 to the Act of 1995 on (*date*) to realise property belonging to [C.D.].

3. That application has been made by petition [*or* note] for an order under paragraph 12 of Schedule 1 to the Act of 1995 (*here set out briefly the nature of the order sought*). A copy of the petition [*or* note] is attached.

4. That you have the right to appear before the court in person or by counsel or other person having a right of audience and make such representations as you may have in respect of the order applied for. The court has fixed (*insert day and date fixed for hearing the application*) at 10 a.m. in the Court of Session, 2 Parliament Square, Edinburgh as the time when you should appear to do this.

5. That if you do not appear or are not represented on the above date, the order applied for may be made in your absence.

IF YOU ARE UNCERTAIN ABOUT THE EFFECT OF THIS NOTICE, you should consult a Solicitor, Citizens Advice Bureau or other local advice agency or adviser immediately.

(*Signed*)

Messenger-at-Arms
[*or* Solicitor [*or* Agent] for petitioner [*or* noter]]
(*Address*)

---

[1] Form 76.9 amended by SI 1994/2901 (minor correction).
[2] Form 76.9 amended by SI 1996/2168 (consolidating enactment).

Form 76.36A

Form 76.36A revoked by S.S.I. 2019 No. 405 (effective 28th December 2019).]   **C1.2A.248.1**

Form 77.10

C1.2A.249 Rule 77.10(1)

Rule 77.10(1)   FORM 77.10

Form of joint minute to transfer summary trial petition to another Lord Ordinary because of death, disability or absence

IN THE COURT OF SESSION

JOINT MINUTE

for the Parties

in the PETITION of

[A.B.] and [C.D.] (*designations and addresses*)

Petitioners

[E.F.] and [G.H.] for the parties concur in craving the court that the cause shall be remitted to Lord (*name*) for determination by him because of the death [*or* disability *or* absence] of Lord (*name*).

IN RESPECT WHEREOF

(*Signed by counsel or other person having a right of audience*)

Form 77.11

Rule 77.11(1)

Rule 77.11(1) [1] FORM 77.11

Form of joint minute to adopt summary trial procedure in action in dependence

IN THE COURT OF SESSION

JOINT MINUTE

for the Parties

in the cause

[A.B.] (*designation and address*)

Pursuer

against

[C.D.] (*designation and address*)

Defender

[E.F.] and [G.H.] for the parties concur in craving the court that the cause shall be remitted to Lord (*name*) for determination by him under section 26 of the Court of Session Act 1988.

IN RESPECT WHEREOF

(*Signed by counsel or other person having* a right of audience)

---

[1] Form 77.11 amended by SI 1997/1050 (minor amendment, effective 6th April 1997).

Form 81.5

Rule 81.5(1)

Rule 81.5(1) FORM 81.5

Form of agreement under section 30(5) of the Human Fertilisation and Embryology Act 1990

[*Omitted by S.S.I. 2010 No. 136 (effective 6th April 2010).*]

Form 81.9

Rule 81.9(1)

Rule 81.9(1) FORM 81.9

Form of petition for parental order under section 30 of the Human Fertilisation and Embryology Act 1990

[*Omitted by S.S.I. 2010 No. 136 (effective 6th April 2010).*]

Form 81.12

C1.2A.253   Rule 81.12(3)

Rule 81.12(3)   FORM 81.12

Form of intimation of hearing of application for a parental order under section 30 of the Human Fertilisation and Embryology Act 1990

[*Omitted by S.S.I. 2010 No. 136 (effective 6th April 2010).*]

Form 82.3-A

C1.2A.254

[1] FORM 82.3–A

Form of notice to Crown under section 5(1) of the Human Rights Act 1998

IN THE COURT OF SESSION

in causa

[A.B.] (*designation and address*)

Pursuer [*or* Petitioner]

against

[C.D.] (*designation and address*)

Defender [*or* Respondent]

Date: (*date of posting or other method of service*)

To: (*specify Minister or other person on whom notice is to be served*)

TAKE NOTICE

That the court is considering whether or not to [*Or:* That (*specify party*) is seeking that the court] make a declaration under section (*specify section 4(2), in relation to primary legislation or section 4(4) in relation to subordinate legislation*) of the Human Rights Act 1998 that (*specify the primary or subordinate legislation which is the subject of the proposed declaration*) is incompatible with (*specify the Convention right*) for the following reasons:

(*set out the reasons in summary*).

You may apply to become a party to the proceedings. If you wish to do so you should notify the Deputy Principal Clerk of Session in Form 82.3-B.

(Signed)

Deputy Principal Clerk of Session

[*or* Solicitor [*or* Agent] for (*specify*)]

---

[1] Form 82.3–A inserted by S.S.I. 2000 No. 316 and amended by S.S.I. 2004 No. 52 and amended by S.S.I. 2006 No. 83 (effective 17th March 2006).

Form 82.3-B

[1] FORM 82.3–B

Form of notice to court under section 5(2) of the Human Rights Act 1998

IN THE COURT OF SESSION

in causa

[A.B.] (*designation and address*)

Pursuer [*or* Petitioner]

against

[C.D.] (*designation and address*)

Defender [*or* Respondent]

To the Deputy Principal Clerk of Session

The (*specify Minister or other person*) intends to join as a party to these proceedings.

(Signed)

Solicitor for (*specify Minister or other person*)
(*Address*)

---

[1] Form 82.3–B inserted by S.S.I. 2000 No. 316 (effective 2nd October 2000) and amended by S.S.I. 2004 No. 52.

Form 82.4

C1.2A.256   Rule 82.4

Rule 82.4   [1] FORM 82.4

Form of minute under rule 82.4

IN THE COURT OF SESSION

MINUTE

By

[E.F.], (designation and address)

Minuter

in causa

[A.B.], (designation and address)

Pursuer [*or* Petitioner]

against

[C.D., (designation and address)

Defender [*or* Respondent]

1. The Minuter lodged a Notice under section 5(2) of the Human Rights Act 1998 on (*date*).

2. The position of the Minuter as to the proposed declaration of incompatibility is as follows—

(here specify the position of the Minuter including where appropriate a summary of any facts on which the Minuter proposes to rely, of any propositions of law which the Minuter proposes to advance and of any argument which the Minuter proposes to make)

(Signed)

Solicitor for (*specify Minister or other person*)

---

[1] Form 82.4 inserted by S.S.I. 2000 No. 316 and substituted by S.S.I. 2006 No. 83 (effective 17th March 2006).

Form 85.5

Rule 85.5

Rule 85.5 [1] FORM 85.5

Form of certificate of delivery of documents to chief constable

(*Insert place and date*) I,   hereby certify that upon the   day of   I duly delivered to (*insert name and address*) chief constable of (*insert name of constabulary*) (*insert details of the documents delivered*). This I did by (*state method of delivery*).

(Signed)

Solicitor/sheriff officer
(add designation and business address)

---

[1] Form 85.5 inserted by S.S.I. 2002 No. 514.

Form 85A.2

Rule 85A.2(8)

Rule 85A.2(8) [1] FORM 85A.2

Form of certificate of sending documents to chief constable

(*Insert place and date*) I,   hereby certify that upon the   day of   I duly sent to (*insert name and address*) chief constable(s) of (*insert name(s) of constabulary*) (*insert details of the documents sent*). This I did by (*state method of sending documents*).

(*Signed*)

(*Insert name and designation of person sending documents*)

---

[1] Form 85A.2 inserted by S.S.I. 2011 No. 288 (effective 21st July 2011).

Form 86.3

C1.2A.259   Rule 86.3(1)

Rule 86.3(1)   [1] FORM 86.3

Form of petition under section 28, 28A, 62, 62A, 63, 65G or 65H of the Competition Act 1998

UNTO THE RIGHT HONOURABLE

THE LORDS OF COUNCIL AND SESSION

PETITION

of

THE OFFICE OF FAIR TRADING ("THE OFT"), (*address*)

Petitioner

for a warrant under

section 28 [*or* section 28A *or* section 62 *or* section 62A *or* section 63 *or* section 65G *or* section 65H] of the Competition Act 1998

in respect of

(*insert name and address or as the case may be*)

HUMBLY SHEWETH:—

1. That (*here set out in this and the following numbered paragraphs the matters mentioned in rule 86.3.(2)*).

MAY IT THEREFORE please your Lordships to (*insert prayer*)

According to Justice, etc.

(Signed)

---

[1] Form 86.3 inserted by S.S.I. 2004 No. 331 (effective 6th August 2004).

Form 87.1

Rule 87.1(2)

Rule 87.1(2) [1] FORM 87.1

Form of notice of intimation to the Office of Fair Trading

Date: (*date of posting or other method of intimation*)

To: The Office of Fair Trading

TAKE NOTICE

(*Name and address of pursuer or defender*) has brought an action against [*or* has defended an action brought by] (*name and address of defender or pursuer*) [*or* (*name and address of petitioner or respondent*) has raised a petition [*or* responded to a petition raised by] (*name and address of respondent or petitioner*)]. The action raises issues under Article 81 or 82 of the Treaty establishing the European Community. A copy of the summons [*or* petition] is [*or* pleadings and interlocutor allowing intimation are] attached.

You may apply to the court by motion for leave to be sisted as a party in the action. You must do so at the Office of Court, Court of Session, 2 Parliament Square, Edinburgh, EH1 1RQ within [21] days after the date of intimation to you of this notice [*or* *if the warrant for intimation is executed before the calling of the summons*, within [7] days after the summons calls in court. The summons will not call in court earlier than [21] days after the date of intimation to you of the summons]. The date of intimation is the date stated at the top of this notice unless intimation has been made by post in which case the date of intimation is the day after that date.

(*Signed*)

Messenger-at-arms

[*or* Solicitor [*or* Agent] for Pursuer [*or* Petitioner *or* Defender *or* Respondent]]

(*Address*)

---

[1] Form 87.1 inserted by S.S.I. 2004 No. 514, Art.2(8) (effective 30th November 2004).

Form 88.5

C1.2A.261   Rule 88.5(3)

Rule 88.5(3)   FORM 88.5

Form of notice of intimation of a hearing to determine jurisdiction under Article 15 of Council Regulation (E.C.) No. 2201/2003 of 27th November 2003

Date: (*date of posting or other method of intimation*)

To: (*name and address*)

TAKE NOTICE

(*Name and address of pursuer*) has lodged a summons in the Court of Session against (*name and address of defender*).

The parties are presently engaged in proceedings involving matters of parental responsibility in (*specify court in other Member State where proceedings are ongoing*) and a request has been made to the Court of Session to accept jurisdiction of these proceedings and for the action to be dealt with in the Court of Session.

A hearing has been fixed on (*date*) at (*time*) within the Court of Session to determine the issue of jurisdiction.

You may appear or be represented by a person having a right of audience before the Court of Session at the hearing.

You or your representative will be asked whether you agree to jurisdiction being accepted by the Court of Session and the proceedings involving matters of parental responsibility being dealt with in the Court of Session.

If you do not appear or are not represented at the hearing the court may decide whether to accept jurisdiction in your absence.

(*Signed*)

Solicitor [*or* Agent] for Pursuer

[*or as the case may be*]

(*Address*)

----

[1] Form 88.5 inserted by S.S.I. 2005 No. 135, para.3 (effective 2nd March 2005).

Form 88.7

Rule 88.7(1)

Rule 88.7(1) ¹ FORM 88.7

Form of request for consent to placement of child under Article 56 of Council Regulation (E.C.) No. 2201/2003 of 27th November 2003

Date: (*date of request*)

To: (*to be inserted by Scottish Central Authority*)

The Court of Session has jurisdiction in matters of parental responsibility under the Council Regulation (E.C.) No. 2201/2003 of 27th November 2003 in respect of (*name and address of child*). The court is contemplating the placement of (*name of child*) in (*name and address of institution*) [*or* with (*name and address of foster family*)] and requests your consent to the placement in accordance with Article 56 of Council Regulation.

(*Signed*)

Deputy Principal Clerk of Session

N.B. To be sent to: Scottish Central Authority,
Civil Justice and International Division,
2nd Floor West,
St Andrew's House,
Regent Road,
Edinburgh,
EH1 3DG.

Form 94.3

Paragraph 2(13)
Rule 94.3

Paragraph 2(13) ¹ FORM 94.3

Rule 94.3

Form of minute of intervention by the Commission for Equality and Human Rights

APPLICATION FOR LEAVE TO INTERVENE BY THE COMMISSION FOR EQUALITY AND HUMAN RIGHTS

in the cause

[A.B.] (*designation and address*), Pursuer [*or* Petitioner]

against

[C.D.] (*designation and address*), Defender [*or* Respondent]

[*Here set out briefly:*
(a) the Commission's reasons for believing that the proceedings are relevant to a matter in connection with which the Commission has a function;
(b) the issue in the proceedings which the Commission wishes to address; and
(c) the propositions to be advanced by the Commission and the Commission's reasons for believing that they are relevant to the proceedings and that they will assist the court.]

---

¹Inserted by S.S.I. 2007 No. 449 (effective 25th October 2007).

Form 95.3

C1.2A.264   Rule 95.3

Rule 95.3   FORM 95.3

Form of minute of intervention by the Scottish Commission for Human Rights

FORM OF MINUTE OF INTERVENTION BY THE SCOTTISH COMMISSION FOR HUMAN RIGHTS

in the cause

[A.B.] (designation and address), Pursuer [*or Petitioner*]

against

[C.D.] (designation and address), Defender [*or Respondent*]

[*Here set out briefly*:
   (*a*) the issue arising in the proceedings which the Commission intends to address; and
   (*b*) a summary of the submission that the Commission intends to make.]

---

[1] Form 95.3 inserted by S.S.I. 2008 No. 123, r. 4 (effective April 1st 2008).

Form 95.4

C1.2A.265   Rule 95.4

Rule 95.4   FORM 95.4

Invitation to the Scottish Commission for Human Rights to intervene

INVITATION TO THE SCOTTISH COMMISSION FOR HUMAN RIGHTS TO INTERVENE

in the cause

[A.B.] (designation and address), Pursuer [*or Petitioner*]

against

[C.D.] (designation and address), Defender [*or Respondent*]

[*Here set out briefly*:
   (*a*) the facts, procedural history and issues in the proceedings;
   (*b*) the issue in the proceedings on which the court seeks a submission.]

---

[1] Form 95.4 inserted by S.S.I. 2008 No. 123, r. 4 (effective April 1st 2008).

Form 97.3

C1.2A.266   Rule 97.3(1)

Form of petition for parental order under section 54 or 54A of the Human Fertilisation and Embryology Act 2008

UNTO THE RIGHT HONOURABLE THE LORDS OF COUNCIL AND SESSION

PETITION

Of

[A.B.] (*designation and address*)*

and

[C.D.] (*designation and address*)*

[*or serial number where one has been assigned*]

Petitioners

for

a parental order under section 54 [*or* 54A] of the Human Fertilisation and Embryology Act 2008

in respect of

[E.F.] (*name as in the birth certificate*]

HUMBLY SHEWETH:—

1. That the petitioners are—

    i.

    spouses*;

    ii.

    civil partners of each other*; or

    iii. two persons who are living as partners in an enduring family relationship and are not within prohibited degrees of relationship to each other*

    (**delete as appropriate*)

    domiciled in the [United Kingdom] [Channel Islands] *or* [Isle of Man] and reside at (*state full address*).

2. That the petitioners are respectively .... and .... years of age.

3. That (*state name of child, the subject of the petition*) is [male] *or* [female] and is [months] *or* [years] old having been born .... on at ....

4. That [a court has not previously refused the petitioners' application for a parental order in respect of the child] *or* [a court has previously refused the petitioners' application for a parental order in respect of the child but the court directed that section 33(1) of the Adoption and Children (Scotland) Act 2007 as modified, should not apply] *or* [a court has previously refused the petitioners' application for a parental order in respect of the child but the petitioners aver that it is proper for the court to hear the application because (*give full details*)].

5. That the child is not and never has been married or a civil partner.

6. That the child's home is with the petitioners.

7. That the child was carried by a woman who is not one of the petitioners as the result of [the placing in her of an embryo] *or* [the placing in her of sperm and eggs] *or* [her artificial insemination].

8. That the gametes of (*state which petitioner or if both state both petitioners*) were used to bring about the creation of the embryo of the child.

9. That the child is not the subject of any other pending or completed court proceedings (*if the child is so subject give full details*)—

[[10.] That (*state full name and address of the other parent of the child*), who is [the father of the child by virtue of sections 35 or 36 of the Human Fertilisation and Embryology Act 2008] *or* [the other parent of the child by virtue of sections 42 or 43 of the Human Fertilisation and Embryology

Act 2008] *or* [the other parent of the child by virtue of (*specify*)], where he or she is not one of the petitioners has freely and with full understanding of what is involved, agreed unconditionally to the making of the order sought.]

[[11.] That (*state full name and address of the woman who carried the child*), is the woman who carried the child and has freely and with full understanding of what is involved, agreed unconditionally to the making of the order sought.]

[12.] That no money or benefit, other than for expenses reasonably incurred, has been given or received by the petitioners for or in consideration of—

(a) the making of the order sought,

(b) any agreement required for the making of the order sought,

(c) the handing over of the child to the petitioners, or

(d) the making of any arrangements with a view to the making of the order,

[other than (*state any money or other benefit given or received by authority of the court and specify such authority*)].

[[13.] That [the father of the child by virtue of sections 35 or 36 of the Human Fertilisation and Embryology Act 2008] *or* [the other parent of the child by virtue of sections 42 or 43 of the Human Fertilisation and Embryology Act 2008] *or* [the other parent of the child by virtue of (*specify*)], [and] [or] [the woman who carried the child] [cannot be found (*state the efforts which have been made to find the person(s) concerned*)] *or* [is [*or are*] incapable of giving agreement by reason of (*state reasons*)].]

MAY IT THEREFORE please your Lordships to dispense with intimation and to order notice of

the petition to be served on such person or persons as the court thinks fit; to appoint a reporting officer and curator ad litem, to the child and direct them to report; [to dispense with the agreement of the [other parent of the child] [*and*] [*or*] [the woman who carried the child] [who cannot be found *or* [who is [*or are*] incapable of giving agreement];] on resuming consideration of this petition and the reports by the reporting officer and the curator ad litem, to make a parental order in their favour under section 54 [*or* 54A] of the Human Fertilisation and Embryology Act 2008 in respect of the child; to direct the Registrar General for Scotland to make an entry regarding the parental order in the Parental Order Register in the form prescribed by him giving [*insert forename(s)*] as the forename(s) and .... [*insert surname*] as the surname of the child; and upon proof to the satisfaction of the court in the course of the proceedings to follow hereon, to find that the child was born on the [*insert date*] day of [*insert month*] in the year [*insert year*] and is identical with the child to whom an entry numbered [*insert entry number*] and made on the [*insert date*] .... day of [*insert month*] in the year [*insert year*], in the Register of Births for the registration district of [*insert district*] relates; and to direct the Registrar General for Scotland to cause such birth entry to be marked with the words "Parental Order" and to include the above mentioned date of birth in the entry recording the parental order in the manner indicated in that form; to pronounce such other or further orders or directions upon such matters, including the expenses of this petition, as the court thinks fit.

ACCORDING TO
JUSTICE ETC.
(*Signed*)
Solicitor [*or* Agent] for
petitioners
(*Address*)
[*or* (*Signed*)
Counsel or other
person having a right
of audience]
or (*Signed*)
(*Signed*)
Petitioners]

[*Note – where the petitioner is a single applicant under section 54A of the Human Fertilisation and Embryology Act 2008, references throughout this form to "the petitioners" should be amended to "the petitioner". Paragraph 1 of the statement of facts should be omitted in petitions by a single applicant. Text in other paragraphs and the signing docquet should be amended as appropriate.*]

Form 97.10

Rule 97.10(1)

C1.2A.267

Form of agreement to a parental order under section 54(6) or 54A(5) of the Human Fertilisation and Embryology Act 2008

IN THE COURT OF SESSION

in the PETITION of

[A.B.] (*designation and address*)*

and

[C.D.] (*designation and address*)*

[*or serial number where one has been assigned*]

for

a parental order under section 54 *or* [54A] of the Human Fertilisation and Embryology Act 2008

in respect of

[E.F.] (*full name as given in the birth certificate*]

I, (*insert name and address*), confirm that I am [the woman who carried the child] *or* [the father of the child by virtue of sections 35 or 36 of the Human Fertilisation and Embryology Act 2008] *or* [the other parent of the child by virtue of sections 42 or 43 of the Human Fertilisation and Embryology Act 2008] *or* [the other parent of the child by virtue of (*specify*)], state—

1. That I fully understand that the effect of the making of a parental order in respect of the child will be to extinguish all the parental responsibilities and parental rights which I have at present in respect of the child.

2. That I understand that the court cannot make a parental order in relation to the child without my agreement [and the agreement of [the woman who carried the child] *or* [the father of the child by virtue of sections 35 or 36 of the Human Fertilisation and Embryology Act 2008] *or* [the other parent of the child by virtue of sections 42 or 43 of the Human Fertilisation and Embryology Act 2008] *or* [the other parent of the child by virtue of (*specify*)], where

he or she is not one of the petitioners] unless the court dispenses with agreement on the ground that the person concerned cannot be found or is incapable of giving agreement.

3. That I understand that when the hearing of the petition to determine the application for a parental order in relation to the child is heard, this document may be used as evidence of my agreement to the making of the order unless I inform the court that I no longer agree.

4. That I freely, and with full understanding of what is involved, agree unconditionally to the making of a parental order in relation to the child.

5. That I have not received or given any money or benefit, other than for expenses reasonably incurred, for or in consideration of—
    (a) the making of the parental order,
    (b) the execution of this agreement,
    (c) the handing over of the child to the petitioners, or
    (d) the making of any arrangements with a view to the making of a parental order,

[other than (*state any money or other benefit given or received by authority of the court and specify such authority*)].

I have signed this agreement at (place of signing) on the .... day of .... Two thousand and ....

(*Signed by the [woman who carried the child] [the father] or [other parent of the child]*)

This agreement was signed in the presence of:—

(*Signed*)
(*Insert full name and address of witness*)

[*Note – where the petition is made by a single applicant under section 54A of the Human Fertilisation and Embryology Act 2008, references throughout this form to "the petitioners" should be amended to "the petitioner".*]

Form 97.12

C1.2A.268   Rule 97.12(3)
Form of intimation of hearing of application for a parental order under section 54 or 54A of the Human Fertilisation and Embryology Act 2008
IN THE COURT OF SESSION
in the PETITION of
[A.B.] (*designation and address*)*
and
[C.D.] (*designation and address*)*
[*or serial number where one has been assigned*]
for
a parental order under section 54 [*or 54A*] of the Human Fertilisation and Embryology Act 2008
in respect of
[E.F.] (*name as given in the birth certificate*]
Date: (*date of posting or other method of intimation*)
To: (*name and address*)

TAKE NOTICE

1. That the hearing on this petition to determine the application for a parental order will come before the Lord Ordinary in the Court of Session, Parliament House, Edinburgh on the [*insert date*], at [*insert time*] and that you may then appear and be heard personally or by counsel or other person having a right of audience on the question whether a parental order should be made.

2. That you are [*not*] obliged to attend the hearing [unless you wish to do so].

[3. That while the petition is pending you must not, except with the leave of the court, remove the child from the care of the petitioners [*or* petitioner].]

[4. That the court has been requested to dispense with your agreement to the making of an order on the ground[s] that (*specify ground(s)*).]

> (*Signed*)
> Messenger-at-Arms
> [or *Solicitor* [or Agent] for petitioners [*or* petitioner]] or [*Deputy Principal Clerk**] or [*Petitioner*[s]]
> (*Address*)
> **where serial number assigned*

Form 102.1A¹

C1.2A.268A   Rule 102.1A(2)

Form of application for an order restricting the reporting of proceedings

(*Cause reference number (insert)*)

IN THE COURT OF SESSION

APPLICATION

For

AN ORDER RESTRICTING THE REPORTING OF PROCEEDINGS

in the cause

[A.B.] (*designation and address*)

Pursuer [*or* Petitioner]

Against

[C.D.] (*designation and address*)

Defender [*or* Respondent]

1. The applicant is the Pursuer [*or* Petitioner] *or* Defender [*or* Respondent].

2. The applicant considers that it is necessary for the court to make an order restricting the reporting of proceedings in the cause of [A.B.] (*designation and address*) against [C.D.] (*designation and address*) because:

    (*state briefly in numbered paragraphs the reasons which, where applicable, should include the following information:*

    (a)   *details of any person (including their designation and address), or any other matter, in relation to whom or to which anonymity is sought,*

    (b)   *details of any enactments relied upon to apply for an order and the reasons why the applicant considers an order should be granted, [with reference to enactments and/or authority,]*

---

¹ Inserted by S.S.I. 2023 No. 196 r. 2(2) Sched. 1 (effective 2nd October 2023).

(c)   details of any other legal basis relied upon to apply for an order and the reasons why the applicant considers an order should be granted, [with reference to enactments and/or authority.]

(d)   whether anonymity has previously been waived by the person in respect of whom anonymity is sought, [and/or in relation to any other matter], and if so, the details of that waiver).

Date (*insert date*)

(*Signed*)

[A.B.] [*or* C.D.], Applicant

[*or* X.Y.], Solicitor for Applicant

(*insert the business address of solicitor*)

Form 105.3-A

Rule 105.3(1)   C1.2A.269

Form of warrant to place [or renew] a caveat under section 67(3) [or 69(2)] of the Land Registration etc. (Scotland) Act 2012

Cause reference no. (*insert reference*)

IN THE COURT OF SESSION

WARRANT TO PLACE [*or* RENEW] CAVEAT

in the cause

[A.B.] (*designation and address*)

Pursuer

against

[C.D.] (*designation and address*)

Defender

Date: (*date of interlocutor*)

To the Keeper of the Registers of Scotland

THE COURT, having considered the application of the pursuer [*or* defender] and being satisfied as to the matters mentioned in section 67(4) [*or* 69(3)] of the Land Registration etc. (Scotland) Act 2012,

GRANTS warrant to place [*or* renew] a caveat on the title sheet of the plot of land—

(a)   at (*state description of the plot(s) of land*);

(b)   registered under title number (*state title number(s)*);

(c)   registered in the name of (*state name and address of proprietor*).

(*Signed*)

NOTE: append a copy of any plan of the plot(s) of land lodged in accordance with rule 105.2(2)(c).

Form 105.3-A as inserted by S.S.I. 2014 No. 291 r. 2(6) (effective 8th December 2014).

Form 105.3-B

C1.2A.270 *Rule 105.3(2)*

Form of order restricting a caveat under section 70(2) of the Land Registration etc. (Scotland) Act 2012

Cause reference no. (*insert reference*)

IN THE COURT OF SESSION

ORDER RESTRICTING A CAVEAT

in the cause

[A.B.] (*designation and address*)

Pursuer

against

[C.D.] (*designation and address*)

Defender

Date: (*date of interlocutor*)

To the Keeper of the Registers of Scotland

THE COURT, having considered the application of the pursuer [or defender], being satisfied—

(a) as to the matters mentioned in section 70(3) of the Land Registration etc. (Scotland) Act 2012; and

(b) that it is reasonable in all the circumstances to do so,

ORDERS that the caveat on the title sheet of the plot of land—

(a) at (*state description of the plot(s) of land*);

(b) registered under title number (*state title number(s)*);

(c) registered in the name of (*state name and address of proprietor*), be restricted as follows:

(*specify nature and extent of restriction*)

(*Signed*)

Form 105.3-B as inserted by S.S.I. 2014 No. 291 r. 2(6) (effective 8th December 2014).

Form 105.3-C

C1.2A.271 *Rule 105.3(3)*

Form of order recalling a caveat under section 71(2) of the Land Registration etc. (Scotland) Act 2012

Cause reference no. (*insert reference*)

IN THE COURT OF SESSION

ORDER RECALLING A CAVEAT

in the cause

[A.B.] (*designation and address*)

Pursuer

against

[C.D.] (*designation and address*)

Defender

Date: (*date of interlocutor*)

To the Keeper of the Registers of Scotland

THE COURT, having considered the application of the pursuer [*or* defender] and no longer being satisfied as to the matters mentioned in section 71(3) of the Land Registration etc. (Scotland) Act 2012,

ORDERS that the caveat on the title sheet of the plot of land—

(a)   at (*state description of the plot(s) of land*);

(b)   registered under title number (*state title number(s)*);

(c)   registered in the name of (*state name and address of proprietor*), be recalled.

(*Signed*)

Form 105.3-C inserted by S.S.I. 2014 No. 291 r. 2(6) (effective 8 December 2014).

Form 105.5

Rule 105.5

C1.2A.272

Form of decree of reduction in terms of section 46A of the Conveyancing (Scotland) Act 1924

[*Cause reference no. and name of cause*]

[*Date*] Lord [*name*]

The Lord Ordinary, on the motion of the pursuer, holds production to be satisfied, [in absence], reduces the [*insert type of deed, parties to the deed and date of registration in the Land Register of Scotland*] registered in the Land Register of Scotland under title number [*insert title number and, if applicable, lease title number*], [recalls the interim interdict dated [*date*]] and decerns; finds the pursuer [*or* defender] liable to the defender [*or* pursuer] in the expenses of the action, remits the account thereof, when lodged, to the Auditor of Court to tax.

Form 105.5 inserted by S.S.I. 2014 No. 291 r. 2(6) (effective 8 December 2014).

Form 105.6

Rule 105.6

C1.2A.273

Form of order for rectification of a document to which section 8A of the Law Reform (Miscellaneous Provisions) (Scotland) Act 1985 applies

[*Cause reference no. and name of cause*]

[*Date*] Lord [*name*]

The Lord Ordinary, on the motion of the pursuer, orders the rectification of [*insert type of deed, parties to the deed and date of registration in the Land Register of Scotland*] registered in the Land Register of Scotland under title number [*state title number and, if applicable, lease title number*] to the extent of [*insert details of the rectification including, if applicable, a statement in terms of section 8(3A) of the Law Reform (Miscellaneous Provisions) (Scotland) Act 1985 (i.e.statement of consent)*].

(*Signed*)

Form 105.6 inserted by S.S.I. 2014 No. 291 r. 2(6) (effective 8 December 2014).

Form 106.2

Rule 106.2

C1.2A.274

APPLICATION FOR A CERTIFICATE UNDER ARTICLE 5 OF REGULA-TION (EU) NO. 606/2013 OF THE EUROPEAN PARLIAMENT AND OF THE

COUNCIL OF 12TH JUNE 2013 ON MUTUAL RECOGNITION OF PROTECTION MEASURES IN CIVIL MATTERS

[Omitted by S.S.I. 2022 No. 329 para.2 (effective 1 December 2022).]

Form 106.5–A

C1.2A.275   *Rule 106.5(2)(a)*

NOTICE OF ISSUE OF CERTIFICATE UNDER ARTICLE 5 OF REGULATION (EU) NO. 606/2013 OF THE EUROPEAN PARLIAMENT AND OF THE COUNCIL OF 12TH JUNE 2013 ON MUTUAL RECOGNITION OF PROTECTION MEASURES IN CIVIL MATTERS

[Omitted by S.S.I. 2022 No. 329 para.2 (effective 1 December 2022).]

Form 106.5–B

C1.2A.276   *Rule 106.5(4)*

NOTICE FOR WALLS OF COURT OF ISSUE OF CERTIFICATE UNDER ARTICLE 5 OF REGULATION (EU) NO. 606/2013 OF THE EUROPEAN PARLIAMENT AND OF THE COUNCIL OF 12TH JUNE 2013 ON MUTUAL RECOGNITION OF PROTECTION MEASURES IN CIVIL MATTERS

[Omitted by S.S.I. 2022 No. 329 para.2 (effective 1 December 2022).]

Form 106.7

C1.2A.277   *Rule 106.7(1)*

APPLICATION FOR RECTIFICATION OR WITHDRAWAL OF A CERTIFICATE ISSUED UNDER ARTICLE 5 OF REGULATION (EU) NO. 606/2013 OF THE EUROPEAN PARLIAMENT AND OF THE COUNCIL OF 12TH JUNE 2013 ON MUTUAL RECOGNITION OF PROTECTION MEASURES IN CIVIL MATTERS

[Omitted by S.S.I. 2022 No. 329 para.2 (effective 1 December 2022).]

Form 106.10–A

C1.2A.278   *Rule 106.10(5)(a)*

NOTICE OF ADJUSTMENT OF A PROTECTION MEASURE UNDER ARTICLE 11 OF REGULATION (EU) NO. 606/2013 OF THE EUROPEAN PARLIAMENT AND OF THE COUNCIL OF 12TH JUNE 2013 ON MUTUAL RECOGNITION OF PROTECTION MEASURES IN CIVIL MATTERS

Date: (*date of posting or other method of intimation*)

To: (*name and designation of party to whom notice is to be given*)

TAKE NOTICE

This notice relates to a protection measure ordered by (*insert name of issuing authority in participating Member State*) in respect of which (*insert name of protected person*) is the protected person and you are the person causing the risk.

You are hereby given notice that, in exercise of the power conferred by Article 11(1) of Regulation (EU) No. 606/2013 of the European Parliament and of the Council of 12th June 2013 on mutual recognition of protection measures in civil matters, the Court of Session has adjusted the factual elements of the protection measure. A copy of the order adjusting the protection measure accompanies this notice.

As a result of the adjustment, the protection measure falls to be recognised and enforced in Scotland subject to the adjustment.

If you consider that the order adjusting the protection measure was wrongly granted, you have the right to appeal. If you are considering appealing, you are advised to consult a solicitor who will be able to give advice.

(*Signed*)

Deputy Principal Clerk
of Session

Form 106.10-A inserted by S.S.I. 2014 No. 371 (effective 11 January 2015).

Form 106.10-A as amended by S.S.I. 2022 No. 329 para.2 (effective 1 December 2022).

Form 106.10–B

Rule 106.10(7)

C1.2A.279

NOTICE FOR WALLS OF COURT OF A PROTECTION MEASURE UNDER ARTICLE 5 OF REGULATION (EU) NO. 606/2013 OF THE EUROPEAN PARLIAMENT AND OF THE COUNCIL OF 12TH JUNE 2013 ON MUTUAL RECOGNITION OF PROTECTION MEASURES IN CIVIL MATTERS

Date: (*insert date*)

To: (*insert name of person causing the risk*)

TAKE NOTICE

This notice relates to a protection measure ordered by (*insert name of issuing authority in participating Member State*) in respect of which (insert name of protected person) is the protected person and (*insert name of person causing the risk*) is the person causing the risk. That person's last known address is (*insert last known address of person causing the risk*).

(*Insert name of person causing the risk*) is hereby given notice that, in exercise of the power conferred by Article 11(1) of Regulation (EU) No. 606/2013 of the European Parliament and of the Council of 12th June 2013 on mutual recognition of protection measures in civil matters, the Court of Session has adjusted the factual elements of the protection measure.

As a result of the adjustment, the protection measure falls to be recognised and enforced in Scotland subject to the adjustment.

If (*insert name of person causing the risk*) wishes to obtain a copy of the order adjusting the protection measure, that person should immediately contact the Deputy Principal Clerk of Session at the Court of Session, 11 Parliament Square, Edinburgh, EH1 1RQ (telephone (0131) 225 2595).

If (*insert name of person causing the risk*) considers that the order adjusting the protection measure was wrongly granted, that person has the right to appeal. If that person is considering appealing, that person is advised to consult a solicitor who will be able to give advice.

(*Signed*)

Deputy Principal Clerk
of Session

Form 106.10-B inserted by S.S.I. 2014 No. 371 (effective 11 January 2015).

Form 106.10-B as amended by S.S.I. 2022 No. 329 para.2 (effective 1 December 2022).

Form 106.11

C1.2A.280   *Rule 106.11(7)*

FORM OF CERTIFICATE OF DELIVERY OF DOCUMENTS TO CHIEF CONSTABLE

(*insert place and date*) I, hereby certify that upon the day of I duly delivered to the chief constable of the Police Service of Scotland (*insert details of documents delivered*). This I did by (*state method of delivery*).

(Signed)

(*insert name and designation of person delivering documents*)

Form 106.11 inserted by S.S.I. 2014 No. 371 (effective 11 January 2015).

Form 106.12

C1.2A.281   *Rule 106.12(5)*

FORM OF CERTIFICATE OF SENDING OF DOCUMENTS TO CHIEF CONSTABLE

(*insert place and date*) I, ... hereby certify that upon theday of .... I duly sent to the chief constable of the Police Service of Scotland (*insert details of documents sent*). This I did by (*state method of delivery*).

(Signed)

(*insert name and designation of person sending documents*)

Form 106.12 inserted by S.S.I. 2014 No. 371 (effective 11 January 2015).

Form 108.2-A[1]

C1.2A.282   Rule 108.2(a)

Form of notice to relevant UK authorities under regulation 5 of the Challenges to Validity of EU Instruments (EU Exit) Regulations 2019

IN THE COURT OF SESSION

in causa

[A.B.], (*designation and address*)

Pursuer [*or* Petitioner]

against

[C.D.], (*designation and address*)

Defender [*or* Respondent]

Date: (*date of posting or other method of service*)

To: (*specify the relevant UK authority*)

TAKE NOTICE

That the court is considering whether or not to [*Or*: That (*specify party*) is seeking that the court] make a declaration under regulation 4 of the Challenges to Validity of EU Instruments (EU Exit) Regulations 2019 that (*specify the EU instrument which is the subject of the proposed declaration*) was invalid on the following grounds:

---

[1] Form 108.2-A inserted by S.S.I. 2019 No. 328 (not yet in force; effective on exit day).

(*set out the grounds in summary*)

If you wish to become a party to the proceedings, you should notify the Deputy Principal Clerk of Session in Form 108.3-A.

(Signed)

Deputy Principal Clerk of Session

[*or* Solicitor [*or* Agent] for (*specify*)]

Form 108.3-A¹

Rule 108.3

C1.2A.283

Form of notice to court under regulation 6 of the Challenges to Validity of EU Instruments (EU Exit) Regulations 2019

IN THE COURT OF SESSION

in causa

[A.B.], (*designation and address*)

Pursuer [*or* Petitioner]

against

[C.D.], (*designation and address*)

Defender [*or* Respondent]

To the Deputy Principal Clerk of Session

The (*specify the relevant UK authority or person nominated by a Minister of the Crown*) intends to join as a party to the proceedings.

(Signed)

Solicitor for (*specify the relevant UK authority or person nominated by a Minister of the Crown*)

(*Address*)

---

¹ Form 108.3-A inserted by S.S.I. 2019 No. 328 (not yet in force; effective on exit day).

SCHEDULE 3: AMENDMENT TO ENACTMENT

SCHEDULE 3

AMENDMENT TO ENACTMENT

Paragraph 3(1)

Presumption of Death (Scotland) Act 1977 (c.27)

In section 4(3) of the Presumption of Death (Scotland) Act 1977 (person having an interest seeking determination or appointment in application for variation order), for the words "lodge a minute", substitute the words "make an application to the court".

SCHEDULE 4

ENACTMENTS REPEALED

Paragraph 3(2)

Year of Session and Chapter	Short title	Extent of repeal	Rules of the Court of Session 1994
c.10 (S.)	Citation Act 1540	The whole Act	r.16.1
c.21 (S.)	Citation Act 1693	The whole Act	Ch. 16
6 Geo. 4, c.120	Court of Session Act 1825	Section 53	r. 16.12(4)
1 & 2 Vict., c.114	Debtors (Scotland) Act 1838	Sections 16, 18 and 20	r. 13.6(c)
			r. 3.5(4)
			r. 13.11
31 & 32 Vict., c.100	Court of Session Act 1868	Section 39	r. 29.1(2)(b)
31 & 32 Vict., c.101	Titles to Land Consolidation Act 1868	Section 158 and Schedule QQ	r. 13.11
			r. 59.1
45 & 46 Vict., c.77	Citation Amendment (Scotland) Act 1882	Sections 3, 4(1) to (4), 5 and 6 and Schedules 1 and 2 in their application to any cause or proceedings in the Court of Session	4. 16.4
57 & 58 Vict., c.40	Nautical Assessors (Scotland) Act 1894	Sections 2, 3 4 and 5 in their application to the Court of Session	r. 12.1(3)
			r.12.8
			r. 12.5
			r. 12.9
58 & 59 Vict., c.19	Court of Session Consignations (Scotland) Act 1895	In section 3, the words from ", and the Clerk of Court" to "such Clerk"	r. 35.11(2)

SCHEDULE 5: ACTS OF SEDERUNT REVOKED

SCHEDULE 5

ACTS OF SEDERUNT REVOKED

Paragraph 3(3)

Statutory Instrument Year and Number	Title of Act of Sederunt	Extent of Revocation
1949/1896	Act of Sederunt (Court of Session Jury Trials) 1949	The whole of the Act of Sederunt
1964/1901	Act of Sederunt (Rules of Court Amendment No. 5)	The whole of the Act of Sederunt
1965/321	Act of Sederunt (Rules of Court, consolidation and amendment) 1965	The whole of the Act of Sederunt
1965/1090	Act of Sederunt (Rules of Court Amendment No.1) 1965	The whole of the Act of Sederunt
1965/1266	Act of Sederunt (Rules of Court Amendment No.2) 1965	The whole of the Act of Sederunt
1965/1405	Act of Sederunt (Rules of Court Amendment No.3) 1965	The whole of the Act of Sederunt
1966/335	Act of Sederunt (Rules of Court Amendment No.1) 1966	The whole of the Act of Sederunt
1966/868	Act of Sederunt (Rules of Court Amendment No.21 1966	The whole of the Act of Sederunt
1966/1283	Act of Sederunt (Rules of Court Amendment No.3) 1966	The whole of the Act of Sederunt
1966/1531	Act of Sederunt (Rules of Court Amendment No.4) 1966	The whole of the Act of Sederunt
1966/1620	Act of Sederunt (Rules of Court Amendment No.5) 1966	The whole of the Act of Sederunt
1967/387	Act of Sederunt (Rules of Court Amendment No.1) 1967	The whole of the Act of Sederunt
1967/487	Act of Sederunt (Appointment of Judicial Factors and Rules of Court Amendment No.2) 1967	Paragraphs 5, 6, 7 and 8
1967/1090	Act of Sederunt (Rules of Court Amendment No.3) 1967	The whole of the Act of Sederunt
1967/1789	Act of Sederunt (Rules of Court Amendment No.4) 1967	The whole of the Act of Sederunt
1968/1016	Act of Sederunt (Rules of Court Amendment No.1) 1968	The whole of the Act of Sederunt
1968/1122	Act of Sederunt (Form of Extract Decree of Divorce) 1968	The whole of the Act of Sederunt

Statutory Instrument Year and Number	Title of Act of Sederunt	Extent of Revocation
1968/1150	Act of Sederunt (Rules of Court Amendment No.2) 1968	The whole of the Act of Sederunt
1968/1602	Act of Sederunt (Rules of Court Amendment No.3) 1968	The whole of the Act of Sederunt
1968/1759	Act of Sederunt (Rules of Court Amendment No.4) 1968	The whole of the Act of Sederunt
1968/1760	Act of Sederunt (Rules of Court Amendment No.5) 1968	The whole of the Act of Sederunt
1969/474	Act of Sederunt (Rules of Court Amendment No.1) 1969	The whole of the Act of Sederunt
1969/475	Act of Sederunt (Rules of Court Amendment No.2) 1969	The whole of the Act of Sederunt
1969/1702	Act of Sederunt (Rules of Court Amendment No.3) 1969	The whole of the Act of Sederunt
1969/1703	Act of Sederunt (Rules of Court Amendment No.4) 1969	The whole of the Act of Sederunt
1969/1819	Act of Sederunt (Rules of Court Amendment No.5) 1969	The whole of the Act of Sederunt
1970/96	Act of Sederunt (Rules of Court Amendment No.1) 1970	The whole of the Act of Sederunt
1970/134	Act of Sederunt (Rules of Court Amendment No.2) 1970	The whole of the Act of Sederunt
1970/682	Act of Sederunt (Rules of Court Amendment No.3) 1970	The whole of the Act of Sederunt
1970/1058	Act of Sederunt (Rules of Court Amendment No.4) 1970	The whole of the Act of Sederunt
1970/1746	Act of Sederunt (Rules of Court Amendment No.5) 1970	The whole of the Act of Sederunt
1971/66	Act of Sederunt (Rules of Court Amendment No.1) 1971	The whole of the Act of Sederunt
1971/201	Act of Sederunt (Rules of Court Amendment No.1) (Alteration of Operative Date) 1971	The whole of the Act of Sederunt
1971/202	Act of Sederunt (Rules of Court Amendment No.2) 1971	The whole of the Act of Sederunt
1971/203	Act of Sederunt (Rules of Court Amendment No.3) 1971	The whole of the Act of Sederunt
1971/265	Act of Sederunt (Rules of Court Amendment No.4) 1971	The whole of the Act of Sederunt
1971/1161	Act of Sederunt (Rules of Court Amendment No.5) 1971	The whole of the Act of Sederunt
1971/198	Act of Sederunt (Rules of Court Amendment No.5) 1970 (Alteration of Fees to Shorthand Writers) 1971	The whole of the Act of Sederunt

Statutory Instrument Year and Number	Title of Act of Sederunt	Extent of Revocation
1971/1162	Act of Sederunt (Rules of Court Amendment No.6) 1971	The whole of the Act of Sederunt
1971/1165	Act of Sederunt (Edictal Citations, Commissary Petitions and Petitions of Service) 1971	Paragraph 1
1971/1215	Act of Sederunt (Rules of Court Amendment No.7) 1971	The whole of the Act of Sederunt
1971/1714	Act of Sederunt (Rules of Court Amendment No.8) 1971	The whole of the Act of Sederunt
1971/1797	Act of Sederunt (Rules of Court Amendment No.9) 1971	The whole of the Act of Sederunt
1971/1809	Act of Sederunt (Rules of Court Amendment No.10) 1971	The whole of the Act of Sederunt
1972/164	Act of Sederunt (Rules of Court Amendment No.1) 1972	The whole of the Act of Sederunt
1972/1530	Act of Sederunt (Rules of Court Amendment No.2) 1972	The whole of the Act of Sederunt
1972/1672	Act of Sederunt (Rules of Court Amendment No. 3) 1972 (Alteration of Fees to Shorthand Writers) 1972	The whole of the Act of Sederunt
1972/1835	Act of Sederunt (Rules of Court Amendment No.4) 1972	The whole of the Act of Sederunt
1972/1981	Act of Sederunt (Rules of Court Amendment No.5) 1972	The whole of the Act of Sederunt
1972/1982	Act of Sederunt (Rules of Court Amendment No.6) 1972	The whole of the Act of Sederunt
1972/2021	Act of Sederunt (Rules of Court Amendment No.7) 1972	The whole of the Act of Sederunt
1972/2022	Act of Sederunt (Rules of Court Amendment No.8) 1972	The whole of the Act of Sederunt
1973/145	Act of Sederunt (Rules of Court Amendment No.1) 1973	The whole of the Act of Sederunt
1973/360	Act of Sederunt (Rules of Court Amendment No.2) 1973	The whole of the Act of Sederunt
1973/540	Act of Sederunt (Rules of Court Amendment No.3) 1973	The whole of the Act of Sederunt
1973/541	Act of Sederunt (Rules of Court Amendment No.4) 1973	The whole of the Act of Sederunt
1973/984	Act of Sederunt (Rules of Court Amendment No.5 1973) (Alteration of fees to Shorthand Writers) 1973	The whole of the Act of Sederunt
1973/1991	Act of Sederunt (Rules of Court Amendment No.6) 1973	The whole of the Act of Sederunt

Statutory Instrument Year and Number	Title of Act of Sederunt	Extent of Revocation
1974/845	Act of Sederunt (Rules of Court Amendment) 1974	The whole of the Act of Sederunt
1974/945	Act of Sederunt (Rules of Court Amendment No.2) 1974	The whole of the Act of Sederunt
1974/946	Act of Sederunt (Rules of Court Amendment No.3) 1974	The whole of the Act of Sederunt
1974/1603	Act of Sederunt (Rules of Court Amendment No.4) 1974	The whole of the Act of Sederunt
1974/1628	Act of Sederunt (Rules of Court Amendment No.5) (Alteration of Fees to Shorthand Writers) 1974	The whole of the Act of Sederunt
1974/1686	Act of Sederunt (Rules of Court Amendment No.6) 1974	The whole of the Act of Sederunt
1974/2090	Act of Sederunt (Rules of Court Amendment No.7) 1974	The whole of the Act of Sederunt
1975/89	Act of Sederunt (Rules of Court Amendment) 1975	The whole of the Act of Sederunt
1975/1106	Act of Sederunt (Rules of Court Amendment No.2) 1975	The whole of the Act of Sederunt
1975/1585	Act of Sederunt (Rules of Court Amendment No.3) (Alteration of Fees to Shorthand Writers) 1975	The whole of the Act of Sederunt
1976/137	Act of Sederunt (Rules of Court Amendment) 1976	The whole of the Act of Sederunt
1976/282	Act of Sederunt (Rules of Court Amendment No.2) 1976	The whole of the Act of Sederunt
1976/372	Act of Sederunt (Rules of Court Amendment No.3) (Alteration of Fees to Shorthand Writers) 1976	The whole of the Act of Sederunt
1976/745	Act of Sederunt (Rules of Court Amendment No.4) (Transmission of Records) 1976	The whole of the Act of Sederunt
1976/779	Act of Sederunt (Rules of Court Amendment No.5) (Appeals under Social Security Acts) 1976	The whole of the Act of Sederunt
1976/847	Act of Sederunt (Rules of Court Amendment No.6) (Appeals under Consumer Credit Act 1974) 1976	The whole of the Act of Sederunt
1976/867	Act of Sederunt (Rules of Court Amendment No.7)	The whole of the Act of Sederunt

Statutory Instrument Year and Number	Title of Act of Sederunt	Extent of Revocation
	(Solicitor's Admission Fees) 1976	
1976/1605	Act of Sederunt (Rules of Court Amendment No.9) (Alteration of Fees to Shorthand Writers No. 2) 1976	The whole of the Act of Sederunt
1976/1849	Act of Sederunt (Rules of Court Amendment No.10) (Revenue Appeals) 1976	The whole of the Act of Sederunt
1976/1994	Act of Sederunt (Rules of Court Amendment No.11) (Consistorial Actions) 1976	The whole of the Act of Sederunt
1976/2196	Act of Sederunt (Rules of Court Amendment No.13) (Medical Witnesses' Fees) 1976	The whole of the Act of Sederunt
1976/2197	Act of Sederunt (Rules of Court Amendment No.14) (Third Party Procedure) 1976	The whole of the Act of Sederunt
1977/472	Act of Sederunt (Rules of Court Amendment No.2) (Adoption Proceedings) 1977	The whole of the Act of Sederunt
1977/974	Act of Sederunt (Rules of Court Amendment No.3) (Applications under Companies and Insolvency Acts 1976) 1977	The whole of the Act of Sederunt
1977/978	Act of Sederunt (Rules of Court Amendment No.4) (Shorthand Writers' Fees) 1977	The whole of the Act of Sederunt
1977/1621	Act of Sederunt (Rules of Court Amendment No.5) (Miscellaneous Amendments) 1977	The whole of the Act of Sederunt
1978/106	Act of Sederunt (Rules of Court Amendment No.1) (Consistorial Causes) 1978	The whole of the Act of Sederunt
1978/161	Act of Sederunt (Rules of Court Amendment No.3) (Presumption of Death) 1978	The whole of the Act of Sederunt
1978/690	Act of Sederunt (Rules of Court Amendment No.4) (Commercial Causes) 1978	The whole of the Act of Sederunt
1978/799	Act of Sederunt (Rules of Court Amendment No.5) (Depute Clerks of Session) 1978	The whole of the Act of Sederunt

Statutory Instrument Year and Number	Title of Act of Sederunt	Extent of Revocation
1978/925	Act of Sederunt (Rules of Court Amendment No.6) (Shorthand Writers' Fees) 1978	The whole of the Act of Sederunt
1978/955	Act of Sederunt (Rules of Court Amendment No.8) (Patent Rules) 1978	The whole of the Act of Sederunt
1978/1373	Act of Sederunt (Rules of Court Amendmen No.9) (Convention Adoption Rules) 1978	The whole of the Act of Sederunt
1978/1804	Act of Sederunt (Rules of Court Amendment No.10) (Induciae) 1978	The whole of the Act of Sederunt
1979/516	Act of Sederunt (Rules of Court Amendment No.2) (European Assembly Election Petitions) 1979	The whole of the Act of Sederunt
1979/670	Act of Sederunt (Rules of Court Amendment No.3) (International Oil Pollution Compensation Fund)1979	The whole of the Act of Sederunt
1979/1033	Act of Sederunt (Rules of Court Amendment No.4) (Shorthand Writers' Fees) 1979	The whole of the Act of Sederunt
1979/1410	Act of Sederunt (Rules of Court Amendment No.5) 1979	The whole of the Act of Sederunt
1980/290	Act of Sederunt (Rules of Court Amendment No.1) (Adoption Proceedings) 1980	The whole of the Act of Sederunt
1980/891	Act of Sederunt (Rules of Court Amendment No.3) (Protection of Trading Interests Act 1980) 1980	The whole of the Act of Sederunt
1980/892	Act of Sederunt (Rules of Court Amendment No.4) (Applications under section 85 of Fair Trading Act 1973) 1980	The whole of the Act of Sederunt
1980/909	Act of Sederunt (Rules of Court Amendment No.5) (Witnesses' Fees) 1980	The whole of the Act of Sederunt
1980/1016	Act of Sederunt (Rules of Court Amendment No.6) (Shorthand Writers' Fees) 1980	The whole of the Act of Sederunt
1980/1144	Act of Sederunt (Rules of Court Amendment No.7) (Miscellaneous Amendments) 1980	The whole of the Act of Sederunt

Statutory Instrument Year and Number	Title of Act of Sederunt	Extent of Revocation
1980/1754	Act of Sederunt (Rules of Court Amendment No.8) (Leave to appeal and appeals from Social Security Commissioners) 1980	The whole of the Act of Sederunt
1980/1801	Act of Sederunt (Rules of Court Amendment No.9) (Remits from Sheriff Court) 1980	The whole of the Act of Sederunt
1981/1137	Act of Sederunt (Rules of Court Amendment No.3) (Shorthand Writers' Fees) 1981	The whole of the Act of Sederunt
1982/654	Act of Sederunt (Rules of Court Amendment No.3) (Court Fees) 1982	The whole of the Act of Sederunt
1982/804	Act of Sederunt (Rules of Court Amendment No.4) (Shorthand Writers' Fees) 1982	The whole of the Act of Sederunt
1982/1381	Act of Sederunt (Rules of Court Amendment No.5) (Applications under Matrimonial Homes (Family Protection) (Scotland) Act 1981) 1982	The whole of the Act of Sederunt
1982/1679	Act of Sederunt (Rules of Court Amendment No.6) (Simplified Divorce Procedure) 1982	The whole of the Act of Sederunt
1982/1723	Act of Sederunt (Rules of Court Amendment No.7) (Witnesses' Fees) 1982	The whole of the Act of Sederunt
1982/1824	Act of Sederunt (Rules of Court Amendment No.8) (Court Fees in Simplified Divorce Procedure) 1982	The whole of the Act of Sederunt
1982/1825	Act of Sederunt (Rules of Court Amendment No.9) (Miscellaneous Amendments) 1982	The whole of the Act of Sederunt
1983/397	Act of Sederunt (Rules of Court Amendment No.1) (Appeals under Social Security Acts) 1983	The whole of the Act of Sederunt
1983/398	Act of Sederunt (Rules of Court Amendment No.2) (Interest in Decrees or Extracts) 1983	The whole of the Act of Sederunt

Statutory Instrument Year and Number	Title of Act of Sederunt	Extent of Revocation
1983/656	Act of Sederunt (Rules of Court Amendment No.3) (Letters of Request) 1983	The whole of the Act of Sederunt
1983/826	Act of Sederunt (Rules of Court Amendment No.4) (Taxation of Accounts) 1983	The whole of the Act of Sederunt
1983/1210	Act of Sederunt (Rules of Court Amendment No.6) (Simplified Divorce Procedure) 1983	The whole of the Act of Sederunt
1983/1642	Act of Sederunt (Rules of Court Amendment No.7) (Shorthand Writers' Fees) 1983	The whole of the Act of Sederunt
1984/235	Act of Sederunt (Rules of Court Amendment No.1) (Court Fees) 1984	The whole of the Act of Sederunt
1984/472	Act of Sederunt (Rules of Court Amendment No.2) (Miscellaneous) 1984	The whole of the Act of Sederunt
1984/499	Act of Sederunt (Rules of Court Amendment No.3) (Summary Decree and Other Amendments) 1984	The whole of the Act of Sederunt
1984/919	Act of Sederunt (Amendment of Rules of Court No.4) (Provisional Damages) 1984	The whole of the Act of Sederunt
1984/920	Act of Sederunt (Amendment of Rules of Court No.5) (Intimation in fatal accident cases) 1984	The whole of the Act of Sederunt
1984/997	Act of Sederunt (Rules of Court Amendment No.6) (Adoption Proceedings) 1984	The whole of the Act of Sederunt
1984/1133	Act of Sederunt (Rules of Court Amendment No.8) (Shorthand Writers' Fees) 1984	The whole of the Act of Sederunt
1985/227	Act of Sederunt (Rules of Court Amendment No.1) (Optional Procedure in Certain Actions of Renaration) 1985	The whole of the Act of Sederunt
1985/500	Act of Sederunt (Rules of Court Amendment No.2) (Judicial Review) 1985	The whole of the Act of Sederunt
1985/760	Act of Sederunt (Rules of Court Amendment No.4) (Shorthand Writers' Fees) 1985	The whole of the Act of Sederunt

Statutory Instrument Year and Number	Title of Act of Sederunt	Extent of Revocation
1985/1178	Act of Sederunt (Rules of Court Amendment No.5) (Interest in Decrees or Extracts) 1985	The whole of the Act of Sederunt
1985/1426	Act of Sederunt (Rules of Court Amendment No.6) (Election Petitions) 1985	The whole of the Act of Sederunt
1985/1600	Act of Sederunt (Rules of Court Amendment No.7) (Miscellaneous Amendments) 1985	The whole of the Act of Sederunt
1986/514	Act of Sederunt (Rules of Court Amendment No.1) (Bankruptcy Forms) 1986	The whole of the Act of Sederunt
1986/515	Act of Sederunt (Rules of Court Amendment No.2) (Custody of Children) 1986	The whole of the Act of Sederunt
1986/694	Act of Sederunt (Rules of Court Amendment No.3) (Companies and Insolvency) 1986	The whole of the Act of Sederunt
1986/799	Act of Sederunt (Rules of Court Amendment No.4) (Liner Conferences) 1986	The whole of the Act of Sederunt
1986/967	Act of Sederunt (Rules of Court Amendment No.5) (Solicitors' Fees) 1986	The whole of the Act of Sederunt
1986/1128	Act of Sederunt (Rules of Court Amendment No.6) (Shorthand Writers' Fees) 1986	The whole of the Act of Sederunt
1986/1231	Act of Sederunt (Rules of Court Amendment No.7) (Consistorial Causes) 1986	The whole of the Act of Sederunt
1986/1937	Act of Sederunt (Rules of Court Amendment No.8) (Miscellaneous) 1986	The whole of the Act of Sederunt
1986/1941	Act of Sederunt (Rules of Court Amendment No.9) (Jurisdiction and Enforcement) 1986	The whole of the Act of Sederunt
1986/1955	Act of Sederunt (Rules of Court Amendment No.10) (Miscellaneous Amendments) 1986	The whole of the Act of Sederunt
1986/2298	Act of Sederunt (Rules of Court Amendment No.11) (Companies) 1986	The whole of the Act of Sederunt

Statutory Instrument Year and Number	Title of Act of Sederunt	Extent of Revocation
1987/12	Act of Sederunt (Rules of Court Amendment No.1) (Drug Trafficking) 1987	The whole of the Act of Sederunt
1987/871	Act of Sederunt (Rules of Court Amendment No.2) (Solicitors' Fees) 1987	The whole of the Act of Sederunt
1987/1079	Act of Sederunt (Rules of Court Amendment No.3) (Shorthand Writers' Fees) 1987	The whole of the Act of Sederunt
1987/1206	Act of Sederunt (Rules of Court Amendment No.4) (Miscellaneous) 1987	The whole of the Act of Sederunt
1987/2160	Act of Sederunt (Rules of Court Amendment No.5) (Miscellaneous) 1987	The whole of the Act of Sederunt
1988/615	Act of Sederunt (Rules of the Court of Session Amendment No.1) (Family Law) 1988	The whole of the Act of Sederunt
1988/684	Act of Sederunt (Rules of the Court of Session Amendment No.2) (Solicitors' Fees) 1988	The whole of the Act of Sederunt
1988/1032	Act of Sederunt (Rules of the Court of Session Amendment No.3) (Shorthand Writers' Fees) 1988	The whole of the Act of Sederunt
1988/1521	Act of Sederunt (Rules of the Court of Session Amendment No.4) (Commercial Actions) 1988	The whole of the Act of Sederunt
1988/2059	Act of Sederunt (Form of charge for payment) 1988	The whole of the Act of Sederunt in its application to the Court of Session
1988/2060	Act of Sederunt (Rules of the Court of Session Amendment No.5) (Time to pay directions) 1988	The whole of the Act of Sederunt
1989/435	Act of Sederunt (Rules of the Court of Session Amendment No.1) (Written Statements) 1989	The whole of the Act of Sederunt
1989/445	Act of Sederunt (Rules of the Court of Session Amendment No.2) (Solicitors' Fees) 1989	The whole of the Act of Sederunt
1989/778	Act of Sederunt (Rules of Court of Session Amendment	The whole of the Act of Sederunt

Statutory Instrument Year and Number	Title of Act of Sederunt	Extent of Revocation
	No.3) Shorthand Writers' Fees) 1989	
1990/705	Act of Sederunt (Rules of Court of Session Amendment No.1) (Miscellaneous) 1990	The whole of the Act of Sederunt
1990/717	Act of Sederunt (Rules of Court of the Session Amendment No.2) (Solicitors' Fees) 1990	The whole of the Act of Sederunt
1990/798	Act of Sederunt (Rules of Court of the Session Amendment No.3) (Shorthand Writers' Fees) 1990	The whole of the Act of Sederunt
1990/1262	Act of Sederunt (Rules of Court of the Session Amendment No.4) (Solicitors' Fees) 1990	The whole of the Act of Sederunt
1991/272	Act of Sederunt (Rules of the Court of Session Amendment No.1) (Fees of Solicitors) 1991	The whole of the Act of Sederunt
1991/1157	Act of Sederunt (Rules of the Court of Session Amendment No.2) (Miscellaneous) 1991	The whole of the Act of Sederunt
1991/846	Act of Sederunt (Rules of the Court of Session Amendment No.3) (Solicitors' Fees) 1991	The whole of the Act of Sederunt
1991/1158	Act of Sederunt (Rules of the Court of Session Amendment No.4) (Shorthand Writers' Fees) 1991	The whole of the Act of Sederunt
1991/1183	Act of Sederunt (Rules of the Court of Session Amendment No.5) (Prevention of Terrorism) 1991	The whole of the Act of Sederunt
1991/1621	Act of Sederunt (Rules of the Court of Session Amendment No.7) (Patents Rules) 1991	The whole of the Act of Sederunt
1991/1915	Act of Sederunt (Rules of the Court of Session Amendment No.8) (Discharge of Judicial Factors) 1991	The whole of the Act of Sederunt
1991/2213	Act of Sederunt (Rules of the Court of Session Amendment No.9) (International Commercial Arbitration) 1991	The whole of the Act of Sederunt

Statutory Instrument Year and Number	Title of Act of Sederunt	Extent of Revocation
1991/2483	Act of Sederunt (Rules of the Court of Session Amendment No.10) (Miscellaneous) 1991	The whole of the Act of Sederunt
1991/2652	Act of Sederunt (Rules of the Court of Session Amendment No.11) (Applications under the Access to Health Records Act 1990) 1991	The whole of the Act of Sederunt
1992/88	Act of Sederunt (Rules of the Court of Session Amendment) (Optional Procedure and Miscellaneous) 1992	The whole of the Act of Sederunt
1992/894	Act of Sederunt (Rules of the Court of Session Amendment No.2) (Solicitors' Fees) 1992	The whole of the Act of Sederunt
1992/1433	Act of Sederunt (Rules of the Court of Session Amendment No.3) (Taxation of Accounts) 1992	The whole of the Act of Sederunt
1992/1422	Act of Sederunt (Rules of the Court of Session Amendment No.4) (Solicitors, Notaries Public, Qualified Conveyancers and Executry Practitioners) 1992	The whole of the Act of Sederunt
1992/1533	Act of Sederunt (Rules of the Court of Session Amendment No.5) (Public Trusts) 1992	The whole of the Act of Sederunt
1992/1905	Act of Sederunt (Rules of the Court of Session Amendment No.6) (Shorthand Writers' Fees) 1992	The whole of the Act of Sederunt
1992/1906	Act of Sederunt (Rules of the Court of Session Amendment No.7) (Witnesses' Fees) 1992	The whole of the Act of Sederunt
1992/1898	Act of Sederunt (Rules of the Court of Session Amendment No.8) (Fees of Solicitors in Speculative Actions) 1992	The whole of the Act of Sederunt
1992/2289	Act of Sederunt (Rules of the Court of Session Amendment No.9) (Miscellaneous) 1992	The whole of the Act of Sederunt
1993/770	Act of Sederunt (Rules of the Court of Session Amendment) (Interest in Decrees and Extracts) 1993	The Whole of the Act of Sederunt

Statutory Instrument Year and Number	Title of Act of Sederunt	Extent of Revocation
1993/899	Act of Sederunt (Rules of the Court of Session Amendment) (Register of Insolvencies) 1993	The whole of the Act of Sederunt
1993/900	Act of Sederunt (Rules of the Court of Session Amendment No.2) (Fees of Solicitors) 1993	The whole of the Act of Sederunt
1993/1357	Act of Sederunt (Rules of the Court of Session Amendment No.3) (Shorthand Writers' Fees) 1993	The whole of the Act of Sederunt
1994/1139	Act of Sederunt (Rules of the Court of Session Amendment No.1) (Fees of Solicitors) 1994	The whole of the Act of Sederunt
1994/1140	Act of Sederunt (Rules of the Court of Session Amendment No.2) (Shorthand Writers' Fees) 1994	The whole of the Act of Sederunt